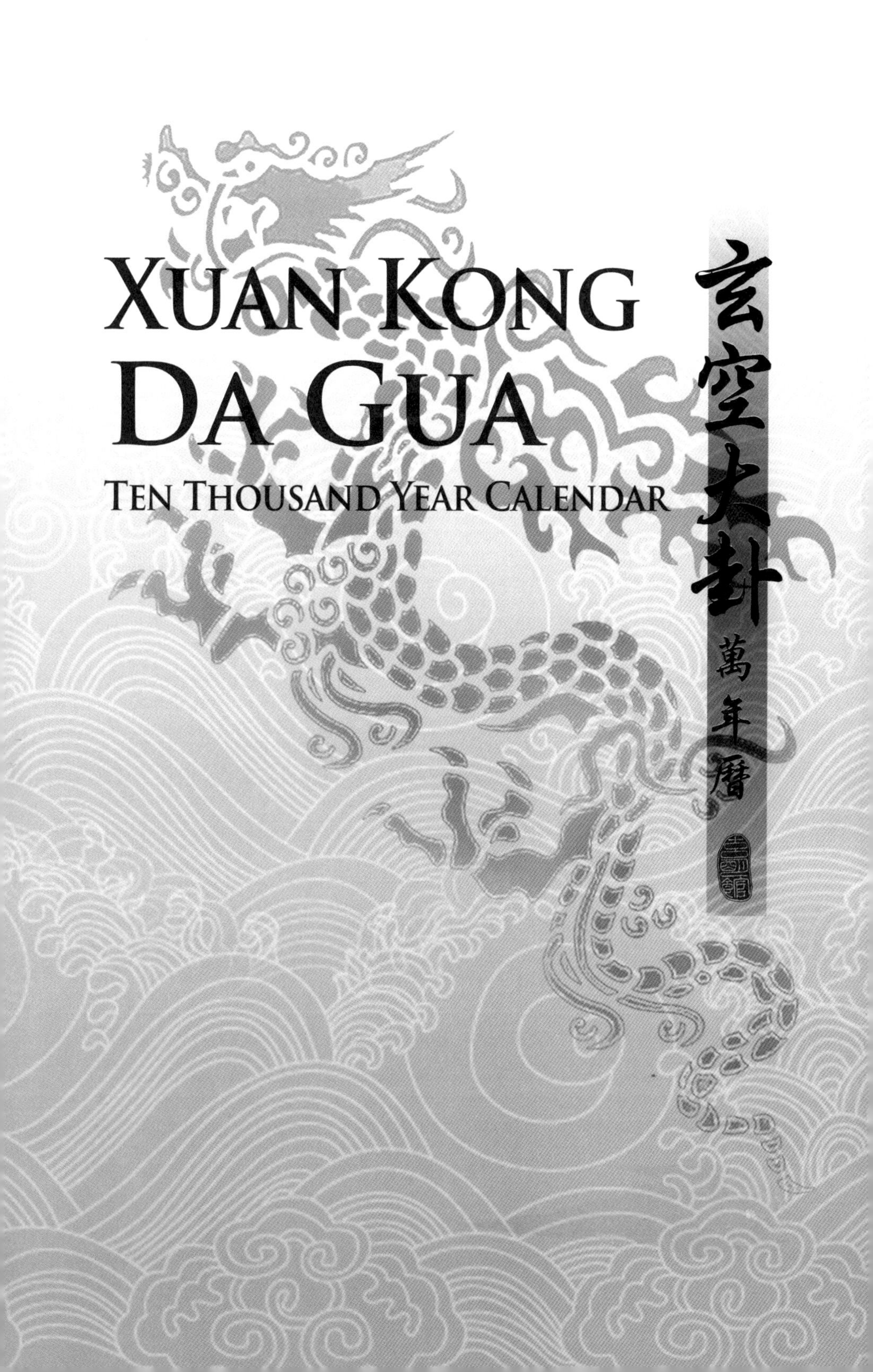

Xuan Kong Da Gua

Ten Thousand Year Calendar

玄空大卦

萬年曆

Xuan Kong Da Gua Ten Thousand Year Calendar

First Edition August 2008

The author can be reached at:

Mastery Academy of Chinese Metaphysics Sdn. Bhd. (611143-A)
19-3, The Boulevard, Mid Valley City,
59200 Kuala Lumpur, Malaysia.
Tel : +603-2284 8080
Fax : +603-2284 1218
Email : info@masteryacademy.com
Website: www.masteryacademy.com

Published by JY Books Sdn. Bhd. (659134-T)

INDEX

About The Chinese Metaphysics Reference Series

The Chinese Metaphysics Reference Series of books are designed primarily to be used as complimentary textbooks for scholars, students, researchers, teachers and practitioners of Chinese Metaphysics.

The goal is to provide quick easy reference tables, diagrams and charts, facilitating the study and practice of various Chinese Metaphysics subjects including Feng Shui, BaZi, Yi Jing, Zi Wei, Liu Ren, Ze Ri, Ta Yi, Qi Men and Mian Xiang.

This series of books are intended as reference text and educational materials principally for the academic syllabuses of the **Mastery Academy of Chinese Metaphysics**. The contents have also been formatted so that Feng Shui Masters and other teachers of Chinese Metaphysics will always have a definitive source of reference at hand, when teaching or applying their art.

Because each school of Chinese Metaphysics is different, the Reference Series of books usually do not contain any specific commentaries, application methods or explanations on the theory behind the formulas presented in its contents. This is to ensure that the contents can be used freely and independently by all Feng Shui Masters and teachers of Chinese Metaphysics without conflict.

If you would like to study or learn the applications of any of the formulas presented in the Reference Series of books, we recommend that you undertake the courses offered by Joey Yap and his team of Instructors at the Mastery Academy of Chinese Metaphysics.

Titles offers in the Reference Series as of Autumn 2008:

1. The Chinese Metaphysics Compendium
2. Dong Gong Date Selection
3. Earth Study Discern Truth
4. Xuan Kong Da Gua Structure Reference Book
5. San Yuan's Dragon Gate Eight Formation Water Method
6. Plum Blossoms Divination Book
7. Xuan Kong Da Gua Ten Thousand Year Calendar

Preface

While the study of Chinese Metaphysics is a rich and rewarding practice, it must be acknowledged that its sources of information are vast, and one might be tempted to say, sprawling. From my experience as a teacher and practitioner, the biggest hindrance towards effective knowledge accumulation in this field seems to be directly related to the difficulty most people have in obtaining organized, updated, and streamlined versions of the classics.

This ***Xuan Kong Da Gua Ten Thousand Year Calendar*** that you have in your hands is part of my ***Chinese Metaphysics Reference Series***, a series of books that are designed primarily to be used as reference texts for students, teachers, and practitioners of Chinese Metaphysics. Please note that it is different from the regular Ten Thousand Year Calendar.

The Xuan Kong Da Gua has three subsystems within it: Xuan Kong Da Gua Feng Shui, Xuan Kong Da Gua Date Selection, and Xuan Kong Da Gua Divination. This book facilitates the practice of Xuan Kong Date Selection and Divination. Xuan Kong Da Gua Date Selection is an extremely sophisticated method of date selection because it has intrinsic divinatory attributes that allows one to predict underlying occurrences of an event – or to put it simply, it is able to give you the 'big picture.' One is able to derive a specific result, as opposed to ascertaining a 'general' good date that doesn't take into account particularities of an event or situation.

As such, this book was conceived primarily as a supplementary text for the Mastery Academy's ZeRi Mastery Series Module 2 class, which focuses on the Xuan Kong Da Gua Date Selection technique. However, it can be used by all students and teachers of Xuan Kong Da Gua Date Selection, regardless of school or affiliation. For that same reason, I encourage you to use this book under the guidance of a trained teacher in order to make the best use of it, and to learn the proper modes of application. While it comes with an explanatory Introduction chapter, it will always be of great help to have an experienced teacher guide you through any questions or difficulties that might arise. Alternatively, you can always attend our Date Selection – the ZeRi Mastery Series in order to learn more.

The selection in Xuan Kong Da Gua Ten Thousand Year Calendar covers a vast 100 years from 1950 to 2050, and it is my wish that you're able to receive many years of use from this handy reference book!

In the meantime, I wish you all the best in your pursuit of further knowledge in Chinese Metaphysics.

Joey Yap
August 2008

Author's personal website: www.joeyyap.com | www.fengshuilogy.com
Academy website:
www.masteryacademy.com | www.masteryjournal.com | www.maelearning.com

MASTERY ACADEMY
OF CHINESE METAPHYSICS™

At **www.masteryacademy.com**, you will find some useful tools to ascertain key information about the Feng Shui of a property or for the study of Astrology.

The Joey Yap Flying Stars Calculator can be utilised to plot your home or office Flying Stars chart. To find out your personal best directions, use the 8 Mansions Calculator. To learn more about your personal Destiny, you can use the Joey Yap BaZi Ming Pan Calculator to plot your Four Pillars of Destiny – you just need to have your date of birth (day, month, year) and time of birth.

For more information about BaZi, Xuan Kong or Flying Star Feng Shui, or if you wish to learn more about these subjects with Joey Yap, logon to the Mastery Academy of Chinese Metaphysics website at **www.masteryacademy.com.**

www.maelearning.com

Bookmark this address on your computer, and visit this newly-launched website today. With the E-Learning Center, knowledge of Chinese Metaphysics is a mere 'click' away!

Our E-Learning Center consists of 3 distinct components.

1. Online Courses

These shall comprise of 3 Programs: our Online Feng Shui Program, Online BaZi Program, and Online Mian Xiang Program. Each lesson contains a video lecture, slide presentation and downloadable course notes.

2. MA Live!

With MA Live!, Joey Yap's workshops, tutorials, courses and seminars on various Chinese Metaphysics subjects broadcasted right to your computer screen. Better still, participants will not only get to see and hear Joey talk 'live', but also get to engage themselves directly in the event and more importantly, TALK to Joey via the MA Live! interface. All the benefits of a live class, minus the hassle of actually having to attend one!

3. Video-On-Demand (VOD)

Get immediate streaming-downloads of the Mastery Academy's wide range of educational DVDs, right on your computer screen. No more shipping costs and waiting time to be incurred!

Study at your own pace, and interact with your Instructor and fellow students worldwide... at your own convenience and privacy. With our E-Learning Center, knowledge of Chinese Metaphysics is brought DIRECTLY to you in all its clarity, with illustrated presentations and comprehensive notes expediting your learning curve!

Welcome to the Mastery Academy's E-LEARNING CENTER...YOUR virtual gateway to Chinese Metaphysics mastery!

Using the Xuan Kong Da Gua Ten Thousand Year Calendar

Every year, month, day, and hour can be converted into a specific 'Hexagram' format. This set of four Hexagrams forms the Xuan Kong Da Gua (XKDG) date.

What is Xuan Kong, and what is Da Gua?

The system of Xuan Kong is divided into Xuan Kong Flying Stars, Xuan Kong Da Gua Feng Shui, and then Xuan Kong Da Gua Date Selection. 'Da Gua' refers to 'Greater Hexagrams'.

XKDG Date Selection is considered by many to be one of the most sophisticated methods of date selection. Like all techniques available in Xuan Kong, XKDG date selection is first and foremost superior for its predictive and divinatory attributes. Using one date for a certain purpose can give you an entire story about the people involved, as well as other underlying events – things that are to come and things that have passed.

Conventional XKDG Date Selection might not seem too complicated. Since each the year, month, day, and hour can be converted into individual hexagrams, and since each hexagram then has its own 'Xuan Kong Element' number and 'Period Luck' number, various 'Structures' can be formed.

Here is how a 'One Gua Pure Formation' looks like. Aside from sharing the same XK Element number, all the hexagrams belong to the Gen Trigram Group:

Gen Pure Gua Structure 艮卦一卦純清

Date	BaZi			
	Hour	Day	Month	Year
3 May 2006 壬 辰 Water Dragon	丁 未 Fire Goat (水) 6 7 山風蠱 Poison	壬 辰 Water Dragon (水) 6 4 山天大畜 Big Livestock	壬 辰 Water Dragon (水) 6 4 山天大畜 Big Livestock	丙 戌 Fire Dog (水) 6 1 艮爲山 Mountain

This is how a 'Tan Lang' Structure looks like, by matching all the 'Period Luck' numbers to 1, which represents Tan Lang:

貪狼格 Tan Lang (Greedy Wolf) Structure

Date	BaZi			
	Hour	Day	Month	Year
4 Jul 2006 甲 午 Wood Horse	甲 子 Wood Rat (水) 1 1 坤爲地 Earth	甲 午 Wood Horse (金) 9 1 乾爲天 Heaven	甲 午 Wood Horse (金) 9 1 乾爲天 Heaven	丙 戌 Fire Dog (水) 6 1 艮爲山 Mountain

Another conventional structure is the Five Element Structure. In this case, notice the XK Element numbers 1 and 6 form the 'Water Element' Structure:

Date	BaZi			
	Hour	Day	Month	Year
2 Nov 2000 甲 子 Earth Rat	丙 子 Fire Rat (水) 6 3 山雷頤 Nourish	甲 子 Wood Rat (水) 1 1 坤爲地 Earth	丙 戌 Fire Dog (水) 6 1 艮爲山 Mountain	庚 辰 Metal Dragon (水) 1 9 地天泰 Unity

Other conventional structures include He Tu Structures, Combination of Ten Structures, Five Element He Tu & Combination of 10 Structures, and Family Gua Structures.

Being sophisticated also means that XKDG date selection can be taken one step further to become highly precise. It can be, if so required, location-based, person-based, action-based, as well as result-based.

Each of the 64 Hexagrams as found in this Ten Thousand Year Calendar – for example: 'Well', 'Following', 'Mountain', 'Accomplished', 'Sincerity' – has its own unique function to create a desired outcome. Then, a 'Hexagram relationship' can be established with a specific person, a specific location, a specific land formation, or a specific action, to collectively induce a specific outcome. This is how XKDG Date Selection distinguishes itself from so many other Date Selection methods out there today, thru its ability to create specific results, and not merely a 'general good date'.

Using a XKDG date requires knowledge of the following:

- BaZi, its fundamentals, 'Pillars', Stems & Branches interactions
- Five Elements (五行) relationships
- Yi Jing, or the 64 Hexagrams
- Other fundamental Date Selection techniques like the 12 Day Officers, Dong Gong, and Auxiliary Stars

The ZeRi Mastery Module 2 (ZRM2) is a complete class that instructs on finding, matching, and using the XKDG Date Selection technique. For example, every Hexagram can be grouped by its Element, Star, or Palace. This determines what goes where within a certain building or property, and when.

While this XKDG Ten Thousand Year Calendar does not instruct on application, a general guide to using this reference book will be provided in the following pages.

The format of the XKDG Ten Thousand Year Calendar is multi-layered. Each year 'Chapter' comes with its respective 12 individual months, complete with the 'Pillar' (Stem & Branch) alongside the Hexagram. This is the same format given to every single day within each month. On the start of each 'Year Chapter' there is also the 'Monthly Flying Stars' as well as the monthly 'Three Killings' location for easy reference.

Each Hexagram is further completed with their individual 'Xuan Kong Element' and 'Period Luck' number.

To plot the Hour Hexagram, refer to the 'Five Rats Chasing Day Establishing Hour' Table at the appendix.

Last but not least, bear in mind that the Chinese Solar Calendar enters each New Year cycle on Feb 4th, which marks the 'Coming of Spring' (Li Chun). All days prior to Feb 4th will belong to the previous year. The Transition Dates of every month is highlighted as well in the respective months.

How To Use This Book

1. A Date is plot from right to left – starting from the Year, then Month, Day, and Hour.

Date	BaZi			
	Hour	Day	Month	Year

2. The Hexagram for the YEAR is indicated at the start of each Year Chapter.
3. The Month Hexagram can be found on the following page, as well as each individual Month Table
4. Every Day Hexagram in contained within the respective 12 Month Tables.
5. The Hour Hexagram is determined by using the 'Five Rats Chasing Day' Table at the appendix
6. Note the Xuan Kong Element and Period Luck number

Example 1

30 April 2008, 0700 hrs

1. Refer to the Year Chapter of 2008.

The Hexagram for the YEAR is indicated at the start of each Year Chapter.

Date	BaZi			
30 April 2008	Hour	Day	Month	Year

The Hexagram of the Wu Zi Year is 'Beginning'. Write this next to the Pillar, with the Xuan Kong Element number 7 on top, and the Period Luck number 4 below the Hexagram

Date	BaZi			
	Hour	Day	Month	Year
30 April 2008				戊子 Earth Rat — (火) 7 水雷屯 4 Beginning

2. To identify the Hexagram for the MONTH, the upper right-hand corner of each Month Table shows the Hexagram for the month. Here, it is the 'Marsh' hexagram.

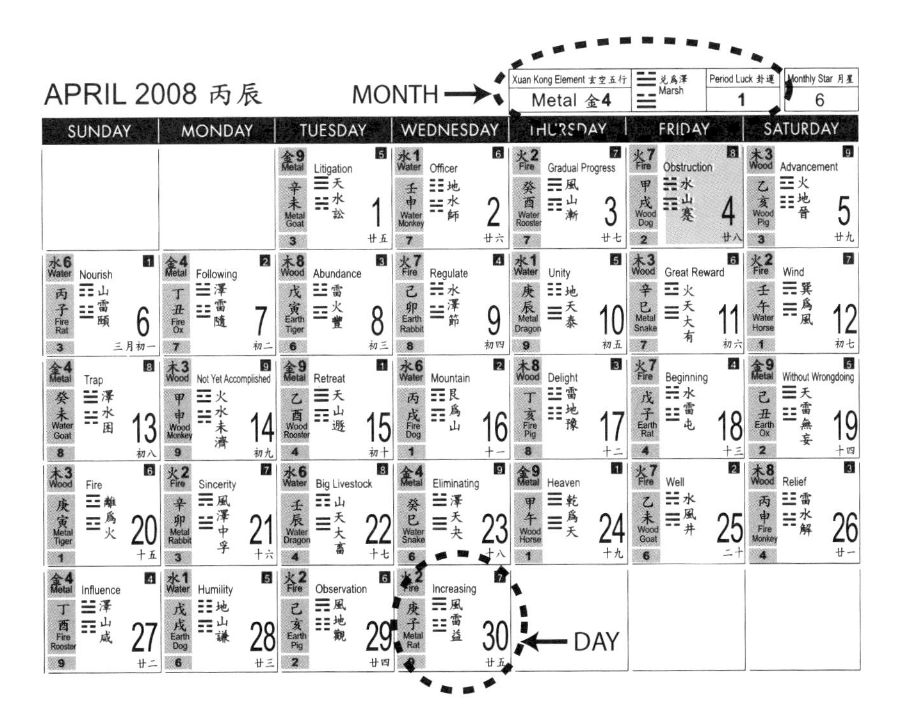

APRIL 2008 丙辰

MONTH → Xuan Kong Element 玄空五行: Metal 金4 | 兑為澤 Marsh | Period Luck 卦運: 1 | Monthly Star 月星: 6

SUNDAY	MONDAY	TUESDAY	WEDNESDAY	THURSDAY	FRIDAY	SATURDAY
		金9 Metal 5 Litigation 天水訟 辛未 Metal Goat 3 **1** 廿五	水1 Water 6 Officer 地水師 壬申 Water Monkey 7 **2** 廿六	火2 Fire 7 Gradual Progress 風山漸 癸酉 Water Rooster 7 **3** 廿七	火7 Fire 8 Obstruction 水山蹇 甲戌 Wood Dog 2 **4** 廿八	木3 Wood 9 Advancement 火地晉 乙亥 Wood Pig 3 **5** 廿九
水6 Water 1 Nourish 山雷頤 丙子 Fire Rat 3 **6** 三月初一	金4 Metal 2 Following 澤雷隨 丁丑 Fire Ox 7 **7** 初二	木8 Wood 3 Abundance 雷火豐 戊寅 Earth Tiger 6 **8** 初三	火7 Fire 4 Regulate 水澤節 己卯 Earth Rabbit 8 **9** 初四	水1 Water 5 Unity 地天泰 庚辰 Metal Dragon 9 **10** 初五	木3 Wood 6 Great Reward 火天大有 辛巳 Metal Snake 7 **11** 初六	火2 Fire 7 Wind 巽為風 壬午 Water Horse 1 **12** 初七
金4 Metal 8 Trap 澤水困 癸未 Water Goat 8 **13** 初八	木3 Wood 9 Not Yet Accomplished 火水未濟 甲申 Wood Monkey 9 **14** 初九	金9 Metal 1 Retreat 天山遯 乙酉 Wood Rooster 4 **15** 初十	水6 Water 2 Mountain 艮為山 丙戌 Fire Dog 1 **16** 十一	木8 Wood 3 Delight 雷地豫 丁亥 Fire Pig 8 **17** 十二	火7 Fire 4 Beginning 水雷屯 戊子 Earth Rat 4 **18** 十三	金9 Metal 5 Without Wrongdoing 天雷無妄 己丑 Earth Ox 2 **19** 十四
木3 Wood 6 Fire 離為火 庚寅 Metal Tiger 1 **20** 十五	火2 Fire 7 Sincerity 風澤中孚 辛卯 Metal Rabbit 3 **21** 十六	水6 Water 8 Big Livestock 山天大畜 壬辰 Water Dragon 4 **22** 十七	金4 Metal 9 Eliminating 澤天夬 癸巳 Water Snake 6 **23** 十八	金9 Metal 1 Heaven 乾為天 甲午 Wood Horse 1 **24** 十九	火7 Fire 2 Well 水風井 乙未 Wood Goat 6 **25** 二十	木8 Wood 3 Relief 雷水解 丙申 Fire Monkey 4 **26** 廿一
金4 Metal 4 Influence 澤山咸 丁酉 Fire Rooster 9 **27** 廿二	水1 Water 5 Humility 地山謙 戊戌 Earth Dog 6 **28** 廿三	火2 Fire 6 Observation 風地觀 己亥 Earth Pig 2 **29** 廿四	火2 Fire 7 Increasing 風雷益 庚子 Metal Rat **30** 廿五			

← DAY

Next to the Bing Chen Month Pillar, write the Hexagram 'Marsh' next to it, with the XK Element 4 above, and the Period Luck number 1 below

3. The same process is used to identify the Hexagram for the day

Date	BaZi			
	Hour	Day	Month	Year
30 April 2008 庚 子 Metal Rat	庚辰 Metal Dragon (水) 1 9 地天泰 Unity	庚子 Metal Rat (火) 2 9 風雷益 Increasing	丙辰 Fire Dragon (金) 4 1 兑爲澤 Marsh	戊子 Earth Rat (火) 7 4 水雷屯 Beginning

The Day pillar is Geng Zi, which is the 'Increasing' Hexagram. The XK Element is Fire (2), and the Period Luck number is 9. Write these down next to the Day Pillar.

Date	BaZi			
	Hour	Day	Month	Year
30 April 2008 庚 子 Metal Rat		庚子 Metal Rat (火) 2 9 風雷益 Increasing	丙辰 Fire Dragon (金) 4 1 兑爲澤 Marsh	戊子 Earth Rat (火) 7 4 水雷屯 Beginning

4. Finally, to plot the Hour Hexagram, refer to the Hour Table at the start of the Ten Thousand Year Calendar, appendix ix.

HOUR

戊 *Wu* Yang Earth / 癸 *Gui* Yin Water	丁 *Ding* Yin Fire / 壬 *Ren* Yang Water	丙 *Bing* Yang Fire / 辛 *Xin* Yin Metal	乙 *Yi* Yin Wood / 庚 *Geng* Yang Metal	甲 *Jia* Yang Wood / 己 *Ji* Yin Earth	日 Day / 時 Hour	
甲子 Wood Rat (水) 1 / 1 坤爲地 Earth	壬子 Water Rat (木) 8 / 1 震爲雷 Thunder	庚子 Metal Rat (火) 2 / 9 風雷益 Increasing	戊子 Earth Rat (火) 7 / 4 水雷屯 Beginning	丙子 Fire Rat (水) 6 / 3 山雷頤 Nourish	夜子 *Ye Zi* Late Rat	11 pm - 11.59 pm
壬子 Water Rat (木) 8 / 1 震爲雷 Thunder	庚子 Metal Rat (火) 2 / 9 風雷益 Increasing	戊子 Earth Rat (火) 7 / 4 水雷屯 Beginning	丙子 Fire Rat (水) 6 / 3 山雷頤 Nourish	甲子 Wood Rat (水) 1 / 1 坤爲地 Earth	子 *Zi* Early Rat	12 am - 12.59 am
癸丑 Water Ox (水) 6 / 8 山火賁 Beauty	辛丑 Metal Ox (水) 1 / 3 地火明夷 Dimming Light	己丑 Earth Ox (金) 9 / 2 天雷無妄 Without Wrongdoing	丁丑 Fire Ox (金) 4 / 7 澤雷隨 Following	乙丑 Wood Ox (木) 3 / 6 火雷噬嗑 Biting	丑 *Chou* Ox	1 am - 2.59 am
甲寅 Wood Tiger (火) 7 / 9 水火既濟 Accomplished	壬寅 Water Tiger (金) 9 / 7 天火同人 Fellowship	庚寅 Metal Tiger (木) 3 / 1 離爲火 Fire	戊寅 Earth Tiger (木) 8 / 6 雷火豐 Abundance	丙寅 Fire Tiger (火) 2 / 4 風火家人 Family	寅 *Yin* Tiger	3 am - 4.59 am
乙卯 Wood Rabbit (水) 1 / 4 地澤臨 Arriving	癸卯 Water Rabbit (木) 8 / 7 雷澤歸妹 Marrying Maiden	辛卯 Metal Rabbit (火) 2 / 3 風澤中孚 Sincerity	己卯 Earth Rabbit (火) 7 / 8 水澤節 Regulate	丁卯 Fire Rabbit (水) 6 / 9 山澤損 Decreasing	卯 *Mao* Rabbit	5 am - 6.59 am
丙辰 Fire Dragon (金) 4 / 1 兑爲澤 Marsh	甲辰 Wood Dragon (木) 3 / 2 火澤睽 Opposition	壬辰 Water Dragon (水) 6 / 4 山天大畜 Big Livestock	庚辰 Metal Dragon (水) 1 / 9 地天泰 Unity	戊辰 Earth Dragon (金) 9 / 6 天澤履 Tread	辰 *Chen* Dragon	7 am - 8.59 am
丁巳 Fire Snake (火) 2 / 8 風天小畜 Small Livestock	乙巳 Wood Snake (火) 7 / 3 水天需 Waiting	癸巳 Water Snake (金) 4 / 6 澤天夬 Eliminating	辛巳 Metal Snake (木) 3 / 7 火天大有 Great Reward	己巳 Earth Snake (木) 8 / 2 雷天大壯 Great Strength	巳 *Si* Snake	9 am - 10.59 am
戊午 Earth Horse (木) 3 / 4 火風鼎 The Cauldron	丙午 Fire Horse (金) 4 / 3 澤風大過 Great Exceeding	甲午 Wood Horse (金) 9 / 1 乾爲天 Heaven	壬午 Water Horse (火) 2 / 1 巽爲風 Wind	庚午 Metal Horse (木) 8 / 9 雷風恆 Consistency	午 *Wu* Horse	11 am - 12.59 am
己未 Earth Goat (水) 1 / 2 地風升 Rising	丁未 Fire Goat (水) 6 / 7 山風蠱 Poison	乙未 Wood Goat (火) 7 / 6 水風井 Well	癸未 Water Goat (金) 4 / 8 澤水困 Trap	辛未 Metal Goat (金) 9 / 3 天水訟 Litigation	未 *Wei* Goat	1 pm - 2.59 pm
庚申 Metal Monkey (火) 7 / 1 坎爲水 Water	戊申 Earth Monkey (火) 2 / 6 風水渙 Dispersing	丙申 Fire Monkey (木) 8 / 4 雷水解 Relief	甲申 Wood Monkey (木) 3 / 9 火水未濟 Not Yet Accomplished	壬申 Water Monkey (水) 1 / 7 地水師 Officer	申 *Shen* Monkey	3 pm - 4.59 pm
辛酉 Metal Rooster (木) 8 / 3 雷山小過 Lesser Exceeding	己酉 Earth Rooster (木) 3 / 8 火山旅 Travelling	丁酉 Fire Rooster (金) 4 / 9 澤山咸 Influence	乙酉 Wood Rooster (金) 9 / 4 天山遯 Retreat	癸酉 Water Rooster (火) 2 / 7 風山漸 Gradual Progress	酉 *You* Rooster	5 pm - 6.59pm
壬戌 Water Dog (金) 4 / 4 澤地萃 Gathering	庚戌 Metal Dog (金) 9 / 9 天地否 Stagnation	戊戌 Earth Dog (水) 1 / 6 地山謙 Humility	丙戌 Fire Dog (水) 6 / 1 艮爲山 Mountain	甲戌 Wood Dog (火) 7 / 2 水山蹇 Obstruction	戌 *Xu* Dog	7 pm - 8.59 pm
癸亥 Water Pig (水) 6 / 6 山地剝 Peel	辛亥 Metal Pig (火) 7 / 7 水地比 Alliance	己亥 Earth Pig (火) 2 / 2 風地觀 Observation	丁亥 Fire Pig (木) 8 / 8 雷地豫 Delight	乙亥 Wood Pig (木) 3 / 3 火地晉 Advancement	亥 *Hai* Pig	9 pm - 10.59 pm

The Hexagram for Geng Chen is 'Unity'. Write this next to the Hour Pillar, along with the XK Element number 1 above, and the Period Luck number 9 below the Hexagram. Here is what a complete Xuan Kong Da Gua Date will look like:

Date	BaZi			
	Hour	Day	Month	Year
30 April 2008 庚 子 Metal Rat	庚辰 Metal Dragon (水) 1 9 地天泰 Unity	庚子 Metal Rat (火) 2 9 風雷益 Increasing	丙辰 Fire Dragon (金) 4 1 兑爲澤 Marsh	戊子 Earth Rat (火) 7 4 水雷屯 Beginning

Example 2

1 Feb 1961, 1600 hrs

1. Refer to the Year Chapter of 1961 in the XK Ten Thousand Year Calendar

Date	BaZi			
	Hour	Day	Month	Year
1 Feb 1961				

The Year 1961 is Xin Chou, Metal Ox. The Hexagram is 'Dimming Light'. The XK Element number is 1. The Period Luck number is 3.

HOWEVER, because the Transition Date for every Solar Year is Feb 4th (Li Chun), Feb 1st of 1961 actually belongs to the previous year.

Therefore, we refer to 1960 instead.

1960 is a Geng Zi, Metal Rat year. The Hexagram is 'Increasing'. The XK Element number is 2. The Period Luck number is 9.

Write all these information in the Year column:

Date	BaZi			
	Hour	Day	Month	Year
1 Feb 1961 乙 丑 Wood Ox				庚 子 Metal Rat (火) 2 9 風雷益 Increasing

2. Since Feb 1st has not transited into the Tiger month, it belongs to the Ox month (January of 1961) – Ji Chou, Earth Ox. The Hexagram is 'Without Wrongdoing'. The XK Element number is 9. The Period Luck number is 2.

Write these in the Month column:

Date	BaZi			
	Hour	Day	Month	Year
1 Feb 1961 乙 丑 Wood Ox			己 丑 Earth Ox (金) 9 2 天雷無妄 Without Wrongdoing	庚 子 Metal Rat (火) 2 9 風雷益 Increasing

3. The Day of Feb 1st is indicated by the Table:

Date	BaZi			
	Hour	Day	Month	Year
1 Feb 1961 乙 丑 Wood Ox	甲 申 Wood Monkey (木) 3 9 火水未濟 Not Yet Accomplished	乙 丑 Wood Ox (木) 3 6 火雷噬嗑 Biting	己 丑 Earth Ox (金) 9 2 天雷無妄 Without Wrongdoing	庚 子 Metal Rat (火) 2 9 風雷益 Increasing

It is a Yi Chou Day, Wood Ox. The Hexagram is 'Biting'. The XK Element number is 3. The Period Luck number is 6.

APRIL 2008 丙辰

MONTH → | Xuan Kong Element 玄空五行: Metal 金4 | 兌為澤 Marsh | Period Luck 卦運: 1 | Monthly Star 月星: 6

SUNDAY	MONDAY	TUESDAY	WEDNESDAY	THURSDAY	FRIDAY	SATURDAY
		金9 Metal 5 Litigation 天水訟 辛未 Metal Goat 1 3 廿五	水1 Water 6 Officer 地水師 壬申 Water Monkey 2 7 廿六	火2 Fire 7 Gradual Progress 風山漸 癸酉 Water Rooster 3 7 廿七	火7 Fire 8 Obstruction 水山蹇 甲戌 Wood Dog 4 2 廿八	木3 Wood 9 Advancement 火地晉 乙亥 Wood Pig 5 3 廿九
水6 Water 1 Nourish 山雷頤 丙子 Fire Rat 6 3 三月初一	金4 Metal 2 Following 澤雷隨 丁丑 Fire Ox 7 7 初二	木8 Wood 3 Abundance 雷火豐 戊寅 Earth Tiger 8 6 初三	火7 Fire 4 Regulate 水澤節 己卯 Earth Rabbit 9 8 初四	水1 Water 5 Unity 地天泰 庚辰 Metal Dragon 10 9 初五	木3 Wood 6 Great Reward 火天大有 辛巳 Metal Snake 11 7 初六	火2 Fire 7 Wind 巽為風 壬午 Water Horse 12 1 初七
金4 Metal 8 Trap 澤水困 癸未 Water Goat 13 8 初八	木3 Wood 9 Not Yet Accomplished 火水未濟 甲申 Wood Monkey 14 9 初九	金9 Metal 1 Retreat 天山遯 乙酉 Wood Rooster 15 4 初十	水6 Water 2 Mountain 艮為山 丙戌 Fire Dog 16 1 十一	木8 Wood 3 Delight 雷地豫 丁亥 Fire Pig 17 8 十二	火7 Fire 4 Beginning 水雷屯 戊子 Earth Rat 18 4 十三	金9 Metal 5 Without Wrongdoing 天雷無妄 己丑 Earth Ox 19 2 十四
木3 Wood 6 Fire 離為火 庚寅 Metal Tiger 20 1 十五	火2 Fire 7 Sincerity 風澤中孚 辛卯 Metal Rabbit 21 3 十六	水6 Water 8 Big Livestock 山天大畜 壬辰 Water Dragon 22 4 十七	金4 Metal 9 Eliminating 澤天夬 癸巳 Water Snake 23 6 十八	金9 Metal 1 Heaven 乾為天 甲午 Wood Horse 24 1 十九	火7 Fire 2 Well 水風井 乙未 Wood Goat 25 6 二十	木8 Wood 3 Relief 雷水解 丙申 Fire Monkey 26 4 廿一
金4 Metal 4 Influence 澤山咸 丁酉 Fire Rooster 27 9 廿二	水1 Water 5 Humility 地山謙 戊戌 Earth Dog 28 6 廿三	火2 Fire 6 Observation 風地觀 己亥 Earth Pig 29 2 廿四	火2 Fire 7 Increasing 風雷益 庚子 Metal Rat 30 9 廿五	← DAY		

Write these in the Day column:

Date	BaZi			
	Hour	Day	Month	Year
1 Feb 1961 乙 丑 Wood Ox		乙丑 Wood Ox (木) 3 / 6 火雷噬嗑 Biting	己丑 Earth Ox (金) 9 / 2 天雷無妄 Without Wrongdoing	庚子 Metal Rat (火) 2 / 9 風雷益 Increasing

4. To plot the Hour, refer to the 'Five Rats Chasing Day' to establish the Hour Pillar and Hexagram on appendix ix:

戊 *Wu* Yang Earth 癸 *Gui* Yin Water	丁 *Ding* Yin Fire 壬 *Ren* Yang Water	丙 *Bing* Yang Fire 辛 *Xin* Yin Metal	乙 *Yi* Yin Wood 庚 *Geng* Yang Metal	甲 *Jia* Yang Wood 己 *Ji* Yin Earth	日 Day / 時 Hour	
(水) 1 甲子 Wood Rat 1 坤爲地 Earth	(木) 8 壬子 Water Rat 1 震爲雷 Thunder	(火) 2 庚子 Metal Rat 9 風雷益 Increasing	(火) 7 戊子 Earth Rat 4 水雷屯 Beginning	(水) 6 丙子 Fire Rat 3 山雷頤 Nourish	夜子 *Ye Zi* Late Rat	11 pm - 11.59 pm
(木) 8 壬子 Water Rat 1 震爲雷 Thunder	(火) 2 庚子 Metal Rat 9 風雷益 Increasing	(火) 7 戊子 Earth Rat 4 水雷屯 Beginning	(水) 6 丙子 Fire Rat 3 山雷頤 Nourish	(水) 1 甲子 Wood Rat 1 坤爲地 Earth	子 *Zi* Early Rat	12 am - 12.59 am
(水) 6 癸丑 Water Ox 8 山火賁 Beauty	(水) 1 辛丑 Metal Ox 3 地火明夷 Dimming Light	(金) 9 己丑 Earth Ox 2 天雷無妄 Without Wrongdoing	(金) 4 丁丑 Fire Ox 7 澤雷隨 Following	(木) 3 乙丑 Wood Ox 6 火雷噬嗑 Biting	丑 *Chou* Ox	1 am - 2.59 am
(火) 7 甲寅 Wood Tiger 9 水火既濟 Accomplished	(金) 9 壬寅 Water Tiger 7 天火同人 Fellowship	(木) 3 庚寅 Metal Tiger 1 離爲火 Fire	(木) 8 戊寅 Earth Tiger 6 雷火豐 Abundance	(火) 2 丙寅 Fire Tiger 4 風火家人 Family	寅 *Yin* Tiger	3 am - 4.59 am
(水) 1 乙卯 Wood Rabbit 4 地澤臨 Arriving	(木) 8 癸卯 Water Rabbit 7 雷澤歸妹 Marrying Maiden	(火) 2 辛卯 Metal Rabbit 3 風澤中孚 Sincerity	(火) 7 己卯 Earth Rabbit 8 水澤節 Regulate	(水) 6 丁卯 Fire Rabbit 9 山澤損 Decreasing	卯 *Mao* Rabbit	5 am - 6.59 am
(金) 4 丙辰 Fire Dragon 1 兌爲澤 Marsh	(木) 3 甲辰 Wood Dragon 2 火澤睽 Opposition	(水) 6 壬辰 Water Dragon 4 山天大畜 Big Livestock	(水) 1 庚辰 Metal Dragon 9 地天泰 Unity	(金) 9 戊辰 Earth Dragon 6 天澤履 Tread	辰 *Chen* Dragon	7 am - 8.59 am
(火) 2 丁巳 Fire Snake 8 風天小畜 Small Livestock	(火) 7 乙巳 Wood Snake 3 水天需 Waiting	(金) 4 癸巳 Water Snake 6 澤天夬 Eliminating	(木) 3 辛巳 Metal Snake 7 火天大有 Great Reward	(木) 8 己巳 Earth Snake 2 雷天大壯 Great Strength	巳 *Si* Snake	9 am - 10.59 am
(木) 3 戊午 Earth Horse 4 火風鼎 The Cauldron	(金) 4 丙午 Fire Horse 3 澤風大過 Great Exceeding	(金) 9 甲午 Wood Horse 1 乾爲天 Heaven	(火) 2 壬午 Water Horse 1 巽爲風 Wind	(木) 8 庚午 Metal Horse 9 雷風恒 Consistency	午 *Wu* Horse	11 am - 12.59 am
(水) 1 己未 Earth Goat 2 地風升 Rising	(水) 6 丁未 Fire Goat 7 山風蠱 Poison	(火) 7 乙未 Wood Goat 6 水風井 Well	(金) 4 癸未 Water Goat 8 澤水困 Trap	(金) 9 辛未 Metal Goat 3 天水訟 Litigation	未 *Wei* Goat	1 pm - 2.59 pm
(火) 7 庚申 Metal Monkey 1 坎爲水 Water	(火) 2 戊申 Earth Monkey 6 風水渙 Dispersing	(木) 8 丙申 Fire Monkey 4 雷水解 Relief	(木) 3 甲申 Wood Monkey 9 火水未濟 Not Yet Accomplished	(水) 1 壬申 Water Monkey 7 地水師 Officer	申 *Shen* Monkey	3 pm - 4.59 pm
(木) 8 辛酉 Metal Rooster 3 雷山小過 Lesser Exceeding	(木) 3 己酉 Earth Rooster 8 火山旅 Travelling	(金) 4 丁酉 Fire Rooster 9 澤山咸 Influence	(金) 9 乙酉 Wood Rooster 4 天山遯 Retreat	(火) 2 癸酉 Water Rooster 7 風山漸 Gradual Progress	酉 *You* Rooster	5 pm - 6.59pm
(金) 4 壬戌 Water Dog 4 澤地萃 Gathering	(金) 9 庚戌 Metal Dog 9 天地否 Stagnation	(水) 1 戊戌 Earth Dog 6 地山謙 Humility	(水) 6 丙戌 Fire Dog 1 艮爲山 Mountain	(火) 7 甲戌 Wood Dog 2 水山蹇 Obstruction	戌 *Xu* Dog	7 pm - 8.59 pm
(水) 6 癸亥 Water Pig 6 山地剝 Peel	(火) 7 辛亥 Metal Pig 7 水地比 Alliance	(火) 2 己亥 Earth Pig 2 風地觀 Observation	(木) 8 丁亥 Fire Pig 8 雷地豫 Delight	(木) 3 乙亥 Wood Pig 3 火地晉 Advancement	亥 *Hai* Pig	9 pm - 10.59 pm

HOUR

It is the Jia Shen, Wood Monkey Hour. The Hexagram is 'Not Accomplished'. The XK Element Number is 3. The Period Luck number is 9.

Here is what the complete Xuan Kong Da Gua Date will look like:

Date	BaZi			
	Hour	Day	Month	Year
1 Feb 1961 乙 丑 Wood Ox	甲 申 Wood Monkey (木) 3 9 火水未濟 Not Yet Accomplished	乙 丑 Wood Ox (木) 3 6 火雷噬嗑 Biting	己 丑 Earth Ox (金) 9 2 天雷無妄 Without Wrongdoing	庚 子 Metal Rat (火) 2 9 風雷益 Increasing

Xuan Kong Da Gua Ten Thousand Year Calendar 1950 - 2050

1950 庚寅

(*Geng Yin*) Metal Tiger

1950 庚寅 *(Geng Yin)* Metal Tiger

January 6 - February 3

February 4 - March 5

SE	S	SW
1	6	8
9	**2**	4
5	7	3

木**8** Wood
戊寅 Earth Tiger
6
Abundance
雷火豐

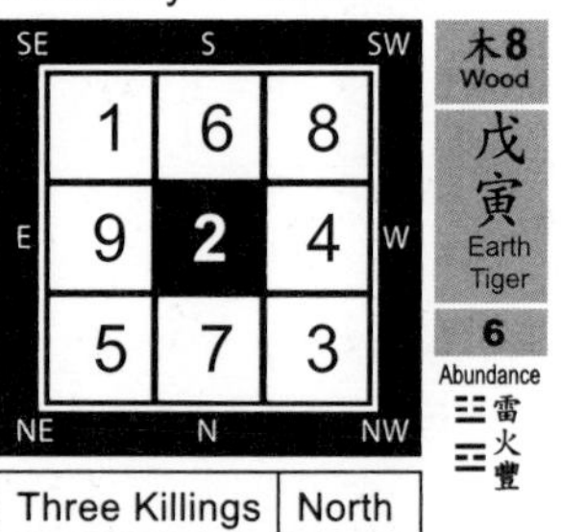

March 6 - April 4

SE	S	SW
9	5	7
8	**1**	3
4	6	2

火**7** Fire
己卯 Earth Rabbit
8
Regulate
水澤節

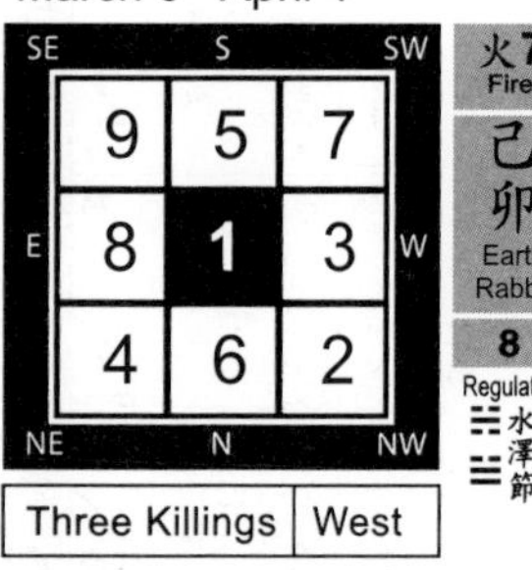

April 5 - May 5

SE	S	SW
8	4	6
7	**9**	2
3	5	1

水**1** Water
庚辰 Metal Dragon
9
Unity
地天泰

May 6 - June 5

SE	S	SW
7	3	5
6	**8**	1
2	4	9

木**3** Wood
辛巳 Metal Snake
7
Great Reward
火天大有

June 6 - July 7

SE	S	SW
6	2	4
5	**7**	9
1	3	8

火**2** Fire
壬午 Water Horse
1
Wind
巽爲風

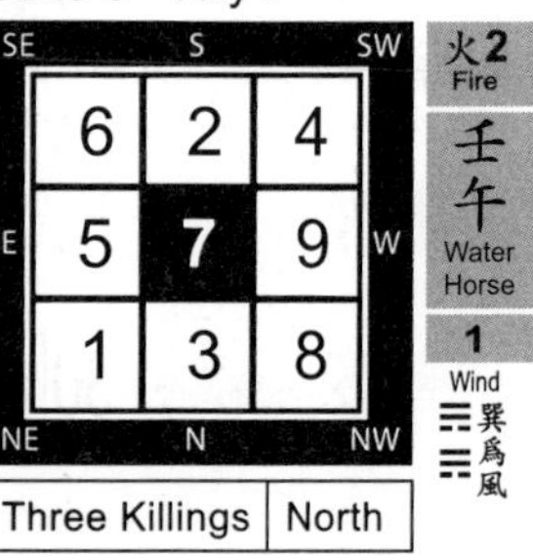

July 8 - August 7

SE	S	SW
5	1	3
4	**6**	8
9	2	7

金**4** Metal
癸未 Water Goat
8
Trap
澤水困

August 8 - September 7

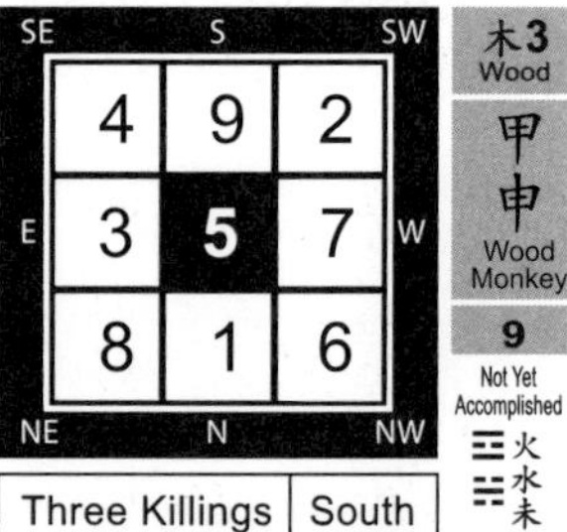

September 8 - October 8

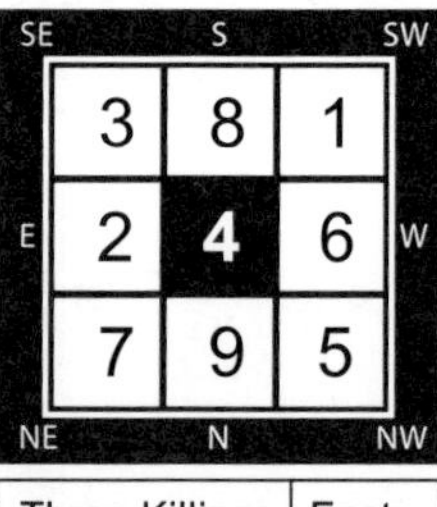

October 9 - November 7

SE	S	SW
2	7	9
1	**3**	5
6	8	4

水**6** Water
丙戌 Fire Dog
1
Mountain
艮爲山

November 8 - December 7

December 8 - January 5

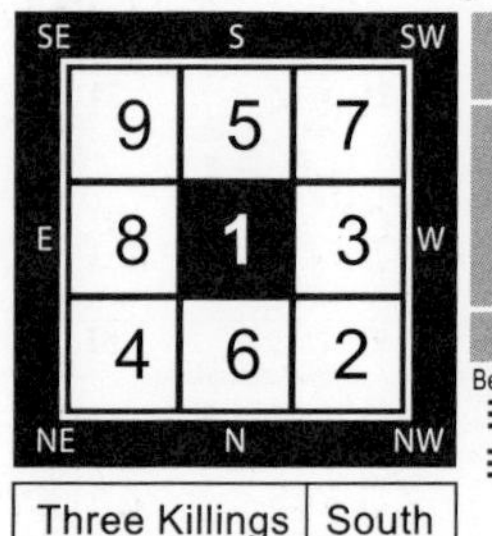

JANUARY 1950 丁丑

Xuan Kong Element 玄空五行	澤雷隨 Following	Period Luck 卦運	Monthly Star 月星
Metal 金4		7	3

SUNDAY	MONDAY	TUESDAY	WEDNESDAY	THURSDAY	FRIDAY	SATURDAY
木8 Wood Relief 9 丙申 Fire Monkey 雷水解 **1** 4 十三	金4 Metal Influence 1 丁酉 Fire Rooster 澤山咸 **2** 9 十四	水1 Water Humility 2 戊戌 Earth Dog 地山謙 **3** 6 十五	火2 Fire Observation 3 己亥 Earth Pig 風地觀 **4** 2 十六	火2 Fire Increasing 4 庚子 Metal Rat 風雷益 **5** 9 十七	水1 Water Dimming Light 5 辛丑 Metal Ox 地火明夷 **6** 3 十八	金9 Metal Fellowship 6 壬寅 Water Tiger 天火同人 **7** 7 十九
木8 Wood Marrying Maiden 7 癸卯 Water Rabbit 雷澤歸妹 **8** 7 二十	木3 Wood Opposition 8 甲辰 Wood Dragon 火澤睽 **9** 2 廿一	火7 Fire Waiting 9 乙巳 Wood Snake 水天需 **10** 3 廿二	金4 Metal Great Exceeding 1 丙午 Fire Horse 澤風大過 **11** 3 廿三	水6 Water Poison 2 丁未 Fire Goat 山風蠱 **12** 7 廿四	火2 Fire Dispersing 3 戊申 Earth Monkey 風水渙 **13** 6 廿五	木3 Wood Travelling 4 己酉 Earth Rooster 火山旅 **14** 8 廿六
金9 Metal Stagnation 5 庚戌 Metal Dog 天地否 **15** 9 廿七	火7 Fire Alliance 6 辛亥 Metal Pig 水地比 **16** 7 廿八	木8 Wood Thunder 7 壬子 Water Rat 震爲雷 **17** 1 廿九	水6 Water Beauty 8 癸丑 Water Ox 山火賁 **18** 8 十二月初一	火7 Fire Accomplished 9 甲寅 Wood Tiger 水火既濟 **19** 9 初二	水1 Water Arriving 1 乙卯 Wood Rabbit 地澤臨 **20** 4 初三	金4 Metal Marsh 2 丙辰 Fire Dragon 兌爲澤 **21** 1 初四
火2 Fire Small Livestock 3 丁巳 Fire Snake 風天小畜 **22** 8 初五	木3 Wood The Cauldron 4 戊午 Earth Horse 火風鼎 **23** 4 初六	水1 Water Rising 5 己未 Earth Goat 地風升 **24** 2 初七	火7 Fire Water 6 庚申 Metal Monkey 坎爲水 **25** 1 初八	木8 Wood Lesser Exceeding 7 辛酉 Metal Rooster 雷山小過 **26** 3 初九	金4 Metal Gathering 8 壬戌 Water Dog 澤地萃 **27** 4 初十	水6 Water Peel 9 癸亥 Water Pig 山地剝 **28** 6 十一
水1 Water Earth 1 甲子 Wood Rat 坤爲地 **29** 1 十二	木3 Wood Biting 2 乙丑 Wood Ox 火雷噬嗑 **30** 6 十三	火2 Fire Family 3 丙寅 Fire Tiger 風火家人 **31** 4 十四				

FEBRUARY 1950 戊寅

Xuan Kong Element 玄空五行	雷火豐 Abundance	Period Luck 卦運	Monthly Star 月星
Wood 木8		6	2

SUNDAY	MONDAY	TUESDAY	WEDNESDAY	THURSDAY	FRIDAY	SATURDAY
			水6 Water Decreasing 4 丁卯 Fire Rabbit 山澤損 **1** 9 十五	金9 Metal Tread 5 戊辰 Earth Dragon 天澤履 **2** 6 十六	木8 Wood Great Strength 6 己巳 Earth Snake 雷天大壯 **3** 2 十七	木8 Wood Consistency 7 庚午 Metal Horse 雷風恆 **4** 9 十八
金9 Metal Litigation 8 辛未 Metal Goat 天水訟 **5** 3 十九	水1 Water Officer 9 壬申 Water Monkey 地水師 **6** 7 二十	火2 Fire Gradual Progress 1 癸酉 Water Rooster 風山漸 **7** 7 廿一	火7 Fire Obstruction 2 甲戌 Wood Dog 水山蹇 **8** 2 廿二	木3 Wood Advancement 3 乙亥 Wood Pig 火地晉 **9** 3 廿三	水6 Water Nourish 4 丙子 Fire Rat 山雷頤 **10** 3 廿四	金4 Metal Following 5 丁丑 Fire Ox 澤雷隨 **11** 7 廿五
木8 Wood Abundance 6 戊寅 Earth Tiger 雷火豐 **12** 6 廿六	火7 Fire Regulate 7 己卯 Earth Rabbit 水澤節 **13** 8 廿七	水1 Water Unity 8 庚辰 Metal Dragon 地天泰 **14** 9 廿八	木3 Wood Great Reward 9 辛巳 Metal Snake 火天大有 **15** 7 廿九	火2 Fire Wind 1 壬午 Water Horse 巽爲風 **16** 1 三十	金4 Metal Trap 2 癸未 Water Goat 澤水困 **17** 8 正月初一	木3 Wood Not Yet Accomplished 3 甲申 Wood Monkey 火水未濟 **18** 9 初二
金9 Metal Retreat 4 乙酉 Wood Rooster 天山遯 **19** 4 初三	水6 Water Mountain 5 丙戌 Fire Dog 艮爲山 **20** 1 初四	木8 Wood Delight 6 丁亥 Fire Pig 雷地豫 **21** 8 初五	火7 Fire Beginning 7 戊子 Earth Rat 水雷屯 **22** 4 初六	金9 Metal Without Wrongdoing 8 己丑 Earth Ox 天雷無妄 **23** 2 初七	木3 Wood Fire 9 庚寅 Metal Tiger 離爲火 **24** 1 初八	火2 Fire Sincerity 1 辛卯 Metal Rabbit 風澤中孚 **25** 3 初九
水6 Water Big Livestock 2 壬辰 Water Dragon 山天大畜 **26** 4 初十	金4 Metal Eliminating 3 癸巳 Water Snake 澤天夬 **27** 6 十一	金9 Metal Heaven 4 甲午 Wood Horse 乾爲天 **28** 1 十二				

MARCH 1950 己卯

Xuan Kong Element 玄空五行	水澤節 Regulate	Period Luck 卦運	Monthly Star 月星
Fire 火7		8	1

SUNDAY	MONDAY	TUESDAY	WEDNESDAY	THURSDAY	FRIDAY	SATURDAY
			火7 Fire 5 Well 水風井 乙未 Wood Goat 1 十三 6	木8 Wood 6 Relief 雷水解 丙申 Fire Monkey 2 十四 4	金4 Metal 7 Influence 澤山咸 丁酉 Fire Rooster 3 十五 9	水1 Water 8 Humility 地山謙 戊戌 Earth Dog 4 十六 6
火2 Fire 9 Observation 風地觀 己亥 Earth Pig 5 十七 2	火2 Fire 1 Increasing 風雷益 庚子 Metal Rat 6 十八 9	水1 Water 2 Dimming Light 地火明夷 辛丑 Metal Ox 7 十九 3	金9 Metal 3 Fellowship 天火同人 壬寅 Water Tiger 8 二十 7	木8 Wood 4 Marrying Maiden 雷澤歸妹 癸卯 Water Rabbit 9 廿一 7	木3 Wood 5 Opposition 火澤睽 甲辰 Wood Dragon 10 廿二 2	火7 Fire 6 Waiting 水天需 乙巳 Wood Snake 11 廿三 3
金4 Metal 7 Great Exceeding 澤風大過 丙午 Fire Horse 12 廿四 3	水6 Water 8 Poison 山風蠱 丁未 Fire Goat 13 廿五 7	火2 Fire 9 Dispersing 風水渙 戊申 Earth Monkey 14 廿六 6	木3 Wood 1 Travelling 火山旅 己酉 Earth Rooster 15 廿七 8	金9 Metal 2 Stagnation 天地否 庚戌 Metal Dog 16 廿八 9	火7 Fire 3 Alliance 水地比 辛亥 Metal Pig 17 廿九 7	木8 Wood 4 Thunder 震爲雷 壬子 Water Rat 18 二月初一 1
水6 Water 5 Beauty 山火賁 癸丑 Water Ox 19 初二 8	火7 Fire 6 Accomplished 水火既濟 甲寅 Wood Tiger 20 初三 9	水1 Water 7 Arriving 地澤臨 乙卯 Wood Rabbit 21 初四 4	金4 Metal 8 Marsh 兑爲澤 丙辰 Fire Dragon 22 初五 1	火2 Fire 9 Small Livestock 風天小畜 丁巳 Fire Snake 23 初六 8	木3 Wood 1 The Cauldron 火風鼎 戊午 Earth Horse 24 初七 4	水1 Water 2 Rising 地風升 己未 Earth Goat 25 初八 2
火7 Fire 3 Water 坎爲水 庚申 Metal Monkey 26 初九 1	木8 Wood 4 Lesser Exceeding 雷山小過 辛酉 Metal Rooster 27 初十 3	金4 Metal 5 Gathering 澤地萃 壬戌 Water Dog 28 十一 4	水6 Water 6 Peel 山地剝 癸亥 Water Pig 29 十二 6	水1 Water 7 Earth 坤爲地 甲子 Wood Rat 30 十三 1	木3 Wood 8 Biting 火雷噬嗑 乙丑 Wood Ox 31 十四 6	

APRIL 1950 庚辰

Xuan Kong Element 玄空五行	地天泰 Unity	Period Luck 卦運	Monthly Star 月星
Water 水1		9	9

SUNDAY	MONDAY	TUESDAY	WEDNESDAY	THURSDAY	FRIDAY	SATURDAY
火7 Fire 2 Well 水風井 乙未 Wood Goat 30 十四 6						火2 Fire 9 Family 風火家人 丙寅 Fire Tiger 1 十五 4
水6 Water 1 Decreasing 山澤損 丁卯 Fire Rabbit 2 十六 9	金9 Metal 2 Tread 天澤履 戊辰 Earth Dragon 3 十七 6	木8 Wood 3 Great Strength 雷天大壯 己巳 Earth Snake 4 十八 2	木8 Wood 4 Consistency 雷風恒 庚午 Metal Horse 5 十九 9	金9 Metal 5 Litigation 天水訟 辛未 Metal Goat 6 二十 3	水1 Water 6 Officer 地水師 壬申 Water Monkey 7 廿一 7	火2 Fire 7 Gradual Progress 風山漸 癸酉 Water Rooster 8 廿二 7
火7 Fire 8 Obstruction 水山蹇 甲戌 Wood Dog 9 廿三 2	木3 Wood 9 Advancement 火地晉 乙亥 Wood Pig 10 廿四 3	水6 Water 1 Nourish 山雷頤 丙子 Fire Rat 11 廿五 3	金4 Metal 2 Following 澤雷隨 丁丑 Fire Ox 12 廿六 7	木8 Wood 3 Abundance 雷火豐 戊寅 Earth Tiger 13 廿七 6	火7 Fire 4 Regulate 水澤節 己卯 Earth Rabbit 14 廿八 8	水1 Water 5 Unity 地天泰 庚辰 Metal Dragon 15 廿九 9
木3 Wood 6 Great Reward 火天大有 辛巳 Metal Snake 16 三十 7	火2 Fire 7 Wind 巽爲風 壬午 Water Horse 17 三月初一 1	金4 Metal 8 Trap 澤水困 癸未 Water Goat 18 初二 8	木3 Wood 9 Not Yet Accomplished 火水未濟 甲申 Wood Monkey 19 初三 9	金9 Metal 1 Retreat 天山遯 乙酉 Wood Rooster 20 初四 4	水6 Water 2 Mountain 艮爲山 丙戌 Fire Dog 21 初五 1	木8 Wood 3 Delight 雷地豫 丁亥 Fire Pig 22 初六 8
火7 Fire 4 Beginning 水雷屯 戊子 Earth Rat 23 初七 4	金9 Metal 5 Without Wrongdoing 天雷無妄 己丑 Earth Ox 24 初八 2	木3 Wood 6 Fire 離爲火 庚寅 Metal Tiger 25 初九 1	火2 Fire 7 Sincerity 風澤中孚 辛卯 Metal Rabbit 26 初十 3	水6 Water 8 Big Livestock 山天大畜 壬辰 Water Dragon 27 十一 4	金4 Metal 9 Eliminating 澤天夬 癸巳 Water Snake 28 十二 6	金9 Metal 1 Heaven 乾爲天 甲午 Wood Horse 29 十三 1

MAY 1950 辛巳

Xuan Kong Element 玄空五行	火天大有 Great Reward	Period Luck 卦運	Monthly Star 月星
Wood 木3		7	8

SUNDAY	MONDAY	TUESDAY	WEDNESDAY	THURSDAY	FRIDAY	SATURDAY
	木8 Wood 3 Relief 雷水解 丙申 Fire Monkey 1 4 十五	金4 Metal 4 Influence 澤山咸 丁酉 Fire Rooster 2 9 十六	水1 Water 5 Humility 地山謙 戊戌 Earth Dog 3 6 十七	火2 Fire 6 Observation 風地觀 己亥 Earth Pig 4 2 十八	火2 Fire 7 Increasing 風雷益 庚子 Metal Rat 5 9 十九	水1 Water 8 Dimming Light 地火明夷 辛丑 Metal Ox 6 3 二十
金9 Metal 9 Fellowship 天火同人 壬寅 Water Tiger 7 7 廿一	木8 Wood 1 Marrying Maiden 雷澤歸妹 癸卯 Water Rabbit 8 7 廿二	木3 Wood 2 Opposition 火澤睽 甲辰 Wood Dragon 9 2 廿三	火7 Fire 3 Waiting 水天需 乙巳 Wood Snake 10 3 廿四	金4 Metal 4 Great Exceeding 澤風大過 丙午 Fire Horse 11 3 廿五	水6 Water 5 Poison 山風蠱 丁未 Fire Goat 12 7 廿六	火2 Fire 6 Dispersing 風水渙 戊申 Earth Monkey 13 6 廿七
木3 Wood 7 Travelling 火山旅 己酉 Earth Rooster 14 8 廿八	金9 Metal 8 Stagnation 天地否 庚戌 Metal Dog 15 9 廿九	火7 Fire 9 Alliance 水地比 辛亥 Metal Pig 16 7 三十	木8 Wood 1 Thunder 震爲雷 壬子 Water Rat 17 1 四月初一	水6 Water 2 Beauty 山火賁 癸丑 Water Ox 18 8 初二	火7 Fire 3 Accomplished 水火既濟 甲寅 Wood Tiger 19 9 初三	水1 Water 4 Arriving 地澤臨 乙卯 Wood Rabbit 20 4 初四
金4 Metal 5 Marsh 兌爲澤 丙辰 Fire Dragon 21 1 初五	火2 Fire 6 Small Livestock 風天小畜 丁巳 Fire Snake 22 8 初六	木3 Wood 7 The Cauldron 火風鼎 戊午 Earth Horse 23 4 初七	水1 Water 8 Rising 地風升 己未 Earth Goat 24 2 初八	火7 Fire 9 Water 坎爲水 庚申 Metal Monkey 25 1 初九	木8 Wood 1 Lesser Exceeding 雷山小過 辛酉 Metal Rooster 26 3 初十	金4 Metal 2 Gathering 澤地萃 壬戌 Water Dog 27 4 十一
水6 Water 3 Peel 山地剝 癸亥 Water Pig 28 6 十二	水1 Water 4 Earth 坤爲地 甲子 Wood Rat 29 1 十三	木3 Wood 5 Biting 火雷噬嗑 乙丑 Wood Ox 30 6 十四	火2 Fire 6 Family 風火家人 丙寅 Fire Tiger 31 4 十五			

JUNE 1950 壬午

Xuan Kong Element 玄空五行	巽爲風 Wind	Period Luck 卦運	Monthly Star 月星
Fire 火2		1	7

SUNDAY	MONDAY	TUESDAY	WEDNESDAY	THURSDAY	FRIDAY	SATURDAY
				水6 Water 7 Decreasing 山澤損 丁卯 Fire Rabbit 1 9 十六	金9 Metal 8 Tread 天澤履 戊辰 Earth Dragon 2 6 十七	木8 Wood 9 Great Strength 雷天大壯 己巳 Earth Snake 3 2 十八
木8 Wood 1 Consistency 雷風恆 庚午 Metal Horse 4 9 十九	金9 Metal 2 Litigation 天水訟 辛未 Metal Goat 5 3 二十	水1 Water 3 Officer 地水師 壬申 Water Monkey 6 7 廿一	火2 Fire 4 Gradual Progress 風山漸 癸酉 Water Rooster 7 7 廿二	火7 Fire 5 Obstruction 水山蹇 甲戌 Wood Dog 8 2 廿三	木3 Wood 6 Advancement 火地晉 乙亥 Wood Pig 9 3 廿四	水6 Water 7 Nourish 山雷頤 丙子 Fire Rat 10 3 廿五
金4 Metal 8 Following 澤雷隨 丁丑 Fire Ox 11 7 廿六	木8 Wood 9 Abundance 雷火豐 戊寅 Earth Tiger 12 6 廿七	火7 Fire 1 Regulate 水澤節 己卯 Earth Rabbit 13 8 廿八	水1 Water 2 Unity 地天泰 庚辰 Metal Dragon 14 9 廿九	木3 Wood 3 Great Reward 火天大有 辛巳 Metal Snake 15 7 五月初一	火2 Fire 4 Wind 巽爲風 壬午 Water Horse 16 1 初二	金4 Metal 5 Trap 澤水困 癸未 Water Goat 17 8 初三
木3 Wood 6 Not Yet Accomplished 火水未濟 甲申 Wood Monkey 18 9 初四	金9 Metal 7 Retreat 天山遯 乙酉 Wood Rooster 19 4 初五	水6 Water 8 Mountain 艮爲山 丙戌 Fire Dog 20 1 初六	木8 Wood 9 Delight 雷地豫 丁亥 Fire Pig 21 8 初七	火7 Fire 1/9 Beginning 水雷屯 戊子 Earth Rat 22 4 初八	金9 Metal 8 Without Wrongdoing 天雷無妄 己丑 Earth Ox 23 2 初九	木3 Wood 7 Fire 離爲火 庚寅 Metal Tiger 24 1 初十
火2 Fire 6 Sincerity 風澤中孚 辛卯 Metal Rabbit 25 3 十一	水6 Water 5 Big Livestock 山天大畜 壬辰 Water Dragon 26 4 十二	金4 Metal 4 Eliminating 澤天夬 癸巳 Water Snake 27 6 十三	金9 Metal 3 Heaven 乾爲天 甲午 Wood Horse 28 1 十四	火7 Fire 2 Well 水風井 乙未 Wood Goat 29 6 十五	木8 Wood 1 Relief 雷水解 丙申 Fire Monkey 30 4 十六	

JULY 1950 癸未

Xuan Kong Element 玄空五行	澤水困 Trap	Period Luck 卦運	Monthly Star 月星
Metal 金4		8	6

SUNDAY	MONDAY	TUESDAY	WEDNESDAY	THURSDAY	FRIDAY	SATURDAY
火2 Fire 7 Family 風火家人 丙寅 Fire Tiger 4 30 十六	水6 Water 6 Decreasing 山澤損 丁卯 Fire Rabbit 9 31 十七					金4 Metal 9 Influence 澤山咸 丁酉 Fire Rooster 9 1 十七
水1 Water 8 Humility 地山謙 戊戌 Earth Dog 6 2 十八	火2 Fire 7 Observation 風地觀 己亥 Earth Pig 2 3 十九	火2 Fire 6 Increasing 風雷益 庚子 Metal Rat 9 4 二十	水1 Water 5 Dimming Light 地火明夷 辛丑 Metal Ox 3 5 廿一	金9 Metal 4 Fellowship 天火同人 壬寅 Water Tiger 7 6 廿二	木8 Wood 3 Marrying Maiden 雷澤歸妹 癸卯 Water Rabbit 7 7 廿三	木3 Wood 2 Opposition 火澤睽 甲辰 Wood Dragon 2 8 廿四
火7 Fire 1 Waiting 水天需 乙巳 Wood Snake 3 9 廿五	金4 Metal 9 Great Exceeding 澤風大過 丙午 Fire Horse 3 10 廿六	水6 Water 8 Poison 山風蠱 丁未 Fire Goat 7 11 廿七	火2 Fire 7 Dispersing 風水渙 戊申 Earth Monkey 6 12 廿八	木3 Wood 6 Travelling 火山旅 己酉 Earth Rooster 8 13 廿九	金9 Metal 5 Stagnation 天地否 庚戌 Metal Dog 9 14 三十	火7 Fire 4 Alliance 水地比 辛亥 Metal Pig 7 15 六月初一
木8 Wood 3 Thunder 震爲雷 壬子 Water Rat 1 16 初二	水6 Water 2 Beauty 山火賁 癸丑 Water Ox 8 17 初三	火7 Fire 1 Accomplished 水火既濟 甲寅 Wood Tiger 9 18 初四	水1 Water 9 Arriving 地澤臨 乙卯 Wood Rabbit 4 19 初五	金4 Metal 8 Marsh 兑爲澤 丙辰 Fire Dragon 1 20 初六	火2 Fire 7 Small Livestock 風天小畜 丁巳 Fire Snake 8 21 初七	木3 Wood 6 The Cauldron 火風鼎 戊午 Earth Horse 4 22 初八
水1 Water 5 Rising 地風升 己未 Earth Goat 2 23 初九	火7 Fire 4 Water 坎爲水 庚申 Metal Monkey 1 24 初十	木8 Wood 3 Lesser Exceeding 雷山小過 辛酉 Metal Rooster 3 25 十一	金4 Metal 2 Gathering 澤地萃 壬戌 Water Dog 4 26 十二	水6 Water 1 Peel 山地剝 癸亥 Water Pig 6 27 十三	水1 Water 9 Earth 坤爲地 甲子 Wood Rat 1 28 十四	木3 Wood 8 Biting 火雷噬嗑 乙丑 Wood Ox 6 29 十五

AUGUST 1950 甲申

Xuan Kong Element 玄空五行	火水未濟 Not Yet Accomplished	Period Luck 卦運	Monthly Star 月星
Wood 木3		9	5

SUNDAY	MONDAY	TUESDAY	WEDNESDAY	THURSDAY	FRIDAY	SATURDAY
		金9 Metal 5 Tread 天澤履 戊辰 Earth Dragon 6 1 十八	木8 Wood 4 Great Strength 雷天大壯 己巳 Earth Snake 2 2 十九	木8 Wood 3 Consistency 雷風恆 庚午 Metal Horse 9 3 二十	金9 Metal 2 Litigation 天水訟 辛未 Metal Goat 3 4 廿一	水1 Water 1 Officer 地水師 壬申 Water Monkey 7 5 廿二
火2 Fire 9 Gradual Progress 風山漸 癸酉 Water Rooster 7 6 廿三	火7 Fire 8 Obstruction 水山蹇 甲戌 Wood Dog 2 7 廿四	木3 Wood 7 Advancement 火地晉 乙亥 Wood Pig 3 8 廿五	水6 Water 6 Nourish 山雷頤 丙子 Fire Rat 3 9 廿六	金4 Metal 5 Following 澤雷隨 丁丑 Fire Ox 7 10 廿七	木8 Wood 4 Abundance 雷火豐 戊寅 Earth Tiger 6 11 廿八	火7 Fire 3 Regulate 水澤節 己卯 Earth Rabbit 8 12 廿九
水1 Water 2 Unity 地天泰 庚辰 Metal Dragon 9 13 三十	木3 Wood 1 Great Reward 火天大有 辛巳 Metal Snake 7 14 七月初一	火2 Fire 9 Wind 巽爲風 壬午 Water Horse 1 15 初二	金4 Metal 8 Trap 澤水困 癸未 Water Goat 8 16 初三	木3 Wood 7 Not Yet Accomplished 火水未濟 甲申 Wood Monkey 9 17 初四	金9 Metal 6 Retreat 天山遯 乙酉 Wood Rooster 4 18 初五	水6 Water 5 Mountain 艮爲山 丙戌 Fire Dog 1 19 初六
木8 Wood 4 Delight 雷地豫 丁亥 Fire Pig 8 20 初七	火7 Fire 3 Beginning 水雷屯 戊子 Earth Rat 4 21 初八	金9 Metal 2 Without Wrongdoing 天雷無妄 己丑 Earth Ox 2 22 初九	木3 Wood 1 Fire 離爲火 庚寅 Metal Tiger 1 23 初十	火2 Fire 9 Sincerity 風澤中孚 辛卯 Metal Rabbit 3 24 十一	水6 Water 8 Big Livestock 山天大畜 壬辰 Water Dragon 4 25 十二	金4 Metal 7 Eliminating 澤天夬 癸巳 Water Snake 6 26 十三
金9 Metal 6 Heaven 乾爲天 甲午 Wood Horse 1 27 十四	火7 Fire 5 Well 水風井 乙未 Wood Goat 6 28 十五	木8 Wood 4 Relief 雷水解 丙申 Fire Monkey 4 29 十六	金4 Metal 3 Influence 澤山咸 丁酉 Fire Rooster 9 30 十七	水1 Water 2 Humility 地山謙 戊戌 Earth Dog 6 31 十八		

SEPTEMBER 1950 乙酉

Xuan Kong Element 玄空五行	天山遯 Retreat	Period Luck 卦運	Monthly Star 月星
Metal 金9		4	4

SUNDAY	MONDAY	TUESDAY	WEDNESDAY	THURSDAY	FRIDAY	SATURDAY
					1 十九 火2 Fire [1] Observation 風地觀 己亥 Earth Pig 2	**2** 二十 火2 Fire [9] Increasing 風雷益 庚子 Metal Rat 9
3 廿一 水1 Water [8] Dimming Light 地火明夷 辛丑 Metal Ox 3	**4** 廿二 金9 Metal [7] Fellowship 天火同人 壬寅 Water Tiger 7	**5** 廿三 木8 Wood [6] Marrying Maiden 雷澤歸妹 癸卯 Water Rabbit 7	**6** 廿四 木3 Wood [5] Opposition 火澤睽 甲辰 Wood Dragon 2	**7** 廿五 火7 Fire [4] Waiting 水天需 乙巳 Wood Snake 3	**8** 廿六 金4 Metal [3] Great Exceeding 澤風大過 丙午 Fire Horse 3	**9** 廿七 水6 Water [2] Poison 山風蠱 丁未 Fire Goat 7
10 廿八 火2 Fire [1] Dispersing 風水渙 戊申 Earth Monkey 6	**11** 廿九 木3 Wood [9] Travelling 火山旅 己酉 Earth Rooster 8	**12** 八月初一 金9 Metal [8] Stagnation 天地否 庚戌 Metal Dog 9	**13** 初二 火7 Fire [7] Alliance 水地比 辛亥 Metal Pig 7	**14** 初三 木8 Wood [6] Thunder 震爲雷 壬子 Water Rat 1	**15** 初四 水6 Water [5] Beauty 山火賁 癸丑 Water Ox 8	**16** 初五 火7 Fire [4] Accomplished 水火既濟 甲寅 Wood Tiger 9
17 初六 水1 Water [3] Arriving 地澤臨 乙卯 Wood Rabbit 4	**18** 初七 金4 Metal [2] Marsh 兌爲澤 丙辰 Fire Dragon 1	**19** 初八 火2 Fire [1] Small Livestock 風天小畜 丁巳 Fire Snake 8	**20** 初九 木3 Wood [9] The Cauldron 火風鼎 戊午 Earth Horse 4	**21** 初十 水1 Water [8] Rising 地風升 己未 Earth Goat 2	**22** 十一 火7 Fire [7] Water 坎爲水 庚申 Metal Monkey 1	**23** 十二 木8 Wood [6] Lesser Exceeding 雷山小過 辛酉 Metal Rooster 3
24 十三 金4 Metal [5] Gathering 澤地萃 壬戌 Water Dog 4	**25** 十四 水6 Water [4] Peel 山地剝 癸亥 Water Pig 6	**26** 十五 水1 Water [3] Earth 坤爲地 甲子 Wood Rat 1	**27** 十六 木3 Wood [2] Biting 火雷噬嗑 乙丑 Wood Ox 6	**28** 十七 火2 Fire [1] Family 風火家人 丙寅 Fire Tiger 4	**29** 十八 水6 Water [9] Decreasing 山澤損 丁卯 Fire Rabbit 9	**30** 十九 金9 Metal [8] Tread 天澤履 戊辰 Earth Dragon 6

OCTOBER 1950 丙戌

Xuan Kong Element 玄空五行	艮爲山 Mountain	Period Luck 卦運	Monthly Star 月星
Water 水6		1	3

SUNDAY	MONDAY	TUESDAY	WEDNESDAY	THURSDAY	FRIDAY	SATURDAY
1 二十 木8 Wood [7] Great Strength 雷天大壯 己巳 Earth Snake 2	**2** 廿一 木8 Wood [6] Consistency 雷風恒 庚午 Metal Horse 9	**3** 廿二 金9 Metal [5] Litigation 天水訟 辛未 Metal Goat 3	**4** 廿三 水1 Water [4] Officer 地水師 壬申 Water Monkey 7	**5** 廿四 火2 Fire [3] Gradual Progress 風山漸 癸酉 Water Rooster 7	**6** 廿五 火7 Fire [2] Obstruction 水山蹇 甲戌 Wood Dog 2	**7** 廿六 木3 Wood [1] Advancement 火地晉 乙亥 Wood Pig 3
8 廿七 水6 Water [9] Nourish 山雷頤 丙子 Fire Rat 3	**9** 廿八 金4 Metal [8] Following 澤雷隨 丁丑 Fire Ox 7	**10** 廿九 木8 Wood [7] Abundance 雷火豐 戊寅 Earth Tiger 6	**11** 九月初一 火7 Fire [6] Regulate 水澤節 己卯 Earth Rabbit 8	**12** 初二 水1 Water [5] Unity 地天泰 庚辰 Metal Dragon 9	**13** 初三 木3 Wood [4] Great Reward 火天大有 辛巳 Metal Snake 7	**14** 初四 火2 Fire [3] Wind 巽爲風 壬午 Water Horse 1
15 初五 金4 Metal [2] Trap 澤水困 癸未 Water Goat 8	**16** 初六 木3 Wood [1] Not Yet Accomplished 火水未濟 甲申 Wood Monkey 9	**17** 初七 金9 Metal [9] Retreat 天山遯 乙酉 Wood Rooster 4	**18** 初八 水6 Water [8] Mountain 艮爲山 丙戌 Fire Dog 1	**19** 初九 木8 Wood [7] Delight 雷地豫 丁亥 Fire Pig 8	**20** 初十 火7 Fire [6] Beginning 水雷屯 戊子 Earth Rat 4	**21** 十一 金9 Metal [5] Without Wrongdoing 天雷無妄 己丑 Earth Ox 2
22 十二 木3 Wood [4] Fire 離爲火 庚寅 Metal Tiger 1	**23** 十三 火2 Fire [3] Sincerity 風澤中孚 辛卯 Metal Rabbit 3	**24** 十四 水6 Water [2] Big Livestock 山天大畜 壬辰 Water Dragon 4	**25** 十五 金4 Metal [1] Eliminating 澤天夬 癸巳 Water Snake 6	**26** 十六 金9 Metal [9] Heaven 乾爲天 甲午 Wood Horse 1	**27** 十七 火7 Fire [8] Well 水風井 乙未 Wood Goat 6	**28** 十八 木8 Wood [7] Relief 雷水解 丙申 Fire Monkey 4
29 十九 金4 Metal [6] Influence 澤山咸 丁酉 Fire Rooster 9	**30** 二十 水1 Water [5] Humility 地山謙 戊戌 Earth Dog 6	**31** 廿一 火2 Fire [4] Observation 風地觀 己亥 Earth Pig 2				

NOVEMBER 1950 丁亥

Xuan Kong Element 玄空五行	雷地豫 Delight	Period Luck 卦運	Monthly Star 月星
Wood 木8		8	2

SUNDAY	MONDAY	TUESDAY	WEDNESDAY	THURSDAY	FRIDAY	SATURDAY
			火2 Fire 3 Increasing 庚子 Metal Rat 風雷益 1 廿二 9	水1 Water 2 Dimming Light 辛丑 Metal Ox 地火明夷 2 廿三 3	金9 Metal 1 Fellowship 壬寅 Water Tiger 天火同人 3 廿四 7	木8 Wood 9 Marrying Maiden 癸卯 Water Rabbit 雷澤歸妹 4 廿五 7
木3 Wood 8 Opposition 甲辰 Wood Dragon 火澤睽 5 廿六 2	火7 Fire 7 Waiting 乙巳 Wood Snake 水天需 6 廿七 3	金4 Metal 6 Great Exceeding 丙午 Fire Horse 澤風大過 7 廿八 3	水6 Water 5 Poison 丁未 Fire Goat 山風蠱 8 廿九 7	火2 Fire 4 Dispersing 戊申 Earth Monkey 風水渙 9 三十 6	木3 Wood 3 Travelling 己酉 Earth Rooster 火山旅 10 十月初一 8	金9 Metal 2 Stagnation 庚戌 Metal Dog 天地否 11 初二 9
火7 Fire 1 Alliance 辛亥 Metal Pig 水地比 12 初三 7	木8 Wood 9 Thunder 壬子 Water Rat 震爲雷 13 初四 1	水6 Water 8 Beauty 癸丑 Water Ox 山火賁 14 初五 8	火7 Fire 7 Accomplished 甲寅 Wood Tiger 水火既濟 15 初六 9	水1 Water 6 Arriving 乙卯 Wood Rabbit 地澤臨 16 初七 4	金4 Metal 5 Marsh 丙辰 Fire Dragon 兌爲澤 17 初八 1	火2 Fire 4 Small Livestock 丁巳 Fire Snake 風天小畜 18 初九 8
木3 Wood 3 The Cauldron 戊午 Earth Horse 火風鼎 19 初十 4	水1 Water 2 Rising 己未 Earth Goat 地風升 20 十一 2	火7 Fire 1 Water 庚申 Metal Monkey 坎爲水 21 十二 1	木8 Wood 9 Lesser Exceeding 辛酉 Metal Rooster 雷山小過 22 十三 3	金4 Metal 8 Gathering 壬戌 Water Dog 澤地萃 23 十四 4	水6 Water 7 Peel 癸亥 Water Pig 山地剝 24 十五 6	水1 Water 6 Earth 甲子 Wood Rat 坤爲地 25 十六 1
木3 Wood 5 Biting 乙丑 Wood Ox 火雷噬嗑 26 十七 6	火2 Fire 4 Family 丙寅 Fire Tiger 風火家人 27 十八 4	水6 Water 3 Decreasing 丁卯 Fire Rabbit 山澤損 28 十九 9	金9 Metal 2 Tread 戊辰 Earth Dragon 天澤履 29 二十 6	木8 Wood 1 Great Strength 己巳 Earth Snake 雷天大壯 30 廿一 2		

DECEMBER 1950 戊子

Xuan Kong Element 玄空五行	水雷屯 Beginning	Period Luck 卦運	Monthly Star 月星
Fire 火7		4	1

SUNDAY	MONDAY	TUESDAY	WEDNESDAY	THURSDAY	FRIDAY	SATURDAY
火2 Fire 4 Increasing 庚子 Metal Rat 風雷益 31 廿三 9					木8 Wood 9 Consistency 庚午 Metal Horse 雷風恆 1 廿二 9	金9 Metal 8 Litigation 辛未 Metal Goat 天水訟 2 廿三 3
水1 Water 7 Officer 壬申 Water Monkey 地水師 3 廿四 7	火2 Fire 6 Gradual Progress 癸酉 Water Rooster 風山漸 4 廿五 7	火7 Fire 5 Obstruction 甲戌 Wood Dog 水山蹇 5 廿六 2	木3 Wood 4 Advancement 乙亥 Wood Pig 火地晉 6 廿七 3	水6 Water 3 Nourish 丙子 Fire Rat 山雷頤 7 廿八 3	金4 Metal 2 Following 丁丑 Fire Ox 澤雷隨 8 廿九 7	木8 Wood 1 Abundance 戊寅 Earth Tiger 雷火豐 9 十一月初一 6
火7 Fire 9 Regulate 己卯 Earth Rabbit 水澤節 10 初二 8	水1 Water 8 Unity 庚辰 Metal Dragon 地天泰 11 初三 9	木3 Wood 7 Great Reward 辛巳 Metal Snake 火天大有 12 初四 7	火2 Fire 6 Wind 壬午 Water Horse 巽爲風 13 初五 1	金4 Metal 5 Trap 癸未 Water Goat 澤水困 14 初六 8	木3 Wood 4 Not Yet Accomplished 甲申 Wood Monkey 火水未濟 15 初七 9	金9 Metal 3 Retreat 乙酉 Wood Rooster 天山遯 16 初八 4
水6 Water 2 Mountain 丙戌 Fire Dog 艮爲山 17 初九 1	木8 Wood 1 Delight 丁亥 Fire Pig 雷地豫 18 初十 8	火7 Fire 9 Beginning 戊子 Earth Rat 水雷屯 19 十一 4	金9 Metal 8 Without Wrongdoing 己丑 Earth Ox 天雷無妄 20 十二 2	木3 Wood 7 Fire 庚寅 Metal Tiger 離爲火 21 十三 1	火2 Fire 6/4 Sincerity 辛卯 Metal Rabbit 風澤中孚 22 十四 3	水6 Water 5 Big Livestock 壬辰 Water Dragon 山天大畜 23 十五 4
金4 Metal 6 Eliminating 癸巳 Water Snake 澤天夬 24 十六 6	金9 Metal 7 Heaven 甲午 Wood Horse 乾爲天 25 十七 1	火7 Fire 8 Well 乙未 Wood Goat 水風井 26 十八 6	木8 Wood 9 Relief 丙申 Fire Monkey 雷水解 27 十九 4	金4 Metal 1 Influence 丁酉 Fire Rooster 澤山咸 28 二十 9	水1 Water 2 Humility 戊戌 Earth Dog 地山謙 29 廿一 6	火2 Fire 3 Observation 己亥 Earth Pig 風地觀 30 廿二 2

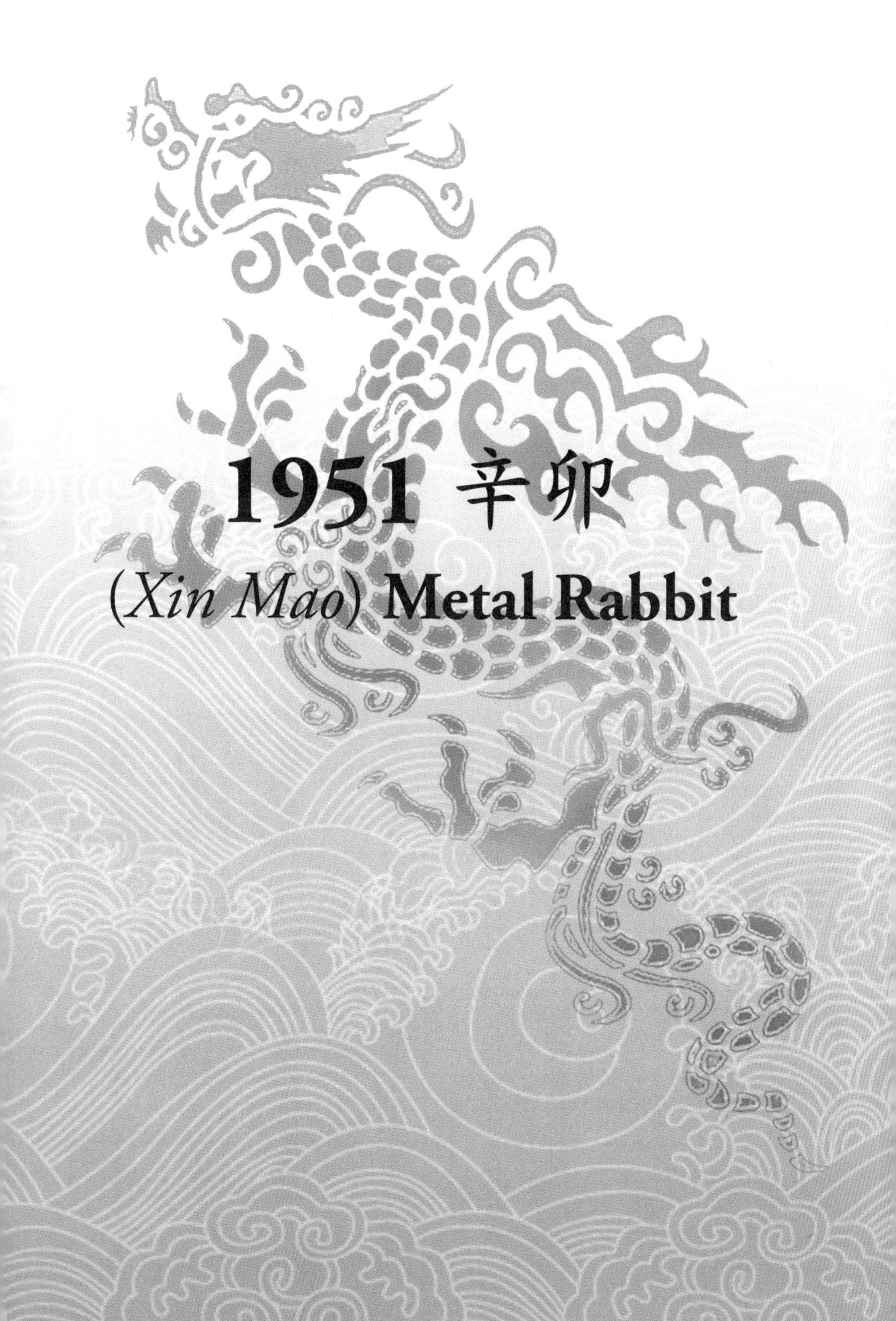

1951 辛卯

(*Xin Mao*) Metal Rabbit

1951 辛卯 *(Xin Mao)* Metal Rabbit

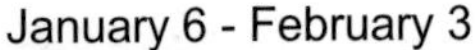

January 6 - February 3

February 4 - March 5

March 6 - April 4

April 5 - May 5

May 6 - June 5

June 6 - July 7

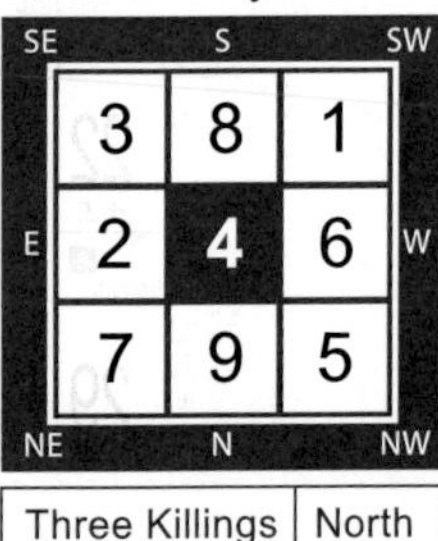

July 8 - August 7

August 8 - September 7

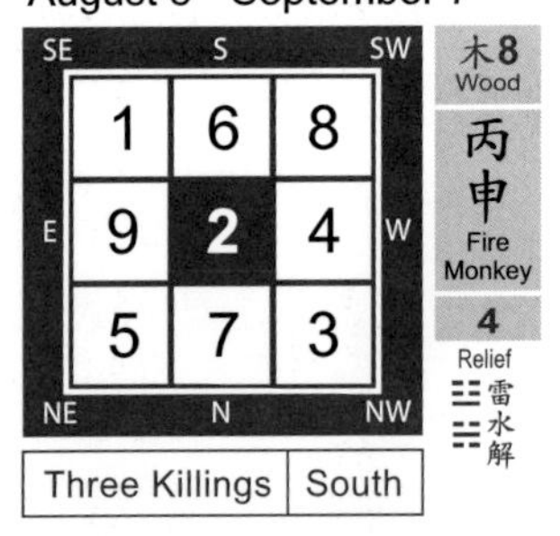

September 8 - October 8

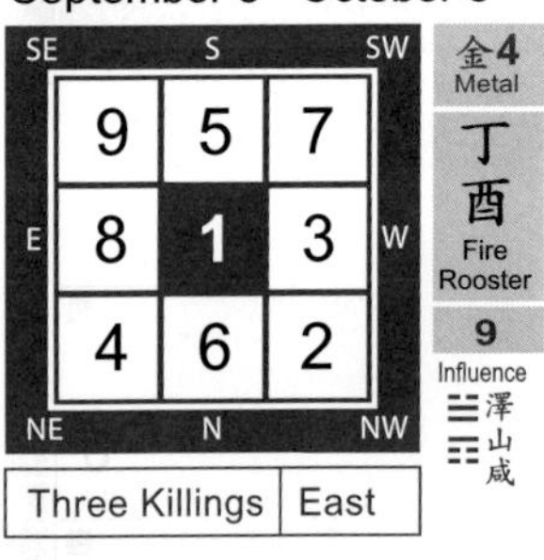

October 9 - November 7

November 8 - December 7

December 8 - January 5

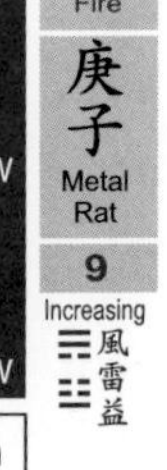

JANUARY 1951 己丑

Xuan Kong Element 玄空五行	天雷無妄 Without Wrongdoing	Period Luck 卦運	Monthly Star 月星
Metal 金9		2	9

SUNDAY	MONDAY	TUESDAY	WEDNESDAY	THURSDAY	FRIDAY	SATURDAY
	水1 Water 5 Dimming Light 辛丑 Metal Ox 地火明夷 1 廿四 3	金9 Metal 6 Fellowship 壬寅 Water Tiger 天火同人 2 廿五 7	木8 Wood 7 Marrying Maiden 癸卯 Water Rabbit 雷澤歸妹 3 廿六 7	木3 Wood 8 Opposition 甲辰 Wood Dragon 火澤睽 4 廿七 2	火7 Fire 9 Waiting 乙巳 Wood Snake 水天需 5 廿八 3	金4 Metal 1 Great Exceeding 丙午 Fire Horse 澤風大過 6 廿九 3
水6 Water 2 Poison 丁未 Fire Goat 山風蠱 7 三十 7	火2 Fire 3 Dispersing 戊申 Earth Monkey 風水渙 8 十二月初一 6	木3 Wood 4 Travelling 己酉 Earth Rooster 火山旅 9 初二 8	金9 Metal 5 Stagnation 庚戌 Metal Dog 天地否 10 初三 9	火7 Fire 6 Alliance 辛亥 Metal Pig 水地比 11 初四 7	木8 Wood 7 Thunder 壬子 Water Rat 震爲雷 12 初五 1	水6 Water 8 Beauty 癸丑 Water Ox 山火賁 13 初六 8
火7 Fire 9 Accomplished 甲寅 Wood Tiger 水火既濟 14 初七 9	水1 Water 1 Arriving 乙卯 Wood Rabbit 地澤臨 15 初八 4	金4 Metal 2 Marsh 丙辰 Fire Dragon 兌爲澤 16 初九 1	火2 Fire 3 Small Livestock 丁巳 Fire Snake 風天小畜 17 初十 8	木3 Wood 4 The Cauldron 戊午 Earth Horse 火風鼎 18 十一 4	水1 Water 5 Rising 己未 Earth Goat 地風升 19 十二 2	火7 Fire 6 Water 庚申 Metal Monkey 坎爲水 20 十三 1
木8 Wood 7 Lesser Exceeding 辛酉 Metal Rooster 雷山小過 21 十四 3	金4 Metal 8 Gathering 壬戌 Water Dog 澤地萃 22 十五 4	水6 Water 9 Peel 癸亥 Water Pig 山地剝 23 十六 6	水1 Water 1 Earth 甲子 Wood Rat 坤爲地 24 十七 1	木3 Wood 2 Biting 乙丑 Wood Ox 火雷噬嗑 25 十八 6	火2 Fire 3 Family 丙寅 Fire Tiger 風火家人 26 十九 4	水6 Water 4 Decreasing 丁卯 Fire Rabbit 山澤損 27 二十 9
金9 Metal 5 Tread 戊辰 Earth Dragon 天澤履 28 廿一 6	木8 Wood 6 Great Strength 己巳 Earth Snake 雷天大壯 29 廿二 2	木8 Wood 7 Consistency 庚午 Metal Horse 雷風恆 30 廿三 9	金9 Metal 8 Litigation 辛未 Metal Goat 天水訟 31 廿四 3			

FEBRUARY 1951 庚寅

Xuan Kong Element 玄空五行	離爲火 Fire	Period Luck 卦運	Monthly Star 月星
Wood 木3		1	8

SUNDAY	MONDAY	TUESDAY	WEDNESDAY	THURSDAY	FRIDAY	SATURDAY
				水1 Water 9 Officer 壬申 Water Monkey 地水師 1 廿五 7	火2 Fire 1 Gradual Progress 癸酉 Water Rooster 風山漸 2 廿六 7	火7 Fire 2 Obstruction 甲戌 Wood Dog 水山蹇 3 廿七 2
木3 Wood 3 Advancement 乙亥 Wood Pig 火地晉 4 廿八 3	水6 Water 4 Nourish 丙子 Fire Rat 山雷頤 5 廿九 3	金4 Metal 5 Following 丁丑 Fire Ox 澤雷隨 6 正月初一 7	木8 Wood 6 Abundance 戊寅 Earth Tiger 雷火豐 7 初二 6	火7 Fire 7 Regulate 己卯 Earth Rabbit 水澤節 8 初三 8	水1 Water 8 Unity 庚辰 Metal Dragon 地天泰 9 初四 9	木3 Wood 9 Great Reward 辛巳 Metal Snake 火天大有 10 初五 7
火2 Fire 1 Wind 壬午 Water Horse 巽爲風 11 初六 1	金4 Metal 2 Trap 癸未 Water Goat 澤水困 12 初七 8	木3 Wood 3 Not Yet Accomplished 甲申 Wood Monkey 火水未濟 13 初八 9	金9 Metal 4 Retreat 乙酉 Wood Rooster 天山遯 14 初九 4	水6 Water 5 Mountain 丙戌 Fire Dog 艮爲山 15 初十 1	木8 Wood 6 Delight 丁亥 Fire Pig 雷地豫 16 十一 8	火7 Fire 7 Beginning 戊子 Earth Rat 水雷屯 17 十二 4
金9 Metal 8 Without Wrongdoing 己丑 Earth Ox 天雷無妄 18 十三 2	木3 Wood 9 Fire 庚寅 Metal Tiger 離爲火 19 十四 1	火2 Fire 1 Sincerity 辛卯 Metal Rabbit 風澤中孚 20 十五 3	水6 Water 2 Big Livestock 壬辰 Water Dragon 山天大畜 21 十六 4	金4 Metal 3 Eliminating 癸巳 Water Snake 澤天夬 22 十七 6	金9 Metal 4 Heaven 甲午 Wood Horse 乾爲天 23 十八 1	火7 Fire 5 Well 乙未 Wood Goat 水風井 24 十九 6
木8 Wood 6 Relief 丙申 Fire Monkey 雷水解 25 二十 4	金4 Metal 7 Influence 丁酉 Fire Rooster 澤山咸 26 廿一 9	水1 Water 8 Humility 戊戌 Earth Dog 地山謙 27 廿二 6	火2 Fire 9 Observation 己亥 Earth Pig 風地觀 28 廿三 2			

MARCH 1951 辛卯

Xuan Kong Element 玄空五行	風澤中孚 Sincerity	Period Luck 卦運	Monthly Star 月星
Fire 火2		3	7

SUNDAY	MONDAY	TUESDAY	WEDNESDAY	THURSDAY	FRIDAY	SATURDAY
				火2 Fire 1 Increasing 風雷益 庚子 Metal Rat **1** 9 廿四	水1 Water 2 Dimming Light 地火明夷 辛丑 Metal Ox **2** 3 廿五	金9 Metal 3 Fellowship 天火同人 壬寅 Water Tiger **3** 7 廿六
木8 Wood 4 Marrying Maiden 雷澤歸妹 癸卯 Water Rabbit **4** 7 廿七	木3 Wood 5 Opposition 火澤睽 甲辰 Wood Dragon **5** 2 廿八	火7 Fire 6 Waiting 水天需 乙巳 Wood Snake **6** 3 廿九	金4 Metal 7 Great Exceeding 澤風大過 丙午 Fire Horse **7** 3 三十	水6 Water 8 Poison 山風蠱 丁未 Fire Goat **8** 7 二月初一	火2 Fire 9 Dispersing 風水渙 戊申 Earth Monkey **9** 6 初二	木3 Wood 1 Travelling 火山旅 己酉 Earth Rooster **10** 8 初三
金9 Metal 2 Stagnation 天地否 庚戌 Metal Dog **11** 9 初四	火7 Fire 3 Alliance 水地比 辛亥 Metal Pig **12** 7 初五	木8 Wood 4 Thunder 震為雷 壬子 Water Rat **13** 1 初六	水6 Water 5 Beauty 山火賁 癸丑 Water Ox **14** 8 初七	火7 Fire 6 Accomplished 水火既濟 甲寅 Wood Tiger **15** 9 初八	水1 Water 7 Arriving 地澤臨 乙卯 Wood Rabbit **16** 4 初九	金4 Metal 8 Marsh 兌為澤 丙辰 Fire Dragon **17** 1 初十
火2 Fire 9 Small Livestock 風天小畜 丁巳 Fire Snake **18** 8 十一	木3 Wood 1 The Cauldron 火風鼎 戊午 Earth Horse **19** 4 十二	水1 Water 2 Rising 地風升 己未 Earth Goat **20** 2 十三	火7 Fire 3 Water 坎為水 庚申 Metal Monkey **21** 1 十四	木8 Wood 4 Lesser Exceeding 雷山小過 辛酉 Metal Rooster **22** 3 十五	金4 Metal 5 Gathering 澤地萃 壬戌 Water Dog **23** 4 十六	水6 Water 6 Peel 山地剝 癸亥 Water Pig **24** 6 十七
水1 Water 7 Earth 坤為地 甲子 Wood Rat **25** 1 十八	木3 Wood 8 Biting 火雷噬嗑 乙丑 Wood Ox **26** 6 十九	火2 Fire 9 Family 風火家人 丙寅 Fire Tiger **27** 4 二十	水6 Water 1 Decreasing 山澤損 丁卯 Fire Rabbit **28** 9 廿一	金9 Metal 2 Tread 天澤履 戊辰 Earth Dragon **29** 6 廿二	木8 Wood 3 Great Strength 雷天大壯 己巳 Earth Snake **30** 2 廿三	木8 Wood 4 Consistency 雷風恒 庚午 Metal Horse **31** 9 廿四

APRIL 1951 壬辰

Xuan Kong Element 玄空五行	山天大畜 Big Livestock	Period Luck 卦運	Monthly Star 月星
Water 水6		4	6

SUNDAY	MONDAY	TUESDAY	WEDNESDAY	THURSDAY	FRIDAY	SATURDAY
金9 Metal 5 Litigation 天水訟 辛未 Metal Goat **1** 3 廿五	水1 Water 6 Officer 地水師 壬申 Water Monkey **2** 7 廿六	火2 Fire 7 Gradual Progress 風山漸 癸酉 Water Rooster **3** 7 廿七	火7 Fire 8 Obstruction 水山蹇 甲戌 Wood Dog **4** 2 廿八	木3 Wood 9 Advancement 火地晉 乙亥 Wood Pig **5** 3 廿九	水6 Water 1 Nourish 山雷頤 丙子 Fire Rat **6** 3 三月初一	金4 Metal 2 Following 澤雷隨 丁丑 Fire Ox **7** 7 初二
木8 Wood 3 Abundance 雷火豐 戊寅 Earth Tiger **8** 6 初三	火7 Fire 4 Regulate 水澤節 己卯 Earth Rabbit **9** 8 初四	水1 Water 5 Unity 地天泰 庚辰 Metal Dragon **10** 9 初五	木3 Wood 6 Great Reward 火天大有 辛巳 Metal Snake **11** 7 初六	火2 Fire 7 Wind 巽為風 壬午 Water Horse **12** 1 初七	金4 Metal 8 Trap 澤水困 癸未 Water Goat **13** 8 初八	木3 Wood 9 Not Yet Accomplished 火水未濟 甲申 Wood Monkey **14** 9 初九
金9 Metal 1 Retreat 天山遯 乙酉 Wood Rooster **15** 4 初十	水6 Water 2 Mountain 艮為山 丙戌 Fire Dog **16** 1 十一	木8 Wood 3 Delight 雷地豫 丁亥 Fire Pig **17** 8 十二	火7 Fire 4 Beginning 水雷屯 戊子 Earth Rat **18** 4 十三	金9 Metal 5 Without Wrongdoing 天雷無妄 己丑 Earth Ox **19** 2 十四	木3 Wood 6 Fire 離為火 庚寅 Metal Tiger **20** 1 十五	火2 Fire 7 Sincerity 風澤中孚 辛卯 Metal Rabbit **21** 3 十六
水6 Water 8 Big Livestock 山天大畜 壬辰 Water Dragon **22** 4 十七	金4 Metal 9 Eliminating 澤天夬 癸巳 Water Snake **23** 6 十八	金9 Metal 1 Heaven 乾為天 甲午 Wood Horse **24** 1 十九	火7 Fire 2 Well 水風井 乙未 Wood Goat **25** 6 二十	木8 Wood 3 Relief 雷水解 丙申 Fire Monkey **26** 4 廿一	金4 Metal 4 Influence 澤山咸 丁酉 Fire Rooster **27** 9 廿二	水1 Water 5 Humility 地山謙 戊戌 Earth Dog **28** 6 廿三
火2 Fire 6 Observation 風地觀 己亥 Earth Pig **29** 2 廿四	火2 Fire 7 Increasing 風雷益 庚子 Metal Rat **30** 9 廿五					

MAY 1951 癸巳

Xuan Kong Element 玄空五行	澤天夬 Eliminating	Period Luck 卦運	Monthly Star 月星
Metal 金4		6	5

SUNDAY	MONDAY	TUESDAY	WEDNESDAY	THURSDAY	FRIDAY	SATURDAY
		水1 Water Dimming Light 8 辛丑 Metal Ox 地火明夷 **1** 廿六 3	金9 Metal Fellowship 9 壬寅 Water Tiger 天火同人 **2** 廿七 7	木8 Wood Marrying Maiden 1 癸卯 Water Rabbit 雷澤歸妹 **3** 廿八 7	木3 Wood Opposition 2 甲辰 Wood Dragon 火澤睽 **4** 廿九 2	火7 Fire Waiting 3 乙巳 Wood Snake 水天需 **5** 三十 3
金4 Metal Great Exceeding 4 丙午 Fire Horse 澤風大過 **6** 四月初一 3	水6 Water Poison 5 丁未 Fire Goat 山風蠱 **7** 初二 7	火2 Fire Dispersing 6 戊申 Earth Monkey 風水渙 **8** 初三 6	木3 Wood Travelling 7 己酉 Earth Rooster 火山旅 **9** 初四 8	金9 Metal Stagnation 8 庚戌 Metal Dog 天地否 **10** 初五 9	火7 Fire Alliance 9 辛亥 Metal Pig 水地比 **11** 初六 7	木8 Wood Thunder 1 壬子 Water Rat 震爲雷 **12** 初七 1
水6 Water Beauty 2 癸丑 Water Ox 山火賁 **13** 初八 8	火7 Fire Accomplished 3 甲寅 Wood Tiger 水火既濟 **14** 初九 9	水1 Water Arriving 4 乙卯 Wood Rabbit 地澤臨 **15** 初十 4	金4 Metal Marsh 5 丙辰 Fire Dragon 兑爲澤 **16** 十一 1	火2 Fire Small Livestock 6 丁巳 Fire Snake 風天小畜 **17** 十二 8	木3 Wood The Cauldron 7 戊午 Earth Horse 火風鼎 **18** 十三 4	水1 Water Rising 8 己未 Earth Goat 地風升 **19** 十四 2
火7 Fire Water 9 庚申 Metal Monkey 坎爲水 **20** 十五 1	木8 Wood Lesser Exceeding 1 辛酉 Metal Rooster 雷山小過 **21** 十六 3	金4 Metal Gathering 2 壬戌 Water Dog 澤地萃 **22** 十七 4	水6 Water Peel 3 癸亥 Water Pig 山地剝 **23** 十八 6	水1 Water Earth 4 甲子 Wood Rat 坤爲地 **24** 十九 1	木3 Wood Biting 5 乙丑 Wood Ox 火雷噬嗑 **25** 二十 6	火2 Fire Family 6 丙寅 Fire Tiger 風火家人 **26** 廿一 4
水6 Water Decreasing 7 丁卯 Fire Rabbit 山澤損 **27** 廿二 9	金9 Metal Tread 8 戊辰 Earth Dragon 天澤履 **28** 廿三 6	木8 Wood Great Strength 9 己巳 Earth Snake 雷天大壯 **29** 廿四 2	木8 Wood Consistency 1 庚午 Metal Horse 雷風恆 **30** 廿五 9	金9 Metal Litigation 2 辛未 Metal Goat 天水訟 **31** 廿六 3		

JUNE 1951 甲午

Xuan Kong Element 玄空五行	乾爲天 Heaven	Period Luck 卦運	Monthly Star 月星
Metal 金9		1	4

SUNDAY	MONDAY	TUESDAY	WEDNESDAY	THURSDAY	FRIDAY	SATURDAY
					水1 Water Officer 3 壬申 Water Monkey 地水師 **1** 廿七 7	火2 Fire Gradual Progress 4 癸酉 Water Rooster 風山漸 **2** 廿八 7
火7 Fire Obstruction 5 甲戌 Wood Dog 水山蹇 **3** 廿九 2	木3 Wood Advancement 6 乙亥 Wood Pig 火地晉 **4** 三十 3	水6 Water Nourish 7 丙子 Fire Rat 山雷頤 **5** 五月初一 3	金4 Metal Following 8 丁丑 Fire Ox 澤雷隨 **6** 初二 7	木8 Wood Abundance 9 戊寅 Earth Tiger 雷火豐 **7** 初三 6	火7 Fire Regulate 1 己卯 Earth Rabbit 水澤節 **8** 初四 8	水1 Water Unity 2 庚辰 Metal Dragon 地天泰 **9** 初五 9
木3 Wood Great Reward 3 辛巳 Metal Snake 火天大有 **10** 初六 7	火2 Fire Wind 4 壬午 Water Horse 巽爲風 **11** 初七 1	金4 Metal Trap 5 癸未 Water Goat 澤水困 **12** 初八 8	木3 Wood Not Yet Accomplished 6 甲申 Wood Monkey 火水未濟 **13** 初九 9	金9 Metal Retreat 7 乙酉 Wood Rooster 天山遯 **14** 初十 4	水6 Water Mountain 8 丙戌 Fire Dog 艮爲山 **15** 十一 1	木8 Wood Delight 9 丁亥 Fire Pig 雷地豫 **16** 十二 8
火7 Fire Beginning 1 戊子 Earth Rat 水雷屯 **17** 十三 4	金9 Metal Without Wrongdoing 2 己丑 Earth Ox 天雷無妄 **18** 十四 2	木3 Wood Fire 3 庚寅 Metal Tiger 離爲火 **19** 十五 1	火2 Fire Sincerity 4 辛卯 Metal Rabbit 風澤中孚 **20** 十六 3	水6 Water Big Livestock 5 壬辰 Water Dragon 山天大畜 **21** 十七 4	金4 Metal Eliminating 3/4 癸巳 Water Snake 澤天夬 **22** 十八 6	金9 Metal Heaven 3 甲午 Wood Horse 乾爲天 **23** 十九 1
火7 Fire Well 2 乙未 Wood Goat 水風井 **24** 二十 6	木8 Wood Relief 1 丙申 Fire Monkey 雷水解 **25** 廿一 4	金4 Metal Influence 9 丁酉 Fire Rooster 澤山咸 **26** 廿二 9	水1 Water Humility 8 戊戌 Earth Dog 地山謙 **27** 廿三 6	火2 Fire Observation 7 己亥 Earth Pig 風地觀 **28** 廿四 2	火2 Fire Increasing 6 庚子 Metal Rat 風雷益 **29** 廿五 9	水1 Water Dimming Light 5 辛丑 Metal Ox 地火明夷 **30** 廿六 3

JULY 1951 乙未

Xuan Kong Element 玄空五行	水風井 Well	Period Luck 卦運	Monthly Star 月星
Fire 火7		6	3

SUNDAY	MONDAY	TUESDAY	WEDNESDAY	THURSDAY	FRIDAY	SATURDAY
金9 Metal 4 Fellowship 壬寅 Water Tiger 天火同人 1 廿七 7	木8 Wood 3 Marrying Maiden 癸卯 Water Rabbit 雷澤歸妹 2 廿八 7	木3 Wood 2 Opposition 甲辰 Wood Dragon 火澤睽 3 廿九 2	火7 Fire 1 Waiting 乙巳 Wood Snake 水天需 4 六月初一 3	金4 Metal 9 Great Exceeding 丙午 Fire Horse 澤風大過 5 初二 3	水6 Water 8 Poison 丁未 Fire Goat 山風蠱 6 初三 7	火2 Fire 7 Dispersing 戊申 Earth Monkey 風水渙 7 初四 6
木3 Wood 6 Travelling 己酉 Earth Rooster 火山旅 8 初五 8	金9 Metal 5 Stagnation 庚戌 Metal Dog 天地否 9 初六 9	火7 Fire 4 Alliance 辛亥 Metal Pig 水地比 10 初七 7	木8 Wood 3 Thunder 壬子 Water Rat 震為雷 11 初八 1	水6 Water 2 Beauty 癸丑 Water Ox 山火賁 12 初九 8	火7 Fire 1 Accomplished 甲寅 Wood Tiger 水火既濟 13 初十 9	水1 Water 9 Arriving 乙卯 Wood Rabbit 地澤臨 14 十一 4
金4 Metal 8 Marsh 丙辰 Fire Dragon 兌為澤 15 十二 1	火2 Fire 7 Small Livestock 丁巳 Fire Snake 風天小畜 16 十三 8	木3 Wood 6 The Cauldron 戊午 Earth Horse 火風鼎 17 十四 4	水1 Water 5 Rising 己未 Earth Goat 地風升 18 十五 2	火7 Fire 4 Water 庚申 Metal Monkey 坎為水 19 十六 1	木8 Wood 3 Lesser Exceeding 辛酉 Metal Rooster 雷山小過 20 十七 3	金4 Metal 2 Gathering 壬戌 Water Dog 澤地萃 21 十八 4
水6 Water 1 Peel 癸亥 Water Pig 山地剝 22 十九 6	水1 Water 9 Earth 甲子 Wood Rat 坤為地 23 二十 1	木3 Wood 8 Biting 乙丑 Wood Ox 火雷噬嗑 24 廿一 6	火2 Fire 7 Family 丙寅 Fire Tiger 風火家人 25 廿二 4	水6 Water 6 Decreasing 丁卯 Fire Rabbit 山澤損 26 廿三 9	金9 Metal 5 Tread 戊辰 Earth Dragon 天澤履 27 廿四 6	木8 Wood 4 Great Strength 己巳 Earth Snake 雷天大壯 28 廿五 2
木8 Wood 3 Consistency 庚午 Metal Horse 雷風恒 29 廿六 9	金9 Metal 2 Litigation 辛未 Metal Goat 天水訟 30 廿七 3	水1 Water 1 Officer 壬申 Water Monkey 地水師 31 廿八 7				

AUGUST 1951 丙申

Xuan Kong Element 玄空五行	雷水解 Relief	Period Luck 卦運	Monthly Star 月星
Wood 木8		4	2

SUNDAY	MONDAY	TUESDAY	WEDNESDAY	THURSDAY	FRIDAY	SATURDAY
			火2 Fire 9 Gradual Progress 癸酉 Water Rooster 風山漸 1 廿九 7	火7 Fire 8 Obstruction 甲戌 Wood Dog 水山蹇 2 三十 2	木3 Wood 7 Advancement 乙亥 Wood Pig 火地晉 3 七月初一 3	水6 Water 6 Nourish 丙子 Fire Rat 山雷頤 4 初二 3
金4 Metal 5 Following 丁丑 Fire Ox 澤雷隨 5 初三 7	木8 Wood 4 Abundance 戊寅 Earth Tiger 雷火豐 6 初四 6	火7 Fire 3 Regulate 己卯 Earth Rabbit 水澤節 7 初五 8	水1 Water 2 Unity 庚辰 Metal Dragon 地天泰 8 初六 9	木3 Wood 1 Great Reward 辛巳 Metal Snake 火天大有 9 初七 7	火2 Fire 9 Wind 壬午 Water Horse 巽為風 10 初八 1	金4 Metal 8 Trap 癸未 Water Goat 澤水困 11 初九 8
木3 Wood 7 Not Yet Accomplished 甲申 Wood Monkey 火水未濟 12 初十 9	金9 Metal 6 Retreat 乙酉 Wood Rooster 天山遯 13 十一 4	水6 Water 5 Mountain 丙戌 Fire Dog 艮為山 14 十二 1	木8 Wood 4 Delight 丁亥 Fire Pig 雷地豫 15 十三 8	火7 Fire 3 Beginning 戊子 Earth Rat 水雷屯 16 十四 4	金9 Metal 2 Without Wrongdoing 己丑 Earth Ox 天雷無妄 17 十五 2	木3 Wood 1 Fire 庚寅 Metal Tiger 離為火 18 十六 1
火2 Fire 9 Sincerity 辛卯 Metal Rabbit 風澤中孚 19 十七 3	水6 Water 8 Big Livestock 壬辰 Water Dragon 山天大畜 20 十八 4	金4 Metal 7 Eliminating 癸巳 Water Snake 澤天夬 21 十九 6	金9 Metal 6 Heaven 甲午 Wood Horse 乾為天 22 二十 1	火7 Fire 5 Well 乙未 Wood Goat 水風井 23 廿一 6	木8 Wood 4 Relief 丙申 Fire Monkey 雷水解 24 廿二 4	金4 Metal 3 Influence 丁酉 Fire Rooster 澤山咸 25 廿三 9
水1 Water 2 Humility 戊戌 Earth Dog 地山謙 26 廿四 6	火2 Fire 1 Observation 己亥 Earth Pig 風地觀 27 廿五 2	火2 Fire 9 Increasing 庚子 Metal Rat 風雷益 28 廿六 9	水1 Water 8 Dimming Light 辛丑 Metal Ox 地火明夷 29 廿七 3	金9 Metal 7 Fellowship 壬寅 Water Tiger 天火同人 30 廿八 7	木8 Wood 6 Marrying Maiden 癸卯 Water Rabbit 雷澤歸妹 31 廿九 7	

SEPTEMBER 1951 丁酉

Xuan Kong Element 玄空五行	澤山咸 Influence	Period Luck 卦運	Monthly Star 月星
Metal 金4		9	1

SUNDAY	MONDAY	TUESDAY	WEDNESDAY	THURSDAY	FRIDAY	SATURDAY
火2 Fire 3 Gradual Progress 癸酉 Water Rooster 風山漸 30 三十 7						木3 Wood 5 Opposition 甲辰 Wood Dragon 火澤睽 1 八月初一 2
火7 Fire 4 Waiting 乙巳 Wood Snake 水天需 2 初二 3	金4 Metal 3 Great Exceeding 丙午 Fire Horse 澤風大過 3 初三 3	水6 Water 2 Poison 丁未 Fire Goat 山風蠱 4 初四 7	火2 Fire 1 Dispersing 戊申 Earth Monkey 風水渙 5 初五 6	木3 Wood 9 Travelling 己酉 Earth Rooster 火山旅 6 初六 8	金9 Metal 8 Stagnation 庚戌 Metal Dog 天地否 7 初七 9	火7 Fire 7 Alliance 辛亥 Metal Pig 水地比 8 初八 7
木8 Wood 6 Thunder 壬子 Water Rat 震爲雷 9 初九 1	水6 Water 5 Beauty 癸丑 Water Ox 山火賁 10 初十 8	火7 Fire 4 Accomplished 甲寅 Wood Tiger 水火既濟 11 十一 9	水1 Water 3 Arriving 乙卯 Wood Rabbit 地澤臨 12 十二 4	金4 Metal 2 Marsh 丙辰 Fire Dragon 兌爲澤 13 十三 1	火2 Fire 1 Small Livestock 丁巳 Fire Snake 風天小畜 14 十四 8	木3 Wood 9 The Cauldron 戊午 Earth Horse 火風鼎 15 十五 4
水1 Water 8 Rising 己未 Earth Goat 地風升 16 十六 2	火7 Fire 7 Water 庚申 Metal Monkey 坎爲水 17 十七 1	木8 Wood 6 Lesser Exceeding 辛酉 Metal Rooster 雷山小過 18 十八 3	金4 Metal 5 Gathering 壬戌 Water Dog 澤地萃 19 十九 4	水6 Water 4 Peel 癸亥 Water Pig 山地剝 20 二十 6	水1 Water 3 Earth 甲子 Wood Rat 坤爲地 21 廿一 1	木3 Wood 2 Biting 乙丑 Wood Ox 火雷噬嗑 22 廿二 6
火2 Fire 1 Family 丙寅 Fire Tiger 風火家人 23 廿三 4	水6 Water 9 Decreasing 丁卯 Fire Rabbit 山澤損 24 廿四 9	金9 Metal 8 Tread 戊辰 Earth Dragon 天澤履 25 廿五 6	木8 Wood 7 Great Strength 己巳 Earth Snake 雷天大壯 26 廿六 2	木8 Wood 6 Consistency 庚午 Metal Horse 雷風恒 27 廿七 9	金9 Metal 5 Litigation 辛未 Metal Goat 天水訟 28 廿八 3	水1 Water 4 Officer 壬申 Water Monkey 地水師 29 廿九 7

OCTOBER 1951 戊戌

Xuan Kong Element 玄空五行	地山謙 Humility	Period Luck 卦運	Monthly Star 月星
Water 水1		6	9

SUNDAY	MONDAY	TUESDAY	WEDNESDAY	THURSDAY	FRIDAY	SATURDAY
	火7 Fire 2 Obstruction 甲戌 Wood Dog 水山蹇 1 九月初一 2	木3 Wood 1 Advancement 乙亥 Wood Pig 火地晉 2 初二 3	水6 Water 9 Nourish 丙子 Fire Rat 山雷頤 3 初三 3	金4 Metal 8 Following 丁丑 Fire Ox 澤雷隨 4 初四 7	木8 Wood 7 Abundance 戊寅 Earth Tiger 雷火豐 5 初五 6	火7 Fire 6 Regulate 己卯 Earth Rabbit 水澤節 6 初六 8
水1 Water 5 Unity 庚辰 Metal Dragon 地天泰 7 初七 9	木3 Wood 4 Great Reward 辛巳 Metal Snake 火天大有 8 初八 7	火2 Fire 3 Wind 壬午 Water Horse 巽爲風 9 初九 1	金4 Metal 2 Trap 癸未 Water Goat 澤水困 10 初十 8	木3 Wood 1 Not Yet Accomplished 甲申 Wood Monkey 火水未濟 11 十一 9	金9 Metal 9 Retreat 乙酉 Wood Rooster 天山遯 12 十二 4	水6 Water 8 Mountain 丙戌 Fire Dog 艮爲山 13 十三 1
木8 Wood 7 Delight 丁亥 Fire Pig 雷地豫 14 十四 8	火7 Fire 6 Beginning 戊子 Earth Rat 水雷屯 15 十五 4	金9 Metal 5 Without Wrongdoing 己丑 Earth Ox 天雷無妄 16 十六 2	木3 Wood 4 Fire 庚寅 Metal Tiger 離爲火 17 十七 1	火2 Fire 3 Sincerity 辛卯 Metal Rabbit 風澤中孚 18 十八 3	水6 Water 2 Big Livestock 壬辰 Water Dragon 山天大畜 19 十九 4	金4 Metal 1 Eliminating 癸巳 Water Snake 澤天夬 20 二十 6
金9 Metal 9 Heaven 甲午 Wood Horse 乾爲天 21 廿一 1	火7 Fire 8 Well 乙未 Wood Goat 水風井 22 廿二 6	木8 Wood 7 Relief 丙申 Fire Monkey 雷水解 23 廿三 4	金4 Metal 6 Influence 丁酉 Fire Rooster 澤山咸 24 廿四 9	水1 Water 5 Humility 戊戌 Earth Dog 地山謙 25 廿五 6	火2 Fire 4 Observation 己亥 Earth Pig 風地觀 26 廿六 2	火2 Fire 3 Increasing 庚子 Metal Rat 風雷益 27 廿七 9
水1 Water 2 Dimming Light 辛丑 Metal Ox 地火明夷 28 廿八 3	金9 Metal 1 Fellowship 壬寅 Water Tiger 天火同人 29 廿九 7	木8 Wood 9 Marrying Maiden 癸卯 Water Rabbit 雷澤歸妹 30 十月初一 7	木3 Wood 8 Opposition 甲辰 Wood Dragon 火澤睽 31 初二 2			

NOVEMBER 1951 己亥

Xuan Kong Element 玄空五行	風地觀 Observation	Period Luck 卦運	Monthly Star 月星
Fire 火2		2	8

SUNDAY	MONDAY	TUESDAY	WEDNESDAY	THURSDAY	FRIDAY	SATURDAY
				火7 Fire Waiting 7 乙巳 Wood Snake 水天需 1 初三 3	金4 Metal Great Exceeding 6 丙午 Fire Horse 澤風大過 2 初四 3	水6 Water Poison 5 丁未 Fire Goat 山風蠱 3 初五 7
火2 Fire Dispersing 4 戊申 Earth Monkey 風水渙 4 初六 6	木3 Wood Travelling 3 己酉 Earth Rooster 火山旅 5 初七 8	金9 Metal Stagnation 2 庚戌 Metal Dog 天地否 6 初八 9	火7 Fire Alliance 1 辛亥 Metal Pig 水地比 7 初九 7	木8 Wood Thunder 9 壬子 Water Rat 震爲雷 8 初十 1	水6 Water Beauty 8 癸丑 Water Ox 山火賁 9 十一 8	火7 Fire Accomplished 7 甲寅 Wood Tiger 水火既濟 10 十二 9
水1 Water Arriving 6 乙卯 Wood Rabbit 地澤臨 11 十三 4	金4 Metal Marsh 5 丙辰 Fire Dragon 兑爲澤 12 十四 1	火2 Fire Small Livestock 4 丁巳 Fire Snake 風天小畜 13 十五 8	木3 Wood The Cauldron 3 戊午 Earth Horse 火風鼎 14 十六 4	水1 Water Rising 2 己未 Earth Goat 地風升 15 十七 2	火7 Fire Water 1 庚申 Metal Monkey 坎爲水 16 十八 1	木8 Wood Lesser Exceeding 9 辛酉 Metal Rooster 雷山小過 17 十九 3
金4 Metal Gathering 8 壬戌 Water Dog 澤地萃 18 二十 4	水6 Water Peel 7 癸亥 Water Pig 山地剝 19 廿一 6	水1 Water Earth 6 甲子 Wood Rat 坤爲地 20 廿二 1	木3 Wood Biting 5 乙丑 Wood Ox 火雷噬嗑 21 廿三 6	火2 Fire Family 4 丙寅 Fire Tiger 風火家人 22 廿四 4	水6 Water Decreasing 3 丁卯 Fire Rabbit 山澤損 23 廿五 9	金9 Metal Tread 2 戊辰 Earth Dragon 天澤履 24 廿六 6
木8 Wood Great Strength 1 己巳 Earth Snake 雷天大壯 25 廿七 2	木8 Wood Consistency 9 庚午 Metal Horse 雷風恒 26 廿八 9	金9 Metal Litigation 8 辛未 Metal Goat 天水訟 27 廿九 3	水1 Water Officer 7 壬申 Water Monkey 地水師 28 三十 7	火2 Fire Gradual Progress 6 癸酉 Water Rooster 風山漸 29 十一月初一 7	火7 Fire Obstruction 5 甲戌 Wood Dog 水山蹇 30 初二 2	

DECEMBER 1951 庚子

Xuan Kong Element 玄空五行	風雷益 Increasing	Period Luck 卦運	Monthly Star 月星
Fire 火2		9	7

SUNDAY	MONDAY	TUESDAY	WEDNESDAY	THURSDAY	FRIDAY	SATURDAY
木3 Wood Opposition 8 甲辰 Wood Dragon 火澤睽 30 初三 2	火7 Fire Waiting 9 乙巳 Wood Snake 水天需 31 初四 3					木3 Wood Advancement 4 乙亥 Wood Pig 火地晉 1 初三 3
水6 Water Nourish 3 丙子 Fire Rat 山雷頤 2 初四 3	金4 Metal Following 2 丁丑 Fire Ox 澤雷隨 3 初五 7	木8 Wood Abundance 1 戊寅 Earth Tiger 雷火豐 4 初六 6	火7 Fire Regulate 9 己卯 Earth Rabbit 水澤節 5 初七 8	水1 Water Unity 8 庚辰 Metal Dragon 地天泰 6 初八 9	木3 Wood Great Reward 7 辛巳 Metal Snake 火天大有 7 初九 7	火2 Fire Wind 6 壬午 Water Horse 巽爲風 8 初十 1
金4 Metal Trap 5 癸未 Water Goat 澤水困 9 十一 8	木3 Wood Not Yet Accomplished 4 甲申 Wood Monkey 火水未濟 10 十二 9	金9 Metal Retreat 3 乙酉 Wood Rooster 天山遯 11 十三 4	水6 Water Mountain 2 丙戌 Fire Dog 艮爲山 12 十四 1	木8 Wood Delight 1 丁亥 Fire Pig 雷地豫 13 十五 8	火7 Fire Beginning 9 戊子 Earth Rat 水雷屯 14 十六 4	金9 Metal Without Wrongdoing 8 己丑 Earth Ox 天雷無妄 15 十七 2
木3 Wood Fire 7 庚寅 Metal Tiger 離爲火 16 十八 1	火2 Fire Sincerity 6 辛卯 Metal Rabbit 風澤中孚 17 十九 3	水6 Water Big Livestock 5 壬辰 Water Dragon 山天大畜 18 二十 4	金4 Metal Eliminating 4 癸巳 Water Snake 澤天夬 19 廿一 6	金9 Metal Heaven 3 甲午 Wood Horse 乾爲天 20 廿二 1	火7 Fire Well 2 乙未 Wood Goat 水風井 21 廿三 6	木8 Wood Relief 1 丙申 Fire Monkey 雷水解 22 廿四 4
金4 Metal Influence 9/1 丁酉 Fire Rooster 澤山咸 23 廿五 9	水1 Water Humility 2 戊戌 Earth Dog 地山謙 24 廿六 6	火2 Fire Observation 3 己亥 Earth Pig 風地觀 25 廿七 2	火2 Fire Increasing 4 庚子 Metal Rat 風雷益 26 廿八 9	水1 Water Dimming Light 5 辛丑 Metal Ox 地火明夷 27 廿九 3	金9 Metal Fellowship 6 壬寅 Water Tiger 天火同人 28 十二月初一 7	木8 Wood Marrying Maiden 7 癸卯 Water Rabbit 雷澤歸妹 29 初二 7

1952 壬辰

(*Ren Chen*) Water Dragon

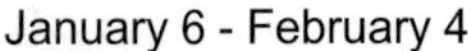

1952 壬辰 *(Ren Chen)* Water Dragon

January 6 - February 4

February 5 - March 4

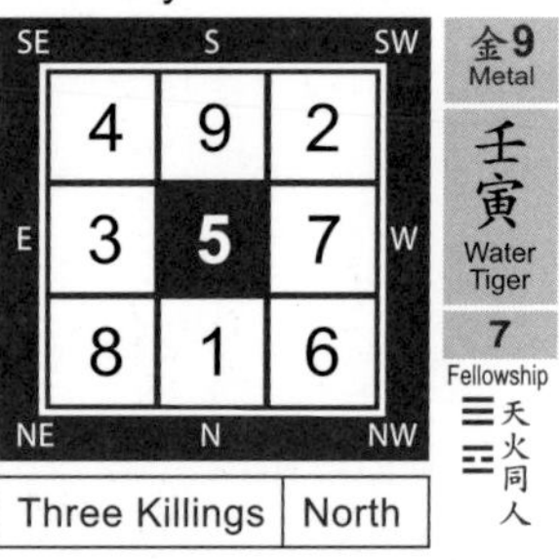

March 5 - April 4

April 5 - May 4

May 5 - June 5

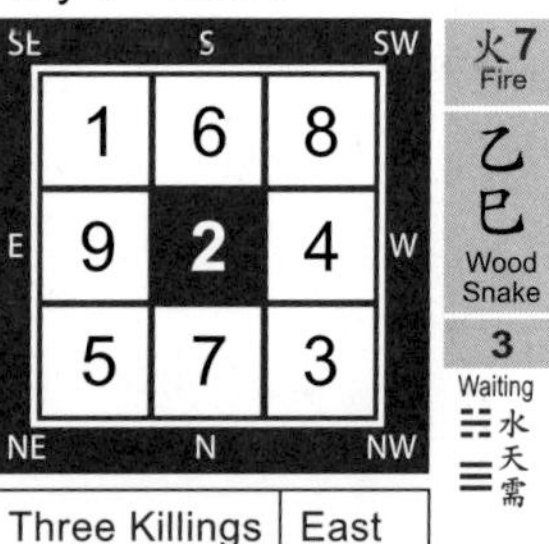

June 6 - July 6

July 7 - August 6

August 7 - September 7

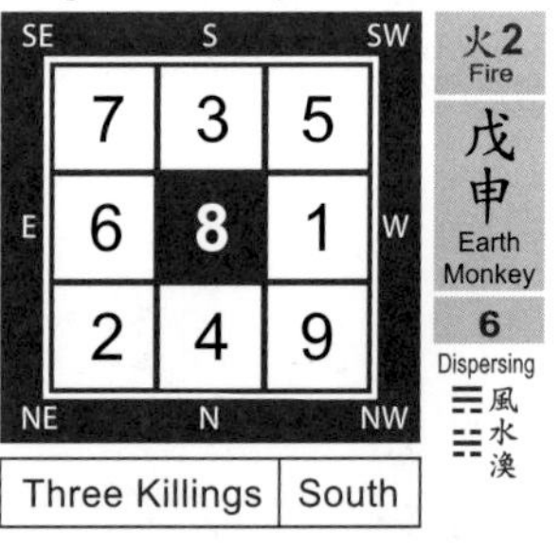

September 8 - October 7

October 8 - November 6

November 7 - December 6

December 7 - January 4

JANUARY 1952 辛丑

Xuan Kong Element 玄空五行	地火明夷 Dimming Light	Period Luck 卦運	Monthly Star 月星
Water 水1		3	6

SUNDAY	MONDAY	TUESDAY	WEDNESDAY	THURSDAY	FRIDAY	SATURDAY
		金4 Metal · Great Exceeding 1 丙午 Fire Horse 澤風大過 **1** 初五 3	水6 Water · Poison 2 丁未 Fire Goat 山風蠱 **2** 初六 7	火2 Fire · Dispersing 3 戊申 Earth Monkey 風水渙 **3** 初七 6	木3 Wood · Travelling 4 己酉 Earth Rooster 火山旅 **4** 初八 8	金9 Metal · Stagnation 5 庚戌 Metal Dog 天地否 **5** 初九 9
火7 Fire · Alliance 6 辛亥 Metal Pig 水地比 **6** 初十 7	木8 Wood · Thunder 7 壬子 Water Rat 震爲雷 **7** 十一 1	水6 Water · Beauty 8 癸丑 Water Ox 山火賁 **8** 十二 8	火7 Fire · Accomplished 9 甲寅 Wood Tiger 水火既濟 **9** 十三 9	水1 Water · Arriving 1 乙卯 Wood Rabbit 地澤臨 **10** 十四 4	金4 Metal · Marsh 2 丙辰 Fire Dragon 兑爲澤 **11** 十五 1	火2 Fire · Small Livestock 3 丁巳 Fire Snake 風天小畜 **12** 十六 8
木3 Wood · The Cauldron 4 戊午 Earth Horse 火風鼎 **13** 十七 4	水1 Water · Rising 5 己未 Earth Goat 地風升 **14** 十八 2	火7 Fire · Water 6 庚申 Metal Monkey 坎爲水 **15** 十九 1	木8 Wood · Lesser Exceeding 7 辛酉 Metal Rooster 雷山小過 **16** 二十 3	金4 Metal · Gathering 8 壬戌 Water Dog 澤地萃 **17** 廿一 4	水6 Water · Peel 9 癸亥 Water Pig 山地剝 **18** 廿二 6	水1 Water · Earth 1 甲子 Wood Rat 坤爲地 **19** 廿三 1
木3 Wood · Biting 2 乙丑 Wood Ox 火雷噬嗑 **20** 廿四 6	火2 Fire · Family 3 丙寅 Fire Tiger 風火家人 **21** 廿五 4	水6 Water · Decreasing 4 丁卯 Fire Rabbit 山澤損 **22** 廿六 9	金9 Metal · Tread 5 戊辰 Earth Dragon 天澤履 **23** 廿七 6	木8 Wood · Great Strength 6 己巳 Earth Snake 雷天大壯 **24** 廿八 2	木8 Wood · Consistency 7 庚午 Metal Horse 雷風恒 **25** 廿九 9	金9 Metal · Litigation 8 辛未 Metal Goat 天水訟 **26** 三十 3
水1 Water · Officer 9 壬申 Water Monkey 地水師 **27** 正月初一 7	火2 Fire · Gradual Progress 1 癸酉 Water Rooster 風山漸 **28** 初二 7	火7 Fire · Obstruction 2 甲戌 Wood Dog 水山蹇 **29** 初三 2	木3 Wood · Advancement 3 乙亥 Wood Pig 火地晉 **30** 初四 3	水6 Water · Nourish 4 丙子 Fire Rat 山雷頤 **31** 初五 3		

FEBRUARY 1952 壬寅

Xuan Kong Element 玄空五行	天火同人 Fellowship	Period Luck 卦運	Monthly Star 月星
Metal 金9		7	5

SUNDAY	MONDAY	TUESDAY	WEDNESDAY	THURSDAY	FRIDAY	SATURDAY
					金4 Metal · Following 5 丁丑 Fire Ox 澤雷隨 **1** 初六 7	木8 Wood · Abundance 6 戊寅 Earth Tiger 雷火豐 **2** 初七 6
火7 Fire · Regulate 7 己卯 Earth Rabbit 水澤節 **3** 初八 8	水1 Water · Unity 8 庚辰 Metal Dragon 地天泰 **4** 初九 9	木3 Wood · Great Reward 9 辛巳 Metal Snake 火天大有 **5** 初十 7	火2 Fire · Wind 1 壬午 Water Horse 巽爲風 **6** 十一 1	金4 Metal · Trap 2 癸未 Water Goat 澤水困 **7** 十二 8	木3 Wood · Not Yet Accomplished 3 甲申 Wood Monkey 火水未濟 **8** 十三 9	金9 Metal · Retreat 4 乙酉 Wood Rooster 天山遯 **9** 十四 4
水6 Water · Mountain 5 丙戌 Fire Dog 艮爲山 **10** 十五 1	木8 Wood · Delight 6 丁亥 Fire Pig 雷地豫 **11** 十六 8	火7 Fire · Beginning 7 戊子 Earth Rat 水雷屯 **12** 十七 4	金9 Metal · Without Wrongdoing 8 己丑 Earth Ox 天雷無妄 **13** 十八 2	木3 Wood · Fire 9 庚寅 Metal Tiger 離爲火 **14** 十九 1	火2 Fire · Sincerity 1 辛卯 Metal Rabbit 風澤中孚 **15** 二十 3	水6 Water · Big Livestock 2 壬辰 Water Dragon 山天大畜 **16** 廿一 4
金4 Metal · Eliminating 3 癸巳 Water Snake 澤天夬 **17** 廿二 6	金9 Metal · Heaven 4 甲午 Wood Horse 乾爲天 **18** 廿三 1	火7 Fire · Well 5 乙未 Wood Goat 水風井 **19** 廿四 6	木8 Wood · Relief 6 丙申 Fire Monkey 雷水解 **20** 廿五 4	金4 Metal · Influence 7 丁酉 Fire Rooster 澤山咸 **21** 廿六 9	水1 Water · Humility 8 戊戌 Earth Dog 地山謙 **22** 廿七 6	火2 Fire · Observation 9 己亥 Earth Pig 風地觀 **23** 廿八 2
火2 Fire · Increasing 1 庚子 Metal Rat 風雷益 **24** 廿九 9	水1 Water · Dimming Light 2 辛丑 Metal Ox 地火明夷 **25** 二月初一 3	金9 Metal · Fellowship 3 壬寅 Water Tiger 天火同人 **26** 初二 7	木8 Wood · Marrying Maiden 4 癸卯 Water Rabbit 雷澤歸妹 **27** 初三 7	木3 Wood · Opposition 5 甲辰 Wood Dragon 火澤睽 **28** 初四 2	火7 Fire · Waiting 6 乙巳 Wood Snake 水天需 **29** 初五 3	

MARCH 1952 癸卯

Xuan Kong Element 玄空五行	雷澤歸妹 Marrying Maiden	Period Luck 卦運	Monthly Star 月星
Wood 木8		7	4

SUNDAY	MONDAY	TUESDAY	WEDNESDAY	THURSDAY	FRIDAY	SATURDAY
木3 Wood 9 Advancement 乙亥 Wood Pig 火地晉 30 初五 3	水6 Water 1 Nourish 丙子 Fire Rat 山雷頤 31 初六 3					金4 Metal 7 Great Exceeding 丙午 Fire Horse 澤風大過 1 初六 3
水6 Water 8 Poison 丁未 Fire Goat 山風蠱 2 初七 7	火2 Fire 9 Dispersing 戊申 Earth Monkey 風水渙 3 初八 6	木3 Wood 1 Travelling 己酉 Earth Rooster 火山旅 4 初九 8	金9 Metal 2 Stagnation 庚戌 Metal Dog 天地否 5 初十 9	火7 Fire 3 Alliance 辛亥 Metal Pig 水地比 6 十一 7	木8 Wood 4 Thunder 壬子 Water Rat 震爲雷 7 十二 1	水6 Water 5 Beauty 癸丑 Water Ox 山火賁 8 十三 8
火7 Fire 6 Accomplished 甲寅 Wood Tiger 水火既濟 9 十四 9	水1 Water 7 Arriving 乙卯 Wood Rabbit 地澤臨 10 十五 4	金4 Metal 8 Marsh 丙辰 Fire Dragon 兌爲澤 11 十六 1	火2 Fire 9 Small Livestock 丁巳 Fire Snake 風天小畜 12 十七 8	木3 Wood 1 The Cauldron 戊午 Earth Horse 火風鼎 13 十八 4	水1 Water 2 Rising 己未 Earth Goat 地風升 14 十九 2	火7 Fire 3 Water 庚申 Metal Monkey 坎爲水 15 二十 1
木8 Wood 4 Lesser Exceeding 辛酉 Metal Rooster 雷山小過 16 廿一 3	金4 Metal 5 Gathering 壬戌 Water Dog 澤地萃 17 廿二 4	水6 Water 6 Peel 癸亥 Water Pig 山地剝 18 廿三 6	水1 Water 7 Earth 甲子 Wood Rat 坤爲地 19 廿四 1	木3 Wood 8 Biting 乙丑 Wood Ox 火雷噬嗑 20 廿五 6	火2 Fire 9 Family 丙寅 Fire Tiger 風火家人 21 廿六 4	水6 Water 1 Decreasing 丁卯 Fire Rabbit 山澤損 22 廿七 9
金9 Metal 2 Tread 戊辰 Earth Dragon 天澤履 23 廿八 6	木8 Wood 3 Great Strength 己巳 Earth Snake 雷天大壯 24 廿九 2	木8 Wood 4 Consistency 庚午 Metal Horse 雷風恒 25 三十 9	金9 Metal 5 Litigation 辛未 Metal Goat 天水訟 26 三月初一 3	水1 Water 6 Officer 壬申 Water Monkey 地水師 27 初二 7	火2 Fire 7 Gradual Progress 癸酉 Water Rooster 風山漸 28 初三 7	火7 Fire 8 Obstruction 甲戌 Wood Dog 水山蹇 29 初四 2

APRIL 1952 甲辰

Xuan Kong Element 玄空五行	火澤睽 Opposition	Period Luck 卦運	Monthly Star 月星
Wood 木3		2	3

SUNDAY	MONDAY	TUESDAY	WEDNESDAY	THURSDAY	FRIDAY	SATURDAY
		金4 Metal 2 Following 丁丑 Fire Ox 澤雷隨 1 初七 7	木8 Wood 3 Abundance 戊寅 Earth Tiger 雷火豐 2 初八 6	火7 Fire 4 Regulate 己卯 Earth Rabbit 水澤節 3 初九 8	水1 Water 5 Unity 庚辰 Metal Dragon 地天泰 4 初十 9	木3 Wood 6 Great Reward 辛巳 Metal Snake 火天大有 5 十一 7
火2 Fire 7 Wind 壬午 Water Horse 巽爲風 6 十二 1	金4 Metal 8 Trap 癸未 Water Goat 澤水困 7 十三 8	木3 Wood 9 Not Yet Accomplished 甲申 Wood Monkey 火水未濟 8 十四 9	金9 Metal 1 Retreat 乙酉 Wood Rooster 天山遯 9 十五 4	水6 Water 2 Mountain 丙戌 Fire Dog 艮爲山 10 十六 1	木8 Wood 3 Delight 丁亥 Fire Pig 雷地豫 11 十七 8	火7 Fire 4 Beginning 戊子 Earth Rat 水雷屯 12 十八 4
金9 Metal 5 Without Wrongdoing 己丑 Earth Ox 天雷無妄 13 十九 2	木3 Wood 6 Fire 庚寅 Metal Tiger 離爲火 14 二十 1	火2 Fire 7 Sincerity 辛卯 Metal Rabbit 風澤中孚 15 廿一 3	水6 Water 8 Big Livestock 壬辰 Water Dragon 山天大畜 16 廿二 4	金4 Metal 9 Eliminating 癸巳 Water Snake 澤天夬 17 廿三 6	金9 Metal 1 Heaven 甲午 Wood Horse 乾爲天 18 廿四 1	火7 Fire 2 Well 乙未 Wood Goat 水風井 19 廿五 6
木8 Wood 3 Relief 丙申 Fire Monkey 雷水解 20 廿六 4	金4 Metal 4 Influence 丁酉 Fire Rooster 澤山咸 21 廿七 9	水1 Water 5 Humility 戊戌 Earth Dog 地山謙 22 廿八 6	火2 Fire 6 Observation 己亥 Earth Pig 風地觀 23 廿九 2	火2 Fire 7 Increasing 庚子 Metal Rat 風雷益 24 四月初一 9	水1 Water 8 Dimming Light 辛丑 Metal Ox 地火明夷 25 初二 3	金9 Metal 9 Fellowship 壬寅 Water Tiger 天火同人 26 初三 7
木8 Wood 1 Marrying Maiden 癸卯 Water Rabbit 雷澤歸妹 27 初四 7	木3 Wood 2 Opposition 甲辰 Wood Dragon 火澤睽 28 初五 2	火7 Fire 3 Waiting 乙巳 Wood Snake 水天需 29 初六 3	金4 Metal 4 Great Exceeding 丙午 Fire Horse 澤風大過 30 初七 3			

MAY 1952 乙巳

Xuan Kong Element 玄空五行	水天需 Waiting	Period Luck 卦運	Monthly Star 月星
Fire 火7		3	2

SUNDAY	MONDAY	TUESDAY	WEDNESDAY	THURSDAY	FRIDAY	SATURDAY
				水6 Water 5 Poison 丁未 Fire Goat 山風蠱 1 7 初八	火2 Fire 6 Dispersing 戊申 Earth Monkey 風水渙 2 6 初九	木3 Wood 7 Travelling 己酉 Earth Rooster 火山旅 3 8 初十
金9 Metal 8 Stagnation 庚戌 Metal Dog 天地否 4 9 十一	火7 Fire 9 Alliance 辛亥 Metal Pig 水地比 5 7 十二	木8 Wood 1 Thunder 壬子 Water Rat 震爲雷 6 1 十三	水6 Water 2 Beauty 癸丑 Water Ox 山火賁 7 8 十四	火7 Fire 3 Accomplished 甲寅 Wood Tiger 水火既濟 8 9 十五	水1 Water 4 Arriving 乙卯 Wood Rabbit 地澤臨 9 4 十六	金4 Metal 5 Marsh 丙辰 Fire Dragon 兑爲澤 10 1 十七
火2 Fire 6 Small Livestock 丁巳 Fire Snake 風天小畜 11 8 十八	木3 Wood 7 The Cauldron 戊午 Earth Horse 火風鼎 12 4 十九	水1 Water 8 Rising 己未 Earth Goat 地風升 13 2 二十	火7 Fire 9 Water 庚申 Metal Monkey 坎爲水 14 1 廿一	木8 Wood 1 Lesser Exceeding 辛酉 Metal Rooster 雷山小過 15 3 廿二	金4 Metal 2 Gathering 壬戌 Water Dog 澤地萃 16 4 廿三	水6 Water 3 Peel 癸亥 Water Pig 山地剝 17 6 廿四
水1 Water 4 Earth 甲子 Wood Rat 坤爲地 18 1 廿五	木3 Wood 5 Biting 乙丑 Wood Ox 火雷噬嗑 19 6 廿六	火2 Fire 6 Family 丙寅 Fire Tiger 風火家人 20 4 廿七	水6 Water 7 Decreasing 丁卯 Fire Rabbit 山澤損 21 9 廿八	金9 Metal 8 Tread 戊辰 Earth Dragon 天澤履 22 6 廿九	木8 Wood 9 Great Strength 己巳 Earth Snake 雷天大壯 23 2 三十	木8 Wood 1 Consistency 庚午 Metal Horse 雷風恆 24 9 五月初一
金9 Metal 2 Litigation 辛未 Metal Goat 天水訟 25 3 初二	水1 Water 3 Officer 壬申 Water Monkey 地水師 26 7 初三	火2 Fire 4 Gradual Progress 癸酉 Water Rooster 風山漸 27 7 初四	火7 Fire 5 Obstruction 甲戌 Wood Dog 水山蹇 28 2 初五	木3 Wood 6 Advancement 乙亥 Wood Pig 火地晉 29 3 初六	水6 Water 7 Nourish 丙子 Fire Rat 山雷頤 30 3 初七	金4 Metal 8 Following 丁丑 Fire Ox 澤雷隨 31 7 初八

JUNE 1952 丙午

Xuan Kong Element 玄空五行	澤風大過 Great Exceeding	Period Luck 卦運	Monthly Star 月星
Metal 金4		3	1

SUNDAY	MONDAY	TUESDAY	WEDNESDAY	THURSDAY	FRIDAY	SATURDAY
木8 Wood 9 Abundance 戊寅 Earth Tiger 雷火豐 1 6 初九	火7 Fire 1 Regulate 己卯 Earth Rabbit 水澤節 2 8 初十	水1 Water 2 Unity 庚辰 Metal Dragon 地天泰 3 9 十一	木3 Wood 3 Great Reward 辛巳 Metal Snake 火天大有 4 7 十二	火2 Fire 4 Wind 壬午 Water Horse 巽爲風 5 1 十三	金4 Metal 5 Trap 癸未 Water Goat 澤水困 6 8 十四	木3 Wood 6 Not Yet Accomplished 甲申 Wood Monkey 火水未濟 7 9 十五
金9 Metal 7 Retreat 乙酉 Wood Rooster 天山遯 8 4 十六	水6 Water 8 Mountain 丙戌 Fire Dog 艮爲山 9 1 十七	木8 Wood 9 Delight 丁亥 Fire Pig 雷地豫 10 8 十八	火7 Fire 1 Beginning 戊子 Earth Rat 水雷屯 11 4 十九	金9 Metal 2 Without Wrongdoing 己丑 Earth Ox 天雷無妄 12 2 二十	木3 Wood 3 Fire 庚寅 Metal Tiger 離爲火 13 1 廿一	火2 Fire 4 Sincerity 辛卯 Metal Rabbit 風澤中孚 14 3 廿二
水6 Water 5 Big Livestock 壬辰 Water Dragon 山天大畜 15 4 廿三	金4 Metal 6 Eliminating 癸巳 Water Snake 澤天夬 16 6 廿四	金9 Metal 7 Heaven 甲午 Wood Horse 乾爲天 17 1 廿五	火7 Fire 8 Well 乙未 Wood Goat 水風井 18 6 廿六	木8 Wood 9 Relief 丙申 Fire Monkey 雷水解 19 4 廿七	金4 Metal 1 Influence 丁酉 Fire Rooster 澤山咸 20 9 廿八	水1 Water 28 Humility 戊戌 Earth Dog 地山謙 21 6 廿九
火2 Fire 7 Observation 己亥 Earth Pig 風地觀 22 2 閏五月初一	火2 Fire 6 Increasing 庚子 Metal Rat 風雷益 23 9 初二	水1 Water 5 Dimming Light 辛丑 Metal Ox 地火明夷 24 3 初三	金9 Metal 4 Fellowship 壬寅 Water Tiger 天火同人 25 7 初四	木8 Wood 3 Marrying Maiden 癸卯 Water Rabbit 雷澤歸妹 26 7 初五	木3 Wood 2 Opposition 甲辰 Wood Dragon 火澤睽 27 2 初六	火7 Fire 1 Waiting 乙巳 Wood Snake 水天需 28 3 初七
金4 Metal 9 Great Exceeding 丙午 Fire Horse 澤風大過 29 3 初八	水6 Water 8 Poison 丁未 Fire Goat 山風蠱 30 7 初九					

JULY 1952 丁未

Xuan Kong Element 玄空五行	山風蠱 Poison	Period Luck 卦運	Monthly Star 月星
Water 水6		7	9

SUNDAY	MONDAY	TUESDAY	WEDNESDAY	THURSDAY	FRIDAY	SATURDAY
		火2 Fire Dispersing 風水渙 7 戊申 Earth Monkey **1** 初十 6	木3 Wood Travelling 火山旅 6 己酉 Earth Rooster **2** 十一 8	金9 Metal Stagnation 天地否 5 庚戌 Metal Dog **3** 十二 9	火7 Fire Alliance 水地比 4 辛亥 Metal Pig **4** 十三 7	木8 Wood Thunder 震為雷 3 壬子 Water Rat **5** 十四 1
水6 Water Beauty 山火賁 2 癸丑 Water Ox **6** 十五 8	火7 Fire Accomplished 水火既濟 1 甲寅 Wood Tiger **7** 十六 9	水1 Water Arriving 地澤臨 9 乙卯 Wood Rabbit **8** 十七 4	金4 Metal Marsh 兑為澤 8 丙辰 Fire Dragon **9** 十八 1	火2 Fire Small Livestock 風天小畜 7 丁巳 Fire Snake **10** 十九 8	木3 Wood The Cauldron 火風鼎 6 戊午 Earth Horse **11** 二十 4	水1 Water Rising 地風升 5 己未 Earth Goat **12** 廿一 2
火7 Fire Water 坎為水 4 庚申 Metal Monkey **13** 廿二 1	木8 Wood Lesser Exceeding 雷山小過 3 辛酉 Metal Rooster **14** 廿三 3	金4 Metal Gathering 澤地萃 2 壬戌 Water Dog **15** 廿四 4	水6 Water Peel 山地剝 1 癸亥 Water Pig **16** 廿五 6	水1 Water Earth 坤為地 9 甲子 Wood Rat **17** 廿六 1	木3 Wood Biting 火雷噬嗑 8 乙丑 Wood Ox **18** 廿七 6	火2 Fire Family 風火家人 7 丙寅 Fire Tiger **19** 廿八 4
水6 Water Decreasing 山澤損 6 丁卯 Fire Rabbit **20** 廿九 9	金9 Metal Tread 天澤履 5 戊辰 Earth Dragon **21** 三十 6	木8 Wood Great Strength 雷天大壯 4 己巳 Earth Snake **22** 六月初一 2	木8 Wood Consistency 雷風恆 3 庚午 Metal Horse **23** 初二 9	金9 Metal Litigation 天水訟 2 辛未 Metal Goat **24** 初三 3	水1 Water Officer 地水師 1 壬申 Water Monkey **25** 初四 7	火2 Fire Gradual Progress 風山漸 9 癸酉 Water Rooster **26** 初五 7
火7 Fire Obstruction 水山蹇 8 甲戌 Wood Dog **27** 初六 2	木3 Wood Advancement 火地晉 7 乙亥 Wood Pig **28** 初七 3	水6 Water Nourish 山雷頤 6 丙子 Fire Rat **29** 初八 3	金4 Metal Following 澤雷隨 5 丁丑 Fire Ox **30** 初九 7	木8 Wood Abundance 雷火豐 4 戊寅 Earth Tiger **31** 初十 6		

AUGUST 1952 戊申

Xuan Kong Element 玄空五行	風水渙 Dispersing	Period Luck 卦運	Monthly Star 月星
Fire 火2		6	8

SUNDAY	MONDAY	TUESDAY	WEDNESDAY	THURSDAY	FRIDAY	SATURDAY
木3 Wood Travelling 火山旅 9 己酉 Earth Rooster **31** 十二 8					火7 Fire Regulate 水澤節 3 己卯 Earth Rabbit **1** 十一 8	水1 Water Unity 地天泰 2 庚辰 Metal Dragon **2** 十二 9
木3 Wood Great Reward 火天大有 1 辛巳 Metal Snake **3** 十三 7	火2 Fire Wind 巽為風 9 壬午 Water Horse **4** 十四 1	金4 Metal Trap 澤水困 8 癸未 Water Goat **5** 十五 8	木3 Wood Not Yet Accomplished 火水未濟 7 甲申 Wood Monkey **6** 十六 9	金9 Metal Retreat 天山遯 6 乙酉 Wood Rooster **7** 十七 4	水6 Water Mountain 艮為山 5 丙戌 Fire Dog **8** 十八 1	木8 Wood Delight 雷地豫 4 丁亥 Fire Pig **9** 十九 8
火7 Fire Beginning 水雷屯 3 戊子 Earth Rat **10** 二十 4	金9 Metal Without Wrongdoing 天雷無妄 2 己丑 Earth Ox **11** 廿一 2	木3 Wood Fire 離為火 1 庚寅 Metal Tiger **12** 廿二 1	火2 Fire Sincerity 風澤中孚 9 辛卯 Metal Rabbit **13** 廿三 3	水6 Water Big Livestock 山天大畜 8 壬辰 Water Dragon **14** 廿四 4	金4 Metal Eliminating 澤天夬 7 癸巳 Water Snake **15** 廿五 6	金9 Metal Heaven 乾為天 6 甲午 Wood Horse **16** 廿六 1
火7 Fire Well 水風井 5 乙未 Wood Goat **17** 廿七 6	木8 Wood Relief 雷水解 4 丙申 Fire Monkey **18** 廿八 4	金4 Metal Influence 澤山咸 3 丁酉 Fire Rooster **19** 廿九 9	水1 Water Humility 地山謙 2 戊戌 Earth Dog **20** 七月初一 6	火2 Fire Observation 風地觀 1 己亥 Earth Pig **21** 初二 2	火2 Fire Increasing 風雷益 9 庚子 Metal Rat **22** 初三 9	水1 Water Dimming Light 地火明夷 8 辛丑 Metal Ox **23** 初四 3
金9 Metal Fellowship 天火同人 7 壬寅 Water Tiger **24** 初五 7	木8 Wood Marrying Maiden 雷澤歸妹 6 癸卯 Water Rabbit **25** 初六 7	木3 Wood Opposition 火澤睽 5 甲辰 Wood Dragon **26** 初七 2	火7 Fire Waiting 水天需 4 乙巳 Wood Snake **27** 初八 3	金4 Metal Great Exceeding 澤風大過 3 丙午 Fire Horse **28** 初九 3	水6 Water Poison 山風蠱 2 丁未 Fire Goat **29** 初十 7	火2 Fire Dispersing 風水渙 1 戊申 Earth Monkey **30** 十一 6

SEPTEMBER 1952 己酉

Xuan Kong Element 玄空五行	火山旅 Travelling	Period Luck 卦運	Monthly Star 月星
Wood 木3		8	7

SUNDAY	MONDAY	TUESDAY	WEDNESDAY	THURSDAY	FRIDAY	SATURDAY
	1 金9 Metal · 8 Stagnation 庚戌 Metal Dog 天地否 十三 · 9	**2** 火7 Fire · 7 Alliance 辛亥 Metal Pig 水地比 十四 · 7	**3** 木8 Wood · 6 Thunder 壬子 Water Rat 震爲雷 十五 · 1	**4** 水6 Water · 5 Beauty 癸丑 Water Ox 山火賁 十六 · 8	**5** 火7 Fire · 4 Accomplished 甲寅 Wood Tiger 水火既濟 十七 · 9	**6** 水1 Water · 3 Arriving 乙卯 Wood Rabbit 地澤臨 十八 · 4
7 金4 Metal · 2 Marsh 丙辰 Fire Dragon 兑爲澤 十九 · 1	**8** 火2 Fire · 1 Small Livestock 丁巳 Fire Snake 風天小畜 二十 · 8	**9** 木3 Wood · 9 The Cauldron 戊午 Earth Horse 火風鼎 廿一 · 4	**10** 水1 Water · 8 Rising 己未 Earth Goat 地風升 廿二 · 2	**11** 火7 Fire · 7 Water 庚申 Metal Monkey 坎爲水 廿三 · 1	**12** 木8 Wood · 6 Lesser Exceeding 辛酉 Metal Rooster 雷山小過 廿四 · 3	**13** 金4 Metal · 5 Gathering 壬戌 Water Dog 澤地萃 廿五 · 4
14 水6 Water · 4 Peel 癸亥 Water Pig 山地剝 廿六 · 6	**15** 水1 Water · 3 Earth 甲子 Wood Rat 坤爲地 廿七 · 1	**16** 木3 Wood · 2 Biting 乙丑 Wood Ox 火雷噬嗑 廿八 · 6	**17** 火2 Fire · 1 Family 丙寅 Fire Tiger 風火家人 廿九 · 4	**18** 水6 Water · 9 Decreasing 丁卯 Fire Rabbit 山澤損 三十 · 9	**19** 金9 Metal · 8 Tread 戊辰 Earth Dragon 天澤履 八月初一 · 6	**20** 木8 Wood · 7 Great Strength 己巳 Earth Snake 雷天大壯 初二 · 2
21 木8 Wood · 6 Consistency 庚午 Metal Horse 雷風恆 初三 · 9	**22** 金9 Metal · 5 Litigation 辛未 Metal Goat 天水訟 初四 · 3	**23** 水1 Water · 4 Officer 壬申 Water Monkey 地水師 初五 · 7	**24** 火2 Fire · 3 Gradual Progress 癸酉 Water Rooster 風山漸 初六 · 7	**25** 火7 Fire · 2 Obstruction 甲戌 Wood Dog 水山蹇 初七 · 2	**26** 木3 Wood · 1 Advancement 乙亥 Wood Pig 火地晉 初八 · 3	**27** 水6 Water · 9 Nourish 丙子 Fire Rat 山雷頤 初九 · 3
28 金4 Metal · 8 Following 丁丑 Fire Ox 澤雷隨 初十 · 7	**29** 木8 Wood · 7 Abundance 戊寅 Earth Tiger 雷火豐 十一 · 6	**30** 火7 Fire · 6 Regulate 己卯 Earth Rabbit 水澤節 十二 · 8				

OCTOBER 1952 庚戌

Xuan Kong Element 玄空五行	天地否 Stagnation	Period Luck 卦運	Monthly Star 月星
Metal 金9		9	6

SUNDAY	MONDAY	TUESDAY	WEDNESDAY	THURSDAY	FRIDAY	SATURDAY
			1 水1 Water · 5 Unity 庚辰 Metal Dragon 地天泰 十三 · 9	**2** 木3 Wood · 4 Great Reward 辛巳 Metal Snake 火天大有 十四 · 7	**3** 火2 Fire · 3 Wind 壬午 Water Horse 巽爲風 十五 · 1	**4** 金4 Metal · 2 Trap 癸未 Water Goat 澤水困 十六 · 8
5 木3 Wood · 1 Not Yet Accomplished 甲申 Wood Monkey 火水未濟 十七 · 9	**6** 金9 Metal · 9 Retreat 乙酉 Wood Rooster 天山遯 十八 · 4	**7** 水6 Water · 8 Mountain 丙戌 Fire Dog 艮爲山 十九 · 1	**8** 木8 Wood · 7 Delight 丁亥 Fire Pig 雷地豫 二十 · 8	**9** 火7 Fire · 6 Beginning 戊子 Earth Rat 水雷屯 廿一 · 4	**10** 金9 Metal · 5 Without Wrongdoing 己丑 Earth Ox 天雷無妄 廿二 · 2	**11** 木3 Wood · 4 Fire 庚寅 Metal Tiger 離爲火 廿三 · 1
12 火2 Fire · 3 Sincerity 辛卯 Metal Rabbit 風澤中孚 廿四 · 3	**13** 水6 Water · 2 Big Livestock 壬辰 Water Dragon 山天大畜 廿五 · 4	**14** 金4 Metal · 1 Eliminating 癸巳 Water Snake 澤天夬 廿六 · 6	**15** 金9 Metal · 9 Heaven 甲午 Wood Horse 乾爲天 廿七 · 1	**16** 火7 Fire · 8 Well 乙未 Wood Goat 水風井 廿八 · 6	**17** 木8 Wood · 7 Relief 丙申 Fire Monkey 雷水解 廿九 · 4	**18** 金4 Metal · 6 Influence 丁酉 Fire Rooster 澤山咸 三十 · 9
19 水1 Water · 5 Humility 戊戌 Earth Dog 地山謙 九月初一 · 6	**20** 火2 Fire · 4 Observation 己亥 Earth Pig 風地觀 初二 · 2	**21** 火2 Fire · 3 Increasing 庚子 Metal Rat 風雷益 初三 · 9	**22** 水1 Water · 2 Dimming Light 辛丑 Metal Ox 地火明夷 初四 · 3	**23** 金9 Metal · 1 Fellowship 壬寅 Water Tiger 天火同人 初五 · 7	**24** 木8 Wood · 9 Marrying Maiden 癸卯 Water Rabbit 雷澤歸妹 初六 · 7	**25** 木3 Wood · 8 Opposition 甲辰 Wood Dragon 火澤睽 初七 · 2
26 火7 Fire · 7 Waiting 乙巳 Wood Snake 水天需 初八 · 3	**27** 金4 Metal · 6 Great Exceeding 丙午 Fire Horse 澤風大過 初九 · 3	**28** 水6 Water · 5 Poison 丁未 Fire Goat 山風蠱 初十 · 7	**29** 火2 Fire · 4 Dispersing 戊申 Earth Monkey 風水渙 十一 · 6	**30** 木3 Wood · 3 Travelling 己酉 Earth Rooster 火山旅 十二 · 8	**31** 金9 Metal · 2 Stagnation 庚戌 Metal Dog 天地否 十三 · 9	

NOVEMBER 1952 辛亥

Xuan Kong Element 玄空五行	水地比 Alliance	Period Luck 卦運	Monthly Star 月星
Fire 火7		7	5

SUNDAY	MONDAY	TUESDAY	WEDNESDAY	THURSDAY	FRIDAY	SATURDAY
水1 Water 8 Unity 地天泰 庚辰 Metal Dragon 30 十四 9						火7 Fire 1 Alliance 水地比 辛亥 Metal Pig 1 十四 7
木8 Wood 9 Thunder 震為雷 壬子 Water Rat 2 十五 1	水6 Water 8 Beauty 山火賁 癸丑 Water Ox 3 十六 8	火7 Fire 7 Accomplished 水火既濟 甲寅 Wood Tiger 4 十七 9	水1 Water 6 Arriving 地澤臨 乙卯 Wood Rabbit 5 十八 4	金4 Metal 5 Marsh 兌為澤 丙辰 Fire Dragon 6 十九 1	火2 Fire 4 Small Livestock 風天小畜 丁巳 Fire Snake 7 二十 8	木3 Wood 3 The Cauldron 火風鼎 戊午 Earth Horse 8 廿一 4
水1 Water 2 Rising 地風升 己未 Earth Goat 9 廿二 2	火7 Fire 1 Water 坎為水 庚申 Metal Monkey 10 廿三 1	木8 Wood 9 Lesser Exceeding 雷山小過 辛酉 Metal Rooster 11 廿四 3	金4 Metal 8 Gathering 澤地萃 壬戌 Water Dog 12 廿五 4	水6 Water 7 Peel 山地剝 癸亥 Water Pig 13 廿六 6	水1 Water 6 Earth 坤為地 甲子 Wood Rat 14 廿七 1	木3 Wood 5 Biting 火雷噬嗑 乙丑 Wood Ox 15 廿八 6
火2 Fire 4 Family 風火家人 丙寅 Fire Tiger 16 廿九 4	水6 Water 3 Decreasing 山澤損 丁卯 Fire Rabbit 17 十月初一 9	金9 Metal 2 Tread 天澤履 戊辰 Earth Dragon 18 初二 6	木8 Wood 1 Great Strength 雷天大壯 己巳 Earth Snake 19 初三 2	木8 Wood 9 Consistency 雷風恆 庚午 Metal Horse 20 初四 9	金9 Metal 8 Litigation 天水訟 辛未 Metal Goat 21 初五 3	水1 Water 7 Officer 地水師 壬申 Water Monkey 22 初六 7
火2 Fire 6 Gradual Progress 風山漸 癸酉 Water Rooster 23 初七 7	火7 Fire 5 Obstruction 水山蹇 甲戌 Wood Dog 24 初八 2	木3 Wood 4 Advancement 火地晉 乙亥 Wood Pig 25 初九 3	水6 Water 3 Nourish 山雷頤 丙子 Fire Rat 26 初十 3	金4 Metal 2 Following 澤雷隨 丁丑 Fire Ox 27 十一 7	木8 Wood 1 Abundance 雷火豐 戊寅 Earth Tiger 28 十二 6	火7 Fire 9 Regulate 水澤節 己卯 Earth Rabbit 29 十三 8

DECEMBER 1952 壬子

Xuan Kong Element 玄空五行	震為雷 Thunder	Period Luck 卦運	Monthly Star 月星
Wood 木8		1	4

SUNDAY	MONDAY	TUESDAY	WEDNESDAY	THURSDAY	FRIDAY	SATURDAY
	木3 Wood 7 Great Reward 火天大有 辛巳 Metal Snake 1 十五 7	火2 Fire 6 Wind 巽為風 壬午 Water Horse 2 十六 1	金4 Metal 5 Trap 澤水困 癸未 Water Goat 3 十七 8	木3 Wood 4 Not Yet Accomplished 火水未濟 甲申 Wood Monkey 4 十八 9	金9 Metal 3 Retreat 天山遯 乙酉 Wood Rooster 5 十九 4	水6 Water 2 Mountain 艮為山 丙戌 Fire Dog 6 二十 1
木8 Wood 1 Delight 雷地豫 丁亥 Fire Pig 7 廿一 8	火7 Fire 9 Beginning 水雷屯 戊子 Earth Rat 8 廿二 4	金9 Metal 8 Without Wrongdoing 天雷無妄 己丑 Earth Ox 9 廿三 2	木3 Wood 7 Fire 離為火 庚寅 Metal Tiger 10 廿四 1	火2 Fire 6 Sincerity 風澤中孚 辛卯 Metal Rabbit 11 廿五 3	水6 Water 5 Big Livestock 山天大畜 壬辰 Water Dragon 12 廿六 4	金4 Metal 4 Eliminating 澤天夬 癸巳 Water Snake 13 廿七 6
金9 Metal 3 Heaven 乾為天 甲午 Wood Horse 14 廿八 1	火7 Fire 2 Well 水風井 乙未 Wood Goat 15 廿九 6	木8 Wood 1 Relief 雷水解 丙申 Fire Monkey 16 三十 4	金4 Metal 9 Influence 澤山咸 丁酉 Fire Rooster 17 十一月初一 9	水1 Water 8 Humility 地山謙 戊戌 Earth Dog 18 初二 6	火2 Fire 7 Observation 風地觀 己亥 Earth Pig 19 初三 2	火2 Fire 6 Increasing 風雷益 庚子 Metal Rat 20 初四 9
水1 Water 5 Dimming Light 地火明夷 辛丑 Metal Ox 21 初五 3	金9 Metal 4/6 Fellowship 天火同人 壬寅 Water Tiger 22 初六 7	木8 Wood 7 Marrying Maiden 雷澤歸妹 癸卯 Water Rabbit 23 初七 7	木3 Wood 8 Opposition 火澤睽 甲辰 Wood Dragon 24 初八 2	火7 Fire 9 Waiting 水天需 乙巳 Wood Snake 25 初九 3	金4 Metal 1 Great Exceeding 澤風大過 丙午 Fire Horse 26 初十 3	水6 Water 2 Poison 山風蠱 丁未 Fire Goat 27 十一 7
火2 Fire 3 Dispersing 風水渙 戊申 Earth Monkey 28 十二 6	木3 Wood 4 Travelling 火山旅 己酉 Earth Rooster 29 十三 8	金9 Metal 5 Stagnation 天地否 庚戌 Metal Dog 30 十四 9	火7 Fire 6 Alliance 水地比 辛亥 Metal Pig 31 十五 7			

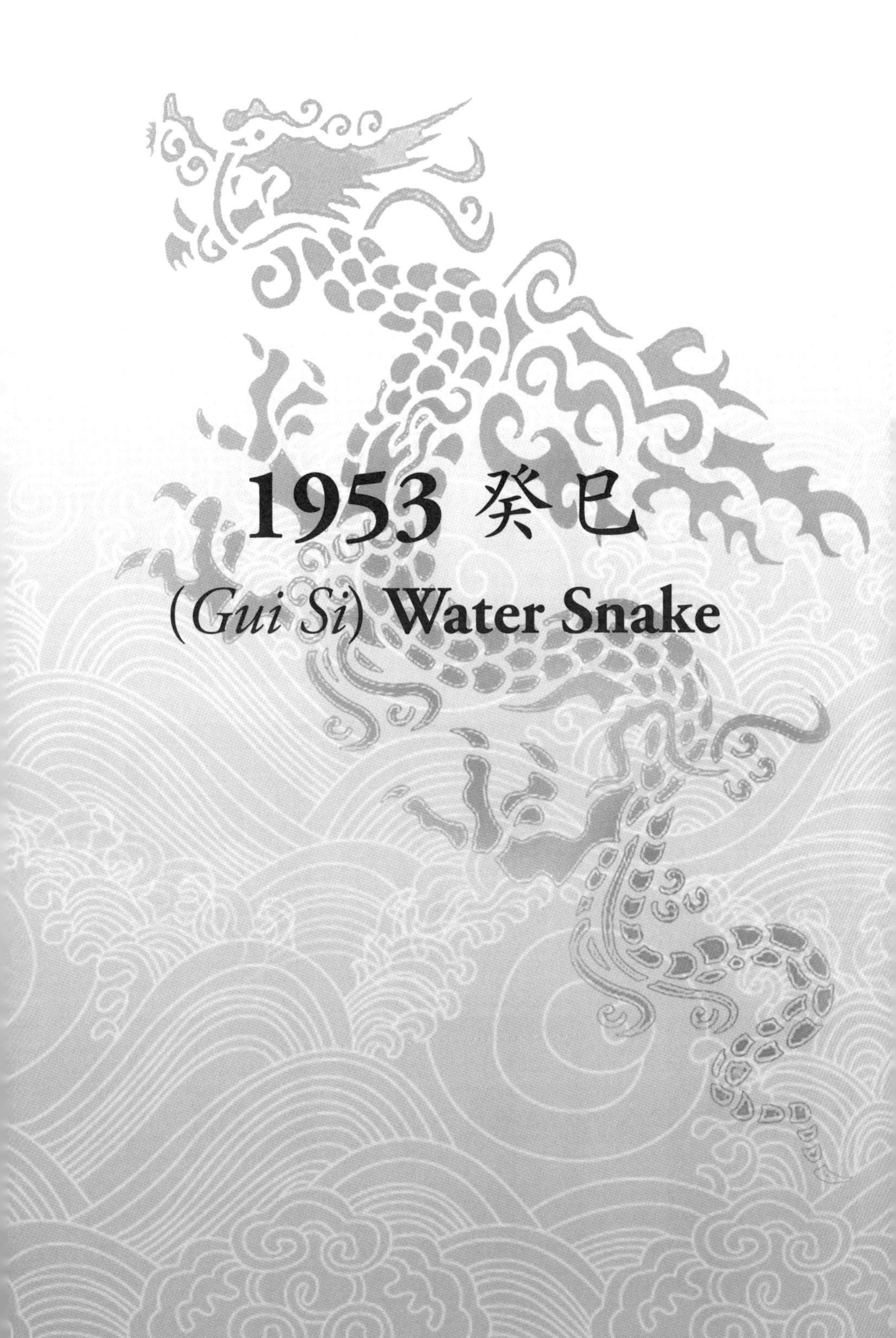

1953 癸巳

(*Gui Si*) Water Snake

1953 癸巳 *(Gui Si)* Water Snake

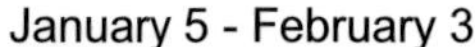

January 5 - February 3

February 4 - March 5

March 6 - April 4

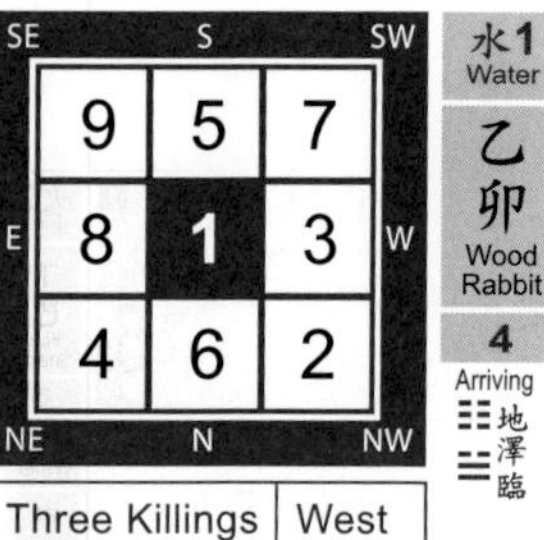

April 5 - May 5

May 6 - June 5

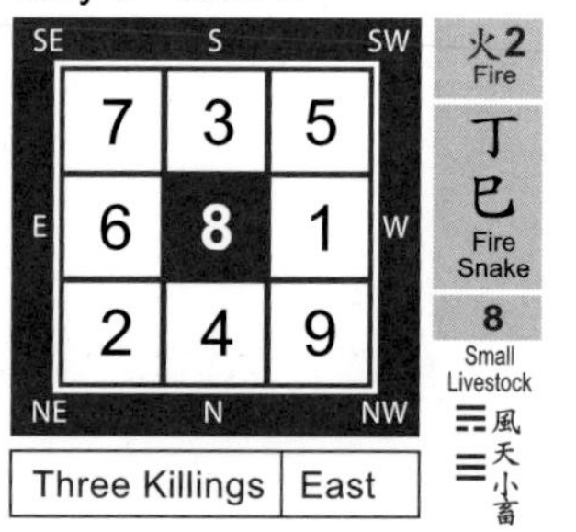

June 6 - July 6

July 7 - August 7

August 8 - September 7

September 8 - October 7

October 8 - November 7

November 8 - December 6

December 7 - January 5

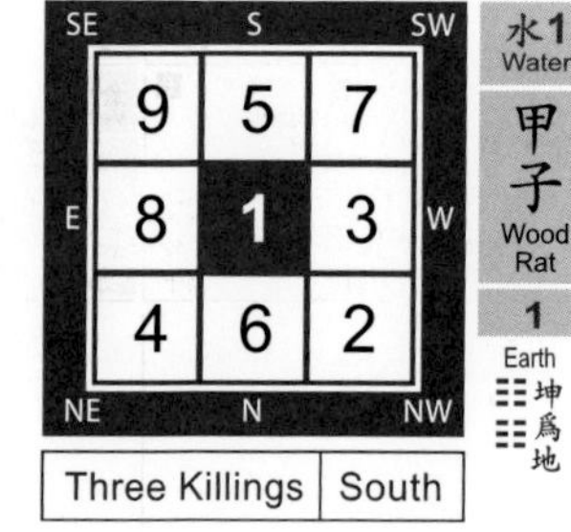

JANUARY 1953 癸丑

Xuan Kong Element 玄空五行	山火賁 Beauty	Period Luck 卦運	Monthly Star 月星
Water 水6		8	3

SUNDAY	MONDAY	TUESDAY	WEDNESDAY	THURSDAY	FRIDAY	SATURDAY
				木8 Wood 7 Thunder 壬子 Water Rat 震爲雷 **1** 十六 1	水6 Water 8 Beauty 癸丑 Water Ox 山火賁 **2** 十七 8	火7 Fire 9 Accomplished 甲寅 Wood Tiger 水火既濟 **3** 十八 9
水1 Water 1 Arriving 乙卯 Wood Rabbit 地澤臨 **4** 十九 4	金4 Metal 2 Marsh 丙辰 Fire Dragon 兌爲澤 **5** 二十 1	火2 Fire 3 Small Livestock 丁巳 Fire Snake 風天小畜 **6** 廿一 8	木3 Wood 4 The Cauldron 戊午 Earth Horse 火風鼎 **7** 廿二 4	水1 Water 5 Rising 己未 Earth Goat 地風升 **8** 廿三 2	火7 Fire 6 Water 庚申 Metal Monkey 坎爲水 **9** 廿四 1	木8 Wood 7 Lesser Exceeding 辛酉 Metal Rooster 雷山小過 **10** 廿五 3
金4 Metal 8 Gathering 壬戌 Water Dog 澤地萃 **11** 廿六 4	水6 Water 9 Peel 癸亥 Water Pig 山地剝 **12** 廿七 6	水1 Water 1 Earth 甲子 Wood Rat 坤爲地 **13** 廿八 1	木3 Wood 2 Biting 乙丑 Wood Ox 火雷噬嗑 **14** 廿九 6	火2 Fire 3 Family 丙寅 Fire Tiger 風火家人 **15** 十二月初一 4	水6 Water 4 Decreasing 丁卯 Fire Rabbit 山澤損 **16** 初二 9	金9 Metal 5 Tread 戊辰 Earth Dragon 天澤履 **17** 初三 6
木8 Wood 6 Great Strength 己巳 Earth Snake 雷天大壯 **18** 初四 2	木8 Wood 7 Consistency 庚午 Metal Horse 雷風恆 **19** 初五 9	金9 Metal 8 Litigation 辛未 Metal Goat 天水訟 **20** 初六 3	水1 Water 9 Officer 壬申 Water Monkey 地水師 **21** 初七 7	火2 Fire 1 Gradual Progress 癸酉 Water Rooster 風山漸 **22** 初八 7	火7 Fire 2 Obstruction 甲戌 Wood Dog 水山蹇 **23** 初九 2	木3 Wood 3 Advancement 乙亥 Wood Pig 火地晉 **24** 初十 3
水6 Water 4 Nourish 丙子 Fire Rat 山雷頤 **25** 十一 3	金4 Metal 5 Following 丁丑 Fire Ox 澤雷隨 **26** 十二 7	木8 Wood 6 Abundance 戊寅 Earth Tiger 雷火豐 **27** 十三 6	火7 Fire 7 Regulate 己卯 Earth Rabbit 水澤節 **28** 十四 8	水1 Water 8 Unity 庚辰 Metal Dragon 地天泰 **29** 十五 9	木3 Wood 9 Great Reward 辛巳 Metal Snake 火天大有 **30** 十六 7	火2 Fire 1 Wind 壬午 Water Horse 巽爲風 **31** 十七 1

FEBRUARY 1953 甲寅

Xuan Kong Element 玄空五行	水火既濟 Accomplished	Period Luck 卦運	Monthly Star 月星
Fire 火7		9	2

SUNDAY	MONDAY	TUESDAY	WEDNESDAY	THURSDAY	FRIDAY	SATURDAY
金4 Metal 2 Trap 癸未 Water Goat 澤水困 **1** 十八 8	木3 Wood 3 Not Yet Accomplished 甲申 Wood Monkey 火水未濟 **2** 十九 9	金9 Metal 4 Retreat 乙酉 Wood Rooster 天山遯 **3** 二十 4	水6 Water 5 Mountain 丙戌 Fire Dog 艮爲山 **4** 廿一 1	木8 Wood 6 Delight 丁亥 Fire Pig 雷地豫 **5** 廿二 8	火7 Fire 7 Beginning 戊子 Earth Rat 水雷屯 **6** 廿三 4	金9 Metal 8 Without Wrongdoing 己丑 Earth Ox 天雷無妄 **7** 廿四 2
木3 Wood 9 Fire 庚寅 Metal Tiger 離爲火 **8** 廿五 1	火2 Fire 1 Sincerity 辛卯 Metal Rabbit 風澤中孚 **9** 廿六 3	水6 Water 2 Big Livestock 壬辰 Water Dragon 山天大畜 **10** 廿七 4	金4 Metal 3 Eliminating 癸巳 Water Snake 澤天夬 **11** 廿八 6	金9 Metal 4 Heaven 甲午 Wood Horse 乾爲天 **12** 廿九 1	火7 Fire 5 Well 乙未 Wood Goat 水風井 **13** 三十 6	木8 Wood 6 Relief 丙申 Fire Monkey 雷水解 **14** 正月初一 4
金4 Metal 7 Influence 丁酉 Fire Rooster 澤山咸 **15** 初二 9	水1 Water 8 Humility 戊戌 Earth Dog 地山謙 **16** 初三 6	火2 Fire 9 Observation 己亥 Earth Pig 風地觀 **17** 初四 2	火2 Fire 1 Increasing 庚子 Metal Rat 風雷益 **18** 初五 9	水1 Water 2 Dimming Light 辛丑 Metal Ox 地火明夷 **19** 初六 3	金9 Metal 3 Fellowship 壬寅 Water Tiger 天火同人 **20** 初七 7	木8 Wood 4 Marrying Maiden 癸卯 Water Rabbit 雷澤歸妹 **21** 初八 7
木3 Wood 5 Opposition 甲辰 Wood Dragon 火澤睽 **22** 初九 2	火7 Fire 6 Waiting 乙巳 Wood Snake 水天需 **23** 初十 3	金4 Metal 7 Great Exceeding 丙午 Fire Horse 澤風大過 **24** 十一 3	水6 Water 8 Poison 丁未 Fire Goat 山風蠱 **25** 十二 7	火2 Fire 9 Dispersing 戊申 Earth Monkey 風水渙 **26** 十三 6	木3 Wood 1 Travelling 己酉 Earth Rooster 火山旅 **27** 十四 8	金9 Metal 2 Stagnation 庚戌 Metal Dog 天地否 **28** 十五 9

MARCH 1953 乙卯

Xuan Kong Element 玄空五行	地澤臨 Arriving	Period Luck 卦運	Monthly Star 月星
Water 水1		4	1

SUNDAY	MONDAY	TUESDAY	WEDNESDAY	THURSDAY	FRIDAY	SATURDAY
火7 Fire 3 Alliance 辛亥 Metal Pig 水地比 1 十六 7	木8 Wood 4 Thunder 壬子 Water Rat 震爲雷 2 十七 1	水6 Water 5 Beauty 癸丑 Water Ox 山火賁 3 十八 8	火7 Fire 6 Accomplished 甲寅 Wood Tiger 水火既濟 4 十九 9	水1 Water 7 Arriving 乙卯 Wood Rabbit 地澤臨 5 二十 4	金4 Metal 8 Marsh 丙辰 Fire Dragon 兌爲澤 6 廿一 1	火2 Fire 9 Small Livestock 丁巳 Fire Snake 風天小畜 7 廿二 8
木3 Wood 1 The Cauldron 戊午 Earth Horse 火風鼎 8 廿三 4	水1 Water 2 Rising 己未 Earth Goat 地風升 9 廿四 2	火7 Fire 3 Water 庚申 Metal Monkey 坎爲水 10 廿五 1	木8 Wood 4 Lesser Exceeding 辛酉 Metal Rooster 雷山小過 11 廿六 3	金4 Metal 5 Gathering 壬戌 Water Dog 澤地萃 12 廿七 4	水6 Water 6 Peel 癸亥 Water Pig 山地剝 13 廿八 6	水1 Water 7 Earth 甲子 Wood Rat 坤爲地 14 廿九 1
木3 Wood 8 Biting 乙丑 Wood Ox 火雷噬嗑 15 二月初一 6	火2 Fire 9 Family 丙寅 Fire Tiger 風火家人 16 初二 4	水6 Water 1 Decreasing 丁卯 Fire Rabbit 山澤損 17 初三 9	金9 Metal 2 Tread 戊辰 Earth Dragon 天澤履 18 初四 6	木8 Wood 3 Great Strength 己巳 Earth Snake 雷天大壯 19 初五 2	木8 Wood 4 Consistency 庚午 Metal Horse 雷風恆 20 初六 9	金9 Metal 5 Litigation 辛未 Metal Goat 天水訟 21 初七 3
水1 Water 6 Officer 壬申 Water Monkey 地水師 22 初八 7	火2 Fire 7 Gradual Progress 癸酉 Water Rooster 風山漸 23 初九 7	火7 Fire 8 Obstruction 甲戌 Wood Dog 水山蹇 24 初十 2	木3 Wood 9 Advancement 乙亥 Wood Pig 火地晉 25 十一 3	水6 Water 1 Nourish 丙子 Fire Rat 山雷頤 26 十二 3	金4 Metal 2 Following 丁丑 Fire Ox 澤雷隨 27 十三 7	木8 Wood 3 Abundance 戊寅 Earth Tiger 雷火豐 28 十四 6
火7 Fire 4 Regulate 己卯 Earth Rabbit 水澤節 29 十五 8	水1 Water 5 Unity 庚辰 Metal Dragon 地天泰 30 十六 9	木3 Wood 6 Great Reward 辛巳 Metal Snake 火天大有 31 十七 7				

APRIL 1953 丙辰

Xuan Kong Element 玄空五行	兌爲澤 Marsh	Period Luck 卦運	Monthly Star 月星
Metal 金4		1	9

SUNDAY	MONDAY	TUESDAY	WEDNESDAY	THURSDAY	FRIDAY	SATURDAY
			火2 Fire 7 Wind 壬午 Water Horse 巽爲風 1 十八 1	金4 Metal 8 Trap 癸未 Water Goat 澤水困 2 十九 8	木3 Wood 9 Not Yet Accomplished 甲申 Wood Monkey 火水未濟 3 二十 9	金9 Metal 1 Retreat 乙酉 Wood Rooster 天山遯 4 廿一 4
水6 Water 2 Mountain 丙戌 Fire Dog 艮爲山 5 廿二 1	木8 Wood 3 Delight 丁亥 Fire Pig 雷地豫 6 廿三 8	火7 Fire 4 Beginning 戊子 Earth Rat 水雷屯 7 廿四 4	金9 Metal 5 Without Wrongdoing 己丑 Earth Ox 天雷無妄 8 廿五 2	木3 Wood 6 Fire 庚寅 Metal Tiger 離爲火 9 廿六 1	火2 Fire 7 Sincerity 辛卯 Metal Rabbit 風澤中孚 10 廿七 3	水6 Water 8 Big Livestock 壬辰 Water Dragon 山天大畜 11 廿八 4
金4 Metal 9 Eliminating 癸巳 Water Snake 澤天夬 12 廿九 6	金9 Metal 1 Heaven 甲午 Wood Horse 乾爲天 13 三十 1	火7 Fire 2 Well 乙未 Wood Goat 水風井 14 三月初一 6	木8 Wood 3 Relief 丙申 Fire Monkey 雷水解 15 初二 4	金4 Metal 4 Influence 丁酉 Fire Rooster 澤山咸 16 初三 9	水1 Water 5 Humility 戊戌 Earth Dog 地山謙 17 初四 6	火2 Fire 6 Observation 己亥 Earth Pig 風地觀 18 初五 2
火2 Fire 7 Increasing 庚子 Metal Rat 風雷益 19 初六 9	水1 Water 8 Dimming Light 辛丑 Metal Ox 地火明夷 20 初七 3	金9 Metal 9 Fellowship 壬寅 Water Tiger 天火同人 21 初八 7	木8 Wood 1 Marrying Maiden 癸卯 Water Rabbit 雷澤歸妹 22 初九 7	木3 Wood 2 Opposition 甲辰 Wood Dragon 火澤睽 23 初十 2	火7 Fire 3 Waiting 乙巳 Wood Snake 水天需 24 十一 3	金4 Metal 4 Great Exceeding 丙午 Fire Horse 澤風大過 25 十二 3
水6 Water 5 Poison 丁未 Fire Goat 山風蠱 26 十三 7	火2 Fire 6 Dispersing 戊申 Earth Monkey 風水渙 27 十四 6	木3 Wood 7 Travelling 己酉 Earth Rooster 火山旅 28 十五 8	金9 Metal 8 Stagnation 庚戌 Metal Dog 天地否 29 十六 9	火7 Fire 9 Alliance 辛亥 Metal Pig 水地比 30 十七 7		

MAY 1953 丁巳

Xuan Kong Element 玄空五行	風天小畜 Small Livestock	Period Luck 卦運	Monthly Star 月星
Fire 火2		8	8

SUNDAY	MONDAY	TUESDAY	WEDNESDAY	THURSDAY	FRIDAY	SATURDAY
31 十九 火2 Fire [4] Wind 巽為風 壬午 Water Horse 1					**1** 十八 木8 Wood [1] Thunder 震為雷 壬子 Water Rat 1	**2** 十九 水6 Water [2] Beauty 山火賁 癸丑 Water Ox 8
3 二十 火7 Fire [3] Accomplished 水火既濟 甲寅 Wood Tiger 9	**4** 廿一 水1 Water [4] Arriving 地澤臨 乙卯 Wood Rabbit 4	**5** 廿二 金4 Metal [5] Marsh 兌為澤 丙辰 Fire Dragon 1	**6** 廿三 火2 Fire [6] Small Livestock 風天小畜 丁巳 Fire Snake 8	**7** 廿四 木3 Wood [7] The Cauldron 火風鼎 戊午 Earth Horse 4	**8** 廿五 水1 Water [8] Rising 地風升 己未 Earth Goat 2	**9** 廿六 火7 Fire [9] Water 坎為水 庚申 Metal Monkey 1
10 廿七 木8 Wood [1] Lesser Exceeding 雷山小過 辛酉 Metal Rooster 3	**11** 廿八 金4 Metal [2] Gathering 澤地萃 壬戌 Water Dog 4	**12** 廿九 水6 Water [3] Peel 山地剝 癸亥 Water Pig 6	**13** 四月初一 水1 Water [4] Earth 坤為地 甲子 Wood Rat 1	**14** 初二 木3 Wood [5] Biting 火雷噬嗑 乙丑 Wood Ox 6	**15** 初三 火2 Fire [6] Family 風火家人 丙寅 Fire Tiger 4	**16** 初四 水6 Water [7] Decreasing 山澤損 丁卯 Fire Rabbit 9
17 初五 金9 Metal [8] Tread 天澤履 戊辰 Earth Dragon 6	**18** 初六 木8 Wood [9] Great Strength 雷天大壯 己巳 Earth Snake 2	**19** 初七 木8 Wood [1] Consistency 雷風恆 庚午 Metal Horse 9	**20** 初八 金9 Metal [2] Litigation 天水訟 辛未 Metal Goat 3	**21** 初九 水1 Water [3] Officer 地水師 壬申 Water Monkey 7	**22** 初十 火2 Fire [4] Gradual Progress 風山漸 癸酉 Water Rooster 7	**23** 十一 火7 Fire [5] Obstruction 水山蹇 甲戌 Wood Dog 2
24 十二 木3 Wood [6] Advancement 火地晉 乙亥 Wood Pig 3	**25** 十三 水6 Water [7] Nourish 山雷頤 丙子 Fire Rat 3	**26** 十四 金4 Metal [8] Following 澤雷隨 丁丑 Fire Ox 7	**27** 十五 木8 Wood [9] Abundance 雷火豐 戊寅 Earth Tiger 6	**28** 十六 火7 Fire [1] Regulate 水澤節 己卯 Earth Rabbit 8	**29** 十七 水1 Water [2] Unity 地天泰 庚辰 Metal Dragon 9	**30** 十八 木3 Wood [3] Great Reward 火天大有 辛巳 Metal Snake 7

JUNE 1953 戊午

Xuan Kong Element 玄空五行	火風鼎 The Cauldron	Period Luck 卦運	Monthly Star 月星
Wood 木3		4	7

SUNDAY	MONDAY	TUESDAY	WEDNESDAY	THURSDAY	FRIDAY	SATURDAY
	1 二十 金4 Metal [5] Trap 澤水困 癸未 Water Goat 8	**2** 廿一 木3 Wood [6] Not Yet Accomplished 火水未濟 甲申 Wood Monkey 9	**3** 廿二 金9 Metal [7] Retreat 天山遯 乙酉 Wood Rooster 4	**4** 廿三 水6 Water [8] Mountain 艮為山 丙戌 Fire Dog 1	**5** 廿四 木8 Wood [9] Delight 雷地豫 丁亥 Fire Pig 8	**6** 廿五 火7 Fire [1] Beginning 水雷屯 戊子 Earth Rat 4
7 廿六 金9 Metal [2] Without Wrongdoing 天雷無妄 己丑 Earth Ox 2	**8** 廿七 木3 Wood [3] Fire 離為火 庚寅 Metal Tiger 1	**9** 廿八 火2 Fire [4] Sincerity 風澤中孚 辛卯 Metal Rabbit 3	**10** 廿九 水6 Water [5] Big Livestock 山天大畜 壬辰 Water Dragon 4	**11** 五月初一 金4 Metal [6] Eliminating 澤天夬 癸巳 Water Snake 6	**12** 初二 金9 Metal [7] Heaven 乾為天 甲午 Wood Horse 1	**13** 初三 火7 Fire [8] Well 水風井 乙未 Wood Goat 6
14 初四 木8 Wood [9] Relief 雷水解 丙申 Fire Monkey 4	**15** 初五 金4 Metal [1] Influence 澤山咸 丁酉 Fire Rooster 9	**16** 初六 水1 Water [2] Humility 地山謙 戊戌 Earth Dog 6	**17** 初七 火2 Fire [3] Observation 風地觀 己亥 Earth Pig 2	**18** 初八 火2 Fire [4] Increasing 風雷益 庚子 Metal Rat 9	**19** 初九 水1 Water [5] Dimming Light 地火明夷 辛丑 Metal Ox 3	**20** 初十 金9 Metal [6] Fellowship 天火同人 壬寅 Water Tiger 7
21 十一 木8 Wood [7] Marrying Maiden 雷澤歸妹 癸卯 Water Rabbit 7	**22** 十二 木3 Wood [8/2] Opposition 火澤睽 甲辰 Wood Dragon 2	**23** 十三 火7 Fire [1] Waiting 水天需 乙巳 Wood Snake 3	**24** 十四 金4 Metal [9] Great Exceeding 澤風大過 丙午 Fire Horse 3	**25** 十五 水6 Water [8] Poison 山風蠱 丁未 Fire Goat 7	**26** 十六 火2 Fire [7] Dispersing 風水渙 戊申 Earth Monkey 6	**27** 十七 木3 Wood [6] Travelling 火山旅 己酉 Earth Rooster 8
28 十八 金9 Metal [5] Stagnation 天地否 庚戌 Metal Dog 9	**29** 十九 火7 Fire [4] Alliance 水地比 辛亥 Metal Pig 7	**30** 二十 木8 Wood [3] Thunder 震為雷 壬子 Water Rat 1				

JULY 1953 己未

Xuan Kong Element 玄空五行	地風升 Rising	Period Luck 卦運	Monthly Star 月星
Water 水1		2	6

SUNDAY	MONDAY	TUESDAY	WEDNESDAY	THURSDAY	FRIDAY	SATURDAY
			水6 Water Beauty 2 山火賁 癸丑 Water Ox **1** 廿一 8	火7 Fire Accomplished 1 水火既濟 甲寅 Wood Tiger **2** 廿二 9	水1 Water Arriving 9 地澤臨 乙卯 Wood Rabbit **3** 廿三 4	金4 Metal Marsh 8 兌爲澤 丙辰 Fire Dragon **4** 廿四 1
火2 Fire Small Livestock 7 風天小畜 丁巳 Fire Snake **5** 廿五 8	木3 Wood The Cauldron 6 火風鼎 戊午 Earth Horse **6** 廿六 4	水1 Water Rising 5 地風升 己未 Earth Goat **7** 廿七 2	火7 Fire Water 4 坎爲水 庚申 Metal Monkey **8** 廿八 1	木8 Wood Lesser Exceeding 3 雷山小過 辛酉 Metal Rooster **9** 廿九 3	金4 Metal Gathering 2 澤地萃 壬戌 Water Dog **10** 三十 4	水6 Water Peel 1 山地剝 癸亥 Water Pig **11** 六月初一 6
水1 Water Earth 9 坤爲地 甲子 Wood Rat **12** 初二 1	木3 Wood Biting 8 火雷噬嗑 乙丑 Wood Ox **13** 初三 6	火2 Fire Family 7 風火家人 丙寅 Fire Tiger **14** 初四 4	水6 Water Decreasing 6 山澤損 丁卯 Fire Rabbit **15** 初五 9	金9 Metal Tread 5 天澤履 戊辰 Earth Dragon **16** 初六 6	木8 Wood Great Strength 4 雷天大壯 己巳 Earth Snake **17** 初七 2	木8 Wood Consistency 3 雷風恆 庚午 Metal Horse **18** 初八 9
金9 Metal Litigation 2 天水訟 辛未 Metal Goat **19** 初九 3	水1 Water Officer 1 地水師 壬申 Water Monkey **20** 初十 7	火2 Fire Gradual Progress 9 風山漸 癸酉 Water Rooster **21** 十一 7	火7 Fire Obstruction 8 水山蹇 甲戌 Wood Dog **22** 十二 2	木3 Wood Advancement 7 火地晉 乙亥 Wood Pig **23** 十三 3	水6 Water Nourish 6 山雷頤 丙子 Fire Rat **24** 十四 3	金4 Metal Following 5 澤雷隨 丁丑 Fire Ox **25** 十五 7
木8 Wood Abundance 4 雷火豐 戊寅 Earth Tiger **26** 十六 6	火7 Fire Regulate 3 水澤節 己卯 Earth Rabbit **27** 十七 8	水1 Water Unity 2 地天泰 庚辰 Metal Dragon **28** 十八 9	木3 Wood Great Reward 1 火天大有 辛巳 Metal Snake **29** 十九 7	火2 Fire Wind 9 巽爲風 壬午 Water Horse **30** 二十 1	金4 Metal Trap 8 澤水困 癸未 Water Goat **31** 廿一 8	

AUGUST 1953 庚申

Xuan Kong Element 玄空五行	坎爲水 Water	Period Luck 卦運	Monthly Star 月星
Fire 火7		1	5

SUNDAY	MONDAY	TUESDAY	WEDNESDAY	THURSDAY	FRIDAY	SATURDAY
水6 Water Beauty 5 山火賁 癸丑 Water Ox **30** 廿一 8	火7 Fire Accomplished 4 水火既濟 甲寅 Wood Tiger **31** 廿二 9					木3 Wood Not Yet Accomplished 7 火水未濟 甲申 Wood Monkey **1** 廿二 9
金9 Metal Retreat 6 天山遯 乙酉 Wood Rooster **2** 廿三 4	水6 Water Mountain 5 艮爲山 丙戌 Fire Dog **3** 廿四 1	木8 Wood Delight 4 雷地豫 丁亥 Fire Pig **4** 廿五 8	火7 Fire Beginning 3 水雷屯 戊子 Earth Rat **5** 廿六 4	金9 Metal Without Wrongdoing 2 天雷無妄 己丑 Earth Ox **6** 廿七 2	木3 Wood Fire 1 離爲火 庚寅 Metal Tiger **7** 廿八 1	火2 Fire Sincerity 9 風澤中孚 辛卯 Metal Rabbit **8** 廿九 3
水6 Water Big Livestock 8 山天大畜 壬辰 Water Dragon **9** 三十 4	金4 Metal Eliminating 7 澤天夬 癸巳 Water Snake **10** 七月初一 6	金9 Metal Heaven 6 乾爲天 甲午 Wood Horse **11** 初二 1	火7 Fire Well 5 水風井 乙未 Wood Goat **12** 初三 6	木8 Wood Relief 4 雷水解 丙申 Fire Monkey **13** 初四 4	金4 Metal Influence 3 澤山咸 丁酉 Fire Rooster **14** 初五 9	水1 Water Humility 2 地山謙 戊戌 Earth Dog **15** 初六 6
火2 Fire Observation 1 風地觀 己亥 Earth Pig **16** 初七 2	火2 Fire Increasing 9 風雷益 庚子 Metal Rat **17** 初八 9	水1 Water Dimming Light 8 地火明夷 辛丑 Metal Ox **18** 初九 3	金9 Metal Fellowship 7 天火同人 壬寅 Water Tiger **19** 初十 7	木8 Wood Marrying Maiden 6 雷澤歸妹 癸卯 Water Rabbit **20** 十一 7	木3 Wood Opposition 5 火澤睽 甲辰 Wood Dragon **21** 十二 2	火7 Fire Waiting 4 水天需 乙巳 Wood Snake **22** 十三 3
金4 Metal Great Exceeding 3 澤風大過 丙午 Fire Horse **23** 十四 3	水6 Water Poison 2 山風蠱 丁未 Fire Goat **24** 十五 7	火2 Fire Dispersing 1 風水渙 戊申 Earth Monkey **25** 十六 6	木3 Wood Travelling 9 火山旅 己酉 Earth Rooster **26** 十七 8	金9 Metal Stagnation 8 天地否 庚戌 Metal Dog **27** 十八 9	火7 Fire Alliance 7 水地比 辛亥 Metal Pig **28** 十九 7	木8 Wood Thunder 6 震爲雷 壬子 Water Rat **29** 二十 1

SEPTEMBER 1953 辛酉

Xuan Kong Element 玄空五行	雷山小過 Lesser Exceeding	Period Luck 卦運	Monthly Star 月星
Wood 木8		3	4

SUNDAY	MONDAY	TUESDAY	WEDNESDAY	THURSDAY	FRIDAY	SATURDAY
		水1 Water 3 Arriving 地澤臨 乙卯 Wood Rabbit 1 4 廿三	金4 Metal 2 Marsh 兌爲澤 丙辰 Fire Dragon 2 1 廿四	火2 Fire 1 Small Livestock 風天小畜 丁巳 Fire Snake 3 8 廿五	木3 Wood 9 The Cauldron 火風鼎 戊午 Earth Horse 4 4 廿六	水1 Water 8 Rising 地風升 己未 Earth Goat 5 2 廿七
火7 Fire 7 Water 坎爲水 庚申 Metal Monkey 6 1 廿八	木8 Wood 6 Lesser Exceeding 雷山小過 辛酉 Metal Rooster 7 3 廿九	金4 Metal 5 Gathering 澤地萃 壬戌 Water Dog 8 4 八月初一	水6 Water 4 Peel 山地剝 癸亥 Water Pig 9 6 初二	水1 Water 3 Earth 坤爲地 甲子 Wood Rat 10 1 初三	木3 Wood 2 Biting 火雷噬嗑 乙丑 Wood Ox 11 6 初四	火2 Fire 1 Family 風火家人 丙寅 Fire Tiger 12 4 初五
水6 Water 9 Decreasing 山澤損 丁卯 Fire Rabbit 13 9 初六	金9 Metal 8 Tread 天澤履 戊辰 Earth Dragon 14 6 初七	木8 Wood 7 Great Strength 雷天大壯 己巳 Earth Snake 15 2 初八	木8 Wood 6 Consistency 雷風恒 庚午 Metal Horse 16 9 初九	金9 Metal 5 Litigation 天水訟 辛未 Metal Goat 17 3 初十	水1 Water 4 Officer 地水師 壬申 Water Monkey 18 7 十一	火2 Fire 3 Gradual Progress 風山漸 癸酉 Water Rooster 19 7 十二
火7 Fire 2 Obstruction 水山蹇 甲戌 Wood Dog 20 2 十三	木3 Wood 1 Advancement 火地晉 乙亥 Wood Pig 21 3 十四	水6 Water 9 Nourish 山雷頤 丙子 Fire Rat 22 3 十五	金4 Metal 8 Following 澤雷隨 丁丑 Fire Ox 23 7 十六	木8 Wood 7 Abundance 雷火豐 戊寅 Earth Tiger 24 6 十七	火7 Fire 6 Regulate 水澤節 己卯 Earth Rabbit 25 8 十八	水1 Water 5 Unity 地天泰 庚辰 Metal Dragon 26 9 十九
木3 Wood 4 Great Reward 火天大有 辛巳 Metal Snake 27 7 二十	火2 Fire 3 Wind 巽爲風 壬午 Water Horse 28 1 廿一	金4 Metal 2 Trap 澤水困 癸未 Water Goat 29 8 廿二	木3 Wood 1 Not Yet Accomplished 火水未濟 甲申 Wood Monkey 30 9 廿三			

OCTOBER 1953 壬戌

Xuan Kong Element 玄空五行	澤地萃 Gathering	Period Luck 卦運	Monthly Star 月星
Metal 金4		4	3

SUNDAY	MONDAY	TUESDAY	WEDNESDAY	THURSDAY	FRIDAY	SATURDAY
				金9 Metal 9 Retreat 天山遯 乙酉 Wood Rooster 1 4 廿四	水6 Water 8 Mountain 艮爲山 丙戌 Fire Dog 2 1 廿五	木8 Wood 7 Delight 雷地豫 丁亥 Fire Pig 3 8 廿六
火7 Fire 6 Beginning 水雷屯 戊子 Earth Rat 4 4 廿七	金9 Metal 5 Without Wrongdoing 天雷無妄 己丑 Earth Ox 5 2 廿八	木3 Wood 4 Fire 離爲火 庚寅 Metal Tiger 6 1 廿九	火2 Fire 3 Sincerity 風澤中孚 辛卯 Metal Rabbit 7 3 三十	水6 Water 2 Big Livestock 山天大畜 壬辰 Water Dragon 8 4 九月初一	金4 Metal 1 Eliminating 澤天夬 癸巳 Water Snake 9 6 初二	金9 Metal 9 Heaven 乾爲天 甲午 Wood Horse 10 1 初三
火7 Fire 8 Well 水風井 乙未 Wood Goat 11 6 初四	木8 Wood 7 Relief 雷水解 丙申 Fire Monkey 12 4 初五	金4 Metal 6 Influence 澤山咸 丁酉 Fire Rooster 13 9 初六	水1 Water 5 Humility 地山謙 戊戌 Earth Dog 14 6 初七	火2 Fire 4 Observation 風地觀 己亥 Earth Pig 15 2 初八	火2 Fire 3 Increasing 風雷益 庚子 Metal Rat 16 9 初九	水1 Water 2 Dimming Light 地火明夷 辛丑 Metal Ox 17 3 初十
金9 Metal 1 Fellowship 天火同人 壬寅 Water Tiger 18 7 十一	木8 Wood 9 Marrying Maiden 雷澤歸妹 癸卯 Water Rabbit 19 7 十二	木3 Wood 8 Opposition 火澤睽 甲辰 Wood Dragon 20 2 十三	火7 Fire 7 Waiting 水天需 乙巳 Wood Snake 21 3 十四	金4 Metal 6 Great Exceeding 澤風大過 丙午 Fire Horse 22 3 十五	水6 Water 5 Poison 山風蠱 丁未 Fire Goat 23 7 十六	火2 Fire 4 Dispersing 風水渙 戊申 Earth Monkey 24 6 十七
木3 Wood 3 Travelling 火山旅 己酉 Earth Rooster 25 8 十八	金9 Metal 2 Stagnation 天地否 庚戌 Metal Dog 26 9 十九	火7 Fire 1 Alliance 水地比 辛亥 Metal Pig 27 7 二十	木8 Wood 9 Thunder 震爲雷 壬子 Water Rat 28 1 廿一	水6 Water 8 Beauty 山火賁 癸丑 Water Ox 29 8 廿二	火7 Fire 7 Accomplished 水火既濟 甲寅 Wood Tiger 30 9 廿三	水1 Water 6 Arriving 地澤臨 乙卯 Wood Rabbit 31 4 廿四

NOVEMBER 1953 癸亥

Xuan Kong Element 玄空五行	山地剝 Peel	Period Luck 卦運	Monthly Star 月星
Water 水6		6	2

SUNDAY	MONDAY	TUESDAY	WEDNESDAY	THURSDAY	FRIDAY	SATURDAY
1 廿五 金4 Metal · 5 Marsh 兌為澤 丙辰 Fire Dragon · 1	**2** 廿六 火2 Fire · 4 Small Livestock 風天小畜 丁巳 Fire Snake · 8	**3** 廿七 木3 Wood · 3 The Cauldron 火風鼎 戊午 Earth Horse · 4	**4** 廿八 水1 Water · 2 Rising 地風升 己未 Earth Goat · 2	**5** 廿九 火7 Fire · 1 Water 坎為水 庚申 Metal Monkey · 1	**6** 三十 木8 Wood · 9 Lesser Exceeding 雷山小過 辛酉 Metal Rooster · 3	**7** 十月初一 金4 Metal · 8 Gathering 澤地萃 壬戌 Water Dog · 4
8 初二 水6 Water · 7 Peel 山地剝 癸亥 Water Pig · 6	**9** 初三 水1 Water · 6 Earth 坤為地 甲子 Wood Rat · 1	**10** 初四 木3 Wood · 5 Biting 火雷噬嗑 乙丑 Wood Ox · 6	**11** 初五 火2 Fire · 4 Family 風火家人 丙寅 Fire Tiger · 4	**12** 初六 水6 Water · 3 Decreasing 山澤損 丁卯 Fire Rabbit · 9	**13** 初七 金9 Metal · 2 Tread 天澤履 戊辰 Earth Dragon · 6	**14** 初八 木8 Wood · 1 Great Strength 雷天大壯 己巳 Earth Snake · 2
15 初九 木8 Wood · 9 Consistency 雷風恆 庚午 Metal Horse · 9	**16** 初十 金9 Metal · 8 Litigation 天水訟 辛未 Metal Goat · 3	**17** 十一 水1 Water · 7 Officer 地水師 壬申 Water Monkey · 7	**18** 十二 火2 Fire · 6 Gradual Progress 風山漸 癸酉 Water Rooster · 7	**19** 十三 火7 Fire · 5 Obstruction 水山蹇 甲戌 Wood Dog · 2	**20** 十四 木3 Wood · 4 Advancement 火地晉 乙亥 Wood Pig · 3	**21** 十五 水6 Water · 3 Nourish 山雷頤 丙子 Fire Rat · 3
22 十六 金4 Metal · 2 Following 澤雷隨 丁丑 Fire Ox · 7	**23** 十七 木8 Wood · 1 Abundance 雷火豐 戊寅 Earth Tiger · 6	**24** 十八 火7 Fire · 9 Regulate 水澤節 己卯 Earth Rabbit · 8	**25** 十九 水1 Water · 8 Unity 地天泰 庚辰 Metal Dragon · 9	**26** 二十 木3 Wood · 7 Great Reward 火天大有 辛巳 Metal Snake · 7	**27** 廿一 火2 Fire · 6 Wind 巽為風 壬午 Water Horse · 1	**28** 廿二 金4 Metal · 5 Trap 澤水困 癸未 Water Goat · 8
29 廿三 木3 Wood · 4 Not Yet Accomplished 火水未濟 甲申 Wood Monkey · 9	**30** 廿四 金9 Metal · 3 Retreat 天山遯 乙酉 Wood Rooster · 4					

DECEMBER 1953 甲子

Xuan Kong Element 玄空五行	坤為地 Earth	Period Luck 卦運	Monthly Star 月星
Water 水1		1	1

SUNDAY	MONDAY	TUESDAY	WEDNESDAY	THURSDAY	FRIDAY	SATURDAY
		1 廿五 水6 Water · 2 Mountain 艮為山 丙戌 Fire Dog · 1	**2** 廿六 木8 Wood · 1 Delight 雷地豫 丁亥 Fire Pig · 8	**3** 廿七 火7 Fire · 9 Beginning 水雷屯 戊子 Earth Rat · 4	**4** 廿八 金9 Metal · 8 Without Wrongdoing 天雷無妄 己丑 Earth Ox · 2	**5** 廿九 木3 Wood · 7 Fire 離為火 庚寅 Metal Tiger · 1
6 十一月初一 火2 Fire · 6 Sincerity 風澤中孚 辛卯 Metal Rabbit · 3	**7** 初二 水6 Water · 5 Big Livestock 山天大畜 壬辰 Water Dragon · 4	**8** 初三 金4 Metal · 4 Eliminating 澤天夬 癸巳 Water Snake · 6	**9** 初四 金9 Metal · 3 Heaven 乾為天 甲午 Wood Horse · 1	**10** 初五 火7 Fire · 2 Well 水風井 乙未 Wood Goat · 6	**11** 初六 木8 Wood · 1 Relief 雷水解 丙申 Fire Monkey · 4	**12** 初七 金4 Metal · 9 Influence 澤山咸 丁酉 Fire Rooster · 9
13 初八 水1 Water · 8 Humility 地山謙 戊戌 Earth Dog · 6	**14** 初九 火2 Fire · 7 Observation 風地觀 己亥 Earth Pig · 2	**15** 初十 火2 Fire · 6 Increasing 風雷益 庚子 Metal Rat · 9	**16** 十一 水1 Water · 5 Dimming Light 地火明夷 辛丑 Metal Ox · 3	**17** 十二 金9 Metal · 4 Fellowship 天火同人 壬寅 Water Tiger · 7	**18** 十三 木8 Wood · 3 Marrying Maiden 雷澤歸妹 癸卯 Water Rabbit · 7	**19** 十四 木3 Wood · 2 Opposition 火澤睽 甲辰 Wood Dragon · 2
20 十五 火7 Fire · 1 Waiting 水天需 乙巳 Wood Snake · 3	**21** 十六 金4 Metal · 9 Great Exceeding 澤風大過 丙午 Fire Horse · 3	**22** 十七 水6 Water · 8/2 Poison 山風蠱 丁未 Fire Goat · 7	**23** 十八 火2 Fire · 3 Dispersing 風水渙 戊申 Earth Monkey · 6	**24** 十九 木3 Wood · 4 Travelling 火山旅 己酉 Earth Rooster · 8	**25** 二十 金9 Metal · 5 Stagnation 天地否 庚戌 Metal Dog · 9	**26** 廿一 火7 Fire · 6 Alliance 水地比 辛亥 Metal Pig · 7
27 廿二 木8 Wood · 7 Thunder 震為雷 壬子 Water Rat · 1	**28** 廿三 水6 Water · 8 Beauty 山火賁 癸丑 Water Ox · 8	**29** 廿四 火7 Fire · 9 Accomplished 水火既濟 甲寅 Wood Tiger · 9	**30** 廿五 水1 Water · 1 Arriving 地澤臨 乙卯 Wood Rabbit · 4	**31** 廿六 金4 Metal · 2 Marsh 兌為澤 丙辰 Fire Dragon · 1		

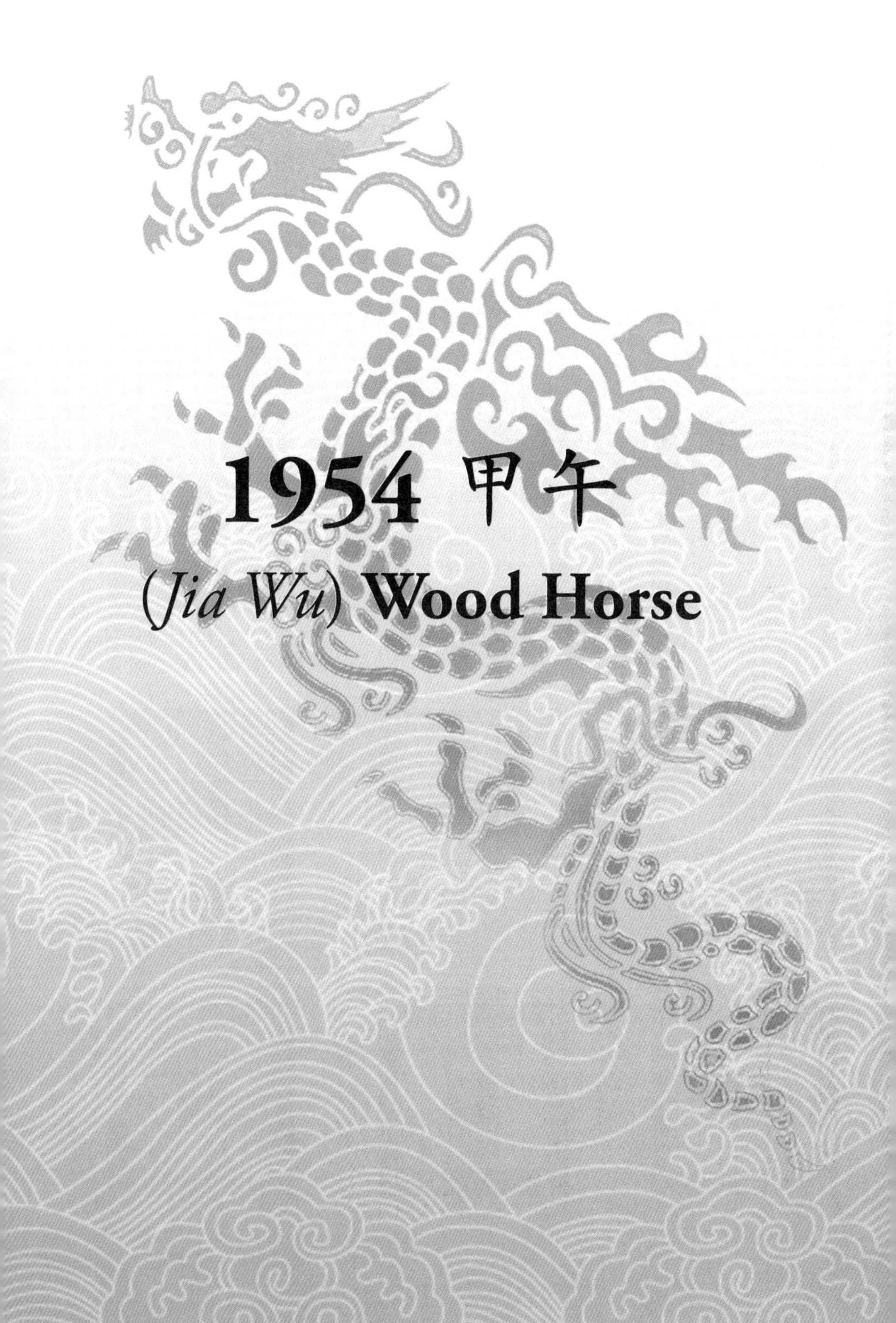

1954 甲午

(*Jia Wu*) Wood Horse

1954 甲午 *(Jia Wu)* Wood Horse

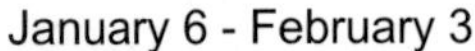
January 6 - February 3

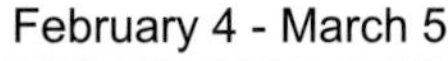
February 4 - March 5

March 6 - April 4

April 5 - May 5

May 6 - June 5

June 6 - July 7

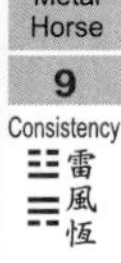

July 8 - August 7

August 8 - September 7

September 8 - October 8

October 9 - November 7

November 8 - December 6

December 7 - January 5

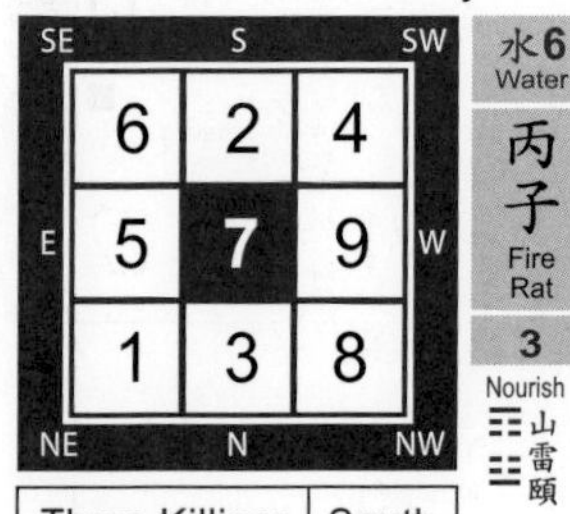

JANUARY 1954 乙丑

Xuan Kong Element 玄空五行	火雷噬嗑 Biting	Period Luck 卦運	Monthly Star 月星
Wood 木3		6	9

SUNDAY	MONDAY	TUESDAY	WEDNESDAY	THURSDAY	FRIDAY	SATURDAY
木8 Wood 6 Delight 雷地豫 丁亥 Fire Pig 31 廿七 8					火2 Fire 3 Small Livestock 風天小畜 丁巳 Fire Snake 1 廿七 8	木3 Wood 4 The Cauldron 火風鼎 戊午 Earth Horse 2 廿八 4
水1 Water 5 Rising 地風升 己未 Earth Goat 3 廿九 2	火7 Fire 6 Water 坎爲水 庚申 Metal Monkey 4 三十 1	木8 Wood 7 Lesser Exceeding 雷山小過 辛酉 Metal Rooster 5 十二月初一 3	金4 Metal 8 Gathering 澤地萃 壬戌 Water Dog 6 初二 4	水6 Water 9 Peel 山地剝 癸亥 Water Pig 7 初三 6	水1 Water 1 Earth 坤爲地 甲子 Wood Rat 8 初四 1	木3 Wood 2 Biting 火雷噬嗑 乙丑 Wood Ox 9 初五 6
火2 Fire 3 Family 風火家人 丙寅 Fire Tiger 10 初六 4	水6 Water 4 Decreasing 山澤損 丁卯 Fire Rabbit 11 初七 9	金9 Metal 5 Tread 天澤履 戊辰 Earth Dragon 12 初八 6	木8 Wood 6 Great Strength 雷天大壯 己巳 Earth Snake 13 初九 2	木8 Wood 7 Consistency 雷風恆 庚午 Metal Horse 14 初十 9	金9 Metal 8 Litigation 天水訟 辛未 Metal Goat 15 十一 3	水1 Water 9 Officer 地水師 壬申 Water Monkey 16 十二 7
火2 Fire 1 Gradual Progress 風山漸 癸酉 Water Rooster 17 十三 7	火7 Fire 2 Obstruction 水山蹇 甲戌 Wood Dog 18 十四 2	木3 Wood 3 Advancement 火地晉 乙亥 Wood Pig 19 十五 3	水6 Water 4 Nourish 山雷頤 丙子 Fire Rat 20 十六 3	金4 Metal 5 Following 澤雷隨 丁丑 Fire Ox 21 十七 7	木8 Wood 6 Abundance 雷火豐 戊寅 Earth Tiger 22 十八 6	火7 Fire 7 Regulate 水澤節 己卯 Earth Rabbit 23 十九 8
水1 Water 8 Unity 地天泰 庚辰 Metal Dragon 24 二十 9	木3 Wood 9 Great Reward 火天大有 辛巳 Metal Snake 25 廿一 7	火2 Fire 1 Wind 巽爲風 壬午 Water Horse 26 廿二 1	金4 Metal 2 Trap 澤水困 癸未 Water Goat 27 廿三 8	木3 Wood 3 Not Yet Accomplished 火水未濟 甲申 Wood Monkey 28 廿四 9	金9 Metal 4 Retreat 天山遯 乙酉 Wood Rooster 29 廿五 4	水6 Water 5 Mountain 艮爲山 丙戌 Fire Dog 30 廿六 1

FEBRUARY 1954 丙寅

Xuan Kong Element 玄空五行	風火家人 Family	Period Luck 卦運	Monthly Star 月星
Fire 火2		4	8

SUNDAY	MONDAY	TUESDAY	WEDNESDAY	THURSDAY	FRIDAY	SATURDAY
	火7 Fire 7 Beginning 水雷屯 戊子 Earth Rat 1 廿八 4	金9 Metal 8 Without Wrongdoing 天雷無妄 己丑 Earth Ox 2 廿九 2	木3 Wood 9 Fire 離爲火 庚寅 Metal Tiger 3 正月初一 1	火2 Fire 1 Sincerity 風澤中孚 辛卯 Metal Rabbit 4 初二 3	水6 Water 2 Big Livestock 山天大畜 壬辰 Water Dragon 5 初三 4	金4 Metal 3 Eliminating 澤天夬 癸巳 Water Snake 6 初四 6
金9 Metal 4 Heaven 乾爲天 甲午 Wood Horse 7 初五 1	火7 Fire 5 Well 水風井 乙未 Wood Goat 8 初六 6	木8 Wood 6 Relief 雷水解 丙申 Fire Monkey 9 初七 4	金4 Metal 7 Influence 澤山咸 丁酉 Fire Rooster 10 初八 9	水1 Water 8 Humility 地山謙 戊戌 Earth Dog 11 初九 6	火2 Fire 9 Observation 風地觀 己亥 Earth Pig 12 初十 2	火2 Fire 1 Increasing 風雷益 庚子 Metal Rat 13 十一 9
水1 Water 2 Dimming Light 地火明夷 辛丑 Metal Ox 14 十二 3	金9 Metal 3 Fellowship 天火同人 壬寅 Water Tiger 15 十三 7	木8 Wood 4 Marrying Maiden 雷澤歸妹 癸卯 Water Rabbit 16 十四 7	木3 Wood 5 Opposition 火澤睽 甲辰 Wood Dragon 17 十五 2	火7 Fire 6 Waiting 水天需 乙巳 Wood Snake 18 十六 3	金4 Metal 7 Great Exceeding 澤風大過 丙午 Fire Horse 19 十七 3	水6 Water 8 Poison 山風蠱 丁未 Fire Goat 20 十八 7
火2 Fire 9 Dispersing 風水渙 戊申 Earth Monkey 21 十九 6	木3 Wood 1 Travelling 火山旅 己酉 Earth Rooster 22 二十 8	金9 Metal 2 Stagnation 天地否 庚戌 Metal Dog 23 廿一 9	火7 Fire 3 Alliance 水地比 辛亥 Metal Pig 24 廿二 7	木8 Wood 4 Thunder 震爲雷 壬子 Water Rat 25 廿三 1	水6 Water 5 Beauty 山火賁 癸丑 Water Ox 26 廿四 8	火7 Fire 6 Accomplished 水火既濟 甲寅 Wood Tiger 27 廿五 9
水1 Water 7 Arriving 地澤臨 乙卯 Wood Rabbit 28 廿六 4						

MARCH 1954 丁卯

Xuan Kong Element 玄空五行	山澤損 Decreasing	Period Luck 卦運	Monthly Star 月星
Water 水6		9	7

SUNDAY	MONDAY	TUESDAY	WEDNESDAY	THURSDAY	FRIDAY	SATURDAY
	金4 Metal Marsh 8 丙辰 Fire Dragon 兑為澤 1 廿七 1	火2 Fire Small Livestock 9 丁巳 Fire Snake 風天小畜 2 廿八 8	木3 Wood The Cauldron 1 戊午 Earth Horse 火風鼎 3 廿九 4	水1 Water Rising 2 己未 Earth Goat 地風升 4 三十 2	火7 Fire Water 3 庚申 Metal Monkey 坎為水 5 二月初一 1	木8 Wood Lesser Exceeding 4 辛酉 Metal Rooster 雷山小過 6 初二 3
金4 Metal Gathering 5 壬戌 Water Dog 澤地萃 7 初三 4	水6 Water Peel 6 癸亥 Water Pig 山地剝 8 初四 6	水1 Water Earth 7 甲子 Wood Rat 坤為地 9 初五 1	木3 Wood Biting 8 乙丑 Wood Ox 火雷噬嗑 10 初六 6	火2 Fire Family 9 丙寅 Fire Tiger 風火家人 11 初七 4	水6 Water Decreasing 1 丁卯 Fire Rabbit 山澤損 12 初八 9	金9 Metal Tread 2 戊辰 Earth Dragon 天澤履 13 初九 6
木8 Wood Great Strength 3 己巳 Earth Snake 雷天大壯 14 初十 2	木8 Wood Consistency 4 庚午 Metal Horse 雷風恒 15 十一 9	金9 Metal Litigation 5 辛未 Metal Goat 天水訟 16 十二 3	水1 Water Officer 6 壬申 Water Monkey 地水師 17 十三 7	火2 Fire Gradual Progress 7 癸酉 Water Rooster 風山漸 18 十四 7	火7 Fire Obstruction 8 甲戌 Wood Dog 水山蹇 19 十五 2	木3 Wood Advancement 9 乙亥 Wood Pig 火地晉 20 十六 3
水6 Water Nourish 1 丙子 Fire Rat 山雷頤 21 十七 3	金4 Metal Following 2 丁丑 Fire Ox 澤雷隨 22 十八 7	木8 Wood Abundance 3 戊寅 Earth Tiger 雷火豐 23 十九 6	火7 Fire Regulate 4 己卯 Earth Rabbit 水澤節 24 二十 8	水1 Water Unity 5 庚辰 Metal Dragon 地天泰 25 廿一 9	木3 Wood Great Reward 6 辛巳 Metal Snake 火天大有 26 廿二 7	火2 Fire Wind 7 壬午 Water Horse 巽為風 27 廿三 1
金4 Metal Trap 8 癸未 Water Goat 澤水困 28 廿四 8	木3 Wood Not Yet Accomplished 9 甲申 Wood Monkey 火水未濟 29 廿五 9	金9 Metal Retreat 1 乙酉 Wood Rooster 天山遯 30 廿六 4	水6 Water Mountain 2 丙戌 Fire Dog 艮為山 31 廿七 1			

APRIL 1954 戊辰

Xuan Kong Element 玄空五行	天澤履 Tread	Period Luck 卦運	Monthly Star 月星
Metal 金9		6	6

SUNDAY	MONDAY	TUESDAY	WEDNESDAY	THURSDAY	FRIDAY	SATURDAY
				木8 Wood Delight 3 丁亥 Fire Pig 雷地豫 1 廿八 8	火7 Fire Beginning 4 戊子 Earth Rat 水雷屯 2 廿九 4	金9 Metal Without Wrongdoing 5 己丑 Earth Ox 天雷無妄 3 三月初一 2
木3 Wood Fire 6 庚寅 Metal Tiger 離為火 4 初二 1	火2 Fire Sincerity 7 辛卯 Metal Rabbit 風澤中孚 5 初三 3	水6 Water Big Livestock 8 壬辰 Water Dragon 山天大畜 6 初四 4	金4 Metal Eliminating 9 癸巳 Water Snake 澤天夬 7 初五 6	金9 Metal Heaven 1 甲午 Wood Horse 乾為天 8 初六 1	火7 Fire Well 2 乙未 Wood Goat 水風井 9 初七 6	木8 Wood Relief 3 丙申 Fire Monkey 雷水解 10 初八 4
金4 Metal Influence 4 丁酉 Fire Rooster 澤山咸 11 初九 9	水1 Water Humility 5 戊戌 Earth Dog 地山謙 12 初十 6	火2 Fire Observation 6 己亥 Earth Pig 風地觀 13 十一 2	火2 Fire Increasing 7 庚子 Metal Rat 風雷益 14 十二 9	水1 Water Dimming Light 8 辛丑 Metal Ox 地火明夷 15 十三 3	金9 Metal Fellowship 9 壬寅 Water Tiger 天火同人 16 十四 7	木8 Wood Marrying Maiden 1 癸卯 Water Rabbit 雷澤歸妹 17 十五 7
木3 Wood Opposition 2 甲辰 Wood Dragon 火澤睽 18 十六 2	火7 Fire Waiting 3 乙巳 Wood Snake 水天需 19 十七 3	金4 Metal Great Exceeding 4 丙午 Fire Horse 澤風大過 20 十八 3	水6 Water Poison 5 丁未 Fire Goat 山風蠱 21 十九 7	火2 Fire Dispersing 6 戊申 Earth Monkey 風水渙 22 二十 6	木3 Wood Travelling 7 己酉 Earth Rooster 火山旅 23 廿一 8	金9 Metal Stagnation 8 庚戌 Metal Dog 天地否 24 廿二 9
火7 Fire Alliance 9 辛亥 Metal Pig 水地比 25 廿三 7	木8 Wood Thunder 1 壬子 Water Rat 震為雷 26 廿四 1	水6 Water Beauty 2 癸丑 Water Ox 山火賁 27 廿五 8	火7 Fire Accomplished 3 甲寅 Wood Tiger 水火既濟 28 廿六 9	水1 Water Arriving 4 乙卯 Wood Rabbit 地澤臨 29 廿七 4	金4 Metal Marsh 5 丙辰 Fire Dragon 兑為澤 30 廿八 1	

MAY 1954 己巳

Xuan Kong Element 玄空五行	雷天大壯	Period Luck 卦運	Monthly Star 月星
Wood 木8	Great Strength	2	5

SUNDAY	MONDAY	TUESDAY	WEDNESDAY	THURSDAY	FRIDAY	SATURDAY
水6 Water 8 Mountain 丙戌 Fire Dog 艮爲山 30 1 廿八	木8 Wood 9 Delight 丁亥 Fire Pig 雷地豫 31 8 廿九					火2 Fire 6 Small Livestock 丁巳 Fire Snake 風天小畜 1 8 廿九
木3 Wood 7 The Cauldron 戊午 Earth Horse 火風鼎 2 4 三十	水1 Water 8 Rising 己未 Earth Goat 地風升 3 2 四月初一	火7 Fire 9 Water 庚申 Metal Monkey 坎爲水 4 1 初二	木8 Wood 1 Lesser Exceeding 辛酉 Metal Rooster 雷山小過 5 3 初三	金4 Metal 2 Gathering 壬戌 Water Dog 澤地萃 6 4 初四	水6 Water 3 Peel 癸亥 Water Pig 山地剝 7 6 初五	水1 Water 4 Earth 甲子 Wood Rat 坤爲地 8 1 初六
木3 Wood 5 Biting 乙丑 Wood Ox 火雷噬嗑 9 6 初七	火2 Fire 6 Family 丙寅 Fire Tiger 風火家人 10 4 初八	水6 Water 7 Decreasing 丁卯 Fire Rabbit 山澤損 11 9 初九	金9 Metal 8 Tread 戊辰 Earth Dragon 天澤履 12 6 初十	木8 Wood 9 Great Strength 己巳 Earth Snake 雷天大壯 13 2 十一	木8 Wood 1 Consistency 庚午 Metal Horse 雷風恆 14 9 十二	金9 Metal 2 Litigation 辛未 Metal Goat 天水訟 15 3 十三
水1 Water 3 Officer 壬申 Water Monkey 地水師 16 7 十四	火2 Fire 4 Gradual Progress 癸酉 Water Rooster 風山漸 17 7 十五	火7 Fire 5 Obstruction 甲戌 Wood Dog 水山蹇 18 2 十六	木3 Wood 6 Advancement 乙亥 Wood Pig 火地晉 19 3 十七	水6 Water 7 Nourish 丙子 Fire Rat 山雷頤 20 3 十八	金4 Metal 8 Following 丁丑 Fire Ox 澤雷隨 21 7 十九	木8 Wood 9 Abundance 戊寅 Earth Tiger 雷火豐 22 6 二十
火7 Fire 1 Regulate 己卯 Earth Rabbit 水澤節 23 8 廿一	水1 Water 2 Unity 庚辰 Metal Dragon 地天泰 24 9 廿二	木3 Wood 3 Great Reward 辛巳 Metal Snake 火天大有 25 7 廿三	火2 Fire 4 Wind 壬午 Water Horse 巽爲風 26 1 廿四	金4 Metal 5 Trap 癸未 Water Goat 澤水困 27 8 廿五	木3 Wood 6 Not Yet Accomplished 甲申 Wood Monkey 火水未濟 28 9 廿六	金9 Metal 7 Retreat 乙酉 Wood Rooster 天山遯 29 4 廿七

JUNE 1954 庚午

Xuan Kong Element 玄空五行	雷風恆	Period Luck 卦運	Monthly Star 月星
Wood 木8	Consistency	9	4

SUNDAY	MONDAY	TUESDAY	WEDNESDAY	THURSDAY	FRIDAY	SATURDAY
		火7 Fire 1 Beginning 戊子 Earth Rat 水雷屯 1 4 五月初一	金9 Metal 2 Without Wrongdoing 己丑 Earth Ox 天雷無妄 2 2 初二	木3 Wood 3 Fire 庚寅 Metal Tiger 離爲火 3 1 初三	火2 Fire 4 Sincerity 辛卯 Metal Rabbit 風澤中孚 4 3 初四	水6 Water 5 Big Livestock 壬辰 Water Dragon 山天大畜 5 4 初五
金4 Metal 6 Eliminating 癸巳 Water Snake 澤天夬 6 6 初六	金9 Metal 7 Heaven 甲午 Wood Horse 乾爲天 7 1 初七	火7 Fire 8 Well 乙未 Wood Goat 水風井 8 6 初八	木8 Wood 9 Relief 丙申 Fire Monkey 雷水解 9 4 初九	金4 Metal 1 Influence 丁酉 Fire Rooster 澤山咸 10 9 初十	水1 Water 2 Humility 戊戌 Earth Dog 地山謙 11 6 十一	火2 Fire 3 Observation 己亥 Earth Pig 風地觀 12 2 十二
火2 Fire 4 Increasing 庚子 Metal Rat 風雷益 13 9 十三	水1 Water 5 Dimming Light 辛丑 Metal Ox 地火明夷 14 3 十四	金9 Metal 6 Fellowship 壬寅 Water Tiger 天火同人 15 7 十五	木8 Wood 7 Marrying Maiden 癸卯 Water Rabbit 雷澤歸妹 16 7 十六	木3 Wood 8 Opposition 甲辰 Wood Dragon 火澤睽 17 2 十七	火7 Fire 9 Waiting 乙巳 Wood Snake 水天需 18 3 十八	金4 Metal 1 Great Exceeding 丙午 Fire Horse 澤風大過 19 3 十九
水6 Water 2 Poison 丁未 Fire Goat 山風蠱 20 7 二十	火2 Fire 3 Dispersing 戊申 Earth Monkey 風水渙 21 6 廿一	木3 Wood 4/6 Travelling 己酉 Earth Rooster 火山旅 22 8 廿二	金9 Metal 5 Stagnation 庚戌 Metal Dog 天地否 23 9 廿三	火7 Fire 4 Alliance 辛亥 Metal Pig 水地比 24 7 廿四	木8 Wood 3 Thunder 壬子 Water Rat 震爲雷 25 1 廿五	水6 Water 2 Beauty 癸丑 Water Ox 山火賁 26 8 廿六
火7 Fire 1 Accomplished 甲寅 Wood Tiger 水火既濟 27 9 廿七	水1 Water 9 Arriving 乙卯 Wood Rabbit 地澤臨 28 4 廿八	金4 Metal 8 Marsh 丙辰 Fire Dragon 兌爲澤 29 1 廿九	火2 Fire 7 Small Livestock 丁巳 Fire Snake 風天小畜 30 8 六月初一			

JULY 1954 辛未

Xuan Kong Element 玄空五行	天水訟 Litigation	Period Luck 卦運	Monthly Star 月星
Metal 金9		3	3

SUNDAY	MONDAY	TUESDAY	WEDNESDAY	THURSDAY	FRIDAY	SATURDAY
				木3 Wood The Cauldron 6 火風鼎 戊午 Earth Horse 4 1 初二	水1 Water Rising 5 地風升 己未 Earth Goat 2 2 初三	火7 Fire Water 4 坎爲水 庚申 Metal Monkey 1 3 初四
木8 Wood Lesser Exceeding 3 雷山小過 辛酉 Metal Rooster 3 4 初五	金4 Metal Gathering 2 澤地萃 壬戌 Water Dog 4 5 初六	水6 Water Peel 1 山地剝 癸亥 Water Pig 6 6 初七	水1 Water Earth 9 坤爲地 甲子 Wood Rat 1 7 初八	木3 Wood Biting 8 火雷噬嗑 乙丑 Wood Ox 6 8 初九	火2 Fire Family 7 風火家人 丙寅 Fire Tiger 4 9 初十	水6 Water Decreasing 6 山澤損 丁卯 Fire Rabbit 9 10 十一
金9 Metal Tread 5 天澤履 戊辰 Earth Dragon 6 11 十二	木8 Wood Great Strength 4 雷天大壯 己巳 Earth Snake 2 12 十三	木8 Wood Consistency 3 雷風恆 庚午 Metal Horse 9 13 十四	金9 Metal Litigation 2 天水訟 辛未 Metal Goat 3 14 十五	水1 Water Officer 1 地水師 壬申 Water Monkey 7 15 十六	火2 Fire Gradual Progress 9 風山漸 癸酉 Water Rooster 7 16 十七	火7 Fire Obstruction 8 水山蹇 甲戌 Wood Dog 2 17 十八
木3 Wood Advancement 7 火地晉 乙亥 Wood Pig 3 18 十九	水6 Water Nourish 6 山雷頤 丙子 Fire Rat 3 19 二十	金4 Metal Following 5 澤雷隨 丁丑 Fire Ox 7 20 廿一	木8 Wood Abundance 4 雷火豐 戊寅 Earth Tiger 6 21 廿二	火7 Fire Regulate 3 水澤節 己卯 Earth Rabbit 8 22 廿三	水1 Water Unity 2 地天泰 庚辰 Metal Dragon 9 23 廿四	木3 Wood Great Reward 1 火天大有 辛巳 Metal Snake 7 24 廿五
火2 Fire Wind 9 巽爲風 壬午 Water Horse 1 25 廿六	金4 Metal Trap 8 澤水困 癸未 Water Goat 8 26 廿七	木3 Wood Not Yet Accomplished 7 火水未濟 甲申 Wood Monkey 9 27 廿八	金9 Metal Retreat 6 天山遯 乙酉 Wood Rooster 4 28 廿九	水6 Water Mountain 5 艮爲山 丙戌 Fire Dog 1 29 三十	木8 Wood Delight 4 雷地豫 丁亥 Fire Pig 8 30 七月初一	火7 Fire Beginning 3 水雷屯 戊子 Earth Rat 4 31 初二

AUGUST 1954 壬申

Xuan Kong Element 玄空五行	地水師 Officer	Period Luck 卦運	Monthly Star 月星
Water 水1		7	2

SUNDAY	MONDAY	TUESDAY	WEDNESDAY	THURSDAY	FRIDAY	SATURDAY
金9 Metal Without Wrongdoing 2 天雷無妄 己丑 Earth Ox 2 1 初三	木3 Wood Fire 1 離爲火 庚寅 Metal Tiger 1 2 初四	火2 Fire Sincerity 9 風澤中孚 辛卯 Metal Rabbit 3 3 初五	水6 Water Big Livestock 8 山天大畜 壬辰 Water Dragon 4 4 初六	金4 Metal Eliminating 7 澤天夬 癸巳 Water Snake 6 5 初七	金9 Metal Heaven 6 乾爲天 甲午 Wood Horse 1 6 初八	火7 Fire Well 5 水風井 乙未 Wood Goat 6 7 初九
木8 Wood Relief 4 雷水解 丙申 Fire Monkey 4 8 初十	金4 Metal Influence 3 澤山咸 丁酉 Fire Rooster 9 9 十一	水1 Water Humility 2 地山謙 戊戌 Earth Dog 6 10 十二	火2 Fire Observation 1 風地觀 己亥 Earth Pig 2 11 十三	火2 Fire Increasing 9 風雷益 庚子 Metal Rat 9 12 十四	水1 Water Dimming Light 8 地火明夷 辛丑 Metal Ox 3 13 十五	金9 Metal Fellowship 7 天火同人 壬寅 Water Tiger 7 14 十六
木8 Wood Marrying Maiden 6 雷澤歸妹 癸卯 Water Rabbit 7 15 十七	木3 Wood Opposition 5 火澤睽 甲辰 Wood Dragon 2 16 十八	火7 Fire Waiting 4 水天需 乙巳 Wood Snake 3 17 十九	金4 Metal Great Exceeding 3 澤風大過 丙午 Fire Horse 3 18 二十	水6 Water Poison 2 山風蠱 丁未 Fire Goat 7 19 廿一	火2 Fire Dispersing 1 風水渙 戊申 Earth Monkey 6 20 廿二	木3 Wood Travelling 9 火山旅 己酉 Earth Rooster 8 21 廿三
金9 Metal Stagnation 8 天地否 庚戌 Metal Dog 9 22 廿四	火7 Fire Alliance 7 水地比 辛亥 Metal Pig 7 23 廿五	木8 Wood Thunder 6 震爲雷 壬子 Water Rat 1 24 廿六	水6 Water Beauty 5 山火賁 癸丑 Water Ox 8 25 廿七	火7 Fire Accomplished 4 水火既濟 甲寅 Wood Tiger 9 26 廿八	水1 Water Arriving 3 地澤臨 乙卯 Wood Rabbit 4 27 廿九	金4 Metal Marsh 2 兑爲澤 丙辰 Fire Dragon 1 28 八月初一
火2 Fire Small Livestock 1 風天小畜 丁巳 Fire Snake 8 29 初二	木3 Wood The Cauldron 9 火風鼎 戊午 Earth Horse 4 30 初三	水1 Water Rising 8 地風升 己未 Earth Goat 2 31 初四				

SEPTEMBER 1954 癸酉

Xuan Kong Element 玄空五行	風山漸 Gradual Progress	Period Luck 卦運	Monthly Star 月星
Fire 火2		7	1

SUNDAY	MONDAY	TUESDAY	WEDNESDAY	THURSDAY	FRIDAY	SATURDAY
			火7 Fire Water 坎爲水 庚申 Metal Monkey **1** 初五 1 · 7	木8 Wood Lesser Exceeding 雷山小過 辛酉 Metal Rooster **2** 初六 3 · 6	金4 Metal Gathering 澤地萃 壬戌 Water Dog **3** 初七 4 · 5	水6 Water Peel 山地剝 癸亥 Water Pig **4** 初八 6 · 4
水1 Water Earth 坤爲地 甲子 Wood Rat **5** 初九 1 · 3	木3 Wood Biting 火雷噬嗑 乙丑 Wood Ox **6** 初十 6 · 2	火2 Fire Family 風火家人 丙寅 Fire Tiger **7** 十一 4 · 1	水6 Water Decreasing 山澤損 丁卯 Fire Rabbit **8** 十二 9 · 9	金9 Metal Tread 天澤履 戊辰 Earth Dragon **9** 十三 6 · 8	木8 Wood Great Strength 雷天大壯 己巳 Earth Snake **10** 十四 2 · 7	木8 Wood Consistency 雷風恒 庚午 Metal Horse **11** 十五 9 · 6
金9 Metal Litigation 天水訟 辛未 Metal Goat **12** 十六 3 · 5	水1 Water Officer 地水師 壬申 Water Monkey **13** 十七 7 · 4	火2 Fire Gradual Progress 風山漸 癸酉 Water Rooster **14** 十八 7 · 3	火7 Fire Obstruction 水山蹇 甲戌 Wood Dog **15** 十九 2 · 2	木3 Wood Advancement 火地晉 乙亥 Wood Pig **16** 二十 3 · 1	水6 Water Nourish 山雷頤 丙子 Fire Rat **17** 廿一 3 · 9	金4 Metal Following 澤雷隨 丁丑 Fire Ox **18** 廿二 7 · 8
木8 Wood Abundance 雷火豐 戊寅 Earth Tiger **19** 廿三 6 · 7	火7 Fire Regulate 水澤節 己卯 Earth Rabbit **20** 廿四 8 · 6	水1 Water Unity 地天泰 庚辰 Metal Dragon **21** 廿五 9 · 5	木3 Wood Great Reward 火天大有 辛巳 Metal Snake **22** 廿六 7 · 4	火2 Fire Wind 巽爲風 壬午 Water Horse **23** 廿七 1 · 3	金4 Metal Trap 澤水困 癸未 Water Goat **24** 廿八 8 · 2	木3 Wood Not Yet Accomplished 火水未濟 甲申 Wood Monkey **25** 廿九 9 · 1
金9 Metal Retreat 天山遯 乙酉 Wood Rooster **26** 三十 4 · 9	水6 Water Mountain 艮爲山 丙戌 Fire Dog **27** 九月初一 1 · 8	木8 Wood Delight 雷地豫 丁亥 Fire Pig **28** 初二 8 · 7	火7 Fire Beginning 水雷屯 戊子 Earth Rat **29** 初三 4 · 6	金9 Metal Without Wrongdoing 天雷無妄 己丑 Earth Ox **30** 初四 2 · 5		

OCTOBER 1954 甲戌

Xuan Kong Element 玄空五行	水山蹇 Obstruction	Period Luck 卦運	Monthly Star 月星
Fire 火7		2	9

SUNDAY	MONDAY	TUESDAY	WEDNESDAY	THURSDAY	FRIDAY	SATURDAY
火7 Fire Water 坎爲水 庚申 Metal Monkey **31** 初五 1 · 1					木3 Wood Fire 離爲火 庚寅 Metal Tiger **1** 初五 1 · 4	火2 Fire Sincerity 風澤中孚 辛卯 Metal Rabbit **2** 初六 3 · 3
水6 Water Big Livestock 山天大畜 壬辰 Water Dragon **3** 初七 4 · 2	金4 Metal Eliminating 澤天夬 癸巳 Water Snake **4** 初八 6 · 1	金9 Metal Heaven 乾爲天 甲午 Wood Horse **5** 初九 1 · 9	火7 Fire Well 水風井 乙未 Wood Goat **6** 初十 6 · 8	木8 Wood Relief 雷水解 丙申 Fire Monkey **7** 十一 4 · 7	金4 Metal Influence 澤山咸 丁酉 Fire Rooster **8** 十二 9 · 6	水1 Water Humility 地山謙 戊戌 Earth Dog **9** 十三 6 · 5
火2 Fire Observation 風地觀 己亥 Earth Pig **10** 十四 2 · 4	火2 Fire Increasing 風雷益 庚子 Metal Rat **11** 十五 9 · 3	水1 Water Dimming Light 地火明夷 辛丑 Metal Ox **12** 十六 3 · 2	金9 Metal Fellowship 天火同人 壬寅 Water Tiger **13** 十七 7 · 1	木8 Wood Marrying Maiden 雷澤歸妹 癸卯 Water Rabbit **14** 十八 7 · 9	木3 Wood Opposition 火澤睽 甲辰 Wood Dragon **15** 十九 2 · 8	火7 Fire Waiting 水天需 乙巳 Wood Snake **16** 二十 3 · 7
金4 Metal Great Exceeding 澤風大過 丙午 Fire Horse **17** 廿一 3 · 6	水6 Water Poison 山風蠱 丁未 Fire Goat **18** 廿二 7 · 5	火2 Fire Dispersing 風水渙 戊申 Earth Monkey **19** 廿三 6 · 4	木3 Wood Travelling 火山旅 己酉 Earth Rooster **20** 廿四 8 · 3	金9 Metal Stagnation 天地否 庚戌 Metal Dog **21** 廿五 9 · 2	火7 Fire Alliance 水地比 辛亥 Metal Pig **22** 廿六 7 · 1	木8 Wood Thunder 震爲雷 壬子 Water Rat **23** 廿七 1 · 9
水6 Water Beauty 山火賁 癸丑 Water Ox **24** 廿八 8 · 8	火7 Fire Accomplished 水火既濟 甲寅 Wood Tiger **25** 廿九 9 · 7	水1 Water Arriving 地澤臨 乙卯 Wood Rabbit **26** 三十 4 · 6	金4 Metal Marsh 兑爲澤 丙辰 Fire Dragon **27** 十月初一 1 · 5	火2 Fire Small Livestock 風天小畜 丁巳 Fire Snake **28** 初二 8 · 4	木3 Wood The Cauldron 火風鼎 戊午 Earth Horse **29** 初三 4 · 3	水1 Water Rising 地風升 己未 Earth Goat **30** 初四 2 · 2

NOVEMBER 1954 乙亥

Xuan Kong Element 玄空五行	火地晉 Advancement	Period Luck 卦運	Monthly Star 月星
Wood 木3		3	8

SUNDAY	MONDAY	TUESDAY	WEDNESDAY	THURSDAY	FRIDAY	SATURDAY
	木8 Wood 9 Lesser Exceeding 辛酉 Metal Rooster 雷山小過 1 初六 3	金4 Metal 8 Gathering 壬戌 Water Dog 澤地萃 2 初七 4	水6 Water 7 Peel 癸亥 Water Pig 山地剝 3 初八 6	水1 Water 6 Earth 甲子 Wood Rat 坤爲地 4 初九 1	木3 Wood 5 Biting 乙丑 Wood Ox 火雷噬嗑 5 初十 6	火2 Fire 4 Family 丙寅 Fire Tiger 風火家人 6 十一 4
水6 Water 3 Decreasing 丁卯 Fire Rabbit 山澤損 7 十二 9	金9 Metal 2 Tread 戊辰 Earth Dragon 天澤履 8 十三 6	木8 Wood 1 Great Strength 己巳 Earth Snake 雷天大壯 9 十四 2	木8 Wood 9 Consistency 庚午 Metal Horse 雷風恆 10 十五 9	金9 Metal 8 Litigation 辛未 Metal Goat 天水訟 11 十六 3	水1 Water 7 Officer 壬申 Water Monkey 地水師 12 十七 7	火2 Fire 6 Gradual Progress 癸酉 Water Rooster 風山漸 13 十八 7
火7 Fire 5 Obstruction 甲戌 Wood Dog 水山蹇 14 十九 2	木3 Wood 4 Advancement 乙亥 Wood Pig 火地晉 15 二十 3	水6 Water 3 Nourish 丙子 Fire Rat 山雷頤 16 廿一 3	金4 Metal 2 Following 丁丑 Fire Ox 澤雷隨 17 廿二 7	木8 Wood 1 Abundance 戊寅 Earth Tiger 雷火豐 18 廿三 6	火7 Fire 9 Regulate 己卯 Earth Rabbit 水澤節 19 廿四 8	水1 Water 8 Unity 庚辰 Metal Dragon 地天泰 20 廿五 9
木3 Wood 7 Great Reward 辛巳 Metal Snake 火天大有 21 廿六 7	火2 Fire 6 Wind 壬午 Water Horse 巽爲風 22 廿七 1	金4 Metal 5 Trap 癸未 Water Goat 澤水困 23 廿八 8	木3 Wood 4 Not Yet Accomplished 甲申 Wood Monkey 火水未濟 24 廿九 9	金9 Metal 3 Retreat 乙酉 Wood Rooster 天山遯 25 十一月初一 4	水6 Water 2 Mountain 丙戌 Fire Dog 艮爲山 26 初二 1	木8 Wood 1 Delight 丁亥 Fire Pig 雷地豫 27 初三 8
火7 Fire 9 Beginning 戊子 Earth Rat 水雷屯 28 初四 4	金9 Metal 8 Without Wrongdoing 己丑 Earth Ox 天雷無妄 29 初五 2	木3 Wood 7 Fire 庚寅 Metal Tiger 離爲火 30 初六 1				

DECEMBER 1954 丙子

Xuan Kong Element 玄空五行	山雷頤 Nourish	Period Luck 卦運	Monthly Star 月星
Water 水6		3	7

SUNDAY	MONDAY	TUESDAY	WEDNESDAY	THURSDAY	FRIDAY	SATURDAY
			火2 Fire 6 Sincerity 辛卯 Metal Rabbit 風澤中孚 1 初七 3	水6 Water 5 Big Livestock 壬辰 Water Dragon 山天大畜 2 初八 4	金4 Metal 4 Eliminating 癸巳 Water Snake 澤天夬 3 初九 6	金9 Metal 3 Heaven 甲午 Wood Horse 乾爲天 4 初十 1
火7 Fire 2 Well 乙未 Wood Goat 水風井 5 十一 6	木8 Wood 1 Relief 丙申 Fire Monkey 雷水解 6 十二 4	金4 Metal 9 Influence 丁酉 Fire Rooster 澤山咸 7 十三 9	水1 Water 8 Humility 戊戌 Earth Dog 地山謙 8 十四 6	火2 Fire 7 Observation 己亥 Earth Pig 風地觀 9 十五 2	火2 Fire 6 Increasing 庚子 Metal Rat 風雷益 10 十六 9	水1 Water 5 Dimming Light 辛丑 Metal Ox 地火明夷 11 十七 3
金9 Metal 4 Fellowship 壬寅 Water Tiger 天火同人 12 十八 7	木8 Wood 3 Marrying Maiden 癸卯 Water Rabbit 雷澤歸妹 13 十九 7	木3 Wood 2 Opposition 甲辰 Wood Dragon 火澤睽 14 二十 2	火7 Fire 1 Waiting 乙巳 Wood Snake 水天需 15 廿一 3	金4 Metal 9 Great Exceeding 丙午 Fire Horse 澤風大過 16 廿二 3	水6 Water 8 Poison 丁未 Fire Goat 山風蠱 17 廿三 7	火2 Fire 7 Dispersing 戊申 Earth Monkey 風水渙 18 廿四 6
木3 Wood 6 Travelling 己酉 Earth Rooster 火山旅 19 廿五 8	金9 Metal 5 Stagnation 庚戌 Metal Dog 天地否 20 廿六 9	火7 Fire 4 Alliance 辛亥 Metal Pig 水地比 21 廿七 7	木8 Wood 3/7 Thunder 壬子 Water Rat 震爲雷 22 廿八 1	水6 Water 8 Beauty 癸丑 Water Ox 山火賁 23 廿九 8	火7 Fire 9 Accomplished 甲寅 Wood Tiger 水火既濟 24 三十 9	水1 Water 1 Arriving 乙卯 Wood Rabbit 地澤臨 25 十二月初一 4
金4 Metal 2 Marsh 丙辰 Fire Dragon 兌爲澤 26 初二 1	火2 Fire 3 Small Livestock 丁巳 Fire Snake 風天小畜 27 初三 8	木3 Wood 4 The Cauldron 戊午 Earth Horse 火風鼎 28 初四 4	水1 Water 5 Rising 己未 Earth Goat 地風升 29 初五 2	火7 Fire 6 Water 庚申 Metal Monkey 坎爲水 30 初六 1	木8 Wood 7 Lesser Exceeding 辛酉 Metal Rooster 雷山小過 31 初七 3	

1955 乙未

(*Yi Wei*) Wood Goat

1955 乙未 *(Yi Wei)* Wood Goat

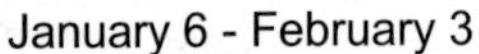

January 6 - February 3

Three Killings | East

February 4 - March 5

Three Killings | North

March 6 - April 4

Three Killings | West

April 5 - May 5

Three Killings | South

May 6 - June 5

Three Killings | East

June 6 - July 7

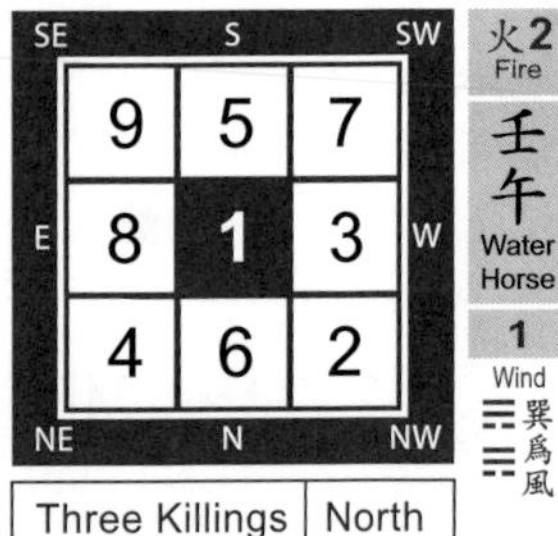

Three Killings | North

July 8 - August 7

Three Killings | West

August 8 - September 7

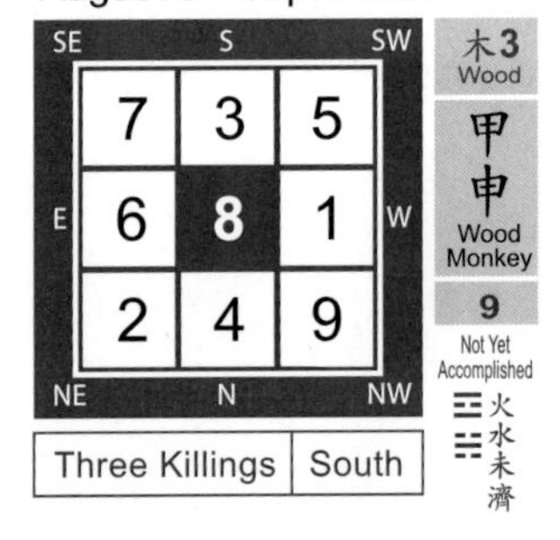

Three Killings | South

September 8 - October 8

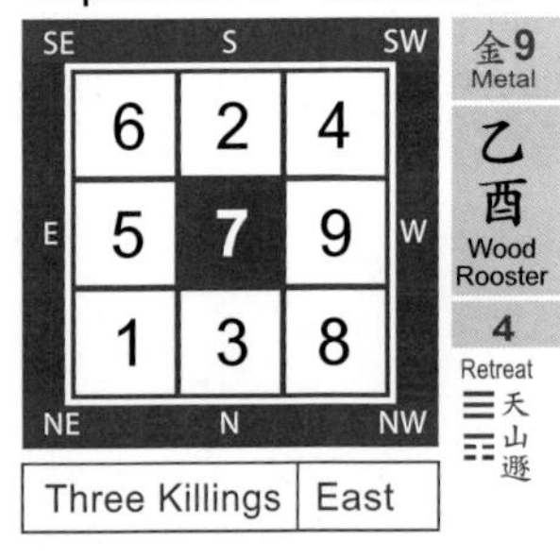

Three Killings | East

October 9 - November 7

Three Killings | North

November 8 - December 7

Three Killings | West

December 8 - January 5

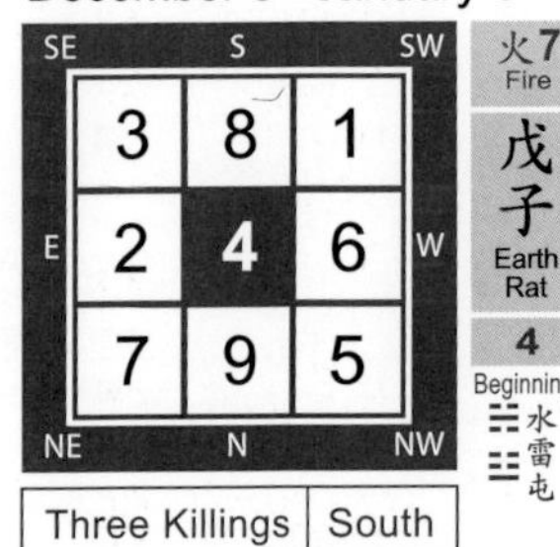

Three Killings | South

JANUARY 1955 丁丑

Xuan Kong Element 玄空五行	澤雷隨 Following	Period Luck 卦運	Monthly Star 月星
Metal 金4		7	6

SUNDAY	MONDAY	TUESDAY	WEDNESDAY	THURSDAY	FRIDAY	SATURDAY
火2 Fire 1 Sincerity 風澤中孚 辛卯 Metal Rabbit 30 初七 3	水6 Water 2 Big Livestock 山天大畜 壬辰 Water Dragon 31 初八 4					金4 Metal 8 Gathering 澤地萃 壬戌 Water Dog 1 初八 4
水6 Water 9 Peel 山地剝 癸亥 Water Pig 2 初九 6	水1 Water 1 Earth 坤爲地 甲子 Wood Rat 3 初十 1	木3 Wood 2 Biting 火雷噬嗑 乙丑 Wood Ox 4 十一 6	火2 Fire 3 Family 風火家人 丙寅 Fire Tiger 5 十二 4	水6 Water 4 Decreasing 山澤損 丁卯 Fire Rabbit 6 十三 9	金9 Metal 5 Tread 天澤履 戊辰 Earth Dragon 7 十四 6	木8 Wood 6 Great Strength 雷天大壯 己巳 Earth Snake 8 十五 2
木8 Wood 7 Consistency 雷風恒 庚午 Metal Horse 9 十六 9	金9 Metal 8 Litigation 天水訟 辛未 Metal Goat 10 十七 3	水1 Water 9 Officer 地水師 壬申 Water Monkey 11 十八 7	火2 Fire 1 Gradual Progress 風山漸 癸酉 Water Rooster 12 十九 7	火7 Fire 2 Obstruction 水山蹇 甲戌 Wood Dog 13 二十 2	木3 Wood 3 Advancement 火地晉 乙亥 Wood Pig 14 廿一 3	水6 Water 4 Nourish 山雷頤 丙子 Fire Rat 15 廿二 3
金4 Metal 5 Following 澤雷隨 丁丑 Fire Ox 16 廿三 7	木8 Wood 6 Abundance 雷火豐 戊寅 Earth Tiger 17 廿四 6	火7 Fire 7 Regulate 水澤節 己卯 Earth Rabbit 18 廿五 8	水1 Water 8 Unity 地天泰 庚辰 Metal Dragon 19 廿六 9	木3 Wood 9 Great Reward 火天大有 辛巳 Metal Snake 20 廿七 7	火2 Fire 1 Wind 巽爲風 壬午 Water Horse 21 廿八 1	金4 Metal 2 Trap 澤水困 癸未 Water Goat 22 廿九 8
木3 Wood 3 Not Yet Accomplished 火水未濟 甲申 Wood Monkey 23 三十 9	金9 Metal 4 Retreat 天山遯 乙酉 Wood Rooster 24 正月初一 4	水6 Water 5 Mountain 艮爲山 丙戌 Fire Dog 25 初二 1	木8 Wood 6 Delight 雷地豫 丁亥 Fire Pig 26 初三 8	火7 Fire 7 Beginning 水雷屯 戊子 Earth Rat 27 初四 4	金9 Metal 8 Without Wrongdoing 天雷無妄 己丑 Earth Ox 28 初五 2	木3 Wood 9 Fire 離爲火 庚寅 Metal Tiger 29 初六 1

FEBRUARY 1955 戊寅

Xuan Kong Element 玄空五行	雷火豐 Abundance	Period Luck 卦運	Monthly Star 月星
Wood 木8		6	5

SUNDAY	MONDAY	TUESDAY	WEDNESDAY	THURSDAY	FRIDAY	SATURDAY
		金4 Metal 3 Eliminating 澤天夬 癸巳 Water Snake 1 初九 6	金9 Metal 4 Heaven 乾爲天 甲午 Wood Horse 2 初十 1	火7 Fire 5 Well 水風井 乙未 Wood Goat 3 十一 6	木8 Wood 6 Relief 雷水解 丙申 Fire Monkey 4 十二 4	金4 Metal 7 Influence 澤山咸 丁酉 Fire Rooster 5 十三 9
水1 Water 8 Humility 地山謙 戊戌 Earth Dog 6 十四 6	火2 Fire 9 Observation 風地觀 己亥 Earth Pig 7 十五 2	火2 Fire 1 Increasing 風雷益 庚子 Metal Rat 8 十六 9	水1 Water 2 Dimming Light 地火明夷 辛丑 Metal Ox 9 十七 3	金9 Metal 3 Fellowship 天火同人 壬寅 Water Tiger 10 十八 7	木8 Wood 4 Marrying Maiden 雷澤歸妹 癸卯 Water Rabbit 11 十九 7	木3 Wood 5 Opposition 火澤睽 甲辰 Wood Dragon 12 二十 2
火7 Fire 6 Waiting 水天需 乙巳 Wood Snake 13 廿一 3	金4 Metal 7 Great Exceeding 澤風大過 丙午 Fire Horse 14 廿二 3	水6 Water 8 Poison 山風蠱 丁未 Fire Goat 15 廿三 7	火2 Fire 9 Dispersing 風水渙 戊申 Earth Monkey 16 廿四 6	木3 Wood 1 Travelling 火山旅 己酉 Earth Rooster 17 廿五 8	金9 Metal 2 Stagnation 天地否 庚戌 Metal Dog 18 廿六 9	火7 Fire 3 Alliance 水地比 辛亥 Metal Pig 19 廿七 7
木8 Wood 4 Thunder 震爲雷 壬子 Water Rat 20 廿八 1	水6 Water 5 Beauty 山火賁 癸丑 Water Ox 21 廿九 8	火7 Fire 6 Accomplished 水火既濟 甲寅 Wood Tiger 22 二月初一 9	水1 Water 7 Arriving 地澤臨 乙卯 Wood Rabbit 23 初二 4	金4 Metal 8 Marsh 兌爲澤 丙辰 Fire Dragon 24 初三 1	火2 Fire 9 Small Livestock 風天小畜 丁巳 Fire Snake 25 初四 8	木3 Wood 1 The Cauldron 火風鼎 戊午 Earth Horse 26 初五 4
水1 Water 2 Rising 地風升 己未 Earth Goat 27 初六 2	火7 Fire 3 Water 坎爲水 庚申 Metal Monkey 28 初七 1					

MARCH 1955 己卯

Xuan Kong Element 玄空五行	水澤節 Regulate	Period Luck 卦運	Monthly Star 月星
Fire 火7		8	4

SUNDAY	MONDAY	TUESDAY	WEDNESDAY	THURSDAY	FRIDAY	SATURDAY
		木8 Wood 辛酉 Metal Rooster 3 Lesser Exceeding 雷山小過 4 1 初八	金4 Metal 壬戌 Water Dog 4 Gathering 澤地萃 5 2 初九	水6 Water 癸亥 Water Pig 6 Peel 山地剝 6 3 初十	水1 Water 甲子 Wood Rat 1 Earth 坤爲地 7 4 十一	木3 Wood 乙丑 Wood Ox 6 Biting 火雷噬嗑 8 5 十二
火2 Fire 丙寅 Fire Tiger 4 Family 風火家人 9 6 十三	水6 Water 丁卯 Fire Rabbit 9 Decreasing 山澤損 1 7 十四	金9 Metal 戊辰 Earth Dragon 6 Tread 天澤履 2 8 十五	木8 Wood 己巳 Earth Snake 2 Great Strength 雷天大壯 3 9 十六	木8 Wood 庚午 Metal Horse 9 Consistency 雷風恒 4 10 十七	金9 Metal 辛未 Metal Goat 3 Litigation 天水訟 5 11 十八	水1 Water 壬申 Water Monkey 7 Officer 地水師 6 12 十九
火2 Fire 癸酉 Water Rooster 7 Gradual Progress 風山漸 7 13 二十	火7 Fire 甲戌 Wood Dog 2 Obstruction 水山蹇 8 14 廿一	木3 Wood 乙亥 Wood Pig 3 Advancement 火地晉 9 15 廿二	水6 Water 丙子 Fire Rat 3 Nourish 山雷頤 1 16 廿三	金4 Metal 丁丑 Fire Ox 7 Following 澤雷隨 2 17 廿四	木8 Wood 戊寅 Earth Tiger 6 Abundance 雷火豐 3 18 廿五	火7 Fire 己卯 Earth Rabbit 8 Regulate 水澤節 4 19 廿六
水1 Water 庚辰 Metal Dragon 9 Unity 地天泰 5 20 廿七	木3 Wood 辛巳 Metal Snake 7 Great Reward 火天大有 6 21 廿八	火2 Fire 壬午 Water Horse 1 Wind 巽爲風 7 22 廿九	金4 Metal 癸未 Water Goat 8 Trap 澤水困 8 23 三十	木3 Wood 甲申 Wood Monkey 9 Not Yet Accomplished 火水未濟 9 24 三月初一	金9 Metal 乙酉 Wood Rooster 4 Retreat 天山遯 1 25 初二	水6 Water 丙戌 Fire Dog 1 Mountain 艮爲山 2 26 初三
木8 Wood 丁亥 Fire Pig 8 Delight 雷地豫 3 27 初四	火7 Fire 戊子 Earth Rat 4 Beginning 水雷屯 4 28 初五	金9 Metal 己丑 Earth Ox 2 Without Wrongdoing 天雷無妄 5 29 初六	木3 Wood 庚寅 Metal Tiger 1 Fire 離爲火 6 30 初七	火2 Fire 辛卯 Metal Rabbit 3 Sincerity 風澤中孚 7 31 初八		

APRIL 1955 庚辰

Xuan Kong Element 玄空五行	地天泰 Unity	Period Luck 卦運	Monthly Star 月星
Water 水1		9	3

SUNDAY	MONDAY	TUESDAY	WEDNESDAY	THURSDAY	FRIDAY	SATURDAY
					水6 Water 壬辰 Water Dragon 4 Big Livestock 山天大畜 8 1 初九	金4 Metal 癸巳 Water Snake 6 Eliminating 澤天夬 9 2 初十
金9 Metal 甲午 Wood Horse 1 Heaven 乾爲天 1 3 十一	火7 Fire 乙未 Wood Goat 6 Well 水風井 2 4 十二	木8 Wood 丙申 Fire Monkey 4 Relief 雷水解 3 5 十三	金4 Metal 丁酉 Fire Rooster 9 Influence 澤山咸 4 6 十四	水1 Water 戊戌 Earth Dog 6 Humility 地山謙 5 7 十五	火2 Fire 己亥 Earth Pig 2 Observation 風地觀 6 8 十六	火2 Fire 庚子 Metal Rat 9 Increasing 風雷益 7 9 十七
水1 Water 辛丑 Metal Ox 3 Dimming Light 地火明夷 8 10 十八	金9 Metal 壬寅 Water Tiger 7 Fellowship 天火同人 9 11 十九	木8 Wood 癸卯 Water Rabbit 7 Marrying Maiden 雷澤歸妹 1 12 二十	木3 Wood 甲辰 Wood Dragon 2 Opposition 火澤睽 2 13 廿一	火7 Fire 乙巳 Wood Snake 3 Waiting 水天需 3 14 廿二	金4 Metal 丙午 Fire Horse 3 Great Exceeding 澤風大過 4 15 廿三	水6 Water 丁未 Fire Goat 7 Poison 山風蠱 5 16 廿四
火2 Fire 戊申 Earth Monkey 6 Dispersing 風水渙 6 17 廿五	木3 Wood 己酉 Earth Rooster 8 Travelling 火山旅 7 18 廿六	金9 Metal 庚戌 Metal Dog 9 Stagnation 天地否 8 19 廿七	火7 Fire 辛亥 Metal Pig 7 Alliance 水地比 9 20 廿八	木8 Wood 壬子 Water Rat 1 Thunder 震爲雷 1 21 廿九	水6 Water 癸丑 Water Ox 8 Beauty 山火賁 2 22 閏三月初一	火7 Fire 甲寅 Wood Tiger 9 Accomplished 水火既濟 3 23 初二
水1 Water 乙卯 Wood Rabbit 4 Arriving 地澤臨 4 24 初三	金4 Metal 丙辰 Fire Dragon 1 Marsh 兑爲澤 5 25 初四	火2 Fire 丁巳 Fire Snake 8 Small Livestock 風天小畜 6 26 初五	木3 Wood 戊午 Earth Horse 4 The Cauldron 火風鼎 7 27 初六	水1 Water 己未 Earth Goat 2 Rising 地風升 8 28 初七	火7 Fire 庚申 Metal Monkey 1 Water 坎爲水 9 29 初八	木8 Wood 辛酉 Metal Rooster 3 Lesser Exceeding 雷山小過 1 30 初九

MAY 1955 辛巳

Xuan Kong Element 玄空五行	火天大有 Great Reward	Period Luck 卦運	Monthly Star 月星
Wood 木3		7	2

SUNDAY	MONDAY	TUESDAY	WEDNESDAY	THURSDAY	FRIDAY	SATURDAY
1 初十 金4 Metal 壬戌 Water Dog Gathering 澤地萃 2 / 4	**2** 十一 水6 Water 癸亥 Water Pig Peel 山地剝 3 / 6	**3** 十二 水1 Water 甲子 Wood Rat Earth 坤爲地 4 / 1	**4** 十三 木3 Wood 乙丑 Wood Ox Biting 火雷噬嗑 5 / 6	**5** 十四 火2 Fire 丙寅 Fire Tiger Family 風火家人 6 / 4	**6** 十五 水6 Water 丁卯 Fire Rabbit Decreasing 山澤損 7 / 9	**7** 十六 金9 Metal 戊辰 Earth Dragon Tread 天澤履 8 / 6
8 十七 木8 Wood 己巳 Earth Snake Great Strength 雷天大壯 9 / 2	**9** 十八 木8 Wood 庚午 Metal Horse Consistency 雷風恆 1 / 9	**10** 十九 金9 Metal 辛未 Metal Goat Litigation 天水訟 2 / 3	**11** 二十 水1 Water 壬申 Water Monkey Officer 地水師 3 / 7	**12** 廿一 火2 Fire 癸酉 Water Rooster Gradual Progress 風山漸 4 / 7	**13** 廿二 火7 Fire 甲戌 Wood Dog Obstruction 水山蹇 5 / 2	**14** 廿三 木3 Wood 乙亥 Wood Pig Advancement 火地晉 6 / 3
15 廿四 水6 Water 丙子 Fire Rat Nourish 山雷頤 7 / 3	**16** 廿五 金4 Metal 丁丑 Fire Ox Following 澤雷隨 8 / 7	**17** 廿六 木8 Wood 戊寅 Earth Tiger Abundance 雷火豐 9 / 6	**18** 廿七 火7 Fire 己卯 Earth Rabbit Regulate 水澤節 1 / 8	**19** 廿八 水1 Water 庚辰 Metal Dragon Unity 地天泰 2 / 9	**20** 廿九 木3 Wood 辛巳 Metal Snake Great Reward 火天大有 3 / 7	**21** 三十 火2 Fire 壬午 Water Horse Wind 巽爲風 4 / 1
22 四月初一 金4 Metal 癸未 Water Goat Trap 澤水困 5 / 8	**23** 初二 木3 Wood 甲申 Wood Monkey Not Yet Accomplished 火水未濟 6 / 9	**24** 初三 金9 Metal 乙酉 Wood Rooster Retreat 天山遯 7 / 4	**25** 初四 水6 Water 丙戌 Fire Dog Mountain 艮爲山 8 / 1	**26** 初五 木8 Wood 丁亥 Fire Pig Delight 雷地豫 9 / 8	**27** 初六 火7 Fire 戊子 Earth Rat Beginning 水雷屯 1 / 4	**28** 初七 金9 Metal 己丑 Earth Ox Without Wrongdoing 天雷無妄 2 / 2
29 初八 木3 Wood 庚寅 Metal Tiger Fire 離爲火 3 / 1	**30** 初九 火2 Fire 辛卯 Metal Rabbit Sincerity 風澤中孚 4 / 3	**31** 初十 水6 Water 壬辰 Water Dragon Big Livestock 山天大畜 5 / 4				

JUNE 1955 壬午

Xuan Kong Element 玄空五行	巽爲風 Wind	Period Luck 卦運	Monthly Star 月星
Fire 火2		1	1

SUNDAY	MONDAY	TUESDAY	WEDNESDAY	THURSDAY	FRIDAY	SATURDAY
			1 十一 金4 Metal 癸巳 Water Snake Eliminating 澤天夬 6 / 6	**2** 十二 金9 Metal 甲午 Wood Horse Heaven 乾爲天 7 / 1	**3** 十三 火7 Fire 乙未 Wood Goat Well 水風井 8 / 6	**4** 十四 木8 Wood 丙申 Fire Monkey Relief 雷水解 9 / 4
5 十五 金4 Metal 丁酉 Fire Rooster Influence 澤山咸 1 / 9	**6** 十六 水1 Water 戊戌 Earth Dog Humility 地山謙 2 / 6	**7** 十七 火2 Fire 己亥 Earth Pig Observation 風地觀 3 / 2	**8** 十八 火2 Fire 庚子 Metal Rat Increasing 風雷益 4 / 9	**9** 十九 水1 Water 辛丑 Metal Ox Dimming Light 地火明夷 5 / 3	**10** 二十 金9 Metal 壬寅 Water Tiger Fellowship 天火同人 6 / 7	**11** 廿一 木8 Wood 癸卯 Water Rabbit Marrying Maiden 雷澤歸妹 7 / 7
12 廿二 木3 Wood 甲辰 Wood Dragon Opposition 火澤睽 8 / 2	**13** 廿三 火7 Fire 乙巳 Wood Snake Waiting 水天需 9 / 3	**14** 廿四 金4 Metal 丙午 Fire Horse Great Exceeding 澤風大過 1 / 3	**15** 廿五 水6 Water 丁未 Fire Goat Poison 山風蠱 2 / 7	**16** 廿六 火2 Fire 戊申 Earth Monkey Dispersing 風水渙 3 / 6	**17** 廿七 木3 Wood 己酉 Earth Rooster Travelling 火山旅 4 / 8	**18** 廿八 金9 Metal 庚戌 Metal Dog Stagnation 天地否 5 / 9
19 廿九 火7 Fire 辛亥 Metal Pig Alliance 水地比 6 / 7	**20** 五月初一 木8 Wood 壬子 Water Rat Thunder 震爲雷 7 / 1	**21** 初二 水6 Water 癸丑 Water Ox Beauty 山火賁 8 / 8	**22** 初三 火7 Fire 甲寅 Wood Tiger Accomplished 水火既濟 9/1 / 9	**23** 初四 水1 Water 乙卯 Wood Rabbit Arriving 地澤臨 9 / 4	**24** 初五 金4 Metal 丙辰 Fire Dragon Marsh 兌爲澤 8 / 1	**25** 初六 火2 Fire 丁巳 Fire Snake Small Livestock 風天小畜 7 / 8
26 初七 木3 Wood 戊午 Earth Horse The Cauldron 火風鼎 6 / 4	**27** 初八 水1 Water 己未 Earth Goat Rising 地風升 5 / 2	**28** 初九 火7 Fire 庚申 Metal Monkey Water 坎爲水 4 / 1	**29** 初十 木8 Wood 辛酉 Metal Rooster Lesser Exceeding 雷山小過 3 / 3	**30** 十一 金4 Metal 壬戌 Water Dog Gathering 澤地萃 2 / 4		

JULY 1955 癸未

Xuan Kong Element 玄空五行	澤水困 Trap	Period Luck 卦運	Monthly Star 月星
Metal 金4		8	9

SUNDAY	MONDAY	TUESDAY	WEDNESDAY	THURSDAY	FRIDAY	SATURDAY
金4 Metal 7 Eliminating 澤天夬 癸巳 Water Snake 31 十三 6					水6 Water 1 Peel 山地剝 癸亥 Water Pig 1 十二 6	水1 Water 9 Earth 坤爲地 甲子 Wood Rat 2 十三 1
木3 Wood 8 Biting 火雷噬嗑 乙丑 Wood Ox 3 十四 6	火2 Fire 7 Family 風火家人 丙寅 Fire Tiger 4 十五 4	水6 Water 6 Decreasing 山澤損 丁卯 Fire Rabbit 5 十六 9	金9 Metal 5 Tread 天澤履 戊辰 Earth Dragon 6 十七 6	木8 Wood 4 Great Strength 雷天大壯 己巳 Earth Snake 7 十八 2	木8 Wood 3 Consistency 雷風恆 庚午 Metal Horse 8 十九 9	金9 Metal 2 Litigation 天水訟 辛未 Metal Goat 9 二十 3
水1 Water 1 Officer 地水師 壬申 Water Monkey 10 廿一 7	火2 Fire 9 Gradual Progress 風山漸 癸酉 Water Rooster 11 廿二 7	火7 Fire 8 Obstruction 水山蹇 甲戌 Wood Dog 12 廿三 2	木3 Wood 7 Advancement 火地晉 乙亥 Wood Pig 13 廿四 3	水6 Water 6 Nourish 山雷頤 丙子 Fire Rat 14 廿五 3	金4 Metal 5 Following 澤雷隨 丁丑 Fire Ox 15 廿六 7	木8 Wood 4 Abundance 雷火豐 戊寅 Earth Tiger 16 廿七 6
火7 Fire 3 Regulate 水澤節 己卯 Earth Rabbit 17 廿八 8	水1 Water 2 Unity 地天泰 庚辰 Metal Dragon 18 廿九 9	木3 Wood 1 Great Reward 火天大有 辛巳 Metal Snake 19 六月初一 7	火2 Fire 9 Wind 巽爲風 壬午 Water Horse 20 初二 1	金4 Metal 8 Trap 澤水困 癸未 Water Goat 21 初三 8	木3 Wood 7 Not Yet Accomplished 火水未濟 甲申 Wood Monkey 22 初四 9	金9 Metal 6 Retreat 天山遯 乙酉 Wood Rooster 23 初五 4
水6 Water 5 Mountain 艮爲山 丙戌 Fire Dog 24 初六 1	木8 Wood 4 Delight 雷地豫 丁亥 Fire Pig 25 初七 8	火7 Fire 3 Beginning 水雷屯 戊子 Earth Rat 26 初八 4	金9 Metal 2 Without Wrongdoing 天雷無妄 己丑 Earth Ox 27 初九 2	木3 Wood 1 Fire 離爲火 庚寅 Metal Tiger 28 初十 1	火2 Fire 9 Sincerity 風澤中孚 辛卯 Metal Rabbit 29 十一 3	水6 Water 8 Big Livestock 山天大畜 壬辰 Water Dragon 30 十二 4

AUGUST 1955 甲申

Xuan Kong Element 玄空五行	火水未濟 Not Yet Accomplished	Period Luck 卦運	Monthly Star 月星
Wood 木3		9	8

SUNDAY	MONDAY	TUESDAY	WEDNESDAY	THURSDAY	FRIDAY	SATURDAY
	金9 Metal 6 Heaven 乾爲天 甲午 Wood Horse 1 十四 1	火7 Fire 5 Well 水風井 乙未 Wood Goat 2 十五 6	木8 Wood 4 Relief 雷水解 丙申 Fire Monkey 3 十六 4	金4 Metal 3 Influence 澤山咸 丁酉 Fire Rooster 4 十七 9	水1 Water 2 Humility 地山謙 戊戌 Earth Dog 5 十八 6	火2 Fire 1 Observation 風地觀 己亥 Earth Pig 6 十九 2
火2 Fire 9 Increasing 風雷益 庚子 Metal Rat 7 二十 9	水1 Water 8 Dimming Light 地火明夷 辛丑 Metal Ox 8 廿一 3	金9 Metal 7 Fellowship 天火同人 壬寅 Water Tiger 9 廿二 7	木8 Wood 6 Marrying Maiden 雷澤歸妹 癸卯 Water Rabbit 10 廿三 7	木3 Wood 5 Opposition 火澤睽 甲辰 Wood Dragon 11 廿四 2	火7 Fire 4 Waiting 水天需 乙巳 Wood Snake 12 廿五 3	金4 Metal 3 Great Exceeding 澤風大過 丙午 Fire Horse 13 廿六 3
水6 Water 2 Poison 山風蠱 丁未 Fire Goat 14 廿七 7	火2 Fire 1 Dispersing 風水渙 戊申 Earth Monkey 15 廿八 6	木3 Wood 9 Travelling 火山旅 己酉 Earth Rooster 16 廿九 8	金9 Metal 8 Stagnation 天地否 庚戌 Metal Dog 17 三十 9	火7 Fire 7 Alliance 水地比 辛亥 Metal Pig 18 七月初一 7	木8 Wood 6 Thunder 震爲雷 壬子 Water Rat 19 初二 1	水6 Water 5 Beauty 山火賁 癸丑 Water Ox 20 初三 8
火7 Fire 4 Accomplished 水火既濟 甲寅 Wood Tiger 21 初四 9	水1 Water 3 Arriving 地澤臨 乙卯 Wood Rabbit 22 初五 4	金4 Metal 2 Marsh 兌爲澤 丙辰 Fire Dragon 23 初六 1	火2 Fire 1 Small Livestock 風天小畜 丁巳 Fire Snake 24 初七 8	木3 Wood 9 The Cauldron 火風鼎 戊午 Earth Horse 25 初八 4	水1 Water 8 Rising 地風升 己未 Earth Goat 26 初九 2	火7 Fire 7 Water 坎爲水 庚申 Metal Monkey 27 初十 1
木8 Wood 6 Lesser Exceeding 雷山小過 辛酉 Metal Rooster 28 十一 3	金4 Metal 5 Gathering 澤地萃 壬戌 Water Dog 29 十二 4	水6 Water 4 Peel 山地剝 癸亥 Water Pig 30 十三 6	水1 Water 3 Earth 坤爲地 甲子 Wood Rat 31 十四 1			

SEPTEMBER 1955 乙酉

Xuan Kong Element 玄空五行	天山遯 Retreat	Period Luck 卦運	Monthly Star 月星
Metal 金9		4	7

SUNDAY	MONDAY	TUESDAY	WEDNESDAY	THURSDAY	FRIDAY	SATURDAY
				1 十五 木3 Wood · 2 Biting 火雷噬嗑 乙丑 Wood Ox · 6	**2** 十六 火2 Fire · 1 Family 風火家人 丙寅 Fire Tiger · 4	**3** 十七 水6 Water · 9 Decreasing 山澤損 丁卯 Fire Rabbit · 9
4 十八 金9 Metal · 8 Tread 天澤履 戊辰 Earth Dragon · 6	**5** 十九 木8 Wood · 7 Great Strength 雷天大壯 己巳 Earth Snake · 2	**6** 二十 木8 Wood · 6 Consistency 雷風恒 庚午 Metal Horse · 9	**7** 廿一 金9 Metal · 5 Litigation 天水訟 辛未 Metal Goat · 3	**8** 廿二 水1 Water · 4 Officer 地水師 壬申 Water Monkey · 7	**9** 廿三 火2 Fire · 3 Gradual Progress 風山漸 癸酉 Water Rooster · 7	**10** 廿四 火7 Fire · 2 Obstruction 水山蹇 甲戌 Wood Dog · 2
11 廿五 木3 Wood · 1 Advancement 火地晉 乙亥 Wood Pig · 3	**12** 廿六 水6 Water · 9 Nourish 山雷頤 丙子 Fire Rat · 3	**13** 廿七 金4 Metal · 8 Following 澤雷隨 丁丑 Fire Ox · 7	**14** 廿八 木8 Wood · 7 Abundance 雷火豐 戊寅 Earth Tiger · 6	**15** 廿九 火7 Fire · 6 Regulate 水澤節 己卯 Earth Rabbit · 8	**16** 八月初一 水1 Water · 5 Unity 地天泰 庚辰 Metal Dragon · 9	**17** 初二 木3 Wood · 4 Great Reward 火天大有 辛巳 Metal Snake · 7
18 初三 火2 Fire · 3 Wind 巽爲風 壬午 Water Horse · 1	**19** 初四 金4 Metal · 2 Trap 澤水困 癸未 Water Goat · 8	**20** 初五 木3 Wood · 1 Not Yet Accomplished 火水未濟 甲申 Wood Monkey · 9	**21** 初六 金9 Metal · 9 Retreat 天山遯 乙酉 Wood Rooster · 4	**22** 初七 水6 Water · 8 Mountain 艮爲山 丙戌 Fire Dog · 1	**23** 初八 木8 Wood · 7 Delight 雷地豫 丁亥 Fire Pig · 8	**24** 初九 火7 Fire · 6 Beginning 水雷屯 戊子 Earth Rat · 4
25 初十 金9 Metal · 5 Without Wrongdoing 天雷無妄 己丑 Earth Ox · 2	**26** 十一 木3 Wood · 4 Fire 離爲火 庚寅 Metal Tiger · 1	**27** 十二 火2 Fire · 3 Sincerity 風澤中孚 辛卯 Metal Rabbit · 3	**28** 十三 水6 Water · 2 Big Livestock 山天大畜 壬辰 Water Dragon · 4	**29** 十四 金4 Metal · 1 Eliminating 澤天夬 癸巳 Water Snake · 6	**30** 十五 金9 Metal · 9 Heaven 乾爲天 甲午 Wood Horse · 1	

OCTOBER 1955 丙戌

Xuan Kong Element 玄空五行	艮爲山 Mountain	Period Luck 卦運	Monthly Star 月星
Water 水6		1	6

SUNDAY	MONDAY	TUESDAY	WEDNESDAY	THURSDAY	FRIDAY	SATURDAY
30 十五 水1 Water · 6 Earth 坤爲地 甲子 Wood Rat · 1	**31** 十六 木3 Wood · 5 Biting 火雷噬嗑 乙丑 Wood Ox · 6					**1** 十六 火7 Fire · 8 Well 水風井 乙未 Wood Goat · 6
2 十七 木8 Wood · 7 Relief 雷水解 丙申 Fire Monkey · 4	**3** 十八 金4 Metal · 6 Influence 澤山咸 丁酉 Fire Rooster · 9	**4** 十九 水1 Water · 5 Humility 地山謙 戊戌 Earth Dog · 6	**5** 二十 火2 Fire · 4 Observation 風地觀 己亥 Earth Pig · 2	**6** 廿一 火2 Fire · 3 Increasing 風雷益 庚子 Metal Rat · 9	**7** 廿二 水1 Water · 2 Dimming Light 地火明夷 辛丑 Metal Ox · 3	**8** 廿三 金9 Metal · 1 Fellowship 天火同人 壬寅 Water Tiger · 7
9 廿四 木8 Wood · 9 Marrying Maiden 雷澤歸妹 癸卯 Water Rabbit · 7	**10** 廿五 木3 Wood · 8 Opposition 火澤睽 甲辰 Wood Dragon · 2	**11** 廿六 火7 Fire · 7 Waiting 水天需 乙巳 Wood Snake · 3	**12** 廿七 金4 Metal · 6 Great Exceeding 澤風大過 丙午 Fire Horse · 3	**13** 廿八 水6 Water · 5 Poison 山風蠱 丁未 Fire Goat · 7	**14** 廿九 火2 Fire · 4 Dispersing 風水渙 戊申 Earth Monkey · 6	**15** 三十 木3 Wood · 3 Travelling 火山旅 己酉 Earth Rooster · 8
16 九月初一 金9 Metal · 2 Stagnation 天地否 庚戌 Metal Dog · 9	**17** 初二 火7 Fire · 1 Alliance 水地比 辛亥 Metal Pig · 7	**18** 初三 木8 Wood · 9 Thunder 震爲雷 壬子 Water Rat · 1	**19** 初四 水6 Water · 8 Beauty 山火賁 癸丑 Water Ox · 8	**20** 初五 火7 Fire · 7 Accomplished 水火既濟 甲寅 Wood Tiger · 9	**21** 初六 水1 Water · 6 Arriving 地澤臨 乙卯 Wood Rabbit · 4	**22** 初七 金4 Metal · 5 Marsh 兌爲澤 丙辰 Fire Dragon · 1
23 初八 火2 Fire · 4 Small Livestock 風天小畜 丁巳 Fire Snake · 8	**24** 初九 木3 Wood · 3 The Cauldron 火風鼎 戊午 Earth Horse · 4	**25** 初十 水1 Water · 2 Rising 地風升 己未 Earth Goat · 2	**26** 十一 火7 Fire · 1 Water 坎爲水 庚申 Metal Monkey · 1	**27** 十二 木8 Wood · 9 Lesser Exceeding 雷山小過 辛酉 Metal Rooster · 3	**28** 十三 金4 Metal · 8 Gathering 澤地萃 壬戌 Water Dog · 4	**29** 十四 水6 Water · 7 Peel 山地剝 癸亥 Water Pig · 6

NOVEMBER 1955 丁亥

Xuan Kong Element 玄空五行	雷地豫 Delight	Period Luck 卦運	Monthly Star 月星
Wood 木8		8	5

SUNDAY	MONDAY	TUESDAY	WEDNESDAY	THURSDAY	FRIDAY	SATURDAY
		火2 Fire [4] Family 風火家人 丙寅 Fire Tiger 1 十七 4	水6 Water [3] Decreasing 山澤損 丁卯 Fire Rabbit 2 十八 9	金9 Metal [2] Tread 天澤履 戊辰 Earth Dragon 3 十九 6	木8 Wood [1] Great Strength 雷天大壯 己巳 Earth Snake 4 二十 2	木8 Wood [9] Consistency 雷風恆 庚午 Metal Horse 5 廿一 9
金9 Metal [8] Litigation 天水訟 辛未 Metal Goat 6 廿二 3	水1 Water [7] Officer 地水師 壬申 Water Monkey 7 廿三 7	火2 Fire [6] Gradual Progress 風山漸 癸酉 Water Rooster 8 廿四 7	火7 Fire [5] Obstruction 水山蹇 甲戌 Wood Dog 9 廿五 2	木3 Wood [4] Advancement 火地晉 乙亥 Wood Pig 10 廿六 3	水6 Water [3] Nourish 山雷頤 丙子 Fire Rat 11 廿七 3	金4 Metal [2] Following 澤雷隨 丁丑 Fire Ox 12 廿八 7
木8 Wood [1] Abundance 雷火豐 戊寅 Earth Tiger 13 廿九 6	火7 Fire [9] Regulate 水澤節 己卯 Earth Rabbit 14 十月初一 8	水1 Water [8] Unity 地天泰 庚辰 Metal Dragon 15 初二 9	木3 Wood [7] Great Reward 火天大有 辛巳 Metal Snake 16 初三 7	火2 Fire [6] Wind 巽爲風 壬午 Water Horse 17 初四 1	金4 Metal [5] Trap 澤水困 癸未 Water Goat 18 初五 8	木3 Wood [4] Not Yet Accomplished 火水未濟 甲申 Wood Monkey 19 初六 9
金9 Metal [3] Retreat 天山遯 乙酉 Wood Rooster 20 初七 4	水6 Water [2] Mountain 艮爲山 丙戌 Fire Dog 21 初八 1	木8 Wood [1] Delight 雷地豫 丁亥 Fire Pig 22 初九 8	火7 Fire [9] Beginning 水雷屯 戊子 Earth Rat 23 初十 4	金9 Metal [8] Without Wrongdoing 天雷無妄 己丑 Earth Ox 24 十一 2	木3 Wood [7] Fire 離爲火 庚寅 Metal Tiger 25 十二 1	火2 Fire [6] Sincerity 風澤中孚 辛卯 Metal Rabbit 26 十三 3
水6 Water [5] Big Livestock 山天大畜 壬辰 Water Dragon 27 十四 4	金4 Metal [4] Eliminating 澤天夬 癸巳 Water Snake 28 十五 6	金9 Metal [3] Heaven 乾爲天 甲午 Wood Horse 29 十六 1	火7 Fire [2] Well 水風井 乙未 Wood Goat 30 十七 6			

DECEMBER 1955 戊子

Xuan Kong Element 玄空五行	水雷屯 Beginning	Period Luck 卦運	Monthly Star 月星
Fire 火7		4	4

SUNDAY	MONDAY	TUESDAY	WEDNESDAY	THURSDAY	FRIDAY	SATURDAY
				木8 Wood [1] Relief 雷水解 丙申 Fire Monkey 1 十八 4	金4 Metal [9] Influence 澤山咸 丁酉 Fire Rooster 2 十九 9	水1 Water [8] Humility 地山謙 戊戌 Earth Dog 3 二十 6
火2 Fire [7] Observation 風地觀 己亥 Earth Pig 4 廿一 2	火2 Fire [6] Increasing 風雷益 庚子 Metal Rat 5 廿二 9	水1 Water [5] Dimming Light 地火明夷 辛丑 Metal Ox 6 廿三 3	金9 Metal [4] Fellowship 天火同人 壬寅 Water Tiger 7 廿四 7	木8 Wood [3] Marrying Maiden 雷澤歸妹 癸卯 Water Rabbit 8 廿五 7	木3 Wood [2] Opposition 火澤睽 甲辰 Wood Dragon 9 廿六 2	火7 Fire [1] Waiting 水天需 乙巳 Wood Snake 10 廿七 3
金4 Metal [9] Great Exceeding 澤風大過 丙午 Fire Horse 11 廿八 3	水6 Water [8] Poison 山風蠱 丁未 Fire Goat 12 廿九 7	火2 Fire [7] Dispersing 風水渙 戊申 Earth Monkey 13 三十 6	木3 Wood [6] Travelling 火山旅 己酉 Earth Rooster 14 十一月初一 8	金9 Metal [5] Stagnation 天地否 庚戌 Metal Dog 15 初二 9	火7 Fire [4] Alliance 水地比 辛亥 Metal Pig 16 初三 7	木8 Wood [3] Thunder 震爲雷 壬子 Water Rat 17 初四 1
水6 Water [2] Beauty 山火賁 癸丑 Water Ox 18 初五 8	火7 Fire [1] Accomplished 水火既濟 甲寅 Wood Tiger 19 初六 9	水1 Water [9] Arriving 地澤臨 乙卯 Wood Rabbit 20 初七 4	金4 Metal [8] Marsh 兌爲澤 丙辰 Fire Dragon 21 初八 1	火2 Fire [7/3] Small Livestock 風天小畜 丁巳 Fire Snake 22 初九 8	木3 Wood [4] The Cauldron 火風鼎 戊午 Earth Horse 23 初十 4	水1 Water [5] Rising 地風升 己未 Earth Goat 24 十一 2
火7 Fire [6] Water 坎爲水 庚申 Metal Monkey 25 十二 1	木8 Wood [7] Lesser Exceeding 雷山小過 辛酉 Metal Rooster 26 十三 3	金4 Metal [8] Gathering 澤地萃 壬戌 Water Dog 27 十四 4	水6 Water [9] Peel 山地剝 癸亥 Water Pig 28 十五 6	水1 Water [1] Earth 坤爲地 甲子 Wood Rat 29 十六 1	木3 Wood [2] Biting 火雷噬嗑 乙丑 Wood Ox 30 十七 6	火2 Fire [3] Family 風火家人 丙寅 Fire Tiger 31 十八 4

1956 丙申

(*Bing Shen*) Fire Monkey

1956 丙申 *(Bing Shen)* Fire Monkey

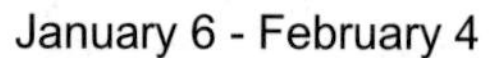

January 6 - February 4

February 5 - March 4

March 5 - April 4

April 5 - May 4

May 5 - June 5

June 6 - July 6

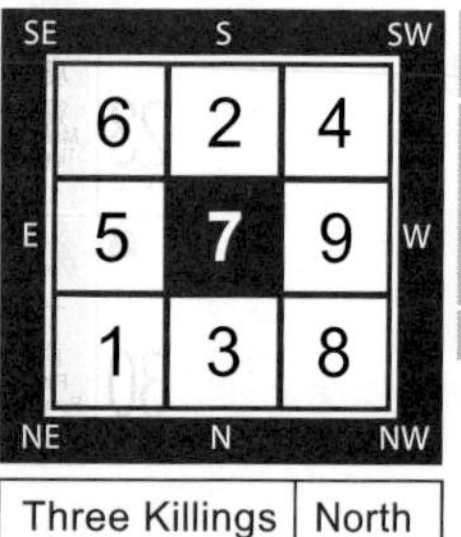

July 7 - August 6

August 7 - September 7

September 8 - October 7

October 8 - November 6

November 7 - December 6

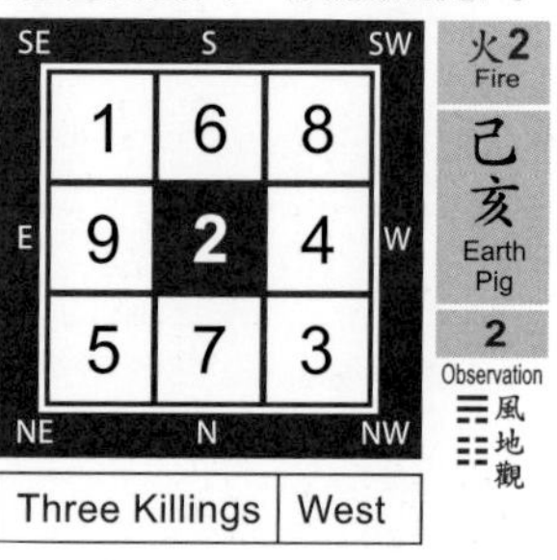

December 7 - January 4

JANUARY 1956 己丑

Xuan Kong Element 玄空五行	天雷無妄 Without Wrongdoing	Period Luck 卦運	Monthly Star 月星
Metal 金9		2	3

SUNDAY	MONDAY	TUESDAY	WEDNESDAY	THURSDAY	FRIDAY	SATURDAY
1 十九 水6 Water · 4 Decreasing 山澤損 丁卯 Fire Rabbit · 9	**2** 二十 金9 Metal · 5 Tread 天澤履 戊辰 Earth Dragon · 6	**3** 廿一 木8 Wood · 6 Great Strength 雷天大壯 己巳 Earth Snake · 2	**4** 廿二 木8 Wood · 7 Consistency 雷風恆 庚午 Metal Horse · 9	**5** 廿三 金9 Metal · 8 Litigation 天水訟 辛未 Metal Goat · 3	**6** 廿四 水1 Water · 9 Officer 地水師 壬申 Water Monkey · 7	**7** 廿五 火2 Fire · 1 Gradual Progress 風山漸 癸酉 Water Rooster · 7
8 廿六 火7 Fire · 2 Obstruction 水山蹇 甲戌 Wood Dog · 2	**9** 廿七 木3 Wood · 3 Advancement 火地晉 乙亥 Wood Pig · 3	**10** 廿八 水6 Water · 4 Nourish 山雷頤 丙子 Fire Rat · 3	**11** 廿九 金4 Metal · 5 Following 澤雷隨 丁丑 Fire Ox · 7	**12** 三十 木8 Wood · 6 Abundance 雷火豐 戊寅 Earth Tiger · 6	**13** 十二月初一 火7 Fire · 7 Regulate 水澤節 己卯 Earth Rabbit · 8	**14** 初二 水1 Water · 8 Unity 地天泰 庚辰 Metal Dragon · 9
15 初三 木3 Wood · 9 Great Reward 火天大有 辛巳 Metal Snake · 7	**16** 初四 火2 Fire · 1 Wind 巽爲風 壬午 Water Horse · 1	**17** 初五 金4 Metal · 2 Trap 澤水困 癸未 Water Goat · 8	**18** 初六 木3 Wood · 3 Not Yet Accomplished 火水未濟 甲申 Wood Monkey · 9	**19** 初七 金9 Metal · 4 Retreat 天山遯 乙酉 Wood Rooster · 4	**20** 初八 水6 Water · 5 Mountain 艮爲山 丙戌 Fire Dog · 1	**21** 初九 木8 Wood · 6 Delight 雷地豫 丁亥 Fire Pig · 8
22 初十 火7 Fire · 7 Beginning 水雷屯 戊子 Earth Rat · 4	**23** 十一 金9 Metal · 8 Without Wrongdoing 天雷無妄 己丑 Earth Ox · 2	**24** 十二 木3 Wood · 9 Fire 離爲火 庚寅 Metal Tiger · 1	**25** 十三 火2 Fire · 1 Sincerity 風澤中孚 辛卯 Metal Rabbit · 3	**26** 十四 水6 Water · 2 Big Livestock 山天大畜 壬辰 Water Dragon · 4	**27** 十五 金4 Metal · 3 Eliminating 澤天夬 癸巳 Water Snake · 6	**28** 十六 金9 Metal · 4 Heaven 乾爲天 甲午 Wood Horse · 1
29 十七 火7 Fire · 5 Well 水風井 乙未 Wood Goat · 6	**30** 十八 木8 Wood · 6 Relief 雷水解 丙申 Fire Monkey · 4	**31** 十九 金4 Metal · 7 Influence 澤山咸 丁酉 Fire Rooster · 9				

FEBRUARY 1956 庚寅

Xuan Kong Element 玄空五行	離爲火 Fire	Period Luck 卦運	Monthly Star 月星
Wood 木3		1	2

SUNDAY	MONDAY	TUESDAY	WEDNESDAY	THURSDAY	FRIDAY	SATURDAY
			1 二十 水1 Water · 8 Humility 地山謙 戊戌 Earth Dog · 6	**2** 廿一 火2 Fire · 9 Observation 風地觀 己亥 Earth Pig · 2	**3** 廿二 火2 Fire · 1 Increasing 風雷益 庚子 Metal Rat · 9	**4** 廿三 水1 Water · 2 Dimming Light 地火明夷 辛丑 Metal Ox · 3
5 廿四 金9 Metal · 3 Fellowship 天火同人 壬寅 Water Tiger · 7	**6** 廿五 木8 Wood · 4 Marrying Maiden 雷澤歸妹 癸卯 Water Rabbit · 7	**7** 廿六 木3 Wood · 5 Opposition 火澤睽 甲辰 Wood Dragon · 2	**8** 廿七 火7 Fire · 6 Waiting 水天需 乙巳 Wood Snake · 3	**9** 廿八 金4 Metal · 7 Great Exceeding 澤風大過 丙午 Fire Horse · 3	**10** 廿九 水6 Water · 8 Poison 山風蠱 丁未 Fire Goat · 7	**11** 三十 火2 Fire · 9 Dispersing 風水渙 戊申 Earth Monkey · 6
12 正月初一 木3 Wood · 1 Travelling 火山旅 己酉 Earth Rooster · 8	**13** 初二 金9 Metal · 2 Stagnation 天地否 庚戌 Metal Dog · 9	**14** 初三 火7 Fire · 3 Alliance 水地比 辛亥 Metal Pig · 7	**15** 初四 木8 Wood · 4 Thunder 震爲雷 壬子 Water Rat · 1	**16** 初五 水6 Water · 5 Beauty 山火賁 癸丑 Water Ox · 8	**17** 初六 火7 Fire · 6 Accomplished 水火既濟 甲寅 Wood Tiger · 9	**18** 初七 水1 Water · 7 Arriving 地澤臨 乙卯 Wood Rabbit · 4
19 初八 金4 Metal · 8 Marsh 兌爲澤 丙辰 Fire Dragon · 1	**20** 初九 火2 Fire · 9 Small Livestock 風天小畜 丁巳 Fire Snake · 8	**21** 初十 木3 Wood · 1 The Cauldron 火風鼎 戊午 Earth Horse · 4	**22** 十一 水1 Water · 2 Rising 地風升 己未 Earth Goat · 2	**23** 十二 火7 Fire · 3 Water 坎爲水 庚申 Metal Monkey · 1	**24** 十三 木8 Wood · 4 Lesser Exceeding 雷山小過 辛酉 Metal Rooster · 3	**25** 十四 金4 Metal · 5 Gathering 澤地萃 壬戌 Water Dog · 4
26 十五 水6 Water · 6 Peel 山地剝 癸亥 Water Pig · 6	**27** 十六 水1 Water · 7 Earth 坤爲地 甲子 Wood Rat · 1	**28** 十七 木3 Wood · 8 Biting 火雷噬嗑 乙丑 Wood Ox · 6	**29** 十八 火2 Fire · 9 Family 風火家人 丙寅 Fire Tiger · 4			

MARCH 1956 辛卯

Xuan Kong Element 玄空五行	風澤中孚 Sincerity	Period Luck 卦運	Monthly Star 月星
Fire 火2		3	1

SUNDAY	MONDAY	TUESDAY	WEDNESDAY	THURSDAY	FRIDAY	SATURDAY
				水6 Water Decreasing 1 丁卯 Fire Rabbit 山澤損 1 十九 9	金9 Metal Tread 2 戊辰 Earth Dragon 天澤履 2 二十 6	木8 Wood Great Strength 3 己巳 Earth Snake 雷天大壯 3 廿一 2
木8 Wood Consistency 4 庚午 Metal Horse 雷風恒 4 廿二 9	金9 Metal Litigation 5 辛未 Metal Goat 天水訟 5 廿三 3	水1 Water Officer 6 壬申 Water Monkey 地水師 6 廿四 7	火2 Fire Gradual Progress 7 癸酉 Water Rooster 風山漸 7 廿五 7	火7 Fire Obstruction 8 甲戌 Wood Dog 水山蹇 8 廿六 2	木3 Wood Advancement 9 乙亥 Wood Pig 火地晉 9 廿七 3	水6 Water Nourish 1 丙子 Fire Rat 山雷頤 10 廿八 3
金4 Metal Following 2 丁丑 Fire Ox 澤雷隨 11 廿九 7	木8 Wood Abundance 3 戊寅 Earth Tiger 雷火豐 12 二月初一 6	火7 Fire Regulate 4 己卯 Earth Rabbit 水澤節 13 初二 8	水1 Water Unity 5 庚辰 Metal Dragon 地天泰 14 初三 9	木3 Wood Great Reward 6 辛巳 Metal Snake 火天大有 15 初四 7	火2 Fire Wind 7 壬午 Water Horse 巽爲風 16 初五 1	金4 Metal Trap 8 癸未 Water Goat 澤水困 17 初六 8
木3 Wood Not Yet Accomplished 9 甲申 Wood Monkey 火水未濟 18 初七 9	金9 Metal Retreat 1 乙酉 Wood Rooster 天山遯 19 初八 4	水6 Water Mountain 2 丙戌 Fire Dog 艮爲山 20 初九 1	木8 Wood Delight 3 丁亥 Fire Pig 雷地豫 21 初十 8	火7 Fire Beginning 4 戊子 Earth Rat 水雷屯 22 十一 4	金9 Metal Without Wrongdoing 5 己丑 Earth Ox 天雷無妄 23 十二 2	木3 Wood Fire 6 庚寅 Metal Tiger 離爲火 24 十三 1
火2 Fire Sincerity 7 辛卯 Metal Rabbit 風澤中孚 25 十四 3	水6 Water Big Livestock 8 壬辰 Water Dragon 山天大畜 26 十五 4	金4 Metal Eliminating 9 癸巳 Water Snake 澤天夬 27 十六 6	金9 Metal Heaven 1 甲午 Wood Horse 乾爲天 28 十七 1	火7 Fire Well 2 乙未 Wood Goat 水風井 29 十八 6	木8 Wood Relief 3 丙申 Fire Monkey 雷水解 30 十九 4	金4 Metal Influence 4 丁酉 Fire Rooster 澤山咸 31 二十 9

APRIL 1956 壬辰

Xuan Kong Element 玄空五行	山天大畜 Big Livestock	Period Luck 卦運	Monthly Star 月星
Water 水6		4	9

SUNDAY	MONDAY	TUESDAY	WEDNESDAY	THURSDAY	FRIDAY	SATURDAY
水1 Water Humility 5 戊戌 Earth Dog 地山謙 1 廿一 6	火2 Fire Observation 6 己亥 Earth Pig 風地觀 2 廿二 2	火2 Fire Increasing 7 庚子 Metal Rat 風雷益 3 廿三 9	水1 Water Dimming Light 8 辛丑 Metal Ox 地火明夷 4 廿四 3	金9 Metal Fellowship 9 壬寅 Water Tiger 天火同人 5 廿五 7	木8 Wood Marrying Maiden 1 癸卯 Water Rabbit 雷澤歸妹 6 廿六 7	木3 Wood Opposition 2 甲辰 Wood Dragon 火澤睽 7 廿七 2
火7 Fire Waiting 3 乙巳 Wood Snake 水天需 8 廿八 3	金4 Metal Great Exceeding 4 丙午 Fire Horse 澤風大過 9 廿九 3	水6 Water Poison 5 丁未 Fire Goat 山風蠱 10 三十 7	火2 Fire Dispersing 6 戊申 Earth Monkey 風水渙 11 三月初一 6	木3 Wood Travelling 7 己酉 Earth Rooster 火山旅 12 初二 8	金9 Metal Stagnation 8 庚戌 Metal Dog 天地否 13 初三 9	火7 Fire Alliance 9 辛亥 Metal Pig 水地比 14 初四 7
木8 Wood Thunder 1 壬子 Water Rat 震爲雷 15 初五 1	水6 Water Beauty 2 癸丑 Water Ox 山火賁 16 初六 8	火7 Fire Accomplished 3 甲寅 Wood Tiger 水火既濟 17 初七 9	水1 Water Arriving 4 乙卯 Wood Rabbit 地澤臨 18 初八 4	金4 Metal Marsh 5 丙辰 Fire Dragon 兌爲澤 19 初九 1	火2 Fire Small Livestock 6 丁巳 Fire Snake 風天小畜 20 初十 8	木3 Wood The Cauldron 7 戊午 Earth Horse 火風鼎 21 十一 4
水1 Water Rising 8 己未 Earth Goat 地風升 22 十二 2	火7 Fire Water 9 庚申 Metal Monkey 坎爲水 23 十三 1	木8 Wood Lesser Exceeding 1 辛酉 Metal Rooster 雷山小過 24 十四 3	金4 Metal Gathering 2 壬戌 Water Dog 澤地萃 25 十五 4	水6 Water Peel 3 癸亥 Water Pig 山地剝 26 十六 6	水1 Water Earth 4 甲子 Wood Rat 坤爲地 27 十七 1	木3 Wood Biting 5 乙丑 Wood Ox 火雷噬嗑 28 十八 6
火2 Fire Family 6 丙寅 Fire Tiger 風火家人 29 十九 4	水6 Water Decreasing 7 丁卯 Fire Rabbit 山澤損 30 二十 9					

MAY 1956 癸巳

Xuan Kong Element 玄空五行	澤天夬 Eliminating	Period Luck 卦運	Monthly Star 月星
Metal 金4		6	8

SUNDAY	MONDAY	TUESDAY	WEDNESDAY	THURSDAY	FRIDAY	SATURDAY
		金9 Metal 8 Tread 戊辰 Earth Dragon 天澤履 **1** 廿一 6	木8 Wood 9 Great Strength 己巳 Earth Snake 雷天大壯 **2** 廿二 2	木8 Wood 1 Consistency 庚午 Metal Horse 雷風恆 **3** 廿三 9	金9 Metal 2 Litigation 辛未 Metal Goat 天水訟 **4** 廿四 3	水1 Water 3 Officer 壬申 Water Monkey 地水師 **5** 廿五 7
火2 Fire 4 Gradual Progress 癸酉 Water Rooster 風山漸 **6** 廿六 7	火7 Fire 5 Obstruction 甲戌 Wood Dog 水山蹇 **7** 廿七 2	木3 Wood 6 Advancement 乙亥 Wood Pig 火地晉 **8** 廿八 3	水6 Water 7 Nourish 丙子 Fire Rat 山雷頤 **9** 廿九 3	金4 Metal 8 Following 丁丑 Fire Ox 澤雷隨 **10** 四月初一 7	木8 Wood 9 Abundance 戊寅 Earth Tiger 雷火豐 **11** 初二 6	火7 Fire 1 Regulate 己卯 Earth Rabbit 水澤節 **12** 初三 8
水1 Water 2 Unity 庚辰 Metal Dragon 地天泰 **13** 初四 9	木3 Wood 3 Great Reward 辛巳 Metal Snake 火天大有 **14** 初五 7	火2 Fire 4 Wind 壬午 Water Horse 巽爲風 **15** 初六 1	金4 Metal 5 Trap 癸未 Water Goat 澤水困 **16** 初七 8	木3 Wood 6 Not Yet Accomplished 甲申 Wood Monkey 火水未濟 **17** 初八 9	金9 Metal 7 Retreat 乙酉 Wood Rooster 天山遯 **18** 初九 4	水6 Water 8 Mountain 丙戌 Fire Dog 艮爲山 **19** 初十 1
木8 Wood 9 Delight 丁亥 Fire Pig 雷地豫 **20** 十一 8	火7 Fire 1 Beginning 戊子 Earth Rat 水雷屯 **21** 十二 4	金9 Metal 2 Without Wrongdoing 己丑 Earth Ox 天雷無妄 **22** 十三 2	木3 Wood 3 Fire 庚寅 Metal Tiger 離爲火 **23** 十四 1	火2 Fire 4 Sincerity 辛卯 Metal Rabbit 風澤中孚 **24** 十五 3	水6 Water 5 Big Livestock 壬辰 Water Dragon 山天大畜 **25** 十六 4	金4 Metal 6 Eliminating 癸巳 Water Snake 澤天夬 **26** 十七 6
金9 Metal 7 Heaven 甲午 Wood Horse 乾爲天 **27** 十八 1	火7 Fire 8 Well 乙未 Wood Goat 水風井 **28** 十九 6	木8 Wood 9 Relief 丙申 Fire Monkey 雷水解 **29** 二十 4	金4 Metal 1 Influence 丁酉 Fire Rooster 澤山咸 **30** 廿一 9	水1 Water 2 Humility 戊戌 Earth Dog 地山謙 **31** 廿二 6		

JUNE 1956 甲午

Xuan Kong Element 玄空五行	乾爲天 Heaven	Period Luck 卦運	Monthly Star 月星
Metal 金9		1	7

SUNDAY	MONDAY	TUESDAY	WEDNESDAY	THURSDAY	FRIDAY	SATURDAY
					火2 Fire 3 Observation 己亥 Earth Pig 風地觀 **1** 廿三 2	火2 Fire 4 Increasing 庚子 Metal Rat 風雷益 **2** 廿四 9
水1 Water 5 Dimming Light 辛丑 Metal Ox 地火明夷 **3** 廿五 3	金9 Metal 6 Fellowship 壬寅 Water Tiger 天火同人 **4** 廿六 7	木8 Wood 7 Marrying Maiden 癸卯 Water Rabbit 雷澤歸妹 **5** 廿七 7	木3 Wood 8 Opposition 甲辰 Wood Dragon 火澤睽 **6** 廿八 2	火7 Fire 9 Waiting 乙巳 Wood Snake 水天需 **7** 廿九 3	金4 Metal 1 Great Exceeding 丙午 Fire Horse 澤風大過 **8** 三十 3	水6 Water 2 Poison 丁未 Fire Goat 山風蠱 **9** 五月初一 7
火2 Fire 3 Dispersing 戊申 Earth Monkey 風水渙 **10** 初二 6	木3 Wood 4 Travelling 己酉 Earth Rooster 火山旅 **11** 初三 8	金9 Metal 5 Stagnation 庚戌 Metal Dog 天地否 **12** 初四 9	火7 Fire 6 Alliance 辛亥 Metal Pig 水地比 **13** 初五 7	木8 Wood 7 Thunder 壬子 Water Rat 震爲雷 **14** 初六 1	水6 Water 8 Beauty 癸丑 Water Ox 山火賁 **15** 初七 8	火7 Fire 9 Accomplished 甲寅 Wood Tiger 水火既濟 **16** 初八 9
水1 Water 1 Arriving 乙卯 Wood Rabbit 地澤臨 **17** 初九 4	金4 Metal 2 Marsh 丙辰 Fire Dragon 兌爲澤 **18** 初十 1	火2 Fire 3 Small Livestock 丁巳 Fire Snake 風天小畜 **19** 十一 8	木3 Wood 4 The Cauldron 戊午 Earth Horse 火風鼎 **20** 十二 4	水1 Water 5/5 Rising 己未 Earth Goat 地風升 **21** 十三 2	火7 Fire 4 Water 庚申 Metal Monkey 坎爲水 **22** 十四 1	木8 Wood 3 Lesser Exceeding 辛酉 Metal Rooster 雷山小過 **23** 十五 3
金4 Metal 2 Gathering 壬戌 Water Dog 澤地萃 **24** 十六 4	水6 Water 1 Peel 癸亥 Water Pig 山地剝 **25** 十七 6	水1 Water 9 Earth 甲子 Wood Rat 坤爲地 **26** 十八 1	木3 Wood 8 Biting 乙丑 Wood Ox 火雷噬嗑 **27** 十九 6	火2 Fire 7 Family 丙寅 Fire Tiger 風火家人 **28** 二十 4	水6 Water 6 Decreasing 丁卯 Fire Rabbit 山澤損 **29** 廿一 9	金9 Metal 5 Tread 戊辰 Earth Dragon 天澤履 **30** 廿二 6

JULY 1956 乙未

Xuan Kong Element 玄空五行	水風井 Well	Period Luck 卦運	Monthly Star 月星
Fire 火7		6	6

SUNDAY	MONDAY	TUESDAY	WEDNESDAY	THURSDAY	FRIDAY	SATURDAY
木8 Wood 4 Great Strength 己巳 Earth Snake 雷天大壯 **1** 廿三 2	木8 Wood 3 Consistency 庚午 Metal Horse 雷風恆 **2** 廿四 9	金9 Metal 2 Litigation 辛未 Metal Goat 天水訟 **3** 廿五 3	水1 Water 1 Officer 壬申 Water Monkey 地水師 **4** 廿六 7	火2 Fire 9 Gradual Progress 癸酉 Water Rooster 風山漸 **5** 廿七 7	火7 Fire 8 Obstruction 甲戌 Wood Dog 水山蹇 **6** 廿八 2	木3 Wood 7 Advancement 乙亥 Wood Pig 火地晉 **7** 廿九 3
水6 Water 6 Nourish 丙子 Fire Rat 山雷頤 **8** 六月初一 3	金4 Metal 5 Following 丁丑 Fire Ox 澤雷隨 **9** 初二 7	木8 Wood 4 Abundance 戊寅 Earth Tiger 雷火豐 **10** 初三 6	火7 Fire 3 Regulate 己卯 Earth Rabbit 水澤節 **11** 初四 8	水1 Water 2 Unity 庚辰 Metal Dragon 地天泰 **12** 初五 9	木3 Wood 1 Great Reward 辛巳 Metal Snake 火天大有 **13** 初六 7	火2 Fire 9 Wind 壬午 Water Horse 巽為風 **14** 初七 1
金4 Metal 8 Trap 癸未 Water Goat 澤水困 **15** 初八 8	木3 Wood 7 Not Yet Accomplished 甲申 Wood Monkey 火水未濟 **16** 初九 9	金9 Metal 6 Retreat 乙酉 Wood Rooster 天山遯 **17** 初十 4	水6 Water 5 Mountain 丙戌 Fire Dog 艮為山 **18** 十一 1	木8 Wood 4 Delight 丁亥 Fire Pig 雷地豫 **19** 十二 8	火7 Fire 3 Beginning 戊子 Earth Rat 水雷屯 **20** 十三 4	金9 Metal 2 Without Wrongdoing 己丑 Earth Ox 天雷無妄 **21** 十四 2
木3 Wood 1 Fire 庚寅 Metal Tiger 離為火 **22** 十五 1	火2 Fire 9 Sincerity 辛卯 Metal Rabbit 風澤中孚 **23** 十六 3	水6 Water 8 Big Livestock 壬辰 Water Dragon 山天大畜 **24** 十七 4	金4 Metal 7 Eliminating 癸巳 Water Snake 澤天夬 **25** 十八 6	金9 Metal 6 Heaven 甲午 Wood Horse 乾為天 **26** 十九 1	火7 Fire 5 Well 乙未 Wood Goat 水風井 **27** 二十 6	木8 Wood 4 Relief 丙申 Fire Monkey 雷水解 **28** 廿一 4
金4 Metal 3 Influence 丁酉 Fire Rooster 澤山咸 **29** 廿二 9	水1 Water 2 Humility 戊戌 Earth Dog 地山謙 **30** 廿三 6	火2 Fire 1 Observation 己亥 Earth Pig 風地觀 **31** 廿四 2				

AUGUST 1956 丙申

Xuan Kong Element 玄空五行	雷水解 Relief	Period Luck 卦運	Monthly Star 月星
Wood 木8		4	5

SUNDAY	MONDAY	TUESDAY	WEDNESDAY	THURSDAY	FRIDAY	SATURDAY
			火2 Fire 9 Increasing 庚子 Metal Rat 風雷益 **1** 廿五 9	水1 Water 8 Dimming Light 辛丑 Metal Ox 地火明夷 **2** 廿六 3	金9 Metal 7 Fellowship 壬寅 Water Tiger 天火同人 **3** 廿七 7	木8 Wood 6 Marrying Maiden 癸卯 Water Rabbit 雷澤歸妹 **4** 廿八 7
木3 Wood 5 Opposition 甲辰 Wood Dragon 火澤睽 **5** 廿九 2	火7 Fire 4 Waiting 乙巳 Wood Snake 水天需 **6** 七月初一 3	金4 Metal 3 Great Exceeding 丙午 Fire Horse 澤風大過 **7** 初二 3	水6 Water 2 Poison 丁未 Fire Goat 山風蠱 **8** 初三 7	火2 Fire 1 Dispersing 戊申 Earth Monkey 風水渙 **9** 初四 6	木3 Wood 9 Travelling 己酉 Earth Rooster 火山旅 **10** 初五 8	金9 Metal 8 Stagnation 庚戌 Metal Dog 天地否 **11** 初六 9
火7 Fire 7 Alliance 辛亥 Metal Pig 水地比 **12** 初七 7	木8 Wood 6 Thunder 壬子 Water Rat 震為雷 **13** 初八 1	水6 Water 5 Beauty 癸丑 Water Ox 山火賁 **14** 初九 8	火7 Fire 4 Accomplished 甲寅 Wood Tiger 水火既濟 **15** 初十 9	水1 Water 3 Arriving 乙卯 Wood Rabbit 地澤臨 **16** 十一 4	金4 Metal 2 Marsh 丙辰 Fire Dragon 兌為澤 **17** 十二 1	火2 Fire 1 Small Livestock 丁巳 Fire Snake 風天小畜 **18** 十三 8
木3 Wood 9 The Cauldron 戊午 Earth Horse 火風鼎 **19** 十四 4	水1 Water 8 Rising 己未 Earth Goat 地風升 **20** 十五 2	火7 Fire 7 Water 庚申 Metal Monkey 坎為水 **21** 十六 1	木8 Wood 6 Lesser Exceeding 辛酉 Metal Rooster 雷山小過 **22** 十七 3	金4 Metal 5 Gathering 壬戌 Water Dog 澤地萃 **23** 十八 4	水6 Water 4 Peel 癸亥 Water Pig 山地剝 **24** 十九 6	水1 Water 3 Earth 甲子 Wood Rat 坤為地 **25** 二十 1
木3 Wood 2 Biting 乙丑 Wood Ox 火雷噬嗑 **26** 廿一 6	火2 Fire 1 Family 丙寅 Fire Tiger 風火家人 **27** 廿二 4	水6 Water 9 Decreasing 丁卯 Fire Rabbit 山澤損 **28** 廿三 9	金9 Metal 8 Tread 戊辰 Earth Dragon 天澤履 **29** 廿四 6	木8 Wood 7 Great Strength 己巳 Earth Snake 雷天大壯 **30** 廿五 2	木8 Wood 6 Consistency 庚午 Metal Horse 雷風恆 **31** 廿六 9	

SEPTEMBER 1956 丁酉

Xuan Kong Element 玄空五行	澤山咸 Influence	Period Luck 卦運	Monthly Star 月星
Metal 金4		9	4

SUNDAY	MONDAY	TUESDAY	WEDNESDAY	THURSDAY	FRIDAY	SATURDAY
火2 Fire 3 Increasing 風雷益 庚子 Metal Rat 30 廿六 9						金9 Metal 5 Litigation 天水訟 辛未 Metal Goat 1 廿七 3
水1 Water 4 Officer 地水師 壬申 Water Monkey 2 廿八 7	火2 Fire 3 Gradual Progress 風山漸 癸酉 Water Rooster 3 廿九 7	火7 Fire 2 Obstruction 水山蹇 甲戌 Wood Dog 4 三十 2	木3 Wood 1 Advancement 火地晉 乙亥 Wood Pig 5 八月初一 3	水6 Water 9 Nourish 山雷頤 丙子 Fire Rat 6 初二 3	金4 Metal 8 Following 澤雷隨 丁丑 Fire Ox 7 初三 7	木8 Wood 7 Abundance 雷火豐 戊寅 Earth Tiger 8 初四 6
火7 Fire 6 Regulate 水澤節 己卯 Earth Rabbit 9 初五 8	水1 Water 5 Unity 地天泰 庚辰 Metal Dragon 10 初六 9	木3 Wood 4 Great Reward 火天大有 辛巳 Metal Snake 11 初七 7	火2 Fire 3 Wind 巽爲風 壬午 Water Horse 12 初八 1	金4 Metal 2 Trap 澤水困 癸未 Water Goat 13 初九 8	木3 Wood 1 Not Yet Accomplished 火水未濟 甲申 Wood Monkey 14 初十 9	金9 Metal 9 Retreat 天山遯 乙酉 Wood Rooster 15 十一 4
水6 Water 8 Mountain 艮爲山 丙戌 Fire Dog 16 十二 1	木8 Wood 7 Delight 雷地豫 丁亥 Fire Pig 17 十三 8	火7 Fire 6 Beginning 水雷屯 戊子 Earth Rat 18 十四 4	金9 Metal 5 Without Wrongdoing 天雷無妄 己丑 Earth Ox 19 十五 2	木3 Wood 4 Fire 離爲火 庚寅 Metal Tiger 20 十六 1	火2 Fire 3 Sincerity 風澤中孚 辛卯 Metal Rabbit 21 十七 3	水6 Water 2 Big Livestock 山天大畜 壬辰 Water Dragon 22 十八 4
金4 Metal 1 Eliminating 澤天夬 癸巳 Water Snake 23 十九 6	金9 Metal 9 Heaven 乾爲天 甲午 Wood Horse 24 二十 1	火7 Fire 8 Well 水風井 乙未 Wood Goat 25 廿一 6	木8 Wood 7 Relief 雷水解 丙申 Fire Monkey 26 廿二 4	金4 Metal 6 Influence 澤山咸 丁酉 Fire Rooster 27 廿三 9	水1 Water 5 Humility 地山謙 戊戌 Earth Dog 28 廿四 6	火2 Fire 4 Observation 風地觀 己亥 Earth Pig 29 廿五 2

OCTOBER 1956 戊戌

Xuan Kong Element 玄空五行	地山謙 Humility	Period Luck 卦運	Monthly Star 月星
Water 水1		6	3

SUNDAY	MONDAY	TUESDAY	WEDNESDAY	THURSDAY	FRIDAY	SATURDAY
	水1 Water 2 Dimming Light 地火明夷 辛丑 Metal Ox 1 廿七 3	金9 Metal 1 Fellowship 天火同人 壬寅 Water Tiger 2 廿八 7	木8 Wood 9 Marrying Maiden 雷澤歸妹 癸卯 Water Rabbit 3 廿九 7	木3 Wood 8 Opposition 火澤睽 甲辰 Wood Dragon 4 九月初一 2	火7 Fire 7 Waiting 水天需 乙巳 Wood Snake 5 初二 3	金4 Metal 6 Great Exceeding 澤風大過 丙午 Fire Horse 6 初三 3
水6 Water 5 Poison 山風蠱 丁未 Fire Goat 7 初四 7	火2 Fire 4 Dispersing 風水渙 戊申 Earth Monkey 8 初五 6	木3 Wood 3 Travelling 火山旅 己酉 Earth Rooster 9 初六 8	金9 Metal 2 Stagnation 天地否 庚戌 Metal Dog 10 初七 9	火7 Fire 1 Alliance 水地比 辛亥 Metal Pig 11 初八 7	木8 Wood 9 Thunder 震爲雷 壬子 Water Rat 12 初九 1	水6 Water 8 Beauty 山火賁 癸丑 Water Ox 13 初十 8
火7 Fire 7 Accomplished 水火既濟 甲寅 Wood Tiger 14 十一 9	水1 Water 6 Arriving 地澤臨 乙卯 Wood Rabbit 15 十二 4	金4 Metal 5 Marsh 兑爲澤 丙辰 Fire Dragon 16 十三 1	火2 Fire 4 Small Livestock 風天小畜 丁巳 Fire Snake 17 十四 8	木3 Wood 3 The Cauldron 火風鼎 戊午 Earth Horse 18 十五 4	水1 Water 2 Rising 地風升 己未 Earth Goat 19 十六 2	火7 Fire 1 Water 坎爲水 庚申 Metal Monkey 20 十七 1
木8 Wood 9 Lesser Exceeding 雷山小過 辛酉 Metal Rooster 21 十八 3	金4 Metal 8 Gathering 澤地萃 壬戌 Water Dog 22 十九 4	水6 Water 7 Peel 山地剝 癸亥 Water Pig 23 二十 6	水1 Water 6 Earth 坤爲地 甲子 Wood Rat 24 廿一 1	木3 Wood 5 Biting 火雷噬嗑 乙丑 Wood Ox 25 廿二 6	火2 Fire 4 Family 風火家人 丙寅 Fire Tiger 26 廿三 4	水6 Water 3 Decreasing 山澤損 丁卯 Fire Rabbit 27 廿四 9
金9 Metal 2 Tread 天澤履 戊辰 Earth Dragon 28 廿五 6	木8 Wood 1 Great Strength 雷天大壯 己巳 Earth Snake 29 廿六 2	木8 Wood 9 Consistency 雷風恆 庚午 Metal Horse 30 廿七 9	金9 Metal 8 Litigation 天水訟 辛未 Metal Goat 31 廿八 3			

NOVEMBER 1956 己亥

Xuan Kong Element 玄空五行	風地觀 Observation	Period Luck 卦運	Monthly Star 月星
Fire 火2		2	2

SUNDAY	MONDAY	TUESDAY	WEDNESDAY	THURSDAY	FRIDAY	SATURDAY
				水1 Water Officer 7 壬申 Water Monkey 地水師 1 廿九 7	火2 Fire Gradual Progress 6 癸酉 Water Rooster 風山漸 2 三十 7	火7 Fire Obstruction 5 甲戌 Wood Dog 水山蹇 3 十月初一 2
木3 Wood Advancement 4 乙亥 Wood Pig 火地晉 4 初二 3	水6 Water Nourish 3 丙子 Fire Rat 山雷頤 5 初三 3	金4 Metal Following 2 丁丑 Fire Ox 澤雷隨 6 初四 7	木8 Wood Abundance 1 戊寅 Earth Tiger 雷火豐 7 初五 6	火7 Fire Regulate 9 己卯 Earth Rabbit 水澤節 8 初六 8	水1 Water Unity 8 庚辰 Metal Dragon 地天泰 9 初七 9	木3 Wood Great Reward 7 辛巳 Metal Snake 火天大有 10 初八 7
火2 Fire Wind 6 壬午 Water Horse 巽爲風 11 初九 1	金4 Metal Trap 5 癸未 Water Goat 澤水困 12 初十 8	木3 Wood Not Yet Accomplished 4 甲申 Wood Monkey 火水未濟 13 十一 9	金9 Metal Retreat 3 乙酉 Wood Rooster 天山遯 14 十二 4	水6 Water Mountain 2 丙戌 Fire Dog 艮爲山 15 十三 1	木8 Wood Delight 1 丁亥 Fire Pig 雷地豫 16 十四 8	火7 Fire Beginning 9 戊子 Earth Rat 水雷屯 17 十五 4
金9 Metal Without Wrongdoing 8 己丑 Earth Ox 天雷無妄 18 十六 2	木3 Wood Fire 7 庚寅 Metal Tiger 離爲火 19 十七 1	火2 Fire Sincerity 6 辛卯 Metal Rabbit 風澤中孚 20 十八 3	水6 Water Big Livestock 5 壬辰 Water Dragon 山天大畜 21 十九 4	金4 Metal Eliminating 4 癸巳 Water Snake 澤天夬 22 二十 6	金9 Metal Heaven 3 甲午 Wood Horse 乾爲天 23 廿一 1	火7 Fire Well 2 乙未 Wood Goat 水風井 24 廿二 6
木8 Wood Relief 1 丙申 Fire Monkey 雷水解 25 廿三 4	金4 Metal Influence 9 丁酉 Fire Rooster 澤山咸 26 廿四 9	水1 Water Humility 8 戊戌 Earth Dog 地山謙 27 廿五 6	火2 Fire Observation 7 己亥 Earth Pig 風地觀 28 廿六 2	火2 Fire Increasing 6 庚子 Metal Rat 風雷益 29 廿七 9	水1 Water Dimming Light 5 辛丑 Metal Ox 地火明夷 30 廿八 3	

DECEMBER 1956 庚子

Xuan Kong Element 玄空五行	風雷益 Increasing	Period Luck 卦運	Monthly Star 月星
Fire 火2		9	1

SUNDAY	MONDAY	TUESDAY	WEDNESDAY	THURSDAY	FRIDAY	SATURDAY
金9 Metal Litigation 8 辛未 Metal Goat 天水訟 30 廿九 3	水1 Water Officer 9 壬申 Water Monkey 地水師 31 三十 7					金9 Metal Fellowship 4 壬寅 Water Tiger 天火同人 1 廿九 7
木8 Wood Marrying Maiden 3 癸卯 Water Rabbit 雷澤歸妹 2 十一月初一 7	木3 Wood Opposition 2 甲辰 Wood Dragon 火澤睽 3 初二 2	火7 Fire Waiting 1 乙巳 Wood Snake 水天需 4 初三 3	金4 Metal Great Exceeding 9 丙午 Fire Horse 澤風大過 5 初四 3	水6 Water Poison 8 丁未 Fire Goat 山風蠱 6 初五 7	火2 Fire Dispersing 7 戊申 Earth Monkey 風水渙 7 初六 6	木3 Wood Travelling 6 己酉 Earth Rooster 火山旅 8 初七 8
金9 Metal Stagnation 5 庚戌 Metal Dog 天地否 9 初八 9	火7 Fire Alliance 4 辛亥 Metal Pig 水地比 10 初九 7	木8 Wood Thunder 3 壬子 Water Rat 震爲雷 11 初十 1	水6 Water Beauty 2 癸丑 Water Ox 山火賁 12 十一 8	火7 Fire Accomplished 1 甲寅 Wood Tiger 水火既濟 13 十二 9	水1 Water Arriving 9 乙卯 Wood Rabbit 地澤臨 14 十三 4	金4 Metal Marsh 8 丙辰 Fire Dragon 兑爲澤 15 十四 1
火2 Fire Small Livestock 7 丁巳 Fire Snake 風天小畜 16 十五 8	木3 Wood The Cauldron 6 戊午 Earth Horse 火風鼎 17 十六 4	水1 Water Rising 5 己未 Earth Goat 地風升 18 十七 2	火7 Fire Water 4 庚申 Metal Monkey 坎爲水 19 十八 1	木8 Wood Lesser Exceeding 3 辛酉 Metal Rooster 雷山小過 20 十九 3	金4 Metal Gathering 2 壬戌 Water Dog 澤地萃 21 二十 4	水6 Water Peel 1/9 癸亥 Water Pig 山地剝 22 廿一 6
水1 Water Earth 1 甲子 Wood Rat 坤爲地 23 廿二 1	木3 Wood Biting 2 乙丑 Wood Ox 火雷噬嗑 24 廿三 6	火2 Fire Family 3 丙寅 Fire Tiger 風火家人 25 廿四 4	水6 Water Decreasing 4 丁卯 Fire Rabbit 山澤損 26 廿五 9	金9 Metal Tread 5 戊辰 Earth Dragon 天澤履 27 廿六 6	木8 Wood Great Strength 6 己巳 Earth Snake 雷天大壯 28 廿七 2	木8 Wood Consistency 7 庚午 Metal Horse 雷風恒 29 廿八 9

1957 丁酉

(*Ding You*) Fire Rooster

1957 丁酉 *(Ding You)* Fire Rooster

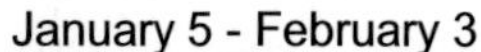

January 5 - February 3

February 4 - March 5

March 6 - April 4

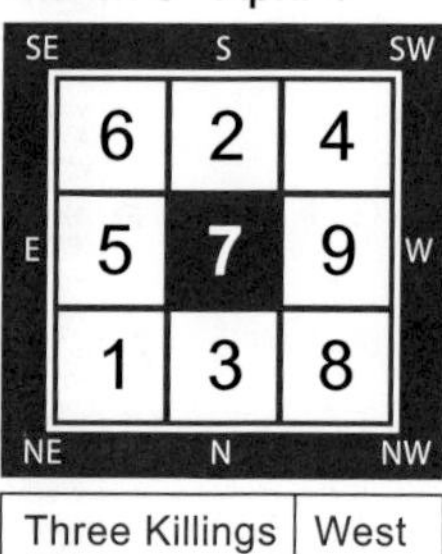

April 5 - May 5

May 6 - June 5

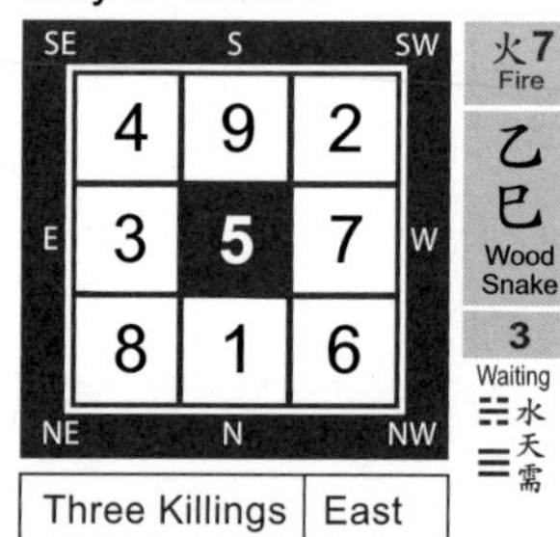

June 6 - July 6

July 7 - August 7

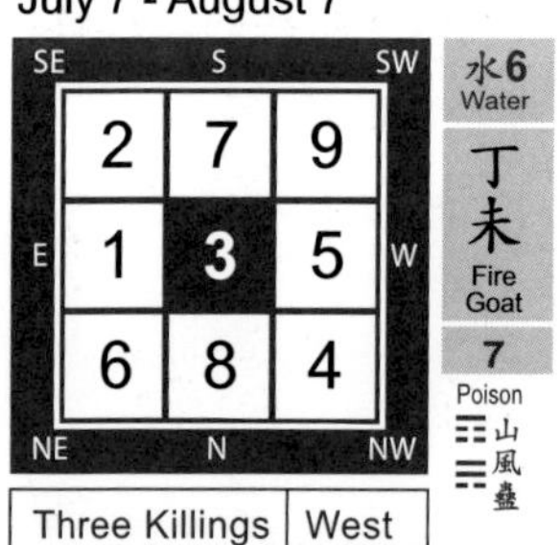

August 8 - September 7

September 8 - October 7

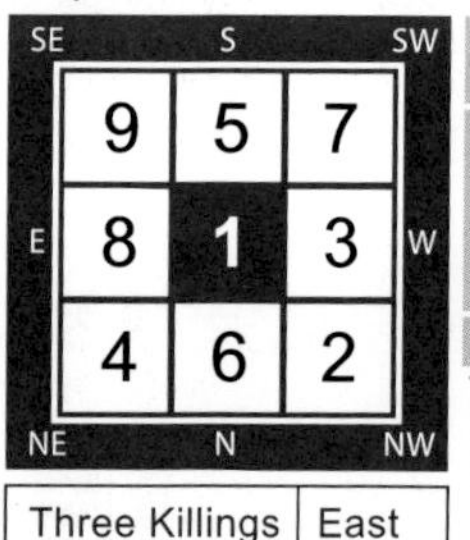

October 8 - November 7

November 8 - December 6

December 7 - January 5

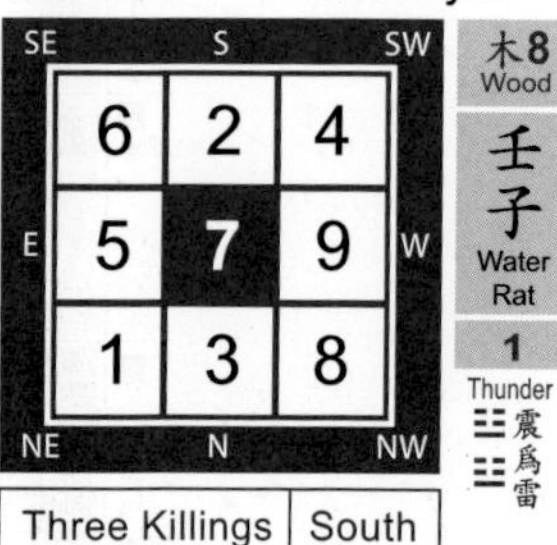

JANUARY 1957 辛丑

Xuan Kong Element 玄空五行	地火明夷 Dimming Light	Period Luck 卦運	Monthly Star 月星
Water 水1		3	9

SUNDAY	MONDAY	TUESDAY	WEDNESDAY	THURSDAY	FRIDAY	SATURDAY
		1 火2 Fire [1] Gradual Progress 癸酉 Water Rooster 風山漸 十二月初一 7	**2** 火7 Fire [2] Obstruction 甲戌 Wood Dog 水山蹇 初二 2	**3** 木3 Wood [3] Advancement 乙亥 Wood Pig 火地晉 初三 3	**4** 水6 Water [4] Nourish 丙子 Fire Rat 山雷頤 初四 3	**5** 金4 Metal [5] Following 丁丑 Fire Ox 澤雷隨 初五 7
6 木8 Wood [6] Abundance 戊寅 Earth Tiger 雷火豐 初六 6	**7** 火7 Fire [7] Regulate 己卯 Earth Rabbit 水澤節 初七 8	**8** 水1 Water [8] Unity 庚辰 Metal Dragon 地天泰 初八 9	**9** 木3 Wood [9] Great Reward 辛巳 Metal Snake 火天大有 初九 7	**10** 火2 Fire [1] Wind 壬午 Water Horse 巽爲風 初十 1	**11** 金4 Metal [2] Trap 癸未 Water Goat 澤水困 十一 8	**12** 木3 Wood [3] Not Yet Accomplished 甲申 Wood Monkey 火水未濟 十二 9
13 金9 Metal [4] Retreat 乙酉 Wood Rooster 天山遯 十三 4	**14** 水6 Water [5] Mountain 丙戌 Fire Dog 艮爲山 十四 1	**15** 木8 Wood [6] Delight 丁亥 Fire Pig 雷地豫 十五 8	**16** 火7 Fire [7] Beginning 戊子 Earth Rat 水雷屯 十六 4	**17** 金9 Metal [8] Without Wrongdoing 己丑 Earth Ox 天雷無妄 十七 2	**18** 木3 Wood [9] Fire 庚寅 Metal Tiger 離爲火 十八 1	**19** 火2 Fire [1] Sincerity 辛卯 Metal Rabbit 風澤中孚 十九 3
20 水6 Water [2] Big Livestock 壬辰 Water Dragon 山天大畜 二十 4	**21** 金4 Metal [3] Eliminating 癸巳 Water Snake 澤天夬 廿一 6	**22** 金9 Metal [4] Heaven 甲午 Wood Horse 乾爲天 廿二 1	**23** 火7 Fire [5] Well 乙未 Wood Goat 水風井 廿三 6	**24** 木8 Wood [6] Relief 丙申 Fire Monkey 雷水解 廿四 4	**25** 金4 Metal [7] Influence 丁酉 Fire Rooster 澤山咸 廿五 9	**26** 水1 Water [8] Humility 戊戌 Earth Dog 地山謙 廿六 6
27 火2 Fire [9] Observation 己亥 Earth Pig 風地觀 廿七 2	**28** 火2 Fire [1] Increasing 庚子 Metal Rat 風雷益 廿八 9	**29** 水1 Water [2] Dimming Light 辛丑 Metal Ox 地火明夷 廿九 3	**30** 金9 Metal [3] Fellowship 壬寅 Water Tiger 天火同人 三十 7	**31** 木8 Wood [4] Marrying Maiden 癸卯 Water Rabbit 雷澤歸妹 正月初一 7		

FEBRUARY 1957 壬寅

Xuan Kong Element 玄空五行	天火同人 Fellowship	Period Luck 卦運	Monthly Star 月星
Metal 金9		7	8

SUNDAY	MONDAY	TUESDAY	WEDNESDAY	THURSDAY	FRIDAY	SATURDAY
					1 木3 Wood [5] Opposition 甲辰 Wood Dragon 火澤睽 初二 2	**2** 火7 Fire [6] Waiting 乙巳 Wood Snake 水天需 初三 3
3 金4 Metal [7] Great Exceeding 丙午 Fire Horse 澤風大過 初四 3	**4** 水6 Water [8] Poison 丁未 Fire Goat 山風蠱 初五 7	**5** 火2 Fire [9] Dispersing 戊申 Earth Monkey 風水渙 初六 6	**6** 木3 Wood [1] Travelling 己酉 Earth Rooster 火山旅 初七 8	**7** 金9 Metal [2] Stagnation 庚戌 Metal Dog 天地否 初八 9	**8** 火7 Fire [3] Alliance 辛亥 Metal Pig 水地比 初九 7	**9** 木8 Wood [4] Thunder 壬子 Water Rat 震爲雷 初十 1
10 水6 Water [5] Beauty 癸丑 Water Ox 山火賁 十一 8	**11** 火7 Fire [6] Accomplished 甲寅 Wood Tiger 水火既濟 十二 9	**12** 水1 Water [7] Arriving 乙卯 Wood Rabbit 地澤臨 十三 4	**13** 金4 Metal [8] Marsh 丙辰 Fire Dragon 兌爲澤 十四 1	**14** 火2 Fire [9] Small Livestock 丁巳 Fire Snake 風天小畜 十五 8	**15** 木3 Wood [1] The Cauldron 戊午 Earth Horse 火風鼎 十六 4	**16** 水1 Water [2] Rising 己未 Earth Goat 地風升 十七 2
17 火7 Fire [3] Water 庚申 Metal Monkey 坎爲水 十八 1	**18** 木8 Wood [4] Lesser Exceeding 辛酉 Metal Rooster 雷山小過 十九 3	**19** 金4 Metal [5] Gathering 壬戌 Water Dog 澤地萃 二十 4	**20** 水6 Water [6] Peel 癸亥 Water Pig 山地剝 廿一 6	**21** 水1 Water [7] Earth 甲子 Wood Rat 坤爲地 廿二 1	**22** 木3 Wood [8] Biting 乙丑 Wood Ox 火雷噬嗑 廿三 6	**23** 火2 Fire [9] Family 丙寅 Fire Tiger 風火家人 廿四 4
24 水6 Water [1] Decreasing 丁卯 Fire Rabbit 山澤損 廿五 9	**25** 金9 Metal [2] Tread 戊辰 Earth Dragon 天澤履 廿六 6	**26** 木8 Wood [3] Great Strength 己巳 Earth Snake 雷天大壯 廿七 2	**27** 木8 Wood [4] Consistency 庚午 Metal Horse 雷風恒 廿八 9	**28** 金9 Metal [5] Litigation 辛未 Metal Goat 天水訟 廿九 3		

MARCH 1957 癸卯

Xuan Kong Element 玄空五行	雷澤歸妹 Marrying Maiden	Period Luck 卦運	Monthly Star 月星
Wood 木8		7	7

SUNDAY	MONDAY	TUESDAY	WEDNESDAY	THURSDAY	FRIDAY	SATURDAY
31 三月初一 金9 Metal · Fellowship 天火同人 · 9 壬寅 Water Tiger · 7					1 三十 水1 Water · Officer 地水師 · 6 壬申 Water Monkey · 7	2 二月初一 火2 Fire · Gradual Progress 風山漸 · 7 癸酉 Water Rooster · 7
3 初二 火7 Fire · Obstruction 水山蹇 · 8 甲戌 Wood Dog · 2	4 初三 木3 Wood · Advancement 火地晉 · 9 乙亥 Wood Pig · 3	5 初四 水6 Water · Nourish 山雷頤 · 1 丙子 Fire Rat · 3	6 初五 金4 Metal · Following 澤雷隨 · 2 丁丑 Fire Ox · 7	7 初六 木8 Wood · Abundance 雷火豐 · 3 戊寅 Earth Tiger · 6	8 初七 火7 Fire · Regulate 水澤節 · 4 己卯 Earth Rabbit · 8	9 初八 水1 Water · Unity 地天泰 · 5 庚辰 Metal Dragon · 9
10 初九 木3 Wood · Great Reward 火天大有 · 6 辛巳 Metal Snake · 7	11 初十 火2 Fire · Wind 巽爲風 · 7 壬午 Water Horse · 1	12 十一 金4 Metal · Trap 澤水困 · 8 癸未 Water Goat · 8	13 十二 木3 Wood · Not Yet Accomplished 火水未濟 · 9 甲申 Wood Monkey · 9	14 十三 金9 Metal · Retreat 天山遯 · 1 乙酉 Wood Rooster · 4	15 十四 水6 Water · Mountain 艮爲山 · 2 丙戌 Fire Dog · 1	16 十五 木8 Wood · Delight 雷地豫 · 3 丁亥 Fire Pig · 8
17 十六 火7 Fire · Beginning 水雷屯 · 4 戊子 Earth Rat · 4	18 十七 金9 Metal · Without Wrongdoing 天雷無妄 · 5 己丑 Earth Ox · 2	19 十八 木3 Wood · Fire 離爲火 · 6 庚寅 Metal Tiger · 1	20 十九 火2 Fire · Sincerity 風澤中孚 · 7 辛卯 Metal Rabbit · 3	21 二十 水6 Water · Big Livestock 山天大畜 · 8 壬辰 Water Dragon · 4	22 廿一 金4 Metal · Eliminating 澤天夬 · 9 癸巳 Water Snake · 6	23 廿二 金9 Metal · Heaven 乾爲天 · 1 甲午 Wood Horse · 1
24 廿三 火7 Fire · Well 水風井 · 2 乙未 Wood Goat · 6	25 廿四 木8 Wood · Relief 雷水解 · 3 丙申 Fire Monkey · 4	26 廿五 金4 Metal · Influence 澤山咸 · 4 丁酉 Fire Rooster · 9	27 廿六 水1 Water · Humility 地山謙 · 5 戊戌 Earth Dog · 6	28 廿七 火2 Fire · Observation 風地觀 · 6 己亥 Earth Pig · 2	29 廿八 火2 Fire · Increasing 風雷益 · 7 庚子 Metal Rat · 9	30 廿九 水1 Water · Dimming Light 地火明夷 · 8 辛丑 Metal Ox · 3

APRIL 1957 甲辰

Xuan Kong Element 玄空五行	火澤睽 Opposition	Period Luck 卦運	Monthly Star 月星
Wood 木3		2	6

SUNDAY	MONDAY	TUESDAY	WEDNESDAY	THURSDAY	FRIDAY	SATURDAY
	1 初二 木8 Wood · Marrying Maiden 雷澤歸妹 · 1 癸卯 Water Rabbit · 7	2 初三 木3 Wood · Opposition 火澤睽 · 2 甲辰 Wood Dragon · 2	3 初四 火7 Fire · Waiting 水天需 · 3 乙巳 Wood Snake · 3	4 初五 金4 Metal · Great Exceeding 澤風大過 · 4 丙午 Fire Horse · 3	5 初六 水6 Water · Poison 山風蠱 · 5 丁未 Fire Goat · 7	6 初七 火2 Fire · Dispersing 風水渙 · 6 戊申 Earth Monkey · 6
7 初八 木3 Wood · Travelling 火山旅 · 7 己酉 Earth Rooster · 8	8 初九 金9 Metal · Stagnation 天地否 · 8 庚戌 Metal Dog · 9	9 初十 火7 Fire · Alliance 水地比 · 9 辛亥 Metal Pig · 7	10 十一 木8 Wood · Thunder 震爲雷 · 1 壬子 Water Rat · 1	11 十二 水6 Water · Beauty 山火賁 · 2 癸丑 Water Ox · 8	12 十三 火7 Fire · Accomplished 水火既濟 · 3 甲寅 Wood Tiger · 9	13 十四 水1 Water · Arriving 地澤臨 · 4 乙卯 Wood Rabbit · 4
14 十五 金4 Metal · Marsh 兑爲澤 · 5 丙辰 Fire Dragon · 1	15 十六 火2 Fire · Small Livestock 風天小畜 · 6 丁巳 Fire Snake · 8	16 十七 木3 Wood · The Cauldron 火風鼎 · 7 戊午 Earth Horse · 4	17 十八 水1 Water · Rising 地風升 · 8 己未 Earth Goat · 2	18 十九 火7 Fire · Water 坎爲水 · 9 庚申 Metal Monkey · 1	19 二十 木8 Wood · Lesser Exceeding 雷山小過 · 1 辛酉 Metal Rooster · 3	20 廿一 金4 Metal · Gathering 澤地萃 · 2 壬戌 Water Dog · 4
21 廿二 水6 Water · Peel 山地剝 · 3 癸亥 Water Pig · 6	22 廿三 水1 Water · Earth 坤爲地 · 4 甲子 Wood Rat · 1	23 廿四 木3 Wood · Biting 火雷噬嗑 · 5 乙丑 Wood Ox · 6	24 廿五 火2 Fire · Family 風火家人 · 6 丙寅 Fire Tiger · 4	25 廿六 水6 Water · Decreasing 山澤損 · 7 丁卯 Fire Rabbit · 9	26 廿七 金9 Metal · Tread 天澤履 · 8 戊辰 Earth Dragon · 6	27 廿八 木8 Wood · Great Strength 雷天大壯 · 9 己巳 Earth Snake · 2
28 廿九 木8 Wood · Consistency 雷風恆 · 1 庚午 Metal Horse · 9	29 三十 金9 Metal · Litigation 天水訟 · 2 辛未 Metal Goat · 3	30 四月初一 水1 Water · Officer 地水師 · 3 壬申 Water Monkey · 7				

MAY 1957 乙巳

Xuan Kong Element 玄空五行	水天需 Waiting	Period Luck 卦運	Monthly Star 月星
Fire 火7		3	5

SUNDAY	MONDAY	TUESDAY	WEDNESDAY	THURSDAY	FRIDAY	SATURDAY
			火2 Fire 癸酉 Water Rooster 7 · 4 Gradual Progress 風山漸 · 1 初二	火7 Fire 甲戌 Wood Dog 2 · 5 Obstruction 水山蹇 · 2 初三	木3 Wood 乙亥 Wood Pig 3 · 6 Advancement 火地晉 · 3 初四	水6 Water 丙子 Fire Rat 3 · 7 Nourish 山雷頤 · 4 初五
金4 Metal 丁丑 Fire Ox 7 · 8 Following 澤雷隨 · 5 初六	木8 Wood 戊寅 Earth Tiger 6 · 9 Abundance 雷火豐 · 6 初七	火7 Fire 己卯 Earth Rabbit 8 · 1 Regulate 水澤節 · 7 初八	水1 Water 庚辰 Metal Dragon 9 · 2 Unity 地天泰 · 8 初九	木3 Wood 辛巳 Metal Snake 7 · 3 Great Reward 火天大有 · 9 初十	火2 Fire 壬午 Water Horse 1 · 4 Wind 巽爲風 · 10 十一	金4 Metal 癸未 Water Goat 8 · 5 Trap 澤水困 · 11 十二
木3 Wood 甲申 Wood Monkey 9 · 6 Not Yet Accomplished 火水未濟 · 12 十三	金9 Metal 乙酉 Wood Rooster 4 · 7 Retreat 天山遯 · 13 十四	水6 Water 丙戌 Fire Dog 1 · 8 Mountain 艮爲山 · 14 十五	木8 Wood 丁亥 Fire Pig 8 · 9 Delight 雷地豫 · 15 十六	火7 Fire 戊子 Earth Rat 4 · 1 Beginning 水雷屯 · 16 十七	金9 Metal 己丑 Earth Ox 2 · 2 Without Wrongdoing 天雷無妄 · 17 十八	木3 Wood 庚寅 Metal Tiger 1 · 3 Fire 離爲火 · 18 十九
火2 Fire 辛卯 Metal Rabbit 3 · 4 Sincerity 風澤中孚 · 19 二十	水6 Water 壬辰 Water Dragon 4 · 5 Big Livestock 山天大畜 · 20 廿一	金4 Metal 癸巳 Water Snake 6 · 6 Eliminating 澤天夬 · 21 廿二	金9 Metal 甲午 Wood Horse 1 · 7 Heaven 乾爲天 · 22 廿三	火7 Fire 乙未 Wood Goat 6 · 8 Well 水風井 · 23 廿四	木8 Wood 丙申 Fire Monkey 4 · 9 Relief 雷水解 · 24 廿五	金4 Metal 丁酉 Fire Rooster 9 · 1 Influence 澤山咸 · 25 廿六
水1 Water 戊戌 Earth Dog 6 · 2 Humility 地山謙 · 26 廿七	火2 Fire 己亥 Earth Pig 2 · 3 Observation 風地觀 · 27 廿八	火2 Fire 庚子 Metal Rat 9 · 4 Increasing 風雷益 · 28 廿九	水1 Water 辛丑 Metal Ox 3 · 5 Dimming Light 地火明夷 · 29 五月初一	金9 Metal 壬寅 Water Tiger 7 · 6 Fellowship 天火同人 · 30 初二	木8 Wood 癸卯 Water Rabbit 7 · 7 Marrying Maiden 雷澤歸妹 · 31 初三	

JUNE 1957 丙午

Xuan Kong Element 玄空五行	澤風大過 Great Exceeding	Period Luck 卦運	Monthly Star 月星
Metal 金4		3	4

SUNDAY	MONDAY	TUESDAY	WEDNESDAY	THURSDAY	FRIDAY	SATURDAY
火2 Fire 癸酉 Water Rooster 7 · 6 Gradual Progress 風山漸 · 30 初三						木3 Wood 甲辰 Wood Dragon 2 · 8 Opposition 火澤睽 · 1 初四
火7 Fire 乙巳 Wood Snake 3 · 9 Waiting 水天需 · 2 初五	金4 Metal 丙午 Fire Horse 3 · 1 Great Exceeding 澤風大過 · 3 初六	水6 Water 丁未 Fire Goat 7 · 2 Poison 山風蠱 · 4 初七	火2 Fire 戊申 Earth Monkey 6 · 3 Dispersing 風水渙 · 5 初八	木3 Wood 己酉 Earth Rooster 8 · 4 Travelling 火山旅 · 6 初九	金9 Metal 庚戌 Metal Dog 9 · 5 Stagnation 天地否 · 7 初十	火7 Fire 辛亥 Metal Pig 7 · 6 Alliance 水地比 · 8 十一
木8 Wood 壬子 Water Rat 1 · 7 Thunder 震爲雷 · 9 十二	水6 Water 癸丑 Water Ox 8 · 8 Beauty 山火賁 · 10 十三	火7 Fire 甲寅 Wood Tiger 9 · 9 Accomplished 水火既濟 · 11 十四	水1 Water 乙卯 Wood Rabbit 4 · 1 Arriving 地澤臨 · 12 十五	金4 Metal 丙辰 Fire Dragon 1 · 2 Marsh 兑爲澤 · 13 十六	火2 Fire 丁巳 Fire Snake 8 · 3 Small Livestock 風天小畜 · 14 十七	木3 Wood 戊午 Earth Horse 4 · 4 The Cauldron 火風鼎 · 15 十八
水1 Water 己未 Earth Goat 2 · 5 Rising 地風升 · 16 十九	火7 Fire 庚申 Metal Monkey 1 · 6 Water 坎爲水 · 17 二十	木8 Wood 辛酉 Metal Rooster 3 · 7 Lesser Exceeding 雷山小過 · 18 廿一	金4 Metal 壬戌 Water Dog 4 · 8 Gathering 澤地萃 · 19 廿二	水6 Water 癸亥 Water Pig 6 · 9 Peel 山地剝 · 20 廿三	水1 Water 甲子 Wood Rat 1 · 1 Earth 坤爲地 · 21 廿四	木3 Wood 乙丑 Wood Ox 6 · 2/5 Biting 火雷噬嗑 · 22 廿五
火2 Fire 丙寅 Fire Tiger 4 · 4 Family 風火家人 · 23 廿六	水6 Water 丁卯 Fire Rabbit 9 · 3 Decreasing 山澤損 · 24 廿七	金9 Metal 戊辰 Earth Dragon 6 · 2 Tread 天澤履 · 25 廿八	木8 Wood 己巳 Earth Snake 2 · 1 Great Strength 雷天大壯 · 26 廿九	木8 Wood 庚午 Metal Horse 9 · 9 Consistency 雷風恒 · 27 三十	金9 Metal 辛未 Metal Goat 3 · 8 Litigation 天水訟 · 28 六月初一	水1 Water 壬申 Water Monkey 7 · 7 Officer 地水師 · 29 初二

JULY 1957 丁未

Xuan Kong Element 玄空五行	山風蠱 Poison	Period Luck 卦運	Monthly Star 月星
Water 水6		7	3

SUNDAY	MONDAY	TUESDAY	WEDNESDAY	THURSDAY	FRIDAY	SATURDAY
	火7 Fire Obstruction 5 甲戌 Wood Dog 水山蹇 **1** 初四 2	木3 Wood Advancement 4 乙亥 Wood Pig 火地晉 **2** 初五 3	水6 Water Nourish 3 丙子 Fire Rat 山雷頤 **3** 初六 3	金4 Metal Following 2 丁丑 Fire Ox 澤雷隨 **4** 初七 7	木8 Wood Abundance 1 戊寅 Earth Tiger 雷火豐 **5** 初八 6	火7 Fire Regulate 9 己卯 Earth Rabbit 水澤節 **6** 初九 8
水1 Water Unity 8 庚辰 Metal Dragon 地天泰 **7** 初十 9	木3 Wood Great Reward 7 辛巳 Metal Snake 火天大有 **8** 十一 7	火2 Fire Wind 6 壬午 Water Horse 巽為風 **9** 十二 1	金4 Metal Trap 5 癸未 Water Goat 澤水困 **10** 十三 8	木3 Wood Not Yet Accomplished 4 甲申 Wood Monkey 火水未濟 **11** 十四 9	金9 Metal Retreat 3 乙酉 Wood Rooster 天山遯 **12** 十五 4	水6 Water Mountain 2 丙戌 Fire Dog 艮為山 **13** 十六 1
木8 Wood Delight 1 丁亥 Fire Pig 雷地豫 **14** 十七 8	火7 Fire Beginning 9 戊子 Earth Rat 水雷屯 **15** 十八 4	金9 Metal Without Wrongdoing 8 己丑 Earth Ox 天雷無妄 **16** 十九 2	木3 Wood Fire 7 庚寅 Metal Tiger 離為火 **17** 二十 1	火2 Fire Sincerity 6 辛卯 Metal Rabbit 風澤中孚 **18** 廿一 3	水6 Water Big Livestock 5 壬辰 Water Dragon 山天大畜 **19** 廿二 4	金4 Metal Eliminating 4 癸巳 Water Snake 澤天夬 **20** 廿三 6
金9 Metal Heaven 3 甲午 Wood Horse 乾為天 **21** 廿四 1	火7 Fire Well 2 乙未 Wood Goat 水風井 **22** 廿五 6	木8 Wood Relief 1 丙申 Fire Monkey 雷水解 **23** 廿六 4	金4 Metal Influence 9 丁酉 Fire Rooster 澤山咸 **24** 廿七 9	水1 Water Humility 8 戊戌 Earth Dog 地山謙 **25** 廿八 6	火2 Fire Observation 7 己亥 Earth Pig 風地觀 **26** 廿九 2	火2 Fire Increasing 6 庚子 Metal Rat 風雷益 **27** 七月初一 9
水1 Water Dimming Light 5 辛丑 Metal Ox 地火明夷 **28** 初二 3	金9 Metal Fellowship 4 壬寅 Water Tiger 天火同人 **29** 初三 7	木8 Wood Marrying Maiden 3 癸卯 Water Rabbit 雷澤歸妹 **30** 初四 7	木3 Wood Opposition 2 甲辰 Wood Dragon 火澤睽 **31** 初五 2			

AUGUST 1957 戊申

Xuan Kong Element 玄空五行	風水渙 Dispersing	Period Luck 卦運	Monthly Star 月星
Fire 火2		6	2

SUNDAY	MONDAY	TUESDAY	WEDNESDAY	THURSDAY	FRIDAY	SATURDAY
				火7 Fire Waiting 1 乙巳 Wood Snake 水天需 **1** 初六 3	金4 Metal Great Exceeding 9 丙午 Fire Horse 澤風大過 **2** 初七 3	水6 Water Poison 8 丁未 Fire Goat 山風蠱 **3** 初八 7
火2 Fire Dispersing 7 戊申 Earth Monkey 風水渙 **4** 初九 6	木3 Wood Travelling 6 己酉 Earth Rooster 火山旅 **5** 初十 8	金9 Metal Stagnation 5 庚戌 Metal Dog 天地否 **6** 十一 9	火7 Fire Alliance 4 辛亥 Metal Pig 水地比 **7** 十二 7	木8 Wood Thunder 3 壬子 Water Rat 震為雷 **8** 十三 1	水6 Water Beauty 2 癸丑 Water Ox 山火賁 **9** 十四 8	火7 Fire Accomplished 1 甲寅 Wood Tiger 水火既濟 **10** 十五 9
水1 Water Arriving 9 乙卯 Wood Rabbit 地澤臨 **11** 十六 4	金4 Metal Marsh 8 丙辰 Fire Dragon 兌為澤 **12** 十七 1	火2 Fire Small Livestock 7 丁巳 Fire Snake 風天小畜 **13** 十八 8	木3 Wood The Cauldron 6 戊午 Earth Horse 火風鼎 **14** 十九 4	水1 Water Rising 5 己未 Earth Goat 地風升 **15** 二十 2	火7 Fire Water 4 庚申 Metal Monkey 坎為水 **16** 廿一 1	木8 Wood Lesser Exceeding 3 辛酉 Metal Rooster 雷山小過 **17** 廿二 3
金4 Metal Gathering 2 壬戌 Water Dog 澤地萃 **18** 廿三 4	水6 Water Peel 1 癸亥 Water Pig 山地剝 **19** 廿四 6	水1 Water Earth 9 甲子 Wood Rat 坤為地 **20** 廿五 1	木3 Wood Biting 8 乙丑 Wood Ox 火雷噬嗑 **21** 廿六 6	火2 Fire Family 7 丙寅 Fire Tiger 風火家人 **22** 廿七 4	水6 Water Decreasing 6 丁卯 Fire Rabbit 山澤損 **23** 廿八 9	金9 Metal Tread 5 戊辰 Earth Dragon 天澤履 **24** 廿九 6
木8 Wood Great Strength 4 己巳 Earth Snake 雷天大壯 **25** 八月初一 2	木8 Wood Consistency 3 庚午 Metal Horse 雷風恆 **26** 初二 9	金9 Metal Litigation 2 辛未 Metal Goat 天水訟 **27** 初三 3	水1 Water Officer 1 壬申 Water Monkey 地水師 **28** 初四 7	火2 Fire Gradual Progress 9 癸酉 Water Rooster 風山漸 **29** 初五 7	火7 Fire Obstruction 8 甲戌 Wood Dog 水山蹇 **30** 初六 2	木3 Wood Advancement 7 乙亥 Wood Pig 火地晉 **31** 初七 3

SEPTEMBER 1957 己酉

Xuan Kong Element 玄空五行	火山旅 Travelling	Period Luck 卦運	Monthly Star 月星
Wood 木3		8	1

SUNDAY	MONDAY	TUESDAY	WEDNESDAY	THURSDAY	FRIDAY	SATURDAY
水6 Water 丙子 Fire Rat 3 Nourish 6 山雷頤 1 初八	金4 Metal 丁丑 Fire Ox 7 Following 5 澤雷隨 2 初九	木8 Wood 戊寅 Earth Tiger 6 Abundance 4 雷火豐 3 初十	火7 Fire 己卯 Earth Rabbit 8 Regulate 3 水澤節 4 十一	水1 Water 庚辰 Metal Dragon 9 Unity 2 地天泰 5 十二	木3 Wood 辛巳 Metal Snake 7 Great Reward 1 火天大有 6 十三	火2 Fire 壬午 Water Horse 1 Wind 9 巽爲風 7 十四
金4 Metal 癸未 Water Goat 8 Trap 8 澤水困 8 十五	木3 Wood 甲申 Wood Monkey 9 Not Yet Accomplished 7 火水未濟 9 十六	金9 Metal 乙酉 Wood Rooster 4 Retreat 6 天山遯 10 十七	水6 Water 丙戌 Fire Dog 1 Mountain 5 艮爲山 11 十八	木8 Wood 丁亥 Fire Pig 8 Delight 4 雷地豫 12 十九	火7 Fire 戊子 Earth Rat 4 Beginning 3 水雷屯 13 二十	金9 Metal 己丑 Earth Ox 2 Without Wrongdoing 2 天雷無妄 14 廿一
木3 Wood 庚寅 Metal Tiger 1 Fire 1 離爲火 15 廿二	火2 Fire 辛卯 Metal Rabbit 3 Sincerity 9 風澤中孚 16 廿三	水6 Water 壬辰 Water Dragon 4 Big Livestock 8 山天大畜 17 廿四	金4 Metal 癸巳 Water Snake 6 Eliminating 7 澤天夬 18 廿五	金9 Metal 甲午 Wood Horse 1 Heaven 6 乾爲天 19 廿六	火7 Fire 乙未 Wood Goat 6 Well 5 水風井 20 廿七	木8 Wood 丙申 Fire Monkey 4 Relief 4 雷水解 21 廿八
金4 Metal 丁酉 Fire Rooster 9 Influence 3 澤山咸 22 廿九	水1 Water 戊戌 Earth Dog 6 Humility 2 地山謙 23 三十	火2 Fire 己亥 Earth Pig 2 Observation 1 風地觀 24 閏八月初一	火2 Fire 庚子 Metal Rat 9 Increasing 9 風雷益 25 初二	水1 Water 辛丑 Metal Ox 3 Dimming Light 8 地火明夷 26 初三	金9 Metal 壬寅 Water Tiger 7 Fellowship 7 天火同人 27 初四	木8 Wood 癸卯 Water Rabbit 7 Marrying Maiden 6 雷澤歸妹 28 初五
木3 Wood 甲辰 Wood Dragon 2 Opposition 5 火澤睽 29 初六	火7 Fire 乙巳 Wood Snake 3 Waiting 4 水天需 30 初七					

OCTOBER 1957 庚戌

Xuan Kong Element 玄空五行	天地否 Stagnation	Period Luck 卦運	Monthly Star 月星
Metal 金9		9	9

SUNDAY	MONDAY	TUESDAY	WEDNESDAY	THURSDAY	FRIDAY	SATURDAY
		金4 Metal 丙午 Fire Horse 3 Great Exceeding 3 澤風大過 1 初八	水6 Water 丁未 Fire Goat 7 Poison 2 山風蠱 2 初九	火2 Fire 戊申 Earth Monkey 6 Dispersing 1 風水渙 3 初十	木3 Wood 己酉 Earth Rooster 8 Travelling 9 火山旅 4 十一	金9 Metal 庚戌 Metal Dog 9 Stagnation 8 天地否 5 十二
火7 Fire 辛亥 Metal Pig 7 Alliance 7 水地比 6 十三	木8 Wood 壬子 Water Rat 1 Thunder 6 震爲雷 7 十四	水6 Water 癸丑 Water Ox 8 Beauty 5 山火賁 8 十五	火7 Fire 甲寅 Wood Tiger 9 Accomplished 4 水火既濟 9 十六	水1 Water 乙卯 Wood Rabbit 4 Arriving 3 地澤臨 10 十七	金4 Metal 丙辰 Fire Dragon 1 Marsh 2 兌爲澤 11 十八	火2 Fire 丁巳 Fire Snake 8 Small Livestock 1 風天小畜 12 十九
木3 Wood 戊午 Earth Horse 4 The Cauldron 9 火風鼎 13 二十	水1 Water 己未 Earth Goat 2 Rising 8 地風升 14 廿一	火7 Fire 庚申 Metal Monkey 1 Water 7 坎爲水 15 廿二	木8 Wood 辛酉 Metal Rooster 3 Lesser Exceeding 6 雷山小過 16 廿三	金4 Metal 壬戌 Water Dog 4 Gathering 5 澤地萃 17 廿四	水6 Water 癸亥 Water Pig 6 Peel 4 山地剝 18 廿五	水1 Water 甲子 Wood Rat 1 Earth 3 坤爲地 19 廿六
木3 Wood 乙丑 Wood Ox 6 Biting 2 火雷噬嗑 20 廿七	火2 Fire 丙寅 Fire Tiger 4 Family 1 風火家人 21 廿八	水6 Water 丁卯 Fire Rabbit 9 Decreasing 9 山澤損 22 廿九	金9 Metal 戊辰 Earth Dragon 6 Tread 8 天澤履 23 九月初一	木8 Wood 己巳 Earth Snake 2 Great Strength 7 雷天大壯 24 初二	木8 Wood 庚午 Metal Horse 9 Consistency 6 雷風恒 25 初三	金9 Metal 辛未 Metal Goat 3 Litigation 5 天水訟 26 初四
水1 Water 壬申 Water Monkey 7 Officer 4 地水師 27 初五	火2 Fire 癸酉 Water Rooster 7 Gradual Progress 3 風山漸 28 初六	火7 Fire 甲戌 Wood Dog 2 Obstruction 2 水山蹇 29 初七	木3 Wood 乙亥 Wood Pig 3 Advancement 1 火地晉 30 初八	水6 Water 丙子 Fire Rat 3 Nourish 9 山雷頤 31 初九		

NOVEMBER 1957 辛亥

Xuan Kong Element 玄空五行	水地比 Alliance	Period Luck 卦運	Monthly Star 月星
Fire 火7		7	8

SUNDAY	MONDAY	TUESDAY	WEDNESDAY	THURSDAY	FRIDAY	SATURDAY
					金4 Metal [8] Following 澤雷隨 丁丑 Fire Ox 1 初十 7	木8 Wood [7] Abundance 雷火豐 戊寅 Earth Tiger 2 十一 6
火7 Fire [6] Regulate 水澤節 己卯 Earth Rabbit 3 十二 8	水1 Water [5] Unity 地天泰 庚辰 Metal Dragon 4 十三 9	木3 Wood [4] Great Reward 火天大有 辛巳 Metal Snake 5 十四 7	火2 Fire [3] Wind 巽爲風 壬午 Water Horse 6 十五 1	金4 Metal [2] Trap 澤水困 癸未 Water Goat 7 十六 8	木3 Wood [1] Not Yet Accomplished 火水未濟 甲申 Wood Monkey 8 十七 9	金9 Metal [9] Retreat 天山遯 乙酉 Wood Rooster 9 十八 4
水6 Water [8] Mountain 艮爲山 丙戌 Fire Dog 10 十九 1	木8 Wood [7] Delight 雷地豫 丁亥 Fire Pig 11 二十 8	火7 Fire [6] Beginning 水雷屯 戊子 Earth Rat 12 廿一 4	金9 Metal [5] Without Wrongdoing 天雷無妄 己丑 Earth Ox 13 廿二 2	木3 Wood [4] Fire 離爲火 庚寅 Metal Tiger 14 廿三 1	火2 Fire [3] Sincerity 風澤中孚 辛卯 Metal Rabbit 15 廿四 3	水6 Water [2] Big Livestock 山天大畜 壬辰 Water Dragon 16 廿五 4
金4 Metal [1] Eliminating 澤天夬 癸巳 Water Snake 17 廿六 6	金9 Metal [9] Heaven 乾爲天 甲午 Wood Horse 18 廿七 1	火7 Fire [8] Well 水風井 乙未 Wood Goat 19 廿八 6	木8 Wood [7] Relief 雷水解 丙申 Fire Monkey 20 廿九 4	金4 Metal [6] Influence 澤山咸 丁酉 Fire Rooster 21 三十 9	水1 Water [5] Humility 地山謙 戊戌 Earth Dog 22 十月初一 6	火2 Fire [4] Observation 風地觀 己亥 Earth Pig 23 初二 2
火2 Fire [3] Increasing 風雷益 庚子 Metal Rat 24 初三 9	水1 Water [2] Dimming Light 地火明夷 辛丑 Metal Ox 25 初四 3	金9 Metal [1] Fellowship 天火同人 壬寅 Water Tiger 26 初五 7	木8 Wood [9] Marrying Maiden 雷澤歸妹 癸卯 Water Rabbit 27 初六 7	木3 Wood [8] Opposition 火澤睽 甲辰 Wood Dragon 28 初七 2	火7 Fire [7] Waiting 水天需 乙巳 Wood Snake 29 初八 3	金4 Metal [6] Great Exceeding 澤風大過 丙午 Fire Horse 30 初九 3

DECEMBER 1957 壬子

Xuan Kong Element 玄空五行	震爲雷 Thunder	Period Luck 卦運	Monthly Star 月星
Wood 木8		1	7

SUNDAY	MONDAY	TUESDAY	WEDNESDAY	THURSDAY	FRIDAY	SATURDAY
水6 Water [5] Poison 山風蠱 丁未 Fire Goat 1 初十 7	火2 Fire [4] Dispersing 風水渙 戊申 Earth Monkey 2 十一 6	木3 Wood [3] Travelling 火山旅 己酉 Earth Rooster 3 十二 8	金9 Metal [2] Stagnation 天地否 庚戌 Metal Dog 4 十三 9	火7 Fire [1] Alliance 水地比 辛亥 Metal Pig 5 十四 7	木8 Wood [9] Thunder 震爲雷 壬子 Water Rat 6 十五 1	水6 Water [8] Beauty 山火賁 癸丑 Water Ox 7 十六 8
火7 Fire [7] Accomplished 水火既濟 甲寅 Wood Tiger 8 十七 9	水1 Water [6] Arriving 地澤臨 乙卯 Wood Rabbit 9 十八 4	金4 Metal [5] Marsh 兑爲澤 丙辰 Fire Dragon 10 十九 1	火2 Fire [4] Small Livestock 風天小畜 丁巳 Fire Snake 11 二十 8	木3 Wood [3] The Cauldron 火風鼎 戊午 Earth Horse 12 廿一 4	水1 Water [2] Rising 地風升 己未 Earth Goat 13 廿二 2	火7 Fire [1] Water 坎爲水 庚申 Metal Monkey 14 廿三 1
木8 Wood [9] Lesser Exceeding 雷山小過 辛酉 Metal Rooster 15 廿四 3	金4 Metal [8] Gathering 澤地萃 壬戌 Water Dog 16 廿五 4	水6 Water [7] Peel 山地剝 癸亥 Water Pig 17 廿六 6	水1 Water [6] Earth 坤爲地 甲子 Wood Rat 18 廿七 1	木3 Wood [5] Biting 火雷噬嗑 乙丑 Wood Ox 19 廿八 6	火2 Fire [4] Family 風火家人 丙寅 Fire Tiger 20 廿九 4	水6 Water [3] Decreasing 山澤損 丁卯 Fire Rabbit 21 十月一初一 9
金9 Metal [2/8] Tread 天澤履 戊辰 Earth Dragon 22 初二 6	木8 Wood [9] Great Strength 雷天大壯 己巳 Earth Snake 23 初三 2	木8 Wood [1] Consistency 雷風恒 庚午 Metal Horse 24 初四 9	金9 Metal [2] Litigation 天水訟 辛未 Metal Goat 25 初五 3	水1 Water [3] Officer 地水師 壬申 Water Monkey 26 初六 7	火2 Fire [4] Gradual Progress 風山漸 癸酉 Water Rooster 27 初七 7	火7 Fire [5] Obstruction 水山蹇 甲戌 Wood Dog 28 初八 2
木3 Wood [6] Advancement 火地晉 乙亥 Wood Pig 29 初九 3	水6 Water [7] Nourish 山雷頤 丙子 Fire Rat 30 初十 3	金4 Metal [8] Following 澤雷隨 丁丑 Fire Ox 31 十一 7				

1958 戊戌

(*Wu Xu*) Earth Dog

1958 戊戌 *(Wu Xu)* Earth Dog

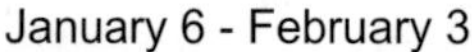

February 4 - March 5

March 6 - April 4

April 5 - May 5

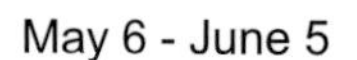

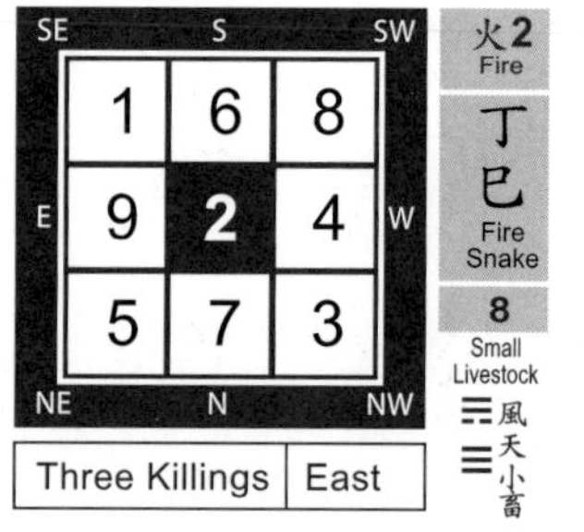

June 6 - July 6

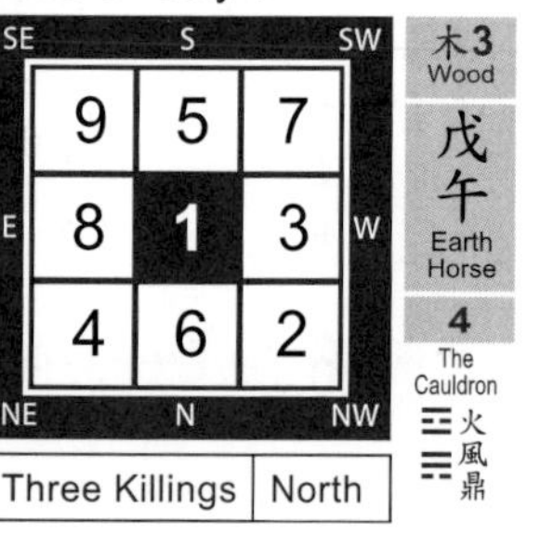

July 7 - August 7

August 8 - September 7

September 8 - October 8

October 9 - November 7

November 8 - December 6

December 7 - January 5

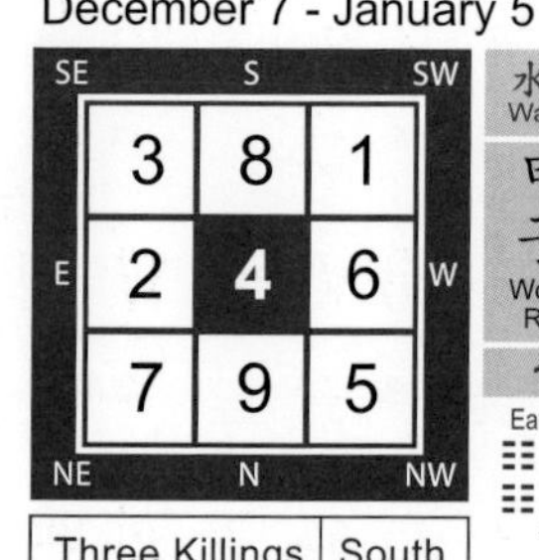

JANUARY 1958 癸丑

Xuan Kong Element 玄空五行	山火賁 Beauty	Period Luck 卦運	Monthly Star 月星
Water 水6		8	6

SUNDAY	MONDAY	TUESDAY	WEDNESDAY	THURSDAY	FRIDAY	SATURDAY
			木8 Wood 9 Abundance 雷火豐 戊寅 Earth Tiger **1** 十二 6	火7 Fire 1 Regulate 水澤節 己卯 Earth Rabbit **2** 十三 8	水1 Water 2 Unity 地天泰 庚辰 Metal Dragon **3** 十四 9	木3 Wood 3 Great Reward 火天大有 辛巳 Metal Snake **4** 十五 7
火2 Fire 4 Wind 巽爲風 壬午 Water Horse **5** 十六 1	金4 Metal 5 Trap 澤水困 癸未 Water Goat **6** 十七 8	木3 Wood 6 Not Yet Accomplished 火水未濟 甲申 Wood Monkey **7** 十八 9	金9 Metal 7 Retreat 天山遯 乙酉 Wood Rooster **8** 十九 4	水6 Water 8 Mountain 艮爲山 丙戌 Fire Dog **9** 二十 1	木8 Wood 9 Delight 雷地豫 丁亥 Fire Pig **10** 廿一 8	火7 Fire 1 Beginning 水雷屯 戊子 Earth Rat **11** 廿二 4
金9 Metal 2 Without Wrongdoing 天雷無妄 己丑 Earth Ox **12** 廿三 2	木3 Wood 3 Fire 離爲火 庚寅 Metal Tiger **13** 廿四 1	火2 Fire 4 Sincerity 風澤中孚 辛卯 Metal Rabbit **14** 廿五 3	水6 Water 5 Big Livestock 山天大畜 壬辰 Water Dragon **15** 廿六 4	金4 Metal 6 Eliminating 澤天夬 癸巳 Water Snake **16** 廿七 6	金9 Metal 7 Heaven 乾爲天 甲午 Wood Horse **17** 廿八 1	火7 Fire 8 Well 水風井 乙未 Wood Goat **18** 廿九 6
木8 Wood 9 Relief 雷水解 丙申 Fire Monkey **19** 三十 4	金4 Metal 1 Influence 澤山咸 丁酉 Fire Rooster **20** 十二月初一 9	水1 Water 2 Humility 地山謙 戊戌 Earth Dog **21** 初二 6	火2 Fire 3 Observation 風地觀 己亥 Earth Pig **22** 初三 2	火2 Fire 4 Increasing 風雷益 庚子 Metal Rat **23** 初四 9	水1 Water 5 Dimming Light 地火明夷 辛丑 Metal Ox **24** 初五 3	金9 Metal 6 Fellowship 天火同人 壬寅 Water Tiger **25** 初六 7
木8 Wood 7 Marrying Maiden 雷澤歸妹 癸卯 Water Rabbit **26** 初七 7	木3 Wood 8 Opposition 火澤睽 甲辰 Wood Dragon **27** 初八 2	火7 Fire 9 Waiting 水天需 乙巳 Wood Snake **28** 初九 3	金4 Metal 1 Great Exceeding 澤風大過 丙午 Fire Horse **29** 初十 9	水6 Water 2 Poison 山風蠱 丁未 Fire Goat **30** 十一 7	火2 Fire 3 Dispersing 風水渙 戊申 Earth Monkey **31** 十二 6	

FEBRUARY 1958 甲寅

Xuan Kong Element 玄空五行	水火既濟 Accomplished	Period Luck 卦運	Monthly Star 月星
Fire 火7		9	5

SUNDAY	MONDAY	TUESDAY	WEDNESDAY	THURSDAY	FRIDAY	SATURDAY
						木3 Wood 4 Travelling 火山旅 己酉 Earth Rooster **1** 十三 8
金9 Metal 5 Stagnation 天地否 庚戌 Metal Dog **2** 十四 9	火7 Fire 6 Alliance 水地比 辛亥 Metal Pig **3** 十五 7	木8 Wood 7 Thunder 震爲雷 壬子 Water Rat **4** 十六 1	水6 Water 8 Beauty 山火賁 癸丑 Water Ox **5** 十七 8	火7 Fire 9 Accomplished 水火既濟 甲寅 Wood Tiger **6** 十八 9	水1 Water 1 Arriving 地澤臨 乙卯 Wood Rabbit **7** 十九 4	金4 Metal 2 Marsh 兌爲澤 丙辰 Fire Dragon **8** 二十 1
火2 Fire 3 Small Livestock 風天小畜 丁巳 Fire Snake **9** 廿一 8	木3 Wood 4 The Cauldron 火風鼎 戊午 Earth Horse **10** 廿二 4	水1 Water 5 Rising 地風升 己未 Earth Goat **11** 廿三 2	火7 Fire 6 Water 坎爲水 庚申 Metal Monkey **12** 廿四 1	木8 Wood 7 Lesser Exceeding 雷山小過 辛酉 Metal Rooster **13** 廿五 3	金4 Metal 8 Gathering 澤地萃 壬戌 Water Dog **14** 廿六 4	水6 Water 9 Peel 山地剝 癸亥 Water Pig **15** 廿七 6
水1 Water 1 Earth 坤爲地 甲子 Wood Rat **16** 廿八 1	木3 Wood 2 Biting 火雷噬嗑 乙丑 Wood Ox **17** 廿九 6	火2 Fire 3 Family 風火家人 丙寅 Fire Tiger **18** 正月初一 4	水6 Water 4 Decreasing 山澤損 丁卯 Fire Rabbit **19** 初二 9	金9 Metal 5 Tread 天澤履 戊辰 Earth Dragon **20** 初三 6	木8 Wood 6 Great Strength 雷天大壯 己巳 Earth Snake **21** 初四 2	木8 Wood 7 Consistency 雷風恒 庚午 Metal Horse **22** 初五 9
金9 Metal 8 Litigation 天水訟 辛未 Metal Goat **23** 初六 3	水1 Water 9 Officer 地水師 壬申 Water Monkey **24** 初七 7	火2 Fire 1 Gradual Progress 風山漸 癸酉 Water Rooster **25** 初八 7	火7 Fire 2 Obstruction 水山蹇 甲戌 Wood Dog **26** 初九 2	木3 Wood 3 Advancement 火地晉 乙亥 Wood Pig **27** 初十 3	水6 Water 4 Nourish 山雷頤 丙子 Fire Rat **28** 十一 3	

MARCH 1958 乙卯

Xuan Kong Element 玄空五行	地澤臨 Arriving	Period Luck 卦運	Monthly Star 月星
Water 水1		4	4

SUNDAY	MONDAY	TUESDAY	WEDNESDAY	THURSDAY	FRIDAY	SATURDAY
金4 Metal Great Exceeding 7 丙午 Fire Horse 澤風大過 30 十一 3	水6 Water Poison 8 丁未 Fire Goat 山風蠱 31 十二 7					金4 Metal Following 5 丁丑 Fire Ox 澤雷隨 1 十二 7
木8 Wood Abundance 6 戊寅 Earth Tiger 雷火豐 2 十三 6	火7 Fire Regulate 7 己卯 Earth Rabbit 水澤節 3 十四 8	水1 Water Unity 8 庚辰 Metal Dragon 地天泰 4 十五 9	木3 Wood Great Reward 9 辛巳 Metal Snake 火天大有 5 十六 7	火2 Fire Wind 1 壬午 Water Horse 巽為風 6 十七 1	金4 Metal Trap 2 癸未 Water Goat 澤水困 7 十八 8	木3 Wood Not Yet Accomplished 3 甲申 Wood Monkey 火水未濟 8 十九 9
金9 Metal Retreat 4 乙酉 Wood Rooster 天山遯 9 二十 4	水6 Water Mountain 5 丙戌 Fire Dog 艮為山 10 廿一 1	木8 Wood Delight 6 丁亥 Fire Pig 雷地豫 11 廿二 8	火7 Fire Beginning 7 戊子 Earth Rat 水雷屯 12 廿三 4	金9 Metal Without Wrongdoing 8 己丑 Earth Ox 天雷無妄 13 廿四 2	木3 Wood Fire 9 庚寅 Metal Tiger 離為火 14 廿五 1	火2 Fire Sincerity 1 辛卯 Metal Rabbit 風澤中孚 15 廿六 3
水6 Water Big Livestock 2 壬辰 Water Dragon 山天大畜 16 廿七 4	金4 Metal Eliminating 3 癸巳 Water Snake 澤天夬 17 廿八 6	金9 Metal Heaven 4 甲午 Wood Horse 乾為天 18 廿九 1	火7 Fire Well 5 乙未 Wood Goat 水風井 19 三十 6	木8 Wood Relief 6 丙申 Fire Monkey 雷水解 20 二月初一 4	金4 Metal Influence 7 丁酉 Fire Rooster 澤山咸 21 初二 9	水1 Water Humility 8 戊戌 Earth Dog 地山謙 22 初三 6
火2 Fire Observation 9 己亥 Earth Pig 風地觀 23 初四 2	火2 Fire Increasing 1 庚子 Metal Rat 風雷益 24 初五 9	水1 Water Dimming Light 2 辛丑 Metal Ox 地火明夷 25 初六 3	金9 Metal Fellowship 3 壬寅 Water Tiger 天火同人 26 初七 7	木8 Wood Marrying Maiden 4 癸卯 Water Rabbit 雷澤歸妹 27 初八 7	木3 Wood Opposition 5 甲辰 Wood Dragon 火澤睽 28 初九 2	火7 Fire Waiting 6 乙巳 Wood Snake 水天需 29 初十 3

APRIL 1958 丙辰

Xuan Kong Element 玄空五行	兌為澤 Marsh	Period Luck 卦運	Monthly Star 月星
Metal 金4		1	3

SUNDAY	MONDAY	TUESDAY	WEDNESDAY	THURSDAY	FRIDAY	SATURDAY
		火2 Fire Dispersing 9 戊申 Earth Monkey 風水渙 1 十三 6	木3 Wood Travelling 1 己酉 Earth Rooster 火山旅 2 十四 8	金9 Metal Stagnation 2 庚戌 Metal Dog 天地否 3 十五 9	火7 Fire Alliance 3 辛亥 Metal Pig 水地比 4 十六 7	木8 Wood Thunder 4 壬子 Water Rat 震為雷 5 十七 1
水6 Water Beauty 5 癸丑 Water Ox 山火賁 6 十八 8	火7 Fire Accomplished 6 甲寅 Wood Tiger 水火既濟 7 十九 9	水1 Water Arriving 7 乙卯 Wood Rabbit 地澤臨 8 二十 4	金4 Metal Marsh 8 丙辰 Fire Dragon 兌為澤 9 廿一 1	火2 Fire Small Livestock 9 丁巳 Fire Snake 風天小畜 10 廿二 8	木3 Wood The Cauldron 1 戊午 Earth Horse 火風鼎 11 廿三 4	水1 Water Rising 2 己未 Earth Goat 地風升 12 廿四 2
火7 Fire Water 3 庚申 Metal Monkey 坎為水 13 廿五 1	木8 Wood Lesser Exceeding 4 辛酉 Metal Rooster 雷山小過 14 廿六 3	金4 Metal Gathering 5 壬戌 Water Dog 澤地萃 15 廿七 4	水6 Water Peel 6 癸亥 Water Pig 山地剝 16 廿八 6	水1 Water Earth 7 甲子 Wood Rat 坤為地 17 廿九 1	木3 Wood Biting 8 乙丑 Wood Ox 火雷噬嗑 18 三十 6	火2 Fire Family 9 丙寅 Fire Tiger 風火家人 19 三月初一 4
水6 Water Decreasing 1 丁卯 Fire Rabbit 山澤損 20 初二 9	金9 Metal Tread 2 戊辰 Earth Dragon 天澤履 21 初三 6	木8 Wood Great Strength 3 己巳 Earth Snake 雷天大壯 22 初四 2	木8 Wood Consistency 4 庚午 Metal Horse 雷風恆 23 初五 9	金9 Metal Litigation 5 辛未 Metal Goat 天水訟 24 初六 3	水1 Water Officer 6 壬申 Water Monkey 地水師 25 初七 7	火2 Fire Gradual Progress 7 癸酉 Water Rooster 風山漸 26 初八 7
火7 Fire Obstruction 8 甲戌 Wood Dog 水山蹇 27 初九 2	木3 Wood Advancement 9 乙亥 Wood Pig 火地晉 28 初十 3	水6 Water Nourish 1 丙子 Fire Rat 山雷頤 29 十一 3	金4 Metal Following 2 丁丑 Fire Ox 澤雷隨 30 十二 7			

MAY 1958 丁巳

Xuan Kong Element 玄空五行	風天小畜 Small Livestock	Period Luck 卦運	Monthly Star 月星
Fire 火2		8	2

SUNDAY	MONDAY	TUESDAY	WEDNESDAY	THURSDAY	FRIDAY	SATURDAY
				木8 Wood · 3 Abundance 雷火豐 戊寅 Earth Tiger · 6 1 十三	火7 Fire · 4 Regulate 水澤節 己卯 Earth Rabbit · 8 2 十四	水1 Water · 5 Unity 地天泰 庚辰 Metal Dragon · 9 3 十五
木3 Wood · 6 Great Reward 火天大有 辛巳 Metal Snake · 7 4 十六	火2 Fire · 7 Wind 巽爲風 壬午 Water Horse · 1 5 十七	金4 Metal · 8 Trap 澤水困 癸未 Water Goat · 8 6 十八	木3 Wood · 9 Not Yet Accomplished 火水未濟 甲申 Wood Monkey · 9 7 十九	金9 Metal · 1 Retreat 天山遯 乙酉 Wood Rooster · 4 8 二十	水6 Water · 2 Mountain 艮爲山 丙戌 Fire Dog · 1 9 廿一	木8 Wood · 3 Delight 雷地豫 丁亥 Fire Pig · 8 10 廿二
火7 Fire · 4 Beginning 水雷屯 戊子 Earth Rat · 4 11 廿三	金9 Metal · 5 Without Wrongdoing 天雷無妄 己丑 Earth Ox · 2 12 廿四	木3 Wood · 6 Fire 離爲火 庚寅 Metal Tiger · 1 13 廿五	火2 Fire · 7 Sincerity 風澤中孚 辛卯 Metal Rabbit · 3 14 廿六	水6 Water · 8 Big Livestock 山天大畜 壬辰 Water Dragon · 4 15 廿七	金4 Metal · 9 Eliminating 澤天夬 癸巳 Water Snake · 6 16 廿八	金9 Metal · 1 Heaven 乾爲天 甲午 Wood Horse · 1 17 廿九
火7 Fire · 2 Well 水風井 乙未 Wood Goat · 6 18 三十	木8 Wood · 3 Relief 雷水解 丙申 Fire Monkey · 4 19 四月初一	金4 Metal · 4 Influence 澤山咸 丁酉 Fire Rooster · 9 20 初二	水1 Water · 5 Humility 地山謙 戊戌 Earth Dog · 6 21 初三	火2 Fire · 6 Observation 風地觀 己亥 Earth Pig · 2 22 初四	火2 Fire · 7 Increasing 風雷益 庚子 Metal Rat · 9 23 初五	水1 Water · 8 Dimming Light 地火明夷 辛丑 Metal Ox · 3 24 初六
金9 Metal · 9 Fellowship 天火同人 壬寅 Water Tiger · 7 25 初七	木8 Wood · 1 Marrying Maiden 雷澤歸妹 癸卯 Water Rabbit · 7 26 初八	木3 Wood · 2 Opposition 火澤睽 甲辰 Wood Dragon · 2 27 初九	火7 Fire · 3 Waiting 水天需 乙巳 Wood Snake · 3 28 初十	金4 Metal · 4 Great Exceeding 澤風大過 丙午 Fire Horse · 3 29 十一	水6 Water · 5 Poison 山風蠱 丁未 Fire Goat · 7 30 十二	火2 Fire · 6 Dispersing 風水渙 戊申 Earth Monkey · 6 31 十三

JUNE 1958 戊午

Xuan Kong Element 玄空五行	火風鼎 The Cauldron	Period Luck 卦運	Monthly Star 月星
Wood 木3		4	1

SUNDAY	MONDAY	TUESDAY	WEDNESDAY	THURSDAY	FRIDAY	SATURDAY
木3 Wood · 7 Travelling 火山旅 己酉 Earth Rooster · 8 1 十四	金9 Metal · 8 Stagnation 天地否 庚戌 Metal Dog · 9 2 十五	火7 Fire · 9 Alliance 水地比 辛亥 Metal Pig · 7 3 十六	木8 Wood · 1 Thunder 震爲雷 壬子 Water Rat · 1 4 十七	水6 Water · 2 Beauty 山火賁 癸丑 Water Ox · 8 5 十八	火7 Fire · 3 Accomplished 水火既濟 甲寅 Wood Tiger · 9 6 十九	水1 Water · 4 Arriving 地澤臨 乙卯 Wood Rabbit · 4 7 二十
金4 Metal · 5 Marsh 兑爲澤 丙辰 Fire Dragon · 1 8 廿一	火2 Fire · 6 Small Livestock 風天小畜 丁巳 Fire Snake · 8 9 廿二	木3 Wood · 7 The Cauldron 火風鼎 戊午 Earth Horse · 4 10 廿三	水1 Water · 8 Rising 地風升 己未 Earth Goat · 2 11 廿四	火7 Fire · 9 Water 坎爲水 庚申 Metal Monkey · 1 12 廿五	木8 Wood · 1 Lesser Exceeding 雷山小過 辛酉 Metal Rooster · 3 13 廿六	金4 Metal · 2 Gathering 澤地萃 壬戌 Water Dog · 4 14 廿七
水6 Water · 3 Peel 山地剝 癸亥 Water Pig · 6 15 廿八	水1 Water · 4 Earth 坤爲地 甲子 Wood Rat · 1 16 廿九	木3 Wood · 5 Biting 火雷噬嗑 乙丑 Wood Ox · 6 17 五月初一	火2 Fire · 6 Family 風火家人 丙寅 Fire Tiger · 4 18 初二	水6 Water · 7 Decreasing 山澤損 丁卯 Fire Rabbit · 9 19 初三	金9 Metal · 8 Tread 天澤履 戊辰 Earth Dragon · 6 20 初四	木8 Wood · 9 Great Strength 雷天大壯 己巳 Earth Snake · 2 21 初五
木8 Wood · 1/9 Consistency 雷風恆 庚午 Metal Horse · 9 22 初六	金9 Metal · 8 Litigation 天水訟 辛未 Metal Goat · 3 23 初七	水1 Water · 7 Officer 地水師 壬申 Water Monkey · 7 24 初八	火2 Fire · 6 Gradual Progress 風山漸 癸酉 Water Rooster · 7 25 初九	火7 Fire · 5 Obstruction 水山蹇 甲戌 Wood Dog · 2 26 初十	木3 Wood · 4 Advancement 火地晉 乙亥 Wood Pig · 3 27 十一	水6 Water · 3 Nourish 山雷頤 丙子 Fire Rat · 3 28 十二
金4 Metal · 2 Following 澤雷隨 丁丑 Fire Ox · 7 29 十三	木8 Wood · 1 Abundance 雷火豐 戊寅 Earth Tiger · 6 30 十四					

JULY 1958 己未

Xuan Kong Element 玄空五行	地風升 Rising	Period Luck 卦運	Monthly Star 月星
Water 水1		2	9

SUNDAY	MONDAY	TUESDAY	WEDNESDAY	THURSDAY	FRIDAY	SATURDAY
		火7 Fire [9] Regulate 己卯 Earth Rabbit 水澤節 **1** 十五 8	水1 Water [8] Unity 庚辰 Metal Dragon 地天泰 **2** 十六 9	木3 Wood [7] Great Reward 辛巳 Metal Snake 火天大有 **3** 十七 7	火2 Fire [6] Wind 壬午 Water Horse 巽爲風 **4** 十八 1	金4 Metal [5] Trap 癸未 Water Goat 澤水困 **5** 十九 8
木3 Wood [4] Not Yet Accomplished 甲申 Wood Monkey 火水未濟 **6** 二十 9	金9 Metal [3] Retreat 乙酉 Wood Rooster 天山遯 **7** 廿一 4	水6 Water [2] Mountain 丙戌 Fire Dog 艮爲山 **8** 廿二 1	木8 Wood [1] Delight 丁亥 Fire Pig 雷地豫 **9** 廿三 8	火7 Fire [9] Beginning 戊子 Earth Rat 水雷屯 **10** 廿四 4	金9 Metal [8] Without Wrongdoing 己丑 Earth Ox 天雷無妄 **11** 廿五 2	木3 Wood [7] Fire 庚寅 Metal Tiger 離爲火 **12** 廿六 1
火2 Fire [6] Sincerity 辛卯 Metal Rabbit 風澤中孚 **13** 廿七 3	水6 Water [5] Big Livestock 壬辰 Water Dragon 山天大畜 **14** 廿八 4	金4 Metal [4] Eliminating 癸巳 Water Snake 澤天夬 **15** 廿九 6	金9 Metal [3] Heaven 甲午 Wood Horse 乾爲天 **16** 三十 1	火7 Fire [2] Well 乙未 Wood Goat 水風井 **17** 六月初一 6	木8 Wood [1] Relief 丙申 Fire Monkey 雷水解 **18** 初二 4	金4 Metal [9] Influence 丁酉 Fire Rooster 澤山咸 **19** 初三 9
水1 Water [8] Humility 戊戌 Earth Dog 地山謙 **20** 初四 6	火2 Fire [7] Observation 己亥 Earth Pig 風地觀 **21** 初五 2	火2 Fire [6] Increasing 庚子 Metal Rat 風雷益 **22** 初六 9	水1 Water [5] Dimming Light 辛丑 Metal Ox 地火明夷 **23** 初七 3	金9 Metal [4] Fellowship 壬寅 Water Tiger 天火同人 **24** 初八 7	木8 Wood [3] Marrying Maiden 癸卯 Water Rabbit 雷澤歸妹 **25** 初九 7	木3 Wood [2] Opposition 甲辰 Wood Dragon 火澤睽 **26** 初十 2
火7 Fire [1] Waiting 乙巳 Wood Snake 水天需 **27** 十一 3	金4 Metal [9] Great Exceeding 丙午 Fire Horse 澤風大過 **28** 十二 3	水6 Water [8] Poison 丁未 Fire Goat 山風蠱 **29** 十三 7	火2 Fire [7] Dispersing 戊申 Earth Monkey 風水渙 **30** 十四 6	木3 Wood [6] Travelling 己酉 Earth Rooster 火山旅 **31** 十五 8		

AUGUST 1958 庚申

Xuan Kong Element 玄空五行	坎爲水 Water	Period Luck 卦運	Monthly Star 月星
Fire 火7		1	8

SUNDAY	MONDAY	TUESDAY	WEDNESDAY	THURSDAY	FRIDAY	SATURDAY
水1 Water [2] Unity 庚辰 Metal Dragon 地天泰 **31** 十七 9					金9 Metal [5] Stagnation 庚戌 Metal Dog 天地否 **1** 十六 9	火7 Fire [4] Alliance 辛亥 Metal Pig 水地比 **2** 十七 7
木8 Wood [3] Thunder 壬子 Water Rat 震爲雷 **3** 十八 1	水6 Water [2] Beauty 癸丑 Water Ox 山火賁 **4** 十九 8	火7 Fire [1] Accomplished 甲寅 Wood Tiger 水火既濟 **5** 二十 9	水1 Water [9] Arriving 乙卯 Wood Rabbit 地澤臨 **6** 廿一 4	金4 Metal [8] Marsh 丙辰 Fire Dragon 兑爲澤 **7** 廿二 1	火2 Fire [7] Small Livestock 丁巳 Fire Snake 風天小畜 **8** 廿三 8	木3 Wood [6] The Cauldron 戊午 Earth Horse 火風鼎 **9** 廿四 4
水1 Water [5] Rising 己未 Earth Goat 地風升 **10** 廿五 2	火7 Fire [4] Water 庚申 Metal Monkey 坎爲水 **11** 廿六 1	木8 Wood [3] Lesser Exceeding 辛酉 Metal Rooster 雷山小過 **12** 廿七 3	金4 Metal [2] Gathering 壬戌 Water Dog 澤地萃 **13** 廿八 4	水6 Water [1] Peel 癸亥 Water Pig 山地剝 **14** 廿九 6	水1 Water [9] Earth 甲子 Wood Rat 坤爲地 **15** 七月初一 1	木3 Wood [8] Biting 乙丑 Wood Ox 火雷噬嗑 **16** 初二 6
火2 Fire [7] Family 丙寅 Fire Tiger 風火家人 **17** 初三 4	水6 Water [6] Decreasing 丁卯 Fire Rabbit 山澤損 **18** 初四 9	金9 Metal [5] Tread 戊辰 Earth Dragon 天澤履 **19** 初五 6	木8 Wood [4] Great Strength 己巳 Earth Snake 雷天大壯 **20** 初六 2	木8 Wood [3] Consistency 庚午 Metal Horse 雷風恆 **21** 初七 9	金9 Metal [2] Litigation 辛未 Metal Goat 天水訟 **22** 初八 3	水1 Water [1] Officer 壬申 Water Monkey 地水師 **23** 初九 7
火2 Fire [9] Gradual Progress 癸酉 Water Rooster 風山漸 **24** 初十 7	火7 Fire [8] Obstruction 甲戌 Wood Dog 水山蹇 **25** 十一 2	木3 Wood [7] Advancement 乙亥 Wood Pig 火地晉 **26** 十二 3	水6 Water [6] Nourish 丙子 Fire Rat 山雷頤 **27** 十三 3	金4 Metal [5] Following 丁丑 Fire Ox 澤雷隨 **28** 十四 7	木8 Wood [4] Abundance 戊寅 Earth Tiger 雷火豐 **29** 十五 6	火7 Fire [3] Regulate 己卯 Earth Rabbit 水澤節 **30** 十六 8

SEPTEMBER 1958 辛酉

Xuan Kong Element 玄空五行	雷山小過	Period Luck 卦運	Monthly Star 月星
Wood 木8	Lesser Exceeding	3	7

SUNDAY	MONDAY	TUESDAY	WEDNESDAY	THURSDAY	FRIDAY	SATURDAY
	1 十八 木3 Wood · 1 Great Reward 火天大有 辛巳 Metal Snake 7	2 十九 火2 Fire · 9 Wind 巽爲風 壬午 Water Horse 1	3 二十 金4 Metal · 8 Trap 澤水困 癸未 Water Goat 8	4 廿一 木3 Wood · 7 Not Yet Accomplished 火水未濟 甲申 Wood Monkey 9	5 廿二 金9 Metal · 6 Retreat 天山遯 乙酉 Wood Rooster 4	6 廿三 水6 Water · 5 Mountain 艮爲山 丙戌 Fire Dog 1
7 廿四 木8 Wood · 4 Delight 雷地豫 丁亥 Fire Pig 8	8 廿五 火7 Fire · 3 Beginning 水雷屯 戊子 Earth Rat 4	9 廿六 金9 Metal · 2 Without Wrongdoing 天雷無妄 己丑 Earth Ox 2	10 廿七 木3 Wood · 1 Fire 離爲火 庚寅 Metal Tiger 1	11 廿八 火2 Fire · 9 Sincerity 風澤中孚 辛卯 Metal Rabbit 3	12 廿九 水6 Water · 8 Big Livestock 山天大畜 壬辰 Water Dragon 4	13 八月初一 金4 Metal · 7 Eliminating 澤天夬 癸巳 Water Snake 6
14 初二 金9 Metal · 6 Heaven 乾爲天 甲午 Wood Horse 1	15 初三 火7 Fire · 5 Well 水風井 乙未 Wood Goat 6	16 初四 木8 Wood · 4 Relief 雷水解 丙申 Fire Monkey 4	17 初五 金4 Metal · 3 Influence 澤山咸 丁酉 Fire Rooster 9	18 初六 水1 Water · 2 Humility 地山謙 戊戌 Earth Dog 6	19 初七 火2 Fire · 1 Observation 風地觀 己亥 Earth Pig 2	20 初八 火2 Fire · 9 Increasing 風雷益 庚子 Metal Rat 9
21 初九 水1 Water · 8 Dimming Light 地火明夷 辛丑 Metal Ox 3	22 初十 金9 Metal · 7 Fellowship 天火同人 壬寅 Water Tiger 7	23 十一 木8 Wood · 6 Marrying Maiden 雷澤歸妹 癸卯 Water Rabbit 7	24 十二 木3 Wood · 5 Opposition 火澤睽 甲辰 Wood Dragon 2	25 十三 火7 Fire · 4 Waiting 水天需 乙巳 Wood Snake 3	26 十四 金4 Metal · 3 Great Exceeding 澤風大過 丙午 Fire Horse 3	27 十五 水6 Water · 2 Poison 山風蠱 丁未 Fire Goat 7
28 十六 火2 Fire · 1 Dispersing 風水渙 戊申 Earth Monkey 6	29 十七 木3 Wood · 9 Travelling 火山旅 己酉 Earth Rooster 8	30 十八 金9 Metal · 8 Stagnation 天地否 庚戌 Metal Dog 9				

OCTOBER 1958 壬戌

Xuan Kong Element 玄空五行	澤地萃	Period Luck 卦運	Monthly Star 月星
Metal 金4	Gathering	4	6

SUNDAY	MONDAY	TUESDAY	WEDNESDAY	THURSDAY	FRIDAY	SATURDAY
			1 十九 火7 Fire · 7 Alliance 水地比 辛亥 Metal Pig 7	2 二十 木8 Wood · 6 Thunder 震爲雷 壬子 Water Rat 1	3 廿一 水6 Water · 5 Beauty 山火賁 癸丑 Water Ox 8	4 廿二 火7 Fire · 4 Accomplished 水火既濟 甲寅 Wood Tiger 9
5 廿三 水1 Water · 3 Arriving 地澤臨 乙卯 Wood Rabbit 4	6 廿四 金4 Metal · 2 Marsh 兑爲澤 丙辰 Fire Dragon 1	7 廿五 火2 Fire · 1 Small Livestock 風天小畜 丁巳 Fire Snake 8	8 廿六 木3 Wood · 9 The Cauldron 火風鼎 戊午 Earth Horse 4	9 廿七 水1 Water · 8 Rising 地風升 己未 Earth Goat 2	10 廿八 火7 Fire · 7 Water 坎爲水 庚申 Metal Monkey 1	11 廿九 木8 Wood · 6 Lesser Exceeding 雷山小過 辛酉 Metal Rooster 3
12 三十 金4 Metal · 5 Gathering 澤地萃 壬戌 Water Dog 4	13 九月初一 水6 Water · 4 Peel 山地剝 癸亥 Water Pig 6	14 初二 水1 Water · 3 Earth 坤爲地 甲子 Wood Rat 1	15 初三 木3 Wood · 2 Biting 火雷噬嗑 乙丑 Wood Ox 6	16 初四 火2 Fire · 1 Family 風火家人 丙寅 Fire Tiger 4	17 初五 水6 Water · 9 Decreasing 山澤損 丁卯 Fire Rabbit 9	18 初六 金9 Metal · 8 Tread 天澤履 戊辰 Earth Dragon 6
19 初七 木8 Wood · 7 Great Strength 雷天大壯 己巳 Earth Snake 2	20 初八 木8 Wood · 6 Consistency 雷風恒 庚午 Metal Horse 9	21 初九 金9 Metal · 5 Litigation 天水訟 辛未 Metal Goat 3	22 初十 水1 Water · 4 Officer 地水師 壬申 Water Monkey 7	23 十一 火2 Fire · 3 Gradual Progress 風山漸 癸酉 Water Rooster 7	24 十二 火7 Fire · 2 Obstruction 水山蹇 甲戌 Wood Dog 2	25 十三 木3 Wood · 1 Advancement 火地晋 乙亥 Wood Pig 3
26 十四 水6 Water · 9 Nourish 山雷頤 丙子 Fire Rat 3	27 十五 金4 Metal · 8 Following 澤雷隨 丁丑 Fire Ox 7	28 十六 木8 Wood · 7 Abundance 雷火豐 戊寅 Earth Tiger 6	29 十七 火7 Fire · 6 Regulate 水澤節 己卯 Earth Rabbit 8	30 十八 水1 Water · 5 Unity 地天泰 庚辰 Metal Dragon 9	31 十九 木3 Wood · 4 Great Reward 火天大有 辛巳 Metal Snake 7	

NOVEMBER 1958 癸亥

Xuan Kong Element 玄空五行	山地剝 Peel	Period Luck 卦運	Monthly Star 月星
Water 水6		6	5

SUNDAY	MONDAY	TUESDAY	WEDNESDAY	THURSDAY	FRIDAY	SATURDAY
火7 Fire 1 Alliance 辛亥 Metal Pig 水地比 30 二十 7						火2 Fire 3 Wind 壬午 Water Horse 巽爲風 1 二十 1
金4 Metal 2 Trap 癸未 Water Goat 澤水困 2 廿一 8	木3 Wood 1 Not Yet Accomplished 甲申 Wood Monkey 火水未濟 3 廿二 9	金9 Metal 9 Retreat 乙酉 Wood Rooster 天山遯 4 廿三 4	水6 Water 8 Mountain 丙戌 Fire Dog 艮爲山 5 廿四 1	木8 Wood 7 Delight 丁亥 Fire Pig 雷地豫 6 廿五 8	火7 Fire 6 Beginning 戊子 Earth Rat 水雷屯 7 廿六 4	金9 Metal 5 Without Wrongdoing 己丑 Earth Ox 天雷無妄 8 廿七 2
木3 Wood 4 Fire 庚寅 Metal Tiger 離爲火 9 廿八 1	火2 Fire 3 Sincerity 辛卯 Metal Rabbit 風澤中孚 10 廿九 3	水6 Water 2 Big Livestock 壬辰 Water Dragon 山天大畜 11 十月初一 4	金4 Metal 1 Eliminating 癸巳 Water Snake 澤天夬 12 初二 6	金9 Metal 9 Heaven 甲午 Wood Horse 乾爲天 13 初三 1	火7 Fire 8 Well 乙未 Wood Goat 水風井 14 初四 6	木8 Wood 7 Relief 丙申 Fire Monkey 雷水解 15 初五 4
金4 Metal 6 Influence 丁酉 Fire Rooster 澤山咸 16 初六 9	水1 Water 5 Humility 戊戌 Earth Dog 地山謙 17 初七 6	火2 Fire 4 Observation 己亥 Earth Pig 風地觀 18 初八 2	火2 Fire 3 Increasing 庚子 Metal Rat 風雷益 19 初九 9	水1 Water 2 Dimming Light 辛丑 Metal Ox 地火明夷 20 初十 3	金9 Metal 1 Fellowship 壬寅 Water Tiger 天火同人 21 十一 7	木8 Wood 9 Marrying Maiden 癸卯 Water Rabbit 雷澤歸妹 22 十二 7
木3 Wood 8 Opposition 甲辰 Wood Dragon 火澤睽 23 十三 2	火7 Fire 7 Waiting 乙巳 Wood Snake 水天需 24 十四 3	金4 Metal 6 Great Exceeding 丙午 Fire Horse 澤風大過 25 十五 3	水6 Water 5 Poison 丁未 Fire Goat 山風蠱 26 十六 7	火2 Fire 4 Dispersing 戊申 Earth Monkey 風水渙 27 十七 6	木3 Wood 3 Travelling 己酉 Earth Rooster 火山旅 28 十八 8	金9 Metal 2 Stagnation 庚戌 Metal Dog 天地否 29 十九 9

DECEMBER 1958 甲子

Xuan Kong Element 玄空五行	坤爲地 Earth	Period Luck 卦運	Monthly Star 月星
Water 水1		1	4

SUNDAY	MONDAY	TUESDAY	WEDNESDAY	THURSDAY	FRIDAY	SATURDAY
	木8 Wood 9 Thunder 壬子 Water Rat 震爲雷 1 廿一 1	水6 Water 8 Beauty 癸丑 Water Ox 山火賁 2 廿二 8	火7 Fire 7 Accomplished 甲寅 Wood Tiger 水火既濟 3 廿三 9	水1 Water 6 Arriving 乙卯 Wood Rabbit 地澤臨 4 廿四 4	金4 Metal 5 Marsh 丙辰 Fire Dragon 兌爲澤 5 廿五 1	火2 Fire 4 Small Livestock 丁巳 Fire Snake 風天小畜 6 廿六 8
木3 Wood 3 The Cauldron 戊午 Earth Horse 火風鼎 7 廿七 4	水1 Water 2 Rising 己未 Earth Goat 地風升 8 廿八 2	火7 Fire 1 Water 庚申 Metal Monkey 坎爲水 9 廿九 1	木8 Wood 9 Lesser Exceeding 辛酉 Metal Rooster 雷山小過 10 三十 3	金4 Metal 8 Gathering 壬戌 Water Dog 澤地萃 11 十一月初一 4	水6 Water 7 Peel 癸亥 Water Pig 山地剝 12 初二 6	水1 Water 6 Earth 甲子 Wood Rat 坤爲地 13 初三 1
木3 Wood 5 Biting 乙丑 Wood Ox 火雷噬嗑 14 初四 6	火2 Fire 4 Family 丙寅 Fire Tiger 風火家人 15 初五 4	水6 Water 3 Decreasing 丁卯 Fire Rabbit 山澤損 16 初六 9	金9 Metal 2 Tread 戊辰 Earth Dragon 天澤履 17 初七 6	木8 Wood 1 Great Strength 己巳 Earth Snake 雷天大壯 18 初八 2	木8 Wood 9 Consistency 庚午 Metal Horse 雷風恒 19 初九 9	金9 Metal 8 Litigation 辛未 Metal Goat 天水訟 20 初十 3
水1 Water 7 Officer 壬申 Water Monkey 地水師 21 十一 7	火2 Fire 6/4 Gradual Progress 癸酉 Water Rooster 風山漸 22 十二 7	火7 Fire 5 Obstruction 甲戌 Wood Dog 水山蹇 23 十三 2	木3 Wood 6 Advancement 乙亥 Wood Pig 火地晉 24 十四 3	水6 Water 7 Nourish 丙子 Fire Rat 山雷頤 25 十五 3	金4 Metal 8 Following 丁丑 Fire Ox 澤雷隨 26 十六 7	木8 Wood 9 Abundance 戊寅 Earth Tiger 雷火豐 27 十七 6
火7 Fire 1 Regulate 己卯 Earth Rabbit 水澤節 28 十八 8	水1 Water 2 Unity 庚辰 Metal Dragon 地天泰 29 十九 9	木3 Wood 3 Great Reward 辛巳 Metal Snake 火天大有 30 二十 7	火2 Fire 4 Wind 壬午 Water Horse 巽爲風 31 廿一 1			

1959 己亥

(*Ji Hai*) Earth Pig

1959 己亥 *(Ji Hai)* Earth Pig

January 6 - February 3

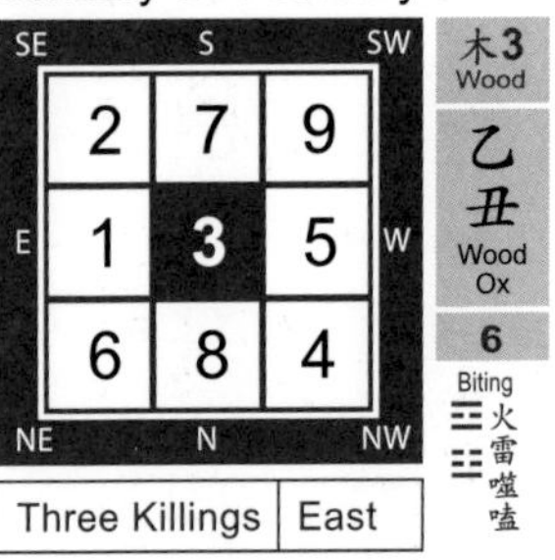

February 4 - March 5

March 6 - April 4

April 5 - May 5

May 6 - June 5

June 6 - July 7

July 8 - August 7

August 8 - September 7

September 8 - October 8

October 9 - November 7

November 8 - December 7

December 8 - January 5

JANUARY 1959 乙丑

Xuan Kong Element 玄空五行	火雷噬嗑 Biting	Period Luck 卦運	Monthly Star 月星
Wood 木3		6	3

SUNDAY	MONDAY	TUESDAY	WEDNESDAY	THURSDAY	FRIDAY	SATURDAY
				1 廿二 金4 Metal · Trap 澤水困 · 5 癸未 Water Goat 8	**2** 廿三 木3 Wood · Not Yet Accomplished 火水未濟 · 6 甲申 Wood Monkey 9	**3** 廿四 金9 Metal · Retreat 天山遯 · 7 乙酉 Wood Rooster 4
4 廿五 水6 Water · Mountain 艮爲山 · 8 丙戌 Fire Dog 1	**5** 廿六 木8 Wood · Delight 雷地豫 · 9 丁亥 Fire Pig 8	**6** 廿七 火7 Fire · Beginning 水雷屯 · 1 戊子 Earth Rat 4	**7** 廿八 金9 Metal · Without Wrongdoing 天雷無妄 · 2 己丑 Earth Ox 2	**8** 廿九 木3 Wood · Fire 離爲火 · 3 庚寅 Metal Tiger 1	**9** 十二月初一 火2 Fire · Sincerity 風澤中孚 · 4 辛卯 Metal Rabbit 3	**10** 初二 水6 Water · Big Livestock 山天大畜 · 5 壬辰 Water Dragon 4
11 初三 金4 Metal · Eliminating 澤天夬 · 6 癸巳 Water Snake 6	**12** 初四 金9 Metal · Heaven 乾爲天 · 7 甲午 Wood Horse 1	**13** 初五 火7 Fire · Well 水風井 · 8 乙未 Wood Goat 6	**14** 初六 木8 Wood · Relief 雷水解 · 9 丙申 Fire Monkey 4	**15** 初七 金4 Metal · Influence 澤山咸 · 1 丁酉 Fire Rooster 9	**16** 初八 水1 Water · Humility 地山謙 · 2 戊戌 Earth Dog 6	**17** 初九 火2 Fire · Observation 風地觀 · 3 己亥 Earth Pig 2
18 初十 火2 Fire · Increasing 風雷益 · 4 庚子 Metal Rat 9	**19** 十一 水1 Water · Dimming Light 地火明夷 · 5 辛丑 Metal Ox 3	**20** 十二 金9 Metal · Fellowship 天火同人 · 6 壬寅 Water Tiger 7	**21** 十三 木8 Wood · Marrying Maiden 雷澤歸妹 · 7 癸卯 Water Rabbit 7	**22** 十四 木3 Wood · Opposition 火澤睽 · 8 甲辰 Wood Dragon 2	**23** 十五 火7 Fire · Waiting 水天需 · 9 乙巳 Wood Snake 3	**24** 十六 金4 Metal · Great Exceeding 澤風大過 · 1 丙午 Fire Horse 3
25 十七 水6 Water · Poison 山風蠱 · 2 丁未 Fire Goat 7	**26** 十八 火2 Fire · Dispersing 風水渙 · 3 戊申 Earth Monkey 6	**27** 十九 木3 Wood · Travelling 火山旅 · 4 己酉 Earth Rooster 8	**28** 二十 金9 Metal · Stagnation 天地否 · 5 庚戌 Metal Dog 9	**29** 廿一 火7 Fire · Alliance 水地比 · 6 辛亥 Metal Pig 7	**30** 廿二 木8 Wood · Thunder 震爲雷 · 7 壬子 Water Rat 1	**31** 廿三 水6 Water · Beauty 山火賁 · 8 癸丑 Water Ox 8

FEBRUARY 1959 丙寅

Xuan Kong Element 玄空五行	風火家人 Family	Period Luck 卦運	Monthly Star 月星
Fire 火2		4	2

SUNDAY	MONDAY	TUESDAY	WEDNESDAY	THURSDAY	FRIDAY	SATURDAY
1 廿四 火7 Fire · Accomplished 水火既濟 · 9 甲寅 Wood Tiger 9	**2** 廿五 水1 Water · Arriving 地澤臨 · 1 乙卯 Wood Rabbit 4	**3** 廿六 金4 Metal · Marsh 兌爲澤 · 2 丙辰 Fire Dragon 1	**4** 廿七 火2 Fire · Small Livestock 風天小畜 · 3 丁巳 Fire Snake 8	**5** 廿八 木3 Wood · The Cauldron 火風鼎 · 4 戊午 Earth Horse 4	**6** 廿九 水1 Water · Rising 地風升 · 5 己未 Earth Goat 2	**7** 三十 火7 Fire · Water 坎爲水 · 6 庚申 Metal Monkey 1
8 正月初一 木8 Wood · Lesser Exceeding 雷山小過 · 7 辛酉 Metal Rooster 3	**9** 初二 金4 Metal · Gathering 澤地萃 · 8 壬戌 Water Dog 4	**10** 初三 水6 Water · Peel 山地剝 · 9 癸亥 Water Pig 6	**11** 初四 水1 Water · Earth 坤爲地 · 1 甲子 Wood Rat 1	**12** 初五 木3 Wood · Biting 火雷噬嗑 · 2 乙丑 Wood Ox 6	**13** 初六 火2 Fire · Family 風火家人 · 3 丙寅 Fire Tiger 4	**14** 初七 水6 Water · Decreasing 山澤損 · 4 丁卯 Fire Rabbit 9
15 初八 金9 Metal · Tread 天澤履 · 5 戊辰 Earth Dragon 6	**16** 初九 木8 Wood · Great Strength 雷天大壯 · 6 己巳 Earth Snake 2	**17** 初十 木8 Wood · Consistency 雷風恆 · 7 庚午 Metal Horse 9	**18** 十一 金9 Metal · Litigation 天水訟 · 8 辛未 Metal Goat 3	**19** 十二 水1 Water · Officer 地水師 · 9 壬申 Water Monkey 7	**20** 十三 火2 Fire · Gradual Progress 風山漸 · 1 癸酉 Water Rooster 7	**21** 十四 火7 Fire · Obstruction 水山蹇 · 2 甲戌 Wood Dog 2
22 十五 木3 Wood · Advancement 火地晉 · 3 乙亥 Wood Pig 3	**23** 十六 水6 Water · Nourish 山雷頤 · 4 丙子 Fire Rat 3	**24** 十七 金4 Metal · Following 澤雷隨 · 5 丁丑 Fire Ox 7	**25** 十八 木8 Wood · Abundance 雷火豐 · 6 戊寅 Earth Tiger 6	**26** 十九 火7 Fire · Regulate 水澤節 · 7 己卯 Earth Rabbit 8	**27** 二十 水1 Water · Unity 地天泰 · 8 庚辰 Metal Dragon 9	**28** 廿一 木3 Wood · Great Reward 火天大有 · 9 辛巳 Metal Snake 7

MARCH 1959 丁卯

Xuan Kong Element 玄空五行	山澤損 Decreasing	Period Luck 卦運	Monthly Star 月星
Water 水6		9	1

SUNDAY	MONDAY	TUESDAY	WEDNESDAY	THURSDAY	FRIDAY	SATURDAY
火2 Fire 1 Wind 巽爲風 壬午 Water Horse 1 廿二 1	金4 Metal 2 Trap 澤水困 癸未 Water Goat 2 廿三 8	木3 Wood 3 Not Yet Accomplished 火水未濟 甲申 Wood Monkey 3 廿四 9	金9 Metal 4 Retreat 天山遯 乙酉 Wood Rooster 4 廿五 4	水6 Water 5 Mountain 艮爲山 丙戌 Fire Dog 5 廿六 1	木8 Wood 6 Delight 雷地豫 丁亥 Fire Pig 6 廿七 8	火7 Fire 7 Beginning 水雷屯 戊子 Earth Rat 7 廿八 4
金9 Metal 8 Without Wrongdoing 天雷無妄 己丑 Earth Ox 8 廿九 2	木3 Wood 9 Fire 離爲火 庚寅 Metal Tiger 9 二月初一 1	火2 Fire 1 Sincerity 風澤中孚 辛卯 Metal Rabbit 10 初二 3	水6 Water 2 Big Livestock 山天大畜 壬辰 Water Dragon 11 初三 4	金4 Metal 3 Eliminating 澤天夬 癸巳 Water Snake 12 初四 6	金9 Metal 4 Heaven 乾爲天 甲午 Wood Horse 13 初五 1	火7 Fire 5 Well 水風井 乙未 Wood Goat 14 初六 6
木8 Wood 6 Relief 雷水解 丙申 Fire Monkey 15 初七 4	金4 Metal 7 Influence 澤山咸 丁酉 Fire Rooster 16 初八 9	水1 Water 8 Humility 地山謙 戊戌 Earth Dog 17 初九 6	火2 Fire 9 Observation 風地觀 己亥 Earth Pig 18 初十 2	火2 Fire 1 Increasing 風雷益 庚子 Metal Rat 19 十一 9	水1 Water 2 Dimming Light 地火明夷 辛丑 Metal Ox 20 十二 3	金9 Metal 3 Fellowship 天火同人 壬寅 Water Tiger 21 十三 7
木8 Wood 4 Marrying Maiden 雷澤歸妹 癸卯 Water Rabbit 22 十四 7	木3 Wood 5 Opposition 火澤睽 甲辰 Wood Dragon 23 十五 2	火7 Fire 6 Waiting 水天需 乙巳 Wood Snake 24 十六 3	金4 Metal 7 Great Exceeding 澤風大過 丙午 Fire Horse 25 十七 3	水6 Water 8 Poison 山風蠱 丁未 Fire Goat 26 十八 7	火2 Fire 9 Dispersing 風水渙 戊申 Earth Monkey 27 十九 6	木3 Wood 1 Travelling 火山旅 己酉 Earth Rooster 28 二十 8
金9 Metal 2 Stagnation 天地否 庚戌 Metal Dog 29 廿一 9	火7 Fire 3 Alliance 水地比 辛亥 Metal Pig 30 廿二 7	木8 Wood 4 Thunder 震爲雷 壬子 Water Rat 31 廿三 1				

APRIL 1959 戊辰

Xuan Kong Element 玄空五行	天澤履 Tread	Period Luck 卦運	Monthly Star 月星
Metal 金9		6	9

SUNDAY	MONDAY	TUESDAY	WEDNESDAY	THURSDAY	FRIDAY	SATURDAY
			水6 Water 5 Beauty 山火賁 癸丑 Water Ox 1 廿四 8	火7 Fire 6 Accomplished 水火既濟 甲寅 Wood Tiger 2 廿五 9	水1 Water 7 Arriving 地澤臨 乙卯 Wood Rabbit 3 廿六 4	金4 Metal 8 Marsh 兑爲澤 丙辰 Fire Dragon 4 廿七 1
火2 Fire 9 Small Livestock 風天小畜 丁巳 Fire Snake 5 廿八 8	木3 Wood 1 The Cauldron 火風鼎 戊午 Earth Horse 6 廿九 4	水1 Water 2 Rising 地風升 己未 Earth Goat 7 三十 2	火7 Fire 3 Water 坎爲水 庚申 Metal Monkey 8 三月初一 1	木8 Wood 4 Lesser Exceeding 雷山小過 辛酉 Metal Rooster 9 初二 3	金4 Metal 5 Gathering 澤地萃 壬戌 Water Dog 10 初三 4	水6 Water 6 Peel 山地剝 癸亥 Water Pig 11 初四 6
水1 Water 7 Earth 坤爲地 甲子 Wood Rat 12 初五 1	木3 Wood 8 Biting 火雷噬嗑 乙丑 Wood Ox 13 初六 6	火2 Fire 9 Family 風火家人 丙寅 Fire Tiger 14 初七 4	水6 Water 1 Decreasing 山澤損 丁卯 Fire Rabbit 15 初八 9	金9 Metal 2 Tread 天澤履 戊辰 Earth Dragon 16 初九 6	木8 Wood 3 Great Strength 雷天大壯 己巳 Earth Snake 17 初十 2	木8 Wood 4 Consistency 雷風恆 庚午 Metal Horse 18 十一 9
金9 Metal 5 Litigation 天水訟 辛未 Metal Goat 19 十二 3	水1 Water 6 Officer 地水師 壬申 Water Monkey 20 十三 7	火2 Fire 7 Gradual Progress 風山漸 癸酉 Water Rooster 21 十四 7	火7 Fire 8 Obstruction 水山蹇 甲戌 Wood Dog 22 十五 2	木3 Wood 9 Advancement 火地晉 乙亥 Wood Pig 23 十六 3	水6 Water 1 Nourish 山雷頤 丙子 Fire Rat 24 十七 3	金4 Metal 2 Following 澤雷隨 丁丑 Fire Ox 25 十八 7
木8 Wood 3 Abundance 雷火豐 戊寅 Earth Tiger 26 十九 6	火7 Fire 4 Regulate 水澤節 己卯 Earth Rabbit 27 二十 8	水1 Water 5 Unity 地天泰 庚辰 Metal Dragon 28 廿一 9	木3 Wood 6 Great Reward 火天大有 辛巳 Metal Snake 29 廿二 7	火2 Fire 7 Wind 巽爲風 壬午 Water Horse 30 廿三 1		

MAY 1959 己巳

Xuan Kong Element 玄空五行	雷天大壯 Great Strength	Period Luck 卦運	Monthly Star 月星
Wood 木8		2	8

SUNDAY	MONDAY	TUESDAY	WEDNESDAY	THURSDAY	FRIDAY	SATURDAY
水6 Water Beauty 2 癸丑 Water Ox 山火賁 31 廿四 8					金4 Metal Trap 8 癸未 Water Goat 澤水困 1 廿四 8	木3 Wood Not Yet Accomplished 9 甲申 Wood Monkey 火水未濟 2 廿五 9
金9 Metal Retreat 1 乙酉 Wood Rooster 天山遯 3 廿六 4	水6 Water Mountain 2 丙戌 Fire Dog 艮爲山 4 廿七 1	木8 Wood Delight 3 丁亥 Fire Pig 雷地豫 5 廿八 8	火7 Fire Beginning 4 戊子 Earth Rat 水雷屯 6 廿九 4	金9 Metal Without Wrongdoing 5 己丑 Earth Ox 天雷無妄 7 三十 2	木3 Wood Fire 6 庚寅 Metal Tiger 離爲火 8 四月初一 1	火2 Fire Sincerity 7 辛卯 Metal Rabbit 風澤中孚 9 初二 3
水6 Water Big Livestock 8 壬辰 Water Dragon 山天大畜 10 初三 4	金4 Metal Eliminating 9 癸巳 Water Snake 澤天夬 11 初四 6	金9 Metal Heaven 1 甲午 Wood Horse 乾爲天 12 初五 1	火7 Fire Well 2 乙未 Wood Goat 水風井 13 初六 6	木8 Wood Relief 3 丙申 Fire Monkey 雷水解 14 初七 4	金4 Metal Influence 4 丁酉 Fire Rooster 澤山咸 15 初八 9	水1 Water Humility 5 戊戌 Earth Dog 地山謙 16 初九 6
火2 Fire Observation 6 己亥 Earth Pig 風地觀 17 初十 2	火2 Fire Increasing 7 庚子 Metal Rat 風雷益 18 十一 9	水1 Water Dimming Light 8 辛丑 Metal Ox 地火明夷 19 十二 3	金9 Metal Fellowship 9 壬寅 Water Tiger 天火同人 20 十三 7	木8 Wood Marrying Maiden 1 癸卯 Water Rabbit 雷澤歸妹 21 十四 7	木3 Wood Opposition 2 甲辰 Wood Dragon 火澤睽 22 十五 2	火7 Fire Waiting 3 乙巳 Wood Snake 水天需 23 十六 3
金4 Metal Great Exceeding 4 丙午 Fire Horse 澤風大過 24 十七 3	水6 Water Poison 5 丁未 Fire Goat 山風蠱 25 十八 7	火2 Fire Dispersing 6 戊申 Earth Monkey 風水渙 26 十九 6	木3 Wood Travelling 7 己酉 Earth Rooster 火山旅 27 二十 8	金9 Metal Stagnation 8 庚戌 Metal Dog 天地否 28 廿一 9	火7 Fire Alliance 9 辛亥 Metal Pig 水地比 29 廿二 7	木8 Wood Thunder 1 壬子 Water Rat 震爲雷 30 廿三 1

JUNE 1959 庚午

Xuan Kong Element 玄空五行	雷風恆 Consistency	Period Luck 卦運	Monthly Star 月星
Wood 木8		9	7

SUNDAY	MONDAY	TUESDAY	WEDNESDAY	THURSDAY	FRIDAY	SATURDAY
	火7 Fire Accomplished 3 甲寅 Wood Tiger 水火既濟 1 廿五 9	水1 Water Arriving 4 乙卯 Wood Rabbit 地澤臨 2 廿六 4	金4 Metal Marsh 5 丙辰 Fire Dragon 兑爲澤 3 廿七 1	火2 Fire Small Livestock 6 丁巳 Fire Snake 風天小畜 4 廿八 8	木3 Wood The Cauldron 7 戊午 Earth Horse 火風鼎 5 廿九 4	水1 Water Rising 8 己未 Earth Goat 地風升 6 五月初一 2
火7 Fire Water 9 庚申 Metal Monkey 坎爲水 7 初二 1	木8 Wood Lesser Exceeding 1 辛酉 Metal Rooster 雷山小過 8 初三 3	金4 Metal Gathering 2 壬戌 Water Dog 澤地萃 9 初四 4	水6 Water Peel 3 癸亥 Water Pig 山地剝 10 初五 6	水1 Water Earth 4 甲子 Wood Rat 坤爲地 11 初六 1	木3 Wood Biting 5 乙丑 Wood Ox 火雷噬嗑 12 初七 6	火2 Fire Family 6 丙寅 Fire Tiger 風火家人 13 初八 4
水6 Water Decreasing 7 丁卯 Fire Rabbit 山澤損 14 初九 9	金9 Metal Tread 8 戊辰 Earth Dragon 天澤履 15 初十 6	木8 Wood Great Strength 9 己巳 Earth Snake 雷天大壯 16 十一 2	木8 Wood Consistency 1 庚午 Metal Horse 雷風恆 17 十二 9	金9 Metal Litigation 2 辛未 Metal Goat 天水訟 18 十三 3	水1 Water Officer 3 壬申 Water Monkey 地水師 19 十四 7	火2 Fire Gradual Progress 4 癸酉 Water Rooster 風山漸 20 十五 7
火7 Fire Obstruction 5 甲戌 Wood Dog 水山蹇 21 十六 2	木3 Wood Advancement 6/4 乙亥 Wood Pig 火地晉 22 十七 3	水6 Water Nourish 3 丙子 Fire Rat 山雷頤 23 十八 3	金4 Metal Following 2 丁丑 Fire Ox 澤雷隨 24 十九 7	木8 Wood Abundance 1 戊寅 Earth Tiger 雷火豐 25 二十 6	火7 Fire Regulate 9 己卯 Earth Rabbit 水澤節 26 廿一 8	水1 Water Unity 8 庚辰 Metal Dragon 地天泰 27 廿二 9
木3 Wood Great Reward 7 辛巳 Metal Snake 火天大有 28 廿三 7	火2 Fire Wind 6 壬午 Water Horse 巽爲風 29 廿四 1	金4 Metal Trap 5 癸未 Water Goat 澤水困 30 廿五 8				

JULY 1959 辛未

Xuan Kong Element 玄空五行	天水訟 Litigation	Period Luck 卦運	Monthly Star 月星
Metal 金9		3	6

SUNDAY	MONDAY	TUESDAY	WEDNESDAY	THURSDAY	FRIDAY	SATURDAY
			木3 Wood 4 Not Yet Accomplished 甲申 Wood Monkey 火水未濟 1 廿六 9	金9 Metal 3 Retreat 乙酉 Wood Rooster 天山遯 2 廿七 4	水6 Water 2 Mountain 丙戌 Fire Dog 艮爲山 3 廿八 1	木8 Wood 1 Delight 丁亥 Fire Pig 雷地豫 4 廿九 8
火7 Fire 9 Beginning 戊子 Earth Rat 水雷屯 5 三十 4	金9 Metal 8 Without Wrongdoing 己丑 Earth Ox 天雷無妄 6 六月初一 2	木3 Wood 7 Fire 庚寅 Metal Tiger 離爲火 7 初二 1	火2 Fire 6 Sincerity 辛卯 Metal Rabbit 風澤中孚 8 初三 3	水6 Water 5 Big Livestock 壬辰 Water Dragon 山天大畜 9 初四 4	金4 Metal 4 Eliminating 癸巳 Water Snake 澤天夬 10 初五 6	金9 Metal 3 Heaven 甲午 Wood Horse 乾爲天 11 初六 1
火7 Fire 2 Well 乙未 Wood Goat 水風井 12 初七 6	木8 Wood 1 Relief 丙申 Fire Monkey 雷水解 13 初八 4	金4 Metal 9 Influence 丁酉 Fire Rooster 澤山咸 14 初九 9	水1 Water 8 Humility 戊戌 Earth Dog 地山謙 15 初十 6	火2 Fire 7 Observation 己亥 Earth Pig 風地觀 16 十一 2	火2 Fire 6 Increasing 庚子 Metal Rat 風雷益 17 十二 9	水1 Water 5 Dimming Light 辛丑 Metal Ox 地火明夷 18 十三 3
金9 Metal 4 Fellowship 壬寅 Water Tiger 天火同人 19 十四 7	木8 Wood 3 Marrying Maiden 癸卯 Water Rabbit 雷澤歸妹 20 十五 7	木3 Wood 2 Opposition 甲辰 Wood Dragon 火澤睽 21 十六 2	火7 Fire 1 Waiting 乙巳 Wood Snake 水天需 22 十七 3	金4 Metal 9 Great Exceeding 丙午 Fire Horse 澤風大過 23 十八 3	水6 Water 8 Poison 丁未 Fire Goat 山風蠱 24 十九 7	火2 Fire 7 Dispersing 戊申 Earth Monkey 風水渙 25 二十 6
木3 Wood 6 Travelling 己酉 Earth Rooster 火山旅 26 廿一 8	金9 Metal 5 Stagnation 庚戌 Metal Dog 天地否 27 廿二 9	火7 Fire 4 Alliance 辛亥 Metal Pig 水地比 28 廿三 7	木8 Wood 3 Thunder 壬子 Water Rat 震爲雷 29 廿四 1	水6 Water 2 Beauty 癸丑 Water Ox 山火賁 30 廿五 8	火7 Fire 1 Accomplished 甲寅 Wood Tiger 水火既濟 31 廿六 9	

AUGUST 1959 壬申

Xuan Kong Element 玄空五行	地水師 Officer	Period Luck 卦運	Monthly Star 月星
Water 水1		7	5

SUNDAY	MONDAY	TUESDAY	WEDNESDAY	THURSDAY	FRIDAY	SATURDAY
木3 Wood 7 Not Yet Accomplished 甲申 Wood Monkey 火水未濟 30 廿七 9	金9 Metal 6 Retreat 乙酉 Wood Rooster 天山遯 31 廿八 4					水1 Water 9 Arriving 乙卯 Wood Rabbit 地澤臨 1 廿七 4
金4 Metal 8 Marsh 丙辰 Fire Dragon 兌爲澤 2 廿八 1	火2 Fire 7 Small Livestock 丁巳 Fire Snake 風天小畜 3 廿九 8	木3 Wood 6 The Cauldron 戊午 Earth Horse 火風鼎 4 七月初一 4	水1 Water 5 Rising 己未 Earth Goat 地風升 5 初二 2	火7 Fire 4 Water 庚申 Metal Monkey 坎爲水 6 初三 1	木8 Wood 3 Lesser Exceeding 辛酉 Metal Rooster 雷山小過 7 初四 3	金4 Metal 2 Gathering 壬戌 Water Dog 澤地萃 8 初五 4
水6 Water 1 Peel 癸亥 Water Pig 山地剝 9 初六 6	水1 Water 9 Earth 甲子 Wood Rat 坤爲地 10 初七 1	木3 Wood 8 Biting 乙丑 Wood Ox 火雷噬嗑 11 初八 6	火2 Fire 7 Family 丙寅 Fire Tiger 風火家人 12 初九 4	水6 Water 6 Decreasing 丁卯 Fire Rabbit 山澤損 13 初十 9	金9 Metal 5 Tread 戊辰 Earth Dragon 天澤履 14 十一 6	木8 Wood 4 Great Strength 己巳 Earth Snake 雷天大壯 15 十二 2
木8 Wood 3 Consistency 庚午 Metal Horse 雷風恒 16 十三 9	金9 Metal 2 Litigation 辛未 Metal Goat 天水訟 17 十四 3	水1 Water 1 Officer 壬申 Water Monkey 地水師 18 十五 7	火2 Fire 9 Gradual Progress 癸酉 Water Rooster 風山漸 19 十六 7	火7 Fire 8 Obstruction 甲戌 Wood Dog 水山蹇 20 十七 2	木3 Wood 7 Advancement 乙亥 Wood Pig 火地晉 21 十八 3	水6 Water 6 Nourish 丙子 Fire Rat 山雷頤 22 十九 3
金4 Metal 5 Following 丁丑 Fire Ox 澤雷隨 23 二十 7	木8 Wood 4 Abundance 戊寅 Earth Tiger 雷火豐 24 廿一 6	火7 Fire 3 Regulate 己卯 Earth Rabbit 水澤節 25 廿二 8	水1 Water 2 Unity 庚辰 Metal Dragon 地天泰 26 廿三 9	木3 Wood 1 Great Reward 辛巳 Metal Snake 火天大有 27 廿四 7	火2 Fire 9 Wind 壬午 Water Horse 巽爲風 28 廿五 1	金4 Metal 8 Trap 癸未 Water Goat 澤水困 29 廿六 8

SEPTEMBER 1959 癸酉

Xuan Kong Element 玄空五行	風山漸 Gradual Progress	Period Luck 卦運	Monthly Star 月星
Fire 火2		7	4

SUNDAY	MONDAY	TUESDAY	WEDNESDAY	THURSDAY	FRIDAY	SATURDAY
		水6 Water 5 Mountain 艮爲山 丙戌 Fire Dog **1** 廿九 1	木8 Wood 4 Delight 雷地豫 丁亥 Fire Pig **2** 三十 8	火7 Fire 3 Beginning 水雷屯 戊子 Earth Rat **3** 八月初一 4	金9 Metal 2 Without Wrongdoing 天雷無妄 己丑 Earth Ox **4** 初二 2	木3 Wood 1 Fire 離爲火 庚寅 Metal Tiger **5** 初三 1
火2 Fire 9 Sincerity 風澤中孚 辛卯 Metal Rabbit **6** 初四 3	水6 Water 8 Big Livestock 山天大畜 壬辰 Water Dragon **7** 初五 4	金4 Metal 7 Eliminating 澤天夬 癸巳 Water Snake **8** 初六 6	金9 Metal 6 Heaven 乾爲天 甲午 Wood Horse **9** 初七 1	火7 Fire 5 Well 水風井 乙未 Wood Goat **10** 初八 6	木8 Wood 4 Relief 雷水解 丙申 Fire Monkey **11** 初九 4	金4 Metal 3 Influence 澤山咸 丁酉 Fire Rooster **12** 初十 9
水1 Water 2 Humility 地山謙 戊戌 Earth Dog **13** 十一 6	火2 Fire 1 Observation 風地觀 己亥 Earth Pig **14** 十二 2	火2 Fire 9 Increasing 風雷益 庚子 Metal Rat **15** 十三 9	水1 Water 8 Dimming Light 地火明夷 辛丑 Metal Ox **16** 十四 3	金9 Metal 7 Fellowship 天火同人 壬寅 Water Tiger **17** 十五 7	木8 Wood 6 Marrying Maiden 雷澤歸妹 癸卯 Water Rabbit **18** 十六 7	木3 Wood 5 Opposition 火澤睽 甲辰 Wood Dragon **19** 十七 2
火7 Fire 4 Waiting 水天需 乙巳 Wood Snake **20** 十八 3	金4 Metal 3 Great Exceeding 澤風大過 丙午 Fire Horse **21** 十九 3	水6 Water 2 Poison 山風蠱 丁未 Fire Goat **22** 二十 7	火2 Fire 1 Dispersing 風水渙 戊申 Earth Monkey **23** 廿一 6	木3 Wood 9 Travelling 火山旅 己酉 Earth Rooster **24** 廿二 8	金9 Metal 8 Stagnation 天地否 庚戌 Metal Dog **25** 廿三 9	火7 Fire 7 Alliance 水地比 辛亥 Metal Pig **26** 廿四 7
木8 Wood 6 Thunder 震爲雷 壬子 Water Rat **27** 廿五 1	水6 Water 5 Beauty 山火賁 癸丑 Water Ox **28** 廿六 8	火7 Fire 4 Accomplished 水火既濟 甲寅 Wood Tiger **29** 廿七 9	水1 Water 3 Arriving 地澤臨 乙卯 Wood Rabbit **30** 廿八 4			

OCTOBER 1959 甲戌

Xuan Kong Element 玄空五行	水山蹇 Obstruction	Period Luck 卦運	Monthly Star 月星
Fire 火7		2	3

SUNDAY	MONDAY	TUESDAY	WEDNESDAY	THURSDAY	FRIDAY	SATURDAY
				金4 Metal 2 Marsh 兌爲澤 丙辰 Fire Dragon **1** 廿九 1	火2 Fire 1 Small Livestock 風天小畜 丁巳 Fire Snake **2** 九月初一 8	木3 Wood 9 The Cauldron 火風鼎 戊午 Earth Horse **3** 初二 4
水1 Water 8 Rising 地風升 己未 Earth Goat **4** 初三 2	火7 Fire 7 Water 坎爲水 庚申 Metal Monkey **5** 初四 1	木8 Wood 6 Lesser Exceeding 雷山小過 辛酉 Metal Rooster **6** 初五 3	金4 Metal 5 Gathering 澤地萃 壬戌 Water Dog **7** 初六 4	水6 Water 4 Peel 山地剝 癸亥 Water Pig **8** 初七 6	水1 Water 3 Earth 坤爲地 甲子 Wood Rat **9** 初八 1	木3 Wood 2 Biting 火雷噬嗑 乙丑 Wood Ox **10** 初九 6
火2 Fire 1 Family 風火家人 丙寅 Fire Tiger **11** 初十 4	水6 Water 9 Decreasing 山澤損 丁卯 Fire Rabbit **12** 十一 9	金9 Metal 8 Tread 天澤履 戊辰 Earth Dragon **13** 十二 6	木8 Wood 7 Great Strength 雷天大壯 己巳 Earth Snake **14** 十三 2	木8 Wood 6 Consistency 雷風恆 庚午 Metal Horse **15** 十四 9	金9 Metal 5 Litigation 天水訟 辛未 Metal Goat **16** 十五 3	水1 Water 4 Officer 地水師 壬申 Water Monkey **17** 十六 7
火2 Fire 3 Gradual Progress 風山漸 癸酉 Water Rooster **18** 十七 7	火7 Fire 2 Obstruction 水山蹇 甲戌 Wood Dog **19** 十八 2	木3 Wood 1 Advancement 火地晉 乙亥 Wood Pig **20** 十九 3	水6 Water 9 Nourish 山雷頤 丙子 Fire Rat **21** 二十 3	金4 Metal 8 Following 澤雷隨 丁丑 Fire Ox **22** 廿一 7	木8 Wood 7 Abundance 雷火豐 戊寅 Earth Tiger **23** 廿二 6	火7 Fire 6 Regulate 水澤節 己卯 Earth Rabbit **24** 廿三 8
水1 Water 5 Unity 地天泰 庚辰 Metal Dragon **25** 廿四 9	木3 Wood 4 Great Reward 火天大有 辛巳 Metal Snake **26** 廿五 7	火2 Fire 3 Wind 巽爲風 壬午 Water Horse **27** 廿六 1	金4 Metal 2 Trap 澤水困 癸未 Water Goat **28** 廿七 8	木3 Wood 1 Not Yet Accomplished 火水未濟 甲申 Wood Monkey **29** 廿八 9	金9 Metal 9 Retreat 天山遯 乙酉 Wood Rooster **30** 廿九 4	水6 Water 8 Mountain 艮爲山 丙戌 Fire Dog **31** 三十 1

NOVEMBER 1959 乙亥

Xuan Kong Element 玄空五行	火地晉 Advancement	Period Luck 卦運	Monthly Star 月星
Wood 木3		3	2

SUNDAY	MONDAY	TUESDAY	WEDNESDAY	THURSDAY	FRIDAY	SATURDAY
1 十月初一 木8 Wood · 7 Delight 雷地豫 丁亥 Fire Pig · 8	**2** 初二 火7 Fire · 6 Beginning 水雷屯 戊子 Earth Rat · 4	**3** 初三 金9 Metal · 5 Without Wrongdoing 天雷無妄 己丑 Earth Ox · 2	**4** 初四 木3 Wood · 4 Fire 離爲火 庚寅 Metal Tiger · 1	**5** 初五 火2 Fire · 3 Sincerity 風澤中孚 辛卯 Metal Rabbit · 3	**6** 初六 水6 Water · 2 Big Livestock 山天大畜 壬辰 Water Dragon · 4	**7** 初七 金4 Metal · 1 Eliminating 澤天夬 癸巳 Water Snake · 6
8 初八 金9 Metal · 9 Heaven 乾爲天 甲午 Wood Horse · 1	**9** 初九 火7 Fire · 8 Well 水風井 乙未 Wood Goat · 6	**10** 初十 木8 Wood · 7 Relief 雷水解 丙申 Fire Monkey · 4	**11** 十一 金4 Metal · 6 Influence 澤山咸 丁酉 Fire Rooster · 9	**12** 十二 水1 Water · 5 Humility 地山謙 戊戌 Earth Dog · 6	**13** 十三 火2 Fire · 4 Observation 風地觀 己亥 Earth Pig · 2	**14** 十四 火2 Fire · 3 Increasing 風雷益 庚子 Metal Rat · 9
15 十五 水1 Water · 2 Dimming Light 地火明夷 辛丑 Metal Ox · 3	**16** 十六 金9 Metal · 1 Fellowship 天火同人 壬寅 Water Tiger · 7	**17** 十七 木8 Wood · 9 Marrying Maiden 雷澤歸妹 癸卯 Water Rabbit · 7	**18** 十八 木3 Wood · 8 Opposition 火澤睽 甲辰 Wood Dragon · 2	**19** 十九 火7 Fire · 7 Waiting 水天需 乙巳 Wood Snake · 3	**20** 二十 金4 Metal · 6 Great Exceeding 澤風大過 丙午 Fire Horse · 3	**21** 廿一 水6 Water · 5 Poison 山風蠱 丁未 Fire Goat · 7
22 廿二 火2 Fire · 4 Dispersing 風水渙 戊申 Earth Monkey · 6	**23** 廿三 木3 Wood · 3 Travelling 火山旅 己酉 Earth Rooster · 8	**24** 廿四 金9 Metal · 2 Stagnation 天地否 庚戌 Metal Dog · 9	**25** 廿五 火7 Fire · 1 Alliance 水地比 辛亥 Metal Pig · 7	**26** 廿六 木8 Wood · 9 Thunder 震爲雷 壬子 Water Rat · 1	**27** 廿七 水6 Water · 8 Beauty 山火賁 癸丑 Water Ox · 8	**28** 廿八 火7 Fire · 7 Accomplished 水火既濟 甲寅 Wood Tiger · 9
29 廿九 水1 Water · 6 Arriving 地澤臨 乙卯 Wood Rabbit · 4	**30** 十一月初一 金4 Metal · 5 Marsh 兑爲澤 丙辰 Fire Dragon · 1					

DECEMBER 1959 丙子

Xuan Kong Element 玄空五行	山雷頤 Nourish	Period Luck 卦運	Monthly Star 月星
Water 水6		3	1

SUNDAY	MONDAY	TUESDAY	WEDNESDAY	THURSDAY	FRIDAY	SATURDAY
		1 初二 火2 Fire · 4 Small Livestock 風天小畜 丁巳 Fire Snake · 8	**2** 初三 木3 Wood · 3 The Cauldron 火風鼎 戊午 Earth Horse · 4	**3** 初四 水1 Water · 2 Rising 地風升 己未 Earth Goat · 2	**4** 初五 火7 Fire · 1 Water 坎爲水 庚申 Metal Monkey · 1	**5** 初六 木8 Wood · 9 Lesser Exceeding 雷山小過 辛酉 Metal Rooster · 3
6 初七 金4 Metal · 8 Gathering 澤地萃 壬戌 Water Dog · 4	**7** 初八 水6 Water · 7 Peel 山地剝 癸亥 Water Pig · 6	**8** 初九 水1 Water · 6 Earth 坤爲地 甲子 Wood Rat · 1	**9** 初十 木3 Wood · 5 Biting 火雷噬嗑 乙丑 Wood Ox · 6	**10** 十一 火2 Fire · 4 Family 風火家人 丙寅 Fire Tiger · 4	**11** 十二 水6 Water · 3 Decreasing 山澤損 丁卯 Fire Rabbit · 9	**12** 十三 金9 Metal · 2 Tread 天澤履 戊辰 Earth Dragon · 6
13 十四 木8 Wood · 1 Great Strength 雷天大壯 己巳 Earth Snake · 2	**14** 十五 木8 Wood · 9 Consistency 雷風恒 庚午 Metal Horse · 9	**15** 十六 金9 Metal · 8 Litigation 天水訟 辛未 Metal Goat · 3	**16** 十七 水1 Water · 7 Officer 地水師 壬申 Water Monkey · 7	**17** 十八 火2 Fire · 6 Gradual Progress 風山漸 癸酉 Water Rooster · 7	**18** 十九 火7 Fire · 5 Obstruction 水山蹇 甲戌 Wood Dog · 2	**19** 二十 木3 Wood · 4 Advancement 火地晉 乙亥 Wood Pig · 3
20 廿一 水6 Water · 3 Nourish 山雷頤 丙子 Fire Rat · 3	**21** 廿二 金4 Metal · 2 Following 澤雷隨 丁丑 Fire Ox · 7	**22** 廿三 木8 Wood · 1/9 Abundance 雷火豐 戊寅 Earth Tiger · 6	**23** 廿四 火7 Fire · 1 Regulate 水澤節 己卯 Earth Rabbit · 8	**24** 廿五 水1 Water · 2 Unity 地天泰 庚辰 Metal Dragon · 9	**25** 廿六 木3 Wood · 3 Great Reward 火天大有 辛巳 Metal Snake · 7	**26** 廿七 火2 Fire · 4 Wind 巽爲風 壬午 Water Horse · 1
27 廿八 金4 Metal · 5 Trap 澤水困 癸未 Water Goat · 8	**28** 廿九 木3 Wood · 6 Not Yet Accomplished 火水未濟 甲申 Wood Monkey · 9	**29** 三十 金9 Metal · 7 Retreat 天山遯 乙酉 Wood Rooster · 4	**30** 十二月初一 水6 Water · 8 Mountain 艮爲山 丙戌 Fire Dog · 1	**31** 初二 木8 Wood · 9 Delight 雷地豫 丁亥 Fire Pig · 8		

1960 庚子

(*Geng Zi*) Metal Rat

1960 庚子 *(Geng Zi)* Metal Rat

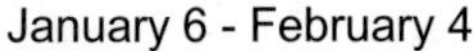

January 6 - February 4

February 5 - March 4

March 5 - April 4

April 5 - May 4

May 5 - June 5

June 6 - July 6

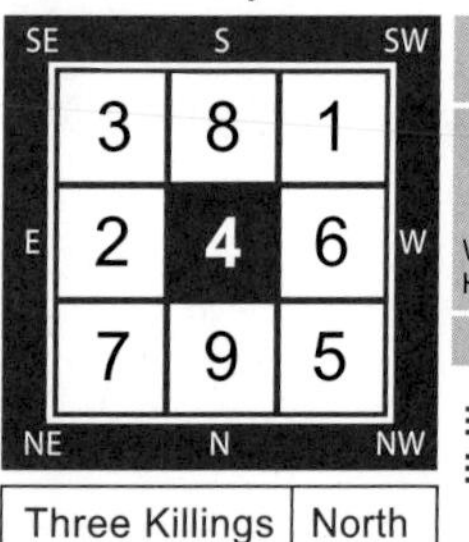

July 7 - August 6

August 7 - September 6

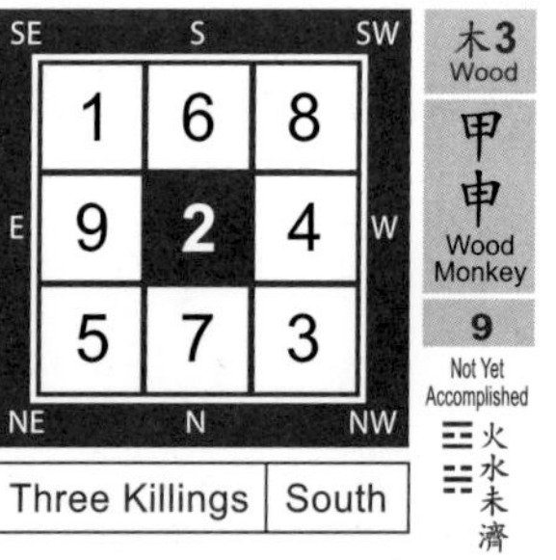

September 7 - October 7

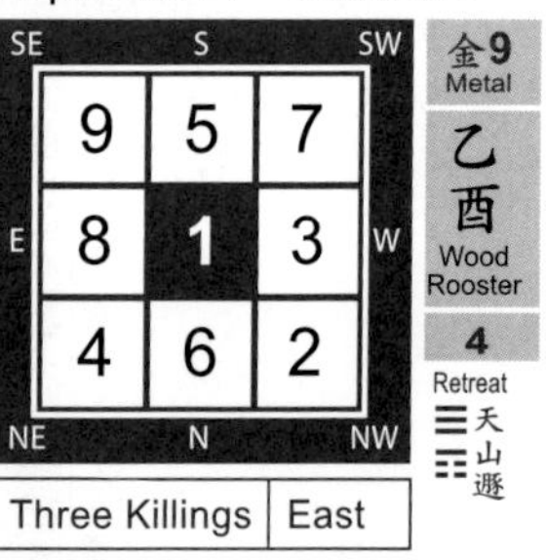

October 8 - November 6

November 7 - December 6

December 7 - January 4

JANUARY 1960 丁丑

Xuan Kong Element 玄空五行	澤雷隨 Following	Period Luck 卦運	Monthly Star 月星
Metal 金4		7	9

SUNDAY	MONDAY	TUESDAY	WEDNESDAY	THURSDAY	FRIDAY	SATURDAY
木3 Wood · The Cauldron · 4 戊午 Earth Horse · 火風鼎 **31** 初四 4					火7 Fire · Beginning · 1 戊子 Earth Rat · 水雷屯 **1** 初三 4	金9 Metal · Without Wrongdoing · 2 己丑 Earth Ox · 天雷無妄 **2** 初四 2
木3 Wood · Fire · 3 庚寅 Metal Tiger · 離爲火 **3** 初五 1	火2 Fire · Sincerity · 4 辛卯 Metal Rabbit · 風澤中孚 **4** 初六 3	水6 Water · Big Livestock · 5 壬辰 Water Dragon · 山天大畜 **5** 初七 4	金4 Metal · Eliminating · 6 癸巳 Water Snake · 澤天夬 **6** 初八 6	金9 Metal · Heaven · 7 甲午 Wood Horse · 乾爲天 **7** 初九 1	火7 Fire · Well · 8 乙未 Wood Goat · 水風井 **8** 初十 6	木8 Wood · Relief · 9 丙申 Fire Monkey · 雷水解 **9** 十一 4
金4 Metal · Influence · 1 丁酉 Fire Rooster · 澤山咸 **10** 十二 9	水1 Water · Humility · 2 戊戌 Earth Dog · 地山謙 **11** 十三 6	火2 Fire · Observation · 3 己亥 Earth Pig · 風地觀 **12** 十四 2	火2 Fire · Increasing · 4 庚子 Metal Rat · 風雷益 **13** 十五 9	水1 Water · Dimming Light · 5 辛丑 Metal Ox · 地火明夷 **14** 十六 3	金9 Metal · Fellowship · 6 壬寅 Water Tiger · 天火同人 **15** 十七 7	木8 Wood · Marrying Maiden · 7 癸卯 Water Rabbit · 雷澤歸妹 **16** 十八 7
木3 Wood · Opposition · 8 甲辰 Wood Dragon · 火澤睽 **17** 十九 2	火7 Fire · Waiting · 9 乙巳 Wood Snake · 水天需 **18** 二十 3	金4 Metal · Great Exceeding · 1 丙午 Fire Horse · 澤風大過 **19** 廿一 3	水6 Water · Poison · 2 丁未 Fire Goat · 山風蠱 **20** 廿二 7	火2 Fire · Dispersing · 3 戊申 Earth Monkey · 風水渙 **21** 廿三 6	木3 Wood · Travelling · 4 己酉 Earth Rooster · 火山旅 **22** 廿四 8	金9 Metal · Stagnation · 5 庚戌 Metal Dog · 天地否 **23** 廿五 9
火7 Fire · Alliance · 6 辛亥 Metal Pig · 水地比 **24** 廿六 7	木8 Wood · Thunder · 7 壬子 Water Rat · 震爲雷 **25** 廿七 1	水6 Water · Beauty · 8 癸丑 Water Ox · 山火賁 **26** 廿八 8	火7 Fire · Accomplished · 9 甲寅 Wood Tiger · 水火既濟 **27** 廿九 9	水1 Water · Arriving · 1 乙卯 Wood Rabbit · 地澤臨 **28** 正月初一 4	金4 Metal · Marsh · 2 丙辰 Fire Dragon · 兌爲澤 **29** 初二 1	火2 Fire · Small Livestock · 3 丁巳 Fire Snake · 風天小畜 **30** 初三 8

FEBRUARY 1960 戊寅

Xuan Kong Element 玄空五行	雷火豐 Abundance	Period Luck 卦運	Monthly Star 月星
Wood 木8		6	8

SUNDAY	MONDAY	TUESDAY	WEDNESDAY	THURSDAY	FRIDAY	SATURDAY
	水1 Water · Rising · 5 己未 Earth Goat · 地風升 **1** 初五 2	火7 Fire · Water · 6 庚申 Metal Monkey · 坎爲水 **2** 初六 1	木8 Wood · Lesser Exceeding · 7 辛酉 Metal Rooster · 雷山小過 **3** 初七 3	金4 Metal · Gathering · 8 壬戌 Water Dog · 澤地萃 **4** 初八 4	水6 Water · Peel · 9 癸亥 Water Pig · 山地剝 **5** 初九 6	水1 Water · Earth · 1 甲子 Wood Rat · 坤爲地 **6** 初十 1
木3 Wood · Biting · 2 乙丑 Wood Ox · 火雷噬嗑 **7** 十一 6	火2 Fire · Family · 3 丙寅 Fire Tiger · 風火家人 **8** 十二 4	水6 Water · Decreasing · 4 丁卯 Fire Rabbit · 山澤損 **9** 十三 9	金9 Metal · Tread · 5 戊辰 Earth Dragon · 天澤履 **10** 十四 6	木8 Wood · Great Strength · 6 己巳 Earth Snake · 雷天大壯 **11** 十五 2	木8 Wood · Consistency · 7 庚午 Metal Horse · 雷風恒 **12** 十六 9	金9 Metal · Litigation · 8 辛未 Metal Goat · 天水訟 **13** 十七 3
水1 Water · Officer · 9 壬申 Water Monkey · 地水師 **14** 十八 7	火2 Fire · Gradual Progress · 1 癸酉 Water Rooster · 風山漸 **15** 十九 7	火7 Fire · Obstruction · 2 甲戌 Wood Dog · 水山蹇 **16** 二十 2	木3 Wood · Advancement · 3 乙亥 Wood Pig · 火地晉 **17** 廿一 3	水6 Water · Nourish · 4 丙子 Fire Rat · 山雷頤 **18** 廿二 3	金4 Metal · Following · 5 丁丑 Fire Ox · 澤雷隨 **19** 廿三 7	木8 Wood · Abundance · 6 戊寅 Earth Tiger · 雷火豐 **20** 廿四 6
火7 Fire · Regulate · 7 己卯 Earth Rabbit · 水澤節 **21** 廿五 8	水1 Water · Unity · 8 庚辰 Metal Dragon · 地天泰 **22** 廿六 9	木3 Wood · Great Reward · 9 辛巳 Metal Snake · 火天大有 **23** 廿七 7	火2 Fire · Wind · 1 壬午 Water Horse · 巽爲風 **24** 廿八 1	金4 Metal · Trap · 2 癸未 Water Goat · 澤水困 **25** 廿九 8	木3 Wood · Not Yet Accomplished · 3 甲申 Wood Monkey · 火水未濟 **26** 三十 9	金9 Metal · Retreat · 4 乙酉 Wood Rooster · 天山遯 **27** 二月初一 4
水6 Water · Mountain · 5 丙戌 Fire Dog · 艮爲山 **28** 初二 1	木8 Wood · Delight · 6 丁亥 Fire Pig · 雷地豫 **29** 初三 8					

MARCH 1960 己卯

Xuan Kong Element 玄空五行	水澤節 Regulate	Period Luck 卦運	Monthly Star 月星
Fire 火7		8	7

SUNDAY	MONDAY	TUESDAY	WEDNESDAY	THURSDAY	FRIDAY	SATURDAY
		火7 Fire 7 Beginning 水雷屯 戊子 Earth Rat 1 初四 4	金9 Metal 8 Without Wrongdoing 天雷無妄 己丑 Earth Ox 2 初五 2	木3 Wood 9 Fire 離爲火 庚寅 Metal Tiger 3 初六 1	火2 Fire 1 Sincerity 風澤中孚 辛卯 Metal Rabbit 4 初七 3	水6 Water 2 Big Livestock 山天大畜 壬辰 Water Dragon 5 初八 4
金4 Metal 3 Eliminating 澤天夬 癸巳 Water Snake 6 初九 6	金9 Metal 4 Heaven 乾爲天 甲午 Wood Horse 7 初十 1	火7 Fire 5 Well 水風井 乙未 Wood Goat 8 十一 6	木8 Wood 6 Relief 雷水解 丙申 Fire Monkey 9 十二 4	金4 Metal 7 Influence 澤山咸 丁酉 Fire Rooster 10 十三 9	水1 Water 8 Humility 地山謙 戊戌 Earth Dog 11 十四 6	火2 Fire 9 Observation 風地觀 己亥 Earth Pig 12 十五 2
火2 Fire 1 Increasing 風雷益 庚子 Metal Rat 13 十六 9	水1 Water 2 Dimming Light 地火明夷 辛丑 Metal Ox 14 十七 3	金9 Metal 3 Fellowship 天火同人 壬寅 Water Tiger 15 十八 7	木8 Wood 4 Marrying Maiden 雷澤歸妹 癸卯 Water Rabbit 16 十九 7	木3 Wood 5 Opposition 火澤睽 甲辰 Wood Dragon 17 二十 2	火7 Fire 6 Waiting 水天需 乙巳 Wood Snake 18 廿一 3	金4 Metal 7 Great Exceeding 澤風大過 丙午 Fire Horse 19 廿二 3
水6 Water 8 Poison 山風蠱 丁未 Fire Goat 20 廿三 7	火2 Fire 9 Dispersing 風水渙 戊申 Earth Monkey 21 廿四 6	木3 Wood 1 Travelling 火山旅 己酉 Earth Rooster 22 廿五 8	金9 Metal 2 Stagnation 天地否 庚戌 Metal Dog 23 廿六 9	火7 Fire 3 Alliance 水地比 辛亥 Metal Pig 24 廿七 7	木8 Wood 4 Thunder 震爲雷 壬子 Water Rat 25 廿八 1	水6 Water 5 Beauty 山火賁 癸丑 Water Ox 26 廿九 8
火7 Fire 6 Accomplished 水火既濟 甲寅 Wood Tiger 27 三月初一 9	水1 Water 7 Arriving 地澤臨 乙卯 Wood Rabbit 28 初二 4	金4 Metal 8 Marsh 兌爲澤 丙辰 Fire Dragon 29 初三 1	火2 Fire 9 Small Livestock 風天小畜 丁巳 Fire Snake 30 初四 8	木3 Wood 1 The Cauldron 火風鼎 戊午 Earth Horse 31 初五 4		

APRIL 1960 庚辰

Xuan Kong Element 玄空五行	地天泰 Unity	Period Luck 卦運	Monthly Star 月星
Water 水1		9	6

SUNDAY	MONDAY	TUESDAY	WEDNESDAY	THURSDAY	FRIDAY	SATURDAY
					水1 Water 2 Rising 地風升 己未 Earth Goat 1 初六 2	火7 Fire 3 Water 坎爲水 庚申 Metal Monkey 2 初七 1
木8 Wood 4 Lesser Exceeding 雷山小過 辛酉 Metal Rooster 3 初八 3	金4 Metal 5 Gathering 澤地萃 壬戌 Water Dog 4 初九 4	水6 Water 6 Peel 山地剝 癸亥 Water Pig 5 初十 6	水1 Water 7 Earth 坤爲地 甲子 Wood Rat 6 十一 1	木3 Wood 8 Biting 火雷噬嗑 乙丑 Wood Ox 7 十二 6	火2 Fire 9 Family 風火家人 丙寅 Fire Tiger 8 十三 4	水6 Water 1 Decreasing 山澤損 丁卯 Fire Rabbit 9 十四 9
金9 Metal 2 Tread 天澤履 戊辰 Earth Dragon 10 十五 6	木8 Wood 3 Great Strength 雷天大壯 己巳 Earth Snake 11 十六 2	木8 Wood 4 Consistency 雷風恆 庚午 Metal Horse 12 十七 9	金9 Metal 5 Litigation 天水訟 辛未 Metal Goat 13 十八 3	水1 Water 6 Officer 地水師 壬申 Water Monkey 14 十九 7	火2 Fire 7 Gradual Progress 風山漸 癸酉 Water Rooster 15 二十 7	火7 Fire 8 Obstruction 水山蹇 甲戌 Wood Dog 16 廿一 2
木3 Wood 9 Advancement 火地晉 乙亥 Wood Pig 17 廿二 3	水6 Water 1 Nourish 山雷頤 丙子 Fire Rat 18 廿三 3	金4 Metal 2 Following 澤雷隨 丁丑 Fire Ox 19 廿四 7	木8 Wood 3 Abundance 雷火豐 戊寅 Earth Tiger 20 廿五 6	火7 Fire 4 Regulate 水澤節 己卯 Earth Rabbit 21 廿六 8	水1 Water 5 Unity 地天泰 庚辰 Metal Dragon 22 廿七 9	木3 Wood 6 Great Reward 火天大有 辛巳 Metal Snake 23 廿八 7
火2 Fire 7 Wind 巽爲風 壬午 Water Horse 24 廿九 1	金4 Metal 8 Trap 澤水困 癸未 Water Goat 25 三十 8	木3 Wood 9 Not Yet Accomplished 火水未濟 甲申 Wood Monkey 26 四月初一 9	金9 Metal 1 Retreat 天山遯 乙酉 Wood Rooster 27 初二 4	水6 Water 2 Mountain 艮爲山 丙戌 Fire Dog 28 初三 1	木8 Wood 3 Delight 雷地豫 丁亥 Fire Pig 29 初四 8	火7 Fire 4 Beginning 水雷屯 戊子 Earth Rat 30 初五 4

MAY 1960 辛巳

Xuan Kong Element 玄空五行	火天大有 Great Reward	Period Luck 卦運	Monthly Star 月星
Wood 木3		7	5

SUNDAY	MONDAY	TUESDAY	WEDNESDAY	THURSDAY	FRIDAY	SATURDAY
金9 Metal 5 Without Wrongdoing 天雷無妄 己丑 Earth Ox **1** 初六 2	木3 Wood 6 Fire 離爲火 庚寅 Metal Tiger **2** 初七 1	火2 Fire 7 Sincerity 風澤中孚 辛卯 Metal Rabbit **3** 初八 3	水6 Water 8 Big Livestock 山天大畜 壬辰 Water Dragon **4** 初九 4	金4 Metal 9 Eliminating 澤天夬 癸巳 Water Snake **5** 初十 6	金9 Metal 1 Heaven 乾爲天 甲午 Wood Horse **6** 十一 1	火7 Fire 2 Well 水風井 乙未 Wood Goat **7** 十二 6
木8 Wood 3 Relief 雷水解 丙申 Fire Monkey **8** 十三 4	金4 Metal 4 Influence 澤山咸 丁酉 Fire Rooster **9** 十四 9	水1 Water 5 Humility 地山謙 戊戌 Earth Dog **10** 十五 6	火2 Fire 6 Observation 風地觀 己亥 Earth Pig **11** 十六 2	火2 Fire 7 Increasing 風雷益 庚子 Metal Rat **12** 十七 9	水1 Water 8 Dimming Light 地火明夷 辛丑 Metal Ox **13** 十八 3	金9 Metal 9 Fellowship 天火同人 壬寅 Water Tiger **14** 十九 7
木8 Wood 1 Marrying Maiden 雷澤歸妹 癸卯 Water Rabbit **15** 二十 7	木3 Wood 2 Opposition 火澤睽 甲辰 Wood Dragon **16** 廿一 2	火7 Fire 3 Waiting 水天需 乙巳 Wood Snake **17** 廿二 3	金4 Metal 4 Great Exceeding 澤風大過 丙午 Fire Horse **18** 廿三 3	水6 Water 5 Poison 山風蠱 丁未 Fire Goat **19** 廿四 7	火2 Fire 6 Dispersing 風水渙 戊申 Earth Monkey **20** 廿五 6	木3 Wood 7 Travelling 火山旅 己酉 Earth Rooster **21** 廿六 8
金9 Metal 8 Stagnation 天地否 庚戌 Metal Dog **22** 廿七 9	火7 Fire 9 Alliance 水地比 辛亥 Metal Pig **23** 廿八 7	木8 Wood 1 Thunder 震爲雷 壬子 Water Rat **24** 廿九 1	水6 Water 2 Beauty 山火賁 癸丑 Water Ox **25** 五月初一 8	火7 Fire 3 Accomplished 水火既濟 甲寅 Wood Tiger **26** 初二 9	水1 Water 4 Arriving 地澤臨 乙卯 Wood Rabbit **27** 初三 4	金4 Metal 5 Marsh 兌爲澤 丙辰 Fire Dragon **28** 初四 1
火2 Fire 6 Small Livestock 風天小畜 丁巳 Fire Snake **29** 初五 8	木3 Wood 7 The Cauldron 火風鼎 戊午 Earth Horse **30** 初六 4	水1 Water 8 Rising 地風升 己未 Earth Goat **31** 初七 2				

JUNE 1960 壬午

Xuan Kong Element 玄空五行	巽爲風 Wind	Period Luck 卦運	Monthly Star 月星
Fire 火2		1	4

SUNDAY	MONDAY	TUESDAY	WEDNESDAY	THURSDAY	FRIDAY	SATURDAY
			火7 Fire 9 Water 坎爲水 庚申 Metal Monkey **1** 初八 1	木8 Wood 1 Lesser Exceeding 雷山小過 辛酉 Metal Rooster **2** 初九 3	金4 Metal 2 Gathering 澤地萃 壬戌 Water Dog **3** 初十 4	水6 Water 3 Peel 山地剝 癸亥 Water Pig **4** 十一 6
水1 Water 4 Earth 坤爲地 甲子 Wood Rat **5** 十二 1	木3 Wood 5 Biting 火雷噬嗑 乙丑 Wood Ox **6** 十三 6	火2 Fire 6 Family 風火家人 丙寅 Fire Tiger **7** 十四 4	水6 Water 7 Decreasing 山澤損 丁卯 Fire Rabbit **8** 十五 9	金9 Metal 8 Tread 天澤履 戊辰 Earth Dragon **9** 十六 6	木8 Wood 9 Great Strength 雷天大壯 己巳 Earth Snake **10** 十七 2	木8 Wood 1 Consistency 雷風恆 庚午 Metal Horse **11** 十八 9
金9 Metal 2 Litigation 天水訟 辛未 Metal Goat **12** 十九 3	水1 Water 3 Officer 地水師 壬申 Water Monkey **13** 二十 7	火2 Fire 4 Gradual Progress 風山漸 癸酉 Water Rooster **14** 廿一 7	火7 Fire 5 Obstruction 水山蹇 甲戌 Wood Dog **15** 廿二 2	木3 Wood 6 Advancement 火地晉 乙亥 Wood Pig **16** 廿三 3	水6 Water 7 Nourish 山雷頤 丙子 Fire Rat **17** 廿四 3	金4 Metal 8 Following 澤雷隨 丁丑 Fire Ox **18** 廿五 7
木8 Wood 9 Abundance 雷火豐 戊寅 Earth Tiger **19** 廿六 6	火7 Fire 1 Regulate 水澤節 己卯 Earth Rabbit **20** 廿七 8	水1 Water 2/8 Unity 地天泰 庚辰 Metal Dragon **21** 廿八 9	木3 Wood 7 Great Reward 火天大有 辛巳 Metal Snake **22** 廿九 7	火2 Fire 6 Wind 巽爲風 壬午 Water Horse **23** 三十 1	金4 Metal 5 Trap 澤水困 癸未 Water Goat **24** 六月初一 8	木3 Wood 4 Not Yet Accomplished 火水未濟 甲申 Wood Monkey **25** 初二 9
金9 Metal 3 Retreat 天山遯 乙酉 Wood Rooster **26** 初三 4	水6 Water 2 Mountain 艮爲山 丙戌 Fire Dog **27** 初四 1	木8 Wood 1 Delight 雷地豫 丁亥 Fire Pig **28** 初五 8	火7 Fire 9 Beginning 水雷屯 戊子 Earth Rat **29** 初六 4	金9 Metal 8 Without Wrongdoing 天雷無妄 己丑 Earth Ox **30** 初七 2		

JULY 1960 癸未

Xuan Kong Element 玄空五行	澤水困 Trap	Period Luck 卦運	Monthly Star 月星
Metal 金4		8	3

SUNDAY	MONDAY	TUESDAY	WEDNESDAY	THURSDAY	FRIDAY	SATURDAY
火7 Fire 4 Water 庚申 Metal Monkey 坎爲水 **31** 初八 1					木3 Wood 7 Fire 庚寅 Metal Tiger 離爲火 **1** 初八 1	火2 Fire 6 Sincerity 辛卯 Metal Rabbit 風澤中孚 **2** 初九 3
水6 Water 5 Big Livestock 壬辰 Water Dragon 山天大畜 **3** 初十 4	金4 Metal 4 Eliminating 癸巳 Water Snake 澤天夬 **4** 十一 6	金9 Metal 3 Heaven 甲午 Wood Horse 乾爲天 **5** 十二 1	火7 Fire 2 Well 乙未 Wood Goat 水風井 **6** 十三 6	木8 Wood 1 Relief 丙申 Fire Monkey 雷水解 **7** 十四 4	金4 Metal 9 Influence 丁酉 Fire Rooster 澤山咸 **8** 十五 9	水1 Water 8 Humility 戊戌 Earth Dog 地山謙 **9** 十六 6
火2 Fire 7 Observation 己亥 Earth Pig 風地觀 **10** 十七 2	火2 Fire 6 Increasing 庚子 Metal Rat 風雷益 **11** 十八 9	水1 Water 5 Dimming Light 辛丑 Metal Ox 地火明夷 **12** 十九 3	金9 Metal 4 Fellowship 壬寅 Water Tiger 天火同人 **13** 二十 7	木8 Wood 3 Marrying Maiden 癸卯 Water Rabbit 雷澤歸妹 **14** 廿一 7	木3 Wood 2 Opposition 甲辰 Wood Dragon 火澤睽 **15** 廿二 2	火7 Fire 1 Waiting 乙巳 Wood Snake 水天需 **16** 廿三 3
金4 Metal 9 Great Exceeding 丙午 Fire Horse 澤風大過 **17** 廿四 3	水6 Water 8 Poison 丁未 Fire Goat 山風蠱 **18** 廿五 7	火2 Fire 7 Dispersing 戊申 Earth Monkey 風水渙 **19** 廿六 6	木3 Wood 6 Travelling 己酉 Earth Rooster 火山旅 **20** 廿七 8	金9 Metal 5 Stagnation 庚戌 Metal Dog 天地否 **21** 廿八 9	火7 Fire 4 Alliance 辛亥 Metal Pig 水地比 **22** 廿九 7	木8 Wood 3 Thunder 壬子 Water Rat 震爲雷 **23** 三十 1
水6 Water 2 Beauty 癸丑 Water Ox 山火賁 **24** 閏六月初一 8	火7 Fire 1 Accomplished 甲寅 Wood Tiger 水火既濟 **25** 初二 9	水1 Water 9 Arriving 乙卯 Wood Rabbit 地澤臨 **26** 初三 4	金4 Metal 8 Marsh 丙辰 Fire Dragon 兌爲澤 **27** 初四 1	火2 Fire 7 Small Livestock 丁巳 Fire Snake 風天小畜 **28** 初五 8	木3 Wood 6 The Cauldron 戊午 Earth Horse 火風鼎 **29** 初六 4	水1 Water 5 Rising 己未 Earth Goat 地風升 **30** 初七 2

AUGUST 1960 甲申

Xuan Kong Element 玄空五行	火水未濟 Not Yet Accomplished	Period Luck 卦運	Monthly Star 月星
Wood 木3		9	2

SUNDAY	MONDAY	TUESDAY	WEDNESDAY	THURSDAY	FRIDAY	SATURDAY
	木8 Wood 3 Lesser Exceeding 辛酉 Metal Rooster 雷山小過 **1** 初九 3	金4 Metal 2 Gathering 壬戌 Water Dog 澤地萃 **2** 初十 4	水6 Water 1 Peel 癸亥 Water Pig 山地剝 **3** 十一 6	水1 Water 9 Earth 甲子 Wood Rat 坤爲地 **4** 十二 1	木3 Wood 8 Biting 乙丑 Wood Ox 火雷噬嗑 **5** 十三 6	火2 Fire 7 Family 丙寅 Fire Tiger 風火家人 **6** 十四 4
水6 Water 6 Decreasing 丁卯 Fire Rabbit 山澤損 **7** 十五 9	金9 Metal 5 Tread 戊辰 Earth Dragon 天澤履 **8** 十六 6	木8 Wood 4 Great Strength 己巳 Earth Snake 雷天大壯 **9** 十七 2	木8 Wood 3 Consistency 庚午 Metal Horse 雷風恒 **10** 十八 9	金9 Metal 2 Litigation 辛未 Metal Goat 天水訟 **11** 十九 3	水1 Water 1 Officer 壬申 Water Monkey 地水師 **12** 二十 7	火2 Fire 9 Gradual Progress 癸酉 Water Rooster 風山漸 **13** 廿一 7
火7 Fire 8 Obstruction 甲戌 Wood Dog 水山蹇 **14** 廿二 2	木3 Wood 7 Advancement 乙亥 Wood Pig 火地晉 **15** 廿三 3	水6 Water 6 Nourish 丙子 Fire Rat 山雷頤 **16** 廿四 3	金4 Metal 5 Following 丁丑 Fire Ox 澤雷隨 **17** 廿五 7	木8 Wood 4 Abundance 戊寅 Earth Tiger 雷火豐 **18** 廿六 6	火7 Fire 3 Regulate 己卯 Earth Rabbit 水澤節 **19** 廿七 8	水1 Water 2 Unity 庚辰 Metal Dragon 地天泰 **20** 廿八 9
木3 Wood 1 Great Reward 辛巳 Metal Snake 火天大有 **21** 廿九 7	火2 Fire 9 Wind 壬午 Water Horse 巽爲風 **22** 七月初一 1	金4 Metal 8 Trap 癸未 Water Goat 澤水困 **23** 初二 8	木3 Wood 7 Not Yet Accomplished 甲申 Wood Monkey 火水未濟 **24** 初三 9	金9 Metal 6 Retreat 乙酉 Wood Rooster 天山遯 **25** 初四 4	水6 Water 5 Mountain 丙戌 Fire Dog 艮爲山 **26** 初五 1	木8 Wood 4 Delight 丁亥 Fire Pig 雷地豫 **27** 初六 8
火7 Fire 3 Beginning 戊子 Earth Rat 水雷屯 **28** 初七 4	金9 Metal 2 Without Wrongdoing 己丑 Earth Ox 天雷無妄 **29** 初八 2	木3 Wood 1 Fire 庚寅 Metal Tiger 離爲火 **30** 初九 1	火2 Fire 9 Sincerity 辛卯 Metal Rabbit 風澤中孚 **31** 初十 3			

SEPTEMBER 1960 乙酉

Xuan Kong Element 玄空五行	天山遯 Retreat	Period Luck 卦運	Monthly Star 月星
Metal 金9		4	1

SUNDAY	MONDAY	TUESDAY	WEDNESDAY	THURSDAY	FRIDAY	SATURDAY
				水6 Water Big Livestock 8 壬辰 Water Dragon 山天大畜 **1** 十一 4	金4 Metal Eliminating 7 癸巳 Water Snake 澤天夬 **2** 十二 6	金9 Metal Heaven 6 甲午 Wood Horse 乾爲天 **3** 十三 1
火7 Fire Well 5 乙未 Wood Goat 水風井 **4** 十四 6	木8 Wood Relief 4 丙申 Fire Monkey 雷水解 **5** 十五 4	金4 Metal Influence 3 丁酉 Fire Rooster 澤山咸 **6** 十六 9	水1 Water Humility 2 戊戌 Earth Dog 地山謙 **7** 十七 6	火2 Fire Observation 1 己亥 Earth Pig 風地觀 **8** 十八 2	火2 Fire Increasing 9 庚子 Metal Rat 風雷益 **9** 十九 9	水1 Water Dimming Light 8 辛丑 Metal Ox 地火明夷 **10** 二十 3
金9 Metal Fellowship 7 壬寅 Water Tiger 天火同人 **11** 廿一 7	木8 Wood Marrying Maiden 6 癸卯 Water Rabbit 雷澤歸妹 **12** 廿二 7	木3 Wood Opposition 5 甲辰 Wood Dragon 火澤睽 **13** 廿三 2	火7 Fire Waiting 4 乙巳 Wood Snake 水天需 **14** 廿四 3	金4 Metal Great Exceeding 3 丙午 Fire Horse 澤風大過 **15** 廿五 3	水6 Water Poison 2 丁未 Fire Goat 山風蠱 **16** 廿六 7	火2 Fire Dispersing 1 戊申 Earth Monkey 風水渙 **17** 廿七 6
木3 Wood Travelling 9 己酉 Earth Rooster 火山旅 **18** 廿八 8	金9 Metal Stagnation 8 庚戌 Metal Dog 天地否 **19** 廿九 9	火7 Fire Alliance 7 辛亥 Metal Pig 水地比 **20** 三十 7	木8 Wood Thunder 6 壬子 Water Rat 震爲雷 **21** 八月初一 1	水6 Water Beauty 5 癸丑 Water Ox 山火賁 **22** 初二 8	火7 Fire Accomplished 4 甲寅 Wood Tiger 水火既濟 **23** 初三 9	水1 Water Arriving 3 乙卯 Wood Rabbit 地澤臨 **24** 初四 4
金4 Metal Marsh 2 丙辰 Fire Dragon 兑爲澤 **25** 初五 1	火2 Fire Small Livestock 1 丁巳 Fire Snake 風天小畜 **26** 初六 8	木3 Wood The Cauldron 9 戊午 Earth Horse 火風鼎 **27** 初七 4	水1 Water Rising 8 己未 Earth Goat 地風升 **28** 初八 2	火7 Fire Water 7 庚申 Metal Monkey 坎爲水 **29** 初九 1	木8 Wood Lesser Exceeding 6 辛酉 Metal Rooster 雷山小過 **30** 初十 3	

OCTOBER 1960 丙戌

Xuan Kong Element 玄空五行	艮爲山 Mountain	Period Luck 卦運	Monthly Star 月星
Water 水6		1	9

SUNDAY	MONDAY	TUESDAY	WEDNESDAY	THURSDAY	FRIDAY	SATURDAY
火2 Fire Sincerity 3 辛卯 Metal Rabbit 風澤中孚 **30** 十一 3	水6 Water Big Livestock 2 壬辰 Water Dragon 山天大畜 **31** 十二 4					金4 Metal Gathering 5 壬戌 Water Dog 澤地萃 **1** 十一 4
水6 Water Peel 4 癸亥 Water Pig 山地剝 **2** 十二 6	水1 Water Earth 3 甲子 Wood Rat 坤爲地 **3** 十三 1	木3 Wood Biting 2 乙丑 Wood Ox 火雷噬嗑 **4** 十四 6	火2 Fire Family 1 丙寅 Fire Tiger 風火家人 **5** 十五 4	水6 Water Decreasing 9 丁卯 Fire Rabbit 山澤損 **6** 十六 9	金9 Metal Tread 8 戊辰 Earth Dragon 天澤履 **7** 十七 6	木8 Wood Great Strength 7 己巳 Earth Snake 雷天大壯 **8** 十八 2
木8 Wood Consistency 6 庚午 Metal Horse 雷風恆 **9** 十九 9	金9 Metal Litigation 5 辛未 Metal Goat 天水訟 **10** 二十 3	水1 Water Officer 4 壬申 Water Monkey 地水師 **11** 廿一 7	火2 Fire Gradual Progress 3 癸酉 Water Rooster 風山漸 **12** 廿二 7	火7 Fire Obstruction 2 甲戌 Wood Dog 水山蹇 **13** 廿三 2	木3 Wood Advancement 1 乙亥 Wood Pig 火地晉 **14** 廿四 3	水6 Water Nourish 9 丙子 Fire Rat 山雷頤 **15** 廿五 3
金4 Metal Following 8 丁丑 Fire Ox 澤雷隨 **16** 廿六 7	木8 Wood Abundance 7 戊寅 Earth Tiger 雷火豐 **17** 廿七 6	火7 Fire Regulate 6 己卯 Earth Rabbit 水澤節 **18** 廿八 8	水1 Water Unity 5 庚辰 Metal Dragon 地天泰 **19** 廿九 9	木3 Wood Great Reward 4 辛巳 Metal Snake 火天大有 **20** 九月初一 7	火2 Fire Wind 3 壬午 Water Horse 巽爲風 **21** 初二 1	金4 Metal Trap 2 癸未 Water Goat 澤水困 **22** 初三 8
木3 Wood Not Yet Accomplished 1 甲申 Wood Monkey 火水未濟 **23** 初四 9	金9 Metal Retreat 9 乙酉 Wood Rooster 天山遯 **24** 初五 4	水6 Water Mountain 8 丙戌 Fire Dog 艮爲山 **25** 初六 1	木8 Wood Delight 7 丁亥 Fire Pig 雷地豫 **26** 初七 8	火7 Fire Beginning 6 戊子 Earth Rat 水雷屯 **27** 初八 4	金9 Metal Without Wrongdoing 5 己丑 Earth Ox 天雷無妄 **28** 初九 2	木3 Wood Fire 4 庚寅 Metal Tiger 離爲火 **29** 初十 1

NOVEMBER 1960 丁亥

Xuan Kong Element 玄空五行	雷地豫 Delight	Period Luck 卦運	Monthly Star 月星
Wood 木8		8	8

SUNDAY	MONDAY	TUESDAY	WEDNESDAY	THURSDAY	FRIDAY	SATURDAY
		金4 Metal [1] Eliminating 癸巳 Water Snake 澤天夬 1 十三 6	金9 Metal [9] Heaven 甲午 Wood Horse 乾爲天 2 十四 1	火7 Fire [8] Well 乙未 Wood Goat 水風井 3 十五 6	木8 Wood [7] Relief 丙申 Fire Monkey 雷水解 4 十六 4	金4 Metal [6] Influence 丁酉 Fire Rooster 澤山咸 5 十七 9
水1 Water [5] Humility 戊戌 Earth Dog 地山謙 6 十八 6	火2 Fire [4] Observation 己亥 Earth Pig 風地觀 7 十九 2	火2 Fire [3] Increasing 庚子 Metal Rat 風雷益 8 二十 9	水1 Water [2] Dimming Light 辛丑 Metal Ox 地火明夷 9 廿一 3	金9 Metal [1] Fellowship 壬寅 Water Tiger 天火同人 10 廿二 7	木8 Wood [9] Marrying Maiden 癸卯 Water Rabbit 雷澤歸妹 11 廿三 7	木3 Wood [8] Opposition 甲辰 Wood Dragon 火澤睽 12 廿四 2
火7 Fire [7] Waiting 乙巳 Wood Snake 水天需 13 廿五 3	金4 Metal [6] Great Exceeding 丙午 Fire Horse 澤風大過 14 廿六 3	水6 Water [5] Poison 丁未 Fire Goat 山風蠱 15 廿七 7	火2 Fire [4] Dispersing 戊申 Earth Monkey 風水渙 16 廿八 6	木3 Wood [3] Travelling 己酉 Earth Rooster 火山旅 17 廿九 8	金9 Metal [2] Stagnation 庚戌 Metal Dog 天地否 18 三十 9	火7 Fire [1] Alliance 辛亥 Metal Pig 水地比 19 十月初一 7
木8 Wood [9] Thunder 壬子 Water Rat 震爲雷 20 初二 1	水6 Water [8] Beauty 癸丑 Water Ox 山火賁 21 初三 8	火7 Fire [7] Accomplished 甲寅 Wood Tiger 水火既濟 22 初四 9	水1 Water [6] Arriving 乙卯 Wood Rabbit 地澤臨 23 初五 4	金4 Metal [5] Marsh 丙辰 Fire Dragon 兑爲澤 24 初六 1	火2 Fire [4] Small Livestock 丁巳 Fire Snake 風天小畜 25 初七 8	木3 Wood [3] The Cauldron 戊午 Earth Horse 火風鼎 26 初八 4
水1 Water [2] Rising 己未 Earth Goat 地風升 27 初九 2	火7 Fire [1] Water 庚申 Metal Monkey 坎爲水 28 初十 1	木8 Wood [9] Lesser Exceeding 辛酉 Metal Rooster 雷山小過 29 十一 3	金4 Metal [8] Gathering 壬戌 Water Dog 澤地萃 30 十二 4			

DECEMBER 1960 戊子

Xuan Kong Element 玄空五行	水雷屯 Beginning	Period Luck 卦運	Monthly Star 月星
Fire 火7		4	7

SUNDAY	MONDAY	TUESDAY	WEDNESDAY	THURSDAY	FRIDAY	SATURDAY
				水6 Water [7] Peel 癸亥 Water Pig 山地剝 1 十三 6	水1 Water [6] Earth 甲子 Wood Rat 坤爲地 2 十四 1	木3 Wood [5] Biting 乙丑 Wood Ox 火雷噬嗑 3 十五 6
火2 Fire [4] Family 丙寅 Fire Tiger 風火家人 4 十六 4	水6 Water [3] Decreasing 丁卯 Fire Rabbit 山澤損 5 十七 9	金9 Metal [2] Tread 戊辰 Earth Dragon 天澤履 6 十八 6	木8 Wood [1] Great Strength 己巳 Earth Snake 雷天大壯 7 十九 2	木8 Wood [9] Consistency 庚午 Metal Horse 雷風恆 8 二十 9	金9 Metal [8] Litigation 辛未 Metal Goat 天水訟 9 廿一 3	水1 Water [7] Officer 壬申 Water Monkey 地水師 10 廿二 7
火2 Fire [6] Gradual Progress 癸酉 Water Rooster 風山漸 11 廿三 7	火7 Fire [5] Obstruction 甲戌 Wood Dog 水山蹇 12 廿四 2	木3 Wood [4] Advancement 乙亥 Wood Pig 火地晉 13 廿五 3	水6 Water [3] Nourish 丙子 Fire Rat 山雷頤 14 廿六 3	金4 Metal [2] Following 丁丑 Fire Ox 澤雷隨 15 廿七 7	木8 Wood [1] Abundance 戊寅 Earth Tiger 雷火豐 16 廿八 6	火7 Fire [9] Regulate 己卯 Earth Rabbit 水澤節 17 廿九 8
水1 Water [8] Unity 庚辰 Metal Dragon 地天泰 18 十一月初一 9	木3 Wood [7] Great Reward 辛巳 Metal Snake 火天大有 19 初二 7	火2 Fire [6] Wind 壬午 Water Horse 巽爲風 20 初三 1	金4 Metal [5] Trap 癸未 Water Goat 澤水困 21 初四 8	木3 Wood [4/6] Not Yet Accomplished 甲申 Wood Monkey 火水未濟 22 初五 9	金9 Metal [7] Retreat 乙酉 Wood Rooster 天山遯 23 初六 4	水6 Water [8] Mountain 丙戌 Fire Dog 艮爲山 24 初七 1
木8 Wood [9] Delight 丁亥 Fire Pig 雷地豫 25 初八 8	火7 Fire [1] Beginning 戊子 Earth Rat 水雷屯 26 初九 4	金9 Metal [2] Without Wrongdoing 己丑 Earth Ox 天雷無妄 27 初十 2	木3 Wood [3] Fire 庚寅 Metal Tiger 離爲火 28 十一 1	火2 Fire [4] Sincerity 辛卯 Metal Rabbit 風澤中孚 29 十二 3	水6 Water [5] Big Livestock 壬辰 Water Dragon 山天大畜 30 十三 4	金4 Metal [6] Eliminating 癸巳 Water Snake 澤天夬 31 十四 6

1961 辛丑

(*Xin Chou*) Metal Ox

1961 辛丑 *(Xin Chou)* Metal Ox

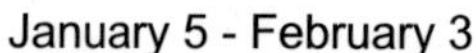

February 4 - March 5

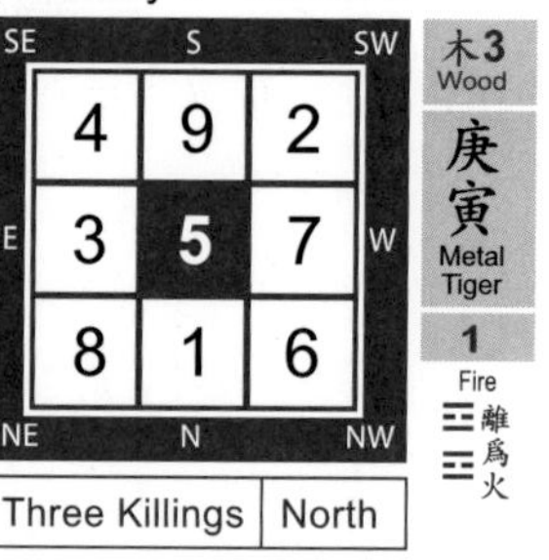

March 6 - April 4

April 5 - May 5

June 6 - July 6

July 7 - August 7

August 8 - September 7

September 8 - October 7

October 8 - November 6

November 7 - December 6

December 7 - January 5

JANUARY 1961 己丑

Xuan Kong Element 玄空五行	天雷無妄 Without Wrongdoing	Period Luck 卦運	Monthly Star 月星
Metal 金9		2	6

SUNDAY	MONDAY	TUESDAY	WEDNESDAY	THURSDAY	FRIDAY	SATURDAY
1 十五 金9 Metal Heaven 7 甲午 Wood Horse 乾爲天 1	**2** 十六 火7 Fire Well 8 乙未 Wood Goat 水風井 6	**3** 十七 木8 Wood Relief 9 丙申 Fire Monkey 雷水解 4	**4** 十八 金4 Metal Influence 1 丁酉 Fire Rooster 澤山咸 9	**5** 十九 水1 Water Humility 2 戊戌 Earth Dog 地山謙 6	**6** 二十 火2 Fire Observation 3 己亥 Earth Pig 風地觀 2	**7** 廿一 火2 Fire Increasing 4 庚子 Metal Rat 風雷益 9
8 廿二 水1 Water Dimming Light 5 辛丑 Metal Ox 地火明夷 3	**9** 廿三 金9 Metal Fellowship 6 壬寅 Water Tiger 天火同人 7	**10** 廿四 木8 Wood Marrying Maiden 7 癸卯 Water Rabbit 雷澤歸妹 7	**11** 廿五 木3 Wood Opposition 8 甲辰 Wood Dragon 火澤睽 2	**12** 廿六 火7 Fire Waiting 9 乙巳 Wood Snake 水天需 3	**13** 廿七 金4 Metal Great Exceeding 1 丙午 Fire Horse 澤風大過 3	**14** 廿八 水6 Water Poison 2 丁未 Fire Goat 山風蠱 7
15 廿九 火2 Fire Dispersing 3 戊申 Earth Monkey 風水渙 6	**16** 三十 木3 Wood Travelling 4 己酉 Earth Rooster 火山旅 8	**17** 十二月初一 金9 Metal Stagnation 5 庚戌 Metal Dog 天地否 9	**18** 初二 火7 Fire Alliance 6 辛亥 Metal Pig 水地比 7	**19** 初三 木8 Wood Thunder 7 壬子 Water Rat 震爲雷 1	**20** 初四 水6 Water Beauty 8 癸丑 Water Ox 山火賁 8	**21** 初五 火7 Fire Accomplished 9 甲寅 Wood Tiger 水火既濟 9
22 初六 水1 Water Arriving 1 乙卯 Wood Rabbit 地澤臨 4	**23** 初七 金4 Metal Marsh 2 丙辰 Fire Dragon 兌爲澤 1	**24** 初八 火2 Fire Small Livestock 3 丁巳 Fire Snake 風天小畜 8	**25** 初九 木3 Wood The Cauldron 4 戊午 Earth Horse 火風鼎 4	**26** 初十 水1 Water Rising 5 己未 Earth Goat 地風升 2	**27** 十一 火7 Fire Water 6 庚申 Metal Monkey 坎爲水 1	**28** 十二 木8 Wood Lesser Exceeding 7 辛酉 Metal Rooster 雷山小過 3
29 十三 金4 Metal Gathering 8 壬戌 Water Dog 澤地萃 4	**30** 十四 水6 Water Peel 9 癸亥 Water Pig 山地剝 6	**31** 十五 水1 Water Earth 1 甲子 Wood Rat 坤爲地 1				

FEBRUARY 1961 庚寅

Xuan Kong Element 玄空五行	離爲火 Fire	Period Luck 卦運	Monthly Star 月星
Wood 木3		1	5

SUNDAY	MONDAY	TUESDAY	WEDNESDAY	THURSDAY	FRIDAY	SATURDAY
			1 十六 木3 Wood Biting 2 乙丑 Wood Ox 火雷噬嗑 6	**2** 十七 火2 Fire Family 3 丙寅 Fire Tiger 風火家人 4	**3** 十八 水6 Water Decreasing 4 丁卯 Fire Rabbit 山澤損 9	**4** 十九 金9 Metal Tread 5 戊辰 Earth Dragon 天澤履 6
5 二十 木8 Wood Great Strength 6 己巳 Earth Snake 雷天大壯 2	**6** 廿一 木8 Wood Consistency 7 庚午 Metal Horse 雷風恆 9	**7** 廿二 金9 Metal Litigation 8 辛未 Metal Goat 天水訟 3	**8** 廿三 水1 Water Officer 9 壬申 Water Monkey 地水師 7	**9** 廿四 火2 Fire Gradual Progress 1 癸酉 Water Rooster 風山漸 7	**10** 廿五 火7 Fire Obstruction 2 甲戌 Wood Dog 水山蹇 2	**11** 廿六 木3 Wood Advancement 3 乙亥 Wood Pig 火地晉 3
12 廿七 水6 Water Nourish 4 丙子 Fire Rat 山雷頤 3	**13** 廿八 金4 Metal Following 5 丁丑 Fire Ox 澤雷隨 7	**14** 廿九 木8 Wood Abundance 6 戊寅 Earth Tiger 雷火豐 6	**15** 正月初一 火7 Fire Regulate 7 己卯 Earth Rabbit 水澤節 8	**16** 初二 水1 Water Unity 8 庚辰 Metal Dragon 地天泰 9	**17** 初三 木3 Wood Great Reward 9 辛巳 Metal Snake 火天大有 7	**18** 初四 火2 Fire Wind 1 壬午 Water Horse 巽爲風 1
19 初五 金4 Metal Trap 2 癸未 Water Goat 澤水困 8	**20** 初六 木3 Wood Not Yet Accomplished 3 甲申 Wood Monkey 火水未濟 9	**21** 初七 金9 Metal Retreat 4 乙酉 Wood Rooster 天山遯 4	**22** 初八 水6 Water Mountain 5 丙戌 Fire Dog 艮爲山 1	**23** 初九 木8 Wood Delight 6 丁亥 Fire Pig 雷地豫 8	**24** 初十 火7 Fire Beginning 7 戊子 Earth Rat 水雷屯 4	**25** 十一 金9 Metal Without Wrongdoing 8 己丑 Earth Ox 天雷無妄 2
26 十二 木3 Wood Fire 9 庚寅 Metal Tiger 離爲火 1	**27** 十三 火2 Fire Sincerity 1 辛卯 Metal Rabbit 風澤中孚 3	**28** 十四 水6 Water Big Livestock 2 壬辰 Water Dragon 山天大畜 4				

MARCH 1961 辛卯

Xuan Kong Element 玄空五行	風澤中孚 Sincerity	Period Luck 卦運	Monthly Star 月星
Fire 火2		3	4

SUNDAY	MONDAY	TUESDAY	WEDNESDAY	THURSDAY	FRIDAY	SATURDAY
			金4 Metal · Eliminating · 3 澤天夬 癸巳 Water Snake · 6 1 十五	金9 Metal · Heaven · 4 乾爲天 甲午 Wood Horse · 1 2 十六	火7 Fire · Well · 5 水風井 乙未 Wood Goat · 6 3 十七	木8 Wood · Relief · 6 雷水解 丙申 Fire Monkey · 4 4 十八
金4 Metal · Influence · 7 澤山咸 丁酉 Fire Rooster · 9 5 十九	水1 Water · Humility · 8 地山謙 戊戌 Earth Dog · 6 6 二十	火2 Fire · Observation · 9 風地觀 己亥 Earth Pig · 2 7 廿一	火2 Fire · Increasing · 1 風雷益 庚子 Metal Rat · 9 8 廿二	水1 Water · Dimming Light · 2 地火明夷 辛丑 Metal Ox · 3 9 廿三	金9 Metal · Fellowship · 3 天火同人 壬寅 Water Tiger · 7 10 廿四	木8 Wood · Marrying Maiden · 4 雷澤歸妹 癸卯 Water Rabbit · 7 11 廿五
木3 Wood · Opposition · 5 火澤睽 甲辰 Wood Dragon · 2 12 廿六	火7 Fire · Waiting · 6 水天需 乙巳 Wood Snake · 3 13 廿七	金4 Metal · Great Exceeding · 7 澤風大過 丙午 Fire Horse · 3 14 廿八	水6 Water · Poison · 8 山風蠱 丁未 Fire Goat · 7 15 廿九	火2 Fire · Dispersing · 9 風水渙 戊申 Earth Monkey · 6 16 三十	木3 Wood · Travelling · 1 火山旅 己酉 Earth Rooster · 8 17 二月初一	金9 Metal · Stagnation · 2 天地否 庚戌 Metal Dog · 9 18 初二
火7 Fire · Alliance · 3 水地比 辛亥 Metal Pig · 7 19 初三	木8 Wood · Thunder · 4 震爲雷 壬子 Water Rat · 1 20 初四	水6 Water · Beauty · 5 山火賁 癸丑 Water Ox · 8 21 初五	火7 Fire · Accomplished · 6 水火既濟 甲寅 Wood Tiger · 9 22 初六	水1 Water · Arriving · 7 地澤臨 乙卯 Wood Rabbit · 4 23 初七	金4 Metal · Marsh · 8 兌爲澤 丙辰 Fire Dragon · 1 24 初八	火2 Fire · Small Livestock · 9 風天小畜 丁巳 Fire Snake · 8 25 初九
木3 Wood · The Cauldron · 1 火風鼎 戊午 Earth Horse · 4 26 初十	水1 Water · Rising · 2 地風升 己未 Earth Goat · 2 27 十一	火7 Fire · Water · 3 坎爲水 庚申 Metal Monkey · 1 28 十二	木8 Wood · Lesser Exceeding · 4 雷山小過 辛酉 Metal Rooster · 3 29 十三	金4 Metal · Gathering · 5 澤地萃 壬戌 Water Dog · 4 30 十四	水6 Water · Peel · 6 山地剝 癸亥 Water Pig · 6 31 十五	

APRIL 1961 壬辰

Xuan Kong Element 玄空五行	山天大畜 Big Livestock	Period Luck 卦運	Monthly Star 月星
Water 水6		4	3

SUNDAY	MONDAY	TUESDAY	WEDNESDAY	THURSDAY	FRIDAY	SATURDAY
金4 Metal · Eliminating · 9 澤天夬 癸巳 Water Snake · 6 30 十六						水1 Water · Earth · 7 坤爲地 甲子 Wood Rat · 1 1 十六
木3 Wood · Biting · 8 火雷噬嗑 乙丑 Wood Ox · 6 2 十七	火2 Fire · Family · 9 風火家人 丙寅 Fire Tiger · 4 3 十八	水6 Water · Decreasing · 1 山澤損 丁卯 Fire Rabbit · 9 4 十九	金9 Metal · Tread · 2 天澤履 戊辰 Earth Dragon · 6 5 二十	木8 Wood · Great Strength · 3 雷天大壯 己巳 Earth Snake · 2 6 廿一	木8 Wood · Consistency · 4 雷風恆 庚午 Metal Horse · 9 7 廿二	金9 Metal · Litigation · 5 天水訟 辛未 Metal Goat · 3 8 廿三
水1 Water · Officer · 6 地水師 壬申 Water Monkey · 7 9 廿四	火2 Fire · Gradual Progress · 7 風山漸 癸酉 Water Rooster · 7 10 廿五	火7 Fire · Obstruction · 8 水山蹇 甲戌 Wood Dog · 2 11 廿六	木3 Wood · Advancement · 9 火地晉 乙亥 Wood Pig · 3 12 廿七	水6 Water · Nourish · 1 山雷頤 丙子 Fire Rat · 3 13 廿八	金4 Metal · Following · 2 澤雷隨 丁丑 Fire Ox · 7 14 廿九	木8 Wood · Abundance · 3 雷火豐 戊寅 Earth Tiger · 6 15 三月初一
火7 Fire · Regulate · 4 水澤節 己卯 Earth Rabbit · 8 16 初二	水1 Water · Unity · 5 地天泰 庚辰 Metal Dragon · 9 17 初三	木3 Wood · Great Reward · 6 火天大有 辛巳 Metal Snake · 7 18 初四	火2 Fire · Wind · 7 巽爲風 壬午 Water Horse · 1 19 初五	金4 Metal · Trap · 8 澤水困 癸未 Water Goat · 8 20 初六	木3 Wood · Not Yet Accomplished · 9 火水未濟 甲申 Wood Monkey · 9 21 初七	金9 Metal · Retreat · 1 天山遯 乙酉 Wood Rooster · 4 22 初八
水6 Water · Mountain · 2 艮爲山 丙戌 Fire Dog · 1 23 初九	木8 Wood · Delight · 3 雷地豫 丁亥 Fire Pig · 8 24 初十	火7 Fire · Beginning · 4 水雷屯 戊子 Earth Rat · 4 25 十一	金9 Metal · Without Wrongdoing · 5 天雷無妄 己丑 Earth Ox · 2 26 十二	木3 Wood · Fire · 6 離爲火 庚寅 Metal Tiger · 1 27 十三	火2 Fire · Sincerity · 7 風澤中孚 辛卯 Metal Rabbit · 3 28 十四	水6 Water · Big Livestock · 8 山天大畜 壬辰 Water Dragon · 4 29 十五

MAY 1961 癸巳

Xuan Kong Element 玄空五行	澤天夬 Eliminating	Period Luck 卦運	Monthly Star 月星
Metal 金4		6	2

SUNDAY	MONDAY	TUESDAY	WEDNESDAY	THURSDAY	FRIDAY	SATURDAY
	金9 Metal · Heaven · 1 甲午 Wood Horse · 乾爲天 **1** 十七 1	火7 Fire · Well · 2 乙未 Wood Goat · 水風井 **2** 十八 6	木8 Wood · Relief · 3 丙申 Fire Monkey · 雷水解 **3** 十九 4	金4 Metal · Influence · 4 丁酉 Fire Rooster · 澤山咸 **4** 二十 9	水1 Water · Humility · 5 戊戌 Earth Dog · 地山謙 **5** 廿一 6	火2 Fire · Observation · 6 己亥 Earth Pig · 風地觀 **6** 廿二 2
火2 Fire · Increasing · 7 庚子 Metal Rat · 風雷益 **7** 廿三 9	水1 Water · Dimming Light · 8 辛丑 Metal Ox · 地火明夷 **8** 廿四 3	金9 Metal · Fellowship · 9 壬寅 Water Tiger · 天火同人 **9** 廿五 7	木8 Wood · Marrying Maiden · 1 癸卯 Water Rabbit · 雷澤歸妹 **10** 廿六 7	木3 Wood · Opposition · 2 甲辰 Wood Dragon · 火澤睽 **11** 廿七 2	火7 Fire · Waiting · 3 乙巳 Wood Snake · 水天需 **12** 廿八 3	金4 Metal · Great Exceeding · 4 丙午 Fire Horse · 澤風大過 **13** 廿九 3
水6 Water · Poison · 5 丁未 Fire Goat · 山風蠱 **14** 三十 7	火2 Fire · Dispersing · 6 戊申 Earth Monkey · 風水渙 **15** 四月初一 6	木3 Wood · Travelling · 7 己酉 Earth Rooster · 火山旅 **16** 初二 8	金9 Metal · Stagnation · 8 庚戌 Metal Dog · 天地否 **17** 初三 9	火7 Fire · Alliance · 9 辛亥 Metal Pig · 水地比 **18** 初四 7	木8 Wood · Thunder · 1 壬子 Water Rat · 震爲雷 **19** 初五 1	水6 Water · Beauty · 2 癸丑 Water Ox · 山火賁 **20** 初六 8
火7 Fire · Accomplished · 3 甲寅 Wood Tiger · 水火既濟 **21** 初七 9	水1 Water · Arriving · 4 乙卯 Wood Rabbit · 地澤臨 **22** 初八 4	金4 Metal · Marsh · 5 丙辰 Fire Dragon · 兌爲澤 **23** 初九 1	火2 Fire · Small Livestock · 6 丁巳 Fire Snake · 風天小畜 **24** 初十 8	木3 Wood · The Cauldron · 7 戊午 Earth Horse · 火風鼎 **25** 十一 4	水1 Water · Rising · 8 己未 Earth Goat · 地風升 **26** 十二 2	火7 Fire · Water · 9 庚申 Metal Monkey · 坎爲水 **27** 十三 1
木8 Wood · Lesser Exceeding · 1 辛酉 Metal Rooster · 雷山小過 **28** 十四 3	金4 Metal · Gathering · 2 壬戌 Water Dog · 澤地萃 **29** 十五 4	水6 Water · Peel · 3 癸亥 Water Pig · 山地剝 **30** 十六 6	水1 Water · Earth · 4 甲子 Wood Rat · 坤爲地 **31** 十七 1			

JUNE 1961 甲午

Xuan Kong Element 玄空五行	乾爲天 Heaven	Period Luck 卦運	Monthly Star 月星
Metal 金9		1	1

SUNDAY	MONDAY	TUESDAY	WEDNESDAY	THURSDAY	FRIDAY	SATURDAY
				木3 Wood · Biting · 5 乙丑 Wood Ox · 火雷噬嗑 **1** 十八 6	火2 Fire · Family · 6 丙寅 Fire Tiger · 風火家人 **2** 十九 4	水6 Water · Decreasing · 7 丁卯 Fire Rabbit · 山澤損 **3** 二十 9
金9 Metal · Tread · 8 戊辰 Earth Dragon · 天澤履 **4** 廿一 6	木8 Wood · Great Strength · 9 己巳 Earth Snake · 雷天大壯 **5** 廿二 2	木8 Wood · Consistency · 1 庚午 Metal Horse · 雷風恆 **6** 廿三 9	金9 Metal · Litigation · 2 辛未 Metal Goat · 天水訟 **7** 廿四 3	水1 Water · Officer · 3 壬申 Water Monkey · 地水師 **8** 廿五 7	火2 Fire · Gradual Progress · 4 癸酉 Water Rooster · 風山漸 **9** 廿六 7	火7 Fire · Obstruction · 5 甲戌 Wood Dog · 水山蹇 **10** 廿七 2
木3 Wood · Advancement · 6 乙亥 Wood Pig · 火地晉 **11** 廿八 3	水6 Water · Nourish · 7 丙子 Fire Rat · 山雷頤 **12** 廿九 3	金4 Metal · Following · 8 丁丑 Fire Ox · 澤雷隨 **13** 五月初一 7	木8 Wood · Abundance · 9 戊寅 Earth Tiger · 雷火豐 **14** 初二 6	火7 Fire · Regulate · 1 己卯 Earth Rabbit · 水澤節 **15** 初三 8	水1 Water · Unity · 2 庚辰 Metal Dragon · 地天泰 **16** 初四 9	木3 Wood · Great Reward · 3 辛巳 Metal Snake · 火天大有 **17** 初五 7
火2 Fire · Wind · 4 壬午 Water Horse · 巽爲風 **18** 初六 1	金4 Metal · Trap · 5 癸未 Water Goat · 澤水困 **19** 初七 8	木3 Wood · Not Yet Accomplished · 6 甲申 Wood Monkey · 火水未濟 **20** 初八 9	金9 Metal · Retreat · 7/3 乙酉 Wood Rooster · 天山遯 **21** 初九 4	水6 Water · Mountain · 2 丙戌 Fire Dog · 艮爲山 **22** 初十 1	木8 Wood · Delight · 1 丁亥 Fire Pig · 雷地豫 **23** 十一 8	火7 Fire · Beginning · 9 戊子 Earth Rat · 水雷屯 **24** 十二 4
金9 Metal · Without Wrongdoing · 8 己丑 Earth Ox · 天雷無妄 **25** 十三 2	木3 Wood · Fire · 7 庚寅 Metal Tiger · 離爲火 **26** 十四 1	火2 Fire · Sincerity · 6 辛卯 Metal Rabbit · 風澤中孚 **27** 十五 3	水6 Water · Big Livestock · 5 壬辰 Water Dragon · 山天大畜 **28** 十六 4	金4 Metal · Eliminating · 4 癸巳 Water Snake · 澤天夬 **29** 十七 6	金9 Metal · Heaven · 3 甲午 Wood Horse · 乾爲天 **30** 十八 1	

JULY 1961 乙未

Xuan Kong Element 玄空五行	水風井 Well	Period Luck 卦運	Monthly Star 月星
Fire 火7		6	9

SUNDAY	MONDAY	TUESDAY	WEDNESDAY	THURSDAY	FRIDAY	SATURDAY
水1 Water 9 Earth 坤爲地 甲子 Wood Rat 30 十八 1	木3 Wood 8 Biting 火雷噬嗑 乙丑 Wood Ox 31 十九 6					火7 Fire 2 Well 水風井 乙未 Wood Goat 1 十九 6
木8 Wood 1 Relief 雷水解 丙申 Fire Monkey 2 二十 4	金4 Metal 9 Influence 澤山咸 丁酉 Fire Rooster 3 廿一 9	水1 Water 8 Humility 地山謙 戊戌 Earth Dog 4 廿二 6	火2 Fire 7 Observation 風地觀 己亥 Earth Pig 5 廿三 2	火2 Fire 6 Increasing 風雷益 庚子 Metal Rat 6 廿四 9	水1 Water 5 Dimming Light 地火明夷 辛丑 Metal Ox 7 廿五 3	金9 Metal 4 Fellowship 天火同人 壬寅 Water Tiger 8 廿六 7
木8 Wood 3 Marrying Maiden 雷澤歸妹 癸卯 Water Rabbit 9 廿七 7	木3 Wood 2 Opposition 火澤睽 甲辰 Wood Dragon 10 廿八 2	火7 Fire 1 Waiting 水天需 乙巳 Wood Snake 11 廿九 3	金4 Metal 9 Great Exceeding 澤風大過 丙午 Fire Horse 12 三十 3	水6 Water 8 Poison 山風蠱 丁未 Fire Goat 13 六月初一 7	火2 Fire 7 Dispersing 風水渙 戊申 Earth Monkey 14 初二 6	木3 Wood 6 Travelling 火山旅 己酉 Earth Rooster 15 初三 8
金9 Metal 5 Stagnation 天地否 庚戌 Metal Dog 16 初四 9	火7 Fire 4 Alliance 水地比 辛亥 Metal Pig 17 初五 7	木8 Wood 3 Thunder 震爲雷 壬子 Water Rat 18 初六 1	水6 Water 2 Beauty 山火賁 癸丑 Water Ox 19 初七 8	火7 Fire 1 Accomplished 水火既濟 甲寅 Wood Tiger 20 初八 9	水1 Water 9 Arriving 地澤臨 乙卯 Wood Rabbit 21 初九 4	金4 Metal 8 Marsh 兑爲澤 丙辰 Fire Dragon 22 初十 1
火2 Fire 7 Small Livestock 風天小畜 丁巳 Fire Snake 23 十一 8	木3 Wood 6 The Cauldron 火風鼎 戊午 Earth Horse 24 十二 4	水1 Water 5 Rising 地風升 己未 Earth Goat 25 十三 2	火7 Fire 4 Water 坎爲水 庚申 Metal Monkey 26 十四 1	木8 Wood 3 Lesser Exceeding 雷山小過 辛酉 Metal Rooster 27 十五 3	金4 Metal 2 Gathering 澤地萃 壬戌 Water Dog 28 十六 4	水6 Water 1 Peel 山地剝 癸亥 Water Pig 29 十七 6

AUGUST 1961 丙申

Xuan Kong Element 玄空五行	雷水解 Relief	Period Luck 卦運	Monthly Star 月星
Wood 木8		4	8

SUNDAY	MONDAY	TUESDAY	WEDNESDAY	THURSDAY	FRIDAY	SATURDAY
		火2 Fire 7 Family 風火家人 丙寅 Fire Tiger 1 二十 4	水6 Water 6 Decreasing 山澤損 丁卯 Fire Rabbit 2 廿一 9	金9 Metal 5 Tread 天澤履 戊辰 Earth Dragon 3 廿二 6	木8 Wood 4 Great Strength 雷天大壯 己巳 Earth Snake 4 廿三 2	木8 Wood 3 Consistency 雷風恆 庚午 Metal Horse 5 廿四 9
金9 Metal 2 Litigation 天水訟 辛未 Metal Goat 6 廿五 3	水1 Water 1 Officer 地水師 壬申 Water Monkey 7 廿六 7	火2 Fire 9 Gradual Progress 風山漸 癸酉 Water Rooster 8 廿七 7	火7 Fire 8 Obstruction 水山蹇 甲戌 Wood Dog 9 廿八 2	木3 Wood 7 Advancement 火地晉 乙亥 Wood Pig 10 廿九 3	水6 Water 6 Nourish 山雷頤 丙子 Fire Rat 11 七月初一 3	金4 Metal 5 Following 澤雷隨 丁丑 Fire Ox 12 初二 7
木8 Wood 4 Abundance 雷火豐 戊寅 Earth Tiger 13 初三 6	火7 Fire 3 Regulate 水澤節 己卯 Earth Rabbit 14 初四 8	水1 Water 2 Unity 地天泰 庚辰 Metal Dragon 15 初五 9	木3 Wood 1 Great Reward 火天大有 辛巳 Metal Snake 16 初六 7	火2 Fire 9 Wind 巽爲風 壬午 Water Horse 17 初七 1	金4 Metal 8 Trap 澤水困 癸未 Water Goat 18 初八 8	木3 Wood 7 Not Yet Accomplished 火水未濟 甲申 Wood Monkey 19 初九 9
金9 Metal 6 Retreat 天山遯 乙酉 Wood Rooster 20 初十 4	水6 Water 5 Mountain 艮爲山 丙戌 Fire Dog 21 十一 1	木8 Wood 4 Delight 雷地豫 丁亥 Fire Pig 22 十二 8	火7 Fire 3 Beginning 水雷屯 戊子 Earth Rat 23 十三 4	金9 Metal 2 Without Wrongdoing 天雷無妄 己丑 Earth Ox 24 十四 2	木3 Wood 1 Fire 離爲火 庚寅 Metal Tiger 25 十五 1	火2 Fire 9 Sincerity 風澤中孚 辛卯 Metal Rabbit 26 十六 3
水6 Water 8 Big Livestock 山天大畜 壬辰 Water Dragon 27 十七 4	金4 Metal 7 Eliminating 澤天夬 癸巳 Water Snake 28 十八 6	金9 Metal 6 Heaven 乾爲天 甲午 Wood Horse 29 十九 1	火7 Fire 5 Well 水風井 乙未 Wood Goat 30 二十 6	木8 Wood 4 Relief 雷水解 丙申 Fire Monkey 31 廿一 4		

SEPTEMBER 1961 丁酉

Xuan Kong Element 玄空五行	澤山咸 Influence	Period Luck 卦運	Monthly Star 月星
Metal 金4		9	7

SUNDAY	MONDAY	TUESDAY	WEDNESDAY	THURSDAY	FRIDAY	SATURDAY
					金4 Metal Influence 3 丁酉 Fire Rooster 澤山咸 1 廿二 9	水1 Water Humility 2 戊戌 Earth Dog 地山謙 2 廿三 6
火2 Fire Observation 1 己亥 Earth Pig 風地觀 3 廿四 2	火2 Fire Increasing 9 庚子 Metal Rat 風雷益 4 廿五 9	水1 Water Dimming Light 8 辛丑 Metal Ox 地火明夷 5 廿六 3	金9 Metal Fellowship 7 壬寅 Water Tiger 天火同人 6 廿七 7	木8 Wood Marrying Maiden 6 癸卯 Water Rabbit 雷澤歸妹 7 廿八 7	木3 Wood Opposition 5 甲辰 Wood Dragon 火澤睽 8 廿九 2	火7 Fire Waiting 4 乙巳 Wood Snake 水天需 9 三十 3
金4 Metal Great Exceeding 3 丙午 Fire Horse 澤風大過 10 八月初一 3	水6 Water Poison 2 丁未 Fire Goat 山風蠱 11 初二 7	火2 Fire Dispersing 1 戊申 Earth Monkey 風水渙 12 初三 6	木3 Wood Travelling 9 己酉 Earth Rooster 火山旅 13 初四 8	金9 Metal Stagnation 8 庚戌 Metal Dog 天地否 14 初五 9	火7 Fire Alliance 7 辛亥 Metal Pig 水地比 15 初六 7	木8 Wood Thunder 6 壬子 Water Rat 震爲雷 16 初七 1
水6 Water Beauty 5 癸丑 Water Ox 山火賁 17 初八 8	火7 Fire Accomplished 4 甲寅 Wood Tiger 水火既濟 18 初九 9	水1 Water Arriving 3 乙卯 Wood Rabbit 地澤臨 19 初十 4	金4 Metal Marsh 2 丙辰 Fire Dragon 兑爲澤 20 十一 1	火2 Fire Small Livestock 1 丁巳 Fire Snake 風天小畜 21 十二 8	木3 Wood The Cauldron 9 戊午 Earth Horse 火風鼎 22 十三 4	水1 Water Rising 8 己未 Earth Goat 地風升 23 十四 2
火7 Fire Water 7 庚申 Metal Monkey 坎爲水 24 十五 1	木8 Wood Lesser Exceeding 6 辛酉 Metal Rooster 雷山小過 25 十六 3	金4 Metal Gathering 5 壬戌 Water Dog 澤地萃 26 十七 4	水6 Water Peel 4 癸亥 Water Pig 山地剝 27 十八 6	水1 Water Earth 3 甲子 Wood Rat 坤爲地 28 十九 1	木3 Wood Biting 2 乙丑 Wood Ox 火雷噬嗑 29 二十 6	火2 Fire Family 1 丙寅 Fire Tiger 風火家人 30 廿一 4

OCTOBER 1961 戊戌

Xuan Kong Element 玄空五行	地山謙 Humility	Period Luck 卦運	Monthly Star 月星
Water 水1		6	6

SUNDAY	MONDAY	TUESDAY	WEDNESDAY	THURSDAY	FRIDAY	SATURDAY
水6 Water Decreasing 9 丁卯 Fire Rabbit 山澤損 1 廿二 9	金9 Metal Tread 8 戊辰 Earth Dragon 天澤履 2 廿三 6	木8 Wood Great Strength 7 己巳 Earth Snake 雷天大壯 3 廿四 2	木8 Wood Consistency 6 庚午 Metal Horse 雷風恆 4 廿五 9	金9 Metal Litigation 5 辛未 Metal Goat 天水訟 5 廿六 3	水1 Water Officer 4 壬申 Water Monkey 地水師 6 廿七 7	火2 Fire Gradual Progress 3 癸酉 Water Rooster 風山漸 7 廿八 7
火7 Fire Obstruction 2 甲戌 Wood Dog 水山蹇 8 廿九 2	木3 Wood Advancement 1 乙亥 Wood Pig 火地晉 9 三十 3	水6 Water Nourish 9 丙子 Fire Rat 山雷頤 10 九月初一 3	金4 Metal Following 8 丁丑 Fire Ox 澤雷隨 11 初二 7	木8 Wood Abundance 7 戊寅 Earth Tiger 雷火豐 12 初三 6	火7 Fire Regulate 6 己卯 Earth Rabbit 水澤節 13 初四 8	水1 Water Unity 5 庚辰 Metal Dragon 地天泰 14 初五 9
木3 Wood Great Reward 4 辛巳 Metal Snake 火天大有 15 初六 7	火2 Fire Wind 3 壬午 Water Horse 巽爲風 16 初七 1	金4 Metal Trap 2 癸未 Water Goat 澤水困 17 初八 8	木3 Wood Not Yet Accomplished 1 甲申 Wood Monkey 火水未濟 18 初九 9	金9 Metal Retreat 9 乙酉 Wood Rooster 天山遯 19 初十 4	水6 Water Mountain 8 丙戌 Fire Dog 艮爲山 20 十一 1	木8 Wood Delight 7 丁亥 Fire Pig 雷地豫 21 十二 8
火7 Fire Beginning 6 戊子 Earth Rat 水雷屯 22 十三 4	金9 Metal Without Wrongdoing 5 己丑 Earth Ox 天雷無妄 23 十四 2	木3 Wood Fire 4 庚寅 Metal Tiger 離爲火 24 十五 1	火2 Fire Sincerity 3 辛卯 Metal Rabbit 風澤中孚 25 十六 3	水6 Water Big Livestock 2 壬辰 Water Dragon 山天大畜 26 十七 4	金4 Metal Eliminating 1 癸巳 Water Snake 澤天夬 27 十八 6	金9 Metal Heaven 9 甲午 Wood Horse 乾爲天 28 十九 1
火7 Fire Well 8 乙未 Wood Goat 水風井 29 二十 6	木8 Wood Relief 7 丙申 Fire Monkey 雷水解 30 廿一 4	金4 Metal Influence 6 丁酉 Fire Rooster 澤山咸 31 廿二 9				

NOVEMBER 1961 己亥

Xuan Kong Element 玄空五行	風地觀 Observation	Period Luck 卦運	Monthly Star 月星
Fire 火2		2	5

SUNDAY	MONDAY	TUESDAY	WEDNESDAY	THURSDAY	FRIDAY	SATURDAY
			水1 Water 5 Humility 地山謙 戊戌 Earth Dog 1 廿三 6	火2 Fire 4 Observation 風地觀 己亥 Earth Pig 2 廿四 2	火2 Fire 3 Increasing 風雷益 庚子 Metal Rat 3 廿五 9	水1 Water 2 Dimming Light 地火明夷 辛丑 Metal Ox 4 廿六 3
金9 Metal 1 Fellowship 天火同人 壬寅 Water Tiger 5 廿七 7	木8 Wood 9 Marrying Maiden 雷澤歸妹 癸卯 Water Rabbit 6 廿八 7	木3 Wood 8 Opposition 火澤睽 甲辰 Wood Dragon 7 廿九 2	火7 Fire 7 Waiting 水天需 乙巳 Wood Snake 8 十月初一 3	金4 Metal 6 Great Exceeding 澤風大過 丙午 Fire Horse 9 初二 3	水6 Water 5 Poison 山風蠱 丁未 Fire Goat 10 初三 7	火2 Fire 4 Dispersing 風水渙 戊申 Earth Monkey 11 初四 6
木3 Wood 3 Travelling 火山旅 己酉 Earth Rooster 12 初五 8	金9 Metal 2 Stagnation 天地否 庚戌 Metal Dog 13 初六 9	火7 Fire 1 Alliance 水地比 辛亥 Metal Pig 14 初七 7	木8 Wood 9 Thunder 震爲雷 壬子 Water Rat 15 初八 1	水6 Water 8 Beauty 山火賁 癸丑 Water Ox 16 初九 8	火7 Fire 7 Accomplished 水火既濟 甲寅 Wood Tiger 17 初十 9	水1 Water 6 Arriving 地澤臨 乙卯 Wood Rabbit 18 十一 4
金4 Metal 5 Marsh 兑爲澤 丙辰 Fire Dragon 19 十二 1	火2 Fire 4 Small Livestock 風天小畜 丁巳 Fire Snake 20 十三 8	木3 Wood 3 The Cauldron 火風鼎 戊午 Earth Horse 21 十四 4	水1 Water 2 Rising 地風升 己未 Earth Goat 22 十五 2	火7 Fire 1 Water 坎爲水 庚申 Metal Monkey 23 十六 1	木8 Wood 9 Lesser Exceeding 雷山小過 辛酉 Metal Rooster 24 十七 3	金4 Metal 8 Gathering 澤地萃 壬戌 Water Dog 25 十八 4
水6 Water 7 Peel 山地剝 癸亥 Water Pig 26 十九 6	水1 Water 6 Earth 坤爲地 甲子 Wood Rat 27 二十 1	木3 Wood 5 Biting 火雷噬嗑 乙丑 Wood Ox 28 廿一 6	火2 Fire 4 Family 風火家人 丙寅 Fire Tiger 29 廿二 4	水6 Water 3 Decreasing 山澤損 丁卯 Fire Rabbit 30 廿三 9		

DECEMBER 1961 庚子

Xuan Kong Element 玄空五行	風雷益 Increasing	Period Luck 卦運	Monthly Star 月星
Fire 火2		9	4

SUNDAY	MONDAY	TUESDAY	WEDNESDAY	THURSDAY	FRIDAY	SATURDAY
水1 Water 2 Humility 地山謙 戊戌 Earth Dog 31 廿四 6					金9 Metal 2 Tread 天澤履 戊辰 Earth Dragon 1 廿四 6	木8 Wood 1 Great Strength 雷天大壯 己巳 Earth Snake 2 廿五 2
木8 Wood 9 Consistency 雷風恆 庚午 Metal Horse 3 廿六 9	金9 Metal 8 Litigation 天水訟 辛未 Metal Goat 4 廿七 3	水1 Water 7 Officer 地水師 壬申 Water Monkey 5 廿八 7	火2 Fire 6 Gradual Progress 風山漸 癸酉 Water Rooster 6 廿九 7	火7 Fire 5 Obstruction 水山蹇 甲戌 Wood Dog 7 三十 2	木3 Wood 4 Advancement 火地晉 乙亥 Wood Pig 8 十一月初一 3	水6 Water 3 Nourish 山雷頤 丙子 Fire Rat 9 初二 3
金4 Metal 2 Following 澤雷隨 丁丑 Fire Ox 10 初三 7	木8 Wood 1 Abundance 雷火豐 戊寅 Earth Tiger 11 初四 6	火7 Fire 9 Regulate 水澤節 己卯 Earth Rabbit 12 初五 8	水1 Water 8 Unity 地天泰 庚辰 Metal Dragon 13 初六 9	木3 Wood 7 Great Reward 火天大有 辛巳 Metal Snake 14 初七 7	火2 Fire 6 Wind 巽爲風 壬午 Water Horse 15 初八 1	金4 Metal 5 Trap 澤水困 癸未 Water Goat 16 初九 8
木3 Wood 4 Not Yet Accomplished 火水未濟 甲申 Wood Monkey 17 初十 9	金9 Metal 3 Retreat 天山遯 乙酉 Wood Rooster 18 十一 4	水6 Water 2 Mountain 艮爲山 丙戌 Fire Dog 19 十二 1	木8 Wood 1 Delight 雷地豫 丁亥 Fire Pig 20 十三 8	火7 Fire 9 Beginning 水雷屯 戊子 Earth Rat 21 十四 4	金9 Metal 8/2 Without Wrongdoing 天雷無妄 己丑 Earth Ox 22 十五 2	木3 Wood 3 Fire 離爲火 庚寅 Metal Tiger 23 十六 1
火2 Fire 4 Sincerity 風澤中孚 辛卯 Metal Rabbit 24 十七 3	水6 Water 5 Big Livestock 山天大畜 壬辰 Water Dragon 25 十八 4	金4 Metal 6 Eliminating 澤天夬 癸巳 Water Snake 26 十九 6	金9 Metal 7 Heaven 乾爲天 甲午 Wood Horse 27 二十 1	火7 Fire 8 Well 水風井 乙未 Wood Goat 28 廿一 6	木8 Wood 9 Relief 雷水解 丙申 Fire Monkey 29 廿二 4	金4 Metal 1 Influence 澤山咸 丁酉 Fire Rooster 30 廿三 9

1962 壬寅

(*Ren Yin*) Water Tiger

1962 壬寅 *(Ren Yin)* Water Tiger

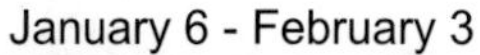

January 6 - February 3

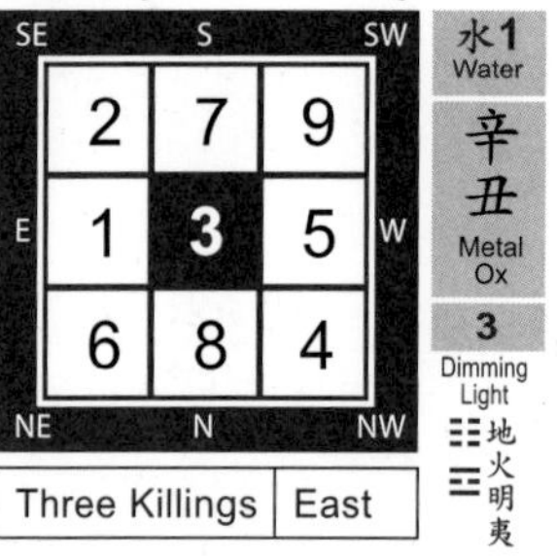

February 4 - March 5

金**9** Metal
壬寅 Water Tiger
7 Fellowship
天火同人

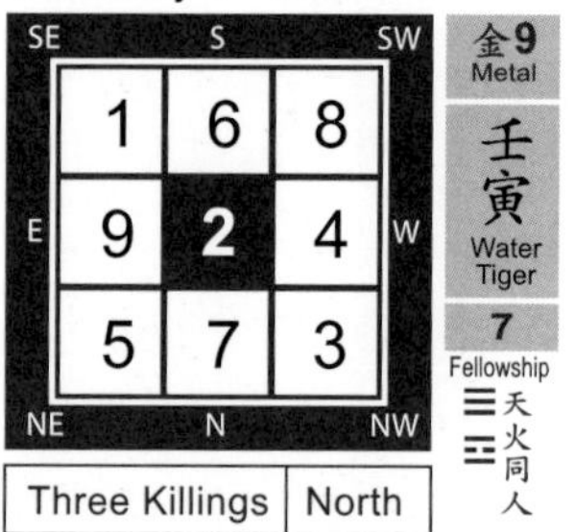

March 6 - April 4

木**8** Wood
癸卯 Water Rabbit
7 Marrying Maiden
雷澤歸妹

April 5 - May 5

木**3** Wood
甲辰 Wood Dragon
2 Opposition
火澤睽

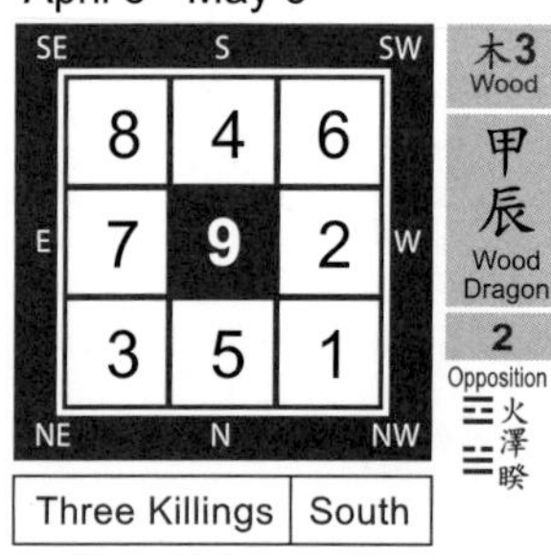

May 6 - June 5

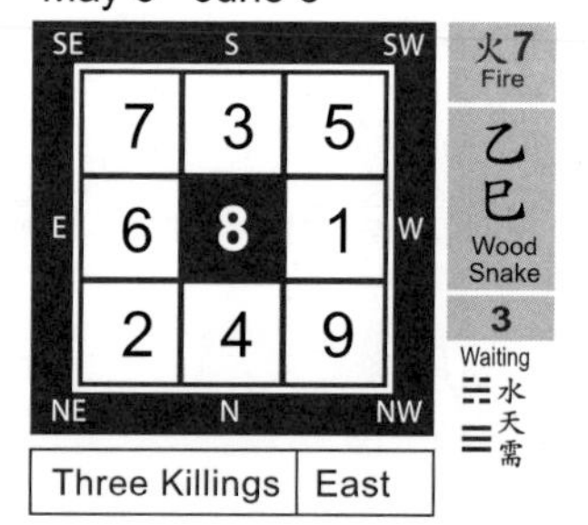

火**7** Fire
乙巳 Wood Snake
3 Waiting
水天需

June 6 - July 6

金**4** Metal
丙午 Fire Horse
3 Great Exceeding
澤風大過

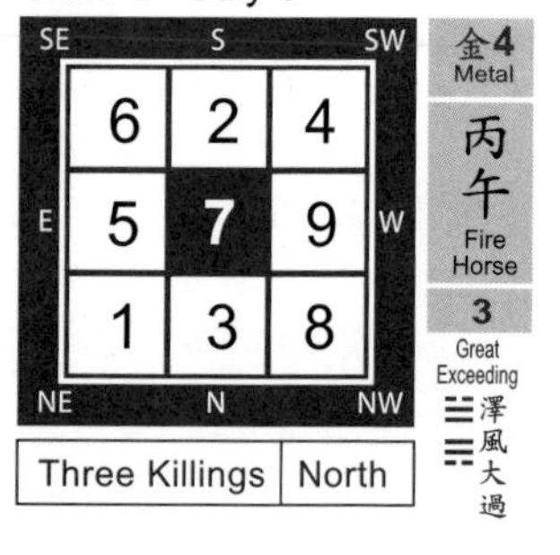

July 7 - August 7

水**6** Water
丁未 Fire Goat
7 Poison
山風蠱

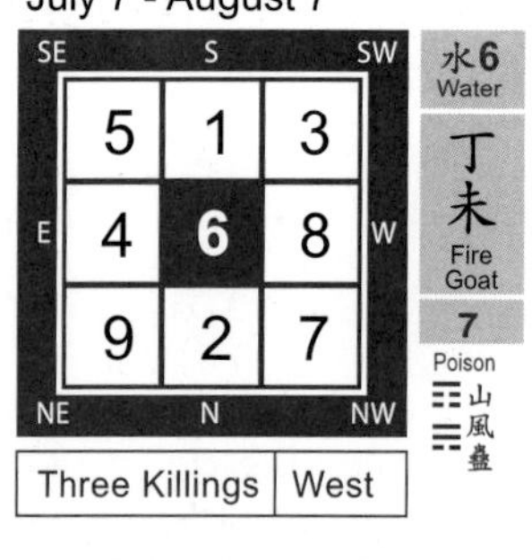

August 8 - September 7

火**2** Fire
戊申 Earth Monkey
6 Dispersing
風水渙

September 8 - October 8

木**3** Wood
己酉 Earth Rooster
8 Travelling
火山旅

October 9 - November 7

金**9** Metal
庚戌 Metal Dog
9 Stagnation
天地否

November 8 - December 6

December 7 - January 5

木**8** Wood
壬子 Water Rat
1 Thunder
震為雷

JANUARY 1962 辛丑

Xuan Kong Element 玄空五行	地火明夷 Dimming Light	Period Luck 卦運	Monthly Star 月星
Water 水1		3	3

SUNDAY	MONDAY	TUESDAY	WEDNESDAY	THURSDAY	FRIDAY	SATURDAY
	火2 Fire [3] Observation 風地觀 己亥 Earth Pig **1** 廿五 2	火2 Fire [4] Increasing 風雷益 庚子 Metal Rat **2** 廿六 9	水1 Water [5] Dimming Light 地火明夷 辛丑 Metal Ox **3** 廿七 3	金9 Metal [6] Fellowship 天火同人 壬寅 Water Tiger **4** 廿八 7	木8 Wood [7] Marrying Maiden 雷澤歸妹 癸卯 Water Rabbit **5** 廿九 7	木3 Wood [8] Opposition 火澤睽 甲辰 Wood Dragon **6** 十二月初一 2
火7 Fire [9] Waiting 水天需 乙巳 Wood Snake **7** 初二 3	金4 Metal [1] Great Exceeding 澤風大過 丙午 Fire Horse **8** 初三 3	水6 Water [2] Poison 山風蠱 丁未 Fire Goat **9** 初四 7	火2 Fire [3] Dispersing 風水渙 戊申 Earth Monkey **10** 初五 6	木3 Wood [4] Travelling 火山旅 己酉 Earth Rooster **11** 初六 8	金9 Metal [5] Stagnation 天地否 庚戌 Metal Dog **12** 初七 9	火7 Fire [6] Alliance 水地比 辛亥 Metal Pig **13** 初八 7
木8 Wood [7] Thunder 震爲雷 壬子 Water Rat **14** 初九 1	水6 Water [8] Beauty 山火賁 癸丑 Water Ox **15** 初十 8	火7 Fire [9] Accomplished 水火既濟 甲寅 Wood Tiger **16** 十一 9	水1 Water [1] Arriving 地澤臨 乙卯 Wood Rabbit **17** 十二 4	金4 Metal [2] Marsh 兑爲澤 丙辰 Fire Dragon **18** 十三 1	火2 Fire [3] Small Livestock 風天小畜 丁巳 Fire Snake **19** 十四 8	木3 Wood [4] The Cauldron 火風鼎 戊午 Earth Horse **20** 十五 4
水1 Water [5] Rising 地風升 己未 Earth Goat **21** 十六 2	火7 Fire [6] Water 坎爲水 庚申 Metal Monkey **22** 十七 1	木8 Wood [7] Lesser Exceeding 雷山小過 辛酉 Metal Rooster **23** 十八 3	金4 Metal [8] Gathering 澤地萃 壬戌 Water Dog **24** 十九 4	水6 Water [9] Peel 山地剝 癸亥 Water Pig **25** 二十 6	水1 Water [1] Earth 坤爲地 甲子 Wood Rat **26** 廿一 1	木3 Wood [2] Biting 火雷噬嗑 乙丑 Wood Ox **27** 廿二 6
火2 Fire [3] Family 風火家人 丙寅 Fire Tiger **28** 廿三 4	水6 Water [4] Decreasing 山澤損 丁卯 Fire Rabbit **29** 廿四 9	金9 Metal [5] Tread 天澤履 戊辰 Earth Dragon **30** 廿五 6	木8 Wood [6] Great Strength 雷天大壯 己巳 Earth Snake **31** 廿六 2			

FEBRUARY 1962 壬寅

Xuan Kong Element 玄空五行	天火同人 Fellowship	Period Luck 卦運	Monthly Star 月星
Metal 金9		7	2

SUNDAY	MONDAY	TUESDAY	WEDNESDAY	THURSDAY	FRIDAY	SATURDAY
				木8 Wood [7] Consistency 雷風恆 庚午 Metal Horse **1** 廿七 9	金9 Metal [8] Litigation 天水訟 辛未 Metal Goat **2** 廿八 3	水1 Water [9] Officer 地水師 壬申 Water Monkey **3** 廿九 7
火2 Fire [1] Gradual Progress 風山漸 癸酉 Water Rooster **4** 三十 7	火7 Fire [2] Obstruction 水山蹇 甲戌 Wood Dog **5** 正月初一 2	木3 Wood [3] Advancement 火地晉 乙亥 Wood Pig **6** 初二 3	水6 Water [4] Nourish 山雷頤 丙子 Fire Rat **7** 初三 3	金4 Metal [5] Following 澤雷隨 丁丑 Fire Ox **8** 初四 7	木8 Wood [6] Abundance 雷火豐 戊寅 Earth Tiger **9** 初五 6	火7 Fire [7] Regulate 水澤節 己卯 Earth Rabbit **10** 初六 8
水1 Water [8] Unity 地天泰 庚辰 Metal Dragon **11** 初七 9	木3 Wood [9] Great Reward 火天大有 辛巳 Metal Snake **12** 初八 7	火2 Fire [1] Wind 巽爲風 壬午 Water Horse **13** 初九 1	金4 Metal [2] Trap 澤水困 癸未 Water Goat **14** 初十 8	木3 Wood [3] Not Yet Accomplished 火水未濟 甲申 Wood Monkey **15** 十一 9	金9 Metal [4] Retreat 天山遯 乙酉 Wood Rooster **16** 十二 4	水6 Water [5] Mountain 艮爲山 丙戌 Fire Dog **17** 十三 1
木8 Wood [6] Delight 雷地豫 丁亥 Fire Pig **18** 十四 8	火7 Fire [7] Beginning 水雷屯 戊子 Earth Rat **19** 十五 4	金9 Metal [8] Without Wrongdoing 天雷無妄 己丑 Earth Ox **20** 十六 2	木3 Wood [9] Fire 離爲火 庚寅 Metal Tiger **21** 十七 1	火2 Fire [1] Sincerity 風澤中孚 辛卯 Metal Rabbit **22** 十八 3	水6 Water [2] Big Livestock 山天大畜 壬辰 Water Dragon **23** 十九 4	金4 Metal [3] Eliminating 澤天夬 癸巳 Water Snake **24** 二十 6
金9 Metal [4] Heaven 乾爲天 甲午 Wood Horse **25** 廿一 1	火7 Fire [5] Well 水風井 乙未 Wood Goat **26** 廿二 6	木8 Wood [6] Relief 雷水解 丙申 Fire Monkey **27** 廿三 4	金4 Metal [7] Influence 澤山咸 丁酉 Fire Rooster **28** 廿四 9			

MARCH 1962 癸卯

Xuan Kong Element 玄空五行	雷澤歸妹 Marrying Maiden	Period Luck 卦運	Monthly Star 月星
Wood 木8		7	1

SUNDAY	MONDAY	TUESDAY	WEDNESDAY	THURSDAY	FRIDAY	SATURDAY
				水1 Water 8 Humility 地山謙 1 戊戌 Earth Dog 6 廿五	火2 Fire 9 Observation 風地觀 2 己亥 Earth Pig 2 廿六	火2 Fire 1 Increasing 風雷益 3 庚子 Metal Rat 9 廿七
水1 Water 2 Dimming Light 地火明夷 4 辛丑 Metal Ox 3 廿八	金9 Metal 3 Fellowship 天火同人 5 壬寅 Water Tiger 7 廿九	木8 Wood 4 Marrying Maiden 雷澤歸妹 6 癸卯 Water Rabbit 7 二月初一	木3 Wood 5 Opposition 火澤睽 7 甲辰 Wood Dragon 2 初二	火7 Fire 6 Waiting 水天需 8 乙巳 Wood Snake 3 初三	金4 Metal 7 Great Exceeding 澤風大過 9 丙午 Fire Horse 3 初四	水6 Water 8 Poison 山風蠱 10 丁未 Fire Goat 7 初五
火2 Fire 9 Dispersing 風水渙 11 戊申 Earth Monkey 6 初六	木3 Wood 1 Travelling 火山旅 12 己酉 Earth Rooster 8 初七	金9 Metal 2 Stagnation 天地否 13 庚戌 Metal Dog 9 初八	火7 Fire 3 Alliance 水地比 14 辛亥 Metal Pig 7 初九	木8 Wood 4 Thunder 震爲雷 15 壬子 Water Rat 1 初十	水6 Water 5 Beauty 山火賁 16 癸丑 Water Ox 8 十一	火7 Fire 6 Accomplished 水火既濟 17 甲寅 Wood Tiger 9 十二
水1 Water 7 Arriving 地澤臨 18 乙卯 Wood Rabbit 4 十三	金4 Metal 8 Marsh 兌爲澤 19 丙辰 Fire Dragon 1 十四	火2 Fire 9 Small Livestock 風天小畜 20 丁巳 Fire Snake 8 十五	木3 Wood 1 The Cauldron 火風鼎 21 戊午 Earth Horse 4 十六	水1 Water 2 Rising 地風升 22 己未 Earth Goat 2 十七	火7 Fire 3 Water 坎爲水 23 庚申 Metal Monkey 1 十八	木8 Wood 4 Lesser Exceeding 雷山小過 24 辛酉 Metal Rooster 3 十九
金4 Metal 5 Gathering 澤地萃 25 壬戌 Water Dog 4 二十	水6 Water 6 Peel 山地剝 26 癸亥 Water Pig 6 廿一	水1 Water 7 Earth 坤爲地 27 甲子 Wood Rat 1 廿二	木3 Wood 8 Biting 火雷噬嗑 28 乙丑 Wood Ox 6 廿三	火2 Fire 9 Family 風火家人 29 丙寅 Fire Tiger 4 廿四	水6 Water 1 Decreasing 山澤損 30 丁卯 Fire Rabbit 9 廿五	金9 Metal 2 Tread 天澤履 31 戊辰 Earth Dragon 6 廿六

APRIL 1962 甲辰

Xuan Kong Element 玄空五行	火澤睽 Opposition	Period Luck 卦運	Monthly Star 月星
Wood 木3		2	9

SUNDAY	MONDAY	TUESDAY	WEDNESDAY	THURSDAY	FRIDAY	SATURDAY
木8 Wood 3 Great Strength 雷天大壯 1 己巳 Earth Snake 2 廿七	木8 Wood 4 Consistency 雷風恆 2 庚午 Metal Horse 9 廿八	金9 Metal 5 Litigation 天水訟 3 辛未 Metal Goat 3 廿九	水1 Water 6 Officer 地水師 4 壬申 Water Monkey 7 三十	火2 Fire 7 Gradual Progress 風山漸 5 癸酉 Water Rooster 7 四月初一	火7 Fire 8 Obstruction 水山蹇 6 甲戌 Wood Dog 2 初二	木3 Wood 9 Advancement 火地晉 7 乙亥 Wood Pig 3 初三
水6 Water 1 Nourish 山雷頤 8 丙子 Fire Rat 3 初四	金4 Metal 2 Following 澤雷隨 9 丁丑 Fire Ox 7 初五	木8 Wood 3 Abundance 雷火豐 10 戊寅 Earth Tiger 6 初六	火7 Fire 4 Regulate 水澤節 11 己卯 Earth Rabbit 8 初七	水1 Water 5 Unity 地天泰 12 庚辰 Metal Dragon 9 初八	木3 Wood 6 Great Reward 火天大有 13 辛巳 Metal Snake 7 初九	火2 Fire 7 Wind 巽爲風 14 壬午 Water Horse 1 初十
金4 Metal 8 Trap 澤水困 15 癸未 Water Goat 8 十一	木3 Wood 9 Not Yet Accomplished 火水未濟 16 甲申 Wood Monkey 9 十二	金9 Metal 1 Retreat 天山遯 17 乙酉 Wood Rooster 4 十三	水6 Water 2 Mountain 艮爲山 18 丙戌 Fire Dog 1 十四	木8 Wood 3 Delight 雷地豫 19 丁亥 Fire Pig 8 十五	火7 Fire 4 Beginning 水雷屯 20 戊子 Earth Rat 4 十六	金9 Metal 5 Without Wrongdoing 天雷無妄 21 己丑 Earth Ox 2 十七
木3 Wood 6 Fire 離爲火 22 庚寅 Metal Tiger 1 十八	火2 Fire 7 Sincerity 風澤中孚 23 辛卯 Metal Rabbit 3 十九	水6 Water 8 Big Livestock 山天大畜 24 壬辰 Water Dragon 4 二十	金4 Metal 9 Eliminating 澤天夬 25 癸巳 Water Snake 6 廿一	金9 Metal 1 Heaven 乾爲天 26 甲午 Wood Horse 1 廿二	火7 Fire 2 Well 水風井 27 乙未 Wood Goat 6 廿三	木8 Wood 3 Relief 雷水解 28 丙申 Fire Monkey 4 廿四
金4 Metal 4 Influence 澤山咸 29 丁酉 Fire Rooster 9 廿五	水1 Water 5 Humility 地山謙 30 戊戌 Earth Dog 6 廿六					

MAY 1962 乙巳

Xuan Kong Element 玄空五行	水天需 Waiting	Period Luck 卦運	Monthly Star 月星
Fire 火7		3	8

SUNDAY	MONDAY	TUESDAY	WEDNESDAY	THURSDAY	FRIDAY	SATURDAY
		火2 Fire 6 Observation 風地觀 己亥 Earth Pig 1 廿七 2	火2 Fire 7 Increasing 風雷益 庚子 Metal Rat 2 廿八 9	水1 Water 8 Dimming Light 地火明夷 辛丑 Metal Ox 3 廿九 3	金9 Metal 9 Fellowship 天火同人 壬寅 Water Tiger 4 四月初一 7	木8 Wood 1 Marrying Maiden 雷澤歸妹 癸卯 Water Rabbit 5 初二 7
木3 Wood 2 Opposition 火澤睽 甲辰 Wood Dragon 6 初三 2	火7 Fire 3 Waiting 水天需 乙巳 Wood Snake 7 初四 3	金4 Metal 4 Great Exceeding 澤風大過 丙午 Fire Horse 8 初五 3	水6 Water 5 Poison 山風蠱 丁未 Fire Goat 9 初六 7	火2 Fire 6 Dispersing 風水渙 戊申 Earth Monkey 10 初七 6	木3 Wood 7 Travelling 火山旅 己酉 Earth Rooster 11 初八 8	金9 Metal 8 Stagnation 天地否 庚戌 Metal Dog 12 初九 9
火7 Fire 9 Alliance 水地比 辛亥 Metal Pig 13 初十 7	木8 Wood 1 Thunder 震爲雷 壬子 Water Rat 14 十一 1	水6 Water 2 Beauty 山火賁 癸丑 Water Ox 15 十二 8	火7 Fire 3 Accomplished 水火既濟 甲寅 Wood Tiger 16 十三 9	水1 Water 4 Arriving 地澤臨 乙卯 Wood Rabbit 17 十四 4	金4 Metal 5 Marsh 兑爲澤 丙辰 Fire Dragon 18 十五 1	火2 Fire 6 Small Livestock 風天小畜 丁巳 Fire Snake 19 十六 8
木3 Wood 7 The Cauldron 火風鼎 戊午 Earth Horse 20 十七 4	水1 Water 8 Rising 地風升 己未 Earth Goat 21 十八 2	火7 Fire 9 Water 坎爲水 庚申 Metal Monkey 22 十九 1	木8 Wood 1 Lesser Exceeding 雷山小過 辛酉 Metal Rooster 23 二十 3	金4 Metal 2 Gathering 澤地萃 壬戌 Water Dog 24 廿一 4	水6 Water 3 Peel 山地剝 癸亥 Water Pig 25 廿二 6	水1 Water 4 Earth 坤爲地 甲子 Wood Rat 26 廿三 1
木3 Wood 5 Biting 火雷噬嗑 乙丑 Wood Ox 27 廿四 6	火2 Fire 6 Family 風火家人 丙寅 Fire Tiger 28 廿五 4	水6 Water 7 Decreasing 山澤損 丁卯 Fire Rabbit 29 廿六 9	金9 Metal 8 Tread 天澤履 戊辰 Earth Dragon 30 廿七 6	木8 Wood 9 Great Strength 雷天大壯 己巳 Earth Snake 31 廿八 2		

JUNE 1962 丙午

Xuan Kong Element 玄空五行	澤風大過 Great Exceeding	Period Luck 卦運	Monthly Star 月星
Metal 金4		3	7

SUNDAY	MONDAY	TUESDAY	WEDNESDAY	THURSDAY	FRIDAY	SATURDAY
					木8 Wood 1 Consistency 雷風恆 庚午 Metal Horse 1 廿九 9	金9 Metal 2 Litigation 天水訟 辛未 Metal Goat 2 五月初一 3
水1 Water 3 Officer 地水師 壬申 Water Monkey 3 初二 7	火2 Fire 4 Gradual Progress 風山漸 癸酉 Water Rooster 4 初三 7	火7 Fire 5 Obstruction 水山蹇 甲戌 Wood Dog 5 初四 2	木3 Wood 6 Advancement 火地晉 乙亥 Wood Pig 6 初五 3	水6 Water 7 Nourish 山雷頤 丙子 Fire Rat 7 初六 3	金4 Metal 8 Following 澤雷隨 丁丑 Fire Ox 8 初七 7	木8 Wood 9 Abundance 雷火豐 戊寅 Earth Tiger 9 初八 6
火7 Fire 1 Regulate 水澤節 己卯 Earth Rabbit 10 初九 8	水1 Water 2 Unity 地天泰 庚辰 Metal Dragon 11 初十 9	木3 Wood 3 Great Reward 火天大有 辛巳 Metal Snake 12 十一 7	火2 Fire 4 Wind 巽爲風 壬午 Water Horse 13 十二 1	金4 Metal 5 Trap 澤水困 癸未 Water Goat 14 十三 8	木3 Wood 6 Not Yet Accomplished 火水未濟 甲申 Wood Monkey 15 十四 9	金9 Metal 7 Retreat 天山遯 乙酉 Wood Rooster 16 十五 4
水6 Water 8 Mountain 艮爲山 丙戌 Fire Dog 17 十六 1	木8 Wood 9 Delight 雷地豫 丁亥 Fire Pig 18 十七 8	火7 Fire 1 Beginning 水雷屯 戊子 Earth Rat 19 十八 4	金9 Metal 2 Without Wrongdoing 天雷無妄 己丑 Earth Ox 20 十九 2	木3 Wood 3 Fire 離爲火 庚寅 Metal Tiger 21 二十 1	火2 Fire 4/6 Sincerity 風澤中孚 辛卯 Metal Rabbit 22 廿一 3	水6 Water 5 Big Livestock 山天大畜 壬辰 Water Dragon 23 廿二 4
金4 Metal 4 Eliminating 澤天夬 癸巳 Water Snake 24 廿三 6	金9 Metal 3 Heaven 乾爲天 甲午 Wood Horse 25 廿四 1	火7 Fire 2 Well 水風井 乙未 Wood Goat 26 廿五 6	木8 Wood 1 Relief 雷水解 丙申 Fire Monkey 27 廿六 4	金4 Metal 9 Influence 澤山咸 丁酉 Fire Rooster 28 廿七 9	水1 Water 8 Humility 地山謙 戊戌 Earth Dog 29 廿八 6	火2 Fire 7 Observation 風地觀 己亥 Earth Pig 30 廿九 2

JULY 1962 丁未

Xuan Kong Element 玄空五行	山風蠱 Poison	Period Luck 卦運	Monthly Star 月星
Water 水6		7	6

SUNDAY	MONDAY	TUESDAY	WEDNESDAY	THURSDAY	FRIDAY	SATURDAY
火2 Fire 6 Increasing 風雷益 庚子 Metal Rat **1** 三十 9	水1 Water 5 Dimming Light 地火明夷 辛丑 Metal Ox **2** 六月初一 3	金9 Metal 4 Fellowship 天火同人 壬寅 Water Tiger **3** 初二 7	木8 Wood 3 Marrying Maiden 雷澤歸妹 癸卯 Water Rabbit **4** 初三 7	木3 Wood 2 Opposition 火澤睽 甲辰 Wood Dragon **5** 初四 2	火7 Fire 1 Waiting 水天需 乙巳 Wood Snake **6** 初五 3	金4 Metal 9 Great Exceeding 澤風大過 丙午 Fire Horse **7** 初六 3
水6 Water 8 Poison 山風蠱 丁未 Fire Goat **8** 初七 7	火2 Fire 7 Dispersing 風水渙 戊申 Earth Monkey **9** 初八 6	木3 Wood 6 Travelling 火山旅 己酉 Earth Rooster **10** 初九 8	金9 Metal 5 Stagnation 天地否 庚戌 Metal Dog **11** 初十 9	火7 Fire 4 Alliance 水地比 辛亥 Metal Pig **12** 十一 7	木8 Wood 3 Thunder 震爲雷 壬子 Water Rat **13** 十二 1	水6 Water 2 Beauty 山火賁 癸丑 Water Ox **14** 十三 8
火7 Fire 1 Accomplished 水火既濟 甲寅 Wood Tiger **15** 十四 9	水1 Water 9 Arriving 地澤臨 乙卯 Wood Rabbit **16** 十五 4	金4 Metal 8 Marsh 兌爲澤 丙辰 Fire Dragon **17** 十六 1	火2 Fire 7 Small Livestock 風天小畜 丁巳 Fire Snake **18** 十七 8	木3 Wood 6 The Cauldron 火風鼎 戊午 Earth Horse **19** 十八 4	水1 Water 5 Rising 地風升 己未 Earth Goat **20** 十九 2	火7 Fire 4 Water 坎爲水 庚申 Metal Monkey **21** 二十 1
木8 Wood 3 Lesser Exceeding 雷山小過 辛酉 Metal Rooster **22** 廿一 3	金4 Metal 2 Gathering 澤地萃 壬戌 Water Dog **23** 廿二 4	水6 Water 1 Peel 山地剝 癸亥 Water Pig **24** 廿三 6	水1 Water 9 Earth 坤爲地 甲子 Wood Rat **25** 廿四 1	木3 Wood 8 Biting 火雷噬嗑 乙丑 Wood Ox **26** 廿五 6	火2 Fire 7 Family 風火家人 丙寅 Fire Tiger **27** 廿六 4	水6 Water 6 Decreasing 山澤損 丁卯 Fire Rabbit **28** 廿七 9
金9 Metal 5 Tread 天澤履 戊辰 Earth Dragon **29** 廿八 6	木8 Wood 4 Great Strength 雷天大壯 己巳 Earth Snake **30** 廿九 2	木8 Wood 3 Consistency 雷風恆 庚午 Metal Horse **31** 七月初一 9				

AUGUST 1962 戊申

Xuan Kong Element 玄空五行	風水渙 Dispersing	Period Luck 卦運	Monthly Star 月星
Fire 火2		6	5

SUNDAY	MONDAY	TUESDAY	WEDNESDAY	THURSDAY	FRIDAY	SATURDAY
			金9 Metal 2 Litigation 天水訟 辛未 Metal Goat **1** 初二 3	水1 Water 1 Officer 地水師 壬申 Water Monkey **2** 初三 7	火2 Fire 9 Gradual Progress 風山漸 癸酉 Water Rooster **3** 初四 7	火7 Fire 8 Obstruction 水山蹇 甲戌 Wood Dog **4** 初五 2
木3 Wood 7 Advancement 火地晉 乙亥 Wood Pig **5** 初六 3	水6 Water 6 Nourish 山雷頤 丙子 Fire Rat **6** 初七 3	金4 Metal 5 Following 澤雷隨 丁丑 Fire Ox **7** 初八 7	木8 Wood 4 Abundance 雷火豐 戊寅 Earth Tiger **8** 初九 6	火7 Fire 3 Regulate 水澤節 己卯 Earth Rabbit **9** 初十 8	水1 Water 2 Unity 地天泰 庚辰 Metal Dragon **10** 十一 9	木3 Wood 1 Great Reward 火天大有 辛巳 Metal Snake **11** 十二 7
火2 Fire 9 Wind 巽爲風 壬午 Water Horse **12** 十三 1	金4 Metal 8 Trap 澤水困 癸未 Water Goat **13** 十四 8	木3 Wood 7 Not Yet Accomplished 火水未濟 甲申 Wood Monkey **14** 十五 9	金9 Metal 6 Retreat 天山遯 乙酉 Wood Rooster **15** 十六 4	水6 Water 5 Mountain 艮爲山 丙戌 Fire Dog **16** 十七 1	木8 Wood 4 Delight 雷地豫 丁亥 Fire Pig **17** 十八 8	火7 Fire 3 Beginning 水雷屯 戊子 Earth Rat **18** 十九 4
金9 Metal 2 Without Wrongdoing 天雷無妄 己丑 Earth Ox **19** 二十 2	木3 Wood 1 Fire 離爲火 庚寅 Metal Tiger **20** 廿一 1	火2 Fire 9 Sincerity 風澤中孚 辛卯 Metal Rabbit **21** 廿二 3	水6 Water 8 Big Livestock 山天大畜 壬辰 Water Dragon **22** 廿三 4	金4 Metal 7 Eliminating 澤天夬 癸巳 Water Snake **23** 廿四 6	金9 Metal 6 Heaven 乾爲天 甲午 Wood Horse **24** 廿五 1	火7 Fire 5 Well 水風井 乙未 Wood Goat **25** 廿六 6
木8 Wood 4 Relief 雷水解 丙申 Fire Monkey **26** 廿七 4	金4 Metal 3 Influence 澤山咸 丁酉 Fire Rooster **27** 廿八 9	水1 Water 2 Humility 地山謙 戊戌 Earth Dog **28** 廿九 6	火2 Fire 1 Observation 風地觀 己亥 Earth Pig **29** 三十 2	火2 Fire 9 Increasing 風雷益 庚子 Metal Rat **30** 八月初一 9	水1 Water 8 Dimming Light 地火明夷 辛丑 Metal Ox **31** 初二 3	

SEPTEMBER 1962 己酉

Xuan Kong Element 玄空五行	火山旅 Travelling	Period Luck 卦運	Monthly Star 月星
Wood 木3		8	4

SUNDAY	MONDAY	TUESDAY	WEDNESDAY	THURSDAY	FRIDAY	SATURDAY
金9 Metal 5 Litigation 天水訟 辛未 Metal Goat 3 30 初二						金9 Metal 7 Fellowship 天火同人 壬寅 Water Tiger 7 1 初三
木8 Wood 6 Marrying Maiden 雷澤歸妹 癸卯 Water Rabbit 7 2 初四	木3 Wood 5 Opposition 火澤睽 甲辰 Wood Dragon 2 3 初五	火7 Fire 4 Waiting 水天需 乙巳 Wood Snake 3 4 初六	金4 Metal 3 Great Exceeding 澤風大過 丙午 Fire Horse 3 5 初七	水6 Water 2 Poison 山風蠱 丁未 Fire Goat 7 6 初八	火2 Fire 1 Dispersing 風水渙 戊申 Earth Monkey 6 7 初九	木3 Wood 9 Travelling 火山旅 己酉 Earth Rooster 8 8 初十
金9 Metal 8 Stagnation 天地否 庚戌 Metal Dog 9 9 十一	火7 Fire 7 Alliance 水地比 辛亥 Metal Pig 7 10 十二	木8 Wood 6 Thunder 震爲雷 壬子 Water Rat 1 11 十三	水6 Water 5 Beauty 山火賁 癸丑 Water Ox 8 12 十四	火7 Fire 4 Accomplished 水火既濟 甲寅 Wood Tiger 9 13 十五	水1 Water 3 Arriving 地澤臨 乙卯 Wood Rabbit 4 14 十六	金4 Metal 2 Marsh 兑爲澤 丙辰 Fire Dragon 1 15 十七
火2 Fire 1 Small Livestock 風天小畜 丁巳 Fire Snake 8 16 十八	木3 Wood 9 The Cauldron 火風鼎 戊午 Earth Horse 4 17 十九	水1 Water 8 Rising 地風升 己未 Earth Goat 2 18 二十	火7 Fire 7 Water 坎爲水 庚申 Metal Monkey 1 19 廿一	木8 Wood 6 Lesser Exceeding 雷山小過 辛酉 Metal Rooster 3 20 廿二	金4 Metal 5 Gathering 澤地萃 壬戌 Water Dog 4 21 廿三	水6 Water 4 Peel 山地剝 癸亥 Water Pig 6 22 廿四
水1 Water 3 Earth 坤爲地 甲子 Wood Rat 1 23 廿五	木3 Wood 2 Biting 火雷噬嗑 乙丑 Wood Ox 6 24 廿六	火2 Fire 1 Family 風火家人 丙寅 Fire Tiger 4 25 廿七	水6 Water 9 Decreasing 山澤損 丁卯 Fire Rabbit 9 26 廿八	金9 Metal 8 Tread 天澤履 戊辰 Earth Dragon 6 27 廿九	木8 Wood 7 Great Strength 雷天大壯 己巳 Earth Snake 2 28 三十	木8 Wood 6 Consistency 雷風恒 庚午 Metal Horse 9 29 九月初一

OCTOBER 1962 庚戌

Xuan Kong Element 玄空五行	天地否 Stagnation	Period Luck 卦運	Monthly Star 月星
Metal 金9		9	3

SUNDAY	MONDAY	TUESDAY	WEDNESDAY	THURSDAY	FRIDAY	SATURDAY
	水1 Water 4 Officer 地水師 壬申 Water Monkey 7 1 初三	火2 Fire 3 Gradual Progress 風山漸 癸酉 Water Rooster 7 2 初四	火7 Fire 2 Obstruction 水山蹇 甲戌 Wood Dog 2 3 初五	木3 Wood 1 Advancement 火地晉 乙亥 Wood Pig 3 4 初六	水6 Water 9 Nourish 山雷頤 丙子 Fire Rat 3 5 初七	金4 Metal 8 Following 澤雷隨 丁丑 Fire Ox 7 6 初八
木8 Wood 7 Abundance 雷火豐 戊寅 Earth Tiger 6 7 初九	火7 Fire 6 Regulate 水澤節 己卯 Earth Rabbit 8 8 初十	水1 Water 5 Unity 地天泰 庚辰 Metal Dragon 9 9 十一	木3 Wood 4 Great Reward 火天大有 辛巳 Metal Snake 7 10 十二	火2 Fire 3 Wind 巽爲風 壬午 Water Horse 1 11 十三	金4 Metal 2 Trap 澤水困 癸未 Water Goat 8 12 十四	木3 Wood 1 Not Yet Accomplished 火水未濟 甲申 Wood Monkey 9 13 十五
金9 Metal 9 Retreat 天山遯 乙酉 Wood Rooster 4 14 十六	水6 Water 8 Mountain 艮爲山 丙戌 Fire Dog 1 15 十七	木8 Wood 7 Delight 雷地豫 丁亥 Fire Pig 8 16 十八	火7 Fire 6 Beginning 水雷屯 戊子 Earth Rat 4 17 十九	金9 Metal 5 Without Wrongdoing 天雷無妄 己丑 Earth Ox 2 18 二十	木3 Wood 4 Fire 離爲火 庚寅 Metal Tiger 1 19 廿一	火2 Fire 3 Sincerity 風澤中孚 辛卯 Metal Rabbit 3 20 廿二
水6 Water 2 Big Livestock 山天大畜 壬辰 Water Dragon 4 21 廿三	金4 Metal 1 Eliminating 澤天夬 癸巳 Water Snake 6 22 廿四	金9 Metal 9 Heaven 乾爲天 甲午 Wood Horse 1 23 廿五	火7 Fire 8 Well 水風井 乙未 Wood Goat 6 24 廿六	木8 Wood 7 Relief 雷水解 丙申 Fire Monkey 4 25 廿七	金4 Metal 6 Influence 澤山咸 丁酉 Fire Rooster 9 26 廿八	水1 Water 5 Humility 地山謙 戊戌 Earth Dog 6 27 廿九
火2 Fire 4 Observation 風地觀 己亥 Earth Pig 2 28 十月初一	火2 Fire 3 Increasing 風雷益 庚子 Metal Rat 9 29 初二	水1 Water 2 Dimming Light 地火明夷 辛丑 Metal Ox 3 30 初三	金9 Metal 1 Fellowship 天火同人 壬寅 Water Tiger 7 31 初四			

NOVEMBER 1962 辛亥

Xuan Kong Element 玄空五行	水地比 Alliance	Period Luck 卦運	Monthly Star 月星
Fire 火7		7	2

SUNDAY	MONDAY	TUESDAY	WEDNESDAY	THURSDAY	FRIDAY	SATURDAY
				木8 Wood 9 Marrying Maiden 癸卯 Water Rabbit 雷澤歸妹 1 初五 7	木3 Wood 8 Opposition 甲辰 Wood Dragon 火澤睽 2 初六 2	火7 Fire 7 Waiting 乙巳 Wood Snake 水天需 3 初七 3
金4 Metal 6 Great Exceeding 丙午 Fire Horse 澤風大過 4 初八 3	水6 Water 5 Poison 丁未 Fire Goat 山風蠱 5 初九 7	火2 Fire 4 Dispersing 戊申 Earth Monkey 風水渙 6 初十 6	木3 Wood 3 Travelling 己酉 Earth Rooster 火山旅 7 十一 8	金9 Metal 2 Stagnation 庚戌 Metal Dog 天地否 8 十二 9	火7 Fire 1 Alliance 辛亥 Metal Pig 水地比 9 十三 7	木8 Wood 9 Thunder 壬子 Water Rat 震為雷 10 十四 1
水6 Water 8 Beauty 癸丑 Water Ox 山火賁 11 十五 8	火7 Fire 7 Accomplished 甲寅 Wood Tiger 水火既濟 12 十六 9	水1 Water 6 Arriving 乙卯 Wood Rabbit 地澤臨 13 十七 4	金4 Metal 5 Marsh 丙辰 Fire Dragon 兌為澤 14 十八 1	火2 Fire 4 Small Livestock 丁巳 Fire Snake 風天小畜 15 十九 8	木3 Wood 3 The Cauldron 戊午 Earth Horse 火風鼎 16 二十 4	水1 Water 2 Rising 己未 Earth Goat 地風升 17 廿一 2
火7 Fire 1 Water 庚申 Metal Monkey 坎為水 18 廿二 1	木8 Wood 9 Lesser Exceeding 辛酉 Metal Rooster 雷山小過 19 廿三 3	金4 Metal 8 Gathering 壬戌 Water Dog 澤地萃 20 廿四 4	水6 Water 7 Peel 癸亥 Water Pig 山地剝 21 廿五 6	水1 Water 6 Earth 甲子 Wood Rat 坤為地 22 廿六 1	木3 Wood 5 Biting 乙丑 Wood Ox 火雷噬嗑 23 廿七 6	火2 Fire 4 Family 丙寅 Fire Tiger 風火家人 24 廿八 4
水6 Water 3 Decreasing 丁卯 Fire Rabbit 山澤損 25 廿九 9	金9 Metal 2 Tread 戊辰 Earth Dragon 天澤履 26 三十 6	木8 Wood 1 Great Strength 己巳 Earth Snake 雷天大壯 27 十一月初一 2	木8 Wood 9 Consistency 庚午 Metal Horse 雷風恆 28 初二 9	金9 Metal 8 Litigation 辛未 Metal Goat 天水訟 29 初三 3	水1 Water 7 Officer 壬申 Water Monkey 地水師 30 初四 7	

DECEMBER 1962 壬子

Xuan Kong Element 玄空五行	震為雷 Thunder	Period Luck 卦運	Monthly Star 月星
Wood 木8		1	1

SUNDAY	MONDAY	TUESDAY	WEDNESDAY	THURSDAY	FRIDAY	SATURDAY
金9 Metal 6 Fellowship 壬寅 Water Tiger 天火同人 30 初四 7	木8 Wood 7 Marrying Maiden 癸卯 Water Rabbit 雷澤歸妹 31 初五 7					火2 Fire 6 Gradual Progress 癸酉 Water Rooster 風山漸 1 初五 7
火7 Fire 5 Obstruction 甲戌 Wood Dog 水山蹇 2 初六 2	木3 Wood 4 Advancement 乙亥 Wood Pig 火地晉 3 初七 3	水6 Water 3 Nourish 丙子 Fire Rat 山雷頤 4 初八 3	金4 Metal 2 Following 丁丑 Fire Ox 澤雷隨 5 初九 7	木8 Wood 1 Abundance 戊寅 Earth Tiger 雷火豐 6 初十 6	火7 Fire 9 Regulate 己卯 Earth Rabbit 水澤節 7 十一 8	水1 Water 8 Unity 庚辰 Metal Dragon 地天泰 8 十二 9
木3 Wood 7 Great Reward 辛巳 Metal Snake 火天大有 9 十三 7	火2 Fire 6 Wind 壬午 Water Horse 巽為風 10 十四 1	金4 Metal 5 Trap 癸未 Water Goat 澤水困 11 十五 8	木3 Wood 4 Not Yet Accomplished 甲申 Wood Monkey 火水未濟 12 十六 9	金9 Metal 3 Retreat 乙酉 Wood Rooster 天山遯 13 十七 4	水6 Water 2 Mountain 丙戌 Fire Dog 艮為山 14 十八 1	木8 Wood 1 Delight 丁亥 Fire Pig 雷地豫 15 十九 8
火7 Fire 9 Beginning 戊子 Earth Rat 水雷屯 16 二十 4	金9 Metal 8 Without Wrongdoing 己丑 Earth Ox 天雷無妄 17 廿一 2	木3 Wood 7 Fire 庚寅 Metal Tiger 離為火 18 廿二 1	火2 Fire 6 Sincerity 辛卯 Metal Rabbit 風澤中孚 19 廿三 3	水6 Water 5 Big Livestock 壬辰 Water Dragon 山天大畜 20 廿四 4	金4 Metal 4 Eliminating 癸巳 Water Snake 澤天夬 21 廿五 6	金9 Metal 3/7 Heaven 甲午 Wood Horse 乾為天 22 廿六 1
火7 Fire 8 Well 乙未 Wood Goat 水風井 23 廿七 6	木8 Wood 9 Relief 丙申 Fire Monkey 雷水解 24 廿八 4	金4 Metal 1 Influence 丁酉 Fire Rooster 澤山咸 25 廿九 9	水1 Water 2 Humility 戊戌 Earth Dog 地山謙 26 三十 6	火2 Fire 3 Observation 己亥 Earth Pig 風地觀 27 十二月初一 2	火2 Fire 4 Increasing 庚子 Metal Rat 風雷益 28 初二 9	水1 Water 5 Dimming Light 辛丑 Metal Ox 地火明夷 29 初三 3

1963 癸卯

(*Gui Mao*) Water Rabbit

1963 癸卯 *(Gui Mao)* Water Rabbit

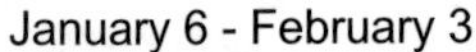

January 6 - February 3

February 4 - March 5

March 6 - April 4

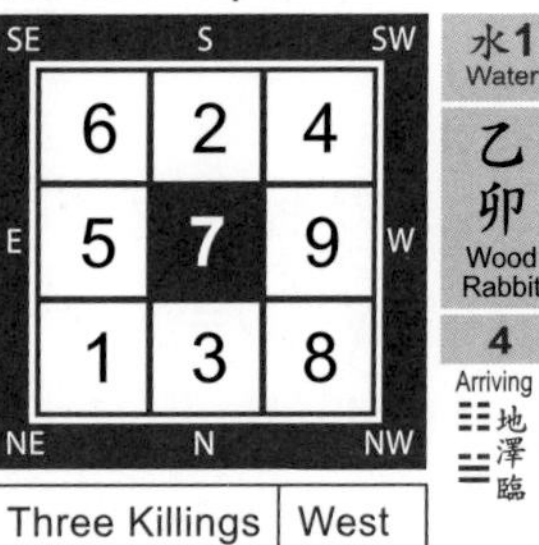

April 5 - May 5

May 6 - June 5

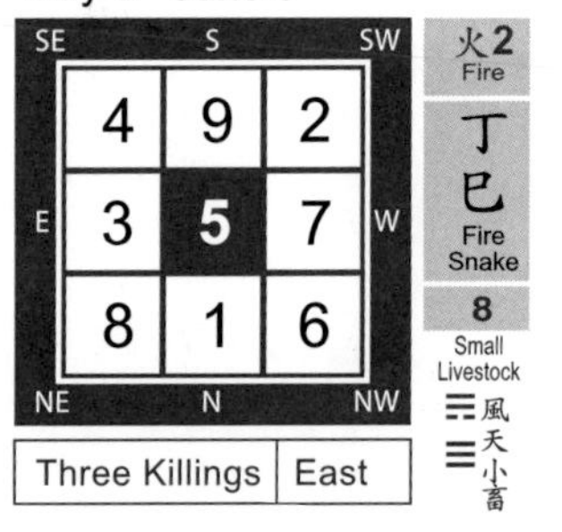

June 6 - July 7

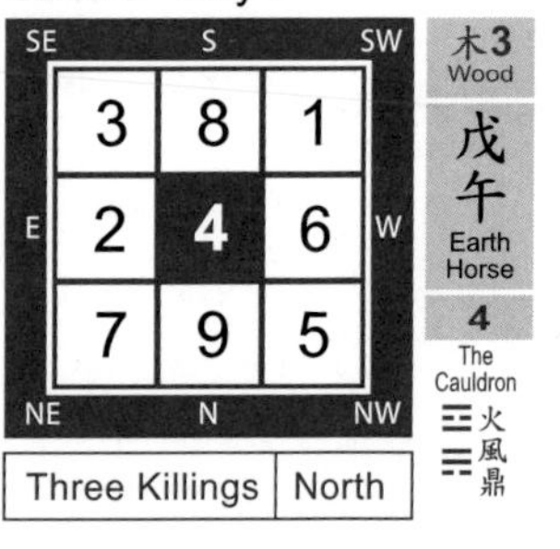

July 8 - August 7

August 8 - September 7

September 8 - October 8

October 9 - November 7

November 8 - December 7

December 8 - January 5

JANUARY 1963 癸丑

Xuan Kong Element 玄空五行	山火賁 Beauty	Period Luck 卦運	Monthly Star 月星
Water 水6		8	9

SUNDAY	MONDAY	TUESDAY	WEDNESDAY	THURSDAY	FRIDAY	SATURDAY
		木3 Wood Opposition 8 甲辰 Wood Dragon 火澤睽 1 初六 2	火7 Fire Waiting 9 乙巳 Wood Snake 水天需 2 初七 3	金4 Metal Great Exceeding 1 丙午 Fire Horse 澤風大過 3 初八 3	水6 Water Poison 2 丁未 Fire Goat 山風蠱 4 初九 7	火2 Fire Dispersing 3 戊申 Earth Monkey 風水渙 5 初十 6
木3 Wood Travelling 4 己酉 Earth Rooster 火山旅 6 十一 8	金9 Metal Stagnation 5 庚戌 Metal Dog 天地否 7 十二 9	火7 Fire Alliance 6 辛亥 Metal Pig 水地比 8 十三 7	木8 Wood Thunder 7 壬子 Water Rat 震爲雷 9 十四 1	水6 Water Beauty 8 癸丑 Water Ox 山火賁 10 十五 8	火7 Fire Accomplished 9 甲寅 Wood Tiger 水火既濟 11 十六 9	水1 Water Arriving 1 乙卯 Wood Rabbit 地澤臨 12 十七 4
金4 Metal Marsh 2 丙辰 Fire Dragon 兌爲澤 13 十八 1	火2 Fire Small Livestock 3 丁巳 Fire Snake 風天小畜 14 十九 8	木3 Wood The Cauldron 4 戊午 Earth Horse 火風鼎 15 二十 4	水1 Water Rising 5 己未 Earth Goat 地風升 16 廿一 2	火7 Fire Water 6 庚申 Metal Monkey 坎爲水 17 廿二 1	木8 Wood Lesser Exceeding 7 辛酉 Metal Rooster 雷山小過 18 廿三 3	金4 Metal Gathering 8 壬戌 Water Dog 澤地萃 19 廿四 4
水6 Water Peel 9 癸亥 Water Pig 山地剝 20 廿五 6	水1 Water Earth 1 甲子 Wood Rat 坤爲地 21 廿六 1	木3 Wood Biting 2 乙丑 Wood Ox 火雷噬嗑 22 廿七 6	火2 Fire Family 3 丙寅 Fire Tiger 風火家人 23 廿八 4	水6 Water Decreasing 4 丁卯 Fire Rabbit 山澤損 24 廿九 9	金9 Metal Tread 5 戊辰 Earth Dragon 天澤履 25 正月初一 6	木8 Wood Great Strength 6 己巳 Earth Snake 雷天大壯 26 初二 2
木8 Wood Consistency 7 庚午 Metal Horse 雷風恒 27 初三 9	金9 Metal Litigation 8 辛未 Metal Goat 天水訟 28 初四 3	水1 Water Officer 9 壬申 Water Monkey 地水師 29 初五 7	火2 Fire Gradual Progress 1 癸酉 Water Rooster 風山漸 30 初六 7	火7 Fire Obstruction 2 甲戌 Wood Dog 水山蹇 31 初七 2		

FEBRUARY 1963 甲寅

Xuan Kong Element 玄空五行	水火既濟 Accomplished	Period Luck 卦運	Monthly Star 月星
Fire 火7		9	8

SUNDAY	MONDAY	TUESDAY	WEDNESDAY	THURSDAY	FRIDAY	SATURDAY
					木3 Wood Advancement 3 乙亥 Wood Pig 火地晉 1 初八 3	水6 Water Nourish 4 丙子 Fire Rat 山雷頤 2 初九 3
金4 Metal Following 5 丁丑 Fire Ox 澤雷隨 3 初十 7	木8 Wood Abundance 6 戊寅 Earth Tiger 雷火豐 4 十一 6	火7 Fire Regulate 7 己卯 Earth Rabbit 水澤節 5 十二 8	水1 Water Unity 8 庚辰 Metal Dragon 地天泰 6 十三 9	木3 Wood Great Reward 9 辛巳 Metal Snake 火天大有 7 十四 7	火2 Fire Wind 1 壬午 Water Horse 巽爲風 8 十五 1	金4 Metal Trap 2 癸未 Water Goat 澤水困 9 十六 8
木3 Wood Not Yet Accomplished 3 甲申 Wood Monkey 火水未濟 10 十七 9	金9 Metal Retreat 4 乙酉 Wood Rooster 天山遯 11 十八 4	水6 Water Mountain 5 丙戌 Fire Dog 艮爲山 12 十九 1	木8 Wood Delight 6 丁亥 Fire Pig 雷地豫 13 二十 8	火7 Fire Beginning 7 戊子 Earth Rat 水雷屯 14 廿一 4	金9 Metal Without Wrongdoing 8 己丑 Earth Ox 天雷無妄 15 廿二 2	木3 Wood Fire 9 庚寅 Metal Tiger 離爲火 16 廿三 1
火2 Fire Sincerity 1 辛卯 Metal Rabbit 風澤中孚 17 廿四 3	水6 Water Big Livestock 2 壬辰 Water Dragon 山天大畜 18 廿五 4	金4 Metal Eliminating 3 癸巳 Water Snake 澤天夬 19 廿六 6	金9 Metal Heaven 4 甲午 Wood Horse 乾爲天 20 廿七 1	火7 Fire Well 5 乙未 Wood Goat 水風井 21 廿八 6	木8 Wood Relief 6 丙申 Fire Monkey 雷水解 22 廿九 4	金4 Metal Influence 7 丁酉 Fire Rooster 澤山咸 23 三十 9
水1 Water Humility 8 戊戌 Earth Dog 地山謙 24 二月初一 6	火2 Fire Observation 9 己亥 Earth Pig 風地觀 25 初二 2	火2 Fire Increasing 1 庚子 Metal Rat 風雷益 26 初三 9	水1 Water Dimming Light 2 辛丑 Metal Ox 地火明夷 27 初四 3	金9 Metal Fellowship 3 壬寅 Water Tiger 天火同人 28 初五 7		

MARCH 1963 乙卯

Xuan Kong Element 玄空五行	地澤臨 Arriving	Period Luck 卦運	Monthly Star 月星
Water 水1		4	7

SUNDAY	MONDAY	TUESDAY	WEDNESDAY	THURSDAY	FRIDAY	SATURDAY
火2 Fire 癸酉 Water Rooster 7 7 Gradual Progress 風山漸 31 初七					木8 Wood 癸卯 Water Rabbit 7 4 Marrying Maiden 雷澤歸妹 1 初六	木3 Wood 甲辰 Wood Dragon 2 5 Opposition 火澤睽 2 初七
火7 Fire 乙巳 Wood Snake 3 6 Waiting 水天需 3 初八	金4 Metal 丙午 Fire Horse 3 7 Great Exceeding 澤風大過 4 初九	水6 Water 丁未 Fire Goat 7 8 Poison 山風蠱 5 初十	火2 Fire 戊申 Earth Monkey 6 9 Dispersing 風水渙 6 十一	木3 Wood 己酉 Earth Rooster 8 1 Travelling 火山旅 7 十二	金9 Metal 庚戌 Metal Dog 9 2 Stagnation 天地否 8 十三	火7 Fire 辛亥 Metal Pig 7 3 Alliance 水地比 9 十四
木8 Wood 壬子 Water Rat 1 4 Thunder 震爲雷 10 十五	水6 Water 癸丑 Water Ox 8 5 Beauty 山火賁 11 十六	火7 Fire 甲寅 Wood Tiger 9 6 Accomplished 水火既濟 12 十七	水1 Water 乙卯 Wood Rabbit 4 7 Arriving 地澤臨 13 十八	金4 Metal 丙辰 Fire Dragon 1 8 Marsh 兌爲澤 14 十九	火2 Fire 丁巳 Fire Snake 8 9 Small Livestock 風天小畜 15 二十	木3 Wood 戊午 Earth Horse 4 1 The Cauldron 火風鼎 16 廿一
水1 Water 己未 Earth Goat 2 2 Rising 地風升 17 廿二	火7 Fire 庚申 Metal Monkey 1 3 Water 坎爲水 18 廿三	木8 Wood 辛酉 Metal Rooster 3 4 Lesser Exceeding 雷山小過 19 廿四	金4 Metal 壬戌 Water Dog 4 5 Gathering 澤地萃 20 廿五	水6 Water 癸亥 Water Pig 6 6 Peel 山地剝 21 廿六	水1 Water 甲子 Wood Rat 1 7 Earth 坤爲地 22 廿七	木3 Wood 乙丑 Wood Ox 6 8 Biting 火雷噬嗑 23 廿八
火2 Fire 丙寅 Fire Tiger 4 9 Family 風火家人 24 廿九	水6 Water 丁卯 Fire Rabbit 9 1 Decreasing 山澤損 25 三月初一	金9 Metal 戊辰 Earth Dragon 6 2 Tread 天澤履 26 初二	木8 Wood 己巳 Earth Snake 2 3 Great Strength 雷天大壯 27 初三	木8 Wood 庚午 Metal Horse 9 4 Consistency 雷風恆 28 初四	金9 Metal 辛未 Metal Goat 3 5 Litigation 天水訟 29 初五	水1 Water 壬申 Water Monkey 7 6 Officer 地水師 30 初六

APRIL 1963 丙辰

Xuan Kong Element 玄空五行	兌爲澤 Marsh	Period Luck 卦運	Monthly Star 月星
Metal 金4		1	6

SUNDAY	MONDAY	TUESDAY	WEDNESDAY	THURSDAY	FRIDAY	SATURDAY
	火7 Fire 甲戌 Wood Dog 2 8 Obstruction 水山蹇 1 初八	木3 Wood 乙亥 Wood Pig 3 9 Advancement 火地晉 2 初九	水6 Water 丙子 Fire Rat 3 1 Nourish 山雷頤 3 初十	金4 Metal 丁丑 Fire Ox 7 2 Following 澤雷隨 4 十一	木8 Wood 戊寅 Earth Tiger 6 3 Abundance 雷火豐 5 十二	火7 Fire 己卯 Earth Rabbit 8 4 Regulate 水澤節 6 十三
水1 Water 庚辰 Metal Dragon 9 5 Unity 地天泰 7 十四	木3 Wood 辛巳 Metal Snake 7 6 Great Reward 火天大有 8 十五	火2 Fire 壬午 Water Horse 1 7 Wind 巽爲風 9 十六	金4 Metal 癸未 Water Goat 8 8 Trap 澤水困 10 十七	木3 Wood 甲申 Wood Monkey 9 9 Not Yet Accomplished 火水未濟 11 十八	金9 Metal 乙酉 Wood Rooster 4 1 Retreat 天山遯 12 十九	水6 Water 丙戌 Fire Dog 1 2 Mountain 艮爲山 13 二十
木8 Wood 丁亥 Fire Pig 8 3 Delight 雷地豫 14 廿一	火7 Fire 戊子 Earth Rat 4 4 Beginning 水雷屯 15 廿二	金9 Metal 己丑 Earth Ox 2 5 Without Wrongdoing 天雷無妄 16 廿三	木3 Wood 庚寅 Metal Tiger 1 6 Fire 離爲火 17 廿四	火2 Fire 辛卯 Metal Rabbit 3 7 Sincerity 風澤中孚 18 廿五	水6 Water 壬辰 Water Dragon 4 8 Big Livestock 山天大畜 19 廿六	金4 Metal 癸巳 Water Snake 6 9 Eliminating 澤天夬 20 廿七
金9 Metal 甲午 Wood Horse 1 1 Heaven 乾爲天 21 廿八	火7 Fire 乙未 Wood Goat 6 2 Well 水風井 22 廿九	木8 Wood 丙申 Fire Monkey 4 3 Relief 雷水解 23 三十	金4 Metal 丁酉 Fire Rooster 9 4 Influence 澤山咸 24 四月初一	水1 Water 戊戌 Earth Dog 6 5 Humility 地山謙 25 初二	火2 Fire 己亥 Earth Pig 2 6 Observation 風地觀 26 初三	火2 Fire 庚子 Metal Rat 9 7 Increasing 風雷益 27 初四
水1 Water 辛丑 Metal Ox 3 8 Dimming Light 地火明夷 28 初五	金9 Metal 壬寅 Water Tiger 7 9 Fellowship 天火同人 29 初六	木8 Wood 癸卯 Water Rabbit 7 1 Marrying Maiden 雷澤歸妹 30 初七				

MAY 1963 丁巳

Xuan Kong Element 玄空五行	風天小畜 Small Livestock	Period Luck 卦運	Monthly Star 月星
Fire 火2		8	5

SUNDAY	MONDAY	TUESDAY	WEDNESDAY	THURSDAY	FRIDAY	SATURDAY
			木3 Wood Opposition 2 甲辰 Wood Dragon 火澤睽 1 初八 2	火7 Fire Waiting 3 乙巳 Wood Snake 水天需 2 初九 3	金4 Metal Great Exceeding 4 丙午 Fire Horse 澤風大過 3 初十 3	水6 Water Poison 5 丁未 Fire Goat 山風蠱 4 十一 7
火2 Fire Dispersing 6 戊申 Earth Monkey 風水渙 5 十二 6	木3 Wood Travelling 7 己酉 Earth Rooster 火山旅 6 十三 8	金9 Metal Stagnation 8 庚戌 Metal Dog 天地否 7 十四 9	火7 Fire Alliance 9 辛亥 Metal Pig 水地比 8 十五 7	木8 Wood Thunder 1 壬子 Water Rat 震爲雷 9 十六 1	水6 Water Beauty 2 癸丑 Water Ox 山火賁 10 十七 8	火7 Fire Accomplished 3 甲寅 Wood Tiger 水火既濟 11 十八 9
水1 Water Arriving 4 乙卯 Wood Rabbit 地澤臨 12 十九 4	金4 Metal Marsh 5 丙辰 Fire Dragon 兑爲澤 13 二十 1	火2 Fire Small Livestock 6 丁巳 Fire Snake 風天小畜 14 廿一 8	木3 Wood The Cauldron 7 戊午 Earth Horse 火風鼎 15 廿二 4	水1 Water Rising 8 己未 Earth Goat 地風升 16 廿三 2	火7 Fire Water 9 庚申 Metal Monkey 坎爲水 17 廿四 1	木8 Wood Lesser Exceeding 1 辛酉 Metal Rooster 雷山小過 18 廿五 3
金4 Metal Gathering 2 壬戌 Water Dog 澤地萃 19 廿六 4	水6 Water Peel 3 癸亥 Water Pig 山地剝 20 廿七 6	水1 Water Earth 4 甲子 Wood Rat 坤爲地 21 廿八 1	木3 Wood Biting 5 乙丑 Wood Ox 火雷噬嗑 22 廿九 6	火2 Fire Family 6 丙寅 Fire Tiger 風火家人 23 閏四月初一 4	水6 Water Decreasing 7 丁卯 Fire Rabbit 山澤損 24 初二 9	金9 Metal Tread 8 戊辰 Earth Dragon 天澤履 25 初三 6
木8 Wood Great Strength 9 己巳 Earth Snake 雷天大壯 26 初四 2	木8 Wood Consistency 1 庚午 Metal Horse 雷風恆 27 初五 9	金9 Metal Litigation 2 辛未 Metal Goat 天水訟 28 初六 3	水1 Water Officer 3 壬申 Water Monkey 地水師 29 初七 7	火2 Fire Gradual Progress 4 癸酉 Water Rooster 風山漸 30 初八 7	火7 Fire Obstruction 5 甲戌 Wood Dog 水山蹇 31 初九 2	

JUNE 1963 戊午

Xuan Kong Element 玄空五行	火風鼎 The Cauldron	Period Luck 卦運	Monthly Star 月星
Wood 木3		4	4

SUNDAY	MONDAY	TUESDAY	WEDNESDAY	THURSDAY	FRIDAY	SATURDAY
木3 Wood Opposition 2 甲辰 Wood Dragon 火澤睽 30 初十 2						木3 Wood Advancement 6 乙亥 Wood Pig 火地晉 1 初十 3
水6 Water Nourish 7 丙子 Fire Rat 山雷頤 2 十一 3	金4 Metal Following 8 丁丑 Fire Ox 澤雷隨 3 十二 7	木8 Wood Abundance 9 戊寅 Earth Tiger 雷火豐 4 十三 6	火7 Fire Regulate 1 己卯 Earth Rabbit 水澤節 5 十四 8	水1 Water Unity 2 庚辰 Metal Dragon 地天泰 6 十五 9	木3 Wood Great Reward 3 辛巳 Metal Snake 火天大有 7 十六 7	火2 Fire Wind 4 壬午 Water Horse 巽爲風 8 十七 1
金4 Metal Trap 5 癸未 Water Goat 澤水困 9 十八 8	木3 Wood Not Yet Accomplished 6 甲申 Wood Monkey 火水未濟 10 十九 9	金9 Metal Retreat 7 乙酉 Wood Rooster 天山遯 11 二十 4	水6 Water Mountain 8 丙戌 Fire Dog 艮爲山 12 廿一 1	木8 Wood Delight 9 丁亥 Fire Pig 雷地豫 13 廿二 8	火7 Fire Beginning 1 戊子 Earth Rat 水雷屯 14 廿三 4	金9 Metal Without Wrongdoing 2 己丑 Earth Ox 天雷無妄 15 廿四 2
木3 Wood Fire 3 庚寅 Metal Tiger 離爲火 16 廿五 1	火2 Fire Sincerity 4 辛卯 Metal Rabbit 風澤中孚 17 廿六 3	水6 Water Big Livestock 5 壬辰 Water Dragon 山天大畜 18 廿七 4	金4 Metal Eliminating 6 癸巳 Water Snake 澤天夬 19 廿八 6	金9 Metal Heaven 7 甲午 Wood Horse 乾爲天 20 廿九 1	火7 Fire Well 8 乙未 Wood Goat 水風井 21 五月初一 6	木8 Wood Relief 9/1 丙申 Fire Monkey 雷水解 22 初二 4
金4 Metal Influence 9 丁酉 Fire Rooster 澤山咸 23 初三 9	水1 Water Humility 8 戊戌 Earth Dog 地山謙 24 初四 6	火2 Fire Observation 7 己亥 Earth Pig 風地觀 25 初五 2	火2 Fire Increasing 6 庚子 Metal Rat 風雷益 26 初六 9	水1 Water Dimming Light 5 辛丑 Metal Ox 地火明夷 27 初七 3	金9 Metal Fellowship 4 壬寅 Water Tiger 天火同人 28 初八 7	木8 Wood Marrying Maiden 3 癸卯 Water Rabbit 雷澤歸妹 29 初九 7

JULY 1963 己未

Xuan Kong Element 玄空五行	地風升 Rising	Period Luck 卦運	Monthly Star 月星
Water 水1		2	3

SUNDAY	MONDAY	TUESDAY	WEDNESDAY	THURSDAY	FRIDAY	SATURDAY
	火7 Fire 1 Waiting 乙巳 Wood Snake 水天需 1 十一 3	金4 Metal 9 Great Exceeding 丙午 Fire Horse 澤風大過 2 十二 3	水6 Water 8 Poison 丁未 Fire Goat 山風蠱 3 十三 7	火2 Fire 7 Dispersing 戊申 Earth Monkey 風水渙 4 十四 6	木3 Wood 6 Travelling 己酉 Earth Rooster 火山旅 5 十五 8	金9 Metal 5 Stagnation 庚戌 Metal Dog 天地否 6 十六 9
火7 Fire 4 Alliance 辛亥 Metal Pig 水地比 7 十七 7	木8 Wood 3 Thunder 壬子 Water Rat 震爲雷 8 十八 1	水6 Water 2 Beauty 癸丑 Water Ox 山火賁 9 十九 8	火7 Fire 1 Accomplished 甲寅 Wood Tiger 水火既濟 10 二十 9	水1 Water 9 Arriving 乙卯 Wood Rabbit 地澤臨 11 廿一 4	金4 Metal 8 Marsh 丙辰 Fire Dragon 兑爲澤 12 廿二 1	火2 Fire 7 Small Livestock 丁巳 Fire Snake 風天小畜 13 廿三 8
木3 Wood 6 The Cauldron 戊午 Earth Horse 火風鼎 14 廿四 4	水1 Water 5 Rising 己未 Earth Goat 地風升 15 廿五 2	火7 Fire 4 Water 庚申 Metal Monkey 坎爲水 16 廿六 1	木8 Wood 3 Lesser Exceeding 辛酉 Metal Rooster 雷山小過 17 廿七 3	金4 Metal 2 Gathering 壬戌 Water Dog 澤地萃 18 廿八 4	水6 Water 1 Peel 癸亥 Water Pig 山地剝 19 廿九 6	水1 Water 9 Earth 甲子 Wood Rat 坤爲地 20 三十 1
木3 Wood 8 Biting 乙丑 Wood Ox 火雷噬嗑 21 六月初一 6	火2 Fire 7 Family 丙寅 Fire Tiger 風火家人 22 初二 4	水6 Water 6 Decreasing 丁卯 Fire Rabbit 山澤損 23 初三 9	金9 Metal 5 Tread 戊辰 Earth Dragon 天澤履 24 初四 6	木8 Wood 4 Great Strength 己巳 Earth Snake 雷天大壯 25 初五 2	木8 Wood 3 Consistency 庚午 Metal Horse 雷風恆 26 初六 9	金9 Metal 2 Litigation 辛未 Metal Goat 天水訟 27 初七 3
水1 Water 1 Officer 壬申 Water Monkey 地水師 28 初八 7	火2 Fire 9 Gradual Progress 癸酉 Water Rooster 風山漸 29 初九 7	火7 Fire 8 Obstruction 甲戌 Wood Dog 水山蹇 30 初十 2	木3 Wood 7 Advancement 乙亥 Wood Pig 火地晉 31 十一 3			

AUGUST 1963 庚申

Xuan Kong Element 玄空五行	坎爲水 Water	Period Luck 卦運	Monthly Star 月星
Fire 火7		1	2

SUNDAY	MONDAY	TUESDAY	WEDNESDAY	THURSDAY	FRIDAY	SATURDAY
				水6 Water 6 Nourish 丙子 Fire Rat 山雷頤 1 十二 3	金4 Metal 5 Following 丁丑 Fire Ox 澤雷隨 2 十三 7	木8 Wood 4 Abundance 戊寅 Earth Tiger 雷火豐 3 十四 6
火7 Fire 3 Regulate 己卯 Earth Rabbit 水澤節 4 十五 8	水1 Water 2 Unity 庚辰 Metal Dragon 地天泰 5 十六 9	木3 Wood 1 Great Reward 辛巳 Metal Snake 火天大有 6 十七 7	火2 Fire 9 Wind 壬午 Water Horse 巽爲風 7 十八 1	金4 Metal 8 Trap 癸未 Water Goat 澤水困 8 十九 8	木3 Wood 7 Not Yet Accomplished 甲申 Wood Monkey 火水未濟 9 二十 9	金9 Metal 6 Retreat 乙酉 Wood Rooster 天山遯 10 廿一 4
水6 Water 5 Mountain 丙戌 Fire Dog 艮爲山 11 廿二 1	木8 Wood 4 Delight 丁亥 Fire Pig 雷地豫 12 廿三 8	火7 Fire 3 Beginning 戊子 Earth Rat 水雷屯 13 廿四 4	金9 Metal 2 Without Wrongdoing 己丑 Earth Ox 天雷無妄 14 廿五 2	木3 Wood 1 Fire 庚寅 Metal Tiger 離爲火 15 廿六 1	火2 Fire 9 Sincerity 辛卯 Metal Rabbit 風澤中孚 16 廿七 3	水6 Water 8 Big Livestock 壬辰 Water Dragon 山天大畜 17 廿八 4
金4 Metal 7 Eliminating 癸巳 Water Snake 澤天夬 18 廿九 6	金9 Metal 6 Heaven 甲午 Wood Horse 乾爲天 19 七月初一 1	火7 Fire 5 Well 乙未 Wood Goat 水風井 20 初二 6	木8 Wood 4 Relief 丙申 Fire Monkey 雷水解 21 初三 4	金4 Metal 3 Influence 丁酉 Fire Rooster 澤山咸 22 初四 9	水1 Water 2 Humility 戊戌 Earth Dog 地山謙 23 初五 6	火2 Fire 1 Observation 己亥 Earth Pig 風地觀 24 初六 2
火2 Fire 9 Increasing 庚子 Metal Rat 風雷益 25 初七 9	水1 Water 8 Dimming Light 辛丑 Metal Ox 地火明夷 26 初八 3	金9 Metal 7 Fellowship 壬寅 Water Tiger 天火同人 27 初九 7	木8 Wood 6 Marrying Maiden 癸卯 Water Rabbit 雷澤歸妹 28 初十 7	木3 Wood 5 Opposition 甲辰 Wood Dragon 火澤睽 29 十一 2	火7 Fire 4 Waiting 乙巳 Wood Snake 水天需 30 十二 3	金4 Metal 3 Great Exceeding 丙午 Fire Horse 澤風大過 31 十三 3

SEPTEMBER 1963 辛酉

Xuan Kong Element 玄空五行	雷山小過 Lesser Exceeding	Period Luck 卦運	Monthly Star 月星
Wood 木8		3	1

SUNDAY	MONDAY	TUESDAY	WEDNESDAY	THURSDAY	FRIDAY	SATURDAY
水6 Water 2 Poison 丁未 Fire Goat 山風蠱 1 十四 7	火2 Fire 1 Dispersing 戊申 Earth Monkey 風水渙 2 十五 6	木3 Wood 9 Travelling 己酉 Earth Rooster 火山旅 3 十六 8	金9 Metal 8 Stagnation 庚戌 Metal Dog 天地否 4 十七 9	火7 Fire 7 Alliance 辛亥 Metal Pig 水地比 5 十八 7	木8 Wood 6 Thunder 壬子 Water Rat 震爲雷 6 十九 1	水6 Water 5 Beauty 癸丑 Water Ox 山火賁 7 二十 8
火7 Fire 4 Accomplished 甲寅 Wood Tiger 水火既濟 8 廿一 9	水1 Water 3 Arriving 乙卯 Wood Rabbit 地澤臨 9 廿二 4	金4 Metal 2 Marsh 丙辰 Fire Dragon 兌爲澤 10 廿三 1	火2 Fire 1 Small Livestock 丁巳 Fire Snake 風天小畜 11 廿四 8	木3 Wood 9 The Cauldron 戊午 Earth Horse 火風鼎 12 廿五 4	水1 Water 8 Rising 己未 Earth Goat 地風升 13 廿六 2	火7 Fire 7 Water 庚申 Metal Monkey 坎爲水 14 廿七 1
木8 Wood 6 Lesser Exceeding 辛酉 Metal Rooster 雷山小過 15 廿八 3	金4 Metal 5 Gathering 壬戌 Water Dog 澤地萃 16 廿九 4	水6 Water 4 Peel 癸亥 Water Pig 山地剝 17 三十 6	水1 Water 3 Earth 甲子 Wood Rat 坤爲地 18 八月初一 1	木3 Wood 2 Biting 乙丑 Wood Ox 火雷噬嗑 19 初二 6	火2 Fire 1 Family 丙寅 Fire Tiger 風火家人 20 初三 4	水6 Water 9 Decreasing 丁卯 Fire Rabbit 山澤損 21 初四 9
金9 Metal 8 Tread 戊辰 Earth Dragon 天澤履 22 初五 6	木8 Wood 7 Great Strength 己巳 Earth Snake 雷天大壯 23 初六 2	木8 Wood 6 Consistency 庚午 Metal Horse 雷風恆 24 初七 9	金9 Metal 5 Litigation 辛未 Metal Goat 天水訟 25 初八 3	水1 Water 4 Officer 壬申 Water Monkey 地水師 26 初九 7	火2 Fire 3 Gradual Progress 癸酉 Water Rooster 風山漸 27 初十 7	火7 Fire 2 Obstruction 甲戌 Wood Dog 水山蹇 28 十一 2
木3 Wood 1 Advancement 乙亥 Wood Pig 火地晉 29 十二 3	水6 Water 9 Nourish 丙子 Fire Rat 山雷頤 30 十三 3					

OCTOBER 1963 壬戌

Xuan Kong Element 玄空五行	澤地萃 Gathering	Period Luck 卦運	Monthly Star 月星
Metal 金4		4	9

SUNDAY	MONDAY	TUESDAY	WEDNESDAY	THURSDAY	FRIDAY	SATURDAY
		金4 Metal 8 Following 丁丑 Fire Ox 澤雷隨 1 十四 7	木8 Wood 7 Abundance 戊寅 Earth Tiger 雷火豐 2 十五 6	火7 Fire 6 Regulate 己卯 Earth Rabbit 水澤節 3 十六 8	水1 Water 5 Unity 庚辰 Metal Dragon 地天泰 4 十七 9	木3 Wood 4 Great Reward 辛巳 Metal Snake 火天大有 5 十八 7
火2 Fire 3 Wind 壬午 Water Horse 巽爲風 6 十九 1	金4 Metal 2 Trap 癸未 Water Goat 澤水困 7 二十 8	木3 Wood 1 Not Yet Accomplished 甲申 Wood Monkey 火水未濟 8 廿一 9	金9 Metal 9 Retreat 乙酉 Wood Rooster 天山遯 9 廿二 4	水6 Water 8 Mountain 丙戌 Fire Dog 艮爲山 10 廿三 1	木8 Wood 7 Delight 丁亥 Fire Pig 雷地豫 11 廿四 8	火7 Fire 6 Beginning 戊子 Earth Rat 水雷屯 12 廿五 4
金9 Metal 5 Without Wrongdoing 己丑 Earth Ox 天雷無妄 13 廿六 2	木3 Wood 4 Fire 庚寅 Metal Tiger 離爲火 14 廿七 1	火2 Fire 3 Sincerity 辛卯 Metal Rabbit 風澤中孚 15 廿八 3	水6 Water 2 Big Livestock 壬辰 Water Dragon 山天大畜 16 廿九 4	金4 Metal 1 Eliminating 癸巳 Water Snake 澤天夬 17 九月初一 6	金9 Metal 9 Heaven 甲午 Wood Horse 乾爲天 18 初二 1	火7 Fire 8 Well 乙未 Wood Goat 水風井 19 初三 6
木8 Wood 7 Relief 丙申 Fire Monkey 雷水解 20 初四 4	金4 Metal 6 Influence 丁酉 Fire Rooster 澤山咸 21 初五 9	水1 Water 5 Humility 戊戌 Earth Dog 地山謙 22 初六 6	火2 Fire 4 Observation 己亥 Earth Pig 風地觀 23 初七 2	火2 Fire 3 Increasing 庚子 Metal Rat 風雷益 24 初八 9	水1 Water 2 Dimming Light 辛丑 Metal Ox 地火明夷 25 初九 3	金9 Metal 1 Fellowship 壬寅 Water Tiger 天火同人 26 初十 7
木8 Wood 9 Marrying Maiden 癸卯 Water Rabbit 雷澤歸妹 27 十一 7	木3 Wood 8 Opposition 甲辰 Wood Dragon 火澤睽 28 十二 2	火7 Fire 7 Waiting 乙巳 Wood Snake 水天需 29 十三 3	金4 Metal 6 Great Exceeding 丙午 Fire Horse 澤風大過 30 十四 3	水6 Water 5 Poison 丁未 Fire Goat 山風蠱 31 十五 7		

NOVEMBER 1963 癸亥

Xuan Kong Element 玄空五行	山地剝 Peel	Period Luck 卦運	Monthly Star 月星
Water 水6		6	8

SUNDAY	MONDAY	TUESDAY	WEDNESDAY	THURSDAY	FRIDAY	SATURDAY
					火2 Fire · Dispersing · 4 · 風水渙 · 戊申 Earth Monkey · **1** 十六 · 6	木3 Wood · Travelling · 3 · 火山旅 · 己酉 Earth Rooster · **2** 十七 · 8
金9 Metal · Stagnation · 2 · 天地否 · 庚戌 Metal Dog · **3** 十八 · 9	火7 Fire · Alliance · 1 · 水地比 · 辛亥 Metal Pig · **4** 十九 · 7	木8 Wood · Thunder · 9 · 震爲雷 · 壬子 Water Rat · **5** 二十 · 1	水6 Water · Beauty · 8 · 山火賁 · 癸丑 Water Ox · **6** 廿一 · 8	火7 Fire · Accomplished · 7 · 水火既濟 · 甲寅 Wood Tiger · **7** 廿二 · 9	水1 Water · Arriving · 6 · 地澤臨 · 乙卯 Wood Rabbit · **8** 廿三 · 4	金4 Metal · Marsh · 5 · 兌爲澤 · 丙辰 Fire Dragon · **9** 廿四 · 1
火2 Fire · Small Livestock · 4 · 風天小畜 · 丁巳 Fire Snake · **10** 廿五 · 8	木3 Wood · The Cauldron · 3 · 火風鼎 · 戊午 Earth Horse · **11** 廿六 · 4	水1 Water · Rising · 2 · 地風升 · 己未 Earth Goat · **12** 廿七 · 2	火7 Fire · Water · 1 · 坎爲水 · 庚申 Metal Monkey · **13** 廿八 · 1	木8 Wood · Lesser Exceeding · 9 · 雷山小過 · 辛酉 Metal Rooster · **14** 廿九 · 3	金4 Metal · Gathering · 8 · 澤地萃 · 壬戌 Water Dog · **15** 三十 · 4	水6 Water · Peel · 7 · 山地剝 · 癸亥 Water Pig · **16** 十月初一 · 6
水1 Water · Earth · 6 · 坤爲地 · 甲子 Wood Rat · **17** 初二 · 1	木3 Wood · Biting · 5 · 火雷噬嗑 · 乙丑 Wood Ox · **18** 初三 · 6	火2 Fire · Family · 4 · 風火家人 · 丙寅 Fire Tiger · **19** 初四 · 4	水6 Water · Decreasing · 3 · 山澤損 · 丁卯 Fire Rabbit · **20** 初五 · 9	金9 Metal · Tread · 2 · 天澤履 · 戊辰 Earth Dragon · **21** 初六 · 6	木8 Wood · Great Strength · 1 · 雷天大壯 · 己巳 Earth Snake · **22** 初七 · 2	木8 Wood · Consistency · 9 · 雷風恆 · 庚午 Metal Horse · **23** 初八 · 9
金9 Metal · Litigation · 8 · 天水訟 · 辛未 Metal Goat · **24** 初九 · 3	水1 Water · Officer · 7 · 地水師 · 壬申 Water Monkey · **25** 初十 · 7	火2 Fire · Gradual Progress · 6 · 風山漸 · 癸酉 Water Rooster · **26** 十一 · 7	火7 Fire · Obstruction · 5 · 水山蹇 · 甲戌 Wood Dog · **27** 十二 · 2	木3 Wood · Advancement · 4 · 火地晉 · 乙亥 Wood Pig · **28** 十三 · 3	水6 Water · Nourish · 3 · 山雷頤 · 丙子 Fire Rat · **29** 十四 · 3	金4 Metal · Following · 2 · 澤雷隨 · 丁丑 Fire Ox · **30** 十五 · 7

DECEMBER 1963 甲子

Xuan Kong Element 玄空五行	坤爲地 Earth	Period Luck 卦運	Monthly Star 月星
Water 水1		1	7

SUNDAY	MONDAY	TUESDAY	WEDNESDAY	THURSDAY	FRIDAY	SATURDAY
木8 Wood · Abundance · 1 · 雷火豐 · 戊寅 Earth Tiger · **1** 十六 · 6	火7 Fire · Regulate · 9 · 水澤節 · 己卯 Earth Rabbit · **2** 十七 · 8	水1 Water · Unity · 8 · 地天泰 · 庚辰 Metal Dragon · **3** 十八 · 9	木3 Wood · Great Reward · 7 · 火天大有 · 辛巳 Metal Snake · **4** 十九 · 7	火2 Fire · Wind · 6 · 巽爲風 · 壬午 Water Horse · **5** 二十 · 1	金4 Metal · Trap · 5 · 澤水困 · 癸未 Water Goat · **6** 廿一 · 8	木3 Wood · Not Yet Accomplished · 4 · 火水未濟 · 甲申 Wood Monkey · **7** 廿二 · 9
金9 Metal · Retreat · 3 · 天山遯 · 乙酉 Wood Rooster · **8** 廿三 · 4	水6 Water · Mountain · 2 · 艮爲山 · 丙戌 Fire Dog · **9** 廿四 · 1	木8 Wood · Delight · 1 · 雷地豫 · 丁亥 Fire Pig · **10** 廿五 · 8	火7 Fire · Beginning · 9 · 水雷屯 · 戊子 Earth Rat · **11** 廿六 · 4	金9 Metal · Without Wrongdoing · 8 · 天雷無妄 · 己丑 Earth Ox · **12** 廿七 · 2	木3 Wood · Fire · 7 · 離爲火 · 庚寅 Metal Tiger · **13** 廿八 · 1	火2 Fire · Sincerity · 6 · 風澤中孚 · 辛卯 Metal Rabbit · **14** 廿九 · 3
水6 Water · Big Livestock · 5 · 山天大畜 · 壬辰 Water Dragon · **15** 三十 · 4	金4 Metal · Eliminating · 4 · 澤天夬 · 癸巳 Water Snake · **16** 十一月初一 · 6	金9 Metal · Heaven · 3 · 乾爲天 · 甲午 Wood Horse · **17** 初二 · 1	火7 Fire · Well · 2 · 水風井 · 乙未 Wood Goat · **18** 初三 · 6	木8 Wood · Relief · 1 · 雷水解 · 丙申 Fire Monkey · **19** 初四 · 4	金4 Metal · Influence · 9 · 澤山咸 · 丁酉 Fire Rooster · **20** 初五 · 9	水1 Water · Humility · 8 · 地山謙 · 戊戌 Earth Dog · **21** 初六 · 6
火2 Fire · Observation · 7/3 · 風地觀 · 己亥 Earth Pig · **22** 初七 · 2	火2 Fire · Increasing · 4 · 風雷益 · 庚子 Metal Rat · **23** 初八 · 9	水1 Water · Dimming Light · 5 · 地火明夷 · 辛丑 Metal Ox · **24** 初九 · 3	金9 Metal · Fellowship · 6 · 天火同人 · 壬寅 Water Tiger · **25** 初十 · 7	木8 Wood · Marrying Maiden · 7 · 雷澤歸妹 · 癸卯 Water Rabbit · **26** 十一 · 7	木3 Wood · Opposition · 8 · 火澤睽 · 甲辰 Wood Dragon · **27** 十二 · 2	火7 Fire · Waiting · 9 · 水天需 · 乙巳 Wood Snake · **28** 十三 · 3
金4 Metal · Great Exceeding · 1 · 澤風大過 · 丙午 Fire Horse · **29** 十四 · 3	水6 Water · Poison · 2 · 山風蠱 · 丁未 Fire Goat · **30** 十五 · 7	火2 Fire · Dispersing · 3 · 風水渙 · 戊申 Earth Monkey · **31** 十六 · 6				

1964 甲辰

(*Jia Chen*) Wood Dragon

1964 甲辰 *(Jia Chen)* Wood Dragon

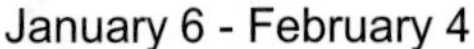

January 6 - February 4

February 5 - March 4

March 5 - April 4

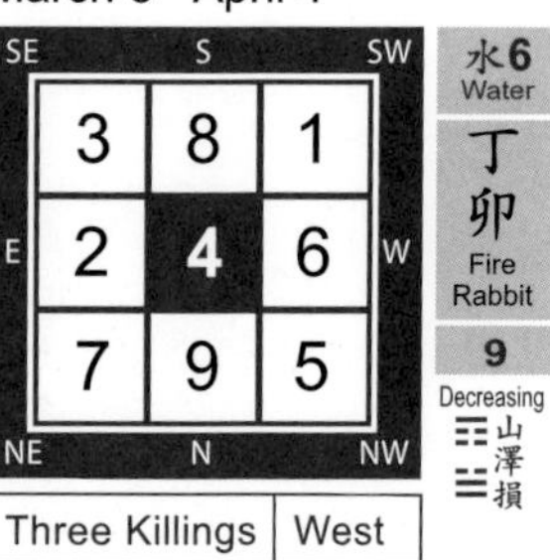

April 5 - May 4

May 5 - June 5

June 6 - July 6

July 7 - August 6

August 7 - September 6

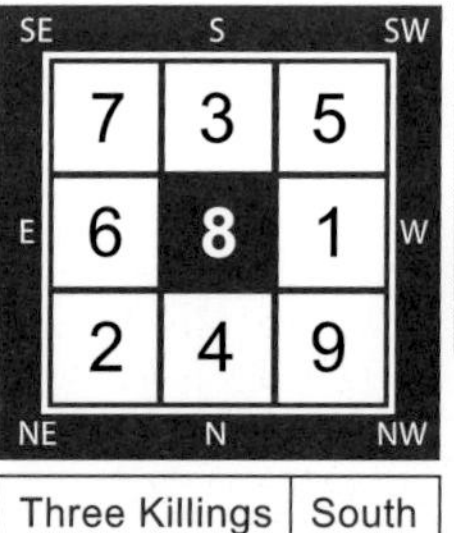

September 7 - October 7

October 8 - November 6

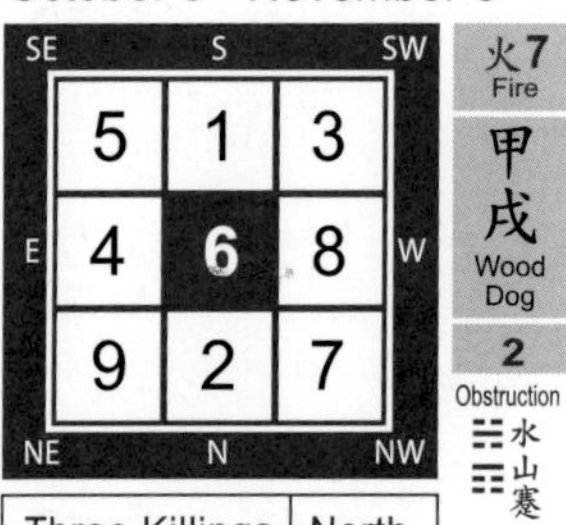

November 7 - December 6

December 7 - January 4

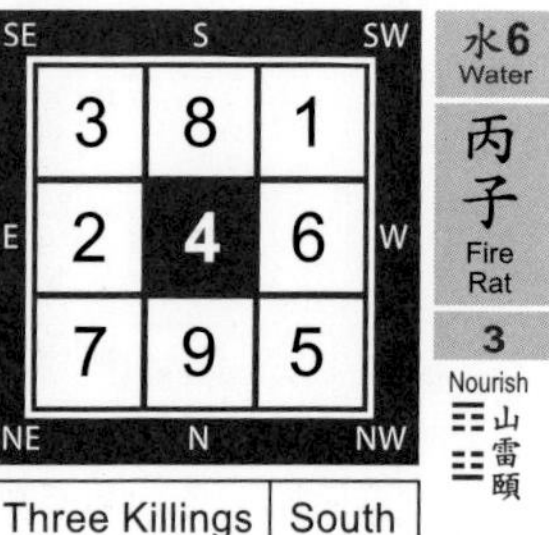

JANUARY 1964 乙丑

Xuan Kong Element 玄空五行	火雷噬嗑 Biting	Period Luck 卦運	Monthly Star 月星
Wood 木3		6	6

SUNDAY	MONDAY	TUESDAY	WEDNESDAY	THURSDAY	FRIDAY	SATURDAY
			木3 Wood Travelling 4 己酉 Earth Rooster 火山旅 1 十七 8	金9 Metal Stagnation 5 庚戌 Metal Dog 天地否 2 十八 9	火7 Fire Alliance 6 辛亥 Metal Pig 水地比 3 十九 7	木8 Wood Thunder 7 壬子 Water Rat 震爲雷 4 二十 1
水6 Water Beauty 8 癸丑 Water Ox 山火賁 5 廿一 8	火7 Fire Accomplished 9 甲寅 Wood Tiger 水火既濟 6 廿二 9	水1 Water Arriving 1 乙卯 Wood Rabbit 地澤臨 7 廿三 4	金4 Metal Marsh 2 丙辰 Fire Dragon 兌爲澤 8 廿四 1	火2 Fire Small Livestock 3 丁巳 Fire Snake 風天小畜 9 廿五 8	木3 Wood The Cauldron 4 戊午 Earth Horse 火風鼎 10 廿六 4	水1 Water Rising 5 己未 Earth Goat 地風升 11 廿七 2
火7 Fire Water 6 庚申 Metal Monkey 坎爲水 12 廿八 1	木8 Wood Lesser Exceeding 7 辛酉 Metal Rooster 雷山小過 13 廿九 3	金4 Metal Gathering 8 壬戌 Water Dog 澤地萃 14 三十 4	水6 Water Peel 9 癸亥 Water Pig 山地剝 15 十二月初一 6	水1 Water Earth 1 甲子 Wood Rat 坤爲地 16 初二 1	木3 Wood Biting 2 乙丑 Wood Ox 火雷噬嗑 17 初三 6	火2 Fire Family 3 丙寅 Fire Tiger 風火家人 18 初四 4
水6 Water Decreasing 4 丁卯 Fire Rabbit 山澤損 19 初五 9	金9 Metal Tread 5 戊辰 Earth Dragon 天澤履 20 初六 6	木8 Wood Great Strength 6 己巳 Earth Snake 雷天大壯 21 初七 2	木8 Wood Consistency 7 庚午 Metal Horse 雷風恆 22 初八 9	金9 Metal Litigation 8 辛未 Metal Goat 天水訟 23 初九 3	水1 Water Officer 9 壬申 Water Monkey 地水師 24 初十 7	火2 Fire Gradual Progress 1 癸酉 Water Rooster 風山漸 25 十一 7
火7 Fire Obstruction 2 甲戌 Wood Dog 水山蹇 26 十二 2	木3 Wood Advancement 3 乙亥 Wood Pig 火地晉 27 十三 3	水6 Water Nourish 4 丙子 Fire Rat 山雷頤 28 十四 3	金4 Metal Following 5 丁丑 Fire Ox 澤雷隨 29 十五 7	木8 Wood Abundance 6 戊寅 Earth Tiger 雷火豐 30 十六 6	火7 Fire Regulate 7 己卯 Earth Rabbit 水澤節 31 十七 8	

FEBRUARY 1964 丙寅

Xuan Kong Element 玄空五行	風火家人 Family	Period Luck 卦運	Monthly Star 月星
Fire 火2		4	5

SUNDAY	MONDAY	TUESDAY	WEDNESDAY	THURSDAY	FRIDAY	SATURDAY
						水1 Water Unity 8 庚辰 Metal Dragon 地天泰 1 十八 9
木3 Wood Great Reward 9 辛巳 Metal Snake 火天大有 2 十九 7	火2 Fire Wind 1 壬午 Water Horse 巽爲風 3 二十 1	金4 Metal Trap 2 癸未 Water Goat 澤水困 4 廿一 8	木3 Wood Not Yet Accomplished 3 甲申 Wood Monkey 火水未濟 5 廿二 9	金9 Metal Retreat 4 乙酉 Wood Rooster 天山遯 6 廿三 4	水6 Water Mountain 5 丙戌 Fire Dog 艮爲山 7 廿四 1	木8 Wood Delight 6 丁亥 Fire Pig 雷地豫 8 廿五 8
火7 Fire Beginning 7 戊子 Earth Rat 水雷屯 9 廿六 4	金9 Metal Without Wrongdoing 8 己丑 Earth Ox 天雷無妄 10 廿七 2	木3 Wood Fire 9 庚寅 Metal Tiger 離爲火 11 廿八 1	火2 Fire Sincerity 1 辛卯 Metal Rabbit 風澤中孚 12 廿九 3	水6 Water Big Livestock 2 壬辰 Water Dragon 山天大畜 13 正月初一 4	金4 Metal Eliminating 3 癸巳 Water Snake 澤天夬 14 初二 6	金9 Metal Heaven 4 甲午 Wood Horse 乾爲天 15 初三 1
火7 Fire Well 5 乙未 Wood Goat 水風井 16 初四 6	木8 Wood Relief 6 丙申 Fire Monkey 雷水解 17 初五 4	金4 Metal Influence 7 丁酉 Fire Rooster 澤山咸 18 初六 9	水1 Water Humility 8 戊戌 Earth Dog 地山謙 19 初七 6	火2 Fire Observation 9 己亥 Earth Pig 風地觀 20 初八 2	火2 Fire Increasing 1 庚子 Metal Rat 風雷益 21 初九 9	水1 Water Dimming Light 2 辛丑 Metal Ox 地火明夷 22 初十 3
金9 Metal Fellowship 3 壬寅 Water Tiger 天火同人 23 十一 7	木8 Wood Marrying Maiden 4 癸卯 Water Rabbit 雷澤歸妹 24 十二 7	木3 Wood Opposition 5 甲辰 Wood Dragon 火澤睽 25 十三 2	火7 Fire Waiting 6 乙巳 Wood Snake 水天需 26 十四 3	金4 Metal Great Exceeding 7 丙午 Fire Horse 澤風大過 27 十五 3	水6 Water Poison 8 丁未 Fire Goat 山風蠱 28 十六 7	火2 Fire Dispersing 9 戊申 Earth Monkey 風水渙 29 十七 6

MARCH 1964 丁卯

Xuan Kong Element 玄空五行	山澤損 Decreasing	Period Luck 卦運	Monthly Star 月星
Water 水6		9	4

SUNDAY	MONDAY	TUESDAY	WEDNESDAY	THURSDAY	FRIDAY	SATURDAY
1 十八 [1] Travelling 火山旅 木3 Wood 己酉 Earth Rooster 8	**2** 十九 [2] Stagnation 天地否 金9 Metal 庚戌 Metal Dog 9	**3** 二十 [3] Alliance 水地比 火7 Fire 辛亥 Metal Pig 7	**4** 廿一 [4] Thunder 震爲雷 木8 Wood 壬子 Water Rat 1	**5** 廿二 [5] Beauty 山火賁 水6 Water 癸丑 Water Ox 8	**6** 廿三 [6] Accomplished 水火既濟 火7 Fire 甲寅 Wood Tiger 9	**7** 廿四 [7] Arriving 地澤臨 水1 Water 乙卯 Wood Rabbit 4
8 廿五 [8] Marsh 兌爲澤 金4 Metal 丙辰 Fire Dragon 1	**9** 廿六 [9] Small Livestock 風天小畜 火2 Fire 丁巳 Fire Snake 8	**10** 廿七 [1] The Cauldron 火風鼎 木3 Wood 戊午 Earth Horse 4	**11** 廿八 [2] Rising 地風升 水1 Water 己未 Earth Goat 2	**12** 廿九 [3] Water 坎爲水 火7 Fire 庚申 Metal Monkey 1	**13** 三十 [4] Lesser Exceeding 雷山小過 木8 Wood 辛酉 Metal Rooster 3	**14** 二月初一 [5] Gathering 澤地萃 金4 Metal 壬戌 Water Dog 4
15 初二 [6] Peel 山地剝 水6 Water 癸亥 Water Pig 6	**16** 初三 [7] Earth 坤爲地 水1 Water 甲子 Wood Rat 1	**17** 初四 [8] Biting 火雷噬嗑 木3 Wood 乙丑 Wood Ox 6	**18** 初五 [9] Family 風火家人 火2 Fire 丙寅 Fire Tiger 4	**19** 初六 [1] Decreasing 山澤損 水6 Water 丁卯 Fire Rabbit 9	**20** 初七 [2] Tread 天澤履 金9 Metal 戊辰 Earth Dragon 6	**21** 初八 [3] Great Strength 雷天大壯 木8 Wood 己巳 Earth Snake 2
22 初九 [4] Consistency 雷風恒 木8 Wood 庚午 Metal Horse 9	**23** 初十 [5] Litigation 天水訟 金9 Metal 辛未 Metal Goat 3	**24** 十一 [6] Officer 地水師 水1 Water 壬申 Water Monkey 7	**25** 十二 [7] Gradual Progress 風山漸 火2 Fire 癸酉 Water Rooster 7	**26** 十三 [8] Obstruction 水山蹇 火7 Fire 甲戌 Wood Dog 2	**27** 十四 [9] Advancement 火地晉 木3 Wood 乙亥 Wood Pig 3	**28** 十五 [1] Nourish 山雷頤 水6 Water 丙子 Fire Rat 3
29 十六 [2] Following 澤雷隨 金4 Metal 丁丑 Fire Ox 7	**30** 十七 [3] Abundance 雷火豐 木8 Wood 戊寅 Earth Tiger 6	**31** 十八 [4] Regulate 水澤節 火7 Fire 己卯 Earth Rabbit 8				

APRIL 1964 戊辰

Xuan Kong Element 玄空五行	天澤履 Tread	Period Luck 卦運	Monthly Star 月星
Metal 金9		6	3

SUNDAY	MONDAY	TUESDAY	WEDNESDAY	THURSDAY	FRIDAY	SATURDAY
			1 十九 [5] Unity 地天泰 水1 Water 庚辰 Metal Dragon 9	**2** 二十 [6] Great Reward 火天大有 木3 Wood 辛巳 Metal Snake 7	**3** 廿一 [7] Wind 巽爲風 火2 Fire 壬午 Water Horse 1	**4** 廿二 [8] Trap 澤水困 金4 Metal 癸未 Water Goat 8
5 廿三 [9] Not Yet Accomplished 火水未濟 木3 Wood 甲申 Wood Monkey 9	**6** 廿四 [1] Retreat 天山遯 金9 Metal 乙酉 Wood Rooster 4	**7** 廿五 [2] Mountain 艮爲山 水6 Water 丙戌 Fire Dog 1	**8** 廿六 [3] Delight 雷地豫 木8 Wood 丁亥 Fire Pig 8	**9** 廿七 [4] Beginning 水雷屯 火7 Fire 戊子 Earth Rat 4	**10** 廿八 [5] Without Wrongdoing 天雷無妄 金9 Metal 己丑 Earth Ox 2	**11** 廿九 [6] Fire 離爲火 木3 Wood 庚寅 Metal Tiger 1
12 三月初一 [7] Sincerity 風澤中孚 火2 Fire 辛卯 Metal Rabbit 3	**13** 初二 [8] Big Livestock 山天大畜 水6 Water 壬辰 Water Dragon 4	**14** 初三 [9] Eliminating 澤天夬 金4 Metal 癸巳 Water Snake 6	**15** 初四 [1] Heaven 乾爲天 金9 Metal 甲午 Wood Horse 1	**16** 初五 [2] Well 水風井 火7 Fire 乙未 Wood Goat 6	**17** 初六 [3] Relief 雷水解 木8 Wood 丙申 Fire Monkey 4	**18** 初七 [4] Influence 澤山咸 金4 Metal 丁酉 Fire Rooster 9
19 初八 [5] Humility 地山謙 水1 Water 戊戌 Earth Dog 6	**20** 初九 [6] Observation 風地觀 火2 Fire 己亥 Earth Pig 2	**21** 初十 [7] Increasing 風雷益 火2 Fire 庚子 Metal Rat 9	**22** 十一 [8] Dimming Light 地火明夷 水1 Water 辛丑 Metal Ox 3	**23** 十二 [9] Fellowship 天火同人 金9 Metal 壬寅 Water Tiger 7	**24** 十三 [1] Marrying Maiden 雷澤歸妹 木8 Wood 癸卯 Water Rabbit 7	**25** 十四 [2] Opposition 火澤睽 木3 Wood 甲辰 Wood Dragon 2
26 十五 [3] Waiting 水天需 火7 Fire 乙巳 Wood Snake 3	**27** 十六 [4] Great Exceeding 澤風大過 金4 Metal 丙午 Fire Horse 3	**28** 十七 [5] Poison 山風蠱 水6 Water 丁未 Fire Goat 7	**29** 十八 [6] Dispersing 風水渙 火2 Fire 戊申 Earth Monkey 6	**30** 十九 [7] Travelling 火山旅 木3 Wood 己酉 Earth Rooster 8		

MAY 1964 己巳

Xuan Kong Element 玄空五行	雷天大壯 Great Strength	Period Luck 卦運	Monthly Star 月星
Wood 木8		2	2

SUNDAY	MONDAY	TUESDAY	WEDNESDAY	THURSDAY	FRIDAY	SATURDAY
水1 Water Unity 2 庚辰 Metal Dragon 地天泰 31 二十 9					金9 Metal Stagnation 8 庚戌 Metal Dog 天地否 1 二十 9	火7 Fire Alliance 9 辛亥 Metal Pig 水地比 2 廿一 7
木8 Wood Thunder 1 壬子 Water Rat 震爲雷 3 廿二 1	水6 Water Beauty 2 癸丑 Water Ox 山火賁 4 廿三 8	火7 Fire Accomplished 3 甲寅 Wood Tiger 水火既濟 5 廿四 9	水1 Water Arriving 4 乙卯 Wood Rabbit 地澤臨 6 廿五 4	金4 Metal Marsh 5 丙辰 Fire Dragon 兌爲澤 7 廿六 1	火2 Fire Small Livestock 6 丁巳 Fire Snake 風天小畜 8 廿七 8	木3 Wood The Cauldron 7 戊午 Earth Horse 火風鼎 9 廿八 4
水1 Water Rising 8 己未 Earth Goat 地風升 10 廿九 2	火7 Fire Water 9 庚申 Metal Monkey 坎爲水 11 三十 1	木8 Wood Lesser Exceeding 1 辛酉 Metal Rooster 雷山小過 12 四月初一 3	金4 Metal Gathering 2 壬戌 Water Dog 澤地萃 13 初二 4	水6 Water Peel 3 癸亥 Water Pig 山地剝 14 初三 6	水1 Water Earth 4 甲子 Wood Rat 坤爲地 15 初四 1	木3 Wood Biting 5 乙丑 Wood Ox 火雷噬嗑 16 初五 6
火2 Fire Family 6 丙寅 Fire Tiger 風火家人 17 初六 4	水6 Water Decreasing 7 丁卯 Fire Rabbit 山澤損 18 初七 9	金9 Metal Tread 8 戊辰 Earth Dragon 天澤履 19 初八 6	木8 Wood Great Strength 9 己巳 Earth Snake 雷天大壯 20 初九 2	木8 Wood Consistency 1 庚午 Metal Horse 雷風恆 21 初十 9	金9 Metal Litigation 2 辛未 Metal Goat 天水訟 22 十一 3	水1 Water Officer 3 壬申 Water Monkey 地水師 23 十二 7
火2 Fire Gradual Progress 4 癸酉 Water Rooster 風山漸 24 十三 7	火7 Fire Obstruction 5 甲戌 Wood Dog 水山蹇 25 十四 2	木3 Wood Advancement 6 乙亥 Wood Pig 火地晉 26 十五 3	水6 Water Nourish 7 丙子 Fire Rat 山雷頤 27 十六 3	金4 Metal Following 8 丁丑 Fire Ox 澤雷隨 28 十七 7	木8 Wood Abundance 9 戊寅 Earth Tiger 雷火豐 29 十八 6	火7 Fire Regulate 1 己卯 Earth Rabbit 水澤節 30 十九 8

JUNE 1964 庚午

Xuan Kong Element 玄空五行	雷風恆 Consistency	Period Luck 卦運	Monthly Star 月星
Wood 木8		9	1

SUNDAY	MONDAY	TUESDAY	WEDNESDAY	THURSDAY	FRIDAY	SATURDAY
	木3 Wood Great Reward 3 辛巳 Metal Snake 火天大有 1 廿一 7	火2 Fire Wind 4 壬午 Water Horse 巽爲風 2 廿二 1	金4 Metal Trap 5 癸未 Water Goat 澤水困 3 廿三 8	木3 Wood Not Yet Accomplished 6 甲申 Wood Monkey 火水未濟 4 廿四 9	金9 Metal Retreat 7 乙酉 Wood Rooster 天山遯 5 廿五 4	水6 Water Mountain 8 丙戌 Fire Dog 艮爲山 6 廿六 1
木8 Wood Delight 9 丁亥 Fire Pig 雷地豫 7 廿七 8	火7 Fire Beginning 1 戊子 Earth Rat 水雷屯 8 廿八 4	金9 Metal Without Wrongdoing 2 己丑 Earth Ox 天雷無妄 9 廿九 2	木3 Wood Fire 3 庚寅 Metal Tiger 離爲火 10 五月初一 1	火2 Fire Sincerity 4 辛卯 Metal Rabbit 風澤中孚 11 初二 3	水6 Water Big Livestock 5 壬辰 Water Dragon 山天大畜 12 初三 4	金4 Metal Eliminating 6 癸巳 Water Snake 澤天夬 13 初四 6
金9 Metal Heaven 7 甲午 Wood Horse 乾爲天 14 初五 1	火7 Fire Well 8 乙未 Wood Goat 水風井 15 初六 6	木8 Wood Relief 9 丙申 Fire Monkey 雷水解 16 初七 4	金4 Metal Influence 1 丁酉 Fire Rooster 澤山咸 17 初八 9	水1 Water Humility 2 戊戌 Earth Dog 地山謙 18 初九 6	火2 Fire Observation 3 己亥 Earth Pig 風地觀 19 初十 2	火2 Fire Increasing 4 庚子 Metal Rat 風雷益 20 十一 9
水1 Water Dimming Light 5/5 辛丑 Metal Ox 地火明夷 21 十二 3	金9 Metal Fellowship 4 壬寅 Water Tiger 天火同人 22 十三 7	木8 Wood Marrying Maiden 3 癸卯 Water Rabbit 雷澤歸妹 23 十四 7	木3 Wood Opposition 2 甲辰 Wood Dragon 火澤睽 24 十五 2	火7 Fire Waiting 1 乙巳 Wood Snake 水天需 25 十六 3	金4 Metal Great Exceeding 9 丙午 Fire Horse 澤風大過 26 十七 3	水6 Water Poison 8 丁未 Fire Goat 山風蠱 27 十八 7
火2 Fire Dispersing 7 戊申 Earth Monkey 風水渙 28 十九 6	木3 Wood Travelling 6 己酉 Earth Rooster 火山旅 29 二十 8	金9 Metal Stagnation 5 庚戌 Metal Dog 天地否 30 廿一 9				

JULY 1964 辛未

Xuan Kong Element 玄空五行	天水訟 Litigation	Period Luck 卦運	Monthly Star 月星
Metal 金9		3	9

SUNDAY	MONDAY	TUESDAY	WEDNESDAY	THURSDAY	FRIDAY	SATURDAY
			1 廿二 火7 Fire Alliance 水地比 辛亥 Metal Pig 7 [4]	**2** 廿三 木8 Wood Thunder 震爲雷 壬子 Water Rat 1 [3]	**3** 廿四 水6 Water Beauty 山火賁 癸丑 Water Ox 8 [2]	**4** 廿五 火7 Fire Accomplished 水火既濟 甲寅 Wood Tiger 9 [1]
5 廿六 水1 Water Arriving 地澤臨 乙卯 Wood Rabbit 4 [9]	**6** 廿七 金4 Metal Marsh 兌爲澤 丙辰 Fire Dragon 1 [8]	**7** 廿八 火2 Fire Small Livestock 風天小畜 丁巳 Fire Snake 8 [7]	**8** 廿九 木3 Wood The Cauldron 火風鼎 戊午 Earth Horse 4 [6]	**9** 六月初一 水1 Water Rising 地風升 己未 Earth Goat 2 [5]	**10** 初二 火7 Fire Water 坎爲水 庚申 Metal Monkey 1 [4]	**11** 初三 木8 Wood Lesser Exceeding 雷山小過 辛酉 Metal Rooster 3 [3]
12 初四 金4 Metal Gathering 澤地萃 壬戌 Water Dog 4 [2]	**13** 初五 水6 Water Peel 山地剝 癸亥 Water Pig 6 [1]	**14** 初六 水1 Water Earth 坤爲地 甲子 Wood Rat 1 [9]	**15** 初七 木3 Wood Biting 火雷噬嗑 乙丑 Wood Ox 6 [8]	**16** 初八 火2 Fire Family 風火家人 丙寅 Fire Tiger 4 [7]	**17** 初九 水6 Water Decreasing 山澤損 丁卯 Fire Rabbit 9 [6]	**18** 初十 金9 Metal Tread 天澤履 戊辰 Earth Dragon 6 [5]
19 十一 木8 Wood Great Strength 雷天大壯 己巳 Earth Snake 2 [4]	**20** 十二 木8 Wood Consistency 雷風恆 庚午 Metal Horse 9 [3]	**21** 十三 金9 Metal Litigation 天水訟 辛未 Metal Goat 3 [2]	**22** 十四 水1 Water Officer 地水師 壬申 Water Monkey 7 [1]	**23** 十五 火2 Fire Gradual Progress 風山漸 癸酉 Water Rooster 7 [9]	**24** 十六 火7 Fire Obstruction 水山蹇 甲戌 Wood Dog 2 [8]	**25** 十七 木3 Wood Advancement 火地晉 乙亥 Wood Pig 3 [7]
26 十八 水6 Water Nourish 山雷頤 丙子 Fire Rat 3 [6]	**27** 十九 金4 Metal Following 澤雷隨 丁丑 Fire Ox 7 [5]	**28** 二十 木8 Wood Abundance 雷火豐 戊寅 Earth Tiger 6 [4]	**29** 廿一 火7 Fire Regulate 水澤節 己卯 Earth Rabbit 8 [3]	**30** 廿二 水1 Water Unity 地天泰 庚辰 Metal Dragon 9 [2]	**31** 廿三 木3 Wood Great Reward 火天大有 辛巳 Metal Snake 7 [1]	

AUGUST 1964 壬申

Xuan Kong Element 玄空五行	地水師 Officer	Period Luck 卦運	Monthly Star 月星
Water 水1		7	8

SUNDAY	MONDAY	TUESDAY	WEDNESDAY	THURSDAY	FRIDAY	SATURDAY
30 廿三 火7 Fire Alliance 水地比 辛亥 Metal Pig 7 [7]	**31** 廿四 木8 Wood Thunder 震爲雷 壬子 Water Rat 1 [6]					**1** 廿四 火2 Fire Wind 巽爲風 壬午 Water Horse 1 [9]
2 廿五 金4 Metal Trap 澤水困 癸未 Water Goat 8 [8]	**3** 廿六 木3 Wood Not Yet Accomplished 火水未濟 甲申 Wood Monkey 9 [7]	**4** 廿七 金9 Metal Retreat 天山遯 乙酉 Wood Rooster 4 [6]	**5** 廿八 水6 Water Mountain 艮爲山 丙戌 Fire Dog 1 [5]	**6** 廿九 木8 Wood Delight 雷地豫 丁亥 Fire Pig 8 [4]	**7** 三十 火7 Fire Beginning 水雷屯 戊子 Earth Rat 4 [3]	**8** 七月初一 金9 Metal Without Wrongdoing 天雷無妄 己丑 Earth Ox 2 [2]
9 初二 木3 Wood Fire 離爲火 庚寅 Metal Tiger 1 [1]	**10** 初三 火2 Fire Sincerity 風澤中孚 辛卯 Metal Rabbit 3 [9]	**11** 初四 水6 Water Big Livestock 山天大畜 壬辰 Water Dragon 4 [8]	**12** 初五 金4 Metal Eliminating 澤天夬 癸巳 Water Snake 6 [7]	**13** 初六 金9 Metal Heaven 乾爲天 甲午 Wood Horse 1 [6]	**14** 初七 火7 Fire Well 水風井 乙未 Wood Goat 6 [5]	**15** 初八 木8 Wood Relief 雷水解 丙申 Fire Monkey 4 [4]
16 初九 金4 Metal Influence 澤山咸 丁酉 Fire Rooster 9 [3]	**17** 初十 水1 Water Humility 地山謙 戊戌 Earth Dog 6 [2]	**18** 十一 火2 Fire Observation 風地觀 己亥 Earth Pig 2 [1]	**19** 十二 火2 Fire Increasing 風雷益 庚子 Metal Rat 9 [9]	**20** 十三 水1 Water Dimming Light 地火明夷 辛丑 Metal Ox 3 [8]	**21** 十四 金9 Metal Fellowship 天火同人 壬寅 Water Tiger 7 [7]	**22** 十五 木8 Wood Marrying Maiden 雷澤歸妹 癸卯 Water Rabbit 7 [6]
23 十六 木3 Wood Opposition 火澤睽 甲辰 Wood Dragon 2 [5]	**24** 十七 火7 Fire Waiting 水天需 乙巳 Wood Snake 3 [4]	**25** 十八 金4 Metal Great Exceeding 澤風大過 丙午 Fire Horse 3 [3]	**26** 十九 水6 Water Poison 山風蠱 丁未 Fire Goat 7 [2]	**27** 二十 火2 Fire Dispersing 風水渙 戊申 Earth Monkey 6 [1]	**28** 廿一 木3 Wood Travelling 火山旅 己酉 Earth Rooster 8 [9]	**29** 廿二 金9 Metal Stagnation 天地否 庚戌 Metal Dog 9 [8]

SEPTEMBER 1964 癸酉

Xuan Kong Element 玄空五行	風山漸 Gradual Progress	Period Luck 卦運	Monthly Star 月星
Fire 火2		7	7

SUNDAY	MONDAY	TUESDAY	WEDNESDAY	THURSDAY	FRIDAY	SATURDAY
		水6 Water 5 Beauty 癸丑 Water Ox 山火賁 1 廿五 8	火7 Fire 4 Accomplished 甲寅 Wood Tiger 水火既濟 2 廿六 9	水1 Water 3 Arriving 乙卯 Wood Rabbit 地澤臨 3 廿七 4	金4 Metal 2 Marsh 丙辰 Fire Dragon 兑爲澤 4 廿八 1	火2 Fire 1 Small Livestock 丁巳 Fire Snake 風天小畜 5 廿九 8
木3 Wood 9 The Cauldron 戊午 Earth Horse 火風鼎 6 八月初一 4	水1 Water 8 Rising 己未 Earth Goat 地風升 7 初二 2	火7 Fire 7 Water 庚申 Metal Monkey 坎爲水 8 初三 1	木8 Wood 6 Lesser Exceeding 辛酉 Metal Rooster 雷山小過 9 初四 3	金4 Metal 5 Gathering 壬戌 Water Dog 澤地萃 10 初五 4	水6 Water 4 Peel 癸亥 Water Pig 山地剝 11 初六 6	水1 Water 3 Earth 甲子 Wood Rat 坤爲地 12 初七 1
木3 Wood 2 Biting 乙丑 Wood Ox 火雷噬嗑 13 初八 6	火2 Fire 1 Family 丙寅 Fire Tiger 風火家人 14 初九 4	水6 Water 9 Decreasing 丁卯 Fire Rabbit 山澤損 15 初十 9	金9 Metal 8 Tread 戊辰 Earth Dragon 天澤履 16 十一 6	木8 Wood 7 Great Strength 己巳 Earth Snake 雷天大壯 17 十二 2	木8 Wood 6 Consistency 庚午 Metal Horse 雷風恆 18 十三 9	金9 Metal 5 Litigation 辛未 Metal Goat 天水訟 19 十四 3
水1 Water 4 Officer 壬申 Water Monkey 地水師 20 十五 7	火2 Fire 3 Gradual Progress 癸酉 Water Rooster 風山漸 21 十六 7	火7 Fire 2 Obstruction 甲戌 Wood Dog 水山蹇 22 十七 2	木3 Wood 1 Advancement 乙亥 Wood Pig 火地晉 23 十八 3	水6 Water 9 Nourish 丙子 Fire Rat 山雷頤 24 十九 3	金4 Metal 8 Following 丁丑 Fire Ox 澤雷隨 25 二十 7	木8 Wood 7 Abundance 戊寅 Earth Tiger 雷火豐 26 廿一 6
火7 Fire 6 Regulate 己卯 Earth Rabbit 水澤節 27 廿二 8	水1 Water 5 Unity 庚辰 Metal Dragon 地天泰 28 廿三 9	木3 Wood 4 Great Reward 辛巳 Metal Snake 火天大有 29 廿四 7	火2 Fire 3 Wind 壬午 Water Horse 巽爲風 30 廿五 1			

OCTOBER 1964 甲戌

Xuan Kong Element 玄空五行	水山蹇 Obstruction	Period Luck 卦運	Monthly Star 月星
Fire 火7		2	6

SUNDAY	MONDAY	TUESDAY	WEDNESDAY	THURSDAY	FRIDAY	SATURDAY
				金4 Metal 2 Trap 癸未 Water Goat 澤水困 1 廿六 8	木3 Wood 1 Not Yet Accomplished 甲申 Wood Monkey 火水未濟 2 廿七 9	金9 Metal 9 Retreat 乙酉 Wood Rooster 天山遯 3 廿八 4
水6 Water 8 Mountain 丙戌 Fire Dog 艮爲山 4 廿九 1	木8 Wood 7 Delight 丁亥 Fire Pig 雷地豫 5 三十 8	火7 Fire 6 Beginning 戊子 Earth Rat 水雷屯 6 九月初一 4	金9 Metal 5 Without Wrongdoing 己丑 Earth Ox 天雷無妄 7 初二 2	木3 Wood 4 Fire 庚寅 Metal Tiger 離爲火 8 初三 1	火2 Fire 3 Sincerity 辛卯 Metal Rabbit 風澤中孚 9 初四 3	水6 Water 2 Big Livestock 壬辰 Water Dragon 山天大畜 10 初五 4
金4 Metal 1 Eliminating 癸巳 Water Snake 澤天夬 11 初六 6	金9 Metal 9 Heaven 甲午 Wood Horse 乾爲天 12 初七 1	火7 Fire 8 Well 乙未 Wood Goat 水風井 13 初八 6	木8 Wood 7 Relief 丙申 Fire Monkey 雷水解 14 初九 4	金4 Metal 6 Influence 丁酉 Fire Rooster 澤山咸 15 初十 9	水1 Water 5 Humility 戊戌 Earth Dog 地山謙 16 十一 6	火2 Fire 4 Observation 己亥 Earth Pig 風地觀 17 十二 2
火2 Fire 3 Increasing 庚子 Metal Rat 風雷益 18 十三 9	水1 Water 2 Dimming Light 辛丑 Metal Ox 地火明夷 19 十四 3	金9 Metal 1 Fellowship 壬寅 Water Tiger 天火同人 20 十五 7	木8 Wood 9 Marrying Maiden 癸卯 Water Rabbit 雷澤歸妹 21 十六 7	木3 Wood 8 Opposition 甲辰 Wood Dragon 火澤睽 22 十七 2	火7 Fire 7 Waiting 乙巳 Wood Snake 水天需 23 十八 3	金4 Metal 6 Great Exceeding 丙午 Fire Horse 澤風大過 24 十九 3
水6 Water 5 Poison 丁未 Fire Goat 山風蠱 25 二十 7	火2 Fire 4 Dispersing 戊申 Earth Monkey 風水渙 26 廿一 6	木3 Wood 3 Travelling 己酉 Earth Rooster 火山旅 27 廿二 8	金9 Metal 2 Stagnation 庚戌 Metal Dog 天地否 28 廿三 9	火7 Fire 1 Alliance 辛亥 Metal Pig 水地比 29 廿四 7	木8 Wood 9 Thunder 壬子 Water Rat 震爲雷 30 廿五 1	水6 Water 8 Beauty 癸丑 Water Ox 山火賁 31 廿六 8

NOVEMBER 1964 乙亥

Xuan Kong Element 玄空五行	火地晉 Advancement	Period Luck 卦運	Monthly Star 月星
Wood 木3		3	5

SUNDAY	MONDAY	TUESDAY	WEDNESDAY	THURSDAY	FRIDAY	SATURDAY
火7 Fire 7 Accomplished 水火既濟 甲寅 Wood Tiger 1 廿七 9	水1 Water 6 Arriving 地澤臨 乙卯 Wood Rabbit 2 廿八 4	金4 Metal 5 Marsh 兌爲澤 丙辰 Fire Dragon 3 廿九 1	火2 Fire 4 Small Livestock 風天小畜 丁巳 Fire Snake 4 十月初一 8	木3 Wood 3 The Cauldron 火風鼎 戊午 Earth Horse 5 初二 4	水1 Water 2 Rising 地風升 己未 Earth Goat 6 初三 2	火7 Fire 1 Water 坎爲水 庚申 Metal Monkey 7 初四 1
木8 Wood 9 Lesser Exceeding 雷山小過 辛酉 Metal Rooster 8 初五 3	金4 Metal 8 Gathering 澤地萃 壬戌 Water Dog 9 初六 4	水6 Water 7 Peel 山地剝 癸亥 Water Pig 10 初七 6	水1 Water 6 Earth 坤爲地 甲子 Wood Rat 11 初八 1	木3 Wood 5 Biting 火雷噬嗑 乙丑 Wood Ox 12 初九 6	火2 Fire 4 Family 風火家人 丙寅 Fire Tiger 13 初十 4	水6 Water 3 Decreasing 山澤損 丁卯 Fire Rabbit 14 十一 9
金9 Metal 2 Tread 天澤履 戊辰 Earth Dragon 15 十二 6	木8 Wood 1 Great Strength 雷天大壯 己巳 Earth Snake 16 十三 2	木8 Wood 9 Consistency 雷風恆 庚午 Metal Horse 17 十四 9	金9 Metal 8 Litigation 天水訟 辛未 Metal Goat 18 十五 3	水1 Water 7 Officer 地水師 壬申 Water Monkey 19 十六 7	火2 Fire 6 Gradual Progress 風山漸 癸酉 Water Rooster 20 十七 7	火7 Fire 5 Obstruction 水山蹇 甲戌 Wood Dog 21 十八 2
木3 Wood 4 Advancement 火地晉 乙亥 Wood Pig 22 十九 3	水6 Water 3 Nourish 山雷頤 丙子 Fire Rat 23 二十 3	金4 Metal 2 Following 澤雷隨 丁丑 Fire Ox 24 廿一 7	木8 Wood 1 Abundance 雷火豐 戊寅 Earth Tiger 25 廿二 6	火7 Fire 9 Regulate 水澤節 己卯 Earth Rabbit 26 廿三 8	水1 Water 8 Unity 地天泰 庚辰 Metal Dragon 27 廿四 9	木3 Wood 7 Great Reward 火天大有 辛巳 Metal Snake 28 廿五 7
火2 Fire 6 Wind 巽爲風 壬午 Water Horse 29 廿六 1	金4 Metal 5 Trap 澤水困 癸未 Water Goat 30 廿七 8					

DECEMBER 1964 丙子

Xuan Kong Element 玄空五行	山雷頤 Nourish	Period Luck 卦運	Monthly Star 月星
Water 水6		3	4

SUNDAY	MONDAY	TUESDAY	WEDNESDAY	THURSDAY	FRIDAY	SATURDAY
		木3 Wood 4 Not Yet Accomplished 火水未濟 甲申 Wood Monkey 1 廿八 9	金9 Metal 3 Retreat 天山遯 乙酉 Wood Rooster 2 廿九 4	水6 Water 2 Mountain 艮爲山 丙戌 Fire Dog 3 三十 1	木8 Wood 1 Delight 雷地豫 丁亥 Fire Pig 4 十一月初一 8	火7 Fire 9 Beginning 水雷屯 戊子 Earth Rat 5 初二 4
金9 Metal 8 Without Wrongdoing 天雷無妄 己丑 Earth Ox 6 初三 2	木3 Wood 7 Fire 離爲火 庚寅 Metal Tiger 7 初四 1	火2 Fire 6 Sincerity 風澤中孚 辛卯 Metal Rabbit 8 初五 3	水6 Water 5 Big Livestock 山天大畜 壬辰 Water Dragon 9 初六 4	金4 Metal 4 Eliminating 澤天夬 癸巳 Water Snake 10 初七 6	金9 Metal 3 Heaven 乾爲天 甲午 Wood Horse 11 初八 1	火7 Fire 2 Well 水風井 乙未 Wood Goat 12 初九 6
木8 Wood 1 Relief 雷水解 丙申 Fire Monkey 13 初十 4	金4 Metal 9 Influence 澤山咸 丁酉 Fire Rooster 14 十一 9	水1 Water 8 Humility 地山謙 戊戌 Earth Dog 15 十二 6	火2 Fire 7 Observation 風地觀 己亥 Earth Pig 16 十三 2	火2 Fire 6 Increasing 風雷益 庚子 Metal Rat 17 十四 9	水1 Water 5 Dimming Light 地火明夷 辛丑 Metal Ox 18 十五 3	金9 Metal 4 Fellowship 天火同人 壬寅 Water Tiger 19 十六 7
木8 Wood 3 Marrying Maiden 雷澤歸妹 癸卯 Water Rabbit 20 十七 7	木3 Wood 2 Opposition 火澤睽 甲辰 Wood Dragon 21 十八 2	火7 Fire 1/9 Waiting 水天需 乙巳 Wood Snake 22 十九 3	金4 Metal 1 Great Exceeding 澤風大過 丙午 Fire Horse 23 二十 3	水6 Water 2 Poison 山風蠱 丁未 Fire Goat 24 廿一 7	火2 Fire 3 Dispersing 風水渙 戊申 Earth Monkey 25 廿二 6	木3 Wood 4 Travelling 火山旅 己酉 Earth Rooster 26 廿三 8
金9 Metal 5 Stagnation 天地否 庚戌 Metal Dog 27 廿四 9	火7 Fire 6 Alliance 水地比 辛亥 Metal Pig 28 廿五 7	木8 Wood 7 Thunder 震爲雷 壬子 Water Rat 29 廿六 1	水6 Water 8 Beauty 山火賁 癸丑 Water Ox 30 廿七 8	火7 Fire 9 Accomplished 水火既濟 甲寅 Wood Tiger 31 廿八 9		

1965 乙巳

(*Yi Si*) Wood Snake

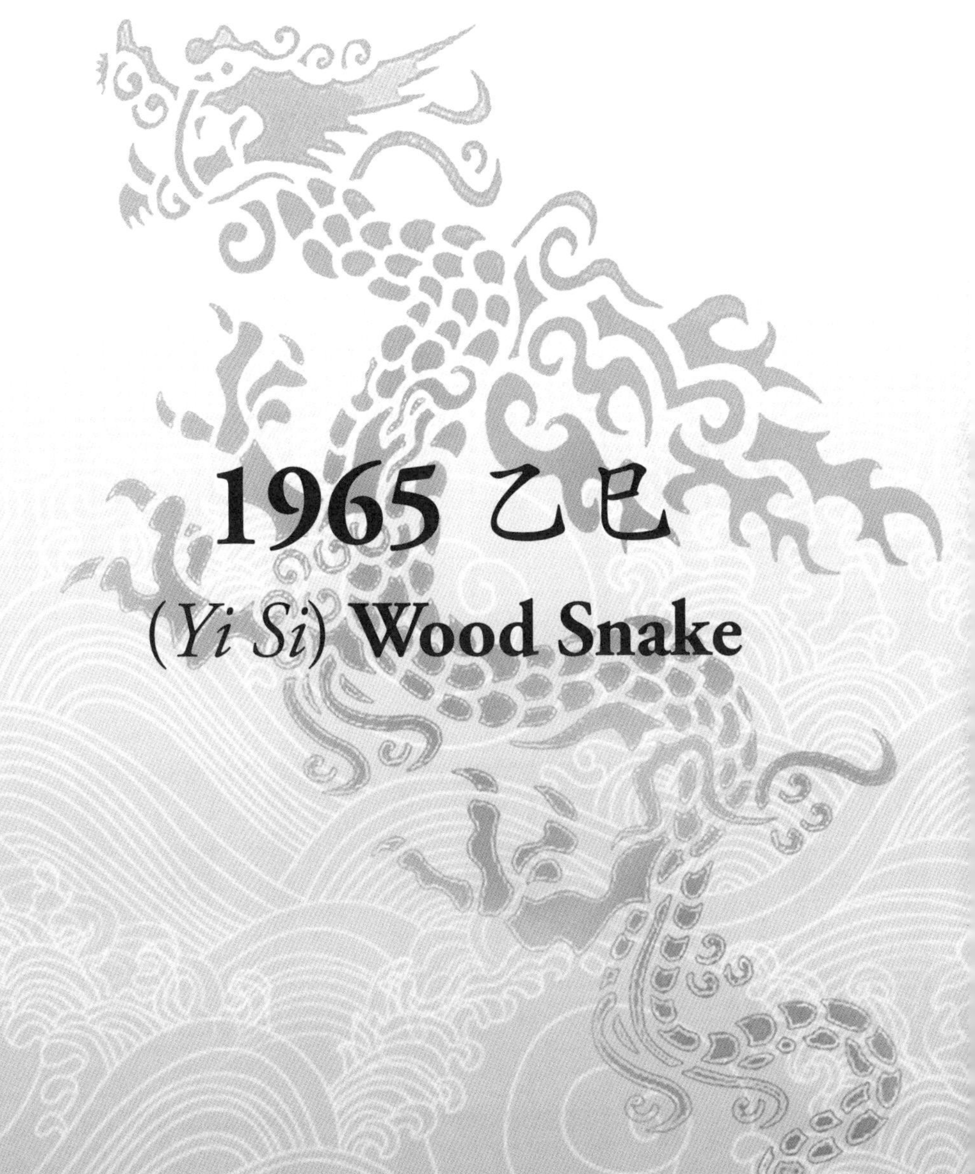

1965 乙巳 (*Yi Si*) Wood Snake

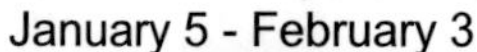

January 5 - February 3

February 4 - March 5

March 6 - April 4

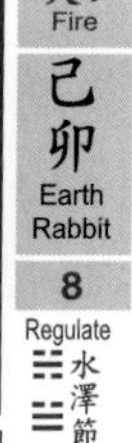

April 5 - May 5

May 6 - June 5

June 6 - July 6

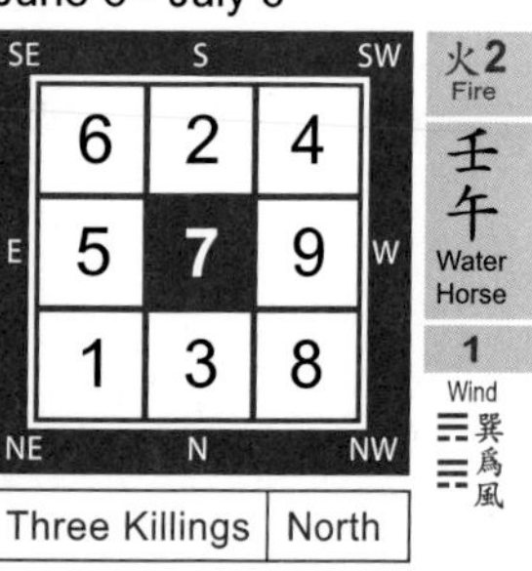

July 7 - August 7

August 8 - September 7

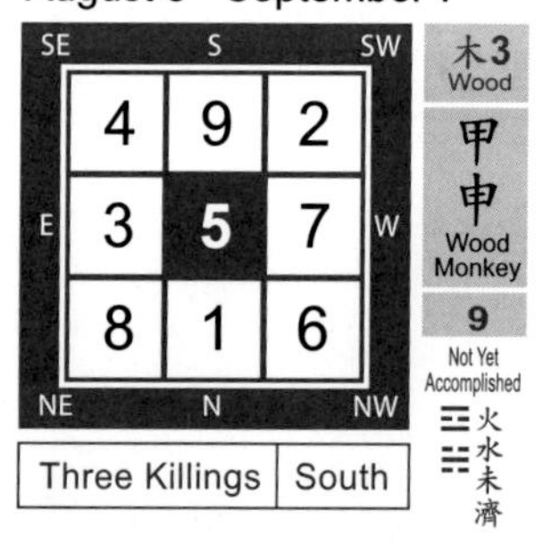

September 8 - October 7

October 8 - November 6

November 7 - December 6

December 7 - January 5

JANUARY 1965 丁丑

Xuan Kong Element 玄空五行	澤雷隨 Following	Period Luck 卦運	Monthly Star 月星
Metal 金4		7	3

SUNDAY	MONDAY	TUESDAY	WEDNESDAY	THURSDAY	FRIDAY	SATURDAY
金9 Metal 4 Retreat 乙酉 Wood Rooster 天山遯 31 廿九 4					水1 Water 1 Arriving 乙卯 Wood Rabbit 地澤臨 1 廿九 4	金4 Metal 2 Marsh 丙辰 Fire Dragon 兌爲澤 2 三十 1
火2 Fire 3 Small Livestock 丁巳 Fire Snake 風天小畜 3 十二月初 8	木3 Wood 4 The Cauldron 戊午 Earth Horse 火風鼎 4 初二 4	水1 Water 5 Rising 己未 Earth Goat 地風升 5 初三 2	火7 Fire 6 Water 庚申 Metal Monkey 坎爲水 6 初四 1	木8 Wood 7 Lesser Exceeding 辛酉 Metal Rooster 雷山小過 7 初五 3	金4 Metal 8 Gathering 壬戌 Water Dog 澤地萃 8 初六 4	水6 Water 9 Peel 癸亥 Water Pig 山地剝 9 初七 6
水1 Water 1 Earth 甲子 Wood Rat 坤爲地 10 初八 1	木3 Wood 2 Biting 乙丑 Wood Ox 火雷噬嗑 11 初九 6	火2 Fire 3 Family 丙寅 Fire Tiger 風火家人 12 初十 4	水6 Water 4 Decreasing 丁卯 Fire Rabbit 山澤損 13 十一 9	金9 Metal 5 Tread 戊辰 Earth Dragon 天澤履 14 十二 6	木8 Wood 6 Great Strength 己巳 Earth Snake 雷天大壯 15 十三 2	木8 Wood 7 Consistency 庚午 Metal Horse 雷風恆 16 十四 9
金9 Metal 8 Litigation 辛未 Metal Goat 天水訟 17 十五 3	水1 Water 9 Officer 壬申 Water Monkey 地水師 18 十六 7	火2 Fire 1 Gradual Progress 癸酉 Water Rooster 風山漸 19 十七 7	火7 Fire 2 Obstruction 甲戌 Wood Dog 水山蹇 20 十八 2	木3 Wood 3 Advancement 乙亥 Wood Pig 火地晉 21 十九 3	水6 Water 4 Nourish 丙子 Fire Rat 山雷頤 22 二十 3	金4 Metal 5 Following 丁丑 Fire Ox 澤雷隨 23 廿一 7
木8 Wood 6 Abundance 戊寅 Earth Tiger 雷火豐 24 廿二 6	火7 Fire 7 Regulate 己卯 Earth Rabbit 水澤節 25 廿三 8	水1 Water 8 Unity 庚辰 Metal Dragon 地天泰 26 廿四 9	木3 Wood 9 Great Reward 辛巳 Metal Snake 火天大有 27 廿五 7	火2 Fire 1 Wind 壬午 Water Horse 巽爲風 28 廿六 1	金4 Metal 2 Trap 癸未 Water Goat 澤水困 29 廿七 8	木3 Wood 3 Not Yet Accomplished 甲申 Wood Monkey 火水未濟 30 廿八 9

FEBRUARY 1965 戊寅

Xuan Kong Element 玄空五行	雷火豐 Abundance	Period Luck 卦運	Monthly Star 月星
Wood 木8		6	2

SUNDAY	MONDAY	TUESDAY	WEDNESDAY	THURSDAY	FRIDAY	SATURDAY
	水6 Water 5 Mountain 丙戌 Fire Dog 艮爲山 1 三十 1	木8 Wood 6 Delight 丁亥 Fire Pig 雷地豫 2 正月初一 8	火7 Fire 7 Beginning 戊子 Earth Rat 水雷屯 3 初二 4	金9 Metal 8 Without Wrongdoing 己丑 Earth Ox 天雷無妄 4 初三 2	木3 Wood 9 Fire 庚寅 Metal Tiger 離爲火 5 初四 1	火2 Fire 1 Sincerity 辛卯 Metal Rabbit 風澤中孚 6 初五 3
水6 Water 2 Big Livestock 壬辰 Water Dragon 山天大畜 7 初六 4	金4 Metal 3 Eliminating 癸巳 Water Snake 澤天夬 8 初七 6	金9 Metal 4 Heaven 甲午 Wood Horse 乾爲天 9 初八 1	火7 Fire 5 Well 乙未 Wood Goat 水風井 10 初九 6	木8 Wood 6 Relief 丙申 Fire Monkey 雷水解 11 初十 4	金4 Metal 7 Influence 丁酉 Fire Rooster 澤山咸 12 十一 9	水1 Water 8 Humility 戊戌 Earth Dog 地山謙 13 十二 6
火2 Fire 9 Observation 己亥 Earth Pig 風地觀 14 十三 2	火2 Fire 1 Increasing 庚子 Metal Rat 風雷益 15 十四 9	水1 Water 2 Dimming Light 辛丑 Metal Ox 地火明夷 16 十五 3	金9 Metal 3 Fellowship 壬寅 Water Tiger 天火同人 17 十六 7	木8 Wood 4 Marrying Maiden 癸卯 Water Rabbit 雷澤歸妹 18 十七 7	木3 Wood 5 Opposition 甲辰 Wood Dragon 火澤睽 19 十八 2	火7 Fire 6 Waiting 乙巳 Wood Snake 水天需 20 十九 3
金4 Metal 7 Great Exceeding 丙午 Fire Horse 澤風大過 21 二十 3	水6 Water 8 Poison 丁未 Fire Goat 山風蠱 22 廿一 7	火2 Fire 9 Dispersing 戊申 Earth Monkey 風水渙 23 廿二 6	木3 Wood 1 Travelling 己酉 Earth Rooster 火山旅 24 廿三 8	金9 Metal 2 Stagnation 庚戌 Metal Dog 天地否 25 廿四 9	火7 Fire 3 Alliance 辛亥 Metal Pig 水地比 26 廿五 7	木8 Wood 4 Thunder 壬子 Water Rat 震爲雷 27 廿六 1
水6 Water 5 Beauty 癸丑 Water Ox 山火賁 28 廿七 8						

MARCH 1965 己卯

Xuan Kong Element 玄空五行	水澤節 Regulate	Period Luck 卦運	Monthly Star 月星
Fire 火7		8	1

SUNDAY	MONDAY	TUESDAY	WEDNESDAY	THURSDAY	FRIDAY	SATURDAY
	火7 Fire 6 甲寅 Wood Tiger Accomplished 水火既濟 1 廿八 9	水1 Water 7 乙卯 Wood Rabbit Arriving 地澤臨 2 廿九 4	金4 Metal 8 丙辰 Fire Dragon Marsh 兌爲澤 3 二月初一 1	火2 Fire 9 丁巳 Fire Snake Small Livestock 風天小畜 4 初二 8	木3 Wood 1 戊午 Earth Horse The Cauldron 火風鼎 5 初三 4	水1 Water 2 己未 Earth Goat Rising 地風升 6 初四 2
火7 Fire 3 庚申 Metal Monkey Water 坎爲水 7 初五 1	木8 Wood 4 辛酉 Metal Rooster Lesser Exceeding 雷山小過 8 初六 3	金4 Metal 5 壬戌 Water Dog Gathering 澤地萃 9 初七 4	水6 Water 6 癸亥 Water Pig Peel 山地剝 10 初八 6	水1 Water 7 甲子 Wood Rat Earth 坤爲地 11 初九 1	木3 Wood 8 乙丑 Wood Ox Biting 火雷噬嗑 12 初十 6	火2 Fire 9 丙寅 Fire Tiger Family 風火家人 13 十一 4
水6 Water 1 丁卯 Fire Rabbit Decreasing 山澤損 14 十二 9	金9 Metal 2 戊辰 Earth Dragon Tread 天澤履 15 十三 6	木8 Wood 3 己巳 Earth Snake Great Strength 雷天大壯 16 十四 2	木8 Wood 4 庚午 Metal Horse Consistency 雷風恒 17 十五 9	金9 Metal 5 辛未 Metal Goat Litigation 天水訟 18 十六 3	水1 Water 6 壬申 Water Monkey Officer 地水師 19 十七 7	火2 Fire 7 癸酉 Water Rooster Gradual Progress 風山漸 20 十八 7
火7 Fire 8 甲戌 Wood Dog Obstruction 水山蹇 21 十九 2	木3 Wood 9 乙亥 Wood Pig Advancement 火地晉 22 二十 3	水6 Water 1 丙子 Fire Rat Nourish 山雷頤 23 廿一 3	金4 Metal 2 丁丑 Fire Ox Following 澤雷隨 24 廿二 7	木8 Wood 3 戊寅 Earth Tiger Abundance 雷火豐 25 廿三 6	火7 Fire 4 己卯 Earth Rabbit Regulate 水澤節 26 廿四 8	水1 Water 5 庚辰 Metal Dragon Unity 地天泰 27 廿五 9
木3 Wood 6 辛巳 Metal Snake Great Reward 火天大有 28 廿六 7	火2 Fire 7 壬午 Water Horse Wind 巽爲風 29 廿七 1	金4 Metal 8 癸未 Water Goat Trap 澤水困 30 廿八 8	木3 Wood 9 甲申 Wood Monkey Not Yet Accomplished 火水未濟 31 廿九 9			

APRIL 1965 庚辰

Xuan Kong Element 玄空五行	地天泰 Unity	Period Luck 卦運	Monthly Star 月星
Water 水1		9	9

SUNDAY	MONDAY	TUESDAY	WEDNESDAY	THURSDAY	FRIDAY	SATURDAY
				金9 Metal 1 乙酉 Wood Rooster Retreat 天山遯 1 三十 4	水6 Water 2 丙戌 Fire Dog Mountain 艮爲山 2 三月初一 1	木8 Wood 3 丁亥 Fire Pig Delight 雷地豫 3 初二 8
火7 Fire 4 戊子 Earth Rat Beginning 水雷屯 4 初三 4	金9 Metal 5 己丑 Earth Ox Without Wrongdoing 天雷無妄 5 初四 2	木3 Wood 6 庚寅 Metal Tiger Fire 離爲火 6 初五 1	火2 Fire 7 辛卯 Metal Rabbit Sincerity 風澤中孚 7 初六 3	水6 Water 8 壬辰 Water Dragon Big Livestock 山天大畜 8 初七 4	金4 Metal 9 癸巳 Water Snake Eliminating 澤天夬 9 初八 6	金9 Metal 1 甲午 Wood Horse Heaven 乾爲天 10 初九 1
火7 Fire 2 乙未 Wood Goat Well 水風井 11 初十 6	木8 Wood 3 丙申 Fire Monkey Relief 雷水解 12 十一 4	金4 Metal 4 丁酉 Fire Rooster Influence 澤山咸 13 十二 9	水1 Water 5 戊戌 Earth Dog Humility 地山謙 14 十三 6	火2 Fire 6 己亥 Earth Pig Observation 風地觀 15 十四 2	火2 Fire 7 庚子 Metal Rat Increasing 風雷益 16 十五 9	水1 Water 8 辛丑 Metal Ox Dimming Light 地火明夷 17 十六 3
金9 Metal 9 壬寅 Water Tiger Fellowship 天火同人 18 十七 7	木8 Wood 1 癸卯 Water Rabbit Marrying Maiden 雷澤歸妹 19 十八 7	木3 Wood 2 甲辰 Wood Dragon Opposition 火澤睽 20 十九 2	火7 Fire 3 乙巳 Wood Snake Waiting 水天需 21 二十 3	金4 Metal 4 丙午 Fire Horse Great Exceeding 澤風大過 22 廿一 3	水6 Water 5 丁未 Fire Goat Poison 山風蠱 23 廿二 7	火2 Fire 6 戊申 Earth Monkey Dispersing 風水渙 24 廿三 6
木3 Wood 7 己酉 Earth Rooster Travelling 火山旅 25 廿四 8	金9 Metal 8 庚戌 Metal Dog Stagnation 天地否 26 廿五 9	火7 Fire 9 辛亥 Metal Pig Alliance 水地比 27 廿六 7	木8 Wood 1 壬子 Water Rat Thunder 震爲雷 28 廿七 1	水6 Water 2 癸丑 Water Ox Beauty 山火賁 29 廿八 8	火7 Fire 3 甲寅 Wood Tiger Accomplished 水火既濟 30 廿九 9	

MAY 1965 辛巳

Xuan Kong Element 玄空五行	火天大有 Great Reward	Period Luck 卦運	Monthly Star 月星
Wood 木3		7	8

SUNDAY	MONDAY	TUESDAY	WEDNESDAY	THURSDAY	FRIDAY	SATURDAY
木3 Wood 6 Not Yet Accomplished 甲申 Wood Monkey 火水未濟 30 三十 9	金9 Metal 7 Retreat 乙酉 Wood Rooster 天山遯 31 五月初一 4					水1 Water 4 Arriving 乙卯 Wood Rabbit 地澤臨 1 四月初一 4
金4 Metal 5 Marsh 丙辰 Fire Dragon 兌爲澤 2 初二 1	火2 Fire 6 Small Livestock 丁巳 Fire Snake 風天小畜 3 初三 8	木3 Wood 7 The Cauldron 戊午 Earth Horse 火風鼎 4 初四 4	水1 Water 8 Rising 己未 Earth Goat 地風升 5 初五 2	火7 Fire 9 Water 庚申 Metal Monkey 坎爲水 6 初六 1	木8 Wood 1 Lesser Exceeding 辛酉 Metal Rooster 雷山小過 7 初七 3	金4 Metal 2 Gathering 壬戌 Water Dog 澤地萃 8 初八 4
水6 Water 3 Peel 癸亥 Water Pig 山地剝 9 初九 6	水1 Water 4 Earth 甲子 Wood Rat 坤爲地 10 初十 1	木3 Wood 5 Biting 乙丑 Wood Ox 火雷噬嗑 11 十一 6	火2 Fire 6 Family 丙寅 Fire Tiger 風火家人 12 十二 4	水6 Water 7 Decreasing 丁卯 Fire Rabbit 山澤損 13 十三 9	金9 Metal 8 Tread 戊辰 Earth Dragon 天澤履 14 十四 6	木8 Wood 9 Great Strength 己巳 Earth Snake 雷天大壯 15 十五 2
木8 Wood 1 Consistency 庚午 Metal Horse 雷風恆 16 十六 9	金9 Metal 2 Litigation 辛未 Metal Goat 天水訟 17 十七 3	水1 Water 3 Officer 壬申 Water Monkey 地水師 18 十八 7	火2 Fire 4 Gradual Progress 癸酉 Water Rooster 風山漸 19 十九 7	火7 Fire 5 Obstruction 甲戌 Wood Dog 水山蹇 20 二十 2	木3 Wood 6 Advancement 乙亥 Wood Pig 火地晉 21 廿一 3	水6 Water 7 Nourish 丙子 Fire Rat 山雷頤 22 廿二 3
金4 Metal 8 Following 丁丑 Fire Ox 澤雷隨 23 廿三 7	木8 Wood 9 Abundance 戊寅 Earth Tiger 雷火豐 24 廿四 6	火7 Fire 1 Regulate 己卯 Earth Rabbit 水澤節 25 廿五 8	水1 Water 2 Unity 庚辰 Metal Dragon 地天泰 26 廿六 9	木3 Wood 3 Great Reward 辛巳 Metal Snake 火天大有 27 廿七 7	火2 Fire 4 Wind 壬午 Water Horse 巽爲風 28 廿八 1	金4 Metal 5 Trap 癸未 Water Goat 澤水困 29 廿九 8

JUNE 1965 壬午

Xuan Kong Element 玄空五行	巽爲風 Wind	Period Luck 卦運	Monthly Star 月星
Fire 火2		1	7

SUNDAY	MONDAY	TUESDAY	WEDNESDAY	THURSDAY	FRIDAY	SATURDAY
		水6 Water 8 Mountain 丙戌 Fire Dog 艮爲山 1 初二 1	木8 Wood 9 Delight 丁亥 Fire Pig 雷地豫 2 初三 8	火7 Fire 1 Beginning 戊子 Earth Rat 水雷屯 3 初四 4	金9 Metal 2 Without Wrongdoing 己丑 Earth Ox 天雷無妄 4 初五 2	木3 Wood 3 Fire 庚寅 Metal Tiger 離爲火 5 初六 1
火2 Fire 4 Sincerity 辛卯 Metal Rabbit 風澤中孚 6 初七 3	水6 Water 5 Big Livestock 壬辰 Water Dragon 山天大畜 7 初八 4	金4 Metal 6 Eliminating 癸巳 Water Snake 澤天夬 8 初九 6	金9 Metal 7 Heaven 甲午 Wood Horse 乾爲天 9 初十 1	火7 Fire 8 Well 乙未 Wood Goat 水風井 10 十一 6	木8 Wood 9 Relief 丙申 Fire Monkey 雷水解 11 十二 4	金4 Metal 1 Influence 丁酉 Fire Rooster 澤山咸 12 十三 9
水1 Water 2 Humility 戊戌 Earth Dog 地山謙 13 十四 6	火2 Fire 3 Observation 己亥 Earth Pig 風地觀 14 十五 2	火2 Fire 4 Increasing 庚子 Metal Rat 風雷益 15 十六 9	水1 Water 5 Dimming Light 辛丑 Metal Ox 地火明夷 16 十七 3	金9 Metal 6 Fellowship 壬寅 Water Tiger 天火同人 17 十八 7	木8 Wood 7 Marrying Maiden 癸卯 Water Rabbit 雷澤歸妹 18 十九 7	木3 Wood 8 Opposition 甲辰 Wood Dragon 火澤睽 19 二十 2
火7 Fire 9 Waiting 乙巳 Wood Snake 水天需 20 廿一 3	金4 Metal 1/9 Great Exceeding 丙午 Fire Horse 澤風大過 21 廿二 3	水6 Water 8 Poison 丁未 Fire Goat 山風蠱 22 廿三 7	火2 Fire 7 Dispersing 戊申 Earth Monkey 風水渙 23 廿四 6	木3 Wood 6 Travelling 己酉 Earth Rooster 火山旅 24 廿五 8	金9 Metal 5 Stagnation 庚戌 Metal Dog 天地否 25 廿六 9	火7 Fire 4 Alliance 辛亥 Metal Pig 水地比 26 廿七 7
木8 Wood 3 Thunder 壬子 Water Rat 震爲雷 27 廿八 1	水6 Water 2 Beauty 癸丑 Water Ox 山火賁 28 廿九 8	火7 Fire 1 Accomplished 甲寅 Wood Tiger 水火既濟 29 六月初一 9	水1 Water 9 Arriving 乙卯 Wood Rabbit 地澤臨 30 初二 4			

JULY 1965 癸未

Xuan Kong Element 玄空五行	澤水困 Trap	Period Luck 卦運	Monthly Star 月星
Metal 金4		8	6

SUNDAY	MONDAY	TUESDAY	WEDNESDAY	THURSDAY	FRIDAY	SATURDAY
				金4 Metal 8 Marsh 丙辰 Fire Dragon 兑爲澤 1 初三 1	火2 Fire 7 Small Livestock 丁巳 Fire Snake 風天小畜 2 初四 8	木3 Wood 6 The Cauldron 戊午 Earth Horse 火風鼎 3 初五 4
水1 Water 5 Rising 己未 Earth Goat 地風升 4 初六 2	火7 Fire 4 Water 庚申 Metal Monkey 坎爲水 5 初七 1	木8 Wood 3 Lesser Exceeding 辛酉 Metal Rooster 雷山小過 6 初八 3	金4 Metal 2 Gathering 壬戌 Water Dog 澤地萃 7 初九 4	水6 Water 1 Peel 癸亥 Water Pig 山地剝 8 初十 6	水1 Water 9 Earth 甲子 Wood Rat 坤爲地 9 十一 1	木3 Wood 8 Biting 乙丑 Wood Ox 火雷噬嗑 10 十二 6
火2 Fire 7 Family 丙寅 Fire Tiger 風火家人 11 十三 4	水6 Water 6 Decreasing 丁卯 Fire Rabbit 山澤損 12 十四 9	金9 Metal 5 Tread 戊辰 Earth Dragon 天澤履 13 十五 6	木8 Wood 4 Great Strength 己巳 Earth Snake 雷天大壯 14 十六 2	木8 Wood 3 Consistency 庚午 Metal Horse 雷風恆 15 十七 9	金9 Metal 2 Litigation 辛未 Metal Goat 天水訟 16 十八 3	水1 Water 1 Officer 壬申 Water Monkey 地水師 17 十九 7
火2 Fire 9 Gradual Progress 癸酉 Water Rooster 風山漸 18 二十 7	火7 Fire 8 Obstruction 甲戌 Wood Dog 水山蹇 19 廿一 2	木3 Wood 7 Advancement 乙亥 Wood Pig 火地晉 20 廿二 3	水6 Water 6 Nourish 丙子 Fire Rat 山雷頤 21 廿三 3	金4 Metal 5 Following 丁丑 Fire Ox 澤雷隨 22 廿四 7	木8 Wood 4 Abundance 戊寅 Earth Tiger 雷火豐 23 廿五 6	火7 Fire 3 Regulate 己卯 Earth Rabbit 水澤節 24 廿六 8
水1 Water 2 Unity 庚辰 Metal Dragon 地天泰 25 廿七 9	木3 Wood 1 Great Reward 辛巳 Metal Snake 火天大有 26 廿八 7	火2 Fire 9 Wind 壬午 Water Horse 巽爲風 27 廿九 1	金4 Metal 8 Trap 癸未 Water Goat 澤水困 28 七月初一 8	木3 Wood 7 Not Yet Accomplished 甲申 Wood Monkey 火水未濟 29 初二 9	金9 Metal 6 Retreat 乙酉 Wood Rooster 天山遯 30 初三 4	水6 Water 5 Mountain 丙戌 Fire Dog 艮爲山 31 初四 1

AUGUST 1965 甲申

Xuan Kong Element 玄空五行	火水未濟 Not Yet Accomplished	Period Luck 卦運	Monthly Star 月星
Wood 木3		9	5

SUNDAY	MONDAY	TUESDAY	WEDNESDAY	THURSDAY	FRIDAY	SATURDAY
木8 Wood 4 Delight 丁亥 Fire Pig 雷地豫 1 初五 8	火7 Fire 3 Beginning 戊子 Earth Rat 水雷屯 2 初六 4	金9 Metal 2 Without Wrongdoing 己丑 Earth Ox 天雷無妄 3 初七 2	木3 Wood 1 Fire 庚寅 Metal Tiger 離爲火 4 初八 1	火2 Fire 9 Sincerity 辛卯 Metal Rabbit 風澤中孚 5 初九 3	水6 Water 8 Big Livestock 壬辰 Water Dragon 山天大畜 6 初十 4	金4 Metal 7 Eliminating 癸巳 Water Snake 澤天夬 7 十一 6
金9 Metal 6 Heaven 甲午 Wood Horse 乾爲天 8 十二 1	火7 Fire 5 Well 乙未 Wood Goat 水風井 9 十三 6	木8 Wood 4 Relief 丙申 Fire Monkey 雷水解 10 十四 4	金4 Metal 3 Influence 丁酉 Fire Rooster 澤山咸 11 十五 9	水1 Water 2 Humility 戊戌 Earth Dog 地山謙 12 十六 6	火2 Fire 1 Observation 己亥 Earth Pig 風地觀 13 十七 2	火2 Fire 9 Increasing 庚子 Metal Rat 風雷益 14 十八 9
水1 Water 8 Dimming Light 辛丑 Metal Ox 地火明夷 15 十九 3	金9 Metal 7 Fellowship 壬寅 Water Tiger 天火同人 16 二十 7	木8 Wood 6 Marrying Maiden 癸卯 Water Rabbit 雷澤歸妹 17 廿一 7	木3 Wood 5 Opposition 甲辰 Wood Dragon 火澤睽 18 廿二 2	火7 Fire 4 Waiting 乙巳 Wood Snake 水天需 19 廿三 3	金4 Metal 3 Great Exceeding 丙午 Fire Horse 澤風大過 20 廿四 3	水6 Water 2 Poison 丁未 Fire Goat 山風蠱 21 廿五 7
火2 Fire 1 Dispersing 戊申 Earth Monkey 風水渙 22 廿六 6	木3 Wood 9 Travelling 己酉 Earth Rooster 火山旅 23 廿七 8	金9 Metal 8 Stagnation 庚戌 Metal Dog 天地否 24 廿八 9	火7 Fire 7 Alliance 辛亥 Metal Pig 水地比 25 廿九 7	木8 Wood 6 Thunder 壬子 Water Rat 震爲雷 26 三十 1	水6 Water 5 Beauty 癸丑 Water Ox 山火賁 27 八月初一 8	火7 Fire 4 Accomplished 甲寅 Wood Tiger 水火既濟 28 初二 9
水1 Water 3 Arriving 乙卯 Wood Rabbit 地澤臨 29 初三 4	金4 Metal 2 Marsh 丙辰 Fire Dragon 兑爲澤 30 初四 1	火2 Fire 1 Small Livestock 丁巳 Fire Snake 風天小畜 31 初五 8				

SEPTEMBER 1965 乙酉

Xuan Kong Element 玄空五行	天山遯 Retreat	Period Luck 卦運	Monthly Star 月星
Metal 金9		4	4

SUNDAY	MONDAY	TUESDAY	WEDNESDAY	THURSDAY	FRIDAY	SATURDAY
			木3 Wood 9 The Cauldron 火風鼎 戊午 Earth Horse 1 初六 4	水1 Water 8 Rising 地風升 己未 Earth Goat 2 初七 2	火7 Fire 7 Water 坎爲水 庚申 Metal Monkey 3 初八 1	木8 Wood 6 Lesser Exceeding 雷山小過 辛酉 Metal Rooster 4 初九 3
金4 Metal 5 Gathering 澤地萃 壬戌 Water Dog 5 初十 4	水6 Water 4 Peel 山地剝 癸亥 Water Pig 6 十一 6	水1 Water 3 Earth 坤爲地 甲子 Wood Rat 7 十二 1	木3 Wood 2 Biting 火雷噬嗑 乙丑 Wood Ox 8 十三 6	火2 Fire 1 Family 風火家人 丙寅 Fire Tiger 9 十四 4	水6 Water 9 Decreasing 山澤損 丁卯 Fire Rabbit 10 十五 9	金9 Metal 8 Tread 天澤履 戊辰 Earth Dragon 11 十六 6
木8 Wood 7 Great Strength 雷天大壯 己巳 Earth Snake 12 十七 2	木8 Wood 6 Consistency 雷風恆 庚午 Metal Horse 13 十八 9	金9 Metal 5 Litigation 天水訟 辛未 Metal Goat 14 十九 3	水1 Water 4 Officer 地水師 壬申 Water Monkey 15 二十 7	火2 Fire 3 Gradual Progress 風山漸 癸酉 Water Rooster 16 廿一 7	火7 Fire 2 Obstruction 水山蹇 甲戌 Wood Dog 17 廿二 2	木3 Wood 1 Advancement 火地晉 乙亥 Wood Pig 18 廿三 3
水6 Water 9 Nourish 山雷頤 丙子 Fire Rat 19 廿四 3	金4 Metal 8 Following 澤雷隨 丁丑 Fire Ox 20 廿五 7	木8 Wood 7 Abundance 雷火豐 戊寅 Earth Tiger 21 廿六 6	火7 Fire 6 Regulate 水澤節 己卯 Earth Rabbit 22 廿七 8	水1 Water 5 Unity 地天泰 庚辰 Metal Dragon 23 廿八 9	木3 Wood 4 Great Reward 火天大有 辛巳 Metal Snake 24 廿九 7	火2 Fire 3 Wind 巽爲風 壬午 Water Horse 25 九月初一 1
金4 Metal 2 Trap 澤水困 癸未 Water Goat 26 初二 8	木3 Wood 1 Not Yet Accomplished 火水未濟 甲申 Wood Monkey 27 初三 9	金9 Metal 9 Retreat 天山遯 乙酉 Wood Rooster 28 初四 4	水6 Water 8 Mountain 艮爲山 丙戌 Fire Dog 29 初五 1	木8 Wood 7 Delight 雷地豫 丁亥 Fire Pig 30 初六 8		

OCTOBER 1965 丙戌

Xuan Kong Element 玄空五行	艮爲山 Mountain	Period Luck 卦運	Monthly Star 月星
Water 水6		1	3

SUNDAY	MONDAY	TUESDAY	WEDNESDAY	THURSDAY	FRIDAY	SATURDAY
木3 Wood 3 The Cauldron 火風鼎 戊午 Earth Horse 31 初八 4					火7 Fire 6 Beginning 水雷屯 戊子 Earth Rat 1 初七 4	金9 Metal 5 Without Wrongdoing 天雷無妄 己丑 Earth Ox 2 初八 2
木3 Wood 4 Fire 離爲火 庚寅 Metal Tiger 3 初九 1	火2 Fire 3 Sincerity 風澤中孚 辛卯 Metal Rabbit 4 初十 3	水6 Water 2 Big Livestock 山天大畜 壬辰 Water Dragon 5 十一 4	金4 Metal 1 Eliminating 澤天夬 癸巳 Water Snake 6 十二 6	金9 Metal 9 Heaven 乾爲天 甲午 Wood Horse 7 十三 1	火7 Fire 8 Well 水風井 乙未 Wood Goat 8 十四 6	木8 Wood 7 Relief 雷水解 丙申 Fire Monkey 9 十五 4
金4 Metal 6 Influence 澤山咸 丁酉 Fire Rooster 10 十六 9	水1 Water 5 Humility 地山謙 戊戌 Earth Dog 11 十七 6	火2 Fire 4 Observation 風地觀 己亥 Earth Pig 12 十八 2	火2 Fire 3 Increasing 風雷益 庚子 Metal Rat 13 十九 9	水1 Water 2 Dimming Light 地火明夷 辛丑 Metal Ox 14 二十 3	金9 Metal 1 Fellowship 天火同人 壬寅 Water Tiger 15 廿一 7	木8 Wood 9 Marrying Maiden 雷澤歸妹 癸卯 Water Rabbit 16 廿二 7
木3 Wood 8 Opposition 火澤睽 甲辰 Wood Dragon 17 廿三 2	火7 Fire 7 Waiting 水天需 乙巳 Wood Snake 18 廿四 3	金4 Metal 6 Great Exceeding 澤風大過 丙午 Fire Horse 19 廿五 3	水6 Water 5 Poison 山風蠱 丁未 Fire Goat 20 廿六 7	火2 Fire 4 Dispersing 風水渙 戊申 Earth Monkey 21 廿七 6	木3 Wood 3 Travelling 火山旅 己酉 Earth Rooster 22 廿八 8	金9 Metal 2 Stagnation 天地否 庚戌 Metal Dog 23 廿九 9
火7 Fire 1 Alliance 水地比 辛亥 Metal Pig 24 十月初一 7	木8 Wood 9 Thunder 震爲雷 壬子 Water Rat 25 初二 1	水6 Water 8 Beauty 山火賁 癸丑 Water Ox 26 初三 8	火7 Fire 7 Accomplished 水火既濟 甲寅 Wood Tiger 27 初四 9	水1 Water 6 Arriving 地澤臨 乙卯 Wood Rabbit 28 初五 4	金4 Metal 5 Marsh 兌爲澤 丙辰 Fire Dragon 29 初六 1	火2 Fire 4 Small Livestock 風天小畜 丁巳 Fire Snake 30 初七 8

NOVEMBER 1965 丁亥

Xuan Kong Element 玄空五行	雷地豫 Delight	Period Luck 卦運	Monthly Star 月星
Wood 木8		8	2

SUNDAY	MONDAY	TUESDAY	WEDNESDAY	THURSDAY	FRIDAY	SATURDAY
	水1 Water 2 Rising 地風升 己未 Earth Goat 1 初九 2	火7 Fire 1 Water 坎爲水 庚申 Metal Monkey 2 初十 1	木8 Wood 9 Lesser Exceeding 雷山小過 辛酉 Metal Rooster 3 十一 3	金4 Metal 8 Gathering 澤地萃 壬戌 Water Dog 4 十二 4	水6 Water 7 Peel 山地剝 癸亥 Water Pig 5 十三 6	水1 Water 6 Earth 坤爲地 甲子 Wood Rat 6 十四 1
木3 Wood 5 Biting 火雷噬嗑 乙丑 Wood Ox 7 十五 6	火2 Fire 4 Family 風火家人 丙寅 Fire Tiger 8 十六 4	水6 Water 3 Decreasing 山澤損 丁卯 Fire Rabbit 9 十七 9	金9 Metal 2 Tread 天澤履 戊辰 Earth Dragon 10 十八 6	木8 Wood 1 Great Strength 雷天大壯 己巳 Earth Snake 11 十九 2	木8 Wood 9 Consistency 雷風恆 庚午 Metal Horse 12 二十 9	金9 Metal 8 Litigation 天水訟 辛未 Metal Goat 13 廿一 3
水1 Water 7 Officer 地水師 壬申 Water Monkey 14 廿二 7	火2 Fire 6 Gradual Progress 風山漸 癸酉 Water Rooster 15 廿三 7	火7 Fire 5 Obstruction 水山蹇 甲戌 Wood Dog 16 廿四 2	木3 Wood 4 Advancement 火地晉 乙亥 Wood Pig 17 廿五 3	水6 Water 3 Nourish 山雷頤 丙子 Fire Rat 18 廿六 3	金4 Metal 2 Following 澤雷隨 丁丑 Fire Ox 19 廿七 7	木8 Wood 1 Abundance 雷火豐 戊寅 Earth Tiger 20 廿八 6
火7 Fire 9 Regulate 水澤節 己卯 Earth Rabbit 21 廿九 8	水1 Water 8 Unity 地天泰 庚辰 Metal Dragon 22 三十 9	木3 Wood 7 Great Reward 火天大有 辛巳 Metal Snake 23 十一月初一 7	火2 Fire 6 Wind 巽爲風 壬午 Water Horse 24 初二 1	金4 Metal 5 Trap 澤水困 癸未 Water Goat 25 初三 8	木3 Wood 4 Not Yet Accomplished 火水未濟 甲申 Wood Monkey 26 初四 9	金9 Metal 3 Retreat 天山遯 乙酉 Wood Rooster 27 初五 4
水6 Water 2 Mountain 艮爲山 丙戌 Fire Dog 28 初六 1	木8 Wood 1 Delight 雷地豫 丁亥 Fire Pig 29 初七 8	火7 Fire 9 Beginning 水雷屯 戊子 Earth Rat 30 初八 4				

DECEMBER 1965 戊子

Xuan Kong Element 玄空五行	水雷屯 Beginning	Period Luck 卦運	Monthly Star 月星
Fire 火7		4	1

SUNDAY	MONDAY	TUESDAY	WEDNESDAY	THURSDAY	FRIDAY	SATURDAY
			金9 Metal 8 Without Wrongdoing 天雷無妄 己丑 Earth Ox 1 初九 2	木3 Wood 7 Fire 離爲火 庚寅 Metal Tiger 2 初十 1	火2 Fire 6 Sincerity 風澤中孚 辛卯 Metal Rabbit 3 十一 3	水6 Water 5 Big Livestock 山天大畜 壬辰 Water Dragon 4 十二 4
金4 Metal 4 Eliminating 澤天夬 癸巳 Water Snake 5 十三 6	金9 Metal 3 Heaven 乾爲天 甲午 Wood Horse 6 十四 1	火7 Fire 2 Well 水風井 乙未 Wood Goat 7 十五 6	木8 Wood 1 Relief 雷水解 丙申 Fire Monkey 8 十六 4	金4 Metal 9 Influence 澤山咸 丁酉 Fire Rooster 9 十七 9	水1 Water 8 Humility 地山謙 戊戌 Earth Dog 10 十八 6	火2 Fire 7 Observation 風地觀 己亥 Earth Pig 11 十九 2
火2 Fire 6 Increasing 風雷益 庚子 Metal Rat 12 二十 9	水1 Water 5 Dimming Light 地火明夷 辛丑 Metal Ox 13 廿一 3	金9 Metal 4 Fellowship 天火同人 壬寅 Water Tiger 14 廿二 7	木8 Wood 3 Marrying Maiden 雷澤歸妹 癸卯 Water Rabbit 15 廿三 7	木3 Wood 2 Opposition 火澤睽 甲辰 Wood Dragon 16 廿四 2	火7 Fire 1 Waiting 水天需 乙巳 Wood Snake 17 廿五 3	金4 Metal 9 Great Exceeding 澤風大過 丙午 Fire Horse 18 廿六 3
水6 Water 8 Poison 山風蠱 丁未 Fire Goat 19 廿七 7	火2 Fire 7 Dispersing 風水渙 戊申 Earth Monkey 20 廿八 6	木3 Wood 6 Travelling 火山旅 己酉 Earth Rooster 21 廿九 8	金9 Metal 5/5 Stagnation 天地否 庚戌 Metal Dog 22 三十 9	火7 Fire 6 Alliance 水地比 辛亥 Metal Pig 23 十二月初一 7	木8 Wood 7 Thunder 震爲雷 壬子 Water Rat 24 初二 1	水6 Water 8 Beauty 山火賁 癸丑 Water Ox 25 初三 8
火7 Fire 9 Accomplished 水火既濟 甲寅 Wood Tiger 26 初四 9	水1 Water 1 Arriving 地澤臨 乙卯 Wood Rabbit 27 初五 4	金4 Metal 2 Marsh 兌爲澤 丙辰 Fire Dragon 28 初六 1	火2 Fire 3 Small Livestock 風天小畜 丁巳 Fire Snake 29 初七 8	木3 Wood 4 The Cauldron 火風鼎 戊午 Earth Horse 30 初八 4	水1 Water 5 Rising 地風升 己未 Earth Goat 31 初九 2	

1966 丙午

(*Bing Wu*) Fire Horse

1966 丙午 *(Bing Wu)* Fire Horse

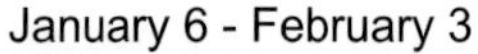

January 6 - February 3

February 4 - March 5

March 6 - April 4

April 5 - May 5

May 6 - June 5

June 6 - July 6

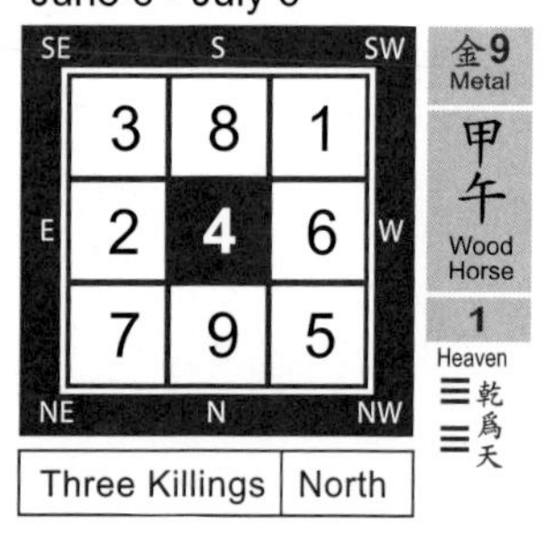

July 7 - August 7

August 8 - September 7

September 8 - October 8

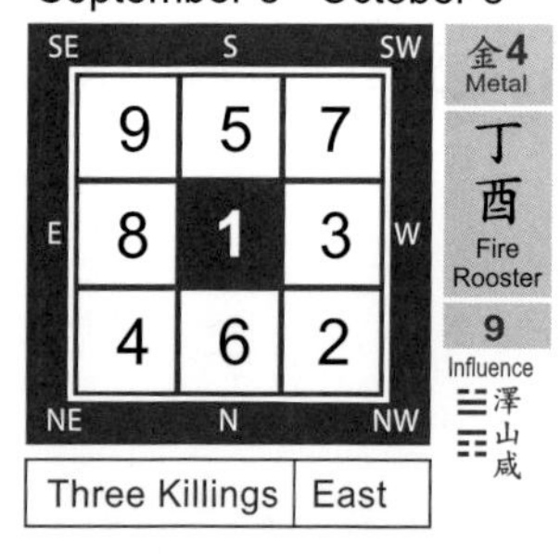

October 9 - November 7

November 8 - December 6

December 7 - January 5

JANUARY 1966 己丑

Xuan Kong Element 玄空五行	天雷無妄 Without Wrongdoing	Period Luck 卦運	Monthly Star 月星
Metal 金9		2	9

SUNDAY	MONDAY	TUESDAY	WEDNESDAY	THURSDAY	FRIDAY	SATURDAY
金9 Metal Without Wrongdoing 8 己丑 Earth Ox 天雷無妄 **30** 2 初十	木3 Wood Fire 9 庚寅 Metal Tiger 離為火 **31** 1 十一					火7 Fire Water 6 庚申 Metal Monkey 坎為水 **1** 1 初十
木8 Wood Lesser Exceeding 7 辛酉 Metal Rooster 雷山小過 **2** 3 十一	金4 Metal Gathering 8 壬戌 Water Dog 澤地萃 **3** 4 十二	水6 Water Peel 9 癸亥 Water Pig 山地剝 **4** 6 十三	水1 Water Earth 1 甲子 Wood Rat 坤為地 **5** 1 十四	木3 Wood Biting 2 乙丑 Wood Ox 火雷噬嗑 **6** 6 十五	火2 Fire Family 3 丙寅 Fire Tiger 風火家人 **7** 4 十六	水6 Water Decreasing 4 丁卯 Fire Rabbit 山澤損 **8** 9 十七
金9 Metal Tread 5 戊辰 Earth Dragon 天澤履 **9** 6 十八	木8 Wood Great Strength 6 己巳 Earth Snake 雷天大壯 **10** 2 十九	木8 Wood Consistency 7 庚午 Metal Horse 雷風恆 **11** 9 二十	金9 Metal Litigation 8 辛未 Metal Goat 天水訟 **12** 3 廿一	水1 Water Officer 9 壬申 Water Monkey 地水師 **13** 7 廿二	火2 Fire Gradual Progress 1 癸酉 Water Rooster 風山漸 **14** 7 廿三	火7 Fire Obstruction 2 甲戌 Wood Dog 水山蹇 **15** 2 廿四
木3 Wood Advancement 3 乙亥 Wood Pig 火地晉 **16** 3 廿五	水6 Water Nourish 4 丙子 Fire Rat 山雷頤 **17** 3 廿六	金4 Metal Following 5 丁丑 Fire Ox 澤雷隨 **18** 7 廿七	木8 Wood Abundance 6 戊寅 Earth Tiger 雷火豐 **19** 6 廿八	火7 Fire Regulate 7 己卯 Earth Rabbit 水澤節 **20** 8 廿九	水1 Water Unity 8 庚辰 Metal Dragon 地天泰 **21** 9 正月初一	木3 Wood Great Reward 9 辛巳 Metal Snake 火天大有 **22** 7 初二
火2 Fire Wind 1 壬午 Water Horse 巽為風 **23** 1 初三	金4 Metal Trap 2 癸未 Water Goat 澤水困 **24** 8 初四	木3 Wood Not Yet Accomplished 3 甲申 Wood Monkey 火水未濟 **25** 9 初五	金9 Metal Retreat 4 乙酉 Wood Rooster 天山遯 **26** 4 初六	水6 Water Mountain 5 丙戌 Fire Dog 艮為山 **27** 1 初七	木8 Wood Delight 6 丁亥 Fire Pig 雷地豫 **28** 8 初八	火7 Fire Beginning 7 戊子 Earth Rat 水雷屯 **29** 4 初九

FEBRUARY 1966 庚寅

Xuan Kong Element 玄空五行	離為火 Fire	Period Luck 卦運	Monthly Star 月星
Wood 木3		1	8

SUNDAY	MONDAY	TUESDAY	WEDNESDAY	THURSDAY	FRIDAY	SATURDAY
		火2 Fire Sincerity 1 辛卯 Metal Rabbit 風澤中孚 **1** 3 十二	水6 Water Big Livestock 2 壬辰 Water Dragon 山天大畜 **2** 4 十三	金4 Metal Eliminating 3 癸巳 Water Snake 澤天夬 **3** 6 十四	金9 Metal Heaven 4 甲午 Wood Horse 乾為天 **4** 1 十五	火7 Fire Well 5 乙未 Wood Goat 水風井 **5** 6 十六
木8 Wood Relief 6 丙申 Fire Monkey 雷水解 **6** 4 十七	金4 Metal Influence 7 丁酉 Fire Rooster 澤山咸 **7** 9 十八	水1 Water Humility 8 戊戌 Earth Dog 地山謙 **8** 6 十九	火2 Fire Observation 9 己亥 Earth Pig 風地觀 **9** 2 二十	火2 Fire Increasing 1 庚子 Metal Rat 風雷益 **10** 9 廿一	水1 Water Dimming Light 2 辛丑 Metal Ox 地火明夷 **11** 3 廿二	金9 Metal Fellowship 3 壬寅 Water Tiger 天火同人 **12** 7 廿三
木8 Wood Marrying Maiden 4 癸卯 Water Rabbit 雷澤歸妹 **13** 7 廿四	木3 Wood Opposition 5 甲辰 Wood Dragon 火澤睽 **14** 2 廿五	火7 Fire Waiting 6 乙巳 Wood Snake 水天需 **15** 3 廿六	金4 Metal Great Exceeding 7 丙午 Fire Horse 澤風大過 **16** 3 廿七	水6 Water Poison 8 丁未 Fire Goat 山風蠱 **17** 7 廿八	火2 Fire Dispersing 9 戊申 Earth Monkey 風水渙 **18** 6 廿九	木3 Wood Travelling 1 己酉 Earth Rooster 火山旅 **19** 8 三十
金9 Metal Stagnation 2 庚戌 Metal Dog 天地否 **20** 9 二月初一	火7 Fire Alliance 3 辛亥 Metal Pig 水地比 **21** 7 初二	木8 Wood Thunder 4 壬子 Water Rat 震為雷 **22** 1 初三	水6 Water Beauty 5 癸丑 Water Ox 山火賁 **23** 8 初四	火7 Fire Accomplished 6 甲寅 Wood Tiger 水火既濟 **24** 9 初五	水1 Water Arriving 7 乙卯 Wood Rabbit 地澤臨 **25** 4 初六	金4 Metal Marsh 8 丙辰 Fire Dragon 兌為澤 **26** 1 初七
火2 Fire Small Livestock 9 丁巳 Fire Snake 風天小畜 **27** 8 初八	木3 Wood The Cauldron 1 戊午 Earth Horse 火風鼎 **28** 4 初九					

MARCH 1966 辛卯

Xuan Kong Element 玄空五行	風澤中孚 Sincerity	Period Luck 卦運	Monthly Star 月星
Fire 火2		3	7

SUNDAY	MONDAY	TUESDAY	WEDNESDAY	THURSDAY	FRIDAY	SATURDAY
		水1 Water 2 Rising 地風升 己未 Earth Goat 1 初十 2	火7 Fire 3 Water 坎爲水 庚申 Metal Monkey 2 十一 1	木8 Wood 4 Lesser Exceeding 雷山小過 辛酉 Metal Rooster 3 十二 3	金4 Metal 5 Gathering 澤地萃 壬戌 Water Dog 4 十三 4	水6 Water 6 Peel 山地剝 癸亥 Water Pig 5 十四 6
水1 Water 7 Earth 坤爲地 甲子 Wood Rat 6 十五 1	木3 Wood 8 Biting 火雷噬嗑 乙丑 Wood Ox 7 十六 6	火2 Fire 9 Family 風火家人 丙寅 Fire Tiger 8 十七 4	水6 Water 1 Decreasing 山澤損 丁卯 Fire Rabbit 9 十八 9	金9 Metal 2 Tread 天澤履 戊辰 Earth Dragon 10 十九 6	木8 Wood 3 Great Strength 雷天大壯 己巳 Earth Snake 11 二十 2	木8 Wood 4 Consistency 雷風恆 庚午 Metal Horse 12 廿一 9
金9 Metal 5 Litigation 天水訟 辛未 Metal Goat 13 廿二 3	水1 Water 6 Officer 地水師 壬申 Water Monkey 14 廿三 7	火2 Fire 7 Gradual Progress 風山漸 癸酉 Water Rooster 15 廿四 7	火7 Fire 8 Obstruction 水山蹇 甲戌 Wood Dog 16 廿五 2	木3 Wood 9 Advancement 火地晉 乙亥 Wood Pig 17 廿六 3	水6 Water 1 Nourish 山雷頤 丙子 Fire Rat 18 廿七 3	金4 Metal 2 Following 澤雷隨 丁丑 Fire Ox 19 廿八 7
木8 Wood 3 Abundance 雷火豐 戊寅 Earth Tiger 20 廿九 6	火7 Fire 4 Regulate 水澤節 己卯 Earth Rabbit 21 三十 8	水1 Water 5 Unity 地天泰 庚辰 Metal Dragon 22 三月初一 9	木3 Wood 6 Great Reward 火天大有 辛巳 Metal Snake 23 初二 7	火2 Fire 7 Wind 巽爲風 壬午 Water Horse 24 初三 1	金4 Metal 8 Trap 澤水困 癸未 Water Goat 25 初四 8	木3 Wood 9 Not Yet Accomplished 火水未濟 甲申 Wood Monkey 26 初五 9
金9 Metal 1 Retreat 天山遯 乙酉 Wood Rooster 27 初六 4	水6 Water 2 Mountain 艮爲山 丙戌 Fire Dog 28 初七 1	木8 Wood 3 Delight 雷地豫 丁亥 Fire Pig 29 初八 8	火7 Fire 4 Beginning 水雷屯 戊子 Earth Rat 30 初九 4	金9 Metal 5 Without Wrongdoing 天雷無妄 己丑 Earth Ox 31 初十 2		

APRIL 1966 壬辰

Xuan Kong Element 玄空五行	山天大畜 Big Livestock	Period Luck 卦運	Monthly Star 月星
Water 水6		4	6

SUNDAY	MONDAY	TUESDAY	WEDNESDAY	THURSDAY	FRIDAY	SATURDAY
					木3 Wood 6 Fire 離爲火 庚寅 Metal Tiger 1 十一 1	火2 Fire 7 Sincerity 風澤中孚 辛卯 Metal Rabbit 2 十二 3
水6 Water 8 Big Livestock 山天大畜 壬辰 Water Dragon 3 十三 4	金4 Metal 9 Eliminating 澤天夬 癸巳 Water Snake 4 十四 6	金9 Metal 1 Heaven 乾爲天 甲午 Wood Horse 5 十五 1	火7 Fire 2 Well 水風井 乙未 Wood Goat 6 十六 6	木8 Wood 3 Relief 雷水解 丙申 Fire Monkey 7 十七 4	金4 Metal 4 Influence 澤山咸 丁酉 Fire Rooster 8 十八 9	水1 Water 5 Humility 地山謙 戊戌 Earth Dog 9 十九 6
火2 Fire 6 Observation 風地觀 己亥 Earth Pig 10 二十 2	火2 Fire 7 Increasing 風雷益 庚子 Metal Rat 11 廿一 9	水1 Water 8 Dimming Light 地火明夷 辛丑 Metal Ox 12 廿二 3	金9 Metal 9 Fellowship 天火同人 壬寅 Water Tiger 13 廿三 7	木8 Wood 1 Marrying Maiden 雷澤歸妹 癸卯 Water Rabbit 14 廿四 7	木3 Wood 2 Opposition 火澤睽 甲辰 Wood Dragon 15 廿五 2	火7 Fire 3 Waiting 水天需 乙巳 Wood Snake 16 廿六 3
金4 Metal 4 Great Exceeding 澤風大過 丙午 Fire Horse 17 廿七 3	水6 Water 5 Poison 山風蠱 丁未 Fire Goat 18 廿八 7	火2 Fire 6 Dispersing 風水渙 戊申 Earth Monkey 19 廿九 6	木3 Wood 7 Travelling 火山旅 己酉 Earth Rooster 20 三十 8	金9 Metal 8 Stagnation 天地否 庚戌 Metal Dog 21 閏三月初一 9	火7 Fire 9 Alliance 水地比 辛亥 Metal Pig 22 初二 7	木8 Wood 1 Thunder 震爲雷 壬子 Water Rat 23 初三 1
水6 Water 2 Beauty 山火賁 癸丑 Water Ox 24 初四 8	火7 Fire 3 Accomplished 水火既濟 甲寅 Wood Tiger 25 初五 9	水1 Water 4 Arriving 地澤臨 乙卯 Wood Rabbit 26 初六 4	金4 Metal 5 Marsh 兌爲澤 丙辰 Fire Dragon 27 初七 1	火2 Fire 6 Small Livestock 風天小畜 丁巳 Fire Snake 28 初八 8	木3 Wood 7 The Cauldron 火風鼎 戊午 Earth Horse 29 初九 4	水1 Water 8 Rising 地風升 己未 Earth Goat 30 初十 2

MAY 1966 癸巳

Xuan Kong Element 玄空五行	澤天夬 Eliminating	Period Luck 卦運	Monthly Star 月星
Metal 金4		6	5

SUNDAY	MONDAY	TUESDAY	WEDNESDAY	THURSDAY	FRIDAY	SATURDAY
火7 Fire 9 Water 庚申 Metal Monkey 坎爲水 1 十一 1	木8 Wood 1 Lesser Exceeding 辛酉 Metal Rooster 雷山小過 2 十二 3	金4 Metal 2 Gathering 壬戌 Water Dog 澤地萃 3 十三 4	水6 Water 3 Peel 癸亥 Water Pig 山地剝 4 十四 6	水1 Water 4 Earth 甲子 Wood Rat 坤爲地 5 十五 1	木3 Wood 5 Biting 乙丑 Wood Ox 火雷噬嗑 6 十六 6	火2 Fire 6 Family 丙寅 Fire Tiger 風火家人 7 十七 4
水6 Water 7 Decreasing 丁卯 Fire Rabbit 山澤損 8 十八 9	金9 Metal 8 Tread 戊辰 Earth Dragon 天澤履 9 十九 6	木8 Wood 9 Great Strength 己巳 Earth Snake 雷天大壯 10 二十 2	木8 Wood 1 Consistency 庚午 Metal Horse 雷風恒 11 廿一 9	金9 Metal 2 Litigation 辛未 Metal Goat 天水訟 12 廿二 3	水1 Water 3 Officer 壬申 Water Monkey 地水師 13 廿三 7	火2 Fire 4 Gradual Progress 癸酉 Water Rooster 風山漸 14 廿四 7
火7 Fire 5 Obstruction 甲戌 Wood Dog 水山蹇 15 廿五 2	木3 Wood 6 Advancement 乙亥 Wood Pig 火地晉 16 廿六 3	水6 Water 7 Nourish 丙子 Fire Rat 山雷頤 17 廿七 3	金4 Metal 8 Following 丁丑 Fire Ox 澤雷隨 18 廿八 7	木8 Wood 9 Abundance 戊寅 Earth Tiger 雷火豐 19 廿九 6	火7 Fire 1 Regulate 己卯 Earth Rabbit 水澤節 20 四月初一 8	水1 Water 2 Unity 庚辰 Metal Dragon 地天泰 21 初二 9
木3 Wood 3 Great Reward 辛巳 Metal Snake 火天大有 22 初三 7	火2 Fire 4 Wind 壬午 Water Horse 巽爲風 23 初四 1	金4 Metal 5 Trap 癸未 Water Goat 澤水困 24 初五 8	木3 Wood 6 Not Yet Accomplished 甲申 Wood Monkey 火水未濟 25 初六 9	金9 Metal 7 Retreat 乙酉 Wood Rooster 天山遯 26 初七 4	水6 Water 8 Mountain 丙戌 Fire Dog 艮爲山 27 初八 1	木8 Wood 9 Delight 丁亥 Fire Pig 雷地豫 28 初九 8
火7 Fire 1 Beginning 戊子 Earth Rat 水雷屯 29 初十 4	金9 Metal 2 Without Wrongdoing 己丑 Earth Ox 天雷無妄 30 十一 2	木3 Wood 3 Fire 庚寅 Metal Tiger 離爲火 31 十二 1				

JUNE 1966 甲午

Xuan Kong Element 玄空五行	乾爲天 Heaven	Period Luck 卦運	Monthly Star 月星
Metal 金9		1	4

SUNDAY	MONDAY	TUESDAY	WEDNESDAY	THURSDAY	FRIDAY	SATURDAY
			火2 Fire 4 Sincerity 辛卯 Metal Rabbit 風澤中孚 1 十三 3	水6 Water 5 Big Livestock 壬辰 Water Dragon 山天大畜 2 十四 4	金4 Metal 6 Eliminating 癸巳 Water Snake 澤天夬 3 十五 6	金9 Metal 7 Heaven 甲午 Wood Horse 乾爲天 4 十六 1
火7 Fire 8 Well 乙未 Wood Goat 水風井 5 十七 6	木8 Wood 9 Relief 丙申 Fire Monkey 雷水解 6 十八 4	金4 Metal 1 Influence 丁酉 Fire Rooster 澤山咸 7 十九 9	水1 Water 2 Humility 戊戌 Earth Dog 地山謙 8 二十 6	火2 Fire 3 Observation 己亥 Earth Pig 風地觀 9 廿一 2	火2 Fire 4 Increasing 庚子 Metal Rat 風雷益 10 廿二 9	水1 Water 5 Dimming Light 辛丑 Metal Ox 地火明夷 11 廿三 3
金9 Metal 6 Fellowship 壬寅 Water Tiger 天火同人 12 廿四 7	木8 Wood 7 Marrying Maiden 癸卯 Water Rabbit 雷澤歸妹 13 廿五 7	木3 Wood 8 Opposition 甲辰 Wood Dragon 火澤睽 14 廿六 2	火7 Fire 9 Waiting 乙巳 Wood Snake 水天需 15 廿七 3	金4 Metal 1 Great Exceeding 丙午 Fire Horse 澤風大過 16 廿八 3	水6 Water 2 Poison 丁未 Fire Goat 山風蠱 17 廿九 7	火2 Fire 3 Dispersing 戊申 Earth Monkey 風水渙 18 三十 6
木3 Wood 4 Travelling 己酉 Earth Rooster 火山旅 19 五月初一 8	金9 Metal 5 Stagnation 庚戌 Metal Dog 天地否 20 初二 9	火7 Fire 6 Alliance 辛亥 Metal Pig 水地比 21 初三 7	木8 Wood 7/3 Thunder 壬子 Water Rat 震爲雷 22 初四 1	水6 Water 2 Beauty 癸丑 Water Ox 山火賁 23 初五 8	火7 Fire 1 Accomplished 甲寅 Wood Tiger 水火既濟 24 初六 9	水1 Water 9 Arriving 乙卯 Wood Rabbit 地澤臨 25 初七 4
金4 Metal 8 Marsh 丙辰 Fire Dragon 兌爲澤 26 初八 1	火2 Fire 7 Small Livestock 丁巳 Fire Snake 風天小畜 27 初九 8	木3 Wood 6 The Cauldron 戊午 Earth Horse 火風鼎 28 初十 4	水1 Water 5 Rising 己未 Earth Goat 地風升 29 十一 2	火7 Fire 4 Water 庚申 Metal Monkey 坎爲水 30 十二 1		

JULY 1966 乙未

Xuan Kong Element 玄空五行	水風井 Well	Period Luck 卦運	Monthly Star 月星
Fire 火7		6	3

SUNDAY	MONDAY	TUESDAY	WEDNESDAY	THURSDAY	FRIDAY	SATURDAY
火2 Fire 9 Sincerity 風澤中孚 辛卯 Metal Rabbit **31** 十四 3					木8 Wood 3 Lesser Exceeding 雷山小過 辛酉 Metal Rooster **1** 十三 3	金4 Metal 2 Gathering 澤地萃 壬戌 Water Dog **2** 十四 4
水6 Water 1 Peel 山地剝 癸亥 Water Pig **3** 十五 6	水1 Water 9 Earth 坤爲地 甲子 Wood Rat **4** 十六 1	木3 Wood 8 Biting 火雷噬嗑 乙丑 Wood Ox **5** 十七 6	火2 Fire 7 Family 風火家人 丙寅 Fire Tiger **6** 十八 4	水6 Water 6 Decreasing 山澤損 丁卯 Fire Rabbit **7** 十九 9	金9 Metal 5 Tread 天澤履 戊辰 Earth Dragon **8** 二十 6	木8 Wood 4 Great Strength 雷天大壯 己巳 Earth Snake **9** 廿一 2
木8 Wood 3 Consistency 雷風恆 庚午 Metal Horse **10** 廿二 9	金9 Metal 2 Litigation 天水訟 辛未 Metal Goat **11** 廿三 3	水1 Water 1 Officer 地水師 壬申 Water Monkey **12** 廿四 7	火2 Fire 9 Gradual Progress 風山漸 癸酉 Water Rooster **13** 廿五 7	火7 Fire 8 Obstruction 水山蹇 甲戌 Wood Dog **14** 廿六 2	木3 Wood 7 Advancement 火地晉 乙亥 Wood Pig **15** 廿七 3	水6 Water 6 Nourish 山雷頤 丙子 Fire Rat **16** 廿八 3
金4 Metal 5 Following 澤雷隨 丁丑 Fire Ox **17** 廿九 7	木8 Wood 4 Abundance 雷火豐 戊寅 Earth Tiger **18** 六月初一 6	火7 Fire 3 Regulate 水澤節 己卯 Earth Rabbit **19** 初二 8	水1 Water 2 Unity 地天泰 庚辰 Metal Dragon **20** 初三 9	木3 Wood 1 Great Reward 火天大有 辛巳 Metal Snake **21** 初四 7	火2 Fire 9 Wind 巽爲風 壬午 Water Horse **22** 初五 1	金4 Metal 8 Trap 澤水困 癸未 Water Goat **23** 初六 8
木3 Wood 7 Not Yet Accomplished 火水未濟 甲申 Wood Monkey **24** 初七 9	金9 Metal 6 Retreat 天山遯 乙酉 Wood Rooster **25** 初八 4	水6 Water 5 Mountain 艮爲山 丙戌 Fire Dog **26** 初九 1	木8 Wood 4 Delight 雷地豫 丁亥 Fire Pig **27** 初十 8	火7 Fire 3 Beginning 水雷屯 戊子 Earth Rat **28** 十一 4	金9 Metal 2 Without Wrongdoing 天雷無妄 己丑 Earth Ox **29** 十二 2	木3 Wood 1 Fire 離爲火 庚寅 Metal Tiger **30** 十三 1

AUGUST 1966 丙申

Xuan Kong Element 玄空五行	雷水解 Relief	Period Luck 卦運	Monthly Star 月星
Wood 木8		4	2

SUNDAY	MONDAY	TUESDAY	WEDNESDAY	THURSDAY	FRIDAY	SATURDAY
	水6 Water 8 Big Livestock 山天大畜 壬辰 Water Dragon **1** 十五 4	金4 Metal 7 Eliminating 澤天夬 癸巳 Water Snake **2** 十六 6	金9 Metal 6 Heaven 乾爲天 甲午 Wood Horse **3** 十七 1	火7 Fire 5 Well 水風井 乙未 Wood Goat **4** 十八 6	木8 Wood 4 Relief 雷水解 丙申 Fire Monkey **5** 十九 4	金4 Metal 3 Influence 澤山咸 丁酉 Fire Rooster **6** 二十 9
水1 Water 2 Humility 地山謙 戊戌 Earth Dog **7** 廿一 6	火2 Fire 1 Observation 風地觀 己亥 Earth Pig **8** 廿二 2	火2 Fire 9 Increasing 風雷益 庚子 Metal Rat **9** 廿三 9	水1 Water 8 Dimming Light 地火明夷 辛丑 Metal Ox **10** 廿四 3	金9 Metal 7 Fellowship 天火同人 壬寅 Water Tiger **11** 廿五 7	木8 Wood 6 Marrying Maiden 雷澤歸妹 癸卯 Water Rabbit **12** 廿六 7	木3 Wood 5 Opposition 火澤睽 甲辰 Wood Dragon **13** 廿七 2
火7 Fire 4 Waiting 水天需 乙巳 Wood Snake **14** 廿八 3	金4 Metal 3 Great Exceeding 澤風大過 丙午 Fire Horse **15** 廿九 3	水6 Water 2 Poison 山風蠱 丁未 Fire Goat **16** 七月初一 7	火2 Fire 1 Dispersing 風水渙 戊申 Earth Monkey **17** 初二 6	木3 Wood 9 Travelling 火山旅 己酉 Earth Rooster **18** 初三 8	金9 Metal 8 Stagnation 天地否 庚戌 Metal Dog **19** 初四 9	火7 Fire 7 Alliance 水地比 辛亥 Metal Pig **20** 初五 7
木8 Wood 6 Thunder 震爲雷 壬子 Water Rat **21** 初六 1	水6 Water 5 Beauty 山火賁 癸丑 Water Ox **22** 初七 8	火7 Fire 4 Accomplished 水火既濟 甲寅 Wood Tiger **23** 初八 9	水1 Water 3 Arriving 地澤臨 乙卯 Wood Rabbit **24** 初九 4	金4 Metal 2 Marsh 兑爲澤 丙辰 Fire Dragon **25** 初十 1	火2 Fire 1 Small Livestock 風天小畜 丁巳 Fire Snake **26** 十一 8	木3 Wood 9 The Cauldron 火風鼎 戊午 Earth Horse **27** 十二 4
水1 Water 8 Rising 地風升 己未 Earth Goat **28** 十三 2	火7 Fire 7 Water 坎爲水 庚申 Metal Monkey **29** 十四 1	木8 Wood 6 Lesser Exceeding 雷山小過 辛酉 Metal Rooster **30** 十五 3	金4 Metal 5 Gathering 澤地萃 壬戌 Water Dog **31** 十六 4			

SEPTEMBER 1966 丁酉

Xuan Kong Element 玄空五行	澤山咸 Influence	Period Luck 卦運	Monthly Star 月星
Metal 金4		9	1

SUNDAY	MONDAY	TUESDAY	WEDNESDAY	THURSDAY	FRIDAY	SATURDAY
				水6 Water 4 癸亥 Water Pig Peel 山地剝 **1** 十七 6	水1 Water 3 甲子 Wood Rat Earth 坤爲地 **2** 十八 1	木3 Wood 2 乙丑 Wood Ox Biting 火雷噬嗑 **3** 十九 6
火2 Fire 1 丙寅 Fire Tiger Family 風火家人 **4** 二十 4	水6 Water 9 丁卯 Fire Rabbit Decreasing 山澤損 **5** 廿一 9	金9 Metal 8 戊辰 Earth Dragon Tread 天澤履 **6** 廿二 6	木8 Wood 7 己巳 Earth Snake Great Strength 雷天大壯 **7** 廿三 2	木8 Wood 6 庚午 Metal Horse Consistency 雷風恆 **8** 廿四 9	金9 Metal 5 辛未 Metal Goat Litigation 天水訟 **9** 廿五 3	水1 Water 4 壬申 Water Monkey Officer 地水師 **10** 廿六 7
火2 Fire 3 癸酉 Water Rooster Gradual Progress 風山漸 **11** 廿七 7	火7 Fire 2 甲戌 Wood Dog Obstruction 水山蹇 **12** 廿八 2	木3 Wood 1 乙亥 Wood Pig Advancement 火地晉 **13** 廿九 3	水6 Water 9 丙子 Fire Rat Nourish 山雷頤 **14** 三十 3	金4 Metal 8 丁丑 Fire Ox Following 澤雷隨 **15** 八月初一 7	木8 Wood 7 戊寅 Earth Tiger Abundance 雷火豐 **16** 初二 6	火7 Fire 6 己卯 Earth Rabbit Regulate 水澤節 **17** 初三 8
水1 Water 5 庚辰 Metal Dragon Unity 地天泰 **18** 初四 9	木3 Wood 4 辛巳 Metal Snake Great Reward 火天大有 **19** 初五 7	火2 Fire 3 壬午 Water Horse Wind 巽爲風 **20** 初六 1	金4 Metal 2 癸未 Water Goat Trap 澤水困 **21** 初七 8	木3 Wood 1 甲申 Wood Monkey Not Yet Accomplished 火水未濟 **22** 初八 9	金9 Metal 9 乙酉 Wood Rooster Retreat 天山遯 **23** 初九 4	水6 Water 8 丙戌 Fire Dog Mountain 艮爲山 **24** 初十 1
木8 Wood 7 丁亥 Fire Pig Delight 雷地豫 **25** 十一 8	火7 Fire 6 戊子 Earth Rat Beginning 水雷屯 **26** 十二 4	金9 Metal 5 己丑 Earth Ox Without Wrongdoing 天雷無妄 **27** 十三 2	木3 Wood 4 庚寅 Metal Tiger Fire 離爲火 **28** 十四 1	火2 Fire 3 辛卯 Metal Rabbit Sincerity 風澤中孚 **29** 十五 3	水6 Water 2 壬辰 Water Dragon Big Livestock 山天大畜 **30** 十六 4	

OCTOBER 1966 戊戌

Xuan Kong Element 玄空五行	地山謙 Humility	Period Luck 卦運	Monthly Star 月星
Water 水1		6	9

SUNDAY	MONDAY	TUESDAY	WEDNESDAY	THURSDAY	FRIDAY	SATURDAY
金4 Metal 8 壬戌 Water Dog Gathering 澤地萃 **30** 十七 4	水6 Water 7 癸亥 Water Pig Peel 山地剝 **31** 十八 6					金4 Metal 1 癸巳 Water Snake Eliminating 澤天夬 **1** 十七 6
金9 Metal 9 甲午 Wood Horse Heaven 乾爲天 **2** 十八 1	火7 Fire 8 乙未 Wood Goat Well 水風井 **3** 十九 6	木8 Wood 7 丙申 Fire Monkey Relief 雷水解 **4** 二十 4	金4 Metal 6 丁酉 Fire Rooster Influence 澤山咸 **5** 廿一 9	水1 Water 5 戊戌 Earth Dog Humility 地山謙 **6** 廿二 6	火2 Fire 4 己亥 Earth Pig Observation 風地觀 **7** 廿三 2	火2 Fire 3 庚子 Metal Rat Increasing 風雷益 **8** 廿四 9
水1 Water 2 辛丑 Metal Ox Dimming Light 地火明夷 **9** 廿五 3	金9 Metal 1 壬寅 Water Tiger Fellowship 天火同人 **10** 廿六 7	木8 Wood 9 癸卯 Water Rabbit Marrying Maiden 雷澤歸妹 **11** 廿七 7	木3 Wood 8 甲辰 Wood Dragon Opposition 火澤睽 **12** 廿八 2	火7 Fire 7 乙巳 Wood Snake Waiting 水天需 **13** 廿九 3	金4 Metal 6 丙午 Fire Horse Great Exceeding 澤風大過 **14** 九月初一 3	水6 Water 5 丁未 Fire Goat Poison 山風蠱 **15** 初二 7
火2 Fire 4 戊申 Earth Monkey Dispersing 風水渙 **16** 初三 6	木3 Wood 3 己酉 Earth Rooster Travelling 火山旅 **17** 初四 8	金9 Metal 2 庚戌 Metal Dog Stagnation 天地否 **18** 初五 9	火7 Fire 1 辛亥 Metal Pig Alliance 水地比 **19** 初六 7	木8 Wood 9 壬子 Water Rat Thunder 震爲雷 **20** 初七 1	水6 Water 8 癸丑 Water Ox Beauty 山火賁 **21** 初八 8	火7 Fire 7 甲寅 Wood Tiger Accomplished 水火既濟 **22** 初九 9
水1 Water 6 乙卯 Wood Rabbit Arriving 地澤臨 **23** 初十 4	金4 Metal 5 丙辰 Fire Dragon Marsh 兑爲澤 **24** 十一 1	火2 Fire 4 丁巳 Fire Snake Small Livestock 風天小畜 **25** 十二 8	木3 Wood 3 戊午 Earth Horse The Cauldron 火風鼎 **26** 十三 4	水1 Water 2 己未 Earth Goat Rising 地風升 **27** 十四 2	火7 Fire 1 庚申 Metal Monkey Water 坎爲水 **28** 十五 1	木8 Wood 9 辛酉 Metal Rooster Lesser Exceeding 雷山小過 **29** 十六 3

NOVEMBER 1966 己亥

Xuan Kong Element 玄空五行	風地觀 Observation	Period Luck 卦運	Monthly Star 月星
Fire 火2		2	8

SUNDAY	MONDAY	TUESDAY	WEDNESDAY	THURSDAY	FRIDAY	SATURDAY
		水1 Water 6 Earth 坤爲地 甲子 Wood Rat 1 十九 1	木3 Wood 5 Biting 火雷噬嗑 乙丑 Wood Ox 2 二十 6	火2 Fire 4 Family 風火家人 丙寅 Fire Tiger 3 廿一 4	水6 Water 3 Decreasing 山澤損 丁卯 Fire Rabbit 4 廿二 9	金9 Metal 2 Tread 天澤履 戊辰 Earth Dragon 5 廿三 6
木8 Wood 1 Great Strength 雷天大壯 己巳 Earth Snake 6 廿四 2	木8 Wood 9 Consistency 雷風恆 庚午 Metal Horse 7 廿五 9	金9 Metal 8 Litigation 天水訟 辛未 Metal Goat 8 廿六 3	水1 Water 7 Officer 地水師 壬申 Water Monkey 9 廿七 7	火2 Fire 6 Gradual Progress 風山漸 癸酉 Water Rooster 10 廿八 7	火7 Fire 5 Obstruction 水山蹇 甲戌 Wood Dog 11 廿九 2	木3 Wood 4 Advancement 火地晉 乙亥 Wood Pig 12 十月初一 3
水6 Water 3 Nourish 山雷頤 丙子 Fire Rat 13 初二 3	金4 Metal 2 Following 澤雷隨 丁丑 Fire Ox 14 初三 7	木8 Wood 1 Abundance 雷火豐 戊寅 Earth Tiger 15 初四 6	火7 Fire 9 Regulate 水澤節 己卯 Earth Rabbit 16 初五 8	水1 Water 8 Unity 地天泰 庚辰 Metal Dragon 17 初六 9	木3 Wood 7 Great Reward 火天大有 辛巳 Metal Snake 18 初七 7	火2 Fire 6 Wind 巽爲風 壬午 Water Horse 19 初八 1
金4 Metal 5 Trap 澤水困 癸未 Water Goat 20 初九 8	木3 Wood 4 Not Yet Accomplished 火水未濟 甲申 Wood Monkey 21 初十 9	金9 Metal 3 Retreat 天山遯 乙酉 Wood Rooster 22 十一 4	水6 Water 2 Mountain 艮爲山 丙戌 Fire Dog 23 十二 1	木8 Wood 1 Delight 雷地豫 丁亥 Fire Pig 24 十三 8	火7 Fire 9 Beginning 水雷屯 戊子 Earth Rat 25 十四 4	金9 Metal 8 Without Wrongdoing 天雷無妄 己丑 Earth Ox 26 十五 2
木3 Wood 7 Fire 離爲火 庚寅 Metal Tiger 27 十六 1	火2 Fire 6 Sincerity 風澤中孚 辛卯 Metal Rabbit 28 十七 3	水6 Water 5 Big Livestock 山天大畜 壬辰 Water Dragon 29 十八 4	金4 Metal 4 Eliminating 澤天夬 癸巳 Water Snake 30 十九 6			

DECEMBER 1966 庚子

Xuan Kong Element 玄空五行	風雷益 Increasing	Period Luck 卦運	Monthly Star 月星
Fire 火2		9	7

SUNDAY	MONDAY	TUESDAY	WEDNESDAY	THURSDAY	FRIDAY	SATURDAY
				金9 Metal 3 Heaven 乾爲天 甲午 Wood Horse 1 二十 1	火7 Fire 2 Well 水風井 乙未 Wood Goat 2 廿一 6	木8 Wood 1 Relief 雷水解 丙申 Fire Monkey 3 廿二 4
金4 Metal 9 Influence 澤山咸 丁酉 Fire Rooster 4 廿三 9	水1 Water 8 Humility 地山謙 戊戌 Earth Dog 5 廿四 6	火2 Fire 7 Observation 風地觀 己亥 Earth Pig 6 廿五 2	火2 Fire 6 Increasing 風雷益 庚子 Metal Rat 7 廿六 9	水1 Water 5 Dimming Light 地火明夷 辛丑 Metal Ox 8 廿七 3	金9 Metal 4 Fellowship 天火同人 壬寅 Water Tiger 9 廿八 7	木8 Wood 3 Marrying Maiden 雷澤歸妹 癸卯 Water Rabbit 10 廿九 7
木3 Wood 2 Opposition 火澤睽 甲辰 Wood Dragon 11 三十 2	火7 Fire 1 Waiting 水天需 乙巳 Wood Snake 12 十一月初一 3	金4 Metal 9 Great Exceeding 澤風大過 丙午 Fire Horse 13 初二 3	水6 Water 8 Poison 山風蠱 丁未 Fire Goat 14 初三 7	火2 Fire 7 Dispersing 風水渙 戊申 Earth Monkey 15 初四 6	木3 Wood 6 Travelling 火山旅 己酉 Earth Rooster 16 初五 8	金9 Metal 5 Stagnation 天地否 庚戌 Metal Dog 17 初六 9
火7 Fire 4 Alliance 水地比 辛亥 Metal Pig 18 初七 7	木8 Wood 3 Thunder 震爲雷 壬子 Water Rat 19 初八 1	水6 Water 2 Beauty 山火賁 癸丑 Water Ox 20 初九 8	火7 Fire 1 Accomplished 水火既濟 甲寅 Wood Tiger 21 初十 9	水1 Water 9/1 Arriving 地澤臨 乙卯 Wood Rabbit 22 十一 4	金4 Metal 2 Marsh 兌爲澤 丙辰 Fire Dragon 23 十二 1	火2 Fire 3 Small Livestock 風天小畜 丁巳 Fire Snake 24 十三 8
木3 Wood 4 The Cauldron 火風鼎 戊午 Earth Horse 25 十四 4	水1 Water 5 Rising 地風升 己未 Earth Goat 26 十五 2	火7 Fire 6 Water 坎爲水 庚申 Metal Monkey 27 十六 1	木8 Wood 7 Lesser Exceeding 雷山小過 辛酉 Metal Rooster 28 十七 3	金4 Metal 8 Gathering 澤地萃 壬戌 Water Dog 29 十八 4	水6 Water 9 Peel 山地剝 癸亥 Water Pig 30 十九 6	水1 Water 1 Earth 坤爲地 甲子 Wood Rat 31 二十 1

1967 丁未

(*Ding Wei*) Fire Goat

1967 丁未 (*Ding Wei*) Fire Goat

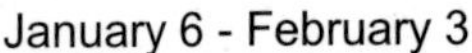

January 6 - February 3

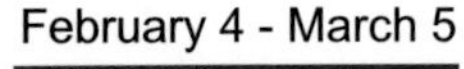

February 4 - March 5

March 6 - April 4

April 5 - May 5

May 6 - June 5

June 6 - July 7

July 8 - August 7

August 8 - September 7

September 8 - October 8

October 9 - November 7

November 8 - December 7

December 8 - January 5

JANUARY 1967 辛丑

Xuan Kong Element 玄空五行	地火明夷 Dimming Light	Period Luck 卦運	Monthly Star 月星
Water 水1		3	6

SUNDAY	MONDAY	TUESDAY	WEDNESDAY	THURSDAY	FRIDAY	SATURDAY
木3 Wood 2 Biting 乙丑 Wood Ox 火雷噬嗑 1 廿一 6	火2 Fire 3 Family 丙寅 Fire Tiger 風火家人 2 廿二 4	水6 Water 4 Decreasing 丁卯 Fire Rabbit 山澤損 3 廿三 9	金9 Metal 5 Tread 戊辰 Earth Dragon 天澤履 4 廿四 6	木8 Wood 6 Great Strength 己巳 Earth Snake 雷天大壯 5 廿五 2	木8 Wood 7 Consistency 庚午 Metal Horse 雷風恆 6 廿六 9	金9 Metal 8 Litigation 辛未 Metal Goat 天水訟 7 廿七 3
水1 Water 9 Officer 壬申 Water Monkey 地水師 8 廿八 7	火2 Fire 1 Gradual Progress 癸酉 Water Rooster 風山漸 9 廿九 7	火7 Fire 2 Obstruction 甲戌 Wood Dog 水山蹇 10 三十 2	木3 Wood 3 Advancement 乙亥 Wood Pig 火地晉 11 十二月初一 3	水6 Water 4 Nourish 丙子 Fire Rat 山雷頤 12 初二 3	金4 Metal 5 Following 丁丑 Fire Ox 澤雷隨 13 初三 7	木8 Wood 6 Abundance 戊寅 Earth Tiger 雷火豐 14 初四 6
火7 Fire 7 Regulate 己卯 Earth Rabbit 水澤節 15 初五 8	水1 Water 8 Unity 庚辰 Metal Dragon 地天泰 16 初六 9	木3 Wood 9 Great Reward 辛巳 Metal Snake 火天大有 17 初七 7	火2 Fire 1 Wind 壬午 Water Horse 巽爲風 18 初八 1	金4 Metal 2 Trap 癸未 Water Goat 澤水困 19 初九 8	木3 Wood 3 Not Yet Accomplished 甲申 Wood Monkey 火水未濟 20 初十 9	金9 Metal 4 Retreat 乙酉 Wood Rooster 天山遯 21 十一 4
水6 Water 5 Mountain 丙戌 Fire Dog 艮爲山 22 十二 1	木8 Wood 6 Delight 丁亥 Fire Pig 雷地豫 23 十三 8	火7 Fire 7 Beginning 戊子 Earth Rat 水雷屯 24 十四 4	金9 Metal 8 Without Wrongdoing 己丑 Earth Ox 天雷無妄 25 十五 2	木3 Wood 9 Fire 庚寅 Metal Tiger 離爲火 26 十六 1	火2 Fire 1 Sincerity 辛卯 Metal Rabbit 風澤中孚 27 十七 3	水6 Water 2 Big Livestock 壬辰 Water Dragon 山天大畜 28 十八 4
金4 Metal 3 Eliminating 癸巳 Water Snake 澤天夬 29 十九 6	金9 Metal 4 Heaven 甲午 Wood Horse 乾爲天 30 二十 1	火7 Fire 5 Well 乙未 Wood Goat 水風井 31 廿一 6				

FEBRUARY 1967 壬寅

Xuan Kong Element 玄空五行	天火同人 Fellowship	Period Luck 卦運	Monthly Star 月星
Metal 金9		7	5

SUNDAY	MONDAY	TUESDAY	WEDNESDAY	THURSDAY	FRIDAY	SATURDAY
			木8 Wood 6 Relief 丙申 Fire Monkey 雷水解 1 廿二 4	金4 Metal 7 Influence 丁酉 Fire Rooster 澤山咸 2 廿三 9	水1 Water 8 Humility 戊戌 Earth Dog 地山謙 3 廿四 6	火2 Fire 9 Observation 己亥 Earth Pig 風地觀 4 廿五 2
火2 Fire 1 Increasing 庚子 Metal Rat 風雷益 5 廿六 9	水1 Water 2 Dimming Light 辛丑 Metal Ox 地火明夷 6 廿七 3	金9 Metal 3 Fellowship 壬寅 Water Tiger 天火同人 7 廿八 7	木8 Wood 4 Marrying Maiden 癸卯 Water Rabbit 雷澤歸妹 8 廿九 7	木3 Wood 5 Opposition 甲辰 Wood Dragon 火澤睽 9 正月初一 2	火7 Fire 6 Waiting 乙巳 Wood Snake 水天需 10 初二 3	金4 Metal 7 Great Exceeding 丙午 Fire Horse 澤風大過 11 初三 3
水6 Water 8 Poison 丁未 Fire Goat 山風蠱 12 初四 7	火2 Fire 9 Dispersing 戊申 Earth Monkey 風水渙 13 初五 6	木3 Wood 1 Travelling 己酉 Earth Rooster 火山旅 14 初六 8	金9 Metal 2 Stagnation 庚戌 Metal Dog 天地否 15 初七 9	火7 Fire 3 Alliance 辛亥 Metal Pig 水地比 16 初八 7	木8 Wood 4 Thunder 壬子 Water Rat 震爲雷 17 初九 1	水6 Water 5 Beauty 癸丑 Water Ox 山火賁 18 初十 8
火7 Fire 6 Accomplished 甲寅 Wood Tiger 水火既濟 19 十一 9	水1 Water 7 Arriving 乙卯 Wood Rabbit 地澤臨 20 十二 4	金4 Metal 8 Marsh 丙辰 Fire Dragon 兌爲澤 21 十三 1	火2 Fire 9 Small Livestock 丁巳 Fire Snake 風天小畜 22 十四 8	木3 Wood 1 The Cauldron 戊午 Earth Horse 火風鼎 23 十五 4	水1 Water 2 Rising 己未 Earth Goat 地風升 24 十六 2	火7 Fire 3 Water 庚申 Metal Monkey 坎爲水 25 十七 1
木8 Wood 4 Lesser Exceeding 辛酉 Metal Rooster 雷山小過 26 十八 3	金4 Metal 5 Gathering 壬戌 Water Dog 澤地萃 27 十九 4	水6 Water 6 Peel 癸亥 Water Pig 山地剝 28 二十 6				

MARCH 1967 癸卯

Xuan Kong Element 玄空五行	雷澤歸妹 Marrying Maiden	Period Luck 卦運	Monthly Star 月星
Wood 木8		7	4

SUNDAY	MONDAY	TUESDAY	WEDNESDAY	THURSDAY	FRIDAY	SATURDAY
			水1 Water Earth 坤爲地 7 甲子 Wood Rat 1 廿一 1	木3 Wood Biting 火雷噬嗑 8 乙丑 Wood Ox 2 廿二 6	火2 Fire Family 風火家人 9 丙寅 Fire Tiger 3 廿三 4	水6 Water Decreasing 山澤損 1 丁卯 Fire Rabbit 4 廿四 9
金9 Metal Tread 天澤履 2 戊辰 Earth Dragon 5 廿五 6	木8 Wood Great Strength 雷天大壯 3 己巳 Earth Snake 6 廿六 2	木8 Wood Consistency 雷風恆 4 庚午 Metal Horse 7 廿七 9	金9 Metal Litigation 天水訟 5 辛未 Metal Goat 8 廿八 3	水1 Water Officer 地水師 6 壬申 Water Monkey 9 廿九 7	火2 Fire Gradual Progress 風山漸 7 癸酉 Water Rooster 10 三十 7	火7 Fire Obstruction 水山蹇 8 甲戌 Wood Dog 11 二月初一 2
木3 Wood Advancement 火地晉 9 乙亥 Wood Pig 12 初二 3	水6 Water Nourish 山雷頤 1 丙子 Fire Rat 13 初三 3	金4 Metal Following 澤雷隨 2 丁丑 Fire Ox 14 初四 7	木8 Wood Abundance 雷火豐 3 戊寅 Earth Tiger 15 初五 6	火7 Fire Regulate 水澤節 4 己卯 Earth Rabbit 16 初六 8	水1 Water Unity 地天泰 5 庚辰 Metal Dragon 17 初七 9	木3 Wood Great Reward 火天大有 6 辛巳 Metal Snake 18 初八 7
火2 Fire Wind 巽爲風 7 壬午 Water Horse 19 初九 1	金4 Metal Trap 澤水困 8 癸未 Water Goat 20 初十 8	木3 Wood Not Yet Accomplished 火水未濟 9 甲申 Wood Monkey 21 十一 9	金9 Metal Retreat 天山遯 1 乙酉 Wood Rooster 22 十二 4	水6 Water Mountain 艮爲山 2 丙戌 Fire Dog 23 十三 1	木8 Wood Delight 雷地豫 3 丁亥 Fire Pig 24 十四 8	火7 Fire Beginning 水雷屯 4 戊子 Earth Rat 25 十五 4
金9 Metal Without Wrongdoing 天雷無妄 5 己丑 Earth Ox 26 十六 2	木3 Wood Fire 離爲火 6 庚寅 Metal Tiger 27 十七 1	火2 Fire Sincerity 風澤中孚 7 辛卯 Metal Rabbit 28 十八 3	水6 Water Big Livestock 山天大畜 8 壬辰 Water Dragon 29 十九 4	金4 Metal Eliminating 澤天夬 9 癸巳 Water Snake 30 二十 6	金9 Metal Heaven 乾爲天 1 甲午 Wood Horse 31 廿一 1	

APRIL 1967 甲辰

Xuan Kong Element 玄空五行	火澤睽 Opposition	Period Luck 卦運	Monthly Star 月星
Wood 木3		2	3

SUNDAY	MONDAY	TUESDAY	WEDNESDAY	THURSDAY	FRIDAY	SATURDAY
水1 Water Earth 坤爲地 4 甲子 Wood Rat 30 廿一 1						火7 Fire Well 水風井 2 乙未 Wood Goat 1 廿二 6
木8 Wood Relief 雷水解 3 丙申 Fire Monkey 2 廿三 4	金4 Metal Influence 澤山咸 4 丁酉 Fire Rooster 3 廿四 9	水1 Water Humility 地山謙 5 戊戌 Earth Dog 4 廿五 6	火2 Fire Observation 風地觀 6 己亥 Earth Pig 5 廿六 2	火2 Fire Increasing 風雷益 7 庚子 Metal Rat 6 廿七 9	水1 Water Dimming Light 地火明夷 8 辛丑 Metal Ox 7 廿八 3	金9 Metal Fellowship 天火同人 9 壬寅 Water Tiger 8 廿九 7
木8 Wood Marrying Maiden 雷澤歸妹 1 癸卯 Water Rabbit 9 三十 7	木3 Wood Opposition 火澤睽 2 甲辰 Wood Dragon 10 三月初一 2	火7 Fire Waiting 水天需 3 乙巳 Wood Snake 11 初二 3	金4 Metal Great Exceeding 澤風大過 4 丙午 Fire Horse 12 初三 3	水6 Water Poison 山風蠱 5 丁未 Fire Goat 13 初四 7	火2 Fire Dispersing 風水渙 6 戊申 Earth Monkey 14 初五 6	木3 Wood Travelling 火山旅 7 己酉 Earth Rooster 15 初六 8
金9 Metal Stagnation 天地否 8 庚戌 Metal Dog 16 初七 9	火7 Fire Alliance 水地比 9 辛亥 Metal Pig 17 初八 7	木8 Wood Thunder 震爲雷 1 壬子 Water Rat 18 初九 1	水6 Water Beauty 山火賁 2 癸丑 Water Ox 19 初十 8	火7 Fire Accomplished 水火既濟 3 甲寅 Wood Tiger 20 十一 9	水1 Water Arriving 地澤臨 4 乙卯 Wood Rabbit 21 十二 4	金4 Metal Marsh 兌爲澤 5 丙辰 Fire Dragon 22 十三 1
火2 Fire Small Livestock 風天小畜 6 丁巳 Fire Snake 23 十四 8	木3 Wood The Cauldron 火風鼎 7 戊午 Earth Horse 24 十五 4	水1 Water Rising 地風升 8 己未 Earth Goat 25 十六 2	火7 Fire Water 坎爲水 9 庚申 Metal Monkey 26 十七 1	木8 Wood Lesser Exceeding 雷山小過 1 辛酉 Metal Rooster 27 十八 3	金4 Metal Gathering 澤地萃 2 壬戌 Water Dog 28 十九 4	水6 Water Peel 山地剝 3 癸亥 Water Pig 29 二十 6

MAY 1967 乙巳

Xuan Kong Element 玄空五行	水天需 Waiting	Period Luck 卦運	Monthly Star 月星
Fire 火7		3	2

SUNDAY	MONDAY	TUESDAY	WEDNESDAY	THURSDAY	FRIDAY	SATURDAY
	木3 Wood Biting 5 乙丑 Wood Ox 火雷噬嗑 1 廿二 6	火2 Fire Family 6 丙寅 Fire Tiger 風火家人 2 廿三 4	水6 Water Decreasing 7 丁卯 Fire Rabbit 山澤損 3 廿四 9	金9 Metal Tread 8 戊辰 Earth Dragon 天澤履 4 廿五 6	木8 Wood Great Strength 9 己巳 Earth Snake 雷天大壯 5 廿六 2	木8 Wood Consistency 1 庚午 Metal Horse 雷風恆 6 廿七 9
金9 Metal Litigation 2 辛未 Metal Goat 天水訟 7 廿八 3	水1 Water Officer 3 壬申 Water Monkey 地水師 8 廿九 7	火2 Fire Gradual Progress 4 癸酉 Water Rooster 風山漸 9 四月初一 7	火7 Fire Obstruction 5 甲戌 Wood Dog 水山蹇 10 初二 2	木3 Wood Advancement 6 乙亥 Wood Pig 火地晉 11 初三 3	水6 Water Nourish 7 丙子 Fire Rat 山雷頤 12 初四 3	金4 Metal Following 8 丁丑 Fire Ox 澤雷隨 13 初五 7
木8 Wood Abundance 9 戊寅 Earth Tiger 雷火豐 14 初六 6	火7 Fire Regulate 1 己卯 Earth Rabbit 水澤節 15 初七 8	水1 Water Unity 2 庚辰 Metal Dragon 地天泰 16 初八 9	木3 Wood Great Reward 3 辛巳 Metal Snake 火天大有 17 初九 7	火2 Fire Wind 4 壬午 Water Horse 巽爲風 18 初十 1	金4 Metal Trap 5 癸未 Water Goat 澤水困 19 十一 8	木3 Wood Not Yet Accomplished 6 甲申 Wood Monkey 火水未濟 20 十二 9
金9 Metal Retreat 7 乙酉 Wood Rooster 天山遯 21 十三 4	水6 Water Mountain 8 丙戌 Fire Dog 艮爲山 22 十四 1	木8 Wood Delight 9 丁亥 Fire Pig 雷地豫 23 十五 8	火7 Fire Beginning 1 戊子 Earth Rat 水雷屯 24 十六 4	金9 Metal Without Wrongdoing 2 己丑 Earth Ox 天雷無妄 25 十七 2	木3 Wood Fire 3 庚寅 Metal Tiger 離爲火 26 十八 1	火2 Fire Sincerity 4 辛卯 Metal Rabbit 風澤中孚 27 十九 3
水6 Water Big Livestock 5 壬辰 Water Dragon 山天大畜 28 二十 4	金4 Metal Eliminating 6 癸巳 Water Snake 澤天夬 29 廿一 6	金9 Metal Heaven 7 甲午 Wood Horse 乾爲天 30 廿二 1	火7 Fire Well 8 乙未 Wood Goat 水風井 31 廿三 6			

JUNE 1967 丙午

Xuan Kong Element 玄空五行	澤風大過 Great Exceeding	Period Luck 卦運	Monthly Star 月星
Metal 金4		3	1

SUNDAY	MONDAY	TUESDAY	WEDNESDAY	THURSDAY	FRIDAY	SATURDAY
				木8 Wood Relief 9 丙申 Fire Monkey 雷水解 1 廿四 4	金4 Metal Influence 1 丁酉 Fire Rooster 澤山咸 2 廿五 9	水1 Water Humility 2 戊戌 Earth Dog 地山謙 3 廿六 6
火2 Fire Observation 3 己亥 Earth Pig 風地觀 4 廿七 2	火2 Fire Increasing 4 庚子 Metal Rat 風雷益 5 廿八 9	水1 Water Dimming Light 5 辛丑 Metal Ox 地火明夷 6 廿九 3	金9 Metal Fellowship 6 壬寅 Water Tiger 天火同人 7 三十 7	木8 Wood Marrying Maiden 7 癸卯 Water Rabbit 雷澤歸妹 8 五月初一 7	木3 Wood Opposition 8 甲辰 Wood Dragon 火澤睽 9 初二 2	火7 Fire Waiting 9 乙巳 Wood Snake 水天需 10 初三 3
金4 Metal Great Exceeding 1 丙午 Fire Horse 澤風大過 11 初四 3	水6 Water Poison 2 丁未 Fire Goat 山風蠱 12 初五 7	火2 Fire Dispersing 3 戊申 Earth Monkey 風水渙 13 初六 6	木3 Wood Travelling 4 己酉 Earth Rooster 火山旅 14 初七 8	金9 Metal Stagnation 5 庚戌 Metal Dog 天地否 15 初八 9	火7 Fire Alliance 6 辛亥 Metal Pig 水地比 16 初九 7	木8 Wood Thunder 7 壬子 Water Rat 震爲雷 17 初十 1
水6 Water Beauty 8 癸丑 Water Ox 山火賁 18 十一 8	火7 Fire Accomplished 9 甲寅 Wood Tiger 水火既濟 19 十二 9	水1 Water Arriving 1 乙卯 Wood Rabbit 地澤臨 20 十三 4	金4 Metal Marsh 2 丙辰 Fire Dragon 兑爲澤 21 十四 1	火2 Fire Small Livestock 3/7 丁巳 Fire Snake 風天小畜 22 十五 8	木3 Wood The Cauldron 6 戊午 Earth Horse 火風鼎 23 十六 4	水1 Water Rising 5 己未 Earth Goat 地風升 24 十七 2
火7 Fire Water 4 庚申 Metal Monkey 坎爲水 25 十八 1	木8 Wood Lesser Exceeding 3 辛酉 Metal Rooster 雷山小過 26 十九 3	金4 Metal Gathering 2 壬戌 Water Dog 澤地萃 27 二十 4	水6 Water Peel 1 癸亥 Water Pig 山地剝 28 廿一 6	水1 Water Earth 9 甲子 Wood Rat 坤爲地 29 廿二 1	木3 Wood Biting 8 乙丑 Wood Ox 火雷噬嗑 30 廿三 6	

JULY 1967 丁未

Xuan Kong Element 玄空五行	山風蠱 Poison	Period Luck 卦運	Monthly Star 月星
Water 水6		7	9

SUNDAY	MONDAY	TUESDAY	WEDNESDAY	THURSDAY	FRIDAY	SATURDAY
火7 Fire Well 5 乙未 Wood Goat 水風井 30 廿三 6	木8 Wood Relief 4 丙申 Fire Monkey 雷水解 31 廿四 4					火2 Fire Family 7 丙寅 Fire Tiger 風火家人 1 廿四 4
水6 Water Decreasing 6 丁卯 Fire Rabbit 山澤損 2 廿五 9	金9 Metal Tread 5 戊辰 Earth Dragon 天澤履 3 廿六 6	木8 Wood Great Strength 4 己巳 Earth Snake 雷天大壯 4 廿七 2	木8 Wood Consistency 3 庚午 Metal Horse 雷風恆 5 廿八 9	金9 Metal Litigation 2 辛未 Metal Goat 天水訟 6 廿九 3	水1 Water Officer 1 壬申 Water Monkey 地水師 7 三十 7	火2 Fire Gradual Progress 9 癸酉 Water Rooster 風山漸 8 六月初一 7
火7 Fire Obstruction 8 甲戌 Wood Dog 水山蹇 9 初二 2	木3 Wood Advancement 7 乙亥 Wood Pig 火地晉 10 初三 3	水6 Water Nourish 6 丙子 Fire Rat 山雷頤 11 初四 3	金4 Metal Following 5 丁丑 Fire Ox 澤雷隨 12 初五 7	木8 Wood Abundance 4 戊寅 Earth Tiger 雷火豐 13 初六 6	火7 Fire Regulate 3 己卯 Earth Rabbit 水澤節 14 初七 8	水1 Water Unity 2 庚辰 Metal Dragon 地天泰 15 初八 9
木3 Wood Great Reward 1 辛巳 Metal Snake 火天大有 16 初九 7	火2 Fire Wind 9 壬午 Water Horse 巽爲風 17 初十 1	金4 Metal Trap 8 癸未 Water Goat 澤水困 18 十一 2	木3 Wood Not Yet Accomplished 7 甲申 Wood Monkey 火水未濟 19 十二 9	金9 Metal Retreat 6 乙酉 Wood Rooster 天山遯 20 十三 4	水6 Water Mountain 5 丙戌 Fire Dog 艮爲山 21 十四 1	木8 Wood Delight 4 丁亥 Fire Pig 雷地豫 22 十五 8
火7 Fire Beginning 3 戊子 Earth Rat 水雷屯 23 十六 4	金9 Metal Without Wrongdoing 2 己丑 Earth Ox 天雷無妄 24 十七 2	木3 Wood Fire 1 庚寅 Metal Tiger 離爲火 25 十八 1	火2 Fire Sincerity 9 辛卯 Metal Rabbit 風澤中孚 26 十九 3	水6 Water Big Livestock 8 壬辰 Water Dragon 山天大畜 27 二十 4	金4 Metal Eliminating 7 癸巳 Water Snake 澤天夬 28 廿一 6	金9 Metal Heaven 6 甲午 Wood Horse 乾爲天 29 廿二 1

AUGUST 1967 戊申

Xuan Kong Element 玄空五行	風水渙 Dispersing	Period Luck 卦運	Monthly Star 月星
Fire 火2		6	8

SUNDAY	MONDAY	TUESDAY	WEDNESDAY	THURSDAY	FRIDAY	SATURDAY
		金4 Metal Influence 3 丁酉 Fire Rooster 澤山咸 1 廿五 9	水1 Water Humility 2 戊戌 Earth Dog 地山謙 2 廿六 6	火2 Fire Observation 1 己亥 Earth Pig 風地觀 3 廿七 2	火2 Fire Increasing 9 庚子 Metal Rat 風雷益 4 廿八 9	水1 Water Dimming Light 8 辛丑 Metal Ox 地火明夷 5 廿九 3
金9 Metal Fellowship 7 壬寅 Water Tiger 天火同人 6 七月初一 7	木8 Wood Marrying Maiden 6 癸卯 Water Rabbit 雷澤歸妹 7 初二 7	木3 Wood Opposition 5 甲辰 Wood Dragon 火澤睽 8 初三 2	火7 Fire Waiting 4 乙巳 Wood Snake 水天需 9 初四 3	金4 Metal Great Exceeding 3 丙午 Fire Horse 澤風大過 10 初五 3	水6 Water Poison 2 丁未 Fire Goat 山風蠱 11 初六 7	火2 Fire Dispersing 1 戊申 Earth Monkey 風水渙 12 初七 6
木3 Wood Travelling 9 己酉 Earth Rooster 火山旅 13 初八 8	金9 Metal Stagnation 8 庚戌 Metal Dog 天地否 14 初九 9	火7 Fire Alliance 7 辛亥 Metal Pig 水地比 15 初十 7	木8 Wood Thunder 6 壬子 Water Rat 震爲雷 16 十一 1	水6 Water Beauty 5 癸丑 Water Ox 山火賁 17 十二 8	火7 Fire Accomplished 4 甲寅 Wood Tiger 水火既濟 18 十三 9	水1 Water Arriving 3 乙卯 Wood Rabbit 地澤臨 19 十四 4
金4 Metal Marsh 2 丙辰 Fire Dragon 兌爲澤 20 十五 1	火2 Fire Small Livestock 1 丁巳 Fire Snake 風天小畜 21 十六 8	木3 Wood The Cauldron 9 戊午 Earth Horse 火風鼎 22 十七 4	水1 Water Rising 8 己未 Earth Goat 地風升 23 十八 2	火7 Fire Water 7 庚申 Metal Monkey 坎爲水 24 十九 1	木8 Wood Lesser Exceeding 6 辛酉 Metal Rooster 雷山小過 25 二十 3	金4 Metal Gathering 5 壬戌 Water Dog 澤地萃 26 廿一 4
水6 Water Peel 4 癸亥 Water Pig 山地剝 27 廿二 6	水1 Water Earth 3 甲子 Wood Rat 坤爲地 28 廿三 1	木3 Wood Biting 2 乙丑 Wood Ox 火雷噬嗑 29 廿四 6	火2 Fire Family 1 丙寅 Fire Tiger 風火家人 30 廿五 4	水6 Water Decreasing 9 丁卯 Fire Rabbit 山澤損 31 廿六 9		

SEPTEMBER 1967 己酉

Xuan Kong Element 玄空五行	火山旅 Travelling	Period Luck 卦運	Monthly Star 月星
Wood 木3		8	7

SUNDAY	MONDAY	TUESDAY	WEDNESDAY	THURSDAY	FRIDAY	SATURDAY
					1 廿七 金9 Metal Tread 天澤履 戊辰 Earth Dragon 8 / 6	2 廿八 木8 Wood Great Strength 雷天大壯 己巳 Earth Snake 7 / 2
3 廿九 木8 Wood Consistency 雷風恆 庚午 Metal Horse 6 / 9	4 八月初一 金9 Metal Litigation 天水訟 辛未 Metal Goat 5 / 3	5 初二 水1 Water Officer 地水師 壬申 Water Monkey 4 / 7	6 初三 火2 Fire Gradual Progress 風山漸 癸酉 Water Rooster 3 / 7	7 初四 火7 Fire Obstruction 水山蹇 甲戌 Wood Dog 2 / 2	8 初五 木3 Wood Advancement 火地晉 乙亥 Wood Pig 1 / 3	9 初六 水6 Water Nourish 山雷頤 丙子 Fire Rat 9 / 3
10 初七 金4 Metal Following 澤雷隨 丁丑 Fire Ox 8 / 7	11 初八 木8 Wood Abundance 雷火豐 戊寅 Earth Tiger 7 / 6	12 初九 火7 Fire Regulate 水澤節 己卯 Earth Rabbit 6 / 8	13 初十 水1 Water Unity 地天泰 庚辰 Metal Dragon 5 / 9	14 十一 木3 Wood Great Reward 火天大有 辛巳 Metal Snake 4 / 7	15 十二 火2 Fire Wind 巽爲風 壬午 Water Horse 3 / 1	16 十三 金4 Metal Trap 澤水困 癸未 Water Goat 2 / 8
17 十四 木3 Wood Not Yet Accomplished 火水未濟 甲申 Wood Monkey 1 / 9	18 十五 金9 Metal Retreat 天山遯 乙酉 Wood Rooster 9 / 4	19 十六 水6 Water Mountain 艮爲山 丙戌 Fire Dog 8 / 1	20 十七 木8 Wood Delight 雷地豫 丁亥 Fire Pig 7 / 8	21 十八 火7 Fire Beginning 水雷屯 戊子 Earth Rat 6 / 4	22 十九 金9 Metal Without Wrongdoing 天雷無妄 己丑 Earth Ox 5 / 2	23 二十 木3 Wood Fire 離爲火 庚寅 Metal Tiger 4 / 1
24 廿一 火2 Fire Sincerity 風澤中孚 辛卯 Metal Rabbit 3 / 3	25 廿二 水6 Water Big Livestock 山天大畜 壬辰 Water Dragon 2 / 4	26 廿三 金4 Metal Eliminating 澤天夬 癸巳 Water Snake 1 / 6	27 廿四 金9 Metal Heaven 乾爲天 甲午 Wood Horse 9 / 1	28 廿五 火7 Fire Well 水風井 乙未 Wood Goat 8 / 6	29 廿六 木8 Wood Relief 雷水解 丙申 Fire Monkey 7 / 4	30 廿七 金4 Metal Influence 澤山咸 丁酉 Fire Rooster 6 / 9

OCTOBER 1967 庚戌

Xuan Kong Element 玄空五行	天地否 Stagnation	Period Luck 卦運	Monthly Star 月星
Metal 金9		9	6

SUNDAY	MONDAY	TUESDAY	WEDNESDAY	THURSDAY	FRIDAY	SATURDAY
1 廿八 水1 Water Humility 地山謙 戊戌 Earth Dog 5 / 6	2 廿九 火2 Fire Observation 風地觀 己亥 Earth Pig 4 / 2	3 三十 火2 Fire Increasing 風雷益 庚子 Metal Rat 3 / 9	4 九月初一 水1 Water Dimming Light 地火明夷 辛丑 Metal Ox 2 / 3	5 初二 金9 Metal Fellowship 天火同人 壬寅 Water Tiger 1 / 7	6 初三 木8 Wood Marrying Maiden 雷澤歸妹 癸卯 Water Rabbit 9 / 7	7 初四 木3 Wood Opposition 火澤睽 甲辰 Wood Dragon 8 / 2
8 初五 火7 Fire Waiting 水天需 乙巳 Wood Snake 7 / 3	9 初六 金4 Metal Great Exceeding 澤風大過 丙午 Fire Horse 6 / 3	10 初七 水6 Water Poison 山風蠱 丁未 Fire Goat 5 / 7	11 初八 火2 Fire Dispersing 風水渙 戊申 Earth Monkey 4 / 6	12 初九 木3 Wood Travelling 火山旅 己酉 Earth Rooster 3 / 8	13 初十 金9 Metal Stagnation 天地否 庚戌 Metal Dog 2 / 9	14 十一 火7 Fire Alliance 水地比 辛亥 Metal Pig 1 / 7
15 十二 木8 Wood Thunder 震爲雷 壬子 Water Rat 9 / 1	16 十三 水6 Water Beauty 山火賁 癸丑 Water Ox 8 / 8	17 十四 火7 Fire Accomplished 水火既濟 甲寅 Wood Tiger 7 / 9	18 十五 水1 Water Arriving 地澤臨 乙卯 Wood Rabbit 6 / 4	19 十六 金4 Metal Marsh 兌爲澤 丙辰 Fire Dragon 5 / 1	20 十七 火2 Fire Small Livestock 風天小畜 丁巳 Fire Snake 4 / 8	21 十八 木3 Wood The Cauldron 火風鼎 戊午 Earth Horse 3 / 4
22 十九 水1 Water Rising 地風升 己未 Earth Goat 2 / 2	23 二十 火7 Fire Water 坎爲水 庚申 Metal Monkey 1 / 1	24 廿一 木8 Wood Lesser Exceeding 雷山小過 辛酉 Metal Rooster 9 / 3	25 廿二 金4 Metal Gathering 澤地萃 壬戌 Water Dog 8 / 4	26 廿三 水6 Water Peel 山地剝 癸亥 Water Pig 7 / 6	27 廿四 水1 Water Earth 坤爲地 甲子 Wood Rat 6 / 1	28 廿五 木3 Wood Biting 火雷噬嗑 乙丑 Wood Ox 5 / 6
29 廿六 火2 Fire Family 風火家人 丙寅 Fire Tiger 4 / 4	30 廿七 水6 Water Decreasing 山澤損 丁卯 Fire Rabbit 3 / 9	31 廿八 金9 Metal Tread 天澤履 戊辰 Earth Dragon 2 / 6				

NOVEMBER 1967 辛亥

Xuan Kong Element 玄空五行	水地比 Alliance	Period Luck 卦運	Monthly Star 月星
Fire 火7		7	5

SUNDAY	MONDAY	TUESDAY	WEDNESDAY	THURSDAY	FRIDAY	SATURDAY
			木8 Wood 1 Great Strength 雷天大壯 己巳 Earth Snake 1 廿九 2	木8 Wood 9 Consistency 雷風恆 庚午 Metal Horse 2 十月初一 9	金9 Metal 8 Litigation 天水訟 辛未 Metal Goat 3 初二 3	水1 Water 7 Officer 地水師 壬申 Water Monkey 4 初三 7
火2 Fire 6 Gradual Progress 風山漸 癸酉 Water Rooster 5 初四 7	火7 Fire 5 Obstruction 水山蹇 甲戌 Wood Dog 6 初五 2	木3 Wood 4 Advancement 火地晉 乙亥 Wood Pig 7 初六 3	水6 Water 3 Nourish 山雷頤 丙子 Fire Rat 8 初七 3	金4 Metal 2 Following 澤雷隨 丁丑 Fire Ox 9 初八 7	木8 Wood 1 Abundance 雷火豐 戊寅 Earth Tiger 10 初九 6	火7 Fire 9 Regulate 水澤節 己卯 Earth Rabbit 11 初十 8
水1 Water 8 Unity 地天泰 庚辰 Metal Dragon 12 十一 9	木3 Wood 7 Great Reward 火天大有 辛巳 Metal Snake 13 十二 7	火2 Fire 6 Wind 巽爲風 壬午 Water Horse 14 十三 1	金4 Metal 5 Trap 澤水困 癸未 Water Goat 15 十四 8	木3 Wood 4 Not Yet Accomplished 火水未濟 甲申 Wood Monkey 16 十五 9	金9 Metal 3 Retreat 天山遯 乙酉 Wood Rooster 17 十六 4	水6 Water 2 Mountain 艮爲山 丙戌 Fire Dog 18 十七 1
木8 Wood 1 Delight 雷地豫 丁亥 Fire Pig 19 十八 8	火7 Fire 9 Beginning 水雷屯 戊子 Earth Rat 20 十九 4	金9 Metal 8 Without Wrongdoing 天雷無妄 己丑 Earth Ox 21 二十 2	木3 Wood 7 Fire 離爲火 庚寅 Metal Tiger 22 廿一 1	火2 Fire 6 Sincerity 風澤中孚 辛卯 Metal Rabbit 23 廿二 3	水6 Water 5 Big Livestock 山天大畜 壬辰 Water Dragon 24 廿三 4	金4 Metal 4 Eliminating 澤天夬 癸巳 Water Snake 25 廿四 6
金9 Metal 3 Heaven 乾爲天 甲午 Wood Horse 26 廿五 1	火7 Fire 2 Well 水風井 乙未 Wood Goat 27 廿六 6	木8 Wood 1 Relief 雷水解 丙申 Fire Monkey 28 廿七 4	金4 Metal 9 Influence 澤山咸 丁酉 Fire Rooster 29 廿八 9	水1 Water 8 Humility 地山謙 戊戌 Earth Dog 30 廿九 6		

DECEMBER 1967 壬子

Xuan Kong Element 玄空五行	震爲雷 Thunder	Period Luck 卦運	Monthly Star 月星
Wood 木8		1	4

SUNDAY	MONDAY	TUESDAY	WEDNESDAY	THURSDAY	FRIDAY	SATURDAY
木8 Wood 6 Great Strength 雷天大壯 己巳 Earth Snake 31 十二月初一 2					火2 Fire 7 Observation 風地觀 己亥 Earth Pig 1 三十 2	火2 Fire 6 Increasing 風雷益 庚子 Metal Rat 2 十一月初一 9
水1 Water 5 Dimming Light 地火明夷 辛丑 Metal Ox 3 初二 3	金9 Metal 4 Fellowship 天火同人 壬寅 Water Tiger 4 初三 7	木8 Wood 3 Marrying Maiden 雷澤歸妹 癸卯 Water Rabbit 5 初四 7	木3 Wood 2 Opposition 火澤睽 甲辰 Wood Dragon 6 初五 2	火7 Fire 1 Waiting 水天需 乙巳 Wood Snake 7 初六 3	金4 Metal 9 Great Exceeding 澤風大過 丙午 Fire Horse 8 初七 3	水6 Water 8 Poison 山風蠱 丁未 Fire Goat 9 初八 7
火2 Fire 7 Dispersing 風水渙 戊申 Earth Monkey 10 初九 6	木3 Wood 6 Travelling 火山旅 己酉 Earth Rooster 11 初十 8	金9 Metal 5 Stagnation 天地否 庚戌 Metal Dog 12 十一 9	火7 Fire 4 Alliance 水地比 辛亥 Metal Pig 13 十二 7	木8 Wood 3 Thunder 震爲雷 壬子 Water Rat 14 十三 1	水6 Water 2 Beauty 山火賁 癸丑 Water Ox 15 十四 8	火7 Fire 1 Accomplished 水火既濟 甲寅 Wood Tiger 16 十五 9
水1 Water 9 Arriving 地澤臨 乙卯 Wood Rabbit 17 十六 4	金4 Metal 8 Marsh 兌爲澤 丙辰 Fire Dragon 18 十七 1	火2 Fire 7 Small Livestock 風天小畜 丁巳 Fire Snake 19 十八 8	木3 Wood 6 The Cauldron 火風鼎 戊午 Earth Horse 20 十九 4	水1 Water 5 Rising 地風升 己未 Earth Goat 21 二十 2	火7 Fire 4/6 Water 坎爲水 庚申 Metal Monkey 22 廿一 1	木8 Wood 7 Lesser Exceeding 雷山小過 辛酉 Metal Rooster 23 廿二 3
金4 Metal 8 Gathering 澤地萃 壬戌 Water Dog 24 廿三 4	水6 Water 9 Peel 山地剝 癸亥 Water Pig 25 廿四 6	水1 Water 1 Earth 坤爲地 甲子 Wood Rat 26 廿五 1	木3 Wood 2 Biting 火雷噬嗑 乙丑 Wood Ox 27 廿六 6	火2 Fire 3 Family 風火家人 丙寅 Fire Tiger 28 廿七 4	水6 Water 4 Decreasing 山澤損 丁卯 Fire Rabbit 29 廿八 9	金9 Metal 5 Tread 天澤履 戊辰 Earth Dragon 30 廿九 6

1968 戊申

(*Wu Shen*) Earth Monkey

1968 戊申 *(Wu Shen)* Earth Monkey

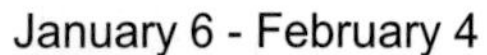

January 6 - February 4

February 5 - March 4

March 5 - April 4

April 5 - May 4

May 5 - June 4

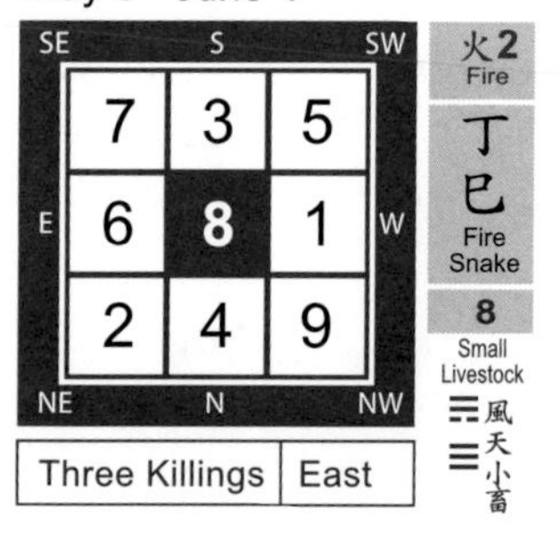

June 5 - July 6

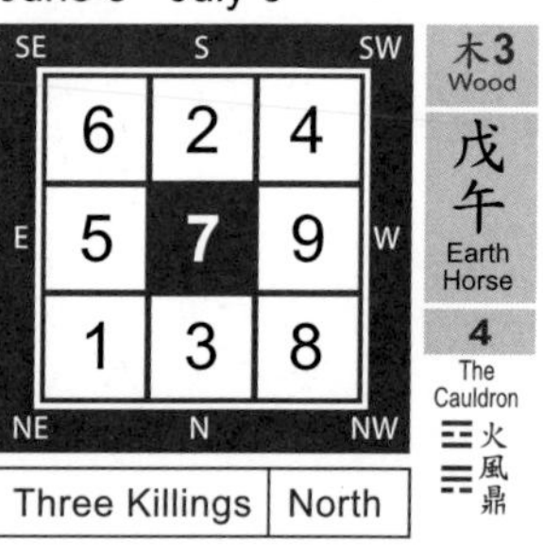

July 7 - August 6

August 7 - September 6

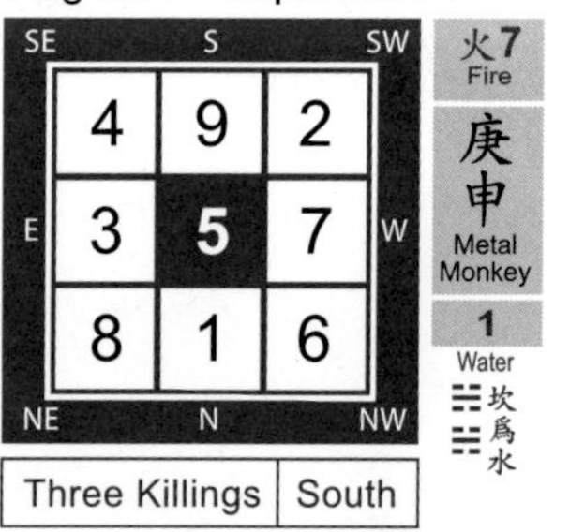

September 7 - October 7

October 8 - November 6

November 7 - December 6

December 7 - January 4

JANUARY 1968 癸丑

Xuan Kong Element 玄空五行	山火賁 Beauty	Period Luck 卦運	Monthly Star 月星
Water 水6		8	3

SUNDAY	MONDAY	TUESDAY	WEDNESDAY	THURSDAY	FRIDAY	SATURDAY
	木8 Wood · 7 · Consistency · 庚午 Metal Horse · 雷風恆 · **1** · 初二 · 9	金9 Metal · 8 · Litigation · 辛未 Metal Goat · 天水訟 · **2** · 初三 · 3	水1 Water · 9 · Officer · 壬申 Water Monkey · 地水師 · **3** · 初四 · 7	火2 Fire · 1 · Gradual Progress · 癸酉 Water Rooster · 風山漸 · **4** · 初五 · 7	火7 Fire · 2 · Obstruction · 甲戌 Wood Dog · 水山蹇 · **5** · 初六 · 2	木3 Wood · 3 · Advancement · 乙亥 Wood Pig · 火地晉 · **6** · 初七 · 3
水6 Water · 4 · Nourish · 丙子 Fire Rat · 山雷頤 · **7** · 初八 · 3	金4 Metal · 5 · Following · 丁丑 Fire Ox · 澤雷隨 · **8** · 初九 · 7	木8 Wood · 6 · Abundance · 戊寅 Earth Tiger · 雷火豐 · **9** · 初十 · 6	火7 Fire · 7 · Regulate · 己卯 Earth Rabbit · 水澤節 · **10** · 十一 · 8	水1 Water · 8 · Unity · 庚辰 Metal Dragon · 地天泰 · **11** · 十二 · 9	木3 Wood · 9 · Great Reward · 辛巳 Metal Snake · 火天大有 · **12** · 十三 · 7	火2 Fire · 1 · Wind · 壬午 Water Horse · 巽為風 · **13** · 十四 · 1
金4 Metal · 2 · Trap · 癸未 Water Goat · 澤水困 · **14** · 十五 · 8	木3 Wood · 3 · Not Yet Accomplished · 甲申 Wood Monkey · 火水未濟 · **15** · 十六 · 9	金9 Metal · 4 · Retreat · 乙酉 Wood Rooster · 天山遯 · **16** · 十七 · 4	水6 Water · 5 · Mountain · 丙戌 Fire Dog · 艮為山 · **17** · 十八 · 1	木8 Wood · 6 · Delight · 丁亥 Fire Pig · 雷地豫 · **18** · 十九 · 8	火7 Fire · 7 · Beginning · 戊子 Earth Rat · 水雷屯 · **19** · 二十 · 4	金9 Metal · 8 · Without Wrongdoing · 己丑 Earth Ox · 天雷無妄 · **20** · 廿一 · 2
木3 Wood · 9 · Fire · 庚寅 Metal Tiger · 離為火 · **21** · 廿二 · 1	火2 Fire · 1 · Sincerity · 辛卯 Metal Rabbit · 風澤中孚 · **22** · 廿三 · 3	水6 Water · 2 · Big Livestock · 壬辰 Water Dragon · 山天大畜 · **23** · 廿四 · 4	金4 Metal · 3 · Eliminating · 癸巳 Water Snake · 澤天夬 · **24** · 廿五 · 6	金9 Metal · 4 · Heaven · 甲午 Wood Horse · 乾為天 · **25** · 廿六 · 1	火7 Fire · 5 · Well · 乙未 Wood Goat · 水風井 · **26** · 廿七 · 6	木8 Wood · 6 · Relief · 丙申 Fire Monkey · 雷水解 · **27** · 廿八 · 4
金4 Metal · 7 · Influence · 丁酉 Fire Rooster · 澤山咸 · **28** · 廿九 · 9	水1 Water · 8 · Humility · 戊戌 Earth Dog · 地山謙 · **29** · 三十 · 6	火2 Fire · 9 · Observation · 己亥 Earth Pig · 風地觀 · **30** · 正月初一 · 2	火2 Fire · 1 · Increasing · 庚子 Metal Rat · 風雷益 · **31** · 初二 · 9			

FEBRUARY 1968 甲寅

Xuan Kong Element 玄空五行	水火既濟 Accomplished	Period Luck 卦運	Monthly Star 月星
Fire 火7		9	2

SUNDAY	MONDAY	TUESDAY	WEDNESDAY	THURSDAY	FRIDAY	SATURDAY
				水1 Water · 2 · Dimming Light · 辛丑 Metal Ox · 地火明夷 · **1** · 初三 · 3	金9 Metal · 3 · Fellowship · 壬寅 Water Tiger · 天火同人 · **2** · 初四 · 7	木8 Wood · 4 · Marrying Maiden · 癸卯 Water Rabbit · 雷澤歸妹 · **3** · 初五 · 7
木3 Wood · 5 · Opposition · 甲辰 Wood Dragon · 火澤睽 · **4** · 初六 · 2	火7 Fire · 6 · Waiting · 乙巳 Wood Snake · 水天需 · **5** · 初七 · 3	金4 Metal · 7 · Great Exceeding · 丙午 Fire Horse · 澤風大過 · **6** · 初八 · 3	水6 Water · 8 · Poison · 丁未 Fire Goat · 山風蠱 · **7** · 初九 · 7	火2 Fire · 9 · Dispersing · 戊申 Earth Monkey · 風水渙 · **8** · 初十 · 6	木3 Wood · 1 · Travelling · 己酉 Earth Rooster · 火山旅 · **9** · 十一 · 8	金9 Metal · 2 · Stagnation · 庚戌 Metal Dog · 天地否 · **10** · 十二 · 9
火7 Fire · 3 · Alliance · 辛亥 Metal Pig · 水地比 · **11** · 十三 · 7	木8 Wood · 4 · Thunder · 壬子 Water Rat · 震為雷 · **12** · 十四 · 1	水6 Water · 5 · Beauty · 癸丑 Water Ox · 山火賁 · **13** · 十五 · 8	火7 Fire · 6 · Accomplished · 甲寅 Wood Tiger · 水火既濟 · **14** · 十六 · 9	水1 Water · 7 · Arriving · 乙卯 Wood Rabbit · 地澤臨 · **15** · 十七 · 4	金4 Metal · 8 · Marsh · 丙辰 Fire Dragon · 兌為澤 · **16** · 十八 · 1	火2 Fire · 9 · Small Livestock · 丁巳 Fire Snake · 風天小畜 · **17** · 十九 · 8
木3 Wood · 1 · The Cauldron · 戊午 Earth Horse · 火風鼎 · **18** · 二十 · 4	水1 Water · 2 · Rising · 己未 Earth Goat · 地風升 · **19** · 廿一 · 2	火7 Fire · 3 · Water · 庚申 Metal Monkey · 坎為水 · **20** · 廿二 · 1	木8 Wood · 4 · Lesser Exceeding · 辛酉 Metal Rooster · 雷山小過 · **21** · 廿三 · 3	金4 Metal · 5 · Gathering · 壬戌 Water Dog · 澤地萃 · **22** · 廿四 · 4	水6 Water · 6 · Peel · 癸亥 Water Pig · 山地剝 · **23** · 廿五 · 6	水1 Water · 7 · Earth · 甲子 Wood Rat · 坤為地 · **24** · 廿六 · 1
木3 Wood · 8 · Biting · 乙丑 Wood Ox · 火雷噬嗑 · **25** · 廿七 · 6	火2 Fire · 9 · Family · 丙寅 Fire Tiger · 風火家人 · **26** · 廿八 · 4	水6 Water · 1 · Decreasing · 丁卯 Fire Rabbit · 山澤損 · **27** · 廿九 · 9	金9 Metal · 2 · Tread · 戊辰 Earth Dragon · 天澤履 · **28** · 二月初一 · 6	木8 Wood · 3 · Great Strength · 己巳 Earth Snake · 雷天大壯 · **29** · 初二 · 2		

MARCH 1968 乙卯

Xuan Kong Element 玄空五行	地澤臨 Arriving	Period Luck 卦運	Monthly Star 月星
Water 水1		4	1

SUNDAY	MONDAY	TUESDAY	WEDNESDAY	THURSDAY	FRIDAY	SATURDAY
31 初三 Increasing 風雷益 火2 Fire · 庚子 Metal Rat 9 · 7					1 初三 Consistency 雷風恆 木8 Wood · 庚午 Metal Horse 9 · 4	2 初四 Litigation 天水訟 金9 Metal · 辛未 Metal Goat 3 · 5
3 初五 Officer 地水師 水1 Water · 壬申 Water Monkey 7 · 6	4 初六 Gradual Progress 風山漸 火2 Fire · 癸酉 Water Rooster 7 · 7	5 初七 Obstruction 水山蹇 火7 Fire · 甲戌 Wood Dog 2 · 8	6 初八 Advancement 火地晉 木3 Wood · 乙亥 Wood Pig 3 · 9	7 初九 Nourish 山雷頤 水6 Water · 丙子 Fire Rat 3 · 1	8 初十 Following 澤雷隨 金4 Metal · 丁丑 Fire Ox 7 · 2	9 十一 Abundance 雷火豐 木8 Wood · 戊寅 Earth Tiger 6 · 3
10 十二 Regulate 水澤節 火7 Fire · 己卯 Earth Rabbit 8 · 4	11 十三 Unity 地天泰 水1 Water · 庚辰 Metal Dragon 9 · 5	12 十四 Great Reward 火天大有 木3 Wood · 辛巳 Metal Snake 7 · 6	13 十五 Wind 巽為風 火2 Fire · 壬午 Water Horse 1 · 7	14 十六 Trap 澤水困 金4 Metal · 癸未 Water Goat 8 · 8	15 十七 Not Yet Accomplished 火水未濟 木3 Wood · 甲申 Wood Monkey 9 · 9	16 十八 Retreat 天山遯 金9 Metal · 乙酉 Wood Rooster 4 · 1
17 十九 Mountain 艮為山 水6 Water · 丙戌 Fire Dog 1 · 2	18 二十 Delight 雷地豫 木8 Wood · 丁亥 Fire Pig 8 · 3	19 廿一 Beginning 水雷屯 火7 Fire · 戊子 Earth Rat 4 · 4	20 廿二 Without Wrongdoing 天雷無妄 金9 Metal · 己丑 Earth Ox 2 · 5	21 廿三 Fire 離為火 木3 Wood · 庚寅 Metal Tiger 1 · 6	22 廿四 Sincerity 風澤中孚 火2 Fire · 辛卯 Metal Rabbit 3 · 7	23 廿五 Big Livestock 山天大畜 水6 Water · 壬辰 Water Dragon 4 · 8
24 廿六 Eliminating 澤天夬 金4 Metal · 癸巳 Water Snake 6 · 9	25 廿七 Heaven 乾為天 金9 Metal · 甲午 Wood Horse 1 · 1	26 廿八 Well 水風井 火7 Fire · 乙未 Wood Goat 6 · 2	27 廿九 Relief 雷水解 木8 Wood · 丙申 Fire Monkey 4 · 3	28 三十 Influence 澤山咸 金4 Metal · 丁酉 Fire Rooster 9 · 4	29 三月初一 Humility 地山謙 水1 Water · 戊戌 Earth Dog 6 · 5	30 初二 Observation 風地觀 火2 Fire · 己亥 Earth Pig 2 · 6

APRIL 1968 丙辰

Xuan Kong Element 玄空五行	兑為澤 Marsh	Period Luck 卦運	Monthly Star 月星
Metal 金4		1	9

SUNDAY	MONDAY	TUESDAY	WEDNESDAY	THURSDAY	FRIDAY	SATURDAY
	1 初四 Dimming Light 地火明夷 水1 Water · 辛丑 Metal Ox 3 · 8	2 初五 Fellowship 天火同人 金9 Metal · 壬寅 Water Tiger 7 · 9	3 初六 Marrying Maiden 雷澤歸妹 木8 Wood · 癸卯 Water Rabbit 7 · 1	4 初七 Opposition 火澤睽 木3 Wood · 甲辰 Wood Dragon 2 · 2	5 初八 Waiting 水天需 火7 Fire · 乙巳 Wood Snake 3 · 3	6 初九 Great Exceeding 澤風大過 金4 Metal · 丙午 Fire Horse 3 · 4
7 初十 Poison 山風蠱 水6 Water · 丁未 Fire Goat 7 · 5	8 十一 Dispersing 風水渙 火2 Fire · 戊申 Earth Monkey 6 · 6	9 十二 Travelling 火山旅 木3 Wood · 己酉 Earth Rooster 8 · 7	10 十三 Stagnation 天地否 金9 Metal · 庚戌 Metal Dog 9 · 8	11 十四 Alliance 水地比 火7 Fire · 辛亥 Metal Pig 7 · 9	12 十五 Thunder 震為雷 木8 Wood · 壬子 Water Rat 1 · 1	13 十六 Beauty 山火賁 水6 Water · 癸丑 Water Ox 8 · 2
14 十七 Accomplished 水火既濟 火7 Fire · 甲寅 Wood Tiger 9 · 3	15 十八 Arriving 地澤臨 水1 Water · 乙卯 Wood Rabbit 4 · 4	16 十九 Marsh 兑為澤 金4 Metal · 丙辰 Fire Dragon 1 · 5	17 二十 Small Livestock 風天小畜 火2 Fire · 丁巳 Fire Snake 8 · 6	18 廿一 The Cauldron 火風鼎 木3 Wood · 戊午 Earth Horse 4 · 7	19 廿二 Rising 地風升 水1 Water · 己未 Earth Goat 2 · 8	20 廿三 Water 坎為水 火7 Fire · 庚申 Metal Monkey 1 · 9
21 廿四 Lesser Exceeding 雷山小過 木8 Wood · 辛酉 Metal Rooster 3 · 1	22 廿五 Gathering 澤地萃 金4 Metal · 壬戌 Water Dog 4 · 2	23 廿六 Peel 山地剝 水6 Water · 癸亥 Water Pig 6 · 3	24 廿七 Earth 坤為地 水1 Water · 甲子 Wood Rat 1 · 4	25 廿八 Biting 火雷噬嗑 木3 Wood · 乙丑 Wood Ox 6 · 5	26 廿九 Family 風火家人 火2 Fire · 丙寅 Fire Tiger 4 · 6	27 四月初一 Decreasing 山澤損 水6 Water · 丁卯 Fire Rabbit 9 · 7
28 初二 Tread 天澤履 金9 Metal · 戊辰 Earth Dragon 6 · 8	29 初三 Great Strength 雷天大壯 木8 Wood · 己巳 Earth Snake 2 · 9	30 初四 Consistency 雷風恆 木8 Wood · 庚午 Metal Horse 9 · 1				

MAY 1968 丁巳

Xuan Kong Element 玄空五行	風天小畜 Small Livestock	Period Luck 卦運	Monthly Star 月星
Fire 火2		8	8

SUNDAY	MONDAY	TUESDAY	WEDNESDAY	THURSDAY	FRIDAY	SATURDAY
			1 金9 Metal Litigation 2 天水訟 辛未 Metal Goat 初五 3	2 水1 Water Officer 3 地水師 壬申 Water Monkey 初六 7	3 火2 Fire Gradual Progress 4 風山漸 癸酉 Water Rooster 初七 7	4 火7 Fire Obstruction 5 水山蹇 甲戌 Wood Dog 初八 2
5 木3 Wood Advancement 6 火地晉 乙亥 Wood Pig 初九 3	6 水6 Water Nourish 7 山雷頤 丙子 Fire Rat 初十 3	7 金4 Metal Following 8 澤雷隨 丁丑 Fire Ox 十一 7	8 木8 Wood Abundance 9 雷火豐 戊寅 Earth Tiger 十二 6	9 火7 Fire Regulate 1 水澤節 己卯 Earth Rabbit 十三 8	10 水1 Water Unity 2 地天泰 庚辰 Metal Dragon 十四 9	11 木3 Wood Great Reward 3 火天大有 辛巳 Metal Snake 十五 7
12 火2 Fire Wind 4 巽為風 壬午 Water Horse 十六 1	13 金4 Metal Trap 5 澤水困 癸未 Water Goat 十七 8	14 木3 Wood Not Yet Accomplished 6 火水未濟 甲申 Wood Monkey 十八 9	15 金9 Metal Retreat 7 天山遯 乙酉 Wood Rooster 十九 4	16 水6 Water Mountain 8 艮為山 丙戌 Fire Dog 二十 1	17 木8 Wood Delight 9 雷地豫 丁亥 Fire Pig 廿一 8	18 火7 Fire Beginning 1 水雷屯 戊子 Earth Rat 廿二 4
19 金9 Metal Without Wrongdoing 2 天雷無妄 己丑 Earth Ox 廿三 2	20 木3 Wood Fire 3 離為火 庚寅 Metal Tiger 廿四 1	21 火2 Fire Sincerity 4 風澤中孚 辛卯 Metal Rabbit 廿五 3	22 水6 Water Big Livestock 5 山天大畜 壬辰 Water Dragon 廿六 4	23 金4 Metal Eliminating 6 澤天夬 癸巳 Water Snake 廿七 6	24 金9 Metal Heaven 7 乾為天 甲午 Wood Horse 廿八 1	25 火7 Fire Well 8 水風井 乙未 Wood Goat 廿九 6
26 木8 Wood Relief 9 雷水解 丙申 Fire Monkey 三十 4	27 金4 Metal Influence 1 澤山咸 丁酉 Fire Rooster 五月初一 9	28 水1 Water Humility 2 地山謙 戊戌 Earth Dog 初二 6	29 火2 Fire Observation 3 風地觀 己亥 Earth Pig 初三 2	30 火2 Fire Increasing 4 風雷益 庚子 Metal Rat 初四 9	31 水1 Water Dimming Light 5 地火明夷 辛丑 Metal Ox 初五 3	

JUNE 1968 戊午

Xuan Kong Element 玄空五行	火風鼎 The Cauldron	Period Luck 卦運	Monthly Star 月星
Wood 木3		4	7

SUNDAY	MONDAY	TUESDAY	WEDNESDAY	THURSDAY	FRIDAY	SATURDAY
30 金9 Metal Litigation 2 天水訟 辛未 Metal Goat 初五 3						1 金9 Metal Fellowship 6 天火同人 壬寅 Water Tiger 初六 7
2 木8 Wood Marrying Maiden 7 雷澤歸妹 癸卯 Water Rabbit 初七 7	3 木3 Wood Opposition 8 火澤睽 甲辰 Wood Dragon 初八 2	4 火7 Fire Waiting 9 水天需 乙巳 Wood Snake 初九 3	5 金4 Metal Great Exceeding 1 澤風大過 丙午 Fire Horse 初十 3	6 水6 Water Poison 2 山風蠱 丁未 Fire Goat 十一 7	7 火2 Fire Dispersing 3 風水渙 戊申 Earth Monkey 十二 6	8 木3 Wood Travelling 4 火山旅 己酉 Earth Rooster 十三 8
9 金9 Metal Stagnation 5 天地否 庚戌 Metal Dog 十四 9	10 火7 Fire Alliance 6 水地比 辛亥 Metal Pig 十五 7	11 木8 Wood Thunder 7 震為雷 壬子 Water Rat 十六 1	12 水6 Water Beauty 8 山火賁 癸丑 Water Ox 十七 8	13 火7 Fire Accomplished 9 水火既濟 甲寅 Wood Tiger 十八 9	14 水1 Water Arriving 1 地澤臨 乙卯 Wood Rabbit 十九 4	15 金4 Metal Marsh 2 兌為澤 丙辰 Fire Dragon 二十 1
16 火2 Fire Small Livestock 3 風天小畜 丁巳 Fire Snake 廿一 8	17 木3 Wood The Cauldron 4 火風鼎 戊午 Earth Horse 廿二 4	18 水1 Water Rising 5 地風升 己未 Earth Goat 廿三 2	19 火7 Fire Water 6 坎為水 庚申 Metal Monkey 廿四 1	20 木8 Wood Lesser Exceeding 7 雷山小過 辛酉 Metal Rooster 廿五 3	21 金4 Metal Gathering 8/2 澤地萃 壬戌 Water Dog 廿六 4	22 水6 Water Peel 1 山地剝 癸亥 Water Pig 廿七 6
23 水1 Water Earth 9 坤為地 甲子 Wood Rat 廿八 1	24 木3 Wood Biting 8 火雷噬嗑 乙丑 Wood Ox 廿九 6	25 火2 Fire Family 7 風火家人 丙寅 Fire Tiger 三十 4	26 水6 Water Decreasing 6 山澤損 丁卯 Fire Rabbit 六月初一 9	27 金9 Metal Tread 5 天澤履 戊辰 Earth Dragon 初二 6	28 木8 Wood Great Strength 4 雷天大壯 己巳 Earth Snake 初三 2	29 木8 Wood Consistency 3 雷風恆 庚午 Metal Horse 初四 9

JULY 1968 己未

Xuan Kong Element 玄空五行	地風升 Rising	Period Luck 卦運	Monthly Star 月星
Water 水1		2	6

SUNDAY	MONDAY	TUESDAY	WEDNESDAY	THURSDAY	FRIDAY	SATURDAY
	水1 Water 1 Officer 壬申 Water Monkey 地水師 **1** 初六 7	火2 Fire 9 Gradual Progress 癸酉 Water Rooster 風山漸 **2** 初七 7	火7 Fire 8 Obstruction 甲戌 Wood Dog 水山蹇 **3** 初八 2	木3 Wood 7 Advancement 乙亥 Wood Pig 火地晉 **4** 初九 3	水6 Water 6 Nourish 丙子 Fire Rat 山雷頤 **5** 初十 3	金4 Metal 5 Following 丁丑 Fire Ox 澤雷隨 **6** 十一 7
木8 Wood 4 Abundance 戊寅 Earth Tiger 雷火豐 **7** 十二 6	火7 Fire 3 Regulate 己卯 Earth Rabbit 水澤節 **8** 十三 8	水1 Water 2 Unity 庚辰 Metal Dragon 地天泰 **9** 十四 9	木3 Wood 1 Great Reward 辛巳 Metal Snake 火天大有 **10** 十五 7	火2 Fire 9 Wind 壬午 Water Horse 巽爲風 **11** 十六 1	金4 Metal 8 Trap 癸未 Water Goat 澤水困 **12** 十七 8	木3 Wood 7 Not Yet Accomplished 甲申 Wood Monkey 火水未濟 **13** 十八 9
金9 Metal 6 Retreat 乙酉 Wood Rooster 天山遯 **14** 十九 4	水6 Water 5 Mountain 丙戌 Fire Dog 艮爲山 **15** 二十 1	木8 Wood 4 Delight 丁亥 Fire Pig 雷地豫 **16** 廿一 8	火7 Fire 3 Beginning 戊子 Earth Rat 水雷屯 **17** 廿二 4	金9 Metal 2 Without Wrongdoing 己丑 Earth Ox 天雷無妄 **18** 廿三 2	木3 Wood 1 Fire 庚寅 Metal Tiger 離爲火 **19** 廿四 1	火2 Fire 9 Sincerity 辛卯 Metal Rabbit 風澤中孚 **20** 廿五 3
水6 Water 8 Big Livestock 壬辰 Water Dragon 山天大畜 **21** 廿六 4	金4 Metal 7 Eliminating 癸巳 Water Snake 澤天夬 **22** 廿七 6	金9 Metal 6 Heaven 甲午 Wood Horse 乾爲天 **23** 廿八 1	火7 Fire 5 Well 乙未 Wood Goat 水風井 **24** 廿九 6	木8 Wood 4 Relief 丙申 Fire Monkey 雷水解 **25** 七月初一 4	金4 Metal 3 Influence 丁酉 Fire Rooster 澤山咸 **26** 初二 9	水1 Water 2 Humility 戊戌 Earth Dog 地山謙 **27** 初三 6
火2 Fire 1 Observation 己亥 Earth Pig 風地觀 **28** 初四 2	火2 Fire 9 Increasing 庚子 Metal Rat 風雷益 **29** 初五 9	水1 Water 8 Dimming Light 辛丑 Metal Ox 地火明夷 **30** 初六 3	金9 Metal 7 Fellowship 壬寅 Water Tiger 天火同人 **31** 初七 7			

AUGUST 1968 庚申

Xuan Kong Element 玄空五行	坎爲水 Water	Period Luck 卦運	Monthly Star 月星
Fire 火7		1	5

SUNDAY	MONDAY	TUESDAY	WEDNESDAY	THURSDAY	FRIDAY	SATURDAY
				木8 Wood 6 Marrying Maiden 癸卯 Water Rabbit 雷澤歸妹 **1** 初八 7	木3 Wood 5 Opposition 甲辰 Wood Dragon 火澤睽 **2** 初九 2	火7 Fire 4 Waiting 乙巳 Wood Snake 水天需 **3** 初十 3
金4 Metal 3 Great Exceeding 丙午 Fire Horse 澤風大過 **4** 十一 3	水6 Water 2 Poison 丁未 Fire Goat 山風蠱 **5** 十二 7	火2 Fire 1 Dispersing 戊申 Earth Monkey 風水渙 **6** 十三 6	木3 Wood 9 Travelling 己酉 Earth Rooster 火山旅 **7** 十四 8	金9 Metal 8 Stagnation 庚戌 Metal Dog 天地否 **8** 十五 9	火7 Fire 7 Alliance 辛亥 Metal Pig 水地比 **9** 十六 7	木8 Wood 6 Thunder 壬子 Water Rat 震爲雷 **10** 十七 1
水6 Water 5 Beauty 癸丑 Water Ox 山火賁 **11** 十八 8	火7 Fire 4 Accomplished 甲寅 Wood Tiger 水火既濟 **12** 十九 9	水1 Water 3 Arriving 乙卯 Wood Rabbit 地澤臨 **13** 二十 4	金4 Metal 2 Marsh 丙辰 Fire Dragon 兑爲澤 **14** 廿一 1	火2 Fire 1 Small Livestock 丁巳 Fire Snake 風天小畜 **15** 廿二 8	木3 Wood 9 The Cauldron 戊午 Earth Horse 火風鼎 **16** 廿三 4	水1 Water 8 Rising 己未 Earth Goat 地風升 **17** 廿四 2
火7 Fire 7 Water 庚申 Metal Monkey 坎爲水 **18** 廿五 1	木8 Wood 6 Lesser Exceeding 辛酉 Metal Rooster 雷山小過 **19** 廿六 3	金4 Metal 5 Gathering 壬戌 Water Dog 澤地萃 **20** 廿七 4	水6 Water 4 Peel 癸亥 Water Pig 山地剝 **21** 廿八 6	水1 Water 3 Earth 甲子 Wood Rat 坤爲地 **22** 廿九 1	木3 Wood 2 Biting 乙丑 Wood Ox 火雷噬嗑 **23** 三十 6	火2 Fire 1 Family 丙寅 Fire Tiger 風火家人 **24** 閏七月初一 4
水6 Water 9 Decreasing 丁卯 Fire Rabbit 山澤損 **25** 初二 9	金9 Metal 8 Tread 戊辰 Earth Dragon 天澤履 **26** 初三 6	木8 Wood 7 Great Strength 己巳 Earth Snake 雷天大壯 **27** 初四 2	木8 Wood 6 Consistency 庚午 Metal Horse 雷風恆 **28** 初五 9	金9 Metal 5 Litigation 辛未 Metal Goat 天水訟 **29** 初六 3	水1 Water 4 Officer 壬申 Water Monkey 地水師 **30** 初七 7	火2 Fire 3 Gradual Progress 癸酉 Water Rooster 風山漸 **31** 初八 7

SEPTEMBER 1968 辛酉

Xuan Kong Element 玄空五行	雷山小過	Period Luck 卦運	Monthly Star 月星
Wood 木8	Lesser Exceeding	3	4

SUNDAY	MONDAY	TUESDAY	WEDNESDAY	THURSDAY	FRIDAY	SATURDAY
火7 Fire 2 Obstruction 甲戌 Wood Dog 水山蹇 **1** 初九 2	木3 Wood 1 Advancement 乙亥 Wood Pig 火地晉 **2** 初十 3	水6 Water 9 Nourish 丙子 Fire Rat 山雷頤 **3** 十一 3	金4 Metal 8 Following 丁丑 Fire Ox 澤雷隨 **4** 十二 7	木8 Wood 7 Abundance 戊寅 Earth Tiger 雷火豐 **5** 十三 6	火7 Fire 6 Regulate 己卯 Earth Rabbit 水澤節 **6** 十四 8	水1 Water 5 Unity 庚辰 Metal Dragon 地天泰 **7** 十五 9
木3 Wood 4 Great Reward 辛巳 Metal Snake 火天大有 **8** 十六 7	火2 Fire 3 Wind 壬午 Water Horse 巽爲風 **9** 十七 1	金4 Metal 2 Trap 癸未 Water Goat 澤水困 **10** 十八 8	木3 Wood 1 Not Yet Accomplished 甲申 Wood Monkey 火水未濟 **11** 十九 9	金9 Metal 9 Retreat 乙酉 Wood Rooster 天山遯 **12** 二十 4	水6 Water 8 Mountain 丙戌 Fire Dog 艮爲山 **13** 廿一 1	木8 Wood 7 Delight 丁亥 Fire Pig 雷地豫 **14** 廿二 8
火7 Fire 6 Beginning 戊子 Earth Rat 水雷屯 **15** 廿三 4	金9 Metal 5 Without Wrongdoing 己丑 Earth Ox 天雷無妄 **16** 廿四 2	木3 Wood 4 Fire 庚寅 Metal Tiger 離爲火 **17** 廿五 1	火2 Fire 3 Sincerity 辛卯 Metal Rabbit 風澤中孚 **18** 廿六 3	水6 Water 2 Big Livestock 壬辰 Water Dragon 山天大畜 **19** 廿七 4	金4 Metal 1 Eliminating 癸巳 Water Snake 澤天夬 **20** 廿八 6	金9 Metal 9 Heaven 甲午 Wood Horse 乾爲天 **21** 廿九 1
火7 Fire 8 Well 乙未 Wood Goat 水風井 **22** 八月初一 6	木8 Wood 7 Relief 丙申 Fire Monkey 雷水解 **23** 初二 4	金4 Metal 6 Influence 丁酉 Fire Rooster 澤山咸 **24** 初三 9	水1 Water 5 Humility 戊戌 Earth Dog 地山謙 **25** 初四 6	火2 Fire 4 Observation 己亥 Earth Pig 風地觀 **26** 初五 2	火2 Fire 3 Increasing 庚子 Metal Rat 風雷益 **27** 初六 9	水1 Water 2 Dimming Light 辛丑 Metal Ox 地火明夷 **28** 初七 3
金9 Metal 1 Fellowship 壬寅 Water Tiger 天火同人 **29** 初八 7	木8 Wood 9 Marrying Maiden 癸卯 Water Rabbit 雷澤歸妹 **30** 初九 7					

OCTOBER 1968 壬戌

Xuan Kong Element 玄空五行	澤地萃	Period Luck 卦運	Monthly Star 月星
Metal 金4	Gathering	4	3

SUNDAY	MONDAY	TUESDAY	WEDNESDAY	THURSDAY	FRIDAY	SATURDAY
		木3 Wood 8 Opposition 甲辰 Wood Dragon 火澤睽 **1** 初十 2	火7 Fire 7 Waiting 乙巳 Wood Snake 水天需 **2** 十一 3	金4 Metal 6 Great Exceeding 丙午 Fire Horse 澤風大過 **3** 十二 3	水6 Water 5 Poison 丁未 Fire Goat 山風蠱 **4** 十三 7	火2 Fire 4 Dispersing 戊申 Earth Monkey 風水渙 **5** 十四 6
木3 Wood 3 Travelling 己酉 Earth Rooster 火山旅 **6** 十五 8	金9 Metal 2 Stagnation 庚戌 Metal Dog 天地否 **7** 十六 9	火7 Fire 1 Alliance 辛亥 Metal Pig 水地比 **8** 十七 7	木8 Wood 9 Thunder 壬子 Water Rat 震爲雷 **9** 十八 1	水6 Water 8 Beauty 癸丑 Water Ox 山火賁 **10** 十九 8	火7 Fire 7 Accomplished 甲寅 Wood Tiger 水火既濟 **11** 二十 9	水1 Water 6 Arriving 乙卯 Wood Rabbit 地澤臨 **12** 廿一 4
金4 Metal 5 Marsh 丙辰 Fire Dragon 兌爲澤 **13** 廿二 1	火2 Fire 4 Small Livestock 丁巳 Fire Snake 風天小畜 **14** 廿三 8	木3 Wood 3 The Cauldron 戊午 Earth Horse 火風鼎 **15** 廿四 4	水1 Water 2 Rising 己未 Earth Goat 地風升 **16** 廿五 2	火7 Fire 1 Water 庚申 Metal Monkey 坎爲水 **17** 廿六 1	木8 Wood 9 Lesser Exceeding 辛酉 Metal Rooster 雷山小過 **18** 廿七 3	金4 Metal 8 Gathering 壬戌 Water Dog 澤地萃 **19** 廿八 4
水6 Water 7 Peel 癸亥 Water Pig 山地剝 **20** 廿九 6	水1 Water 6 Earth 甲子 Wood Rat 坤爲地 **21** 三十 1	木3 Wood 5 Biting 乙丑 Wood Ox 火雷噬嗑 **22** 九月初一 6	火2 Fire 4 Family 丙寅 Fire Tiger 風火家人 **23** 初二 4	水6 Water 3 Decreasing 丁卯 Fire Rabbit 山澤損 **24** 初三 9	金9 Metal 2 Tread 戊辰 Earth Dragon 天澤履 **25** 初四 6	木8 Wood 1 Great Strength 己巳 Earth Snake 雷天大壯 **26** 初五 2
木8 Wood 9 Consistency 庚午 Metal Horse 雷風恆 **27** 初六 9	金9 Metal 8 Litigation 辛未 Metal Goat 天水訟 **28** 初七 3	水1 Water 7 Officer 壬申 Water Monkey 地水師 **29** 初八 7	火2 Fire 6 Gradual Progress 癸酉 Water Rooster 風山漸 **30** 初九 7	火7 Fire 5 Obstruction 甲戌 Wood Dog 水山蹇 **31** 初十 2		

NOVEMBER 1968 癸亥

Xuan Kong Element 玄空五行	山地剝 Peel	Period Luck 卦運	Monthly Star 月星
Water 水6		6	2

SUNDAY	MONDAY	TUESDAY	WEDNESDAY	THURSDAY	FRIDAY	SATURDAY
					木3 Wood 4 Advancement 乙亥 Wood Pig 火地晉 1 十一 3	水6 Water 3 Nourish 丙子 Fire Rat 山雷頤 2 十二 3
金4 Metal 2 Following 丁丑 Fire Ox 澤雷隨 3 十三 7	木8 Wood 1 Abundance 戊寅 Earth Tiger 雷火豐 4 十四 6	火7 Fire 9 Regulate 己卯 Earth Rabbit 水澤節 5 十五 8	水1 Water 8 Unity 庚辰 Metal Dragon 地天泰 6 十六 9	木3 Wood 7 Great Reward 辛巳 Metal Snake 火天大有 7 十七 7	火2 Fire 6 Wind 壬午 Water Horse 巽為風 8 十八 1	金4 Metal 5 Trap 癸未 Water Goat 澤水困 9 十九 8
木3 Wood 4 Not Yet Accomplished 甲申 Wood Monkey 火水未濟 10 二十 9	金9 Metal 3 Retreat 乙酉 Wood Rooster 天山遯 11 廿一 4	水6 Water 2 Mountain 丙戌 Fire Dog 艮為山 12 廿二 1	木8 Wood 1 Delight 丁亥 Fire Pig 雷地豫 13 廿三 8	火7 Fire 9 Beginning 戊子 Earth Rat 水雷屯 14 廿四 4	金9 Metal 8 Without Wrongdoing 己丑 Earth Ox 天雷無妄 15 廿五 2	木3 Wood 7 Fire 庚寅 Metal Tiger 離為火 16 廿六 1
火2 Fire 6 Sincerity 辛卯 Metal Rabbit 風澤中孚 17 廿七 3	水6 Water 5 Big Livestock 壬辰 Water Dragon 山天大畜 18 廿八 4	金4 Metal 4 Eliminating 癸巳 Water Snake 澤天夬 19 廿九 6	金9 Metal 3 Heaven 甲午 Wood Horse 乾為天 20 十月初一 1	火7 Fire 2 Well 乙未 Wood Goat 水風井 21 初二 6	木8 Wood 1 Relief 丙申 Fire Monkey 雷水解 22 初三 4	金4 Metal 9 Influence 丁酉 Fire Rooster 澤山咸 23 初四 9
水1 Water 8 Humility 戊戌 Earth Dog 地山謙 24 初五 6	火2 Fire 7 Observation 己亥 Earth Pig 風地觀 25 初六 2	火2 Fire 6 Increasing 庚子 Metal Rat 風雷益 26 初七 9	水1 Water 5 Dimming Light 辛丑 Metal Ox 地火明夷 27 初八 3	金9 Metal 4 Fellowship 壬寅 Water Tiger 天火同人 28 初九 7	木8 Wood 3 Marrying Maiden 癸卯 Water Rabbit 雷澤歸妹 29 初十 7	木3 Wood 2 Opposition 甲辰 Wood Dragon 火澤睽 30 十一 2

DECEMBER 1968 甲子

Xuan Kong Element 玄空五行	坤為地 Earth	Period Luck 卦運	Monthly Star 月星
Water 水1		1	1

SUNDAY	MONDAY	TUESDAY	WEDNESDAY	THURSDAY	FRIDAY	SATURDAY
火7 Fire 1 Waiting 乙巳 Wood Snake 水天需 1 十二 3	金4 Metal 9 Great Exceeding 丙午 Fire Horse 澤風大過 2 十三 3	水6 Water 8 Poison 丁未 Fire Goat 山風蠱 3 十四 7	火2 Fire 7 Dispersing 戊申 Earth Monkey 風水渙 4 十五 6	木3 Wood 6 Travelling 己酉 Earth Rooster 火山旅 5 十六 8	金9 Metal 5 Stagnation 庚戌 Metal Dog 天地否 6 十七 9	火7 Fire 4 Alliance 辛亥 Metal Pig 水地比 7 十八 7
木8 Wood 3 Thunder 壬子 Water Rat 震為雷 8 十九 1	水6 Water 2 Beauty 癸丑 Water Ox 山火賁 9 二十 8	火7 Fire 1 Accomplished 甲寅 Wood Tiger 水火既濟 10 廿一 9	水1 Water 9 Arriving 乙卯 Wood Rabbit 地澤臨 11 廿二 4	金4 Metal 8 Marsh 丙辰 Fire Dragon 兌為澤 12 廿三 1	火2 Fire 7 Small Livestock 丁巳 Fire Snake 風天小畜 13 廿四 8	木3 Wood 6 The Cauldron 戊午 Earth Horse 火風鼎 14 廿五 4
水1 Water 5 Rising 己未 Earth Goat 地風升 15 廿六 2	火7 Fire 4 Water 庚申 Metal Monkey 坎為水 16 廿七 1	木8 Wood 3 Lesser Exceeding 辛酉 Metal Rooster 雷山小過 17 廿八 3	金4 Metal 2 Gathering 壬戌 Water Dog 澤地萃 18 廿九 4	水6 Water 1 Peel 癸亥 Water Pig 山地剝 19 三十 6	水1 Water 9 Earth 甲子 Wood Rat 坤為地 20 十一月初一 1	木3 Wood 8 Biting 乙丑 Wood Ox 火雷噬嗑 21 初二 6
火2 Fire 7/6 Family 丙寅 Fire Tiger 風火家人 22 初三 4	水6 Water 7 Decreasing 丁卯 Fire Rabbit 山澤損 23 初四 9	金9 Metal 8 Tread 戊辰 Earth Dragon 天澤履 24 初五 6	木8 Wood 9 Great Strength 己巳 Earth Snake 雷天大壯 25 初六 2	木8 Wood 1 Consistency 庚午 Metal Horse 雷風恆 26 初七 9	金9 Metal 2 Litigation 辛未 Metal Goat 天水訟 27 初八 3	水1 Water 3 Officer 壬申 Water Monkey 地水師 28 初九 7
火2 Fire 4 Gradual Progress 癸酉 Water Rooster 風山漸 29 初十 7	火7 Fire 5 Obstruction 甲戌 Wood Dog 水山蹇 30 十一 2	木3 Wood 6 Advancement 乙亥 Wood Pig 火地晉 31 十二 3				

1969 己酉

(*Ji You*) Earth Rooster

1969 己酉 *(Ji You)* Earth Rooster

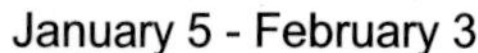

January 5 - February 3

February 4 - March 5

March 6 - April 4

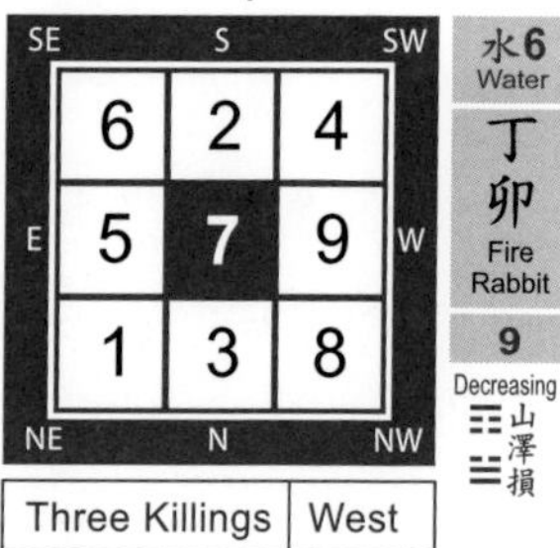

April 5 - May 5

May 6 - June 5

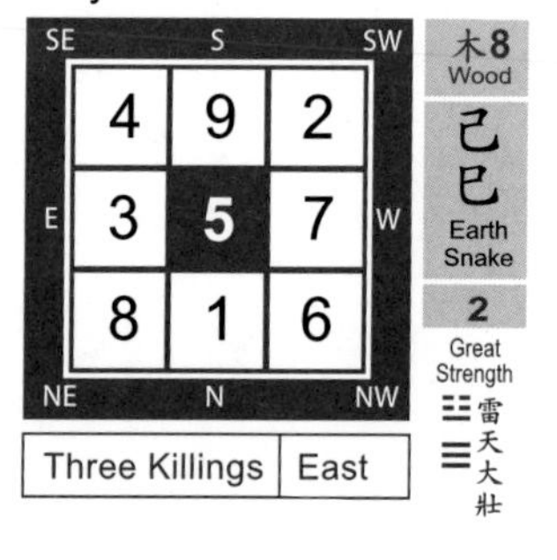

June 6 - July 6

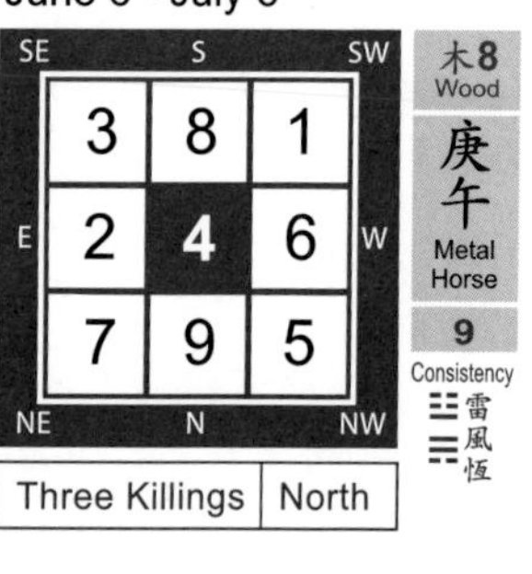

July 7 - August 7

August 8 - September 7

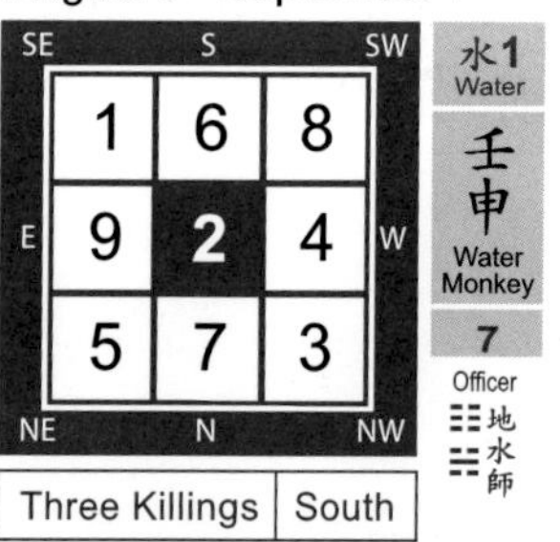

September 8 - October 7

October 8 - November 6

November 7 - December 6

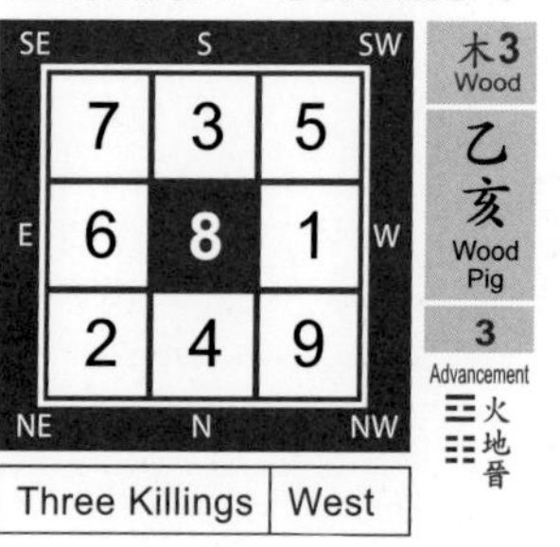

December 7 - January 5

JANUARY 1969 乙丑

Xuan Kong Element 玄空五行	火雷噬嗑 Biting	Period Luck 卦運	Monthly Star 月星
Wood 木3		6	9

SUNDAY	MONDAY	TUESDAY	WEDNESDAY	THURSDAY	FRIDAY	SATURDAY
			水6 Water 7 Nourish 丙子 Fire Rat 山雷頤 1 十三 3	金4 Metal 8 Following 丁丑 Fire Ox 澤雷隨 2 十四 7	木8 Wood 9 Abundance 戊寅 Earth Tiger 雷火豐 3 十五 6	火7 Fire 1 Regulate 己卯 Earth Rabbit 水澤節 4 十六 8
水1 Water 2 Unity 庚辰 Metal Dragon 地天泰 5 十七 9	木3 Wood 3 Great Reward 辛巳 Metal Snake 火天大有 6 十八 7	火2 Fire 4 Wind 壬午 Water Horse 巽爲風 7 十九 1	金4 Metal 5 Trap 癸未 Water Goat 澤水困 8 二十 8	木3 Wood 6 Not Yet Accomplished 甲申 Wood Monkey 火水未濟 9 廿一 9	金9 Metal 7 Retreat 乙酉 Wood Rooster 天山遯 10 廿二 4	水6 Water 8 Mountain 丙戌 Fire Dog 艮爲山 11 廿三 1
木8 Wood 9 Delight 丁亥 Fire Pig 雷地豫 12 廿四 8	火7 Fire 1 Beginning 戊子 Earth Rat 水雷屯 13 廿五 4	金9 Metal 2 Without Wrongdoing 己丑 Earth Ox 天雷無妄 14 廿六 2	木3 Wood 3 Fire 庚寅 Metal Tiger 離爲火 15 廿七 1	火2 Fire 4 Sincerity 辛卯 Metal Rabbit 風澤中孚 16 廿八 3	水6 Water 5 Big Livestock 壬辰 Water Dragon 山天大畜 17 廿九 4	金4 Metal 6 Eliminating 癸巳 Water Snake 澤天夬 18 十二月初一 6
金9 Metal 7 Heaven 甲午 Wood Horse 乾爲天 19 初二 1	火7 Fire 8 Well 乙未 Wood Goat 水風井 20 初三 6	木8 Wood 9 Relief 丙申 Fire Monkey 雷水解 21 初四 4	金4 Metal 1 Influence 丁酉 Fire Rooster 澤山咸 22 初五 9	水1 Water 2 Humility 戊戌 Earth Dog 地山謙 23 初六 6	火2 Fire 3 Observation 己亥 Earth Pig 風地觀 24 初七 2	火2 Fire 4 Increasing 庚子 Metal Rat 風雷益 25 初八 9
水1 Water 5 Dimming Light 辛丑 Metal Ox 地火明夷 26 初九 3	金9 Metal 6 Fellowship 壬寅 Water Tiger 天火同人 27 初十 7	木8 Wood 7 Marrying Maiden 癸卯 Water Rabbit 雷澤歸妹 28 十一 7	木3 Wood 8 Opposition 甲辰 Wood Dragon 火澤睽 29 十二 2	火7 Fire 9 Waiting 乙巳 Wood Snake 水天需 30 十三 3	金4 Metal 1 Great Exceeding 丙午 Fire Horse 澤風大過 31 十四 3	

FEBRUARY 1969 丙寅

Xuan Kong Element 玄空五行	風火家人 Family	Period Luck 卦運	Monthly Star 月星
Fire 火2		4	8

SUNDAY	MONDAY	TUESDAY	WEDNESDAY	THURSDAY	FRIDAY	SATURDAY
						水6 Water 2 Poison 丁未 Fire Goat 山風蠱 1 十五 7
火2 Fire 3 Dispersing 戊申 Earth Monkey 風水渙 2 十六 6	木3 Wood 4 Travelling 己酉 Earth Rooster 火山旅 3 十七 8	金9 Metal 5 Stagnation 庚戌 Metal Dog 天地否 4 十八 9	火7 Fire 6 Alliance 辛亥 Metal Pig 水地比 5 十九 7	木8 Wood 7 Thunder 壬子 Water Rat 震爲雷 6 二十 1	水6 Water 8 Beauty 癸丑 Water Ox 山火賁 7 廿一 8	火7 Fire 9 Accomplished 甲寅 Wood Tiger 水火既濟 8 廿二 9
水1 Water 1 Arriving 乙卯 Wood Rabbit 地澤臨 9 廿三 4	金4 Metal 2 Marsh 丙辰 Fire Dragon 兌爲澤 10 廿四 1	火2 Fire 3 Small Livestock 丁巳 Fire Snake 風天小畜 11 廿五 8	木3 Wood 4 The Cauldron 戊午 Earth Horse 火風鼎 12 廿六 4	水1 Water 5 Rising 己未 Earth Goat 地風升 13 廿七 2	火7 Fire 6 Water 庚申 Metal Monkey 坎爲水 14 廿八 1	木8 Wood 7 Lesser Exceeding 辛酉 Metal Rooster 雷山小過 15 廿九 3
金4 Metal 8 Gathering 壬戌 Water Dog 澤地萃 16 三十 4	水6 Water 9 Peel 癸亥 Water Pig 山地剝 17 正月初一 6	水1 Water 1 Earth 甲子 Wood Rat 坤爲地 18 初二 1	木3 Wood 2 Biting 乙丑 Wood Ox 火雷噬嗑 19 初三 6	火2 Fire 3 Family 丙寅 Fire Tiger 風火家人 20 初四 4	水6 Water 4 Decreasing 丁卯 Fire Rabbit 山澤損 21 初五 9	金9 Metal 5 Tread 戊辰 Earth Dragon 天澤履 22 初六 6
木8 Wood 6 Great Strength 己巳 Earth Snake 雷天大壯 23 初七 2	木8 Wood 7 Consistency 庚午 Metal Horse 雷風恒 24 初八 9	金9 Metal 8 Litigation 辛未 Metal Goat 天水訟 25 初九 3	水1 Water 9 Officer 壬申 Water Monkey 地水師 26 初十 7	火2 Fire 1 Gradual Progress 癸酉 Water Rooster 風山漸 27 十一 7	火7 Fire 2 Obstruction 甲戌 Wood Dog 水山蹇 28 十二 2	

MARCH 1969 丁卯

Xuan Kong Element 玄空五行	山澤損 Decreasing	Period Luck 卦運	Monthly Star 月星
Water 水6		9	7

SUNDAY	MONDAY	TUESDAY	WEDNESDAY	THURSDAY	FRIDAY	SATURDAY
木3 Wood 5 Opposition 甲辰 Wood Dragon 火澤睽 30 十三 2	火7 Fire 6 Waiting 乙巳 Wood Snake 水天需 31 十四 3					木3 Wood 3 Advancement 乙亥 Wood Pig 火地晉 1 十三 3
水6 Water 4 Nourish 丙子 Fire Rat 山雷頤 2 十四 3	金4 Metal 5 Following 丁丑 Fire Ox 澤雷隨 3 十五 7	木8 Wood 6 Abundance 戊寅 Earth Tiger 雷火豐 4 十六 6	火7 Fire 7 Regulate 己卯 Earth Rabbit 水澤節 5 十七 8	水1 Water 8 Unity 庚辰 Metal Dragon 地天泰 6 十八 9	木3 Wood 9 Great Reward 辛巳 Metal Snake 火天大有 7 十九 7	火2 Fire 1 Wind 壬午 Water Horse 巽為風 8 二十 1
金4 Metal 2 Trap 癸未 Water Goat 澤水困 9 廿一 8	木3 Wood 3 Not Yet Accomplished 甲申 Wood Monkey 火水未濟 10 廿二 9	金9 Metal 4 Retreat 乙酉 Wood Rooster 天山遯 11 廿三 4	水6 Water 5 Mountain 丙戌 Fire Dog 艮為山 12 廿四 1	木8 Wood 6 Delight 丁亥 Fire Pig 雷地豫 13 廿五 8	火7 Fire 7 Beginning 戊子 Earth Rat 水雷屯 14 廿六 4	金9 Metal 8 Without Wrongdoing 己丑 Earth Ox 天雷無妄 15 廿七 2
木3 Wood 9 Fire 庚寅 Metal Tiger 離為火 16 廿八 1	火2 Fire 1 Sincerity 辛卯 Metal Rabbit 風澤中孚 17 廿九 3	水6 Water 2 Big Livestock 壬辰 Water Dragon 山天大畜 18 二月初一 4	金4 Metal 3 Eliminating 癸巳 Water Snake 澤天夬 19 初二 6	金9 Metal 4 Heaven 甲午 Wood Horse 乾為天 20 初三 1	火7 Fire 5 Well 乙未 Wood Goat 水風井 21 初四 6	木8 Wood 6 Relief 丙申 Fire Monkey 雷水解 22 初五 4
金4 Metal 7 Influence 丁酉 Fire Rooster 澤山咸 23 初六 9	水1 Water 8 Humility 戊戌 Earth Dog 地山謙 24 初七 6	火2 Fire 9 Observation 己亥 Earth Pig 風地觀 25 初八 2	火2 Fire 1 Increasing 庚子 Metal Rat 風雷益 26 初九 9	水1 Water 2 Dimming Light 辛丑 Metal Ox 地火明夷 27 初十 3	金9 Metal 3 Fellowship 壬寅 Water Tiger 天火同人 28 十一 7	木8 Wood 4 Marrying Maiden 癸卯 Water Rabbit 雷澤歸妹 29 十二 7

APRIL 1969 戊辰

Xuan Kong Element 玄空五行	天澤履 Tread	Period Luck 卦運	Monthly Star 月星
Metal 金9		6	6

SUNDAY	MONDAY	TUESDAY	WEDNESDAY	THURSDAY	FRIDAY	SATURDAY
		金4 Metal 7 Great Exceeding 丙午 Fire Horse 澤風大過 1 十五 3	水6 Water 8 Poison 丁未 Fire Goat 山風蠱 2 十六 7	火2 Fire 9 Dispersing 戊申 Earth Monkey 風水渙 3 十七 6	木3 Wood 1 Travelling 己酉 Earth Rooster 火山旅 4 十八 8	金9 Metal 2 Stagnation 庚戌 Metal Dog 天地否 5 十九 9
火7 Fire 3 Alliance 辛亥 Metal Pig 水地比 6 二十 7	木8 Wood 4 Thunder 壬子 Water Rat 震為雷 7 廿一 1	水6 Water 5 Beauty 癸丑 Water Ox 山火賁 8 廿二 8	火7 Fire 6 Accomplished 甲寅 Wood Tiger 水火既濟 9 廿三 9	水1 Water 7 Arriving 乙卯 Wood Rabbit 地澤臨 10 廿四 3	金4 Metal 8 Marsh 丙辰 Fire Dragon 兌為澤 11 廿五 1	火2 Fire 9 Small Livestock 丁巳 Fire Snake 風天小畜 12 廿六 8
木3 Wood 1 The Cauldron 戊午 Earth Horse 火風鼎 13 廿七 4	水1 Water 2 Rising 己未 Earth Goat 地風升 14 廿八 2	火7 Fire 3 Water 庚申 Metal Monkey 坎為水 15 廿九 1	木8 Wood 4 Lesser Exceeding 辛酉 Metal Rooster 雷山小過 16 三十 3	金4 Metal 5 Gathering 壬戌 Water Dog 澤地萃 17 三月初一 4	水6 Water 6 Peel 癸亥 Water Pig 山地剝 18 初二 6	水1 Water 7 Earth 甲子 Wood Rat 坤為地 19 初三 1
木3 Wood 8 Biting 乙丑 Wood Ox 火雷噬嗑 20 初四 6	火2 Fire 9 Family 丙寅 Fire Tiger 風火家人 21 初五 4	水6 Water 1 Decreasing 丁卯 Fire Rabbit 山澤損 22 初六 9	金9 Metal 2 Tread 戊辰 Earth Dragon 天澤履 23 初七 6	木8 Wood 3 Great Strength 己巳 Earth Snake 雷天大壯 24 初八 2	木8 Wood 4 Consistency 庚午 Metal Horse 雷風恆 25 初九 9	金9 Metal 5 Litigation 辛未 Metal Goat 天水訟 26 初十 3
水1 Water 6 Officer 壬申 Water Monkey 地水師 27 十一 7	火2 Fire 7 Gradual Progress 癸酉 Water Rooster 風山漸 28 十二 7	火7 Fire 8 Obstruction 甲戌 Wood Dog 水山蹇 29 十三 2	木3 Wood 9 Advancement 乙亥 Wood Pig 火地晉 30 十四 3			

MAY 1969 己巳

Xuan Kong Element 玄空五行	雷天大壯 Great Strength	Period Luck 卦運	Monthly Star 月星
Wood 木8		2	5

SUNDAY	MONDAY	TUESDAY	WEDNESDAY	THURSDAY	FRIDAY	SATURDAY
				1 十五 水6 Water Nourish 1 丙子 Fire Rat 山雷頤 3	**2** 十六 金4 Metal Following 2 丁丑 Fire Ox 澤雷隨 7	**3** 十七 木8 Wood Abundance 3 戊寅 Earth Tiger 雷火豐 6
4 十八 火7 Fire Regulate 4 己卯 Earth Rabbit 水澤節 8	**5** 十九 水1 Water Unity 5 庚辰 Metal Dragon 地天泰 9	**6** 二十 木3 Wood Great Reward 6 辛巳 Metal Snake 火天大有 7	**7** 廿一 火2 Fire Wind 7 壬午 Water Horse 巽為風 1	**8** 廿二 金4 Metal Trap 8 癸未 Water Goat 澤水困 8	**9** 廿三 木3 Wood Not Yet Accomplished 9 甲申 Wood Monkey 火水未濟 9	**10** 廿四 金9 Metal Retreat 1 乙酉 Wood Rooster 天山遯 4
11 廿五 水6 Water Mountain 2 丙戌 Fire Dog 艮為山 1	**12** 廿六 木8 Wood Delight 3 丁亥 Fire Pig 雷地豫 8	**13** 廿七 火7 Fire Beginning 4 戊子 Earth Rat 水雷屯 4	**14** 廿八 金9 Metal Without Wrongdoing 5 己丑 Earth Ox 天雷無妄 2	**15** 廿九 木3 Wood Fire 6 庚寅 Metal Tiger 離為火 1	**16** 四月初一 火2 Fire Sincerity 7 辛卯 Metal Rabbit 風澤中孚 3	**17** 初二 水6 Water Big Livestock 8 壬辰 Water Dragon 山天大畜 4
18 初三 金4 Metal Eliminating 9 癸巳 Water Snake 澤天夬 6	**19** 初四 金9 Metal Heaven 1 甲午 Wood Horse 乾為天 1	**20** 初五 火7 Fire Well 2 乙未 Wood Goat 水風井 6	**21** 初六 木8 Wood Relief 3 丙申 Fire Monkey 雷水解 4	**22** 初七 金4 Metal Influence 4 丁酉 Fire Rooster 澤山咸 9	**23** 初八 水1 Water Humility 5 戊戌 Earth Dog 地山謙 6	**24** 初九 火2 Fire Observation 6 己亥 Earth Pig 風地觀 2
25 初十 火2 Fire Increasing 7 庚子 Metal Rat 風雷益 9	**26** 十一 水1 Water Dimming Light 8 辛丑 Metal Ox 地火明夷 3	**27** 十二 金9 Metal Fellowship 9 壬寅 Water Tiger 天火同人 7	**28** 十三 木8 Wood Marrying Maiden 1 癸卯 Water Rabbit 雷澤歸妹 7	**29** 十四 木3 Wood Opposition 2 甲辰 Wood Dragon 火澤睽 2	**30** 十五 火7 Fire Waiting 3 乙巳 Wood Snake 水天需 3	**31** 十六 金4 Metal Great Exceeding 4 丙午 Fire Horse 澤風大過 3

JUNE 1969 庚午

Xuan Kong Element 玄空五行	雷風恆 Consistency	Period Luck 卦運	Monthly Star 月星
Wood 木8		9	4

SUNDAY	MONDAY	TUESDAY	WEDNESDAY	THURSDAY	FRIDAY	SATURDAY
1 十七 水6 Water Poison 5 丁未 Fire Goat 山風蠱 7	**2** 十八 火2 Fire Dispersing 6 戊申 Earth Monkey 風水渙 6	**3** 十九 木3 Wood Travelling 7 己酉 Earth Rooster 火山旅 8	**4** 二十 金9 Metal Stagnation 8 庚戌 Metal Dog 天地否 9	**5** 廿一 火7 Fire Alliance 9 辛亥 Metal Pig 水地比 7	**6** 廿二 木8 Wood Thunder 1 壬子 Water Rat 震為雷 1	**7** 廿三 水6 Water Beauty 2 癸丑 Water Ox 山火賁 8
8 廿四 火7 Fire Accomplished 3 甲寅 Wood Tiger 水火既濟 9	**9** 廿五 水1 Water Arriving 4 乙卯 Wood Rabbit 地澤臨 4	**10** 廿六 金4 Metal Marsh 5 丙辰 Fire Dragon 兑為澤 1	**11** 廿七 火2 Fire Small Livestock 6 丁巳 Fire Snake 風天小畜 8	**12** 廿八 木3 Wood The Cauldron 7 戊午 Earth Horse 火風鼎 4	**13** 廿九 水1 Water Rising 8 己未 Earth Goat 地風升 2	**14** 三十 火7 Fire Water 9 庚申 Metal Monkey 坎為水 1
15 五月初一 木8 Wood Lesser Exceeding 1 辛酉 Metal Rooster 雷山小過 3	**16** 初二 金4 Metal Gathering 2 壬戌 Water Dog 澤地萃 4	**17** 初三 水6 Water Peel 3 癸亥 Water Pig 山地剝 6	**18** 初四 水1 Water Earth 4 甲子 Wood Rat 坤為地 1	**19** 初五 木3 Wood Biting 5 乙丑 Wood Ox 火雷噬嗑 6	**20** 初六 火2 Fire Family 6 丙寅 Fire Tiger 風火家人 4	**21** 初七 水6 Water Decreasing 7/3 丁卯 Fire Rabbit 山澤損 9
22 初八 金9 Metal Tread 2 戊辰 Earth Dragon 天澤履 6	**23** 初九 木8 Wood Great Strength 1 己巳 Earth Snake 雷天大壯 2	**24** 初十 木8 Wood Consistency 9 庚午 Metal Horse 雷風恆 9	**25** 十一 金9 Metal Litigation 8 辛未 Metal Goat 天水訟 3	**26** 十二 水1 Water Officer 7 壬申 Water Monkey 地水師 7	**27** 十三 火2 Fire Gradual Progress 6 癸酉 Water Rooster 風山漸 7	**28** 十四 火7 Fire Obstruction 5 甲戌 Wood Dog 水山蹇 2
29 十五 木3 Wood Advancement 4 乙亥 Wood Pig 火地晉 3	**30** 十六 水6 Water Nourish 3 丙子 Fire Rat 山雷頤 3					

JULY 1969 辛未

Xuan Kong Element 玄空五行	天水訟 Litigation	Period Luck 卦運	Monthly Star 月星
Metal 金9		3	3

SUNDAY	MONDAY	TUESDAY	WEDNESDAY	THURSDAY	FRIDAY	SATURDAY
		1 十七 金4 Metal 丁丑 Fire Ox 7 Following 澤雷隨 2	2 十八 木8 Wood 戊寅 Earth Tiger 6 Abundance 雷火豐 1	3 十九 火7 Fire 己卯 Earth Rabbit 8 Regulate 水澤節 9	4 二十 水1 Water 庚辰 Metal Dragon 9 Unity 地天泰 8	5 廿一 木3 Wood 辛巳 Metal Snake 7 Great Reward 火天大有 7
6 廿二 火2 Fire 壬午 Water Horse 1 Wind 巽為風 6	7 廿三 金4 Metal 癸未 Water Goat 8 Trap 澤水困 5	8 廿四 木3 Wood 甲申 Wood Monkey 9 Not Yet Accomplished 火水未濟 4	9 廿五 金9 Metal 乙酉 Wood Rooster 4 Retreat 天山遯 3	10 廿六 水6 Water 丙戌 Fire Dog 1 Mountain 艮為山 2	11 廿七 木8 Wood 丁亥 Fire Pig 8 Delight 雷地豫 1	12 廿八 火7 Fire 戊子 Earth Rat 4 Beginning 水雷屯 9
13 廿九 金9 Metal 己丑 Earth Ox 2 Without Wrongdoing 天雷無妄 8	14 六月初一 木3 Wood 庚寅 Metal Tiger 1 Fire 離為火 7	15 初二 火2 Fire 辛卯 Metal Rabbit 3 Sincerity 風澤中孚 6	16 初三 水6 Water 壬辰 Water Dragon 4 Big Livestock 山天大畜 5	17 初四 金4 Metal 癸巳 Water Snake 6 Eliminating 澤天夬 4	18 初五 金9 Metal 甲午 Wood Horse 1 Heaven 乾為天 3	19 初六 火7 Fire 乙未 Wood Goat 6 Well 水風井 2
20 初七 木8 Wood 丙申 Fire Monkey 4 Relief 雷水解 1	21 初八 金4 Metal 丁酉 Fire Rooster 9 Influence 澤山咸 9	22 初九 水1 Water 戊戌 Earth Dog 6 Humility 地山謙 8	23 初十 火2 Fire 己亥 Earth Pig 2 Observation 風地觀 7	24 十一 火2 Fire 庚子 Metal Rat 9 Increasing 風雷益 6	25 十二 水1 Water 辛丑 Metal Ox 3 Dimming Light 地火明夷 5	26 十三 金9 Metal 壬寅 Water Tiger 7 Fellowship 天火同人 4
27 十四 木8 Wood 癸卯 Water Rabbit 7 Marrying Maiden 雷澤歸妹 3	28 十五 木3 Wood 甲辰 Wood Dragon 2 Opposition 火澤睽 2	29 十六 火7 Fire 乙巳 Wood Snake 3 Waiting 水天需 1	30 十七 金4 Metal 丙午 Fire Horse 3 Great Exceeding 澤風大過 9	31 十八 水6 Water 丁未 Fire Goat 7 Poison 山風蠱 8		

AUGUST 1969 壬申

Xuan Kong Element 玄空五行	地水師 Officer	Period Luck 卦運	Monthly Star 月星
Water 水1		7	2

SUNDAY	MONDAY	TUESDAY	WEDNESDAY	THURSDAY	FRIDAY	SATURDAY
31 十九 木8 Wood 戊寅 Earth Tiger 6 Abundance 雷火豐 4					1 十九 火2 Fire 戊申 Earth Monkey 6 Dispersing 風水渙 7	2 二十 木3 Wood 己酉 Earth Rooster 8 Travelling 火山旅 6
3 廿一 金9 Metal 庚戌 Metal Dog 9 Stagnation 天地否 5	4 廿二 火7 Fire 辛亥 Metal Pig 7 Alliance 水地比 4	5 廿三 木8 Wood 壬子 Water Rat 1 Thunder 震為雷 3	6 廿四 水6 Water 癸丑 Water Ox 8 Beauty 山火賁 2	7 廿五 火7 Fire 甲寅 Wood Tiger 9 Accomplished 水火既濟 1	8 廿六 水1 Water 乙卯 Wood Rabbit 4 Arriving 地澤臨 9	9 廿七 金4 Metal 丙辰 Fire Dragon 1 Marsh 兌為澤 8
10 廿八 火2 Fire 丁巳 Fire Snake 8 Small Livestock 風天小畜 7	11 廿九 木3 Wood 戊午 Earth Horse 4 The Cauldron 火風鼎 6	12 三十 水1 Water 己未 Earth Goat 2 Rising 地風升 5	13 七月初一 火7 Fire 庚申 Metal Monkey 1 Water 坎為水 4	14 初二 木8 Wood 辛酉 Metal Rooster 3 Lesser Exceeding 雷山小過 3	15 初三 金4 Metal 壬戌 Water Dog 4 Gathering 澤地萃 2	16 初四 水6 Water 癸亥 Water Pig 6 Peel 山地剝 1
17 初五 水1 Water 甲子 Wood Rat 1 Earth 坤為地 9	18 初六 木3 Wood 乙丑 Wood Ox 6 Biting 火雷噬嗑 8	19 初七 火2 Fire 丙寅 Fire Tiger 4 Family 風火家人 7	20 初八 水6 Water 丁卯 Fire Rabbit 9 Decreasing 山澤損 6	21 初九 金9 Metal 戊辰 Earth Dragon 6 Tread 天澤履 5	22 初十 木8 Wood 己巳 Earth Snake 2 Great Strength 雷天大壯 4	23 十一 木8 Wood 庚午 Metal Horse 9 Consistency 雷風恆 3
24 十二 金9 Metal 辛未 Metal Goat 3 Litigation 天水訟 2	25 十三 水1 Water 壬申 Water Monkey 7 Officer 地水師 1	26 十四 火2 Fire 癸酉 Water Rooster 7 Gradual Progress 風山漸 9	27 十五 火7 Fire 甲戌 Wood Dog 2 Obstruction 水山蹇 8	28 十六 木3 Wood 乙亥 Wood Pig 3 Advancement 火地晉 7	29 十七 水6 Water 丙子 Fire Rat 3 Nourish 山雷頤 6	30 十八 金4 Metal 丁丑 Fire Ox 7 Following 澤雷隨 5

SEPTEMBER 1969 癸酉

Xuan Kong Element 玄空五行	風山漸 Gradual Progress	Period Luck 卦運	Monthly Star 月星
Fire 火2		7	1

SUNDAY	MONDAY	TUESDAY	WEDNESDAY	THURSDAY	FRIDAY	SATURDAY
	火7 Fire 3 Regulate 水澤節 己卯 Earth Rabbit 1 二十 8	水1 Water 2 Unity 地天泰 庚辰 Metal Dragon 2 廿一 9	木3 Wood 1 Great Reward 火天大有 辛巳 Metal Snake 3 廿二 7	火2 Fire 9 Wind 巽爲風 壬午 Water Horse 4 廿三 1	金4 Metal 8 Trap 澤水困 癸未 Water Goat 5 廿四 8	木3 Wood 7 Not Yet Accomplished 火水未濟 甲申 Wood Monkey 6 廿五 9
金9 Metal 6 Retreat 天山遯 乙酉 Wood Rooster 7 廿六 4	水6 Water 5 Mountain 艮爲山 丙戌 Fire Dog 8 廿七 1	木8 Wood 4 Delight 雷地豫 丁亥 Fire Pig 9 廿八 8	火7 Fire 3 Beginning 水雷屯 戊子 Earth Rat 10 廿九 4	金9 Metal 2 Without Wrongdoing 天雷無妄 己丑 Earth Ox 11 三十 2	木3 Wood 1 Fire 離爲火 庚寅 Metal Tiger 12 八月初一 1	火2 Fire 9 Sincerity 風澤中孚 辛卯 Metal Rabbit 13 初二 3
水6 Water 8 Big Livestock 山天大畜 壬辰 Water Dragon 14 初三 4	金4 Metal 7 Eliminating 澤天夬 癸巳 Water Snake 15 初四 6	金9 Metal 6 Heaven 乾爲天 甲午 Wood Horse 16 初五 1	火7 Fire 5 Well 水風井 乙未 Wood Goat 17 初六 6	木8 Wood 4 Relief 雷水解 丙申 Fire Monkey 18 初七 4	金4 Metal 3 Influence 澤山咸 丁酉 Fire Rooster 19 初八 9	水1 Water 2 Humility 地山謙 戊戌 Earth Dog 20 初九 6
火2 Fire 1 Observation 風地觀 己亥 Earth Pig 21 初十 2	火2 Fire 9 Increasing 風雷益 庚子 Metal Rat 22 十一 9	水1 Water 8 Dimming Light 地火明夷 辛丑 Metal Ox 23 十二 3	金9 Metal 7 Fellowship 天火同人 壬寅 Water Tiger 24 十三 7	木8 Wood 6 Marrying Maiden 雷澤歸妹 癸卯 Water Rabbit 25 十四 7	木3 Wood 5 Opposition 火澤睽 甲辰 Wood Dragon 26 十五 2	火7 Fire 4 Waiting 水天需 乙巳 Wood Snake 27 十六 3
金4 Metal 3 Great Exceeding 澤風大過 丙午 Fire Horse 28 十七 3	水6 Water 2 Poison 山風蠱 丁未 Fire Goat 29 十八 7	火2 Fire 1 Dispersing 風水渙 戊申 Earth Monkey 30 十九 6				

OCTOBER 1969 甲戌

Xuan Kong Element 玄空五行	水山蹇 Obstruction	Period Luck 卦運	Monthly Star 月星
Fire 火7		2	9

SUNDAY	MONDAY	TUESDAY	WEDNESDAY	THURSDAY	FRIDAY	SATURDAY
			木3 Wood 9 Travelling 火山旅 己酉 Earth Rooster 1 二十 8	金9 Metal 8 Stagnation 天地否 庚戌 Metal Dog 2 廿一 9	火7 Fire 7 Alliance 水地比 辛亥 Metal Pig 3 廿二 7	木8 Wood 6 Thunder 震爲雷 壬子 Water Rat 4 廿三 1
水6 Water 5 Beauty 山火賁 癸丑 Water Ox 5 廿四 8	火7 Fire 4 Accomplished 水火既濟 甲寅 Wood Tiger 6 廿五 9	水1 Water 3 Arriving 地澤臨 乙卯 Wood Rabbit 7 廿六 4	金4 Metal 2 Marsh 兑爲澤 丙辰 Fire Dragon 8 廿七 1	火2 Fire 1 Small Livestock 風天小畜 丁巳 Fire Snake 9 廿八 8	木3 Wood 9 The Cauldron 火風鼎 戊午 Earth Horse 10 廿九 4	水1 Water 8 Rising 地風升 己未 Earth Goat 11 九月初一 2
火7 Fire 7 Water 坎爲水 庚申 Metal Monkey 12 初二 1	木8 Wood 6 Lesser Exceeding 雷山小過 辛酉 Metal Rooster 13 初三 3	金4 Metal 5 Gathering 澤地萃 壬戌 Water Dog 14 初四 4	水6 Water 4 Peel 山地剝 癸亥 Water Pig 15 初五 6	水1 Water 3 Earth 坤爲地 甲子 Wood Rat 16 初六 1	木3 Wood 2 Biting 火雷噬嗑 乙丑 Wood Ox 17 初七 6	火2 Fire 1 Family 風火家人 丙寅 Fire Tiger 18 初八 4
水6 Water 9 Decreasing 山澤損 丁卯 Fire Rabbit 19 初九 9	金9 Metal 8 Tread 天澤履 戊辰 Earth Dragon 20 初十 6	木8 Wood 7 Great Strength 雷天大壯 己巳 Earth Snake 21 十一 2	木8 Wood 6 Consistency 雷風恒 庚午 Metal Horse 22 十二 9	金9 Metal 5 Litigation 天水訟 辛未 Metal Goat 23 十三 3	水1 Water 4 Officer 地水師 壬申 Water Monkey 24 十四 7	火2 Fire 3 Gradual Progress 風山漸 癸酉 Water Rooster 25 十五 7
火7 Fire 2 Obstruction 水山蹇 甲戌 Wood Dog 26 十六 2	木3 Wood 1 Advancement 火地晉 乙亥 Wood Pig 27 十七 3	水6 Water 9 Nourish 山雷頤 丙子 Fire Rat 28 十八 3	金4 Metal 8 Following 澤雷隨 丁丑 Fire Ox 29 十九 7	木8 Wood 7 Abundance 雷火豐 戊寅 Earth Tiger 30 二十 6	火7 Fire 6 Regulate 水澤節 己卯 Earth Rabbit 31 廿一 8	

NOVEMBER 1969 乙亥

Xuan Kong Element 玄空五行	火地晉 Advancement	Period Luck 卦運	Monthly Star 月星
Wood 木3		3	8

SUNDAY	MONDAY	TUESDAY	WEDNESDAY	THURSDAY	FRIDAY	SATURDAY
木3 Wood 3 Travelling 火山旅 己酉 Earth Rooster 30 廿一 8						水1 Water 5 Unity 地天泰 庚辰 Metal Dragon 1 廿二 9
木3 Wood 4 Great Reward 火天大有 辛巳 Metal Snake 2 廿三 7	火2 Fire 3 Wind 巽爲風 壬午 Water Horse 3 廿四 1	金4 Metal 2 Trap 澤水困 癸未 Water Goat 4 廿五 8	木3 Wood 1 Not Yet Accomplished 火水未濟 甲申 Wood Monkey 5 廿六 9	金9 Metal 9 Retreat 天山遯 乙酉 Wood Rooster 6 廿七 4	水6 Water 8 Mountain 艮爲山 丙戌 Fire Dog 7 廿八 1	木8 Wood 7 Delight 雷地豫 丁亥 Fire Pig 8 廿九 8
火7 Fire 6 Beginning 水雷屯 戊子 Earth Rat 9 三十 4	金9 Metal 5 Without Wrongdoing 天雷無妄 己丑 Earth Ox 10 十月初一 2	木3 Wood 4 Fire 離爲火 庚寅 Metal Tiger 11 初二 1	火2 Fire 3 Sincerity 風澤中孚 辛卯 Metal Rabbit 12 初三 3	水6 Water 2 Big Livestock 山天大畜 壬辰 Water Dragon 13 初四 4	金4 Metal 1 Eliminating 澤天夬 癸巳 Water Snake 14 初五 6	金9 Metal 9 Heaven 乾爲天 甲午 Wood Horse 15 初六 1
火7 Fire 8 Well 水風井 乙未 Wood Goat 16 初七 6	木8 Wood 7 Relief 雷水解 丙申 Fire Monkey 17 初八 4	金4 Metal 6 Influence 澤山咸 丁酉 Fire Rooster 18 初九 9	水1 Water 5 Humility 地山謙 戊戌 Earth Dog 19 初十 6	火2 Fire 4 Observation 風地觀 己亥 Earth Pig 20 十一 2	火2 Fire 3 Increasing 風雷益 庚子 Metal Rat 21 十二 9	水1 Water 2 Dimming Light 地火明夷 辛丑 Metal Ox 22 十三 3
金9 Metal 1 Fellowship 天火同人 壬寅 Water Tiger 23 十四 7	木8 Wood 9 Marrying Maiden 雷澤歸妹 癸卯 Water Rabbit 24 十五 7	木3 Wood 8 Opposition 火澤睽 甲辰 Wood Dragon 25 十六 2	火7 Fire 7 Waiting 水天需 乙巳 Wood Snake 26 十七 3	金4 Metal 6 Great Exceeding 澤風大過 丙午 Fire Horse 27 十八 3	水6 Water 5 Poison 山風蠱 丁未 Fire Goat 28 十九 7	火2 Fire 4 Dispersing 風水渙 戊申 Earth Monkey 29 二十 6

DECEMBER 1969 丙子

Xuan Kong Element 玄空五行	山雷頤 Nourish	Period Luck 卦運	Monthly Star 月星
Water 水6		3	7

SUNDAY	MONDAY	TUESDAY	WEDNESDAY	THURSDAY	FRIDAY	SATURDAY
	金9 Metal 2 Stagnation 天地否 庚戌 Metal Dog 1 廿二 9	火7 Fire 1 Alliance 水地比 辛亥 Metal Pig 2 廿三 7	木8 Wood 9 Thunder 震爲雷 壬子 Water Rat 3 廿四 1	水6 Water 8 Beauty 山火賁 癸丑 Water Ox 4 廿五 8	火7 Fire 7 Accomplished 水火既濟 甲寅 Wood Tiger 5 廿六 9	水1 Water 6 Arriving 地澤臨 乙卯 Wood Rabbit 6 廿七 4
金4 Metal 5 Marsh 兌爲澤 丙辰 Fire Dragon 7 廿八 1	火2 Fire 4 Small Livestock 風天小畜 丁巳 Fire Snake 8 廿九 8	木3 Wood 3 The Cauldron 火風鼎 戊午 Earth Horse 9 十一月初一 4	水1 Water 2 Rising 地風升 己未 Earth Goat 10 初二 2	火7 Fire 1 Water 坎爲水 庚申 Metal Monkey 11 初三 1	木8 Wood 9 Lesser Exceeding 雷山小過 辛酉 Metal Rooster 12 初四 3	金4 Metal 8 Gathering 澤地萃 壬戌 Water Dog 13 初五 4
水6 Water 7 Peel 山地剝 癸亥 Water Pig 14 初六 6	水1 Water 6 Earth 坤爲地 甲子 Wood Rat 15 初七 1	木3 Wood 5 Biting 火雷噬嗑 乙丑 Wood Ox 16 初八 6	火2 Fire 4 Family 風火家人 丙寅 Fire Tiger 17 初九 4	水6 Water 3 Decreasing 山澤損 丁卯 Fire Rabbit 18 初十 9	金9 Metal 2 Tread 天澤履 戊辰 Earth Dragon 19 十一 6	木8 Wood 1 Great Strength 雷天大壯 己巳 Earth Snake 20 十二 2
木8 Wood 9 Consistency 雷風恒 庚午 Metal Horse 21 十三 9	金9 Metal 8/2 Litigation 天水訟 辛未 Metal Goat 22 十四 3	水1 Water 3 Officer 地水師 壬申 Water Monkey 23 十五 7	火2 Fire 4 Gradual Progress 風山漸 癸酉 Water Rooster 24 十六 7	火7 Fire 5 Obstruction 水山蹇 甲戌 Wood Dog 25 十七 2	木3 Wood 6 Advancement 火地晉 乙亥 Wood Pig 26 十八 3	水6 Water 7 Nourish 山雷頤 丙子 Fire Rat 27 十九 3
金4 Metal 8 Following 澤雷隨 丁丑 Fire Ox 28 二十 7	木8 Wood 9 Abundance 雷火豐 戊寅 Earth Tiger 29 廿一 6	火7 Fire 1 Regulate 水澤節 己卯 Earth Rabbit 30 廿二 8	水1 Water 2 Unity 地天泰 庚辰 Metal Dragon 31 廿三 9			

1970 庚戌

(*Geng Xu*) Metal Dog

1970 庚戌 *(Geng Xu)* Metal Dog

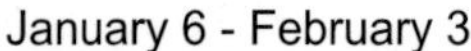

January 6 - February 3

February 4 - March 5

March 6 - April 4

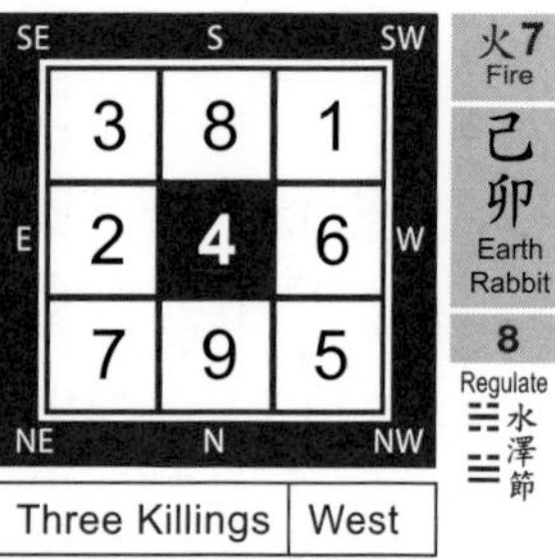

April 5 - May 5

May 6 - June 5

June 6 - July 6

July 7 - August 7

August 8 - September 7

7	3	5
6	**8**	1
2	4	9

木**3** Wood

甲申 Wood Monkey

9

Not Yet Accomplished
火水未濟

September 8 - October 8

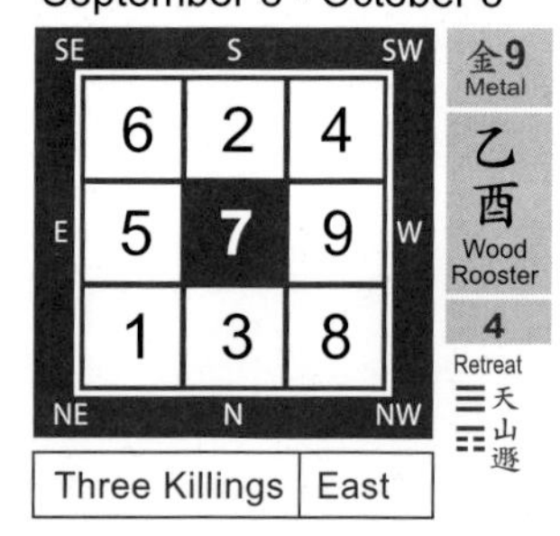

October 9 - November 7

November 8 - December 6

December 7 - January 5

JANUARY 1970 丁丑

Xuan Kong Element 玄空五行	澤雷隨 Following	Period Luck 卦運	Monthly Star 月星
Metal 金4		7	6

SUNDAY	MONDAY	TUESDAY	WEDNESDAY	THURSDAY	FRIDAY	SATURDAY
				1 廿四 木3 Wood · 3 Great Reward 火天大有 辛巳 Metal Snake · 7	**2** 廿五 火2 Fire · 4 Wind 巽爲風 壬午 Water Horse · 1	**3** 廿六 金4 Metal · 5 Trap 澤水困 癸未 Water Goat · 8
4 廿七 木3 Wood · 6 Not Yet Accomplished 火水未濟 甲申 Wood Monkey · 9	**5** 廿八 金9 Metal · 7 Retreat 天山遯 乙酉 Wood Rooster · 4	**6** 廿九 水6 Water · 8 Mountain 艮爲山 丙戌 Fire Dog · 1	**7** 三十 木8 Wood · 9 Delight 雷地豫 丁亥 Fire Pig · 8	**8** 十二月初一 火7 Fire · 1 Beginning 水雷屯 戊子 Earth Rat · 4	**9** 初二 金9 Metal · 2 Without Wrongdoing 天雷無妄 己丑 Earth Ox · 2	**10** 初三 木3 Wood · 3 Fire 離爲火 庚寅 Metal Tiger · 1
11 初四 火2 Fire · 4 Sincerity 風澤中孚 辛卯 Metal Rabbit · 3	**12** 初五 水6 Water · 5 Big Livestock 山天大畜 壬辰 Water Dragon · 4	**13** 初六 金4 Metal · 6 Eliminating 澤天夬 癸巳 Water Snake · 6	**14** 初七 金9 Metal · 7 Heaven 乾爲天 甲午 Wood Horse · 1	**15** 初八 火7 Fire · 8 Well 水風井 乙未 Wood Goat · 6	**16** 初九 木8 Wood · 9 Relief 雷水解 丙申 Fire Monkey · 4	**17** 初十 金4 Metal · 1 Influence 澤山咸 丁酉 Fire Rooster · 9
18 十一 水1 Water · 2 Humility 地山謙 戊戌 Earth Dog · 6	**19** 十二 火2 Fire · 3 Observation 風地觀 己亥 Earth Pig · 2	**20** 十三 火2 Fire · 4 Increasing 風雷益 庚子 Metal Rat · 9	**21** 十四 水1 Water · 5 Dimming Light 地火明夷 辛丑 Metal Ox · 3	**22** 十五 金9 Metal · 6 Fellowship 天火同人 壬寅 Water Tiger · 7	**23** 十六 木8 Wood · 7 Marrying Maiden 雷澤歸妹 癸卯 Water Rabbit · 7	**24** 十七 木3 Wood · 8 Opposition 火澤睽 甲辰 Wood Dragon · 2
25 十八 火7 Fire · 9 Waiting 水天需 乙巳 Wood Snake · 3	**26** 十九 金4 Metal · 1 Great Exceeding 澤風大過 丙午 Fire Horse · 3	**27** 二十 水6 Water · 2 Poison 山風蠱 丁未 Fire Goat · 7	**28** 廿一 火2 Fire · 3 Dispersing 風水渙 戊申 Earth Monkey · 6	**29** 廿二 木3 Wood · 4 Travelling 火山旅 己酉 Earth Rooster · 8	**30** 廿三 金9 Metal · 5 Stagnation 天地否 庚戌 Metal Dog · 9	**31** 廿四 火7 Fire · 6 Alliance 水地比 辛亥 Metal Pig · 7

FEBRUARY 1970 戊寅

Xuan Kong Element 玄空五行	雷火豐 Abundance	Period Luck 卦運	Monthly Star 月星
Wood 木8		6	5

SUNDAY	MONDAY	TUESDAY	WEDNESDAY	THURSDAY	FRIDAY	SATURDAY
1 廿五 木8 Wood · 7 Thunder 震爲雷 壬子 Water Rat · 1	**2** 廿六 水6 Water · 8 Beauty 山火賁 癸丑 Water Ox · 8	**3** 廿七 火7 Fire · 9 Accomplished 水火既濟 甲寅 Wood Tiger · 9	**4** 廿八 水1 Water · 1 Arriving 地澤臨 乙卯 Wood Rabbit · 4	**5** 廿九 金4 Metal · 2 Marsh 兌爲澤 丙辰 Fire Dragon · 1	**6** 正月初一 火2 Fire · 3 Small Livestock 風天小畜 丁巳 Fire Snake · 8	**7** 初二 木3 Wood · 4 The Cauldron 火風鼎 戊午 Earth Horse · 4
8 初三 水1 Water · 5 Rising 地風升 己未 Earth Goat · 2	**9** 初四 火7 Fire · 6 Water 坎爲水 庚申 Metal Monkey · 1	**10** 初五 木8 Wood · 7 Lesser Exceeding 雷山小過 辛酉 Metal Rooster · 3	**11** 初六 金4 Metal · 8 Gathering 澤地萃 壬戌 Water Dog · 4	**12** 初七 水6 Water · 9 Peel 山地剝 癸亥 Water Pig · 6	**13** 初八 水1 Water · 1 Earth 坤爲地 甲子 Wood Rat · 1	**14** 初九 木3 Wood · 2 Biting 火雷噬嗑 乙丑 Wood Ox · 6
15 初十 火2 Fire · 3 Family 風火家人 丙寅 Fire Tiger · 4	**16** 十一 水6 Water · 4 Decreasing 山澤損 丁卯 Fire Rabbit · 9	**17** 十二 金9 Metal · 5 Tread 天澤履 戊辰 Earth Dragon · 6	**18** 十三 木8 Wood · 6 Great Strength 雷天大壯 己巳 Earth Snake · 2	**19** 十四 木8 Wood · 7 Consistency 雷風恆 庚午 Metal Horse · 9	**20** 十五 金9 Metal · 8 Litigation 天水訟 辛未 Metal Goat · 3	**21** 十六 水1 Water · 9 Officer 地水師 壬申 Water Monkey · 7
22 十七 火2 Fire · 1 Gradual Progress 風山漸 癸酉 Water Rooster · 7	**23** 十八 火7 Fire · 2 Obstruction 水山蹇 甲戌 Wood Dog · 2	**24** 十九 木3 Wood · 3 Advancement 火地晉 乙亥 Wood Pig · 3	**25** 二十 水6 Water · 4 Nourish 山雷頤 丙子 Fire Rat · 3	**26** 廿一 金4 Metal · 5 Following 澤雷隨 丁丑 Fire Ox · 7	**27** 廿二 木8 Wood · 6 Abundance 雷火豐 戊寅 Earth Tiger · 6	**28** 廿三 火7 Fire · 7 Regulate 水澤節 己卯 Earth Rabbit · 8

MARCH 1970 己卯

Xuan Kong Element 玄空五行	水澤節 Regulate	Period Luck 卦運	Monthly Star 月星
Fire 火7		8	4

SUNDAY	MONDAY	TUESDAY	WEDNESDAY	THURSDAY	FRIDAY	SATURDAY
水1 Water 8 Unity 地天泰 庚辰 Metal Dragon 1 廿四 9	木3 Wood 9 Great Reward 火天大有 辛巳 Metal Snake 2 廿五 7	火2 Fire 1 Wind 巽爲風 壬午 Water Horse 3 廿六 1	金4 Metal 2 Trap 澤水困 癸未 Water Goat 4 廿七 8	木3 Wood 3 Not Yet Accomplished 火水未濟 甲申 Wood Monkey 5 廿八 9	金9 Metal 4 Retreat 天山遯 乙酉 Wood Rooster 6 廿九 4	水6 Water 5 Mountain 艮爲山 丙戌 Fire Dog 7 三十 1
木8 Wood 6 Delight 雷地豫 丁亥 Fire Pig 8 二月初一 8	火7 Fire 7 Beginning 水雷屯 戊子 Earth Rat 9 初二 4	金9 Metal 8 Without Wrongdoing 天雷無妄 己丑 Earth Ox 10 初三 2	木3 Wood 9 Fire 離爲火 庚寅 Metal Tiger 11 初四 1	火2 Fire 1 Sincerity 風澤中孚 辛卯 Metal Rabbit 12 初五 3	水6 Water 2 Big Livestock 山天大畜 壬辰 Water Dragon 13 初六 4	金4 Metal 3 Eliminating 澤天夬 癸巳 Water Snake 14 初七 6
金9 Metal 4 Heaven 乾爲天 甲午 Wood Horse 15 初八 1	火7 Fire 5 Well 水風井 乙未 Wood Goat 16 初九 6	木8 Wood 6 Relief 雷水解 丙申 Fire Monkey 17 初十 4	金4 Metal 7 Influence 澤山咸 丁酉 Fire Rooster 18 十一 9	水1 Water 8 Humility 地山謙 戊戌 Earth Dog 19 十二 6	火2 Fire 9 Observation 風地觀 己亥 Earth Pig 20 十三 2	火2 Fire 1 Increasing 風雷益 庚子 Metal Rat 21 十四 9
水1 Water 2 Dimming Light 地火明夷 辛丑 Metal Ox 22 十五 3	金9 Metal 3 Fellowship 天火同人 壬寅 Water Tiger 23 十六 7	木8 Wood 4 Marrying Maiden 雷澤歸妹 癸卯 Water Rabbit 24 十七 7	木3 Wood 5 Opposition 火澤睽 甲辰 Wood Dragon 25 十八 2	火7 Fire 6 Waiting 水天需 乙巳 Wood Snake 26 十九 3	金4 Metal 7 Great Exceeding 澤風大過 丙午 Fire Horse 27 二十 3	水6 Water 8 Poison 山風蠱 丁未 Fire Goat 28 廿一 7
火2 Fire 9 Dispersing 風水渙 戊申 Earth Monkey 29 廿二 6	木3 Wood 1 Travelling 火山旅 己酉 Earth Rooster 30 廿三 8	金9 Metal 2 Stagnation 天地否 庚戌 Metal Dog 31 廿四 9				

APRIL 1970 庚辰

Xuan Kong Element 玄空五行	地天泰 Unity	Period Luck 卦運	Monthly Star 月星
Water 水1		9	3

SUNDAY	MONDAY	TUESDAY	WEDNESDAY	THURSDAY	FRIDAY	SATURDAY
			火7 Fire 3 Alliance 水地比 辛亥 Metal Pig 1 廿五 7	木8 Wood 4 Thunder 震爲雷 壬子 Water Rat 2 廿六 1	水6 Water 5 Beauty 山火賁 癸丑 Water Ox 3 廿七 8	火7 Fire 6 Accomplished 水火既濟 甲寅 Wood Tiger 4 廿八 9
水1 Water 7 Arriving 地澤臨 乙卯 Wood Rabbit 5 廿九 4	金4 Metal 8 Marsh 兌爲澤 丙辰 Fire Dragon 6 三月初一 1	火2 Fire 9 Small Livestock 風天小畜 丁巳 Fire Snake 7 初二 8	木3 Wood 1 The Cauldron 火風鼎 戊午 Earth Horse 8 初三 4	水1 Water 2 Rising 地風升 己未 Earth Goat 9 初四 2	火7 Fire 3 Water 坎爲水 庚申 Metal Monkey 10 初五 1	木8 Wood 4 Lesser Exceeding 雷山小過 辛酉 Metal Rooster 11 初六 3
金4 Metal 5 Gathering 澤地萃 壬戌 Water Dog 12 初七 4	水6 Water 6 Peel 山地剝 癸亥 Water Pig 13 初八 6	水1 Water 7 Earth 坤爲地 甲子 Wood Rat 14 初九 1	木3 Wood 8 Biting 火雷噬嗑 乙丑 Wood Ox 15 初十 6	火2 Fire 9 Family 風火家人 丙寅 Fire Tiger 16 十一 4	水6 Water 1 Decreasing 山澤損 丁卯 Fire Rabbit 17 十二 9	金9 Metal 2 Tread 天澤履 戊辰 Earth Dragon 18 十三 6
木8 Wood 3 Great Strength 雷天大壯 己巳 Earth Snake 19 十四 2	木8 Wood 4 Consistency 雷風恆 庚午 Metal Horse 20 十五 9	金9 Metal 5 Litigation 天水訟 辛未 Metal Goat 21 十六 3	水1 Water 6 Officer 地水師 壬申 Water Monkey 22 十七 7	火2 Fire 7 Gradual Progress 風山漸 癸酉 Water Rooster 23 十八 7	火7 Fire 8 Obstruction 水山蹇 甲戌 Wood Dog 24 十九 2	木3 Wood 9 Advancement 火地晉 乙亥 Wood Pig 25 二十 3
水6 Water 1 Nourish 山雷頤 丙子 Fire Rat 26 廿一 3	金4 Metal 2 Following 澤雷隨 丁丑 Fire Ox 27 廿二 7	木8 Wood 3 Abundance 雷火豐 戊寅 Earth Tiger 28 廿三 6	火7 Fire 4 Regulate 水澤節 己卯 Earth Rabbit 29 廿四 8	水1 Water 5 Unity 地天泰 庚辰 Metal Dragon 30 廿五 9		

MAY 1970 辛巳

Xuan Kong Element 玄空五行	火天大有 Great Reward	Period Luck 卦運	Monthly Star 月星
Wood 木3		7	2

SUNDAY	MONDAY	TUESDAY	WEDNESDAY	THURSDAY	FRIDAY	SATURDAY
火7 Fire Alliance 9 水地比 辛亥 Metal Pig 7 31 廿七					木3 Wood Great Reward 6 火天大有 辛巳 Metal Snake 7 1 廿六	火2 Fire Wind 7 巽為風 壬午 Water Horse 1 2 廿七
金4 Metal Trap 8 澤水困 癸未 Water Goat 8 3 廿八	木3 Wood Not Yet Accomplished 9 火水未濟 甲申 Wood Monkey 9 4 廿九	金9 Metal Retreat 1 天山遯 乙酉 Wood Rooster 4 5 四月初一	水6 Water Mountain 2 艮為山 丙戌 Fire Dog 1 6 初二	木8 Wood Delight 3 雷地豫 丁亥 Fire Pig 8 7 初三	火7 Fire Beginning 4 水雷屯 戊子 Earth Rat 4 8 初四	金9 Metal Without Wrongdoing 5 天雷無妄 己丑 Earth Ox 2 9 初五
木3 Wood Fire 6 離為火 庚寅 Metal Tiger 1 10 初六	火2 Fire Sincerity 7 風澤中孚 辛卯 Metal Rabbit 3 11 初七	水6 Water Big Livestock 8 山天大畜 壬辰 Water Dragon 4 12 初八	金4 Metal Eliminating 9 澤天夬 癸巳 Water Snake 6 13 初九	金9 Metal Heaven 1 乾為天 甲午 Wood Horse 1 14 初十	火7 Fire Well 2 水風井 乙未 Wood Goat 6 15 十一	木8 Wood Relief 3 雷水解 丙申 Fire Monkey 4 16 十二
金4 Metal Influence 4 澤山咸 丁酉 Fire Rooster 9 17 十三	水1 Water Humility 5 地山謙 戊戌 Earth Dog 6 18 十四	火2 Fire Observation 6 風地觀 己亥 Earth Pig 2 19 十五	火2 Fire Increasing 7 風雷益 庚子 Metal Rat 9 20 十六	水1 Water Dimming Light 8 地火明夷 辛丑 Metal Ox 3 21 十七	金9 Metal Fellowship 9 天火同人 壬寅 Water Tiger 7 22 十八	木8 Wood Marrying Maiden 1 雷澤歸妹 癸卯 Water Rabbit 7 23 十九
木3 Wood Opposition 2 火澤睽 甲辰 Wood Dragon 2 24 二十	火7 Fire Waiting 3 水天需 乙巳 Wood Snake 3 25 廿一	金4 Metal Great Exceeding 4 澤風大過 丙午 Fire Horse 3 26 廿二	水6 Water Poison 5 山風蠱 丁未 Fire Goat 7 27 廿三	火2 Fire Dispersing 6 風水渙 戊申 Earth Monkey 6 28 廿四	木3 Wood Travelling 7 火山旅 己酉 Earth Rooster 8 29 廿五	金9 Metal Stagnation 8 天地否 庚戌 Metal Dog 9 30 廿六

JUNE 1970 壬午

Xuan Kong Element 玄空五行	巽為風 Wind	Period Luck 卦運	Monthly Star 月星
Fire 火2		1	1

SUNDAY	MONDAY	TUESDAY	WEDNESDAY	THURSDAY	FRIDAY	SATURDAY
	木8 Wood Thunder 1 震為雷 壬子 Water Rat 1 1 廿八	水6 Water Beauty 2 山火賁 癸丑 Water Ox 8 2 廿九	火7 Fire Accomplished 3 水火既濟 甲寅 Wood Tiger 9 3 三十	水1 Water Arriving 4 地澤臨 乙卯 Wood Rabbit 4 4 五月初一	金4 Metal Marsh 5 兌為澤 丙辰 Fire Dragon 1 5 初二	火2 Fire Small Livestock 6 風天小畜 丁巳 Fire Snake 8 6 初三
木3 Wood The Cauldron 7 火風鼎 戊午 Earth Horse 4 7 初四	水1 Water Rising 8 地風升 己未 Earth Goat 2 8 初五	火7 Fire Water 9 坎為水 庚申 Metal Monkey 1 9 初六	木8 Wood Lesser Exceeding 1 雷山小過 辛酉 Metal Rooster 3 10 初七	金4 Metal Gathering 2 澤地萃 壬戌 Water Dog 4 11 初八	水6 Water Peel 3 山地剝 癸亥 Water Pig 6 12 初九	水1 Water Earth 4 坤為地 甲子 Wood Rat 1 13 初十
木3 Wood Biting 5 火雷噬嗑 乙丑 Wood Ox 6 14 十一	火2 Fire Family 6 風火家人 丙寅 Fire Tiger 4 15 十二	水6 Water Decreasing 7 山澤損 丁卯 Fire Rabbit 9 16 十三	金9 Metal Tread 8 天澤履 戊辰 Earth Dragon 6 17 十四	木8 Wood Great Strength 9 雷天大壯 己巳 Earth Snake 2 18 十五	木8 Wood Consistency 1 雷風恆 庚午 Metal Horse 9 19 十六	金9 Metal Litigation 2 天水訟 辛未 Metal Goat 3 20 十七
水1 Water Officer 3 地水師 壬申 Water Monkey 7 21 十八	火2 Fire Gradual Progress 4/6 風山漸 癸酉 Water Rooster 7 22 十九	火7 Fire Obstruction 5 水山蹇 甲戌 Wood Dog 2 23 二十	木3 Wood Advancement 4 火地晉 乙亥 Wood Pig 3 24 廿一	水6 Water Nourish 3 山雷頤 丙子 Fire Rat 3 25 廿二	金4 Metal Following 2 澤雷隨 丁丑 Fire Ox 7 26 廿三	木8 Wood Abundance 1 雷火豐 戊寅 Earth Tiger 6 27 廿四
火7 Fire Regulate 9 水澤節 己卯 Earth Rabbit 8 28 廿五	水1 Water Unity 8 地天泰 庚辰 Metal Dragon 9 29 廿六	木3 Wood Great Reward 7 火天大有 辛巳 Metal Snake 7 30 廿七				

JULY 1970 癸未

Xuan Kong Element 玄空五行	澤水困 Trap	Period Luck 卦運	Monthly Star 月星
Metal 金4		8	9

SUNDAY	MONDAY	TUESDAY	WEDNESDAY	THURSDAY	FRIDAY	SATURDAY
			火2 Fire 6 Wind 巽爲風 壬午 Water Horse 1 **1** 廿八	金4 Metal 5 Trap 澤水困 癸未 Water Goat 8 **2** 廿九	木3 Wood 4 Not Yet Accomplished 火水未濟 甲申 Wood Monkey 9 **3** 六月初一	金9 Metal 3 Retreat 天山遯 乙酉 Wood Rooster 4 **4** 初二
水6 Water 2 Mountain 艮爲山 丙戌 Fire Dog 1 **5** 初三	木8 Wood 1 Delight 雷地豫 丁亥 Fire Pig 8 **6** 初四	火7 Fire 9 Beginning 水雷屯 戊子 Earth Rat 4 **7** 初五	金9 Metal 8 Without Wrongdoing 天雷無妄 己丑 Earth Ox 2 **8** 初六	木3 Wood 7 Fire 離爲火 庚寅 Metal Tiger 1 **9** 初七	火2 Fire 6 Sincerity 風澤中孚 辛卯 Metal Rabbit 3 **10** 初八	水6 Water 5 Big Livestock 山天大畜 壬辰 Water Dragon 4 **11** 初九
金4 Metal 4 Eliminating 澤天夬 癸巳 Water Snake 6 **12** 初十	金9 Metal 3 Heaven 乾爲天 甲午 Wood Horse 1 **13** 十一	火7 Fire 2 Well 水風井 乙未 Wood Goat 6 **14** 十二	木8 Wood 1 Relief 雷水解 丙申 Fire Monkey 4 **15** 十三	金4 Metal 9 Influence 澤山咸 丁酉 Fire Rooster 9 **16** 十四	水1 Water 8 Humility 地山謙 戊戌 Earth Dog 6 **17** 十五	火2 Fire 7 Observation 風地觀 己亥 Earth Pig 2 **18** 十六
火2 Fire 6 Increasing 風雷益 庚子 Metal Rat 9 **19** 十七	水1 Water 5 Dimming Light 地火明夷 辛丑 Metal Ox 3 **20** 十八	金9 Metal 4 Fellowship 天火同人 壬寅 Water Tiger 7 **21** 十九	木8 Wood 3 Marrying Maiden 雷澤歸妹 癸卯 Water Rabbit 7 **22** 二十	木3 Wood 2 Opposition 火澤睽 甲辰 Wood Dragon 2 **23** 廿一	火7 Fire 1 Waiting 水天需 乙巳 Wood Snake 3 **24** 廿二	金4 Metal 9 Great Exceeding 澤風大過 丙午 Fire Horse 3 **25** 廿三
水6 Water 8 Poison 山風蠱 丁未 Fire Goat 7 **26** 廿四	火2 Fire 7 Dispersing 風水渙 戊申 Earth Monkey 6 **27** 廿五	木3 Wood 6 Travelling 火山旅 己酉 Earth Rooster 8 **28** 廿六	金9 Metal 5 Stagnation 天地否 庚戌 Metal Dog 9 **29** 廿七	火7 Fire 4 Alliance 水地比 辛亥 Metal Pig 7 **30** 廿八	木8 Wood 3 Thunder 震爲雷 壬子 Water Rat 1 **31** 廿九	

AUGUST 1970 甲申

Xuan Kong Element 玄空五行	火水未濟 Not Yet Accomplished	Period Luck 卦運	Monthly Star 月星
Wood 木3		9	8

SUNDAY	MONDAY	TUESDAY	WEDNESDAY	THURSDAY	FRIDAY	SATURDAY
火2 Fire 9 Wind 巽爲風 壬午 Water Horse 1 **30** 廿九	金4 Metal 8 Trap 澤水困 癸未 Water Goat 8 **31** 三十					水6 Water 2 Beauty 山火賁 癸丑 Water Ox 8 **1** 三十
火7 Fire 1 Accomplished 水火既濟 甲寅 Wood Tiger 9 **2** 七月初一	水1 Water 9 Arriving 地澤臨 乙卯 Wood Rabbit 4 **3** 初二	金4 Metal 8 Marsh 兑爲澤 丙辰 Fire Dragon 1 **4** 初三	火2 Fire 7 Small Livestock 風天小畜 丁巳 Fire Snake 8 **5** 初四	木3 Wood 6 The Cauldron 火風鼎 戊午 Earth Horse 4 **6** 初五	水1 Water 5 Rising 地風升 己未 Earth Goat 2 **7** 初六	火7 Fire 4 Water 坎爲水 庚申 Metal Monkey 1 **8** 初七
木8 Wood 3 Lesser Exceeding 雷山小過 辛酉 Metal Rooster 3 **9** 初八	金4 Metal 2 Gathering 澤地萃 壬戌 Water Dog 4 **10** 初九	水6 Water 1 Peel 山地剝 癸亥 Water Pig 6 **11** 初十	水1 Water 9 Earth 坤爲地 甲子 Wood Rat 1 **12** 十一	木3 Wood 8 Biting 火雷噬嗑 乙丑 Wood Ox 6 **13** 十二	火2 Fire 7 Family 風火家人 丙寅 Fire Tiger 4 **14** 十三	水6 Water 6 Decreasing 山澤損 丁卯 Fire Rabbit 9 **15** 十四
金9 Metal 5 Tread 天澤履 戊辰 Earth Dragon 6 **16** 十五	木8 Wood 4 Great Strength 雷天大壯 己巳 Earth Snake 2 **17** 十六	木8 Wood 3 Consistency 雷風恆 庚午 Metal Horse 9 **18** 十七	金9 Metal 2 Litigation 天水訟 辛未 Metal Goat 3 **19** 十八	水1 Water 1 Officer 地水師 壬申 Water Monkey 7 **20** 十九	火2 Fire 9 Gradual Progress 風山漸 癸酉 Water Rooster 7 **21** 二十	火7 Fire 8 Obstruction 水山蹇 甲戌 Wood Dog 2 **22** 廿一
木3 Wood 7 Advancement 火地晉 乙亥 Wood Pig 3 **23** 廿二	水6 Water 6 Nourish 山雷頤 丙子 Fire Rat 3 **24** 廿三	金4 Metal 5 Following 澤雷隨 丁丑 Fire Ox 7 **25** 廿四	木8 Wood 4 Abundance 雷火豐 戊寅 Earth Tiger 6 **26** 廿五	火7 Fire 3 Regulate 水澤節 己卯 Earth Rabbit 8 **27** 廿六	水1 Water 2 Unity 地天泰 庚辰 Metal Dragon 9 **28** 廿七	木3 Wood 1 Great Reward 火天大有 辛巳 Metal Snake 7 **29** 廿八

SEPTEMBER 1970 乙酉

Xuan Kong Element 玄空五行	天山遯 Retreat	Period Luck 卦運	Monthly Star 月星
Metal 金9		4	7

SUNDAY	MONDAY	TUESDAY	WEDNESDAY	THURSDAY	FRIDAY	SATURDAY
		木3 Wood 7 Not Yet Accomplished 甲申 Wood Monkey 火水未濟 1 八月初一 9	金9 Metal 6 Retreat 乙酉 Wood Rooster 天山遯 2 初二 4	水6 Water 5 Mountain 丙戌 Fire Dog 艮爲山 3 初三 1	木8 Wood 4 Delight 丁亥 Fire Pig 雷地豫 4 初四 8	火7 Fire 3 Beginning 戊子 Earth Rat 水雷屯 5 初五 4
金9 Metal 2 Without Wrongdoing 己丑 Earth Ox 天雷無妄 6 初六 2	木3 Wood 1 Fire 庚寅 Metal Tiger 離爲火 7 初七 1	火2 Fire 9 Sincerity 辛卯 Metal Rabbit 風澤中孚 8 初八 3	水6 Water 8 Big Livestock 壬辰 Water Dragon 山天大畜 9 初九 4	金4 Metal 7 Eliminating 癸巳 Water Snake 澤天夬 10 初十 6	金9 Metal 6 Heaven 甲午 Wood Horse 乾爲天 11 十一 1	火7 Fire 5 Well 乙未 Wood Goat 水風井 12 十二 6
木8 Wood 4 Relief 丙申 Fire Monkey 雷水解 13 十三 4	金4 Metal 3 Influence 丁酉 Fire Rooster 澤山咸 14 十四 9	水1 Water 2 Humility 戊戌 Earth Dog 地山謙 15 十五 6	火2 Fire 1 Observation 己亥 Earth Pig 風地觀 16 十六 2	火2 Fire 9 Increasing 庚子 Metal Rat 風雷益 17 十七 9	水1 Water 8 Dimming Light 辛丑 Metal Ox 地火明夷 18 十八 3	金9 Metal 7 Fellowship 壬寅 Water Tiger 天火同人 19 十九 7
木8 Wood 6 Marrying Maiden 癸卯 Water Rabbit 雷澤歸妹 20 二十 7	木3 Wood 5 Opposition 甲辰 Wood Dragon 火澤睽 21 廿一 2	火7 Fire 4 Waiting 乙巳 Wood Snake 水天需 22 廿二 3	金4 Metal 3 Great Exceeding 丙午 Fire Horse 澤風大過 23 廿三 3	水6 Water 2 Poison 丁未 Fire Goat 山風蠱 24 廿四 7	火2 Fire 1 Dispersing 戊申 Earth Monkey 風水渙 25 廿五 6	木3 Wood 9 Travelling 己酉 Earth Rooster 火山旅 26 廿六 8
金9 Metal 8 Stagnation 庚戌 Metal Dog 天地否 27 廿七 9	火7 Fire 7 Alliance 辛亥 Metal Pig 水地比 28 廿八 7	木8 Wood 6 Thunder 壬子 Water Rat 震爲雷 29 廿九 1	水6 Water 5 Beauty 癸丑 Water Ox 山火賁 30 九月初一 8			

OCTOBER 1970 丙戌

Xuan Kong Element 玄空五行	艮爲山 Mountain	Period Luck 卦運	Monthly Star 月星
Water 水6		1	6

SUNDAY	MONDAY	TUESDAY	WEDNESDAY	THURSDAY	FRIDAY	SATURDAY
				火7 Fire 4 Accomplished 甲寅 Wood Tiger 水火既濟 1 初二 9	水1 Water 3 Arriving 乙卯 Wood Rabbit 地澤臨 2 初三 4	金4 Metal 2 Marsh 丙辰 Fire Dragon 兌爲澤 3 初四 1
火2 Fire 1 Small Livestock 丁巳 Fire Snake 風天小畜 4 初五 8	木3 Wood 9 The Cauldron 戊午 Earth Horse 火風鼎 5 初六 4	水1 Water 8 Rising 己未 Earth Goat 地風升 6 初七 2	火7 Fire 7 Water 庚申 Metal Monkey 坎爲水 7 初八 1	木8 Wood 6 Lesser Exceeding 辛酉 Metal Rooster 雷山小過 8 初九 3	金4 Metal 5 Gathering 壬戌 Water Dog 澤地萃 9 初十 4	水6 Water 4 Peel 癸亥 Water Pig 山地剝 10 十一 6
水1 Water 3 Earth 甲子 Wood Rat 坤爲地 11 十二 1	木3 Wood 2 Biting 乙丑 Wood Ox 火雷噬嗑 12 十三 6	火2 Fire 1 Family 丙寅 Fire Tiger 風火家人 13 十四 4	水6 Water 9 Decreasing 丁卯 Fire Rabbit 山澤損 14 十五 9	金9 Metal 8 Tread 戊辰 Earth Dragon 天澤履 15 十六 6	木8 Wood 7 Great Strength 己巳 Earth Snake 雷天大壯 16 十七 2	木8 Wood 6 Consistency 庚午 Metal Horse 雷風恆 17 十八 9
金9 Metal 5 Litigation 辛未 Metal Goat 天水訟 18 十九 3	水1 Water 4 Officer 壬申 Water Monkey 地水師 19 二十 7	火2 Fire 3 Gradual Progress 癸酉 Water Rooster 風山漸 20 廿一 7	火7 Fire 2 Obstruction 甲戌 Wood Dog 水山蹇 21 廿二 2	木3 Wood 1 Advancement 乙亥 Wood Pig 火地晉 22 廿三 3	水6 Water 9 Nourish 丙子 Fire Rat 山雷頤 23 廿四 3	金4 Metal 8 Following 丁丑 Fire Ox 澤雷隨 24 廿五 7
木8 Wood 7 Abundance 戊寅 Earth Tiger 雷火豐 25 廿六 6	火7 Fire 6 Regulate 己卯 Earth Rabbit 水澤節 26 廿七 8	水1 Water 5 Unity 庚辰 Metal Dragon 地天泰 27 廿八 9	木3 Wood 4 Great Reward 辛巳 Metal Snake 火天大有 28 廿九 7	火2 Fire 3 Wind 壬午 Water Horse 巽爲風 29 三十 1	金4 Metal 2 Trap 癸未 Water Goat 澤水困 30 十月初一 8	木3 Wood 1 Not Yet Accomplished 甲申 Wood Monkey 火水未濟 31 初二 9

NOVEMBER 1970 丁亥

Xuan Kong Element 玄空五行	雷地豫 Delight	Period Luck 卦運	Monthly Star 月星
Wood 木8		8	5

SUNDAY	MONDAY	TUESDAY	WEDNESDAY	THURSDAY	FRIDAY	SATURDAY
金9 Metal 9 Retreat 乙酉 Wood Rooster 天山遯 1 初三 4	水6 Water 8 Mountain 丙戌 Fire Dog 艮為山 2 初四 1	木8 Wood 7 Delight 丁亥 Fire Pig 雷地豫 3 初五 8	火7 Fire 6 Beginning 戊子 Earth Rat 水雷屯 4 初六 4	金9 Metal 5 Without Wrongdoing 己丑 Earth Ox 天雷無妄 5 初七 2	木3 Wood 4 Fire 庚寅 Metal Tiger 離為火 6 初八 1	火2 Fire 3 Sincerity 辛卯 Metal Rabbit 風澤中孚 7 初九 3
水6 Water 2 Big Livestock 壬辰 Water Dragon 山天大畜 8 初十 4	金4 Metal 1 Eliminating 癸巳 Water Snake 澤天夬 9 十一 6	金9 Metal 9 Heaven 甲午 Wood Horse 乾為天 10 十二 1	火7 Fire 8 Well 乙未 Wood Goat 水風井 11 十三 6	木8 Wood 7 Relief 丙申 Fire Monkey 雷水解 12 十四 4	金4 Metal 6 Influence 丁酉 Fire Rooster 澤山咸 13 十五 9	水1 Water 5 Humility 戊戌 Earth Dog 地山謙 14 十六 6
火2 Fire 4 Observation 己亥 Earth Pig 風地觀 15 十七 2	火2 Fire 3 Increasing 庚子 Metal Rat 風雷益 16 十八 9	水1 Water 2 Dimming Light 辛丑 Metal Ox 地火明夷 17 十九 3	金9 Metal 1 Fellowship 壬寅 Water Tiger 天火同人 18 二十 7	木8 Wood 9 Marrying Maiden 癸卯 Water Rabbit 雷澤歸妹 19 廿一 7	木3 Wood 8 Opposition 甲辰 Wood Dragon 火澤睽 20 廿二 2	火7 Fire 7 Waiting 乙巳 Wood Snake 水天需 21 廿三 3
金4 Metal 6 Great Exceeding 丙午 Fire Horse 澤風大過 22 廿四 3	水6 Water 5 Poison 丁未 Fire Goat 山風蠱 23 廿五 7	火2 Fire 4 Dispersing 戊申 Earth Monkey 風水渙 24 廿六 6	木3 Wood 3 Travelling 己酉 Earth Rooster 火山旅 25 廿七 8	金9 Metal 2 Stagnation 庚戌 Metal Dog 天地否 26 廿八 9	火7 Fire 1 Alliance 辛亥 Metal Pig 水地比 27 廿九 7	木8 Wood 9 Thunder 壬子 Water Rat 震為雷 28 三十 1
水6 Water 8 Beauty 癸丑 Water Ox 山火賁 29 十一月初一 8	火7 Fire 7 Accomplished 甲寅 Wood Tiger 水火既濟 30 初二 9					

DECEMBER 1970 戊子

Xuan Kong Element 玄空五行	水雷屯 Beginning	Period Luck 卦運	Monthly Star 月星
Fire 火7		4	4

SUNDAY	MONDAY	TUESDAY	WEDNESDAY	THURSDAY	FRIDAY	SATURDAY
		水1 Water 6 Arriving 乙卯 Wood Rabbit 地澤臨 1 初三 4	金4 Metal 5 Marsh 丙辰 Fire Dragon 兌為澤 2 初四 1	火2 Fire 4 Small Livestock 丁巳 Fire Snake 風天小畜 3 初五 8	木3 Wood 3 The Cauldron 戊午 Earth Horse 火風鼎 4 初六 4	水1 Water 2 Rising 己未 Earth Goat 地風升 5 初七 2
火7 Fire 1 Water 庚申 Metal Monkey 坎為水 6 初八 1	木8 Wood 9 Lesser Exceeding 辛酉 Metal Rooster 雷山小過 7 初九 3	金4 Metal 8 Gathering 壬戌 Water Dog 澤地萃 8 初十 4	水6 Water 7 Peel 癸亥 Water Pig 山地剝 9 十一 6	水1 Water 6 Earth 甲子 Wood Rat 坤為地 10 十二 1	木3 Wood 5 Biting 乙丑 Wood Ox 火雷噬嗑 11 十三 6	火2 Fire 4 Family 丙寅 Fire Tiger 風火家人 12 十四 4
水6 Water 3 Decreasing 丁卯 Fire Rabbit 山澤損 13 十五 9	金9 Metal 2 Tread 戊辰 Earth Dragon 天澤履 14 十六 6	木8 Wood 1 Great Strength 己巳 Earth Snake 雷天大壯 15 十七 2	木8 Wood 9 Consistency 庚午 Metal Horse 雷風恆 16 十八 9	金9 Metal 8 Litigation 辛未 Metal Goat 天水訟 17 十九 3	水1 Water 7 Officer 壬申 Water Monkey 地水師 18 二十 7	火2 Fire 6 Gradual Progress 癸酉 Water Rooster 風山漸 19 廿一 7
火7 Fire 5 Obstruction 甲戌 Wood Dog 水山蹇 20 廿二 2	木3 Wood 4 Advancement 乙亥 Wood Pig 火地晉 21 廿三 3	水6 Water 3/7 Nourish 丙子 Fire Rat 山雷頤 22 廿四 3	金4 Metal 8 Following 丁丑 Fire Ox 澤雷隨 23 廿五 7	木8 Wood 9 Abundance 戊寅 Earth Tiger 雷火豐 24 廿六 6	火7 Fire 1 Regulate 己卯 Earth Rabbit 水澤節 25 廿七 8	水1 Water 2 Unity 庚辰 Metal Dragon 地天泰 26 廿八 9
木3 Wood 3 Great Reward 辛巳 Metal Snake 火天大有 27 廿九 7	火2 Fire 4 Wind 壬午 Water Horse 巽為風 28 十二月初一 1	金4 Metal 5 Trap 癸未 Water Goat 澤水困 29 初二 8	木3 Wood 6 Not Yet Accomplished 甲申 Wood Monkey 火水未濟 30 初三 9	金9 Metal 7 Retreat 乙酉 Wood Rooster 天山遯 31 初四 4		

1971 辛亥

(*Xin Hai*) Metal Pig

1971 辛亥 *(Xin Hai)* Metal Pig

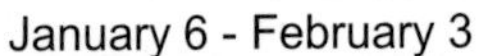

January 6 - February 3

February 4 - March 5

March 6 - April 4

April 5 - May 5

May 6 - June 5

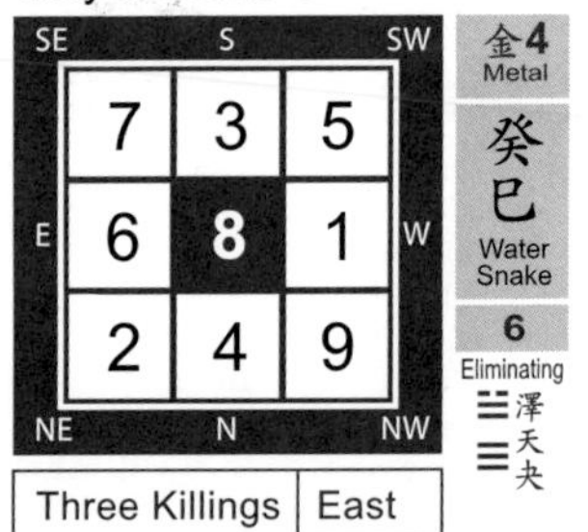

June 6 - July 7

July 8 - August 7

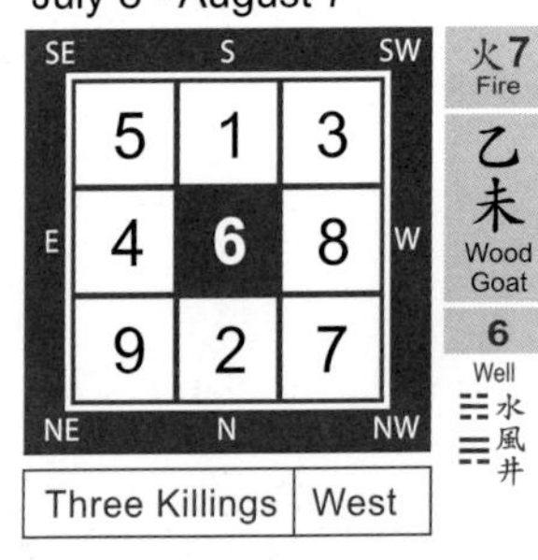

August 8 - September 7

September 8 - October 8

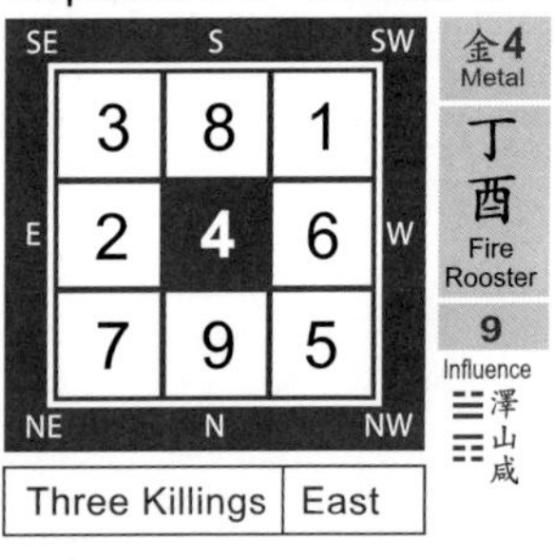

October 9 - November 7

November 8 - December 7

December 8 - January 5

JANUARY 1971 己丑

Xuan Kong Element 玄空五行	天雷無妄 Without Wrongdoing	Period Luck 卦運	Monthly Star 月星
Metal 金9		2	3

SUNDAY	MONDAY	TUESDAY	WEDNESDAY	THURSDAY	FRIDAY	SATURDAY
金4 Metal Marsh 2 兑爲澤 丙辰 Fire Dragon 31 初五 1					水6 Water Mountain 8 艮爲山 丙戌 Fire Dog 1 初五 1	木8 Wood Delight 9 雷地豫 丁亥 Fire Pig 2 初六 8
火7 Fire Beginning 1 水雷屯 戊子 Earth Rat 3 初七 4	金9 Metal Without Wrongdoing 2 天雷無妄 己丑 Earth Ox 4 初八 2	木3 Wood Fire 3 離爲火 庚寅 Metal Tiger 5 初九 1	火2 Fire Sincerity 4 風澤中孚 辛卯 Metal Rabbit 6 初十 3	水6 Water Big Livestock 5 山天大畜 壬辰 Water Dragon 7 十一 4	金4 Metal Eliminating 6 澤天夬 癸巳 Water Snake 8 十二 6	金9 Metal Heaven 7 乾爲天 甲午 Wood Horse 9 十三 1
火7 Fire Well 8 水風井 乙未 Wood Goat 10 十四 6	木8 Wood Relief 9 雷水解 丙申 Fire Monkey 11 十五 4	金4 Metal Influence 1 澤山咸 丁酉 Fire Rooster 12 十六 9	水1 Water Humility 2 地山謙 戊戌 Earth Dog 13 十七 6	火2 Fire Observation 3 風地觀 己亥 Earth Pig 14 十八 2	火2 Fire Increasing 4 風雷益 庚子 Metal Rat 15 十九 9	水1 Water Dimming Light 5 地火明夷 辛丑 Metal Ox 16 二十 3
金9 Metal Fellowship 6 天火同人 壬寅 Water Tiger 17 廿一 7	木8 Wood Marrying Maiden 7 雷澤歸妹 癸卯 Water Rabbit 18 廿二 7	木3 Wood Opposition 8 火澤睽 甲辰 Wood Dragon 19 廿三 2	火7 Fire Waiting 9 水天需 乙巳 Wood Snake 20 廿四 3	金4 Metal Great Exceeding 1 澤風大過 丙午 Fire Horse 21 廿五 3	水6 Water Poison 2 山風蠱 丁未 Fire Goat 22 廿六 7	火2 Fire Dispersing 3 風水渙 戊申 Earth Monkey 23 廿七 6
木3 Wood Travelling 4 火山旅 己酉 Earth Rooster 24 廿八 8	金9 Metal Stagnation 5 天地否 庚戌 Metal Dog 25 廿九 9	火7 Fire Alliance 6 水地比 辛亥 Metal Pig 26 三十 7	木8 Wood Thunder 7 震爲雷 壬子 Water Rat 27 正月初一 1	水6 Water Beauty 8 山火賁 癸丑 Water Ox 28 初二 8	火7 Fire Accomplished 9 水火既濟 甲寅 Wood Tiger 29 初三 9	水1 Water Arriving 1 地澤臨 乙卯 Wood Rabbit 30 初四 4

FEBRUARY 1971 庚寅

Xuan Kong Element 玄空五行	離爲火 Fire	Period Luck 卦運	Monthly Star 月星
Wood 木3		1	2

SUNDAY	MONDAY	TUESDAY	WEDNESDAY	THURSDAY	FRIDAY	SATURDAY
	火2 Fire Small Livestock 3 風天小畜 丁巳 Fire Snake 1 初六 8	木3 Wood The Cauldron 4 火風鼎 戊午 Earth Horse 2 初七 4	水1 Water Rising 5 地風升 己未 Earth Goat 3 初八 2	火7 Fire Water 6 坎爲水 庚申 Metal Monkey 4 初九 1	木8 Wood Lesser Exceeding 7 雷山小過 辛酉 Metal Rooster 5 初十 3	金4 Metal Gathering 8 澤地萃 壬戌 Water Dog 6 十一 4
水6 Water Peel 9 山地剝 癸亥 Water Pig 7 十二 6	水1 Water Earth 1 坤爲地 甲子 Wood Rat 8 十三 1	木3 Wood Biting 2 火雷噬嗑 乙丑 Wood Ox 9 十四 6	火2 Fire Family 3 風火家人 丙寅 Fire Tiger 10 十五 4	水6 Water Decreasing 4 山澤損 丁卯 Fire Rabbit 11 十六 9	金9 Metal Tread 5 天澤履 戊辰 Earth Dragon 12 十七 6	木8 Wood Great Strength 6 雷天大壯 己巳 Earth Snake 13 十八 2
木8 Wood Consistency 7 雷風恆 庚午 Metal Horse 14 十九 9	金9 Metal Litigation 8 天水訟 辛未 Metal Goat 15 二十 3	水1 Water Officer 9 地水師 壬申 Water Monkey 16 廿一 7	火2 Fire Gradual Progress 1 風山漸 癸酉 Water Rooster 17 廿二 7	火7 Fire Obstruction 2 水山蹇 甲戌 Wood Dog 18 廿三 2	木3 Wood Advancement 3 火地晉 乙亥 Wood Pig 19 廿四 3	水6 Water Nourish 4 山雷頤 丙子 Fire Rat 20 廿五 3
金4 Metal Following 5 澤雷隨 丁丑 Fire Ox 21 廿六 7	木8 Wood Abundance 6 雷火豐 戊寅 Earth Tiger 22 廿七 6	火7 Fire Regulate 7 水澤節 己卯 Earth Rabbit 23 廿八 8	水1 Water Unity 8 地天泰 庚辰 Metal Dragon 24 廿九 9	木3 Wood Great Reward 9 火天大有 辛巳 Metal Snake 25 二月初一 7	火2 Fire Wind 1 巽爲風 壬午 Water Horse 26 初二 1	金4 Metal Trap 2 澤水困 癸未 Water Goat 27 初三 8
木3 Wood Not Yet Accomplished 3 火水未濟 甲申 Wood Monkey 28 初四 9						

MARCH 1971 辛卯

Xuan Kong Element 玄空五行	風澤中孚 Sincerity	Period Luck 卦運	Monthly Star 月星
Fire 火2		3	1

SUNDAY	MONDAY	TUESDAY	WEDNESDAY	THURSDAY	FRIDAY	SATURDAY
	1 初五 金9 Metal Retreat 天山遯 [4] 乙酉 Wood Rooster 4	**2** 初六 水6 Water Mountain 艮爲山 [5] 丙戌 Fire Dog 1	**3** 初七 木8 Wood Delight 雷地豫 [6] 丁亥 Fire Pig 8	**4** 初八 火7 Fire Beginning 水雷屯 [7] 戊子 Earth Rat 4	**5** 初九 金9 Metal Without Wrongdoing 天雷無妄 [8] 己丑 Earth Ox 2	**6** 初十 木3 Wood Fire 離爲火 [9] 庚寅 Metal Tiger 1
7 十一 火2 Fire Sincerity 風澤中孚 [1] 辛卯 Metal Rabbit 3	**8** 十二 水6 Water Big Livestock 山天大畜 [2] 壬辰 Water Dragon 4	**9** 十三 金4 Metal Eliminating 澤天夬 [3] 癸巳 Water Snake 6	**10** 十四 金9 Metal Heaven 乾爲天 [4] 甲午 Wood Horse 1	**11** 十五 火7 Fire Well 水風井 [5] 乙未 Wood Goat 6	**12** 十六 木8 Wood Relief 雷水解 [6] 丙申 Fire Monkey 4	**13** 十七 金4 Metal Influence 澤山咸 [7] 丁酉 Fire Rooster 9
14 十八 水1 Water Humility 地山謙 [8] 戊戌 Earth Dog 6	**15** 十九 火2 Fire Observation 風地觀 [9] 己亥 Earth Pig 2	**16** 二十 火2 Fire Increasing 風雷益 [1] 庚子 Metal Rat 9	**17** 廿一 水1 Water Dimming Light 地火明夷 [2] 辛丑 Metal Ox 3	**18** 廿二 金9 Metal Fellowship 天火同人 [3] 壬寅 Water Tiger 7	**19** 廿三 木8 Wood Marrying Maiden 雷澤歸妹 [4] 癸卯 Water Rabbit 7	**20** 廿四 木3 Wood Opposition 火澤睽 [5] 甲辰 Wood Dragon 2
21 廿五 火7 Fire Waiting 水天需 [6] 乙巳 Wood Snake 3	**22** 廿六 金4 Metal Great Exceeding 澤風大過 [7] 丙午 Fire Horse 3	**23** 廿七 水6 Water Poison 山風蠱 [8] 丁未 Fire Goat 7	**24** 廿八 火2 Fire Dispersing 風水渙 [9] 戊申 Earth Monkey 6	**25** 廿九 木3 Wood Travelling 火山旅 [1] 己酉 Earth Rooster 8	**26** 三十 金9 Metal Stagnation 天地否 [2] 庚戌 Metal Dog 9	**27** 三月初一 火7 Fire Alliance 水地比 [3] 辛亥 Metal Pig 7
28 初二 木8 Wood Thunder 震爲雷 [4] 壬子 Water Rat 1	**29** 初三 水6 Water Beauty 山火賁 [5] 癸丑 Water Ox 8	**30** 初四 火7 Fire Accomplished 水火既濟 [6] 甲寅 Wood Tiger 9	**31** 初五 水1 Water Arriving 地澤臨 [7] 乙卯 Wood Rabbit 4			

APRIL 1971 壬辰

Xuan Kong Element 玄空五行	山天大畜 Big Livestock	Period Luck 卦運	Monthly Star 月星
Water 水6		4	9

SUNDAY	MONDAY	TUESDAY	WEDNESDAY	THURSDAY	FRIDAY	SATURDAY
				1 初六 金4 Metal Marsh 兌爲澤 [8] 丙辰 Fire Dragon 1	**2** 初七 火2 Fire Small Livestock 風天小畜 [9] 丁巳 Fire Snake 8	**3** 初八 木3 Wood The Cauldron 火風鼎 [1] 戊午 Earth Horse 4
4 初九 水1 Water Rising 地風升 [2] 己未 Earth Goat 2	**5** 初十 火7 Fire Water 坎爲水 [3] 庚申 Metal Monkey 1	**6** 十一 木8 Wood Lesser Exceeding 雷山小過 [4] 辛酉 Metal Rooster 3	**7** 十二 金4 Metal Gathering 澤地萃 [5] 壬戌 Water Dog 4	**8** 十三 水6 Water Peel 山地剝 [6] 癸亥 Water Pig 6	**9** 十四 水1 Water Earth 坤爲地 [7] 甲子 Wood Rat 1	**10** 十五 木3 Wood Biting 火雷噬嗑 [8] 乙丑 Wood Ox 6
11 十六 火2 Fire Family 風火家人 [9] 丙寅 Fire Tiger 4	**12** 十七 水6 Water Decreasing 山澤損 [1] 丁卯 Fire Rabbit 9	**13** 十八 金9 Metal Tread 天澤履 [2] 戊辰 Earth Dragon 6	**14** 十九 木8 Wood Great Strength 雷天大壯 [3] 己巳 Earth Snake 2	**15** 二十 木8 Wood Consistency 雷風恆 [4] 庚午 Metal Horse 9	**16** 廿一 金9 Metal Litigation 天水訟 [5] 辛未 Metal Goat 3	**17** 廿二 水1 Water Officer 地水師 [6] 壬申 Water Monkey 7
18 廿三 火2 Fire Gradual Progress 風山漸 [7] 癸酉 Water Rooster 7	**19** 廿四 火7 Fire Obstruction 水山蹇 [8] 甲戌 Wood Dog 2	**20** 廿五 木3 Wood Advancement 火地晉 [9] 乙亥 Wood Pig 3	**21** 廿六 水6 Water Nourish 山雷頤 [1] 丙子 Fire Rat 3	**22** 廿七 金4 Metal Following 澤雷隨 [2] 丁丑 Fire Ox 7	**23** 廿八 木8 Wood Abundance 雷火豐 [3] 戊寅 Earth Tiger 6	**24** 廿九 火7 Fire Regulate 水澤節 [4] 己卯 Earth Rabbit 8
25 四月初一 水1 Water Unity 地天泰 [5] 庚辰 Metal Dragon 9	**26** 初二 木3 Wood Great Reward 火天大有 [6] 辛巳 Metal Snake 7	**27** 初三 火2 Fire Wind 巽爲風 [7] 壬午 Water Horse 1	**28** 初四 金4 Metal Trap 澤水困 [8] 癸未 Water Goat 8	**29** 初五 木3 Wood Not Yet Accomplished 火水未濟 [9] 甲申 Wood Monkey 9	**30** 初六 金9 Metal Retreat 天山遯 [1] 乙酉 Wood Rooster 4	

MAY 1971 癸巳

Xuan Kong Element 玄空五行	澤天夬 Eliminating	Period Luck 卦運	Monthly Star 月星
Metal 金4		6	8

SUNDAY	MONDAY	TUESDAY	WEDNESDAY	THURSDAY	FRIDAY	SATURDAY
水1 Water 4 Arriving 地澤臨 乙卯 Wood Rabbit 30 初七 4	金4 Metal 5 Marsh 兌爲澤 丙辰 Fire Dragon 31 初八 1					水6 Water 2 Mountain 艮爲山 丙戌 Fire Dog 1 初七 1
木8 Wood 3 Delight 雷地豫 丁亥 Fire Pig 2 初八 8	火7 Fire 4 Beginning 水雷屯 戊子 Earth Rat 3 初九 4	金9 Metal 5 Without Wrongdoing 天雷無妄 己丑 Earth Ox 4 初十 2	木3 Wood 6 Fire 離爲火 庚寅 Metal Tiger 5 十一 1	火2 Fire 7 Sincerity 風澤中孚 辛卯 Metal Rabbit 6 十二 3	水6 Water 8 Big Livestock 山天大畜 壬辰 Water Dragon 7 十三 4	金4 Metal 9 Eliminating 澤天夬 癸巳 Water Snake 8 十四 6
金9 Metal 1 Heaven 乾爲天 甲午 Wood Horse 9 十五 1	火7 Fire 2 Well 水風井 乙未 Wood Goat 10 十六 6	木8 Wood 3 Relief 雷水解 丙申 Fire Monkey 11 十七 4	金4 Metal 4 Influence 澤山咸 丁酉 Fire Rooster 12 十八 9	水1 Water 5 Humility 地山謙 戊戌 Earth Dog 13 十九 6	火2 Fire 6 Observation 風地觀 己亥 Earth Pig 14 二十 2	火2 Fire 7 Increasing 風雷益 庚子 Metal Rat 15 廿一 9
水1 Water 8 Dimming Light 地火明夷 辛丑 Metal Ox 16 廿二 3	金9 Metal 9 Fellowship 天火同人 壬寅 Water Tiger 17 廿三 7	木8 Wood 1 Marrying Maiden 雷澤歸妹 癸卯 Water Rabbit 18 廿四 7	木3 Wood 2 Opposition 火澤睽 甲辰 Wood Dragon 19 廿五 2	火7 Fire 3 Waiting 水天需 乙巳 Wood Snake 20 廿六 3	金4 Metal 4 Great Exceeding 澤風大過 丙午 Fire Horse 21 廿七 3	水6 Water 5 Poison 山風蠱 丁未 Fire Goat 22 廿八 7
火2 Fire 6 Dispersing 風水渙 戊申 Earth Monkey 23 廿九 6	木3 Wood 7 Travelling 火山旅 己酉 Earth Rooster 24 五月初一 8	金9 Metal 8 Stagnation 天地否 庚戌 Metal Dog 25 初二 9	火7 Fire 9 Alliance 水地比 辛亥 Metal Pig 26 初三 7	木8 Wood 1 Thunder 震爲雷 壬子 Water Rat 27 初四 1	水6 Water 2 Beauty 山火賁 癸丑 Water Ox 28 初五 8	火7 Fire 3 Accomplished 水火既濟 甲寅 Wood Tiger 29 初六 9

JUNE 1971 甲午

Xuan Kong Element 玄空五行	乾爲天 Heaven	Period Luck 卦運	Monthly Star 月星
Metal 金9		1	7

SUNDAY	MONDAY	TUESDAY	WEDNESDAY	THURSDAY	FRIDAY	SATURDAY
		火2 Fire 6 Small Livestock 風天小畜 丁巳 Fire Snake 1 初九 8	木3 Wood 7 The Cauldron 火風鼎 戊午 Earth Horse 2 初十 4	水1 Water 8 Rising 地風升 己未 Earth Goat 3 十一 2	火7 Fire 9 Water 坎爲水 庚申 Metal Monkey 4 十二 1	木8 Wood 1 Lesser Exceeding 雷山小過 辛酉 Metal Rooster 5 十三 3
金4 Metal 2 Gathering 澤地萃 壬戌 Water Dog 6 十四 4	水6 Water 3 Peel 山地剝 癸亥 Water Pig 7 十五 6	水1 Water 4 Earth 坤爲地 甲子 Wood Rat 8 十六 1	木3 Wood 5 Biting 火雷噬嗑 乙丑 Wood Ox 9 十七 6	火2 Fire 6 Family 風火家人 丙寅 Fire Tiger 10 十八 4	水6 Water 7 Decreasing 山澤損 丁卯 Fire Rabbit 11 十九 9	金9 Metal 8 Tread 天澤履 戊辰 Earth Dragon 12 二十 6
木8 Wood 9 Great Strength 雷天大壯 己巳 Earth Snake 13 廿一 2	木8 Wood 1 Consistency 雷風恆 庚午 Metal Horse 14 廿二 9	金9 Metal 2 Litigation 天水訟 辛未 Metal Goat 15 廿三 3	水1 Water 3 Officer 地水師 壬申 Water Monkey 16 廿四 7	火2 Fire 4 Gradual Progress 風山漸 癸酉 Water Rooster 17 廿五 7	火7 Fire 5 Obstruction 水山蹇 甲戌 Wood Dog 18 廿六 2	木3 Wood 6 Advancement 火地晉 乙亥 Wood Pig 19 廿七 3
水6 Water 7 Nourish 山雷頤 丙子 Fire Rat 20 廿八 3	金4 Metal 8 Following 澤雷隨 丁丑 Fire Ox 21 廿九 7	木8 Wood 9/1 Abundance 雷火豐 戊寅 Earth Tiger 22 三十 6	火7 Fire 9 Regulate 水澤節 己卯 Earth Rabbit 23 閏五月初一 8	水1 Water 8 Unity 地天泰 庚辰 Metal Dragon 24 初二 9	木3 Wood 7 Great Reward 火天大有 辛巳 Metal Snake 25 初三 7	火2 Fire 6 Wind 巽爲風 壬午 Water Horse 26 初四 1
金4 Metal 5 Trap 澤水困 癸未 Water Goat 27 初五 8	木3 Wood 4 Not Yet Accomplished 火水未濟 甲申 Wood Monkey 28 初六 9	金9 Metal 3 Retreat 天山遯 乙酉 Wood Rooster 29 初七 4	水6 Water 2 Mountain 艮爲山 丙戌 Fire Dog 30 初八 1			

JULY 1971 乙未

Xuan Kong Element 玄空五行	水風井 Well	Period Luck 卦運	Monthly Star 月星
Fire 火7		6	6

SUNDAY	MONDAY	TUESDAY	WEDNESDAY	THURSDAY	FRIDAY	SATURDAY
				木8 Wood 1 Delight 丁亥 Fire Pig 雷地豫 1 初九 8	火7 Fire 9 Beginning 戊子 Earth Rat 水雷屯 2 初十 4	金9 Metal 8 Without Wrongdoing 己丑 Earth Ox 天雷無妄 3 十一 2
木3 Wood 7 Fire 庚寅 Metal Tiger 離爲火 4 十二 1	火2 Fire 6 Sincerity 辛卯 Metal Rabbit 風澤中孚 5 十三 3	水6 Water 5 Big Livestock 壬辰 Water Dragon 山天大畜 6 十四 4	金4 Metal 4 Eliminating 癸巳 Water Snake 澤天夬 7 十五 6	金9 Metal 3 Heaven 甲午 Wood Horse 乾爲天 8 十六 1	火7 Fire 2 Well 乙未 Wood Goat 水風井 9 十七 6	木8 Wood 1 Relief 丙申 Fire Monkey 雷水解 10 十八 4
金4 Metal 9 Influence 丁酉 Fire Rooster 澤山咸 11 十九 9	水1 Water 8 Humility 戊戌 Earth Dog 地山謙 12 二十 6	火2 Fire 7 Observation 己亥 Earth Pig 風地觀 13 廿一 2	火2 Fire 6 Increasing 庚子 Metal Rat 風雷益 14 廿二 9	水1 Water 5 Dimming Light 辛丑 Metal Ox 地火明夷 15 廿三 3	金9 Metal 4 Fellowship 壬寅 Water Tiger 天火同人 16 廿四 7	木8 Wood 3 Marrying Maiden 癸卯 Water Rabbit 雷澤歸妹 17 廿五 7
木3 Wood 2 Opposition 甲辰 Wood Dragon 火澤睽 18 廿六 2	火7 Fire 1 Waiting 乙巳 Wood Snake 水天需 19 廿七 3	金4 Metal 9 Great Exceeding 丙午 Fire Horse 澤風大過 20 廿八 3	水6 Water 8 Poison 丁未 Fire Goat 山風蠱 21 廿九 7	火2 Fire 7 Dispersing 戊申 Earth Monkey 風水渙 22 六月初一 6	木3 Wood 6 Travelling 己酉 Earth Rooster 火山旅 23 初二 8	金9 Metal 5 Stagnation 庚戌 Metal Dog 天地否 24 初三 9
火7 Fire 4 Alliance 辛亥 Metal Pig 水地比 25 初四 7	木8 Wood 3 Thunder 壬子 Water Rat 震爲雷 26 初五 1	水6 Water 2 Beauty 癸丑 Water Ox 山火賁 27 初六 8	火7 Fire 1 Accomplished 甲寅 Wood Tiger 水火既濟 28 初七 9	水1 Water 9 Arriving 乙卯 Wood Rabbit 地澤臨 29 初八 4	金4 Metal 8 Marsh 丙辰 Fire Dragon 兑爲澤 30 初九 1	火2 Fire 7 Small Livestock 丁巳 Fire Snake 風天小畜 31 初十 8

AUGUST 1971 丙申

Xuan Kong Element 玄空五行	雷水解 Relief	Period Luck 卦運	Monthly Star 月星
Wood 木8		4	5

SUNDAY	MONDAY	TUESDAY	WEDNESDAY	THURSDAY	FRIDAY	SATURDAY
木3 Wood 6 The Cauldron 戊午 Earth Horse 火風鼎 1 十一 4	水1 Water 5 Rising 己未 Earth Goat 地風升 2 十二 2	火7 Fire 4 Water 庚申 Metal Monkey 坎爲水 3 十三 1	木8 Wood 3 Lesser Exceeding 辛酉 Metal Rooster 雷山小過 4 十四 3	金4 Metal 2 Gathering 壬戌 Water Dog 澤地萃 5 十五 4	水6 Water 1 Peel 癸亥 Water Pig 山地剝 6 十六 6	水1 Water 9 Earth 甲子 Wood Rat 坤爲地 7 十七 1
木3 Wood 8 Biting 乙丑 Wood Ox 火雷噬嗑 8 十八 6	火2 Fire 7 Family 丙寅 Fire Tiger 風火家人 9 十九 4	水6 Water 6 Decreasing 丁卯 Fire Rabbit 山澤損 10 二十 9	金9 Metal 5 Tread 戊辰 Earth Dragon 天澤履 11 廿一 6	木8 Wood 4 Great Strength 己巳 Earth Snake 雷天大壯 12 廿二 2	木8 Wood 3 Consistency 庚午 Metal Horse 雷風恆 13 廿三 9	金9 Metal 2 Litigation 辛未 Metal Goat 天水訟 14 廿四 3
水1 Water 1 Officer 壬申 Water Monkey 地水師 15 廿五 7	火2 Fire 9 Gradual Progress 癸酉 Water Rooster 風山漸 16 廿六 7	火7 Fire 8 Obstruction 甲戌 Wood Dog 水山蹇 17 廿七 2	木3 Wood 7 Advancement 乙亥 Wood Pig 火地晉 18 廿八 3	水6 Water 6 Nourish 丙子 Fire Rat 山雷頤 19 廿九 3	金4 Metal 5 Following 丁丑 Fire Ox 澤雷隨 20 三十 7	木8 Wood 4 Abundance 戊寅 Earth Tiger 雷火豐 21 七月初一 6
火7 Fire 3 Regulate 己卯 Earth Rabbit 水澤節 22 初二 8	水1 Water 2 Unity 庚辰 Metal Dragon 地天泰 23 初三 9	木3 Wood 1 Great Reward 辛巳 Metal Snake 火天大有 24 初四 7	火2 Fire 9 Wind 壬午 Water Horse 巽爲風 25 初五 1	金4 Metal 8 Trap 癸未 Water Goat 澤水困 26 初六 8	木3 Wood 7 Not Yet Accomplished 甲申 Wood Monkey 火水未濟 27 初七 9	金9 Metal 6 Retreat 乙酉 Wood Rooster 天山遯 28 初八 4
水6 Water 5 Mountain 丙戌 Fire Dog 艮爲山 29 初九 1	木8 Wood 4 Delight 丁亥 Fire Pig 雷地豫 30 初十 8	火7 Fire 3 Beginning 戊子 Earth Rat 水雷屯 31 十一 4				

SEPTEMBER 1971 丁酉

Xuan Kong Element 玄空五行	澤山咸 Influence	Period Luck 卦運	Monthly Star 月星
Metal 金4		9	4

SUNDAY	MONDAY	TUESDAY	WEDNESDAY	THURSDAY	FRIDAY	SATURDAY
			金9 Metal Without Wrongdoing 天雷無妄 2 己丑 Earth Ox 1 十二 2	木3 Wood Fire 離爲火 1 庚寅 Metal Tiger 2 十三 1	火2 Fire Sincerity 風澤中孚 9 辛卯 Metal Rabbit 3 十四 3	水6 Water Big Livestock 山天大畜 8 壬辰 Water Dragon 4 十五 4
金4 Metal Eliminating 澤天夬 7 癸巳 Water Snake 5 十六 6	金9 Metal Heaven 乾爲天 6 甲午 Wood Horse 6 十七 1	火7 Fire Well 水風井 5 乙未 Wood Goat 7 十八 6	木8 Wood Relief 雷水解 4 丙申 Fire Monkey 8 十九 4	金4 Metal Influence 澤山咸 3 丁酉 Fire Rooster 9 二十 9	水1 Water Humility 地山謙 2 戊戌 Earth Dog 10 廿一 6	火2 Fire Observation 風地觀 1 己亥 Earth Pig 11 廿二 2
火2 Fire Increasing 風雷益 9 庚子 Metal Rat 12 廿三 9	水1 Water Dimming Light 地火明夷 8 辛丑 Metal Ox 13 廿四 3	金9 Metal Fellowship 天火同人 7 壬寅 Water Tiger 14 廿五 7	木8 Wood Marrying Maiden 雷澤歸妹 6 癸卯 Water Rabbit 15 廿六 7	木3 Wood Opposition 火澤睽 5 甲辰 Wood Dragon 16 廿七 2	火7 Fire Waiting 水天需 4 乙巳 Wood Snake 17 廿八 3	金4 Metal Great Exceeding 澤風大過 3 丙午 Fire Horse 18 廿九 3
水6 Water Poison 山風蠱 2 丁未 Fire Goat 19 八月初一 7	火2 Fire Dispersing 風水渙 1 戊申 Earth Monkey 20 初二 6	木3 Wood Travelling 火山旅 9 己酉 Earth Rooster 21 初三 8	金9 Metal Stagnation 天地否 8 庚戌 Metal Dog 22 初四 9	火7 Fire Alliance 水地比 7 辛亥 Metal Pig 23 初五 7	木8 Wood Thunder 震爲雷 6 壬子 Water Rat 24 初六 1	水6 Water Beauty 山火賁 5 癸丑 Water Ox 25 初七 8
火7 Fire Accomplished 水火既濟 4 甲寅 Wood Tiger 26 初八 9	水1 Water Arriving 地澤臨 3 乙卯 Wood Rabbit 27 初九 4	金4 Metal Marsh 兌爲澤 2 丙辰 Fire Dragon 28 初十 1	火2 Fire Small Livestock 風天小畜 1 丁巳 Fire Snake 29 十一 8	木3 Wood The Cauldron 火風鼎 9 戊午 Earth Horse 30 十二 4		

OCTOBER 1971 戊戌

Xuan Kong Element 玄空五行	地山謙 Humility	Period Luck 卦運	Monthly Star 月星
Water 水1		6	3

SUNDAY	MONDAY	TUESDAY	WEDNESDAY	THURSDAY	FRIDAY	SATURDAY
金9 Metal Without Wrongdoing 天雷無妄 5 己丑 Earth Ox 31 十三 2					水1 Water Rising 地風升 8 己未 Earth Goat 1 十三 2	火7 Fire Water 坎爲水 7 庚申 Metal Monkey 2 十四 1
木8 Wood Lesser Exceeding 雷山小過 6 辛酉 Metal Rooster 3 十五 3	金4 Metal Gathering 澤地萃 5 壬戌 Water Dog 4 十六 4	水6 Water Peel 山地剝 4 癸亥 Water Pig 5 十七 6	水1 Water Earth 坤爲地 3 甲子 Wood Rat 6 十八 1	木3 Wood Biting 火雷噬嗑 2 乙丑 Wood Ox 7 十九 6	火2 Fire Family 風火家人 1 丙寅 Fire Tiger 8 二十 4	水6 Water Decreasing 山澤損 9 丁卯 Fire Rabbit 9 廿一 9
金9 Metal Tread 天澤履 8 戊辰 Earth Dragon 10 廿二 6	木8 Wood Great Strength 雷天大壯 7 己巳 Earth Snake 11 廿三 2	木8 Wood Consistency 雷風恆 6 庚午 Metal Horse 12 廿四 9	金9 Metal Litigation 天水訟 5 辛未 Metal Goat 13 廿五 3	水1 Water Officer 地水師 4 壬申 Water Monkey 14 廿六 7	火2 Fire Gradual Progress 風山漸 3 癸酉 Water Rooster 15 廿七 7	火7 Fire Obstruction 水山蹇 2 甲戌 Wood Dog 16 廿八 2
木3 Wood Advancement 火地晉 1 乙亥 Wood Pig 17 廿九 3	水6 Water Nourish 山雷頤 9 丙子 Fire Rat 18 三十 3	金4 Metal Following 澤雷隨 8 丁丑 Fire Ox 19 九月初一 7	木8 Wood Abundance 雷火豐 7 戊寅 Earth Tiger 20 初二 6	火7 Fire Regulate 水澤節 6 己卯 Earth Rabbit 21 初三 8	水1 Water Unity 地天泰 5 庚辰 Metal Dragon 22 初四 9	木3 Wood Great Reward 火天大有 4 辛巳 Metal Snake 23 初五 7
火2 Fire Wind 巽爲風 3 壬午 Water Horse 24 初六 1	金4 Metal Trap 澤水困 2 癸未 Water Goat 25 初七 8	木3 Wood Not Yet Accomplished 火水未濟 1 甲申 Wood Monkey 26 初八 9	金9 Metal Retreat 天山遯 9 乙酉 Wood Rooster 27 初九 4	水6 Water Mountain 艮爲山 8 丙戌 Fire Dog 28 初十 1	木8 Wood Delight 雷地豫 7 丁亥 Fire Pig 29 十一 8	火7 Fire Beginning 水雷屯 6 戊子 Earth Rat 30 十二 4

NOVEMBER 1971 己亥

Xuan Kong Element 玄空五行	風地觀 Observation	Period Luck 卦運	Monthly Star 月星
Fire 火2		2	2

SUNDAY	MONDAY	TUESDAY	WEDNESDAY	THURSDAY	FRIDAY	SATURDAY
	木3 Wood 4 Fire 離爲火 庚寅 Metal Tiger 1 1 十四	火2 Fire 3 Sincerity 風澤中孚 辛卯 Metal Rabbit 3 2 十五	水6 Water 2 Big Livestock 山天大畜 壬辰 Water Dragon 4 3 十六	金4 Metal 1 Eliminating 澤天夬 癸巳 Water Snake 6 4 十七	金9 Metal 9 Heaven 乾爲天 甲午 Wood Horse 1 5 十八	火7 Fire 8 Well 水風井 乙未 Wood Goat 6 6 十九
木8 Wood 7 Relief 雷水解 丙申 Fire Monkey 4 7 二十	金4 Metal 6 Influence 澤山咸 丁酉 Fire Rooster 9 8 廿一	水1 Water 5 Humility 地山謙 戊戌 Earth Dog 6 9 廿二	火2 Fire 4 Observation 風地觀 己亥 Earth Pig 2 10 廿三	火2 Fire 3 Increasing 風雷益 庚子 Metal Rat 9 11 廿四	水1 Water 2 Dimming Light 地火明夷 辛丑 Metal Ox 3 12 廿五	金9 Metal 1 Fellowship 天火同人 壬寅 Water Tiger 7 13 廿六
木8 Wood 9 Marrying Maiden 雷澤歸妹 癸卯 Water Rabbit 7 14 廿七	木3 Wood 8 Opposition 火澤睽 甲辰 Wood Dragon 2 15 廿八	火7 Fire 7 Waiting 水天需 乙巳 Wood Snake 3 16 廿九	金4 Metal 6 Great Exceeding 澤風大過 丙午 Fire Horse 3 17 三十	水6 Water 5 Poison 山風蠱 丁未 Fire Goat 7 18 十月初一	火2 Fire 4 Dispersing 風水渙 戊申 Earth Monkey 6 19 初二	木3 Wood 3 Travelling 火山旅 己酉 Earth Rooster 8 20 初三
金9 Metal 2 Stagnation 天地否 庚戌 Metal Dog 9 21 初四	火7 Fire 1 Alliance 水地比 辛亥 Metal Pig 7 22 初五	木8 Wood 9 Thunder 震爲雷 壬子 Water Rat 1 23 初六	水6 Water 8 Beauty 山火賁 癸丑 Water Ox 8 24 初七	火7 Fire 7 Accomplished 水火既濟 甲寅 Wood Tiger 9 25 初八	水1 Water 6 Arriving 地澤臨 乙卯 Wood Rabbit 4 26 初九	金4 Metal 5 Marsh 兌爲澤 丙辰 Fire Dragon 1 27 初十
火2 Fire 4 Small Livestock 風天小畜 丁巳 Fire Snake 8 28 十一	木3 Wood 3 The Cauldron 火風鼎 戊午 Earth Horse 4 29 十二	水1 Water 2 Rising 地風升 己未 Earth Goat 2 30 十三				

DECEMBER 1971 庚子

Xuan Kong Element 玄空五行	風雷益 Increasing	Period Luck 卦運	Monthly Star 月星
Fire 火2		9	1

SUNDAY	MONDAY	TUESDAY	WEDNESDAY	THURSDAY	FRIDAY	SATURDAY
			火7 Fire 1 Water 坎爲水 庚申 Metal Monkey 1 1 十四	木8 Wood 9 Lesser Exceeding 雷山小過 辛酉 Metal Rooster 3 2 十五	金4 Metal 8 Gathering 澤地萃 壬戌 Water Dog 4 3 十六	水6 Water 7 Peel 山地剝 癸亥 Water Pig 6 4 十七
水1 Water 6 Earth 坤爲地 甲子 Wood Rat 1 5 十八	木3 Wood 5 Biting 火雷噬嗑 乙丑 Wood Ox 6 6 十九	火2 Fire 4 Family 風火家人 丙寅 Fire Tiger 4 7 二十	水6 Water 3 Decreasing 山澤損 丁卯 Fire Rabbit 9 8 廿一	金9 Metal 2 Tread 天澤履 戊辰 Earth Dragon 6 9 廿二	木8 Wood 1 Great Strength 雷天大壯 己巳 Earth Snake 2 10 廿三	木8 Wood 9 Consistency 雷風恆 庚午 Metal Horse 9 11 廿四
金9 Metal 8 Litigation 天水訟 辛未 Metal Goat 3 12 廿五	水1 Water 7 Officer 地水師 壬申 Water Monkey 7 13 廿六	火2 Fire 6 Gradual Progress 風山漸 癸酉 Water Rooster 7 14 廿七	火7 Fire 5 Obstruction 水山蹇 甲戌 Wood Dog 2 15 廿八	木3 Wood 4 Advancement 火地晉 乙亥 Wood Pig 3 16 廿九	水6 Water 3 Nourish 山雷頤 丙子 Fire Rat 3 17 三十	金4 Metal 2 Following 澤雷隨 丁丑 Fire Ox 7 18 十一月初一
木8 Wood 1 Abundance 雷火豐 戊寅 Earth Tiger 6 19 初二	火7 Fire 9 Regulate 水澤節 己卯 Earth Rabbit 8 20 初三	水1 Water 8 Unity 地天泰 庚辰 Metal Dragon 9 21 初四	木3 Wood 7/3 Great Reward 火天大有 辛巳 Metal Snake 7 22 初五	火2 Fire 4 Wind 巽爲風 壬午 Water Horse 1 23 初六	金4 Metal 5 Trap 澤水困 癸未 Water Goat 8 24 初七	木3 Wood 6 Not Yet Accomplished 火水未濟 甲申 Wood Monkey 9 25 初八
金9 Metal 7 Retreat 天山遯 乙酉 Wood Rooster 4 26 初九	水6 Water 8 Mountain 艮爲山 丙戌 Fire Dog 1 27 初十	木8 Wood 9 Delight 雷地豫 丁亥 Fire Pig 8 28 十一	火7 Fire 1 Beginning 水雷屯 戊子 Earth Rat 4 29 十二	金9 Metal 2 Without Wrongdoing 天雷無妄 己丑 Earth Ox 2 30 十三	木3 Wood 3 Fire 離爲火 庚寅 Metal Tiger 1 31 十四	

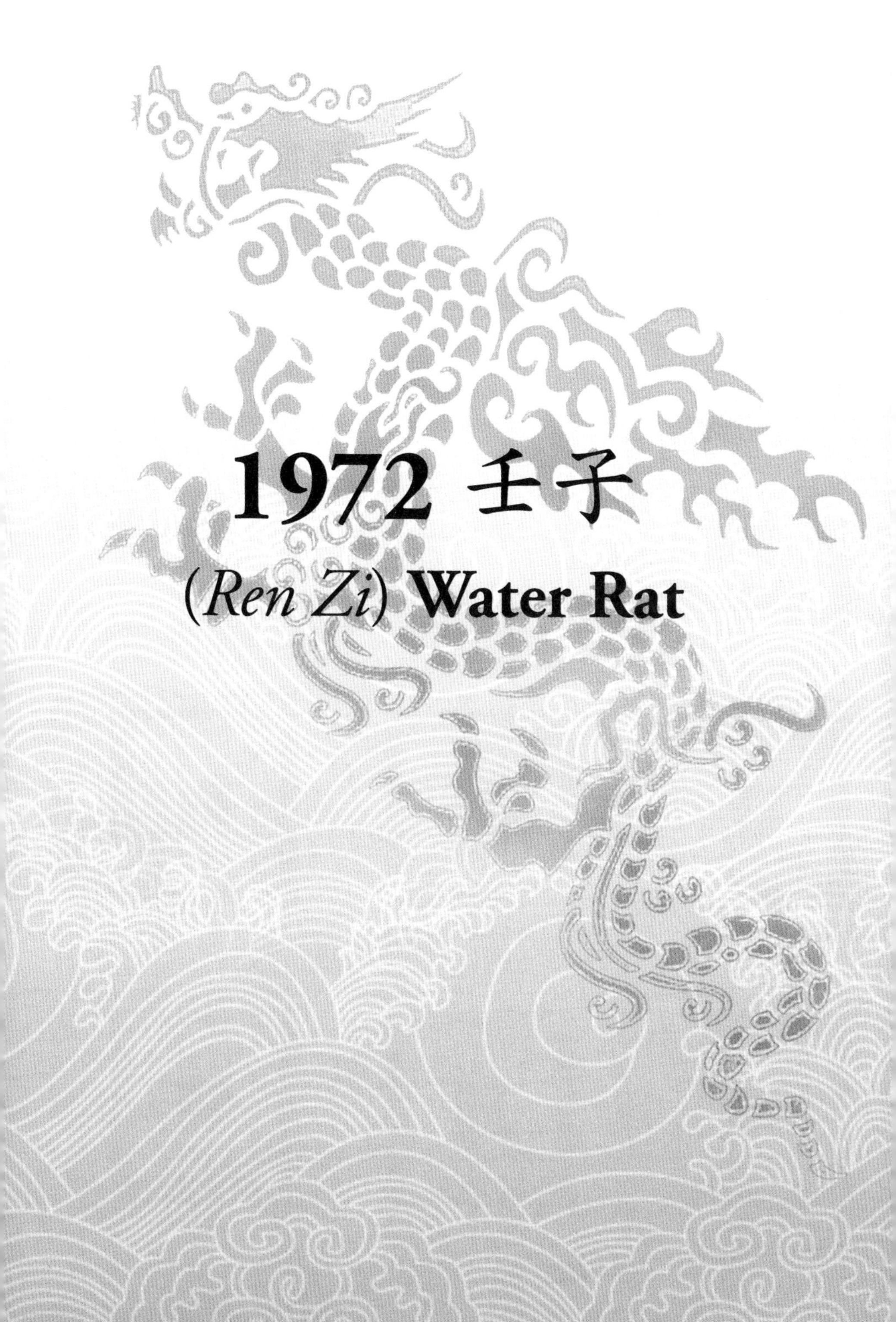

1972 壬子

(*Ren Zi*) Water Rat

1972 壬子 *(Ren Zi)* Water Rat

January 6 - February 4

SE	S	SW
8	4	6
7	**9**	2
3	5	1
NE	N	NW

水1 Water · 辛丑 Metal Ox · 3 Dimming Light 地火明夷

Three Killings | East

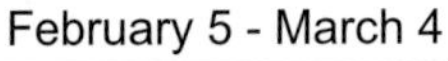

February 5 - March 4

SE	S	SW
7	3	5
6	**8**	1
2	4	9
NE	N	NW

金9 Metal · 壬寅 Water Tiger · 7 Fellowship 天火同人

Three Killings | North

March 5 - April 4

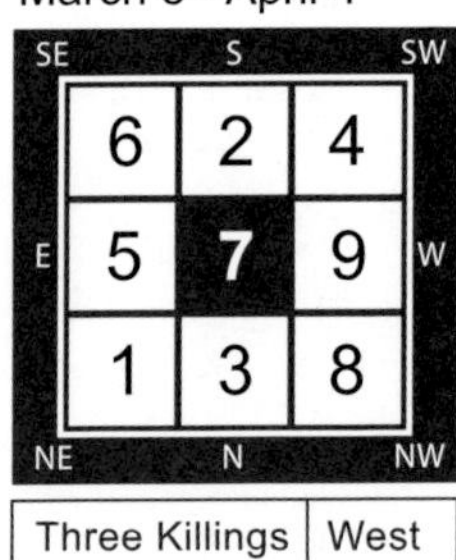

SE	S	SW
6	2	4
5	**7**	9
1	3	8
NE	N	NW

木8 Wood · 癸卯 Water Rabbit · 7 Marrying Maiden 雷澤歸妹

Three Killings | West

April 5 - May 4

SE	S	SW
5	1	3
4	**6**	8
9	2	7
NE	N	NW

木3 Wood · 甲辰 Wood Dragon · 2 Opposition 火澤睽

Three Killings | South

May 5 - June 4

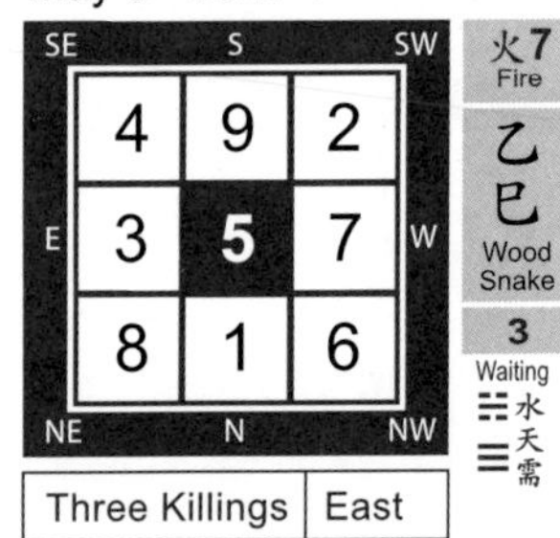

SE	S	SW
4	9	2
3	**5**	7
8	1	6
NE	N	NW

火7 Fire · 乙巳 Wood Snake · 3 Waiting 水天需

Three Killings | East

June 5 - July 6

SE	S	SW
3	8	1
2	**4**	6
7	9	5
NE	N	NW

金4 Metal · 丙午 Fire Horse · 3 Great Exceeding 澤風大過

Three Killings | North

July 7 - August 6

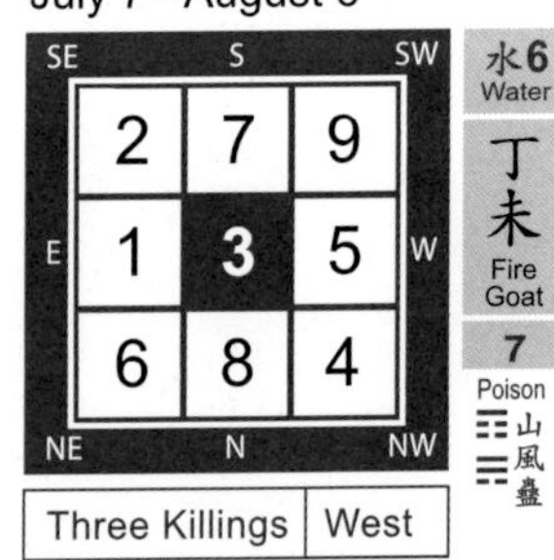

SE	S	SW
2	7	9
1	**3**	5
6	8	4
NE	N	NW

水6 Water · 丁未 Fire Goat · 7 Poison 山風蠱

Three Killings | West

August 7 - September 6

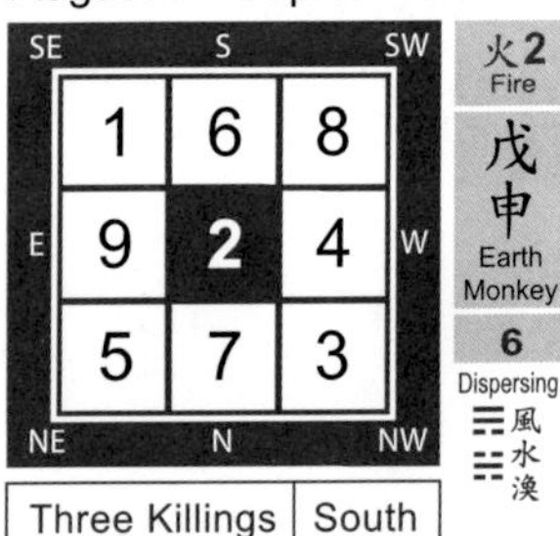

SE	S	SW
1	6	8
9	**2**	4
5	7	3
NE	N	NW

火2 Fire · 戊申 Earth Monkey · 6 Dispersing 風水渙

Three Killings | South

September 7 - October 7

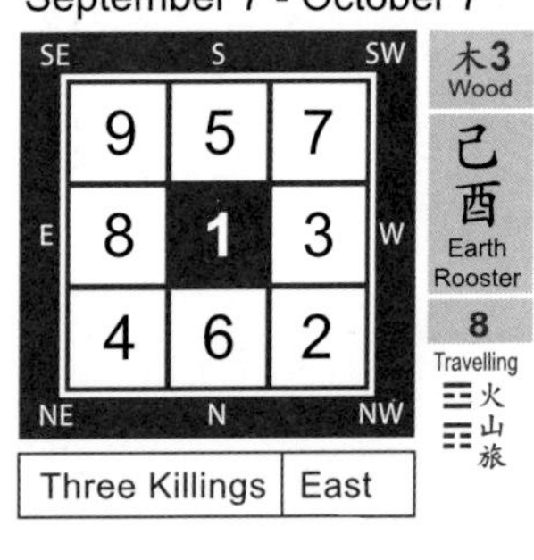

SE	S	SW
9	5	7
8	**1**	3
4	6	2
NE	N	NW

木3 Wood · 己酉 Earth Rooster · 8 Travelling 火山旅

Three Killings | East

October 8 - November 6

SE	S	SW
8	4	6
7	**9**	2
3	5	1
NE	N	NW

金9 Metal · 庚戌 Metal Dog · 9 Stagnation 天地否

Three Killings | North

November 7 - December 6

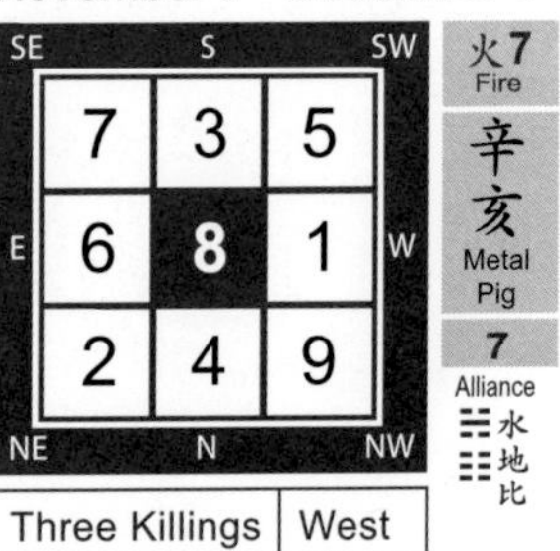

SE	S	SW
7	3	5
6	**8**	1
2	4	9
NE	N	NW

火7 Fire · 辛亥 Metal Pig · 7 Alliance 水地比

Three Killings | West

December 7 - January 4

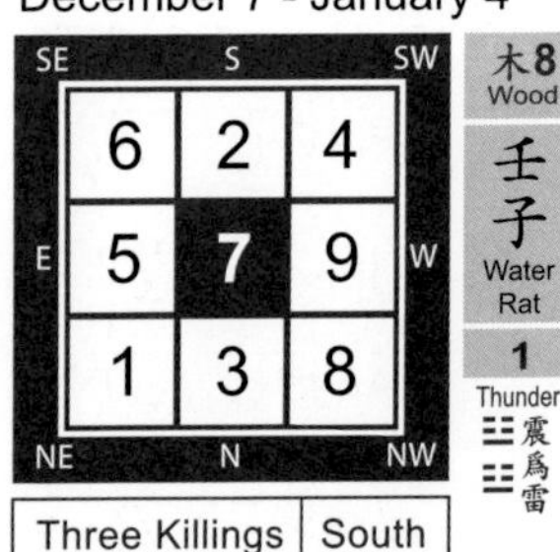

SE	S	SW
6	2	4
5	**7**	9
1	3	8
NE	N	NW

木8 Wood · 壬子 Water Rat · 1 Thunder 震爲雷

Three Killings | South

JANUARY 1972 辛丑

Xuan Kong Element 玄空五行	地火明夷 Dimming Light	Period Luck 卦運	Monthly Star 月星
Water 水1		3	9

SUNDAY	MONDAY	TUESDAY	WEDNESDAY	THURSDAY	FRIDAY	SATURDAY
火7 Fire 6 Water 庚申 Metal Monkey 坎爲水 30 十五 1	木8 Wood 7 Lesser Exceeding 辛酉 Metal Rooster 雷山小過 31 十六 3					火2 Fire 4 Sincerity 辛卯 Metal Rabbit 風澤中孚 1 十五 3
水6 Water 5 Big Livestock 壬辰 Water Dragon 山天大畜 2 十六 4	金4 Metal 6 Eliminating 癸巳 Water Snake 澤天夬 3 十七 6	金9 Metal 7 Heaven 甲午 Wood Horse 乾爲天 4 十八 1	火7 Fire 8 Well 乙未 Wood Goat 水風井 5 十九 6	木8 Wood 9 Relief 丙申 Fire Monkey 雷水解 6 二十 4	金4 Metal 1 Influence 丁酉 Fire Rooster 澤山咸 7 廿一 9	水1 Water 2 Humility 戊戌 Earth Dog 地山謙 8 廿二 6
火2 Fire 3 Observation 己亥 Earth Pig 風地觀 9 廿三 2	火2 Fire 4 Increasing 庚子 Metal Rat 風雷益 10 廿四 9	水1 Water 5 Dimming Light 辛丑 Metal Ox 地火明夷 11 廿五 3	金9 Metal 6 Fellowship 壬寅 Water Tiger 天火同人 12 廿六 7	木8 Wood 7 Marrying Maiden 癸卯 Water Rabbit 雷澤歸妹 13 廿七 7	木3 Wood 8 Opposition 甲辰 Wood Dragon 火澤睽 14 廿八 2	火7 Fire 9 Waiting 乙巳 Wood Snake 水天需 15 廿九 3
金4 Metal 1 Great Exceeding 丙午 Fire Horse 澤風大過 16 十二月初一 3	水6 Water 2 Poison 丁未 Fire Goat 山風蠱 17 初二 7	火2 Fire 3 Dispersing 戊申 Earth Monkey 風水渙 18 初三 6	木3 Wood 4 Travelling 己酉 Earth Rooster 火山旅 19 初四 8	金9 Metal 5 Stagnation 庚戌 Metal Dog 天地否 20 初五 9	火7 Fire 6 Alliance 辛亥 Metal Pig 水地比 21 初六 7	木8 Wood 7 Thunder 壬子 Water Rat 震爲雷 22 初七 1
水6 Water 8 Beauty 癸丑 Water Ox 山火賁 23 初八 8	火7 Fire 9 Accomplished 甲寅 Wood Tiger 水火既濟 24 初九 9	水1 Water 1 Arriving 乙卯 Wood Rabbit 地澤臨 25 初十 4	金4 Metal 2 Marsh 丙辰 Fire Dragon 兌爲澤 26 十一 1	火2 Fire 3 Small Livestock 丁巳 Fire Snake 風天小畜 27 十二 8	木3 Wood 4 The Cauldron 戊午 Earth Horse 火風鼎 28 十三 4	水1 Water 5 Rising 己未 Earth Goat 地風升 29 十四 2

FEBRUARY 1972 壬寅

Xuan Kong Element 玄空五行	天火同人 Fellowship	Period Luck 卦運	Monthly Star 月星
Metal 金9		7	8

SUNDAY	MONDAY	TUESDAY	WEDNESDAY	THURSDAY	FRIDAY	SATURDAY
		金4 Metal 8 Gathering 壬戌 Water Dog 澤地萃 1 十七 4	水6 Water 9 Peel 癸亥 Water Pig 山地剝 2 十八 6	水1 Water 1 Earth 甲子 Wood Rat 坤爲地 3 十九 1	木3 Wood 2 Biting 乙丑 Wood Ox 火雷噬嗑 4 二十 6	火2 Fire 3 Family 丙寅 Fire Tiger 風火家人 5 廿一 4
水6 Water 4 Decreasing 丁卯 Fire Rabbit 山澤損 6 廿二 9	金9 Metal 5 Tread 戊辰 Earth Dragon 天澤履 7 廿三 6	木8 Wood 6 Great Strength 己巳 Earth Snake 雷天大壯 8 廿四 2	木8 Wood 7 Consistency 庚午 Metal Horse 雷風恒 9 廿五 9	金9 Metal 8 Litigation 辛未 Metal Goat 天水訟 10 廿六 3	水1 Water 9 Officer 壬申 Water Monkey 地水師 11 廿七 7	火2 Fire 1 Gradual Progress 癸酉 Water Rooster 風山漸 12 廿八 7
火7 Fire 2 Obstruction 甲戌 Wood Dog 水山蹇 13 廿九 2	木3 Wood 3 Advancement 乙亥 Wood Pig 火地晉 14 三十 3	水6 Water 4 Nourish 丙子 Fire Rat 山雷頤 15 正月初一 3	金4 Metal 5 Following 丁丑 Fire Ox 澤雷隨 16 初二 7	木8 Wood 6 Abundance 戊寅 Earth Tiger 雷火豐 17 初三 6	火7 Fire 7 Regulate 己卯 Earth Rabbit 水澤節 18 初四 8	水1 Water 8 Unity 庚辰 Metal Dragon 地天泰 19 初五 9
木3 Wood 9 Great Reward 辛巳 Metal Snake 火天大有 20 初六 7	火2 Fire 1 Wind 壬午 Water Horse 巽爲風 21 初七 1	金4 Metal 2 Trap 癸未 Water Goat 澤水困 22 初八 8	木3 Wood 3 Not Yet Accomplished 甲申 Wood Monkey 火水未濟 23 初九 9	金9 Metal 4 Retreat 乙酉 Wood Rooster 天山遯 24 初十 4	水6 Water 5 Mountain 丙戌 Fire Dog 艮爲山 25 十一 1	木8 Wood 6 Delight 丁亥 Fire Pig 雷地豫 26 十二 8
火7 Fire 7 Beginning 戊子 Earth Rat 水雷屯 27 十三 4	金9 Metal 8 Without Wrongdoing 己丑 Earth Ox 天雷無妄 28 十四 2	木3 Wood 9 Fire 庚寅 Metal Tiger 離爲火 29 十五 1				

MARCH 1972 癸卯

Xuan Kong Element 玄空五行	雷澤歸妹 Marrying Maiden	Period Luck 卦運	Monthly Star 月星
Wood 木8		7	7

SUNDAY	MONDAY	TUESDAY	WEDNESDAY	THURSDAY	FRIDAY	SATURDAY
			火2 Fire Sincerity 1 辛卯 Metal Rabbit 風澤中孚 1 十六 3	水6 Water Big Livestock 2 壬辰 Water Dragon 山天大畜 2 十七 4	金4 Metal Eliminating 3 癸巳 Water Snake 澤天夬 3 十八 6	金9 Metal Heaven 4 甲午 Wood Horse 乾爲天 4 十九 1
火7 Fire Well 5 乙未 Wood Goat 水風井 5 二十 6	木8 Wood Relief 6 丙申 Fire Monkey 雷水解 6 廿一 4	金4 Metal Influence 7 丁酉 Fire Rooster 澤山咸 7 廿二 9	水1 Water Humility 8 戊戌 Earth Dog 地山謙 8 廿三 6	火2 Fire Observation 9 己亥 Earth Pig 風地觀 9 廿四 2	火2 Fire Increasing 1 庚子 Metal Rat 風雷益 10 廿五 9	水1 Water Dimming Light 2 辛丑 Metal Ox 地火明夷 11 廿六 3
金9 Metal Fellowship 3 壬寅 Water Tiger 天火同人 12 廿七 7	木8 Wood Marrying Maiden 4 癸卯 Water Rabbit 雷澤歸妹 13 廿八 7	木3 Wood Opposition 5 甲辰 Wood Dragon 火澤睽 14 廿九 2	火7 Fire Waiting 6 乙巳 Wood Snake 水天需 15 二月初一 3	金4 Metal Great Exceeding 7 丙午 Fire Horse 澤風大過 16 初二 3	水6 Water Poison 8 丁未 Fire Goat 山風蠱 17 初三 7	火2 Fire Dispersing 9 戊申 Earth Monkey 風水渙 18 初四 6
木3 Wood Travelling 1 己酉 Earth Rooster 火山旅 19 初五 8	金9 Metal Stagnation 2 庚戌 Metal Dog 天地否 20 初六 9	火7 Fire Alliance 3 辛亥 Metal Pig 水地比 21 初七 7	木8 Wood Thunder 4 壬子 Water Rat 震爲雷 22 初八 1	水6 Water Beauty 5 癸丑 Water Ox 山火賁 23 初九 8	火7 Fire Accomplished 6 甲寅 Wood Tiger 水火既濟 24 初十 9	水1 Water Arriving 7 乙卯 Wood Rabbit 地澤臨 25 十一 4
金4 Metal Marsh 8 丙辰 Fire Dragon 兌爲澤 26 十二 1	火2 Fire Small Livestock 9 丁巳 Fire Snake 風天小畜 27 十三 8	木3 Wood The Cauldron 1 戊午 Earth Horse 火風鼎 28 十四 4	水1 Water Rising 2 己未 Earth Goat 地風升 29 十五 2	火7 Fire Water 3 庚申 Metal Monkey 坎爲水 30 十六 1	木8 Wood Lesser Exceeding 4 辛酉 Metal Rooster 雷山小過 31 十七 3	

APRIL 1972 甲辰

Xuan Kong Element 玄空五行	火澤睽 Opposition	Period Luck 卦運	Monthly Star 月星
Wood 木3		2	6

SUNDAY	MONDAY	TUESDAY	WEDNESDAY	THURSDAY	FRIDAY	SATURDAY
火2 Fire Sincerity 7 辛卯 Metal Rabbit 風澤中孚 30 十七 3						金4 Metal Gathering 5 壬戌 Water Dog 澤地萃 1 十八 4
水6 Water Peel 6 癸亥 Water Pig 山地剝 2 十九 6	水1 Water Earth 7 甲子 Wood Rat 坤爲地 3 二十 1	木3 Wood Biting 8 乙丑 Wood Ox 火雷噬嗑 4 廿一 6	火2 Fire Family 9 丙寅 Fire Tiger 風火家人 5 廿二 4	水6 Water Decreasing 1 丁卯 Fire Rabbit 山澤損 6 廿三 9	金9 Metal Tread 2 戊辰 Earth Dragon 天澤履 7 廿四 6	木8 Wood Great Strength 3 己巳 Earth Snake 雷天大壯 8 廿五 2
木8 Wood Consistency 4 庚午 Metal Horse 雷風恆 9 廿六 9	金9 Metal Litigation 5 辛未 Metal Goat 天水訟 10 廿七 3	水1 Water Officer 6 壬申 Water Monkey 地水師 11 廿八 7	火2 Fire Gradual Progress 7 癸酉 Water Rooster 風山漸 12 廿九 7	火7 Fire Obstruction 8 甲戌 Wood Dog 水山蹇 13 三十 2	木3 Wood Advancement 9 乙亥 Wood Pig 火地晉 14 三月初一 3	水6 Water Nourish 1 丙子 Fire Rat 山雷頤 15 初二 3
金4 Metal Following 2 丁丑 Fire Ox 澤雷隨 16 初三 7	木8 Wood Abundance 3 戊寅 Earth Tiger 雷火豐 17 初四 6	火7 Fire Regulate 4 己卯 Earth Rabbit 水澤節 18 初五 8	水1 Water Unity 5 庚辰 Metal Dragon 地天泰 19 初六 9	木3 Wood Great Reward 6 辛巳 Metal Snake 火天大有 20 初七 7	火2 Fire Wind 7 壬午 Water Horse 巽爲風 21 初八 1	金4 Metal Trap 8 癸未 Water Goat 澤水困 22 初九 8
木3 Wood Not Yet Accomplished 9 甲申 Wood Monkey 火水未濟 23 初十 9	金9 Metal Retreat 1 乙酉 Wood Rooster 天山遯 24 十一 4	水6 Water Mountain 2 丙戌 Fire Dog 艮爲山 25 十二 1	木8 Wood Delight 3 丁亥 Fire Pig 雷地豫 26 十三 8	火7 Fire Beginning 4 戊子 Earth Rat 水雷屯 27 十四 4	金9 Metal Without Wrongdoing 5 己丑 Earth Ox 天雷無妄 28 十五 2	木3 Wood Fire 6 庚寅 Metal Tiger 離爲火 29 十六 1

MAY 1972 乙巳

Xuan Kong Element 玄空五行	水天需 Waiting	Period Luck 卦運	Monthly Star 月星
Fire 火7		3	5

SUNDAY	MONDAY	TUESDAY	WEDNESDAY	THURSDAY	FRIDAY	SATURDAY
	水6 Water 8 Big Livestock 山天大畜 壬辰 Water Dragon **1** 十八 4	金4 Metal 9 Eliminating 澤天夬 癸巳 Water Snake **2** 十九 6	金9 Metal 1 Heaven 乾為天 甲午 Wood Horse **3** 二十 1	火7 Fire 2 Well 水風井 乙未 Wood Goat **4** 廿一 6	木8 Wood 3 Relief 雷水解 丙申 Fire Monkey **5** 廿二 4	金4 Metal 4 Influence 澤山咸 丁酉 Fire Rooster **6** 廿三 9
水1 Water 5 Humility 地山謙 戊戌 Earth Dog **7** 廿四 6	火2 Fire 6 Observation 風地觀 己亥 Earth Pig **8** 廿五 2	火2 Fire 7 Increasing 風雷益 庚子 Metal Rat **9** 廿六 9	水1 Water 8 Dimming Light 地火明夷 辛丑 Metal Ox **10** 廿七 3	金9 Metal 9 Fellowship 天火同人 壬寅 Water Tiger **11** 廿八 7	木8 Wood 1 Marrying Maiden 雷澤歸妹 癸卯 Water Rabbit **12** 廿九 7	木3 Wood 2 Opposition 火澤睽 甲辰 Wood Dragon **13** 四月初一 2
火7 Fire 3 Waiting 水天需 乙巳 Wood Snake **14** 初二 3	金4 Metal 4 Great Exceeding 澤風大過 丙午 Fire Horse **15** 初三 3	水6 Water 5 Poison 山風蠱 丁未 Fire Goat **16** 初四 7	火2 Fire 6 Dispersing 風水渙 戊申 Earth Monkey **17** 初五 6	木3 Wood 7 Travelling 火山旅 己酉 Earth Rooster **18** 初六 8	金9 Metal 8 Stagnation 天地否 庚戌 Metal Dog **19** 初七 9	火7 Fire 9 Alliance 水地比 辛亥 Metal Pig **20** 初八 7
木8 Wood 1 Thunder 震為雷 壬子 Water Rat **21** 初九 1	水6 Water 2 Beauty 山火賁 癸丑 Water Ox **22** 初十 8	火7 Fire 3 Accomplished 水火既濟 甲寅 Wood Tiger **23** 十一 9	水1 Water 4 Arriving 地澤臨 乙卯 Wood Rabbit **24** 十二 4	金4 Metal 5 Marsh 兌為澤 丙辰 Fire Dragon **25** 十三 1	火2 Fire 6 Small Livestock 風天小畜 丁巳 Fire Snake **26** 十四 8	木3 Wood 7 The Cauldron 火風鼎 戊午 Earth Horse **27** 十五 4
水1 Water 8 Rising 地風升 己未 Earth Goat **28** 十六 2	火7 Fire 9 Water 坎為水 庚申 Metal Monkey **29** 十七 1	木8 Wood 1 Lesser Exceeding 雷山小過 辛酉 Metal Rooster **30** 十八 3	金4 Metal 2 Gathering 澤地萃 壬戌 Water Dog **31** 十九 4			

JUNE 1972 丙午

Xuan Kong Element 玄空五行	澤風大過 Great Exceeding	Period Luck 卦運	Monthly Star 月星
Metal 金4		3	4

SUNDAY	MONDAY	TUESDAY	WEDNESDAY	THURSDAY	FRIDAY	SATURDAY
				水6 Water 3 Peel 山地剝 癸亥 Water Pig **1** 二十 6	水1 Water 4 Earth 坤為地 甲子 Wood Rat **2** 廿一 1	木3 Wood 5 Biting 火雷噬嗑 乙丑 Wood Ox **3** 廿二 6
火2 Fire 6 Family 風火家人 丙寅 Fire Tiger **4** 廿三 4	水6 Water 7 Decreasing 山澤損 丁卯 Fire Rabbit **5** 廿四 9	金9 Metal 8 Tread 天澤履 戊辰 Earth Dragon **6** 廿五 6	木8 Wood 9 Great Strength 雷天大壯 己巳 Earth Snake **7** 廿六 2	木8 Wood 1 Consistency 雷風恒 庚午 Metal Horse **8** 廿七 9	金9 Metal 2 Litigation 天水訟 辛未 Metal Goat **9** 廿八 3	水1 Water 3 Officer 地水師 壬申 Water Monkey **10** 廿九 7
火2 Fire 4 Gradual Progress 風山漸 癸酉 Water Rooster **11** 五月初一 7	火7 Fire 5 Obstruction 水山蹇 甲戌 Wood Dog **12** 初二 2	木3 Wood 6 Advancement 火地晉 乙亥 Wood Pig **13** 初三 3	水6 Water 7 Nourish 山雷頤 丙子 Fire Rat **14** 初四 3	金4 Metal 8 Following 澤雷隨 丁丑 Fire Ox **15** 初五 7	木8 Wood 9 Abundance 雷火豐 戊寅 Earth Tiger **16** 初六 6	火7 Fire 1 Regulate 水澤節 己卯 Earth Rabbit **17** 初七 8
水1 Water 2 Unity 地天泰 庚辰 Metal Dragon **18** 初八 9	木3 Wood 3 Great Reward 火天大有 辛巳 Metal Snake **19** 初九 7	火2 Fire 4 Wind 巽為風 壬午 Water Horse **20** 初十 1	金4 Metal 5/5 Trap 澤水困 癸未 Water Goat **21** 十一 8	木3 Wood 4 Not Yet Accomplished 火水未濟 甲申 Wood Monkey **22** 十二 9	金9 Metal 3 Retreat 天山遯 乙酉 Wood Rooster **23** 十三 4	水6 Water 2 Mountain 艮為山 丙戌 Fire Dog **24** 十四 1
木8 Wood 1 Delight 雷地豫 丁亥 Fire Pig **25** 十五 8	火7 Fire 9 Beginning 水雷屯 戊子 Earth Rat **26** 十六 4	金9 Metal 8 Without Wrongdoing 天雷無妄 己丑 Earth Ox **27** 十七 2	木3 Wood 7 Fire 離為火 庚寅 Metal Tiger **28** 十八 1	火2 Fire 6 Sincerity 風澤中孚 辛卯 Metal Rabbit **29** 十九 3	水6 Water 5 Big Livestock 山天大畜 壬辰 Water Dragon **30** 二十 4	

JULY 1972 丁未

Xuan Kong Element 玄空五行	山風蠱 Poison	Period Luck 卦運	Monthly Star 月星
Water 水6		7	3

SUNDAY	MONDAY	TUESDAY	WEDNESDAY	THURSDAY	FRIDAY	SATURDAY
金4 Metal 2 Gathering 澤地萃 壬戌 Water Dog 30 二十 4	水6 Water 1 Peel 山地剝 癸亥 Water Pig 31 廿一 6					金4 Metal 4 Eliminating 澤天夬 癸巳 Water Snake 1 廿一 6
金9 Metal 3 Heaven 乾爲天 甲午 Wood Horse 2 廿二 1	火7 Fire 2 Well 水風井 乙未 Wood Goat 3 廿三 6	木8 Wood 1 Relief 雷水解 丙申 Fire Monkey 4 廿四 4	金4 Metal 9 Influence 澤山咸 丁酉 Fire Rooster 5 廿五 9	水1 Water 8 Humility 地山謙 戊戌 Earth Dog 6 廿六 6	火2 Fire 7 Observation 風地觀 己亥 Earth Pig 7 廿七 2	火2 Fire 6 Increasing 風雷益 庚子 Metal Rat 8 廿八 9
水1 Water 5 Dimming Light 地火明夷 辛丑 Metal Ox 9 廿九 3	金9 Metal 4 Fellowship 天火同人 壬寅 Water Tiger 10 三十 7	木8 Wood 3 Marrying Maiden 雷澤歸妹 癸卯 Water Rabbit 11 六月初一 7	木3 Wood 2 Opposition 火澤睽 甲辰 Wood Dragon 12 初二 2	火7 Fire 1 Waiting 水天需 乙巳 Wood Snake 13 初三 3	金4 Metal 9 Great Exceeding 澤風大過 丙午 Fire Horse 14 初四 3	水6 Water 8 Poison 山風蠱 丁未 Fire Goat 15 初五 7
火2 Fire 7 Dispersing 風水渙 戊申 Earth Monkey 16 初六 6	木3 Wood 6 Travelling 火山旅 己酉 Earth Rooster 17 初七 8	金9 Metal 5 Stagnation 天地否 庚戌 Metal Dog 18 初八 9	火7 Fire 4 Alliance 水地比 辛亥 Metal Pig 19 初九 7	木8 Wood 3 Thunder 震爲雷 壬子 Water Rat 20 初十 1	水6 Water 2 Beauty 山火賁 癸丑 Water Ox 21 十一 8	火7 Fire 1 Accomplished 水火既濟 甲寅 Wood Tiger 22 十二 9
水1 Water 9 Arriving 地澤臨 乙卯 Wood Rabbit 23 十三 4	金4 Metal 8 Marsh 兌爲澤 丙辰 Fire Dragon 24 十四 1	火2 Fire 7 Small Livestock 風天小畜 丁巳 Fire Snake 25 十五 8	木3 Wood 6 The Cauldron 火風鼎 戊午 Earth Horse 26 十六 4	水1 Water 5 Rising 地風升 己未 Earth Goat 27 十七 2	火7 Fire 4 Water 坎爲水 庚申 Metal Monkey 28 十八 1	木8 Wood 3 Lesser Exceeding 雷山小過 辛酉 Metal Rooster 29 十九 3

AUGUST 1972 戊申

Xuan Kong Element 玄空五行	風水渙 Dispersing	Period Luck 卦運	Monthly Star 月星
Fire 火2		6	2

SUNDAY	MONDAY	TUESDAY	WEDNESDAY	THURSDAY	FRIDAY	SATURDAY
		水1 Water 9 Earth 坤爲地 甲子 Wood Rat 1 廿二 1	木3 Wood 8 Biting 火雷噬嗑 乙丑 Wood Ox 2 廿三 6	火2 Fire 7 Family 風火家人 丙寅 Fire Tiger 3 廿四 4	水6 Water 6 Decreasing 山澤損 丁卯 Fire Rabbit 4 廿五 9	金9 Metal 5 Tread 天澤履 戊辰 Earth Dragon 5 廿六 6
木8 Wood 4 Great Strength 雷天大壯 己巳 Earth Snake 6 廿七 2	木8 Wood 3 Consistency 雷風恆 庚午 Metal Horse 7 廿八 9	金9 Metal 2 Litigation 天水訟 辛未 Metal Goat 8 廿九 3	水1 Water 1 Officer 地水師 壬申 Water Monkey 9 七月初一 7	火2 Fire 9 Gradual Progress 風山漸 癸酉 Water Rooster 10 初二 7	火7 Fire 8 Obstruction 水山蹇 甲戌 Wood Dog 11 初三 2	木3 Wood 7 Advancement 火地晉 乙亥 Wood Pig 12 初四 3
水6 Water 6 Nourish 山雷頤 丙子 Fire Rat 13 初五 3	金4 Metal 5 Following 澤雷隨 丁丑 Fire Ox 14 初六 7	木8 Wood 4 Abundance 雷火豐 戊寅 Earth Tiger 15 初七 6	火7 Fire 3 Regulate 水澤節 己卯 Earth Rabbit 16 初八 8	水1 Water 2 Unity 地天泰 庚辰 Metal Dragon 17 初九 9	木3 Wood 1 Great Reward 火天大有 辛巳 Metal Snake 18 初十 7	火2 Fire 9 Wind 巽爲風 壬午 Water Horse 19 十一 1
金4 Metal 8 Trap 澤水困 癸未 Water Goat 20 十二 8	木3 Wood 7 Not Yet Accomplished 火水未濟 甲申 Wood Monkey 21 十三 9	金9 Metal 6 Retreat 天山遯 乙酉 Wood Rooster 22 十四 4	水6 Water 5 Mountain 艮爲山 丙戌 Fire Dog 23 十五 1	木8 Wood 4 Delight 雷地豫 丁亥 Fire Pig 24 十六 8	火7 Fire 3 Beginning 水雷屯 戊子 Earth Rat 25 十七 4	金9 Metal 2 Without Wrongdoing 天雷無妄 己丑 Earth Ox 26 十八 2
木3 Wood 1 Fire 離爲火 庚寅 Metal Tiger 27 十九 1	火2 Fire 9 Sincerity 風澤中孚 辛卯 Metal Rabbit 28 二十 3	水6 Water 8 Big Livestock 山天大畜 壬辰 Water Dragon 29 廿一 4	金4 Metal 7 Eliminating 澤天夬 癸巳 Water Snake 30 廿二 6	金9 Metal 6 Heaven 乾爲天 甲午 Wood Horse 31 廿三 1		

SEPTEMBER 1972 己酉

Xuan Kong Element 玄空五行	火山旅 Travelling	Period Luck 卦運	Monthly Star 月星
Wood 木3		8	1

SUNDAY	MONDAY	TUESDAY	WEDNESDAY	THURSDAY	FRIDAY	SATURDAY
					火7 Fire Well 5 乙未 Wood Goat 水風井 1 廿四 6	木8 Wood Relief 4 丙申 Fire Monkey 雷水解 2 廿五 4
金4 Metal Influence 3 丁酉 Fire Rooster 澤山咸 3 廿六 9	水1 Water Humility 2 戊戌 Earth Dog 地山謙 4 廿七 6	火2 Fire Observation 1 己亥 Earth Pig 風地觀 5 廿八 2	火2 Fire Increasing 9 庚子 Metal Rat 風雷益 6 廿九 9	水1 Water Dimming Light 8 辛丑 Metal Ox 地火明夷 7 三十 3	金9 Metal Fellowship 7 壬寅 Water Tiger 天火同人 8 八月初一 7	木8 Wood Marrying Maiden 6 癸卯 Water Rabbit 雷澤歸妹 9 初二 7
木3 Wood Opposition 5 甲辰 Wood Dragon 火澤睽 10 初三 2	火7 Fire Waiting 4 乙巳 Wood Snake 水天需 11 初四 3	金4 Metal Great Exceeding 3 丙午 Fire Horse 澤風大過 12 初五 3	水6 Water Poison 2 丁未 Fire Goat 山風蠱 13 初六 7	火2 Fire Dispersing 1 戊申 Earth Monkey 風水渙 14 初七 6	木3 Wood Travelling 9 己酉 Earth Rooster 火山旅 15 初八 8	金9 Metal Stagnation 8 庚戌 Metal Dog 天地否 16 初九 9
火7 Fire Alliance 7 辛亥 Metal Pig 水地比 17 初十 7	木8 Wood Thunder 6 壬子 Water Rat 震爲雷 18 十一 1	水6 Water Beauty 5 癸丑 Water Ox 山火賁 19 十二 8	火7 Fire Accomplished 4 甲寅 Wood Tiger 水火既濟 20 十三 9	水1 Water Arriving 3 乙卯 Wood Rabbit 地澤臨 21 十四 4	金4 Metal Marsh 2 丙辰 Fire Dragon 兑爲澤 22 十五 1	火2 Fire Small Livestock 1 丁巳 Fire Snake 風天小畜 23 十六 8
木3 Wood The Cauldron 9 戊午 Earth Horse 火風鼎 24 十七 4	水1 Water Rising 8 己未 Earth Goat 地風升 25 十八 2	火7 Fire Water 7 庚申 Metal Monkey 坎爲水 26 十九 1	木8 Wood Lesser Exceeding 6 辛酉 Metal Rooster 雷山小過 27 二十 3	金4 Metal Gathering 5 壬戌 Water Dog 澤地萃 28 廿一 4	水6 Water Peel 4 癸亥 Water Pig 山地剝 29 廿二 6	水1 Water Earth 3 甲子 Wood Rat 坤爲地 30 廿三 1

OCTOBER 1972 庚戌

Xuan Kong Element 玄空五行	天地否 Stagnation	Period Luck 卦運	Monthly Star 月星
Metal 金9		9	9

SUNDAY	MONDAY	TUESDAY	WEDNESDAY	THURSDAY	FRIDAY	SATURDAY
木3 Wood Biting 2 乙丑 Wood Ox 火雷噬嗑 1 廿四 6	火2 Fire Family 1 丙寅 Fire Tiger 風火家人 2 廿五 4	水6 Water Decreasing 9 丁卯 Fire Rabbit 山澤損 3 廿六 9	金9 Metal Tread 8 戊辰 Earth Dragon 天澤履 4 廿七 6	木8 Wood Great Strength 7 己巳 Earth Snake 雷天大壯 5 廿八 2	木8 Wood Consistency 6 庚午 Metal Horse 雷風恆 6 廿九 9	金9 Metal Litigation 5 辛未 Metal Goat 天水訟 7 九月初一 3
水1 Water Officer 4 壬申 Water Monkey 地水師 8 初二 7	火2 Fire Gradual Progress 3 癸酉 Water Rooster 風山漸 9 初三 7	火7 Fire Obstruction 2 甲戌 Wood Dog 水山蹇 10 初四 2	木3 Wood Advancement 1 乙亥 Wood Pig 火地晉 11 初五 3	水6 Water Nourish 9 丙子 Fire Rat 山雷頤 12 初六 3	金4 Metal Following 8 丁丑 Fire Ox 澤雷隨 13 初七 7	木8 Wood Abundance 7 戊寅 Earth Tiger 雷火豐 14 初八 6
火7 Fire Regulate 6 己卯 Earth Rabbit 水澤節 15 初九 8	水1 Water Unity 5 庚辰 Metal Dragon 地天泰 16 初十 9	木3 Wood Great Reward 4 辛巳 Metal Snake 火天大有 17 十一 7	火2 Fire Wind 3 壬午 Water Horse 巽爲風 18 十二 1	金4 Metal Trap 2 癸未 Water Goat 澤水困 19 十三 8	木3 Wood Not Yet Accomplished 1 甲申 Wood Monkey 火水未濟 20 十四 9	金9 Metal Retreat 9 乙酉 Wood Rooster 天山遯 21 十五 4
水6 Water Mountain 8 丙戌 Fire Dog 艮爲山 22 十六 1	木8 Wood Delight 7 丁亥 Fire Pig 雷地豫 23 十七 8	火7 Fire Beginning 6 戊子 Earth Rat 水雷屯 24 十八 4	金9 Metal Without Wrongdoing 5 己丑 Earth Ox 天雷無妄 25 十九 2	木3 Wood Fire 4 庚寅 Metal Tiger 離爲火 26 二十 1	火2 Fire Sincerity 3 辛卯 Metal Rabbit 風澤中孚 27 廿一 3	水6 Water Big Livestock 2 壬辰 Water Dragon 山天大畜 28 廿二 4
金4 Metal Eliminating 1 癸巳 Water Snake 澤天夬 29 廿三 6	金9 Metal Heaven 9 甲午 Wood Horse 乾爲天 30 廿四 1	火7 Fire Well 8 乙未 Wood Goat 水風井 31 廿五 6				

NOVEMBER 1972 辛亥

Xuan Kong Element 玄空五行	水地比 Alliance	Period Luck 卦運	Monthly Star 月星
Fire 火7		7	8

SUNDAY	MONDAY	TUESDAY	WEDNESDAY	THURSDAY	FRIDAY	SATURDAY
			木8 Wood Relief 7 丙申 Fire Monkey 雷水解 1 廿六 4	金4 Metal Influence 6 丁酉 Fire Rooster 澤山咸 2 廿七 9	水1 Water Humility 5 戊戌 Earth Dog 地山謙 3 廿八 6	火2 Fire Observation 4 己亥 Earth Pig 風地觀 4 廿九 2
火2 Fire Increasing 3 庚子 Metal Rat 風雷益 5 三十 9	水1 Water Dimming Light 2 辛丑 Metal Ox 地火明夷 6 十月初一 3	金9 Metal Fellowship 1 壬寅 Water Tiger 天火同人 7 初二 7	木8 Wood Marrying Maiden 9 癸卯 Water Rabbit 雷澤歸妹 8 初三 7	木3 Wood Opposition 8 甲辰 Wood Dragon 火澤睽 9 初四 2	火7 Fire Waiting 7 乙巳 Wood Snake 水天需 10 初五 3	金4 Metal Great Exceeding 6 丙午 Fire Horse 澤風大過 11 初六 3
水6 Water Poison 5 丁未 Fire Goat 山風蠱 12 初七 7	火2 Fire Dispersing 4 戊申 Earth Monkey 風水渙 13 初八 6	木3 Wood Travelling 3 己酉 Earth Rooster 火山旅 14 初九 8	金9 Metal Stagnation 2 庚戌 Metal Dog 天地否 15 初十 9	火7 Fire Alliance 1 辛亥 Metal Pig 水地比 16 十一 7	木8 Wood Thunder 9 壬子 Water Rat 震爲雷 17 十二 1	水6 Water Beauty 8 癸丑 Water Ox 山火賁 18 十三 8
火7 Fire Accomplished 7 甲寅 Wood Tiger 水火既濟 19 十四 9	水1 Water Arriving 6 乙卯 Wood Rabbit 地澤臨 20 十五 4	金4 Metal Marsh 5 丙辰 Fire Dragon 兑爲澤 21 十六 1	火2 Fire Small Livestock 4 丁巳 Fire Snake 風天小畜 22 十七 8	木3 Wood The Cauldron 3 戊午 Earth Horse 火風鼎 23 十八 4	水1 Water Rising 2 己未 Earth Goat 地風升 24 十九 2	火7 Fire Water 1 庚申 Metal Monkey 坎爲水 25 二十 1
木8 Wood Lesser Exceeding 9 辛酉 Metal Rooster 雷山小過 26 廿一 3	金4 Metal Gathering 8 壬戌 Water Dog 澤地萃 27 廿二 4	水6 Water Peel 7 癸亥 Water Pig 山地剝 28 廿三 6	水1 Water Earth 6 甲子 Wood Rat 坤爲地 29 廿四 1	木3 Wood Biting 5 乙丑 Wood Ox 火雷噬嗑 30 廿五 6		

DECEMBER 1972 壬子

Xuan Kong Element 玄空五行	震爲雷 Thunder	Period Luck 卦運	Monthly Star 月星
Wood 木8		1	7

SUNDAY	MONDAY	TUESDAY	WEDNESDAY	THURSDAY	FRIDAY	SATURDAY
木8 Wood Relief 9 丙申 Fire Monkey 雷水解 31 廿六 4					火2 Fire Family 4 丙寅 Fire Tiger 風火家人 1 廿六 4	水6 Water Decreasing 3 丁卯 Fire Rabbit 山澤損 2 廿七 9
金9 Metal Tread 2 戊辰 Earth Dragon 天澤履 3 廿八 6	木8 Wood Great Strength 1 己巳 Earth Snake 雷天大壯 4 廿九 2	木8 Wood Consistency 9 庚午 Metal Horse 雷風恒 5 三十 9	金9 Metal Litigation 8 辛未 Metal Goat 天水訟 6 十一月初一 3	水1 Water Officer 7 壬申 Water Monkey 地水師 7 初二 7	火2 Fire Gradual Progress 6 癸酉 Water Rooster 風山漸 8 初三 7	火7 Fire Obstruction 5 甲戌 Wood Dog 水山蹇 9 初四 2
木3 Wood Advancement 4 乙亥 Wood Pig 火地晉 10 初五 3	水6 Water Nourish 3 丙子 Fire Rat 山雷頤 11 初六 3	金4 Metal Following 2 丁丑 Fire Ox 澤雷隨 12 初七 7	木8 Wood Abundance 1 戊寅 Earth Tiger 雷火豐 13 初八 6	火7 Fire Regulate 9 己卯 Earth Rabbit 水澤節 14 初九 8	水1 Water Unity 8 庚辰 Metal Dragon 地天泰 15 初十 9	木3 Wood Great Reward 7 辛巳 Metal Snake 火天大有 16 十一 7
火2 Fire Wind 6 壬午 Water Horse 巽爲風 17 十二 1	金4 Metal Trap 5 癸未 Water Goat 澤水困 18 十三 8	木3 Wood Not Yet Accomplished 4 甲申 Wood Monkey 火水未濟 19 十四 9	金9 Metal Retreat 3 乙酉 Wood Rooster 天山遯 20 十五 4	水6 Water Mountain 2 丙戌 Fire Dog 艮爲山 21 十六 1	木8 Wood Delight 1/9 丁亥 Fire Pig 雷地豫 22 十七 8	火7 Fire Beginning 1 戊子 Earth Rat 水雷屯 23 十八 4
金9 Metal Without Wrongdoing 2 己丑 Earth Ox 天雷無妄 24 十九 2	木3 Wood Fire 3 庚寅 Metal Tiger 離爲火 25 二十 1	火2 Fire Sincerity 4 辛卯 Metal Rabbit 風澤中孚 26 廿一 3	水6 Water Big Livestock 5 壬辰 Water Dragon 山天大畜 27 廿二 4	金4 Metal Eliminating 6 癸巳 Water Snake 澤天夬 28 廿三 6	金9 Metal Heaven 7 甲午 Wood Horse 乾爲天 29 廿四 1	火7 Fire Well 8 乙未 Wood Goat 水風井 30 廿五 6

1973 癸丑

(*Gui Chou*) Water Ox

1973 癸丑 *(Gui Chou)* Water Ox

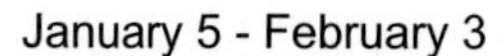

January 5 - February 3

	SE	S	SW	
	5	1	3	
E	4	6	8	W
	9	2	7	
	NE	N	NW	

水6 Water
癸丑 Water Ox
8 Beauty
山火賁

Three Killings	East

February 4 - March 5

	SE	S	SW	
	4	9	2	
E	3	5	7	W
	8	1	6	
	NE	N	NW	

火7 Fire
甲寅 Wood Tiger
9 Accomplished
水火既濟

Three Killings	North

March 6 - April 4

	SE	S	SW	
	3	8	1	
E	2	4	6	W
	7	9	5	
	NE	N	NW	

水1 Water
乙卯 Wood Rabbit
4 Arriving
地澤臨

Three Killings	West

April 5 - May 4

	SE	S	SW	
	2	7	9	
E	1	3	5	W
	6	8	4	
	NE	N	NW	

金4 Metal
丙辰 Fire Dragon
1 Marsh
兌為澤

Three Killings	South

May 5 - June 5

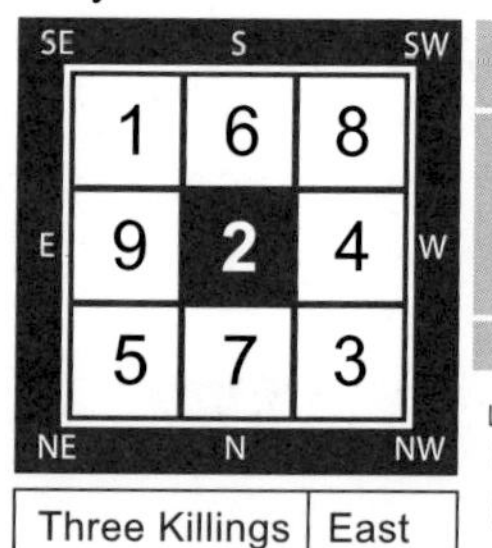

	SE	S	SW	
	1	6	8	
E	9	2	4	W
	5	7	3	
	NE	N	NW	

火2 Fire
丁巳 Fire Snake
8 Small Livestock
風天小畜

Three Killings	East

June 6 - July 6

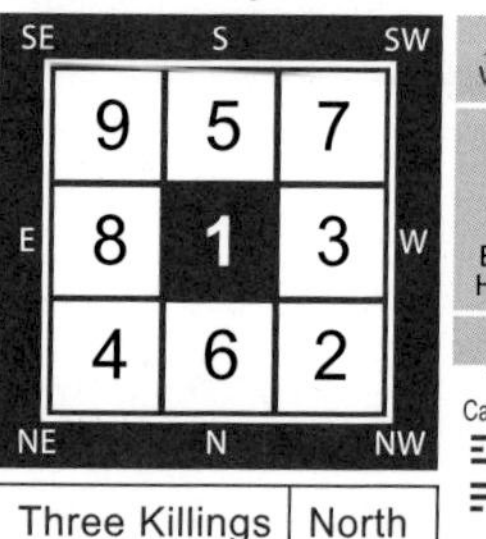

	SE	S	SW	
	9	5	7	
E	8	1	3	W
	4	6	2	
	NE	N	NW	

木3 Wood
戊午 Earth Horse
4 The Cauldron
火風鼎

Three Killings	North

July 7 - August 7

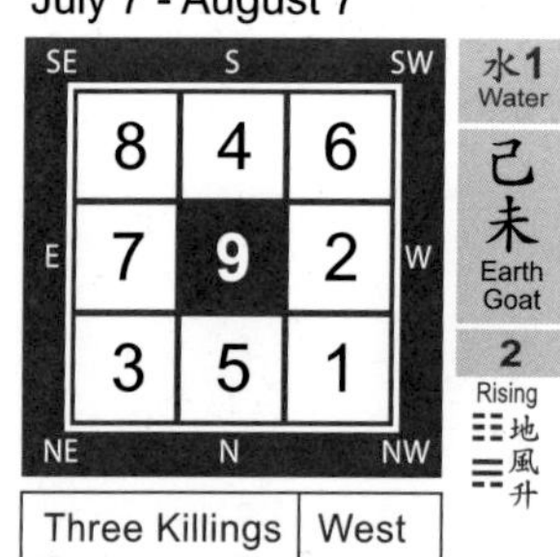

	SE	S	SW	
	8	4	6	
E	7	9	2	W
	3	5	1	
	NE	N	NW	

水1 Water
己未 Earth Goat
2 Rising
地風升

Three Killings	West

August 8 - September 7

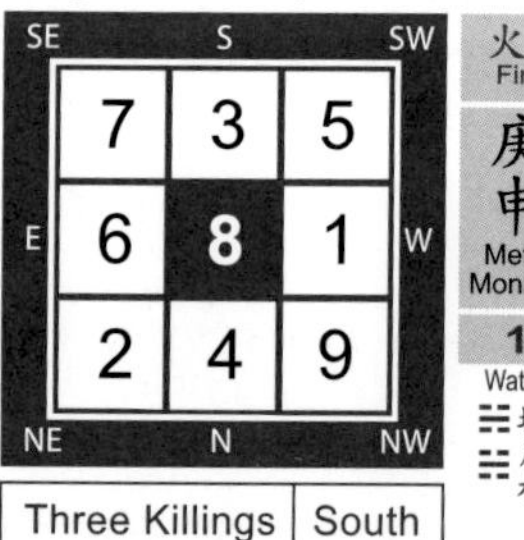

	SE	S	SW	
	7	3	5	
E	6	8	1	W
	2	4	9	
	NE	N	NW	

火7 Fire
庚申 Metal Monkey
1 Water
坎為水

Three Killings	South

September 8 - October 7

	SE	S	SW	
	6	2	4	
E	5	7	9	W
	1	3	8	
	NE	N	NW	

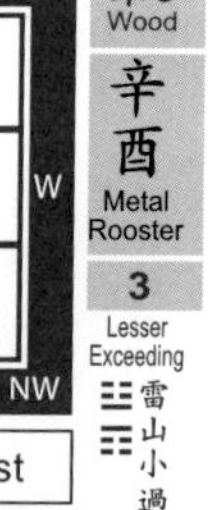

木8 Wood
辛酉 Metal Rooster
3 Lesser Exceeding
雷山小過

Three Killings	East

October 8 - November 6

	SE	S	SW	
	5	1	3	
E	4	6	8	W
	9	2	7	
	NE	N	NW	

金4 Metal
壬戌 Water Dog
4 Gathering
澤地萃

Three Killings	North

November 7 - December 6

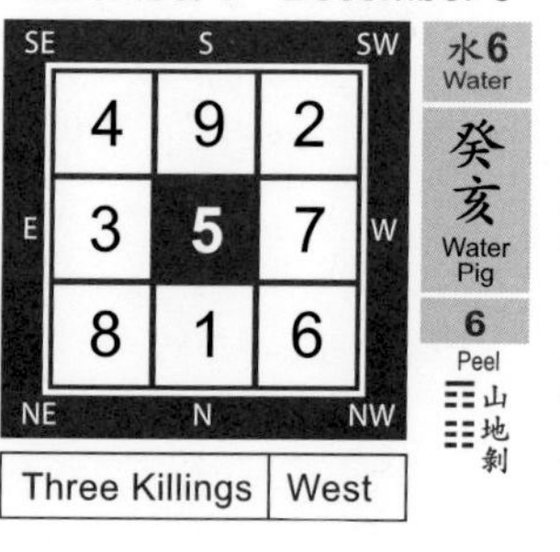

	SE	S	SW	
	4	9	2	
E	3	5	7	W
	8	1	6	
	NE	N	NW	

水6 Water
癸亥 Water Pig
6 Peel
山地剝

Three Killings	West

December 7 - January 5

	SE	S	SW	
	3	8	1	
E	2	4	6	W
	7	9	5	
	NE	N	NW	

水1 Water
甲子 Wood Rat
1 Earth
坤為地

Three Killings	South

JANUARY 1973 癸丑

Xuan Kong Element 玄空五行	山火賁 Beauty	Period Luck 卦運	Monthly Star 月星
Water 水6		8	6

SUNDAY	MONDAY	TUESDAY	WEDNESDAY	THURSDAY	FRIDAY	SATURDAY
	金4 Metal 1 Influence 丁酉 Fire Rooster 澤山咸 1 廿七 9	水1 Water 2 Humility 戊戌 Earth Dog 地山謙 2 廿八 6	火2 Fire 3 Observation 己亥 Earth Pig 風地觀 3 廿九 2	火2 Fire 4 Increasing 庚子 Metal Rat 風雷益 4 十二月初一 9	水1 Water 5 Dimming Light 辛丑 Metal Ox 地火明夷 5 初二 3	金9 Metal 6 Fellowship 壬寅 Water Tiger 天火同人 6 初三 7
木8 Wood 7 Marrying Maiden 癸卯 Water Rabbit 雷澤歸妹 7 初四 7	木3 Wood 8 Opposition 甲辰 Wood Dragon 火澤睽 8 初五 2	火7 Fire 9 Waiting 乙巳 Wood Snake 水天需 9 初六 3	金4 Metal 1 Great Exceeding 丙午 Fire Horse 澤風大過 10 初七 3	水6 Water 2 Poison 丁未 Fire Goat 山風蠱 11 初八 7	火2 Fire 3 Dispersing 戊申 Earth Monkey 風水渙 12 初九 6	木3 Wood 4 Travelling 己酉 Earth Rooster 火山旅 13 初十 8
金9 Metal 5 Stagnation 庚戌 Metal Dog 天地否 14 十一 9	火7 Fire 6 Alliance 辛亥 Metal Pig 水地比 15 十二 7	木8 Wood 7 Thunder 壬子 Water Rat 震爲雷 16 十三 1	水6 Water 8 Beauty 癸丑 Water Ox 山火賁 17 十四 8	火7 Fire 9 Accomplished 甲寅 Wood Tiger 水火既濟 18 十五 9	水1 Water 1 Arriving 乙卯 Wood Rabbit 地澤臨 19 十六 4	金4 Metal 2 Marsh 丙辰 Fire Dragon 兑爲澤 20 十七 1
火2 Fire 3 Small Livestock 丁巳 Fire Snake 風天小畜 21 十八 8	木3 Wood 4 The Cauldron 戊午 Earth Horse 火風鼎 22 十九 4	水1 Water 5 Rising 己未 Earth Goat 地風升 23 二十 2	火7 Fire 6 Water 庚申 Metal Monkey 坎爲水 24 廿一 1	木8 Wood 7 Lesser Exceeding 辛酉 Metal Rooster 雷山小過 25 廿二 3	金4 Metal 8 Gathering 壬戌 Water Dog 澤地萃 26 廿三 4	水6 Water 9 Peel 癸亥 Water Pig 山地剝 27 廿四 6
水1 Water 1 Earth 甲子 Wood Rat 坤爲地 28 廿五 1	木3 Wood 2 Biting 乙丑 Wood Ox 火雷噬嗑 29 廿六 6	火2 Fire 3 Family 丙寅 Fire Tiger 風火家人 30 廿七 4	水6 Water 4 Decreasing 丁卯 Fire Rabbit 山澤損 31 廿八 9			

FEBRUARY 1973 甲寅

Xuan Kong Element 玄空五行	水火既濟 Accomplished	Period Luck 卦運	Monthly Star 月星
Fire 火7		9	5

SUNDAY	MONDAY	TUESDAY	WEDNESDAY	THURSDAY	FRIDAY	SATURDAY
				金9 Metal 5 Tread 戊辰 Earth Dragon 天澤履 1 廿九 6	木8 Wood 6 Great Strength 己巳 Earth Snake 雷天大壯 2 三十 2	木8 Wood 7 Consistency 庚午 Metal Horse 雷風恆 3 正月初一 9
金9 Metal 8 Litigation 辛未 Metal Goat 天水訟 4 初二 3	水1 Water 9 Officer 壬申 Water Monkey 地水師 5 初三 7	火2 Fire 1 Gradual Progress 癸酉 Water Rooster 風山漸 6 初四 7	火7 Fire 2 Obstruction 甲戌 Wood Dog 水山蹇 7 初五 2	木3 Wood 3 Advancement 乙亥 Wood Pig 火地晉 8 初六 3	水6 Water 4 Nourish 丙子 Fire Rat 山雷頤 9 初七 3	金4 Metal 5 Following 丁丑 Fire Ox 澤雷隨 10 初八 7
木8 Wood 6 Abundance 戊寅 Earth Tiger 雷火豐 11 初九 6	火7 Fire 7 Regulate 己卯 Earth Rabbit 水澤節 12 初十 8	水1 Water 8 Unity 庚辰 Metal Dragon 地天泰 13 十一 9	木3 Wood 9 Great Reward 辛巳 Metal Snake 火天大有 14 十二 7	火2 Fire 1 Wind 壬午 Water Horse 巽爲風 15 十三 1	金4 Metal 2 Trap 癸未 Water Goat 澤水困 16 十四 8	木3 Wood 3 Not Yet Accomplished 甲申 Wood Monkey 火水未濟 17 十五 9
金9 Metal 4 Retreat 乙酉 Wood Rooster 天山遯 18 十六 4	水6 Water 5 Mountain 丙戌 Fire Dog 艮爲山 19 十七 1	木8 Wood 6 Delight 丁亥 Fire Pig 雷地豫 20 十八 8	火7 Fire 7 Beginning 戊子 Earth Rat 水雷屯 21 十九 4	金9 Metal 8 Without Wrongdoing 己丑 Earth Ox 天雷無妄 22 二十 2	木3 Wood 9 Fire 庚寅 Metal Tiger 離爲火 23 廿一 1	火2 Fire 1 Sincerity 辛卯 Metal Rabbit 風澤中孚 24 廿二 3
水6 Water 2 Big Livestock 壬辰 Water Dragon 山天大畜 25 廿三 4	金4 Metal 3 Eliminating 癸巳 Water Snake 澤天夬 26 廿四 6	金9 Metal 4 Heaven 甲午 Wood Horse 乾爲天 27 廿五 1	火7 Fire 5 Well 乙未 Wood Goat 水風井 28 廿六 6			

MARCH 1973 乙卯

Xuan Kong Element 玄空五行	地澤臨 Arriving	Period Luck 卦運	Monthly Star 月星
Water 水1		4	4

SUNDAY	MONDAY	TUESDAY	WEDNESDAY	THURSDAY	FRIDAY	SATURDAY
				1 廿七 木8 Wood Relief 雷水解 丙申 Fire Monkey 4 · 6	**2** 廿八 金4 Metal Influence 澤山咸 丁酉 Fire Rooster 9 · 7	**3** 廿九 水1 Water Humility 地山謙 戊戌 Earth Dog 6 · 8
4 三十 火2 Fire Observation 風地觀 己亥 Earth Pig 2 · 9	**5** 二月初一 火2 Fire Increasing 風雷益 庚子 Metal Rat 9 · 1	**6** 初二 水1 Water Dimming Light 地火明夷 辛丑 Metal Ox 3 · 2	**7** 初三 金9 Metal Fellowship 天火同人 壬寅 Water Tiger 7 · 3	**8** 初四 木8 Wood Marrying Maiden 雷澤歸妹 癸卯 Water Rabbit 7 · 4	**9** 初五 木3 Wood Opposition 火澤睽 甲辰 Wood Dragon 2 · 5	**10** 初六 火7 Fire Waiting 水天需 乙巳 Wood Snake 3 · 6
11 初七 金4 Metal Great Exceeding 澤風大過 丙午 Fire Horse 3 · 7	**12** 初八 水6 Water Poison 山風蠱 丁未 Fire Goat 7 · 8	**13** 初九 火2 Fire Dispersing 風水渙 戊申 Earth Monkey 6 · 9	**14** 初十 木3 Wood Travelling 火山旅 己酉 Earth Rooster 8 · 1	**15** 十一 金9 Metal Stagnation 天地否 庚戌 Metal Dog 9 · 2	**16** 十二 火7 Fire Alliance 水地比 辛亥 Metal Pig 7 · 3	**17** 十三 木8 Wood Thunder 震為雷 壬子 Water Rat 1 · 4
18 十四 水6 Water Beauty 山火賁 癸丑 Water Ox 8 · 5	**19** 十五 火7 Fire Accomplished 水火既濟 甲寅 Wood Tiger 9 · 6	**20** 十六 水1 Water Arriving 地澤臨 乙卯 Wood Rabbit 4 · 7	**21** 十七 金4 Metal Marsh 兑為澤 丙辰 Fire Dragon 1 · 8	**22** 十八 火2 Fire Small Livestock 風天小畜 丁巳 Fire Snake 8 · 9	**23** 十九 木3 Wood The Cauldron 火風鼎 戊午 Earth Horse 4 · 1	**24** 二十 水1 Water Rising 地風升 己未 Earth Goat 2 · 2
25 廿一 火7 Fire Water 坎為水 庚申 Metal Monkey 1 · 3	**26** 廿二 木8 Wood Lesser Exceeding 雷山小過 辛酉 Metal Rooster 3 · 4	**27** 廿三 金4 Metal Gathering 澤地萃 壬戌 Water Dog 4 · 5	**28** 廿四 水6 Water Peel 山地剝 癸亥 Water Pig 6 · 6	**29** 廿五 水1 Water Earth 坤為地 甲子 Wood Rat 1 · 7	**30** 廿六 木3 Wood Biting 火雷噬嗑 乙丑 Wood Ox 6 · 8	**31** 廿七 火2 Fire Family 風火家人 丙寅 Fire Tiger 4 · 9

APRIL 1973 丙辰

Xuan Kong Element 玄空五行	兑為澤 Marsh	Period Luck 卦運	Monthly Star 月星
Metal 金4		1	3

SUNDAY	MONDAY	TUESDAY	WEDNESDAY	THURSDAY	FRIDAY	SATURDAY
1 廿八 水6 Water Decreasing 山澤損 丁卯 Fire Rabbit 9 · 1	**2** 廿九 金9 Metal Tread 天澤履 戊辰 Earth Dragon 6 · 2	**3** 三月初一 木8 Wood Great Strength 雷天大壯 己巳 Earth Snake 2 · 3	**4** 初二 木8 Wood Consistency 雷風恆 庚午 Metal Horse 9 · 4	**5** 初三 金9 Metal Litigation 天水訟 辛未 Metal Goat 3 · 5	**6** 初四 水1 Water Officer 地水師 壬申 Water Monkey 7 · 6	**7** 初五 火2 Fire Gradual Progress 風山漸 癸酉 Water Rooster 7 · 7
8 初六 火7 Fire Obstruction 水山蹇 甲戌 Wood Dog 2 · 8	**9** 初七 木3 Wood Advancement 火地晉 乙亥 Wood Pig 3 · 9	**10** 初八 水6 Water Nourish 山雷頤 丙子 Fire Rat 3 · 1	**11** 初九 金4 Metal Following 澤雷隨 丁丑 Fire Ox 7 · 2	**12** 初十 木8 Wood Abundance 雷火豐 戊寅 Earth Tiger 6 · 3	**13** 十一 火7 Fire Regulate 水澤節 己卯 Earth Rabbit 8 · 4	**14** 十二 水1 Water Unity 地天泰 庚辰 Metal Dragon 9 · 5
15 十三 木3 Wood Great Reward 火天大有 辛巳 Metal Snake 7 · 6	**16** 十四 火2 Fire Wind 巽為風 壬午 Water Horse 1 · 7	**17** 十五 金4 Metal Trap 澤水困 癸未 Water Goat 8 · 8	**18** 十六 木3 Wood Not Yet Accomplished 火水未濟 甲申 Wood Monkey 9 · 9	**19** 十七 金9 Metal Retreat 天山遯 乙酉 Wood Rooster 4 · 1	**20** 十八 水6 Water Mountain 艮為山 丙戌 Fire Dog 1 · 2	**21** 十九 木8 Wood Delight 雷地豫 丁亥 Fire Pig 8 · 3
22 二十 火7 Fire Beginning 水雷屯 戊子 Earth Rat 4 · 4	**23** 廿一 金9 Metal Without Wrongdoing 天雷無妄 己丑 Earth Ox 2 · 5	**24** 廿二 木3 Wood Fire 離為火 庚寅 Metal Tiger 1 · 6	**25** 廿三 火2 Fire Sincerity 風澤中孚 辛卯 Metal Rabbit 3 · 7	**26** 廿四 水6 Water Big Livestock 山天大畜 壬辰 Water Dragon 4 · 8	**27** 廿五 金4 Metal Eliminating 澤天夬 癸巳 Water Snake 6 · 9	**28** 廿六 金9 Metal Heaven 乾為天 甲午 Wood Horse 1 · 1
29 廿七 火7 Fire Well 水風井 乙未 Wood Goat 6 · 2	**30** 廿八 木8 Wood Relief 雷水解 丙申 Fire Monkey 4 · 3					

MAY 1973 丁巳

Xuan Kong Element 玄空五行	風天小畜 Small Livestock	Period Luck 卦運	Monthly Star 月星
Fire 火2		8	2

SUNDAY	MONDAY	TUESDAY	WEDNESDAY	THURSDAY	FRIDAY	SATURDAY
		金4 Metal [4] Influence 丁酉 Fire Rooster 澤山咸 1 廿九 9	水1 Water [5] Humility 戊戌 Earth Dog 地山謙 2 三十 6	火2 Fire [6] Observation 己亥 Earth Pig 風地觀 3 四月初一 2	火2 Fire [7] Increasing 庚子 Metal Rat 風雷益 4 初二 9	水1 Water [8] Dimming Light 辛丑 Metal Ox 地火明夷 5 初三 3
金9 Metal [9] Fellowship 壬寅 Water Tiger 天火同人 6 初四 7	木8 Wood [1] Marrying Maiden 癸卯 Water Rabbit 雷澤歸妹 7 初五 7	木3 Wood [2] Opposition 甲辰 Wood Dragon 火澤睽 8 初六 2	火7 Fire [3] Waiting 乙巳 Wood Snake 水天需 9 初七 3	金4 Metal [4] Great Exceeding 丙午 Fire Horse 澤風大過 10 初八 3	水6 Water [5] Poison 丁未 Fire Goat 山風蠱 11 初九 7	火2 Fire [6] Dispersing 戊申 Earth Monkey 風水渙 12 初十 6
木3 Wood [7] Travelling 己酉 Earth Rooster 火山旅 13 十一 8	金9 Metal [8] Stagnation 庚戌 Metal Dog 天地否 14 十二 9	火7 Fire [9] Alliance 辛亥 Metal Pig 水地比 15 十三 7	木8 Wood [1] Thunder 壬子 Water Rat 震為雷 16 十四 1	水6 Water [2] Beauty 癸丑 Water Ox 山火賁 17 十五 8	火7 Fire [3] Accomplished 甲寅 Wood Tiger 水火既濟 18 十六 9	水1 Water [4] Arriving 乙卯 Wood Rabbit 地澤臨 19 十七 4
金4 Metal [5] Marsh 丙辰 Fire Dragon 兌為澤 20 十八 1	火2 Fire [6] Small Livestock 丁巳 Fire Snake 風天小畜 21 十九 8	木3 Wood [7] The Cauldron 戊午 Earth Horse 火風鼎 22 二十 4	水1 Water [8] Rising 己未 Earth Goat 地風升 23 廿一 2	火7 Fire [9] Water 庚申 Metal Monkey 坎為水 24 廿二 1	木8 Wood [1] Lesser Exceeding 辛酉 Metal Rooster 雷山小過 25 廿三 3	金4 Metal [2] Gathering 壬戌 Water Dog 澤地萃 26 廿四 4
水6 Water [3] Peel 癸亥 Water Pig 山地剝 27 廿五 6	水1 Water [4] Earth 甲子 Wood Rat 坤為地 28 廿六 1	木3 Wood [5] Biting 乙丑 Wood Ox 火雷噬嗑 29 廿七 6	火2 Fire [6] Family 丙寅 Fire Tiger 風火家人 30 廿八 4	水6 Water [7] Decreasing 丁卯 Fire Rabbit 山澤損 31 廿九 9		

JUNE 1973 戊午

Xuan Kong Element 玄空五行	火風鼎 The Cauldron	Period Luck 卦運	Monthly Star 月星
Wood 木3		4	1

SUNDAY	MONDAY	TUESDAY	WEDNESDAY	THURSDAY	FRIDAY	SATURDAY
					金9 Metal [8] Tread 戊辰 Earth Dragon 天澤履 1 五月初一 6	木8 Wood [9] Great Strength 己巳 Earth Snake 雷天大壯 2 初二 2
木8 Wood [1] Consistency 庚午 Metal Horse 雷風恒 3 初三 9	金9 Metal [2] Litigation 辛未 Metal Goat 天水訟 4 初四 3	水1 Water [3] Officer 壬申 Water Monkey 地水師 5 初五 7	火2 Fire [4] Gradual Progress 癸酉 Water Rooster 風山漸 6 初六 7	火7 Fire [5] Obstruction 甲戌 Wood Dog 水山蹇 7 初七 2	木3 Wood [6] Advancement 乙亥 Wood Pig 火地晉 8 初八 3	水6 Water [7] Nourish 丙子 Fire Rat 山雷頤 9 初九 3
金4 Metal [8] Following 丁丑 Fire Ox 澤雷隨 10 初十 7	木8 Wood [9] Abundance 戊寅 Earth Tiger 雷火豐 11 十一 6	火7 Fire [1] Regulate 己卯 Earth Rabbit 水澤節 12 十二 8	水1 Water [2] Unity 庚辰 Metal Dragon 地天泰 13 十三 9	木3 Wood [3] Great Reward 辛巳 Metal Snake 火天大有 14 十四 7	火2 Fire [4] Wind 壬午 Water Horse 巽為風 15 十五 1	金4 Metal [5] Trap 癸未 Water Goat 澤水困 16 十六 8
木3 Wood [6] Not Yet Accomplished 甲申 Wood Monkey 火水未濟 17 十七 9	金9 Metal [7] Retreat 乙酉 Wood Rooster 天山遯 18 十八 4	水6 Water [8] Mountain 丙戌 Fire Dog 艮為山 19 十九 1	木8 Wood [9] Delight 丁亥 Fire Pig 雷地豫 20 二十 8	火7 Fire [1/9] Beginning 戊子 Earth Rat 水雷屯 21 廿一 4	金9 Metal [8] Without Wrongdoing 己丑 Earth Ox 天雷無妄 22 廿二 2	木3 Wood [7] Fire 庚寅 Metal Tiger 離為火 23 廿三 1
火2 Fire [6] Sincerity 辛卯 Metal Rabbit 風澤中孚 24 廿四 3	水6 Water [5] Big Livestock 壬辰 Water Dragon 山天大畜 25 廿五 4	金4 Metal [4] Eliminating 癸巳 Water Snake 澤天夬 26 廿六 6	金9 Metal [3] Heaven 甲午 Wood Horse 乾為天 27 廿七 1	火7 Fire [2] Well 乙未 Wood Goat 水風井 28 廿八 6	木8 Wood [1] Relief 丙申 Fire Monkey 雷水解 29 廿九 4	金4 Metal [9] Influence 丁酉 Fire Rooster 澤山咸 30 六月初一 9

JULY 1973 己未

Xuan Kong Element 玄空五行	地風升 Rising	Period Luck 卦運	Monthly Star 月星
Water 水1		2	9

SUNDAY	MONDAY	TUESDAY	WEDNESDAY	THURSDAY	FRIDAY	SATURDAY
水1 Water 8 Humility 地山謙 戊戌 Earth Dog 1 初二 6	火2 Fire 7 Observation 風地觀 己亥 Earth Pig 2 初三 2	火2 Fire 6 Increasing 風雷益 庚子 Metal Rat 3 初四 9	水1 Water 5 Dimming Light 地火明夷 辛丑 Metal Ox 4 初五 3	金9 Metal 4 Fellowship 天火同人 壬寅 Water Tiger 5 初六 7	木8 Wood 3 Marrying Maiden 雷澤歸妹 癸卯 Water Rabbit 6 初七 7	木3 Wood 2 Opposition 火澤睽 甲辰 Wood Dragon 7 初八 2
火7 Fire 1 Waiting 水天需 乙巳 Wood Snake 8 初九 3	金4 Metal 9 Great Exceeding 澤風大過 丙午 Fire Horse 9 初十 3	水6 Water 8 Poison 山風蠱 丁未 Fire Goat 10 十一 7	火2 Fire 7 Dispersing 風水渙 戊申 Earth Monkey 11 十二 6	木3 Wood 6 Travelling 火山旅 己酉 Earth Rooster 12 十三 8	金9 Metal 5 Stagnation 天地否 庚戌 Metal Dog 13 十四 9	火7 Fire 4 Alliance 水地比 辛亥 Metal Pig 14 十五 7
木8 Wood 3 Thunder 震為雷 壬子 Water Rat 15 十六 1	水6 Water 2 Beauty 山火賁 癸丑 Water Ox 16 十七 8	火7 Fire 1 Accomplished 水火既濟 甲寅 Wood Tiger 17 十八 9	水1 Water 9 Arriving 地澤臨 乙卯 Wood Rabbit 18 十九 4	金4 Metal 8 Marsh 兑為澤 丙辰 Fire Dragon 19 二十 1	火2 Fire 7 Small Livestock 風天小畜 丁巳 Fire Snake 20 廿一 8	木3 Wood 6 The Cauldron 火風鼎 戊午 Earth Horse 21 廿二 4
水1 Water 5 Rising 地風升 己未 Earth Goat 22 廿三 2	火7 Fire 4 Water 坎為水 庚申 Metal Monkey 23 廿四 1	木8 Wood 3 Lesser Exceeding 雷山小過 辛酉 Metal Rooster 24 廿五 3	金4 Metal 2 Gathering 澤地萃 壬戌 Water Dog 25 廿六 4	水6 Water 1 Peel 山地剝 癸亥 Water Pig 26 廿七 6	水1 Water 9 Earth 坤為地 甲子 Wood Rat 27 廿八 1	木3 Wood 8 Biting 火雷噬嗑 乙丑 Wood Ox 28 廿九 6
火2 Fire 7 Family 風火家人 丙寅 Fire Tiger 29 三十 4	水6 Water 6 Decreasing 山澤損 丁卯 Fire Rabbit 30 七月初一 9	金9 Metal 5 Tread 天澤履 戊辰 Earth Dragon 31 初二 6				

AUGUST 1973 庚申

Xuan Kong Element 玄空五行	坎為水 Water	Period Luck 卦運	Monthly Star 月星
Fire 火7		1	8

SUNDAY	MONDAY	TUESDAY	WEDNESDAY	THURSDAY	FRIDAY	SATURDAY
			木8 Wood 4 Great Strength 雷天大壯 己巳 Earth Snake 1 初三 2	木8 Wood 3 Consistency 雷風恆 庚午 Metal Horse 2 初四 9	金9 Metal 2 Litigation 天水訟 辛未 Metal Goat 3 初五 3	水1 Water 1 Officer 地水師 壬申 Water Monkey 4 初六 7
火2 Fire 9 Gradual Progress 風山漸 癸酉 Water Rooster 5 初七 7	火7 Fire 8 Obstruction 水山蹇 甲戌 Wood Dog 6 初八 2	木3 Wood 7 Advancement 火地晉 乙亥 Wood Pig 7 初九 3	水6 Water 6 Nourish 山雷頤 丙子 Fire Rat 8 初十 3	金4 Metal 5 Following 澤雷隨 丁丑 Fire Ox 9 十一 7	木8 Wood 4 Abundance 雷火豐 戊寅 Earth Tiger 10 十二 6	火7 Fire 3 Regulate 水澤節 己卯 Earth Rabbit 11 十三 8
水1 Water 2 Unity 地天泰 庚辰 Metal Dragon 12 十四 9	木3 Wood 1 Great Reward 火天大有 辛巳 Metal Snake 13 十五 7	火2 Fire 9 Wind 巽為風 壬午 Water Horse 14 十六 1	金4 Metal 8 Trap 澤水困 癸未 Water Goat 15 十七 8	木3 Wood 7 Not Yet Accomplished 火水未濟 甲申 Wood Monkey 16 十八 9	金9 Metal 6 Retreat 天山遯 乙酉 Wood Rooster 17 十九 4	水6 Water 5 Mountain 艮為山 丙戌 Fire Dog 18 二十 1
木8 Wood 4 Delight 雷地豫 丁亥 Fire Pig 19 廿一 8	火7 Fire 3 Beginning 水雷屯 戊子 Earth Rat 20 廿二 4	金9 Metal 2 Without Wrongdoing 天雷無妄 己丑 Earth Ox 21 廿三 2	木3 Wood 1 Fire 離為火 庚寅 Metal Tiger 22 廿四 1	火2 Fire 9 Sincerity 風澤中孚 辛卯 Metal Rabbit 23 廿五 3	水6 Water 8 Big Livestock 山天大畜 壬辰 Water Dragon 24 廿六 4	金4 Metal 7 Eliminating 澤天夬 癸巳 Water Snake 25 廿七 6
金9 Metal 6 Heaven 乾為天 甲午 Wood Horse 26 廿八 1	火7 Fire 5 Well 水風井 乙未 Wood Goat 27 廿九 6	木8 Wood 4 Relief 雷水解 丙申 Fire Monkey 28 八月初一 4	金4 Metal 3 Influence 澤山咸 丁酉 Fire Rooster 29 初二 9	水1 Water 2 Humility 地山謙 戊戌 Earth Dog 30 初三 6	火2 Fire 1 Observation 風地觀 己亥 Earth Pig 31 初四 2	

SEPTEMBER 1973 辛酉

Xuan Kong Element 玄空五行	雷山小過 Lesser Exceeding	Period Luck 卦運	Monthly Star 月星
Wood 木8		3	7

SUNDAY	MONDAY	TUESDAY	WEDNESDAY	THURSDAY	FRIDAY	SATURDAY
木8 Wood 7 Great Strength 己巳 Earth Snake 雷天大壯 2 **30** 初五						火2 Fire 9 Increasing 庚子 Metal Rat 風雷益 9 **1** 初五
水1 Water 8 Dimming Light 辛丑 Metal Ox 地火明夷 3 **2** 初六	金9 Metal 7 Fellowship 壬寅 Water Tiger 天火同人 7 **3** 初七	木8 Wood 6 Marrying Maiden 癸卯 Water Rabbit 雷澤歸妹 7 **4** 初八	木3 Wood 5 Opposition 甲辰 Wood Dragon 火澤睽 2 **5** 初九	火7 Fire 4 Waiting 乙巳 Wood Snake 水天需 3 **6** 初十	金4 Metal 3 Great Exceeding 丙午 Fire Horse 澤風大過 3 **7** 十一	水6 Water 2 Poison 丁未 Fire Goat 山風蠱 7 **8** 十二
火2 Fire 1 Dispersing 戊申 Earth Monkey 風水渙 6 **9** 十三	木3 Wood 9 Travelling 己酉 Earth Rooster 火山旅 8 **10** 十四	金9 Metal 8 Stagnation 庚戌 Metal Dog 天地否 9 **11** 十五	火7 Fire 7 Alliance 辛亥 Metal Pig 水地比 7 **12** 十六	木8 Wood 6 Thunder 壬子 Water Rat 震爲雷 1 **13** 十七	水6 Water 5 Beauty 癸丑 Water Ox 山火賁 8 **14** 十八	火7 Fire 4 Accomplished 甲寅 Wood Tiger 水火既濟 9 **15** 十九
水1 Water 3 Arriving 乙卯 Wood Rabbit 地澤臨 4 **16** 二十	金4 Metal 2 Marsh 丙辰 Fire Dragon 兑爲澤 1 **17** 廿一	火2 Fire 1 Small Livestock 丁巳 Fire Snake 風天小畜 8 **18** 廿二	木3 Wood 9 The Cauldron 戊午 Earth Horse 火風鼎 4 **19** 廿三	水1 Water 8 Rising 己未 Earth Goat 地風升 2 **20** 廿四	火7 Fire 7 Water 庚申 Metal Monkey 坎爲水 1 **21** 廿五	木8 Wood 6 Lesser Exceeding 辛酉 Metal Rooster 雷山小過 3 **22** 廿六
金4 Metal 5 Gathering 壬戌 Water Dog 澤地萃 4 **23** 廿七	水6 Water 4 Peel 癸亥 Water Pig 山地剝 6 **24** 廿八	水1 Water 3 Earth 甲子 Wood Rat 坤爲地 1 **25** 廿九	木3 Wood 2 Biting 乙丑 Wood Ox 火雷噬嗑 6 **26** 九月初一	火2 Fire 1 Family 丙寅 Fire Tiger 風火家人 4 **27** 初二	水6 Water 9 Decreasing 丁卯 Fire Rabbit 山澤損 9 **28** 初三	金9 Metal 8 Tread 戊辰 Earth Dragon 天澤履 6 **29** 初四

OCTOBER 1973 壬戌

Xuan Kong Element 玄空五行	澤地萃 Gathering	Period Luck 卦運	Monthly Star 月星
Metal 金4		4	6

SUNDAY	MONDAY	TUESDAY	WEDNESDAY	THURSDAY	FRIDAY	SATURDAY
	木8 Wood 6 Consistency 庚午 Metal Horse 雷風恆 9 **1** 初六	金9 Metal 5 Litigation 辛未 Metal Goat 天水訟 3 **2** 初七	水1 Water 4 Officer 壬申 Water Monkey 地水師 7 **3** 初八	火2 Fire 3 Gradual Progress 癸酉 Water Rooster 風山漸 7 **4** 初九	火7 Fire 2 Obstruction 甲戌 Wood Dog 水山蹇 2 **5** 初十	木3 Wood 1 Advancement 乙亥 Wood Pig 火地晉 3 **6** 十一
水6 Water 9 Nourish 丙子 Fire Rat 山雷頤 3 **7** 十二	金4 Metal 8 Following 丁丑 Fire Ox 澤雷隨 7 **8** 十三	木8 Wood 7 Abundance 戊寅 Earth Tiger 雷火豐 6 **9** 十四	火7 Fire 6 Regulate 己卯 Earth Rabbit 水澤節 8 **10** 十五	水1 Water 5 Unity 庚辰 Metal Dragon 地天泰 9 **11** 十六	木3 Wood 4 Great Reward 辛巳 Metal Snake 火天大有 7 **12** 十七	火2 Fire 3 Wind 壬午 Water Horse 巽爲風 1 **13** 十八
金4 Metal 2 Trap 癸未 Water Goat 澤水困 8 **14** 十九	木3 Wood 1 Not Yet Accomplished 甲申 Wood Monkey 火水未濟 9 **15** 二十	金9 Metal 9 Retreat 乙酉 Wood Rooster 天山遯 4 **16** 廿一	水6 Water 8 Mountain 丙戌 Fire Dog 艮爲山 1 **17** 廿二	木8 Wood 7 Delight 丁亥 Fire Pig 雷地豫 8 **18** 廿三	火7 Fire 6 Beginning 戊子 Earth Rat 水雷屯 4 **19** 廿四	金9 Metal 5 Without Wrongdoing 己丑 Earth Ox 天雷無妄 2 **20** 廿五
木3 Wood 4 Fire 庚寅 Metal Tiger 離爲火 1 **21** 廿六	火2 Fire 3 Sincerity 辛卯 Metal Rabbit 風澤中孚 3 **22** 廿七	水6 Water 2 Big Livestock 壬辰 Water Dragon 山天大畜 4 **23** 廿八	金4 Metal 1 Eliminating 癸巳 Water Snake 澤天夬 6 **24** 廿九	金9 Metal 9 Heaven 甲午 Wood Horse 乾爲天 1 **25** 三十	火7 Fire 8 Well 乙未 Wood Goat 水風井 6 **26** 十月初一	木8 Wood 7 Relief 丙申 Fire Monkey 雷水解 4 **27** 初二
金4 Metal 6 Influence 丁酉 Fire Rooster 澤山咸 9 **28** 初三	水1 Water 5 Humility 戊戌 Earth Dog 地山謙 6 **29** 初四	火2 Fire 4 Observation 己亥 Earth Pig 風地觀 2 **30** 初五	火2 Fire 3 Increasing 庚子 Metal Rat 風雷益 9 **31** 初六			

NOVEMBER 1973 癸亥

Xuan Kong Element 玄空五行	山地剝 Peel	Period Luck 卦運	Monthly Star 月星
Water 水6		6	5

SUNDAY	MONDAY	TUESDAY	WEDNESDAY	THURSDAY	FRIDAY	SATURDAY
				水1 Water 2 Dimming Light 辛丑 Metal Ox 地火明夷 **1** 初七 3	金9 Metal 1 Fellowship 壬寅 Water Tiger 天火同人 **2** 初八 7	木8 Wood 9 Marrying Maiden 癸卯 Water Rabbit 雷澤歸妹 **3** 初九 7
木3 Wood 8 Opposition 甲辰 Wood Dragon 火澤睽 **4** 初十 2	火7 Fire 7 Waiting 乙巳 Wood Snake 水天需 **5** 十一 3	金4 Metal 6 Great Exceeding 丙午 Fire Horse 澤風大過 **6** 十二 3	水6 Water 5 Poison 丁未 Fire Goat 山風蠱 **7** 十三 7	火2 Fire 4 Dispersing 戊申 Earth Monkey 風水渙 **8** 十四 6	木3 Wood 3 Travelling 己酉 Earth Rooster 火山旅 **9** 十五 8	金9 Metal 2 Stagnation 庚戌 Metal Dog 天地否 **10** 十六 9
火7 Fire 1 Alliance 辛亥 Metal Pig 水地比 **11** 十七 7	木8 Wood 9 Thunder 壬子 Water Rat 震爲雷 **12** 十八 1	水6 Water 8 Beauty 癸丑 Water Ox 山火賁 **13** 十九 8	火7 Fire 7 Accomplished 甲寅 Wood Tiger 水火既濟 **14** 二十 9	水1 Water 6 Arriving 乙卯 Wood Rabbit 地澤臨 **15** 廿一 4	金4 Metal 5 Marsh 丙辰 Fire Dragon 兌爲澤 **16** 廿二 1	火2 Fire 4 Small Livestock 丁巳 Fire Snake 風天小畜 **17** 廿三 8
木3 Wood 3 The Cauldron 戊午 Earth Horse 火風鼎 **18** 廿四 4	水1 Water 2 Rising 己未 Earth Goat 地風升 **19** 廿五 2	火7 Fire 1 Water 庚申 Metal Monkey 坎爲水 **20** 廿六 1	木8 Wood 9 Lesser Exceeding 辛酉 Metal Rooster 雷山小過 **21** 廿七 3	金4 Metal 8 Gathering 壬戌 Water Dog 澤地萃 **22** 廿八 4	水6 Water 7 Peel 癸亥 Water Pig 山地剝 **23** 廿九 6	水1 Water 6 Earth 甲子 Wood Rat 坤爲地 **24** 三十 1
木3 Wood 5 Biting 乙丑 Wood Ox 火雷噬嗑 **25** 十一月初一 6	火2 Fire 4 Family 丙寅 Fire Tiger 風火家人 **26** 初二 4	水6 Water 3 Decreasing 丁卯 Fire Rabbit 山澤損 **27** 初三 9	金9 Metal 2 Tread 戊辰 Earth Dragon 天澤履 **28** 初四 6	木8 Wood 1 Great Strength 己巳 Earth Snake 雷天大壯 **29** 初五 2	木8 Wood 9 Consistency 庚午 Metal Horse 雷風恆 **30** 初六 9	

DECEMBER 1973 甲子

Xuan Kong Element 玄空五行	坤爲地 Earth	Period Luck 卦運	Monthly Star 月星
Water 水1		1	4

SUNDAY	MONDAY	TUESDAY	WEDNESDAY	THURSDAY	FRIDAY	SATURDAY
火2 Fire 4 Increasing 庚子 Metal Rat 風雷益 **30** 初七 9	水1 Water 5 Dimming Light 辛丑 Metal Ox 地火明夷 **31** 初八 3					金9 Metal 8 Litigation 辛未 Metal Goat 天水訟 **1** 初七 3
水1 Water 7 Officer 壬申 Water Monkey 地水師 **2** 初八 7	火2 Fire 6 Gradual Progress 癸酉 Water Rooster 風山漸 **3** 初九 7	火7 Fire 5 Obstruction 甲戌 Wood Dog 水山蹇 **4** 初十 2	木3 Wood 4 Advancement 乙亥 Wood Pig 火地晉 **5** 十一 3	水6 Water 3 Nourish 丙子 Fire Rat 山雷頤 **6** 十二 3	金4 Metal 2 Following 丁丑 Fire Ox 澤雷隨 **7** 十三 7	木8 Wood 1 Abundance 戊寅 Earth Tiger 雷火豐 **8** 十四 6
火7 Fire 9 Regulate 己卯 Earth Rabbit 水澤節 **9** 十五 8	水1 Water 8 Unity 庚辰 Metal Dragon 地天泰 **10** 十六 9	木3 Wood 7 Great Reward 辛巳 Metal Snake 火天大有 **11** 十七 7	火2 Fire 6 Wind 壬午 Water Horse 巽爲風 **12** 十八 1	金4 Metal 5 Trap 癸未 Water Goat 澤水困 **13** 十九 8	木3 Wood 4 Not Yet Accomplished 甲申 Wood Monkey 火水未濟 **14** 二十 9	金9 Metal 3 Retreat 乙酉 Wood Rooster 天山遯 **15** 廿一 4
水6 Water 2 Mountain 丙戌 Fire Dog 艮爲山 **16** 廿二 1	木8 Wood 1 Delight 丁亥 Fire Pig 雷地豫 **17** 廿三 8	火7 Fire 9 Beginning 戊子 Earth Rat 水雷屯 **18** 廿四 4	金9 Metal 8 Without Wrongdoing 己丑 Earth Ox 天雷無妄 **19** 廿五 2	木3 Wood 7 Fire 庚寅 Metal Tiger 離爲火 **20** 廿六 1	火2 Fire 6 Sincerity 辛卯 Metal Rabbit 風澤中孚 **21** 廿七 3	水6 Water 5 5 Big Livestock 壬辰 Water Dragon 山天大畜 **22** 廿八 4
金4 Metal 6 Eliminating 癸巳 Water Snake 澤天夬 **23** 廿九 6	金9 Metal 7 Heaven 甲午 Wood Horse 乾爲天 **24** 十二月初一 1	火7 Fire 8 Well 乙未 Wood Goat 水風井 **25** 初二 6	木8 Wood 9 Relief 丙申 Fire Monkey 雷水解 **26** 初三 4	金4 Metal 1 Influence 丁酉 Fire Rooster 澤山咸 **27** 初四 9	水1 Water 2 Humility 戊戌 Earth Dog 地山謙 **28** 初五 6	火2 Fire 3 Observation 己亥 Earth Pig 風地觀 **29** 初六 2

1974 甲寅

(*Jia Yin*) Wood Tiger

1974 甲寅 *(Jia Yin)* Wood Tiger

January 6 - February 3

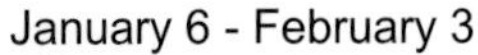

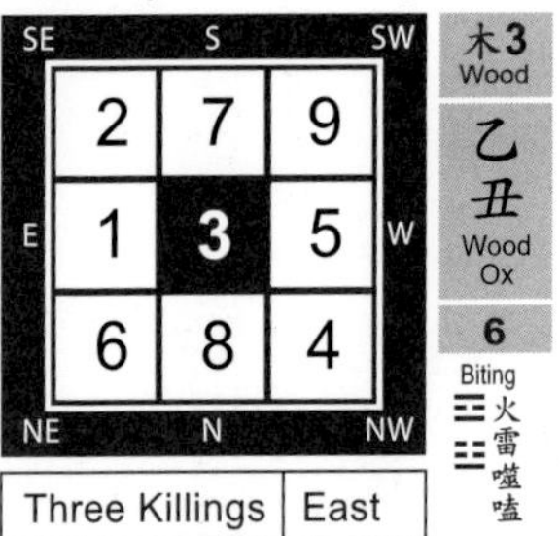

SE S SW E W NE N NW
2 7 9
1 3 5
6 8 4
木3 Wood
乙丑 Wood Ox
6
Biting
火雷噬嗑
Three Killings East

February 4 - March 5

SE	S	SW
1	6	8
9	**2**	4
5	7	3

火**2** Fire
丙寅 Fire Tiger
4 Family
風火家人

March 6 - April 4

SE	S	SW
9	5	7
8	**1**	3
4	6	2

水**6** Water
丁卯 Fire Rabbit
9 Decreasing
山澤損

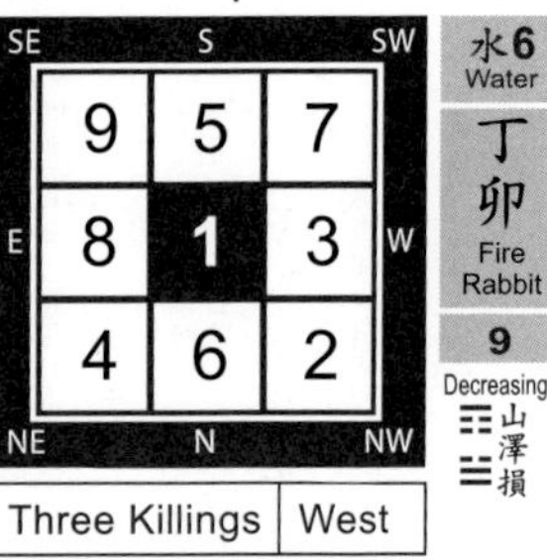

April 5 - May 5
戊辰 Earth Dragon
6 Tread
天澤履

May 6 - June 5

SE	S	SW
7	3	5
6	**8**	1
2	4	9

木**8** Wood
己巳 Earth Snake
2 Great Strength
雷天大壯

June 6 - July 6

July 7 - August 7

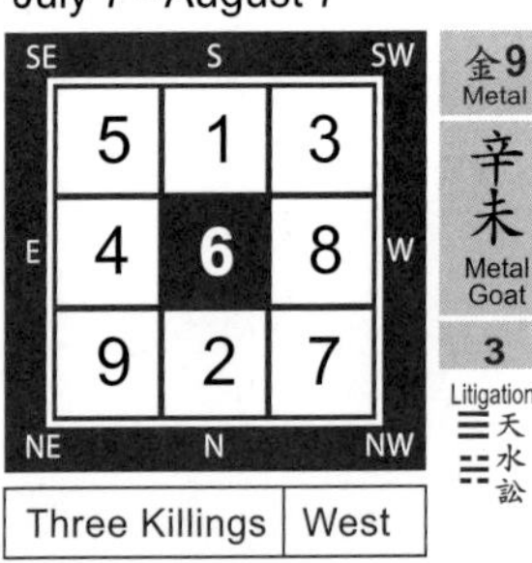

SE S SW E W NE N NW
5 1 3
4 6 8
9 2 7
金9 Metal
辛未 Metal Goat
3
Litigation
天水訟
Three Killings West

August 8 - September 7

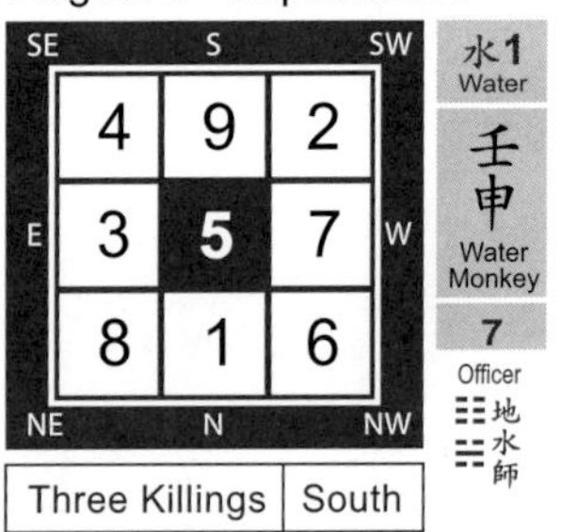

September 8 - October 8

SE	S	SW
3	8	1
2	**4**	6
7	9	5

火**2** Fire
癸酉 Water Rooster
7 Gradual Progress
風山漸

October 9 - November 7

November 8 - December 6
乙亥 Wood Pig
3 Advancement
火地晉

December 7 - January 5

JANUARY 1974 乙丑

Xuan Kong Element 玄空五行	火雷噬嗑 Biting	Period Luck 卦運	Monthly Star 月星
Wood 木3		6	3

SUNDAY	MONDAY	TUESDAY	WEDNESDAY	THURSDAY	FRIDAY	SATURDAY
		金9 Metal Fellowship 6 壬寅 Water Tiger 天火同人 1 初九 7	木8 Wood Marrying Maiden 7 癸卯 Water Rabbit 雷澤歸妹 2 初十 7	木3 Wood Opposition 8 甲辰 Wood Dragon 火澤睽 3 十一 2	火7 Fire Waiting 9 乙巳 Wood Snake 水天需 4 十二 3	金4 Metal Great Exceeding 1 丙午 Fire Horse 澤風大過 5 十三 3
水6 Water Poison 2 丁未 Fire Goat 山風蠱 6 十四 7	火2 Fire Dispersing 3 戊申 Earth Monkey 風水渙 7 十五 6	木3 Wood Travelling 4 己酉 Earth Rooster 火山旅 8 十六 8	金9 Metal Stagnation 5 庚戌 Metal Dog 天地否 9 十七 9	火7 Fire Alliance 6 辛亥 Metal Pig 水地比 10 十八 7	木8 Wood Thunder 7 壬子 Water Rat 震爲雷 11 十九 1	水6 Water Beauty 8 癸丑 Water Ox 山火賁 12 二十 8
火7 Fire Accomplished 9 甲寅 Wood Tiger 水火既濟 13 廿一 9	水1 Water Arriving 1 乙卯 Wood Rabbit 地澤臨 14 廿二 4	金4 Metal Marsh 2 丙辰 Fire Dragon 兌爲澤 15 廿三 1	火2 Fire Small Livestock 3 丁巳 Fire Snake 風天小畜 16 廿四 8	木3 Wood The Cauldron 4 戊午 Earth Horse 火風鼎 17 廿五 4	水1 Water Rising 5 己未 Earth Goat 地風升 18 廿六 2	火7 Fire Water 6 庚申 Metal Monkey 坎爲水 19 廿七 1
木8 Wood Lesser Exceeding 7 辛酉 Metal Rooster 雷山小過 20 廿八 3	金4 Metal Gathering 8 壬戌 Water Dog 澤地萃 21 廿九 4	水6 Water Peel 9 癸亥 Water Pig 山地剝 22 三十 6	水1 Water Earth 1 甲子 Wood Rat 坤爲地 23 正月初一 1	木3 Wood Biting 2 乙丑 Wood Ox 火雷噬嗑 24 初二 6	火2 Fire Family 3 丙寅 Fire Tiger 風火家人 25 初三 4	水6 Water Decreasing 4 丁卯 Fire Rabbit 山澤損 26 初四 9
金9 Metal Tread 5 戊辰 Earth Dragon 天澤履 27 初五 6	木8 Wood Great Strength 6 己巳 Earth Snake 雷天大壯 28 初六 2	木8 Wood Consistency 7 庚午 Metal Horse 雷風恒 29 初七 9	金9 Metal Litigation 8 辛未 Metal Goat 天水訟 30 初八 3	水1 Water Officer 9 壬申 Water Monkey 地水師 31 初九 7		

FEBRUARY 1974 丙寅

Xuan Kong Element 玄空五行	風火家人 Family	Period Luck 卦運	Monthly Star 月星
Fire 火2		4	2

SUNDAY	MONDAY	TUESDAY	WEDNESDAY	THURSDAY	FRIDAY	SATURDAY
					火2 Fire Gradual Progress 1 癸酉 Water Rooster 風山漸 1 初十 7	火7 Fire Obstruction 2 甲戌 Wood Dog 水山蹇 2 十一 2
木3 Wood Advancement 3 乙亥 Wood Pig 火地晉 3 十二 3	水6 Water Nourish 4 丙子 Fire Rat 山雷頤 4 十三 3	金4 Metal Following 5 丁丑 Fire Ox 澤雷隨 5 十四 7	木8 Wood Abundance 6 戊寅 Earth Tiger 雷火豐 6 十五 6	火7 Fire Regulate 7 己卯 Earth Rabbit 水澤節 7 十六 8	水1 Water Unity 8 庚辰 Metal Dragon 地天泰 8 十七 9	木3 Wood Great Reward 9 辛巳 Metal Snake 火天大有 9 十八 7
火2 Fire Wind 1 壬午 Water Horse 巽爲風 10 十九 1	金4 Metal Trap 2 癸未 Water Goat 澤水困 11 二十 8	木3 Wood Not Yet Accomplished 3 甲申 Wood Monkey 火水未濟 12 廿一 9	金9 Metal Retreat 4 乙酉 Wood Rooster 天山遯 13 廿二 4	水6 Water Mountain 5 丙戌 Fire Dog 艮爲山 14 廿三 1	木8 Wood Delight 6 丁亥 Fire Pig 雷地豫 15 廿四 8	火7 Fire Beginning 7 戊子 Earth Rat 水雷屯 16 廿五 4
金9 Metal Without Wrongdoing 8 己丑 Earth Ox 天雷無妄 17 廿六 2	木3 Wood Fire 9 庚寅 Metal Tiger 離爲火 18 廿七 1	火2 Fire Sincerity 1 辛卯 Metal Rabbit 風澤中孚 19 廿八 3	水6 Water Big Livestock 2 壬辰 Water Dragon 山天大畜 20 廿九 4	金4 Metal Eliminating 3 癸巳 Water Snake 澤天夬 21 三十 6	金9 Metal Heaven 4 甲午 Wood Horse 乾爲天 22 二月初一 1	火7 Fire Well 5 乙未 Wood Goat 水風井 23 初二 6
木8 Wood Relief 6 丙申 Fire Monkey 雷水解 24 初三 4	金4 Metal Influence 7 丁酉 Fire Rooster 澤山咸 25 初四 9	水1 Water Humility 8 戊戌 Earth Dog 地山謙 26 初五 6	火2 Fire Observation 9 己亥 Earth Pig 風地觀 27 初六 2	火2 Fire Increasing 1 庚子 Metal Rat 風雷益 28 初七 9		

MARCH 1974 丁卯

Xuan Kong Element 玄空五行	山澤損 Decreasing	Period Luck 卦運	Monthly Star 月星
Water 水6		9	1

SUNDAY	MONDAY	TUESDAY	WEDNESDAY	THURSDAY	FRIDAY	SATURDAY
金9 Metal 5 Litigation 天水訟 辛未 Metal Goat 3 31 初八					水1 Water 2 Dimming Light 地火明夷 辛丑 Metal Ox 3 1 初八	金9 Metal 3 Fellowship 天火同人 壬寅 Water Tiger 7 2 初九
木8 Wood 4 Marrying Maiden 雷澤歸妹 癸卯 Water Rabbit 7 3 初十	木3 Wood 5 Opposition 火澤睽 甲辰 Wood Dragon 2 4 十一	火7 Fire 6 Waiting 水天需 乙巳 Wood Snake 3 5 十二	金4 Metal 7 Great Exceeding 澤風大過 丙午 Fire Horse 3 6 十三	水6 Water 8 Poison 山風蠱 丁未 Fire Goat 7 7 十四	火2 Fire 9 Dispersing 風水渙 戊申 Earth Monkey 6 8 十五	木3 Wood 1 Travelling 火山旅 己酉 Earth Rooster 8 9 十六
金9 Metal 2 Stagnation 天地否 庚戌 Metal Dog 9 10 十七	火7 Fire 3 Alliance 水地比 辛亥 Metal Pig 7 11 十八	木8 Wood 4 Thunder 震爲雷 壬子 Water Rat 1 12 十九	水6 Water 5 Beauty 山火賁 癸丑 Water Ox 8 13 二十	火7 Fire 6 Accomplished 水火既濟 甲寅 Wood Tiger 9 14 廿一	水1 Water 7 Arriving 地澤臨 乙卯 Wood Rabbit 4 15 廿二	金4 Metal 8 Marsh 兑爲澤 丙辰 Fire Dragon 1 16 廿三
火2 Fire 9 Small Livestock 風天小畜 丁巳 Fire Snake 8 17 廿四	木3 Wood 1 The Cauldron 火風鼎 戊午 Earth Horse 4 18 廿五	水1 Water 2 Rising 地風升 己未 Earth Goat 2 19 廿六	火7 Fire 3 Water 坎爲水 庚申 Metal Monkey 1 20 廿七	木8 Wood 4 Lesser Exceeding 雷山小過 辛酉 Metal Rooster 3 21 廿八	金4 Metal 5 Gathering 澤地萃 壬戌 Water Dog 4 22 廿九	水6 Water 6 Peel 山地剝 癸亥 Water Pig 6 23 三十
水1 Water 7 Earth 坤爲地 甲子 Wood Rat 1 24 三月初一	木3 Wood 8 Biting 火雷噬嗑 乙丑 Wood Ox 6 25 初二	火2 Fire 9 Family 風火家人 丙寅 Fire Tiger 4 26 初三	水6 Water 1 Decreasing 山澤損 丁卯 Fire Rabbit 9 27 初四	金9 Metal 2 Tread 天澤履 戊辰 Earth Dragon 6 28 初五	木8 Wood 3 Great Strength 雷天大壯 己巳 Earth Snake 2 29 初六	木8 Wood 4 Consistency 雷風恆 庚午 Metal Horse 9 30 初七

APRIL 1974 戊辰

Xuan Kong Element 玄空五行	天澤履 Tread	Period Luck 卦運	Monthly Star 月星
Metal 金9		6	9

SUNDAY	MONDAY	TUESDAY	WEDNESDAY	THURSDAY	FRIDAY	SATURDAY
	水1 Water 6 Officer 地水師 壬申 Water Monkey 7 1 初九	火2 Fire 7 Gradual Progress 風山漸 癸酉 Water Rooster 7 2 初十	火7 Fire 8 Obstruction 水山蹇 甲戌 Wood Dog 2 3 十一	木3 Wood 9 Advancement 火地晉 乙亥 Wood Pig 3 4 十二	水6 Water 1 Nourish 山雷頤 丙子 Fire Rat 3 5 十三	金4 Metal 2 Following 澤雷隨 丁丑 Fire Ox 7 6 十四
木8 Wood 3 Abundance 雷火豐 戊寅 Earth Tiger 6 7 十五	火7 Fire 4 Regulate 水澤節 己卯 Earth Rabbit 8 8 十六	水1 Water 5 Unity 地天泰 庚辰 Metal Dragon 9 9 十七	木3 Wood 6 Great Reward 火天大有 辛巳 Metal Snake 7 10 十八	火2 Fire 7 Wind 巽爲風 壬午 Water Horse 1 11 十九	金4 Metal 8 Trap 澤水困 癸未 Water Goat 8 12 二十	木3 Wood 9 Not Yet Accomplished 火水未濟 甲申 Wood Monkey 9 13 廿一
金9 Metal 1 Retreat 天山遯 乙酉 Wood Rooster 4 14 廿二	水6 Water 2 Mountain 艮爲山 丙戌 Fire Dog 1 15 廿三	木8 Wood 3 Delight 雷地豫 丁亥 Fire Pig 8 16 廿四	火7 Fire 4 Beginning 水雷屯 戊子 Earth Rat 4 17 廿五	金9 Metal 5 Without Wrongdoing 天雷無妄 己丑 Earth Ox 2 18 廿六	木3 Wood 6 Fire 離爲火 庚寅 Metal Tiger 1 19 廿七	火2 Fire 7 Sincerity 風澤中孚 辛卯 Metal Rabbit 3 20 廿八
水6 Water 8 Big Livestock 山天大畜 壬辰 Water Dragon 4 21 廿九	金4 Metal 9 Eliminating 澤天夬 癸巳 Water Snake 6 22 四月初一	金9 Metal 1 Heaven 乾爲天 甲午 Wood Horse 1 23 初二	火7 Fire 2 Well 水風井 乙未 Wood Goat 6 24 初三	木8 Wood 3 Relief 雷水解 丙申 Fire Monkey 4 25 初四	金4 Metal 4 Influence 澤山咸 丁酉 Fire Rooster 9 26 初五	水1 Water 5 Humility 地山謙 戊戌 Earth Dog 6 27 初六
火2 Fire 6 Observation 風地觀 己亥 Earth Pig 2 28 初七	火2 Fire 7 Increasing 風雷益 庚子 Metal Rat 9 29 初八	水1 Water 8 Dimming Light 地火明夷 辛丑 Metal Ox 3 30 初九				

MAY 1974 己巳

Xuan Kong Element 玄空五行	雷天大壯 Great Strength	Period Luck 卦運	Monthly Star 月星
Wood 木8		2	8

SUNDAY	MONDAY	TUESDAY	WEDNESDAY	THURSDAY	FRIDAY	SATURDAY
			金9 Metal 壬寅 Water Tiger 7 Fellowship 天火同人 9 1 初十	木8 Wood 癸卯 Water Rabbit 7 Marrying Maiden 雷澤歸妹 1 2 十一	木3 Wood 甲辰 Wood Dragon 2 Opposition 火澤睽 2 3 十二	火7 Fire 乙巳 Wood Snake 3 Waiting 水天需 3 4 十三
金4 Metal 丙午 Fire Horse 3 Great Exceeding 澤風大過 4 5 十四	水6 Water 丁未 Fire Goat 7 Poison 山風蠱 5 6 十五	火2 Fire 戊申 Earth Monkey 6 Dispersing 風水渙 6 7 十六	木3 Wood 己酉 Earth Rooster 8 Travelling 火山旅 7 8 十七	金9 Metal 庚戌 Metal Dog 9 Stagnation 天地否 8 9 十八	火7 Fire 辛亥 Metal Pig 7 Alliance 水地比 9 10 十九	木8 Wood 壬子 Water Rat 1 Thunder 震爲雷 1 11 二十
水6 Water 癸丑 Water Ox 8 Beauty 山火賁 2 12 廿一	火7 Fire 甲寅 Wood Tiger 9 Accomplished 水火既濟 3 13 廿二	水1 Water 乙卯 Wood Rabbit 4 Arriving 地澤臨 4 14 廿三	金4 Metal 丙辰 Fire Dragon 1 Marsh 兌爲澤 5 15 廿四	火2 Fire 丁巳 Fire Snake 8 Small Livestock 風天小畜 6 16 廿五	木3 Wood 戊午 Earth Horse 4 The Cauldron 火風鼎 7 17 廿六	水1 Water 己未 Earth Goat 2 Rising 地風升 8 18 廿七
火7 Fire 庚申 Metal Monkey 1 Water 坎爲水 9 19 廿八	木8 Wood 辛酉 Metal Rooster 3 Lesser Exceeding 雷山小過 1 20 廿九	金4 Metal 壬戌 Water Dog 4 Gathering 澤地萃 2 21 三十	水6 Water 癸亥 Water Pig 6 Peel 山地剝 3 22 閏四月初一	水1 Water 甲子 Wood Rat 1 Earth 坤爲地 4 23 初二	木3 Wood 乙丑 Wood Ox 6 Biting 火雷噬嗑 5 24 初三	火2 Fire 丙寅 Fire Tiger 4 Family 風火家人 6 25 初四
水6 Water 丁卯 Fire Rabbit 9 Decreasing 山澤損 7 26 初五	金9 Metal 戊辰 Earth Dragon 6 Tread 天澤履 8 27 初六	木8 Wood 己巳 Earth Snake 2 Great Strength 雷天大壯 9 28 初七	木8 Wood 庚午 Metal Horse 9 Consistency 雷風恒 1 29 初八	金9 Metal 辛未 Metal Goat 3 Litigation 天水訟 2 30 初九	水1 Water 壬申 Water Monkey 7 Officer 地水師 3 31 初十	

JUNE 1974 庚午

Xuan Kong Element 玄空五行	雷風恒 Consistency	Period Luck 卦運	Monthly Star 月星
Wood 木8		9	7

SUNDAY	MONDAY	TUESDAY	WEDNESDAY	THURSDAY	FRIDAY	SATURDAY
金9 Metal 壬寅 Water Tiger 7 Fellowship 天火同人 4 30 十一						火2 Fire 癸酉 Water Rooster 7 Gradual Progress 風山漸 4 1 十一
火7 Fire 甲戌 Wood Dog 2 Obstruction 水山蹇 5 2 十二	木3 Wood 乙亥 Wood Pig 3 Advancement 火地晉 6 3 十三	水6 Water 丙子 Fire Rat 3 Nourish 山雷頤 7 4 十四	金4 Metal 丁丑 Fire Ox 7 Following 澤雷隨 8 5 十五	木8 Wood 戊寅 Earth Tiger 6 Abundance 雷火豐 9 6 十六	火7 Fire 己卯 Earth Rabbit 8 Regulate 水澤節 1 7 十七	水1 Water 庚辰 Metal Dragon 9 Unity 地天泰 2 8 十八
木3 Wood 辛巳 Metal Snake 7 Great Reward 火天大有 3 9 十九	火2 Fire 壬午 Water Horse 1 Wind 巽爲風 4 10 二十	金4 Metal 癸未 Water Goat 8 Trap 澤水困 5 11 廿一	木3 Wood 甲申 Wood Monkey 9 Not Yet Accomplished 火水未濟 6 12 廿二	金9 Metal 乙酉 Wood Rooster 4 Retreat 天山遯 7 13 廿三	水6 Water 丙戌 Fire Dog 1 Mountain 艮爲山 8 14 廿四	木8 Wood 丁亥 Fire Pig 8 Delight 雷地豫 9 15 廿五
火7 Fire 戊子 Earth Rat 4 Beginning 水雷屯 1 16 廿六	金9 Metal 己丑 Earth Ox 2 Without Wrongdoing 天雷無妄 2 17 廿七	木3 Wood 庚寅 Metal Tiger 1 Fire 離爲火 3 18 廿八	火2 Fire 辛卯 Metal Rabbit 3 Sincerity 風澤中孚 4 19 廿九	水6 Water 壬辰 Water Dragon 4 Big Livestock 山天大畜 5 20 五月初一	金4 Metal 癸巳 Water Snake 6 Eliminating 澤天夬 6 21 初二	金9 Metal 甲午 Wood Horse 1 Heaven 乾爲天 7/3 22 初三
火7 Fire 乙未 Wood Goat 6 Well 水風井 2 23 初四	木8 Wood 丙申 Fire Monkey 4 Relief 雷水解 1 24 初五	金4 Metal 丁酉 Fire Rooster 9 Influence 澤山咸 9 25 初六	水1 Water 戊戌 Earth Dog 6 Humility 地山謙 8 26 初七	火2 Fire 己亥 Earth Pig 2 Observation 風地觀 7 27 初八	火2 Fire 庚子 Metal Rat 9 Increasing 風雷益 6 28 初九	水1 Water 辛丑 Metal Ox 3 Dimming Light 地火明夷 5 29 初十

JULY 1974 辛未

Xuan Kong Element 玄空五行	天水訟 Litigation	Period Luck 卦運	Monthly Star 月星
Metal 金9		3	6

SUNDAY	MONDAY	TUESDAY	WEDNESDAY	THURSDAY	FRIDAY	SATURDAY
	木8 Wood 3 Marrying Maiden 癸卯 Water Rabbit 雷澤歸妹 1 十二 7	木3 Wood 2 Opposition 甲辰 Wood Dragon 火澤睽 2 十三 2	火7 Fire 1 Waiting 乙巳 Wood Snake 水天需 3 十四 3	金4 Metal 9 Great Exceeding 丙午 Fire Horse 澤風大過 4 十五 3	水6 Water 8 Poison 丁未 Fire Goat 山風蠱 5 十六 7	火2 Fire 7 Dispersing 戊申 Earth Monkey 風水渙 6 十七 6
木3 Wood 6 Travelling 己酉 Earth Rooster 火山旅 7 十八 8	金9 Metal 5 Stagnation 庚戌 Metal Dog 天地否 8 十九 9	火7 Fire 4 Alliance 辛亥 Metal Pig 水地比 9 二十 7	木8 Wood 3 Thunder 壬子 Water Rat 震爲雷 10 廿一 1	水6 Water 2 Beauty 癸丑 Water Ox 山火賁 11 廿二 8	火7 Fire 1 Accomplished 甲寅 Wood Tiger 水火既濟 12 廿三 9	水1 Water 9 Arriving 乙卯 Wood Rabbit 地澤臨 13 廿四 4
金4 Metal 8 Marsh 丙辰 Fire Dragon 兑爲澤 14 廿五 1	火2 Fire 7 Small Livestock 丁巳 Fire Snake 風天小畜 15 廿六 8	木3 Wood 6 The Cauldron 戊午 Earth Horse 火風鼎 16 廿七 4	水1 Water 5 Rising 己未 Earth Goat 地風升 17 廿八 2	火7 Fire 4 Water 庚申 Metal Monkey 坎爲水 18 廿九 1	木8 Wood 3 Lesser Exceeding 辛酉 Metal Rooster 雷山小過 19 六月初一 3	金4 Metal 2 Gathering 壬戌 Water Dog 澤地萃 20 初二 4
水6 Water 1 Peel 癸亥 Water Pig 山地剝 21 初三 6	水1 Water 9 Earth 甲子 Wood Rat 坤爲地 22 初四 1	木3 Wood 8 Biting 乙丑 Wood Ox 火雷噬嗑 23 初五 6	火2 Fire 7 Family 丙寅 Fire Tiger 風火家人 24 初六 4	水6 Water 6 Decreasing 丁卯 Fire Rabbit 山澤損 25 初七 9	金9 Metal 5 Tread 戊辰 Earth Dragon 天澤履 26 初八 6	木8 Wood 4 Great Strength 己巳 Earth Snake 雷天大壯 27 初九 2
木8 Wood 3 Consistency 庚午 Metal Horse 雷風恒 28 初十 9	金9 Metal 2 Litigation 辛未 Metal Goat 天水訟 29 十一 3	水1 Water 1 Officer 壬申 Water Monkey 地水師 30 十二 7	火2 Fire 9 Gradual Progress 癸酉 Water Rooster 風山漸 31 十三 7			

AUGUST 1974 壬申

Xuan Kong Element 玄空五行	地水師 Officer	Period Luck 卦運	Monthly Star 月星
Water 水1		7	5

SUNDAY	MONDAY	TUESDAY	WEDNESDAY	THURSDAY	FRIDAY	SATURDAY
				火7 Fire 8 Obstruction 甲戌 Wood Dog 水山蹇 1 十四 2	木3 Wood 7 Advancement 乙亥 Wood Pig 火地晉 2 十五 3	水6 Water 6 Nourish 丙子 Fire Rat 山雷頤 3 十六 3
金4 Metal 5 Following 丁丑 Fire Ox 澤雷隨 4 十七 7	木8 Wood 4 Abundance 戊寅 Earth Tiger 雷火豐 5 十八 6	火7 Fire 3 Regulate 己卯 Earth Rabbit 水澤節 6 十九 8	水1 Water 2 Unity 庚辰 Metal Dragon 地天泰 7 二十 9	木3 Wood 1 Great Reward 辛巳 Metal Snake 火天大有 8 廿一 7	火2 Fire 9 Wind 壬午 Water Horse 巽爲風 9 廿二 1	金4 Metal 8 Trap 癸未 Water Goat 澤水困 10 廿三 8
木3 Wood 7 Not Yet Accomplished 甲申 Wood Monkey 火水未濟 11 廿四 9	金9 Metal 6 Retreat 乙酉 Wood Rooster 天山遯 12 廿五 4	水6 Water 5 Mountain 丙戌 Fire Dog 艮爲山 13 廿六 1	木8 Wood 4 Delight 丁亥 Fire Pig 雷地豫 14 廿七 8	火7 Fire 3 Beginning 戊子 Earth Rat 水雷屯 15 廿八 4	金9 Metal 2 Without Wrongdoing 己丑 Earth Ox 天雷無妄 16 廿九 2	木3 Wood 1 Fire 庚寅 Metal Tiger 離爲火 17 三十 1
火2 Fire 9 Sincerity 辛卯 Metal Rabbit 風澤中孚 18 七月初一 3	水6 Water 8 Big Livestock 壬辰 Water Dragon 山天大畜 19 初二 4	金4 Metal 7 Eliminating 癸巳 Water Snake 澤天夬 20 初三 6	金9 Metal 6 Heaven 甲午 Wood Horse 乾爲天 21 初四 1	火7 Fire 5 Well 乙未 Wood Goat 水風井 22 初五 6	木8 Wood 4 Relief 丙申 Fire Monkey 雷水解 23 初六 4	金4 Metal 3 Influence 丁酉 Fire Rooster 澤山咸 24 初七 9
水1 Water 2 Humility 戊戌 Earth Dog 地山謙 25 初八 6	火2 Fire 1 Observation 己亥 Earth Pig 風地觀 26 初九 2	火2 Fire 9 Increasing 庚子 Metal Rat 風雷益 27 初十 9	水1 Water 8 Dimming Light 辛丑 Metal Ox 地火明夷 28 十一 3	金9 Metal 7 Fellowship 壬寅 Water Tiger 天火同人 29 十二 7	木8 Wood 6 Marrying Maiden 癸卯 Water Rabbit 雷澤歸妹 30 十三 7	木3 Wood 5 Opposition 甲辰 Wood Dragon 火澤睽 31 十四 2

SEPTEMBER 1974 癸酉

Xuan Kong Element 玄空五行	風山漸 Gradual Progress	Period Luck 卦運	Monthly Star 月星
Fire 火2		7	4

SUNDAY	MONDAY	TUESDAY	WEDNESDAY	THURSDAY	FRIDAY	SATURDAY
火7 Fire 4 Waiting 水天需 乙巳 Wood Snake 1 十五 3	金4 Metal 3 Great Exceeding 澤風大過 丙午 Fire Horse 2 十六 3	水6 Water 2 Poison 山風蠱 丁未 Fire Goat 3 十七 7	火2 Fire 1 Dispersing 風水渙 戊申 Earth Monkey 4 十八 6	木3 Wood 9 Travelling 火山旅 己酉 Earth Rooster 5 十九 8	金9 Metal 8 Stagnation 天地否 庚戌 Metal Dog 6 二十 9	火7 Fire 7 Alliance 水地比 辛亥 Metal Pig 7 廿一 7
木8 Wood 6 Thunder 震爲雷 壬子 Water Rat 8 廿二 1	水6 Water 5 Beauty 山火賁 癸丑 Water Ox 9 廿三 8	火7 Fire 4 Accomplished 水火既濟 甲寅 Wood Tiger 10 廿四 9	水1 Water 3 Arriving 地澤臨 乙卯 Wood Rabbit 11 廿五 4	金4 Metal 2 Marsh 兌爲澤 丙辰 Fire Dragon 12 廿六 1	火2 Fire 1 Small Livestock 風天小畜 丁巳 Fire Snake 13 廿七 8	木3 Wood 9 The Cauldron 火風鼎 戊午 Earth Horse 14 廿八 4
水1 Water 8 Rising 地風升 己未 Earth Goat 15 廿九 2	火7 Fire 7 Water 坎爲水 庚申 Metal Monkey 16 八月初一 1	木8 Wood 6 Lesser Exceeding 雷山小過 辛酉 Metal Rooster 17 初二 3	金4 Metal 5 Gathering 澤地萃 壬戌 Water Dog 18 初三 4	水6 Water 4 Peel 山地剝 癸亥 Water Pig 19 初四 6	水1 Water 3 Earth 坤爲地 甲子 Wood Rat 20 初五 1	木3 Wood 2 Biting 火雷噬嗑 乙丑 Wood Ox 21 初六 6
火2 Fire 1 Family 風火家人 丙寅 Fire Tiger 22 初七 4	水6 Water 9 Decreasing 山澤損 丁卯 Fire Rabbit 23 初八 9	金9 Metal 8 Tread 天澤履 戊辰 Earth Dragon 24 初九 6	木8 Wood 7 Great Strength 雷天大壯 己巳 Earth Snake 25 初十 2	木8 Wood 6 Consistency 雷風恆 庚午 Metal Horse 26 十一 9	金9 Metal 5 Litigation 天水訟 辛未 Metal Goat 27 十二 3	水1 Water 4 Officer 地水師 壬申 Water Monkey 28 十三 7
火2 Fire 3 Gradual Progress 風山漸 癸酉 Water Rooster 29 十四 7	火7 Fire 2 Obstruction 水山蹇 甲戌 Wood Dog 30 十五 2					

OCTOBER 1974 甲戌

Xuan Kong Element 玄空五行	水山蹇 Obstruction	Period Luck 卦運	Monthly Star 月星
Fire 火7		2	3

SUNDAY	MONDAY	TUESDAY	WEDNESDAY	THURSDAY	FRIDAY	SATURDAY
		木3 Wood 1 Advancement 火地晉 乙亥 Wood Pig 1 十六 3	水6 Water 9 Nourish 山雷頤 丙子 Fire Rat 2 十七 3	金4 Metal 8 Following 澤雷隨 丁丑 Fire Ox 3 十八 7	木8 Wood 7 Abundance 雷火豐 戊寅 Earth Tiger 4 十九 6	火7 Fire 6 Regulate 水澤節 己卯 Earth Rabbit 5 二十 8
水1 Water 5 Unity 地天泰 庚辰 Metal Dragon 6 廿一 9	木3 Wood 4 Great Reward 火天大有 辛巳 Metal Snake 7 廿二 7	火2 Fire 3 Wind 巽爲風 壬午 Water Horse 8 廿三 1	金4 Metal 2 Trap 澤水困 癸未 Water Goat 9 廿四 8	木3 Wood 1 Not Yet Accomplished 火水未濟 甲申 Wood Monkey 10 廿五 9	金9 Metal 9 Retreat 天山遯 乙酉 Wood Rooster 11 廿六 4	水6 Water 8 Mountain 艮爲山 丙戌 Fire Dog 12 廿七 1
木8 Wood 7 Delight 雷地豫 丁亥 Fire Pig 13 廿八 8	火7 Fire 6 Beginning 水雷屯 戊子 Earth Rat 14 廿九 4	金9 Metal 5 Without Wrongdoing 天雷無妄 己丑 Earth Ox 15 九月初一 2	木3 Wood 4 Fire 離爲火 庚寅 Metal Tiger 16 初二 1	火2 Fire 3 Sincerity 風澤中孚 辛卯 Metal Rabbit 17 初三 3	水6 Water 2 Big Livestock 山天大畜 壬辰 Water Dragon 18 初四 4	金4 Metal 1 Eliminating 澤天夬 癸巳 Water Snake 19 初五 6
金9 Metal 9 Heaven 乾爲天 甲午 Wood Horse 20 初六 1	火7 Fire 8 Well 水風井 乙未 Wood Goat 21 初七 6	木8 Wood 7 Relief 雷水解 丙申 Fire Monkey 22 初八 4	金4 Metal 6 Influence 澤山咸 丁酉 Fire Rooster 23 初九 9	水1 Water 5 Humility 地山謙 戊戌 Earth Dog 24 初十 6	火2 Fire 4 Observation 風地觀 己亥 Earth Pig 25 十一 2	火2 Fire 3 Increasing 風雷益 庚子 Metal Rat 26 十二 9
水1 Water 2 Dimming Light 地火明夷 辛丑 Metal Ox 27 十三 3	金9 Metal 1 Fellowship 天火同人 壬寅 Water Tiger 28 十四 7	木8 Wood 9 Marrying Maiden 雷澤歸妹 癸卯 Water Rabbit 29 十五 7	木3 Wood 8 Opposition 火澤睽 甲辰 Wood Dragon 30 十六 2	火7 Fire 7 Waiting 水天需 乙巳 Wood Snake 31 十七 3		

NOVEMBER 1974 乙亥

Xuan Kong Element 玄空五行	火地晉 Advancement	Period Luck 卦運	Monthly Star 月星
Wood 木3		3	2

SUNDAY	MONDAY	TUESDAY	WEDNESDAY	THURSDAY	FRIDAY	SATURDAY
					金4 Metal Great Exceeding 6 澤風大過 丙午 Fire Horse 1 十八 3	水6 Water Poison 5 山風蠱 丁未 Fire Goat 2 十九 7
火2 Fire Dispersing 4 風水渙 戊申 Earth Monkey 3 二十 6	木3 Wood Travelling 3 火山旅 己酉 Earth Rooster 4 廿一 8	金9 Metal Stagnation 2 天地否 庚戌 Metal Dog 5 廿二 9	火7 Fire Alliance 1 水地比 辛亥 Metal Pig 6 廿三 7	木8 Wood Thunder 9 震爲雷 壬子 Water Rat 7 廿四 1	水6 Water Beauty 8 山火賁 癸丑 Water Ox 8 廿五 8	火7 Fire Accomplished 7 水火既濟 甲寅 Wood Tiger 9 廿六 9
水1 Water Arriving 6 地澤臨 乙卯 Wood Rabbit 10 廿七 4	金4 Metal Marsh 5 兌爲澤 丙辰 Fire Dragon 11 廿八 1	火2 Fire Small Livestock 4 風天小畜 丁巳 Fire Snake 12 廿九 8	木3 Wood The Cauldron 3 火風鼎 戊午 Earth Horse 13 三十 4	水1 Water Rising 2 地風升 己未 Earth Goat 14 十月初一 2	火7 Fire Water 1 坎爲水 庚申 Metal Monkey 15 初二 1	木8 Wood Lesser Exceeding 9 雷山小過 辛酉 Metal Rooster 16 初三 3
金4 Metal Gathering 8 澤地萃 壬戌 Water Dog 17 初四 4	水6 Water Peel 7 山地剝 癸亥 Water Pig 18 初五 6	水1 Water Earth 6 坤爲地 甲子 Wood Rat 19 初六 1	木3 Wood Biting 5 火雷噬嗑 乙丑 Wood Ox 20 初七 6	火2 Fire Family 4 風火家人 丙寅 Fire Tiger 21 初八 4	水6 Water Decreasing 3 山澤損 丁卯 Fire Rabbit 22 初九 9	金9 Metal Tread 2 天澤履 戊辰 Earth Dragon 23 初十 6
木8 Wood Great Strength 1 雷天大壯 己巳 Earth Snake 24 十一 2	木8 Wood Consistency 9 雷風恆 庚午 Metal Horse 25 十二 9	金9 Metal Litigation 8 天水訟 辛未 Metal Goat 26 十三 3	水1 Water Officer 7 地水師 壬申 Water Monkey 27 十四 7	火2 Fire Gradual Progress 6 風山漸 癸酉 Water Rooster 28 十五 7	火7 Fire Obstruction 5 水山蹇 甲戌 Wood Dog 29 十六 2	木3 Wood Advancement 4 火地晉 乙亥 Wood Pig 30 十七 3

DECEMBER 1974 丙子

Xuan Kong Element 玄空五行	山雷頤 Nourish	Period Luck 卦運	Monthly Star 月星
Water 水6		3	1

SUNDAY	MONDAY	TUESDAY	WEDNESDAY	THURSDAY	FRIDAY	SATURDAY
水6 Water Nourish 3 山雷頤 丙子 Fire Rat 1 十八 3	金4 Metal Following 2 澤雷隨 丁丑 Fire Ox 2 十九 7	木8 Wood Abundance 1 雷火豐 戊寅 Earth Tiger 3 二十 6	火7 Fire Regulate 9 水澤節 己卯 Earth Rabbit 4 廿一 8	水1 Water Unity 8 地天泰 庚辰 Metal Dragon 5 廿二 9	木3 Wood Great Reward 7 火天大有 辛巳 Metal Snake 6 廿三 7	火2 Fire Wind 6 巽爲風 壬午 Water Horse 7 廿四 1
金4 Metal Trap 5 澤水困 癸未 Water Goat 8 廿五 8	木3 Wood Not Yet Accomplished 4 火水未濟 甲申 Wood Monkey 9 廿六 9	金9 Metal Retreat 3 天山遯 乙酉 Wood Rooster 10 廿七 4	水6 Water Mountain 2 艮爲山 丙戌 Fire Dog 11 廿八 1	木8 Wood Delight 1 雷地豫 丁亥 Fire Pig 12 廿九 8	火7 Fire Beginning 9 水雷屯 戊子 Earth Rat 13 三十 4	金9 Metal Without Wrongdoing 8 天雷無妄 己丑 Earth Ox 14 十一月初一 2
木3 Wood Fire 7 離爲火 庚寅 Metal Tiger 15 初二 1	火2 Fire Sincerity 6 風澤中孚 辛卯 Metal Rabbit 16 初三 3	水6 Water Big Livestock 5 山天大畜 壬辰 Water Dragon 17 初四 4	金4 Metal Eliminating 4 澤天夬 癸巳 Water Snake 18 初五 6	金9 Metal Heaven 3 乾爲天 甲午 Wood Horse 19 初六 1	火7 Fire Well 2 水風井 乙未 Wood Goat 20 初七 6	木8 Wood Relief 1 雷水解 丙申 Fire Monkey 21 初八 4
金4 Metal Influence 9/1 澤山咸 丁酉 Fire Rooster 22 初九 9	水1 Water Humility 2 地山謙 戊戌 Earth Dog 23 初十 6	火2 Fire Observation 3 風地觀 己亥 Earth Pig 24 十一 2	火2 Fire Increasing 4 風雷益 庚子 Metal Rat 25 十二 9	水1 Water Dimming Light 5 地火明夷 辛丑 Metal Ox 26 十三 3	金9 Metal Fellowship 6 天火同人 壬寅 Water Tiger 27 十四 7	木8 Wood Marrying Maiden 7 雷澤歸妹 癸卯 Water Rabbit 28 十五 7
木3 Wood Opposition 8 火澤睽 甲辰 Wood Dragon 29 十六 2	火7 Fire Waiting 9 水天需 乙巳 Wood Snake 30 十七 3	金4 Metal Great Exceeding 1 澤風大過 丙午 Fire Horse 31 十八 3				

1975 乙卯

(*Yi Mao*) Wood Rabbit

1975 乙卯 *(Yi Mao)* Wood Rabbit

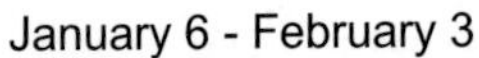

January 6 - February 3

Three Killings	East

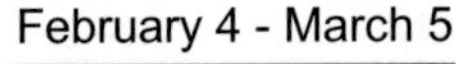

February 4 - March 5

Three Killings	North

March 6 - April 4

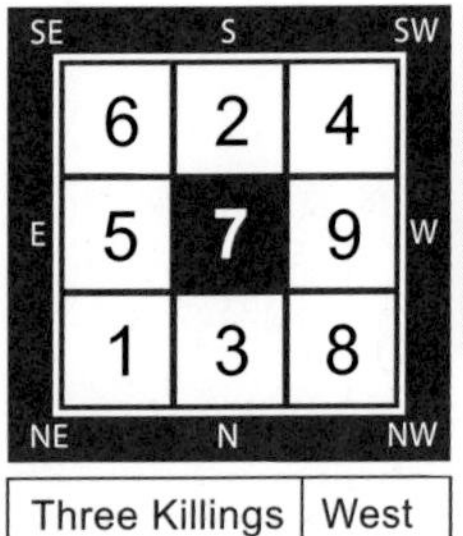

Three Killings	West

April 5 - May 5

Three Killings	South

May 6 - June 5

Three Killings	East

June 6 - July 5

Three Killings	North

July 6 - August 7

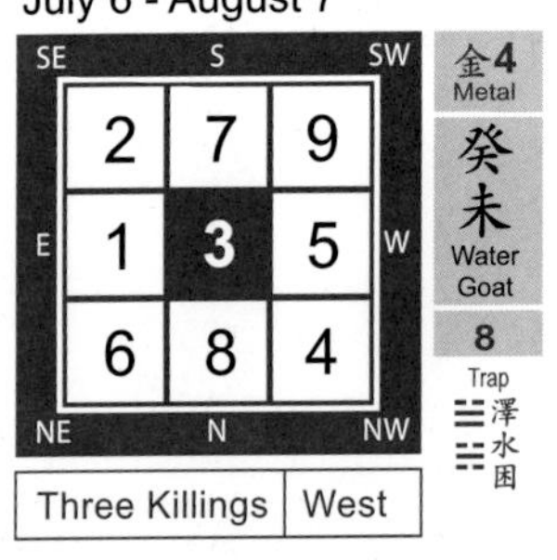

Three Killings	West

August 8 - September 7

Three Killings	South

September 8 - October 8

Three Killings	East

October 9 - November 7

Three Killings	North

November 8 - December 7

Three Killings	West

December 8 - January 5

Three Killings	South

JANUARY 1975 丁丑

Xuan Kong Element 玄空五行	澤雷隨 Following	Period Luck 卦運	Monthly Star 月星
Metal 金4		7	9

SUNDAY	MONDAY	TUESDAY	WEDNESDAY	THURSDAY	FRIDAY	SATURDAY
			水6 Water 2 Poison 山風蠱 丁未 Fire Goat 7 1 十九	火2 Fire 3 Dispersing 風水渙 戊申 Earth Monkey 6 2 二十	木3 Wood 4 Travelling 火山旅 己酉 Earth Rooster 8 3 廿一	金9 Metal 5 Stagnation 天地否 庚戌 Metal Dog 9 4 廿二
火7 Fire 6 Alliance 水地比 辛亥 Metal Pig 7 5 廿三	木8 Wood 7 Thunder 震爲雷 壬子 Water Rat 1 6 廿四	水6 Water 8 Beauty 山火賁 癸丑 Water Ox 8 7 廿五	火7 Fire 9 Accomplished 水火既濟 甲寅 Wood Tiger 9 8 廿六	水1 Water 1 Arriving 地澤臨 乙卯 Wood Rabbit 4 9 廿七	金4 Metal 2 Marsh 兑爲澤 丙辰 Fire Dragon 1 10 廿八	火2 Fire 3 Small Livestock 風天小畜 丁巳 Fire Snake 8 11 廿九
木3 Wood 4 The Cauldron 火風鼎 戊午 Earth Horse 4 12 十二月初一	水1 Water 5 Rising 地風升 己未 Earth Goat 2 13 初二	火7 Fire 6 Water 坎爲水 庚申 Metal Monkey 1 14 初三	木8 Wood 7 Lesser Exceeding 雷山小過 辛酉 Metal Rooster 3 15 初四	金4 Metal 8 Gathering 澤地萃 壬戌 Water Dog 4 16 初五	水6 Water 9 Peel 山地剝 癸亥 Water Pig 6 17 初六	水1 Water 1 Earth 坤爲地 甲子 Wood Rat 1 18 初七
木3 Wood 2 Biting 火雷噬嗑 乙丑 Wood Ox 6 19 初八	火2 Fire 3 Family 風火家人 丙寅 Fire Tiger 4 20 初九	水6 Water 4 Decreasing 山澤損 丁卯 Fire Rabbit 9 21 初十	金9 Metal 5 Tread 天澤履 戊辰 Earth Dragon 6 22 十一	木8 Wood 6 Great Strength 雷天大壯 己巳 Earth Snake 2 23 十二	木8 Wood 7 Consistency 雷風恆 庚午 Metal Horse 9 24 十三	金9 Metal 8 Litigation 天水訟 辛未 Metal Goat 3 25 十四
水1 Water 9 Officer 地水師 壬申 Water Monkey 7 26 十五	火2 Fire 1 Gradual Progress 風山漸 癸酉 Water Rooster 7 27 十六	火7 Fire 2 Obstruction 水山蹇 甲戌 Wood Dog 2 28 十七	木3 Wood 3 Advancement 火地晉 乙亥 Wood Pig 3 29 十八	水6 Water 4 Nourish 山雷頤 丙子 Fire Rat 3 30 十九	金4 Metal 5 Following 澤雷隨 丁丑 Fire Ox 7 31 二十	

FEBRUARY 1975 戊寅

Xuan Kong Element 玄空五行	雷火豐 Abundance	Period Luck 卦運	Monthly Star 月星
Wood 木8		6	8

SUNDAY	MONDAY	TUESDAY	WEDNESDAY	THURSDAY	FRIDAY	SATURDAY
						木8 Wood 6 Abundance 雷火豐 戊寅 Earth Tiger 6 1 廿一
火7 Fire 7 Regulate 水澤節 己卯 Earth Rabbit 8 2 廿二	水1 Water 8 Unity 地天泰 庚辰 Metal Dragon 9 3 廿三	木3 Wood 9 Great Reward 火天大有 辛巳 Metal Snake 7 4 廿四	火2 Fire 1 Wind 巽爲風 壬午 Water Horse 1 5 廿五	金4 Metal 2 Trap 澤水困 癸未 Water Goat 8 6 廿六	木3 Wood 3 Not Yet Accomplished 火水未濟 甲申 Wood Monkey 9 7 廿七	金9 Metal 4 Retreat 天山遯 乙酉 Wood Rooster 3 8 廿八
水6 Water 5 Mountain 艮爲山 丙戌 Fire Dog 1 9 廿九	木8 Wood 6 Delight 雷地豫 丁亥 Fire Pig 8 10 三十	火7 Fire 7 Beginning 水雷屯 戊子 Earth Rat 4 11 正月初一	金9 Metal 8 Without Wrongdoing 天雷無妄 己丑 Earth Ox 2 12 初二	木3 Wood 9 Fire 離爲火 庚寅 Metal Tiger 1 13 初三	火2 Fire 1 Sincerity 風澤中孚 辛卯 Metal Rabbit 3 14 初四	水6 Water 2 Big Livestock 山天大畜 壬辰 Water Dragon 4 15 初五
金4 Metal 3 Eliminating 澤天夬 癸巳 Water Snake 6 16 初六	金9 Metal 4 Heaven 乾爲天 甲午 Wood Horse 1 17 初七	火7 Fire 5 Well 水風井 乙未 Wood Goat 6 18 初八	木8 Wood 6 Relief 雷水解 丙申 Fire Monkey 4 19 初九	金4 Metal 7 Influence 澤山咸 丁酉 Fire Rooster 9 20 初十	水1 Water 8 Humility 地山謙 戊戌 Earth Dog 6 21 十一	火2 Fire 9 Observation 風地觀 己亥 Earth Pig 2 22 十二
火2 Fire 1 Increasing 風雷益 庚子 Metal Rat 9 23 十三	水1 Water 2 Dimming Light 地火明夷 辛丑 Metal Ox 3 24 十四	金9 Metal 3 Fellowship 天火同人 壬寅 Water Tiger 7 25 十五	木8 Wood 4 Marrying Maiden 雷澤歸妹 癸卯 Water Rabbit 7 26 十六	木3 Wood 5 Opposition 火澤睽 甲辰 Wood Dragon 2 27 十七	火7 Fire 6 Waiting 水天需 乙巳 Wood Snake 3 28 十八	

MARCH 1975 己卯

Xuan Kong Element 玄空五行	水澤節 Regulate	Period Luck 卦運	Monthly Star 月星
Fire 火7		8	7

SUNDAY	MONDAY	TUESDAY	WEDNESDAY	THURSDAY	FRIDAY	SATURDAY
木3 Wood 9 Advancement 火地晉 乙亥 Wood Pig 30 十八 3	水6 Water 1 Nourish 山雷頤 丙子 Fire Rat 31 十九 3					金4 Metal 7 Great Exceeding 澤風大過 丙午 Fire Horse 1 十九 3
水6 Water 8 Poison 山風蠱 丁未 Fire Goat 2 二十 7	火2 Fire 9 Dispersing 風水渙 戊申 Earth Monkey 3 廿一 6	木3 Wood 1 Travelling 火山旅 己酉 Earth Rooster 4 廿二 8	金9 Metal 2 Stagnation 天地否 庚戌 Metal Dog 5 廿三 9	火7 Fire 3 Alliance 水地比 辛亥 Metal Pig 6 廿四 7	木8 Wood 4 Thunder 震為雷 壬子 Water Rat 7 廿五 1	水6 Water 5 Beauty 山火賁 癸丑 Water Ox 8 廿六 8
火7 Fire 6 Accomplished 水火既濟 甲寅 Wood Tiger 9 廿七 9	水1 Water 7 Arriving 地澤臨 乙卯 Wood Rabbit 10 廿八 4	金4 Metal 8 Marsh 兌為澤 丙辰 Fire Dragon 11 廿九 1	火2 Fire 9 Small Livestock 風天小畜 丁巳 Fire Snake 12 三十 8	木3 Wood 1 The Cauldron 火風鼎 戊午 Earth Horse 13 二月初一 4	水1 Water 2 Rising 地風升 己未 Earth Goat 14 初二 2	火7 Fire 3 Water 坎為水 庚申 Metal Monkey 15 初三 1
木8 Wood 4 Lesser Exceeding 雷山小過 辛酉 Metal Rooster 16 初四 3	金4 Metal 5 Gathering 澤地萃 壬戌 Water Dog 17 初五 4	水6 Water 6 Peel 山地剝 癸亥 Water Pig 18 初六 6	水1 Water 7 Earth 坤為地 甲子 Wood Rat 19 初七 1	木3 Wood 8 Biting 火雷噬嗑 乙丑 Wood Ox 20 初八 6	火2 Fire 9 Family 風火家人 丙寅 Fire Tiger 21 初九 4	水6 Water 1 Decreasing 山澤損 丁卯 Fire Rabbit 22 初十 9
金9 Metal 2 Tread 天澤履 戊辰 Earth Dragon 23 十一 6	木8 Wood 3 Great Strength 雷天大壯 己巳 Earth Snake 24 十二 2	木8 Wood 4 Consistency 雷風恒 庚午 Metal Horse 25 十三 9	金9 Metal 5 Litigation 天水訟 辛未 Metal Goat 26 十四 3	水1 Water 6 Officer 地水師 壬申 Water Monkey 27 十五 7	火2 Fire 7 Gradual Progress 風山漸 癸酉 Water Rooster 28 十六 7	火7 Fire 8 Obstruction 水山蹇 甲戌 Wood Dog 29 十七 2

APRIL 1975 庚辰

Xuan Kong Element 玄空五行	地天泰 Unity	Period Luck 卦運	Monthly Star 月星
Water 水1		9	6

SUNDAY	MONDAY	TUESDAY	WEDNESDAY	THURSDAY	FRIDAY	SATURDAY
		金4 Metal 2 Following 澤雷隨 丁丑 Fire Ox 1 二十 7	木8 Wood 3 Abundance 雷火豐 戊寅 Earth Tiger 2 廿一 6	火7 Fire 4 Regulate 水澤節 己卯 Earth Rabbit 3 廿二 8	水1 Water 5 Unity 地天泰 庚辰 Metal Dragon 4 廿三 9	木3 Wood 6 Great Reward 火天大有 辛巳 Metal Snake 5 廿四 7
火2 Fire 7 Wind 巽為風 壬午 Water Horse 6 廿五 1	金4 Metal 8 Trap 澤水困 癸未 Water Goat 7 廿六 8	木3 Wood 9 Not Yet Accomplished 火水未濟 甲申 Wood Monkey 8 廿七 9	金9 Metal 1 Retreat 天山遯 乙酉 Wood Rooster 9 廿八 4	水6 Water 2 Mountain 艮為山 丙戌 Fire Dog 10 廿九 1	木8 Wood 3 Delight 雷地豫 丁亥 Fire Pig 11 三十 8	火7 Fire 4 Beginning 水雷屯 戊子 Earth Rat 12 三月初一 4
金9 Metal 5 Without Wrongdoing 天雷無妄 己丑 Earth Ox 13 初二 2	木3 Wood 6 Fire 離為火 庚寅 Metal Tiger 14 初三 1	火2 Fire 7 Sincerity 風澤中孚 辛卯 Metal Rabbit 15 初四 3	水6 Water 8 Big Livestock 山天大畜 壬辰 Water Dragon 16 初五 4	金4 Metal 9 Eliminating 澤天夬 癸巳 Water Snake 17 初六 6	金9 Metal 1 Heaven 乾為天 甲午 Wood Horse 18 初七 1	火7 Fire 2 Well 水風井 乙未 Wood Goat 19 初八 6
木8 Wood 3 Relief 雷水解 丙申 Fire Monkey 20 初九 4	金4 Metal 4 Influence 澤山咸 丁酉 Fire Rooster 21 初十 9	水1 Water 5 Humility 地山謙 戊戌 Earth Dog 22 十一 6	火2 Fire 6 Observation 風地觀 己亥 Earth Pig 23 十二 2	火2 Fire 7 Increasing 風雷益 庚子 Metal Rat 24 十三 9	水1 Water 8 Dimming Light 地火明夷 辛丑 Metal Ox 25 十四 3	金9 Metal 9 Fellowship 天火同人 壬寅 Water Tiger 26 十五 7
木8 Wood 1 Marrying Maiden 雷澤歸妹 癸卯 Water Rabbit 27 十六 7	木3 Wood 2 Opposition 火澤睽 甲辰 Wood Dragon 28 十七 2	火7 Fire 3 Waiting 水天需 乙巳 Wood Snake 29 十八 3	金4 Metal 4 Great Exceeding 澤風大過 丙午 Fire Horse 30 十九 3			

MAY 1975 辛巳

Xuan Kong Element 玄空五行	火天大有 Great Reward	Period Luck 卦運	Monthly Star 月星
Wood 木3		7	5

SUNDAY	MONDAY	TUESDAY	WEDNESDAY	THURSDAY	FRIDAY	SATURDAY
				水6 Water Poison 5 丁未 Fire Goat 山風蠱 1 二十 7	火2 Fire Dispersing 6 戊申 Earth Monkey 風水渙 2 廿一 6	木3 Wood Travelling 7 己酉 Earth Rooster 火山旅 3 廿二 8
金9 Metal Stagnation 8 庚戌 Metal Dog 天地否 4 廿三 9	火7 Fire Alliance 9 辛亥 Metal Pig 水地比 5 廿四 7	木8 Wood Thunder 1 壬子 Water Rat 震爲雷 6 廿五 1	水6 Water Beauty 2 癸丑 Water Ox 山火賁 7 廿六 8	火7 Fire Accomplished 3 甲寅 Wood Tiger 水火既濟 8 廿七 9	水1 Water Arriving 4 乙卯 Wood Rabbit 地澤臨 9 廿八 4	金4 Metal Marsh 5 丙辰 Fire Dragon 兌爲澤 10 廿九 1
火2 Fire Small Livestock 6 丁巳 Fire Snake 風天小畜 11 四月初一 8	木3 Wood The Cauldron 7 戊午 Earth Horse 火風鼎 12 初二 4	水1 Water Rising 8 己未 Earth Goat 地風升 13 初三 2	火7 Fire Water 9 庚申 Metal Monkey 坎爲水 14 初四 1	木8 Wood Lesser Exceeding 1 辛酉 Metal Rooster 雷山小過 15 初五 3	金4 Metal Gathering 2 壬戌 Water Dog 澤地萃 16 初六 4	水6 Water Peel 3 癸亥 Water Pig 山地剝 17 初七 6
水1 Water Earth 4 甲子 Wood Rat 坤爲地 18 初八 1	木3 Wood Biting 5 乙丑 Wood Ox 火雷噬嗑 19 初九 6	火2 Fire Family 6 丙寅 Fire Tiger 風火家人 20 初十 4	水6 Water Decreasing 7 丁卯 Fire Rabbit 山澤損 21 十一 9	金9 Metal Tread 8 戊辰 Earth Dragon 天澤履 22 十二 6	木8 Wood Great Strength 9 己巳 Earth Snake 雷天大壯 23 十三 2	木8 Wood Consistency 1 庚午 Metal Horse 雷風恆 24 十四 9
金9 Metal Litigation 2 辛未 Metal Goat 天水訟 25 十五 3	水1 Water Officer 3 壬申 Water Monkey 地水師 26 十六 7	火2 Fire Gradual Progress 4 癸酉 Water Rooster 風山漸 27 十七 7	火7 Fire Obstruction 5 甲戌 Wood Dog 水山蹇 28 十八 2	木3 Wood Advancement 6 乙亥 Wood Pig 火地晉 29 十九 3	水6 Water Nourish 7 丙子 Fire Rat 山雷頤 30 二十 3	金4 Metal Following 8 丁丑 Fire Ox 澤雷隨 31 廿一 7

JUNE 1975 壬午

Xuan Kong Element 玄空五行	巽爲風 Wind	Period Luck 卦運	Monthly Star 月星
Fire 火2		1	4

SUNDAY	MONDAY	TUESDAY	WEDNESDAY	THURSDAY	FRIDAY	SATURDAY
木8 Wood Abundance 9 戊寅 Earth Tiger 雷火豐 1 廿二 6	火7 Fire Regulate 1 己卯 Earth Rabbit 水澤節 2 廿三 8	水1 Water Unity 2 庚辰 Metal Dragon 地天泰 3 廿四 9	木3 Wood Great Reward 3 辛巳 Metal Snake 火天大有 4 廿五 7	火2 Fire Wind 4 壬午 Water Horse 巽爲風 5 廿六 1	金4 Metal Trap 5 癸未 Water Goat 澤水困 6 廿七 8	木3 Wood Not Yet Accomplished 6 甲申 Wood Monkey 火水未濟 7 廿八 9
金9 Metal Retreat 7 乙酉 Wood Rooster 天山遯 8 廿九 4	水6 Water Mountain 8 丙戌 Fire Dog 艮爲山 9 三十 1	木8 Wood Delight 9 丁亥 Fire Pig 雷地豫 10 五月初一 8	火7 Fire Beginning 1 戊子 Earth Rat 水雷屯 11 初二 4	金9 Metal Without Wrongdoing 2 己丑 Earth Ox 天雷無妄 12 初三 2	木3 Wood Fire 3 庚寅 Metal Tiger 離爲火 13 初四 1	火2 Fire Sincerity 4 辛卯 Metal Rabbit 風澤中孚 14 初五 3
水6 Water Big Livestock 5 壬辰 Water Dragon 山天大畜 15 初六 4	金4 Metal Eliminating 6 癸巳 Water Snake 澤天夬 16 初七 6	金9 Metal Heaven 7 甲午 Wood Horse 乾爲天 17 初八 1	火7 Fire Well 8 乙未 Wood Goat 水風井 18 初九 6	木8 Wood Relief 9 丙申 Fire Monkey 雷水解 19 初十 4	金4 Metal Influence 1 丁酉 Fire Rooster 澤山咸 20 十一 9	水1 Water Humility 2 戊戌 Earth Dog 地山謙 21 十二 6
火2 Fire Observation 3/7 己亥 Earth Pig 風地觀 22 十三 2	火2 Fire Increasing 6 庚子 Metal Rat 風雷益 23 十四 9	水1 Water Dimming Light 5 辛丑 Metal Ox 地火明夷 24 十五 3	金9 Metal Fellowship 4 壬寅 Water Tiger 天火同人 25 十六 7	木8 Wood Marrying Maiden 3 癸卯 Water Rabbit 雷澤歸妹 26 十七 7	木3 Wood Opposition 2 甲辰 Wood Dragon 火澤睽 27 十八 2	火7 Fire Waiting 1 乙巳 Wood Snake 水天需 28 十九 3
金4 Metal Great Exceeding 9 丙午 Fire Horse 澤風大過 29 二十 3	水6 Water Poison 8 丁未 Fire Goat 山風蠱 30 廿一 7					

JULY 1975 癸未

Xuan Kong Element 玄空五行	澤水困 Trap	Period Luck 卦運	Monthly Star 月星
Metal 金4		8	3

SUNDAY	MONDAY	TUESDAY	WEDNESDAY	THURSDAY	FRIDAY	SATURDAY
		火2 Fire Dispersing 7 戊申 Earth Monkey 風水渙 1 廿二 6	木3 Wood Travelling 6 己酉 Earth Rooster 火山旅 2 廿三 8	金9 Metal Stagnation 5 庚戌 Metal Dog 天地否 3 廿四 9	火7 Fire Alliance 4 辛亥 Metal Pig 水地比 4 廿五 7	木8 Wood Thunder 3 壬子 Water Rat 震爲雷 5 廿六 1
水6 Water Beauty 2 癸丑 Water Ox 山火賁 6 廿七 8	火7 Fire Accomplished 1 甲寅 Wood Tiger 水火既濟 7 廿八 9	水1 Water Arriving 9 乙卯 Wood Rabbit 地澤臨 8 廿九 4	金4 Metal Marsh 8 丙辰 Fire Dragon 兌爲澤 9 六月初一 1	火2 Fire Small Livestock 7 丁巳 Fire Snake 風天小畜 10 初二 8	木3 Wood The Cauldron 6 戊午 Earth Horse 火風鼎 11 初三 4	水1 Water Rising 5 己未 Earth Goat 地風升 12 初四 2
火7 Fire Water 4 庚申 Metal Monkey 坎爲水 13 初五 1	木8 Wood Lesser Exceeding 3 辛酉 Metal Rooster 雷山小過 14 初六 3	金4 Metal Gathering 2 壬戌 Water Dog 澤地萃 15 初七 4	水6 Water Peel 1 癸亥 Water Pig 山地剝 16 初八 6	水1 Water Earth 9 甲子 Wood Rat 坤爲地 17 初九 1	木3 Wood Biting 8 乙丑 Wood Ox 火雷噬嗑 18 初十 6	火2 Fire Family 7 丙寅 Fire Tiger 風火家人 19 十一 4
水6 Water Decreasing 6 丁卯 Fire Rabbit 山澤損 20 十二 9	金9 Metal Tread 5 戊辰 Earth Dragon 天澤履 21 十三 6	木8 Wood Great Strength 4 己巳 Earth Snake 雷天大壯 22 十四 2	木8 Wood Consistency 3 庚午 Metal Horse 雷風恆 23 十五 9	金9 Metal Litigation 2 辛未 Metal Goat 天水訟 24 十六 3	水1 Water Officer 1 壬申 Water Monkey 地水師 25 十七 7	火2 Fire Gradual Progress 9 癸酉 Water Rooster 風山漸 26 十八 7
火7 Fire Obstruction 8 甲戌 Wood Dog 水山蹇 27 十九 2	木3 Wood Advancement 7 乙亥 Wood Pig 火地晉 28 二十 3	水6 Water Nourish 6 丙子 Fire Rat 山雷頤 29 廿一 3	金4 Metal Following 5 丁丑 Fire Ox 澤雷隨 30 廿二 7	木8 Wood Abundance 4 戊寅 Earth Tiger 雷火豐 31 廿三 6		

AUGUST 1975 甲申

Xuan Kong Element 玄空五行	火水未濟 Not Yet Accomplished	Period Luck 卦運	Monthly Star 月星
Wood 木3		9	2

SUNDAY	MONDAY	TUESDAY	WEDNESDAY	THURSDAY	FRIDAY	SATURDAY
木3 Wood Travelling 9 己酉 Earth Rooster 火山旅 31 廿五 8					火7 Fire Regulate 3 己卯 Earth Rabbit 水澤節 1 廿四 8	水1 Water Unity 2 庚辰 Metal Dragon 地天泰 2 廿五 9
木3 Wood Great Reward 1 辛巳 Metal Snake 火天大有 3 廿六 7	火2 Fire Wind 9 壬午 Water Horse 巽爲風 4 廿七 1	金4 Metal Trap 8 癸未 Water Goat 澤水困 5 廿八 8	木3 Wood Not Yet Accomplished 7 甲申 Wood Monkey 火水未濟 6 廿九 9	金9 Metal Retreat 6 乙酉 Wood Rooster 天山遯 7 七月初一 4	水6 Water Mountain 5 丙戌 Fire Dog 艮爲山 8 初二 1	木8 Wood Delight 4 丁亥 Fire Pig 雷地豫 9 初三 8
火7 Fire Beginning 3 戊子 Earth Rat 水雷屯 10 初四 4	金9 Metal Without Wrongdoing 2 己丑 Earth Ox 天雷無妄 11 初五 2	木3 Wood Fire 1 庚寅 Metal Tiger 離爲火 12 初六 1	火2 Fire Sincerity 9 辛卯 Metal Rabbit 風澤中孚 13 初七 3	水6 Water Big Livestock 8 壬辰 Water Dragon 山天大畜 14 初八 4	金4 Metal Eliminating 7 癸巳 Water Snake 澤天夬 15 初九 6	金9 Metal Heaven 6 甲午 Wood Horse 乾爲天 16 初十 1
火7 Fire Well 5 乙未 Wood Goat 水風井 17 十一 6	木8 Wood Relief 4 丙申 Fire Monkey 雷水解 18 十二 4	金4 Metal Influence 3 丁酉 Fire Rooster 澤山咸 19 十三 9	水1 Water Humility 2 戊戌 Earth Dog 地山謙 20 十四 6	火2 Fire Observation 1 己亥 Earth Pig 風地觀 21 十五 2	火2 Fire Increasing 9 庚子 Metal Rat 風雷益 22 十六 9	水1 Water Dimming Light 8 辛丑 Metal Ox 地火明夷 23 十七 3
金9 Metal Fellowship 7 壬寅 Water Tiger 天火同人 24 十八 7	木8 Wood Marrying Maiden 6 癸卯 Water Rabbit 雷澤歸妹 25 十九 7	木3 Wood Opposition 5 甲辰 Wood Dragon 火澤睽 26 二十 2	火7 Fire Waiting 4 乙巳 Wood Snake 水天需 27 廿一 3	金4 Metal Great Exceeding 3 丙午 Fire Horse 澤風大過 28 廿二 3	水6 Water Poison 2 丁未 Fire Goat 山風蠱 29 廿三 7	火2 Fire Dispersing 1 戊申 Earth Monkey 風水渙 30 廿四 6

SEPTEMBER 1975 乙酉

Xuan Kong Element 玄空五行	天山遯 Retreat	Period Luck 卦運	Monthly Star 月星
Metal 金9		4	1

SUNDAY	MONDAY	TUESDAY	WEDNESDAY	THURSDAY	FRIDAY	SATURDAY
	金9 Metal Stagnation 8 庚戌 Metal Dog 天地否 9 1 廿六	火7 Fire Alliance 7 辛亥 Metal Pig 水地比 7 2 廿七	木8 Wood Thunder 6 壬子 Water Rat 震爲雷 1 3 廿八	水6 Water Beauty 5 癸丑 Water Ox 山火賁 8 4 廿九	火7 Fire Accomplished 4 甲寅 Wood Tiger 水火既濟 9 5 三十	水1 Water Arriving 3 乙卯 Wood Rabbit 地澤臨 4 6 八月初一
金4 Metal Marsh 2 丙辰 Fire Dragon 兑爲澤 1 7 初二	火2 Fire Small Livestock 1 丁巳 Fire Snake 風天小畜 8 8 初三	木3 Wood The Cauldron 9 戊午 Earth Horse 火風鼎 4 9 初四	水1 Water Rising 8 己未 Earth Goat 地風升 2 10 初五	火7 Fire Water 7 庚申 Metal Monkey 坎爲水 1 11 初六	木8 Wood Lesser Exceeding 6 辛酉 Metal Rooster 雷山小過 3 12 初七	金4 Metal Gathering 5 壬戌 Water Dog 澤地萃 4 13 初八
水6 Water Peel 4 癸亥 Water Pig 山地剝 6 14 初九	水1 Water Earth 3 甲子 Wood Rat 坤爲地 1 15 初十	木3 Wood Biting 2 乙丑 Wood Ox 火雷噬嗑 6 16 十一	火2 Fire Family 1 丙寅 Fire Tiger 風火家人 4 17 十二	水6 Water Decreasing 9 丁卯 Fire Rabbit 山澤損 9 18 十三	金9 Metal Tread 8 戊辰 Earth Dragon 天澤履 6 19 十四	木8 Wood Great Strength 7 己巳 Earth Snake 雷天大壯 2 20 十五
木8 Wood Consistency 6 庚午 Metal Horse 雷風恆 9 21 十六	金9 Metal Litigation 5 辛未 Metal Goat 天水訟 3 22 十七	水1 Water Officer 4 壬申 Water Monkey 地水師 7 23 十八	火2 Fire Gradual Progress 3 癸酉 Water Rooster 風山漸 7 24 十九	火7 Fire Obstruction 2 甲戌 Wood Dog 水山蹇 2 25 二十	木3 Wood Advancement 1 乙亥 Wood Pig 火地晉 3 26 廿一	水6 Water Nourish 9 丙子 Fire Rat 山雷頤 3 27 廿二
金4 Metal Following 8 丁丑 Fire Ox 澤雷隨 7 28 廿三	木8 Wood Abundance 7 戊寅 Earth Tiger 雷火豐 6 29 廿四	火7 Fire Regulate 6 己卯 Earth Rabbit 水澤節 8 30 廿五				

OCTOBER 1975 丙戌

Xuan Kong Element 玄空五行	艮爲山 Mountain	Period Luck 卦運	Monthly Star 月星
Water 水6		1	9

SUNDAY	MONDAY	TUESDAY	WEDNESDAY	THURSDAY	FRIDAY	SATURDAY
			水1 Water Unity 5 庚辰 Metal Dragon 地天泰 9 1 廿六	木3 Wood Great Reward 4 辛巳 Metal Snake 火天大有 7 2 廿七	火2 Fire Wind 3 壬午 Water Horse 巽爲風 1 3 廿八	金4 Metal Trap 2 癸未 Water Goat 澤水困 8 4 廿九
木3 Wood Not Yet Accomplished 1 甲申 Wood Monkey 火水未濟 9 5 九月初一	金9 Metal Retreat 9 乙酉 Wood Rooster 天山遯 4 6 初二	水6 Water Mountain 8 丙戌 Fire Dog 艮爲山 1 7 初三	木8 Wood Delight 7 丁亥 Fire Pig 雷地豫 8 8 初四	火7 Fire Beginning 6 戊子 Earth Rat 水雷屯 4 9 初五	金9 Metal Without Wrongdoing 5 己丑 Earth Ox 天雷無妄 2 10 初六	木3 Wood Fire 4 庚寅 Metal Tiger 離爲火 1 11 初七
火2 Fire Sincerity 3 辛卯 Metal Rabbit 風澤中孚 3 12 初八	水6 Water Big Livestock 2 壬辰 Water Dragon 山天大畜 4 13 初九	金4 Metal Eliminating 1 癸巳 Water Snake 澤天夬 6 14 初十	金9 Metal Heaven 9 甲午 Wood Horse 乾爲天 1 15 十一	火7 Fire Well 8 乙未 Wood Goat 水風井 6 16 十二	木8 Wood Relief 7 丙申 Fire Monkey 雷水解 4 17 十三	金4 Metal Influence 6 丁酉 Fire Rooster 澤山咸 9 18 十四
水1 Water Humility 5 戊戌 Earth Dog 地山謙 6 19 十五	火2 Fire Observation 4 己亥 Earth Pig 風地觀 2 20 十六	火2 Fire Increasing 3 庚子 Metal Rat 風雷益 9 21 十七	水1 Water Dimming Light 2 辛丑 Metal Ox 地火明夷 3 22 十八	金9 Metal Fellowship 1 壬寅 Water Tiger 天火同人 7 23 十九	木8 Wood Marrying Maiden 9 癸卯 Water Rabbit 雷澤歸妹 7 24 二十	木3 Wood Opposition 8 甲辰 Wood Dragon 火澤睽 2 25 廿一
火7 Fire Waiting 7 乙巳 Wood Snake 水天需 3 26 廿二	金4 Metal Great Exceeding 6 丙午 Fire Horse 澤風大過 3 27 廿三	水6 Water Poison 5 丁未 Fire Goat 山風蠱 7 28 廿四	火2 Fire Dispersing 4 戊申 Earth Monkey 風水渙 6 29 廿五	木3 Wood Travelling 3 己酉 Earth Rooster 火山旅 8 30 廿六	金9 Metal Stagnation 2 庚戌 Metal Dog 天地否 9 31 廿七	

NOVEMBER 1975 丁亥

Xuan Kong Element 玄空五行	雷地豫 Delight	Period Luck 卦運	Monthly Star 月星
Wood 木8		8	8

SUNDAY	MONDAY	TUESDAY	WEDNESDAY	THURSDAY	FRIDAY	SATURDAY
水1 Water 8 Unity 庚辰 Metal Dragon 地天泰 30 廿八 9						火7 Fire 1 Alliance 辛亥 Metal Pig 水地比 1 廿八 7
木8 Wood 9 Thunder 壬子 Water Rat 震為雷 2 廿九 1	水6 Water 8 Beauty 癸丑 Water Ox 山火賁 3 十月初一 8	火7 Fire 7 Accomplished 甲寅 Wood Tiger 水火既濟 4 初二 9	水1 Water 6 Arriving 乙卯 Wood Rabbit 地澤臨 5 初三 4	金4 Metal 5 Marsh 丙辰 Fire Dragon 兌為澤 6 初四 1	火2 Fire 4 Small Livestock 丁巳 Fire Snake 風天小畜 7 初五 8	木3 Wood 3 The Cauldron 戊午 Earth Horse 火風鼎 8 初六 4
水1 Water 2 Rising 己未 Earth Goat 地風升 9 初七 2	火7 Fire 1 Water 庚申 Metal Monkey 坎為水 10 初八 1	木8 Wood 9 Lesser Exceeding 辛酉 Metal Rooster 雷山小過 11 初九 3	金4 Metal 8 Gathering 壬戌 Water Dog 澤地萃 12 初十 4	水6 Water 7 Peel 癸亥 Water Pig 山地剝 13 十一 6	水1 Water 6 Earth 甲子 Wood Rat 坤為地 14 十二 1	木3 Wood 5 Biting 乙丑 Wood Ox 火雷噬嗑 15 十三 6
火2 Fire 4 Family 丙寅 Fire Tiger 風火家人 16 十四 4	水6 Water 3 Decreasing 丁卯 Fire Rabbit 山澤損 17 十五 9	金9 Metal 2 Tread 戊辰 Earth Dragon 天澤履 18 十六 6	木8 Wood 1 Great Strength 己巳 Earth Snake 雷天大壯 19 十七 2	木8 Wood 9 Consistency 庚午 Metal Horse 雷風恆 20 十八 9	金9 Metal 8 Litigation 辛未 Metal Goat 天水訟 21 十九 3	水1 Water 7 Officer 壬申 Water Monkey 地水師 22 二十 7
火2 Fire 6 Gradual Progress 癸酉 Water Rooster 風山漸 23 廿一 7	火7 Fire 5 Obstruction 甲戌 Wood Dog 水山蹇 24 廿二 2	木3 Wood 4 Advancement 乙亥 Wood Pig 火地晉 25 廿三 3	水6 Water 3 Nourish 丙子 Fire Rat 山雷頤 26 廿四 3	金4 Metal 2 Following 丁丑 Fire Ox 澤雷隨 27 廿五 7	木8 Wood 1 Abundance 戊寅 Earth Tiger 雷火豐 28 廿六 6	火7 Fire 9 Regulate 己卯 Earth Rabbit 水澤節 29 廿七 8

DECEMBER 1975 戊子

Xuan Kong Element 玄空五行	水雷屯 Beginning	Period Luck 卦運	Monthly Star 月星
Fire 火7		4	7

SUNDAY	MONDAY	TUESDAY	WEDNESDAY	THURSDAY	FRIDAY	SATURDAY
	木3 Wood 7 Great Reward 辛巳 Metal Snake 火天大有 1 廿九 7	火2 Fire 6 Wind 壬午 Water Horse 巽為風 2 三十 1	金4 Metal 5 Trap 癸未 Water Goat 澤水困 3 十一月初一 8	木3 Wood 4 Not Yet Accomplished 甲申 Wood Monkey 火水未濟 4 初二 9	金9 Metal 3 Retreat 乙酉 Wood Rooster 天山遯 5 初三 4	水6 Water 2 Mountain 丙戌 Fire Dog 艮為山 6 初四 1
木8 Wood 1 Delight 丁亥 Fire Pig 雷地豫 7 初五 8	火7 Fire 9 Beginning 戊子 Earth Rat 水雷屯 8 初六 4	金9 Metal 8 Without Wrongdoing 己丑 Earth Ox 天雷無妄 9 初七 2	木3 Wood 7 Fire 庚寅 Metal Tiger 離為火 10 初八 1	火2 Fire 6 Sincerity 辛卯 Metal Rabbit 風澤中孚 11 初九 3	水6 Water 5 Big Livestock 壬辰 Water Dragon 山天大畜 12 初十 4	金4 Metal 4 Eliminating 癸巳 Water Snake 澤天夬 13 十一 6
金9 Metal 3 Heaven 甲午 Wood Horse 乾為天 14 十二 1	火7 Fire 2 Well 乙未 Wood Goat 水風井 15 十三 6	木8 Wood 1 Relief 丙申 Fire Monkey 雷水解 16 十四 4	金4 Metal 9 Influence 丁酉 Fire Rooster 澤山咸 17 十五 9	水1 Water 8 Humility 戊戌 Earth Dog 地山謙 18 十六 6	火2 Fire 7 Observation 己亥 Earth Pig 風地觀 19 十七 2	火2 Fire 6 Increasing 庚子 Metal Rat 風雷益 20 十八 9
水1 Water 5 Dimming Light 辛丑 Metal Ox 地火明夷 21 十九 3	金9 Metal 4/6 Fellowship 壬寅 Water Tiger 天火同人 22 二十 7	木8 Wood 7 Marrying Maiden 癸卯 Water Rabbit 雷澤歸妹 23 廿一 7	木3 Wood 8 Opposition 甲辰 Wood Dragon 火澤睽 24 廿二 2	火7 Fire 9 Waiting 乙巳 Wood Snake 水天需 25 廿三 3	金4 Metal 1 Great Exceeding 丙午 Fire Horse 澤風大過 26 廿四 3	水6 Water 2 Poison 丁未 Fire Goat 山風蠱 27 廿五 7
火2 Fire 3 Dispersing 戊申 Earth Monkey 風水渙 28 廿六 6	木3 Wood 4 Travelling 己酉 Earth Rooster 火山旅 29 廿七 8	金9 Metal 5 Stagnation 庚戌 Metal Dog 天地否 30 廿八 9	火7 Fire 6 Alliance 辛亥 Metal Pig 水地比 31 廿九 7			

1976 丙辰

(*Bing Chen*) Fire Dragon

1976 丙辰 *(Bing Chen)* Fire Dragon

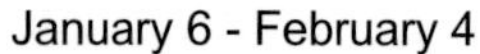
January 6 - February 4

February 5 - March 4

March 5 - April 3

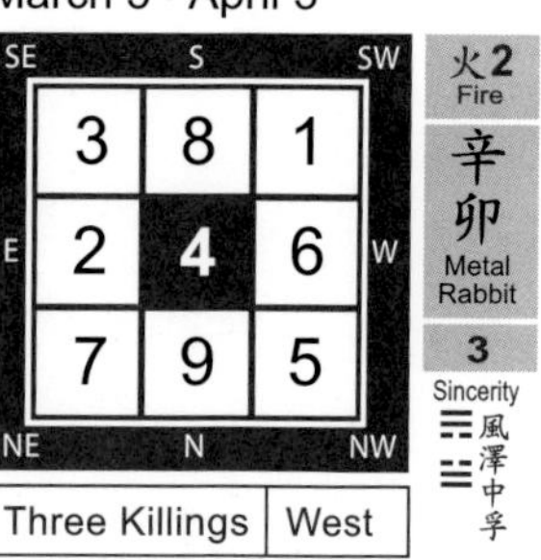

April 4 - May 4

May 5 - June 4

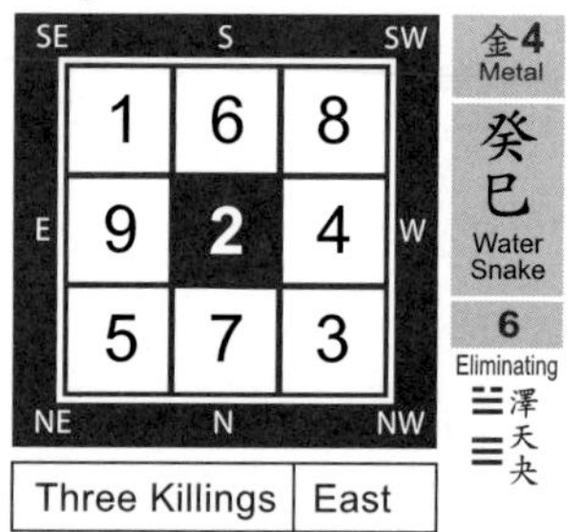

June 5 - July 6

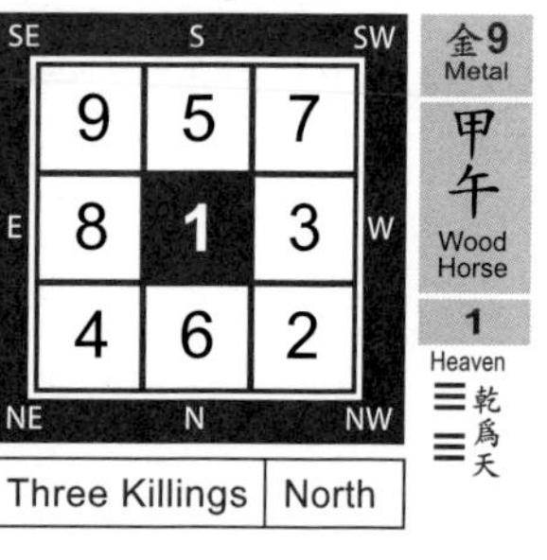

July 7 - August 6

August 7 - September 6

September 7 - October 7

October 8 - November 6

November 7 - December 6

December 7 - January 4

JANUARY 1976 己丑

Xuan Kong Element 玄空五行	天雷無妄 Without Wrongdoing	Period Luck 卦運	Monthly Star 月星
Metal 金9		2	6

SUNDAY	MONDAY	TUESDAY	WEDNESDAY	THURSDAY	FRIDAY	SATURDAY
				木8 Wood 7 Thunder 震為雷 壬子 Water Rat 1 **1** 十二月初一	水6 Water 8 Beauty 山火賁 癸丑 Water Ox 8 **2** 初二	火7 Fire 9 Accomplished 水火既濟 甲寅 Wood Tiger 9 **3** 初三
水1 Water 1 Arriving 地澤臨 乙卯 Wood Rabbit 4 **4** 初四	金4 Metal 2 Marsh 兌為澤 丙辰 Fire Dragon 1 **5** 初五	火2 Fire 3 Small Livestock 風天小畜 丁巳 Fire Snake 8 **6** 初六	木3 Wood 4 The Cauldron 火風鼎 戊午 Earth Horse 4 **7** 初七	水1 Water 5 Rising 地風升 己未 Earth Goat 2 **8** 初八	火7 Fire 6 Water 坎為水 庚申 Metal Monkey 1 **9** 初九	木8 Wood 7 Lesser Exceeding 雷山小過 辛酉 Metal Rooster 3 **10** 初十
金4 Metal 8 Gathering 澤地萃 壬戌 Water Dog 4 **11** 十一	水6 Water 9 Peel 山地剝 癸亥 Water Pig 6 **12** 十二	水1 Water 1 Earth 坤為地 甲子 Wood Rat 1 **13** 十三	木3 Wood 2 Biting 火雷噬嗑 乙丑 Wood Ox 6 **14** 十四	火2 Fire 3 Family 風火家人 丙寅 Fire Tiger 4 **15** 十五	水6 Water 4 Decreasing 山澤損 丁卯 Fire Rabbit 9 **16** 十六	金9 Metal 5 Tread 天澤履 戊辰 Earth Dragon 6 **17** 十七
木8 Wood 6 Great Strength 雷天大壯 己巳 Earth Snake 2 **18** 十八	木8 Wood 7 Consistency 雷風恆 庚午 Metal Horse 9 **19** 十九	金9 Metal 8 Litigation 天水訟 辛未 Metal Goat 3 **20** 二十	水1 Water 9 Officer 地水師 壬申 Water Monkey 7 **21** 廿一	火2 Fire 1 Gradual Progress 風山漸 癸酉 Water Rooster 7 **22** 廿二	火7 Fire 2 Obstruction 水山蹇 甲戌 Wood Dog 2 **23** 廿三	木3 Wood 3 Advancement 火地晉 乙亥 Wood Pig 3 **24** 廿四
水6 Water 4 Nourish 山雷頤 丙子 Fire Rat 3 **25** 廿五	金4 Metal 5 Following 澤雷隨 丁丑 Fire Ox 7 **26** 廿六	木8 Wood 6 Abundance 雷火豐 戊寅 Earth Tiger 6 **27** 廿七	火7 Fire 7 Regulate 水澤節 己卯 Earth Rabbit 8 **28** 廿八	水1 Water 8 Unity 地天泰 庚辰 Metal Dragon 9 **29** 廿九	木3 Wood 9 Great Reward 火天大有 辛巳 Metal Snake 7 **30** 三十	火2 Fire 1 Wind 巽為風 壬午 Water Horse 1 **31** 正月初一

FEBRUARY 1976 庚寅

Xuan Kong Element 玄空五行	離為火 Fire	Period Luck 卦運	Monthly Star 月星
Wood 木3		1	5

SUNDAY	MONDAY	TUESDAY	WEDNESDAY	THURSDAY	FRIDAY	SATURDAY
金4 Metal 2 Trap 澤水困 癸未 Water Goat 8 **1** 初二	木3 Wood 3 Not Yet Accomplished 火水未濟 甲申 Wood Monkey 9 **2** 初三	金9 Metal 4 Retreat 天山遯 乙酉 Wood Rooster 4 **3** 初四	水6 Water 5 Mountain 艮為山 丙戌 Fire Dog 1 **4** 初五	木8 Wood 6 Delight 雷地豫 丁亥 Fire Pig 8 **5** 初六	火7 Fire 7 Beginning 水雷屯 戊子 Earth Rat 4 **6** 初七	金9 Metal 8 Without Wrongdoing 天雷無妄 己丑 Earth Ox 2 **7** 初八
木3 Wood 9 Fire 離為火 庚寅 Metal Tiger 1 **8** 初九	火2 Fire 1 Sincerity 風澤中孚 辛卯 Metal Rabbit 3 **9** 初十	水6 Water 2 Big Livestock 山天大畜 壬辰 Water Dragon 4 **10** 十一	金4 Metal 3 Eliminating 澤天夬 癸巳 Water Snake 6 **11** 十二	金9 Metal 4 Heaven 乾為天 甲午 Wood Horse 1 **12** 十三	火7 Fire 5 Well 水風井 乙未 Wood Goat 6 **13** 十四	木8 Wood 6 Relief 雷水解 丙申 Fire Monkey 4 **14** 十五
金4 Metal 7 Influence 澤山咸 丁酉 Fire Rooster 9 **15** 十六	水1 Water 8 Humility 地山謙 戊戌 Earth Dog 6 **16** 十七	火2 Fire 9 Observation 風地觀 己亥 Earth Pig 2 **17** 十八	火2 Fire 1 Increasing 風雷益 庚子 Metal Rat 9 **18** 十九	水1 Water 2 Dimming Light 地火明夷 辛丑 Metal Ox 3 **19** 二十	金9 Metal 3 Fellowship 天火同人 壬寅 Water Tiger 7 **20** 廿一	木8 Wood 4 Marrying Maiden 雷澤歸妹 癸卯 Water Rabbit 7 **21** 廿二
木3 Wood 5 Opposition 火澤睽 甲辰 Wood Dragon 2 **22** 廿三	火7 Fire 6 Waiting 水天需 乙巳 Wood Snake 3 **23** 廿四	金4 Metal 7 Great Exceeding 澤風大過 丙午 Fire Horse 3 **24** 廿五	水6 Water 8 Poison 山風蠱 丁未 Fire Goat 7 **25** 廿六	火2 Fire 9 Dispersing 風水渙 戊申 Earth Monkey 6 **26** 廿七	木3 Wood 1 Travelling 火山旅 己酉 Earth Rooster 8 **27** 廿八	金9 Metal 2 Stagnation 天地否 庚戌 Metal Dog 9 **28** 廿九
火7 Fire 3 Alliance 水地比 辛亥 Metal Pig 7 **29** 三十						

MARCH 1976 辛卯

Xuan Kong Element 玄空五行	風澤中孚 Sincerity	Period Luck 卦運	Monthly Star 月星
Fire 火2		3	4

SUNDAY	MONDAY	TUESDAY	WEDNESDAY	THURSDAY	FRIDAY	SATURDAY
	木8 Wood 4 Thunder 壬子 Water Rat 震爲雷 1 二月初一 1	水6 Water 5 Beauty 癸丑 Water Ox 山火賁 2 初二 8	火7 Fire 6 Accomplished 甲寅 Wood Tiger 水火既濟 3 初三 9	水1 Water 7 Arriving 乙卯 Wood Rabbit 地澤臨 4 初四 4	金4 Metal 8 Marsh 丙辰 Fire Dragon 兌爲澤 5 初五 1	火2 Fire 9 Small Livestock 丁巳 Fire Snake 風天小畜 6 初六 8
木3 Wood 1 The Cauldron 戊午 Earth Horse 火風鼎 7 初七 4	水1 Water 2 Rising 己未 Earth Goat 地風升 8 初八 2	火7 Fire 3 Water 庚申 Metal Monkey 坎爲水 9 初九 1	木8 Wood 4 Lesser Exceeding 辛酉 Metal Rooster 雷山小過 10 初十 3	金4 Metal 5 Gathering 壬戌 Water Dog 澤地萃 11 十一 4	水6 Water 6 Peel 癸亥 Water Pig 山地剝 12 十二 6	水1 Water 7 Earth 甲子 Wood Rat 坤爲地 13 十三 1
木3 Wood 8 Biting 乙丑 Wood Ox 火雷噬嗑 14 十四 6	火2 Fire 9 Family 丙寅 Fire Tiger 風火家人 15 十五 4	水6 Water 1 Decreasing 丁卯 Fire Rabbit 山澤損 16 十六 9	金9 Metal 2 Tread 戊辰 Earth Dragon 天澤履 17 十七 6	木8 Wood 3 Great Strength 己巳 Earth Snake 雷天大壯 18 十八 2	木8 Wood 4 Consistency 庚午 Metal Horse 雷風恆 19 十九 9	金9 Metal 5 Litigation 辛未 Metal Goat 天水訟 20 二十 3
水1 Water 6 Officer 壬申 Water Monkey 地水師 21 廿一 7	火2 Fire 7 Gradual Progress 癸酉 Water Rooster 風山漸 22 廿二 7	火7 Fire 8 Obstruction 甲戌 Wood Dog 水山蹇 23 廿三 2	木3 Wood 9 Advancement 乙亥 Wood Pig 火地晉 24 廿四 3	水6 Water 1 Nourish 丙子 Fire Rat 山雷頤 25 廿五 3	金4 Metal 2 Following 丁丑 Fire Ox 澤雷隨 26 廿六 7	木8 Wood 3 Abundance 戊寅 Earth Tiger 雷火豐 27 廿七 6
火7 Fire 4 Regulate 己卯 Earth Rabbit 水澤節 28 廿八 8	水1 Water 5 Unity 庚辰 Metal Dragon 地天泰 29 廿九 9	木3 Wood 6 Great Reward 辛巳 Metal Snake 火天大有 30 三十 7	火2 Fire 7 Wind 壬午 Water Horse 巽爲風 31 三月初一 1			

APRIL 1976 壬辰

Xuan Kong Element 玄空五行	山天大畜 Big Livestock	Period Luck 卦運	Monthly Star 月星
Water 水6		4	3

SUNDAY	MONDAY	TUESDAY	WEDNESDAY	THURSDAY	FRIDAY	SATURDAY
				金4 Metal 8 Trap 癸未 Water Goat 澤水困 1 初二 8	木3 Wood 9 Not Yet Accomplished 甲申 Wood Monkey 火水未濟 2 初三 9	金9 Metal 1 Retreat 乙酉 Wood Rooster 天山遯 3 初四 4
水6 Water 2 Mountain 丙戌 Fire Dog 艮爲山 4 初五 1	木8 Wood 3 Delight 丁亥 Fire Pig 雷地豫 5 初六 8	火7 Fire 4 Beginning 戊子 Earth Rat 水雷屯 6 初七 4	金9 Metal 5 Without Wrongdoing 己丑 Earth Ox 天雷無妄 7 初八 2	木3 Wood 6 Fire 庚寅 Metal Tiger 離爲火 8 初九 1	火2 Fire 7 Sincerity 辛卯 Metal Rabbit 風澤中孚 9 初十 3	水6 Water 8 Big Livestock 壬辰 Water Dragon 山天大畜 10 十一 4
金4 Metal 9 Eliminating 癸巳 Water Snake 澤天夬 11 十二 6	金9 Metal 1 Heaven 甲午 Wood Horse 乾爲天 12 十三 1	火7 Fire 2 Well 乙未 Wood Goat 水風井 13 十四 6	木8 Wood 3 Relief 丙申 Fire Monkey 雷水解 14 十五 4	金4 Metal 4 Influence 丁酉 Fire Rooster 澤山咸 15 十六 9	水1 Water 5 Humility 戊戌 Earth Dog 地山謙 16 十七 6	火2 Fire 6 Observation 己亥 Earth Pig 風地觀 17 十八 2
火2 Fire 7 Increasing 庚子 Metal Rat 風雷益 18 十九 9	水1 Water 8 Dimming Light 辛丑 Metal Ox 地火明夷 19 二十 3	金9 Metal 9 Fellowship 壬寅 Water Tiger 天火同人 20 廿一 7	木8 Wood 1 Marrying Maiden 癸卯 Water Rabbit 雷澤歸妹 21 廿二 7	木3 Wood 2 Opposition 甲辰 Wood Dragon 火澤睽 22 廿三 2	火7 Fire 3 Waiting 乙巳 Wood Snake 水天需 23 廿四 3	金4 Metal 4 Great Exceeding 丙午 Fire Horse 澤風大過 24 廿五 3
水6 Water 5 Poison 丁未 Fire Goat 山風蠱 25 廿六 7	火2 Fire 6 Dispersing 戊申 Earth Monkey 風水渙 26 廿七 6	木3 Wood 7 Travelling 己酉 Earth Rooster 火山旅 27 廿八 8	金9 Metal 8 Stagnation 庚戌 Metal Dog 天地否 28 廿九 9	火7 Fire 9 Alliance 辛亥 Metal Pig 水地比 29 四月初一 7	木8 Wood 1 Thunder 壬子 Water Rat 震爲雷 30 初二 1	

MAY 1976 癸巳

Xuan Kong Element 玄空五行	澤天夬 Eliminating	Period Luck 卦運	Monthly Star 月星
Metal 金4		6	2

SUNDAY	MONDAY	TUESDAY	WEDNESDAY	THURSDAY	FRIDAY	SATURDAY
火2 Fire 4 Wind 巽爲風 壬午 Water Horse 30 初二 1	金4 Metal 5 Trap 澤水困 癸未 Water Goat 31 初三 8					水6 Water 2 Beauty 山火賁 癸丑 Water Ox 1 初三 8
火7 Fire 3 Accomplished 水火既濟 甲寅 Wood Tiger 2 初四 9	水1 Water 4 Arriving 地澤臨 乙卯 Wood Rabbit 3 初五 4	金4 Metal 5 Marsh 兌爲澤 丙辰 Fire Dragon 4 初六 1	火2 Fire 6 Small Livestock 風天小畜 丁巳 Fire Snake 5 初七 8	木3 Wood 7 The Cauldron 火風鼎 戊午 Earth Horse 6 初八 4	水1 Water 8 Rising 地風升 己未 Earth Goat 7 初九 2	火7 Fire 9 Water 坎爲水 庚申 Metal Monkey 8 初十 1
木8 Wood 1 Lesser Exceeding 雷山小過 辛酉 Metal Rooster 9 十一 3	金4 Metal 2 Gathering 澤地萃 壬戌 Water Dog 10 十二 4	水6 Water 3 Peel 山地剝 癸亥 Water Pig 11 十三 6	水1 Water 4 Earth 坤爲地 甲子 Wood Rat 12 十四 1	木3 Wood 5 Biting 火雷噬嗑 乙丑 Wood Ox 13 十五 6	火2 Fire 6 Family 風火家人 丙寅 Fire Tiger 14 十六 4	水6 Water 7 Decreasing 山澤損 丁卯 Fire Rabbit 15 十七 9
金9 Metal 8 Tread 天澤履 戊辰 Earth Dragon 16 十八 6	木8 Wood 9 Great Strength 雷天大壯 己巳 Earth Snake 17 十九 2	木8 Wood 1 Consistency 雷風恒 庚午 Metal Horse 18 二十 9	金9 Metal 2 Litigation 天水訟 辛未 Metal Goat 19 廿一 3	水1 Water 3 Officer 地水師 壬申 Water Monkey 20 廿二 7	火2 Fire 4 Gradual Progress 風山漸 癸酉 Water Rooster 21 廿三 7	火7 Fire 5 Obstruction 水山蹇 甲戌 Wood Dog 22 廿四 2
木3 Wood 6 Advancement 火地晉 乙亥 Wood Pig 23 廿五 3	水6 Water 7 Nourish 山雷頤 丙子 Fire Rat 24 廿六 3	金4 Metal 8 Following 澤雷隨 丁丑 Fire Ox 25 廿七 7	木8 Wood 9 Abundance 雷火豐 戊寅 Earth Tiger 26 廿八 6	火7 Fire 1 Regulate 水澤節 己卯 Earth Rabbit 27 廿九 8	水1 Water 2 Unity 地天泰 庚辰 Metal Dragon 28 三十 9	木3 Wood 3 Great Reward 火天大有 辛巳 Metal Snake 29 五月初一 7

JUNE 1976 甲午

Xuan Kong Element 玄空五行	乾爲天 Heaven	Period Luck 卦運	Monthly Star 月星
Metal 金9		1	1

SUNDAY	MONDAY	TUESDAY	WEDNESDAY	THURSDAY	FRIDAY	SATURDAY
		木3 Wood 6 Not Yet Accomplished 火水未濟 甲申 Wood Monkey 1 初四 9	金9 Metal 7 Retreat 天山遯 乙酉 Wood Rooster 2 初五 4	水6 Water 8 Mountain 艮爲山 丙戌 Fire Dog 3 初六 1	木8 Wood 9 Delight 雷地豫 丁亥 Fire Pig 4 初七 8	火7 Fire 1 Beginning 水雷屯 戊子 Earth Rat 5 初八 4
金9 Metal 2 Without Wrongdoing 天雷無妄 己丑 Earth Ox 6 初九 2	木3 Wood 3 Fire 離爲火 庚寅 Metal Tiger 7 初十 1	火2 Fire 4 Sincerity 風澤中孚 辛卯 Metal Rabbit 8 十一 3	水6 Water 5 Big Livestock 山天大畜 壬辰 Water Dragon 9 十二 4	金4 Metal 6 Eliminating 澤天夬 癸巳 Water Snake 10 十三 6	金9 Metal 7 Heaven 乾爲天 甲午 Wood Horse 11 十四 1	火7 Fire 8 Well 水風井 乙未 Wood Goat 12 十五 6
木8 Wood 9 Relief 雷水解 丙申 Fire Monkey 13 十六 4	金4 Metal 1 Influence 澤山咸 丁酉 Fire Rooster 14 十七 9	水1 Water 2 Humility 地山謙 戊戌 Earth Dog 15 十八 6	火2 Fire 3 Observation 風地觀 己亥 Earth Pig 16 十九 2	火2 Fire 4 Increasing 風雷益 庚子 Metal Rat 17 二十 9	水1 Water 5 Dimming Light 地火明夷 辛丑 Metal Ox 18 廿一 3	金9 Metal 6 Fellowship 天火同人 壬寅 Water Tiger 19 廿二 7
木8 Wood 7 Marrying Maiden 雷澤歸妹 癸卯 Water Rabbit 20 廿三 7	木3 Wood 8/2 Opposition 火澤睽 甲辰 Wood Dragon 21 廿四 2	火7 Fire 1 Waiting 水天需 乙巳 Wood Snake 22 廿五 3	金4 Metal 9 Great Exceeding 澤風大過 丙午 Fire Horse 23 廿六 3	水6 Water 8 Poison 山風蠱 丁未 Fire Goat 24 廿七 7	火2 Fire 7 Dispersing 風水渙 戊申 Earth Monkey 25 廿八 6	木3 Wood 6 Travelling 火山旅 己酉 Earth Rooster 26 廿九 8
金9 Metal 5 Stagnation 天地否 庚戌 Metal Dog 27 六月初一 9	火7 Fire 4 Alliance 水地比 辛亥 Metal Pig 28 初二 7	木8 Wood 3 Thunder 震爲雷 壬子 Water Rat 29 初三 1	水6 Water 2 Beauty 山火賁 癸丑 Water Ox 30 初四 8			

JULY 1976 乙未

Xuan Kong Element 玄空五行	水風井 Well	Period Luck 卦運	Monthly Star 月星
Fire 火7		6	9

SUNDAY	MONDAY	TUESDAY	WEDNESDAY	THURSDAY	FRIDAY	SATURDAY
				火7 Fire [1] Accomplished 甲寅 Wood Tiger 水火既濟 **1** 初五 9	水1 Water [9] Arriving 乙卯 Wood Rabbit 地澤臨 **2** 初六 4	金4 Metal [8] Marsh 丙辰 Fire Dragon 兌爲澤 **3** 初七 1
火2 Fire [7] Small Livestock 丁巳 Fire Snake 風天小畜 **4** 初八 8	木3 Wood [6] The Cauldron 戊午 Earth Horse 火風鼎 **5** 初九 4	水1 Water [5] Rising 己未 Earth Goat 地風升 **6** 初十 2	火7 Fire [4] Water 庚申 Metal Monkey 坎爲水 **7** 十一 1	木8 Wood [3] Lesser Exceeding 辛酉 Metal Rooster 雷山小過 **8** 十二 3	金4 Metal [2] Gathering 壬戌 Water Dog 澤地萃 **9** 十三 4	水6 Water [1] Peel 癸亥 Water Pig 山地剝 **10** 十四 6
水1 Water [9] Earth 甲子 Wood Rat 坤爲地 **11** 十五 1	木3 Wood [8] Biting 乙丑 Wood Ox 火雷噬嗑 **12** 十六 6	火2 Fire [7] Family 丙寅 Fire Tiger 風火家人 **13** 十七 4	水6 Water [6] Decreasing 丁卯 Fire Rabbit 山澤損 **14** 十八 9	金9 Metal [5] Tread 戊辰 Earth Dragon 天澤履 **15** 十九 6	木8 Wood [4] Great Strength 己巳 Earth Snake 雷天大壯 **16** 二十 2	木8 Wood [3] Consistency 庚午 Metal Horse 雷風恒 **17** 廿一 9
金9 Metal [2] Litigation 辛未 Metal Goat 天水訟 **18** 廿二 3	水1 Water [1] Officer 壬申 Water Monkey 地水師 **19** 廿三 7	火2 Fire [9] Gradual Progress 癸酉 Water Rooster 風山漸 **20** 廿四 7	火7 Fire [8] Obstruction 甲戌 Wood Dog 水山蹇 **21** 廿五 2	木3 Wood [7] Advancement 乙亥 Wood Pig 火地晉 **22** 廿六 3	水6 Water [6] Nourish 丙子 Fire Rat 山雷頤 **23** 廿七 3	金4 Metal [5] Following 丁丑 Fire Ox 澤雷隨 **24** 廿八 7
木8 Wood [4] Abundance 戊寅 Earth Tiger 雷火豐 **25** 廿九 6	火7 Fire [3] Regulate 己卯 Earth Rabbit 水澤節 **26** 三十 8	水1 Water [2] Unity 庚辰 Metal Dragon 地天泰 **27** 七月初一 9	木3 Wood [1] Great Reward 辛巳 Metal Snake 火天大有 **28** 初二 7	火2 Fire [9] Wind 壬午 Water Horse 巽爲風 **29** 初三 1	金4 Metal [8] Trap 癸未 Water Goat 澤水困 **30** 初四 8	木3 Wood [7] Not Yet Accomplished 甲申 Wood Monkey 火水未濟 **31** 初五 9

AUGUST 1976 丙申

Xuan Kong Element 玄空五行	雷水解 Relief	Period Luck 卦運	Monthly Star 月星
Wood 木8		4	8

SUNDAY	MONDAY	TUESDAY	WEDNESDAY	THURSDAY	FRIDAY	SATURDAY
金9 Metal [6] Retreat 乙酉 Wood Rooster 天山遯 **1** 初六 4	水6 Water [5] Mountain 丙戌 Fire Dog 艮爲山 **2** 初七 1	木8 Wood [4] Delight 丁亥 Fire Pig 雷地豫 **3** 初八 8	火7 Fire [3] Beginning 戊子 Earth Rat 水雷屯 **4** 初九 4	金9 Metal [2] Without Wrongdoing 己丑 Earth Ox 天雷無妄 **5** 初十 2	木3 Wood [1] Fire 庚寅 Metal Tiger 離爲火 **6** 十一 1	火2 Fire [9] Sincerity 辛卯 Metal Rabbit 風澤中孚 **7** 十二 3
水6 Water [8] Big Livestock 壬辰 Water Dragon 山天大畜 **8** 十三 4	金4 Metal [7] Eliminating 癸巳 Water Snake 澤天夬 **9** 十四 6	金9 Metal [6] Heaven 甲午 Wood Horse 乾爲天 **10** 十五 1	火7 Fire [5] Well 乙未 Wood Goat 水風井 **11** 十六 6	木8 Wood [4] Relief 丙申 Fire Monkey 雷水解 **12** 十七 4	金4 Metal [3] Influence 丁酉 Fire Rooster 澤山咸 **13** 十八 9	水1 Water [2] Humility 戊戌 Earth Dog 地山謙 **14** 十九 6
火2 Fire [1] Observation 己亥 Earth Pig 風地觀 **15** 二十 2	火2 Fire [9] Increasing 庚子 Metal Rat 風雷益 **16** 廿一 9	水1 Water [8] Dimming Light 辛丑 Metal Ox 地火明夷 **17** 廿二 3	金9 Metal [7] Fellowship 壬寅 Water Tiger 天火同人 **18** 廿三 7	木8 Wood [6] Marrying Maiden 癸卯 Water Rabbit 雷澤歸妹 **19** 廿四 7	木3 Wood [5] Opposition 甲辰 Wood Dragon 火澤睽 **20** 廿五 2	火7 Fire [4] Waiting 乙巳 Wood Snake 水天需 **21** 廿六 3
金4 Metal [3] Great Exceeding 丙午 Fire Horse 澤風大過 **22** 廿七 3	水6 Water [2] Poison 丁未 Fire Goat 山風蠱 **23** 廿八 7	火2 Fire [1] Dispersing 戊申 Earth Monkey 風水渙 **24** 廿九 6	木3 Wood [9] Travelling 己酉 Earth Rooster 火山旅 **25** 八月初一 8	金9 Metal [8] Stagnation 庚戌 Metal Dog 天地否 **26** 初二 9	火7 Fire [7] Alliance 辛亥 Metal Pig 水地比 **27** 初三 7	木8 Wood [6] Thunder 壬子 Water Rat 震爲雷 **28** 初四 1
水6 Water [5] Beauty 癸丑 Water Ox 山火賁 **29** 初五 8	火7 Fire [4] Accomplished 甲寅 Wood Tiger 水火既濟 **30** 初六 9	水1 Water [3] Arriving 乙卯 Wood Rabbit 地澤臨 **31** 初七 4				

SEPTEMBER 1976 丁酉

Xuan Kong Element 玄空五行	澤山咸 Influence	Period Luck 卦運	Monthly Star 月星
Metal 金4		9	7

SUNDAY	MONDAY	TUESDAY	WEDNESDAY	THURSDAY	FRIDAY	SATURDAY
			金4 Metal 2 Marsh 丙辰 Fire Dragon 兌爲澤 1 初八 1	火2 Fire 1 Small Livestock 丁巳 Fire Snake 風天小畜 2 初九 8	木3 Wood 9 The Cauldron 戊午 Earth Horse 火風鼎 3 初十 4	水1 Water 8 Rising 己未 Earth Goat 地風升 4 十一 2
火7 Fire 7 Water 庚申 Metal Monkey 坎爲水 5 十二 1	木8 Wood 6 Lesser Exceeding 辛酉 Metal Rooster 雷山小過 6 十三 3	金4 Metal 5 Gathering 壬戌 Water Dog 澤地萃 7 十四 4	水6 Water 4 Peel 癸亥 Water Pig 山地剝 8 十五 6	水1 Water 3 Earth 甲子 Wood Rat 坤爲地 9 十六 1	木3 Wood 2 Biting 乙丑 Wood Ox 火雷噬嗑 10 十七 6	火2 Fire 1 Family 丙寅 Fire Tiger 風火家人 11 十八 4
水6 Water 9 Decreasing 丁卯 Fire Rabbit 山澤損 12 十九 9	金9 Metal 8 Tread 戊辰 Earth Dragon 天澤履 13 二十 6	木8 Wood 7 Great Strength 己巳 Earth Snake 雷天大壯 14 廿一 2	木8 Wood 6 Consistency 庚午 Metal Horse 雷風恆 15 廿二 9	金9 Metal 5 Litigation 辛未 Metal Goat 天水訟 16 廿三 3	水1 Water 4 Officer 壬申 Water Monkey 地水師 17 廿四 7	火2 Fire 3 Gradual Progress 癸酉 Water Rooster 風山漸 18 廿五 7
火7 Fire 2 Obstruction 甲戌 Wood Dog 水山蹇 19 廿六 2	木3 Wood 1 Advancement 乙亥 Wood Pig 火地晉 20 廿七 3	水6 Water 9 Nourish 丙子 Fire Rat 山雷頤 21 廿八 3	金4 Metal 8 Following 丁丑 Fire Ox 澤雷隨 22 廿九 7	木8 Wood 7 Abundance 戊寅 Earth Tiger 雷火豐 23 三十 6	火7 Fire 6 Regulate 己卯 Earth Rabbit 水澤節 24 閏八月初一 8	水1 Water 5 Unity 庚辰 Metal Dragon 地天泰 25 初一 9
木3 Wood 4 Great Reward 辛巳 Metal Snake 火天大有 26 初三 7	火2 Fire 3 Wind 壬午 Water Horse 巽爲風 27 初四 1	金4 Metal 2 Trap 癸未 Water Goat 澤水困 28 初五 8	木3 Wood 1 Not Yet Accomplished 甲申 Wood Monkey 火水未濟 29 初六 9	金9 Metal 9 Retreat 乙酉 Wood Rooster 天山遯 30 初七 4		

OCTOBER 1976 戊戌

Xuan Kong Element 玄空五行	地山謙 Humility	Period Luck 卦運	Monthly Star 月星
Water 水1		6	6

SUNDAY	MONDAY	TUESDAY	WEDNESDAY	THURSDAY	FRIDAY	SATURDAY
金4 Metal 5 Marsh 丙辰 Fire Dragon 兌爲澤 31 初九 1					水6 Water 8 Mountain 丙戌 Fire Dog 艮爲山 1 初八 1	木8 Wood 7 Delight 丁亥 Fire Pig 雷地豫 2 初九 8
火7 Fire 6 Beginning 戊子 Earth Rat 水雷屯 3 初十 4	金9 Metal 5 Without Wrongdoing 己丑 Earth Ox 天雷無妄 4 十一 2	木3 Wood 4 Fire 庚寅 Metal Tiger 離爲火 5 十二 1	火2 Fire 3 Sincerity 辛卯 Metal Rabbit 風澤中孚 6 十三 3	水6 Water 2 Big Livestock 壬辰 Water Dragon 山天大畜 7 十四 4	金4 Metal 1 Eliminating 癸巳 Water Snake 澤天夬 8 十五 6	金9 Metal 9 Heaven 甲午 Wood Horse 乾爲天 9 十六 1
火7 Fire 8 Well 乙未 Wood Goat 水風井 10 十七 6	木8 Wood 7 Relief 丙申 Fire Monkey 雷水解 11 十八 4	金4 Metal 6 Influence 丁酉 Fire Rooster 澤山咸 12 十九 9	水1 Water 5 Humility 戊戌 Earth Dog 地山謙 13 二十 6	火2 Fire 4 Observation 己亥 Earth Pig 風地觀 14 廿一 2	火2 Fire 3 Increasing 庚子 Metal Rat 風雷益 15 廿二 9	水1 Water 2 Dimming Light 辛丑 Metal Ox 地火明夷 16 廿三 3
金9 Metal 1 Fellowship 壬寅 Water Tiger 天火同人 17 廿四 7	木8 Wood 9 Marrying Maiden 癸卯 Water Rabbit 雷澤歸妹 18 廿五 7	木3 Wood 8 Opposition 甲辰 Wood Dragon 火澤睽 19 廿六 2	火7 Fire 7 Waiting 乙巳 Wood Snake 水天需 20 廿七 3	金4 Metal 6 Great Exceeding 丙午 Fire Horse 澤風大過 21 廿八 3	水6 Water 5 Poison 丁未 Fire Goat 山風蠱 22 廿九 7	火2 Fire 4 Dispersing 戊申 Earth Monkey 風水渙 23 九月初一 6
木3 Wood 3 Travelling 己酉 Earth Rooster 火山旅 24 初二 8	金9 Metal 2 Stagnation 庚戌 Metal Dog 天地否 25 初三 9	火7 Fire 1 Alliance 辛亥 Metal Pig 水地比 26 初四 7	木8 Wood 9 Thunder 壬子 Water Rat 震爲雷 27 初五 1	水6 Water 8 Beauty 癸丑 Water Ox 山火賁 28 初六 8	火7 Fire 7 Accomplished 甲寅 Wood Tiger 水火既濟 29 初七 9	水1 Water 6 Arriving 乙卯 Wood Rabbit 地澤臨 30 初八 4

NOVEMBER 1976 己亥

Xuan Kong Element 玄空五行	風地觀 Observation	Period Luck 卦運	Monthly Star 月星
Fire 火2		2	5

SUNDAY	MONDAY	TUESDAY	WEDNESDAY	THURSDAY	FRIDAY	SATURDAY
	火2 Fire Small Livestock 4 丁巳 Fire Snake 風天小畜 1 初十 8	木3 Wood The Cauldron 3 戊午 Earth Horse 火風鼎 2 十一 4	水1 Water Rising 2 己未 Earth Goat 地風升 3 十二 2	火7 Fire Water 1 庚申 Metal Monkey 坎爲水 4 十三 1	木8 Wood Lesser Exceeding 9 辛酉 Metal Rooster 雷山小過 5 十四 3	金4 Metal Gathering 8 壬戌 Water Dog 澤地萃 6 十五 4
水6 Water Peel 7 癸亥 Water Pig 山地剝 7 十六 6	水1 Water Earth 6 甲子 Wood Rat 坤爲地 8 十七 1	木3 Wood Biting 5 乙丑 Wood Ox 火雷噬嗑 9 十八 6	火2 Fire Family 4 丙寅 Fire Tiger 風火家人 10 十九 4	水6 Water Decreasing 3 丁卯 Fire Rabbit 山澤損 11 二十 9	金9 Metal Tread 2 戊辰 Earth Dragon 天澤履 12 廿一 6	木8 Wood Great Strength 1 己巳 Earth Snake 雷天大壯 13 廿二 2
木8 Wood Consistency 9 庚午 Metal Horse 雷風恆 14 廿三 9	金9 Metal Litigation 8 辛未 Metal Goat 天水訟 15 廿四 3	水1 Water Officer 7 壬申 Water Monkey 地水師 16 廿五 7	火2 Fire Gradual Progress 6 癸酉 Water Rooster 風山漸 17 廿六 7	火7 Fire Obstruction 5 甲戌 Wood Dog 水山蹇 18 廿七 2	木3 Wood Advancement 4 乙亥 Wood Pig 火地晉 19 廿八 3	水6 Water Nourish 3 丙子 Fire Rat 山雷頤 20 廿九 3
金4 Metal Following 2 丁丑 Fire Ox 澤雷隨 21 十月初一 7	木8 Wood Abundance 1 戊寅 Earth Tiger 雷火豐 22 初二 6	火7 Fire Regulate 9 己卯 Earth Rabbit 水澤節 23 初三 8	水1 Water Unity 8 庚辰 Metal Dragon 地天泰 24 初四 9	木3 Wood Great Reward 7 辛巳 Metal Snake 火天大有 25 初五 7	火2 Fire Wind 6 壬午 Water Horse 巽爲風 26 初六 1	金4 Metal Trap 5 癸未 Water Goat 澤水困 27 初七 8
木3 Wood Not Yet Accomplished 4 甲申 Wood Monkey 火水未濟 28 初八 9	金9 Metal Retreat 3 乙酉 Wood Rooster 天山遯 29 初九 4	水6 Water Mountain 2 丙戌 Fire Dog 艮爲山 30 初十 1				

DECEMBER 1976 庚子

Xuan Kong Element 玄空五行	風雷益 Increasing	Period Luck 卦運	Monthly Star 月星
Fire 火2		9	4

SUNDAY	MONDAY	TUESDAY	WEDNESDAY	THURSDAY	FRIDAY	SATURDAY
			木8 Wood Delight 1 丁亥 Fire Pig 雷地豫 1 十一 8	火7 Fire Beginning 9 戊子 Earth Rat 水雷屯 2 十二 4	金9 Metal Without Wrongdoing 8 己丑 Earth Ox 天雷無妄 3 十三 2	木3 Wood Fire 7 庚寅 Metal Tiger 離爲火 4 十四 1
火2 Fire Sincerity 6 辛卯 Metal Rabbit 風澤中孚 5 十五 3	水6 Water Big Livestock 5 壬辰 Water Dragon 山天大畜 6 十六 4	金4 Metal Eliminating 4 癸巳 Water Snake 澤天夬 7 十七 6	金9 Metal Heaven 3 甲午 Wood Horse 乾爲天 8 十八 1	火7 Fire Well 2 乙未 Wood Goat 水風井 9 十九 6	木8 Wood Relief 1 丙申 Fire Monkey 雷水解 10 二十 4	金4 Metal Influence 9 丁酉 Fire Rooster 澤山咸 11 廿一 9
水1 Water Humility 8 戊戌 Earth Dog 地山謙 12 廿二 6	火2 Fire Observation 7 己亥 Earth Pig 風地觀 13 廿三 2	火2 Fire Increasing 6 庚子 Metal Rat 風雷益 14 廿四 9	水1 Water Dimming Light 5 辛丑 Metal Ox 地火明夷 15 廿五 3	金9 Metal Fellowship 4 壬寅 Water Tiger 天火同人 16 廿六 7	木8 Wood Marrying Maiden 3 癸卯 Water Rabbit 雷澤歸妹 17 廿七 7	木3 Wood Opposition 2 甲辰 Wood Dragon 火澤睽 18 廿八 2
火7 Fire Waiting 1 乙巳 Wood Snake 水天需 19 廿九 3	金4 Metal Great Exceeding 9 丙午 Fire Horse 澤風大過 20 三十 3	水6 Water Poison 8 丁未 Fire Goat 山風蠱 21 十一月初一 7	火2 Fire Dispersing 7/3 戊申 Earth Monkey 風水渙 22 初二 6	木3 Wood Travelling 4 己酉 Earth Rooster 火山旅 23 初三 8	金9 Metal Stagnation 5 庚戌 Metal Dog 天地否 24 初四 9	火7 Fire Alliance 6 辛亥 Metal Pig 水地比 25 初五 7
木8 Wood Thunder 7 壬子 Water Rat 震爲雷 26 初六 1	水6 Water Beauty 8 癸丑 Water Ox 山火賁 27 初七 8	火7 Fire Accomplished 9 甲寅 Wood Tiger 水火既濟 28 初八 9	水1 Water Arriving 1 乙卯 Wood Rabbit 地澤臨 29 初九 4	金4 Metal Marsh 2 丙辰 Fire Dragon 兌爲澤 30 初十 1	火2 Fire Small Livestock 3 丁巳 Fire Snake 風天小畜 31 十一 8	

1977 丁巳

(*Ding Si*) Fire Snake

1977 丁巳 *(Ding Si)* Fire Snake

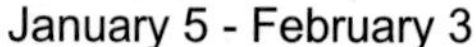

January 5 - February 3

February 4 - March 5

March 6 - April 4

April 5 - May 4

May 5 - June 5

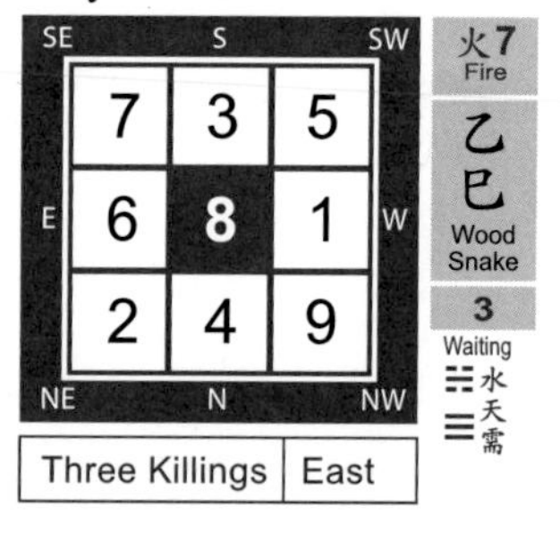

June 6 - July 6

July 7 - August 6

August 7 - September 7

September 8 - October 7

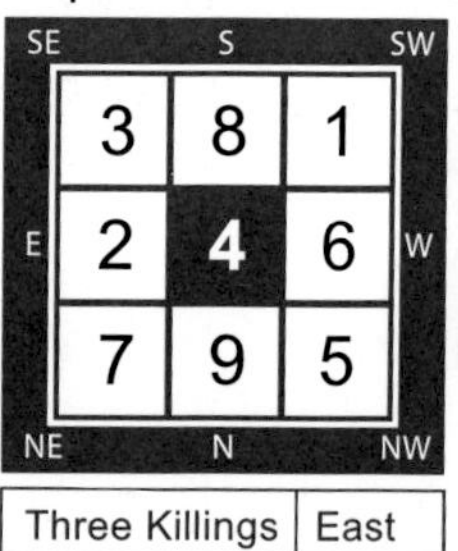

October 8 - November 6

November 7 - December 6

December 7 - January 5

JANUARY 1977 辛丑

Xuan Kong Element 玄空五行	地火明夷 Dimming Light	Period Luck 卦運	Monthly Star 月星
Water 水1		3	3

SUNDAY	MONDAY	TUESDAY	WEDNESDAY	THURSDAY	FRIDAY	SATURDAY
木8 Wood 6 Delight 雷地豫 丁亥 Fire Pig 8 30 十二	火7 Fire 7 Beginning 水雷屯 戊子 Earth Rat 4 31 十三					木3 Wood 4 The Cauldron 火風鼎 戊午 Earth Horse 4 1 十二
水1 Water 5 Rising 地風升 己未 Earth Goat 2 2 十三	火7 Fire 6 Water 坎爲水 庚申 Metal Monkey 1 3 十四	木8 Wood 7 Lesser Exceeding 雷山小過 辛酉 Metal Rooster 3 4 十五	金4 Metal 8 Gathering 澤地萃 壬戌 Water Dog 4 5 十六	水6 Water 9 Peel 山地剝 癸亥 Water Pig 6 6 十七	水1 Water 1 Earth 坤爲地 甲子 Wood Rat 1 7 十八	木3 Wood 2 Biting 火雷噬嗑 乙丑 Wood Ox 6 8 十九
火2 Fire 3 Family 風火家人 丙寅 Fire Tiger 4 9 二十	水6 Water 4 Decreasing 山澤損 丁卯 Fire Rabbit 9 10 廿一	金9 Metal 5 Tread 天澤履 戊辰 Earth Dragon 6 11 廿二	木8 Wood 6 Great Strength 雷天大壯 己巳 Earth Snake 2 12 廿三	木8 Wood 7 Consistency 雷風恆 庚午 Metal Horse 9 13 廿四	金9 Metal 8 Litigation 天水訟 辛未 Metal Goat 3 14 廿五	水1 Water 9 Officer 地水師 壬申 Water Monkey 7 15 廿六
火2 Fire 1 Gradual Progress 風山漸 癸酉 Water Rooster 7 16 廿七	火7 Fire 2 Obstruction 水山蹇 甲戌 Wood Dog 2 17 廿八	木3 Wood 3 Advancement 火地晉 乙亥 Wood Pig 3 18 廿九	水6 Water 4 Nourish 山雷頤 丙子 Fire Rat 3 19 十二月初一	金4 Metal 5 Following 澤雷隨 丁丑 Fire Ox 7 20 初二	木8 Wood 6 Abundance 雷火豐 戊寅 Earth Tiger 6 21 初三	火7 Fire 7 Regulate 水澤節 己卯 Earth Rabbit 8 22 初四
水1 Water 8 Unity 地天泰 庚辰 Metal Dragon 9 23 初五	木3 Wood 9 Great Reward 火天大有 辛巳 Metal Snake 7 24 初六	火2 Fire 1 Wind 巽爲風 壬午 Water Horse 1 25 初七	金4 Metal 2 Trap 澤水困 癸未 Water Goat 8 26 初八	木3 Wood 3 Not Yet Accomplished 火水未濟 甲申 Wood Monkey 9 27 初九	金9 Metal 4 Retreat 天山遯 乙酉 Wood Rooster 4 28 初十	水6 Water 5 Mountain 艮爲山 丙戌 Fire Dog 1 29 十一

FEBRUARY 1977 壬寅

Xuan Kong Element 玄空五行	天火同人 Fellowship	Period Luck 卦運	Monthly Star 月星
Metal 金9		7	2

SUNDAY	MONDAY	TUESDAY	WEDNESDAY	THURSDAY	FRIDAY	SATURDAY
		金9 Metal 8 Without Wrongdoing 天雷無妄 己丑 Earth Ox 2 1 十四	木3 Wood 9 Fire 離爲火 庚寅 Metal Tiger 1 2 十五	火2 Fire 1 Sincerity 風澤中孚 辛卯 Metal Rabbit 3 3 十六	水6 Water 2 Big Livestock 山天大畜 壬辰 Water Dragon 4 4 十七	金4 Metal 3 Eliminating 澤天夬 癸巳 Water Snake 6 5 十八
金9 Metal 4 Heaven 乾爲天 甲午 Wood Horse 1 6 十九	火7 Fire 5 Well 水風井 乙未 Wood Goat 6 7 二十	木8 Wood 6 Relief 雷水解 丙申 Fire Monkey 4 8 廿一	金4 Metal 7 Influence 澤山咸 丁酉 Fire Rooster 9 9 廿二	水1 Water 8 Humility 地山謙 戊戌 Earth Dog 6 10 廿三	火2 Fire 9 Observation 風地觀 己亥 Earth Pig 2 11 廿四	火2 Fire 1 Increasing 風雷益 庚子 Metal Rat 9 12 廿五
水1 Water 2 Dimming Light 地火明夷 辛丑 Metal Ox 3 13 廿六	金9 Metal 3 Fellowship 天火同人 壬寅 Water Tiger 7 14 廿七	木8 Wood 4 Marrying Maiden 雷澤歸妹 癸卯 Water Rabbit 7 15 廿八	木3 Wood 5 Opposition 火澤睽 甲辰 Wood Dragon 2 16 廿九	火7 Fire 6 Waiting 水天需 乙巳 Wood Snake 3 17 三十	金4 Metal 7 Great Exceeding 澤風大過 丙午 Fire Horse 3 18 正月初一	水6 Water 8 Poison 山風蠱 丁未 Fire Goat 7 19 初二
火2 Fire 9 Dispersing 風水渙 戊申 Earth Monkey 6 20 初三	木3 Wood 1 Travelling 火山旅 己酉 Earth Rooster 8 21 初四	金9 Metal 2 Stagnation 天地否 庚戌 Metal Dog 9 22 初五	火7 Fire 3 Alliance 水地比 辛亥 Metal Pig 7 23 初六	木8 Wood 4 Thunder 震爲雷 壬子 Water Rat 1 24 初七	水6 Water 5 Beauty 山火賁 癸丑 Water Ox 8 25 初八	火7 Fire 6 Accomplished 水火既濟 甲寅 Wood Tiger 9 26 初九
水1 Water 7 Arriving 地澤臨 乙卯 Wood Rabbit 4 27 初十	金4 Metal 8 Marsh 兌爲澤 丙辰 Fire Dragon 1 28 十一					

MARCH 1977 癸卯

Xuan Kong Element 玄空五行	雷澤歸妹 Marrying Maiden	Period Luck 卦運	Monthly Star 月星
Wood 木8		7	1

SUNDAY	MONDAY	TUESDAY	WEDNESDAY	THURSDAY	FRIDAY	SATURDAY
		火2 Fire 9 Small Livestock 風天小畜 丁巳 Fire Snake 1 十二 8	木3 Wood 1 The Cauldron 火風鼎 戊午 Earth Horse 2 十三 4	水1 Water 2 Rising 地風升 己未 Earth Goat 3 十四 2	火7 Fire 3 Water 坎爲水 庚申 Metal Monkey 4 十五 1	木8 Wood 4 Lesser Exceeding 雷山小過 辛酉 Metal Rooster 5 十六 3
金4 Metal 5 Gathering 澤地萃 壬戌 Water Dog 6 十七 4	水6 Water 6 Peel 山地剝 癸亥 Water Pig 7 十八 6	水1 Water 7 Earth 坤爲地 甲子 Wood Rat 8 十九 1	木3 Wood 8 Biting 火雷噬嗑 乙丑 Wood Ox 9 二十 6	火2 Fire 9 Family 風火家人 丙寅 Fire Tiger 10 廿一 4	水6 Water 1 Decreasing 山澤損 丁卯 Fire Rabbit 11 廿二 9	金9 Metal 2 Tread 天澤履 戊辰 Earth Dragon 12 廿三 6
木8 Wood 3 Great Strength 雷天大壯 己巳 Earth Snake 13 廿四 2	木8 Wood 4 Consistency 雷風恆 庚午 Metal Horse 14 廿五 9	金9 Metal 5 Litigation 天水訟 辛未 Metal Goat 15 廿六 3	水1 Water 6 Officer 地水師 壬申 Water Monkey 16 廿七 7	火2 Fire 7 Gradual Progress 風山漸 癸酉 Water Rooster 17 廿八 7	火7 Fire 8 Obstruction 水山蹇 甲戌 Wood Dog 18 廿九 2	木3 Wood 9 Advancement 火地晉 乙亥 Wood Pig 19 三十 3
水6 Water 1 Nourish 山雷頤 丙子 Fire Rat 20 二月初一 3	金4 Metal 2 Following 澤雷隨 丁丑 Fire Ox 21 初二 7	木8 Wood 3 Abundance 雷火豐 戊寅 Earth Tiger 22 初三 6	火7 Fire 4 Regulate 水澤節 己卯 Earth Rabbit 23 初四 8	水1 Water 5 Unity 地天泰 庚辰 Metal Dragon 24 初五 9	木3 Wood 6 Great Reward 火天大有 辛巳 Metal Snake 25 初六 7	火2 Fire 7 Wind 巽爲風 壬午 Water Horse 26 初七 1
金4 Metal 8 Trap 澤水困 癸未 Water Goat 27 初八 8	木3 Wood 9 Not Yet Accomplished 火水未濟 甲申 Wood Monkey 28 初九 9	金9 Metal 1 Retreat 天山遯 乙酉 Wood Rooster 29 初十 4	水6 Water 2 Mountain 艮爲山 丙戌 Fire Dog 30 十一 1	木8 Wood 3 Delight 雷地豫 丁亥 Fire Pig 31 十二 8		

APRIL 1977 甲辰

Xuan Kong Element 玄空五行	火澤睽 Opposition	Period Luck 卦運	Monthly Star 月星
Wood 木3		2	9

SUNDAY	MONDAY	TUESDAY	WEDNESDAY	THURSDAY	FRIDAY	SATURDAY
					火7 Fire 4 Beginning 水雷屯 戊子 Earth Rat 1 十三 4	金9 Metal 5 Without Wrongdoing 天雷無妄 己丑 Earth Ox 2 十四 2
木3 Wood 6 Fire 離爲火 庚寅 Metal Tiger 3 十五 1	火2 Fire 7 Sincerity 風澤中孚 辛卯 Metal Rabbit 4 十六 3	水6 Water 8 Big Livestock 山天大畜 壬辰 Water Dragon 5 十七 4	金4 Metal 9 Eliminating 澤天夬 癸巳 Water Snake 6 十八 6	金9 Metal 1 Heaven 乾爲天 甲午 Wood Horse 7 十九 1	火7 Fire 2 Well 水風井 乙未 Wood Goat 8 二十 6	木8 Wood 3 Relief 雷水解 丙申 Fire Monkey 9 廿一 4
金4 Metal 4 Influence 澤山咸 丁酉 Fire Rooster 10 廿二 9	水1 Water 5 Humility 地山謙 戊戌 Earth Dog 11 廿三 6	火2 Fire 6 Observation 風地觀 己亥 Earth Pig 12 廿四 2	火2 Fire 7 Increasing 風雷益 庚子 Metal Rat 13 廿五 9	水1 Water 8 Dimming Light 地火明夷 辛丑 Metal Ox 14 廿六 3	金9 Metal 9 Fellowship 天火同人 壬寅 Water Tiger 15 廿七 7	木8 Wood 1 Marrying Maiden 雷澤歸妹 癸卯 Water Rabbit 16 廿八 7
木3 Wood 2 Opposition 火澤睽 甲辰 Wood Dragon 17 廿九 2	火7 Fire 3 Waiting 水天需 乙巳 Wood Snake 18 三月初一 3	金4 Metal 4 Great Exceeding 澤風大過 丙午 Fire Horse 19 初二 3	水6 Water 5 Poison 山風蠱 丁未 Fire Goat 20 初三 7	火2 Fire 6 Dispersing 風水渙 戊申 Earth Monkey 21 初四 6	木3 Wood 7 Travelling 火山旅 己酉 Earth Rooster 22 初五 8	金9 Metal 8 Stagnation 天地否 庚戌 Metal Dog 23 初六 9
火7 Fire 9 Alliance 水地比 辛亥 Metal Pig 24 初七 7	木8 Wood 1 Thunder 震爲雷 壬子 Water Rat 25 初八 1	水6 Water 2 Beauty 山火賁 癸丑 Water Ox 26 初九 8	火7 Fire 3 Accomplished 水火既濟 甲寅 Wood Tiger 27 初十 9	水1 Water 4 Arriving 地澤臨 乙卯 Wood Rabbit 28 十一 4	金4 Metal 5 Marsh 兌爲澤 丙辰 Fire Dragon 29 十二 1	火2 Fire 6 Small Livestock 風天小畜 丁巳 Fire Snake 30 十三 8

MAY 1977 乙巳

Xuan Kong Element 玄空五行	水天需 Waiting	Period Luck 卦運	Monthly Star 月星
Fire 火7		3	8

SUNDAY	MONDAY	TUESDAY	WEDNESDAY	THURSDAY	FRIDAY	SATURDAY
木3 Wood 7 The Cauldron 戊午 Earth Horse 火風鼎 1 十四 4	水1 Water 8 Rising 己未 Earth Goat 地風升 2 十五 2	火7 Fire 9 Water 庚申 Metal Monkey 坎為水 3 十六 1	木8 Wood 1 Lesser Exceeding 辛酉 Metal Rooster 雷山小過 4 十七 3	金4 Metal 2 Gathering 壬戌 Water Dog 澤地萃 5 十八 4	水6 Water 3 Peel 癸亥 Water Pig 山地剝 6 十九 6	水1 Water 4 Earth 甲子 Wood Rat 坤為地 7 二十 1
木3 Wood 5 Biting 乙丑 Wood Ox 火雷噬嗑 8 廿一 6	火2 Fire 6 Family 丙寅 Fire Tiger 風火家人 9 廿二 4	水6 Water 7 Decreasing 丁卯 Fire Rabbit 山澤損 10 廿三 9	金9 Metal 8 Tread 戊辰 Earth Dragon 天澤履 11 廿四 6	木8 Wood 9 Great Strength 己巳 Earth Snake 雷天大壯 12 廿五 2	木8 Wood 1 Consistency 庚午 Metal Horse 雷風恆 13 廿六 9	金9 Metal 2 Litigation 辛未 Metal Goat 天水訟 14 廿七 3
水1 Water 3 Officer 壬申 Water Monkey 地水師 15 廿八 7	火2 Fire 4 Gradual Progress 癸酉 Water Rooster 風山漸 16 廿九 7	火7 Fire 5 Obstruction 甲戌 Wood Dog 水山蹇 17 三十 2	木3 Wood 6 Advancement 乙亥 Wood Pig 火地晉 18 四月初一 3	水6 Water 7 Nourish 丙子 Fire Rat 山雷頤 19 初二 3	金4 Metal 8 Following 丁丑 Fire Ox 澤雷隨 20 初三 7	木8 Wood 9 Abundance 戊寅 Earth Tiger 雷火豐 21 初四 6
火7 Fire 1 Regulate 己卯 Earth Rabbit 水澤節 22 初五 8	水1 Water 2 Unity 庚辰 Metal Dragon 地天泰 23 初六 9	木3 Wood 3 Great Reward 辛巳 Metal Snake 火天大有 24 初七 7	火2 Fire 4 Wind 壬午 Water Horse 巽為風 25 初八 1	金4 Metal 5 Trap 癸未 Water Goat 澤水困 26 初九 8	木3 Wood 6 Not Yet Accomplished 甲申 Wood Monkey 火水未濟 27 初十 9	金9 Metal 7 Retreat 乙酉 Wood Rooster 天山遯 28 十一 4
水6 Water 8 Mountain 丙戌 Fire Dog 艮為山 29 十二 1	木8 Wood 9 Delight 丁亥 Fire Pig 雷地豫 30 十三 8	火7 Fire 1 Beginning 戊子 Earth Rat 水雷屯 31 十四 4				

JUNE 1977 丙午

Xuan Kong Element 玄空五行	澤風大過 Great Exceeding	Period Luck 卦運	Monthly Star 月星
Metal 金4		3	7

SUNDAY	MONDAY	TUESDAY	WEDNESDAY	THURSDAY	FRIDAY	SATURDAY
			金9 Metal 2 Without Wrongdoing 己丑 Earth Ox 天雷無妄 1 十五 2	木3 Wood 3 Fire 庚寅 Metal Tiger 離為火 2 十六 1	火2 Fire 4 Sincerity 辛卯 Metal Rabbit 風澤中孚 3 十七 3	水6 Water 5 Big Livestock 壬辰 Water Dragon 山天大畜 4 十八 4
金4 Metal 6 Eliminating 癸巳 Water Snake 澤天夬 5 十九 6	金9 Metal 7 Heaven 甲午 Wood Horse 乾為天 6 二十 1	火7 Fire 8 Well 乙未 Wood Goat 水風井 7 廿一 6	木8 Wood 9 Relief 丙申 Fire Monkey 雷水解 8 廿二 4	金4 Metal 1 Influence 丁酉 Fire Rooster 澤山咸 9 廿三 9	水1 Water 2 Humility 戊戌 Earth Dog 地山謙 10 廿四 6	火2 Fire 3 Observation 己亥 Earth Pig 風地觀 11 廿五 2
火2 Fire 4 Increasing 庚子 Metal Rat 風雷益 12 廿六 9	水1 Water 5 Dimming Light 辛丑 Metal Ox 地火明夷 13 廿七 3	金9 Metal 6 Fellowship 壬寅 Water Tiger 天火同人 14 廿八 7	木8 Wood 7 Marrying Maiden 癸卯 Water Rabbit 雷澤歸妹 15 廿九 7	木3 Wood 8 Opposition 甲辰 Wood Dragon 火澤睽 16 三十 2	火7 Fire 9 Waiting 乙巳 Wood Snake 水天需 17 五月初一 3	金4 Metal 1 Great Exceeding 丙午 Fire Horse 澤風大過 18 初二 3
水6 Water 2 Poison 丁未 Fire Goat 山風蠱 19 初三 7	火2 Fire 3 Dispersing 戊申 Earth Monkey 風水渙 20 初四 6	木3 Wood 4/6 Travelling 己酉 Earth Rooster 火山旅 21 初五 8	金9 Metal 5 Stagnation 庚戌 Metal Dog 天地否 22 初六 9	火7 Fire 4 Alliance 辛亥 Metal Pig 水地比 23 初七 7	木8 Wood 3 Thunder 壬子 Water Rat 震為雷 24 初八 1	水6 Water 2 Beauty 癸丑 Water Ox 山火賁 25 初九 8
火7 Fire 1 Accomplished 甲寅 Wood Tiger 水火既濟 26 初十 9	水1 Water 9 Arriving 乙卯 Wood Rabbit 地澤臨 27 十一 4	金4 Metal 8 Marsh 丙辰 Fire Dragon 兌為澤 28 十二 1	火2 Fire 7 Small Livestock 丁巳 Fire Snake 風天小畜 29 十三 8	木3 Wood 6 The Cauldron 戊午 Earth Horse 火風鼎 30 十四 4		

JULY 1977 丁未

Xuan Kong Element 玄空五行	山風蠱 Poison	Period Luck 卦運	Monthly Star 月星
Water 水6		7	6

SUNDAY	MONDAY	TUESDAY	WEDNESDAY	THURSDAY	FRIDAY	SATURDAY
金9 Metal 2 Without Wrongdoing 天雷無妄 己丑 Earth Ox 31 十六 2					水1 Water 5 Rising 地風升 己未 Earth Goat 1 十五 2	火7 Fire 4 Water 坎為水 庚申 Metal Monkey 2 十六 1
木8 Wood 3 Lesser Exceeding 雷山小過 辛酉 Metal Rooster 3 十七 3	金4 Metal 2 Gathering 澤地萃 壬戌 Water Dog 4 十八 4	水6 Water 1 Peel 山地剝 癸亥 Water Pig 5 十九 6	水1 Water 9 Earth 坤為地 甲子 Wood Rat 6 二十 1	木3 Wood 8 Biting 火雷噬嗑 乙丑 Wood Ox 7 廿一 6	火2 Fire 7 Family 風火家人 丙寅 Fire Tiger 8 廿二 4	水6 Water 6 Decreasing 山澤損 丁卯 Fire Rabbit 9 廿三 9
金9 Metal 5 Tread 天澤履 戊辰 Earth Dragon 10 廿四 6	木8 Wood 4 Great Strength 雷天大壯 己巳 Earth Snake 11 廿五 2	木8 Wood 3 Consistency 雷風恆 庚午 Metal Horse 12 廿六 9	金9 Metal 2 Litigation 天水訟 辛未 Metal Goat 13 廿七 3	水1 Water 1 Officer 地水師 壬申 Water Monkey 14 廿八 7	火2 Fire 9 Gradual Progress 風山漸 癸酉 Water Rooster 15 廿九 7	火7 Fire 8 Obstruction 水山蹇 甲戌 Wood Dog 16 六月初一 2
木3 Wood 7 Advancement 火地晉 乙亥 Wood Pig 17 初二 3	水6 Water 6 Nourish 山雷頤 丙子 Fire Rat 18 初三 3	金4 Metal 5 Following 澤雷隨 丁丑 Fire Ox 19 初四 7	木8 Wood 4 Abundance 雷火豐 戊寅 Earth Tiger 20 初五 6	火7 Fire 3 Regulate 水澤節 己卯 Earth Rabbit 21 初六 8	水1 Water 2 Unity 地天泰 庚辰 Metal Dragon 22 初七 9	木3 Wood 1 Great Reward 火天大有 辛巳 Metal Snake 23 初八 7
火2 Fire 9 Wind 巽為風 壬午 Water Horse 24 初九 1	金4 Metal 8 Trap 澤水困 癸未 Water Goat 25 初十 8	木3 Wood 7 Not Yet Accomplished 火水未濟 甲申 Wood Monkey 26 十一 9	金9 Metal 6 Retreat 天山遯 乙酉 Wood Rooster 27 十二 4	水6 Water 5 Mountain 艮為山 丙戌 Fire Dog 28 十三 1	木8 Wood 4 Delight 雷地豫 丁亥 Fire Pig 29 十四 8	火7 Fire 3 Beginning 水雷屯 戊子 Earth Rat 30 十五 4

AUGUST 1977 戊申

Xuan Kong Element 玄空五行	風水渙 Dispersing	Period Luck 卦運	Monthly Star 月星
Fire 火2		6	5

SUNDAY	MONDAY	TUESDAY	WEDNESDAY	THURSDAY	FRIDAY	SATURDAY
	木3 Wood 1 Fire 離為火 庚寅 Metal Tiger 1 十七 1	火2 Fire 9 Sincerity 風澤中孚 辛卯 Metal Rabbit 2 十八 3	水6 Water 8 Big Livestock 山天大畜 壬辰 Water Dragon 3 十九 4	金4 Metal 7 Eliminating 澤天夬 癸巳 Water Snake 4 二十 6	金9 Metal 6 Heaven 乾為天 甲午 Wood Horse 5 廿一 1	火7 Fire 5 Well 水風井 乙未 Wood Goat 6 廿二 6
木8 Wood 4 Relief 雷水解 丙申 Fire Monkey 7 廿三 4	金4 Metal 3 Influence 澤山咸 丁酉 Fire Rooster 8 廿四 9	水1 Water 2 Humility 地山謙 戊戌 Earth Dog 9 廿五 6	火2 Fire 1 Observation 風地觀 己亥 Earth Pig 10 廿六 2	火2 Fire 9 Increasing 風雷益 庚子 Metal Rat 11 廿七 9	水1 Water 8 Dimming Light 地火明夷 辛丑 Metal Ox 12 廿八 3	金9 Metal 7 Fellowship 天火同人 壬寅 Water Tiger 13 廿九 7
木8 Wood 6 Marrying Maiden 雷澤歸妹 癸卯 Water Rabbit 14 三十 7	木3 Wood 5 Opposition 火澤睽 甲辰 Wood Dragon 15 七月初一 2	火7 Fire 4 Waiting 水天需 乙巳 Wood Snake 16 初二 3	金4 Metal 3 Great Exceeding 澤風大過 丙午 Fire Horse 17 初三 3	水6 Water 2 Poison 山風蠱 丁未 Fire Goat 18 初四 7	火2 Fire 1 Dispersing 風水渙 戊申 Earth Monkey 19 初五 6	木3 Wood 9 Travelling 火山旅 己酉 Earth Rooster 20 初六 8
金9 Metal 8 Stagnation 天地否 庚戌 Metal Dog 21 初七 9	火7 Fire 7 Alliance 水地比 辛亥 Metal Pig 22 初八 7	木8 Wood 6 Thunder 震為雷 壬子 Water Rat 23 初九 1	水6 Water 5 Beauty 山火賁 癸丑 Water Ox 24 初十 8	火7 Fire 4 Accomplished 水火既濟 甲寅 Wood Tiger 25 十一 9	水1 Water 3 Arriving 地澤臨 乙卯 Wood Rabbit 26 十二 4	金4 Metal 2 Marsh 兌為澤 丙辰 Fire Dragon 27 十三 1
火2 Fire 1 Small Livestock 風天小畜 丁巳 Fire Snake 28 十四 8	木3 Wood 9 The Cauldron 火風鼎 戊午 Earth Horse 29 十五 4	水1 Water 8 Rising 地風升 己未 Earth Goat 30 十六 2	火7 Fire 7 Water 坎為水 庚申 Metal Monkey 31 十七 1			

SEPTEMBER 1977 己酉

Xuan Kong Element 玄空五行	火山旅 Travelling	Period Luck 卦運	Monthly Star 月星
Wood 木3		8	4

SUNDAY	MONDAY	TUESDAY	WEDNESDAY	THURSDAY	FRIDAY	SATURDAY
				木8 Wood Lesser Exceeding 6 辛酉 Metal Rooster 雷山小過 1 十八 3	金4 Metal Gathering 5 壬戌 Water Dog 澤地萃 2 十九 4	水6 Water Peel 4 癸亥 Water Pig 山地剝 3 二十 6
水1 Water Earth 3 甲子 Wood Rat 坤爲地 4 廿一 1	木3 Wood Biting 2 乙丑 Wood Ox 火雷噬嗑 5 廿二 6	火2 Fire Family 1 丙寅 Fire Tiger 風火家人 6 廿三 4	水6 Water Decreasing 9 丁卯 Fire Rabbit 山澤損 7 廿四 9	金9 Metal Tread 8 戊辰 Earth Dragon 天澤履 8 廿五 6	木8 Wood Great Strength 7 己巳 Earth Snake 雷天大壯 9 廿六 2	木8 Wood Consistency 6 庚午 Metal Horse 雷風恆 10 廿七 9
金9 Metal Litigation 5 辛未 Metal Goat 天水訟 11 廿八 3	水1 Water Officer 4 壬申 Water Monkey 地水師 12 廿九 7	火2 Fire Gradual Progress 3 癸酉 Water Rooster 風山漸 13 八月初一 7	火7 Fire Obstruction 2 甲戌 Wood Dog 水山蹇 14 初二 2	木3 Wood Advancement 1 乙亥 Wood Pig 火地晉 15 初三 3	水6 Water Nourish 9 丙子 Fire Rat 山雷頤 16 初四 3	金4 Metal Following 8 丁丑 Fire Ox 澤雷隨 17 初五 7
木8 Wood Abundance 7 戊寅 Earth Tiger 雷火豐 18 初六 6	火7 Fire Regulate 6 己卯 Earth Rabbit 水澤節 19 初七 8	水1 Water Unity 5 庚辰 Metal Dragon 地天泰 20 初八 9	木3 Wood Great Reward 4 辛巳 Metal Snake 火天大有 21 初九 7	火2 Fire Wind 3 壬午 Water Horse 巽爲風 22 初十 1	金4 Metal Trap 2 癸未 Water Goat 澤水困 23 十一 8	木3 Wood Not Yet Accomplished 1 甲申 Wood Monkey 火水未濟 24 十二 9
金9 Metal Retreat 9 乙酉 Wood Rooster 天山遯 25 十三 4	水6 Water Mountain 8 丙戌 Fire Dog 艮爲山 26 十四 1	木8 Wood Delight 7 丁亥 Fire Pig 雷地豫 27 十五 8	火7 Fire Beginning 6 戊子 Earth Rat 水雷屯 28 十六 4	金9 Metal Without Wrongdoing 5 己丑 Earth Ox 天雷無妄 29 十七 2	木3 Wood Fire 4 庚寅 Metal Tiger 離爲火 30 十八 1	

OCTOBER 1977 庚戌

Xuan Kong Element 玄空五行	天地否 Stagnation	Period Luck 卦運	Monthly Star 月星
Metal 金9		9	3

SUNDAY	MONDAY	TUESDAY	WEDNESDAY	THURSDAY	FRIDAY	SATURDAY
火7 Fire Water 1 庚申 Metal Monkey 坎爲水 30 十八 1	木8 Wood Lesser Exceeding 9 辛酉 Metal Rooster 雷山小過 31 十九 3					火2 Fire Sincerity 3 辛卯 Metal Rabbit 風澤中孚 1 十九 3
水6 Water Big Livestock 2 壬辰 Water Dragon 山天大畜 2 二十 4	金4 Metal Eliminating 1 癸巳 Water Snake 澤天夬 3 廿一 6	金9 Metal Heaven 9 甲午 Wood Horse 乾爲天 4 廿二 1	火7 Fire Well 8 乙未 Wood Goat 水風井 5 廿三 6	木8 Wood Relief 7 丙申 Fire Monkey 雷水解 6 廿四 4	金4 Metal Influence 6 丁酉 Fire Rooster 澤山咸 7 廿五 9	水1 Water Humility 5 戊戌 Earth Dog 地山謙 8 廿六 6
火2 Fire Observation 4 己亥 Earth Pig 風地觀 9 廿七 2	火2 Fire Increasing 3 庚子 Metal Rat 風雷益 10 廿八 9	水1 Water Dimming Light 2 辛丑 Metal Ox 地火明夷 11 廿九 3	金9 Metal Fellowship 1 壬寅 Water Tiger 天火同人 12 三十 7	木8 Wood Marrying Maiden 9 癸卯 Water Rabbit 雷澤歸妹 13 九月初一 7	木3 Wood Opposition 8 甲辰 Wood Dragon 火澤睽 14 初二 2	火7 Fire Waiting 7 乙巳 Wood Snake 水天需 15 初三 3
金4 Metal Great Exceeding 6 丙午 Fire Horse 澤風大過 16 初四 3	水6 Water Poison 5 丁未 Fire Goat 山風蠱 17 初五 7	火2 Fire Dispersing 4 戊申 Earth Monkey 風水渙 18 初六 6	木3 Wood Travelling 3 己酉 Earth Rooster 火山旅 19 初七 8	金9 Metal Stagnation 2 庚戌 Metal Dog 天地否 20 初八 9	火7 Fire Alliance 1 辛亥 Metal Pig 水地比 21 初九 7	木8 Wood Thunder 9 壬子 Water Rat 震爲雷 22 初十 1
水6 Water Beauty 8 癸丑 Water Ox 山火賁 23 十一 8	火7 Fire Accomplished 7 甲寅 Wood Tiger 水火既濟 24 十二 9	水1 Water Arriving 6 乙卯 Wood Rabbit 地澤臨 25 十三 4	金4 Metal Marsh 5 丙辰 Fire Dragon 兌爲澤 26 十四 1	火2 Fire Small Livestock 4 丁巳 Fire Snake 風天小畜 27 十五 8	木3 Wood The Cauldron 3 戊午 Earth Horse 火風鼎 28 十六 4	水1 Water Rising 2 己未 Earth Goat 地風升 29 十七 2

NOVEMBER 1977 辛亥

Xuan Kong Element 玄空五行	水地比 Alliance	Period Luck 卦運	Monthly Star 月星
Fire 火7		7	2

SUNDAY	MONDAY	TUESDAY	WEDNESDAY	THURSDAY	FRIDAY	SATURDAY
		金4 Metal 8 Gathering 澤地萃 壬戌 Water Dog 4 1 二十	水6 Water 7 Peel 山地剝 癸亥 Water Pig 6 2 廿一	水1 Water 6 Earth 坤爲地 甲子 Wood Rat 1 3 廿二	木3 Wood 5 Biting 火雷噬嗑 乙丑 Wood Ox 6 4 廿三	火2 Fire 4 Family 風火家人 丙寅 Fire Tiger 4 5 廿四
水6 Water 3 Decreasing 山澤損 丁卯 Fire Rabbit 9 6 廿五	金9 Metal 2 Tread 天澤履 戊辰 Earth Dragon 6 7 廿六	木8 Wood 1 Great Strength 雷天大壯 己巳 Earth Snake 2 8 廿七	木8 Wood 9 Consistency 雷風恆 庚午 Metal Horse 9 9 廿八	金9 Metal 8 Litigation 天水訟 辛未 Metal Goat 3 10 廿九	水1 Water 7 Officer 地水師 壬申 Water Monkey 7 11 十月初一	火2 Fire 6 Gradual Progress 風山漸 癸酉 Water Rooster 7 12 初二
火7 Fire 5 Obstruction 水山蹇 甲戌 Wood Dog 2 13 初三	木3 Wood 4 Advancement 火地晉 乙亥 Wood Pig 3 14 初四	水6 Water 3 Nourish 山雷頤 丙子 Fire Rat 3 15 初五	金4 Metal 2 Following 澤雷隨 丁丑 Fire Ox 7 16 初六	木8 Wood 1 Abundance 雷火豐 戊寅 Earth Tiger 6 17 初七	火7 Fire 9 Regulate 水澤節 己卯 Earth Rabbit 8 18 初八	水1 Water 8 Unity 地天泰 庚辰 Metal Dragon 9 19 初九
木3 Wood 7 Great Reward 火天大有 辛巳 Metal Snake 7 20 初十	火2 Fire 6 Wind 巽爲風 壬午 Water Horse 1 21 十一	金4 Metal 5 Trap 澤水困 癸未 Water Goat 8 22 十二	木3 Wood 4 Not Yet Accomplished 火水未濟 甲申 Wood Monkey 9 23 十三	金9 Metal 3 Retreat 天山遯 乙酉 Wood Rooster 4 24 十四	水6 Water 2 Mountain 艮爲山 丙戌 Fire Dog 1 25 十五	木8 Wood 1 Delight 雷地豫 丁亥 Fire Pig 8 26 十六
火7 Fire 9 Beginning 水雷屯 戊子 Earth Rat 4 27 十七	金9 Metal 8 Without Wrongdoing 天雷無妄 己丑 Earth Ox 2 28 十八	木3 Wood 7 Fire 離爲火 庚寅 Metal Tiger 1 29 十九	火2 Fire 6 Sincerity 風澤中孚 辛卯 Metal Rabbit 3 30 二十			

DECEMBER 1977 壬子

Xuan Kong Element 玄空五行	震爲雷 Thunder	Period Luck 卦運	Monthly Star 月星
Wood 木8		1	1

SUNDAY	MONDAY	TUESDAY	WEDNESDAY	THURSDAY	FRIDAY	SATURDAY
				水6 Water 5 Big Livestock 山天大畜 壬辰 Water Dragon 4 1 廿一	金4 Metal 4 Eliminating 澤天夬 癸巳 Water Snake 6 2 廿二	金9 Metal 3 Heaven 乾爲天 甲午 Wood Horse 1 3 廿三
火7 Fire 2 Well 水風井 乙未 Wood Goat 6 4 廿四	木8 Wood 1 Relief 雷水解 丙申 Fire Monkey 4 5 廿五	金4 Metal 9 Influence 澤山咸 丁酉 Fire Rooster 9 6 廿六	水1 Water 8 Humility 地山謙 戊戌 Earth Dog 6 7 廿七	火2 Fire 7 Observation 風地觀 己亥 Earth Pig 2 8 廿八	火2 Fire 6 Increasing 風雷益 庚子 Metal Rat 9 9 廿九	水1 Water 5 Dimming Light 地火明夷 辛丑 Metal Ox 3 10 三十
金9 Metal 4 Fellowship 天火同人 壬寅 Water Tiger 7 11 十一月初一	木8 Wood 3 Marrying Maiden 雷澤歸妹 癸卯 Water Rabbit 7 12 初二	木3 Wood 2 Opposition 火澤睽 甲辰 Wood Dragon 2 13 初三	火7 Fire 1 Waiting 水天需 乙巳 Wood Snake 3 14 初四	金4 Metal 9 Great Exceeding 澤風大過 丙午 Fire Horse 3 15 初五	水6 Water 8 Poison 山風蠱 丁未 Fire Goat 7 16 初六	火2 Fire 7 Dispersing 風水渙 戊申 Earth Monkey 6 17 初七
木3 Wood 6 Travelling 火山旅 己酉 Earth Rooster 8 18 初八	金9 Metal 5 Stagnation 天地否 庚戌 Metal Dog 9 19 初九	火7 Fire 4 Alliance 水地比 辛亥 Metal Pig 7 20 初十	木8 Wood 3 Thunder 震爲雷 壬子 Water Rat 1 21 十一	水6 Water 2/8 Beauty 山火賁 癸丑 Water Ox 8 22 十二	火7 Fire 9 Accomplished 水火既濟 甲寅 Wood Tiger 9 23 十三	水1 Water 1 Arriving 地澤臨 乙卯 Wood Rabbit 4 24 十四
金4 Metal 2 Marsh 兌爲澤 丙辰 Fire Dragon 1 25 十五	火2 Fire 3 Small Livestock 風天小畜 丁巳 Fire Snake 8 26 十六	木3 Wood 4 The Cauldron 火風鼎 戊午 Earth Horse 4 27 十七	水1 Water 5 Rising 地風升 己未 Earth Goat 2 28 十八	火7 Fire 6 Water 坎爲水 庚申 Metal Monkey 1 29 十九	木8 Wood 7 Lesser Exceeding 雷山小過 辛酉 Metal Rooster 3 30 二十	金4 Metal 8 Gathering 澤地萃 壬戌 Water Dog 4 31 廿一

1978 戊午

(*Wu Wu*) Earth Horse

1978 戊午 *(Wu Wu)* Earth Horse

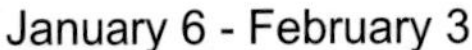
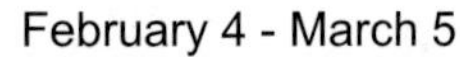

January 6 - February 3

	SE	S	SW	
	8	4	6	
E	7	9	2	W
	3	5	1	
	NE	N	NW	

水6 Water
癸丑 Water Ox
8 Beauty
山火賁

Three Killings	East

February 4 - March 5

	SE	S	SW	
	7	3	5	
E	6	8	1	W
	2	4	9	
	NE	N	NW	

火7 Fire
甲寅 Wood Tiger
9 Accomplished
水火既濟

Three Killings	North

March 6 - April 4

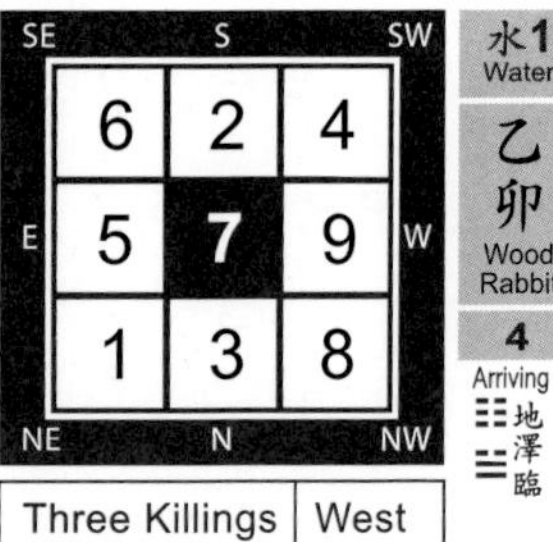

	SE	S	SW	
	6	2	4	
E	5	7	9	W
	1	3	8	
	NE	N	NW	

水1 Water
乙卯 Wood Rabbit
4 Arriving
地澤臨

Three Killings	West

April 5 - May 5

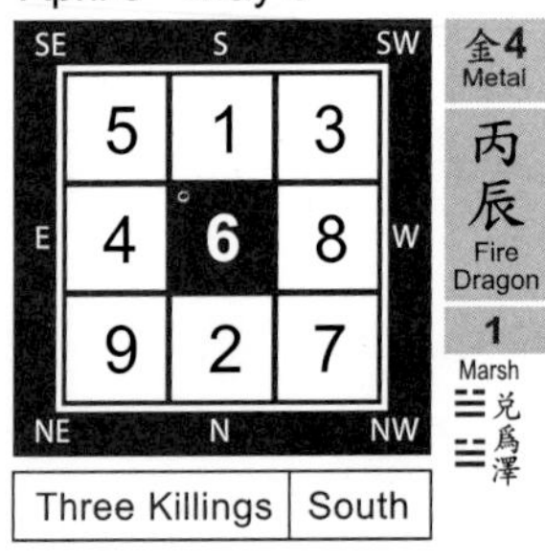

	SE	S	SW	
	5	1	3	
E	4	6	8	W
	9	2	7	
	NE	N	NW	

金4 Metal
丙辰 Fire Dragon
1 Marsh
兑為澤

Three Killings	South

May 6 - June 5

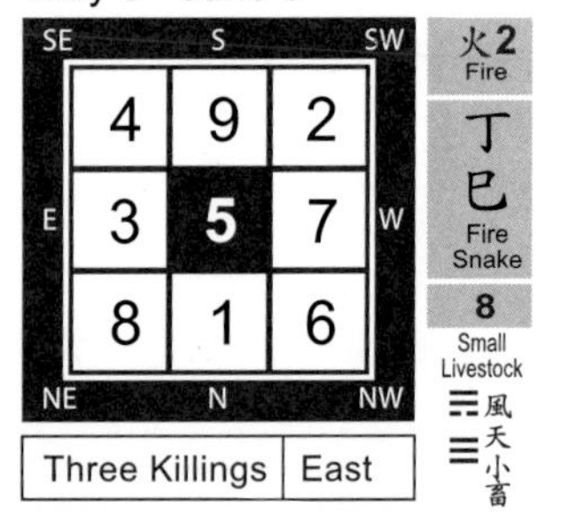

	SE	S	SW	
	4	9	2	
E	3	5	7	W
	8	1	6	
	NE	N	NW	

火2 Fire
丁巳 Fire Snake
8 Small Livestock
風天小畜

Three Killings	East

June 6 - July 6

	SE	S	SW	
	3	8	1	
E	2	4	6	W
	7	9	5	
	NE	N	NW	

木3 Wood
戊午 Earth Horse
4 The Cauldron
火風鼎

Three Killings	North

July 7 - August 7

	SE	S	SW	
	2	7	9	
E	1	3	5	W
	6	8	4	
	NE	N	NW	

水1 Water
己未 Earth Goat
2 Rising
地風升

Three Killings	West

August 8 - September 7

	SE	S	SW	
	1	6	8	
E	9	2	4	W
	5	7	3	
	NE	N	NW	

火7 Fire
庚申 Metal Monkey
1 Water
坎為水

Three Killings	South

September 8 - October 7

	SE	S	SW	
	9	5	7	
E	8	1	3	W
	4	6	2	
	NE	N	NW	

木8 Wood
辛酉 Metal Rooster
3 Lesser Exceeding
雷山小過

Three Killings	East

October 8 - November 7

	SE	S	SW	
	8	4	6	
E	7	9	2	W
	3	5	1	
	NE	N	NW	

金4 Metal
壬戌 Water Dog
4 Gathering
澤地萃

Three Killings	North

November 8 - December 6

	SE	S	SW	
	7	3	5	
E	6	8	1	W
	2	4	9	
	NE	N	NW	

水6 Water
癸亥 Water Pig
6 Peel
山地剝

Three Killings	West

December 7 - January 5

	SE	S	SW	
	6	2	4	
E	5	7	9	W
	1	3	8	
	NE	N	NW	

水1 Water
甲子 Wood Rat
1 Earth
坤為地

Three Killings	South

JANUARY 1978 癸丑

Xuan Kong Element 玄空五行	山火賁 Beauty	Period Luck 卦運	Monthly Star 月星
Water 水6		8	9

SUNDAY	MONDAY	TUESDAY	WEDNESDAY	THURSDAY	FRIDAY	SATURDAY
水6 Water 9 Peel 山地剝 癸亥 Water Pig **1** 廿二 6	水1 Water 1 Earth 坤爲地 甲子 Wood Rat **2** 廿三 1	木3 Wood 2 Biting 火雷噬嗑 乙丑 Wood Ox **3** 廿四 6	火2 Fire 3 Family 風火家人 丙寅 Fire Tiger **4** 廿五 4	水6 Water 4 Decreasing 山澤損 丁卯 Fire Rabbit **5** 廿六 9	金9 Metal 5 Tread 天澤履 戊辰 Earth Dragon **6** 廿七 6	木8 Wood 6 Great Strength 雷天大壯 己巳 Earth Snake **7** 廿八 2
木8 Wood 7 Consistency 雷風恒 庚午 Metal Horse **8** 廿九 9	金9 Metal 8 Litigation 天水訟 辛未 Metal Goat **9** 十二月初一 3	水1 Water 9 Officer 地水師 壬申 Water Monkey **10** 初二 7	火2 Fire 1 Gradual Progress 風山漸 癸酉 Water Rooster **11** 初三 7	火7 Fire 2 Obstruction 水山蹇 甲戌 Wood Dog **12** 初四 2	木3 Wood 3 Advancement 火地晉 乙亥 Wood Pig **13** 初五 3	水6 Water 4 Nourish 山雷頤 丙子 Fire Rat **14** 初六 3
金4 Metal 5 Following 澤雷隨 丁丑 Fire Ox **15** 初七 7	木8 Wood 6 Abundance 雷火豐 戊寅 Earth Tiger **16** 初八 6	火7 Fire 7 Regulate 水澤節 己卯 Earth Rabbit **17** 初九 8	水1 Water 8 Unity 地天泰 庚辰 Metal Dragon **18** 初十 9	木3 Wood 9 Great Reward 火天大有 辛巳 Metal Snake **19** 十一 7	火2 Fire 1 Wind 巽爲風 壬午 Water Horse **20** 十二 1	金4 Metal 2 Trap 澤水困 癸未 Water Goat **21** 十三 8
木3 Wood 3 Not Yet Accomplished 火水未濟 甲申 Wood Monkey **22** 十四 9	金9 Metal 4 Retreat 天山遯 乙酉 Wood Rooster **23** 十五 4	水6 Water 5 Mountain 艮爲山 丙戌 Fire Dog **24** 十六 1	木8 Wood 6 Delight 雷地豫 丁亥 Fire Pig **25** 十七 8	火7 Fire 7 Beginning 水雷屯 戊子 Earth Rat **26** 十八 4	金9 Metal 8 Without Wrongdoing 天雷無妄 己丑 Earth Ox **27** 十九 2	木3 Wood 9 Fire 離爲火 庚寅 Metal Tiger **28** 二十 1
火2 Fire 1 Sincerity 風澤中孚 辛卯 Metal Rabbit **29** 廿一 3	水6 Water 2 Big Livestock 山天大畜 壬辰 Water Dragon **30** 廿二 4	金4 Metal 3 Eliminating 澤天夬 癸巳 Water Snake **31** 廿三 6				

FEBRUARY 1978 甲寅

Xuan Kong Element 玄空五行	水火既濟 Accomplished	Period Luck 卦運	Monthly Star 月星
Fire 火7		9	8

SUNDAY	MONDAY	TUESDAY	WEDNESDAY	THURSDAY	FRIDAY	SATURDAY
			金9 Metal 4 Heaven 乾爲天 甲午 Wood Horse **1** 廿四 1	火7 Fire 5 Well 水風井 乙未 Wood Goat **2** 廿五 6	木8 Wood 6 Relief 雷水解 丙申 Fire Monkey **3** 廿六 4	金4 Metal 7 Influence 澤山咸 丁酉 Fire Rooster **4** 廿七 9
水1 Water 8 Humility 地山謙 戊戌 Earth Dog **5** 廿八 6	火2 Fire 9 Observation 風地觀 己亥 Earth Pig **6** 廿九 2	火2 Fire 1 Increasing 風雷益 庚子 Metal Rat **7** 正月初一 9	水1 Water 2 Dimming Light 地火明夷 辛丑 Metal Ox **8** 初二 3	金9 Metal 3 Fellowship 天火同人 壬寅 Water Tiger **9** 初三 7	木8 Wood 4 Marrying Maiden 雷澤歸妹 癸卯 Water Rabbit **10** 初四 7	木3 Wood 5 Opposition 火澤睽 甲辰 Wood Dragon **11** 初五 2
火7 Fire 6 Waiting 水天需 乙巳 Wood Snake **12** 初六 3	金4 Metal 7 Great Exceeding 澤風大過 丙午 Fire Horse **13** 初七 3	水6 Water 8 Poison 山風蠱 丁未 Fire Goat **14** 初八 7	火2 Fire 9 Dispersing 風水渙 戊申 Earth Monkey **15** 初九 6	木3 Wood 1 Travelling 火山旅 己酉 Earth Rooster **16** 初十 8	金9 Metal 2 Stagnation 天地否 庚戌 Metal Dog **17** 十一 9	火7 Fire 3 Alliance 水地比 辛亥 Metal Pig **18** 十二 7
木8 Wood 4 Thunder 震爲雷 壬子 Water Rat **19** 十三 1	水6 Water 5 Beauty 山火賁 癸丑 Water Ox **20** 十四 8	火7 Fire 6 Accomplished 水火既濟 甲寅 Wood Tiger **21** 十五 9	水1 Water 7 Arriving 地澤臨 乙卯 Wood Rabbit **22** 十六 4	金4 Metal 8 Marsh 兌爲澤 丙辰 Fire Dragon **23** 十七 1	火2 Fire 9 Small Livestock 風天小畜 丁巳 Fire Snake **24** 十八 8	木3 Wood 1 The Cauldron 火風鼎 戊午 Earth Horse **25** 十九 4
水1 Water 2 Rising 地風升 己未 Earth Goat **26** 二十 2	火7 Fire 3 Water 坎爲水 庚申 Metal Monkey **27** 廿一 1	木8 Wood 4 Lesser Exceeding 雷山小過 辛酉 Metal Rooster **28** 廿二 3				

MARCH 1978 乙卯

Xuan Kong Element 玄空五行	地澤臨 Arriving	Period Luck 卦運	Monthly Star 月星
Water 水1		4	7

SUNDAY	MONDAY	TUESDAY	WEDNESDAY	THURSDAY	FRIDAY	SATURDAY
			金4 Metal · Gathering 5 澤地萃 壬戌 Water Dog **1** 廿三 4	水6 Water · Peel 6 山地剝 癸亥 Water Pig **2** 廿四 6	水1 Water · Earth 7 坤爲地 甲子 Wood Rat **3** 廿五 1	木3 Wood · Biting 8 火雷噬嗑 乙丑 Wood Ox **4** 廿六 6
火2 Fire · Family 9 風火家人 丙寅 Fire Tiger **5** 廿七 4	水6 Water · Decreasing 1 山澤損 丁卯 Fire Rabbit **6** 廿八 9	金9 Metal · Tread 2 天澤履 戊辰 Earth Dragon **7** 廿九 6	木8 Wood · Great Strength 3 雷天大壯 己巳 Earth Snake **8** 三十 2	木8 Wood · Consistency 4 雷風恆 庚午 Metal Horse **9** 二月初一 9	金9 Metal · Litigation 5 天水訟 辛未 Metal Goat **10** 初二 3	水1 Water · Officer 6 地水師 壬申 Water Monkey **11** 初三 7
火2 Fire · Gradual Progress 7 風山漸 癸酉 Water Rooster **12** 初四 7	火7 Fire · Obstruction 8 水山蹇 甲戌 Wood Dog **13** 初五 2	木3 Wood · Advancement 9 火地晉 乙亥 Wood Pig **14** 初六 3	水6 Water · Nourish 1 山雷頤 丙子 Fire Rat **15** 初七 3	金4 Metal · Following 2 澤雷隨 丁丑 Fire Ox **16** 初八 7	木8 Wood · Abundance 3 雷火豐 戊寅 Earth Tiger **17** 初九 6	火7 Fire · Regulate 4 水澤節 己卯 Earth Rabbit **18** 初十 8
水1 Water · Unity 5 地天泰 庚辰 Metal Dragon **19** 十一 9	木3 Wood · Great Reward 6 火天大有 辛巳 Metal Snake **20** 十二 7	火2 Fire · Wind 7 巽爲風 壬午 Water Horse **21** 十三 1	金4 Metal · Trap 8 澤水困 癸未 Water Goat **22** 十四 8	木3 Wood · Not Yet Accomplished 9 火水未濟 甲申 Wood Monkey **23** 十五 9	金9 Metal · Retreat 1 天山遯 乙酉 Wood Rooster **24** 十六 4	水6 Water · Mountain 2 艮爲山 丙戌 Fire Dog **25** 十七 1
木8 Wood · Delight 3 雷地豫 丁亥 Fire Pig **26** 十八 8	火7 Fire · Beginning 4 水雷屯 戊子 Earth Rat **27** 十九 4	金9 Metal · Without Wrongdoing 5 天雷無妄 己丑 Earth Ox **28** 二十 2	木3 Wood · Fire 6 離爲火 庚寅 Metal Tiger **29** 廿一 1	火2 Fire · Sincerity 7 風澤中孚 辛卯 Metal Rabbit **30** 廿二 3	水6 Water · Big Livestock 8 山天大畜 壬辰 Water Dragon **31** 廿三 4	

APRIL 1978 丙辰

Xuan Kong Element 玄空五行	兌爲澤 Marsh	Period Luck 卦運	Monthly Star 月星
Metal 金4		1	6

SUNDAY	MONDAY	TUESDAY	WEDNESDAY	THURSDAY	FRIDAY	SATURDAY
金4 Metal · Gathering 2 澤地萃 壬戌 Water Dog **30** 廿四 4						金4 Metal · Eliminating 9 澤天夬 癸巳 Water Snake **1** 廿四 6
金9 Metal · Heaven 1 乾爲天 甲午 Wood Horse **2** 廿五 1	火7 Fire · Well 2 水風井 乙未 Wood Goat **3** 廿六 6	木8 Wood · Relief 3 雷水解 丙申 Fire Monkey **4** 廿七 4	金4 Metal · Influence 4 澤山咸 丁酉 Fire Rooster **5** 廿八 9	水1 Water · Humility 5 地山謙 戊戌 Earth Dog **6** 廿九 6	火2 Fire · Observation 6 風地觀 己亥 Earth Pig **7** 三月初一 2	火2 Fire · Increasing 7 風雷益 庚子 Metal Rat **8** 初二 9
水1 Water · Dimming Light 8 地火明夷 辛丑 Metal Ox **9** 初三 3	金9 Metal · Fellowship 9 天火同人 壬寅 Water Tiger **10** 初四 7	木8 Wood · Marrying Maiden 1 雷澤歸妹 癸卯 Water Rabbit **11** 初五 7	木3 Wood · Opposition 2 火澤睽 甲辰 Wood Dragon **12** 初六 2	火7 Fire · Waiting 3 水天需 乙巳 Wood Snake **13** 初七 3	金4 Metal · Great Exceeding 4 澤風大過 丙午 Fire Horse **14** 初八 3	水6 Water · Poison 5 山風蠱 丁未 Fire Goat **15** 初九 7
火2 Fire · Dispersing 6 風水渙 戊申 Earth Monkey **16** 初十 6	木3 Wood · Travelling 7 火山旅 己酉 Earth Rooster **17** 十一 8	金9 Metal · Stagnation 8 天地否 庚戌 Metal Dog **18** 十二 9	火7 Fire · Alliance 9 水地比 辛亥 Metal Pig **19** 十三 7	木8 Wood · Thunder 1 震爲雷 壬子 Water Rat **20** 十四 1	水6 Water · Beauty 2 山火賁 癸丑 Water Ox **21** 十五 8	火7 Fire · Accomplished 3 水火既濟 甲寅 Wood Tiger **22** 十六 9
水1 Water · Arriving 4 地澤臨 乙卯 Wood Rabbit **23** 十七 4	金4 Metal · Marsh 5 兌爲澤 丙辰 Fire Dragon **24** 十八 1	火2 Fire · Small Livestock 6 風天小畜 丁巳 Fire Snake **25** 十九 8	木3 Wood · The Cauldron 7 火風鼎 戊午 Earth Horse **26** 二十 4	水1 Water · Rising 8 地風升 己未 Earth Goat **27** 廿一 2	火7 Fire · Water 9 坎爲水 庚申 Metal Monkey **28** 廿二 1	木8 Wood · Lesser Exceeding 1 雷山小過 辛酉 Metal Rooster **29** 廿三 3

MAY 1978 丁巳

Xuan Kong Element 玄空五行	風天小畜	Period Luck 卦運	Monthly Star 月星
Fire 火2	Small Livestock	8	5

SUNDAY	MONDAY	TUESDAY	WEDNESDAY	THURSDAY	FRIDAY	SATURDAY
	水6 Water Peel 3 癸亥 Water Pig 山地剝 1 廿五 6	水1 Water Earth 4 甲子 Wood Rat 坤爲地 2 廿六 1	木3 Wood Biting 5 乙丑 Wood Ox 火雷噬嗑 3 廿七 6	火2 Fire Family 6 丙寅 Fire Tiger 風火家人 4 廿八 4	水6 Water Decreasing 7 丁卯 Fire Rabbit 山澤損 5 廿九 9	金9 Metal Tread 8 戊辰 Earth Dragon 天澤履 6 三十 6
木8 Wood Great Strength 9 己巳 Earth Snake 雷天大壯 7 四月初一 2	木8 Wood Consistency 1 庚午 Metal Horse 雷風恆 8 初二 9	金9 Metal Litigation 2 辛未 Metal Goat 天水訟 9 初三 3	水1 Water Officer 3 壬申 Water Monkey 地水師 10 初四 7	火2 Fire Gradual Progress 4 癸酉 Water Rooster 風山漸 11 初五 7	火7 Fire Obstruction 5 甲戌 Wood Dog 水山蹇 12 初六 2	木3 Wood Advancement 6 乙亥 Wood Pig 火地晉 13 初七 3
水6 Water Nourish 7 丙子 Fire Rat 山雷頤 14 初八 3	金4 Metal Following 8 丁丑 Fire Ox 澤雷隨 15 初九 7	木8 Wood Abundance 9 戊寅 Earth Tiger 雷火豐 16 初十 6	火7 Fire Regulate 1 己卯 Earth Rabbit 水澤節 17 十一 8	水1 Water Unity 2 庚辰 Metal Dragon 地天泰 18 十二 9	木3 Wood Great Reward 3 辛巳 Metal Snake 火天大有 19 十三 7	火2 Fire Wind 4 壬午 Water Horse 巽爲風 20 十四 1
金4 Metal Trap 5 癸未 Water Goat 澤水困 21 十五 8	木3 Wood Not Yet Accomplished 6 甲申 Wood Monkey 火水未濟 22 十六 9	金9 Metal Retreat 7 乙酉 Wood Rooster 天山遯 23 十七 4	水6 Water Mountain 8 丙戌 Fire Dog 艮爲山 24 十八 1	木8 Wood Delight 9 丁亥 Fire Pig 雷地豫 25 十九 8	火7 Fire Beginning 1 戊子 Earth Rat 水雷屯 26 二十 4	金9 Metal Without Wrongdoing 2 己丑 Earth Ox 天雷無妄 27 廿一 2
木3 Wood Fire 3 庚寅 Metal Tiger 離爲火 28 廿二 1	火2 Fire Sincerity 4 辛卯 Metal Rabbit 風澤中孚 29 廿三 3	水6 Water Big Livestock 5 壬辰 Water Dragon 山天大畜 30 廿四 4	金4 Metal Eliminating 6 癸巳 Water Snake 澤天夬 31 廿五 6			

JUNE 1978 戊午

Xuan Kong Element 玄空五行	火風鼎	Period Luck 卦運	Monthly Star 月星
Wood 木3	The Cauldron	4	4

SUNDAY	MONDAY	TUESDAY	WEDNESDAY	THURSDAY	FRIDAY	SATURDAY
				金9 Metal Heaven 7 甲午 Wood Horse 乾爲天 1 廿六 1	火7 Fire Well 8 乙未 Wood Goat 水風井 2 廿七 6	木8 Wood Relief 9 丙申 Fire Monkey 雷水解 3 廿八 4
金4 Metal Influence 1 丁酉 Fire Rooster 澤山咸 4 廿九 9	水1 Water Humility 2 戊戌 Earth Dog 地山謙 5 三十 6	火2 Fire Observation 3 己亥 Earth Pig 風地觀 6 五月初一 2	火2 Fire Increasing 4 庚子 Metal Rat 風雷益 7 初二 9	水1 Water Dimming Light 5 辛丑 Metal Ox 地火明夷 8 初三 3	金9 Metal Fellowship 6 壬寅 Water Tiger 天火同人 9 初四 7	木8 Wood Marrying Maiden 7 癸卯 Water Rabbit 雷澤歸妹 10 初五 7
木3 Wood Opposition 8 甲辰 Wood Dragon 火澤睽 11 初六 2	火7 Fire Waiting 9 乙巳 Wood Snake 水天需 12 初七 3	金4 Metal Great Exceeding 1 丙午 Fire Horse 澤風大過 13 初八 3	水6 Water Poison 2 丁未 Fire Goat 山風蠱 14 初九 7	火2 Fire Dispersing 3 戊申 Earth Monkey 風水渙 15 初十 6	木3 Wood Travelling 4 己酉 Earth Rooster 火山旅 16 十一 8	金9 Metal Stagnation 5 庚戌 Metal Dog 天地否 17 十二 9
火7 Fire Alliance 6 辛亥 Metal Pig 水地比 18 十三 7	木8 Wood Thunder 7 壬子 Water Rat 震爲雷 19 十四 1	水6 Water Beauty 8 癸丑 Water Ox 山火賁 20 十五 8	火7 Fire Accomplished 9 甲寅 Wood Tiger 水火既濟 21 十六 9	水1 Water Arriving 1/9 乙卯 Wood Rabbit 地澤臨 22 十七 4	金4 Metal Marsh 8 丙辰 Fire Dragon 兌爲澤 23 十八 1	火2 Fire Small Livestock 7 丁巳 Fire Snake 風天小畜 24 十九 8
木3 Wood The Cauldron 6 戊午 Earth Horse 火風鼎 25 二十 4	水1 Water Rising 5 己未 Earth Goat 地風升 26 廿一 2	火7 Fire Water 4 庚申 Metal Monkey 坎爲水 27 廿二 1	木8 Wood Lesser Exceeding 3 辛酉 Metal Rooster 雷山小過 28 廿三 3	金4 Metal Gathering 2 壬戌 Water Dog 澤地萃 29 廿四 4	水6 Water Peel 1 癸亥 Water Pig 山地剝 30 廿五 6	

JULY 1978 己未

Xuan Kong Element 玄空五行	地風升 Rising	Period Luck 卦運	Monthly Star 月星
Water 水1		2	3

SUNDAY	MONDAY	TUESDAY	WEDNESDAY	THURSDAY	FRIDAY	SATURDAY
金4 Metal 7 Eliminating 澤天夬 癸巳 Water Snake 30 廿六 6	金9 Metal 6 Heaven 乾爲天 甲午 Wood Horse 31 廿七 1					水1 Water 9 Earth 坤爲地 甲子 Wood Rat 1 廿六 1
木3 Wood 8 Biting 火雷噬嗑 乙丑 Wood Ox 2 廿七 6	火2 Fire 7 Family 風火家人 丙寅 Fire Tiger 3 廿八 4	水6 Water 6 Decreasing 山澤損 丁卯 Fire Rabbit 4 廿九 9	金9 Metal 5 Tread 天澤履 戊辰 Earth Dragon 5 六月初一 6	木8 Wood 4 Great Strength 雷天大壯 己巳 Earth Snake 6 初二 2	木8 Wood 3 Consistency 雷風恆 庚午 Metal Horse 7 初三 9	金9 Metal 2 Litigation 天水訟 辛未 Metal Goat 8 初四 3
水1 Water 1 Officer 地水師 壬申 Water Monkey 9 初五 7	火2 Fire 9 Gradual Progress 風山漸 癸酉 Water Rooster 10 初六 7	火7 Fire 8 Obstruction 水山蹇 甲戌 Wood Dog 11 初七 2	木3 Wood 7 Advancement 火地晉 乙亥 Wood Pig 12 初八 3	水6 Water 6 Nourish 山雷頤 丙子 Fire Rat 13 初九 3	金4 Metal 5 Following 澤雷隨 丁丑 Fire Ox 14 初十 7	木8 Wood 4 Abundance 雷火豐 戊寅 Earth Tiger 15 十一 6
火7 Fire 3 Regulate 水澤節 己卯 Earth Rabbit 16 十二 8	水1 Water 2 Unity 地天泰 庚辰 Metal Dragon 17 十三 9	木3 Wood 1 Great Reward 火天大有 辛巳 Metal Snake 18 十四 7	火2 Fire 9 Wind 巽爲風 壬午 Water Horse 19 十五 1	金4 Metal 8 Trap 澤水困 癸未 Water Goat 20 十六 8	木3 Wood 7 Not Yet Accomplished 火水未濟 甲申 Wood Monkey 21 十七 9	金9 Metal 6 Retreat 天山遯 乙酉 Wood Rooster 22 十八 4
水6 Water 5 Mountain 艮爲山 丙戌 Fire Dog 23 十九 1	木8 Wood 4 Delight 雷地豫 丁亥 Fire Pig 24 二十 8	火7 Fire 3 Beginning 水雷屯 戊子 Earth Rat 25 廿一 4	金9 Metal 2 Without Wrongdoing 天雷無妄 己丑 Earth Ox 26 廿二 2	木3 Wood 1 Fire 離爲火 庚寅 Metal Tiger 27 廿三 1	火2 Fire 9 Sincerity 風澤中孚 辛卯 Metal Rabbit 28 廿四 3	水6 Water 8 Big Livestock 山天大畜 壬辰 Water Dragon 29 廿五 4

AUGUST 1978 庚申

Xuan Kong Element 玄空五行	坎爲水 Water	Period Luck 卦運	Monthly Star 月星
Fire 火7		1	2

SUNDAY	MONDAY	TUESDAY	WEDNESDAY	THURSDAY	FRIDAY	SATURDAY
		火7 Fire 5 Well 水風井 乙未 Wood Goat 1 廿八 6	木8 Wood 4 Relief 雷水解 丙申 Fire Monkey 2 廿九 4	金4 Metal 3 Influence 澤山咸 丁酉 Fire Rooster 3 三十 9	水1 Water 2 Humility 地山謙 戊戌 Earth Dog 4 七月初一 6	火2 Fire 1 Observation 風地觀 己亥 Earth Pig 5 初二 2
火2 Fire 9 Increasing 風雷益 庚子 Metal Rat 6 初三 9	水1 Water 8 Dimming Light 地火明夷 辛丑 Metal Ox 7 初四 3	金9 Metal 7 Fellowship 天火同人 壬寅 Water Tiger 8 初五 7	木8 Wood 6 Marrying Maiden 雷澤歸妹 癸卯 Water Rabbit 9 初六 7	木3 Wood 5 Opposition 火澤睽 甲辰 Wood Dragon 10 初七 2	火7 Fire 4 Waiting 水天需 乙巳 Wood Snake 11 初八 3	金4 Metal 3 Great Exceeding 澤風大過 丙午 Fire Horse 12 初九 3
水6 Water 2 Poison 山風蠱 丁未 Fire Goat 13 初十 7	火2 Fire 1 Dispersing 風水渙 戊申 Earth Monkey 14 十一 6	木3 Wood 9 Travelling 火山旅 己酉 Earth Rooster 15 十二 8	金9 Metal 8 Stagnation 天地否 庚戌 Metal Dog 16 十三 9	火7 Fire 7 Alliance 水地比 辛亥 Metal Pig 17 十四 7	木8 Wood 6 Thunder 震爲雷 壬子 Water Rat 18 十五 1	水6 Water 5 Beauty 山火賁 癸丑 Water Ox 19 十六 8
火7 Fire 4 Accomplished 水火既濟 甲寅 Wood Tiger 20 十七 9	水1 Water 3 Arriving 地澤臨 乙卯 Wood Rabbit 21 十八 4	金4 Metal 2 Marsh 兌爲澤 丙辰 Fire Dragon 22 十九 1	火2 Fire 1 Small Livestock 風天小畜 丁巳 Fire Snake 23 二十 8	木3 Wood 9 The Cauldron 火風鼎 戊午 Earth Horse 24 廿一 4	水1 Water 8 Rising 地風升 己未 Earth Goat 25 廿二 2	火7 Fire 7 Water 坎爲水 庚申 Metal Monkey 26 廿三 1
木8 Wood 6 Lesser Exceeding 雷山小過 辛酉 Metal Rooster 27 廿四 3	金4 Metal 5 Gathering 澤地萃 壬戌 Water Dog 28 廿五 4	水6 Water 4 Peel 山地剝 癸亥 Water Pig 29 廿六 6	水1 Water 3 Earth 坤爲地 甲子 Wood Rat 30 廿七 1	木3 Wood 2 Biting 火雷噬嗑 乙丑 Wood Ox 31 廿八 6		

SEPTEMBER 1978 辛酉

Xuan Kong Element 玄空五行	雷山小過 Lesser Exceeding	Period Luck 卦運	Monthly Star 月星
Wood 木8		3	1

SUNDAY	MONDAY	TUESDAY	WEDNESDAY	THURSDAY	FRIDAY	SATURDAY
					火2 Fire 1 Family 丙寅 Fire Tiger 風火家人 1 廿九 4	水6 Water 9 Decreasing 丁卯 Fire Rabbit 山澤損 2 三十 9
金9 Metal 8 Tread 戊辰 Earth Dragon 天澤履 3 八月初一 6	木8 Wood 7 Great Strength 己巳 Earth Snake 雷天大壯 4 初二 2	木8 Wood 6 Consistency 庚午 Metal Horse 雷風恆 5 初三 9	金9 Metal 5 Litigation 辛未 Metal Goat 天水訟 6 初四 3	水1 Water 4 Officer 壬申 Water Monkey 地水師 7 初五 7	火2 Fire 3 Gradual Progress 癸酉 Water Rooster 風山漸 8 初六 7	火7 Fire 2 Obstruction 甲戌 Wood Dog 水山蹇 9 初七 2
木3 Wood 1 Advancement 乙亥 Wood Pig 火地晉 10 初八 3	水6 Water 9 Nourish 丙子 Fire Rat 山雷頤 11 初九 3	金4 Metal 8 Following 丁丑 Fire Ox 澤雷隨 12 初十 7	木8 Wood 7 Abundance 戊寅 Earth Tiger 雷火豐 13 十一 6	火7 Fire 6 Regulate 己卯 Earth Rabbit 水澤節 14 十二 8	水1 Water 5 Unity 庚辰 Metal Dragon 地天泰 15 十三 9	木3 Wood 4 Great Reward 辛巳 Metal Snake 火天大有 16 十四 7
火2 Fire 3 Wind 壬午 Water Horse 巽爲風 17 十五 1	金4 Metal 2 Trap 癸未 Water Goat 澤水困 18 十六 8	木3 Wood 1 Not Yet Accomplished 甲申 Wood Monkey 火水未濟 19 十七 9	金9 Metal 9 Retreat 乙酉 Wood Rooster 天山遯 20 十八 4	水6 Water 8 Mountain 丙戌 Fire Dog 艮爲山 21 十九 1	木8 Wood 7 Delight 丁亥 Fire Pig 雷地豫 22 二十 8	火7 Fire 6 Beginning 戊子 Earth Rat 水雷屯 23 廿一 4
金9 Metal 5 Without Wrongdoing 己丑 Earth Ox 天雷無妄 24 廿二 2	木3 Wood 4 Fire 庚寅 Metal Tiger 離爲火 25 廿三 1	火2 Fire 3 Sincerity 辛卯 Metal Rabbit 風澤中孚 26 廿四 3	水6 Water 2 Big Livestock 壬辰 Water Dragon 山天大畜 27 廿五 4	金4 Metal 1 Eliminating 癸巳 Water Snake 澤天夬 28 廿六 6	金9 Metal 9 Heaven 甲午 Wood Horse 乾爲天 29 廿七 1	火7 Fire 8 Well 乙未 Wood Goat 水風井 30 廿八 6

OCTOBER 1978 壬戌

Xuan Kong Element 玄空五行	澤地萃 Gathering	Period Luck 卦運	Monthly Star 月星
Metal 金4		4	9

SUNDAY	MONDAY	TUESDAY	WEDNESDAY	THURSDAY	FRIDAY	SATURDAY
木8 Wood 7 Relief 丙申 Fire Monkey 雷水解 1 廿九 4	金4 Metal 6 Influence 丁酉 Fire Rooster 澤山咸 2 九月初一 9	水1 Water 5 Humility 戊戌 Earth Dog 地山謙 3 初二 6	火2 Fire 4 Observation 己亥 Earth Pig 風地觀 4 初三 2	火2 Fire 3 Increasing 庚子 Metal Rat 風雷益 5 初四 9	水1 Water 2 Dimming Light 辛丑 Metal Ox 地火明夷 6 初五 3	金9 Metal 1 Fellowship 壬寅 Water Tiger 天火同人 7 初六 7
木8 Wood 9 Marrying Maiden 癸卯 Water Rabbit 雷澤歸妹 8 初七 7	木3 Wood 8 Opposition 甲辰 Wood Dragon 火澤睽 9 初八 2	火7 Fire 7 Waiting 乙巳 Wood Snake 水天需 10 初九 3	金4 Metal 6 Great Exceeding 丙午 Fire Horse 澤風大過 11 初十 3	水6 Water 5 Poison 丁未 Fire Goat 山風蠱 12 十一 7	火2 Fire 4 Dispersing 戊申 Earth Monkey 風水渙 13 十二 6	木3 Wood 3 Travelling 己酉 Earth Rooster 火山旅 14 十三 8
金9 Metal 2 Stagnation 庚戌 Metal Dog 天地否 15 十四 9	火7 Fire 1 Alliance 辛亥 Metal Pig 水地比 16 十五 7	木8 Wood 9 Thunder 壬子 Water Rat 震爲雷 17 十六 1	水6 Water 8 Beauty 癸丑 Water Ox 山火賁 18 十七 8	火7 Fire 7 Accomplished 甲寅 Wood Tiger 水火既濟 19 十八 9	水1 Water 6 Arriving 乙卯 Wood Rabbit 地澤臨 20 十九 4	金4 Metal 5 Marsh 丙辰 Fire Dragon 兌爲澤 21 二十 1
火2 Fire 4 Small Livestock 丁巳 Fire Snake 風天小畜 22 廿一 8	木3 Wood 3 The Cauldron 戊午 Earth Horse 火風鼎 23 廿二 4	水1 Water 2 Rising 己未 Earth Goat 地風升 24 廿三 2	火7 Fire 1 Water 庚申 Metal Monkey 坎爲水 25 廿四 1	木8 Wood 9 Lesser Exceeding 辛酉 Metal Rooster 雷山小過 26 廿五 3	金4 Metal 8 Gathering 壬戌 Water Dog 澤地萃 27 廿六 4	水6 Water 7 Peel 癸亥 Water Pig 山地剝 28 廿七 6
水1 Water 6 Earth 甲子 Wood Rat 坤爲地 29 廿八 1	木3 Wood 5 Biting 乙丑 Wood Ox 火雷噬嗑 30 廿九 6	火2 Fire 4 Family 丙寅 Fire Tiger 風火家人 31 三十 4				

NOVEMBER 1978 癸亥

Xuan Kong Element 玄空五行	山地剝 Peel	Period Luck 卦運	Monthly Star 月星
Water 水6		6	8

SUNDAY	MONDAY	TUESDAY	WEDNESDAY	THURSDAY	FRIDAY	SATURDAY
			水6 Water 3 Decreasing 丁卯 Fire Rabbit 山澤損 **1** 十月初一 9	金9 Metal 2 Tread 戊辰 Earth Dragon 天澤履 **2** 初二 6	木8 Wood 1 Great Strength 己巳 Earth Snake 雷天大壯 **3** 初三 2	木8 Wood 9 Consistency 庚午 Metal Horse 雷風恒 **4** 初四 9
金9 Metal 8 Litigation 辛未 Metal Goat 天水訟 **5** 初五 3	水1 Water 7 Officer 壬申 Water Monkey 地水師 **6** 初六 7	火2 Fire 6 Gradual Progress 癸酉 Water Rooster 風山漸 **7** 初七 7	火7 Fire 5 Obstruction 甲戌 Wood Dog 水山蹇 **8** 初八 2	木3 Wood 4 Advancement 乙亥 Wood Pig 火地晉 **9** 初九 3	水6 Water 3 Nourish 丙子 Fire Rat 山雷頤 **10** 初十 3	金4 Metal 2 Following 丁丑 Fire Ox 澤雷隨 **11** 十一 7
木8 Wood 1 Abundance 戊寅 Earth Tiger 雷火豐 **12** 十二 6	火7 Fire 9 Regulate 己卯 Earth Rabbit 水澤節 **13** 十三 8	水1 Water 8 Unity 庚辰 Metal Dragon 地天泰 **14** 十四 9	木3 Wood 7 Great Reward 辛巳 Metal Snake 火天大有 **15** 十五 7	火2 Fire 6 Wind 壬午 Water Horse 巽爲風 **16** 十六 1	金4 Metal 5 Trap 癸未 Water Goat 澤水困 **17** 十七 8	木3 Wood 4 Not Yet Accomplished 甲申 Wood Monkey 火水未濟 **18** 十八 9
金9 Metal 3 Retreat 乙酉 Wood Rooster 天山遯 **19** 十九 4	水6 Water 2 Mountain 丙戌 Fire Dog 艮爲山 **20** 二十 1	木8 Wood 1 Delight 丁亥 Fire Pig 雷地豫 **21** 廿一 8	火7 Fire 9 Beginning 戊子 Earth Rat 水雷屯 **22** 廿二 4	金9 Metal 8 Without Wrongdoing 己丑 Earth Ox 天雷無妄 **23** 廿三 2	木3 Wood 7 Fire 庚寅 Metal Tiger 離爲火 **24** 廿四 1	火2 Fire 6 Sincerity 辛卯 Metal Rabbit 風澤中孚 **25** 廿五 3
水6 Water 5 Big Livestock 壬辰 Water Dragon 山天大畜 **26** 廿六 4	金4 Metal 4 Eliminating 癸巳 Water Snake 澤天夬 **27** 廿七 6	金9 Metal 3 Heaven 甲午 Wood Horse 乾爲天 **28** 廿八 1	火7 Fire 2 Well 乙未 Wood Goat 水風井 **29** 廿九 6	木8 Wood 1 Relief 丙申 Fire Monkey 雷水解 **30** 十一月初一 4		

DECEMBER 1978 甲子

Xuan Kong Element 玄空五行	坤爲地 Earth	Period Luck 卦運	Monthly Star 月星
Water 水1		1	7

SUNDAY	MONDAY	TUESDAY	WEDNESDAY	THURSDAY	FRIDAY	SATURDAY
水6 Water 4 Decreasing 丁卯 Fire Rabbit 山澤損 **31** 初二 9					金4 Metal 9 Influence 丁酉 Fire Rooster 澤山咸 **1** 初二 9	水1 Water 8 Humility 戊戌 Earth Dog 地山謙 **2** 初三 6
火2 Fire 7 Observation 己亥 Earth Pig 風地觀 **3** 初四 2	火2 Fire 6 Increasing 庚子 Metal Rat 風雷益 **4** 初五 9	水1 Water 5 Dimming Light 辛丑 Metal Ox 地火明夷 **5** 初六 3	金9 Metal 4 Fellowship 壬寅 Water Tiger 天火同人 **6** 初七 7	木8 Wood 3 Marrying Maiden 癸卯 Water Rabbit 雷澤歸妹 **7** 初八 7	木3 Wood 2 Opposition 甲辰 Wood Dragon 火澤睽 **8** 初九 2	火7 Fire 1 Waiting 乙巳 Wood Snake 水天需 **9** 初十 3
金4 Metal 9 Great Exceeding 丙午 Fire Horse 澤風大過 **10** 十一 3	水6 Water 8 Poison 丁未 Fire Goat 山風蠱 **11** 十二 7	火2 Fire 7 Dispersing 戊申 Earth Monkey 風水渙 **12** 十三 6	木3 Wood 6 Travelling 己酉 Earth Rooster 火山旅 **13** 十四 8	金9 Metal 5 Stagnation 庚戌 Metal Dog 天地否 **14** 十五 9	火7 Fire 4 Alliance 辛亥 Metal Pig 水地比 **15** 十六 7	木8 Wood 3 Thunder 壬子 Water Rat 震爲雷 **16** 十七 1
水6 Water 2 Beauty 癸丑 Water Ox 山火賁 **17** 十八 8	火7 Fire 1 Accomplished 甲寅 Wood Tiger 水火既濟 **18** 十九 9	水1 Water 9 Arriving 乙卯 Wood Rabbit 地澤臨 **19** 二十 4	金4 Metal 8 Marsh 丙辰 Fire Dragon 兌爲澤 **20** 廿一 1	火2 Fire 7 Small Livestock 丁巳 Fire Snake 風天小畜 **21** 廿二 8	木3 Wood 6/4 The Cauldron 戊午 Earth Horse 火風鼎 **22** 廿三 4	水1 Water 5 Rising 己未 Earth Goat 地風升 **23** 廿四 2
火7 Fire 6 Water 庚申 Metal Monkey 坎爲水 **24** 廿五 1	木8 Wood 7 Lesser Exceeding 辛酉 Metal Rooster 雷山小過 **25** 廿六 3	金4 Metal 8 Gathering 壬戌 Water Dog 澤地萃 **26** 廿七 4	水6 Water 9 Peel 癸亥 Water Pig 山地剝 **27** 廿八 6	水1 Water 1 Earth 甲子 Wood Rat 坤爲地 **28** 廿九 1	木3 Wood 2 Biting 乙丑 Wood Ox 火雷噬嗑 **29** 三十 6	火2 Fire 3 Family 丙寅 Fire Tiger 風火家人 **30** 十二月初一 4

1979 己未

(*Ji Wei*) Earth Goat

1979 己未 *(Ji Wei)* Earth Goat

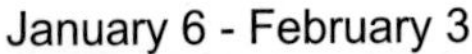

January 6 - February 3

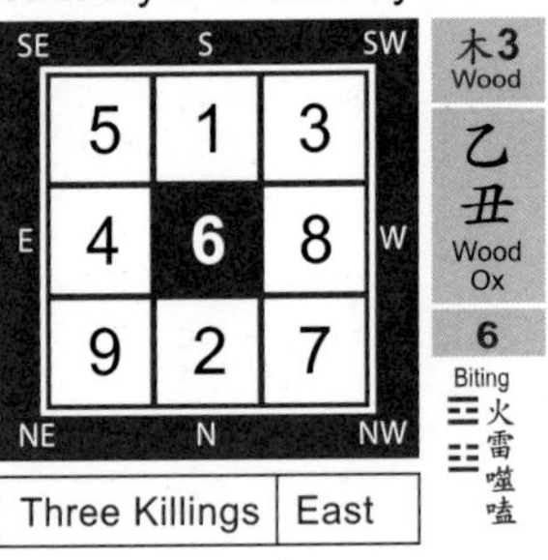

February 4 - March 5

March 6 - April 4

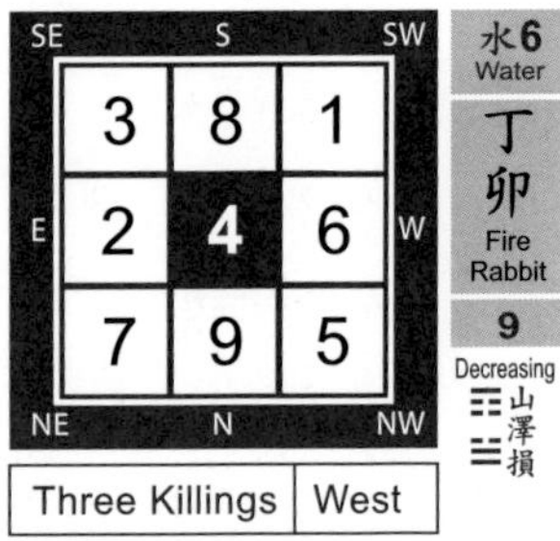

April 5 - May 5

May 6 - June 5

June 6 - July 7

July 8 - August 7

August 8 - September 7

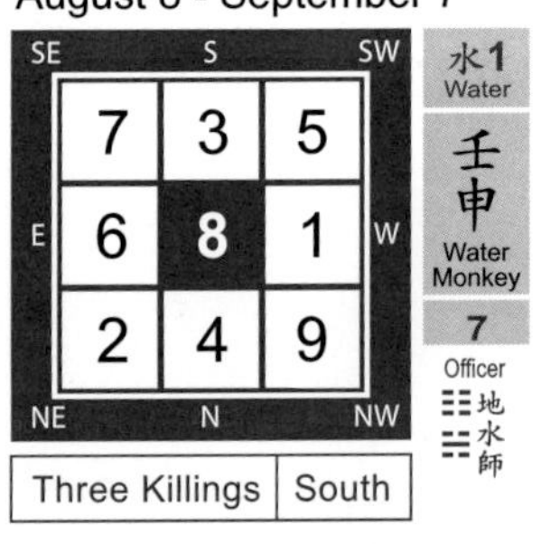

September 8 - October 8

October 9 - November 7

November 8 - December 7

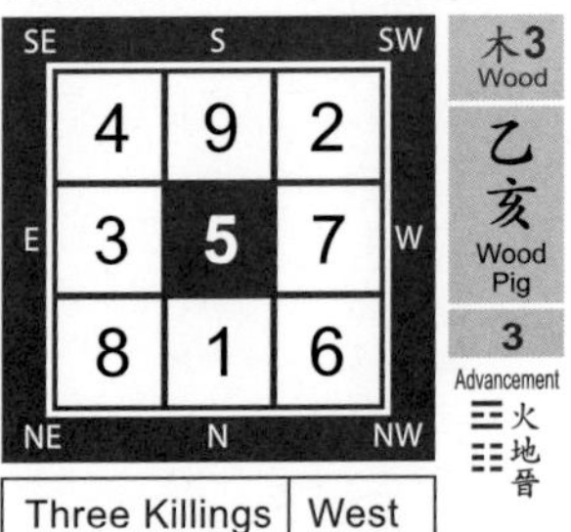

December 8 - January 5

JANUARY 1979 乙丑

Xuan Kong Element 玄空五行	火雷噬嗑 Biting	Period Luck 卦運	Monthly Star 月星
Wood 木3		6	6

SUNDAY	MONDAY	TUESDAY	WEDNESDAY	THURSDAY	FRIDAY	SATURDAY
	金9 Metal · 5 Tread 天澤履 戊辰 Earth Dragon **1** 初三 6	木8 Wood · 6 Great Strength 雷天大壯 己巳 Earth Snake **2** 初四 2	木8 Wood · 7 Consistency 雷風恆 庚午 Metal Horse **3** 初五 9	金9 Metal · 8 Litigation 天水訟 辛未 Metal Goat **4** 初六 3	水1 Water · 9 Officer 地水師 壬申 Water Monkey **5** 初七 7	火2 Fire · 1 Gradual Progress 風山漸 癸酉 Water Rooster **6** 初八 7
火7 Fire · 2 Obstruction 水山蹇 甲戌 Wood Dog **7** 初九 2	木3 Wood · 3 Advancement 火地晉 乙亥 Wood Pig **8** 初十 3	水6 Water · 4 Nourish 山雷頤 丙子 Fire Rat **9** 十一 3	金4 Metal · 5 Following 澤雷隨 丁丑 Fire Ox **10** 十二 7	木8 Wood · 6 Abundance 雷火豐 戊寅 Earth Tiger **11** 十三 6	火7 Fire · 7 Regulate 水澤節 己卯 Earth Rabbit **12** 十四 8	水1 Water · 8 Unity 地天泰 庚辰 Metal Dragon **13** 十五 9
木3 Wood · 9 Great Reward 火天大有 辛巳 Metal Snake **14** 十六 7	火2 Fire · 1 Wind 巽爲風 壬午 Water Horse **15** 十七 1	金4 Metal · 2 Trap 澤水困 癸未 Water Goat **16** 十八 8	木3 Wood · 3 Not Yet Accomplished 火水未濟 甲申 Wood Monkey **17** 十九 9	金9 Metal · 4 Retreat 天山遯 乙酉 Wood Rooster **18** 二十 4	水6 Water · 5 Mountain 艮爲山 丙戌 Fire Dog **19** 廿一 1	木8 Wood · 6 Delight 雷地豫 丁亥 Fire Pig **20** 廿二 8
火7 Fire · 7 Beginning 水雷屯 戊子 Earth Rat **21** 廿三 4	金9 Metal · 8 Without Wrongdoing 天雷無妄 己丑 Earth Ox **22** 廿四 2	木3 Wood · 9 Fire 離爲火 庚寅 Metal Tiger **23** 廿五 1	火2 Fire · 1 Sincerity 風澤中孚 辛卯 Metal Rabbit **24** 廿六 3	水6 Water · 2 Big Livestock 山天大畜 壬辰 Water Dragon **25** 廿七 4	金4 Metal · 3 Eliminating 澤天夬 癸巳 Water Snake **26** 廿八 6	金9 Metal · 4 Heaven 乾爲天 甲午 Wood Horse **27** 廿九 1
火7 Fire · 5 Well 水風井 乙未 Wood Goat **28** 正月初一 6	木8 Wood · 6 Relief 雷水解 丙申 Fire Monkey **29** 初二 4	金4 Metal · 7 Influence 澤山咸 丁酉 Fire Rooster **30** 初三 9	水1 Water · 8 Humility 地山謙 戊戌 Earth Dog **31** 初四 6			

FEBRUARY 1979 丙寅

Xuan Kong Element 玄空五行	風火家人 Family	Period Luck 卦運	Monthly Star 月星
Fire 火2		4	5

SUNDAY	MONDAY	TUESDAY	WEDNESDAY	THURSDAY	FRIDAY	SATURDAY
				火2 Fire · 9 Observation 風地觀 己亥 Earth Pig **1** 初五 2	火2 Fire · 1 Increasing 風雷益 庚子 Metal Rat **2** 初六 9	水1 Water · 2 Dimming Light 地火明夷 辛丑 Metal Ox **3** 初七 3
金9 Metal · 3 Fellowship 天火同人 壬寅 Water Tiger **4** 初八 7	木8 Wood · 4 Marrying Maiden 雷澤歸妹 癸卯 Water Rabbit **5** 初九 7	木3 Wood · 5 Opposition 火澤睽 甲辰 Wood Dragon **6** 初十 2	火7 Fire · 6 Waiting 水天需 乙巳 Wood Snake **7** 十一 3	金4 Metal · 7 Great Exceeding 澤風大過 丙午 Fire Horse **8** 十二 3	水6 Water · 8 Poison 山風蠱 丁未 Fire Goat **9** 十三 7	火2 Fire · 9 Dispersing 風水渙 戊申 Earth Monkey **10** 十四 6
木3 Wood · 1 Travelling 火山旅 己酉 Earth Rooster **11** 十五 8	金9 Metal · 2 Stagnation 天地否 庚戌 Metal Dog **12** 十六 9	火7 Fire · 3 Alliance 水地比 辛亥 Metal Pig **13** 十七 7	木8 Wood · 4 Thunder 震爲雷 壬子 Water Rat **14** 十八 1	水6 Water · 5 Beauty 山火賁 癸丑 Water Ox **15** 十九 8	火7 Fire · 6 Accomplished 水火既濟 甲寅 Wood Tiger **16** 二十 9	水1 Water · 7 Arriving 地澤臨 乙卯 Wood Rabbit **17** 廿一 4
金4 Metal · 8 Marsh 兌爲澤 丙辰 Fire Dragon **18** 廿二 1	火2 Fire · 9 Small Livestock 風天小畜 丁巳 Fire Snake **19** 廿三 8	木3 Wood · 1 The Cauldron 火風鼎 戊午 Earth Horse **20** 廿四 4	水1 Water · 2 Rising 地風升 己未 Earth Goat **21** 廿五 2	火7 Fire · 3 Water 坎爲水 庚申 Metal Monkey **22** 廿六 1	木8 Wood · 4 Lesser Exceeding 雷山小過 辛酉 Metal Rooster **23** 廿七 3	金4 Metal · 5 Gathering 澤地萃 壬戌 Water Dog **24** 廿八 4
水6 Water · 6 Peel 山地剝 癸亥 Water Pig **25** 廿九 6	水1 Water · 7 Earth 坤爲地 甲子 Wood Rat **26** 三十 1	木3 Wood · 8 Biting 火雷噬嗑 乙丑 Wood Ox **27** 二月初一 6	火2 Fire · 9 Family 風火家人 丙寅 Fire Tiger **28** 初二 4			

MARCH 1979 丁卯

Xuan Kong Element 玄空五行	山澤損 Decreasing	Period Luck 卦運	Monthly Star 月星
Water 水6		9	4

SUNDAY	MONDAY	TUESDAY	WEDNESDAY	THURSDAY	FRIDAY	SATURDAY
				水6 Water Decreasing 1 丁卯 Fire Rabbit 山澤損 1 初三 9	金9 Metal Tread 2 戊辰 Earth Dragon 天澤履 2 初四 6	木8 Wood Great Strength 3 己巳 Earth Snake 雷天大壯 3 初五 2
木8 Wood Consistency 4 庚午 Metal Horse 雷風恆 4 初六 9	金9 Metal Litigation 5 辛未 Metal Goat 天水訟 5 初七 3	水1 Water Officer 6 壬申 Water Monkey 地水師 6 初八 7	火2 Fire Gradual Progress 7 癸酉 Water Rooster 風山漸 7 初九 7	火7 Fire Obstruction 8 甲戌 Wood Dog 水山蹇 8 初十 2	木3 Wood Advancement 9 乙亥 Wood Pig 火地晉 9 十一 3	水6 Water Nourish 1 丙子 Fire Rat 山雷頤 10 十二 3
金4 Metal Following 2 丁丑 Fire Ox 澤雷隨 11 十三 7	木8 Wood Abundance 3 戊寅 Earth Tiger 雷火豐 12 十四 6	火7 Fire Regulate 4 己卯 Earth Rabbit 水澤節 13 十五 8	水1 Water Unity 5 庚辰 Metal Dragon 地天泰 14 十六 9	木3 Wood Great Reward 6 辛巳 Metal Snake 火天大有 15 十七 7	火2 Fire Wind 7 壬午 Water Horse 巽爲風 16 十八 1	金4 Metal Trap 8 癸未 Water Goat 澤水困 17 十九 8
木3 Wood Not Yet Accomplished 9 甲申 Wood Monkey 火水未濟 18 二十 9	金9 Metal Retreat 1 乙酉 Wood Rooster 天山遯 19 廿一 4	水6 Water Mountain 2 丙戌 Fire Dog 艮爲山 20 廿二 1	木8 Wood Delight 3 丁亥 Fire Pig 雷地豫 21 廿三 8	火7 Fire Beginning 4 戊子 Earth Rat 水雷屯 22 廿四 4	金9 Metal Without Wrongdoing 5 己丑 Earth Ox 天雷無妄 23 廿五 2	木3 Wood Fire 6 庚寅 Metal Tiger 離爲火 24 廿六 1
火2 Fire Sincerity 7 辛卯 Metal Rabbit 風澤中孚 25 廿七 3	水6 Water Big Livestock 8 壬辰 Water Dragon 山天大畜 26 廿八 4	金4 Metal Eliminating 9 癸巳 Water Snake 澤天夬 27 廿九 6	金9 Metal Heaven 1 甲午 Wood Horse 乾爲天 28 三月初一 1	火7 Fire Well 2 乙未 Wood Goat 水風井 29 初二 6	木8 Wood Relief 3 丙申 Fire Monkey 雷水解 30 初三 4	金4 Metal Influence 4 丁酉 Fire Rooster 澤山咸 31 初四 9

APRIL 1979 戊辰

Xuan Kong Element 玄空五行	天澤履 Tread	Period Luck 卦運	Monthly Star 月星
Metal 金9		6	3

SUNDAY	MONDAY	TUESDAY	WEDNESDAY	THURSDAY	FRIDAY	SATURDAY
水1 Water Humility 5 戊戌 Earth Dog 地山謙 1 初五 6	火2 Fire Observation 6 己亥 Earth Pig 風地觀 2 初六 2	火2 Fire Increasing 7 庚子 Metal Rat 風雷益 3 初七 9	水1 Water Dimming Light 8 辛丑 Metal Ox 地火明夷 4 初八 3	金9 Metal Fellowship 9 壬寅 Water Tiger 天火同人 5 初九 7	木8 Wood Marrying Maiden 1 癸卯 Water Rabbit 雷澤歸妹 6 初十 7	木3 Wood Opposition 2 甲辰 Wood Dragon 火澤睽 7 十一 2
火7 Fire Waiting 3 乙巳 Wood Snake 水天需 8 十二 3	金4 Metal Great Exceeding 4 丙午 Fire Horse 澤風大過 9 十三 3	水6 Water Poison 5 丁未 Fire Goat 山風蠱 10 十四 7	火2 Fire Dispersing 6 戊申 Earth Monkey 風水渙 11 十五 6	木3 Wood Travelling 7 己酉 Earth Rooster 火山旅 12 十六 8	金9 Metal Stagnation 8 庚戌 Metal Dog 天地否 13 十七 9	火7 Fire Alliance 9 辛亥 Metal Pig 水地比 14 十八 7
木8 Wood Thunder 1 壬子 Water Rat 震爲雷 15 十九 1	水6 Water Beauty 2 癸丑 Water Ox 山火賁 16 二十 8	火7 Fire Accomplished 3 甲寅 Wood Tiger 水火既濟 17 廿一 9	水1 Water Arriving 4 乙卯 Wood Rabbit 地澤臨 18 廿二 4	金4 Metal Marsh 5 丙辰 Fire Dragon 兌爲澤 19 廿三 1	火2 Fire Small Livestock 6 丁巳 Fire Snake 風天小畜 20 廿四 8	木3 Wood The Cauldron 7 戊午 Earth Horse 火風鼎 21 廿五 4
水1 Water Rising 8 己未 Earth Goat 地風升 22 廿六 2	火7 Fire Water 9 庚申 Metal Monkey 坎爲水 23 廿七 1	木8 Wood Lesser Exceeding 1 辛酉 Metal Rooster 雷山小過 24 廿八 3	金4 Metal Gathering 2 壬戌 Water Dog 澤地萃 25 廿九 4	水6 Water Peel 3 癸亥 Water Pig 山地剝 26 四月初一 6	水1 Water Earth 4 甲子 Wood Rat 坤爲地 27 初二 1	木3 Wood Biting 5 乙丑 Wood Ox 火雷噬嗑 28 初三 6
火2 Fire Family 6 丙寅 Fire Tiger 風火家人 29 初四 4	水6 Water Decreasing 7 丁卯 Fire Rabbit 山澤損 30 初五 9					

MAY 1979 己巳

Xuan Kong Element 玄空五行	雷天大壯	Period Luck 卦運	Monthly Star 月星
Wood 木8	Great Strength	2	2

SUNDAY	MONDAY	TUESDAY	WEDNESDAY	THURSDAY	FRIDAY	SATURDAY
		金9 Metal 8 Tread 天澤履 戊辰 Earth Dragon 6 1 初六	木8 Wood 9 Great Strength 雷天大壯 己巳 Earth Snake 2 2 初七	木8 Wood 1 Consistency 雷風恆 庚午 Metal Horse 9 3 初八	金9 Metal 2 Litigation 天水訟 辛未 Metal Goat 3 4 初九	水1 Water 3 Officer 地水師 壬申 Water Monkey 7 5 初十
火2 Fire 4 Gradual Progress 風山漸 癸酉 Water Rooster 7 6 十一	火7 Fire 5 Obstruction 水山蹇 甲戌 Wood Dog 2 7 十二	木3 Wood 6 Advancement 火地晉 乙亥 Wood Pig 3 8 十三	水6 Water 7 Nourish 山雷頤 丙子 Fire Rat 3 9 十四	金4 Metal 8 Following 澤雷隨 丁丑 Fire Ox 7 10 十五	木8 Wood 9 Abundance 雷火豐 戊寅 Earth Tiger 6 11 十六	火7 Fire 1 Regulate 水澤節 己卯 Earth Rabbit 8 12 十七
水1 Water 2 Unity 地天泰 庚辰 Metal Dragon 9 13 十八	木3 Wood 3 Great Reward 火天大有 辛巳 Metal Snake 7 14 十九	火2 Fire 4 Wind 巽為風 壬午 Water Horse 1 15 二十	金4 Metal 5 Trap 澤水困 癸未 Water Goat 8 16 廿一	木3 Wood 6 Not Yet Accomplished 火水未濟 甲申 Wood Monkey 9 17 廿二	金9 Metal 7 Retreat 天山遯 乙酉 Wood Rooster 4 18 廿三	水6 Water 8 Mountain 艮為山 丙戌 Fire Dog 1 19 廿四
木8 Wood 9 Delight 雷地豫 丁亥 Fire Pig 8 20 廿五	火7 Fire 1 Beginning 水雷屯 戊子 Earth Rat 4 21 廿六	金9 Metal 2 Without Wrongdoing 天雷無妄 己丑 Earth Ox 2 22 廿七	木3 Wood 3 Fire 離為火 庚寅 Metal Tiger 1 23 廿八	火2 Fire 4 Sincerity 風澤中孚 辛卯 Metal Rabbit 3 24 廿九	水6 Water 5 Big Livestock 山天大畜 壬辰 Water Dragon 4 25 三十	金4 Metal 6 Eliminating 澤天夬 癸巳 Water Snake 6 26 五月初一
金9 Metal 7 Heaven 乾為天 甲午 Wood Horse 1 27 初二	火7 Fire 8 Well 水風井 乙未 Wood Goat 6 28 初三	木8 Wood 9 Relief 雷水解 丙申 Fire Monkey 4 29 初四	金4 Metal 1 Influence 澤山咸 丁酉 Fire Rooster 9 30 初五	水1 Water 2 Humility 地山謙 戊戌 Earth Dog 6 31 初六		

JUNE 1979 庚午

Xuan Kong Element 玄空五行	雷風恆	Period Luck 卦運	Monthly Star 月星
Wood 木8	Consistency	9	1

SUNDAY	MONDAY	TUESDAY	WEDNESDAY	THURSDAY	FRIDAY	SATURDAY
					火2 Fire 3 Observation 風地觀 己亥 Earth Pig 2 1 初七	火2 Fire 4 Increasing 風雷益 庚子 Metal Rat 9 2 初八
水1 Water 5 Dimming Light 地火明夷 辛丑 Metal Ox 3 3 初九	金9 Metal 6 Fellowship 天火同人 壬寅 Water Tiger 7 4 初十	木8 Wood 7 Marrying Maiden 雷澤歸妹 癸卯 Water Rabbit 7 5 十一	木3 Wood 8 Opposition 火澤睽 甲辰 Wood Dragon 2 6 十二	火7 Fire 9 Waiting 水天需 乙巳 Wood Snake 3 7 十三	金4 Metal 1 Great Exceeding 澤風大過 丙午 Fire Horse 3 8 十四	水6 Water 2 Poison 山風蠱 丁未 Fire Goat 7 9 十五
火2 Fire 3 Dispersing 風水渙 戊申 Earth Monkey 6 10 十六	木3 Wood 4 Travelling 火山旅 己酉 Earth Rooster 8 11 十七	金9 Metal 5 Stagnation 天地否 庚戌 Metal Dog 9 12 十八	火7 Fire 6 Alliance 水地比 辛亥 Metal Pig 7 13 十九	木8 Wood 7 Thunder 震為雷 壬子 Water Rat 1 14 二十	水6 Water 8 Beauty 山火賁 癸丑 Water Ox 8 15 廿一	火7 Fire 9 Accomplished 水火既濟 甲寅 Wood Tiger 9 16 廿二
水1 Water 1 Arriving 地澤臨 乙卯 Wood Rabbit 4 17 廿三	金4 Metal 2 Marsh 兌為澤 丙辰 Fire Dragon 1 18 廿四	火2 Fire 3 Small Livestock 風天小畜 丁巳 Fire Snake 8 19 廿五	木3 Wood 4 The Cauldron 火風鼎 戊午 Earth Horse 4 20 廿六	水1 Water 5 Rising 地風升 己未 Earth Goat 2 21 廿七	火7 Fire 6/4 Water 坎為水 庚申 Metal Monkey 1 22 廿八	木8 Wood 3 Lesser Exceeding 雷山小過 辛酉 Metal Rooster 3 23 廿九
金4 Metal 2 Gathering 澤地萃 壬戌 Water Dog 4 24 六月初一	水6 Water 1 Peel 山地剝 癸亥 Water Pig 6 25 初二	水1 Water 9 Earth 坤為地 甲子 Wood Rat 1 26 初三	木3 Wood 8 Biting 火雷噬嗑 乙丑 Wood Ox 6 27 初四	火2 Fire 7 Family 風火家人 丙寅 Fire Tiger 4 28 初五	水6 Water 6 Decreasing 山澤損 丁卯 Fire Rabbit 9 29 初六	金9 Metal 5 Tread 天澤履 戊辰 Earth Dragon 6 30 初七

JULY 1979 辛未

Xuan Kong Element 玄空五行	天水訟 Litigation	Period Luck 卦運	Monthly Star 月星
Metal 金9		3	9

SUNDAY	MONDAY	TUESDAY	WEDNESDAY	THURSDAY	FRIDAY	SATURDAY
木8 Wood 4 Great Strength 雷天大壯 己巳 Earth Snake 1 初八 2	木8 Wood 3 Consistency 雷風恆 庚午 Metal Horse 2 初九 9	金9 Metal 2 Litigation 天水訟 辛未 Metal Goat 3 初十 3	水1 Water 1 Officer 地水師 壬申 Water Monkey 4 十一 7	火2 Fire 9 Gradual Progress 風山漸 癸酉 Water Rooster 5 十二 7	火7 Fire 8 Obstruction 水山蹇 甲戌 Wood Dog 6 十三 2	木3 Wood 7 Advancement 火地晉 乙亥 Wood Pig 7 十四 3
水6 Water 6 Nourish 山雷頤 丙子 Fire Rat 8 十五 3	金4 Metal 5 Following 澤雷隨 丁丑 Fire Ox 9 十六 7	木8 Wood 4 Abundance 雷火豐 戊寅 Earth Tiger 10 十七 6	火7 Fire 3 Regulate 水澤節 己卯 Earth Rabbit 11 十八 8	水1 Water 2 Unity 地天泰 庚辰 Metal Dragon 12 十九 9	木3 Wood 1 Great Reward 火天大有 辛巳 Metal Snake 13 二十 7	火2 Fire 9 Wind 巽為風 壬午 Water Horse 14 廿一 1
金4 Metal 8 Trap 澤水困 癸未 Water Goat 15 廿二 8	木3 Wood 7 Not Yet Accomplished 火水未濟 甲申 Wood Monkey 16 廿三 9	金9 Metal 6 Retreat 天山遯 乙酉 Wood Rooster 17 廿四 4	水6 Water 5 Mountain 艮為山 丙戌 Fire Dog 18 廿五 1	木8 Wood 4 Delight 雷地豫 丁亥 Fire Pig 19 廿六 8	火7 Fire 3 Beginning 水雷屯 戊子 Earth Rat 20 廿七 4	金9 Metal 2 Without Wrongdoing 天雷無妄 己丑 Earth Ox 21 廿八 2
木3 Wood 1 Fire 離為火 庚寅 Metal Tiger 22 廿九 1	火2 Fire 9 Sincerity 風澤中孚 辛卯 Metal Rabbit 23 三十 3	水6 Water 8 Big Livestock 山天大畜 壬辰 Water Dragon 24 閏六月初一 4	金4 Metal 7 Eliminating 澤天夬 癸巳 Water Snake 25 初二 6	金9 Metal 6 Heaven 乾為天 甲午 Wood Horse 26 初三 1	火7 Fire 5 Well 水風井 乙未 Wood Goat 27 初四 6	木8 Wood 4 Relief 雷水解 丙申 Fire Monkey 28 初五 4
金4 Metal 3 Influence 澤山咸 丁酉 Fire Rooster 29 初六 9	水1 Water 2 Humility 地山謙 戊戌 Earth Dog 30 初七 6	火2 Fire 1 Observation 風地觀 己亥 Earth Pig 31 初八 2				

AUGUST 1979 壬申

Xuan Kong Element 玄空五行	地水師 Officer	Period Luck 卦運	Monthly Star 月星
Water 水1		7	8

SUNDAY	MONDAY	TUESDAY	WEDNESDAY	THURSDAY	FRIDAY	SATURDAY
			火2 Fire 9 Increasing 風雷益 庚子 Metal Rat 1 初九 9	水1 Water 8 Dimming Light 地火明夷 辛丑 Metal Ox 2 初十 3	金9 Metal 7 Fellowship 天火同人 壬寅 Water Tiger 3 十一 7	木8 Wood 6 Marrying Maiden 雷澤歸妹 癸卯 Water Rabbit 4 十二 7
木3 Wood 5 Opposition 火澤睽 甲辰 Wood Dragon 5 十三 2	火7 Fire 4 Waiting 水天需 乙巳 Wood Snake 6 十四 3	金4 Metal 3 Great Exceeding 澤風大過 丙午 Fire Horse 7 十五 3	水6 Water 2 Poison 山風蠱 丁未 Fire Goat 8 十六 7	火2 Fire 1 Dispersing 風水渙 戊申 Earth Monkey 9 十七 6	木3 Wood 9 Travelling 火山旅 己酉 Earth Rooster 10 十八 8	金9 Metal 8 Stagnation 天地否 庚戌 Metal Dog 11 十九 9
火7 Fire 7 Alliance 水地比 辛亥 Metal Pig 12 二十 7	木8 Wood 6 Thunder 震為雷 壬子 Water Rat 13 廿一 1	水6 Water 5 Beauty 山火賁 癸丑 Water Ox 14 廿二 8	火7 Fire 4 Accomplished 水火既濟 甲寅 Wood Tiger 15 廿三 9	水1 Water 3 Arriving 地澤臨 乙卯 Wood Rabbit 16 廿四 4	金4 Metal 2 Marsh 兌為澤 丙辰 Fire Dragon 17 廿五 1	火2 Fire 1 Small Livestock 風天小畜 丁巳 Fire Snake 18 廿六 8
木3 Wood 9 The Cauldron 火風鼎 戊午 Earth Horse 19 廿七 4	水1 Water 8 Rising 地風升 己未 Earth Goat 20 廿八 2	火7 Fire 7 Water 坎為水 庚申 Metal Monkey 21 廿九 1	木8 Wood 6 Lesser Exceeding 雷山小過 辛酉 Metal Rooster 22 三十 3	金4 Metal 5 Gathering 澤地萃 壬戌 Water Dog 23 七月初一 4	水6 Water 4 Peel 山地剝 癸亥 Water Pig 24 初二 6	水1 Water 3 Earth 坤為地 甲子 Wood Rat 25 初三 1
木3 Wood 2 Biting 火雷噬嗑 乙丑 Wood Ox 26 初四 6	火2 Fire 1 Family 風火家人 丙寅 Fire Tiger 27 初五 4	水6 Water 9 Decreasing 山澤損 丁卯 Fire Rabbit 28 初六 9	金9 Metal 8 Tread 天澤履 戊辰 Earth Dragon 29 初七 6	木8 Wood 7 Great Strength 雷天大壯 己巳 Earth Snake 30 初八 2	木8 Wood 6 Consistency 雷風恆 庚午 Metal Horse 31 初九 9	

SEPTEMBER 1979 癸酉

Xuan Kong Element 玄空五行	風山漸 Gradual Progress	Period Luck 卦運	Monthly Star 月星
Fire 火2		7	7

SUNDAY	MONDAY	TUESDAY	WEDNESDAY	THURSDAY	FRIDAY	SATURDAY
火2 Fire 3 Increasing 風雷益 庚子 Metal Rat 30 初十 9						金9 Metal 5 Litigation 天水訟 辛未 Metal Goat 1 初十 3
水1 Water 4 Officer 地水師 壬申 Water Monkey 2 十一 7	火2 Fire 3 Gradual Progress 風山漸 癸酉 Water Rooster 3 十二 7	火7 Fire 2 Obstruction 水山蹇 甲戌 Wood Dog 4 十三 2	木3 Wood 1 Advancement 火地晉 乙亥 Wood Pig 5 十四 3	水6 Water 9 Nourish 山雷頤 丙子 Fire Rat 6 十五 3	金4 Metal 8 Following 澤雷隨 丁丑 Fire Ox 7 十六 7	木8 Wood 7 Abundance 雷火豐 戊寅 Earth Tiger 8 十七 6
火7 Fire 6 Regulate 水澤節 己卯 Earth Rabbit 9 十八 8	水1 Water 5 Unity 地天泰 庚辰 Metal Dragon 10 十九 9	木3 Wood 4 Great Reward 火天大有 辛巳 Metal Snake 11 二十 7	火2 Fire 3 Wind 巽為風 壬午 Water Horse 12 廿一 1	金4 Metal 2 Trap 澤水困 癸未 Water Goat 13 廿二 8	木3 Wood 1 Not Yet Accomplished 火水未濟 甲申 Wood Monkey 14 廿三 9	金9 Metal 9 Retreat 天山遯 乙酉 Wood Rooster 15 廿四 4
水6 Water 8 Mountain 艮為山 丙戌 Fire Dog 16 廿五 1	木8 Wood 7 Delight 雷地豫 丁亥 Fire Pig 17 廿六 8	火7 Fire 6 Beginning 水雷屯 戊子 Earth Rat 18 廿七 4	金9 Metal 5 Without Wrongdoing 天雷無妄 己丑 Earth Ox 19 廿八 2	木3 Wood 4 Fire 離為火 庚寅 Metal Tiger 20 廿九 1	火2 Fire 3 Sincerity 風澤中孚 辛卯 Metal Rabbit 21 九月初一 3	水6 Water 2 Big Livestock 山天大畜 壬辰 Water Dragon 22 初二 4
金4 Metal 1 Eliminating 澤天夬 癸巳 Water Snake 23 初三 6	金9 Metal 9 Heaven 乾為天 甲午 Wood Horse 24 初四 1	火7 Fire 8 Well 水風井 乙未 Wood Goat 25 初五 6	木8 Wood 7 Relief 雷水解 丙申 Fire Monkey 26 初六 4	金4 Metal 6 Influence 澤山咸 丁酉 Fire Rooster 27 初七 9	水1 Water 5 Humility 地山謙 戊戌 Earth Dog 28 初八 6	火2 Fire 4 Observation 風地觀 己亥 Earth Pig 29 初九 2

OCTOBER 1979 甲戌

Xuan Kong Element 玄空五行	水山蹇 Obstruction	Period Luck 卦運	Monthly Star 月星
Fire 火7		2	6

SUNDAY	MONDAY	TUESDAY	WEDNESDAY	THURSDAY	FRIDAY	SATURDAY
	水1 Water 2 Dimming Light 地火明夷 辛丑 Metal Ox 1 十一 3	金9 Metal 1 Fellowship 天火同人 壬寅 Water Tiger 2 十二 7	木8 Wood 9 Marrying Maiden 雷澤歸妹 癸卯 Water Rabbit 3 十三 7	木3 Wood 8 Opposition 火澤睽 甲辰 Wood Dragon 4 十四 2	火7 Fire 7 Waiting 水天需 乙巳 Wood Snake 5 十五 3	金4 Metal 6 Great Exceeding 澤風大過 丙午 Fire Horse 6 十六 3
水6 Water 5 Poison 山風蠱 丁未 Fire Goat 7 十七 7	火2 Fire 4 Dispersing 風水渙 戊申 Earth Monkey 8 十八 6	木3 Wood 3 Travelling 火山旅 己酉 Earth Rooster 9 十九 8	金9 Metal 2 Stagnation 天地否 庚戌 Metal Dog 10 二十 9	火7 Fire 1 Alliance 水地比 辛亥 Metal Pig 11 廿一 7	木8 Wood 9 Thunder 震為雷 壬子 Water Rat 12 廿二 1	水6 Water 8 Beauty 山火賁 癸丑 Water Ox 13 廿三 8
火7 Fire 7 Accomplished 水火既濟 甲寅 Wood Tiger 14 廿四 9	水1 Water 6 Arriving 地澤臨 乙卯 Wood Rabbit 15 廿五 4	金4 Metal 5 Marsh 兌為澤 丙辰 Fire Dragon 16 廿六 1	火2 Fire 4 Small Livestock 風天小畜 丁巳 Fire Snake 17 廿七 8	木3 Wood 3 The Cauldron 火風鼎 戊午 Earth Horse 18 廿八 4	水1 Water 2 Rising 地風升 己未 Earth Goat 19 廿九 2	火7 Fire 1 Water 坎為水 庚申 Metal Monkey 20 三十 1
木8 Wood 9 Lesser Exceeding 雷山小過 辛酉 Metal Rooster 21 九月初一 3	金4 Metal 8 Gathering 澤地萃 壬戌 Water Dog 22 初二 4	水6 Water 7 Peel 山地剝 癸亥 Water Pig 23 初三 6	水1 Water 6 Earth 坤為地 甲子 Wood Rat 24 初四 1	木3 Wood 5 Biting 火雷噬嗑 乙丑 Wood Ox 25 初五 6	火2 Fire 4 Family 風火家人 丙寅 Fire Tiger 26 初六 4	水6 Water 3 Decreasing 山澤損 丁卯 Fire Rabbit 27 初七 9
金9 Metal 2 Tread 天澤履 戊辰 Earth Dragon 28 初八 6	木8 Wood 1 Great Strength 雷天大壯 己巳 Earth Snake 29 初九 2	木8 Wood 9 Consistency 雷風恆 庚午 Metal Horse 30 初十 9	金9 Metal 8 Litigation 天水訟 辛未 Metal Goat 31 十一 3			

NOVEMBER 1979 乙亥

Xuan Kong Element 玄空五行	火地晉 Advancement	Period Luck 卦運	Monthly Star 月星
Wood 木3		3	5

SUNDAY	MONDAY	TUESDAY	WEDNESDAY	THURSDAY	FRIDAY	SATURDAY
				水1 Water 7 Officer 地水師 壬申 Water Monkey 1 十二 7	火2 Fire 6 Gradual Progress 風山漸 癸酉 Water Rooster 2 十三 7	火7 Fire 5 Obstruction 水山蹇 甲戌 Wood Dog 3 十四 2
木3 Wood 4 Advancement 火地晉 乙亥 Wood Pig 4 十五 3	水6 Water 3 Nourish 山雷頤 丙子 Fire Rat 5 十六 3	金4 Metal 2 Following 澤雷隨 丁丑 Fire Ox 6 十七 7	木8 Wood 1 Abundance 雷火豐 戊寅 Earth Tiger 7 十八 6	火7 Fire 9 Regulate 水澤節 己卯 Earth Rabbit 8 十九 8	水1 Water 8 Unity 地天泰 庚辰 Metal Dragon 9 二十 9	木3 Wood 7 Great Reward 火天大有 辛巳 Metal Snake 10 廿一 7
火2 Fire 6 Wind 巽為風 壬午 Water Horse 11 廿二 1	金4 Metal 5 Trap 澤水困 癸未 Water Goat 12 廿三 8	木3 Wood 4 Not Yet Accomplished 火水未濟 甲申 Wood Monkey 13 廿四 9	金9 Metal 3 Retreat 天山遯 乙酉 Wood Rooster 14 廿五 4	水6 Water 2 Mountain 艮為山 丙戌 Fire Dog 15 廿六 1	木8 Wood 1 Delight 雷地豫 丁亥 Fire Pig 16 廿七 8	火7 Fire 9 Beginning 水雷屯 戊子 Earth Rat 17 廿八 4
金9 Metal 8 Without Wrongdoing 天雷無妄 己丑 Earth Ox 18 廿九 2	木3 Wood 7 Fire 離為火 庚寅 Metal Tiger 19 三十 1	火2 Fire 6 Sincerity 風澤中孚 辛卯 Metal Rabbit 20 十月初一 3	水6 Water 5 Big Livestock 山天大畜 壬辰 Water Dragon 21 初二 4	金4 Metal 4 Eliminating 澤天夬 癸巳 Water Snake 22 初三 6	金9 Metal 3 Heaven 乾為天 甲午 Wood Horse 23 初四 1	火7 Fire 2 Well 水風井 乙未 Wood Goat 24 初五 6
木8 Wood 1 Relief 雷水解 丙申 Fire Monkey 25 初六 4	金4 Metal 9 Influence 澤山咸 丁酉 Fire Rooster 26 初七 9	水1 Water 8 Humility 地山謙 戊戌 Earth Dog 27 初八 6	火2 Fire 7 Observation 風地觀 己亥 Earth Pig 28 初九 2	火2 Fire 6 Increasing 風雷益 庚子 Metal Rat 29 初十 9	水1 Water 5 Dimming Light 地火明夷 辛丑 Metal Ox 30 十一 3	

DECEMBER 1979 丙子

Xuan Kong Element 玄空五行	山雷頤 Nourish	Period Luck 卦運	Monthly Star 月星
Water 水6		3	4

SUNDAY	MONDAY	TUESDAY	WEDNESDAY	THURSDAY	FRIDAY	SATURDAY
金9 Metal 8 Litigation 天水訟 辛未 Metal Goat 30 十二 3	水1 Water 9 Officer 地水師 壬申 Water Monkey 31 十三 7					金9 Metal 4 Fellowship 天火同人 壬寅 Water Tiger 1 十二 7
木8 Wood 3 Marrying Maiden 雷澤歸妹 癸卯 Water Rabbit 2 十三 7	木3 Wood 2 Opposition 火澤睽 甲辰 Wood Dragon 3 十四 2	火7 Fire 1 Waiting 水天需 乙巳 Wood Snake 4 十五 3	金4 Metal 9 Great Exceeding 澤風大過 丙午 Fire Horse 5 十六 3	水6 Water 8 Poison 山風蠱 丁未 Fire Goat 6 十七 7	火2 Fire 7 Dispersing 風水渙 戊申 Earth Monkey 7 十八 6	木3 Wood 6 Travelling 火山旅 己酉 Earth Rooster 8 十九 8
金9 Metal 5 Stagnation 天地否 庚戌 Metal Dog 9 二十 9	火7 Fire 4 Alliance 水地比 辛亥 Metal Pig 10 廿一 7	木8 Wood 3 Thunder 震為雷 壬子 Water Rat 11 廿二 1	水6 Water 2 Beauty 山火賁 癸丑 Water Ox 12 廿三 8	火7 Fire 1 Accomplished 水火既濟 甲寅 Wood Tiger 13 廿四 9	水1 Water 9 Arriving 地澤臨 乙卯 Wood Rabbit 14 廿五 4	金4 Metal 8 Marsh 兌為澤 丙辰 Fire Dragon 15 廿六 1
火2 Fire 7 Small Livestock 風天小畜 丁巳 Fire Snake 16 廿七 8	木3 Wood 6 The Cauldron 火風鼎 戊午 Earth Horse 17 廿八 4	水1 Water 5 Rising 地風升 己未 Earth Goat 18 廿九 2	火7 Fire 4 Water 坎為水 庚申 Metal Monkey 19 十一月初一 1	木8 Wood 3 Lesser Exceeding 雷山小過 辛酉 Metal Rooster 20 初二 3	金4 Metal 2 Gathering 澤地萃 壬戌 Water Dog 21 初三 4	水6 Water 1/9 Peel 山地剝 癸亥 Water Pig 22 初四 6
水1 Water 1 Earth 坤為地 甲子 Wood Rat 23 初五 1	木3 Wood 2 Biting 火雷噬嗑 乙丑 Wood Ox 24 初六 6	火2 Fire 3 Family 風火家人 丙寅 Fire Tiger 25 初七 4	水6 Water 4 Decreasing 山澤損 丁卯 Fire Rabbit 26 初八 9	金9 Metal 5 Tread 天澤履 戊辰 Earth Dragon 27 初九 6	木8 Wood 6 Great Strength 雷天大壯 己巳 Earth Snake 28 初十 2	木8 Wood 7 Consistency 雷風恆 庚午 Metal Horse 29 十一 9

1980 庚申

(*Geng Shen*) Metal Monkey

1980 庚申 *(Geng Shen)* Metal Monkey

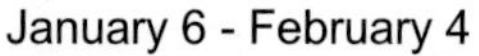

January 6 - February 4

February 5 - March 4

March 5 - April 3

April 4 - May 4

May 5 - June 4

June 5 - July 6

July 7 - August 6

August 7 - September 6

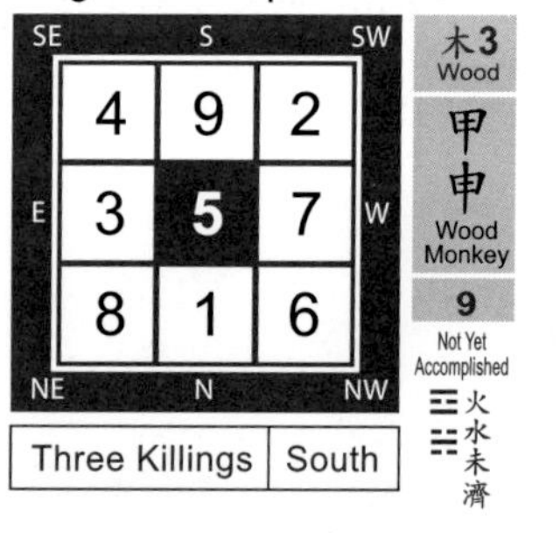

September 7 - October 7

October 8 - November 6

November 7 - December 6

December 7 - January 4

JANUARY 1980 丁丑

Xuan Kong Element 玄空五行	澤雷隨 Following	Period Luck 卦運	Monthly Star 月星
Metal 金4		7	3

SUNDAY	MONDAY	TUESDAY	WEDNESDAY	THURSDAY	FRIDAY	SATURDAY
		火2 Fire 1 Gradual Progress 風山漸 癸酉 Water Rooster **1** 十四 7	火7 Fire 2 Obstruction 水山蹇 甲戌 Wood Dog **2** 十五 2	木3 Wood 3 Advancement 火地晉 乙亥 Wood Pig **3** 十六 3	水6 Water 4 Nourish 山雷頤 丙子 Fire Rat **4** 十七 3	金4 Metal 5 Following 澤雷隨 丁丑 Fire Ox **5** 十八 7
木8 Wood 6 Abundance 雷火豐 戊寅 Earth Tiger **6** 十九 6	火7 Fire 7 Regulate 水澤節 己卯 Earth Rabbit **7** 二十 8	水1 Water 8 Unity 地天泰 庚辰 Metal Dragon **8** 廿一 9	木3 Wood 9 Great Reward 火天大有 辛巳 Metal Snake **9** 廿二 7	火2 Fire 1 Wind 巽為風 壬午 Water Horse **10** 廿三 1	金4 Metal 2 Trap 澤水困 癸未 Water Goat **11** 廿四 8	木3 Wood 3 Not Yet Accomplished 火水未濟 甲申 Wood Monkey **12** 廿五 9
金9 Metal 4 Retreat 天山遯 乙酉 Wood Rooster **13** 廿六 4	水6 Water 5 Mountain 艮為山 丙戌 Fire Dog **14** 廿七 1	木8 Wood 6 Delight 雷地豫 丁亥 Fire Pig **15** 廿八 8	火7 Fire 7 Beginning 水雷屯 戊子 Earth Rat **16** 廿九 4	金9 Metal 8 Without Wrongdoing 天雷無妄 己丑 Earth Ox **17** 三十 2	木3 Wood 9 Fire 離為火 庚寅 Metal Tiger **18** 十二月初一 1	火2 Fire 1 Sincerity 風澤中孚 辛卯 Metal Rabbit **19** 初二 3
水6 Water 2 Big Livestock 山天大畜 壬辰 Water Dragon **20** 初三 4	金4 Metal 3 Eliminating 澤天夬 癸巳 Water Snake **21** 初四 6	金9 Metal 4 Heaven 乾為天 甲午 Wood Horse **22** 初五 1	火7 Fire 5 Well 水風井 乙未 Wood Goat **23** 初六 6	木8 Wood 6 Relief 雷水解 丙申 Fire Monkey **24** 初七 4	金4 Metal 7 Influence 澤山咸 丁酉 Fire Rooster **25** 初八 9	水1 Water 8 Humility 地山謙 戊戌 Earth Dog **26** 初九 6
火2 Fire 9 Observation 風地觀 己亥 Earth Pig **27** 初十 2	火2 Fire 1 Increasing 風雷益 庚子 Metal Rat **28** 十一 9	水1 Water 2 Dimming Light 地火明夷 辛丑 Metal Ox **29** 十二 3	金9 Metal 3 Fellowship 天火同人 壬寅 Water Tiger **30** 十三 7	木8 Wood 4 Marrying Maiden 雷澤歸妹 癸卯 Water Rabbit **31** 十四 7		

FEBRUARY 1980 戊寅

Xuan Kong Element 玄空五行	雷火豐 Abundance	Period Luck 卦運	Monthly Star 月星
Wood 木8		6	2

SUNDAY	MONDAY	TUESDAY	WEDNESDAY	THURSDAY	FRIDAY	SATURDAY
					木3 Wood 5 Opposition 火澤睽 甲辰 Wood Dragon **1** 十五 2	火7 Fire 6 Waiting 水天需 乙巳 Wood Snake **2** 十六 3
金4 Metal 7 Great Exceeding 澤風大過 丙午 Fire Horse **3** 十七 3	水6 Water 8 Poison 山風蠱 丁未 Fire Goat **4** 十八 7	火2 Fire 9 Dispersing 風水渙 戊申 Earth Monkey **5** 十九 6	木3 Wood 1 Travelling 火山旅 己酉 Earth Rooster **6** 二十 8	金9 Metal 2 Stagnation 天地否 庚戌 Metal Dog **7** 廿一 9	火7 Fire 3 Alliance 水地比 辛亥 Metal Pig **8** 廿二 7	木8 Wood 4 Thunder 震為雷 壬子 Water Rat **9** 廿三 1
水6 Water 5 Beauty 山火賁 癸丑 Water Ox **10** 廿四 8	火7 Fire 6 Accomplished 水火既濟 甲寅 Wood Tiger **11** 廿五 9	水1 Water 7 Arriving 地澤臨 乙卯 Wood Rabbit **12** 廿六 4	金4 Metal 8 Marsh 兌為澤 丙辰 Fire Dragon **13** 廿七 1	火2 Fire 9 Small Livestock 風天小畜 丁巳 Fire Snake **14** 廿八 8	木3 Wood 1 The Cauldron 火風鼎 戊午 Earth Horse **15** 廿九 4	水1 Water 2 Rising 地風升 己未 Earth Goat **16** 正月初一 2
火7 Fire 3 Water 坎為水 庚申 Metal Monkey **17** 初二 1	木8 Wood 4 Lesser Exceeding 雷山小過 辛酉 Metal Rooster **18** 初三 3	金4 Metal 5 Gathering 澤地萃 壬戌 Water Dog **19** 初四 4	水6 Water 6 Peel 山地剝 癸亥 Water Pig **20** 初五 6	水1 Water 7 Earth 坤為地 甲子 Wood Rat **21** 初六 1	木3 Wood 8 Biting 火雷噬嗑 乙丑 Wood Ox **22** 初七 6	火2 Fire 9 Family 風火家人 丙寅 Fire Tiger **23** 初八 4
水6 Water 1 Decreasing 山澤損 丁卯 Fire Rabbit **24** 初九 9	金9 Metal 2 Tread 天澤履 戊辰 Earth Dragon **25** 初十 6	木8 Wood 3 Great Strength 雷天大壯 己巳 Earth Snake **26** 十一 2	木8 Wood 4 Consistency 雷風恆 庚午 Metal Horse **27** 十二 9	金9 Metal 5 Litigation 天水訟 辛未 Metal Goat **28** 十三 3	水1 Water 6 Officer 地水師 壬申 Water Monkey **29** 十四 7	

MARCH 1980 己卯

Xuan Kong Element 玄空五行	水澤節 Regulate	Period Luck 卦運	Monthly Star 月星
Fire 火7		8	1

SUNDAY	MONDAY	TUESDAY	WEDNESDAY	THURSDAY	FRIDAY	SATURDAY
金9 Metal 9 Fellowship 壬寅 Water Tiger 天火同人 30 十四 7	木8 Wood 1 Marrying Maiden 癸卯 Water Rabbit 雷澤歸妹 31 十五 7					火2 Fire 7 Gradual Progress 癸酉 Water Rooster 風山漸 1 十五 7
火7 Fire 8 Obstruction 甲戌 Wood Dog 水山蹇 2 十六 2	木3 Wood 9 Advancement 乙亥 Wood Pig 火地晉 3 十七 3	水6 Water 1 Nourish 丙子 Fire Rat 山雷頤 4 十八 3	金4 Metal 2 Following 丁丑 Fire Ox 澤雷隨 5 十九 7	木8 Wood 3 Abundance 戊寅 Earth Tiger 雷火豐 6 二十 6	火7 Fire 4 Regulate 己卯 Earth Rabbit 水澤節 7 廿一 8	水1 Water 5 Unity 庚辰 Metal Dragon 地天泰 8 廿二 9
木3 Wood 6 Great Reward 辛巳 Metal Snake 火天大有 9 廿三 7	火2 Fire 7 Wind 壬午 Water Horse 巽爲風 10 廿四 1	金4 Metal 8 Trap 癸未 Water Goat 澤水困 11 廿五 8	木3 Wood 9 Not Yet Accomplished 甲申 Wood Monkey 火水未濟 12 廿六 9	金9 Metal 1 Retreat 乙酉 Wood Rooster 天山遯 13 廿七 4	水6 Water 2 Mountain 丙戌 Fire Dog 艮爲山 14 廿八 1	木8 Wood 3 Delight 丁亥 Fire Pig 雷地豫 15 廿九 8
火7 Fire 4 Beginning 戊子 Earth Rat 水雷屯 16 三十 4	金9 Metal 5 Without Wrongdoing 己丑 Earth Ox 天雷無妄 17 二月初一 2	木3 Wood 6 Fire 庚寅 Metal Tiger 離爲火 18 初二 1	火2 Fire 7 Sincerity 辛卯 Metal Rabbit 風澤中孚 19 初三 3	水6 Water 8 Big Livestock 壬辰 Water Dragon 山天大畜 20 初四 4	金4 Metal 9 Eliminating 癸巳 Water Snake 澤天夬 21 初五 6	金9 Metal 1 Heaven 甲午 Wood Horse 乾爲天 22 初六 1
火7 Fire 2 Well 乙未 Wood Goat 水風井 23 初七 6	木8 Wood 3 Relief 丙申 Fire Monkey 雷水解 24 初八 4	金4 Metal 4 Influence 丁酉 Fire Rooster 澤山咸 25 初九 9	水1 Water 5 Humility 戊戌 Earth Dog 地山謙 26 初十 6	火2 Fire 6 Observation 己亥 Earth Pig 風地觀 27 十一 2	火2 Fire 7 Increasing 庚子 Metal Rat 風雷益 28 十二 9	水1 Water 8 Dimming Light 辛丑 Metal Ox 地火明夷 29 十三 3

APRIL 1980 庚辰

Xuan Kong Element 玄空五行	地天泰 Unity	Period Luck 卦運	Monthly Star 月星
Water 水1		9	9

SUNDAY	MONDAY	TUESDAY	WEDNESDAY	THURSDAY	FRIDAY	SATURDAY
		木3 Wood 2 Opposition 甲辰 Wood Dragon 火澤睽 1 十六 2	火7 Fire 3 Waiting 乙巳 Wood Snake 水天需 2 十七 3	金4 Metal 4 Great Exceeding 丙午 Fire Horse 澤風大過 3 十八 3	水6 Water 5 Poison 丁未 Fire Goat 山風蠱 4 十九 7	火2 Fire 6 Dispersing 戊申 Earth Monkey 風水渙 5 二十 6
木3 Wood 7 Travelling 己酉 Earth Rooster 火山旅 6 廿一 8	金9 Metal 8 Stagnation 庚戌 Metal Dog 天地否 7 廿二 9	火7 Fire 9 Alliance 辛亥 Metal Pig 水地比 8 廿三 7	木8 Wood 1 Thunder 壬子 Water Rat 震爲雷 9 廿四 1	水6 Water 2 Beauty 癸丑 Water Ox 山火賁 10 廿五 8	火7 Fire 3 Accomplished 甲寅 Wood Tiger 水火既濟 11 廿六 9	水1 Water 4 Arriving 乙卯 Wood Rabbit 地澤臨 12 廿七 4
金4 Metal 5 Marsh 丙辰 Fire Dragon 兌爲澤 13 廿八 1	火2 Fire 6 Small Livestock 丁巳 Fire Snake 風天小畜 14 廿九 8	木3 Wood 7 The Cauldron 戊午 Earth Horse 火風鼎 15 三月初一 4	水1 Water 8 Rising 己未 Earth Goat 地風升 16 初二 2	火7 Fire 9 Water 庚申 Metal Monkey 坎爲水 17 初三 1	木8 Wood 1 Lesser Exceeding 辛酉 Metal Rooster 雷山小過 18 初四 3	金4 Metal 2 Gathering 壬戌 Water Dog 澤地萃 19 初五 4
水6 Water 3 Peel 癸亥 Water Pig 山地剝 20 初六 6	水1 Water 4 Earth 甲子 Wood Rat 坤爲地 21 初七 1	木3 Wood 5 Biting 乙丑 Wood Ox 火雷噬嗑 22 初八 6	火2 Fire 6 Family 丙寅 Fire Tiger 風火家人 23 初九 4	水6 Water 7 Decreasing 丁卯 Fire Rabbit 山澤損 24 初十 9	金9 Metal 8 Tread 戊辰 Earth Dragon 天澤履 25 十一 6	木8 Wood 9 Great Strength 己巳 Earth Snake 雷天大壯 26 十二 2
木8 Wood 1 Consistency 庚午 Metal Horse 雷風恆 27 十三 9	金9 Metal 2 Litigation 辛未 Metal Goat 天水訟 28 十四 3	水1 Water 3 Officer 壬申 Water Monkey 地水師 29 十五 7	火2 Fire 4 Gradual Progress 癸酉 Water Rooster 風山漸 30 十六 7			

MAY 1980 辛巳

Xuan Kong Element 玄空五行	火天大有 Great Reward	Period Luck 卦運	Monthly Star 月星
Wood 木3		7	8

SUNDAY	MONDAY	TUESDAY	WEDNESDAY	THURSDAY	FRIDAY	SATURDAY
				火7 Fire 5 Obstruction 甲戌 Wood Dog 水山蹇 1 十七 2	木3 Wood 6 Advancement 乙亥 Wood Pig 火地晉 2 十八 3	水6 Water 7 Nourish 丙子 Fire Rat 山雷頤 3 十九 3
金4 Metal 8 Following 丁丑 Fire Ox 澤雷隨 4 二十 7	木8 Wood 9 Abundance 戊寅 Earth Tiger 雷火豐 5 廿一 6	火7 Fire 1 Regulate 己卯 Earth Rabbit 水澤節 6 廿二 8	水1 Water 2 Unity 庚辰 Metal Dragon 地天泰 7 廿三 9	木3 Wood 3 Great Reward 辛巳 Metal Snake 火天大有 8 廿四 7	火2 Fire 4 Wind 壬午 Water Horse 巽爲風 9 廿五 1	金4 Metal 5 Trap 癸未 Water Goat 澤水困 10 廿六 8
木3 Wood 6 Not Yet Accomplished 甲申 Wood Monkey 火水未濟 11 廿七 9	金9 Metal 7 Retreat 乙酉 Wood Rooster 天山遯 12 廿八 4	水6 Water 8 Mountain 丙戌 Fire Dog 艮爲山 13 廿九 1	木8 Wood 9 Delight 丁亥 Fire Pig 雷地豫 14 四月初一 8	火7 Fire 1 Beginning 戊子 Earth Rat 水雷屯 15 初二 4	金9 Metal 2 Without Wrongdoing 己丑 Earth Ox 天雷無妄 16 初三 2	木3 Wood 3 Fire 庚寅 Metal Tiger 離爲火 17 初四 1
火2 Fire 4 Sincerity 辛卯 Metal Rabbit 風澤中孚 18 初五 3	水6 Water 5 Big Livestock 壬辰 Water Dragon 山天大畜 19 初六 4	金4 Metal 6 Eliminating 癸巳 Water Snake 澤天夬 20 初七 6	金9 Metal 7 Heaven 甲午 Wood Horse 乾爲天 21 初八 1	火7 Fire 8 Well 乙未 Wood Goat 水風井 22 初九 6	木8 Wood 9 Relief 丙申 Fire Monkey 雷水解 23 初十 4	金4 Metal 1 Influence 丁酉 Fire Rooster 澤山咸 24 十一 9
水1 Water 2 Humility 戊戌 Earth Dog 地山謙 25 十二 6	火2 Fire 3 Observation 己亥 Earth Pig 風地觀 26 十三 2	火2 Fire 4 Increasing 庚子 Metal Rat 風雷益 27 十四 9	水1 Water 5 Dimming Light 辛丑 Metal Ox 地火明夷 28 十五 3	金9 Metal 6 Fellowship 壬寅 Water Tiger 天火同人 29 十六 7	木8 Wood 7 Marrying Maiden 癸卯 Water Rabbit 雷澤歸妹 30 十七 7	木3 Wood 8 Opposition 甲辰 Wood Dragon 火澤睽 31 十八 2

JUNE 1980 壬午

Xuan Kong Element 玄空五行	巽爲風 Wind	Period Luck 卦運	Monthly Star 月星
Fire 火2		1	7

SUNDAY	MONDAY	TUESDAY	WEDNESDAY	THURSDAY	FRIDAY	SATURDAY
火7 Fire 9 Waiting 乙巳 Wood Snake 水天需 1 十九 3	金4 Metal 1 Great Exceeding 丙午 Fire Horse 澤風大過 2 二十 3	水6 Water 2 Poison 丁未 Fire Goat 山風蠱 3 廿一 7	火2 Fire 3 Dispersing 戊申 Earth Monkey 風水渙 4 廿二 6	木3 Wood 4 Travelling 己酉 Earth Rooster 火山旅 5 廿三 8	金9 Metal 5 Stagnation 庚戌 Metal Dog 天地否 6 廿四 9	火7 Fire 6 Alliance 辛亥 Metal Pig 水地比 7 廿五 7
木8 Wood 7 Thunder 壬子 Water Rat 震爲雷 8 廿六 1	水6 Water 8 Beauty 癸丑 Water Ox 山火賁 9 廿七 8	火7 Fire 9 Accomplished 甲寅 Wood Tiger 水火既濟 10 廿八 9	水1 Water 1 Arriving 乙卯 Wood Rabbit 地澤臨 11 廿九 4	金4 Metal 2 Marsh 丙辰 Fire Dragon 兌爲澤 12 三十 1	火2 Fire 3 Small Livestock 丁巳 Fire Snake 風天小畜 13 五月初一 8	木3 Wood 4 The Cauldron 戊午 Earth Horse 火風鼎 14 初二 4
水1 Water 5 Rising 己未 Earth Goat 地風升 15 初三 2	火7 Fire 6 Water 庚申 Metal Monkey 坎爲水 16 初四 1	木8 Wood 7 Lesser Exceeding 辛酉 Metal Rooster 雷山小過 17 初五 3	金4 Metal 8 Gathering 壬戌 Water Dog 澤地萃 18 初六 4	水6 Water 9 Peel 癸亥 Water Pig 山地剝 19 初七 6	水1 Water 1 Earth 甲子 Wood Rat 坤爲地 20 初八 1	木3 Wood 2/5 Biting 乙丑 Wood Ox 火雷噬嗑 21 初九 6
火2 Fire 4 Family 丙寅 Fire Tiger 風火家人 22 初十 4	水6 Water 3 Decreasing 丁卯 Fire Rabbit 山澤損 23 十一 9	金9 Metal 2 Tread 戊辰 Earth Dragon 天澤履 24 十二 6	木8 Wood 1 Great Strength 己巳 Earth Snake 雷天大壯 25 十三 2	木8 Wood 9 Consistency 庚午 Metal Horse 雷風恆 26 十四 9	金9 Metal 8 Litigation 辛未 Metal Goat 天水訟 27 十五 3	水1 Water 7 Officer 壬申 Water Monkey 地水師 28 十六 7
火2 Fire 6 Gradual Progress 癸酉 Water Rooster 風山漸 29 十七 7	火7 Fire 5 Obstruction 甲戌 Wood Dog 水山蹇 30 十八 2					

JULY 1980 癸未

Xuan Kong Element 玄空五行	澤水困 Trap	Period Luck 卦運	Monthly Star 月星
Metal 金4		8	6

SUNDAY	MONDAY	TUESDAY	WEDNESDAY	THURSDAY	FRIDAY	SATURDAY
		木3 Wood 4 Advancement 乙亥 Wood Pig 火地晉 1 十九 3	水6 Water 3 Nourish 丙子 Fire Rat 山雷頤 2 二十 3	金4 Metal 2 Following 丁丑 Fire Ox 澤雷隨 3 廿一 7	木8 Wood 1 Abundance 戊寅 Earth Tiger 雷火豐 4 廿二 6	火7 Fire 9 Regulate 己卯 Earth Rabbit 水澤節 5 廿三 8
水1 Water 8 Unity 庚辰 Metal Dragon 地天泰 6 廿四 9	木3 Wood 7 Great Reward 辛巳 Metal Snake 火天大有 7 廿五 7	火2 Fire 6 Wind 壬午 Water Horse 巽為風 8 廿六 1	金4 Metal 5 Trap 癸未 Water Goat 澤水困 9 廿七 8	木3 Wood 4 Not Yet Accomplished 甲申 Wood Monkey 火水未濟 10 廿八 9	金9 Metal 3 Retreat 乙酉 Wood Rooster 天山遯 11 廿九 4	水6 Water 2 Mountain 丙戌 Fire Dog 艮為山 12 六月初一 1
木8 Wood 1 Delight 丁亥 Fire Pig 雷地豫 13 初二 8	火7 Fire 9 Beginning 戊子 Earth Rat 水雷屯 14 初三 4	金9 Metal 8 Without Wrongdoing 己丑 Earth Ox 天雷無妄 15 初四 2	木3 Wood 7 Fire 庚寅 Metal Tiger 離為火 16 初五 1	火2 Fire 6 Sincerity 辛卯 Metal Rabbit 風澤中孚 17 初六 3	水6 Water 5 Big Livestock 壬辰 Water Dragon 山天大畜 18 初七 4	金4 Metal 4 Eliminating 癸巳 Water Snake 澤天夬 19 初八 6
金9 Metal 3 Heaven 甲午 Wood Horse 乾為天 20 初九 1	火7 Fire 2 Well 乙未 Wood Goat 水風井 21 初十 6	木8 Wood 1 Relief 丙申 Fire Monkey 雷水解 22 十一 4	金4 Metal 9 Influence 丁酉 Fire Rooster 澤山咸 23 十二 9	水1 Water 8 Humility 戊戌 Earth Dog 地山謙 24 十三 6	火2 Fire 7 Observation 己亥 Earth Pig 風地觀 25 十四 2	火2 Fire 6 Increasing 庚子 Metal Rat 風雷益 26 十五 9
水1 Water 5 Dimming Light 辛丑 Metal Ox 地火明夷 27 十六 3	金9 Metal 4 Fellowship 壬寅 Water Tiger 天火同人 28 十七 7	木8 Wood 3 Marrying Maiden 癸卯 Water Rabbit 雷澤歸妹 29 十八 7	木3 Wood 2 Opposition 甲辰 Wood Dragon 火澤睽 30 十九 2	火7 Fire 1 Waiting 乙巳 Wood Snake 水天需 31 二十 3		

AUGUST 1980 甲申

Xuan Kong Element 玄空五行	火水未濟 Not Yet Accomplished	Period Luck 卦運	Monthly Star 月星
Wood 木3		9	5

SUNDAY	MONDAY	TUESDAY	WEDNESDAY	THURSDAY	FRIDAY	SATURDAY
水6 Water 6 Nourish 丙子 Fire Rat 山雷頤 31 廿一 3					金4 Metal 9 Great Exceeding 丙午 Fire Horse 澤風大過 1 廿一 3	水6 Water 8 Poison 丁未 Fire Goat 山風蠱 2 廿二 7
火2 Fire 7 Dispersing 戊申 Earth Monkey 風水渙 3 廿三 6	木3 Wood 6 Travelling 己酉 Earth Rooster 火山旅 4 廿四 8	金9 Metal 5 Stagnation 庚戌 Metal Dog 天地否 5 廿五 9	火7 Fire 4 Alliance 辛亥 Metal Pig 水地比 6 廿六 7	木8 Wood 3 Thunder 壬子 Water Rat 震為雷 7 廿七 1	水6 Water 2 Beauty 癸丑 Water Ox 山火賁 8 廿八 8	火7 Fire 1 Accomplished 甲寅 Wood Tiger 水火既濟 9 廿九 9
水1 Water 9 Arriving 乙卯 Wood Rabbit 地澤臨 10 三十 4	金4 Metal 8 Marsh 丙辰 Fire Dragon 兌為澤 11 七月初一 1	火2 Fire 7 Small Livestock 丁巳 Fire Snake 風天小畜 12 初二 8	木3 Wood 6 The Cauldron 戊午 Earth Horse 火風鼎 13 初三 4	水1 Water 5 Rising 己未 Earth Goat 地風升 14 初四 2	火7 Fire 4 Water 庚申 Metal Monkey 坎為水 15 初五 1	木8 Wood 3 Lesser Exceeding 辛酉 Metal Rooster 雷山小過 16 初六 3
金4 Metal 2 Gathering 壬戌 Water Dog 澤地萃 17 初七 4	水6 Water 1 Peel 癸亥 Water Pig 山地剝 18 初八 6	水1 Water 9 Earth 甲子 Wood Rat 坤為地 19 初九 1	木3 Wood 8 Biting 乙丑 Wood Ox 火雷噬嗑 20 初十 6	火2 Fire 7 Family 丙寅 Fire Tiger 風火家人 21 十一 4	水6 Water 6 Decreasing 丁卯 Fire Rabbit 山澤損 22 十二 9	金9 Metal 5 Tread 戊辰 Earth Dragon 天澤履 23 十三 6
木8 Wood 4 Great Strength 己巳 Earth Snake 雷天大壯 24 十四 2	木8 Wood 3 Consistency 庚午 Metal Horse 雷風恆 25 十五 9	金9 Metal 2 Litigation 辛未 Metal Goat 天水訟 26 十六 3	水1 Water 1 Officer 壬申 Water Monkey 地水師 27 十七 7	火2 Fire 9 Gradual Progress 癸酉 Water Rooster 風山漸 28 十八 7	火7 Fire 8 Obstruction 甲戌 Wood Dog 水山蹇 29 十九 2	木3 Wood 7 Advancement 乙亥 Wood Pig 火地晉 30 二十 3

SEPTEMBER 1980 乙酉

Xuan Kong Element 玄空五行	天山遯 Retreat	Period Luck 卦運	Monthly Star 月星
Metal 金9		4	4

SUNDAY	MONDAY	TUESDAY	WEDNESDAY	THURSDAY	FRIDAY	SATURDAY
	金4 Metal 5 丁丑 Fire Ox Following 澤雷隨 1 廿二 7	木8 Wood 4 戊寅 Earth Tiger Abundance 雷火豐 2 廿三 6	火7 Fire 3 己卯 Earth Rabbit Regulate 水澤節 3 廿四 8	水1 Water 2 庚辰 Metal Dragon Unity 地天泰 4 廿五 9	木3 Wood 1 辛巳 Metal Snake Great Reward 火天大有 5 廿六 7	火2 Fire 9 壬午 Water Horse Wind 巽爲風 6 廿七 1
金4 Metal 8 癸未 Water Goat Trap 澤水困 7 廿八 8	木3 Wood 7 甲申 Wood Monkey Not Yet Accomplished 火水未濟 8 廿九 9	金9 Metal 6 乙酉 Wood Rooster Retreat 天山遯 9 八月初一 4	水6 Water 5 丙戌 Fire Dog Mountain 艮爲山 10 初二 1	木8 Wood 4 丁亥 Fire Pig Delight 雷地豫 11 初三 8	火7 Fire 3 戊子 Earth Rat Beginning 水雷屯 12 初四 4	金9 Metal 2 己丑 Earth Ox Without Wrongdoing 天雷無妄 13 初五 2
木3 Wood 1 庚寅 Metal Tiger Fire 離爲火 14 初六 1	火2 Fire 9 辛卯 Metal Rabbit Sincerity 風澤中孚 15 初七 3	水6 Water 8 壬辰 Water Dragon Big Livestock 山天大畜 16 初八 4	金4 Metal 7 癸巳 Water Snake Eliminating 澤天夬 17 初九 6	金9 Metal 6 甲午 Wood Horse Heaven 乾爲天 18 初十 1	火7 Fire 5 乙未 Wood Goat Well 水風井 19 十一 6	木8 Wood 4 丙申 Fire Monkey Relief 雷水解 20 十二 4
金4 Metal 3 丁酉 Fire Rooster Influence 澤山咸 21 十三 9	水1 Water 2 戊戌 Earth Dog Humility 地山謙 22 十四 6	火2 Fire 1 己亥 Earth Pig Observation 風地觀 23 十五 2	火2 Fire 9 庚子 Metal Rat Increasing 風雷益 24 十六 9	水1 Water 8 辛丑 Metal Ox Dimming Light 地火明夷 25 十七 3	金9 Metal 7 壬寅 Water Tiger Fellowship 天火同人 26 十八 7	木8 Wood 6 癸卯 Water Rabbit Marrying Maiden 雷澤歸妹 27 十九 7
木3 Wood 5 甲辰 Wood Dragon Opposition 火澤睽 28 二十 2	火7 Fire 4 乙巳 Wood Snake Waiting 水天需 29 廿一 3	金4 Metal 3 丙午 Fire Horse Great Exceeding 澤風大過 30 廿二 3				

OCTOBER 1980 丙戌

Xuan Kong Element 玄空五行	艮爲山 Mountain	Period Luck 卦運	Monthly Star 月星
Water 水6		1	3

SUNDAY	MONDAY	TUESDAY	WEDNESDAY	THURSDAY	FRIDAY	SATURDAY
			水6 Water 2 丁未 Fire Goat Poison 山風蠱 1 廿三 7	火2 Fire 1 戊申 Earth Monkey Dispersing 風水渙 2 廿四 6	木3 Wood 9 己酉 Earth Rooster Travelling 火山旅 3 廿五 8	金9 Metal 8 庚戌 Metal Dog Stagnation 天地否 4 廿六 9
火7 Fire 7 辛亥 Metal Pig Alliance 水地比 5 廿七 7	木8 Wood 6 壬子 Water Rat Thunder 震爲雷 6 廿八 1	水6 Water 5 癸丑 Water Ox Beauty 山火賁 7 廿九 8	火7 Fire 4 甲寅 Wood Tiger Accomplished 水火既濟 8 三十 9	水1 Water 3 乙卯 Wood Rabbit Arriving 地澤臨 9 九月初一 4	金4 Metal 2 丙辰 Fire Dragon Marsh 兑爲澤 10 初二 1	火2 Fire 1 丁巳 Fire Snake Small Livestock 風天小畜 11 初三 8
木3 Wood 9 戊午 Earth Horse The Cauldron 火風鼎 12 初四 4	水1 Water 8 己未 Earth Goat Rising 地風升 13 初五 2	火7 Fire 7 庚申 Metal Monkey Water 坎爲水 14 初六 1	木8 Wood 6 辛酉 Metal Rooster Lesser Exceeding 雷山小過 15 初七 3	金4 Metal 5 壬戌 Water Dog Gathering 澤地萃 16 初八 4	水6 Water 4 癸亥 Water Pig Peel 山地剝 17 初九 6	水1 Water 3 甲子 Wood Rat Earth 坤爲地 18 初十 1
木3 Wood 2 乙丑 Wood Ox Biting 火雷噬嗑 19 十一 6	火2 Fire 1 丙寅 Fire Tiger Family 風火家人 20 十二 4	水6 Water 9 丁卯 Fire Rabbit Decreasing 山澤損 21 十三 9	金9 Metal 8 戊辰 Earth Dragon Tread 天澤履 22 十四 6	木8 Wood 7 己巳 Earth Snake Great Strength 雷天大壯 23 十五 2	木8 Wood 6 庚午 Metal Horse Consistency 雷風恒 24 十六 9	金9 Metal 5 辛未 Metal Goat Litigation 天水訟 25 十七 3
水1 Water 4 壬申 Water Monkey Officer 地水師 26 十八 7	火2 Fire 3 癸酉 Water Rooster Gradual Progress 風山漸 27 十九 7	火7 Fire 2 甲戌 Wood Dog Obstruction 水山蹇 28 二十 2	木3 Wood 1 乙亥 Wood Pig Advancement 火地晉 29 廿一 3	水6 Water 9 丙子 Fire Rat Nourish 山雷頤 30 廿二 3	金4 Metal 8 丁丑 Fire Ox Following 澤雷隨 31 廿三 7	

NOVEMBER 1980 丁亥

Xuan Kong Element 玄空五行	雷地豫 Delight	Period Luck 卦運	Monthly Star 月星
Wood 木8		8	2

SUNDAY	MONDAY	TUESDAY	WEDNESDAY	THURSDAY	FRIDAY	SATURDAY
水6 Water 5 Poison 山風蠱 丁未 Fire Goat 30 廿三 7						木8 Wood 7 Abundance 雷火豐 戊寅 Earth Tiger 1 廿四 6
火7 Fire 6 Regulate 水澤節 己卯 Earth Rabbit 2 廿五 8	水1 Water 5 Unity 地天泰 庚辰 Metal Dragon 3 廿六 9	木3 Wood 4 Great Reward 火天大有 辛巳 Metal Snake 4 廿七 7	火2 Fire 3 Wind 巽爲風 壬午 Water Horse 5 廿八 1	金4 Metal 2 Trap 澤水困 癸未 Water Goat 6 廿九 8	木3 Wood 1 Not Yet Accomplished 火水未濟 甲申 Wood Monkey 7 三十 9	金9 Metal 9 Retreat 天山遯 乙酉 Wood Rooster 8 十月初一 4
水6 Water 8 Mountain 艮爲山 丙戌 Fire Dog 9 初二 1	木8 Wood 7 Delight 雷地豫 丁亥 Fire Pig 10 初三 8	火7 Fire 6 Beginning 水雷屯 戊子 Earth Rat 11 初四 4	金9 Metal 5 Without Wrongdoing 天雷無妄 己丑 Earth Ox 12 初五 2	木3 Wood 4 Fire 離爲火 庚寅 Metal Tiger 13 初六 1	火2 Fire 3 Sincerity 風澤中孚 辛卯 Metal Rabbit 14 初七 3	水6 Water 2 Big Livestock 山天大畜 壬辰 Water Dragon 15 初八 4
金4 Metal 1 Eliminating 澤天夬 癸巳 Water Snake 16 初九 6	金9 Metal 9 Heaven 乾爲天 甲午 Wood Horse 17 初十 1	火7 Fire 8 Well 水風井 乙未 Wood Goat 18 十一 6	木8 Wood 7 Relief 雷水解 丙申 Fire Monkey 19 十二 4	金4 Metal 6 Influence 澤山咸 丁酉 Fire Rooster 20 十三 9	水1 Water 5 Humility 地山謙 戊戌 Earth Dog 21 十四 6	火2 Fire 4 Observation 風地觀 己亥 Earth Pig 22 十五 2
火2 Fire 3 Increasing 風雷益 庚子 Metal Rat 23 十六 9	水1 Water 2 Dimming Light 地火明夷 辛丑 Metal Ox 24 十七 3	金9 Metal 1 Fellowship 天火同人 壬寅 Water Tiger 25 十八 7	木8 Wood 9 Marrying Maiden 雷澤歸妹 癸卯 Water Rabbit 26 十九 7	木3 Wood 8 Opposition 火澤睽 甲辰 Wood Dragon 27 二十 2	火7 Fire 7 Waiting 水天需 乙巳 Wood Snake 28 廿一 3	金4 Metal 6 Great Exceeding 澤風大過 丙午 Fire Horse 29 廿二 3

DECEMBER 1980 戊子

Xuan Kong Element 玄空五行	水雷屯 Beginning	Period Luck 卦運	Monthly Star 月星
Fire 火7		4	1

SUNDAY	MONDAY	TUESDAY	WEDNESDAY	THURSDAY	FRIDAY	SATURDAY
	火2 Fire 4 Dispersing 風水渙 戊申 Earth Monkey 1 廿四 6	木3 Wood 3 Travelling 火山旅 己酉 Earth Rooster 2 廿五 8	金9 Metal 2 Stagnation 天地否 庚戌 Metal Dog 3 廿六 9	火7 Fire 1 Alliance 水地比 辛亥 Metal Pig 4 廿七 7	木8 Wood 9 Thunder 震爲雷 壬子 Water Rat 5 廿八 1	水6 Water 8 Beauty 山火賁 癸丑 Water Ox 6 廿九 8
火7 Fire 7 Accomplished 水火既濟 甲寅 Wood Tiger 7 十一月初一 9	水1 Water 6 Arriving 地澤臨 乙卯 Wood Rabbit 8 初二 4	金4 Metal 5 Marsh 兌爲澤 丙辰 Fire Dragon 9 初三 1	火2 Fire 4 Small Livestock 風天小畜 丁巳 Fire Snake 10 初四 8	木3 Wood 3 The Cauldron 火風鼎 戊午 Earth Horse 11 初五 4	水1 Water 2 Rising 地風升 己未 Earth Goat 12 初六 2	火7 Fire 1 Water 坎爲水 庚申 Metal Monkey 13 初七 1
木8 Wood 9 Lesser Exceeding 雷山小過 辛酉 Metal Rooster 14 初八 3	金4 Metal 8 Gathering 澤地萃 壬戌 Water Dog 15 初九 4	水6 Water 7 Peel 山地剝 癸亥 Water Pig 16 初十 6	水1 Water 6 Earth 坤爲地 甲子 Wood Rat 17 十一 1	木3 Wood 5 Biting 火雷噬嗑 乙丑 Wood Ox 18 十二 6	火2 Fire 4 Family 風火家人 丙寅 Fire Tiger 19 十三 4	水6 Water 3 Decreasing 山澤損 丁卯 Fire Rabbit 20 十四 9
金9 Metal 2 Tread 天澤履 戊辰 Earth Dragon 21 十五 6	木8 Wood 1/9 Great Strength 雷天大壯 己巳 Earth Snake 22 十六 2	木8 Wood 1 Consistency 雷風恒 庚午 Metal Horse 23 十七 9	金9 Metal 2 Litigation 天水訟 辛未 Metal Goat 24 十八 3	水1 Water 3 Officer 地水師 壬申 Water Monkey 25 十九 7	火2 Fire 4 Gradual Progress 風山漸 癸酉 Water Rooster 26 二十 7	火7 Fire 5 Obstruction 水山蹇 甲戌 Wood Dog 27 廿一 2
木3 Wood 6 Advancement 火地晉 乙亥 Wood Pig 28 廿二 3	水6 Water 7 Nourish 山雷頤 丙子 Fire Rat 29 廿三 3	金4 Metal 8 Following 澤雷隨 丁丑 Fire Ox 30 廿四 7	木8 Wood 9 Abundance 雷火豐 戊寅 Earth Tiger 31 廿五 6			

1981 辛酉

(*Xin You*) Metal Rooster

1981 辛酉 *(Xin You)* Metal Rooster

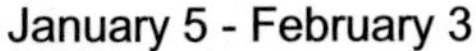

January 5 - February 3

February 4 - March 5

March 6 - April 4

April 5 - May 4

May 5 - June 5

June 6 - July 6

July 7 - August 6

August 7 - September 7

September 8 - October 7

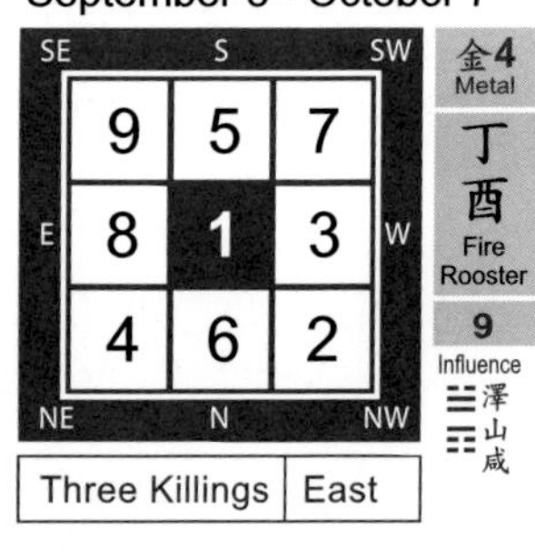

October 8 - November 6

November 7 - December 6

December 7 - January 5

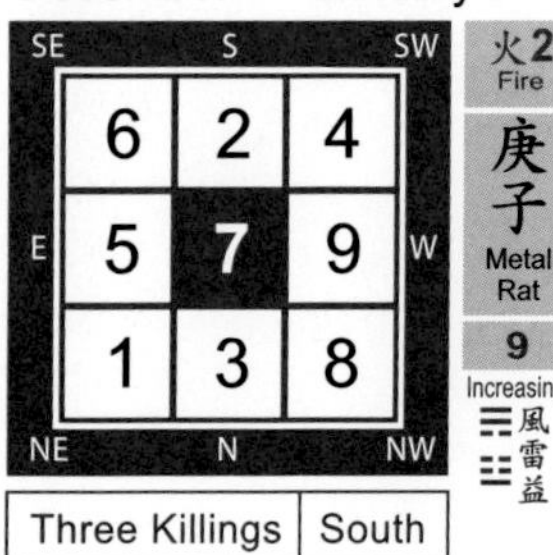

JANUARY 1981 己丑

Xuan Kong Element 玄空五行	天雷無妄 Without Wrongdoing	Period Luck 卦運	Monthly Star 月星
Metal 金9		2	9

SUNDAY	MONDAY	TUESDAY	WEDNESDAY	THURSDAY	FRIDAY	SATURDAY
				火7 Fire · 1 Regulate 己卯 Earth Rabbit 水澤節 **1** 廿六 8	水1 Water · 2 Unity 庚辰 Metal Dragon 地天泰 **2** 廿七 9	木3 Wood · 3 Great Reward 辛巳 Metal Snake 火天大有 **3** 廿八 7
火2 Fire · 4 Wind 壬午 Water Horse 巽爲風 **4** 廿九 1	金4 Metal · 5 Trap 癸未 Water Goat 澤水困 **5** 三十 8	木3 Wood · 6 Not Yet Accomplished 甲申 Wood Monkey 火水未濟 **6** 十二月初一 9	金9 Metal · 7 Retreat 乙酉 Wood Rooster 天山遯 **7** 初二 4	水6 Water · 8 Mountain 丙戌 Fire Dog 艮爲山 **8** 初三 1	木8 Wood · 9 Delight 丁亥 Fire Pig 雷地豫 **9** 初四 8	火7 Fire · 1 Beginning 戊子 Earth Rat 水雷屯 **10** 初五 4
金9 Metal · 2 Without Wrongdoing 己丑 Earth Ox 天雷無妄 **11** 初六 2	木3 Wood · 3 Fire 庚寅 Metal Tiger 離爲火 **12** 初七 1	火2 Fire · 4 Sincerity 辛卯 Metal Rabbit 風澤中孚 **13** 初八 3	水6 Water · 5 Big Livestock 壬辰 Water Dragon 山天大畜 **14** 初九 4	金4 Metal · 6 Eliminating 癸巳 Water Snake 澤天夬 **15** 初十 6	金9 Metal · 7 Heaven 甲午 Wood Horse 乾爲天 **16** 十一 1	火7 Fire · 8 Well 乙未 Wood Goat 水風井 **17** 十二 6
木8 Wood · 9 Relief 丙申 Fire Monkey 雷水解 **18** 十三 4	金4 Metal · 1 Influence 丁酉 Fire Rooster 澤山咸 **19** 十四 9	水1 Water · 2 Humility 戊戌 Earth Dog 地山謙 **20** 十五 6	火2 Fire · 3 Observation 己亥 Earth Pig 風地觀 **21** 十六 2	火2 Fire · 4 Increasing 庚子 Metal Rat 風雷益 **22** 十七 9	水1 Water · 5 Dimming Light 辛丑 Metal Ox 地火明夷 **23** 十八 3	金9 Metal · 6 Fellowship 壬寅 Water Tiger 天火同人 **24** 十九 7
木8 Wood · 7 Marrying Maiden 癸卯 Water Rabbit 雷澤歸妹 **25** 二十 7	木3 Wood · 8 Opposition 甲辰 Wood Dragon 火澤睽 **26** 廿一 2	火7 Fire · 9 Waiting 乙巳 Wood Snake 水天需 **27** 廿二 3	金4 Metal · 1 Great Exceeding 丙午 Fire Horse 澤風大過 **28** 廿三 3	水6 Water · 2 Poison 丁未 Fire Goat 山風蠱 **29** 廿四 7	火2 Fire · 3 Dispersing 戊申 Earth Monkey 風水渙 **30** 廿五 6	木3 Wood · 4 Travelling 己酉 Earth Rooster 火山旅 **31** 廿六 8

FEBRUARY 1981 庚寅

Xuan Kong Element 玄空五行	離爲火 Fire	Period Luck 卦運	Monthly Star 月星
Wood 木3		1	8

SUNDAY	MONDAY	TUESDAY	WEDNESDAY	THURSDAY	FRIDAY	SATURDAY
金9 Metal · 5 Stagnation 庚戌 Metal Dog 天地否 **1** 廿七 9	火7 Fire · 6 Alliance 辛亥 Metal Pig 水地比 **2** 廿八 7	木8 Wood · 7 Thunder 壬子 Water Rat 震爲雷 **3** 廿九 1	水6 Water · 8 Beauty 癸丑 Water Ox 山火賁 **4** 三十 8	火7 Fire · 9 Accomplished 甲寅 Wood Tiger 水火既濟 **5** 正月初一 9	水1 Water · 1 Arriving 乙卯 Wood Rabbit 地澤臨 **6** 初二 4	金4 Metal · 2 Marsh 丙辰 Fire Dragon 兌爲澤 **7** 初三 1
火2 Fire · 3 Small Livestock 丁巳 Fire Snake 風天小畜 **8** 初四 8	木3 Wood · 4 The Cauldron 戊午 Earth Horse 火風鼎 **9** 初五 4	水1 Water · 5 Rising 己未 Earth Goat 地風升 **10** 初六 2	火7 Fire · 6 Water 庚申 Metal Monkey 坎爲水 **11** 初七 1	木8 Wood · 7 Lesser Exceeding 辛酉 Metal Rooster 雷山小過 **12** 初八 3	金4 Metal · 8 Gathering 壬戌 Water Dog 澤地萃 **13** 初九 4	水6 Water · 9 Peel 癸亥 Water Pig 山地剝 **14** 初十 6
水1 Water · 1 Earth 甲子 Wood Rat 坤爲地 **15** 十一 1	木3 Wood · 2 Biting 乙丑 Wood Ox 火雷噬嗑 **16** 十二 6	火2 Fire · 3 Family 丙寅 Fire Tiger 風火家人 **17** 十三 4	水6 Water · 4 Decreasing 丁卯 Fire Rabbit 山澤損 **18** 十四 9	金9 Metal · 5 Tread 戊辰 Earth Dragon 天澤履 **19** 十五 6	木8 Wood · 6 Great Strength 己巳 Earth Snake 雷天大壯 **20** 十六 2	木8 Wood · 7 Consistency 庚午 Metal Horse 雷風恒 **21** 十七 9
金9 Metal · 8 Litigation 辛未 Metal Goat 天水訟 **22** 十八 3	水1 Water · 9 Officer 壬申 Water Monkey 地水師 **23** 十九 7	火2 Fire · 1 Gradual Progress 癸酉 Water Rooster 風山漸 **24** 二十 7	火7 Fire · 2 Obstruction 甲戌 Wood Dog 水山蹇 **25** 廿一 2	木3 Wood · 3 Advancement 乙亥 Wood Pig 火地晉 **26** 廿二 3	水6 Water · 4 Nourish 丙子 Fire Rat 山雷頤 **27** 廿三 3	金4 Metal · 5 Following 丁丑 Fire Ox 澤雷隨 **28** 廿四 7

MARCH 1981 辛卯

Xuan Kong Element 玄空五行	風澤中孚 Sincerity	Period Luck 卦運	Monthly Star 月星
Fire 火2		3	7

SUNDAY	MONDAY	TUESDAY	WEDNESDAY	THURSDAY	FRIDAY	SATURDAY
木8 Wood 6 Abundance 雷火豐 戊寅 Earth Tiger 1 廿五 6	火7 Fire 7 Regulate 水澤節 己卯 Earth Rabbit 2 廿六 8	水1 Water 8 Unity 地天泰 庚辰 Metal Dragon 3 廿七 9	木3 Wood 9 Great Reward 火天大有 辛巳 Metal Snake 4 廿八 7	火2 Fire 1 Wind 巽為風 壬午 Water Horse 5 廿九 1	金4 Metal 2 Trap 澤水困 癸未 Water Goat 6 二月初一 8	木3 Wood 3 Not Yet Accomplished 火水未濟 甲申 Wood Monkey 7 初二 9
金9 Metal 4 Retreat 天山遯 乙酉 Wood Rooster 8 初三 4	水6 Water 5 Mountain 艮為山 丙戌 Fire Dog 9 初四 1	木8 Wood 6 Delight 雷地豫 丁亥 Fire Pig 10 初五 8	火7 Fire 7 Beginning 水雷屯 戊子 Earth Rat 11 初六 4	金9 Metal 8 Without Wrongdoing 天雷無妄 己丑 Earth Ox 12 初七 2	木3 Wood 9 Fire 離為火 庚寅 Metal Tiger 13 初八 1	火2 Fire 1 Sincerity 風澤中孚 辛卯 Metal Rabbit 14 初九 3
水6 Water 2 Big Livestock 山天大畜 壬辰 Water Dragon 15 初十 4	金4 Metal 3 Eliminating 澤天夬 癸巳 Water Snake 16 十一 6	金9 Metal 4 Heaven 乾為天 甲午 Wood Horse 17 十二 1	火7 Fire 5 Well 水風井 乙未 Wood Goat 18 十三 6	木8 Wood 6 Relief 雷水解 丙申 Fire Monkey 19 十四 4	金4 Metal 7 Influence 澤山咸 丁酉 Fire Rooster 20 十五 9	水1 Water 8 Humility 地山謙 戊戌 Earth Dog 21 十六 6
火2 Fire 9 Observation 風地觀 己亥 Earth Pig 22 十七 2	火2 Fire 1 Increasing 風雷益 庚子 Metal Rat 23 十八 9	水1 Water 2 Dimming Light 地火明夷 辛丑 Metal Ox 24 十九 3	金9 Metal 3 Fellowship 天火同人 壬寅 Water Tiger 25 二十 7	木8 Wood 4 Marrying Maiden 雷澤歸妹 癸卯 Water Rabbit 26 廿一 7	木3 Wood 5 Opposition 火澤睽 甲辰 Wood Dragon 27 廿二 2	火7 Fire 6 Waiting 水天需 乙巳 Wood Snake 28 廿三 3
金4 Metal 7 Great Exceeding 澤風大過 丙午 Fire Horse 29 廿四 3	水6 Water 8 Poison 山風蠱 丁未 Fire Goat 30 廿五 7	火2 Fire 9 Dispersing 風水渙 戊申 Earth Monkey 31 廿六 6				

APRIL 1981 壬辰

Xuan Kong Element 玄空五行	山天大畜 Big Livestock	Period Luck 卦運	Monthly Star 月星
Water 水6		4	6

SUNDAY	MONDAY	TUESDAY	WEDNESDAY	THURSDAY	FRIDAY	SATURDAY
			木3 Wood 1 Travelling 火山旅 己酉 Earth Rooster 1 廿七 8	金9 Metal 2 Stagnation 天地否 庚戌 Metal Dog 2 廿八 9	火7 Fire 3 Alliance 水地比 辛亥 Metal Pig 3 廿九 7	木8 Wood 4 Thunder 震為雷 壬子 Water Rat 4 三十 1
水6 Water 5 Beauty 山火賁 癸丑 Water Ox 5 三月初一 8	火7 Fire 6 Accomplished 水火既濟 甲寅 Wood Tiger 6 初二 9	水1 Water 7 Arriving 地澤臨 乙卯 Wood Rabbit 7 初三 4	金4 Metal 8 Marsh 兌為澤 丙辰 Fire Dragon 8 初四 1	火2 Fire 9 Small Livestock 風天小畜 丁巳 Fire Snake 9 初五 8	木3 Wood 1 The Cauldron 火風鼎 戊午 Earth Horse 10 初六 4	水1 Water 2 Rising 地風升 己未 Earth Goat 11 初七 2
火7 Fire 3 Water 坎為水 庚申 Metal Monkey 12 初八 1	木8 Wood 4 Lesser Exceeding 雷山小過 辛酉 Metal Rooster 13 初九 3	金4 Metal 5 Gathering 澤地萃 壬戌 Water Dog 14 初十 4	水6 Water 6 Peel 山地剝 癸亥 Water Pig 15 十一 6	水1 Water 7 Earth 坤為地 甲子 Wood Rat 16 十二 1	木3 Wood 8 Biting 火雷噬嗑 乙丑 Wood Ox 17 十三 6	火2 Fire 9 Family 風火家人 丙寅 Fire Tiger 18 十四 4
水6 Water 1 Decreasing 山澤損 丁卯 Fire Rabbit 19 十五 9	金9 Metal 2 Tread 天澤履 戊辰 Earth Dragon 20 十六 6	木8 Wood 3 Great Strength 雷天大壯 己巳 Earth Snake 21 十七 2	木8 Wood 4 Consistency 雷風恆 庚午 Metal Horse 22 十八 9	金9 Metal 5 Litigation 天水訟 辛未 Metal Goat 23 十九 3	水1 Water 6 Officer 地水師 壬申 Water Monkey 24 二十 7	火2 Fire 7 Gradual Progress 風山漸 癸酉 Water Rooster 25 廿一 7
火7 Fire 8 Obstruction 水山蹇 甲戌 Wood Dog 26 廿二 2	木3 Wood 9 Advancement 火地晉 乙亥 Wood Pig 27 廿三 3	水6 Water 1 Nourish 山雷頤 丙子 Fire Rat 28 廿四 3	金4 Metal 2 Following 澤雷隨 丁丑 Fire Ox 29 廿五 7	木8 Wood 3 Abundance 雷火豐 戊寅 Earth Tiger 30 廿六 6		

MAY 1981 癸巳

Xuan Kong Element 玄空五行	澤天夬 Eliminating	Period Luck 卦運	Monthly Star 月星
Metal 金4		6	5

SUNDAY	MONDAY	TUESDAY	WEDNESDAY	THURSDAY	FRIDAY	SATURDAY
木3 Wood 7 Travelling 火山旅 己酉 Earth Rooster 8 31 廿八					火7 Fire 4 Regulate 水澤節 己卯 Earth Rabbit 8 1 廿七	水1 Water 5 Unity 地天泰 庚辰 Metal Dragon 9 2 廿八
木3 Wood 6 Great Reward 火天大有 辛巳 Metal Snake 7 3 廿九	火2 Fire 7 Wind 巽爲風 壬午 Water Horse 1 4 四月初一	金4 Metal 8 Trap 澤水困 癸未 Water Goat 8 5 初二	木3 Wood 9 Not Yet Accomplished 火水未濟 甲申 Wood Monkey 9 6 初三	金9 Metal 1 Retreat 天山遯 乙酉 Wood Rooster 4 7 初四	水6 Water 2 Mountain 艮爲山 丙戌 Fire Dog 1 8 初五	木8 Wood 3 Delight 雷地豫 丁亥 Fire Pig 8 9 初六
火7 Fire 4 Beginning 水雷屯 戊子 Earth Rat 4 10 初七	金9 Metal 5 Without Wrongdoing 天雷無妄 己丑 Earth Ox 2 11 初八	木3 Wood 6 Fire 離爲火 庚寅 Metal Tiger 1 12 初九	火2 Fire 7 Sincerity 風澤中孚 辛卯 Metal Rabbit 3 13 初十	水6 Water 8 Big Livestock 山天大畜 壬辰 Water Dragon 4 14 十一	金4 Metal 9 Eliminating 澤天夬 癸巳 Water Snake 6 15 十二	金9 Metal 1 Heaven 乾爲天 甲午 Wood Horse 1 16 十三
火7 Fire 2 Well 水風井 乙未 Wood Goat 6 17 十四	木8 Wood 3 Relief 雷水解 丙申 Fire Monkey 4 18 十五	金4 Metal 4 Influence 澤山咸 丁酉 Fire Rooster 9 19 十六	水1 Water 5 Humility 地山謙 戊戌 Earth Dog 6 20 十七	火2 Fire 6 Observation 風地觀 己亥 Earth Pig 2 21 十八	火2 Fire 7 Increasing 風雷益 庚子 Metal Rat 9 22 十九	水1 Water 8 Dimming Light 地火明夷 辛丑 Metal Ox 3 23 二十
金9 Metal 9 Fellowship 天火同人 壬寅 Water Tiger 7 24 廿一	木8 Wood 1 Marrying Maiden 雷澤歸妹 癸卯 Water Rabbit 7 25 廿二	木3 Wood 2 Opposition 火澤睽 甲辰 Wood Dragon 2 26 廿三	火7 Fire 3 Waiting 水天需 乙巳 Wood Snake 3 27 廿四	金4 Metal 4 Great Exceeding 澤風大過 丙午 Fire Horse 3 28 廿五	水6 Water 5 Poison 山風蠱 丁未 Fire Goat 7 29 廿六	火2 Fire 6 Dispersing 風水渙 戊申 Earth Monkey 6 30 廿七

JUNE 1981 甲午

Xuan Kong Element 玄空五行	乾爲天 Heaven	Period Luck 卦運	Monthly Star 月星
Metal 金9		1	4

SUNDAY	MONDAY	TUESDAY	WEDNESDAY	THURSDAY	FRIDAY	SATURDAY
	金9 Metal 8 Stagnation 天地否 庚戌 Metal Dog 9 1 廿九	火7 Fire 9 Alliance 水地比 辛亥 Metal Pig 7 2 五月初一	木8 Wood 1 Thunder 震爲雷 壬子 Water Rat 1 3 初二	水6 Water 2 Beauty 山火賁 癸丑 Water Ox 8 4 初三	火7 Fire 3 Accomplished 水火既濟 甲寅 Wood Tiger 9 5 初四	水1 Water 4 Arriving 地澤臨 乙卯 Wood Rabbit 4 6 初五
金4 Metal 5 Marsh 兑爲澤 丙辰 Fire Dragon 1 7 初六	火2 Fire 6 Small Livestock 風天小畜 丁巳 Fire Snake 8 8 初七	木3 Wood 7 The Cauldron 火風鼎 戊午 Earth Horse 4 9 初八	水1 Water 8 Rising 地風升 己未 Earth Goat 2 10 初九	火7 Fire 9 Water 坎爲水 庚申 Metal Monkey 1 11 初十	木8 Wood 1 Lesser Exceeding 雷山小過 辛酉 Metal Rooster 3 12 十一	金4 Metal 2 Gathering 澤地萃 壬戌 Water Dog 4 13 十二
水6 Water 3 Peel 山地剝 癸亥 Water Pig 6 14 十三	水1 Water 4 Earth 坤爲地 甲子 Wood Rat 1 15 十四	木3 Wood 5 Biting 火雷噬嗑 乙丑 Wood Ox 6 16 十五	火2 Fire 6 Family 風火家人 丙寅 Fire Tiger 4 17 十六	水6 Water 7 Decreasing 山澤損 丁卯 Fire Rabbit 9 18 十七	金9 Metal 8 Tread 天澤履 戊辰 Earth Dragon 6 19 十八	木8 Wood 9 Great Strength 雷天大壯 己巳 Earth Snake 2 20 十九
木8 Wood 1/9 Consistency 雷風恒 庚午 Metal Horse 9 21 二十	金9 Metal 8 Litigation 天水訟 辛未 Metal Goat 3 22 廿一	水1 Water 7 Officer 地水師 壬申 Water Monkey 7 23 廿二	火2 Fire 6 Gradual Progress 風山漸 癸酉 Water Rooster 7 24 廿三	火7 Fire 5 Obstruction 水山蹇 甲戌 Wood Dog 2 25 廿四	木3 Wood 4 Advancement 火地晉 乙亥 Wood Pig 3 26 廿五	水6 Water 3 Nourish 山雷頤 丙子 Fire Rat 3 27 廿六
金4 Metal 2 Following 澤雷隨 丁丑 Fire Ox 7 28 廿七	木8 Wood 1 Abundance 雷火豐 戊寅 Earth Tiger 6 29 廿八	火7 Fire 9 Regulate 水澤節 己卯 Earth Rabbit 8 30 廿九				

JULY 1981 乙未

Xuan Kong Element 玄空五行	水風井 Well	Period Luck 卦運	Monthly Star 月星
Fire 火7		6	3

SUNDAY	MONDAY	TUESDAY	WEDNESDAY	THURSDAY	FRIDAY	SATURDAY
			水1 Water Unity 8 庚辰 Metal Dragon 地天泰 1 三十 9	木3 Wood Great Reward 7 辛巳 Metal Snake 火天大有 2 六月初一 7	火2 Fire Wind 6 壬午 Water Horse 巽爲風 3 初二 1	金4 Metal Trap 5 癸未 Water Goat 澤水困 4 初三 8
木3 Wood Not Yet Accomplished 4 甲申 Wood Monkey 火水未濟 5 初四 9	金9 Metal Retreat 3 乙酉 Wood Rooster 天山遯 6 初五 4	水6 Water Mountain 2 丙戌 Fire Dog 艮爲山 7 初六 1	木8 Wood Delight 1 丁亥 Fire Pig 雷地豫 8 初七 8	火7 Fire Beginning 9 戊子 Earth Rat 水雷屯 9 初八 4	金9 Metal Without Wrongdoing 8 己丑 Earth Ox 天雷無妄 10 初九 2	木3 Wood Fire 7 庚寅 Metal Tiger 離爲火 11 初十 1
火2 Fire Sincerity 6 辛卯 Metal Rabbit 風澤中孚 12 十一 3	水6 Water Big Livestock 5 壬辰 Water Dragon 山天大畜 13 十二 4	金4 Metal Eliminating 4 癸巳 Water Snake 澤天夬 14 十三 6	金9 Metal Heaven 3 甲午 Wood Horse 乾爲天 15 十四 1	火7 Fire Well 2 乙未 Wood Goat 水風井 16 十五 6	木8 Wood Relief 1 丙申 Fire Monkey 雷水解 17 十六 4	金4 Metal Influence 9 丁酉 Fire Rooster 澤山咸 18 十七 9
水1 Water Humility 8 戊戌 Earth Dog 地山謙 19 十八 6	火2 Fire Observation 7 己亥 Earth Pig 風地觀 20 十九 2	火2 Fire Increasing 6 庚子 Metal Rat 風雷益 21 二十 9	水1 Water Dimming Light 5 辛丑 Metal Ox 地火明夷 22 廿一 3	金9 Metal Fellowship 4 壬寅 Water Tiger 天火同人 23 廿二 7	木8 Wood Marrying Maiden 3 癸卯 Water Rabbit 雷澤歸妹 24 廿三 7	木3 Wood Opposition 2 甲辰 Wood Dragon 火澤睽 25 廿四 2
火7 Fire Waiting 1 乙巳 Wood Snake 水天需 26 廿五 3	金4 Metal Great Exceeding 9 丙午 Fire Horse 澤風大過 27 廿六 3	水6 Water Poison 8 丁未 Fire Goat 山風蠱 28 廿七 7	火2 Fire Dispersing 7 戊申 Earth Monkey 風水渙 29 廿八 6	木3 Wood Travelling 6 己酉 Earth Rooster 火山旅 30 廿九 8	金9 Metal Stagnation 5 庚戌 Metal Dog 天地否 31 七月初一 9	

AUGUST 1981 丙申

Xuan Kong Element 玄空五行	雷水解 Relief	Period Luck 卦運	Monthly Star 月星
Wood 木8		4	2

SUNDAY	MONDAY	TUESDAY	WEDNESDAY	THURSDAY	FRIDAY	SATURDAY
水1 Water Unity 2 庚辰 Metal Dragon 地天泰 30 初二 9	木3 Wood Great Reward 1 辛巳 Metal Snake 火天大有 31 初三 7					火7 Fire Alliance 4 辛亥 Metal Pig 水地比 1 初二 7
木8 Wood Thunder 3 壬子 Water Rat 震爲雷 2 初三 1	水6 Water Beauty 2 癸丑 Water Ox 山火賁 3 初四 8	火7 Fire Accomplished 1 甲寅 Wood Tiger 水火既濟 4 初五 9	水1 Water Arriving 9 乙卯 Wood Rabbit 地澤臨 5 初六 4	金4 Metal Marsh 8 丙辰 Fire Dragon 兑爲澤 6 初七 1	火2 Fire Small Livestock 7 丁巳 Fire Snake 風天小畜 7 初八 8	木3 Wood The Cauldron 6 戊午 Earth Horse 火風鼎 8 初九 4
水1 Water Rising 5 己未 Earth Goat 地風升 9 初十 2	火7 Fire Water 4 庚申 Metal Monkey 坎爲水 10 十一 1	木8 Wood Lesser Exceeding 3 辛酉 Metal Rooster 雷山小過 11 十二 3	金4 Metal Gathering 2 壬戌 Water Dog 澤地萃 12 十三 4	水6 Water Peel 1 癸亥 Water Pig 山地剝 13 十四 6	水1 Water Earth 9 甲子 Wood Rat 坤爲地 14 十五 1	木3 Wood Biting 8 乙丑 Wood Ox 火雷噬嗑 15 十六 6
火2 Fire Family 7 丙寅 Fire Tiger 風火家人 16 十七 4	水6 Water Decreasing 6 丁卯 Fire Rabbit 山澤損 17 十八 9	金9 Metal Tread 5 戊辰 Earth Dragon 天澤履 18 十九 6	木8 Wood Great Strength 4 己巳 Earth Snake 雷天大壯 19 二十 2	木8 Wood Consistency 3 庚午 Metal Horse 雷風恆 20 廿一 9	金9 Metal Litigation 2 辛未 Metal Goat 天水訟 21 廿二 3	水1 Water Officer 1 壬申 Water Monkey 地水師 22 廿三 7
火2 Fire Gradual Progress 9 癸酉 Water Rooster 風山漸 23 廿四 7	火7 Fire Obstruction 8 甲戌 Wood Dog 水山蹇 24 廿五 2	木3 Wood Advancement 7 乙亥 Wood Pig 火地晉 25 廿六 3	水6 Water Nourish 6 丙子 Fire Rat 山雷頤 26 廿七 3	金4 Metal Following 5 丁丑 Fire Ox 澤雷隨 27 廿八 7	木8 Wood Abundance 4 戊寅 Earth Tiger 雷火豐 28 廿九 6	火7 Fire Regulate 3 己卯 Earth Rabbit 水澤節 29 八月初一 8

SEPTEMBER 1981 丁酉

Xuan Kong Element 玄空五行	澤山咸 Influence	Period Luck 卦運	Monthly Star 月星
Metal 金4		9	1

SUNDAY	MONDAY	TUESDAY	WEDNESDAY	THURSDAY	FRIDAY	SATURDAY
		火2 Fire Wind 9 壬午 Water Horse 巽為風 1 初四 1	金4 Metal Trap 8 癸未 Water Goat 澤水困 2 初五 8	木3 Wood Not Yet Accomplished 7 甲申 Wood Monkey 火水未濟 3 初六 9	金9 Metal Retreat 6 乙酉 Wood Rooster 天山遯 4 初七 4	水6 Water Mountain 5 丙戌 Fire Dog 艮為山 5 初八 1
木8 Wood Delight 4 丁亥 Fire Pig 雷地豫 6 初九 8	火7 Fire Beginning 3 戊子 Earth Rat 水雷屯 7 初十 4	金9 Metal Without Wrongdoing 2 己丑 Earth Ox 天雷無妄 8 十一 2	木3 Wood Fire 1 庚寅 Metal Tiger 離為火 9 十二 1	火2 Fire Sincerity 9 辛卯 Metal Rabbit 風澤中孚 10 十三 3	水6 Water Big Livestock 8 壬辰 Water Dragon 山天大畜 11 十四 4	金4 Metal Eliminating 7 癸巳 Water Snake 澤天夬 12 十五 6
金9 Metal Heaven 6 甲午 Wood Horse 乾為天 13 十六 1	火7 Fire Well 5 乙未 Wood Goat 水風井 14 十七 6	木8 Wood Relief 4 丙申 Fire Monkey 雷水解 15 十八 4	金4 Metal Influence 3 丁酉 Fire Rooster 澤山咸 16 十九 9	水1 Water Humility 2 戊戌 Earth Dog 地山謙 17 二十 6	火2 Fire Observation 1 己亥 Earth Pig 風地觀 18 廿一 2	火2 Fire Increasing 9 庚子 Metal Rat 風雷益 19 廿二 9
水1 Water Dimming Light 8 辛丑 Metal Ox 地火明夷 20 廿三 3	金9 Metal Fellowship 7 壬寅 Water Tiger 天火同人 21 廿四 7	木8 Wood Marrying Maiden 6 癸卯 Water Rabbit 雷澤歸妹 22 廿五 7	木3 Wood Opposition 5 甲辰 Wood Dragon 火澤睽 23 廿六 2	火7 Fire Waiting 4 乙巳 Wood Snake 水天需 24 廿七 3	金4 Metal Great Exceeding 3 丙午 Fire Horse 澤風大過 25 廿八 3	水6 Water Poison 2 丁未 Fire Goat 山風蠱 26 廿九 7
火2 Fire Dispersing 1 戊申 Earth Monkey 風水渙 27 三十 6	木3 Wood Travelling 9 己酉 Earth Rooster 火山旅 28 九月初一 8	金9 Metal Stagnation 8 庚戌 Metal Dog 天地否 29 初二 9	火7 Fire Alliance 7 辛亥 Metal Pig 水地比 30 初三 7			

OCTOBER 1981 戊戌

Xuan Kong Element 玄空五行	地山謙 Humility	Period Luck 卦運	Monthly Star 月星
Water 水1		6	9

SUNDAY	MONDAY	TUESDAY	WEDNESDAY	THURSDAY	FRIDAY	SATURDAY
				木8 Wood Thunder 6 壬子 Water Rat 震為雷 1 初四 1	水6 Water Beauty 5 癸丑 Water Ox 山火賁 2 初五 8	火7 Fire Accomplished 4 甲寅 Wood Tiger 水火既濟 3 初六 9
水1 Water Arriving 3 乙卯 Wood Rabbit 地澤臨 4 初七 4	金4 Metal Marsh 2 丙辰 Fire Dragon 兌為澤 5 初八 1	火2 Fire Small Livestock 1 丁巳 Fire Snake 風天小畜 6 初九 8	木3 Wood The Cauldron 9 戊午 Earth Horse 火風鼎 7 初十 4	水1 Water Rising 8 己未 Earth Goat 地風升 8 十一 2	火7 Fire Water 7 庚申 Metal Monkey 坎為水 9 十二 1	木8 Wood Lesser Exceeding 6 辛酉 Metal Rooster 雷山小過 10 十三 3
金4 Metal Gathering 5 壬戌 Water Dog 澤地萃 11 十四 4	水6 Water Peel 4 癸亥 Water Pig 山地剝 12 十五 6	水1 Water Earth 3 甲子 Wood Rat 坤為地 13 十六 1	木3 Wood Biting 2 乙丑 Wood Ox 火雷噬嗑 14 十七 6	火2 Fire Family 1 丙寅 Fire Tiger 風火家人 15 十八 4	水6 Water Decreasing 9 丁卯 Fire Rabbit 山澤損 16 十九 9	金9 Metal Tread 8 戊辰 Earth Dragon 天澤履 17 二十 6
木8 Wood Great Strength 7 己巳 Earth Snake 雷天大壯 18 廿一 2	木8 Wood Consistency 6 庚午 Metal Horse 雷風恆 19 廿二 9	金9 Metal Litigation 5 辛未 Metal Goat 天水訟 20 廿三 3	水1 Water Officer 4 壬申 Water Monkey 地水師 21 廿四 7	火2 Fire Gradual Progress 3 癸酉 Water Rooster 風山漸 22 廿五 7	火7 Fire Obstruction 2 甲戌 Wood Dog 水山蹇 23 廿六 2	木3 Wood Advancement 1 乙亥 Wood Pig 火地晉 24 廿七 3
水6 Water Nourish 9 丙子 Fire Rat 山雷頤 25 廿八 3	金4 Metal Following 8 丁丑 Fire Ox 澤雷隨 26 廿九 7	木8 Wood Abundance 7 戊寅 Earth Tiger 雷火豐 27 三十 6	火7 Fire Regulate 6 己卯 Earth Rabbit 水澤節 28 十月初一 8	水1 Water Unity 5 庚辰 Metal Dragon 地天泰 29 初二 9	木3 Wood Great Reward 4 辛巳 Metal Snake 火天大有 30 初三 7	火2 Fire Wind 3 壬午 Water Horse 巽為風 31 初四 1

NOVEMBER 1981 己亥

Xuan Kong Element 玄空五行	風地觀 Observation	Period Luck 卦運	Monthly Star 月星
Fire 火2		2	8

SUNDAY	MONDAY	TUESDAY	WEDNESDAY	THURSDAY	FRIDAY	SATURDAY
金4 Metal 2 Trap 澤水困 癸未 Water Goat 1 初五 8	木3 Wood 1 Not Yet Accomplished 火水未濟 甲申 Wood Monkey 2 初六 9	金9 Metal 9 Retreat 天山遯 乙酉 Wood Rooster 3 初七 4	水6 Water 8 Mountain 艮爲山 丙戌 Fire Dog 4 初八 1	木8 Wood 7 Delight 雷地豫 丁亥 Fire Pig 5 初九 8	火7 Fire 6 Beginning 水雷屯 戊子 Earth Rat 6 初十 4	金9 Metal 5 Without Wrongdoing 天雷無妄 己丑 Earth Ox 7 十一 2
木3 Wood 4 Fire 離爲火 庚寅 Metal Tiger 8 十二 1	火2 Fire 3 Sincerity 風澤中孚 辛卯 Metal Rabbit 9 十三 3	水6 Water 2 Big Livestock 山天大畜 壬辰 Water Dragon 10 十四 4	金4 Metal 1 Eliminating 澤天夬 癸巳 Water Snake 11 十五 6	金9 Metal 9 Heaven 乾爲天 甲午 Wood Horse 12 十六 1	火7 Fire 8 Well 水風井 乙未 Wood Goat 13 十七 6	木8 Wood 7 Relief 雷水解 丙申 Fire Monkey 14 十八 4
金4 Metal 6 Influence 澤山咸 丁酉 Fire Rooster 15 十九 9	水1 Water 5 Humility 地山謙 戊戌 Earth Dog 16 二十 6	火2 Fire 4 Observation 風地觀 己亥 Earth Pig 17 廿一 2	火2 Fire 3 Increasing 風雷益 庚子 Metal Rat 18 廿二 9	水1 Water 2 Dimming Light 地火明夷 辛丑 Metal Ox 19 廿三 3	金9 Metal 1 Fellowship 天火同人 壬寅 Water Tiger 20 廿四 7	木8 Wood 9 Marrying Maiden 雷澤歸妹 癸卯 Water Rabbit 21 廿五 7
木3 Wood 8 Opposition 火澤睽 甲辰 Wood Dragon 22 廿六 2	火7 Fire 7 Waiting 水天需 乙巳 Wood Snake 23 廿七 3	金4 Metal 6 Great Exceeding 澤風大過 丙午 Fire Horse 24 廿八 3	水6 Water 5 Poison 山風蠱 丁未 Fire Goat 25 廿九 7	火2 Fire 4 Dispersing 風水渙 戊申 Earth Monkey 26 十一月初一 6	木3 Wood 3 Travelling 火山旅 己酉 Earth Rooster 27 初二 8	金9 Metal 2 Stagnation 天地否 庚戌 Metal Dog 28 初三 9
火7 Fire 1 Alliance 水地比 辛亥 Metal Pig 29 初四 7	木8 Wood 9 Thunder 震爲雷 壬子 Water Rat 30 初五 1					

DECEMBER 1981 庚子

Xuan Kong Element 玄空五行	風雷益 Increasing	Period Luck 卦運	Monthly Star 月星
Fire 火2		9	7

SUNDAY	MONDAY	TUESDAY	WEDNESDAY	THURSDAY	FRIDAY	SATURDAY
		水6 Water 8 Beauty 山火賁 癸丑 Water Ox 1 初六 8	火7 Fire 7 Accomplished 水火既濟 甲寅 Wood Tiger 2 初七 9	水1 Water 6 Arriving 地澤臨 乙卯 Wood Rabbit 3 初八 4	金4 Metal 5 Marsh 兌爲澤 丙辰 Fire Dragon 4 初九 1	火2 Fire 4 Small Livestock 風天小畜 丁巳 Fire Snake 5 初十 8
木3 Wood 3 The Cauldron 火風鼎 戊午 Earth Horse 6 十一 4	水1 Water 2 Rising 地風升 己未 Earth Goat 7 十二 2	火7 Fire 1 Water 坎爲水 庚申 Metal Monkey 8 十三 1	木8 Wood 9 Lesser Exceeding 雷山小過 辛酉 Metal Rooster 9 十四 3	金4 Metal 8 Gathering 澤地萃 壬戌 Water Dog 10 十五 4	水6 Water 7 Peel 山地剝 癸亥 Water Pig 11 十六 6	水1 Water 6 Earth 坤爲地 甲子 Wood Rat 12 十七 1
木3 Wood 5 Biting 火雷噬嗑 乙丑 Wood Ox 13 十八 6	火2 Fire 4 Family 風火家人 丙寅 Fire Tiger 14 十九 4	水6 Water 3 Decreasing 山澤損 丁卯 Fire Rabbit 15 二十 9	金9 Metal 2 Tread 天澤履 戊辰 Earth Dragon 16 廿一 6	木8 Wood 1 Great Strength 雷天大壯 己巳 Earth Snake 17 廿二 2	木8 Wood 9 Consistency 雷風恆 庚午 Metal Horse 18 廿三 9	金9 Metal 8 Litigation 天水訟 辛未 Metal Goat 19 廿四 3
水1 Water 7 Officer 地水師 壬申 Water Monkey 20 廿五 7	火2 Fire 6 Gradual Progress 風山漸 癸酉 Water Rooster 21 廿六 7	火7 Fire 5/5 Obstruction 水山蹇 甲戌 Wood Dog 22 廿七 2	木3 Wood 6 Advancement 火地晉 乙亥 Wood Pig 23 廿八 3	水6 Water 7 Nourish 山雷頤 丙子 Fire Rat 24 廿九 3	金4 Metal 8 Following 澤雷隨 丁丑 Fire Ox 25 三十 7	木8 Wood 9 Abundance 雷火豐 戊寅 Earth Tiger 26 十二月初一 6
火7 Fire 1 Regulate 水澤節 己卯 Earth Rabbit 27 初二 8	水1 Water 2 Unity 地天泰 庚辰 Metal Dragon 28 初三 9	木3 Wood 3 Great Reward 火天大有 辛巳 Metal Snake 29 初四 7	火2 Fire 4 Wind 巽爲風 壬午 Water Horse 30 初五 1	金4 Metal 5 Trap 澤水困 癸未 Water Goat 31 初六 8		

1982 壬戌

(*Ren Xu*) Water Dog

1982 壬戌 *(Ren Xu)* Water Dog

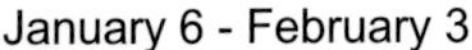

January 6 - February 3

February 4 - March 5

March 6 - April 4

April 5 - May 5

May 6 - June 5

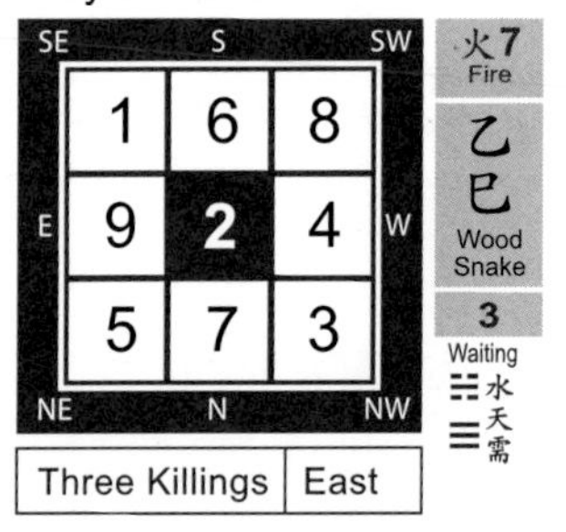

June 6 - July 6

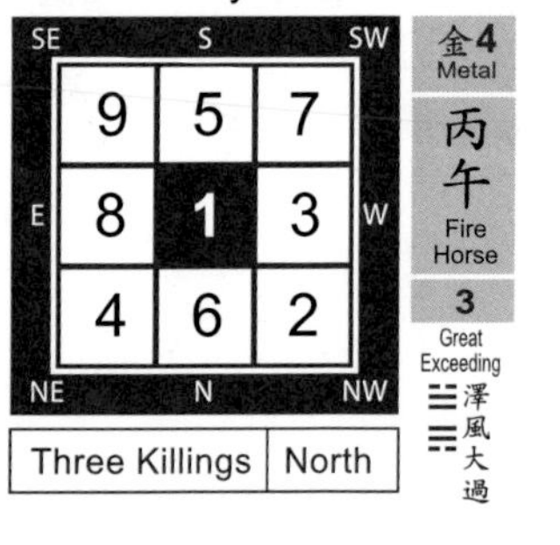

July 7 - August 7

August 8 - September 7

7	3	5
6	**8**	1
2	4	9

火**2** Fire
戊申 Earth Monkey
6 Dispersing
風水渙

September 8 - October 7

6	2	4
5	**7**	9
1	3	8

木**3** Wood
己酉 Earth Rooster
8 Travelling
火山旅

October 8 - November 7

November 8 - December 6

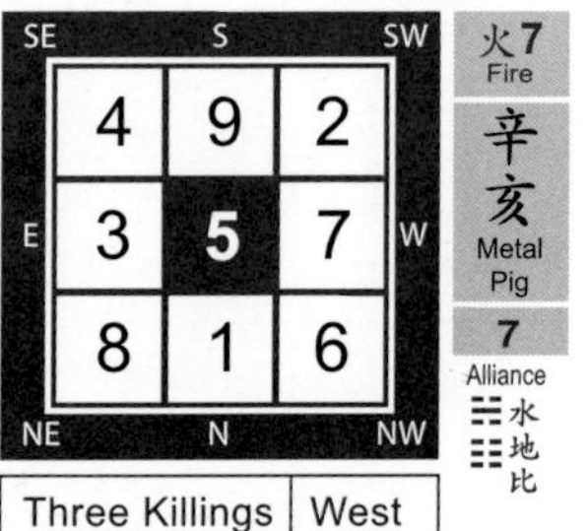

December 7 - January 5

3	8	1
2	**4**	6
7	9	5

木**8** Wood
壬子 Water Rat
1 Thunder
震為雷

JANUARY 1982 辛丑

Xuan Kong Element 玄空五行	地火明夷 Dimming Light	Period Luck 卦運	Monthly Star 月星
Water 水1		3	6

SUNDAY	MONDAY	TUESDAY	WEDNESDAY	THURSDAY	FRIDAY	SATURDAY
火7 Fire 9 Accomplished 甲寅 Wood Tiger 水火既濟 31 初七 9					木3 Wood 6 Not Yet Accomplished 甲申 Wood Monkey 火水未濟 1 初七 9	金9 Metal 7 Retreat 乙酉 Wood Rooster 天山遯 2 初八 4
水6 Water 8 Mountain 丙戌 Fire Dog 艮爲山 3 初九 1	木8 Wood 9 Delight 丁亥 Fire Pig 雷地豫 4 初十 8	火7 Fire 1 Beginning 戊子 Earth Rat 水雷屯 5 十一 4	金9 Metal 2 Without Wrongdoing 己丑 Earth Ox 天雷無妄 6 十二 2	木3 Wood 3 Fire 庚寅 Metal Tiger 離爲火 7 十三 1	火2 Fire 4 Sincerity 辛卯 Metal Rabbit 風澤中孚 8 十四 3	水6 Water 5 Big Livestock 壬辰 Water Dragon 山天大畜 9 十五 4
金4 Metal 6 Eliminating 癸巳 Water Snake 澤天夬 10 十六 6	金9 Metal 7 Heaven 甲午 Wood Horse 乾爲天 11 十七 1	火7 Fire 8 Well 乙未 Wood Goat 水風井 12 十八 6	木8 Wood 9 Relief 丙申 Fire Monkey 雷水解 13 十九 4	金4 Metal 1 Influence 丁酉 Fire Rooster 澤山咸 14 二十 9	水1 Water 2 Humility 戊戌 Earth Dog 地山謙 15 廿一 6	火2 Fire 3 Observation 己亥 Earth Pig 風地觀 16 廿二 2
火2 Fire 4 Increasing 庚子 Metal Rat 風雷益 17 廿三 9	水1 Water 5 Dimming Light 辛丑 Metal Ox 地火明夷 18 廿四 3	金9 Metal 6 Fellowship 壬寅 Water Tiger 天火同人 19 廿五 7	木8 Wood 7 Marrying Maiden 癸卯 Water Rabbit 雷澤歸妹 20 廿六 7	木3 Wood 8 Opposition 甲辰 Wood Dragon 火澤睽 21 廿七 2	火7 Fire 9 Waiting 乙巳 Wood Snake 水天需 22 廿八 3	金4 Metal 1 Great Exceeding 丙午 Fire Horse 澤風大過 23 廿九 3
水6 Water 2 Poison 丁未 Fire Goat 山風蠱 24 三十 7	火2 Fire 3 Dispersing 戊申 Earth Monkey 風水渙 25 正月初一 6	木3 Wood 4 Travelling 己酉 Earth Rooster 火山旅 26 初二 8	金9 Metal 5 Stagnation 庚戌 Metal Dog 天地否 27 初三 9	火7 Fire 6 Alliance 辛亥 Metal Pig 水地比 28 初四 7	木8 Wood 7 Thunder 壬子 Water Rat 震爲雷 29 初五 1	水6 Water 8 Beauty 癸丑 Water Ox 山火賁 30 初六 8

FEBRUARY 1982 壬寅

Xuan Kong Element 玄空五行	天火同人 Fellowship	Period Luck 卦運	Monthly Star 月星
Metal 金9		7	5

SUNDAY	MONDAY	TUESDAY	WEDNESDAY	THURSDAY	FRIDAY	SATURDAY
	水1 Water 1 Arriving 乙卯 Wood Rabbit 地澤臨 1 初八 4	金4 Metal 2 Marsh 丙辰 Fire Dragon 兌爲澤 2 初九 1	火2 Fire 3 Small Livestock 丁巳 Fire Snake 風天小畜 3 初十 8	木3 Wood 4 The Cauldron 戊午 Earth Horse 火風鼎 4 十一 4	水1 Water 5 Rising 己未 Earth Goat 地風升 5 十二 2	火7 Fire 6 Water 庚申 Metal Monkey 坎爲水 6 十三 1
木8 Wood 7 Lesser Exceeding 辛酉 Metal Rooster 雷山小過 7 十四 3	金4 Metal 8 Gathering 壬戌 Water Dog 澤地萃 8 十五 4	水6 Water 9 Peel 癸亥 Water Pig 山地剝 9 十六 6	水1 Water 1 Earth 甲子 Wood Rat 坤爲地 10 十七 1	木3 Wood 2 Biting 乙丑 Wood Ox 火雷噬嗑 11 十八 6	火2 Fire 3 Family 丙寅 Fire Tiger 風火家人 12 十九 4	水6 Water 4 Decreasing 丁卯 Fire Rabbit 山澤損 13 二十 9
金9 Metal 5 Tread 戊辰 Earth Dragon 天澤履 14 廿一 6	木8 Wood 6 Great Strength 己巳 Earth Snake 雷天大壯 15 廿二 2	木8 Wood 7 Consistency 庚午 Metal Horse 雷風恆 16 廿三 9	金9 Metal 8 Litigation 辛未 Metal Goat 天水訟 17 廿四 3	水1 Water 9 Officer 壬申 Water Monkey 地水師 18 廿五 7	火2 Fire 1 Gradual Progress 癸酉 Water Rooster 風山漸 19 廿六 7	火7 Fire 2 Obstruction 甲戌 Wood Dog 水山蹇 20 廿七 2
木3 Wood 3 Advancement 乙亥 Wood Pig 火地晉 21 廿八 3	水6 Water 4 Nourish 丙子 Fire Rat 山雷頤 22 廿九 3	金4 Metal 5 Following 丁丑 Fire Ox 澤雷隨 23 三十 7	木8 Wood 6 Abundance 戊寅 Earth Tiger 雷火豐 24 二月初一 6	火7 Fire 7 Regulate 己卯 Earth Rabbit 水澤節 25 初二 8	水1 Water 8 Unity 庚辰 Metal Dragon 地天泰 26 初三 9	木3 Wood 9 Great Reward 辛巳 Metal Snake 火天大有 27 初四 7
火2 Fire 1 Wind 壬午 Water Horse 巽爲風 28 初五 1						

MARCH 1982 癸卯

Xuan Kong Element 玄空五行	雷澤歸妹 Marrying Maiden	Period Luck 卦運	Monthly Star 月星
Wood 木8		7	4

SUNDAY	MONDAY	TUESDAY	WEDNESDAY	THURSDAY	FRIDAY	SATURDAY
	金4 Metal 2 癸未 Water Goat 8 Trap 澤水困 1 初六	木3 Wood 3 甲申 Wood Monkey 9 Not Yet Accomplished 火水未濟 2 初七	金9 Metal 4 乙酉 Wood Rooster 4 Retreat 天山遯 3 初八	水6 Water 5 丙戌 Fire Dog 1 Mountain 艮為山 4 初九	木8 Wood 6 丁亥 Fire Pig 8 Delight 雷地豫 5 初十	火7 Fire 7 戊子 Earth Rat 4 Beginning 水雷屯 6 十一
金9 Metal 8 己丑 Earth Ox 2 Without Wrongdoing 天雷無妄 7 十二	木3 Wood 9 庚寅 Metal Tiger 1 Fire 離為火 8 十三	火2 Fire 1 辛卯 Metal Rabbit 3 Sincerity 風澤中孚 9 十四	水6 Water 2 壬辰 Water Dragon 4 Big Livestock 山天大畜 10 十五	金4 Metal 3 癸巳 Water Snake 6 Eliminating 澤天夬 11 十六	金9 Metal 4 甲午 Wood Horse 1 Heaven 乾為天 12 十七	火7 Fire 5 乙未 Wood Goat 6 Well 水風井 13 十八
木8 Wood 6 丙申 Fire Monkey 4 Relief 雷水解 14 十九	金4 Metal 7 丁酉 Fire Rooster 9 Influence 澤山咸 15 二十	水1 Water 8 戊戌 Earth Dog 6 Humility 地山謙 16 廿一	火2 Fire 9 己亥 Earth Pig 2 Observation 風地觀 17 廿二	火2 Fire 1 庚子 Metal Rat 9 Increasing 風雷益 18 廿三	水1 Water 2 辛丑 Metal Ox 3 Dimming Light 地火明夷 19 廿四	金9 Metal 3 壬寅 Water Tiger 7 Fellowship 天火同人 20 廿五
木8 Wood 4 癸卯 Water Rabbit 7 Marrying Maiden 雷澤歸妹 21 廿六	木3 Wood 5 甲辰 Wood Dragon 2 Opposition 火澤睽 22 廿七	火7 Fire 6 乙巳 Wood Snake 3 Waiting 水天需 23 廿八	金4 Metal 7 丙午 Fire Horse 3 Great Exceeding 澤風大過 24 廿九	水6 Water 8 丁未 Fire Goat 7 Poison 山風蠱 25 三月初一	火2 Fire 9 戊申 Earth Monkey 6 Dispersing 風水渙 26 初二	木3 Wood 1 己酉 Earth Rooster 8 Travelling 火山旅 27 初三
金9 Metal 2 庚戌 Metal Dog 9 Stagnation 天地否 28 初四	火7 Fire 3 辛亥 Metal Pig 7 Alliance 水地比 29 初五	木8 Wood 4 壬子 Water Rat 1 Thunder 震為雷 30 初六	水6 Water 5 癸丑 Water Ox 8 Beauty 山火賁 31 初七			

APRIL 1982 甲辰

Xuan Kong Element 玄空五行	火澤睽 Opposition	Period Luck 卦運	Monthly Star 月星
Wood 木3		2	3

SUNDAY	MONDAY	TUESDAY	WEDNESDAY	THURSDAY	FRIDAY	SATURDAY
				火7 Fire 6 甲寅 Wood Tiger 9 Accomplished 水火既濟 1 初八	水1 Water 7 乙卯 Wood Rabbit 4 Arriving 地澤臨 2 初九	金4 Metal 8 丙辰 Fire Dragon 1 Marsh 兌為澤 3 初十
火2 Fire 9 丁巳 Fire Snake 8 Small Livestock 風天小畜 4 十一	木3 Wood 1 戊午 Earth Horse 4 The Cauldron 火風鼎 5 十二	水1 Water 2 己未 Earth Goat 2 Rising 地風升 6 十三	火7 Fire 3 庚申 Metal Monkey 1 Water 坎為水 7 十四	木8 Wood 4 辛酉 Metal Rooster 3 Lesser Exceeding 雷山小過 8 十五	金4 Metal 5 壬戌 Water Dog 4 Gathering 澤地萃 9 十六	水6 Water 6 癸亥 Water Pig 6 Peel 山地剝 10 十七
水1 Water 7 甲子 Wood Rat 1 Earth 坤為地 11 十八	木3 Wood 8 乙丑 Wood Ox 6 Biting 火雷噬嗑 12 十九	火2 Fire 9 丙寅 Fire Tiger 4 Family 風火家人 13 二十	水6 Water 1 丁卯 Fire Rabbit 9 Decreasing 山澤損 14 廿一	金9 Metal 2 戊辰 Earth Dragon 6 Tread 天澤履 15 廿二	木8 Wood 3 己巳 Earth Snake 2 Great Strength 雷天大壯 16 廿三	木8 Wood 4 庚午 Metal Horse 9 Consistency 雷風恒 17 廿四
金9 Metal 5 辛未 Metal Goat 3 Litigation 天水訟 18 廿五	水1 Water 6 壬申 Water Monkey 7 Officer 地水師 19 廿六	火2 Fire 7 癸酉 Water Rooster 7 Gradual Progress 風山漸 20 廿七	火7 Fire 8 甲戌 Wood Dog 2 Obstruction 水山蹇 21 廿八	木3 Wood 9 乙亥 Wood Pig 3 Advancement 火地晉 22 廿九	水6 Water 1 丙子 Fire Rat 3 Nourish 山雷頤 23 三十	金4 Metal 2 丁丑 Fire Ox 7 Following 澤雷隨 24 四月初一
木8 Wood 3 戊寅 Earth Tiger 6 Abundance 雷火豐 25 初二	火7 Fire 4 己卯 Earth Rabbit 8 Regulate 水澤節 26 初三	水1 Water 5 庚辰 Metal Dragon 9 Unity 地天泰 27 初四	木3 Wood 6 辛巳 Metal Snake 7 Great Reward 火天大有 28 初五	火2 Fire 7 壬午 Water Horse 1 Wind 巽為風 29 初六	金4 Metal 8 癸未 Water Goat 8 Trap 澤水困 30 初七	

MAY 1982 乙巳

Xuan Kong Element 玄空五行	水天需 Waiting	Period Luck 卦運	Monthly Star 月星
Fire 火7		3	2

SUNDAY	MONDAY	TUESDAY	WEDNESDAY	THURSDAY	FRIDAY	SATURDAY
水6 Water Beauty 2 癸丑 Water Ox 山火賁 30 初八 8	火7 Fire Accomplished 3 甲寅 Wood Tiger 水火既濟 31 初九 9					木3 Wood Not Yet Accomplished 9 甲申 Wood Monkey 火水未濟 1 初八 9
金9 Metal Retreat 1 乙酉 Wood Rooster 天山遯 2 初九 4	水6 Water Mountain 2 丙戌 Fire Dog 艮爲山 3 初十 1	木8 Wood Delight 3 丁亥 Fire Pig 雷地豫 4 十一 8	火7 Fire Beginning 4 戊子 Earth Rat 水雷屯 5 十二 4	金9 Metal Without Wrongdoing 5 己丑 Earth Ox 天雷無妄 6 十三 2	木3 Wood Fire 6 庚寅 Metal Tiger 離爲火 7 十四 1	火2 Fire Sincerity 7 辛卯 Metal Rabbit 風澤中孚 8 十五 3
水6 Water Big Livestock 8 壬辰 Water Dragon 山天大畜 9 十六 4	金4 Metal Eliminating 9 癸巳 Water Snake 澤天夬 10 十七 6	金9 Metal Heaven 1 甲午 Wood Horse 乾爲天 11 十八 1	火7 Fire Well 2 乙未 Wood Goat 水風井 12 十九 6	木8 Wood Relief 3 丙申 Fire Monkey 雷水解 13 二十 4	金4 Metal Influence 4 丁酉 Fire Rooster 澤山咸 14 廿一 9	水1 Water Humility 5 戊戌 Earth Dog 地山謙 15 廿二 6
火2 Fire Observation 6 己亥 Earth Pig 風地觀 16 廿三 2	火2 Fire Increasing 7 庚子 Metal Rat 風雷益 17 廿四 9	水1 Water Dimming Light 8 辛丑 Metal Ox 地火明夷 18 廿五 3	金9 Metal Fellowship 9 壬寅 Water Tiger 天火同人 19 廿六 7	木8 Wood Marrying Maiden 1 癸卯 Water Rabbit 雷澤歸妹 20 廿七 7	木3 Wood Opposition 2 甲辰 Wood Dragon 火澤睽 21 廿八 2	火7 Fire Waiting 3 乙巳 Wood Snake 水天需 22 廿九 3
金4 Metal Great Exceeding 4 丙午 Fire Horse 澤風大過 23 閏四月初一 3	水6 Water Poison 5 丁未 Fire Goat 山風蠱 24 初二 7	火2 Fire Dispersing 6 戊申 Earth Monkey 風水渙 25 初三 6	木3 Wood Travelling 7 己酉 Earth Rooster 火山旅 26 初四 8	金9 Metal Stagnation 8 庚戌 Metal Dog 天地否 27 初五 9	火7 Fire Alliance 9 辛亥 Metal Pig 水地比 28 初六 7	木8 Wood Thunder 1 壬子 Water Rat 震爲雷 29 初七 1

JUNE 1982 丙午

Xuan Kong Element 玄空五行	澤風大過 Great Exceeding	Period Luck 卦運	Monthly Star 月星
Metal 金4		3	1

SUNDAY	MONDAY	TUESDAY	WEDNESDAY	THURSDAY	FRIDAY	SATURDAY
		水1 Water Arriving 4 乙卯 Wood Rabbit 地澤臨 1 初十 4	金4 Metal Marsh 5 丙辰 Fire Dragon 兑爲澤 2 十一 1	火2 Fire Small Livestock 6 丁巳 Fire Snake 風天小畜 3 十二 8	木3 Wood The Cauldron 7 戊午 Earth Horse 火風鼎 4 十三 4	水1 Water Rising 8 己未 Earth Goat 地風升 5 十四 2
火7 Fire Water 9 庚申 Metal Monkey 坎爲水 6 十五 1	木8 Wood Lesser Exceeding 1 辛酉 Metal Rooster 雷山小過 7 十六 3	金4 Metal Gathering 2 壬戌 Water Dog 澤地萃 8 十七 4	水6 Water Peel 3 癸亥 Water Pig 山地剝 9 十八 6	水1 Water Earth 4 甲子 Wood Rat 坤爲地 10 十九 1	木3 Wood Biting 5 乙丑 Wood Ox 火雷噬嗑 11 二十 6	火2 Fire Family 6 丙寅 Fire Tiger 風火家人 12 廿一 4
水6 Water Decreasing 7 丁卯 Fire Rabbit 山澤損 13 廿二 9	金9 Metal Tread 8 戊辰 Earth Dragon 天澤履 14 廿三 6	木8 Wood Great Strength 9 己巳 Earth Snake 雷天大壯 15 廿四 2	木8 Wood Consistency 1 庚午 Metal Horse 雷風恒 16 廿五 9	金9 Metal Litigation 2 辛未 Metal Goat 天水訟 17 廿六 3	水1 Water Officer 3 壬申 Water Monkey 地水師 18 廿七 7	火2 Fire Gradual Progress 4 癸酉 Water Rooster 風山漸 19 廿八 7
火7 Fire Obstruction 5 甲戌 Wood Dog 水山蹇 20 廿九 2	木3 Wood Advancement 6 乙亥 Wood Pig 火地晉 21 五月初一 3	水6 Water Nourish 7/3 丙子 Fire Rat 山雷頤 22 初二 3	金4 Metal Following 2 丁丑 Fire Ox 澤雷隨 23 初三 7	木8 Wood Abundance 1 戊寅 Earth Tiger 雷火豐 24 初四 6	火7 Fire Regulate 9 己卯 Earth Rabbit 水澤節 25 初五 8	水1 Water Unity 8 庚辰 Metal Dragon 地天泰 26 初六 9
木3 Wood Great Reward 7 辛巳 Metal Snake 火天大有 27 初七 7	火2 Fire Wind 6 壬午 Water Horse 巽爲風 28 初八 1	金4 Metal Trap 5 癸未 Water Goat 澤水困 29 初九 8	木3 Wood Not Yet Accomplished 4 甲申 Wood Monkey 火水未濟 30 初十 9			

JULY 1982 丁未

Xuan Kong Element 玄空五行	山風蠱 Poison	Period Luck 卦運	Monthly Star 月星
Water 水6		7	9

SUNDAY	MONDAY	TUESDAY	WEDNESDAY	THURSDAY	FRIDAY	SATURDAY
				金9 Metal Retreat 3 乙酉 Wood Rooster 天山遯 1 十一 4	水6 Water Mountain 2 丙戌 Fire Dog 艮爲山 2 十二 1	木8 Wood Delight 1 丁亥 Fire Pig 雷地豫 3 十三 8
火7 Fire Beginning 9 戊子 Earth Rat 水雷屯 4 十四 4	金9 Metal Without Wrongdoing 8 己丑 Earth Ox 天雷無妄 5 十五 2	木3 Wood Fire 7 庚寅 Metal Tiger 離爲火 6 十六 1	火2 Fire Sincerity 6 辛卯 Metal Rabbit 風澤中孚 7 十七 3	水6 Water Big Livestock 5 壬辰 Water Dragon 山天大畜 8 十八 4	金4 Metal Eliminating 4 癸巳 Water Snake 澤天夬 9 十九 6	金9 Metal Heaven 3 甲午 Wood Horse 乾爲天 10 二十 1
火7 Fire Well 2 乙未 Wood Goat 水風井 11 廿一 6	木8 Wood Relief 1 丙申 Fire Monkey 雷水解 12 廿二 4	金4 Metal Influence 9 丁酉 Fire Rooster 澤山咸 13 廿三 9	水1 Water Humility 8 戊戌 Earth Dog 地山謙 14 廿四 6	火2 Fire Observation 7 己亥 Earth Pig 風地觀 15 廿五 2	火2 Fire Increasing 6 庚子 Metal Rat 風雷益 16 廿六 9	水1 Water Dimming Light 5 辛丑 Metal Ox 地火明夷 17 廿七 3
金9 Metal Fellowship 4 壬寅 Water Tiger 天火同人 18 廿八 7	木8 Wood Marrying Maiden 3 癸卯 Water Rabbit 雷澤歸妹 19 廿九 7	木3 Wood Opposition 2 甲辰 Wood Dragon 火澤睽 20 三十 2	火7 Fire Waiting 1 乙巳 Wood Snake 水天需 21 六月初一 3	金4 Metal Great Exceeding 9 丙午 Fire Horse 澤風大過 22 初二 3	水6 Water Poison 8 丁未 Fire Goat 山風蠱 23 初三 7	火2 Fire Dispersing 7 戊申 Earth Monkey 風水渙 24 初四 6
木3 Wood Travelling 6 己酉 Earth Rooster 火山旅 25 初五 8	金9 Metal Stagnation 5 庚戌 Metal Dog 天地否 26 初六 9	火7 Fire Alliance 4 辛亥 Metal Pig 水地比 27 初七 7	木8 Wood Thunder 3 壬子 Water Rat 震爲雷 28 初八 1	水6 Water Beauty 2 癸丑 Water Ox 山火賁 29 初九 8	火7 Fire Accomplished 1 甲寅 Wood Tiger 水火既濟 30 初十 9	水1 Water Arriving 9 乙卯 Wood Rabbit 地澤臨 31 十一 4

AUGUST 1982 戊申

Xuan Kong Element 玄空五行	風水渙 Dispersing	Period Luck 卦運	Monthly Star 月星
Fire 火2		6	8

SUNDAY	MONDAY	TUESDAY	WEDNESDAY	THURSDAY	FRIDAY	SATURDAY
金4 Metal Marsh 8 丙辰 Fire Dragon 兌爲澤 1 十二 1	火2 Fire Small Livestock 7 丁巳 Fire Snake 風天小畜 2 十三 8	木3 Wood The Cauldron 6 戊午 Earth Horse 火風鼎 3 十四 4	水1 Water Rising 5 己未 Earth Goat 地風升 4 十五 2	火7 Fire Water 4 庚申 Metal Monkey 坎爲水 5 十六 1	木8 Wood Lesser Exceeding 3 辛酉 Metal Rooster 雷山小過 6 十七 3	金4 Metal Gathering 2 壬戌 Water Dog 澤地萃 7 十八 4
水6 Water Peel 1 癸亥 Water Pig 山地剝 8 十九 6	水1 Water Earth 9 甲子 Wood Rat 坤爲地 9 二十 1	木3 Wood Biting 8 乙丑 Wood Ox 火雷噬嗑 10 廿一 6	火2 Fire Family 7 丙寅 Fire Tiger 風火家人 11 廿二 4	水6 Water Decreasing 6 丁卯 Fire Rabbit 山澤損 12 廿三 9	金9 Metal Tread 5 戊辰 Earth Dragon 天澤履 13 廿四 6	木8 Wood Great Strength 4 己巳 Earth Snake 雷天大壯 14 廿五 2
木8 Wood Consistency 3 庚午 Metal Horse 雷風恆 15 廿六 9	金9 Metal Litigation 2 辛未 Metal Goat 天水訟 16 廿七 3	水1 Water Officer 1 壬申 Water Monkey 地水師 17 廿八 7	火2 Fire Gradual Progress 9 癸酉 Water Rooster 風山漸 18 廿九 7	火7 Fire Obstruction 8 甲戌 Wood Dog 水山蹇 19 七月初一 2	木3 Wood Advancement 7 乙亥 Wood Pig 火地晉 20 初二 3	水6 Water Nourish 6 丙子 Fire Rat 山雷頤 21 初三 3
金4 Metal Following 5 丁丑 Fire Ox 澤雷隨 22 初四 7	木8 Wood Abundance 4 戊寅 Earth Tiger 雷火豐 23 初五 6	火7 Fire Regulate 3 己卯 Earth Rabbit 水澤節 24 初六 8	水1 Water Unity 2 庚辰 Metal Dragon 地天泰 25 初七 9	木3 Wood Great Reward 1 辛巳 Metal Snake 火天大有 26 初八 7	火2 Fire Wind 9 壬午 Water Horse 巽爲風 27 初九 1	金4 Metal Trap 8 癸未 Water Goat 澤水困 28 初十 8
木3 Wood Not Yet Accomplished 7 甲申 Wood Monkey 火水未濟 29 十一 9	金9 Metal Retreat 6 乙酉 Wood Rooster 天山遯 30 十二 4	水6 Water Mountain 5 丙戌 Fire Dog 艮爲山 31 十三 1				

SEPTEMBER 1982 己酉

Xuan Kong Element 玄空五行	火山旅 Travelling	Period Luck 卦運	Monthly Star 月星
Wood 木3		8	7

SUNDAY	MONDAY	TUESDAY	WEDNESDAY	THURSDAY	FRIDAY	SATURDAY
			木8 Wood 4 Delight 雷地豫 丁亥 Fire Pig 8 1 十四	火7 Fire 3 Beginning 水雷屯 戊子 Earth Rat 4 2 十五	金9 Metal 2 Without Wrongdoing 天雷無妄 己丑 Earth Ox 2 3 十六	木3 Wood 1 Fire 離爲火 庚寅 Metal Tiger 1 4 十七
火2 Fire 9 Sincerity 風澤中孚 辛卯 Metal Rabbit 3 5 十八	水6 Water 8 Big Livestock 山天大畜 壬辰 Water Dragon 4 6 十九	金4 Metal 7 Eliminating 澤天夬 癸巳 Water Snake 6 7 二十	金9 Metal 6 Heaven 乾爲天 甲午 Wood Horse 1 8 廿一	火7 Fire 5 Well 水風井 乙未 Wood Goat 6 9 廿二	木8 Wood 4 Relief 雷水解 丙申 Fire Monkey 4 10 廿三	金4 Metal 3 Influence 澤山咸 丁酉 Fire Rooster 9 11 廿四
水1 Water 2 Humility 地山謙 戊戌 Earth Dog 6 12 廿五	火2 Fire 1 Observation 風地觀 己亥 Earth Pig 2 13 廿六	火2 Fire 9 Increasing 風雷益 庚子 Metal Rat 9 14 廿七	水1 Water 8 Dimming Light 地火明夷 辛丑 Metal Ox 3 15 廿八	金9 Metal 7 Fellowship 天火同人 壬寅 Water Tiger 7 16 廿九	木8 Wood 6 Marrying Maiden 雷澤歸妹 癸卯 Water Rabbit 7 17 八月初一	木3 Wood 5 Opposition 火澤睽 甲辰 Wood Dragon 2 18 初二
火7 Fire 4 Waiting 水天需 乙巳 Wood Snake 3 19 初三	金4 Metal 3 Great Exceeding 澤風大過 丙午 Fire Horse 3 20 初四	水6 Water 2 Poison 山風蠱 丁未 Fire Goat 7 21 初五	火2 Fire 1 Dispersing 風水渙 戊申 Earth Monkey 6 22 初六	木3 Wood 9 Travelling 火山旅 己酉 Earth Rooster 8 23 初七	金9 Metal 8 Stagnation 天地否 庚戌 Metal Dog 9 24 初八	火7 Fire 7 Alliance 水地比 辛亥 Metal Pig 7 25 初九
木8 Wood 6 Thunder 震爲雷 壬子 Water Rat 1 26 初十	水6 Water 5 Beauty 山火賁 癸丑 Water Ox 8 27 十一	火7 Fire 4 Accomplished 水火既濟 甲寅 Wood Tiger 9 28 十二	水1 Water 3 Arriving 地澤臨 乙卯 Wood Rabbit 4 29 十三	金4 Metal 2 Marsh 兌爲澤 丙辰 Fire Dragon 1 30 十四		

OCTOBER 1982 庚戌

Xuan Kong Element 玄空五行	天地否 Stagnation	Period Luck 卦運	Monthly Star 月星
Metal 金9		9	6

SUNDAY	MONDAY	TUESDAY	WEDNESDAY	THURSDAY	FRIDAY	SATURDAY
木8 Wood 7 Delight 雷地豫 丁亥 Fire Pig 8 31 十五					火2 Fire 1 Small Livestock 風天小畜 丁巳 Fire Snake 8 1 十五	木3 Wood 9 The Cauldron 火風鼎 戊午 Earth Horse 4 2 十六
水1 Water 8 Rising 地風升 己未 Earth Goat 2 3 十七	火7 Fire 7 Water 坎爲水 庚申 Metal Monkey 1 4 十八	木8 Wood 6 Lesser Exceeding 雷山小過 辛酉 Metal Rooster 3 5 十九	金4 Metal 5 Gathering 澤地萃 壬戌 Water Dog 4 6 二十	水6 Water 4 Peel 山地剝 癸亥 Water Pig 6 7 廿一	水1 Water 3 Earth 坤爲地 甲子 Wood Rat 1 8 廿二	木3 Wood 2 Biting 火雷噬嗑 乙丑 Wood Ox 6 9 廿三
火2 Fire 1 Family 風火家人 丙寅 Fire Tiger 4 10 廿四	水6 Water 9 Decreasing 山澤損 丁卯 Fire Rabbit 9 11 廿五	金9 Metal 8 Tread 天澤履 戊辰 Earth Dragon 6 12 廿六	木8 Wood 7 Great Strength 雷天大壯 己巳 Earth Snake 2 13 廿七	木8 Wood 6 Consistency 雷風恆 庚午 Metal Horse 9 14 廿八	金9 Metal 5 Litigation 天水訟 辛未 Metal Goat 3 15 廿九	水1 Water 4 Officer 地水師 壬申 Water Monkey 7 16 三十
火2 Fire 3 Gradual Progress 風山漸 癸酉 Water Rooster 7 17 九月初一	火7 Fire 2 Obstruction 水山蹇 甲戌 Wood Dog 2 18 初二	木3 Wood 1 Advancement 火地晉 乙亥 Wood Pig 3 19 初三	水6 Water 9 Nourish 山雷頤 丙子 Fire Rat 3 20 初四	金4 Metal 8 Following 澤雷隨 丁丑 Fire Ox 7 21 初五	木8 Wood 7 Abundance 雷火豐 戊寅 Earth Tiger 6 22 初六	火7 Fire 6 Regulate 水澤節 己卯 Earth Rabbit 8 23 初七
水1 Water 5 Unity 地天泰 庚辰 Metal Dragon 9 24 初八	木3 Wood 4 Great Reward 火天大有 辛巳 Metal Snake 7 25 初九	火2 Fire 3 Wind 巽爲風 壬午 Water Horse 1 26 初十	金4 Metal 2 Trap 澤水困 癸未 Water Goat 8 27 十一	木3 Wood 1 Not Yet Accomplished 火水未濟 甲申 Wood Monkey 9 28 十二	金9 Metal 9 Retreat 天山遯 乙酉 Wood Rooster 4 29 十三	水6 Water 8 Mountain 艮爲山 丙戌 Fire Dog 1 30 十四

NOVEMBER 1982 辛亥

Xuan Kong Element 玄空五行	水地比 Alliance	Period Luck 卦運	Monthly Star 月星
Fire 火7		7	5

SUNDAY	MONDAY	TUESDAY	WEDNESDAY	THURSDAY	FRIDAY	SATURDAY
	火7 Fire [6] Beginning 水雷屯 戊子 Earth Rat 1 十六 4	金9 Metal [5] Without Wrongdoing 天雷無妄 己丑 Earth Ox 2 十七 2	木3 Wood [4] Fire 離爲火 庚寅 Metal Tiger 3 十八 1	火2 Fire [3] Sincerity 風澤中孚 辛卯 Metal Rabbit 4 十九 3	水6 Water [2] Big Livestock 山天大畜 壬辰 Water Dragon 5 二十 4	金4 Metal [1] Eliminating 澤天夬 癸巳 Water Snake 6 廿一 6
金9 Metal [9] Heaven 乾爲天 甲午 Wood Horse 7 廿二 1	火7 Fire [8] Well 水風井 乙未 Wood Goat 8 廿三 6	木8 Wood [7] Relief 雷水解 丙申 Fire Monkey 9 廿四 4	金4 Metal [6] Influence 澤山咸 丁酉 Fire Rooster 10 廿五 9	水1 Water [5] Humility 地山謙 戊戌 Earth Dog 11 廿六 6	火2 Fire [4] Observation 風地觀 己亥 Earth Pig 12 廿七 2	火2 Fire [3] Increasing 風雷益 庚子 Metal Rat 13 廿八 9
水1 Water [2] Dimming Light 地火明夷 辛丑 Metal Ox 14 廿九 3	金9 Metal [1] Fellowship 天火同人 壬寅 Water Tiger 15 十月初一 7	木8 Wood [9] Marrying Maiden 雷澤歸妹 癸卯 Water Rabbit 16 初二 7	木3 Wood [8] Opposition 火澤睽 甲辰 Wood Dragon 17 初三 2	火7 Fire [7] Waiting 水天需 乙巳 Wood Snake 18 初四 3	金4 Metal [6] Great Exceeding 澤風大過 丙午 Fire Horse 19 初五 3	水6 Water [5] Poison 山風蠱 丁未 Fire Goat 20 初六 7
火2 Fire [4] Dispersing 風水渙 戊申 Earth Monkey 21 初七 6	木3 Wood [3] Travelling 火山旅 己酉 Earth Rooster 22 初八 8	金9 Metal [2] Stagnation 天地否 庚戌 Metal Dog 23 初九 9	火7 Fire [1] Alliance 水地比 辛亥 Metal Pig 24 初十 7	木8 Wood [9] Thunder 震爲雷 壬子 Water Rat 25 十一 1	水6 Water [8] Beauty 山火賁 癸丑 Water Ox 26 十二 8	火7 Fire [7] Accomplished 水火既濟 甲寅 Wood Tiger 27 十三 9
水1 Water [6] Arriving 地澤臨 乙卯 Wood Rabbit 28 十四 4	金4 Metal [5] Marsh 兑爲澤 丙辰 Fire Dragon 29 十五 1	火2 Fire [4] Small Livestock 風天小畜 丁巳 Fire Snake 30 十六 8				

DECEMBER 1982 壬子

Xuan Kong Element 玄空五行	震爲雷 Thunder	Period Luck 卦運	Monthly Star 月星
Wood 木8		1	4

SUNDAY	MONDAY	TUESDAY	WEDNESDAY	THURSDAY	FRIDAY	SATURDAY
			木3 Wood [3] The Cauldron 火風鼎 戊午 Earth Horse 1 十七 4	水1 Water [2] Rising 地風升 己未 Earth Goat 2 十八 2	火7 Fire [1] Water 坎爲水 庚申 Metal Monkey 3 十九 1	木8 Wood [9] Lesser Exceeding 雷山小過 辛酉 Metal Rooster 4 二十 3
金4 Metal [8] Gathering 澤地萃 壬戌 Water Dog 5 廿一 4	水6 Water [7] Peel 山地剝 癸亥 Water Pig 6 廿二 6	水1 Water [6] Earth 坤爲地 甲子 Wood Rat 7 廿三 1	木3 Wood [5] Biting 火雷噬嗑 乙丑 Wood Ox 8 廿四 6	火2 Fire [4] Family 風火家人 丙寅 Fire Tiger 9 廿五 4	水6 Water [3] Decreasing 山澤損 丁卯 Fire Rabbit 10 廿六 9	金9 Metal [2] Tread 天澤履 戊辰 Earth Dragon 11 廿七 6
木8 Wood [1] Great Strength 雷天大壯 己巳 Earth Snake 12 廿八 2	木8 Wood [9] Consistency 雷風恆 庚午 Metal Horse 13 廿九 9	金9 Metal [8] Litigation 天水訟 辛未 Metal Goat 14 三十 3	水1 Water [7] Officer 地水師 壬申 Water Monkey 15 十一月初一 7	火2 Fire [6] Gradual Progress 風山漸 癸酉 Water Rooster 16 初二 7	火7 Fire [5] Obstruction 水山蹇 甲戌 Wood Dog 17 初三 2	木3 Wood [4] Advancement 火地晉 乙亥 Wood Pig 18 初四 3
水6 Water [3] Nourish 山雷頤 丙子 Fire Rat 19 初五 3	金4 Metal [2] Following 澤雷隨 丁丑 Fire Ox 20 初六 7	木8 Wood [1] Abundance 雷火豐 戊寅 Earth Tiger 21 初七 6	火7 Fire [9/1] Regulate 水澤節 己卯 Earth Rabbit 22 初八 8	水1 Water [2] Unity 地天泰 庚辰 Metal Dragon 23 初九 9	木3 Wood [3] Great Reward 火天大有 辛巳 Metal Snake 24 初十 7	火2 Fire [4] Wind 巽爲風 壬午 Water Horse 25 十一 1
金4 Metal [5] Trap 澤水困 癸未 Water Goat 26 十二 8	木3 Wood [6] Not Yet Accomplished 火水未濟 甲申 Wood Monkey 27 十三 9	金9 Metal [7] Retreat 天山遯 乙酉 Wood Rooster 28 十四 4	水6 Water [8] Mountain 艮爲山 丙戌 Fire Dog 29 十五 1	木8 Wood [9] Delight 雷地豫 丁亥 Fire Pig 30 十六 8	火7 Fire [1] Beginning 水雷屯 戊子 Earth Rat 31 十七 4	

1983 癸亥

(*Gui Hai*) Water Pig

1983 癸亥 *(Gui Hai)* Water Pig

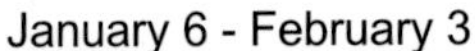

January 6 - February 3

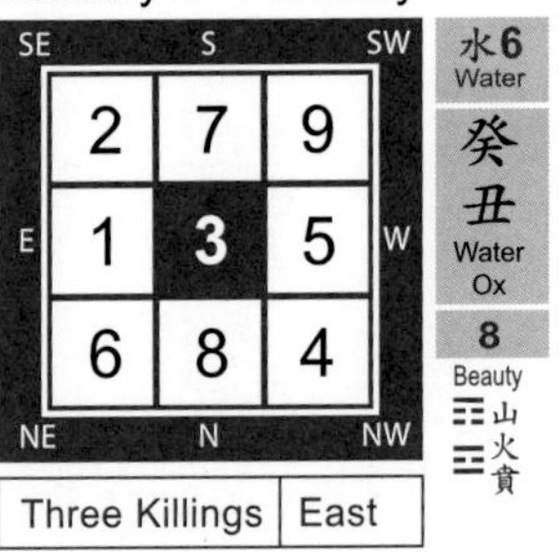

February 4 - March 5

March 6 - April 4

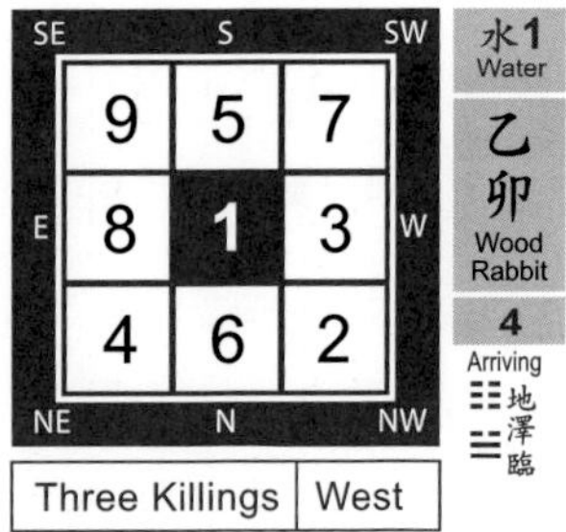

April 5 - May 5

May 6 - June 5

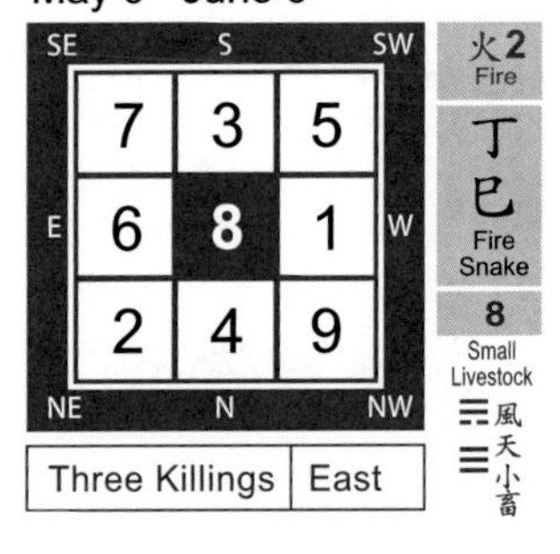

June 6 - July 7

July 8 - August 7

August 8 - September 7

September 8 - October 8

October 9 - November 7

November 8 - December 7

December 8 - January 5

JANUARY 1983 癸丑

Xuan Kong Element 玄空五行	山火賁 Beauty	Period Luck 卦運	Monthly Star 月星
Water 水6		8	3

SUNDAY	MONDAY	TUESDAY	WEDNESDAY	THURSDAY	FRIDAY	SATURDAY
木3 Wood The Cauldron 4 戊午 Earth Horse 火風鼎 30 十七 4	水1 Water Rising 5 己未 Earth Goat 地風升 31 十八 2					金9 Metal Without Wrongdoing 2 己丑 Earth Ox 天雷無妄 1 十八 2
木3 Wood Fire 3 庚寅 Metal Tiger 離爲火 2 十九 1	火2 Fire Sincerity 4 辛卯 Metal Rabbit 風澤中孚 3 二十 3	水6 Water Big Livestock 5 壬辰 Water Dragon 山天大畜 4 廿一 4	金4 Metal Eliminating 6 癸巳 Water Snake 澤天夬 5 廿二 6	金9 Metal Heaven 7 甲午 Wood Horse 乾爲天 6 廿三 1	火7 Fire Well 8 乙未 Wood Goat 水風井 7 廿四 6	木8 Wood Relief 9 丙申 Fire Monkey 雷水解 8 廿五 4
金4 Metal Influence 1 丁酉 Fire Rooster 澤山咸 9 廿六 9	水1 Water Humility 2 戊戌 Earth Dog 地山謙 10 廿七 6	火2 Fire Observation 3 己亥 Earth Pig 風地觀 11 廿八 2	火2 Fire Increasing 4 庚子 Metal Rat 風雷益 12 廿九 9	水1 Water Dimming Light 5 辛丑 Metal Ox 地火明夷 13 三十 3	金9 Metal Fellowship 6 壬寅 Water Tiger 天火同人 14 十二月初一 7	木8 Wood Marrying Maiden 7 癸卯 Water Rabbit 雷澤歸妹 15 初二 7
木3 Wood Opposition 8 甲辰 Wood Dragon 火澤睽 16 初三 2	火7 Fire Waiting 9 乙巳 Wood Snake 水天需 17 初四 3	金4 Metal Great Exceeding 1 丙午 Fire Horse 澤風大過 18 初五 3	水6 Water Poison 2 丁未 Fire Goat 山風蠱 19 初六 7	火2 Fire Dispersing 3 戊申 Earth Monkey 風水渙 20 初七 6	木3 Wood Travelling 4 己酉 Earth Rooster 火山旅 21 初八 8	金9 Metal Stagnation 5 庚戌 Metal Dog 天地否 22 初九 9
火7 Fire Alliance 6 辛亥 Metal Pig 水地比 23 初十 7	木8 Wood Thunder 7 壬子 Water Rat 震爲雷 24 十一 1	水6 Water Beauty 8 癸丑 Water Ox 山火賁 25 十二 8	火7 Fire Accomplished 9 甲寅 Wood Tiger 水火既濟 26 十三 9	水1 Water Arriving 1 乙卯 Wood Rabbit 地澤臨 27 十四 4	金4 Metal Marsh 2 丙辰 Fire Dragon 兑爲澤 28 十五 1	火2 Fire Small Livestock 3 丁巳 Fire Snake 風天小畜 29 十六 8

FEBRUARY 1983 甲寅

Xuan Kong Element 玄空五行	水火既濟 Accomplished	Period Luck 卦運	Monthly Star 月星
Fire 火7		9	2

SUNDAY	MONDAY	TUESDAY	WEDNESDAY	THURSDAY	FRIDAY	SATURDAY
		火7 Fire Water 6 庚申 Metal Monkey 坎爲水 1 十九 1	木8 Wood Lesser Exceeding 7 辛酉 Metal Rooster 雷山小過 2 二十 3	金4 Metal Gathering 8 壬戌 Water Dog 澤地萃 3 廿一 4	水6 Water Peel 9 癸亥 Water Pig 山地剝 4 廿二 6	水1 Water Earth 1 甲子 Wood Rat 坤爲地 5 廿三 1
木3 Wood Biting 2 乙丑 Wood Ox 火雷噬嗑 6 廿四 6	火2 Fire Family 3 丙寅 Fire Tiger 風火家人 7 廿五 4	水6 Water Decreasing 4 丁卯 Fire Rabbit 山澤損 8 廿六 9	金9 Metal Tread 5 戊辰 Earth Dragon 天澤履 9 廿七 6	木8 Wood Great Strength 6 己巳 Earth Snake 雷天大壯 10 廿八 2	木8 Wood Consistency 7 庚午 Metal Horse 雷風恆 11 廿九 9	金9 Metal Litigation 8 辛未 Metal Goat 天水訟 12 三十 3
水1 Water Officer 9 壬申 Water Monkey 地水師 13 正月初一 7	火2 Fire Gradual Progress 1 癸酉 Water Rooster 風山漸 14 初二 7	火7 Fire Obstruction 2 甲戌 Wood Dog 水山蹇 15 初三 2	木3 Wood Advancement 3 乙亥 Wood Pig 火地晉 16 初四 3	水6 Water Nourish 4 丙子 Fire Rat 山雷頤 17 初五 3	金4 Metal Following 5 丁丑 Fire Ox 澤雷隨 18 初六 7	木8 Wood Abundance 6 戊寅 Earth Tiger 雷火豐 19 初七 6
火7 Fire Regulate 7 己卯 Earth Rabbit 水澤節 20 初八 8	水1 Water Unity 8 庚辰 Metal Dragon 地天泰 21 初九 9	木3 Wood Great Reward 9 辛巳 Metal Snake 火天大有 22 初十 7	火2 Fire Wind 1 壬午 Water Horse 巽爲風 23 十一 1	金4 Metal Trap 2 癸未 Water Goat 澤水困 24 十二 8	木3 Wood Not Yet Accomplished 3 甲申 Wood Monkey 火水未濟 25 十三 9	金9 Metal Retreat 4 乙酉 Wood Rooster 天山遯 26 十四 4
水6 Water Mountain 5 丙戌 Fire Dog 艮爲山 27 十五 1	木8 Wood Delight 6 丁亥 Fire Pig 雷地豫 28 十六 8					

MARCH 1983 乙卯

Xuan Kong Element 玄空五行	地澤臨 Arriving	Period Luck 卦運	Monthly Star 月星
Water 水1		4	1

SUNDAY	MONDAY	TUESDAY	WEDNESDAY	THURSDAY	FRIDAY	SATURDAY
		1 十七 火7 Fire · 7 Beginning 水雷屯 戊子 Earth Rat 4	**2** 十八 金9 Metal · 8 Without Wrongdoing 天雷無妄 己丑 Earth Ox 2	**3** 十九 木3 Wood · 9 Fire 離爲火 庚寅 Metal Tiger 1	**4** 二十 火2 Fire · 1 Sincerity 風澤中孚 辛卯 Metal Rabbit 3	**5** 廿一 水6 Water · 2 Big Livestock 山天大畜 壬辰 Water Dragon 4
6 廿二 金4 Metal · 3 Eliminating 澤天夬 癸巳 Water Snake 6	**7** 廿三 金9 Metal · 4 Heaven 乾爲天 甲午 Wood Horse 1	**8** 廿四 火7 Fire · 5 Well 水風井 乙未 Wood Goat 6	**9** 廿五 木8 Wood · 6 Relief 雷水解 丙申 Fire Monkey 4	**10** 廿六 金4 Metal · 7 Influence 澤山咸 丁酉 Fire Rooster 9	**11** 廿七 水1 Water · 8 Humility 地山謙 戊戌 Earth Dog 6	**12** 廿八 火2 Fire · 9 Observation 風地觀 己亥 Earth Pig 2
13 廿九 火2 Fire · 1 Increasing 風雷益 庚子 Metal Rat 9	**14** 三十 水1 Water · 2 Dimming Light 地火明夷 辛丑 Metal Ox 3	**15** 二月初一 金9 Metal · 3 Fellowship 天火同人 壬寅 Water Tiger 7	**16** 初二 木8 Wood · 4 Marrying Maiden 雷澤歸妹 癸卯 Water Rabbit 7	**17** 初三 木3 Wood · 5 Opposition 火澤睽 甲辰 Wood Dragon 2	**18** 初四 火7 Fire · 6 Waiting 水天需 乙巳 Wood Snake 3	**19** 初五 金4 Metal · 7 Great Exceeding 澤風大過 丙午 Fire Horse 3
20 初六 水6 Water · 8 Poison 山風蠱 丁未 Fire Goat 7	**21** 初七 火2 Fire · 9 Dispersing 風水渙 戊申 Earth Monkey 6	**22** 初八 木3 Wood · 1 Travelling 火山旅 己酉 Earth Rooster 8	**23** 初九 金9 Metal · 2 Stagnation 天地否 庚戌 Metal Dog 9	**24** 初十 火7 Fire · 3 Alliance 水地比 辛亥 Metal Pig 7	**25** 十一 木8 Wood · 4 Thunder 震爲雷 壬子 Water Rat 1	**26** 十二 水6 Water · 5 Beauty 山火賁 癸丑 Water Ox 8
27 十三 火7 Fire · 6 Accomplished 水火既濟 甲寅 Wood Tiger 9	**28** 十四 水1 Water · 7 Arriving 地澤臨 乙卯 Wood Rabbit 4	**29** 十五 金4 Metal · 8 Marsh 兑爲澤 丙辰 Fire Dragon 1	**30** 十六 火2 Fire · 9 Small Livestock 風天小畜 丁巳 Fire Snake 8	**31** 十七 木3 Wood · 1 The Cauldron 火風鼎 戊午 Earth Horse 4		

APRIL 1983 丙辰

Xuan Kong Element 玄空五行	兑爲澤 Marsh	Period Luck 卦運	Monthly Star 月星
Metal 金4		1	9

SUNDAY	MONDAY	TUESDAY	WEDNESDAY	THURSDAY	FRIDAY	SATURDAY
					1 十八 水1 Water · 2 Rising 地風升 己未 Earth Goat 2	**2** 十九 火7 Fire · 3 Water 坎爲水 庚申 Metal Monkey 1
3 二十 木8 Wood · 4 Lesser Exceeding 雷山小過 辛酉 Metal Rooster 3	**4** 廿一 金4 Metal · 5 Gathering 澤地萃 壬戌 Water Dog 4	**5** 廿二 水6 Water · 6 Peel 山地剝 癸亥 Water Pig 6	**6** 廿三 水1 Water · 7 Earth 坤爲地 甲子 Wood Rat 1	**7** 廿四 木3 Wood · 8 Biting 火雷噬嗑 乙丑 Wood Ox 6	**8** 廿五 火2 Fire · 9 Family 風火家人 丙寅 Fire Tiger 4	**9** 廿六 水6 Water · 1 Decreasing 山澤損 丁卯 Fire Rabbit 9
10 廿七 金9 Metal · 2 Tread 天澤履 戊辰 Earth Dragon 6	**11** 廿八 木8 Wood · 3 Great Strength 雷天大壯 己巳 Earth Snake 2	**12** 廿九 木8 Wood · 4 Consistency 雷風恒 庚午 Metal Horse 9	**13** 三月初一 金9 Metal · 5 Litigation 天水訟 辛未 Metal Goat 3	**14** 初二 水1 Water · 6 Officer 地水師 壬申 Water Monkey 7	**15** 初三 火2 Fire · 7 Gradual Progress 風山漸 癸酉 Water Rooster 7	**16** 初四 火7 Fire · 8 Obstruction 水山蹇 甲戌 Wood Dog 2
17 初五 木3 Wood · 9 Advancement 火地晉 乙亥 Wood Pig 3	**18** 初六 水6 Water · 1 Nourish 山雷頤 丙子 Fire Rat 3	**19** 初七 金4 Metal · 2 Following 澤雷隨 丁丑 Fire Ox 7	**20** 初八 木8 Wood · 3 Abundance 雷火豐 戊寅 Earth Tiger 6	**21** 初九 火7 Fire · 4 Regulate 水澤節 己卯 Earth Rabbit 8	**22** 初十 水1 Water · 5 Unity 地天泰 庚辰 Metal Dragon 9	**23** 十一 木3 Wood · 6 Great Reward 火天大有 辛巳 Metal Snake 7
24 十二 火2 Fire · 7 Wind 巽爲風 壬午 Water Horse 1	**25** 十三 金4 Metal · 8 Trap 澤水困 癸未 Water Goat 8	**26** 十四 木3 Wood · 9 Not Yet Accomplished 火水未濟 甲申 Wood Monkey 9	**27** 十五 金9 Metal · 1 Retreat 天山遯 乙酉 Wood Rooster 4	**28** 十六 水6 Water · 2 Mountain 艮爲山 丙戌 Fire Dog 1	**29** 十七 木8 Wood · 3 Delight 雷地豫 丁亥 Fire Pig 8	**30** 十八 火7 Fire · 4 Beginning 水雷屯 戊子 Earth Rat 4

MAY 1983 丁巳

Xuan Kong Element 玄空五行	風天小畜 Small Livestock	Period Luck 卦運	Monthly Star 月星
Fire 火2		8	8

SUNDAY	MONDAY	TUESDAY	WEDNESDAY	THURSDAY	FRIDAY	SATURDAY
金9 Metal 5 Without Wrongdoing 己丑 Earth Ox 天雷無妄 1 十九 2	木3 Wood 6 Fire 庚寅 Metal Tiger 離爲火 2 二十 1	火2 Fire 7 Sincerity 辛卯 Metal Rabbit 風澤中孚 3 廿一 3	水6 Water 8 Big Livestock 壬辰 Water Dragon 山天大畜 4 廿二 4	金4 Metal 9 Eliminating 癸巳 Water Snake 澤天夬 5 廿三 6	金9 Metal 1 Heaven 甲午 Wood Horse 乾爲天 6 廿四 1	火7 Fire 2 Well 乙未 Wood Goat 水風井 7 廿五 6
木8 Wood 3 Relief 丙申 Fire Monkey 雷水解 8 廿六 4	金4 Metal 4 Influence 丁酉 Fire Rooster 澤山咸 9 廿七 9	水1 Water 5 Humility 戊戌 Earth Dog 地山謙 10 廿八 6	火2 Fire 6 Observation 己亥 Earth Pig 風地觀 11 廿九 2	火2 Fire 7 Increasing 庚子 Metal Rat 風雷益 12 三十 9	水1 Water 8 Dimming Light 辛丑 Metal Ox 地火明夷 13 四月初一 3	金9 Metal 9 Fellowship 壬寅 Water Tiger 天火同人 14 初二 7
木8 Wood 1 Marrying Maiden 癸卯 Water Rabbit 雷澤歸妹 15 初三 7	木3 Wood 2 Opposition 甲辰 Wood Dragon 火澤睽 16 初四 2	火7 Fire 3 Waiting 乙巳 Wood Snake 水天需 17 初五 3	金4 Metal 4 Great Exceeding 丙午 Fire Horse 澤風大過 18 初六 3	水6 Water 5 Poison 丁未 Fire Goat 山風蠱 19 初七 7	火2 Fire 6 Dispersing 戊申 Earth Monkey 風水渙 20 初八 6	木3 Wood 7 Travelling 己酉 Earth Rooster 火山旅 21 初九 8
金9 Metal 8 Stagnation 庚戌 Metal Dog 天地否 22 初十 9	火7 Fire 9 Alliance 辛亥 Metal Pig 水地比 23 十一 7	木8 Wood 1 Thunder 壬子 Water Rat 震爲雷 24 十二 1	水6 Water 2 Beauty 癸丑 Water Ox 山火賁 25 十三 8	火7 Fire 3 Accomplished 甲寅 Wood Tiger 水火既濟 26 十四 9	水1 Water 4 Arriving 乙卯 Wood Rabbit 地澤臨 27 十五 4	金4 Metal 5 Marsh 丙辰 Fire Dragon 兌爲澤 28 十六 1
火2 Fire 6 Small Livestock 丁巳 Fire Snake 風天小畜 29 十七 8	木3 Wood 7 The Cauldron 戊午 Earth Horse 火風鼎 30 十八 4	水1 Water 8 Rising 己未 Earth Goat 地風升 31 十九 2				

JUNE 1983 戊午

Xuan Kong Element 玄空五行	火風鼎 The Cauldron	Period Luck 卦運	Monthly Star 月星
Wood 木3		4	7

SUNDAY	MONDAY	TUESDAY	WEDNESDAY	THURSDAY	FRIDAY	SATURDAY
			火7 Fire 9 Water 庚申 Metal Monkey 坎爲水 1 二十 1	木8 Wood 1 Lesser Exceeding 辛酉 Metal Rooster 雷山小過 2 廿一 3	金4 Metal 2 Gathering 壬戌 Water Dog 澤地萃 3 廿二 4	水6 Water 3 Peel 癸亥 Water Pig 山地剝 4 廿三 6
水1 Water 4 Earth 甲子 Wood Rat 坤爲地 5 廿四 1	木3 Wood 5 Biting 乙丑 Wood Ox 火雷噬嗑 6 廿五 6	火2 Fire 6 Family 丙寅 Fire Tiger 風火家人 7 廿六 4	水6 Water 7 Decreasing 丁卯 Fire Rabbit 山澤損 8 廿七 9	金9 Metal 8 Tread 戊辰 Earth Dragon 天澤履 9 廿八 6	木8 Wood 9 Great Strength 己巳 Earth Snake 雷天大壯 10 廿九 2	木8 Wood 1 Consistency 庚午 Metal Horse 雷風恆 11 五月初一 9
金9 Metal 2 Litigation 辛未 Metal Goat 天水訟 12 初二 3	水1 Water 3 Officer 壬申 Water Monkey 地水師 13 初三 7	火2 Fire 4 Gradual Progress 癸酉 Water Rooster 風山漸 14 初四 7	火7 Fire 5 Obstruction 甲戌 Wood Dog 水山蹇 15 初五 2	木3 Wood 6 Advancement 乙亥 Wood Pig 火地晉 16 初六 3	水6 Water 7 Nourish 丙子 Fire Rat 山雷頤 17 初七 3	金4 Metal 8 Following 丁丑 Fire Ox 澤雷隨 18 初八 7
木8 Wood 9 Abundance 戊寅 Earth Tiger 雷火豐 19 初九 6	火7 Fire 1 Regulate 己卯 Earth Rabbit 水澤節 20 初十 8	水1 Water 2 Unity 庚辰 Metal Dragon 地天泰 21 十一 9	木3 Wood 3/7 Great Reward 辛巳 Metal Snake 火天大有 22 十二 7	火2 Fire 6 Wind 壬午 Water Horse 巽爲風 23 十三 1	金4 Metal 5 Trap 癸未 Water Goat 澤水困 24 十四 8	木3 Wood 4 Not Yet Accomplished 甲申 Wood Monkey 火水未濟 25 十五 9
金9 Metal 3 Retreat 乙酉 Wood Rooster 天山遯 26 十六 4	水6 Water 2 Mountain 丙戌 Fire Dog 艮爲山 27 十七 1	木8 Wood 1 Delight 丁亥 Fire Pig 雷地豫 28 十八 8	火7 Fire 9 Beginning 戊子 Earth Rat 水雷屯 29 十九 4	金9 Metal 8 Without Wrongdoing 己丑 Earth Ox 天雷無妄 30 二十 2		

JULY 1983 己未

Xuan Kong Element 玄空五行	地風升 Rising	Period Luck 卦運	Monthly Star 月星
Water 水1		2	6

SUNDAY	MONDAY	TUESDAY	WEDNESDAY	THURSDAY	FRIDAY	SATURDAY
火7 Fire Water 4 庚申 Metal Monkey 坎爲水 31 廿二 1					木3 Wood Fire 7 庚寅 Metal Tiger 離爲火 1 廿一 1	火2 Fire Sincerity 6 辛卯 Metal Rabbit 風澤中孚 2 廿二 3
水6 Water Big Livestock 5 壬辰 Water Dragon 山天大畜 3 廿三 4	金4 Metal Eliminating 4 癸巳 Water Snake 澤天夬 4 廿四 6	金9 Metal Heaven 3 甲午 Wood Horse 乾爲天 5 廿五 1	火7 Fire Well 2 乙未 Wood Goat 水風井 6 廿六 6	木8 Wood Relief 1 丙申 Fire Monkey 雷水解 7 廿七 4	金4 Metal Influence 9 丁酉 Fire Rooster 澤山咸 8 廿八 9	水1 Water Humility 8 戊戌 Earth Dog 地山謙 9 廿九 6
火2 Fire Observation 7 己亥 Earth Pig 風地觀 10 六月初一 2	火2 Fire Increasing 6 庚子 Metal Rat 風雷益 11 初二 9	水1 Water Dimming Light 5 辛丑 Metal Ox 地火明夷 12 初三 3	金9 Metal Fellowship 4 壬寅 Water Tiger 天火同人 13 初四 7	木8 Wood Marrying Maiden 3 癸卯 Water Rabbit 雷澤歸妹 14 初五 7	木3 Wood Opposition 2 甲辰 Wood Dragon 火澤睽 15 初六 2	火7 Fire Waiting 1 乙巳 Wood Snake 水天需 16 初七 3
金4 Metal Great Exceeding 9 丙午 Fire Horse 澤風大過 17 初八 3	水6 Water Poison 8 丁未 Fire Goat 山風蠱 18 初九 7	火2 Fire Dispersing 7 戊申 Earth Monkey 風水渙 19 初十 6	木3 Wood Travelling 6 己酉 Earth Rooster 火山旅 20 十一 8	金9 Metal Stagnation 5 庚戌 Metal Dog 天地否 21 十二 9	火7 Fire Alliance 4 辛亥 Metal Pig 水地比 22 十三 7	木8 Wood Thunder 3 壬子 Water Rat 震爲雷 23 十四 1
水6 Water Beauty 2 癸丑 Water Ox 山火賁 24 十五 8	火7 Fire Accomplished 1 甲寅 Wood Tiger 水火既濟 25 十六 9	水1 Water Arriving 9 乙卯 Wood Rabbit 地澤臨 26 十七 4	金4 Metal Marsh 8 丙辰 Fire Dragon 兑爲澤 27 十八 1	火2 Fire Small Livestock 7 丁巳 Fire Snake 風天小畜 28 十九 8	木3 Wood The Cauldron 6 戊午 Earth Horse 火風鼎 29 二十 4	水1 Water Rising 5 己未 Earth Goat 地風升 30 廿一 2

AUGUST 1983 庚申

Xuan Kong Element 玄空五行	坎爲水 Water	Period Luck 卦運	Monthly Star 月星
Fire 火7		1	5

SUNDAY	MONDAY	TUESDAY	WEDNESDAY	THURSDAY	FRIDAY	SATURDAY
	木8 Wood Lesser Exceeding 3 辛酉 Metal Rooster 雷山小過 1 廿三 3	金4 Metal Gathering 2 壬戌 Water Dog 澤地萃 2 廿四 4	水6 Water Peel 1 癸亥 Water Pig 山地剝 3 廿五 6	水1 Water Earth 9 甲子 Wood Rat 坤爲地 4 廿六 1	木3 Wood Biting 8 乙丑 Wood Ox 火雷噬嗑 5 廿七 6	火2 Fire Family 7 丙寅 Fire Tiger 風火家人 6 廿八 4
水6 Water Decreasing 6 丁卯 Fire Rabbit 山澤損 7 廿九 9	金9 Metal Tread 5 戊辰 Earth Dragon 天澤履 8 三十 6	木8 Wood Great Strength 4 己巳 Earth Snake 雷天大壯 9 七月初一 2	木8 Wood Consistency 3 庚午 Metal Horse 雷風恆 10 初二 9	金9 Metal Litigation 2 辛未 Metal Goat 天水訟 11 初三 3	水1 Water Officer 1 壬申 Water Monkey 地水師 12 初四 7	火2 Fire Gradual Progress 9 癸酉 Water Rooster 風山漸 13 初五 7
火7 Fire Obstruction 8 甲戌 Wood Dog 水山蹇 14 初六 2	木3 Wood Advancement 7 乙亥 Wood Pig 火地晉 15 初七 3	水6 Water Nourish 6 丙子 Fire Rat 山雷頤 16 初八 3	金4 Metal Following 5 丁丑 Fire Ox 澤雷隨 17 初九 7	木8 Wood Abundance 4 戊寅 Earth Tiger 雷火豐 18 初十 6	火7 Fire Regulate 3 己卯 Earth Rabbit 水澤節 19 十一 8	水1 Water Unity 2 庚辰 Metal Dragon 地天泰 20 十二 9
木3 Wood Great Reward 1 辛巳 Metal Snake 火天大有 21 十三 7	火2 Fire Wind 9 壬午 Water Horse 巽爲風 22 十四 1	金4 Metal Trap 8 癸未 Water Goat 澤水困 23 十五 8	木3 Wood Not Yet Accomplished 7 甲申 Wood Monkey 火水未濟 24 十六 9	金9 Metal Retreat 6 乙酉 Wood Rooster 天山遯 25 十七 4	水6 Water Mountain 5 丙戌 Fire Dog 艮爲山 26 十八 1	木8 Wood Delight 4 丁亥 Fire Pig 雷地豫 27 十九 8
火7 Fire Beginning 3 戊子 Earth Rat 水雷屯 28 二十 4	金9 Metal Without Wrongdoing 2 己丑 Earth Ox 天雷無妄 29 廿一 2	木3 Wood Fire 1 庚寅 Metal Tiger 離爲火 30 廿二 1	火2 Fire Sincerity 9 辛卯 Metal Rabbit 風澤中孚 31 廿三 3			

SEPTEMBER 1983 辛酉

Xuan Kong Element 玄空五行	雷山小過 Lesser Exceeding	Period Luck 卦運	Monthly Star 月星
Wood 木8		3	4

SUNDAY	MONDAY	TUESDAY	WEDNESDAY	THURSDAY	FRIDAY	SATURDAY
				水6 Water 8 Big Livestock 壬辰 Water Dragon 山天大畜 1 廿四 4	金4 Metal 7 Eliminating 癸巳 Water Snake 澤天夬 2 廿五 6	金9 Metal 6 Heaven 甲午 Wood Horse 乾為天 3 廿六 1
火7 Fire 5 Well 乙未 Wood Goat 水風井 4 廿七 6	木8 Wood 4 Relief 丙申 Fire Monkey 雷水解 5 廿八 4	金4 Metal 3 Influence 丁酉 Fire Rooster 澤山咸 6 廿九 9	水1 Water 2 Humility 戊戌 Earth Dog 地山謙 7 八月初一 6	火2 Fire 1 Observation 己亥 Earth Pig 風地觀 8 初二 2	火2 Fire 9 Increasing 庚子 Metal Rat 風雷益 9 初三 9	水1 Water 8 Dimming Light 辛丑 Metal Ox 地火明夷 10 初四 3
金9 Metal 7 Fellowship 壬寅 Water Tiger 天火同人 11 初五 7	木8 Wood 6 Marrying Maiden 癸卯 Water Rabbit 雷澤歸妹 12 初六 7	木3 Wood 5 Opposition 甲辰 Wood Dragon 火澤睽 13 初七 2	火7 Fire 4 Waiting 乙巳 Wood Snake 水天需 14 初八 3	金4 Metal 3 Great Exceeding 丙午 Fire Horse 澤風大過 15 初九 3	水6 Water 2 Poison 丁未 Fire Goat 山風蠱 16 初十 7	火2 Fire 1 Dispersing 戊申 Earth Monkey 風水渙 17 十一 6
木3 Wood 9 Travelling 己酉 Earth Rooster 火山旅 18 十二 8	金9 Metal 8 Stagnation 庚戌 Metal Dog 天地否 19 十三 9	火7 Fire 7 Alliance 辛亥 Metal Pig 水地比 20 十四 7	木8 Wood 6 Thunder 壬子 Water Rat 震為雷 21 十五 1	水6 Water 5 Beauty 癸丑 Water Ox 山火賁 22 十六 8	火7 Fire 4 Accomplished 甲寅 Wood Tiger 水火既濟 23 十七 9	水1 Water 3 Arriving 乙卯 Wood Rabbit 地澤臨 24 十八 4
金4 Metal 2 Marsh 丙辰 Fire Dragon 兑為澤 25 十九 1	火2 Fire 1 Small Livestock 丁巳 Fire Snake 風天小畜 26 二十 8	木3 Wood 9 The Cauldron 戊午 Earth Horse 火風鼎 27 廿一 4	水1 Water 8 Rising 己未 Earth Goat 地風升 28 廿二 2	火7 Fire 7 Water 庚申 Metal Monkey 坎為水 29 廿三 1	木8 Wood 6 Lesser Exceeding 辛酉 Metal Rooster 雷山小過 30 廿四 3	

OCTOBER 1983 壬戌

Xuan Kong Element 玄空五行	澤地萃 Gathering	Period Luck 卦運	Monthly Star 月星
Metal 金4		4	3

SUNDAY	MONDAY	TUESDAY	WEDNESDAY	THURSDAY	FRIDAY	SATURDAY
火2 Fire 3 Sincerity 辛卯 Metal Rabbit 風澤中孚 30 廿五 3	水6 Water 2 Big Livestock 壬辰 Water Dragon 山天大畜 31 廿六 4					金4 Metal 5 Gathering 壬戌 Water Dog 澤地萃 1 廿五 4
水6 Water 4 Peel 癸亥 Water Pig 山地剝 2 廿六 6	水1 Water 3 Earth 甲子 Wood Rat 坤為地 3 廿七 1	木3 Wood 2 Biting 乙丑 Wood Ox 火雷噬嗑 4 廿八 6	火2 Fire 1 Family 丙寅 Fire Tiger 風火家人 5 廿九 4	水6 Water 9 Decreasing 丁卯 Fire Rabbit 山澤損 6 九月初一 9	金9 Metal 8 Tread 戊辰 Earth Dragon 天澤履 7 初二 6	木8 Wood 7 Great Strength 己巳 Earth Snake 雷天大壯 8 初三 2
木8 Wood 6 Consistency 庚午 Metal Horse 雷風恆 9 初四 9	金9 Metal 5 Litigation 辛未 Metal Goat 天水訟 10 初五 3	水1 Water 4 Officer 壬申 Water Monkey 地水師 11 初六 7	火2 Fire 3 Gradual Progress 癸酉 Water Rooster 風山漸 12 初七 7	火7 Fire 2 Obstruction 甲戌 Wood Dog 水山蹇 13 初八 2	木3 Wood 1 Advancement 乙亥 Wood Pig 火地晉 14 初九 3	水6 Water 9 Nourish 丙子 Fire Rat 山雷頤 15 初十 3
金4 Metal 8 Following 丁丑 Fire Ox 澤雷隨 16 十一 7	木8 Wood 7 Abundance 戊寅 Earth Tiger 雷火豐 17 十二 6	火7 Fire 6 Regulate 己卯 Earth Rabbit 水澤節 18 十三 8	水1 Water 5 Unity 庚辰 Metal Dragon 地天泰 19 十四 9	木3 Wood 4 Great Reward 辛巳 Metal Snake 火天大有 20 十五 7	火2 Fire 3 Wind 壬午 Water Horse 巽為風 21 十六 1	金4 Metal 2 Trap 癸未 Water Goat 澤水困 22 十七 8
木3 Wood 1 Not Yet Accomplished 甲申 Wood Monkey 火水未濟 23 十八 9	金9 Metal 9 Retreat 乙酉 Wood Rooster 天山遯 24 十九 4	水6 Water 8 Mountain 丙戌 Fire Dog 艮為山 25 二十 1	木8 Wood 7 Delight 丁亥 Fire Pig 雷地豫 26 廿一 8	火7 Fire 6 Beginning 戊子 Earth Rat 水雷屯 27 廿二 4	金9 Metal 5 Without Wrongdoing 己丑 Earth Ox 天雷無妄 28 廿三 2	木3 Wood 4 Fire 庚寅 Metal Tiger 離為火 29 廿四 1

NOVEMBER 1983 癸亥

Xuan Kong Element 玄空五行	山地剝 Peel	Period Luck 卦運	Monthly Star 月星
Water 水6		6	2

SUNDAY	MONDAY	TUESDAY	WEDNESDAY	THURSDAY	FRIDAY	SATURDAY
		金4 Metal 1 Eliminating 澤天夬 癸巳 Water Snake **1** 廿七 6	金9 Metal 9 Heaven 乾爲天 甲午 Wood Horse **2** 廿八 1	火7 Fire 8 Well 水風井 乙未 Wood Goat **3** 廿九 6	木8 Wood 7 Relief 雷水解 丙申 Fire Monkey **4** 三十 4	金4 Metal 6 Influence 澤山咸 丁酉 Fire Rooster **5** 十月初一 9
水1 Water 5 Humility 地山謙 戊戌 Earth Dog **6** 初二 6	火2 Fire 4 Observation 風地觀 己亥 Earth Pig **7** 初三 2	火2 Fire 3 Increasing 風雷益 庚子 Metal Rat **8** 初四 9	水1 Water 2 Dimming Light 地火明夷 辛丑 Metal Ox **9** 初五 3	金9 Metal 1 Fellowship 天火同人 壬寅 Water Tiger **10** 初六 7	木8 Wood 9 Marrying Maiden 雷澤歸妹 癸卯 Water Rabbit **11** 初七 7	木3 Wood 8 Opposition 火澤睽 甲辰 Wood Dragon **12** 初八 2
火7 Fire 7 Waiting 水天需 乙巳 Wood Snake **13** 初九 3	金4 Metal 6 Great Exceeding 澤風大過 丙午 Fire Horse **14** 初十 3	水6 Water 5 Poison 山風蠱 丁未 Fire Goat **15** 十一 7	火2 Fire 4 Dispersing 風水渙 戊申 Earth Monkey **16** 十二 6	木3 Wood 3 Travelling 火山旅 己酉 Earth Rooster **17** 十三 8	金9 Metal 2 Stagnation 天地否 庚戌 Metal Dog **18** 十四 9	火7 Fire 1 Alliance 水地比 辛亥 Metal Pig **19** 十五 7
木8 Wood 9 Thunder 震爲雷 壬子 Water Rat **20** 十六 1	水6 Water 8 Beauty 山火賁 癸丑 Water Ox **21** 十七 8	火7 Fire 7 Accomplished 水火既濟 甲寅 Wood Tiger **22** 十八 9	水1 Water 6 Arriving 地澤臨 乙卯 Wood Rabbit **23** 十九 4	金4 Metal 5 Marsh 兑爲澤 丙辰 Fire Dragon **24** 二十 1	火2 Fire 4 Small Livestock 風天小畜 丁巳 Fire Snake **25** 廿一 8	木3 Wood 3 The Cauldron 火風鼎 戊午 Earth Horse **26** 廿二 4
水1 Water 2 Rising 地風升 己未 Earth Goat **27** 廿三 2	火7 Fire 1 Water 坎爲水 庚申 Metal Monkey **28** 廿四 1	木8 Wood 9 Lesser Exceeding 雷山小過 辛酉 Metal Rooster **29** 廿五 3	金4 Metal 8 Gathering 澤地萃 壬戌 Water Dog **30** 廿六 4			

DECEMBER 1983 甲子

Xuan Kong Element 玄空五行	坤爲地 Earth	Period Luck 卦運	Monthly Star 月星
Water 水1		1	1

SUNDAY	MONDAY	TUESDAY	WEDNESDAY	THURSDAY	FRIDAY	SATURDAY
				水6 Water 7 Peel 山地剝 癸亥 Water Pig **1** 廿七 6	水1 Water 6 Earth 坤爲地 甲子 Wood Rat **2** 廿八 1	木3 Wood 5 Biting 火雷噬嗑 乙丑 Wood Ox **3** 廿九 6
火2 Fire 4 Family 風火家人 丙寅 Fire Tiger **4** 十一月初一 4	水6 Water 3 Decreasing 山澤損 丁卯 Fire Rabbit **5** 初二 9	金9 Metal 2 Tread 天澤履 戊辰 Earth Dragon **6** 初三 6	木8 Wood 1 Great Strength 雷天大壯 己巳 Earth Snake **7** 初四 2	木8 Wood 9 Consistency 雷風恒 庚午 Metal Horse **8** 初五 9	金9 Metal 8 Litigation 天水訟 辛未 Metal Goat **9** 初六 3	水1 Water 7 Officer 地水師 壬申 Water Monkey **10** 初七 7
火2 Fire 6 Gradual Progress 風山漸 癸酉 Water Rooster **11** 初八 7	火7 Fire 5 Obstruction 水山蹇 甲戌 Wood Dog **12** 初九 2	木3 Wood 4 Advancement 火地晉 乙亥 Wood Pig **13** 初十 3	水6 Water 3 Nourish 山雷頤 丙子 Fire Rat **14** 十一 3	金4 Metal 2 Following 澤雷隨 丁丑 Fire Ox **15** 十二 7	木8 Wood 1 Abundance 雷火豐 戊寅 Earth Tiger **16** 十三 6	火7 Fire 9 Regulate 水澤節 己卯 Earth Rabbit **17** 十四 8
水1 Water 8 Unity 地天泰 庚辰 Metal Dragon **18** 十五 9	木3 Wood 7 Great Reward 火天大有 辛巳 Metal Snake **19** 十六 7	火2 Fire 6 Wind 巽爲風 壬午 Water Horse **20** 十七 1	金4 Metal 5 Trap 澤水困 癸未 Water Goat **21** 十八 8	木3 Wood 4/6 Not Yet Accomplished 火水未濟 甲申 Wood Monkey **22** 十九 9	金9 Metal 7 Retreat 天山遯 乙酉 Wood Rooster **23** 二十 4	水6 Water 8 Mountain 艮爲山 丙戌 Fire Dog **24** 廿一 1
木8 Wood 9 Delight 雷地豫 丁亥 Fire Pig **25** 廿二 8	火7 Fire 1 Beginning 水雷屯 戊子 Earth Rat **26** 廿三 4	金9 Metal 2 Without Wrongdoing 天雷無妄 己丑 Earth Ox **27** 廿四 2	木3 Wood 3 Fire 離爲火 庚寅 Metal Tiger **28** 廿五 1	火2 Fire 4 Sincerity 風澤中孚 辛卯 Metal Rabbit **29** 廿六 3	水6 Water 5 Big Livestock 山天大畜 壬辰 Water Dragon **30** 廿七 4	金4 Metal 6 Eliminating 澤天夬 癸巳 Water Snake **31** 廿八 6

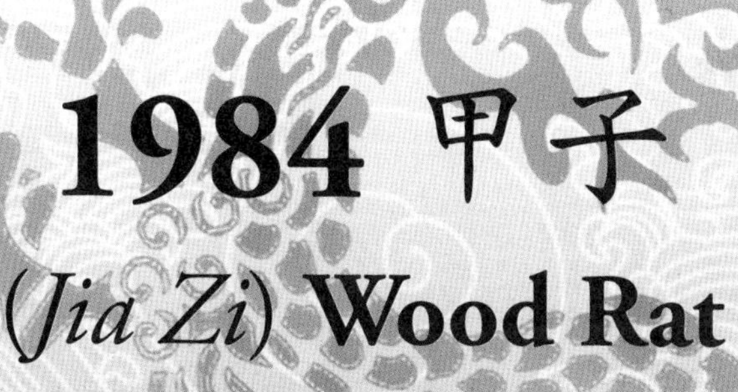

1984 甲子

(*Jia Zi*) Wood Rat

1984 甲子 *(Jia Zi)* Wood Rat

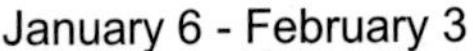

January 6 - February 3

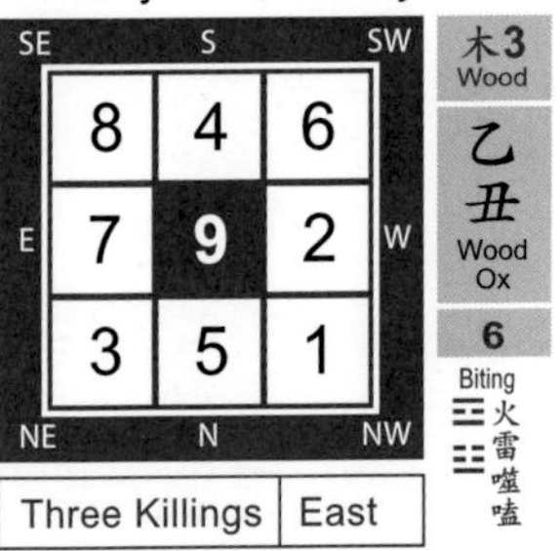

February 4 - March 4

March 5 - April 3

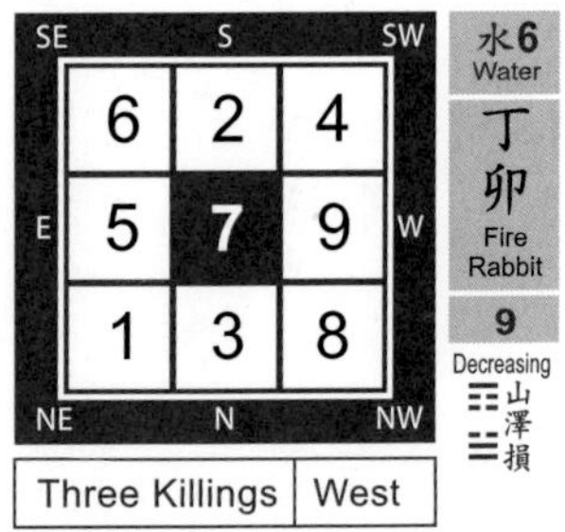

April 4 - May 4

May 5 - June 4

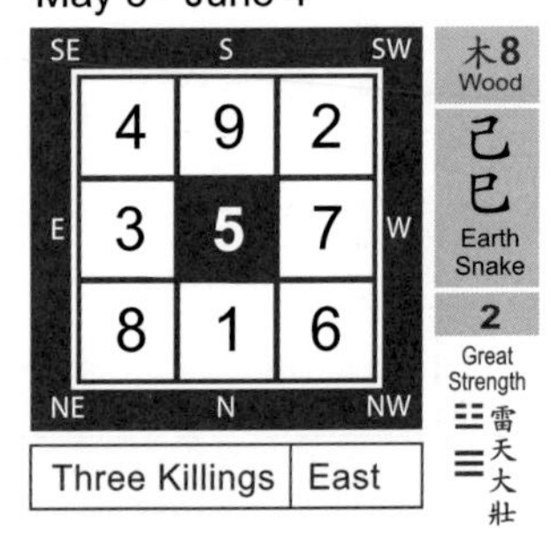

June 5 - July 6

July 7 - August 6

August 7 - September 6

September 7 - October 7

October 8 - November 6

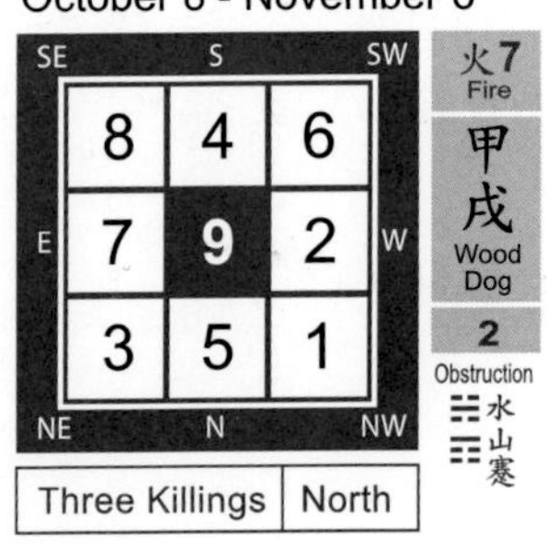

November 7 - December 6

December 7 - January 4

JANUARY 1984 乙丑

Xuan Kong Element 玄空五行	火雷噬嗑 Biting	Period Luck 卦運	Monthly Star 月星
Wood 木3		6	9

SUNDAY	MONDAY	TUESDAY	WEDNESDAY	THURSDAY	FRIDAY	SATURDAY
金9 Metal Heaven 7 甲午 Wood Horse 乾爲天 1 廿九 1	火7 Fire Well 8 乙未 Wood Goat 水風井 2 三十 6	木8 Wood Relief 9 丙申 Fire Monkey 雷水解 3 十二月初一 4	金4 Metal Influence 1 丁酉 Fire Rooster 澤山咸 4 初二 9	水1 Water Humility 2 戊戌 Earth Dog 地山謙 5 初三 6	火2 Fire Observation 3 己亥 Earth Pig 風地觀 6 初四 2	火2 Fire Increasing 4 庚子 Metal Rat 風雷益 7 初五 9
水1 Water Dimming Light 5 辛丑 Metal Ox 地火明夷 8 初六 3	金9 Metal Fellowship 6 壬寅 Water Tiger 天火同人 9 初七 7	木8 Wood Marrying Maiden 7 癸卯 Water Rabbit 雷澤歸妹 10 初八 7	木3 Wood Opposition 8 甲辰 Wood Dragon 火澤睽 11 初九 2	火7 Fire Waiting 9 乙巳 Wood Snake 水天需 12 初十 3	金4 Metal Great Exceeding 1 丙午 Fire Horse 澤風大過 13 十一 3	水6 Water Poison 2 丁未 Fire Goat 山風蠱 14 十二 7
火2 Fire Dispersing 3 戊申 Earth Monkey 風水渙 15 十三 6	木3 Wood Travelling 4 己酉 Earth Rooster 火山旅 16 十四 8	金9 Metal Stagnation 5 庚戌 Metal Dog 天地否 17 十五 9	火7 Fire Alliance 6 辛亥 Metal Pig 水地比 18 十六 7	木8 Wood Thunder 7 壬子 Water Rat 震爲雷 19 十七 1	水6 Water Beauty 8 癸丑 Water Ox 山火賁 20 十八 8	火7 Fire Accomplished 9 甲寅 Wood Tiger 水火既濟 21 十九 9
水1 Water Arriving 1 乙卯 Wood Rabbit 地澤臨 22 二十 4	金4 Metal Marsh 2 丙辰 Fire Dragon 兑爲澤 23 廿一 1	火2 Fire Small Livestock 3 丁巳 Fire Snake 風天小畜 24 廿二 8	木3 Wood The Cauldron 4 戊午 Earth Horse 火風鼎 25 廿三 4	水1 Water Rising 5 己未 Earth Goat 地風升 26 廿四 2	火7 Fire Water 6 庚申 Metal Monkey 坎爲水 27 廿五 1	木8 Wood Lesser Exceeding 7 辛酉 Metal Rooster 雷山小過 28 廿六 3
金4 Metal Gathering 8 壬戌 Water Dog 澤地萃 29 廿七 4	水6 Water Peel 9 癸亥 Water Pig 山地剝 30 廿八 6	水1 Water Earth 1 甲子 Wood Rat 坤爲地 31 廿九 1				

FEBRUARY 1984 丙寅

Xuan Kong Element 玄空五行	風火家人 Family	Period Luck 卦運	Monthly Star 月星
Fire 火2		4	8

SUNDAY	MONDAY	TUESDAY	WEDNESDAY	THURSDAY	FRIDAY	SATURDAY
			木3 Wood Biting 2 乙丑 Wood Ox 火雷噬嗑 1 三十 6	火2 Fire Family 3 丙寅 Fire Tiger 風火家人 2 正月初一 4	水6 Water Decreasing 4 丁卯 Fire Rabbit 山澤損 3 初二 9	金9 Metal Tread 5 戊辰 Earth Dragon 天澤履 4 初三 6
木8 Wood Great Strength 6 己巳 Earth Snake 雷天大壯 5 初四 2	木8 Wood Consistency 7 庚午 Metal Horse 雷風恒 6 初五 9	金9 Metal Litigation 8 辛未 Metal Goat 天水訟 7 初六 3	水1 Water Officer 9 壬申 Water Monkey 地水師 8 初七 7	火2 Fire Gradual Progress 1 癸酉 Water Rooster 風山漸 9 初八 7	火7 Fire Obstruction 2 甲戌 Wood Dog 水山蹇 10 初九 2	木3 Wood Advancement 3 乙亥 Wood Pig 火地晉 11 初十 3
水6 Water Nourish 4 丙子 Fire Rat 山雷頤 12 十一 3	金4 Metal Following 5 丁丑 Fire Ox 澤雷隨 13 十二 7	木8 Wood Abundance 6 戊寅 Earth Tiger 雷火豐 14 十三 6	火7 Fire Regulate 7 己卯 Earth Rabbit 水澤節 15 十四 8	水1 Water Unity 8 庚辰 Metal Dragon 地天泰 16 十五 9	木3 Wood Great Reward 9 辛巳 Metal Snake 火天大有 17 十六 7	火2 Fire Wind 1 壬午 Water Horse 巽爲風 18 十七 1
金4 Metal Trap 2 癸未 Water Goat 澤水困 19 十八 8	木3 Wood Not Yet Accomplished 3 甲申 Wood Monkey 火水未濟 20 十九 9	金9 Metal Retreat 4 乙酉 Wood Rooster 天山遯 21 二十 4	水6 Water Mountain 5 丙戌 Fire Dog 艮爲山 22 廿一 1	木8 Wood Delight 6 丁亥 Fire Pig 雷地豫 23 廿二 8	火7 Fire Beginning 7 戊子 Earth Rat 水雷屯 24 廿三 4	金9 Metal Without Wrongdoing 8 己丑 Earth Ox 天雷無妄 25 廿四 2
木3 Wood Fire 9 庚寅 Metal Tiger 離爲火 26 廿五 1	火2 Fire Sincerity 1 辛卯 Metal Rabbit 風澤中孚 27 廿六 3	水6 Water Big Livestock 2 壬辰 Water Dragon 山天大畜 28 廿七 4	金4 Metal Eliminating 3 癸巳 Water Snake 澤天夬 29 廿八 6			

MARCH 1984 丁卯

Xuan Kong Element 玄空五行	山澤損 Decreasing	Period Luck 卦運	Monthly Star 月星
Water 水6		9	7

SUNDAY	MONDAY	TUESDAY	WEDNESDAY	THURSDAY	FRIDAY	SATURDAY
				金9 Metal Heaven 4 甲午 Wood Horse 乾爲天 1 廿九 1	火7 Fire Well 5 乙未 Wood Goat 水風井 2 三十 6	木8 Wood Relief 6 丙申 Fire Monkey 雷水解 3 二月初一 4
金4 Metal Influence 7 丁酉 Fire Rooster 澤山咸 4 初二 9	水1 Water Humility 8 戊戌 Earth Dog 地山謙 5 初三 6	火2 Fire Observation 9 己亥 Earth Pig 風地觀 6 初四 2	火2 Fire Increasing 1 庚子 Metal Rat 風雷益 7 初五 9	水1 Water Dimming Light 2 辛丑 Metal Ox 地火明夷 8 初六 3	金9 Metal Fellowship 3 壬寅 Water Tiger 天火同人 9 初七 7	木8 Wood Marrying Maiden 4 癸卯 Water Rabbit 雷澤歸妹 10 初八 7
木3 Wood Opposition 5 甲辰 Wood Dragon 火澤睽 11 初九 2	火7 Fire Waiting 6 乙巳 Wood Snake 水天需 12 初十 3	金4 Metal Great Exceeding 7 丙午 Fire Horse 澤風大過 13 十一 3	水6 Water Poison 8 丁未 Fire Goat 山風蠱 14 十二 7	火2 Fire Dispersing 9 戊申 Earth Monkey 風水渙 15 十三 6	木3 Wood Travelling 1 己酉 Earth Rooster 火山旅 16 十四 8	金9 Metal Stagnation 2 庚戌 Metal Dog 天地否 17 十五 9
火7 Fire Alliance 3 辛亥 Metal Pig 水地比 18 十六 7	木8 Wood Thunder 4 壬子 Water Rat 震爲雷 19 十七 1	水6 Water Beauty 5 癸丑 Water Ox 山火賁 20 十八 8	火7 Fire Accomplished 6 甲寅 Wood Tiger 水火既濟 21 十九 9	水1 Water Arriving 7 乙卯 Wood Rabbit 地澤臨 22 二十 4	金4 Metal Marsh 8 丙辰 Fire Dragon 兑爲澤 23 廿一 1	火2 Fire Small Livestock 9 丁巳 Fire Snake 風天小畜 24 廿二 8
木3 Wood The Cauldron 1 戊午 Earth Horse 火風鼎 25 廿三 4	水1 Water Rising 2 己未 Earth Goat 地風升 26 廿四 2	火7 Fire Water 3 庚申 Metal Monkey 坎爲水 27 廿五 1	木8 Wood Lesser Exceeding 4 辛酉 Metal Rooster 雷山小過 28 廿六 3	金4 Metal Gathering 5 壬戌 Water Dog 澤地萃 29 廿七 4	水6 Water Peel 6 癸亥 Water Pig 山地剝 30 廿八 6	水1 Water Earth 7 甲子 Wood Rat 坤爲地 31 廿九 1

APRIL 1984 戊辰

Xuan Kong Element 玄空五行	天澤履 Tread	Period Luck 卦運	Monthly Star 月星
Metal 金9		6	6

SUNDAY	MONDAY	TUESDAY	WEDNESDAY	THURSDAY	FRIDAY	SATURDAY
木3 Wood Biting 8 乙丑 Wood Ox 火雷噬嗑 1 三月初一 6	火2 Fire Family 9 丙寅 Fire Tiger 風火家人 2 初二 4	水6 Water Decreasing 1 丁卯 Fire Rabbit 山澤損 3 初三 9	金9 Metal Tread 2 戊辰 Earth Dragon 天澤履 4 初四 6	木8 Wood Great Strength 3 己巳 Earth Snake 雷天大壯 5 初五 2	木8 Wood Consistency 4 庚午 Metal Horse 雷風恆 6 初六 9	金9 Metal Litigation 5 辛未 Metal Goat 天水訟 7 初七 3
水1 Water Officer 6 壬申 Water Monkey 地水師 8 初八 7	火2 Fire Gradual Progress 7 癸酉 Water Rooster 風山漸 9 初九 7	火7 Fire Obstruction 8 甲戌 Wood Dog 水山蹇 10 初十 2	木3 Wood Advancement 9 乙亥 Wood Pig 火地晉 11 十一 3	水6 Water Nourish 1 丙子 Fire Rat 山雷頤 12 十二 3	金4 Metal Following 2 丁丑 Fire Ox 澤雷隨 13 十三 7	木8 Wood Abundance 3 戊寅 Earth Tiger 雷火豐 14 十四 6
火7 Fire Regulate 4 己卯 Earth Rabbit 水澤節 15 十五 8	水1 Water Unity 5 庚辰 Metal Dragon 地天泰 16 十六 9	木3 Wood Great Reward 6 辛巳 Metal Snake 火天大有 17 十七 7	火2 Fire Wind 7 壬午 Water Horse 巽爲風 18 十八 1	金4 Metal Trap 8 癸未 Water Goat 澤水困 19 十九 8	木3 Wood Not Yet Accomplished 9 甲申 Wood Monkey 火水未濟 20 二十 9	金9 Metal Retreat 1 乙酉 Wood Rooster 天山遯 21 廿一 4
水6 Water Mountain 2 丙戌 Fire Dog 艮爲山 22 廿二 1	木8 Wood Delight 3 丁亥 Fire Pig 雷地豫 23 廿三 8	火7 Fire Beginning 4 戊子 Earth Rat 水雷屯 24 廿四 4	金9 Metal Without Wrongdoing 5 己丑 Earth Ox 天雷無妄 25 廿五 2	木3 Wood Fire 6 庚寅 Metal Tiger 離爲火 26 廿六 1	火2 Fire Sincerity 7 辛卯 Metal Rabbit 風澤中孚 27 廿七 3	水6 Water Big Livestock 8 壬辰 Water Dragon 山天大畜 28 廿八 4
金4 Metal Eliminating 9 癸巳 Water Snake 澤天夬 29 廿九 6	金9 Metal Heaven 1 甲午 Wood Horse 乾爲天 30 三十 1					

MAY 1984 己巳

Xuan Kong Element 玄空五行	雷天大壯	Period Luck 卦運	Monthly Star 月星
Wood 木8	Great Strength	2	5

SUNDAY	MONDAY	TUESDAY	WEDNESDAY	THURSDAY	FRIDAY	SATURDAY
		1 火7 Fire · 2 Well 乙未 Wood Goat 水風井 四月初一 6	2 木8 Wood · 3 Relief 丙申 Fire Monkey 雷水解 初二 4	3 金4 Metal · 4 Influence 丁酉 Fire Rooster 澤山咸 初三 9	4 水1 Water · 5 Humility 戊戌 Earth Dog 地山謙 初四 6	5 火2 Fire · 6 Observation 己亥 Earth Pig 風地觀 初五 2
6 火2 Fire · 7 Increasing 庚子 Metal Rat 風雷益 初六 9	7 水1 Water · 8 Dimming Light 辛丑 Metal Ox 地火明夷 初七 3	8 金9 Metal · 9 Fellowship 壬寅 Water Tiger 天火同人 初八 7	9 木8 Wood · 1 Marrying Maiden 癸卯 Water Rabbit 雷澤歸妹 初九 7	10 木3 Wood · 2 Opposition 甲辰 Wood Dragon 火澤睽 初十 2	11 火7 Fire · 3 Waiting 乙巳 Wood Snake 水天需 十一 3	12 金4 Metal · 4 Great Exceeding 丙午 Fire Horse 澤風大過 十二 3
13 水6 Water · 5 Poison 丁未 Fire Goat 山風蠱 十三 7	14 火2 Fire · 6 Dispersing 戊申 Earth Monkey 風水渙 十四 6	15 木3 Wood · 7 Travelling 己酉 Earth Rooster 火山旅 十五 8	16 金9 Metal · 8 Stagnation 庚戌 Metal Dog 天地否 十六 9	17 火7 Fire · 9 Alliance 辛亥 Metal Pig 水地比 十七 7	18 木8 Wood · 1 Thunder 壬子 Water Rat 震為雷 十八 1	19 水6 Water · 2 Beauty 癸丑 Water Ox 山火賁 十九 8
20 火7 Fire · 3 Accomplished 甲寅 Wood Tiger 水火既濟 二十 9	21 水1 Water · 4 Arriving 乙卯 Wood Rabbit 地澤臨 廿一 4	22 金4 Metal · 5 Marsh 丙辰 Fire Dragon 兑為澤 廿二 1	23 火2 Fire · 6 Small Livestock 丁巳 Fire Snake 風天小畜 廿三 8	24 木3 Wood · 7 The Cauldron 戊午 Earth Horse 火風鼎 廿四 4	25 水1 Water · 8 Rising 己未 Earth Goat 地風升 廿五 2	26 火7 Fire · 9 Water 庚申 Metal Monkey 坎為水 廿六 1
27 木8 Wood · 1 Lesser Exceeding 辛酉 Metal Rooster 雷山小過 廿七 3	28 金4 Metal · 2 Gathering 壬戌 Water Dog 澤地萃 廿八 4	29 水6 Water · 3 Peel 癸亥 Water Pig 山地剝 廿九 6	30 水1 Water · 4 Earth 甲子 Wood Rat 坤為地 三十 1	31 木3 Wood · 5 Biting 乙丑 Wood Ox 火雷噬嗑 五月初一 6		

JUNE 1984 庚午

Xuan Kong Element 玄空五行	雷風恆	Period Luck 卦運	Monthly Star 月星
Wood 木8	Consistency	9	4

SUNDAY	MONDAY	TUESDAY	WEDNESDAY	THURSDAY	FRIDAY	SATURDAY
					1 火2 Fire · 6 Family 丙寅 Fire Tiger 風火家人 初二 4	2 水6 Water · 7 Decreasing 丁卯 Fire Rabbit 山澤損 初三 9
3 金9 Metal · 8 Tread 戊辰 Earth Dragon 天澤履 初四 6	4 木8 Wood · 9 Great Strength 己巳 Earth Snake 雷天大壯 初五 2	5 木8 Wood · 1 Consistency 庚午 Metal Horse 雷風恆 初六 9	6 金9 Metal · 2 Litigation 辛未 Metal Goat 天水訟 初七 3	7 水1 Water · 3 Officer 壬申 Water Monkey 地水師 初八 7	8 火2 Fire · 4 Gradual Progress 癸酉 Water Rooster 風山漸 初九 7	9 火7 Fire · 5 Obstruction 甲戌 Wood Dog 水山蹇 初十 2
10 木3 Wood · 6 Advancement 乙亥 Wood Pig 火地晉 十一 3	11 水6 Water · 7 Nourish 丙子 Fire Rat 山雷頤 十二 3	12 金4 Metal · 8 Following 丁丑 Fire Ox 澤雷隨 十三 7	13 木8 Wood · 9 Abundance 戊寅 Earth Tiger 雷火豐 十四 6	14 火7 Fire · 1 Regulate 己卯 Earth Rabbit 水澤節 十五 8	15 水1 Water · 2 Unity 庚辰 Metal Dragon 地天泰 十六 9	16 木3 Wood · 3 Great Reward 辛巳 Metal Snake 火天大有 十七 7
17 火2 Fire · 4 Wind 壬午 Water Horse 巽為風 十八 1	18 金4 Metal · 5 Trap 癸未 Water Goat 澤水困 十九 8	19 木3 Wood · 6 Not Yet Accomplished 甲申 Wood Monkey 火水未濟 二十 9	20 金9 Metal · 7 Retreat 乙酉 Wood Rooster 天山遯 廿一 4	21 水6 Water · 8/2 Mountain 丙戌 Fire Dog 艮為山 廿二 1	22 木8 Wood · 1 Delight 丁亥 Fire Pig 雷地豫 廿三 8	23 火7 Fire · 9 Beginning 戊子 Earth Rat 水雷屯 廿四 4
24 金9 Metal · 8 Without Wrongdoing 己丑 Earth Ox 天雷無妄 廿五 2	25 木3 Wood · 7 Fire 庚寅 Metal Tiger 離為火 廿六 1	26 火2 Fire · 6 Sincerity 辛卯 Metal Rabbit 風澤中孚 廿七 3	27 水6 Water · 5 Big Livestock 壬辰 Water Dragon 山天大畜 廿八 4	28 金4 Metal · 4 Eliminating 癸巳 Water Snake 澤天夬 廿九 6	29 金9 Metal · 3 Heaven 甲午 Wood Horse 乾為天 六月初一 1	30 火7 Fire · 2 Well 乙未 Wood Goat 水風井 初二 6

JULY 1984 辛未

Xuan Kong Element 玄空五行	天水訟 Litigation	Period Luck 卦運	Monthly Star 月星
Metal 金9		3	3

SUNDAY	MONDAY	TUESDAY	WEDNESDAY	THURSDAY	FRIDAY	SATURDAY
1 初三 木8 Wood 丙申 Fire Monkey Relief 雷水解 4 / 1	**2** 初四 金4 Metal 丁酉 Fire Rooster Influence 澤山咸 9 / 9	**3** 初五 水1 Water 戊戌 Earth Dog Humility 地山謙 6 / 8	**4** 初六 火2 Fire 己亥 Earth Pig Observation 風地觀 2 / 7	**5** 初七 火2 Fire 庚子 Metal Rat Increasing 風雷益 9 / 6	**6** 初八 水1 Water 辛丑 Metal Ox Dimming Light 地火明夷 3 / 5	**7** 初九 金9 Metal 壬寅 Water Tiger Fellowship 天火同人 7 / 4
8 初十 木8 Wood 癸卯 Water Rabbit Marrying Maiden 雷澤歸妹 7 / 3	**9** 十一 木3 Wood 甲辰 Wood Dragon Opposition 火澤睽 2 / 2	**10** 十二 火7 Fire 乙巳 Wood Snake Waiting 水天需 3 / 1	**11** 十三 金4 Metal 丙午 Fire Horse Great Exceeding 澤風大過 3 / 9	**12** 十四 水6 Water 丁未 Fire Goat Poison 山風蠱 7 / 8	**13** 十五 火2 Fire 戊申 Earth Monkey Dispersing 風水渙 6 / 7	**14** 十六 木3 Wood 己酉 Earth Rooster Travelling 火山旅 8 / 6
15 十七 金9 Metal 庚戌 Metal Dog Stagnation 天地否 9 / 5	**16** 十八 火7 Fire 辛亥 Metal Pig Alliance 水地比 7 / 4	**17** 十九 木8 Wood 壬子 Water Rat Thunder 震爲雷 1 / 3	**18** 二十 水6 Water 癸丑 Water Ox Beauty 山火賁 8 / 2	**19** 廿一 火7 Fire 甲寅 Wood Tiger Accomplished 水火既濟 9 / 1	**20** 廿二 水1 Water 乙卯 Wood Rabbit Arriving 地澤臨 4 / 9	**21** 廿三 金4 Metal 丙辰 Fire Dragon Marsh 兑爲澤 1 / 8
22 廿四 火2 Fire 丁巳 Fire Snake Small Livestock 風天小畜 8 / 7	**23** 廿五 木3 Wood 戊午 Earth Horse The Cauldron 火風鼎 4 / 6	**24** 廿六 水1 Water 己未 Earth Goat Rising 地風升 2 / 5	**25** 廿七 火7 Fire 庚申 Metal Monkey Water 坎爲水 1 / 4	**26** 廿八 木8 Wood 辛酉 Metal Rooster Lesser Exceeding 雷山小過 3 / 3	**27** 廿九 金4 Metal 壬戌 Water Dog Gathering 澤地萃 4 / 2	**28** 七月初一 水6 Water 癸亥 Water Pig Peel 山地剝 6 / 1
29 初二 水1 Water 甲子 Wood Rat Earth 坤爲地 1 / 9	**30** 初三 木3 Wood 乙丑 Wood Ox Biting 火雷噬嗑 6 / 8	**31** 初四 火2 Fire 丙寅 Fire Tiger Family 風火家人 4 / 7				

AUGUST 1984 壬申

Xuan Kong Element 玄空五行	地水師 Officer	Period Luck 卦運	Monthly Star 月星
Water 水1		7	2

SUNDAY	MONDAY	TUESDAY	WEDNESDAY	THURSDAY	FRIDAY	SATURDAY
			1 初五 水6 Water 丁卯 Fire Rabbit Decreasing 山澤損 9 / 6	**2** 初六 金9 Metal 戊辰 Earth Dragon Tread 天澤履 6 / 5	**3** 初七 木8 Wood 己巳 Earth Snake Great Strength 雷天大壯 2 / 4	**4** 初八 木8 Wood 庚午 Metal Horse Consistency 雷風恒 9 / 3
5 初九 金9 Metal 辛未 Metal Goat Litigation 天水訟 3 / 2	**6** 初十 水1 Water 壬申 Water Monkey Officer 地水師 7 / 1	**7** 十一 火2 Fire 癸酉 Water Rooster Gradual Progress 風山漸 7 / 9	**8** 十二 火7 Fire 甲戌 Wood Dog Obstruction 水山蹇 2 / 8	**9** 十三 木3 Wood 乙亥 Wood Pig Advancement 火地晉 3 / 7	**10** 十四 水6 Water 丙子 Fire Rat Nourish 山雷頤 3 / 6	**11** 十五 金4 Metal 丁丑 Fire Ox Following 澤雷隨 7 / 5
12 十六 木8 Wood 戊寅 Earth Tiger Abundance 雷火豐 6 / 4	**13** 十七 火7 Fire 己卯 Earth Rabbit Regulate 水澤節 8 / 3	**14** 十八 水1 Water 庚辰 Metal Dragon Unity 地天泰 9 / 2	**15** 十九 木3 Wood 辛巳 Metal Snake Great Reward 火天大有 7 / 1	**16** 二十 火2 Fire 壬午 Water Horse Wind 巽爲風 1 / 9	**17** 廿一 金4 Metal 癸未 Water Goat Trap 澤水困 8 / 8	**18** 廿二 木3 Wood 甲申 Wood Monkey Not Yet Accomplished 火水未濟 9 / 7
19 廿三 金9 Metal 乙酉 Wood Rooster Retreat 天山遯 4 / 6	**20** 廿四 水6 Water 丙戌 Fire Dog Mountain 艮爲山 1 / 5	**21** 廿五 木8 Wood 丁亥 Fire Pig Delight 雷地豫 8 / 4	**22** 廿六 火7 Fire 戊子 Earth Rat Beginning 水雷屯 4 / 3	**23** 廿七 金9 Metal 己丑 Earth Ox Without Wrongdoing 天雷無妄 2 / 2	**24** 廿八 木3 Wood 庚寅 Metal Tiger Fire 離爲火 1 / 1	**25** 廿九 火2 Fire 辛卯 Metal Rabbit Sincerity 風澤中孚 3 / 9
26 三十 水6 Water 壬辰 Water Dragon Big Livestock 山天大畜 4 / 8	**27** 八月初一 金4 Metal 癸巳 Water Snake Eliminating 澤天夬 6 / 7	**28** 初二 金9 Metal 甲午 Wood Horse Heaven 乾爲天 1 / 6	**29** 初三 火7 Fire 乙未 Wood Goat Well 水風井 6 / 5	**30** 初四 木8 Wood 丙申 Fire Monkey Relief 雷水解 4 / 4	**31** 初五 金4 Metal 丁酉 Fire Rooster Influence 澤山咸 9 / 3	

SEPTEMBER 1984 癸酉

Xuan Kong Element 玄空五行	風山漸 Gradual Progress	Period Luck 卦運	Monthly Star 月星
Fire 火2		7	1

SUNDAY	MONDAY	TUESDAY	WEDNESDAY	THURSDAY	FRIDAY	SATURDAY
水6 Water · Decreasing 山澤損 · 丁卯 Fire Rabbit · 9 · **30** 初六 · [9]						水1 Water · Humility 地山謙 · 戊戌 Earth Dog · 6 · **1** 初六 · [2]
火2 Fire · Observation 風地觀 · 己亥 Earth Pig · 2 · **2** 初七 · [1]	火2 Fire · Increasing 風雷益 · 庚子 Metal Rat · 9 · **3** 初八 · [9]	水1 Water · Dimming Light 地火明夷 · 辛丑 Metal Ox · 3 · **4** 初九 · [8]	金9 Metal · Fellowship 天火同人 · 壬寅 Water Tiger · 7 · **5** 初十 · [7]	木8 Wood · Marrying Maiden 雷澤歸妹 · 癸卯 Water Rabbit · 7 · **6** 十一 · [6]	木3 Wood · Opposition 火澤睽 · 甲辰 Wood Dragon · 2 · **7** 十二 · [5]	火7 Fire · Waiting 水天需 · 乙巳 Wood Snake · 3 · **8** 十三 · [4]
金4 Metal · Great Exceeding 澤風大過 · 丙午 Fire Horse · 3 · **9** 十四 · [3]	水6 Water · Poison 山風蠱 · 丁未 Fire Goat · 7 · **10** 十五 · [2]	火2 Fire · Dispersing 風水渙 · 戊申 Earth Monkey · 6 · **11** 十六 · [1]	木3 Wood · Travelling 火山旅 · 己酉 Earth Rooster · 8 · **12** 十七 · [9]	金9 Metal · Stagnation 天地否 · 庚戌 Metal Dog · 9 · **13** 十八 · [8]	火7 Fire · Alliance 水地比 · 辛亥 Metal Pig · 7 · **14** 十九 · [7]	木8 Wood · Thunder 震爲雷 · 壬子 Water Rat · 1 · **15** 二十 · [6]
水6 Water · Beauty 山火賁 · 癸丑 Water Ox · 8 · **16** 廿一 · [5]	火7 Fire · Accomplished 水火既濟 · 甲寅 Wood Tiger · 9 · **17** 廿二 · [4]	水1 Water · Arriving 地澤臨 · 乙卯 Wood Rabbit · 4 · **18** 廿三 · [3]	金4 Metal · Marsh 兑爲澤 · 丙辰 Fire Dragon · 1 · **19** 廿四 · [2]	火2 Fire · Small Livestock 風天小畜 · 丁巳 Fire Snake · 8 · **20** 廿五 · [1]	木3 Wood · The Cauldron 火風鼎 · 戊午 Earth Horse · 4 · **21** 廿六 · [9]	水1 Water · Rising 地風升 · 己未 Earth Goat · 2 · **22** 廿七 · [8]
火7 Fire · Water 坎爲水 · 庚申 Metal Monkey · 1 · **23** 廿八 · [7]	木8 Wood · Lesser Exceeding 雷山小過 · 辛酉 Metal Rooster · 3 · **24** 廿九 · [6]	金4 Metal · Gathering 澤地萃 · 壬戌 Water Dog · 4 · **25** 九月初一 · [5]	水6 Water · Peel 山地剝 · 癸亥 Water Pig · 6 · **26** 初二 · [4]	水1 Water · Earth 坤爲地 · 甲子 Wood Rat · 1 · **27** 初三 · [3]	木3 Wood · Biting 火雷噬嗑 · 乙丑 Wood Ox · 6 · **28** 初四 · [2]	火2 Fire · Family 風火家人 · 丙寅 Fire Tiger · 4 · **29** 初五 · [1]

OCTOBER 1984 甲戌

Xuan Kong Element 玄空五行	水山蹇 Obstruction	Period Luck 卦運	Monthly Star 月星
Fire 火7		2	9

SUNDAY	MONDAY	TUESDAY	WEDNESDAY	THURSDAY	FRIDAY	SATURDAY
	金9 Metal · Tread 天澤履 · 戊辰 Earth Dragon · 6 · **1** 初七 · [8]	木8 Wood · Great Strength 雷天大壯 · 己巳 Earth Snake · 2 · **2** 初八 · [7]	木8 Wood · Consistency 雷風恆 · 庚午 Metal Horse · 9 · **3** 初九 · [6]	金9 Metal · Litigation 天水訟 · 辛未 Metal Goat · 3 · **4** 初十 · [5]	水1 Water · Officer 地水師 · 壬申 Water Monkey · 7 · **5** 十一 · [4]	火2 Fire · Gradual Progress 風山漸 · 癸酉 Water Rooster · 7 · **6** 十二 · [3]
火7 Fire · Obstruction 水山蹇 · 甲戌 Wood Dog · 2 · **7** 十三 · [2]	木3 Wood · Advancement 火地晉 · 乙亥 Wood Pig · 3 · **8** 十四 · [1]	水6 Water · Nourish 山雷頤 · 丙子 Fire Rat · 3 · **9** 十五 · [9]	金4 Metal · Following 澤雷隨 · 丁丑 Fire Ox · 7 · **10** 十六 · [8]	木8 Wood · Abundance 雷火豐 · 戊寅 Earth Tiger · 6 · **11** 十七 · [7]	火7 Fire · Regulate 水澤節 · 己卯 Earth Rabbit · 8 · **12** 十八 · [6]	水1 Water · Unity 地天泰 · 庚辰 Metal Dragon · 9 · **13** 十九 · [5]
木3 Wood · Great Reward 火天大有 · 辛巳 Metal Snake · 7 · **14** 二十 · [4]	火2 Fire · Wind 巽爲風 · 壬午 Water Horse · 1 · **15** 廿一 · [3]	金4 Metal · Trap 澤水困 · 癸未 Water Goat · 8 · **16** 廿二 · [2]	木3 Wood · Not Yet Accomplished 火水未濟 · 甲申 Wood Monkey · 9 · **17** 廿三 · [1]	金9 Metal · Retreat 天山遯 · 乙酉 Wood Rooster · 4 · **18** 廿四 · [9]	水6 Water · Mountain 艮爲山 · 丙戌 Fire Dog · 1 · **19** 廿五 · [8]	木8 Wood · Delight 雷地豫 · 丁亥 Fire Pig · 8 · **20** 廿六 · [7]
火7 Fire · Beginning 水雷屯 · 戊子 Earth Rat · 4 · **21** 廿七 · [6]	金9 Metal · Without Wrongdoing 天雷無妄 · 己丑 Earth Ox · 2 · **22** 廿八 · [5]	木3 Wood · Fire 離爲火 · 庚寅 Metal Tiger · 1 · **23** 廿九 · [4]	火2 Fire · Sincerity 風澤中孚 · 辛卯 Metal Rabbit · 3 · **24** 十月初一 · [3]	水6 Water · Big Livestock 山天大畜 · 壬辰 Water Dragon · 4 · **25** 初二 · [2]	金4 Metal · Eliminating 澤天夬 · 癸巳 Water Snake · 6 · **26** 初三 · [1]	金9 Metal · Heaven 乾爲天 · 甲午 Wood Horse · 1 · **27** 初四 · [9]
火7 Fire · Well 水風井 · 乙未 Wood Goat · 6 · **28** 初五 · [8]	木8 Wood · Relief 雷水解 · 丙申 Fire Monkey · 4 · **29** 初六 · [7]	金4 Metal · Influence 澤山咸 · 丁酉 Fire Rooster · 9 · **30** 初七 · [6]	水1 Water · Humility 地山謙 · 戊戌 Earth Dog · 6 · **31** 初八 · [5]			

NOVEMBER 1984 乙亥

Xuan Kong Element 玄空五行	火地晉 Advancement	Period Luck 卦運	Monthly Star 月星
Wood 木3		3	8

SUNDAY	MONDAY	TUESDAY	WEDNESDAY	THURSDAY	FRIDAY	SATURDAY
				火2 Fire 4 Observation 己亥 Earth Pig 風地觀 1 初九 2	火2 Fire 3 Increasing 庚子 Metal Rat 風雷益 2 初十 9	水1 Water 2 Dimming Light 辛丑 Metal Ox 地火明夷 3 十一 3
金9 Metal 1 Fellowship 壬寅 Water Tiger 天火同人 4 十二 7	木8 Wood 9 Marrying Maiden 癸卯 Water Rabbit 雷澤歸妹 5 十三 7	木3 Wood 8 Opposition 甲辰 Wood Dragon 火澤睽 6 十四 2	火7 Fire 7 Waiting 乙巳 Wood Snake 水天需 7 十五 3	金4 Metal 6 Great Exceeding 丙午 Fire Horse 澤風大過 8 十六 3	水6 Water 5 Poison 丁未 Fire Goat 山風蠱 9 十七 7	火2 Fire 4 Dispersing 戊申 Earth Monkey 風水渙 10 十八 6
木3 Wood 3 Travelling 己酉 Earth Rooster 火山旅 11 十九 8	金9 Metal 2 Stagnation 庚戌 Metal Dog 天地否 12 二十 9	火7 Fire 1 Alliance 辛亥 Metal Pig 水地比 13 廿一 7	木8 Wood 9 Thunder 壬子 Water Rat 震爲雷 14 廿二 1	水6 Water 8 Beauty 癸丑 Water Ox 山火賁 15 廿三 8	火7 Fire 7 Accomplished 甲寅 Wood Tiger 水火既濟 16 廿四 9	水1 Water 6 Arriving 乙卯 Wood Rabbit 地澤臨 17 廿五 4
金4 Metal 5 Marsh 丙辰 Fire Dragon 兌爲澤 18 廿六 1	火2 Fire 4 Small Livestock 丁巳 Fire Snake 風天小畜 19 廿七 8	木3 Wood 3 The Cauldron 戊午 Earth Horse 火風鼎 20 廿八 4	水1 Water 2 Rising 己未 Earth Goat 地風升 21 廿九 2	火7 Fire 1 Water 庚申 Metal Monkey 坎爲水 22 三十 1	木8 Wood 9 Lesser Exceeding 辛酉 Metal Rooster 雷山小過 23 閏十月初一 3	金4 Metal 8 Gathering 壬戌 Water Dog 澤地萃 24 初二 4
水6 Water 7 Peel 癸亥 Water Pig 山地剝 25 初三 6	水1 Water 6 Earth 甲子 Wood Rat 坤爲地 26 初四 1	木3 Wood 5 Biting 乙丑 Wood Ox 火雷噬嗑 27 初五 6	火2 Fire 4 Family 丙寅 Fire Tiger 風火家人 28 初六 4	水6 Water 3 Decreasing 丁卯 Fire Rabbit 山澤損 29 初七 9	金9 Metal 2 Tread 戊辰 Earth Dragon 天澤履 30 初八 6	

DECEMBER 1984 丙子

Xuan Kong Element 玄空五行	山雷頤 Nourish	Period Luck 卦運	Monthly Star 月星
Water 水6		3	7

SUNDAY	MONDAY	TUESDAY	WEDNESDAY	THURSDAY	FRIDAY	SATURDAY
水1 Water 2 Humility 戊戌 Earth Dog 地山謙 30 初九 6	火2 Fire 3 Observation 己亥 Earth Pig 風地觀 31 初十 2					木8 Wood 1 Great Strength 己巳 Earth Snake 雷天大壯 1 初九 2
木8 Wood 9 Consistency 庚午 Metal Horse 雷風恆 2 初十 9	金9 Metal 8 Litigation 辛未 Metal Goat 天水訟 3 十一 3	水1 Water 7 Officer 壬申 Water Monkey 地水師 4 十二 7	火2 Fire 6 Gradual Progress 癸酉 Water Rooster 風山漸 5 十三 7	火7 Fire 5 Obstruction 甲戌 Wood Dog 水山蹇 6 十四 2	木3 Wood 4 Advancement 乙亥 Wood Pig 火地晉 7 十五 3	水6 Water 3 Nourish 丙子 Fire Rat 山雷頤 8 十六 3
金4 Metal 2 Following 丁丑 Fire Ox 澤雷隨 9 十七 7	木8 Wood 1 Abundance 戊寅 Earth Tiger 雷火豐 10 十八 6	火7 Fire 9 Regulate 己卯 Earth Rabbit 水澤節 11 十九 8	水1 Water 8 Unity 庚辰 Metal Dragon 地天泰 12 二十 9	木3 Wood 7 Great Reward 辛巳 Metal Snake 火天大有 13 廿一 7	火2 Fire 6 Wind 壬午 Water Horse 巽爲風 14 廿二 1	金4 Metal 5 Trap 癸未 Water Goat 澤水困 15 廿三 8
木3 Wood 4 Not Yet Accomplished 甲申 Wood Monkey 火水未濟 16 廿四 9	金9 Metal 3 Retreat 乙酉 Wood Rooster 天山遯 17 廿五 4	水6 Water 2 Mountain 丙戌 Fire Dog 艮爲山 18 廿六 1	木8 Wood 1 Delight 丁亥 Fire Pig 雷地豫 19 廿七 8	火7 Fire 9 Beginning 戊子 Earth Rat 水雷屯 20 廿八 4	金9 Metal 8 Without Wrongdoing 己丑 Earth Ox 天雷無妄 21 廿九 2	木3 Wood 7/3 Fire 庚寅 Metal Tiger 離爲火 22 十一月初一 1
火2 Fire 4 Sincerity 辛卯 Metal Rabbit 風澤中孚 23 初二 3	水6 Water 5 Big Livestock 壬辰 Water Dragon 山天大畜 24 初三 4	金4 Metal 6 Eliminating 癸巳 Water Snake 澤天夬 25 初四 6	金9 Metal 7 Heaven 甲午 Wood Horse 乾爲天 26 初五 1	火7 Fire 8 Well 乙未 Wood Goat 水風井 27 初六 6	木8 Wood 9 Relief 丙申 Fire Monkey 雷水解 28 初七 4	金4 Metal 1 Influence 丁酉 Fire Rooster 澤山咸 29 初八 9

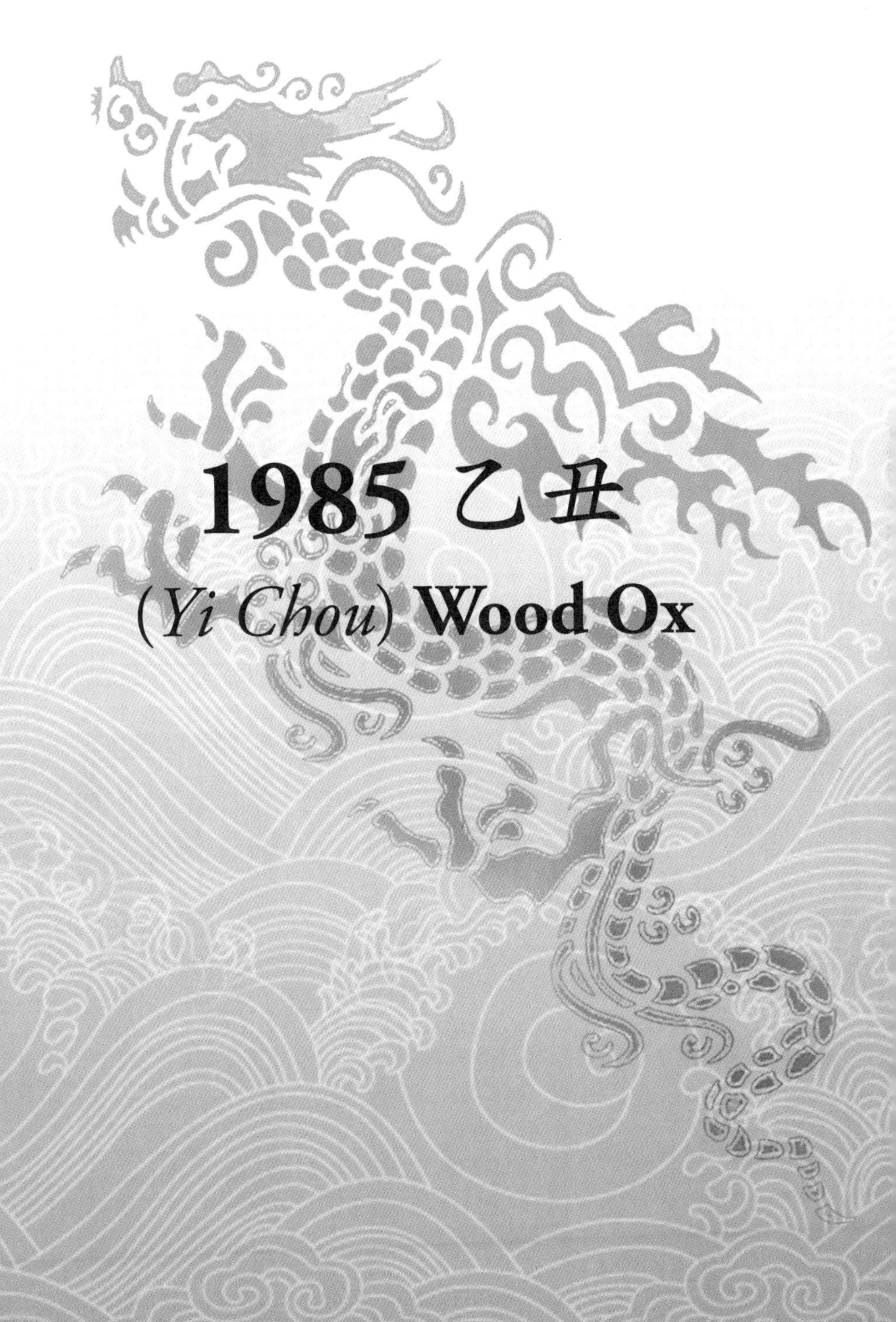

1985 乙丑

(*Yi Chou*) Wood Ox

1985 乙丑 *(Yi Chou)* Wood Ox

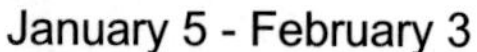

January 5 - February 3

February 4 - March 4

March 5 - April 4

April 5 - May 4

May 5 - June 5

June 6 - July 6

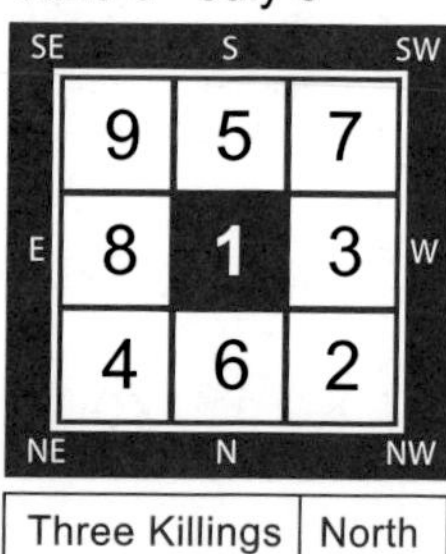

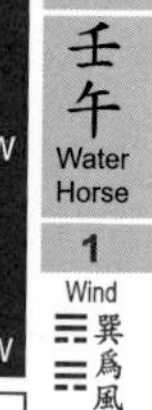

July 7 - August 6

August 7 - September 7

7	3	5
6	**8**	1
2	4	9

木 **3** Wood
甲申 Wood Monkey
9 Not Yet Accomplished 火水未濟

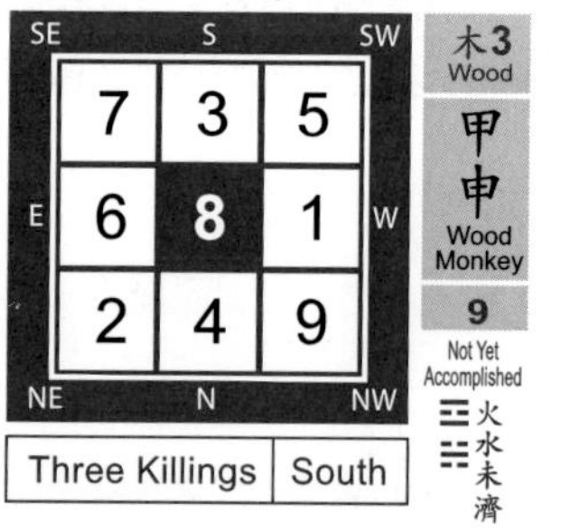

September 8 - October 7

6	2	4
5	**7**	9
1	3	8

金 **9** Metal
乙酉 Wood Rooster
4 Retreat 天山遯

October 8 - November 6

November 7 - December 6

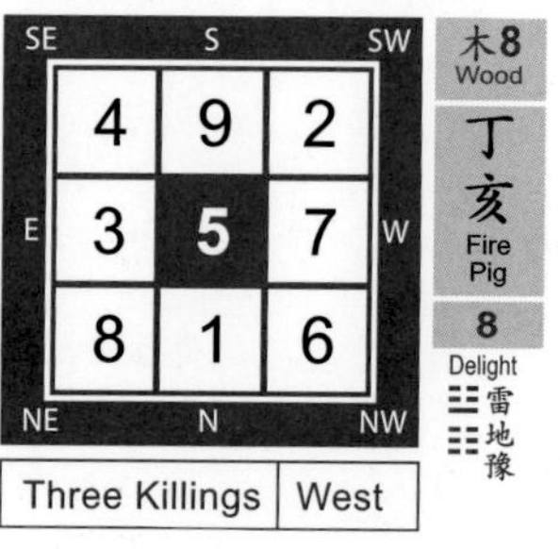

December 7 - January 4

JANUARY 1985 丁丑

Xuan Kong Element 玄空五行	澤雷隨 Following	Period Luck 卦運	Monthly Star 月星
Metal 金4		7	6

SUNDAY	MONDAY	TUESDAY	WEDNESDAY	THURSDAY	FRIDAY	SATURDAY
		火2 Fire 4 Increasing 風雷益 庚子 Metal Rat 1 十一 9	水1 Water 5 Dimming Light 地火明夷 辛丑 Metal Ox 2 十二 3	金9 Metal 6 Fellowship 天火同人 壬寅 Water Tiger 3 十三 7	木8 Wood 7 Marrying Maiden 雷澤歸妹 癸卯 Water Rabbit 4 十四 7	木3 Wood 8 Opposition 火澤睽 甲辰 Wood Dragon 5 十五 2
火7 Fire 9 Waiting 水天需 乙巳 Wood Snake 6 十六 3	金4 Metal 1 Great Exceeding 澤風大過 丙午 Fire Horse 7 十七 3	水6 Water 2 Poison 山風蠱 丁未 Fire Goat 8 十八 7	火2 Fire 3 Dispersing 風水渙 戊申 Earth Monkey 9 十九 6	木3 Wood 4 Travelling 火山旅 己酉 Earth Rooster 10 二十 8	金9 Metal 5 Stagnation 天地否 庚戌 Metal Dog 11 廿一 9	火7 Fire 6 Alliance 水地比 辛亥 Metal Pig 12 廿二 7
木8 Wood 7 Thunder 震為雷 壬子 Water Rat 13 廿三 1	水6 Water 8 Beauty 山火賁 癸丑 Water Ox 14 廿四 8	火7 Fire 9 Accomplished 水火既濟 甲寅 Wood Tiger 15 廿五 9	水1 Water 1 Arriving 地澤臨 乙卯 Wood Rabbit 16 廿六 4	金4 Metal 2 Marsh 兌為澤 丙辰 Fire Dragon 17 廿七 1	火2 Fire 3 Small Livestock 風天小畜 丁巳 Fire Snake 18 廿八 8	木3 Wood 4 The Cauldron 火風鼎 戊午 Earth Horse 19 廿九 4
水1 Water 5 Rising 地風升 己未 Earth Goat 20 三十 2	火7 Fire 6 Water 坎為水 庚申 Metal Monkey 21 十二月初一 1	木8 Wood 7 Lesser Exceeding 雷山小過 辛酉 Metal Rooster 22 初二 3	金4 Metal 8 Gathering 澤地萃 壬戌 Water Dog 23 初三 4	水6 Water 9 Peel 山地剝 癸亥 Water Pig 24 初四 6	水1 Water 1 Earth 坤為地 甲子 Wood Rat 25 初五 1	木3 Wood 2 Biting 火雷噬嗑 乙丑 Wood Ox 26 初六 6
火2 Fire 3 Family 風火家人 丙寅 Fire Tiger 27 初七 4	水6 Water 4 Decreasing 山澤損 丁卯 Fire Rabbit 28 初八 9	金9 Metal 5 Tread 天澤履 戊辰 Earth Dragon 29 初九 6	木8 Wood 6 Great Strength 雷天大壯 己巳 Earth Snake 30 初十 2	木8 Wood 7 Consistency 雷風恆 庚午 Metal Horse 31 十一 9		

FEBRUARY 1985 戊寅

Xuan Kong Element 玄空五行	雷火豐 Abundance	Period Luck 卦運	Monthly Star 月星
Wood 木8		6	5

SUNDAY	MONDAY	TUESDAY	WEDNESDAY	THURSDAY	FRIDAY	SATURDAY
					金9 Metal 8 Litigation 天水訟 辛未 Metal Goat 1 十二 3	水1 Water 9 Officer 地水師 壬申 Water Monkey 2 十三 7
火2 Fire 1 Gradual Progress 風山漸 癸酉 Water Rooster 3 十四 7	火7 Fire 2 Obstruction 水山蹇 甲戌 Wood Dog 4 十五 2	木3 Wood 3 Advancement 火地晉 乙亥 Wood Pig 5 十六 3	水6 Water 4 Nourish 山雷頤 丙子 Fire Rat 6 十七 3	金4 Metal 5 Following 澤雷隨 丁丑 Fire Ox 7 十八 7	木8 Wood 6 Abundance 雷火豐 戊寅 Earth Tiger 8 十九 6	火7 Fire 7 Regulate 水澤節 己卯 Earth Rabbit 9 二十 8
水1 Water 8 Unity 地天泰 庚辰 Metal Dragon 10 廿一 9	木3 Wood 9 Great Reward 火天大有 辛巳 Metal Snake 11 廿二 7	火2 Fire 1 Wind 巽為風 壬午 Water Horse 12 廿三 1	金4 Metal 2 Trap 澤水困 癸未 Water Goat 13 廿四 8	木3 Wood 3 Not Yet Accomplished 火水未濟 甲申 Wood Monkey 14 廿五 9	金9 Metal 4 Retreat 天山遯 乙酉 Wood Rooster 15 廿六 4	水6 Water 5 Mountain 艮為山 丙戌 Fire Dog 16 廿七 1
木8 Wood 6 Delight 雷地豫 丁亥 Fire Pig 17 廿八 8	火7 Fire 7 Beginning 水雷屯 戊子 Earth Rat 18 廿九 4	金9 Metal 8 Without Wrongdoing 天雷無妄 己丑 Earth Ox 19 三十 2	木3 Wood 9 Fire 離為火 庚寅 Metal Tiger 20 正月初一 1	火2 Fire 1 Sincerity 風澤中孚 辛卯 Metal Rabbit 21 初二 3	水6 Water 2 Big Livestock 山天大畜 壬辰 Water Dragon 22 初三 4	金4 Metal 3 Eliminating 澤天夬 癸巳 Water Snake 23 初四 6
金9 Metal 4 Heaven 乾為天 甲午 Wood Horse 24 初五 1	火7 Fire 5 Well 水風井 乙未 Wood Goat 25 初六 6	木8 Wood 6 Relief 雷水解 丙申 Fire Monkey 26 初七 4	金4 Metal 7 Influence 澤山咸 丁酉 Fire Rooster 27 初八 9	水1 Water 8 Humility 地山謙 戊戌 Earth Dog 28 初九 6		

MARCH 1985 己卯

Xuan Kong Element 玄空五行	水澤節 Regulate	Period Luck 卦運	Monthly Star 月星
Fire 火7		8	4

SUNDAY	MONDAY	TUESDAY	WEDNESDAY	THURSDAY	FRIDAY	SATURDAY
木8 Wood 3 Great Strength 己巳 Earth Snake 雷天大壯 31 十一 2					火2 Fire 9 Observation 己亥 Earth Pig 風地觀 1 初十 2	火2 Fire 1 Increasing 庚子 Metal Rat 風雷益 2 十一 9
水1 Water 2 Dimming Light 辛丑 Metal Ox 地火明夷 3 十二 3	金9 Metal 3 Fellowship 壬寅 Water Tiger 天火同人 4 十三 7	木8 Wood 4 Marrying Maiden 癸卯 Water Rabbit 雷澤歸妹 5 十四 7	木3 Wood 5 Opposition 甲辰 Wood Dragon 火澤睽 6 十五 2	火7 Fire 6 Waiting 乙巳 Wood Snake 水天需 7 十六 3	金4 Metal 7 Great Exceeding 丙午 Fire Horse 澤風大過 8 十七 3	水6 Water 8 Poison 丁未 Fire Goat 山風蠱 9 十八 7
火2 Fire 9 Dispersing 戊申 Earth Monkey 風水渙 10 十九 6	木3 Wood 1 Travelling 己酉 Earth Rooster 火山旅 11 二十 8	金9 Metal 2 Stagnation 庚戌 Metal Dog 天地否 12 廿一 9	火7 Fire 3 Alliance 辛亥 Metal Pig 水地比 13 廿二 7	木8 Wood 4 Thunder 壬子 Water Rat 震爲雷 14 廿三 1	水6 Water 5 Beauty 癸丑 Water Ox 山火賁 15 廿四 8	火7 Fire 6 Accomplished 甲寅 Wood Tiger 水火既濟 16 廿五 9
水1 Water 7 Arriving 乙卯 Wood Rabbit 地澤臨 17 廿六 4	金4 Metal 8 Marsh 丙辰 Fire Dragon 兑爲澤 18 廿七 1	火2 Fire 9 Small Livestock 丁巳 Fire Snake 風天小畜 19 廿八 8	木3 Wood 1 The Cauldron 戊午 Earth Horse 火風鼎 20 廿九 4	水1 Water 2 Rising 己未 Earth Goat 地風升 21 二月初一 2	火7 Fire 3 Water 庚申 Metal Monkey 坎爲水 22 初二 1	木8 Wood 4 Lesser Exceeding 辛酉 Metal Rooster 雷山小過 23 初三 3
金4 Metal 5 Gathering 壬戌 Water Dog 澤地萃 24 初四 4	水6 Water 6 Peel 癸亥 Water Pig 山地剝 25 初五 6	水1 Water 7 Earth 甲子 Wood Rat 坤爲地 26 初六 1	木3 Wood 8 Biting 乙丑 Wood Ox 火雷噬嗑 27 初七 6	火2 Fire 9 Family 丙寅 Fire Tiger 風火家人 28 初八 4	水6 Water 1 Decreasing 丁卯 Fire Rabbit 山澤損 29 初九 9	金9 Metal 2 Tread 戊辰 Earth Dragon 天澤履 30 初十 6

APRIL 1985 庚辰

Xuan Kong Element 玄空五行	地天泰 Unity	Period Luck 卦運	Monthly Star 月星
Water 水1		9	3

SUNDAY	MONDAY	TUESDAY	WEDNESDAY	THURSDAY	FRIDAY	SATURDAY
	木8 Wood 4 Consistency 庚午 Metal Horse 雷風恆 1 十二 9	金9 Metal 5 Litigation 辛未 Metal Goat 天水訟 2 十三 3	水1 Water 6 Officer 壬申 Water Monkey 地水師 3 十四 7	火2 Fire 7 Gradual Progress 癸酉 Water Rooster 風山漸 4 十五 7	火7 Fire 8 Obstruction 甲戌 Wood Dog 水山蹇 5 十六 2	木3 Wood 9 Advancement 乙亥 Wood Pig 火地晉 6 十七 3
水6 Water 1 Nourish 丙子 Fire Rat 山雷頤 7 十八 3	金4 Metal 2 Following 丁丑 Fire Ox 澤雷隨 8 十九 7	木8 Wood 3 Abundance 戊寅 Earth Tiger 雷火豐 9 二十 6	火7 Fire 4 Regulate 己卯 Earth Rabbit 水澤節 10 廿一 8	水1 Water 5 Unity 庚辰 Metal Dragon 地天泰 11 廿二 9	木3 Wood 6 Great Reward 辛巳 Metal Snake 火天大有 12 廿三 7	火2 Fire 7 Wind 壬午 Water Horse 巽爲風 13 廿四 1
金4 Metal 8 Trap 癸未 Water Goat 澤水困 14 廿五 8	木3 Wood 9 Not Yet Accomplished 甲申 Wood Monkey 火水未濟 15 廿六 9	金9 Metal 1 Retreat 乙酉 Wood Rooster 天山遯 16 廿七 4	水6 Water 2 Mountain 丙戌 Fire Dog 艮爲山 17 廿八 1	木8 Wood 3 Delight 丁亥 Fire Pig 雷地豫 18 廿九 8	火7 Fire 4 Beginning 戊子 Earth Rat 水雷屯 19 三十 4	金9 Metal 5 Without Wrongdoing 己丑 Earth Ox 天雷無妄 20 三月初一 2
木3 Wood 6 Fire 庚寅 Metal Tiger 離爲火 21 初二 1	火2 Fire 7 Sincerity 辛卯 Metal Rabbit 風澤中孚 22 初三 3	水6 Water 8 Big Livestock 壬辰 Water Dragon 山天大畜 23 初四 4	金4 Metal 9 Eliminating 癸巳 Water Snake 澤天夬 24 初五 6	金9 Metal 1 Heaven 甲午 Wood Horse 乾爲天 25 初六 1	火7 Fire 2 Well 乙未 Wood Goat 水風井 26 初七 6	木8 Wood 3 Relief 丙申 Fire Monkey 雷水解 27 初八 4
金4 Metal 4 Influence 丁酉 Fire Rooster 澤山咸 28 初九 9	水1 Water 5 Humility 戊戌 Earth Dog 地山謙 29 初十 6	火2 Fire 6 Observation 己亥 Earth Pig 風地觀 30 十一 2				

MAY 1985 辛巳

Xuan Kong Element 玄空五行	火天大有 Great Reward	Period Luck 卦運	Monthly Star 月星
Wood 木3		7	2

SUNDAY	MONDAY	TUESDAY	WEDNESDAY	THURSDAY	FRIDAY	SATURDAY
			1 十二 火2 Fire [7] Increasing 風雷益 庚子 Metal Rat 9	2 十三 水1 Water [8] Dimming Light 地火明夷 辛丑 Metal Ox 3	3 十四 金9 Metal [9] Fellowship 天火同人 壬寅 Water Tiger 7	4 十五 木8 Wood [1] Marrying Maiden 雷澤歸妹 癸卯 Water Rabbit 7
5 十六 木3 Wood [2] Opposition 火澤睽 甲辰 Wood Dragon 2	6 十七 火7 Fire [3] Waiting 水天需 乙巳 Wood Snake 3	7 十八 金4 Metal [4] Great Exceeding 澤風大過 丙午 Fire Horse 3	8 十九 水6 Water [5] Poison 山風蠱 丁未 Fire Goat 7	9 二十 火2 Fire [6] Dispersing 風水渙 戊申 Earth Monkey 6	10 廿一 木3 Wood [7] Travelling 火山旅 己酉 Earth Rooster 8	11 廿二 金9 Metal [8] Stagnation 天地否 庚戌 Metal Dog 9
12 廿三 火7 Fire [9] Alliance 水地比 辛亥 Metal Pig 7	13 廿四 木8 Wood [1] Thunder 震爲雷 壬子 Water Rat 1	14 廿五 水6 Water [2] Beauty 山火賁 癸丑 Water Ox 8	15 廿六 火7 Fire [3] Accomplished 水火既濟 甲寅 Wood Tiger 9	16 廿七 水1 Water [4] Arriving 地澤臨 乙卯 Wood Rabbit 4	17 廿八 金4 Metal [5] Marsh 兑爲澤 丙辰 Fire Dragon 1	18 廿九 火2 Fire [6] Small Livestock 風天小畜 丁巳 Fire Snake 8
19 三十 木3 Wood [7] The Cauldron 火風鼎 戊午 Earth Horse 4	20 四月初一 水1 Water [8] Rising 地風升 己未 Earth Goat 2	21 初二 火7 Fire [9] Water 坎爲水 庚申 Metal Monkey 1	22 初三 木8 Wood [1] Lesser Exceeding 雷山小過 辛酉 Metal Rooster 3	23 初四 金4 Metal [2] Gathering 澤地萃 壬戌 Water Dog 4	24 初五 水6 Water [3] Peel 山地剝 癸亥 Water Pig 6	25 初六 水1 Water [4] Earth 坤爲地 甲子 Wood Rat 1
26 初七 木3 Wood [5] Biting 火雷噬嗑 乙丑 Wood Ox 6	27 初八 火2 Fire [6] Family 風火家人 丙寅 Fire Tiger 4	28 初九 水6 Water [7] Decreasing 山澤損 丁卯 Fire Rabbit 9	29 初十 金9 Metal [8] Tread 天澤履 戊辰 Earth Dragon 6	30 十一 木8 Wood [9] Great Strength 雷天大壯 己巳 Earth Snake 2	31 十二 木8 Wood [1] Consistency 雷風恒 庚午 Metal Horse 9	

JUNE 1985 壬午

Xuan Kong Element 玄空五行	巽爲風 Wind	Period Luck 卦運	Monthly Star 月星
Fire 火2		1	1

SUNDAY	MONDAY	TUESDAY	WEDNESDAY	THURSDAY	FRIDAY	SATURDAY
30 十三 火2 Fire [6] Increasing 風雷益 庚子 Metal Rat 9						1 十三 金9 Metal [2] Litigation 天水訟 辛未 Metal Goat 3
2 十四 水1 Water [3] Officer 地水師 壬申 Water Monkey 7	3 十五 火2 Fire [4] Gradual Progress 風山漸 癸酉 Water Rooster 7	4 十六 火7 Fire [5] Obstruction 水山蹇 甲戌 Wood Dog 2	5 十七 木3 Wood [6] Advancement 火地晉 乙亥 Wood Pig 3	6 十八 水6 Water [7] Nourish 山雷頤 丙子 Fire Rat 3	7 十九 金4 Metal [8] Following 澤雷隨 丁丑 Fire Ox 7	8 二十 木8 Wood [9] Abundance 雷火豐 戊寅 Earth Tiger 6
9 廿一 火7 Fire [1] Regulate 水澤節 己卯 Earth Rabbit 8	10 廿二 水1 Water [2] Unity 地天泰 庚辰 Metal Dragon 9	11 廿三 木3 Wood [3] Great Reward 火天大有 辛巳 Metal Snake 7	12 廿四 火2 Fire [4] Wind 巽爲風 壬午 Water Horse 1	13 廿五 金4 Metal [5] Trap 澤水困 癸未 Water Goat 8	14 廿六 木3 Wood [6] Not Yet Accomplished 火水未濟 甲申 Wood Monkey 9	15 廿七 金9 Metal [7] Retreat 天山遯 乙酉 Wood Rooster 4
16 廿八 水6 Water [8] Mountain 艮爲山 丙戌 Fire Dog 1	17 廿九 木8 Wood [9] Delight 雷地豫 丁亥 Fire Pig 8	18 五月初一 火7 Fire [1] Beginning 水雷屯 戊子 Earth Rat 4	19 初二 金9 Metal [2] Without Wrongdoing 天雷無妄 己丑 Earth Ox 2	20 初三 木3 Wood [3] Fire 離爲火 庚寅 Metal Tiger 1	21 初四 火2 Fire [4/6] Sincerity 風澤中孚 辛卯 Metal Rabbit 3	22 初五 水6 Water [5] Big Livestock 山天大畜 壬辰 Water Dragon 4
23 初六 金4 Metal [4] Eliminating 澤天夬 癸巳 Water Snake 6	24 初七 金9 Metal [3] Heaven 乾爲天 甲午 Wood Horse 1	25 初八 火7 Fire [2] Well 水風井 乙未 Wood Goat 6	26 初九 木8 Wood [1] Relief 雷水解 丙申 Fire Monkey 4	27 初十 金4 Metal [9] Influence 澤山咸 丁酉 Fire Rooster 9	28 十一 水1 Water [8] Humility 地山謙 戊戌 Earth Dog 6	29 十二 火2 Fire [7] Observation 風地觀 己亥 Earth Pig 2

JULY 1985 癸未

Xuan Kong Element 玄空五行	澤水困 Trap	Period Luck 卦運	Monthly Star 月星
Metal 金4		8	9

SUNDAY	MONDAY	TUESDAY	WEDNESDAY	THURSDAY	FRIDAY	SATURDAY
	水1 Water 5 Dimming Light 地火明夷 辛丑 Metal Ox 3 1 十四	金9 Metal 4 Fellowship 天火同人 壬寅 Water Tiger 7 2 十五	木8 Wood 3 Marrying Maiden 雷澤歸妹 癸卯 Water Rabbit 7 3 十六	木3 Wood 2 Opposition 火澤睽 甲辰 Wood Dragon 2 4 十七	火7 Fire 1 Waiting 水天需 乙巳 Wood Snake 3 5 十八	金4 Metal 9 Great Exceeding 澤風大過 丙午 Fire Horse 3 6 十九
水6 Water 8 Poison 山風蠱 丁未 Fire Goat 7 7 二十	火2 Fire 7 Dispersing 風水渙 戊申 Earth Monkey 6 8 廿一	木3 Wood 6 Travelling 火山旅 己酉 Earth Rooster 8 9 廿二	金9 Metal 5 Stagnation 天地否 庚戌 Metal Dog 9 10 廿三	火7 Fire 4 Alliance 水地比 辛亥 Metal Pig 7 11 廿四	木8 Wood 3 Thunder 震爲雷 壬子 Water Rat 1 12 廿五	水6 Water 2 Beauty 山火賁 癸丑 Water Ox 8 13 廿六
火7 Fire 1 Accomplished 水火既濟 甲寅 Wood Tiger 9 14 廿七	水1 Water 9 Arriving 地澤臨 乙卯 Wood Rabbit 4 15 廿八	金4 Metal 8 Marsh 兑爲澤 丙辰 Fire Dragon 1 16 廿九	火2 Fire 7 Small Livestock 風天小畜 丁巳 Fire Snake 8 17 三十	木3 Wood 6 The Cauldron 火風鼎 戊午 Earth Horse 4 18 六月初一	水1 Water 5 Rising 地風升 己未 Earth Goat 2 19 初二	火7 Fire 4 Water 坎爲水 庚申 Metal Monkey 1 20 初三
木8 Wood 3 Lesser Exceeding 雷山小過 辛酉 Metal Rooster 3 21 初四	金4 Metal 2 Gathering 澤地萃 壬戌 Water Dog 4 22 初五	水6 Water 1 Peel 山地剝 癸亥 Water Pig 6 23 初六	水1 Water 9 Earth 坤爲地 甲子 Wood Rat 1 24 初七	木3 Wood 8 Biting 火雷噬嗑 乙丑 Wood Ox 6 25 初八	火2 Fire 7 Family 風火家人 丙寅 Fire Tiger 4 26 初九	水6 Water 6 Decreasing 山澤損 丁卯 Fire Rabbit 9 27 初十
金9 Metal 5 Tread 天澤履 戊辰 Earth Dragon 6 28 十一	木8 Wood 4 Great Strength 雷天大壯 己巳 Earth Snake 2 29 十二	木8 Wood 3 Consistency 雷風恆 庚午 Metal Horse 9 30 十三	金9 Metal 2 Litigation 天水訟 辛未 Metal Goat 3 31 十四			

AUGUST 1985 甲申

Xuan Kong Element 玄空五行	火水未濟 Not Yet Accomplished	Period Luck 卦運	Monthly Star 月星
Wood 木3		9	8

SUNDAY	MONDAY	TUESDAY	WEDNESDAY	THURSDAY	FRIDAY	SATURDAY
				水1 Water 1 Officer 地水師 壬申 Water Monkey 7 1 十五	火2 Fire 9 Gradual Progress 風山漸 癸酉 Water Rooster 7 2 十六	火7 Fire 8 Obstruction 水山蹇 甲戌 Wood Dog 2 3 十七
木3 Wood 7 Advancement 火地晉 乙亥 Wood Pig 3 4 十八	水6 Water 6 Nourish 山雷頤 丙子 Fire Rat 3 5 十九	金4 Metal 5 Following 澤雷隨 丁丑 Fire Ox 7 6 二十	木8 Wood 4 Abundance 雷火豐 戊寅 Earth Tiger 6 7 廿一	火7 Fire 3 Regulate 水澤節 己卯 Earth Rabbit 8 8 廿二	水1 Water 2 Unity 地天泰 庚辰 Metal Dragon 9 9 廿三	木3 Wood 1 Great Reward 火天大有 辛巳 Metal Snake 7 10 廿四
火2 Fire 9 Wind 巽爲風 壬午 Water Horse 1 11 廿五	金4 Metal 8 Trap 澤水困 癸未 Water Goat 8 12 廿六	木3 Wood 7 Not Yet Accomplished 火水未濟 甲申 Wood Monkey 9 13 廿七	金9 Metal 6 Retreat 天山遯 乙酉 Wood Rooster 4 14 廿八	水6 Water 5 Mountain 艮爲山 丙戌 Fire Dog 1 15 廿九	木8 Wood 4 Delight 雷地豫 丁亥 Fire Pig 8 16 七月初一	火7 Fire 3 Beginning 水雷屯 戊子 Earth Rat 4 17 初二
金9 Metal 2 Without Wrongdoing 天雷無妄 己丑 Earth Ox 2 18 初三	木3 Wood 1 Fire 離爲火 庚寅 Metal Tiger 1 19 初四	火2 Fire 9 Sincerity 風澤中孚 辛卯 Metal Rabbit 3 20 初五	水6 Water 8 Big Livestock 山天大畜 壬辰 Water Dragon 4 21 初六	金4 Metal 7 Eliminating 澤天夬 癸巳 Water Snake 6 22 初七	金9 Metal 6 Heaven 乾爲天 甲午 Wood Horse 1 23 初八	火7 Fire 5 Well 水風井 乙未 Wood Goat 6 24 初九
木8 Wood 4 Relief 雷水解 丙申 Fire Monkey 4 25 初十	金4 Metal 3 Influence 澤山咸 丁酉 Fire Rooster 9 26 十一	水1 Water 2 Humility 地山謙 戊戌 Earth Dog 6 27 十二	火2 Fire 1 Observation 風地觀 己亥 Earth Pig 2 28 十三	火2 Fire 9 Increasing 風雷益 庚子 Metal Rat 9 29 十四	水1 Water 8 Dimming Light 地火明夷 辛丑 Metal Ox 3 30 十五	金9 Metal 7 Fellowship 天火同人 壬寅 Water Tiger 7 31 十六

SEPTEMBER 1985 乙酉

Xuan Kong Element 玄空五行	天山遯 Retreat	Period Luck 卦運	Monthly Star 月星
Metal 金9		4	7

SUNDAY	MONDAY	TUESDAY	WEDNESDAY	THURSDAY	FRIDAY	SATURDAY
木8 Wood 6 Marrying Maiden 癸卯 Water Rabbit 雷澤歸妹 1 十七 7	木3 Wood 5 Opposition 甲辰 Wood Dragon 火澤睽 2 十八 2	火7 Fire 4 Waiting 乙巳 Wood Snake 水天需 3 十九 3	金4 Metal 3 Great Exceeding 丙午 Fire Horse 澤風大過 4 二十 3	水6 Water 2 Poison 丁未 Fire Goat 山風蠱 5 廿一 7	火2 Fire 1 Dispersing 戊申 Earth Monkey 風水渙 6 廿二 6	木3 Wood 9 Travelling 己酉 Earth Rooster 火山旅 7 廿三 8
金9 Metal 8 Stagnation 庚戌 Metal Dog 天地否 8 廿四 9	火7 Fire 7 Alliance 辛亥 Metal Pig 水地比 9 廿五 7	木8 Wood 6 Thunder 壬子 Water Rat 震爲雷 10 廿六 1	水6 Water 5 Beauty 癸丑 Water Ox 山火賁 11 廿七 8	火7 Fire 4 Accomplished 甲寅 Wood Tiger 水火既濟 12 廿八 9	水1 Water 3 Arriving 乙卯 Wood Rabbit 地澤臨 13 廿九 4	金4 Metal 2 Marsh 丙辰 Fire Dragon 兑爲澤 14 三十 1
火2 Fire 1 Small Livestock 丁巳 Fire Snake 風天小畜 15 八月初一 8	木3 Wood 9 The Cauldron 戊午 Earth Horse 火風鼎 16 初二 4	水1 Water 8 Rising 己未 Earth Goat 地風升 17 初三 2	火7 Fire 7 Water 庚申 Metal Monkey 坎爲水 18 初四 1	木8 Wood 6 Lesser Exceeding 辛酉 Metal Rooster 雷山小過 19 初五 3	金4 Metal 5 Gathering 壬戌 Water Dog 澤地萃 20 初六 4	水6 Water 4 Peel 癸亥 Water Pig 山地剝 21 初七 6
水1 Water 3 Earth 甲子 Wood Rat 坤爲地 22 初八 1	木3 Wood 2 Biting 乙丑 Wood Ox 火雷噬嗑 23 初九 6	火2 Fire 1 Family 丙寅 Fire Tiger 風火家人 24 初十 4	水6 Water 9 Decreasing 丁卯 Fire Rabbit 山澤損 25 十一 9	金9 Metal 8 Tread 戊辰 Earth Dragon 天澤履 26 十二 6	木8 Wood 7 Great Strength 己巳 Earth Snake 雷天大壯 27 十三 2	木8 Wood 6 Consistency 庚午 Metal Horse 雷風恆 28 十四 9
金9 Metal 5 Litigation 辛未 Metal Goat 天水訟 29 十五 3	水1 Water 4 Officer 壬申 Water Monkey 地水師 30 十六 7					

OCTOBER 1985 丙戌

Xuan Kong Element 玄空五行	艮爲山 Mountain	Period Luck 卦運	Monthly Star 月星
Water 水6		1	6

SUNDAY	MONDAY	TUESDAY	WEDNESDAY	THURSDAY	FRIDAY	SATURDAY
		火2 Fire 3 Gradual Progress 癸酉 Water Rooster 風山漸 1 十七 7	火7 Fire 2 Obstruction 甲戌 Wood Dog 水山蹇 2 十八 2	木3 Wood 1 Advancement 乙亥 Wood Pig 火地晉 3 十九 3	水6 Water 9 Nourish 丙子 Fire Rat 山雷頤 4 二十 3	金4 Metal 8 Following 丁丑 Fire Ox 澤雷隨 5 廿一 7
木8 Wood 7 Abundance 戊寅 Earth Tiger 雷火豐 6 廿二 6	火7 Fire 6 Regulate 己卯 Earth Rabbit 水澤節 7 廿三 8	水1 Water 5 Unity 庚辰 Metal Dragon 地天泰 8 廿四 9	木3 Wood 4 Great Reward 辛巳 Metal Snake 火天大有 9 廿五 7	火2 Fire 3 Wind 壬午 Water Horse 巽爲風 10 廿六 1	金4 Metal 2 Trap 癸未 Water Goat 澤水困 11 廿七 8	木3 Wood 1 Not Yet Accomplished 甲申 Wood Monkey 火水未濟 12 廿八 9
金9 Metal 9 Retreat 乙酉 Wood Rooster 天山遯 13 廿九 4	水6 Water 8 Mountain 丙戌 Fire Dog 艮爲山 14 九月初一 1	木8 Wood 7 Delight 丁亥 Fire Pig 雷地豫 15 初二 8	火7 Fire 6 Beginning 戊子 Earth Rat 水雷屯 16 初三 4	金9 Metal 5 Without Wrongdoing 己丑 Earth Ox 天雷無妄 17 初四 2	木3 Wood 4 Fire 庚寅 Metal Tiger 離爲火 18 初五 1	火2 Fire 3 Sincerity 辛卯 Metal Rabbit 風澤中孚 19 初六 3
水6 Water 2 Big Livestock 壬辰 Water Dragon 山天大畜 20 初七 4	金4 Metal 1 Eliminating 癸巳 Water Snake 澤天夬 21 初八 6	金9 Metal 9 Heaven 甲午 Wood Horse 乾爲天 22 初九 1	火7 Fire 8 Well 乙未 Wood Goat 水風井 23 初十 6	木8 Wood 7 Relief 丙申 Fire Monkey 雷水解 24 十一 4	金4 Metal 6 Influence 丁酉 Fire Rooster 澤山咸 25 十二 9	水1 Water 5 Humility 戊戌 Earth Dog 地山謙 26 十三 6
火2 Fire 4 Observation 己亥 Earth Pig 風地觀 27 十四 2	火2 Fire 3 Increasing 庚子 Metal Rat 風雷益 28 十五 9	水1 Water 2 Dimming Light 辛丑 Metal Ox 地火明夷 29 十六 3	金9 Metal 1 Fellowship 壬寅 Water Tiger 天火同人 30 十七 7	木8 Wood 9 Marrying Maiden 癸卯 Water Rabbit 雷澤歸妹 31 十八 7		

NOVEMBER 1985 丁亥

Xuan Kong Element 玄空五行	雷地豫 Delight	Period Luck 卦運	Monthly Star 月星
Wood 木8		8	5

SUNDAY	MONDAY	TUESDAY	WEDNESDAY	THURSDAY	FRIDAY	SATURDAY
					木3 Wood Opposition 8 甲辰 Wood Dragon 火澤睽 1 十九 2	火7 Fire Waiting 7 乙巳 Wood Snake 水天需 2 二十 3
金4 Metal Great Exceeding 6 丙午 Fire Horse 澤風大過 3 廿一 3	水6 Water Poison 5 丁未 Fire Goat 山風蠱 4 廿二 7	火2 Fire Dispersing 4 戊申 Earth Monkey 風水渙 5 廿三 6	木3 Wood Travelling 3 己酉 Earth Rooster 火山旅 6 廿四 8	金9 Metal Stagnation 2 庚戌 Metal Dog 天地否 7 廿五 9	火7 Fire Alliance 1 辛亥 Metal Pig 水地比 8 廿六 7	木8 Wood Thunder 9 壬子 Water Rat 震為雷 9 廿七 1
水6 Water Beauty 8 癸丑 Water Ox 山火賁 10 廿八 8	火7 Fire Accomplished 7 甲寅 Wood Tiger 水火既濟 11 廿九 9	水1 Water Arriving 6 乙卯 Wood Rabbit 地澤臨 12 十月初一 4	金4 Metal Marsh 5 丙辰 Fire Dragon 兌為澤 13 初二 1	火2 Fire Small Livestock 4 丁巳 Fire Snake 風天小畜 14 初三 8	木3 Wood The Cauldron 3 戊午 Earth Horse 火風鼎 15 初四 4	水1 Water Rising 2 己未 Earth Goat 地風升 16 初五 2
火7 Fire Water 1 庚申 Metal Monkey 坎為水 17 初六 1	木8 Wood Lesser Exceeding 9 辛酉 Metal Rooster 雷山小過 18 初七 3	金4 Metal Gathering 8 壬戌 Water Dog 澤地萃 19 初八 4	水6 Water Peel 7 癸亥 Water Pig 山地剝 20 初九 6	水1 Water Earth 6 甲子 Wood Rat 坤為地 21 初十 1	木3 Wood Biting 5 乙丑 Wood Ox 火雷噬嗑 22 十一 6	火2 Fire Family 4 丙寅 Fire Tiger 風火家人 23 十二 4
水6 Water Decreasing 3 丁卯 Fire Rabbit 山澤損 24 十三 9	金9 Metal Tread 2 戊辰 Earth Dragon 天澤履 25 十四 6	木8 Wood Great Strength 1 己巳 Earth Snake 雷天大壯 26 十五 2	木8 Wood Consistency 9 庚午 Metal Horse 雷風恒 27 十六 9	金9 Metal Litigation 8 辛未 Metal Goat 天水訟 28 十七 3	水1 Water Officer 7 壬申 Water Monkey 地水師 29 十八 7	火2 Fire Gradual Progress 6 癸酉 Water Rooster 風山漸 30 十九 7

DECEMBER 1985 戊子

Xuan Kong Element 玄空五行	水雷屯 Beginning	Period Luck 卦運	Monthly Star 月星
Fire 火7		4	4

SUNDAY	MONDAY	TUESDAY	WEDNESDAY	THURSDAY	FRIDAY	SATURDAY
火7 Fire Obstruction 5 甲戌 Wood Dog 水山蹇 1 二十 2	木3 Wood Advancement 4 乙亥 Wood Pig 火地晉 2 廿一 3	水6 Water Nourish 3 丙子 Fire Rat 山雷頤 3 廿二 3	金4 Metal Following 2 丁丑 Fire Ox 澤雷隨 4 廿三 7	木8 Wood Abundance 1 戊寅 Earth Tiger 雷火豐 5 廿四 6	火7 Fire Regulate 9 己卯 Earth Rabbit 水澤節 6 廿五 8	水1 Water Unity 8 庚辰 Metal Dragon 地天泰 7 廿六 9
木3 Wood Great Reward 7 辛巳 Metal Snake 火天大有 8 廿七 7	火2 Fire Wind 6 壬午 Water Horse 巽為風 9 廿八 1	金4 Metal Trap 5 癸未 Water Goat 澤水困 10 廿九 8	木3 Wood Not Yet Accomplished 4 甲申 Wood Monkey 火水未濟 11 三十 9	金9 Metal Retreat 3 乙酉 Wood Rooster 天山遯 12 十一月初一 4	水6 Water Mountain 2 丙戌 Fire Dog 艮為山 13 初二 1	木8 Wood Delight 1 丁亥 Fire Pig 雷地豫 14 初三 8
火7 Fire Beginning 9 戊子 Earth Rat 水雷屯 15 初四 4	金9 Metal Without Wrongdoing 8 己丑 Earth Ox 天雷無妄 16 初五 2	木3 Wood Fire 7 庚寅 Metal Tiger 離為火 17 初六 1	火2 Fire Sincerity 6 辛卯 Metal Rabbit 風澤中孚 18 初七 3	水6 Water Big Livestock 5 壬辰 Water Dragon 山天大畜 19 初八 4	金4 Metal Eliminating 4 癸巳 Water Snake 澤天夬 20 初九 6	金9 Metal Heaven 3 甲午 Wood Horse 乾為天 21 初十 1
火7 Fire Well 2/8 乙未 Wood Goat 水風井 22 十一 6	木8 Wood Relief 9 丙申 Fire Monkey 雷水解 23 十二 4	金4 Metal Influence 1 丁酉 Fire Rooster 澤山咸 24 十三 9	水1 Water Humility 2 戊戌 Earth Dog 地山謙 25 十四 6	火2 Fire Observation 3 己亥 Earth Pig 風地觀 26 十五 2	火2 Fire Increasing 4 庚子 Metal Rat 風雷益 27 十六 9	水1 Water Dimming Light 5 辛丑 Metal Ox 地火明夷 28 十七 3
金9 Metal Fellowship 6 壬寅 Water Tiger 天火同人 29 十八 7	木8 Wood Marrying Maiden 7 癸卯 Water Rabbit 雷澤歸妹 30 十九 7	木3 Wood Opposition 8 甲辰 Wood Dragon 火澤睽 31 二十 2				

1986 丙寅

(*Bing Yin*) Fire Tiger

1986 丙寅 *(Bing Yin)* Fire Tiger

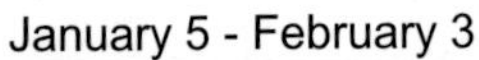

January 5 - February 3

February 4 - March 5

March 6 - April 4

April 5 - May 5

May 6 - June 5

June 6 - July 6

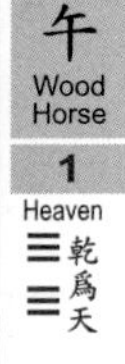

July 7 - August 7

August 8 - September 7

September 8 - October 7

October 8 - November 7

November 8 - December 6

December 7 - January 5

JANUARY 1986 己丑

Xuan Kong Element 玄空五行	天雷無妄 Without Wrongdoing	Period Luck 卦運	Monthly Star 月星
Metal 金9		2	3

SUNDAY	MONDAY	TUESDAY	WEDNESDAY	THURSDAY	FRIDAY	SATURDAY
			火7 Fire Waiting 9 乙巳 Wood Snake 水天需 1 廿一 3	金4 Metal Great Exceeding 1 丙午 Fire Horse 澤風大過 2 廿二 3	水6 Water Poison 2 丁未 Fire Goat 山風蠱 3 廿三 7	火2 Fire Dispersing 3 戊申 Earth Monkey 風水渙 4 廿四 6
木3 Wood Travelling 4 己酉 Earth Rooster 火山旅 5 廿五 8	金9 Metal Stagnation 5 庚戌 Metal Dog 天地否 6 廿六 9	火7 Fire Alliance 6 辛亥 Metal Pig 水地比 7 廿七 7	木8 Wood Thunder 7 壬子 Water Rat 震為雷 8 廿八 1	水6 Water Beauty 8 癸丑 Water Ox 山火賁 9 廿九 8	火7 Fire Accomplished 9 甲寅 Wood Tiger 水火既濟 10 十二月初一 9	水1 Water Arriving 1 乙卯 Wood Rabbit 地澤臨 11 初二 4
金4 Metal Marsh 2 丙辰 Fire Dragon 兌為澤 12 初三 1	火2 Fire Small Livestock 3 丁巳 Fire Snake 風天小畜 13 初四 8	木3 Wood The Cauldron 4 戊午 Earth Horse 火風鼎 14 初五 4	水1 Water Rising 5 己未 Earth Goat 地風升 15 初六 2	火7 Fire Water 6 庚申 Metal Monkey 坎為水 16 初七 1	木8 Wood Lesser Exceeding 7 辛酉 Metal Rooster 雷山小過 17 初八 3	金4 Metal Gathering 8 壬戌 Water Dog 澤地萃 18 初九 4
水6 Water Peel 9 癸亥 Water Pig 山地剝 19 初十 6	水1 Water Earth 1 甲子 Wood Rat 坤為地 20 十一 1	木3 Wood Biting 2 乙丑 Wood Ox 火雷噬嗑 21 十二 6	火2 Fire Family 3 丙寅 Fire Tiger 風火家人 22 十三 4	水6 Water Decreasing 4 丁卯 Fire Rabbit 山澤損 23 十四 9	金9 Metal Tread 5 戊辰 Earth Dragon 天澤履 24 十五 6	木8 Wood Great Strength 6 己巳 Earth Snake 雷天大壯 25 十六 2
木8 Wood Consistency 7 庚午 Metal Horse 雷風恆 26 十七 9	金9 Metal Litigation 8 辛未 Metal Goat 天水訟 27 十八 3	水1 Water Officer 9 壬申 Water Monkey 地水師 28 十九 7	火2 Fire Gradual Progress 1 癸酉 Water Rooster 風山漸 29 二十 7	火7 Fire Obstruction 2 甲戌 Wood Dog 水山蹇 30 廿一 2	木3 Wood Advancement 3 乙亥 Wood Pig 火地晉 31 廿二 3	

FEBRUARY 1986 庚寅

Xuan Kong Element 玄空五行	離為火 Fire	Period Luck 卦運	Monthly Star 月星
Wood 木3		1	2

SUNDAY	MONDAY	TUESDAY	WEDNESDAY	THURSDAY	FRIDAY	SATURDAY
						水6 Water Nourish 4 丙子 Fire Rat 山雷頤 1 十三 3
金4 Metal Following 5 丁丑 Fire Ox 澤雷隨 2 廿四 7	木8 Wood Abundance 6 戊寅 Earth Tiger 雷火豐 3 廿五 6	火7 Fire Regulate 7 己卯 Earth Rabbit 水澤節 4 廿六 8	水1 Water Unity 8 庚辰 Metal Dragon 地天泰 5 廿七 9	木3 Wood Great Reward 9 辛巳 Metal Snake 火天大有 6 廿八 7	火2 Fire Wind 1 壬午 Water Horse 巽為風 7 廿九 1	金4 Metal Trap 2 癸未 Water Goat 澤水困 8 三十 8
木3 Wood Not Yet Accomplished 3 甲申 Wood Monkey 火水未濟 9 正月初一 9	金9 Metal Retreat 4 乙酉 Wood Rooster 天山遯 10 初二 4	水6 Water Mountain 5 丙戌 Fire Dog 艮為山 11 初三 1	木8 Wood Delight 6 丁亥 Fire Pig 雷地豫 12 初四 8	火7 Fire Beginning 7 戊子 Earth Rat 水雷屯 13 初五 4	金9 Metal Without Wrongdoing 8 己丑 Earth Ox 天雷無妄 14 初六 2	木3 Wood Fire 9 庚寅 Metal Tiger 離為火 15 初七 1
火2 Fire Sincerity 1 辛卯 Metal Rabbit 風澤中孚 16 初八 3	水6 Water Big Livestock 2 壬辰 Water Dragon 山天大畜 17 初九 4	金4 Metal Eliminating 3 癸巳 Water Snake 澤天夬 18 初十 6	金9 Metal Heaven 4 甲午 Wood Horse 乾為天 19 十一 1	火7 Fire Well 5 乙未 Wood Goat 水風井 20 十二 6	木8 Wood Relief 6 丙申 Fire Monkey 雷水解 21 十三 4	金4 Metal Influence 7 丁酉 Fire Rooster 澤山咸 22 十四 9
水1 Water Humility 8 戊戌 Earth Dog 地山謙 23 十五 6	火2 Fire Observation 9 己亥 Earth Pig 風地觀 24 十六 2	火2 Fire Increasing 1 庚子 Metal Rat 風雷益 25 十七 9	水1 Water Dimming Light 2 辛丑 Metal Ox 地火明夷 26 十八 3	金9 Metal Fellowship 3 壬寅 Water Tiger 天火同人 27 十九 7	木8 Wood Marrying Maiden 4 癸卯 Water Rabbit 雷澤歸妹 28 二十 7	

MARCH 1986 辛卯

Xuan Kong Element 玄空五行	風澤中孚 Sincerity	Period Luck 卦運	Monthly Star 月星
Fire 火2		3	1

SUNDAY	MONDAY	TUESDAY	WEDNESDAY	THURSDAY	FRIDAY	SATURDAY
火2 Fire 7 Gradual Progress 風山漸 癸酉 Water Rooster 7 30 廿一	火7 Fire 8 Obstruction 水山蹇 甲戌 Wood Dog 2 31 廿二					木3 Wood 5 Opposition 火澤睽 甲辰 Wood Dragon 2 1 廿一
火7 Fire 6 Waiting 水天需 乙巳 Wood Snake 3 2 廿二	金4 Metal 7 Great Exceeding 澤風大過 丙午 Fire Horse 3 3 廿三	水6 Water 8 Poison 山風蠱 丁未 Fire Goat 7 4 廿四	火2 Fire 9 Dispersing 風水渙 戊申 Earth Monkey 6 5 廿五	木3 Wood 1 Travelling 火山旅 己酉 Earth Rooster 8 6 廿六	金9 Metal 2 Stagnation 天地否 庚戌 Metal Dog 9 7 廿七	火7 Fire 3 Alliance 水地比 辛亥 Metal Pig 7 8 廿八
木8 Wood 4 Thunder 震爲雷 壬子 Water Rat 1 9 廿九	水6 Water 5 Beauty 山火賁 癸丑 Water Ox 8 10 二月初一	火7 Fire 6 Accomplished 水火既濟 甲寅 Wood Tiger 9 11 初二	水1 Water 7 Arriving 地澤臨 乙卯 Wood Rabbit 4 12 初三	金4 Metal 8 Marsh 兌爲澤 丙辰 Fire Dragon 1 13 初四	火2 Fire 9 Small Livestock 風天小畜 丁巳 Fire Snake 8 14 初五	木3 Wood 1 The Cauldron 火風鼎 戊午 Earth Horse 4 15 初六
水1 Water 2 Rising 地風升 己未 Earth Goat 2 16 初七	火7 Fire 3 Water 坎爲水 庚申 Metal Monkey 1 17 初八	木8 Wood 4 Lesser Exceeding 雷山小過 辛酉 Metal Rooster 3 18 初九	金4 Metal 5 Gathering 澤地萃 壬戌 Water Dog 4 19 初十	水6 Water 6 Peel 山地剝 癸亥 Water Pig 6 20 十一	水1 Water 7 Earth 坤爲地 甲子 Wood Rat 1 21 十二	木3 Wood 8 Biting 火雷噬嗑 乙丑 Wood Ox 6 22 十三
火2 Fire 9 Family 風火家人 丙寅 Fire Tiger 4 23 十四	水6 Water 1 Decreasing 山澤損 丁卯 Fire Rabbit 9 24 十五	金9 Metal 2 Tread 天澤履 戊辰 Earth Dragon 6 25 十六	木8 Wood 3 Great Strength 雷天大壯 己巳 Earth Snake 2 26 十七	木8 Wood 4 Consistency 雷風恆 庚午 Metal Horse 9 27 十八	金9 Metal 5 Litigation 天水訟 辛未 Metal Goat 3 28 十九	水1 Water 6 Officer 地水師 壬申 Water Monkey 7 29 二十

APRIL 1986 壬辰

Xuan Kong Element 玄空五行	山天大畜 Big Livestock	Period Luck 卦運	Monthly Star 月星
Water 水6		4	9

SUNDAY	MONDAY	TUESDAY	WEDNESDAY	THURSDAY	FRIDAY	SATURDAY
		木3 Wood 9 Advancement 火地晉 乙亥 Wood Pig 3 1 廿三	水6 Water 1 Nourish 山雷頤 丙子 Fire Rat 3 2 廿四	金4 Metal 2 Following 澤雷隨 丁丑 Fire Ox 7 3 廿五	木8 Wood 3 Abundance 雷火豐 戊寅 Earth Tiger 6 4 廿六	火7 Fire 4 Regulate 水澤節 己卯 Earth Rabbit 8 5 廿七
水1 Water 5 Unity 地天泰 庚辰 Metal Dragon 9 6 廿八	木3 Wood 6 Great Reward 火天大有 辛巳 Metal Snake 7 7 廿九	火2 Fire 7 Wind 巽爲風 壬午 Water Horse 1 8 三十	金4 Metal 8 Trap 澤水困 癸未 Water Goat 8 9 三月初一	木3 Wood 9 Not Yet Accomplished 火水未濟 甲申 Wood Monkey 9 10 初二	金9 Metal 1 Retreat 天山遯 乙酉 Wood Rooster 4 11 初三	水6 Water 2 Mountain 艮爲山 丙戌 Fire Dog 1 12 初四
木8 Wood 3 Delight 雷地豫 丁亥 Fire Pig 8 13 初五	火7 Fire 4 Beginning 水雷屯 戊子 Earth Rat 4 14 初六	金9 Metal 5 Without Wrongdoing 天雷無妄 己丑 Earth Ox 2 15 初七	木3 Wood 6 Fire 離爲火 庚寅 Metal Tiger 1 16 初八	火2 Fire 7 Sincerity 風澤中孚 辛卯 Metal Rabbit 3 17 初九	水6 Water 8 Big Livestock 山天大畜 壬辰 Water Dragon 4 18 初十	金4 Metal 9 Eliminating 澤天夬 癸巳 Water Snake 6 19 十一
金9 Metal 1 Heaven 乾爲天 甲午 Wood Horse 1 20 十二	火7 Fire 2 Well 水風井 乙未 Wood Goat 6 21 十三	木8 Wood 3 Relief 雷水解 丙申 Fire Monkey 4 22 十四	金4 Metal 4 Influence 澤山咸 丁酉 Fire Rooster 9 23 十五	水1 Water 5 Humility 地山謙 戊戌 Earth Dog 6 24 十六	火2 Fire 6 Observation 風地觀 己亥 Earth Pig 2 25 十七	火2 Fire 7 Increasing 風雷益 庚子 Metal Rat 9 26 十八
水1 Water 8 Dimming Light 地火明夷 辛丑 Metal Ox 3 27 十九	金9 Metal 9 Fellowship 天火同人 壬寅 Water Tiger 7 28 二十	木8 Wood 1 Marrying Maiden 雷澤歸妹 癸卯 Water Rabbit 7 29 廿一	木3 Wood 2 Opposition 火澤睽 甲辰 Wood Dragon 2 30 廿二			

MAY 1986 癸巳

Xuan Kong Element 玄空五行	澤天夬 Eliminating	Period Luck 卦運	Monthly Star 月星
Metal 金4		6	8

SUNDAY	MONDAY	TUESDAY	WEDNESDAY	THURSDAY	FRIDAY	SATURDAY
				火7 Fire 3 Waiting 水天需 乙巳 Wood Snake 1 廿三 3	金4 Metal 4 Great Exceeding 澤風大過 丙午 Fire Horse 2 廿四 3	水6 Water 5 Poison 山風蠱 丁未 Fire Goat 3 廿五 7
火2 Fire 6 Dispersing 風水渙 戊申 Earth Monkey 4 廿六 6	木3 Wood 7 Travelling 火山旅 己酉 Earth Rooster 5 廿七 8	金9 Metal 8 Stagnation 天地否 庚戌 Metal Dog 6 廿八 9	火7 Fire 9 Alliance 水地比 辛亥 Metal Pig 7 廿九 7	木8 Wood 1 Thunder 震爲雷 壬子 Water Rat 8 三十 1	水6 Water 2 Beauty 山火賁 癸丑 Water Ox 9 四月初一 8	火7 Fire 3 Accomplished 水火既濟 甲寅 Wood Tiger 10 初二 9
水1 Water 4 Arriving 地澤臨 乙卯 Wood Rabbit 11 初三 4	金4 Metal 5 Marsh 兌爲澤 丙辰 Fire Dragon 12 初四 1	火2 Fire 6 Small Livestock 風天小畜 丁巳 Fire Snake 13 初五 8	木3 Wood 7 The Cauldron 火風鼎 戊午 Earth Horse 14 初六 4	水1 Water 8 Rising 地風升 己未 Earth Goat 15 初七 2	火7 Fire 9 Water 坎爲水 庚申 Metal Monkey 16 初八 1	木8 Wood 1 Lesser Exceeding 雷山小過 辛酉 Metal Rooster 17 初九 3
金4 Metal 2 Gathering 澤地萃 壬戌 Water Dog 18 初十 4	水6 Water 3 Peel 山地剝 癸亥 Water Pig 19 十一 6	水1 Water 4 Earth 坤爲地 甲子 Wood Rat 20 十二 1	木3 Wood 5 Biting 火雷噬嗑 乙丑 Wood Ox 21 十三 6	火2 Fire 6 Family 風火家人 丙寅 Fire Tiger 22 十四 4	水6 Water 7 Decreasing 山澤損 丁卯 Fire Rabbit 23 十五 9	金9 Metal 8 Tread 天澤履 戊辰 Earth Dragon 24 十六 6
木8 Wood 9 Great Strength 雷天大壯 己巳 Earth Snake 25 十七 2	木8 Wood 1 Consistency 雷風恒 庚午 Metal Horse 26 十八 9	金9 Metal 2 Litigation 天水訟 辛未 Metal Goat 27 十九 3	水1 Water 3 Officer 地水師 壬申 Water Monkey 28 二十 7	火2 Fire 4 Gradual Progress 風山漸 癸酉 Water Rooster 29 廿一 7	火7 Fire 5 Obstruction 水山蹇 甲戌 Wood Dog 30 廿二 2	木3 Wood 6 Advancement 火地晉 乙亥 Wood Pig 31 廿三 3

JUNE 1986 甲午

Xuan Kong Element 玄空五行	乾爲天 Heaven	Period Luck 卦運	Monthly Star 月星
Metal 金9		1	7

SUNDAY	MONDAY	TUESDAY	WEDNESDAY	THURSDAY	FRIDAY	SATURDAY
水6 Water 7 Nourish 山雷頤 丙子 Fire Rat 1 廿四 3	金4 Metal 8 Following 澤雷隨 丁丑 Fire Ox 2 廿五 7	木8 Wood 9 Abundance 雷火豐 戊寅 Earth Tiger 3 廿六 6	火7 Fire 1 Regulate 水澤節 己卯 Earth Rabbit 4 廿七 8	水1 Water 2 Unity 地天泰 庚辰 Metal Dragon 5 廿八 9	木3 Wood 3 Great Reward 火天大有 辛巳 Metal Snake 6 廿九 7	火2 Fire 4 Wind 巽爲風 壬午 Water Horse 7 五月初一 1
金4 Metal 5 Trap 澤水困 癸未 Water Goat 8 初二 8	木3 Wood 6 Not Yet Accomplished 火水未濟 甲申 Wood Monkey 9 初三 9	金9 Metal 7 Retreat 天山遯 乙酉 Wood Rooster 10 初四 4	水6 Water 8 Mountain 艮爲山 丙戌 Fire Dog 11 初五 1	木8 Wood 9 Delight 雷地豫 丁亥 Fire Pig 12 初六 8	火7 Fire 1 Beginning 水雷屯 戊子 Earth Rat 13 初七 4	金9 Metal 2 Without Wrongdoing 天雷無妄 己丑 Earth Ox 14 初八 2
木3 Wood 3 Fire 離爲火 庚寅 Metal Tiger 15 初九 1	火2 Fire 4 Sincerity 風澤中孚 辛卯 Metal Rabbit 16 初十 3	水6 Water 5 Big Livestock 山天大畜 壬辰 Water Dragon 17 十一 4	金4 Metal 6 Eliminating 澤天夬 癸巳 Water Snake 18 十二 6	金9 Metal 7 Heaven 乾爲天 甲午 Wood Horse 19 十三 1	火7 Fire 8 Well 水風井 乙未 Wood Goat 20 十四 6	木8 Wood 9 Relief 雷水解 丙申 Fire Monkey 21 十五 4
金4 Metal 1/9 Influence 澤山咸 丁酉 Fire Rooster 22 十六 9	水1 Water 8 Humility 地山謙 戊戌 Earth Dog 23 十七 6	火2 Fire 7 Observation 風地觀 己亥 Earth Pig 24 十八 2	火2 Fire 6 Increasing 風雷益 庚子 Metal Rat 25 十九 9	水1 Water 5 Dimming Light 地火明夷 辛丑 Metal Ox 26 二十 3	金9 Metal 4 Fellowship 天火同人 壬寅 Water Tiger 27 廿一 7	木8 Wood 3 Marrying Maiden 雷澤歸妹 癸卯 Water Rabbit 28 廿二 7
木3 Wood 2 Opposition 火澤睽 甲辰 Wood Dragon 29 廿三 2	火7 Fire 1 Waiting 水天需 乙巳 Wood Snake 30 廿四 3					

JULY 1986 乙未

Xuan Kong Element 玄空五行	水風井 Well	Period Luck 卦運	Monthly Star 月星
Fire 火7		6	6

SUNDAY	MONDAY	TUESDAY	WEDNESDAY	THURSDAY	FRIDAY	SATURDAY
		金4 Metal · 9 Great Exceeding 澤風大過 丙午 Fire Horse **1** 廿五 3	水6 Water · 8 Poison 山風蠱 丁未 Fire Goat **2** 廿六 7	火2 Fire · 7 Dispersing 風水渙 戊申 Earth Monkey **3** 廿七 6	木3 Wood · 6 Travelling 火山旅 己酉 Earth Rooster **4** 廿八 8	金9 Metal · 5 Stagnation 天地否 庚戌 Metal Dog **5** 廿九 9
火7 Fire · 4 Alliance 水地比 辛亥 Metal Pig **6** 三十 7	木8 Wood · 3 Thunder 震爲雷 壬子 Water Rat **7** 六月初一 1	水6 Water · 2 Beauty 山火賁 癸丑 Water Ox **8** 初二 8	火7 Fire · 1 Accomplished 水火既濟 甲寅 Wood Tiger **9** 初三 9	水1 Water · 9 Arriving 地澤臨 乙卯 Wood Rabbit **10** 初四 4	金4 Metal · 8 Marsh 兌爲澤 丙辰 Fire Dragon **11** 初五 1	火2 Fire · 7 Small Livestock 風天小畜 丁巳 Fire Snake **12** 初六 8
木3 Wood · 6 The Cauldron 火風鼎 戊午 Earth Horse **13** 初七 4	水1 Water · 5 Rising 地風升 己未 Earth Goat **14** 初八 2	火7 Fire · 4 Water 坎爲水 庚申 Metal Monkey **15** 初九 1	木8 Wood · 3 Lesser Exceeding 雷山小過 辛酉 Metal Rooster **16** 初十 3	金4 Metal · 2 Gathering 澤地萃 壬戌 Water Dog **17** 十一 4	水6 Water · 1 Peel 山地剝 癸亥 Water Pig **18** 十二 6	水1 Water · 9 Earth 坤爲地 甲子 Wood Rat **19** 十三 1
木3 Wood · 8 Biting 火雷噬嗑 乙丑 Wood Ox **20** 十四 6	火2 Fire · 7 Family 風火家人 丙寅 Fire Tiger **21** 十五 4	水6 Water · 6 Decreasing 山澤損 丁卯 Fire Rabbit **22** 十六 9	金9 Metal · 5 Tread 天澤履 戊辰 Earth Dragon **23** 十七 6	木8 Wood · 4 Great Strength 雷天大壯 己巳 Earth Snake **24** 十八 2	木8 Wood · 3 Consistency 雷風恒 庚午 Metal Horse **25** 十九 9	金9 Metal · 2 Litigation 天水訟 辛未 Metal Goat **26** 二十 3
水1 Water · 1 Officer 地水師 壬申 Water Monkey **27** 廿一 7	火2 Fire · 9 Gradual Progress 風山漸 癸酉 Water Rooster **28** 廿二 7	火7 Fire · 8 Obstruction 水山蹇 甲戌 Wood Dog **29** 廿三 2	木3 Wood · 7 Advancement 火地晉 乙亥 Wood Pig **30** 廿四 3	水6 Water · 6 Nourish 山雷頤 丙子 Fire Rat **31** 廿五 3		

AUGUST 1986 丙申

Xuan Kong Element 玄空五行	雷水解 Relief	Period Luck 卦運	Monthly Star 月星
Wood 木8		4	5

SUNDAY	MONDAY	TUESDAY	WEDNESDAY	THURSDAY	FRIDAY	SATURDAY
水6 Water · 2 Poison 山風蠱 丁未 Fire Goat **31** 廿六 7					金4 Metal · 5 Following 澤雷隨 丁丑 Fire Ox **1** 廿六 7	木8 Wood · 4 Abundance 雷火豐 戊寅 Earth Tiger **2** 廿七 6
火7 Fire · 3 Regulate 水澤節 己卯 Earth Rabbit **3** 廿八 8	水1 Water · 2 Unity 地天泰 庚辰 Metal Dragon **4** 廿九 9	木3 Wood · 1 Great Reward 火天大有 辛巳 Metal Snake **5** 三十 7	火2 Fire · 9 Wind 巽爲風 壬午 Water Horse **6** 七月初一 1	金4 Metal · 8 Trap 澤水困 癸未 Water Goat **7** 初二 8	木3 Wood · 7 Not Yet Accomplished 火水未濟 甲申 Wood Monkey **8** 初三 9	金9 Metal · 6 Retreat 天山遯 乙酉 Wood Rooster **9** 初四 4
水6 Water · 5 Mountain 艮爲山 丙戌 Fire Dog **10** 初五 1	木8 Wood · 4 Delight 雷地豫 丁亥 Fire Pig **11** 初六 8	火7 Fire · 3 Beginning 水雷屯 戊子 Earth Rat **12** 初七 4	金9 Metal · 2 Without Wrongdoing 天雷無妄 己丑 Earth Ox **13** 初八 2	木3 Wood · 1 Fire 離爲火 庚寅 Metal Tiger **14** 初九 1	火2 Fire · 9 Sincerity 風澤中孚 辛卯 Metal Rabbit **15** 初十 3	水6 Water · 8 Big Livestock 山天大畜 壬辰 Water Dragon **16** 十一 4
金4 Metal · 7 Eliminating 澤天夬 癸巳 Water Snake **17** 十二 6	金9 Metal · 6 Heaven 乾爲天 甲午 Wood Horse **18** 十三 1	火7 Fire · 5 Well 水風井 乙未 Wood Goat **19** 十四 6	木8 Wood · 4 Relief 雷水解 丙申 Fire Monkey **20** 十五 4	金4 Metal · 3 Influence 澤山咸 丁酉 Fire Rooster **21** 十六 9	水1 Water · 2 Humility 地山謙 戊戌 Earth Dog **22** 十七 6	火2 Fire · 1 Observation 風地觀 己亥 Earth Pig **23** 十八 2
火2 Fire · 9 Increasing 風雷益 庚子 Metal Rat **24** 十九 9	水1 Water · 8 Dimming Light 地火明夷 辛丑 Metal Ox **25** 二十 3	金9 Metal · 7 Fellowship 天火同人 壬寅 Water Tiger **26** 廿一 7	木8 Wood · 6 Marrying Maiden 雷澤歸妹 癸卯 Water Rabbit **27** 廿二 7	木3 Wood · 5 Opposition 火澤睽 甲辰 Wood Dragon **28** 廿三 2	火7 Fire · 4 Waiting 水天需 乙巳 Wood Snake **29** 廿四 3	金4 Metal · 3 Great Exceeding 澤風大過 丙午 Fire Horse **30** 廿五 3

SEPTEMBER 1986 丁酉

Xuan Kong Element 玄空五行	澤山咸 Influence	Period Luck 卦運	Monthly Star 月星
Metal 金4		9	4

SUNDAY	MONDAY	TUESDAY	WEDNESDAY	THURSDAY	FRIDAY	SATURDAY
	火2 Fire 1 Dispersing 風水渙 戊申 Earth Monkey **1** 廿七 6	木3 Wood 9 Travelling 火山旅 己酉 Earth Rooster **2** 廿八 8	金9 Metal 8 Stagnation 天地否 庚戌 Metal Dog **3** 廿九 9	火7 Fire 7 Alliance 水地比 辛亥 Metal Pig **4** 八月初一 7	木8 Wood 6 Thunder 震爲雷 壬子 Water Rat **5** 初二 1	水6 Water 5 Beauty 山火賁 癸丑 Water Ox **6** 初三 8
火7 Fire 4 Accomplished 水火既濟 甲寅 Wood Tiger **7** 初四 9	水1 Water 3 Arriving 地澤臨 乙卯 Wood Rabbit **8** 初五 4	金4 Metal 2 Marsh 兌爲澤 丙辰 Fire Dragon **9** 初六 1	火2 Fire 1 Small Livestock 風天小畜 丁巳 Fire Snake **10** 初七 8	木3 Wood 9 The Cauldron 火風鼎 戊午 Earth Horse **11** 初八 4	水1 Water 8 Rising 地風升 己未 Earth Goat **12** 初九 2	火7 Fire 7 Water 坎爲水 庚申 Metal Monkey **13** 初十 1
木8 Wood 6 Lesser Exceeding 雷山小過 辛酉 Metal Rooster **14** 十一 3	金4 Metal 5 Gathering 澤地萃 壬戌 Water Dog **15** 十二 4	水6 Water 4 Peel 山地剝 癸亥 Water Pig **16** 十三 6	水1 Water 3 Earth 坤爲地 甲子 Wood Rat **17** 十四 1	木3 Wood 2 Biting 火雷噬嗑 乙丑 Wood Ox **18** 十五 6	火2 Fire 1 Family 風火家人 丙寅 Fire Tiger **19** 十六 4	水6 Water 9 Decreasing 山澤損 丁卯 Fire Rabbit **20** 十七 9
金9 Metal 8 Tread 天澤履 戊辰 Earth Dragon **21** 十八 6	木8 Wood 7 Great Strength 雷天大壯 己巳 Earth Snake **22** 十九 2	木8 Wood 6 Consistency 雷風恆 庚午 Metal Horse **23** 二十 9	金9 Metal 5 Litigation 天水訟 辛未 Metal Goat **24** 廿一 3	水1 Water 4 Officer 地水師 壬申 Water Monkey **25** 廿二 7	火2 Fire 3 Gradual Progress 風山漸 癸酉 Water Rooster **26** 廿三 7	火7 Fire 2 Obstruction 水山蹇 甲戌 Wood Dog **27** 廿四 2
木3 Wood 1 Advancement 火地晉 乙亥 Wood Pig **28** 廿五 3	水6 Water 9 Nourish 山雷頤 丙子 Fire Rat **29** 廿六 3	金4 Metal 8 Following 澤雷隨 丁丑 Fire Ox **30** 廿七 7				

OCTOBER 1986 戊戌

Xuan Kong Element 玄空五行	地山謙 Humility	Period Luck 卦運	Monthly Star 月星
Water 水1		6	3

SUNDAY	MONDAY	TUESDAY	WEDNESDAY	THURSDAY	FRIDAY	SATURDAY
			木8 Wood 7 Abundance 雷火豐 戊寅 Earth Tiger **1** 廿八 6	火7 Fire 6 Regulate 水澤節 己卯 Earth Rabbit **2** 廿九 8	水1 Water 5 Unity 地天泰 庚辰 Metal Dragon **3** 三十 9	木3 Wood 4 Great Reward 火天大有 辛巳 Metal Snake **4** 九月初一 7
火2 Fire 3 Wind 巽爲風 壬午 Water Horse **5** 初二 1	金4 Metal 2 Trap 澤水困 癸未 Water Goat **6** 初三 8	木3 Wood 1 Not Yet Accomplished 火水未濟 甲申 Wood Monkey **7** 初四 9	金9 Metal 9 Retreat 天山遯 乙酉 Wood Rooster **8** 初五 4	水6 Water 8 Mountain 艮爲山 丙戌 Fire Dog **9** 初六 1	木8 Wood 7 Delight 雷地豫 丁亥 Fire Pig **10** 初七 8	火7 Fire 6 Beginning 水雷屯 戊子 Earth Rat **11** 初八 4
金9 Metal 5 Without Wrongdoing 天雷無妄 己丑 Earth Ox **12** 初九 2	木3 Wood 4 Fire 離爲火 庚寅 Metal Tiger **13** 初十 1	火2 Fire 3 Sincerity 風澤中孚 辛卯 Metal Rabbit **14** 十一 3	水6 Water 2 Big Livestock 山天大畜 壬辰 Water Dragon **15** 十二 4	金4 Metal 1 Eliminating 澤天夬 癸巳 Water Snake **16** 十三 6	金9 Metal 9 Heaven 乾爲天 甲午 Wood Horse **17** 十四 1	火7 Fire 8 Well 水風井 乙未 Wood Goat **18** 十五 6
木8 Wood 7 Relief 雷水解 丙申 Fire Monkey **19** 十六 4	金4 Metal 6 Influence 澤山咸 丁酉 Fire Rooster **20** 十七 9	水1 Water 5 Humility 地山謙 戊戌 Earth Dog **21** 十八 6	火2 Fire 4 Observation 風地觀 己亥 Earth Pig **22** 十九 2	火2 Fire 3 Increasing 風雷益 庚子 Metal Rat **23** 二十 9	水1 Water 2 Dimming Light 地火明夷 辛丑 Metal Ox **24** 廿一 3	金9 Metal 1 Fellowship 天火同人 壬寅 Water Tiger **25** 廿二 7
木8 Wood 9 Marrying Maiden 雷澤歸妹 癸卯 Water Rabbit **26** 廿三 7	木3 Wood 8 Opposition 火澤睽 甲辰 Wood Dragon **27** 廿四 2	火7 Fire 7 Waiting 水天需 乙巳 Wood Snake **28** 廿五 3	金4 Metal 6 Great Exceeding 澤風大過 丙午 Fire Horse **29** 廿六 3	水6 Water 5 Poison 山風蠱 丁未 Fire Goat **30** 廿七 7	火2 Fire 4 Dispersing 風水渙 戊申 Earth Monkey **31** 廿八 6	

NOVEMBER 1986 己亥

Xuan Kong Element 玄空五行	風地觀 Observation	Period Luck 卦運	Monthly Star 月星
Fire 火2		2	2

SUNDAY	MONDAY	TUESDAY	WEDNESDAY	THURSDAY	FRIDAY	SATURDAY
30 廿九 Abundance 雷火豐 1 木8 Wood 戊寅 Earth Tiger 6						1 廿九 Travelling 火山旅 3 木3 Wood 己酉 Earth Rooster 8
2 十月初一 Stagnation 天地否 2 金9 Metal 庚戌 Metal Dog 9	3 初二 Alliance 水地比 1 火7 Fire 辛亥 Metal Pig 7	4 初三 Thunder 震為雷 9 木8 Wood 壬子 Water Rat 1	5 初四 Beauty 山火賁 8 水6 Water 癸丑 Water Ox 8	6 初五 Accomplished 水火既濟 7 火7 Fire 甲寅 Wood Tiger 9	7 初六 Arriving 地澤臨 6 水1 Water 乙卯 Wood Rabbit 4	8 初七 Marsh 兌為澤 5 金4 Metal 丙辰 Fire Dragon 1
9 初八 Small Livestock 風天小畜 4 火2 Fire 丁巳 Fire Snake 8	10 初九 The Cauldron 火風鼎 3 木3 Wood 戊午 Earth Horse 4	11 初十 Rising 地風升 2 水1 Water 己未 Earth Goat 2	12 十一 Water 坎為水 1 火7 Fire 庚申 Metal Monkey 1	13 十二 Lesser Exceeding 雷山小過 9 木8 Wood 辛酉 Metal Rooster 3	14 十三 Gathering 澤地萃 8 金4 Metal 壬戌 Water Dog 4	15 十四 Peel 山地剝 7 水6 Water 癸亥 Water Pig 6
16 十五 Earth 坤為地 6 水1 Water 甲子 Wood Rat 1	17 十六 Biting 火雷噬嗑 5 木3 Wood 乙丑 Wood Ox 6	18 十七 Family 風火家人 4 火2 Fire 丙寅 Fire Tiger 4	19 十八 Decreasing 山澤損 3 水6 Water 丁卯 Fire Rabbit 9	20 十九 Tread 天澤履 2 金9 Metal 戊辰 Earth Dragon 6	21 二十 Great Strength 雷天大壯 1 木8 Wood 己巳 Earth Snake 2	22 廿一 Consistency 雷風恆 9 木8 Wood 庚午 Metal Horse 9
23 廿二 Litigation 天水訟 8 金9 Metal 辛未 Metal Goat 3	24 廿三 Officer 地水師 7 水1 Water 壬申 Water Monkey 7	25 廿四 Gradual Progress 風山漸 6 火2 Fire 癸酉 Water Rooster 7	26 廿五 Obstruction 水山蹇 5 火7 Fire 甲戌 Wood Dog 2	27 廿六 Advancement 火地晉 4 木3 Wood 乙亥 Wood Pig 3	28 廿七 Nourish 山雷頤 3 水6 Water 丙子 Fire Rat 3	29 廿八 Following 澤雷隨 2 金4 Metal 丁丑 Fire Ox 7

DECEMBER 1986 庚子

Xuan Kong Element 玄空五行	風雷益 Increasing	Period Luck 卦運	Monthly Star 月星
Fire 火2		9	1

SUNDAY	MONDAY	TUESDAY	WEDNESDAY	THURSDAY	FRIDAY	SATURDAY
	1 三十 Regulate 水澤節 9 火7 Fire 己卯 Earth Rabbit 8	2 十一月初一 Unity 地天泰 8 水1 Water 庚辰 Metal Dragon 9	3 初二 Great Reward 火天大有 7 木3 Wood 辛巳 Metal Snake 7	4 初三 Wind 巽為風 6 火2 Fire 壬午 Water Horse 1	5 初四 Trap 澤水困 5 金4 Metal 癸未 Water Goat 8	6 初五 Not Yet Accomplished 火水未濟 4 木3 Wood 甲申 Wood Monkey 9
7 初六 Retreat 天山遯 3 金9 Metal 乙酉 Wood Rooster 4	8 初七 Mountain 艮為山 2 水6 Water 丙戌 Fire Dog 1	9 初八 Delight 雷地豫 1 木8 Wood 丁亥 Fire Pig 8	10 初九 Beginning 水雷屯 9 火7 Fire 戊子 Earth Rat 4	11 初十 Without Wrongdoing 天雷無妄 8 金9 Metal 己丑 Earth Ox 2	12 十一 Fire 離為火 7 木3 Wood 庚寅 Metal Tiger 1	13 十二 Sincerity 風澤中孚 6 火2 Fire 辛卯 Metal Rabbit 3
14 十三 Big Livestock 山天大畜 5 水6 Water 壬辰 Water Dragon 4	15 十四 Eliminating 澤天夬 4 金4 Metal 癸巳 Water Snake 6	16 十五 Heaven 乾為天 3 金9 Metal 甲午 Wood Horse 1	17 十六 Well 水風井 2 火7 Fire 乙未 Wood Goat 6	18 十七 Relief 雷水解 1 木8 Wood 丙申 Fire Monkey 4	19 十八 Influence 澤山咸 9 金4 Metal 丁酉 Fire Rooster 9	20 十九 Humility 地山謙 8 水1 Water 戊戌 Earth Dog 6
21 二十 Observation 風地觀 7 火2 Fire 己亥 Earth Pig 2	22 廿一 Increasing 風雷益 6/4 火2 Fire 庚子 Metal Rat 9	23 廿二 Dimming Light 地火明夷 5 水1 Water 辛丑 Metal Ox 3	24 廿三 Fellowship 天火同人 6 金9 Metal 壬寅 Water Tiger 7	25 廿四 Marrying Maiden 雷澤歸妹 7 木8 Wood 癸卯 Water Rabbit 7	26 廿五 Opposition 火澤睽 8 木3 Wood 甲辰 Wood Dragon 2	27 廿六 Waiting 水天需 9 火7 Fire 乙巳 Wood Snake 3
28 廿七 Great Exceeding 澤風大過 1 金4 Metal 丙午 Fire Horse 3	29 廿八 Poison 山風蠱 2 水6 Water 丁未 Fire Goat 7	30 廿九 Dispersing 風水渙 3 火2 Fire 戊申 Earth Monkey 6	31 十二月初一 Travelling 火山旅 4 木3 Wood 己酉 Earth Rooster 8			

1987 丁卯

(*Ding Mao*) Fire Rabbit

1987 丁卯 *(Ding Mao)* Fire Rabbit

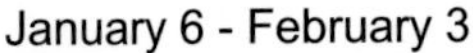

January 6 - February 3

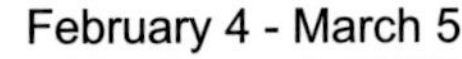

February 4 - March 5

March 6 - April 4

April 5 - May 5

May 6 - June 5

June 6 - July 6

July 7 - August 7

August 8 - September 7

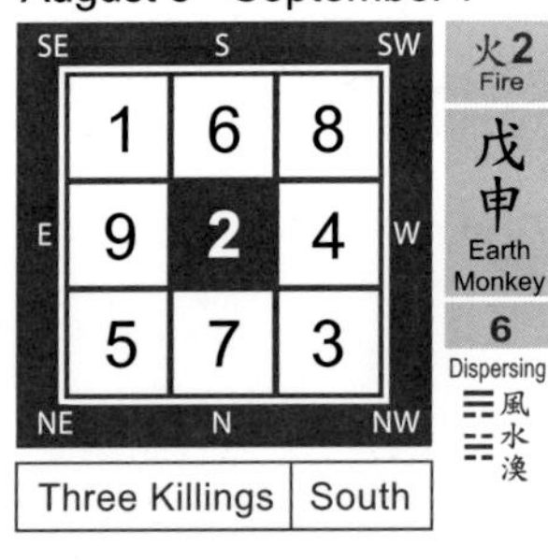

September 8 - October 8

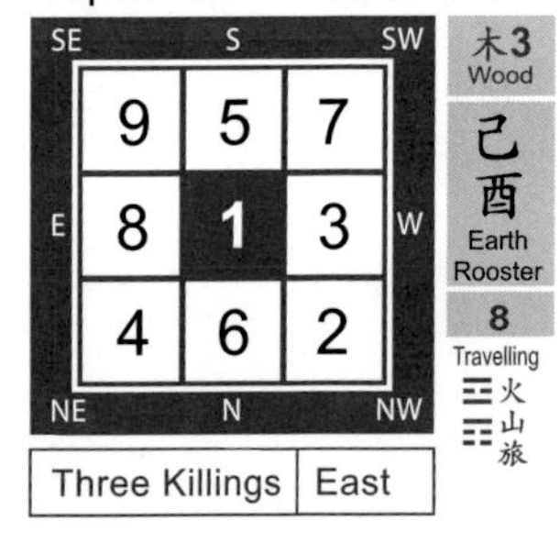

October 9 - November 7

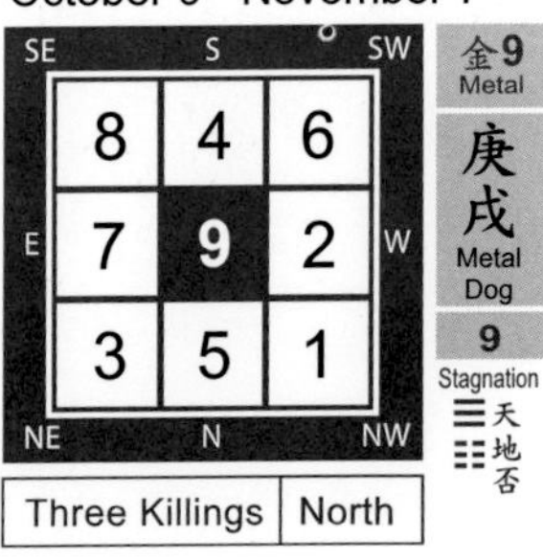

November 8 - December 6

December 7 - January 5

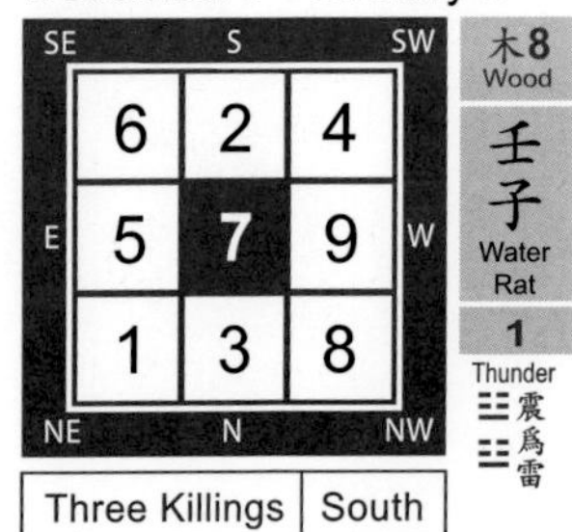

JANUARY 1987 辛丑

Xuan Kong Element 玄空五行	地火明夷 Dimming Light	Period Luck 卦運	Monthly Star 月星
Water 水1		3	9

SUNDAY	MONDAY	TUESDAY	WEDNESDAY	THURSDAY	FRIDAY	SATURDAY
				金9 Metal Stagnation 5 庚戌 Metal Dog 天地否 1 初二 9	火7 Fire Alliance 6 辛亥 Metal Pig 水地比 2 初三 7	木8 Wood Thunder 7 壬子 Water Rat 震為雷 3 初四 1
水6 Water Beauty 8 癸丑 Water Ox 山火賁 4 初五 8	火7 Fire Accomplished 9 甲寅 Wood Tiger 水火既濟 5 初六 9	水1 Water Arriving 1 乙卯 Wood Rabbit 地澤臨 6 初七 4	金4 Metal Marsh 2 丙辰 Fire Dragon 兌為澤 7 初八 1	火2 Fire Small Livestock 3 丁巳 Fire Snake 風天小畜 8 初九 8	木3 Wood The Cauldron 4 戊午 Earth Horse 火風鼎 9 初十 4	水1 Water Rising 5 己未 Earth Goat 地風升 10 十一 2
火7 Fire Water 6 庚申 Metal Monkey 坎為水 11 十二 1	木8 Wood Lesser Exceeding 7 辛酉 Metal Rooster 雷山小過 12 十三 3	金4 Metal Gathering 8 壬戌 Water Dog 澤地萃 13 十四 4	水6 Water Peel 9 癸亥 Water Pig 山地剝 14 十五 6	水1 Water Earth 1 甲子 Wood Rat 坤為地 15 十六 1	木3 Wood Biting 2 乙丑 Wood Ox 火雷噬嗑 16 十七 6	火2 Fire Family 3 丙寅 Fire Tiger 風火家人 17 十八 4
水6 Water Decreasing 4 丁卯 Fire Rabbit 山澤損 18 十九 9	金9 Metal Tread 5 戊辰 Earth Dragon 天澤履 19 二十 6	木8 Wood Great Strength 6 己巳 Earth Snake 雷天大壯 20 廿一 2	木8 Wood Consistency 7 庚午 Metal Horse 雷風恆 21 廿二 9	金9 Metal Litigation 8 辛未 Metal Goat 天水訟 22 廿三 3	水1 Water Officer 9 壬申 Water Monkey 地水師 23 廿四 7	火2 Fire Gradual Progress 1 癸酉 Water Rooster 風山漸 24 廿五 7
火7 Fire Obstruction 2 甲戌 Wood Dog 水山蹇 25 廿六 2	木3 Wood Advancement 3 乙亥 Wood Pig 火地晉 26 廿七 3	水6 Water Nourish 4 丙子 Fire Rat 山雷頤 27 廿八 3	金4 Metal Following 5 丁丑 Fire Ox 澤雷隨 28 廿九 7	木8 Wood Abundance 6 戊寅 Earth Tiger 雷火豐 29 正月初一 6	火7 Fire Regulate 7 己卯 Earth Rabbit 水澤節 30 初二 8	水1 Water Unity 8 庚辰 Metal Dragon 地天泰 31 初三 9

FEBRUARY 1987 壬寅

Xuan Kong Element 玄空五行	天火同人 Fellowship	Period Luck 卦運	Monthly Star 月星
Metal 金9		7	8

SUNDAY	MONDAY	TUESDAY	WEDNESDAY	THURSDAY	FRIDAY	SATURDAY
木3 Wood Great Reward 9 辛巳 Metal Snake 火天大有 1 初四 7	火2 Fire Wind 1 壬午 Water Horse 巽為風 2 初五 1	金4 Metal Trap 2 癸未 Water Goat 澤水困 3 初六 8	木3 Wood Not Yet Accomplished 3 甲申 Wood Monkey 火水未濟 4 初七 9	金9 Metal Retreat 4 乙酉 Wood Rooster 天山遯 5 初八 4	水6 Water Mountain 5 丙戌 Fire Dog 艮為山 6 初九 1	木8 Wood Delight 6 丁亥 Fire Pig 雷地豫 7 初十 8
火7 Fire Beginning 7 戊子 Earth Rat 水雷屯 8 十一 4	金9 Metal Without Wrongdoing 8 己丑 Earth Ox 天雷無妄 9 十二 2	木3 Wood Fire 9 庚寅 Metal Tiger 離為火 10 十三 1	火2 Fire Sincerity 1 辛卯 Metal Rabbit 風澤中孚 11 十四 3	水6 Water Big Livestock 2 壬辰 Water Dragon 山天大畜 12 十五 4	金4 Metal Eliminating 3 癸巳 Water Snake 澤天夬 13 十六 6	金9 Metal Heaven 4 甲午 Wood Horse 乾為天 14 十七 1
火7 Fire Well 5 乙未 Wood Goat 水風井 15 十八 6	木8 Wood Relief 6 丙申 Fire Monkey 雷水解 16 十九 4	金4 Metal Influence 7 丁酉 Fire Rooster 澤山咸 17 二十 9	水1 Water Humility 8 戊戌 Earth Dog 地山謙 18 廿一 6	火2 Fire Observation 9 己亥 Earth Pig 風地觀 19 廿二 2	火2 Fire Increasing 1 庚子 Metal Rat 風雷益 20 廿三 9	水1 Water Dimming Light 2 辛丑 Metal Ox 地火明夷 21 廿四 3
金9 Metal Fellowship 3 壬寅 Water Tiger 天火同人 22 廿五 7	木8 Wood Marrying Maiden 4 癸卯 Water Rabbit 雷澤歸妹 23 廿六 7	木3 Wood Opposition 5 甲辰 Wood Dragon 火澤睽 24 廿七 2	火7 Fire Waiting 6 乙巳 Wood Snake 水天需 25 廿八 3	金4 Metal Great Exceeding 7 丙午 Fire Horse 澤風大過 26 廿九 3	水6 Water Poison 8 丁未 Fire Goat 山風蠱 27 三十 7	火2 Fire Dispersing 9 戊申 Earth Monkey 風水渙 28 二月初一 6

MARCH 1987 癸卯

Xuan Kong Element 玄空五行	雷澤歸妹 Marrying Maiden	Period Luck 卦運	Monthly Star 月星
Wood 木8		7	7

SUNDAY	MONDAY	TUESDAY	WEDNESDAY	THURSDAY	FRIDAY	SATURDAY
木3 Wood 己酉 Earth Rooster 8 · Travelling 火山旅 · 1 初二 · [1]	金9 Metal 庚戌 Metal Dog 9 · Stagnation 天地否 · 2 初三 · [2]	火7 Fire 辛亥 Metal Pig 7 · Alliance 水地比 · 3 初四 · [3]	木8 Wood 壬子 Water Rat 1 · Thunder 震爲雷 · 4 初五 · [4]	水6 Water 癸丑 Water Ox 8 · Beauty 山火賁 · 5 初六 · [5]	火7 Fire 甲寅 Wood Tiger 9 · Accomplished 水火既濟 · 6 初七 · [6]	水1 Water 乙卯 Wood Rabbit 4 · Arriving 地澤臨 · 7 初八 · [7]
金4 Metal 丙辰 Fire Dragon 1 · Marsh 兌爲澤 · 8 初九 · [8]	火2 Fire 丁巳 Fire Snake 8 · Small Livestock 風天小畜 · 9 初十 · [9]	木3 Wood 戊午 Earth Horse 4 · The Cauldron 火風鼎 · 10 十一 · [1]	水1 Water 己未 Earth Goat 2 · Rising 地風升 · 11 十二 · [2]	火7 Fire 庚申 Metal Monkey 1 · Water 坎爲水 · 12 十三 · [3]	木8 Wood 辛酉 Metal Rooster 3 · Lesser Exceeding 雷山小過 · 13 十四 · [4]	金4 Metal 壬戌 Water Dog 4 · Gathering 澤地萃 · 14 十五 · [5]
水6 Water 癸亥 Water Pig 6 · Peel 山地剝 · 15 十六 · [6]	水1 Water 甲子 Wood Rat 1 · Earth 坤爲地 · 16 十七 · [7]	木3 Wood 乙丑 Wood Ox 6 · Biting 火雷噬嗑 · 17 十八 · [8]	火2 Fire 丙寅 Fire Tiger 4 · Family 風火家人 · 18 十九 · [9]	水6 Water 丁卯 Fire Rabbit 9 · Decreasing 山澤損 · 19 二十 · [1]	金9 Metal 戊辰 Earth Dragon 6 · Tread 天澤履 · 20 廿一 · [2]	木8 Wood 己巳 Earth Snake 2 · Great Strength 雷天大壯 · 21 廿二 · [3]
木8 Wood 庚午 Metal Horse 9 · Consistency 雷風恒 · 22 廿三 · [4]	金9 Metal 辛未 Metal Goat 3 · Litigation 天水訟 · 23 廿四 · [5]	水1 Water 壬申 Water Monkey 7 · Officer 地水師 · 24 廿五 · [6]	火2 Fire 癸酉 Water Rooster 7 · Gradual Progress 風山漸 · 25 廿六 · [7]	火7 Fire 甲戌 Wood Dog 2 · Obstruction 水山蹇 · 26 廿七 · [8]	木3 Wood 乙亥 Wood Pig 3 · Advancement 火地晉 · 27 廿八 · [9]	水6 Water 丙子 Fire Rat 3 · Nourish 山雷頤 · 28 廿九 · [1]
金4 Metal 丁丑 Fire Ox 7 · Following 澤雷隨 · 29 三月初一 · [2]	木8 Wood 戊寅 Earth Tiger 6 · Abundance 雷火豐 · 30 初二 · [3]	火7 Fire 己卯 Earth Rabbit 8 · Regulate 水澤節 · 31 初三 · [4]				

APRIL 1987 甲辰

Xuan Kong Element 玄空五行	火澤睽 Opposition	Period Luck 卦運	Monthly Star 月星
Wood 木3		2	6

SUNDAY	MONDAY	TUESDAY	WEDNESDAY	THURSDAY	FRIDAY	SATURDAY
			水1 Water 庚辰 Metal Dragon 9 · Unity 地天泰 · 1 初四 · [5]	木3 Wood 辛巳 Metal Snake 7 · Great Reward 火天大有 · 2 初五 · [6]	火2 Fire 壬午 Water Horse 1 · Wind 巽爲風 · 3 初六 · [7]	金4 Metal 癸未 Water Goat 8 · Trap 澤水困 · 4 初七 · [8]
木3 Wood 甲申 Wood Monkey 9 · Not Yet Accomplished 火水未濟 · 5 初八 · [9]	金9 Metal 乙酉 Wood Rooster 4 · Retreat 天山遯 · 6 初九 · [1]	水6 Water 丙戌 Fire Dog 1 · Mountain 艮爲山 · 7 初十 · [2]	木8 Wood 丁亥 Fire Pig 8 · Delight 雷地豫 · 8 十一 · [3]	火7 Fire 戊子 Earth Rat 4 · Beginning 水雷屯 · 9 十二 · [4]	金9 Metal 己丑 Earth Ox 2 · Without Wrongdoing 天雷無妄 · 10 十三 · [5]	木3 Wood 庚寅 Metal Tiger 1 · Fire 離爲火 · 11 十四 · [6]
火2 Fire 辛卯 Metal Rabbit 3 · Sincerity 風澤中孚 · 12 十五 · [7]	水6 Water 壬辰 Water Dragon 4 · Big Livestock 山天大畜 · 13 十六 · [8]	金4 Metal 癸巳 Water Snake 6 · Eliminating 澤天夬 · 14 十七 · [9]	金9 Metal 甲午 Wood Horse 1 · Heaven 乾爲天 · 15 十八 · [1]	火7 Fire 乙未 Wood Goat 6 · Well 水風井 · 16 十九 · [2]	木8 Wood 丙申 Fire Monkey 4 · Relief 雷水解 · 17 二十 · [3]	金4 Metal 丁酉 Fire Rooster 9 · Influence 澤山咸 · 18 廿一 · [4]
水1 Water 戊戌 Earth Dog 6 · Humility 地山謙 · 19 廿二 · [5]	火2 Fire 己亥 Earth Pig 2 · Observation 風地觀 · 20 廿三 · [6]	火2 Fire 庚子 Metal Rat 9 · Increasing 風雷益 · 21 廿四 · [7]	水1 Water 辛丑 Metal Ox 3 · Dimming Light 地火明夷 · 22 廿五 · [8]	金9 Metal 壬寅 Water Tiger 7 · Fellowship 天火同人 · 23 廿六 · [9]	木8 Wood 癸卯 Water Rabbit 7 · Marrying Maiden 雷澤歸妹 · 24 廿七 · [1]	木3 Wood 甲辰 Wood Dragon 2 · Opposition 火澤睽 · 25 廿八 · [2]
火7 Fire 乙巳 Wood Snake 3 · Waiting 水天需 · 26 廿九 · [3]	金4 Metal 丙午 Fire Horse 3 · Great Exceeding 澤風大過 · 27 三十 · [4]	水6 Water 丁未 Fire Goat 7 · Poison 山風蠱 · 28 四月初一 · [5]	火2 Fire 戊申 Earth Monkey 6 · Dispersing 風水渙 · 29 初二 · [6]	木3 Wood 己酉 Earth Rooster 8 · Travelling 火山旅 · 30 初三 · [7]		

MAY 1987 乙巳

Xuan Kong Element 玄空五行	水天需 Waiting	Period Luck 卦運	Monthly Star 月星
Fire 火7		3	5

SUNDAY	MONDAY	TUESDAY	WEDNESDAY	THURSDAY	FRIDAY	SATURDAY
水1 Water 2 Unity 庚辰 Metal Dragon 地天泰 31 初五 9					金9 Metal 8 Stagnation 庚戌 Metal Dog 天地否 1 初四 9	火7 Fire 9 Alliance 辛亥 Metal Pig 水地比 2 初五 7
木8 Wood 1 Thunder 壬子 Water Rat 震爲雷 3 初六 1	水6 Water 2 Beauty 癸丑 Water Ox 山火賁 4 初七 8	火7 Fire 3 Accomplished 甲寅 Wood Tiger 水火既濟 5 初八 9	水1 Water 4 Arriving 乙卯 Wood Rabbit 地澤臨 6 初九 4	金4 Metal 5 Marsh 丙辰 Fire Dragon 兌爲澤 7 初十 1	火2 Fire 6 Small Livestock 丁巳 Fire Snake 風天小畜 8 十一 8	木3 Wood 7 The Cauldron 戊午 Earth Horse 火風鼎 9 十二 4
水1 Water 8 Rising 己未 Earth Goat 地風升 10 十三 2	火7 Fire 9 Water 庚申 Metal Monkey 坎爲水 11 十四 1	木8 Wood 1 Lesser Exceeding 辛酉 Metal Rooster 雷山小過 12 十五 3	金4 Metal 2 Gathering 壬戌 Water Dog 澤地萃 13 十六 4	水6 Water 3 Peel 癸亥 Water Pig 山地剝 14 十七 6	水1 Water 4 Earth 甲子 Wood Rat 坤爲地 15 十八 1	木3 Wood 5 Biting 乙丑 Wood Ox 火雷噬嗑 16 十九 6
火2 Fire 6 Family 丙寅 Fire Tiger 風火家人 17 二十 4	水6 Water 7 Decreasing 丁卯 Fire Rabbit 山澤損 18 廿一 9	金9 Metal 8 Tread 戊辰 Earth Dragon 天澤履 19 廿二 6	木8 Wood 9 Great Strength 己巳 Earth Snake 雷天大壯 20 廿三 2	木8 Wood 1 Consistency 庚午 Metal Horse 雷風恆 21 廿四 9	金9 Metal 2 Litigation 辛未 Metal Goat 天水訟 22 廿五 3	水1 Water 3 Officer 壬申 Water Monkey 地水師 23 廿六 7
火2 Fire 4 Gradual Progress 癸酉 Water Rooster 風山漸 24 廿七 7	火7 Fire 5 Obstruction 甲戌 Wood Dog 水山蹇 25 廿八 2	木3 Wood 6 Advancement 乙亥 Wood Pig 火地晉 26 廿九 3	水6 Water 7 Nourish 丙子 Fire Rat 山雷頤 27 五月初一 3	金4 Metal 8 Following 丁丑 Fire Ox 澤雷隨 28 初二 7	木8 Wood 9 Abundance 戊寅 Earth Tiger 雷火豐 29 初三 6	火7 Fire 1 Regulate 己卯 Earth Rabbit 水澤節 30 初四 8

JUNE 1987 丙午

Xuan Kong Element 玄空五行	澤風大過 Great Exceeding	Period Luck 卦運	Monthly Star 月星
Metal 金4		3	4

SUNDAY	MONDAY	TUESDAY	WEDNESDAY	THURSDAY	FRIDAY	SATURDAY
	木3 Wood 3 Great Reward 辛巳 Metal Snake 火天大有 1 初六 7	火2 Fire 4 Wind 壬午 Water Horse 巽爲風 2 初七 1	金4 Metal 5 Trap 癸未 Water Goat 澤水困 3 初八 8	木3 Wood 6 Not Yet Accomplished 甲申 Wood Monkey 火水未濟 4 初九 9	金9 Metal 7 Retreat 乙酉 Wood Rooster 天山遯 5 初十 4	水6 Water 8 Mountain 丙戌 Fire Dog 艮爲山 6 十一 1
木8 Wood 9 Delight 丁亥 Fire Pig 雷地豫 7 十二 8	火7 Fire 1 Beginning 戊子 Earth Rat 水雷屯 8 十三 4	金9 Metal 2 Without Wrongdoing 己丑 Earth Ox 天雷無妄 9 十四 2	木3 Wood 3 Fire 庚寅 Metal Tiger 離爲火 10 十五 1	火2 Fire 4 Sincerity 辛卯 Metal Rabbit 風澤中孚 11 十六 3	水6 Water 5 Big Livestock 壬辰 Water Dragon 山天大畜 12 十七 4	金4 Metal 6 Eliminating 癸巳 Water Snake 澤天夬 13 十八 6
金9 Metal 7 Heaven 甲午 Wood Horse 乾爲天 14 十九 1	火7 Fire 8 Well 乙未 Wood Goat 水風井 15 二十 6	木8 Wood 9 Relief 丙申 Fire Monkey 雷水解 16 廿一 4	金4 Metal 1 Influence 丁酉 Fire Rooster 澤山咸 17 廿二 9	水1 Water 2 Humility 戊戌 Earth Dog 地山謙 18 廿三 6	火2 Fire 3 Observation 己亥 Earth Pig 風地觀 19 廿四 2	火2 Fire 4 Increasing 庚子 Metal Rat 風雷益 20 廿五 9
水1 Water 5 Dimming Light 辛丑 Metal Ox 地火明夷 21 廿六 3	金9 Metal 6/4 Fellowship 壬寅 Water Tiger 天火同人 22 廿七 7	木8 Wood 3 Marrying Maiden 癸卯 Water Rabbit 雷澤歸妹 23 廿八 7	木3 Wood 2 Opposition 甲辰 Wood Dragon 火澤睽 24 廿九 2	火7 Fire 1 Waiting 乙巳 Wood Snake 水天需 25 三十 3	金4 Metal 9 Great Exceeding 丙午 Fire Horse 澤風大過 26 六月初一 3	水6 Water 8 Poison 丁未 Fire Goat 山風蠱 27 初二 7
火2 Fire 7 Dispersing 戊申 Earth Monkey 風水渙 28 初三 6	木3 Wood 6 Travelling 己酉 Earth Rooster 火山旅 29 初四 8	金9 Metal 5 Stagnation 庚戌 Metal Dog 天地否 30 初五 9				

JULY 1987 丁未

Xuan Kong Element 玄空五行	山風蠱 Poison	Period Luck 卦運	Monthly Star 月星
Water 水6		7	3

SUNDAY	MONDAY	TUESDAY	WEDNESDAY	THURSDAY	FRIDAY	SATURDAY
			火7 Fire Alliance 4 辛亥 Metal Pig 水地比 1 初六 7	木8 Wood Thunder 3 壬子 Water Rat 震爲雷 2 初七 1	水6 Water Beauty 2 癸丑 Water Ox 山火賁 3 初八 8	火7 Fire Accomplished 1 甲寅 Wood Tiger 水火既濟 4 初九 9
水1 Water Arriving 9 乙卯 Wood Rabbit 地澤臨 5 初十 4	金4 Metal Marsh 8 丙辰 Fire Dragon 兌爲澤 6 十一 1	火2 Fire Small Livestock 7 丁巳 Fire Snake 風天小畜 7 十二 8	木3 Wood The Cauldron 6 戊午 Earth Horse 火風鼎 8 十三 4	水1 Water Rising 5 己未 Earth Goat 地風升 9 十四 2	火7 Fire Water 4 庚申 Metal Monkey 坎爲水 10 十五 1	木8 Wood Lesser Exceeding 3 辛酉 Metal Rooster 雷山小過 11 十六 3
金4 Metal Gathering 2 壬戌 Water Dog 澤地萃 12 十七 4	水6 Water Peel 1 癸亥 Water Pig 山地剝 13 十八 6	水1 Water Earth 9 甲子 Wood Rat 坤爲地 14 十九 1	木3 Wood Biting 8 乙丑 Wood Ox 火雷噬嗑 15 二十 6	火2 Fire Family 7 丙寅 Fire Tiger 風火家人 16 廿一 4	水6 Water Decreasing 6 丁卯 Fire Rabbit 山澤損 17 廿二 9	金9 Metal Tread 5 戊辰 Earth Dragon 天澤履 18 廿三 6
木8 Wood Great Strength 4 己巳 Earth Snake 雷天大壯 19 廿四 2	木8 Wood Consistency 3 庚午 Metal Horse 雷風恆 20 廿五 9	金9 Metal Litigation 2 辛未 Metal Goat 天水訟 21 廿六 3	水1 Water Officer 1 壬申 Water Monkey 地水師 22 廿七 7	火2 Fire Gradual Progress 9 癸酉 Water Rooster 風山漸 23 廿八 7	火7 Fire Obstruction 8 甲戌 Wood Dog 水山蹇 24 廿九 2	木3 Wood Advancement 7 乙亥 Wood Pig 火地晉 25 三十 3
水6 Water Nourish 6 丙子 Fire Rat 山雷頤 26 閏六月初一 3	金4 Metal Following 5 丁丑 Fire Ox 澤雷隨 27 初二 7	木8 Wood Abundance 4 戊寅 Earth Tiger 雷火豐 28 初三 6	火7 Fire Regulate 3 己卯 Earth Rabbit 水澤節 29 初四 8	水1 Water Unity 2 庚辰 Metal Dragon 地天泰 30 初五 9	木3 Wood Great Reward 1 辛巳 Metal Snake 火天大有 31 初六 7	

AUGUST 1987 戊申

Xuan Kong Element 玄空五行	風水渙 Dispersing	Period Luck 卦運	Monthly Star 月星
Fire 火2		6	2

SUNDAY	MONDAY	TUESDAY	WEDNESDAY	THURSDAY	FRIDAY	SATURDAY
火7 Fire Alliance 7 辛亥 Metal Pig 水地比 30 初七 7	木8 Wood Thunder 6 壬子 Water Rat 震爲雷 31 初八 1					火2 Fire Wind 9 壬午 Water Horse 巽爲風 1 初七 1
金4 Metal Trap 8 癸未 Water Goat 澤水困 2 初八 8	木3 Wood Not Yet Accomplished 7 甲申 Wood Monkey 火水未濟 3 初九 9	金9 Metal Retreat 6 乙酉 Wood Rooster 天山遯 4 初十 4	水6 Water Mountain 5 丙戌 Fire Dog 艮爲山 5 十一 1	木8 Wood Delight 4 丁亥 Fire Pig 雷地豫 6 十二 8	火7 Fire Beginning 3 戊子 Earth Rat 水雷屯 7 十三 4	金9 Metal Without Wrongdoing 2 己丑 Earth Ox 天雷無妄 8 十四 2
木3 Wood Fire 1 庚寅 Metal Tiger 離爲火 9 十五 1	火2 Fire Sincerity 9 辛卯 Metal Rabbit 風澤中孚 10 十六 3	水6 Water Big Livestock 8 壬辰 Water Dragon 山天大畜 11 十七 4	金4 Metal Eliminating 7 癸巳 Water Snake 澤天夬 12 十八 6	金9 Metal Heaven 6 甲午 Wood Horse 乾爲天 13 十九 1	火7 Fire Well 5 乙未 Wood Goat 水風井 14 二十 6	木8 Wood Relief 4 丙申 Fire Monkey 雷水解 15 廿一 4
金4 Metal Influence 3 丁酉 Fire Rooster 澤山咸 16 廿二 9	水1 Water Humility 2 戊戌 Earth Dog 地山謙 17 廿三 6	火2 Fire Observation 1 己亥 Earth Pig 風地觀 18 廿四 2	火2 Fire Increasing 9 庚子 Metal Rat 風雷益 19 廿五 9	水1 Water Dimming Light 8 辛丑 Metal Ox 地火明夷 20 廿六 3	金9 Metal Fellowship 7 壬寅 Water Tiger 天火同人 21 廿七 7	木8 Wood Marrying Maiden 6 癸卯 Water Rabbit 雷澤歸妹 22 廿八 7
木3 Wood Opposition 5 甲辰 Wood Dragon 火澤睽 23 廿九 2	火7 Fire Waiting 4 乙巳 Wood Snake 水天需 24 七月初一 3	金4 Metal Great Exceeding 3 丙午 Fire Horse 澤風大過 25 初二 3	水6 Water Poison 2 丁未 Fire Goat 山風蠱 26 初三 7	火2 Fire Dispersing 1 戊申 Earth Monkey 風水渙 27 初四 6	木3 Wood Travelling 9 己酉 Earth Rooster 火山旅 28 初五 8	金9 Metal Stagnation 8 庚戌 Metal Dog 天地否 29 初六 9

SEPTEMBER 1987 己酉

Xuan Kong Element 玄空五行	火山旅 Travelling	Period Luck 卦運	Monthly Star 月星
Wood 木3		8	1

SUNDAY	MONDAY	TUESDAY	WEDNESDAY	THURSDAY	FRIDAY	SATURDAY
		水6 Water 5 Beauty 癸丑 Water Ox 山火賁 1 初九 8	火7 Fire 4 Accomplished 甲寅 Wood Tiger 水火既濟 2 初十 9	水1 Water 3 Arriving 乙卯 Wood Rabbit 地澤臨 3 十一 4	金4 Metal 2 Marsh 丙辰 Fire Dragon 兌爲澤 4 十二 1	火2 Fire 1 Small Livestock 丁巳 Fire Snake 風天小畜 5 十三 8
木3 Wood 9 The Cauldron 戊午 Earth Horse 火風鼎 6 十四 4	水1 Water 8 Rising 己未 Earth Goat 地風升 7 十五 2	火7 Fire 7 Water 庚申 Metal Monkey 坎爲水 8 十六 1	木8 Wood 6 Lesser Exceeding 辛酉 Metal Rooster 雷山小過 9 十七 3	金4 Metal 5 Gathering 壬戌 Water Dog 澤地萃 10 十八 4	水6 Water 4 Peel 癸亥 Water Pig 山地剝 11 十九 6	水1 Water 3 Earth 甲子 Wood Rat 坤爲地 12 二十 1
木3 Wood 2 Biting 乙丑 Wood Ox 火雷噬嗑 13 廿一 6	火2 Fire 1 Family 丙寅 Fire Tiger 風火家人 14 廿二 4	水6 Water 9 Decreasing 丁卯 Fire Rabbit 山澤損 15 廿三 9	金9 Metal 8 Tread 戊辰 Earth Dragon 天澤履 16 廿四 6	木8 Wood 7 Great Strength 己巳 Earth Snake 雷天大壯 17 廿五 2	木8 Wood 6 Consistency 庚午 Metal Horse 雷風恒 18 廿六 9	金9 Metal 5 Litigation 辛未 Metal Goat 天水訟 19 廿七 3
水1 Water 4 Officer 壬申 Water Monkey 地水師 20 廿八 7	火2 Fire 3 Gradual Progress 癸酉 Water Rooster 風山漸 21 廿九 7	火7 Fire 2 Obstruction 甲戌 Wood Dog 水山蹇 22 三十 2	木3 Wood 1 Advancement 乙亥 Wood Pig 火地晉 23 八月初一 3	水6 Water 9 Nourish 丙子 Fire Rat 山雷頤 24 初二 3	金4 Metal 8 Following 丁丑 Fire Ox 澤雷隨 25 初三 7	木8 Wood 7 Abundance 戊寅 Earth Tiger 雷火豐 26 初四 6
火7 Fire 6 Regulate 己卯 Earth Rabbit 水澤節 27 初五 8	水1 Water 5 Unity 庚辰 Metal Dragon 地天泰 28 初六 9	木3 Wood 4 Great Reward 辛巳 Metal Snake 火天大有 29 初七 7	火2 Fire 3 Wind 壬午 Water Horse 巽爲風 30 初八 1			

OCTOBER 1987 庚戌

Xuan Kong Element 玄空五行	天地否 Stagnation	Period Luck 卦運	Monthly Star 月星
Metal 金9		9	9

SUNDAY	MONDAY	TUESDAY	WEDNESDAY	THURSDAY	FRIDAY	SATURDAY
				金4 Metal 2 Trap 癸未 Water Goat 澤水困 1 初九 8	木3 Wood 1 Not Yet Accomplished 甲申 Wood Monkey 火水未濟 2 初十 9	金9 Metal 9 Retreat 乙酉 Wood Rooster 天山遯 3 十一 4
水6 Water 8 Mountain 丙戌 Fire Dog 艮爲山 4 十二 1	木8 Wood 7 Delight 丁亥 Fire Pig 雷地豫 5 十三 8	火7 Fire 6 Beginning 戊子 Earth Rat 水雷屯 6 十四 4	金9 Metal 5 Without Wrongdoing 己丑 Earth Ox 天雷無妄 7 十五 2	木3 Wood 4 Fire 庚寅 Metal Tiger 離爲火 8 十六 1	火2 Fire 3 Sincerity 辛卯 Metal Rabbit 風澤中孚 9 十七 3	水6 Water 2 Big Livestock 壬辰 Water Dragon 山天大畜 10 十八 4
金4 Metal 1 Eliminating 癸巳 Water Snake 澤天夬 11 十九 6	金9 Metal 9 Heaven 甲午 Wood Horse 乾爲天 12 二十 1	火7 Fire 8 Well 乙未 Wood Goat 水風井 13 廿一 6	木8 Wood 7 Relief 丙申 Fire Monkey 雷水解 14 廿二 4	金4 Metal 6 Influence 丁酉 Fire Rooster 澤山咸 15 廿三 9	水1 Water 5 Humility 戊戌 Earth Dog 地山謙 16 廿四 6	火2 Fire 4 Observation 己亥 Earth Pig 風地觀 17 廿五 2
火2 Fire 3 Increasing 庚子 Metal Rat 風雷益 18 廿六 9	水1 Water 2 Dimming Light 辛丑 Metal Ox 地火明夷 19 廿七 3	金9 Metal 1 Fellowship 壬寅 Water Tiger 天火同人 20 廿八 7	木8 Wood 9 Marrying Maiden 癸卯 Water Rabbit 雷澤歸妹 21 廿九 7	木3 Wood 8 Opposition 甲辰 Wood Dragon 火澤睽 22 三十 2	火7 Fire 7 Waiting 乙巳 Wood Snake 水天需 23 九月初一 3	金4 Metal 6 Great Exceeding 丙午 Fire Horse 澤風大過 24 初二 3
水6 Water 5 Poison 丁未 Fire Goat 山風蠱 25 初三 7	火2 Fire 4 Dispersing 戊申 Earth Monkey 風水渙 26 初四 6	木3 Wood 3 Travelling 己酉 Earth Rooster 火山旅 27 初五 8	金9 Metal 2 Stagnation 庚戌 Metal Dog 天地否 28 初六 9	火7 Fire 1 Alliance 辛亥 Metal Pig 水地比 29 初七 7	木8 Wood 9 Thunder 壬子 Water Rat 震爲雷 30 初八 1	水6 Water 8 Beauty 癸丑 Water Ox 山火賁 31 初九 8

NOVEMBER 1987 辛亥

Xuan Kong Element 玄空五行	水地比 Alliance	Period Luck 卦運	Monthly Star 月星
Fire 火7		7	8

SUNDAY	MONDAY	TUESDAY	WEDNESDAY	THURSDAY	FRIDAY	SATURDAY
火7 Fire · 7 Accomplished 水火既濟 甲寅 Wood Tiger **1** 初十 9	水1 Water · 6 Arriving 地澤臨 乙卯 Wood Rabbit **2** 十一 4	金4 Metal · 5 Marsh 兑爲澤 丙辰 Fire Dragon **3** 十二 1	火2 Fire · 4 Small Livestock 風天小畜 丁巳 Fire Snake **4** 十三 8	木3 Wood · 3 The Cauldron 火風鼎 戊午 Earth Horse **5** 十四 4	水1 Water · 2 Rising 地風升 己未 Earth Goat **6** 十五 2	火7 Fire · 1 Water 坎爲水 庚申 Metal Monkey **7** 十六 1
木8 Wood · 9 Lesser Exceeding 雷山小過 辛酉 Metal Rooster **8** 十七 3	金4 Metal · 8 Gathering 澤地萃 壬戌 Water Dog **9** 十八 4	水6 Water · 7 Peel 山地剝 癸亥 Water Pig **10** 十九 6	水1 Water · 6 Earth 坤爲地 甲子 Wood Rat **11** 二十 1	木3 Wood · 5 Biting 火雷噬嗑 乙丑 Wood Ox **12** 廿一 6	火2 Fire · 4 Family 風火家人 丙寅 Fire Tiger **13** 廿二 4	水6 Water · 3 Decreasing 山澤損 丁卯 Fire Rabbit **14** 廿三 9
金9 Metal · 2 Tread 天澤履 戊辰 Earth Dragon **15** 廿四 6	木8 Wood · 1 Great Strength 雷天大壯 己巳 Earth Snake **16** 廿五 2	木8 Wood · 9 Consistency 雷風恆 庚午 Metal Horse **17** 廿六 9	金9 Metal · 8 Litigation 天水訟 辛未 Metal Goat **18** 廿七 3	水1 Water · 7 Officer 地水師 壬申 Water Monkey **19** 廿八 7	火2 Fire · 6 Gradual Progress 風山漸 癸酉 Water Rooster **20** 廿九 7	火7 Fire · 5 Obstruction 水山蹇 甲戌 Wood Dog **21** 十月初一 2
木3 Wood · 4 Advancement 火地晉 乙亥 Wood Pig **22** 初二 3	水6 Water · 3 Nourish 山雷頤 丙子 Fire Rat **23** 初三 3	金4 Metal · 2 Following 澤雷隨 丁丑 Fire Ox **24** 初四 7	木8 Wood · 1 Abundance 雷火豐 戊寅 Earth Tiger **25** 初五 6	火7 Fire · 9 Regulate 水澤節 己卯 Earth Rabbit **26** 初六 8	水1 Water · 8 Unity 地天泰 庚辰 Metal Dragon **27** 初七 9	木3 Wood · 7 Great Reward 火天大有 辛巳 Metal Snake **28** 初八 7
火2 Fire · 6 Wind 巽爲風 壬午 Water Horse **29** 初九 1	金4 Metal · 5 Trap 澤水困 癸未 Water Goat **30** 初十 8					

DECEMBER 1987 壬子

Xuan Kong Element 玄空五行	震爲雷 Thunder	Period Luck 卦運	Monthly Star 月星
Wood 木8		1	7

SUNDAY	MONDAY	TUESDAY	WEDNESDAY	THURSDAY	FRIDAY	SATURDAY
		木3 Wood · 4 Not Yet Accomplished 火水未濟 甲申 Wood Monkey **1** 十一 9	金9 Metal · 3 Retreat 天山遯 乙酉 Wood Rooster **2** 十二 4	水6 Water · 2 Mountain 艮爲山 丙戌 Fire Dog **3** 十三 1	木8 Wood · 1 Delight 雷地豫 丁亥 Fire Pig **4** 十四 8	火7 Fire · 9 Beginning 水雷屯 戊子 Earth Rat **5** 十五 4
金9 Metal · 8 Without Wrongdoing 天雷無妄 己丑 Earth Ox **6** 十六 2	木3 Wood · 7 Fire 離爲火 庚寅 Metal Tiger **7** 十七 1	火2 Fire · 6 Sincerity 風澤中孚 辛卯 Metal Rabbit **8** 十八 3	水6 Water · 5 Big Livestock 山天大畜 壬辰 Water Dragon **9** 十九 4	金4 Metal · 4 Eliminating 澤天夬 癸巳 Water Snake **10** 二十 6	金9 Metal · 3 Heaven 乾爲天 甲午 Wood Horse **11** 廿一 1	火7 Fire · 2 Well 水風井 乙未 Wood Goat **12** 廿二 6
木8 Wood · 1 Relief 雷水解 丙申 Fire Monkey **13** 廿三 4	金4 Metal · 9 Influence 澤山咸 丁酉 Fire Rooster **14** 廿四 9	水1 Water · 8 Humility 地山謙 戊戌 Earth Dog **15** 廿五 6	火2 Fire · 7 Observation 風地觀 己亥 Earth Pig **16** 廿六 2	火2 Fire · 6 Increasing 風雷益 庚子 Metal Rat **17** 廿七 9	水1 Water · 5 Dimming Light 地火明夷 辛丑 Metal Ox **18** 廿八 3	金9 Metal · 4 Fellowship 天火同人 壬寅 Water Tiger **19** 廿九 7
木8 Wood · 3 Marrying Maiden 雷澤歸妹 癸卯 Water Rabbit **20** 三十 7	木3 Wood · 2 Opposition 火澤睽 甲辰 Wood Dragon **21** 十一月初一 2	火7 Fire · 1/9 Waiting 水天需 乙巳 Wood Snake **22** 初二 3	金4 Metal · 1 Great Exceeding 澤風大過 丙午 Fire Horse **23** 初三 3	水6 Water · 2 Poison 山風蠱 丁未 Fire Goat **24** 初四 7	火2 Fire · 3 Dispersing 風水渙 戊申 Earth Monkey **25** 初五 6	木3 Wood · 4 Travelling 火山旅 己酉 Earth Rooster **26** 初六 8
金9 Metal · 5 Stagnation 天地否 庚戌 Metal Dog **27** 初七 9	火7 Fire · 6 Alliance 水地比 辛亥 Metal Pig **28** 初八 7	木8 Wood · 7 Thunder 震爲雷 壬子 Water Rat **29** 初九 1	水6 Water · 8 Beauty 山火賁 癸丑 Water Ox **30** 初十 8	火7 Fire · 9 Accomplished 水火既濟 甲寅 Wood Tiger **31** 十一 9		

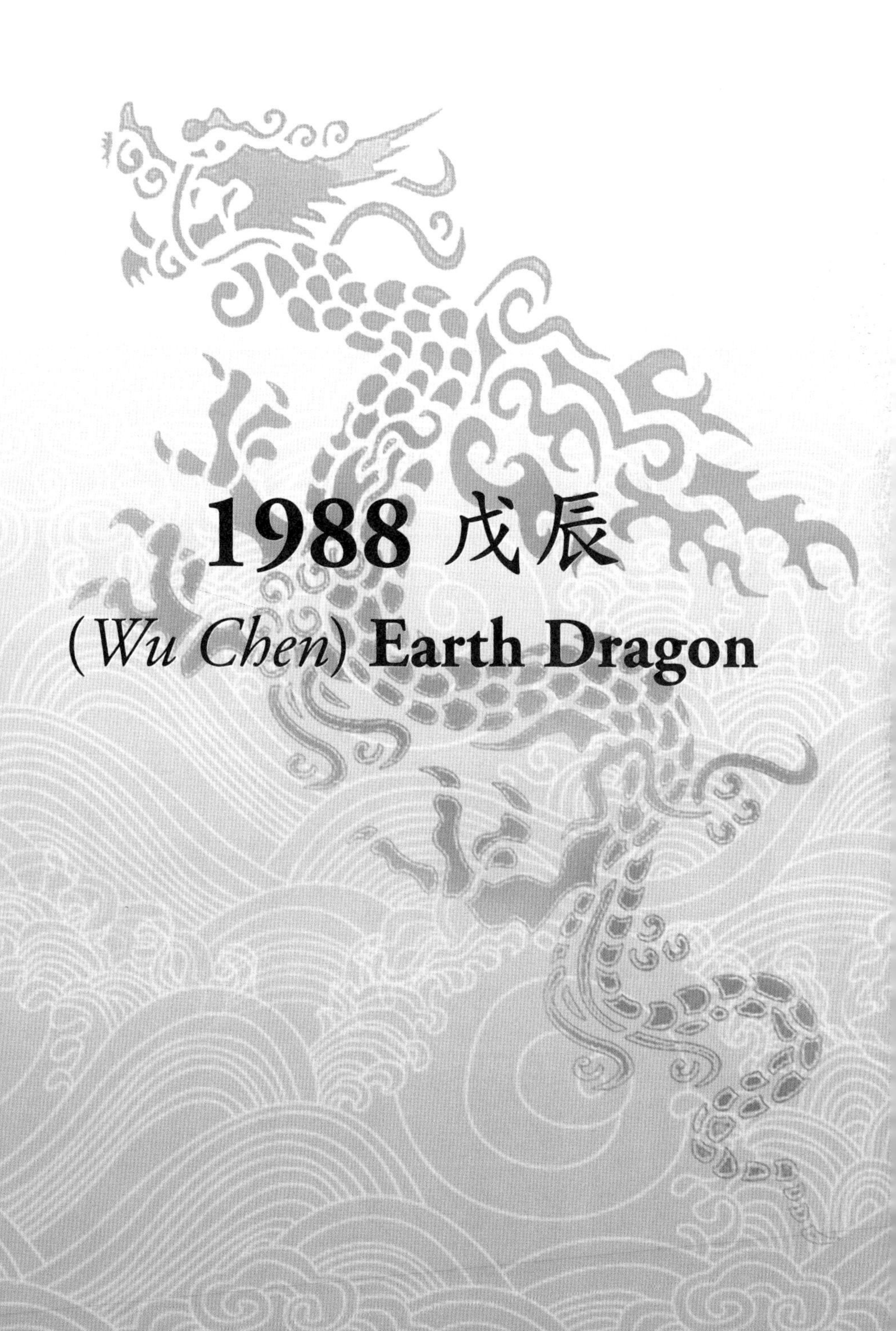

1988 戊辰

(*Wu Chen*) Earth Dragon

1988 戊辰 *(Wu Chen)* Earth Dragon

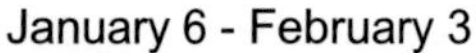

January 6 - February 3

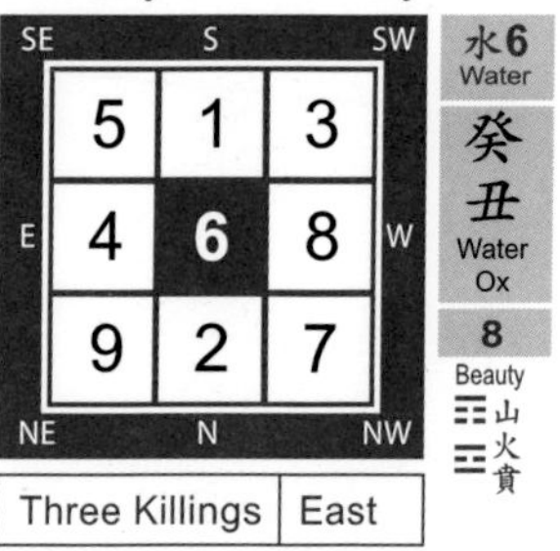

Three Killings | East

February 4 - March 4

SE S SW
4 9 2
E 3 5 7 W
8 1 6
NE N NW
火7 Fire
甲寅 Wood Tiger
9 Accomplished
水火既濟

Three Killings | North

March 5 - April 3

Three Killings | West

April 4 - May 4

Three Killings | South

May 5 - June 4

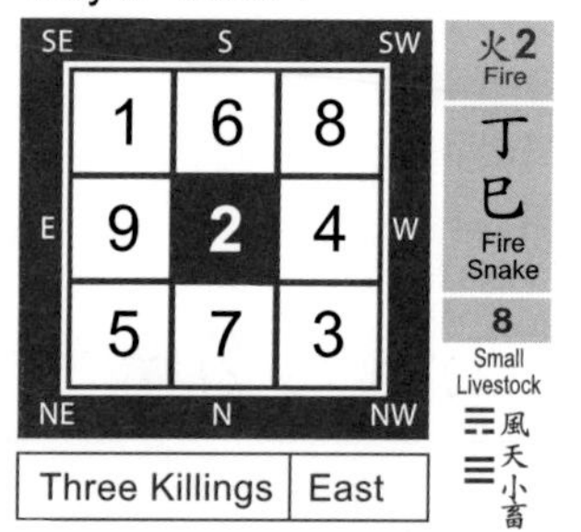

Three Killings | East

June 5 - July 6

Three Killings | North

July 7 - August 6

SE S SW
8 4 6
E 7 9 2 W
3 5 1
NE N NW
水1 Water
己未 Earth Goat
2 Rising
地風升

Three Killings | West

August 7 - September 6

Three Killings | South

September 7 - October 7

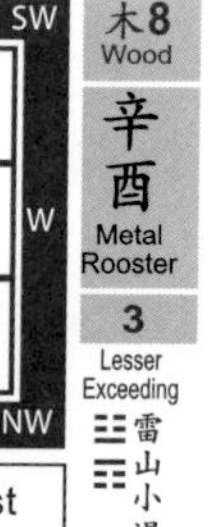

Three Killings | East

October 8 - November 6

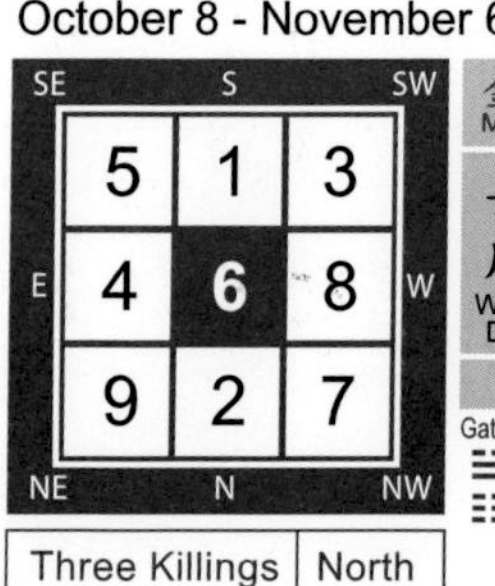

Three Killings | North

November 7 - December 6

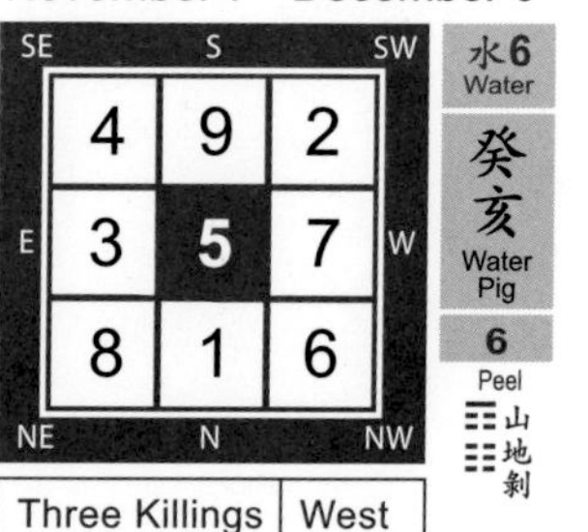

Three Killings | West

December 7 - January 4

Three Killings | South

JANUARY 1988 癸丑

Xuan Kong Element 玄空五行	山火賁 Beauty	Period Luck 卦運	Monthly Star 月星
Water 水6		8	6

SUNDAY	MONDAY	TUESDAY	WEDNESDAY	THURSDAY	FRIDAY	SATURDAY
31 十三 金9 Metal [4] Retreat 天山遯 乙酉 Wood Rooster 4					1 十二 火7 Fire [1] Regulate 水澤節 己卯 Earth Rabbit 8	2 十三 金4 Metal [2] Marsh 兑爲澤 丙辰 Fire Dragon 1
3 十四 火2 Fire [3] Small Livestock 風天小畜 丁巳 Fire Snake 8	4 十五 木3 Wood [4] The Cauldron 火風鼎 戊午 Earth Horse 4	5 十六 水1 Water [5] Rising 地風升 己未 Earth Goat 2	6 十七 火7 Fire [6] Water 坎爲水 庚申 Metal Monkey 1	7 十八 木8 Wood [7] Lesser Exceeding 雷山小過 辛酉 Metal Rooster 3	8 十九 金4 Metal [8] Gathering 澤地萃 壬戌 Water Dog 4	9 二十 水6 Water [9] Peel 山地剝 癸亥 Water Pig 6
10 廿一 水1 Water [1] Earth 坤爲地 甲子 Wood Rat 1	11 廿二 木3 Wood [2] Biting 火雷噬嗑 乙丑 Wood Ox 6	12 廿三 火2 Fire [3] Family 風火家人 丙寅 Fire Tiger 4	13 廿四 水6 Water [4] Decreasing 山澤損 丁卯 Fire Rabbit 9	14 廿五 金9 Metal [5] Tread 天澤履 戊辰 Earth Dragon 6	15 廿六 木8 Wood [6] Great Strength 雷天大壯 己巳 Earth Snake 2	16 廿七 木8 Wood [7] Consistency 雷風恆 庚午 Metal Horse 9
17 廿八 金9 Metal [8] Litigation 天水訟 辛未 Metal Goat 3	18 廿九 水1 Water [9] Officer 地水師 壬申 Water Monkey 7	19 十二月初一 火2 Fire [1] Gradual Progress 風山漸 癸酉 Water Rooster 7	20 初二 火7 Fire [2] Obstruction 水山蹇 甲戌 Wood Dog 2	21 初三 木3 Wood [3] Advancement 火地晉 乙亥 Wood Pig 3	22 初四 水6 Water [4] Nourish 山雷頤 丙子 Fire Rat 3	23 初五 金4 Metal [5] Following 澤雷隨 丁丑 Fire Ox 7
24 初六 木8 Wood [6] Abundance 雷火豐 戊寅 Earth Tiger 6	25 初七 火7 Fire [7] Regulate 水澤節 己卯 Earth Rabbit 8	26 初八 水1 Water [8] Unity 地天泰 庚辰 Metal Dragon 9	27 初九 木3 Wood [9] Great Reward 火天大有 辛巳 Metal Snake 7	28 初十 火2 Fire [1] Wind 巽爲風 壬午 Water Horse 1	29 十一 金4 Metal [2] Trap 澤水困 癸未 Water Goat 8	30 十二 木3 Wood [3] Not Yet Accomplished 火水未濟 甲申 Wood Monkey 9

FEBRUARY 1988 甲寅

Xuan Kong Element 玄空五行	水火既濟 Accomplished	Period Luck 卦運	Monthly Star 月星
Fire 火7		9	5

SUNDAY	MONDAY	TUESDAY	WEDNESDAY	THURSDAY	FRIDAY	SATURDAY
	1 十四 水6 Water [5] Mountain 艮爲山 丙戌 Fire Dog 1	2 十五 木8 Wood [6] Delight 雷地豫 丁亥 Fire Pig 8	3 十六 火7 Fire [7] Beginning 水雷屯 戊子 Earth Rat 4	4 十七 金9 Metal [8] Without Wrongdoing 天雷無妄 己丑 Earth Ox 2	5 十八 木3 Wood [9] Fire 離爲火 庚寅 Metal Tiger 1	6 十九 火2 Fire [1] Sincerity 風澤中孚 辛卯 Metal Rabbit 3
7 二十 水6 Water [2] Big Livestock 山天大畜 壬辰 Water Dragon 4	8 廿一 金4 Metal [3] Eliminating 澤天夬 癸巳 Water Snake 6	9 廿二 金9 Metal [4] Heaven 乾爲天 甲午 Wood Horse 1	10 廿三 火7 Fire [5] Well 水風井 乙未 Wood Goat 6	11 廿四 木8 Wood [6] Relief 雷水解 丙申 Fire Monkey 4	12 廿五 金4 Metal [7] Influence 澤山咸 丁酉 Fire Rooster 9	13 廿六 水1 Water [8] Humility 地山謙 戊戌 Earth Dog 6
14 廿七 火2 Fire [9] Observation 風地觀 己亥 Earth Pig 2	15 廿八 火2 Fire [1] Increasing 風雷益 庚子 Metal Rat 9	16 廿九 水1 Water [2] Dimming Light 地火明夷 辛丑 Metal Ox 3	17 正月初一 金9 Metal [3] Fellowship 天火同人 壬寅 Water Tiger 7	18 初二 木8 Wood [4] Marrying Maiden 雷澤歸妹 癸卯 Water Rabbit 7	19 初三 木3 Wood [5] Opposition 火澤睽 甲辰 Wood Dragon 2	20 初四 火7 Fire [6] Waiting 水天需 乙巳 Wood Snake 3
21 初五 金4 Metal [7] Great Exceeding 澤風大過 丙午 Fire Horse 3	22 初六 水6 Water [8] Poison 山風蠱 丁未 Fire Goat 7	23 初七 火2 Fire [9] Dispersing 風水渙 戊申 Earth Monkey 6	24 初八 木3 Wood [1] Travelling 火山旅 己酉 Earth Rooster 8	25 初九 金9 Metal [2] Stagnation 天地否 庚戌 Metal Dog 9	26 初十 火7 Fire [3] Alliance 水地比 辛亥 Metal Pig 7	27 十一 木8 Wood [4] Thunder 震爲雷 壬子 Water Rat 1
28 十二 水6 Water [5] Beauty 山火賁 癸丑 Water Ox 8	29 十三 火7 Fire [6] Accomplished 水火既濟 甲寅 Wood Tiger 9					

MARCH 1988 乙卯

Xuan Kong Element 玄空五行	地澤臨 Arriving	Period Luck 卦運	Monthly Star 月星
Water 水1		4	4

SUNDAY	MONDAY	TUESDAY	WEDNESDAY	THURSDAY	FRIDAY	SATURDAY
		水1 Water 7 Arriving 地澤臨 乙卯 Wood Rabbit **1** 十四 4	金4 Metal 8 Marsh 兑爲澤 丙辰 Fire Dragon **2** 十五 1	火2 Fire 9 Small Livestock 風天小畜 丁巳 Fire Snake **3** 十六 8	木3 Wood 1 The Cauldron 火風鼎 戊午 Earth Horse **4** 十七 4	水1 Water 2 Rising 地風升 己未 Earth Goat **5** 十八 2
火7 Fire 3 Water 坎爲水 庚申 Metal Monkey **6** 十九 1	木8 Wood 4 Lesser Exceeding 雷山小過 辛酉 Metal Rooster **7** 二十 3	金4 Metal 5 Gathering 澤地萃 壬戌 Water Dog **8** 廿一 4	水6 Water 6 Peel 山地剝 癸亥 Water Pig **9** 廿二 6	水1 Water 7 Earth 坤爲地 甲子 Wood Rat **10** 廿三 1	木3 Wood 8 Biting 火雷噬嗑 乙丑 Wood Ox **11** 廿四 6	火2 Fire 9 Family 風火家人 丙寅 Fire Tiger **12** 廿五 4
水6 Water 1 Decreasing 山澤損 丁卯 Fire Rabbit **13** 廿六 9	金9 Metal 2 Tread 天澤履 戊辰 Earth Dragon **14** 廿七 6	木8 Wood 3 Great Strength 雷天大壯 己巳 Earth Snake **15** 廿八 2	木8 Wood 4 Consistency 雷風恒 庚午 Metal Horse **16** 廿九 9	金9 Metal 5 Litigation 天水訟 辛未 Metal Goat **17** 三十 3	水1 Water 6 Officer 地水師 壬申 Water Monkey **18** 二月初一 7	火2 Fire 7 Gradual Progress 風山漸 癸酉 Water Rooster **19** 初二 7
火7 Fire 8 Obstruction 水山蹇 甲戌 Wood Dog **20** 初三 2	木3 Wood 9 Advancement 火地晉 乙亥 Wood Pig **21** 初四 3	水6 Water 1 Nourish 山雷頤 丙子 Fire Rat **22** 初五 3	金4 Metal 2 Following 澤雷隨 丁丑 Fire Ox **23** 初六 7	木8 Wood 3 Abundance 雷火豐 戊寅 Earth Tiger **24** 初七 6	火7 Fire 4 Regulate 水澤節 己卯 Earth Rabbit **25** 初八 8	水1 Water 5 Unity 地天泰 庚辰 Metal Dragon **26** 初九 9
木3 Wood 6 Great Reward 火天大有 辛巳 Metal Snake **27** 初十 7	火2 Fire 7 Wind 巽爲風 壬午 Water Horse **28** 十一 1	金4 Metal 8 Trap 澤水困 癸未 Water Goat **29** 十二 8	木3 Wood 9 Not Yet Accomplished 火水未濟 甲申 Wood Monkey **30** 十三 9	金9 Metal 1 Retreat 天山遯 乙酉 Wood Rooster **31** 十四 4		

APRIL 1988 丙辰

Xuan Kong Element 玄空五行	兑爲澤 Marsh	Period Luck 卦運	Monthly Star 月星
Metal 金4		1	3

SUNDAY	MONDAY	TUESDAY	WEDNESDAY	THURSDAY	FRIDAY	SATURDAY
					水6 Water 2 Mountain 艮爲山 丙戌 Fire Dog **1** 十五 1	木8 Wood 3 Delight 雷地豫 丁亥 Fire Pig **2** 十六 8
火7 Fire 4 Beginning 水雷屯 戊子 Earth Rat **3** 十七 4	金9 Metal 5 Without Wrongdoing 天雷無妄 己丑 Earth Ox **4** 十八 2	木3 Wood 6 Fire 離爲火 庚寅 Metal Tiger **5** 十九 1	火2 Fire 7 Sincerity 風澤中孚 辛卯 Metal Rabbit **6** 二十 3	水6 Water 8 Big Livestock 山天大畜 壬辰 Water Dragon **7** 廿一 4	金4 Metal 9 Eliminating 澤天夬 癸巳 Water Snake **8** 廿二 6	金9 Metal 1 Heaven 乾爲天 甲午 Wood Horse **9** 廿三 1
火7 Fire 2 Well 水風井 乙未 Wood Goat **10** 廿四 6	木8 Wood 3 Relief 雷水解 丙申 Fire Monkey **11** 廿五 4	金4 Metal 4 Influence 澤山咸 丁酉 Fire Rooster **12** 廿六 9	水1 Water 5 Humility 地山謙 戊戌 Earth Dog **13** 廿七 6	火2 Fire 6 Observation 風地觀 己亥 Earth Pig **14** 廿八 2	火2 Fire 7 Increasing 風雷益 庚子 Metal Rat **15** 廿九 9	水1 Water 8 Dimming Light 地火明夷 辛丑 Metal Ox **16** 三月初一 3
金9 Metal 9 Fellowship 天火同人 壬寅 Water Tiger **17** 初二 7	木8 Wood 1 Marrying Maiden 雷澤歸妹 癸卯 Water Rabbit **18** 初三 7	木3 Wood 2 Opposition 火澤睽 甲辰 Wood Dragon **19** 初四 2	火7 Fire 3 Waiting 水天需 乙巳 Wood Snake **20** 初五 3	金4 Metal 4 Great Exceeding 澤風大過 丙午 Fire Horse **21** 初六 3	水6 Water 5 Poison 山風蠱 丁未 Fire Goat **22** 初七 7	火2 Fire 6 Dispersing 風水渙 戊申 Earth Monkey **23** 初八 6
木3 Wood 7 Travelling 火山旅 己酉 Earth Rooster **24** 初九 8	金9 Metal 8 Stagnation 天地否 庚戌 Metal Dog **25** 初十 9	火7 Fire 9 Alliance 水地比 辛亥 Metal Pig **26** 十一 7	木8 Wood 1 Thunder 震爲雷 壬子 Water Rat **27** 十二 1	水6 Water 2 Beauty 山火賁 癸丑 Water Ox **28** 十三 8	火7 Fire 3 Accomplished 水火既濟 甲寅 Wood Tiger **29** 十四 9	水1 Water 4 Arriving 地澤臨 乙卯 Wood Rabbit **30** 十五 4

MAY 1988 丁巳

Xuan Kong Element 玄空五行	風天小畜	Period Luck 卦運	Monthly Star 月星
Fire 火2	Small Livestock	8	2

SUNDAY	MONDAY	TUESDAY	WEDNESDAY	THURSDAY	FRIDAY	SATURDAY
金4 Metal · 5 Marsh 兑爲澤 丙辰 Fire Dragon **1** 十六 1	火2 Fire · 6 Small Livestock 風天小畜 丁巳 Fire Snake **2** 十七 8	木3 Wood · 7 The Cauldron 火風鼎 戊午 Earth Horse **3** 十八 4	水1 Water · 8 Rising 地風升 己未 Earth Goat **4** 十九 2	火7 Fire · 9 Water 坎爲水 庚申 Metal Monkey **5** 二十 1	木8 Wood · 1 Lesser Exceeding 雷山小過 辛酉 Metal Rooster **6** 廿一 3	金4 Metal · 2 Gathering 澤地萃 壬戌 Water Dog **7** 廿二 4
水6 Water · 3 Peel 山地剝 癸亥 Water Pig **8** 廿三 6	水1 Water · 4 Earth 坤爲地 甲子 Wood Rat **9** 廿四 1	木3 Wood · 5 Biting 火雷噬嗑 乙丑 Wood Ox **10** 廿五 6	火2 Fire · 6 Family 風火家人 丙寅 Fire Tiger **11** 廿六 4	水6 Water · 7 Decreasing 山澤損 丁卯 Fire Rabbit **12** 廿七 9	金9 Metal · 8 Tread 天澤履 戊辰 Earth Dragon **13** 廿八 6	木8 Wood · 9 Great Strength 雷天大壯 己巳 Earth Snake **14** 廿九 2
木8 Wood · 1 Consistency 雷風恆 庚午 Metal Horse **15** 三十 9	金9 Metal · 2 Litigation 天水訟 辛未 Metal Goat **16** 四月初一 3	水1 Water · 3 Officer 地水師 壬申 Water Monkey **17** 初二 7	火2 Fire · 4 Gradual Progress 風山漸 癸酉 Water Rooster **18** 初三 7	火7 Fire · 5 Obstruction 水山蹇 甲戌 Wood Dog **19** 初四 2	木3 Wood · 6 Advancement 火地晉 乙亥 Wood Pig **20** 初五 3	水6 Water · 7 Nourish 山雷頤 丙子 Fire Rat **21** 初六 3
金4 Metal · 8 Following 澤雷隨 丁丑 Fire Ox **22** 初七 7	木8 Wood · 9 Abundance 雷火豐 戊寅 Earth Tiger **23** 初八 6	火7 Fire · 1 Regulate 水澤節 己卯 Earth Rabbit **24** 初九 8	水1 Water · 2 Unity 地天泰 庚辰 Metal Dragon **25** 初十 9	木3 Wood · 3 Great Reward 火天大有 辛巳 Metal Snake **26** 十一 7	火2 Fire · 4 Wind 巽爲風 壬午 Water Horse **27** 十二 1	金4 Metal · 5 Trap 澤水困 癸未 Water Goat **28** 十三 8
木3 Wood · 6 Not Yet Accomplished 火水未濟 甲申 Wood Monkey **29** 十四 9	金9 Metal · 7 Retreat 天山遯 乙酉 Wood Rooster **30** 十五 4	水6 Water · 8 Mountain 艮爲山 丙戌 Fire Dog **31** 十六 1				

JUNE 1988 戊午

Xuan Kong Element 玄空五行	火風鼎	Period Luck 卦運	Monthly Star 月星
Wood 木3	The Cauldron	4	1

SUNDAY	MONDAY	TUESDAY	WEDNESDAY	THURSDAY	FRIDAY	SATURDAY
			木8 Wood · 9 Delight 雷地豫 丁亥 Fire Pig **1** 十七 8	火7 Fire · 1 Beginning 水雷屯 戊子 Earth Rat **2** 十八 4	金9 Metal · 2 Without Wrongdoing 天雷無妄 己丑 Earth Ox **3** 十九 2	木3 Wood · 3 Fire 離爲火 庚寅 Metal Tiger **4** 二十 1
火2 Fire · 4 Sincerity 風澤中孚 辛卯 Metal Rabbit **5** 廿一 3	水6 Water · 5 Big Livestock 山天大畜 壬辰 Water Dragon **6** 廿二 4	金4 Metal · 6 Eliminating 澤天夬 癸巳 Water Snake **7** 廿三 6	金9 Metal · 7 Heaven 乾爲天 甲午 Wood Horse **8** 廿四 1	火7 Fire · 8 Well 水風井 乙未 Wood Goat **9** 廿五 6	木8 Wood · 9 Relief 雷水解 丙申 Fire Monkey **10** 廿六 4	金4 Metal · 1 Influence 澤山咸 丁酉 Fire Rooster **11** 廿七 9
水1 Water · 2 Humility 地山謙 戊戌 Earth Dog **12** 廿八 6	火2 Fire · 3 Observation 風地觀 己亥 Earth Pig **13** 廿九 2	火2 Fire · 4 Increasing 風雷益 庚子 Metal Rat **14** 五月初一 9	水1 Water · 5 Dimming Light 地火明夷 辛丑 Metal Ox **15** 初二 3	金9 Metal · 6 Fellowship 天火同人 壬寅 Water Tiger **16** 初三 7	木8 Wood · 7 Marrying Maiden 雷澤歸妹 癸卯 Water Rabbit **17** 初四 7	木3 Wood · 8 Opposition 火澤睽 甲辰 Wood Dragon **18** 初五 2
火7 Fire · 9 Waiting 水天需 乙巳 Wood Snake **19** 初六 3	金4 Metal · 1 Great Exceeding 澤風大過 丙午 Fire Horse **20** 初七 3	水6 Water · 2/8 Poison 山風蠱 丁未 Fire Goat **21** 初八 7	火2 Fire · 7 Dispersing 風水渙 戊申 Earth Monkey **22** 初九 6	木3 Wood · 6 Travelling 火山旅 己酉 Earth Rooster **23** 初十 8	金9 Metal · 5 Stagnation 天地否 庚戌 Metal Dog **24** 十一 9	火7 Fire · 4 Alliance 水地比 辛亥 Metal Pig **25** 十二 7
木8 Wood · 3 Thunder 震爲雷 壬子 Water Rat **26** 十三 1	水6 Water · 2 Beauty 山火賁 癸丑 Water Ox **27** 十四 8	火7 Fire · 1 Accomplished 水火既濟 甲寅 Wood Tiger **28** 十五 9	水1 Water · 9 Arriving 地澤臨 乙卯 Wood Rabbit **29** 十六 4	金4 Metal · 8 Marsh 兑爲澤 丙辰 Fire Dragon **30** 十七 1		

JULY 1988 己未

Xuan Kong Element 玄空五行	地風升 Rising	Period Luck 卦運	Monthly Star 月星
Water 水1		2	9

SUNDAY	MONDAY	TUESDAY	WEDNESDAY	THURSDAY	FRIDAY	SATURDAY
木8 Wood Delight 4 雷地豫 丁亥 Fire Pig 31 8 十八					火2 Fire Small Livestock 7 風天小畜 丁巳 Fire Snake 1 8 十八	木3 Wood The Cauldron 6 火風鼎 戊午 Earth Horse 2 4 十九
水1 Water Rising 5 地風升 己未 Earth Goat 3 2 二十	火7 Fire Water 4 坎爲水 庚申 Metal Monkey 4 1 廿一	木8 Wood Lesser Exceeding 3 雷山小過 辛酉 Metal Rooster 5 3 廿二	金4 Metal Gathering 2 澤地萃 壬戌 Water Dog 6 4 廿三	水6 Water Peel 1 山地剝 癸亥 Water Pig 7 6 廿四	水1 Water Earth 9 坤爲地 甲子 Wood Rat 8 1 廿五	木3 Wood Biting 8 火雷噬嗑 乙丑 Wood Ox 9 6 廿六
火2 Fire Family 7 風火家人 丙寅 Fire Tiger 10 4 廿七	水6 Water Decreasing 6 山澤損 丁卯 Fire Rabbit 11 9 廿八	金9 Metal Tread 5 天澤履 戊辰 Earth Dragon 12 6 廿九	木8 Wood Great Strength 4 雷天大壯 己巳 Earth Snake 13 2 三十	木8 Wood Consistency 3 雷風恒 庚午 Metal Horse 14 9 六月初一	金9 Metal Litigation 2 天水訟 辛未 Metal Goat 15 3 初二	水1 Water Officer 1 地水師 壬申 Water Monkey 16 7 初三
火2 Fire Gradual Progress 9 風山漸 癸酉 Water Rooster 17 7 初四	火7 Fire Obstruction 8 水山蹇 甲戌 Wood Dog 18 2 初五	木3 Wood Advancement 7 火地晋 乙亥 Wood Pig 19 3 初六	水6 Water Nourish 6 山雷頤 丙子 Fire Rat 20 3 初七	金4 Metal Following 5 澤雷隨 丁丑 Fire Ox 21 7 初八	木8 Wood Abundance 4 雷火豐 戊寅 Earth Tiger 22 6 初九	火7 Fire Regulate 3 水澤節 己卯 Earth Rabbit 23 8 初十
水1 Water Unity 2 地天泰 庚辰 Metal Dragon 24 9 十一	木3 Wood Great Reward 1 火天大有 辛巳 Metal Snake 25 7 十二	火2 Fire Wind 9 巽爲風 壬午 Water Horse 26 1 十三	金4 Metal Trap 8 澤水困 癸未 Water Goat 27 8 十四	木3 Wood Not Yet Accomplished 7 火水未濟 甲申 Wood Monkey 28 9 十五	金9 Metal Retreat 6 天山遯 乙酉 Wood Rooster 29 4 十六	水6 Water Mountain 5 艮爲山 丙戌 Fire Dog 30 1 十七

AUGUST 1988 庚申

Xuan Kong Element 玄空五行	坎爲水 Water	Period Luck 卦運	Monthly Star 月星
Fire 火7		1	8

SUNDAY	MONDAY	TUESDAY	WEDNESDAY	THURSDAY	FRIDAY	SATURDAY
	火7 Fire Beginning 3 水雷屯 戊子 Earth Rat 1 4 十九	金9 Metal Without Wrongdoing 2 天雷無妄 己丑 Earth Ox 2 2 二十	木3 Wood Fire 1 離爲火 庚寅 Metal Tiger 3 1 廿一	火2 Fire Sincerity 9 風澤中孚 辛卯 Metal Rabbit 4 3 廿二	水6 Water Big Livestock 8 山天大畜 壬辰 Water Dragon 5 4 廿三	金4 Metal Eliminating 7 澤天夬 癸巳 Water Snake 6 6 廿四
金9 Metal Heaven 6 乾爲天 甲午 Wood Horse 7 1 廿五	火7 Fire Well 5 水風井 乙未 Wood Goat 8 6 廿六	木8 Wood Relief 4 雷水解 丙申 Fire Monkey 9 4 廿七	金4 Metal Influence 3 澤山咸 丁酉 Fire Rooster 10 9 廿八	水1 Water Humility 2 地山謙 戊戌 Earth Dog 11 6 廿九	火2 Fire Observation 1 風地觀 己亥 Earth Pig 12 2 七月初一	火2 Fire Increasing 9 風雷益 庚子 Metal Rat 13 9 初二
水1 Water Dimming Light 8 地火明夷 辛丑 Metal Ox 14 3 初三	金9 Metal Fellowship 7 天火同人 壬寅 Water Tiger 15 7 初四	木8 Wood Marrying Maiden 6 雷澤歸妹 癸卯 Water Rabbit 16 7 初五	木3 Wood Opposition 5 火澤睽 甲辰 Wood Dragon 17 2 初六	火7 Fire Waiting 4 水天需 乙巳 Wood Snake 18 3 初七	金4 Metal Great Exceeding 3 澤風大過 丙午 Fire Horse 19 3 初八	水6 Water Poison 2 山風蠱 丁未 Fire Goat 20 7 初九
火2 Fire Dispersing 1 風水渙 戊申 Earth Monkey 21 6 初十	木3 Wood Travelling 9 火山旅 己酉 Earth Rooster 22 8 十一	金9 Metal Stagnation 8 天地否 庚戌 Metal Dog 23 9 十二	火7 Fire Alliance 7 水地比 辛亥 Metal Pig 24 7 十三	木8 Wood Thunder 6 震爲雷 壬子 Water Rat 25 1 十四	水6 Water Beauty 5 山火賁 癸丑 Water Ox 26 8 十五	火7 Fire Accomplished 4 水火既濟 甲寅 Wood Tiger 27 9 十六
水1 Water Arriving 3 地澤臨 乙卯 Wood Rabbit 28 4 十七	金4 Metal Marsh 2 兌爲澤 丙辰 Fire Dragon 29 1 十八	火2 Fire Small Livestock 1 風天小畜 丁巳 Fire Snake 30 8 十九	木3 Wood The Cauldron 9 火風鼎 戊午 Earth Horse 31 4 二十			

SEPTEMBER 1988 辛酉

Xuan Kong Element 玄空五行	雷山小過	Period Luck 卦運	Monthly Star 月星
Wood 木8	Lesser Exceeding	3	7

SUNDAY	MONDAY	TUESDAY	WEDNESDAY	THURSDAY	FRIDAY	SATURDAY
				水1 Water 8 Rising 己未 Earth Goat 地風升 **1** 廿一 2	火7 Fire 7 Water 庚申 Metal Monkey 坎爲水 **2** 廿二 1	木8 Wood 6 Lesser Exceeding 辛酉 Metal Rooster 雷山小過 **3** 廿三 3
金4 Metal 5 Gathering 壬戌 Water Dog 澤地萃 **4** 廿四 4	水6 Water 4 Peel 癸亥 Water Pig 山地剝 **5** 廿五 6	水1 Water 3 Earth 甲子 Wood Rat 坤爲地 **6** 廿六 1	木3 Wood 2 Biting 乙丑 Wood Ox 火雷噬嗑 **7** 廿七 6	火2 Fire 1 Family 丙寅 Fire Tiger 風火家人 **8** 廿八 4	水6 Water 9 Decreasing 丁卯 Fire Rabbit 山澤損 **9** 廿九 9	金9 Metal 8 Tread 戊辰 Earth Dragon 天澤履 **10** 三十 6
木8 Wood 7 Great Strength 己巳 Earth Snake 雷天大壯 **11** 八月初一 2	木8 Wood 6 Consistency 庚午 Metal Horse 雷風恒 **12** 初二 9	金9 Metal 5 Litigation 辛未 Metal Goat 天水訟 **13** 初三 3	水1 Water 4 Officer 壬申 Water Monkey 地水師 **14** 初四 7	火2 Fire 3 Gradual Progress 癸酉 Water Rooster 風山漸 **15** 初五 7	火7 Fire 2 Obstruction 甲戌 Wood Dog 水山蹇 **16** 初六 2	木3 Wood 1 Advancement 乙亥 Wood Pig 火地晉 **17** 初七 3
水6 Water 9 Nourish 丙子 Fire Rat 山雷頤 **18** 初八 3	金4 Metal 8 Following 丁丑 Fire Ox 澤雷隨 **19** 初九 7	木8 Wood 7 Abundance 戊寅 Earth Tiger 雷火豐 **20** 初十 6	火7 Fire 6 Regulate 己卯 Earth Rabbit 水澤節 **21** 十一 8	水1 Water 5 Unity 庚辰 Metal Dragon 地天泰 **22** 十二 9	木3 Wood 4 Great Reward 辛巳 Metal Snake 火天大有 **23** 十三 7	火2 Fire 3 Wind 壬午 Water Horse 巽爲風 **24** 十四 1
金4 Metal 2 Trap 癸未 Water Goat 澤水困 **25** 十五 8	木3 Wood 1 Not Yet Accomplished 甲申 Wood Monkey 火水未濟 **26** 十六 9	金9 Metal 9 Retreat 乙酉 Wood Rooster 天山遯 **27** 十七 4	水6 Water 8 Mountain 丙戌 Fire Dog 艮爲山 **28** 十八 1	木8 Wood 7 Delight 丁亥 Fire Pig 雷地豫 **29** 十九 8	火7 Fire 6 Beginning 戊子 Earth Rat 水雷屯 **30** 二十 4	

OCTOBER 1988 壬戌

Xuan Kong Element 玄空五行	澤地萃	Period Luck 卦運	Monthly Star 月星
Metal 金4	Gathering	4	6

SUNDAY	MONDAY	TUESDAY	WEDNESDAY	THURSDAY	FRIDAY	SATURDAY
木3 Wood 3 The Cauldron 戊午 Earth Horse 火風鼎 **30** 二十 4	水1 Water 2 Rising 己未 Earth Goat 地風升 **31** 廿一 2					金9 Metal 5 Without Wrongdoing 己丑 Earth Ox 天雷無妄 **1** 廿一 2
木3 Wood 4 Fire 庚寅 Metal Tiger 離爲火 **2** 廿二 1	火2 Fire 3 Sincerity 辛卯 Metal Rabbit 風澤中孚 **3** 廿三 3	水6 Water 2 Big Livestock 壬辰 Water Dragon 山天大畜 **4** 廿四 4	金4 Metal 1 Eliminating 癸巳 Water Snake 澤天夬 **5** 廿五 6	金9 Metal 9 Heaven 甲午 Wood Horse 乾爲天 **6** 廿六 1	火7 Fire 8 Well 乙未 Wood Goat 水風井 **7** 廿七 6	木8 Wood 7 Relief 丙申 Fire Monkey 雷水解 **8** 廿八 4
金4 Metal 6 Influence 丁酉 Fire Rooster 澤山咸 **9** 廿九 9	水1 Water 5 Humility 戊戌 Earth Dog 地山謙 **10** 三十 6	火2 Fire 4 Observation 己亥 Earth Pig 風地觀 **11** 九月初一 2	火2 Fire 3 Increasing 庚子 Metal Rat 風雷益 **12** 初二 9	水1 Water 2 Dimming Light 辛丑 Metal Ox 地火明夷 **13** 初三 3	金9 Metal 1 Fellowship 壬寅 Water Tiger 天火同人 **14** 初四 7	木8 Wood 9 Marrying Maiden 癸卯 Water Rabbit 雷澤歸妹 **15** 初五 7
木3 Wood 8 Opposition 甲辰 Wood Dragon 火澤睽 **16** 初六 2	火7 Fire 7 Waiting 乙巳 Wood Snake 水天需 **17** 初七 3	金4 Metal 6 Great Exceeding 丙午 Fire Horse 澤風大過 **18** 初八 3	水6 Water 5 Poison 丁未 Fire Goat 山風蠱 **19** 初九 7	火2 Fire 4 Dispersing 戊申 Earth Monkey 風水渙 **20** 初十 6	木3 Wood 3 Travelling 己酉 Earth Rooster 火山旅 **21** 十一 8	金9 Metal 2 Stagnation 庚戌 Metal Dog 天地否 **22** 十二 9
火7 Fire 1 Alliance 辛亥 Metal Pig 水地比 **23** 十三 7	木8 Wood 9 Thunder 壬子 Water Rat 震爲雷 **24** 十四 1	水6 Water 8 Beauty 癸丑 Water Ox 山火賁 **25** 十五 8	火7 Fire 7 Accomplished 甲寅 Wood Tiger 水火既濟 **26** 十六 9	水1 Water 6 Arriving 乙卯 Wood Rabbit 地澤臨 **27** 十七 4	金4 Metal 5 Marsh 丙辰 Fire Dragon 兑爲澤 **28** 十八 1	火2 Fire 4 Small Livestock 丁巳 Fire Snake 風天小畜 **29** 十九 8

NOVEMBER 1988 癸亥

Xuan Kong Element 玄空五行	山地剝 Peel	Period Luck 卦運	Monthly Star 月星
Water 水6		6	5

SUNDAY	MONDAY	TUESDAY	WEDNESDAY	THURSDAY	FRIDAY	SATURDAY
		火7 Fire 庚申 Metal Monkey 1 Water 坎爲水 7 **1** 廿二	木8 Wood 辛酉 Metal Rooster 3 Lesser Exceeding 雷山小過 8 **2** 廿三	金4 Metal 壬戌 Water Dog 4 Gathering 澤地萃 8 **3** 廿四	水6 Water 癸亥 Water Pig 6 Peel 山地剝 7 **4** 廿五	水1 Water 甲子 Wood Rat 1 Earth 坤爲地 6 **5** 廿六
木3 Wood 乙丑 Wood Ox 6 Biting 火雷噬嗑 5 **6** 廿七	火2 Fire 丙寅 Fire Tiger 4 Family 風火家人 4 **7** 廿八	水6 Water 丁卯 Fire Rabbit 9 Decreasing 山澤損 3 **8** 廿九	金9 Metal 戊辰 Earth Dragon 6 Tread 天澤履 2 **9** 十月初一	木8 Wood 己巳 Earth Snake 2 Great Strength 雷天大壯 1 **10** 初二	木8 Wood 庚午 Metal Horse 9 Consistency 雷風恆 9 **11** 初三	金9 Metal 辛未 Metal Goat 3 Litigation 天水訟 8 **12** 初四
水1 Water 壬申 Water Monkey 7 Officer 地水師 7 **13** 初五	火2 Fire 癸酉 Water Rooster 7 Gradual Progress 風山漸 6 **14** 初六	火7 Fire 甲戌 Wood Dog 2 Obstruction 水山蹇 5 **15** 初七	木3 Wood 乙亥 Wood Pig 3 Advancement 火地晉 4 **16** 初八	水6 Water 丙子 Fire Rat 3 Nourish 山雷頤 3 **17** 初九	金4 Metal 丁丑 Fire Ox 7 Following 澤雷隨 2 **18** 初十	木8 Wood 戊寅 Earth Tiger 6 Abundance 雷火豐 1 **19** 十一
火7 Fire 己卯 Earth Rabbit 8 Regulate 水澤節 9 **20** 十二	水1 Water 庚辰 Metal Dragon 9 Unity 地天泰 8 **21** 十三	木3 Wood 辛巳 Metal Snake 7 Great Reward 火天大有 7 **22** 十四	火2 Fire 壬午 Water Horse 1 Wind 巽爲風 6 **23** 十五	金4 Metal 癸未 Water Goat 8 Trap 澤水困 5 **24** 十六	木3 Wood 甲申 Wood Monkey 9 Not Yet Accomplished 火水未濟 4 **25** 十七	金9 Metal 乙酉 Wood Rooster 4 Retreat 天山遯 3 **26** 十八
水6 Water 丙戌 Fire Dog 1 Mountain 艮爲山 2 **27** 十九	木8 Wood 丁亥 Fire Pig 8 Delight 雷地豫 1 **28** 二十	火7 Fire 戊子 Earth Rat 4 Beginning 水雷屯 9 **29** 廿一	金9 Metal 己丑 Earth Ox 2 Without Wrongdoing 天雷無妄 8 **30** 廿二			

DECEMBER 1988 甲子

Xuan Kong Element 玄空五行	坤爲地 Earth	Period Luck 卦運	Monthly Star 月星
Water 水1		1	4

SUNDAY	MONDAY	TUESDAY	WEDNESDAY	THURSDAY	FRIDAY	SATURDAY
				木3 Wood 庚寅 Metal Tiger 1 Fire 離爲火 7 **1** 廿三	火2 Fire 辛卯 Metal Rabbit 3 Sincerity 風澤中孚 6 **2** 廿四	水6 Water 壬辰 Water Dragon 4 Big Livestock 山天大畜 5 **3** 廿五
金4 Metal 癸巳 Water Snake 6 Eliminating 澤天夬 4 **4** 廿六	金9 Metal 甲午 Wood Horse 1 Heaven 乾爲天 3 **5** 廿七	火7 Fire 乙未 Wood Goat 6 Well 水風井 2 **6** 廿八	木8 Wood 丙申 Fire Monkey 4 Relief 雷水解 1 **7** 廿九	金4 Metal 丁酉 Fire Rooster 9 Influence 澤山咸 9 **8** 三十	水1 Water 戊戌 Earth Dog 6 Humility 地山謙 8 **9** 十一月初一	火2 Fire 己亥 Earth Pig 2 Observation 風地觀 7 **10** 初二
火2 Fire 庚子 Metal Rat 9 Increasing 風雷益 6 **11** 初三	水1 Water 辛丑 Metal Ox 3 Dimming Light 地火明夷 5 **12** 初四	金9 Metal 壬寅 Water Tiger 7 Fellowship 天火同人 4 **13** 初五	木8 Wood 癸卯 Water Rabbit 7 Marrying Maiden 雷澤歸妹 3 **14** 初六	木3 Wood 甲辰 Wood Dragon 2 Opposition 火澤睽 2 **15** 初七	火7 Fire 乙巳 Wood Snake 3 Waiting 水天需 1 **16** 初八	金4 Metal 丙午 Fire Horse 3 Great Exceeding 澤風大過 9 **17** 初九
水6 Water 丁未 Fire Goat 7 Poison 山風蠱 8 **18** 初十	火2 Fire 戊申 Earth Monkey 6 Dispersing 風水渙 7 **19** 十一	木3 Wood 己酉 Earth Rooster 8 Travelling 火山旅 6 **20** 十二	金9 Metal 庚戌 Metal Dog 9 Stagnation 天地否 5 **21** 十三	火7 Fire 辛亥 Metal Pig 7 Alliance 水地比 6 **22** 十四	木8 Wood 壬子 Water Rat 1 Thunder 震爲雷 7 **23** 十五	水6 Water 癸丑 Water Ox 8 Beauty 山火賁 8 **24** 十六
火7 Fire 甲寅 Wood Tiger 9 Accomplished 水火既濟 9 **25** 十七	水1 Water 乙卯 Wood Rabbit 4 Arriving 地澤臨 1 **26** 十八	金4 Metal 丙辰 Fire Dragon 1 Marsh 兌爲澤 2 **27** 十九	火2 Fire 丁巳 Fire Snake 8 Small Livestock 風天小畜 3 **28** 二十	木3 Wood 戊午 Earth Horse 4 The Cauldron 火風鼎 4 **29** 廿一	水1 Water 己未 Earth Goat 2 Rising 地風升 5 **30** 廿二	火7 Fire 庚申 Metal Monkey 1 Water 坎爲水 6 **31** 廿三

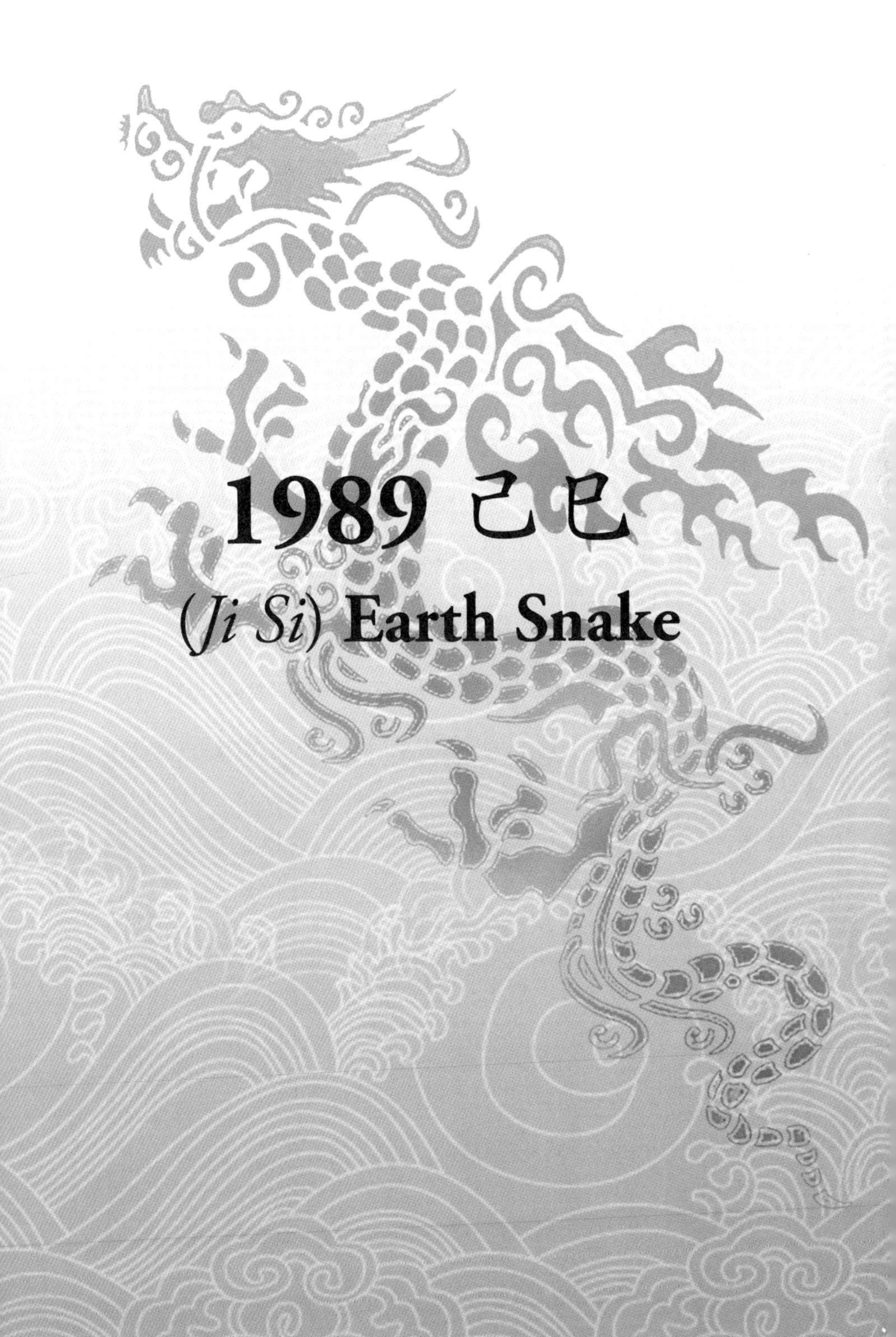

1989 己巳

(*Ji Si*) Earth Snake

1989 己巳 *(Ji Si)* Earth Snake

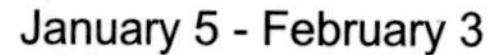

January 5 - February 3

February 4 - March 4

March 5 - April 4

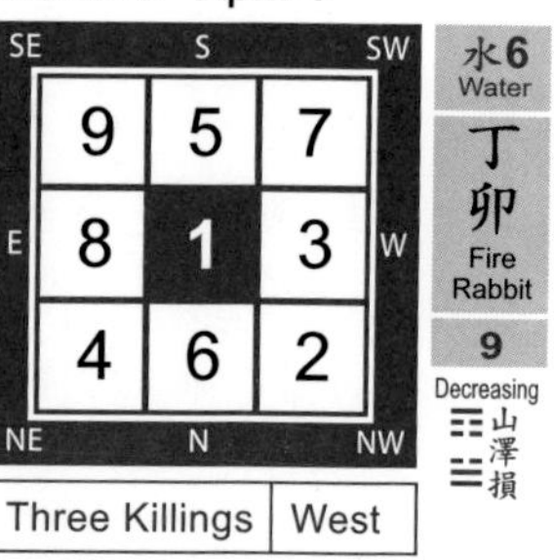

April 5 - May 4

May 5 - June 5

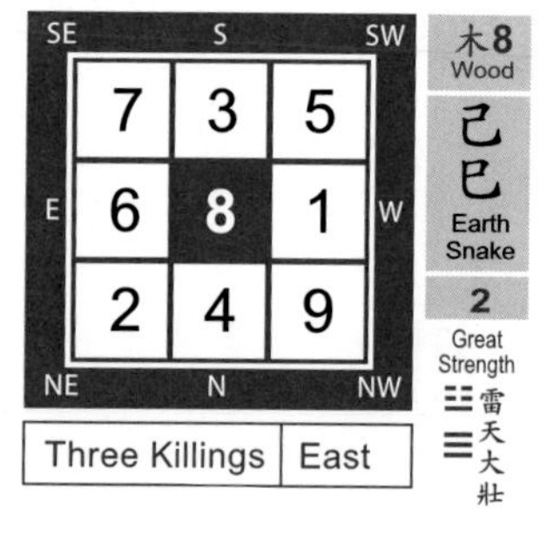

June 6 - July 6

July 7 - August 6

August 7 - September 6

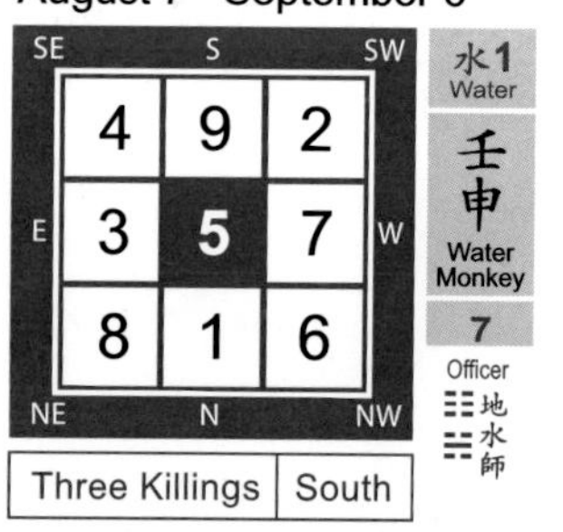

September 7 - October 7

October 8 - November 6

November 7 - December 6

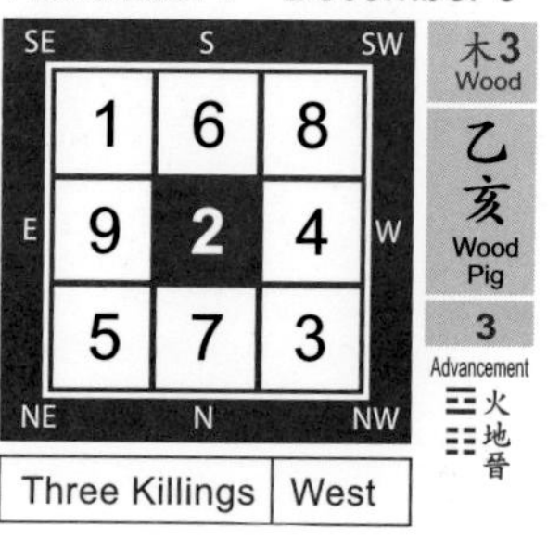

December 7 - January 4

JANUARY 1989 乙丑

Xuan Kong Element 玄空五行	火雷噬嗑 Biting	Period Luck 卦運	Monthly Star 月星
Wood 木3		6	3

SUNDAY	MONDAY	TUESDAY	WEDNESDAY	THURSDAY	FRIDAY	SATURDAY
木8 Wood · 7 Lesser Exceeding 雷山小過 辛酉 Metal Rooster **1** 廿四 · 3	金4 Metal · 8 Gathering 澤地萃 壬戌 Water Dog **2** 廿五 · 4	水6 Water · 9 Peel 山地剝 癸亥 Water Pig **3** 廿六 · 6	水1 Water · 1 Earth 坤爲地 甲子 Wood Rat **4** 廿七 · 1	木3 Wood · 2 Biting 火雷噬嗑 乙丑 Wood Ox **5** 廿八 · 6	火2 Fire · 3 Family 風火家人 丙寅 Fire Tiger **6** 廿九 · 4	水6 Water · 4 Decreasing 山澤損 丁卯 Fire Rabbit **7** 三十 · 9
金9 Metal · 5 Tread 天澤履 戊辰 Earth Dragon **8** 十二月初一 · 6	木8 Wood · 6 Great Strength 雷天大壯 己巳 Earth Snake **9** 初二 · 2	木8 Wood · 7 Consistency 雷風恆 庚午 Metal Horse **10** 初三 · 9	金9 Metal · 8 Litigation 天水訟 辛未 Metal Goat **11** 初四 · 3	水1 Water · 9 Officer 地水師 壬申 Water Monkey **12** 初五 · 7	火2 Fire · 1 Gradual Progress 風山漸 癸酉 Water Rooster **13** 初六 · 7	火7 Fire · 2 Obstruction 水山蹇 甲戌 Wood Dog **14** 初七 · 2
木3 Wood · 3 Advancement 火地晉 乙亥 Wood Pig **15** 初八 · 3	水6 Water · 4 Nourish 山雷頤 丙子 Fire Rat **16** 初九 · 3	金4 Metal · 5 Following 澤雷隨 丁丑 Fire Ox **17** 初十 · 7	木8 Wood · 6 Abundance 雷火豐 戊寅 Earth Tiger **18** 十一 · 6	火7 Fire · 7 Regulate 水澤節 己卯 Earth Rabbit **19** 十二 · 8	水1 Water · 8 Unity 地天泰 庚辰 Metal Dragon **20** 十三 · 9	木3 Wood · 9 Great Reward 火天大有 辛巳 Metal Snake **21** 十四 · 7
火2 Fire · 1 Wind 巽爲風 壬午 Water Horse **22** 十五 · 1	金4 Metal · 2 Trap 澤水困 癸未 Water Goat **23** 十六 · 8	木3 Wood · 3 Not Yet Accomplished 火水未濟 甲申 Wood Monkey **24** 十七 · 9	金9 Metal · 4 Retreat 天山遯 乙酉 Wood Rooster **25** 十八 · 4	水6 Water · 5 Mountain 艮爲山 丙戌 Fire Dog **26** 十九 · 1	木8 Wood · 6 Delight 雷地豫 丁亥 Fire Pig **27** 二十 · 8	火7 Fire · 7 Beginning 水雷屯 戊子 Earth Rat **28** 廿一 · 4
金9 Metal · 8 Without Wrongdoing 天雷無妄 己丑 Earth Ox **29** 廿二 · 2	木3 Wood · 9 Fire 離爲火 庚寅 Metal Tiger **30** 廿三 · 1	火2 Fire · 1 Sincerity 風澤中孚 辛卯 Metal Rabbit **31** 廿四 · 3				

FEBRUARY 1989 丙寅

Xuan Kong Element 玄空五行	風火家人 Family	Period Luck 卦運	Monthly Star 月星
Fire 火2		4	2

SUNDAY	MONDAY	TUESDAY	WEDNESDAY	THURSDAY	FRIDAY	SATURDAY
			水6 Water · 2 Big Livestock 山天大畜 壬辰 Water Dragon **1** 廿五 · 4	金4 Metal · 3 Eliminating 澤天夬 癸巳 Water Snake **2** 廿六 · 6	金9 Metal · 4 Heaven 乾爲天 甲午 Wood Horse **3** 廿七 · 1	火7 Fire · 5 Well 水風井 乙未 Wood Goat **4** 廿八 · 6
木8 Wood · 6 Relief 雷水解 丙申 Fire Monkey **5** 廿九 · 4	金4 Metal · 7 Influence 澤山咸 丁酉 Fire Rooster **6** 正月初一 · 9	水1 Water · 8 Humility 地山謙 戊戌 Earth Dog **7** 初二 · 6	火2 Fire · 9 Observation 風地觀 己亥 Earth Pig **8** 初三 · 2	火2 Fire · 1 Increasing 風雷益 庚子 Metal Rat **9** 初四 · 9	水1 Water · 2 Dimming Light 地火明夷 辛丑 Metal Ox **10** 初五 · 3	金9 Metal · 4 Fellowship 天火同人 壬寅 Water Tiger **11** 初六 · 7
木8 Wood · 4 Marrying Maiden 雷澤歸妹 癸卯 Water Rabbit **12** 初七 · 7	木3 Wood · 5 Opposition 火澤睽 甲辰 Wood Dragon **13** 初八 · 2	火7 Fire · 6 Waiting 水天需 乙巳 Wood Snake **14** 初九 · 3	金4 Metal · 7 Great Exceeding 澤風大過 丙午 Fire Horse **15** 初十 · 3	水6 Water · 8 Poison 山風蠱 丁未 Fire Goat **16** 十一 · 7	火2 Fire · 9 Dispersing 風水渙 戊申 Earth Monkey **17** 十二 · 6	木3 Wood · 1 Travelling 火山旅 己酉 Earth Rooster **18** 十三 · 8
金9 Metal · 2 Stagnation 天地否 庚戌 Metal Dog **19** 十四 · 9	火7 Fire · 3 Alliance 水地比 辛亥 Metal Pig **20** 十五 · 7	木8 Wood · 4 Thunder 震爲雷 壬子 Water Rat **21** 十六 · 1	水6 Water · 5 Beauty 山火賁 癸丑 Water Ox **22** 十七 · 8	火7 Fire · 6 Accomplished 水火既濟 甲寅 Wood Tiger **23** 十八 · 9	水1 Water · 7 Arriving 地澤臨 乙卯 Wood Rabbit **24** 十九 · 4	金4 Metal · 8 Marsh 兌爲澤 丙辰 Fire Dragon **25** 二十 · 1
火2 Fire · 9 Small Livestock 風天小畜 丁巳 Fire Snake **26** 廿一 · 8	木3 Wood · 1 The Cauldron 火風鼎 戊午 Earth Horse **27** 廿二 · 4	水1 Water · 2 Rising 地風升 己未 Earth Goat **28** 廿三 · 2				

MARCH 1989 丁卯

Xuan Kong Element 玄空五行	山澤損 Decreasing	Period Luck 卦運	Monthly Star 月星
Water 水6		9	1

SUNDAY	MONDAY	TUESDAY	WEDNESDAY	THURSDAY	FRIDAY	SATURDAY
			1 廿四 火7 Fire Water 坎爲水 庚申 Metal Monkey 1 / 3	2 廿五 木8 Wood Lesser Exceeding 雷山小過 辛酉 Metal Rooster 3 / 4	3 廿六 金4 Metal Gathering 澤地萃 壬戌 Water Dog 4 / 5	4 廿七 水6 Water Peel 山地剝 癸亥 Water Pig 6 / 6
5 廿八 水1 Water Earth 坤爲地 甲子 Wood Rat 1 / 7	6 廿九 木3 Wood Biting 火雷噬嗑 乙丑 Wood Ox 6 / 8	7 三十 火2 Fire Family 風火家人 丙寅 Fire Tiger 4 / 9	8 二月初一 水6 Water Decreasing 山澤損 丁卯 Fire Rabbit 9 / 1	9 初二 金9 Metal Tread 天澤履 戊辰 Earth Dragon 6 / 2	10 初三 木8 Wood Great Strength 雷天大壯 己巳 Earth Snake 2 / 3	11 初四 木8 Wood Consistency 雷風恆 庚午 Metal Horse 9 / 4
12 初五 金9 Metal Litigation 天水訟 辛未 Metal Goat 3 / 5	13 初六 水1 Water Officer 地水師 壬申 Water Monkey 7 / 6	14 初七 火2 Fire Gradual Progress 風山漸 癸酉 Water Rooster 7 / 7	15 初八 火7 Fire Obstruction 水山蹇 甲戌 Wood Dog 2 / 8	16 初九 木3 Wood Advancement 火地晉 乙亥 Wood Pig 3 / 9	17 初十 水6 Water Nourish 山雷頤 丙子 Fire Rat 3 / 1	18 十一 金4 Metal Following 澤雷隨 丁丑 Fire Ox 7 / 2
19 十二 木8 Wood Abundance 雷火豐 戊寅 Earth Tiger 6 / 3	20 十三 火7 Fire Regulate 水澤節 己卯 Earth Rabbit 8 / 4	21 十四 水1 Water Unity 地天泰 庚辰 Metal Dragon 9 / 5	22 十五 木3 Wood Great Reward 火天大有 辛巳 Metal Snake 7 / 6	23 十六 火2 Fire Wind 巽爲風 壬午 Water Horse 1 / 7	24 十七 金4 Metal Trap 澤水困 癸未 Water Goat 8 / 8	25 十八 木3 Wood Not Yet Accomplished 火水未濟 甲申 Wood Monkey 9 / 9
26 十九 金9 Metal Retreat 天山遯 乙酉 Wood Rooster 4 / 1	27 二十 水6 Water Mountain 艮爲山 丙戌 Fire Dog 1 / 2	28 廿一 木8 Wood Delight 雷地豫 丁亥 Fire Pig 8 / 3	29 廿二 火7 Fire Beginning 水雷屯 戊子 Earth Rat 4 / 4	30 廿三 金9 Metal Without Wrongdoing 天雷無妄 己丑 Earth Ox 2 / 5	31 廿四 木3 Wood Fire 離爲火 庚寅 Metal Tiger 1 / 6	

APRIL 1989 戊辰

Xuan Kong Element 玄空五行	天澤履 Tread	Period Luck 卦運	Monthly Star 月星
Metal 金9		6	9

SUNDAY	MONDAY	TUESDAY	WEDNESDAY	THURSDAY	FRIDAY	SATURDAY
30 廿五 火7 Fire Water 坎爲水 庚申 Metal Monkey 1 / 9						1 廿五 火2 Fire Sincerity 風澤中孚 辛卯 Metal Rabbit 3 / 7
2 廿六 水6 Water Big Livestock 山天大畜 壬辰 Water Dragon 4 / 8	3 廿七 金4 Metal Eliminating 澤天夬 癸巳 Water Snake 6 / 9	4 廿八 金9 Metal Heaven 乾爲天 甲午 Wood Horse 1 / 1	5 廿九 火7 Fire Well 水風井 乙未 Wood Goat 6 / 2	6 三月初一 木8 Wood Relief 雷水解 丙申 Fire Monkey 4 / 3	7 初二 金4 Metal Influence 澤山咸 丁酉 Fire Rooster 9 / 4	8 初三 水1 Water Humility 地山謙 戊戌 Earth Dog 6 / 5
9 初四 火2 Fire Observation 風地觀 己亥 Earth Pig 2 / 6	10 初五 火2 Fire Increasing 風雷益 庚子 Metal Rat 9 / 7	11 初六 水1 Water Dimming Light 地火明夷 辛丑 Metal Ox 3 / 8	12 初七 金9 Metal Fellowship 天火同人 壬寅 Water Tiger 7 / 9	13 初八 木8 Wood Marrying Maiden 雷澤歸妹 癸卯 Water Rabbit 7 / 1	14 初九 木3 Wood Opposition 火澤睽 甲辰 Wood Dragon 2 / 2	15 初十 火7 Fire Waiting 水天需 乙巳 Wood Snake 3 / 3
16 十一 金4 Metal Great Exceeding 澤風大過 丙午 Fire Horse 3 / 4	17 十二 水6 Water Poison 山風蠱 丁未 Fire Goat 7 / 5	18 十三 火2 Fire Dispersing 風水渙 戊申 Earth Monkey 6 / 6	19 十四 木3 Wood Travelling 火山旅 己酉 Earth Rooster 8 / 7	20 十五 金9 Metal Stagnation 天地否 庚戌 Metal Dog 9 / 8	21 十六 火7 Fire Alliance 水地比 辛亥 Metal Pig 7 / 9	22 十七 木8 Wood Thunder 震爲雷 壬子 Water Rat 1 / 1
23 十八 水6 Water Beauty 山火賁 癸丑 Water Ox 8 / 2	24 十九 火7 Fire Accomplished 水火既濟 甲寅 Wood Tiger 9 / 3	25 二十 水1 Water Arriving 地澤臨 乙卯 Wood Rabbit 4 / 4	26 廿一 金4 Metal Marsh 兌爲澤 丙辰 Fire Dragon 1 / 5	27 廿二 火2 Fire Small Livestock 風天小畜 丁巳 Fire Snake 8 / 6	28 廿三 木3 Wood The Cauldron 火風鼎 戊午 Earth Horse 4 / 7	29 廿四 水1 Water Rising 地風升 己未 Earth Goat 2 / 8

MAY 1989 己巳

Xuan Kong Element 玄空五行	雷天大壯 Great Strength	Period Luck 卦運	Monthly Star 月星
Wood 木8		2	8

SUNDAY	MONDAY	TUESDAY	WEDNESDAY	THURSDAY	FRIDAY	SATURDAY
	木8 Wood 1 Lesser Exceeding 雷山小過 辛酉 Metal Rooster **1** 廿六 3	金4 Metal 2 Gathering 澤地萃 壬戌 Water Dog **2** 廿七 4	水6 Water 3 Peel 山地剝 癸亥 Water Pig **3** 廿八 6	水1 Water 4 Earth 坤爲地 甲子 Wood Rat **4** 廿九 1	木3 Wood 5 Biting 火雷噬嗑 乙丑 Wood Ox **5** 三月初一 6	火2 Fire 6 Family 風火家人 丙寅 Fire Tiger **6** 初二 4
水6 Water 7 Decreasing 山澤損 丁卯 Fire Rabbit **7** 初三 9	金9 Metal 8 Tread 天澤履 戊辰 Earth Dragon **8** 初四 6	木8 Wood 9 Great Strength 雷天大壯 己巳 Earth Snake **9** 初五 2	木8 Wood 1 Consistency 雷風恆 庚午 Metal Horse **10** 初六 9	金9 Metal 2 Litigation 天水訟 辛未 Metal Goat **11** 初七 3	水1 Water 3 Officer 地水師 壬申 Water Monkey **12** 初八 7	火2 Fire 4 Gradual Progress 風山漸 癸酉 Water Rooster **13** 初九 7
火7 Fire 5 Obstruction 水山蹇 甲戌 Wood Dog **14** 初十 2	木3 Wood 6 Advancement 火地晉 乙亥 Wood Pig **15** 十一 3	水6 Water 7 Nourish 山雷頤 丙子 Fire Rat **16** 十二 3	金4 Metal 8 Following 澤雷隨 丁丑 Fire Ox **17** 十三 7	木8 Wood 9 Abundance 雷火豐 戊寅 Earth Tiger **18** 十四 6	火7 Fire 1 Regulate 水澤節 己卯 Earth Rabbit **19** 十五 8	水1 Water 2 Unity 地天泰 庚辰 Metal Dragon **20** 十六 9
木3 Wood 3 Great Reward 火天大有 辛巳 Metal Snake **21** 十七 7	火2 Fire 4 Wind 巽爲風 壬午 Water Horse **22** 十八 1	金4 Metal 5 Trap 澤水困 癸未 Water Goat **23** 十九 8	木3 Wood 6 Not Yet Accomplished 火水未濟 甲申 Wood Monkey **24** 二十 9	金9 Metal 7 Retreat 天山遯 乙酉 Wood Rooster **25** 廿一 4	水6 Water 8 Mountain 艮爲山 丙戌 Fire Dog **26** 廿二 1	木8 Wood 9 Delight 雷地豫 丁亥 Fire Pig **27** 廿三 8
火7 Fire 1 Beginning 水雷屯 戊子 Earth Rat **28** 廿四 4	金9 Metal 2 Without Wrongdoing 天雷無妄 己丑 Earth Ox **29** 廿五 2	木3 Wood 3 Fire 離爲火 庚寅 Metal Tiger **30** 廿六 1	火2 Fire 4 Sincerity 風澤中孚 辛卯 Metal Rabbit **31** 廿七 3			

JUNE 1989 庚午

Xuan Kong Element 玄空五行	雷風恆 Consistency	Period Luck 卦運	Monthly Star 月星
Wood 木8		9	7

SUNDAY	MONDAY	TUESDAY	WEDNESDAY	THURSDAY	FRIDAY	SATURDAY
				水6 Water 5 Big Livestock 山天大畜 壬辰 Water Dragon **1** 廿八 4	金4 Metal 6 Eliminating 澤天夬 癸巳 Water Snake **2** 廿九 6	金9 Metal 7 Heaven 乾爲天 甲午 Wood Horse **3** 三十 1
火7 Fire 8 Well 水風井 乙未 Wood Goat **4** 五月初一 6	木8 Wood 9 Relief 雷水解 丙申 Fire Monkey **5** 初二 4	金4 Metal 1 Influence 澤山咸 丁酉 Fire Rooster **6** 初三 9	水1 Water 2 Humility 地山謙 戊戌 Earth Dog **7** 初四 6	火2 Fire 3 Observation 風地觀 己亥 Earth Pig **8** 初五 2	火2 Fire 4 Increasing 風雷益 庚子 Metal Rat **9** 初六 9	水1 Water 5 Dimming Light 地火明夷 辛丑 Metal Ox **10** 初七 3
金9 Metal 6 Fellowship 天火同人 壬寅 Water Tiger **11** 初八 7	木8 Wood 7 Marrying Maiden 雷澤歸妹 癸卯 Water Rabbit **12** 初九 7	木3 Wood 8 Opposition 火澤睽 甲辰 Wood Dragon **13** 初十 2	火7 Fire 9 Waiting 水天需 乙巳 Wood Snake **14** 十一 3	金4 Metal 1 Great Exceeding 澤風大過 丙午 Fire Horse **15** 十二 3	水6 Water 2 Poison 山風蠱 丁未 Fire Goat **16** 十三 7	火2 Fire 3 Dispersing 風水渙 戊申 Earth Monkey **17** 十四 6
木3 Wood 4 Travelling 火山旅 己酉 Earth Rooster **18** 十五 8	金9 Metal 5 Stagnation 天地否 庚戌 Metal Dog **19** 十六 9	火7 Fire 6 Alliance 水地比 辛亥 Metal Pig **20** 十七 7	木8 Wood 7/3 Thunder 震爲雷 壬子 Water Rat **21** 十八 1	水6 Water 2 Beauty 山火賁 癸丑 Water Ox **22** 十九 8	火7 Fire 1 Accomplished 水火既濟 甲寅 Wood Tiger **23** 二十 9	水1 Water 9 Arriving 地澤臨 乙卯 Wood Rabbit **24** 廿一 4
金4 Metal 8 Marsh 兑爲澤 丙辰 Fire Dragon **25** 廿二 1	火2 Fire 7 Small Livestock 風天小畜 丁巳 Fire Snake **26** 廿三 8	木3 Wood 6 The Cauldron 火風鼎 戊午 Earth Horse **27** 廿四 4	水1 Water 5 Rising 地風升 己未 Earth Goat **28** 廿五 2	火7 Fire 4 Water 坎爲水 庚申 Metal Monkey **29** 廿六 1	木8 Wood 3 Lesser Exceeding 雷山小過 辛酉 Metal Rooster **30** 廿七 3	

JULY 1989 辛未

Xuan Kong Element 玄空五行	天水訟 Litigation	Period Luck 卦運	Monthly Star 月星
Metal 金9		3	6

SUNDAY	MONDAY	TUESDAY	WEDNESDAY	THURSDAY	FRIDAY	SATURDAY
火2 Fire 9 Sincerity 辛卯 Metal Rabbit 風澤中孚 30 廿八 3	水6 Water 8 Big Livestock 壬辰 Water Dragon 山天大畜 31 廿九 4					金4 Metal 2 Gathering 壬戌 Water Dog 澤地萃 1 廿八 4
水6 Water 1 Peel 癸亥 Water Pig 山地剝 2 廿九 6	水1 Water 9 Earth 甲子 Wood Rat 坤爲地 3 六月初一 1	木3 Wood 8 Biting 乙丑 Wood Ox 火雷噬嗑 4 初二 6	火2 Fire 7 Family 丙寅 Fire Tiger 風火家人 5 初三 4	水6 Water 6 Decreasing 丁卯 Fire Rabbit 山澤損 6 初四 9	金9 Metal 5 Tread 戊辰 Earth Dragon 天澤履 7 初五 6	木8 Wood 4 Great Strength 己巳 Earth Snake 雷天大壯 8 初六 2
木8 Wood 3 Consistency 庚午 Metal Horse 雷風恆 9 初七 9	金9 Metal 2 Litigation 辛未 Metal Goat 天水訟 10 初八 3	水1 Water 1 Officer 壬申 Water Monkey 地水師 11 初九 7	火2 Fire 9 Gradual Progress 癸酉 Water Rooster 風山漸 12 初十 7	火7 Fire 8 Obstruction 甲戌 Wood Dog 水山蹇 13 十一 2	木3 Wood 7 Advancement 乙亥 Wood Pig 火地晉 14 十二 3	水6 Water 6 Nourish 丙子 Fire Rat 山雷頤 15 十三 3
金4 Metal 5 Following 丁丑 Fire Ox 澤雷隨 16 十四 7	木8 Wood 4 Abundance 戊寅 Earth Tiger 雷火豐 17 十五 6	火7 Fire 3 Regulate 己卯 Earth Rabbit 水澤節 18 十六 8	水1 Water 2 Unity 庚辰 Metal Dragon 地天泰 19 十七 9	木3 Wood 1 Great Reward 辛巳 Metal Snake 火天大有 20 十八 7	火2 Fire 9 Wind 壬午 Water Horse 巽爲風 21 十九 1	金4 Metal 8 Trap 癸未 Water Goat 澤水困 22 二十 8
木3 Wood 7 Not Yet Accomplished 甲申 Wood Monkey 火水未濟 23 廿一 9	金9 Metal 6 Retreat 乙酉 Wood Rooster 天山遯 24 廿二 4	水6 Water 5 Mountain 丙戌 Fire Dog 艮爲山 25 廿三 1	木8 Wood 4 Delight 丁亥 Fire Pig 雷地豫 26 廿四 8	火7 Fire 3 Beginning 戊子 Earth Rat 水雷屯 27 廿五 4	金9 Metal 2 Without Wrongdoing 己丑 Earth Ox 天雷無妄 28 廿六 2	木3 Wood 1 Fire 庚寅 Metal Tiger 離爲火 29 廿七 1

AUGUST 1989 壬申

Xuan Kong Element 玄空五行	地水師 Officer	Period Luck 卦運	Monthly Star 月星
Water 水1		7	5

SUNDAY	MONDAY	TUESDAY	WEDNESDAY	THURSDAY	FRIDAY	SATURDAY
		金4 Metal 7 Eliminating 癸巳 Water Snake 澤天夬 1 三十 6	金9 Metal 6 Heaven 甲午 Wood Horse 乾爲天 2 七月初一 1	火7 Fire 5 Well 乙未 Wood Goat 水風井 3 初二 6	木8 Wood 4 Relief 丙申 Fire Monkey 雷水解 4 初三 4	金4 Metal 3 Influence 丁酉 Fire Rooster 澤山咸 5 初四 9
水1 Water 2 Humility 戊戌 Earth Dog 地山謙 6 初五 6	火2 Fire 1 Observation 己亥 Earth Pig 風地觀 7 初六 2	火2 Fire 9 Increasing 庚子 Metal Rat 風雷益 8 初七 9	水1 Water 8 Dimming Light 辛丑 Metal Ox 地火明夷 9 初八 3	金9 Metal 7 Fellowship 壬寅 Water Tiger 天火同人 10 初九 7	木8 Wood 6 Marrying Maiden 癸卯 Water Rabbit 雷澤歸妹 11 初十 7	木3 Wood 5 Opposition 甲辰 Wood Dragon 火澤睽 12 十一 2
火7 Fire 4 Waiting 乙巳 Wood Snake 水天需 13 十二 3	金4 Metal 3 Great Exceeding 丙午 Fire Horse 澤風大過 14 十三 3	水6 Water 2 Poison 丁未 Fire Goat 山風蠱 15 十四 7	火2 Fire 1 Dispersing 戊申 Earth Monkey 風水渙 16 十五 6	木3 Wood 9 Travelling 己酉 Earth Rooster 火山旅 17 十六 8	金9 Metal 8 Stagnation 庚戌 Metal Dog 天地否 18 十七 9	火7 Fire 7 Alliance 辛亥 Metal Pig 水地比 19 十八 7
木8 Wood 6 Thunder 壬子 Water Rat 震爲雷 20 十九 1	水6 Water 5 Beauty 癸丑 Water Ox 山火賁 21 二十 8	火7 Fire 4 Accomplished 甲寅 Wood Tiger 水火既濟 22 廿一 9	水1 Water 3 Arriving 乙卯 Wood Rabbit 地澤臨 23 廿二 4	金4 Metal 2 Marsh 丙辰 Fire Dragon 兑爲澤 24 廿三 1	火2 Fire 1 Small Livestock 丁巳 Fire Snake 風天小畜 25 廿四 8	木3 Wood 9 The Cauldron 戊午 Earth Horse 火風鼎 26 廿五 4
水1 Water 8 Rising 己未 Earth Goat 地風升 27 廿六 2	火7 Fire 7 Water 庚申 Metal Monkey 坎爲水 28 廿七 1	木8 Wood 6 Lesser Exceeding 辛酉 Metal Rooster 雷山小過 29 廿八 3	金4 Metal 5 Gathering 壬戌 Water Dog 澤地萃 30 廿九 4	水6 Water 4 Peel 癸亥 Water Pig 山地剝 31 八月初一 6		

SEPTEMBER 1989 癸酉

Xuan Kong Element 玄空五行	風山漸 Gradual Progress	Period Luck 卦運	Monthly Star 月星
Fire 火2		7	4

SUNDAY	MONDAY	TUESDAY	WEDNESDAY	THURSDAY	FRIDAY	SATURDAY
					水1 Water 3 Earth 甲子 Wood Rat 坤爲地 1 初二 1	木3 Wood 2 Biting 乙丑 Wood Ox 火雷噬嗑 2 初三 6
火2 Fire 1 Family 丙寅 Fire Tiger 風火家人 3 初四 4	水6 Water 9 Decreasing 丁卯 Fire Rabbit 山澤損 4 初五 9	金9 Metal 8 Tread 戊辰 Earth Dragon 天澤履 5 初六 6	木8 Wood 7 Great Strength 己巳 Earth Snake 雷天大壯 6 初七 2	木8 Wood 6 Consistency 庚午 Metal Horse 雷風恆 7 初八 9	金9 Metal 5 Litigation 辛未 Metal Goat 天水訟 8 初九 3	水1 Water 4 Officer 壬申 Water Monkey 地水師 9 初十 7
火2 Fire 3 Gradual Progress 癸酉 Water Rooster 風山漸 10 十一 7	火7 Fire 2 Obstruction 甲戌 Wood Dog 水山蹇 11 十二 2	木3 Wood 1 Advancement 乙亥 Wood Pig 火地晉 12 十三 3	水6 Water 9 Nourish 丙子 Fire Rat 山雷頤 13 十四 3	金4 Metal 8 Following 丁丑 Fire Ox 澤雷隨 14 十五 7	木8 Wood 7 Abundance 戊寅 Earth Tiger 雷火豐 15 十六 6	火7 Fire 6 Regulate 己卯 Earth Rabbit 水澤節 16 十七 8
水1 Water 5 Unity 庚辰 Metal Dragon 地天泰 17 十八 9	木3 Wood 4 Great Reward 辛巳 Metal Snake 火天大有 18 十九 7	火2 Fire 3 Wind 壬午 Water Horse 巽爲風 19 二十 1	金4 Metal 2 Trap 癸未 Water Goat 澤水困 20 廿一 8	木3 Wood 1 Not Yet Accomplished 甲申 Wood Monkey 火水未濟 21 廿二 9	金9 Metal 9 Retreat 乙酉 Wood Rooster 天山遯 22 廿三 4	水6 Water 8 Mountain 丙戌 Fire Dog 艮爲山 23 廿四 1
木8 Wood 7 Delight 丁亥 Fire Pig 雷地豫 24 廿五 8	火7 Fire 6 Beginning 戊子 Earth Rat 水雷屯 25 廿六 4	金9 Metal 5 Without Wrongdoing 己丑 Earth Ox 天雷無妄 26 廿七 2	木3 Wood 4 Fire 庚寅 Metal Tiger 離爲火 27 廿八 1	火2 Fire 3 Sincerity 辛卯 Metal Rabbit 風澤中孚 28 廿九 3	水6 Water 2 Big Livestock 壬辰 Water Dragon 山天大畜 29 三十 4	金4 Metal 1 Eliminating 癸巳 Water Snake 澤天夬 30 九月初一 6

OCTOBER 1989 甲戌

Xuan Kong Element 玄空五行	水山蹇 Obstruction	Period Luck 卦運	Monthly Star 月星
Fire 火7		2	3

SUNDAY	MONDAY	TUESDAY	WEDNESDAY	THURSDAY	FRIDAY	SATURDAY
金9 Metal 9 Heaven 甲午 Wood Horse 乾爲天 1 初二 1	火7 Fire 8 Well 乙未 Wood Goat 水風井 2 初三 6	木8 Wood 7 Relief 丙申 Fire Monkey 雷水解 3 初四 4	金4 Metal 6 Influence 丁酉 Fire Rooster 澤山咸 4 初五 9	水1 Water 5 Humility 戊戌 Earth Dog 地山謙 5 初六 6	火2 Fire 4 Observation 己亥 Earth Pig 風地觀 6 初七 2	火2 Fire 3 Increasing 庚子 Metal Rat 風雷益 7 初八 9
水1 Water 2 Dimming Light 辛丑 Metal Ox 地火明夷 8 初九 3	金9 Metal 1 Fellowship 壬寅 Water Tiger 天火同人 9 初十 7	木8 Wood 9 Marrying Maiden 癸卯 Water Rabbit 雷澤歸妹 10 十一 7	木3 Wood 8 Opposition 甲辰 Wood Dragon 火澤睽 11 十二 2	火7 Fire 7 Waiting 乙巳 Wood Snake 水天需 12 十三 3	金4 Metal 6 Great Exceeding 丙午 Fire Horse 澤風大過 13 十四 3	水6 Water 5 Poison 丁未 Fire Goat 山風蠱 14 十五 7
火2 Fire 4 Dispersing 戊申 Earth Monkey 風水渙 15 十六 6	木3 Wood 3 Travelling 己酉 Earth Rooster 火山旅 16 十七 8	金9 Metal 2 Stagnation 庚戌 Metal Dog 天地否 17 十八 9	火7 Fire 1 Alliance 辛亥 Metal Pig 水地比 18 十九 7	木8 Wood 9 Thunder 壬子 Water Rat 震爲雷 19 二十 1	水6 Water 8 Beauty 癸丑 Water Ox 山火賁 20 廿一 8	火7 Fire 7 Accomplished 甲寅 Wood Tiger 水火既濟 21 廿二 9
水1 Water 6 Arriving 乙卯 Wood Rabbit 地澤臨 22 廿三 4	金4 Metal 5 Marsh 丙辰 Fire Dragon 兌爲澤 23 廿四 1	火2 Fire 4 Small Livestock 丁巳 Fire Snake 風天小畜 24 廿五 8	木3 Wood 3 The Cauldron 戊午 Earth Horse 火風鼎 25 廿六 4	水1 Water 2 Rising 己未 Earth Goat 地風升 26 廿七 2	火7 Fire 1 Water 庚申 Metal Monkey 坎爲水 27 廿八 1	木8 Wood 9 Lesser Exceeding 辛酉 Metal Rooster 雷山小過 28 廿九 3
金4 Metal 8 Gathering 壬戌 Water Dog 澤地萃 29 十月初一 4	水6 Water 7 Peel 癸亥 Water Pig 山地剝 30 初二 6	水1 Water 6 Earth 甲子 Wood Rat 坤爲地 31 初三 1				

NOVEMBER 1989 乙亥

Xuan Kong Element 玄空五行	火地晉 Advancement	Period Luck 卦運	Monthly Star 月星
Wood 木3		3	2

SUNDAY	MONDAY	TUESDAY	WEDNESDAY	THURSDAY	FRIDAY	SATURDAY
			木3 Wood 5 Biting 乙丑 Wood Ox 火雷噬嗑 1 初四 6	火2 Fire 4 Family 丙寅 Fire Tiger 風火家人 2 初五 4	水6 Water 3 Decreasing 丁卯 Fire Rabbit 山澤損 3 初六 9	金9 Metal 2 Tread 戊辰 Earth Dragon 天澤履 4 初七 6
木8 Wood 1 Great Strength 己巳 Earth Snake 雷天大壯 5 初八 2	木8 Wood 9 Consistency 庚午 Metal Horse 雷風恒 6 初九 9	金9 Metal 8 Litigation 辛未 Metal Goat 天水訟 7 初十 3	水1 Water 7 Officer 壬申 Water Monkey 地水師 8 十一 7	火2 Fire 6 Gradual Progress 癸酉 Water Rooster 風山漸 9 十二 7	火7 Fire 5 Obstruction 甲戌 Wood Dog 水山蹇 10 十三 2	木3 Wood 4 Advancement 乙亥 Wood Pig 火地晉 11 十四 3
水6 Water 3 Nourish 丙子 Fire Rat 山雷頤 12 十五 3	金4 Metal 2 Following 丁丑 Fire Ox 澤雷隨 13 十六 7	木8 Wood 1 Abundance 戊寅 Earth Tiger 雷火豐 14 十七 6	火7 Fire 9 Regulate 己卯 Earth Rabbit 水澤節 15 十八 8	水1 Water 8 Unity 庚辰 Metal Dragon 地天泰 16 十九 9	木3 Wood 7 Great Reward 辛巳 Metal Snake 火天大有 17 二十 7	火2 Fire 6 Wind 壬午 Water Horse 巽爲風 18 廿一 1
金4 Metal 5 Trap 癸未 Water Goat 澤水困 19 廿二 8	木3 Wood 4 Not Yet Accomplished 甲申 Wood Monkey 火水未濟 20 廿三 9	金9 Metal 3 Retreat 乙酉 Wood Rooster 天山遯 21 廿四 4	水6 Water 2 Mountain 丙戌 Fire Dog 艮爲山 22 廿五 1	木8 Wood 1 Delight 丁亥 Fire Pig 雷地豫 23 廿六 8	火7 Fire 9 Beginning 戊子 Earth Rat 水雷屯 24 廿七 4	金9 Metal 8 Without Wrongdoing 己丑 Earth Ox 天雷無妄 25 廿八 2
木3 Wood 7 Fire 庚寅 Metal Tiger 離爲火 26 廿九 1	火2 Fire 6 Sincerity 辛卯 Metal Rabbit 風澤中孚 27 三十 3	水6 Water 5 Big Livestock 壬辰 Water Dragon 山天大畜 28 十一月初一 4	金4 Metal 4 Eliminating 癸巳 Water Snake 澤天夬 29 初二 6	金9 Metal 3 Heaven 甲午 Wood Horse 乾爲天 30 初三 1		

DECEMBER 1989 丙子

Xuan Kong Element 玄空五行	山雷頤 Nourish	Period Luck 卦運	Monthly Star 月星
Water 水6		3	1

SUNDAY	MONDAY	TUESDAY	WEDNESDAY	THURSDAY	FRIDAY	SATURDAY
木3 Wood 2 Biting 乙丑 Wood Ox 火雷噬嗑 31 初四 6					火7 Fire 2 Well 乙未 Wood Goat 水風井 1 初四 6	木8 Wood 1 Relief 丙申 Fire Monkey 雷水解 2 初五 4
金4 Metal 9 Influence 丁酉 Fire Rooster 澤山咸 3 初六 9	水1 Water 8 Humility 戊戌 Earth Dog 地山謙 4 初七 6	火2 Fire 7 Observation 己亥 Earth Pig 風地觀 5 初八 2	火2 Fire 6 Increasing 庚子 Metal Rat 風雷益 6 初九 9	水1 Water 5 Dimming Light 辛丑 Metal Ox 地火明夷 7 初十 3	金9 Metal 4 Fellowship 壬寅 Water Tiger 天火同人 8 十一 7	木8 Wood 3 Marrying Maiden 癸卯 Water Rabbit 雷澤歸妹 9 十二 7
木3 Wood 2 Opposition 甲辰 Wood Dragon 火澤睽 10 十三 2	火7 Fire 1 Waiting 乙巳 Wood Snake 水天需 11 十四 3	金4 Metal 9 Great Exceeding 丙午 Fire Horse 澤風大過 12 十五 3	水6 Water 8 Poison 丁未 Fire Goat 山風蠱 13 十六 7	火2 Fire 7 Dispersing 戊申 Earth Monkey 風水渙 14 十七 6	木3 Wood 6 Travelling 己酉 Earth Rooster 火山旅 15 十八 8	金9 Metal 5 Stagnation 庚戌 Metal Dog 天地否 16 十九 9
火7 Fire 4 Alliance 辛亥 Metal Pig 水地比 17 二十 7	木8 Wood 3 Thunder 壬子 Water Rat 震爲雷 18 廿一 1	水6 Water 2 Beauty 癸丑 Water Ox 山火賁 19 廿二 8	火7 Fire 1 Accomplished 甲寅 Wood Tiger 水火既濟 20 廿三 9	水1 Water 9 Arriving 乙卯 Wood Rabbit 地澤臨 21 廿四 4	金4 Metal 8/2 Marsh 丙辰 Fire Dragon 兌爲澤 22 廿五 1	火2 Fire 3 Small Livestock 丁巳 Fire Snake 風天小畜 23 廿六 8
木3 Wood 4 The Cauldron 戊午 Earth Horse 火風鼎 24 廿七 4	水1 Water 5 Rising 己未 Earth Goat 地風升 25 廿八 2	火7 Fire 6 Water 庚申 Metal Monkey 坎爲水 26 廿九 1	木8 Wood 7 Lesser Exceeding 辛酉 Metal Rooster 雷山小過 27 三十 3	金4 Metal 8 Gathering 壬戌 Water Dog 澤地萃 28 十二月初一 4	水6 Water 9 Peel 癸亥 Water Pig 山地剝 29 初二 6	水1 Water 1 Earth 甲子 Wood Rat 坤爲地 30 初三 1

1990 庚午

(*Geng Wu*) Metal Horse

1990 庚午 *(Geng Wu)* Metal Horse

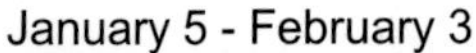

January 5 - February 3

February 4 - March 5

March 6 - April 4

April 5 - May 5

May 6 - June 5

June 6 - July 6

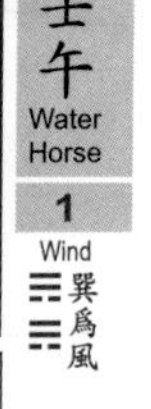

July 7 - August 7

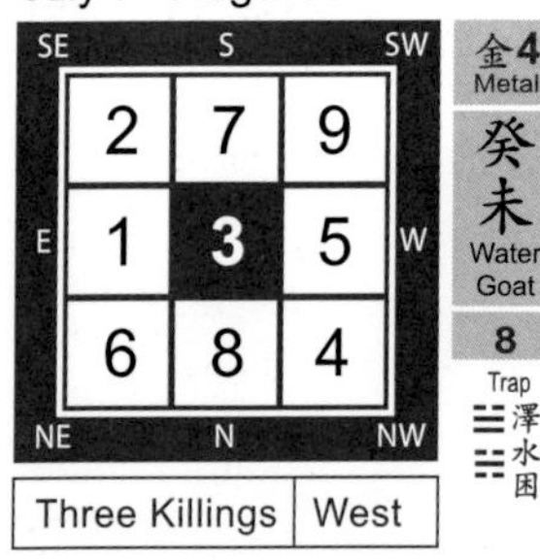

August 8 - September 7

September 8 - October 7

October 8 - November 7

November 8 - December 6

December 7 - January 5

JANUARY 1990 丁丑

Xuan Kong Element 玄空五行	澤雷隨 Following	Period Luck 卦運	Monthly Star 月星
Metal 金4		7	9

SUNDAY	MONDAY	TUESDAY	WEDNESDAY	THURSDAY	FRIDAY	SATURDAY
	1 火2 Fire · 3 Family 丙寅 Fire Tiger 風火家人 初五 4	2 水6 Water · 4 Decreasing 丁卯 Fire Rabbit 山澤損 初六 9	3 金9 Metal · 5 Tread 戊辰 Earth Dragon 天澤履 初七 6	4 木8 Wood · 6 Great Strength 己巳 Earth Snake 雷天大壯 初八 2	5 木8 Wood · 7 Consistency 庚午 Metal Horse 雷風恆 初九 9	6 金9 Metal · 8 Litigation 辛未 Metal Goat 天水訟 初十 3
7 水1 Water · 9 Officer 壬申 Water Monkey 地水師 十一 7	8 火2 Fire · 1 Gradual Progress 癸酉 Water Rooster 風山漸 十二 7	9 火7 Fire · 2 Obstruction 甲戌 Wood Dog 水山蹇 十三 2	10 木3 Wood · 3 Advancement 乙亥 Wood Pig 火地晉 十四 3	11 水6 Water · 4 Nourish 丙子 Fire Rat 山雷頤 十五 3	12 金4 Metal · 5 Following 丁丑 Fire Ox 澤雷隨 十六 7	13 木8 Wood · 6 Abundance 戊寅 Earth Tiger 雷火豐 十七 6
14 火7 Fire · 7 Regulate 己卯 Earth Rabbit 水澤節 十八 8	15 水1 Water · 8 Unity 庚辰 Metal Dragon 地天泰 十九 9	16 木3 Wood · 9 Great Reward 辛巳 Metal Snake 火天大有 二十 7	17 火2 Fire · 1 Wind 壬午 Water Horse 巽爲風 廿一 1	18 金4 Metal · 2 Trap 癸未 Water Goat 澤水困 廿二 8	19 木3 Wood · 3 Not Yet Accomplished 甲申 Wood Monkey 火水未濟 廿三 9	20 金9 Metal · 4 Retreat 乙酉 Wood Rooster 天山遯 廿四 4
21 水6 Water · 5 Mountain 丙戌 Fire Dog 艮爲山 廿五 1	22 木8 Wood · 6 Delight 丁亥 Fire Pig 雷地豫 廿六 8	23 火7 Fire · 7 Beginning 戊子 Earth Rat 水雷屯 廿七 4	24 金9 Metal · 8 Without Wrongdoing 己丑 Earth Ox 天雷無妄 廿八 2	25 木3 Wood · 9 Fire 庚寅 Metal Tiger 離爲火 廿九 1	26 火2 Fire · 1 Sincerity 辛卯 Metal Rabbit 風澤中孚 三十 3	27 水6 Water · 2 Big Livestock 壬辰 Water Dragon 山天大畜 正月初一 4
28 金4 Metal · 3 Eliminating 癸巳 Water Snake 澤天夬 初二 6	29 金9 Metal · 4 Heaven 甲午 Wood Horse 乾爲天 初三 1	30 火7 Fire · 5 Well 乙未 Wood Goat 水風井 初四 6	31 木8 Wood · 6 Relief 丙申 Fire Monkey 雷水解 初五 4			

FEBRUARY 1990 戊寅

Xuan Kong Element 玄空五行	雷火豐 Abundance	Period Luck 卦運	Monthly Star 月星
Wood 木8		6	8

SUNDAY	MONDAY	TUESDAY	WEDNESDAY	THURSDAY	FRIDAY	SATURDAY
				1 金4 Metal · 7 Influence 丁酉 Fire Rooster 澤山咸 初六 9	2 水1 Water · 8 Humility 戊戌 Earth Dog 地山謙 初七 6	3 火2 Fire · 9 Observation 己亥 Earth Pig 風地觀 初八 2
4 火2 Fire · 1 Increasing 庚子 Metal Rat 風雷益 初九 9	5 水1 Water · 2 Dimming Light 辛丑 Metal Ox 地火明夷 初十 3	6 金9 Metal · 3 Fellowship 壬寅 Water Tiger 天火同人 十一 7	7 木8 Wood · 4 Marrying Maiden 癸卯 Water Rabbit 雷澤歸妹 十二 7	8 木3 Wood · 5 Opposition 甲辰 Wood Dragon 火澤睽 十三 2	9 火7 Fire · 6 Waiting 乙巳 Wood Snake 水天需 十四 3	10 金4 Metal · 7 Great Exceeding 丙午 Fire Horse 澤風大過 十五 3
11 水6 Water · 8 Poison 丁未 Fire Goat 山風蠱 十六 7	12 火2 Fire · 9 Dispersing 戊申 Earth Monkey 風水渙 十七 6	13 木3 Wood · 1 Travelling 己酉 Earth Rooster 火山旅 十八 8	14 金9 Metal · 2 Stagnation 庚戌 Metal Dog 天地否 十九 9	15 火7 Fire · 3 Alliance 辛亥 Metal Pig 水地比 二十 7	16 木8 Wood · 4 Thunder 壬子 Water Rat 震爲雷 廿一 1	17 水6 Water · 5 Beauty 癸丑 Water Ox 山火賁 廿二 8
18 火7 Fire · 6 Accomplished 甲寅 Wood Tiger 水火既濟 廿三 9	19 水1 Water · 7 Arriving 乙卯 Wood Rabbit 地澤臨 廿四 4	20 金4 Metal · 8 Marsh 丙辰 Fire Dragon 兑爲澤 廿五 1	21 火2 Fire · 9 Small Livestock 丁巳 Fire Snake 風天小畜 廿六 8	22 木3 Wood · 1 The Cauldron 戊午 Earth Horse 火風鼎 廿七 4	23 水1 Water · 2 Rising 己未 Earth Goat 地風升 廿八 2	24 火7 Fire · 3 Water 庚申 Metal Monkey 坎爲水 廿九 1
25 木8 Wood · 4 Lesser Exceeding 辛酉 Metal Rooster 雷山小過 二月初一 3	26 金4 Metal · 5 Gathering 壬戌 Water Dog 澤地萃 初二 4	27 水6 Water · 6 Peel 癸亥 Water Pig 山地剝 初三 6	28 水1 Water · 7 Earth 甲子 Wood Rat 坤爲地 初四 1			

MARCH 1990 己卯

Xuan Kong Element 玄空五行	水澤節 Regulate	Period Luck 卦運	Monthly Star 月星
Fire 火7		8	7

SUNDAY	MONDAY	TUESDAY	WEDNESDAY	THURSDAY	FRIDAY	SATURDAY
				1 初五 木3 Wood Biting 8 火雷噬嗑 乙丑 Wood Ox 6	2 初六 火2 Fire Family 7 風火家人 丙寅 Fire Tiger 4	3 初七 水6 Water Decreasing 1 山澤損 丁卯 Fire Rabbit 9
4 初八 金9 Metal Tread 2 天澤履 戊辰 Earth Dragon 6	5 初九 木8 Wood Great Strength 3 雷天大壯 己巳 Earth Snake 2	6 初十 木8 Wood Consistency 4 雷風恆 庚午 Metal Horse 9	7 十一 金9 Metal Litigation 5 天水訟 辛未 Metal Goat 3	8 十二 水1 Water Officer 6 地水師 壬申 Water Monkey 7	9 十三 火2 Fire Gradual Progress 7 風山漸 癸酉 Water Rooster 7	10 十四 火7 Fire Obstruction 8 水山蹇 甲戌 Wood Dog 2
11 十五 木3 Wood Advancement 9 火地晉 乙亥 Wood Pig 3	12 十六 水6 Water Nourish 1 山雷頤 丙子 Fire Rat 3	13 十七 金4 Metal Following 2 澤雷隨 丁丑 Fire Ox 7	14 十八 木8 Wood Abundance 3 雷火豐 戊寅 Earth Tiger 6	15 十九 火7 Fire Regulate 4 水澤節 己卯 Earth Rabbit 8	16 二十 水1 Water Unity 5 地天泰 庚辰 Metal Dragon 9	17 廿一 木3 Wood Great Reward 6 火天大有 辛巳 Metal Snake 7
18 廿二 火2 Fire Wind 7 巽爲風 壬午 Water Horse 1	19 廿三 金4 Metal Trap 8 澤水困 癸未 Water Goat 8	20 廿四 木3 Wood Not Yet Accomplished 9 火水未濟 甲申 Wood Monkey 9	21 廿五 金9 Metal Retreat 1 天山遯 乙酉 Wood Rooster 4	22 廿六 水6 Water Mountain 2 艮爲山 丙戌 Fire Dog 1	23 廿七 木8 Wood Delight 3 雷地豫 丁亥 Fire Pig 8	24 廿八 火7 Fire Beginning 4 水雷屯 戊子 Earth Rat 4
25 廿九 金9 Metal Without Wrongdoing 5 天雷無妄 己丑 Earth Ox 2	26 三十 木3 Wood Fire 6 離爲火 庚寅 Metal Tiger 1	27 三月初一 火2 Fire Sincerity 7 風澤中孚 辛卯 Metal Rabbit 3	28 初二 水6 Water Big Livestock 8 山天大畜 壬辰 Water Dragon 4	29 初三 金4 Metal Eliminating 9 澤天夬 癸巳 Water Snake 6	30 初四 金9 Metal Heaven 1 乾爲天 甲午 Wood Horse 1	31 初五 火7 Fire Well 2 水風井 乙未 Wood Goat 6

APRIL 1990 庚辰

Xuan Kong Element 玄空五行	地天泰 Unity	Period Luck 卦運	Monthly Star 月星
Water 水1		9	6

SUNDAY	MONDAY	TUESDAY	WEDNESDAY	THURSDAY	FRIDAY	SATURDAY
1 初六 木8 Wood Relief 3 雷水解 丙申 Fire Monkey 4	2 初七 金4 Metal Influence 4 澤山咸 丁酉 Fire Rooster 9	3 初八 水1 Water Humility 5 地山謙 戊戌 Earth Dog 6	4 初九 火2 Fire Observation 6 風地觀 己亥 Earth Pig 2	5 初十 火2 Fire Increasing 7 風雷益 庚子 Metal Rat 9	6 十一 水1 Water Dimming Light 8 地火明夷 辛丑 Metal Ox 3	7 十二 金9 Metal Fellowship 9 天火同人 壬寅 Water Tiger 7
8 十三 木8 Wood Marrying Maiden 1 雷澤歸妹 癸卯 Water Rabbit 7	9 十四 木3 Wood Opposition 2 火澤睽 甲辰 Wood Dragon 2	10 十五 火7 Fire Waiting 3 水天需 乙巳 Wood Snake 3	11 十六 金4 Metal Great Exceeding 4 澤風大過 丙午 Fire Horse 3	12 十七 水6 Water Poison 5 山風蠱 丁未 Fire Goat 7	13 十八 火2 Fire Dispersing 6 風水渙 戊申 Earth Monkey 6	14 十九 木3 Wood Travelling 7 火山旅 己酉 Earth Rooster 8
15 二十 金9 Metal Stagnation 8 天地否 庚戌 Metal Dog 9	16 廿一 火7 Fire Alliance 9 水地比 辛亥 Metal Pig 7	17 廿二 木8 Wood Thunder 1 震爲雷 壬子 Water Rat 1	18 廿三 水6 Water Beauty 2 山火賁 癸丑 Water Ox 8	19 廿四 火7 Fire Accomplished 3 水火既濟 甲寅 Wood Tiger 9	20 廿五 水1 Water Arriving 4 地澤臨 乙卯 Wood Rabbit 4	21 廿六 金4 Metal Marsh 5 兌爲澤 丙辰 Fire Dragon 1
22 廿七 火2 Fire Small Livestock 6 風天小畜 丁巳 Fire Snake 8	23 廿八 木3 Wood The Cauldron 7 火風鼎 戊午 Earth Horse 4	24 廿九 水1 Water Rising 8 地風升 己未 Earth Goat 2	25 四月初一 火7 Fire Water 9 坎爲水 庚申 Metal Monkey 1	26 初二 木8 Wood Lesser Exceeding 1 雷山小過 辛酉 Metal Rooster 3	27 初三 金4 Metal Gathering 2 澤地萃 壬戌 Water Dog 4	28 初四 水6 Water Peel 3 山地剝 癸亥 Water Pig 6
29 初五 水1 Water Earth 4 坤爲地 甲子 Wood Rat 1	30 初六 木3 Wood Biting 5 火雷噬嗑 乙丑 Wood Ox 6					

MAY 1990 辛巳

Xuan Kong Element 玄空五行	火天大有 Great Reward	Period Luck 卦運	Monthly Star 月星
Wood 木3		7	5

SUNDAY	MONDAY	TUESDAY	WEDNESDAY	THURSDAY	FRIDAY	SATURDAY
		火2 Fire · 6 Family 風火家人 丙寅 Fire Tiger 4 **1** 初七	水6 Water · 7 Decreasing 山澤損 丁卯 Fire Rabbit 9 **2** 初八	金9 Metal · 8 Tread 天澤履 戊辰 Earth Dragon 6 **3** 初九	木8 Wood · 9 Great Strength 雷天大壯 己巳 Earth Snake 2 **4** 初十	木8 Wood · 1 Consistency 雷風恆 庚午 Metal Horse 9 **5** 十一
金9 Metal · 2 Litigation 天水訟 辛未 Metal Goat 3 **6** 十二	水1 Water · 3 Officer 地水師 壬申 Water Monkey 7 **7** 十三	火2 Fire · 4 Gradual Progress 風山漸 癸酉 Water Rooster 7 **8** 十四	火7 Fire · 5 Obstruction 水山蹇 甲戌 Wood Dog 2 **9** 十五	木3 Wood · 6 Advancement 火地晉 乙亥 Wood Pig 3 **10** 十六	水6 Water · 7 Nourish 山雷頤 丙子 Fire Rat 3 **11** 十七	金4 Metal · 8 Following 澤雷隨 丁丑 Fire Ox 7 **12** 十八
木8 Wood · 9 Abundance 雷火豐 戊寅 Earth Tiger 6 **13** 十九	火7 Fire · 1 Regulate 水澤節 己卯 Earth Rabbit 8 **14** 二十	水1 Water · 2 Unity 地天泰 庚辰 Metal Dragon 9 **15** 廿一	木3 Wood · 3 Great Reward 火天大有 辛巳 Metal Snake 7 **16** 廿二	火2 Fire · 4 Wind 巽爲風 壬午 Water Horse 1 **17** 廿三	金4 Metal · 5 Trap 澤水困 癸未 Water Goat 8 **18** 廿四	木3 Wood · 6 Not Yet Accomplished 火水未濟 甲申 Wood Monkey 9 **19** 廿五
金9 Metal · 7 Retreat 天山遯 乙酉 Wood Rooster 4 **20** 廿六	水6 Water · 8 Mountain 艮爲山 丙戌 Fire Dog 1 **21** 廿七	木8 Wood · 9 Delight 雷地豫 丁亥 Fire Pig 8 **22** 廿八	火7 Fire · 1 Beginning 水雷屯 戊子 Earth Rat 4 **23** 廿九	金9 Metal · 2 Without Wrongdoing 天雷無妄 己丑 Earth Ox 2 **24** 五月初一	木3 Wood · 3 Fire 離爲火 庚寅 Metal Tiger 1 **25** 初二	火2 Fire · 4 Sincerity 風澤中孚 辛卯 Metal Rabbit 3 **26** 初三
水6 Water · 5 Big Livestock 山天大畜 壬辰 Water Dragon 4 **27** 初四	金4 Metal · 6 Eliminating 澤天夬 癸巳 Water Snake 6 **28** 初五	金9 Metal · 7 Heaven 乾爲天 甲午 Wood Horse 1 **29** 初六	火7 Fire · 8 Well 水風井 乙未 Wood Goat 6 **30** 初七	木8 Wood · 9 Relief 雷水解 丙申 Fire Monkey 4 **31** 初八		

JUNE 1990 壬午

Xuan Kong Element 玄空五行	巽爲風 Wind	Period Luck 卦運	Monthly Star 月星
Fire 火2		1	4

SUNDAY	MONDAY	TUESDAY	WEDNESDAY	THURSDAY	FRIDAY	SATURDAY
					金4 Metal · 1 Influence 澤山咸 丁酉 Fire Rooster 9 **1** 初九	水1 Water · 2 Humility 地山謙 戊戌 Earth Dog 6 **2** 初十
火2 Fire · 3 Observation 風地觀 己亥 Earth Pig 2 **3** 十一	火2 Fire · 4 Increasing 風雷益 庚子 Metal Rat 9 **4** 十二	水1 Water · 5 Dimming Light 地火明夷 辛丑 Metal Ox 3 **5** 十三	金9 Metal · 6 Fellowship 天火同人 壬寅 Water Tiger 7 **6** 十四	木8 Wood · 7 Marrying Maiden 雷澤歸妹 癸卯 Water Rabbit 7 **7** 十五	木3 Wood · 8 Opposition 火澤睽 甲辰 Wood Dragon 2 **8** 十六	火7 Fire · 9 Waiting 水天需 乙巳 Wood Snake 3 **9** 十七
金4 Metal · 1 Great Exceeding 澤風大過 丙午 Fire Horse 3 **10** 十八	水6 Water · 2 Poison 山風蠱 丁未 Fire Goat 7 **11** 十九	火2 Fire · 3 Dispersing 風水渙 戊申 Earth Monkey 6 **12** 二十	木3 Wood · 4 Travelling 火山旅 己酉 Earth Rooster 8 **13** 廿一	金9 Metal · 5 Stagnation 天地否 庚戌 Metal Dog 9 **14** 廿二	火7 Fire · 6 Alliance 水地比 辛亥 Metal Pig 7 **15** 廿三	木8 Wood · 7 Thunder 震爲雷 壬子 Water Rat 1 **16** 廿四
水6 Water · 8 Beauty 山火賁 癸丑 Water Ox 8 **17** 廿五	火7 Fire · 9 Accomplished 水火既濟 甲寅 Wood Tiger 9 **18** 廿六	水1 Water · 1 Arriving 地澤臨 乙卯 Wood Rabbit 4 **19** 廿七	金4 Metal · 2 Marsh 兌爲澤 丙辰 Fire Dragon 1 **20** 廿八	火2 Fire · 3/7 Small Livestock 風天小畜 丁巳 Fire Snake 8 **21** 廿九	木3 Wood · 6 The Cauldron 火風鼎 戊午 Earth Horse 4 **22** 三十	水1 Water · 5 Rising 地風升 己未 Earth Goat 2 **23** 閏五月初一
火7 Fire · 4 Water 坎爲水 庚申 Metal Monkey 1 **24** 初二	木8 Wood · 3 Lesser Exceeding 雷山小過 辛酉 Metal Rooster 3 **25** 初三	金4 Metal · 2 Gathering 澤地萃 壬戌 Water Dog 4 **26** 初四	水6 Water · 1 Peel 山地剝 癸亥 Water Pig 6 **27** 初五	水1 Water · 9 Earth 坤爲地 甲子 Wood Rat 1 **28** 初六	木3 Wood · 8 Biting 火雷噬嗑 乙丑 Wood Ox 6 **29** 初七	火2 Fire · 7 Family 風火家人 丙寅 Fire Tiger 4 **30** 初八

JULY 1990 癸未

Xuan Kong Element 玄空五行	澤水困 Trap	Period Luck 卦運	Monthly Star 月星
Metal 金4		8	3

SUNDAY	MONDAY	TUESDAY	WEDNESDAY	THURSDAY	FRIDAY	SATURDAY
水6 Water Decreasing 6 山澤損 丁卯 Fire Rabbit **1** 初九 9	金9 Metal Tread 5 天澤履 戊辰 Earth Dragon **2** 初十 6	木8 Wood Great Strength 4 雷天大壯 己巳 Earth Snake **3** 十一 2	木8 Wood Consistency 3 雷風恒 庚午 Metal Horse **4** 十二 9	金9 Metal Litigation 2 天水訟 辛未 Metal Goat **5** 十三 3	水1 Water Officer 1 地水師 壬申 Water Monkey **6** 十四 7	火2 Fire Gradual Progress 9 風山漸 癸酉 Water Rooster **7** 十五 7
火7 Fire Obstruction 8 水山蹇 甲戌 Wood Dog **8** 十六 2	木3 Wood Advancement 7 火地晉 乙亥 Wood Pig **9** 十七 3	水6 Water Nourish 6 山雷頤 丙子 Fire Rat **10** 十八 3	金4 Metal Following 5 澤雷隨 丁丑 Fire Ox **11** 十九 7	木8 Wood Abundance 4 雷火豐 戊寅 Earth Tiger **12** 二十 6	火7 Fire Regulate 3 水澤節 己卯 Earth Rabbit **13** 廿一 8	水1 Water Unity 2 地天泰 庚辰 Metal Dragon **14** 廿二 9
木3 Wood Great Reward 1 火天大有 辛巳 Metal Snake **15** 廿三 7	火2 Fire Wind 9 巽爲風 壬午 Water Horse **16** 廿四 1	金4 Metal Trap 8 澤水困 癸未 Water Goat **17** 廿五 8	木3 Wood Not Yet Accomplished 7 火水未濟 甲申 Wood Monkey **18** 廿六 9	金9 Metal Retreat 6 天山遯 乙酉 Wood Rooster **19** 廿七 4	水6 Water Mountain 5 艮爲山 丙戌 Fire Dog **20** 廿八 1	木8 Wood Delight 4 雷地豫 丁亥 Fire Pig **21** 廿九 8
火7 Fire Beginning 3 水雷屯 戊子 Earth Rat **22** 六月初一 4	金9 Metal Without Wrongdoing 2 天雷無妄 己丑 Earth Ox **23** 初二 2	木3 Wood Fire 1 離爲火 庚寅 Metal Tiger **24** 初三 1	火2 Fire Sincerity 9 風澤中孚 辛卯 Metal Rabbit **25** 初四 3	水6 Water Big Livestock 8 山天大畜 壬辰 Water Dragon **26** 初五 4	金4 Metal Eliminating 7 澤天夬 癸巳 Water Snake **27** 初六 6	金9 Metal Heaven 6 乾爲天 甲午 Wood Horse **28** 初七 1
火7 Fire Well 5 水風井 乙未 Wood Goat **29** 初八 6	木8 Wood Relief 4 雷水解 丙申 Fire Monkey **30** 初九 4	金4 Metal Influence 3 澤山咸 丁酉 Fire Rooster **31** 初十 9				

AUGUST 1990 甲申

Xuan Kong Element 玄空五行	火水未濟 Not Yet Accomplished	Period Luck 卦運	Monthly Star 月星
Wood 木3		9	2

SUNDAY	MONDAY	TUESDAY	WEDNESDAY	THURSDAY	FRIDAY	SATURDAY
			水1 Water Humility 2 地山謙 戊戌 Earth Dog **1** 十一 6	火2 Fire Observation 1 風地觀 己亥 Earth Pig **2** 十二 2	火2 Fire Increasing 9 風雷益 庚子 Metal Rat **3** 十三 9	水1 Water Dimming Light 8 地火明夷 辛丑 Metal Ox **4** 十四 3
金9 Metal Fellowship 7 天火同人 壬寅 Water Tiger **5** 十五 7	木8 Wood Marrying Maiden 6 雷澤歸妹 癸卯 Water Rabbit **6** 十六 7	木3 Wood Opposition 5 火澤睽 甲辰 Wood Dragon **7** 十七 2	火7 Fire Waiting 4 水天需 乙巳 Wood Snake **8** 十八 3	金4 Metal Great Exceeding 3 澤風大過 丙午 Fire Horse **9** 十九 3	水6 Water Poison 2 山風蠱 丁未 Fire Goat **10** 二十 7	火2 Fire Dispersing 1 風水渙 戊申 Earth Monkey **11** 廿一 6
木3 Wood Travelling 9 火山旅 己酉 Earth Rooster **12** 廿二 8	金9 Metal Stagnation 8 天地否 庚戌 Metal Dog **13** 廿三 9	火7 Fire Alliance 7 水地比 辛亥 Metal Pig **14** 廿四 7	木8 Wood Thunder 6 震爲雷 壬子 Water Rat **15** 廿五 1	水6 Water Beauty 5 山火賁 癸丑 Water Ox **16** 廿六 8	火7 Fire Accomplished 4 水火既濟 甲寅 Wood Tiger **17** 廿七 9	水1 Water Arriving 3 地澤臨 乙卯 Wood Rabbit **18** 廿八 4
金4 Metal Marsh 2 兌爲澤 丙辰 Fire Dragon **19** 廿九 1	火2 Fire Small Livestock 1 風天小畜 丁巳 Fire Snake **20** 七月初一 8	木3 Wood The Cauldron 9 火風鼎 戊午 Earth Horse **21** 初二 4	水1 Water Rising 8 地風升 己未 Earth Goat **22** 初三 2	火7 Fire Water 7 坎爲水 庚申 Metal Monkey **23** 初四 1	木8 Wood Lesser Exceeding 6 雷山小過 辛酉 Metal Rooster **24** 初五 3	金4 Metal Gathering 5 澤地萃 壬戌 Water Dog **25** 初六 4
水6 Water Peel 4 山地剝 癸亥 Water Pig **26** 初七 6	水1 Water Earth 3 坤爲地 甲子 Wood Rat **27** 初八 1	木3 Wood Biting 2 火雷噬嗑 乙丑 Wood Ox **28** 初九 6	火2 Fire Family 1 風火家人 丙寅 Fire Tiger **29** 初十 4	水6 Water Decreasing 9 山澤損 丁卯 Fire Rabbit **30** 十一 9	金9 Metal Tread 8 天澤履 戊辰 Earth Dragon **31** 十二 6	

SEPTEMBER 1990 乙酉

Xuan Kong Element 玄空五行	天山遯 Retreat	Period Luck 卦運	Monthly Star 月星
Metal 金9		4	1

SUNDAY	MONDAY	TUESDAY	WEDNESDAY	THURSDAY	FRIDAY	SATURDAY
水1 Water · 5 Humility 地山謙 戊戌 Earth Dog 30 十二 6						木8 Wood · 7 Great Strength 雷天大壯 己巳 Earth Snake 1 十三 2
木8 Wood · 6 Consistency 雷風恆 庚午 Metal Horse 2 十四 9	金9 Metal · 5 Litigation 天水訟 辛未 Metal Goat 3 十五 3	水1 Water · 4 Officer 地水師 壬申 Water Monkey 4 十六 7	火2 Fire · 3 Gradual Progress 風山漸 癸酉 Water Rooster 5 十七 7	火7 Fire · 2 Obstruction 水山蹇 甲戌 Wood Dog 6 十八 2	木3 Wood · 1 Advancement 火地晉 乙亥 Wood Pig 7 十九 3	水6 Water · 9 Nourish 山雷頤 丙子 Fire Rat 8 二十 3
金4 Metal · 8 Following 澤雷隨 丁丑 Fire Ox 9 廿一 7	木8 Wood · 7 Abundance 雷火豐 戊寅 Earth Tiger 10 廿二 6	火7 Fire · 6 Regulate 水澤節 己卯 Earth Rabbit 11 廿三 8	水1 Water · 5 Unity 地天泰 庚辰 Metal Dragon 12 廿四 9	木3 Wood · 4 Great Reward 火天大有 辛巳 Metal Snake 13 廿五 7	火2 Fire · 3 Wind 巽為風 壬午 Water Horse 14 廿六 1	金4 Metal · 2 Trap 澤水困 癸未 Water Goat 15 廿七 8
木3 Wood · 1 Not Yet Accomplished 火水未濟 甲申 Wood Monkey 16 廿八 9	金9 Metal · 9 Retreat 天山遯 乙酉 Wood Rooster 17 廿九 4	水6 Water · 8 Mountain 艮為山 丙戌 Fire Dog 18 三十 1	木8 Wood · 7 Delight 雷地豫 丁亥 Fire Pig 19 八月初一 8	火7 Fire · 6 Beginning 水雷屯 戊子 Earth Rat 20 初二 4	金9 Metal · 5 Without Wrongdoing 天雷無妄 己丑 Earth Ox 21 初三 2	木3 Wood · 4 Fire 離為火 庚寅 Metal Tiger 22 初四 1
火2 Fire · 3 Sincerity 風澤中孚 辛卯 Metal Rabbit 23 初五 3	水6 Water · 2 Big Livestock 山天大畜 壬辰 Water Dragon 24 初六 4	金4 Metal · 1 Eliminating 澤天夬 癸巳 Water Snake 25 初七 6	金9 Metal · 9 Heaven 乾為天 甲午 Wood Horse 26 初八 1	火7 Fire · 8 Well 水風井 乙未 Wood Goat 27 初九 6	木8 Wood · 7 Relief 雷水解 丙申 Fire Monkey 28 初十 4	金4 Metal · 6 Influence 澤山咸 丁酉 Fire Rooster 29 十一 9

OCTOBER 1990 丙戌

Xuan Kong Element 玄空五行	艮為山 Mountain	Period Luck 卦運	Monthly Star 月星
Water 水6		1	9

SUNDAY	MONDAY	TUESDAY	WEDNESDAY	THURSDAY	FRIDAY	SATURDAY
	火2 Fire · 4 Observation 風地觀 己亥 Earth Pig 1 十三 2	火2 Fire · 3 Increasing 風雷益 庚子 Metal Rat 2 十四 9	水1 Water · 2 Dimming Light 地火明夷 辛丑 Metal Ox 3 十五 3	金9 Metal · 1 Fellowship 天火同人 壬寅 Water Tiger 4 十六 7	木8 Wood · 9 Marrying Maiden 雷澤歸妹 癸卯 Water Rabbit 5 十七 7	木3 Wood · 8 Opposition 火澤睽 甲辰 Wood Dragon 6 十八 2
火7 Fire · 7 Waiting 水天需 乙巳 Wood Snake 7 十九 3	金4 Metal · 6 Great Exceeding 澤風大過 丙午 Fire Horse 8 二十 3	水6 Water · 5 Poison 山風蠱 丁未 Fire Goat 9 廿一 7	火2 Fire · 4 Dispersing 風水渙 戊申 Earth Monkey 10 廿二 6	木3 Wood · 3 Travelling 火山旅 己酉 Earth Rooster 11 廿三 8	金9 Metal · 2 Stagnation 天地否 庚戌 Metal Dog 12 廿四 9	火7 Fire · 1 Alliance 水地比 辛亥 Metal Pig 13 廿五 7
木8 Wood · 9 Thunder 震為雷 壬子 Water Rat 14 廿六 1	水6 Water · 8 Beauty 山火賁 癸丑 Water Ox 15 廿七 8	火7 Fire · 7 Accomplished 水火既濟 甲寅 Wood Tiger 16 廿八 9	水1 Water · 6 Arriving 地澤臨 乙卯 Wood Rabbit 17 廿九 4	金4 Metal · 5 Marsh 兑為澤 丙辰 Fire Dragon 18 九月初一 1	火2 Fire · 4 Small Livestock 風天小畜 丁巳 Fire Snake 19 初二 8	木3 Wood · 3 The Cauldron 火風鼎 戊午 Earth Horse 20 初三 4
水1 Water · 2 Rising 地風升 己未 Earth Goat 21 初四 2	火7 Fire · 1 Water 坎為水 庚申 Metal Monkey 22 初五 1	木8 Wood · 9 Lesser Exceeding 雷山小過 辛酉 Metal Rooster 23 初六 3	金4 Metal · 8 Gathering 澤地萃 壬戌 Water Dog 24 初七 4	水6 Water · 7 Peel 山地剝 癸亥 Water Pig 25 初八 6	水1 Water · 6 Earth 坤為地 甲子 Wood Rat 26 初九 1	木3 Wood · 5 Biting 火雷噬嗑 乙丑 Wood Ox 27 初十 6
火2 Fire · 4 Family 風火家人 丙寅 Fire Tiger 28 十一 4	水6 Water · 3 Decreasing 山澤損 丁卯 Fire Rabbit 29 十二 9	金9 Metal · 2 Tread 天澤履 戊辰 Earth Dragon 30 十三 6	木8 Wood · 1 Great Strength 雷天大壯 己巳 Earth Snake 31 十四 2			

NOVEMBER 1990 丁亥

Xuan Kong Element 玄空五行	雷地豫 Delight	Period Luck 卦運	Monthly Star 月星
Wood 木8		8	8

SUNDAY	MONDAY	TUESDAY	WEDNESDAY	THURSDAY	FRIDAY	SATURDAY
				木8 Wood · Consistency · 9 庚午 Metal Horse 雷風恆 1 十五 9	金9 Metal · Litigation · 8 辛未 Metal Goat 天水訟 2 十六 3	水1 Water · Officer · 7 壬申 Water Monkey 地水師 3 十七 7
火2 Fire · Gradual Progress · 6 癸酉 Water Rooster 風山漸 4 十八 7	火7 Fire · Obstruction · 5 甲戌 Wood Dog 水山蹇 5 十九 2	木3 Wood · Advancement · 4 乙亥 Wood Pig 火地晉 6 二十 3	水6 Water · Nourish · 3 丙子 Fire Rat 山雷頤 7 廿一 3	金4 Metal · Following · 2 丁丑 Fire Ox 澤雷隨 8 廿二 7	木8 Wood · Abundance · 1 戊寅 Earth Tiger 雷火豐 9 廿三 6	火7 Fire · Regulate · 9 己卯 Earth Rabbit 水澤節 10 廿四 8
水1 Water · Unity · 8 庚辰 Metal Dragon 地天泰 11 廿五 9	木3 Wood · Great Reward · 7 辛巳 Metal Snake 火天大有 12 廿六 7	火2 Fire · Wind · 6 壬午 Water Horse 巽爲風 13 廿七 1	金4 Metal · Trap · 5 癸未 Water Goat 澤水困 14 廿八 8	木3 Wood · Not Yet Accomplished · 4 甲申 Wood Monkey 火水未濟 15 廿九 9	金9 Metal · Retreat · 3 乙酉 Wood Rooster 天山遯 16 三十 4	水6 Water · Mountain · 2 丙戌 Fire Dog 艮爲山 17 十月初一 1
木8 Wood · Delight · 1 丁亥 Fire Pig 雷地豫 18 初二 8	火7 Fire · Beginning · 9 戊子 Earth Rat 水雷屯 19 初三 4	金9 Metal · Without Wrongdoing · 8 己丑 Earth Ox 天雷無妄 20 初四 2	木3 Wood · Fire · 7 庚寅 Metal Tiger 離爲火 21 初五 1	火2 Fire · Sincerity · 6 辛卯 Metal Rabbit 風澤中孚 22 初六 3	水6 Water · Big Livestock · 5 壬辰 Water Dragon 山天大畜 23 初七 4	金4 Metal · Eliminating · 4 癸巳 Water Snake 澤天夬 24 初八 6
金9 Metal · Heaven · 3 甲午 Wood Horse 乾爲天 25 初九 1	火7 Fire · Well · 2 乙未 Wood Goat 水風井 26 初十 6	木8 Wood · Relief · 1 丙申 Fire Monkey 雷水解 27 十一 4	金4 Metal · Influence · 9 丁酉 Fire Rooster 澤山咸 28 十二 9	水1 Water · Humility · 8 戊戌 Earth Dog 地山謙 29 十三 6	火2 Fire · Observation · 7 己亥 Earth Pig 風地觀 30 十四 2	

DECEMBER 1990 戊子

Xuan Kong Element 玄空五行	水雷屯 Beginning	Period Luck 卦運	Monthly Star 月星
Fire 火7		4	7

SUNDAY	MONDAY	TUESDAY	WEDNESDAY	THURSDAY	FRIDAY	SATURDAY
木8 Wood · Great Strength · 6 己巳 Earth Snake 雷天大壯 30 十四 2	木8 Wood · Consistency · 7 庚午 Metal Horse 雷風恆 31 十五 9					火2 Fire · Increasing · 6 庚子 Metal Rat 風雷益 1 十五 9
水1 Water · Dimming Light · 5 辛丑 Metal Ox 地火明夷 2 十六 3	金9 Metal · Fellowship · 4 壬寅 Water Tiger 天火同人 3 十七 7	木8 Wood · Marrying Maiden · 3 癸卯 Water Rabbit 雷澤歸妹 4 十八 7	木3 Wood · Opposition · 2 甲辰 Wood Dragon 火澤睽 5 十九 2	火7 Fire · Waiting · 1 乙巳 Wood Snake 水天需 6 二十 3	金4 Metal · Great Exceeding · 9 丙午 Fire Horse 澤風大過 7 廿一 3	水6 Water · Poison · 8 丁未 Fire Goat 山風蠱 8 廿二 7
火2 Fire · Dispersing · 7 戊申 Earth Monkey 風水渙 9 廿三 6	木3 Wood · Travelling · 6 己酉 Earth Rooster 火山旅 10 廿四 8	金9 Metal · Stagnation · 5 庚戌 Metal Dog 天地否 11 廿五 9	火7 Fire · Alliance · 4 辛亥 Metal Pig 水地比 12 廿六 7	木8 Wood · Thunder · 3 壬子 Water Rat 震爲雷 13 廿七 1	水6 Water · Beauty · 2 癸丑 Water Ox 山火賁 14 廿八 8	火7 Fire · Accomplished · 1 甲寅 Wood Tiger 水火既濟 15 廿九 9
水1 Water · Arriving · 9 乙卯 Wood Rabbit 地澤臨 16 三十 4	金4 Metal · Marsh · 8 丙辰 Fire Dragon 兌爲澤 17 十一月初一 1	火2 Fire · Small Livestock · 7 丁巳 Fire Snake 風天小畜 18 初二 8	木3 Wood · The Cauldron · 6 戊午 Earth Horse 火風鼎 19 初三 4	水1 Water · Rising · 5 己未 Earth Goat 地風升 20 初四 2	火7 Fire · Water · 4 庚申 Metal Monkey 坎爲水 21 初五 1	木8 Wood · Lesser Exceeding · 37 辛酉 Metal Rooster 雷山小過 22 初六 3
金4 Metal · Gathering · 8 壬戌 Water Dog 澤地萃 23 初七 4	水6 Water · Peel · 9 癸亥 Water Pig 山地剝 24 初八 6	水1 Water · Earth · 1 甲子 Wood Rat 坤爲地 25 初九 1	木3 Wood · Biting · 2 乙丑 Wood Ox 火雷噬嗑 26 初十 6	火2 Fire · Family · 3 丙寅 Fire Tiger 風火家人 27 十一 4	水6 Water · Decreasing · 4 丁卯 Fire Rabbit 山澤損 28 十二 9	金9 Metal · Tread · 5 戊辰 Earth Dragon 天澤履 29 十三 6

1991 辛未

(*Xin Wei*) Metal Goat

1991 辛未 *(Xin Wei)* Metal Goat

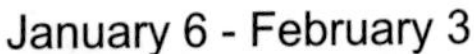

January 6 - February 3

金9 Metal · 己丑 Earth Ox · 2 Without Wrongdoing · 天雷無妄

SE	S	SW
5	1	3
4	**6**	8
9	2	7

February 4 - March 5

木3 Wood · 庚寅 Metal Tiger · 1 Fire · 離為火

SE	S	SW
4	9	2
3	**5**	7
8	1	6

March 6 - April 4

火2 Fire · 辛卯 Metal Rabbit · 3 Sincerity · 風澤中孚

SE	S	SW
3	8	1
2	**4**	6
7	9	5

April 5 - May 5

水6 Water · 壬辰 Water Dragon · 4 Big Livestock · 山天大畜

SE	S	SW
2	7	9
1	**3**	5
6	8	4

May 6 - June 5

金4 Metal · 癸巳 Water Snake · 6 Eliminating · 澤天夬

SE	S	SW
1	6	8
9	**2**	4
5	7	3

June 6 - July 6

SE	S	SW
9	5	7
8	**1**	3
4	6	2

July 7 - August 7

火7 Fire · 乙未 Wood Goat · 6 Well · 水風井

SE	S	SW
8	4	6
7	**9**	2
3	5	1

August 8 - September 7

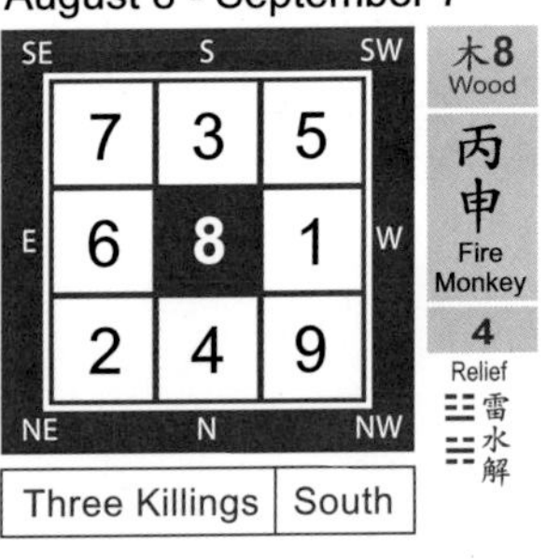

木8 Wood · 丙申 Fire Monkey · 4 Relief · 雷水解

SE	S	SW
7	3	5
6	**8**	1
2	4	9

September 8 - October 8

金4 Metal · 丁酉 Fire Rooster · 9 Influence · 澤山咸

SE	S	SW
6	2	4
5	**7**	9
1	3	8

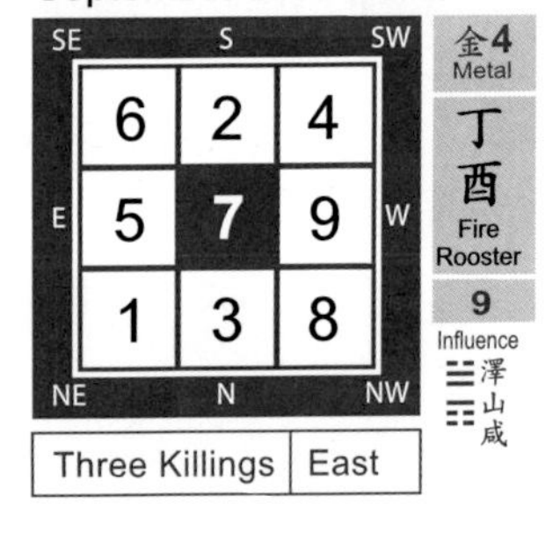

October 9 - November 7

水1 Water · 戊戌 Earth Dog · 6 Humility · 地山謙

SE	S	SW
5	1	3
4	**6**	8
9	2	7

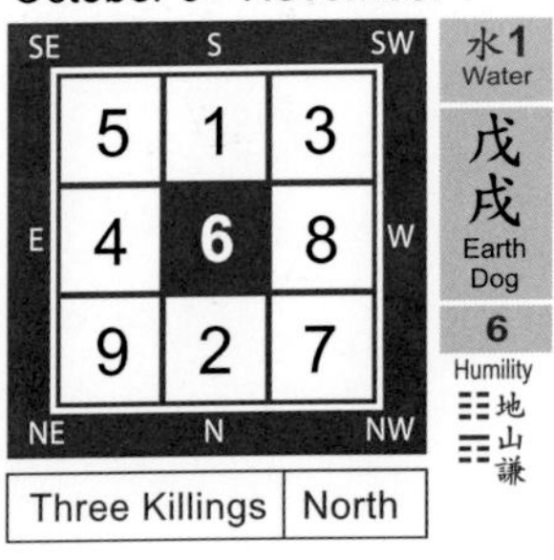

November 8 - December 6

火2 Fire · 己亥 Earth Pig · 2 Observation · 風地觀

SE	S	SW
4	9	2
3	**5**	7
8	1	6

December 7 - January 5

火2 Fire · 庚子 Metal Rat · 9 Increasing · 風雷益

SE	S	SW
3	8	1
2	**4**	6
7	9	5

JANUARY 1991 己丑

Xuan Kong Element 玄空五行	天雷無妄 Without Wrongdoing	Period Luck 卦運	Monthly Star 月星
Metal 金9		2	6

SUNDAY	MONDAY	TUESDAY	WEDNESDAY	THURSDAY	FRIDAY	SATURDAY
		金9 Metal 8 Litigation 天水訟 辛未 Metal Goat 3 1 十六	水1 Water 9 Officer 地水師 壬申 Water Monkey 7 2 十七	火2 Fire 1 Gradual Progress 風山漸 癸酉 Water Rooster 7 3 十八	火7 Fire 2 Obstruction 水山蹇 甲戌 Wood Dog 2 4 十九	木3 Wood 3 Advancement 火地晉 乙亥 Wood Pig 3 5 二十
水6 Water 4 Nourish 山雷頤 丙子 Fire Rat 3 6 廿一	金4 Metal 5 Following 澤雷隨 丁丑 Fire Ox 7 7 廿二	木8 Wood 6 Abundance 雷火豐 戊寅 Earth Tiger 6 8 廿三	火7 Fire 7 Regulate 水澤節 己卯 Earth Rabbit 8 9 廿四	水1 Water 8 Unity 地天泰 庚辰 Metal Dragon 9 10 廿五	木3 Wood 9 Great Reward 火天大有 辛巳 Metal Snake 7 11 廿六	火2 Fire 1 Wind 巽爲風 壬午 Water Horse 1 12 廿七
金4 Metal 2 Trap 澤水困 癸未 Water Goat 8 13 廿八	木3 Wood 3 Not Yet Accomplished 火水未濟 甲申 Wood Monkey 9 14 廿九	金9 Metal 4 Retreat 天山遯 乙酉 Wood Rooster 4 15 三十	水6 Water 5 Mountain 艮爲山 丙戌 Fire Dog 1 16 十二月初一	木8 Wood 6 Delight 雷地豫 丁亥 Fire Pig 8 17 初二	火7 Fire 7 Beginning 水雷屯 戊子 Earth Rat 4 18 初三	金9 Metal 8 Without Wrongdoing 天雷無妄 己丑 Earth Ox 2 19 初四
木3 Wood 9 Fire 離爲火 庚寅 Metal Tiger 1 20 初五	火2 Fire 1 Sincerity 風澤中孚 辛卯 Metal Rabbit 3 21 初六	水6 Water 2 Big Livestock 山天大畜 壬辰 Water Dragon 4 22 初七	金4 Metal 3 Eliminating 澤天夬 癸巳 Water Snake 6 23 初八	金9 Metal 4 Heaven 乾爲天 甲午 Wood Horse 1 24 初九	火7 Fire 5 Well 水風井 乙未 Wood Goat 6 25 初十	木8 Wood 6 Relief 雷水解 丙申 Fire Monkey 4 26 十一
金4 Metal 7 Influence 澤山咸 丁酉 Fire Rooster 9 27 十二	水1 Water 8 Humility 地山謙 戊戌 Earth Dog 6 28 十三	火2 Fire 9 Observation 風地觀 己亥 Earth Pig 2 29 十四	火2 Fire 1 Increasing 風雷益 庚子 Metal Rat 9 30 十五	水1 Water 2 Dimming Light 地火明夷 辛丑 Metal Ox 3 31 十六		

FEBRUARY 1991 庚寅

Xuan Kong Element 玄空五行	離爲火 Fire	Period Luck 卦運	Monthly Star 月星
Wood 木3		1	5

SUNDAY	MONDAY	TUESDAY	WEDNESDAY	THURSDAY	FRIDAY	SATURDAY
					金9 Metal 3 Fellowship 天火同人 壬寅 Water Tiger 7 1 十七	木8 Wood 4 Marrying Maiden 雷澤歸妹 癸卯 Water Rabbit 7 2 十八
木3 Wood 5 Opposition 火澤睽 甲辰 Wood Dragon 2 3 十九	火7 Fire 6 Waiting 水天需 乙巳 Wood Snake 3 4 二十	金4 Metal 7 Great Exceeding 澤風大過 丙午 Fire Horse 3 5 廿一	水6 Water 8 Poison 山風蠱 丁未 Fire Goat 7 6 廿二	火2 Fire 9 Dispersing 風水渙 戊申 Earth Monkey 6 7 廿三	木3 Wood 1 Travelling 火山旅 己酉 Earth Rooster 8 8 廿四	金9 Metal 2 Stagnation 天地否 庚戌 Metal Dog 9 9 廿五
火7 Fire 3 Alliance 水地比 辛亥 Metal Pig 7 10 廿六	木8 Wood 4 Thunder 震爲雷 壬子 Water Rat 1 11 廿七	水6 Water 5 Beauty 山火賁 癸丑 Water Ox 8 12 廿八	火7 Fire 6 Accomplished 水火既濟 甲寅 Wood Tiger 9 13 廿九	水1 Water 7 Arriving 地澤臨 乙卯 Wood Rabbit 4 14 三十	金4 Metal 8 Marsh 兑爲澤 丙辰 Fire Dragon 1 15 正月初一	火2 Fire 9 Small Livestock 風天小畜 丁巳 Fire Snake 8 16 初二
木3 Wood 1 The Cauldron 火風鼎 戊午 Earth Horse 4 17 初三	水1 Water 2 Rising 地風升 己未 Earth Goat 2 18 初四	火7 Fire 3 Water 坎爲水 庚申 Metal Monkey 1 19 初五	木8 Wood 4 Lesser Exceeding 雷山小過 辛酉 Metal Rooster 3 20 初六	金4 Metal 5 Gathering 澤地萃 壬戌 Water Dog 4 21 初七	水6 Water 6 Peel 山地剝 癸亥 Water Pig 6 22 初八	水1 Water 7 Earth 坤爲地 甲子 Wood Rat 1 23 初九
木3 Wood 8 Biting 火雷噬嗑 乙丑 Wood Ox 6 24 初十	火2 Fire 9 Family 風火家人 丙寅 Fire Tiger 4 25 十一	水6 Water 1 Decreasing 山澤損 丁卯 Fire Rabbit 9 26 十二	金9 Metal 2 Tread 天澤履 戊辰 Earth Dragon 6 27 十三	木8 Wood 3 Great Strength 雷天大壯 己巳 Earth Snake 2 28 十四		

MARCH 1991 辛卯

Xuan Kong Element 玄空五行	風澤中孚 Sincerity	Period Luck 卦運	Monthly Star 月星
Fire 火2		3	4

SUNDAY	MONDAY	TUESDAY	WEDNESDAY	THURSDAY	FRIDAY	SATURDAY
火2 Fire 7 Increasing 風雷益 庚子 Metal Rat 31 十六 9					木8 Wood 4 Consistency 雷風恆 庚午 Metal Horse 1 十五 9	金9 Metal 5 Litigation 天水訟 辛未 Metal Goat 2 十六 3
水1 Water 6 Officer 地水師 壬申 Water Monkey 3 十七 7	火2 Fire 7 Gradual Progress 風山漸 癸酉 Water Rooster 4 十八 7	火7 Fire 8 Obstruction 水山蹇 甲戌 Wood Dog 5 十九 2	木3 Wood 9 Advancement 火地晉 乙亥 Wood Pig 6 二十 3	水6 Water 1 Nourish 山雷頤 丙子 Fire Rat 7 廿一 3	金4 Metal 2 Following 澤雷隨 丁丑 Fire Ox 8 廿二 7	木8 Wood 3 Abundance 雷火豐 戊寅 Earth Tiger 9 廿三 6
火7 Fire 4 Regulate 水澤節 己卯 Earth Rabbit 10 廿四 8	水1 Water 5 Unity 地天泰 庚辰 Metal Dragon 11 廿五 9	木3 Wood 6 Great Reward 火天大有 辛巳 Metal Snake 12 廿六 7	火2 Fire 7 Wind 巽為風 壬午 Water Horse 13 廿七 1	金4 Metal 8 Trap 澤水困 癸未 Water Goat 14 廿八 8	木3 Wood 9 Not Yet Accomplished 火水未濟 甲申 Wood Monkey 15 廿九 9	金9 Metal 1 Retreat 天山遯 乙酉 Wood Rooster 16 二月初一 4
水6 Water 2 Mountain 艮為山 丙戌 Fire Dog 17 初二 1	木8 Wood 3 Delight 雷地豫 丁亥 Fire Pig 18 初三 8	火7 Fire 4 Beginning 水雷屯 戊子 Earth Rat 19 初四 4	金9 Metal 5 Without Wrongdoing 天雷無妄 己丑 Earth Ox 20 初五 2	木3 Wood 6 Fire 離為火 庚寅 Metal Tiger 21 初六 1	火2 Fire 7 Sincerity 風澤中孚 辛卯 Metal Rabbit 22 初七 3	水6 Water 8 Big Livestock 山天大畜 壬辰 Water Dragon 23 初八 4
金4 Metal 9 Eliminating 澤天夬 癸巳 Water Snake 24 初九 6	金9 Metal 1 Heaven 乾為天 甲午 Wood Horse 25 初十 1	火7 Fire 2 Well 水風井 乙未 Wood Goat 26 十一 6	木8 Wood 3 Relief 雷水解 丙申 Fire Monkey 27 十二 4	金4 Metal 4 Influence 澤山咸 丁酉 Fire Rooster 28 十三 9	水1 Water 5 Humility 地山謙 戊戌 Earth Dog 29 十四 6	火2 Fire 6 Observation 風地觀 己亥 Earth Pig 30 十五 2

APRIL 1991 壬辰

Xuan Kong Element 玄空五行	山天大畜 Big Livestock	Period Luck 卦運	Monthly Star 月星
Water 水6		4	3

SUNDAY	MONDAY	TUESDAY	WEDNESDAY	THURSDAY	FRIDAY	SATURDAY
	水1 Water 8 Dimming Light 地火明夷 辛丑 Metal Ox 1 十七 3	金9 Metal 9 Fellowship 天火同人 壬寅 Water Tiger 2 十八 7	木8 Wood 1 Marrying Maiden 雷澤歸妹 癸卯 Water Rabbit 3 十九 7	木3 Wood 2 Opposition 火澤睽 甲辰 Wood Dragon 4 二十 2	火7 Fire 3 Waiting 水天需 乙巳 Wood Snake 5 廿一 3	金4 Metal 4 Great Exceeding 澤風大過 丙午 Fire Horse 6 廿二 3
水6 Water 5 Poison 山風蠱 丁未 Fire Goat 7 廿三 7	火2 Fire 6 Dispersing 風水渙 戊申 Earth Monkey 8 廿四 6	木3 Wood 7 Travelling 火山旅 己酉 Earth Rooster 9 廿五 8	金9 Metal 8 Stagnation 天地否 庚戌 Metal Dog 10 廿六 9	火7 Fire 9 Alliance 水地比 辛亥 Metal Pig 11 廿七 7	木8 Wood 1 Thunder 震為雷 壬子 Water Rat 12 廿八 1	水6 Water 2 Beauty 山火賁 癸丑 Water Ox 13 廿九 8
火7 Fire 3 Accomplished 水火既濟 甲寅 Wood Tiger 14 三十 9	水1 Water 4 Arriving 地澤臨 乙卯 Wood Rabbit 15 三月初一 4	金4 Metal 5 Marsh 兌為澤 丙辰 Fire Dragon 16 初二 1	火2 Fire 6 Small Livestock 風天小畜 丁巳 Fire Snake 17 初三 8	木3 Wood 7 The Cauldron 火風鼎 戊午 Earth Horse 18 初四 4	水1 Water 8 Rising 地風升 己未 Earth Goat 19 初五 2	火7 Fire 9 Water 坎為水 庚申 Metal Monkey 20 初六 1
木8 Wood 1 Lesser Exceeding 雷山小過 辛酉 Metal Rooster 21 初七 3	金4 Metal 2 Gathering 澤地萃 壬戌 Water Dog 22 初八 4	水6 Water 3 Peel 山地剝 癸亥 Water Pig 23 初九 6	水1 Water 4 Earth 坤為地 甲子 Wood Rat 24 初十 1	木3 Wood 5 Biting 火雷噬嗑 乙丑 Wood Ox 25 十一 6	火2 Fire 6 Family 風火家人 丙寅 Fire Tiger 26 十二 4	水6 Water 7 Decreasing 山澤損 丁卯 Fire Rabbit 27 十三 9
金9 Metal 8 Tread 天澤履 戊辰 Earth Dragon 28 十四 6	木8 Wood 9 Great Strength 雷天大壯 己巳 Earth Snake 29 十五 2	木8 Wood 1 Consistency 雷風恆 庚午 Metal Horse 30 十六 9				

MAY 1991 癸巳

Xuan Kong Element 玄空五行	澤天夬 Eliminating	Period Luck 卦運	Monthly Star 月星
Metal 金4		6	2

SUNDAY	MONDAY	TUESDAY	WEDNESDAY	THURSDAY	FRIDAY	SATURDAY
			[2] 金9 Metal Litigation 天水訟 辛未 Metal Goat 3 **1** 十七	[3] 水1 Water Officer 地水師 壬申 Water Monkey 7 **2** 十八	[4] 火2 Fire Gradual Progress 風山漸 癸酉 Water Rooster 7 **3** 十九	[5] 火7 Fire Obstruction 水山蹇 甲戌 Wood Dog 2 **4** 二十
[6] 木3 Wood Advancement 火地晉 乙亥 Wood Pig 3 **5** 廿一	[7] 水6 Water Nourish 山雷頤 丙子 Fire Rat 3 **6** 廿二	[8] 金4 Metal Following 澤雷隨 丁丑 Fire Ox 7 **7** 廿三	[9] 木8 Wood Abundance 雷火豐 戊寅 Earth Tiger 6 **8** 廿四	[1] 火7 Fire Regulate 水澤節 己卯 Earth Rabbit 8 **9** 廿五	[2] 水1 Water Unity 地天泰 庚辰 Metal Dragon 9 **10** 廿六	[3] 木3 Wood Great Reward 火天大有 辛巳 Metal Snake 7 **11** 廿七
[4] 火2 Fire Wind 巽為風 壬午 Water Horse 1 **12** 廿八	[5] 金4 Metal Trap 澤水困 癸未 Water Goat 8 **13** 廿九	[6] 木3 Wood Not Yet Accomplished 火水未濟 甲申 Wood Monkey 9 **14** 四月初一	[7] 金9 Metal Retreat 天山遯 乙酉 Wood Rooster 4 **15** 初二	[8] 水6 Water Mountain 艮為山 丙戌 Fire Dog 1 **16** 初三	[9] 木8 Wood Delight 雷地豫 丁亥 Fire Pig 8 **17** 初四	[1] 火7 Fire Beginning 水雷屯 戊子 Earth Rat 4 **18** 初五
[2] 金9 Metal Without Wrongdoing 天雷無妄 己丑 Earth Ox 2 **19** 初六	[3] 木3 Wood Fire 離為火 庚寅 Metal Tiger 1 **20** 初七	[4] 火2 Fire Sincerity 風澤中孚 辛卯 Metal Rabbit 3 **21** 初八	[5] 水6 Water Big Livestock 山天大畜 壬辰 Water Dragon 4 **22** 初九	[6] 金4 Metal Eliminating 澤天夬 癸巳 Water Snake 6 **23** 初十	[7] 金9 Metal Heaven 乾為天 甲午 Wood Horse 1 **24** 十一	[8] 火7 Fire Well 水風井 乙未 Wood Goat 6 **25** 十二
[9] 木8 Wood Relief 雷水解 丙申 Fire Monkey 4 **26** 十三	[1] 金4 Metal Influence 澤山咸 丁酉 Fire Rooster 9 **27** 十四	[2] 水1 Water Humility 地山謙 戊戌 Earth Dog 6 **28** 十五	[3] 火2 Fire Observation 風地觀 己亥 Earth Pig 2 **29** 十六	[4] 火2 Fire Increasing 風雷益 庚子 Metal Rat 9 **30** 十七	[5] 水1 Water Dimming Light 地火明夷 辛丑 Metal Ox 3 **31** 十八	

JUNE 1991 甲午

Xuan Kong Element 玄空五行	乾為天 Heaven	Period Luck 卦運	Monthly Star 月星
Metal 金9		1	1

SUNDAY	MONDAY	TUESDAY	WEDNESDAY	THURSDAY	FRIDAY	SATURDAY
[2] 金9 Metal Litigation 天水訟 辛未 Metal Goat 3 **30** 十九						[6] 金9 Metal Fellowship 天火同人 壬寅 Water Tiger 7 **1** 十九
[7] 木8 Wood Marrying Maiden 雷澤歸妹 癸卯 Water Rabbit 7 **2** 二十	[8] 木3 Wood Opposition 火澤睽 甲辰 Wood Dragon 2 **3** 廿一	[9] 火7 Fire Waiting 水天需 乙巳 Wood Snake 3 **4** 廿二	[1] 金4 Metal Great Exceeding 澤風大過 丙午 Fire Horse 3 **5** 廿三	[2] 水6 Water Poison 山風蠱 丁未 Fire Goat 7 **6** 廿四	[3] 火2 Fire Dispersing 風水渙 戊申 Earth Monkey 6 **7** 廿五	[4] 木3 Wood Travelling 火山旅 己酉 Earth Rooster 8 **8** 廿六
[5] 金9 Metal Stagnation 天地否 庚戌 Metal Dog 9 **9** 廿七	[6] 火7 Fire Alliance 水地比 辛亥 Metal Pig 7 **10** 廿八	[7] 木8 Wood Thunder 震為雷 壬子 Water Rat 1 **11** 廿九	[8] 水6 Water Beauty 山火賁 癸丑 Water Ox 8 **12** 五月初一	[9] 火7 Fire Accomplished 水火既濟 甲寅 Wood Tiger 9 **13** 初二	[1] 水1 Water Arriving 地澤臨 乙卯 Wood Rabbit 4 **14** 初三	[2] 金4 Metal Marsh 兌為澤 丙辰 Fire Dragon 1 **15** 初四
[3] 火2 Fire Small Livestock 風天小畜 丁巳 Fire Snake 8 **16** 初五	[4] 木3 Wood The Cauldron 火風鼎 戊午 Earth Horse 4 **17** 初六	[5] 水1 Water Rising 地風升 己未 Earth Goat 2 **18** 初七	[6] 火7 Fire Water 坎為水 庚申 Metal Monkey 1 **19** 初八	[7] 木8 Wood Lesser Exceeding 雷山小過 辛酉 Metal Rooster 3 **20** 初九	[8] 金4 Metal Gathering 澤地萃 壬戌 Water Dog 4 **21** 初十	[9/1] 水6 Water Peel 山地剝 癸亥 Water Pig 6 **22** 十一
[9] 水1 Water Earth 坤為地 甲子 Wood Rat 1 **23** 十二	[8] 木3 Wood Biting 火雷噬嗑 乙丑 Wood Ox 6 **24** 十三	[7] 火2 Fire Family 風火家人 丙寅 Fire Tiger 4 **25** 十四	[6] 水6 Water Decreasing 山澤損 丁卯 Fire Rabbit 9 **26** 十五	[5] 金9 Metal Tread 天澤履 戊辰 Earth Dragon 6 **27** 十六	[4] 木8 Wood Great Strength 雷天大壯 己巳 Earth Snake 2 **28** 十七	[3] 木8 Wood Consistency 雷風恆 庚午 Metal Horse 9 **29** 十八

JULY 1991 乙未

Xuan Kong Element 玄空五行	水風井 Well	Period Luck 卦運	Monthly Star 月星
Fire 火7		6	9

SUNDAY	MONDAY	TUESDAY	WEDNESDAY	THURSDAY	FRIDAY	SATURDAY
	水1 Water 1 Officer 地水師 壬申 Water Monkey 1 二十 7	火2 Fire 9 Gradual Progress 風山漸 癸酉 Water Rooster 2 廿一 7	火7 Fire 8 Obstruction 水山蹇 甲戌 Wood Dog 3 廿二 2	木3 Wood 7 Advancement 火地晉 乙亥 Wood Pig 4 廿三 3	水6 Water 6 Nourish 山雷頤 丙子 Fire Rat 5 廿四 3	金4 Metal 5 Following 澤雷隨 丁丑 Fire Ox 6 廿五 7
木8 Wood 4 Abundance 雷火豐 戊寅 Earth Tiger 7 廿六 6	火7 Fire 3 Regulate 水澤節 己卯 Earth Rabbit 8 廿七 8	水1 Water 2 Unity 地天泰 庚辰 Metal Dragon 9 廿八 9	木3 Wood 1 Great Reward 火天大有 辛巳 Metal Snake 10 廿九 7	火2 Fire 9 Wind 巽爲風 壬午 Water Horse 11 三十 1	金4 Metal 8 Trap 澤水困 癸未 Water Goat 12 六月初一 8	木3 Wood 7 Not Yet Accomplished 火水未濟 甲申 Wood Monkey 13 初二 9
金9 Metal 6 Retreat 天山遯 乙酉 Wood Rooster 14 初三 4	水6 Water 5 Mountain 艮爲山 丙戌 Fire Dog 15 初四 1	木8 Wood 4 Delight 雷地豫 丁亥 Fire Pig 16 初五 8	火7 Fire 3 Beginning 水雷屯 戊子 Earth Rat 17 初六 4	金9 Metal 2 Without Wrongdoing 天雷無妄 己丑 Earth Ox 18 初七 2	木3 Wood 1 Fire 離爲火 庚寅 Metal Tiger 19 初八 1	火2 Fire 9 Sincerity 風澤中孚 辛卯 Metal Rabbit 20 初九 3
水6 Water 8 Big Livestock 山天大畜 壬辰 Water Dragon 21 初十 4	金4 Metal 7 Eliminating 澤天夬 癸巳 Water Snake 22 十一 6	金9 Metal 6 Heaven 乾爲天 甲午 Wood Horse 23 十二 1	火7 Fire 5 Well 水風井 乙未 Wood Goat 24 十三 6	木8 Wood 4 Relief 雷水解 丙申 Fire Monkey 25 十四 4	金4 Metal 3 Influence 澤山咸 丁酉 Fire Rooster 26 十五 9	水1 Water 2 Humility 地山謙 戊戌 Earth Dog 27 十六 6
火2 Fire 1 Observation 風地觀 己亥 Earth Pig 28 十七 2	火2 Fire 9 Increasing 風雷益 庚子 Metal Rat 29 十八 9	水1 Water 8 Dimming Light 地火明夷 辛丑 Metal Ox 30 十九 3	金9 Metal 7 Fellowship 天火同人 壬寅 Water Tiger 31 二十 7			

AUGUST 1991 丙申

Xuan Kong Element 玄空五行	雷水解 Relief	Period Luck 卦運	Monthly Star 月星
Wood 木8		4	8

SUNDAY	MONDAY	TUESDAY	WEDNESDAY	THURSDAY	FRIDAY	SATURDAY
				木8 Wood 6 Marrying Maiden 雷澤歸妹 癸卯 Water Rabbit 1 廿一 7	木3 Wood 5 Opposition 火澤睽 甲辰 Wood Dragon 2 廿二 2	火7 Fire 4 Waiting 水天需 乙巳 Wood Snake 3 廿三 3
金4 Metal 3 Great Exceeding 澤風大過 丙午 Fire Horse 4 廿四 3	水6 Water 2 Poison 山風蠱 丁未 Fire Goat 5 廿五 7	火2 Fire 1 Dispersing 風水渙 戊申 Earth Monkey 6 廿六 6	木3 Wood 9 Travelling 火山旅 己酉 Earth Rooster 7 廿七 8	金9 Metal 8 Stagnation 天地否 庚戌 Metal Dog 8 廿八 9	火7 Fire 7 Alliance 水地比 辛亥 Metal Pig 9 廿九 7	木8 Wood 6 Thunder 震爲雷 壬子 Water Rat 10 七月初一 1
水6 Water 5 Beauty 山火賁 癸丑 Water Ox 11 初二 8	火7 Fire 4 Accomplished 水火既濟 甲寅 Wood Tiger 12 初三 9	水1 Water 3 Arriving 地澤臨 乙卯 Wood Rabbit 13 初四 4	金4 Metal 2 Marsh 兌爲澤 丙辰 Fire Dragon 14 初五 1	火2 Fire 1 Small Livestock 風天小畜 丁巳 Fire Snake 15 初六 8	木3 Wood 9 The Cauldron 火風鼎 戊午 Earth Horse 16 初七 4	水1 Water 8 Rising 地風升 己未 Earth Goat 17 初八 2
火7 Fire 7 Water 坎爲水 庚申 Metal Monkey 18 初九 1	木8 Wood 6 Lesser Exceeding 雷山小過 辛酉 Metal Rooster 19 初十 3	金4 Metal 5 Gathering 澤地萃 壬戌 Water Dog 20 十一 4	水6 Water 4 Peel 山地剝 癸亥 Water Pig 21 十二 6	水1 Water 3 Earth 坤爲地 甲子 Wood Rat 22 十三 1	木3 Wood 2 Biting 火雷噬嗑 乙丑 Wood Ox 23 十四 6	火2 Fire 1 Family 風火家人 丙寅 Fire Tiger 24 十五 4
水6 Water 9 Decreasing 山澤損 丁卯 Fire Rabbit 25 十六 9	金9 Metal 8 Tread 天澤履 戊辰 Earth Dragon 26 十七 6	木8 Wood 7 Great Strength 雷天大壯 己巳 Earth Snake 27 十八 2	木8 Wood 6 Consistency 雷風恆 庚午 Metal Horse 28 十九 9	金9 Metal 5 Litigation 天水訟 辛未 Metal Goat 29 二十 3	水1 Water 4 Officer 地水師 壬申 Water Monkey 30 廿一 7	火2 Fire 3 Gradual Progress 風山漸 癸酉 Water Rooster 31 廿二 7

SEPTEMBER 1991 丁酉

Xuan Kong Element 玄空五行	澤山咸 Influence	Period Luck 卦運	Monthly Star 月星
Metal 金4		9	7

SUNDAY	MONDAY	TUESDAY	WEDNESDAY	THURSDAY	FRIDAY	SATURDAY
火7 Fire 2 Obstruction 水山蹇 甲戌 Wood Dog 1 廿三 2	木3 Wood 1 Advancement 火地晉 乙亥 Wood Pig 2 廿四 3	水6 Water 9 Nourish 山雷頤 丙子 Fire Rat 3 廿五 3	金4 Metal 8 Following 澤雷隨 丁丑 Fire Ox 4 廿六 7	木8 Wood 7 Abundance 雷火豐 戊寅 Earth Tiger 5 廿七 6	火7 Fire 6 Regulate 水澤節 己卯 Earth Rabbit 6 廿八 8	水1 Water 5 Unity 地天泰 庚辰 Metal Dragon 7 廿九 9
木3 Wood 4 Great Reward 火天大有 辛巳 Metal Snake 8 八月初一 7	火2 Fire 3 Wind 巽為風 壬午 Water Horse 9 初二 1	金4 Metal 2 Trap 澤水困 癸未 Water Goat 10 初三 8	木3 Wood 1 Not Yet Accomplished 火水未濟 甲申 Wood Monkey 11 初四 9	金9 Metal 9 Retreat 天山遯 乙酉 Wood Rooster 12 初五 4	水6 Water 8 Mountain 艮為山 丙戌 Fire Dog 13 初六 1	木8 Wood 7 Delight 雷地豫 丁亥 Fire Pig 14 初七 8
火7 Fire 6 Beginning 水雷屯 戊子 Earth Rat 15 初八 4	金9 Metal 5 Without Wrongdoing 天雷無妄 己丑 Earth Ox 16 初九 2	木3 Wood 4 Fire 離為火 庚寅 Metal Tiger 17 初十 1	火2 Fire 3 Sincerity 風澤中孚 辛卯 Metal Rabbit 18 十一 3	水6 Water 2 Big Livestock 山天大畜 壬辰 Water Dragon 19 十二 4	金4 Metal 1 Eliminating 澤天夬 癸巳 Water Snake 20 十三 6	金9 Metal 9 Heaven 乾為天 甲午 Wood Horse 21 十四 1
火7 Fire 8 Well 水風井 乙未 Wood Goat 22 十五 6	木8 Wood 7 Relief 雷水解 丙申 Fire Monkey 23 十六 4	金4 Metal 6 Influence 澤山咸 丁酉 Fire Rooster 24 十七 9	水1 Water 5 Humility 地山謙 戊戌 Earth Dog 25 十八 6	火2 Fire 4 Observation 風地觀 己亥 Earth Pig 26 十九 2	火2 Fire 3 Increasing 風雷益 庚子 Metal Rat 27 二十 9	水1 Water 2 Dimming Light 地火明夷 辛丑 Metal Ox 28 廿一 3
金9 Metal 1 Fellowship 天火同人 壬寅 Water Tiger 29 廿二 7	木8 Wood 9 Marrying Maiden 雷澤歸妹 癸卯 Water Rabbit 30 廿三 7					

OCTOBER 1991 戊戌

Xuan Kong Element 玄空五行	地山謙 Humility	Period Luck 卦運	Monthly Star 月星
Water 水1		6	6

SUNDAY	MONDAY	TUESDAY	WEDNESDAY	THURSDAY	FRIDAY	SATURDAY
		木3 Wood 8 Opposition 火澤睽 甲辰 Wood Dragon 1 廿四 2	火7 Fire 7 Waiting 水天需 乙巳 Wood Snake 2 廿五 3	金4 Metal 6 Great Exceeding 澤風大過 丙午 Fire Horse 3 廿六 3	水6 Water 5 Poison 山風蠱 丁未 Fire Goat 4 廿七 7	火2 Fire 4 Dispersing 風水渙 戊申 Earth Monkey 5 廿八 6
木3 Wood 3 Travelling 火山旅 己酉 Earth Rooster 6 廿九 8	金9 Metal 2 Stagnation 天地否 庚戌 Metal Dog 7 三十 9	火7 Fire 1 Alliance 水地比 辛亥 Metal Pig 8 九月初一 7	木8 Wood 9 Thunder 震為雷 壬子 Water Rat 9 初二 1	水6 Water 8 Beauty 山火賁 癸丑 Water Ox 10 初三 8	火7 Fire 7 Accomplished 水火既濟 甲寅 Wood Tiger 11 初四 9	水1 Water 6 Arriving 地澤臨 乙卯 Wood Rabbit 12 初五 4
金4 Metal 5 Marsh 兌為澤 丙辰 Fire Dragon 13 初六 1	火2 Fire 4 Small Livestock 風天小畜 丁巳 Fire Snake 14 初七 8	木3 Wood 3 The Cauldron 火風鼎 戊午 Earth Horse 15 初八 4	水1 Water 2 Rising 地風升 己未 Earth Goat 16 初九 2	火7 Fire 1 Water 坎為水 庚申 Metal Monkey 17 初十 1	木8 Wood 9 Lesser Exceeding 雷山小過 辛酉 Metal Rooster 18 十一 3	金4 Metal 8 Gathering 澤地萃 壬戌 Water Dog 19 十二 4
水6 Water 7 Peel 山地剝 癸亥 Water Pig 20 十三 6	水1 Water 6 Earth 坤為地 甲子 Wood Rat 21 十四 1	木3 Wood 5 Biting 火雷噬嗑 乙丑 Wood Ox 22 十五 6	火2 Fire 4 Family 風火家人 丙寅 Fire Tiger 23 十六 4	水6 Water 3 Decreasing 山澤損 丁卯 Fire Rabbit 24 十七 9	金9 Metal 2 Tread 天澤履 戊辰 Earth Dragon 25 十八 6	木8 Wood 1 Great Strength 雷天大壯 己巳 Earth Snake 26 十九 2
木8 Wood 9 Consistency 雷風恆 庚午 Metal Horse 27 二十 9	金9 Metal 8 Litigation 天水訟 辛未 Metal Goat 28 廿一 3	水1 Water 7 Officer 地水師 壬申 Water Monkey 29 廿二 7	火2 Fire 6 Gradual Progress 風山漸 癸酉 Water Rooster 30 廿三 7	火7 Fire 5 Obstruction 水山蹇 甲戌 Wood Dog 31 廿四 2		

NOVEMBER 1991 己亥

Xuan Kong Element 玄空五行	風地觀 Observation	Period Luck 卦運	Monthly Star 月星
Fire 火2		2	5

SUNDAY	MONDAY	TUESDAY	WEDNESDAY	THURSDAY	FRIDAY	SATURDAY
					木3 Wood Advancement 4 乙亥 Wood Pig 火地晉 1 廿五 3	水6 Water Nourish 3 丙子 Fire Rat 山雷頤 2 廿六 3
金4 Metal Following 2 丁丑 Fire Ox 澤雷隨 3 廿七 7	木8 Wood Abundance 1 戊寅 Earth Tiger 雷火豐 4 廿八 6	火7 Fire Regulate 9 己卯 Earth Rabbit 水澤節 5 廿九 8	水1 Water Unity 8 庚辰 Metal Dragon 地天泰 6 十月初一 9	木3 Wood Great Reward 7 辛巳 Metal Snake 火天大有 7 初二 7	火2 Fire Wind 6 壬午 Water Horse 巽爲風 8 初三 1	金4 Metal Trap 5 癸未 Water Goat 澤水困 9 初四 8
木3 Wood Not Yet Accomplished 4 甲申 Wood Monkey 火水未濟 10 初五 9	金9 Metal Retreat 3 乙酉 Wood Rooster 天山遯 11 初六 4	水6 Water Mountain 2 丙戌 Fire Dog 艮爲山 12 初七 1	木8 Wood Delight 1 丁亥 Fire Pig 雷地豫 13 初八 8	火7 Fire Beginning 9 戊子 Earth Rat 水雷屯 14 初九 4	金9 Metal Without Wrongdoing 8 己丑 Earth Ox 天雷無妄 15 初十 2	木3 Wood Fire 7 庚寅 Metal Tiger 離爲火 16 十一 1
火2 Fire Sincerity 6 辛卯 Metal Rabbit 風澤中孚 17 十二 3	水6 Water Big Livestock 5 壬辰 Water Dragon 山天大畜 18 十三 4	金4 Metal Eliminating 4 癸巳 Water Snake 澤天夬 19 十四 6	金9 Metal Heaven 3 甲午 Wood Horse 乾爲天 20 十五 1	火7 Fire Well 2 乙未 Wood Goat 水風井 21 十六 6	木8 Wood Relief 1 丙申 Fire Monkey 雷水解 22 十七 4	金4 Metal Influence 9 丁酉 Fire Rooster 澤山咸 23 十八 9
水1 Water Humility 8 戊戌 Earth Dog 地山謙 24 十九 6	火2 Fire Observation 7 己亥 Earth Pig 風地觀 25 二十 2	火2 Fire Increasing 6 庚子 Metal Rat 風雷益 26 廿一 9	水1 Water Dimming Light 5 辛丑 Metal Ox 地火明夷 27 廿二 3	金9 Metal Fellowship 4 壬寅 Water Tiger 天火同人 28 廿三 7	木8 Wood Marrying Maiden 3 癸卯 Water Rabbit 雷澤歸妹 29 廿四 7	木3 Wood Opposition 2 甲辰 Wood Dragon 火澤睽 30 廿五 2

DECEMBER 1991 庚子

Xuan Kong Element 玄空五行	風雷益 Increasing	Period Luck 卦運	Monthly Star 月星
Fire 火2		9	4

SUNDAY	MONDAY	TUESDAY	WEDNESDAY	THURSDAY	FRIDAY	SATURDAY
火7 Fire Waiting 1 乙巳 Wood Snake 水天需 1 廿六 3	金4 Metal Great Exceeding 9 丙午 Fire Horse 澤風大過 2 廿七 3	水6 Water Poison 8 丁未 Fire Goat 山風蠱 3 廿八 7	火2 Fire Dispersing 7 戊申 Earth Monkey 風水渙 4 廿九 6	木3 Wood Travelling 6 己酉 Earth Rooster 火山旅 5 三十 8	金9 Metal Stagnation 5 庚戌 Metal Dog 天地否 6 十一月初一 9	火7 Fire Alliance 4 辛亥 Metal Pig 水地比 7 初二 7
木8 Wood Thunder 3 壬子 Water Rat 震爲雷 8 初三 1	水6 Water Beauty 2 癸丑 Water Ox 山火賁 9 初四 8	火7 Fire Accomplished 1 甲寅 Wood Tiger 水火既濟 10 初五 9	水1 Water Arriving 9 乙卯 Wood Rabbit 地澤臨 11 初六 4	金4 Metal Marsh 8 丙辰 Fire Dragon 兑爲澤 12 初七 1	火2 Fire Small Livestock 7 丁巳 Fire Snake 風天小畜 13 初八 8	木3 Wood The Cauldron 6 戊午 Earth Horse 火風鼎 14 初九 4
水1 Water Rising 5 己未 Earth Goat 地風升 15 初十 2	火7 Fire Water 4 庚申 Metal Monkey 坎爲水 16 十一 1	木8 Wood Lesser Exceeding 3 辛酉 Metal Rooster 雷山小過 17 十二 3	金4 Metal Gathering 2 壬戌 Water Dog 澤地萃 18 十三 4	水6 Water Peel 1 癸亥 Water Pig 山地剝 19 十四 6	水1 Water Earth 9 甲子 Wood Rat 坤爲地 20 十五 1	木3 Wood Biting 8 乙丑 Wood Ox 火雷噬嗑 21 十六 6
火2 Fire Family 7/6 丙寅 Fire Tiger 風火家人 22 十七 4	水6 Water Decreasing 7 丁卯 Fire Rabbit 山澤損 23 十八 9	金9 Metal Tread 8 戊辰 Earth Dragon 天澤履 24 十九 6	木8 Wood Great Strength 9 己巳 Earth Snake 雷天大壯 25 二十 2	木8 Wood Consistency 1 庚午 Metal Horse 雷風恆 26 廿一 9	金9 Metal Litigation 2 辛未 Metal Goat 天水訟 27 廿二 3	水1 Water Officer 3 壬申 Water Monkey 地水師 28 廿三 7
火2 Fire Gradual Progress 4 癸酉 Water Rooster 風山漸 29 廿四 7	火7 Fire Obstruction 5 甲戌 Wood Dog 水山蹇 30 廿五 2	木3 Wood Advancement 6 乙亥 Wood Pig 火地晉 31 廿六 3				

1992 壬申

(*Ren Shen*) Water Monkey

1992 壬申 *(Ren Shen)* Water Monkey

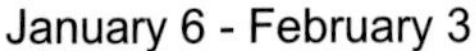

January 6 - February 3

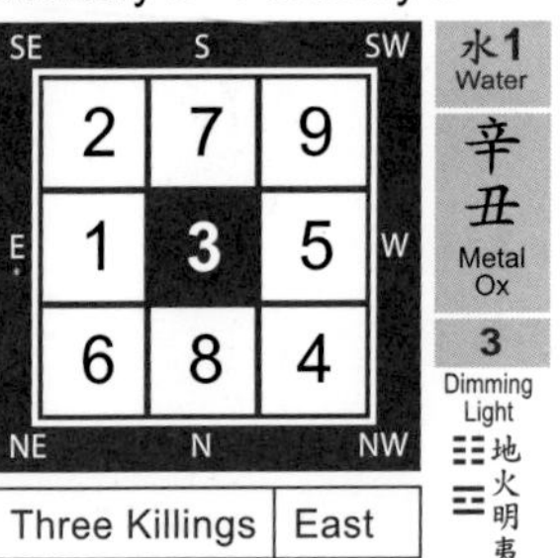

February 4 - March 4

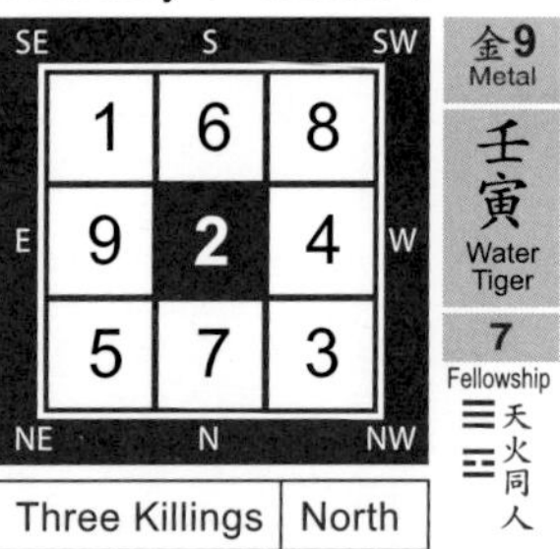

March 5 - April 3

April 4 - May 4

May 5 - June 4

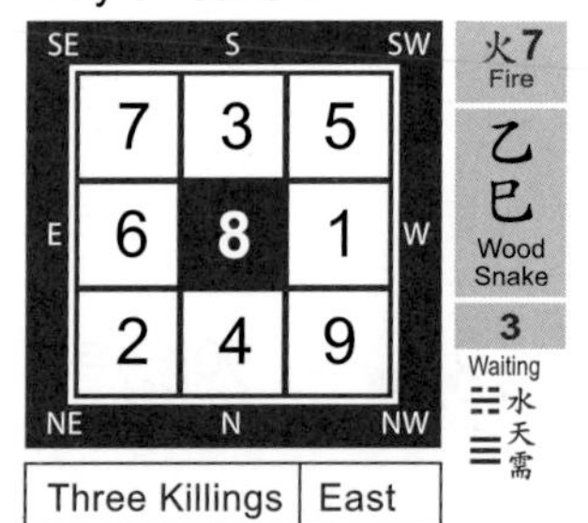

June 5 - July 6

July 7 - August 6

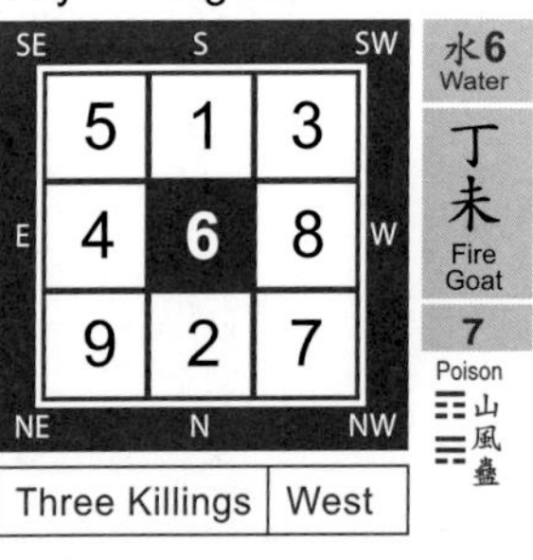

August 7 - September 6

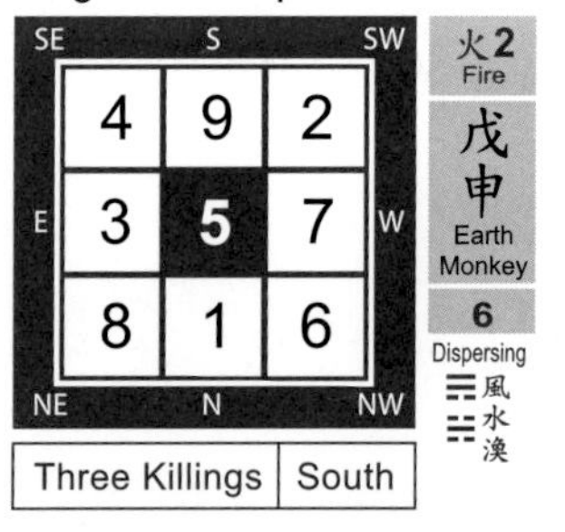

September 7 - October 7

October 8 - November 6

November 7 - December 6

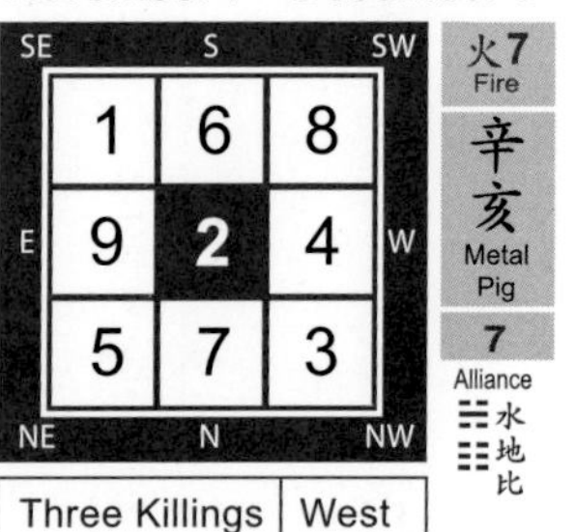

December 7 - January 4

JANUARY 1992 辛丑

Xuan Kong Element 玄空五行	地火明夷 Dimming Light	Period Luck 卦運	Monthly Star 月星
Water 水1		3	3

SUNDAY	MONDAY	TUESDAY	WEDNESDAY	THURSDAY	FRIDAY	SATURDAY
			水6 Water 7 Nourish 山雷頤 丙子 Fire Rat 3 **1** 廿七	金4 Metal 8 Following 澤雷隨 丁丑 Fire Ox 7 **2** 廿八	木8 Wood 9 Abundance 雷火豐 戊寅 Earth Tiger 6 **3** 廿九	火7 Fire 1 Regulate 水澤節 己卯 Earth Rabbit 8 **4** 三十
水1 Water 2 Unity 地天泰 庚辰 Metal Dragon 9 **5** 十二月初一	木3 Wood 3 Great Reward 火天大有 辛巳 Metal Snake 7 **6** 初二	火2 Fire 4 Wind 巽爲風 壬午 Water Horse 1 **7** 初三	金4 Metal 5 Trap 澤水困 癸未 Water Goat 8 **8** 初四	木3 Wood 6 Not Yet Accomplished 火水未濟 甲申 Wood Monkey 9 **9** 初五	金9 Metal 7 Retreat 天山遯 乙酉 Wood Rooster 4 **10** 初六	水6 Water 8 Mountain 艮爲山 丙戌 Fire Dog 1 **11** 初七
木8 Wood 9 Delight 雷地豫 丁亥 Fire Pig 8 **12** 初八	火7 Fire 1 Beginning 水雷屯 戊子 Earth Rat 4 **13** 初九	金9 Metal 2 Without Wrongdoing 天雷無妄 己丑 Earth Ox 2 **14** 初十	木3 Wood 3 Fire 離爲火 庚寅 Metal Tiger 1 **15** 十一	火2 Fire 4 Sincerity 風澤中孚 辛卯 Metal Rabbit 3 **16** 十二	水6 Water 5 Big Livestock 山天大畜 壬辰 Water Dragon 4 **17** 十三	金4 Metal 6 Eliminating 澤天夬 癸巳 Water Snake 6 **18** 十四
金9 Metal 7 Heaven 乾爲天 甲午 Wood Horse 1 **19** 十五	火7 Fire 8 Well 水風井 乙未 Wood Goat 6 **20** 十六	木8 Wood 9 Relief 雷水解 丙申 Fire Monkey 4 **21** 十七	金4 Metal 1 Influence 澤山咸 丁酉 Fire Rooster 9 **22** 十八	水1 Water 2 Humility 地山謙 戊戌 Earth Dog 6 **23** 十九	火2 Fire 3 Observation 風地觀 己亥 Earth Pig 2 **24** 二十	火2 Fire 4 Increasing 風雷益 庚子 Metal Rat 9 **25** 廿一
水1 Water 5 Dimming Light 地火明夷 辛丑 Metal Ox 3 **26** 廿二	金9 Metal 6 Fellowship 天火同人 壬寅 Water Tiger 7 **27** 廿三	木8 Wood 7 Marrying Maiden 雷澤歸妹 癸卯 Water Rabbit 7 **28** 廿四	木3 Wood 8 Opposition 火澤睽 甲辰 Wood Dragon 2 **29** 廿五	火7 Fire 9 Waiting 水天需 乙巳 Wood Snake 3 **30** 廿六	金4 Metal 1 Great Exceeding 澤風大過 丙午 Fire Horse 3 **31** 廿七	

FEBRUARY 1992 壬寅

Xuan Kong Element 玄空五行	天火同人 Fellowship	Period Luck 卦運	Monthly Star 月星
Metal 金9		7	2

SUNDAY	MONDAY	TUESDAY	WEDNESDAY	THURSDAY	FRIDAY	SATURDAY
						水6 Water 2 Poison 山風蠱 丁未 Fire Goat 7 **1** 廿八
火2 Fire 3 Dispersing 風水渙 戊申 Earth Monkey 6 **2** 廿九	木3 Wood 4 Travelling 火山旅 己酉 Earth Rooster 8 **3** 三十	金9 Metal 5 Stagnation 天地否 庚戌 Metal Dog 9 **4** 正月初一	火7 Fire 6 Alliance 水地比 辛亥 Metal Pig 7 **5** 初二	木8 Wood 7 Thunder 震爲雷 壬子 Water Rat 1 **6** 初三	水6 Water 8 Beauty 山火賁 癸丑 Water Ox 8 **7** 初四	火7 Fire 9 Accomplished 水火既濟 甲寅 Wood Tiger 9 **8** 初五
水1 Water 1 Arriving 地澤臨 乙卯 Wood Rabbit 4 **9** 初六	金4 Metal 2 Marsh 兌爲澤 丙辰 Fire Dragon 1 **10** 初七	火2 Fire 3 Small Livestock 風天小畜 丁巳 Fire Snake 8 **11** 初八	木3 Wood 4 The Cauldron 火風鼎 戊午 Earth Horse 4 **12** 初九	水1 Water 5 Rising 地風升 己未 Earth Goat 2 **13** 初十	火7 Fire 6 Water 坎爲水 庚申 Metal Monkey 1 **14** 十一	木8 Wood 7 Lesser Exceeding 雷山小過 辛酉 Metal Rooster 3 **15** 十二
金4 Metal 8 Gathering 澤地萃 壬戌 Water Dog 4 **16** 十三	水6 Water 9 Peel 山地剝 癸亥 Water Pig 6 **17** 十四	水1 Water 1 Earth 坤爲地 甲子 Wood Rat 1 **18** 十五	木3 Wood 2 Biting 火雷噬嗑 乙丑 Wood Ox 6 **19** 十六	火2 Fire 3 Family 風火家人 丙寅 Fire Tiger 4 **20** 十七	水6 Water 4 Decreasing 山澤損 丁卯 Fire Rabbit 9 **21** 十八	金9 Metal 5 Tread 天澤履 戊辰 Earth Dragon 6 **22** 十九
木8 Wood 6 Great Strength 雷天大壯 己巳 Earth Snake 2 **23** 二十	木8 Wood 7 Consistency 雷風恆 庚午 Metal Horse 9 **24** 廿一	金9 Metal 8 Litigation 天水訟 辛未 Metal Goat 3 **25** 廿二	水1 Water 9 Officer 地水師 壬申 Water Monkey 7 **26** 廿三	火2 Fire 1 Gradual Progress 風山漸 癸酉 Water Rooster 7 **27** 廿四	火7 Fire 2 Obstruction 水山蹇 甲戌 Wood Dog 2 **28** 廿五	木3 Wood 3 Advancement 火地晉 乙亥 Wood Pig 3 **29** 廿六

MARCH 1992 癸卯

Xuan Kong Element 玄空五行	雷澤歸妹 Marrying Maiden	Period Luck 卦運	Monthly Star 月星
Wood 木8		7	1

SUNDAY	MONDAY	TUESDAY	WEDNESDAY	THURSDAY	FRIDAY	SATURDAY
水6 Water 4 Nourish 山雷頤 丙子 Fire Rat 3 1 廿七	金4 Metal 5 Following 澤雷隨 丁丑 Fire Ox 7 2 廿八	木8 Wood 6 Abundance 雷火豐 戊寅 Earth Tiger 6 3 廿九	火7 Fire 7 Regulate 水澤節 己卯 Earth Rabbit 8 4 二月初一	水1 Water 8 Unity 地天泰 庚辰 Metal Dragon 9 5 初二	木3 Wood 9 Great Reward 火天大有 辛巳 Metal Snake 7 6 初三	火2 Fire 1 Wind 巽爲風 壬午 Water Horse 1 7 初四
金4 Metal 2 Trap 澤水困 癸未 Water Goat 8 8 初五	木3 Wood 3 Not Yet Accomplished 火水未濟 甲申 Wood Monkey 9 9 初六	金9 Metal 4 Retreat 天山遯 乙酉 Wood Rooster 4 10 初七	水6 Water 5 Mountain 艮爲山 丙戌 Fire Dog 1 11 初八	木8 Wood 6 Delight 雷地豫 丁亥 Fire Pig 8 12 初九	火7 Fire 7 Beginning 水雷屯 戊子 Earth Rat 4 13 初十	金9 Metal 8 Without Wrongdoing 天雷無妄 己丑 Earth Ox 2 14 十一
木3 Wood 9 Fire 離爲火 庚寅 Metal Tiger 1 15 十二	火2 Fire 1 Sincerity 風澤中孚 辛卯 Metal Rabbit 3 16 十三	水6 Water 2 Big Livestock 山天大畜 壬辰 Water Dragon 4 17 十四	金4 Metal 3 Eliminating 澤天夬 癸巳 Water Snake 6 18 十五	金9 Metal 4 Heaven 乾爲天 甲午 Wood Horse 1 19 十六	火7 Fire 5 Well 水風井 乙未 Wood Goat 6 20 十七	木8 Wood 6 Relief 雷水解 丙申 Fire Monkey 4 21 十八
金4 Metal 7 Influence 澤山咸 丁酉 Fire Rooster 9 22 十九	水1 Water 8 Humility 地山謙 戊戌 Earth Dog 6 23 二十	火2 Fire 9 Observation 風地觀 己亥 Earth Pig 2 24 廿一	火2 Fire 1 Increasing 風雷益 庚子 Metal Rat 9 25 廿二	水1 Water 2 Dimming Light 地火明夷 辛丑 Metal Ox 3 26 廿三	金9 Metal 3 Fellowship 天火同人 壬寅 Water Tiger 7 27 廿四	木8 Wood 4 Marrying Maiden 雷澤歸妹 癸卯 Water Rabbit 7 28 廿五
木3 Wood 5 Opposition 火澤睽 甲辰 Wood Dragon 2 29 廿六	火7 Fire 6 Waiting 水天需 乙巳 Wood Snake 3 30 廿七	金4 Metal 7 Great Exceeding 澤風大過 丙午 Fire Horse 3 31 廿八				

APRIL 1992 甲辰

Xuan Kong Element 玄空五行	火澤睽 Opposition	Period Luck 卦運	Monthly Star 月星
Wood 木3		2	9

SUNDAY	MONDAY	TUESDAY	WEDNESDAY	THURSDAY	FRIDAY	SATURDAY
			水6 Water 8 Poison 山風蠱 丁未 Fire Goat 7 1 廿九	火2 Fire 9 Dispersing 風水渙 戊申 Earth Monkey 6 2 三十	木3 Wood 1 Travelling 火山旅 己酉 Earth Rooster 8 3 三月初一	金9 Metal 2 Stagnation 天地否 庚戌 Metal Dog 9 4 初二
火7 Fire 3 Alliance 水地比 辛亥 Metal Pig 7 5 初三	木8 Wood 4 Thunder 震爲雷 壬子 Water Rat 1 6 初四	水6 Water 5 Beauty 山火賁 癸丑 Water Ox 8 7 初五	火7 Fire 6 Accomplished 水火既濟 甲寅 Wood Tiger 9 8 初六	水1 Water 7 Arriving 地澤臨 乙卯 Wood Rabbit 4 9 初七	金4 Metal 8 Marsh 兑爲澤 丙辰 Fire Dragon 1 10 初八	火2 Fire 9 Small Livestock 風天小畜 丁巳 Fire Snake 8 11 初九
木3 Wood 1 The Cauldron 火風鼎 戊午 Earth Horse 4 12 初十	水1 Water 2 Rising 地風升 己未 Earth Goat 2 13 十一	火7 Fire 3 Water 坎爲水 庚申 Metal Monkey 1 14 十二	木8 Wood 4 Lesser Exceeding 雷山小過 辛酉 Metal Rooster 3 15 十三	金4 Metal 5 Gathering 澤地萃 壬戌 Water Dog 4 16 十四	水6 Water 6 Peel 山地剝 癸亥 Water Pig 6 17 十五	水1 Water 7 Earth 坤爲地 甲子 Wood Rat 1 18 十六
木3 Wood 8 Biting 火雷噬嗑 乙丑 Wood Ox 6 19 十七	火2 Fire 9 Family 風火家人 丙寅 Fire Tiger 4 20 十八	水6 Water 1 Decreasing 山澤損 丁卯 Fire Rabbit 9 21 十九	金9 Metal 2 Tread 天澤履 戊辰 Earth Dragon 6 22 二十	木8 Wood 3 Great Strength 雷天大壯 己巳 Earth Snake 2 23 廿一	木8 Wood 4 Consistency 雷風恒 庚午 Metal Horse 9 24 廿二	金9 Metal 5 Litigation 天水訟 辛未 Metal Goat 3 25 廿三
水1 Water 6 Officer 地水師 壬申 Water Monkey 7 26 廿四	火2 Fire 7 Gradual Progress 風山漸 癸酉 Water Rooster 7 27 廿五	火7 Fire 8 Obstruction 水山蹇 甲戌 Wood Dog 2 28 廿六	木3 Wood 9 Advancement 火地晉 乙亥 Wood Pig 3 29 廿七	水6 Water 1 Nourish 山雷頤 丙子 Fire Rat 3 30 廿八		

MAY 1992 乙巳

Xuan Kong Element 玄空五行	水天需 Waiting	Period Luck 卦運	Monthly Star 月星
Fire 火7		3	8

SUNDAY	MONDAY	TUESDAY	WEDNESDAY	THURSDAY	FRIDAY	SATURDAY
水6 Water · 5 Poison 山風蠱 丁未 Fire Goat **31** 廿九 7					金4 Metal · 2 Following 澤雷隨 丁丑 Fire Ox **1** 廿九 7	木8 Wood · 3 Abundance 雷火豐 戊寅 Earth Tiger **2** 三十 6
火7 Fire · 4 Regulate 水澤節 己卯 Earth Rabbit **3** 四月初一 8	水1 Water · 5 Unity 地天泰 庚辰 Metal Dragon **4** 初二 9	木3 Wood · 6 Great Reward 火天大有 辛巳 Metal Snake **5** 初三 7	火2 Fire · 7 Wind 巽爲風 壬午 Water Horse **6** 初四 1	金4 Metal · 8 Trap 澤水困 癸未 Water Goat **7** 初五 8	木3 Wood · 9 Not Yet Accomplished 火水未濟 甲申 Wood Monkey **8** 初六 9	金9 Metal · 1 Retreat 天山遯 乙酉 Wood Rooster **9** 初七 4
水6 Water · 2 Mountain 艮爲山 丙戌 Fire Dog **10** 初八 1	木8 Wood · 3 Delight 雷地豫 丁亥 Fire Pig **11** 初九 8	火7 Fire · 4 Beginning 水雷屯 戊子 Earth Rat **12** 初十 4	金9 Metal · 5 Without Wrongdoing 天雷無妄 己丑 Earth Ox **13** 十一 2	木3 Wood · 6 Fire 離爲火 庚寅 Metal Tiger **14** 十二 1	火2 Fire · 7 Sincerity 風澤中孚 辛卯 Metal Rabbit **15** 十三 3	水6 Water · 8 Big Livestock 山天大畜 壬辰 Water Dragon **16** 十四 4
金4 Metal · 9 Eliminating 澤天夬 癸巳 Water Snake **17** 十五 6	金9 Metal · 1 Heaven 乾爲天 甲午 Wood Horse **18** 十六 1	火7 Fire · 2 Well 水風井 乙未 Wood Goat **19** 十七 6	木8 Wood · 3 Relief 雷水解 丙申 Fire Monkey **20** 十八 4	金4 Metal · 4 Influence 澤山咸 丁酉 Fire Rooster **21** 十九 9	水1 Water · 5 Humility 地山謙 戊戌 Earth Dog **22** 二十 6	火2 Fire · 6 Observation 風地觀 己亥 Earth Pig **23** 廿一 2
火2 Fire · 7 Increasing 風雷益 庚子 Metal Rat **24** 廿二 9	水1 Water · 8 Dimming Light 地火明夷 辛丑 Metal Ox **25** 廿三 3	金9 Metal · 9 Fellowship 天火同人 壬寅 Water Tiger **26** 廿四 7	木8 Wood · 1 Marrying Maiden 雷澤歸妹 癸卯 Water Rabbit **27** 廿五 7	木3 Wood · 2 Opposition 火澤睽 甲辰 Wood Dragon **28** 廿六 2	火7 Fire · 3 Waiting 水天需 乙巳 Wood Snake **29** 廿七 3	金4 Metal · 4 Great Exceeding 澤風大過 丙午 Fire Horse **30** 廿八 3

JUNE 1992 丙午

Xuan Kong Element 玄空五行	澤風大過 Great Exceeding	Period Luck 卦運	Monthly Star 月星
Metal 金4		3	7

SUNDAY	MONDAY	TUESDAY	WEDNESDAY	THURSDAY	FRIDAY	SATURDAY
	火2 Fire · 6 Dispersing 風水渙 戊申 Earth Monkey **1** 五月初一 6	木3 Wood · 7 Travelling 火山旅 己酉 Earth Rooster **2** 初二 8	金9 Metal · 8 Stagnation 天地否 庚戌 Metal Dog **3** 初三 9	火7 Fire · 9 Alliance 水地比 辛亥 Metal Pig **4** 初四 7	木8 Wood · 1 Thunder 震爲雷 壬子 Water Rat **5** 初五 1	水6 Water · 2 Beauty 山火賁 癸丑 Water Ox **6** 初六 8
火7 Fire · 3 Accomplished 水火既濟 甲寅 Wood Tiger **7** 初七 9	水1 Water · 4 Arriving 地澤臨 乙卯 Wood Rabbit **8** 初八 4	金4 Metal · 5 Marsh 兌爲澤 丙辰 Fire Dragon **9** 初九 1	火2 Fire · 6 Small Livestock 風天小畜 丁巳 Fire Snake **10** 初十 8	木3 Wood · 7 The Cauldron 火風鼎 戊午 Earth Horse **11** 十一 4	水1 Water · 8 Rising 地風升 己未 Earth Goat **12** 十二 2	火7 Fire · 9 Water 坎爲水 庚申 Metal Monkey **13** 十三 1
木8 Wood · 1 Lesser Exceeding 雷山小過 辛酉 Metal Rooster **14** 十四 3	金4 Metal · 2 Gathering 澤地萃 壬戌 Water Dog **15** 十五 4	水6 Water · 3 Peel 山地剝 癸亥 Water Pig **16** 十六 6	水1 Water · 4 Earth 坤爲地 甲子 Wood Rat **17** 十七 1	木3 Wood · 5 Biting 火雷噬嗑 乙丑 Wood Ox **18** 十八 6	火2 Fire · 6 Family 風火家人 丙寅 Fire Tiger **19** 十九 4	水6 Water · 7 Decreasing 山澤損 丁卯 Fire Rabbit **20** 二十 9
金9 Metal · 8/2 Tread 天澤履 戊辰 Earth Dragon **21** 廿一 6	木8 Wood · 1 Great Strength 雷天大壯 己巳 Earth Snake **22** 廿二 2	木8 Wood · 9 Consistency 雷風恆 庚午 Metal Horse **23** 廿三 9	金9 Metal · 8 Litigation 天水訟 辛未 Metal Goat **24** 廿四 3	水1 Water · 7 Officer 地水師 壬申 Water Monkey **25** 廿五 7	火2 Fire · 6 Gradual Progress 風山漸 癸酉 Water Rooster **26** 廿六 7	火7 Fire · 5 Obstruction 水山蹇 甲戌 Wood Dog **27** 廿七 2
木3 Wood · 4 Advancement 火地晉 乙亥 Wood Pig **28** 廿八 3	水6 Water · 3 Nourish 山雷頤 丙子 Fire Rat **29** 廿九 3	金4 Metal · 2 Following 澤雷隨 丁丑 Fire Ox **30** 六月初一 7				

JULY 1992 丁未

Xuan Kong Element 玄空五行	山風蠱 Poison	Period Luck 卦運	Monthly Star 月星
Water 水6		7	6

SUNDAY	MONDAY	TUESDAY	WEDNESDAY	THURSDAY	FRIDAY	SATURDAY
			木8 Wood 1 Abundance 雷火豐 戊寅 Earth Tiger 1 初二 6	火7 Fire 9 Regulate 水澤節 己卯 Earth Rabbit 2 初三 8	水1 Water 8 Unity 地天泰 庚辰 Metal Dragon 3 初四 9	木3 Wood 7 Great Reward 火天大有 辛巳 Metal Snake 4 初五 7
火2 Fire 6 Wind 巽爲風 壬午 Water Horse 5 初六 1	金4 Metal 5 Trap 澤水困 癸未 Water Goat 6 初七 8	木3 Wood 4 Not Yet Accomplished 火水未濟 甲申 Wood Monkey 7 初八 9	金9 Metal 3 Retreat 天山遯 乙酉 Wood Rooster 8 初九 4	水6 Water 2 Mountain 艮爲山 丙戌 Fire Dog 9 初十 1	木8 Wood 1 Delight 雷地豫 丁亥 Fire Pig 10 十一 8	火7 Fire 9 Beginning 水雷屯 戊子 Earth Rat 11 十二 4
金9 Metal 8 Without Wrongdoing 天雷無妄 己丑 Earth Ox 12 十三 2	木3 Wood 7 Fire 離爲火 庚寅 Metal Tiger 13 十四 1	火2 Fire 6 Sincerity 風澤中孚 辛卯 Metal Rabbit 14 十五 3	水6 Water 5 Big Livestock 山天大畜 壬辰 Water Dragon 15 十六 4	金4 Metal 4 Eliminating 澤天夬 癸巳 Water Snake 16 十七 6	金9 Metal 3 Heaven 乾爲天 甲午 Wood Horse 17 十八 1	火7 Fire 2 Well 水風井 乙未 Wood Goat 18 十九 6
木8 Wood 1 Relief 雷水解 丙申 Fire Monkey 19 二十 4	金4 Metal 9 Influence 澤山咸 丁酉 Fire Rooster 20 廿一 9	水1 Water 8 Humility 地山謙 戊戌 Earth Dog 21 廿二 6	火2 Fire 7 Observation 風地觀 己亥 Earth Pig 22 廿三 2	火2 Fire 6 Increasing 風雷益 庚子 Metal Rat 23 廿四 9	水1 Water 5 Dimming Light 地火明夷 辛丑 Metal Ox 24 廿五 3	金9 Metal 4 Fellowship 天火同人 壬寅 Water Tiger 25 廿六 7
木8 Wood 3 Marrying Maiden 雷澤歸妹 癸卯 Water Rabbit 26 廿七 7	木3 Wood 2 Opposition 火澤睽 甲辰 Wood Dragon 27 廿八 2	火7 Fire 1 Waiting 水天需 乙巳 Wood Snake 28 廿九 3	金4 Metal 9 Great Exceeding 澤風大過 丙午 Fire Horse 29 三十 3	水6 Water 8 Poison 山風蠱 丁未 Fire Goat 30 七月初一 7	火2 Fire 7 Dispersing 風水渙 戊申 Earth Monkey 31 初二 6	

AUGUST 1992 戊申

Xuan Kong Element 玄空五行	風水渙 Dispersing	Period Luck 卦運	Monthly Star 月星
Fire 火2		6	5

SUNDAY	MONDAY	TUESDAY	WEDNESDAY	THURSDAY	FRIDAY	SATURDAY
木8 Wood 4 Abundance 雷火豐 戊寅 Earth Tiger 30 初三 6	火7 Fire 3 Regulate 水澤節 己卯 Earth Rabbit 31 初四 8					木3 Wood 6 Travelling 火山旅 己酉 Earth Rooster 1 初三 8
金9 Metal 5 Stagnation 天地否 庚戌 Metal Dog 2 初四 9	火7 Fire 4 Alliance 水地比 辛亥 Metal Pig 3 初五 7	木8 Wood 3 Thunder 震爲雷 壬子 Water Rat 4 初六 1	水6 Water 2 Beauty 山火賁 癸丑 Water Ox 5 初七 8	火7 Fire 1 Accomplished 水火既濟 甲寅 Wood Tiger 6 初八 9	水1 Water 9 Arriving 地澤臨 乙卯 Wood Rabbit 7 初九 4	金4 Metal 8 Marsh 兑爲澤 丙辰 Fire Dragon 8 初十 1
火2 Fire 7 Small Livestock 風天小畜 丁巳 Fire Snake 9 十一 8	木3 Wood 6 The Cauldron 火風鼎 戊午 Earth Horse 10 十二 4	水1 Water 5 Rising 地風升 己未 Earth Goat 11 十三 2	火7 Fire 4 Water 坎爲水 庚申 Metal Monkey 12 十四 1	木8 Wood 3 Lesser Exceeding 雷山小過 辛酉 Metal Rooster 13 十五 3	金4 Metal 2 Gathering 澤地萃 壬戌 Water Dog 14 十六 4	水6 Water 1 Peel 山地剝 癸亥 Water Pig 15 十七 6
水1 Water 9 Earth 坤爲地 甲子 Wood Rat 16 十八 1	木3 Wood 8 Biting 火雷噬嗑 乙丑 Wood Ox 17 十九 6	火2 Fire 7 Family 風火家人 丙寅 Fire Tiger 18 二十 4	水6 Water 6 Decreasing 山澤損 丁卯 Fire Rabbit 19 廿一 9	金9 Metal 5 Tread 天澤履 戊辰 Earth Dragon 20 廿二 6	木8 Wood 4 Great Strength 雷天大壯 己巳 Earth Snake 21 廿三 2	木8 Wood 3 Consistency 雷風恒 庚午 Metal Horse 22 廿四 9
金9 Metal 2 Litigation 天水訟 辛未 Metal Goat 23 廿五 3	水1 Water 1 Officer 地水師 壬申 Water Monkey 24 廿六 7	火2 Fire 9 Gradual Progress 風山漸 癸酉 Water Rooster 25 廿七 7	火7 Fire 8 Obstruction 水山蹇 甲戌 Wood Dog 26 廿八 2	木3 Wood 7 Advancement 火地晉 乙亥 Wood Pig 27 廿九 3	水6 Water 6 Nourish 山雷頤 丙子 Fire Rat 28 八月初一 3	金4 Metal 5 Following 澤雷隨 丁丑 Fire Ox 29 初二 7

SEPTEMBER 1992 己酉

Xuan Kong Element 玄空五行	火山旅 Travelling	Period Luck 卦運	Monthly Star 月星
Wood 木3		8	4

SUNDAY	MONDAY	TUESDAY	WEDNESDAY	THURSDAY	FRIDAY	SATURDAY
		水1 Water Unity [2] 地天泰 庚辰 Metal Dragon 1 初五 9	木3 Wood Great Reward [1] 火天大有 辛巳 Metal Snake 2 初六 7	火2 Fire Wind [8] 巽爲風 壬午 Water Horse 3 初七 1	金4 Metal Trap [8] 澤水困 癸未 Water Goat 4 初八 8	木3 Wood Not Yet Accomplished [7] 火水未濟 甲申 Wood Monkey 5 初九 9
金9 Metal Retreat [6] 天山遯 乙酉 Wood Rooster 6 初十 4	水6 Water Mountain [5] 艮爲山 丙戌 Fire Dog 7 十一 1	木8 Wood Delight [4] 雷地豫 丁亥 Fire Pig 8 十二 8	火7 Fire Beginning [3] 水雷屯 戊子 Earth Rat 9 十三 4	金9 Metal Without Wrongdoing [2] 天雷無妄 己丑 Earth Ox 10 十四 2	木3 Wood Fire [1] 離爲火 庚寅 Metal Tiger 11 十五 1	火2 Fire Sincerity [9] 風澤中孚 辛卯 Metal Rabbit 12 十六 3
水6 Water Big Livestock [8] 山天大畜 壬辰 Water Dragon 13 十七 4	金4 Metal Eliminating [7] 澤天夬 癸巳 Water Snake 14 十八 6	金9 Metal Heaven [6] 乾爲天 甲午 Wood Horse 15 十九 1	火7 Fire Well [5] 水風井 乙未 Wood Goat 16 二十 6	木8 Wood Relief [4] 雷水解 丙申 Fire Monkey 17 廿一 4	金4 Metal Influence [3] 澤山咸 丁酉 Fire Rooster 18 廿二 9	水1 Water Humility [2] 地山謙 戊戌 Earth Dog 19 廿三 6
火2 Fire Observation [1] 風地觀 己亥 Earth Pig 20 廿四 2	火2 Fire Increasing [9] 風雷益 庚子 Metal Rat 21 廿五 9	水1 Water Dimming Light [8] 地火明夷 辛丑 Metal Ox 22 廿六 3	金9 Metal Fellowship [7] 天火同人 壬寅 Water Tiger 23 廿七 7	木8 Wood Marrying Maiden [6] 雷澤歸妹 癸卯 Water Rabbit 24 廿八 7	木3 Wood Opposition [5] 火澤睽 甲辰 Wood Dragon 25 廿九 2	火7 Fire Waiting [4] 水天需 乙巳 Wood Snake 26 九月初一 3
金4 Metal Great Exceeding [3] 澤風大過 丙午 Fire Horse 27 初二 3	水6 Water Poison [2] 山風蠱 丁未 Fire Goat 28 初三 7	火2 Fire Dispersing [1] 風水渙 戊申 Earth Monkey 29 初四 6	木3 Wood Travelling [9] 火山旅 己酉 Earth Rooster 30 初五 8			

OCTOBER 1992 庚戌

Xuan Kong Element 玄空五行	天地否 Stagnation	Period Luck 卦運	Monthly Star 月星
Metal 金9		9	3

SUNDAY	MONDAY	TUESDAY	WEDNESDAY	THURSDAY	FRIDAY	SATURDAY
				金9 Metal Stagnation [8] 天地否 庚戌 Metal Dog 1 初六 9	火7 Fire Alliance [7] 水地比 辛亥 Metal Pig 2 初七 7	木8 Wood Thunder [6] 震爲雷 壬子 Water Rat 3 初八 1
水6 Water Beauty [5] 山火賁 癸丑 Water Ox 4 初九 8	火7 Fire Accomplished [4] 水火既濟 甲寅 Wood Tiger 5 初十 9	水1 Water Arriving [3] 地澤臨 乙卯 Wood Rabbit 6 十一 4	金4 Metal Marsh [2] 兌爲澤 丙辰 Fire Dragon 7 十二 1	火2 Fire Small Livestock [1] 風天小畜 丁巳 Fire Snake 8 十三 8	木3 Wood The Cauldron [9] 火風鼎 戊午 Earth Horse 9 十四 4	水1 Water Rising [8] 地風升 己未 Earth Goat 10 十五 2
火7 Fire Water [7] 坎爲水 庚申 Metal Monkey 11 十六 1	木8 Wood Lesser Exceeding [6] 雷山小過 辛酉 Metal Rooster 12 十七 3	金4 Metal Gathering [5] 澤地萃 壬戌 Water Dog 13 十八 4	水6 Water Peel [4] 山地剝 癸亥 Water Pig 14 十九 6	水1 Water Earth [3] 坤爲地 甲子 Wood Rat 15 二十 1	木3 Wood Biting [2] 火雷噬嗑 乙丑 Wood Ox 16 廿一 6	火2 Fire Family [1] 風火家人 丙寅 Fire Tiger 17 廿二 4
水6 Water Decreasing [9] 山澤損 丁卯 Fire Rabbit 18 廿三 9	金9 Metal Tread [8] 天澤履 戊辰 Earth Dragon 19 廿四 6	木8 Wood Great Strength [7] 雷天大壯 己巳 Earth Snake 20 廿五 2	木8 Wood Consistency [6] 雷風恆 庚午 Metal Horse 21 廿六 9	金9 Metal Litigation [5] 天水訟 辛未 Metal Goat 22 廿七 3	水1 Water Officer [4] 地水師 壬申 Water Monkey 23 廿八 7	火2 Fire Gradual Progress [3] 風山漸 癸酉 Water Rooster 24 廿九 7
火7 Fire Obstruction [2] 水山蹇 甲戌 Wood Dog 25 三十 2	木3 Wood Advancement [1] 火地晉 乙亥 Wood Pig 26 十月初一 3	水6 Water Nourish [9] 山雷頤 丙子 Fire Rat 27 初二 3	金4 Metal Following [8] 澤雷隨 丁丑 Fire Ox 28 初三 7	木8 Wood Abundance [7] 雷火豐 戊寅 Earth Tiger 29 初四 6	火7 Fire Regulate [6] 水澤節 己卯 Earth Rabbit 30 初五 8	水1 Water Unity [5] 地天泰 庚辰 Metal Dragon 31 初六 9

NOVEMBER 1992 辛亥

Xuan Kong Element 玄空五行	水地比 Alliance	Period Luck 卦運	Monthly Star 月星
Fire 火7		7	2

SUNDAY	MONDAY	TUESDAY	WEDNESDAY	THURSDAY	FRIDAY	SATURDAY
木3 Wood 4 Great Reward 辛巳 Metal Snake 火天大有 1 初七 7	火2 Fire 3 Wind 壬午 Water Horse 巽為風 2 初八 1	金4 Metal 2 Trap 癸未 Water Goat 澤水困 3 初九 8	木3 Wood 1 Not Yet Accomplished 甲申 Wood Monkey 火水未濟 4 初十 9	金9 Metal 9 Retreat 乙酉 Wood Rooster 天山遯 5 十一 4	水6 Water 8 Mountain 丙戌 Fire Dog 艮為山 6 十二 1	木8 Wood 7 Delight 丁亥 Fire Pig 雷地豫 7 十三 8
火7 Fire 6 Beginning 戊子 Earth Rat 水雷屯 8 十四 4	金9 Metal 5 Without Wrongdoing 己丑 Earth Ox 天雷無妄 9 十五 2	木3 Wood 4 Fire 庚寅 Metal Tiger 離為火 10 十六 1	火2 Fire 3 Sincerity 辛卯 Metal Rabbit 風澤中孚 11 十七 3	水6 Water 2 Big Livestock 壬辰 Water Dragon 山天大畜 12 十八 4	金4 Metal 1 Eliminating 癸巳 Water Snake 澤天夬 13 十九 6	金9 Metal 9 Heaven 甲午 Wood Horse 乾為天 14 二十 1
火7 Fire 8 Well 乙未 Wood Goat 水風井 15 廿一 6	木8 Wood 7 Relief 丙申 Fire Monkey 雷水解 16 廿二 4	金4 Metal 6 Influence 丁酉 Fire Rooster 澤山咸 17 廿三 9	水1 Water 5 Humility 戊戌 Earth Dog 地山謙 18 廿四 6	火2 Fire 4 Observation 己亥 Earth Pig 風地觀 19 廿五 2	火2 Fire 3 Increasing 庚子 Metal Rat 風雷益 20 廿六 9	水1 Water 2 Dimming Light 辛丑 Metal Ox 地火明夷 21 廿七 3
金9 Metal 1 Fellowship 壬寅 Water Tiger 天火同人 22 廿八 7	木8 Wood 9 Marrying Maiden 癸卯 Water Rabbit 雷澤歸妹 23 廿九 7	木3 Wood 8 Opposition 甲辰 Wood Dragon 火澤睽 24 十一月初一 2	火7 Fire 7 Waiting 乙巳 Wood Snake 水天需 25 初二 3	金4 Metal 6 Great Exceeding 丙午 Fire Horse 澤風大過 26 初三 3	水6 Water 5 Poison 丁未 Fire Goat 山風蠱 27 初四 7	火2 Fire 4 Dispersing 戊申 Earth Monkey 風水渙 28 初五 6
木3 Wood 3 Travelling 己酉 Earth Rooster 火山旅 29 初六 8	金9 Metal 2 Stagnation 庚戌 Metal Dog 天地否 30 初七 9					

DECEMBER 1992 壬子

Xuan Kong Element 玄空五行	震為雷 Thunder	Period Luck 卦運	Monthly Star 月星
Wood 木8		1	1

SUNDAY	MONDAY	TUESDAY	WEDNESDAY	THURSDAY	FRIDAY	SATURDAY
		火7 Fire 1 Alliance 辛亥 Metal Pig 水地比 1 初八 7	木8 Wood 9 Thunder 壬子 Water Rat 震為雷 2 初九 1	水6 Water 8 Beauty 癸丑 Water Ox 山火賁 3 初十 8	火7 Fire 7 Accomplished 甲寅 Wood Tiger 水火既濟 4 十一 9	水1 Water 6 Arriving 乙卯 Wood Rabbit 地澤臨 5 十二 4
金4 Metal 5 Marsh 丙辰 Fire Dragon 兌為澤 6 十三 1	火2 Fire 4 Small Livestock 丁巳 Fire Snake 風天小畜 7 十四 8	木3 Wood 3 The Cauldron 戊午 Earth Horse 火風鼎 8 十五 4	水1 Water 2 Rising 己未 Earth Goat 地風升 9 十六 2	火7 Fire 1 Water 庚申 Metal Monkey 坎為水 10 十七 1	木8 Wood 9 Lesser Exceeding 辛酉 Metal Rooster 雷山小過 11 十八 3	金4 Metal 8 Gathering 壬戌 Water Dog 澤地萃 12 十九 4
水6 Water 7 Peel 癸亥 Water Pig 山地剝 13 二十 6	水1 Water 6 Earth 甲子 Wood Rat 坤為地 14 廿一 1	木3 Wood 5 Biting 乙丑 Wood Ox 火雷噬嗑 15 廿二 6	火2 Fire 4 Family 丙寅 Fire Tiger 風火家人 16 廿三 4	水6 Water 3 Decreasing 丁卯 Fire Rabbit 山澤損 17 廿四 9	金9 Metal 2 Tread 戊辰 Earth Dragon 天澤履 18 廿五 6	木8 Wood 1 Great Strength 己巳 Earth Snake 雷天大壯 19 廿六 2
木8 Wood 9 Consistency 庚午 Metal Horse 雷風恒 20 廿七 9	金9 Metal 8/2 Litigation 辛未 Metal Goat 天水訟 21 廿八 3	水1 Water 3 Officer 壬申 Water Monkey 地水師 22 廿九 7	火2 Fire 4 Gradual Progress 癸酉 Water Rooster 風山漸 23 三十 7	火7 Fire 5 Obstruction 甲戌 Wood Dog 水山蹇 24 十二月初一 2	木3 Wood 6 Advancement 乙亥 Wood Pig 火地晉 25 初二 3	水6 Water 7 Nourish 丙子 Fire Rat 山雷頤 26 初三 3
金4 Metal 8 Following 丁丑 Fire Ox 澤雷隨 27 初四 7	木8 Wood 9 Abundance 戊寅 Earth Tiger 雷火豐 28 初五 6	火7 Fire 1 Regulate 己卯 Earth Rabbit 水澤節 29 初六 8	水1 Water 2 Unity 庚辰 Metal Dragon 地天泰 30 初七 9	木3 Wood 3 Great Reward 辛巳 Metal Snake 火天大有 31 初八 7		

1993 癸酉

(*Gui You*) Water Rooster

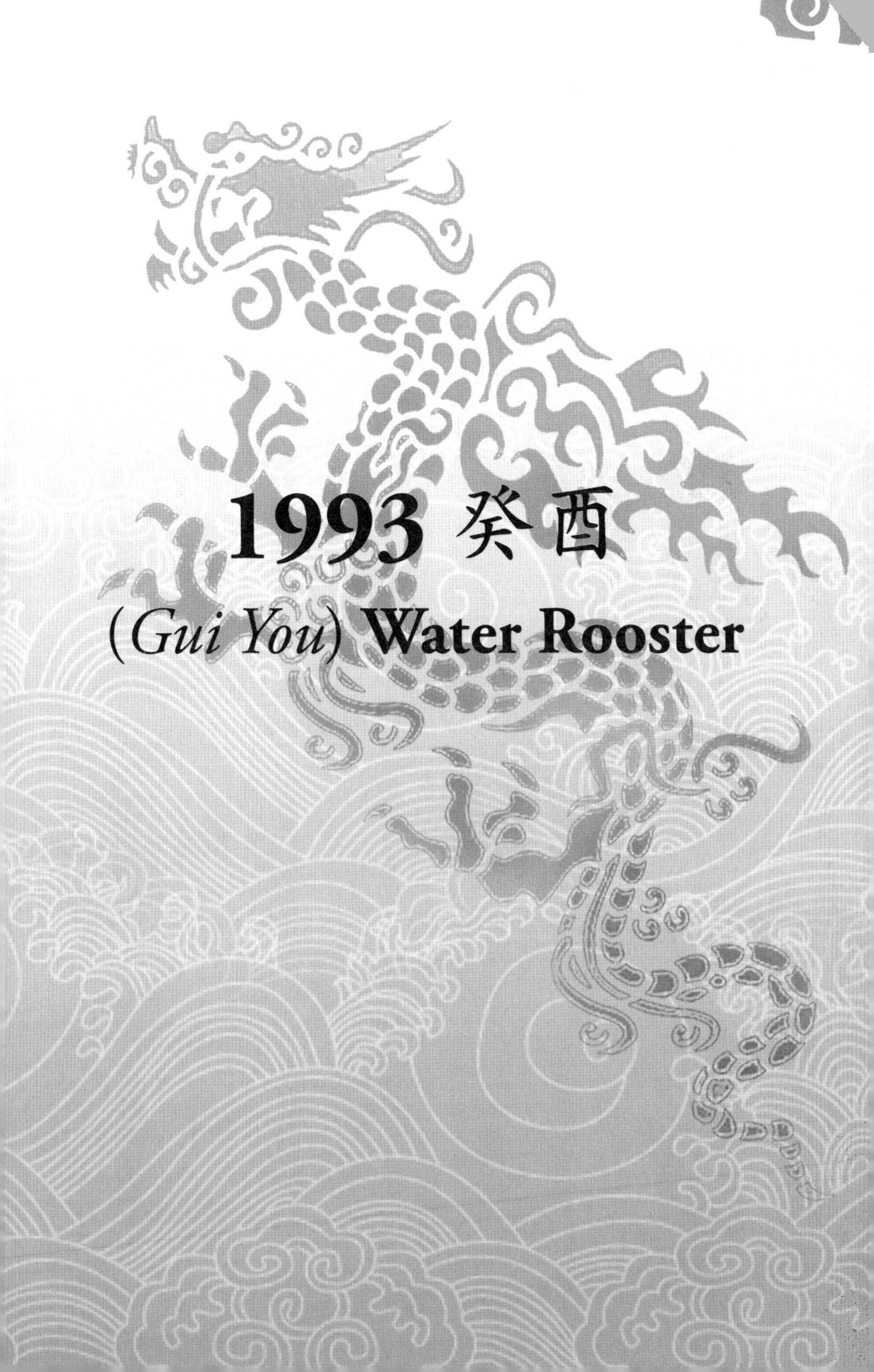

1993 癸酉 *(Gui You)* Water Rooster

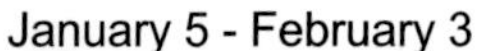

January 5 - February 3

February 4 - March 4

March 5 - April 4

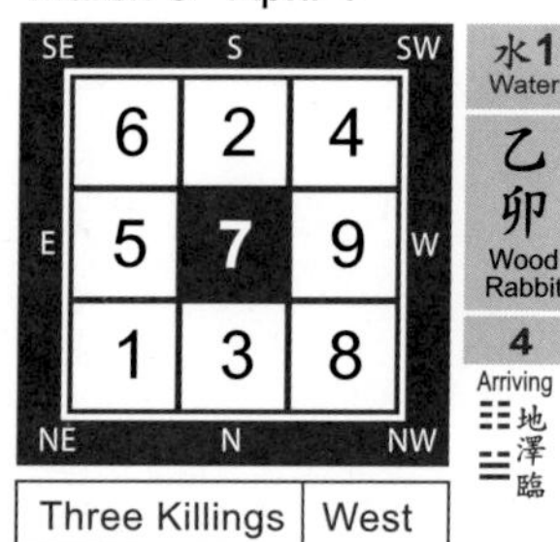

April 5 - May 4

May 5 - June 5

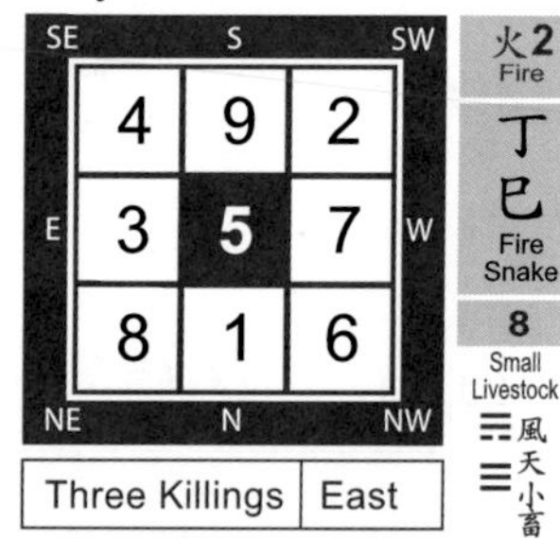

June 6 - July 6

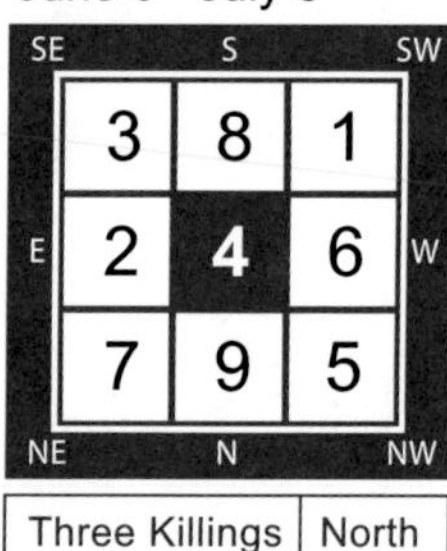

SE S SW
3 8 1
E 2 4 6 W
7 9 5
NE N NW
木3 Wood
戊午 Earth Horse
4 The Cauldron
Three Killings North

July 7 - August 6

August 7 - September 6

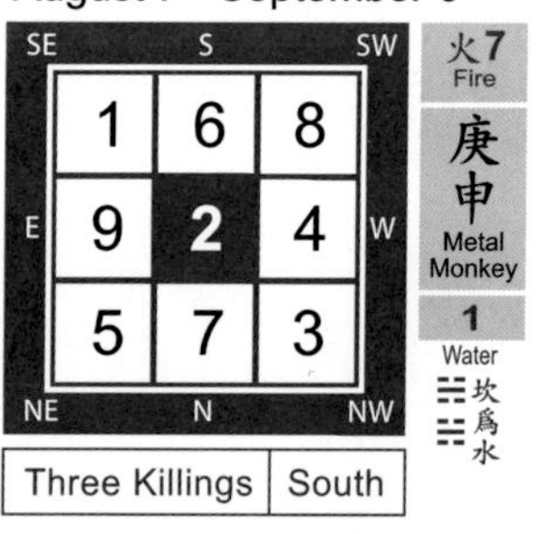

September 7 - October 7

October 8 - November 6

November 7 - December 6

December 7 - January 4

JANUARY 1993 癸丑

Xuan Kong Element 玄空五行	山火賁 Beauty	Period Luck 卦運	Monthly Star 月星
Water 水6		8	9

SUNDAY	MONDAY	TUESDAY	WEDNESDAY	THURSDAY	FRIDAY	SATURDAY
木8 Wood 7 Thunder 震爲雷 壬子 Water Rat 31 初九 1					火2 Fire 4 Wind 巽爲風 壬午 Water Horse 1 初九 1	金4 Metal 5 Trap 澤水困 癸未 Water Goat 2 初十 8
木3 Wood 6 Not Yet Accomplished 火水未濟 甲申 Wood Monkey 3 十一 9	金9 Metal 7 Retreat 天山遯 乙酉 Wood Rooster 4 十二 4	水6 Water 8 Mountain 艮爲山 丙戌 Fire Dog 5 十三 1	木8 Wood 9 Delight 雷地豫 丁亥 Fire Pig 6 十四 8	火7 Fire 1 Beginning 水雷屯 戊子 Earth Rat 7 十五 4	金9 Metal 2 Without Wrongdoing 天雷無妄 己丑 Earth Ox 8 十六 2	木3 Wood 3 Fire 離爲火 庚寅 Metal Tiger 9 十七 1
火2 Fire 4 Sincerity 風澤中孚 辛卯 Metal Rabbit 10 十八 3	水6 Water 5 Big Livestock 山天大畜 壬辰 Water Dragon 11 十九 4	金4 Metal 6 Eliminating 澤天夬 癸巳 Water Snake 12 二十 6	金9 Metal 7 Heaven 乾爲天 甲午 Wood Horse 13 廿一 1	火7 Fire 8 Well 水風井 乙未 Wood Goat 14 廿二 6	木8 Wood 9 Relief 雷水解 丙申 Fire Monkey 15 廿三 4	金4 Metal 1 Influence 澤山咸 丁酉 Fire Rooster 16 廿四 9
水1 Water 2 Humility 地山謙 戊戌 Earth Dog 17 廿五 6	火2 Fire 3 Observation 風地觀 己亥 Earth Pig 18 廿六 2	火2 Fire 4 Increasing 風雷益 庚子 Metal Rat 19 廿七 9	水1 Water 5 Dimming Light 地火明夷 辛丑 Metal Ox 20 廿八 3	金9 Metal 6 Fellowship 天火同人 壬寅 Water Tiger 21 廿九 7	木8 Wood 7 Marrying Maiden 雷澤歸妹 癸卯 Water Rabbit 22 三十 7	木3 Wood 8 Opposition 火澤睽 甲辰 Wood Dragon 23 正月初一 2
火7 Fire 9 Waiting 水天需 乙巳 Wood Snake 24 初二 3	金4 Metal 1 Great Exceeding 澤風大過 丙午 Fire Horse 25 初三 3	水6 Water 2 Poison 山風蠱 丁未 Fire Goat 26 初四 7	火2 Fire 3 Dispersing 風水渙 戊申 Earth Monkey 27 初五 6	木3 Wood 4 Travelling 火山旅 己酉 Earth Rooster 28 初六 8	金9 Metal 5 Stagnation 天地否 庚戌 Metal Dog 29 初七 9	火7 Fire 6 Alliance 水地比 辛亥 Metal Pig 30 初八 7

FEBRUARY 1993 甲寅

Xuan Kong Element 玄空五行	水火既濟 Accomplished	Period Luck 卦運	Monthly Star 月星
Fire 火7		9	8

SUNDAY	MONDAY	TUESDAY	WEDNESDAY	THURSDAY	FRIDAY	SATURDAY
	水6 Water 8 Beauty 山火賁 癸丑 Water Ox 1 初十 8	火7 Fire 9 Accomplished 水火既濟 甲寅 Wood Tiger 2 十一 9	水1 Water 1 Arriving 地澤臨 乙卯 Wood Rabbit 3 十二 4	金4 Metal 2 Marsh 兌爲澤 丙辰 Fire Dragon 4 十三 1	火2 Fire 3 Small Livestock 風天小畜 丁巳 Fire Snake 5 十四 8	木3 Wood 4 The Cauldron 火風鼎 戊午 Earth Horse 6 十五 4
水1 Water 5 Rising 地風升 己未 Earth Goat 7 十六 2	火7 Fire 6 Water 坎爲水 庚申 Metal Monkey 8 十七 1	木8 Wood 7 Lesser Exceeding 雷山小過 辛酉 Metal Rooster 9 十八 3	金4 Metal 8 Gathering 澤地萃 壬戌 Water Dog 10 十九 4	水6 Water 9 Peel 山地剝 癸亥 Water Pig 11 二十 6	水1 Water 1 Earth 坤爲地 甲子 Wood Rat 12 廿一 1	木3 Wood 2 Biting 火雷噬嗑 乙丑 Wood Ox 13 廿二 6
火2 Fire 3 Family 風火家人 丙寅 Fire Tiger 14 廿三 4	水6 Water 4 Decreasing 山澤損 丁卯 Fire Rabbit 15 廿四 9	金9 Metal 5 Tread 天澤履 戊辰 Earth Dragon 16 廿五 6	木8 Wood 6 Great Strength 雷天大壯 己巳 Earth Snake 17 廿六 2	木8 Wood 7 Consistency 雷風恆 庚午 Metal Horse 18 廿七 9	金9 Metal 8 Litigation 天水訟 辛未 Metal Goat 19 廿八 3	水1 Water 9 Officer 地水師 壬申 Water Monkey 20 廿九 7
火2 Fire 1 Gradual Progress 風山漸 癸酉 Water Rooster 21 二月初一 7	火7 Fire 2 Obstruction 水山蹇 甲戌 Wood Dog 22 初二 2	木3 Wood 3 Advancement 火地晉 乙亥 Wood Pig 23 初三 3	水6 Water 4 Nourish 山雷頤 丙子 Fire Rat 24 初四 3	金4 Metal 5 Following 澤雷隨 丁丑 Fire Ox 25 初五 7	木8 Wood 6 Abundance 雷火豐 戊寅 Earth Tiger 26 初六 6	火7 Fire 7 Regulate 水澤節 己卯 Earth Rabbit 27 初七 8
水1 Water 8 Unity 地天泰 庚辰 Metal Dragon 28 初八 9						

MARCH 1993 乙卯

Xuan Kong Element 玄空五行	地澤臨 Arriving	Period Luck 卦運	Monthly Star 月星
Water 水1		4	7

SUNDAY	MONDAY	TUESDAY	WEDNESDAY	THURSDAY	FRIDAY	SATURDAY
	木3 Wood Great Reward 9 辛巳 Metal Snake 火天大有 1 初九 7	火2 Fire Wind 1 壬午 Water Horse 巽為風 2 初十 1	金4 Metal Trap 2 癸未 Water Goat 澤水困 3 十一 8	木3 Wood Not Yet Accomplished 3 甲申 Wood Monkey 火水未濟 4 十二 9	金9 Metal Retreat 4 乙酉 Wood Rooster 天山遯 5 十三 4	水6 Water Mountain 5 丙戌 Fire Dog 艮為山 6 十四 1
木8 Wood Delight 6 丁亥 Fire Pig 雷地豫 7 十五 8	火7 Fire Beginning 7 戊子 Earth Rat 水雷屯 8 十六 4	金9 Metal Without Wrongdoing 8 己丑 Earth Ox 天雷無妄 9 十七 2	木3 Wood Fire 9 庚寅 Metal Tiger 離為火 10 十八 1	火2 Fire Sincerity 1 辛卯 Metal Rabbit 風澤中孚 11 十九 3	水6 Water Big Livestock 2 壬辰 Water Dragon 山天大畜 12 二十 4	金4 Metal Eliminating 3 癸巳 Water Snake 澤天夬 13 廿一 6
金9 Metal Heaven 4 甲午 Wood Horse 乾為天 14 廿二 1	火7 Fire Well 5 乙未 Wood Goat 水風井 15 廿三 6	木8 Wood Relief 6 丙申 Fire Monkey 雷水解 16 廿四 4	金4 Metal Influence 7 丁酉 Fire Rooster 澤山咸 17 廿五 9	水1 Water Humility 8 戊戌 Earth Dog 地山謙 18 廿六 6	火2 Fire Observation 9 己亥 Earth Pig 風地觀 19 廿七 2	火2 Fire Increasing 1 庚子 Metal Rat 風雷益 20 廿八 9
水1 Water Dimming Light 2 辛丑 Metal Ox 地火明夷 21 廿九 3	金9 Metal Fellowship 3 壬寅 Water Tiger 天火同人 22 三十 7	木8 Wood Marrying Maiden 4 癸卯 Water Rabbit 雷澤歸妹 23 三月初一 7	木3 Wood Opposition 5 甲辰 Wood Dragon 火澤睽 24 初二 2	火7 Fire Waiting 6 乙巳 Wood Snake 水天需 25 初三 3	金4 Metal Great Exceeding 7 丙午 Fire Horse 澤風大過 26 初四 3	水6 Water Poison 8 丁未 Fire Goat 山風蠱 27 初五 7
火2 Fire Dispersing 9 戊申 Earth Monkey 風水渙 28 初六 6	木3 Wood Travelling 1 己酉 Earth Rooster 火山旅 29 初七 8	金9 Metal Stagnation 2 庚戌 Metal Dog 天地否 30 初八 9	火7 Fire Alliance 3 辛亥 Metal Pig 水地比 31 初九 7			

APRIL 1993 丙辰

Xuan Kong Element 玄空五行	兑為澤 Marsh	Period Luck 卦運	Monthly Star 月星
Metal 金4		1	6

SUNDAY	MONDAY	TUESDAY	WEDNESDAY	THURSDAY	FRIDAY	SATURDAY
				木8 Wood Thunder 4 壬子 Water Rat 震為雷 1 初十 1	水6 Water Beauty 5 癸丑 Water Ox 山火賁 2 十一 8	火7 Fire Accomplished 6 甲寅 Wood Tiger 水火既濟 3 十二 9
水1 Water Arriving 7 乙卯 Wood Rabbit 地澤臨 4 十三 4	金4 Metal Marsh 8 丙辰 Fire Dragon 兑為澤 5 十四 1	火2 Fire Small Livestock 9 丁巳 Fire Snake 風天小畜 6 十五 8	木3 Wood The Cauldron 1 戊午 Earth Horse 火風鼎 7 十六 4	水1 Water Rising 2 己未 Earth Goat 地風升 8 十七 2	火7 Fire Water 3 庚申 Metal Monkey 坎為水 9 十八 1	木8 Wood Lesser Exceeding 4 辛酉 Metal Rooster 雷山小過 10 十九 3
金4 Metal Gathering 5 壬戌 Water Dog 澤地萃 11 二十 4	水6 Water Peel 6 癸亥 Water Pig 山地剝 12 廿一 6	水1 Water Earth 7 甲子 Wood Rat 坤為地 13 廿二 1	木3 Wood Biting 8 乙丑 Wood Ox 火雷噬嗑 14 廿三 6	火2 Fire Family 9 丙寅 Fire Tiger 風火家人 15 廿四 4	水6 Water Decreasing 1 丁卯 Fire Rabbit 山澤損 16 廿五 9	金9 Metal Tread 2 戊辰 Earth Dragon 天澤履 17 廿六 6
木8 Wood Great Strength 3 己巳 Earth Snake 雷天大壯 18 廿七 2	木8 Wood Consistency 4 庚午 Metal Horse 雷風恆 19 廿八 9	金9 Metal Litigation 5 辛未 Metal Goat 天水訟 20 廿九 3	水1 Water Officer 6 壬申 Water Monkey 地水師 21 三十 7	火2 Fire Gradual Progress 7 癸酉 Water Rooster 風山漸 22 閏三月初一 7	火7 Fire Obstruction 8 甲戌 Wood Dog 水山蹇 23 初二 2	木3 Wood Advancement 9 乙亥 Wood Pig 火地晉 24 初三 3
水6 Water Nourish 1 丙子 Fire Rat 山雷頤 25 初四 3	金4 Metal Following 2 丁丑 Fire Ox 澤雷隨 26 初五 7	木8 Wood Abundance 3 戊寅 Earth Tiger 雷火豐 27 初六 6	火7 Fire Regulate 4 己卯 Earth Rabbit 水澤節 28 初七 8	水1 Water Unity 5 庚辰 Metal Dragon 地天泰 29 初八 9	木3 Wood Great Reward 6 辛巳 Metal Snake 火天大有 30 初九 7	

MAY 1993 丁巳

Xuan Kong Element 玄空五行	風天小畜 Small Livestock	Period Luck 卦運	Monthly Star 月星
Fire 火2		8	5

SUNDAY	MONDAY	TUESDAY	WEDNESDAY	THURSDAY	FRIDAY	SATURDAY
30 火7 Fire 9 Alliance 水地比 辛亥 Metal Pig 7 初十	31 木8 Wood 1 Thunder 震爲雷 壬子 Water Rat 1 十一					1 火2 Fire 7 Wind 巽爲風 壬午 Water Horse 1 初十
2 金4 Metal 8 Trap 澤水困 癸未 Water Goat 8 十一	3 木3 Wood 9 Not Yet Accomplished 火水未濟 甲申 Wood Monkey 9 十二	4 金9 Metal 1 Retreat 天山遯 乙酉 Wood Rooster 4 十三	5 水6 Water 2 Mountain 艮爲山 丙戌 Fire Dog 1 十四	6 木8 Wood 3 Delight 雷地豫 丁亥 Fire Pig 8 十五	7 火7 Fire 4 Beginning 水雷屯 戊子 Earth Rat 4 十六	8 金9 Metal 5 Without Wrongdoing 天雷無妄 己丑 Earth Ox 2 十七
9 木3 Wood 6 Fire 離爲火 庚寅 Metal Tiger 1 十八	10 火2 Fire 7 Sincerity 風澤中孚 辛卯 Metal Rabbit 3 十九	11 水6 Water 8 Big Livestock 山天大畜 壬辰 Water Dragon 4 二十	12 金4 Metal 9 Eliminating 澤天夬 癸巳 Water Snake 6 廿一	13 金9 Metal 1 Heaven 乾爲天 甲午 Wood Horse 1 廿二	14 火7 Fire 2 Well 水風井 乙未 Wood Goat 6 廿三	15 木8 Wood 3 Relief 雷水解 丙申 Fire Monkey 4 廿四
16 金4 Metal 4 Influence 澤山咸 丁酉 Fire Rooster 9 廿五	17 水1 Water 5 Humility 地山謙 戊戌 Earth Dog 6 廿六	18 火2 Fire 6 Observation 風地觀 己亥 Earth Pig 2 廿七	19 火2 Fire 7 Increasing 風雷益 庚子 Metal Rat 9 廿八	20 水1 Water 8 Dimming Light 地火明夷 辛丑 Metal Ox 3 廿九	21 金9 Metal 9 Fellowship 天火同人 壬寅 Water Tiger 7 四月初一	22 木8 Wood 1 Marrying Maiden 雷澤歸妹 癸卯 Water Rabbit 7 初二
23 木3 Wood 2 Opposition 火澤睽 甲辰 Wood Dragon 2 初三	24 火7 Fire 3 Waiting 水天需 乙巳 Wood Snake 3 初四	25 金4 Metal 4 Great Exceeding 澤風大過 丙午 Fire Horse 3 初五	26 水6 Water 5 Poison 山風蠱 丁未 Fire Goat 7 初六	27 火2 Fire 6 Dispersing 風水渙 戊申 Earth Monkey 6 初七	28 木3 Wood 7 Travelling 火山旅 己酉 Earth Rooster 8 初八	29 金9 Metal 8 Stagnation 天地否 庚戌 Metal Dog 9 初九

JUNE 1993 戊午

Xuan Kong Element 玄空五行	火風鼎 The Cauldron	Period Luck 卦運	Monthly Star 月星
Wood 木3		4	4

SUNDAY	MONDAY	TUESDAY	WEDNESDAY	THURSDAY	FRIDAY	SATURDAY
		1 水6 Water 2 Beauty 山火賁 癸丑 Water Ox 8 十二	2 火7 Fire 3 Accomplished 水火既濟 甲寅 Wood Tiger 9 十三	3 水1 Water 4 Arriving 地澤臨 乙卯 Wood Rabbit 4 十四	4 金4 Metal 5 Marsh 兌爲澤 丙辰 Fire Dragon 1 十五	5 火2 Fire 6 Small Livestock 風天小畜 丁巳 Fire Snake 8 十六
6 木3 Wood 7 The Cauldron 火風鼎 戊午 Earth Horse 4 十七	7 水1 Water 8 Rising 地風升 己未 Earth Goat 2 十八	8 火7 Fire 9 Water 坎爲水 庚申 Metal Monkey 1 十九	9 木8 Wood 1 Lesser Exceeding 雷山小過 辛酉 Metal Rooster 3 二十	10 金4 Metal 2 Gathering 澤地萃 壬戌 Water Dog 4 廿一	11 水6 Water 3 Peel 山地剝 癸亥 Water Pig 6 廿二	12 水1 Water 4 Earth 坤爲地 甲子 Wood Rat 1 廿三
13 木3 Wood 5 Biting 火雷噬嗑 乙丑 Wood Ox 6 廿四	14 火2 Fire 6 Family 風火家人 丙寅 Fire Tiger 4 廿五	15 水6 Water 7 Decreasing 山澤損 丁卯 Fire Rabbit 9 廿六	16 金9 Metal 8 Tread 天澤履 戊辰 Earth Dragon 6 廿七	17 木8 Wood 9 Great Strength 雷天大壯 己巳 Earth Snake 2 廿八	18 木8 Wood 1 Consistency 雷風恒 庚午 Metal Horse 9 廿九	19 金9 Metal 2 Litigation 天水訟 辛未 Metal Goat 3 三十
20 水1 Water 3 Officer 地水師 壬申 Water Monkey 7 五月初一	21 火2 Fire 4/6 Gradual Progress 風山漸 癸酉 Water Rooster 7 初二	22 火7 Fire 5 Obstruction 水山蹇 甲戌 Wood Dog 2 初三	23 木3 Wood 4 Advancement 火地晉 乙亥 Wood Pig 3 初四	24 水6 Water 3 Nourish 山雷頤 丙子 Fire Rat 3 初五	25 金4 Metal 2 Following 澤雷隨 丁丑 Fire Ox 7 初六	26 木8 Wood 1 Abundance 雷火豐 戊寅 Earth Tiger 6 初七
27 火7 Fire 9 Regulate 水澤節 己卯 Earth Rabbit 8 初八	28 水1 Water 8 Unity 地天泰 庚辰 Metal Dragon 9 初九	29 木3 Wood 7 Great Reward 火天大有 辛巳 Metal Snake 7 初十	30 火2 Fire 6 Wind 巽爲風 壬午 Water Horse 1 十一			

JULY 1993 己未

Xuan Kong Element 玄空五行	地風升 Rising	Period Luck 卦運	Monthly Star 月星
Water 水1		2	3

SUNDAY	MONDAY	TUESDAY	WEDNESDAY	THURSDAY	FRIDAY	SATURDAY
				金4 Metal Trap 5 澤水困 癸未 Water Goat 1 十二 8	木3 Wood Not Yet Accomplished 4 火水未濟 甲申 Wood Monkey 2 十三 9	金9 Metal Retreat 3 天山遯 乙酉 Wood Rooster 3 十四 4
水6 Water Mountain 2 艮爲山 丙戌 Fire Dog 4 十五 1	木8 Wood Delight 1 雷地豫 丁亥 Fire Pig 5 十六 8	火7 Fire Beginning 9 水雷屯 戊子 Earth Rat 6 十七 4	金9 Metal Without Wrongdoing 8 天雷無妄 己丑 Earth Ox 7 十八 2	木3 Wood Fire 7 離爲火 庚寅 Metal Tiger 8 十九 1	火2 Fire Sincerity 6 風澤中孚 辛卯 Metal Rabbit 9 二十 3	水6 Water Big Livestock 5 山天大畜 壬辰 Water Dragon 10 廿一 4
金4 Metal Eliminating 4 澤天夬 癸巳 Water Snake 11 廿二 6	金9 Metal Heaven 3 乾爲天 甲午 Wood Horse 12 廿三 1	火7 Fire Well 2 水風井 乙未 Wood Goat 13 廿四 6	木8 Wood Relief 1 雷水解 丙申 Fire Monkey 14 廿五 4	金4 Metal Influence 9 澤山咸 丁酉 Fire Rooster 15 廿六 9	水1 Water Humility 8 地山謙 戊戌 Earth Dog 16 廿七 6	火2 Fire Observation 7 風地觀 己亥 Earth Pig 17 廿八 2
火2 Fire Increasing 6 風雷益 庚子 Metal Rat 18 廿九 9	水1 Water Dimming Light 5 地火明夷 辛丑 Metal Ox 19 六月初一 3	金9 Metal Fellowship 4 天火同人 壬寅 Water Tiger 20 初二 7	木8 Wood Marrying Maiden 3 雷澤歸妹 癸卯 Water Rabbit 21 初三 7	木3 Wood Opposition 2 火澤睽 甲辰 Wood Dragon 22 初四 2	火7 Fire Waiting 1 水天需 乙巳 Wood Snake 23 初五 3	金4 Metal Great Exceeding 9 澤風大過 丙午 Fire Horse 24 初六 3
水6 Water Poison 8 山風蠱 丁未 Fire Goat 25 初七 7	火2 Fire Dispersing 7 風水渙 戊申 Earth Monkey 26 初八 6	木3 Wood Travelling 6 火山旅 己酉 Earth Rooster 27 初九 8	金9 Metal Stagnation 5 天地否 庚戌 Metal Dog 28 初十 9	火7 Fire Alliance 4 水地比 辛亥 Metal Pig 29 十一 7	木8 Wood Thunder 3 震爲雷 壬子 Water Rat 30 十二 1	水6 Water Beauty 2 山火賁 癸丑 Water Ox 31 十三 8

AUGUST 1993 庚申

Xuan Kong Element 玄空五行	坎爲水 Water	Period Luck 卦運	Monthly Star 月星
Fire 火7		1	2

SUNDAY	MONDAY	TUESDAY	WEDNESDAY	THURSDAY	FRIDAY	SATURDAY
火7 Fire Accomplished 1 水火既濟 甲寅 Wood Tiger 1 十四 9	水1 Water Arriving 9 地澤臨 乙卯 Wood Rabbit 2 十五 4	金4 Metal Marsh 8 兌爲澤 丙辰 Fire Dragon 3 十六 1	火2 Fire Small Livestock 7 風天小畜 丁巳 Fire Snake 4 十七 8	木3 Wood The Cauldron 6 火風鼎 戊午 Earth Horse 5 十八 4	水1 Water Rising 5 地風升 己未 Earth Goat 6 十九 2	火7 Fire Water 4 坎爲水 庚申 Metal Monkey 7 二十 1
木8 Wood Lesser Exceeding 3 雷山小過 辛酉 Metal Rooster 8 廿一 3	金4 Metal Gathering 2 澤地萃 壬戌 Water Dog 9 廿二 4	水6 Water Peel 1 山地剝 癸亥 Water Pig 10 廿三 6	水1 Water Earth 9 坤爲地 甲子 Wood Rat 11 廿四 1	木3 Wood Biting 8 火雷噬嗑 乙丑 Wood Ox 12 廿五 6	火2 Fire Family 7 風火家人 丙寅 Fire Tiger 13 廿六 4	水6 Water Decreasing 6 山澤損 丁卯 Fire Rabbit 14 廿七 9
金9 Metal Tread 5 天澤履 戊辰 Earth Dragon 15 廿八 6	木8 Wood Great Strength 4 雷天大壯 己巳 Earth Snake 16 廿九 2	木8 Wood Consistency 3 雷風恆 庚午 Metal Horse 17 三十 9	金9 Metal Litigation 2 天水訟 辛未 Metal Goat 18 七月初一 3	水1 Water Officer 1 地水師 壬申 Water Monkey 19 初二 7	火2 Fire Gradual Progress 9 風山漸 癸酉 Water Rooster 20 初三 7	火7 Fire Obstruction 8 水山蹇 甲戌 Wood Dog 21 初四 2
木3 Wood Advancement 7 火地晉 乙亥 Wood Pig 22 初五 3	水6 Water Nourish 6 山雷頤 丙子 Fire Rat 23 初六 3	金4 Metal Following 5 澤雷隨 丁丑 Fire Ox 24 初七 7	木8 Wood Abundance 4 雷火豐 戊寅 Earth Tiger 25 初八 6	火7 Fire Regulate 3 水澤節 己卯 Earth Rabbit 26 初九 8	水1 Water Unity 2 地天泰 庚辰 Metal Dragon 27 初十 9	木3 Wood Great Reward 1 火天大有 辛巳 Metal Snake 28 十一 7
火2 Fire Wind 9 巽爲風 壬午 Water Horse 29 十二 1	金4 Metal Trap 8 澤水困 癸未 Water Goat 30 十三 8	木3 Wood Not Yet Accomplished 7 火水未濟 甲申 Wood Monkey 31 十四 9				

SEPTEMBER 1993 辛酉

Xuan Kong Element 玄空五行	雷山小過 Lesser Exceeding	Period Luck 卦運	Monthly Star 月星
Wood 木8		3	1

SUNDAY	MONDAY	TUESDAY	WEDNESDAY	THURSDAY	FRIDAY	SATURDAY
			金9 Metal 6 Retreat 天山遯 乙酉 Wood Rooster **1** 十五 4	水6 Water 5 Mountain 艮爲山 丙戌 Fire Dog **2** 十六 1	木8 Wood 4 Delight 雷地豫 丁亥 Fire Pig **3** 十七 8	火7 Fire 3 Beginning 水雷屯 戊子 Earth Rat **4** 十八 4
金9 Metal 2 Without Wrongdoing 天雷無妄 己丑 Earth Ox **5** 十九 2	木3 Wood 1 Fire 離爲火 庚寅 Metal Tiger **6** 二十 1	火2 Fire 9 Sincerity 風澤中孚 辛卯 Metal Rabbit **7** 廿一 3	水6 Water 8 Big Livestock 山天大畜 壬辰 Water Dragon **8** 廿二 4	金4 Metal 7 Eliminating 澤天夬 癸巳 Water Snake **9** 廿三 6	金9 Metal 6 Heaven 乾爲天 甲午 Wood Horse **10** 廿四 1	火7 Fire 5 Well 水風井 乙未 Wood Goat **11** 廿五 6
木8 Wood 4 Relief 雷水解 丙申 Fire Monkey **12** 廿六 4	金4 Metal 3 Influence 澤山咸 丁酉 Fire Rooster **13** 廿七 9	水1 Water 2 Humility 地山謙 戊戌 Earth Dog **14** 廿八 6	火2 Fire 1 Observation 風地觀 己亥 Earth Pig **15** 廿九 2	火2 Fire 9 Increasing 風雷益 庚子 Metal Rat **16** 八月初一 9	水1 Water 8 Dimming Light 地火明夷 辛丑 Metal Ox **17** 初二 3	金9 Metal 7 Fellowship 天火同人 壬寅 Water Tiger **18** 初三 7
木8 Wood 6 Marrying Maiden 雷澤歸妹 癸卯 Water Rabbit **19** 初四 7	木3 Wood 5 Opposition 火澤睽 甲辰 Wood Dragon **20** 初五 2	火7 Fire 4 Waiting 水天需 乙巳 Wood Snake **21** 初六 3	金4 Metal 3 Great Exceeding 澤風大過 丙午 Fire Horse **22** 初七 3	水6 Water 2 Poison 山風蠱 丁未 Fire Goat **23** 初八 7	火2 Fire 1 Dispersing 風水渙 戊申 Earth Monkey **24** 初九 6	木3 Wood 9 Travelling 火山旅 己酉 Earth Rooster **25** 初十 8
金9 Metal 8 Stagnation 天地否 庚戌 Metal Dog **26** 十一 9	火7 Fire 7 Alliance 水地比 辛亥 Metal Pig **27** 十二 7	木8 Wood 6 Thunder 震爲雷 壬子 Water Rat **28** 十三 1	水6 Water 5 Beauty 山火賁 癸丑 Water Ox **29** 十四 8	火7 Fire 4 Accomplished 水火既濟 甲寅 Wood Tiger **30** 十五 9		

OCTOBER 1993 壬戌

Xuan Kong Element 玄空五行	澤地萃 Gathering	Period Luck 卦運	Monthly Star 月星
Metal 金4		4	9

SUNDAY	MONDAY	TUESDAY	WEDNESDAY	THURSDAY	FRIDAY	SATURDAY
金9 Metal 9 Retreat 天山遯 乙酉 Wood Rooster **31** 十七 4					水1 Water 3 Arriving 地澤臨 乙卯 Wood Rabbit **1** 十六 4	金4 Metal 2 Marsh 兌爲澤 丙辰 Fire Dragon **2** 十七 1
火2 Fire 1 Small Livestock 風天小畜 丁巳 Fire Snake **3** 十八 8	木3 Wood 9 The Cauldron 火風鼎 戊午 Earth Horse **4** 十九 4	水1 Water 8 Rising 地風升 己未 Earth Goat **5** 二十 2	火7 Fire 7 Water 坎爲水 庚申 Metal Monkey **6** 廿一 1	木8 Wood 6 Lesser Exceeding 雷山小過 辛酉 Metal Rooster **7** 廿二 3	金4 Metal 5 Gathering 澤地萃 壬戌 Water Dog **8** 廿三 4	水6 Water 4 Peel 山地剝 癸亥 Water Pig **9** 廿四 6
水1 Water 3 Earth 坤爲地 甲子 Wood Rat **10** 廿五 1	木3 Wood 2 Biting 火雷噬嗑 乙丑 Wood Ox **11** 廿六 6	火2 Fire 1 Family 風火家人 丙寅 Fire Tiger **12** 廿七 4	水6 Water 9 Decreasing 山澤損 丁卯 Fire Rabbit **13** 廿八 9	金9 Metal 8 Tread 天澤履 戊辰 Earth Dragon **14** 廿九 6	木8 Wood 7 Great Strength 雷天大壯 己巳 Earth Snake **15** 九月初一 2	木8 Wood 6 Consistency 雷風恆 庚午 Metal Horse **16** 初二 9
金9 Metal 5 Litigation 天水訟 辛未 Metal Goat **17** 初三 3	水1 Water 4 Officer 地水師 壬申 Water Monkey **18** 初四 7	火2 Fire 3 Gradual Progress 風山漸 癸酉 Water Rooster **19** 初五 7	火7 Fire 2 Obstruction 水山蹇 甲戌 Wood Dog **20** 初六 2	木3 Wood 1 Advancement 火地晉 乙亥 Wood Pig **21** 初七 3	水6 Water 9 Nourish 山雷頤 丙子 Fire Rat **22** 初八 3	金4 Metal 8 Following 澤雷隨 丁丑 Fire Ox **23** 初九 7
木8 Wood 7 Abundance 雷火豐 戊寅 Earth Tiger **24** 初十 6	火7 Fire 6 Regulate 水澤節 己卯 Earth Rabbit **25** 十一 8	水1 Water 5 Unity 地天泰 庚辰 Metal Dragon **26** 十二 9	木3 Wood 4 Great Reward 火天大有 辛巳 Metal Snake **27** 十三 7	火2 Fire 3 Wind 巽爲風 壬午 Water Horse **28** 十四 1	金4 Metal 2 Trap 澤水困 癸未 Water Goat **29** 十五 8	木3 Wood 1 Not Yet Accomplished 火水未濟 甲申 Wood Monkey **30** 十六 9

NOVEMBER 1993 癸亥

Xuan Kong Element 玄空五行	山地剝 Peel	Period Luck 卦運	Monthly Star 月星
Water 水6		6	8

SUNDAY	MONDAY	TUESDAY	WEDNESDAY	THURSDAY	FRIDAY	SATURDAY
	水6 Water 8 Mountain 丙戌 Fire Dog 艮為山 1 十八 1	木8 Wood 7 Delight 丁亥 Fire Pig 雷地豫 2 十九 8	火7 Fire 6 Beginning 戊子 Earth Rat 水雷屯 3 二十 4	金9 Metal 5 Without Wrongdoing 己丑 Earth Ox 天雷無妄 4 廿一 2	木3 Wood 4 Fire 庚寅 Metal Tiger 離為火 5 廿二 1	火2 Fire 3 Sincerity 辛卯 Metal Rabbit 風澤中孚 6 廿三 3
水6 Water 2 Big Livestock 壬辰 Water Dragon 山天大畜 7 廿四 4	金4 Metal 1 Eliminating 癸巳 Water Snake 澤天夬 8 廿五 6	金9 Metal 9 Heaven 甲午 Wood Horse 乾為天 9 廿六 1	火7 Fire 8 Well 乙未 Wood Goat 水風井 10 廿七 6	木8 Wood 7 Relief 丙申 Fire Monkey 雷水解 11 廿八 4	金4 Metal 6 Influence 丁酉 Fire Rooster 澤山咸 12 廿九 9	水1 Water 5 Humility 戊戌 Earth Dog 地山謙 13 三十 6
火2 Fire 4 Observation 己亥 Earth Pig 風地觀 14 十月初一 2	火2 Fire 3 Increasing 庚子 Metal Rat 風雷益 15 初二 9	水1 Water 2 Dimming Light 辛丑 Metal Ox 地火明夷 16 初三 3	金9 Metal 1 Fellowship 壬寅 Water Tiger 天火同人 17 初四 7	木8 Wood 9 Marrying Maiden 癸卯 Water Rabbit 雷澤歸妹 18 初五 7	木3 Wood 8 Opposition 甲辰 Wood Dragon 火澤睽 19 初六 2	火7 Fire 7 Waiting 乙巳 Wood Snake 水天需 20 初七 3
金4 Metal 6 Great Exceeding 丙午 Fire Horse 澤風大過 21 初八 3	水6 Water 5 Poison 丁未 Fire Goat 山風蠱 22 初九 7	火2 Fire 4 Dispersing 戊申 Earth Monkey 風水渙 23 初十 6	木3 Wood 3 Travelling 己酉 Earth Rooster 火山旅 24 十一 8	金9 Metal 2 Stagnation 庚戌 Metal Dog 天地否 25 十二 9	火7 Fire 1 Alliance 辛亥 Metal Pig 水地比 26 十三 7	木8 Wood 9 Thunder 壬子 Water Rat 震為雷 27 十四 1
水6 Water 8 Beauty 癸丑 Water Ox 山火賁 28 十五 8	火7 Fire 7 Accomplished 甲寅 Wood Tiger 水火既濟 29 十六 9	水1 Water 6 Arriving 乙卯 Wood Rabbit 地澤臨 30 十七 4				

DECEMBER 1993 甲子

Xuan Kong Element 玄空五行	坤為地 Earth	Period Luck 卦運	Monthly Star 月星
Water 水1		1	7

SUNDAY	MONDAY	TUESDAY	WEDNESDAY	THURSDAY	FRIDAY	SATURDAY
			金4 Metal 5 Marsh 丙辰 Fire Dragon 兌為澤 1 十八 1	火2 Fire 4 Small Livestock 丁巳 Fire Snake 風天小畜 2 十九 8	木3 Wood 3 The Cauldron 戊午 Earth Horse 火風鼎 3 二十 4	水1 Water 2 Rising 己未 Earth Goat 地風升 4 廿一 2
火7 Fire 1 Water 庚申 Metal Monkey 坎為水 5 廿二 1	木8 Wood 9 Lesser Exceeding 辛酉 Metal Rooster 雷山小過 6 廿三 3	金4 Metal 8 Gathering 壬戌 Water Dog 澤地萃 7 廿四 4	水6 Water 7 Peel 癸亥 Water Pig 山地剝 8 廿五 6	水1 Water 6 Earth 甲子 Wood Rat 坤為地 9 廿六 1	木3 Wood 5 Biting 乙丑 Wood Ox 火雷噬嗑 10 廿七 6	火2 Fire 4 Family 丙寅 Fire Tiger 風火家人 11 廿八 4
水6 Water 3 Decreasing 丁卯 Fire Rabbit 山澤損 12 廿九 9	金9 Metal 2 Tread 戊辰 Earth Dragon 天澤履 13 十一月初一 6	木8 Wood 1 Great Strength 己巳 Earth Snake 雷天大壯 14 初二 2	木8 Wood 9 Consistency 庚午 Metal Horse 雷風恒 15 初三 9	金9 Metal 8 Litigation 辛未 Metal Goat 天水訟 16 初四 3	水1 Water 7 Officer 壬申 Water Monkey 地水師 17 初五 7	火2 Fire 6 Gradual Progress 癸酉 Water Rooster 風山漸 18 初六 7
火7 Fire 5 Obstruction 甲戌 Wood Dog 水山蹇 19 初七 2	木3 Wood 4 Advancement 乙亥 Wood Pig 火地晉 20 初八 3	水6 Water 3 Nourish 丙子 Fire Rat 山雷頤 21 初九 3	金4 Metal 2/8 Following 丁丑 Fire Ox 澤雷隨 22 初十 7	木8 Wood 9 Abundance 戊寅 Earth Tiger 雷火豐 23 十一 6	火7 Fire 1 Regulate 己卯 Earth Rabbit 水澤節 24 十二 8	水1 Water 2 Unity 庚辰 Metal Dragon 地天泰 25 十三 9
木3 Wood 3 Great Reward 辛巳 Metal Snake 火天大有 26 十四 7	火2 Fire 4 Wind 壬午 Water Horse 巽為風 27 十五 1	金4 Metal 5 Trap 癸未 Water Goat 澤水困 28 十六 8	木3 Wood 6 Not Yet Accomplished 甲申 Wood Monkey 火水未濟 29 十七 9	金9 Metal 7 Retreat 乙酉 Wood Rooster 天山遯 30 十八 4	水6 Water 8 Mountain 丙戌 Fire Dog 艮為山 31 十九 1	

1994 甲戌

(*Jia Xu*) Wood Dog

1994 甲戌 *(Jia Xu)* Wood Dog

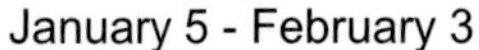

January 5 - February 3

February 4 - March 5

March 6 - April 4

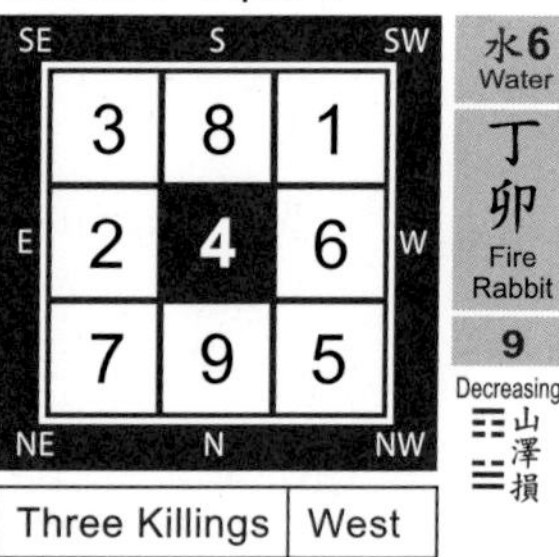

April 5 - May 5

May 6 - June 5

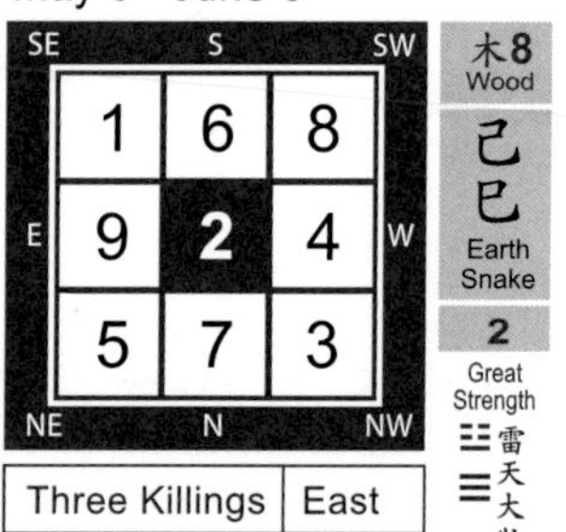

June 6 - July 6

July 7 - August 7

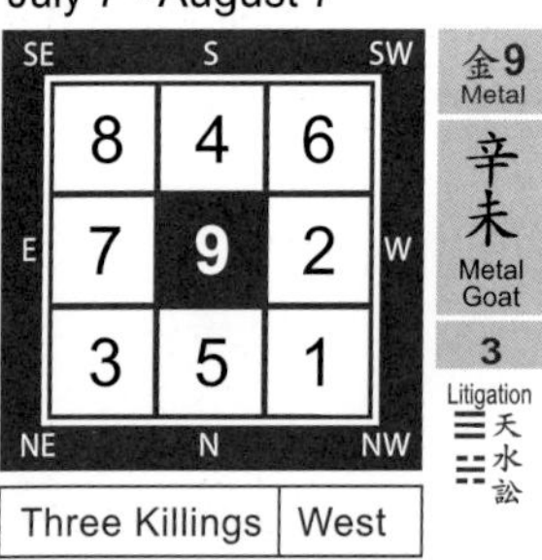

August 8 - September 7

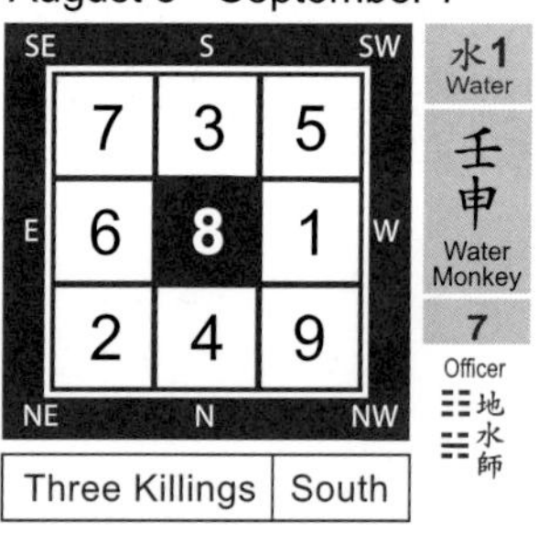

September 8 - October 7

October 8 - November 6

November 7 - December 6

December 7 - January 5

JANUARY 1994 乙丑

Xuan Kong Element 玄空五行	火雷噬嗑 Biting	Period Luck 卦運	Monthly Star 月星
Wood 木3		6	6

SUNDAY	MONDAY	TUESDAY	WEDNESDAY	THURSDAY	FRIDAY	SATURDAY
金4 Metal 丙辰 Fire Dragon 1 Marsh 兑爲澤 [2] **30** 十九	火2 Fire 丁巳 Fire Snake 8 Small Livestock 風天小畜 [3] **31** 二十					木8 Wood 丁亥 Fire Pig 8 Delight 雷地豫 [9] **1** 二十
火7 Fire 戊子 Earth Rat 4 Beginning 水雷屯 [1] **2** 廿一	金9 Metal 己丑 Earth Ox 2 Without Wrongdoing 天雷無妄 [2] **3** 廿二	木3 Wood 庚寅 Metal Tiger 1 Fire 離爲火 [3] **4** 廿三	火2 Fire 辛卯 Metal Rabbit 3 Sincerity 風澤中孚 [4] **5** 廿四	水6 Water 壬辰 Water Dragon 4 Big Livestock 山天大畜 [5] **6** 廿五	金4 Metal 癸巳 Water Snake 6 Eliminating 澤天夬 [6] **7** 廿六	金9 Metal 甲午 Wood Horse 1 Heaven 乾爲天 [7] **8** 廿七
火7 Fire 乙未 Wood Goat 6 Well 水風井 [8] **9** 廿八	木8 Wood 丙申 Fire Monkey 4 Relief 雷水解 [9] **10** 廿九	金4 Metal 丁酉 Fire Rooster 9 Influence 澤山咸 [1] **11** 三十	水1 Water 戊戌 Earth Dog 6 Humility 地山謙 [2] **12** 十二月初一	火2 Fire 己亥 Earth Pig 2 Observation 風地觀 [3] **13** 初二	火2 Fire 庚子 Metal Rat 9 Increasing 風雷益 [4] **14** 初三	水1 Water 辛丑 Metal Ox 3 Dimming Light 地火明夷 [5] **15** 初四
金9 Metal 壬寅 Water Tiger 7 Fellowship 天火同人 [6] **16** 初五	木8 Wood 癸卯 Water Rabbit 7 Marrying Maiden 雷澤歸妹 [7] **17** 初六	木3 Wood 甲辰 Wood Dragon 2 Opposition 火澤睽 [8] **18** 初七	火7 Fire 乙巳 Wood Snake 3 Waiting 水天需 [9] **19** 初八	金4 Metal 丙午 Fire Horse 3 Great Exceeding 澤風大過 [1] **20** 初九	水6 Water 丁未 Fire Goat 7 Poison 山風蠱 [2] **21** 初十	火2 Fire 戊申 Earth Monkey 6 Dispersing 風水渙 [3] **22** 十一
木3 Wood 己酉 Earth Rooster 8 Travelling 火山旅 [4] **23** 十二	金9 Metal 庚戌 Metal Dog 9 Stagnation 天地否 [5] **24** 十三	火7 Fire 辛亥 Metal Pig 7 Alliance 水地比 [6] **25** 十四	木8 Wood 壬子 Water Rat 1 Thunder 震爲雷 [7] **26** 十五	水6 Water 癸丑 Water Ox 8 Beauty 山火賁 [8] **27** 十六	火7 Fire 甲寅 Wood Tiger 9 Accomplished 水火既濟 [9] **28** 十七	水1 Water 乙卯 Wood Rabbit 4 Arriving 地澤臨 [1] **29** 十八

FEBRUARY 1994 丙寅

Xuan Kong Element 玄空五行	風火家人 Family	Period Luck 卦運	Monthly Star 月星
Fire 火2		4	5

SUNDAY	MONDAY	TUESDAY	WEDNESDAY	THURSDAY	FRIDAY	SATURDAY
		木3 Wood 戊午 Earth Horse 4 The Cauldron 火風鼎 [4] **1** 廿一	水1 Water 己未 Earth Goat 2 Rising 地風升 [5] **2** 廿二	火7 Fire 庚申 Metal Monkey 1 Water 坎爲水 [6] **3** 廿三	木8 Wood 辛酉 Metal Rooster 3 Lesser Exceeding 雷山小過 [7] **4** 廿四	金4 Metal 壬戌 Water Dog 4 Gathering 澤地萃 [8] **5** 廿五
水6 Water 癸亥 Water Pig 6 Peel 山地剝 [9] **6** 廿六	水1 Water 甲子 Wood Rat 1 Earth 坤爲地 [1] **7** 廿七	木3 Wood 乙丑 Wood Ox 6 Biting 火雷噬嗑 [2] **8** 廿八	火2 Fire 丙寅 Fire Tiger 4 Family 風火家人 [3] **9** 廿九	水6 Water 丁卯 Fire Rabbit 9 Decreasing 山澤損 [4] **10** 正月初一	金9 Metal 戊辰 Earth Dragon 6 Tread 天澤履 [5] **11** 初二	木8 Wood 己巳 Earth Snake 2 Great Strength 雷天大壯 [6] **12** 初三
木8 Wood 庚午 Metal Horse 9 Consistency 雷風恆 [7] **13** 初四	金9 Metal 辛未 Metal Goat 3 Litigation 天水訟 [8] **14** 初五	水1 Water 壬申 Water Monkey 7 Officer 地水師 [9] **15** 初六	火2 Fire 癸酉 Water Rooster 7 Gradual Progress 風山漸 [1] **16** 初七	火7 Fire 甲戌 Wood Dog 2 Obstruction 水山蹇 [2] **17** 初八	木3 Wood 乙亥 Wood Pig 3 Advancement 火地晉 [3] **18** 初九	水6 Water 丙子 Fire Rat 3 Nourish 山雷頤 [4] **19** 初十
金4 Metal 丁丑 Fire Ox 7 Following 澤雷隨 [5] **20** 十一	木8 Wood 戊寅 Earth Tiger 6 Abundance 雷火豐 [6] **21** 十二	火7 Fire 己卯 Earth Rabbit 8 Regulate 水澤節 [7] **22** 十三	水1 Water 庚辰 Metal Dragon 9 Unity 地天泰 [8] **23** 十四	木3 Wood 辛巳 Metal Snake 7 Great Reward 火天大有 [9] **24** 十五	火2 Fire 壬午 Water Horse 1 Wind 巽爲風 [1] **25** 十六	金4 Metal 癸未 Water Goat 8 Trap 澤水困 [2] **26** 十七
木3 Wood 甲申 Wood Monkey 9 Not Yet Accomplished 火水未濟 [3] **27** 十八	金9 Metal 乙酉 Wood Rooster 4 Retreat 天山遯 [4] **28** 十九					

MARCH 1994 丁卯

Xuan Kong Element 玄空五行	山澤損 Decreasing	Period Luck 卦運	Monthly Star 月星
Water 水6		9	4

SUNDAY	MONDAY	TUESDAY	WEDNESDAY	THURSDAY	FRIDAY	SATURDAY
		水6 Water 5 Mountain 艮爲山 丙戌 Fire Dog 1 **1** 二十	木8 Wood 6 Delight 雷地豫 丁亥 Fire Pig 8 **2** 廿一	火7 Fire 3 Beginning 水雷屯 戊子 Earth Rat 4 **3** 廿二	金9 Metal 8 Without Wrongdoing 天雷無妄 己丑 Earth Ox 2 **4** 廿三	木3 Wood 9 Fire 離爲火 庚寅 Metal Tiger 1 **5** 廿四
火2 Fire 1 Sincerity 風澤中孚 辛卯 Metal Rabbit 3 **6** 廿五	水6 Water 2 Big Livestock 山天大畜 壬辰 Water Dragon 4 **7** 廿六	金4 Metal 3 Eliminating 澤天夬 癸巳 Water Snake 6 **8** 廿七	金9 Metal 4 Heaven 乾爲天 甲午 Wood Horse 1 **9** 廿八	火7 Fire 5 Well 水風井 乙未 Wood Goat 6 **10** 廿九	木8 Wood 6 Relief 雷水解 丙申 Fire Monkey 4 **11** 三十	金4 Metal 7 Influence 澤山咸 丁酉 Fire Rooster 9 **12** 二月初一
水1 Water 8 Humility 地山謙 戊戌 Earth Dog 6 **13** 初二	火2 Fire 9 Observation 風地觀 己亥 Earth Pig 2 **14** 初三	火2 Fire 1 Increasing 風雷益 庚子 Metal Rat 9 **15** 初四	水1 Water 2 Dimming Light 地火明夷 辛丑 Metal Ox 3 **16** 初五	金9 Metal 3 Fellowship 天火同人 壬寅 Water Tiger 7 **17** 初六	木8 Wood 4 Marrying Maiden 雷澤歸妹 癸卯 Water Rabbit 7 **18** 初七	木3 Wood 5 Opposition 火澤睽 甲辰 Wood Dragon 2 **19** 初八
火7 Fire 6 Waiting 水天需 乙巳 Wood Snake 3 **20** 初九	金4 Metal 7 Great Exceeding 澤風大過 丙午 Fire Horse 3 **21** 初十	水6 Water 8 Poison 山風蠱 丁未 Fire Goat 7 **22** 十一	火2 Fire 9 Dispersing 風水渙 戊申 Earth Monkey 6 **23** 十二	木3 Wood 1 Travelling 火山旅 己酉 Earth Rooster 8 **24** 十三	金9 Metal 2 Stagnation 天地否 庚戌 Metal Dog 9 **25** 十四	火7 Fire 3 Alliance 水地比 辛亥 Metal Pig 7 **26** 十五
木8 Wood 4 Thunder 震爲雷 壬子 Water Rat 1 **27** 十六	水6 Water 5 Beauty 山火賁 癸丑 Water Ox 8 **28** 十七	火7 Fire 6 Accomplished 水火既濟 甲寅 Wood Tiger 9 **29** 十八	水1 Water 7 Arriving 地澤臨 乙卯 Wood Rabbit 4 **30** 十九	金4 Metal 8 Marsh 兌爲澤 丙辰 Fire Dragon 1 **31** 二十		

APRIL 1994 戊辰

Xuan Kong Element 玄空五行	天澤履 Tread	Period Luck 卦運	Monthly Star 月星
Metal 金9		6	3

SUNDAY	MONDAY	TUESDAY	WEDNESDAY	THURSDAY	FRIDAY	SATURDAY
					火2 Fire 9 Small Livestock 風天小畜 丁巳 Fire Snake 8 **1** 廿一	木3 Wood 1 The Cauldron 火風鼎 戊午 Earth Horse 4 **2** 廿二
水1 Water 2 Rising 地風升 己未 Earth Goat 2 **3** 廿三	火7 Fire 3 Water 坎爲水 庚申 Metal Monkey 1 **4** 廿四	木8 Wood 4 Lesser Exceeding 雷山小過 辛酉 Metal Rooster 3 **5** 廿五	金4 Metal 5 Gathering 澤地萃 壬戌 Water Dog 4 **6** 廿六	水6 Water 6 Peel 山地剝 癸亥 Water Pig 6 **7** 廿七	水1 Water 7 Earth 坤爲地 甲子 Wood Rat 1 **8** 廿八	木3 Wood 8 Biting 火雷噬嗑 乙丑 Wood Ox 6 **9** 廿九
火2 Fire 9 Family 風火家人 丙寅 Fire Tiger 4 **10** 三十	水6 Water 1 Decreasing 山澤損 丁卯 Fire Rabbit 9 **11** 三月初一	金9 Metal 2 Tread 天澤履 戊辰 Earth Dragon 6 **12** 初二	木8 Wood 3 Great Strength 雷天大壯 己巳 Earth Snake 2 **13** 初三	木8 Wood 4 Consistency 雷風恒 庚午 Metal Horse 9 **14** 初四	金9 Metal 5 Litigation 天水訟 辛未 Metal Goat 3 **15** 初五	水1 Water 6 Officer 地水師 壬申 Water Monkey 7 **16** 初六
火2 Fire 7 Gradual Progress 風山漸 癸酉 Water Rooster 7 **17** 初七	火7 Fire 8 Obstruction 水山蹇 甲戌 Wood Dog 2 **18** 初八	木3 Wood 9 Advancement 火地晉 乙亥 Wood Pig 3 **19** 初九	水6 Water 1 Nourish 山雷頤 丙子 Fire Rat 3 **20** 初十	金4 Metal 2 Following 澤雷隨 丁丑 Fire Ox 7 **21** 十一	木8 Wood 3 Abundance 雷火豐 戊寅 Earth Tiger 6 **22** 十二	火7 Fire 4 Regulate 水澤節 己卯 Earth Rabbit 8 **23** 十三
水1 Water 5 Unity 地天泰 庚辰 Metal Dragon 9 **24** 十四	木3 Wood 6 Great Reward 火天大有 辛巳 Metal Snake 7 **25** 十五	火2 Fire 7 Wind 巽爲風 壬午 Water Horse 1 **26** 十六	金4 Metal 8 Trap 澤水困 癸未 Water Goat 8 **27** 十七	木3 Wood 9 Not Yet Accomplished 火水未濟 甲申 Wood Monkey 9 **28** 十八	金9 Metal 1 Retreat 天山遯 乙酉 Wood Rooster 4 **29** 十九	水6 Water 2 Mountain 艮爲山 丙戌 Fire Dog 1 **30** 二十

MAY 1994 己巳

Xuan Kong Element 玄空五行	雷天大壯	Period Luck 卦運	Monthly Star 月星
Wood 木8	Great Strength	2	2

SUNDAY	MONDAY	TUESDAY	WEDNESDAY	THURSDAY	FRIDAY	SATURDAY
1 廿一 木8 Wood · 3 Delight 雷地豫 丁亥 Fire Pig · 8	**2** 廿二 火7 Fire · 4 Beginning 水雷屯 戊子 Earth Rat · 4	**3** 廿三 金9 Metal · 5 Without Wrongdoing 天雷無妄 己丑 Earth Ox · 2	**4** 廿四 木3 Wood · 6 Fire 離爲火 庚寅 Metal Tiger · 1	**5** 廿五 火2 Fire · 7 Sincerity 風澤中孚 辛卯 Metal Rabbit · 3	**6** 廿六 水6 Water · 8 Big Livestock 山天大畜 壬辰 Water Dragon · 4	**7** 廿七 金4 Metal · 9 Eliminating 澤天夬 癸巳 Water Snake · 6
8 廿八 金9 Metal · 1 Heaven 乾爲天 甲午 Wood Horse · 1	**9** 廿九 火7 Fire · 2 Well 水風井 乙未 Wood Goat · 6	**10** 三十 木8 Wood · 3 Relief 雷水解 丙申 Fire Monkey · 4	**11** 四月初一 金4 Metal · 4 Influence 澤山咸 丁酉 Fire Rooster · 9	**12** 初二 水1 Water · 5 Humility 地山謙 戊戌 Earth Dog · 6	**13** 初三 火2 Fire · 6 Observation 風地觀 己亥 Earth Pig · 2	**14** 初四 火2 Fire · 7 Increasing 風雷益 庚子 Metal Rat · 9
15 初五 水1 Water · 8 Dimming Light 地火明夷 辛丑 Metal Ox · 3	**16** 初六 金9 Metal · 9 Fellowship 天火同人 壬寅 Water Tiger · 7	**17** 初七 木8 Wood · 1 Marrying Maiden 雷澤歸妹 癸卯 Water Rabbit · 7	**18** 初八 木3 Wood · 2 Opposition 火澤睽 甲辰 Wood Dragon · 2	**19** 初九 火7 Fire · 3 Waiting 水天需 乙巳 Wood Snake · 3	**20** 初十 金4 Metal · 4 Great Exceeding 澤風大過 丙午 Fire Horse · 3	**21** 十一 水6 Water · 5 Poison 山風蠱 丁未 Fire Goat · 7
22 十二 火2 Fire · 6 Dispersing 風水渙 戊申 Earth Monkey · 6	**23** 十三 木3 Wood · 7 Travelling 火山旅 己酉 Earth Rooster · 8	**24** 十四 金9 Metal · 8 Stagnation 天地否 庚戌 Metal Dog · 9	**25** 十五 火7 Fire · 9 Alliance 水地比 辛亥 Metal Pig · 7	**26** 十六 木8 Wood · 1 Thunder 震爲雷 壬子 Water Rat · 1	**27** 十七 水6 Water · 2 Beauty 山火賁 癸丑 Water Ox · 8	**28** 十八 火7 Fire · 3 Accomplished 水火既濟 甲寅 Wood Tiger · 9
29 十九 水1 Water · 4 Arriving 地澤臨 乙卯 Wood Rabbit · 4	**30** 二十 金4 Metal · 5 Marsh 兌爲澤 丙辰 Fire Dragon · 1	**31** 廿一 火2 Fire · 6 Small Livestock 風天小畜 丁巳 Fire Snake · 8				

JUNE 1994 庚午

Xuan Kong Element 玄空五行	雷風恆	Period Luck 卦運	Monthly Star 月星
Wood 木8	Consistency	9	1

SUNDAY	MONDAY	TUESDAY	WEDNESDAY	THURSDAY	FRIDAY	SATURDAY
			1 廿二 木3 Wood · 7 The Cauldron 火風鼎 戊午 Earth Horse · 4	**2** 廿三 水1 Water · 8 Rising 地風升 己未 Earth Goat · 2	**3** 廿四 火7 Fire · 9 Water 坎爲水 庚申 Metal Monkey · 1	**4** 廿五 木8 Wood · 1 Lesser Exceeding 雷山小過 辛酉 Metal Rooster · 3
5 廿六 金4 Metal · 2 Gathering 澤地萃 壬戌 Water Dog · 4	**6** 廿七 水6 Water · 3 Peel 山地剝 癸亥 Water Pig · 6	**7** 廿八 水1 Water · 4 Earth 坤爲地 甲子 Wood Rat · 1	**8** 廿九 木3 Wood · 5 Biting 火雷噬嗑 乙丑 Wood Ox · 6	**9** 五月初一 火2 Fire · 6 Family 風火家人 丙寅 Fire Tiger · 4	**10** 初二 水6 Water · 7 Decreasing 山澤損 丁卯 Fire Rabbit · 9	**11** 初三 金9 Metal · 8 Tread 天澤履 戊辰 Earth Dragon · 6
12 初四 木8 Wood · 9 Great Strength 雷天大壯 己巳 Earth Snake · 2	**13** 初五 木8 Wood · 1 Consistency 雷風恆 庚午 Metal Horse · 9	**14** 初六 金9 Metal · 2 Litigation 天水訟 辛未 Metal Goat · 3	**15** 初七 水1 Water · 3 Officer 地水師 壬申 Water Monkey · 7	**16** 初八 火2 Fire · 4 Gradual Progress 風山漸 癸酉 Water Rooster · 7	**17** 初九 火7 Fire · 5 Obstruction 水山蹇 甲戌 Wood Dog · 2	**18** 初十 木3 Wood · 6 Advancement 火地晉 乙亥 Wood Pig · 3
19 十一 水6 Water · 7 Nourish 山雷頤 丙子 Fire Rat · 3	**20** 十二 金4 Metal · 8 Following 澤雷隨 丁丑 Fire Ox · 7	**21** 十三 木8 Wood · 9/1 Abundance 雷火豐 戊寅 Earth Tiger · 6	**22** 十四 火7 Fire · 9 Regulate 水澤節 己卯 Earth Rabbit · 8	**23** 十五 水1 Water · 8 Unity 地天泰 庚辰 Metal Dragon · 9	**24** 十六 木3 Wood · 7 Great Reward 火天大有 辛巳 Metal Snake · 7	**25** 十七 火2 Fire · 6 Wind 巽爲風 壬午 Water Horse · 1
26 十八 金4 Metal · 5 Trap 澤水困 癸未 Water Goat · 8	**27** 十九 木3 Wood · 4 Not Yet Accomplished 火水未濟 甲申 Wood Monkey · 9	**28** 二十 金9 Metal · 3 Retreat 天山遯 乙酉 Wood Rooster · 4	**29** 廿一 水6 Water · 2 Mountain 艮爲山 丙戌 Fire Dog · 1	**30** 廿二 木8 Wood · 1 Delight 雷地豫 丁亥 Fire Pig · 8		

JULY 1994 辛未

Xuan Kong Element 玄空五行	天水訟 Litigation	Period Luck 卦運	Monthly Star 月星
Metal 金9		3	9

SUNDAY	MONDAY	TUESDAY	WEDNESDAY	THURSDAY	FRIDAY	SATURDAY
木3 Wood 6 The Cauldron 火風鼎 戊午 Earth Horse **31** 廿三 4					火7 Fire 9 Beginning 水雷屯 戊子 Earth Rat **1** 廿三 4	金9 Metal 8 Without Wrongdoing 天雷無妄 己丑 Earth Ox **2** 廿四 2
木3 Wood 7 Fire 離為火 庚寅 Metal Tiger **3** 廿五 1	火2 Fire 6 Sincerity 風澤中孚 辛卯 Metal Rabbit **4** 廿六 3	水6 Water 5 Big Livestock 山天大畜 壬辰 Water Dragon **5** 廿七 4	金4 Metal 4 Eliminating 澤天夬 癸巳 Water Snake **6** 廿八 6	金9 Metal 3 Heaven 乾為天 甲午 Wood Horse **7** 廿九 1	火7 Fire 2 Well 水風井 乙未 Wood Goat **8** 三十 6	木8 Wood 1 Relief 雷水解 丙申 Fire Monkey **9** 六月初一 4
金4 Metal 9 Influence 澤山咸 丁酉 Fire Rooster **10** 初二 9	水1 Water 8 Humility 地山謙 戊戌 Earth Dog **11** 初三 6	火2 Fire 7 Observation 風地觀 己亥 Earth Pig **12** 初四 2	火2 Fire 6 Increasing 風雷益 庚子 Metal Rat **13** 初五 9	水1 Water 5 Dimming Light 地火明夷 辛丑 Metal Ox **14** 初六 3	金9 Metal 4 Fellowship 天火同人 壬寅 Water Tiger **15** 初七 7	木8 Wood 3 Marrying Maiden 雷澤歸妹 癸卯 Water Rabbit **16** 初八 7
木3 Wood 2 Opposition 火澤睽 甲辰 Wood Dragon **17** 初九 2	火7 Fire 1 Waiting 水天需 乙巳 Wood Snake **18** 初十 3	金4 Metal 9 Great Exceeding 澤風大過 丙午 Fire Horse **19** 十一 3	水6 Water 8 Poison 山風蠱 丁未 Fire Goat **20** 十二 7	火2 Fire 7 Dispersing 風水渙 戊申 Earth Monkey **21** 十三 6	木3 Wood 6 Travelling 火山旅 己酉 Earth Rooster **22** 十四 8	金9 Metal 5 Stagnation 天地否 庚戌 Metal Dog **23** 十五 9
火7 Fire 4 Alliance 水地比 辛亥 Metal Pig **24** 十六 7	木8 Wood 3 Thunder 震為雷 壬子 Water Rat **25** 十七 1	水6 Water 2 Beauty 山火賁 癸丑 Water Ox **26** 十八 8	火7 Fire 1 Accomplished 水火既濟 甲寅 Wood Tiger **27** 十九 9	水1 Water 9 Arriving 地澤臨 乙卯 Wood Rabbit **28** 二十 4	金4 Metal 8 Marsh 兌為澤 丙辰 Fire Dragon **29** 廿一 1	火2 Fire 7 Small Livestock 風天小畜 丁巳 Fire Snake **30** 廿二 8

AUGUST 1994 壬申

Xuan Kong Element 玄空五行	地水師 Officer	Period Luck 卦運	Monthly Star 月星
Water 水1		7	8

SUNDAY	MONDAY	TUESDAY	WEDNESDAY	THURSDAY	FRIDAY	SATURDAY
	水1 Water 5 Rising 地風升 己未 Earth Goat **1** 廿四 2	火7 Fire 4 Water 坎為水 庚申 Metal Monkey **2** 廿五 1	木8 Wood 3 Lesser Exceeding 雷山小過 辛酉 Metal Rooster **3** 廿六 3	金4 Metal 2 Gathering 澤地萃 壬戌 Water Dog **4** 廿七 4	水6 Water 1 Peel 山地剝 癸亥 Water Pig **5** 廿八 6	水1 Water 9 Earth 坤為地 甲子 Wood Rat **6** 廿九 1
木3 Wood 8 Biting 火雷噬嗑 乙丑 Wood Ox **7** 七月初一 6	火2 Fire 7 Family 風火家人 丙寅 Fire Tiger **8** 初二 4	水6 Water 6 Decreasing 山澤損 丁卯 Fire Rabbit **9** 初三 9	金9 Metal 5 Tread 天澤履 戊辰 Earth Dragon **10** 初四 6	木8 Wood 4 Great Strength 雷天大壯 己巳 Earth Snake **11** 初五 2	木8 Wood 3 Consistency 雷風恆 庚午 Metal Horse **12** 初六 9	金9 Metal 2 Litigation 天水訟 辛未 Metal Goat **13** 初七 3
水1 Water 1 Officer 地水師 壬申 Water Monkey **14** 初八 7	火2 Fire 9 Gradual Progress 風山漸 癸酉 Water Rooster **15** 初九 7	火7 Fire 8 Obstruction 水山蹇 甲戌 Wood Dog **16** 初十 2	木3 Wood 7 Advancement 火地晉 乙亥 Wood Pig **17** 十一 3	水6 Water 6 Nourish 山雷頤 丙子 Fire Rat **18** 十二 3	金4 Metal 5 Following 澤雷隨 丁丑 Fire Ox **19** 十三 7	木8 Wood 4 Abundance 雷火豐 戊寅 Earth Tiger **20** 十四 6
火7 Fire 3 Regulate 水澤節 己卯 Earth Rabbit **21** 十五 8	水1 Water 2 Unity 地天泰 庚辰 Metal Dragon **22** 十六 9	木3 Wood 1 Great Reward 火天大有 辛巳 Metal Snake **23** 十七 7	火2 Fire 9 Wind 巽為風 壬午 Water Horse **24** 十八 1	金4 Metal 8 Trap 澤水困 癸未 Water Goat **25** 十九 8	木3 Wood 7 Not Yet Accomplished 火水未濟 甲申 Wood Monkey **26** 二十 9	金9 Metal 6 Retreat 天山遯 乙酉 Wood Rooster **27** 廿一 4
水6 Water 5 Mountain 艮為山 丙戌 Fire Dog **28** 廿二 1	木8 Wood 4 Delight 雷地豫 丁亥 Fire Pig **29** 廿三 8	火7 Fire 3 Beginning 水雷屯 戊子 Earth Rat **30** 廿四 4	金9 Metal 2 Without Wrongdoing 天雷無妄 己丑 Earth Ox **31** 廿五 2			

SEPTEMBER 1994 癸酉

Xuan Kong Element 玄空五行	風山漸 Gradual Progress	Period Luck 卦運	Monthly Star 月星
Fire 火2		7	7

SUNDAY	MONDAY	TUESDAY	WEDNESDAY	THURSDAY	FRIDAY	SATURDAY
				木3 Wood 1 Fire 離爲火 庚寅 Metal Tiger 1 1 廿六	火2 Fire 9 Sincerity 風澤中孚 辛卯 Metal Rabbit 3 2 廿七	水6 Water 8 Big Livestock 山天大畜 壬辰 Water Dragon 4 3 廿八
金4 Metal 7 Eliminating 澤天夬 癸巳 Water Snake 6 4 廿九	金9 Metal 6 Heaven 乾爲天 甲午 Wood Horse 1 5 三十	火7 Fire 5 Well 水風井 乙未 Wood Goat 6 6 八月初一	木8 Wood 4 Relief 雷水解 丙申 Fire Monkey 4 7 初二	金4 Metal 3 Influence 澤山咸 丁酉 Fire Rooster 9 8 初三	水1 Water 2 Humility 地山謙 戊戌 Earth Dog 6 9 初四	火2 Fire 1 Observation 風地觀 己亥 Earth Pig 2 10 初五
火2 Fire 9 Increasing 風雷益 庚子 Metal Rat 9 11 初六	水1 Water 8 Dimming Light 地火明夷 辛丑 Metal Ox 3 12 初七	金9 Metal 7 Fellowship 天火同人 壬寅 Water Tiger 7 13 初八	木8 Wood 6 Marrying Maiden 雷澤歸妹 癸卯 Water Rabbit 7 14 初九	木3 Wood 5 Opposition 火澤睽 甲辰 Wood Dragon 2 15 初十	火7 Fire 4 Waiting 水天需 乙巳 Wood Snake 3 16 十一	金4 Metal 3 Great Exceeding 澤風大過 丙午 Fire Horse 3 17 十二
水6 Water 2 Poison 山風蠱 丁未 Fire Goat 7 18 十三	火2 Fire 1 Dispersing 風水渙 戊申 Earth Monkey 6 19 十四	木3 Wood 9 Travelling 火山旅 己酉 Earth Rooster 8 20 十五	金9 Metal 8 Stagnation 天地否 庚戌 Metal Dog 9 21 十六	火7 Fire 7 Alliance 水地比 辛亥 Metal Pig 7 22 十七	木8 Wood 6 Thunder 震爲雷 壬子 Water Rat 1 23 十八	水6 Water 5 Beauty 山火賁 癸丑 Water Ox 8 24 十九
火7 Fire 4 Accomplished 水火既濟 甲寅 Wood Tiger 9 25 二十	水1 Water 3 Arriving 地澤臨 乙卯 Wood Rabbit 4 26 廿一	金4 Metal 2 Marsh 兌爲澤 丙辰 Fire Dragon 1 27 廿二	火2 Fire 1 Small Livestock 風天小畜 丁巳 Fire Snake 8 28 廿三	木3 Wood 9 The Cauldron 火風鼎 戊午 Earth Horse 4 29 廿四	水1 Water 8 Rising 地風升 己未 Earth Goat 2 30 廿五	

OCTOBER 1994 甲戌

Xuan Kong Element 玄空五行	水山蹇 Obstruction	Period Luck 卦運	Monthly Star 月星
Fire 火7		2	6

SUNDAY	MONDAY	TUESDAY	WEDNESDAY	THURSDAY	FRIDAY	SATURDAY
金9 Metal 5 Without Wrongdoing 天雷無妄 己丑 Earth Ox 2 30 廿六	木3 Wood 4 Fire 離爲火 庚寅 Metal Tiger 1 31 廿七					火7 Fire 7 Water 坎爲水 庚申 Metal Monkey 1 1 廿六
木8 Wood 6 Lesser Exceeding 雷山小過 辛酉 Metal Rooster 3 2 廿七	金4 Metal 5 Gathering 澤地萃 壬戌 Water Dog 4 3 廿八	水6 Water 4 Peel 山地剝 癸亥 Water Pig 6 4 廿九	水1 Water 3 Earth 坤爲地 甲子 Wood Rat 1 5 九月初一	木3 Wood 2 Biting 火雷噬嗑 乙丑 Wood Ox 6 6 初二	火2 Fire 1 Family 風火家人 丙寅 Fire Tiger 4 7 初三	水6 Water 9 Decreasing 山澤損 丁卯 Fire Rabbit 9 8 初四
金9 Metal 8 Tread 天澤履 戊辰 Earth Dragon 6 9 初五	木8 Wood 7 Great Strength 雷天大壯 己巳 Earth Snake 2 10 初六	木8 Wood 6 Consistency 雷風恆 庚午 Metal Horse 9 11 初七	金9 Metal 5 Litigation 天水訟 辛未 Metal Goat 3 12 初八	水1 Water 4 Officer 地水師 壬申 Water Monkey 7 13 初九	火2 Fire 3 Gradual Progress 風山漸 癸酉 Water Rooster 7 14 初十	火7 Fire 2 Obstruction 水山蹇 甲戌 Wood Dog 2 15 十一
木3 Wood 1 Advancement 火地晉 乙亥 Wood Pig 3 16 十二	水6 Water 9 Nourish 山雷頤 丙子 Fire Rat 3 17 十三	金4 Metal 8 Following 澤雷隨 丁丑 Fire Ox 7 18 十四	木8 Wood 7 Abundance 雷火豐 戊寅 Earth Tiger 6 19 十五	火7 Fire 6 Regulate 水澤節 己卯 Earth Rabbit 8 20 十六	水1 Water 5 Unity 地天泰 庚辰 Metal Dragon 9 21 十七	木3 Wood 4 Great Reward 火天大有 辛巳 Metal Snake 7 22 十八
火2 Fire 3 Wind 巽爲風 壬午 Water Horse 1 23 十九	金4 Metal 2 Trap 澤水困 癸未 Water Goat 8 24 二十	木3 Wood 1 Not Yet Accomplished 火水未濟 甲申 Wood Monkey 9 25 廿一	金9 Metal 9 Retreat 天山遯 乙酉 Wood Rooster 4 26 廿二	水6 Water 8 Mountain 艮爲山 丙戌 Fire Dog 1 27 廿三	木8 Wood 7 Delight 雷地豫 丁亥 Fire Pig 8 28 廿四	火7 Fire 6 Beginning 水雷屯 戊子 Earth Rat 4 29 廿五

NOVEMBER 1994 乙亥

Xuan Kong Element 玄空五行	火地晉 Advancement	Period Luck 卦運	Monthly Star 月星
Wood 木3		3	5

Date	Day	Element	Hexagram	卦	Stem-Branch	Lunar Date	Period Number	Star
1	Tuesday	火2 Fire	Sincerity	風澤中孚	辛卯 Metal Rabbit	廿八	3	3
2	Wednesday	水6 Water	Big Livestock	山天大畜	壬辰 Water Dragon	廿九	4	2
3	Thursday	金4 Metal	Eliminating	澤天夬	癸巳 Water Snake	十月初一	6	1
4	Friday	金9 Metal	Heaven	乾爲天	甲午 Wood Horse	初二	1	9
5	Saturday	火7 Fire	Well	水風井	乙未 Wood Goat	初三	6	8
6	Sunday	木8 Wood	Relief	雷水解	丙申 Fire Monkey	初四	4	7
7	Monday	金4 Metal	Influence	澤山咸	丁酉 Fire Rooster	初五	9	6
8	Tuesday	水1 Water	Humility	地山謙	戊戌 Earth Dog	初六	6	5
9	Wednesday	火2 Fire	Observation	風地觀	己亥 Earth Pig	初七	2	4
10	Thursday	火2 Fire	Increasing	風雷益	庚子 Metal Rat	初八	9	3
11	Friday	水1 Water	Dimming Light	地火明夷	辛丑 Metal Ox	初九	3	2
12	Saturday	金9 Metal	Fellowship	天火同人	壬寅 Water Tiger	初十	7	1
13	Sunday	木8 Wood	Marrying Maiden	雷澤歸妹	癸卯 Water Rabbit	十一	7	9
14	Monday	木3 Wood	Opposition	火澤睽	甲辰 Wood Dragon	十二	2	8
15	Tuesday	火7 Fire	Waiting	水天需	乙巳 Wood Snake	十三	3	7
16	Wednesday	金4 Metal	Great Exceeding	澤風大過	丙午 Fire Horse	十四	3	6
17	Thursday	水6 Water	Poison	山風蠱	丁未 Fire Goat	十五	7	5
18	Friday	火2 Fire	Dispersing	風水渙	戊申 Earth Monkey	十六	6	4
19	Saturday	木3 Wood	Travelling	火山旅	己酉 Earth Rooster	十七	8	3
20	Sunday	金9 Metal	Stagnation	天地否	庚戌 Metal Dog	十八	9	2
21	Monday	火7 Fire	Alliance	水地比	辛亥 Metal Pig	十九	7	1
22	Tuesday	木8 Wood	Thunder	震爲雷	壬子 Water Rat	二十	1	9
23	Wednesday	水6 Water	Beauty	山火賁	癸丑 Water Ox	廿一	8	8
24	Thursday	火7 Fire	Accomplished	水火既濟	甲寅 Wood Tiger	廿二	9	7
25	Friday	水1 Water	Arriving	地澤臨	乙卯 Wood Rabbit	廿三	4	6
26	Saturday	金4 Metal	Marsh	兑爲澤	丙辰 Fire Dragon	廿四	1	5
27	Sunday	火2 Fire	Small Livestock	風天小畜	丁巳 Fire Snake	廿五	8	4
28	Monday	木3 Wood	The Cauldron	火風鼎	戊午 Earth Horse	廿六	4	3
29	Tuesday	水1 Water	Rising	地風升	己未 Earth Goat	廿七	2	2
30	Wednesday	火7 Fire	Water	坎爲水	庚申 Metal Monkey	廿八	1	1

DECEMBER 1994 丙子

Xuan Kong Element 玄空五行	山雷頤 Nourish	Period Luck 卦運	Monthly Star 月星
Water 水6		3	4

Date	Day	Element	Hexagram	卦	Stem-Branch	Lunar Date	Period Number	Star
1	Thursday	木8 Wood	Lesser Exceeding	雷山小過	辛酉 Metal Rooster	廿九	3	9
2	Friday	金4 Metal	Gathering	澤地萃	壬戌 Water Dog	三十	4	8
3	Saturday	水6 Water	Peel	山地剝	癸亥 Water Pig	十一月初一	6	7
4	Sunday	水1 Water	Earth	坤爲地	甲子 Wood Rat	初二	1	6
5	Monday	木3 Wood	Biting	火雷噬嗑	乙丑 Wood Ox	初三	6	5
6	Tuesday	火2 Fire	Family	風火家人	丙寅 Fire Tiger	初四	4	4
7	Wednesday	水6 Water	Decreasing	山澤損	丁卯 Fire Rabbit	初五	9	3
8	Thursday	金9 Metal	Tread	天澤履	戊辰 Earth Dragon	初六	6	2
9	Friday	木8 Wood	Great Strength	雷天大壯	己巳 Earth Snake	初七	2	1
10	Saturday	木8 Wood	Consistency	雷風恆	庚午 Metal Horse	初八	9	9
11	Sunday	金9 Metal	Litigation	天水訟	辛未 Metal Goat	初九	3	8
12	Monday	水1 Water	Officer	地水師	壬申 Water Monkey	初十	7	7
13	Tuesday	火2 Fire	Gradual Progress	風山漸	癸酉 Water Rooster	十一	7	6
14	Wednesday	火7 Fire	Obstruction	水山蹇	甲戌 Wood Dog	十二	2	5
15	Thursday	木3 Wood	Advancement	火地晉	乙亥 Wood Pig	十三	3	4
16	Friday	水6 Water	Nourish	山雷頤	丙子 Fire Rat	十四	3	3
17	Saturday	金4 Metal	Following	澤雷隨	丁丑 Fire Ox	十五	7	2
18	Sunday	木8 Wood	Abundance	雷火豐	戊寅 Earth Tiger	十六	6	1
19	Monday	火7 Fire	Regulate	水澤節	己卯 Earth Rabbit	十七	8	9
20	Tuesday	水1 Water	Unity	地天泰	庚辰 Metal Dragon	十八	9	8
21	Wednesday	木3 Wood	Great Reward	火天大有	辛巳 Metal Snake	十九	7	7
22	Thursday	火2 Fire	Wind	巽爲風	壬午 Water Horse	二十	1	6/4
23	Friday	金4 Metal	Trap	澤水困	癸未 Water Goat	廿一	8	5
24	Saturday	木3 Wood	Not Yet Accomplished	火水未濟	甲申 Wood Monkey	廿二	9	6
25	Sunday	金9 Metal	Retreat	天山遯	乙酉 Wood Rooster	廿三	4	7
26	Monday	水6 Water	Mountain	艮爲山	丙戌 Fire Dog	廿四	1	8
27	Tuesday	木8 Wood	Delight	雷地豫	丁亥 Fire Pig	廿五	8	9
28	Wednesday	火7 Fire	Beginning	水雷屯	戊子 Earth Rat	廿六	4	1
29	Thursday	金9 Metal	Without Wrongdoing	天雷無妄	己丑 Earth Ox	廿七	2	2
30	Friday	木3 Wood	Fire	離爲火	庚寅 Metal Tiger	廿八	1	3
31	Saturday	火2 Fire	Sincerity	風澤中孚	辛卯 Metal Rabbit	廿九	3	4

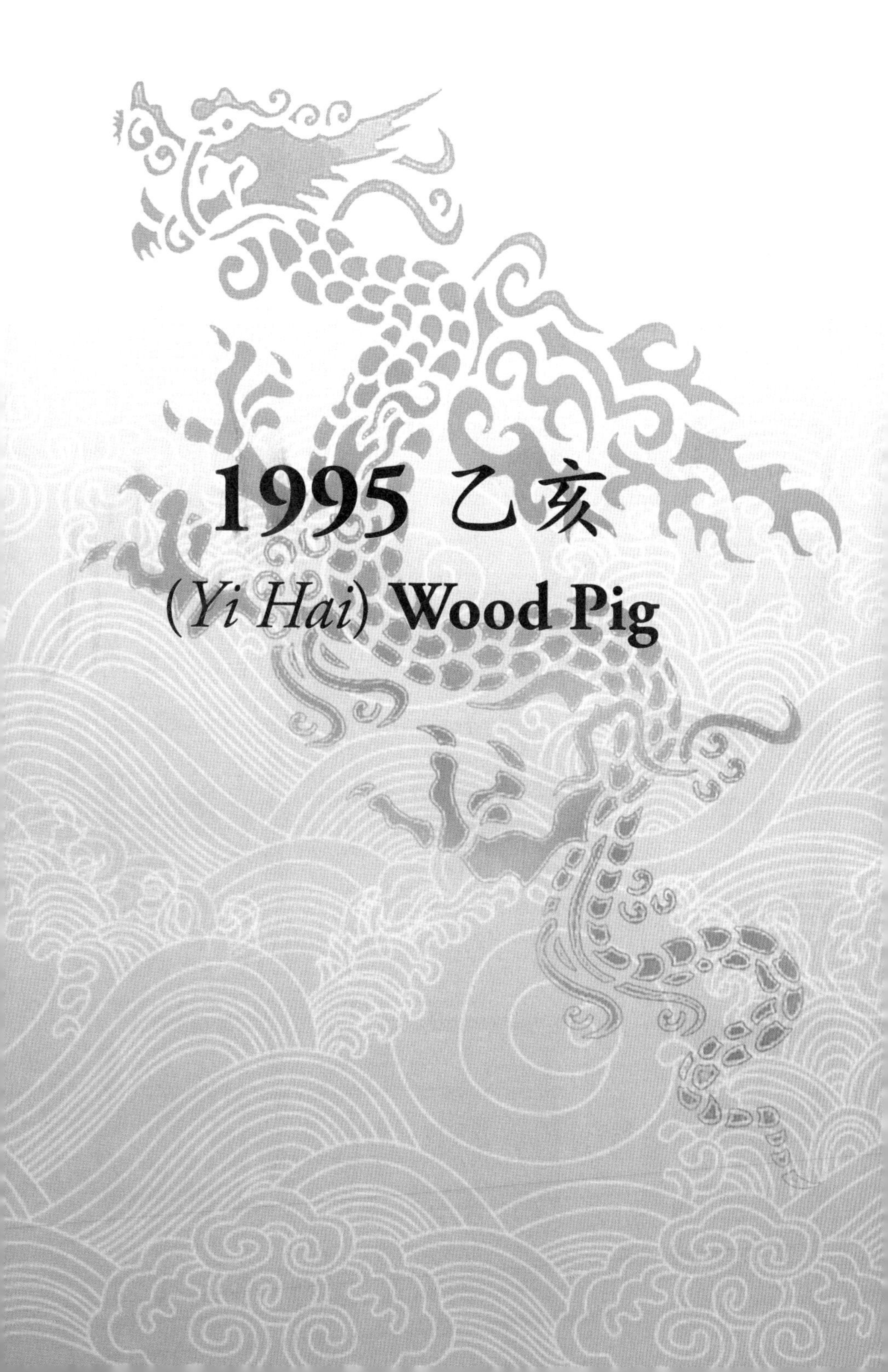

1995 乙亥

(*Yi Hai*) Wood Pig

1995 乙亥 *(Yi Hai)* Wood Pig

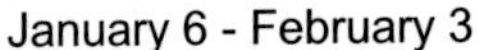

January 6 - February 3

金**4** Metal
丁丑 Fire Ox
7
Following
☱ 澤雷隨

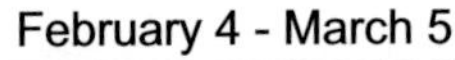

February 4 - March 5

木**8** Wood
戊寅 Earth Tiger
6
Abundance
☳ 雷火豐

March 6 - April 4

火**7** Fire
己卯 Earth Rabbit
8
Regulate
☵ 水澤節

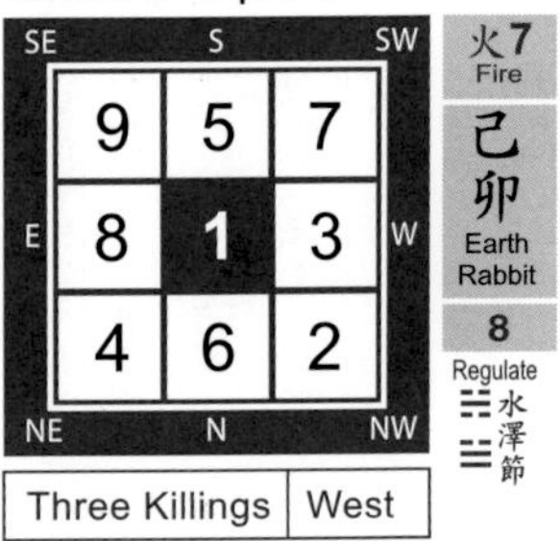

April 5 - May 5

SE S SW
E W
NE N NW
8 4 6
7 9 2
3 5 1
水1 Water
庚辰 Metal Dragon
9
Unity 地天泰
Three Killings South

May 6 - June 5

June 6 - July 6

July 7 - August 7

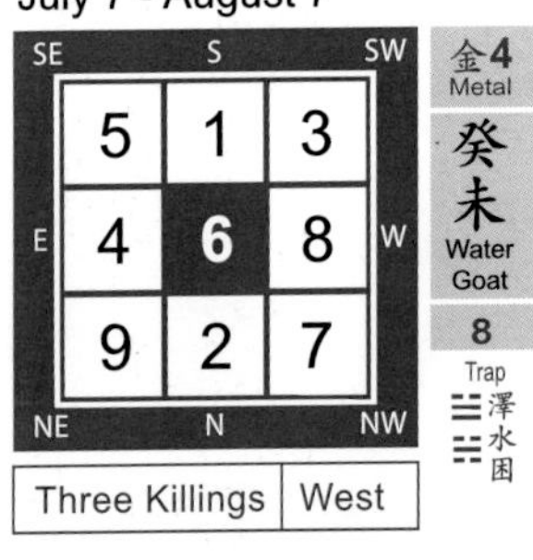

August 8 - September 7

September 8 - October 8

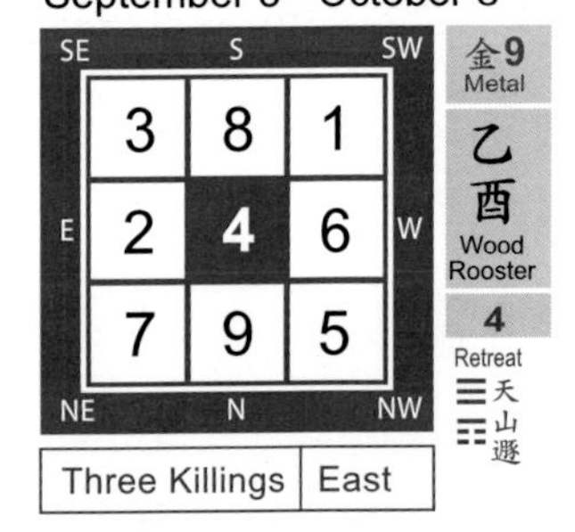

October 9 - November 7

November 8 - December 6

December 7 - January 5

JANUARY 1995 丁丑

Xuan Kong Element 玄空五行	澤雷隨 Following	Period Luck 卦運	Monthly Star 月星
Metal 金4		7	3

SUNDAY	MONDAY	TUESDAY	WEDNESDAY	THURSDAY	FRIDAY	SATURDAY
水6 Water 5 Big Livestock 山天大畜 壬辰 Water Dragon 1 十二月初一 4	金4 Metal 6 Eliminating 澤天夬 癸巳 Water Snake 2 初二 6	金9 Metal 7 Heaven 乾爲天 甲午 Wood Horse 3 初三 1	火7 Fire 8 Well 水風井 乙未 Wood Goat 4 初四 6	木8 Wood 9 Relief 雷水解 丙申 Fire Monkey 5 初五 4	金4 Metal 1 Influence 澤山咸 丁酉 Fire Rooster 6 初六 9	水1 Water 2 Humility 地山謙 戊戌 Earth Dog 7 初七 6
火2 Fire 3 Observation 風地觀 己亥 Earth Pig 8 初八 2	火2 Fire 4 Increasing 風雷益 庚子 Metal Rat 9 初九 9	水1 Water 5 Dimming Light 地火明夷 辛丑 Metal Ox 10 初十 3	金9 Metal 6 Fellowship 天火同人 壬寅 Water Tiger 11 十一 7	木8 Wood 7 Marrying Maiden 雷澤歸妹 癸卯 Water Rabbit 12 十二 7	木3 Wood 8 Opposition 火澤睽 甲辰 Wood Dragon 13 十三 2	火7 Fire 9 Waiting 水天需 乙巳 Wood Snake 14 十四 3
金4 Metal 1 Great Exceeding 澤風大過 丙午 Fire Horse 15 十五 3	水6 Water 2 Poison 山風蠱 丁未 Fire Goat 16 十六 7	火2 Fire 3 Dispersing 風水渙 戊申 Earth Monkey 17 十七 6	木3 Wood 4 Travelling 火山旅 己酉 Earth Rooster 18 十八 8	金9 Metal 5 Stagnation 天地否 庚戌 Metal Dog 19 十九 9	火7 Fire 6 Alliance 水地比 辛亥 Metal Pig 20 二十 7	木8 Wood 7 Thunder 震爲雷 壬子 Water Rat 21 廿一 1
水6 Water 8 Beauty 山火賁 癸丑 Water Ox 22 廿二 8	火7 Fire 9 Accomplished 水火既濟 甲寅 Wood Tiger 23 廿三 9	水1 Water 1 Arriving 地澤臨 乙卯 Wood Rabbit 24 廿四 4	金4 Metal 2 Marsh 兑爲澤 丙辰 Fire Dragon 25 廿五 1	火2 Fire 3 Small Livestock 風天小畜 丁巳 Fire Snake 26 廿六 8	木3 Wood 4 The Cauldron 火風鼎 戊午 Earth Horse 27 廿七 4	水1 Water 5 Rising 地風升 己未 Earth Goat 28 廿八 2
火7 Fire 6 Water 坎爲水 庚申 Metal Monkey 29 廿九 1	木8 Wood 7 Lesser Exceeding 雷山小過 辛酉 Metal Rooster 30 三十 3	金4 Metal 8 Gathering 澤地萃 壬戌 Water Dog 31 正月初一 4				

FEBRUARY 1995 戊寅

Xuan Kong Element 玄空五行	雷火豐 Abundance	Period Luck 卦運	Monthly Star 月星
Wood 木8		6	2

SUNDAY	MONDAY	TUESDAY	WEDNESDAY	THURSDAY	FRIDAY	SATURDAY
			水6 Water 9 Peel 山地剝 癸亥 Water Pig 1 初二 6	水1 Water 1 Earth 坤爲地 甲子 Wood Rat 2 初三 1	木3 Wood 2 Biting 火雷噬嗑 乙丑 Wood Ox 3 初四 6	火2 Fire 3 Family 風火家人 丙寅 Fire Tiger 4 初五 4
水6 Water 4 Decreasing 山澤損 丁卯 Fire Rabbit 5 初六 9	金9 Metal 5 Tread 天澤履 戊辰 Earth Dragon 6 初七 6	木8 Wood 6 Great Strength 雷天大壯 己巳 Earth Snake 7 初八 2	木8 Wood 7 Consistency 雷風恆 庚午 Metal Horse 8 初九 9	金9 Metal 8 Litigation 天水訟 辛未 Metal Goat 9 初十 3	水1 Water 9 Officer 地水師 壬申 Water Monkey 10 十一 7	火2 Fire 1 Gradual Progress 風山漸 癸酉 Water Rooster 11 十二 7
火7 Fire 2 Obstruction 水山蹇 甲戌 Wood Dog 12 十三 2	木3 Wood 3 Advancement 火地晉 乙亥 Wood Pig 13 十四 3	水6 Water 4 Nourish 山雷頤 丙子 Fire Rat 14 十五 3	金4 Metal 5 Following 澤雷隨 丁丑 Fire Ox 15 十六 7	木8 Wood 6 Abundance 雷火豐 戊寅 Earth Tiger 16 十七 6	火7 Fire 7 Regulate 水澤節 己卯 Earth Rabbit 17 十八 8	水1 Water 8 Unity 地天泰 庚辰 Metal Dragon 18 十九 9
木3 Wood 9 Great Reward 火天大有 辛巳 Metal Snake 19 二十 7	火2 Fire 1 Wind 巽爲風 壬午 Water Horse 20 廿一 1	金4 Metal 2 Trap 澤水困 癸未 Water Goat 21 廿二 8	木3 Wood 3 Not Yet Accomplished 火水未濟 甲申 Wood Monkey 22 廿三 9	金9 Metal 4 Retreat 天山遯 乙酉 Wood Rooster 23 廿四 4	水6 Water 5 Mountain 艮爲山 丙戌 Fire Dog 24 廿五 1	木8 Wood 6 Delight 雷地豫 丁亥 Fire Pig 25 廿六 8
火7 Fire 7 Beginning 水雷屯 戊子 Earth Rat 26 廿七 4	金9 Metal 8 Without Wrongdoing 天雷無妄 己丑 Earth Ox 27 廿八 2	木3 Wood 9 Fire 離爲火 庚寅 Metal Tiger 28 廿九 1				

MARCH 1995 己卯

Xuan Kong Element 玄空五行	水澤節 Regulate	Period Luck 卦運	Monthly Star 月星
Fire 火7		8	1

SUNDAY	MONDAY	TUESDAY	WEDNESDAY	THURSDAY	FRIDAY	SATURDAY
			火2 Fire 辛卯 Metal Rabbit Sincerity 風澤中孚 **1** 二月初一 3 [1]	水6 Water 壬辰 Water Dragon Big Livestock 山天大畜 **2** 初二 4 [2]	金4 Metal 癸巳 Water Snake Eliminating 澤天夬 **3** 初三 6 [3]	金9 Metal 甲午 Wood Horse Heaven 乾爲天 **4** 初四 1 [4]
火7 Fire 乙未 Wood Goat Well 水風井 **5** 初五 6 [5]	木8 Wood 丙申 Fire Monkey Relief 雷水解 **6** 初六 4 [6]	金4 Metal 丁酉 Fire Rooster Influence 澤山咸 **7** 初七 9 [7]	水1 Water 戊戌 Earth Dog Humility 地山謙 **8** 初八 6 [8]	火2 Fire 己亥 Earth Pig Observation 風地觀 **9** 初九 2 [9]	火2 Fire 庚子 Metal Rat Increasing 風雷益 **10** 初十 9 [1]	水1 Water 辛丑 Metal Ox Dimming Light 地火明夷 **11** 十一 3 [2]
金9 Metal 壬寅 Water Tiger Fellowship 天火同人 **12** 十二 7 [3]	木8 Wood 癸卯 Water Rabbit Marrying Maiden 雷澤歸妹 **13** 十三 7 [4]	木3 Wood 甲辰 Wood Dragon Opposition 火澤睽 **14** 十四 2 [5]	火7 Fire 乙巳 Wood Snake Waiting 水天需 **15** 十五 3 [6]	金4 Metal 丙午 Fire Horse Great Exceeding 澤風大過 **16** 十六 3 [7]	水6 Water 丁未 Fire Goat Poison 山風蠱 **17** 十七 7 [8]	火2 Fire 戊申 Earth Monkey Dispersing 風水渙 **18** 十八 6 [9]
木3 Wood 己酉 Earth Rooster Travelling 火山旅 **19** 十九 8 [1]	金9 Metal 庚戌 Metal Dog Stagnation 天地否 **20** 二十 9 [2]	火7 Fire 辛亥 Metal Pig Alliance 水地比 **21** 廿一 7 [3]	木8 Wood 壬子 Water Rat Thunder 震爲雷 **22** 廿二 1 [4]	水6 Water 癸丑 Water Ox Beauty 山火賁 **23** 廿三 8 [5]	火7 Fire 甲寅 Wood Tiger Accomplished 水火既濟 **24** 廿四 9 [6]	水1 Water 乙卯 Wood Rabbit Arriving 地澤臨 **25** 廿五 4 [7]
金4 Metal 丙辰 Fire Dragon Marsh 兑爲澤 **26** 廿六 1 [8]	火2 Fire 丁巳 Fire Snake Small Livestock 風天小畜 **27** 廿七 8 [9]	木3 Wood 戊午 Earth Horse The Cauldron 火風鼎 **28** 廿八 4 [1]	水1 Water 己未 Earth Goat Rising 地風升 **29** 廿九 2 [2]	火7 Fire 庚申 Metal Monkey Water 坎爲水 **30** 三十 1 [3]	木8 Wood 辛酉 Metal Rooster Lesser Exceeding 雷山小過 **31** 三月初一 3 [4]	

APRIL 1995 庚辰

Xuan Kong Element 玄空五行	地天泰 Unity	Period Luck 卦運	Monthly Star 月星
Water 水1		9	9

SUNDAY	MONDAY	TUESDAY	WEDNESDAY	THURSDAY	FRIDAY	SATURDAY
火2 Fire 辛卯 Metal Rabbit Sincerity 風澤中孚 **30** 四月初一 3 [7]						金4 Metal 壬戌 Water Dog Gathering 澤地萃 **1** 初二 4 [5]
水6 Water 癸亥 Water Pig Peel 山地剝 **2** 初三 6 [6]	水1 Water 甲子 Wood Rat Earth 坤爲地 **3** 初四 1 [7]	木3 Wood 乙丑 Wood Ox Biting 火雷噬嗑 **4** 初五 6 [8]	火2 Fire 丙寅 Fire Tiger Family 風火家人 **5** 初六 4 [9]	水6 Water 丁卯 Fire Rabbit Decreasing 山澤損 **6** 初七 9 [1]	金9 Metal 戊辰 Earth Dragon Tread 天澤履 **7** 初八 6 [2]	木8 Wood 己巳 Earth Snake Great Strength 雷天大壯 **8** 初九 2 [3]
木8 Wood 庚午 Metal Horse Consistency 雷風恆 **9** 初十 9 [4]	金9 Metal 辛未 Metal Goat Litigation 天水訟 **10** 十一 3 [5]	水1 Water 壬申 Water Monkey Officer 地水師 **11** 十二 7 [6]	火2 Fire 癸酉 Water Rooster Gradual Progress 風山漸 **12** 十三 7 [7]	火7 Fire 甲戌 Wood Dog Obstruction 水山蹇 **13** 十四 2 [8]	木3 Wood 乙亥 Wood Pig Advancement 火地晉 **14** 十五 3 [9]	水6 Water 丙子 Fire Rat Nourish 山雷頤 **15** 十六 3 [1]
金4 Metal 丁丑 Fire Ox Following 澤雷隨 **16** 十七 7 [2]	木8 Wood 戊寅 Earth Tiger Abundance 雷火豐 **17** 十八 6 [3]	火7 Fire 己卯 Earth Rabbit Regulate 水澤節 **18** 十九 8 [4]	水1 Water 庚辰 Metal Dragon Unity 地天泰 **19** 二十 9 [5]	木3 Wood 辛巳 Metal Snake Great Reward 火天大有 **20** 廿一 7 [6]	火2 Fire 壬午 Water Horse Wind 巽爲風 **21** 廿二 1 [7]	金4 Metal 癸未 Water Goat Trap 澤水困 **22** 廿三 8 [8]
木3 Wood 甲申 Wood Monkey Not Yet Accomplished 火水未濟 **23** 廿四 9 [9]	金9 Metal 乙酉 Wood Rooster Retreat 天山遯 **24** 廿五 4 [1]	水6 Water 丙戌 Fire Dog Mountain 艮爲山 **25** 廿六 1 [2]	木8 Wood 丁亥 Fire Pig Delight 雷地豫 **26** 廿七 8 [3]	火7 Fire 戊子 Earth Rat Beginning 水雷屯 **27** 廿八 4 [4]	金9 Metal 己丑 Earth Ox Without Wrongdoing 天雷無妄 **28** 廿九 2 [5]	木3 Wood 庚寅 Metal Tiger Fire 離爲火 **29** 三十 1 [6]

MAY 1995 辛巳

Xuan Kong Element 玄空五行	火天大有 Great Reward	Period Luck 卦運	Monthly Star 月星
Wood 木3		7	8

SUNDAY	MONDAY	TUESDAY	WEDNESDAY	THURSDAY	FRIDAY	SATURDAY
	水6 Water 8 Big Livestock 壬辰 Water Dragon 山天大畜 1 初二 4	金4 Metal 9 Eliminating 癸巳 Water Snake 澤天夬 2 初三 6	金9 Metal 1 Heaven 甲午 Wood Horse 乾爲天 3 初四 1	火7 Fire 2 Well 乙未 Wood Goat 水風井 4 初五 6	木8 Wood 3 Relief 丙申 Fire Monkey 雷水解 5 初六 4	金4 Metal 4 Influence 丁酉 Fire Rooster 澤山咸 6 初七 9
水1 Water 5 Humility 戊戌 Earth Dog 地山謙 7 初八 6	火2 Fire 6 Observation 己亥 Earth Pig 風地觀 8 初九 2	火2 Fire 7 Increasing 庚子 Metal Rat 風雷益 9 初十 9	水1 Water 8 Dimming Light 辛丑 Metal Ox 地火明夷 10 十一 3	金9 Metal 9 Fellowship 壬寅 Water Tiger 天火同人 11 十二 7	木8 Wood 1 Marrying Maiden 癸卯 Water Rabbit 雷澤歸妹 12 十三 7	木3 Wood 2 Opposition 甲辰 Wood Dragon 火澤睽 13 十四 2
火7 Fire 3 Waiting 乙巳 Wood Snake 水天需 14 十五 3	金4 Metal 4 Great Exceeding 丙午 Fire Horse 澤風大過 15 十六 3	水6 Water 5 Poison 丁未 Fire Goat 山風蠱 16 十七 7	火2 Fire 6 Dispersing 戊申 Earth Monkey 風水渙 17 十八 6	木3 Wood 7 Travelling 己酉 Earth Rooster 火山旅 18 十九 8	金9 Metal 8 Stagnation 庚戌 Metal Dog 天地否 19 二十 9	火7 Fire 9 Alliance 辛亥 Metal Pig 水地比 20 廿一 7
木8 Wood 1 Thunder 壬子 Water Rat 震爲雷 21 廿二 1	水6 Water 2 Beauty 癸丑 Water Ox 山火賁 22 廿三 8	火7 Fire 3 Accomplished 甲寅 Wood Tiger 水火既濟 23 廿四 9	水1 Water 4 Arriving 乙卯 Wood Rabbit 地澤臨 24 廿五 4	金4 Metal 5 Marsh 丙辰 Fire Dragon 兑爲澤 25 廿六 1	火2 Fire 6 Small Livestock 丁巳 Fire Snake 風天小畜 26 廿七 8	木3 Wood 7 The Cauldron 戊午 Earth Horse 火風鼎 27 廿八 4
水1 Water 8 Rising 己未 Earth Goat 地風升 28 廿九 2	火7 Fire 9 Water 庚申 Metal Monkey 坎爲水 29 五月初一 1	木8 Wood 1 Lesser Exceeding 辛酉 Metal Rooster 雷山小過 30 初二 3	金4 Metal 2 Gathering 壬戌 Water Dog 澤地萃 31 初三 4			

JUNE 1995 壬午

Xuan Kong Element 玄空五行	巽爲風 Wind	Period Luck 卦運	Monthly Star 月星
Fire 火2		1	7

SUNDAY	MONDAY	TUESDAY	WEDNESDAY	THURSDAY	FRIDAY	SATURDAY
				水6 Water 3 Peel 癸亥 Water Pig 山地剝 1 初四 6	水1 Water 4 Earth 甲子 Wood Rat 坤爲地 2 初五 1	木3 Wood 5 Biting 乙丑 Wood Ox 火雷噬嗑 3 初六 6
火2 Fire 6 Family 丙寅 Fire Tiger 風火家人 4 初七 4	水6 Water 7 Decreasing 丁卯 Fire Rabbit 山澤損 5 初八 9	金9 Metal 8 Tread 戊辰 Earth Dragon 天澤履 6 初九 6	木8 Wood 9 Great Strength 己巳 Earth Snake 雷天大壯 7 初十 2	木8 Wood 1 Consistency 庚午 Metal Horse 雷風恒 8 十一 9	金9 Metal 2 Litigation 辛未 Metal Goat 天水訟 9 十二 3	水1 Water 3 Officer 壬申 Water Monkey 地水師 10 十三 7
火2 Fire 4 Gradual Progress 癸酉 Water Rooster 風山漸 11 十四 7	火7 Fire 5 Obstruction 甲戌 Wood Dog 水山蹇 12 十五 2	木3 Wood 6 Advancement 乙亥 Wood Pig 火地晉 13 十六 3	水6 Water 7 Nourish 丙子 Fire Rat 山雷頤 14 十七 3	金4 Metal 8 Following 丁丑 Fire Ox 澤雷隨 15 十八 7	木8 Wood 9 Abundance 戊寅 Earth Tiger 雷火豐 16 十九 6	火7 Fire 1 Regulate 己卯 Earth Rabbit 水澤節 17 二十 8
水1 Water 2 Unity 庚辰 Metal Dragon 地天泰 18 廿一 9	木3 Wood 3 Great Reward 辛巳 Metal Snake 火天大有 19 廿二 7	火2 Fire 4 Wind 壬午 Water Horse 巽爲風 20 廿三 1	金4 Metal 5 Trap 癸未 Water Goat 澤水困 21 廿四 8	木3 Wood 4/6 Not Yet Accomplished 甲申 Wood Monkey 火水未濟 22 廿五 9	金9 Metal 3 Retreat 乙酉 Wood Rooster 天山遯 23 廿六 4	水6 Water 2 Mountain 丙戌 Fire Dog 艮爲山 24 廿七 1
木8 Wood 1 Delight 丁亥 Fire Pig 雷地豫 25 廿八 8	火7 Fire 9 Beginning 戊子 Earth Rat 水雷屯 26 廿九 4	金9 Metal 8 Without Wrongdoing 己丑 Earth Ox 天雷無妄 27 三十 2	木3 Wood 7 Fire 庚寅 Metal Tiger 離爲火 28 六月初一 1	火2 Fire 6 Sincerity 辛卯 Metal Rabbit 風澤中孚 29 初二 3	水6 Water 5 Big Livestock 壬辰 Water Dragon 山天大畜 30 初三 4	

JULY 1995 癸未

Xuan Kong Element 玄空五行	澤水困 Trap	Period Luck 卦運	Monthly Star 月星
Metal 金4		8	6

SUNDAY	MONDAY	TUESDAY	WEDNESDAY	THURSDAY	FRIDAY	SATURDAY
30 初四 Gathering 澤地萃 金4 Metal 壬戌 Water Dog [2] · 4	**31** 初五 Peel 山地剝 水6 Water 癸亥 Water Pig [1] · 6					**1** 初四 Eliminating 澤天夬 金4 Metal 癸巳 Water Snake [4] · 6
2 初五 Heaven 乾爲天 金9 Metal 甲午 Wood Horse [3] · 1	**3** 初六 Well 水風井 火7 Fire 乙未 Wood Goat [2] · 6	**4** 初七 Relief 雷水解 木8 Wood 丙申 Fire Monkey [1] · 4	**5** 初八 Influence 澤山咸 金4 Metal 丁酉 Fire Rooster [9] · 9	**6** 初九 Humility 地山謙 水1 Water 戊戌 Earth Dog [8] · 6	**7** 初十 Observation 風地觀 火2 Fire 己亥 Earth Pig [7] · 2	**8** 十一 Increasing 風雷益 火2 Fire 庚子 Metal Rat [6] · 9
9 十二 Dimming Light 地火明夷 水1 Water 辛丑 Metal Ox [5] · 3	**10** 十三 Fellowship 天火同人 金9 Metal 壬寅 Water Tiger [4] · 7	**11** 十四 Marrying Maiden 雷澤歸妹 木8 Wood 癸卯 Water Rabbit [3] · 7	**12** 十五 Opposition 火澤睽 木3 Wood 甲辰 Wood Dragon [2] · 2	**13** 十六 Waiting 水天需 火7 Fire 乙巳 Wood Snake [1] · 3	**14** 十七 Great Exceeding 澤風大過 金4 Metal 丙午 Fire Horse [9] · 3	**15** 十八 Poison 山風蠱 水6 Water 丁未 Fire Goat [8] · 7
16 十九 Dispersing 風水渙 火2 Fire 戊申 Earth Monkey [7] · 6	**17** 二十 Travelling 火山旅 木3 Wood 己酉 Earth Rooster [6] · 8	**18** 廿一 Stagnation 天地否 金9 Metal 庚戌 Metal Dog [5] · 9	**19** 廿二 Alliance 水地比 火7 Fire 辛亥 Metal Pig [4] · 7	**20** 廿三 Thunder 震爲雷 木8 Wood 壬子 Water Rat [3] · 1	**21** 廿四 Beauty 山火賁 水6 Water 癸丑 Water Ox [2] · 8	**22** 廿五 Accomplished 水火既濟 火7 Fire 甲寅 Wood Tiger [1] · 9
23 廿六 Arriving 地澤臨 水1 Water 乙卯 Wood Rabbit [9] · 4	**24** 廿七 Marsh 兌爲澤 金4 Metal 丙辰 Fire Dragon [8] · 1	**25** 廿八 Small Livestock 風天小畜 火2 Fire 丁巳 Fire Snake [7] · 8	**26** 廿九 The Cauldron 火風鼎 木3 Wood 戊午 Earth Horse [6] · 4	**27** 七月初一 Rising 地風升 水1 Water 己未 Earth Goat [5] · 2	**28** 初二 Water 坎爲水 火7 Fire 庚申 Metal Monkey [4] · 1	**29** 初三 Lesser Exceeding 雷山小過 木8 Wood 辛酉 Metal Rooster [3] · 3

AUGUST 1995 甲申

Xuan Kong Element 玄空五行	火水未濟 Not Yet Accomplished	Period Luck 卦運	Monthly Star 月星
Wood 木3		9	5

SUNDAY	MONDAY	TUESDAY	WEDNESDAY	THURSDAY	FRIDAY	SATURDAY
		1 初六 Earth 坤爲地 水1 Water 甲子 Wood Rat [9] · 1	**2** 初七 Biting 火雷噬嗑 木3 Wood 乙丑 Wood Ox [8] · 6	**3** 初八 Family 風火家人 火2 Fire 丙寅 Fire Tiger [7] · 4	**4** 初九 Decreasing 山澤損 水6 Water 丁卯 Fire Rabbit [6] · 9	**5** 初十 Tread 天澤履 金9 Metal 戊辰 Earth Dragon [5] · 6
6 十一 Great Strength 雷天大壯 木8 Wood 己巳 Earth Snake [4] · 2	**7** 十二 Consistency 雷風恆 木8 Wood 庚午 Metal Horse [3] · 9	**8** 十三 Litigation 天水訟 金9 Metal 辛未 Metal Goat [2] · 3	**9** 十四 Officer 地水師 水1 Water 壬申 Water Monkey [1] · 7	**10** 十五 Gradual Progress 風山漸 火2 Fire 癸酉 Water Rooster [9] · 7	**11** 十六 Obstruction 水山蹇 火7 Fire 甲戌 Wood Dog [8] · 2	**12** 十七 Advancement 火地晉 木3 Wood 乙亥 Wood Pig [7] · 3
13 十八 Nourish 山雷頤 水6 Water 丙子 Fire Rat [6] · 3	**14** 十九 Following 澤雷隨 金4 Metal 丁丑 Fire Ox [5] · 7	**15** 二十 Abundance 雷火豐 木8 Wood 戊寅 Earth Tiger [4] · 6	**16** 廿一 Regulate 水澤節 火7 Fire 己卯 Earth Rabbit [3] · 8	**17** 廿二 Unity 地天泰 水1 Water 庚辰 Metal Dragon [2] · 9	**18** 廿三 Great Reward 火天大有 木3 Wood 辛巳 Metal Snake [1] · 7	**19** 廿四 Wind 巽爲風 火2 Fire 壬午 Water Horse [9] · 1
20 廿五 Trap 澤水困 金4 Metal 癸未 Water Goat [8] · 8	**21** 廿六 Not Yet Accomplished 火水未濟 木3 Wood 甲申 Wood Monkey [7] · 9	**22** 廿七 Retreat 天山遯 金9 Metal 乙酉 Wood Rooster [65] · 4	**23** 廿八 Mountain 艮爲山 水6 Water 丙戌 Fire Dog [8] · 1	**24** 廿九 Delight 雷地豫 木8 Wood 丁亥 Fire Pig [4] · 8	**25** 三十 Beginning 水雷屯 火7 Fire 戊子 Earth Rat [3] · 4	**26** 八月初一 Without Wrongdoing 天雷無妄 金9 Metal 己丑 Earth Ox [2] · 2
27 初二 Fire 離爲火 木3 Wood 庚寅 Metal Tiger [1] · 1	**28** 初三 Sincerity 風澤中孚 火2 Fire 辛卯 Metal Rabbit [9] · 3	**29** 初四 Big Livestock 山天大畜 水6 Water 壬辰 Water Dragon [8] · 4	**30** 初五 Eliminating 澤天夬 金4 Metal 癸巳 Water Snake [7] · 6	**31** 初六 Heaven 乾爲天 金9 Metal 甲午 Wood Horse [6] · 1		

SEPTEMBER 1995 乙酉

Xuan Kong Element 玄空五行	天山遯 Retreat	Period Luck 卦運	Monthly Star 月星
Metal 金9		4	4

SUNDAY	MONDAY	TUESDAY	WEDNESDAY	THURSDAY	FRIDAY	SATURDAY
					火7 Fire · Well · 5 乙未 Wood Goat · 水風井 **1** 初七 · 6	木8 Wood · Relief · 4 丙申 Fire Monkey · 雷水解 **2** 初八 · 4
金4 Metal · Influence · 3 丁酉 Fire Rooster · 澤山咸 **3** 初九 · 9	水1 Water · Humility · 2 戊戌 Earth Dog · 地山謙 **4** 初十 · 6	火2 Fire · Observation · 1 己亥 Earth Pig · 風地觀 **5** 十一 · 2	火2 Fire · Increasing · 9 庚子 Metal Rat · 風雷益 **6** 十二 · 9	水1 Water · Dimming Light · 8 辛丑 Metal Ox · 地火明夷 **7** 十三 · 3	金9 Metal · Fellowship · 7 壬寅 Water Tiger · 天火同人 **8** 十四 · 7	木8 Wood · Marrying Maiden · 6 癸卯 Water Rabbit · 雷澤歸妹 **9** 十五 · 7
木3 Wood · Opposition · 5 甲辰 Wood Dragon · 火澤睽 **10** 十六 · 2	火7 Fire · Waiting · 4 乙巳 Wood Snake · 水天需 **11** 十七 · 3	金4 Metal · Great Exceeding · 3 丙午 Fire Horse · 澤風大過 **12** 十八 · 3	水6 Water · Poison · 2 丁未 Fire Goat · 山風蠱 **13** 十九 · 7	火2 Fire · Dispersing · 1 戊申 Earth Monkey · 風水渙 **14** 二十 · 6	木3 Wood · Travelling · 9 己酉 Earth Rooster · 火山旅 **15** 廿一 · 8	金9 Metal · Stagnation · 8 庚戌 Metal Dog · 天地否 **16** 廿二 · 9
火7 Fire · Alliance · 7 辛亥 Metal Pig · 水地比 **17** 廿三 · 7	木8 Wood · Thunder · 6 壬子 Water Rat · 震爲雷 **18** 廿四 · 1	水6 Water · Beauty · 5 癸丑 Water Ox · 山火賁 **19** 廿五 · 8	火7 Fire · Accomplished · 4 甲寅 Wood Tiger · 水火既濟 **20** 廿六 · 9	水1 Water · Arriving · 3 乙卯 Wood Rabbit · 地澤臨 **21** 廿七 · 4	金4 Metal · Marsh · 2 丙辰 Fire Dragon · 兑爲澤 **22** 廿八 · 1	火2 Fire · Small Livestock · 1 丁巳 Fire Snake · 風天小畜 **23** 廿九 · 8
木3 Wood · The Cauldron · 9 戊午 Earth Horse · 火風鼎 **24** 三十 · 4	水1 Water · Rising · 8 己未 Earth Goat · 地風升 **25** 閏八月初一 · 2	火7 Fire · Water · 7 庚申 Metal Monkey · 坎爲水 **26** 初二 · 1	木8 Wood · Lesser Exceeding · 6 辛酉 Metal Rooster · 雷山小過 **27** 初三 · 3	金4 Metal · Gathering · 5 壬戌 Water Dog · 澤地萃 **28** 初四 · 4	水6 Water · Peel · 4 癸亥 Water Pig · 山地剝 **29** 初五 · 6	水1 Water · Earth · 3 甲子 Wood Rat · 坤爲地 **30** 初六 · 1

OCTOBER 1995 丙戌

Xuan Kong Element 玄空五行	艮爲山 Mountain	Period Luck 卦運	Monthly Star 月星
Water 水6		1	3

SUNDAY	MONDAY	TUESDAY	WEDNESDAY	THURSDAY	FRIDAY	SATURDAY
木3 Wood · Biting · 2 乙丑 Wood Ox · 火雷噬嗑 **1** 初七 · 6	火2 Fire · Family · 1 丙寅 Fire Tiger · 風火家人 **2** 初八 · 4	水6 Water · Decreasing · 9 丁卯 Fire Rabbit · 山澤損 **3** 初九 · 9	金9 Metal · Tread · 8 戊辰 Earth Dragon · 天澤履 **4** 初十 · 6	木8 Wood · Great Strength · 7 己巳 Earth Snake · 雷天大壯 **5** 十一 · 2	木8 Wood · Consistency · 6 庚午 Metal Horse · 雷風恆 **6** 十二 · 9	金9 Metal · Litigation · 5 辛未 Metal Goat · 天水訟 **7** 十三 · 3
水1 Water · Officer · 4 壬申 Water Monkey · 地水師 **8** 十四 · 7	火2 Fire · Gradual Progress · 3 癸酉 Water Rooster · 風山漸 **9** 十五 · 7	火7 Fire · Obstruction · 2 甲戌 Wood Dog · 水山蹇 **10** 十六 · 2	木3 Wood · Advancement · 1 乙亥 Wood Pig · 火地晉 **11** 十七 · 3	水6 Water · Nourish · 9 丙子 Fire Rat · 山雷頤 **12** 十八 · 3	金4 Metal · Following · 8 丁丑 Fire Ox · 澤雷隨 **13** 十九 · 7	木8 Wood · Abundance · 7 戊寅 Earth Tiger · 雷火豐 **14** 二十 · 6
火7 Fire · Regulate · 6 己卯 Earth Rabbit · 水澤節 **15** 廿一 · 8	水1 Water · Unity · 5 庚辰 Metal Dragon · 地天泰 **16** 廿二 · 9	木3 Wood · Great Reward · 4 辛巳 Metal Snake · 火天大有 **17** 廿三 · 7	火2 Fire · Wind · 3 壬午 Water Horse · 巽爲風 **18** 廿四 · 1	金4 Metal · Trap · 2 癸未 Water Goat · 澤水困 **19** 廿五 · 8	木3 Wood · Not Yet Accomplished · 1 甲申 Wood Monkey · 火水未濟 **20** 廿六 · 9	金9 Metal · Retreat · 9 乙酉 Wood Rooster · 天山遯 **21** 廿七 · 4
水6 Water · Mountain · 8 丙戌 Fire Dog · 艮爲山 **22** 廿八 · 1	木8 Wood · Delight · 7 丁亥 Fire Pig · 雷地豫 **23** 廿九 · 8	火7 Fire · Beginning · 6 戊子 Earth Rat · 水雷屯 **24** 九月初一 · 4	金9 Metal · Without Wrongdoing · 5 己丑 Earth Ox · 天雷無妄 **25** 初二 · 2	木3 Wood · Fire · 4 庚寅 Metal Tiger · 離爲火 **26** 初三 · 1	火2 Fire · Sincerity · 3 辛卯 Metal Rabbit · 風澤中孚 **27** 初四 · 3	水6 Water · Big Livestock · 2 壬辰 Water Dragon · 山天大畜 **28** 初五 · 4
金4 Metal · Eliminating · 1 癸巳 Water Snake · 澤天夬 **29** 初六 · 6	金9 Metal · Heaven · 9 甲午 Wood Horse · 乾爲天 **30** 初七 · 1	火7 Fire · Well · 8 乙未 Wood Goat · 水風井 **31** 初八 · 6				

NOVEMBER 1995 丁亥

Xuan Kong Element 玄空五行	雷地豫 Delight	Period Luck 卦運	Monthly Star 月星
Wood 木8		8	2

SUNDAY	MONDAY	TUESDAY	WEDNESDAY	THURSDAY	FRIDAY	SATURDAY
			木8 Wood 7 Relief 丙申 Fire Monkey 雷水解 1 初九 4	金4 Metal 6 Influence 丁酉 Fire Rooster 澤山咸 2 初十 9	水1 Water 5 Humility 戊戌 Earth Dog 地山謙 3 十一 6	火2 Fire 4 Observation 己亥 Earth Pig 風地觀 4 十二 2
火2 Fire 3 Increasing 庚子 Metal Rat 風雷益 5 十三 9	水1 Water 2 Dimming Light 辛丑 Metal Ox 地火明夷 6 十四 3	金9 Metal 1 Fellowship 壬寅 Water Tiger 天火同人 7 十五 7	木8 Wood 9 Marrying Maiden 癸卯 Water Rabbit 雷澤歸妹 8 十六 7	木3 Wood 8 Opposition 甲辰 Wood Dragon 火澤睽 9 十七 2	火7 Fire 7 Waiting 乙巳 Wood Snake 水天需 10 十八 3	金4 Metal 6 Great Exceeding 丙午 Fire Horse 澤風大過 11 十九 3
水6 Water 5 Poison 丁未 Fire Goat 山風蠱 12 二十 7	火2 Fire 4 Dispersing 戊申 Earth Monkey 風水渙 13 廿一 6	木3 Wood 3 Travelling 己酉 Earth Rooster 火山旅 14 廿二 8	金9 Metal 2 Stagnation 庚戌 Metal Dog 天地否 15 廿三 9	火7 Fire 1 Alliance 辛亥 Metal Pig 水地比 16 廿四 7	木8 Wood 9 Thunder 壬子 Water Rat 震為雷 17 廿五 1	水6 Water 8 Beauty 癸丑 Water Ox 山火賁 18 廿六 8
火7 Fire 7 Accomplished 甲寅 Wood Tiger 水火既濟 19 廿七 9	水1 Water 6 Arriving 乙卯 Wood Rabbit 地澤臨 20 廿八 4	金4 Metal 5 Marsh 丙辰 Fire Dragon 兌為澤 21 廿九 1	火2 Fire 4 Small Livestock 丁巳 Fire Snake 風天小畜 22 十月初一 8	木3 Wood 3 The Cauldron 戊午 Earth Horse 火風鼎 23 初二 4	水1 Water 2 Rising 己未 Earth Goat 地風升 24 初三 2	火7 Fire 1 Water 庚申 Metal Monkey 坎為水 25 初四 1
木8 Wood 9 Lesser Exceeding 辛酉 Metal Rooster 雷山小過 26 初五 3	金4 Metal 8 Gathering 壬戌 Water Dog 澤地萃 27 初六 4	水6 Water 7 Peel 癸亥 Water Pig 山地剝 28 初七 6	水1 Water 6 Earth 甲子 Wood Rat 坤為地 29 初八 1	木3 Wood 5 Biting 乙丑 Wood Ox 火雷噬嗑 30 初九 6		

DECEMBER 1995 戊子

Xuan Kong Element 玄空五行	水雷屯 Beginning	Period Luck 卦運	Monthly Star 月星
Fire 火7		4	1

SUNDAY	MONDAY	TUESDAY	WEDNESDAY	THURSDAY	FRIDAY	SATURDAY
木8 Wood 9 Relief 丙申 Fire Monkey 雷水解 31 初十 4					火2 Fire 4 Family 丙寅 Fire Tiger 風火家人 1 初十 4	水6 Water 3 Decreasing 丁卯 Fire Rabbit 山澤損 2 十一 9
金9 Metal 2 Tread 戊辰 Earth Dragon 天澤履 3 十二 6	木8 Wood 1 Great Strength 己巳 Earth Snake 雷天大壯 4 十三 2	木8 Wood 9 Consistency 庚午 Metal Horse 雷風恆 5 十四 9	金9 Metal 8 Litigation 辛未 Metal Goat 天水訟 6 十五 3	水1 Water 7 Officer 壬申 Water Monkey 地水師 7 十六 7	火2 Fire 6 Gradual Progress 癸酉 Water Rooster 風山漸 8 十七 7	火7 Fire 5 Obstruction 甲戌 Wood Dog 水山蹇 9 十八 2
木3 Wood 4 Advancement 乙亥 Wood Pig 火地晉 10 十九 3	水6 Water 3 Nourish 丙子 Fire Rat 山雷頤 11 二十 3	金4 Metal 2 Following 丁丑 Fire Ox 澤雷隨 12 廿一 7	木8 Wood 1 Abundance 戊寅 Earth Tiger 雷火豐 13 廿二 6	火7 Fire 9 Regulate 己卯 Earth Rabbit 水澤節 14 廿三 8	水1 Water 8 Unity 庚辰 Metal Dragon 地天泰 15 廿四 9	木3 Wood 7 Great Reward 辛巳 Metal Snake 火天大有 16 廿五 7
火2 Fire 6 Wind 壬午 Water Horse 巽為風 17 廿六 1	金4 Metal 5 Trap 癸未 Water Goat 澤水困 18 廿七 8	木3 Wood 4 Not Yet Accomplished 甲申 Wood Monkey 火水未濟 19 廿八 9	金9 Metal 3 Retreat 乙酉 Wood Rooster 天山遯 20 廿九 4	水6 Water 2 Mountain 丙戌 Fire Dog 艮為山 21 三十 1	木8 Wood 1/9 Delight 丁亥 Fire Pig 雷地豫 22 十一月初一 8	火7 Fire 1 Beginning 戊子 Earth Rat 水雷屯 23 初二 4
金9 Metal 2 Without Wrongdoing 己丑 Earth Ox 天雷無妄 24 初三 2	木3 Wood 3 Fire 庚寅 Metal Tiger 離為火 25 初四 1	火2 Fire 4 Sincerity 辛卯 Metal Rabbit 風澤中孚 26 初五 3	水6 Water 5 Big Livestock 壬辰 Water Dragon 山天大畜 27 初六 4	金4 Metal 6 Eliminating 癸巳 Water Snake 澤天夬 28 初七 6	金9 Metal 7 Heaven 甲午 Wood Horse 乾為天 29 初八 1	火7 Fire 8 Well 乙未 Wood Goat 水風井 30 初九 6

1996 丙子

(*Bing Zi*) Fire Rat

1996 丙子 *(Bing Zi)* Fire Rat

January 6 - February 3

February 4 - March 4

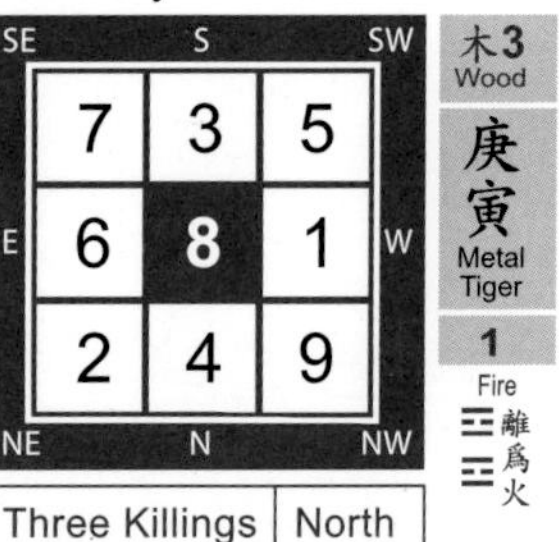

SE S SW
7 3 5
E 6 8 1 W
2 4 9
NE N NW
木3 Wood
庚寅 Metal Tiger
1
Fire
離為火
Three Killings North

March 5 - April 3

April 4 - May 4

May 5 - June 4

June 5 - July 6

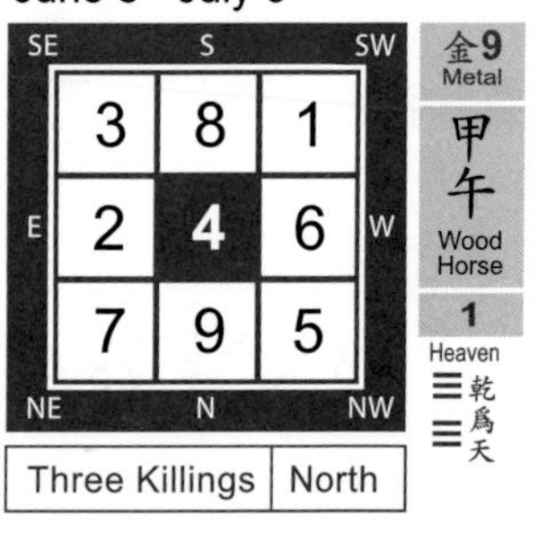

July 7 - August 6

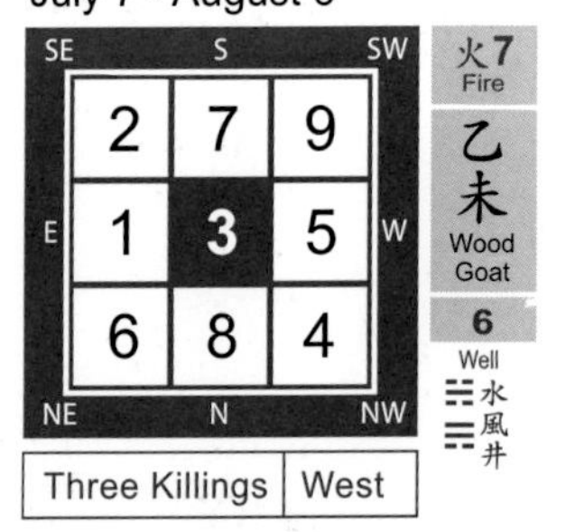

August 7 - September 6

September 7 - October 7

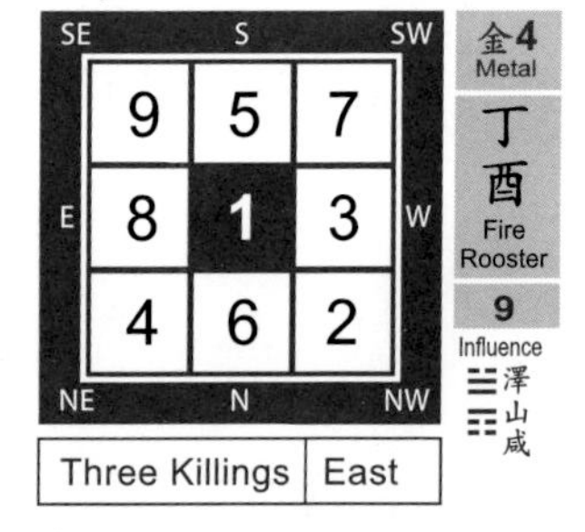

October 8 - November 6

November 7 - December 6

December 7 - January 4

JANUARY 1996 己丑

Xuan Kong Element 玄空五行	天雷無妄 Without Wrongdoing	Period Luck 卦運	Monthly Star 月星
Metal 金9		2	9

SUNDAY	MONDAY	TUESDAY	WEDNESDAY	THURSDAY	FRIDAY	SATURDAY
	1 十一 金4 Metal · 1 Influence 澤山咸 丁酉 Fire Rooster · 9	**2** 十二 水1 Water · 2 Humility 地山謙 戊戌 Earth Dog · 6	**3** 十三 火2 Fire · 3 Observation 風地觀 己亥 Earth Pig · 2	**4** 十四 火2 Fire · 4 Increasing 風雷益 庚子 Metal Rat · 9	**5** 十五 水1 Water · 5 Dimming Light 地火明夷 辛丑 Metal Ox · 3	**6** 十六 金9 Metal · 6 Fellowship 天火同人 壬寅 Water Tiger · 7
7 十七 木8 Wood · 7 Marrying Maiden 雷澤歸妹 癸卯 Water Rabbit · 7	**8** 十八 木3 Wood · 8 Opposition 火澤睽 甲辰 Wood Dragon · 2	**9** 十九 火7 Fire · 9 Waiting 水天需 乙巳 Wood Snake · 3	**10** 二十 金4 Metal · 1 Great Exceeding 澤風大過 丙午 Fire Horse · 3	**11** 廿一 水6 Water · 2 Poison 山風蠱 丁未 Fire Goat · 7	**12** 廿二 火2 Fire · 3 Dispersing 風水渙 戊申 Earth Monkey · 6	**13** 廿三 木3 Wood · 4 Travelling 火山旅 己酉 Earth Rooster · 8
14 廿四 金9 Metal · 5 Stagnation 天地否 庚戌 Metal Dog · 9	**15** 廿五 火7 Fire · 6 Alliance 水地比 辛亥 Metal Pig · 7	**16** 廿六 木8 Wood · 7 Thunder 震爲雷 壬子 Water Rat · 1	**17** 廿七 水6 Water · 8 Beauty 山火賁 癸丑 Water Ox · 8	**18** 廿八 火7 Fire · 9 Accomplished 水火既濟 甲寅 Wood Tiger · 9	**19** 廿九 水1 Water · 1 Arriving 地澤臨 乙卯 Wood Rabbit · 4	**20** 十二月初一 金4 Metal · 2 Marsh 兌爲澤 丙辰 Fire Dragon · 1
21 初二 火2 Fire · 3 Small Livestock 風天小畜 丁巳 Fire Snake · 8	**22** 初三 木3 Wood · 4 The Cauldron 火風鼎 戊午 Earth Horse · 4	**23** 初四 水1 Water · 5 Rising 地風升 己未 Earth Goat · 2	**24** 初五 火7 Fire · 6 Water 坎爲水 庚申 Metal Monkey · 1	**25** 初六 木8 Wood · 7 Lesser Exceeding 雷山小過 辛酉 Metal Rooster · 3	**26** 初七 金4 Metal · 8 Gathering 澤地萃 壬戌 Water Dog · 4	**27** 初八 水6 Water · 9 Peel 山地剝 癸亥 Water Pig · 6
28 初九 水1 Water · 1 Earth 坤爲地 甲子 Wood Rat · 1	**29** 初十 木3 Wood · 2 Biting 火雷噬嗑 乙丑 Wood Ox · 6	**30** 十一 火2 Fire · 3 Family 風火家人 丙寅 Fire Tiger · 4	**31** 十二 水6 Water · 4 Decreasing 山澤損 丁卯 Fire Rabbit · 9			

FEBRUARY 1996 庚寅

Xuan Kong Element 玄空五行	離爲火 Fire	Period Luck 卦運	Monthly Star 月星
Wood 木3		1	8

SUNDAY	MONDAY	TUESDAY	WEDNESDAY	THURSDAY	FRIDAY	SATURDAY
				1 十三 金9 Metal · 5 Tread 天澤履 戊辰 Earth Dragon · 6	**2** 十四 木8 Wood · 6 Great Strength 雷天大壯 己巳 Earth Snake · 2	**3** 十五 木8 Wood · 7 Consistency 雷風恆 庚午 Metal Horse · 9
4 十六 金9 Metal · 8 Litigation 天水訟 辛未 Metal Goat · 3	**5** 十七 水1 Water · 9 Officer 地水師 壬申 Water Monkey · 7	**6** 十八 火2 Fire · 1 Gradual Progress 風山漸 癸酉 Water Rooster · 7	**7** 十九 火7 Fire · 2 Obstruction 水山蹇 甲戌 Wood Dog · 2	**8** 二十 木3 Wood · 3 Advancement 火地晉 乙亥 Wood Pig · 3	**9** 廿一 水6 Water · 4 Nourish 山雷頤 丙子 Fire Rat · 3	**10** 廿二 金4 Metal · 5 Following 澤雷隨 丁丑 Fire Ox · 7
11 廿三 木8 Wood · 6 Abundance 雷火豐 戊寅 Earth Tiger · 6	**12** 廿四 火7 Fire · 7 Regulate 水澤節 己卯 Earth Rabbit · 8	**13** 廿五 水1 Water · 8 Unity 地天泰 庚辰 Metal Dragon · 9	**14** 廿六 木3 Wood · 9 Great Reward 火天大有 辛巳 Metal Snake · 7	**15** 廿七 火2 Fire · 1 Wind 巽爲風 壬午 Water Horse · 1	**16** 廿八 金4 Metal · 2 Trap 澤水困 癸未 Water Goat · 8	**17** 廿九 木3 Wood · 3 Not Yet Accomplished 火水未濟 甲申 Wood Monkey · 9
18 三十 金9 Metal · 4 Retreat 天山遯 乙酉 Wood Rooster · 4	**19** 正月初一 水6 Water · 5 Mountain 艮爲山 丙戌 Fire Dog · 1	**20** 初二 木8 Wood · 6 Delight 雷地豫 丁亥 Fire Pig · 8	**21** 初三 火7 Fire · 7 Beginning 水雷屯 戊子 Earth Rat · 4	**22** 初四 金9 Metal · 8 Without Wrongdoing 天雷無妄 己丑 Earth Ox · 2	**23** 初五 木3 Wood · 9 Fire 離爲火 庚寅 Metal Tiger · 1	**24** 初六 火2 Fire · 1 Sincerity 風澤中孚 辛卯 Metal Rabbit · 3
25 初七 水6 Water · 2 Big Livestock 山天大畜 壬辰 Water Dragon · 4	**26** 初八 金4 Metal · 3 Eliminating 澤天夬 癸巳 Water Snake · 6	**27** 初九 金9 Metal · 4 Heaven 乾爲天 甲午 Wood Horse · 1	**28** 初十 火7 Fire · 5 Well 水風井 乙未 Wood Goat · 6	**29** 十一 木8 Wood · 6 Relief 雷水解 丙申 Fire Monkey · 4		

MARCH 1996 辛卯

Xuan Kong Element 玄空五行	風澤中孚 Sincerity	Period Luck 卦運	Monthly Star 月星
Fire 火2		3	7

SUNDAY	MONDAY	TUESDAY	WEDNESDAY	THURSDAY	FRIDAY	SATURDAY
水6 Water Decreasing 山澤損 丁卯 Fire Rabbit 31 十三 9 / 1					金4 Metal Influence 澤山咸 丁酉 Fire Rooster 1 十二 9 / 7	水1 Water Humility 地山謙 戊戌 Earth Dog 2 十三 6 / 8
火2 Fire Observation 風地觀 己亥 Earth Pig 3 十四 2 / 9	火2 Fire Increasing 風雷益 庚子 Metal Rat 4 十五 9 / 1	水1 Water Dimming Light 地火明夷 辛丑 Metal Ox 5 十六 3 / 2	金9 Metal Fellowship 天火同人 壬寅 Water Tiger 6 十七 7 / 3	木8 Wood Marrying Maiden 雷澤歸妹 癸卯 Water Rabbit 7 十八 7 / 4	木3 Wood Opposition 火澤睽 甲辰 Wood Dragon 8 十九 2 / 5	火7 Fire Waiting 水天需 乙巳 Wood Snake 9 二十 3 / 6
金4 Metal Great Exceeding 澤風大過 丙午 Fire Horse 10 廿一 3 / 7	水6 Water Poison 山風蠱 丁未 Fire Goat 11 廿二 7 / 8	火2 Fire Dispersing 風水渙 戊申 Earth Monkey 12 廿三 6 / 9	木3 Wood Travelling 火山旅 己酉 Earth Rooster 13 廿四 8 / 1	金9 Metal Stagnation 天地否 庚戌 Metal Dog 14 廿五 9 / 2	火7 Fire Alliance 水地比 辛亥 Metal Pig 15 廿六 7 / 3	木8 Wood Thunder 震爲雷 壬子 Water Rat 16 廿七 1 / 4
水6 Water Beauty 山火賁 癸丑 Water Ox 17 廿八 8 / 5	火7 Fire Accomplished 水火既濟 甲寅 Wood Tiger 18 廿九 9 / 6	水1 Water Arriving 地澤臨 乙卯 Wood Rabbit 19 二月初一 4 / 7	金4 Metal Marsh 兑爲澤 丙辰 Fire Dragon 20 初二 1 / 8	火2 Fire Small Livestock 風天小畜 丁巳 Fire Snake 21 初三 8 / 9	木3 Wood The Cauldron 火風鼎 戊午 Earth Horse 22 初四 4 / 1	水1 Water Rising 地風升 己未 Earth Goat 23 初五 2 / 2
火7 Fire Water 坎爲水 庚申 Metal Monkey 24 初六 1 / 3	木8 Wood Lesser Exceeding 雷山小過 辛酉 Metal Rooster 25 初七 3 / 4	金4 Metal Gathering 澤地萃 壬戌 Water Dog 26 初八 4 / 5	水6 Water Peel 山地剝 癸亥 Water Pig 27 初九 6 / 6	水1 Water Earth 坤爲地 甲子 Wood Rat 28 初十 1 / 7	木3 Wood Biting 火雷噬嗑 乙丑 Wood Ox 29 十一 6 / 8	火2 Fire Family 風火家人 丙寅 Fire Tiger 30 十二 4 / 9

APRIL 1996 壬辰

Xuan Kong Element 玄空五行	山天大畜 Big Livestock	Period Luck 卦運	Monthly Star 月星
Water 水6		4	6

SUNDAY	MONDAY	TUESDAY	WEDNESDAY	THURSDAY	FRIDAY	SATURDAY
	金9 Metal Tread 天澤履 戊辰 Earth Dragon 1 十四 6 / 2	木8 Wood Great Strength 雷天大壯 己巳 Earth Snake 2 十五 2 / 3	木8 Wood Consistency 雷風恆 庚午 Metal Horse 3 十六 9 / 4	金9 Metal Litigation 天水訟 辛未 Metal Goat 4 十七 3 / 5	水1 Water Officer 地水師 壬申 Water Monkey 5 十八 7 / 6	火2 Fire Gradual Progress 風山漸 癸酉 Water Rooster 6 十九 7 / 7
火7 Fire Obstruction 水山蹇 甲戌 Wood Dog 7 二十 2 / 8	木3 Wood Advancement 火地晉 乙亥 Wood Pig 8 廿一 3 / 9	水6 Water Nourish 山雷頤 丙子 Fire Rat 9 廿二 3 / 1	金4 Metal Following 澤雷隨 丁丑 Fire Ox 10 廿三 7 / 2	木8 Wood Abundance 雷火豐 戊寅 Earth Tiger 11 廿四 6 / 3	火7 Fire Regulate 水澤節 己卯 Earth Rabbit 12 廿五 8 / 4	水1 Water Unity 地天泰 庚辰 Metal Dragon 13 廿六 9 / 5
木3 Wood Great Reward 火天大有 辛巳 Metal Snake 14 廿七 7 / 6	火2 Fire Wind 巽爲風 壬午 Water Horse 15 廿八 1 / 7	金4 Metal Trap 澤水困 癸未 Water Goat 16 廿九 8 / 8	木3 Wood Not Yet Accomplished 火水未濟 甲申 Wood Monkey 17 三十 9 / 9	金9 Metal Retreat 天山遯 乙酉 Wood Rooster 18 三月初一 4 / 1	水6 Water Mountain 艮爲山 丙戌 Fire Dog 19 初二 1 / 2	木8 Wood Delight 雷地豫 丁亥 Fire Pig 20 初三 8 / 3
火7 Fire Beginning 水雷屯 戊子 Earth Rat 21 初四 4 / 4	金9 Metal Without Wrongdoing 天雷無妄 己丑 Earth Ox 22 初五 2 / 5	木3 Wood Fire 離爲火 庚寅 Metal Tiger 23 初六 1 / 6	火2 Fire Sincerity 風澤中孚 辛卯 Metal Rabbit 24 初七 3 / 7	水6 Water Big Livestock 山天大畜 壬辰 Water Dragon 25 初八 4 / 8	金4 Metal Eliminating 澤天夬 癸巳 Water Snake 26 初九 6 / 9	金9 Metal Heaven 乾爲天 甲午 Wood Horse 27 初十 1 / 1
火7 Fire Well 水風井 乙未 Wood Goat 28 十一 6 / 2	木8 Wood Relief 雷水解 丙申 Fire Monkey 29 十二 4 / 3	金4 Metal Influence 澤山咸 丁酉 Fire Rooster 30 十三 9 / 4				

MAY 1996 癸巳

Xuan Kong Element 玄空五行	澤天夬 Eliminating	Period Luck 卦運	Monthly Star 月星
Metal 金4		6	5

SUNDAY	MONDAY	TUESDAY	WEDNESDAY	THURSDAY	FRIDAY	SATURDAY
			水1 Water Humility 5 戊戌 Earth Dog 地山謙 1 十四 6	火2 Fire Observation 6 己亥 Earth Pig 風地觀 2 十五 2	火2 Fire Increasing 7 庚子 Metal Rat 風雷益 3 十六 9	水1 Water Dimming Light 8 辛丑 Metal Ox 地火明夷 4 十七 3
金9 Metal Fellowship 9 壬寅 Water Tiger 天火同人 5 十八 7	木8 Wood Marrying Maiden 1 癸卯 Water Rabbit 雷澤歸妹 6 十九 7	木3 Wood Opposition 2 甲辰 Wood Dragon 火澤睽 7 二十 2	火7 Fire Waiting 3 乙巳 Wood Snake 水天需 8 廿一 3	金4 Metal Great Exceeding 4 丙午 Fire Horse 澤風大過 9 廿二 3	水6 Water Poison 5 丁未 Fire Goat 山風蠱 10 廿三 7	火2 Fire Dispersing 6 戊申 Earth Monkey 風水渙 11 廿四 6
木3 Wood Travelling 7 己酉 Earth Rooster 火山旅 12 廿五 8	金9 Metal Stagnation 8 庚戌 Metal Dog 天地否 13 廿六 9	火7 Fire Alliance 9 辛亥 Metal Pig 水地比 14 廿七 7	木8 Wood Thunder 1 壬子 Water Rat 震爲雷 15 廿八 1	水6 Water Beauty 2 癸丑 Water Ox 山火賁 16 廿九 8	火7 Fire Accomplished 3 甲寅 Wood Tiger 水火既濟 17 四月初一 9	水1 Water Arriving 4 乙卯 Wood Rabbit 地澤臨 18 初二 4
金4 Metal Marsh 5 丙辰 Fire Dragon 兌爲澤 19 初三 1	火2 Fire Small Livestock 6 丁巳 Fire Snake 風天小畜 20 初四 8	木3 Wood The Cauldron 7 戊午 Earth Horse 火風鼎 21 初五 4	水1 Water Rising 8 己未 Earth Goat 地風升 22 初六 2	火7 Fire Water 9 庚申 Metal Monkey 坎爲水 23 初七 1	木8 Wood Lesser Exceeding 1 辛酉 Metal Rooster 雷山小過 24 初八 3	金4 Metal Gathering 2 壬戌 Water Dog 澤地萃 25 初九 4
水6 Water Peel 3 癸亥 Water Pig 山地剝 26 初十 6	水1 Water Earth 4 甲子 Wood Rat 坤爲地 27 十一 1	木3 Wood Biting 5 乙丑 Wood Ox 火雷噬嗑 28 十二 6	火2 Fire Family 6 丙寅 Fire Tiger 風火家人 29 十三 4	水6 Water Decreasing 7 丁卯 Fire Rabbit 山澤損 30 十四 9	金9 Metal Tread 8 戊辰 Earth Dragon 天澤履 31 十五 6	

JUNE 1996 甲午

Xuan Kong Element 玄空五行	乾爲天 Heaven	Period Luck 卦運	Monthly Star 月星
Metal 金9		1	4

SUNDAY	MONDAY	TUESDAY	WEDNESDAY	THURSDAY	FRIDAY	SATURDAY
水1 Water Humility 8 戊戌 Earth Dog 地山謙 30 十五 6						木8 Wood Great Strength 9 己巳 Earth Snake 雷天大壯 1 十六 2
木8 Wood Consistency 1 庚午 Metal Horse 雷風恆 2 十七 9	金9 Metal Litigation 2 辛未 Metal Goat 天水訟 3 十八 3	水1 Water Officer 3 壬申 Water Monkey 地水師 4 十九 7	火2 Fire Gradual Progress 4 癸酉 Water Rooster 風山漸 5 二十 7	火7 Fire Obstruction 5 甲戌 Wood Dog 水山蹇 6 廿一 2	木3 Wood Advancement 6 乙亥 Wood Pig 火地晉 7 廿二 3	水6 Water Nourish 7 丙子 Fire Rat 山雷頤 8 廿三 3
金4 Metal Following 8 丁丑 Fire Ox 澤雷隨 9 廿四 7	木8 Wood Abundance 9 戊寅 Earth Tiger 雷火豐 10 廿五 6	火7 Fire Regulate 1 己卯 Earth Rabbit 水澤節 11 廿六 8	水1 Water Unity 2 庚辰 Metal Dragon 地天泰 12 廿七 9	木3 Wood Great Reward 3 辛巳 Metal Snake 火天大有 13 廿八 7	火2 Fire Wind 4 壬午 Water Horse 巽爲風 14 廿九 1	金4 Metal Trap 5 癸未 Water Goat 澤水困 15 三十 8
木3 Wood Not Yet Accomplished 6 甲申 Wood Monkey 火水未濟 16 五月初一 9	金9 Metal Retreat 7 乙酉 Wood Rooster 天山遯 17 初二 4	水6 Water Mountain 8 丙戌 Fire Dog 艮爲山 18 初三 1	木8 Wood Delight 9 丁亥 Fire Pig 雷地豫 19 初四 8	火7 Fire Beginning 1 戊子 Earth Rat 水雷屯 20 初五 4	金9 Metal Without Wrongdoing 2/8 己丑 Earth Ox 天雷無妄 21 初六 2	木3 Wood Fire 7 庚寅 Metal Tiger 離爲火 22 初七 1
火2 Fire Sincerity 6 辛卯 Metal Rabbit 風澤中孚 23 初八 3	水6 Water Big Livestock 5 壬辰 Water Dragon 山天大畜 24 初九 4	金4 Metal Eliminating 4 癸巳 Water Snake 澤天夬 25 初十 6	金9 Metal Heaven 3 甲午 Wood Horse 乾爲天 26 十一 1	火7 Fire Well 2 乙未 Wood Goat 水風井 27 十二 6	木8 Wood Relief 1 丙申 Fire Monkey 雷水解 28 十三 4	金4 Metal Influence 9 丁酉 Fire Rooster 澤山咸 29 十四 9

JULY 1996 乙未

Xuan Kong Element 玄空五行	水風井 Well	Period Luck 卦運	Monthly Star 月星
Fire 火7		6	3

SUNDAY	MONDAY	TUESDAY	WEDNESDAY	THURSDAY	FRIDAY	SATURDAY
	火2 Fire 7 Observation 風地觀 己亥 Earth Pig 1 十六 2	火2 Fire 6 Increasing 風雷益 庚子 Metal Rat 2 十七 9	水1 Water 5 Dimming Light 地火明夷 辛丑 Metal Ox 3 十八 3	金9 Metal 4 Fellowship 天火同人 壬寅 Water Tiger 4 十九 7	木8 Wood 3 Marrying Maiden 雷澤歸妹 癸卯 Water Rabbit 5 二十 7	木3 Wood 2 Opposition 火澤睽 甲辰 Wood Dragon 6 廿一 2
火7 Fire 1 Waiting 水天需 乙巳 Wood Snake 7 廿二 3	金4 Metal 9 Great Exceeding 澤風大過 丙午 Fire Horse 8 廿三 3	水6 Water 8 Poison 山風蠱 丁未 Fire Goat 9 廿四 7	火2 Fire 7 Dispersing 風水渙 戊申 Earth Monkey 10 廿五 6	木3 Wood 6 Travelling 火山旅 己酉 Earth Rooster 11 廿六 8	金9 Metal 5 Stagnation 天地否 庚戌 Metal Dog 12 廿七 9	火7 Fire 4 Alliance 水地比 辛亥 Metal Pig 13 廿八 7
木8 Wood 3 Thunder 震爲雷 壬子 Water Rat 14 廿九 1	水6 Water 2 Beauty 山火賁 癸丑 Water Ox 15 三十 8	火7 Fire 1 Accomplished 水火既濟 甲寅 Wood Tiger 16 六月初一 9	水1 Water 9 Arriving 地澤臨 乙卯 Wood Rabbit 17 初二 4	金4 Metal 8 Marsh 兌爲澤 丙辰 Fire Dragon 18 初三 1	火2 Fire 7 Small Livestock 風天小畜 丁巳 Fire Snake 19 初四 8	木3 Wood 6 The Cauldron 火風鼎 戊午 Earth Horse 20 初五 4
水1 Water 5 Rising 地風升 己未 Earth Goat 21 初六 2	火7 Fire 4 Water 坎爲水 庚申 Metal Monkey 22 初七 1	木8 Wood 3 Lesser Exceeding 雷山小過 辛酉 Metal Rooster 23 初八 3	金4 Metal 2 Gathering 澤地萃 壬戌 Water Dog 24 初九 4	水6 Water 1 Peel 山地剝 癸亥 Water Pig 25 初十 6	水1 Water 9 Earth 坤爲地 甲子 Wood Rat 26 十一 1	木3 Wood 8 Biting 火雷噬嗑 乙丑 Wood Ox 27 十二 6
火2 Fire 7 Family 風火家人 丙寅 Fire Tiger 28 十三 4	水6 Water 6 Decreasing 山澤損 丁卯 Fire Rabbit 29 十四 9	金9 Metal 5 Tread 天澤履 戊辰 Earth Dragon 30 十五 6	木8 Wood 4 Great Strength 雷天大壯 己巳 Earth Snake 31 十六 2			

AUGUST 1996 丙申

Xuan Kong Element 玄空五行	雷水解 Relief	Period Luck 卦運	Monthly Star 月星
Wood 木8		4	2

SUNDAY	MONDAY	TUESDAY	WEDNESDAY	THURSDAY	FRIDAY	SATURDAY
				木8 Wood 3 Consistency 雷風恆 庚午 Metal Horse 1 十七 9	金9 Metal 2 Litigation 天水訟 辛未 Metal Goat 2 十八 3	水1 Water 1 Officer 地水師 壬申 Water Monkey 3 十九 7
火2 Fire 9 Gradual Progress 風山漸 癸酉 Water Rooster 4 二十 7	火7 Fire 8 Obstruction 水山蹇 甲戌 Wood Dog 5 廿一 2	木3 Wood 7 Advancement 火地晉 乙亥 Wood Pig 6 廿二 3	水6 Water 6 Nourish 山雷頤 丙子 Fire Rat 7 廿三 3	金4 Metal 5 Following 澤雷隨 丁丑 Fire Ox 8 廿四 7	木8 Wood 4 Abundance 雷火豐 戊寅 Earth Tiger 9 廿五 6	火7 Fire 3 Regulate 水澤節 己卯 Earth Rabbit 10 廿六 8
水1 Water 2 Unity 地天泰 庚辰 Metal Dragon 11 廿七 9	木3 Wood 1 Great Reward 火天大有 辛巳 Metal Snake 12 廿八 7	火2 Fire 9 Wind 巽爲風 壬午 Water Horse 13 廿九 1	金4 Metal 8 Trap 澤水困 癸未 Water Goat 14 六月初一 8	木3 Wood 7 Not Yet Accomplished 火水未濟 甲申 Wood Monkey 15 初二 9	金9 Metal 6 Retreat 天山遯 乙酉 Wood Rooster 16 初三 4	水6 Water 5 Mountain 艮爲山 丙戌 Fire Dog 17 初四 1
木8 Wood 4 Delight 雷地豫 丁亥 Fire Pig 18 初五 8	火7 Fire 3 Beginning 水雷屯 戊子 Earth Rat 19 初六 4	金9 Metal 2 Without Wrongdoing 天雷無妄 己丑 Earth Ox 20 初七 2	木3 Wood 1 Fire 離爲火 庚寅 Metal Tiger 21 初八 1	火2 Fire 9 Sincerity 風澤中孚 辛卯 Metal Rabbit 22 初九 3	水6 Water 8 Big Livestock 山天大畜 壬辰 Water Dragon 23 初十 4	金4 Metal 7 Eliminating 澤天夬 癸巳 Water Snake 24 十一 6
金9 Metal 6 Heaven 乾爲天 甲午 Wood Horse 25 十二 1	火7 Fire 5 Well 水風井 乙未 Wood Goat 26 十三 6	木8 Wood 4 Relief 雷水解 丙申 Fire Monkey 27 十四 4	金4 Metal 3 Influence 澤山咸 丁酉 Fire Rooster 28 十五 9	水1 Water 2 Humility 地山謙 戊戌 Earth Dog 29 十六 6	火2 Fire 1 Observation 風地觀 己亥 Earth Pig 30 十七 2	火2 Fire 9 Increasing 風雷益 庚子 Metal Rat 31 十八 9

SEPTEMBER 1996 丁酉

Xuan Kong Element 玄空五行	☱☶ 澤山咸 Influence	Period Luck 卦運	Monthly Star 月星
Metal 金4		9	1

SUNDAY	MONDAY	TUESDAY	WEDNESDAY	THURSDAY	FRIDAY	SATURDAY
水1 Water 8 Dimming Light 地火明夷 辛丑 Metal Ox **1** 十九 3	金9 Metal 7 Fellowship 天火同人 壬寅 Water Tiger **2** 二十 7	木8 Wood 6 Marrying Maiden 雷澤歸妹 癸卯 Water Rabbit **3** 廿一 7	木3 Wood 5 Opposition 火澤睽 甲辰 Wood Dragon **4** 廿二 2	火7 Fire 4 Waiting 水天需 乙巳 Wood Snake **5** 廿三 3	金4 Metal 3 Great Exceeding 澤風大過 丙午 Fire Horse **6** 廿四 3	水6 Water 2 Poison 山風蠱 丁未 Fire Goat **7** 廿五 7
火2 Fire 1 Dispersing 風水渙 戊申 Earth Monkey **8** 廿六 6	木3 Wood 9 Travelling 火山旅 己酉 Earth Rooster **9** 廿七 8	金9 Metal 8 Stagnation 天地否 庚戌 Metal Dog **10** 廿八 9	火7 Fire 7 Alliance 水地比 辛亥 Metal Pig **11** 廿九 7	木8 Wood 6 Thunder 震為雷 壬子 Water Rat **12** 三十 1	水6 Water 5 Beauty 山火賁 癸丑 Water Ox **13** 八月初一 8	火7 Fire 4 Accomplished 水火既濟 甲寅 Wood Tiger **14** 初二 9
水1 Water 3 Arriving 地澤臨 乙卯 Wood Rabbit **15** 初三 4	金4 Metal 2 Marsh 兑為澤 丙辰 Fire Dragon **16** 初四 1	火2 Fire 1 Small Livestock 風天小畜 丁巳 Fire Snake **17** 初五 8	木3 Wood 9 The Cauldron 火風鼎 戊午 Earth Horse **18** 初六 4	水1 Water 8 Rising 地風升 己未 Earth Goat **19** 初七 2	火7 Fire 7 Water 坎為水 庚申 Metal Monkey **20** 初八 1	木8 Wood 6 Lesser Exceeding 雷山小過 辛酉 Metal Rooster **21** 初九 3
金4 Metal 5 Gathering 澤地萃 壬戌 Water Dog **22** 初十 4	水6 Water 4 Peel 山地剝 癸亥 Water Pig **23** 十一 6	水1 Water 3 Earth 坤為地 甲子 Wood Rat **24** 十二 1	木3 Wood 2 Biting 火雷噬嗑 乙丑 Wood Ox **25** 十三 6	火2 Fire 1 Family 風火家人 丙寅 Fire Tiger **26** 十四 4	水6 Water 9 Decreasing 山澤損 丁卯 Fire Rabbit **27** 十五 9	金9 Metal 8 Tread 天澤履 戊辰 Earth Dragon **28** 十六 6
木8 Wood 7 Great Strength 雷天大壯 己巳 Earth Snake **29** 十七 2	木8 Wood 6 Consistency 雷風恆 庚午 Metal Horse **30** 十八 9					

OCTOBER 1996 戊戌

Xuan Kong Element 玄空五行	☷☶ 地山謙 Humility	Period Luck 卦運	Monthly Star 月星
Water 水1		6	9

SUNDAY	MONDAY	TUESDAY	WEDNESDAY	THURSDAY	FRIDAY	SATURDAY
		金9 Metal 5 Litigation 天水訟 辛未 Metal Goat **1** 十九 3	水1 Water 4 Officer 地水師 壬申 Water Monkey **2** 二十 7	火2 Fire 3 Gradual Progress 風山漸 癸酉 Water Rooster **3** 廿一 7	火7 Fire 2 Obstruction 水山蹇 甲戌 Wood Dog **4** 廿二 2	木3 Wood 1 Advancement 火地晉 乙亥 Wood Pig **5** 廿三 3
水6 Water 9 Nourish 山雷頤 丙子 Fire Rat **6** 廿四 3	金4 Metal 8 Following 澤雷隨 丁丑 Fire Ox **7** 廿五 7	木8 Wood 7 Abundance 雷火豐 戊寅 Earth Tiger **8** 廿六 6	火7 Fire 6 Regulate 水澤節 己卯 Earth Rabbit **9** 廿七 8	水1 Water 5 Unity 地天泰 庚辰 Metal Dragon **10** 廿八 9	木3 Wood 4 Great Reward 火天大有 辛巳 Metal Snake **11** 廿九 7	火2 Fire 3 Wind 巽為風 壬午 Water Horse **12** 九月初一 1
金4 Metal 2 Trap 澤水困 癸未 Water Goat **13** 初二 8	木3 Wood 1 Not Yet Accomplished 火水未濟 甲申 Wood Monkey **14** 初三 9	金9 Metal 9 Retreat 天山遯 乙酉 Wood Rooster **15** 初四 4	水6 Water 8 Mountain 艮為山 丙戌 Fire Dog **16** 初五 1	木8 Wood 7 Delight 雷地豫 丁亥 Fire Pig **17** 初六 8	火7 Fire 6 Beginning 水雷屯 戊子 Earth Rat **18** 初七 4	金9 Metal 5 Without Wrongdoing 天雷無妄 己丑 Earth Ox **19** 初八 2
木3 Wood 4 Fire 離為火 庚寅 Metal Tiger **20** 初九 1	火2 Fire 3 Sincerity 風澤中孚 辛卯 Metal Rabbit **21** 初十 3	水6 Water 2 Big Livestock 山天大畜 壬辰 Water Dragon **22** 十一 4	金4 Metal 1 Eliminating 澤天夬 癸巳 Water Snake **23** 十二 6	金9 Metal 9 Heaven 乾為天 甲午 Wood Horse **24** 十三 1	火7 Fire 8 Well 水風井 乙未 Wood Goat **25** 十四 6	木8 Wood 7 Relief 雷水解 丙申 Fire Monkey **26** 十五 4
金4 Metal 6 Influence 澤山咸 丁酉 Fire Rooster **27** 十六 9	水1 Water 5 Humility 地山謙 戊戌 Earth Dog **28** 十七 6	火2 Fire 4 Observation 風地觀 己亥 Earth Pig **29** 十八 2	火2 Fire 3 Increasing 風雷益 庚子 Metal Rat **30** 十九 9	水1 Water 2 Dimming Light 地火明夷 辛丑 Metal Ox **31** 二十 3		

NOVEMBER 1996 己亥

Xuan Kong Element 玄空五行	風地觀 Observation	Period Luck 卦運	Monthly Star 月星
Fire 火2		2	8

SUNDAY	MONDAY	TUESDAY	WEDNESDAY	THURSDAY	FRIDAY	SATURDAY
					金9 Metal · Fellowship · 1 壬寅 Water Tiger 天火同人 1 廿一 7	木8 Wood · Marrying Maiden · 9 癸卯 Water Rabbit 雷澤歸妹 2 廿二 7
木3 Wood · Opposition · 8 甲辰 Wood Dragon 火澤睽 3 廿三 2	火7 Fire · Waiting · 7 乙巳 Wood Snake 水天需 4 廿四 3	金4 Metal · Great Exceeding · 6 丙午 Fire Horse 澤風大過 5 廿五 3	水6 Water · Poison · 5 丁未 Fire Goat 山風蠱 6 廿六 7	火2 Fire · Dispersing · 4 戊申 Earth Monkey 風水渙 7 廿七 6	木3 Wood · Travelling · 3 己酉 Earth Rooster 火山旅 8 廿八 8	金9 Metal · Stagnation · 2 庚戌 Metal Dog 天地否 9 廿九 9
火7 Fire · Alliance · 1 辛亥 Metal Pig 水地比 10 三十 7	木8 Wood · Thunder · 9 壬子 Water Rat 震爲雷 11 十月初一 1	水6 Water · Beauty · 8 癸丑 Water Ox 山火賁 12 初二 8	火7 Fire · Accomplished · 7 甲寅 Wood Tiger 水火既濟 13 初三 9	水1 Water · Arriving · 6 乙卯 Wood Rabbit 地澤臨 14 初四 4	金4 Metal · Marsh · 5 丙辰 Fire Dragon 兌爲澤 15 初五 1	火2 Fire · Small Livestock · 4 丁巳 Fire Snake 風天小畜 16 初六 8
木3 Wood · The Cauldron · 3 戊午 Earth Horse 火風鼎 17 初七 4	水1 Water · Rising · 2 己未 Earth Goat 地風升 18 初八 2	火7 Fire · Water · 1 庚申 Metal Monkey 坎爲水 19 初九 1	木8 Wood · Lesser Exceeding · 9 辛酉 Metal Rooster 雷山小過 20 初十 3	金4 Metal · Gathering · 8 壬戌 Water Dog 澤地萃 21 十一 4	水6 Water · Peel · 7 癸亥 Water Pig 山地剝 22 十二 6	水1 Water · Earth · 6 甲子 Wood Rat 坤爲地 23 十三 1
木3 Wood · Biting · 5 乙丑 Wood Ox 火雷噬嗑 24 十四 6	火2 Fire · Family · 4 丙寅 Fire Tiger 風火家人 25 十五 4	水6 Water · Decreasing · 3 丁卯 Fire Rabbit 山澤損 26 十六 9	金9 Metal · Tread · 2 戊辰 Earth Dragon 天澤履 27 十七 6	木8 Wood · Great Strength · 1 己巳 Earth Snake 雷天大壯 28 十八 2	木8 Wood · Consistency · 9 庚午 Metal Horse 雷風恆 29 十九 9	金9 Metal · Litigation · 8 辛未 Metal Goat 天水訟 30 二十 3

DECEMBER 1996 庚子

Xuan Kong Element 玄空五行	風雷益 Increasing	Period Luck 卦運	Monthly Star 月星
Fire 火2		9	7

SUNDAY	MONDAY	TUESDAY	WEDNESDAY	THURSDAY	FRIDAY	SATURDAY
水1 Water · Officer · 7 壬申 Water Monkey 地水師 1 廿一 7	火2 Fire · Gradual Progress · 6 癸酉 Water Rooster 風山漸 2 廿二 7	火7 Fire · Obstruction · 5 甲戌 Wood Dog 水山蹇 3 廿三 2	木3 Wood · Advancement · 4 乙亥 Wood Pig 火地晉 4 廿四 3	水6 Water · Nourish · 3 丙子 Fire Rat 山雷頤 5 廿五 3	金4 Metal · Following · 2 丁丑 Fire Ox 澤雷隨 6 廿六 7	木8 Wood · Abundance · 1 戊寅 Earth Tiger 雷火豐 7 廿七 6
火7 Fire · Regulate · 9 己卯 Earth Rabbit 水澤節 8 廿八 8	水1 Water · Unity · 8 庚辰 Metal Dragon 地天泰 9 廿九 9	木3 Wood · Great Reward · 7 辛巳 Metal Snake 火天大有 10 三十 7	火2 Fire · Wind · 6 壬午 Water Horse 巽爲風 11 十一月初一 1	金4 Metal · Trap · 5 癸未 Water Goat 澤水困 12 初二 8	木3 Wood · Not Yet Accomplished · 4 甲申 Wood Monkey 火水未濟 13 初三 9	金9 Metal · Retreat · 3 乙酉 Wood Rooster 天山遯 14 初四 4
水6 Water · Mountain · 2 丙戌 Fire Dog 艮爲山 15 初五 1	木8 Wood · Delight · 1 丁亥 Fire Pig 雷地豫 16 初六 8	火7 Fire · Beginning · 9 戊子 Earth Rat 水雷屯 17 初七 4	金9 Metal · Without Wrongdoing · 8 己丑 Earth Ox 天雷無妄 18 初八 2	木3 Wood · Fire · 7 庚寅 Metal Tiger 離爲火 19 初九 1	火2 Fire · Sincerity · 6 辛卯 Metal Rabbit 風澤中孚 20 初十 3	水6 Water · Big Livestock · 5 5 壬辰 Water Dragon 山天大畜 21 十一 4
金4 Metal · Eliminating · 6 癸巳 Water Snake 澤天夬 22 十二 6	金9 Metal · Heaven · 7 甲午 Wood Horse 乾爲天 23 十三 1	火7 Fire · Well · 8 乙未 Wood Goat 水風井 24 十四 6	木8 Wood · Relief · 9 丙申 Fire Monkey 雷水解 25 十五 4	金4 Metal · Influence · 1 丁酉 Fire Rooster 澤山咸 26 十六 9	水1 Water · Humility · 2 戊戌 Earth Dog 地山謙 27 十七 6	火2 Fire · Observation · 3 己亥 Earth Pig 風地觀 28 十八 2
火2 Fire · Increasing · 4 庚子 Metal Rat 風雷益 29 十九 9	水1 Water · Dimming Light · 5 辛丑 Metal Ox 地火明夷 30 二十 3	金9 Metal · Fellowship · 6 壬寅 Water Tiger 天火同人 31 廿一 7				

1997 丁丑

(*Ding Chou*) Fire Ox

1997 丁丑 *(Ding Chou)* Fire Ox

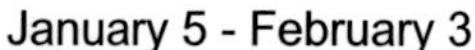

January 5 - February 3

February 4 - March 4

March 5 - April 4

April 5 - May 4

May 5 - June 4

June 5 - July 6

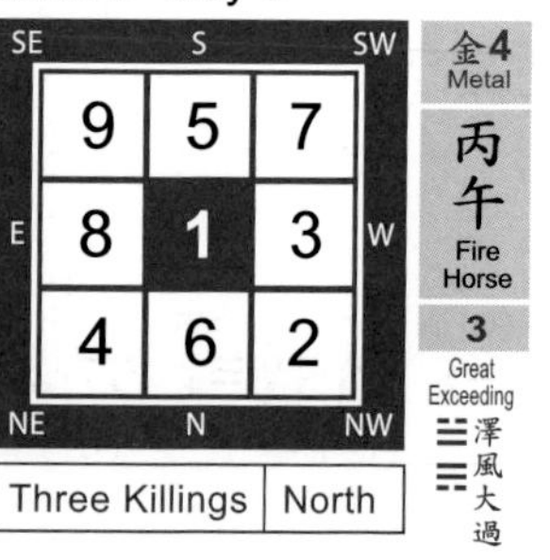

July 7 - August 6

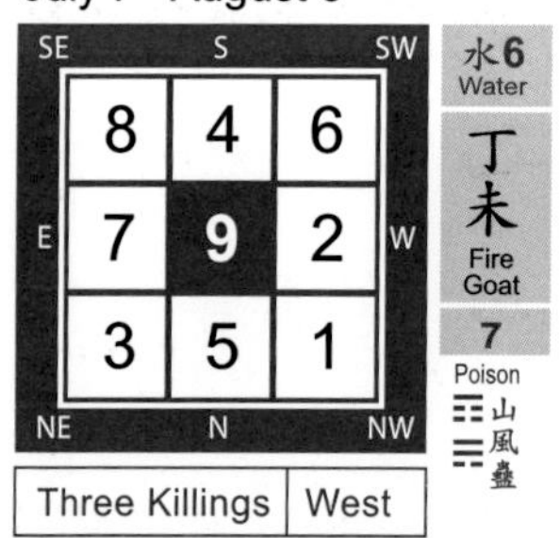

August 7 - September 6

September 7 - October 7

October 8 - November 6

November 7 - December 6

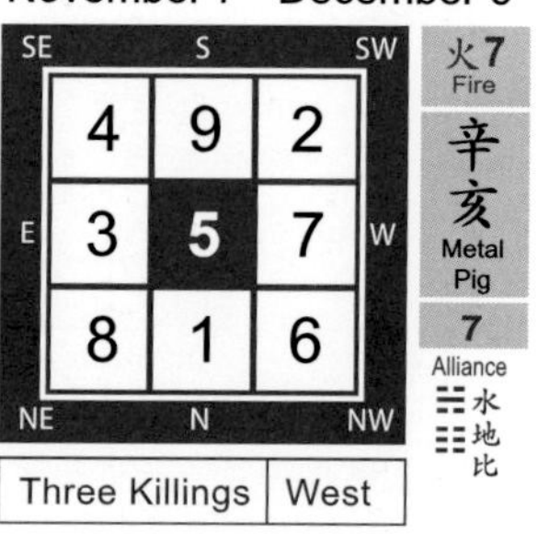

December 7 - January 4

JANUARY 1997 辛丑

Xuan Kong Element 玄空五行	地火明夷 Dimming Light	Period Luck 卦運	Monthly Star 月星
Water 水1		3	6

SUNDAY	MONDAY	TUESDAY	WEDNESDAY	THURSDAY	FRIDAY	SATURDAY
			1 廿二 木8 Wood · 7 Marrying Maiden 雷澤歸妹 癸卯 Water Rabbit 7	**2** 廿三 木3 Wood · 8 Opposition 火澤睽 甲辰 Wood Dragon 2	**3** 廿四 火7 Fire · 9 Waiting 水天需 乙巳 Wood Snake 3	**4** 廿五 金4 Metal · 1 Great Exceeding 澤風大過 丙午 Fire Horse 3
5 廿六 水6 Water · 2 Poison 山風蠱 丁未 Fire Goat 7	**6** 廿七 火2 Fire · 3 Dispersing 風水渙 戊申 Earth Monkey 6	**7** 廿八 木3 Wood · 4 Travelling 火山旅 己酉 Earth Rooster 8	**8** 廿九 金9 Metal · 5 Stagnation 天地否 庚戌 Metal Dog 9	**9** 十二月初一 火7 Fire · 6 Alliance 水地比 辛亥 Metal Pig 7	**10** 初二 木8 Wood · 7 Thunder 震爲雷 壬子 Water Rat 1	**11** 初三 水6 Water · 8 Beauty 山火賁 癸丑 Water Ox 8
12 初四 火7 Fire · 9 Accomplished 水火既濟 甲寅 Wood Tiger 9	**13** 初五 水1 Water · 1 Arriving 地澤臨 乙卯 Wood Rabbit 4	**14** 初六 金4 Metal · 2 Marsh 兑爲澤 丙辰 Fire Dragon 1	**15** 初七 火2 Fire · 3 Small Livestock 風天小畜 丁巳 Fire Snake 8	**16** 初八 木3 Wood · 4 The Cauldron 火風鼎 戊午 Earth Horse 4	**17** 初九 水1 Water · 5 Rising 地風升 己未 Earth Goat 2	**18** 初十 火7 Fire · 6 Water 坎爲水 庚申 Metal Monkey 1
19 十一 木8 Wood · 7 Lesser Exceeding 雷山小過 辛酉 Metal Rooster 3	**20** 十二 金4 Metal · 8 Gathering 澤地萃 壬戌 Water Dog 4	**21** 十三 水6 Water · 9 Peel 山地剝 癸亥 Water Pig 6	**22** 十四 水1 Water · 1 Earth 坤爲地 甲子 Wood Rat 1	**23** 十五 木3 Wood · 2 Biting 火雷噬嗑 乙丑 Wood Ox 6	**24** 十六 火2 Fire · 3 Family 風火家人 丙寅 Fire Tiger 4	**25** 十七 水6 Water · 4 Decreasing 山澤損 丁卯 Fire Rabbit 9
26 十八 金9 Metal · 5 Tread 天澤履 戊辰 Earth Dragon 6	**27** 十九 木8 Wood · 6 Great Strength 雷天大壯 己巳 Earth Snake 2	**28** 二十 木8 Wood · 7 Consistency 雷風恆 庚午 Metal Horse 9	**29** 廿一 金9 Metal · 8 Litigation 天水訟 辛未 Metal Goat 3	**30** 廿二 水1 Water · 9 Officer 地水師 壬申 Water Monkey 7	**31** 廿三 火2 Fire · 1 Gradual Progress 風山漸 癸酉 Water Rooster 7	

FEBRUARY 1997 壬寅

Xuan Kong Element 玄空五行	天火同人 Fellowship	Period Luck 卦運	Monthly Star 月星
Metal 金9		7	5

SUNDAY	MONDAY	TUESDAY	WEDNESDAY	THURSDAY	FRIDAY	SATURDAY
						1 廿四 火7 Fire · 2 Obstruction 水山蹇 甲戌 Wood Dog 2
2 廿五 木3 Wood · 3 Advancement 火地晉 乙亥 Wood Pig 3	**3** 廿六 水6 Water · 4 Nourish 山雷頤 丙子 Fire Rat 3	**4** 廿七 金4 Metal · 5 Following 澤雷隨 丁丑 Fire Ox 7	**5** 廿八 木8 Wood · 6 Abundance 雷火豐 戊寅 Earth Tiger 6	**6** 廿九 火7 Fire · 7 Regulate 水澤節 己卯 Earth Rabbit 8	**7** 正月初一 水1 Water · 8 Unity 地天泰 庚辰 Metal Dragon 9	**8** 初二 木3 Wood · 9 Great Reward 火天大有 辛巳 Metal Snake 7
9 初三 火2 Fire · 1 Wind 巽爲風 壬午 Water Horse 1	**10** 初四 金4 Metal · 2 Trap 澤水困 癸未 Water Goat 8	**11** 初五 木3 Wood · 3 Not Yet Accomplished 火水未濟 甲申 Wood Monkey 9	**12** 初六 金9 Metal · 4 Retreat 天山遯 乙酉 Wood Rooster 4	**13** 初七 水6 Water · 5 Mountain 艮爲山 丙戌 Fire Dog 1	**14** 初八 木8 Wood · 6 Delight 雷地豫 丁亥 Fire Pig 8	**15** 初九 火7 Fire · 7 Beginning 水雷屯 戊子 Earth Rat 4
16 初十 金9 Metal · 8 Without Wrongdoing 天雷無妄 己丑 Earth Ox 2	**17** 十一 木3 Wood · 9 Fire 離爲火 庚寅 Metal Tiger 1	**18** 十二 火2 Fire · 1 Sincerity 風澤中孚 辛卯 Metal Rabbit 3	**19** 十三 水6 Water · 2 Big Livestock 山天大畜 壬辰 Water Dragon 4	**20** 十四 金4 Metal · 3 Eliminating 澤天夬 癸巳 Water Snake 6	**21** 十五 金9 Metal · 4 Heaven 乾爲天 甲午 Wood Horse 1	**22** 十六 火7 Fire · 5 Well 水風井 乙未 Wood Goat 6
23 十七 木8 Wood · 6 Relief 雷水解 丙申 Fire Monkey 4	**24** 十八 金4 Metal · 7 Influence 澤山咸 丁酉 Fire Rooster 9	**25** 十九 水1 Water · 8 Humility 地山謙 戊戌 Earth Dog 6	**26** 二十 火2 Fire · 9 Observation 風地觀 己亥 Earth Pig 2	**27** 廿一 火2 Fire · 1 Increasing 風雷益 庚子 Metal Rat 9	**28** 廿二 水1 Water · 2 Dimming Light 地火明夷 辛丑 Metal Ox 3	

MARCH 1997 癸卯

Xuan Kong Element 玄空五行	雷澤歸妹 Marrying Maiden	Period Luck 卦運	Monthly Star 月星
Wood 木8		7	4

SUNDAY	MONDAY	TUESDAY	WEDNESDAY	THURSDAY	FRIDAY	SATURDAY
金9 Metal · 5 Litigation 天水訟 辛未 Metal Goat **30** 廿二 3	水1 Water · 6 Officer 地水師 壬申 Water Monkey **31** 廿三 7					金9 Metal · 3 Fellowship 天火同人 壬寅 Water Tiger **1** 廿三 7
木8 Wood · 4 Marrying Maiden 雷澤歸妹 癸卯 Water Rabbit **2** 廿四 7	木3 Wood · 5 Opposition 火澤睽 甲辰 Wood Dragon **3** 廿五 2	火7 Fire · 6 Waiting 水天需 乙巳 Wood Snake **4** 廿六 3	金4 Metal · 7 Great Exceeding 澤風大過 丙午 Fire Horse **5** 廿七 3	水6 Water · 8 Poison 山風蠱 丁未 Fire Goat **6** 廿八 7	火2 Fire · 9 Dispersing 風水渙 戊申 Earth Monkey **7** 廿九 6	木3 Wood · 1 Travelling 火山旅 己酉 Earth Rooster **8** 三十 8
金9 Metal · 2 Stagnation 天地否 庚戌 Metal Dog **9** 二月初一 9	火7 Fire · 3 Alliance 水地比 辛亥 Metal Pig **10** 初二 7	木8 Wood · 4 Thunder 震爲雷 壬子 Water Rat **11** 初三 1	水6 Water · 5 Beauty 山火賁 癸丑 Water Ox **12** 初四 8	火7 Fire · 6 Accomplished 水火既濟 甲寅 Wood Tiger **13** 初五 9	水1 Water · 7 Arriving 地澤臨 乙卯 Wood Rabbit **14** 初六 4	金4 Metal · 8 Marsh 兑爲澤 丙辰 Fire Dragon **15** 初七 1
火2 Fire · 9 Small Livestock 風天小畜 丁巳 Fire Snake **16** 初八 8	木3 Wood · 1 The Cauldron 火風鼎 戊午 Earth Horse **17** 初九 4	水1 Water · 2 Rising 地風升 己未 Earth Goat **18** 初十 2	火7 Fire · 3 Water 坎爲水 庚申 Metal Monkey **19** 十一 1	木8 Wood · 4 Lesser Exceeding 雷山小過 辛酉 Metal Rooster **20** 十二 3	金4 Metal · 5 Gathering 澤地萃 壬戌 Water Dog **21** 十三 4	水6 Water · 6 Peel 山地剝 癸亥 Water Pig **22** 十四 6
水1 Water · 7 Earth 坤爲地 甲子 Wood Rat **23** 十五 1	木3 Wood · 8 Biting 火雷噬嗑 乙丑 Wood Ox **24** 十六 6	火2 Fire · 9 Family 風火家人 丙寅 Fire Tiger **25** 十七 4	水6 Water · 1 Decreasing 山澤損 丁卯 Fire Rabbit **26** 十八 9	金9 Metal · 2 Tread 天澤履 戊辰 Earth Dragon **27** 十九 6	木8 Wood · 3 Great Strength 雷天大壯 己巳 Earth Snake **28** 二十 2	木8 Wood · 4 Consistency 雷風恒 庚午 Metal Horse **29** 廿一 9

APRIL 1997 甲辰

Xuan Kong Element 玄空五行	火澤睽 Opposition	Period Luck 卦運	Monthly Star 月星
Wood 木3		2	3

SUNDAY	MONDAY	TUESDAY	WEDNESDAY	THURSDAY	FRIDAY	SATURDAY
		火2 Fire · 7 Gradual Progress 風山漸 癸酉 Water Rooster **1** 廿四 7	火7 Fire · 8 Obstruction 水山蹇 甲戌 Wood Dog **2** 廿五 2	木3 Wood · 9 Advancement 火地晉 乙亥 Wood Pig **3** 廿六 3	水6 Water · 1 Nourish 山雷頤 丙子 Fire Rat **4** 廿七 3	金4 Metal · 2 Following 澤雷隨 丁丑 Fire Ox **5** 廿八 7
木8 Wood · 3 Abundance 雷火豐 戊寅 Earth Tiger **6** 廿九 6	火7 Fire · 4 Regulate 水澤節 己卯 Earth Rabbit **7** 三月初一 8	水1 Water · 5 Unity 地天泰 庚辰 Metal Dragon **8** 初二 9	木3 Wood · 6 Great Reward 火天大有 辛巳 Metal Snake **9** 初三 7	火2 Fire · 7 Wind 巽爲風 壬午 Water Horse **10** 初四 1	金4 Metal · 8 Trap 澤水困 癸未 Water Goat **11** 初五 8	木3 Wood · 9 Not Yet Accomplished 火水未濟 甲申 Wood Monkey **12** 初六 9
金9 Metal · 1 Retreat 天山遯 乙酉 Wood Rooster **13** 初七 4	水6 Water · 2 Mountain 艮爲山 丙戌 Fire Dog **14** 初八 1	木8 Wood · 3 Delight 雷地豫 丁亥 Fire Pig **15** 初九 8	火7 Fire · 4 Beginning 水雷屯 戊子 Earth Rat **16** 初十 4	金9 Metal · 5 Without Wrongdoing 天雷無妄 己丑 Earth Ox **17** 十一 2	木3 Wood · 6 Fire 離爲火 庚寅 Metal Tiger **18** 十二 1	火2 Fire · 7 Sincerity 風澤中孚 辛卯 Metal Rabbit **19** 十三 3
水6 Water · 8 Big Livestock 山天大畜 壬辰 Water Dragon **20** 十四 4	金4 Metal · 9 Eliminating 澤天夬 癸巳 Water Snake **21** 十五 6	金9 Metal · 1 Heaven 乾爲天 甲午 Wood Horse **22** 十六 1	火7 Fire · 2 Well 水風井 乙未 Wood Goat **23** 十七 6	木8 Wood · 3 Relief 雷水解 丙申 Fire Monkey **24** 十八 4	金4 Metal · 4 Influence 澤山咸 丁酉 Fire Rooster **25** 十九 9	水1 Water · 5 Humility 地山謙 戊戌 Earth Dog **26** 二十 6
火2 Fire · 6 Observation 風地觀 己亥 Earth Pig **27** 廿一 2	火2 Fire · 7 Increasing 風雷益 庚子 Metal Rat **28** 廿二 9	水1 Water · 8 Dimming Light 地火明夷 辛丑 Metal Ox **29** 廿三 3	金9 Metal · 9 Fellowship 天火同人 壬寅 Water Tiger **30** 廿四 7			

MAY 1997 乙巳

Xuan Kong Element 玄空五行	水天需 Waiting	Period Luck 卦運	Monthly Star 月星
Fire 火7		3	2

SUNDAY	MONDAY	TUESDAY	WEDNESDAY	THURSDAY	FRIDAY	SATURDAY
				木8 Wood 1 Marrying Maiden 雷澤歸妹 癸卯 Water Rabbit **1** 廿五 7	木3 Wood 2 Opposition 火澤睽 甲辰 Wood Dragon **2** 廿六 2	火7 Fire 3 Waiting 水天需 乙巳 Wood Snake **3** 廿七 3
金4 Metal 4 Great Exceeding 澤風大過 丙午 Fire Horse **4** 廿八 3	水6 Water 5 Poison 山風蠱 丁未 Fire Goat **5** 廿九 7	火2 Fire 6 Dispersing 風水渙 戊申 Earth Monkey **6** 三十 6	木3 Wood 7 Travelling 火山旅 己酉 Earth Rooster **7** 四月初一 8	金9 Metal 8 Stagnation 天地否 庚戌 Metal Dog **8** 初二 9	火7 Fire 9 Alliance 水地比 辛亥 Metal Pig **9** 初三 7	木8 Wood 1 Thunder 震為雷 壬子 Water Rat **10** 初四 1
水6 Water 2 Beauty 山火賁 癸丑 Water Ox **11** 初五 8	火7 Fire 3 Accomplished 水火既濟 甲寅 Wood Tiger **12** 初六 9	水1 Water 4 Arriving 地澤臨 乙卯 Wood Rabbit **13** 初七 4	金4 Metal 5 Marsh 兑為澤 丙辰 Fire Dragon **14** 初八 1	火2 Fire 6 Small Livestock 風天小畜 丁巳 Fire Snake **15** 初九 8	木3 Wood 7 The Cauldron 火風鼎 戊午 Earth Horse **16** 初十 4	水1 Water 8 Rising 地風升 己未 Earth Goat **17** 十一 2
火7 Fire 9 Water 坎為水 庚申 Metal Monkey **18** 十二 1	木8 Wood 1 Lesser Exceeding 雷山小過 辛酉 Metal Rooster **19** 十三 3	金4 Metal 2 Gathering 澤地萃 壬戌 Water Dog **20** 十四 4	水6 Water 3 Peel 山地剝 癸亥 Water Pig **21** 十五 6	水1 Water 4 Earth 坤為地 甲子 Wood Rat **22** 十六 1	木3 Wood 5 Biting 火雷噬嗑 乙丑 Wood Ox **23** 十七 6	火2 Fire 6 Family 風火家人 丙寅 Fire Tiger **24** 十八 4
水6 Water 7 Decreasing 山澤損 丁卯 Fire Rabbit **25** 十九 9	金9 Metal 8 Tread 天澤履 戊辰 Earth Dragon **26** 二十 6	木8 Wood 9 Great Strength 雷天大壯 己巳 Earth Snake **27** 廿一 2	木8 Wood 1 Consistency 雷風恆 庚午 Metal Horse **28** 廿二 9	金9 Metal 2 Litigation 天水訟 辛未 Metal Goat **29** 廿三 3	水1 Water 3 Officer 地水師 壬申 Water Monkey **30** 廿四 7	火2 Fire 4 Gradual Progress 風山漸 癸酉 Water Rooster **31** 廿五 7

JUNE 1997 丙午

Xuan Kong Element 玄空五行	澤風大過 Great Exceeding	Period Luck 卦運	Monthly Star 月星
Metal 金4		3	1

SUNDAY	MONDAY	TUESDAY	WEDNESDAY	THURSDAY	FRIDAY	SATURDAY
火7 Fire 5 Obstruction 水山蹇 甲戌 Wood Dog **1** 廿六 2	木3 Wood 6 Advancement 火地晉 乙亥 Wood Pig **2** 廿七 3	水6 Water 7 Nourish 山雷頤 丙子 Fire Rat **3** 廿八 3	金4 Metal 8 Following 澤雷隨 丁丑 Fire Ox **4** 廿九 7	木8 Wood 9 Abundance 雷火豐 戊寅 Earth Tiger **5** 三月初一 6	火7 Fire 1 Regulate 水澤節 己卯 Earth Rabbit **6** 初二 8	水1 Water 2 Unity 地天泰 庚辰 Metal Dragon **7** 初三 9
木3 Wood 3 Great Reward 火天大有 辛巳 Metal Snake **8** 初四 7	火2 Fire 4 Wind 巽為風 壬午 Water Horse **9** 初五 1	金4 Metal 5 Trap 澤水困 癸未 Water Goat **10** 初六 8	木3 Wood 6 Not Yet Accomplished 火水未濟 甲申 Wood Monkey **11** 初七 9	金9 Metal 7 Retreat 天山遯 乙酉 Wood Rooster **12** 初八 4	水6 Water 8 Mountain 艮為山 丙戌 Fire Dog **13** 初九 1	木8 Wood 9 Delight 雷地豫 丁亥 Fire Pig **14** 初十 8
火7 Fire 1 Beginning 水雷屯 戊子 Earth Rat **15** 十一 4	金9 Metal 2 Without Wrongdoing 天雷無妄 己丑 Earth Ox **16** 十二 2	木3 Wood 3 Fire 離為火 庚寅 Metal Tiger **17** 十三 1	火2 Fire 4 Sincerity 風澤中孚 辛卯 Metal Rabbit **18** 十四 3	水6 Water 5 Big Livestock 山天大畜 壬辰 Water Dragon **19** 十五 4	金4 Metal 6 Eliminating 澤天夬 癸巳 Water Snake **20** 十六 6	金9 Metal 7/3 Heaven 乾為天 甲午 Wood Horse **21** 十七 1
火7 Fire 2 Well 水風井 乙未 Wood Goat **22** 十八 6	木8 Wood 1 Relief 雷水解 丙申 Fire Monkey **23** 十九 4	金4 Metal 9 Influence 澤山咸 丁酉 Fire Rooster **24** 二十 9	水1 Water 8 Humility 地山謙 戊戌 Earth Dog **25** 廿一 6	火2 Fire 7 Observation 風地觀 己亥 Earth Pig **26** 廿二 2	火2 Fire 6 Increasing 風雷益 庚子 Metal Rat **27** 廿三 9	水1 Water 5 Dimming Light 地火明夷 辛丑 Metal Ox **28** 廿四 3
金9 Metal 4 Fellowship 天火同人 壬寅 Water Tiger **29** 廿五 7	木8 Wood 3 Marrying Maiden 雷澤歸妹 癸卯 Water Rabbit **30** 廿六 7					

JULY 1997 丁未

Xuan Kong Element 玄空五行	山風蠱 Poison	Period Luck 卦運	Monthly Star 月星
Water 水6		7	9

SUNDAY	MONDAY	TUESDAY	WEDNESDAY	THURSDAY	FRIDAY	SATURDAY
		木3 Wood 2 Opposition 甲辰 Wood Dragon 火澤睽 1 廿七 2	火7 Fire 1 Waiting 乙巳 Wood Snake 水天需 2 廿八 3	金4 Metal 9 Great Exceeding 丙午 Fire Horse 澤風大過 3 廿九 3	水6 Water 8 Poison 丁未 Fire Goat 山風蠱 4 三十 7	火2 Fire 7 Dispersing 戊申 Earth Monkey 風水渙 5 六月初一 6
木3 Wood 6 Travelling 己酉 Earth Rooster 火山旅 6 初二 8	金9 Metal 5 Stagnation 庚戌 Metal Dog 天地否 7 初三 9	火7 Fire 4 Alliance 辛亥 Metal Pig 水地比 8 初四 7	木8 Wood 3 Thunder 壬子 Water Rat 震爲雷 9 初五 1	水6 Water 2 Beauty 癸丑 Water Ox 山火賁 10 初六 8	火7 Fire 1 Accomplished 甲寅 Wood Tiger 水火既濟 11 初七 9	水1 Water 9 Arriving 乙卯 Wood Rabbit 地澤臨 12 初八 4
金4 Metal 8 Marsh 丙辰 Fire Dragon 兑爲澤 13 初九 1	火2 Fire 7 Small Livestock 丁巳 Fire Snake 風天小畜 14 初十 8	木3 Wood 6 The Cauldron 戊午 Earth Horse 火風鼎 15 十一 4	水1 Water 5 Rising 己未 Earth Goat 地風升 16 十二 2	火7 Fire 4 Water 庚申 Metal Monkey 坎爲水 17 十三 1	木8 Wood 3 Lesser Exceeding 辛酉 Metal Rooster 雷山小過 18 十四 3	金4 Metal 2 Gathering 壬戌 Water Dog 澤地萃 19 十五 4
水6 Water 1 Peel 癸亥 Water Pig 山地剝 20 十六 6	水1 Water 9 Earth 甲子 Wood Rat 坤爲地 21 十七 1	木3 Wood 8 Biting 乙丑 Wood Ox 火雷噬嗑 22 十八 6	火2 Fire 7 Family 丙寅 Fire Tiger 風火家人 23 十九 4	水6 Water 6 Decreasing 丁卯 Fire Rabbit 山澤損 24 二十 9	金9 Metal 5 Tread 戊辰 Earth Dragon 天澤履 25 廿一 6	木8 Wood 4 Great Strength 己巳 Earth Snake 雷天大壯 26 廿二 2
木8 Wood 3 Consistency 庚午 Metal Horse 雷風恒 27 廿三 9	金9 Metal 2 Litigation 辛未 Metal Goat 天水訟 28 廿四 3	水1 Water 1 Officer 壬申 Water Monkey 地水師 29 廿五 7	火2 Fire 9 Gradual Progress 癸酉 Water Rooster 風山漸 30 廿六 7	火7 Fire 8 Obstruction 甲戌 Wood Dog 水山蹇 31 廿七 2		

AUGUST 1997 戊申

Xuan Kong Element 玄空五行	風水渙 Dispersing	Period Luck 卦運	Monthly Star 月星
Fire 火2		6	8

SUNDAY	MONDAY	TUESDAY	WEDNESDAY	THURSDAY	FRIDAY	SATURDAY
火7 Fire 4 Waiting 乙巳 Wood Snake 水天需 31 廿九 3					木3 Wood 7 Advancement 乙亥 Wood Pig 火地晉 1 廿八 3	水6 Water 6 Nourish 丙子 Fire Rat 山雷頤 2 廿九 3
金4 Metal 5 Following 丁丑 Fire Ox 澤雷隨 3 七月初一 7	木8 Wood 4 Abundance 戊寅 Earth Tiger 雷火豐 4 初二 6	火7 Fire 3 Regulate 己卯 Earth Rabbit 水澤節 5 初三 8	水1 Water 2 Unity 庚辰 Metal Dragon 地天泰 6 初四 9	木3 Wood 1 Great Reward 辛巳 Metal Snake 火天大有 7 初五 7	火2 Fire 9 Wind 壬午 Water Horse 巽爲風 8 初六 1	金4 Metal 8 Trap 癸未 Water Goat 澤水困 9 初七 8
木3 Wood 7 Not Yet Accomplished 甲申 Wood Monkey 火水未濟 10 初八 9	金9 Metal 6 Retreat 乙酉 Wood Rooster 天山遯 11 初九 4	水6 Water 5 Mountain 丙戌 Fire Dog 艮爲山 12 初十 1	木8 Wood 4 Delight 丁亥 Fire Pig 雷地豫 13 十一 8	火7 Fire 3 Beginning 戊子 Earth Rat 水雷屯 14 十二 4	金9 Metal 2 Without Wrongdoing 己丑 Earth Ox 天雷無妄 15 十三 2	木3 Wood 1 Fire 庚寅 Metal Tiger 離爲火 16 十四 1
火2 Fire 9 Sincerity 辛卯 Metal Rabbit 風澤中孚 17 十五 3	水6 Water 8 Big Livestock 壬辰 Water Dragon 山天大畜 18 十六 4	金4 Metal 7 Eliminating 癸巳 Water Snake 澤天夬 19 十七 6	金9 Metal 6 Heaven 甲午 Wood Horse 乾爲天 20 十八 1	火7 Fire 5 Well 乙未 Wood Goat 水風井 21 十九 6	木8 Wood 4 Relief 丙申 Fire Monkey 雷水解 22 二十 4	金4 Metal 3 Influence 丁酉 Fire Rooster 澤山咸 23 廿一 9
水1 Water 2 Humility 戊戌 Earth Dog 地山謙 24 廿二 6	火2 Fire 1 Observation 己亥 Earth Pig 風地觀 25 廿三 2	火2 Fire 9 Increasing 庚子 Metal Rat 風雷益 26 廿四 9	水1 Water 8 Dimming Light 辛丑 Metal Ox 地火明夷 27 廿五 3	金9 Metal 7 Fellowship 壬寅 Water Tiger 天火同人 28 廿六 7	木8 Wood 6 Marrying Maiden 癸卯 Water Rabbit 雷澤歸妹 29 廿七 7	木3 Wood 5 Opposition 甲辰 Wood Dragon 火澤睽 30 廿八 2

SEPTEMBER 1997 己酉

Xuan Kong Element 玄空五行	火山旅 Travelling	Period Luck 卦運	Monthly Star 月星
Wood 木3		8	7

SUNDAY	MONDAY	TUESDAY	WEDNESDAY	THURSDAY	FRIDAY	SATURDAY
	金4 Metal 3 Great Exceeding 丙午 Fire Horse 澤風大過 1 三十 3	水6 Water 2 Poison 丁未 Fire Goat 山風蠱 2 八月初一 7	火2 Fire 1 Dispersing 戊申 Earth Monkey 風水渙 3 初二 6	木3 Wood 9 Travelling 己酉 Earth Rooster 火山旅 4 初三 8	金9 Metal 8 Stagnation 庚戌 Metal Dog 天地否 5 初四 9	火7 Fire 7 Alliance 辛亥 Metal Pig 水地比 6 初五 7
木8 Wood 6 Thunder 壬子 Water Rat 震爲雷 7 初六 1	水6 Water 5 Beauty 癸丑 Water Ox 山火賁 8 初七 8	火7 Fire 4 Accomplished 甲寅 Wood Tiger 水火既濟 9 初八 9	水1 Water 3 Arriving 乙卯 Wood Rabbit 地澤臨 10 初九 4	金4 Metal 2 Marsh 丙辰 Fire Dragon 兑爲澤 11 初十 1	火2 Fire 1 Small Livestock 丁巳 Fire Snake 風天小畜 12 十一 8	木3 Wood 9 The Cauldron 戊午 Earth Horse 火風鼎 13 十二 4
水1 Water 8 Rising 己未 Earth Goat 地風升 14 十三 2	火7 Fire 7 Water 庚申 Metal Monkey 坎爲水 15 十四 1	木8 Wood 6 Lesser Exceeding 辛酉 Metal Rooster 雷山小過 16 十五 3	金4 Metal 5 Gathering 壬戌 Water Dog 澤地萃 17 十六 4	水6 Water 4 Peel 癸亥 Water Pig 山地剝 18 十七 6	水1 Water 3 Earth 甲子 Wood Rat 坤爲地 19 十八 1	木3 Wood 2 Biting 乙丑 Wood Ox 火雷噬嗑 20 十九 6
火2 Fire 1 Family 丙寅 Fire Tiger 風火家人 21 二十 4	水6 Water 9 Decreasing 丁卯 Fire Rabbit 山澤損 22 廿一 9	金9 Metal 8 Tread 戊辰 Earth Dragon 天澤履 23 廿二 6	木8 Wood 7 Great Strength 己巳 Earth Snake 雷天大壯 24 廿三 2	木8 Wood 6 Consistency 庚午 Metal Horse 雷風恆 25 廿四 9	金9 Metal 5 Litigation 辛未 Metal Goat 天水訟 26 廿五 3	水1 Water 4 Officer 壬申 Water Monkey 地水師 27 廿六 7
火2 Fire 3 Gradual Progress 癸酉 Water Rooster 風山漸 28 廿七 7	火7 Fire 2 Obstruction 甲戌 Wood Dog 水山蹇 29 廿八 2	木3 Wood 1 Advancement 乙亥 Wood Pig 火地晉 30 廿九 3				

OCTOBER 1997 庚戌

Xuan Kong Element 玄空五行	天地否 Stagnation	Period Luck 卦運	Monthly Star 月星
Metal 金9		9	6

SUNDAY	MONDAY	TUESDAY	WEDNESDAY	THURSDAY	FRIDAY	SATURDAY
			水6 Water 9 Nourish 丙子 Fire Rat 山雷頤 1 三十 3	金4 Metal 8 Following 丁丑 Fire Ox 澤雷隨 2 九月初一 7	木8 Wood 7 Abundance 戊寅 Earth Tiger 雷火豐 3 初二 6	火7 Fire 6 Regulate 己卯 Earth Rabbit 水澤節 4 初三 8
水1 Water 5 Unity 庚辰 Metal Dragon 地天泰 5 初四 9	木3 Wood 4 Great Reward 辛巳 Metal Snake 火天大有 6 初五 7	火2 Fire 3 Wind 壬午 Water Horse 巽爲風 7 初六 1	金4 Metal 2 Trap 癸未 Water Goat 澤水困 8 初七 8	木3 Wood 1 Not Yet Accomplished 甲申 Wood Monkey 火水未濟 9 初八 9	金9 Metal 9 Retreat 乙酉 Wood Rooster 天山遯 10 初九 4	水6 Water 8 Mountain 丙戌 Fire Dog 艮爲山 11 初十 1
木8 Wood 7 Delight 丁亥 Fire Pig 雷地豫 12 十一 8	火7 Fire 6 Beginning 戊子 Earth Rat 水雷屯 13 十二 4	金9 Metal 5 Without Wrongdoing 己丑 Earth Ox 天雷無妄 14 十三 2	木3 Wood 4 Fire 庚寅 Metal Tiger 離爲火 15 十四 1	火2 Fire 3 Sincerity 辛卯 Metal Rabbit 風澤中孚 16 十五 3	水6 Water 2 Big Livestock 壬辰 Water Dragon 山天大畜 17 十六 4	金4 Metal 1 Eliminating 癸巳 Water Snake 澤天夬 18 十七 6
金9 Metal 9 Heaven 甲午 Wood Horse 乾爲天 19 十八 1	火7 Fire 8 Well 乙未 Wood Goat 水風井 20 十九 6	木8 Wood 7 Relief 丙申 Fire Monkey 雷水解 21 二十 4	金4 Metal 6 Influence 丁酉 Fire Rooster 澤山咸 22 廿一 9	水1 Water 5 Humility 戊戌 Earth Dog 地山謙 23 廿二 6	火2 Fire 4 Observation 己亥 Earth Pig 風地觀 24 廿三 2	火2 Fire 3 Increasing 庚子 Metal Rat 風雷益 25 廿四 9
水1 Water 2 Dimming Light 辛丑 Metal Ox 地火明夷 26 廿五 3	金9 Metal 1 Fellowship 壬寅 Water Tiger 天火同人 27 廿六 7	木8 Wood 9 Marrying Maiden 癸卯 Water Rabbit 雷澤歸妹 28 廿七 7	木3 Wood 8 Opposition 甲辰 Wood Dragon 火澤睽 29 廿八 2	火7 Fire 7 Waiting 乙巳 Wood Snake 水天需 30 廿九 3	金4 Metal 6 Great Exceeding 丙午 Fire Horse 澤風大過 31 十月初 3	

NOVEMBER 1997 辛亥

Xuan Kong Element 玄空五行	水地比 Alliance	Period Luck 卦運	Monthly Star 月星
Fire 火7		7	5

SUNDAY	MONDAY	TUESDAY	WEDNESDAY	THURSDAY	FRIDAY	SATURDAY
水6 Water 丙子 Fire Rat Nourish 山雷頤 [3] **30** 十一月初一 3						水6 Water 丁未 Fire Goat Poison 山風蠱 [5] **1** 初二 7
火2 Fire 戊申 Earth Monkey Dispersing 風水渙 [4] **2** 初三 6	木3 Wood 己酉 Earth Rooster Travelling 火山旅 [3] **3** 初四 8	金9 Metal 庚戌 Metal Dog Stagnation 天地否 [2] **4** 初五 9	火7 Fire 辛亥 Metal Pig Alliance 水地比 [1] **5** 初六 7	木8 Wood 壬子 Water Rat Thunder 震爲雷 [9] **6** 初七 1	水6 Water 癸丑 Water Ox Beauty 山火賁 [8] **7** 初八 8	火7 Fire 甲寅 Wood Tiger Accomplished 水火既濟 [7] **8** 初九 9
水1 Water 乙卯 Wood Rabbit Arriving 地澤臨 [6] **9** 初十 4	金4 Metal 丙辰 Fire Dragon Marsh 兑爲澤 [5] **10** 十一 1	火2 Fire 丁巳 Fire Snake Small Livestock 風天小畜 [4] **11** 十二 8	木3 Wood 戊午 Earth Horse The Cauldron 火風鼎 [3] **12** 十三 4	水1 Water 己未 Earth Goat Rising 地風升 [2] **13** 十四 2	火7 Fire 庚申 Metal Monkey Water 坎爲水 [1] **14** 十五 1	木8 Wood 辛酉 Metal Rooster Lesser Exceeding 雷山小過 [9] **15** 十六 3
金4 Metal 壬戌 Water Dog Gathering 澤地萃 [8] **16** 十七 4	水6 Water 癸亥 Water Pig Peel 山地剝 [7] **17** 十八 6	水1 Water 甲子 Wood Rat Earth 坤爲地 [6] **18** 十九 1	木3 Wood 乙丑 Wood Ox Biting 火雷噬嗑 [5] **19** 二十 6	火2 Fire 丙寅 Fire Tiger Family 風火家人 [4] **20** 廿一 4	水6 Water 丁卯 Fire Rabbit Decreasing 山澤損 [3] **21** 廿二 9	金9 Metal 戊辰 Earth Dragon Tread 天澤履 [2] **22** 廿三 6
木8 Wood 己巳 Earth Snake Great Strength 雷天大壯 [1] **23** 廿四 2	木8 Wood 庚午 Metal Horse Consistency 雷風恒 [9] **24** 廿五 9	金9 Metal 辛未 Metal Goat Litigation 天水訟 [8] **25** 廿六 3	水1 Water 壬申 Water Monkey Officer 地水師 [7] **26** 廿七 7	火2 Fire 癸酉 Water Rooster Gradual Progress 風山漸 [6] **27** 廿八 7	火7 Fire 甲戌 Wood Dog Obstruction 水山蹇 [5] **28** 廿九 2	木3 Wood 乙亥 Wood Pig Advancement 火地晉 [4] **29** 三十 3

DECEMBER 1997 壬子

Xuan Kong Element 玄空五行	震爲雷 Thunder	Period Luck 卦運	Monthly Star 月星
Wood 木8		1	4

SUNDAY	MONDAY	TUESDAY	WEDNESDAY	THURSDAY	FRIDAY	SATURDAY
	金4 Metal 丁丑 Fire Ox Following 澤雷隨 [2] **1** 初二 7	木8 Wood 戊寅 Earth Tiger Abundance 雷火豐 [1] **2** 初三 6	火7 Fire 己卯 Earth Rabbit Regulate 水澤節 [9] **3** 初四 8	水1 Water 庚辰 Metal Dragon Unity 地天泰 [8] **4** 初五 9	木3 Wood 辛巳 Metal Snake Great Reward 火天大有 [7] **5** 初六 7	火2 Fire 壬午 Water Horse Wind 巽爲風 [6] **6** 初七 1
金4 Metal 癸未 Water Goat Trap 澤水困 [5] **7** 初八 8	木3 Wood 甲申 Wood Monkey Not Yet Accomplished 火水未濟 [4] **8** 初九 9	金9 Metal 乙酉 Wood Rooster Retreat 天山遯 [3] **9** 初十 4	水6 Water 丙戌 Fire Dog Mountain 艮爲山 [2] **10** 十一 1	木8 Wood 丁亥 Fire Pig Delight 雷地豫 [1] **11** 十二 8	火7 Fire 戊子 Earth Rat Beginning 水雷屯 [9] **12** 十三 4	金9 Metal 己丑 Earth Ox Without Wrongdoing 天雷無妄 [8] **13** 十四 2
木3 Wood 庚寅 Metal Tiger Fire 離爲火 [7] **14** 十五 1	火2 Fire 辛卯 Metal Rabbit Sincerity 風澤中孚 [6] **15** 十六 3	水6 Water 壬辰 Water Dragon Big Livestock 山天大畜 [5] **16** 十七 4	金4 Metal 癸巳 Water Snake Eliminating 澤天夬 [4] **17** 十八 6	金9 Metal 甲午 Wood Horse Heaven 乾爲天 [3] **18** 十九 1	火7 Fire 乙未 Wood Goat Well 水風井 [2] **19** 二十 6	木8 Wood 丙申 Fire Monkey Relief 雷水解 [1] **20** 廿一 4
金4 Metal 丁酉 Fire Rooster Influence 澤山咸 [9] **21** 廿二 9	水1 Water 戊戌 Earth Dog Humility 地山謙 [8/2] **22** 廿三 6	火2 Fire 己亥 Earth Pig Observation 風地觀 [3] **23** 廿四 2	火2 Fire 庚子 Metal Rat Increasing 風雷益 [4] **24** 廿五 9	水1 Water 辛丑 Metal Ox Dimming Light 地火明夷 [5] **25** 廿六 3	金9 Metal 壬寅 Water Tiger Fellowship 天火同人 [6] **26** 廿七 7	木8 Wood 癸卯 Water Rabbit Marrying Maiden 雷澤歸妹 [7] **27** 廿八 7
木3 Wood 甲辰 Wood Dragon Opposition 火澤睽 [8] **28** 廿九 2	火7 Fire 乙巳 Wood Snake Waiting 水天需 [9] **29** 三十 3	金4 Metal 丙午 Fire Horse Great Exceeding 澤風大過 [1] **30** 十二月初一 3	水6 Water 丁未 Fire Goat Poison 山風蠱 [2] **31** 初二 7			

1998 戊寅

(*Wu Yin*) Earth Tiger

1998 戊寅 *(Wu Yin)* Earth Tiger

January 5 - February 3

水6 Water
癸丑 Water Ox
8 Beauty
山火賁

Three Killings	East

February 4 - March 5

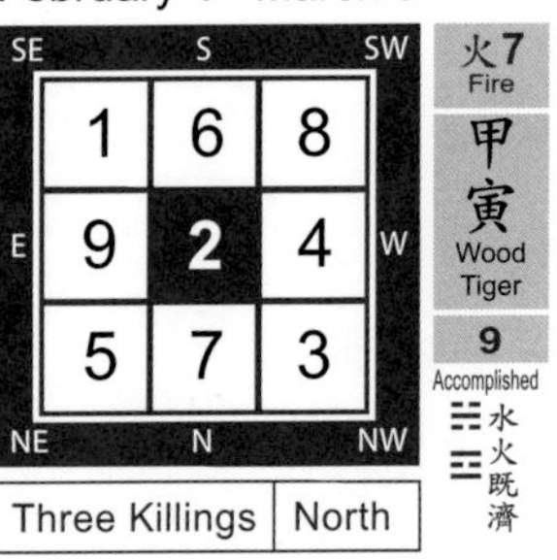

火7 Fire
甲寅 Wood Tiger
9 Accomplished
水火既濟

Three Killings	North

March 6 - April 4

Three Killings	West

April 5 - May 5

金4 Metal
丙辰 Fire Dragon
1 Marsh
兌爲澤

Three Killings	South

May 6 - June 5

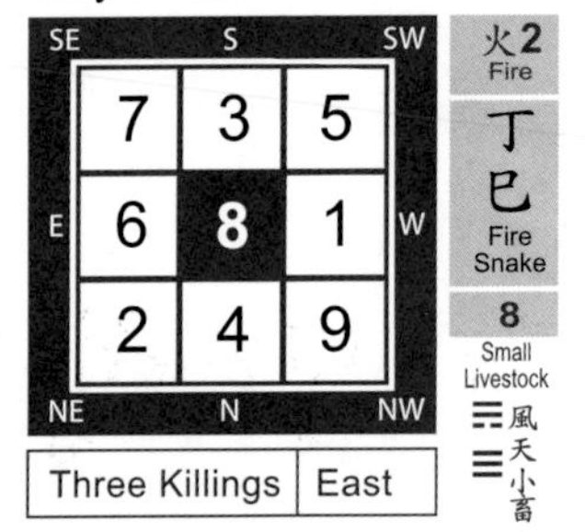

火2 Fire
丁巳 Fire Snake
8 Small Livestock
風天小畜

Three Killings	East

June 6 - July 6

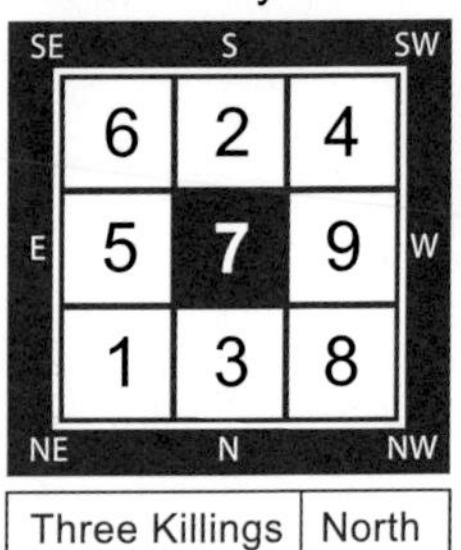

Three Killings	North

July 7 - August 7

水1 Water
己未 Earth Goat
2 Rising
地風升

Three Killings	West

August 8 - September 7

火7 Fire
庚申 Metal Monkey
1 Water
坎爲水

Three Killings	South

September 8 - October 7

Three Killings	East

October 8 - November 6

金4 Metal
壬戌 Water Dog
4 Gathering
澤地萃

Three Killings	North

November 7 - December 6

水6 Water
癸亥 Water Pig
6 Peel
山地剝

Three Killings	West

December 7 - January 5

水1 Water
甲子 Wood Rat
1 Earth
坤爲地

Three Killings	South

JANUARY 1998 癸丑

Xuan Kong Element 玄空五行	山火賁 Beauty	Period Luck 卦運	Monthly Star 月星
Water 水6		8	3

SUNDAY	MONDAY	TUESDAY	WEDNESDAY	THURSDAY	FRIDAY	SATURDAY
				火2 Fire · Dispersing · 3 戊申 Earth Monkey 風水渙 **1** 初三 6	木3 Wood · Travelling · 4 己酉 Earth Rooster 火山旅 **2** 初四 8	金9 Metal · Stagnation · 5 庚戌 Metal Dog 天地否 **3** 初五 9
火7 Fire · Alliance · 6 辛亥 Metal Pig 水地比 **4** 初六 7	木8 Wood · Thunder · 7 壬子 Water Rat 震爲雷 **5** 初七 1	水6 Water · Beauty · 8 癸丑 Water Ox 山火賁 **6** 初八 8	火7 Fire · Accomplished · 9 甲寅 Wood Tiger 水火既濟 **7** 初九 9	水1 Water · Arriving · 1 乙卯 Wood Rabbit 地澤臨 **8** 初十 4	金4 Metal · Marsh · 2 丙辰 Fire Dragon 兑爲澤 **9** 十一 1	火2 Fire · Small Livestock · 3 丁巳 Fire Snake 風天小畜 **10** 十二 8
木3 Wood · The Cauldron · 4 戊午 Earth Horse 火風鼎 **11** 十三 4	水1 Water · Rising · 5 己未 Earth Goat 地風升 **12** 十四 2	火7 Fire · Water · 6 庚申 Metal Monkey 坎爲水 **13** 十五 1	木8 Wood · Lesser Exceeding · 7 辛酉 Metal Rooster 雷山小過 **14** 十六 3	金4 Metal · Gathering · 8 壬戌 Water Dog 澤地萃 **15** 十七 4	水6 Water · Peel · 9 癸亥 Water Pig 山地剝 **16** 十八 6	水1 Water · Earth · 1 甲子 Wood Rat 坤爲地 **17** 十九 1
木3 Wood · Biting · 2 乙丑 Wood Ox 火雷噬嗑 **18** 二十 6	火2 Fire · Family · 3 丙寅 Fire Tiger 風火家人 **19** 廿一 4	水6 Water · Decreasing · 4 丁卯 Fire Rabbit 山澤損 **20** 廿二 9	金9 Metal · Tread · 5 戊辰 Earth Dragon 天澤履 **21** 廿三 6	木8 Wood · Great Strength · 6 己巳 Earth Snake 雷天大壯 **22** 廿四 2	木8 Wood · Consistency · 7 庚午 Metal Horse 雷風恆 **23** 廿五 9	金9 Metal · Litigation · 8 辛未 Metal Goat 天水訟 **24** 廿六 3
水1 Water · Officer · 9 壬申 Water Monkey 地水師 **25** 廿七 7	火2 Fire · Gradual Progress · 1 癸酉 Water Rooster 風山漸 **26** 廿八 7	火7 Fire · Obstruction · 2 甲戌 Wood Dog 水山蹇 **27** 廿九 2	木3 Wood · Advancement · 3 乙亥 Wood Pig 火地晉 **28** 正月初一 3	水6 Water · Nourish · 4 丙子 Fire Rat 山雷頤 **29** 初二 3	金4 Metal · Following · 5 丁丑 Fire Ox 澤雷隨 **30** 初三 7	木8 Wood · Abundance · 6 戊寅 Earth Tiger 雷火豐 **31** 初四 6

FEBRUARY 1998 甲寅

Xuan Kong Element 玄空五行	水火既濟 Accomplished	Period Luck 卦運	Monthly Star 月星
Fire 火7		9	2

SUNDAY	MONDAY	TUESDAY	WEDNESDAY	THURSDAY	FRIDAY	SATURDAY
火7 Fire · Regulate · 7 己卯 Earth Rabbit 水澤節 **1** 初五 8	水1 Water · Unity · 8 庚辰 Metal Dragon 地天泰 **2** 初六 9	木3 Wood · Great Reward · 9 辛巳 Metal Snake 火天大有 **3** 初七 7	火2 Fire · Wind · 1 壬午 Water Horse 巽爲風 **4** 初八 1	金4 Metal · Trap · 2 癸未 Water Goat 澤水困 **5** 初九 8	木3 Wood · Not Yet Accomplished · 3 甲申 Wood Monkey 火水未濟 **6** 初十 9	金9 Metal · Retreat · 4 乙酉 Wood Rooster 天山遯 **7** 十一 4
水6 Water · Mountain · 5 丙戌 Fire Dog 艮爲山 **8** 十二 1	木8 Wood · Delight · 6 丁亥 Fire Pig 雷地豫 **9** 十三 8	火7 Fire · Beginning · 7 戊子 Earth Rat 水雷屯 **10** 十四 4	金9 Metal · Without Wrongdoing · 8 己丑 Earth Ox 天雷無妄 **11** 十五 2	木3 Wood · Fire · 9 庚寅 Metal Tiger 離爲火 **12** 十六 1	火2 Fire · Sincerity · 1 辛卯 Metal Rabbit 風澤中孚 **13** 十七 3	水6 Water · Big Livestock · 2 壬辰 Water Dragon 山天大畜 **14** 十八 4
金4 Metal · Eliminating · 3 癸巳 Water Snake 澤天夬 **15** 十九 6	金9 Metal · Heaven · 4 甲午 Wood Horse 乾爲天 **16** 二十 1	火7 Fire · Well · 5 乙未 Wood Goat 水風井 **17** 廿一 6	木8 Wood · Relief · 6 丙申 Fire Monkey 雷水解 **18** 廿二 4	金4 Metal · Influence · 7 丁酉 Fire Rooster 澤山咸 **19** 廿三 9	水1 Water · Humility · 8 戊戌 Earth Dog 地山謙 **20** 廿四 6	火2 Fire · Observation · 9 己亥 Earth Pig 風地觀 **21** 廿五 2
火2 Fire · Increasing · 1 庚子 Metal Rat 風雷益 **22** 廿六 9	水1 Water · Dimming Light · 2 辛丑 Metal Ox 地火明夷 **23** 廿七 3	金9 Metal · Fellowship · 3 壬寅 Water Tiger 天火同人 **24** 廿八 7	木8 Wood · Marrying Maiden · 4 癸卯 Water Rabbit 雷澤歸妹 **25** 廿九 7	木3 Wood · Opposition · 5 甲辰 Wood Dragon 火澤睽 **26** 三十 2	火7 Fire · Waiting · 6 乙巳 Wood Snake 水天需 **27** 二月初一 3	金4 Metal · Great Exceeding · 7 丙午 Fire Horse 澤風大過 **28** 初二 3

MARCH 1998 乙卯

Xuan Kong Element 玄空五行	地澤臨 Arriving	Period Luck 卦運	Monthly Star 月星
Water 水1		4	1

SUNDAY	MONDAY	TUESDAY	WEDNESDAY	THURSDAY	FRIDAY	SATURDAY
8 水6 Water Poison 山風蠱 丁未 Fire Goat **1** 初三 7	9 火2 Fire Dispersing 風水渙 戊申 Earth Monkey **2** 初四 6	1 木3 Wood Travelling 火山旅 己酉 Earth Rooster **3** 初五 8	2 金9 Metal Stagnation 天地否 庚戌 Metal Dog **4** 初六 9	3 火7 Fire Alliance 水地比 辛亥 Metal Pig **5** 初七 7	4 木8 Wood Thunder 震為雷 壬子 Water Rat **6** 初八 1	5 水6 Water Beauty 山火賁 癸丑 Water Ox **7** 初九 8
6 火7 Fire Accomplished 水火既濟 甲寅 Wood Tiger **8** 初十 9	7 水1 Water Arriving 地澤臨 乙卯 Wood Rabbit **9** 十一 4	8 金4 Metal Marsh 兌為澤 丙辰 Fire Dragon **10** 十二 1	9 火2 Fire Small Livestock 風天小畜 丁巳 Fire Snake **11** 十三 8	1 木3 Wood The Cauldron 火風鼎 戊午 Earth Horse **12** 十四 4	2 水1 Water Rising 地風升 己未 Earth Goat **13** 十五 2	3 火7 Fire Water 坎為水 庚申 Metal Monkey **14** 十六 1
4 木8 Wood Lesser Exceeding 雷山小過 辛酉 Metal Rooster **15** 十七 3	5 金4 Metal Gathering 澤地萃 壬戌 Water Dog **16** 十八 4	6 水6 Water Peel 山地剝 癸亥 Water Pig **17** 十九 6	7 水1 Water Earth 坤為地 甲子 Wood Rat **18** 二十 1	8 木3 Wood Biting 火雷噬嗑 乙丑 Wood Ox **19** 廿一 6	9 火2 Fire Family 風火家人 丙寅 Fire Tiger **20** 廿二 4	1 水6 Water Decreasing 山澤損 丁卯 Fire Rabbit **21** 廿三 9
2 金9 Metal Tread 天澤履 戊辰 Earth Dragon **22** 廿四 6	3 木8 Wood Great Strength 雷天大壯 己巳 Earth Snake **23** 廿五 2	4 木8 Wood Consistency 雷風恆 庚午 Metal Horse **24** 廿六 9	5 金9 Metal Litigation 天水訟 辛未 Metal Goat **25** 廿七 3	6 水1 Water Officer 地水師 壬申 Water Monkey **26** 廿八 7	7 火2 Fire Gradual Progress 風山漸 癸酉 Water Rooster **27** 廿九 7	8 火7 Fire Obstruction 水山蹇 甲戌 Wood Dog **28** 三月初一 2
9 木3 Wood Advancement 火地晉 乙亥 Wood Pig **29** 初二 3	1 水6 Water Nourish 山雷頤 丙子 Fire Rat **30** 初三 3	2 金4 Metal Following 澤雷隨 丁丑 Fire Ox **31** 初四 7				

APRIL 1998 丙辰

Xuan Kong Element 玄空五行	兌為澤 Marsh	Period Luck 卦運	Monthly Star 月星
Metal 金4		1	9

SUNDAY	MONDAY	TUESDAY	WEDNESDAY	THURSDAY	FRIDAY	SATURDAY
			3 木8 Wood Abundance 雷火豐 戊寅 Earth Tiger **1** 初五 6	4 火7 Fire Regulate 水澤節 己卯 Earth Rabbit **2** 初六 8	5 水1 Water Unity 地天泰 庚辰 Metal Dragon **3** 初七 9	6 木3 Wood Great Reward 火天大有 辛巳 Metal Snake **4** 初八 7
7 火2 Fire Wind 巽為風 壬午 Water Horse **5** 初九 1	8 金4 Metal Trap 澤水困 癸未 Water Goat **6** 初十 8	9 木3 Wood Not Yet Accomplished 火水未濟 甲申 Wood Monkey **7** 十一 9	1 金9 Metal Retreat 天山遯 乙酉 Wood Rooster **8** 十二 4	2 水6 Water Mountain 艮為山 丙戌 Fire Dog **9** 十三 1	3 木8 Wood Delight 雷地豫 丁亥 Fire Pig **10** 十四 8	4 火7 Fire Beginning 水雷屯 戊子 Earth Rat **11** 十五 4
5 金9 Metal Without Wrongdoing 天雷無妄 己丑 Earth Ox **12** 十六 2	6 木3 Wood Fire 離為火 庚寅 Metal Tiger **13** 十七 1	7 火2 Fire Sincerity 風澤中孚 辛卯 Metal Rabbit **14** 十八 3	8 水6 Water Big Livestock 山天大畜 壬辰 Water Dragon **15** 十九 4	9 金4 Metal Eliminating 澤天夬 癸巳 Water Snake **16** 二十 6	1 金9 Metal Heaven 乾為天 甲午 Wood Horse **17** 廿一 1	2 火7 Fire Well 水風井 乙未 Wood Goat **18** 廿二 6
3 木8 Wood Relief 雷水解 丙申 Fire Monkey **19** 廿三 4	4 金4 Metal Influence 澤山咸 丁酉 Fire Rooster **20** 廿四 9	5 水1 Water Humility 地山謙 戊戌 Earth Dog **21** 廿五 6	6 火2 Fire Observation 風地觀 己亥 Earth Pig **22** 廿六 2	7 火2 Fire Increasing 風雷益 庚子 Metal Rat **23** 廿七 9	8 水1 Water Dimming Light 地火明夷 辛丑 Metal Ox **24** 廿八 3	9 金9 Metal Fellowship 天火同人 壬寅 Water Tiger **25** 廿九 7
1 木8 Wood Marrying Maiden 雷澤歸妹 癸卯 Water Rabbit **26** 四月初一 7	2 木3 Wood Opposition 火澤睽 甲辰 Wood Dragon **27** 初二 2	3 火7 Fire Waiting 水天需 乙巳 Wood Snake **28** 初三 3	4 金4 Metal Great Exceeding 澤風大過 丙午 Fire Horse **29** 初四 3	5 水6 Water Poison 山風蠱 丁未 Fire Goat **30** 初五 7		

MAY 1998 丁巳

Xuan Kong Element 玄空五行	風天小畜 Small Livestock	Period Luck 卦運	Monthly Star 月星
Fire 火2		8	8

SUNDAY	MONDAY	TUESDAY	WEDNESDAY	THURSDAY	FRIDAY	SATURDAY
木8 Wood 戊寅 Earth Tiger Abundance 雷火豐 31 初六 6 / 9					火2 Fire 戊申 Earth Monkey Dispersing 風水渙 1 初六 6 / 6	木3 Wood 己酉 Earth Rooster Travelling 火山旅 2 初七 8 / 7
金9 Metal 庚戌 Metal Dog Stagnation 天地否 3 初八 9 / 8	火7 Fire 辛亥 Metal Pig Alliance 水地比 4 初九 7 / 9	木8 Wood 壬子 Water Rat Thunder 震為雷 5 初十 1 / 1	水6 Water 癸丑 Water Ox Beauty 山火賁 6 十一 8 / 2	火7 Fire 甲寅 Wood Tiger Accomplished 水火既濟 7 十二 9 / 3	水1 Water 乙卯 Wood Rabbit Arriving 地澤臨 8 十三 4 / 4	金4 Metal 丙辰 Fire Dragon Marsh 兌為澤 9 十四 1 / 5
火2 Fire 丁巳 Fire Snake Small Livestock 風天小畜 10 十五 8 / 6	木3 Wood 戊午 Earth Horse The Cauldron 火風鼎 11 十六 4 / 7	水1 Water 己未 Earth Goat Rising 地風升 12 十七 2 / 8	火7 Fire 庚申 Metal Monkey Water 坎為水 13 十八 1 / 9	木8 Wood 辛酉 Metal Rooster Lesser Exceeding 雷山小過 14 十九 3 / 1	金4 Metal 壬戌 Water Dog Gathering 澤地萃 15 二十 4 / 2	水6 Water 癸亥 Water Pig Peel 山地剝 16 廿一 6 / 3
水1 Water 甲子 Wood Rat Earth 坤為地 17 廿二 1 / 4	木3 Wood 乙丑 Wood Ox Biting 火雷噬嗑 18 廿三 6 / 5	火2 Fire 丙寅 Fire Tiger Family 風火家人 19 廿四 4 / 6	水6 Water 丁卯 Fire Rabbit Decreasing 山澤損 20 廿五 9 / 7	金9 Metal 戊辰 Earth Dragon Tread 天澤履 21 廿六 6 / 8	木8 Wood 己巳 Earth Snake Great Strength 雷天大壯 22 廿七 2 / 9	木8 Wood 庚午 Metal Horse Consistency 雷風恆 23 廿八 9 / 1
金9 Metal 辛未 Metal Goat Litigation 天水訟 24 廿九 3 / 2	水1 Water 壬申 Water Monkey Officer 地水師 25 三十 7 / 3	火2 Fire 癸酉 Water Rooster Gradual Progress 風山漸 26 五月初一 7 / 4	火7 Fire 甲戌 Wood Dog Obstruction 水山蹇 27 初二 2 / 5	木3 Wood 乙亥 Wood Pig Advancement 火地晉 28 初三 3 / 6	水6 Water 丙子 Fire Rat Nourish 山雷頤 29 初四 3 / 7	金4 Metal 丁丑 Fire Ox Following 澤雷隨 30 初五 7 / 8

JUNE 1998 戊午

Xuan Kong Element 玄空五行	火風鼎 The Cauldron	Period Luck 卦運	Monthly Star 月星
Wood 木3		4	7

SUNDAY	MONDAY	TUESDAY	WEDNESDAY	THURSDAY	FRIDAY	SATURDAY
	火7 Fire 己卯 Earth Rabbit Regulate 水澤節 1 初七 8 / 1	水1 Water 庚辰 Metal Dragon Unity 地天泰 2 初八 9 / 2	木3 Wood 辛巳 Metal Snake Great Reward 火天大有 3 初九 7 / 3	火2 Fire 壬午 Water Horse Wind 巽為風 4 初十 1 / 4	金4 Metal 癸未 Water Goat Trap 澤水困 5 十一 8 / 5	木3 Wood 甲申 Wood Monkey Not Yet Accomplished 火水未濟 6 十二 9 / 6
金9 Metal 乙酉 Wood Rooster Retreat 天山遯 7 十三 4 / 7	水6 Water 丙戌 Fire Dog Mountain 艮為山 8 十四 1 / 8	木8 Wood 丁亥 Fire Pig Delight 雷地豫 9 十五 8 / 9	火7 Fire 戊子 Earth Rat Beginning 水雷屯 10 十六 4 / 1	金9 Metal 己丑 Earth Ox Without Wrongdoing 天雷無妄 11 十七 2 / 2	木3 Wood 庚寅 Metal Tiger Fire 離為火 12 十八 1 / 3	火2 Fire 辛卯 Metal Rabbit Sincerity 風澤中孚 13 十九 3 / 4
水6 Water 壬辰 Water Dragon Big Livestock 山天大畜 14 二十 4 / 5	金4 Metal 癸巳 Water Snake Eliminating 澤天夬 15 廿一 6 / 6	金9 Metal 甲午 Wood Horse Heaven 乾為天 16 廿二 1 / 7	火7 Fire 乙未 Wood Goat Well 水風井 17 廿三 6 / 8	木8 Wood 丙申 Fire Monkey Relief 雷水解 18 廿四 4 / 9	金4 Metal 丁酉 Fire Rooster Influence 澤山咸 19 廿五 9 / 1	水1 Water 戊戌 Earth Dog Humility 地山謙 20 廿六 6 / 2
火2 Fire 己亥 Earth Pig Observation 風地觀 21 廿七 2 / 3/7	火2 Fire 庚子 Metal Rat Increasing 風雷益 22 廿八 9 / 6	水1 Water 辛丑 Metal Ox Dimming Light 地火明夷 23 廿九 3 / 5	金9 Metal 壬寅 Water Tiger Fellowship 天火同人 24 閏五月初一 7 / 4	木8 Wood 癸卯 Water Rabbit Marrying Maiden 雷澤歸妹 25 初二 7 / 3	木3 Wood 甲辰 Wood Dragon Opposition 火澤睽 26 初三 2 / 2	火7 Fire 乙巳 Wood Snake Waiting 水天需 27 初四 3 / 1
金4 Metal 丙午 Fire Horse Great Exceeding 澤風大過 28 初五 3 / 9	水6 Water 丁未 Fire Goat Poison 山風蠱 29 初六 7 / 8	火2 Fire 戊申 Earth Monkey Dispersing 風水渙 30 初七 6 / 7				

JULY 1998 己未

Xuan Kong Element 玄空五行	地風升 Rising	Period Luck 卦運	Monthly Star 月星
Water 水1		2	6

SUNDAY	MONDAY	TUESDAY	WEDNESDAY	THURSDAY	FRIDAY	SATURDAY
			木3 Wood [6] Travelling 火山旅 己酉 Earth Rooster 1 初八 8	金9 Metal [5] Stagnation 天地否 庚戌 Metal Dog 2 初九 9	火7 Fire [4] Alliance 水地比 辛亥 Metal Pig 3 初十 7	木8 Wood [3] Thunder 震爲雷 壬子 Water Rat 4 十一 1
水6 Water [2] Beauty 山火賁 癸丑 Water Ox 5 十二 8	火7 Fire [1] Accomplished 水火既濟 甲寅 Wood Tiger 6 十三 9	水1 Water [9] Arriving 地澤臨 乙卯 Wood Rabbit 7 十四 4	金4 Metal [8] Marsh 兌爲澤 丙辰 Fire Dragon 8 十五 1	火2 Fire [7] Small Livestock 風天小畜 丁巳 Fire Snake 9 十六 8	木3 Wood [6] The Cauldron 火風鼎 戊午 Earth Horse 10 十七 4	水1 Water [5] Rising 地風升 己未 Earth Goat 11 十八 2
火7 Fire [4] Water 坎爲水 庚申 Metal Monkey 12 十九 1	木8 Wood [3] Lesser Exceeding 雷山小過 辛酉 Metal Rooster 13 二十 3	金4 Metal [2] Gathering 澤地萃 壬戌 Water Dog 14 廿一 4	水6 Water [1] Peel 山地剝 癸亥 Water Pig 15 廿二 6	水1 Water [9] Earth 坤爲地 甲子 Wood Rat 16 廿三 1	木3 Wood [8] Biting 火雷噬嗑 乙丑 Wood Ox 17 廿四 6	火2 Fire [7] Family 風火家人 丙寅 Fire Tiger 18 廿五 4
水6 Water [6] Decreasing 山澤損 丁卯 Fire Rabbit 19 廿六 9	金9 Metal [5] Tread 天澤履 戊辰 Earth Dragon 20 廿七 6	木8 Wood [4] Great Strength 雷天大壯 己巳 Earth Snake 21 廿八 2	木8 Wood [3] Consistency 雷風恒 庚午 Metal Horse 22 廿九 9	金9 Metal [2] Litigation 天水訟 辛未 Metal Goat 23 六月初一 3	水1 Water [1] Officer 地水師 壬申 Water Monkey 24 初二 7	火2 Fire [9] Gradual Progress 風山漸 癸酉 Water Rooster 25 初三 7
火7 Fire [8] Obstruction 水山蹇 甲戌 Wood Dog 26 初四 2	木3 Wood [7] Advancement 火地晉 乙亥 Wood Pig 27 初五 3	水6 Water [6] Nourish 山雷頤 丙子 Fire Rat 28 初六 3	金4 Metal [5] Following 澤雷隨 丁丑 Fire Ox 29 初七 7	木8 Wood [4] Abundance 雷火豐 戊寅 Earth Tiger 30 初八 6	火7 Fire [3] Regulate 水澤節 己卯 Earth Rabbit 31 初九 8	

AUGUST 1998 庚申

Xuan Kong Element 玄空五行	坎爲水 Water	Period Luck 卦運	Monthly Star 月星
Fire 火7		1	5

SUNDAY	MONDAY	TUESDAY	WEDNESDAY	THURSDAY	FRIDAY	SATURDAY
木3 Wood [9] Travelling 火山旅 己酉 Earth Rooster 30 初九 8	金9 Metal [8] Stagnation 天地否 庚戌 Metal Dog 31 初十 9					水1 Water [2] Unity 地天泰 庚辰 Metal Dragon 1 初十 9
木3 Wood [1] Great Reward 火天大有 辛巳 Metal Snake 2 十一 7	火2 Fire [9] Wind 巽爲風 壬午 Water Horse 3 十二 1	金4 Metal [8] Trap 澤水困 癸未 Water Goat 4 十三 8	木3 Wood [7] Not Yet Accomplished 火水未濟 甲申 Wood Monkey 5 十四 9	金9 Metal [6] Retreat 天山遯 乙酉 Wood Rooster 6 十五 4	水6 Water [5] Mountain 艮爲山 丙戌 Fire Dog 7 十六 1	木8 Wood [4] Delight 雷地豫 丁亥 Fire Pig 8 十七 8
火7 Fire [3] Beginning 水雷屯 戊子 Earth Rat 9 十八 4	金9 Metal [2] Without Wrongdoing 天雷無妄 己丑 Earth Ox 10 十九 2	木3 Wood [1] Fire 離爲火 庚寅 Metal Tiger 11 二十 1	火2 Fire [9] Sincerity 風澤中孚 辛卯 Metal Rabbit 12 廿一 3	水6 Water [8] Big Livestock 山天大畜 壬辰 Water Dragon 13 廿二 4	金4 Metal [7] Eliminating 澤天夬 癸巳 Water Snake 14 廿三 6	金9 Metal [6] Heaven 乾爲天 甲午 Wood Horse 15 廿四 1
火7 Fire [5] Well 水風井 乙未 Wood Goat 16 廿五 6	木8 Wood [4] Relief 雷水解 丙申 Fire Monkey 17 廿六 4	金4 Metal [3] Influence 澤山咸 丁酉 Fire Rooster 18 廿七 9	水1 Water [2] Humility 地山謙 戊戌 Earth Dog 19 廿八 6	火2 Fire [1] Observation 風地觀 己亥 Earth Pig 20 廿九 2	火2 Fire [9] Increasing 風雷益 庚子 Metal Rat 21 三十 9	水1 Water [8] Dimming Light 地火明夷 辛丑 Metal Ox 22 七月初一 3
金9 Metal [7] Fellowship 天火同人 壬寅 Water Tiger 23 初二 7	木8 Wood [6] Marrying Maiden 雷澤歸妹 癸卯 Water Rabbit 24 初三 7	木3 Wood [5] Opposition 火澤睽 甲辰 Wood Dragon 25 初四 2	火7 Fire [4] Waiting 水天需 乙巳 Wood Snake 26 初五 3	金4 Metal [3] Great Exceeding 澤風大過 丙午 Fire Horse 27 初六 3	水6 Water [2] Poison 山風蠱 丁未 Fire Goat 28 初七 7	火2 Fire [1] Dispersing 風水渙 戊申 Earth Monkey 29 初八 6

SEPTEMBER 1998 辛酉

Xuan Kong Element 玄空五行	雷山小過 Lesser Exceeding	Period Luck 卦運	Monthly Star 月星
Wood 木8		3	4

SUNDAY	MONDAY	TUESDAY	WEDNESDAY	THURSDAY	FRIDAY	SATURDAY
		火7 Fire [7] Alliance 水地比 辛亥 Metal Pig 7 1 十一	木8 Wood [6] Thunder 震為雷 壬子 Water Rat 1 2 十二	水6 Water [5] Beauty 山火賁 癸丑 Water Ox 8 3 十三	火7 Fire [4] Accomplished 水火既濟 甲寅 Wood Tiger 9 4 十四	水1 Water [3] Arriving 地澤臨 乙卯 Wood Rabbit 4 5 十五
金4 Metal [2] Marsh 兌為澤 丙辰 Fire Dragon 1 6 十六	火2 Fire [1] Small Livestock 風天小畜 丁巳 Fire Snake 8 7 十七	木3 Wood [9] The Cauldron 火風鼎 戊午 Earth Horse 4 8 十八	水1 Water [8] Rising 地風升 己未 Earth Goat 2 9 十九	火7 Fire [7] Water 坎為水 庚申 Metal Monkey 1 10 二十	木8 Wood [6] Lesser Exceeding 雷山小過 辛酉 Metal Rooster 3 11 廿一	金4 Metal [5] Gathering 澤地萃 壬戌 Water Dog 4 12 廿二
水6 Water [4] Peel 山地剝 癸亥 Water Pig 6 13 廿三	水1 Water [3] Earth 坤為地 甲子 Wood Rat 1 14 廿四	木3 Wood [2] Biting 火雷噬嗑 乙丑 Wood Ox 6 15 廿五	火2 Fire [1] Family 風火家人 丙寅 Fire Tiger 4 16 廿六	水6 Water [9] Decreasing 山澤損 丁卯 Fire Rabbit 9 17 廿七	金9 Metal [8] Tread 天澤履 戊辰 Earth Dragon 6 18 廿八	木8 Wood [7] Great Strength 雷天大壯 己巳 Earth Snake 2 19 廿九
木8 Wood [6] Consistency 雷風恒 庚午 Metal Horse 9 20 三十	金9 Metal [5] Litigation 天水訟 辛未 Metal Goat 3 21 八月初一	水1 Water [4] Officer 地水師 壬申 Water Monkey 7 22 初二	火2 Fire [3] Gradual Progress 風山漸 癸酉 Water Rooster 7 23 初三	火7 Fire [2] Obstruction 水山蹇 甲戌 Wood Dog 2 24 初四	木3 Wood [1] Advancement 火地晉 乙亥 Wood Pig 3 25 初五	水6 Water [9] Nourish 山雷頤 丙子 Fire Rat 3 26 初六
金4 Metal [8] Following 澤雷隨 丁丑 Fire Ox 7 27 初七	木8 Wood [7] Abundance 雷火豐 戊寅 Earth Tiger 6 28 初八	火7 Fire [6] Regulate 水澤節 己卯 Earth Rabbit 8 29 初九	水1 Water [5] Unity 地天泰 庚辰 Metal Dragon 9 30 初十			

OCTOBER 1998 壬戌

Xuan Kong Element 玄空五行	澤地萃 Gathering	Period Luck 卦運	Monthly Star 月星
Metal 金4		4	3

SUNDAY	MONDAY	TUESDAY	WEDNESDAY	THURSDAY	FRIDAY	SATURDAY
				木3 Wood [4] Great Reward 火天大有 辛巳 Metal Snake 7 1 十一	火2 Fire [3] Wind 巽為風 壬午 Water Horse 1 2 十二	金4 Metal [2] Trap 澤水困 癸未 Water Goat 8 3 十三
木3 Wood [1] Not Yet Accomplished 火水未濟 甲申 Wood Monkey 9 4 十四	金9 Metal [9] Retreat 天山遯 乙酉 Wood Rooster 4 5 十五	水6 Water [8] Mountain 艮為山 丙戌 Fire Dog 1 6 十六	木8 Wood [7] Delight 雷地豫 丁亥 Fire Pig 8 7 十七	火7 Fire [6] Beginning 水雷屯 戊子 Earth Rat 4 8 十八	金9 Metal [5] Without Wrongdoing 天雷無妄 己丑 Earth Ox 2 9 十九	木3 Wood [4] Fire 離為火 庚寅 Metal Tiger 1 10 二十
火2 Fire [3] Sincerity 風澤中孚 辛卯 Metal Rabbit 3 11 廿一	水6 Water [2] Big Livestock 山天大畜 壬辰 Water Dragon 4 12 廿二	金4 Metal [1] Eliminating 澤天夬 癸巳 Water Snake 6 13 廿三	金9 Metal [9] Heaven 乾為天 甲午 Wood Horse 1 14 廿四	火7 Fire [8] Well 水風井 乙未 Wood Goat 6 15 廿五	木8 Wood [7] Relief 雷水解 丙申 Fire Monkey 4 16 廿六	金4 Metal [6] Influence 澤山咸 丁酉 Fire Rooster 9 17 廿七
水1 Water [5] Humility 地山謙 戊戌 Earth Dog 6 18 廿八	火2 Fire [4] Observation 風地觀 己亥 Earth Pig 2 19 廿九	火2 Fire [3] Increasing 風雷益 庚子 Metal Rat 9 20 九月初一	水1 Water [2] Dimming Light 地火明夷 辛丑 Metal Ox 3 21 初二	金9 Metal [1] Fellowship 天火同人 壬寅 Water Tiger 7 22 初三	木8 Wood [9] Marrying Maiden 雷澤歸妹 癸卯 Water Rabbit 7 23 初四	木3 Wood [8] Opposition 火澤睽 甲辰 Wood Dragon 2 24 初五
火7 Fire [7] Waiting 水天需 乙巳 Wood Snake 3 25 初六	金4 Metal [6] Great Exceeding 澤風大過 丙午 Fire Horse 3 26 初七	水6 Water [5] Poison 山風蠱 丁未 Fire Goat 7 27 初八	火2 Fire [4] Dispersing 風水渙 戊申 Earth Monkey 6 28 初九	木3 Wood [3] Travelling 火山旅 己酉 Earth Rooster 8 29 初十	金9 Metal [2] Stagnation 天地否 庚戌 Metal Dog 9 30 十一	火7 Fire [1] Alliance 水地比 辛亥 Metal Pig 7 31 十二

NOVEMBER 1998 癸亥

Xuan Kong Element 玄空五行	山地剝 Peel	Period Luck 卦運	Monthly Star 月星
Water 水6		6	2

SUNDAY	MONDAY	TUESDAY	WEDNESDAY	THURSDAY	FRIDAY	SATURDAY
1 十三 木8 Wood [9] Thunder 震爲雷 壬子 Water Rat 1	**2** 十四 水6 Water [8] Beauty 山火賁 癸丑 Water Ox 8	**3** 十五 火7 Fire [7] Accomplished 水火既濟 甲寅 Wood Tiger 9	**4** 十六 水1 Water [6] Arriving 地澤臨 乙卯 Wood Rabbit 4	**5** 十七 金4 Metal [5] Marsh 兌爲澤 丙辰 Fire Dragon 1	**6** 十八 火2 Fire [4] Small Livestock 風天小畜 丁巳 Fire Snake 8	**7** 十九 木3 Wood [3] The Cauldron 火風鼎 戊午 Earth Horse 4
8 二十 水1 Water [2] Rising 地風升 己未 Earth Goat 2	**9** 廿一 火7 Fire [1] Water 坎爲水 庚申 Metal Monkey 1	**10** 廿二 木8 Wood [9] Lesser Exceeding 雷山小過 辛酉 Metal Rooster 3	**11** 廿三 金4 Metal [8] Gathering 澤地萃 壬戌 Water Dog 4	**12** 廿四 水6 Water [7] Peel 山地剝 癸亥 Water Pig 6	**13** 廿五 水1 Water [6] Earth 坤爲地 甲子 Wood Rat 1	**14** 廿六 木3 Wood [5] Biting 火雷噬嗑 乙丑 Wood Ox 6
15 廿七 火2 Fire [4] Family 風火家人 丙寅 Fire Tiger 4	**16** 廿八 水6 Water [3] Decreasing 山澤損 丁卯 Fire Rabbit 9	**17** 廿九 金9 Metal [2] Tread 天澤履 戊辰 Earth Dragon 6	**18** 三十 木8 Wood [1] Great Strength 雷天大壯 己巳 Earth Snake 2	**19** 十月初一 木8 Wood [9] Consistency 雷風恆 庚午 Metal Horse 9	**20** 初二 金9 Metal [8] Litigation 天水訟 辛未 Metal Goat 3	**21** 初三 水1 Water [7] Officer 地水師 壬申 Water Monkey 7
22 初四 火2 Fire [6] Gradual Progress 風山漸 癸酉 Water Rooster 7	**23** 初五 火7 Fire [5] Obstruction 水山蹇 甲戌 Wood Dog 2	**24** 初六 木3 Wood [4] Advancement 火地晉 乙亥 Wood Pig 3	**25** 初七 水6 Water [3] Nourish 山雷頤 丙子 Fire Rat 3	**26** 初八 金4 Metal [2] Following 澤雷隨 丁丑 Fire Ox 7	**27** 初九 木8 Wood [1] Abundance 雷火豐 戊寅 Earth Tiger 6	**28** 初十 火7 Fire [9] Regulate 水澤節 己卯 Earth Rabbit 8
29 十一 水1 Water [8] Unity 地天泰 庚辰 Metal Dragon 9	**30** 十二 木3 Wood [7] Great Reward 火天大有 辛巳 Metal Snake 7					

DECEMBER 1998 甲子

Xuan Kong Element 玄空五行	坤爲地 Earth	Period Luck 卦運	Monthly Star 月星
Water 水1		1	1

SUNDAY	MONDAY	TUESDAY	WEDNESDAY	THURSDAY	FRIDAY	SATURDAY
		1 十三 火2 Fire [6] Wind 巽爲風 壬午 Water Horse 1	**2** 十四 金4 Metal [5] Trap 澤水困 癸未 Water Goat 8	**3** 十五 木3 Wood [4] Not Yet Accomplished 火水未濟 甲申 Wood Monkey 9	**4** 十六 金9 Metal [3] Retreat 天山遯 乙酉 Wood Rooster 4	**5** 十七 水6 Water [2] Mountain 艮爲山 丙戌 Fire Dog 1
6 十八 木8 Wood [1] Delight 雷地豫 丁亥 Fire Pig 8	**7** 十九 火7 Fire [9] Beginning 水雷屯 戊子 Earth Rat 4	**8** 二十 金9 Metal [8] Without Wrongdoing 天雷無妄 己丑 Earth Ox 2	**9** 廿一 木3 Wood [7] Fire 離爲火 庚寅 Metal Tiger 1	**10** 廿二 火2 Fire [6] Sincerity 風澤中孚 辛卯 Metal Rabbit 3	**11** 廿三 水6 Water [5] Big Livestock 山天大畜 壬辰 Water Dragon 4	**12** 廿四 金4 Metal [4] Eliminating 澤天夬 癸巳 Water Snake 6
13 廿五 金9 Metal [3] Heaven 乾爲天 甲午 Wood Horse 1	**14** 廿六 火7 Fire [2] Well 水風井 乙未 Wood Goat 6	**15** 廿七 木8 Wood [1] Relief 雷水解 丙申 Fire Monkey 4	**16** 廿八 金4 Metal [9] Influence 澤山咸 丁酉 Fire Rooster 9	**17** 廿九 水1 Water [8] Humility 地山謙 戊戌 Earth Dog 6	**18** 三十 火2 Fire [7] Observation 風地觀 己亥 Earth Pig 2	**19** 十一月初一 火2 Fire [6] Increasing 風雷益 庚子 Metal Rat 9
20 初二 水1 Water [5] Dimming Light 地火明夷 辛丑 Metal Ox 3	**21** 初三 金9 Metal [4] Fellowship 天火同人 壬寅 Water Tiger 7	**22** 初四 木8 Wood [3/7] Marrying Maiden 雷澤歸妹 癸卯 Water Rabbit 7	**23** 初五 木3 Wood [8] Opposition 火澤睽 甲辰 Wood Dragon 2	**24** 初六 火7 Fire [9] Waiting 水天需 乙巳 Wood Snake 3	**25** 初七 金4 Metal [1] Great Exceeding 澤風大過 丙午 Fire Horse 3	**26** 初八 水6 Water [2] Poison 山風蠱 丁未 Fire Goat 7
27 初九 火2 Fire [3] Dispersing 風水渙 戊申 Earth Monkey 6	**28** 初十 木3 Wood [4] Travelling 火山旅 己酉 Earth Rooster 8	**29** 十一 金9 Metal [5] Stagnation 天地否 庚戌 Metal Dog 9	**30** 十二 火7 Fire [6] Alliance 水地比 辛亥 Metal Pig 7	**31** 十三 木8 Wood [7] Thunder 震爲雷 壬子 Water Rat 1		

1999 己卯

(*Ji Mao*) Earth Rabbit

1999 己卯 *(Ji Mao)* Earth Rabbit

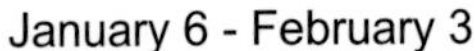

January 6 - February 3

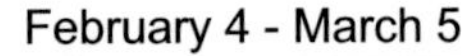

February 4 - March 5

March 6 - April 4

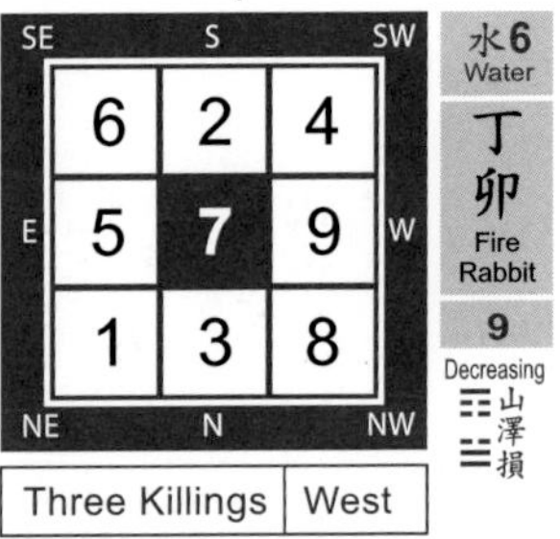

April 5 - May 5

May 6 - June 5

June 6 - July 6

July 7 - August 7

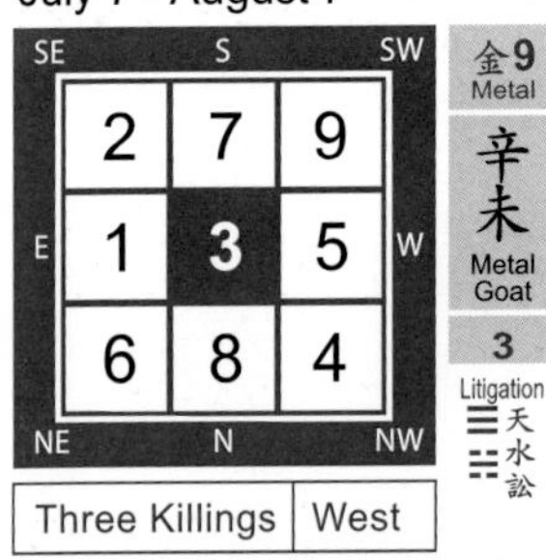

August 8 - September 7

September 8 - October 8

October 9 - November 7

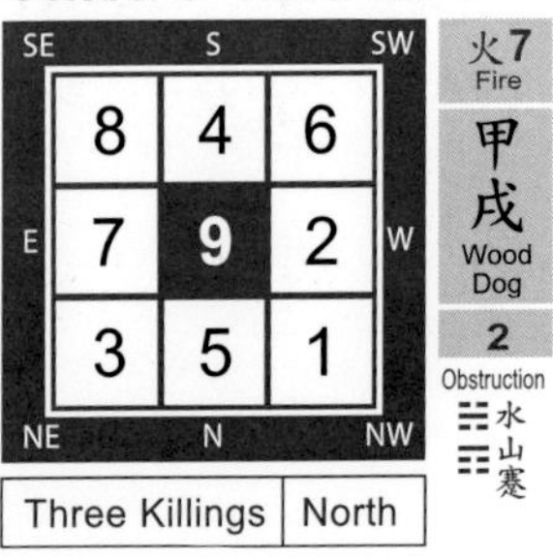

November 8 - December 6

December 7 - January 5

JANUARY 1999 乙丑

Xuan Kong Element 玄空五行	火雷噬嗑 Biting	Period Luck 卦運	Monthly Star 月星
Wood 木3		6	9

SUNDAY	MONDAY	TUESDAY	WEDNESDAY	THURSDAY	FRIDAY	SATURDAY
金4 Metal · Trap 2 · 澤水困 · 癸未 Water Goat · **31** 十五 · 8					水6 Water · Beauty 8 · 山火賁 · 癸丑 Water Ox · **1** 十四 · 8	火7 Fire · Accomplished 9 · 水火既濟 · 甲寅 Wood Tiger · **2** 十五 · 9
水1 Water · Arriving 1 · 地澤臨 · 乙卯 Wood Rabbit · **3** 十六 · 4	金4 Metal · Marsh 2 · 兌爲澤 · 丙辰 Fire Dragon · **4** 十七 · 1	火2 Fire · Small Livestock 3 · 風天小畜 · 丁巳 Fire Snake · **5** 十八 · 8	木3 Wood · The Cauldron 4 · 火風鼎 · 戊午 Earth Horse · **6** 十九 · 4	水1 Water · Rising 5 · 地風升 · 己未 Earth Goat · **7** 二十 · 2	火7 Fire · Water 6 · 坎爲水 · 庚申 Metal Monkey · **8** 廿一 · 1	木8 Wood · Lesser Exceeding 7 · 雷山小過 · 辛酉 Metal Rooster · **9** 廿二 · 3
金4 Metal · Gathering 8 · 澤地萃 · 壬戌 Water Dog · **10** 廿三 · 4	水6 Water · Peel 9 · 山地剝 · 癸亥 Water Pig · **11** 廿四 · 6	水1 Water · Earth 1 · 坤爲地 · 甲子 Wood Rat · **12** 廿五 · 1	木3 Wood · Biting 2 · 火雷噬嗑 · 乙丑 Wood Ox · **13** 廿六 · 6	火2 Fire · Family 3 · 風火家人 · 丙寅 Fire Tiger · **14** 廿七 · 4	水6 Water · Decreasing 4 · 山澤損 · 丁卯 Fire Rabbit · **15** 廿八 · 9	金9 Metal · Tread 5 · 天澤履 · 戊辰 Earth Dragon · **16** 廿九 · 6
木8 Wood · Great Strength 6 · 雷天大壯 · 己巳 Earth Snake · **17** 十二月初一 · 2	木8 Wood · Consistency 7 · 雷風恆 · 庚午 Metal Horse · **18** 初二 · 9	金9 Metal · Litigation 8 · 天水訟 · 辛未 Metal Goat · **19** 初三 · 3	水1 Water · Officer 9 · 地水師 · 壬申 Water Monkey · **20** 初四 · 7	火2 Fire · Gradual Progress 1 · 風山漸 · 癸酉 Water Rooster · **21** 初五 · 7	火7 Fire · Obstruction 2 · 水山蹇 · 甲戌 Wood Dog · **22** 初六 · 2	木3 Wood · Advancement 3 · 火地晉 · 乙亥 Wood Pig · **23** 初七 · 3
水6 Water · Nourish 4 · 山雷頤 · 丙子 Fire Rat · **24** 初八 · 3	金4 Metal · Following 5 · 澤雷隨 · 丁丑 Fire Ox · **25** 初九 · 7	木8 Wood · Abundance 6 · 雷火豐 · 戊寅 Earth Tiger · **26** 初十 · 6	火7 Fire · Regulate 7 · 水澤節 · 己卯 Earth Rabbit · **27** 十一 · 8	水1 Water · Unity 8 · 地天泰 · 庚辰 Metal Dragon · **28** 十二 · 9	木3 Wood · Great Reward 9 · 火天大有 · 辛巳 Metal Snake · **29** 十三 · 7	火2 Fire · Wind 1 · 巽爲風 · 壬午 Water Horse · **30** 十四 · 1

FEBRUARY 1999 丙寅

Xuan Kong Element 玄空五行	風火家人 Family	Period Luck 卦運	Monthly Star 月星
Fire 火2		4	8

SUNDAY	MONDAY	TUESDAY	WEDNESDAY	THURSDAY	FRIDAY	SATURDAY
	木3 Wood · Not Yet Accomplished 3 · 火水未濟 · 甲申 Wood Monkey · **1** 十六 · 9	金9 Metal · Retreat 4 · 天山遯 · 乙酉 Wood Rooster · **2** 十七 · 4	水6 Water · Mountain 5 · 艮爲山 · 丙戌 Fire Dog · **3** 十八 · 1	木8 Wood · Delight 6 · 雷地豫 · 丁亥 Fire Pig · **4** 十九 · 8	火7 Fire · Beginning 7 · 水雷屯 · 戊子 Earth Rat · **5** 二十 · 4	金9 Metal · Without Wrongdoing 8 · 天雷無妄 · 己丑 Earth Ox · **6** 廿一 · 2
木3 Wood · Fire 9 · 離爲火 · 庚寅 Metal Tiger · **7** 廿二 · 1	火2 Fire · Sincerity 1 · 風澤中孚 · 辛卯 Metal Rabbit · **8** 廿三 · 3	水6 Water · Big Livestock 2 · 山天大畜 · 壬辰 Water Dragon · **9** 廿四 · 4	金4 Metal · Eliminating 3 · 澤天夬 · 癸巳 Water Snake · **10** 廿五 · 6	金9 Metal · Heaven 4 · 乾爲天 · 甲午 Wood Horse · **11** 廿六 · 1	火7 Fire · Well 5 · 水風井 · 乙未 Wood Goat · **12** 廿七 · 6	木8 Wood · Relief 6 · 雷水解 · 丙申 Fire Monkey · **13** 廿八 · 4
金4 Metal · Influence 7 · 澤山咸 · 丁酉 Fire Rooster · **14** 廿九 · 9	水1 Water · Humility 8 · 地山謙 · 戊戌 Earth Dog · **15** 三十 · 6	火2 Fire · Observation 9 · 風地觀 · 己亥 Earth Pig · **16** 正月初一 · 2	火2 Fire · Increasing 1 · 風雷益 · 庚子 Metal Rat · **17** 初二 · 9	水1 Water · Dimming Light 2 · 地火明夷 · 辛丑 Metal Ox · **18** 初三 · 3	金9 Metal · Fellowship 3 · 天火同人 · 壬寅 Water Tiger · **19** 初四 · 7	木8 Wood · Marrying Maiden 4 · 雷澤歸妹 · 癸卯 Water Rabbit · **20** 初五 · 7
木3 Wood · Opposition 5 · 火澤睽 · 甲辰 Wood Dragon · **21** 初六 · 2	火7 Fire · Waiting 6 · 水天需 · 乙巳 Wood Snake · **22** 初七 · 3	金4 Metal · Great Exceeding 7 · 澤風大過 · 丙午 Fire Horse · **23** 初八 · 3	水6 Water · Poison 8 · 山風蠱 · 丁未 Fire Goat · **24** 初九 · 7	火2 Fire · Dispersing 9 · 風水渙 · 戊申 Earth Monkey · **25** 初十 · 6	木3 Wood · Travelling 1 · 火山旅 · 己酉 Earth Rooster · **26** 十一 · 8	金9 Metal · Stagnation 2 · 天地否 · 庚戌 Metal Dog · **27** 十二 · 9
火7 Fire · Alliance 3 · 水地比 · 辛亥 Metal Pig · **28** 十三 · 7						

MARCH 1999 丁卯

Xuan Kong Element 玄空五行	山澤損 Decreasing	Period Luck 卦運	Monthly Star 月星
Water 水6		9	7

SUNDAY	MONDAY	TUESDAY	WEDNESDAY	THURSDAY	FRIDAY	SATURDAY
	1 十四 木8 Wood · 4 Thunder 震爲雷 壬子 Water Rat 1	**2** 十五 水6 Water · 5 Beauty 山火賁 癸丑 Water Ox 8	**3** 十六 火7 Fire · 6 Accomplished 水火既濟 甲寅 Wood Tiger 9	**4** 十七 水1 Water · 7 Arriving 地澤臨 乙卯 Wood Rabbit 4	**5** 十八 金4 Metal · 8 Marsh 兑爲澤 丙辰 Fire Dragon 1	**6** 十九 火2 Fire · 9 Small Livestock 風天小畜 丁巳 Fire Snake 8
7 二十 木3 Wood · 1 The Cauldron 火風鼎 戊午 Earth Horse 4	**8** 廿一 水1 Water · 2 Rising 地風升 己未 Earth Goat 2	**9** 廿二 火7 Fire · 3 Water 坎爲水 庚申 Metal Monkey 1	**10** 廿三 木8 Wood · 4 Lesser Exceeding 雷山小過 辛酉 Metal Rooster 3	**11** 廿四 金4 Metal · 5 Gathering 澤地萃 壬戌 Water Dog 4	**12** 廿五 水6 Water · 6 Peel 山地剝 癸亥 Water Pig 6	**13** 廿六 水1 Water · 7 Earth 坤爲地 甲子 Wood Rat 1
14 廿七 木3 Wood · 8 Biting 火雷噬嗑 乙丑 Wood Ox 6	**15** 廿八 火2 Fire · 9 Family 風火家人 丙寅 Fire Tiger 4	**16** 廿九 水6 Water · 1 Decreasing 山澤損 丁卯 Fire Rabbit 9	**17** 三十 金9 Metal · 2 Tread 天澤履 戊辰 Earth Dragon 6	**18** 二月初一 木8 Wood · 3 Great Strength 雷天大壯 己巳 Earth Snake 2	**19** 初二 木8 Wood · 4 Consistency 雷風恒 庚午 Metal Horse 9	**20** 初三 金9 Metal · 5 Litigation 天水訟 辛未 Metal Goat 3
21 初四 水1 Water · 6 Officer 地水師 壬申 Water Monkey 7	**22** 初五 火2 Fire · 7 Gradual Progress 風山漸 癸酉 Water Rooster 7	**23** 初六 火7 Fire · 8 Obstruction 水山蹇 甲戌 Wood Dog 2	**24** 初七 木3 Wood · 9 Advancement 火地晉 乙亥 Wood Pig 3	**25** 初八 水6 Water · 1 Nourish 山雷頤 丙子 Fire Rat 3	**26** 初九 金4 Metal · 2 Following 澤雷隨 丁丑 Fire Ox 7	**27** 初十 木8 Wood · 3 Abundance 雷火豐 戊寅 Earth Tiger 6
28 十一 火7 Fire · 4 Regulate 水澤節 己卯 Earth Rabbit 8	**29** 十二 水1 Water · 5 Unity 地天泰 庚辰 Metal Dragon 9	**30** 十三 木3 Wood · 6 Great Reward 火天大有 辛巳 Metal Snake 7	**31** 十四 火2 Fire · 7 Wind 巽爲風 壬午 Water Horse 1			

APRIL 1999 戊辰

Xuan Kong Element 玄空五行	天澤履 Tread	Period Luck 卦運	Monthly Star 月星
Metal 金9		6	6

SUNDAY	MONDAY	TUESDAY	WEDNESDAY	THURSDAY	FRIDAY	SATURDAY
				1 十五 金4 Metal · 8 Trap 澤水困 癸未 Water Goat 8	**2** 十六 木3 Wood · 9 Not Yet Accomplished 火水未濟 甲申 Wood Monkey 9	**3** 十七 金9 Metal · 1 Retreat 天山遯 乙酉 Wood Rooster 4
4 十八 水6 Water · 2 Mountain 艮爲山 丙戌 Fire Dog 1	**5** 十九 木8 Wood · 3 Delight 雷地豫 丁亥 Fire Pig 8	**6** 二十 火7 Fire · 4 Beginning 水雷屯 戊子 Earth Rat 4	**7** 廿一 金9 Metal · 5 Without Wrongdoing 天雷無妄 己丑 Earth Ox 2	**8** 廿二 木3 Wood · 6 Fire 離爲火 庚寅 Metal Tiger 1	**9** 廿三 火2 Fire · 7 Sincerity 風澤中孚 辛卯 Metal Rabbit 3	**10** 廿四 水6 Water · 8 Big Livestock 山天大畜 壬辰 Water Dragon 4
11 廿五 金4 Metal · 9 Eliminating 澤天夬 癸巳 Water Snake 6	**12** 廿六 金9 Metal · 1 Heaven 乾爲天 甲午 Wood Horse 1	**13** 廿七 火7 Fire · 2 Well 水風井 乙未 Wood Goat 6	**14** 廿八 木8 Wood · 3 Relief 雷水解 丙申 Fire Monkey 4	**15** 廿九 金4 Metal · 4 Influence 澤山咸 丁酉 Fire Rooster 9	**16** 三月初一 水1 Water · 5 Humility 地山謙 戊戌 Earth Dog 6	**17** 初二 火2 Fire · 6 Observation 風地觀 己亥 Earth Pig 2
18 初三 火2 Fire · 7 Increasing 風雷益 庚子 Metal Rat 9	**19** 初四 水1 Water · 8 Dimming Light 地火明夷 辛丑 Metal Ox 3	**20** 初五 金9 Metal · 9 Fellowship 天火同人 壬寅 Water Tiger 7	**21** 初六 木8 Wood · 1 Marrying Maiden 雷澤歸妹 癸卯 Water Rabbit 7	**22** 初七 木3 Wood · 2 Opposition 火澤睽 甲辰 Wood Dragon 2	**23** 初八 火7 Fire · 3 Waiting 水天需 乙巳 Wood Snake 3	**24** 初九 金4 Metal · 4 Great Exceeding 澤風大過 丙午 Fire Horse 3
25 初十 水6 Water · 5 Poison 山風蠱 丁未 Fire Goat 7	**26** 十一 火2 Fire · 6 Dispersing 風水渙 戊申 Earth Monkey 6	**27** 十二 木3 Wood · 7 Travelling 火山旅 己酉 Earth Rooster 8	**28** 十三 金9 Metal · 8 Stagnation 天地否 庚戌 Metal Dog 9	**29** 十四 火7 Fire · 9 Alliance 水地比 辛亥 Metal Pig 7	**30** 十五 木8 Wood · 1 Thunder 震爲雷 壬子 Water Rat 1	

MAY 1999 己巳

Xuan Kong Element 玄空五行	雷天大壯 Great Strength	Period Luck 卦運	Monthly Star 月星
Wood 木8		2	5

SUNDAY	MONDAY	TUESDAY	WEDNESDAY	THURSDAY	FRIDAY	SATURDAY
30 十六 火2 Fire · 4 壬午 Water Horse · 1 Wind 巽爲風	**31** 十七 金4 Metal · 5 癸未 Water Goat · 8 Trap 澤水困					**1** 十六 水6 Water · 2 癸丑 Water Ox · 8 Beauty 山火賁
2 十七 火7 Fire · 3 甲寅 Wood Tiger · 9 Accomplished 水火既濟	**3** 十八 水1 Water · 4 乙卯 Wood Rabbit · 4 Arriving 地澤臨	**4** 十九 金4 Metal · 5 丙辰 Fire Dragon · 1 Marsh 兌爲澤	**5** 二十 火2 Fire · 6 丁巳 Fire Snake · 8 Small Livestock 風天小畜	**6** 廿一 木3 Wood · 7 戊午 Earth Horse · 4 The Cauldron 火風鼎	**7** 廿二 水1 Water · 8 己未 Earth Goat · 2 Rising 地風升	**8** 廿三 火7 Fire · 9 庚申 Metal Monkey · 1 Water 坎爲水
9 廿四 木8 Wood · 1 辛酉 Metal Rooster · 3 Lesser Exceeding 雷山小過	**10** 廿五 金4 Metal · 2 壬戌 Water Dog · 4 Gathering 澤地萃	**11** 廿六 水6 Water · 3 癸亥 Water Pig · 6 Peel 山地剝	**12** 廿七 水1 Water · 4 甲子 Wood Rat · 1 Earth 坤爲地	**13** 廿八 木3 Wood · 5 乙丑 Wood Ox · 6 Biting 火雷噬嗑	**14** 廿九 火2 Fire · 6 丙寅 Fire Tiger · 4 Family 風火家人	**15** 四月初一 水6 Water · 7 丁卯 Fire Rabbit · 9 Decreasing 山澤損
16 初二 金9 Metal · 8 戊辰 Earth Dragon · 6 Tread 天澤履	**17** 初三 木8 Wood · 9 己巳 Earth Snake · 2 Great Strength 雷天大壯	**18** 初四 木8 Wood · 1 庚午 Metal Horse · 9 Consistency 雷風恆	**19** 初五 金9 Metal · 2 辛未 Metal Goat · 3 Litigation 天水訟	**20** 初六 水1 Water · 3 壬申 Water Monkey · 7 Officer 地水師	**21** 初七 火2 Fire · 4 癸酉 Water Rooster · 7 Gradual Progress 風山漸	**22** 初八 火7 Fire · 5 甲戌 Wood Dog · 2 Obstruction 水山蹇
23 初九 木3 Wood · 6 乙亥 Wood Pig · 3 Advancement 火地晉	**24** 初十 水6 Water · 7 丙子 Fire Rat · 3 Nourish 山雷頤	**25** 十一 金4 Metal · 8 丁丑 Fire Ox · 7 Following 澤雷隨	**26** 十二 木8 Wood · 9 戊寅 Earth Tiger · 6 Abundance 雷火豐	**27** 十三 火7 Fire · 1 己卯 Earth Rabbit · 8 Regulate 水澤節	**28** 十四 水1 Water · 2 庚辰 Metal Dragon · 9 Unity 地天泰	**29** 十五 木3 Wood · 3 辛巳 Metal Snake · 7 Great Reward 火天大有

JUNE 1999 庚午

Xuan Kong Element 玄空五行	雷風恆 Consistency	Period Luck 卦運	Monthly Star 月星
Wood 木8		9	4

SUNDAY	MONDAY	TUESDAY	WEDNESDAY	THURSDAY	FRIDAY	SATURDAY
		1 十八 木3 Wood · 6 甲申 Wood Monkey · 9 Not Yet Accomplished 火水未濟	**2** 十九 金9 Metal · 7 乙酉 Wood Rooster · 4 Retreat 天山遯	**3** 二十 水6 Water · 8 丙戌 Fire Dog · 1 Mountain 艮爲山	**4** 廿一 木8 Wood · 9 丁亥 Fire Pig · 8 Delight 雷地豫	**5** 廿二 火7 Fire · 1 戊子 Earth Rat · 4 Beginning 水雷屯
6 廿三 金9 Metal · 2 己丑 Earth Ox · 2 Without Wrongdoing 天雷無妄	**7** 廿四 木3 Wood · 3 庚寅 Metal Tiger · 1 Fire 離爲火	**8** 廿五 火2 Fire · 4 辛卯 Metal Rabbit · 3 Sincerity 風澤中孚	**9** 廿六 水6 Water · 5 壬辰 Water Dragon · 4 Big Livestock 山天大畜	**10** 廿七 金4 Metal · 6 癸巳 Water Snake · 6 Eliminating 澤天夬	**11** 廿八 金9 Metal · 7 甲午 Wood Horse · 1 Heaven 乾爲天	**12** 廿九 火7 Fire · 8 乙未 Wood Goat · 6 Well 水風井
13 三十 木8 Wood · 9 丙申 Fire Monkey · 4 Relief 雷水解	**14** 五月初一 金4 Metal · 1 丁酉 Fire Rooster · 9 Influence 澤山咸	**15** 初二 水1 Water · 2 戊戌 Earth Dog · 6 Humility 地山謙	**16** 初三 火2 Fire · 3 己亥 Earth Pig · 2 Observation 風地觀	**17** 初四 火2 Fire · 4 庚子 Metal Rat · 9 Increasing 風雷益	**18** 初五 水1 Water · 5 辛丑 Metal Ox · 3 Dimming Light 地火明夷	**19** 初六 金9 Metal · 6 壬寅 Water Tiger · 7 Fellowship 天火同人
20 初七 木8 Wood · 7 癸卯 Water Rabbit · 7 Marrying Maiden 雷澤歸妹	**21** 初八 木3 Wood · 8 甲辰 Wood Dragon · 2 Opposition 火澤睽	**22** 初九 火7 Fire · 9/1 乙巳 Wood Snake · 3 Waiting 水天需	**23** 初十 金4 Metal · 9 丙午 Fire Horse · 3 Great Exceeding 澤風大過	**24** 十一 水6 Water · 8 丁未 Fire Goat · 7 Poison 山風蠱	**25** 十二 火2 Fire · 7 戊申 Earth Monkey · 6 Dispersing 風水渙	**26** 十三 木3 Wood · 6 己酉 Earth Rooster · 8 Travelling 火山旅
27 十四 金9 Metal · 5 庚戌 Metal Dog · 9 Stagnation 天地否	**28** 十五 火7 Fire · 4 辛亥 Metal Pig · 7 Alliance 水地比	**29** 十六 木8 Wood · 3 壬子 Water Rat · 1 Thunder 震爲雷	**30** 十七 水6 Water · 2 癸丑 Water Ox · 8 Beauty 山火賁			

JULY 1999 辛未

Xuan Kong Element 玄空五行	天水訟 Litigation	Period Luck 卦運	Monthly Star 月星
Metal 金9		3	3

SUNDAY	MONDAY	TUESDAY	WEDNESDAY	THURSDAY	FRIDAY	SATURDAY
				火7 Fire Accomplished 1 甲寅 Wood Tiger 水火既濟 1 十八 9	水1 Water Arriving 9 乙卯 Wood Rabbit 地澤臨 2 十九 4	金4 Metal Marsh 8 丙辰 Fire Dragon 兌爲澤 3 二十 1
火2 Fire Small Livestock 7 丁巳 Fire Snake 風天小畜 4 廿一 8	木3 Wood The Cauldron 6 戊午 Earth Horse 火風鼎 5 廿二 4	水1 Water Rising 5 己未 Earth Goat 地風升 6 廿三 2	火7 Fire Water 4 庚申 Metal Monkey 坎爲水 7 廿四 1	木8 Wood Lesser Exceeding 3 辛酉 Metal Rooster 雷山小過 8 廿五 3	金4 Metal Gathering 2 壬戌 Water Dog 澤地萃 9 廿六 4	水6 Water Peel 1 癸亥 Water Pig 山地剝 10 廿七 6
水1 Water Earth 9 甲子 Wood Rat 坤爲地 11 廿八 1	木3 Wood Biting 8 乙丑 Wood Ox 火雷噬嗑 12 廿九 6	火2 Fire Family 7 丙寅 Fire Tiger 風火家人 13 六月初一 4	水6 Water Decreasing 6 丁卯 Fire Rabbit 山澤損 14 初二 9	金9 Metal Tread 5 戊辰 Earth Dragon 天澤履 15 初三 6	木8 Wood Great Strength 4 己巳 Earth Snake 雷天大壯 16 初四 2	木8 Wood Consistency 3 庚午 Metal Horse 雷風恒 17 初五 9
金9 Metal Litigation 2 辛未 Metal Goat 天水訟 18 初六 3	水1 Water Officer 1 壬申 Water Monkey 地水師 19 初七 7	火2 Fire Gradual Progress 9 癸酉 Water Rooster 風山漸 20 初八 7	火7 Fire Obstruction 8 甲戌 Wood Dog 水山蹇 21 初九 2	木3 Wood Advancement 7 乙亥 Wood Pig 火地晉 22 初十 3	水6 Water Nourish 6 丙子 Fire Rat 山雷頤 23 十一 3	金4 Metal Following 5 丁丑 Fire Ox 澤雷隨 24 十二 7
木8 Wood Abundance 4 戊寅 Earth Tiger 雷火豐 25 十三 6	火7 Fire Regulate 3 己卯 Earth Rabbit 水澤節 26 十四 8	水1 Water Unity 2 庚辰 Metal Dragon 地天泰 27 十五 9	木3 Wood Great Reward 1 辛巳 Metal Snake 火天大有 28 十六 7	火2 Fire Wind 9 壬午 Water Horse 巽爲風 29 十七 1	金4 Metal Trap 8 癸未 Water Goat 澤水困 30 十八 8	木3 Wood Not Yet Accomplished 7 甲申 Wood Monkey 火水未濟 31 十九 9

AUGUST 1999 壬申

Xuan Kong Element 玄空五行	地水師 Officer	Period Luck 卦運	Monthly Star 月星
Water 水1		7	2

SUNDAY	MONDAY	TUESDAY	WEDNESDAY	THURSDAY	FRIDAY	SATURDAY
金9 Metal Retreat 6 乙酉 Wood Rooster 天山遯 1 二十 4	水6 Water Mountain 5 丙戌 Fire Dog 艮爲山 2 廿一 1	木8 Wood Delight 4 丁亥 Fire Pig 雷地豫 3 廿二 8	火7 Fire Beginning 3 戊子 Earth Rat 水雷屯 4 廿三 4	金9 Metal Without Wrongdoing 2 己丑 Earth Ox 天雷無妄 5 廿四 2	木3 Wood Fire 1 庚寅 Metal Tiger 離爲火 6 廿五 1	火2 Fire Sincerity 9 辛卯 Metal Rabbit 風澤中孚 7 廿六 3
水6 Water Big Livestock 8 壬辰 Water Dragon 山天大畜 8 廿七 4	金4 Metal Eliminating 7 癸巳 Water Snake 澤天夬 9 廿八 6	金9 Metal Heaven 6 甲午 Wood Horse 乾爲天 10 廿九 1	火7 Fire Well 5 乙未 Wood Goat 水風井 11 七月初一 6	木8 Wood Relief 4 丙申 Fire Monkey 雷水解 12 初二 4	金4 Metal Influence 3 丁酉 Fire Rooster 澤山咸 13 初三 9	水1 Water Humility 2 戊戌 Earth Dog 地山謙 14 初四 6
火2 Fire Observation 1 己亥 Earth Pig 風地觀 15 初五 2	火2 Fire Increasing 9 庚子 Metal Rat 風雷益 16 初六 9	水1 Water Dimming Light 8 辛丑 Metal Ox 地火明夷 17 初七 3	金9 Metal Fellowship 7 壬寅 Water Tiger 天火同人 18 初八 7	木8 Wood Marrying Maiden 6 癸卯 Water Rabbit 雷澤歸妹 19 初九 7	木3 Wood Opposition 5 甲辰 Wood Dragon 火澤睽 20 初十 2	火7 Fire Waiting 4 乙巳 Wood Snake 水天需 21 十一 3
金4 Metal Great Exceeding 3 丙午 Fire Horse 澤風大過 22 十二 3	水6 Water Poison 2 丁未 Fire Goat 山風蠱 23 十三 7	火2 Fire Dispersing 1 戊申 Earth Monkey 風水渙 24 十四 6	木3 Wood Travelling 9 己酉 Earth Rooster 火山旅 25 十五 8	金9 Metal Stagnation 8 庚戌 Metal Dog 天地否 26 十六 9	火7 Fire Alliance 7 辛亥 Metal Pig 水地比 27 十七 7	木8 Wood Thunder 6 壬子 Water Rat 震爲雷 28 十八 1
水6 Water Beauty 5 癸丑 Water Ox 山火賁 29 十九 8	火7 Fire Accomplished 4 甲寅 Wood Tiger 水火既濟 30 二十 9	水1 Water Arriving 3 乙卯 Wood Rabbit 地澤臨 31 廿一 4				

SEPTEMBER 1999 癸酉

Xuan Kong Element 玄空五行	風山漸 Gradual Progress	Period Luck 卦運	Monthly Star 月星
Fire 火2		7	1

SUNDAY	MONDAY	TUESDAY	WEDNESDAY	THURSDAY	FRIDAY	SATURDAY
			金4 Metal · Marsh · 2 丙辰 Fire Dragon 兑爲澤 **1** 廿二 1	火2 Fire · Small Livestock · 1 丁巳 Fire Snake 風天小畜 **2** 廿三 8	木3 Wood · The Cauldron · 9 戊午 Earth Horse 火風鼎 **3** 廿四 4	水1 Water · Rising · 8 己未 Earth Goat 地風升 **4** 廿五 2
火7 Fire · Water · 7 庚申 Metal Monkey 坎爲水 **5** 廿六 1	木8 Wood · Lesser Exceeding · 6 辛酉 Metal Rooster 雷山小過 **6** 廿七 3	金4 Metal · Gathering · 5 壬戌 Water Dog 澤地萃 **7** 廿八 4	水6 Water · Peel · 4 癸亥 Water Pig 山地剝 **8** 廿九 6	水1 Water · Earth · 3 甲子 Wood Rat 坤爲地 **9** 三十 1	木3 Wood · Biting · 2 乙丑 Wood Ox 火雷噬嗑 **10** 八月初一 6	火2 Fire · Family · 1 丙寅 Fire Tiger 風火家人 **11** 初二 4
水6 Water · Decreasing · 9 丁卯 Fire Rabbit 山澤損 **12** 初三 9	金9 Metal · Tread · 8 戊辰 Earth Dragon 天澤履 **13** 初四 6	木8 Wood · Great Strength · 7 己巳 Earth Snake 雷天大壯 **14** 初五 2	木8 Wood · Consistency · 6 庚午 Metal Horse 雷風恆 **15** 初六 9	金9 Metal · Litigation · 5 辛未 Metal Goat 天水訟 **16** 初七 3	水1 Water · Officer · 4 壬申 Water Monkey 地水師 **17** 初八 7	火2 Fire · Gradual Progress · 3 癸酉 Water Rooster 風山漸 **18** 初九 7
火7 Fire · Obstruction · 2 甲戌 Wood Dog 水山蹇 **19** 初十 2	木3 Wood · Advancement · 1 乙亥 Wood Pig 火地晉 **20** 十一 3	水6 Water · Nourish · 9 丙子 Fire Rat 山雷頤 **21** 十二 3	金4 Metal · Following · 8 丁丑 Fire Ox 澤雷隨 **22** 十三 7	木8 Wood · Abundance · 7 戊寅 Earth Tiger 雷火豐 **23** 十四 6	火7 Fire · Regulate · 6 己卯 Earth Rabbit 水澤節 **24** 十五 8	水1 Water · Unity · 5 庚辰 Metal Dragon 地天泰 **25** 十六 9
木3 Wood · Great Reward · 4 辛巳 Metal Snake 火天大有 **26** 十七 7	火2 Fire · Wind · 3 壬午 Water Horse 巽爲風 **27** 十八 1	金4 Metal · Trap · 2 癸未 Water Goat 澤水困 **28** 十九 8	木3 Wood · Not Yet Accomplished · 1 甲申 Wood Monkey 火水未濟 **29** 二十 9	金9 Metal · Retreat · 9 乙酉 Wood Rooster 天山遯 **30** 廿一 4		

OCTOBER 1999 甲戌

Xuan Kong Element 玄空五行	水山蹇 Obstruction	Period Luck 卦運	Monthly Star 月星
Fire 火7		2	9

SUNDAY	MONDAY	TUESDAY	WEDNESDAY	THURSDAY	FRIDAY	SATURDAY
金4 Metal · Marsh · 5 丙辰 Fire Dragon 兑爲澤 **31** 廿三 1					水6 Water · Mountain · 8 丙戌 Fire Dog 艮爲山 **1** 廿二 1	木8 Wood · Delight · 7 丁亥 Fire Pig 雷地豫 **2** 廿三 8
火7 Fire · Beginning · 6 戊子 Earth Rat 水雷屯 **3** 廿四 4	金9 Metal · Without Wrongdoing · 5 己丑 Earth Ox 天雷無妄 **4** 廿五 2	木3 Wood · Fire · 4 庚寅 Metal Tiger 離爲火 **5** 廿六 1	火2 Fire · Sincerity · 3 辛卯 Metal Rabbit 風澤中孚 **6** 廿七 3	水6 Water · Big Livestock · 2 壬辰 Water Dragon 山天大畜 **7** 廿八 4	金4 Metal · Eliminating · 1 癸巳 Water Snake 澤天夬 **8** 廿九 6	金9 Metal · Heaven · 9 甲午 Wood Horse 乾爲天 **9** 九月初一 1
火7 Fire · Well · 8 乙未 Wood Goat 水風井 **10** 初二 6	木8 Wood · Relief · 7 丙申 Fire Monkey 雷水解 **11** 初三 4	金4 Metal · Influence · 6 丁酉 Fire Rooster 澤山咸 **12** 初四 9	水1 Water · Humility · 5 戊戌 Earth Dog 地山謙 **13** 初五 6	火2 Fire · Observation · 4 己亥 Earth Pig 風地觀 **14** 初六 2	火2 Fire · Increasing · 3 庚子 Metal Rat 風雷益 **15** 初七 9	水1 Water · Dimming Light · 2 辛丑 Metal Ox 地火明夷 **16** 初八 3
金9 Metal · Fellowship · 1 壬寅 Water Tiger 天火同人 **17** 初九 7	木8 Wood · Marrying Maiden · 9 癸卯 Water Rabbit 雷澤歸妹 **18** 初十 7	木3 Wood · Opposition · 8 甲辰 Wood Dragon 火澤睽 **19** 十一 2	火7 Fire · Waiting · 7 乙巳 Wood Snake 水天需 **20** 十二 3	金4 Metal · Great Exceeding · 6 丙午 Fire Horse 澤風大過 **21** 十三 3	水6 Water · Poison · 5 丁未 Fire Goat 山風蠱 **22** 十四 7	火2 Fire · Dispersing · 4 戊申 Earth Monkey 風水渙 **23** 十五 6
木3 Wood · Travelling · 3 己酉 Earth Rooster 火山旅 **24** 十六 8	金9 Metal · Stagnation · 2 庚戌 Metal Dog 天地否 **25** 十七 9	火7 Fire · Alliance · 1 辛亥 Metal Pig 水地比 **26** 十八 7	木8 Wood · Thunder · 9 壬子 Water Rat 震爲雷 **27** 十九 1	水6 Water · Beauty · 8 癸丑 Water Ox 山火賁 **28** 二十 8	火7 Fire · Accomplished · 7 甲寅 Wood Tiger 水火既濟 **29** 廿一 9	水1 Water · Arriving · 6 乙卯 Wood Rabbit 地澤臨 **30** 廿二 4

NOVEMBER 1999 乙亥

Xuan Kong Element 玄空五行	火地晉 Advancement	Period Luck 卦運	Monthly Star 月星
Wood 木3		3	8

SUNDAY	MONDAY	TUESDAY	WEDNESDAY	THURSDAY	FRIDAY	SATURDAY
	火2 Fire 4 Small Livestock 丁巳 Fire Snake 風天小畜 1 廿四 8	木3 Wood 3 The Cauldron 戊午 Earth Horse 火風鼎 2 廿五 4	水1 Water 2 Rising 己未 Earth Goat 地風升 3 廿六 2	火7 Fire 1 Water 庚申 Metal Monkey 坎為水 4 廿七 1	木8 Wood 9 Lesser Exceeding 辛酉 Metal Rooster 雷山小過 5 廿八 3	金4 Metal 8 Gathering 壬戌 Water Dog 澤地萃 6 廿九 4
水6 Water 7 Peel 癸亥 Water Pig 山地剝 7 三十 6	水1 Water 6 Earth 甲子 Wood Rat 坤為地 8 十月初一 1	木3 Wood 5 Biting 乙丑 Wood Ox 火雷噬嗑 9 初二 6	火2 Fire 4 Family 丙寅 Fire Tiger 風火家人 10 初三 4	水6 Water 3 Decreasing 丁卯 Fire Rabbit 山澤損 11 初四 9	金9 Metal 2 Tread 戊辰 Earth Dragon 天澤履 12 初五 6	木8 Wood 1 Great Strength 己巳 Earth Snake 雷天大壯 13 初六 2
木8 Wood 9 Consistency 庚午 Metal Horse 雷風恆 14 初七 9	金9 Metal 8 Litigation 辛未 Metal Goat 天水訟 15 初八 3	水1 Water 7 Officer 壬申 Water Monkey 地水師 16 初九 7	火2 Fire 6 Gradual Progress 癸酉 Water Rooster 風山漸 17 初十 7	火7 Fire 5 Obstruction 甲戌 Wood Dog 水山蹇 18 十一 2	木3 Wood 4 Advancement 乙亥 Wood Pig 火地晉 19 十二 3	水6 Water 3 Nourish 丙子 Fire Rat 山雷頤 20 十三 3
金4 Metal 2 Following 丁丑 Fire Ox 澤雷隨 21 十四 7	木8 Wood 1 Abundance 戊寅 Earth Tiger 雷火豐 22 十五 6	火7 Fire 9 Regulate 己卯 Earth Rabbit 水澤節 23 十六 8	水1 Water 8 Unity 庚辰 Metal Dragon 地天泰 24 十七 9	木3 Wood 7 Great Reward 辛巳 Metal Snake 火天大有 25 十八 7	火2 Fire 6 Wind 壬午 Water Horse 巽為風 26 十九 1	金4 Metal 5 Trap 癸未 Water Goat 澤水困 27 二十 8
木3 Wood 4 Not Yet Accomplished 甲申 Wood Monkey 火水未濟 28 廿一 9	金9 Metal 3 Retreat 乙酉 Wood Rooster 天山遯 29 廿二 4	水6 Water 2 Mountain 丙戌 Fire Dog 艮為山 30 廿三 1				

DECEMBER 1999 丙子

Xuan Kong Element 玄空五行	山雷頤 Nourish	Period Luck 卦運	Monthly Star 月星
Water 水6		3	7

SUNDAY	MONDAY	TUESDAY	WEDNESDAY	THURSDAY	FRIDAY	SATURDAY
			木8 Wood 1 Delight 丁亥 Fire Pig 雷地豫 1 廿四 8	火7 Fire 9 Beginning 戊子 Earth Rat 水雷屯 2 廿五 4	金9 Metal 8 Without Wrongdoing 己丑 Earth Ox 天雷無妄 3 廿六 2	木3 Wood 7 Fire 庚寅 Metal Tiger 離為火 4 廿七 1
火2 Fire 6 Sincerity 辛卯 Metal Rabbit 風澤中孚 5 廿八 3	水6 Water 5 Big Livestock 壬辰 Water Dragon 山天大畜 6 廿九 4	金4 Metal 4 Eliminating 癸巳 Water Snake 澤天夬 7 三十 6	金9 Metal 3 Heaven 甲午 Wood Horse 乾為天 8 十一月初一 1	火7 Fire 2 Well 乙未 Wood Goat 水風井 9 初二 6	木8 Wood 1 Relief 丙申 Fire Monkey 雷水解 10 初三 4	金4 Metal 9 Influence 丁酉 Fire Rooster 澤山咸 11 初四 9
水1 Water 8 Humility 戊戌 Earth Dog 地山謙 12 初五 6	火2 Fire 7 Observation 己亥 Earth Pig 風地觀 13 初六 2	火2 Fire 6 Increasing 庚子 Metal Rat 風雷益 14 初七 9	水1 Water 5 Dimming Light 辛丑 Metal Ox 地火明夷 15 初八 3	金9 Metal 4 Fellowship 壬寅 Water Tiger 天火同人 16 初九 7	木8 Wood 3 Marrying Maiden 癸卯 Water Rabbit 雷澤歸妹 17 初十 7	木3 Wood 2 Opposition 甲辰 Wood Dragon 火澤睽 18 十一 2
火7 Fire 1 Waiting 乙巳 Wood Snake 水天需 19 十二 3	金4 Metal 9 Great Exceeding 丙午 Fire Horse 澤風大過 20 十三 3	水6 Water 8 Poison 丁未 Fire Goat 山風蠱 21 十四 7	火2 Fire 7/3 Dispersing 戊申 Earth Monkey 風水渙 22 十五 6	木3 Wood 4 Travelling 己酉 Earth Rooster 火山旅 23 十六 8	金9 Metal 5 Stagnation 庚戌 Metal Dog 天地否 24 十七 9	火7 Fire 6 Alliance 辛亥 Metal Pig 水地比 25 十八 7
木8 Wood 7 Thunder 壬子 Water Rat 震為雷 26 十九 1	水6 Water 8 Beauty 癸丑 Water Ox 山火賁 27 二十 8	火7 Fire 9 Accomplished 甲寅 Wood Tiger 水火既濟 28 廿一 9	水1 Water 1 Arriving 乙卯 Wood Rabbit 地澤臨 29 廿二 4	金4 Metal 2 Marsh 丙辰 Fire Dragon 兌為澤 30 廿三 1	火2 Fire 3 Small Livestock 丁巳 Fire Snake 風天小畜 31 廿四 8	

2000 庚辰

(*Geng Chen*) Metal Dragon

2000 庚辰 *(Geng Chen)* Metal Dragon

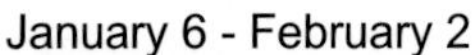

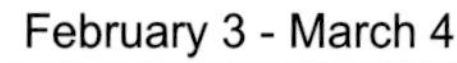

March 5 - April 3

April 4 - May 4

May 5 - June 4

June 5 - July 6

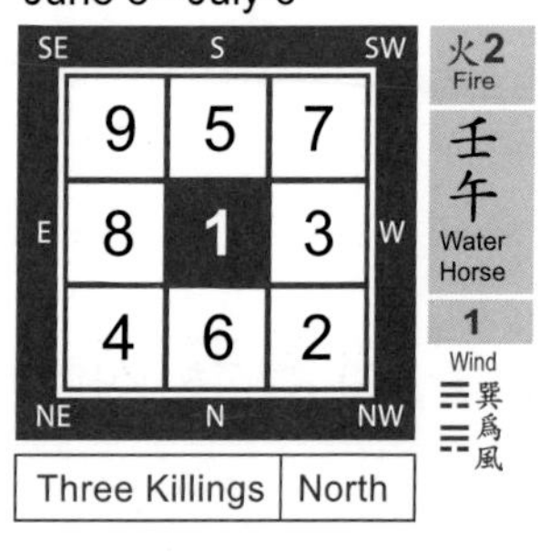

July 7 - August 6

August 7 - September 6

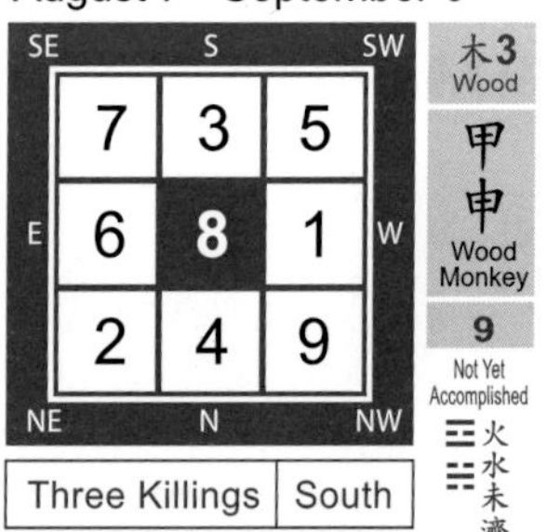

September 7 - October 7

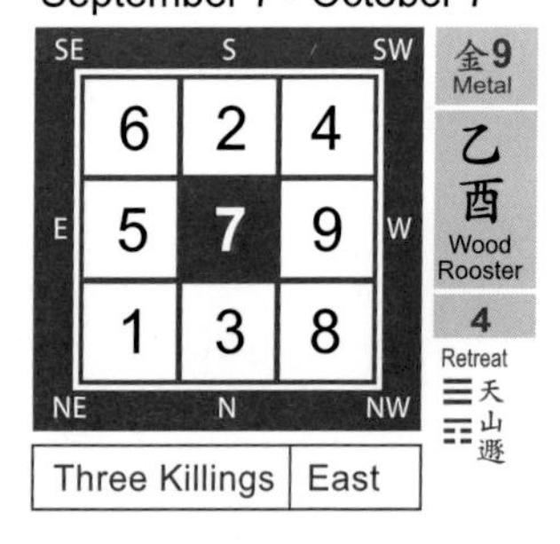

October 8 - November 6

November 7 - December 6

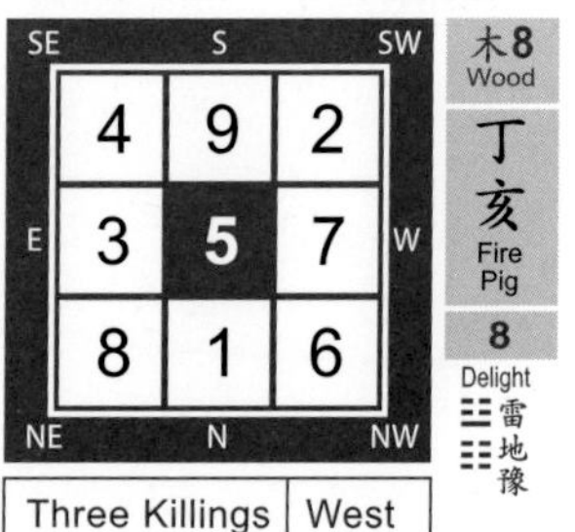

December 7 - January 4

JANUARY 2000 丁丑

Xuan Kong Element 玄空五行	澤雷隨 Following	Period Luck 卦運	Monthly Star 月星
Metal 金4		7	6

SUNDAY	MONDAY	TUESDAY	WEDNESDAY	THURSDAY	FRIDAY	SATURDAY
木8 Wood 6 Delight 雷地豫 丁亥 Fire Pig 30 廿四 8	火7 Fire 7 Beginning 水雷屯 戊子 Earth Rat 31 廿五 4					木3 Wood 4 The Cauldron 火風鼎 戊午 Earth Horse 1 廿五 4
水1 Water 5 Rising 地風升 己未 Earth Goat 2 廿六 2	火7 Fire 6 Water 坎為水 庚申 Metal Monkey 3 廿七 2	木8 Wood 7 Lesser Exceeding 雷山小過 辛酉 Metal Rooster 4 廿八 3	金4 Metal 8 Gathering 澤地萃 壬戌 Water Dog 5 廿九 4	水6 Water 9 Peel 山地剝 癸亥 Water Pig 6 三十 6	水1 Water 1 Earth 坤為地 甲子 Wood Rat 7 十二月初一 1	木3 Wood 2 Biting 火雷噬嗑 乙丑 Wood Ox 8 初二 6
火2 Fire 3 Family 風火家人 丙寅 Fire Tiger 9 初三 4	水6 Water 4 Decreasing 山澤損 丁卯 Fire Rabbit 10 初四 9	金9 Metal 5 Tread 天澤履 戊辰 Earth Dragon 11 初五 6	木8 Wood 6 Great Strength 雷天大壯 己巳 Earth Snake 12 初六 2	木8 Wood 7 Consistency 雷風恆 庚午 Metal Horse 13 初七 9	金9 Metal 8 Litigation 天水訟 辛未 Metal Goat 14 初八 3	水1 Water 9 Officer 地水師 壬申 Water Monkey 15 初九 7
火2 Fire 1 Gradual Progress 風山漸 癸酉 Water Rooster 16 初十 7	火7 Fire 2 Obstruction 水山蹇 甲戌 Wood Dog 17 十一 2	木3 Wood 3 Advancement 火地晉 乙亥 Wood Pig 18 十二 3	水6 Water 4 Nourish 山雷頤 丙子 Fire Rat 19 十三 3	金4 Metal 5 Following 澤雷隨 丁丑 Fire Ox 20 十四 7	木8 Wood 6 Abundance 雷火豐 戊寅 Earth Tiger 21 十五 6	火7 Fire 7 Regulate 水澤節 己卯 Earth Rabbit 22 十六 8
水1 Water 8 Unity 地天泰 庚辰 Metal Dragon 23 十七 9	木3 Wood 9 Great Reward 火天大有 辛巳 Metal Snake 24 十八 7	火2 Fire 1 Wind 巽為風 壬午 Water Horse 25 十九 1	金4 Metal 2 Trap 澤水困 癸未 Water Goat 26 二十 8	木3 Wood 3 Not Yet Accomplished 火水未濟 甲申 Wood Monkey 27 廿一 9	金9 Metal 4 Retreat 天山遯 乙酉 Wood Rooster 28 廿二 4	水6 Water 5 Mountain 艮為山 丙戌 Fire Dog 29 廿三 1

FEBRUARY 2000 戊寅

Xuan Kong Element 玄空五行	雷火豐 Abundance	Period Luck 卦運	Monthly Star 月星
Wood 木8		6	5

SUNDAY	MONDAY	TUESDAY	WEDNESDAY	THURSDAY	FRIDAY	SATURDAY
		金9 Metal 8 Without Wrongdoing 天雷無妄 己丑 Earth Ox 1 廿六 2	木3 Wood 9 Fire 離為火 庚寅 Metal Tiger 2 廿七 1	火2 Fire 1 Sincerity 風澤中孚 辛卯 Metal Rabbit 3 廿八 3	水6 Water 2 Big Livestock 山天大畜 壬辰 Water Dragon 4 廿九 4	金4 Metal 3 Eliminating 澤天夬 癸巳 Water Snake 5 正月初一 6
金9 Metal 4 Heaven 乾為天 甲午 Wood Horse 6 初二 1	火7 Fire 5 Well 水風井 乙未 Wood Goat 7 初三 6	木8 Wood 6 Relief 雷水解 丙申 Fire Monkey 8 初四 4	金4 Metal 7 Influence 澤山咸 丁酉 Fire Rooster 9 初五 9	水1 Water 8 Humility 地山謙 戊戌 Earth Dog 10 初六 6	火2 Fire 9 Observation 風地觀 己亥 Earth Pig 11 初七 2	火2 Fire 1 Increasing 風雷益 庚子 Metal Rat 12 初八 9
水1 Water 2 Dimming Light 地火明夷 辛丑 Metal Ox 13 初九 3	金9 Metal 3 Fellowship 天火同人 壬寅 Water Tiger 14 初十 7	木8 Wood 4 Marrying Maiden 雷澤歸妹 癸卯 Water Rabbit 15 十一 7	木3 Wood 5 Opposition 火澤睽 甲辰 Wood Dragon 16 十二 2	火7 Fire 6 Waiting 水天需 乙巳 Wood Snake 17 十三 3	金4 Metal 7 Great Exceeding 澤風大過 丙午 Fire Horse 18 十四 3	水6 Water 8 Poison 山風蠱 丁未 Fire Goat 19 十五 7
火2 Fire 9 Dispersing 風水渙 戊申 Earth Monkey 20 十六 6	木3 Wood 1 Travelling 火山旅 己酉 Earth Rooster 21 十七 8	金9 Metal 2 Stagnation 天地否 庚戌 Metal Dog 22 十八 9	火7 Fire 3 Alliance 水地比 辛亥 Metal Pig 23 十九 7	木8 Wood 4 Thunder 震為雷 壬子 Water Rat 24 二十 1	水6 Water 5 Beauty 山火賁 癸丑 Water Ox 25 廿一 8	火7 Fire 6 Accomplished 水火既濟 甲寅 Wood Tiger 26 廿二 9
水1 Water 7 Arriving 地澤臨 乙卯 Wood Rabbit 27 廿三 4	金4 Metal 8 Marsh 兌為澤 丙辰 Fire Dragon 28 廿四 1	火2 Fire 9 Small Livestock 風天小畜 丁巳 Fire Snake 29 廿五 8				

MARCH 2000 己卯

Xuan Kong Element 玄空五行	水澤節 Regulate	Period Luck 卦運	Monthly Star 月星
Fire 火7		8	4

SUNDAY	MONDAY	TUESDAY	WEDNESDAY	THURSDAY	FRIDAY	SATURDAY
			木3 Wood [1] The Cauldron 火風鼎 戊午 Earth Horse **1** 廿六 4	水1 Water [2] Rising 地風升 己未 Earth Goat **2** 廿七 2	火7 Fire [3] Water 坎爲水 庚申 Metal Monkey **3** 廿八 1	木8 Wood [4] Lesser Exceeding 雷山小過 辛酉 Metal Rooster **4** 廿九 3
金4 Metal [5] Gathering 澤地萃 壬戌 Water Dog **5** 三十 4	水6 Water [6] Peel 山地剝 癸亥 Water Pig **6** 二月初一 6	水1 Water [7] Earth 坤爲地 甲子 Wood Rat **7** 初二 1	木3 Wood [8] Biting 火雷噬嗑 乙丑 Wood Ox **8** 初三 6	火2 Fire [9] Family 風火家人 丙寅 Fire Tiger **9** 初四 4	水6 Water [1] Decreasing 山澤損 丁卯 Fire Rabbit **10** 初五 9	金9 Metal [2] Tread 天澤履 戊辰 Earth Dragon **11** 初六 6
木8 Wood [3] Great Strength 雷天大壯 己巳 Earth Snake **12** 初七 2	木8 Wood [4] Consistency 雷風恒 庚午 Metal Horse **13** 初八 9	金9 Metal [5] Litigation 天水訟 辛未 Metal Goat **14** 初九 3	水1 Water [6] Officer 地水師 壬申 Water Monkey **15** 初十 7	火2 Fire [7] Gradual Progress 風山漸 癸酉 Water Rooster **16** 十一 7	火7 Fire [8] Obstruction 水山蹇 甲戌 Wood Dog **17** 十二 2	木3 Wood [9] Advancement 火地晉 乙亥 Wood Pig **18** 十三 3
水6 Water [1] Nourish 山雷頤 丙子 Fire Rat **19** 十四 3	金4 Metal [2] Following 澤雷隨 丁丑 Fire Ox **20** 十五 7	木8 Wood [3] Abundance 雷火豐 戊寅 Earth Tiger **21** 十六 6	火7 Fire [4] Regulate 水澤節 己卯 Earth Rabbit **22** 十七 8	水1 Water [5] Unity 地天泰 庚辰 Metal Dragon **23** 十八 9	木3 Wood [6] Great Reward 火天大有 辛巳 Metal Snake **24** 十九 7	火2 Fire [7] Wind 巽爲風 壬午 Water Horse **25** 二十 1
金4 Metal [8] Trap 澤水困 癸未 Water Goat **26** 廿一 8	木3 Wood [9] Not Yet Accomplished 火水未濟 甲申 Wood Monkey **27** 廿二 9	金9 Metal [1] Retreat 天山遯 乙酉 Wood Rooster **28** 廿三 4	水6 Water [2] Mountain 艮爲山 丙戌 Fire Dog **29** 廿四 1	木8 Wood [3] Delight 雷地豫 丁亥 Fire Pig **30** 廿五 8	火7 Fire [4] Beginning 水雷屯 戊子 Earth Rat **31** 廿六 4	

APRIL 2000 庚辰

Xuan Kong Element 玄空五行	地天泰 Unity	Period Luck 卦運	Monthly Star 月星
Water 水1		9	3

SUNDAY	MONDAY	TUESDAY	WEDNESDAY	THURSDAY	FRIDAY	SATURDAY
木3 Wood [7] The Cauldron 火風鼎 戊午 Earth Horse **30** 廿六 4						金9 Metal [5] Without Wrongdoing 天雷無妄 己丑 Earth Ox **1** 廿七 2
木3 Wood [6] Fire 離爲火 庚寅 Metal Tiger **2** 廿八 1	火2 Fire [7] Sincerity 風澤中孚 辛卯 Metal Rabbit **3** 廿九 3	水6 Water [8] Big Livestock 山天大畜 壬辰 Water Dragon **4** 三十 4	金4 Metal [9] Eliminating 澤天夬 癸巳 Water Snake **5** 三月初一 6	金9 Metal [1] Heaven 乾爲天 甲午 Wood Horse **6** 初二 1	火7 Fire [2] Well 水風井 乙未 Wood Goat **7** 初三 6	木8 Wood [3] Relief 雷水解 丙申 Fire Monkey **8** 初四 4
金4 Metal [4] Influence 澤山咸 丁酉 Fire Rooster **9** 初五 9	水1 Water [5] Humility 地山謙 戊戌 Earth Dog **10** 初六 6	火2 Fire [6] Observation 風地觀 己亥 Earth Pig **11** 初七 2	火2 Fire [7] Increasing 風雷益 庚子 Metal Rat **12** 初八 9	水1 Water [8] Dimming Light 地火明夷 辛丑 Metal Ox **13** 初九 3	金9 Metal [9] Fellowship 天火同人 壬寅 Water Tiger **14** 初十 7	木8 Wood [1] Marrying Maiden 雷澤歸妹 癸卯 Water Rabbit **15** 十一 7
木3 Wood [2] Opposition 火澤睽 甲辰 Wood Dragon **16** 十二 2	火7 Fire [3] Waiting 水天需 乙巳 Wood Snake **17** 十三 3	金4 Metal [4] Great Exceeding 澤風大過 丙午 Fire Horse **18** 十四 3	水6 Water [5] Poison 山風蠱 丁未 Fire Goat **19** 十五 7	火2 Fire [6] Dispersing 風水渙 戊申 Earth Monkey **20** 十六 6	木3 Wood [7] Travelling 火山旅 己酉 Earth Rooster **21** 十七 8	金9 Metal [8] Stagnation 天地否 庚戌 Metal Dog **22** 十八 9
火7 Fire [9] Alliance 水地比 辛亥 Metal Pig **23** 十九 7	木8 Wood [1] Thunder 震爲雷 壬子 Water Rat **24** 二十 1	水6 Water [2] Beauty 山火賁 癸丑 Water Ox **25** 廿一 8	火7 Fire [3] Accomplished 水火既濟 甲寅 Wood Tiger **26** 廿二 9	水1 Water [4] Arriving 地澤臨 乙卯 Wood Rabbit **27** 廿三 4	金4 Metal [5] Marsh 兌爲澤 丙辰 Fire Dragon **28** 廿四 1	火2 Fire [6] Small Livestock 風天小畜 丁巳 Fire Snake **29** 廿五 8

MAY 2000 辛巳

Xuan Kong Element 玄空五行	火天大有 Great Reward	Period Luck 卦運	Monthly Star 月星
Wood 木3		7	2

SUNDAY	MONDAY	TUESDAY	WEDNESDAY	THURSDAY	FRIDAY	SATURDAY
	水1 Water 己未 Earth Goat Rising 地風升 8 **1** 廿七 2	火7 Fire 庚申 Metal Monkey Water 坎爲水 9 **2** 廿八 1	木8 Wood 辛酉 Metal Rooster Lesser Exceeding 雷山小過 1 **3** 廿九 3	金4 Metal 壬戌 Water Dog Gathering 澤地萃 2 **4** 四月初一 4	水6 Water 癸亥 Water Pig Peel 山地剝 3 **5** 初二 6	水1 Water 甲子 Wood Rat Earth 坤爲地 4 **6** 初三 1
木3 Wood 乙丑 Wood Ox Biting 火雷噬嗑 5 **7** 初四 6	火2 Fire 丙寅 Fire Tiger Family 風火家人 6 **8** 初五 4	水6 Water 丁卯 Fire Rabbit Decreasing 山澤損 7 **9** 初六 9	金9 Metal 戊辰 Earth Dragon Tread 天澤履 8 **10** 初七 6	木8 Wood 己巳 Earth Snake Great Strength 雷天大壯 9 **11** 初八 2	木8 Wood 庚午 Metal Horse Consistency 雷風恆 1 **12** 初九 9	金9 Metal 辛未 Metal Goat Litigation 天水訟 2 **13** 初十 3
水1 Water 壬申 Water Monkey Officer 地水師 3 **14** 十一 7	火2 Fire 癸酉 Water Rooster Gradual Progress 風山漸 4 **15** 十二 7	火7 Fire 甲戌 Wood Dog Obstruction 水山蹇 5 **16** 十三 2	木3 Wood 乙亥 Wood Pig Advancement 火地晉 6 **17** 十四 3	水6 Water 丙子 Fire Rat Nourish 山雷頤 7 **18** 十五 3	金4 Metal 丁丑 Fire Ox Following 澤雷隨 8 **19** 十六 7	木8 Wood 戊寅 Earth Tiger Abundance 雷火豐 9 **20** 十七 6
火7 Fire 己卯 Earth Rabbit Regulate 水澤節 1 **21** 十八 8	水1 Water 庚辰 Metal Dragon Unity 地天泰 2 **22** 十九 9	木3 Wood 辛巳 Metal Snake Great Reward 火天大有 3 **23** 二十 7	火2 Fire 壬午 Water Horse Wind 巽爲風 4 **24** 廿一 1	金4 Metal 癸未 Water Goat Trap 澤水困 5 **25** 廿二 8	木3 Wood 甲申 Wood Monkey Not Yet Accomplished 火水未濟 6 **26** 廿三 9	金9 Metal 乙酉 Wood Rooster Retreat 天山遯 7 **27** 廿四 4
水6 Water 丙戌 Fire Dog Mountain 艮爲山 8 **28** 廿五 1	木8 Wood 丁亥 Fire Pig Delight 雷地豫 9 **29** 廿六 8	火7 Fire 戊子 Earth Rat Beginning 水雷屯 1 **30** 廿七 4	金9 Metal 己丑 Earth Ox Without Wrongdoing 天雷無妄 2 **31** 廿八 2			

JUNE 2000 壬午

Xuan Kong Element 玄空五行	巽爲風 Wind	Period Luck 卦運	Monthly Star 月星
Fire 火2		1	1

SUNDAY	MONDAY	TUESDAY	WEDNESDAY	THURSDAY	FRIDAY	SATURDAY
				木3 Wood 庚寅 Metal Tiger Fire 離爲火 3 **1** 廿九 1	火2 Fire 辛卯 Metal Rabbit Sincerity 風澤中孚 4 **2** 五月初一 3	水6 Water 壬辰 Water Dragon Big Livestock 山天大畜 5 **3** 初二 4
金4 Metal 癸巳 Water Snake Eliminating 澤天夬 6 **4** 初三 6	金9 Metal 甲午 Wood Horse Heaven 乾爲天 7 **5** 初四 1	火7 Fire 乙未 Wood Goat Well 水風井 8 **6** 初五 6	木8 Wood 丙申 Fire Monkey Relief 雷水解 9 **7** 初六 4	金4 Metal 丁酉 Fire Rooster Influence 澤山咸 1 **8** 初七 9	水1 Water 戊戌 Earth Dog Humility 地山謙 2 **9** 初八 6	火2 Fire 己亥 Earth Pig Observation 風地觀 3 **10** 初九 2
火2 Fire 庚子 Metal Rat Increasing 風雷益 4 **11** 初十 9	水1 Water 辛丑 Metal Ox Dimming Light 地火明夷 5 **12** 十一 3	金9 Metal 壬寅 Water Tiger Fellowship 天火同人 6 **13** 十二 7	木8 Wood 癸卯 Water Rabbit Marrying Maiden 雷澤歸妹 7 **14** 十三 7	木3 Wood 甲辰 Wood Dragon Opposition 火澤睽 8 **15** 十四 2	火7 Fire 乙巳 Wood Snake Waiting 水天需 9 **16** 十五 3	金4 Metal 丙午 Fire Horse Great Exceeding 澤風大過 1 **17** 十六 3
水6 Water 丁未 Fire Goat Poison 山風蠱 2 **18** 十七 7	火2 Fire 戊申 Earth Monkey Dispersing 風水渙 3 **19** 十八 6	木3 Wood 己酉 Earth Rooster Travelling 火山旅 4 **20** 十九 8	金9 Metal 庚戌 Metal Dog Stagnation 天地否 5 **21** 二十 9	火7 Fire 辛亥 Metal Pig Alliance 水地比 4 **22** 廿一 7	木8 Wood 壬子 Water Rat Thunder 震爲雷 3 **23** 廿二 1	水6 Water 癸丑 Water Ox Beauty 山火賁 2 **24** 廿三 8
火7 Fire 甲寅 Wood Tiger Accomplished 水火既濟 1 **25** 廿四 9	水1 Water 乙卯 Wood Rabbit Arriving 地澤臨 9 **26** 廿五 4	金4 Metal 丙辰 Fire Dragon Marsh 兌爲澤 8 **27** 廿六 1	火2 Fire 丁巳 Fire Snake Small Livestock 風天小畜 7 **28** 廿七 8	木3 Wood 戊午 Earth Horse The Cauldron 火風鼎 6 **29** 廿八 4	水1 Water 己未 Earth Goat Rising 地風升 5 **30** 廿九 2	

JULY 2000 癸未

Xuan Kong Element 玄空五行	澤水困 Trap	Period Luck 卦運	Monthly Star 月星
Metal 金4		8	9

SUNDAY	MONDAY	TUESDAY	WEDNESDAY	THURSDAY	FRIDAY	SATURDAY
金9 Metal 2 Without Wrongdoing 己丑 Earth Ox 天雷無妄 30 廿九 2	木3 Wood 1 Fire 庚寅 Metal Tiger 離爲火 31 七月初一 1					火7 Fire 4 Water 庚申 Metal Monkey 坎爲水 1 三十 1
木8 Wood 3 Lesser Exceeding 辛酉 Metal Rooster 雷山小過 2 六月初一 3	金4 Metal 2 Gathering 壬戌 Water Dog 澤地萃 3 初二 4	水6 Water 1 Peel 癸亥 Water Pig 山地剝 4 初三 6	水1 Water 9 Earth 甲子 Wood Rat 坤爲地 5 初四 1	木3 Wood 8 Biting 乙丑 Wood Ox 火雷噬嗑 6 初五 6	火2 Fire 7 Family 丙寅 Fire Tiger 風火家人 7 初六 4	水6 Water 6 Decreasing 丁卯 Fire Rabbit 山澤損 8 初七 9
金9 Metal 5 Tread 戊辰 Earth Dragon 天澤履 9 初八 6	木8 Wood 4 Great Strength 己巳 Earth Snake 雷天大壯 10 初九 2	木8 Wood 3 Consistency 庚午 Metal Horse 雷風恆 11 初十 9	金9 Metal 2 Litigation 辛未 Metal Goat 天水訟 12 十一 3	水1 Water 1 Officer 壬申 Water Monkey 地水師 13 十二 7	火2 Fire 9 Gradual Progress 癸酉 Water Rooster 風山漸 14 十三 7	火7 Fire 8 Obstruction 甲戌 Wood Dog 水山蹇 15 十四 2
木3 Wood 7 Advancement 乙亥 Wood Pig 火地晉 16 十五 3	水6 Water 6 Nourish 丙子 Fire Rat 山雷頤 17 十六 3	金4 Metal 5 Following 丁丑 Fire Ox 澤雷隨 18 十七 7	木8 Wood 4 Abundance 戊寅 Earth Tiger 雷火豐 19 十八 6	火7 Fire 3 Regulate 己卯 Earth Rabbit 水澤節 20 十九 8	水1 Water 2 Unity 庚辰 Metal Dragon 地天泰 21 二十 9	木3 Wood 1 Great Reward 辛巳 Metal Snake 火天大有 22 廿一 7
火2 Fire 9 Wind 壬午 Water Horse 巽爲風 23 廿二 1	金4 Metal 8 Trap 癸未 Water Goat 澤水困 24 廿三 8	木3 Wood 7 Not Yet Accomplished 甲申 Wood Monkey 火水未濟 25 廿四 9	金9 Metal 6 Retreat 乙酉 Wood Rooster 天山遯 26 廿五 4	水6 Water 5 Mountain 丙戌 Fire Dog 艮爲山 27 廿六 1	木8 Wood 4 Delight 丁亥 Fire Pig 雷地豫 28 廿七 8	火7 Fire 3 Beginning 戊子 Earth Rat 水雷屯 29 廿八 4

AUGUST 2000 甲申

Xuan Kong Element 玄空五行	火水未濟 Not Yet Accomplished	Period Luck 卦運	Monthly Star 月星
Wood 木3		9	8

SUNDAY	MONDAY	TUESDAY	WEDNESDAY	THURSDAY	FRIDAY	SATURDAY
		火2 Fire 9 Sincerity 辛卯 Metal Rabbit 風澤中孚 1 初二 3	水6 Water 8 Big Livestock 壬辰 Water Dragon 山天大畜 2 初三 4	金4 Metal 7 Eliminating 癸巳 Water Snake 澤天夬 3 初四 6	金9 Metal 6 Heaven 甲午 Wood Horse 乾爲天 4 初五 1	火7 Fire 5 Well 乙未 Wood Goat 水風井 5 初六 6
木8 Wood 4 Relief 丙申 Fire Monkey 雷水解 6 初七 4	金4 Metal 3 Influence 丁酉 Fire Rooster 澤山咸 7 初八 9	水1 Water 2 Humility 戊戌 Earth Dog 地山謙 8 初九 6	火2 Fire 1 Observation 己亥 Earth Pig 風地觀 9 初十 2	火2 Fire 9 Increasing 庚子 Metal Rat 風雷益 10 十一 9	水1 Water 8 Dimming Light 辛丑 Metal Ox 地火明夷 11 十二 3	金9 Metal 7 Fellowship 壬寅 Water Tiger 天火同人 12 十三 7
木8 Wood 6 Marrying Maiden 癸卯 Water Rabbit 雷澤歸妹 13 十四 7	木3 Wood 5 Opposition 甲辰 Wood Dragon 火澤睽 14 十五 2	火7 Fire 4 Waiting 乙巳 Wood Snake 水天需 15 十六 3	金4 Metal 3 Great Exceeding 丙午 Fire Horse 澤風大過 16 十七 3	水6 Water 2 Poison 丁未 Fire Goat 山風蠱 17 十八 7	火2 Fire 1 Dispersing 戊申 Earth Monkey 風水渙 18 十九 6	木3 Wood 9 Travelling 己酉 Earth Rooster 火山旅 19 二十 8
金9 Metal 8 Stagnation 庚戌 Metal Dog 天地否 20 廿一 9	火7 Fire 7 Alliance 辛亥 Metal Pig 水地比 21 廿二 7	木8 Wood 65 Thunder 壬子 Water Rat 震爲雷 22 廿三 1	水6 Water 8 Beauty 癸丑 Water Ox 山火賁 23 廿四 8	火7 Fire 4 Accomplished 甲寅 Wood Tiger 水火既濟 24 廿五 9	水1 Water 3 Arriving 乙卯 Wood Rabbit 地澤臨 25 廿六 4	金4 Metal 2 Marsh 丙辰 Fire Dragon 兌爲澤 26 廿七 1
火2 Fire 1 Small Livestock 丁巳 Fire Snake 風天小畜 27 廿八 8	木3 Wood 9 The Cauldron 戊午 Earth Horse 火風鼎 28 廿九 4	水1 Water 8 Rising 己未 Earth Goat 地風升 29 八月初一 2	火7 Fire 7 Water 庚申 Metal Monkey 坎爲水 30 初二 1	木8 Wood 6 Lesser Exceeding 辛酉 Metal Rooster 雷山小過 31 初三 3		

SEPTEMBER 2000 乙酉

Xuan Kong Element 玄空五行	天山遯 Retreat	Period Luck 卦運	Monthly Star 月星
Metal 金9		4	7

SUNDAY	MONDAY	TUESDAY	WEDNESDAY	THURSDAY	FRIDAY	SATURDAY
					1 金4 Metal [5] Gathering 澤地萃 壬戌 Water Dog 4 · 初四	**2** 水6 Water [4] Peel 山地剝 癸亥 Water Pig 6 · 初五
3 水1 Water [3] Earth 坤爲地 甲子 Wood Rat 1 · 初六	**4** 木3 Wood [2] Biting 火雷噬嗑 乙丑 Wood Ox 6 · 初七	**5** 火2 Fire [1] Family 風火家人 丙寅 Fire Tiger 4 · 初八	**6** 水6 Water [9] Decreasing 山澤損 丁卯 Fire Rabbit 9 · 初九	**7** 金9 Metal [8] Tread 天澤履 戊辰 Earth Dragon 6 · 初十	**8** 木8 Wood [7] Great Strength 雷天大壯 己巳 Earth Snake 2 · 十一	**9** 木8 Wood [6] Consistency 雷風恒 庚午 Metal Horse 9 · 十二
10 金9 Metal [5] Litigation 天水訟 辛未 Metal Goat 3 · 十三	**11** 水1 Water [4] Officer 地水師 壬申 Water Monkey 7 · 十四	**12** 火2 Fire [3] Gradual Progress 風山漸 癸酉 Water Rooster 7 · 十五	**13** 火7 Fire [2] Obstruction 水山蹇 甲戌 Wood Dog 2 · 十六	**14** 木3 Wood [1] Advancement 火地晉 乙亥 Wood Pig 3 · 十七	**15** 水6 Water [9] Nourish 山雷頤 丙子 Fire Rat 3 · 十八	**16** 金4 Metal [8] Following 澤雷隨 丁丑 Fire Ox 7 · 十九
17 木8 Wood [7] Abundance 雷火豐 戊寅 Earth Tiger 6 · 二十	**18** 火7 Fire [6] Regulate 水澤節 己卯 Earth Rabbit 8 · 廿一	**19** 水1 Water [5] Unity 地天泰 庚辰 Metal Dragon 9 · 廿二	**20** 木3 Wood [4] Great Reward 火天大有 辛巳 Metal Snake 7 · 廿三	**21** 火2 Fire [3] Wind 巽爲風 壬午 Water Horse 1 · 廿四	**22** 金4 Metal [2] Trap 澤水困 癸未 Water Goat 8 · 廿五	**23** 木3 Wood [1] Not Yet Accomplished 火水未濟 甲申 Wood Monkey 9 · 廿六
24 金9 Metal [9] Retreat 天山遯 乙酉 Wood Rooster 4 · 廿七	**25** 水6 Water [8] Mountain 艮爲山 丙戌 Fire Dog 1 · 廿八	**26** 木8 Wood [7] Delight 雷地豫 丁亥 Fire Pig 8 · 廿九	**27** 火7 Fire [6] Beginning 水雷屯 戊子 Earth Rat 4 · 三十	**28** 金9 Metal [5] Without Wrongdoing 天雷無妄 己丑 Earth Ox 2 · 九月初一	**29** 木3 Wood [4] Fire 離爲火 庚寅 Metal Tiger 1 · 初二	**30** 火2 Fire [3] Sincerity 風澤中孚 辛卯 Metal Rabbit 3 · 初三

OCTOBER 2000 丙戌

Xuan Kong Element 玄空五行	艮爲山 Mountain	Period Luck 卦運	Monthly Star 月星
Water 水6		1	6

SUNDAY	MONDAY	TUESDAY	WEDNESDAY	THURSDAY	FRIDAY	SATURDAY
1 水6 Water [2] Big Livestock 山天大畜 壬辰 Water Dragon 4 · 初四	**2** 金4 Metal [1] Eliminating 澤天夬 癸巳 Water Snake 6 · 初五	**3** 金9 Metal [9] Heaven 乾爲天 甲午 Wood Horse 1 · 初六	**4** 火7 Fire [8] Well 水風井 乙未 Wood Goat 6 · 初七	**5** 木8 Wood [7] Relief 雷水解 丙申 Fire Monkey 4 · 初八	**6** 金4 Metal [6] Influence 澤山咸 丁酉 Fire Rooster 9 · 初九	**7** 水1 Water [5] Humility 地山謙 戊戌 Earth Dog 6 · 初十
8 火2 Fire [4] Observation 風地觀 己亥 Earth Pig 2 · 十一	**9** 火2 Fire [3] Increasing 風雷益 庚子 Metal Rat 9 · 十二	**10** 水1 Water [2] Dimming Light 地火明夷 辛丑 Metal Ox 3 · 十三	**11** 金9 Metal [1] Fellowship 天火同人 壬寅 Water Tiger 7 · 十四	**12** 木8 Wood [9] Marrying Maiden 雷澤歸妹 癸卯 Water Rabbit 7 · 十五	**13** 木3 Wood [8] Opposition 火澤睽 甲辰 Wood Dragon 2 · 十六	**14** 火7 Fire [7] Waiting 水天需 乙巳 Wood Snake 3 · 十七
15 金4 Metal [6] Great Exceeding 澤風大過 丙午 Fire Horse 3 · 十八	**16** 水6 Water [5] Poison 山風蠱 丁未 Fire Goat 7 · 十九	**17** 火2 Fire [4] Dispersing 風水渙 戊申 Earth Monkey 6 · 二十	**18** 木3 Wood [3] Travelling 火山旅 己酉 Earth Rooster 8 · 廿一	**19** 金9 Metal [2] Stagnation 天地否 庚戌 Metal Dog 9 · 廿二	**20** 火7 Fire [1] Alliance 水地比 辛亥 Metal Pig 7 · 廿三	**21** 木8 Wood [9] Thunder 震爲雷 壬子 Water Rat 1 · 廿四
22 水6 Water [8] Beauty 山火賁 癸丑 Water Ox 8 · 廿五	**23** 火7 Fire [7] Accomplished 水火既濟 甲寅 Wood Tiger 9 · 廿六	**24** 水1 Water [6] Arriving 地澤臨 乙卯 Wood Rabbit 4 · 廿七	**25** 金4 Metal [5] Marsh 兑爲澤 丙辰 Fire Dragon 1 · 廿八	**26** 火2 Fire [4] Small Livestock 風天小畜 丁巳 Fire Snake 8 · 廿九	**27** 木3 Wood [3] The Cauldron 火風鼎 戊午 Earth Horse 4 · 十月初一	**28** 水1 Water [2] Rising 地風升 己未 Earth Goat 2 · 初二
29 火7 Fire [1] Water 坎爲水 庚申 Metal Monkey 1 · 初三	**30** 木8 Wood [9] Lesser Exceeding 雷山小過 辛酉 Metal Rooster 3 · 初四	**31** 金4 Metal [8] Gathering 澤地萃 壬戌 Water Dog 4 · 初五				

NOVEMBER 2000 丁亥

Xuan Kong Element 玄空五行	雷地豫 Delight	Period Luck 卦運	Monthly Star 月星
Wood 木8		8	5

SUNDAY	MONDAY	TUESDAY	WEDNESDAY	THURSDAY	FRIDAY	SATURDAY
			水6 Water 7 癸亥 Water Pig Peel 山地剝 1 初六 6	水1 Water 6 甲子 Wood Rat Earth 坤爲地 2 初七 1	木3 Wood 5 乙丑 Wood Ox Biting 火雷噬嗑 3 初八 6	火2 Fire 4 丙寅 Fire Tiger Family 風火家人 4 初九 4
水6 Water 3 丁卯 Fire Rabbit Decreasing 山澤損 5 初十 9	金9 Metal 2 戊辰 Earth Dragon Tread 天澤履 6 十一 6	木8 Wood 1 己巳 Earth Snake Great Strength 雷天大壯 7 十二 2	木8 Wood 9 庚午 Metal Horse Consistency 雷風恆 8 十三 9	金9 Metal 8 辛未 Metal Goat Litigation 天水訟 9 十四 3	水1 Water 7 壬申 Water Monkey Officer 地水師 10 十五 7	火2 Fire 6 癸酉 Water Rooster Gradual Progress 風山漸 11 十六 7
火7 Fire 5 甲戌 Wood Dog Obstruction 水山蹇 12 十七 2	木3 Wood 4 乙亥 Wood Pig Advancement 火地晉 13 十八 3	水6 Water 3 丙子 Fire Rat Nourish 山雷頤 14 十九 3	金4 Metal 2 丁丑 Fire Ox Following 澤雷隨 15 二十 7	木8 Wood 1 戊寅 Earth Tiger Abundance 雷火豐 16 廿一 6	火7 Fire 9 己卯 Earth Rabbit Regulate 水澤節 17 廿二 8	水1 Water 8 庚辰 Metal Dragon Unity 地天泰 18 廿三 9
木3 Wood 7 辛巳 Metal Snake Great Reward 火天大有 19 廿四 7	火2 Fire 6 壬午 Water Horse Wind 巽爲風 20 廿五 1	金4 Metal 5 癸未 Water Goat Trap 澤水困 21 廿六 8	木3 Wood 4 甲申 Wood Monkey Not Yet Accomplished 火水未濟 22 廿七 9	金9 Metal 3 乙酉 Wood Rooster Retreat 天山遯 23 廿八 4	水6 Water 2 丙戌 Fire Dog Mountain 艮爲山 24 廿九 1	木8 Wood 1 丁亥 Fire Pig Delight 雷地豫 25 三十 8
火7 Fire 9 戊子 Earth Rat Beginning 水雷屯 26 十一月初一 4	金9 Metal 8 己丑 Earth Ox Without Wrongdoing 天雷無妄 27 初二 2	木3 Wood 7 庚寅 Metal Tiger Fire 離爲火 28 初三 1	火2 Fire 6 辛卯 Metal Rabbit Sincerity 風澤中孚 29 初四 3	水6 Water 5 壬辰 Water Dragon Big Livestock 山天大畜 30 初五 4		

DECEMBER 2000 戊子

Xuan Kong Element 玄空五行	水雷屯 Beginning	Period Luck 卦運	Monthly Star 月星
Fire 火7		4	4

SUNDAY	MONDAY	TUESDAY	WEDNESDAY	THURSDAY	FRIDAY	SATURDAY
水6 Water 9 癸亥 Water Pig Peel 山地剝 31 初六 6					金4 Metal 4 癸巳 Water Snake Eliminating 澤天夬 1 初六 6	金9 Metal 3 甲午 Wood Horse Heaven 乾爲天 2 初七 1
火7 Fire 2 乙未 Wood Goat Well 水風井 3 初八 6	木8 Wood 1 丙申 Fire Monkey Relief 雷水解 4 初九 4	金4 Metal 9 丁酉 Fire Rooster Influence 澤山咸 5 初十 9	水1 Water 8 戊戌 Earth Dog Humility 地山謙 6 十一 6	火2 Fire 7 己亥 Earth Pig Observation 風地觀 7 十二 2	火2 Fire 6 庚子 Metal Rat Increasing 風雷益 8 十三 9	水1 Water 5 辛丑 Metal Ox Dimming Light 地火明夷 9 十四 3
金9 Metal 4 壬寅 Water Tiger Fellowship 天火同人 10 十五 7	木8 Wood 3 癸卯 Water Rabbit Marrying Maiden 雷澤歸妹 11 十六 7	木3 Wood 2 甲辰 Wood Dragon Opposition 火澤睽 12 十七 2	火7 Fire 1 乙巳 Wood Snake Waiting 水天需 13 十八 3	金4 Metal 9 丙午 Fire Horse Great Exceeding 澤風大過 14 十九 3	水6 Water 8 丁未 Fire Goat Poison 山風蠱 15 二十 7	火2 Fire 7 戊申 Earth Monkey Dispersing 風水渙 16 廿一 6
木3 Wood 6 己酉 Earth Rooster Travelling 火山旅 17 廿二 8	金9 Metal 5 庚戌 Metal Dog Stagnation 天地否 18 廿三 9	火7 Fire 4 辛亥 Metal Pig Alliance 水地比 19 廿四 7	木8 Wood 3 壬子 Water Rat Thunder 震爲雷 20 廿五 1	水6 Water 2/8 癸丑 Water Ox Beauty 山火賁 21 廿六 8	火7 Fire 9 甲寅 Wood Tiger Accomplished 水火既濟 22 廿七 9	水1 Water 1 乙卯 Wood Rabbit Arriving 地澤臨 23 廿八 4
金4 Metal 2 丙辰 Fire Dragon Marsh 兌爲澤 24 廿九 1	火2 Fire 3 丁巳 Fire Snake Small Livestock 風天小畜 25 三十 8	木3 Wood 4 戊午 Earth Horse The Cauldron 火風鼎 26 十二月初一 4	水1 Water 5 己未 Earth Goat Rising 地風升 27 初二 2	火7 Fire 6 庚申 Metal Monkey Water 坎爲水 28 初三 1	木8 Wood 7 辛酉 Metal Rooster Lesser Exceeding 雷山小過 29 初四 3	金4 Metal 8 壬戌 Water Dog Gathering 澤地萃 30 初五 4

2001 辛巳

(*Xin Si*) Metal Snake

2001 辛巳 *(Xin Si)* Metal Snake

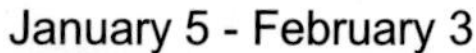

January 5 - February 3

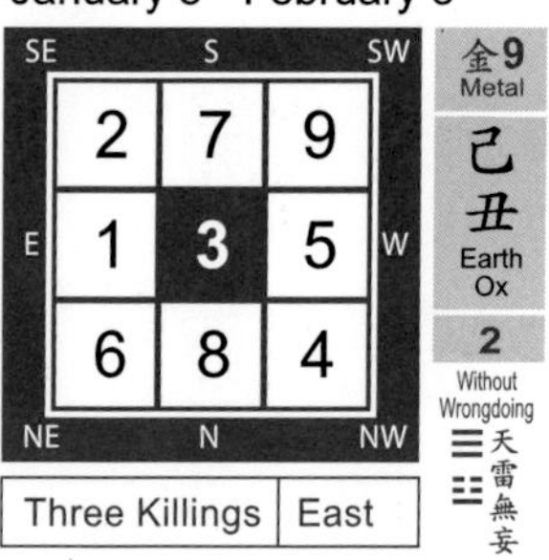

SE	S	SW
2	7	9
1	3	5
6	8	4
NE	N	NW

金9 Metal · 己丑 Earth Ox · 2 Without Wrongdoing · 天雷無妄

Three Killings | East

February 4 - March 4

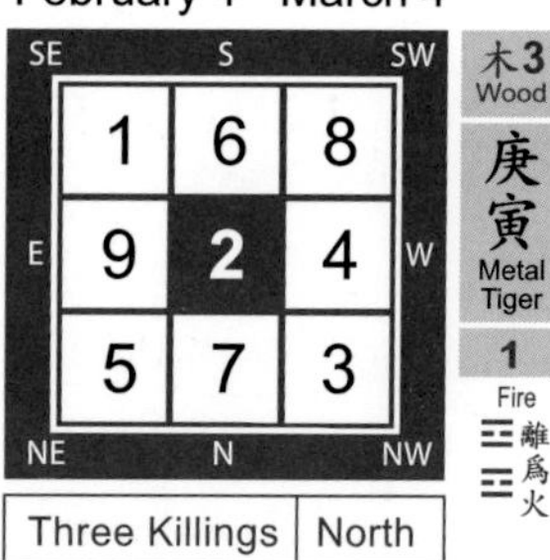

SE	S	SW
1	6	8
9	2	4
5	7	3
NE	N	NW

木3 Wood · 庚寅 Metal Tiger · 1 Fire · 離爲火

Three Killings | North

March 5 - April 4

SE	S	SW
9	5	7
8	1	3
4	6	2
NE	N	NW

火2 Fire · 辛卯 Metal Rabbit · 3 Sincerity · 風澤中孚

Three Killings | West

April 5 - May 4

SE	S	SW
8	4	6
7	9	2
3	5	1
NE	N	NW

水6 Water · 壬辰 Water Dragon · 4 Big Livestock · 山天大畜

Three Killings | South

May 5 - June 4

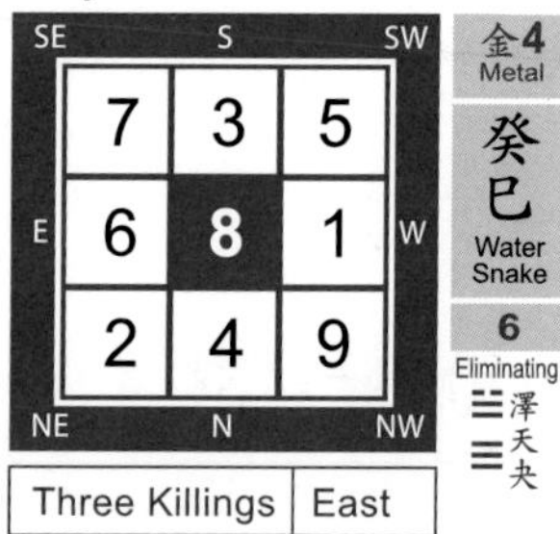

SE	S	SW
7	3	5
6	8	1
2	4	9
NE	N	NW

金4 Metal · 癸巳 Water Snake · 6 Eliminating · 澤天夬

Three Killings | East

June 5 - July 6

SE	S	SW
6	2	4
5	7	9
1	3	8
NE	N	NW

金9 Metal · 甲午 Wood Horse · 1 Heaven · 乾爲天

Three Killings | North

July 7 - August 6

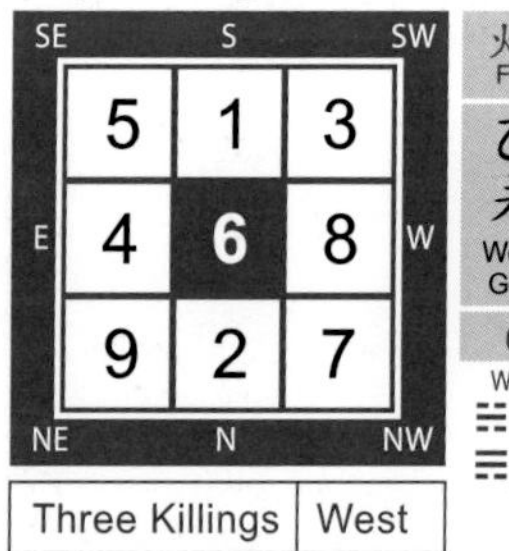

SE	S	SW
5	1	3
4	6	8
9	2	7
NE	N	NW

火7 Fire · 乙未 Wood Goat · 6 Well · 水風井

Three Killings | West

August 7 - September 6

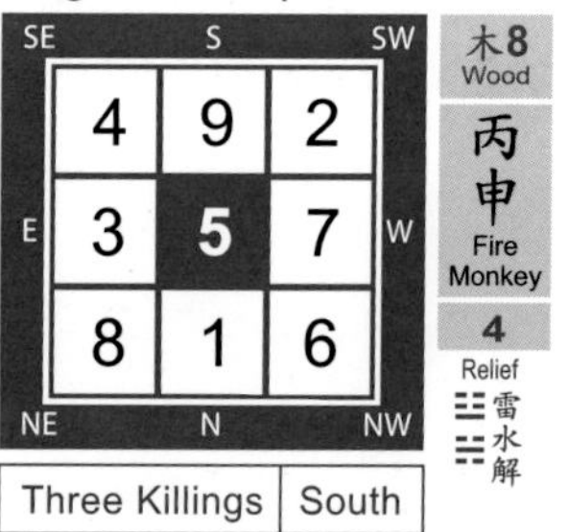

SE	S	SW
4	9	2
3	5	7
8	1	6
NE	N	NW

木8 Wood · 丙申 Fire Monkey · 4 Relief · 雷水解

Three Killings | South

September 7 - October 7

SE	S	SW
3	8	1
2	4	6
7	9	5
NE	N	NW

金4 Metal · 丁酉 Fire Rooster · 9 Influence · 澤山咸

Three Killings | East

October 8 - November 6

SE	S	SW
2	7	9
1	3	5
6	8	4
NE	N	NW

水1 Water · 戊戌 Earth Dog · 6 Humility · 地山謙

Three Killings | North

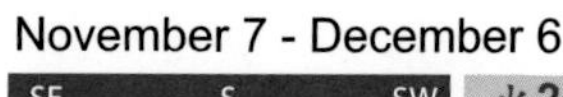

November 7 - December 6

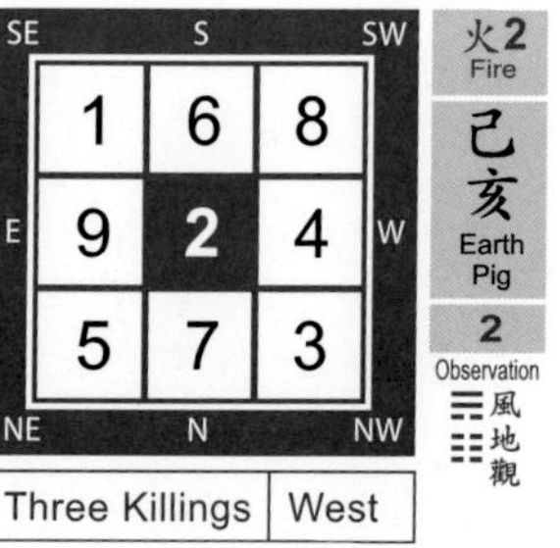

SE	S	SW
1	6	8
9	2	4
5	7	3
NE	N	NW

火2 Fire · 己亥 Earth Pig · 2 Observation · 風地觀

Three Killings | West

December 7 - January 4

SE	S	SW
9	5	7
8	1	3
4	6	2
NE	N	NW

火2 Fire · 庚子 Metal Rat · 9 Increasing · 風雷益

Three Killings | South

JANUARY 2001 己丑

Xuan Kong Element 玄空五行	天雷無妄 Without Wrongdoing	Period Luck 卦運	Monthly Star 月星
Metal 金9		2	3

SUNDAY	MONDAY	TUESDAY	WEDNESDAY	THURSDAY	FRIDAY	SATURDAY
	水1 Water 1 Earth 甲子 Wood Rat 坤為地 1 初七 1	木3 Wood 2 Biting 乙丑 Wood Ox 火雷噬嗑 2 初八 6	火2 Fire 3 Family 丙寅 Fire Tiger 風火家人 3 初九 4	水6 Water 4 Decreasing 丁卯 Fire Rabbit 山澤損 4 初十 9	金9 Metal 5 Tread 戊辰 Earth Dragon 天澤履 5 十一 6	木8 Wood 6 Great Strength 己巳 Earth Snake 雷天大壯 6 十二 2
木8 Wood 7 Consistency 庚午 Metal Horse 雷風恒 7 十三 9	金9 Metal 8 Litigation 辛未 Metal Goat 天水訟 8 十四 3	水1 Water 9 Officer 壬申 Water Monkey 地水師 9 十五 7	火2 Fire 1 Gradual Progress 癸酉 Water Rooster 風山漸 10 十六 7	火7 Fire 2 Obstruction 甲戌 Wood Dog 水山蹇 11 十七 2	木3 Wood 3 Advancement 乙亥 Wood Pig 火地晉 12 十八 3	水6 Water 4 Nourish 丙子 Fire Rat 山雷頤 13 十九 3
金4 Metal 5 Following 丁丑 Fire Ox 澤雷隨 14 二十 7	木8 Wood 6 Abundance 戊寅 Earth Tiger 雷火豐 15 廿一 6	火7 Fire 7 Regulate 己卯 Earth Rabbit 水澤節 16 廿二 8	水1 Water 8 Unity 庚辰 Metal Dragon 地天泰 17 廿三 9	木3 Wood 9 Great Reward 辛巳 Metal Snake 火天大有 18 廿四 7	火2 Fire 1 Wind 壬午 Water Horse 巽為風 19 廿五 1	金4 Metal 2 Trap 癸未 Water Goat 澤水困 20 廿六 8
木3 Wood 3 Not Yet Accomplished 甲申 Wood Monkey 火水未濟 21 廿七 9	金9 Metal 4 Retreat 乙酉 Wood Rooster 天山遯 22 廿八 4	水6 Water 5 Mountain 丙戌 Fire Dog 艮為山 23 廿九 1	木8 Wood 6 Delight 丁亥 Fire Pig 雷地豫 24 正月初一 8	火7 Fire 7 Beginning 戊子 Earth Rat 水雷屯 25 初二 4	金9 Metal 8 Without Wrongdoing 己丑 Earth Ox 天雷無妄 26 初三 2	木3 Wood 9 Fire 庚寅 Metal Tiger 離為火 27 初四 1
火2 Fire 1 Sincerity 辛卯 Metal Rabbit 風澤中孚 28 初五 3	水6 Water 2 Big Livestock 壬辰 Water Dragon 山天大畜 29 初六 4	金4 Metal 3 Eliminating 癸巳 Water Snake 澤天夬 30 初七 6	金9 Metal 4 Heaven 甲午 Wood Horse 乾為天 31 初八 1			

FEBRUARY 2001 庚寅

Xuan Kong Element 玄空五行	離為火 Fire	Period Luck 卦運	Monthly Star 月星
Wood 木3		1	2

SUNDAY	MONDAY	TUESDAY	WEDNESDAY	THURSDAY	FRIDAY	SATURDAY
				火7 Fire 5 Well 乙未 Wood Goat 水風井 1 初九 6	木8 Wood 6 Relief 丙申 Fire Monkey 雷水解 2 初十 4	金4 Metal 7 Influence 丁酉 Fire Rooster 澤山咸 3 十一 9
水1 Water 8 Humility 戊戌 Earth Dog 地山謙 4 十二 6	火2 Fire 9 Observation 己亥 Earth Pig 風地觀 5 十三 2	火2 Fire 1 Increasing 庚子 Metal Rat 風雷益 6 十四 9	水1 Water 2 Dimming Light 辛丑 Metal Ox 地火明夷 7 十五 3	金9 Metal 3 Fellowship 壬寅 Water Tiger 天火同人 8 十六 7	木8 Wood 4 Marrying Maiden 癸卯 Water Rabbit 雷澤歸妹 9 十七 7	木3 Wood 5 Opposition 甲辰 Wood Dragon 火澤睽 10 十八 2
火7 Fire 6 Waiting 乙巳 Wood Snake 水天需 11 十九 3	金4 Metal 7 Great Exceeding 丙午 Fire Horse 澤風大過 12 二十 3	水6 Water 8 Poison 丁未 Fire Goat 山風蠱 13 廿一 7	火2 Fire 9 Dispersing 戊申 Earth Monkey 風水渙 14 廿二 6	木3 Wood 1 Travelling 己酉 Earth Rooster 火山旅 15 廿三 8	金9 Metal 2 Stagnation 庚戌 Metal Dog 天地否 16 廿四 9	火7 Fire 3 Alliance 辛亥 Metal Pig 水地比 17 廿五 7
木8 Wood 4 Thunder 壬子 Water Rat 震為雷 18 廿六 1	水6 Water 5 Beauty 癸丑 Water Ox 山火賁 19 廿七 8	火7 Fire 6 Accomplished 甲寅 Wood Tiger 水火既濟 20 廿八 9	水1 Water 7 Arriving 乙卯 Wood Rabbit 地澤臨 21 廿九 4	金4 Metal 8 Marsh 丙辰 Fire Dragon 兌為澤 22 三十 1	火2 Fire 9 Small Livestock 丁巳 Fire Snake 風天小畜 23 二月初一 8	木3 Wood 1 The Cauldron 戊午 Earth Horse 火風鼎 24 初二 4
水1 Water 2 Rising 己未 Earth Goat 地風升 25 初三 2	火7 Fire 3 Water 庚申 Metal Monkey 坎為水 26 初四 1	木8 Wood 4 Lesser Exceeding 辛酉 Metal Rooster 雷山小過 27 初五 3	金4 Metal 5 Gathering 壬戌 Water Dog 澤地萃 28 初六 4			

MARCH 2001 辛卯

Xuan Kong Element 玄空五行	風澤中孚 Sincerity	Period Luck 卦運	Monthly Star 月星
Fire 火2		3	1

SUNDAY	MONDAY	TUESDAY	WEDNESDAY	THURSDAY	FRIDAY	SATURDAY
				水6 Water Peel 山地剝 癸亥 Water Pig 6 · 6 1 初七	水1 Water Earth 坤爲地 甲子 Wood Rat 1 · 7 2 初八	木3 Wood Biting 火雷噬嗑 乙丑 Wood Ox 6 · 8 3 初九
火2 Fire Family 風火家人 丙寅 Fire Tiger 4 · 9 4 初十	水6 Water Decreasing 山澤損 丁卯 Fire Rabbit 9 · 1 5 十一	金9 Metal Tread 天澤履 戊辰 Earth Dragon 6 · 2 6 十二	木8 Wood Great Strength 雷天大壯 己巳 Earth Snake 2 · 3 7 十三	木8 Wood Consistency 雷風恒 庚午 Metal Horse 9 · 4 8 十四	金9 Metal Litigation 天水訟 辛未 Metal Goat 3 · 5 9 十五	水1 Water Officer 地水師 壬申 Water Monkey 7 · 6 10 十六
火2 Fire Gradual Progress 風山漸 癸酉 Water Rooster 7 · 7 11 十七	火7 Fire Obstruction 水山蹇 甲戌 Wood Dog 2 · 8 12 十八	木3 Wood Advancement 火地晉 乙亥 Wood Pig 3 · 9 13 十九	水6 Water Nourish 山雷頤 丙子 Fire Rat 3 · 1 14 二十	金4 Metal Following 澤雷隨 丁丑 Fire Ox 7 · 2 15 廿一	木8 Wood Abundance 雷火豐 戊寅 Earth Tiger 6 · 3 16 廿二	火7 Fire Regulate 水澤節 己卯 Earth Rabbit 8 · 4 17 廿三
水1 Water Unity 地天泰 庚辰 Metal Dragon 9 · 5 18 廿四	木3 Wood Great Reward 火天大有 辛巳 Metal Snake 7 · 6 19 廿五	火2 Fire Wind 巽爲風 壬午 Water Horse 1 · 7 20 廿六	金4 Metal Trap 澤水困 癸未 Water Goat 8 · 8 21 廿七	木3 Wood Not Yet Accomplished 火水未濟 甲申 Wood Monkey 9 · 9 22 廿八	金9 Metal Retreat 天山遯 乙酉 Wood Rooster 4 · 1 23 廿九	水6 Water Mountain 艮爲山 丙戌 Fire Dog 1 · 2 24 三十
木8 Wood Delight 雷地豫 丁亥 Fire Pig 8 · 3 25 三月初一	火7 Fire Beginning 水雷屯 戊子 Earth Rat 4 · 4 26 初二	金9 Metal Without Wrongdoing 天雷無妄 己丑 Earth Ox 2 · 5 27 初三	木3 Wood Fire 離爲火 庚寅 Metal Tiger 1 · 6 28 初四	火2 Fire Sincerity 風澤中孚 辛卯 Metal Rabbit 3 · 7 29 初五	水6 Water Big Livestock 山天大畜 壬辰 Water Dragon 4 · 8 30 初六	金4 Metal Eliminating 澤天夬 癸巳 Water Snake 6 · 9 31 初七

APRIL 2001 壬辰

Xuan Kong Element 玄空五行	山天大畜 Big Livestock	Period Luck 卦運	Monthly Star 月星
Water 水6		4	9

SUNDAY	MONDAY	TUESDAY	WEDNESDAY	THURSDAY	FRIDAY	SATURDAY
金9 Metal Heaven 乾爲天 甲午 Wood Horse 1 · 1 1 初八	火7 Fire Well 水風井 乙未 Wood Goat 6 · 2 2 初九	木8 Wood Relief 雷水解 丙申 Fire Monkey 4 · 3 3 初十	金4 Metal Influence 澤山咸 丁酉 Fire Rooster 9 · 4 4 十一	水1 Water Humility 地山謙 戊戌 Earth Dog 6 · 5 5 十二	火2 Fire Observation 風地觀 己亥 Earth Pig 2 · 6 6 十三	火2 Fire Increasing 風雷益 庚子 Metal Rat 9 · 7 7 十四
水1 Water Dimming Light 地火明夷 辛丑 Metal Ox 3 · 8 8 十五	金9 Metal Fellowship 天火同人 壬寅 Water Tiger 7 · 9 9 十六	木8 Wood Marrying Maiden 雷澤歸妹 癸卯 Water Rabbit 7 · 1 10 十七	木3 Wood Opposition 火澤睽 甲辰 Wood Dragon 2 · 2 11 十八	火7 Fire Waiting 水天需 乙巳 Wood Snake 3 · 3 12 十九	金4 Metal Great Exceeding 澤風大過 丙午 Fire Horse 3 · 4 13 二十	水6 Water Poison 山風蠱 丁未 Fire Goat 7 · 5 14 廿一
火2 Fire Dispersing 風水渙 戊申 Earth Monkey 6 · 6 15 廿二	木3 Wood Travelling 火山旅 己酉 Earth Rooster 8 · 7 16 廿三	金9 Metal Stagnation 天地否 庚戌 Metal Dog 9 · 8 17 廿四	火7 Fire Alliance 水地比 辛亥 Metal Pig 7 · 9 18 廿五	木8 Wood Thunder 震爲雷 壬子 Water Rat 1 · 1 19 廿六	水6 Water Beauty 山火賁 癸丑 Water Ox 8 · 2 20 廿七	火7 Fire Accomplished 水火既濟 甲寅 Wood Tiger 9 · 3 21 廿八
水1 Water Arriving 地澤臨 乙卯 Wood Rabbit 4 · 4 22 廿九	金4 Metal Marsh 兑爲澤 丙辰 Fire Dragon 1 · 5 23 四月初一	火2 Fire Small Livestock 風天小畜 丁巳 Fire Snake 8 · 6 24 初二	木3 Wood The Cauldron 火風鼎 戊午 Earth Horse 4 · 7 25 初三	水1 Water Rising 地風升 己未 Earth Goat 2 · 8 26 初四	火7 Fire Water 坎爲水 庚申 Metal Monkey 1 · 9 27 初五	木8 Wood Lesser Exceeding 雷山小過 辛酉 Metal Rooster 3 · 1 28 初六
金4 Metal Gathering 澤地萃 壬戌 Water Dog 4 · 2 29 初七	水6 Water Peel 山地剝 癸亥 Water Pig 6 · 3 30 初八					

MAY 2001 癸巳

Xuan Kong Element 玄空五行	澤天夬 Eliminating	Period Luck 卦運	Monthly Star 月星
Metal 金4		6	8

SUNDAY	MONDAY	TUESDAY	WEDNESDAY	THURSDAY	FRIDAY	SATURDAY
		1 初九 水1 Water 甲子 Wood Rat 1 Earth 坤爲地 4	2 初十 木3 Wood 乙丑 Wood Ox 6 Biting 火雷噬嗑 5	3 十一 火2 Fire 丙寅 Fire Tiger 4 Family 風火家人 6	4 十二 水6 Water 丁卯 Fire Rabbit 9 Decreasing 山澤損 7	5 十三 金9 Metal 戊辰 Earth Dragon 6 Tread 天澤履 8
6 十四 木8 Wood 己巳 Earth Snake 2 Great Strength 雷天大壯 9	7 十五 木8 Wood 庚午 Metal Horse 9 Consistency 雷風恆 1	8 十六 金9 Metal 辛未 Metal Goat 3 Litigation 天水訟 2	9 十七 水1 Water 壬申 Water Monkey 7 Officer 地水師 3	10 十八 火2 Fire 癸酉 Water Rooster 7 Gradual Progress 風山漸 4	11 十九 火7 Fire 甲戌 Wood Dog 2 Obstruction 水山蹇 5	12 二十 木3 Wood 乙亥 Wood Pig 3 Advancement 火地晉 6
13 廿一 水6 Water 丙子 Fire Rat 3 Nourish 山雷頤 7	14 廿二 金4 Metal 丁丑 Fire Ox 7 Following 澤雷隨 8	15 廿三 木8 Wood 戊寅 Earth Tiger 6 Abundance 雷火豐 9	16 廿四 火7 Fire 己卯 Earth Rabbit 8 Regulate 水澤節 1	17 廿五 水1 Water 庚辰 Metal Dragon 9 Unity 地天泰 2	18 廿六 木3 Wood 辛巳 Metal Snake 7 Great Reward 火天大有 3	19 廿七 火2 Fire 壬午 Water Horse 1 Wind 巽爲風 4
20 廿八 金4 Metal 癸未 Water Goat 8 Trap 澤水困 5	21 廿九 木3 Wood 甲申 Wood Monkey 9 Not Yet Accomplished 火水未濟 6	22 三十 金9 Metal 乙酉 Wood Rooster 4 Retreat 天山遯 7	23 閏四月初一 水6 Water 丙戌 Fire Dog 1 Mountain 艮爲山 8	24 初二 木8 Wood 丁亥 Fire Pig 8 Delight 雷地豫 9	25 初三 火7 Fire 戊子 Earth Rat 4 Beginning 水雷屯 1	26 初四 金9 Metal 己丑 Earth Ox 2 Without Wrongdoing 天雷無妄 2
27 初五 木3 Wood 庚寅 Metal Tiger 1 Fire 離爲火 3	28 初六 火2 Fire 辛卯 Metal Rabbit 3 Sincerity 風澤中孚 4	29 初七 水6 Water 壬辰 Water Dragon 4 Big Livestock 山天大畜 5	30 初八 金4 Metal 癸巳 Water Snake 6 Eliminating 澤天夬 6	31 初九 金9 Metal 甲午 Wood Horse 1 Heaven 乾爲天 7		

JUNE 2001 甲午

Xuan Kong Element 玄空五行	乾爲天 Heaven	Period Luck 卦運	Monthly Star 月星
Metal 金9		1	7

SUNDAY	MONDAY	TUESDAY	WEDNESDAY	THURSDAY	FRIDAY	SATURDAY
					1 初十 火7 Fire 乙未 Wood Goat 6 Well 水風井 8	2 十一 木8 Wood 丙申 Fire Monkey 4 Relief 雷水解 9
3 十二 金4 Metal 丁酉 Fire Rooster 9 Influence 澤山咸 1	4 十三 水1 Water 戊戌 Earth Dog 6 Humility 地山謙 2	5 十四 火2 Fire 己亥 Earth Pig 2 Observation 風地觀 3	6 十五 火2 Fire 庚子 Metal Rat 9 Increasing 風雷益 4	7 十六 水1 Water 辛丑 Metal Ox 3 Dimming Light 地火明夷 5	8 十七 金9 Metal 壬寅 Water Tiger 7 Fellowship 天火同人 6	9 十八 木8 Wood 癸卯 Water Rabbit 7 Marrying Maiden 雷澤歸妹 7
10 十九 木3 Wood 甲辰 Wood Dragon 2 Opposition 火澤睽 8	11 二十 火7 Fire 乙巳 Wood Snake 3 Waiting 水天需 9	12 廿一 金4 Metal 丙午 Fire Horse 3 Great Exceeding 澤風大過 1	13 廿二 水6 Water 丁未 Fire Goat 7 Poison 山風蠱 2	14 廿三 火2 Fire 戊申 Earth Monkey 6 Dispersing 風水渙 3	15 廿四 木3 Wood 己酉 Earth Rooster 8 Travelling 火山旅 4	16 廿五 金9 Metal 庚戌 Metal Dog 9 Stagnation 天地否 5
17 廿六 火7 Fire 辛亥 Metal Pig 7 Alliance 水地比 6	18 廿七 木8 Wood 壬子 Water Rat 1 Thunder 震爲雷 7	19 廿八 水6 Water 癸丑 Water Ox 8 Beauty 山火賁 8	20 廿九 火7 Fire 甲寅 Wood Tiger 9 Accomplished 水火既濟 9	21 五月初一 水1 Water 乙卯 Wood Rabbit 4 Arriving 地澤臨 1/9	22 初二 金4 Metal 丙辰 Fire Dragon 1 Marsh 兌爲澤 8	23 初三 火2 Fire 丁巳 Fire Snake 8 Small Livestock 風天小畜 7
24 初四 木3 Wood 戊午 Earth Horse 4 The Cauldron 火風鼎 6	25 初五 水1 Water 己未 Earth Goat 2 Rising 地風升 5	26 初六 火7 Fire 庚申 Metal Monkey 1 Water 坎爲水 4	27 初七 木8 Wood 辛酉 Metal Rooster 3 Lesser Exceeding 雷山小過 3	28 初八 金4 Metal 壬戌 Water Dog 4 Gathering 澤地萃 2	29 初九 水6 Water 癸亥 Water Pig 6 Peel 山地剝 1	30 初十 水1 Water 甲子 Wood Rat 1 Earth 坤爲地 9

JULY 2001 乙未

Xuan Kong Element 玄空五行	水風井 Well	Period Luck 卦運	Monthly Star 月星
Fire 火7		6	6

SUNDAY	MONDAY	TUESDAY	WEDNESDAY	THURSDAY	FRIDAY	SATURDAY
木3 Wood 8 Biting 火雷噬嗑 乙丑 Wood Ox **1** 十一 6	火2 Fire 7 Family 風火家人 丙寅 Fire Tiger **2** 十二 4	水6 Water 6 Decreasing 山澤損 丁卯 Fire Rabbit **3** 十三 9	金9 Metal 5 Tread 天澤履 戊辰 Earth Dragon **4** 十四 6	木8 Wood 4 Great Strength 雷天大壯 己巳 Earth Snake **5** 十五 2	木8 Wood 3 Consistency 雷風恆 庚午 Metal Horse **6** 十六 9	金9 Metal 2 Litigation 天水訟 辛未 Metal Goat **7** 十七 3
水1 Water 1 Officer 地水師 壬申 Water Monkey **8** 十八 7	火2 Fire 9 Gradual Progress 風山漸 癸酉 Water Rooster **9** 十九 2	火7 Fire 8 Obstruction 水山蹇 甲戌 Wood Dog **10** 二十 2	木3 Wood 7 Advancement 火地晉 乙亥 Wood Pig **11** 廿一 3	水6 Water 6 Nourish 山雷頤 丙子 Fire Rat **12** 廿二 3	金4 Metal 5 Following 澤雷隨 丁丑 Fire Ox **13** 廿三 7	木8 Wood 4 Abundance 雷火豐 戊寅 Earth Tiger **14** 廿四 6
火7 Fire 3 Regulate 水澤節 己卯 Earth Rabbit **15** 廿五 8	水1 Water 2 Unity 地天泰 庚辰 Metal Dragon **16** 廿六 9	木3 Wood 1 Great Reward 火天大有 辛巳 Metal Snake **17** 廿七 7	火2 Fire 9 Wind 巽爲風 壬午 Water Horse **18** 廿八 1	金4 Metal 8 Trap 澤水困 癸未 Water Goat **19** 廿九 8	木3 Wood 7 Not Yet Accomplished 火水未濟 甲申 Wood Monkey **20** 三十 9	金9 Metal 6 Retreat 天山遯 乙酉 Wood Rooster **21** 六月初一 4
水6 Water 5 Mountain 艮爲山 丙戌 Fire Dog **22** 初二 1	木8 Wood 4 Delight 雷地豫 丁亥 Fire Pig **23** 初三 8	火7 Fire 3 Beginning 水雷屯 戊子 Earth Rat **24** 初四 4	金9 Metal 2 Without Wrongdoing 天雷無妄 己丑 Earth Ox **25** 初五 2	木3 Wood 1 Fire 離爲火 庚寅 Metal Tiger **26** 初六 1	火2 Fire 9 Sincerity 風澤中孚 辛卯 Metal Rabbit **27** 初七 3	水6 Water 8 Big Livestock 山天大畜 壬辰 Water Dragon **28** 初八 4
金4 Metal 7 Eliminating 澤天夬 癸巳 Water Snake **29** 初九 6	金9 Metal 6 Heaven 乾爲天 甲午 Wood Horse **30** 初十 1	火7 Fire 5 Well 水風井 乙未 Wood Goat **31** 十一 6				

AUGUST 2001 丙申

Xuan Kong Element 玄空五行	雷水解 Relief	Period Luck 卦運	Monthly Star 月星
Wood 木8		4	5

SUNDAY	MONDAY	TUESDAY	WEDNESDAY	THURSDAY	FRIDAY	SATURDAY
			木8 Wood 4 Relief 雷水解 丙申 Fire Monkey **1** 十二 4	金4 Metal 3 Influence 澤山咸 丁酉 Fire Rooster **2** 十三 9	水1 Water 2 Humility 地山謙 戊戌 Earth Dog **3** 十四 6	火2 Fire 1 Observation 風地觀 己亥 Earth Pig **4** 十五 2
火2 Fire 9 Increasing 風雷益 庚子 Metal Rat **5** 十六 9	水1 Water 8 Dimming Light 地火明夷 辛丑 Metal Ox **6** 十七 3	金9 Metal 7 Fellowship 天火同人 壬寅 Water Tiger **7** 十八 7	木8 Wood 6 Marrying Maiden 雷澤歸妹 癸卯 Water Rabbit **8** 十九 7	木3 Wood 5 Opposition 火澤睽 甲辰 Wood Dragon **9** 二十 2	火7 Fire 4 Waiting 水天需 乙巳 Wood Snake **10** 廿一 3	金4 Metal 3 Great Exceeding 澤風大過 丙午 Fire Horse **11** 廿二 3
水6 Water 2 Poison 山風蠱 丁未 Fire Goat **12** 廿三 7	火2 Fire 1 Dispersing 風水渙 戊申 Earth Monkey **13** 廿四 6	木3 Wood 9 Travelling 火山旅 己酉 Earth Rooster **14** 廿五 8	金9 Metal 8 Stagnation 天地否 庚戌 Metal Dog **15** 廿六 9	火7 Fire 7 Alliance 水地比 辛亥 Metal Pig **16** 廿七 7	木8 Wood 6 Thunder 震爲雷 壬子 Water Rat **17** 廿八 1	水6 Water 5 Beauty 山火賁 癸丑 Water Ox **18** 廿九 8
火7 Fire 4 Accomplished 水火既濟 甲寅 Wood Tiger **19** 七月初一 9	水1 Water 3 Arriving 地澤臨 乙卯 Wood Rabbit **20** 初二 4	金4 Metal 2 Marsh 兌爲澤 丙辰 Fire Dragon **21** 初三 1	火2 Fire 1 Small Livestock 風天小畜 丁巳 Fire Snake **22** 初四 8	木3 Wood 9 The Cauldron 火風鼎 戊午 Earth Horse **23** 初五 4	水1 Water 8 Rising 地風升 己未 Earth Goat **24** 初六 2	火7 Fire 7 Water 坎爲水 庚申 Metal Monkey **25** 初七 1
木8 Wood 6 Lesser Exceeding 雷山小過 辛酉 Metal Rooster **26** 初八 3	金4 Metal 5 Gathering 澤地萃 壬戌 Water Dog **27** 初九 4	水6 Water 4 Peel 山地剝 癸亥 Water Pig **28** 初十 6	水1 Water 3 Earth 坤爲地 甲子 Wood Rat **29** 十一 1	木3 Wood 2 Biting 火雷噬嗑 乙丑 Wood Ox **30** 十二 6	火2 Fire 1 Family 風火家人 丙寅 Fire Tiger **31** 十三 4	

SEPTEMBER 2001 丁酉

Xuan Kong Element 玄空五行	澤山咸 Influence	Period Luck 卦運	Monthly Star 月星
Metal 金4		9	4

SUNDAY	MONDAY	TUESDAY	WEDNESDAY	THURSDAY	FRIDAY	SATURDAY
木8 Wood 7 Relief 雷水解 丙申 Fire Monkey 30 十四 4						水6 Water 9 Decreasing 山澤損 丁卯 Fire Rabbit 1 十四 9
金9 Metal 8 Tread 天澤履 戊辰 Earth Dragon 2 十五 6	木8 Wood 7 Great Strength 雷天大壯 己巳 Earth Snake 3 十六 2	木8 Wood 6 Consistency 雷風恆 庚午 Metal Horse 4 十七 9	金9 Metal 5 Litigation 天水訟 辛未 Metal Goat 5 十八 3	水1 Water 4 Officer 地水師 壬申 Water Monkey 6 十九 7	火2 Fire 3 Gradual Progress 風山漸 癸酉 Water Rooster 7 二十 7	火7 Fire 2 Obstruction 水山蹇 甲戌 Wood Dog 8 廿一 2
木3 Wood 1 Advancement 火地晉 乙亥 Wood Pig 9 廿二 3	水6 Water 9 Nourish 山雷頤 丙子 Fire Rat 10 廿三 3	金4 Metal 8 Following 澤雷隨 丁丑 Fire Ox 11 廿四 7	木8 Wood 7 Abundance 雷火豐 戊寅 Earth Tiger 12 廿五 6	火7 Fire 6 Regulate 水澤節 己卯 Earth Rabbit 13 廿六 8	水1 Water 5 Unity 地天泰 庚辰 Metal Dragon 14 廿七 9	木3 Wood 4 Great Reward 火天大有 辛巳 Metal Snake 15 廿八 7
火2 Fire 3 Wind 巽爲風 壬午 Water Horse 16 廿九 1	金4 Metal 2 Trap 澤水困 癸未 Water Goat 17 八月初一 8	木3 Wood 1 Not Yet Accomplished 火水未濟 甲申 Wood Monkey 18 初二 9	金9 Metal 9 Retreat 天山遯 乙酉 Wood Rooster 19 初三 4	水6 Water 8 Mountain 艮爲山 丙戌 Fire Dog 20 初四 1	木8 Wood 7 Delight 雷地豫 丁亥 Fire Pig 21 初五 8	火7 Fire 6 Beginning 水雷屯 戊子 Earth Rat 22 初六 4
金9 Metal 5 Without Wrongdoing 天雷無妄 己丑 Earth Ox 23 初七 2	木3 Wood 4 Fire 離爲火 庚寅 Metal Tiger 24 初八 1	火2 Fire 3 Sincerity 風澤中孚 辛卯 Metal Rabbit 25 初九 3	水6 Water 2 Big Livestock 山天大畜 壬辰 Water Dragon 26 初十 4	金4 Metal 1 Eliminating 澤天夬 癸巳 Water Snake 27 十一 6	金9 Metal 9 Heaven 乾爲天 甲午 Wood Horse 28 十二 1	火7 Fire 8 Well 水風井 乙未 Wood Goat 29 十三 6

OCTOBER 2001 戊戌

Xuan Kong Element 玄空五行	地山謙 Humility	Period Luck 卦運	Monthly Star 月星
Water 水1		6	3

SUNDAY	MONDAY	TUESDAY	WEDNESDAY	THURSDAY	FRIDAY	SATURDAY
	金4 Metal 6 Influence 澤山咸 丁酉 Fire Rooster 1 十五 9	水1 Water 5 Humility 地山謙 戊戌 Earth Dog 2 十六 6	火2 Fire 4 Observation 風地觀 己亥 Earth Pig 3 十七 2	火2 Fire 3 Increasing 風雷益 庚子 Metal Rat 4 十八 9	水1 Water 2 Dimming Light 地火明夷 辛丑 Metal Ox 5 十九 3	金9 Metal 1 Fellowship 天火同人 壬寅 Water Tiger 6 二十 7
木8 Wood 9 Marrying Maiden 雷澤歸妹 癸卯 Water Rabbit 7 廿一 7	木3 Wood 8 Opposition 火澤睽 甲辰 Wood Dragon 8 廿二 2	火7 Fire 7 Waiting 水天需 乙巳 Wood Snake 9 廿三 3	金4 Metal 6 Great Exceeding 澤風大過 丙午 Fire Horse 10 廿四 3	水6 Water 5 Poison 山風蠱 丁未 Fire Goat 11 廿五 7	火2 Fire 4 Dispersing 風水渙 戊申 Earth Monkey 12 廿六 4	木3 Wood 3 Travelling 火山旅 己酉 Earth Rooster 13 廿七 8
金9 Metal 2 Stagnation 天地否 庚戌 Metal Dog 14 廿八 9	火7 Fire 1 Alliance 水地比 辛亥 Metal Pig 15 廿九 7	木8 Wood 9 Thunder 震爲雷 壬子 Water Rat 16 三十 1	水6 Water 8 Beauty 山火賁 癸丑 Water Ox 17 九月初一 8	火7 Fire 7 Accomplished 水火既濟 甲寅 Wood Tiger 18 初二 9	水1 Water 6 Arriving 地澤臨 乙卯 Wood Rabbit 19 初三 4	金4 Metal 5 Marsh 兌爲澤 丙辰 Fire Dragon 20 初四 1
火2 Fire 4 Small Livestock 風天小畜 丁巳 Fire Snake 21 初五 8	木3 Wood 3 The Cauldron 火風鼎 戊午 Earth Horse 22 初六 4	水1 Water 2 Rising 地風升 己未 Earth Goat 23 初七 2	火7 Fire 1 Water 坎爲水 庚申 Metal Monkey 24 初八 1	木8 Wood 9 Lesser Exceeding 雷山小過 辛酉 Metal Rooster 25 初九 3	金4 Metal 8 Gathering 澤地萃 壬戌 Water Dog 26 初十 4	水6 Water 7 Peel 山地剝 癸亥 Water Pig 27 十一 6
水1 Water 6 Earth 坤爲地 甲子 Wood Rat 28 十二 1	木3 Wood 5 Biting 火雷噬嗑 乙丑 Wood Ox 29 十三 6	火2 Fire 4 Family 風火家人 丙寅 Fire Tiger 30 十四 4	水6 Water 3 Decreasing 山澤損 丁卯 Fire Rabbit 31 十五 9			

NOVEMBER 2001 己亥

Xuan Kong Element 玄空五行	風地觀 Observation	Period Luck 卦運	Monthly Star 月星
Fire 火2		2	2

SUNDAY	MONDAY	TUESDAY	WEDNESDAY	THURSDAY	FRIDAY	SATURDAY
				金9 Metal Tread 2 天澤履 戊辰 Earth Dragon 1 十六 6	木8 Wood Great Strength 1 雷天大壯 己巳 Earth Snake 2 十七 2	木8 Wood Consistency 9 雷風恆 庚午 Metal Horse 3 十八 9
金9 Metal Litigation 8 天水訟 辛未 Metal Goat 4 十九 3	水1 Water Officer 7 地水師 壬申 Water Monkey 5 二十 7	火2 Fire Gradual Progress 6 風山漸 癸酉 Water Rooster 6 廿一 7	火7 Fire Obstruction 5 水山蹇 甲戌 Wood Dog 7 廿二 2	木3 Wood Advancement 4 火地晉 乙亥 Wood Pig 8 廿三 3	水6 Water Nourish 3 山雷頤 丙子 Fire Rat 9 廿四 3	金4 Metal Following 2 澤雷隨 丁丑 Fire Ox 10 廿五 7
木8 Wood Abundance 1 雷火豐 戊寅 Earth Tiger 11 廿六 6	火7 Fire Regulate 9 水澤節 己卯 Earth Rabbit 12 廿七 8	水1 Water Unity 8 地天泰 庚辰 Metal Dragon 13 廿八 9	木3 Wood Great Reward 7 火天大有 辛巳 Metal Snake 14 廿九 7	火2 Fire Wind 6 巽為風 壬午 Water Horse 15 十月初一 1	金4 Metal Trap 5 澤水困 癸未 Water Goat 16 初二 8	木3 Wood Not Yet Accomplished 4 火水未濟 甲申 Wood Monkey 17 初三 9
金9 Metal Retreat 3 天山遯 乙酉 Wood Rooster 18 初四 4	水6 Water Mountain 2 艮為山 丙戌 Fire Dog 19 初五 1	木8 Wood Delight 1 雷地豫 丁亥 Fire Pig 20 初六 8	火7 Fire Beginning 9 水雷屯 戊子 Earth Rat 21 初七 4	金9 Metal Without Wrongdoing 8 天雷無妄 己丑 Earth Ox 22 初八 2	木3 Wood Fire 7 離為火 庚寅 Metal Tiger 23 初九 1	火2 Fire Sincerity 6 風澤中孚 辛卯 Metal Rabbit 24 初十 3
水6 Water Big Livestock 5 山天大畜 壬辰 Water Dragon 25 十一 4	金4 Metal Eliminating 4 澤天夬 癸巳 Water Snake 26 十二 6	金9 Metal Heaven 3 乾為天 甲午 Wood Horse 27 十三 1	火7 Fire Well 2 水風井 乙未 Wood Goat 28 十四 6	木8 Wood Relief 1 雷水解 丙申 Fire Monkey 29 十五 4	金4 Metal Influence 9 澤山咸 丁酉 Fire Rooster 30 十六 9	

DECEMBER 2001 庚子

Xuan Kong Element 玄空五行	風雷益 Increasing	Period Luck 卦運	Monthly Star 月星
Fire 火2		9	1

SUNDAY	MONDAY	TUESDAY	WEDNESDAY	THURSDAY	FRIDAY	SATURDAY
水6 Water Decreasing 4 山澤損 丁卯 Fire Rabbit 30 十六 9	金9 Metal Tread 5 天澤履 戊辰 Earth Dragon 31 十七 6					水1 Water Humility 8 地山謙 戊戌 Earth Dog 1 十七 6
火2 Fire Observation 7 風地觀 己亥 Earth Pig 2 十八 2	火2 Fire Increasing 6 風雷益 庚子 Metal Rat 3 十九 9	水1 Water Dimming Light 5 地火明夷 辛丑 Metal Ox 4 二十 3	金9 Metal Fellowship 4 天火同人 壬寅 Water Tiger 5 廿一 7	木8 Wood Marrying Maiden 3 雷澤歸妹 癸卯 Water Rabbit 6 廿二 7	木3 Wood Opposition 2 火澤睽 甲辰 Wood Dragon 7 廿三 2	火7 Fire Waiting 1 水天需 乙巳 Wood Snake 8 廿四 3
金4 Metal Great Exceeding 9 澤風大過 丙午 Fire Horse 9 廿五 3	水6 Water Poison 8 山風蠱 丁未 Fire Goat 10 廿六 7	火2 Fire Dispersing 7 風水渙 戊申 Earth Monkey 11 廿七 6	木3 Wood Travelling 6 火山旅 己酉 Earth Rooster 12 廿八 8	金9 Metal Stagnation 5 天地否 庚戌 Metal Dog 13 廿九 9	火7 Fire Alliance 4 水地比 辛亥 Metal Pig 14 三十 7	木8 Wood Thunder 3 震為雷 壬子 Water Rat 15 十一月初一 1
水6 Water Beauty 2 山火賁 癸丑 Water Ox 16 初二 8	火7 Fire Accomplished 1 水火既濟 甲寅 Wood Tiger 17 初三 9	水1 Water Arriving 9 地澤臨 乙卯 Wood Rabbit 18 初四 4	金4 Metal Marsh 8 兌為澤 丙辰 Fire Dragon 19 初五 1	火2 Fire Small Livestock 7 風天小畜 丁巳 Fire Snake 20 初六 8	木3 Wood The Cauldron 6 火風鼎 戊午 Earth Horse 21 初七 4	水1 Water Rising 5/5 地風升 己未 Earth Goat 22 初八 2
火7 Fire Water 6 坎為水 庚申 Metal Monkey 23 初九 1	木8 Wood Lesser Exceeding 7 雷山小過 辛酉 Metal Rooster 24 初十 3	金4 Metal Gathering 8 澤地萃 壬戌 Water Dog 25 十一 4	水6 Water Peel 9 山地剝 癸亥 Water Pig 26 十二 6	水1 Water Earth 1 坤為地 甲子 Wood Rat 27 十三 1	木3 Wood Biting 2 火雷噬嗑 乙丑 Wood Ox 28 十四 6	火2 Fire Family 3 風火家人 丙寅 Fire Tiger 29 十五 4

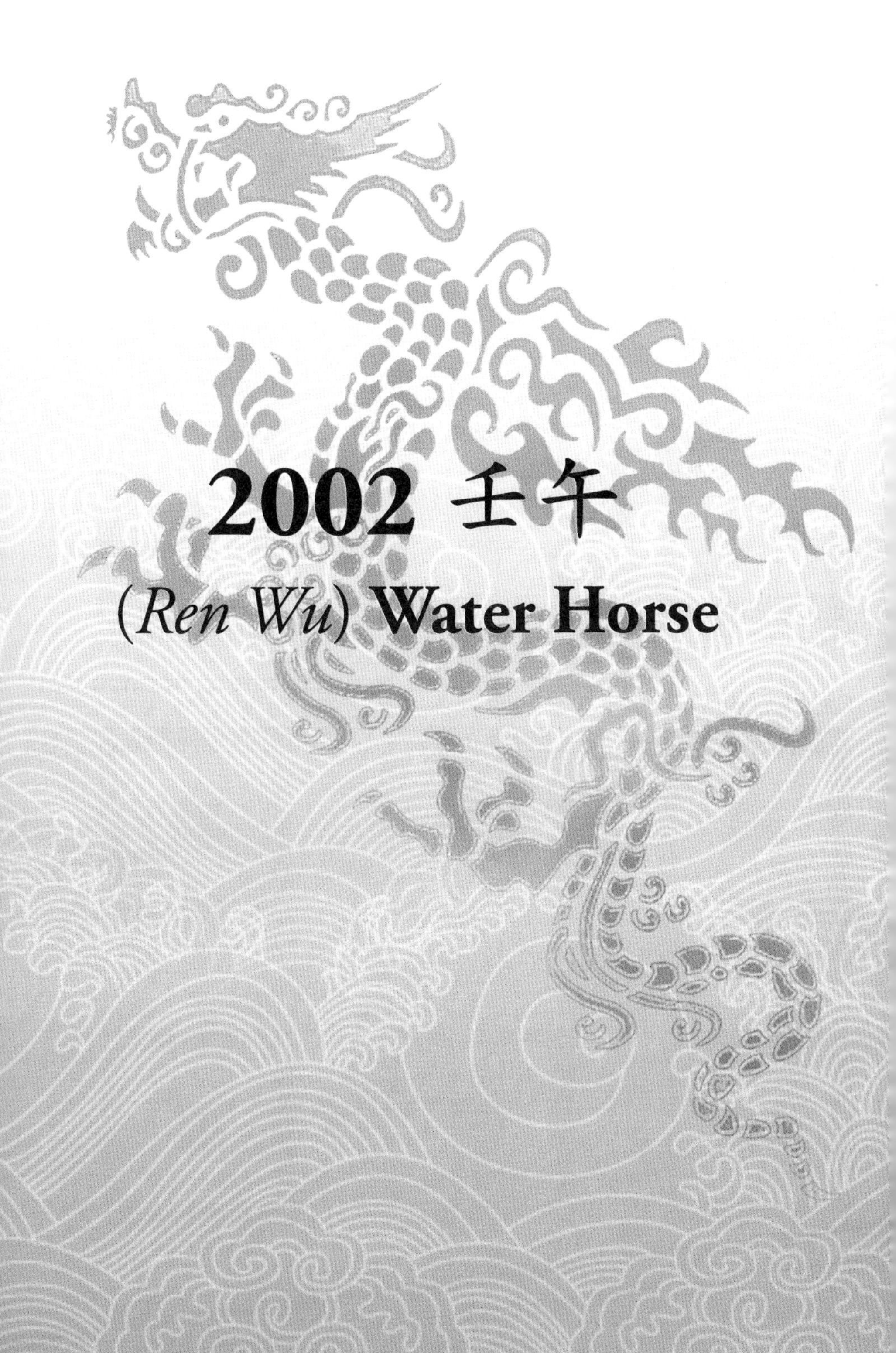

2002 壬午

(*Ren Wu*) Water Horse

2002 壬午 *(Ren Wu)* Water Horse

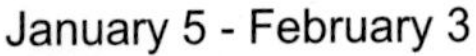

January 5 - February 3

Three Killings | East

水1 Water
辛丑 Metal Ox
3 Dimming Light
地火明夷

February 4 - March 5

Three Killings | North

金9 Metal
壬寅 Water Tiger
7 Fellowship
天火同人

March 6 - April 4

Three Killings | West

April 5 - May 5

Three Killings | South

木3 Wood
甲辰 Wood Dragon
2 Opposition
火澤睽

May 6 - June 5

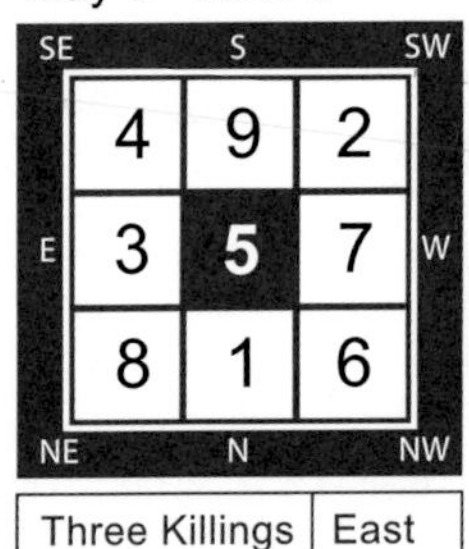

Three Killings | East

火7 Fire
乙巳 Wood Snake
3 Waiting
水天需

June 6 - July 6

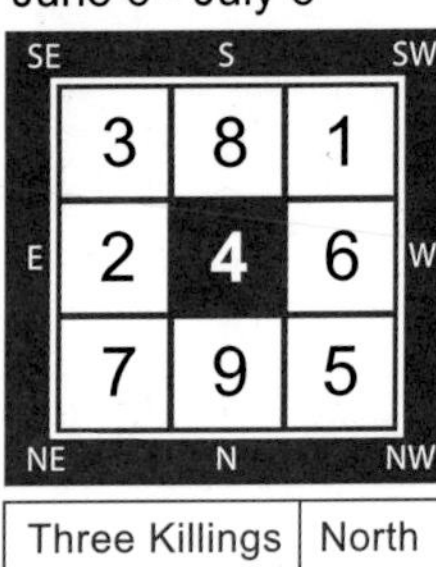

Three Killings | North

July 7 - August 7

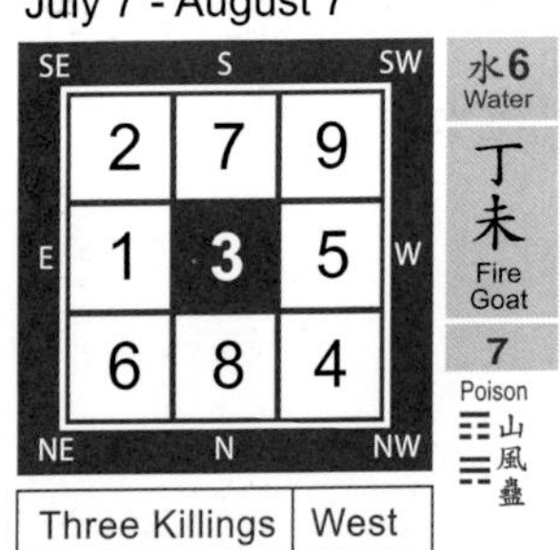

Three Killings | West

水6 Water
丁未 Fire Goat
7 Poison
山風蠱

August 8 - September 7

Three Killings | South

火2 Fire
戊申 Earth Monkey
6 Dispersing
風水渙

September 8 - October 7

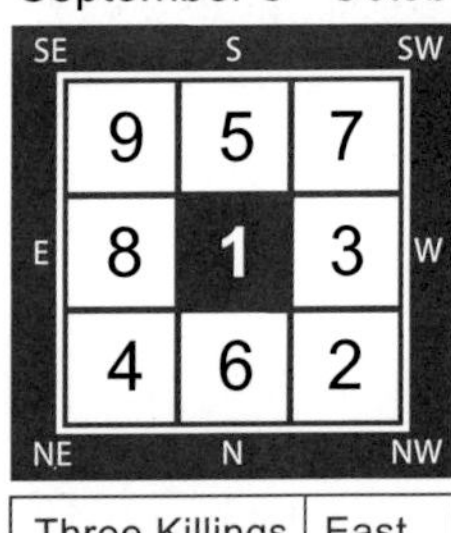

Three Killings | East

October 8 - November 6

Three Killings | North

金9 Metal
庚戌 Metal Dog
9 Stagnation
天地否

November 7 - December 6

Three Killings | West

火7 Fire
辛亥 Metal Pig
7 Alliance
水地比

December 7 - January 5

Three Killings | South

木8 Wood
壬子 Water Rat
1 Thunder
震爲雷

JANUARY 2002 辛丑

Xuan Kong Element 玄空五行	地火明夷 Dimming Light	Period Luck 卦運	Monthly Star 月星
Water 水1		3	9

SUNDAY	MONDAY	TUESDAY	WEDNESDAY	THURSDAY	FRIDAY	SATURDAY
		木8 Wood · Great Strength · 6 己巳 Earth Snake 雷天大壯 **1** 十八 2	木8 Wood · Consistency · 7 庚午 Metal Horse 雷風恆 **2** 十九 9	金9 Metal · Litigation · 8 辛未 Metal Goat 天水訟 **3** 二十 3	水1 Water · Officer · 9 壬申 Water Monkey 地水師 **4** 廿一 7	火2 Fire · Gradual Progress · 1 癸酉 Water Rooster 風山漸 **5** 廿二 7
火7 Fire · Obstruction · 2 甲戌 Wood Dog 水山蹇 **6** 廿三 2	木3 Wood · Advancement · 3 乙亥 Wood Pig 火地晉 **7** 廿四 3	水6 Water · Nourish · 4 丙子 Fire Rat 山雷頤 **8** 廿五 3	金4 Metal · Following · 5 丁丑 Fire Ox 澤雷隨 **9** 廿六 7	木8 Wood · Abundance · 6 戊寅 Earth Tiger 雷火豐 **10** 廿七 6	火7 Fire · Regulate · 7 己卯 Earth Rabbit 水澤節 **11** 廿八 8	水1 Water · Unity · 8 庚辰 Metal Dragon 地天泰 **12** 廿九 9
木3 Wood · Great Reward · 9 辛巳 Metal Snake 火天大有 **13** 十二月初一 7	火2 Fire · Wind · 1 壬午 Water Horse 巽爲風 **14** 初二 1	金4 Metal · Trap · 2 癸未 Water Goat 澤水困 **15** 初三 8	木3 Wood · Not Yet Accomplished · 3 甲申 Wood Monkey 火水未濟 **16** 初四 9	金9 Metal · Retreat · 4 乙酉 Wood Rooster 天山遯 **17** 初五 4	水6 Water · Mountain · 5 丙戌 Fire Dog 艮爲山 **18** 初六 1	木8 Wood · Delight · 6 丁亥 Fire Pig 雷地豫 **19** 初七 8
火7 Fire · Beginning · 7 戊子 Earth Rat 水雷屯 **20** 初八 4	金9 Metal · Without Wrongdoing · 8 己丑 Earth Ox 天雷無妄 **21** 初九 2	木3 Wood · Fire · 9 庚寅 Metal Tiger 離爲火 **22** 初十 1	火2 Fire · Sincerity · 1 辛卯 Metal Rabbit 風澤中孚 **23** 十一 3	水6 Water · Big Livestock · 2 壬辰 Water Dragon 山天大畜 **24** 十二 4	金4 Metal · Eliminating · 3 癸巳 Water Snake 澤天夬 **25** 十三 6	金9 Metal · Heaven · 4 甲午 Wood Horse 乾爲天 **26** 十四 1
火7 Fire · Well · 5 乙未 Wood Goat 水風井 **27** 十五 6	木8 Wood · Relief · 6 丙申 Fire Monkey 雷水解 **28** 十六 4	金4 Metal · Influence · 7 丁酉 Fire Rooster 澤山咸 **29** 十七 9	水1 Water · Humility · 8 戊戌 Earth Dog 地山謙 **30** 十八 6	火2 Fire · Observation · 9 己亥 Earth Pig 風地觀 **31** 十九 2		

FEBRUARY 2002 壬寅

Xuan Kong Element 玄空五行	天火同人 Fellowship	Period Luck 卦運	Monthly Star 月星
Metal 金9		7	8

SUNDAY	MONDAY	TUESDAY	WEDNESDAY	THURSDAY	FRIDAY	SATURDAY
					火2 Fire · Increasing · 1 庚子 Metal Rat 風雷益 **1** 二十 9	水1 Water · Dimming Light · 2 辛丑 Metal Ox 地火明夷 **2** 廿一 3
金9 Metal · Fellowship · 3 壬寅 Water Tiger 天火同人 **3** 廿二 7	木8 Wood · Marrying Maiden · 4 癸卯 Water Rabbit 雷澤歸妹 **4** 廿三 7	木3 Wood · Opposition · 5 甲辰 Wood Dragon 火澤睽 **5** 廿四 2	火7 Fire · Waiting · 6 乙巳 Wood Snake 水天需 **6** 廿五 3	金4 Metal · Great Exceeding · 7 丙午 Fire Horse 澤風大過 **7** 廿六 3	水6 Water · Poison · 8 丁未 Fire Goat 山風蠱 **8** 廿七 7	火2 Fire · Dispersing · 9 戊申 Earth Monkey 風水渙 **9** 廿八 6
木3 Wood · Travelling · 1 己酉 Earth Rooster 火山旅 **10** 廿九 8	金9 Metal · Stagnation · 2 庚戌 Metal Dog 天地否 **11** 三十 9	火7 Fire · Alliance · 3 辛亥 Metal Pig 水地比 **12** 正月初一 7	木8 Wood · Thunder · 4 壬子 Water Rat 震爲雷 **13** 初二 1	水6 Water · Beauty · 5 癸丑 Water Ox 山火賁 **14** 初三 8	火7 Fire · Accomplished · 6 甲寅 Wood Tiger 水火既濟 **15** 初四 9	水1 Water · Arriving · 7 乙卯 Wood Rabbit 地澤臨 **16** 初五 4
金4 Metal · Marsh · 8 丙辰 Fire Dragon 兌爲澤 **17** 初六 1	火2 Fire · Small Livestock · 9 丁巳 Fire Snake 風天小畜 **18** 初七 8	木3 Wood · The Cauldron · 1 戊午 Earth Horse 火風鼎 **19** 初八 4	水1 Water · Rising · 2 己未 Earth Goat 地風升 **20** 初九 2	火7 Fire · Water · 3 庚申 Metal Monkey 坎爲水 **21** 初十 1	木8 Wood · Lesser Exceeding · 4 辛酉 Metal Rooster 雷山小過 **22** 十一 3	金4 Metal · Gathering · 5 壬戌 Water Dog 澤地萃 **23** 十二 4
水6 Water · Peel · 6 癸亥 Water Pig 山地剝 **24** 十三 6	水1 Water · Earth · 7 甲子 Wood Rat 坤爲地 **25** 十四 1	木3 Wood · Biting · 8 乙丑 Wood Ox 火雷噬嗑 **26** 十五 6	火2 Fire · Family · 9 丙寅 Fire Tiger 風火家人 **27** 十六 4	水6 Water · Decreasing · 1 丁卯 Fire Rabbit 山澤損 **28** 十七 9		

MARCH 2002 癸卯

Xuan Kong Element 玄空五行	雷澤歸妹 Marrying Maiden	Period Luck 卦運	Monthly Star 月星
Wood 木8		7	7

SUNDAY	MONDAY	TUESDAY	WEDNESDAY	THURSDAY	FRIDAY	SATURDAY
水1 Water Humility 地山謙 5 戊戌 Earth Dog 31 十八 6					金9 Metal Tread 天澤履 2 戊辰 Earth Dragon 1 十八 6	木8 Wood Great Strength 雷天大壯 3 己巳 Earth Snake 2 十九 2
木8 Wood Consistency 雷風恒 4 庚午 Metal Horse 3 二十 9	金9 Metal Litigation 天水訟 5 辛未 Metal Goat 4 廿一 3	水1 Water Officer 地水師 6 壬申 Water Monkey 5 廿二 7	火2 Fire Gradual Progress 風山漸 7 癸酉 Water Rooster 6 廿三 7	火7 Fire Obstruction 水山蹇 8 甲戌 Wood Dog 7 廿四 2	木3 Wood Advancement 火地晉 9 乙亥 Wood Pig 8 廿五 3	水6 Water Nourish 山雷頤 1 丙子 Fire Rat 9 廿六 3
金4 Metal Following 澤雷隨 2 丁丑 Fire Ox 10 廿七 7	木8 Wood Abundance 雷火豐 3 戊寅 Earth Tiger 11 廿八 6	火7 Fire Regulate 水澤節 4 己卯 Earth Rabbit 12 廿九 8	水1 Water Unity 地天泰 5 庚辰 Metal Dragon 13 三十 9	木3 Wood Great Reward 火天大有 6 辛巳 Metal Snake 14 二月初一 7	火2 Fire Wind 巽爲風 7 壬午 Water Horse 15 初二 1	金4 Metal Trap 澤水困 8 癸未 Water Goat 16 初三 8
木3 Wood Not Yet Accomplished 火水未濟 9 甲申 Wood Monkey 17 初四 9	金9 Metal Retreat 天山遯 1 乙酉 Wood Rooster 18 初五 4	水6 Water Mountain 艮爲山 2 丙戌 Fire Dog 19 初六 1	木8 Wood Delight 雷地豫 3 丁亥 Fire Pig 20 初七 8	火7 Fire Beginning 水雷屯 4 戊子 Earth Rat 21 初八 4	金9 Metal Without Wrongdoing 天雷無妄 5 己丑 Earth Ox 22 初九 2	木3 Wood Fire 離爲火 6 庚寅 Metal Tiger 23 初十 1
火2 Fire Sincerity 風澤中孚 7 辛卯 Metal Rabbit 24 十一 3	水6 Water Big Livestock 山天大畜 8 壬辰 Water Dragon 25 十二 4	金4 Metal Eliminating 澤天夬 9 癸巳 Water Snake 26 十三 6	金9 Metal Heaven 乾爲天 1 甲午 Wood Horse 27 十四 1	火7 Fire Well 水風井 2 乙未 Wood Goat 28 十五 6	木8 Wood Relief 雷水解 3 丙申 Fire Monkey 29 十六 4	金4 Metal Influence 澤山咸 4 丁酉 Fire Rooster 30 十七 9

APRIL 2002 甲辰

Xuan Kong Element 玄空五行	火澤睽 Opposition	Period Luck 卦運	Monthly Star 月星
Wood 木3		2	6

SUNDAY	MONDAY	TUESDAY	WEDNESDAY	THURSDAY	FRIDAY	SATURDAY
	火2 Fire Observation 風地觀 6 己亥 Earth Pig 1 十九 2	火2 Fire Increasing 風雷益 7 庚子 Metal Rat 2 二十 9	水1 Water Dimming Light 地火明夷 8 辛丑 Metal Ox 3 廿一 3	金9 Metal Fellowship 天火同人 9 壬寅 Water Tiger 4 廿二 7	木8 Wood Marrying Maiden 雷澤歸妹 1 癸卯 Water Rabbit 5 廿三 7	木3 Wood Opposition 火澤睽 2 甲辰 Wood Dragon 6 廿四 2
火7 Fire Waiting 水天需 3 乙巳 Wood Snake 7 廿五 3	金4 Metal Great Exceeding 澤風大過 4 丙午 Fire Horse 8 廿六 3	水6 Water Poison 山風蠱 5 丁未 Fire Goat 9 廿七 7	火2 Fire Dispersing 風水渙 6 戊申 Earth Monkey 10 廿八 6	木3 Wood Travelling 火山旅 7 己酉 Earth Rooster 11 廿九 8	金9 Metal Stagnation 天地否 8 庚戌 Metal Dog 12 三十 9	火7 Fire Alliance 水地比 9 辛亥 Metal Pig 13 三月初一 7
木8 Wood Thunder 震爲雷 1 壬子 Water Rat 14 初二 1	水6 Water Beauty 山火賁 2 癸丑 Water Ox 15 初三 8	火7 Fire Accomplished 水火既濟 3 甲寅 Wood Tiger 16 初四 9	水1 Water Arriving 地澤臨 4 乙卯 Wood Rabbit 17 初五 4	金4 Metal Marsh 兌爲澤 5 丙辰 Fire Dragon 18 初六 1	火2 Fire Small Livestock 風天小畜 6 丁巳 Fire Snake 19 初七 8	木3 Wood The Cauldron 火風鼎 7 戊午 Earth Horse 20 初八 4
水1 Water Rising 地風升 8 己未 Earth Goat 21 初九 2	火7 Fire Water 坎爲水 9 庚申 Metal Monkey 22 初十 1	木8 Wood Lesser Exceeding 雷山小過 1 辛酉 Metal Rooster 23 十一 3	金4 Metal Gathering 澤地萃 2 壬戌 Water Dog 24 十二 4	水6 Water Peel 山地剝 3 癸亥 Water Pig 25 十三 6	水1 Water Earth 坤爲地 4 甲子 Wood Rat 26 十四 1	木3 Wood Biting 火雷噬嗑 5 乙丑 Wood Ox 27 十五 6
火2 Fire Family 風火家人 6 丙寅 Fire Tiger 28 十六 4	水6 Water Decreasing 山澤損 7 丁卯 Fire Rabbit 29 十七 9	金9 Metal Tread 天澤履 8 戊辰 Earth Dragon 30 十八 6				

MAY 2002 乙巳

Xuan Kong Element 玄空五行	水天需	Period Luck 卦運	Monthly Star 月星
Fire 火7	Waiting	3	5

SUNDAY	MONDAY	TUESDAY	WEDNESDAY	THURSDAY	FRIDAY	SATURDAY
			木8 Wood 9 Great Strength 己巳 Earth Snake 雷天大壯 1 十九 2	木8 Wood 1 Consistency 庚午 Metal Horse 雷風恆 2 二十 9	金9 Metal 2 Litigation 辛未 Metal Goat 天水訟 3 廿一 3	水1 Water 3 Officer 壬申 Water Monkey 地水師 4 廿二 7
火2 Fire 4 Gradual Progress 癸酉 Water Rooster 風山漸 5 廿三 7	火7 Fire 5 Obstruction 甲戌 Wood Dog 水山蹇 6 廿四 2	木3 Wood 6 Advancement 乙亥 Wood Pig 火地晉 7 廿五 3	水6 Water 7 Nourish 丙子 Fire Rat 山雷頤 8 廿六 3	金4 Metal 8 Following 丁丑 Fire Ox 澤雷隨 9 廿七 7	木8 Wood 9 Abundance 戊寅 Earth Tiger 雷火豐 10 廿八 6	火7 Fire 1 Regulate 己卯 Earth Rabbit 水澤節 11 廿九 8
水1 Water 2 Unity 庚辰 Metal Dragon 地天泰 12 四月初一 9	木3 Wood 3 Great Reward 辛巳 Metal Snake 火天大有 13 初二 7	火2 Fire 4 Wind 壬午 Water Horse 巽爲風 14 初三 1	金4 Metal 5 Trap 癸未 Water Goat 澤水困 15 初四 8	木3 Wood 6 Not Yet Accomplished 甲申 Wood Monkey 火水未濟 16 初五 9	金9 Metal 7 Retreat 乙酉 Wood Rooster 天山遯 17 初六 4	水6 Water 8 Mountain 丙戌 Fire Dog 艮爲山 18 初七 1
木8 Wood 9 Delight 丁亥 Fire Pig 雷地豫 19 初八 8	火7 Fire 1 Beginning 戊子 Earth Rat 水雷屯 20 初九 4	金9 Metal 2 Without Wrongdoing 己丑 Earth Ox 天雷無妄 21 初十 2	木3 Wood 3 Fire 庚寅 Metal Tiger 離爲火 22 十一 1	火2 Fire 4 Sincerity 辛卯 Metal Rabbit 風澤中孚 23 十二 3	水6 Water 5 Big Livestock 壬辰 Water Dragon 山天大畜 24 十三 4	金4 Metal 6 Eliminating 癸巳 Water Snake 澤天夬 25 十四 6
金9 Metal 7 Heaven 甲午 Wood Horse 乾爲天 26 十五 1	火7 Fire 8 Well 乙未 Wood Goat 水風井 27 十六 6	木8 Wood 9 Relief 丙申 Fire Monkey 雷水解 28 十七 4	金4 Metal 1 Influence 丁酉 Fire Rooster 澤山咸 29 十八 9	水1 Water 2 Humility 戊戌 Earth Dog 地山謙 30 十九 6	火2 Fire 3 Observation 己亥 Earth Pig 風地觀 31 二十 2	

JUNE 2002 丙午

Xuan Kong Element 玄空五行	澤風大過	Period Luck 卦運	Monthly Star 月星
Metal 金4	Great Exceeding	3	4

SUNDAY	MONDAY	TUESDAY	WEDNESDAY	THURSDAY	FRIDAY	SATURDAY
木8 Wood 4 Great Strength 己巳 Earth Snake 雷天大壯 30 二十 2						火2 Fire 4 Increasing 庚子 Metal Rat 風雷益 1 廿一 9
水1 Water 5 Dimming Light 辛丑 Metal Ox 地火明夷 2 廿二 3	金9 Metal 6 Fellowship 壬寅 Water Tiger 天火同人 3 廿三 7	木8 Wood 7 Marrying Maiden 癸卯 Water Rabbit 雷澤歸妹 4 廿四 7	木3 Wood 8 Opposition 甲辰 Wood Dragon 火澤睽 5 廿五 2	火7 Fire 9 Waiting 乙巳 Wood Snake 水天需 6 廿六 3	金4 Metal 1 Great Exceeding 丙午 Fire Horse 澤風大過 7 廿七 3	水6 Water 2 Poison 丁未 Fire Goat 山風蠱 8 廿八 7
火2 Fire 3 Dispersing 戊申 Earth Monkey 風水渙 9 廿九 6	木3 Wood 4 Travelling 己酉 Earth Rooster 火山旅 10 三十 8	金9 Metal 5 Stagnation 庚戌 Metal Dog 天地否 11 五月初一 9	火7 Fire 6 Alliance 辛亥 Metal Pig 水地比 12 初二 7	木8 Wood 7 Thunder 壬子 Water Rat 震爲雷 13 初三 1	水6 Water 8 Beauty 癸丑 Water Ox 山火賁 14 初四 8	火7 Fire 9 Accomplished 甲寅 Wood Tiger 水火既濟 15 初五 9
水1 Water 1 Arriving 乙卯 Wood Rabbit 地澤臨 16 初六 4	金4 Metal 2 Marsh 丙辰 Fire Dragon 兌爲澤 17 初七 1	火2 Fire 3 Small Livestock 丁巳 Fire Snake 風天小畜 18 初八 8	木3 Wood 4 The Cauldron 戊午 Earth Horse 火風鼎 19 初九 4	水1 Water 5 Rising 己未 Earth Goat 地風升 20 初十 2	火7 Fire 6/4 Water 庚申 Metal Monkey 坎爲水 21 十一 1	木8 Wood 3 Lesser Exceeding 辛酉 Metal Rooster 雷山小過 22 十二 3
金4 Metal 2 Gathering 壬戌 Water Dog 澤地萃 23 十三 4	水6 Water 1 Peel 癸亥 Water Pig 山地剝 24 十四 6	水1 Water 9 Earth 甲子 Wood Rat 坤爲地 25 十五 1	木3 Wood 8 Biting 乙丑 Wood Ox 火雷噬嗑 26 十六 6	火2 Fire 7 Family 丙寅 Fire Tiger 風火家人 27 十七 4	水6 Water 6 Decreasing 丁卯 Fire Rabbit 山澤損 28 十八 9	金9 Metal 5 Tread 戊辰 Earth Dragon 天澤履 29 十九 6

JULY 2002 丁未

Xuan Kong Element 玄空五行	山風蠱 Poison	Period Luck 卦運	Monthly Star 月星
Water 水6		7	3

SUNDAY	MONDAY	TUESDAY	WEDNESDAY	THURSDAY	FRIDAY	SATURDAY
	1 廿一 木8 Wood · 3 Consistency 雷風恒 庚午 Metal Horse 9	**2** 廿二 金9 Metal · 2 Litigation 天水訟 辛未 Metal Goat 3	**3** 廿三 水1 Water · 1 Officer 地水師 壬申 Water Monkey 7	**4** 廿四 火2 Fire · 9 Gradual Progress 風山漸 癸酉 Water Rooster 7	**5** 廿五 火7 Fire · 8 Obstruction 水山蹇 甲戌 Wood Dog 2	**6** 廿六 木3 Wood · 7 Advancement 火地晉 乙亥 Wood Pig 3
7 廿七 水6 Water · 6 Nourish 山雷頤 丙子 Fire Rat 3	**8** 廿八 金4 Metal · 5 Following 澤雷隨 丁丑 Fire Ox 7	**9** 廿九 木8 Wood · 4 Abundance 雷火豐 戊寅 Earth Tiger 6	**10** 六月初一 火7 Fire · 3 Regulate 水澤節 己卯 Earth Rabbit 8	**11** 初二 水1 Water · 2 Unity 地天泰 庚辰 Metal Dragon 9	**12** 初三 木3 Wood · 1 Great Reward 火天大有 辛巳 Metal Snake 7	**13** 初四 火2 Fire · 9 Wind 巽爲風 壬午 Water Horse 1
14 初五 金4 Metal · 8 Trap 澤水困 癸未 Water Goat 8	**15** 初六 木3 Wood · 7 Not Yet Accomplished 火水未濟 甲申 Wood Monkey 9	**16** 初七 金9 Metal · 6 Retreat 天山遯 乙酉 Wood Rooster 4	**17** 初八 水6 Water · 5 Mountain 艮爲山 丙戌 Fire Dog 1	**18** 初九 木8 Wood · 4 Delight 雷地豫 丁亥 Fire Pig 8	**19** 初十 火7 Fire · 3 Beginning 水雷屯 戊子 Earth Rat 4	**20** 十一 金9 Metal · 2 Without Wrongdoing 天雷無妄 己丑 Earth Ox 2
21 十二 木3 Wood · 1 Fire 離爲火 庚寅 Metal Tiger 1	**22** 十三 火2 Fire · 9 Sincerity 風澤中孚 辛卯 Metal Rabbit 3	**23** 十四 水6 Water · 8 Big Livestock 山天大畜 壬辰 Water Dragon 4	**24** 十五 金4 Metal · 7 Eliminating 澤天夬 癸巳 Water Snake 6	**25** 十六 金9 Metal · 6 Heaven 乾爲天 甲午 Wood Horse 1	**26** 十七 火7 Fire · 5 Well 水風井 乙未 Wood Goat 6	**27** 十八 木8 Wood · 4 Relief 雷水解 丙申 Fire Monkey 4
28 十九 金4 Metal · 3 Influence 澤山咸 丁酉 Fire Rooster 9	**29** 二十 水1 Water · 2 Humility 地山謙 戊戌 Earth Dog 6	**30** 廿一 火2 Fire · 1 Observation 風地觀 己亥 Earth Pig 2	**31** 廿二 火2 Fire · 9 Increasing 風雷益 庚子 Metal Rat 9			

AUGUST 2002 戊申

Xuan Kong Element 玄空五行	風水渙 Dispersing	Period Luck 卦運	Monthly Star 月星
Fire 火2		6	2

SUNDAY	MONDAY	TUESDAY	WEDNESDAY	THURSDAY	FRIDAY	SATURDAY
				1 廿三 水1 Water · 8 Dimming Light 地火明夷 辛丑 Metal Ox 3	**2** 廿四 金9 Metal · 7 Fellowship 天火同人 壬寅 Water Tiger 7	**3** 廿五 木8 Wood · 6 Marrying Maiden 雷澤歸妹 癸卯 Water Rabbit 7
4 廿六 木3 Wood · 5 Opposition 火澤睽 甲辰 Wood Dragon 2	**5** 廿七 火7 Fire · 4 Waiting 水天需 乙巳 Wood Snake 3	**6** 廿八 金4 Metal · 3 Great Exceeding 澤風大過 丙午 Fire Horse 3	**7** 廿九 水6 Water · 2 Poison 山風蠱 丁未 Fire Goat 7	**8** 三十 火2 Fire · 1 Dispersing 風水渙 戊申 Earth Monkey 6	**9** 七月初一 木3 Wood · 9 Travelling 火山旅 己酉 Earth Rooster 8	**10** 初二 金9 Metal · 8 Stagnation 天地否 庚戌 Metal Dog 9
11 初三 火7 Fire · 7 Alliance 水地比 辛亥 Metal Pig 7	**12** 初四 木8 Wood · 6 Thunder 震爲雷 壬子 Water Rat 1	**13** 初五 水6 Water · 5 Beauty 山火賁 癸丑 Water Ox 8	**14** 初六 火7 Fire · 4 Accomplished 水火既濟 甲寅 Wood Tiger 9	**15** 初七 水1 Water · 3 Arriving 地澤臨 乙卯 Wood Rabbit 4	**16** 初八 金4 Metal · 2 Marsh 兑爲澤 丙辰 Fire Dragon 1	**17** 初九 火2 Fire · 1 Small Livestock 風天小畜 丁巳 Fire Snake 8
18 初十 木3 Wood · 9 The Cauldron 火風鼎 戊午 Earth Horse 4	**19** 十一 水1 Water · 8 Rising 地風升 己未 Earth Goat 2	**20** 十二 火7 Fire · 7 Water 坎爲水 庚申 Metal Monkey 1	**21** 十三 木8 Wood · 6 Lesser Exceeding 雷山小過 辛酉 Metal Rooster 3	**22** 十四 金4 Metal · 5 Gathering 澤地萃 壬戌 Water Dog 4	**23** 十五 水6 Water · 4 Peel 山地剝 癸亥 Water Pig 6	**24** 十六 水1 Water · 3 Earth 坤爲地 甲子 Wood Rat 1
25 十七 木3 Wood · 2 Biting 火雷噬嗑 乙丑 Wood Ox 6	**26** 十八 火2 Fire · 1 Family 風火家人 丙寅 Fire Tiger 4	**27** 十九 水6 Water · 9 Decreasing 山澤損 丁卯 Fire Rabbit 9	**28** 二十 金9 Metal · 8 Tread 天澤履 戊辰 Earth Dragon 6	**29** 廿一 木8 Wood · 7 Great Strength 雷天大壯 己巳 Earth Snake 2	**30** 廿二 木8 Wood · 6 Consistency 雷風恒 庚午 Metal Horse 9	**31** 廿三 金9 Metal · 5 Litigation 天水訟 辛未 Metal Goat 3

SEPTEMBER 2002 己酉

Xuan Kong Element 玄空五行	火山旅 Travelling	Period Luck 卦運	Monthly Star 月星
Wood 木3		8	1

SUNDAY	MONDAY	TUESDAY	WEDNESDAY	THURSDAY	FRIDAY	SATURDAY
水1 Water 4 Officer 壬申 Water Monkey 地水師 **1** 廿四 7	火2 Fire 3 Gradual Progress 癸酉 Water Rooster 風山漸 **2** 廿五 7	火7 Fire 2 Obstruction 甲戌 Wood Dog 水山蹇 **3** 廿六 2	木3 Wood 1 Advancement 乙亥 Wood Pig 火地晉 **4** 廿七 3	水6 Water 9 Nourish 丙子 Fire Rat 山雷頤 **5** 廿八 3	金4 Metal 8 Following 丁丑 Fire Ox 澤雷隨 **6** 廿九 7	木8 Wood 7 Abundance 戊寅 Earth Tiger 雷火豐 **7** 八月初一 6
火7 Fire 6 Regulate 己卯 Earth Rabbit 水澤節 **8** 初二 8	水1 Water 5 Unity 庚辰 Metal Dragon 地天泰 **9** 初三 9	木3 Wood 4 Great Reward 辛巳 Metal Snake 火天大有 **10** 初四 7	火2 Fire 3 Wind 壬午 Water Horse 巽爲風 **11** 初五 1	金4 Metal 2 Trap 癸未 Water Goat 澤水困 **12** 初六 8	木3 Wood 1 Not Yet Accomplished 甲申 Wood Monkey 火水未濟 **13** 初七 9	金9 Metal 9 Retreat 乙酉 Wood Rooster 天山遯 **14** 初八 4
水6 Water 8 Mountain 丙戌 Fire Dog 艮爲山 **15** 初九 1	木8 Wood 7 Delight 丁亥 Fire Pig 雷地豫 **16** 初十 8	火7 Fire 6 Beginning 戊子 Earth Rat 水雷屯 **17** 十一 4	金9 Metal 5 Without Wrongdoing 己丑 Earth Ox 天雷無妄 **18** 十二 2	木3 Wood 4 Fire 庚寅 Metal Tiger 離爲火 **19** 十三 1	火2 Fire 3 Sincerity 辛卯 Metal Rabbit 風澤中孚 **20** 十四 3	水6 Water 2 Big Livestock 壬辰 Water Dragon 山天大畜 **21** 十五 4
金4 Metal 1 Eliminating 癸巳 Water Snake 澤天夬 **22** 十六 6	金9 Metal 9 Heaven 甲午 Wood Horse 乾爲天 **23** 十七 1	火7 Fire 8 Well 乙未 Wood Goat 水風井 **24** 十八 6	木8 Wood 7 Relief 丙申 Fire Monkey 雷水解 **25** 十九 4	金4 Metal 6 Influence 丁酉 Fire Rooster 澤山咸 **26** 二十 9	水1 Water 5 Humility 戊戌 Earth Dog 地山謙 **27** 廿一 6	火2 Fire 4 Observation 己亥 Earth Pig 風地觀 **28** 廿二 2
火2 Fire 3 Increasing 庚子 Metal Rat 風雷益 **29** 廿三 9	水1 Water 2 Dimming Light 辛丑 Metal Ox 地火明夷 **30** 廿四 3					

OCTOBER 2002 庚戌

Xuan Kong Element 玄空五行	天地否 Stagnation	Period Luck 卦運	Monthly Star 月星
Metal 金9		9	9

SUNDAY	MONDAY	TUESDAY	WEDNESDAY	THURSDAY	FRIDAY	SATURDAY
		金9 Metal 1 Fellowship 壬寅 Water Tiger 天火同人 **1** 廿五 7	木8 Wood 9 Marrying Maiden 癸卯 Water Rabbit 雷澤歸妹 **2** 廿六 7	木3 Wood 8 Opposition 甲辰 Wood Dragon 火澤睽 **3** 廿七 2	火7 Fire 7 Waiting 乙巳 Wood Snake 水天需 **4** 廿八 3	金4 Metal 6 Great Exceeding 丙午 Fire Horse 澤風大過 **5** 廿九 3
水6 Water 5 Poison 丁未 Fire Goat 山風蠱 **6** 九月初一 7	火2 Fire 4 Dispersing 戊申 Earth Monkey 風水渙 **7** 初二 6	木3 Wood 3 Travelling 己酉 Earth Rooster 火山旅 **8** 初三 8	金9 Metal 2 Stagnation 庚戌 Metal Dog 天地否 **9** 初四 9	火7 Fire 1 Alliance 辛亥 Metal Pig 水地比 **10** 初五 7	木8 Wood 9 Thunder 壬子 Water Rat 震爲雷 **11** 初六 1	水6 Water 8 Beauty 癸丑 Water Ox 山火賁 **12** 初七 8
火7 Fire 7 Accomplished 甲寅 Wood Tiger 水火既濟 **13** 初八 9	水1 Water 6 Arriving 乙卯 Wood Rabbit 地澤臨 **14** 初九 4	金4 Metal 5 Marsh 丙辰 Fire Dragon 兌爲澤 **15** 初十 1	火2 Fire 4 Small Livestock 丁巳 Fire Snake 風天小畜 **16** 十一 8	木3 Wood 3 The Cauldron 戊午 Earth Horse 火風鼎 **17** 十二 4	水1 Water 2 Rising 己未 Earth Goat 地風升 **18** 十三 2	火7 Fire 1 Water 庚申 Metal Monkey 坎爲水 **19** 十四 1
木8 Wood 9 Lesser Exceeding 辛酉 Metal Rooster 雷山小過 **20** 十五 3	金4 Metal 8 Gathering 壬戌 Water Dog 澤地萃 **21** 十六 4	水6 Water 7 Peel 癸亥 Water Pig 山地剝 **22** 十七 6	水1 Water 6 Earth 甲子 Wood Rat 坤爲地 **23** 十八 1	木3 Wood 5 Biting 乙丑 Wood Ox 火雷噬嗑 **24** 十九 6	火2 Fire 4 Family 丙寅 Fire Tiger 風火家人 **25** 二十 4	水6 Water 3 Decreasing 丁卯 Fire Rabbit 山澤損 **26** 廿一 9
金9 Metal 2 Tread 戊辰 Earth Dragon 天澤履 **27** 廿二 6	木8 Wood 1 Great Strength 己巳 Earth Snake 雷天大壯 **28** 廿三 2	木8 Wood 9 Consistency 庚午 Metal Horse 雷風恆 **29** 廿四 9	金9 Metal 8 Litigation 辛未 Metal Goat 天水訟 **30** 廿五 3	水1 Water 7 Officer 壬申 Water Monkey 地水師 **31** 廿六 7		

NOVEMBER 2002 辛亥

Xuan Kong Element 玄空五行	水地比 Alliance	Period Luck 卦運	Monthly Star 月星
Fire 火7		7	8

SUNDAY	MONDAY	TUESDAY	WEDNESDAY	THURSDAY	FRIDAY	SATURDAY
					火2 Fire 6 Gradual Progress 風山漸 癸酉 Water Rooster 7 **1** 廿七	火7 Fire 5 Obstruction 水山蹇 甲戌 Wood Dog 2 **2** 廿八
木3 Wood 4 Advancement 火地晉 乙亥 Wood Pig 3 **3** 廿九	水6 Water 3 Nourish 山雷頤 丙子 Fire Rat 3 **4** 三十	金4 Metal 2 Following 澤雷隨 丁丑 Fire Ox 7 **5** 十月初一	木8 Wood 1 Abundance 雷火豐 戊寅 Earth Tiger 6 **6** 初二	火7 Fire 9 Regulate 水澤節 己卯 Earth Rabbit 8 **7** 初三	水1 Water 8 Unity 地天泰 庚辰 Metal Dragon 9 **8** 初四	木3 Wood 7 Great Reward 火天大有 辛巳 Metal Snake 7 **9** 初五
火2 Fire 6 Wind 巽爲風 壬午 Water Horse 1 **10** 初六	金4 Metal 5 Trap 澤水困 癸未 Water Goat 8 **11** 初七	木3 Wood 4 Not Yet Accomplished 火水未濟 甲申 Wood Monkey 9 **12** 初八	金9 Metal 3 Retreat 天山遯 乙酉 Wood Rooster 4 **13** 初九	水6 Water 2 Mountain 艮爲山 丙戌 Fire Dog 1 **14** 初十	木8 Wood 1 Delight 雷地豫 丁亥 Fire Pig 8 **15** 十一	火7 Fire 9 Beginning 水雷屯 戊子 Earth Rat 4 **16** 十二
金9 Metal 8 Without Wrongdoing 天雷無妄 己丑 Earth Ox 2 **17** 十三	木3 Wood 7 Fire 離爲火 庚寅 Metal Tiger 1 **18** 十四	火2 Fire 6 Sincerity 風澤中孚 辛卯 Metal Rabbit 3 **19** 十五	水6 Water 5 Big Livestock 山天大畜 壬辰 Water Dragon 4 **20** 十六	金4 Metal 4 Eliminating 澤天夬 癸巳 Water Snake 6 **21** 十七	金9 Metal 3 Heaven 乾爲天 甲午 Wood Horse 1 **22** 十八	火7 Fire 2 Well 水風井 乙未 Wood Goat 6 **23** 十九
木8 Wood 1 Relief 雷水解 丙申 Fire Monkey 4 **24** 二十	金4 Metal 9 Influence 澤山咸 丁酉 Fire Rooster 9 **25** 廿一	水1 Water 8 Humility 地山謙 戊戌 Earth Dog 6 **26** 廿二	火2 Fire 7 Observation 風地觀 己亥 Earth Pig 2 **27** 廿三	火2 Fire 6 Increasing 風雷益 庚子 Metal Rat 9 **28** 廿四	水1 Water 5 Dimming Light 地火明夷 辛丑 Metal Ox 3 **29** 廿五	金9 Metal 4 Fellowship 天火同人 壬寅 Water Tiger 7 **30** 廿六

DECEMBER 2002 壬子

Xuan Kong Element 玄空五行	震爲雷 Thunder	Period Luck 卦運	Monthly Star 月星
Wood 木8		1	7

SUNDAY	MONDAY	TUESDAY	WEDNESDAY	THURSDAY	FRIDAY	SATURDAY
木8 Wood 3 Marrying Maiden 雷澤歸妹 癸卯 Water Rabbit 7 **1** 廿七	木3 Wood 2 Opposition 火澤睽 甲辰 Wood Dragon 2 **2** 廿八	火7 Fire 1 Waiting 水天需 乙巳 Wood Snake 3 **3** 廿九	金4 Metal 9 Great Exceeding 澤風大過 丙午 Fire Horse 3 **4** 十一月初一	水6 Water 8 Poison 山風蠱 丁未 Fire Goat 7 **5** 初二	火2 Fire 7 Dispersing 風水渙 戊申 Earth Monkey 6 **6** 初三	木3 Wood 6 Travelling 火山旅 己酉 Earth Rooster 8 **7** 初四
金9 Metal 5 Stagnation 天地否 庚戌 Metal Dog 9 **8** 初五	火7 Fire 4 Alliance 水地比 辛亥 Metal Pig 7 **9** 初六	木8 Wood 3 Thunder 震爲雷 壬子 Water Rat 1 **10** 初七	水6 Water 2 Beauty 山火賁 癸丑 Water Ox 8 **11** 初八	火7 Fire 1 Accomplished 水火既濟 甲寅 Wood Tiger 9 **12** 初九	水1 Water 9 Arriving 地澤臨 乙卯 Wood Rabbit 4 **13** 初十	金4 Metal 8 Marsh 兑爲澤 丙辰 Fire Dragon 1 **14** 十一
火2 Fire 7 Small Livestock 風天小畜 丁巳 Fire Snake 8 **15** 十二	木3 Wood 6 The Cauldron 火風鼎 戊午 Earth Horse 4 **16** 十三	水1 Water 5 Rising 地風升 己未 Earth Goat 2 **17** 十四	火7 Fire 4 Water 坎爲水 庚申 Metal Monkey 1 **18** 十五	木8 Wood 3 Lesser Exceeding 雷山小過 辛酉 Metal Rooster 3 **19** 十六	金4 Metal 2 Gathering 澤地萃 壬戌 Water Dog 4 **20** 十七	水6 Water 1 Peel 山地剝 癸亥 Water Pig 6 **21** 十八
水1 Water 9/1 Earth 坤爲地 甲子 Wood Rat 1 **22** 十九	木3 Wood 2 Biting 火雷噬嗑 乙丑 Wood Ox 6 **23** 二十	火2 Fire 3 Family 風火家人 丙寅 Fire Tiger 4 **24** 廿一	水6 Water 4 Decreasing 山澤損 丁卯 Fire Rabbit 9 **25** 廿二	金9 Metal 5 Tread 天澤履 戊辰 Earth Dragon 6 **26** 廿三	木8 Wood 6 Great Strength 雷天大壯 己巳 Earth Snake 2 **27** 廿四	木8 Wood 7 Consistency 雷風恒 庚午 Metal Horse 9 **28** 廿五
金9 Metal 8 Litigation 天水訟 辛未 Metal Goat 3 **29** 廿六	水1 Water 9 Officer 地水師 壬申 Water Monkey 7 **30** 廿七	火2 Fire 1 Gradual Progress 風山漸 癸酉 Water Rooster 7 **31** 廿八				

2003 癸未

(*Gui Wei*) Water Goat

2003 癸未 *(Gui Wei)* Water Goat

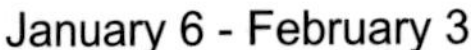

January 6 - February 3

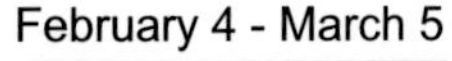

February 4 - March 5

March 6 - April 4

April 5 - May 5

May 6 - June 5

June 6 - July 6

July 7 - August 7

August 8 - September 7

September 8 - October 8

October 9 - November 7

November 8 - December 6

December 7 - January 5

JANUARY 2003 癸丑

Xuan Kong Element 玄空五行	山火賁 Beauty	Period Luck 卦運	Monthly Star 月星
Water 水6		8	6

SUNDAY	MONDAY	TUESDAY	WEDNESDAY	THURSDAY	FRIDAY	SATURDAY
			火7 Fire Obstruction 2 甲戌 Wood Dog 水山蹇 1 廿九 2	木3 Wood Advancement 3 乙亥 Wood Pig 火地晉 2 三十 3	水6 Water Nourish 4 丙子 Fire Rat 山雷頤 3 十二月初一 3	金4 Metal Following 5 丁丑 Fire Ox 澤雷隨 4 初二 7
木8 Wood Abundance 6 戊寅 Earth Tiger 雷火豐 5 初三 6	火7 Fire Regulate 7 己卯 Earth Rabbit 水澤節 6 初四 8	水1 Water Unity 8 庚辰 Metal Dragon 地天泰 7 初五 9	木3 Wood Great Reward 9 辛巳 Metal Snake 火天大有 8 初六 7	火2 Fire Wind 1 壬午 Water Horse 巽爲風 9 初七 1	金4 Metal Trap 2 癸未 Water Goat 澤水困 10 初八 8	木3 Wood Not Yet Accomplished 3 甲申 Wood Monkey 火水未濟 11 初九 9
金9 Metal Retreat 4 乙酉 Wood Rooster 天山遯 12 初十 4	水6 Water Mountain 5 丙戌 Fire Dog 艮爲山 13 十一 1	木8 Wood Delight 6 丁亥 Fire Pig 雷地豫 14 十二 8	火7 Fire Beginning 7 戊子 Earth Rat 水雷屯 15 十三 4	金9 Metal Without Wrongdoing 8 己丑 Earth Ox 天雷無妄 16 十四 2	木3 Wood Fire 9 庚寅 Metal Tiger 離爲火 17 十五 1	火2 Fire Sincerity 1 辛卯 Metal Rabbit 風澤中孚 18 十六 3
水6 Water Big Livestock 2 壬辰 Water Dragon 山天大畜 19 十七 4	金4 Metal Eliminating 3 癸巳 Water Snake 澤天夬 20 十八 6	金9 Metal Heaven 4 甲午 Wood Horse 乾爲天 21 十九 1	火7 Fire Well 5 乙未 Wood Goat 水風井 22 二十 6	木8 Wood Relief 6 丙申 Fire Monkey 雷水解 23 廿一 4	金4 Metal Influence 7 丁酉 Fire Rooster 澤山咸 24 廿二 9	水1 Water Humility 8 戊戌 Earth Dog 地山謙 25 廿三 6
火2 Fire Observation 9 己亥 Earth Pig 風地觀 26 廿四 2	火2 Fire Increasing 1 庚子 Metal Rat 風雷益 27 廿五 9	水1 Water Dimming Light 2 辛丑 Metal Ox 地火明夷 28 廿六 3	金9 Metal Fellowship 3 壬寅 Water Tiger 天火同人 29 廿七 7	木8 Wood Marrying Maiden 4 癸卯 Water Rabbit 雷澤歸妹 30 廿八 7	木3 Wood Opposition 5 甲辰 Wood Dragon 火澤睽 31 廿九 2	

FEBRUARY 2003 甲寅

Xuan Kong Element 玄空五行	水火既濟 Accomplished	Period Luck 卦運	Monthly Star 月星
Fire 火7		9	5

SUNDAY	MONDAY	TUESDAY	WEDNESDAY	THURSDAY	FRIDAY	SATURDAY
						火7 Fire Waiting 6 乙巳 Wood Snake 水天需 1 正月初一 3
金4 Metal Great Exceeding 7 丙午 Fire Horse 澤風大過 2 初二 3	水6 Water Poison 8 丁未 Fire Goat 山風蠱 3 初三 7	火2 Fire Dispersing 9 戊申 Earth Monkey 風水渙 4 初四 6	木3 Wood Travelling 1 己酉 Earth Rooster 火山旅 5 初五 8	金9 Metal Stagnation 2 庚戌 Metal Dog 天地否 6 初六 9	火7 Fire Alliance 3 辛亥 Metal Pig 水地比 7 初七 7	木8 Wood Thunder 4 壬子 Water Rat 震爲雷 8 初八 1
水6 Water Beauty 5 癸丑 Water Ox 山火賁 9 初九 8	火7 Fire Accomplished 6 甲寅 Wood Tiger 水火既濟 10 初十 9	水1 Water Arriving 7 乙卯 Wood Rabbit 地澤臨 11 十一 4	金4 Metal Marsh 8 丙辰 Fire Dragon 兌爲澤 12 十二 1	火2 Fire Small Livestock 9 丁巳 Fire Snake 風天小畜 13 十三 8	木3 Wood The Cauldron 1 戊午 Earth Horse 火風鼎 14 十四 4	水1 Water Rising 2 己未 Earth Goat 地風升 15 十五 2
火7 Fire Water 3 庚申 Metal Monkey 坎爲水 16 十六 1	木8 Wood Lesser Exceeding 4 辛酉 Metal Rooster 雷山小過 17 十七 3	金4 Metal Gathering 5 壬戌 Water Dog 澤地萃 18 十八 4	水6 Water Peel 6 癸亥 Water Pig 山地剝 19 十九 6	水1 Water Earth 7 甲子 Wood Rat 坤爲地 20 二十 1	木3 Wood Biting 8 乙丑 Wood Ox 火雷噬嗑 21 廿一 6	火2 Fire Family 9 丙寅 Fire Tiger 風火家人 22 廿二 4
水6 Water Decreasing 1 丁卯 Fire Rabbit 山澤損 23 廿三 9	金9 Metal Tread 2 戊辰 Earth Dragon 天澤履 24 廿四 6	木8 Wood Great Strength 3 己巳 Earth Snake 雷天大壯 25 廿五 2	木8 Wood Consistency 4 庚午 Metal Horse 雷風恒 26 廿六 9	金9 Metal Litigation 5 辛未 Metal Goat 天水訟 27 廿七 3	水1 Water Officer 6 壬申 Water Monkey 地水師 28 廿八 7	

MARCH 2003 乙卯

Xuan Kong Element 玄空五行	地澤臨 Arriving	Period Luck 卦運	Monthly Star 月星
Water 水1		4	4

SUNDAY	MONDAY	TUESDAY	WEDNESDAY	THURSDAY	FRIDAY	SATURDAY
金9 Metal · Fellowship · 9 壬寅 Water Tiger 天火同人 30 廿八 7	木8 Wood · Marrying Maiden · 1 癸卯 Water Rabbit 雷澤歸妹 31 廿九 7					火2 Fire · Gradual Progress · 7 癸酉 Water Rooster 風山漸 1 廿九 7
火7 Fire · Obstruction · 8 甲戌 Wood Dog 水山蹇 2 三十 2	木3 Wood · Advancement · 9 乙亥 Wood Pig 火地晉 3 二月初一 3	水6 Water · Nourish · 1 丙子 Fire Rat 山雷頤 4 初二 3	金4 Metal · Following · 2 丁丑 Fire Ox 澤雷隨 5 初三 7	木8 Wood · Abundance · 3 戊寅 Earth Tiger 雷火豐 6 初四 6	火7 Fire · Regulate · 4 己卯 Earth Rabbit 水澤節 7 初五 8	水1 Water · Unity · 5 庚辰 Metal Dragon 地天泰 8 初六 9
木3 Wood · Great Reward · 6 辛巳 Metal Snake 火天大有 9 初七 7	火2 Fire · Wind · 7 壬午 Water Horse 巽爲風 10 初八 1	金4 Metal · Trap · 8 癸未 Water Goat 澤水困 11 初九 8	木3 Wood · Not Yet Accomplished · 9 甲申 Wood Monkey 火水未濟 12 初十 9	金9 Metal · Retreat · 1 乙酉 Wood Rooster 天山遯 13 十一 4	水6 Water · Mountain · 2 丙戌 Fire Dog 艮爲山 14 十二 1	木8 Wood · Delight · 3 丁亥 Fire Pig 雷地豫 15 十三 8
火7 Fire · Beginning · 4 戊子 Earth Rat 水雷屯 16 十四 4	金9 Metal · Without Wrongdoing · 5 己丑 Earth Ox 天雷無妄 17 十五 2	木3 Wood · Fire · 6 庚寅 Metal Tiger 離爲火 18 十六 1	火2 Fire · Sincerity · 7 辛卯 Metal Rabbit 風澤中孚 19 十七 3	水6 Water · Big Livestock · 8 壬辰 Water Dragon 山天大畜 20 十八 4	金4 Metal · Eliminating · 9 癸巳 Water Snake 澤天夬 21 十九 6	金9 Metal · Heaven · 1 甲午 Wood Horse 乾爲天 22 二十 1
火7 Fire · Well · 2 乙未 Wood Goat 水風井 23 廿一 6	木8 Wood · Relief · 3 丙申 Fire Monkey 雷水解 24 廿二 4	金4 Metal · Influence · 4 丁酉 Fire Rooster 澤山咸 25 廿三 9	水1 Water · Humility · 5 戊戌 Earth Dog 地山謙 26 廿四 6	火2 Fire · Observation · 6 己亥 Earth Pig 風地觀 27 廿五 2	火2 Fire · Increasing · 7 庚子 Metal Rat 風雷益 28 廿六 9	水1 Water · Dimming Light · 8 辛丑 Metal Ox 地火明夷 29 廿七 3

APRIL 2003 丙辰

Xuan Kong Element 玄空五行	兑爲澤 Marsh	Period Luck 卦運	Monthly Star 月星
Metal 金4		1	3

SUNDAY	MONDAY	TUESDAY	WEDNESDAY	THURSDAY	FRIDAY	SATURDAY
		木3 Wood · Opposition · 2 甲辰 Wood Dragon 火澤睽 1 三十 2	火7 Fire · Waiting · 3 乙巳 Wood Snake 水天需 2 三月初一 3	金4 Metal · Great Exceeding · 4 丙午 Fire Horse 澤風大過 3 初二 3	水6 Water · Poison · 5 丁未 Fire Goat 山風蠱 4 初三 7	火2 Fire · Dispersing · 6 戊申 Earth Monkey 風水渙 5 初四 6
木3 Wood · Travelling · 7 己酉 Earth Rooster 火山旅 6 初五 8	金9 Metal · Stagnation · 8 庚戌 Metal Dog 天地否 7 初六 9	火7 Fire · Alliance · 9 辛亥 Metal Pig 水地比 8 初七 7	木8 Wood · Thunder · 1 壬子 Water Rat 震爲雷 9 初八 1	水6 Water · Beauty · 2 癸丑 Water Ox 山火賁 10 初九 8	火7 Fire · Accomplished · 3 甲寅 Wood Tiger 水火既濟 11 初十 9	水1 Water · Arriving · 4 乙卯 Wood Rabbit 地澤臨 12 十一 4
金4 Metal · Marsh · 5 丙辰 Fire Dragon 兑爲澤 13 十二 1	火2 Fire · Small Livestock · 6 丁巳 Fire Snake 風天小畜 14 十三 8	木3 Wood · The Cauldron · 7 戊午 Earth Horse 火風鼎 15 十四 4	水1 Water · Rising · 8 己未 Earth Goat 地風升 16 十五 2	火7 Fire · Water · 9 庚申 Metal Monkey 坎爲水 17 十六 1	木8 Wood · Lesser Exceeding · 1 辛酉 Metal Rooster 雷山小過 18 十七 3	金4 Metal · Gathering · 2 壬戌 Water Dog 澤地萃 19 十八 4
水6 Water · Peel · 3 癸亥 Water Pig 山地剝 20 十九 6	水1 Water · Earth · 4 甲子 Wood Rat 坤爲地 21 二十 1	木3 Wood · Biting · 5 乙丑 Wood Ox 火雷噬嗑 22 廿一 6	火2 Fire · Family · 6 丙寅 Fire Tiger 風火家人 23 廿二 4	水6 Water · Decreasing · 7 丁卯 Fire Rabbit 山澤損 24 廿三 9	金9 Metal · Tread · 8 戊辰 Earth Dragon 天澤履 25 廿四 6	木8 Wood · Great Strength · 9 己巳 Earth Snake 雷天大壯 26 廿五 2
木8 Wood · Consistency · 1 庚午 Metal Horse 雷風恒 27 廿六 9	金9 Metal · Litigation · 2 辛未 Metal Goat 天水訟 28 廿七 3	水1 Water · Officer · 3 壬申 Water Monkey 地水師 29 廿八 7	火2 Fire · Gradual Progress · 4 癸酉 Water Rooster 風山漸 30 廿九 7			

MAY 2003 丁巳

Xuan Kong Element 玄空五行	風天小畜 Small Livestock	Period Luck 卦運	Monthly Star 月星
Fire 火2		8	2

SUNDAY	MONDAY	TUESDAY	WEDNESDAY	THURSDAY	FRIDAY	SATURDAY
				火7 Fire · 5 Obstruction 水山蹇 甲戌 Wood Dog **1** 四月初一 2	木3 Wood · 6 Advancement 火地晉 乙亥 Wood Pig **2** 初二 3	水6 Water · 7 Nourish 山雷頤 丙子 Fire Rat **3** 初三 3
金4 Metal · 8 Following 澤雷隨 丁丑 Fire Ox **4** 初四 7	木8 Wood · 9 Abundance 雷火豐 戊寅 Earth Tiger **5** 初五 6	火7 Fire · 1 Regulate 水澤節 己卯 Earth Rabbit **6** 初六 8	水1 Water · 2 Unity 地天泰 庚辰 Metal Dragon **7** 初七 9	木3 Wood · 3 Great Reward 火天大有 辛巳 Metal Snake **8** 初八 7	火2 Fire · 4 Wind 巽爲風 壬午 Water Horse **9** 初九 1	金4 Metal · 5 Trap 澤水困 癸未 Water Goat **10** 初十 8
木3 Wood · 6 Not Yet Accomplished 火水未濟 甲申 Wood Monkey **11** 十一 9	金9 Metal · 7 Retreat 天山遯 乙酉 Wood Rooster **12** 十二 4	水6 Water · 8 Mountain 艮爲山 丙戌 Fire Dog **13** 十三 1	木8 Wood · 9 Delight 雷地豫 丁亥 Fire Pig **14** 十四 8	火7 Fire · 1 Beginning 水雷屯 戊子 Earth Rat **15** 十五 4	金9 Metal · 2 Without Wrongdoing 天雷無妄 己丑 Earth Ox **16** 十六 2	木3 Wood · 3 Fire 離爲火 庚寅 Metal Tiger **17** 十七 1
火2 Fire · 4 Sincerity 風澤中孚 辛卯 Metal Rabbit **18** 十八 3	水6 Water · 5 Big Livestock 山天大畜 壬辰 Water Dragon **19** 十九 4	金4 Metal · 6 Eliminating 澤天夬 癸巳 Water Snake **20** 二十 6	金9 Metal · 7 Heaven 乾爲天 甲午 Wood Horse **21** 廿一 1	火7 Fire · 8 Well 水風井 乙未 Wood Goat **22** 廿二 6	木8 Wood · 9 Relief 雷水解 丙申 Fire Monkey **23** 廿三 4	金4 Metal · 1 Influence 澤山咸 丁酉 Fire Rooster **24** 廿四 9
水1 Water · 2 Humility 地山謙 戊戌 Earth Dog **25** 廿五 6	火2 Fire · 3 Observation 風地觀 己亥 Earth Pig **26** 廿六 2	火2 Fire · 4 Increasing 風雷益 庚子 Metal Rat **27** 廿七 9	水1 Water · 5 Dimming Light 地火明夷 辛丑 Metal Ox **28** 廿八 3	金9 Metal · 6 Fellowship 天火同人 壬寅 Water Tiger **29** 廿九 7	木8 Wood · 7 Marrying Maiden 雷澤歸妹 癸卯 Water Rabbit **30** 三十 7	木3 Wood · 8 Opposition 火澤睽 甲辰 Wood Dragon **31** 五月初一 2

JUNE 2003 戊午

Xuan Kong Element 玄空五行	火風鼎 The Cauldron	Period Luck 卦運	Monthly Star 月星
Wood 木3		4	1

SUNDAY	MONDAY	TUESDAY	WEDNESDAY	THURSDAY	FRIDAY	SATURDAY
火7 Fire · 9 Waiting 水天需 乙巳 Wood Snake **1** 初二 3	金4 Metal · 1 Great Exceeding 澤風大過 丙午 Fire Horse **2** 初三 3	水6 Water · 2 Poison 山風蠱 丁未 Fire Goat **3** 初四 7	火2 Fire · 3 Dispersing 風水渙 戊申 Earth Monkey **4** 初五 6	木3 Wood · 4 Travelling 火山旅 己酉 Earth Rooster **5** 初六 8	金9 Metal · 5 Stagnation 天地否 庚戌 Metal Dog **6** 初七 9	火7 Fire · 6 Alliance 水地比 辛亥 Metal Pig **7** 初八 7
木8 Wood · 7 Thunder 震爲雷 壬子 Water Rat **8** 初九 1	水6 Water · 8 Beauty 山火賁 癸丑 Water Ox **9** 初十 8	火7 Fire · 9 Accomplished 水火既濟 甲寅 Wood Tiger **10** 十一 9	水1 Water · 1 Arriving 地澤臨 乙卯 Wood Rabbit **11** 十二 4	金4 Metal · 2 Marsh 兌爲澤 丙辰 Fire Dragon **12** 十三 1	火2 Fire · 3 Small Livestock 風天小畜 丁巳 Fire Snake **13** 十四 8	木3 Wood · 4 The Cauldron 火風鼎 戊午 Earth Horse **14** 十五 4
水1 Water · 5 Rising 地風升 己未 Earth Goat **15** 十六 2	火7 Fire · 6 Water 坎爲水 庚申 Metal Monkey **16** 十七 1	木8 Wood · 7 Lesser Exceeding 雷山小過 辛酉 Metal Rooster **17** 十八 3	金4 Metal · 8 Gathering 澤地萃 壬戌 Water Dog **18** 十九 4	水6 Water · 9 Peel 山地剝 癸亥 Water Pig **19** 二十 6	水1 Water · 1 Earth 坤爲地 甲子 Wood Rat **20** 廿一 1	木3 Wood · 2 Biting 火雷噬嗑 乙丑 Wood Ox **21** 廿二 6
火2 Fire · 3/4 Family 風火家人 丙寅 Fire Tiger **22** 廿三 4	水6 Water · 3 Decreasing 山澤損 丁卯 Fire Rabbit **23** 廿四 9	金9 Metal · 2 Tread 天澤履 戊辰 Earth Dragon **24** 廿五 6	木8 Wood · 1 Great Strength 雷天大壯 己巳 Earth Snake **25** 廿六 2	木8 Wood · 9 Consistency 雷風恆 庚午 Metal Horse **26** 廿七 9	金9 Metal · 8 Litigation 天水訟 辛未 Metal Goat **27** 廿八 3	水1 Water · 7 Officer 地水師 壬申 Water Monkey **28** 廿九 7
火2 Fire · 6 Gradual Progress 風山漸 癸酉 Water Rooster **29** 三十 7	火7 Fire · 5 Obstruction 水山蹇 甲戌 Wood Dog **30** 六月初一 2					

JULY 2003 己未

Xuan Kong Element 玄空五行	地風升 Rising	Period Luck 卦運	Monthly Star 月星
Water 水1		2	9

SUNDAY	MONDAY	TUESDAY	WEDNESDAY	THURSDAY	FRIDAY	SATURDAY
		木3 Wood 4 Advancement 火地晉 乙亥 Wood Pig 1 初二 3	水6 Water 3 Nourish 山雷頤 丙子 Fire Rat 2 初三 3	金4 Metal 2 Following 澤雷隨 丁丑 Fire Ox 3 初四 7	木8 Wood 1 Abundance 雷火豐 戊寅 Earth Tiger 4 初五 6	火7 Fire 9 Regulate 水澤節 己卯 Earth Rabbit 5 初六 8
水1 Water 8 Unity 地天泰 庚辰 Metal Dragon 6 初七 9	木3 Wood 7 Great Reward 火天大有 辛巳 Metal Snake 7 初八 7	火2 Fire 6 Wind 巽為風 壬午 Water Horse 8 初九 1	金4 Metal 5 Trap 澤水困 癸未 Water Goat 9 初十 8	木3 Wood 4 Not Yet Accomplished 火水未濟 甲申 Wood Monkey 10 十一 9	金9 Metal 3 Retreat 天山遯 乙酉 Wood Rooster 11 十二 4	水6 Water 2 Mountain 艮為山 丙戌 Fire Dog 12 十三 1
木8 Wood 1 Delight 雷地豫 丁亥 Fire Pig 13 十四 8	火7 Fire 9 Beginning 水雷屯 戊子 Earth Rat 14 十五 4	金9 Metal 8 Without Wrongdoing 天雷無妄 己丑 Earth Ox 15 十六 2	木3 Wood 7 Fire 離為火 庚寅 Metal Tiger 16 十七 1	火2 Fire 6 Sincerity 風澤中孚 辛卯 Metal Rabbit 17 十八 3	水6 Water 5 Big Livestock 山天大畜 壬辰 Water Dragon 18 十九 4	金4 Metal 4 Eliminating 澤天夬 癸巳 Water Snake 19 二十 6
金9 Metal 3 Heaven 乾為天 甲午 Wood Horse 20 廿一 1	火7 Fire 2 Well 水風井 乙未 Wood Goat 21 廿二 6	木8 Wood 1 Relief 雷水解 丙申 Fire Monkey 22 廿三 4	金4 Metal 9 Influence 澤山咸 丁酉 Fire Rooster 23 廿四 9	水1 Water 8 Humility 地山謙 戊戌 Earth Dog 24 廿五 6	火2 Fire 7 Observation 風地觀 己亥 Earth Pig 25 廿六 2	火2 Fire 6 Increasing 風雷益 庚子 Metal Rat 26 廿七 9
水1 Water 5 Dimming Light 地火明夷 辛丑 Metal Ox 27 廿八 3	金9 Metal 4 Fellowship 天火同人 壬寅 Water Tiger 28 廿九 7	木8 Wood 3 Marrying Maiden 雷澤歸妹 癸卯 Water Rabbit 29 七月初一 7	木3 Wood 2 Opposition 火澤睽 甲辰 Wood Dragon 30 初二 2	火7 Fire 1 Waiting 水天需 乙巳 Wood Snake 31 初三 3		

AUGUST 2003 庚申

Xuan Kong Element 玄空五行	坎為水 Water	Period Luck 卦運	Monthly Star 月星
Fire 火7		1	8

SUNDAY	MONDAY	TUESDAY	WEDNESDAY	THURSDAY	FRIDAY	SATURDAY
水6 Water 6 Nourish 山雷頤 丙子 Fire Rat 31 廿九 3					金4 Metal 9 Great Exceeding 澤風大過 丙午 Fire Horse 1 初四 3	水6 Water 8 Poison 山風蠱 丁未 Fire Goat 2 初五 7
火2 Fire 7 Dispersing 風水渙 戊申 Earth Monkey 3 初六 6	木3 Wood 6 Travelling 火山旅 己酉 Earth Rooster 4 初七 8	金9 Metal 5 Stagnation 天地否 庚戌 Metal Dog 5 初八 9	火7 Fire 4 Alliance 水地比 辛亥 Metal Pig 6 初九 7	木8 Wood 3 Thunder 震為雷 壬子 Water Rat 7 初十 1	水6 Water 2 Beauty 山火賁 癸丑 Water Ox 8 十一 8	火7 Fire 1 Accomplished 水火既濟 甲寅 Wood Tiger 9 十二 9
水1 Water 9 Arriving 地澤臨 乙卯 Wood Rabbit 10 十三 4	金4 Metal 8 Marsh 兌為澤 丙辰 Fire Dragon 11 十四 1	火2 Fire 7 Small Livestock 風天小畜 丁巳 Fire Snake 12 十五 8	木3 Wood 6 The Cauldron 火風鼎 戊午 Earth Horse 13 十六 4	水1 Water 5 Rising 地風升 己未 Earth Goat 14 十七 2	火7 Fire 4 Water 坎為水 庚申 Metal Monkey 15 十八 1	木8 Wood 3 Lesser Exceeding 雷山小過 辛酉 Metal Rooster 16 十九 3
金4 Metal 2 Gathering 澤地萃 壬戌 Water Dog 17 二十 4	水6 Water 1 Peel 山地剝 癸亥 Water Pig 18 廿一 6	水1 Water 9 Earth 坤為地 甲子 Wood Rat 19 廿二 1	木3 Wood 8 Biting 火雷噬嗑 乙丑 Wood Ox 20 廿三 6	火2 Fire 7 Family 風火家人 丙寅 Fire Tiger 21 廿四 4	水6 Water 6 Decreasing 山澤損 丁卯 Fire Rabbit 22 廿五 9	金9 Metal 5 Tread 天澤履 戊辰 Earth Dragon 23 廿六 6
木8 Wood 4 Great Strength 雷天大壯 己巳 Earth Snake 24 廿七 2	木8 Wood 3 Consistency 雷風恒 庚午 Metal Horse 25 廿八 9	金9 Metal 2 Litigation 天水訟 辛未 Metal Goat 26 廿九 3	水1 Water 1 Officer 地水師 壬申 Water Monkey 27 三十 7	火2 Fire 9 Gradual Progress 風山漸 癸酉 Water Rooster 28 八月初一 7	火7 Fire 8 Obstruction 水山蹇 甲戌 Wood Dog 29 初二 2	木3 Wood 7 Advancement 火地晉 乙亥 Wood Pig 30 初三 3

SEPTEMBER 2003 辛酉

Xuan Kong Element 玄空五行	雷山小過 Lesser Exceeding	Period Luck 卦運	Monthly Star 月星
Wood 木8		3	7

SUNDAY	MONDAY	TUESDAY	WEDNESDAY	THURSDAY	FRIDAY	SATURDAY
	1 初五 金4 Metal · 5 Following 澤雷隨 丁丑 Fire Ox · 7	**2** 初六 木8 Wood · 4 Abundance 雷火豐 戊寅 Earth Tiger · 6	**3** 初七 火7 Fire · 3 Regulate 水澤節 己卯 Earth Rabbit · 8	**4** 初八 水1 Water · 2 Unity 地天泰 庚辰 Metal Dragon · 9	**5** 初九 木3 Wood · 1 Great Reward 火天大有 辛巳 Metal Snake · 7	**6** 初十 火2 Fire · 9 Wind 巽爲風 壬午 Water Horse · 1
7 十一 金4 Metal · 8 Trap 澤水困 癸未 Water Goat · 8	**8** 十二 木3 Wood · 7 Not Yet Accomplished 火水未濟 甲申 Wood Monkey · 9	**9** 十三 金9 Metal · 6 Retreat 天山遯 乙酉 Wood Rooster · 4	**10** 十四 水6 Water · 5 Mountain 艮爲山 丙戌 Fire Dog · 1	**11** 十五 木8 Wood · 4 Delight 雷地豫 丁亥 Fire Pig · 8	**12** 十六 火7 Fire · 3 Beginning 水雷屯 戊子 Earth Rat · 4	**13** 十七 金9 Metal · 2 Without Wrongdoing 天雷無妄 己丑 Earth Ox · 2
14 十八 木3 Wood · 1 Fire 離爲火 庚寅 Metal Tiger · 1	**15** 十九 火2 Fire · 9 Sincerity 風澤中孚 辛卯 Metal Rabbit · 3	**16** 二十 水6 Water · 8 Big Livestock 山天大畜 壬辰 Water Dragon · 4	**17** 廿一 金4 Metal · 7 Eliminating 澤天夬 癸巳 Water Snake · 6	**18** 廿二 金9 Metal · 6 Heaven 乾爲天 甲午 Wood Horse · 1	**19** 廿三 火7 Fire · 5 Well 水風井 乙未 Wood Goat · 6	**20** 廿四 木8 Wood · 4 Relief 雷水解 丙申 Fire Monkey · 4
21 廿五 金4 Metal · 3 Influence 澤山咸 丁酉 Fire Rooster · 9	**22** 廿六 水1 Water · 2 Humility 地山謙 戊戌 Earth Dog · 6	**23** 廿七 火2 Fire · 1 Observation 風地觀 己亥 Earth Pig · 2	**24** 廿八 火2 Fire · 9 Increasing 風雷益 庚子 Metal Rat · 9	**25** 廿九 水1 Water · 8 Dimming Light 地火明夷 辛丑 Metal Ox · 3	**26** 九月初一 金9 Metal · 7 Fellowship 天火同人 壬寅 Water Tiger · 7	**27** 初二 木8 Wood · 6 Marrying Maiden 雷澤歸妹 癸卯 Water Rabbit · 7
28 初三 木3 Wood · 5 Opposition 火澤睽 甲辰 Wood Dragon · 2	**29** 初四 火7 Fire · 4 Waiting 水天需 乙巳 Wood Snake · 3	**30** 初五 金4 Metal · 3 Great Exceeding 澤風大過 丙午 Fire Horse · 3				

OCTOBER 2003 壬戌

Xuan Kong Element 玄空五行	澤地萃 Gathering	Period Luck 卦運	Monthly Star 月星
Metal 金4		4	6

SUNDAY	MONDAY	TUESDAY	WEDNESDAY	THURSDAY	FRIDAY	SATURDAY
			1 初六 水6 Water · 2 Poison 山風蠱 丁未 Fire Goat · 7	**2** 初七 火2 Fire · 1 Dispersing 風水渙 戊申 Earth Monkey · 6	**3** 初八 木3 Wood · 9 Travelling 火山旅 己酉 Earth Rooster · 8	**4** 初九 金9 Metal · 8 Stagnation 天地否 庚戌 Metal Dog · 9
5 初十 火7 Fire · 7 Alliance 水地比 辛亥 Metal Pig · 7	**6** 十一 木8 Wood · 6 Thunder 震爲雷 壬子 Water Rat · 1	**7** 十二 水6 Water · 5 Beauty 山火賁 癸丑 Water Ox · 8	**8** 十三 火7 Fire · 4 Accomplished 水火既濟 甲寅 Wood Tiger · 9	**9** 十四 水1 Water · 3 Arriving 地澤臨 乙卯 Wood Rabbit · 4	**10** 十五 金4 Metal · 2 Marsh 兑爲澤 丙辰 Fire Dragon · 1	**11** 十六 火2 Fire · 1 Small Livestock 風天小畜 丁巳 Fire Snake · 8
12 十七 木3 Wood · 9 The Cauldron 火風鼎 戊午 Earth Horse · 4	**13** 十八 水1 Water · 8 Rising 地風升 己未 Earth Goat · 2	**14** 十九 火7 Fire · 7 Water 坎爲水 庚申 Metal Monkey · 1	**15** 二十 木8 Wood · 6 Lesser Exceeding 雷山小過 辛酉 Metal Rooster · 3	**16** 廿一 金4 Metal · 5 Gathering 澤地萃 壬戌 Water Dog · 4	**17** 廿二 水6 Water · 4 Peel 山地剝 癸亥 Water Pig · 6	**18** 廿三 水1 Water · 3 Earth 坤爲地 甲子 Wood Rat · 1
19 廿四 木3 Wood · 2 Biting 火雷噬嗑 乙丑 Wood Ox · 6	**20** 廿五 火2 Fire · 1 Family 風火家人 丙寅 Fire Tiger · 4	**21** 廿六 水6 Water · 9 Decreasing 山澤損 丁卯 Fire Rabbit · 9	**22** 廿七 金9 Metal · 8 Tread 天澤履 戊辰 Earth Dragon · 6	**23** 廿八 木8 Wood · 7 Great Strength 雷天大壯 己巳 Earth Snake · 2	**24** 廿九 木8 Wood · 6 Consistency 雷風恒 庚午 Metal Horse · 9	**25** 十月初一 金9 Metal · 5 Litigation 天水訟 辛未 Metal Goat · 3
26 初二 水1 Water · 4 Officer 地水師 壬申 Water Monkey · 7	**27** 初三 火2 Fire · 3 Gradual Progress 風山漸 癸酉 Water Rooster · 7	**28** 初四 火7 Fire · 2 Obstruction 水山蹇 甲戌 Wood Dog · 2	**29** 初五 木3 Wood · 1 Advancement 火地晉 乙亥 Wood Pig · 3	**30** 初六 水6 Water · 9 Nourish 山雷頤 丙子 Fire Rat · 3	**31** 初七 金4 Metal · 8 Following 澤雷隨 丁丑 Fire Ox · 7	

NOVEMBER 2003 癸亥

Xuan Kong Element 玄空五行	山地剝 Peel	Period Luck 卦運	Monthly Star 月星
Water 水6		6	5

SUNDAY	MONDAY	TUESDAY	WEDNESDAY	THURSDAY	FRIDAY	SATURDAY
水6 Water Poison 山風蠱 5 丁未 Fire Goat 30 初七 7						木8 Wood Abundance 雷火豐 7 戊寅 Earth Tiger 1 初八 6
火7 Fire Regulate 水澤節 6 己卯 Earth Rabbit 2 初九 8	水1 Water Unity 地天泰 5 庚辰 Metal Dragon 3 初十 9	木3 Wood Great Reward 火天大有 4 辛巳 Metal Snake 4 十一 7	火2 Fire Wind 巽爲風 3 壬午 Water Horse 5 十二 1	金4 Metal Trap 澤水困 2 癸未 Water Goat 6 十三 8	木3 Wood Not Yet Accomplished 火水未濟 1 甲申 Wood Monkey 7 十四 9	金9 Metal Retreat 天山遯 9 乙酉 Wood Rooster 8 十五 4
水6 Water Mountain 艮爲山 8 丙戌 Fire Dog 9 十六 1	木8 Wood Delight 雷地豫 7 丁亥 Fire Pig 10 十七 8	火7 Fire Beginning 水雷屯 6 戊子 Earth Rat 11 十八 4	金9 Metal Without Wrongdoing 天雷無妄 5 己丑 Earth Ox 12 十九 2	木3 Wood Fire 離爲火 4 庚寅 Metal Tiger 13 二十 1	火2 Fire Sincerity 風澤中孚 3 辛卯 Metal Rabbit 14 廿一 3	水6 Water Big Livestock 山天大畜 2 壬辰 Water Dragon 15 廿二 4
金4 Metal Eliminating 澤天夬 1 癸巳 Water Snake 16 廿三 6	金9 Metal Heaven 乾爲天 9 甲午 Wood Horse 17 廿四 1	火7 Fire Well 水風井 8 乙未 Wood Goat 18 廿五 6	木8 Wood Relief 雷水解 7 丙申 Fire Monkey 19 廿六 4	金4 Metal Influence 澤山咸 6 丁酉 Fire Rooster 20 廿七 9	水1 Water Humility 地山謙 5 戊戌 Earth Dog 21 廿八 6	火2 Fire Observation 風地觀 4 己亥 Earth Pig 22 廿九 2
火2 Fire Increasing 風雷益 3 庚子 Metal Rat 23 三十 9	水1 Water Dimming Light 地火明夷 2 辛丑 Metal Ox 24 十一月初一 3	金9 Metal Fellowship 天火同人 1 壬寅 Water Tiger 25 初二 7	木8 Wood Marrying Maiden 雷澤歸妹 9 癸卯 Water Rabbit 26 初三 7	木3 Wood Opposition 火澤睽 8 甲辰 Wood Dragon 27 初四 2	火7 Fire Waiting 水天需 7 乙巳 Wood Snake 28 初五 3	金4 Metal Great Exceeding 澤風大過 6 丙午 Fire Horse 29 初六 3

DECEMBER 2003 甲子

Xuan Kong Element 玄空五行	坤爲地 Earth	Period Luck 卦運	Monthly Star 月星
Water 水1		1	4

SUNDAY	MONDAY	TUESDAY	WEDNESDAY	THURSDAY	FRIDAY	SATURDAY
	火2 Fire Dispersing 風水渙 4 戊申 Earth Monkey 1 初八 6	木3 Wood Travelling 火山旅 3 己酉 Earth Rooster 2 初九 8	金9 Metal Stagnation 天地否 2 庚戌 Metal Dog 3 初十 9	火7 Fire Alliance 水地比 1 辛亥 Metal Pig 4 十一 7	木8 Wood Thunder 震爲雷 9 壬子 Water Rat 5 十二 1	水6 Water Beauty 山火賁 8 癸丑 Water Ox 6 十三 8
火7 Fire Accomplished 水火既濟 7 甲寅 Wood Tiger 7 十四 9	水1 Water Arriving 地澤臨 6 乙卯 Wood Rabbit 8 十五 4	金4 Metal Marsh 兌爲澤 5 丙辰 Fire Dragon 9 十六 1	火2 Fire Small Livestock 風天小畜 4 丁巳 Fire Snake 10 十七 8	木3 Wood The Cauldron 火風鼎 3 戊午 Earth Horse 11 十八 4	水1 Water Rising 地風升 2 己未 Earth Goat 12 十九 2	火7 Fire Water 坎爲水 1 庚申 Metal Monkey 13 二十 1
木8 Wood Lesser Exceeding 雷山小過 9 辛酉 Metal Rooster 14 廿一 3	金4 Metal Gathering 澤地萃 8 壬戌 Water Dog 15 廿二 4	水6 Water Peel 山地剝 7 癸亥 Water Pig 16 廿三 6	水1 Water Earth 坤爲地 6 甲子 Wood Rat 17 廿四 1	木3 Wood Biting 火雷噬嗑 5 乙丑 Wood Ox 18 廿五 6	火2 Fire Family 風火家人 4 丙寅 Fire Tiger 19 廿六 4	水6 Water Decreasing 山澤損 3 丁卯 Fire Rabbit 20 廿七 9
金9 Metal Tread 天澤履 2 戊辰 Earth Dragon 21 廿八 6	木8 Wood Great Strength 雷天大壯 1/9 己巳 Earth Snake 22 廿九 2	木8 Wood Consistency 雷風恒 1 庚午 Metal Horse 23 十二月初一 9	金9 Metal Litigation 天水訟 2 辛未 Metal Goat 24 初二 3	水1 Water Officer 地水師 3 壬申 Water Monkey 25 初三 7	火2 Fire Gradual Progress 風山漸 4 癸酉 Water Rooster 26 初四 7	火7 Fire Obstruction 水山蹇 5 甲戌 Wood Dog 27 初五 2
木3 Wood Advancement 火地晉 6 乙亥 Wood Pig 28 初六 3	水6 Water Nourish 山雷頤 7 丙子 Fire Rat 29 初七 3	金4 Metal Following 澤雷隨 8 丁丑 Fire Ox 30 初八 7	木8 Wood Abundance 雷火豐 9 戊寅 Earth Tiger 31 初九 6			

2004 甲申

(*Jia Shen*) Wood Monkey

2004 甲申 *(Jia Shen)* Wood Monkey

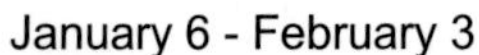

January 6 - February 3

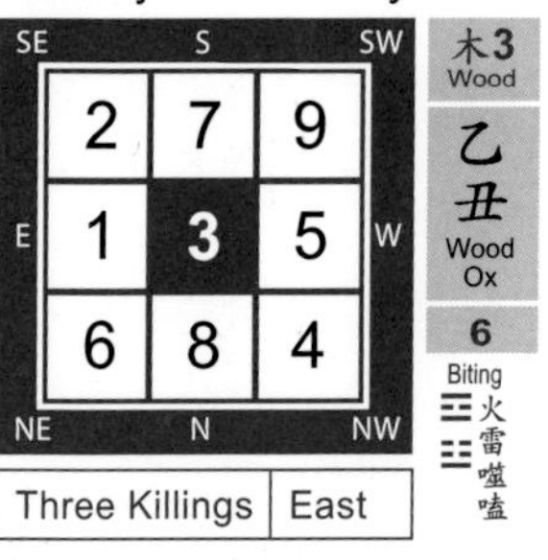

February 4 - March 4

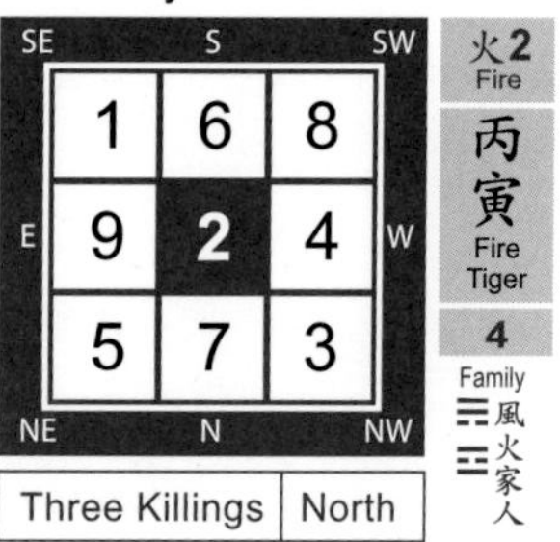

March 5 - April 3

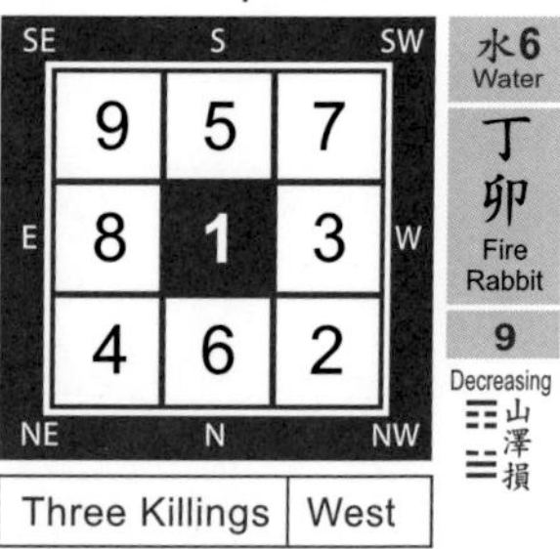

April 4 - May 4

May 5 - June 4

June 5 - July 6

July 7 - August 6

August 7 - September 6

September 7 - October 7

October 8 - November 6

November 7 - December 6

December 7 - January 4

JANUARY 2004 乙丑

Xuan Kong Element 玄空五行	火雷噬嗑 Biting	Period Luck 卦運	Monthly Star 月星
Wood 木3		6	3

SUNDAY	MONDAY	TUESDAY	WEDNESDAY	THURSDAY	FRIDAY	SATURDAY
				火7 Fire 1 Regulate 己卯 Earth Rabbit 水澤節 1 初十 8	水1 Water 2 Unity 庚辰 Metal Dragon 地天泰 2 十一 9	木3 Wood 3 Great Reward 辛巳 Metal Snake 火天大有 3 十二 7
火2 Fire 4 Wind 壬午 Water Horse 巽為風 4 十三 1	金4 Metal 5 Trap 癸未 Water Goat 澤水困 5 十四 8	木3 Wood 6 Not Yet Accomplished 甲申 Wood Monkey 火水未濟 6 十五 9	金9 Metal 7 Retreat 乙酉 Wood Rooster 天山遯 7 十六 4	水6 Water 8 Mountain 丙戌 Fire Dog 艮為山 8 十七 1	木8 Wood 9 Delight 丁亥 Fire Pig 雷地豫 9 十八 8	火7 Fire 1 Beginning 戊子 Earth Rat 水雷屯 10 十九 4
金9 Metal 2 Without Wrongdoing 己丑 Earth Ox 天雷無妄 11 二十 2	木3 Wood 3 Fire 庚寅 Metal Tiger 離為火 12 廿一 1	火2 Fire 4 Sincerity 辛卯 Metal Rabbit 風澤中孚 13 廿二 3	水6 Water 5 Big Livestock 壬辰 Water Dragon 山天大畜 14 廿三 4	金4 Metal 6 Eliminating 癸巳 Water Snake 澤天夬 15 廿四 6	金9 Metal 7 Heaven 甲午 Wood Horse 乾為天 16 廿五 1	火7 Fire 8 Well 乙未 Wood Goat 水風井 17 廿六 6
木8 Wood 9 Relief 丙申 Fire Monkey 雷水解 18 廿七 4	金4 Metal 1 Influence 丁酉 Fire Rooster 澤山咸 19 廿八 9	水1 Water 2 Humility 戊戌 Earth Dog 地山謙 20 廿九 6	火2 Fire 3 Observation 己亥 Earth Pig 風地觀 21 三十 2	火2 Fire 4 Increasing 庚子 Metal Rat 風雷益 22 正月初一 9	水1 Water 5 Dimming Light 辛丑 Metal Ox 地火明夷 23 初二 3	金9 Metal 6 Fellowship 壬寅 Water Tiger 天火同人 24 初三 7
木8 Wood 7 Marrying Maiden 癸卯 Water Rabbit 雷澤歸妹 25 初四 7	木3 Wood 8 Opposition 甲辰 Wood Dragon 火澤睽 26 初五 2	火7 Fire 9 Waiting 乙巳 Wood Snake 水天需 27 初六 3	金4 Metal 1 Great Exceeding 丙午 Fire Horse 澤風大過 28 初七 3	水6 Water 2 Poison 丁未 Fire Goat 山風蠱 29 初八 7	火2 Fire 3 Dispersing 戊申 Earth Monkey 風水渙 30 初九 6	木3 Wood 4 Travelling 己酉 Earth Rooster 火山旅 31 初十 8

FEBRUARY 2004 丙寅

Xuan Kong Element 玄空五行	風火家人 Family	Period Luck 卦運	Monthly Star 月星
Fire 火2		4	2

SUNDAY	MONDAY	TUESDAY	WEDNESDAY	THURSDAY	FRIDAY	SATURDAY
金9 Metal 5 Stagnation 庚戌 Metal Dog 天地否 1 十一 9	火7 Fire 6 Alliance 辛亥 Metal Pig 水地比 2 十二 7	木8 Wood 7 Thunder 壬子 Water Rat 震為雷 3 十三 1	水6 Water 8 Beauty 癸丑 Water Ox 山火賁 4 十四 8	火7 Fire 9 Accomplished 甲寅 Wood Tiger 水火既濟 5 十五 9	水1 Water 1 Arriving 乙卯 Wood Rabbit 地澤臨 6 十六 4	金4 Metal 2 Marsh 丙辰 Fire Dragon 兌為澤 7 十七 1
火2 Fire 3 Small Livestock 丁巳 Fire Snake 風天小畜 8 十八 8	木3 Wood 4 The Cauldron 戊午 Earth Horse 火風鼎 9 十九 4	水1 Water 5 Rising 己未 Earth Goat 地風升 10 二十 2	火7 Fire 6 Water 庚申 Metal Monkey 坎為水 11 廿一 1	木8 Wood 7 Lesser Exceeding 辛酉 Metal Rooster 雷山小過 12 廿二 3	金4 Metal 8 Gathering 壬戌 Water Dog 澤地萃 13 廿三 4	水6 Water 9 Peel 癸亥 Water Pig 山地剝 14 廿四 6
水1 Water 1 Earth 甲子 Wood Rat 坤為地 15 廿五 1	木3 Wood 2 Biting 乙丑 Wood Ox 火雷噬嗑 16 廿六 6	火2 Fire 3 Family 丙寅 Fire Tiger 風火家人 17 廿七 4	水6 Water 4 Decreasing 丁卯 Fire Rabbit 山澤損 18 廿八 9	金9 Metal 5 Tread 戊辰 Earth Dragon 天澤履 19 廿九 6	木8 Wood 6 Great Strength 己巳 Earth Snake 雷天大壯 20 二月初一 2	木8 Wood 7 Consistency 庚午 Metal Horse 雷風恆 21 初二 9
金9 Metal 8 Litigation 辛未 Metal Goat 天水訟 22 初三 3	水1 Water 9 Officer 壬申 Water Monkey 地水師 23 初四 7	火2 Fire 1 Gradual Progress 癸酉 Water Rooster 風山漸 24 初五 7	火7 Fire 2 Obstruction 甲戌 Wood Dog 水山蹇 25 初六 2	木3 Wood 3 Advancement 乙亥 Wood Pig 火地晉 26 初七 3	水6 Water 4 Nourish 丙子 Fire Rat 山雷頤 27 初八 3	金4 Metal 5 Following 丁丑 Fire Ox 澤雷隨 28 初九 7
木8 Wood 6 Abundance 戊寅 Earth Tiger 雷火豐 29 初十 6						

MARCH 2004 丁卯

Xuan Kong Element 玄空五行	山澤損 Decreasing	Period Luck 卦運	Monthly Star 月星
Water 水6		9	1

SUNDAY	MONDAY	TUESDAY	WEDNESDAY	THURSDAY	FRIDAY	SATURDAY
	1 十一 火7 Fire · 己卯 Earth Rabbit · 8 Regulate 水澤節 · 7	**2** 十二 水1 Water · 庚辰 Metal Dragon · 9 Unity 地天泰 · 8	**3** 十三 木3 Wood · 辛巳 Metal Snake · 7 Great Reward 火天大有 · 9	**4** 十四 火2 Fire · 壬午 Water Horse · 1 Wind 巽爲風 · 1	**5** 十五 金4 Metal · 癸未 Water Goat · 8 Trap 澤水困 · 2	**6** 十六 木3 Wood · 甲申 Wood Monkey · 9 Not Yet Accomplished 火水未濟 · 3
7 十七 金9 Metal · 乙酉 Wood Rooster · 4 Retreat 天山遯 · 4	**8** 十八 水6 Water · 丙戌 Fire Dog · 1 Mountain 艮爲山 · 5	**9** 十九 木8 Wood · 丁亥 Fire Pig · 8 Delight 雷地豫 · 6	**10** 二十 火7 Fire · 戊子 Earth Rat · 4 Beginning 水雷屯 · 7	**11** 廿一 金9 Metal · 己丑 Earth Ox · 2 Without Wrongdoing 天雷無妄 · 8	**12** 廿二 木3 Wood · 庚寅 Metal Tiger · 1 Fire 離爲火 · 9	**13** 廿三 火2 Fire · 辛卯 Metal Rabbit · 3 Sincerity 風澤中孚 · 1
14 廿四 水6 Water · 壬辰 Water Dragon · 4 Big Livestock 山天大畜 · 2	**15** 廿五 金4 Metal · 癸巳 Water Snake · 6 Eliminating 澤天夬 · 3	**16** 廿六 金9 Metal · 甲午 Wood Horse · 1 Heaven 乾爲天 · 4	**17** 廿七 火7 Fire · 乙未 Wood Goat · 6 Well 水風井 · 5	**18** 廿八 木8 Wood · 丙申 Fire Monkey · 4 Relief 雷水解 · 6	**19** 廿九 金4 Metal · 丁酉 Fire Rooster · 9 Influence 澤山咸 · 7	**20** 三十 水1 Water · 戊戌 Earth Dog · 6 Humility 地山謙 · 8
21 閏二月初一 火2 Fire · 己亥 Earth Pig · 2 Observation 風地觀 · 9	**22** 初二 火2 Fire · 庚子 Metal Rat · 9 Increasing 風雷益 · 1	**23** 初三 水1 Water · 辛丑 Metal Ox · 3 Dimming Light 地火明夷 · 2	**24** 初四 金9 Metal · 壬寅 Water Tiger · 7 Fellowship 天火同人 · 3	**25** 初五 木8 Wood · 癸卯 Water Rabbit · 7 Marrying Maiden 雷澤歸妹 · 4	**26** 初六 木3 Wood · 甲辰 Wood Dragon · 2 Opposition 火澤睽 · 5	**27** 初七 火7 Fire · 乙巳 Wood Snake · 3 Waiting 水天需 · 6
28 初八 金4 Metal · 丙午 Fire Horse · 3 Great Exceeding 澤風大過 · 7	**29** 初九 水6 Water · 丁未 Fire Goat · 7 Poison 山風蠱 · 8	**30** 初十 火2 Fire · 戊申 Earth Monkey · 6 Dispersing 風水渙 · 9	**31** 十一 木3 Wood · 己酉 Earth Rooster · 8 Travelling 火山旅 · 1			

APRIL 2004 戊辰

Xuan Kong Element 玄空五行	天澤履 Tread	Period Luck 卦運	Monthly Star 月星
Metal 金9		6	9

SUNDAY	MONDAY	TUESDAY	WEDNESDAY	THURSDAY	FRIDAY	SATURDAY
				1 十二 金9 Metal · 庚戌 Metal Dog · 9 Stagnation 天地否 · 2	**2** 十三 火7 Fire · 辛亥 Metal Pig · 7 Alliance 水地比 · 3	**3** 十四 木8 Wood · 壬子 Water Rat · 1 Thunder 震爲雷 · 4
4 十五 水6 Water · 癸丑 Water Ox · 8 Beauty 山火賁 · 5	**5** 十六 火7 Fire · 甲寅 Wood Tiger · 9 Accomplished 水火既濟 · 6	**6** 十七 水1 Water · 乙卯 Wood Rabbit · 4 Arriving 地澤臨 · 7	**7** 十八 金4 Metal · 丙辰 Fire Dragon · 1 Marsh 兑爲澤 · 8	**8** 十九 火2 Fire · 丁巳 Fire Snake · 8 Small Livestock 風天小畜 · 9	**9** 二十 木3 Wood · 戊午 Earth Horse · 4 The Cauldron 火風鼎 · 1	**10** 廿一 水1 Water · 己未 Earth Goat · 2 Rising 地風升 · 2
11 廿二 火7 Fire · 庚申 Metal Monkey · 1 Water 坎爲水 · 3	**12** 廿三 木8 Wood · 辛酉 Metal Rooster · 3 Lesser Exceeding 雷山小過 · 4	**13** 廿四 金4 Metal · 壬戌 Water Dog · 4 Gathering 澤地萃 · 5	**14** 廿五 水6 Water · 癸亥 Water Pig · 6 Peel 山地剝 · 6	**15** 廿六 水1 Water · 甲子 Wood Rat · 1 Earth 坤爲地 · 7	**16** 廿七 木3 Wood · 乙丑 Wood Ox · 6 Biting 火雷噬嗑 · 8	**17** 廿八 火2 Fire · 丙寅 Fire Tiger · 4 Family 風火家人 · 9
18 廿九 水6 Water · 丁卯 Fire Rabbit · 9 Decreasing 山澤損 · 1	**19** 三月初一 金9 Metal · 戊辰 Earth Dragon · 6 Tread 天澤履 · 2	**20** 初二 木8 Wood · 己巳 Earth Snake · 2 Great Strength 雷天大壯 · 3	**21** 初三 木8 Wood · 庚午 Metal Horse · 9 Consistency 雷風恒 · 4	**22** 初四 金9 Metal · 辛未 Metal Goat · 3 Litigation 天水訟 · 5	**23** 初五 水1 Water · 壬申 Water Monkey · 7 Officer 地水師 · 6	**24** 初六 火2 Fire · 癸酉 Water Rooster · 7 Gradual Progress 風山漸 · 7
25 初七 火7 Fire · 甲戌 Wood Dog · 2 Obstruction 水山蹇 · 8	**26** 初八 木3 Wood · 乙亥 Wood Pig · 3 Advancement 火地晉 · 9	**27** 初九 水6 Water · 丙子 Fire Rat · 3 Nourish 山雷頤 · 1	**28** 初十 金4 Metal · 丁丑 Fire Ox · 7 Following 澤雷隨 · 2	**29** 十一 木8 Wood · 戊寅 Earth Tiger · 6 Abundance 雷火豐 · 3	**30** 十二 火7 Fire · 己卯 Earth Rabbit · 8 Regulate 水澤節 · 4	

MAY 2004 己巳

Xuan Kong Element 玄空五行	雷天大壯 Great Strength	Period Luck 卦運	Monthly Star 月星
Wood 木8		2	8

SUNDAY	MONDAY	TUESDAY	WEDNESDAY	THURSDAY	FRIDAY	SATURDAY
木3 Wood 7 Travelling 火山旅 己酉 Earth Rooster 30 十二 8	金9 Metal 8 Stagnation 天地否 庚戌 Metal Dog 31 十三 9					水1 Water 5 Unity 地天泰 庚辰 Metal Dragon 1 十三 9
木3 Wood 6 Great Reward 火天大有 辛巳 Metal Snake 2 十四 7	火2 Fire 7 Wind 巽為風 壬午 Water Horse 3 十五 1	金4 Metal 8 Trap 澤水困 癸未 Water Goat 4 十六 8	木3 Wood 9 Not Yet Accomplished 火水未濟 甲申 Wood Monkey 5 十七 9	金9 Metal 1 Retreat 天山遯 乙酉 Wood Rooster 6 十八 4	水6 Water 2 Mountain 艮為山 丙戌 Fire Dog 7 十九 1	木8 Wood 3 Delight 雷地豫 丁亥 Fire Pig 8 二十 8
火7 Fire 4 Beginning 水雷屯 戊子 Earth Rat 9 廿一 4	金9 Metal 5 Without Wrongdoing 天雷無妄 己丑 Earth Ox 10 廿二 2	木3 Wood 6 Fire 離為火 庚寅 Metal Tiger 11 廿三 1	火2 Fire 7 Sincerity 風澤中孚 辛卯 Metal Rabbit 12 廿四 3	水6 Water 8 Big Livestock 山天大畜 壬辰 Water Dragon 13 廿五 4	金4 Metal 9 Eliminating 澤天夬 癸巳 Water Snake 14 廿六 6	金9 Metal 1 Heaven 乾為天 甲午 Wood Horse 15 廿七 1
火7 Fire 2 Well 水風井 乙未 Wood Goat 16 廿八 6	木8 Wood 3 Relief 雷水解 丙申 Fire Monkey 17 廿九 4	金4 Metal 4 Influence 澤山咸 丁酉 Fire Rooster 18 三十 9	水1 Water 5 Humility 地山謙 戊戌 Earth Dog 19 四月初一 6	火2 Fire 6 Observation 風地觀 己亥 Earth Pig 20 初二 2	火2 Fire 7 Increasing 風雷益 庚子 Metal Rat 21 初三 9	水1 Water 8 Dimming Light 地火明夷 辛丑 Metal Ox 22 初四 3
金9 Metal 9 Fellowship 天火同人 壬寅 Water Tiger 23 初五 7	木8 Wood 1 Marrying Maiden 雷澤歸妹 癸卯 Water Rabbit 24 初六 7	木3 Wood 2 Opposition 火澤睽 甲辰 Wood Dragon 25 初七 2	火7 Fire 3 Waiting 水天需 乙巳 Wood Snake 26 初八 3	金4 Metal 4 Great Exceeding 澤風大過 丙午 Fire Horse 27 初九 3	水6 Water 5 Poison 山風蠱 丁未 Fire Goat 28 初十 7	火2 Fire 6 Dispersing 風水渙 戊申 Earth Monkey 29 十一 6

JUNE 2004 庚午

Xuan Kong Element 玄空五行	雷風恆 Consistency	Period Luck 卦運	Monthly Star 月星
Wood 木8		9	7

SUNDAY	MONDAY	TUESDAY	WEDNESDAY	THURSDAY	FRIDAY	SATURDAY
		火7 Fire 9 Alliance 水地比 辛亥 Metal Pig 1 十四 7	木8 Wood 1 Thunder 震為雷 壬子 Water Rat 2 十五 1	水6 Water 2 Beauty 山火賁 癸丑 Water Ox 3 十六 8	火7 Fire 3 Accomplished 水火既濟 甲寅 Wood Tiger 4 十七 9	水1 Water 4 Arriving 地澤臨 乙卯 Wood Rabbit 5 十八 4
金4 Metal 5 Marsh 兌為澤 丙辰 Fire Dragon 6 十九 1	火2 Fire 6 Small Livestock 風天小畜 丁巳 Fire Snake 7 二十 8	木3 Wood 7 The Cauldron 火風鼎 戊午 Earth Horse 8 廿一 4	水1 Water 8 Rising 地風升 己未 Earth Goat 9 廿二 2	火7 Fire 9 Water 坎為水 庚申 Metal Monkey 10 廿三 1	木8 Wood 1 Lesser Exceeding 雷山小過 辛酉 Metal Rooster 11 廿四 3	金4 Metal 2 Gathering 澤地萃 壬戌 Water Dog 12 廿五 4
水6 Water 3 Peel 山地剝 癸亥 Water Pig 13 廿六 6	水1 Water 4 Earth 坤為地 甲子 Wood Rat 14 廿七 1	木3 Wood 5 Biting 火雷噬嗑 乙丑 Wood Ox 15 廿八 6	火2 Fire 6 Family 風火家人 丙寅 Fire Tiger 16 廿九 4	水6 Water 7 Decreasing 山澤損 丁卯 Fire Rabbit 17 三十 9	金9 Metal 8 Tread 天澤履 戊辰 Earth Dragon 18 五月初一 6	木8 Wood 9 Great Strength 雷天大壯 己巳 Earth Snake 19 初二 2
木8 Wood 1 Consistency 雷風恆 庚午 Metal Horse 20 初三 9	金9 Metal 2/8 Litigation 天水訟 辛未 Metal Goat 21 初四 3	水1 Water 7 Officer 地水師 壬申 Water Monkey 22 初五 7	火2 Fire 6 Gradual Progress 風山漸 癸酉 Water Rooster 23 初六 7	火7 Fire 5 Obstruction 水山蹇 甲戌 Wood Dog 24 初七 2	木3 Wood 4 Advancement 火地晉 乙亥 Wood Pig 25 初八 3	水6 Water 3 Nourish 山雷頤 丙子 Fire Rat 26 初九 3
金4 Metal 2 Following 澤雷隨 丁丑 Fire Ox 27 初十 7	木8 Wood 1 Abundance 雷火豐 戊寅 Earth Tiger 28 十一 6	火7 Fire 9 Regulate 水澤節 己卯 Earth Rabbit 29 十二 8	水1 Water 8 Unity 地天泰 庚辰 Metal Dragon 30 十三 9			

JULY 2004 辛未

Xuan Kong Element 玄空五行	天水訟 Litigation	Period Luck 卦運	Monthly Star 月星
Metal 金9		3	6

SUNDAY	MONDAY	TUESDAY	WEDNESDAY	THURSDAY	FRIDAY	SATURDAY
				1 十四 木3 Wood [7] Great Reward 火天大有 辛巳 Metal Snake 7	2 十五 火2 Fire [6] Wind 巽爲風 壬午 Water Horse 1	3 十六 金4 Metal [5] Trap 澤水困 癸未 Water Goat 8
4 十七 木3 Wood [4] Not Yet Accomplished 火水未濟 甲申 Wood Monkey 9	5 十八 金9 Metal [3] Retreat 天山遯 乙酉 Wood Rooster 4	6 十九 水6 Water [2] Mountain 艮爲山 丙戌 Fire Dog 1	7 二十 木8 Wood [1] Delight 雷地豫 丁亥 Fire Pig 8	8 廿一 火7 Fire [9] Beginning 水雷屯 戊子 Earth Rat 4	9 廿二 金9 Metal [8] Without Wrongdoing 天雷無妄 己丑 Earth Ox 2	10 廿三 木3 Wood [7] Fire 離爲火 庚寅 Metal Tiger 1
11 廿四 火2 Fire [6] Sincerity 風澤中孚 辛卯 Metal Rabbit 3	12 廿五 水6 Water [5] Big Livestock 山天大畜 壬辰 Water Dragon 4	13 廿六 金4 Metal [4] Eliminating 澤天夬 癸巳 Water Snake 6	14 廿七 金9 Metal [3] Heaven 乾爲天 甲午 Wood Horse 1	15 廿八 火7 Fire [2] Well 水風井 乙未 Wood Goat 6	16 廿九 木8 Wood [1] Relief 雷水解 丙申 Fire Monkey 4	17 六月初一 金4 Metal [9] Influence 澤山咸 丁酉 Fire Rooster 9
18 初二 水1 Water [8] Humility 地山謙 戊戌 Earth Dog 6	19 初三 火2 Fire [7] Observation 風地觀 己亥 Earth Pig 2	20 初四 火2 Fire [6] Increasing 風雷益 庚子 Metal Rat 9	21 初五 水1 Water [5] Dimming Light 地火明夷 辛丑 Metal Ox 3	22 初六 金9 Metal [4] Fellowship 天火同人 壬寅 Water Tiger 7	23 初七 木8 Wood [3] Marrying Maiden 雷澤歸妹 癸卯 Water Rabbit 7	24 初八 木3 Wood [2] Opposition 火澤睽 甲辰 Wood Dragon 2
25 初九 火7 Fire [1] Waiting 水天需 乙巳 Wood Snake 3	26 初十 金4 Metal [9] Great Exceeding 澤風大過 丙午 Fire Horse 3	27 十一 水6 Water [8] Poison 山風蠱 丁未 Fire Goat 7	28 十二 火2 Fire [7] Dispersing 風水渙 戊申 Earth Monkey 6	29 十三 木3 Wood [6] Travelling 火山旅 己酉 Earth Rooster 8	30 十四 金9 Metal [5] Stagnation 天地否 庚戌 Metal Dog 9	31 十五 火7 Fire [4] Alliance 水地比 辛亥 Metal Pig 7

AUGUST 2004 壬申

Xuan Kong Element 玄空五行	地水師 Officer	Period Luck 卦運	Monthly Star 月星
Water 水1		7	5

SUNDAY	MONDAY	TUESDAY	WEDNESDAY	THURSDAY	FRIDAY	SATURDAY
1 十六 木8 Wood [3] Thunder 震爲雷 壬子 Water Rat 1	2 十七 水6 Water [2] Beauty 山火賁 癸丑 Water Ox 8	3 十八 火7 Fire [1] Accomplished 水火既濟 甲寅 Wood Tiger 9	4 十九 水1 Water [9] Arriving 地澤臨 乙卯 Wood Rabbit 4	5 二十 金4 Metal [8] Marsh 兑爲澤 丙辰 Fire Dragon 1	6 廿一 火2 Fire [7] Small Livestock 風天小畜 丁巳 Fire Snake 8	7 廿二 木3 Wood [6] The Cauldron 火風鼎 戊午 Earth Horse 4
8 廿三 水1 Water [5] Rising 地風升 己未 Earth Goat 2	9 廿四 火7 Fire [4] Water 坎爲水 庚申 Metal Monkey 1	10 廿五 木8 Wood [3] Lesser Exceeding 雷山小過 辛酉 Metal Rooster 3	11 廿六 金4 Metal [2] Gathering 澤地萃 壬戌 Water Dog 4	12 廿七 水6 Water [1] Peel 山地剝 癸亥 Water Pig 6	13 廿八 水1 Water [9] Earth 坤爲地 甲子 Wood Rat 1	14 廿九 木3 Wood [8] Biting 火雷噬嗑 乙丑 Wood Ox 6
15 三十 火2 Fire [7] Family 風火家人 丙寅 Fire Tiger 4	16 七月初一 水6 Water [6] Decreasing 山澤損 丁卯 Fire Rabbit 9	17 初二 金9 Metal [5] Tread 天澤履 戊辰 Earth Dragon 6	18 初三 木8 Wood [4] Great Strength 雷天大壯 己巳 Earth Snake 2	19 初四 木8 Wood [3] Consistency 雷風恆 庚午 Metal Horse 9	20 初五 金9 Metal [2] Litigation 天水訟 辛未 Metal Goat 3	21 初六 水1 Water [1] Officer 地水師 壬申 Water Monkey 7
22 初七 火2 Fire [9] Gradual Progress 風山漸 癸酉 Water Rooster 7	23 初八 火7 Fire [8] Obstruction 水山蹇 甲戌 Wood Dog 2	24 初九 木3 Wood [7] Advancement 火地晉 乙亥 Wood Pig 3	25 初十 水6 Water [6] Nourish 山雷頤 丙子 Fire Rat 3	26 十一 金4 Metal [5] Following 澤雷隨 丁丑 Fire Ox 7	27 十二 木8 Wood [4] Abundance 雷火豐 戊寅 Earth Tiger 6	28 十三 火7 Fire [3] Regulate 水澤節 己卯 Earth Rabbit 8
29 十四 水1 Water [2] Unity 地天泰 庚辰 Metal Dragon 9	30 十五 木3 Wood [1] Great Reward 火天大有 辛巳 Metal Snake 7	31 十六 火2 Fire [9] Wind 巽爲風 壬午 Water Horse 1				

SEPTEMBER 2004 癸酉

Xuan Kong Element 玄空五行	風山漸 Gradual Progress	Period Luck 卦運	Monthly Star 月星
Fire 火2		7	4

SUNDAY	MONDAY	TUESDAY	WEDNESDAY	THURSDAY	FRIDAY	SATURDAY
			1 金4 Metal · 8 Trap 澤水困 癸未 Water Goat 十七 · 8	**2** 木3 Wood · 7 Not Yet Accomplished 火水未濟 甲申 Wood Monkey 十八 · 9	**3** 金9 Metal · 6 Retreat 天山遯 乙酉 Wood Rooster 十九 · 4	**4** 水6 Water · 5 Mountain 艮爲山 丙戌 Fire Dog 二十 · 1
5 木8 Wood · 4 Delight 雷地豫 丁亥 Fire Pig 廿一 · 8	**6** 火7 Fire · 3 Beginning 水雷屯 戊子 Earth Rat 廿二 · 4	**7** 金9 Metal · 2 Without Wrongdoing 天雷無妄 己丑 Earth Ox 廿三 · 2	**8** 木3 Wood · 1 Fire 離爲火 庚寅 Metal Tiger 廿四 · 1	**9** 火2 Fire · 9 Sincerity 風澤中孚 辛卯 Metal Rabbit 廿五 · 3	**10** 水6 Water · 8 Big Livestock 山天大畜 壬辰 Water Dragon 廿六 · 4	**11** 金4 Metal · 7 Eliminating 澤天夬 癸巳 Water Snake 廿七 · 6
12 金9 Metal · 6 Heaven 乾爲天 甲午 Wood Horse 廿八 · 1	**13** 火7 Fire · 5 Well 水風井 乙未 Wood Goat 廿九 · 6	**14** 木8 Wood · 4 Relief 雷水解 丙申 Fire Monkey 八月初一 · 4	**15** 金4 Metal · 3 Influence 澤山咸 丁酉 Fire Rooster 初二 · 9	**16** 水1 Water · 2 Humility 地山謙 戊戌 Earth Dog 初三 · 6	**17** 火2 Fire · 1 Observation 風地觀 己亥 Earth Pig 初四 · 2	**18** 火2 Fire · 9 Increasing 風雷益 庚子 Metal Rat 初五 · 9
19 水1 Water · 8 Dimming Light 地火明夷 辛丑 Metal Ox 初六 · 3	**20** 金9 Metal · 7 Fellowship 天火同人 壬寅 Water Tiger 初七 · 7	**21** 木8 Wood · 6 Marrying Maiden 雷澤歸妹 癸卯 Water Rabbit 初八 · 7	**22** 木3 Wood · 5 Opposition 火澤睽 甲辰 Wood Dragon 初九 · 2	**23** 火7 Fire · 4 Waiting 水天需 乙巳 Wood Snake 初十 · 3	**24** 金4 Metal · 3 Great Exceeding 澤風大過 丙午 Fire Horse 十一 · 3	**25** 水6 Water · 2 Poison 山風蠱 丁未 Fire Goat 十二 · 7
26 火2 Fire · 1 Dispersing 風水渙 戊申 Earth Monkey 十三 · 6	**27** 木3 Wood · 9 Travelling 火山旅 己酉 Earth Rooster 十四 · 8	**28** 金9 Metal · 8 Stagnation 天地否 庚戌 Metal Dog 十五 · 9	**29** 火7 Fire · 7 Alliance 水地比 辛亥 Metal Pig 十六 · 7	**30** 木8 Wood · 6 Thunder 震爲雷 壬子 Water Rat 十七 · 1		

OCTOBER 2004 甲戌

Xuan Kong Element 玄空五行	水山蹇 Obstruction	Period Luck 卦運	Monthly Star 月星
Fire 火7		2	3

SUNDAY	MONDAY	TUESDAY	WEDNESDAY	THURSDAY	FRIDAY	SATURDAY
31 金4 Metal · 2 Trap 澤水困 癸未 Water Goat 十八 · 8					**1** 水6 Water · 5 Beauty 山火賁 癸丑 Water Ox 十八 · 8	**2** 火7 Fire · 4 Accomplished 水火既濟 甲寅 Wood Tiger 十九 · 9
3 水1 Water · 3 Arriving 地澤臨 乙卯 Wood Rabbit 二十 · 4	**4** 金4 Metal · 2 Marsh 兌爲澤 丙辰 Fire Dragon 廿一 · 1	**5** 火2 Fire · 1 Small Livestock 風天小畜 丁巳 Fire Snake 廿二 · 8	**6** 木3 Wood · 9 The Cauldron 火風鼎 戊午 Earth Horse 廿三 · 4	**7** 水1 Water · 8 Rising 地風升 己未 Earth Goat 廿四 · 2	**8** 火7 Fire · 7 Water 坎爲水 庚申 Metal Monkey 廿五 · 1	**9** 木8 Wood · 6 Lesser Exceeding 雷山小過 辛酉 Metal Rooster 廿六 · 3
10 金4 Metal · 5 Gathering 澤地萃 壬戌 Water Dog 廿七 · 4	**11** 水6 Water · 4 Peel 山地剝 癸亥 Water Pig 廿八 · 6	**12** 水1 Water · 3 Earth 坤爲地 甲子 Wood Rat 廿九 · 1	**13** 木3 Wood · 2 Biting 火雷噬嗑 乙丑 Wood Ox 三十 · 6	**14** 火2 Fire · 1 Family 風火家人 丙寅 Fire Tiger 九月初一 · 4	**15** 水6 Water · 9 Decreasing 山澤損 丁卯 Fire Rabbit 初二 · 9	**16** 金9 Metal · 8 Tread 天澤履 戊辰 Earth Dragon 初三 · 6
17 木8 Wood · 7 Great Strength 雷天大壯 己巳 Earth Snake 初四 · 2	**18** 木8 Wood · 6 Consistency 雷風恆 庚午 Metal Horse 初五 · 9	**19** 金9 Metal · 5 Litigation 天水訟 辛未 Metal Goat 初六 · 3	**20** 水1 Water · 4 Officer 地水師 壬申 Water Monkey 初七 · 7	**21** 火2 Fire · 3 Gradual Progress 風山漸 癸酉 Water Rooster 初八 · 7	**22** 火7 Fire · 2 Obstruction 水山蹇 甲戌 Wood Dog 初九 · 2	**23** 木3 Wood · 1 Advancement 火地晉 乙亥 Wood Pig 初十 · 3
24 水6 Water · 9 Nourish 山雷頤 丙子 Fire Rat 十一 · 3	**25** 金4 Metal · 8 Following 澤雷隨 丁丑 Fire Ox 十二 · 7	**26** 木8 Wood · 7 Abundance 雷火豐 戊寅 Earth Tiger 十三 · 6	**27** 火7 Fire · 6 Regulate 水澤節 己卯 Earth Rabbit 十四 · 8	**28** 水1 Water · 5 Unity 地天泰 庚辰 Metal Dragon 十五 · 9	**29** 木3 Wood · 4 Great Reward 火天大有 辛巳 Metal Snake 十六 · 7	**30** 火2 Fire · 3 Wind 巽爲風 壬午 Water Horse 十七 · 1

NOVEMBER 2004 乙亥

Xuan Kong Element 玄空五行	火地晉 Advancement	Period Luck 卦運	Monthly Star 月星
Wood 木3		3	2

SUNDAY	MONDAY	TUESDAY	WEDNESDAY	THURSDAY	FRIDAY	SATURDAY
	木3 Wood 1 甲申 Wood Monkey Not Yet Accomplished 火水未濟 1 十九 9	金9 Metal 9 乙酉 Wood Rooster Retreat 天山遯 2 二十 4	水6 Water 8 丙戌 Fire Dog Mountain 艮爲山 3 廿一 1	木8 Wood 7 丁亥 Fire Pig Delight 雷地豫 4 廿二 8	火7 Fire 6 戊子 Earth Rat Beginning 水雷屯 5 廿三 4	金9 Metal 5 己丑 Earth Ox Without Wrongdoing 天雷無妄 6 廿四 2
木3 Wood 4 庚寅 Metal Tiger Fire 離爲火 7 廿五 1	火2 Fire 3 辛卯 Metal Rabbit Sincerity 風澤中孚 8 廿六 3	水6 Water 2 壬辰 Water Dragon Big Livestock 山天大畜 9 廿七 4	金4 Metal 1 癸巳 Water Snake Eliminating 澤天夬 10 廿八 6	金9 Metal 9 甲午 Wood Horse Heaven 乾爲天 11 廿九 1	火7 Fire 8 乙未 Wood Goat Well 水風井 12 十月初一 6	木8 Wood 7 丙申 Fire Monkey Relief 雷水解 13 初二 4
金4 Metal 6 丁酉 Fire Rooster Influence 澤山咸 14 初三 9	水1 Water 5 戊戌 Earth Dog Humility 地山謙 15 初四 6	火2 Fire 4 己亥 Earth Pig Observation 風地觀 16 初五 2	火2 Fire 3 庚子 Metal Rat Increasing 風雷益 17 初六 9	水1 Water 2 辛丑 Metal Ox Dimming Light 地火明夷 18 初七 3	金9 Metal 1 壬寅 Water Tiger Fellowship 天火同人 19 初八 7	木8 Wood 9 癸卯 Water Rabbit Marrying Maiden 雷澤歸妹 20 初九 7
木3 Wood 8 甲辰 Wood Dragon Opposition 火澤睽 21 初十 2	火7 Fire 7 乙巳 Wood Snake Waiting 水天需 22 十一 3	金4 Metal 6 丙午 Fire Horse Great Exceeding 澤風大過 23 十二 3	水6 Water 5 丁未 Fire Goat Poison 山風蠱 24 十三 7	火2 Fire 4 戊申 Earth Monkey Dispersing 風水渙 25 十四 6	木3 Wood 3 己酉 Earth Rooster Travelling 火山旅 26 十五 8	金9 Metal 2 庚戌 Metal Dog Stagnation 天地否 27 十六 9
火7 Fire 1 辛亥 Metal Pig Alliance 水地比 28 十七 7	木8 Wood 9 壬子 Water Rat Thunder 震爲雷 29 十八 1	水6 Water 8 癸丑 Water Ox Beauty 山火賁 30 十九 8				

DECEMBER 2004 丙子

Xuan Kong Element 玄空五行	山雷頤 Nourish	Period Luck 卦運	Monthly Star 月星
Water 水6		3	1

SUNDAY	MONDAY	TUESDAY	WEDNESDAY	THURSDAY	FRIDAY	SATURDAY
			火7 Fire 7 甲寅 Wood Tiger Accomplished 水火既濟 1 二十 9	水1 Water 6 乙卯 Wood Rabbit Arriving 地澤臨 2 廿一 4	金4 Metal 5 丙辰 Fire Dragon Marsh 兌爲澤 3 廿二 1	火2 Fire 4 丁巳 Fire Snake Small Livestock 風天小畜 4 廿三 8
木3 Wood 3 戊午 Earth Horse The Cauldron 火風鼎 5 廿四 4	水1 Water 2 己未 Earth Goat Rising 地風升 6 廿五 2	火7 Fire 1 庚申 Metal Monkey Water 坎爲水 7 廿六 1	木8 Wood 9 辛酉 Metal Rooster Lesser Exceeding 雷山小過 8 廿七 3	金4 Metal 8 壬戌 Water Dog Gathering 澤地萃 9 廿八 4	水6 Water 7 癸亥 Water Pig Peel 山地剝 10 廿九 6	水1 Water 6 甲子 Wood Rat Earth 坤爲地 11 三十 1
木3 Wood 5 乙丑 Wood Ox Biting 火雷噬嗑 12 十一月初一 6	火2 Fire 4 丙寅 Fire Tiger Family 風火家人 13 初二 4	水6 Water 3 丁卯 Fire Rabbit Decreasing 山澤損 14 初三 9	金9 Metal 2 戊辰 Earth Dragon Tread 天澤履 15 初四 6	木8 Wood 1 己巳 Earth Snake Great Strength 雷天大壯 16 初五 2	木8 Wood 9 庚午 Metal Horse Consistency 雷風恒 17 初六 9	金9 Metal 8 辛未 Metal Goat Litigation 天水訟 18 初七 3
水1 Water 7 壬申 Water Monkey Officer 地水師 19 初八 7	火2 Fire 6 癸酉 Water Rooster Gradual Progress 風山漸 20 初九 7	火7 Fire 5/5 甲戌 Wood Dog Obstruction 水山蹇 21 初十 2	木3 Wood 6 乙亥 Wood Pig Advancement 火地晉 22 十一 3	水6 Water 7 丙子 Fire Rat Nourish 山雷頤 23 十二 3	金4 Metal 8 丁丑 Fire Ox Following 澤雷隨 24 十三 7	木8 Wood 9 戊寅 Earth Tiger Abundance 雷火豐 25 十四 6
火7 Fire 1 己卯 Earth Rabbit Regulate 水澤節 26 十五 8	水1 Water 2 庚辰 Metal Dragon Unity 地天泰 27 十六 9	木3 Wood 3 辛巳 Metal Snake Great Reward 火天大有 28 十七 7	火2 Fire 4 壬午 Water Horse Wind 巽爲風 29 十八 1	金4 Metal 5 癸未 Water Goat Trap 澤水困 30 十九 8	木3 Wood 6 甲申 Wood Monkey Not Yet Accomplished 火水未濟 31 二十 9	

2005 乙酉

(*Yi You*) Wood Rooster

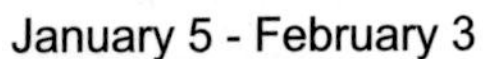

2005 乙酉 *(Yi You)* Wood Rooster

January 5 - February 3

金4 Metal
丁丑 Fire Ox
7 Following
澤雷隨

Three Killings	East

February 4 - March 4

木8 Wood
戊寅 Earth Tiger
6 Abundance
雷火豐

Three Killings	North

March 5 - April 4

火7 Fire
己卯 Earth Rabbit
8 Regulate
水澤節

Three Killings	West

April 5 - May 4

水1 Water
庚辰 Metal Dragon
9 Unity
地天泰

Three Killings	South

May 5 - June 4

木3 Wood
辛巳 Metal Snake
7 Great Reward
火天大有

Three Killings	East

June 5 - July 6

火2 Fire
壬午 Water Horse
1 Wind
巽為風

Three Killings	North

July 7 - August 6

金4 Metal
癸未 Water Goat
8 Trap
澤水困

Three Killings	West

August 7 - September 6

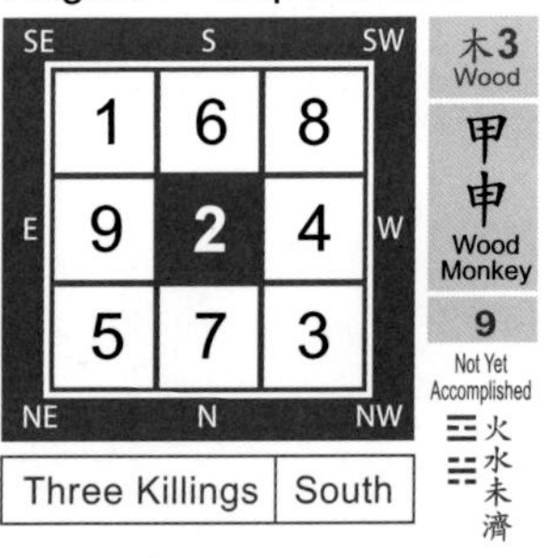

木3 Wood
甲申 Wood Monkey
9 Not Yet Accomplished
火水未濟

Three Killings	South

September 7 - October 7

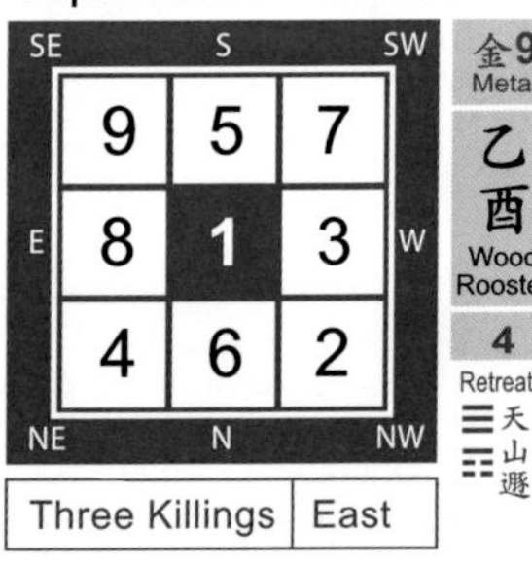

金9 Metal
乙酉 Wood Rooster
4 Retreat
天山遯

Three Killings	East

October 8 - November 6

水6 Water
丙戌 Fire Dog
1 Mountain
艮為山

Three Killings	North

November 7 - December 6

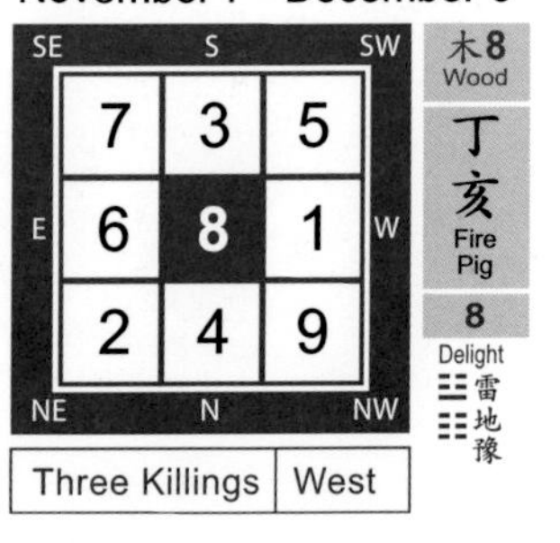

木8 Wood
丁亥 Fire Pig
8 Delight
雷地豫

Three Killings	West

December 7 - January 4

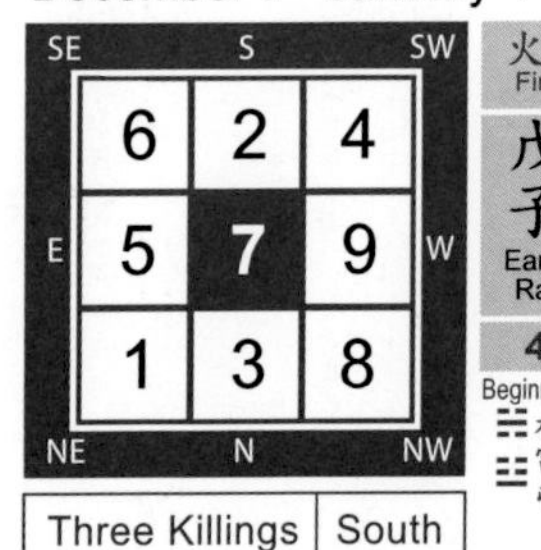

火7 Fire
戊子 Earth Rat
4 Beginning
水雷屯

Three Killings	South

JANUARY 2005 丁丑

Xuan Kong Element 玄空五行	澤雷隨 Following	Period Luck 卦運	Monthly Star 月星
Metal 金4		7	9

SUNDAY	MONDAY	TUESDAY	WEDNESDAY	THURSDAY	FRIDAY	SATURDAY
火7 Fire 甲寅 Wood Tiger Accomplished 水火既濟 **30** 廿一 9 · 9	水1 Water 乙卯 Wood Rabbit Arriving 地澤臨 **31** 廿二 4 · 1					金9 Metal 乙酉 Wood Rooster Retreat 天山遯 **1** 廿一 4 · 7
水6 Water 丙戌 Fire Dog Mountain 艮為山 **2** 廿二 1 · 8	木8 Wood 丁亥 Fire Pig Delight 雷地豫 **3** 廿三 8 · 9	火7 Fire 戊子 Earth Rat Beginning 水雷屯 **4** 廿四 4 · 1	金9 Metal 己丑 Earth Ox Without Wrongdoing 天雷無妄 **5** 廿五 2 · 2	木3 Wood 庚寅 Metal Tiger Fire 離為火 **6** 廿六 1 · 3	火2 Fire 辛卯 Metal Rabbit Sincerity 風澤中孚 **7** 廿七 3 · 4	水6 Water 壬辰 Water Dragon Big Livestock 山天大畜 **8** 廿八 4 · 5
金4 Metal 癸巳 Water Snake Eliminating 澤天夬 **9** 廿九 6 · 6	金9 Metal 甲午 Wood Horse Heaven 乾為天 **10** 十二月初一 1 · 7	火7 Fire 乙未 Wood Goat Well 水風井 **11** 初二 6 · 8	木8 Wood 丙申 Fire Monkey Relief 雷水解 **12** 初三 4 · 9	金4 Metal 丁酉 Fire Rooster Influence 澤山咸 **13** 初四 9 · 1	水1 Water 戊戌 Earth Dog Humility 地山謙 **14** 初五 6 · 2	火2 Fire 己亥 Earth Pig Observation 風地觀 **15** 初六 2 · 3
火2 Fire 庚子 Metal Rat Increasing 風雷益 **16** 初七 9 · 4	水1 Water 辛丑 Metal Ox Dimming Light 地火明夷 **17** 初八 3 · 5	金9 Metal 壬寅 Water Tiger Fellowship 天火同人 **18** 初九 7 · 6	木8 Wood 癸卯 Water Rabbit Marrying Maiden 雷澤歸妹 **19** 初十 7 · 7	木3 Wood 甲辰 Wood Dragon Opposition 火澤睽 **20** 十一 2 · 8	火7 Fire 乙巳 Wood Snake Waiting 水天需 **21** 十二 3 · 9	金4 Metal 丙午 Fire Horse Great Exceeding 澤風大過 **22** 十三 3 · 1
水6 Water 丁未 Fire Goat Poison 山風蠱 **23** 十四 7 · 2	火2 Fire 戊申 Earth Monkey Dispersing 風水渙 **24** 十五 6 · 3	木3 Wood 己酉 Earth Rooster Travelling 火山旅 **25** 十六 8 · 4	金9 Metal 庚戌 Metal Dog Stagnation 天地否 **26** 十七 9 · 5	火7 Fire 辛亥 Metal Pig Alliance 水地比 **27** 十八 7 · 6	木8 Wood 壬子 Water Rat Thunder 震為雷 **28** 十九 1 · 7	水6 Water 癸丑 Water Ox Beauty 山火賁 **29** 二十 8 · 8

FEBRUARY 2005 戊寅

Xuan Kong Element 玄空五行	雷火豐 Abundance	Period Luck 卦運	Monthly Star 月星
Wood 木8		6	8

SUNDAY	MONDAY	TUESDAY	WEDNESDAY	THURSDAY	FRIDAY	SATURDAY
		金4 Metal 丙辰 Fire Dragon Marsh 兑為澤 **1** 廿三 1 · 2	火2 Fire 丁巳 Fire Snake Small Livestock 風天小畜 **2** 廿四 8 · 3	木3 Wood 戊午 Earth Horse The Cauldron 火風鼎 **3** 廿五 4 · 4	水1 Water 己未 Earth Goat Rising 地風升 **4** 廿六 2 · 5	火7 Fire 庚申 Metal Monkey Water 坎為水 **5** 廿七 1 · 6
木8 Wood 辛酉 Metal Rooster Lesser Exceeding 雷山小過 **6** 廿八 3 · 7	金4 Metal 壬戌 Water Dog Gathering 澤地萃 **7** 廿九 4 · 8	水6 Water 癸亥 Water Pig Peel 山地剝 **8** 三十 6 · 9	水1 Water 甲子 Wood Rat Earth 坤為地 **9** 正月初一 1 · 1	木3 Wood 乙丑 Wood Ox Biting 火雷噬嗑 **10** 初二 6 · 2	火2 Fire 丙寅 Fire Tiger Family 風火家人 **11** 初三 4 · 3	水6 Water 丁卯 Fire Rabbit Decreasing 山澤損 **12** 初四 9 · 4
金9 Metal 戊辰 Earth Dragon Tread 天澤履 **13** 初五 6 · 5	木8 Wood 己巳 Earth Snake Great Strength 雷天大壯 **14** 初六 2 · 6	木8 Wood 庚午 Metal Horse Consistency 雷風恆 **15** 初七 9 · 7	金9 Metal 辛未 Metal Goat Litigation 天水訟 **16** 初八 3 · 8	水1 Water 壬申 Water Monkey Officer 地水師 **17** 初九 7 · 9	火2 Fire 癸酉 Water Rooster Gradual Progress 風山漸 **18** 初十 7 · 1	火7 Fire 甲戌 Wood Dog Obstruction 水山蹇 **19** 十一 2 · 2
木3 Wood 乙亥 Wood Pig Advancement 火地晉 **20** 十二 3 · 3	水6 Water 丙子 Fire Rat Nourish 山雷頤 **21** 十三 3 · 4	金4 Metal 丁丑 Fire Ox Following 澤雷隨 **22** 十四 7 · 5	木8 Wood 戊寅 Earth Tiger Abundance 雷火豐 **23** 十五 6 · 6	火7 Fire 己卯 Earth Rabbit Regulate 水澤節 **24** 十六 8 · 7	水1 Water 庚辰 Metal Dragon Unity 地天泰 **25** 十七 9 · 8	木3 Wood 辛巳 Metal Snake Great Reward 火天大有 **26** 十八 7 · 9
火2 Fire 壬午 Water Horse Wind 巽為風 **27** 十九 1 · 1	金4 Metal 癸未 Water Goat Trap 澤水困 **28** 二十 8 · 2					

MARCH 2005 己卯

Xuan Kong Element 玄空五行	水澤節 Regulate	Period Luck 卦運	Monthly Star 月星
Fire 火7		8	7

SUNDAY	MONDAY	TUESDAY	WEDNESDAY	THURSDAY	FRIDAY	SATURDAY
		木3 Wood · 3 Not Yet Accomplished 甲申 Wood Monkey 火水未濟 **1** 廿一 9	金9 Metal · 4 Retreat 乙酉 Wood Rooster 天山遯 **2** 廿二 4	水6 Water · 5 Mountain 丙戌 Fire Dog 艮爲山 **3** 廿三 1	木8 Wood · 6 Delight 丁亥 Fire Pig 雷地豫 **4** 廿四 8	火7 Fire · 7 Beginning 戊子 Earth Rat 水雷屯 **5** 廿五 4
金9 Metal · 8 Without Wrongdoing 己丑 Earth Ox 天雷無妄 **6** 廿六 2	木3 Wood · 9 Fire 庚寅 Metal Tiger 離爲火 **7** 廿七 1	火2 Fire · 1 Sincerity 辛卯 Metal Rabbit 風澤中孚 **8** 廿八 3	水6 Water · 2 Big Livestock 壬辰 Water Dragon 山天大畜 **9** 廿九 4	金4 Metal · 3 Eliminating 癸巳 Water Snake 澤天夬 **10** 二月初一 6	金9 Metal · 4 Heaven 甲午 Wood Horse 乾爲天 **11** 初二 1	火7 Fire · 5 Well 乙未 Wood Goat 水風井 **12** 初三 6
木8 Wood · 6 Relief 丙申 Fire Monkey 雷水解 **13** 初四 4	金4 Metal · 7 Influence 丁酉 Fire Rooster 澤山咸 **14** 初五 9	水1 Water · 8 Humility 戊戌 Earth Dog 地山謙 **15** 初六 6	火2 Fire · 9 Observation 己亥 Earth Pig 風地觀 **16** 初七 2	火2 Fire · 1 Increasing 庚子 Metal Rat 風雷益 **17** 初八 9	水1 Water · 2 Dimming Light 辛丑 Metal Ox 地火明夷 **18** 初九 3	金9 Metal · 3 Fellowship 壬寅 Water Tiger 天火同人 **19** 初十 7
木8 Wood · 4 Marrying Maiden 癸卯 Water Rabbit 雷澤歸妹 **20** 十一 7	木3 Wood · 5 Opposition 甲辰 Wood Dragon 火澤睽 **21** 十二 2	火7 Fire · 6 Waiting 乙巳 Wood Snake 水天需 **22** 十三 3	金4 Metal · 7 Great Exceeding 丙午 Fire Horse 澤風大過 **23** 十四 3	水6 Water · 8 Poison 丁未 Fire Goat 山風蠱 **24** 十五 7	火2 Fire · 9 Dispersing 戊申 Earth Monkey 風水渙 **25** 十六 6	木3 Wood · 1 Travelling 己酉 Earth Rooster 火山旅 **26** 十七 8
金9 Metal · 2 Stagnation 庚戌 Metal Dog 天地否 **27** 十八 9	火7 Fire · 3 Alliance 辛亥 Metal Pig 水地比 **28** 十九 7	木8 Wood · 4 Thunder 壬子 Water Rat 震爲雷 **29** 二十 1	水6 Water · 5 Beauty 癸丑 Water Ox 山火賁 **30** 廿一 8	火7 Fire · 6 Accomplished 甲寅 Wood Tiger 水火既濟 **31** 廿二 9		

APRIL 2005 庚辰

Xuan Kong Element 玄空五行	地天泰 Unity	Period Luck 卦運	Monthly Star 月星
Water 水1		9	6

SUNDAY	MONDAY	TUESDAY	WEDNESDAY	THURSDAY	FRIDAY	SATURDAY
					水1 Water · 7 Arriving 乙卯 Wood Rabbit 地澤臨 **1** 廿三 4	金4 Metal · 8 Marsh 丙辰 Fire Dragon 兌爲澤 **2** 廿四 1
火2 Fire · 9 Small Livestock 丁巳 Fire Snake 風天小畜 **3** 廿五 8	木3 Wood · 1 The Cauldron 戊午 Earth Horse 火風鼎 **4** 廿六 4	水1 Water · 2 Rising 己未 Earth Goat 地風升 **5** 廿七 2	火7 Fire · 3 Water 庚申 Metal Monkey 坎爲水 **6** 廿八 1	木8 Wood · 4 Lesser Exceeding 辛酉 Metal Rooster 雷山小過 **7** 廿九 3	金4 Metal · 5 Gathering 壬戌 Water Dog 澤地萃 **8** 三十 4	水6 Water · 6 Peel 癸亥 Water Pig 山地剝 **9** 三月初一 6
水1 Water · 7 Earth 甲子 Wood Rat 坤爲地 **10** 初二 1	木3 Wood · 8 Biting 乙丑 Wood Ox 火雷噬嗑 **11** 初三 6	火2 Fire · 9 Family 丙寅 Fire Tiger 風火家人 **12** 初四 4	水6 Water · 1 Decreasing 丁卯 Fire Rabbit 山澤損 **13** 初五 9	金9 Metal · 2 Tread 戊辰 Earth Dragon 天澤履 **14** 初六 6	木8 Wood · 3 Great Strength 己巳 Earth Snake 雷天大壯 **15** 初七 2	木8 Wood · 4 Consistency 庚午 Metal Horse 雷風恆 **16** 初八 9
金9 Metal · 5 Litigation 辛未 Metal Goat 天水訟 **17** 初九 3	水1 Water · 6 Officer 壬申 Water Monkey 地水師 **18** 初十 7	火2 Fire · 7 Gradual Progress 癸酉 Water Rooster 風山漸 **19** 十一 7	火7 Fire · 8 Obstruction 甲戌 Wood Dog 水山蹇 **20** 十二 2	木3 Wood · 9 Advancement 乙亥 Wood Pig 火地晉 **21** 十三 3	水6 Water · 1 Nourish 丙子 Fire Rat 山雷頤 **22** 十四 7	金4 Metal · 2 Following 丁丑 Fire Ox 澤雷隨 **23** 十五 7
木8 Wood · 3 Abundance 戊寅 Earth Tiger 雷火豐 **24** 十六 6	火7 Fire · 4 Regulate 己卯 Earth Rabbit 水澤節 **25** 十七 8	水1 Water · 5 Unity 庚辰 Metal Dragon 地天泰 **26** 十八 9	木3 Wood · 6 Great Reward 辛巳 Metal Snake 火天大有 **27** 十九 7	火2 Fire · 7 Wind 壬午 Water Horse 巽爲風 **28** 二十 1	金4 Metal · 8 Trap 癸未 Water Goat 澤水困 **29** 廿一 8	木3 Wood · 9 Not Yet Accomplished 甲申 Wood Monkey 火水未濟 **30** 廿二 9

MAY 2005 辛巳

Xuan Kong Element 玄空五行	火天大有 Great Reward	Period Luck 卦運	Monthly Star 月星
Wood 木3		7	5

SUNDAY	MONDAY	TUESDAY	WEDNESDAY	THURSDAY	FRIDAY	SATURDAY
金9 Metal [1] Retreat 天山遯 乙酉 Wood Rooster **1** 廿三 4	水6 Water [2] Mountain 艮爲山 丙戌 Fire Dog **2** 廿四 1	木8 Wood [3] Delight 雷地豫 丁亥 Fire Pig **3** 廿五 8	火7 Fire [4] Beginning 水雷屯 戊子 Earth Rat **4** 廿六 4	金9 Metal [5] Without Wrongdoing 天雷無妄 己丑 Earth Ox **5** 廿七 2	木3 Wood [6] Fire 離爲火 庚寅 Metal Tiger **6** 廿八 1	火2 Fire [7] Sincerity 風澤中孚 辛卯 Metal Rabbit **7** 廿九 3
水6 Water [8] Big Livestock 山天大畜 壬辰 Water Dragon **8** 四月初一 4	金4 Metal [9] Eliminating 澤天夬 癸巳 Water Snake **9** 初二 6	金9 Metal [1] Heaven 乾爲天 甲午 Wood Horse **10** 初三 1	火7 Fire [2] Well 水風井 乙未 Wood Goat **11** 初四 6	木8 Wood [3] Relief 雷水解 丙申 Fire Monkey **12** 初五 4	金4 Metal [4] Influence 澤山咸 丁酉 Fire Rooster **13** 初六 9	水1 Water [5] Humility 地山謙 戊戌 Earth Dog **14** 初七 6
火2 Fire [6] Observation 風地觀 己亥 Earth Pig **15** 初八 2	火2 Fire [7] Increasing 風雷益 庚子 Metal Rat **16** 初九 9	水1 Water [8] Dimming Light 地火明夷 辛丑 Metal Ox **17** 初十 3	金9 Metal [9] Fellowship 天火同人 壬寅 Water Tiger **18** 十一 7	木8 Wood [1] Marrying Maiden 雷澤歸妹 癸卯 Water Rabbit **19** 十二 7	木3 Wood [2] Opposition 火澤睽 甲辰 Wood Dragon **20** 十三 2	火7 Fire [3] Waiting 水天需 乙巳 Wood Snake **21** 十四 3
金4 Metal [4] Great Exceeding 澤風大過 丙午 Fire Horse **22** 十五 3	水6 Water [5] Poison 山風蠱 丁未 Fire Goat **23** 十六 7	火2 Fire [6] Dispersing 風水渙 戊申 Earth Monkey **24** 十七 6	木3 Wood [7] Travelling 火山旅 己酉 Earth Rooster **25** 十八 8	金9 Metal [8] Stagnation 天地否 庚戌 Metal Dog **26** 十九 9	火7 Fire [9] Alliance 水地比 辛亥 Metal Pig **27** 二十 7	木8 Wood [1] Thunder 震爲雷 壬子 Water Rat **28** 廿一 1
水6 Water [2] Beauty 山火賁 癸丑 Water Ox **29** 廿二 8	火7 Fire [3] Accomplished 水火既濟 甲寅 Wood Tiger **30** 廿三 9	水1 Water [4] Arriving 地澤臨 乙卯 Wood Rabbit **31** 廿四 4				

JUNE 2005 壬午

Xuan Kong Element 玄空五行	巽爲風 Wind	Period Luck 卦運	Monthly Star 月星
Fire 火2		1	4

SUNDAY	MONDAY	TUESDAY	WEDNESDAY	THURSDAY	FRIDAY	SATURDAY
			金4 Metal [5] Marsh 兑爲澤 丙辰 Fire Dragon **1** 廿五 1	火2 Fire [6] Small Livestock 風天小畜 丁巳 Fire Snake **2** 廿六 8	木3 Wood [7] The Cauldron 火風鼎 戊午 Earth Horse **3** 廿七 4	水1 Water [8] Rising 地風升 己未 Earth Goat **4** 廿八 2
火7 Fire [9] Water 坎爲水 庚申 Metal Monkey **5** 廿九 1	木8 Wood [1] Lesser Exceeding 雷山小過 辛酉 Metal Rooster **6** 三十 3	金4 Metal [2] Gathering 澤地萃 壬戌 Water Dog **7** 五月初一 4	水6 Water [3] Peel 山地剝 癸亥 Water Pig **8** 初二 6	水1 Water [4] Earth 坤爲地 甲子 Wood Rat **9** 初三 1	木3 Wood [5] Biting 火雷噬嗑 乙丑 Wood Ox **10** 初四 6	火2 Fire [6] Family 風火家人 丙寅 Fire Tiger **11** 初五 4
水6 Water [7] Decreasing 山澤損 丁卯 Fire Rabbit **12** 初六 9	金9 Metal [8] Tread 天澤履 戊辰 Earth Dragon **13** 初七 6	木8 Wood [9] Great Strength 雷天大壯 己巳 Earth Snake **14** 初八 2	木8 Wood [1] Consistency 雷風恒 庚午 Metal Horse **15** 初九 9	金9 Metal [2] Litigation 天水訟 辛未 Metal Goat **16** 初十 3	水1 Water [3] Officer 地水師 壬申 Water Monkey **17** 十一 7	火2 Fire [4] Gradual Progress 風山漸 癸酉 Water Rooster **18** 十二 7
火7 Fire [5] Obstruction 水山蹇 甲戌 Wood Dog **19** 十三 2	木3 Wood [6] Advancement 火地晉 乙亥 Wood Pig **20** 十四 3	水6 Water [7/3] Nourish 山雷頤 丙子 Fire Rat **21** 十五 3	金4 Metal [2] Following 澤雷隨 丁丑 Fire Ox **22** 十六 7	木8 Wood [1] Abundance 雷火豐 戊寅 Earth Tiger **23** 十七 6	火7 Fire [9] Regulate 水澤節 己卯 Earth Rabbit **24** 十八 8	水1 Water [8] Unity 地天泰 庚辰 Metal Dragon **25** 十九 9
木3 Wood [7] Great Reward 火天大有 辛巳 Metal Snake **26** 二十 7	火2 Fire [6] Wind 巽爲風 壬午 Water Horse **27** 廿一 1	金4 Metal [5] Trap 澤水困 癸未 Water Goat **28** 廿二 8	木3 Wood [4] Not Yet Accomplished 火水未濟 甲申 Wood Monkey **29** 廿三 9	金9 Metal [3] Retreat 天山遯 乙酉 Wood Rooster **30** 廿四 4		

JULY 2005 癸未

Xuan Kong Element 玄空五行	澤水困 Trap	Period Luck 卦運	Monthly Star 月星
Metal 金4		8	3

SUNDAY	MONDAY	TUESDAY	WEDNESDAY	THURSDAY	FRIDAY	SATURDAY
金4 Metal Marsh 兑為澤 8 丙辰 Fire Dragon 1 31 廿六					水6 Water Mountain 艮為山 2 丙戌 Fire Dog 1 1 廿五	木8 Wood Delight 雷地豫 1 丁亥 Fire Pig 8 2 廿六
火7 Fire Beginning 水雷屯 9 戊子 Earth Rat 4 3 廿七	金9 Metal Without Wrongdoing 天雷無妄 8 己丑 Earth Ox 2 4 廿八	木3 Wood Fire 離為火 7 庚寅 Metal Tiger 1 5 廿九	火2 Fire Sincerity 風澤中孚 6 辛卯 Metal Rabbit 3 6 六月初一	水6 Water Big Livestock 山天大畜 5 壬辰 Water Dragon 4 7 初二	金4 Metal Eliminating 澤天夬 4 癸巳 Water Snake 6 8 初三	金9 Metal Heaven 乾為天 3 甲午 Wood Horse 1 9 初四
火7 Fire Well 水風井 2 乙未 Wood Goat 6 10 初五	木8 Wood Relief 雷水解 1 丙申 Fire Monkey 4 11 初六	金4 Metal Influence 澤山咸 9 丁酉 Fire Rooster 9 12 初七	水1 Water Humility 地山謙 8 戊戌 Earth Dog 6 13 初八	火2 Fire Observation 風地觀 7 己亥 Earth Pig 2 14 初九	火2 Fire Increasing 風雷益 6 庚子 Metal Rat 9 15 初十	水1 Water Dimming Light 地火明夷 5 辛丑 Metal Ox 3 16 十一
金9 Metal Fellowship 天火同人 4 壬寅 Water Tiger 7 17 十二	木8 Wood Marrying Maiden 雷澤歸妹 3 癸卯 Water Rabbit 7 18 十三	木3 Wood Opposition 火澤睽 2 甲辰 Wood Dragon 2 19 十四	火7 Fire Waiting 水天需 1 乙巳 Wood Snake 3 20 十五	金4 Metal Great Exceeding 澤風大過 9 丙午 Fire Horse 3 21 十六	水6 Water Poison 山風蠱 8 丁未 Fire Goat 7 22 十七	火2 Fire Dispersing 風水渙 7 戊申 Earth Monkey 6 23 十八
木3 Wood Travelling 火山旅 6 己酉 Earth Rooster 8 24 十九	金9 Metal Stagnation 天地否 5 庚戌 Metal Dog 9 25 二十	火7 Fire Alliance 水地比 4 辛亥 Metal Pig 7 26 廿一	木8 Wood Thunder 震為雷 3 壬子 Water Rat 1 27 廿二	水6 Water Beauty 山火賁 2 癸丑 Water Ox 8 28 廿三	火7 Fire Accomplished 水火既濟 1 甲寅 Wood Tiger 9 29 廿四	水1 Water Arriving 地澤臨 9 乙卯 Wood Rabbit 4 30 廿五

AUGUST 2005 甲申

Xuan Kong Element 玄空五行	火水未濟 Not Yet Accomplished	Period Luck 卦運	Monthly Star 月星
Wood 木3		9	2

SUNDAY	MONDAY	TUESDAY	WEDNESDAY	THURSDAY	FRIDAY	SATURDAY
	火2 Fire Small Livestock 風天小畜 7 丁巳 Fire Snake 8 1 廿七	木3 Wood The Cauldron 火風鼎 6 戊午 Earth Horse 4 2 廿八	水1 Water Rising 地風升 5 己未 Earth Goat 2 3 廿九	火7 Fire Water 坎為水 4 庚申 Metal Monkey 1 4 三十	木8 Wood Lesser Exceeding 雷山小過 3 辛酉 Metal Rooster 3 5 七月初一	金4 Metal Gathering 澤地萃 2 壬戌 Water Dog 4 6 初二
水6 Water Peel 山地剝 1 癸亥 Water Pig 6 7 初三	水1 Water Earth 坤為地 9 甲子 Wood Rat 1 8 初四	木3 Wood Biting 火雷噬嗑 8 乙丑 Wood Ox 6 9 初五	火2 Fire Family 風火家人 7 丙寅 Fire Tiger 4 10 初六	水6 Water Decreasing 山澤損 6 丁卯 Fire Rabbit 9 11 初七	金9 Metal Tread 天澤履 5 戊辰 Earth Dragon 6 12 初八	木8 Wood Great Strength 雷天大壯 4 己巳 Earth Snake 2 13 初九
木8 Wood Consistency 雷風恒 3 庚午 Metal Horse 9 14 初十	金9 Metal Litigation 天水訟 2 辛未 Metal Goat 3 15 十一	水1 Water Officer 地水師 1 壬申 Water Monkey 7 16 十二	火2 Fire Gradual Progress 風山漸 9 癸酉 Water Rooster 7 17 十三	火7 Fire Obstruction 水山蹇 8 甲戌 Wood Dog 2 18 十四	木3 Wood Advancement 火地晉 7 乙亥 Wood Pig 3 19 十五	水6 Water Nourish 山雷頤 6 丙子 Fire Rat 3 20 十六
金4 Metal Following 澤雷隨 5 丁丑 Fire Ox 7 21 十七	木8 Wood Abundance 雷火豐 4 戊寅 Earth Tiger 6 22 十八	火7 Fire Regulate 水澤節 3 己卯 Earth Rabbit 8 23 十九	水1 Water Unity 地天泰 2 庚辰 Metal Dragon 9 24 二十	木3 Wood Great Reward 火天大有 1 辛巳 Metal Snake 7 25 廿一	火2 Fire Wind 巽為風 9 壬午 Water Horse 1 26 廿二	金4 Metal Trap 澤水困 8 癸未 Water Goat 8 27 廿三
木3 Wood Not Yet Accomplished 火水未濟 7 甲申 Wood Monkey 9 28 廿四	金9 Metal Retreat 天山遯 6 乙酉 Wood Rooster 4 29 廿五	水6 Water Mountain 艮為山 5 丙戌 Fire Dog 1 30 廿六	木8 Wood Delight 雷地豫 4 丁亥 Fire Pig 8 31 廿七			

SEPTEMBER 2005 乙酉

Xuan Kong Element 玄空五行	天山遯 Retreat	Period Luck 卦運	Monthly Star 月星
Metal 金9		4	1

SUNDAY	MONDAY	TUESDAY	WEDNESDAY	THURSDAY	FRIDAY	SATURDAY
				火7 Fire 3 Beginning 戊子 Earth Rat 水雷屯 1 廿八 4	金9 Metal 2 Without Wrongdoing 己丑 Earth Ox 天雷無妄 2 廿九 2	木3 Wood 1 Fire 庚寅 Metal Tiger 離爲火 3 三十 1
火2 Fire 9 Sincerity 辛卯 Metal Rabbit 風澤中孚 4 八月初一 3	水6 Water 8 Big Livestock 壬辰 Water Dragon 山天大畜 5 初二 4	金4 Metal 7 Eliminating 癸巳 Water Snake 澤天夬 6 初三 6	金9 Metal 6 Heaven 甲午 Wood Horse 乾爲天 7 初四 1	火7 Fire 5 Well 乙未 Wood Goat 水風井 8 初五 6	木8 Wood 4 Relief 丙申 Fire Monkey 雷水解 9 初六 4	金4 Metal 3 Influence 丁酉 Fire Rooster 澤山咸 10 初七 9
水1 Water 2 Humility 戊戌 Earth Dog 地山謙 11 初八 6	火2 Fire 1 Observation 己亥 Earth Pig 風地觀 12 初九 2	火2 Fire 9 Increasing 庚子 Metal Rat 風雷益 13 初十 9	水1 Water 8 Dimming Light 辛丑 Metal Ox 地火明夷 14 十一 3	金9 Metal 7 Fellowship 壬寅 Water Tiger 天火同人 15 十二 7	木8 Wood 6 Marrying Maiden 癸卯 Water Rabbit 雷澤歸妹 16 十三 7	木3 Wood 5 Opposition 甲辰 Wood Dragon 火澤睽 17 十四 2
火7 Fire 4 Waiting 乙巳 Wood Snake 水天需 18 十五 3	金4 Metal 3 Great Exceeding 丙午 Fire Horse 澤風大過 19 十六 3	水6 Water 2 Poison 丁未 Fire Goat 山風蠱 20 十七 7	火2 Fire 1 Dispersing 戊申 Earth Monkey 風水渙 21 十八 6	木3 Wood 9 Travelling 己酉 Earth Rooster 火山旅 22 十九 8	金9 Metal 8 Stagnation 庚戌 Metal Dog 天地否 23 二十 9	火7 Fire 7 Alliance 辛亥 Metal Pig 水地比 24 廿一 7
木8 Wood 6 Thunder 壬子 Water Rat 震爲雷 25 廿二 1	水6 Water 5 Beauty 癸丑 Water Ox 山火賁 26 廿三 8	火7 Fire 4 Accomplished 甲寅 Wood Tiger 水火既濟 27 廿四 9	水1 Water 3 Arriving 乙卯 Wood Rabbit 地澤臨 28 廿五 4	金4 Metal 2 Marsh 丙辰 Fire Dragon 兑爲澤 29 廿六 1	火2 Fire 1 Small Livestock 丁巳 Fire Snake 風天小畜 30 廿七 8	

OCTOBER 2005 丙戌

Xuan Kong Element 玄空五行	艮爲山 Mountain	Period Luck 卦運	Monthly Star 月星
Water 水6		1	9

SUNDAY	MONDAY	TUESDAY	WEDNESDAY	THURSDAY	FRIDAY	SATURDAY
木8 Wood 7 Delight 丁亥 Fire Pig 雷地豫 30 廿八 8	火7 Fire 6 Beginning 戊子 Earth Rat 水雷屯 31 廿九 4					木3 Wood 9 The Cauldron 戊午 Earth Horse 火風鼎 1 廿八 4
水1 Water 8 Rising 己未 Earth Goat 地風升 2 廿九 2	火7 Fire 7 Water 庚申 Metal Monkey 坎爲水 3 九月初一 1	木8 Wood 6 Lesser Exceeding 辛酉 Metal Rooster 雷山小過 4 初二 3	金4 Metal 5 Gathering 壬戌 Water Dog 澤地萃 5 初三 4	水6 Water 4 Peel 癸亥 Water Pig 山地剝 6 初四 6	水1 Water 3 Earth 甲子 Wood Rat 坤爲地 7 初五 1	木3 Wood 2 Biting 乙丑 Wood Ox 火雷噬嗑 8 初六 6
火2 Fire 1 Family 丙寅 Fire Tiger 風火家人 9 初七 4	水6 Water 9 Decreasing 丁卯 Fire Rabbit 山澤損 10 初八 9	金9 Metal 8 Tread 戊辰 Earth Dragon 天澤履 11 初九 6	木8 Wood 7 Great Strength 己巳 Earth Snake 雷天大壯 12 初十 2	木8 Wood 6 Consistency 庚午 Metal Horse 雷風恆 13 十一 9	金9 Metal 5 Litigation 辛未 Metal Goat 天水訟 14 十二 3	水1 Water 4 Officer 壬申 Water Monkey 地水師 15 十三 7
火2 Fire 3 Gradual Progress 癸酉 Water Rooster 風山漸 16 十四 7	火7 Fire 2 Obstruction 甲戌 Wood Dog 水山蹇 17 十五 2	木3 Wood 1 Advancement 乙亥 Wood Pig 火地晉 18 十六 3	水6 Water 9 Nourish 丙子 Fire Rat 山雷頤 19 十七 3	金4 Metal 8 Following 丁丑 Fire Ox 澤雷隨 20 十八 7	木8 Wood 7 Abundance 戊寅 Earth Tiger 雷火豐 21 十九 6	火7 Fire 6 Regulate 己卯 Earth Rabbit 水澤節 22 二十 8
水1 Water 5 Unity 庚辰 Metal Dragon 地天泰 23 廿一 9	木3 Wood 4 Great Reward 辛巳 Metal Snake 火天大有 24 廿二 7	火2 Fire 3 Wind 壬午 Water Horse 巽爲風 25 廿三 1	金4 Metal 2 Trap 癸未 Water Goat 澤水困 26 廿四 8	木3 Wood 1 Not Yet Accomplished 甲申 Wood Monkey 火水未濟 27 廿五 9	金9 Metal 9 Retreat 乙酉 Wood Rooster 天山遯 28 廿六 4	水6 Water 8 Mountain 丙戌 Fire Dog 艮爲山 29 廿七 1

NOVEMBER 2005 丁亥

Xuan Kong Element 玄空五行	雷地豫 Delight	Period Luck 卦運	Monthly Star 月星
Wood 木8		8	8

SUNDAY	MONDAY	TUESDAY	WEDNESDAY	THURSDAY	FRIDAY	SATURDAY
		金9 Metal 己丑 Earth Ox 2 Without Wrongdoing 天雷無妄 5 1 三十	木3 Wood 庚寅 Metal Tiger 1 Fire 離爲火 4 2 十月初一	火2 Fire 辛卯 Metal Rabbit 3 Sincerity 風澤中孚 3 3 初二	水6 Water 壬辰 Water Dragon 4 Big Livestock 山天大畜 2 4 初三	金4 Metal 癸巳 Water Snake 6 Eliminating 澤天夬 1 5 初四
金9 Metal 甲午 Wood Horse 1 Heaven 乾爲天 9 6 初五	火7 Fire 乙未 Wood Goat 6 Well 水風井 8 7 初六	木8 Wood 丙申 Fire Monkey 4 Relief 雷水解 7 8 初七	金4 Metal 丁酉 Fire Rooster 9 Influence 澤山咸 6 9 初八	水1 Water 戊戌 Earth Dog 6 Humility 地山謙 5 10 初九	火2 Fire 己亥 Earth Pig 2 Observation 風地觀 4 11 初十	火2 Fire 庚子 Metal Rat 9 Increasing 風雷益 3 12 十一
水1 Water 辛丑 Metal Ox 3 Dimming Light 地火明夷 2 13 十二	金9 Metal 壬寅 Water Tiger 7 Fellowship 天火同人 1 14 十三	木8 Wood 癸卯 Water Rabbit 7 Marrying Maiden 雷澤歸妹 9 15 十四	木3 Wood 甲辰 Wood Dragon 2 Opposition 火澤睽 8 16 十五	火7 Fire 乙巳 Wood Snake 3 Waiting 水天需 7 17 十六	金4 Metal 丙午 Fire Horse 3 Great Exceeding 澤風大過 6 18 十七	水6 Water 丁未 Fire Goat 7 Poison 山風蠱 5 19 十八
火2 Fire 戊申 Earth Monkey 6 Dispersing 風水渙 4 20 十九	木3 Wood 己酉 Earth Rooster 8 Travelling 火山旅 3 21 二十	金9 Metal 庚戌 Metal Dog 9 Stagnation 天地否 2 22 廿一	火7 Fire 辛亥 Metal Pig 7 Alliance 水地比 1 23 廿二	木8 Wood 壬子 Water Rat 1 Thunder 震爲雷 9 24 廿三	水6 Water 癸丑 Water Ox 8 Beauty 山火賁 8 25 廿四	火7 Fire 甲寅 Wood Tiger 9 Accomplished 水火既濟 7 26 廿五
水1 Water 乙卯 Wood Rabbit 4 Arriving 地澤臨 6 27 廿六	金4 Metal 丙辰 Fire Dragon 1 Marsh 兌爲澤 5 28 廿七	火2 Fire 丁巳 Fire Snake 8 Small Livestock 風天小畜 4 29 廿八	木3 Wood 戊午 Earth Horse 4 The Cauldron 火風鼎 3 30 廿九			

DECEMBER 2005 戊子

Xuan Kong Element 玄空五行	水雷屯 Beginning	Period Luck 卦運	Monthly Star 月星
Fire 火7		4	7

SUNDAY	MONDAY	TUESDAY	WEDNESDAY	THURSDAY	FRIDAY	SATURDAY
				水1 Water 己未 Earth Goat 2 Rising 地風升 2 1 十一月初一	火7 Fire 庚申 Metal Monkey 1 Water 坎爲水 1 2 初二	木8 Wood 辛酉 Metal Rooster 3 Lesser Exceeding 雷山小過 9 3 初三
金4 Metal 壬戌 Water Dog 4 Gathering 澤地萃 8 4 初四	水6 Water 癸亥 Water Pig 6 Peel 山地剝 7 5 初五	水1 Water 甲子 Wood Rat 1 Earth 坤爲地 6 6 初六	木3 Wood 乙丑 Wood Ox 6 Biting 火雷噬嗑 5 7 初七	火2 Fire 丙寅 Fire Tiger 4 Family 風火家人 4 8 初八	水6 Water 丁卯 Fire Rabbit 9 Decreasing 山澤損 3 9 初九	金9 Metal 戊辰 Earth Dragon 6 Tread 天澤履 2 10 初十
木8 Wood 己巳 Earth Snake 2 Great Strength 雷天大壯 1 11 十一	木8 Wood 庚午 Metal Horse 9 Consistency 雷風恆 9 12 十二	金9 Metal 辛未 Metal Goat 3 Litigation 天水訟 8 13 十三	水1 Water 壬申 Water Monkey 7 Officer 地水師 7 14 十四	火2 Fire 癸酉 Water Rooster 7 Gradual Progress 風山漸 6 15 十五	火7 Fire 甲戌 Wood Dog 2 Obstruction 水山蹇 5 16 十六	木3 Wood 乙亥 Wood Pig 3 Advancement 火地晉 4 17 十七
水6 Water 丙子 Fire Rat 3 Nourish 山雷頤 3 18 十八	金4 Metal 丁丑 Fire Ox 7 Following 澤雷隨 2 19 十九	木8 Wood 戊寅 Earth Tiger 6 Abundance 雷火豐 1 20 二十	火7 Fire 己卯 Earth Rabbit 8 Regulate 水澤節 9 21 廿一	水1 Water 庚辰 Metal Dragon 9 Unity 地天泰 8/2 22 廿二	木3 Wood 辛巳 Metal Snake 7 Great Reward 火天大有 3 23 廿三	火2 Fire 壬午 Water Horse 1 Wind 巽爲風 4 24 廿四
金4 Metal 癸未 Water Goat 8 Trap 澤水困 5 25 廿五	木3 Wood 甲申 Wood Monkey 9 Not Yet Accomplished 火水未濟 6 26 廿六	金9 Metal 乙酉 Wood Rooster 4 Retreat 天山遯 7 27 廿七	水6 Water 丙戌 Fire Dog 1 Mountain 艮爲山 8 28 廿八	木8 Wood 丁亥 Fire Pig 8 Delight 雷地豫 9 29 廿九	火7 Fire 戊子 Earth Rat 4 Beginning 水雷屯 1 30 三十	金9 Metal 己丑 Earth Ox 2 Without Wrongdoing 天雷無妄 2 31 十二月初一

2006 丙戌

(*Bing Xu*) Fire Dog

2006 丙戌 *(Bing Xu)* Fire Dog

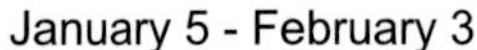

January 5 - February 3

February 4 - March 5

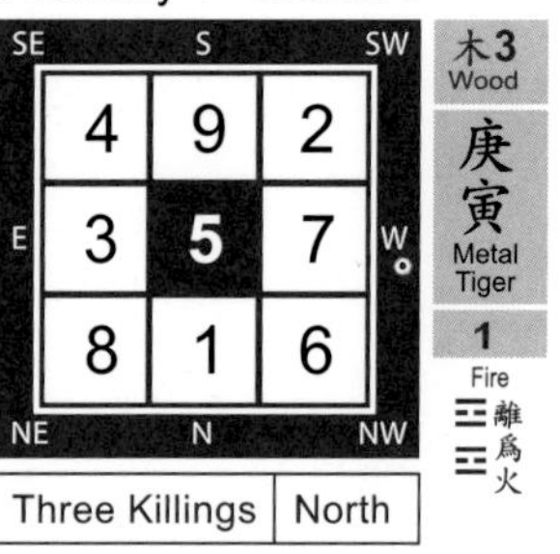

March 6 - April 4

April 5 - May 4

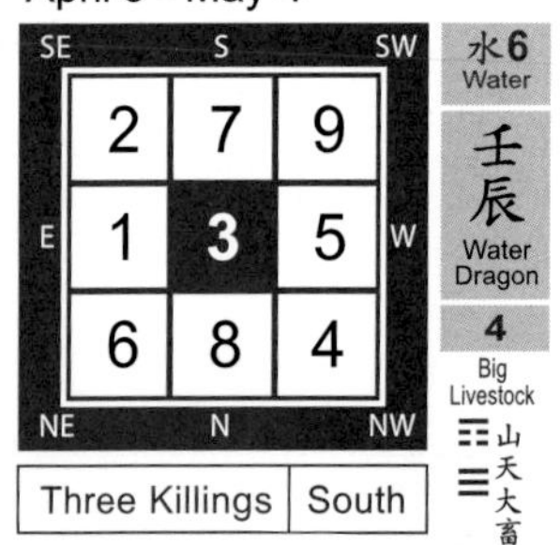

May 5 - June 5

June 6 - July 6

July 7 - August 6

August 7 - September 7

SE	S	SW
7	3	5
6	8	1
2	4	9
NE	N	NW

木8 Wood

丙申 Fire Monkey

4 Relief

雷水解

Three Killings South

September 8 - October 7

October 8 - November 6

November 7 - December 6

December 7 - January 5

JANUARY 2006 己丑

Xuan Kong Element 玄空五行	天雷無妄 Without Wrongdoing	Period Luck 卦運	Monthly Star 月星
Metal 金9		2	6

SUNDAY	MONDAY	TUESDAY	WEDNESDAY	THURSDAY	FRIDAY	SATURDAY
1 初二 木3 Wood [3] Fire 離爲火 庚寅 Metal Tiger 1	**2** 初三 火2 Fire [4] Sincerity 風澤中孚 辛卯 Metal Rabbit 3	**3** 初四 水6 Water [5] Big Livestock 山天大畜 壬辰 Water Dragon 4	**4** 初五 金4 Metal [6] Eliminating 澤天夬 癸巳 Water Snake 6	**5** 初六 金9 Metal [7] Heaven 乾爲天 甲午 Wood Horse 1	**6** 初七 火7 Fire [8] Well 水風井 乙未 Wood Goat 6	**7** 初八 木8 Wood [9] Relief 雷水解 丙申 Fire Monkey 4
8 初九 金4 Metal [1] Influence 澤山咸 丁酉 Fire Rooster 9	**9** 初十 水1 Water [2] Humility 地山謙 戊戌 Earth Dog 6	**10** 十一 火2 Fire [3] Observation 風地觀 己亥 Earth Pig 2	**11** 十二 火2 Fire [4] Increasing 風雷益 庚子 Metal Rat 9	**12** 十三 水1 Water [5] Dimming Light 地火明夷 辛丑 Metal Ox 3	**13** 十四 金9 Metal [6] Fellowship 天火同人 壬寅 Water Tiger 7	**14** 十五 木8 Wood [7] Marrying Maiden 雷澤歸妹 癸卯 Water Rabbit 7
15 十六 木3 Wood [8] Opposition 火澤睽 甲辰 Wood Dragon 2	**16** 十七 火7 Fire [9] Waiting 水天需 乙巳 Wood Snake 3	**17** 十八 金4 Metal [1] Great Exceeding 澤風大過 丙午 Fire Horse 3	**18** 十九 水6 Water [2] Poison 山風蠱 丁未 Fire Goat 7	**19** 二十 火2 Fire [3] Dispersing 風水渙 戊申 Earth Monkey 6	**20** 廿一 木3 Wood [4] Travelling 火山旅 己酉 Earth Rooster 8	**21** 廿二 金9 Metal [5] Stagnation 天地否 庚戌 Metal Dog 9
22 廿三 火7 Fire [6] Alliance 水地比 辛亥 Metal Pig 7	**23** 廿四 木8 Wood [7] Thunder 震爲雷 壬子 Water Rat 1	**24** 廿五 水6 Water [8] Beauty 山火賁 癸丑 Water Ox 8	**25** 廿六 火7 Fire [9] Accomplished 水火既濟 甲寅 Wood Tiger 9	**26** 廿七 水1 Water [1] Arriving 地澤臨 乙卯 Wood Rabbit 4	**27** 廿八 金4 Metal [2] Marsh 兑爲澤 丙辰 Fire Dragon 1	**28** 廿九 火2 Fire [3] Small Livestock 風天小畜 丁巳 Fire Snake 8
29 正月初一 木3 Wood [4] The Cauldron 火風鼎 戊午 Earth Horse 4	**30** 初二 水1 Water [5] Rising 地風升 己未 Earth Goat 2	**31** 初三 火7 Fire [6] Water 坎爲水 庚申 Metal Monkey 1				

FEBRUARY 2006 庚寅

Xuan Kong Element 玄空五行	離爲火 Fire	Period Luck 卦運	Monthly Star 月星
Wood 木3		1	5

SUNDAY	MONDAY	TUESDAY	WEDNESDAY	THURSDAY	FRIDAY	SATURDAY
			1 初四 木8 Wood [7] Lesser Exceeding 雷山小過 辛酉 Metal Rooster 3	**2** 初五 金4 Metal [8] Gathering 澤地萃 壬戌 Water Dog 4	**3** 初六 水6 Water [9] Peel 山地剝 癸亥 Water Pig 6	**4** 初七 水1 Water [1] Earth 坤爲地 甲子 Wood Rat 1
5 初八 木3 Wood [2] Biting 火雷噬嗑 乙丑 Wood Ox 6	**6** 初九 火2 Fire [3] Family 風火家人 丙寅 Fire Tiger 4	**7** 初十 水6 Water [4] Decreasing 山澤損 丁卯 Fire Rabbit 9	**8** 十一 金9 Metal [5] Tread 天澤履 戊辰 Earth Dragon 6	**9** 十二 木8 Wood [6] Great Strength 雷天大壯 己巳 Earth Snake 2	**10** 十三 木8 Wood [7] Consistency 雷風恆 庚午 Metal Horse 9	**11** 十四 金9 Metal [8] Litigation 天水訟 辛未 Metal Goat 3
12 十五 水1 Water [9] Officer 地水師 壬申 Water Monkey 7	**13** 十六 火2 Fire [1] Gradual Progress 風山漸 癸酉 Water Rooster 7	**14** 十七 火7 Fire [2] Obstruction 水山蹇 甲戌 Wood Dog 2	**15** 十八 木3 Wood [3] Advancement 火地晉 乙亥 Wood Pig 3	**16** 十九 水6 Water [4] Nourish 山雷頤 丙子 Fire Rat 3	**17** 二十 金4 Metal [5] Following 澤雷隨 丁丑 Fire Ox 7	**18** 廿一 木8 Wood [6] Abundance 雷火豐 戊寅 Earth Tiger 6
19 廿二 火7 Fire [7] Regulate 水澤節 己卯 Earth Rabbit 8	**20** 廿三 水1 Water [8] Unity 地天泰 庚辰 Metal Dragon 9	**21** 廿四 木3 Wood [9] Great Reward 火天大有 辛巳 Metal Snake 7	**22** 廿五 火2 Fire [1] Wind 巽爲風 壬午 Water Horse 1	**23** 廿六 金4 Metal [2] Trap 澤水困 癸未 Water Goat 8	**24** 廿七 木3 Wood [3] Not Yet Accomplished 火水未濟 甲申 Wood Monkey 9	**25** 廿八 金9 Metal [4] Retreat 天山遯 乙酉 Wood Rooster 4
26 廿九 水6 Water [5] Mountain 艮爲山 丙戌 Fire Dog 1	**27** 三十 木8 Wood [6] Delight 雷地豫 丁亥 Fire Pig 8	**28** 二月初一 火7 Fire [7] Beginning 水雷屯 戊子 Earth Rat 4				

MARCH 2006 辛卯

Xuan Kong Element 玄空五行	風澤中孚 Sincerity	Period Luck 卦運	Monthly Star 月星
Fire 火2		3	4

SUNDAY	MONDAY	TUESDAY	WEDNESDAY	THURSDAY	FRIDAY	SATURDAY
			金9 Metal 8 Without Wrongdoing 天雷無妄 己丑 Earth Ox 2 1 初二	木3 Wood 9 Fire 離爲火 庚寅 Metal Tiger 1 2 初三	火2 Fire 1 Sincerity 風澤中孚 辛卯 Metal Rabbit 3 3 初四	水6 Water 2 Big Livestock 山天大畜 壬辰 Water Dragon 4 4 初五
金4 Metal 3 Eliminating 澤天夬 癸巳 Water Snake 6 5 初六	金9 Metal 4 Heaven 乾爲天 甲午 Wood Horse 1 6 初七	火7 Fire 5 Well 水風井 乙未 Wood Goat 6 7 初八	木8 Wood 6 Relief 雷水解 丙申 Fire Monkey 4 8 初九	金4 Metal 7 Influence 澤山咸 丁酉 Fire Rooster 9 9 初十	水1 Water 8 Humility 地山謙 戊戌 Earth Dog 6 10 十一	火2 Fire 9 Observation 風地觀 己亥 Earth Pig 2 11 十二
火2 Fire 1 Increasing 風雷益 庚子 Metal Rat 9 12 十三	水1 Water 2 Dimming Light 地火明夷 辛丑 Metal Ox 3 13 十四	金9 Metal 3 Fellowship 天火同人 壬寅 Water Tiger 7 14 十五	木8 Wood 4 Marrying Maiden 雷澤歸妹 癸卯 Water Rabbit 7 15 十六	木3 Wood 5 Opposition 火澤睽 甲辰 Wood Dragon 2 16 十七	火7 Fire 6 Waiting 水天需 乙巳 Wood Snake 3 17 十八	金4 Metal 7 Great Exceeding 澤風大過 丙午 Fire Horse 3 18 十九
水6 Water 8 Poison 山風蠱 丁未 Fire Goat 7 19 二十	火2 Fire 9 Dispersing 風水渙 戊申 Earth Monkey 6 20 廿一	木3 Wood 1 Travelling 火山旅 己酉 Earth Rooster 8 21 廿二	金9 Metal 2 Stagnation 天地否 庚戌 Metal Dog 9 22 廿三	火7 Fire 3 Alliance 水地比 辛亥 Metal Pig 7 23 廿四	木8 Wood 4 Thunder 震爲雷 壬子 Water Rat 1 24 廿五	水6 Water 5 Beauty 山火賁 癸丑 Water Ox 8 25 廿六
火7 Fire 6 Accomplished 水火既濟 甲寅 Wood Tiger 9 26 廿七	水1 Water 7 Arriving 地澤臨 乙卯 Wood Rabbit 4 27 廿八	金4 Metal 8 Marsh 兑爲澤 丙辰 Fire Dragon 1 28 廿九	火2 Fire 9 Small Livestock 風天小畜 丁巳 Fire Snake 8 29 三月初一	木3 Wood 1 The Cauldron 火風鼎 戊午 Earth Horse 4 30 初二	水1 Water 2 Rising 地風升 己未 Earth Goat 2 31 初三	

APRIL 2006 壬辰

Xuan Kong Element 玄空五行	山天大畜 Big Livestock	Period Luck 卦運	Monthly Star 月星
Water 水6		4	3

SUNDAY	MONDAY	TUESDAY	WEDNESDAY	THURSDAY	FRIDAY	SATURDAY
金9 Metal 5 Without Wrongdoing 天雷無妄 己丑 Earth Ox 2 30 初三						火7 Fire 3 Water 坎爲水 庚申 Metal Monkey 1 1 初四
木8 Wood 4 Lesser Exceeding 雷山小過 辛酉 Metal Rooster 3 2 初五	金4 Metal 5 Gathering 澤地萃 壬戌 Water Dog 4 3 初六	水6 Water 6 Peel 山地剝 癸亥 Water Pig 6 4 初七	水1 Water 7 Earth 坤爲地 甲子 Wood Rat 1 5 初八	木3 Wood 8 Biting 火雷噬嗑 乙丑 Wood Ox 6 6 初九	火2 Fire 9 Family 風火家人 丙寅 Fire Tiger 4 7 初十	水6 Water 1 Decreasing 山澤損 丁卯 Fire Rabbit 9 8 十一
金9 Metal 2 Tread 天澤履 戊辰 Earth Dragon 6 9 十二	木8 Wood 3 Great Strength 雷天大壯 己巳 Earth Snake 2 10 十三	木8 Wood 4 Consistency 雷風恆 庚午 Metal Horse 9 11 十四	金9 Metal 5 Litigation 天水訟 辛未 Metal Goat 3 12 十五	水1 Water 6 Officer 地水師 壬申 Water Monkey 7 13 十六	火2 Fire 7 Gradual Progress 風山漸 癸酉 Water Rooster 7 14 十七	火7 Fire 8 Obstruction 水山蹇 甲戌 Wood Dog 2 15 十八
木3 Wood 9 Advancement 火地晉 乙亥 Wood Pig 3 16 十九	水6 Water 1 Nourish 山雷頤 丙子 Fire Rat 3 17 二十	金4 Metal 2 Following 澤雷隨 丁丑 Fire Ox 7 18 廿一	木8 Wood 3 Abundance 雷火豐 戊寅 Earth Tiger 6 19 廿二	火7 Fire 4 Regulate 水澤節 己卯 Earth Rabbit 8 20 廿三	水1 Water 5 Unity 地天泰 庚辰 Metal Dragon 9 21 廿四	木3 Wood 6 Great Reward 火天大有 辛巳 Metal Snake 7 22 廿五
火2 Fire 7 Wind 巽爲風 壬午 Water Horse 1 23 廿六	金4 Metal 8 Trap 澤水困 癸未 Water Goat 8 24 廿七	木3 Wood 9 Not Yet Accomplished 火水未濟 甲申 Wood Monkey 9 25 廿八	金9 Metal 1 Retreat 天山遯 乙酉 Wood Rooster 4 26 廿九	水6 Water 2 Mountain 艮爲山 丙戌 Fire Dog 1 27 三十	木8 Wood 3 Delight 雷地豫 丁亥 Fire Pig 8 28 四月初一	火7 Fire 4 Beginning 水雷屯 戊子 Earth Rat 4 29 初二

MAY 2006 癸巳

Xuan Kong Element 玄空五行	澤天夬 Eliminating	Period Luck 卦運	Monthly Star 月星
Metal 金4		6	2

SUNDAY	MONDAY	TUESDAY	WEDNESDAY	THURSDAY	FRIDAY	SATURDAY
	木3 Wood 庚寅 Metal Tiger 1 Fire 離爲火 6 **1** 初四	火2 Fire 辛卯 Metal Rabbit 3 Sincerity 風澤中孚 7 **2** 初五	水6 Water 壬辰 Water Dragon 4 Big Livestock 山天大畜 8 **3** 初六	金4 Metal 癸巳 Water Snake 6 Eliminating 澤天夬 9 **4** 初七	金9 Metal 甲午 Wood Horse 1 Heaven 乾爲天 1 **5** 初八	火7 Fire 乙未 Wood Goat 6 Well 水風井 2 **6** 初九
木8 Wood 丙申 Fire Monkey 4 Relief 雷水解 3 **7** 初十	金4 Metal 丁酉 Fire Rooster 9 Influence 澤山咸 4 **8** 十一	水1 Water 戊戌 Earth Dog 6 Humility 地山謙 5 **9** 十二	火2 Fire 己亥 Earth Pig 2 Observation 風地觀 6 **10** 十三	火2 Fire 庚子 Metal Rat 9 Increasing 風雷益 7 **11** 十四	水1 Water 辛丑 Metal Ox 3 Dimming Light 地火明夷 8 **12** 十五	金9 Metal 壬寅 Water Tiger 7 Fellowship 天火同人 9 **13** 十六
木8 Wood 癸卯 Water Rabbit 7 Marrying Maiden 雷澤歸妹 1 **14** 十七	木3 Wood 甲辰 Wood Dragon 2 Opposition 火澤睽 2 **15** 十八	火7 Fire 乙巳 Wood Snake 3 Waiting 水天需 3 **16** 十九	金4 Metal 丙午 Fire Horse 3 Great Exceeding 澤風大過 4 **17** 二十	水6 Water 丁未 Fire Goat 7 Poison 山風蠱 5 **18** 廿一	火2 Fire 戊申 Earth Monkey 6 Dispersing 風水渙 6 **19** 廿二	木3 Wood 己酉 Earth Rooster 8 Travelling 火山旅 7 **20** 廿三
金9 Metal 庚戌 Metal Dog 9 Stagnation 天地否 8 **21** 廿四	火7 Fire 辛亥 Metal Pig 7 Alliance 水地比 9 **22** 廿五	木8 Wood 壬子 Water Rat 1 Thunder 震爲雷 1 **23** 廿六	水6 Water 癸丑 Water Ox 8 Beauty 山火賁 2 **24** 廿七	火7 Fire 甲寅 Wood Tiger 9 Accomplished 水火既濟 3 **25** 廿八	水1 Water 乙卯 Wood Rabbit 4 Arriving 地澤臨 4 **26** 廿九	金4 Metal 丙辰 Fire Dragon 1 Marsh 兑爲澤 5 **27** 五月初一
火2 Fire 丁巳 Fire Snake 8 Small Livestock 風天小畜 6 **28** 初二	木3 Wood 戊午 Earth Horse 4 The Cauldron 火風鼎 7 **29** 初三	水1 Water 己未 Earth Goat 2 Rising 地風升 8 **30** 初四	火7 Fire 庚申 Metal Monkey 1 Water 坎爲水 9 **31** 初五			

JUNE 2006 甲午

Xuan Kong Element 玄空五行	乾爲天 Heaven	Period Luck 卦運	Monthly Star 月星
Metal 金9		1	1

SUNDAY	MONDAY	TUESDAY	WEDNESDAY	THURSDAY	FRIDAY	SATURDAY
				木8 Wood 辛酉 Metal Rooster 3 Lesser Exceeding 雷山小過 1 **1** 初六	金4 Metal 壬戌 Water Dog 4 Gathering 澤地萃 2 **2** 初七	水6 Water 癸亥 Water Pig 6 Peel 山地剝 3 **3** 初八
水1 Water 甲子 Wood Rat 1 Earth 坤爲地 4 **4** 初九	木3 Wood 乙丑 Wood Ox 6 Biting 火雷噬嗑 5 **5** 初十	火2 Fire 丙寅 Fire Tiger 4 Family 風火家人 6 **6** 十一	水6 Water 丁卯 Fire Rabbit 9 Decreasing 山澤損 7 **7** 十二	金9 Metal 戊辰 Earth Dragon 6 Tread 天澤履 8 **8** 十三	木8 Wood 己巳 Earth Snake 2 Great Strength 雷天大壯 9 **9** 十四	木8 Wood 庚午 Metal Horse 9 Consistency 雷風恒 1 **10** 十五
金9 Metal 辛未 Metal Goat 3 Litigation 天水訟 2 **11** 十六	水1 Water 壬申 Water Monkey 7 Officer 地水師 3 **12** 十七	火2 Fire 癸酉 Water Rooster 7 Gradual Progress 風山漸 4 **13** 十八	火7 Fire 甲戌 Wood Dog 2 Obstruction 水山蹇 5 **14** 十九	木3 Wood 乙亥 Wood Pig 3 Advancement 火地晉 6 **15** 二十	水6 Water 丙子 Fire Rat 3 Nourish 山雷頤 7 **16** 廿一	金4 Metal 丁丑 Fire Ox 7 Following 澤雷隨 8 **17** 廿二
木8 Wood 戊寅 Earth Tiger 6 Abundance 雷火豐 9 **18** 廿三	火7 Fire 己卯 Earth Rabbit 8 Regulate 水澤節 1 **19** 廿四	水1 Water 庚辰 Metal Dragon 9 Unity 地天泰 2 **20** 廿五	木3 Wood 辛巳 Metal Snake 7 Great Reward 火天大有 3/7 **21** 廿六	火2 Fire 壬午 Water Horse 1 Wind 巽爲風 6 **22** 廿七	金4 Metal 癸未 Water Goat 8 Trap 澤水困 5 **23** 廿八	木3 Wood 甲申 Wood Monkey 9 Not Yet Accomplished 火水未濟 4 **24** 廿九
金9 Metal 乙酉 Wood Rooster 4 Retreat 天山遯 3 **25** 三十	水6 Water 丙戌 Fire Dog 1 Mountain 艮爲山 2 **26** 六月初一	木8 Wood 丁亥 Fire Pig 8 Delight 雷地豫 1 **27** 初二	火7 Fire 戊子 Earth Rat 4 Beginning 水雷屯 9 **28** 初三	金9 Metal 己丑 Earth Ox 2 Without Wrongdoing 天雷無妄 8 **29** 初四	木3 Wood 庚寅 Metal Tiger 1 Fire 離爲火 7 **30** 初五	

JULY 2006 乙未

Xuan Kong Element 玄空五行	水風井 Well	Period Luck 卦運	Monthly Star 月星
Fire 火7		6	9

SUNDAY	MONDAY	TUESDAY	WEDNESDAY	THURSDAY	FRIDAY	SATURDAY
火7 Fire · 4 Water 坎爲水 庚申 Metal Monkey 30 初六 1	木8 Wood · 3 Lesser Exceeding 雷山小過 辛酉 Metal Rooster 31 初七 3					火2 Fire · 6 Sincerity 風澤中孚 辛卯 Metal Rabbit 1 初六 3
水6 Water · 5 Big Livestock 山天大畜 壬辰 Water Dragon 2 初七 4	金4 Metal · 4 Eliminating 澤天夬 癸巳 Water Snake 3 初八 6	金9 Metal · 3 Heaven 乾爲天 甲午 Wood Horse 4 初九 1	火7 Fire · 2 Well 水風井 乙未 Wood Goat 5 初十 6	木8 Wood · 1 Relief 雷水解 丙申 Fire Monkey 6 十一 4	金4 Metal · 9 Influence 澤山咸 丁酉 Fire Rooster 7 十二 9	水1 Water · 8 Humility 地山謙 戊戌 Earth Dog 8 十三 6
火2 Fire · 7 Observation 風地觀 己亥 Earth Pig 9 十四 2	火2 Fire · 6 Increasing 風雷益 庚子 Metal Rat 10 十五 9	水1 Water · 5 Dimming Light 地火明夷 辛丑 Metal Ox 11 十六 3	金9 Metal · 4 Fellowship 天火同人 壬寅 Water Tiger 12 十七 7	木8 Wood · 3 Marrying Maiden 雷澤歸妹 癸卯 Water Rabbit 13 十八 7	木3 Wood · 2 Opposition 火澤睽 甲辰 Wood Dragon 14 十九 2	火7 Fire · 1 Waiting 水天需 乙巳 Wood Snake 15 二十 3
金4 Metal · 9 Great Exceeding 澤風大過 丙午 Fire Horse 16 廿一 3	水6 Water · 8 Poison 山風蠱 丁未 Fire Goat 17 廿二 7	火2 Fire · 7 Dispersing 風水渙 戊申 Earth Monkey 18 廿三 6	木3 Wood · 6 Travelling 火山旅 己酉 Earth Rooster 19 廿四 8	金9 Metal · 5 Stagnation 天地否 庚戌 Metal Dog 20 廿五 9	火7 Fire · 4 Alliance 水地比 辛亥 Metal Pig 21 廿六 7	木8 Wood · 3 Thunder 震爲雷 壬子 Water Rat 22 廿七 1
水6 Water · 2 Beauty 山火賁 癸丑 Water Ox 23 廿八 8	火7 Fire · 1 Accomplished 水火既濟 甲寅 Wood Tiger 24 廿九 9	水1 Water · 9 Arriving 地澤臨 乙卯 Wood Rabbit 25 七月初一 4	金4 Metal · 8 Marsh 兌爲澤 丙辰 Fire Dragon 26 初二 1	火2 Fire · 7 Small Livestock 風天小畜 丁巳 Fire Snake 27 初三 8	木3 Wood · 6 The Cauldron 火風鼎 戊午 Earth Horse 28 初四 4	水1 Water · 5 Rising 地風升 己未 Earth Goat 29 初五 2

AUGUST 2006 丙申

Xuan Kong Element 玄空五行	雷水解 Relief	Period Luck 卦運	Monthly Star 月星
Wood 木8		4	8

SUNDAY	MONDAY	TUESDAY	WEDNESDAY	THURSDAY	FRIDAY	SATURDAY
		金4 Metal · 2 Gathering 澤地萃 壬戌 Water Dog 1 初八 4	水6 Water · 1 Peel 山地剝 癸亥 Water Pig 2 初九 6	水1 Water · 9 Earth 坤爲地 甲子 Wood Rat 3 初十 1	木3 Wood · 8 Biting 火雷噬嗑 乙丑 Wood Ox 4 十一 6	火2 Fire · 7 Family 風火家人 丙寅 Fire Tiger 5 十二 4
水6 Water · 6 Decreasing 山澤損 丁卯 Fire Rabbit 6 十三 9	金9 Metal · 5 Tread 天澤履 戊辰 Earth Dragon 7 十四 6	木8 Wood · 4 Great Strength 雷天大壯 己巳 Earth Snake 8 十五 2	木8 Wood · 3 Consistency 雷風恆 庚午 Metal Horse 9 十六 9	金9 Metal · 2 Litigation 天水訟 辛未 Metal Goat 10 十七 3	水1 Water · 1 Officer 地水師 壬申 Water Monkey 11 十八 7	火2 Fire · 9 Gradual Progress 風山漸 癸酉 Water Rooster 12 十九 7
火7 Fire · 8 Obstruction 水山蹇 甲戌 Wood Dog 13 二十 2	木3 Wood · 7 Advancement 火地晉 乙亥 Wood Pig 14 廿一 3	水6 Water · 6 Nourish 山雷頤 丙子 Fire Rat 15 廿二 3	金4 Metal · 5 Following 澤雷隨 丁丑 Fire Ox 16 廿三 7	木8 Wood · 4 Abundance 雷火豐 戊寅 Earth Tiger 17 廿四 6	火7 Fire · 3 Regulate 水澤節 己卯 Earth Rabbit 18 廿五 8	水1 Water · 2 Unity 地天泰 庚辰 Metal Dragon 19 廿六 9
木3 Wood · 1 Great Reward 火天大有 辛巳 Metal Snake 20 廿七 7	火2 Fire · 9 Wind 巽爲風 壬午 Water Horse 21 廿八 1	金4 Metal · 8 Trap 澤水困 癸未 Water Goat 22 廿九 8	木3 Wood · 7 Not Yet Accomplished 火水未濟 甲申 Wood Monkey 23 三十 9	金9 Metal · 6 Retreat 天山遯 乙酉 Wood Rooster 24 閏七月初一 4	水6 Water · 5 Mountain 艮爲山 丙戌 Fire Dog 25 初二 1	木8 Wood · 4 Delight 雷地豫 丁亥 Fire Pig 26 初三 8
火7 Fire · 3 Beginning 水雷屯 戊子 Earth Rat 27 初四 4	金9 Metal · 2 Without Wrongdoing 天雷無妄 己丑 Earth Ox 28 初五 2	木3 Wood · 1 Fire 離爲火 庚寅 Metal Tiger 29 初六 1	火2 Fire · 9 Sincerity 風澤中孚 辛卯 Metal Rabbit 30 初七 3	水6 Water · 8 Big Livestock 山天大畜 壬辰 Water Dragon 31 初八 4		

SEPTEMBER 2006 丁酉

Xuan Kong Element 玄空五行	澤山咸 Influence	Period Luck 卦運	Monthly Star 月星
Metal 金4		9	7

SUNDAY	MONDAY	TUESDAY	WEDNESDAY	THURSDAY	FRIDAY	SATURDAY
					金4 Metal Eliminating 7 澤天夬 癸巳 Water Snake 1 初九 6	金9 Metal Heaven 6 乾爲天 甲午 Wood Horse 2 初十 1
火7 Fire Well 5 水風井 乙未 Wood Goat 3 十一 6	木8 Wood Relief 4 雷水解 丙申 Fire Monkey 4 十二 4	金4 Metal Influence 3 澤山咸 丁酉 Fire Rooster 5 十三 9	水1 Water Humility 2 地山謙 戊戌 Earth Dog 6 十四 6	火2 Fire Observation 1 風地觀 己亥 Earth Pig 7 十五 2	火2 Fire Increasing 9 風雷益 庚子 Metal Rat 8 十六 9	水1 Water Dimming Light 8 地火明夷 辛丑 Metal Ox 9 十七 3
金9 Metal Fellowship 7 天火同人 壬寅 Water Tiger 10 十八 7	木8 Wood Marrying Maiden 6 雷澤歸妹 癸卯 Water Rabbit 11 十九 7	木3 Wood Opposition 5 火澤睽 甲辰 Wood Dragon 12 二十 2	火7 Fire Waiting 4 水天需 乙巳 Wood Snake 13 廿一 3	金4 Metal Great Exceeding 3 澤風大過 丙午 Fire Horse 14 廿二 3	水6 Water Poison 2 山風蠱 丁未 Fire Goat 15 廿三 7	火2 Fire Dispersing 1 風水渙 戊申 Earth Monkey 16 廿四 6
木3 Wood Travelling 9 火山旅 己酉 Earth Rooster 17 廿五 8	金9 Metal Stagnation 8 天地否 庚戌 Metal Dog 18 廿六 9	火7 Fire Alliance 7 水地比 辛亥 Metal Pig 19 廿七 7	木8 Wood Thunder 6 震爲雷 壬子 Water Rat 20 廿八 1	水6 Water Beauty 5 山火賁 癸丑 Water Ox 21 廿九 8	火7 Fire Accomplished 4 水火既濟 甲寅 Wood Tiger 22 八月初一 9	水1 Water Arriving 3 地澤臨 乙卯 Wood Rabbit 23 初二 4
金4 Metal Marsh 2 兌爲澤 丙辰 Fire Dragon 24 初三 1	火2 Fire Small Livestock 1 風天小畜 丁巳 Fire Snake 25 初四 8	木3 Wood The Cauldron 9 火風鼎 戊午 Earth Horse 26 初五 4	水1 Water Rising 8 地風升 己未 Earth Goat 27 初六 2	火7 Fire Water 7 坎爲水 庚申 Metal Monkey 28 初七 1	木8 Wood Lesser Exceeding 6 雷山小過 辛酉 Metal Rooster 29 初八 3	金4 Metal Gathering 5 澤地萃 壬戌 Water Dog 30 初九 4

OCTOBER 2006 戊戌

Xuan Kong Element 玄空五行	地山謙 Humility	Period Luck 卦運	Monthly Star 月星
Water 水1		6	6

SUNDAY	MONDAY	TUESDAY	WEDNESDAY	THURSDAY	FRIDAY	SATURDAY
水6 Water Peel 4 山地剝 癸亥 Water Pig 1 初十 6	水1 Water Earth 3 坤爲地 甲子 Wood Rat 2 十一 1	木3 Wood Biting 2 火雷噬嗑 乙丑 Wood Ox 3 十二 6	火2 Fire Family 1 風火家人 丙寅 Fire Tiger 4 十三 4	水6 Water Decreasing 9 山澤損 丁卯 Fire Rabbit 5 十四 9	金9 Metal Tread 8 天澤履 戊辰 Earth Dragon 6 十五 6	木8 Wood Great Strength 7 雷天大壯 己巳 Earth Snake 7 十六 2
木8 Wood Consistency 6 雷風恆 庚午 Metal Horse 8 十七 9	金9 Metal Litigation 5 天水訟 辛未 Metal Goat 9 十八 3	水1 Water Officer 4 地水師 壬申 Water Monkey 10 十九 7	火2 Fire Gradual Progress 3 風山漸 癸酉 Water Rooster 11 二十 7	火7 Fire Obstruction 2 水山蹇 甲戌 Wood Dog 12 廿一 2	木3 Wood Advancement 1 火地晉 乙亥 Wood Pig 13 廿二 3	水6 Water Nourish 9 山雷頤 丙子 Fire Rat 14 廿三 3
金4 Metal Following 8 澤雷隨 丁丑 Fire Ox 15 廿四 7	木8 Wood Abundance 7 雷火豐 戊寅 Earth Tiger 16 廿五 6	火7 Fire Regulate 6 水澤節 己卯 Earth Rabbit 17 廿六 8	水1 Water Unity 5 地天泰 庚辰 Metal Dragon 18 廿七 9	木3 Wood Great Reward 4 火天大有 辛巳 Metal Snake 19 廿八 7	火2 Fire Wind 3 巽爲風 壬午 Water Horse 20 廿九 1	金4 Metal Trap 2 澤水困 癸未 Water Goat 21 三十 8
木3 Wood Not Yet Accomplished 1 火水未濟 甲申 Wood Monkey 22 九月初一 9	金9 Metal Retreat 9 天山遯 乙酉 Wood Rooster 23 初二 4	水6 Water Mountain 8 艮爲山 丙戌 Fire Dog 24 初三 1	木8 Wood Delight 7 雷地豫 丁亥 Fire Pig 25 初四 8	火7 Fire Beginning 6 水雷屯 戊子 Earth Rat 26 初五 4	金9 Metal Without Wrongdoing 5 天雷無妄 己丑 Earth Ox 27 初六 2	木3 Wood Fire 4 離爲火 庚寅 Metal Tiger 28 初七 1
火2 Fire Sincerity 3 風澤中孚 辛卯 Metal Rabbit 29 初八 3	水6 Water Big Livestock 2 山天大畜 壬辰 Water Dragon 30 初九 4	金4 Metal Eliminating 1 澤天夬 癸巳 Water Snake 31 初十 6				

NOVEMBER 2006 己亥

Xuan Kong Element 玄空五行	風地觀 Observation	Period Luck 卦運	Monthly Star 月星
Fire 火2		2	5

SUNDAY	MONDAY	TUESDAY	WEDNESDAY	THURSDAY	FRIDAY	SATURDAY
			金9 Metal Heaven 9 甲午 Wood Horse 乾爲天 1 十一 1	火7 Fire Well 8 乙未 Wood Goat 水風井 2 十二 6	木8 Wood Relief 7 丙申 Fire Monkey 雷水解 3 十三 4	金4 Metal Influence 6 丁酉 Fire Rooster 澤山咸 4 十四 9
水1 Water Humility 5 戊戌 Earth Dog 地山謙 5 十五 6	火2 Fire Observation 4 己亥 Earth Pig 風地觀 6 十六 2	火2 Fire Increasing 3 庚子 Metal Rat 風雷益 7 十七 9	水1 Water Dimming Light 2 辛丑 Metal Ox 地火明夷 8 十八 3	金9 Metal Fellowship 1 壬寅 Water Tiger 天火同人 9 十九 7	木8 Wood Marrying Maiden 9 癸卯 Water Rabbit 雷澤歸妹 10 二十 7	木3 Wood Opposition 8 甲辰 Wood Dragon 火澤睽 11 廿一 2
火7 Fire Waiting 7 乙巳 Wood Snake 水天需 12 廿二 3	金4 Metal Great Exceeding 6 丙午 Fire Horse 澤風大過 13 廿三 3	水6 Water Poison 5 丁未 Fire Goat 山風蠱 14 廿四 7	火2 Fire Dispersing 4 戊申 Earth Monkey 風水渙 15 廿五 6	木3 Wood Travelling 3 己酉 Earth Rooster 火山旅 16 廿六 8	金9 Metal Stagnation 2 庚戌 Metal Dog 天地否 17 廿七 9	火7 Fire Alliance 1 辛亥 Metal Pig 水地比 18 廿八 7
木8 Wood Thunder 9 壬子 Water Rat 震爲雷 19 廿九 1	水6 Water Beauty 8 癸丑 Water Ox 山火賁 20 三十 8	火7 Fire Accomplished 7 甲寅 Wood Tiger 水火既濟 21 十月初一 9	水1 Water Arriving 6 乙卯 Wood Rabbit 地澤臨 22 初二 4	金4 Metal Marsh 5 丙辰 Fire Dragon 兑爲澤 23 初三 1	火2 Fire Small Livestock 4 丁巳 Fire Snake 風天小畜 24 初四 8	木3 Wood The Cauldron 3 戊午 Earth Horse 火風鼎 25 初五 4
水1 Water Rising 2 己未 Earth Goat 地風升 26 初六 2	火7 Fire Water 1 庚申 Metal Monkey 坎爲水 27 初七 1	木8 Wood Lesser Exceeding 9 辛酉 Metal Rooster 雷山小過 28 初八 3	金4 Metal Gathering 8 壬戌 Water Dog 澤地萃 29 初九 4	水6 Water Peel 7 癸亥 Water Pig 山地剝 30 初十 6		

DECEMBER 2006 庚子

Xuan Kong Element 玄空五行	風雷益 Increasing	Period Luck 卦運	Monthly Star 月星
Fire 火2		9	4

SUNDAY	MONDAY	TUESDAY	WEDNESDAY	THURSDAY	FRIDAY	SATURDAY
金9 Metal Heaven 7 甲午 Wood Horse 乾爲天 31 十二 1					水1 Water Earth 6 甲子 Wood Rat 坤爲地 1 十一 1	木3 Wood Biting 5 乙丑 Wood Ox 火雷噬嗑 2 十二 6
火2 Fire Family 4 丙寅 Fire Tiger 風火家人 3 十三 4	水6 Water Decreasing 3 丁卯 Fire Rabbit 山澤損 4 十四 9	金9 Metal Tread 2 戊辰 Earth Dragon 天澤履 5 十五 6	木8 Wood Great Strength 1 己巳 Earth Snake 雷天大壯 6 十六 2	木8 Wood Consistency 9 庚午 Metal Horse 雷風恆 7 十七 9	金9 Metal Litigation 8 辛未 Metal Goat 天水訟 8 十八 3	水1 Water Officer 7 壬申 Water Monkey 地水師 9 十九 7
火2 Fire Gradual Progress 6 癸酉 Water Rooster 風山漸 10 二十 7	火7 Fire Obstruction 5 甲戌 Wood Dog 水山蹇 11 廿一 2	木3 Wood Advancement 4 乙亥 Wood Pig 火地晉 12 廿二 3	水6 Water Nourish 3 丙子 Fire Rat 山雷頤 13 廿三 3	金4 Metal Following 2 丁丑 Fire Ox 澤雷隨 14 廿四 7	木8 Wood Abundance 1 戊寅 Earth Tiger 雷火豐 15 廿五 6	火7 Fire Regulate 9 己卯 Earth Rabbit 水澤節 16 廿六 8
水1 Water Unity 8 庚辰 Metal Dragon 地天泰 17 廿七 9	木3 Wood Great Reward 7 辛巳 Metal Snake 火天大有 18 廿八 7	火2 Fire Wind 6 壬午 Water Horse 巽爲風 19 廿九 1	金4 Metal Trap 5 癸未 Water Goat 澤水困 20 十一月初一 8	木3 Wood Not Yet Accomplished 4 甲申 Wood Monkey 火水未濟 21 初二 9	金9 Metal Retreat 3/7 乙酉 Wood Rooster 天山遯 22 初三 4	水6 Water Mountain 8 丙戌 Fire Dog 艮爲山 23 初四 1
木8 Wood Delight 9 丁亥 Fire Pig 雷地豫 24 初五 8	火7 Fire Beginning 1 戊子 Earth Rat 水雷屯 25 初六 4	金9 Metal Without Wrongdoing 2 己丑 Earth Ox 天雷無妄 26 初七 2	木3 Wood Fire 3 庚寅 Metal Tiger 離爲火 27 初八 1	火2 Fire Sincerity 4 辛卯 Metal Rabbit 風澤中孚 28 初九 3	水6 Water Big Livestock 5 壬辰 Water Dragon 山天大畜 29 初十 4	金4 Metal Eliminating 6 癸巳 Water Snake 澤天夬 30 十一 6

2007 丁亥

(*Ding Hai*) **Fire Pig**

2007 丁亥 *(Ding Hai)* Fire Pig

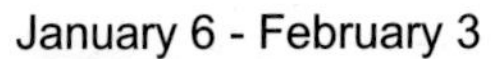

January 6 - February 3

February 4 - March 5

March 6 - April 4

April 5 - May 5

May 6 - June 5

June 6 - July 6

July 7 - August 7

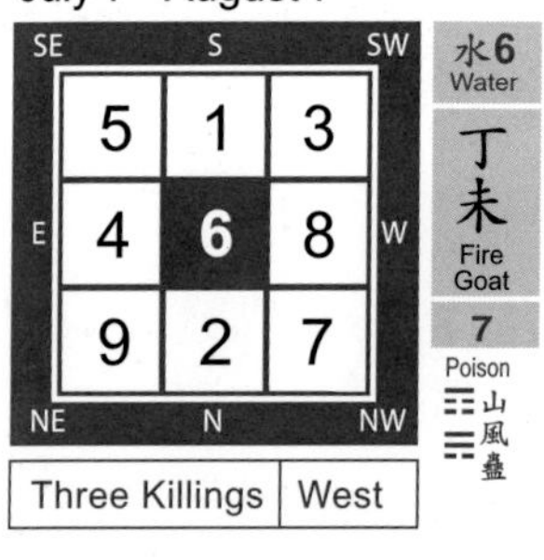

August 8 - September 7

September 8 - October 8

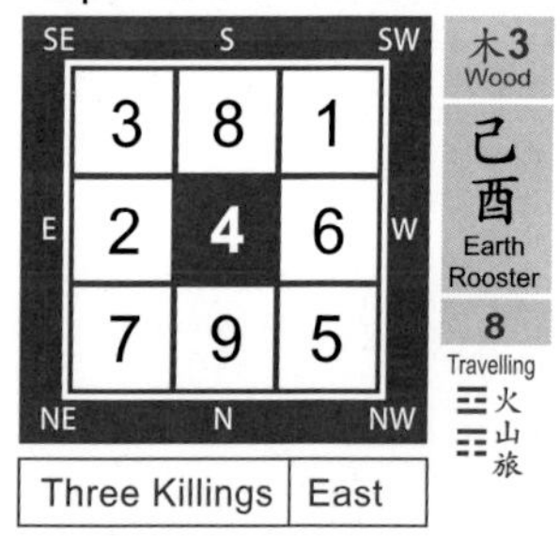

October 9 - November 7

November 8 - December 6

December 7 - January 5

JANUARY 2007 辛丑

Xuan Kong Element 玄空五行	地火明夷 Dimming Light	Period Luck 卦運	Monthly Star 月星
Water 水1		3	3

SUNDAY	MONDAY	TUESDAY	WEDNESDAY	THURSDAY	FRIDAY	SATURDAY
	火7 Fire 8 Well 水風井 乙未 Wood Goat 1 十三 6	木8 Wood 9 Relief 雷水解 丙申 Fire Monkey 2 十四 4	金4 Metal 1 Influence 澤山咸 丁酉 Fire Rooster 3 十五 9	水1 Water 2 Humility 地山謙 戊戌 Earth Dog 4 十六 6	火2 Fire 3 Observation 風地觀 己亥 Earth Pig 5 十七 2	火2 Fire 4 Increasing 風雷益 庚子 Metal Rat 6 十八 9
水1 Water 5 Dimming Light 地火明夷 辛丑 Metal Ox 7 十九 3	金9 Metal 6 Fellowship 天火同人 壬寅 Water Tiger 8 二十 7	木8 Wood 7 Marrying Maiden 雷澤歸妹 癸卯 Water Rabbit 9 廿一 7	木3 Wood 8 Opposition 火澤睽 甲辰 Wood Dragon 10 廿二 2	火7 Fire 9 Waiting 水天需 乙巳 Wood Snake 11 廿三 3	金4 Metal 1 Great Exceeding 澤風大過 丙午 Fire Horse 12 廿四 3	水6 Water 2 Poison 山風蠱 丁未 Fire Goat 13 廿五 7
火2 Fire 3 Dispersing 風水渙 戊申 Earth Monkey 14 廿六 6	木3 Wood 4 Travelling 火山旅 己酉 Earth Rooster 15 廿七 8	金9 Metal 5 Stagnation 天地否 庚戌 Metal Dog 16 廿八 9	火7 Fire 6 Alliance 水地比 辛亥 Metal Pig 17 廿九 7	木8 Wood 7 Thunder 震爲雷 壬子 Water Rat 18 三十 1	水6 Water 8 Beauty 山火賁 癸丑 Water Ox 19 十二月初一 8	火7 Fire 9 Accomplished 水火既濟 甲寅 Wood Tiger 20 初二 9
水1 Water 1 Arriving 地澤臨 乙卯 Wood Rabbit 21 初三 4	金4 Metal 2 Marsh 兌爲澤 丙辰 Fire Dragon 22 初四 1	火2 Fire 3 Small Livestock 風天小畜 丁巳 Fire Snake 23 初五 8	木3 Wood 4 The Cauldron 火風鼎 戊午 Earth Horse 24 初六 4	水1 Water 5 Rising 地風升 己未 Earth Goat 25 初七 2	火7 Fire 6 Water 坎爲水 庚申 Metal Monkey 26 初八 1	木8 Wood 7 Lesser Exceeding 雷山小過 辛酉 Metal Rooster 27 初九 3
金4 Metal 8 Gathering 澤地萃 壬戌 Water Dog 28 初十 4	水6 Water 9 Peel 山地剝 癸亥 Water Pig 29 十一 6	水1 Water 1 Earth 坤爲地 甲子 Wood Rat 30 十二 1	木3 Wood 2 Biting 火雷噬嗑 乙丑 Wood Ox 31 十三 6			

FEBRUARY 2007 壬寅

Xuan Kong Element 玄空五行	天火同人 Fellowship	Period Luck 卦運	Monthly Star 月星
Metal 金9		7	2

SUNDAY	MONDAY	TUESDAY	WEDNESDAY	THURSDAY	FRIDAY	SATURDAY
				火2 Fire 3 Family 風火家人 丙寅 Fire Tiger 1 十四 4	水6 Water 4 Decreasing 山澤損 丁卯 Fire Rabbit 2 十五 9	金9 Metal 5 Tread 天澤履 戊辰 Earth Dragon 3 十六 6
木8 Wood 6 Great Strength 雷天大壯 己巳 Earth Snake 4 十七 2	木8 Wood 7 Consistency 雷風恆 庚午 Metal Horse 5 十八 9	金9 Metal 8 Litigation 天水訟 辛未 Metal Goat 6 十九 3	水1 Water 9 Officer 地水師 壬申 Water Monkey 7 二十 7	火2 Fire 1 Gradual Progress 風山漸 癸酉 Water Rooster 8 廿一 7	火7 Fire 2 Obstruction 水山蹇 甲戌 Wood Dog 9 廿二 2	木3 Wood 3 Advancement 火地晉 乙亥 Wood Pig 10 廿三 3
水6 Water 4 Nourish 山雷頤 丙子 Fire Rat 11 廿四 3	金4 Metal 5 Following 澤雷隨 丁丑 Fire Ox 12 廿五 7	木8 Wood 6 Abundance 雷火豐 戊寅 Earth Tiger 13 廿六 6	火7 Fire 7 Regulate 水澤節 己卯 Earth Rabbit 14 廿七 8	水1 Water 8 Unity 地天泰 庚辰 Metal Dragon 15 廿八 9	木3 Wood 9 Great Reward 火天大有 辛巳 Metal Snake 16 廿九 7	火2 Fire 1 Wind 巽爲風 壬午 Water Horse 17 三十 1
金4 Metal 2 Trap 澤水困 癸未 Water Goat 18 正月初一 8	木3 Wood 3 Not Yet Accomplished 火水未濟 甲申 Wood Monkey 19 初二 9	金9 Metal 4 Retreat 天山遯 乙酉 Wood Rooster 20 初三 4	水6 Water 5 Mountain 艮爲山 丙戌 Fire Dog 21 初四 1	木8 Wood 6 Delight 雷地豫 丁亥 Fire Pig 22 初五 8	火7 Fire 7 Beginning 水雷屯 戊子 Earth Rat 23 初六 4	金9 Metal 8 Without Wrongdoing 天雷無妄 己丑 Earth Ox 24 初七 2
木3 Wood 9 Fire 離爲火 庚寅 Metal Tiger 25 初八 1	火2 Fire 1 Sincerity 風澤中孚 辛卯 Metal Rabbit 26 初九 3	水6 Water 2 Big Livestock 山天大畜 壬辰 Water Dragon 27 初十 4	金4 Metal 3 Eliminating 澤天夬 癸巳 Water Snake 28 十一 6			

MARCH 2007 癸卯

Xuan Kong Element 玄空五行	雷澤歸妹	Period Luck 卦運	Monthly Star 月星
Wood 木8	Marrying Maiden	7	1

SUNDAY	MONDAY	TUESDAY	WEDNESDAY	THURSDAY	FRIDAY	SATURDAY
				金9 Metal Heaven 4 甲午 Wood Horse 乾爲天 1 十二 1	火7 Fire Well 5 乙未 Wood Goat 水風井 2 十三 6	木8 Wood Relief 6 丙申 Fire Monkey 雷水解 3 十四 4
金4 Metal Influence 7 丁酉 Fire Rooster 澤山咸 4 十五 9	水1 Water Humility 8 戊戌 Earth Dog 地山謙 5 十六 6	火2 Fire Observation 9 己亥 Earth Pig 風地觀 6 十七 2	火2 Fire Increasing 1 庚子 Metal Rat 風雷益 7 十八 9	水1 Water Dimming Light 2 辛丑 Metal Ox 地火明夷 8 十九 3	金9 Metal Fellowship 3 壬寅 Water Tiger 天火同人 9 二十 7	木8 Wood Marrying Maiden 4 癸卯 Water Rabbit 雷澤歸妹 10 廿一 7
木3 Wood Opposition 5 甲辰 Wood Dragon 火澤睽 11 廿二 2	火7 Fire Waiting 6 乙巳 Wood Snake 水天需 12 廿三 3	金4 Metal Great Exceeding 7 丙午 Fire Horse 澤風大過 13 廿四 3	水6 Water Poison 8 丁未 Fire Goat 山風蠱 14 廿五 7	火2 Fire Dispersing 9 戊申 Earth Monkey 風水渙 15 廿六 6	木3 Wood Travelling 1 己酉 Earth Rooster 火山旅 16 廿七 8	金9 Metal Stagnation 2 庚戌 Metal Dog 天地否 17 廿八 9
火7 Fire Alliance 3 辛亥 Metal Pig 水地比 18 廿九 7	木8 Wood Thunder 4 壬子 Water Rat 震爲雷 19 二月初一 1	水6 Water Beauty 5 癸丑 Water Ox 山火賁 20 初二 8	火7 Fire Accomplished 6 甲寅 Wood Tiger 水火既濟 21 初三 9	水1 Water Arriving 7 乙卯 Wood Rabbit 地澤臨 22 初四 4	金4 Metal Marsh 8 丙辰 Fire Dragon 兑爲澤 23 初五 1	火2 Fire Small Livestock 9 丁巳 Fire Snake 風天小畜 24 初六 8
木3 Wood The Cauldron 1 戊午 Earth Horse 火風鼎 25 初七 4	水1 Water Rising 2 己未 Earth Goat 地風升 26 初八 2	火7 Fire Water 3 庚申 Metal Monkey 坎爲水 27 初九 1	木8 Wood Lesser Exceeding 4 辛酉 Metal Rooster 雷山小過 28 初十 3	金4 Metal Gathering 5 壬戌 Water Dog 澤地萃 29 十一 4	水6 Water Peel 6 癸亥 Water Pig 山地剝 30 十二 6	水1 Water Earth 7 甲子 Wood Rat 坤爲地 31 十三 1

APRIL 2007 甲辰

Xuan Kong Element 玄空五行	火澤睽	Period Luck 卦運	Monthly Star 月星
Wood 木3	Opposition	2	9

SUNDAY	MONDAY	TUESDAY	WEDNESDAY	THURSDAY	FRIDAY	SATURDAY
木3 Wood Biting 8 乙丑 Wood Ox 火雷噬嗑 1 十四 6	火2 Fire Family 9 丙寅 Fire Tiger 風火家人 2 十五 4	水6 Water Decreasing 1 丁卯 Fire Rabbit 山澤損 3 十六 9	金9 Metal Tread 2 戊辰 Earth Dragon 天澤履 4 十七 6	木8 Wood Great Strength 3 己巳 Earth Snake 雷天大壯 5 十八 2	木8 Wood Consistency 4 庚午 Metal Horse 雷風恆 6 十九 9	金9 Metal Litigation 5 辛未 Metal Goat 天水訟 7 二十 3
水1 Water Officer 6 壬申 Water Monkey 地水師 8 廿一 7	火2 Fire Gradual Progress 7 癸酉 Water Rooster 風山漸 9 廿二 7	火7 Fire Obstruction 8 甲戌 Wood Dog 水山蹇 10 廿三 2	木3 Wood Advancement 9 乙亥 Wood Pig 火地晉 11 廿四 3	水6 Water Nourish 1 丙子 Fire Rat 山雷頤 12 廿五 3	金4 Metal Following 2 丁丑 Fire Ox 澤雷隨 13 廿六 7	木8 Wood Abundance 3 戊寅 Earth Tiger 雷火豐 14 廿七 6
火7 Fire Regulate 4 己卯 Earth Rabbit 水澤節 15 廿八 8	水1 Water Unity 5 庚辰 Metal Dragon 地天泰 16 廿九 9	木3 Wood Great Reward 6 辛巳 Metal Snake 火天大有 17 三月初一 7	火2 Fire Wind 7 壬午 Water Horse 巽爲風 18 初二 1	金4 Metal Trap 8 癸未 Water Goat 澤水困 19 初三 8	木3 Wood Not Yet Accomplished 9 甲申 Wood Monkey 火水未濟 20 初四 9	金9 Metal Retreat 1 乙酉 Wood Rooster 天山遯 21 初五 4
水6 Water Mountain 2 丙戌 Fire Dog 艮爲山 22 初六 1	木8 Wood Delight 3 丁亥 Fire Pig 雷地豫 23 初七 8	火7 Fire Beginning 4 戊子 Earth Rat 水雷屯 24 初八 4	金9 Metal Without Wrongdoing 5 己丑 Earth Ox 天雷無妄 25 初九 2	木3 Wood Fire 6 庚寅 Metal Tiger 離爲火 26 初十 1	火2 Fire Sincerity 7 辛卯 Metal Rabbit 風澤中孚 27 十一 3	水6 Water Big Livestock 8 壬辰 Water Dragon 山天大畜 28 十二 4
金4 Metal Eliminating 9 癸巳 Water Snake 澤天夬 29 十三 6	金9 Metal Heaven 1 甲午 Wood Horse 乾爲天 30 十四 1					

MAY 2007 乙巳

Xuan Kong Element 玄空五行	水天需 Waiting	Period Luck 卦運	Monthly Star 月星
Fire 火7		3	8

SUNDAY	MONDAY	TUESDAY	WEDNESDAY	THURSDAY	FRIDAY	SATURDAY
		火7 Fire Well 水風井 2 乙未 Wood Goat 6 **1** 十五	木8 Wood Relief 雷水解 3 丙申 Fire Monkey 4 **2** 十六	金4 Metal Influence 澤山咸 4 丁酉 Fire Rooster 9 **3** 十七	水1 Water Humility 地山謙 5 戊戌 Earth Dog 6 **4** 十八	火2 Fire Observation 風地觀 6 己亥 Earth Pig 2 **5** 十九
火2 Fire Increasing 風雷益 7 庚子 Metal Rat 9 **6** 二十	水1 Water Dimming Light 地火明夷 8 辛丑 Metal Ox 3 **7** 廿一	金9 Metal Fellowship 天火同人 9 壬寅 Water Tiger 7 **8** 廿二	木8 Wood Marrying Maiden 雷澤歸妹 1 癸卯 Water Rabbit 7 **9** 廿三	木3 Wood Opposition 火澤睽 2 甲辰 Wood Dragon 2 **10** 廿四	火7 Fire Waiting 水天需 3 乙巳 Wood Snake 3 **11** 廿五	金4 Metal Great Exceeding 澤風大過 4 丙午 Fire Horse 3 **12** 廿六
水6 Water Poison 山風蠱 5 丁未 Fire Goat 7 **13** 廿七	火2 Fire Dispersing 風水渙 6 戊申 Earth Monkey 6 **14** 廿八	木3 Wood Travelling 火山旅 7 己酉 Earth Rooster 8 **15** 廿九	金9 Metal Stagnation 天地否 8 庚戌 Metal Dog 9 **16** 三十	火7 Fire Alliance 水地比 9 辛亥 Metal Pig 7 **17** 四月初一	木8 Wood Thunder 震爲雷 1 壬子 Water Rat 1 **18** 初二	水6 Water Beauty 山火賁 2 癸丑 Water Ox 8 **19** 初三
火7 Fire Accomplished 水火既濟 3 甲寅 Wood Tiger 9 **20** 初四	水1 Water Arriving 地澤臨 4 乙卯 Wood Rabbit 4 **21** 初五	金4 Metal Marsh 兌爲澤 5 丙辰 Fire Dragon 1 **22** 初六	火2 Fire Small Livestock 風天小畜 6 丁巳 Fire Snake 8 **23** 初七	木3 Wood The Cauldron 火風鼎 7 戊午 Earth Horse 4 **24** 初八	水1 Water Rising 地風升 8 己未 Earth Goat 2 **25** 初九	火7 Fire Water 坎爲水 9 庚申 Metal Monkey 1 **26** 初十
木8 Wood Lesser Exceeding 雷山小過 1 辛酉 Metal Rooster 3 **27** 十一	金4 Metal Gathering 澤地萃 2 壬戌 Water Dog 4 **28** 十二	水6 Water Peel 山地剝 3 癸亥 Water Pig 6 **29** 十三	水1 Water Earth 坤爲地 4 甲子 Wood Rat 1 **30** 十四	木3 Wood Biting 火雷噬嗑 5 乙丑 Wood Ox 6 **31** 十五		

JUNE 2007 丙午

Xuan Kong Element 玄空五行	澤風大過 Great Exceeding	Period Luck 卦運	Monthly Star 月星
Metal 金4		3	7

SUNDAY	MONDAY	TUESDAY	WEDNESDAY	THURSDAY	FRIDAY	SATURDAY
					火2 Fire Family 風火家人 6 丙寅 Fire Tiger 4 **1** 十六	水6 Water Decreasing 山澤損 7 丁卯 Fire Rabbit 9 **2** 十七
金9 Metal Tread 天澤履 8 戊辰 Earth Dragon 6 **3** 十八	木8 Wood Great Strength 雷天大壯 9 己巳 Earth Snake 2 **4** 十九	木8 Wood Consistency 雷風恆 1 庚午 Metal Horse 9 **5** 二十	金9 Metal Litigation 天水訟 2 辛未 Metal Goat 3 **6** 廿一	水1 Water Officer 地水師 3 壬申 Water Monkey 7 **7** 廿二	火2 Fire Gradual Progress 風山漸 4 癸酉 Water Rooster 7 **8** 廿三	火7 Fire Obstruction 水山蹇 5 甲戌 Wood Dog 2 **9** 廿四
木3 Wood Advancement 火地晉 6 乙亥 Wood Pig 3 **10** 廿五	水6 Water Nourish 山雷頤 7 丙子 Fire Rat 3 **11** 廿六	金4 Metal Following 澤雷隨 8 丁丑 Fire Ox 7 **12** 廿七	木8 Wood Abundance 雷火豐 9 戊寅 Earth Tiger 6 **13** 廿八	火7 Fire Regulate 水澤節 1 己卯 Earth Rabbit 8 **14** 廿九	水1 Water Unity 地天泰 2 庚辰 Metal Dragon 9 **15** 五月初一	木3 Wood Great Reward 火天大有 3 辛巳 Metal Snake 7 **16** 初二
火2 Fire Wind 巽爲風 4 壬午 Water Horse 1 **17** 初三	金4 Metal Trap 澤水困 5 癸未 Water Goat 8 **18** 初四	木3 Wood Not Yet Accomplished 火水未濟 6 甲申 Wood Monkey 9 **19** 初五	金9 Metal Retreat 天山遯 7 乙酉 Wood Rooster 4 **20** 初六	水6 Water Mountain 艮爲山 8 丙戌 Fire Dog 1 **21** 初七	木8 Wood Delight 雷地豫 9/1 丁亥 Fire Pig 8 **22** 初八	火7 Fire Beginning 水雷屯 9 戊子 Earth Rat 4 **23** 初九
金9 Metal Without Wrongdoing 天雷無妄 8 己丑 Earth Ox 2 **24** 初十	木3 Wood Fire 離爲火 7 庚寅 Metal Tiger 1 **25** 十一	火2 Fire Sincerity 風澤中孚 6 辛卯 Metal Rabbit 3 **26** 十二	水6 Water Big Livestock 山天大畜 5 壬辰 Water Dragon 4 **27** 十三	金4 Metal Eliminating 澤天夬 4 癸巳 Water Snake 6 **28** 十四	金9 Metal Heaven 乾爲天 3 甲午 Wood Horse 1 **29** 十五	火7 Fire Well 水風井 2 乙未 Wood Goat 6 **30** 十六

JULY 2007 丁未

Xuan Kong Element 玄空五行	山風蠱 Poison	Period Luck 卦運	Monthly Star 月星
Water 水6		7	6

SUNDAY	MONDAY	TUESDAY	WEDNESDAY	THURSDAY	FRIDAY	SATURDAY
木8 Wood Relief 1 丙申 Fire Monkey 雷水解 **1** 十七 4	金4 Metal Influence 9 丁酉 Fire Rooster 澤山咸 **2** 十八 9	水1 Water Humility 8 戊戌 Earth Dog 地山謙 **3** 十九 6	火2 Fire Observation 7 己亥 Earth Pig 風地觀 **4** 二十 2	火2 Fire Increasing 6 庚子 Metal Rat 風雷益 **5** 廿一 9	水1 Water Dimming Light 5 辛丑 Metal Ox 地火明夷 **6** 廿二 3	金9 Metal Fellowship 4 壬寅 Water Tiger 天火同人 **7** 廿三 7
木8 Wood Marrying Maiden 3 癸卯 Water Rabbit 雷澤歸妹 **8** 廿四 7	木3 Wood Opposition 2 甲辰 Wood Dragon 火澤睽 **9** 廿五 2	火7 Fire Waiting 1 乙巳 Wood Snake 水天需 **10** 廿六 3	金4 Metal Great Exceeding 9 丙午 Fire Horse 澤風大過 **11** 廿七 3	水6 Water Poison 8 丁未 Fire Goat 山風蠱 **12** 廿八 7	火2 Fire Dispersing 7 戊申 Earth Monkey 風水渙 **13** 廿九 6	木3 Wood Travelling 6 己酉 Earth Rooster 火山旅 **14** 六月初一 8
金9 Metal Stagnation 5 庚戌 Metal Dog 天地否 **15** 初二 9	火7 Fire Alliance 4 辛亥 Metal Pig 水地比 **16** 初三 7	木8 Wood Thunder 3 壬子 Water Rat 震爲雷 **17** 初四 1	水6 Water Beauty 2 癸丑 Water Ox 山火賁 **18** 初五 8	火7 Fire Accomplished 1 甲寅 Wood Tiger 水火既濟 **19** 初六 9	水1 Water Arriving 9 乙卯 Wood Rabbit 地澤臨 **20** 初七 4	金4 Metal Marsh 8 丙辰 Fire Dragon 兑爲澤 **21** 初八 1
火2 Fire Small Livestock 7 丁巳 Fire Snake 風天小畜 **22** 初九 8	木3 Wood The Cauldron 6 戊午 Earth Horse 火風鼎 **23** 初十 4	水1 Water Rising 5 己未 Earth Goat 地風升 **24** 十一 2	火7 Fire Water 4 庚申 Metal Monkey 坎爲水 **25** 十二 1	木8 Wood Lesser Exceeding 3 辛酉 Metal Rooster 雷山小過 **26** 十三 3	金4 Metal Gathering 2 壬戌 Water Dog 澤地萃 **27** 十四 4	水6 Water Peel 1 癸亥 Water Pig 山地剝 **28** 十五 6
水1 Water Earth 9 甲子 Wood Rat 坤爲地 **29** 十六 1	木3 Wood Biting 8 乙丑 Wood Ox 火雷噬嗑 **30** 十七 6	火2 Fire Family 7 丙寅 Fire Tiger 風火家人 **31** 十八 4				

AUGUST 2007 戊申

Xuan Kong Element 玄空五行	風水渙 Dispersing	Period Luck 卦運	Monthly Star 月星
Fire 火2		6	5

SUNDAY	MONDAY	TUESDAY	WEDNESDAY	THURSDAY	FRIDAY	SATURDAY
			水6 Water Decreasing 6 丁卯 Fire Rabbit 山澤損 **1** 十九 9	金9 Metal Tread 5 戊辰 Earth Dragon 天澤履 **2** 二十 6	木8 Wood Great Strength 4 己巳 Earth Snake 雷天大壯 **3** 廿一 2	木8 Wood Consistency 3 庚午 Metal Horse 雷風恒 **4** 廿二 9
金9 Metal Litigation 2 辛未 Metal Goat 天水訟 **5** 廿三 3	水1 Water Officer 1 壬申 Water Monkey 地水師 **6** 廿四 7	火2 Fire Gradual Progress 9 癸酉 Water Rooster 風山漸 **7** 廿五 7	火7 Fire Obstruction 8 甲戌 Wood Dog 水山蹇 **8** 廿六 2	木3 Wood Advancement 7 乙亥 Wood Pig 火地晉 **9** 廿七 3	水6 Water Nourish 6 丙子 Fire Rat 山雷頤 **10** 廿八 3	金4 Metal Following 5 丁丑 Fire Ox 澤雷隨 **11** 廿九 7
木8 Wood Abundance 4 戊寅 Earth Tiger 雷火豐 **12** 三十 6	火7 Fire Regulate 3 己卯 Earth Rabbit 水澤節 **13** 七月初一 8	水1 Water Unity 2 庚辰 Metal Dragon 地天泰 **14** 初二 9	木3 Wood Great Reward 1 辛巳 Metal Snake 火天大有 **15** 初三 7	火2 Fire Wind 9 壬午 Water Horse 巽爲風 **16** 初四 1	金4 Metal Trap 8 癸未 Water Goat 澤水困 **17** 初五 8	木3 Wood Not Yet Accomplished 7 甲申 Wood Monkey 火水未濟 **18** 初六 9
金9 Metal Retreat 6 乙酉 Wood Rooster 天山遯 **19** 初七 4	水6 Water Mountain 5 丙戌 Fire Dog 艮爲山 **20** 初八 1	木8 Wood Delight 4 丁亥 Fire Pig 雷地豫 **21** 初九 8	火7 Fire Beginning 3 戊子 Earth Rat 水雷屯 **22** 初十 4	金9 Metal Without Wrongdoing 2 己丑 Earth Ox 天雷無妄 **23** 十一 2	木3 Wood Fire 1 庚寅 Metal Tiger 離爲火 **24** 十二 1	火2 Fire Sincerity 9 辛卯 Metal Rabbit 風澤中孚 **25** 十三 3
水6 Water Big Livestock 8 壬辰 Water Dragon 山天大畜 **26** 十四 4	金4 Metal Eliminating 7 癸巳 Water Snake 澤天夬 **27** 十五 6	金9 Metal Heaven 6 甲午 Wood Horse 乾爲天 **28** 十六 1	火7 Fire Well 5 乙未 Wood Goat 水風井 **29** 十七 6	木8 Wood Relief 4 丙申 Fire Monkey 雷水解 **30** 十八 4	金4 Metal Influence 3 丁酉 Fire Rooster 澤山咸 **31** 十九 9	

SEPTEMBER 2007 己酉

Xuan Kong Element 玄空五行	火山旅 Travelling	Period Luck 卦運	Monthly Star 月星
Wood 木3		8	4

SUNDAY	MONDAY	TUESDAY	WEDNESDAY	THURSDAY	FRIDAY	SATURDAY
水6 Water 9 Decreasing 山澤損 丁卯 Fire Rabbit 9 30 二十						水1 Water 2 Humility 地山謙 戊戌 Earth Dog 6 1 二十
火2 Fire 1 Observation 風地觀 己亥 Earth Pig 2 2 廿一	火2 Fire 9 Increasing 風雷益 庚子 Metal Rat 9 3 廿二	水1 Water 8 Dimming Light 地火明夷 辛丑 Metal Ox 3 4 廿三	金9 Metal 7 Fellowship 天火同人 壬寅 Water Tiger 7 5 廿四	木8 Wood 6 Marrying Maiden 雷澤歸妹 癸卯 Water Rabbit 7 6 廿五	木3 Wood 5 Opposition 火澤睽 甲辰 Wood Dragon 2 7 廿六	火7 Fire 4 Waiting 水天需 乙巳 Wood Snake 3 8 廿七
金4 Metal 3 Great Exceeding 澤風大過 丙午 Fire Horse 3 9 廿八	水6 Water 2 Poison 山風蠱 丁未 Fire Goat 7 10 廿九	火2 Fire 1 Dispersing 風水渙 戊申 Earth Monkey 6 11 八月初一	木3 Wood 9 Travelling 火山旅 己酉 Earth Rooster 8 12 初二	金9 Metal 8 Stagnation 天地否 庚戌 Metal Dog 9 13 初三	火7 Fire 7 Alliance 水地比 辛亥 Metal Pig 7 14 初四	木8 Wood 6 Thunder 震爲雷 壬子 Water Rat 1 15 初五
水6 Water 5 Beauty 山火賁 癸丑 Water Ox 8 16 初六	火7 Fire 4 Accomplished 水火既濟 甲寅 Wood Tiger 9 17 初七	水1 Water 3 Arriving 地澤臨 乙卯 Wood Rabbit 4 18 初八	金4 Metal 2 Marsh 兑爲澤 丙辰 Fire Dragon 1 19 初九	火2 Fire 1 Small Livestock 風天小畜 丁巳 Fire Snake 8 20 初十	木3 Wood 9 The Cauldron 火風鼎 戊午 Earth Horse 4 21 十一	水1 Water 8 Rising 地風升 己未 Earth Goat 2 22 十二
火7 Fire 7 Water 坎爲水 庚申 Metal Monkey 1 23 十三	木8 Wood 6 Lesser Exceeding 雷山小過 辛酉 Metal Rooster 3 24 十四	金4 Metal 5 Gathering 澤地萃 壬戌 Water Dog 4 25 十五	水6 Water 4 Peel 山地剝 癸亥 Water Pig 6 26 十六	水1 Water 3 Earth 坤爲地 甲子 Wood Rat 1 27 十七	木3 Wood 2 Biting 火雷噬嗑 乙丑 Wood Ox 6 28 十八	火2 Fire 1 Family 風火家人 丙寅 Fire Tiger 4 29 十九

OCTOBER 2007 庚戌

Xuan Kong Element 玄空五行	天地否 Stagnation	Period Luck 卦運	Monthly Star 月星
Metal 金9		9	3

SUNDAY	MONDAY	TUESDAY	WEDNESDAY	THURSDAY	FRIDAY	SATURDAY
	金9 Metal 8 Tread 天澤履 戊辰 Earth Dragon 6 1 廿一	木8 Wood 7 Great Strength 雷天大壯 己巳 Earth Snake 2 2 廿二	木8 Wood 6 Consistency 雷風恆 庚午 Metal Horse 9 3 廿三	金9 Metal 5 Litigation 天水訟 辛未 Metal Goat 3 4 廿四	水1 Water 4 Officer 地水師 壬申 Water Monkey 7 5 廿五	火2 Fire 3 Gradual Progress 風山漸 癸酉 Water Rooster 7 6 廿六
火7 Fire 2 Obstruction 水山蹇 甲戌 Wood Dog 2 7 廿七	木3 Wood 1 Advancement 火地晉 乙亥 Wood Pig 3 8 廿八	水6 Water 9 Nourish 山雷頤 丙子 Fire Rat 3 9 廿九	金4 Metal 8 Following 澤雷隨 丁丑 Fire Ox 7 10 三十	木8 Wood 7 Abundance 雷火豐 戊寅 Earth Tiger 6 11 九月初一	火7 Fire 6 Regulate 水澤節 己卯 Earth Rabbit 8 12 初二	水1 Water 5 Unity 地天泰 庚辰 Metal Dragon 9 13 初三
木3 Wood 4 Great Reward 火天大有 辛巳 Metal Snake 7 14 初四	火2 Fire 3 Wind 巽爲風 壬午 Water Horse 1 15 初五	金4 Metal 2 Trap 澤水困 癸未 Water Goat 8 16 初六	木3 Wood 1 Not Yet Accomplished 火水未濟 甲申 Wood Monkey 9 17 初七	金9 Metal 9 Retreat 天山遯 乙酉 Wood Rooster 4 18 初八	水6 Water 8 Mountain 艮爲山 丙戌 Fire Dog 1 19 初九	木8 Wood 7 Delight 雷地豫 丁亥 Fire Pig 8 20 初十
火7 Fire 6 Beginning 水雷屯 戊子 Earth Rat 4 21 十一	金9 Metal 5 Without Wrongdoing 天雷無妄 己丑 Earth Ox 2 22 十二	木3 Wood 4 Fire 離爲火 庚寅 Metal Tiger 1 23 十三	火2 Fire 3 Sincerity 風澤中孚 辛卯 Metal Rabbit 3 24 十四	水6 Water 2 Big Livestock 山天大畜 壬辰 Water Dragon 4 25 十五	金4 Metal 1 Eliminating 澤天夬 癸巳 Water Snake 6 26 十六	金9 Metal 9 Heaven 乾爲天 甲午 Wood Horse 1 27 十七
火7 Fire 8 Well 水風井 乙未 Wood Goat 6 28 十八	木8 Wood 7 Relief 雷水解 丙申 Fire Monkey 4 29 十九	金4 Metal 6 Influence 澤山咸 丁酉 Fire Rooster 9 30 二十	水1 Water 5 Humility 地山謙 戊戌 Earth Dog 6 31 廿一			

NOVEMBER 2007 辛亥

Xuan Kong Element 玄空五行	水地比 Alliance	Period Luck 卦運	Monthly Star 月星
Fire 火7		7	2

SUNDAY	MONDAY	TUESDAY	WEDNESDAY	THURSDAY	FRIDAY	SATURDAY
				火2 Fire 己亥 Earth Pig Observation 風地觀 1 廿二 2 (4)	火2 Fire 庚子 Metal Rat Increasing 風雷益 2 廿三 9 (3)	水1 Water 辛丑 Metal Ox Dimming Light 地火明夷 3 廿四 3 (2)
金9 Metal 壬寅 Water Tiger Fellowship 天火同人 4 廿五 7 (1)	木8 Wood 癸卯 Water Rabbit Marrying Maiden 雷澤歸妹 5 廿六 7 (9)	木3 Wood 甲辰 Wood Dragon Opposition 火澤睽 6 廿七 2 (8)	火7 Fire 乙巳 Wood Snake Waiting 水天需 7 廿八 3 (7)	金4 Metal 丙午 Fire Horse Great Exceeding 澤風大過 8 廿九 3 (6)	水6 Water 丁未 Fire Goat Poison 山風蠱 9 三十 7 (5)	火2 Fire 戊申 Earth Monkey Dispersing 風水渙 10 十月初一 6 (4)
木3 Wood 己酉 Earth Rooster Travelling 火山旅 11 初二 8 (3)	金9 Metal 庚戌 Metal Dog Stagnation 天地否 12 初三 9 (2)	火7 Fire 辛亥 Metal Pig Alliance 水地比 13 初四 7 (1)	木8 Wood 壬子 Water Rat Thunder 震為雷 14 初五 1 (9)	水6 Water 癸丑 Water Ox Beauty 山火賁 15 初六 8 (8)	火7 Fire 甲寅 Wood Tiger Accomplished 水火既濟 16 初七 9 (7)	水1 Water 乙卯 Wood Rabbit Arriving 地澤臨 17 初八 4 (6)
金4 Metal 丙辰 Fire Dragon Marsh 兌為澤 18 初九 1 (5)	火2 Fire 丁巳 Fire Snake Small Livestock 風天小畜 19 初十 8 (4)	木3 Wood 戊午 Earth Horse The Cauldron 火風鼎 20 十一 4 (3)	水1 Water 己未 Earth Goat Rising 地風升 21 十二 2 (2)	火7 Fire 庚申 Metal Monkey Water 坎為水 22 十三 1 (1)	木8 Wood 辛酉 Metal Rooster Lesser Exceeding 雷山小過 23 十四 3 (9)	金4 Metal 壬戌 Water Dog Gathering 澤地萃 24 十五 4 (8)
水6 Water 癸亥 Water Pig Peel 山地剝 25 十六 6 (7)	水1 Water 甲子 Wood Rat Earth 坤為地 26 十七 1 (6)	木3 Wood 乙丑 Wood Ox Biting 火雷噬嗑 27 十八 6 (5)	火2 Fire 丙寅 Fire Tiger Family 風火家人 28 十九 4 (4)	水6 Water 丁卯 Fire Rabbit Decreasing 山澤損 29 二十 9 (3)	金9 Metal 戊辰 Earth Dragon Tread 天澤履 30 廿一 6 (2)	

DECEMBER 2007 壬子

Xuan Kong Element 玄空五行	震為雷 Thunder	Period Luck 卦運	Monthly Star 月星
Wood 木8		1	1

SUNDAY	MONDAY	TUESDAY	WEDNESDAY	THURSDAY	FRIDAY	SATURDAY
水1 Water 戊戌 Earth Dog Humility 地山謙 30 廿一 6 (2)	火2 Fire 己亥 Earth Pig Observation 風地觀 31 廿二 2 (3)					木8 Wood 己巳 Earth Snake Great Strength 雷天大壯 1 廿二 2 (1)
木8 Wood 庚午 Metal Horse Consistency 雷風恆 2 廿三 9 (9)	金9 Metal 辛未 Metal Goat Litigation 天水訟 3 廿四 3 (8)	水1 Water 壬申 Water Monkey Officer 地水師 4 廿五 7 (7)	火2 Fire 癸酉 Water Rooster Gradual Progress 風山漸 5 廿六 7 (6)	火7 Fire 甲戌 Wood Dog Obstruction 水山蹇 6 廿七 2 (5)	木3 Wood 乙亥 Wood Pig Advancement 火地晉 7 廿八 3 (4)	水6 Water 丙子 Fire Rat Nourish 山雷頤 8 廿九 3 (3)
金4 Metal 丁丑 Fire Ox Following 澤雷隨 9 三十 7 (2)	木8 Wood 戊寅 Earth Tiger Abundance 雷火豐 10 十一月初一 6 (1)	火7 Fire 己卯 Earth Rabbit Regulate 水澤節 11 初二 8 (9)	水1 Water 庚辰 Metal Dragon Unity 地天泰 12 初三 9 (8)	木3 Wood 辛巳 Metal Snake Great Reward 火天大有 13 初四 7 (7)	火2 Fire 壬午 Water Horse Wind 巽為風 14 初五 1 (6)	金4 Metal 癸未 Water Goat Trap 澤水困 15 初六 8 (5)
木3 Wood 甲申 Wood Monkey Not Yet Accomplished 火水未濟 16 初七 9 (4)	金9 Metal 乙酉 Wood Rooster Retreat 天山遯 17 初八 4 (3)	水6 Water 丙戌 Fire Dog Mountain 艮為山 18 初九 1 (2)	木8 Wood 丁亥 Fire Pig Delight 雷地豫 19 初十 8 (1)	火7 Fire 戊子 Earth Rat Beginning 水雷屯 20 十一 4 (9)	金9 Metal 己丑 Earth Ox Without Wrongdoing 天雷無妄 21 十二 2 (8)	木3 Wood 庚寅 Metal Tiger Fire 離為火 22 十三 1 (7/3)
火2 Fire 辛卯 Metal Rabbit Sincerity 風澤中孚 23 十四 3 (4)	水6 Water 壬辰 Water Dragon Big Livestock 山天大畜 24 十五 4 (5)	金4 Metal 癸巳 Water Snake Eliminating 澤天夬 25 十六 6 (6)	金9 Metal 甲午 Wood Horse Heaven 乾為天 26 十七 1 (7)	火7 Fire 乙未 Wood Goat Well 水風井 27 十八 6 (8)	木8 Wood 丙申 Fire Monkey Relief 雷水解 28 十九 4 (9)	金4 Metal 丁酉 Fire Rooster Influence 澤山咸 29 二十 9 (1)

2008 戊子

(*Wu Zi*) Earth Rat

2008 戊子 *(Wu Zi)* Earth Rat

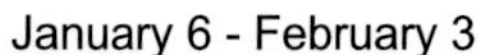

January 6 - February 3

February 4 - March 4

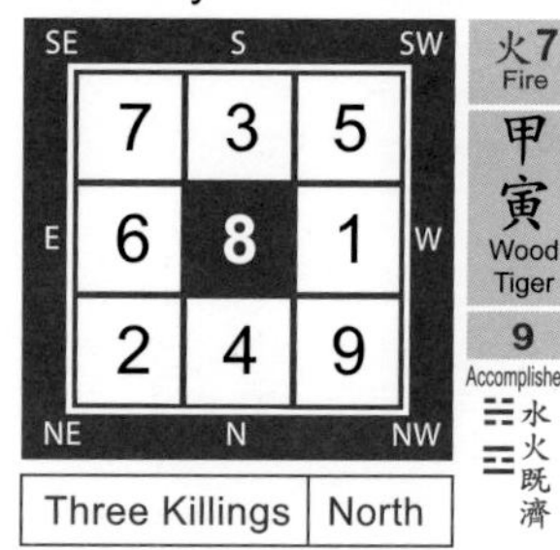

March 5 - April 3

April 4 - May 4

May 5 - June 4

June 5 - July 6

July 7 - August 6

August 7 - September 6

September 7 - October 7

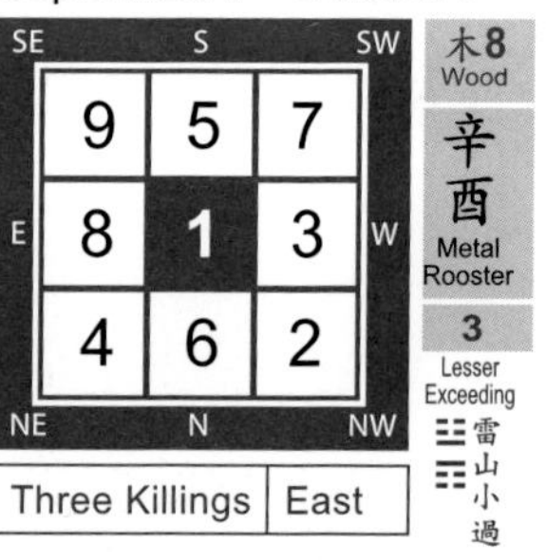

October 8 - November 6

November 7 - December 6

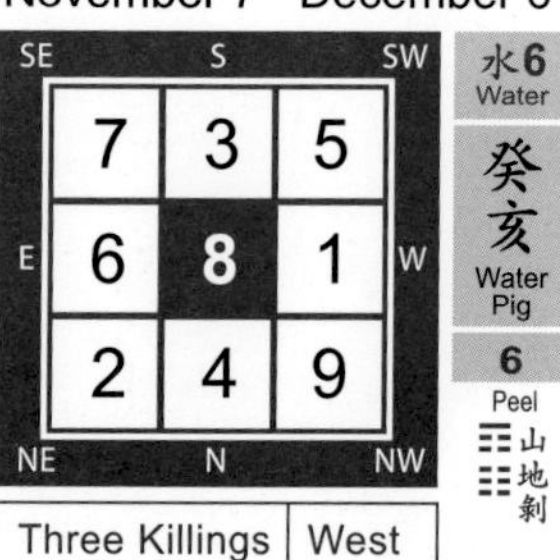

December 7 - January 4

JANUARY 2008 癸丑

Xuan Kong Element 玄空五行	山火賁 Beauty	Period Luck 卦運	Monthly Star 月星
Water 水6	☶☲	8	9

SUNDAY	MONDAY	TUESDAY	WEDNESDAY	THURSDAY	FRIDAY	SATURDAY
		4 火2 Fire Increasing 風雷益 庚子 Metal Rat 1 廿三 9	5 水1 Water Dimming Light 地火明夷 辛丑 Metal Ox 2 廿四 3	6 金9 Metal Fellowship 天火同人 壬寅 Water Tiger 3 廿五 7	7 木8 Wood Marrying Maiden 雷澤歸妹 癸卯 Water Rabbit 4 廿六 7	8 木3 Wood Opposition 火澤睽 甲辰 Wood Dragon 5 廿七 2
9 火7 Fire Waiting 水天需 乙巳 Wood Snake 6 廿八 3	1 金4 Metal Great Exceeding 澤風大過 丙午 Fire Horse 7 廿九 3	2 水6 Water Poison 山風蠱 丁未 Fire Goat 8 十二月初一 7	3 火2 Fire Dispersing 風水渙 戊申 Earth Monkey 9 初二 6	4 木3 Wood Travelling 火山旅 己酉 Earth Rooster 10 初三 8	5 金9 Metal Stagnation 天地否 庚戌 Metal Dog 11 初四 9	6 火7 Fire Alliance 水地比 辛亥 Metal Pig 12 初五 7
7 木8 Wood Thunder 震爲雷 壬子 Water Rat 13 初六 1	8 水6 Water Beauty 山火賁 癸丑 Water Ox 14 初七 8	9 火7 Fire Accomplished 水火既濟 甲寅 Wood Tiger 15 初八 9	1 水1 Water Arriving 地澤臨 乙卯 Wood Rabbit 16 初九 4	2 金4 Metal Marsh 兌爲澤 丙辰 Fire Dragon 17 初十 1	3 火2 Fire Small Livestock 風天小畜 丁巳 Fire Snake 18 十一 8	4 木3 Wood The Cauldron 火風鼎 戊午 Earth Horse 19 十二 4
5 水1 Water Rising 地風升 己未 Earth Goat 20 十三 2	6 火7 Fire Water 坎爲水 庚申 Metal Monkey 21 十四 1	7 木8 Wood Lesser Exceeding 雷山小過 辛酉 Metal Rooster 22 十五 3	8 金4 Metal Gathering 澤地萃 壬戌 Water Dog 23 十六 4	9 水6 Water Peel 山地剝 癸亥 Water Pig 24 十七 6	1 水1 Water Earth 坤爲地 甲子 Wood Rat 25 十八 1	2 木3 Wood Biting 火雷噬嗑 乙丑 Wood Ox 26 十九 6
3 火2 Fire Family 風火家人 丙寅 Fire Tiger 27 二十 4	4 水6 Water Decreasing 山澤損 丁卯 Fire Rabbit 28 廿一 9	5 金9 Metal Tread 天澤履 戊辰 Earth Dragon 29 廿二 6	6 木8 Wood Great Strength 雷天大壯 己巳 Earth Snake 30 廿三 2	7 木8 Wood Consistency 雷風恆 庚午 Metal Horse 31 廿四 9		

FEBRUARY 2008 甲寅

Xuan Kong Element 玄空五行	水火既濟 Accomplished	Period Luck 卦運	Monthly Star 月星
Fire 火7	☵☲	9	8

SUNDAY	MONDAY	TUESDAY	WEDNESDAY	THURSDAY	FRIDAY	SATURDAY
					8 金9 Metal Litigation 天水訟 辛未 Metal Goat 1 廿五 3	9 水1 Water Officer 地水師 壬申 Water Monkey 2 廿六 7
1 火2 Fire Gradual Progress 風山漸 癸酉 Water Rooster 3 廿七 7	2 火7 Fire Obstruction 水山蹇 甲戌 Wood Dog 4 廿八 2	3 木3 Wood Advancement 火地晉 乙亥 Wood Pig 5 廿九 3	4 水6 Water Nourish 山雷頤 丙子 Fire Rat 6 三十 3	5 金4 Metal Following 澤雷隨 丁丑 Fire Ox 7 正月初一 7	6 木8 Wood Abundance 雷火豐 戊寅 Earth Tiger 8 初二 6	7 火7 Fire Regulate 水澤節 己卯 Earth Rabbit 9 初三 8
8 水1 Water Unity 地天泰 庚辰 Metal Dragon 10 初四 9	9 木3 Wood Great Reward 火天大有 辛巳 Metal Snake 11 初五 7	1 火2 Fire Wind 巽爲風 壬午 Water Horse 12 初六 1	2 金4 Metal Trap 澤水困 癸未 Water Goat 13 初七 8	3 木3 Wood Not Yet Accomplished 火水未濟 甲申 Wood Monkey 14 初八 9	4 金9 Metal Retreat 天山遯 乙酉 Wood Rooster 15 初九 4	5 水6 Water Mountain 艮爲山 丙戌 Fire Dog 16 初十 1
6 木8 Wood Delight 雷地豫 丁亥 Fire Pig 17 十一 8	7 火7 Fire Beginning 水雷屯 戊子 Earth Rat 18 十二 4	8 金9 Metal Without Wrongdoing 天雷無妄 己丑 Earth Ox 19 十三 2	9 木3 Wood Fire 離爲火 庚寅 Metal Tiger 20 十四 1	1 火2 Fire Sincerity 風澤中孚 辛卯 Metal Rabbit 21 十五 3	2 水6 Water Big Livestock 山天大畜 壬辰 Water Dragon 22 十六 4	3 金4 Metal Eliminating 澤天夬 癸巳 Water Snake 23 十七 6
4 金9 Metal Heaven 乾爲天 甲午 Wood Horse 24 十八 1	5 火7 Fire Well 水風井 乙未 Wood Goat 25 十九 6	6 木8 Wood Relief 雷水解 丙申 Fire Monkey 26 二十 4	7 金4 Metal Influence 澤山咸 丁酉 Fire Rooster 27 廿一 9	8 水1 Water Humility 地山謙 戊戌 Earth Dog 28 廿二 6	9 火2 Fire Observation 風地觀 己亥 Earth Pig 29 廿三 2	

MARCH 2008 乙卯

Xuan Kong Element 玄空五行	地澤臨 Arriving	Period Luck 卦運	Monthly Star 月星
Water 水1		4	7

SUNDAY	MONDAY	TUESDAY	WEDNESDAY	THURSDAY	FRIDAY	SATURDAY
木8 Wood 3 Great Strength 己巳 Earth Snake 雷天大壯 30 廿三 2	木8 Wood 4 Consistency 庚午 Metal Horse 雷風恆 31 廿四 9					火2 Fire 1 Increasing 庚子 Metal Rat 風雷益 1 廿四 9
水1 Water 2 Dimming Light 辛丑 Metal Ox 地火明夷 2 廿五 3	金9 Metal 3 Fellowship 壬寅 Water Tiger 天火同人 3 廿六 7	木8 Wood 4 Marrying Maiden 癸卯 Water Rabbit 雷澤歸妹 4 廿七 7	木3 Wood 5 Opposition 甲辰 Wood Dragon 火澤睽 5 廿八 2	火7 Fire 6 Waiting 乙巳 Wood Snake 水天需 6 廿九 3	金4 Metal 7 Great Exceeding 丙午 Fire Horse 澤風大過 7 三十 3	水6 Water 8 Poison 丁未 Fire Goat 山風蠱 8 二月初一 7
火2 Fire 9 Dispersing 戊申 Earth Monkey 風水渙 9 初二 6	木3 Wood 1 Travelling 己酉 Earth Rooster 火山旅 10 初三 8	金9 Metal 2 Stagnation 庚戌 Metal Dog 天地否 11 初四 9	火7 Fire 3 Alliance 辛亥 Metal Pig 水地比 12 初五 7	木8 Wood 4 Thunder 壬子 Water Rat 震爲雷 13 初六 1	水6 Water 5 Beauty 癸丑 Water Ox 山火賁 14 初七 8	火7 Fire 6 Accomplished 甲寅 Wood Tiger 水火既濟 15 初八 9
水1 Water 7 Arriving 乙卯 Wood Rabbit 地澤臨 16 初九 4	金4 Metal 8 Marsh 丙辰 Fire Dragon 兑爲澤 17 初十 1	火2 Fire 9 Small Livestock 丁巳 Fire Snake 風天小畜 18 十一 8	木3 Wood 1 The Cauldron 戊午 Earth Horse 火風鼎 19 十二 4	水1 Water 2 Rising 己未 Earth Goat 地風升 20 十三 2	火7 Fire 3 Water 庚申 Metal Monkey 坎爲水 21 十四 1	木8 Wood 4 Lesser Exceeding 辛酉 Metal Rooster 雷山小過 22 十五 3
金4 Metal 5 Gathering 壬戌 Water Dog 澤地萃 23 十六 4	水6 Water 6 Peel 癸亥 Water Pig 山地剝 24 十七 6	水1 Water 7 Earth 甲子 Wood Rat 坤爲地 25 十八 1	木3 Wood 8 Biting 乙丑 Wood Ox 火雷噬嗑 26 十九 6	火2 Fire 9 Family 丙寅 Fire Tiger 風火家人 27 二十 4	水6 Water 1 Decreasing 丁卯 Fire Rabbit 山澤損 28 廿一 9	金9 Metal 2 Tread 戊辰 Earth Dragon 天澤履 29 廿二 6

APRIL 2008 丙辰

Xuan Kong Element 玄空五行	兑爲澤 Marsh	Period Luck 卦運	Monthly Star 月星
Metal 金4		1	6

SUNDAY	MONDAY	TUESDAY	WEDNESDAY	THURSDAY	FRIDAY	SATURDAY
		金9 Metal 5 Litigation 辛未 Metal Goat 天水訟 1 廿五 3	水1 Water 6 Officer 壬申 Water Monkey 地水師 2 廿六 7	火2 Fire 7 Gradual Progress 癸酉 Water Rooster 風山漸 3 廿七 7	火7 Fire 8 Obstruction 甲戌 Wood Dog 水山蹇 4 廿八 2	木3 Wood 9 Advancement 乙亥 Wood Pig 火地晉 5 廿九 3
水6 Water 1 Nourish 丙子 Fire Rat 山雷頤 6 三月初一 3	金4 Metal 2 Following 丁丑 Fire Ox 澤雷隨 7 初二 7	木8 Wood 3 Abundance 戊寅 Earth Tiger 雷火豐 8 初三 6	火7 Fire 4 Regulate 己卯 Earth Rabbit 水澤節 9 初四 8	水1 Water 5 Unity 庚辰 Metal Dragon 地天泰 10 初五 9	木3 Wood 6 Great Reward 辛巳 Metal Snake 火天大有 11 初六 7	火2 Fire 7 Wind 壬午 Water Horse 巽爲風 12 初七 1
金4 Metal 8 Trap 癸未 Water Goat 澤水困 13 初八 8	木3 Wood 9 Not Yet Accomplished 甲申 Wood Monkey 火水未濟 14 初九 9	金9 Metal 1 Retreat 乙酉 Wood Rooster 天山遯 15 初十 4	水6 Water 2 Mountain 丙戌 Fire Dog 艮爲山 16 十一 1	木8 Wood 3 Delight 丁亥 Fire Pig 雷地豫 17 十二 8	火7 Fire 4 Beginning 戊子 Earth Rat 水雷屯 18 十三 4	金9 Metal 5 Without Wrongdoing 己丑 Earth Ox 天雷無妄 19 十四 2
木3 Wood 6 Fire 庚寅 Metal Tiger 離爲火 20 十五 1	火2 Fire 7 Sincerity 辛卯 Metal Rabbit 風澤中孚 21 十六 3	水6 Water 8 Big Livestock 壬辰 Water Dragon 山天大畜 22 十七 4	金4 Metal 9 Eliminating 癸巳 Water Snake 澤天夬 23 十八 6	金9 Metal 1 Heaven 甲午 Wood Horse 乾爲天 24 十九 1	火7 Fire 2 Well 乙未 Wood Goat 水風井 25 二十 6	木8 Wood 3 Relief 丙申 Fire Monkey 雷水解 26 廿一 4
金4 Metal 4 Influence 丁酉 Fire Rooster 澤山咸 27 廿二 9	水1 Water 5 Humility 戊戌 Earth Dog 地山謙 28 廿三 6	火2 Fire 6 Observation 己亥 Earth Pig 風地觀 29 廿四 2	火2 Fire 7 Increasing 庚子 Metal Rat 風雷益 30 廿五 9			

MAY 2008 丁巳

Xuan Kong Element 玄空五行	風天小畜 Small Livestock	Period Luck 卦運	Monthly Star 月星
Fire 火2		8	5

SUNDAY	MONDAY	TUESDAY	WEDNESDAY	THURSDAY	FRIDAY	SATURDAY
				水1 Water 8 Dimming Light 地火明夷 辛丑 Metal Ox 1 廿六 3	金9 Metal 9 Fellowship 天火同人 壬寅 Water Tiger 2 廿七 7	木8 Wood 1 Marrying Maiden 雷澤歸妹 癸卯 Water Rabbit 3 廿八 7
木3 Wood 2 Opposition 火澤睽 甲辰 Wood Dragon 4 廿九 2	火7 Fire 3 Waiting 水天需 乙巳 Wood Snake 5 四月初一 3	金4 Metal 4 Great Exceeding 澤風大過 丙午 Fire Horse 6 初二 3	水6 Water 5 Poison 山風蠱 丁未 Fire Goat 7 初三 7	火2 Fire 6 Dispersing 風水渙 戊申 Earth Monkey 8 初四 6	木3 Wood 7 Travelling 火山旅 己酉 Earth Rooster 9 初五 8	金9 Metal 8 Stagnation 天地否 庚戌 Metal Dog 10 初六 9
火7 Fire 9 Alliance 水地比 辛亥 Metal Pig 11 初七 7	木8 Wood 1 Thunder 震爲雷 壬子 Water Rat 12 初八 1	水6 Water 2 Beauty 山火賁 癸丑 Water Ox 13 初九 8	火7 Fire 3 Accomplished 水火既濟 甲寅 Wood Tiger 14 初十 9	水1 Water 4 Arriving 地澤臨 乙卯 Wood Rabbit 15 十一 4	金4 Metal 5 Marsh 兑爲澤 丙辰 Fire Dragon 16 十二 1	火2 Fire 6 Small Livestock 風天小畜 丁巳 Fire Snake 17 十三 8
木3 Wood 7 The Cauldron 火風鼎 戊午 Earth Horse 18 十四 4	水1 Water 8 Rising 地風升 己未 Earth Goat 19 十五 2	火7 Fire 9 Water 坎爲水 庚申 Metal Monkey 20 十六 1	木8 Wood 1 Lesser Exceeding 雷山小過 辛酉 Metal Rooster 21 十七 3	金4 Metal 2 Gathering 澤地萃 壬戌 Water Dog 22 十八 4	水6 Water 3 Peel 山地剝 癸亥 Water Pig 23 十九 6	水1 Water 4 Earth 坤爲地 甲子 Wood Rat 24 二十 1
木3 Wood 5 Biting 火雷噬嗑 乙丑 Wood Ox 25 廿一 6	火2 Fire 6 Family 風火家人 丙寅 Fire Tiger 26 廿二 4	水6 Water 7 Decreasing 山澤損 丁卯 Fire Rabbit 27 廿三 9	金9 Metal 8 Tread 天澤履 戊辰 Earth Dragon 28 廿四 6	木8 Wood 9 Great Strength 雷天大壯 己巳 Earth Snake 29 廿五 2	木8 Wood 1 Consistency 雷風恆 庚午 Metal Horse 30 廿六 9	金9 Metal 2 Litigation 天水訟 辛未 Metal Goat 31 廿七 3

JUNE 2008 戊午

Xuan Kong Element 玄空五行	火風鼎 The Cauldron	Period Luck 卦運	Monthly Star 月星
Wood 木3		4	4

SUNDAY	MONDAY	TUESDAY	WEDNESDAY	THURSDAY	FRIDAY	SATURDAY
水1 Water 3 Officer 地水師 壬申 Water Monkey 1 廿八 7	火2 Fire 4 Gradual Progress 風山漸 癸酉 Water Rooster 2 廿九 7	火7 Fire 5 Obstruction 水山蹇 甲戌 Wood Dog 3 三十 2	木3 Wood 6 Advancement 火地晉 乙亥 Wood Pig 4 五月初一 3	水6 Water 7 Nourish 山雷頤 丙子 Fire Rat 5 初二 3	金4 Metal 8 Following 澤雷隨 丁丑 Fire Ox 6 初三 7	木8 Wood 9 Abundance 雷火豐 戊寅 Earth Tiger 7 初四 6
火7 Fire 1 Regulate 水澤節 己卯 Earth Rabbit 8 初五 8	水1 Water 2 Unity 地天泰 庚辰 Metal Dragon 9 初六 9	木3 Wood 3 Great Reward 火天大有 辛巳 Metal Snake 10 初七 7	火2 Fire 4 Wind 巽爲風 壬午 Water Horse 11 初八 1	金4 Metal 5 Trap 澤水困 癸未 Water Goat 12 初九 8	木3 Wood 6 Not Yet Accomplished 火水未濟 甲申 Wood Monkey 13 初十 9	金9 Metal 7 Retreat 天山遯 乙酉 Wood Rooster 14 十一 4
水6 Water 8 Mountain 艮爲山 丙戌 Fire Dog 15 十二 1	木8 Wood 9 Delight 雷地豫 丁亥 Fire Pig 16 十三 8	火7 Fire 1 Beginning 水雷屯 戊子 Earth Rat 17 十四 4	金9 Metal 2 Without Wrongdoing 天雷無妄 己丑 Earth Ox 18 十五 2	木3 Wood 3 Fire 離爲火 庚寅 Metal Tiger 19 十六 1	火2 Fire 4 Sincerity 風澤中孚 辛卯 Metal Rabbit 20 十七 3	水6 Water 5/5 Big Livestock 山天大畜 壬辰 Water Dragon 21 十八 4
金4 Metal 4 Eliminating 澤天夬 癸巳 Water Snake 22 十九 6	金9 Metal 3 Heaven 乾爲天 甲午 Wood Horse 23 二十 1	火7 Fire 2 Well 水風井 乙未 Wood Goat 24 廿一 6	木8 Wood 1 Relief 雷水解 丙申 Fire Monkey 25 廿二 4	金4 Metal 9 Influence 澤山咸 丁酉 Fire Rooster 26 廿三 9	水1 Water 8 Humility 地山謙 戊戌 Earth Dog 27 廿四 6	火2 Fire 7 Observation 風地觀 己亥 Earth Pig 28 廿五 2
火2 Fire 6 Increasing 風雷益 庚子 Metal Rat 29 廿六 9	水1 Water 5 Dimming Light 地火明夷 辛丑 Metal Ox 30 廿七 3					

JULY 2008 己未

Xuan Kong Element 玄空五行	地風升 Rising	Period Luck 卦運	Monthly Star 月星
Water 水1		2	3

SUNDAY	MONDAY	TUESDAY	WEDNESDAY	THURSDAY	FRIDAY	SATURDAY
		1 廿八 金9 Metal Fellowship 4 壬寅 Water Tiger 天火同人 7	2 廿九 木8 Wood Marrying Maiden 3 癸卯 Water Rabbit 雷澤歸妹 7	3 六月初一 木3 Wood Opposition 2 甲辰 Wood Dragon 火澤睽 2	4 初二 火7 Fire Waiting 1 乙巳 Wood Snake 水天需 3	5 初三 金4 Metal Great Exceeding 9 丙午 Fire Horse 澤風大過 3
6 初四 水6 Water Poison 8 丁未 Fire Goat 山風蠱 7	7 初五 火2 Fire Dispersing 7 戊申 Earth Monkey 風水渙 6	8 初六 木3 Wood Travelling 6 己酉 Earth Rooster 火山旅 8	9 初七 金9 Metal Stagnation 5 庚戌 Metal Dog 天地否 9	10 初八 火7 Fire Alliance 4 辛亥 Metal Pig 水地比 7	11 初九 木8 Wood Thunder 3 壬子 Water Rat 震爲雷 1	12 初十 水6 Water Beauty 2 癸丑 Water Ox 山火賁 8
13 十一 火7 Fire Accomplished 1 甲寅 Wood Tiger 水火既濟 9	14 十二 水1 Water Arriving 9 乙卯 Wood Rabbit 地澤臨 4	15 十三 金4 Metal Marsh 8 丙辰 Fire Dragon 兑爲澤 1	16 十四 火2 Fire Small Livestock 7 丁巳 Fire Snake 風天小畜 8	17 十五 木3 Wood The Cauldron 6 戊午 Earth Horse 火風鼎 4	18 十六 水1 Water Rising 5 己未 Earth Goat 地風升 2	19 十七 火7 Fire Water 4 庚申 Metal Monkey 坎爲水 1
20 十八 木8 Wood Lesser Exceeding 3 辛酉 Metal Rooster 雷山小過 3	21 十九 金4 Metal Gathering 2 壬戌 Water Dog 澤地萃 4	22 二十 水6 Water Peel 1 癸亥 Water Pig 山地剝 6	23 廿一 水1 Water Earth 9 甲子 Wood Rat 坤爲地 1	24 廿二 木3 Wood Biting 8 乙丑 Wood Ox 火雷噬嗑 6	25 廿三 火2 Fire Family 7 丙寅 Fire Tiger 風火家人 4	26 廿四 水6 Water Decreasing 6 丁卯 Fire Rabbit 山澤損 9
27 廿五 金9 Metal Tread 5 戊辰 Earth Dragon 天澤履 6	28 廿六 木8 Wood Great Strength 4 己巳 Earth Snake 雷天大壯 2	29 廿七 木8 Wood Consistency 3 庚午 Metal Horse 雷風恆 9	30 廿八 金9 Metal Litigation 2 辛未 Metal Goat 天水訟 3	31 廿九 水1 Water Officer 1 壬申 Water Monkey 地水師 7		

AUGUST 2008 庚申

Xuan Kong Element 玄空五行	坎爲水 Water	Period Luck 卦運	Monthly Star 月星
Fire 火7		1	2

SUNDAY	MONDAY	TUESDAY	WEDNESDAY	THURSDAY	FRIDAY	SATURDAY
31 八月初一 木8 Wood Marrying Maiden 6 癸卯 Water Rabbit 雷澤歸妹 7					1 七月初一 火2 Fire Gradual Progress 9 癸酉 Water Rooster 風山漸 7	2 初二 火7 Fire Obstruction 8 甲戌 Wood Dog 水山蹇 2
3 初三 木3 Wood Advancement 7 乙亥 Wood Pig 火地晉 3	4 初四 水6 Water Nourish 6 丙子 Fire Rat 山雷頤 3	5 初五 金4 Metal Following 5 丁丑 Fire Ox 澤雷隨 7	6 初六 木8 Wood Abundance 4 戊寅 Earth Tiger 雷火豐 6	7 初七 火7 Fire Regulate 3 己卯 Earth Rabbit 水澤節 8	8 初八 水1 Water Unity 2 庚辰 Metal Dragon 地天泰 9	9 初九 木3 Wood Great Reward 1 辛巳 Metal Snake 火天大有 7
10 初十 火2 Fire Wind 9 壬午 Water Horse 巽爲風 1	11 十一 金4 Metal Trap 8 癸未 Water Goat 澤水困 8	12 十二 木3 Wood Not Yet Accomplished 7 甲申 Wood Monkey 火水未濟 9	13 十三 金9 Metal Retreat 6 乙酉 Wood Rooster 天山遯 4	14 十四 水6 Water Mountain 5 丙戌 Fire Dog 艮爲山 1	15 十五 木8 Wood Delight 4 丁亥 Fire Pig 雷地豫 8	16 十六 火7 Fire Beginning 3 戊子 Earth Rat 水雷屯 4
17 十七 金9 Metal Without Wrongdoing 2 己丑 Earth Ox 天雷無妄 2	18 十八 木3 Wood Fire 1 庚寅 Metal Tiger 離爲火 1	19 十九 火2 Fire Sincerity 9 辛卯 Metal Rabbit 風澤中孚 3	20 二十 水6 Water Big Livestock 8 壬辰 Water Dragon 山天大畜 4	21 廿一 金4 Metal Eliminating 7 癸巳 Water Snake 澤天夬 6	22 廿二 金9 Metal Heaven 6 甲午 Wood Horse 乾爲天 1	23 廿三 火7 Fire Well 5 乙未 Wood Goat 水風井 6
24 廿四 木8 Wood Relief 4 丙申 Fire Monkey 雷水解 4	25 廿五 金4 Metal Influence 3 丁酉 Fire Rooster 澤山咸 9	26 廿六 水1 Water Humility 2 戊戌 Earth Dog 地山謙 6	27 廿七 火2 Fire Observation 1 己亥 Earth Pig 風地觀 2	28 廿八 火2 Fire Increasing 9 庚子 Metal Rat 風雷益 9	29 廿九 水1 Water Dimming Light 8 辛丑 Metal Ox 地火明夷 3	30 三十 金9 Metal Fellowship 7 壬寅 Water Tiger 天火同人 7

SEPTEMBER 2008 辛酉

Xuan Kong Element 玄空五行	雷山小過 Lesser Exceeding	Period Luck 卦運	Monthly Star 月星
Wood 木8		3	1

SUNDAY	MONDAY	TUESDAY	WEDNESDAY	THURSDAY	FRIDAY	SATURDAY
	木3 Wood 5 Opposition 火澤睽 甲辰 Wood Dragon **1** 初二 2	火7 Fire 4 Waiting 水天需 乙巳 Wood Snake **2** 初三 3	金4 Metal 3 Great Exceeding 澤風大過 丙午 Fire Horse **3** 初四 3	水6 Water 2 Poison 山風蠱 丁未 Fire Goat **4** 初五 7	火2 Fire 1 Dispersing 風水渙 戊申 Earth Monkey **5** 初六 6	木3 Wood 9 Travelling 火山旅 己酉 Earth Rooster **6** 初七 8
金9 Metal 8 Stagnation 天地否 庚戌 Metal Dog **7** 初八 9	火7 Fire 7 Alliance 水地比 辛亥 Metal Pig **8** 初九 7	木8 Wood 6 Thunder 震爲雷 壬子 Water Rat **9** 初十 1	水6 Water 5 Beauty 山火賁 癸丑 Water Ox **10** 十一 8	火7 Fire 4 Accomplished 水火既濟 甲寅 Wood Tiger **11** 十二 9	水1 Water 3 Arriving 地澤臨 乙卯 Wood Rabbit **12** 十三 4	金4 Metal 2 Marsh 兑爲澤 丙辰 Fire Dragon **13** 十四 1
火2 Fire 1 Small Livestock 風天小畜 丁巳 Fire Snake **14** 十五 8	木3 Wood 9 The Cauldron 火風鼎 戊午 Earth Horse **15** 十六 4	水1 Water 8 Rising 地風升 己未 Earth Goat **16** 十七 2	火7 Fire 7 Water 坎爲水 庚申 Metal Monkey **17** 十八 1	木8 Wood 6 Lesser Exceeding 雷山小過 辛酉 Metal Rooster **18** 十九 3	金4 Metal 5 Gathering 澤地萃 壬戌 Water Dog **19** 二十 4	水6 Water 4 Peel 山地剝 癸亥 Water Pig **20** 廿一 6
水1 Water 3 Earth 坤爲地 甲子 Wood Rat **21** 廿二 1	木3 Wood 2 Biting 火雷噬嗑 乙丑 Wood Ox **22** 廿三 6	火2 Fire 1 Family 風火家人 丙寅 Fire Tiger **23** 廿四 4	水6 Water 9 Decreasing 山澤損 丁卯 Fire Rabbit **24** 廿五 9	金9 Metal 8 Tread 天澤履 戊辰 Earth Dragon **25** 廿六 6	木8 Wood 7 Great Strength 雷天大壯 己巳 Earth Snake **26** 廿七 2	木8 Wood 6 Consistency 雷風恆 庚午 Metal Horse **27** 廿八 9
金9 Metal 5 Litigation 天水訟 辛未 Metal Goat **28** 廿九 3	水1 Water 4 Officer 地水師 壬申 Water Monkey **29** 九月初一 7	火2 Fire 3 Gradual Progress 風山漸 癸酉 Water Rooster **30** 初二 7				

OCTOBER 2008 壬戌

Xuan Kong Element 玄空五行	澤地萃 Gathering	Period Luck 卦運	Monthly Star 月星
Metal 金4		4	9

SUNDAY	MONDAY	TUESDAY	WEDNESDAY	THURSDAY	FRIDAY	SATURDAY
			火7 Fire 2 Obstruction 水山蹇 甲戌 Wood Dog **1** 初三 2	木3 Wood 1 Advancement 火地晉 乙亥 Wood Pig **2** 初四 3	水6 Water 9 Nourish 山雷頤 丙子 Fire Rat **3** 初五 3	金4 Metal 8 Following 澤雷隨 丁丑 Fire Ox **4** 初六 7
木8 Wood 7 Abundance 雷火豐 戊寅 Earth Tiger **5** 初七 6	火7 Fire 6 Regulate 水澤節 己卯 Earth Rabbit **6** 初八 8	水1 Water 5 Unity 地天泰 庚辰 Metal Dragon **7** 初九 9	木3 Wood 4 Great Reward 火天大有 辛巳 Metal Snake **8** 初十 7	火2 Fire 3 Wind 巽爲風 壬午 Water Horse **9** 十一 1	金4 Metal 2 Trap 澤水困 癸未 Water Goat **10** 十二 8	木3 Wood 1 Not Yet Accomplished 火水未濟 甲申 Wood Monkey **11** 十三 9
金9 Metal 9 Retreat 天山遯 乙酉 Wood Rooster **12** 十四 4	水6 Water 8 Mountain 艮爲山 丙戌 Fire Dog **13** 十五 1	木8 Wood 7 Delight 雷地豫 丁亥 Fire Pig **14** 十六 8	火7 Fire 6 Beginning 水雷屯 戊子 Earth Rat **15** 十七 4	金9 Metal 5 Without Wrongdoing 天雷無妄 己丑 Earth Ox **16** 十八 2	木3 Wood 4 Fire 離爲火 庚寅 Metal Tiger **17** 十九 1	火2 Fire 3 Sincerity 風澤中孚 辛卯 Metal Rabbit **18** 二十 3
水6 Water 2 Big Livestock 山天大畜 壬辰 Water Dragon **19** 廿一 4	金4 Metal 1 Eliminating 澤天夬 癸巳 Water Snake **20** 廿二 6	金9 Metal 9 Heaven 乾爲天 甲午 Wood Horse **21** 廿三 1	火7 Fire 8 Well 水風井 乙未 Wood Goat **22** 廿四 6	木8 Wood 7 Relief 雷水解 丙申 Fire Monkey **23** 廿五 4	金4 Metal 6 Influence 澤山咸 丁酉 Fire Rooster **24** 廿六 9	水1 Water 5 Humility 地山謙 戊戌 Earth Dog **25** 廿七 6
火2 Fire 4 Observation 風地觀 己亥 Earth Pig **26** 廿八 2	火2 Fire 3 Increasing 風雷益 庚子 Metal Rat **27** 廿九 9	水1 Water 2 Dimming Light 地火明夷 辛丑 Metal Ox **28** 三十 3	金9 Metal 1 Fellowship 天火同人 壬寅 Water Tiger **29** 十月初一 7	木8 Wood 9 Marrying Maiden 雷澤歸妹 癸卯 Water Rabbit **30** 初二 7	木3 Wood 8 Opposition 火澤睽 甲辰 Wood Dragon **31** 初三 2	

NOVEMBER 2008 癸亥

Xuan Kong Element 玄空五行	山地剝 Peel	Period Luck 卦運	Monthly Star 月星
Water 水6		6	8

SUNDAY	MONDAY	TUESDAY	WEDNESDAY	THURSDAY	FRIDAY	SATURDAY
火7 Fire [5] Obstruction 水山蹇 甲戌 Wood Dog 2 30 初三						火7 Fire [7] Waiting 水天需 乙巳 Wood Snake 3 1 初四
金4 Metal [6] Great Exceeding 澤風大過 丙午 Fire Horse 3 2 初五	水6 Water [5] Poison 山風蠱 丁未 Fire Goat 7 3 初六	火2 Fire [4] Dispersing 風水渙 戊申 Earth Monkey 6 4 初七	木3 Wood [3] Travelling 火山旅 己酉 Earth Rooster 8 5 初八	金9 Metal [2] Stagnation 天地否 庚戌 Metal Dog 9 6 初九	火7 Fire [1] Alliance 水地比 辛亥 Metal Pig 7 7 初十	木8 Wood [9] Thunder 震爲雷 壬子 Water Rat 1 8 十一
水6 Water [8] Beauty 山火賁 癸丑 Water Ox 8 9 十二	火7 Fire [7] Accomplished 水火既濟 甲寅 Wood Tiger 9 10 十三	水1 Water [6] Arriving 地澤臨 乙卯 Wood Rabbit 4 11 十四	金4 Metal [5] Marsh 兑爲澤 丙辰 Fire Dragon 1 12 十五	火2 Fire [4] Small Livestock 風天小畜 丁巳 Fire Snake 8 13 十六	木3 Wood [3] The Cauldron 火風鼎 戊午 Earth Horse 4 14 十七	水1 Water [2] Rising 地風升 己未 Earth Goat 2 15 十八
火7 Fire [1] Water 坎爲水 庚申 Metal Monkey 1 16 十九	木8 Wood [9] Lesser Exceeding 雷山小過 辛酉 Metal Rooster 3 17 二十	金4 Metal [8] Gathering 澤地萃 壬戌 Water Dog 4 18 廿一	水6 Water [7] Peel 山地剝 癸亥 Water Pig 6 19 廿二	水1 Water [6] Earth 坤爲地 甲子 Wood Rat 1 20 廿三	木3 Wood [5] Biting 火雷噬嗑 乙丑 Wood Ox 6 21 廿四	火2 Fire [4] Family 風火家人 丙寅 Fire Tiger 4 22 廿五
水6 Water [3] Decreasing 山澤損 丁卯 Fire Rabbit 9 23 廿六	金9 Metal [2] Tread 天澤履 戊辰 Earth Dragon 6 24 廿七	木8 Wood [1] Great Strength 雷天大壯 己巳 Earth Snake 2 25 廿八	木8 Wood [9] Consistency 雷風恒 庚午 Metal Horse 9 26 廿九	金9 Metal [8] Litigation 天水訟 辛未 Metal Goat 3 27 三十	水1 Water [7] Officer 地水師 壬申 Water Monkey 7 28 十一月初一	火2 Fire [6] Gradual Progress 風山漸 癸酉 Water Rooster 7 29 初二

DECEMBER 2008 甲子

Xuan Kong Element 玄空五行	坤爲地 Earth	Period Luck 卦運	Monthly Star 月星
Water 水1		1	7

SUNDAY	MONDAY	TUESDAY	WEDNESDAY	THURSDAY	FRIDAY	SATURDAY
	木3 Wood [4] Advancement 火地晉 乙亥 Wood Pig 3 1 初四	水6 Water [3] Nourish 山雷頤 丙子 Fire Rat 3 2 初五	金4 Metal [2] Following 澤雷隨 丁丑 Fire Ox 7 3 初六	木8 Wood [1] Abundance 雷火豐 戊寅 Earth Tiger 6 4 初七	火7 Fire [9] Regulate 水澤節 己卯 Earth Rabbit 8 5 初八	水1 Water [8] Unity 地天泰 庚辰 Metal Dragon 9 6 初九
木3 Wood [7] Great Reward 火天大有 辛巳 Metal Snake 7 7 初十	火2 Fire [6] Wind 巽爲風 壬午 Water Horse 1 8 十一	金4 Metal [5] Trap 澤水困 癸未 Water Goat 8 9 十二	木3 Wood [4] Not Yet Accomplished 火水未濟 甲申 Wood Monkey 9 10 十三	金9 Metal [3] Retreat 天山遯 乙酉 Wood Rooster 4 11 十四	水6 Water [2] Mountain 艮爲山 丙戌 Fire Dog 1 12 十五	木8 Wood [1] Delight 雷地豫 丁亥 Fire Pig 8 13 十六
火7 Fire [9] Beginning 水雷屯 戊子 Earth Rat 4 14 十七	金9 Metal [8] Without Wrongdoing 天雷無妄 己丑 Earth Ox 2 15 十八	木3 Wood [7] Fire 離爲火 庚寅 Metal Tiger 1 16 十九	火2 Fire [6] Sincerity 風澤中孚 辛卯 Metal Rabbit 3 17 二十	水6 Water [5] Big Livestock 山天大畜 壬辰 Water Dragon 4 18 廿一	金4 Metal [4] Eliminating 澤天夬 癸巳 Water Snake 6 19 廿二	金9 Metal [3] Heaven 乾爲天 甲午 Wood Horse 1 20 廿三
火7 Fire [2/8] Well 水風井 乙未 Wood Goat 6 21 廿四	木8 Wood [9] Relief 雷水解 丙申 Fire Monkey 4 22 廿五	金4 Metal [1] Influence 澤山咸 丁酉 Fire Rooster 9 23 廿六	水1 Water [2] Humility 地山謙 戊戌 Earth Dog 6 24 廿七	火2 Fire [3] Observation 風地觀 己亥 Earth Pig 2 25 廿八	火2 Fire [4] Increasing 風雷益 庚子 Metal Rat 9 26 廿九	水1 Water [5] Dimming Light 地火明夷 辛丑 Metal Ox 3 27 十二月初一
金9 Metal [6] Fellowship 天火同人 壬寅 Water Tiger 7 28 初二	木8 Wood [7] Marrying Maiden 雷澤歸妹 癸卯 Water Rabbit 7 29 初三	木3 Wood [8] Opposition 火澤睽 甲辰 Wood Dragon 2 30 初四	火7 Fire [9] Waiting 水天需 乙巳 Wood Snake 3 31 初五			

2009 己丑

(*Ji Chou*) Earth Ox

2009 己丑 *(Ji Chou)* Earth Ox

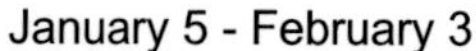

January 5 - February 3

	SE	S	SW	
	5	1	3	
E	4	6	8	W
	9	2	7	
	NE	N	NW	

木3 Wood
乙丑 Wood Ox
6
Biting 火雷噬嗑

Three Killings	East

February 4 - March 4

	SE	S	SW	
	4	9	2	
E	3	5	7	W
	8	1	6	
	NE	N	NW	

火2 Fire
丙寅 Fire Tiger
4
Family 風火家人

Three Killings	North

March 5 - April 3

	SE	S	SW	
	3	8	1	
E	2	4	6	W
	7	9	5	
	NE	N	NW	

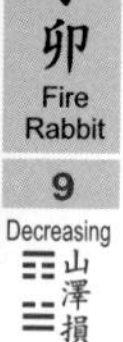

水6 Water
丁卯 Fire Rabbit
9
Decreasing 山澤損

Three Killings	West

April 4 - May 4

	SE	S	SW	
	2	7	9	
E	1	3	5	W
	6	8	4	
	NE	N	NW	

金9 Metal
戊辰 Earth Dragon
6
Tread 天澤履

Three Killings	South

May 5 - June 4

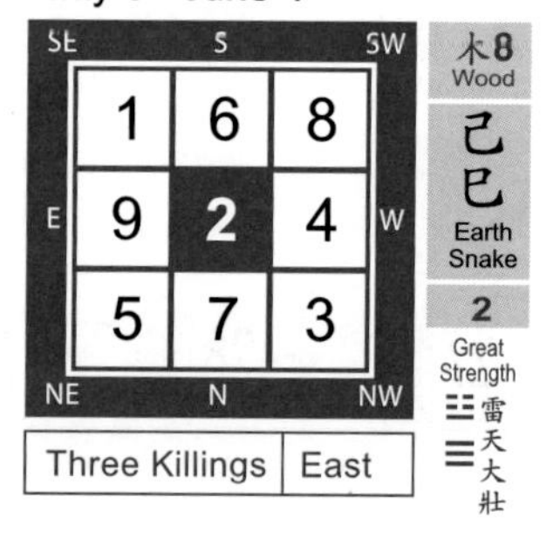

	SE	S	SW	
	1	6	8	
E	9	2	4	W
	5	7	3	
	NE	N	NW	

木8 Wood
己巳 Earth Snake
2
Great Strength 雷天大壯

Three Killings	East

June 5 - July 6

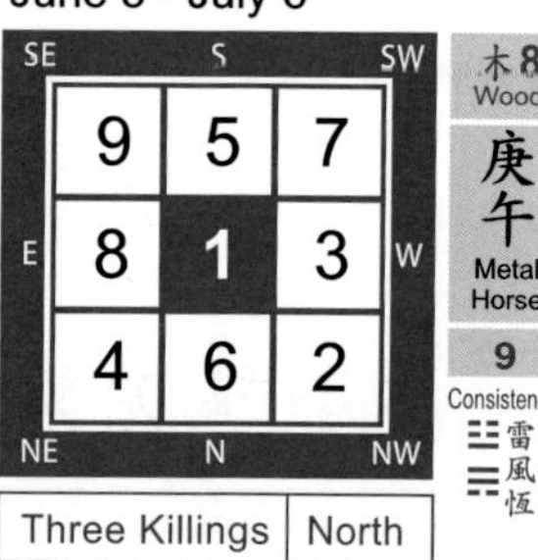

	SE	S	SW	
	9	5	7	
E	8	1	3	W
	4	6	2	
	NE	N	NW	

木8 Wood
庚午 Metal Horse
9
Consistency 雷風恒

Three Killings	North

July 7 - August 6

	SE	S	SW	
	8	4	6	
E	7	9	2	W
	3	5	1	
	NE	N	NW	

金9 Metal
辛未 Metal Goat
3
Litigation 天水訟

Three Killings	West

August 7 - September 6

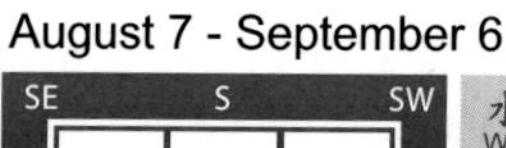

	SE	S	SW	
	7	3	5	
E	6	8	1	W
	2	4	9	
	NE	N	NW	

水1 Water
壬申 Water Monkey
7
Officer 地水師

Three Killings	South

September 7 - October 7

	SE	S	SW	
	6	2	4	
E	5	7	9	W
	1	3	8	
	NE	N	NW	

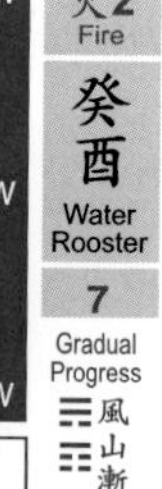

火2 Fire
癸酉 Water Rooster
7
Gradual Progress 風山漸

Three Killings	East

October 8 - November 6

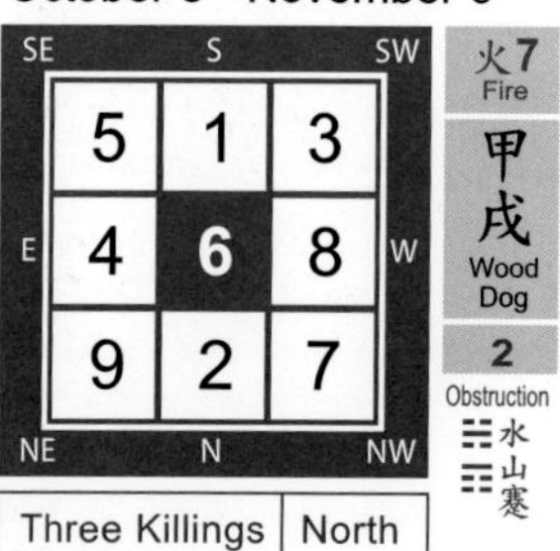

	SE	S	SW	
	5	1	3	
E	4	6	8	W
	9	2	7	
	NE	N	NW	

火7 Fire
甲戌 Wood Dog
2
Obstruction 水山蹇

Three Killings	North

November 7 - December 6

	SE	S	SW	
	4	9	2	
E	3	5	7	W
	8	1	6	
	NE	N	NW	

木3 Wood
乙亥 Wood Pig
3
Advancement 火地晉

Three Killings	West

December 7 - January 4

	SE	S	SW	
	3	8	1	
E	2	4	6	W
	7	9	5	
	NE	N	NW	

水6 Water
丙子 Fire Rat
3
Nourish 山雷頤

Three Killings	South

JANUARY 2009 乙丑

Xuan Kong Element 玄空五行	火雷噬嗑 Biting	Period Luck 卦運	Monthly Star 月星
Wood 木3		6	6

SUNDAY	MONDAY	TUESDAY	WEDNESDAY	THURSDAY	FRIDAY	SATURDAY
				金4 Metal Great Exceeding 1 丙午 Fire Horse 澤風大過 **1** 初六 3	水6 Water Poison 2 丁未 Fire Goat 山風蠱 **2** 初七 7	火2 Fire Dispersing 3 戊申 Earth Monkey 風水渙 **3** 初八 6
木3 Wood Travelling 4 己酉 Earth Rooster 火山旅 **4** 初九 8	金9 Metal Stagnation 5 庚戌 Metal Dog 天地否 **5** 初十 9	火7 Fire Alliance 6 辛亥 Metal Pig 水地比 **6** 十一 7	木8 Wood Thunder 7 壬子 Water Rat 震爲雷 **7** 十二 1	水6 Water Beauty 8 癸丑 Water Ox 山火賁 **8** 十三 8	火7 Fire Accomplished 9 甲寅 Wood Tiger 水火既濟 **9** 十四 9	水1 Water Arriving 1 乙卯 Wood Rabbit 地澤臨 **10** 十五 4
金4 Metal Marsh 2 丙辰 Fire Dragon 兑爲澤 **11** 十六 1	火2 Fire Small Livestock 3 丁巳 Fire Snake 風天小畜 **12** 十七 8	木3 Wood The Cauldron 4 戊午 Earth Horse 火風鼎 **13** 十八 4	水1 Water Rising 5 己未 Earth Goat 地風升 **14** 十九 2	火7 Fire Water 6 庚申 Metal Monkey 坎爲水 **15** 二十 1	木8 Wood Lesser Exceeding 7 辛酉 Metal Rooster 雷山小過 **16** 廿一 3	金4 Metal Gathering 8 壬戌 Water Dog 澤地萃 **17** 廿二 4
水6 Water Peel 9 癸亥 Water Pig 山地剝 **18** 廿三 6	水1 Water Earth 1 甲子 Wood Rat 坤爲地 **19** 廿四 1	木3 Wood Biting 2 乙丑 Wood Ox 火雷噬嗑 **20** 廿五 6	火2 Fire Family 3 丙寅 Fire Tiger 風火家人 **21** 廿六 4	水6 Water Decreasing 4 丁卯 Fire Rabbit 山澤損 **22** 廿七 9	金9 Metal Tread 5 戊辰 Earth Dragon 天澤履 **23** 廿八 6	木8 Wood Great Strength 6 己巳 Earth Snake 雷天大壯 **24** 廿九 2
木8 Wood Consistency 7 庚午 Metal Horse 雷風恆 **25** 三十 9	金9 Metal Litigation 8 辛未 Metal Goat 天水訟 **26** 正月初一 3	水1 Water Officer 9 壬申 Water Monkey 地水師 **27** 初二 7	火2 Fire Gradual Progress 1 癸酉 Water Rooster 風山漸 **28** 初三 7	火7 Fire Obstruction 2 甲戌 Wood Dog 水山蹇 **29** 初四 2	木3 Wood Advancement 3 乙亥 Wood Pig 火地晉 **30** 初五 3	水6 Water Nourish 4 丙子 Fire Rat 山雷頤 **31** 初六 3

FEBRUARY 2009 丙寅

Xuan Kong Element 玄空五行	風火家人 Family	Period Luck 卦運	Monthly Star 月星
Fire 火2		4	5

SUNDAY	MONDAY	TUESDAY	WEDNESDAY	THURSDAY	FRIDAY	SATURDAY
金4 Metal Following 5 丁丑 Fire Ox 澤雷隨 **1** 初七 7	木8 Wood Abundance 6 戊寅 Earth Tiger 雷火豐 **2** 初八 6	火7 Fire Regulate 7 己卯 Earth Rabbit 水澤節 **3** 初九 8	水1 Water Unity 8 庚辰 Metal Dragon 地天泰 **4** 初十 9	木3 Wood Great Reward 9 辛巳 Metal Snake 火天大有 **5** 十一 7	火2 Fire Wind 1 壬午 Water Horse 巽爲風 **6** 十二 1	金4 Metal Trap 2 癸未 Water Goat 澤水困 **7** 十三 8
木3 Wood Not Yet Accomplished 3 甲申 Wood Monkey 火水未濟 **8** 十四 9	金9 Metal Retreat 4 乙酉 Wood Rooster 天山遯 **9** 十五 4	水6 Water Mountain 5 丙戌 Fire Dog 艮爲山 **10** 十六 1	木8 Wood Delight 6 丁亥 Fire Pig 雷地豫 **11** 十七 8	火7 Fire Beginning 7 戊子 Earth Rat 水雷屯 **12** 十八 4	金9 Metal Without Wrongdoing 8 己丑 Earth Ox 天雷無妄 **13** 十九 2	木3 Wood Fire 9 庚寅 Metal Tiger 離爲火 **14** 二十 1
火2 Fire Sincerity 1 辛卯 Metal Rabbit 風澤中孚 **15** 廿一 3	水6 Water Big Livestock 2 壬辰 Water Dragon 山天大畜 **16** 廿二 4	金4 Metal Eliminating 3 癸巳 Water Snake 澤天夬 **17** 廿三 6	金9 Metal Heaven 4 甲午 Wood Horse 乾爲天 **18** 廿四 1	火7 Fire Well 5 乙未 Wood Goat 水風井 **19** 廿五 6	木8 Wood Relief 6 丙申 Fire Monkey 雷水解 **20** 廿六 4	金4 Metal Influence 7 丁酉 Fire Rooster 澤山咸 **21** 廿七 9
水1 Water Humility 8 戊戌 Earth Dog 地山謙 **22** 廿八 6	火2 Fire Observation 9 己亥 Earth Pig 風地觀 **23** 廿九 2	火2 Fire Increasing 1 庚子 Metal Rat 風雷益 **24** 三十 9	水1 Water Dimming Light 2 辛丑 Metal Ox 地火明夷 **25** 二月初一 3	金9 Metal Fellowship 3 壬寅 Water Tiger 天火同人 **26** 初二 7	木8 Wood Marrying Maiden 4 癸卯 Water Rabbit 雷澤歸妹 **27** 初三 7	木3 Wood Opposition 5 甲辰 Wood Dragon 火澤睽 **28** 初四 2

MARCH 2009 丁卯

Xuan Kong Element 玄空五行	山澤損 Decreasing	Period Luck 卦運	Monthly Star 月星
Water 水6		9	4

SUNDAY	MONDAY	TUESDAY	WEDNESDAY	THURSDAY	FRIDAY	SATURDAY
火7 Fire 6 Waiting 水天需 乙巳 Wood Snake 1 初五 3	金4 Metal 7 Great Exceeding 澤風大過 丙午 Fire Horse 2 初六 3	水6 Water 8 Poison 山風蠱 丁未 Fire Goat 3 初七 7	火2 Fire 9 Dispersing 風水渙 戊申 Earth Monkey 4 初八 6	木3 Wood 1 Travelling 火山旅 己酉 Earth Rooster 5 初九 8	金9 Metal 2 Stagnation 天地否 庚戌 Metal Dog 6 初十 9	火7 Fire 3 Alliance 水地比 辛亥 Metal Pig 7 十一 7
木8 Wood 4 Thunder 震爲雷 壬子 Water Rat 8 十二 1	水6 Water 5 Beauty 山火賁 癸丑 Water Ox 9 十三 8	火7 Fire 6 Accomplished 水火既濟 甲寅 Wood Tiger 10 十四 9	水1 Water 7 Arriving 地澤臨 乙卯 Wood Rabbit 11 十五 4	金4 Metal 8 Marsh 兌爲澤 丙辰 Fire Dragon 12 十六 1	火2 Fire 9 Small Livestock 風天小畜 丁巳 Fire Snake 13 十七 8	木3 Wood 1 The Cauldron 火風鼎 戊午 Earth Horse 14 十八 4
水1 Water 2 Rising 地風升 己未 Earth Goat 15 十九 2	火7 Fire 3 Water 坎爲水 庚申 Metal Monkey 16 二十 1	木8 Wood 4 Lesser Exceeding 雷山小過 辛酉 Metal Rooster 17 廿一 3	金4 Metal 5 Gathering 澤地萃 壬戌 Water Dog 18 廿二 4	水6 Water 6 Peel 山地剝 癸亥 Water Pig 19 廿三 6	水1 Water 7 Earth 坤爲地 甲子 Wood Rat 20 廿四 1	木3 Wood 8 Biting 火雷噬嗑 乙丑 Wood Ox 21 廿五 6
火2 Fire 9 Family 風火家人 丙寅 Fire Tiger 22 廿六 4	水6 Water 1 Decreasing 山澤損 丁卯 Fire Rabbit 23 廿七 9	金9 Metal 2 Tread 天澤履 戊辰 Earth Dragon 24 廿八 6	木8 Wood 3 Great Strength 雷天大壯 己巳 Earth Snake 25 廿九 2	木8 Wood 4 Consistency 雷風恆 庚午 Metal Horse 26 三十 9	金9 Metal 5 Litigation 天水訟 辛未 Metal Goat 27 三月初一 3	水1 Water 6 Officer 地水師 壬申 Water Monkey 28 初二 7
火2 Fire 7 Gradual Progress 風山漸 癸酉 Water Rooster 29 初三 7	火7 Fire 8 Obstruction 水山蹇 甲戌 Wood Dog 30 初四 2	木3 Wood 9 Advancement 火地晉 乙亥 Wood Pig 31 初五 3				

APRIL 2009 戊辰

Xuan Kong Element 玄空五行	天澤履 Tread	Period Luck 卦運	Monthly Star 月星
Metal 金9		6	3

SUNDAY	MONDAY	TUESDAY	WEDNESDAY	THURSDAY	FRIDAY	SATURDAY
			水6 Water 1 Nourish 山雷頤 丙子 Fire Rat 1 初六 3	金4 Metal 2 Following 澤雷隨 丁丑 Fire Ox 2 初七 7	木8 Wood 3 Abundance 雷火豐 戊寅 Earth Tiger 3 初八 6	火7 Fire 4 Regulate 水澤節 己卯 Earth Rabbit 4 初九 8
水1 Water 5 Unity 地天泰 庚辰 Metal Dragon 5 初十 9	木3 Wood 6 Great Reward 火天大有 辛巳 Metal Snake 6 十一 7	火2 Fire 7 Wind 巽爲風 壬午 Water Horse 7 十二 1	金4 Metal 8 Trap 澤水困 癸未 Water Goat 8 十三 8	木3 Wood 9 Not Yet Accomplished 火水未濟 甲申 Wood Monkey 9 十四 9	金9 Metal 1 Retreat 天山遯 乙酉 Wood Rooster 10 十五 4	水6 Water 2 Mountain 艮爲山 丙戌 Fire Dog 11 十六 1
木8 Wood 3 Delight 雷地豫 丁亥 Fire Pig 12 十七 8	火7 Fire 4 Beginning 水雷屯 戊子 Earth Rat 13 十八 4	金9 Metal 5 Without Wrongdoing 天雷無妄 己丑 Earth Ox 14 十九 2	木3 Wood 6 Fire 離爲火 庚寅 Metal Tiger 15 二十 1	火2 Fire 7 Sincerity 風澤中孚 辛卯 Metal Rabbit 16 廿一 3	水6 Water 8 Big Livestock 山天大畜 壬辰 Water Dragon 17 廿二 4	金4 Metal 9 Eliminating 澤天夬 癸巳 Water Snake 18 廿三 6
金9 Metal 1 Heaven 乾爲天 甲午 Wood Horse 19 廿四 1	火7 Fire 2 Well 水風井 乙未 Wood Goat 20 廿五 6	木8 Wood 3 Relief 雷水解 丙申 Fire Monkey 21 廿六 4	金4 Metal 4 Influence 澤山咸 丁酉 Fire Rooster 22 廿七 9	水1 Water 5 Humility 地山謙 戊戌 Earth Dog 23 廿八 6	火2 Fire 6 Observation 風地觀 己亥 Earth Pig 24 廿九 2	火2 Fire 7 Increasing 風雷益 庚子 Metal Rat 25 四月初一 9
水1 Water 8 Dimming Light 地火明夷 辛丑 Metal Ox 26 初二 3	金9 Metal 9 Fellowship 天火同人 壬寅 Water Tiger 27 初三 7	木8 Wood 1 Marrying Maiden 雷澤歸妹 癸卯 Water Rabbit 28 初四 7	木3 Wood 2 Opposition 火澤睽 甲辰 Wood Dragon 29 初五 2	火7 Fire 3 Waiting 水天需 乙巳 Wood Snake 30 初六 3		

MAY 2009 癸酉

Xuan Kong Element 玄空五行	風山漸 Gradual Progress	Period Luck 卦運	Monthly Star 月星
Fire 火2		7	2

SUNDAY	MONDAY	TUESDAY	WEDNESDAY	THURSDAY	FRIDAY	SATURDAY
水6 Water · 7 Nourish 丙子 Fire Rat 山雷頤 **31** 初八 3					金4 Metal · 4 Great Exceeding 丙午 Fire Horse 澤風大過 **1** 初七 3	水6 Water · 5 Poison 丁未 Fire Goat 山風蠱 **2** 初八 7
火2 Fire · 6 Dispersing 戊申 Earth Monkey 風水渙 **3** 初九 6	木3 Wood · 7 Travelling 己酉 Earth Rooster 火山旅 **4** 初十 8	金9 Metal · 8 Stagnation 庚戌 Metal Dog 天地否 **5** 十一 9	火7 Fire · 9 Alliance 辛亥 Metal Pig 水地比 **6** 十二 7	木8 Wood · 1 Thunder 壬子 Water Rat 震為雷 **7** 十三 1	水6 Water · 2 Beauty 癸丑 Water Ox 山火賁 **8** 十四 8	火7 Fire · 3 Accomplished 甲寅 Wood Tiger 水火既濟 **9** 十五 9
水1 Water · 4 Arriving 乙卯 Wood Rabbit 地澤臨 **10** 十六 4	金4 Metal · 5 Marsh 丙辰 Fire Dragon 兌為澤 **11** 十七 1	火2 Fire · 6 Small Livestock 丁巳 Fire Snake 風天小畜 **12** 十八 8	木3 Wood · 7 The Cauldron 戊午 Earth Horse 火風鼎 **13** 十九 4	水1 Water · 8 Rising 己未 Earth Goat 地風升 **14** 二十 2	火7 Fire · 9 Water 庚申 Metal Monkey 坎為水 **15** 廿一 1	木8 Wood · 1 Lesser Exceeding 辛酉 Metal Rooster 雷山小過 **16** 廿二 3
金4 Metal · 2 Gathering 壬戌 Water Dog 澤地萃 **17** 廿三 4	水6 Water · 3 Peel 癸亥 Water Pig 山地剝 **18** 廿四 6	水1 Water · 4 Earth 甲子 Wood Rat 坤為地 **19** 廿五 1	木3 Wood · 5 Biting 乙丑 Wood Ox 火雷噬嗑 **20** 廿六 6	火2 Fire · 6 Family 丙寅 Fire Tiger 風火家人 **21** 廿七 4	水6 Water · 7 Decreasing 丁卯 Fire Rabbit 山澤損 **22** 廿八 9	金9 Metal · 8 Tread 戊辰 Earth Dragon 天澤履 **23** 廿九 6
木8 Wood · 9 Great Strength 己巳 Earth Snake 雷天大壯 **24** 五月初一 2	木8 Wood · 1 Consistency 庚午 Metal Horse 雷風恆 **25** 初二 9	金9 Metal · 2 Litigation 辛未 Metal Goat 天水訟 **26** 初三 3	水1 Water · 3 Officer 壬申 Water Monkey 地水師 **27** 初四 7	火2 Fire · 4 Gradual Progress 癸酉 Water Rooster 風山漸 **28** 初五 7	火7 Fire · 5 Obstruction 甲戌 Wood Dog 水山蹇 **29** 初六 2	木3 Wood · 6 Advancement 乙亥 Wood Pig 火地晉 **30** 初七 3

JUNE 2009 甲戌

Xuan Kong Element 玄空五行	水山蹇 Obstruction	Period Luck 卦運	Monthly Star 月星
Fire 火7		2	1

SUNDAY	MONDAY	TUESDAY	WEDNESDAY	THURSDAY	FRIDAY	SATURDAY
	金4 Metal · 8 Following 丁丑 Fire Ox 澤雷隨 **1** 初九 7	木8 Wood · 9 Abundance 戊寅 Earth Tiger 雷火豐 **2** 初十 6	火7 Fire · 1 Regulate 己卯 Earth Rabbit 水澤節 **3** 十一 8	水1 Water · 2 Unity 庚辰 Metal Dragon 地天泰 **4** 十二 9	木3 Wood · 3 Great Reward 辛巳 Metal Snake 火天大有 **5** 十三 7	火2 Fire · 4 Wind 壬午 Water Horse 巽為風 **6** 十四 1
金4 Metal · 5 Trap 癸未 Water Goat 澤水困 **7** 十五 8	木3 Wood · 6 Not Yet Accomplished 甲申 Wood Monkey 火水未濟 **8** 十六 9	金9 Metal · 7 Retreat 乙酉 Wood Rooster 天山遯 **9** 十七 4	水6 Water · 8 Mountain 丙戌 Fire Dog 艮為山 **10** 十八 1	木8 Wood · 9 Delight 丁亥 Fire Pig 雷地豫 **11** 十九 8	火7 Fire · 1 Beginning 戊子 Earth Rat 水雷屯 **12** 二十 4	金9 Metal · 2 Without Wrongdoing 己丑 Earth Ox 天雷無妄 **13** 廿一 2
木3 Wood · 3 Fire 庚寅 Metal Tiger 離為火 **14** 廿二 1	火2 Fire · 4 Sincerity 辛卯 Metal Rabbit 風澤中孚 **15** 廿三 3	水6 Water · 5 Big Livestock 壬辰 Water Dragon 山天大畜 **16** 廿四 4	金4 Metal · 6 Eliminating 癸巳 Water Snake 澤天夬 **17** 廿五 6	金9 Metal · 7 Heaven 甲午 Wood Horse 乾為天 **18** 廿六 1	火7 Fire · 8 Well 乙未 Wood Goat 水風井 **19** 廿七 6	木8 Wood · 9 Relief 丙申 Fire Monkey 雷水解 **20** 廿八 4
金4 Metal · 1/9 Influence 丁酉 Fire Rooster 澤山咸 **21** 廿九 9	水1 Water · 8 Humility 戊戌 Earth Dog 地山謙 **22** 三十 6	火2 Fire · 7 Observation 己亥 Earth Pig 風地觀 **23** 閏五月初一 2	火2 Fire · 6 Increasing 庚子 Metal Rat 風雷益 **24** 初二 9	水1 Water · 5 Dimming Light 辛丑 Metal Ox 地火明夷 **25** 初三 3	金9 Metal · 4 Fellowship 壬寅 Water Tiger 天火同人 **26** 初四 7	木8 Wood · 3 Marrying Maiden 癸卯 Water Rabbit 雷澤歸妹 **27** 初五 7
木3 Wood · 2 Opposition 甲辰 Wood Dragon 火澤睽 **28** 初六 2	火7 Fire · 1 Waiting 乙巳 Wood Snake 水天需 **29** 初七 3	金4 Metal · 9 Great Exceeding 丙午 Fire Horse 澤風大過 **30** 初八 3				

JULY 2009 辛未

Xuan Kong Element 玄空五行	天水訟 Litigation	Period Luck 卦運	Monthly Star 月星
Metal 金9		3	9

SUNDAY	MONDAY	TUESDAY	WEDNESDAY	THURSDAY	FRIDAY	SATURDAY
			水6 Water Poison 8 山風蠱 丁未 Fire Goat 7 1 初九	火2 Fire Dispersing 7 風水渙 戊申 Earth Monkey 6 2 初十	木3 Wood Travelling 6 火山旅 己酉 Earth Rooster 8 3 十一	金9 Metal Stagnation 5 天地否 庚戌 Metal Dog 9 4 十二
火7 Fire Alliance 4 水地比 辛亥 Metal Pig 7 5 十三	木8 Wood Thunder 3 震為雷 壬子 Water Rat 1 6 十四	水6 Water Beauty 2 山火賁 癸丑 Water Ox 8 7 十五	火7 Fire Accomplished 1 水火既濟 甲寅 Wood Tiger 9 8 十六	水1 Water Arriving 9 地澤臨 乙卯 Wood Rabbit 4 9 十七	金4 Metal Marsh 8 兌為澤 丙辰 Fire Dragon 1 10 十八	火2 Fire Small Livestock 7 風天小畜 丁巳 Fire Snake 8 11 十九
木3 Wood The Cauldron 6 火風鼎 戊午 Earth Horse 4 12 二十	水1 Water Rising 5 地風升 己未 Earth Goat 2 13 廿一	火7 Fire Water 4 坎為水 庚申 Metal Monkey 1 14 廿二	木8 Wood Lesser Exceeding 3 雷山小過 辛酉 Metal Rooster 3 15 廿三	金4 Metal Gathering 2 澤地萃 壬戌 Water Dog 4 16 廿四	水6 Water Peel 1 山地剝 癸亥 Water Pig 6 17 廿五	水1 Water Earth 9 坤為地 甲子 Wood Rat 1 18 廿六
木3 Wood Biting 8 火雷噬嗑 乙丑 Wood Ox 6 19 廿七	火2 Fire Family 7 風火家人 丙寅 Fire Tiger 4 20 廿八	水6 Water Decreasing 6 山澤損 丁卯 Fire Rabbit 9 21 廿九	金9 Metal Tread 5 天澤履 戊辰 Earth Dragon 6 22 六月初一	木8 Wood Great Strength 4 雷天大壯 己巳 Earth Snake 2 23 初二	木8 Wood Consistency 3 雷風恆 庚午 Metal Horse 9 24 初三	金9 Metal Litigation 2 天水訟 辛未 Metal Goat 3 25 初四
水1 Water Officer 1 地水師 壬申 Water Monkey 7 26 初五	火2 Fire Gradual Progress 9 風山漸 癸酉 Water Rooster 7 27 初六	火7 Fire Obstruction 8 水山蹇 甲戌 Wood Dog 2 28 初七	木3 Wood Advancement 7 火地晉 乙亥 Wood Pig 3 29 初八	水6 Water Nourish 6 山雷頤 丙子 Fire Rat 3 30 初九	金4 Metal Following 5 澤雷隨 丁丑 Fire Ox 7 31 初十	

AUGUST 2009 壬申

Xuan Kong Element 玄空五行	地水師 Officer	Period Luck 卦運	Monthly Star 月星
Water 水1		7	8

SUNDAY	MONDAY	TUESDAY	WEDNESDAY	THURSDAY	FRIDAY	SATURDAY
水6 Water Poison 2 山風蠱 丁未 Fire Goat 7 30 十一	火2 Fire Dispersing 1 風水渙 戊申 Earth Monkey 6 31 十二					木8 Wood Abundance 4 雷火豐 戊寅 Earth Tiger 6 1 十一
火7 Fire Regulate 3 水澤節 己卯 Earth Rabbit 8 2 十二	水1 Water Unity 2 地天泰 庚辰 Metal Dragon 9 3 十三	木3 Wood Great Reward 1 火天大有 辛巳 Metal Snake 7 4 十四	火2 Fire Wind 9 巽為風 壬午 Water Horse 1 5 十五	金4 Metal Trap 8 澤水困 癸未 Water Goat 8 6 十六	木3 Wood Not Yet Accomplished 7 火水未濟 甲申 Wood Monkey 9 7 十七	金9 Metal Retreat 6 天山遯 乙酉 Wood Rooster 4 8 十八
水6 Water Mountain 5 艮為山 丙戌 Fire Dog 1 9 十九	木8 Wood Delight 4 雷地豫 丁亥 Fire Pig 8 10 二十	火7 Fire Beginning 3 水雷屯 戊子 Earth Rat 4 11 廿一	金9 Metal Without Wrongdoing 2 天雷無妄 己丑 Earth Ox 2 12 廿二	木3 Wood Fire 1 離為火 庚寅 Metal Tiger 1 13 廿三	火2 Fire Sincerity 9 風澤中孚 辛卯 Metal Rabbit 3 14 廿四	水6 Water Big Livestock 8 山天大畜 壬辰 Water Dragon 4 15 廿五
金4 Metal Eliminating 7 澤天夬 癸巳 Water Snake 6 16 廿六	金9 Metal Heaven 6 乾為天 甲午 Wood Horse 1 17 廿七	火7 Fire Well 5 水風井 乙未 Wood Goat 6 18 廿八	木8 Wood Relief 4 雷水解 丙申 Fire Monkey 4 19 廿九	金4 Metal Influence 3 澤山咸 丁酉 Fire Rooster 9 20 七月初一	水1 Water Humility 2 地山謙 戊戌 Earth Dog 6 21 初二	火2 Fire Observation 1 風地觀 己亥 Earth Pig 2 22 初三
火2 Fire Increasing 9 風雷益 庚子 Metal Rat 9 23 初四	水1 Water Dimming Light 8 地火明夷 辛丑 Metal Ox 3 24 初五	金9 Metal Fellowship 7 天火同人 壬寅 Water Tiger 7 25 初六	木8 Wood Marrying Maiden 6 雷澤歸妹 癸卯 Water Rabbit 7 26 初七	木3 Wood Opposition 5 火澤睽 甲辰 Wood Dragon 2 27 初八	火7 Fire Waiting 4 水天需 乙巳 Wood Snake 3 28 初九	金4 Metal Great Exceeding 3 澤風大過 丙午 Fire Horse 3 29 初十

SEPTEMBER 2009 癸酉

Xuan Kong Element 玄空五行	風山漸 Gradual Progress	Period Luck 卦運	Monthly Star 月星
Fire 火2		7	7

SUNDAY	MONDAY	TUESDAY	WEDNESDAY	THURSDAY	FRIDAY	SATURDAY
		木3 Wood 9 Travelling 火山旅 己酉 Earth Rooster 8 1 十三	金9 Metal 8 Stagnation 天地否 庚戌 Metal Dog 9 2 十四	火7 Fire 7 Alliance 水地比 辛亥 Metal Pig 7 3 十五	木8 Wood 6 Thunder 震為雷 壬子 Water Rat 1 4 十六	水6 Water 5 Beauty 山火賁 癸丑 Water Ox 8 5 十七
火7 Fire 4 Accomplished 水火既濟 甲寅 Wood Tiger 9 6 十八	水1 Water 3 Arriving 地澤臨 乙卯 Wood Rabbit 4 7 十九	金4 Metal 2 Marsh 兌為澤 丙辰 Fire Dragon 1 8 二十	火2 Fire 1 Small Livestock 風天小畜 丁巳 Fire Snake 8 9 廿一	木3 Wood 9 The Cauldron 火風鼎 戊午 Earth Horse 4 10 廿二	水1 Water 8 Rising 地風升 己未 Earth Goat 2 11 廿三	火7 Fire 7 Water 坎為水 庚申 Metal Monkey 1 12 廿四
木8 Wood 6 Lesser Exceeding 雷山小過 辛酉 Metal Rooster 3 13 廿五	金4 Metal 5 Gathering 澤地萃 壬戌 Water Dog 4 14 廿六	水6 Water 4 Peel 山地剝 癸亥 Water Pig 6 15 廿七	水1 Water 3 Earth 坤為地 甲子 Wood Rat 1 16 廿八	木3 Wood 2 Biting 火雷噬嗑 乙丑 Wood Ox 6 17 廿九	火2 Fire 1 Family 風火家人 丙寅 Fire Tiger 4 18 三十	水6 Water 9 Decreasing 山澤損 丁卯 Fire Rabbit 9 19 八月初一
金9 Metal 8 Tread 天澤履 戊辰 Earth Dragon 6 20 初二	木8 Wood 7 Great Strength 雷天大壯 己巳 Earth Snake 2 21 初三	木8 Wood 6 Consistency 雷風恆 庚午 Metal Horse 9 22 初四	金9 Metal 5 Litigation 天水訟 辛未 Metal Goat 3 23 初五	水1 Water 4 Officer 地水師 壬申 Water Monkey 7 24 初六	火2 Fire 3 Gradual Progress 風山漸 癸酉 Water Rooster 7 25 初七	火7 Fire 2 Obstruction 水山蹇 甲戌 Wood Dog 2 26 初八
木3 Wood 1 Advancement 火地晉 乙亥 Wood Pig 3 27 初九	水6 Water 9 Nourish 山雷頤 丙子 Fire Rat 3 28 初十	金4 Metal 8 Following 澤雷隨 丁丑 Fire Ox 7 29 十一	木8 Wood 7 Abundance 雷火豐 戊寅 Earth Tiger 6 30 十二			

OCTOBER 2009 甲戌

Xuan Kong Element 玄空五行	水山蹇 Obstruction	Period Luck 卦運	Monthly Star 月星
Fire 火7		2	6

SUNDAY	MONDAY	TUESDAY	WEDNESDAY	THURSDAY	FRIDAY	SATURDAY
				火7 Fire 6 Regulate 水澤節 己卯 Earth Rabbit 8 1 十三	水1 Water 5 Unity 地天泰 庚辰 Metal Dragon 9 2 十四	木3 Wood 4 Great Reward 火天大有 辛巳 Metal Snake 7 3 十五
火2 Fire 3 Wind 巽為風 壬午 Water Horse 1 4 十六	金4 Metal 2 Trap 澤水困 癸未 Water Goat 8 5 十七	木3 Wood 1 Not Yet Accomplished 火水未濟 甲申 Wood Monkey 9 6 十八	金9 Metal 9 Retreat 天山遯 乙酉 Wood Rooster 4 7 十九	水6 Water 8 Mountain 艮為山 丙戌 Fire Dog 1 8 二十	木8 Wood 7 Delight 雷地豫 丁亥 Fire Pig 8 9 廿一	火7 Fire 6 Beginning 水雷屯 戊子 Earth Rat 4 10 廿二
金9 Metal 5 Without Wrongdoing 天雷無妄 己丑 Earth Ox 2 11 廿三	木3 Wood 4 Fire 離為火 庚寅 Metal Tiger 1 12 廿四	火2 Fire 3 Sincerity 風澤中孚 辛卯 Metal Rabbit 3 13 廿五	水6 Water 2 Big Livestock 山天大畜 壬辰 Water Dragon 4 14 廿六	金4 Metal 1 Eliminating 澤天夬 癸巳 Water Snake 6 15 廿七	金9 Metal 9 Heaven 乾為天 甲午 Wood Horse 1 16 廿八	火7 Fire 8 Well 水風井 乙未 Wood Goat 6 17 廿九
木8 Wood 7 Relief 雷水解 丙申 Fire Monkey 4 18 九月初一	金4 Metal 6 Influence 澤山咸 丁酉 Fire Rooster 9 19 初二	水1 Water 5 Humility 地山謙 戊戌 Earth Dog 6 20 初三	火2 Fire 4 Observation 風地觀 己亥 Earth Pig 2 21 初四	火2 Fire 3 Increasing 風雷益 庚子 Metal Rat 9 22 初五	水1 Water 2 Dimming Light 地火明夷 辛丑 Metal Ox 3 23 初六	金9 Metal 1 Fellowship 天火同人 壬寅 Water Tiger 7 24 初七
木8 Wood 9 Marrying Maiden 雷澤歸妹 癸卯 Water Rabbit 7 25 初八	木3 Wood 8 Opposition 火澤睽 甲辰 Wood Dragon 2 26 初九	火7 Fire 7 Waiting 水天需 乙巳 Wood Snake 3 27 初十	金4 Metal 6 Great Exceeding 澤風大過 丙午 Fire Horse 3 28 十一	水6 Water 5 Poison 山風蠱 丁未 Fire Goat 7 29 十二	火2 Fire 4 Dispersing 風水渙 戊申 Earth Monkey 6 30 十三	木3 Wood 3 Travelling 火山旅 己酉 Earth Rooster 8 31 十四

NOVEMBER 2009 乙亥

Xuan Kong Element 玄空五行	火地晉 Advancement	Period Luck 卦運	Monthly Star 月星
Wood 木3		3	5

SUNDAY	MONDAY	TUESDAY	WEDNESDAY	THURSDAY	FRIDAY	SATURDAY
1 十五 金9 Metal · 2 Stagnation 天地否 庚戌 Metal Dog 9	**2** 十六 火7 Fire · 1 Alliance 水地比 辛亥 Metal Pig 7	**3** 十七 木8 Wood · 9 Thunder 震爲雷 壬子 Water Rat 1	**4** 十八 水6 Water · 8 Beauty 山火賁 癸丑 Water Ox 8	**5** 十九 火7 Fire · 7 Accomplished 水火既濟 甲寅 Wood Tiger 9	**6** 二十 水1 Water · 6 Arriving 地澤臨 乙卯 Wood Rabbit 4	**7** 廿一 金4 Metal · 5 Marsh 兑爲澤 丙辰 Fire Dragon 1
8 廿二 火2 Fire · 4 Small Livestock 風天小畜 丁巳 Fire Snake 8	**9** 廿三 木3 Wood · 3 The Cauldron 火風鼎 戊午 Earth Horse 4	**10** 廿四 水1 Water · 2 Rising 地風升 己未 Earth Goat 2	**11** 廿五 火7 Fire · 1 Water 坎爲水 庚申 Metal Monkey 1	**12** 廿六 木8 Wood · 9 Lesser Exceeding 雷山小過 辛酉 Metal Rooster 3	**13** 廿七 金4 Metal · 8 Gathering 澤地萃 壬戌 Water Dog 4	**14** 廿八 水6 Water · 7 Peel 山地剝 癸亥 Water Pig 6
15 廿九 水1 Water · 6 Earth 坤爲地 甲子 Wood Rat 1	**16** 三十 木3 Wood · 5 Biting 火雷噬嗑 乙丑 Wood Ox 6	**17** 十月初一 火2 Fire · 4 Family 風火家人 丙寅 Fire Tiger 4	**18** 初二 水6 Water · 3 Decreasing 山澤損 丁卯 Fire Rabbit 9	**19** 初三 金9 Metal · 2 Tread 天澤履 戊辰 Earth Dragon 6	**20** 初四 木8 Wood · 1 Great Strength 雷天大壯 己巳 Earth Snake 2	**21** 初五 木8 Wood · 9 Consistency 雷風恆 庚午 Metal Horse 9
22 初六 金9 Metal · 8 Litigation 天水訟 辛未 Metal Goat 3	**23** 初七 水1 Water · 7 Officer 地水師 壬申 Water Monkey 7	**24** 初八 火2 Fire · 6 Gradual Progress 風山漸 癸酉 Water Rooster 7	**25** 初九 火7 Fire · 5 Obstruction 水山蹇 甲戌 Wood Dog 2	**26** 初十 木3 Wood · 4 Advancement 火地晉 乙亥 Wood Pig 3	**27** 十一 水6 Water · 3 Nourish 山雷頤 丙子 Fire Rat 3	**28** 十二 金4 Metal · 2 Following 澤雷隨 丁丑 Fire Ox 7
29 十三 木8 Wood · 1 Abundance 雷火豐 戊寅 Earth Tiger 6	**30** 十四 火7 Fire · 9 Regulate 水澤節 己卯 Earth Rabbit 8					

DECEMBER 2009 丙子

Xuan Kong Element 玄空五行	山雷頤 Nourish	Period Luck 卦運	Monthly Star 月星
Water 水6		3	4

SUNDAY	MONDAY	TUESDAY	WEDNESDAY	THURSDAY	FRIDAY	SATURDAY
		1 十五 水1 Water · 8 Unity 地天泰 庚辰 Metal Dragon 9	**2** 十六 木3 Wood · 7 Great Reward 火天大有 辛巳 Metal Snake 7	**3** 十七 火2 Fire · 6 Wind 巽爲風 壬午 Water Horse 1	**4** 十八 金4 Metal · 5 Trap 澤水困 癸未 Water Goat 8	**5** 十九 木3 Wood · 4 Not Yet Accomplished 火水未濟 甲申 Wood Monkey 9
6 二十 金9 Metal · 3 Retreat 天山遯 乙酉 Wood Rooster 4	**7** 廿一 水6 Water · 2 Mountain 艮爲山 丙戌 Fire Dog 1	**8** 廿二 木8 Wood · 1 Delight 雷地豫 丁亥 Fire Pig 8	**9** 廿三 火7 Fire · 9 Beginning 水雷屯 戊子 Earth Rat 4	**10** 廿四 金9 Metal · 8 Without Wrongdoing 天雷無妄 己丑 Earth Ox 2	**11** 廿五 木3 Wood · 7 Fire 離爲火 庚寅 Metal Tiger 1	**12** 廿六 火2 Fire · 6 Sincerity 風澤中孚 辛卯 Metal Rabbit 3
13 廿七 水6 Water · 5 Big Livestock 山天大畜 壬辰 Water Dragon 4	**14** 廿八 金4 Metal · 4 Eliminating 澤天夬 癸巳 Water Snake 6	**15** 廿九 金9 Metal · 3 Heaven 乾爲天 甲午 Wood Horse 1	**16** 十一月初一 火7 Fire · 2 Well 水風井 乙未 Wood Goat 6	**17** 初二 木8 Wood · 1 Relief 雷水解 丙申 Fire Monkey 4	**18** 初三 金4 Metal · 9 Influence 澤山咸 丁酉 Fire Rooster 9	**19** 初四 水1 Water · 8 Humility 地山謙 戊戌 Earth Dog 6
20 初五 火2 Fire · 7 Observation 風地觀 己亥 Earth Pig 2	**21** 初六 火2 Fire · 6 Increasing 風雷益 庚子 Metal Rat 9	**22** 初七 水1 Water · 5/5 Dimming Light 地火明夷 辛丑 Metal Ox 3	**23** 初八 金9 Metal · 6 Fellowship 天火同人 壬寅 Water Tiger 7	**24** 初九 木8 Wood · 7 Marrying Maiden 雷澤歸妹 癸卯 Water Rabbit 7	**25** 初十 木3 Wood · 8 Opposition 火澤睽 甲辰 Wood Dragon 2	**26** 十一 火7 Fire · 9 Waiting 水天需 乙巳 Wood Snake 3
27 十二 金4 Metal · 1 Great Exceeding 澤風大過 丙午 Fire Horse 3	**28** 十三 水6 Water · 2 Poison 山風蠱 丁未 Fire Goat 7	**29** 十四 火2 Fire · 3 Dispersing 風水渙 戊申 Earth Monkey 6	**30** 十五 木3 Wood · 4 Travelling 火山旅 己酉 Earth Rooster 8	**31** 十六 金9 Metal · 5 Stagnation 天地否 庚戌 Metal Dog 9		

2010 庚寅

(*Geng Yin*) Metal Tiger

2010 庚寅 *(Geng Yin)* Metal Tiger

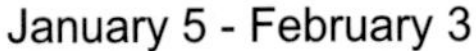

January 5 - February 3

金4 Metal
丁丑 Fire Ox
7 Following
澤雷隨

SE	S	SW
2	7	9
1	**3**	5
6	8	4

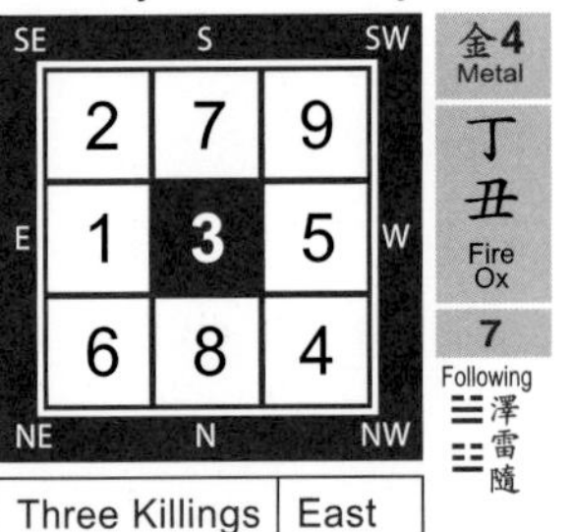

February 4 - March 5

木8 Wood
戊寅 Earth Tiger
6 Abundance
雷火豐

SE	S	SW
1	6	8
9	**2**	4
5	7	3

March 6 - April 4

火7 Fire
己卯 Earth Rabbit
8 Regulate
水澤節

SE	S	SW
9	5	7
8	**1**	3
4	6	2

April 5 - May 4

水1 Water
庚辰 Metal Dragon
9 Unity
地天泰

SE	S	SW
8	4	6
7	**9**	2
3	5	1

May 5 - June 5

木3 Wood
辛巳 Metal Snake
7 Great Reward
火天大有

SE	S	SW
7	3	5
6	**8**	1
2	4	9

June 6 - July 6

火2 Fire
壬午 Water Horse
1 Wind
巽爲風

SE	S	SW
6	2	4
5	**7**	9
1	3	8

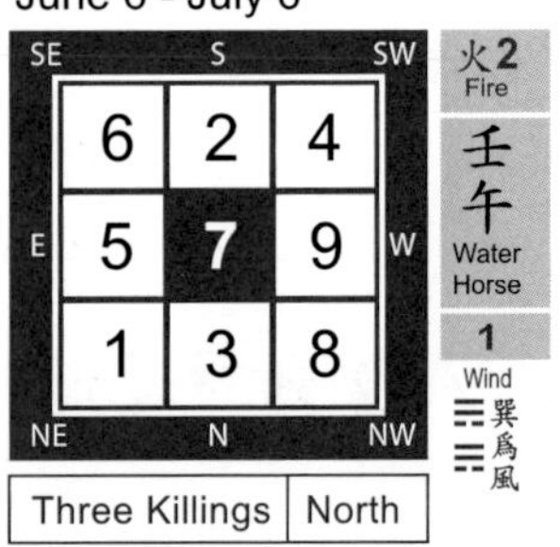

July 7 - August 6

金4 Metal
癸未 Water Goat
8 Trap
澤水困

SE	S	SW
5	1	3
4	**6**	8
9	2	7

August 7 - September 7

木3 Wood
甲申 Wood Monkey
9 Not Yet Accomplished
火水未濟

SE	S	SW
4	9	2
3	**5**	7
8	1	6

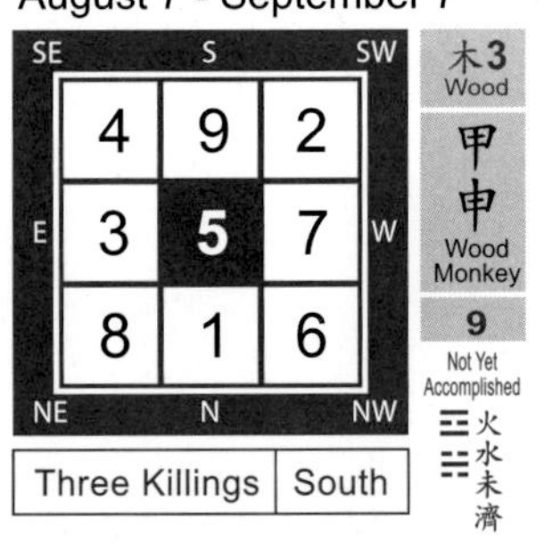

September 8 - October 7

金9 Metal
乙酉 Wood Rooster
4 Retreat
天山遯

SE	S	SW
3	8	1
2	**4**	6
7	9	5

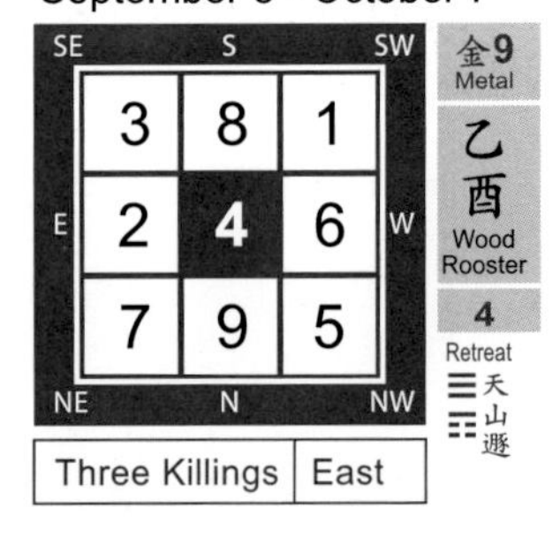

October 8 - November 6

水6 Water
丙戌 Fire Dog
1 Mountain
艮爲山

SE	S	SW
2	7	9
1	**3**	5
6	8	4

November 7 - December 6

木8 Wood
丁亥 Fire Pig
8 Delight
雷地豫

SE	S	SW
1	6	8
9	**2**	4
5	7	3

December 7 - January 5

火7 Fire
戊子 Earth Rat
4 Beginning
水雷屯

SE	S	SW
9	5	7
8	**1**	3
4	6	2

JANUARY 2010 丁丑

Xuan Kong Element 玄空五行	澤雷隨 Following	Period Luck 卦運	Monthly Star 月星
Metal 金4		7	3

SUNDAY	MONDAY	TUESDAY	WEDNESDAY	THURSDAY	FRIDAY	SATURDAY
木3 Wood 9 Great Reward 火天大有 辛巳 Metal Snake 7 31 十七					火7 Fire 6 Alliance 水地比 辛亥 Metal Pig 7 1 十七	木8 Wood 7 Thunder 震爲雷 壬子 Water Rat 1 2 十八
水6 Water 8 Beauty 山火賁 癸丑 Water Ox 8 3 十九	火7 Fire 9 Accomplished 水火既濟 甲寅 Wood Tiger 9 4 二十	水1 Water 1 Arriving 地澤臨 乙卯 Wood Rabbit 4 5 廿一	金4 Metal 2 Marsh 兌爲澤 丙辰 Fire Dragon 1 6 廿二	火2 Fire 3 Small Livestock 風天小畜 丁巳 Fire Snake 8 7 廿三	木3 Wood 4 The Cauldron 火風鼎 戊午 Earth Horse 4 8 廿四	水1 Water 5 Rising 地風升 己未 Earth Goat 2 9 廿五
火7 Fire 6 Water 坎爲水 庚申 Metal Monkey 1 10 廿六	木8 Wood 7 Lesser Exceeding 雷山小過 辛酉 Metal Rooster 3 11 廿七	金4 Metal 8 Gathering 澤地萃 壬戌 Water Dog 4 12 廿八	水6 Water 9 Peel 山地剝 癸亥 Water Pig 6 13 廿九	水1 Water 1 Earth 坤爲地 甲子 Wood Rat 1 14 三十	木3 Wood 2 Biting 火雷噬嗑 乙丑 Wood Ox 6 15 十二月初一	火2 Fire 3 Family 風火家人 丙寅 Fire Tiger 4 16 初二
水6 Water 4 Decreasing 山澤損 丁卯 Fire Rabbit 9 17 初三	金9 Metal 5 Tread 天澤履 戊辰 Earth Dragon 6 18 初四	木8 Wood 6 Great Strength 雷天大壯 己巳 Earth Snake 2 19 初五	木8 Wood 7 Consistency 雷風恆 庚午 Metal Horse 9 20 初六	金9 Metal 8 Litigation 天水訟 辛未 Metal Goat 3 21 初七	水1 Water 9 Officer 地水師 壬申 Water Monkey 7 22 初八	火2 Fire 1 Gradual Progress 風山漸 癸酉 Water Rooster 7 23 初九
火7 Fire 2 Obstruction 水山蹇 甲戌 Wood Dog 2 24 初十	木3 Wood 3 Advancement 火地晉 乙亥 Wood Pig 3 25 十一	水6 Water 4 Nourish 山雷頤 丙子 Fire Rat 3 26 十二	金4 Metal 5 Following 澤雷隨 丁丑 Fire Ox 7 27 十三	木8 Wood 6 Abundance 雷火豐 戊寅 Earth Tiger 6 28 十四	火7 Fire 7 Regulate 水澤節 己卯 Earth Rabbit 8 29 十五	水1 Water 8 Unity 地天泰 庚辰 Metal Dragon 9 30 十六

FEBRUARY 2010 戊寅

Xuan Kong Element 玄空五行	雷火豐 Abundance	Period Luck 卦運	Monthly Star 月星
Wood 木8		6	2

SUNDAY	MONDAY	TUESDAY	WEDNESDAY	THURSDAY	FRIDAY	SATURDAY
	火2 Fire 1 Wind 巽爲風 壬午 Water Horse 1 1 十八	金4 Metal 2 Trap 澤水困 癸未 Water Goat 8 2 十九	木3 Wood 3 Not Yet Accomplished 火水未濟 甲申 Wood Monkey 9 3 二十	金9 Metal 4 Retreat 天山遯 乙酉 Wood Rooster 4 4 廿一	水6 Water 5 Mountain 艮爲山 丙戌 Fire Dog 1 5 廿二	木8 Wood 6 Delight 雷地豫 丁亥 Fire Pig 8 6 廿三
火7 Fire 7 Beginning 水雷屯 戊子 Earth Rat 4 7 廿四	金9 Metal 8 Without Wrongdoing 天雷無妄 己丑 Earth Ox 2 8 廿五	木3 Wood 9 Fire 離爲火 庚寅 Metal Tiger 1 9 廿六	火2 Fire 1 Sincerity 風澤中孚 辛卯 Metal Rabbit 3 10 廿七	水6 Water 2 Big Livestock 山天大畜 壬辰 Water Dragon 4 11 廿八	金4 Metal 3 Eliminating 澤天夬 癸巳 Water Snake 6 12 廿九	金9 Metal 4 Heaven 乾爲天 甲午 Wood Horse 1 13 三十
火7 Fire 5 Well 水風井 乙未 Wood Goat 6 14 正月初一	木8 Wood 6 Relief 雷水解 丙申 Fire Monkey 4 15 初二	金4 Metal 7 Influence 澤山咸 丁酉 Fire Rooster 9 16 初三	水1 Water 8 Humility 地山謙 戊戌 Earth Dog 6 17 初四	火2 Fire 9 Observation 風地觀 己亥 Earth Pig 2 18 初五	火2 Fire 1 Increasing 風雷益 庚子 Metal Rat 9 19 初六	水1 Water 2 Dimming Light 地火明夷 辛丑 Metal Ox 3 20 初七
金9 Metal 3 Fellowship 天火同人 壬寅 Water Tiger 7 21 初八	木8 Wood 4 Marrying Maiden 雷澤歸妹 癸卯 Water Rabbit 7 22 初九	木3 Wood 5 Opposition 火澤睽 甲辰 Wood Dragon 2 23 初十	火7 Fire 6 Waiting 水天需 乙巳 Wood Snake 3 24 十一	金4 Metal 7 Great Exceeding 澤風大過 丙午 Fire Horse 3 25 十二	水6 Water 8 Poison 山風蠱 丁未 Fire Goat 7 26 十三	火2 Fire 9 Dispersing 風水渙 戊申 Earth Monkey 6 27 十四
木3 Wood 1 Travelling 火山旅 己酉 Earth Rooster 8 28 十五						

MARCH 2010 己卯

Xuan Kong Element 玄空五行	水澤節 Regulate	Period Luck 卦運	Monthly Star 月星
Fire 火7		8	1

SUNDAY	MONDAY	TUESDAY	WEDNESDAY	THURSDAY	FRIDAY	SATURDAY
	金9 Metal · 2 Stagnation 天地否 庚戌 Metal Dog **1** 十六 9	火7 Fire · 3 Alliance 水地比 辛亥 Metal Pig **2** 十七 7	木8 Wood · 4 Thunder 震爲雷 壬子 Water Rat **3** 十八 1	水6 Water · 5 Beauty 山火賁 癸丑 Water Ox **4** 十九 8	火7 Fire · 6 Accomplished 水火既濟 甲寅 Wood Tiger **5** 二十 9	水1 Water · 7 Arriving 地澤臨 乙卯 Wood Rabbit **6** 廿一 4
金4 Metal · 8 Marsh 兑爲澤 丙辰 Fire Dragon **7** 廿二 1	火2 Fire · 9 Small Livestock 風天小畜 丁巳 Fire Snake **8** 廿三 8	木3 Wood · 1 The Cauldron 火風鼎 戊午 Earth Horse **9** 廿四 4	水1 Water · 2 Rising 地風升 己未 Earth Goat **10** 廿五 2	火7 Fire · 3 Water 坎爲水 庚申 Metal Monkey **11** 廿六 1	木8 Wood · 4 Lesser Exceeding 雷山小過 辛酉 Metal Rooster **12** 廿七 3	金4 Metal · 5 Gathering 澤地萃 壬戌 Water Dog **13** 廿八 4
水6 Water · 6 Peel 山地剝 癸亥 Water Pig **14** 廿九 6	水1 Water · 7 Earth 坤爲地 甲子 Wood Rat **15** 三十 1	木3 Wood · 8 Biting 火雷噬嗑 乙丑 Wood Ox **16** 二月初一 6	火2 Fire · 9 Family 風火家人 丙寅 Fire Tiger **17** 初二 4	水6 Water · 1 Decreasing 山澤損 丁卯 Fire Rabbit **18** 初三 9	金9 Metal · 2 Tread 天澤履 戊辰 Earth Dragon **19** 初四 6	木8 Wood · 3 Great Strength 雷天大壯 己巳 Earth Snake **20** 初五 2
木8 Wood · 4 Consistency 雷風恆 庚午 Metal Horse **21** 初六 9	金9 Metal · 5 Litigation 天水訟 辛未 Metal Goat **22** 初七 3	水1 Water · 6 Officer 地水師 壬申 Water Monkey **23** 初八 7	火2 Fire · 7 Gradual Progress 風山漸 癸酉 Water Rooster **24** 初九 7	火7 Fire · 8 Obstruction 水山蹇 甲戌 Wood Dog **25** 初十 2	木3 Wood · 9 Advancement 火地晉 乙亥 Wood Pig **26** 十一 3	水6 Water · 1 Nourish 山雷頤 丙子 Fire Rat **27** 十二 3
金4 Metal · 2 Following 澤雷隨 丁丑 Fire Ox **28** 十三 7	木8 Wood · 3 Abundance 雷火豐 戊寅 Earth Tiger **29** 十四 6	火7 Fire · 4 Regulate 水澤節 己卯 Earth Rabbit **30** 十五 8	水1 Water · 5 Unity 地天泰 庚辰 Metal Dragon **31** 十六 9			

APRIL 2010 庚辰

Xuan Kong Element 玄空五行	地天泰 Unity	Period Luck 卦運	Monthly Star 月星
Water 水1		9	9

SUNDAY	MONDAY	TUESDAY	WEDNESDAY	THURSDAY	FRIDAY	SATURDAY
				木3 Wood · 6 Great Reward 火天大有 辛巳 Metal Snake **1** 十七 7	火2 Fire · 7 Wind 巽爲風 壬午 Water Horse **2** 十八 1	金4 Metal · 8 Trap 澤水困 癸未 Water Goat **3** 十九 8
木3 Wood · 9 Not Yet Accomplished 火水未濟 甲申 Wood Monkey **4** 二十 9	金9 Metal · 1 Retreat 天山遯 乙酉 Wood Rooster **5** 廿一 4	水6 Water · 2 Mountain 艮爲山 丙戌 Fire Dog **6** 廿二 1	木8 Wood · 3 Delight 雷地豫 丁亥 Fire Pig **7** 廿三 8	火7 Fire · 4 Beginning 水雷屯 戊子 Earth Rat **8** 廿四 4	金9 Metal · 5 Without Wrongdoing 天雷無妄 己丑 Earth Ox **9** 廿五 2	木3 Wood · 6 Fire 離爲火 庚寅 Metal Tiger **10** 廿六 1
火2 Fire · 7 Sincerity 風澤中孚 辛卯 Metal Rabbit **11** 廿七 3	水6 Water · 8 Big Livestock 山天大畜 壬辰 Water Dragon **12** 廿八 4	金4 Metal · 9 Eliminating 澤天夬 癸巳 Water Snake **13** 廿九 6	金9 Metal · 1 Heaven 乾爲天 甲午 Wood Horse **14** 三月初一 1	火7 Fire · 2 Well 水風井 乙未 Wood Goat **15** 初二 6	木8 Wood · 3 Relief 雷水解 丙申 Fire Monkey **16** 初三 4	金4 Metal · 4 Influence 澤山咸 丁酉 Fire Rooster **17** 初四 9
水1 Water · 5 Humility 地山謙 戊戌 Earth Dog **18** 初五 6	火2 Fire · 6 Observation 風地觀 己亥 Earth Pig **19** 初六 2	火2 Fire · 7 Increasing 風雷益 庚子 Metal Rat **20** 初七 9	水1 Water · 8 Dimming Light 地火明夷 辛丑 Metal Ox **21** 初八 3	金9 Metal · 9 Fellowship 天火同人 壬寅 Water Tiger **22** 初九 7	木8 Wood · 1 Marrying Maiden 雷澤歸妹 癸卯 Water Rabbit **23** 初十 7	木3 Wood · 2 Opposition 火澤睽 甲辰 Wood Dragon **24** 十一 2
火7 Fire · 3 Waiting 水天需 乙巳 Wood Snake **25** 十二 3	金4 Metal · 4 Great Exceeding 澤風大過 丙午 Fire Horse **26** 十三 3	水6 Water · 5 Poison 山風蠱 丁未 Fire Goat **27** 十四 7	火2 Fire · 6 Dispersing 風水渙 戊申 Earth Monkey **28** 十五 6	木3 Wood · 7 Travelling 火山旅 己酉 Earth Rooster **29** 十六 8	金9 Metal · 8 Stagnation 天地否 庚戌 Metal Dog **30** 十七 9	

MAY 2010 辛巳

Xuan Kong Element 玄空五行	火天大有 Great Reward	Period Luck 卦運	Monthly Star 月星
Wood 木3		7	8

SUNDAY	MONDAY	TUESDAY	WEDNESDAY	THURSDAY	FRIDAY	SATURDAY
水1 Water Unity 2 庚辰 Metal Dragon 地天泰 30 十七 9	木3 Wood Great Reward 3 辛巳 Metal Snake 火天大有 31 十八 7					火7 Fire Alliance 9 辛亥 Metal Pig 水地比 1 十八 7
木8 Wood Thunder 1 壬子 Water Rat 震爲雷 2 十九 1	水6 Water Beauty 2 癸丑 Water Ox 山火賁 3 二十 8	火7 Fire Accomplished 3 甲寅 Wood Tiger 水火既濟 4 廿一 9	水1 Water Arriving 4 乙卯 Wood Rabbit 地澤臨 5 廿二 4	金4 Metal Marsh 5 丙辰 Fire Dragon 兑爲澤 6 廿三 1	火2 Fire Small Livestock 6 丁巳 Fire Snake 風天小畜 7 廿四 8	木3 Wood The Cauldron 7 戊午 Earth Horse 火風鼎 8 廿五 4
水1 Water Rising 8 己未 Earth Goat 地風升 9 廿六 2	火7 Fire Water 9 庚申 Metal Monkey 坎爲水 10 廿七 1	木8 Wood Lesser Exceeding 1 辛酉 Metal Rooster 雷山小過 11 廿八 3	金4 Metal Gathering 2 壬戌 Water Dog 澤地萃 12 廿九 4	水6 Water Peel 3 癸亥 Water Pig 山地剝 13 三十 6	水1 Water Earth 4 甲子 Wood Rat 坤爲地 14 四月初一 1	木3 Wood Biting 5 乙丑 Wood Ox 火雷噬嗑 15 初二 6
火2 Fire Family 6 丙寅 Fire Tiger 風火家人 16 初三 4	水6 Water Decreasing 7 丁卯 Fire Rabbit 山澤損 17 初四 9	金9 Metal Tread 8 戊辰 Earth Dragon 天澤履 18 初五 6	木8 Wood Great Strength 9 己巳 Earth Snake 雷天大壯 19 初六 2	木8 Wood Consistency 1 庚午 Metal Horse 雷風恆 20 初七 9	金9 Metal Litigation 2 辛未 Metal Goat 天水訟 21 初八 3	水1 Water Officer 3 壬申 Water Monkey 地水師 22 初九 7
火2 Fire Gradual Progress 4 癸酉 Water Rooster 風山漸 23 初十 7	火7 Fire Obstruction 5 甲戌 Wood Dog 水山蹇 24 十一 2	木3 Wood Advancement 6 乙亥 Wood Pig 火地晉 25 十二 3	水6 Water Nourish 7 丙子 Fire Rat 山雷頤 26 十三 3	金4 Metal Following 8 丁丑 Fire Ox 澤雷隨 27 十四 7	木8 Wood Abundance 9 戊寅 Earth Tiger 雷火豐 28 十五 6	火7 Fire Regulate 1 己卯 Earth Rabbit 水澤節 29 十六 8

JUNE 2010 壬午

Xuan Kong Element 玄空五行	巽爲風 Wind	Period Luck 卦運	Monthly Star 月星
Fire 火2		1	7

SUNDAY	MONDAY	TUESDAY	WEDNESDAY	THURSDAY	FRIDAY	SATURDAY
		火2 Fire Wind 4 壬午 Water Horse 巽爲風 1 十九 1	金4 Metal Trap 5 癸未 Water Goat 澤水困 2 二十 8	木3 Wood Not Yet Accomplished 6 甲申 Wood Monkey 火水未濟 3 廿一 9	金9 Metal Retreat 7 乙酉 Wood Rooster 天山遯 4 廿二 4	水6 Water Mountain 8 丙戌 Fire Dog 艮爲山 5 廿三 1
木8 Wood Delight 9 丁亥 Fire Pig 雷地豫 6 廿四 8	火7 Fire Beginning 1 戊子 Earth Rat 水雷屯 7 廿五 4	金9 Metal Without Wrongdoing 2 己丑 Earth Ox 天雷無妄 8 廿六 2	木3 Wood Fire 3 庚寅 Metal Tiger 離爲火 9 廿七 1	火2 Fire Sincerity 4 辛卯 Metal Rabbit 風澤中孚 10 廿八 3	水6 Water Big Livestock 5 壬辰 Water Dragon 山天大畜 11 廿九 4	金4 Metal Eliminating 6 癸巳 Water Snake 澤天夬 12 五月初一 6
金9 Metal Heaven 7 甲午 Wood Horse 乾爲天 13 初二 1	火7 Fire Well 8 乙未 Wood Goat 水風井 14 初三 6	木8 Wood Relief 9 丙申 Fire Monkey 雷水解 15 初四 4	金4 Metal Influence 1 丁酉 Fire Rooster 澤山咸 16 初五 9	水1 Water Humility 2 戊戌 Earth Dog 地山謙 17 初六 6	火2 Fire Observation 3 己亥 Earth Pig 風地觀 18 初七 2	火2 Fire Increasing 4 庚子 Metal Rat 風雷益 19 初八 9
水1 Water Dimming Light 5 辛丑 Metal Ox 地火明夷 20 初九 3	金9 Metal Fellowship 6/4 壬寅 Water Tiger 天火同人 21 初十 7	木8 Wood Marrying Maiden 3 癸卯 Water Rabbit 雷澤歸妹 22 十一 7	木3 Wood Opposition 2 甲辰 Wood Dragon 火澤睽 23 十二 2	火7 Fire Waiting 1 乙巳 Wood Snake 水天需 24 十三 3	金4 Metal Great Exceeding 9 丙午 Fire Horse 澤風大過 25 十四 3	水6 Water Poison 8 丁未 Fire Goat 山風蠱 26 十五 7
火2 Fire Dispersing 7 戊申 Earth Monkey 風水渙 27 十六 6	木3 Wood Travelling 6 己酉 Earth Rooster 火山旅 28 十七 8	金9 Metal Stagnation 5 庚戌 Metal Dog 天地否 29 十八 9	火7 Fire Alliance 4 辛亥 Metal Pig 水地比 30 十九 7			

JULY 2010 癸未

Xuan Kong Element 玄空五行	澤水困 Trap	Period Luck 卦運	Monthly Star 月星
Metal 金4		8	6

SUNDAY	MONDAY	TUESDAY	WEDNESDAY	THURSDAY	FRIDAY	SATURDAY
				1 二十 木8 Wood · 3 Thunder 震爲雷 壬子 Water Rat 1	**2** 廿一 水6 Water · 2 Beauty 山火賁 癸丑 Water Ox 8	**3** 廿二 火7 Fire · 1 Accomplished 水火既濟 甲寅 Wood Tiger 9
4 廿三 水1 Water · 9 Arriving 地澤臨 乙卯 Wood Rabbit 4	**5** 廿四 金4 Metal · 8 Marsh 兌爲澤 丙辰 Fire Dragon 1	**6** 廿五 火2 Fire · 7 Small Livestock 風天小畜 丁巳 Fire Snake 8	**7** 廿六 木3 Wood · 6 The Cauldron 火風鼎 戊午 Earth Horse 4	**8** 廿七 水1 Water · 5 Rising 地風升 己未 Earth Goat 2	**9** 廿八 火7 Fire · 4 Water 坎爲水 庚申 Metal Monkey 1	**10** 廿九 木8 Wood · 3 Lesser Exceeding 雷山小過 辛酉 Metal Rooster 3
11 三十 金4 Metal · 2 Gathering 澤地萃 壬戌 Water Dog 4	**12** 六月初一 水6 Water · 1 Peel 山地剝 癸亥 Water Pig 6	**13** 初二 水1 Water · 9 Earth 坤爲地 甲子 Wood Rat 1	**14** 初三 木3 Wood · 8 Biting 火雷噬嗑 乙丑 Wood Ox 6	**15** 初四 火2 Fire · 7 Family 風火家人 丙寅 Fire Tiger 4	**16** 初五 水6 Water · 6 Decreasing 山澤損 丁卯 Fire Rabbit 9	**17** 初六 金9 Metal · 5 Tread 天澤履 戊辰 Earth Dragon 6
18 初七 木8 Wood · 4 Great Strength 雷天大壯 己巳 Earth Snake 2	**19** 初八 木8 Wood · 3 Consistency 雷風恆 庚午 Metal Horse 9	**20** 初九 金9 Metal · 2 Litigation 天水訟 辛未 Metal Goat 3	**21** 初十 水1 Water · 1 Officer 地水師 壬申 Water Monkey 7	**22** 十一 火2 Fire · 9 Gradual Progress 風山漸 癸酉 Water Rooster 7	**23** 十二 火7 Fire · 8 Obstruction 水山蹇 甲戌 Wood Dog 2	**24** 十三 木3 Wood · 7 Advancement 火地晉 乙亥 Wood Pig 3
25 十四 水6 Water · 6 Nourish 山雷頤 丙子 Fire Rat 3	**26** 十五 金4 Metal · 5 Following 澤雷隨 丁丑 Fire Ox 7	**27** 十六 木8 Wood · 4 Abundance 雷火豐 戊寅 Earth Tiger 6	**28** 十七 火7 Fire · 3 Regulate 水澤節 己卯 Earth Rabbit 8	**29** 十八 水1 Water · 2 Unity 地天泰 庚辰 Metal Dragon 9	**30** 十九 木3 Wood · 1 Great Reward 火天大有 辛巳 Metal Snake 7	**31** 二十 火2 Fire · 9 Wind 巽爲風 壬午 Water Horse 1

AUGUST 2010 甲申

Xuan Kong Element 玄空五行	火水未濟 Not Yet Accomplished	Period Luck 卦運	Monthly Star 月星
Wood 木3		9	5

SUNDAY	MONDAY	TUESDAY	WEDNESDAY	THURSDAY	FRIDAY	SATURDAY
1 廿一 金4 Metal · 8 Trap 澤水困 癸未 Water Goat 8	**2** 廿二 木3 Wood · 7 Not Yet Accomplished 火水未濟 甲申 Wood Monkey 9	**3** 廿三 金9 Metal · 6 Retreat 天山遯 乙酉 Wood Rooster 4	**4** 廿四 水6 Water · 5 Mountain 艮爲山 丙戌 Fire Dog 1	**5** 廿五 木8 Wood · 4 Delight 雷地豫 丁亥 Fire Pig 8	**6** 廿六 火7 Fire · 3 Beginning 水雷屯 戊子 Earth Rat 4	**7** 廿七 金9 Metal · 2 Without Wrongdoing 天雷無妄 己丑 Earth Ox 2
8 廿八 木3 Wood · 1 Fire 離爲火 庚寅 Metal Tiger 1	**9** 廿九 火2 Fire · 9 Sincerity 風澤中孚 辛卯 Metal Rabbit 3	**10** 七月初一 水6 Water · 8 Big Livestock 山天大畜 壬辰 Water Dragon 4	**11** 初二 金4 Metal · 7 Eliminating 澤天夬 癸巳 Water Snake 6	**12** 初三 金9 Metal · 6 Heaven 乾爲天 甲午 Wood Horse 1	**13** 初四 火7 Fire · 5 Well 水風井 乙未 Wood Goat 6	**14** 初五 木8 Wood · 4 Relief 雷水解 丙申 Fire Monkey 4
15 初六 金4 Metal · 3 Influence 澤山咸 丁酉 Fire Rooster 9	**16** 初七 水1 Water · 2 Humility 地山謙 戊戌 Earth Dog 6	**17** 初八 火2 Fire · 1 Observation 風地觀 己亥 Earth Pig 2	**18** 初九 火2 Fire · 9 Increasing 風雷益 庚子 Metal Rat 9	**19** 初十 水1 Water · 8 Dimming Light 地火明夷 辛丑 Metal Ox 3	**20** 十一 金9 Metal · 7 Fellowship 天火同人 壬寅 Water Tiger 7	**21** 十二 木8 Wood · 6 Marrying Maiden 雷澤歸妹 癸卯 Water Rabbit 7
22 十三 木3 Wood · 5 Opposition 火澤睽 甲辰 Wood Dragon 2	**23** 十四 火7 Fire · 4 Waiting 水天需 乙巳 Wood Snake 3	**24** 十五 金4 Metal · 3 Great Exceeding 澤風大過 丙午 Fire Horse 3	**25** 十六 水6 Water · 2 Poison 山風蠱 丁未 Fire Goat 7	**26** 十七 火2 Fire · 1 Dispersing 風水渙 戊申 Earth Monkey 6	**27** 十八 木3 Wood · 9 Travelling 火山旅 己酉 Earth Rooster 8	**28** 十九 金9 Metal · 8 Stagnation 天地否 庚戌 Metal Dog 9
29 二十 火7 Fire · 7 Alliance 水地比 辛亥 Metal Pig 7	**30** 廿一 木8 Wood · 6 Thunder 震爲雷 壬子 Water Rat 1	**31** 廿二 水6 Water · 5 Beauty 山火賁 癸丑 Water Ox 8				

SEPTEMBER 2010 乙酉

Xuan Kong Element 玄空五行	天山遯 Retreat	Period Luck 卦運	Monthly Star 月星
Metal 金9		4	4

SUNDAY	MONDAY	TUESDAY	WEDNESDAY	THURSDAY	FRIDAY	SATURDAY
			火7 Fire · 4 Accomplished 甲寅 Wood Tiger 水火既濟 **1** 廿三 9	水1 Water · 3 Arriving 乙卯 Wood Rabbit 地澤臨 **2** 廿四 4	金4 Metal · 2 Marsh 丙辰 Fire Dragon 兌爲澤 **3** 廿五 1	火2 Fire · 1 Small Livestock 丁巳 Fire Snake 風天小畜 **4** 廿六 8
木3 Wood · 9 The Cauldron 戊午 Earth Horse 火風鼎 **5** 廿七 4	水1 Water · 8 Rising 己未 Earth Goat 地風升 **6** 廿八 2	火7 Fire · 7 Water 庚申 Metal Monkey 坎爲水 **7** 廿九 1	木8 Wood · 6 Lesser Exceeding 辛酉 Metal Rooster 雷山小過 **8** 六月初一 3	金4 Metal · 5 Gathering 壬戌 Water Dog 澤地萃 **9** 初二 4	水6 Water · 4 Peel 癸亥 Water Pig 山地剝 **10** 初三 6	水1 Water · 3 Earth 甲子 Wood Rat 坤爲地 **11** 初四 1
木3 Wood · 2 Biting 乙丑 Wood Ox 火雷噬嗑 **12** 初五 6	火2 Fire · 1 Family 丙寅 Fire Tiger 風火家人 **13** 初六 4	水6 Water · 9 Decreasing 丁卯 Fire Rabbit 山澤損 **14** 初七 9	金9 Metal · 8 Tread 戊辰 Earth Dragon 天澤履 **15** 初八 6	木8 Wood · 7 Great Strength 己巳 Earth Snake 雷天大壯 **16** 初九 2	木8 Wood · 6 Consistency 庚午 Metal Horse 雷風恆 **17** 初十 9	金9 Metal · 5 Litigation 辛未 Metal Goat 天水訟 **18** 十一 3
水1 Water · 4 Officer 壬申 Water Monkey 地水師 **19** 十二 7	火2 Fire · 3 Gradual Progress 癸酉 Water Rooster 風山漸 **20** 十三 7	火7 Fire · 2 Obstruction 甲戌 Wood Dog 水山蹇 **21** 十四 2	木3 Wood · 1 Advancement 乙亥 Wood Pig 火地晉 **22** 十五 3	水6 Water · 9 Nourish 丙子 Fire Rat 山雷頤 **23** 十六 3	金4 Metal · 8 Following 丁丑 Fire Ox 澤雷隨 **24** 十七 7	木8 Wood · 7 Abundance 戊寅 Earth Tiger 雷火豐 **25** 十八 6
火7 Fire · 6 Regulate 己卯 Earth Rabbit 水澤節 **26** 十九 8	水1 Water · 5 Unity 庚辰 Metal Dragon 地天泰 **27** 二十 9	木3 Wood · 4 Great Reward 辛巳 Metal Snake 火天大有 **28** 廿一 7	火2 Fire · 3 Wind 壬午 Water Horse 巽爲風 **29** 廿二 1	金4 Metal · 2 Trap 癸未 Water Goat 澤水困 **30** 廿三 8		

OCTOBER 2010 丙戌

Xuan Kong Element 玄空五行	艮爲山 Mountain	Period Luck 卦運	Monthly Star 月星
Water 水6		1	3

SUNDAY	MONDAY	TUESDAY	WEDNESDAY	THURSDAY	FRIDAY	SATURDAY
火7 Fire · 7 Accomplished 甲寅 Wood Tiger 水火既濟 **31** 廿四 9					木3 Wood · 1 Not Yet Accomplished 甲申 Wood Monkey 火水未濟 **1** 廿四 9	金9 Metal · 9 Retreat 乙酉 Wood Rooster 天山遯 **2** 廿五 4
水6 Water · 8 Mountain 丙戌 Fire Dog 艮爲山 **3** 廿六 1	木8 Wood · 7 Delight 丁亥 Fire Pig 雷地豫 **4** 廿七 8	火7 Fire · 6 Beginning 戊子 Earth Rat 水雷屯 **5** 廿八 4	金9 Metal · 5 Without Wrongdoing 己丑 Earth Ox 天雷無妄 **6** 廿九 2	木3 Wood · 4 Fire 庚寅 Metal Tiger 離爲火 **7** 三十 1	火2 Fire · 3 Sincerity 辛卯 Metal Rabbit 風澤中孚 **8** 九月初一 3	水6 Water · 2 Big Livestock 壬辰 Water Dragon 山天大畜 **9** 初二 4
金4 Metal · 1 Eliminating 癸巳 Water Snake 澤天夬 **10** 初三 6	金9 Metal · 9 Heaven 甲午 Wood Horse 乾爲天 **11** 初四 1	火7 Fire · 8 Well 乙未 Wood Goat 水風井 **12** 初五 6	木8 Wood · 7 Relief 丙申 Fire Monkey 雷水解 **13** 初六 4	金4 Metal · 6 Influence 丁酉 Fire Rooster 澤山咸 **14** 初七 9	水1 Water · 5 Humility 戊戌 Earth Dog 地山謙 **15** 初八 6	火2 Fire · 4 Observation 己亥 Earth Pig 風地觀 **16** 初九 2
火2 Fire · 3 Increasing 庚子 Metal Rat 風雷益 **17** 初十 9	水1 Water · 2 Dimming Light 辛丑 Metal Ox 地火明夷 **18** 十一 3	金9 Metal · 1 Fellowship 壬寅 Water Tiger 天火同人 **19** 十二 7	木8 Wood · 9 Marrying Maiden 癸卯 Water Rabbit 雷澤歸妹 **20** 十三 7	木3 Wood · 8 Opposition 甲辰 Wood Dragon 火澤睽 **21** 十四 2	火7 Fire · 7 Waiting 乙巳 Wood Snake 水天需 **22** 十五 3	金4 Metal · 6 Great Exceeding 丙午 Fire Horse 澤風大過 **23** 十六 3
水6 Water · 5 Poison 丁未 Fire Goat 山風蠱 **24** 十七 7	火2 Fire · 4 Dispersing 戊申 Earth Monkey 風水渙 **25** 十八 6	木3 Wood · 3 Travelling 己酉 Earth Rooster 火山旅 **26** 十九 8	金9 Metal · 2 Stagnation 庚戌 Metal Dog 天地否 **27** 二十 9	火7 Fire · 1 Alliance 辛亥 Metal Pig 水地比 **28** 廿一 7	木8 Wood · 9 Thunder 壬子 Water Rat 震爲雷 **29** 廿二 1	水6 Water · 8 Beauty 癸丑 Water Ox 山火賁 **30** 廿三 8

NOVEMBER 2010 丁亥

Xuan Kong Element 玄空五行	雷地豫 Delight	Period Luck 卦運	Monthly Star 月星
Wood 木8		8	2

SUNDAY	MONDAY	TUESDAY	WEDNESDAY	THURSDAY	FRIDAY	SATURDAY
	水1 Water Arriving 6 乙卯 Wood Rabbit 地澤臨 4 1 廿五	金4 Metal Marsh 5 丙辰 Fire Dragon 兌爲澤 1 2 廿六	火2 Fire Small Livestock 4 丁巳 Fire Snake 風天小畜 8 3 廿七	木3 Wood The Cauldron 3 戊午 Earth Horse 火風鼎 4 4 廿八	水1 Water Rising 2 己未 Earth Goat 地風升 2 5 廿九	火7 Fire Water 1 庚申 Metal Monkey 坎爲水 1 6 十月初一
木8 Wood Lesser Exceeding 9 辛酉 Metal Rooster 雷山小過 3 7 初二	金4 Metal Gathering 8 壬戌 Water Dog 澤地萃 4 8 初三	水6 Water Peel 7 癸亥 Water Pig 山地剝 6 9 初四	水1 Water Earth 6 甲子 Wood Rat 坤爲地 1 10 初五	木3 Wood Biting 5 乙丑 Wood Ox 火雷噬嗑 6 11 初六	火2 Fire Family 4 丙寅 Fire Tiger 風火家人 4 12 初七	水6 Water Decreasing 3 丁卯 Fire Rabbit 山澤損 9 13 初八
金9 Metal Tread 2 戊辰 Earth Dragon 天澤履 6 14 初九	木8 Wood Great Strength 1 己巳 Earth Snake 雷天大壯 2 15 初十	木8 Wood Consistency 9 庚午 Metal Horse 雷風恆 9 16 十一	金9 Metal Litigation 8 辛未 Metal Goat 天水訟 3 17 十二	水1 Water Officer 7 壬申 Water Monkey 地水師 7 18 十三	火2 Fire Gradual Progress 6 癸酉 Water Rooster 風山漸 7 19 十四	火7 Fire Obstruction 5 甲戌 Wood Dog 水山蹇 2 20 十五
木3 Wood Advancement 4 乙亥 Wood Pig 火地晉 3 21 十六	水6 Water Nourish 3 丙子 Fire Rat 山雷頤 3 22 十七	金4 Metal Following 2 丁丑 Fire Ox 澤雷隨 7 23 十八	木8 Wood Abundance 1 戊寅 Earth Tiger 雷火豐 6 24 十九	火7 Fire Regulate 9 己卯 Earth Rabbit 水澤節 8 25 二十	水1 Water Unity 8 庚辰 Metal Dragon 地天泰 9 26 廿一	木3 Wood Great Reward 7 辛巳 Metal Snake 火天大有 7 27 廿二
火2 Fire Wind 6 壬午 Water Horse 巽爲風 1 28 廿三	金4 Metal Trap 5 癸未 Water Goat 澤水困 8 29 廿四	木3 Wood Not Yet Accomplished 4 甲申 Wood Monkey 火水未濟 9 30 廿五				

DECEMBER 2010 戊子

Xuan Kong Element 玄空五行	水雷屯 Beginning	Period Luck 卦運	Monthly Star 月星
Fire 火7		4	1

SUNDAY	MONDAY	TUESDAY	WEDNESDAY	THURSDAY	FRIDAY	SATURDAY
			金9 Metal Retreat 3 乙酉 Wood Rooster 天山遯 4 1 廿六	水6 Water Mountain 2 丙戌 Fire Dog 艮爲山 1 2 廿七	木8 Wood Delight 1 丁亥 Fire Pig 雷地豫 8 3 廿八	火7 Fire Beginning 9 戊子 Earth Rat 水雷屯 4 4 廿九
金9 Metal Without Wrongdoing 8 己丑 Earth Ox 天雷無妄 2 5 三十	木3 Wood Fire 7 庚寅 Metal Tiger 離爲火 1 6 十一月初一	火2 Fire Sincerity 6 辛卯 Metal Rabbit 風澤中孚 3 7 初二	水6 Water Big Livestock 5 壬辰 Water Dragon 山天大畜 4 8 初三	金4 Metal Eliminating 4 癸巳 Water Snake 澤天夬 6 9 初四	金9 Metal Heaven 3 甲午 Wood Horse 乾爲天 1 10 初五	火7 Fire Well 2 乙未 Wood Goat 水風井 6 11 初六
木8 Wood Relief 1 丙申 Fire Monkey 雷水解 4 12 初七	金4 Metal Influence 9 丁酉 Fire Rooster 澤山咸 9 13 初八	水1 Water Humility 8 戊戌 Earth Dog 地山謙 6 14 初九	火2 Fire Observation 7 己亥 Earth Pig 風地觀 2 15 初十	火2 Fire Increasing 6 庚子 Metal Rat 風雷益 9 16 十一	水1 Water Dimming Light 5 辛丑 Metal Ox 地火明夷 3 17 十二	金9 Metal Fellowship 4 壬寅 Water Tiger 天火同人 7 18 十三
木8 Wood Marrying Maiden 3 癸卯 Water Rabbit 雷澤歸妹 7 19 十四	木3 Wood Opposition 2 甲辰 Wood Dragon 火澤睽 2 20 十五	火7 Fire Waiting 1 乙巳 Wood Snake 水天需 3 21 十六	金4 Metal Great Exceeding 9/1 丙午 Fire Horse 澤風大過 3 22 十七	水6 Water Poison 2 丁未 Fire Goat 山風蠱 7 23 十八	火2 Fire Dispersing 3 戊申 Earth Monkey 風水渙 6 24 十九	木3 Wood Travelling 4 己酉 Earth Rooster 火山旅 8 25 二十
金9 Metal Stagnation 5 庚戌 Metal Dog 天地否 9 26 廿一	火7 Fire Alliance 6 辛亥 Metal Pig 水地比 7 27 廿二	木8 Wood Thunder 7 壬子 Water Rat 震爲雷 1 28 廿三	水6 Water Beauty 8 癸丑 Water Ox 山火賁 8 29 廿四	火7 Fire Accomplished 9 甲寅 Wood Tiger 水火既濟 9 30 廿五	水1 Water Arriving 1 乙卯 Wood Rabbit 地澤臨 4 31 廿六	

2011 辛卯

(*Xin Mao*) Metal Rabbit

2011 辛卯 *(Xin Mao)* Metal Rabbit

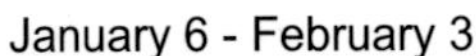

January 6 - February 3

February 4 - March 5

March 6 - April 4

April 5 - May 5

May 6 - June 5

June 6 - July 6

July 7 - August 7

August 8 - September 7

September 8 - October 7

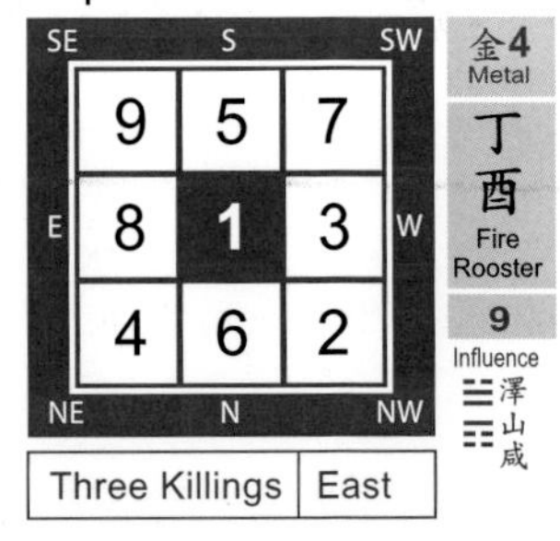

October 8 - November 7

November 8 - December 6

December 7 - January 5

JANUARY 2011 己丑

Xuan Kong Element 玄空五行	天雷無妄 Without Wrongdoing	Period Luck 卦運	Monthly Star 月星
Metal 金9		2	9

SUNDAY	MONDAY	TUESDAY	WEDNESDAY	THURSDAY	FRIDAY	SATURDAY
金9 Metal Retreat 4 天山遯 乙酉 Wood Rooster 30 4 廿七	水6 Water Mountain 5 艮爲山 丙戌 Fire Dog 31 1 廿八					金4 Metal Marsh 2 兑爲澤 丙辰 Fire Dragon 1 1 廿七
火2 Fire Small Livestock 3 風天小畜 丁巳 Fire Snake 2 8 廿八	木3 Wood The Cauldron 4 火風鼎 戊午 Earth Horse 3 4 廿九	水1 Water Rising 5 地風升 己未 Earth Goat 4 2 十二月初一	火7 Fire Water 6 坎爲水 庚申 Metal Monkey 5 1 初二	木8 Wood Lesser Exceeding 7 雷山小過 辛酉 Metal Rooster 6 3 初三	金4 Metal Gathering 8 澤地萃 壬戌 Water Dog 7 4 初四	水6 Water Peel 9 山地剝 癸亥 Water Pig 8 6 初五
水1 Water Earth 1 坤爲地 甲子 Wood Rat 9 1 初六	木3 Wood Biting 2 火雷噬嗑 乙丑 Wood Ox 10 6 初七	火2 Fire Family 3 風火家人 丙寅 Fire Tiger 11 4 初八	水6 Water Decreasing 4 山澤損 丁卯 Fire Rabbit 12 9 初九	金9 Metal Tread 5 天澤履 戊辰 Earth Dragon 13 6 初十	木8 Wood Great Strength 6 雷天大壯 己巳 Earth Snake 14 2 十一	木8 Wood Consistency 7 雷風恆 庚午 Metal Horse 15 9 十二
金9 Metal Litigation 8 天水訟 辛未 Metal Goat 16 3 十三	水1 Water Officer 9 地水師 壬申 Water Monkey 17 7 十四	火2 Fire Gradual Progress 1 風山漸 癸酉 Water Rooster 18 7 十五	火7 Fire Obstruction 2 水山蹇 甲戌 Wood Dog 19 2 十六	木3 Wood Advancement 3 火地晉 乙亥 Wood Pig 20 3 十七	水6 Water Nourish 4 山雷頤 丙子 Fire Rat 21 3 十八	金4 Metal Following 5 澤雷隨 丁丑 Fire Ox 22 7 十九
木8 Wood Abundance 6 雷火豐 戊寅 Earth Tiger 23 6 二十	火7 Fire Regulate 7 水澤節 己卯 Earth Rabbit 24 8 廿一	水1 Water Unity 8 地天泰 庚辰 Metal Dragon 25 9 廿二	木3 Wood Great Reward 9 火天大有 辛巳 Metal Snake 26 7 廿三	火2 Fire Wind 1 巽爲風 壬午 Water Horse 27 1 廿四	金4 Metal Trap 2 澤水困 癸未 Water Goat 28 8 廿五	木3 Wood Not Yet Accomplished 3 火水未濟 甲申 Wood Monkey 29 9 廿六

FEBRUARY 2011 庚寅

Xuan Kong Element 玄空五行	離爲火 Fire	Period Luck 卦運	Monthly Star 月星
Wood 木3		1	8

SUNDAY	MONDAY	TUESDAY	WEDNESDAY	THURSDAY	FRIDAY	SATURDAY
		木8 Wood Delight 6 雷地豫 丁亥 Fire Pig 1 8 廿九	火7 Fire Beginning 7 水雷屯 戊子 Earth Rat 2 4 三十	金9 Metal Without Wrongdoing 8 天雷無妄 己丑 Earth Ox 3 2 正月初一	木3 Wood Fire 9 離爲火 庚寅 Metal Tiger 4 1 初二	火2 Fire Sincerity 1 風澤中孚 辛卯 Metal Rabbit 5 3 初三
水6 Water Big Livestock 2 山天大畜 壬辰 Water Dragon 6 4 初四	金4 Metal Eliminating 3 澤天夬 癸巳 Water Snake 7 6 初五	金9 Metal Heaven 4 乾爲天 甲午 Wood Horse 8 1 初六	火7 Fire Well 5 水風井 乙未 Wood Goat 9 6 初七	木8 Wood Relief 6 雷水解 丙申 Fire Monkey 10 4 初八	金4 Metal Influence 7 澤山咸 丁酉 Fire Rooster 11 9 初九	水1 Water Humility 8 地山謙 戊戌 Earth Dog 12 6 初十
火2 Fire Observation 9 風地觀 己亥 Earth Pig 13 2 十一	火2 Fire Increasing 1 風雷益 庚子 Metal Rat 14 9 十二	水1 Water Dimming Light 2 地火明夷 辛丑 Metal Ox 15 3 十三	金9 Metal Fellowship 3 天火同人 壬寅 Water Tiger 16 7 十四	木8 Wood Marrying Maiden 4 雷澤歸妹 癸卯 Water Rabbit 17 7 十五	木3 Wood Opposition 5 火澤睽 甲辰 Wood Dragon 18 2 十六	火7 Fire Waiting 6 水天需 乙巳 Wood Snake 19 3 十七
金4 Metal Great Exceeding 7 澤風大過 丙午 Fire Horse 20 3 十八	水6 Water Poison 8 山風蠱 丁未 Fire Goat 21 7 十九	火2 Fire Dispersing 9 風水渙 戊申 Earth Monkey 22 6 二十	木3 Wood Travelling 1 火山旅 己酉 Earth Rooster 23 8 廿一	金9 Metal Stagnation 2 天地否 庚戌 Metal Dog 24 9 廿二	火7 Fire Alliance 3 水地比 辛亥 Metal Pig 25 7 廿三	木8 Wood Thunder 4 震爲雷 壬子 Water Rat 26 1 廿四
水6 Water Beauty 5 山火賁 癸丑 Water Ox 27 8 廿五	火7 Fire Accomplished 6 水火既濟 甲寅 Wood Tiger 28 9 廿六					

MARCH 2011 辛卯

Xuan Kong Element 玄空五行	風澤中孚	Period Luck 卦運	Monthly Star 月星
Fire 火2	Sincerity	3	7

SUNDAY	MONDAY	TUESDAY	WEDNESDAY	THURSDAY	FRIDAY	SATURDAY
		水1 Water 7 Arriving 地澤臨 乙卯 Wood Rabbit 1 廿七 4	金4 Metal 8 Marsh 兌爲澤 丙辰 Fire Dragon 2 廿八 1	火2 Fire 9 Small Livestock 風天小畜 丁巳 Fire Snake 3 廿九 8	木3 Wood 1 The Cauldron 火風鼎 戊午 Earth Horse 4 三十 4	水1 Water 2 Rising 地風升 己未 Earth Goat 5 二月初一 2
火7 Fire 3 Water 坎爲水 庚申 Metal Monkey 6 初二 1	木8 Wood 4 Lesser Exceeding 雷山小過 辛酉 Metal Rooster 7 初三 3	金4 Metal 5 Gathering 澤地萃 壬戌 Water Dog 8 初四 4	水6 Water 6 Peel 山地剝 癸亥 Water Pig 9 初五 6	水1 Water 7 Earth 坤爲地 甲子 Wood Rat 10 初六 1	木3 Wood 8 Biting 火雷噬嗑 乙丑 Wood Ox 11 初七 6	火2 Fire 9 Family 風火家人 丙寅 Fire Tiger 12 初八 4
水6 Water 1 Decreasing 山澤損 丁卯 Fire Rabbit 13 初九 9	金9 Metal 2 Tread 天澤履 戊辰 Earth Dragon 14 初十 6	木8 Wood 3 Great Strength 雷天大壯 己巳 Earth Snake 15 十一 2	木8 Wood 4 Consistency 雷風恆 庚午 Metal Horse 16 十二 9	金9 Metal 5 Litigation 天水訟 辛未 Metal Goat 17 十三 3	水1 Water 6 Officer 地水師 壬申 Water Monkey 18 十四 7	火2 Fire 7 Gradual Progress 風山漸 癸酉 Water Rooster 19 十五 7
火7 Fire 8 Obstruction 水山蹇 甲戌 Wood Dog 20 十六 2	木3 Wood 9 Advancement 火地晉 乙亥 Wood Pig 21 十七 3	水6 Water 1 Nourish 山雷頤 丙子 Fire Rat 22 十八 3	金4 Metal 2 Following 澤雷隨 丁丑 Fire Ox 23 十九 7	木8 Wood 3 Abundance 雷火豐 戊寅 Earth Tiger 24 二十 6	火7 Fire 4 Regulate 水澤節 己卯 Earth Rabbit 25 廿一 8	水1 Water 5 Unity 地天泰 庚辰 Metal Dragon 26 廿二 9
木3 Wood 6 Great Reward 火天大有 辛巳 Metal Snake 27 廿三 7	火2 Fire 7 Wind 巽爲風 壬午 Water Horse 28 廿四 1	金4 Metal 8 Trap 澤水困 癸未 Water Goat 29 廿五 8	木3 Wood 9 Not Yet Accomplished 火水未濟 甲申 Wood Monkey 30 廿六 9	金9 Metal 1 Retreat 天山遯 乙酉 Wood Rooster 31 廿七 4		

APRIL 2011 壬辰

Xuan Kong Element 玄空五行	山天大畜	Period Luck 卦運	Monthly Star 月星
Water 水6	Big Livestock	4	6

SUNDAY	MONDAY	TUESDAY	WEDNESDAY	THURSDAY	FRIDAY	SATURDAY
					水6 Water 2 Mountain 艮爲山 丙戌 Fire Dog 1 廿八 1	木8 Wood 3 Delight 雷地豫 丁亥 Fire Pig 2 廿九 8
火7 Fire 4 Beginning 水雷屯 戊子 Earth Rat 3 三月初一 4	金9 Metal 5 Without Wrongdoing 天雷無妄 己丑 Earth Ox 4 初二 2	木3 Wood 6 Fire 離爲火 庚寅 Metal Tiger 5 初三 1	火2 Fire 7 Sincerity 風澤中孚 辛卯 Metal Rabbit 6 初四 3	水6 Water 8 Big Livestock 山天大畜 壬辰 Water Dragon 7 初五 4	金4 Metal 9 Eliminating 澤天夬 癸巳 Water Snake 8 初六 6	金9 Metal 1 Heaven 乾爲天 甲午 Wood Horse 9 初七 1
火7 Fire 2 Well 水風井 乙未 Wood Goat 10 初八 6	木8 Wood 3 Relief 雷水解 丙申 Fire Monkey 11 初九 4	金4 Metal 4 Influence 澤山咸 丁酉 Fire Rooster 12 初十 9	水1 Water 5 Humility 地山謙 戊戌 Earth Dog 13 十一 6	火2 Fire 6 Observation 風地觀 己亥 Earth Pig 14 十二 2	火2 Fire 7 Increasing 風雷益 庚子 Metal Rat 15 十三 9	水1 Water 8 Dimming Light 地火明夷 辛丑 Metal Ox 16 十四 3
金9 Metal 9 Fellowship 天火同人 壬寅 Water Tiger 17 十五 7	木8 Wood 1 Marrying Maiden 雷澤歸妹 癸卯 Water Rabbit 18 十六 7	木3 Wood 2 Opposition 火澤睽 甲辰 Wood Dragon 19 十七 2	火7 Fire 3 Waiting 水天需 乙巳 Wood Snake 20 十八 3	金4 Metal 4 Great Exceeding 澤風大過 丙午 Fire Horse 21 十九 3	水6 Water 5 Poison 山風蠱 丁未 Fire Goat 22 二十 7	火2 Fire 6 Dispersing 風水渙 戊申 Earth Monkey 23 廿一 6
木3 Wood 7 Travelling 火山旅 己酉 Earth Rooster 24 廿二 8	金9 Metal 8 Stagnation 天地否 庚戌 Metal Dog 25 廿三 9	火7 Fire 9 Alliance 水地比 辛亥 Metal Pig 26 廿四 7	木8 Wood 1 Thunder 震爲雷 壬子 Water Rat 27 廿五 1	水6 Water 2 Beauty 山火賁 癸丑 Water Ox 28 廿六 8	火7 Fire 3 Accomplished 水火既濟 甲寅 Wood Tiger 29 廿七 9	水1 Water 4 Arriving 地澤臨 乙卯 Wood Rabbit 30 廿八 4

MAY 2011 癸巳

Xuan Kong Element 玄空五行	澤天夬 Eliminating	Period Luck 卦運	Monthly Star 月星
Metal 金4		6	5

SUNDAY	MONDAY	TUESDAY	WEDNESDAY	THURSDAY	FRIDAY	SATURDAY
金4 Metal 5 Marsh 兌爲澤 丙辰 Fire Dragon 1 1 廿九	火2 Fire 6 Small Livestock 風天小畜 丁巳 Fire Snake 2 8 三十	木3 Wood 7 The Cauldron 火風鼎 戊午 Earth Horse 3 4 四月初一	水1 Water 8 Rising 地風升 己未 Earth Goat 4 2 初二	火7 Fire 9 Water 坎爲水 庚申 Metal Monkey 5 1 初三	木8 Wood 1 Lesser Exceeding 雷山小過 辛酉 Metal Rooster 6 3 初四	金4 Metal 2 Gathering 澤地萃 壬戌 Water Dog 7 4 初五
水6 Water 3 Peel 山地剝 癸亥 Water Pig 8 6 初六	水1 Water 4 Earth 坤爲地 甲子 Wood Rat 9 1 初七	木3 Wood 5 Biting 火雷噬嗑 乙丑 Wood Ox 10 6 初八	火2 Fire 6 Family 風火家人 丙寅 Fire Tiger 11 4 初九	水6 Water 7 Decreasing 山澤損 丁卯 Fire Rabbit 12 9 初十	金9 Metal 8 Tread 天澤履 戊辰 Earth Dragon 13 6 十一	木8 Wood 9 Great Strength 雷天大壯 己巳 Earth Snake 14 2 十二
木8 Wood 1 Consistency 雷風恆 庚午 Metal Horse 15 9 十三	金9 Metal 2 Litigation 天水訟 辛未 Metal Goat 16 3 十四	水1 Water 3 Officer 地水師 壬申 Water Monkey 17 7 十五	火2 Fire 4 Gradual Progress 風山漸 癸酉 Water Rooster 18 7 十六	火7 Fire 5 Obstruction 水山蹇 甲戌 Wood Dog 19 2 十七	木3 Wood 6 Advancement 火地晉 乙亥 Wood Pig 20 3 十八	水6 Water 7 Nourish 山雷頤 丙子 Fire Rat 21 3 十九
金4 Metal 8 Following 澤雷隨 丁丑 Fire Ox 22 7 二十	木8 Wood 9 Abundance 雷火豐 戊寅 Earth Tiger 23 6 廿一	火7 Fire 1 Regulate 水澤節 己卯 Earth Rabbit 24 8 廿二	水1 Water 2 Unity 地天泰 庚辰 Metal Dragon 25 9 廿三	木3 Wood 3 Great Reward 火天大有 辛巳 Metal Snake 26 7 廿四	火2 Fire 4 Wind 巽爲風 壬午 Water Horse 27 1 廿五	金4 Metal 5 Trap 澤水困 癸未 Water Goat 28 8 廿六
木3 Wood 6 Not Yet Accomplished 火水未濟 甲申 Wood Monkey 29 9 廿七	金9 Metal 7 Retreat 天山遯 乙酉 Wood Rooster 30 4 廿八	水6 Water 8 Mountain 艮爲山 丙戌 Fire Dog 31 1 廿九				

JUNE 2011 甲午

Xuan Kong Element 玄空五行	乾爲天 Heaven	Period Luck 卦運	Monthly Star 月星
Metal 金9		1	4

SUNDAY	MONDAY	TUESDAY	WEDNESDAY	THURSDAY	FRIDAY	SATURDAY
			木8 Wood 9 Delight 雷地豫 丁亥 Fire Pig 1 8 三十	火7 Fire 1 Beginning 水雷屯 戊子 Earth Rat 2 4 五月初一	金9 Metal 2 Without Wrongdoing 天雷無妄 己丑 Earth Ox 3 2 初二	木3 Wood 3 Fire 離爲火 庚寅 Metal Tiger 4 1 初三
火2 Fire 4 Sincerity 風澤中孚 辛卯 Metal Rabbit 5 3 初四	水6 Water 5 Big Livestock 山天大畜 壬辰 Water Dragon 6 4 初五	金4 Metal 6 Eliminating 澤天夬 癸巳 Water Snake 7 6 初六	金9 Metal 7 Heaven 乾爲天 甲午 Wood Horse 8 1 初七	火7 Fire 8 Well 水風井 乙未 Wood Goat 9 6 初八	木8 Wood 9 Relief 雷水解 丙申 Fire Monkey 10 4 初九	金4 Metal 1 Influence 澤山咸 丁酉 Fire Rooster 11 9 初十
水1 Water 2 Humility 地山謙 戊戌 Earth Dog 12 6 十一	火2 Fire 3 Observation 風地觀 己亥 Earth Pig 13 2 十二	火2 Fire 4 Increasing 風雷益 庚子 Metal Rat 14 9 十三	水1 Water 5 Dimming Light 地火明夷 辛丑 Metal Ox 15 3 十四	金9 Metal 6 Fellowship 天火同人 壬寅 Water Tiger 16 7 十五	木8 Wood 7 Marrying Maiden 雷澤歸妹 癸卯 Water Rabbit 17 7 十六	木3 Wood 8 Opposition 火澤睽 甲辰 Wood Dragon 18 2 十七
火7 Fire 9 Waiting 水天需 乙巳 Wood Snake 19 3 十八	金4 Metal 1 Great Exceeding 澤風大過 丙午 Fire Horse 20 3 十九	水6 Water 2 Poison 山風蠱 丁未 Fire Goat 21 7 二十	火2 Fire 3/7 Dispersing 風水渙 戊申 Earth Monkey 22 6 廿一	木3 Wood 6 Travelling 火山旅 己酉 Earth Rooster 23 8 廿二	金9 Metal 5 Stagnation 天地否 庚戌 Metal Dog 24 9 廿三	火7 Fire 4 Alliance 水地比 辛亥 Metal Pig 25 7 廿四
木8 Wood 3 Thunder 震爲雷 壬子 Water Rat 26 1 廿五	水6 Water 2 Beauty 山火賁 癸丑 Water Ox 27 8 廿六	火7 Fire 1 Accomplished 水火既濟 甲寅 Wood Tiger 28 9 廿七	水1 Water 9 Arriving 地澤臨 乙卯 Wood Rabbit 29 4 廿八	金4 Metal 8 Marsh 兌爲澤 丙辰 Fire Dragon 30 1 廿九		

JULY 2011 乙未

Xuan Kong Element 玄空五行	水風井 Well	Period Luck 卦運	Monthly Star 月星
Fire 火7		6	3

SUNDAY	MONDAY	TUESDAY	WEDNESDAY	THURSDAY	FRIDAY	SATURDAY
木8 Wood Delight 4 雷地豫 丁亥 Fire Pig 8 31 七月初一					火2 Fire Small Livestock 7 風天小畜 丁巳 Fire Snake 8 1 六月初一	木3 Wood The Cauldron 6 火風鼎 戊午 Earth Horse 4 2 初二
水1 Water Rising 5 地風升 己未 Earth Goat 2 3 初三	火7 Fire Water 4 坎爲水 庚申 Metal Monkey 1 4 初四	木8 Wood Lesser Exceeding 3 雷山小過 辛酉 Metal Rooster 3 5 初五	金4 Metal Gathering 2 澤地萃 壬戌 Water Dog 4 6 初六	水6 Water Peel 1 山地剝 癸亥 Water Pig 6 7 初七	水1 Water Earth 9 坤爲地 甲子 Wood Rat 1 8 初八	木3 Wood Biting 8 火雷噬嗑 乙丑 Wood Ox 6 9 初九
火2 Fire Family 7 風火家人 丙寅 Fire Tiger 4 10 初十	水6 Water Decreasing 6 山澤損 丁卯 Fire Rabbit 9 11 十一	金9 Metal Tread 5 天澤履 戊辰 Earth Dragon 6 12 十二	木8 Wood Great Strength 4 雷天大壯 己巳 Earth Snake 2 13 十三	木8 Wood Consistency 3 雷風恆 庚午 Metal Horse 9 14 十四	金9 Metal Litigation 2 天水訟 辛未 Metal Goat 3 15 十五	水1 Water Officer 1 地水師 壬申 Water Monkey 7 16 十六
火2 Fire Gradual Progress 9 風山漸 癸酉 Water Rooster 7 17 十七	火7 Fire Obstruction 8 水山蹇 甲戌 Wood Dog 2 18 十八	木3 Wood Advancement 7 火地晉 乙亥 Wood Pig 3 19 十九	水6 Water Nourish 6 山雷頤 丙子 Fire Rat 3 20 二十	金4 Metal Following 5 澤雷隨 丁丑 Fire Ox 7 21 廿一	木8 Wood Abundance 4 雷火豐 戊寅 Earth Tiger 6 22 廿二	火7 Fire Regulate 3 水澤節 己卯 Earth Rabbit 8 23 廿三
水1 Water Unity 2 地天泰 庚辰 Metal Dragon 9 24 廿四	木3 Wood Great Reward 1 火天大有 辛巳 Metal Snake 7 25 廿五	火2 Fire Wind 9 巽爲風 壬午 Water Horse 1 26 廿六	金4 Metal Trap 8 澤水困 癸未 Water Goat 8 27 廿七	木3 Wood Not Yet Accomplished 7 火水未濟 甲申 Wood Monkey 9 28 廿八	金9 Metal Retreat 6 天山遯 乙酉 Wood Rooster 4 29 廿九	水6 Water Mountain 5 艮爲山 丙戌 Fire Dog 1 30 三十

AUGUST 2011 丙申

Xuan Kong Element 玄空五行	雷水解 Relief	Period Luck 卦運	Monthly Star 月星
Wood 木8		4	2

SUNDAY	MONDAY	TUESDAY	WEDNESDAY	THURSDAY	FRIDAY	SATURDAY
	火7 Fire Beginning 3 水雷屯 戊子 Earth Rat 4 1 初二	金9 Metal Without Wrongdoing 2 天雷無妄 己丑 Earth Ox 2 2 初三	木3 Wood Fire 1 離爲火 庚寅 Metal Tiger 1 3 初四	火2 Fire Sincerity 9 風澤中孚 辛卯 Metal Rabbit 3 4 初五	水6 Water Big Livestock 8 山天大畜 壬辰 Water Dragon 4 5 初六	金4 Metal Eliminating 7 澤天夬 癸巳 Water Snake 6 6 初七
金9 Metal Heaven 6 乾爲天 甲午 Wood Horse 1 7 初八	火7 Fire Well 5 水風井 乙未 Wood Goat 6 8 初九	木8 Wood Relief 4 雷水解 丙申 Fire Monkey 4 9 初十	金4 Metal Influence 3 澤山咸 丁酉 Fire Rooster 9 10 十一	水1 Water Humility 2 地山謙 戊戌 Earth Dog 6 11 十二	火2 Fire Observation 1 風地觀 己亥 Earth Pig 2 12 十三	火2 Fire Increasing 9 風雷益 庚子 Metal Rat 9 13 十四
水1 Water Dimming Light 8 地火明夷 辛丑 Metal Ox 3 14 十五	金9 Metal Fellowship 7 天火同人 壬寅 Water Tiger 7 15 十六	木8 Wood Marrying Maiden 6 雷澤歸妹 癸卯 Water Rabbit 7 16 十七	木3 Wood Opposition 5 火澤睽 甲辰 Wood Dragon 2 17 十八	火7 Fire Waiting 4 水天需 乙巳 Wood Snake 3 18 十九	金4 Metal Great Exceeding 3 澤風大過 丙午 Fire Horse 3 19 二十	水6 Water Poison 2 山風蠱 丁未 Fire Goat 7 20 廿一
火2 Fire Dispersing 1 風水渙 戊申 Earth Monkey 6 21 廿二	木3 Wood Travelling 9 火山旅 己酉 Earth Rooster 8 22 廿三	金9 Metal Stagnation 8 天地否 庚戌 Metal Dog 9 23 廿四	火7 Fire Alliance 7 水地比 辛亥 Metal Pig 7 24 廿五	木8 Wood Thunder 6 震爲雷 壬子 Water Rat 1 25 廿六	水6 Water Beauty 5 山火賁 癸丑 Water Ox 8 26 廿七	火7 Fire Accomplished 4 水火既濟 甲寅 Wood Tiger 9 27 廿八
水1 Water Arriving 3 地澤臨 乙卯 Wood Rabbit 4 28 廿九	金4 Metal Marsh 2 兌爲澤 丙辰 Fire Dragon 1 29 八月初一	火2 Fire Small Livestock 1 風天小畜 丁巳 Fire Snake 8 30 初二	木3 Wood The Cauldron 9 火風鼎 戊午 Earth Horse 4 31 初三			

SEPTEMBER 2011 丁酉

Xuan Kong Element 玄空五行	澤山咸 Influence	Period Luck 卦運	Monthly Star 月星
Metal 金4		9	1

SUNDAY	MONDAY	TUESDAY	WEDNESDAY	THURSDAY	FRIDAY	SATURDAY
				水1 Water 8 Rising 地風升 己未 Earth Goat **1** 初四 2	火7 Fire 7 Water 坎爲水 庚申 Metal Monkey **2** 初五 1	木8 Wood 6 Lesser Exceeding 雷山小過 辛酉 Metal Rooster **3** 初六 3
金4 Metal 5 Gathering 澤地萃 壬戌 Water Dog **4** 初七 4	水6 Water 4 Peel 山地剝 癸亥 Water Pig **5** 初八 6	水1 Water 3 Earth 坤爲地 甲子 Wood Rat **6** 初九 1	木3 Wood 2 Biting 火雷噬嗑 乙丑 Wood Ox **7** 初十 6	火2 Fire 1 Family 風火家人 丙寅 Fire Tiger **8** 十一 4	水6 Water 9 Decreasing 山澤損 丁卯 Fire Rabbit **9** 十二 9	金9 Metal 8 Tread 天澤履 戊辰 Earth Dragon **10** 十三 6
木8 Wood 7 Great Strength 雷天大壯 己巳 Earth Snake **11** 十四 2	木8 Wood 6 Consistency 雷風恆 庚午 Metal Horse **12** 十五 9	金9 Metal 5 Litigation 天水訟 辛未 Metal Goat **13** 十六 3	水1 Water 4 Officer 地水師 壬申 Water Monkey **14** 十七 7	火2 Fire 3 Gradual Progress 風山漸 癸酉 Water Rooster **15** 十八 7	火7 Fire 2 Obstruction 水山蹇 甲戌 Wood Dog **16** 十九 2	木3 Wood 1 Advancement 火地晉 乙亥 Wood Pig **17** 二十 3
水6 Water 9 Nourish 山雷頤 丙子 Fire Rat **18** 廿一 3	金4 Metal 8 Following 澤雷隨 丁丑 Fire Ox **19** 廿二 7	木8 Wood 7 Abundance 雷火豐 戊寅 Earth Tiger **20** 廿三 6	火7 Fire 6 Regulate 水澤節 己卯 Earth Rabbit **21** 廿四 8	水1 Water 5 Unity 地天泰 庚辰 Metal Dragon **22** 廿五 9	木3 Wood 4 Great Reward 火天大有 辛巳 Metal Snake **23** 廿六 7	火2 Fire 3 Wind 巽爲風 壬午 Water Horse **24** 廿七 1
金4 Metal 2 Trap 澤水困 癸未 Water Goat **25** 廿八 8	木3 Wood 1 Not Yet Accomplished 火水未濟 甲申 Wood Monkey **26** 廿九 9	金9 Metal 9 Retreat 天山遯 乙酉 Wood Rooster **27** 九月初一 4	水6 Water 8 Mountain 艮爲山 丙戌 Fire Dog **28** 初二 1	木8 Wood 7 Delight 雷地豫 丁亥 Fire Pig **29** 初三 8	火7 Fire 6 Beginning 水雷屯 戊子 Earth Rat **30** 初四 4	

OCTOBER 2011 戊戌

Xuan Kong Element 玄空五行	地山謙 Humility	Period Luck 卦運	Monthly Star 月星
Water 水1		6	9

SUNDAY	MONDAY	TUESDAY	WEDNESDAY	THURSDAY	FRIDAY	SATURDAY
木3 Wood 3 The Cauldron 火風鼎 戊午 Earth Horse **30** 初四 4	水1 Water 2 Rising 地風升 己未 Earth Goat **31** 初五 2					金9 Metal 5 Without Wrongdoing 天雷無妄 己丑 Earth Ox **1** 初五 2
木3 Wood 4 Fire 離爲火 庚寅 Metal Tiger **2** 初六 1	火2 Fire 3 Sincerity 風澤中孚 辛卯 Metal Rabbit **3** 初七 3	水6 Water 2 Big Livestock 山天大畜 壬辰 Water Dragon **4** 初八 4	金4 Metal 1 Eliminating 澤天夬 癸巳 Water Snake **5** 初九 6	金9 Metal 9 Heaven 乾爲天 甲午 Wood Horse **6** 初十 1	火7 Fire 8 Well 水風井 乙未 Wood Goat **7** 十一 6	木8 Wood 7 Relief 雷水解 丙申 Fire Monkey **8** 十二 4
金4 Metal 6 Influence 澤山咸 丁酉 Fire Rooster **9** 十三 9	水1 Water 5 Humility 地山謙 戊戌 Earth Dog **10** 十四 6	火2 Fire 4 Observation 風地觀 己亥 Earth Pig **11** 十五 2	火2 Fire 3 Increasing 風雷益 庚子 Metal Rat **12** 十六 9	水1 Water 2 Dimming Light 地火明夷 辛丑 Metal Ox **13** 十七 3	金9 Metal 1 Fellowship 天火同人 壬寅 Water Tiger **14** 十八 7	木8 Wood 9 Marrying Maiden 雷澤歸妹 癸卯 Water Rabbit **15** 十九 7
木3 Wood 8 Opposition 火澤睽 甲辰 Wood Dragon **16** 二十 2	火7 Fire 7 Waiting 水天需 乙巳 Wood Snake **17** 廿一 3	金4 Metal 6 Great Exceeding 澤風大過 丙午 Fire Horse **18** 廿二 3	水6 Water 5 Poison 山風蠱 丁未 Fire Goat **19** 廿三 7	火2 Fire 4 Dispersing 風水渙 戊申 Earth Monkey **20** 廿四 6	木3 Wood 3 Travelling 火山旅 己酉 Earth Rooster **21** 廿五 8	金9 Metal 2 Stagnation 天地否 庚戌 Metal Dog **22** 廿六 9
火7 Fire 1 Alliance 水地比 辛亥 Metal Pig **23** 廿七 7	木8 Wood 9 Thunder 震爲雷 壬子 Water Rat **24** 廿八 1	水6 Water 8 Beauty 山火賁 癸丑 Water Ox **25** 廿九 8	火7 Fire 7 Accomplished 水火既濟 甲寅 Wood Tiger **26** 三十 9	水1 Water 6 Arriving 地澤臨 乙卯 Wood Rabbit **27** 十月初一 4	金4 Metal 5 Marsh 兌爲澤 丙辰 Fire Dragon **28** 初二 1	火2 Fire 4 Small Livestock 風天小畜 丁巳 Fire Snake **29** 初三 8

NOVEMBER 2011 己亥

Xuan Kong Element 玄空五行	風地觀 Observation	Period Luck 卦運	Monthly Star 月星
Fire 火2		2	8

SUNDAY	MONDAY	TUESDAY	WEDNESDAY	THURSDAY	FRIDAY	SATURDAY
		火7 Fire [1] Water 坎爲水 庚申 Metal Monkey **1** 初六 1	木8 Wood [9] Lesser Exceeding 雷山小過 辛酉 Metal Rooster **2** 初七 3	金4 Metal [8] Gathering 澤地萃 壬戌 Water Dog **3** 初八 4	水6 Water [7] Peel 山地剝 癸亥 Water Pig **4** 初九 6	水1 Water [6] Earth 坤爲地 甲子 Wood Rat **5** 初十 1
木3 Wood [5] Biting 火雷噬嗑 乙丑 Wood Ox **6** 十一 6	火2 Fire [4] Family 風火家人 丙寅 Fire Tiger **7** 十二 4	水6 Water [3] Decreasing 山澤損 丁卯 Fire Rabbit **8** 十三 9	金9 Metal [2] Tread 天澤履 戊辰 Earth Dragon **9** 十四 6	木8 Wood [1] Great Strength 雷天大壯 己巳 Earth Snake **10** 十五 2	木8 Wood [9] Consistency 雷風恒 庚午 Metal Horse **11** 十六 9	金9 Metal [8] Litigation 天水訟 辛未 Metal Goat **12** 十七 3
水1 Water [7] Officer 地水師 壬申 Water Monkey **13** 十八 7	火2 Fire [6] Gradual Progress 風山漸 癸酉 Water Rooster **14** 十九 7	火7 Fire [5] Obstruction 水山蹇 甲戌 Wood Dog **15** 二十 2	木3 Wood [4] Advancement 火地晉 乙亥 Wood Pig **16** 廿一 3	水6 Water [3] Nourish 山雷頤 丙子 Fire Rat **17** 廿二 3	金4 Metal [2] Following 澤雷隨 丁丑 Fire Ox **18** 廿三 7	木8 Wood [1] Abundance 雷火豐 戊寅 Earth Tiger **19** 廿四 6
火7 Fire [9] Regulate 水澤節 己卯 Earth Rabbit **20** 廿五 8	水1 Water [8] Unity 地天泰 庚辰 Metal Dragon **21** 廿六 9	木3 Wood [7] Great Reward 火天大有 辛巳 Metal Snake **22** 廿七 7	火2 Fire [6] Wind 巽爲風 壬午 Water Horse **23** 廿八 1	金4 Metal [5] Trap 澤水困 癸未 Water Goat **24** 廿九 8	木3 Wood [4] Not Yet Accomplished 火水未濟 甲申 Wood Monkey **25** 十一月初一 9	金9 Metal [3] Retreat 天山遯 乙酉 Wood Rooster **26** 初二 4
水6 Water [2] Mountain 艮爲山 丙戌 Fire Dog **27** 初三 1	木8 Wood [1] Delight 雷地豫 丁亥 Fire Pig **28** 初四 8	火7 Fire [9] Beginning 水雷屯 戊子 Earth Rat **29** 初五 4	金9 Metal [8] Without Wrongdoing 天雷無妄 己丑 Earth Ox **30** 初六 2			

DECEMBER 2011 庚子

Xuan Kong Element 玄空五行	風雷益 Increasing	Period Luck 卦運	Monthly Star 月星
Fire 火2		9	7

SUNDAY	MONDAY	TUESDAY	WEDNESDAY	THURSDAY	FRIDAY	SATURDAY
				木3 Wood [7] Fire 離爲火 庚寅 Metal Tiger **1** 初七 1	火2 Fire [6] Sincerity 風澤中孚 辛卯 Metal Rabbit **2** 初八 3	水6 Water [5] Big Livestock 山天大畜 壬辰 Water Dragon **3** 初九 4
金4 Metal [4] Eliminating 澤天夬 癸巳 Water Snake **4** 初十 6	金9 Metal [3] Heaven 乾爲天 甲午 Wood Horse **5** 十一 1	火7 Fire [2] Well 水風井 乙未 Wood Goat **6** 十二 6	木8 Wood [1] Relief 雷水解 丙申 Fire Monkey **7** 十三 4	金4 Metal [9] Influence 澤山咸 丁酉 Fire Rooster **8** 十四 9	水1 Water [8] Humility 地山謙 戊戌 Earth Dog **9** 十五 6	火2 Fire [7] Observation 風地觀 己亥 Earth Pig **10** 十六 2
火2 Fire [6] Increasing 風雷益 庚子 Metal Rat **11** 十七 9	水1 Water [5] Dimming Light 地火明夷 辛丑 Metal Ox **12** 十八 3	金9 Metal [4] Fellowship 天火同人 壬寅 Water Tiger **13** 十九 7	木8 Wood [3] Marrying Maiden 雷澤歸妹 癸卯 Water Rabbit **14** 二十 7	木3 Wood [2] Opposition 火澤睽 甲辰 Wood Dragon **15** 廿一 2	火7 Fire [1] Waiting 水天需 乙巳 Wood Snake **16** 廿二 3	金4 Metal [9] Great Exceeding 澤風大過 丙午 Fire Horse **17** 廿三 3
水6 Water [8] Poison 山風蠱 丁未 Fire Goat **18** 廿四 7	火2 Fire [7] Dispersing 風水渙 戊申 Earth Monkey **19** 廿五 6	木3 Wood [6] Travelling 火山旅 己酉 Earth Rooster **20** 廿六 8	金9 Metal [5] Stagnation 天地否 庚戌 Metal Dog **21** 廿七 9	火7 Fire [4/6] Alliance 水地比 辛亥 Metal Pig **22** 廿八 7	木8 Wood [7] Thunder 震爲雷 壬子 Water Rat **23** 廿九 1	水6 Water [8] Beauty 山火賁 癸丑 Water Ox **24** 三十 8
火7 Fire [9] Accomplished 水火既濟 甲寅 Wood Tiger **25** 十二月初一 9	水1 Water [1] Arriving 地澤臨 乙卯 Wood Rabbit **26** 初二 4	金4 Metal [2] Marsh 兌爲澤 丙辰 Fire Dragon **27** 初三 1	火2 Fire [3] Small Livestock 風天小畜 丁巳 Fire Snake **28** 初四 8	木3 Wood [4] The Cauldron 火風鼎 戊午 Earth Horse **29** 初五 4	水1 Water [5] Rising 地風升 己未 Earth Goat **30** 初六 2	火7 Fire [6] Water 坎爲水 庚申 Metal Monkey **31** 初七 1

2012 壬辰

(*Ren Chen*) Water Dragon

2012 壬辰 *(Ren Chen)* Water Dragon

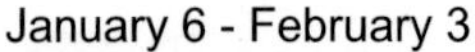

January 6 - February 3

SE	S	SW
5	1	3
4	**6**	8
9	2	7
NE	N	NW

水 **1** Water
辛 丑 Metal Ox
3 Dimming Light
地火明夷

February 4 - March 4

SE	S	SW
4	9	2
3	**5**	7
8	1	6
NE	N	NW

金 **9** Metal
壬 寅 Water Tiger
7 Fellowship
天火同人

March 5 - April 3

SE	S	SW
3	8	1
2	**4**	6
7	9	5
NE	N	NW

木 **8** Wood
癸 卯 Water Rabbit
7 Marrying Maiden
雷澤歸妹

April 4 - May 4

SE	S	SW
2	7	9
1	**3**	5
6	8	4
NE	N	NW

木 **3** Wood
甲 辰 Wood Dragon
2 Opposition
火澤睽

May 5 - June 4

SE	S	SW
1	6	8
9	**2**	4
5	7	3
NE	N	NW

火 **7** Fire
乙 巳 Wood Snake
3 Waiting
水天需

June 5 - July 6

SE	S	SW
9	5	7
8	**1**	3
4	6	2
NE	N	NW

金 **4** Metal
丙 午 Fire Horse
3 Great Exceeding
澤風大過

July 7 - August 6

SE	S	SW
8	4	6
7	**9**	2
3	5	1
NE	N	NW

水 **6** Water
丁 未 Fire Goat
7 Poison
山風蠱

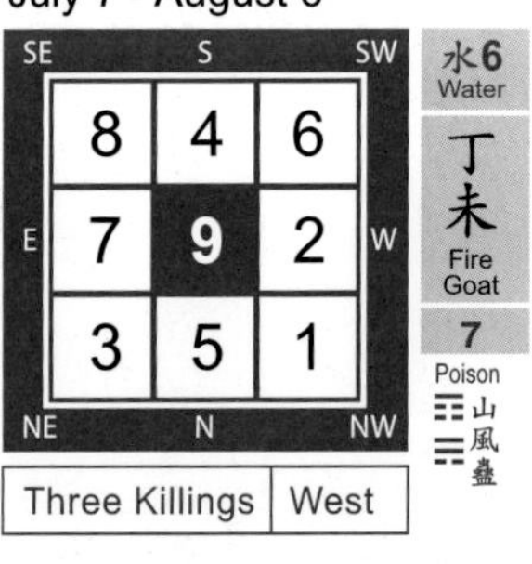

August 7 - September 6

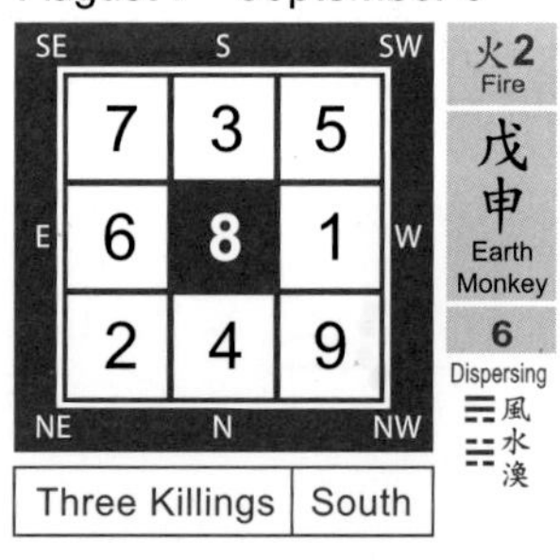

September 7 - October 7

SE	S	SW
6	2	4
5	**7**	9
1	3	8
NE	N	NW

木 **3** Wood
己 酉 Earth Rooster
8 Travelling
火山旅

October 8 - November 6

SE	S	SW
5	1	3
4	**6**	8
9	2	7
NE	N	NW

金 **9** Metal
庚 戌 Metal Dog
9 Stagnation
天地否

November 7 - December 6

SE	S	SW
4	9	2
3	**5**	7
8	1	6
NE	N	NW

火 **7** Fire
辛 亥 Metal Pig
7 Alliance
水地比

December 7 - January 4

SE	S	SW
3	8	1
2	**4**	6
7	9	5
NE	N	NW

木 **8** Wood
壬 子 Water Rat
7 Thunder
震為雷

JANUARY 2012 辛丑

Xuan Kong Element 玄空五行	地火明夷 Dimming Light	Period Luck 卦運	Monthly Star 月星
Water 水1		3	6

SUNDAY	MONDAY	TUESDAY	WEDNESDAY	THURSDAY	FRIDAY	SATURDAY
1 初八 木8 Wood Lesser Exceeding 雷山小過 辛酉 Metal Rooster 7 · 3	**2** 初九 金4 Metal Gathering 澤地萃 壬戌 Water Dog 8 · 4	**3** 初十 水6 Water Peel 山地剝 癸亥 Water Pig 9 · 6	**4** 十一 水1 Water Earth 坤爲地 甲子 Wood Rat 1 · 1	**5** 十二 木3 Wood Biting 火雷噬嗑 乙丑 Wood Ox 2 · 6	**6** 十三 火2 Fire Family 風火家人 丙寅 Fire Tiger 3 · 4	**7** 十四 水6 Water Decreasing 山澤損 丁卯 Fire Rabbit 4 · 9
8 十五 金9 Metal Tread 天澤履 戊辰 Earth Dragon 5 · 6	**9** 十六 木8 Wood Great Strength 雷天大壯 己巳 Earth Snake 6 · 2	**10** 十七 木8 Wood Consistency 雷風恆 庚午 Metal Horse 7 · 9	**11** 十八 金9 Metal Litigation 天水訟 辛未 Metal Goat 8 · 3	**12** 十九 水1 Water Officer 地水師 壬申 Water Monkey 9 · 7	**13** 二十 火2 Fire Gradual Progress 風山漸 癸酉 Water Rooster 1 · 7	**14** 廿一 火7 Fire Obstruction 水山蹇 甲戌 Wood Dog 2 · 2
15 廿二 木3 Wood Advancement 火地晉 乙亥 Wood Pig 3 · 3	**16** 廿三 水6 Water Nourish 山雷頤 丙子 Fire Rat 4 · 3	**17** 廿四 金4 Metal Following 澤雷隨 丁丑 Fire Ox 5 · 7	**18** 廿五 木8 Wood Abundance 雷火豐 戊寅 Earth Tiger 6 · 6	**19** 廿六 火7 Fire Regulate 水澤節 己卯 Earth Rabbit 7 · 8	**20** 廿七 水1 Water Unity 地天泰 庚辰 Metal Dragon 8 · 9	**21** 廿八 木3 Wood Great Reward 火天大有 辛巳 Metal Snake 9 · 7
22 廿九 火2 Fire Wind 巽爲風 壬午 Water Horse 1 · 1	**23** 正月初一 金4 Metal Trap 澤水困 癸未 Water Goat 2 · 8	**24** 初二 木3 Wood Not Yet Accomplished 火水未濟 甲申 Wood Monkey 3 · 9	**25** 初三 金9 Metal Retreat 天山遯 乙酉 Wood Rooster 4 · 4	**26** 初四 水6 Water Mountain 艮爲山 丙戌 Fire Dog 5 · 1	**27** 初五 木8 Wood Delight 雷地豫 丁亥 Fire Pig 6 · 8	**28** 初六 火7 Fire Beginning 水雷屯 戊子 Earth Rat 7 · 4
29 初七 金9 Metal Without Wrongdoing 天雷無妄 己丑 Earth Ox 8 · 2	**30** 初八 木3 Wood Fire 離爲火 庚寅 Metal Tiger 9 · 1	**31** 初九 火2 Fire Sincerity 風澤中孚 辛卯 Metal Rabbit 1 · 3				

FEBRUARY 2012 壬寅

Xuan Kong Element 玄空五行	天火同人 Fellowship	Period Luck 卦運	Monthly Star 月星
Metal 金9		7	5

SUNDAY	MONDAY	TUESDAY	WEDNESDAY	THURSDAY	FRIDAY	SATURDAY
			1 初十 水6 Water Big Livestock 山天大畜 壬辰 Water Dragon 2 · 4	**2** 十一 金4 Metal Eliminating 澤天夬 癸巳 Water Snake 3 · 6	**3** 十二 金9 Metal Heaven 乾爲天 甲午 Wood Horse 4 · 1	**4** 十三 火7 Fire Well 水風井 乙未 Wood Goat 5 · 6
5 十四 木8 Wood Relief 雷水解 丙申 Fire Monkey 6 · 4	**6** 十五 金4 Metal Influence 澤山咸 丁酉 Fire Rooster 7 · 9	**7** 十六 水1 Water Humility 地山謙 戊戌 Earth Dog 8 · 6	**8** 十七 火2 Fire Observation 風地觀 己亥 Earth Pig 9 · 2	**9** 十八 火2 Fire Increasing 風雷益 庚子 Metal Rat 1 · 9	**10** 十九 水1 Water Dimming Light 地火明夷 辛丑 Metal Ox 2 · 3	**11** 二十 金9 Metal Fellowship 天火同人 壬寅 Water Tiger 3 · 7
12 廿一 木8 Wood Marrying Maiden 雷澤歸妹 癸卯 Water Rabbit 4 · 7	**13** 廿二 木3 Wood Opposition 火澤睽 甲辰 Wood Dragon 5 · 2	**14** 廿三 火7 Fire Waiting 水天需 乙巳 Wood Snake 6 · 3	**15** 廿四 金4 Metal Great Exceeding 澤風大過 丙午 Fire Horse 7 · 3	**16** 廿五 水6 Water Poison 山風蠱 丁未 Fire Goat 8 · 7	**17** 廿六 火2 Fire Dispersing 風水渙 戊申 Earth Monkey 9 · 6	**18** 廿七 木3 Wood Travelling 火山旅 己酉 Earth Rooster 1 · 8
19 廿八 金9 Metal Stagnation 天地否 庚戌 Metal Dog 2 · 9	**20** 廿九 火7 Fire Alliance 水地比 辛亥 Metal Pig 3 · 7	**21** 三十 木8 Wood Thunder 震爲雷 壬子 Water Rat 4 · 1	**22** 二月初一 水6 Water Beauty 山火賁 癸丑 Water Ox 5 · 8	**23** 初二 火7 Fire Accomplished 水火既濟 甲寅 Wood Tiger 6 · 9	**24** 初三 水1 Water Arriving 地澤臨 乙卯 Wood Rabbit 7 · 4	**25** 初四 金4 Metal Marsh 兌爲澤 丙辰 Fire Dragon 8 · 1
26 初五 火2 Fire Small Livestock 風天小畜 丁巳 Fire Snake 9 · 8	**27** 初六 木3 Wood The Cauldron 火風鼎 戊午 Earth Horse 1 · 4	**28** 初七 水1 Water Rising 地風升 己未 Earth Goat 2 · 2	**29** 初八 火7 Fire Water 坎爲水 庚申 Metal Monkey 3 · 1			

MARCH 2012 癸卯

Xuan Kong Element 玄空五行	雷澤歸妹 Marrying Maiden	Period Luck 卦運	Monthly Star 月星
Wood 木8		7	4

SUNDAY	MONDAY	TUESDAY	WEDNESDAY	THURSDAY	FRIDAY	SATURDAY
				木8 Wood 4 Lesser Exceeding 雷山小過 辛酉 Metal Rooster 1 初九 3	金4 Metal 5 Gathering 澤地萃 壬戌 Water Dog 2 初十 4	水6 Water 6 Peel 山地剝 癸亥 Water Pig 3 十一 6
水1 Water 7 Earth 坤爲地 甲子 Wood Rat 4 十二 1	木3 Wood 8 Biting 火雷噬嗑 乙丑 Wood Ox 5 十三 6	火2 Fire 9 Family 風火家人 丙寅 Fire Tiger 6 十四 4	水6 Water 1 Decreasing 山澤損 丁卯 Fire Rabbit 7 十五 9	金9 Metal 2 Tread 天澤履 戊辰 Earth Dragon 8 十六 6	木8 Wood 3 Great Strength 雷天大壯 己巳 Earth Snake 9 十七 2	木8 Wood 4 Consistency 雷風恆 庚午 Metal Horse 10 十八 9
金9 Metal 5 Litigation 天水訟 辛未 Metal Goat 11 十九 3	水1 Water 6 Officer 地水師 壬申 Water Monkey 12 二十 7	火2 Fire 7 Gradual Progress 風山漸 癸酉 Water Rooster 13 廿一 7	火7 Fire 8 Obstruction 水山蹇 甲戌 Wood Dog 14 廿二 2	木3 Wood 9 Advancement 火地晉 乙亥 Wood Pig 15 廿三 3	水6 Water 1 Nourish 山雷頤 丙子 Fire Rat 16 廿四 3	金4 Metal 2 Following 澤雷隨 丁丑 Fire Ox 17 廿五 7
木8 Wood 3 Abundance 雷火豐 戊寅 Earth Tiger 18 廿六 6	火7 Fire 4 Regulate 水澤節 己卯 Earth Rabbit 19 廿七 8	水1 Water 5 Unity 地天泰 庚辰 Metal Dragon 20 廿八 9	木3 Wood 6 Great Reward 火天大有 辛巳 Metal Snake 21 廿九 7	火2 Fire 7 Wind 巽爲風 壬午 Water Horse 22 三月初一 1	金4 Metal 8 Trap 澤水困 癸未 Water Goat 23 初二 8	木3 Wood 9 Not Yet Accomplished 火水未濟 甲申 Wood Monkey 24 初三 9
金9 Metal 1 Retreat 天山遯 乙酉 Wood Rooster 25 初四 4	水6 Water 2 Mountain 艮爲山 丙戌 Fire Dog 26 初五 1	木8 Wood 3 Delight 雷地豫 丁亥 Fire Pig 27 初六 8	火7 Fire 4 Beginning 水雷屯 戊子 Earth Rat 28 初七 4	金9 Metal 5 Without Wrongdoing 天雷無妄 己丑 Earth Ox 29 初八 2	木3 Wood 6 Fire 離爲火 庚寅 Metal Tiger 30 初九 1	火2 Fire 7 Sincerity 風澤中孚 辛卯 Metal Rabbit 31 初十 3

APRIL 2012 甲辰

Xuan Kong Element 玄空五行	火澤睽 Opposition	Period Luck 卦運	Monthly Star 月星
Wood 木3		2	3

SUNDAY	MONDAY	TUESDAY	WEDNESDAY	THURSDAY	FRIDAY	SATURDAY
水6 Water 8 Big Livestock 山天大畜 壬辰 Water Dragon 1 十一 4	金4 Metal 9 Eliminating 澤天夬 癸巳 Water Snake 2 十二 6	金9 Metal 1 Heaven 乾爲天 甲午 Wood Horse 3 十三 1	火7 Fire 2 Well 水風井 乙未 Wood Goat 4 十四 6	木8 Wood 3 Relief 雷水解 丙申 Fire Monkey 5 十五 4	金4 Metal 4 Influence 澤山咸 丁酉 Fire Rooster 6 十六 9	水1 Water 5 Humility 地山謙 戊戌 Earth Dog 7 十七 6
火2 Fire 6 Observation 風地觀 己亥 Earth Pig 8 十八 2	火2 Fire 7 Increasing 風雷益 庚子 Metal Rat 9 十九 9	水1 Water 8 Dimming Light 地火明夷 辛丑 Metal Ox 10 二十 3	金9 Metal 9 Fellowship 天火同人 壬寅 Water Tiger 11 廿一 7	木8 Wood 1 Marrying Maiden 雷澤歸妹 癸卯 Water Rabbit 12 廿二 7	木3 Wood 2 Opposition 火澤睽 甲辰 Wood Dragon 13 廿三 2	火7 Fire 3 Waiting 水天需 乙巳 Wood Snake 14 廿四 3
金4 Metal 4 Great Exceeding 澤風大過 丙午 Fire Horse 15 廿五 3	水6 Water 5 Poison 山風蠱 丁未 Fire Goat 16 廿六 7	火2 Fire 6 Dispersing 風水渙 戊申 Earth Monkey 17 廿七 6	木3 Wood 7 Travelling 火山旅 己酉 Earth Rooster 18 廿八 8	金9 Metal 8 Stagnation 天地否 庚戌 Metal Dog 19 廿九 9	火7 Fire 9 Alliance 水地比 辛亥 Metal Pig 20 三十 7	木8 Wood 1 Thunder 震爲雷 壬子 Water Rat 21 四月初一 1
水6 Water 2 Beauty 山火賁 癸丑 Water Ox 22 初二 8	火7 Fire 3 Accomplished 水火既濟 甲寅 Wood Tiger 23 初三 9	水1 Water 4 Arriving 地澤臨 乙卯 Wood Rabbit 24 初四 4	金4 Metal 5 Marsh 兑爲澤 丙辰 Fire Dragon 25 初五 1	火2 Fire 6 Small Livestock 風天小畜 丁巳 Fire Snake 26 初六 8	木3 Wood 7 The Cauldron 火風鼎 戊午 Earth Horse 27 初七 4	水1 Water 8 Rising 地風升 己未 Earth Goat 28 初八 2
火7 Fire 9 Water 坎爲水 庚申 Metal Monkey 29 初九 1	木8 Wood 1 Lesser Exceeding 雷山小過 辛酉 Metal Rooster 30 初十 3					

MAY 2012 乙巳

Xuan Kong Element 玄空五行	水天需 Waiting	Period Luck 卦運	Monthly Star 月星
Fire 火7		3	2

SUNDAY	MONDAY	TUESDAY	WEDNESDAY	THURSDAY	FRIDAY	SATURDAY
		金4 Metal Gathering 澤地萃 2 壬戌 Water Dog 4 **1** 十一	水6 Water Peel 山地剝 3 癸亥 Water Pig 6 **2** 十二	水1 Water Earth 坤爲地 4 甲子 Wood Rat 1 **3** 十三	木3 Wood Biting 火雷噬嗑 5 乙丑 Wood Ox 6 **4** 十四	火2 Fire Family 風火家人 6 丙寅 Fire Tiger 4 **5** 十五
水6 Water Decreasing 山澤損 7 丁卯 Fire Rabbit 9 **6** 十六	金9 Metal Tread 天澤履 8 戊辰 Earth Dragon 6 **7** 十七	木8 Wood Great Strength 雷天大壯 9 己巳 Earth Snake 2 **8** 十八	木8 Wood Consistency 雷風恒 1 庚午 Metal Horse 9 **9** 十九	金9 Metal Litigation 天水訟 2 辛未 Metal Goat 3 **10** 二十	水1 Water Officer 地水師 3 壬申 Water Monkey 7 **11** 廿一	火2 Fire Gradual Progress 風山漸 4 癸酉 Water Rooster 7 **12** 廿二
火7 Fire Obstruction 水山蹇 5 甲戌 Wood Dog 2 **13** 廿三	木3 Wood Advancement 火地晉 6 乙亥 Wood Pig 3 **14** 廿四	水6 Water Nourish 山雷頤 7 丙子 Fire Rat 3 **15** 廿五	金4 Metal Following 澤雷隨 8 丁丑 Fire Ox 7 **16** 廿六	木8 Wood Abundance 雷火豐 9 戊寅 Earth Tiger 6 **17** 廿七	火7 Fire Regulate 水澤節 1 己卯 Earth Rabbit 8 **18** 廿八	水1 Water Unity 地天泰 2 庚辰 Metal Dragon 9 **19** 廿九
木3 Wood Great Reward 火天大有 3 辛巳 Metal Snake 7 **20** 三十	火2 Fire Wind 巽爲風 4 壬午 Water Horse 1 **21** 閏四月初一	金4 Metal Trap 澤水困 5 癸未 Water Goat 8 **22** 初二	木3 Wood Not Yet Accomplished 火水未濟 6 甲申 Wood Monkey 9 **23** 初三	金9 Metal Retreat 天山遯 7 乙酉 Wood Rooster 4 **24** 初四	水6 Water Mountain 艮爲山 8 丙戌 Fire Dog 1 **25** 初五	木8 Wood Delight 雷地豫 9 丁亥 Fire Pig 8 **26** 初六
火7 Fire Beginning 水雷屯 1 戊子 Earth Rat 4 **27** 初七	金9 Metal Without Wrongdoing 天雷無妄 2 己丑 Earth Ox 2 **28** 初八	木3 Wood Fire 離爲火 3 庚寅 Metal Tiger 1 **29** 初九	火2 Fire Sincerity 風澤中孚 4 辛卯 Metal Rabbit 3 **30** 初十	水6 Water Big Livestock 山天大畜 5 壬辰 Water Dragon 4 **31** 十一		

JUNE 2012 丙午

Xuan Kong Element 玄空五行	澤風大過 Great Exceeding	Period Luck 卦運	Monthly Star 月星
Metal 金4		3	1

SUNDAY	MONDAY	TUESDAY	WEDNESDAY	THURSDAY	FRIDAY	SATURDAY
					金4 Metal Eliminating 澤天夬 6 癸巳 Water Snake 6 **1** 十二	金9 Metal Heaven 乾爲天 7 甲午 Wood Horse 1 **2** 十三
火7 Fire Well 水風井 8 乙未 Wood Goat 6 **3** 十四	木8 Wood Relief 雷水解 9 丙申 Fire Monkey 4 **4** 十五	金4 Metal Influence 澤山咸 1 丁酉 Fire Rooster 9 **5** 十六	水1 Water Humility 地山謙 2 戊戌 Earth Dog 6 **6** 十七	火2 Fire Observation 風地觀 3 己亥 Earth Pig 2 **7** 十八	火2 Fire Increasing 風雷益 4 庚子 Metal Rat 9 **8** 十九	水1 Water Dimming Light 地火明夷 5 辛丑 Metal Ox 3 **9** 二十
金9 Metal Fellowship 天火同人 6 壬寅 Water Tiger 7 **10** 廿一	木8 Wood Marrying Maiden 雷澤歸妹 7 癸卯 Water Rabbit 7 **11** 廿二	木3 Wood Opposition 火澤睽 8 甲辰 Wood Dragon 2 **12** 廿三	火7 Fire Waiting 水天需 9 乙巳 Wood Snake 3 **13** 廿四	金4 Metal Great Exceeding 澤風大過 1 丙午 Fire Horse 3 **14** 廿五	水6 Water Poison 山風蠱 2 丁未 Fire Goat 7 **15** 廿六	火2 Fire Dispersing 風水渙 3 戊申 Earth Monkey 6 **16** 廿七
木3 Wood Travelling 火山旅 4 己酉 Earth Rooster 8 **17** 廿八	金9 Metal Stagnation 天地否 5 庚戌 Metal Dog 9 **18** 廿九	火7 Fire Alliance 水地比 6 辛亥 Metal Pig 7 **19** 五月初一	木8 Wood Thunder 震爲雷 7 壬子 Water Rat 1 **20** 初二	水6 Water Beauty 山火賁 8/2 癸丑 Water Ox 8 **21** 初三	火7 Fire Accomplished 水火既濟 1 甲寅 Wood Tiger 9 **22** 初四	水1 Water Arriving 地澤臨 9 乙卯 Wood Rabbit 4 **23** 初五
金4 Metal Marsh 兌爲澤 8 丙辰 Fire Dragon 1 **24** 初六	火2 Fire Small Livestock 風天小畜 7 丁巳 Fire Snake 8 **25** 初七	木3 Wood The Cauldron 火風鼎 6 戊午 Earth Horse 4 **26** 初八	水1 Water Rising 地風升 5 己未 Earth Goat 2 **27** 初九	火7 Fire Water 坎爲水 4 庚申 Metal Monkey 1 **28** 初十	木8 Wood Lesser Exceeding 雷山小過 3 辛酉 Metal Rooster 3 **29** 十一	金4 Metal Gathering 澤地萃 2 壬戌 Water Dog 4 **30** 十二

JULY 2012 丁未

Xuan Kong Element 玄空五行	山風蠱 Poison	Period Luck 卦運	Monthly Star 月星
Water 水6		7	9

SUNDAY	MONDAY	TUESDAY	WEDNESDAY	THURSDAY	FRIDAY	SATURDAY
水6 Water 1 Peel 山地剝 癸亥 Water Pig 6 1 十三	水1 Water 9 Earth 坤爲地 甲子 Wood Rat 1 2 十四	木3 Wood 8 Biting 火雷噬嗑 乙丑 Wood Ox 6 3 十五	火2 Fire 7 Family 風火家人 丙寅 Fire Tiger 4 4 十六	水6 Water 6 Decreasing 山澤損 丁卯 Fire Rabbit 9 5 十七	金9 Metal 5 Tread 天澤履 戊辰 Earth Dragon 6 6 十八	木8 Wood 4 Great Strength 雷天大壯 己巳 Earth Snake 2 7 十九
木8 Wood 3 Consistency 雷風恒 庚午 Metal Horse 9 8 二十	金9 Metal 2 Litigation 天水訟 辛未 Metal Goat 3 9 廿一	水1 Water 1 Officer 地水師 壬申 Water Monkey 7 10 廿二	火2 Fire 9 Gradual Progress 風山漸 癸酉 Water Rooster 7 11 廿三	火7 Fire 8 Obstruction 水山蹇 甲戌 Wood Dog 2 12 廿四	木3 Wood 7 Advancement 火地晉 乙亥 Wood Pig 3 13 廿五	水6 Water 6 Nourish 山雷頤 丙子 Fire Rat 3 14 廿六
金4 Metal 5 Following 澤雷隨 丁丑 Fire Ox 7 15 廿七	木8 Wood 4 Abundance 雷火豐 戊寅 Earth Tiger 6 16 廿八	火7 Fire 3 Regulate 水澤節 己卯 Earth Rabbit 8 17 廿九	水1 Water 2 Unity 地天泰 庚辰 Metal Dragon 9 18 三十	木3 Wood 1 Great Reward 火天大有 辛巳 Metal Snake 7 19 六月初一	火2 Fire 9 Wind 巽爲風 壬午 Water Horse 1 20 初二	金4 Metal 8 Trap 澤水困 癸未 Water Goat 8 21 初三
木3 Wood 7 Not Yet Accomplished 火水未濟 甲申 Wood Monkey 9 22 初四	金9 Metal 6 Retreat 天山遯 乙酉 Wood Rooster 4 23 初五	水6 Water 5 Mountain 艮爲山 丙戌 Fire Dog 1 24 初六	木8 Wood 4 Delight 雷地豫 丁亥 Fire Pig 8 25 初七	火7 Fire 3 Beginning 水雷屯 戊子 Earth Rat 4 26 初八	金9 Metal 2 Without Wrongdoing 天雷無妄 己丑 Earth Ox 2 27 初九	木3 Wood 1 Fire 離爲火 庚寅 Metal Tiger 1 28 初十
火2 Fire 9 Sincerity 風澤中孚 辛卯 Metal Rabbit 3 29 十一	水6 Water 8 Big Livestock 山天大畜 壬辰 Water Dragon 4 30 十二	金4 Metal 7 Eliminating 澤天夬 癸巳 Water Snake 6 31 十三				

AUGUST 2012 戊申

Xuan Kong Element 玄空五行	風水渙 Dispersing	Period Luck 卦運	Monthly Star 月星
Fire 火2		6	8

SUNDAY	MONDAY	TUESDAY	WEDNESDAY	THURSDAY	FRIDAY	SATURDAY
			金9 Metal 6 Heaven 乾爲天 甲午 Wood Horse 1 1 十四	火7 Fire 5 Well 水風井 乙未 Wood Goat 6 2 十五	木8 Wood 4 Relief 雷水解 丙申 Fire Monkey 4 3 十六	金4 Metal 3 Influence 澤山咸 丁酉 Fire Rooster 9 4 十七
水1 Water 2 Humility 地山謙 戊戌 Earth Dog 6 5 十八	火2 Fire 1 Observation 風地觀 己亥 Earth Pig 2 6 十九	火2 Fire 9 Increasing 風雷益 庚子 Metal Rat 9 7 二十	水1 Water 8 Dimming Light 地火明夷 辛丑 Metal Ox 3 8 廿一	金9 Metal 7 Fellowship 天火同人 壬寅 Water Tiger 7 9 廿二	木8 Wood 6 Marrying Maiden 雷澤歸妹 癸卯 Water Rabbit 7 10 廿三	木3 Wood 5 Opposition 火澤睽 甲辰 Wood Dragon 2 11 廿四
火7 Fire 4 Waiting 水天需 乙巳 Wood Snake 3 12 廿五	金4 Metal 3 Great Exceeding 澤風大過 丙午 Fire Horse 3 13 廿六	水6 Water 2 Poison 山風蠱 丁未 Fire Goat 7 14 廿七	火2 Fire 1 Dispersing 風水渙 戊申 Earth Monkey 6 15 廿八	木3 Wood 9 Travelling 火山旅 己酉 Earth Rooster 8 16 廿九	金9 Metal 8 Stagnation 天地否 庚戌 Metal Dog 9 17 七月初一	火7 Fire 7 Alliance 水地比 辛亥 Metal Pig 7 18 初二
木8 Wood 6 Thunder 震爲雷 壬子 Water Rat 1 19 初三	水6 Water 5 Beauty 山火賁 癸丑 Water Ox 8 20 初四	火7 Fire 4 Accomplished 水火既濟 甲寅 Wood Tiger 9 21 初五	水1 Water 3 Arriving 地澤臨 乙卯 Wood Rabbit 4 22 初六	金4 Metal 2 Marsh 兌爲澤 丙辰 Fire Dragon 1 23 初七	火2 Fire 1 Small Livestock 風天小畜 丁巳 Fire Snake 8 24 初八	木3 Wood 9 The Cauldron 火風鼎 戊午 Earth Horse 4 25 初九
水1 Water 8 Rising 地風升 己未 Earth Goat 2 26 初十	火7 Fire 7 Water 坎爲水 庚申 Metal Monkey 1 27 十一	木8 Wood 6 Lesser Exceeding 雷山小過 辛酉 Metal Rooster 3 28 十二	金4 Metal 5 Gathering 澤地萃 壬戌 Water Dog 4 29 十三	水6 Water 4 Peel 山地剝 癸亥 Water Pig 6 30 十四	水1 Water 3 Earth 坤爲地 甲子 Wood Rat 1 31 十五	

SEPTEMBER 2012 己酉

Xuan Kong Element 玄空五行	火山旅 Travelling	Period Luck 卦運	Monthly Star 月星
Wood 木3		8	7

SUNDAY	MONDAY	TUESDAY	WEDNESDAY	THURSDAY	FRIDAY	SATURDAY
金9 Metal 9 Heaven 乾爲天 甲午 Wood Horse 1 30 十五						木3 Wood 2 Biting 火雷噬嗑 乙丑 Wood Ox 6 1 十六
火2 Fire 1 Family 風火家人 丙寅 Fire Tiger 4 2 十七	水6 Water 9 Decreasing 山澤損 丁卯 Fire Rabbit 9 3 十八	金9 Metal 8 Tread 天澤履 戊辰 Earth Dragon 6 4 十九	木8 Wood 7 Great Strength 雷天大壯 己巳 Earth Snake 2 5 二十	木8 Wood 6 Consistency 雷風恒 庚午 Metal Horse 9 6 廿一	金9 Metal 5 Litigation 天水訟 辛未 Metal Goat 3 7 廿二	水1 Water 4 Officer 地水師 壬申 Water Monkey 7 8 廿三
火2 Fire 3 Gradual Progress 風山漸 癸酉 Water Rooster 7 9 廿四	火7 Fire 2 Obstruction 水山蹇 甲戌 Wood Dog 2 10 廿五	木3 Wood 1 Advancement 火地晉 乙亥 Wood Pig 3 11 廿六	水6 Water 9 Nourish 山雷頤 丙子 Fire Rat 3 12 廿七	金4 Metal 8 Following 澤雷隨 丁丑 Fire Ox 7 13 廿八	木8 Wood 7 Abundance 雷火豐 戊寅 Earth Tiger 6 14 廿九	火7 Fire 6 Regulate 水澤節 己卯 Earth Rabbit 8 15 三十
水1 Water 5 Unity 地天泰 庚辰 Metal Dragon 9 16 八月初一	木3 Wood 4 Great Reward 火天大有 辛巳 Metal Snake 7 17 初二	火2 Fire 3 Wind 巽爲風 壬午 Water Horse 1 18 初三	金4 Metal 2 Trap 澤水困 癸未 Water Goat 8 19 初四	木3 Wood 1 Not Yet Accomplished 火水未濟 甲申 Wood Monkey 9 20 初五	金9 Metal 9 Retreat 天山遯 乙酉 Wood Rooster 4 21 初六	水6 Water 8 Mountain 艮爲山 丙戌 Fire Dog 1 22 初七
木8 Wood 7 Delight 雷地豫 丁亥 Fire Pig 8 23 初八	火7 Fire 6 Beginning 水雷屯 戊子 Earth Rat 4 24 初九	金9 Metal 5 Without Wrongdoing 天雷無妄 己丑 Earth Ox 2 25 初十	木3 Wood 4 Fire 離爲火 庚寅 Metal Tiger 1 26 十一	火2 Fire 3 Sincerity 風澤中孚 辛卯 Metal Rabbit 3 27 十二	水6 Water 2 Big Livestock 山天大畜 壬辰 Water Dragon 4 28 十三	金4 Metal 1 Eliminating 澤天夬 癸巳 Water Snake 6 29 十四

OCTOBER 2012 庚戌

Xuan Kong Element 玄空五行	天地否 Stagnation	Period Luck 卦運	Monthly Star 月星
Metal 金9		9	6

SUNDAY	MONDAY	TUESDAY	WEDNESDAY	THURSDAY	FRIDAY	SATURDAY
	火7 Fire 8 Well 水風井 乙未 Wood Goat 6 1 十六	木8 Wood 7 Relief 雷水解 丙申 Fire Monkey 4 2 十七	金4 Metal 6 Influence 澤山咸 丁酉 Fire Rooster 9 3 十八	水1 Water 5 Humility 地山謙 戊戌 Earth Dog 6 4 十九	火2 Fire 4 Observation 風地觀 己亥 Earth Pig 2 5 二十	火2 Fire 3 Increasing 風雷益 庚子 Metal Rat 9 6 廿一
水1 Water 2 Dimming Light 地火明夷 辛丑 Metal Ox 3 7 廿二	金9 Metal 1 Fellowship 天火同人 壬寅 Water Tiger 7 8 廿三	木8 Wood 9 Marrying Maiden 雷澤歸妹 癸卯 Water Rabbit 7 9 廿四	木3 Wood 8 Opposition 火澤睽 甲辰 Wood Dragon 2 10 廿五	火7 Fire 7 Waiting 水天需 乙巳 Wood Snake 3 11 廿六	金4 Metal 6 Great Exceeding 澤風大過 丙午 Fire Horse 3 12 廿七	水6 Water 5 Poison 山風蠱 丁未 Fire Goat 7 13 廿八
火2 Fire 4 Dispersing 風水渙 戊申 Earth Monkey 6 14 廿九	木3 Wood 3 Travelling 火山旅 己酉 Earth Rooster 8 15 九月初一	金9 Metal 2 Stagnation 天地否 庚戌 Metal Dog 9 16 初二	火7 Fire 1 Alliance 水地比 辛亥 Metal Pig 7 17 初三	木8 Wood 9 Thunder 震爲雷 壬子 Water Rat 1 18 初四	水6 Water 8 Beauty 山火賁 癸丑 Water Ox 8 19 初五	火7 Fire 7 Accomplished 水火既濟 甲寅 Wood Tiger 9 20 初六
水1 Water 6 Arriving 地澤臨 乙卯 Wood Rabbit 4 21 初七	金4 Metal 5 Marsh 兑爲澤 丙辰 Fire Dragon 1 22 初八	火2 Fire 4 Small Livestock 風天小畜 丁巳 Fire Snake 8 23 初九	木3 Wood 3 The Cauldron 火風鼎 戊午 Earth Horse 4 24 初十	水1 Water 2 Rising 地風升 己未 Earth Goat 2 25 十一	火7 Fire 1 Water 坎爲水 庚申 Metal Monkey 1 26 十二	木8 Wood 9 Lesser Exceeding 雷山小過 辛酉 Metal Rooster 3 27 十三
金4 Metal 8 Gathering 澤地萃 壬戌 Water Dog 4 28 十四	水6 Water 7 Peel 山地剝 癸亥 Water Pig 6 29 十五	水1 Water 6 Earth 坤爲地 甲子 Wood Rat 1 30 十六	木3 Wood 5 Biting 火雷噬嗑 乙丑 Wood Ox 6 31 十七			

NOVEMBER 2012 辛亥

Xuan Kong Element 玄空五行	水地比 Alliance	Period Luck 卦運	Monthly Star 月星
Fire 火7		7	5

SUNDAY	MONDAY	TUESDAY	WEDNESDAY	THURSDAY	FRIDAY	SATURDAY
				火2 Fire 4 Family 丙寅 Fire Tiger 風火家人 1 十八 4	水6 Water 3 Decreasing 丁卯 Fire Rabbit 山澤損 2 十九 9	金9 Metal 2 Tread 戊辰 Earth Dragon 天澤履 3 二十 6
木8 Wood 1 Great Strength 己巳 Earth Snake 雷天大壯 4 廿一 2	木8 Wood 9 Consistency 庚午 Metal Horse 雷風恒 5 廿二 9	金9 Metal 8 Litigation 辛未 Metal Goat 天水訟 6 廿三 3	水1 Water 7 Officer 壬申 Water Monkey 地水師 7 廿四 7	火2 Fire 6 Gradual Progress 癸酉 Water Rooster 風山漸 8 廿五 7	火7 Fire 5 Obstruction 甲戌 Wood Dog 水山蹇 9 廿六 2	木3 Wood 4 Advancement 乙亥 Wood Pig 火地晉 10 廿七 3
水6 Water 3 Nourish 丙子 Fire Rat 山雷頤 11 廿八 3	金4 Metal 2 Following 丁丑 Fire Ox 澤雷隨 12 廿九 7	木8 Wood 1 Abundance 戊寅 Earth Tiger 雷火豐 13 三十 6	火7 Fire 9 Regulate 己卯 Earth Rabbit 水澤節 14 十月初一 8	水1 Water 8 Unity 庚辰 Metal Dragon 地天泰 15 初二 9	木3 Wood 7 Great Reward 辛巳 Metal Snake 火天大有 16 初三 7	火2 Fire 6 Wind 壬午 Water Horse 巽爲風 17 初四 1
金4 Metal 5 Trap 癸未 Water Goat 澤水困 18 初五 8	木3 Wood 4 Not Yet Accomplished 甲申 Wood Monkey 火水未濟 19 初六 9	金9 Metal 3 Retreat 乙酉 Wood Rooster 天山遯 20 初七 4	水6 Water 2 Mountain 丙戌 Fire Dog 艮爲山 21 初八 1	木8 Wood 1 Delight 丁亥 Fire Pig 雷地豫 22 初九 8	火7 Fire 9 Beginning 戊子 Earth Rat 水雷屯 23 初十 4	金9 Metal 8 Without Wrongdoing 己丑 Earth Ox 天雷無妄 24 十一 2
木3 Wood 7 Fire 庚寅 Metal Tiger 離爲火 25 十二 1	火2 Fire 6 Sincerity 辛卯 Metal Rabbit 風澤中孚 26 十三 3	水6 Water 5 Big Livestock 壬辰 Water Dragon 山天大畜 27 十四 4	金4 Metal 4 Eliminating 癸巳 Water Snake 澤天夬 28 十五 6	金9 Metal 3 Heaven 甲午 Wood Horse 乾爲天 29 十六 1	火7 Fire 2 Well 乙未 Wood Goat 水風井 30 十七 6	

DECEMBER 2012 壬子

Xuan Kong Element 玄空五行	震爲雷 Thunder	Period Luck 卦運	Monthly Star 月星
Wood 木8		1	4

SUNDAY	MONDAY	TUESDAY	WEDNESDAY	THURSDAY	FRIDAY	SATURDAY
木3 Wood 2 Biting 乙丑 Wood Ox 火雷噬嗑 30 十八 6	火2 Fire 3 Family 丙寅 Fire Tiger 風火家人 31 十九 4					木8 Wood 1 Relief 丙申 Fire Monkey 雷水解 1 十八 4
金4 Metal 9 Influence 丁酉 Fire Rooster 澤山咸 2 十九 9	水1 Water 8 Humility 戊戌 Earth Dog 地山謙 3 二十 6	火2 Fire 7 Observation 己亥 Earth Pig 風地觀 4 廿一 2	火2 Fire 6 Increasing 庚子 Metal Rat 風雷益 5 廿二 9	水1 Water 5 Dimming Light 辛丑 Metal Ox 地火明夷 6 廿三 3	金9 Metal 4 Fellowship 壬寅 Water Tiger 天火同人 7 廿四 7	木8 Wood 3 Marrying Maiden 癸卯 Water Rabbit 雷澤歸妹 8 廿五 7
木3 Wood 2 Opposition 甲辰 Wood Dragon 火澤睽 9 廿六 2	火7 Fire 1 Waiting 乙巳 Wood Snake 水天需 10 廿七 3	金4 Metal 9 Great Exceeding 丙午 Fire Horse 澤風大過 11 廿八 3	水6 Water 8 Poison 丁未 Fire Goat 山風蠱 12 廿九 7	火2 Fire 7 Dispersing 戊申 Earth Monkey 風水渙 13 十一月初一 6	木3 Wood 6 Travelling 己酉 Earth Rooster 火山旅 14 初二 8	金9 Metal 5 Stagnation 庚戌 Metal Dog 天地否 15 初三 9
火7 Fire 4 Alliance 辛亥 Metal Pig 水地比 16 初四 7	木8 Wood 3 Thunder 壬子 Water Rat 震爲雷 17 初五 1	水6 Water 2 Beauty 癸丑 Water Ox 山火賁 18 初六 8	火7 Fire 1 Accomplished 甲寅 Wood Tiger 水火既濟 19 初七 9	水1 Water 9 Arriving 乙卯 Wood Rabbit 地澤臨 20 初八 4	金4 Metal 8/2 Marsh 丙辰 Fire Dragon 兑爲澤 21 初九 1	火2 Fire 3 Small Livestock 丁巳 Fire Snake 風天小畜 22 初十 8
木3 Wood 4 The Cauldron 戊午 Earth Horse 火風鼎 23 十一 4	水1 Water 5 Rising 己未 Earth Goat 地風升 24 十二 2	火7 Fire 6 Water 庚申 Metal Monkey 坎爲水 25 十三 1	木8 Wood 7 Lesser Exceeding 辛酉 Metal Rooster 雷山小過 26 十四 3	金4 Metal 8 Gathering 壬戌 Water Dog 澤地萃 27 十五 4	水6 Water 9 Peel 癸亥 Water Pig 山地剝 28 十六 6	水1 Water 1 Earth 甲子 Wood Rat 坤爲地 29 十七 1

2013 癸巳

(*Gui Si*) Water Snake

2013 癸巳 *(Gui Si)* Water Snake

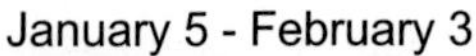

January 5 - February 3

February 4 - March 4

March 5 - April 3

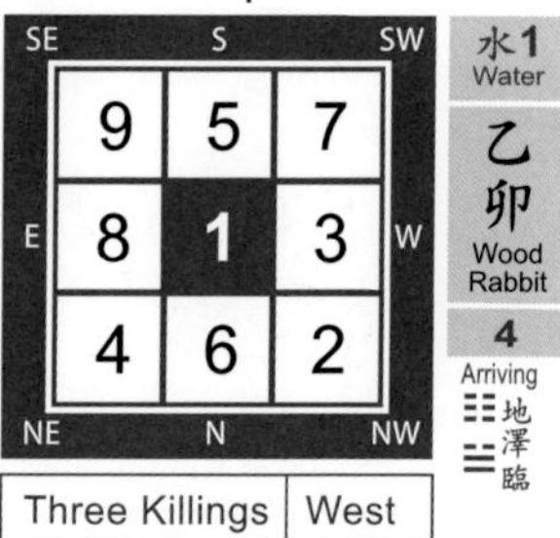

April 4 - May 4

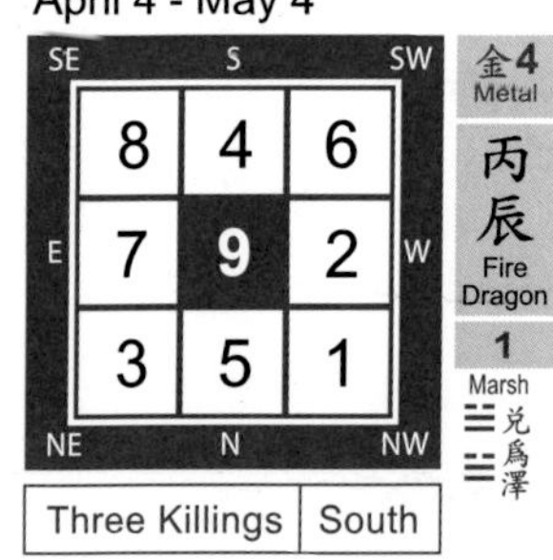

May 5 - June 4

June 5 - July 6

July 7 - August 6

August 7 - September 6

September 7 - October 7

October 8 - November 6

November 7 - December 6

December 7 - January 4

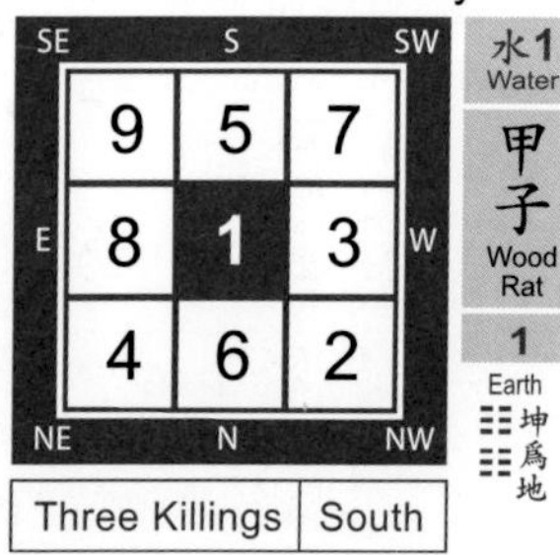

JANUARY 2013 癸丑

Xuan Kong Element 玄空五行	山火賁 Beauty	Period Luck 卦運	Monthly Star 月星
Water 水6		8	3

SUNDAY	MONDAY	TUESDAY	WEDNESDAY	THURSDAY	FRIDAY	SATURDAY
		水6 Water 4 Decreasing 山澤損 丁卯 Fire Rabbit 1 二十 9	金9 Metal 5 Tread 天澤履 戊辰 Earth Dragon 2 廿一 6	木8 Wood 6 Great Strength 雷天大壯 己巳 Earth Snake 3 廿二 2	木8 Wood 7 Consistency 雷風恆 庚午 Metal Horse 4 廿三 9	金9 Metal 8 Litigation 天水訟 辛未 Metal Goat 5 廿四 3
水1 Water 9 Officer 地水師 壬申 Water Monkey 6 廿五 7	火2 Fire 1 Gradual Progress 風山漸 癸酉 Water Rooster 7 廿六 7	火7 Fire 2 Obstruction 水山蹇 甲戌 Wood Dog 8 廿七 2	木3 Wood 3 Advancement 火地晉 乙亥 Wood Pig 9 廿八 3	水6 Water 4 Nourish 山雷頤 丙子 Fire Rat 10 廿九 3	金4 Metal 5 Following 澤雷隨 丁丑 Fire Ox 11 三十 7	木8 Wood 6 Abundance 雷火豐 戊寅 Earth Tiger 12 十二月初一 6
火7 Fire 7 Regulate 水澤節 己卯 Earth Rabbit 13 初二 8	水1 Water 8 Unity 地天泰 庚辰 Metal Dragon 14 初三 9	木3 Wood 9 Great Reward 火天大有 辛巳 Metal Snake 15 初四 7	火2 Fire 1 Wind 巽爲風 壬午 Water Horse 16 初五 1	金4 Metal 2 Trap 澤水困 癸未 Water Goat 17 初六 8	木3 Wood 3 Not Yet Accomplished 火水未濟 甲申 Wood Monkey 18 初七 9	金9 Metal 4 Retreat 天山遯 乙酉 Wood Rooster 19 初八 4
水6 Water 5 Mountain 艮爲山 丙戌 Fire Dog 20 初九 1	木8 Wood 6 Delight 雷地豫 丁亥 Fire Pig 21 初十 8	火7 Fire 7 Beginning 水雷屯 戊子 Earth Rat 22 十一 4	金9 Metal 8 Without Wrongdoing 天雷無妄 己丑 Earth Ox 23 十二 2	木3 Wood 9 Fire 離爲火 庚寅 Metal Tiger 24 十三 1	火2 Fire 1 Sincerity 風澤中孚 辛卯 Metal Rabbit 25 十四 3	水6 Water 2 Big Livestock 山天大畜 壬辰 Water Dragon 26 十五 4
金4 Metal 3 Eliminating 澤天夬 癸巳 Water Snake 27 十六 6	金9 Metal 4 Heaven 乾爲天 甲午 Wood Horse 28 十七 1	火7 Fire 5 Well 水風井 乙未 Wood Goat 29 十八 6	木8 Wood 6 Relief 雷水解 丙申 Fire Monkey 30 十九 4	金4 Metal 7 Influence 澤山咸 丁酉 Fire Rooster 31 二十 9		

FEBRUARY 2013 甲寅

Xuan Kong Element 玄空五行	水火既濟 Accomplished	Period Luck 卦運	Monthly Star 月星
Fire 火7		9	2

SUNDAY	MONDAY	TUESDAY	WEDNESDAY	THURSDAY	FRIDAY	SATURDAY
					水1 Water 8 Humility 地山謙 戊戌 Earth Dog 1 廿一 6	火2 Fire 9 Observation 風地觀 己亥 Earth Pig 2 廿二 2
火2 Fire 1 Increasing 風雷益 庚子 Metal Rat 3 廿三 9	水1 Water 2 Dimming Light 地火明夷 辛丑 Metal Ox 4 廿四 3	金9 Metal 3 Fellowship 天火同人 壬寅 Water Tiger 5 廿五 7	木8 Wood 4 Marrying Maiden 雷澤歸妹 癸卯 Water Rabbit 6 廿六 7	木3 Wood 5 Opposition 火澤睽 甲辰 Wood Dragon 7 廿七 2	火7 Fire 6 Waiting 水天需 乙巳 Wood Snake 8 廿八 3	金4 Metal 7 Great Exceeding 澤風大過 丙午 Fire Horse 9 廿九 3
水6 Water 8 Poison 山風蠱 丁未 Fire Goat 10 正月初一 7	火2 Fire 9 Dispersing 風水渙 戊申 Earth Monkey 11 初二 6	木3 Wood 1 Travelling 火山旅 己酉 Earth Rooster 12 初三 8	金9 Metal 2 Stagnation 天地否 庚戌 Metal Dog 13 初四 9	火7 Fire 3 Alliance 水地比 辛亥 Metal Pig 14 初五 7	木8 Wood 4 Thunder 震爲雷 壬子 Water Rat 15 初六 1	水6 Water 5 Beauty 山火賁 癸丑 Water Ox 16 初七 8
火7 Fire 6 Accomplished 水火既濟 甲寅 Wood Tiger 17 初八 9	水1 Water 7 Arriving 地澤臨 乙卯 Wood Rabbit 18 初九 4	金4 Metal 8 Marsh 兌爲澤 丙辰 Fire Dragon 19 初十 1	火2 Fire 9 Small Livestock 風天小畜 丁巳 Fire Snake 20 十一 8	木3 Wood 1 The Cauldron 火風鼎 戊午 Earth Horse 21 十二 4	水1 Water 2 Rising 地風升 己未 Earth Goat 22 十三 2	火7 Fire 3 Water 坎爲水 庚申 Metal Monkey 23 十四 1
木8 Wood 4 Lesser Exceeding 雷山小過 辛酉 Metal Rooster 24 十五 3	金4 Metal 5 Gathering 澤地萃 壬戌 Water Dog 25 十六 4	水6 Water 6 Peel 山地剝 癸亥 Water Pig 26 十七 6	水1 Water 7 Earth 坤爲地 甲子 Wood Rat 27 十八 1	木3 Wood 8 Biting 火雷噬嗑 乙丑 Wood Ox 28 十九 6		

MARCH 2013 乙卯

Xuan Kong Element 玄空五行	地澤臨 Arriving	Period Luck 卦運	Monthly Star 月星
Water 水1		4	1

SUNDAY	MONDAY	TUESDAY	WEDNESDAY	THURSDAY	FRIDAY	SATURDAY
木8 Wood 3 Relief 雷水解 丙申 Fire Monkey 4 31 二十					火2 Fire 9 Family 風火家人 丙寅 Fire Tiger 4 1 二十	水6 Water 1 Decreasing 山澤損 丁卯 Fire Rabbit 9 2 廿一
金9 Metal 2 Tread 天澤履 戊辰 Earth Dragon 6 3 廿二	木8 Wood 3 Great Strength 雷天大壯 己巳 Earth Snake 2 4 廿三	木8 Wood 4 Consistency 雷風恆 庚午 Metal Horse 9 5 廿四	金9 Metal 5 Litigation 天水訟 辛未 Metal Goat 3 6 廿五	水1 Water 6 Officer 地水師 壬申 Water Monkey 7 7 廿六	火2 Fire 7 Gradual Progress 風山漸 癸酉 Water Rooster 7 8 廿七	火7 Fire 8 Obstruction 水山蹇 甲戌 Wood Dog 2 9 廿八
木3 Wood 9 Advancement 火地晉 乙亥 Wood Pig 3 10 廿九	水6 Water 1 Nourish 山雷頤 丙子 Fire Rat 3 11 三十	金4 Metal 2 Following 澤雷隨 丁丑 Fire Ox 7 12 二月初一	木8 Wood 3 Abundance 雷火豐 戊寅 Earth Tiger 6 13 初二	火7 Fire 4 Regulate 水澤節 己卯 Earth Rabbit 8 14 初三	水1 Water 5 Unity 地天泰 庚辰 Metal Dragon 9 15 初四	木3 Wood 6 Great Reward 火天大有 辛巳 Metal Snake 7 16 初五
火2 Fire 7 Wind 巽爲風 壬午 Water Horse 1 17 初六	金4 Metal 8 Trap 澤水困 癸未 Water Goat 8 18 初七	木3 Wood 9 Not Yet Accomplished 火水未濟 甲申 Wood Monkey 9 19 初八	金9 Metal 1 Retreat 天山遯 乙酉 Wood Rooster 4 20 初九	水6 Water 2 Mountain 艮爲山 丙戌 Fire Dog 1 21 初十	木8 Wood 3 Delight 雷地豫 丁亥 Fire Pig 8 22 十一	火7 Fire 4 Beginning 水雷屯 戊子 Earth Rat 4 23 十二
金9 Metal 5 Without Wrongdoing 天雷無妄 己丑 Earth Ox 2 24 十三	木3 Wood 6 Fire 離爲火 庚寅 Metal Tiger 1 25 十四	火2 Fire 7 Sincerity 風澤中孚 辛卯 Metal Rabbit 3 26 十五	水6 Water 8 Big Livestock 山天大畜 壬辰 Water Dragon 4 27 十六	金4 Metal 9 Eliminating 澤天夬 癸巳 Water Snake 6 28 十七	金9 Metal 1 Heaven 乾爲天 甲午 Wood Horse 1 29 十八	火7 Fire 2 Well 水風井 乙未 Wood Goat 6 30 十九

APRIL 2013 丙辰

Xuan Kong Element 玄空五行	兌爲澤 Marsh	Period Luck 卦運	Monthly Star 月星
Metal 金4		1	9

SUNDAY	MONDAY	TUESDAY	WEDNESDAY	THURSDAY	FRIDAY	SATURDAY
	金4 Metal 4 Influence 澤山咸 丁酉 Fire Rooster 9 1 廿一	水1 Water 5 Humility 地山謙 戊戌 Earth Dog 6 2 廿二	火2 Fire 6 Observation 風地觀 己亥 Earth Pig 2 3 廿三	火2 Fire 7 Increasing 風雷益 庚子 Metal Rat 9 4 廿四	水1 Water 8 Dimming Light 地火明夷 辛丑 Metal Ox 3 5 廿五	金9 Metal 9 Fellowship 天火同人 壬寅 Water Tiger 7 6 廿六
木8 Wood 1 Marrying Maiden 雷澤歸妹 癸卯 Water Rabbit 7 7 廿七	木3 Wood 2 Opposition 火澤睽 甲辰 Wood Dragon 2 8 廿八	火7 Fire 3 Waiting 水天需 乙巳 Wood Snake 3 9 廿九	金4 Metal 4 Great Exceeding 澤風大過 丙午 Fire Horse 3 10 三月初一	水6 Water 5 Poison 山風蠱 丁未 Fire Goat 7 11 初二	火2 Fire 6 Dispersing 風水渙 戊申 Earth Monkey 6 12 初三	木3 Wood 7 Travelling 火山旅 己酉 Earth Rooster 8 13 初四
金9 Metal 8 Stagnation 天地否 庚戌 Metal Dog 9 14 初五	火7 Fire 9 Alliance 水地比 辛亥 Metal Pig 7 15 初六	木8 Wood 1 Thunder 震爲雷 壬子 Water Rat 1 16 初七	水6 Water 2 Beauty 山火賁 癸丑 Water Ox 8 17 初八	火7 Fire 3 Accomplished 水火既濟 甲寅 Wood Tiger 9 18 初九	水1 Water 4 Arriving 地澤臨 乙卯 Wood Rabbit 4 19 初十	金4 Metal 5 Marsh 兌爲澤 丙辰 Fire Dragon 1 20 十一
火2 Fire 6 Small Livestock 風天小畜 丁巳 Fire Snake 8 21 十二	木3 Wood 7 The Cauldron 火風鼎 戊午 Earth Horse 4 22 十三	水1 Water 8 Rising 地風升 己未 Earth Goat 2 23 十四	火7 Fire 9 Water 坎爲水 庚申 Metal Monkey 1 24 十五	木8 Wood 1 Lesser Exceeding 雷山小過 辛酉 Metal Rooster 3 25 十六	金4 Metal 2 Gathering 澤地萃 壬戌 Water Dog 4 26 十七	水6 Water 3 Peel 山地剝 癸亥 Water Pig 6 27 十八
水1 Water 4 Earth 坤爲地 甲子 Wood Rat 1 28 十九	木3 Wood 5 Biting 火雷噬嗑 乙丑 Wood Ox 6 29 二十	火2 Fire 6 Family 風火家人 丙寅 Fire Tiger 4 30 廿一				

MAY 2013 丁巳

Xuan Kong Element 玄空五行	風天小畜	Period Luck 卦運	Monthly Star 月星
Fire 火2	Small Livestock	8	8

SUNDAY	MONDAY	TUESDAY	WEDNESDAY	THURSDAY	FRIDAY	SATURDAY
			水6 Water 7 Decreasing 丁卯 Fire Rabbit 山澤損 1 廿二 9	金9 Metal 8 Tread 戊辰 Earth Dragon 天澤履 2 廿三 6	木8 Wood 9 Great Strength 己巳 Earth Snake 雷天大壯 3 廿四 2	木8 Wood 1 Consistency 庚午 Metal Horse 雷風恆 4 廿五 9
金9 Metal 2 Litigation 辛未 Metal Goat 天水訟 5 廿六 3	水1 Water 3 Officer 壬申 Water Monkey 地水師 6 廿七 7	火2 Fire 4 Gradual Progress 癸酉 Water Rooster 風山漸 7 廿八 7	火7 Fire 5 Obstruction 甲戌 Wood Dog 水山蹇 8 廿九 2	木3 Wood 6 Advancement 乙亥 Wood Pig 火地晉 9 三十 3	水6 Water 7 Nourish 丙子 Fire Rat 山雷頤 10 四月初一 3	金4 Metal 8 Following 丁丑 Fire Ox 澤雷隨 11 初二 7
木8 Wood 9 Abundance 戊寅 Earth Tiger 雷火豐 12 初三 6	火7 Fire 1 Regulate 己卯 Earth Rabbit 水澤節 13 初四 8	水1 Water 2 Unity 庚辰 Metal Dragon 地天泰 14 初五 9	木3 Wood 3 Great Reward 辛巳 Metal Snake 火天大有 15 初六 7	火2 Fire 4 Wind 壬午 Water Horse 巽爲風 16 初七 1	金4 Metal 5 Trap 癸未 Water Goat 澤水困 17 初八 8	木3 Wood 6 Not Yet Accomplished 甲申 Wood Monkey 火水未濟 18 初九 9
金9 Metal 7 Retreat 乙酉 Wood Rooster 天山遯 19 初十 4	水6 Water 8 Mountain 丙戌 Fire Dog 艮爲山 20 十一 1	木8 Wood 9 Delight 丁亥 Fire Pig 雷地豫 21 十二 8	火7 Fire 1 Beginning 戊子 Earth Rat 水雷屯 22 十三 4	金9 Metal 2 Without Wrongdoing 己丑 Earth Ox 天雷無妄 23 十四 2	木3 Wood 3 Fire 庚寅 Metal Tiger 離爲火 24 十五 1	火2 Fire 4 Sincerity 辛卯 Metal Rabbit 風澤中孚 25 十六 3
水6 Water 5 Big Livestock 壬辰 Water Dragon 山天大畜 26 十七 4	金4 Metal 6 Eliminating 癸巳 Water Snake 澤天夬 27 十八 6	金9 Metal 7 Heaven 甲午 Wood Horse 乾爲天 28 十九 1	火7 Fire 8 Well 乙未 Wood Goat 水風井 29 二十 6	木8 Wood 9 Relief 丙申 Fire Monkey 雷水解 30 廿一 4	金4 Metal 1 Influence 丁酉 Fire Rooster 澤山咸 31 廿二 9	

JUNE 3013 戊午

Xuan Kong Element 玄空五行	火風鼎	Period Luck 卦運	Monthly Star 月星
Wood 木3	The Cauldron	4	7

SUNDAY	MONDAY	TUESDAY	WEDNESDAY	THURSDAY	FRIDAY	SATURDAY
水6 Water 6 Decreasing 丁卯 Fire Rabbit 山澤損 30 廿二 9						水1 Water 2 Humility 戊戌 Earth Dog 地山謙 1 廿三 6
火2 Fire 3 Observation 己亥 Earth Pig 風地觀 2 廿四 2	火2 Fire 4 Increasing 庚子 Metal Rat 風雷益 3 廿五 9	水1 Water 5 Dimming Light 辛丑 Metal Ox 地火明夷 4 廿六 3	金9 Metal 6 Fellowship 壬寅 Water Tiger 天火同人 5 廿七 7	木8 Wood 7 Marrying Maiden 癸卯 Water Rabbit 雷澤歸妹 6 廿八 7	木3 Wood 8 Opposition 甲辰 Wood Dragon 火澤睽 7 廿九 2	火7 Fire 9 Waiting 乙巳 Wood Snake 水天需 8 三十 3
金4 Metal 1 Great Exceeding 丙午 Fire Horse 澤風大過 9 五月初一 3	水6 Water 2 Poison 丁未 Fire Goat 山風蠱 10 初二 7	火2 Fire 3 Dispersing 戊申 Earth Monkey 風水渙 11 初三 6	木3 Wood 4 Travelling 己酉 Earth Rooster 火山旅 12 初四 8	金9 Metal 5 Stagnation 庚戌 Metal Dog 天地否 13 初五 9	火7 Fire 6 Alliance 辛亥 Metal Pig 水地比 14 初六 7	木8 Wood 7 Thunder 壬子 Water Rat 震爲雷 15 初七 1
水6 Water 8 Beauty 癸丑 Water Ox 山火賁 16 初八 8	火7 Fire 9 Accomplished 甲寅 Wood Tiger 水火既濟 17 初九 9	水1 Water 1 Arriving 乙卯 Wood Rabbit 地澤臨 18 初十 4	金4 Metal 2 Marsh 丙辰 Fire Dragon 兌爲澤 19 十一 1	火2 Fire 3 Small Livestock 丁巳 Fire Snake 風天小畜 20 十二 8	木3 Wood 4/6 The Cauldron 戊午 Earth Horse 火風鼎 21 十三 4	水1 Water 5 Rising 己未 Earth Goat 地風升 22 十四 2
火7 Fire 4 Water 庚申 Metal Monkey 坎爲水 23 十五 1	木8 Wood 3 Lesser Exceeding 辛酉 Metal Rooster 雷山小過 24 十六 3	金4 Metal 2 Gathering 壬戌 Water Dog 澤地萃 25 十七 4	水6 Water 1 Peel 癸亥 Water Pig 山地剝 26 十八 6	水1 Water 9 Earth 甲子 Wood Rat 坤爲地 27 十九 1	木3 Wood 8 Biting 乙丑 Wood Ox 火雷噬嗑 28 二十 6	火2 Fire 7 Family 丙寅 Fire Tiger 風火家人 29 廿一 4

JULY 2013 己未

Xuan Kong Element 玄空五行	地風升 Rising	Period Luck 卦運	Monthly Star 月星
Water 水1		2	6

SUNDAY	MONDAY	TUESDAY	WEDNESDAY	THURSDAY	FRIDAY	SATURDAY
	金9 Metal · Tread · 5 戊辰 Earth Dragon 天澤履 1 廿三 6	木8 Wood · Great Strength · 4 己巳 Earth Snake 雷天大壯 2 廿四 2	木8 Wood · Consistency · 3 庚午 Metal Horse 雷風恆 3 廿五 9	金9 Metal · Litigation · 2 辛未 Metal Goat 天水訟 4 廿六 3	水1 Water · Officer · 1 壬申 Water Monkey 地水師 5 廿七 7	火2 Fire · Gradual Progress · 9 癸酉 Water Rooster 風山漸 6 廿八 7
火7 Fire · Obstruction · 8 甲戌 Wood Dog 水山蹇 7 廿九 2	木3 Wood · Advancement · 7 乙亥 Wood Pig 火地晉 8 六月初一 3	水6 Water · Nourish · 6 丙子 Fire Rat 山雷頤 9 初二 3	金4 Metal · Following · 5 丁丑 Fire Ox 澤雷隨 10 初三 7	木8 Wood · Abundance · 4 戊寅 Earth Tiger 雷火豐 11 初四 6	火7 Fire · Regulate · 3 己卯 Earth Rabbit 水澤節 12 初五 8	水1 Water · Unity · 2 庚辰 Metal Dragon 地天泰 13 初六 9
木3 Wood · Great Reward · 1 辛巳 Metal Snake 火天大有 14 初七 7	火2 Fire · Wind · 9 壬午 Water Horse 巽爲風 15 初八 1	金4 Metal · Trap · 8 癸未 Water Goat 澤水困 16 初九 8	木3 Wood · Not Yet Accomplished · 7 甲申 Wood Monkey 火水未濟 17 初十 9	金9 Metal · Retreat · 6 乙酉 Wood Rooster 天山遯 18 十一 4	水6 Water · Mountain · 5 丙戌 Fire Dog 艮爲山 19 十二 1	木8 Wood · Delight · 4 丁亥 Fire Pig 雷地豫 20 十三 8
火7 Fire · Beginning · 3 戊子 Earth Rat 水雷屯 21 十四 4	金9 Metal · Without Wrongdoing · 2 己丑 Earth Ox 天雷無妄 22 十五 2	木3 Wood · Fire · 1 庚寅 Metal Tiger 離爲火 23 十六 1	火2 Fire · Sincerity · 9 辛卯 Metal Rabbit 風澤中孚 24 十七 3	水6 Water · Big Livestock · 8 壬辰 Water Dragon 山天大畜 25 十八 4	金4 Metal · Eliminating · 7 癸巳 Water Snake 澤天夬 26 十九 6	金9 Metal · Heaven · 6 甲午 Wood Horse 乾爲天 27 二十 1
火7 Fire · Well · 5 乙未 Wood Goat 水風井 28 廿一 6	木8 Wood · Relief · 4 丙申 Fire Monkey 雷水解 29 廿二 4	金4 Metal · Influence · 3 丁酉 Fire Rooster 澤山咸 30 廿三 9	水1 Water · Humility · 2 戊戌 Earth Dog 地山謙 31 廿四 6			

AUGUST 2013 庚申

Xuan Kong Element 玄空五行	坎爲水 Water	Period Luck 卦運	Monthly Star 月星
Fire 火7		1	5

SUNDAY	MONDAY	TUESDAY	WEDNESDAY	THURSDAY	FRIDAY	SATURDAY
				火2 Fire · Observation · 1 己亥 Earth Pig 風地觀 1 廿五 2	火2 Fire · Increasing · 9 庚子 Metal Rat 風雷益 2 廿六 9	水1 Water · Dimming Light · 8 辛丑 Metal Ox 地火明夷 3 廿七 3
金9 Metal · Fellowship · 7 壬寅 Water Tiger 天火同人 4 廿八 7	木8 Wood · Marrying Maiden · 6 癸卯 Water Rabbit 雷澤歸妹 5 廿九 7	木3 Wood · Opposition · 5 甲辰 Wood Dragon 火澤睽 6 三十 2	火7 Fire · Waiting · 4 乙巳 Wood Snake 水天需 7 七月初一 3	金4 Metal · Great Exceeding · 3 丙午 Fire Horse 澤風大過 8 初二 3	水6 Water · Poison · 2 丁未 Fire Goat 山風蠱 9 初三 7	火2 Fire · Dispersing · 1 戊申 Earth Monkey 風水渙 10 初四 6
木3 Wood · Travelling · 9 己酉 Earth Rooster 火山旅 11 初五 8	金9 Metal · Stagnation · 8 庚戌 Metal Dog 天地否 12 初六 9	火7 Fire · Alliance · 7 辛亥 Metal Pig 水地比 13 初七 7	木8 Wood · Thunder · 6 壬子 Water Rat 震爲雷 14 初八 1	水6 Water · Beauty · 5 癸丑 Water Ox 山火賁 15 初九 8	火7 Fire · Accomplished · 4 甲寅 Wood Tiger 水火既濟 16 初十 9	水1 Water · Arriving · 3 乙卯 Wood Rabbit 地澤臨 17 十一 4
金4 Metal · Marsh · 2 丙辰 Fire Dragon 兌爲澤 18 十二 1	火2 Fire · Small Livestock · 1 丁巳 Fire Snake 風天小畜 19 十三 8	木3 Wood · The Cauldron · 9 戊午 Earth Horse 火風鼎 20 十四 4	水1 Water · Rising · 8 己未 Earth Goat 地風升 21 十五 2	火7 Fire · Water · 7 庚申 Metal Monkey 坎爲水 22 十六 1	木8 Wood · Lesser Exceeding · 6 辛酉 Metal Rooster 雷山小過 23 十七 3	金4 Metal · Gathering · 5 壬戌 Water Dog 澤地萃 24 十八 4
水6 Water · Peel · 4 癸亥 Water Pig 山地剝 25 十九 6	水1 Water · Earth · 3 甲子 Wood Rat 坤爲地 26 二十 1	木3 Wood · Biting · 2 乙丑 Wood Ox 火雷噬嗑 27 廿一 6	火2 Fire · Family · 1 丙寅 Fire Tiger 風火家人 28 廿二 4	水6 Water · Decreasing · 9 丁卯 Fire Rabbit 山澤損 29 廿三 9	金9 Metal · Tread · 8 戊辰 Earth Dragon 天澤履 30 廿四 6	木8 Wood · Great Strength · 7 己巳 Earth Snake 雷天大壯 31 廿五 2

SEPTEMBER 2013 辛酉

Xuan Kong Element 玄空五行	雷山小過 Lesser Exceeding	Period Luck 卦運	Monthly Star 月星
Wood 木8		3	4

SUNDAY	MONDAY	TUESDAY	WEDNESDAY	THURSDAY	FRIDAY	SATURDAY
木8 Wood 6 Consistency 雷風恒 庚午 Metal Horse **1** 廿六 9	金9 Metal 5 Litigation 天水訟 辛未 Metal Goat **2** 廿七 3	水1 Water 4 Officer 地水師 壬申 Water Monkey **3** 廿八 7	火2 Fire 3 Gradual Progress 風山漸 癸酉 Water Rooster **4** 廿九 7	火7 Fire 2 Obstruction 水山蹇 甲戌 Wood Dog **5** 八月初一 2	木3 Wood 1 Advancement 火地晉 乙亥 Wood Pig **6** 初二 3	水6 Water 9 Nourish 山雷頤 丙子 Fire Rat **7** 初三 3
金4 Metal 8 Following 澤雷隨 丁丑 Fire Ox **8** 初四 7	木8 Wood 7 Abundance 雷火豐 戊寅 Earth Tiger **9** 初五 6	火7 Fire 6 Regulate 水澤節 己卯 Earth Rabbit **10** 初六 8	水1 Water 5 Unity 地天泰 庚辰 Metal Dragon **11** 初七 9	木3 Wood 4 Great Reward 火天大有 辛巳 Metal Snake **12** 初八 7	火2 Fire 3 Wind 巽爲風 壬午 Water Horse **13** 初九 1	金4 Metal 2 Trap 澤水困 癸未 Water Goat **14** 初十 8
木3 Wood 1 Not Yet Accomplished 火水未濟 甲申 Wood Monkey **15** 十一 9	金9 Metal 9 Retreat 天山遯 乙酉 Wood Rooster **16** 十二 4	水6 Water 8 Mountain 艮爲山 丙戌 Fire Dog **17** 十三 1	木8 Wood 7 Delight 雷地豫 丁亥 Fire Pig **18** 十四 8	火7 Fire 6 Beginning 水雷屯 戊子 Earth Rat **19** 十五 4	金9 Metal 5 Without Wrongdoing 天雷無妄 己丑 Earth Ox **20** 十六 2	木3 Wood 4 Fire 離爲火 庚寅 Metal Tiger **21** 十七 1
火2 Fire 3 Sincerity 風澤中孚 辛卯 Metal Rabbit **22** 十八 3	水6 Water 2 Big Livestock 山天大畜 壬辰 Water Dragon **23** 十九 4	金4 Metal 1 Eliminating 澤天夬 癸巳 Water Snake **24** 二十 6	金9 Metal 9 Heaven 乾爲天 甲午 Wood Horse **25** 廿一 1	火7 Fire 8 Well 水風井 乙未 Wood Goat **26** 廿二 6	木8 Wood 7 Relief 雷水解 丙申 Fire Monkey **27** 廿三 4	金4 Metal 6 Influence 澤山咸 丁酉 Fire Rooster **28** 廿四 9
水1 Water 5 Humility 地山謙 戊戌 Earth Dog **29** 廿五 6	火2 Fire 4 Observation 風地觀 己亥 Earth Pig **30** 廿六 2					

OCTOBER 2013 壬戌

Xuan Kong Element 玄空五行	澤地萃 Gathering	Period Luck 卦運	Monthly Star 月星
Metal 金4		4	3

SUNDAY	MONDAY	TUESDAY	WEDNESDAY	THURSDAY	FRIDAY	SATURDAY
		火2 Fire 3 Increasing 風雷益 庚子 Metal Rat **1** 廿七 9	水1 Water 2 Dimming Light 地火明夷 辛丑 Metal Ox **2** 廿八 3	金9 Metal 1 Fellowship 天火同人 壬寅 Water Tiger **3** 廿九 7	木8 Wood 9 Marrying Maiden 雷澤歸妹 癸卯 Water Rabbit **4** 三十 7	木3 Wood 8 Opposition 火澤睽 甲辰 Wood Dragon **5** 九月初一 2
火7 Fire 7 Waiting 水天需 乙巳 Wood Snake **6** 初二 3	金4 Metal 6 Great Exceeding 澤風大過 丙午 Fire Horse **7** 初三 3	水6 Water 5 Poison 山風蠱 丁未 Fire Goat **8** 初四 7	火2 Fire 4 Dispersing 風水渙 戊申 Earth Monkey **9** 初五 6	木3 Wood 3 Travelling 火山旅 己酉 Earth Rooster **10** 初六 8	金9 Metal 2 Stagnation 天地否 庚戌 Metal Dog **11** 初七 9	火7 Fire 1 Alliance 水地比 辛亥 Metal Pig **12** 初八 7
木8 Wood 9 Thunder 震爲雷 壬子 Water Rat **13** 初九 1	水6 Water 8 Beauty 山火賁 癸丑 Water Ox **14** 初十 8	火7 Fire 7 Accomplished 水火既濟 甲寅 Wood Tiger **15** 十一 9	水1 Water 6 Arriving 地澤臨 乙卯 Wood Rabbit **16** 十二 4	金4 Metal 5 Marsh 兑爲澤 丙辰 Fire Dragon **17** 十三 1	火2 Fire 4 Small Livestock 風天小畜 丁巳 Fire Snake **18** 十四 8	木3 Wood 3 The Cauldron 火風鼎 戊午 Earth Horse **19** 十五 4
水1 Water 2 Rising 地風升 己未 Earth Goat **20** 十六 2	火7 Fire 1 Water 坎爲水 庚申 Metal Monkey **21** 十七 1	木8 Wood 9 Lesser Exceeding 雷山小過 辛酉 Metal Rooster **22** 十八 3	金4 Metal 8 Gathering 澤地萃 壬戌 Water Dog **23** 十九 4	水6 Water 7 Peel 山地剝 癸亥 Water Pig **24** 二十 6	水1 Water 6 Earth 坤爲地 甲子 Wood Rat **25** 廿一 1	木3 Wood 5 Biting 火雷噬嗑 乙丑 Wood Ox **26** 廿二 6
火2 Fire 4 Family 風火家人 丙寅 Fire Tiger **27** 廿三 4	水6 Water 3 Decreasing 山澤損 丁卯 Fire Rabbit **28** 廿四 9	金9 Metal 2 Tread 天澤履 戊辰 Earth Dragon **29** 廿五 6	木8 Wood 1 Great Strength 雷天大壯 己巳 Earth Snake **30** 廿六 2	木8 Wood 9 Consistency 雷風恒 庚午 Metal Horse **31** 廿七 9		

NOVEMBER 2013 癸亥

Xuan Kong Element 玄空五行	山地剝 Peel	Period Luck 卦運	Monthly Star 月星
Water 水6		6	2

SUNDAY	MONDAY	TUESDAY	WEDNESDAY	THURSDAY	FRIDAY	SATURDAY
					金9 Metal 8 辛未 Metal Goat Litigation 天水訟 1 廿八 3	水1 Water 7 壬申 Water Monkey Officer 地水師 2 廿九 7
火2 Fire 6 癸酉 Water Rooster Gradual Progress 風山漸 3 十月初一 7	火7 Fire 5 甲戌 Wood Dog Obstruction 水山蹇 4 初二 2	木3 Wood 4 乙亥 Wood Pig Advancement 火地晉 5 初三 3	水6 Water 3 丙子 Fire Rat Nourish 山雷頤 6 初四 3	金4 Metal 2 丁丑 Fire Ox Following 澤雷隨 7 初五 7	木8 Wood 1 戊寅 Earth Tiger Abundance 雷火豐 8 初六 6	火7 Fire 9 己卯 Earth Rabbit Regulate 水澤節 9 初七 8
水1 Water 8 庚辰 Metal Dragon Unity 地天泰 10 初八 9	木3 Wood 7 辛巳 Metal Snake Great Reward 火天大有 11 初九 7	火2 Fire 6 壬午 Water Horse Wind 巽為風 12 初十 1	金4 Metal 5 癸未 Water Goat Trap 澤水困 13 十一 8	木3 Wood 4 甲申 Wood Monkey Not Yet Accomplished 火水未濟 14 十二 9	金9 Metal 3 乙酉 Wood Rooster Retreat 天山遯 15 十三 4	水6 Water 2 丙戌 Fire Dog Mountain 艮為山 16 十四 1
木8 Wood 1 丁亥 Fire Pig Delight 雷地豫 17 十五 8	火7 Fire 9 戊子 Earth Rat Beginning 水雷屯 18 十六 4	金9 Metal 8 己丑 Earth Ox Without Wrongdoing 天雷無妄 19 十七 2	木3 Wood 7 庚寅 Metal Tiger Fire 離為火 20 十八 1	火2 Fire 6 辛卯 Metal Rabbit Sincerity 風澤中孚 21 十九 3	水6 Water 5 壬辰 Water Dragon Big Livestock 山天大畜 22 二十 4	金4 Metal 4 癸巳 Water Snake Eliminating 澤天夬 23 廿一 6
金9 Metal 3 甲午 Wood Horse Heaven 乾為天 24 廿二 1	火7 Fire 2 乙未 Wood Goat Well 水風井 25 廿三 6	木8 Wood 1 丙申 Fire Monkey Relief 雷水解 26 廿四 4	金4 Metal 9 丁酉 Fire Rooster Influence 澤山咸 27 廿五 9	水1 Water 8 戊戌 Earth Dog Humility 地山謙 28 廿六 6	火2 Fire 7 己亥 Earth Pig Observation 風地觀 29 廿七 2	火2 Fire 6 庚子 Metal Rat Increasing 風雷益 30 廿八 9

DECEMBER 2013 甲子

Xuan Kong Element 玄空五行	坤為地 Earth	Period Luck 卦運	Monthly Star 月星
Water 水1		1	1

SUNDAY	MONDAY	TUESDAY	WEDNESDAY	THURSDAY	FRIDAY	SATURDAY
水1 Water 5 辛丑 Metal Ox Dimming Light 地火明夷 1 廿九 3	金9 Metal 4 壬寅 Water Tiger Fellowship 天火同人 2 三十 7	木8 Wood 3 癸卯 Water Rabbit Marrying Maiden 雷澤歸妹 3 十一月初一 7	木3 Wood 2 甲辰 Wood Dragon Opposition 火澤睽 4 初二 2	火7 Fire 1 乙巳 Wood Snake Waiting 水天需 5 初三 3	金4 Metal 9 丙午 Fire Horse Great Exceeding 澤風大過 6 初四 3	水6 Water 8 丁未 Fire Goat Poison 山風蠱 7 初五 7
火2 Fire 7 戊申 Earth Monkey Dispersing 風水渙 8 初六 6	木3 Wood 6 己酉 Earth Rooster Travelling 火山旅 9 初七 8	金9 Metal 5 庚戌 Metal Dog Stagnation 天地否 10 初八 9	火7 Fire 4 辛亥 Metal Pig Alliance 水地比 11 初九 7	木8 Wood 3 壬子 Water Rat Thunder 震為雷 12 初十 1	水6 Water 2 癸丑 Water Ox Beauty 山火賁 13 十一 8	火7 Fire 1 甲寅 Wood Tiger Accomplished 水火既濟 14 十二 9
水1 Water 9 乙卯 Wood Rabbit Arriving 地澤臨 15 十三 4	金4 Metal 8 丙辰 Fire Dragon Marsh 兑為澤 16 十四 1	火2 Fire 7 丁巳 Fire Snake Small Livestock 風天小畜 17 十五 8	木3 Wood 6 戊午 Earth Horse The Cauldron 火風鼎 18 十六 4	水1 Water 5 己未 Earth Goat Rising 地風升 19 十七 2	火7 Fire 4 庚申 Metal Monkey Water 坎為水 20 十八 1	木8 Wood 3 辛酉 Metal Rooster Lesser Exceeding 雷山小過 21 十九 3
金4 Metal 2/8 壬戌 Water Dog Gathering 澤地萃 22 二十 4	水6 Water 9 癸亥 Water Pig Peel 山地剝 23 廿一 6	水1 Water 1 甲子 Wood Rat Earth 坤為地 24 廿二 1	木3 Wood 2 乙丑 Wood Ox Biting 火雷噬嗑 25 廿三 6	火2 Fire 3 丙寅 Fire Tiger Family 風火家人 26 廿四 4	水6 Water 4 丁卯 Fire Rabbit Decreasing 山澤損 27 廿五 9	金9 Metal 5 戊辰 Earth Dragon Tread 天澤履 28 廿六 6
木8 Wood 6 己巳 Earth Snake Great Strength 雷天大壯 29 廿七 2	木8 Wood 7 庚午 Metal Horse Consistency 雷風恆 30 廿八 9	金9 Metal 8 辛未 Metal Goat Litigation 天水訟 31 廿九 3				

2014 甲午

(*Jia Wu*) Wood Horse

2014 甲午 *(Jia Wu)* Wood Horse

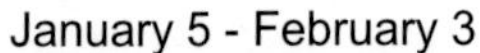

January 5 - February 3

木3 Wood | 乙丑 Wood Ox | 6 | Biting 火雷噬嗑

Three Killings	East

February 4 - March 5

火2 Fire | 丙寅 Fire Tiger | 4 | Family 風火家人

Three Killings	North

March 6 - April 4

9 | Decreasing 山澤損

Three Killings	West

April 5 - May 4

金9 Metal | 戊辰 Earth Dragon | 6 | Tread 天澤履

Three Killings	South

May 5 - June 5

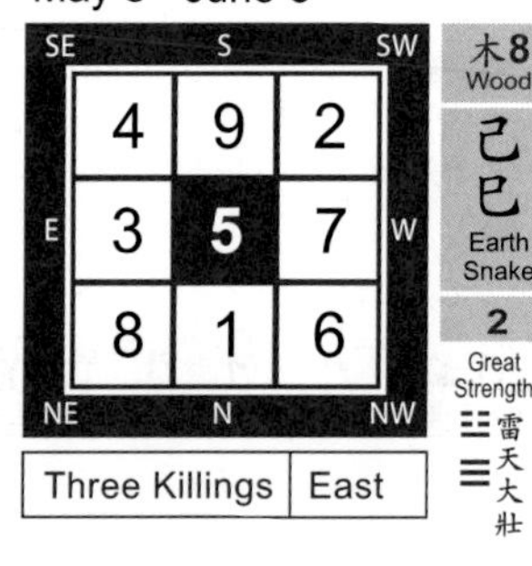

木8 Wood | 己巳 Earth Snake | 2 | Great Strength 雷天大壯

Three Killings	East

June 6 - July 6

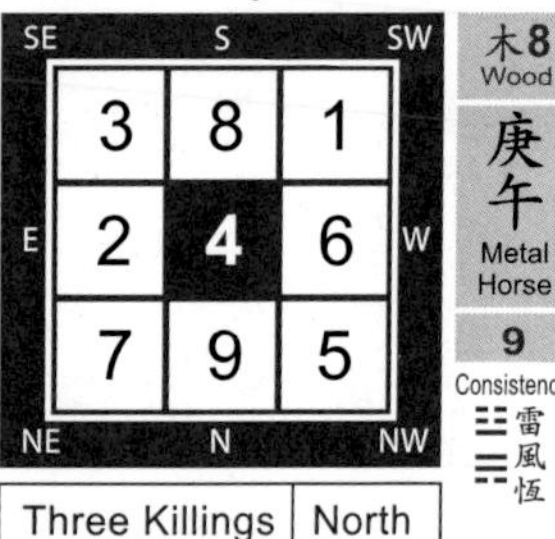

9 | Consistency 雷風恆

Three Killings	North

July 7 - August 6

金9 Metal | 辛未 Metal Goat | 3 | Litigation 天水訟

Three Killings	West

August 7 - September 7

水1 Water | 壬申 Water Monkey | 7 | Officer 地水師

Three Killings	South

September 8 - October 7

火2 Fire | 癸酉 Water Rooster | 7 | Gradual Progress 風山漸

Three Killings	East

October 8 - November 6

火7 Fire | 甲戌 Wood Dog | 2 | Obstruction 水山蹇

Three Killings	North

November 7 - December 6

木3 Wood | 乙亥 Wood Pig | 3 | Advancement 火地晉

Three Killings	West

December 7 - January 5

水6 Water | 丙子 Fire Rat | 3 | Nourish 山雷頤

Three Killings	South

JANUARY 2014 乙丑

Xuan Kong Element 玄空五行	火雷噬嗑 Biting	Period Luck 卦運	Monthly Star 月星
Wood 木3		6	9

SUNDAY	MONDAY	TUESDAY	WEDNESDAY	THURSDAY	FRIDAY	SATURDAY
			水1 Water [9] Officer 壬申 Water Monkey 地水師 1 十二月初一 7	火2 Fire [1] Gradual Progress 癸酉 Water Rooster 風山漸 2 初二 7	火7 Fire [2] Obstruction 甲戌 Wood Dog 水山蹇 3 初三 2	木3 Wood [3] Advancement 乙亥 Wood Pig 火地晉 4 初四 3
水6 Water [4] Nourish 丙子 Fire Rat 山雷頤 5 初五 3	金4 Metal [5] Following 丁丑 Fire Ox 澤雷隨 6 初六 7	木8 Wood [6] Abundance 戊寅 Earth Tiger 雷火豐 7 初七 6	火7 Fire [7] Regulate 己卯 Earth Rabbit 水澤節 8 初八 8	水1 Water [8] Unity 庚辰 Metal Dragon 地天泰 9 初九 9	木3 Wood [9] Great Reward 辛巳 Metal Snake 火天大有 10 初十 7	火2 Fire [1] Wind 壬午 Water Horse 巽為風 11 十一 1
金4 Metal [2] Trap 癸未 Water Goat 澤水困 12 十二 8	木3 Wood [3] Not Yet Accomplished 甲申 Wood Monkey 火水未濟 13 十三 9	金9 Metal [4] Retreat 乙酉 Wood Rooster 天山遯 14 十四 4	水6 Water [5] Mountain 丙戌 Fire Dog 艮為山 15 十五 1	木8 Wood [6] Delight 丁亥 Fire Pig 雷地豫 16 十六 8	火7 Fire [7] Beginning 戊子 Earth Rat 水雷屯 17 十七 4	金9 Metal [8] Without Wrongdoing 己丑 Earth Ox 天雷無妄 18 十八 2
木3 Wood [9] Fire 庚寅 Metal Tiger 離為火 19 十九 1	火2 Fire [1] Sincerity 辛卯 Metal Rabbit 風澤中孚 20 二十 3	水6 Water [2] Big Livestock 壬辰 Water Dragon 山天大畜 21 廿一 4	金4 Metal [3] Eliminating 癸巳 Water Snake 澤天夬 22 廿二 6	金9 Metal [4] Heaven 甲午 Wood Horse 乾為天 23 廿三 1	火7 Fire [5] Well 乙未 Wood Goat 水風井 24 廿四 6	木8 Wood [6] Relief 丙申 Fire Monkey 雷水解 25 廿五 4
金4 Metal [7] Influence 丁酉 Fire Rooster 澤山咸 26 廿六 9	水1 Water [8] Humility 戊戌 Earth Dog 地山謙 27 廿七 6	火2 Fire [9] Observation 己亥 Earth Pig 風地觀 28 廿八 2	火2 Fire [1] Increasing 庚子 Metal Rat 風雷益 29 廿九 9	水1 Water [2] Dimming Light 辛丑 Metal Ox 地火明夷 30 三十 3	金9 Metal [3] Fellowship 壬寅 Water Tiger 天火同人 31 正月初一 7	

FEBRUARY 2014 丙寅

Xuan Kong Element 玄空五行	風火家人 Family	Period Luck 卦運	Monthly Star 月星
Fire 火2		4	8

SUNDAY	MONDAY	TUESDAY	WEDNESDAY	THURSDAY	FRIDAY	SATURDAY
						木8 Wood [4] Marrying Maiden 癸卯 Water Rabbit 雷澤歸妹 1 初二 7
木3 Wood [5] Opposition 甲辰 Wood Dragon 火澤睽 2 初三 2	火7 Fire [6] Waiting 乙巳 Wood Snake 水天需 3 初四 3	金4 Metal [7] Great Exceeding 丙午 Fire Horse 澤風大過 4 初五 3	水6 Water [8] Poison 丁未 Fire Goat 山風蠱 5 初六 7	火2 Fire [9] Dispersing 戊申 Earth Monkey 風水渙 6 初七 6	木3 Wood [1] Travelling 己酉 Earth Rooster 火山旅 7 初八 8	金9 Metal [2] Stagnation 庚戌 Metal Dog 天地否 8 初九 9
火7 Fire [3] Alliance 辛亥 Metal Pig 水地比 9 初十 7	木8 Wood [4] Thunder 壬子 Water Rat 震為雷 10 十一 1	水6 Water [5] Beauty 癸丑 Water Ox 山火賁 11 十二 8	火7 Fire [6] Accomplished 甲寅 Wood Tiger 水火既濟 12 十三 9	水1 Water [7] Arriving 乙卯 Wood Rabbit 地澤臨 13 十四 4	金4 Metal [8] Marsh 丙辰 Fire Dragon 兌為澤 14 十五 1	火2 Fire [9] Small Livestock 丁巳 Fire Snake 風天小畜 15 十六 8
木3 Wood [1] The Cauldron 戊午 Earth Horse 火風鼎 16 十七 4	水1 Water [2] Rising 己未 Earth Goat 地風升 17 十八 2	火7 Fire [3] Water 庚申 Metal Monkey 坎為水 18 十九 1	木8 Wood [4] Lesser Exceeding 辛酉 Metal Rooster 雷山小過 19 二十 3	金4 Metal [5] Gathering 壬戌 Water Dog 澤地萃 20 廿一 4	水6 Water [6] Peel 癸亥 Water Pig 山地剝 21 廿二 6	水1 Water [7] Earth 甲子 Wood Rat 坤為地 22 廿三 1
木3 Wood [8] Biting 乙丑 Wood Ox 火雷噬嗑 23 廿四 6	火2 Fire [9] Family 丙寅 Fire Tiger 風火家人 24 廿五 4	水6 Water [1] Decreasing 丁卯 Fire Rabbit 山澤損 25 廿六 9	金9 Metal [2] Tread 戊辰 Earth Dragon 天澤履 26 廿七 6	木8 Wood [3] Great Strength 己巳 Earth Snake 雷天大壯 27 廿八 2	木8 Wood [4] Consistency 庚午 Metal Horse 雷風恆 28 廿九 9	

MARCH 2014 丁卯

Xuan Kong Element 玄空五行	山澤損 Decreasing	Period Luck 卦運	Monthly Star 月星
Water 水6		9	7

SUNDAY	MONDAY	TUESDAY	WEDNESDAY	THURSDAY	FRIDAY	SATURDAY
火2 Fire 7 Increasing 風雷益 庚子 Metal Rat 30 三十 9	水1 Water 8 Dimming Light 地火明夷 辛丑 Metal Ox 31 三月初一 3					金9 Metal 5 Litigation 天水訟 辛未 Metal Goat 1 二月初一 3
水1 Water 6 Officer 地水師 壬申 Water Monkey 2 初二 7	火2 Fire 7 Gradual Progress 風山漸 癸酉 Water Rooster 3 初三 7	火7 Fire 8 Obstruction 水山蹇 甲戌 Wood Dog 4 初四 2	木3 Wood 9 Advancement 火地晉 乙亥 Wood Pig 5 初五 3	水6 Water 1 Nourish 山雷頤 丙子 Fire Rat 6 初六 3	金4 Metal 2 Following 澤雷隨 丁丑 Fire Ox 7 初七 7	木8 Wood 3 Abundance 雷火豐 戊寅 Earth Tiger 8 初八 6
火7 Fire 4 Regulate 水澤節 己卯 Earth Rabbit 9 初九 8	水1 Water 5 Unity 地天泰 庚辰 Metal Dragon 10 初十 9	木3 Wood 6 Great Reward 火天大有 辛巳 Metal Snake 11 十一 7	火2 Fire 7 Wind 巽為風 壬午 Water Horse 12 十二 1	金4 Metal 8 Trap 澤水困 癸未 Water Goat 13 十三 8	木3 Wood 9 Not Yet Accomplished 火水未濟 甲申 Wood Monkey 14 十四 9	金9 Metal 1 Retreat 天山遯 乙酉 Wood Rooster 15 十五 4
水6 Water 2 Mountain 艮為山 丙戌 Fire Dog 16 十六 1	木8 Wood 3 Delight 雷地豫 丁亥 Fire Pig 17 十七 8	火7 Fire 4 Beginning 水雷屯 戊子 Earth Rat 18 十八 4	金9 Metal 5 Without Wrongdoing 天雷無妄 己丑 Earth Ox 19 十九 2	木3 Wood 6 Fire 離為火 庚寅 Metal Tiger 20 二十 1	火2 Fire 7 Sincerity 風澤中孚 辛卯 Metal Rabbit 21 廿一 3	水6 Water 8 Big Livestock 山天大畜 壬辰 Water Dragon 22 廿二 4
金4 Metal 9 Eliminating 澤天夬 癸巳 Water Snake 23 廿三 6	金9 Metal 1 Heaven 乾為天 甲午 Wood Horse 24 廿四 1	火7 Fire 2 Well 水風井 乙未 Wood Goat 25 廿五 6	木8 Wood 3 Relief 雷水解 丙申 Fire Monkey 26 廿六 4	金4 Metal 4 Influence 澤山咸 丁酉 Fire Rooster 27 廿七 9	水1 Water 5 Humility 地山謙 戊戌 Earth Dog 28 廿八 6	火2 Fire 6 Observation 風地觀 己亥 Earth Pig 29 廿九 2

APRIL 2014 戊辰

Xuan Kong Element 玄空五行	天澤履 Tread	Period Luck 卦運	Monthly Star 月星
Metal 金9		6	6

SUNDAY	MONDAY	TUESDAY	WEDNESDAY	THURSDAY	FRIDAY	SATURDAY
		金9 Metal 9 Fellowship 天火同人 壬寅 Water Tiger 1 初二 7	木8 Wood 1 Marrying Maiden 雷澤歸妹 癸卯 Water Rabbit 2 初三 7	木3 Wood 2 Opposition 火澤睽 甲辰 Wood Dragon 3 初四 2	火7 Fire 3 Waiting 水天需 乙巳 Wood Snake 4 初五 3	金4 Metal 4 Great Exceeding 澤風大過 丙午 Fire Horse 5 初六 3
水6 Water 5 Poison 山風蠱 丁未 Fire Goat 6 初七 7	火2 Fire 6 Dispersing 風水渙 戊申 Earth Monkey 7 初八 6	木3 Wood 7 Travelling 火山旅 己酉 Earth Rooster 8 初九 8	金9 Metal 8 Stagnation 天地否 庚戌 Metal Dog 9 初十 9	火7 Fire 9 Alliance 水地比 辛亥 Metal Pig 10 十一 7	木8 Wood 1 Thunder 震為雷 壬子 Water Rat 11 十二 1	水6 Water 2 Beauty 山火賁 癸丑 Water Ox 12 十三 8
火7 Fire 3 Accomplished 水火既濟 甲寅 Wood Tiger 13 十四 9	水1 Water 4 Arriving 地澤臨 乙卯 Wood Rabbit 14 十五 4	金4 Metal 5 Marsh 兌為澤 丙辰 Fire Dragon 15 十六 1	火2 Fire 6 Small Livestock 風天小畜 丁巳 Fire Snake 16 十七 8	木3 Wood 7 The Cauldron 火風鼎 戊午 Earth Horse 17 十八 4	水1 Water 8 Rising 地風升 己未 Earth Goat 18 十九 2	火7 Fire 9 Water 坎為水 庚申 Metal Monkey 19 二十 1
木8 Wood 1 Lesser Exceeding 雷山小過 辛酉 Metal Rooster 20 廿一 3	金4 Metal 2 Gathering 澤地萃 壬戌 Water Dog 21 廿二 4	水6 Water 3 Peel 山地剝 癸亥 Water Pig 22 廿三 6	水1 Water 4 Earth 坤為地 甲子 Wood Rat 23 廿四 1	木3 Wood 5 Biting 火雷噬嗑 乙丑 Wood Ox 24 廿五 6	火2 Fire 6 Family 風火家人 丙寅 Fire Tiger 25 廿六 4	水6 Water 7 Decreasing 山澤損 丁卯 Fire Rabbit 26 廿七 9
金9 Metal 8 Tread 天澤履 戊辰 Earth Dragon 27 廿八 6	木8 Wood 9 Great Strength 雷天大壯 己巳 Earth Snake 28 廿九 2	木8 Wood 1 Consistency 雷風恒 庚午 Metal Horse 29 四月初一 9	金9 Metal 2 Litigation 天水訟 辛未 Metal Goat 30 初二 3			

MAY 2014 己巳

Xuan Kong Element 玄空五行	雷天大壯 Great Strength	Period Luck 卦運	Monthly Star 月星
Wood 木8		2	5

SUNDAY	MONDAY	TUESDAY	WEDNESDAY	THURSDAY	FRIDAY	SATURDAY
				水1 Water 3 Officer 壬申 Water Monkey 地水師 1 初三 7	火2 Fire 4 Gradual Progress 癸酉 Water Rooster 風山漸 2 初四 7	火7 Fire 5 Obstruction 甲戌 Wood Dog 水山蹇 3 初五 2
木3 Wood 6 Advancement 乙亥 Wood Pig 火地晉 4 初六 3	水6 Water 7 Nourish 丙子 Fire Rat 山雷頤 5 初七 3	金4 Metal 8 Following 丁丑 Fire Ox 澤雷隨 6 初八 7	木8 Wood 9 Abundance 戊寅 Earth Tiger 雷火豐 7 初九 6	火7 Fire 1 Regulate 己卯 Earth Rabbit 水澤節 8 初十 8	水1 Water 2 Unity 庚辰 Metal Dragon 地天泰 9 十一 9	木3 Wood 3 Great Reward 辛巳 Metal Snake 火天大有 10 十二 7
火2 Fire 4 Wind 壬午 Water Horse 巽爲風 11 十三 1	金4 Metal 5 Trap 癸未 Water Goat 澤水困 12 十四 8	木3 Wood 6 Not Yet Accomplished 甲申 Wood Monkey 火水未濟 13 十五 9	金9 Metal 7 Retreat 乙酉 Wood Rooster 天山遯 14 十六 4	水6 Water 8 Mountain 丙戌 Fire Dog 艮爲山 15 十七 1	木8 Wood 9 Delight 丁亥 Fire Pig 雷地豫 16 十八 8	火7 Fire 1 Beginning 戊子 Earth Rat 水雷屯 17 十九 4
金9 Metal 2 Without Wrongdoing 己丑 Earth Ox 天雷無妄 18 二十 2	木3 Wood 3 Fire 庚寅 Metal Tiger 離爲火 19 廿一 1	火2 Fire 4 Sincerity 辛卯 Metal Rabbit 風澤中孚 20 廿二 3	水6 Water 5 Big Livestock 壬辰 Water Dragon 山天大畜 21 廿三 4	金4 Metal 6 Eliminating 癸巳 Water Snake 澤天夬 22 廿四 6	金9 Metal 7 Heaven 甲午 Wood Horse 乾爲天 23 廿五 1	火7 Fire 8 Well 乙未 Wood Goat 水風井 24 廿六 6
木8 Wood 9 Relief 丙申 Fire Monkey 雷水解 25 廿七 4	金4 Metal 1 Influence 丁酉 Fire Rooster 澤山咸 26 廿八 9	水1 Water 2 Humility 戊戌 Earth Dog 地山謙 27 廿九 6	火2 Fire 3 Observation 己亥 Earth Pig 風地觀 28 三十 2	火2 Fire 4 Increasing 庚子 Metal Rat 風雷益 29 五月初一 9	水1 Water 5 Dimming Light 辛丑 Metal Ox 地火明夷 30 初二 3	金9 Metal 6 Fellowship 壬寅 Water Tiger 天火同人 31 初三 7

JUNE 2014 庚午

Xuan Kong Element 玄空五行	雷風恆 Consistency	Period Luck 卦運	Monthly Star 月星
Wood 木8		9	4

SUNDAY	MONDAY	TUESDAY	WEDNESDAY	THURSDAY	FRIDAY	SATURDAY
木8 Wood 7 Marrying Maiden 癸卯 Water Rabbit 雷澤歸妹 1 初四 7	木3 Wood 8 Opposition 甲辰 Wood Dragon 火澤睽 2 初五 2	火7 Fire 9 Waiting 乙巳 Wood Snake 水天需 3 初六 3	金4 Metal 1 Great Exceeding 丙午 Fire Horse 澤風大過 4 初七 3	水6 Water 2 Poison 丁未 Fire Goat 山風蠱 5 初八 7	火2 Fire 3 Dispersing 戊申 Earth Monkey 風水渙 6 初九 6	木3 Wood 4 Travelling 己酉 Earth Rooster 火山旅 7 初十 8
金9 Metal 5 Stagnation 庚戌 Metal Dog 天地否 8 十一 9	火7 Fire 6 Alliance 辛亥 Metal Pig 水地比 9 十二 7	木8 Wood 7 Thunder 壬子 Water Rat 震爲雷 10 十三 1	水6 Water 8 Beauty 癸丑 Water Ox 山火賁 11 十四 8	火7 Fire 9 Accomplished 甲寅 Wood Tiger 水火既濟 12 十五 9	水1 Water 1 Arriving 乙卯 Wood Rabbit 地澤臨 13 十六 4	金4 Metal 2 Marsh 丙辰 Fire Dragon 兌爲澤 14 十七 1
火2 Fire 3 Small Livestock 丁巳 Fire Snake 風天小畜 15 十八 8	木3 Wood 4 The Cauldron 戊午 Earth Horse 火風鼎 16 十九 4	水1 Water 5 Rising 己未 Earth Goat 地風升 17 二十 2	火7 Fire 6 Water 庚申 Metal Monkey 坎爲水 18 廿一 1	木8 Wood 7 Lesser Exceeding 辛酉 Metal Rooster 雷山小過 19 廿二 3	金4 Metal 8 Gathering 壬戌 Water Dog 澤地萃 20 廿三 4	水6 Water 9/1 Peel 癸亥 Water Pig 山地剝 21 廿四 6
水1 Water 9 Earth 甲子 Wood Rat 坤爲地 22 廿五 1	木3 Wood 8 Biting 乙丑 Wood Ox 火雷噬嗑 23 廿六 6	火2 Fire 7 Family 丙寅 Fire Tiger 風火家人 24 廿七 4	水6 Water 6 Decreasing 丁卯 Fire Rabbit 山澤損 25 廿八 9	金9 Metal 5 Tread 戊辰 Earth Dragon 天澤履 26 廿九 6	木8 Wood 4 Great Strength 己巳 Earth Snake 雷天大壯 27 六月初一 2	木8 Wood 3 Consistency 庚午 Metal Horse 雷風恆 28 初二 9
金9 Metal 2 Litigation 辛未 Metal Goat 天水訟 29 初三 3	水1 Water 1 Officer 壬申 Water Monkey 地水師 30 初四 7					

JULY 2014 辛未

Xuan Kong Element 玄空五行	天水訟 Litigation	Period Luck 卦運	Monthly Star 月星
Metal 金9		3	3

SUNDAY	MONDAY	TUESDAY	WEDNESDAY	THURSDAY	FRIDAY	SATURDAY
		火2 Fire Gradual Progress 風山漸 9 癸酉 Water Rooster 7 1 初五	火7 Fire Obstruction 水山蹇 8 甲戌 Wood Dog 2 2 初六	木3 Wood Advancement 火地晉 7 乙亥 Wood Pig 3 3 初七	水6 Water Nourish 山雷頤 6 丙子 Fire Rat 3 4 初八	金4 Metal Following 澤雷隨 5 丁丑 Fire Ox 7 5 初九
木8 Wood Abundance 雷火豐 4 戊寅 Earth Tiger 6 6 初十	火7 Fire Regulate 水澤節 3 己卯 Earth Rabbit 8 7 十一	水1 Water Unity 地天泰 2 庚辰 Metal Dragon 9 8 十二	木3 Wood Great Reward 火天大有 1 辛巳 Metal Snake 7 9 十三	火2 Fire Wind 巽爲風 9 壬午 Water Horse 1 10 十四	金4 Metal Trap 澤水困 8 癸未 Water Goat 8 11 十五	木3 Wood Not Yet Accomplished 火水未濟 7 甲申 Wood Monkey 9 12 十六
金9 Metal Retreat 天山遯 6 乙酉 Wood Rooster 4 13 十七	水6 Water Mountain 艮爲山 5 丙戌 Fire Dog 1 14 十八	木8 Wood Delight 雷地豫 4 丁亥 Fire Pig 8 15 十九	火7 Fire Beginning 水雷屯 3 戊子 Earth Rat 4 16 二十	金9 Metal Without Wrongdoing 天雷無妄 2 己丑 Earth Ox 2 17 廿一	木3 Wood Fire 離爲火 1 庚寅 Metal Tiger 1 18 廿二	火2 Fire Sincerity 風澤中孚 9 辛卯 Metal Rabbit 3 19 廿三
水6 Water Big Livestock 山天大畜 8 壬辰 Water Dragon 4 20 廿四	金4 Metal Eliminating 澤天夬 7 癸巳 Water Snake 6 21 廿五	金9 Metal Heaven 乾爲天 6 甲午 Wood Horse 1 22 廿六	火7 Fire Well 水風井 5 乙未 Wood Goat 6 23 廿七	木8 Wood Relief 雷水解 4 丙申 Fire Monkey 4 24 廿八	金4 Metal Influence 澤山咸 3 丁酉 Fire Rooster 9 25 廿九	水1 Water Humility 地山謙 2 戊戌 Earth Dog 6 26 三十
火2 Fire Observation 風地觀 1 己亥 Earth Pig 2 27 七月初一	火2 Fire Increasing 風雷益 9 庚子 Metal Rat 9 28 初二	水1 Water Dimming Light 地火明夷 8 辛丑 Metal Ox 3 29 初三	金9 Metal Fellowship 天火同人 7 壬寅 Water Tiger 7 30 初四	木8 Wood Marrying Maiden 雷澤歸妹 6 癸卯 Water Rabbit 7 31 初五		

AUGUST 2014 壬申

Xuan Kong Element 玄空五行	地水師 Officer	Period Luck 卦運	Monthly Star 月星
Water 水1		7	2

SUNDAY	MONDAY	TUESDAY	WEDNESDAY	THURSDAY	FRIDAY	SATURDAY
火7 Fire Obstruction 水山蹇 2 甲戌 Wood Dog 2 31 初七					木3 Wood Opposition 火澤睽 5 甲辰 Wood Dragon 2 1 初六	火7 Fire Waiting 水天需 4 乙巳 Wood Snake 3 2 初七
金4 Metal Great Exceeding 澤風大過 3 丙午 Fire Horse 3 3 初八	水6 Water Poison 山風蠱 2 丁未 Fire Goat 7 4 初九	火2 Fire Dispersing 風水渙 1 戊申 Earth Monkey 6 5 初十	木3 Wood Travelling 火山旅 9 己酉 Earth Rooster 8 6 十一	金9 Metal Stagnation 天地否 8 庚戌 Metal Dog 9 7 十二	火7 Fire Alliance 水地比 7 辛亥 Metal Pig 7 8 十三	木8 Wood Thunder 震爲雷 6 壬子 Water Rat 1 9 十四
水6 Water Beauty 山火賁 5 癸丑 Water Ox 8 10 十五	火7 Fire Accomplished 水火既濟 4 甲寅 Wood Tiger 9 11 十六	水1 Water Arriving 地澤臨 3 乙卯 Wood Rabbit 4 12 十七	金4 Metal Marsh 兑爲澤 2 丙辰 Fire Dragon 1 13 十八	火2 Fire Small Livestock 風天小畜 1 丁巳 Fire Snake 8 14 十九	木3 Wood The Cauldron 火風鼎 9 戊午 Earth Horse 4 15 二十	水1 Water Rising 地風升 8 己未 Earth Goat 2 16 廿一
火7 Fire Water 坎爲水 7 庚申 Metal Monkey 1 17 廿二	木8 Wood Lesser Exceeding 雷山小過 6 辛酉 Metal Rooster 3 18 廿三	金4 Metal Gathering 澤地萃 5 壬戌 Water Dog 4 19 廿四	水6 Water Peel 山地剝 4 癸亥 Water Pig 6 20 廿五	水1 Water Earth 坤爲地 3 甲子 Wood Rat 1 21 廿六	木3 Wood Biting 火雷噬嗑 2 乙丑 Wood Ox 6 22 廿七	火2 Fire Family 風火家人 1 丙寅 Fire Tiger 4 23 廿八
水6 Water Decreasing 山澤損 9 丁卯 Fire Rabbit 9 24 廿九	金9 Metal Tread 天澤履 8 戊辰 Earth Dragon 6 25 八月初一	木8 Wood Great Strength 雷天大壯 7 己巳 Earth Snake 2 26 初二	木8 Wood Consistency 雷風恆 6 庚午 Metal Horse 9 27 初三	金9 Metal Litigation 天水訟 5 辛未 Metal Goat 3 28 初四	水1 Water Officer 地水師 4 壬申 Water Monkey 7 29 初五	火2 Fire Gradual Progress 風山漸 3 癸酉 Water Rooster 7 30 初六

SEPTEMBER 2014 癸酉

Xuan Kong Element 玄空五行	風山漸 Gradual Progress	Period Luck 卦運	Monthly Star 月星
Fire 火2		7	1

SUNDAY	MONDAY	TUESDAY	WEDNESDAY	THURSDAY	FRIDAY	SATURDAY
	木3 Wood 1 Advancement 乙亥 Wood Pig 火地晉 1 初八 3	水6 Water 9 Nourish 丙子 Fire Rat 山雷頤 2 初九 3	金4 Metal 8 Following 丁丑 Fire Ox 澤雷隨 3 初十 7	木8 Wood 7 Abundance 戊寅 Earth Tiger 雷火豐 4 十一 6	火7 Fire 6 Regulate 己卯 Earth Rabbit 水澤節 5 十二 8	水1 Water 5 Unity 庚辰 Metal Dragon 地天泰 6 十三 9
木3 Wood 4 Great Reward 辛巳 Metal Snake 火天大有 7 十四 7	火2 Fire 3 Wind 壬午 Water Horse 巽為風 8 十五 1	金4 Metal 2 Trap 癸未 Water Goat 澤水困 9 十六 8	木3 Wood 1 Not Yet Accomplished 甲申 Wood Monkey 火水未濟 10 十七 9	金9 Metal 9 Retreat 乙酉 Wood Rooster 天山遯 11 十八 4	水6 Water 8 Mountain 丙戌 Fire Dog 艮為山 12 十九 1	木8 Wood 7 Delight 丁亥 Fire Pig 雷地豫 13 二十 8
火7 Fire 6 Beginning 戊子 Earth Rat 水雷屯 14 廿一 4	金9 Metal 5 Without Wrongdoing 己丑 Earth Ox 天雷無妄 15 廿二 2	木3 Wood 4 Fire 庚寅 Metal Tiger 離為火 16 廿三 1	火2 Fire 3 Sincerity 辛卯 Metal Rabbit 風澤中孚 17 廿四 3	水6 Water 2 Big Livestock 壬辰 Water Dragon 山天大畜 18 廿五 4	金4 Metal 1 Eliminating 癸巳 Water Snake 澤天夬 19 廿六 6	金9 Metal 9 Heaven 甲午 Wood Horse 乾為天 20 廿七 1
火7 Fire 8 Well 乙未 Wood Goat 水風井 21 廿八 6	木8 Wood 7 Relief 丙申 Fire Monkey 雷水解 22 廿九 4	金4 Metal 6 Influence 丁酉 Fire Rooster 澤山咸 23 三十 9	水1 Water 5 Humility 戊戌 Earth Dog 地山謙 24 九月初一 6	火2 Fire 4 Observation 己亥 Earth Pig 風地觀 25 初二 2	火2 Fire 3 Increasing 庚子 Metal Rat 風雷益 26 初三 9	水1 Water 2 Dimming Light 辛丑 Metal Ox 地火明夷 27 初四 3
金9 Metal 1 Fellowship 壬寅 Water Tiger 天火同人 28 初五 7	木8 Wood 9 Marrying Maiden 癸卯 Water Rabbit 雷澤歸妹 29 初六 7	木3 Wood 8 Opposition 甲辰 Wood Dragon 火澤睽 30 初七 2				

OCTOBER 2014 甲戌

Xuan Kong Element 玄空五行	水山蹇 Obstruction	Period Luck 卦運	Monthly Star 月星
Fire 火7		2	9

SUNDAY	MONDAY	TUESDAY	WEDNESDAY	THURSDAY	FRIDAY	SATURDAY
			火7 Fire 7 Waiting 乙巳 Wood Snake 水天需 1 初八 3	金4 Metal 6 Great Exceeding 丙午 Fire Horse 澤風大過 2 初九 3	水6 Water 5 Poison 丁未 Fire Goat 山風蠱 3 初十 7	火2 Fire 4 Dispersing 戊申 Earth Monkey 風水渙 4 十一 6
木3 Wood 3 Travelling 己酉 Earth Rooster 火山旅 5 十二 8	金9 Metal 2 Stagnation 庚戌 Metal Dog 天地否 6 十三 9	火7 Fire 1 Alliance 辛亥 Metal Pig 水地比 7 十四 7	木8 Wood 9 Thunder 壬子 Water Rat 震為雷 8 十五 1	水6 Water 8 Beauty 癸丑 Water Ox 山火賁 9 十六 8	火7 Fire 7 Accomplished 甲寅 Wood Tiger 水火既濟 10 十七 9	水1 Water 6 Arriving 乙卯 Wood Rabbit 地澤臨 11 十八 4
金4 Metal 5 Marsh 丙辰 Fire Dragon 兌為澤 12 十九 1	火2 Fire 4 Small Livestock 丁巳 Fire Snake 風天小畜 13 二十 8	木3 Wood 3 The Cauldron 戊午 Earth Horse 火風鼎 14 廿一 4	水1 Water 2 Rising 己未 Earth Goat 地風升 15 廿二 2	火7 Fire 1 Water 庚申 Metal Monkey 坎為水 16 廿三 1	木8 Wood 9 Lesser Exceeding 辛酉 Metal Rooster 雷山小過 17 廿四 3	金4 Metal 8 Gathering 壬戌 Water Dog 澤地萃 18 廿五 4
水6 Water 7 Peel 癸亥 Water Pig 山地剝 19 廿六 6	水1 Water 6 Earth 甲子 Wood Rat 坤為地 20 廿七 1	木3 Wood 5 Biting 乙丑 Wood Ox 火雷噬嗑 21 廿八 6	火2 Fire 4 Family 丙寅 Fire Tiger 風火家人 22 廿九 4	水6 Water 3 Decreasing 丁卯 Fire Rabbit 山澤損 23 三十 9	金9 Metal 2 Tread 戊辰 Earth Dragon 天澤履 24 閏九月初一 6	木8 Wood 1 Great Strength 己巳 Earth Snake 雷天大壯 25 初二 2
木8 Wood 9 Consistency 庚午 Metal Horse 雷風恒 26 初三 9	金9 Metal 8 Litigation 辛未 Metal Goat 天水訟 27 初四 3	水1 Water 7 Officer 壬申 Water Monkey 地水師 28 初五 7	火2 Fire 6 Gradual Progress 癸酉 Water Rooster 風山漸 29 初六 7	火7 Fire 5 Obstruction 甲戌 Wood Dog 水山蹇 30 初七 2	木3 Wood 4 Advancement 乙亥 Wood Pig 火地晉 31 初八 3	

NOVEMBER 2014 乙亥

Xuan Kong Element 玄空五行	火地晉 Advancement	Period Luck 卦運	Monthly Star 月星
Wood 木3		3	8

SUNDAY	MONDAY	TUESDAY	WEDNESDAY	THURSDAY	FRIDAY	SATURDAY
火7 Fire Waiting 1 水天需 乙巳 Wood Snake 30 初九 3						水6 Water Nourish 3 山雷頤 丙子 Fire Rat 1 初九 3
金4 Metal Following 2 澤雷隨 丁丑 Fire Ox 2 初十 7	木8 Wood Abundance 1 雷火豐 戊寅 Earth Tiger 3 十一 6	火7 Fire Regulate 9 水澤節 己卯 Earth Rabbit 4 十二 8	水1 Water Unity 8 地天泰 庚辰 Metal Dragon 5 十三 9	木3 Wood Great Reward 7 火天大有 辛巳 Metal Snake 6 十四 7	火2 Fire Wind 6 巽爲風 壬午 Water Horse 7 十五 1	金4 Metal Trap 5 澤水困 癸未 Water Goat 8 十六 8
木3 Wood Not Yet Accomplished 4 火水未濟 甲申 Wood Monkey 9 十七 9	金9 Metal Retreat 3 天山遯 乙酉 Wood Rooster 10 十八 4	水6 Water Mountain 2 艮爲山 丙戌 Fire Dog 11 十九 1	木8 Wood Delight 1 雷地豫 丁亥 Fire Pig 12 二十 8	火7 Fire Beginning 9 水雷屯 戊子 Earth Rat 13 廿一 4	金9 Metal Without Wrongdoing 8 天雷無妄 己丑 Earth Ox 14 廿二 2	木3 Wood Fire 7 離爲火 庚寅 Metal Tiger 15 廿三 1
火2 Fire Sincerity 6 風澤中孚 辛卯 Metal Rabbit 16 廿四 3	水6 Water Big Livestock 5 山天大畜 壬辰 Water Dragon 17 廿五 4	金4 Metal Eliminating 4 澤天夬 癸巳 Water Snake 18 廿六 6	金9 Metal Heaven 3 乾爲天 甲午 Wood Horse 19 廿七 1	火7 Fire Well 2 水風井 乙未 Wood Goat 20 廿八 6	木8 Wood Relief 1 雷水解 丙申 Fire Monkey 21 廿九 4	金4 Metal Influence 9 澤山咸 丁酉 Fire Rooster 22 十月初一 9
水1 Water Humility 8 地山謙 戊戌 Earth Dog 23 初二 6	火2 Fire Observation 7 風地觀 己亥 Earth Pig 24 初三 2	火2 Fire Increasing 6 風雷益 庚子 Metal Rat 25 初四 9	水1 Water Dimming Light 5 地火明夷 辛丑 Metal Ox 26 初五 3	金9 Metal Fellowship 4 天火同人 壬寅 Water Tiger 27 初六 7	木8 Wood Marrying Maiden 3 雷澤歸妹 癸卯 Water Rabbit 28 初七 7	木3 Wood Opposition 2 火澤睽 甲辰 Wood Dragon 29 初八 2

DECEMBER 2014 丙子

Xuan Kong Element 玄空五行	山雷頤 Nourish	Period Luck 卦運	Monthly Star 月星
Water 水6		3	7

SUNDAY	MONDAY	TUESDAY	WEDNESDAY	THURSDAY	FRIDAY	SATURDAY
	金4 Metal Great Exceeding 9 澤風大過 丙午 Fire Horse 1 初十 3	水6 Water Poison 8 山風蠱 丁未 Fire Goat 2 十一 7	火2 Fire Dispersing 7 風水渙 戊申 Earth Monkey 3 十二 6	木3 Wood Travelling 6 火山旅 己酉 Earth Rooster 4 十三 8	金9 Metal Stagnation 5 天地否 庚戌 Metal Dog 5 十四 9	火7 Fire Alliance 4 水地比 辛亥 Metal Pig 6 十五 7
木8 Wood Thunder 3 震爲雷 壬子 Water Rat 7 十六 1	水6 Water Beauty 2 山火賁 癸丑 Water Ox 8 十七 8	火7 Fire Accomplished 1 水火既濟 甲寅 Wood Tiger 9 十八 9	水1 Water Arriving 9 地澤臨 乙卯 Wood Rabbit 10 十九 4	金4 Metal Marsh 8 兌爲澤 丙辰 Fire Dragon 11 二十 1	火2 Fire Small Livestock 7 風天小畜 丁巳 Fire Snake 12 廿一 8	木3 Wood The Cauldron 6 火風鼎 戊午 Earth Horse 13 廿二 4
水1 Water Rising 5 地風升 己未 Earth Goat 14 廿三 2	火7 Fire Water 4 坎爲水 庚申 Metal Monkey 15 廿四 1	木8 Wood Lesser Exceeding 3 雷山小過 辛酉 Metal Rooster 16 廿五 3	金4 Metal Gathering 2 澤地萃 壬戌 Water Dog 17 廿六 4	水6 Water Peel 1 山地剝 癸亥 Water Pig 18 廿七 6	水1 Water Earth 9 坤爲地 甲子 Wood Rat 19 廿八 1	木3 Wood Biting 8 火雷噬嗑 乙丑 Wood Ox 20 廿九 6
火2 Fire Family 7 風火家人 丙寅 Fire Tiger 21 三十 4	水6 Water Decreasing 6/7 山澤損 丁卯 Fire Rabbit 22 十一月初一 9	金9 Metal Tread 8 天澤履 戊辰 Earth Dragon 23 初二 6	木8 Wood Great Strength 9 雷天大壯 己巳 Earth Snake 24 初三 2	木8 Wood Consistency 1 雷風恆 庚午 Metal Horse 25 初四 9	金9 Metal Litigation 2 天水訟 辛未 Metal Goat 26 初五 3	水1 Water Officer 3 地水師 壬申 Water Monkey 27 初六 7
火2 Fire Gradual Progress 4 風山漸 癸酉 Water Rooster 28 初七 7	火7 Fire Obstruction 5 水山蹇 甲戌 Wood Dog 29 初八 2	木3 Wood Advancement 6 火地晉 乙亥 Wood Pig 30 初九 3	水6 Water Nourish 7 山雷頤 丙子 Fire Rat 31 初十 3			

2015 乙未

(*Yi Wei*) Wood Goat

2015 乙未 *(Yi Wei)* Wood Goat

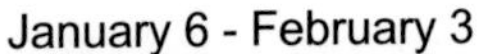

January 6 - February 3

February 4 - March 5

March 6 - April 4

April 5 - May 5

May 6 - June 5

June 6 - July 6

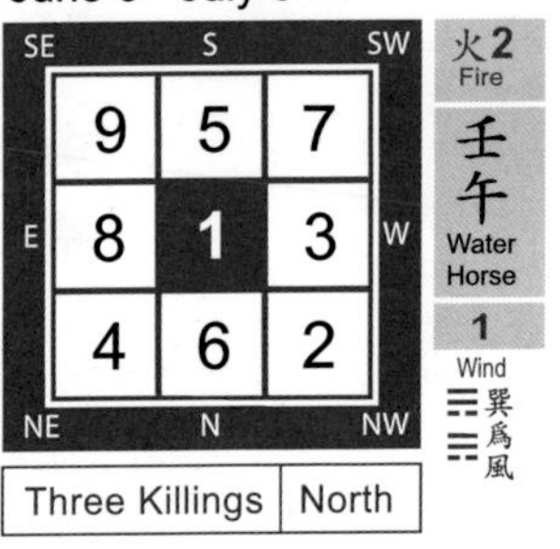

July 7 - August 7

August 8 - September 7

September 8 - October 7

October 8 - November 7

November 8 - December 6

December 7 - January 5

JANUARY 2015 丁丑

Xuan Kong Element 玄空五行	澤雷隨 Following	Period Luck 卦運	Monthly Star 月星
Metal 金4		7	6

SUNDAY	MONDAY	TUESDAY	WEDNESDAY	THURSDAY	FRIDAY	SATURDAY
				金4 Metal · Following 8 · 澤雷隨 · 丁丑 Fire Ox · 7 · **1** 十一	木8 Wood · Abundance 9 · 雷火豐 · 戊寅 Earth Tiger · 6 · **2** 十二	火7 Fire · Regulate 1 · 水澤節 · 己卯 Earth Rabbit · 8 · **3** 十三
水1 Water · Unity 2 · 地天泰 · 庚辰 Metal Dragon · 9 · **4** 十四	木3 Wood · Great Reward 3 · 火天大有 · 辛巳 Metal Snake · 7 · **5** 十五	火2 Fire · Wind 4 · 巽爲風 · 壬午 Water Horse · 1 · **6** 十六	金4 Metal · Trap 5 · 澤水困 · 癸未 Water Goat · 8 · **7** 十七	木3 Wood · Not Yet Accomplished 6 · 火水未濟 · 甲申 Wood Monkey · 9 · **8** 十八	金9 Metal · Retreat 7 · 天山遯 · 乙酉 Wood Rooster · 4 · **9** 十九	水6 Water · Mountain 8 · 艮爲山 · 丙戌 Fire Dog · 1 · **10** 二十
木8 Wood · Delight 9 · 雷地豫 · 丁亥 Fire Pig · 8 · **11** 廿一	火7 Fire · Beginning 1 · 水雷屯 · 戊子 Earth Rat · 4 · **12** 廿二	金9 Metal · Without Wrongdoing 2 · 天雷無妄 · 己丑 Earth Ox · 2 · **13** 廿三	木3 Wood · Fire 3 · 離爲火 · 庚寅 Metal Tiger · 1 · **14** 廿四	火2 Fire · Sincerity 4 · 風澤中孚 · 辛卯 Metal Rabbit · 3 · **15** 廿五	水6 Water · Big Livestock 5 · 山天大畜 · 壬辰 Water Dragon · 4 · **16** 廿六	金4 Metal · Eliminating 6 · 澤天夬 · 癸巳 Water Snake · 6 · **17** 廿七
金9 Metal · Heaven 7 · 乾爲天 · 甲午 Wood Horse · 1 · **18** 廿八	火7 Fire · Well 8 · 水風井 · 乙未 Wood Goat · 6 · **19** 廿九	木8 Wood · Relief 9 · 雷水解 · 丙申 Fire Monkey · 4 · **20** 十二月初一	金4 Metal · Influence 1 · 澤山咸 · 丁酉 Fire Rooster · 9 · **21** 初二	水1 Water · Humility 2 · 地山謙 · 戊戌 Earth Dog · 6 · **22** 初三	火2 Fire · Observation 3 · 風地觀 · 己亥 Earth Pig · 2 · **23** 初四	火2 Fire · Increasing 4 · 風雷益 · 庚子 Metal Rat · 9 · **24** 初五
水1 Water · Dimming Light 5 · 地火明夷 · 辛丑 Metal Ox · 3 · **25** 初六	金9 Metal · Fellowship 6 · 天火同人 · 壬寅 Water Tiger · 7 · **26** 初七	木8 Wood · Marrying Maiden 7 · 雷澤歸妹 · 癸卯 Water Rabbit · 7 · **27** 初八	木3 Wood · Opposition 8 · 火澤睽 · 甲辰 Wood Dragon · 2 · **28** 初九	火7 Fire · Waiting 9 · 水天需 · 乙巳 Wood Snake · 3 · **29** 初十	金4 Metal · Great Exceeding 1 · 澤風大過 · 丙午 Fire Horse · 3 · **30** 十一	水6 Water · Poison 2 · 山風蠱 · 丁未 Fire Goat · 7 · **31** 十二

FEBRUARY 2015 戊寅

Xuan Kong Element 玄空五行	雷火豐 Abundance	Period Luck 卦運	Monthly Star 月星
Wood 木8		6	5

SUNDAY	MONDAY	TUESDAY	WEDNESDAY	THURSDAY	FRIDAY	SATURDAY
火2 Fire · Dispersing 3 · 風水渙 · 戊申 Earth Monkey · 6 · **1** 十三	木3 Wood · Travelling 4 · 火山旅 · 己酉 Earth Rooster · 8 · **2** 十四	金9 Metal · Stagnation 5 · 天地否 · 庚戌 Metal Dog · 9 · **3** 十五	火7 Fire · Alliance 6 · 水地比 · 辛亥 Metal Pig · 7 · **4** 十六	木8 Wood · Thunder 7 · 震爲雷 · 壬子 Water Rat · 1 · **5** 十七	水6 Water · Beauty 8 · 山火賁 · 癸丑 Water Ox · 8 · **6** 十八	火7 Fire · Accomplished 9 · 水火既濟 · 甲寅 Wood Tiger · 9 · **7** 十九
水1 Water · Arriving 1 · 地澤臨 · 乙卯 Wood Rabbit · 4 · **8** 二十	金4 Metal · Marsh 2 · 兌爲澤 · 丙辰 Fire Dragon · 1 · **9** 廿一	火2 Fire · Small Livestock 3 · 風天小畜 · 丁巳 Fire Snake · 8 · **10** 廿二	木3 Wood · The Cauldron 4 · 火風鼎 · 戊午 Earth Horse · 4 · **11** 廿三	水1 Water · Rising 5 · 地風升 · 己未 Earth Goat · 2 · **12** 廿四	火7 Fire · Water 6 · 坎爲水 · 庚申 Metal Monkey · 1 · **13** 廿五	木8 Wood · Lesser Exceeding 7 · 雷山小過 · 辛酉 Metal Rooster · 3 · **14** 廿六
金4 Metal · Gathering 8 · 澤地萃 · 壬戌 Water Dog · 4 · **15** 廿七	水6 Water · Peel 9 · 山地剝 · 癸亥 Water Pig · 6 · **16** 廿八	水1 Water · Earth 1 · 坤爲地 · 甲子 Wood Rat · 1 · **17** 廿九	木3 Wood · Biting 2 · 火雷噬嗑 · 乙丑 Wood Ox · 6 · **18** 三十	火2 Fire · Family 3 · 風火家人 · 丙寅 Fire Tiger · 4 · **19** 正月初一	水6 Water · Decreasing 4 · 山澤損 · 丁卯 Fire Rabbit · 9 · **20** 初二	金9 Metal · Tread 5 · 天澤履 · 戊辰 Earth Dragon · 6 · **21** 初三
木8 Wood · Great Strength 6 · 雷天大壯 · 己巳 Earth Snake · 2 · **22** 初四	木8 Wood · Consistency 7 · 雷風恆 · 庚午 Metal Horse · 9 · **23** 初五	金9 Metal · Litigation 8 · 天水訟 · 辛未 Metal Goat · 3 · **24** 初六	水1 Water · Officer 9 · 地水師 · 壬申 Water Monkey · 7 · **25** 初七	火2 Fire · Gradual Progress 1 · 風山漸 · 癸酉 Water Rooster · 7 · **26** 初八	火7 Fire · Obstruction 2 · 水山蹇 · 甲戌 Wood Dog · 2 · **27** 初九	木3 Wood · Advancement 3 · 火地晉 · 乙亥 Wood Pig · 3 · **28** 初十

MARCH 2015 己卯

Xuan Kong Element 玄空五行	水澤節 Regulate	Period Luck 卦運	Monthly Star 月星
Fire 火7		8	4

SUNDAY	MONDAY	TUESDAY	WEDNESDAY	THURSDAY	FRIDAY	SATURDAY
水6 Water Nourish 4 丙子 Fire Rat 山雷頤 1 十一 3	金4 Metal Following 5 丁丑 Fire Ox 澤雷隨 2 十二 7	木8 Wood Abundance 6 戊寅 Earth Tiger 雷火豐 3 十三 6	火7 Fire Regulate 7 己卯 Earth Rabbit 水澤節 4 十四 8	水1 Water Unity 8 庚辰 Metal Dragon 地天泰 5 十五 9	木3 Wood Great Reward 9 辛巳 Metal Snake 火天大有 6 十六 7	火2 Fire Wind 1 壬午 Water Horse 巽為風 7 十七 1
金4 Metal Trap 2 癸未 Water Goat 澤水困 8 十八 8	木3 Wood Not Yet Accomplished 3 甲申 Wood Monkey 火水未濟 9 十九 9	金9 Metal Retreat 4 乙酉 Wood Rooster 天山遯 10 二十 4	水6 Water Mountain 5 丙戌 Fire Dog 艮為山 11 廿一 1	木8 Wood Delight 6 丁亥 Fire Pig 雷地豫 12 廿二 8	火7 Fire Beginning 7 戊子 Earth Rat 水雷屯 13 廿三 4	金9 Metal Without Wrongdoing 8 己丑 Earth Ox 天雷無妄 14 廿四 2
木3 Wood Fire 9 庚寅 Metal Tiger 離為火 15 廿五 1	火2 Fire Sincerity 1 辛卯 Metal Rabbit 風澤中孚 16 廿六 3	水6 Water Big Livestock 2 壬辰 Water Dragon 山天大畜 17 廿七 4	金4 Metal Eliminating 3 癸巳 Water Snake 澤天夬 18 廿八 6	金9 Metal Heaven 4 甲午 Wood Horse 乾為天 19 廿九 1	火7 Fire Well 5 乙未 Wood Goat 水風井 20 二月初一 6	木8 Wood Relief 6 丙申 Fire Monkey 雷水解 21 初二 4
金4 Metal Influence 7 丁酉 Fire Rooster 澤山咸 22 初三 9	水1 Water Humility 8 戊戌 Earth Dog 地山謙 23 初四 6	火2 Fire Observation 9 己亥 Earth Pig 風地觀 24 初五 2	火2 Fire Increasing 1 庚子 Metal Rat 風雷益 25 初六 9	水1 Water Dimming Light 2 辛丑 Metal Ox 地火明夷 26 初七 3	金9 Metal Fellowship 3 壬寅 Water Tiger 天火同人 27 初八 7	木8 Wood Marrying Maiden 4 癸卯 Water Rabbit 雷澤歸妹 28 初九 7
木3 Wood Opposition 5 甲辰 Wood Dragon 火澤睽 29 初十 2	火7 Fire Waiting 6 乙巳 Wood Snake 水天需 30 十一 3	金4 Metal Great Exceeding 7 丙午 Fire Horse 澤風大過 31 十二 3				

APRIL 2015 庚辰

Xuan Kong Element 玄空五行	地天泰 Unity	Period Luck 卦運	Monthly Star 月星
Water 水1		9	3

SUNDAY	MONDAY	TUESDAY	WEDNESDAY	THURSDAY	FRIDAY	SATURDAY
			水6 Water Poison 8 丁未 Fire Goat 山風蠱 1 十三 7	火2 Fire Dispersing 9 戊申 Earth Monkey 風水渙 2 十四 6	木3 Wood Travelling 1 己酉 Earth Rooster 火山旅 3 十五 8	金9 Metal Stagnation 2 庚戌 Metal Dog 天地否 4 十六 9
火7 Fire Alliance 3 辛亥 Metal Pig 水地比 5 十七 7	木8 Wood Thunder 4 壬子 Water Rat 震為雷 6 十八 1	水6 Water Beauty 5 癸丑 Water Ox 山火賁 7 十九 8	火7 Fire Accomplished 6 甲寅 Wood Tiger 水火既濟 8 二十 9	水1 Water Arriving 7 乙卯 Wood Rabbit 地澤臨 9 廿一 4	金4 Metal Marsh 8 丙辰 Fire Dragon 兑為澤 10 廿二 1	火2 Fire Small Livestock 9 丁巳 Fire Snake 風天小畜 11 廿三 8
木3 Wood The Cauldron 1 戊午 Earth Horse 火風鼎 12 廿四 4	水1 Water Rising 2 己未 Earth Goat 地風升 13 廿五 2	火7 Fire Water 3 庚申 Metal Monkey 坎為水 14 廿六 1	木8 Wood Lesser Exceeding 4 辛酉 Metal Rooster 雷山小過 15 廿七 3	金4 Metal Gathering 5 壬戌 Water Dog 澤地萃 16 廿八 4	水6 Water Peel 6 癸亥 Water Pig 山地剝 17 廿九 6	水1 Water Earth 7 甲子 Wood Rat 坤為地 18 三十 1
木3 Wood Biting 8 乙丑 Wood Ox 火雷噬嗑 19 三月初一 6	火2 Fire Family 9 丙寅 Fire Tiger 風火家人 20 初二 4	水6 Water Decreasing 1 丁卯 Fire Rabbit 山澤損 21 初三 9	金9 Metal Tread 2 戊辰 Earth Dragon 天澤履 22 初四 6	木8 Wood Great Strength 3 己巳 Earth Snake 雷天大壯 23 初五 2	木8 Wood Consistency 4 庚午 Metal Horse 雷風恆 24 初六 9	金9 Metal Litigation 5 辛未 Metal Goat 天水訟 25 初七 3
水1 Water Officer 6 壬申 Water Monkey 地水師 26 初八 7	火2 Fire Gradual Progress 7 癸酉 Water Rooster 風山漸 27 初九 7	火7 Fire Obstruction 8 甲戌 Wood Dog 水山蹇 28 初十 2	木3 Wood Advancement 9 乙亥 Wood Pig 火地晉 29 十一 3	水6 Water Nourish 1 丙子 Fire Rat 山雷頤 30 十二 3		

MAY 2015 辛巳

Xuan Kong Element 玄空五行	火天大有 Great Reward	Period Luck 卦運	Monthly Star 月星
Wood 木3		7	2

SUNDAY	MONDAY	TUESDAY	WEDNESDAY	THURSDAY	FRIDAY	SATURDAY
31 水6 Water Poison 5 丁未 Fire Goat 山風蠱 十四 7					1 金4 Metal Following 2 丁丑 Fire Ox 澤雷隨 十三 7	2 木8 Wood Abundance 3 戊寅 Earth Tiger 雷火豐 十四 6
3 火7 Fire Regulate 4 己卯 Earth Rabbit 水澤節 十五 8	4 水1 Water Unity 5 庚辰 Metal Dragon 地天泰 十六 9	5 木3 Wood Great Reward 6 辛巳 Metal Snake 火天大有 十七 7	6 火2 Fire Wind 7 壬午 Water Horse 巽爲風 十八 1	7 金4 Metal Trap 8 癸未 Water Goat 澤水困 十九 8	8 木3 Wood Not Yet Accomplished 9 甲申 Wood Monkey 火水未濟 二十 9	9 金9 Metal Retreat 1 乙酉 Wood Rooster 天山遯 廿一 4
10 水6 Water Mountain 2 丙戌 Fire Dog 艮爲山 廿二 1	11 木8 Wood Delight 3 丁亥 Fire Pig 雷地豫 廿三 8	12 火7 Fire Beginning 4 戊子 Earth Rat 水雷屯 廿四 4	13 金9 Metal Without Wrongdoing 5 己丑 Earth Ox 天雷無妄 廿五 2	14 木3 Wood Fire 6 庚寅 Metal Tiger 離爲火 廿六 1	15 火2 Fire Sincerity 7 辛卯 Metal Rabbit 風澤中孚 廿七 3	16 水6 Water Big Livestock 8 壬辰 Water Dragon 山天大畜 廿八 4
17 金4 Metal Eliminating 9 癸巳 Water Snake 澤天夬 廿九 6	18 金9 Metal Heaven 1 甲午 Wood Horse 乾爲天 四月初一 1	19 火7 Fire Well 2 乙未 Wood Goat 水風井 初二 6	20 木8 Wood Relief 3 丙申 Fire Monkey 雷水解 初三 4	21 金4 Metal Influence 4 丁酉 Fire Rooster 澤山咸 初四 9	22 水1 Water Humility 5 戊戌 Earth Dog 地山謙 初五 6	23 火2 Fire Observation 6 己亥 Earth Pig 風地觀 初六 2
24 火2 Fire Increasing 7 庚子 Metal Rat 風雷益 初七 9	25 水1 Water Dimming Light 8 辛丑 Metal Ox 地火明夷 初八 3	26 金9 Metal Fellowship 9 壬寅 Water Tiger 天火同人 初九 7	27 木8 Wood Marrying Maiden 1 癸卯 Water Rabbit 雷澤歸妹 初十 7	28 木3 Wood Opposition 2 甲辰 Wood Dragon 火澤睽 十一 2	29 火7 Fire Waiting 3 乙巳 Wood Snake 水天需 十二 3	30 金4 Metal Great Exceeding 4 丙午 Fire Horse 澤風大過 十三 3

JUNE 2015 壬午

Xuan Kong Element 玄空五行	巽爲風 Wind	Period Luck 卦運	Monthly Star 月星
Fire 火2		1	1

SUNDAY	MONDAY	TUESDAY	WEDNESDAY	THURSDAY	FRIDAY	SATURDAY
	1 火2 Fire Dispersing 6 戊申 Earth Monkey 風水渙 十五 6	2 木3 Wood Travelling 7 己酉 Earth Rooster 火山旅 十六 8	3 金9 Metal Stagnation 8 庚戌 Metal Dog 天地否 十七 9	4 火7 Fire Alliance 9 辛亥 Metal Pig 水地比 十八 7	5 木8 Wood Thunder 1 壬子 Water Rat 震爲雷 十九 1	6 水6 Water Beauty 2 癸丑 Water Ox 山火賁 二十 8
7 火7 Fire Accomplished 3 甲寅 Wood Tiger 水火既濟 廿一 9	8 水1 Water Arriving 4 乙卯 Wood Rabbit 地澤臨 廿二 4	9 金4 Metal Marsh 5 丙辰 Fire Dragon 兑爲澤 廿三 1	10 火2 Fire Small Livestock 6 丁巳 Fire Snake 風天小畜 廿四 8	11 木3 Wood The Cauldron 7 戊午 Earth Horse 火風鼎 廿五 4	12 水1 Water Rising 8 己未 Earth Goat 地風升 廿六 2	13 火7 Fire Water 9 庚申 Metal Monkey 坎爲水 廿七 1
14 木8 Wood Lesser Exceeding 1 辛酉 Metal Rooster 雷山小過 廿八 3	15 金4 Metal Gathering 2 壬戌 Water Dog 澤地萃 廿九 4	16 水6 Water Peel 3 癸亥 Water Pig 山地剝 五月初一 6	17 水1 Water Earth 4 甲子 Wood Rat 坤爲地 初二 1	18 木3 Wood Biting 5 乙丑 Wood Ox 火雷噬嗑 初三 6	19 火2 Fire Family 6 丙寅 Fire Tiger 風火家人 初四 4	20 水6 Water Decreasing 7 丁卯 Fire Rabbit 山澤損 初五 9
21 金9 Metal Tread 8 戊辰 Earth Dragon 天澤履 初六 6	22 木8 Wood Great Strength 9/1 己巳 Earth Snake 雷天大壯 初七 2	23 木8 Wood Consistency 9 庚午 Metal Horse 雷風恒 初八 9	24 金9 Metal Litigation 8 辛未 Metal Goat 天水訟 初九 3	25 水1 Water Officer 7 壬申 Water Monkey 地水師 初十 7	26 火2 Fire Gradual Progress 6 癸酉 Water Rooster 風山漸 十一 7	27 火7 Fire Obstruction 5 甲戌 Wood Dog 水山蹇 十二 2
28 木3 Wood Advancement 4 乙亥 Wood Pig 火地晉 十三 3	29 水6 Water Nourish 3 丙子 Fire Rat 山雷頤 十四 3	30 金4 Metal Following 2 丁丑 Fire Ox 澤雷隨 十五 7				

JULY 2015 癸未

Xuan Kong Element 玄空五行	澤水困 Trap	Period Luck 卦運	Monthly Star 月星
Metal 金4		8	9

SUNDAY	MONDAY	TUESDAY	WEDNESDAY	THURSDAY	FRIDAY	SATURDAY
			1 木8 Wood Abundance [1] 戊寅 Earth Tiger 雷火豐 十六 6	**2** 火7 Fire Regulate [9] 己卯 Earth Rabbit 水澤節 十七 8	**3** 水1 Water Unity [8] 庚辰 Metal Dragon 地天泰 十八 9	**4** 木3 Wood Great Reward [7] 辛巳 Metal Snake 火天大有 十九 7
5 火2 Fire Wind [6] 壬午 Water Horse 巽為風 二十 1	**6** 金4 Metal Trap [5] 癸未 Water Goat 澤水困 廿一 8	**7** 木3 Wood Not Yet Accomplished [4] 甲申 Wood Monkey 火水未濟 廿二 9	**8** 金9 Metal Retreat [3] 乙酉 Wood Rooster 天山遯 廿三 4	**9** 水6 Water Mountain [2] 丙戌 Fire Dog 艮為山 廿四 1	**10** 木8 Wood Delight [1] 丁亥 Fire Pig 雷地豫 廿五 8	**11** 火7 Fire Beginning [9] 戊子 Earth Rat 水雷屯 廿六 4
12 金9 Metal Without Wrongdoing [8] 己丑 Earth Ox 天雷無妄 廿七 2	**13** 木3 Wood Fire [7] 庚寅 Metal Tiger 離為火 廿八 1	**14** 火2 Fire Sincerity [6] 辛卯 Metal Rabbit 風澤中孚 廿九 3	**15** 水6 Water Big Livestock [5] 壬辰 Water Dragon 山天大畜 三十 4	**16** 金4 Metal Eliminating [4] 癸巳 Water Snake 澤天夬 六月初一 6	**17** 金9 Metal Heaven [3] 甲午 Wood Horse 乾為天 初二 1	**18** 火7 Fire Well [2] 乙未 Wood Goat 水風井 初三 6
19 木8 Wood Relief [1] 丙申 Fire Monkey 雷水解 初四 4	**20** 金4 Metal Influence [9] 丁酉 Fire Rooster 澤山咸 初五 9	**21** 水1 Water Humility [8] 戊戌 Earth Dog 地山謙 初六 6	**22** 火2 Fire Observation [7] 己亥 Earth Pig 風地觀 初七 2	**23** 火2 Fire Increasing [6] 庚子 Metal Rat 風雷益 初八 9	**24** 水1 Water Dimming Light [5] 辛丑 Metal Ox 地火明夷 初九 3	**25** 金9 Metal Fellowship [4] 壬寅 Water Tiger 天火同人 初十 7
26 木8 Wood Marrying Maiden [3] 癸卯 Water Rabbit 雷澤歸妹 十一 7	**27** 木3 Wood Opposition [2] 甲辰 Wood Dragon 火澤睽 十二 2	**28** 火7 Fire Waiting [1] 乙巳 Wood Snake 水天需 十三 3	**29** 金4 Metal Great Exceeding [9] 丙午 Fire Horse 澤風大過 十四 3	**30** 水6 Water Poison [8] 丁未 Fire Goat 山風蠱 十五 7	**31** 火2 Fire Dispersing [7] 戊申 Earth Monkey 風水渙 十六 6	

AUGUST 2015 甲申

Xuan Kong Element 玄空五行	火水未濟 Not Yet Accomplished	Period Luck 卦運	Monthly Star 月星
Wood 木3		9	8

SUNDAY	MONDAY	TUESDAY	WEDNESDAY	THURSDAY	FRIDAY	SATURDAY
30 木8 Wood Abundance [4] 戊寅 Earth Tiger 雷火豐 十七 6	**31** 火7 Fire Regulate [3] 己卯 Earth Rabbit 水澤節 十八 8					**1** 木3 Wood Travelling [6] 己酉 Earth Rooster 火山旅 十七 8
2 金9 Metal Stagnation [5] 庚戌 Metal Dog 天地否 十八 9	**3** 火7 Fire Alliance [4] 辛亥 Metal Pig 水地比 十九 7	**4** 木8 Wood Thunder [3] 壬子 Water Rat 震為雷 二十 1	**5** 水6 Water Beauty [2] 癸丑 Water Ox 山火賁 廿一 8	**6** 火7 Fire Accomplished [1] 甲寅 Wood Tiger 水火既濟 廿二 9	**7** 水1 Water Arriving [9] 乙卯 Wood Rabbit 地澤臨 廿三 4	**8** 金4 Metal Marsh [8] 丙辰 Fire Dragon 兑為澤 廿四 1
9 火2 Fire Small Livestock [7] 丁巳 Fire Snake 風天小畜 廿五 8	**10** 木3 Wood The Cauldron [6] 戊午 Earth Horse 火風鼎 廿六 4	**11** 水1 Water Rising [5] 己未 Earth Goat 地風升 廿七 2	**12** 火7 Fire Water [4] 庚申 Metal Monkey 坎為水 廿八 1	**13** 木8 Wood Lesser Exceeding [3] 辛酉 Metal Rooster 雷山小過 廿九 3	**14** 金4 Metal Gathering [2] 壬戌 Water Dog 澤地萃 七月初一 4	**15** 水6 Water Peel [1] 癸亥 Water Pig 山地剝 初二 6
16 水1 Water Earth [9] 甲子 Wood Rat 坤為地 初三 1	**17** 木3 Wood Biting [8] 乙丑 Wood Ox 火雷噬嗑 初四 6	**18** 火2 Fire Family [7] 丙寅 Fire Tiger 風火家人 初五 4	**19** 水6 Water Decreasing [6] 丁卯 Fire Rabbit 山澤損 初六 9	**20** 金9 Metal Tread [5] 戊辰 Earth Dragon 天澤履 初七 6	**21** 木8 Wood Great Strength [4] 己巳 Earth Snake 雷天大壯 初八 2	**22** 木8 Wood Consistency [3] 庚午 Metal Horse 雷風恆 初九 9
23 金9 Metal Litigation [2] 辛未 Metal Goat 天水訟 初十 3	**24** 水1 Water Officer [1] 壬申 Water Monkey 地水師 十一 7	**25** 火2 Fire Gradual Progress [9] 癸酉 Water Rooster 風山漸 十二 7	**26** 火7 Fire Obstruction [8] 甲戌 Wood Dog 水山蹇 十三 2	**27** 木3 Wood Advancement [7] 乙亥 Wood Pig 火地晉 十四 3	**28** 水6 Water Nourish [6] 丙子 Fire Rat 山雷頤 十五 3	**29** 金4 Metal Following [5] 丁丑 Fire Ox 澤雷隨 十六 7

SEPTEMBER 2015 乙酉

Xuan Kong Element 玄空五行	天山遯 Retreat	Period Luck 卦運	Monthly Star 月星
Metal 金9		4	7

SUNDAY	MONDAY	TUESDAY	WEDNESDAY	THURSDAY	FRIDAY	SATURDAY
		水1 Water Unity 2 庚辰 Metal Dragon 地天泰 **1** 十九 9	木3 Wood Great Reward 1 辛巳 Metal Snake 火天大有 **2** 二十 7	火2 Fire Wind 9 壬午 Water Horse 巽爲風 **3** 廿一 1	金4 Metal Trap 8 癸未 Water Goat 澤水困 **4** 廿二 8	木3 Wood Not Yet Accomplished 7 甲申 Wood Monkey 火水未濟 **5** 廿三 9
金9 Metal Retreat 6 乙酉 Wood Rooster 天山遯 **6** 廿四 4	水6 Water Mountain 5 丙戌 Fire Dog 艮爲山 **7** 廿五 1	木8 Wood Delight 4 丁亥 Fire Pig 雷地豫 **8** 廿六 8	火7 Fire Beginning 3 戊子 Earth Rat 水雷屯 **9** 廿七 4	金9 Metal Without Wrongdoing 2 己丑 Earth Ox 天雷無妄 **10** 廿八 2	木3 Wood Fire 1 庚寅 Metal Tiger 離爲火 **11** 廿九 1	火2 Fire Sincerity 9 辛卯 Metal Rabbit 風澤中孚 **12** 三十 3
水6 Water Big Livestock 8 壬辰 Water Dragon 山天大畜 **13** 八月初一 4	金4 Metal Eliminating 7 癸巳 Water Snake 澤天夬 **14** 初二 6	金9 Metal Heaven 6 甲午 Wood Horse 乾爲天 **15** 初三 1	火7 Fire Well 5 乙未 Wood Goat 水風井 **16** 初四 6	木8 Wood Relief 4 丙申 Fire Monkey 雷水解 **17** 初五 4	金4 Metal Influence 3 丁酉 Fire Rooster 澤山咸 **18** 初六 9	水1 Water Humility 2 戊戌 Earth Dog 地山謙 **19** 初七 6
火2 Fire Observation 1 己亥 Earth Pig 風地觀 **20** 初八 2	火2 Fire Increasing 9 庚子 Metal Rat 風雷益 **21** 初九 9	水1 Water Dimming Light 8 辛丑 Metal Ox 地火明夷 **22** 初十 3	金9 Metal Fellowship 7 壬寅 Water Tiger 天火同人 **23** 十一 7	木8 Wood Marrying Maiden 6 癸卯 Water Rabbit 雷澤歸妹 **24** 十二 7	木3 Wood Opposition 5 甲辰 Wood Dragon 火澤睽 **25** 十三 2	火7 Fire Waiting 4 乙巳 Wood Snake 水天需 **26** 十四 3
金4 Metal Great Exceeding 3 丙午 Fire Horse 澤風大過 **27** 十五 3	水6 Water Poison 2 丁未 Fire Goat 山風蠱 **28** 十六 7	火2 Fire Dispersing 1 戊申 Earth Monkey 風水渙 **29** 十七 6	木3 Wood Travelling 9 己酉 Earth Rooster 火山旅 **30** 十八 8			

OCTOBER 2015 丙戌

Xuan Kong Element 玄空五行	艮爲山 Mountain	Period Luck 卦運	Monthly Star 月星
Water 水6		1	6

SUNDAY	MONDAY	TUESDAY	WEDNESDAY	THURSDAY	FRIDAY	SATURDAY
				金9 Metal Stagnation 8 庚戌 Metal Dog 天地否 **1** 十九 9	火7 Fire Alliance 7 辛亥 Metal Pig 水地比 **2** 二十 7	木8 Wood Thunder 6 壬子 Water Rat 震爲雷 **3** 廿一 1
水6 Water Beauty 5 癸丑 Water Ox 山火賁 **4** 廿二 8	火7 Fire Accomplished 4 甲寅 Wood Tiger 水火既濟 **5** 廿三 9	水1 Water Arriving 3 乙卯 Wood Rabbit 地澤臨 **6** 廿四 4	金4 Metal Marsh 2 丙辰 Fire Dragon 兌爲澤 **7** 廿五 1	火2 Fire Small Livestock 1 丁巳 Fire Snake 風天小畜 **8** 廿六 8	木3 Wood The Cauldron 9 戊午 Earth Horse 火風鼎 **9** 廿七 4	水1 Water Rising 8 己未 Earth Goat 地風升 **10** 廿八 2
火7 Fire Water 7 庚申 Metal Monkey 坎爲水 **11** 廿八 1	木8 Wood Lesser Exceeding 6 辛酉 Metal Rooster 雷山小過 **12** 廿九 3	金4 Metal Gathering 5 壬戌 Water Dog 澤地萃 **13** 九月初一 4	水6 Water Peel 4 癸亥 Water Pig 山地剝 **14** 初二 6	水1 Water Earth 3 甲子 Wood Rat 坤爲地 **15** 初三 1	木3 Wood Biting 2 乙丑 Wood Ox 火雷噬嗑 **16** 初四 6	火2 Fire Family 1 丙寅 Fire Tiger 風火家人 **17** 初五 4
水6 Water Decreasing 9 丁卯 Fire Rabbit 山澤損 **18** 初六 9	金9 Metal Tread 8 戊辰 Earth Dragon 天澤履 **19** 初七 6	木8 Wood Great Strength 7 己巳 Earth Snake 雷天大壯 **20** 初八 2	木8 Wood Consistency 6 庚午 Metal Horse 雷風恆 **21** 初九 9	金9 Metal Litigation 5 辛未 Metal Goat 天水訟 **22** 初十 3	水1 Water Officer 4 壬申 Water Monkey 地水師 **23** 十一 7	火2 Fire Gradual Progress 3 癸酉 Water Rooster 風山漸 **24** 十二 7
火7 Fire Obstruction 2 甲戌 Wood Dog 水山蹇 **25** 十三 2	木3 Wood Advancement 1 乙亥 Wood Pig 火地晉 **26** 十四 3	水6 Water Nourish 9 丙子 Fire Rat 山雷頤 **27** 十五 3	金4 Metal Following 8 丁丑 Fire Ox 澤雷隨 **28** 十六 7	木8 Wood Abundance 7 戊寅 Earth Tiger 雷火豐 **29** 十七 6	火7 Fire Regulate 6 己卯 Earth Rabbit 水澤節 **30** 十八 8	水1 Water Unity 5 庚辰 Metal Dragon 地天泰 **31** 十九 9

NOVEMBER 2015 丁亥

Xuan Kong Element 玄空五行	雷地豫 Delight	Period Luck 卦運	Monthly Star 月星
Wood 木8		8	5

SUNDAY	MONDAY	TUESDAY	WEDNESDAY	THURSDAY	FRIDAY	SATURDAY
木3 Wood 4 Great Reward 辛巳 Metal Snake 火天大有 **1** 7 二十	火2 Fire 3 Wind 壬午 Water Horse 巽爲風 **2** 1 廿一	金4 Metal 2 Trap 癸未 Water Goat 澤水困 **3** 8 廿二	木3 Wood 1 Not Yet Accomplished 甲申 Wood Monkey 火水未濟 **4** 9 廿三	金9 Metal 9 Retreat 乙酉 Wood Rooster 天山遯 **5** 4 廿四	水6 Water 8 Mountain 丙戌 Fire Dog 艮爲山 **6** 1 廿五	木8 Wood 7 Delight 丁亥 Fire Pig 雷地豫 **7** 8 廿六
火7 Fire 6 Beginning 戊子 Earth Rat 水雷屯 **8** 4 廿七	金9 Metal 5 Without Wrongdoing 己丑 Earth Ox 天雷無妄 **9** 2 廿八	木3 Wood 4 Fire 庚寅 Metal Tiger 離爲火 **10** 1 廿九	火2 Fire 3 Sincerity 辛卯 Metal Rabbit 風澤中孚 **11** 3 三十	水6 Water 2 Big Livestock 壬辰 Water Dragon 山天大畜 **12** 4 十月初一	金4 Metal 1 Eliminating 癸巳 Water Snake 澤天夬 **13** 6 初二	金9 Metal 9 Heaven 甲午 Wood Horse 乾爲天 **14** 1 初三
火7 Fire 8 Well 乙未 Wood Goat 水風井 **15** 6 初四	木8 Wood 7 Relief 丙申 Fire Monkey 雷水解 **16** 4 初五	金4 Metal 6 Influence 丁酉 Fire Rooster 澤山咸 **17** 9 初六	水1 Water 5 Humility 戊戌 Earth Dog 地山謙 **18** 6 初七	火2 Fire 4 Observation 己亥 Earth Pig 風地觀 **19** 2 初八	火2 Fire 3 Increasing 庚子 Metal Rat 風雷益 **20** 9 初九	水1 Water 2 Dimming Light 辛丑 Metal Ox 地火明夷 **21** 3 初十
金9 Metal 1 Fellowship 壬寅 Water Tiger 天火同人 **22** 7 十一	木8 Wood 9 Marrying Maiden 癸卯 Water Rabbit 雷澤歸妹 **23** 7 十二	木3 Wood 8 Opposition 甲辰 Wood Dragon 火澤睽 **24** 2 十三	火7 Fire 7 Waiting 乙巳 Wood Snake 水天需 **25** 3 十四	金4 Metal 6 Great Exceeding 丙午 Fire Horse 澤風大過 **26** 3 十五	水6 Water 5 Poison 丁未 Fire Goat 山風蠱 **27** 7 十六	火2 Fire 4 Dispersing 戊申 Earth Monkey 風水渙 **28** 6 十七
木3 Wood 3 Travelling 己酉 Earth Rooster 火山旅 **29** 8 十八	金9 Metal 2 Stagnation 庚戌 Metal Dog 天地否 **30** 9 十九					

DECEMBER 2015 戊子

Xuan Kong Element 玄空五行	水雷屯 Beginning	Period Luck 卦運	Monthly Star 月星
Fire 火7		4	4

SUNDAY	MONDAY	TUESDAY	WEDNESDAY	THURSDAY	FRIDAY	SATURDAY
		火7 Fire 1 Alliance 辛亥 Metal Pig 水地比 **1** 7 二十	木8 Wood 9 Thunder 壬子 Water Rat 震爲雷 **2** 1 廿一	水6 Water 8 Beauty 癸丑 Water Ox 山火賁 **3** 8 廿二	火7 Fire 7 Accomplished 甲寅 Wood Tiger 水火既濟 **4** 9 廿三	水1 Water 6 Arriving 乙卯 Wood Rabbit 地澤臨 **5** 4 廿四
金4 Metal 5 Marsh 丙辰 Fire Dragon 兌爲澤 **6** 1 廿五	火2 Fire 4 Small Livestock 丁巳 Fire Snake 風天小畜 **7** 8 廿六	木3 Wood 3 The Cauldron 戊午 Earth Horse 火風鼎 **8** 4 廿七	水1 Water 2 Rising 己未 Earth Goat 地風升 **9** 2 廿八	火7 Fire 1 Water 庚申 Metal Monkey 坎爲水 **10** 1 廿九	木8 Wood 9 Lesser Exceeding 辛酉 Metal Rooster 雷山小過 **11** 3 十一月初一	金4 Metal 8 Gathering 壬戌 Water Dog 澤地萃 **12** 4 初二
水6 Water 7 Peel 癸亥 Water Pig 山地剝 **13** 6 初三	水1 Water 6 Earth 甲子 Wood Rat 坤爲地 **14** 1 初四	木3 Wood 5 Biting 乙丑 Wood Ox 火雷噬嗑 **15** 6 初五	火2 Fire 4 Family 丙寅 Fire Tiger 風火家人 **16** 4 初六	水6 Water 3 Decreasing 丁卯 Fire Rabbit 山澤損 **17** 9 初七	金9 Metal 2 Tread 戊辰 Earth Dragon 天澤履 **18** 6 初八	木8 Wood 1 Great Strength 己巳 Earth Snake 雷天大壯 **19** 2 初九
木8 Wood 9 Consistency 庚午 Metal Horse 雷風恒 **20** 9 初十	金9 Metal 8 Litigation 辛未 Metal Goat 天水訟 **21** 3 十一	水1 Water 7/3 Officer 壬申 Water Monkey 地水師 **22** 7 十二	火2 Fire 4 Gradual Progress 癸酉 Water Rooster 風山漸 **23** 7 十三	火7 Fire 5 Obstruction 甲戌 Wood Dog 水山蹇 **24** 2 十四	木3 Wood 6 Advancement 乙亥 Wood Pig 火地晉 **25** 3 十五	水6 Water 7 Nourish 丙子 Fire Rat 山雷頤 **26** 3 十六
金4 Metal 8 Following 丁丑 Fire Ox 澤雷隨 **27** 7 十七	木8 Wood 9 Abundance 戊寅 Earth Tiger 雷火豐 **28** 6 十八	火7 Fire 1 Regulate 己卯 Earth Rabbit 水澤節 **29** 8 十九	水1 Water 2 Unity 庚辰 Metal Dragon 地天泰 **30** 9 二十	木3 Wood 3 Great Reward 辛巳 Metal Snake 火天大有 **31** 7 廿一		

2016 丙申

(*Bing Shen*) Fire Monkey

2016 丙申 *(Bing Shen)* Fire Monkey

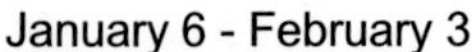

January 6 - February 3

February 4 - March 4

March 5 - April 3

April 4 - May 4

May 5 - June 4

June 5 - July 6

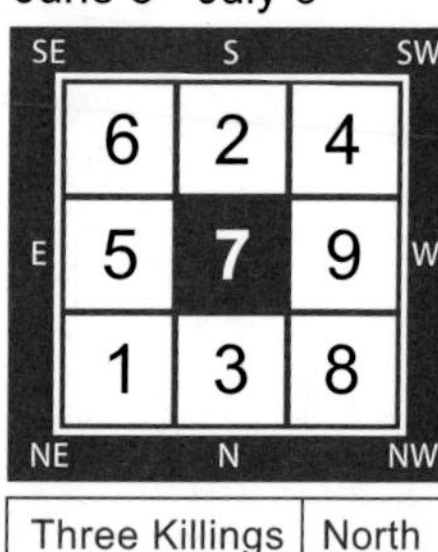

July 7 - August 6

August 7 - September 6

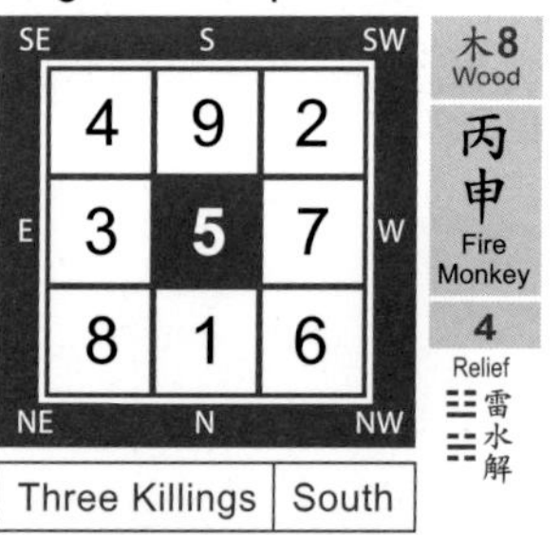

September 7 - October 7

October 8 - November 6

November 7 - December 6

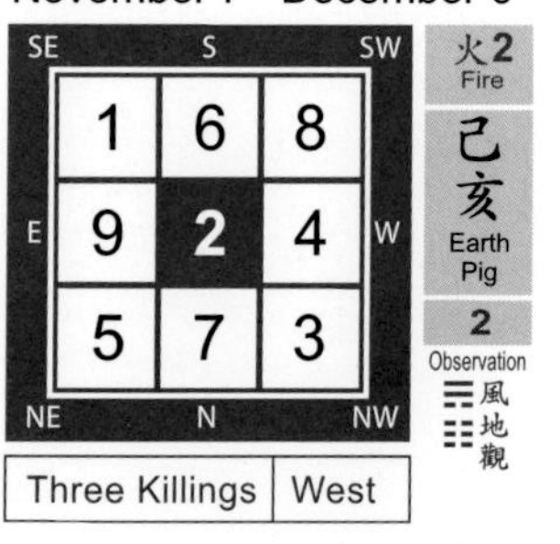

December 7 - January 4

JANUARY 2016 己丑

Xuan Kong Element 玄空五行	天雷無妄 Without Wrongdoing	Period Luck 卦運	Monthly Star 月星
Metal 金9		2	3

SUNDAY	MONDAY	TUESDAY	WEDNESDAY	THURSDAY	FRIDAY	SATURDAY
木8 Wood Thunder 7 震爲雷 壬子 Water Rat 1 31 廿二					火2 Fire Wind 4 巽爲風 壬午 Water Horse 1 1 廿二	金4 Metal Trap 5 澤水困 癸未 Water Goat 8 2 廿三
木3 Wood Not Yet Accomplished 6 火水未濟 甲申 Wood Monkey 9 3 廿四	金9 Metal Retreat 7 天山遯 乙酉 Wood Rooster 4 4 廿五	水6 Water Mountain 8 艮爲山 丙戌 Fire Dog 1 5 廿六	木8 Wood Delight 9 雷地豫 丁亥 Fire Pig 8 6 廿七	火7 Fire Beginning 1 水雷屯 戊子 Earth Rat 4 7 廿八	金9 Metal Without Wrongdoing 2 天雷無妄 己丑 Earth Ox 2 8 廿九	木3 Wood Fire 3 離爲火 庚寅 Metal Tiger 1 9 三十
火2 Fire Sincerity 4 風澤中孚 辛卯 Metal Rabbit 3 10 十二月初一	水6 Water Big Livestock 5 山天大畜 壬辰 Water Dragon 4 11 初二	金4 Metal Eliminating 6 澤天夬 癸巳 Water Snake 6 12 初三	金9 Metal Heaven 7 乾爲天 甲午 Wood Horse 1 13 初四	火7 Fire Well 8 水風井 乙未 Wood Goat 6 14 初五	木8 Wood Relief 9 雷水解 丙申 Fire Monkey 4 15 初六	金4 Metal Influence 1 澤山咸 丁酉 Fire Rooster 9 16 初七
水1 Water Humility 2 地山謙 戊戌 Earth Dog 6 17 初八	火2 Fire Observation 3 風地觀 己亥 Earth Pig 2 18 初九	火2 Fire Increasing 4 風雷益 庚子 Metal Rat 9 19 初十	水1 Water Dimming Light 5 地火明夷 辛丑 Metal Ox 3 20 十一	金9 Metal Fellowship 6 天火同人 壬寅 Water Tiger 7 21 十二	木8 Wood Marrying Maiden 7 雷澤歸妹 癸卯 Water Rabbit 7 22 十三	木3 Wood Opposition 8 火澤睽 甲辰 Wood Dragon 2 23 十四
火7 Fire Waiting 9 水天需 乙巳 Wood Snake 3 24 十五	金4 Metal Great Exceeding 1 澤風大過 丙午 Fire Horse 3 25 十六	水6 Water Poison 2 山風蠱 丁未 Fire Goat 7 26 十七	火2 Fire Dispersing 3 風水渙 戊申 Earth Monkey 6 27 十八	木3 Wood Travelling 4 火山旅 己酉 Earth Rooster 8 28 十九	金9 Metal Stagnation 5 天地否 庚戌 Metal Dog 9 29 二十	火7 Fire Alliance 6 水地比 辛亥 Metal Pig 7 30 廿一

FEBRUARY 2016 庚寅

Xuan Kong Element 玄空五行	離爲火 Fire	Period Luck 卦運	Monthly Star 月星
Wood 木3		1	2

SUNDAY	MONDAY	TUESDAY	WEDNESDAY	THURSDAY	FRIDAY	SATURDAY
	水6 Water Beauty 8 山火賁 癸丑 Water Ox 8 1 廿三	火7 Fire Accomplished 9 水火既濟 甲寅 Wood Tiger 9 2 廿四	水1 Water Arriving 1 地澤臨 乙卯 Wood Rabbit 4 3 廿五	金4 Metal Marsh 2 兑爲澤 丙辰 Fire Dragon 1 4 廿六	火2 Fire Small Livestock 3 風天小畜 丁巳 Fire Snake 8 5 廿七	木3 Wood The Cauldron 4 火風鼎 戊午 Earth Horse 4 6 廿八
水1 Water Rising 5 地風升 己未 Earth Goat 2 7 廿九	火7 Fire Water 6 坎爲水 庚申 Metal Monkey 1 8 正月初一	木8 Wood Lesser Exceeding 7 雷山小過 辛酉 Metal Rooster 3 9 初二	金4 Metal Gathering 8 澤地萃 壬戌 Water Dog 4 10 初三	水6 Water Peel 9 山地剝 癸亥 Water Pig 6 11 初四	水1 Water Earth 1 坤爲地 甲子 Wood Rat 1 12 初五	木3 Wood Biting 2 火雷噬嗑 乙丑 Wood Ox 6 13 初六
火2 Fire Family 3 風火家人 丙寅 Fire Tiger 4 14 初七	水6 Water Decreasing 4 山澤損 丁卯 Fire Rabbit 9 15 初八	金9 Metal Tread 5 天澤履 戊辰 Earth Dragon 6 16 初九	木8 Wood Great Strength 6 雷天大壯 己巳 Earth Snake 2 17 初十	木8 Wood Consistency 7 雷風恆 庚午 Metal Horse 9 18 十一	金9 Metal Litigation 8 天水訟 辛未 Metal Goat 3 19 十二	水1 Water Officer 9 地水師 壬申 Water Monkey 7 20 十三
火2 Fire Gradual Progress 1 風山漸 癸酉 Water Rooster 7 21 十四	火7 Fire Obstruction 2 水山蹇 甲戌 Wood Dog 2 22 十五	木3 Wood Advancement 3 火地晉 乙亥 Wood Pig 3 23 十六	水6 Water Nourish 4 山雷頤 丙子 Fire Rat 3 24 十七	金4 Metal Following 5 澤雷隨 丁丑 Fire Ox 7 25 十八	木8 Wood Abundance 6 雷火豐 戊寅 Earth Tiger 6 26 十九	火7 Fire Regulate 7 水澤節 己卯 Earth Rabbit 8 27 二十
水1 Water Unity 8 地天泰 庚辰 Metal Dragon 9 28 廿一	木3 Wood Great Reward 9 火天大有 辛巳 Metal Snake 7 29 廿二					

MARCH 2016 辛卯

Xuan Kong Element 玄空五行	風澤中孚 Sincerity	Period Luck 卦運	Monthly Star 月星
Fire 火2		3	1

SUNDAY	MONDAY	TUESDAY	WEDNESDAY	THURSDAY	FRIDAY	SATURDAY
		1 廿三 火2 Fire 壬午 Water Horse Wind 巽爲風 ■1 · 1	**2** 廿四 金4 Metal 癸未 Water Goat Trap 澤水困 ■2 · 8	**3** 廿五 木3 Wood 甲申 Wood Monkey Not Yet Accomplished 火水未濟 ■3 · 9	**4** 廿六 金9 Metal 乙酉 Wood Rooster Retreat 天山遯 ■4 · 4	**5** 廿七 水6 Water 丙戌 Fire Dog Mountain 艮爲山 ■5 · 1
6 廿八 木8 Wood 丁亥 Fire Pig Delight 雷地豫 ■6 · 8	**7** 廿九 火7 Fire 戊子 Earth Rat Beginning 水雷屯 ■7 · 4	**8** 三十 金9 Metal 己丑 Earth Ox Without Wrongdoing 天雷無妄 ■8 · 2	**9** 二月初一 木3 Wood 庚寅 Metal Tiger Fire 離爲火 ■9 · 1	**10** 初二 火2 Fire 辛卯 Metal Rabbit Sincerity 風澤中孚 ■1 · 3	**11** 初三 水6 Water 壬辰 Water Dragon Big Livestock 山天大畜 ■2 · 4	**12** 初四 金4 Metal 癸巳 Water Snake Eliminating 澤天夬 ■3 · 6
13 初五 金9 Metal 甲午 Wood Horse Heaven 乾爲天 ■4 · 1	**14** 初六 火7 Fire 乙未 Wood Goat Well 水風井 ■5 · 6	**15** 初七 木8 Wood 丙申 Fire Monkey Relief 雷水解 ■6 · 4	**16** 初八 金4 Metal 丁酉 Fire Rooster Influence 澤山咸 ■7 · 9	**17** 初九 水1 Water 戊戌 Earth Dog Humility 地山謙 ■8 · 6	**18** 初十 火2 Fire 己亥 Earth Pig Observation 風地觀 ■9 · 2	**19** 十一 火2 Fire 庚子 Metal Rat Increasing 風雷益 ■1 · 9
20 十二 水1 Water 辛丑 Metal Ox Dimming Light 地火明夷 ■2 · 3	**21** 十三 金9 Metal 壬寅 Water Tiger Fellowship 天火同人 ■3 · 7	**22** 十四 木8 Wood 癸卯 Water Rabbit Marrying Maiden 雷澤歸妹 ■4 · 7	**23** 十五 木3 Wood 甲辰 Wood Dragon Opposition 火澤睽 ■5 · 2	**24** 十六 火7 Fire 乙巳 Wood Snake Waiting 水天需 ■6 · 3	**25** 十七 金4 Metal 丙午 Fire Horse Great Exceeding 澤風大過 ■7 · 3	**26** 十八 水6 Water 丁未 Fire Goat Poison 山風蠱 ■8 · 7
27 十九 火2 Fire 戊申 Earth Monkey Dispersing 風水渙 ■9 · 6	**28** 二十 木3 Wood 己酉 Earth Rooster Travelling 火山旅 ■1 · 8	**29** 廿一 金9 Metal 庚戌 Metal Dog Stagnation 天地否 ■2 · 9	**30** 廿二 火7 Fire 辛亥 Metal Pig Alliance 水地比 ■3 · 7	**31** 廿三 木8 Wood 壬子 Water Rat Thunder 震爲雷 ■4 · 1		

APRIL 2016 壬辰

Xuan Kong Element 玄空五行	山天大畜 Big Livestock	Period Luck 卦運	Monthly Star 月星
Water 水6		4	9

SUNDAY	MONDAY	TUESDAY	WEDNESDAY	THURSDAY	FRIDAY	SATURDAY
					1 廿四 水6 Water 癸丑 Water Ox Beauty 山火賁 ■5 · 8	**2** 廿五 火7 Fire 甲寅 Wood Tiger Accomplished 水火既濟 ■6 · 9
3 廿六 水1 Water 乙卯 Wood Rabbit Arriving 地澤臨 ■7 · 4	**4** 廿七 金4 Metal 丙辰 Fire Dragon Marsh 兌爲澤 ■8 · 1	**5** 廿八 火2 Fire 丁巳 Fire Snake Small Livestock 風天小畜 ■9 · 8	**6** 廿九 木3 Wood 戊午 Earth Horse The Cauldron 火風鼎 ■1 · 4	**7** 三月初一 水1 Water 己未 Earth Goat Rising 地風升 ■2 · 2	**8** 初二 火7 Fire 庚申 Metal Monkey Water 坎爲水 ■3 · 1	**9** 初三 木8 Wood 辛酉 Metal Rooster Lesser Exceeding 雷山小過 ■4 · 3
10 初四 金4 Metal 壬戌 Water Dog Gathering 澤地萃 ■5 · 4	**11** 初五 水6 Water 癸亥 Water Pig Peel 山地剝 ■6 · 6	**12** 初六 水1 Water 甲子 Wood Rat Earth 坤爲地 ■7 · 1	**13** 初七 木3 Wood 乙丑 Wood Ox Biting 火雷噬嗑 ■8 · 6	**14** 初八 火2 Fire 丙寅 Fire Tiger Family 風火家人 ■9 · 4	**15** 初九 水6 Water 丁卯 Fire Rabbit Decreasing 山澤損 ■1 · 9	**16** 初十 金9 Metal 戊辰 Earth Dragon Tread 天澤履 ■2 · 6
17 十一 木8 Wood 己巳 Earth Snake Great Strength 雷天大壯 ■3 · 2	**18** 十二 木8 Wood 庚午 Metal Horse Consistency 雷風恒 ■4 · 9	**19** 十三 金9 Metal 辛未 Metal Goat Litigation 天水訟 ■5 · 3	**20** 十四 水1 Water 壬申 Water Monkey Officer 地水師 ■6 · 7	**21** 十五 火2 Fire 癸酉 Water Rooster Gradual Progress 風山漸 ■7 · 7	**22** 十六 火7 Fire 甲戌 Wood Dog Obstruction 水山蹇 ■8 · 2	**23** 十七 木3 Wood 乙亥 Wood Pig Advancement 火地晉 ■9 · 3
24 十八 水6 Water 丙子 Fire Rat Nourish 山雷頤 ■1 · 3	**25** 十九 金4 Metal 丁丑 Fire Ox Following 澤雷隨 ■2 · 7	**26** 二十 木8 Wood 戊寅 Earth Tiger Abundance 雷火豐 ■3 · 6	**27** 廿一 火7 Fire 己卯 Earth Rabbit Regulate 水澤節 ■4 · 8	**28** 廿二 水1 Water 庚辰 Metal Dragon Unity 地天泰 ■5 · 9	**29** 廿三 木3 Wood 辛巳 Metal Snake Great Reward 火天大有 ■6 · 7	**30** 廿四 火2 Fire 壬午 Water Horse Wind 巽爲風 ■7 · 1

MAY 2016 癸巳

Xuan Kong Element 玄空五行	澤天夬 Eliminating	Period Luck 卦運	Monthly Star 月星
Metal 金4		6	8

SUNDAY	MONDAY	TUESDAY	WEDNESDAY	THURSDAY	FRIDAY	SATURDAY
金4 Metal · Trap · 8 癸未 Water Goat · 澤水困 **1** 廿五 8	木3 Wood · Not Yet Accomplished · 9 甲申 Wood Monkey · 火水未濟 **2** 廿六 9	金9 Metal · Retreat · 1 乙酉 Wood Rooster · 天山遯 **3** 廿七 4	水6 Water · Mountain · 2 丙戌 Fire Dog · 艮為山 **4** 廿八 1	木8 Wood · Delight · 3 丁亥 Fire Pig · 雷地豫 **5** 廿九 8	火7 Fire · Beginning · 4 戊子 Earth Rat · 水雷屯 **6** 三十 4	金9 Metal · Without Wrongdoing · 5 己丑 Earth Ox · 天雷無妄 **7** 四月初一 2
木3 Wood · Fire · 6 庚寅 Metal Tiger · 離為火 **8** 初二 1	火2 Fire · Sincerity · 7 辛卯 Metal Rabbit · 風澤中孚 **9** 初三 3	水6 Water · Big Livestock · 8 壬辰 Water Dragon · 山天大畜 **10** 初四 4	金4 Metal · Eliminating · 9 癸巳 Water Snake · 澤天夬 **11** 初五 6	金9 Metal · Heaven · 1 甲午 Wood Horse · 乾為天 **12** 初六 1	火7 Fire · Well · 2 乙未 Wood Goat · 水風井 **13** 初七 6	木8 Wood · Relief · 3 丙申 Fire Monkey · 雷水解 **14** 初八 4
金4 Metal · Influence · 4 丁酉 Fire Rooster · 澤山咸 **15** 初九 9	水1 Water · Humility · 5 戊戌 Earth Dog · 地山謙 **16** 初十 6	火2 Fire · Observation · 6 己亥 Earth Pig · 風地觀 **17** 十一 2	火2 Fire · Increasing · 7 庚子 Metal Rat · 風雷益 **18** 十二 9	水1 Water · Dimming Light · 8 辛丑 Metal Ox · 地火明夷 **19** 十三 3	金9 Metal · Fellowship · 9 壬寅 Water Tiger · 天火同人 **20** 十四 7	木8 Wood · Marrying Maiden · 1 癸卯 Water Rabbit · 雷澤歸妹 **21** 十五 7
木3 Wood · Opposition · 2 甲辰 Wood Dragon · 火澤睽 **22** 十六 2	火7 Fire · Waiting · 3 乙巳 Wood Snake · 水天需 **23** 十七 3	金4 Metal · Great Exceeding · 4 丙午 Fire Horse · 澤風大過 **24** 十八 3	水6 Water · Poison · 5 丁未 Fire Goat · 山風蠱 **25** 十九 7	火2 Fire · Dispersing · 6 戊申 Earth Monkey · 風水渙 **26** 二十 6	木3 Wood · Travelling · 7 己酉 Earth Rooster · 火山旅 **27** 廿一 8	金9 Metal · Stagnation · 8 庚戌 Metal Dog · 天地否 **28** 廿二 9
火7 Fire · Alliance · 9 辛亥 Metal Pig · 水地比 **29** 廿三 7	木8 Wood · Thunder · 1 壬子 Water Rat · 震為雷 **30** 廿四 1	水6 Water · Beauty · 2 癸丑 Water Ox · 山火賁 **31** 廿五 8				

JUNE 2016 甲午

Xuan Kong Element 玄空五行	乾為天 Heaven	Period Luck 卦運	Monthly Star 月星
Metal 金9		1	7

SUNDAY	MONDAY	TUESDAY	WEDNESDAY	THURSDAY	FRIDAY	SATURDAY
			火7 Fire · Accomplished · 3 甲寅 Wood Tiger · 水火既濟 **1** 廿六 9	水1 Water · Arriving · 4 乙卯 Wood Rabbit · 地澤臨 **2** 廿七 4	金4 Metal · Marsh · 5 丙辰 Fire Dragon · 兌為澤 **3** 廿八 1	火2 Fire · Small Livestock · 6 丁巳 Fire Snake · 風天小畜 **4** 廿九 8
木3 Wood · The Cauldron · 7 戊午 Earth Horse · 火風鼎 **5** 五月初一 4	水1 Water · Rising · 8 己未 Earth Goat · 地風升 **6** 初二 2	火7 Fire · Water · 9 庚申 Metal Monkey · 坎為水 **7** 初三 1	木8 Wood · Lesser Exceeding · 1 辛酉 Metal Rooster · 雷山小過 **8** 初四 3	金4 Metal · Gathering · 2 壬戌 Water Dog · 澤地萃 **9** 初五 4	水6 Water · Peel · 3 癸亥 Water Pig · 山地剝 **10** 初六 6	水1 Water · Earth · 4 甲子 Wood Rat · 坤為地 **11** 初七 1
木3 Wood · Biting · 5 乙丑 Wood Ox · 火雷噬嗑 **12** 初八 6	火2 Fire · Family · 6 丙寅 Fire Tiger · 風火家人 **13** 初九 4	水6 Water · Decreasing · 7 丁卯 Fire Rabbit · 山澤損 **14** 初十 9	金9 Metal · Tread · 8 戊辰 Earth Dragon · 天澤履 **15** 十一 6	木8 Wood · Great Strength · 9 己巳 Earth Snake · 雷天大壯 **16** 十二 2	木8 Wood · Consistency · 1 庚午 Metal Horse · 雷風恒 **17** 十三 9	金9 Metal · Litigation · 2 辛未 Metal Goat · 天水訟 **18** 十四 3
水1 Water · Officer · 3 壬申 Water Monkey · 地水師 **19** 十五 7	火2 Fire · Gradual Progress · 4 癸酉 Water Rooster · 風山漸 **20** 十六 7	火7 Fire · Obstruction · 5/5 甲戌 Wood Dog · 水山蹇 **21** 十七 2	木3 Wood · Advancement · 4 乙亥 Wood Pig · 火地晉 **22** 十八 3	水6 Water · Nourish · 3 丙子 Fire Rat · 山雷頤 **23** 十九 3	金4 Metal · Following · 2 丁丑 Fire Ox · 澤雷隨 **24** 二十 7	木8 Wood · Abundance · 1 戊寅 Earth Tiger · 雷火豐 **25** 廿一 6
火7 Fire · Regulate · 9 己卯 Earth Rabbit · 水澤節 **26** 廿二 8	水1 Water · Unity · 8 庚辰 Metal Dragon · 地天泰 **27** 廿三 9	木3 Wood · Great Reward · 7 辛巳 Metal Snake · 火天大有 **28** 廿四 7	火2 Fire · Wind · 6 壬午 Water Horse · 巽為風 **29** 廿五 1	金4 Metal · Trap · 5 癸未 Water Goat · 澤水困 **30** 廿六 8		

JULY 2016 乙未

Xuan Kong Element 玄空五行	水風井 Well	Period Luck 卦運	Monthly Star 月星
Fire 火7		6	6

SUNDAY	MONDAY	TUESDAY	WEDNESDAY	THURSDAY	FRIDAY	SATURDAY
火7 Fire 1 Accomplished 甲寅 Wood Tiger 水火既濟 31 廿八 9					木3 Wood 4 Not Yet Accomplished 甲申 Wood Monkey 火水未濟 1 廿七 9	金9 Metal 3 Retreat 乙酉 Wood Rooster 天山遯 2 廿八 4
水6 Water 2 Mountain 丙戌 Fire Dog 艮爲山 3 廿九 1	木8 Wood 1 Delight 丁亥 Fire Pig 雷地豫 4 六月初一 8	火7 Fire 9 Beginning 戊子 Earth Rat 水雷屯 5 初二 4	金9 Metal 8 Without Wrongdoing 己丑 Earth Ox 天雷無妄 6 初三 2	木3 Wood 7 Fire 庚寅 Metal Tiger 離爲火 7 初四 1	火2 Fire 6 Sincerity 辛卯 Metal Rabbit 風澤中孚 8 初五 3	水6 Water 5 Big Livestock 壬辰 Water Dragon 山天大畜 9 初六 4
金4 Metal 4 Eliminating 癸巳 Water Snake 澤天夬 10 初七 6	金9 Metal 3 Heaven 甲午 Wood Horse 乾爲天 11 初八 1	火7 Fire 2 Well 乙未 Wood Goat 水風井 12 初九 6	木8 Wood 1 Relief 丙申 Fire Monkey 雷水解 13 初十 4	金4 Metal 9 Influence 丁酉 Fire Rooster 澤山咸 14 十一 9	水1 Water 8 Humility 戊戌 Earth Dog 地山謙 15 十二 6	火2 Fire 7 Observation 己亥 Earth Pig 風地觀 16 十三 2
火2 Fire 6 Increasing 庚子 Metal Rat 風雷益 17 十四 9	水1 Water 5 Dimming Light 辛丑 Metal Ox 地火明夷 18 十五 3	金9 Metal 4 Fellowship 壬寅 Water Tiger 天火同人 19 十六 7	木8 Wood 3 Marrying Maiden 癸卯 Water Rabbit 雷澤歸妹 20 十七 7	木3 Wood 2 Opposition 甲辰 Wood Dragon 火澤睽 21 十八 2	火7 Fire 1 Waiting 乙巳 Wood Snake 水天需 22 十九 3	金4 Metal 9 Great Exceeding 丙午 Fire Horse 澤風大過 23 二十 3
水6 Water 8 Poison 丁未 Fire Goat 山風蠱 24 廿一 7	火2 Fire 7 Dispersing 戊申 Earth Monkey 風水渙 25 廿二 6	木3 Wood 6 Travelling 己酉 Earth Rooster 火山旅 26 廿三 8	金9 Metal 5 Stagnation 庚戌 Metal Dog 天地否 27 廿四 9	火7 Fire 4 Alliance 辛亥 Metal Pig 水地比 28 廿五 7	木8 Wood 3 Thunder 壬子 Water Rat 震爲雷 29 廿六 1	水6 Water 2 Beauty 癸丑 Water Ox 山火賁 30 廿七 8

AUGUST 2016 丙申

Xuan Kong Element 玄空五行	雷水解 Relief	Period Luck 卦運	Monthly Star 月星
Wood 木8		4	5

SUNDAY	MONDAY	TUESDAY	WEDNESDAY	THURSDAY	FRIDAY	SATURDAY
	水1 Water 9 Arriving 乙卯 Wood Rabbit 地澤臨 1 廿九 4	金4 Metal 8 Marsh 丙辰 Fire Dragon 兑爲澤 2 三十 1	火2 Fire 7 Small Livestock 丁巳 Fire Snake 風天小畜 3 七月初一 8	木3 Wood 6 The Cauldron 戊午 Earth Horse 火風鼎 4 初二 4	水1 Water 5 Rising 己未 Earth Goat 地風升 5 初三 2	火7 Fire 4 Water 庚申 Metal Monkey 坎爲水 6 初四 1
木8 Wood 3 Lesser Exceeding 辛酉 Metal Rooster 雷山小過 7 初五 3	金4 Metal 2 Gathering 壬戌 Water Dog 澤地萃 8 初六 4	水6 Water 1 Peel 癸亥 Water Pig 山地剝 9 初七 6	水1 Water 9 Earth 甲子 Wood Rat 坤爲地 10 初八 1	木3 Wood 8 Biting 乙丑 Wood Ox 火雷噬嗑 11 初九 6	火2 Fire 7 Family 丙寅 Fire Tiger 風火家人 12 初十 4	水6 Water 6 Decreasing 丁卯 Fire Rabbit 山澤損 13 十一 9
金9 Metal 5 Tread 戊辰 Earth Dragon 天澤履 14 十二 6	木8 Wood 4 Great Strength 己巳 Earth Snake 雷天大壯 15 十三 2	木8 Wood 3 Consistency 庚午 Metal Horse 雷風恆 16 十四 9	金9 Metal 2 Litigation 辛未 Metal Goat 天水訟 17 十五 3	水1 Water 1 Officer 壬申 Water Monkey 地水師 18 十六 7	火2 Fire 9 Gradual Progress 癸酉 Water Rooster 風山漸 19 十七 7	火7 Fire 8 Obstruction 甲戌 Wood Dog 水山蹇 20 十八 2
木3 Wood 7 Advancement 乙亥 Wood Pig 火地晉 21 十九 3	水6 Water 6 Nourish 丙子 Fire Rat 山雷頤 22 二十 3	金4 Metal 5 Following 丁丑 Fire Ox 澤雷隨 23 廿一 7	木8 Wood 4 Abundance 戊寅 Earth Tiger 雷火豐 24 廿二 6	火7 Fire 3 Regulate 己卯 Earth Rabbit 水澤節 25 廿三 8	水1 Water 2 Unity 庚辰 Metal Dragon 地天泰 26 廿四 9	木3 Wood 1 Great Reward 辛巳 Metal Snake 火天大有 27 廿五 7
火2 Fire 9 Wind 壬午 Water Horse 巽爲風 28 廿六 1	金4 Metal 8 Trap 癸未 Water Goat 澤水困 29 廿七 8	木3 Wood 7 Not Yet Accomplished 甲申 Wood Monkey 火水未濟 30 廿八 9	金9 Metal 6 Retreat 乙酉 Wood Rooster 天山遯 31 廿九 4			

SEPTEMBER 2016 丁酉

Xuan Kong Element 玄空五行	澤山咸 Influence	Period Luck 卦運	Monthly Star 月星
Metal 金4		9	4

SUNDAY	MONDAY	TUESDAY	WEDNESDAY	THURSDAY	FRIDAY	SATURDAY
				水6 Water Mountain 5 丙戌 Fire Dog 艮爲山 1 八月初一 1	木8 Wood Delight 4 丁亥 Fire Pig 雷地豫 2 初二 8	火7 Fire Beginning 3 戊子 Earth Rat 水雷屯 3 初三 4
金9 Metal Without Wrongdoing 2 己丑 Earth Ox 天雷無妄 4 初四 2	木3 Wood Fire 1 庚寅 Metal Tiger 離爲火 5 初五 1	火2 Fire Sincerity 9 辛卯 Metal Rabbit 風澤中孚 6 初六 3	水6 Water Big Livestock 8 壬辰 Water Dragon 山天大畜 7 初七 4	金4 Metal Eliminating 7 癸巳 Water Snake 澤天夬 8 初八 6	金9 Metal Heaven 6 甲午 Wood Horse 乾爲天 9 初九 1	火7 Fire Well 5 乙未 Wood Goat 水風井 10 初十 6
木8 Wood Relief 4 丙申 Fire Monkey 雷水解 11 十一 4	金4 Metal Influence 3 丁酉 Fire Rooster 澤山咸 12 十二 9	水1 Water Humility 2 戊戌 Earth Dog 地山謙 13 十三 6	火2 Fire Observation 1 己亥 Earth Pig 風地觀 14 十四 2	火2 Fire Increasing 9 庚子 Metal Rat 風雷益 15 十五 9	水1 Water Dimming Light 8 辛丑 Metal Ox 地火明夷 16 十六 3	金9 Metal Fellowship 7 壬寅 Water Tiger 天火同人 17 十七 7
木8 Wood Marrying Maiden 6 癸卯 Water Rabbit 雷澤歸妹 18 十八 7	木3 Wood Opposition 5 甲辰 Wood Dragon 火澤睽 19 十九 2	火7 Fire Waiting 4 乙巳 Wood Snake 水天需 20 二十 3	金4 Metal Great Exceeding 3 丙午 Fire Horse 澤風大過 21 廿一 3	水6 Water Poison 2 丁未 Fire Goat 山風蠱 22 廿二 7	火2 Fire Dispersing 1 戊申 Earth Monkey 風水渙 23 廿三 6	木3 Wood Travelling 9 己酉 Earth Rooster 火山旅 24 廿四 8
金9 Metal Stagnation 8 庚戌 Metal Dog 天地否 25 廿五 9	火7 Fire Alliance 7 辛亥 Metal Pig 水地比 26 廿六 7	木8 Wood Thunder 6 壬子 Water Rat 震爲雷 27 廿七 1	水6 Water Beauty 5 癸丑 Water Ox 山火賁 28 廿八 8	火7 Fire Accomplished 4 甲寅 Wood Tiger 水火既濟 29 廿九 9	水1 Water Arriving 3 乙卯 Wood Rabbit 地澤臨 30 三十 4	

OCTOBER 2016 戊戌

Xuan Kong Element 玄空五行	地山謙 Humility	Period Luck 卦運	Monthly Star 月星
Water 水1		6	3

SUNDAY	MONDAY	TUESDAY	WEDNESDAY	THURSDAY	FRIDAY	SATURDAY
金9 Metal Retreat 9 乙酉 Wood Rooster 天山遯 30 三十 4	水6 Water Mountain 8 丙戌 Fire Dog 艮爲山 31 十月初一 1					金4 Metal Marsh 2 丙辰 Fire Dragon 兌爲澤 1 九月初一 1
火2 Fire Small Livestock 1 丁巳 Fire Snake 風天小畜 2 初二 8	木3 Wood The Cauldron 9 戊午 Earth Horse 火風鼎 3 初三 4	水1 Water Rising 8 己未 Earth Goat 地風升 4 初四 2	火7 Fire Water 7 庚申 Metal Monkey 坎爲水 5 初五 1	木8 Wood Lesser Exceeding 6 辛酉 Metal Rooster 雷山小過 6 初六 3	金4 Metal Gathering 5 壬戌 Water Dog 澤地萃 7 初七 4	水6 Water Peel 4 癸亥 Water Pig 山地剝 8 初八 6
水1 Water Earth 3 甲子 Wood Rat 坤爲地 9 初九 1	木3 Wood Biting 2 乙丑 Wood Ox 火雷噬嗑 10 初十 6	火2 Fire Family 1 丙寅 Fire Tiger 風火家人 11 十一 4	水6 Water Decreasing 9 丁卯 Fire Rabbit 山澤損 12 十二 9	金9 Metal Tread 8 戊辰 Earth Dragon 天澤履 13 十三 6	木8 Wood Great Strength 7 己巳 Earth Snake 雷天大壯 14 十四 2	木8 Wood Consistency 6 庚午 Metal Horse 雷風恆 15 十五 9
金9 Metal Litigation 5 辛未 Metal Goat 天水訟 16 十六 3	水1 Water Officer 4 壬申 Water Monkey 地水師 17 十七 7	火2 Fire Gradual Progress 3 癸酉 Water Rooster 風山漸 18 十八 7	火7 Fire Obstruction 2 甲戌 Wood Dog 水山蹇 19 十九 2	木3 Wood Advancement 1 乙亥 Wood Pig 火地晉 20 二十 3	水6 Water Nourish 9 丙子 Fire Rat 山雷頤 21 廿一 3	金4 Metal Following 8 丁丑 Fire Ox 澤雷隨 22 廿二 7
木8 Wood Abundance 7 戊寅 Earth Tiger 雷火豐 23 廿三 6	火7 Fire Regulate 6 己卯 Earth Rabbit 水澤節 24 廿四 8	水1 Water Unity 5 庚辰 Metal Dragon 地天泰 25 廿五 9	木3 Wood Great Reward 4 辛巳 Metal Snake 火天大有 26 廿六 7	火2 Fire Wind 3 壬午 Water Horse 巽爲風 27 廿七 1	金4 Metal Trap 2 癸未 Water Goat 澤水困 28 廿八 8	木3 Wood Not Yet Accomplished 1 甲申 Wood Monkey 火水未濟 29 廿九 9

NOVEMBER 2016 己亥

Xuan Kong Element 玄空五行	風地觀 Observation	Period Luck 卦運	Monthly Star 月星
Fire 火2		2	2

SUNDAY	MONDAY	TUESDAY	WEDNESDAY	THURSDAY	FRIDAY	SATURDAY
		木8 Wood Delight 7 雷地豫 丁亥 Fire Pig 8 1 初二	火7 Fire Beginning 6 水雷屯 戊子 Earth Rat 4 2 初三	金9 Metal Without Wrongdoing 5 天雷無妄 己丑 Earth Ox 2 3 初四	木3 Wood Fire 4 離爲火 庚寅 Metal Tiger 1 4 初五	火2 Fire Sincerity 3 風澤中孚 辛卯 Metal Rabbit 3 5 初六
水6 Water Big Livestock 2 山天大畜 壬辰 Water Dragon 4 6 初七	金4 Metal Eliminating 1 澤天夬 癸巳 Water Snake 6 7 初八	金9 Metal Heaven 9 乾爲天 甲午 Wood Horse 1 8 初九	火7 Fire Well 8 水風井 乙未 Wood Goat 6 9 初十	木8 Wood Relief 7 雷水解 丙申 Fire Monkey 4 10 十一	金4 Metal Influence 6 澤山咸 丁酉 Fire Rooster 9 11 十二	水1 Water Humility 5 地山謙 戊戌 Earth Dog 6 12 十三
火2 Fire Observation 4 風地觀 己亥 Earth Pig 2 13 十四	火2 Fire Increasing 3 風雷益 庚子 Metal Rat 9 14 十五	水1 Water Dimming Light 2 地火明夷 辛丑 Metal Ox 3 15 十六	金9 Metal Fellowship 1 天火同人 壬寅 Water Tiger 7 16 十七	木8 Wood Marrying Maiden 9 雷澤歸妹 癸卯 Water Rabbit 7 17 十八	木3 Wood Opposition 8 火澤睽 甲辰 Wood Dragon 2 18 十九	火7 Fire Waiting 7 水天需 乙巳 Wood Snake 3 19 二十
金4 Metal Great Exceeding 6 澤風大過 丙午 Fire Horse 3 20 廿一	水6 Water Poison 5 山風蠱 丁未 Fire Goat 7 21 廿二	火2 Fire Dispersing 4 風水渙 戊申 Earth Monkey 6 22 廿三	木3 Wood Travelling 3 火山旅 己酉 Earth Rooster 8 23 廿四	金9 Metal Stagnation 2 天地否 庚戌 Metal Dog 9 24 廿五	火7 Fire Alliance 1 水地比 辛亥 Metal Pig 7 25 廿六	木8 Wood Thunder 9 震爲雷 壬子 Water Rat 1 26 廿七
水6 Water Beauty 8 山火賁 癸丑 Water Ox 8 27 廿八	火7 Fire Accomplished 7 水火既濟 甲寅 Wood Tiger 9 28 廿九	水1 Water Arriving 6 地澤臨 乙卯 Wood Rabbit 4 29 十一月初一	金4 Metal Marsh 5 兑爲澤 丙辰 Fire Dragon 1 30 初二			

DECEMBER 2016 庚子

Xuan Kong Element 玄空五行	風雷益 Increasing	Period Luck 卦運	Monthly Star 月星
Fire 火2		9	1

SUNDAY	MONDAY	TUESDAY	WEDNESDAY	THURSDAY	FRIDAY	SATURDAY
				火2 Fire Small Livestock 4 風天小畜 丁巳 Fire Snake 8 1 初三	木3 Wood The Cauldron 3 火風鼎 戊午 Earth Horse 4 2 初四	水1 Water Rising 2 地風升 己未 Earth Goat 2 3 初五
火7 Fire Water 1 坎爲水 庚申 Metal Monkey 1 4 初六	木8 Wood Lesser Exceeding 9 雷山小過 辛酉 Metal Rooster 3 5 初七	金4 Metal Gathering 8 澤地萃 壬戌 Water Dog 4 6 初八	水6 Water Peel 7 山地剝 癸亥 Water Pig 6 7 初九	水1 Water Earth 6 坤爲地 甲子 Wood Rat 1 8 初十	木3 Wood Biting 5 火雷噬嗑 乙丑 Wood Ox 6 9 十一	火2 Fire Family 4 風火家人 丙寅 Fire Tiger 4 10 十二
水6 Water Decreasing 3 山澤損 丁卯 Fire Rabbit 9 11 十三	金9 Metal Tread 2 天澤履 戊辰 Earth Dragon 6 12 十四	木8 Wood Great Strength 1 雷天大壯 己巳 Earth Snake 2 13 十五	木8 Wood Consistency 9 雷風恒 庚午 Metal Horse 9 14 十六	金9 Metal Litigation 8 天水訟 辛未 Metal Goat 3 15 十七	水1 Water Officer 7 地水師 壬申 Water Monkey 7 16 十八	火2 Fire Gradual Progress 6 風山漸 癸酉 Water Rooster 7 17 十九
火7 Fire Obstruction 5 水山蹇 甲戌 Wood Dog 2 18 二十	木3 Wood Advancement 4 火地晉 乙亥 Wood Pig 3 19 廿一	水6 Water Nourish 3 山雷頤 丙子 Fire Rat 3 20 廿二	金4 Metal Following 2/8 澤雷隨 丁丑 Fire Ox 7 21 廿三	木8 Wood Abundance 9 雷火豐 戊寅 Earth Tiger 6 22 廿四	火7 Fire Regulate 1 水澤節 己卯 Earth Rabbit 8 23 廿五	水1 Water Unity 2 地天泰 庚辰 Metal Dragon 9 24 廿六
木3 Wood Great Reward 3 火天大有 辛巳 Metal Snake 7 25 廿七	火2 Fire Wind 4 巽爲風 壬午 Water Horse 1 26 廿八	金4 Metal Trap 5 澤水困 癸未 Water Goat 8 27 廿九	木3 Wood Not Yet Accomplished 6 火水未濟 甲申 Wood Monkey 9 28 三十	金9 Metal Retreat 7 天山遯 乙酉 Wood Rooster 4 29 十二月初一	水6 Water Mountain 8 艮爲山 丙戌 Fire Dog 1 30 初二	木8 Wood Delight 9 雷地豫 丁亥 Fire Pig 8 31 初三

2017 丁酉

(*Ding You*) Fire Rooster

2017 丁酉 *(Ding You)* Fire Rooster

January 5 - February 2

February 3 - March 4

March 5 - April 3

April 4 - May 4

May 5 - June 4

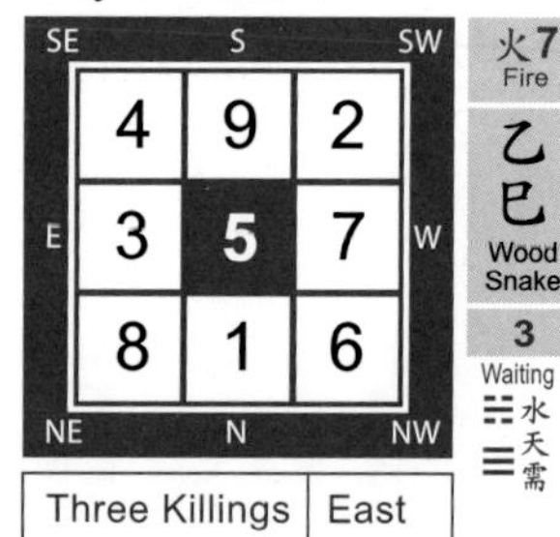

June 5 - July 6

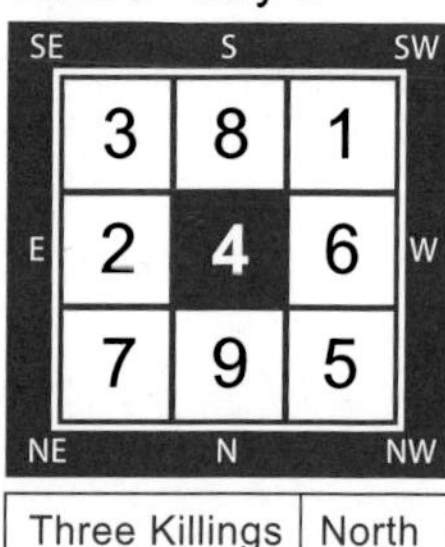

July 7 - August 6

August 7 - September 6

September 7 - October 7

October 8 - November 6

November 7 - December 6

December 7 - January 4

JANUARY 2017 辛丑

Xuan Kong Element 玄空五行	地火明夷 Dimming Light	Period Luck 卦運	Monthly Star 月星
Water 水1		3	9

SUNDAY	MONDAY	TUESDAY	WEDNESDAY	THURSDAY	FRIDAY	SATURDAY
火7 Fire Beginning 1 戊子 Earth Rat 水雷屯 **1** 4 初四	金9 Metal Without Wrongdoing 2 己丑 Earth Ox 天雷無妄 **2** 2 初五	木3 Wood Fire 3 庚寅 Metal Tiger 離爲火 **3** 1 初六	火2 Fire Sincerity 4 辛卯 Metal Rabbit 風澤中孚 **4** 3 初七	水6 Water Big Livestock 5 壬辰 Water Dragon 山天大畜 **5** 4 初八	金4 Metal Eliminating 6 癸巳 Water Snake 澤天夬 **6** 6 初九	金9 Metal Heaven 7 甲午 Wood Horse 乾爲天 **7** 1 初十
火7 Fire Well 8 乙未 Wood Goat 水風井 **8** 6 十一	木8 Wood Relief 9 丙申 Fire Monkey 雷水解 **9** 4 十二	金4 Metal Influence 1 丁酉 Fire Rooster 澤山咸 **10** 9 十三	水1 Water Humility 2 戊戌 Earth Dog 地山謙 **11** 6 十四	火2 Fire Observation 3 己亥 Earth Pig 風地觀 **12** 2 十五	火2 Fire Increasing 4 庚子 Metal Rat 風雷益 **13** 9 十六	水1 Water Dimming Light 5 辛丑 Metal Ox 地火明夷 **14** 3 十七
金9 Metal Fellowship 6 壬寅 Water Tiger 天火同人 **15** 7 十八	木8 Wood Marrying Maiden 7 癸卯 Water Rabbit 雷澤歸妹 **16** 7 十九	木3 Wood Opposition 8 甲辰 Wood Dragon 火澤睽 **17** 2 二十	火7 Fire Waiting 9 乙巳 Wood Snake 水天需 **18** 3 廿一	金4 Metal Great Exceeding 1 丙午 Fire Horse 澤風大過 **19** 3 廿二	水6 Water Poison 2 丁未 Fire Goat 山風蠱 **20** 7 廿三	火2 Fire Dispersing 3 戊申 Earth Monkey 風水渙 **21** 6 廿四
木3 Wood Travelling 4 己酉 Earth Rooster 火山旅 **22** 8 廿五	金9 Metal Stagnation 5 庚戌 Metal Dog 天地否 **23** 9 廿六	火7 Fire Alliance 6 辛亥 Metal Pig 水地比 **24** 7 廿七	木8 Wood Thunder 7 壬子 Water Rat 震爲雷 **25** 1 廿八	水6 Water Beauty 8 癸丑 Water Ox 山火賁 **26** 8 廿九	火7 Fire Accomplished 9 甲寅 Wood Tiger 水火既濟 **27** 9 三十	水1 Water Arriving 1 乙卯 Wood Rabbit 地澤臨 **28** 4 正月初一
金4 Metal Marsh 2 丙辰 Fire Dragon 兑爲澤 **29** 1 初二	火2 Fire Small Livestock 3 丁巳 Fire Snake 風天小畜 **30** 8 初三	木3 Wood The Cauldron 4 戊午 Earth Horse 火風鼎 **31** 4 初四				

FEBRUARY 2017 壬寅

Xuan Kong Element 玄空五行	天火同人 Fellowship	Period Luck 卦運	Monthly Star 月星
Metal 金9		7	8

SUNDAY	MONDAY	TUESDAY	WEDNESDAY	THURSDAY	FRIDAY	SATURDAY
			水1 Water Rising 5 己未 Earth Goat 地風升 **1** 2 初五	火7 Fire Water 6 庚申 Metal Monkey 坎爲水 **2** 1 初六	木8 Wood Lesser Exceeding 7 辛酉 Metal Rooster 雷山小過 **3** 3 初七	金4 Metal Gathering 8 壬戌 Water Dog 澤地萃 **4** 4 初八
水6 Water Peel 9 癸亥 Water Pig 山地剝 **5** 6 初九	水1 Water Earth 1 甲子 Wood Rat 坤爲地 **6** 1 初十	木3 Wood Biting 2 乙丑 Wood Ox 火雷噬嗑 **7** 6 十一	火2 Fire Family 3 丙寅 Fire Tiger 風火家人 **8** 4 十二	水6 Water Decreasing 4 丁卯 Fire Rabbit 山澤損 **9** 9 十三	金9 Metal Tread 5 戊辰 Earth Dragon 天澤履 **10** 6 十四	木8 Wood Great Strength 6 己巳 Earth Snake 雷天大壯 **11** 2 十五
木8 Wood Consistency 7 庚午 Metal Horse 雷風恆 **12** 9 十六	金9 Metal Litigation 8 辛未 Metal Goat 天水訟 **13** 3 十七	水1 Water Officer 9 壬申 Water Monkey 地水師 **14** 7 十八	火2 Fire Gradual Progress 1 癸酉 Water Rooster 風山漸 **15** 7 十九	火7 Fire Obstruction 2 甲戌 Wood Dog 水山蹇 **16** 2 二十	木3 Wood Advancement 3 乙亥 Wood Pig 火地晉 **17** 3 廿一	水6 Water Nourish 4 丙子 Fire Rat 山雷頤 **18** 3 廿二
金4 Metal Following 5 丁丑 Fire Ox 澤雷隨 **19** 7 廿三	木8 Wood Abundance 6 戊寅 Earth Tiger 雷火豐 **20** 6 廿四	火7 Fire Regulate 7 己卯 Earth Rabbit 水澤節 **21** 8 廿五	水1 Water Unity 8 庚辰 Metal Dragon 地天泰 **22** 9 廿六	木3 Wood Great Reward 9 辛巳 Metal Snake 火天大有 **23** 7 廿七	火2 Fire Wind 1 壬午 Water Horse 巽爲風 **24** 1 廿八	金4 Metal Trap 2 癸未 Water Goat 澤水困 **25** 8 廿九
木3 Wood Not Yet Accomplished 3 甲申 Wood Monkey 火水未濟 **26** 9 二月初一	金9 Metal Retreat 4 乙酉 Wood Rooster 天山遯 **27** 4 初二	水6 Water Mountain 5 丙戌 Fire Dog 艮爲山 **28** 1 初三				

MARCH 2017 癸卯

Xuan Kong Element 玄空五行	雷澤歸妹 Marrying Maiden	Period Luck 卦運	Monthly Star 月星
Wood 木8		7	7

SUNDAY	MONDAY	TUESDAY	WEDNESDAY	THURSDAY	FRIDAY	SATURDAY
			木8 Wood 6 Delight 雷地豫 丁亥 Fire Pig 8 **1** 初四	火7 Fire 7 Beginning 水雷屯 戊子 Earth Rat 4 **2** 初五	金9 Metal 8 Without Wrongdoing 天雷無妄 己丑 Earth Ox 2 **3** 初六	木3 Wood 9 Fire 離爲火 庚寅 Metal Tiger 1 **4** 初七
火2 Fire 1 Sincerity 風澤中孚 辛卯 Metal Rabbit 3 **5** 初八	水6 Water 2 Big Livestock 山天大畜 壬辰 Water Dragon 4 **6** 初九	金4 Metal 3 Eliminating 澤天夬 癸巳 Water Snake 6 **7** 初十	金9 Metal 4 Heaven 乾爲天 甲午 Wood Horse 1 **8** 十一	火7 Fire 5 Well 水風井 乙未 Wood Goat 6 **9** 十二	木8 Wood 6 Relief 雷水解 丙申 Fire Monkey 4 **10** 十三	金4 Metal 7 Influence 澤山咸 丁酉 Fire Rooster 9 **11** 十四
水1 Water 8 Humility 地山謙 戊戌 Earth Dog 6 **12** 十五	火2 Fire 9 Observation 風地觀 己亥 Earth Pig 2 **13** 十六	火2 Fire 1 Increasing 風雷益 庚子 Metal Rat 9 **14** 十七	水1 Water 2 Dimming Light 地火明夷 辛丑 Metal Ox 3 **15** 十八	金9 Metal 3 Fellowship 天火同人 壬寅 Water Tiger 7 **16** 十九	木8 Wood 4 Marrying Maiden 雷澤歸妹 癸卯 Water Rabbit 7 **17** 二十	木3 Wood 5 Opposition 火澤睽 甲辰 Wood Dragon 2 **18** 廿一
火7 Fire 6 Waiting 水天需 乙巳 Wood Snake 3 **19** 廿二	金4 Metal 7 Great Exceeding 澤風大過 丙午 Fire Horse 3 **20** 廿三	水6 Water 8 Poison 山風蠱 丁未 Fire Goat 7 **21** 廿四	火2 Fire 9 Dispersing 風水渙 戊申 Earth Monkey 6 **22** 廿五	木3 Wood 1 Travelling 火山旅 己酉 Earth Rooster 8 **23** 廿六	金9 Metal 2 Stagnation 天地否 庚戌 Metal Dog 9 **24** 廿七	火7 Fire 3 Alliance 水地比 辛亥 Metal Pig 7 **25** 廿八
木8 Wood 4 Thunder 震爲雷 壬子 Water Rat 1 **26** 廿九	水6 Water 5 Beauty 山火賁 癸丑 Water Ox 8 **27** 三十	火7 Fire 6 Accomplished 水火既濟 甲寅 Wood Tiger 9 **28** 三月初一	水1 Water 7 Arriving 地澤臨 乙卯 Wood Rabbit 4 **29** 初二	金4 Metal 8 Marsh 兌爲澤 丙辰 Fire Dragon 1 **30** 初三	火2 Fire 9 Small Livestock 風天小畜 丁巳 Fire Snake 8 **31** 初四	

APRIL 2017 甲辰

Xuan Kong Element 玄空五行	火澤睽 Opposition	Period Luck 卦運	Monthly Star 月星
Wood 木3		2	6

SUNDAY	MONDAY	TUESDAY	WEDNESDAY	THURSDAY	FRIDAY	SATURDAY
木8 Wood 3 Delight 雷地豫 丁亥 Fire Pig 8 **30** 初五						木3 Wood 1 The Cauldron 火風鼎 戊午 Earth Horse 4 **1** 初五
水1 Water 2 Rising 地風升 己未 Earth Goat 2 **2** 初六	火7 Fire 3 Water 坎爲水 庚申 Metal Monkey 1 **3** 初七	木8 Wood 4 Lesser Exceeding 雷山小過 辛酉 Metal Rooster 3 **4** 初八	金4 Metal 5 Gathering 澤地萃 壬戌 Water Dog 4 **5** 初九	水6 Water 6 Peel 山地剝 癸亥 Water Pig 6 **6** 初十	水1 Water 7 Earth 坤爲地 甲子 Wood Rat 1 **7** 十一	木3 Wood 8 Biting 火雷噬嗑 乙丑 Wood Ox 6 **8** 十二
火2 Fire 9 Family 風火家人 丙寅 Fire Tiger 4 **9** 十三	水6 Water 1 Decreasing 山澤損 丁卯 Fire Rabbit 9 **10** 十四	金9 Metal 2 Tread 天澤履 戊辰 Earth Dragon 6 **11** 十五	木8 Wood 3 Great Strength 雷天大壯 己巳 Earth Snake 2 **12** 十六	木8 Wood 4 Consistency 雷風恆 庚午 Metal Horse 9 **13** 十七	金9 Metal 5 Litigation 天水訟 辛未 Metal Goat 3 **14** 十八	水1 Water 6 Officer 地水師 壬申 Water Monkey 7 **15** 十九
火2 Fire 7 Gradual Progress 風山漸 癸酉 Water Rooster 7 **16** 二十	火7 Fire 8 Obstruction 水山蹇 甲戌 Wood Dog 2 **17** 廿一	木3 Wood 9 Advancement 火地晉 乙亥 Wood Pig 3 **18** 廿二	水6 Water 1 Nourish 山雷頤 丙子 Fire Rat 3 **19** 廿三	金4 Metal 2 Following 澤雷隨 丁丑 Fire Ox 7 **20** 廿四	木8 Wood 3 Abundance 雷火豐 戊寅 Earth Tiger 6 **21** 廿五	火7 Fire 4 Regulate 水澤節 己卯 Earth Rabbit 8 **22** 廿六
水1 Water 5 Unity 地天泰 庚辰 Metal Dragon 9 **23** 廿七	木3 Wood 6 Great Reward 火天大有 辛巳 Metal Snake 7 **24** 廿八	火2 Fire 7 Wind 巽爲風 壬午 Water Horse 1 **25** 廿九	金4 Metal 8 Trap 澤水困 癸未 Water Goat 8 **26** 四月初一	木3 Wood 9 Not Yet Accomplished 火水未濟 甲申 Wood Monkey 9 **27** 初二	金9 Metal 1 Retreat 天山遯 乙酉 Wood Rooster 4 **28** 初三	水6 Water 2 Mountain 艮爲山 丙戌 Fire Dog 1 **29** 初四

MAY 2017 乙巳

Xuan Kong Element 玄空五行	水天需 Waiting	Period Luck 卦運	Monthly Star 月星
Fire 火7		3	5

SUNDAY	MONDAY	TUESDAY	WEDNESDAY	THURSDAY	FRIDAY	SATURDAY
	火7 Fire 4 Beginning 水雷屯 戊子 Earth Rat 1 4 初六	金9 Metal 5 Without Wrongdoing 天雷無妄 己丑 Earth Ox 2 2 初七	木3 Wood 6 Fire 離為火 庚寅 Metal Tiger 3 1 初八	火2 Fire 7 Sincerity 風澤中孚 辛卯 Metal Rabbit 4 3 初九	水6 Water 8 Big Livestock 山天大畜 壬辰 Water Dragon 5 4 初十	金4 Metal 9 Eliminating 澤天夬 癸巳 Water Snake 6 6 十一
金9 Metal 1 Heaven 乾為天 甲午 Wood Horse 7 1 十二	火7 Fire 2 Well 水風井 乙未 Wood Goat 8 6 十三	木8 Wood 3 Relief 雷水解 丙申 Fire Monkey 9 4 十四	金4 Metal 4 Influence 澤山咸 丁酉 Fire Rooster 10 9 十五	水1 Water 5 Humility 地山謙 戊戌 Earth Dog 11 6 十六	火2 Fire 6 Observation 風地觀 己亥 Earth Pig 12 2 十七	火2 Fire 7 Increasing 風雷益 庚子 Metal Rat 13 9 十八
水1 Water 8 Dimming Light 地火明夷 辛丑 Metal Ox 14 3 十九	金9 Metal 9 Fellowship 天火同人 壬寅 Water Tiger 15 7 二十	木8 Wood 1 Marrying Maiden 雷澤歸妹 癸卯 Water Rabbit 16 7 廿一	木3 Wood 2 Opposition 火澤睽 甲辰 Wood Dragon 17 2 廿二	火7 Fire 3 Waiting 水天需 乙巳 Wood Snake 18 3 廿三	金4 Metal 4 Great Exceeding 澤風大過 丙午 Fire Horse 19 3 廿四	水6 Water 5 Poison 山風蠱 丁未 Fire Goat 20 7 廿五
火2 Fire 6 Dispersing 風水渙 戊申 Earth Monkey 21 6 廿六	木3 Wood 7 Travelling 火山旅 己酉 Earth Rooster 22 8 廿七	金9 Metal 8 Stagnation 天地否 庚戌 Metal Dog 23 9 廿八	火7 Fire 9 Alliance 水地比 辛亥 Metal Pig 24 7 廿九	木8 Wood 1 Thunder 震為雷 壬子 Water Rat 25 1 三十	水6 Water 2 Beauty 山火賁 癸丑 Water Ox 26 8 五月初一	火7 Fire 3 Accomplished 水火既濟 甲寅 Wood Tiger 27 9 初二
水1 Water 4 Arriving 地澤臨 乙卯 Wood Rabbit 28 4 初三	金4 Metal 5 Marsh 兌為澤 丙辰 Fire Dragon 29 1 初四	火2 Fire 6 Small Livestock 風天小畜 丁巳 Fire Snake 30 8 初五	木3 Wood 7 The Cauldron 火風鼎 戊午 Earth Horse 31 4 初六			

JUNE 2017 丙午

Xuan Kong Element 玄空五行	澤風大過 Great Exceeding	Period Luck 卦運	Monthly Star 月星
Metal 金4		3	4

SUNDAY	MONDAY	TUESDAY	WEDNESDAY	THURSDAY	FRIDAY	SATURDAY
				水1 Water 8 Rising 地風升 己未 Earth Goat 1 2 初七	火7 Fire 9 Water 坎為水 庚申 Metal Monkey 2 1 初八	木8 Wood 1 Lesser Exceeding 雷山小過 辛酉 Metal Rooster 3 3 初九
金4 Metal 2 Gathering 澤地萃 壬戌 Water Dog 4 4 初十	水6 Water 3 Peel 山地剝 癸亥 Water Pig 5 6 十一	水1 Water 4 Earth 坤為地 甲子 Wood Rat 6 1 十二	木3 Wood 5 Biting 火雷噬嗑 乙丑 Wood Ox 7 6 十三	火2 Fire 6 Family 風火家人 丙寅 Fire Tiger 8 4 十四	水6 Water 7 Decreasing 山澤損 丁卯 Fire Rabbit 9 9 十五	金9 Metal 8 Tread 天澤履 戊辰 Earth Dragon 10 6 十六
木8 Wood 9 Great Strength 雷天大壯 己巳 Earth Snake 11 2 十七	木8 Wood 1 Consistency 雷風恆 庚午 Metal Horse 12 9 十八	金9 Metal 2 Litigation 天水訟 辛未 Metal Goat 13 3 十九	水1 Water 3 Officer 地水師 壬申 Water Monkey 14 7 二十	火2 Fire 4 Gradual Progress 風山漸 癸酉 Water Rooster 15 7 廿一	火7 Fire 5 Obstruction 水山蹇 甲戌 Wood Dog 16 2 廿二	木3 Wood 6 Advancement 火地晉 乙亥 Wood Pig 17 3 廿三
水6 Water 7 Nourish 山雷頤 丙子 Fire Rat 18 3 廿四	金4 Metal 8 Following 澤雷隨 丁丑 Fire Ox 19 7 廿五	木8 Wood 9 Abundance 雷火豐 戊寅 Earth Tiger 20 6 廿六	火7 Fire 1/9 Regulate 水澤節 己卯 Earth Rabbit 21 8 廿七	水1 Water 8 Unity 地天泰 庚辰 Metal Dragon 22 9 廿八	木3 Wood 7 Great Reward 火天大有 辛巳 Metal Snake 23 7 廿九	火2 Fire 6 Wind 巽為風 壬午 Water Horse 24 1 六月初一
金4 Metal 5 Trap 澤水困 癸未 Water Goat 25 8 初二	木3 Wood 4 Not Yet Accomplished 火水未濟 甲申 Wood Monkey 26 9 初三	金9 Metal 3 Retreat 天山遯 乙酉 Wood Rooster 27 4 初四	水6 Water 2 Mountain 艮為山 丙戌 Fire Dog 28 1 初五	木8 Wood 1 Delight 雷地豫 丁亥 Fire Pig 29 8 初六	火7 Fire 9 Beginning 水雷屯 戊子 Earth Rat 30 4 初七	

JULY 2017 丁未

Xuan Kong Element 玄空五行	山風蠱	Period Luck 卦運	Monthly Star 月星
Water 水6	Poison	7	3

SUNDAY	MONDAY	TUESDAY	WEDNESDAY	THURSDAY	FRIDAY	SATURDAY
30 木3 Wood The Cauldron 6 戊午 Earth Horse 火風鼎 初八 4	31 水1 Water Rising 5 己未 Earth Goat 地風升 初九 2					1 金9 Metal Without Wrongdoing 8 己丑 Earth Ox 天雷無妄 初八 2
2 木3 Wood Fire 7 庚寅 Metal Tiger 離爲火 初九 1	3 火2 Fire Sincerity 6 辛卯 Metal Rabbit 風澤中孚 初十 3	4 水6 Water Big Livestock 5 壬辰 Water Dragon 山天大畜 十一 4	5 金4 Metal Eliminating 4 癸巳 Water Snake 澤天夬 十二 6	6 金9 Metal Heaven 3 甲午 Wood Horse 乾爲天 十三 1	7 火7 Fire Well 2 乙未 Wood Goat 水風井 十四 6	8 木8 Wood Relief 1 丙申 Fire Monkey 雷水解 十五 4
9 金4 Metal Influence 9 丁酉 Fire Rooster 澤山咸 十六 9	10 水1 Water Humility 8 戊戌 Earth Dog 地山謙 十七 6	11 火2 Fire Observation 7 己亥 Earth Pig 風地觀 十八 2	12 火2 Fire Increasing 6 庚子 Metal Rat 風雷益 十九 9	13 水1 Water Dimming Light 5 辛丑 Metal Ox 地火明夷 二十 3	14 金9 Metal Fellowship 4 壬寅 Water Tiger 天火同人 廿一 7	15 木8 Wood Marrying Maiden 3 癸卯 Water Rabbit 雷澤歸妹 廿二 7
16 木3 Wood Opposition 2 甲辰 Wood Dragon 火澤睽 廿三 2	17 火7 Fire Waiting 1 乙巳 Wood Snake 水天需 廿四 3	18 金4 Metal Great Exceeding 9 丙午 Fire Horse 澤風大過 廿五 3	19 水6 Water Poison 8 丁未 Fire Goat 山風蠱 廿六 7	20 火2 Fire Dispersing 7 戊申 Earth Monkey 風水渙 廿七 6	21 木3 Wood Travelling 6 己酉 Earth Rooster 火山旅 廿八 8	22 金9 Metal Stagnation 5 庚戌 Metal Dog 天地否 廿九 9
23 火7 Fire Alliance 4 辛亥 Metal Pig 水地比 閏六月初一 7	24 木8 Wood Thunder 3 壬子 Water Rat 震爲雷 初二 1	25 水6 Water Beauty 2 癸丑 Water Ox 山火賁 初三 8	26 火7 Fire Accomplished 1 甲寅 Wood Tiger 水火既濟 初四 9	27 水1 Water Arriving 9 乙卯 Wood Rabbit 地澤臨 初五 4	28 金4 Metal Marsh 8 丙辰 Fire Dragon 兑爲澤 初六 1	29 火2 Fire Small Livestock 7 丁巳 Fire Snake 風天小畜 初七 8

AUGUST 2017 戊申

Xuan Kong Element 玄空五行	風水渙	Period Luck 卦運	Monthly Star 月星
Fire 火2	Dispersing	6	2

SUNDAY	MONDAY	TUESDAY	WEDNESDAY	THURSDAY	FRIDAY	SATURDAY
		1 火7 Fire Water 4 庚申 Metal Monkey 坎爲水 初十 1	2 木8 Wood Lesser Exceeding 3 辛酉 Metal Rooster 雷山小過 十一 3	3 金4 Metal Gathering 2 壬戌 Water Dog 澤地萃 十二 4	4 水6 Water Peel 1 癸亥 Water Pig 山地剝 十三 6	5 水1 Water Earth 9 甲子 Wood Rat 坤爲地 十四 1
6 木3 Wood Biting 8 乙丑 Wood Ox 火雷噬嗑 十五 6	7 火2 Fire Family 7 丙寅 Fire Tiger 風火家人 十六 4	8 水6 Water Decreasing 6 丁卯 Fire Rabbit 山澤損 十七 9	9 金9 Metal Tread 5 戊辰 Earth Dragon 天澤履 十八 6	10 木8 Wood Great Strength 4 己巳 Earth Snake 雷天大壯 十九 2	11 木8 Wood Consistency 3 庚午 Metal Horse 雷風恆 二十 9	12 金9 Metal Litigation 2 辛未 Metal Goat 天水訟 廿一 3
13 水1 Water Officer 1 壬申 Water Monkey 地水師 廿二 7	14 火2 Fire Gradual Progress 9 癸酉 Water Rooster 風山漸 廿三 7	15 火7 Fire Obstruction 8 甲戌 Wood Dog 水山蹇 廿四 2	16 木3 Wood Advancement 7 乙亥 Wood Pig 火地晉 廿五 3	17 水6 Water Nourish 6 丙子 Fire Rat 山雷頤 廿六 3	18 金4 Metal Following 5 丁丑 Fire Ox 澤雷隨 廿七 7	19 木8 Wood Abundance 4 戊寅 Earth Tiger 雷火豐 廿八 6
20 火7 Fire Regulate 3 己卯 Earth Rabbit 水澤節 廿九 8	21 水1 Water Unity 2 庚辰 Metal Dragon 地天泰 三十 9	22 木3 Wood Great Reward 1 辛巳 Metal Snake 火天大有 七月初一 7	23 火2 Fire Wind 9 壬午 Water Horse 巽爲風 初二 1	24 金4 Metal Trap 8 癸未 Water Goat 澤水困 初三 8	25 木3 Wood Not Yet Accomplished 7 甲申 Wood Monkey 火水未濟 初四 9	26 金9 Metal Retreat 6 乙酉 Wood Rooster 天山遯 初五 4
27 水6 Water Mountain 5 丙戌 Fire Dog 艮爲山 初六 1	28 木8 Wood Delight 4 丁亥 Fire Pig 雷地豫 初七 8	29 火7 Fire Beginning 3 戊子 Earth Rat 水雷屯 初八 4	30 金9 Metal Without Wrongdoing 2 己丑 Earth Ox 天雷無妄 初九 2	31 木3 Wood Fire 1 庚寅 Metal Tiger 離爲火 初十 1		

SEPTEMBER 2017 己酉

Xuan Kong Element 玄空五行	火山旅 Travelling	Period Luck 卦運	Monthly Star 月星
Wood 木3		8	1

SUNDAY	MONDAY	TUESDAY	WEDNESDAY	THURSDAY	FRIDAY	SATURDAY
					火2 Fire 9 Sincerity 辛卯 Metal Rabbit 風澤中孚 1 十一 3	水6 Water 8 Big Livestock 壬辰 Water Dragon 山天大畜 2 十二 4
金4 Metal 7 Eliminating 癸巳 Water Snake 澤天夬 3 十三 6	金9 Metal 6 Heaven 甲午 Wood Horse 乾爲天 4 十四 1	火7 Fire 5 Well 乙未 Wood Goat 水風井 5 十五 6	木8 Wood 4 Relief 丙申 Fire Monkey 雷水解 6 十六 4	金4 Metal 3 Influence 丁酉 Fire Rooster 澤山咸 7 十七 9	水1 Water 2 Humility 戊戌 Earth Dog 地山謙 8 十八 6	火2 Fire 1 Observation 己亥 Earth Pig 風地觀 9 十九 2
火2 Fire 9 Increasing 庚子 Metal Rat 風雷益 10 二十 9	水1 Water 8 Dimming Light 辛丑 Metal Ox 地火明夷 11 廿一 3	金9 Metal 7 Fellowship 壬寅 Water Tiger 天火同人 12 廿二 7	木8 Wood 6 Marrying Maiden 癸卯 Water Rabbit 雷澤歸妹 13 廿三 7	木3 Wood 5 Opposition 甲辰 Wood Dragon 火澤睽 14 廿四 2	火7 Fire 4 Waiting 乙巳 Wood Snake 水天需 15 廿五 3	金4 Metal 3 Great Exceeding 丙午 Fire Horse 澤風大過 16 廿六 3
水6 Water 2 Poison 丁未 Fire Goat 山風蠱 17 廿七 7	火2 Fire 1 Dispersing 戊申 Earth Monkey 風水渙 18 廿八 6	木3 Wood 9 Travelling 己酉 Earth Rooster 火山旅 19 廿九 8	金9 Metal 8 Stagnation 庚戌 Metal Dog 天地否 20 八月初一 9	火7 Fire 7 Alliance 辛亥 Metal Pig 水地比 21 初二 7	木8 Wood 6 Thunder 壬子 Water Rat 震爲雷 22 初三 1	水6 Water 5 Beauty 癸丑 Water Ox 山火賁 23 初四 8
火7 Fire 4 Accomplished 甲寅 Wood Tiger 水火既濟 24 初五 9	水1 Water 3 Arriving 乙卯 Wood Rabbit 地澤臨 25 初六 4	金4 Metal 2 Marsh 丙辰 Fire Dragon 兌爲澤 26 初七 1	火2 Fire 1 Small Livestock 丁巳 Fire Snake 風天小畜 27 初八 8	木3 Wood 9 The Cauldron 戊午 Earth Horse 火風鼎 28 初九 4	水1 Water 8 Rising 己未 Earth Goat 地風升 29 初十 2	火7 Fire 7 Water 庚申 Metal Monkey 坎爲水 30 十一 1

OCTOBER 2017 庚戌

Xuan Kong Element 玄空五行	天地否 Stagnation	Period Luck 卦運	Monthly Star 月星
Metal 金9		9	9

SUNDAY	MONDAY	TUESDAY	WEDNESDAY	THURSDAY	FRIDAY	SATURDAY
木8 Wood 6 Lesser Exceeding 辛酉 Metal Rooster 雷山小過 1 十二 3	金4 Metal 5 Gathering 壬戌 Water Dog 澤地萃 2 十三 4	水6 Water 4 Peel 癸亥 Water Pig 山地剝 3 十四 6	水1 Water 3 Earth 甲子 Wood Rat 坤爲地 4 十五 1	木3 Wood 2 Biting 乙丑 Wood Ox 火雷噬嗑 5 十六 6	火2 Fire 1 Family 丙寅 Fire Tiger 風火家人 6 十七 4	水6 Water 9 Decreasing 丁卯 Fire Rabbit 山澤損 7 十八 9
金9 Metal 8 Tread 戊辰 Earth Dragon 天澤履 8 十九 6	木8 Wood 7 Great Strength 己巳 Earth Snake 雷天大壯 9 二十 2	木8 Wood 6 Consistency 庚午 Metal Horse 雷風恒 10 廿一 9	金9 Metal 5 Litigation 辛未 Metal Goat 天水訟 11 廿二 3	水1 Water 4 Officer 壬申 Water Monkey 地水師 12 廿三 7	火2 Fire 3 Gradual Progress 癸酉 Water Rooster 風山漸 13 廿四 7	火7 Fire 2 Obstruction 甲戌 Wood Dog 水山蹇 14 廿五 2
木3 Wood 1 Advancement 乙亥 Wood Pig 火地晉 15 廿六 3	水6 Water 9 Nourish 丙子 Fire Rat 山雷頤 16 廿七 3	金4 Metal 8 Following 丁丑 Fire Ox 澤雷隨 17 廿八 7	木8 Wood 7 Abundance 戊寅 Earth Tiger 雷火豐 18 廿九 6	火7 Fire 6 Regulate 己卯 Earth Rabbit 水澤節 19 三十 8	水1 Water 5 Unity 庚辰 Metal Dragon 地天泰 20 九月初一 9	木3 Wood 4 Great Reward 辛巳 Metal Snake 火天大有 21 初二 7
火2 Fire 3 Wind 壬午 Water Horse 巽爲風 22 初三 6	金4 Metal 2 Trap 癸未 Water Goat 澤水困 23 初四 8	木3 Wood 1 Not Yet Accomplished 甲申 Wood Monkey 火水未濟 24 初五 9	金9 Metal 9 Retreat 乙酉 Wood Rooster 天山遯 25 初六 4	水6 Water 8 Mountain 丙戌 Fire Dog 艮爲山 26 初七 1	木8 Wood 7 Delight 丁亥 Fire Pig 雷地豫 27 初八 8	火7 Fire 6 Beginning 戊子 Earth Rat 水雷屯 28 初九 4
金9 Metal 5 Without Wrongdoing 己丑 Earth Ox 天雷無妄 29 初十 2	木3 Wood 4 Fire 庚寅 Metal Tiger 離爲火 30 十一 1	火2 Fire 3 Sincerity 辛卯 Metal Rabbit 風澤中孚 31 十二 3				

NOVEMBER 2017 辛亥

Xuan Kong Element 玄空五行	水地比 Alliance	Period Luck 卦運	Monthly Star 月星
Fire 火7		7	8

SUNDAY	MONDAY	TUESDAY	WEDNESDAY	THURSDAY	FRIDAY	SATURDAY
			水6 Water 2 Big Livestock 山天大畜 壬辰 Water Dragon 1 十三 4	金4 Metal 1 Eliminating 澤天夬 癸巳 Water Snake 2 十四 6	金9 Metal 9 Heaven 乾爲天 甲午 Wood Horse 3 十五 1	火7 Fire 8 Well 水風井 乙未 Wood Goat 4 十六 6
木8 Wood 7 Relief 雷水解 丙申 Fire Monkey 5 十七 4	金4 Metal 6 Influence 澤山咸 丁酉 Fire Rooster 6 十八 9	水1 Water 5 Humility 地山謙 戊戌 Earth Dog 7 十九 6	火2 Fire 4 Observation 風地觀 己亥 Earth Pig 8 二十 2	火2 Fire 3 Increasing 風雷益 庚子 Metal Rat 9 廿一 9	水1 Water 2 Dimming Light 地火明夷 辛丑 Metal Ox 10 廿二 3	金9 Metal 1 Fellowship 天火同人 壬寅 Water Tiger 11 廿三 7
木8 Wood 9 Marrying Maiden 雷澤歸妹 癸卯 Water Rabbit 12 廿四 7	木3 Wood 8 Opposition 火澤睽 甲辰 Wood Dragon 13 廿五 2	火7 Fire 7 Waiting 水天需 乙巳 Wood Snake 14 廿六 3	金4 Metal 6 Great Exceeding 澤風大過 丙午 Fire Horse 15 廿七 3	水6 Water 5 Poison 山風蠱 丁未 Fire Goat 16 廿八 7	火2 Fire 4 Dispersing 風水渙 戊申 Earth Monkey 17 廿九 6	木3 Wood 3 Travelling 火山旅 己酉 Earth Rooster 18 十月初一 8
金9 Metal 2 Stagnation 天地否 庚戌 Metal Dog 19 初二 9	火7 Fire 1 Alliance 水地比 辛亥 Metal Pig 20 初三 7	木8 Wood 9 Thunder 震爲雷 壬子 Water Rat 21 初四 1	水6 Water 8 Beauty 山火賁 癸丑 Water Ox 22 初五 8	火7 Fire 7 Accomplished 水火既濟 甲寅 Wood Tiger 23 初六 9	水1 Water 6 Arriving 地澤臨 乙卯 Wood Rabbit 24 初七 4	金4 Metal 5 Marsh 兑爲澤 丙辰 Fire Dragon 25 初八 1
火2 Fire 4 Small Livestock 風天小畜 丁巳 Fire Snake 26 初九 8	木3 Wood 3 The Cauldron 火風鼎 戊午 Earth Horse 27 初十 4	水1 Water 2 Rising 地風升 己未 Earth Goat 28 十一 2	火7 Fire 1 Water 坎爲水 庚申 Metal Monkey 29 十二 1	木8 Wood 9 Lesser Exceeding 雷山小過 辛酉 Metal Rooster 30 十三 3		

DECEMBER 2017 壬子

Xuan Kong Element 玄空五行	震爲雷 Thunder	Period Luck 卦運	Monthly Star 月星
Wood 木8		1	7

SUNDAY	MONDAY	TUESDAY	WEDNESDAY	THURSDAY	FRIDAY	SATURDAY
水6 Water 5 Big Livestock 山天大畜 壬辰 Water Dragon 31 十四 4					金4 Metal 8 Gathering 澤地萃 壬戌 Water Dog 1 十四 4	水6 Water 7 Peel 山地剝 癸亥 Water Pig 2 十五 6
水1 Water 6 Earth 坤爲地 甲子 Wood Rat 3 十六 1	木3 Wood 5 Biting 火雷噬嗑 乙丑 Wood Ox 4 十七 6	火2 Fire 4 Family 風火家人 丙寅 Fire Tiger 5 十八 4	水6 Water 3 Decreasing 山澤損 丁卯 Fire Rabbit 6 十九 9	金9 Metal 2 Tread 天澤履 戊辰 Earth Dragon 7 二十 6	木8 Wood 1 Great Strength 雷天大壯 己巳 Earth Snake 8 廿一 2	木8 Wood 9 Consistency 雷風恆 庚午 Metal Horse 9 廿二 9
金9 Metal 8 Litigation 天水訟 辛未 Metal Goat 10 廿三 3	水1 Water 7 Officer 地水師 壬申 Water Monkey 11 廿四 7	火2 Fire 6 Gradual Progress 風山漸 癸酉 Water Rooster 12 廿五 7	火7 Fire 5 Obstruction 水山蹇 甲戌 Wood Dog 13 廿六 2	木3 Wood 4 Advancement 火地晉 乙亥 Wood Pig 14 廿七 3	水6 Water 3 Nourish 山雷頤 丙子 Fire Rat 15 廿八 3	金4 Metal 2 Following 澤雷隨 丁丑 Fire Ox 16 廿九 7
木8 Wood 1 Abundance 雷火豐 戊寅 Earth Tiger 17 三十 6	火7 Fire 9 Regulate 水澤節 己卯 Earth Rabbit 18 十一月初一 8	水1 Water 8 Unity 地天泰 庚辰 Metal Dragon 19 初二 9	木3 Wood 7 Great Reward 火天大有 辛巳 Metal Snake 20 初三 7	火2 Fire 6 Wind 巽爲風 壬午 Water Horse 21 初四 1	金4 Metal 5/6 Trap 澤水困 癸未 Water Goat 22 初五 8	木3 Wood 6 Not Yet Accomplished 火水未濟 甲申 Wood Monkey 23 初六 9
金9 Metal 7 Retreat 天山遯 乙酉 Wood Rooster 24 初七 4	水6 Water 8 Mountain 艮爲山 丙戌 Fire Dog 25 初八 1	木8 Wood 9 Delight 雷地豫 丁亥 Fire Pig 26 初九 8	火7 Fire 1 Beginning 水雷屯 戊子 Earth Rat 27 初十 4	金9 Metal 2 Without Wrongdoing 天雷無妄 己丑 Earth Ox 28 十一 2	木3 Wood 3 Fire 離爲火 庚寅 Metal Tiger 29 十二 1	火2 Fire 4 Sincerity 風澤中孚 辛卯 Metal Rabbit 30 十三 3

2018 戊戌

(*Wu Xu*) Earth Dog

2018 戊戌 *(Wu Xu)* Earth Dog

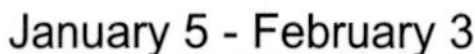

January 5 - February 3

February 4 - March 4

March 5 - April 4

April 5 - May 4

May 5 - June 5

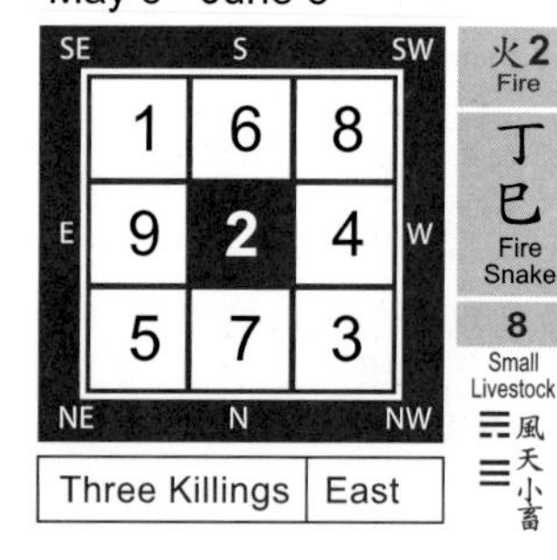

June 6 - July 6

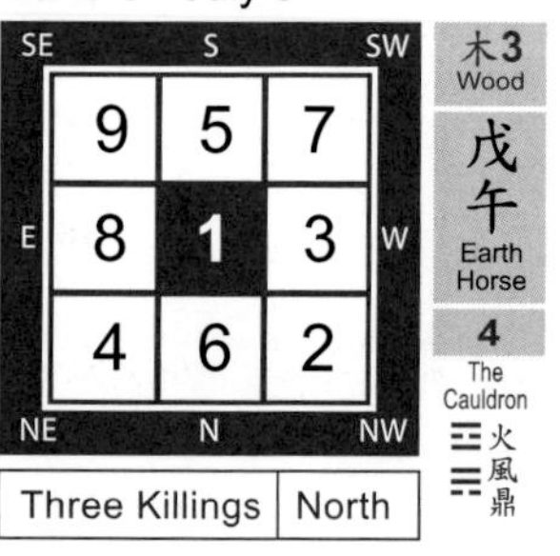

July 7 - August 6

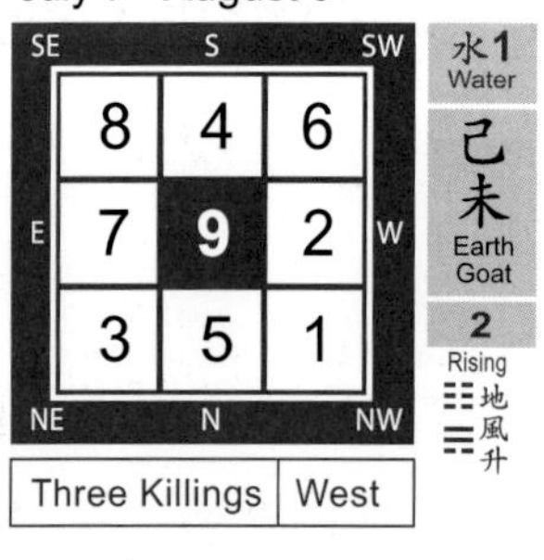

August 7 - September 7

September 8 - October 7

October 8 - November 6

November 7 - December 6

December 7 - January 4

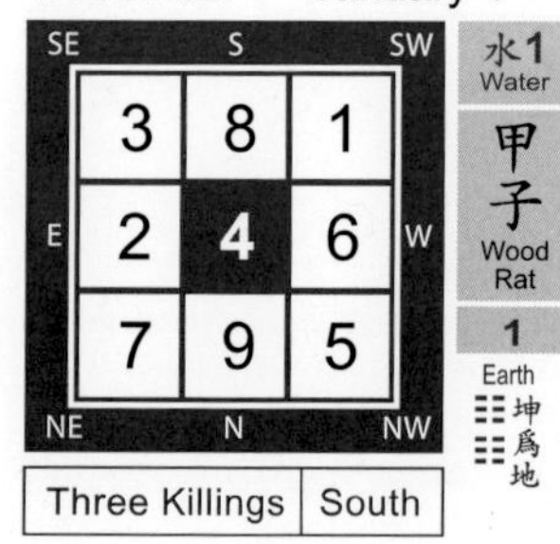

JANUARY 2018 癸丑

Xuan Kong Element 玄空五行	山火賁 Beauty	Period Luck 卦運	Monthly Star 月星
Water 水6		8	6

SUNDAY	MONDAY	TUESDAY	WEDNESDAY	THURSDAY	FRIDAY	SATURDAY
	金4 Metal 6 Eliminating 澤天夬 癸巳 Water Snake **1** 6 十五	金9 Metal 7 Heaven 乾爲天 甲午 Wood Horse **2** 1 十六	火7 Fire 8 Well 水風井 乙未 Wood Goat **3** 6 十七	木8 Wood 9 Relief 雷水解 丙申 Fire Monkey **4** 4 十八	金4 Metal 1 Influence 澤山咸 丁酉 Fire Rooster **5** 9 十九	水1 Water 2 Humility 地山謙 戊戌 Earth Dog **6** 6 二十
火2 Fire 3 Observation 風地觀 己亥 Earth Pig **7** 2 廿一	火2 Fire 4 Increasing 風雷益 庚子 Metal Rat **8** 9 廿二	水1 Water 5 Dimming Light 地火明夷 辛丑 Metal Ox **9** 3 廿三	金9 Metal 6 Fellowship 天火同人 壬寅 Water Tiger **10** 7 廿四	木8 Wood 7 Marrying Maiden 雷澤歸妹 癸卯 Water Rabbit **11** 7 廿五	木3 Wood 8 Opposition 火澤睽 甲辰 Wood Dragon **12** 2 廿六	火7 Fire 9 Waiting 水天需 乙巳 Wood Snake **13** 3 廿七
金4 Metal 1 Great Exceeding 澤風大過 丙午 Fire Horse **14** 3 廿八	水6 Water 2 Poison 山風蠱 丁未 Fire Goat **15** 7 廿九	火2 Fire 3 Dispersing 風水渙 戊申 Earth Monkey **16** 6 三十	木3 Wood 4 Travelling 火山旅 己酉 Earth Rooster **17** 8 十二月初一	金9 Metal 5 Stagnation 天地否 庚戌 Metal Dog **18** 9 初二	火7 Fire 6 Alliance 水地比 辛亥 Metal Pig **19** 7 初三	木8 Wood 7 Thunder 震爲雷 壬子 Water Rat **20** 1 初四
水6 Water 8 Beauty 山火賁 癸丑 Water Ox **21** 8 初五	火7 Fire 9 Accomplished 水火既濟 甲寅 Wood Tiger **22** 9 初六	水1 Water 1 Arriving 地澤臨 乙卯 Wood Rabbit **23** 1 初七	金4 Metal 2 Marsh 兑爲澤 丙辰 Fire Dragon **24** 1 初八	火2 Fire 3 Small Livestock 風天小畜 丁巳 Fire Snake **25** 8 初九	木3 Wood 4 The Cauldron 火風鼎 戊午 Earth Horse **26** 4 初十	水1 Water 5 Rising 地風升 己未 Earth Goat **27** 2 十一
火7 Fire 6 Water 坎爲水 庚申 Metal Monkey **28** 1 十二	木8 Wood 7 Lesser Exceeding 雷山小過 辛酉 Metal Rooster **29** 3 十三	金4 Metal 8 Gathering 澤地萃 壬戌 Water Dog **30** 4 十四	水6 Water 9 Peel 山地剝 癸亥 Water Pig **31** 6 十五			

FEBRUARY 2018 甲寅

Xuan Kong Element 玄空五行	水火既濟 Accomplished	Period Luck 卦運	Monthly Star 月星
Fire 火7		9	5

SUNDAY	MONDAY	TUESDAY	WEDNESDAY	THURSDAY	FRIDAY	SATURDAY
				水1 Water 1 Earth 坤爲地 甲子 Wood Rat **1** 1 十六	木3 Wood 2 Biting 火雷噬嗑 乙丑 Wood Ox **2** 6 十七	火2 Fire 3 Family 風火家人 丙寅 Fire Tiger **3** 4 十八
水6 Water 4 Decreasing 山澤損 丁卯 Fire Rabbit **4** 9 十九	金9 Metal 5 Tread 天澤履 戊辰 Earth Dragon **5** 6 二十	木8 Wood 6 Great Strength 雷天大壯 己巳 Earth Snake **6** 2 廿一	木8 Wood 7 Consistency 雷風恆 庚午 Metal Horse **7** 9 廿二	金9 Metal 8 Litigation 天水訟 辛未 Metal Goat **8** 3 廿三	水1 Water 9 Officer 地水師 壬申 Water Monkey **9** 7 廿四	火2 Fire 1 Gradual Progress 風山漸 癸酉 Water Rooster **10** 7 廿五
火7 Fire 2 Obstruction 水山蹇 甲戌 Wood Dog **11** 2 廿六	木3 Wood 3 Advancement 火地晉 乙亥 Wood Pig **12** 3 廿七	水6 Water 4 Nourish 山雷頤 丙子 Fire Rat **13** 3 廿八	金4 Metal 5 Following 澤雷隨 丁丑 Fire Ox **14** 7 廿九	木8 Wood 6 Abundance 雷火豐 戊寅 Earth Tiger **15** 6 三十	火7 Fire 7 Regulate 水澤節 己卯 Earth Rabbit **16** 8 正月初一	水1 Water 8 Unity 地天泰 庚辰 Metal Dragon **17** 9 初二
木3 Wood 9 Great Reward 火天大有 辛巳 Metal Snake **18** 7 初三	火2 Fire 1 Wind 巽爲風 壬午 Water Horse **19** 1 初四	金4 Metal 2 Trap 澤水困 癸未 Water Goat **20** 8 初五	木3 Wood 3 Not Yet Accomplished 火水未濟 甲申 Wood Monkey **21** 9 初六	金9 Metal 4 Retreat 天山遯 乙酉 Wood Rooster **22** 4 初七	水6 Water 5 Mountain 艮爲山 丙戌 Fire Dog **23** 1 初八	木8 Wood 6 Delight 雷地豫 丁亥 Fire Pig **24** 8 初九
火7 Fire 7 Beginning 水雷屯 戊子 Earth Rat **25** 4 初十	金9 Metal 8 Without Wrongdoing 天雷無妄 己丑 Earth Ox **26** 2 十一	木3 Wood 9 Fire 離爲火 庚寅 Metal Tiger **27** 1 十二	火2 Fire 1 Sincerity 風澤中孚 辛卯 Metal Rabbit **28** 3 十三			

MARCH 2018 乙卯

Xuan Kong Element 玄空五行	地澤臨 Arriving	Period Luck 卦運	Monthly Star 月星
Water 水1		4	4

SUNDAY	MONDAY	TUESDAY	WEDNESDAY	THURSDAY	FRIDAY	SATURDAY
				水6 Water ■2 Big Livestock 山天大畜 壬辰 Water Dragon 4 **1** 十四	金4 Metal ■3 Eliminating 澤天夬 癸巳 Water Snake 6 **2** 十五	金9 Metal ■4 Heaven 乾爲天 甲午 Wood Horse 1 **3** 十六
火7 Fire ■5 Well 水風井 乙未 Wood Goat 6 **4** 十七	木8 Wood ■6 Relief 雷水解 丙申 Fire Monkey 4 **5** 十八	金4 Metal ■7 Influence 澤山咸 丁酉 Fire Rooster 9 **6** 十九	水1 Water ■8 Humility 地山謙 戊戌 Earth Dog 6 **7** 二十	火2 Fire ■9 Observation 風地觀 己亥 Earth Pig 2 **8** 廿一	火2 Fire ■1 Increasing 風雷益 庚子 Metal Rat 9 **9** 廿二	水1 Water ■2 Dimming Light 地火明夷 辛丑 Metal Ox 3 **10** 廿三
金9 Metal ■3 Fellowship 天火同人 壬寅 Water Tiger 7 **11** 廿四	木8 Wood ■4 Marrying Maiden 雷澤歸妹 癸卯 Water Rabbit 7 **12** 廿五	木3 Wood ■5 Opposition 火澤睽 甲辰 Wood Dragon 2 **13** 廿六	火7 Fire ■6 Waiting 水天需 乙巳 Wood Snake 3 **14** 廿七	金4 Metal ■7 Great Exceeding 澤風大過 丙午 Fire Horse 3 **15** 廿八	水6 Water ■8 Poison 山風蠱 丁未 Fire Goat 7 **16** 廿九	火2 Fire ■9 Dispersing 風水渙 戊申 Earth Monkey 6 **17** 二月初一
木3 Wood ■1 Travelling 火山旅 己酉 Earth Rooster 8 **18** 初二	金9 Metal ■2 Stagnation 天地否 庚戌 Metal Dog 9 **19** 初三	火7 Fire ■3 Alliance 水地比 辛亥 Metal Pig 7 **20** 初四	木8 Wood ■4 Thunder 震爲雷 壬子 Water Rat 1 **21** 初五	水6 Water ■5 Beauty 山火賁 癸丑 Water Ox 8 **22** 初六	火7 Fire ■6 Accomplished 水火既濟 甲寅 Wood Tiger 9 **23** 初七	水1 Water ■7 Arriving 地澤臨 乙卯 Wood Rabbit 4 **24** 初八
金4 Metal ■8 Marsh 兑爲澤 丙辰 Fire Dragon 1 **25** 初九	火2 Fire ■9 Small Livestock 風天小畜 丁巳 Fire Snake 8 **26** 初十	木3 Wood ■1 The Cauldron 火風鼎 戊午 Earth Horse 4 **27** 十一	水1 Water ■2 Rising 地風升 己未 Earth Goat 2 **28** 十二	火7 Fire ■3 Water 坎爲水 庚申 Metal Monkey 1 **29** 十三	木8 Wood ■4 Lesser Exceeding 雷山小過 辛酉 Metal Rooster 3 **30** 十四	金4 Metal ■5 Gathering 澤地萃 壬戌 Water Dog 4 **31** 十五

APRIL 2018 丙辰

Xuan Kong Element 玄空五行	兑爲澤 Marsh	Period Luck 卦運	Monthly Star 月星
Metal 金4		1	3

SUNDAY	MONDAY	TUESDAY	WEDNESDAY	THURSDAY	FRIDAY	SATURDAY
水6 Water ■6 Peel 山地剝 癸亥 Water Pig 6 **1** 十六	水1 Water ■7 Earth 坤爲地 甲子 Wood Rat 1 **2** 十七	木3 Wood ■8 Biting 火雷噬嗑 乙丑 Wood Ox 6 **3** 十八	火2 Fire ■9 Family 風火家人 丙寅 Fire Tiger 4 **4** 十九	水6 Water ■1 Decreasing 山澤損 丁卯 Fire Rabbit 9 **5** 二十	金9 Metal ■2 Tread 天澤履 戊辰 Earth Dragon 6 **6** 廿一	木8 Wood ■3 Great Strength 雷天大壯 己巳 Earth Snake 2 **7** 廿二
木8 Wood ■4 Consistency 雷風恒 庚午 Metal Horse 9 **8** 廿三	金9 Metal ■5 Litigation 天水訟 辛未 Metal Goat 3 **9** 廿四	水1 Water ■6 Officer 地水師 壬申 Water Monkey 7 **10** 廿五	火2 Fire ■7 Gradual Progress 風山漸 癸酉 Water Rooster 7 **11** 廿六	火7 Fire ■8 Obstruction 水山蹇 甲戌 Wood Dog 2 **12** 廿七	木3 Wood ■9 Advancement 火地晉 乙亥 Wood Pig 3 **13** 廿八	水6 Water ■1 Nourish 山雷頤 丙子 Fire Rat 3 **14** 廿九
金4 Metal ■2 Following 澤雷隨 丁丑 Fire Ox 7 **15** 三十	木8 Wood ■3 Abundance 雷火豐 戊寅 Earth Tiger 6 **16** 三月初一	火7 Fire ■4 Regulate 水澤節 己卯 Earth Rabbit 8 **17** 初二	水1 Water ■5 Unity 地天泰 庚辰 Metal Dragon 9 **18** 初三	木3 Wood ■6 Great Reward 火天大有 辛巳 Metal Snake 7 **19** 初四	火2 Fire ■7 Wind 巽爲風 壬午 Water Horse 1 **20** 初五	金4 Metal ■8 Trap 澤水困 癸未 Water Goat 8 **21** 初六
木3 Wood ■9 Not Yet Accomplished 火水未濟 甲申 Wood Monkey 9 **22** 初七	金9 Metal ■1 Retreat 天山遯 乙酉 Wood Rooster 4 **23** 初八	水6 Water ■2 Mountain 艮爲山 丙戌 Fire Dog 1 **24** 初九	木8 Wood ■3 Delight 雷地豫 丁亥 Fire Pig 8 **25** 初十	火7 Fire ■4 Beginning 水雷屯 戊子 Earth Rat 4 **26** 十一	金9 Metal ■5 Without Wrongdoing 天雷無妄 己丑 Earth Ox 2 **27** 十二	木3 Wood ■6 Fire 離爲火 庚寅 Metal Tiger 1 **28** 十三
火2 Fire ■7 Sincerity 風澤中孚 辛卯 Metal Rabbit 3 **29** 十四	水6 Water ■8 Big Livestock 山天大畜 壬辰 Water Dragon 4 **30** 十五					

MAY 2018 丁巳

Xuan Kong Element 玄空五行	風天小畜 Small Livestock	Period Luck 卦運	Monthly Star 月星
Fire 火2		8	2

SUNDAY	MONDAY	TUESDAY	WEDNESDAY	THURSDAY	FRIDAY	SATURDAY
		金4 Metal 9 Eliminating 澤天夬 癸巳 Water Snake **1** 十六 6	金9 Metal 1 Heaven 乾爲天 甲午 Wood Horse **2** 十七 1	火7 Fire 2 Well 水風井 乙未 Wood Goat **3** 十八 6	木8 Wood 3 Relief 雷水解 丙申 Fire Monkey **4** 十九 4	金4 Metal 4 Influence 澤山咸 丁酉 Fire Rooster **5** 二十 9
水1 Water 5 Humility 地山謙 戊戌 Earth Dog **6** 廿一 6	火2 Fire 6 Observation 風地觀 己亥 Earth Pig **7** 廿二 2	火2 Fire 7 Increasing 風雷益 庚子 Metal Rat **8** 廿三 9	水1 Water 8 Dimming Light 地火明夷 辛丑 Metal Ox **9** 廿四 3	金9 Metal 9 Fellowship 天火同人 壬寅 Water Tiger **10** 廿五 7	木8 Wood 1 Marrying Maiden 雷澤歸妹 癸卯 Water Rabbit **11** 廿六 7	木3 Wood 2 Opposition 火澤睽 甲辰 Wood Dragon **12** 廿七 2
火7 Fire 3 Waiting 水天需 乙巳 Wood Snake **13** 廿八 3	金4 Metal 4 Great Exceeding 澤風大過 丙午 Fire Horse **14** 廿九 3	水6 Water 5 Poison 山風蠱 丁未 Fire Goat **15** 四月初一 7	火2 Fire 6 Dispersing 風水渙 戊申 Earth Monkey **16** 初二 6	木3 Wood 7 Travelling 火山旅 己酉 Earth Rooster **17** 初三 8	金9 Metal 8 Stagnation 天地否 庚戌 Metal Dog **18** 初四 9	火7 Fire 9 Alliance 水地比 辛亥 Metal Pig **19** 初五 7
木8 Wood 1 Thunder 震爲雷 壬子 Water Rat **20** 初六 1	水6 Water 2 Beauty 山火賁 癸丑 Water Ox **21** 初七 8	火7 Fire 3 Accomplished 水火既濟 甲寅 Wood Tiger **22** 初八 9	水1 Water 4 Arriving 地澤臨 乙卯 Wood Rabbit **23** 初九 4	金4 Metal 5 Marsh 兌爲澤 丙辰 Fire Dragon **24** 初十 1	火2 Fire 6 Small Livestock 風天小畜 丁巳 Fire Snake **25** 十一 8	木3 Wood 7 The Cauldron 火風鼎 戊午 Earth Horse **26** 十二 4
水1 Water 8 Rising 地風升 己未 Earth Goat **27** 十三 2	火7 Fire 9 Water 坎爲水 庚申 Metal Monkey **28** 十四 1	木8 Wood 1 Lesser Exceeding 雷山小過 辛酉 Metal Rooster **29** 十五 3	金4 Metal 2 Gathering 澤地萃 壬戌 Water Dog **30** 十六 4	水6 Water 3 Peel 山地剝 癸亥 Water Pig **31** 十七 6		

JUNE 2018 戊午

Xuan Kong Element 玄空五行	火風鼎 The Cauldron	Period Luck 卦運	Monthly Star 月星
Wood 木3		4	1

SUNDAY	MONDAY	TUESDAY	WEDNESDAY	THURSDAY	FRIDAY	SATURDAY
					水1 Water 4 Earth 坤爲地 甲子 Wood Rat **1** 十八 1	木3 Wood 5 Biting 火雷噬嗑 乙丑 Wood Ox **2** 十九 6
火2 Fire 6 Family 風火家人 丙寅 Fire Tiger **3** 二十 4	水6 Water 7 Decreasing 山澤損 丁卯 Fire Rabbit **4** 廿一 9	金9 Metal 8 Tread 天澤履 戊辰 Earth Dragon **5** 廿二 6	木8 Wood 9 Great Strength 雷天大壯 己巳 Earth Snake **6** 廿三 2	木8 Wood 1 Consistency 雷風恆 庚午 Metal Horse **7** 廿四 9	金9 Metal 2 Litigation 天水訟 辛未 Metal Goat **8** 廿五 3	水1 Water 3 Officer 地水師 壬申 Water Monkey **9** 廿六 7
火2 Fire 4 Gradual Progress 風山漸 癸酉 Water Rooster **10** 廿七 7	火7 Fire 5 Obstruction 水山蹇 甲戌 Wood Dog **11** 廿八 2	木3 Wood 6 Advancement 火地晉 乙亥 Wood Pig **12** 廿九 3	水6 Water 7 Nourish 山雷頤 丙子 Fire Rat **13** 三十 3	金4 Metal 8 Following 澤雷隨 丁丑 Fire Ox **14** 五月初一 7	木8 Wood 9 Abundance 雷火豐 戊寅 Earth Tiger **15** 初二 6	火7 Fire 1 Regulate 水澤節 己卯 Earth Rabbit **16** 初三 8
水1 Water 2 Unity 地天泰 庚辰 Metal Dragon **17** 初四 9	木3 Wood 3 Great Reward 火天大有 辛巳 Metal Snake **18** 初五 7	火2 Fire 4 Wind 巽爲風 壬午 Water Horse **19** 初六 1	金4 Metal 5 Trap 澤水困 癸未 Water Goat **20** 初七 8	木3 Wood 6/4 Not Yet Accomplished 火水未濟 甲申 Wood Monkey **21** 初八 9	金9 Metal 3 Retreat 天山遯 乙酉 Wood Rooster **22** 初九 4	水6 Water 2 Mountain 艮爲山 丙戌 Fire Dog **23** 初十 1
木8 Wood 1 Delight 雷地豫 丁亥 Fire Pig **24** 十一 8	火7 Fire 9 Beginning 水雷屯 戊子 Earth Rat **25** 十二 4	金9 Metal 6 Without Wrongdoing 天雷無妄 己丑 Earth Ox **26** 十三 2	木3 Wood 7 Fire 離爲火 庚寅 Metal Tiger **27** 十四 1	火2 Fire 6 Sincerity 風澤中孚 辛卯 Metal Rabbit **28** 十五 3	水6 Water 5 Big Livestock 山天大畜 壬辰 Water Dragon **29** 十六 4	金4 Metal 4 Eliminating 澤天夬 癸巳 Water Snake **30** 十七 6

JULY 2018 己未

Xuan Kong Element 玄空五行	地風升 Rising	Period Luck 卦運	Monthly Star 月星
Water 水1		2	9

SUNDAY	MONDAY	TUESDAY	WEDNESDAY	THURSDAY	FRIDAY	SATURDAY
1 十八 金9 Metal · 3 Heaven 乾為天 甲午 Wood Horse · 1	**2** 十九 火7 Fire · 2 Well 水風井 乙未 Wood Goat · 6	**3** 二十 木8 Wood · 1 Relief 雷水解 丙申 Fire Monkey · 4	**4** 廿一 金4 Metal · 9 Influence 澤山咸 丁酉 Fire Rooster · 9	**5** 廿二 水1 Water · 8 Humility 地山謙 戊戌 Earth Dog · 6	**6** 廿三 火2 Fire · 7 Observation 風地觀 己亥 Earth Pig · 2	**7** 廿四 火2 Fire · 6 Increasing 風雷益 庚子 Metal Rat · 9
8 廿五 水1 Water · 5 Dimming Light 地火明夷 辛丑 Metal Ox · 3	**9** 廿六 金9 Metal · 4 Fellowship 天火同人 壬寅 Water Tiger · 7	**10** 廿七 木8 Wood · 3 Marrying Maiden 雷澤歸妹 癸卯 Water Rabbit · 7	**11** 廿八 木3 Wood · 2 Opposition 火澤睽 甲辰 Wood Dragon · 2	**12** 廿九 火7 Fire · 1 Waiting 水天需 乙巳 Wood Snake · 3	**13** 六月初一 金4 Metal · 9 Great Exceeding 澤風大過 丙午 Fire Horse · 3	**14** 初二 水6 Water · 8 Poison 山風蠱 丁未 Fire Goat · 7
15 初三 火2 Fire · 7 Dispersing 風水渙 戊申 Earth Monkey · 6	**16** 初四 木3 Wood · 6 Travelling 火山旅 己酉 Earth Rooster · 8	**17** 初五 金9 Metal · 5 Stagnation 天地否 庚戌 Metal Dog · 9	**18** 初六 火7 Fire · 4 Alliance 水地比 辛亥 Metal Pig · 7	**19** 初七 木8 Wood · 3 Thunder 震為雷 壬子 Water Rat · 1	**20** 初八 水6 Water · 2 Beauty 山火賁 癸丑 Water Ox · 8	**21** 初九 火7 Fire · 1 Accomplished 水火既濟 甲寅 Wood Tiger · 9
22 初十 水1 Water · 9 Arriving 地澤臨 乙卯 Wood Rabbit · 4	**23** 十一 金4 Metal · 8 Marsh 兌為澤 丙辰 Fire Dragon · 1	**24** 十二 火2 Fire · 7 Small Livestock 風天小畜 丁巳 Fire Snake · 8	**25** 十三 木3 Wood · 6 The Cauldron 火風鼎 戊午 Earth Horse · 4	**26** 十四 水1 Water · 5 Rising 地風升 己未 Earth Goat · 2	**27** 十五 火7 Fire · 4 Water 坎為水 庚申 Metal Monkey · 1	**28** 十六 木8 Wood · 3 Lesser Exceeding 雷山小過 辛酉 Metal Rooster · 3
29 十七 金4 Metal · 2 Gathering 澤地萃 壬戌 Water Dog · 4	**30** 十八 水6 Water · 1 Peel 山地剝 癸亥 Water Pig · 6	**31** 十九 水1 Water · 9 Earth 坤為地 甲子 Wood Rat · 1				

AUGUST 2018 庚申

Xuan Kong Element 玄空五行	坎為水 Water	Period Luck 卦運	Monthly Star 月星
Fire 火7		1	8

SUNDAY	MONDAY	TUESDAY	WEDNESDAY	THURSDAY	FRIDAY	SATURDAY
			1 二十 木3 Wood · 8 Biting 火雷噬嗑 乙丑 Wood Ox · 6	**2** 廿一 火2 Fire · 7 Family 風火家人 丙寅 Fire Tiger · 4	**3** 廿二 水6 Water · 6 Decreasing 山澤損 丁卯 Fire Rabbit · 9	**4** 廿三 金9 Metal · 5 Tread 天澤履 戊辰 Earth Dragon · 6
5 廿四 木8 Wood · 4 Great Strength 雷天大壯 己巳 Earth Snake · 2	**6** 廿五 木8 Wood · 3 Consistency 雷風恆 庚午 Metal Horse · 9	**7** 廿六 金9 Metal · 2 Litigation 天水訟 辛未 Metal Goat · 3	**8** 廿七 水1 Water · 1 Officer 地水師 壬申 Water Monkey · 7	**9** 廿八 火2 Fire · 9 Gradual Progress 風山漸 癸酉 Water Rooster · 7	**10** 廿九 火7 Fire · 8 Obstruction 水山蹇 甲戌 Wood Dog · 2	**11** 七月初一 木3 Wood · 7 Advancement 火地晉 乙亥 Wood Pig · 3
12 初二 水6 Water · 6 Nourish 山雷頤 丙子 Fire Rat · 3	**13** 初三 金4 Metal · 5 Following 澤雷隨 丁丑 Fire Ox · 7	**14** 初四 木8 Wood · 4 Abundance 雷火豐 戊寅 Earth Tiger · 6	**15** 初五 火7 Fire · 3 Regulate 水澤節 己卯 Earth Rabbit · 8	**16** 初六 水1 Water · 2 Unity 地天泰 庚辰 Metal Dragon · 9	**17** 初七 木3 Wood · 1 Great Reward 火天大有 辛巳 Metal Snake · 7	**18** 初八 火2 Fire · 9 Wind 巽為風 壬午 Water Horse · 1
19 初九 金4 Metal · 8 Trap 澤水困 癸未 Water Goat · 8	**20** 初十 木3 Wood · 7 Not Yet Accomplished 火水未濟 甲申 Wood Monkey · 9	**21** 十一 金9 Metal · 6 Retreat 天山遯 乙酉 Wood Rooster · 4	**22** 十二 水6 Water · 5 Mountain 艮為山 丙戌 Fire Dog · 1	**23** 十三 木8 Wood · 4 Delight 雷地豫 丁亥 Fire Pig · 8	**24** 十四 火7 Fire · 3 Beginning 水雷屯 戊子 Earth Rat · 4	**25** 十五 金9 Metal · 2 Without Wrongdoing 天雷無妄 己丑 Earth Ox · 2
26 十六 木3 Wood · 1 Fire 離為火 庚寅 Metal Tiger · 1	**27** 十七 火2 Fire · 9 Sincerity 風澤中孚 辛卯 Metal Rabbit · 3	**28** 十八 水6 Water · 8 Big Livestock 山天大畜 壬辰 Water Dragon · 4	**29** 十九 金4 Metal · 7 Eliminating 澤天夬 癸巳 Water Snake · 6	**30** 二十 金9 Metal · 6 Heaven 乾為天 甲午 Wood Horse · 1	**31** 廿一 火7 Fire · 5 Well 水風井 乙未 Wood Goat · 6	

SEPTEMBER 2018 辛酉

Xuan Kong Element 玄空五行	雷山小過 Lesser Exceeding	Period Luck 卦運	Monthly Star 月星
Wood 木8		3	7

SUNDAY	MONDAY	TUESDAY	WEDNESDAY	THURSDAY	FRIDAY	SATURDAY
木3 Wood Biting 2 乙丑 Wood Ox 火雷噬嗑 **30** 廿一 6						木8 Wood Relief 4 丙申 Fire Monkey 雷水解 **1** 廿二 4
金4 Metal Influence 3 丁酉 Fire Rooster 澤山咸 **2** 廿三 9	水1 Water Humility 2 戊戌 Earth Dog 地山謙 **3** 廿四 6	火2 Fire Observation 1 己亥 Earth Pig 風地觀 **4** 廿五 2	火2 Fire Increasing 9 庚子 Metal Rat 風雷益 **5** 廿六 9	水1 Water Dimming Light 8 辛丑 Metal Ox 地火明夷 **6** 廿七 3	金9 Metal Fellowship 7 壬寅 Water Tiger 天火同人 **7** 廿八 7	木8 Wood Marrying Maiden 6 癸卯 Water Rabbit 雷澤歸妹 **8** 廿九 7
木3 Wood Opposition 5 甲辰 Wood Dragon 火澤睽 **9** 三十 2	火7 Fire Waiting 4 乙巳 Wood Snake 水天需 **10** 八月初一 3	金4 Metal Great Exceeding 3 丙午 Fire Horse 澤風大過 **11** 初二 3	水6 Water Poison 2 丁未 Fire Goat 山風蠱 **12** 初三 7	火2 Fire Dispersing 1 戊申 Earth Monkey 風水渙 **13** 初四 6	木3 Wood Travelling 9 己酉 Earth Rooster 火山旅 **14** 初五 8	金9 Metal Stagnation 8 庚戌 Metal Dog 天地否 **15** 初六 9
火7 Fire Alliance 7 辛亥 Metal Pig 水地比 **16** 初七 7	木8 Wood Thunder 6 壬子 Water Rat 震爲雷 **17** 初八 1	水6 Water Beauty 5 癸丑 Water Ox 山火賁 **18** 初九 8	火7 Fire Accomplished 4 甲寅 Wood Tiger 水火既濟 **19** 初十 9	水1 Water Arriving 3 乙卯 Wood Rabbit 地澤臨 **20** 十一 4	金4 Metal Marsh 2 丙辰 Fire Dragon 兑爲澤 **21** 十二 1	火2 Fire Small Livestock 1 丁巳 Fire Snake 風天小畜 **22** 十三 8
木3 Wood The Cauldron 9 戊午 Earth Horse 火風鼎 **23** 十四 4	水1 Water Rising 8 己未 Earth Goat 地風升 **24** 十五 2	火7 Fire Water 7 庚申 Metal Monkey 坎爲水 **25** 十六 1	木8 Wood Lesser Exceeding 6 辛酉 Metal Rooster 雷山小過 **26** 十七 3	金4 Metal Gathering 5 壬戌 Water Dog 澤地萃 **27** 十八 4	水6 Water Peel 4 癸亥 Water Pig 山地剝 **28** 十九 6	水1 Water Earth 3 甲子 Wood Rat 坤爲地 **29** 二十 1

OCTOBER 2018 壬戌

Xuan Kong Element 玄空五行	澤地萃 Gathering	Period Luck 卦運	Monthly Star 月星
Metal 金4		4	6

SUNDAY	MONDAY	TUESDAY	WEDNESDAY	THURSDAY	FRIDAY	SATURDAY
	火2 Fire Family 1 丙寅 Fire Tiger 風火家人 **1** 廿二 4	水6 Water Decreasing 9 丁卯 Fire Rabbit 山澤損 **2** 廿三 9	金9 Metal Tread 8 戊辰 Earth Dragon 天澤履 **3** 廿四 6	木8 Wood Great Strength 7 己巳 Earth Snake 雷天大壯 **4** 廿五 2	木8 Wood Consistency 6 庚午 Metal Horse 雷風恆 **5** 廿六 9	金9 Metal Litigation 5 辛未 Metal Goat 天水訟 **6** 廿七 3
水1 Water Officer 4 壬申 Water Monkey 地水師 **7** 廿八 7	火2 Fire Gradual Progress 3 癸酉 Water Rooster 風山漸 **8** 廿九 7	火7 Fire Obstruction 2 甲戌 Wood Dog 水山蹇 **9** 九月初一 2	木3 Wood Advancement 1 乙亥 Wood Pig 火地晉 **10** 初二 3	水6 Water Nourish 9 丙子 Fire Rat 山雷頤 **11** 初三 3	金4 Metal Following 8 丁丑 Fire Ox 澤雷隨 **12** 初四 7	木8 Wood Abundance 7 戊寅 Earth Tiger 雷火豐 **13** 初五 6
火7 Fire Regulate 6 己卯 Earth Rabbit 水澤節 **14** 初六 8	水1 Water Unity 5 庚辰 Metal Dragon 地天泰 **15** 初七 9	木3 Wood Great Reward 4 辛巳 Metal Snake 火天大有 **16** 初八 7	火2 Fire Wind 3 壬午 Water Horse 巽爲風 **17** 初九 1	金4 Metal Trap 2 癸未 Water Goat 澤水困 **18** 初十 8	木3 Wood Not Yet Accomplished 1 甲申 Wood Monkey 火水未濟 **19** 十一 9	金9 Metal Retreat 9 乙酉 Wood Rooster 天山遯 **20** 十二 4
水6 Water Mountain 8 丙戌 Fire Dog 艮爲山 **21** 十三 1	木8 Wood Delight 7 丁亥 Fire Pig 雷地豫 **22** 十四 8	火7 Fire Beginning 6 戊子 Earth Rat 水雷屯 **23** 十五 4	金9 Metal Without Wrongdoing 5 己丑 Earth Ox 天雷無妄 **24** 十六 2	木3 Wood Fire 4 庚寅 Metal Tiger 離爲火 **25** 十七 1	火2 Fire Sincerity 3 辛卯 Metal Rabbit 風澤中孚 **26** 十八 3	水6 Water Big Livestock 2 壬辰 Water Dragon 山天大畜 **27** 十九 4
金4 Metal Eliminating 1 癸巳 Water Snake 澤天夬 **28** 二十 6	金9 Metal Heaven 9 甲午 Wood Horse 乾爲天 **29** 廿一 1	火7 Fire Well 8 乙未 Wood Goat 水風井 **30** 廿二 6	木8 Wood Relief 7 丙申 Fire Monkey 雷水解 **31** 廿三 4			

NOVEMBER 2018 癸亥

Xuan Kong Element 玄空五行	山地剝 Peel	Period Luck 卦運	Monthly Star 月星
Water 水6		6	5

SUNDAY	MONDAY	TUESDAY	WEDNESDAY	THURSDAY	FRIDAY	SATURDAY
				金4 Metal Influence 6 丁酉 Fire Rooster 澤山咸 1 廿四 9	水1 Water Humility 5 戊戌 Earth Dog 地山謙 2 廿五 6	火2 Fire Observation 4 己亥 Earth Pig 風地觀 3 廿六 2
火2 Fire Increasing 3 庚子 Metal Rat 風雷益 4 廿七 9	水1 Water Dimming Light 2 辛丑 Metal Ox 地火明夷 5 廿八 3	金9 Metal Fellowship 1 壬寅 Water Tiger 天火同人 6 廿九 7	木8 Wood Marrying Maiden 9 癸卯 Water Rabbit 雷澤歸妹 7 三十 7	木3 Wood Opposition 8 甲辰 Wood Dragon 火澤睽 8 十月初一 2	火7 Fire Waiting 7 乙巳 Wood Snake 水天需 9 初二 3	金4 Metal Great Exceeding 6 丙午 Fire Horse 澤風大過 10 初三 3
水6 Water Poison 5 丁未 Fire Goat 山風蠱 11 初四 7	火2 Fire Dispersing 4 戊申 Earth Monkey 風水渙 12 初五 6	木3 Wood Travelling 3 己酉 Earth Rooster 火山旅 13 初六 8	金9 Metal Stagnation 2 庚戌 Metal Dog 天地否 14 初七 9	火7 Fire Alliance 1 辛亥 Metal Pig 水地比 15 初八 7	木8 Wood Thunder 9 壬子 Water Rat 震爲雷 16 初九 1	水6 Water Beauty 8 癸丑 Water Ox 山火賁 17 初十 8
火7 Fire Accomplished 7 甲寅 Wood Tiger 水火既濟 18 十一 9	水1 Water Arriving 6 乙卯 Wood Rabbit 地澤臨 19 十二 4	金4 Metal Marsh 5 丙辰 Fire Dragon 兌爲澤 20 十三 1	火2 Fire Small Livestock 4 丁巳 Fire Snake 風天小畜 21 十四 8	木3 Wood The Cauldron 3 戊午 Earth Horse 火風鼎 22 十五 4	水1 Water Rising 2 己未 Earth Goat 地風升 23 十六 2	火7 Fire Water 1 庚申 Metal Monkey 坎爲水 24 十七 1
木8 Wood Lesser Exceeding 9 辛酉 Metal Rooster 雷山小過 25 十八 3	金4 Metal Gathering 8 壬戌 Water Dog 澤地萃 26 十九 4	水6 Water Peel 7 癸亥 Water Pig 山地剝 27 二十 6	水1 Water Earth 6 甲子 Wood Rat 坤爲地 28 廿一 1	木3 Wood Biting 5 乙丑 Wood Ox 火雷噬嗑 29 廿二 6	火2 Fire Family 4 丙寅 Fire Tiger 風火家人 30 廿三 4	

DECEMBER 2018 甲子

Xuan Kong Element 玄空五行	坤爲地 Earth	Period Luck 卦運	Monthly Star 月星
Water 水1		1	4

SUNDAY	MONDAY	TUESDAY	WEDNESDAY	THURSDAY	FRIDAY	SATURDAY
木8 Wood Relief 9 丙申 Fire Monkey 雷水解 30 廿四 4	金4 Metal Influence 1 丁酉 Fire Rooster 澤山咸 31 廿五 9					水6 Water Decreasing 3 丁卯 Fire Rabbit 山澤損 1 廿四 9
金9 Metal Tread 2 戊辰 Earth Dragon 天澤履 2 廿五 6	木8 Wood Great Strength 1 己巳 Earth Snake 雷天大壯 3 廿六 2	木8 Wood Consistency 9 庚午 Metal Horse 雷風恆 4 廿七 9	金9 Metal Litigation 8 辛未 Metal Goat 天水訟 5 廿八 3	水1 Water Officer 7 壬申 Water Monkey 地水師 6 廿九 7	火2 Fire Gradual Progress 6 癸酉 Water Rooster 風山漸 7 十一月初一 7	火7 Fire Obstruction 5 甲戌 Wood Dog 水山蹇 8 初二 2
木3 Wood Advancement 4 乙亥 Wood Pig 火地晉 9 初三 3	水6 Water Nourish 3 丙子 Fire Rat 山雷頤 10 初四 3	金4 Metal Following 2 丁丑 Fire Ox 澤雷隨 11 初五 7	木8 Wood Abundance 1 戊寅 Earth Tiger 雷火豐 12 初六 6	火7 Fire Regulate 9 己卯 Earth Rabbit 水澤節 13 初七 8	水1 Water Unity 8 庚辰 Metal Dragon 地天泰 14 初八 9	木3 Wood Great Reward 7 辛巳 Metal Snake 火天大有 15 初九 7
火2 Fire Wind 6 壬午 Water Horse 巽爲風 16 初十 1	金4 Metal Trap 5 癸未 Water Goat 澤水困 17 十一 8	木3 Wood Not Yet Accomplished 4 甲申 Wood Monkey 火水未濟 18 十二 9	金9 Metal Retreat 3 乙酉 Wood Rooster 天山遯 19 十三 4	水6 Water Mountain 2 丙戌 Fire Dog 艮爲山 20 十四 1	木8 Wood Delight 1 丁亥 Fire Pig 雷地豫 21 十五 8	火7 Fire Beginning 9/1 戊子 Earth Rat 水雷屯 22 十六 4
金9 Metal Without Wrongdoing 2 己丑 Earth Ox 天雷無妄 23 十七 2	木3 Wood Fire 3 庚寅 Metal Tiger 離爲火 24 十八 1	火2 Fire Sincerity 4 辛卯 Metal Rabbit 風澤中孚 25 十九 3	水6 Water Big Livestock 5 壬辰 Water Dragon 山天大畜 26 二十 4	金4 Metal Eliminating 6 癸巳 Water Snake 澤天夬 27 廿一 6	金9 Metal Heaven 7 甲午 Wood Horse 乾爲天 28 廿二 1	火7 Fire Well 8 乙未 Wood Goat 水風井 29 廿三 6

2019 己亥

(*Ji Hai*) Earth Pig

2019 己亥 *(Ji Hai)* Earth Pig

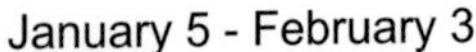

January 5 - February 3

木**3** Wood

乙丑 Wood Ox

6 Biting

火雷噬嗑

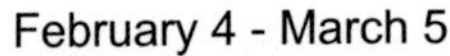

February 4 - March 5

火**2** Fire

丙寅 Fire Tiger

4 Family

風火家人

March 6 - April 4

April 5 - May 5

SE S SW
8 4 6
E 7 9 2 W
3 5 1
NE N NW
Three Killings South
金9 Metal
戊辰
Earth Dragon
6
Tread
天澤履

May 6 - June 5

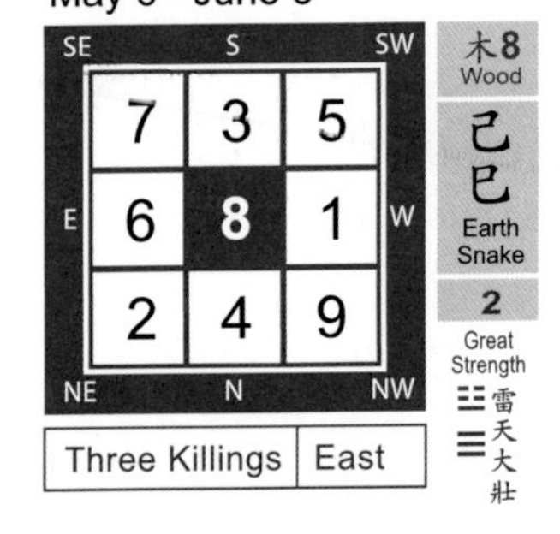

木**8** Wood

己巳 Earth Snake

2 Great Strength

雷天大壯

June 6 - July 6

木**8** Wood

庚午 Metal Horse

9 Consistency

雷風恆

July 7 - August 7

辛未 Metal Goat

3 Litigation

天水訟

August 8 - September 7

水**1** Water

壬申 Water Monkey

7 Officer

地水師

September 8 - October 7

火**2** Fire

癸酉 Water Rooster

7 Gradual Progress

風山漸

October 8 - November 7

November 8 - December 6

December 7 - January 5

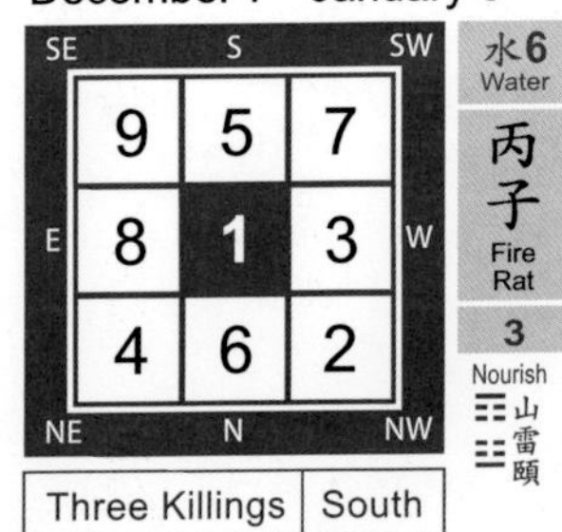

JANUARY 2019 乙丑

Xuan Kong Element 玄空五行	火雷噬嗑 Biting	Period Luck 卦運	Monthly Star 月星
Wood 木3		6	3

SUNDAY	MONDAY	TUESDAY	WEDNESDAY	THURSDAY	FRIDAY	SATURDAY
		水1 Water 2 Humility 地山謙 戊戌 Earth Dog 6 **1** 廿六	火2 Fire 3 Observation 風地觀 己亥 Earth Pig 2 **2** 廿七	火2 Fire 4 Increasing 風雷益 庚子 Metal Rat 9 **3** 廿八	水1 Water 5 Dimming Light 地火明夷 辛丑 Metal Ox 3 **4** 廿九	金9 Metal 6 Fellowship 天火同人 壬寅 Water Tiger 7 **5** 三十
木8 Wood 7 Marrying Maiden 雷澤歸妹 癸卯 Water Rabbit 7 **6** 十二月初一	木3 Wood 8 Opposition 火澤睽 甲辰 Wood Dragon 2 **7** 初二	火7 Fire 9 Waiting 水天需 乙巳 Wood Snake 3 **8** 初三	金4 Metal 1 Great Exceeding 澤風大過 丙午 Fire Horse 3 **9** 初四	水6 Water 2 Poison 山風蠱 丁未 Fire Goat 7 **10** 初五	火2 Fire 3 Dispersing 風水渙 戊申 Earth Monkey 6 **11** 初六	木3 Wood 4 Travelling 火山旅 己酉 Earth Rooster 8 **12** 初七
金9 Metal 5 Stagnation 天地否 庚戌 Metal Dog 9 **13** 初八	火7 Fire 6 Alliance 水地比 辛亥 Metal Pig 7 **14** 初九	木8 Wood 7 Thunder 震爲雷 壬子 Water Rat 1 **15** 初十	水6 Water 8 Beauty 山火賁 癸丑 Water Ox 8 **16** 十一	火7 Fire 9 Accomplished 水火既濟 甲寅 Wood Tiger 9 **17** 十二	水1 Water 1 Arriving 地澤臨 乙卯 Wood Rabbit 4 **18** 十三	金4 Metal 2 Marsh 兑爲澤 丙辰 Fire Dragon 1 **19** 十四
火2 Fire 3 Small Livestock 風天小畜 丁巳 Fire Snake 8 **20** 十五	木3 Wood 4 The Cauldron 火風鼎 戊午 Earth Horse 4 **21** 十六	水1 Water 5 Rising 地風升 己未 Earth Goat 2 **22** 十七	火7 Fire 6 Water 坎爲水 庚申 Metal Monkey 1 **23** 十八	木8 Wood 7 Lesser Exceeding 雷山小過 辛酉 Metal Rooster 3 **24** 十九	金4 Metal 8 Gathering 澤地萃 壬戌 Water Dog 4 **25** 二十	水6 Water 9 Peel 山地剝 癸亥 Water Pig 6 **26** 廿一
水1 Water 1 Earth 坤爲地 甲子 Wood Rat 1 **27** 廿二	木3 Wood 2 Biting 火雷噬嗑 乙丑 Wood Ox 6 **28** 廿三	火2 Fire 3 Family 風火家人 丙寅 Fire Tiger 4 **29** 廿四	水6 Water 4 Decreasing 山澤損 丁卯 Fire Rabbit 9 **30** 廿五	金9 Metal 5 Tread 天澤履 戊辰 Earth Dragon 6 **31** 廿六		

FEBRUARY 2019 丙寅

Xuan Kong Element 玄空五行	風火家人 Family	Period Luck 卦運	Monthly Star 月星
Fire 火2		4	2

SUNDAY	MONDAY	TUESDAY	WEDNESDAY	THURSDAY	FRIDAY	SATURDAY
					木8 Wood 6 Great Strength 雷天大壯 己巳 Earth Snake 2 **1** 廿七	木8 Wood 7 Consistency 雷風恒 庚午 Metal Horse 9 **2** 廿八
金9 Metal 8 Litigation 天水訟 辛未 Metal Goat 3 **3** 廿九	水1 Water 9 Officer 地水師 壬申 Water Monkey 7 **4** 三十	火2 Fire 1 Gradual Progress 風山漸 癸酉 Water Rooster 7 **5** 正月初一	火7 Fire 2 Obstruction 水山蹇 甲戌 Wood Dog 2 **6** 初二	木3 Wood 3 Advancement 火地晉 乙亥 Wood Pig 3 **7** 初三	水6 Water 4 Nourish 山雷頤 丙子 Fire Rat 3 **8** 初四	金4 Metal 5 Following 澤雷隨 丁丑 Fire Ox 7 **9** 初五
木8 Wood 6 Abundance 雷火豐 戊寅 Earth Tiger 6 **10** 初六	火7 Fire 7 Regulate 水澤節 己卯 Earth Rabbit 8 **11** 初七	水1 Water 8 Unity 地天泰 庚辰 Metal Dragon 9 **12** 初八	木3 Wood 9 Great Reward 火天大有 辛巳 Metal Snake 7 **13** 初九	火2 Fire 1 Wind 巽爲風 壬午 Water Horse 1 **14** 初十	金4 Metal 2 Trap 澤水困 癸未 Water Goat 8 **15** 十一	木3 Wood 3 Not Yet Accomplished 火水未濟 甲申 Wood Monkey 9 **16** 十二
金9 Metal 4 Retreat 天山遯 乙酉 Wood Rooster 4 **17** 十三	水6 Water 5 Mountain 艮爲山 丙戌 Fire Dog 1 **18** 十四	木8 Wood 6 Delight 雷地豫 丁亥 Fire Pig 8 **19** 十五	火7 Fire 7 Beginning 水雷屯 戊子 Earth Rat 4 **20** 十六	金9 Metal 8 Without Wrongdoing 天雷無妄 己丑 Earth Ox 2 **21** 十七	木3 Wood 9 Fire 離爲火 庚寅 Metal Tiger 1 **22** 十八	火2 Fire 1 Sincerity 風澤中孚 辛卯 Metal Rabbit 3 **23** 十九
水6 Water 2 Big Livestock 山天大畜 壬辰 Water Dragon 4 **24** 二十	金4 Metal 3 Eliminating 澤天夬 癸巳 Water Snake 6 **25** 廿一	金9 Metal 4 Heaven 乾爲天 甲午 Wood Horse 1 **26** 廿二	火7 Fire 5 Well 水風井 乙未 Wood Goat 6 **27** 廿三	木8 Wood 6 Relief 雷水解 丙申 Fire Monkey 4 **28** 廿四		

MARCH 2019 丁卯

Xuan Kong Element 玄空五行	山澤損 Decreasing	Period Luck 卦運	Monthly Star 月星
Water 水6		9	1

SUNDAY	MONDAY	TUESDAY	WEDNESDAY	THURSDAY	FRIDAY	SATURDAY
水6 Water Decreasing 1 山澤損 丁卯 Fire Rabbit 9 **31** 廿六					金4 Metal Influence 7 澤山咸 丁酉 Fire Rooster 9 **1** 廿五	水1 Water Humility 8 地山謙 戊戌 Earth Dog 6 **2** 廿六
火2 Fire Observation 9 風地觀 己亥 Earth Pig 2 **3** 廿七	火2 Fire Increasing 1 風雷益 庚子 Metal Rat 9 **4** 廿八	水1 Water Dimming Light 2 地火明夷 辛丑 Metal Ox 3 **5** 廿九	金9 Metal Fellowship 3 天火同人 壬寅 Water Tiger 7 **6** 二月初一	木8 Wood Marrying Maiden 4 雷澤歸妹 癸卯 Water Rabbit 7 **7** 初二	木3 Wood Opposition 5 火澤睽 甲辰 Wood Dragon 2 **8** 初三	火7 Fire Waiting 6 水天需 乙巳 Wood Snake 3 **9** 初四
金4 Metal Great Exceeding 7 澤風大過 丙午 Fire Horse 3 **10** 初五	水6 Water Poison 8 山風蠱 丁未 Fire Goat 7 **11** 初六	火2 Fire Dispersing 9 風水渙 戊申 Earth Monkey 6 **12** 初七	木3 Wood Travelling 1 火山旅 己酉 Earth Rooster 8 **13** 初八	金9 Metal Stagnation 2 天地否 庚戌 Metal Dog 9 **14** 初九	火7 Fire Alliance 3 水地比 辛亥 Metal Pig 7 **15** 初十	木8 Wood Thunder 4 震爲雷 壬子 Water Rat 1 **16** 十一
水6 Water Beauty 5 山火賁 癸丑 Water Ox 8 **17** 十二	火7 Fire Accomplished 6 水火既濟 甲寅 Wood Tiger 9 **18** 十三	水1 Water Arriving 7 地澤臨 乙卯 Wood Rabbit 4 **19** 十四	金4 Metal Marsh 8 兑爲澤 丙辰 Fire Dragon 1 **20** 十五	火2 Fire Small Livestock 9 風天小畜 丁巳 Fire Snake 8 **21** 十六	木3 Wood The Cauldron 1 火風鼎 戊午 Earth Horse 4 **22** 十七	水1 Water Rising 2 地風升 己未 Earth Goat 2 **23** 十八
火7 Fire Water 3 坎爲水 庚申 Metal Monkey 1 **24** 十九	木8 Wood Lesser Exceeding 4 雷山小過 辛酉 Metal Rooster 3 **25** 二十	金4 Metal Gathering 5 澤地萃 壬戌 Water Dog 4 **26** 廿一	水6 Water Peel 6 山地剝 癸亥 Water Pig 6 **27** 廿二	水1 Water Earth 7 坤爲地 甲子 Wood Rat 1 **28** 廿三	木3 Wood Biting 8 火雷噬嗑 乙丑 Wood Ox 6 **29** 廿四	火2 Fire Family 9 風火家人 丙寅 Fire Tiger 4 **30** 廿五

APRIL 2019 戊辰

Xuan Kong Element 玄空五行	天澤履 Tread	Period Luck 卦運	Monthly Star 月星
Metal 金9		6	9

SUNDAY	MONDAY	TUESDAY	WEDNESDAY	THURSDAY	FRIDAY	SATURDAY
	金9 Metal Tread 2 天澤履 戊辰 Earth Dragon 6 **1** 廿七	木8 Wood Great Strength 3 雷天大壯 己巳 Earth Snake 2 **2** 廿八	木8 Wood Consistency 4 雷風恆 庚午 Metal Horse 9 **3** 廿九	金9 Metal Litigation 5 天水訟 辛未 Metal Goat 3 **4** 三十	水1 Water Officer 6 地水師 壬申 Water Monkey 7 **5** 三月初一	火2 Fire Gradual Progress 7 風山漸 癸酉 Water Rooster 7 **6** 初二
火7 Fire Obstruction 8 水山蹇 甲戌 Wood Dog 2 **7** 初三	木3 Wood Advancement 9 火地晉 乙亥 Wood Pig 3 **8** 初四	水6 Water Nourish 1 山雷頤 丙子 Fire Rat 3 **9** 初五	金4 Metal Following 2 澤雷隨 丁丑 Fire Ox 7 **10** 初六	木8 Wood Abundance 3 雷火豐 戊寅 Earth Tiger 6 **11** 初七	火7 Fire Regulate 4 水澤節 己卯 Earth Rabbit 8 **12** 初八	水1 Water Unity 5 地天泰 庚辰 Metal Dragon 9 **13** 初九
木3 Wood Great Reward 6 火天大有 辛巳 Metal Snake 7 **14** 初十	火2 Fire Wind 7 巽爲風 壬午 Water Horse 1 **15** 十一	金4 Metal Trap 8 澤水困 癸未 Water Goat 8 **16** 十二	木3 Wood Not Yet Accomplished 9 火水未濟 甲申 Wood Monkey 9 **17** 十三	金9 Metal Retreat 1 天山遯 乙酉 Wood Rooster 4 **18** 十四	水6 Water Mountain 2 艮爲山 丙戌 Fire Dog 1 **19** 十五	木8 Wood Delight 3 雷地豫 丁亥 Fire Pig 8 **20** 十六
火7 Fire Beginning 4 水雷屯 戊子 Earth Rat 4 **21** 十七	金9 Metal Without Wrongdoing 5 天雷無妄 己丑 Earth Ox 2 **22** 十八	木3 Wood Fire 6 離爲火 庚寅 Metal Tiger 1 **23** 十九	火2 Fire Sincerity 7 風澤中孚 辛卯 Metal Rabbit 3 **24** 二十	水6 Water Big Livestock 8 山天大畜 壬辰 Water Dragon 4 **25** 廿一	金4 Metal Eliminating 9 澤天夬 癸巳 Water Snake 6 **26** 廿二	金9 Metal Heaven 1 乾爲天 甲午 Wood Horse 1 **27** 廿三
火7 Fire Well 2 水風井 乙未 Wood Goat 6 **28** 廿四	木8 Wood Relief 3 雷水解 丙申 Fire Monkey 4 **29** 廿五	金4 Metal Influence 4 澤山咸 丁酉 Fire Rooster 9 **30** 廿六				

MAY 2019 己巳

Xuan Kong Element 玄空五行	雷天大壯 Great Strength	Period Luck 卦運	Monthly Star 月星
Wood 木8		2	8

SUNDAY	MONDAY	TUESDAY	WEDNESDAY	THURSDAY	FRIDAY	SATURDAY
			水1 Water · 5 Humility 戊戌 Earth Dog 地山謙 **1** 廿七 6	火2 Fire · 6 Observation 己亥 Earth Pig 風地觀 **2** 廿八 2	火2 Fire · 7 Increasing 庚子 Metal Rat 風雷益 **3** 廿九 9	水1 Water · 8 Dimming Light 辛丑 Metal Ox 地火明夷 **4** 三十 3
金9 Metal · 9 Fellowship 壬寅 Water Tiger 天火同人 **5** 四月初一 7	木8 Wood · 1 Marrying Maiden 癸卯 Water Rabbit 雷澤歸妹 **6** 初二 7	木3 Wood · 2 Opposition 甲辰 Wood Dragon 火澤睽 **7** 初三 2	火7 Fire · 3 Waiting 乙巳 Wood Snake 水天需 **8** 初四 3	金4 Metal · 4 Great Exceeding 丙午 Fire Horse 澤風大過 **9** 初五 3	水6 Water · 5 Poison 丁未 Fire Goat 山風蠱 **10** 初六 7	火2 Fire · 6 Dispersing 戊申 Earth Monkey 風水渙 **11** 初七 6
木3 Wood · 7 Travelling 己酉 Earth Rooster 火山旅 **12** 初八 8	金9 Metal · 8 Stagnation 庚戌 Metal Dog 天地否 **13** 初九 9	火7 Fire · 9 Alliance 辛亥 Metal Pig 水地比 **14** 初十 7	木8 Wood · 1 Thunder 壬子 Water Rat 震爲雷 **15** 十一 1	水6 Water · 2 Beauty 癸丑 Water Ox 山火賁 **16** 十二 8	火7 Fire · 3 Accomplished 甲寅 Wood Tiger 水火既濟 **17** 十三 9	水1 Water · 4 Arriving 乙卯 Wood Rabbit 地澤臨 **18** 十四 4
金4 Metal · 5 Marsh 丙辰 Fire Dragon 兑爲澤 **19** 十五 1	火2 Fire · 6 Small Livestock 丁巳 Fire Snake 風天小畜 **20** 十六 8	木3 Wood · 7 The Cauldron 戊午 Earth Horse 火風鼎 **21** 十七 4	水1 Water · 8 Rising 己未 Earth Goat 地風升 **22** 十八 2	火7 Fire · 9 Water 庚申 Metal Monkey 坎爲水 **23** 十九 1	木8 Wood · 1 Lesser Exceeding 辛酉 Metal Rooster 雷山小過 **24** 二十 3	金4 Metal · 2 Gathering 壬戌 Water Dog 澤地萃 **25** 廿一 4
水6 Water · 3 Peel 癸亥 Water Pig 山地剝 **26** 廿二 6	水1 Water · 4 Earth 甲子 Wood Rat 坤爲地 **27** 廿三 1	木3 Wood · 5 Biting 乙丑 Wood Ox 火雷噬嗑 **28** 廿四 6	火2 Fire · 6 Family 丙寅 Fire Tiger 風火家人 **29** 廿五 4	水6 Water · 7 Decreasing 丁卯 Fire Rabbit 山澤損 **30** 廿六 9	金9 Metal · 8 Tread 戊辰 Earth Dragon 天澤履 **31** 廿七 6	

JUNE 2019 庚午

Xuan Kong Element 玄空五行	雷風恆 Consistency	Period Luck 卦運	Monthly Star 月星
Wood 木8		9	7

SUNDAY	MONDAY	TUESDAY	WEDNESDAY	THURSDAY	FRIDAY	SATURDAY
水1 Water · 8 Humility 戊戌 Earth Dog 地山謙 **30** 廿八 6						木8 Wood · 9 Great Strength 己巳 Earth Snake 雷天大壯 **1** 廿八 2
木8 Wood · 1 Consistency 庚午 Metal Horse 雷風恆 **2** 廿九 9	金9 Metal · 2 Litigation 辛未 Metal Goat 天水訟 **3** 五月初一 3	水1 Water · 3 Officer 壬申 Water Monkey 地水師 **4** 初二 7	火2 Fire · 4 Gradual Progress 癸酉 Water Rooster 風山漸 **5** 初三 7	火7 Fire · 5 Obstruction 甲戌 Wood Dog 水山蹇 **6** 初四 2	木3 Wood · 6 Advancement 乙亥 Wood Pig 火地晉 **7** 初五 3	水6 Water · 7 Nourish 丙子 Fire Rat 山雷頤 **8** 初六 3
金4 Metal · 8 Following 丁丑 Fire Ox 澤雷隨 **9** 初七 7	木8 Wood · 9 Abundance 戊寅 Earth Tiger 雷火豐 **10** 初八 6	火7 Fire · 1 Regulate 己卯 Earth Rabbit 水澤節 **11** 初九 8	水1 Water · 2 Unity 庚辰 Metal Dragon 地天泰 **12** 初十 9	木3 Wood · 3 Great Reward 辛巳 Metal Snake 火天大有 **13** 十一 7	火2 Fire · 4 Wind 壬午 Water Horse 巽爲風 **14** 十二 1	金4 Metal · 5 Trap 癸未 Water Goat 澤水困 **15** 十三 8
木3 Wood · 6 Not Yet Accomplished 甲申 Wood Monkey 火水未濟 **16** 十四 9	金9 Metal · 7 Retreat 乙酉 Wood Rooster 天山遯 **17** 十五 4	水6 Water · 8 Mountain 丙戌 Fire Dog 艮爲山 **18** 十六 1	木8 Wood · 9 Delight 丁亥 Fire Pig 雷地豫 **19** 十七 8	火7 Fire · 1 Beginning 戊子 Earth Rat 水雷屯 **20** 十八 4	金9 Metal · 2/8 Without Wrongdoing 己丑 Earth Ox 天雷無妄 **21** 十九 2	木3 Wood · 7 Fire 庚寅 Metal Tiger 離爲火 **22** 二十 1
火2 Fire · 6 Sincerity 辛卯 Metal Rabbit 風澤中孚 **23** 廿一 3	水6 Water · 5 Big Livestock 壬辰 Water Dragon 山天大畜 **24** 廿二 4	金4 Metal · 4 Eliminating 癸巳 Water Snake 澤天夬 **25** 廿三 6	金9 Metal · 3 Heaven 甲午 Wood Horse 乾爲天 **26** 廿四 1	火7 Fire · 2 Well 乙未 Wood Goat 水風井 **27** 廿五 6	木8 Wood · 1 Relief 丙申 Fire Monkey 雷水解 **28** 廿六 4	金4 Metal · 9 Influence 丁酉 Fire Rooster 澤山咸 **29** 廿七 9

JULY 2019 辛未

Xuan Kong Element 玄空五行	天水訟 Litigation	Period Luck 卦運	Monthly Star 月星
Metal 金9		3	6

SUNDAY	MONDAY	TUESDAY	WEDNESDAY	THURSDAY	FRIDAY	SATURDAY
	火2 Fire · 7 Observation 風地觀 己亥 Earth Pig **1** 廿九 2	火2 Fire · 6 Increasing 風雷益 庚子 Metal Rat **2** 三十 9	水1 Water · 5 Dimming Light 地火明夷 辛丑 Metal Ox **3** 六月初一 3	金9 Metal · 4 Fellowship 天火同人 壬寅 Water Tiger **4** 初二 7	木8 Wood · 3 Marrying Maiden 雷澤歸妹 癸卯 Water Rabbit **5** 初三 7	木3 Wood · 2 Opposition 火澤睽 甲辰 Wood Dragon **6** 初四 2
火7 Fire · 1 Waiting 水天需 乙巳 Wood Snake **7** 初五 3	金4 Metal · 9 Great Exceeding 澤風大過 丙午 Fire Horse **8** 初六 3	水6 Water · 8 Poison 山風蠱 丁未 Fire Goat **9** 初七 7	火2 Fire · 7 Dispersing 風水渙 戊申 Earth Monkey **10** 初八 6	木3 Wood · 6 Travelling 火山旅 己酉 Earth Rooster **11** 初九 8	金9 Metal · 5 Stagnation 天地否 庚戌 Metal Dog **12** 初十 9	火7 Fire · 4 Alliance 水地比 辛亥 Metal Pig **13** 十一 7
木8 Wood · 3 Thunder 震爲雷 壬子 Water Rat **14** 十二 1	水6 Water · 2 Beauty 山火賁 癸丑 Water Ox **15** 十三 8	火7 Fire · 1 Accomplished 水火既濟 甲寅 Wood Tiger **16** 十四 9	水1 Water · 9 Arriving 地澤臨 乙卯 Wood Rabbit **17** 十五 1	金4 Metal · 8 Marsh 兑爲澤 丙辰 Fire Dragon **18** 十六 1	火2 Fire · 7 Small Livestock 風天小畜 丁巳 Fire Snake **19** 十七 8	木3 Wood · 6 The Cauldron 火風鼎 戊午 Earth Horse **20** 十八 4
水1 Water · 5 Rising 地風升 己未 Earth Goat **21** 十九 2	火7 Fire · 4 Water 坎爲水 庚申 Metal Monkey **22** 二十 1	木8 Wood · 3 Lesser Exceeding 雷山小過 辛酉 Metal Rooster **23** 廿一 3	金4 Metal · 2 Gathering 澤地萃 壬戌 Water Dog **24** 廿二 4	水6 Water · 1 Peel 山地剝 癸亥 Water Pig **25** 廿三 6	水1 Water · 9 Earth 坤爲地 甲子 Wood Rat **26** 廿四 1	木3 Wood · 8 Biting 火雷噬嗑 乙丑 Wood Ox **27** 廿五 6
火2 Fire · 7 Family 風火家人 丙寅 Fire Tiger **28** 廿六 4	水6 Water · 6 Decreasing 山澤損 丁卯 Fire Rabbit **29** 廿七 9	金9 Metal · 5 Tread 天澤履 戊辰 Earth Dragon **30** 廿八 6	木8 Wood · 4 Great Strength 雷天大壯 己巳 Earth Snake **31** 廿九 2			

AUGUST 2019 壬申

Xuan Kong Element 玄空五行	地水師 Officer	Period Luck 卦運	Monthly Star 月星
Water 水1		7	5

SUNDAY	MONDAY	TUESDAY	WEDNESDAY	THURSDAY	FRIDAY	SATURDAY
				木8 Wood · 3 Consistency 雷風恆 庚午 Metal Horse **1** 七月初一 9	金9 Metal · 2 Litigation 天水訟 辛未 Metal Goat **2** 初二 3	水1 Water · 1 Officer 地水師 壬申 Water Monkey **3** 初三 7
火2 Fire · 9 Gradual Progress 風山漸 癸酉 Water Rooster **4** 初四 7	火7 Fire · 8 Obstruction 水山蹇 甲戌 Wood Dog **5** 初五 2	木3 Wood · 7 Advancement 火地晉 乙亥 Wood Pig **6** 初六 3	水6 Water · 6 Nourish 山雷頤 丙子 Fire Rat **7** 初七 3	金4 Metal · 5 Following 澤雷隨 丁丑 Fire Ox **8** 初八 7	木8 Wood · 4 Abundance 雷火豐 戊寅 Earth Tiger **9** 初九 6	火7 Fire · 3 Regulate 水澤節 己卯 Earth Rabbit **10** 初十 8
水1 Water · 2 Unity 地天泰 庚辰 Metal Dragon **11** 十一 9	木3 Wood · 1 Great Reward 火天大有 辛巳 Metal Snake **12** 十二 7	火2 Fire · 9 Wind 巽爲風 壬午 Water Horse **13** 十三 1	金4 Metal · 8 Trap 澤水困 癸未 Water Goat **14** 十四 8	木3 Wood · 7 Not Yet Accomplished 火水未濟 甲申 Wood Monkey **15** 十五 9	金9 Metal · 6 Retreat 天山遯 乙酉 Wood Rooster **16** 十六 4	水6 Water · 5 Mountain 艮爲山 丙戌 Fire Dog **17** 十七 1
木8 Wood · 4 Delight 雷地豫 丁亥 Fire Pig **18** 十八 8	火7 Fire · 3 Beginning 水雷屯 戊子 Earth Rat **19** 十九 4	金9 Metal · 2 Without Wrongdoing 天雷無妄 己丑 Earth Ox **20** 二十 2	木3 Wood · 1 Fire 離爲火 庚寅 Metal Tiger **21** 廿一 1	火2 Fire · 9 Sincerity 風澤中孚 辛卯 Metal Rabbit **22** 廿二 3	水6 Water · 8 Big Livestock 山天大畜 壬辰 Water Dragon **23** 廿三 4	金4 Metal · 7 Eliminating 澤天夬 癸巳 Water Snake **24** 廿四 6
金9 Metal · 6 Heaven 乾爲天 甲午 Wood Horse **25** 廿五 1	火7 Fire · 5 Well 水風井 乙未 Wood Goat **26** 廿六 6	木8 Wood · 4 Relief 雷水解 丙申 Fire Monkey **27** 廿七 4	金4 Metal · 3 Influence 澤山咸 丁酉 Fire Rooster **28** 廿八 9	水1 Water · 2 Humility 地山謙 戊戌 Earth Dog **29** 廿九 6	火2 Fire · 1 Observation 風地觀 己亥 Earth Pig **30** 八月初一 2	火2 Fire · 9 Increasing 風雷益 庚子 Metal Rat **31** 初二 9

SEPTEMBER 2019 癸酉

Xuan Kong Element 玄空五行	風山漸 Gradual Progress	Period Luck 卦運	Monthly Star 月星
Fire 火2		7	4

SUNDAY	MONDAY	TUESDAY	WEDNESDAY	THURSDAY	FRIDAY	SATURDAY
水1 Water Dimming Light 8 辛丑 Metal Ox 地火明夷 1 初三 3	金9 Metal Fellowship 7 壬寅 Water Tiger 天火同人 2 初四 7	木8 Wood Marrying Maiden 6 癸卯 Water Rabbit 雷澤歸妹 3 初五 7	木3 Wood Opposition 5 甲辰 Wood Dragon 火澤睽 4 初六 2	火7 Fire Waiting 4 乙巳 Wood Snake 水天需 5 初七 3	金4 Metal Great Exceeding 3 丙午 Fire Horse 澤風大過 6 初八 3	水6 Water Poison 2 丁未 Fire Goat 山風蠱 7 初九 7
火2 Fire Dispersing 1 戊申 Earth Monkey 風水渙 8 初十 6	木3 Wood Travelling 9 己酉 Earth Rooster 火山旅 9 十一 8	金9 Metal Stagnation 8 庚戌 Metal Dog 天地否 10 十二 9	火7 Fire Alliance 7 辛亥 Metal Pig 水地比 11 十三 7	木8 Wood Thunder 6 壬子 Water Rat 震爲雷 12 十四 1	水6 Water Beauty 5 癸丑 Water Ox 山火賁 13 十五 8	火7 Fire Accomplished 4 甲寅 Wood Tiger 水火既濟 14 十六 9
水1 Water Arriving 3 乙卯 Wood Rabbit 地澤臨 15 十七 4	金4 Metal Marsh 2 丙辰 Fire Dragon 兑爲澤 16 十八 1	火2 Fire Small Livestock 1 丁巳 Fire Snake 風天小畜 17 十九 8	木3 Wood The Cauldron 9 戊午 Earth Horse 火風鼎 18 二十 4	水1 Water Rising 8 己未 Earth Goat 地風升 19 廿一 2	火7 Fire Water 7 庚申 Metal Monkey 坎爲水 20 廿二 1	木8 Wood Lesser Exceeding 6 辛酉 Metal Rooster 雷山小過 21 廿三 3
金4 Metal Gathering 5 壬戌 Water Dog 澤地萃 22 廿四 4	水6 Water Peel 4 癸亥 Water Pig 山地剝 23 廿五 6	水1 Water Earth 3 甲子 Wood Rat 坤爲地 24 廿六 1	木3 Wood Biting 2 乙丑 Wood Ox 火雷噬嗑 25 廿七 6	火2 Fire Family 1 丙寅 Fire Tiger 風火家人 26 廿八 4	水6 Water Decreasing 9 丁卯 Fire Rabbit 山澤損 27 廿九 9	金9 Metal Tread 8 戊辰 Earth Dragon 天澤履 28 三十 6
木8 Wood Great Strength 7 己巳 Earth Snake 雷天大壯 29 九月初一 2	木8 Wood Consistency 6 庚午 Metal Horse 雷風恒 30 初二 9					

OCTOBER 2019 甲戌

Xuan Kong Element 玄空五行	水山蹇 Obstruction	Period Luck 卦運	Monthly Star 月星
Fire 火7		2	3

SUNDAY	MONDAY	TUESDAY	WEDNESDAY	THURSDAY	FRIDAY	SATURDAY
		金9 Metal Litigation 5 辛未 Metal Goat 天水訟 1 初三 3	水1 Water Officer 4 壬申 Water Monkey 地水師 2 初四 7	火2 Fire Gradual Progress 3 癸酉 Water Rooster 風山漸 3 初五 7	火7 Fire Obstruction 2 甲戌 Wood Dog 水山蹇 4 初六 2	木3 Wood Advancement 1 乙亥 Wood Pig 火地晉 5 初七 3
水6 Water Nourish 9 丙子 Fire Rat 山雷頤 6 初八 3	金4 Metal Following 8 丁丑 Fire Ox 澤雷隨 7 初九 7	木8 Wood Abundance 7 戊寅 Earth Tiger 雷火豐 8 初十 6	火7 Fire Regulate 6 己卯 Earth Rabbit 水澤節 9 十一 8	水1 Water Unity 5 庚辰 Metal Dragon 地天泰 10 十二 9	木3 Wood Great Reward 4 辛巳 Metal Snake 火天大有 11 十三 7	火2 Fire Wind 3 壬午 Water Horse 巽爲風 12 十四 1
金4 Metal Trap 2 癸未 Water Goat 澤水困 13 十五 8	木3 Wood Not Yet Accomplished 1 甲申 Wood Monkey 火水未濟 14 十六 9	金9 Metal Retreat 9 乙酉 Wood Rooster 天山遯 15 十七 4	水6 Water Mountain 8 丙戌 Fire Dog 艮爲山 16 十八 1	木8 Wood Delight 7 丁亥 Fire Pig 雷地豫 17 十九 8	火7 Fire Beginning 6 戊子 Earth Rat 水雷屯 18 二十 4	金9 Metal Without Wrongdoing 5 己丑 Earth Ox 天雷無妄 19 廿一 2
木3 Wood Fire 4 庚寅 Metal Tiger 離爲火 20 廿二 1	火2 Fire Sincerity 3 辛卯 Metal Rabbit 風澤中孚 21 廿三 3	水6 Water Big Livestock 2 壬辰 Water Dragon 山天大畜 22 廿四 4	金4 Metal Eliminating 1 癸巳 Water Snake 澤天夬 23 廿五 6	金9 Metal Heaven 9 甲午 Wood Horse 乾爲天 24 廿六 1	火7 Fire Well 8 乙未 Wood Goat 水風井 25 廿七 6	木8 Wood Relief 7 丙申 Fire Monkey 雷水解 26 廿八 4
金4 Metal Influence 6 丁酉 Fire Rooster 澤山咸 27 廿九 9	水1 Water Humility 5 戊戌 Earth Dog 地山謙 28 十月初一 6	火2 Fire Observation 4 己亥 Earth Pig 風地觀 29 初二 2	火2 Fire Increasing 3 庚子 Metal Rat 風雷益 30 初三 9	水1 Water Dimming Light 2 辛丑 Metal Ox 地火明夷 31 初四 3		

NOVEMBER 2019 乙亥

Xuan Kong Element 玄空五行	火地晉 Advancement	Period Luck 卦運	Monthly Star 月星
Wood 木3		3	2

SUNDAY	MONDAY	TUESDAY	WEDNESDAY	THURSDAY	FRIDAY	SATURDAY
					金9 Metal Fellowship 1 天火同人 壬寅 Water Tiger 7 1 初五	木8 Wood Marrying Maiden 9 雷澤歸妹 癸卯 Water Rabbit 7 2 初六
木3 Wood Opposition 8 火澤睽 甲辰 Wood Dragon 2 3 初七	火7 Fire Waiting 7 水天需 乙巳 Wood Snake 3 4 初八	金4 Metal Great Exceeding 6 澤風大過 丙午 Fire Horse 3 5 初九	水6 Water Poison 5 山風蠱 丁未 Fire Goat 7 6 初十	火2 Fire Dispersing 4 風水渙 戊申 Earth Monkey 6 7 十一	木3 Wood Travelling 3 火山旅 己酉 Earth Rooster 8 8 十二	金9 Metal Stagnation 2 天地否 庚戌 Metal Dog 9 9 十三
火7 Fire Alliance 1 水地比 辛亥 Metal Pig 7 10 十四	木8 Wood Thunder 9 震爲雷 壬子 Water Rat 1 11 十五	水6 Water Beauty 8 山火賁 癸丑 Water Ox 8 12 十六	火7 Fire Accomplished 7 水火既濟 甲寅 Wood Tiger 9 13 十七	水1 Water Arriving 6 地澤臨 乙卯 Wood Rabbit 4 14 十八	金4 Metal Marsh 5 兌爲澤 丙辰 Fire Dragon 1 15 十九	火2 Fire Small Livestock 4 風天小畜 丁巳 Fire Snake 8 16 二十
木3 Wood The Cauldron 3 火風鼎 戊午 Earth Horse 4 17 廿一	水1 Water Rising 2 地風升 己未 Earth Goat 2 18 廿二	火7 Fire Water 1 坎爲水 庚申 Metal Monkey 1 19 廿三	木8 Wood Lesser Exceeding 9 雷山小過 辛酉 Metal Rooster 3 20 廿四	金4 Metal Gathering 8 澤地萃 壬戌 Water Dog 4 21 廿五	水6 Water Peel 7 山地剝 癸亥 Water Pig 6 22 廿六	水1 Water Earth 6 坤爲地 甲子 Wood Rat 1 23 廿七
木3 Wood Biting 5 火雷噬嗑 乙丑 Wood Ox 6 24 廿八	火2 Fire Family 4 風火家人 丙寅 Fire Tiger 4 25 廿九	水6 Water Decreasing 3 山澤損 丁卯 Fire Rabbit 9 26 十一月初一	金9 Metal Tread 2 天澤履 戊辰 Earth Dragon 6 27 初二	木8 Wood Great Strength 1 雷天大壯 己巳 Earth Snake 2 28 初三	木8 Wood Consistency 9 雷風恒 庚午 Metal Horse 9 29 初四	金9 Metal Litigation 8 天水訟 辛未 Metal Goat 3 30 初五

DECEMBER 2019 丙子

Xuan Kong Element 玄空五行	山雷頤 Nourish	Period Luck 卦運	Monthly Star 月星
Water 水6		3	1

SUNDAY	MONDAY	TUESDAY	WEDNESDAY	THURSDAY	FRIDAY	SATURDAY
水1 Water Officer 7 地水師 壬申 Water Monkey 7 1 初六	火2 Fire Gradual Progress 6 風山漸 癸酉 Water Rooster 7 2 初七	火7 Fire Obstruction 5 水山蹇 甲戌 Wood Dog 2 3 初八	木3 Wood Advancement 4 火地晉 乙亥 Wood Pig 3 4 初九	水6 Water Nourish 3 山雷頤 丙子 Fire Rat 3 5 初十	金4 Metal Following 2 澤雷隨 丁丑 Fire Ox 7 6 十一	木8 Wood Abundance 1 雷火豐 戊寅 Earth Tiger 6 7 十二
火7 Fire Regulate 9 水澤節 己卯 Earth Rabbit 8 8 十三	水1 Water Unity 8 地天泰 庚辰 Metal Dragon 9 9 十四	木3 Wood Great Reward 7 火天大有 辛巳 Metal Snake 7 10 十五	火2 Fire Wind 6 巽爲風 壬午 Water Horse 1 11 十六	金4 Metal Trap 5 澤水困 癸未 Water Goat 8 12 十七	木3 Wood Not Yet Accomplished 4 火水未濟 甲申 Wood Monkey 9 13 十八	金9 Metal Retreat 3 天山遯 乙酉 Wood Rooster 4 14 十九
水6 Water Mountain 2 艮爲山 丙戌 Fire Dog 1 15 二十	木8 Wood Delight 1 雷地豫 丁亥 Fire Pig 8 16 廿一	火7 Fire Beginning 9 水雷屯 戊子 Earth Rat 4 17 廿二	金9 Metal Without Wrongdoing 8 天雷無妄 己丑 Earth Ox 2 18 廿三	木3 Wood Fire 7 離爲火 庚寅 Metal Tiger 1 19 廿四	火2 Fire Sincerity 6 風澤中孚 辛卯 Metal Rabbit 3 20 廿五	水6 Water Big Livestock 5 山天大畜 壬辰 Water Dragon 4 21 廿六
金4 Metal Eliminating 4/6 澤天夬 癸巳 Water Snake 6 22 廿七	金9 Metal Heaven 7 乾爲天 甲午 Wood Horse 1 23 廿八	火7 Fire Well 8 水風井 乙未 Wood Goat 6 24 廿九	木8 Wood Relief 9 雷水解 丙申 Fire Monkey 4 25 三十	金4 Metal Influence 1 澤山咸 丁酉 Fire Rooster 9 26 十一月初一	水1 Water Humility 2 地山謙 戊戌 Earth Dog 6 27 初二	火2 Fire Observation 3 風地觀 己亥 Earth Pig 2 28 初三
火2 Fire Increasing 4 風雷益 庚子 Metal Rat 9 29 初四	水1 Water Dimming Light 5 地火明夷 辛丑 Metal Ox 3 30 初五	金9 Metal Fellowship 6 天火同人 壬寅 Water Tiger 7 31 初六				

2020 庚子

(*Geng Zi*) Metal Rat

2020 庚子 *(Geng Zi)* Metal Rat

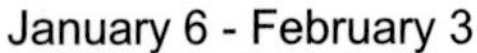

January 6 - February 3

February 4 - March 4

March 5 - April 3

April 4 - May 4

May 5 - June 4

June 5 - July 5

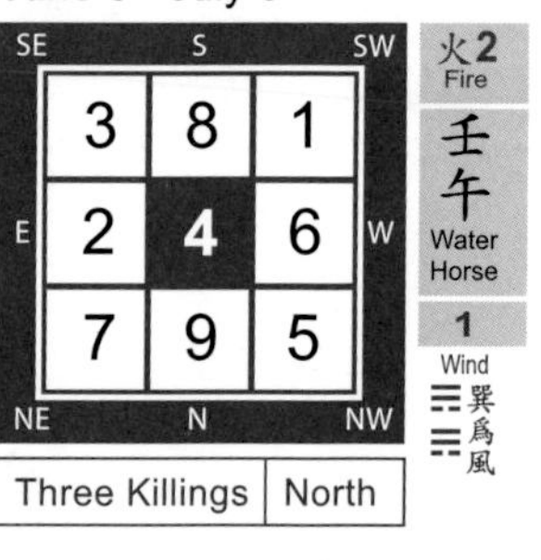

July 6 - August 6

August 7 - September 6

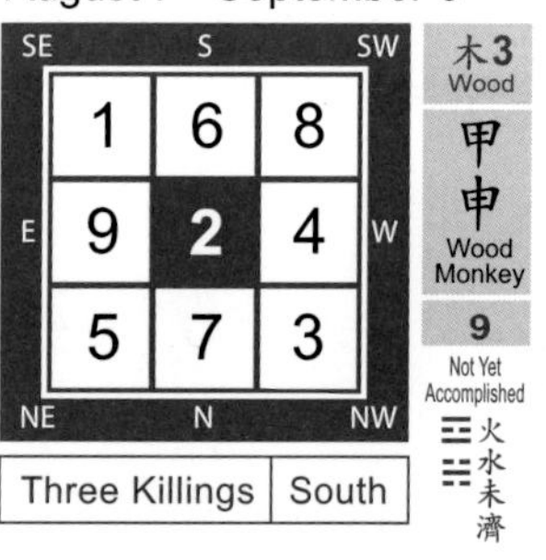

September 7 - October 7

October 8 - November 6

November 7 - December 6

December 7 - January 4

JANUARY 2020 丁丑

Xuan Kong Element 玄空五行	澤雷隨 Following	Period Luck 卦運	Monthly Star 月星
Metal 金4		7	9

SUNDAY	MONDAY	TUESDAY	WEDNESDAY	THURSDAY	FRIDAY	SATURDAY
			1 初七 木8 Wood · 7 Marrying Maiden 雷澤歸妹 癸卯 Water Rabbit 7	**2** 初八 木3 Wood · 8 Opposition 火澤睽 甲辰 Wood Dragon 2	**3** 初九 火7 Fire · 9 Waiting 水天需 乙巳 Wood Snake 3	**4** 初十 金4 Metal · 1 Great Exceeding 澤風大過 丙午 Fire Horse 3
5 十一 水6 Water · 2 Poison 山風蠱 丁未 Fire Goat 7	**6** 十二 火2 Fire · 3 Dispersing 風水渙 戊申 Earth Monkey 6	**7** 十三 木3 Wood · 4 Travelling 火山旅 己酉 Earth Rooster 8	**8** 十四 金9 Metal · 5 Stagnation 天地否 庚戌 Metal Dog 9	**9** 十五 火7 Fire · 6 Alliance 水地比 辛亥 Metal Pig 7	**10** 十六 木8 Wood · 7 Thunder 震為雷 壬子 Water Rat 1	**11** 十七 水6 Water · 8 Beauty 山火賁 癸丑 Water Ox 8
12 十八 火7 Fire · 9 Accomplished 水火既濟 甲寅 Wood Tiger 9	**13** 十九 水1 Water · 1 Arriving 地澤臨 乙卯 Wood Rabbit 4	**14** 二十 金4 Metal · 2 Marsh 兌為澤 丙辰 Fire Dragon 1	**15** 廿一 火2 Fire · 3 Small Livestock 風天小畜 丁巳 Fire Snake 8	**16** 廿二 木3 Wood · 4 The Cauldron 火風鼎 戊午 Earth Horse 4	**17** 廿三 水1 Water · 5 Rising 地風升 己未 Earth Goat 2	**18** 廿四 火7 Fire · 6 Water 坎為水 庚申 Metal Monkey 1
19 廿五 木8 Wood · 7 Lesser Exceeding 雷山小過 辛酉 Metal Rooster 3	**20** 廿六 金4 Metal · 8 Gathering 澤地萃 壬戌 Water Dog 4	**21** 廿七 水6 Water · 9 Peel 山地剝 癸亥 Water Pig 6	**22** 廿八 水1 Water · 1 Earth 坤為地 甲子 Wood Rat 1	**23** 廿九 木3 Wood · 2 Biting 火雷噬嗑 乙丑 Wood Ox 6	**24** 三十 火2 Fire · 3 Family 風火家人 丙寅 Fire Tiger 4	**25** 正月初一 水6 Water · 4 Decreasing 山澤損 丁卯 Fire Rabbit 9
26 初二 金9 Metal · 5 Tread 天澤履 戊辰 Earth Dragon 6	**27** 初三 木8 Wood · 6 Great Strength 雷天大壯 己巳 Earth Snake 2	**28** 初四 木8 Wood · 7 Consistency 雷風恆 庚午 Metal Horse 9	**29** 初五 金9 Metal · 8 Litigation 天水訟 辛未 Metal Goat 3	**30** 初六 水1 Water · 9 Officer 地水師 壬申 Water Monkey 7	**31** 初七 火2 Fire · 1 Gradual Progress 風山漸 癸酉 Water Rooster 7	

FEBRUARY 2020 戊寅

Xuan Kong Element 玄空五行	雷火豐 Abundance	Period Luck 卦運	Monthly Star 月星
Wood 木8		6	8

SUNDAY	MONDAY	TUESDAY	WEDNESDAY	THURSDAY	FRIDAY	SATURDAY
						1 初八 火7 Fire · 2 Obstruction 水山蹇 甲戌 Wood Dog 2
2 初九 木3 Wood · 3 Advancement 火地晉 乙亥 Wood Pig 3	**3** 初十 水6 Water · 4 Nourish 山雷頤 丙子 Fire Rat 3	**4** 十一 金4 Metal · 5 Following 澤雷隨 丁丑 Fire Ox 7	**5** 十二 木8 Wood · 6 Abundance 雷火豐 戊寅 Earth Tiger 6	**6** 十三 火7 Fire · 7 Regulate 水澤節 己卯 Earth Rabbit 8	**7** 十四 水1 Water · 8 Unity 地天泰 庚辰 Metal Dragon 9	**8** 十五 木3 Wood · 9 Great Reward 火天大有 辛巳 Metal Snake 7
9 十六 火2 Fire · 1 Wind 巽為風 壬午 Water Horse 1	**10** 十七 金4 Metal · 2 Trap 澤水困 癸未 Water Goat 8	**11** 十八 木3 Wood · 3 Not Yet Accomplished 火水未濟 甲申 Wood Monkey 9	**12** 十九 金9 Metal · 4 Retreat 天山遯 乙酉 Wood Rooster 4	**13** 二十 水6 Water · 5 Mountain 艮為山 丙戌 Fire Dog 1	**14** 廿一 木8 Wood · 6 Delight 雷地豫 丁亥 Fire Pig 8	**15** 廿二 火7 Fire · 7 Beginning 水雷屯 戊子 Earth Rat 4
16 廿三 金9 Metal · 8 Without Wrongdoing 天雷無妄 己丑 Earth Ox 2	**17** 廿四 木3 Wood · 9 Fire 離為火 庚寅 Metal Tiger 1	**18** 廿五 火2 Fire · 1 Sincerity 風澤中孚 辛卯 Metal Rabbit 3	**19** 廿六 水6 Water · 2 Big Livestock 山天大畜 壬辰 Water Dragon 4	**20** 廿七 金4 Metal · 3 Eliminating 澤天夬 癸巳 Water Snake 6	**21** 廿八 金9 Metal · 4 Heaven 乾為天 甲午 Wood Horse 1	**22** 廿九 火7 Fire · 5 Well 水風井 乙未 Wood Goat 6
23 二月初一 木8 Wood · 6 Relief 雷水解 丙申 Fire Monkey 4	**24** 初二 金4 Metal · 7 Influence 澤山咸 丁酉 Fire Rooster 9	**25** 初三 水1 Water · 8 Humility 地山謙 戊戌 Earth Dog 6	**26** 初四 火2 Fire · 9 Observation 風地觀 己亥 Earth Pig 2	**27** 初五 火2 Fire · 1 Increasing 風雷益 庚子 Metal Rat 9	**28** 初六 水1 Water · 2 Dimming Light 地火明夷 辛丑 Metal Ox 3	**29** 初七 金9 Metal · 3 Fellowship 天火同人 壬寅 Water Tiger 7

MARCH 2020 己卯

Xuan Kong Element 玄空五行	水澤節	Period Luck 卦運	Monthly Star 月星
Fire 火7	Regulate	8	7

SUNDAY	MONDAY	TUESDAY	WEDNESDAY	THURSDAY	FRIDAY	SATURDAY
木8 Wood 4 Marrying Maiden 癸卯 Water Rabbit 雷澤歸妹 1 初八 7	木3 Wood 5 Opposition 甲辰 Wood Dragon 火澤睽 2 初九 2	火7 Fire 6 Waiting 乙巳 Wood Snake 水天需 3 初十 3	金4 Metal 7 Great Exceeding 丙午 Fire Horse 澤風大過 4 十一 3	水6 Water 8 Poison 丁未 Fire Goat 山風蠱 5 十二 7	火2 Fire 9 Dispersing 戊申 Earth Monkey 風水渙 6 十三 6	木3 Wood 1 Travelling 己酉 Earth Rooster 火山旅 7 十四 8
金9 Metal 2 Stagnation 庚戌 Metal Dog 天地否 8 十五 9	火7 Fire 3 Alliance 辛亥 Metal Pig 水地比 9 十六 7	木8 Wood 4 Thunder 壬子 Water Rat 震為雷 10 十七 1	水6 Water 5 Beauty 癸丑 Water Ox 山火賁 11 十八 8	火7 Fire 6 Accomplished 甲寅 Wood Tiger 水火既濟 12 十九 9	水1 Water 7 Arriving 乙卯 Wood Rabbit 地澤臨 13 二十 4	金4 Metal 8 Marsh 丙辰 Fire Dragon 兑為澤 14 廿一 1
火2 Fire 9 Small Livestock 丁巳 Fire Snake 風天小畜 15 廿二 8	木3 Wood 1 The Cauldron 戊午 Earth Horse 火風鼎 16 廿三 4	水1 Water 2 Rising 己未 Earth Goat 地風升 17 廿四 2	火7 Fire 3 Water 庚申 Metal Monkey 坎為水 18 廿五 1	木8 Wood 4 Lesser Exceeding 辛酉 Metal Rooster 雷山小過 19 廿六 3	金4 Metal 5 Gathering 壬戌 Water Dog 澤地萃 20 廿七 4	水6 Water 6 Peel 癸亥 Water Pig 山地剝 21 廿八 6
水1 Water 7 Earth 甲子 Wood Rat 坤為地 22 廿九 1	木3 Wood 8 Biting 乙丑 Wood Ox 火雷噬嗑 23 三十 6	火2 Fire 9 Family 丙寅 Fire Tiger 風火家人 24 三月初一 4	水6 Water 1 Decreasing 丁卯 Fire Rabbit 山澤損 25 初二 9	金9 Metal 2 Tread 戊辰 Earth Dragon 天澤履 26 初三 6	木8 Wood 3 Great Strength 己巳 Earth Snake 雷天大壯 27 初四 2	木8 Wood 4 Consistency 庚午 Metal Horse 雷風恒 28 初五 9
金9 Metal 5 Litigation 辛未 Metal Goat 天水訟 29 初六 3	水1 Water 6 Officer 壬申 Water Monkey 地水師 30 初七 7	火2 Fire 7 Gradual Progress 癸酉 Water Rooster 風山漸 31 初八 7				

APRIL 2020 庚辰

Xuan Kong Element 玄空五行	地天泰	Period Luck 卦運	Monthly Star 月星
Water 水1	Unity	9	6

SUNDAY	MONDAY	TUESDAY	WEDNESDAY	THURSDAY	FRIDAY	SATURDAY
			火7 Fire 8 Obstruction 甲戌 Wood Dog 水山蹇 1 初九 2	木3 Wood 9 Advancement 乙亥 Wood Pig 火地晉 2 初十 3	水6 Water 1 Nourish 丙子 Fire Rat 山雷頤 3 十一 3	金4 Metal 2 Following 丁丑 Fire Ox 澤雷隨 4 十二 7
木8 Wood 3 Abundance 戊寅 Earth Tiger 雷火豐 5 十三 6	火7 Fire 4 Regulate 己卯 Earth Rabbit 水澤節 6 十四 8	水1 Water 5 Unity 庚辰 Metal Dragon 地天泰 7 十五 9	木3 Wood 6 Great Reward 辛巳 Metal Snake 火天大有 8 十六 7	火2 Fire 7 Wind 壬午 Water Horse 巽為風 9 十七 1	金4 Metal 8 Trap 癸未 Water Goat 澤水困 10 十八 8	木3 Wood 9 Not Yet Accomplished 甲申 Wood Monkey 火水未濟 11 十九 9
金9 Metal 1 Retreat 乙酉 Wood Rooster 天山遯 12 二十 4	水6 Water 2 Mountain 丙戌 Fire Dog 艮為山 13 廿一 1	木8 Wood 3 Delight 丁亥 Fire Pig 雷地豫 14 廿二 8	火7 Fire 4 Beginning 戊子 Earth Rat 水雷屯 15 廿三 4	金9 Metal 5 Without Wrongdoing 己丑 Earth Ox 天雷無妄 16 廿四 2	木3 Wood 6 Fire 庚寅 Metal Tiger 離為火 17 廿五 1	火2 Fire 7 Sincerity 辛卯 Metal Rabbit 風澤中孚 18 廿六 3
水6 Water 8 Big Livestock 壬辰 Water Dragon 山天大畜 19 廿七 4	金4 Metal 9 Eliminating 癸巳 Water Snake 澤天夬 20 廿八 6	金9 Metal 1 Heaven 甲午 Wood Horse 乾為天 21 廿九 1	火7 Fire 2 Well 乙未 Wood Goat 水風井 22 三十 6	木8 Wood 3 Relief 丙申 Fire Monkey 雷水解 23 四月初一 4	金4 Metal 4 Influence 丁酉 Fire Rooster 澤山咸 24 初二 9	水1 Water 5 Humility 戊戌 Earth Dog 地山謙 25 初三 6
火2 Fire 6 Observation 己亥 Earth Pig 風地觀 26 初四 2	火2 Fire 7 Increasing 庚子 Metal Rat 風雷益 27 初五 9	水1 Water 8 Dimming Light 辛丑 Metal Ox 地火明夷 28 初六 3	金9 Metal 9 Fellowship 壬寅 Water Tiger 天火同人 29 初七 7	木8 Wood 1 Marrying Maiden 癸卯 Water Rabbit 雷澤歸妹 30 初八 7		

MAY 2020 辛巳

Xuan Kong Element 玄空五行	火天大有 Great Reward	Period Luck 卦運	Monthly Star 月星
Wood 木3		7	5

SUNDAY	MONDAY	TUESDAY	WEDNESDAY	THURSDAY	FRIDAY	SATURDAY
火7 Fire Obstruction 5 甲戌 Wood Dog 水山蹇 **31** 初九 2					木3 Wood Opposition 2 甲辰 Wood Dragon 火澤睽 **1** 初九 2	火7 Fire Waiting 3 乙巳 Wood Snake 水天需 **2** 初十 3
金4 Metal Great Exceeding 4 丙午 Fire Horse 澤風大過 **3** 十一 3	水6 Water Poison 5 丁未 Fire Goat 山風蠱 **4** 十二 7	火2 Fire Dispersing 6 戊申 Earth Monkey 風水渙 **5** 十三 6	木3 Wood Travelling 7 己酉 Earth Rooster 火山旅 **6** 十四 8	金9 Metal Stagnation 8 庚戌 Metal Dog 天地否 **7** 十五 9	火7 Fire Alliance 9 辛亥 Metal Pig 水地比 **8** 十六 7	木8 Wood Thunder 1 壬子 Water Rat 震爲雷 **9** 十七 1
水6 Water Beauty 2 癸丑 Water Ox 山火賁 **10** 十八 8	火7 Fire Accomplished 3 甲寅 Wood Tiger 水火既濟 **11** 十九 9	水1 Water Arriving 4 乙卯 Wood Rabbit 地澤臨 **12** 二十 4	金4 Metal Marsh 5 丙辰 Fire Dragon 兑爲澤 **13** 廿一 1	火2 Fire Small Livestock 6 丁巳 Fire Snake 風天小畜 **14** 廿二 8	木3 Wood The Cauldron 7 戊午 Earth Horse 火風鼎 **15** 廿三 4	水1 Water Rising 8 己未 Earth Goat 地風升 **16** 廿四 2
火7 Fire Water 9 庚申 Metal Monkey 坎爲水 **17** 廿五 1	木8 Wood Lesser Exceeding 1 辛酉 Metal Rooster 雷山小過 **18** 廿六 3	金4 Metal Gathering 2 壬戌 Water Dog 澤地萃 **19** 廿七 4	水6 Water Peel 3 癸亥 Water Pig 山地剝 **20** 廿八 6	水1 Water Earth 4 甲子 Wood Rat 坤爲地 **21** 廿九 1	木3 Wood Biting 5 乙丑 Wood Ox 火雷噬嗑 **22** 三十 6	火2 Fire Family 6 丙寅 Fire Tiger 風火家人 **23** 閏四月初一 4
水6 Water Decreasing 7 丁卯 Fire Rabbit 山澤損 **24** 初二 9	金9 Metal Tread 8 戊辰 Earth Dragon 天澤履 **25** 初三 6	木8 Wood Great Strength 9 己巳 Earth Snake 雷天大壯 **26** 初四 2	木8 Wood Consistency 1 庚午 Metal Horse 雷風恒 **27** 初五 9	金9 Metal Litigation 2 辛未 Metal Goat 天水訟 **28** 初六 3	水1 Water Officer 3 壬申 Water Monkey 地水師 **29** 初七 7	火2 Fire Gradual Progress 4 癸酉 Water Rooster 風山漸 **30** 初八 7

JUNE 2020 壬午

Xuan Kong Element 玄空五行	巽爲風 Wind	Period Luck 卦運	Monthly Star 月星
Fire 火2		1	4

SUNDAY	MONDAY	TUESDAY	WEDNESDAY	THURSDAY	FRIDAY	SATURDAY
	木3 Wood Advancement 6 乙亥 Wood Pig 火地晉 **1** 初十 3	水6 Water Nourish 7 丙子 Fire Rat 山雷頤 **2** 十一 3	金4 Metal Following 8 丁丑 Fire Ox 澤雷隨 **3** 十二 7	木8 Wood Abundance 9 戊寅 Earth Tiger 雷火豐 **4** 十三 6	火7 Fire Regulate 1 己卯 Earth Rabbit 水澤節 **5** 十四 8	水1 Water Unity 2 庚辰 Metal Dragon 地天泰 **6** 十五 9
木3 Wood Great Reward 3 辛巳 Metal Snake 火天大有 **7** 十六 7	火2 Fire Wind 4 壬午 Water Horse 巽爲風 **8** 十七 1	金4 Metal Trap 5 癸未 Water Goat 澤水困 **9** 十八 8	木3 Wood Not Yet Accomplished 6 甲申 Wood Monkey 火水未濟 **10** 十九 9	金9 Metal Retreat 7 乙酉 Wood Rooster 天山遯 **11** 二十 4	水6 Water Mountain 8 丙戌 Fire Dog 艮爲山 **12** 廿一 1	木8 Wood Delight 9 丁亥 Fire Pig 雷地豫 **13** 廿二 8
火7 Fire Beginning 1 戊子 Earth Rat 水雷屯 **14** 廿三 4	金9 Metal Without Wrongdoing 2 己丑 Earth Ox 天雷無妄 **15** 廿四 2	木3 Wood Fire 3 庚寅 Metal Tiger 離爲火 **16** 廿五 1	火2 Fire Sincerity 4 辛卯 Metal Rabbit 風澤中孚 **17** 廿六 3	水6 Water Big Livestock 5 壬辰 Water Dragon 山天大畜 **18** 廿七 4	金4 Metal Eliminating 6 癸巳 Water Snake 澤天夬 **19** 廿八 6	金9 Metal Heaven 7 甲午 Wood Horse 乾爲天 **20** 廿九 1
火7 Fire Well 8/2 乙未 Wood Goat 水風井 **21** 五月初一 6	木8 Wood Relief 1 丙申 Fire Monkey 雷水解 **22** 初二 4	金4 Metal Influence 9 丁酉 Fire Rooster 澤山咸 **23** 初三 9	水1 Water Humility 8 戊戌 Earth Dog 地山謙 **24** 初四 6	火2 Fire Observation 7 己亥 Earth Pig 風地觀 **25** 初五 2	火2 Fire Increasing 6 庚子 Metal Rat 風雷益 **26** 初六 9	水1 Water Dimming Light 5 辛丑 Metal Ox 地火明夷 **27** 初七 3
金9 Metal Fellowship 4 壬寅 Water Tiger 天火同人 **28** 初八 7	木8 Wood Marrying Maiden 3 癸卯 Water Rabbit 雷澤歸妹 **29** 初九 7	木3 Wood Opposition 2 甲辰 Wood Dragon 火澤睽 **30** 初十 2				

JULY 2020 癸未

Xuan Kong Element 玄空五行	澤水困 Trap	Period Luck 卦運	Monthly Star 月星
Metal 金4		8	3

SUNDAY	MONDAY	TUESDAY	WEDNESDAY	THURSDAY	FRIDAY	SATURDAY
			火7 Fire Waiting 1 水天需 乙巳 Wood Snake **1** 十一 3	金4 Metal Great Exceeding 9 澤風大過 丙午 Fire Horse **2** 十二 3	水6 Water Poison 8 山風蠱 丁未 Fire Goat **3** 十三 7	火2 Fire Dispersing 7 風水渙 戊申 Earth Monkey **4** 十四 6
木3 Wood Travelling 6 火山旅 己酉 Earth Rooster **5** 十五 8	金9 Metal Stagnation 5 天地否 庚戌 Metal Dog **6** 十六 9	火7 Fire Alliance 4 水地比 辛亥 Metal Pig **7** 十七 7	木8 Wood Thunder 3 震爲雷 壬子 Water Rat **8** 十八 1	水6 Water Beauty 2 山火賁 癸丑 Water Ox **9** 十九 8	火7 Fire Accomplished 1 水火既濟 甲寅 Wood Tiger **10** 二十 9	水1 Water Arriving 9 地澤臨 乙卯 Wood Rabbit **11** 廿一 4
金4 Metal Marsh 8 兌爲澤 丙辰 Fire Dragon **12** 廿二 1	火2 Fire Small Livestock 7 風天小畜 丁巳 Fire Snake **13** 廿三 8	木3 Wood The Cauldron 6 火風鼎 戊午 Earth Horse **14** 廿四 4	水1 Water Rising 5 地風升 己未 Earth Goat **15** 廿五 2	火7 Fire Water 4 坎爲水 庚申 Metal Monkey **16** 廿六 1	木8 Wood Lesser Exceeding 3 雷山小過 辛酉 Metal Rooster **17** 廿七 3	金4 Metal Gathering 2 澤地萃 壬戌 Water Dog **18** 廿八 4
水6 Water Peel 1 山地剝 癸亥 Water Pig **19** 廿九 6	水1 Water Earth 9 坤爲地 甲子 Wood Rat **20** 三十 1	木3 Wood Biting 8 火雷噬嗑 乙丑 Wood Ox **21** 六月初一 6	火2 Fire Family 7 風火家人 丙寅 Fire Tiger **22** 初二 4	水6 Water Decreasing 6 山澤損 丁卯 Fire Rabbit **23** 初三 9	金9 Metal Tread 5 天澤履 戊辰 Earth Dragon **24** 初四 6	木8 Wood Great Strength 4 雷天大壯 己巳 Earth Snake **25** 初五 2
木8 Wood Consistency 3 雷風恒 庚午 Metal Horse **26** 初六 9	金9 Metal Litigation 2 天水訟 辛未 Metal Goat **27** 初七 3	水1 Water Officer 1 地水師 壬申 Water Monkey **28** 初八 7	火2 Fire Gradual Progress 9 風山漸 癸酉 Water Rooster **29** 初九 7	火7 Fire Obstruction 8 水山蹇 甲戌 Wood Dog **30** 初十 2	木3 Wood Advancement 7 火地晉 乙亥 Wood Pig **31** 十一 3	

AUGUST 2020 甲申

Xuan Kong Element 玄空五行	火水未濟 Not Yet Accomplished	Period Luck 卦運	Monthly Star 月星
Wood 木3		9	2

SUNDAY	MONDAY	TUESDAY	WEDNESDAY	THURSDAY	FRIDAY	SATURDAY
火7 Fire Waiting 4 水天需 乙巳 Wood Snake **30** 十二 3	金4 Metal Great Exceeding 3 澤風大過 丙午 Fire Horse **31** 十三 3					水6 Water Nourish 6 山雷頤 丙子 Fire Rat **1** 十二 3
金4 Metal Following 5 澤雷隨 丁丑 Fire Ox **2** 十三 7	木8 Wood Abundance 4 雷火豐 戊寅 Earth Tiger **3** 十四 6	火7 Fire Regulate 3 水澤節 己卯 Earth Rabbit **4** 十五 8	水1 Water Unity 2 地天泰 庚辰 Metal Dragon **5** 十六 9	木3 Wood Great Reward 1 火天大有 辛巳 Metal Snake **6** 十七 7	火2 Fire Wind 9 巽爲風 壬午 Water Horse **7** 十八 1	金4 Metal Trap 8 澤水困 癸未 Water Goat **8** 十九 8
木3 Wood Not Yet Accomplished 7 火水未濟 甲申 Wood Monkey **9** 二十 9	金9 Metal Retreat 6 天山遯 乙酉 Wood Rooster **10** 廿一 4	水6 Water Mountain 5 艮爲山 丙戌 Fire Dog **11** 廿二 1	木8 Wood Delight 4 雷地豫 丁亥 Fire Pig **12** 廿三 8	火7 Fire Beginning 3 水雷屯 戊子 Earth Rat **13** 廿四 4	金9 Metal Without Wrongdoing 2 天雷無妄 己丑 Earth Ox **14** 廿五 2	木3 Wood Fire 1 離爲火 庚寅 Metal Tiger **15** 廿六 1
火2 Fire Sincerity 9 風澤中孚 辛卯 Metal Rabbit **16** 廿七 3	水6 Water Big Livestock 8 山天大畜 壬辰 Water Dragon **17** 廿八 4	金4 Metal Eliminating 7 澤天夬 癸巳 Water Snake **18** 廿九 6	金9 Metal Heaven 6 乾爲天 甲午 Wood Horse **19** 七月初一 1	火7 Fire Well 5 水風井 乙未 Wood Goat **20** 初二 6	木8 Wood Relief 4 雷水解 丙申 Fire Monkey **21** 初三 4	金4 Metal Influence 3 澤山咸 丁酉 Fire Rooster **22** 初四 9
水1 Water Humility 2 地山謙 戊戌 Earth Dog **23** 初五 6	火2 Fire Observation 1 風地觀 己亥 Earth Pig **24** 初六 2	火2 Fire Increasing 9 風雷益 庚子 Metal Rat **25** 初七 9	水1 Water Dimming Light 8 地火明夷 辛丑 Metal Ox **26** 初八 3	金9 Metal Fellowship 7 天火同人 壬寅 Water Tiger **27** 初九 7	木8 Wood Marrying Maiden 6 雷澤歸妹 癸卯 Water Rabbit **28** 初十 7	木3 Wood Opposition 5 火澤睽 甲辰 Wood Dragon **29** 十一 2

SEPTEMBER 2020 乙酉

Xuan Kong Element 玄空五行	天山遯 Retreat	Period Luck 卦運	Monthly Star 月星
Metal 金9		4	1

SUNDAY	MONDAY	TUESDAY	WEDNESDAY	THURSDAY	FRIDAY	SATURDAY
		水6 Water 2 Poison 丁未 Fire Goat 山風蠱 1 十四 7	火2 Fire 1 Dispersing 戊申 Earth Monkey 風水渙 2 十五 6	木3 Wood 9 Travelling 己酉 Earth Rooster 火山旅 3 十六 8	金9 Metal 8 Stagnation 庚戌 Metal Dog 天地否 4 十七 9	火7 Fire 7 Alliance 辛亥 Metal Pig 水地比 5 十八 7
木8 Wood 6 Thunder 壬子 Water Rat 震爲雷 6 十九 1	水6 Water 5 Beauty 癸丑 Water Ox 山火賁 7 二十 8	火7 Fire 4 Accomplished 甲寅 Wood Tiger 水火既濟 8 廿一 9	水1 Water 3 Arriving 乙卯 Wood Rabbit 地澤臨 9 廿二 4	金4 Metal 2 Marsh 丙辰 Fire Dragon 兑爲澤 10 廿三 1	火2 Fire 1 Small Livestock 丁巳 Fire Snake 風天小畜 11 廿四 8	木3 Wood 9 The Cauldron 戊午 Earth Horse 火風鼎 12 廿五 4
水1 Water 8 Rising 己未 Earth Goat 地風升 13 廿六 2	火7 Fire 7 Water 庚申 Metal Monkey 坎爲水 14 廿七 1	木8 Wood 6 Lesser Exceeding 辛酉 Metal Rooster 雷山小過 15 廿八 3	金4 Metal 5 Gathering 壬戌 Water Dog 澤地萃 16 廿九 4	水6 Water 4 Peel 癸亥 Water Pig 山地剝 17 八月初一 6	水1 Water 3 Earth 甲子 Wood Rat 坤爲地 18 初二 1	木3 Wood 2 Biting 乙丑 Wood Ox 火雷噬嗑 19 初三 6
火2 Fire 1 Family 丙寅 Fire Tiger 風火家人 20 初四 4	水6 Water 9 Decreasing 丁卯 Fire Rabbit 山澤損 21 初五 9	金9 Metal 8 Tread 戊辰 Earth Dragon 天澤履 22 初六 6	木8 Wood 7 Great Strength 己巳 Earth Snake 雷天大壯 23 初七 2	木8 Wood 6 Consistency 庚午 Metal Horse 雷風恒 24 初八 9	金9 Metal 5 Litigation 辛未 Metal Goat 天水訟 25 初九 3	水1 Water 4 Officer 壬申 Water Monkey 地水師 26 初十 7
火2 Fire 3 Gradual Progress 癸酉 Water Rooster 風山漸 27 十一 7	火7 Fire 2 Obstruction 甲戌 Wood Dog 水山蹇 28 十二 2	木3 Wood 1 Advancement 乙亥 Wood Pig 火地晉 29 十三 3	水6 Water 9 Nourish 丙子 Fire Rat 山雷頤 30 十四 3			

OCTOBER 2020 丙戌

Xuan Kong Element 玄空五行	艮爲山 Mountain	Period Luck 卦運	Monthly Star 月星
Water 水6		1	9

SUNDAY	MONDAY	TUESDAY	WEDNESDAY	THURSDAY	FRIDAY	SATURDAY
				金4 Metal 8 Following 丁丑 Fire Ox 澤雷隨 1 十五 7	木8 Wood 7 Abundance 戊寅 Earth Tiger 雷火豐 2 十六 6	火7 Fire 6 Regulate 己卯 Earth Rabbit 水澤節 3 十七 8
水1 Water 5 Unity 庚辰 Metal Dragon 地天泰 4 十八 9	木3 Wood 4 Great Reward 辛巳 Metal Snake 火天大有 5 十九 7	火2 Fire 3 Wind 壬午 Water Horse 巽爲風 6 二十 1	金4 Metal 2 Trap 癸未 Water Goat 澤水困 7 廿一 8	木3 Wood 1 Not Yet Accomplished 甲申 Wood Monkey 火水未濟 8 廿二 9	金9 Metal 9 Retreat 乙酉 Wood Rooster 天山遯 9 廿三 4	水6 Water 8 Mountain 丙戌 Fire Dog 艮爲山 10 廿四 1
木8 Wood 7 Delight 丁亥 Fire Pig 雷地豫 11 廿五 8	火7 Fire 6 Beginning 戊子 Earth Rat 水雷屯 12 廿六 4	金9 Metal 5 Without Wrongdoing 己丑 Earth Ox 天雷無妄 13 廿七 2	木3 Wood 4 Fire 庚寅 Metal Tiger 離爲火 14 廿八 1	火2 Fire 3 Sincerity 辛卯 Metal Rabbit 風澤中孚 15 廿九 3	水6 Water 2 Big Livestock 壬辰 Water Dragon 山天大畜 16 三十 4	金4 Metal 1 Eliminating 癸巳 Water Snake 澤天夬 17 九月初一 6
金9 Metal 9 Heaven 甲午 Wood Horse 乾爲天 18 初二 1	火7 Fire 8 Well 乙未 Wood Goat 水風井 19 初三 6	木8 Wood 7 Relief 丙申 Fire Monkey 雷水解 20 初四 4	金4 Metal 6 Influence 丁酉 Fire Rooster 澤山咸 21 初五 9	水1 Water 5 Humility 戊戌 Earth Dog 地山謙 22 初六 6	火2 Fire 4 Observation 己亥 Earth Pig 風地觀 23 初七 2	火2 Fire 3 Increasing 庚子 Metal Rat 風雷益 24 初八 9
水1 Water 2 Dimming Light 辛丑 Metal Ox 地火明夷 25 初九 3	金9 Metal 1 Fellowship 壬寅 Water Tiger 天火同人 26 初十 7	木8 Wood 9 Marrying Maiden 癸卯 Water Rabbit 雷澤歸妹 27 十一 7	木3 Wood 8 Opposition 甲辰 Wood Dragon 火澤睽 28 十二 2	火7 Fire 7 Waiting 乙巳 Wood Snake 水天需 29 十三 3	金4 Metal 6 Great Exceeding 丙午 Fire Horse 澤風大過 30 十四 3	水6 Water 5 Poison 丁未 Fire Goat 山風蠱 31 十五 7

NOVEMBER 2020 丁亥

Xuan Kong Element 玄空五行	雷地豫	Period Luck 卦運	Monthly Star 月星
Wood 木8	Delight	8	8

SUNDAY	MONDAY	TUESDAY	WEDNESDAY	THURSDAY	FRIDAY	SATURDAY
火2 Fire 4 Dispersing 風水渙 戊申 Earth Monkey **1** 十六 6	木3 Wood 3 Travelling 火山旅 己酉 Earth Rooster **2** 十七 8	金9 Metal 2 Stagnation 天地否 庚戌 Metal Dog **3** 十八 9	火7 Fire 1 Alliance 水地比 辛亥 Metal Pig **4** 十九 7	木8 Wood 9 Thunder 震爲雷 壬子 Water Rat **5** 二十 1	水6 Water 8 Beauty 山火賁 癸丑 Water Ox **6** 廿一 8	火7 Fire 7 Accomplished 水火既濟 甲寅 Wood Tiger **7** 廿二 9
水1 Water 6 Arriving 地澤臨 乙卯 Wood Rabbit **8** 廿三 4	金4 Metal 5 Marsh 兌爲澤 丙辰 Fire Dragon **9** 廿四 1	火2 Fire 4 Small Livestock 風天小畜 丁巳 Fire Snake **10** 廿五 8	木3 Wood 3 The Cauldron 火風鼎 戊午 Earth Horse **11** 廿六 4	水1 Water 2 Rising 地風升 己未 Earth Goat **12** 廿七 2	火7 Fire 1 Water 坎爲水 庚申 Metal Monkey **13** 廿八 1	木8 Wood 9 Lesser Exceeding 雷山小過 辛酉 Metal Rooster **14** 廿九 3
金4 Metal 8 Gathering 澤地萃 壬戌 Water Dog **15** 十月初一 4	水6 Water 7 Peel 山地剝 癸亥 Water Pig **16** 初二 6	水1 Water 6 Earth 坤爲地 甲子 Wood Rat **17** 初三 1	木3 Wood 5 Biting 火雷噬嗑 乙丑 Wood Ox **18** 初四 6	火2 Fire 4 Family 風火家人 丙寅 Fire Tiger **19** 初五 4	水6 Water 3 Decreasing 山澤損 丁卯 Fire Rabbit **20** 初六 9	金9 Metal 2 Tread 天澤履 戊辰 Earth Dragon **21** 初七 6
木8 Wood 1 Great Strength 雷天大壯 己巳 Earth Snake **22** 初八 2	木8 Wood 9 Consistency 雷風恒 庚午 Metal Horse **23** 初九 9	金9 Metal 8 Litigation 天水訟 辛未 Metal Goat **24** 初十 3	水1 Water 7 Officer 地水師 壬申 Water Monkey **25** 十一 7	火2 Fire 6 Gradual Progress 風山漸 癸酉 Water Rooster **26** 十二 7	火7 Fire 5 Obstruction 水山蹇 甲戌 Wood Dog **27** 十三 2	木3 Wood 4 Advancement 火地晉 乙亥 Wood Pig **28** 十四 3
水6 Water 3 Nourish 山雷頤 丙子 Fire Rat **29** 十五 3	金4 Metal 2 Following 澤雷隨 丁丑 Fire Ox **30** 十六 7					

DECEMBER 2020 戊子

Xuan Kong Element 玄空五行	水雷屯	Period Luck 卦運	Monthly Star 月星
Fire 火7	Beginning	4	7

SUNDAY	MONDAY	TUESDAY	WEDNESDAY	THURSDAY	FRIDAY	SATURDAY
		木8 Wood 1 Abundance 雷火豐 戊寅 Earth Tiger **1** 十七 6	火7 Fire 9 Regulate 水澤節 己卯 Earth Rabbit **2** 十八 8	水1 Water 8 Unity 地天泰 庚辰 Metal Dragon **3** 十九 9	木3 Wood 7 Great Reward 火天大有 辛巳 Metal Snake **4** 二十 7	火2 Fire 6 Wind 巽爲風 壬午 Water Horse **5** 廿一 1
金4 Metal 5 Trap 澤水困 癸未 Water Goat **6** 廿二 8	木3 Wood 4 Not Yet Accomplished 火水未濟 甲申 Wood Monkey **7** 廿三 9	金9 Metal 3 Retreat 天山遯 乙酉 Wood Rooster **8** 廿四 4	水6 Water 2 Mountain 艮爲山 丙戌 Fire Dog **9** 廿五 1	木8 Wood 1 Delight 雷地豫 丁亥 Fire Pig **10** 廿六 8	火7 Fire 9 Beginning 水雷屯 戊子 Earth Rat **11** 廿七 4	金9 Metal 8 Without Wrongdoing 天雷無妄 己丑 Earth Ox **12** 廿八 2
木3 Wood 7 Fire 離爲火 庚寅 Metal Tiger **13** 廿九 1	火2 Fire 6 Sincerity 風澤中孚 辛卯 Metal Rabbit **14** 三十 3	水6 Water 5 Big Livestock 山天大畜 壬辰 Water Dragon **15** 十一月初一 4	金4 Metal 4 Eliminating 澤天夬 癸巳 Water Snake **16** 初二 6	金9 Metal 3 Heaven 乾爲天 甲午 Wood Horse **17** 初三 1	火7 Fire 2 Well 水風井 乙未 Wood Goat **18** 初四 6	木8 Wood 1 Relief 雷水解 丙申 Fire Monkey **19** 初五 4
金4 Metal 9 Influence 澤山咸 丁酉 Fire Rooster **20** 初六 9	水1 Water 8/2 Humility 地山謙 戊戌 Earth Dog **21** 初七 6	火2 Fire 3 Observation 風地觀 己亥 Earth Pig **22** 初八 2	火2 Fire 4 Increasing 風雷益 庚子 Metal Rat **23** 初九 9	水1 Water 5 Dimming Light 地火明夷 辛丑 Metal Ox **24** 初十 3	金9 Metal 6 Fellowship 天火同人 壬寅 Water Tiger **25** 十一 7	木8 Wood 7 Marrying Maiden 雷澤歸妹 癸卯 Water Rabbit **26** 十二 7
木3 Wood 8 Opposition 火澤睽 甲辰 Wood Dragon **27** 十三 2	火7 Fire 9 Waiting 水天需 乙巳 Wood Snake **28** 十四 3	金4 Metal 1 Great Exceeding 澤風大過 丙午 Fire Horse **29** 十五 3	水6 Water 2 Poison 山風蠱 丁未 Fire Goat **30** 十六 7	火2 Fire 3 Dispersing 風水渙 戊申 Earth Monkey **31** 十七 6		

2021 辛丑

(*Xin Chou*) Metal Ox

2021 辛丑 *(Xin Chou)* Metal Ox

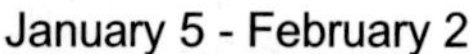

January 5 - February 2

February 3 - March 4

March 5 - April 3

April 4 - May 4

May 5 - June 4

June 5 - July 6

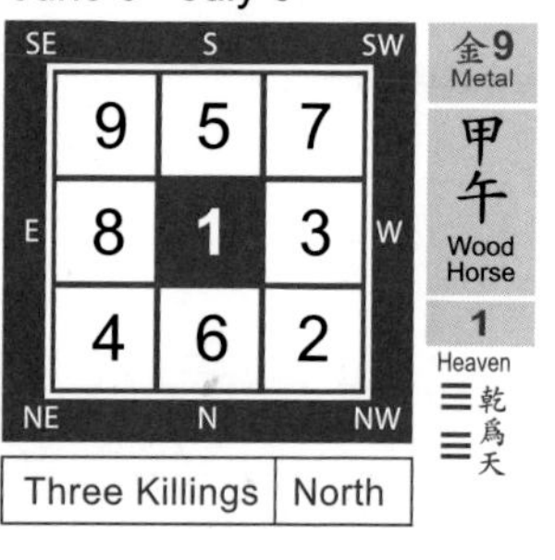

July 7 - August 6

August 7 - September 6

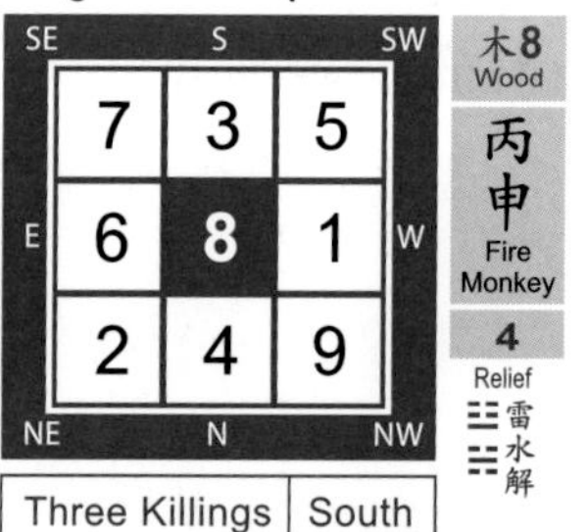

September 7 - October 7

October 8 - November 6

November 7 - December 6

December 7 - January 4

JANUARY 2021 己丑

Xuan Kong Element 玄空五行	天雷無妄 Without Wrongdoing	Period Luck 卦運	Monthly Star 月星
Metal 金9		2	6

SUNDAY	MONDAY	TUESDAY	WEDNESDAY	THURSDAY	FRIDAY	SATURDAY
火7 Fire 7 Regulate 水澤節 己卯 Earth Rabbit 31 十九 8					木3 Wood 4 Travelling 火山旅 己酉 Earth Rooster 1 十八 8	金9 Metal 5 Stagnation 天地否 庚戌 Metal Dog 2 十九 9
火7 Fire 6 Alliance 水地比 辛亥 Metal Pig 3 二十 7	木8 Wood 7 Thunder 震爲雷 壬子 Water Rat 4 廿一 1	水6 Water 8 Beauty 山火賁 癸丑 Water Ox 5 廿二 8	火7 Fire 9 Accomplished 水火既濟 甲寅 Wood Tiger 6 廿三 9	水1 Water 1 Arriving 地澤臨 乙卯 Wood Rabbit 7 廿四 4	金4 Metal 2 Marsh 兑爲澤 丙辰 Fire Dragon 8 廿五 1	火2 Fire 3 Small Livestock 風天小畜 丁巳 Fire Snake 9 廿六 8
木3 Wood 4 The Cauldron 火風鼎 戊午 Earth Horse 10 廿七 4	水1 Water 5 Rising 地風升 己未 Earth Goat 11 廿八 2	火7 Fire 6 Water 坎爲水 庚申 Metal Monkey 12 廿九 1	木8 Wood 7 Lesser Exceeding 雷山小過 辛酉 Metal Rooster 13 十二月初一 3	金4 Metal 8 Gathering 澤地萃 壬戌 Water Dog 14 初二 4	水6 Water 9 Peel 山地剝 癸亥 Water Pig 15 初三 6	水1 Water 1 Earth 坤爲地 甲子 Wood Rat 16 初四 1
木3 Wood 2 Biting 火雷噬嗑 乙丑 Wood Ox 17 初五 6	火2 Fire 3 Family 風火家人 丙寅 Fire Tiger 18 初六 4	水6 Water 4 Decreasing 山澤損 丁卯 Fire Rabbit 19 初七 9	金9 Metal 5 Tread 天澤履 戊辰 Earth Dragon 20 初八 6	木8 Wood 6 Great Strength 雷天大壯 己巳 Earth Snake 21 初九 2	木8 Wood 7 Consistency 雷風恆 庚午 Metal Horse 22 初十 9	金9 Metal 8 Litigation 天水訟 辛未 Metal Goat 23 十一 3
水1 Water 9 Officer 地水師 壬申 Water Monkey 24 十二 7	火2 Fire 1 Gradual Progress 風山漸 癸酉 Water Rooster 25 十三 7	火7 Fire 2 Obstruction 水山蹇 甲戌 Wood Dog 26 十四 2	木3 Wood 3 Advancement 火地晉 乙亥 Wood Pig 27 十五 3	水6 Water 4 Nourish 山雷頤 丙子 Fire Rat 28 十六 3	金4 Metal 5 Following 澤雷隨 丁丑 Fire Ox 29 十七 7	木8 Wood 6 Abundance 雷火豐 戊寅 Earth Tiger 30 十八 6

FEBRUARY 2021 庚寅

Xuan Kong Element 玄空五行	離爲火 Fire	Period Luck 卦運	Monthly Star 月星
Wood 木3		1	5

SUNDAY	MONDAY	TUESDAY	WEDNESDAY	THURSDAY	FRIDAY	SATURDAY
	水1 Water 8 Unity 地天泰 庚辰 Metal Dragon 1 二十 9	木3 Wood 9 Great Reward 火天大有 辛巳 Metal Snake 2 廿一 7	火2 Fire 1 Wind 巽爲風 壬午 Water Horse 3 廿二 1	金4 Metal 2 Trap 澤水困 癸未 Water Goat 4 廿三 8	木3 Wood 3 Not Yet Accomplished 火水未濟 甲申 Wood Monkey 5 廿四 9	金9 Metal 4 Retreat 天山遯 乙酉 Wood Rooster 6 廿五 4
水6 Water 5 Mountain 艮爲山 丙戌 Fire Dog 7 廿六 1	木8 Wood 6 Delight 雷地豫 丁亥 Fire Pig 8 廿七 8	火7 Fire 7 Beginning 水雷屯 戊子 Earth Rat 9 廿八 4	金9 Metal 8 Without Wrongdoing 天雷無妄 己丑 Earth Ox 10 廿九 2	木3 Wood 9 Fire 離爲火 庚寅 Metal Tiger 11 三十 1	火2 Fire 1 Sincerity 風澤中孚 辛卯 Metal Rabbit 12 正月初一 3	水6 Water 2 Big Livestock 山天大畜 壬辰 Water Dragon 13 初二 4
金4 Metal 3 Eliminating 澤天夬 癸巳 Water Snake 14 初三 6	金9 Metal 4 Heaven 乾爲天 甲午 Wood Horse 15 初四 1	火7 Fire 5 Well 水風井 乙未 Wood Goat 16 初五 6	木8 Wood 6 Relief 雷水解 丙申 Fire Monkey 17 初六 4	金4 Metal 7 Influence 澤山咸 丁酉 Fire Rooster 18 初七 9	水1 Water 8 Humility 地山謙 戊戌 Earth Dog 19 初八 6	火2 Fire 9 Observation 風地觀 己亥 Earth Pig 20 初九 2
火2 Fire 1 Increasing 風雷益 庚子 Metal Rat 21 初十 9	水1 Water 2 Dimming Light 地火明夷 辛丑 Metal Ox 22 十一 3	金9 Metal 3 Fellowship 天火同人 壬寅 Water Tiger 23 十二 7	木8 Wood 4 Marrying Maiden 雷澤歸妹 癸卯 Water Rabbit 24 十三 7	木3 Wood 5 Opposition 火澤睽 甲辰 Wood Dragon 25 十四 2	火7 Fire 6 Waiting 水天需 乙巳 Wood Snake 26 十五 3	金4 Metal 7 Great Exceeding 澤風大過 丙午 Fire Horse 27 十六 3
水6 Water 8 Poison 山風蠱 丁未 Fire Goat 28 十七 7						

Xuan Kong Da Gua Ten Thousand Year Calendar 571

MARCH 2021 辛卯

Xuan Kong Element 玄空五行	風澤中孚 Sincerity	Period Luck 卦運	Monthly Star 月星
Fire 火2		3	4

SUNDAY	MONDAY	TUESDAY	WEDNESDAY	THURSDAY	FRIDAY	SATURDAY
	火2 Fire 9 Dispersing 風水渙 戊申 Earth Monkey 1 十八 6	木3 Wood 1 Travelling 火山旅 己酉 Earth Rooster 2 十九 8	金9 Metal 2 Stagnation 天地否 庚戌 Metal Dog 3 二十 9	火7 Fire 3 Alliance 水地比 辛亥 Metal Pig 4 廿一 7	木8 Wood 4 Thunder 震為雷 壬子 Water Rat 5 廿二 1	水6 Water 5 Beauty 山火賁 癸丑 Water Ox 6 廿三 8
火7 Fire 6 Accomplished 水火既濟 甲寅 Wood Tiger 7 廿四 9	水1 Water 7 Arriving 地澤臨 乙卯 Wood Rabbit 8 廿五 4	金4 Metal 8 Marsh 兌為澤 丙辰 Fire Dragon 9 廿六 1	火2 Fire 9 Small Livestock 風天小畜 丁巳 Fire Snake 10 廿七 8	木3 Wood 1 The Cauldron 火風鼎 戊午 Earth Horse 11 廿八 4	水1 Water 2 Rising 地風升 己未 Earth Goat 12 廿九 2	火7 Fire 3 Water 坎為水 庚申 Metal Monkey 13 二月初一 1
木8 Wood 4 Lesser Exceeding 雷山小過 辛酉 Metal Rooster 14 初二 3	金4 Metal 5 Gathering 澤地萃 壬戌 Water Dog 15 初三 4	水6 Water 6 Peel 山地剝 癸亥 Water Pig 16 初四 6	水1 Water 7 Earth 坤為地 甲子 Wood Rat 17 初五 1	木3 Wood 8 Biting 火雷噬嗑 乙丑 Wood Ox 18 初六 6	火2 Fire 9 Family 風火家人 丙寅 Fire Tiger 19 初七 4	水6 Water 1 Decreasing 山澤損 丁卯 Fire Rabbit 20 初八 9
金9 Metal 2 Tread 天澤履 戊辰 Earth Dragon 21 初九 6	木8 Wood 3 Great Strength 雷天大壯 己巳 Earth Snake 22 初十 2	木8 Wood 4 Consistency 雷風恆 庚午 Metal Horse 23 十一 9	金9 Metal 5 Litigation 天水訟 辛未 Metal Goat 24 十二 3	水1 Water 6 Officer 地水師 壬申 Water Monkey 25 十三 7	火2 Fire 7 Gradual Progress 風山漸 癸酉 Water Rooster 26 十四 7	火7 Fire 8 Obstruction 水山蹇 甲戌 Wood Dog 27 十五 2
木3 Wood 9 Advancement 火地晉 乙亥 Wood Pig 28 十六 3	水6 Water 1 Nourish 山雷頤 丙子 Fire Rat 29 十七 3	金4 Metal 2 Following 澤雷隨 丁丑 Fire Ox 30 十八 7	木8 Wood 3 Abundance 雷火豐 戊寅 Earth Tiger 31 十九 6			

APRIL 2021 壬辰

Xuan Kong Element 玄空五行	山天大畜 Big Livestock	Period Luck 卦運	Monthly Star 月星
Water 水6		4	3

SUNDAY	MONDAY	TUESDAY	WEDNESDAY	THURSDAY	FRIDAY	SATURDAY
				火7 Fire 4 Regulate 水澤節 己卯 Earth Rabbit 1 二十 8	水1 Water 5 Unity 地天泰 庚辰 Metal Dragon 2 廿一 9	木3 Wood 6 Great Reward 火天大有 辛巳 Metal Snake 3 廿二 7
火2 Fire 7 Wind 巽為風 壬午 Water Horse 4 廿三 1	金4 Metal 8 Trap 澤水困 癸未 Water Goat 5 廿四 8	木3 Wood 9 Not Yet Accomplished 火水未濟 甲申 Wood Monkey 6 廿五 9	金9 Metal 1 Retreat 天山遯 乙酉 Wood Rooster 7 廿六 4	水6 Water 2 Mountain 艮為山 丙戌 Fire Dog 8 廿七 1	木8 Wood 3 Delight 雷地豫 丁亥 Fire Pig 9 廿八 8	火7 Fire 4 Beginning 水雷屯 戊子 Earth Rat 10 廿九 4
金9 Metal 5 Without Wrongdoing 天雷無妄 己丑 Earth Ox 11 三十 2	木3 Wood 6 Fire 離為火 庚寅 Metal Tiger 12 三月初一 1	火2 Fire 7 Sincerity 風澤中孚 辛卯 Metal Rabbit 13 初二 3	水6 Water 8 Big Livestock 山天大畜 壬辰 Water Dragon 14 初三 4	金4 Metal 9 Eliminating 澤天夬 癸巳 Water Snake 15 初四 6	金9 Metal 1 Heaven 乾為天 甲午 Wood Horse 16 初五 1	火7 Fire 2 Well 水風井 乙未 Wood Goat 17 初六 6
木8 Wood 3 Relief 雷水解 丙申 Fire Monkey 18 初七 4	金4 Metal 4 Influence 澤山咸 丁酉 Fire Rooster 19 初八 9	水1 Water 5 Humility 地山謙 戊戌 Earth Dog 20 初九 6	火2 Fire 6 Observation 風地觀 己亥 Earth Pig 21 初十 2	火2 Fire 7 Increasing 風雷益 庚子 Metal Rat 22 十一 9	水1 Water 8 Dimming Light 地火明夷 辛丑 Metal Ox 23 十二 3	金9 Metal 9 Fellowship 天火同人 壬寅 Water Tiger 24 十三 7
木8 Wood 1 Marrying Maiden 雷澤歸妹 癸卯 Water Rabbit 25 十四 7	木3 Wood 2 Opposition 火澤睽 甲辰 Wood Dragon 26 十五 2	火7 Fire 3 Waiting 水天需 乙巳 Wood Snake 27 十六 3	金4 Metal 4 Great Exceeding 澤風大過 丙午 Fire Horse 28 十七 3	水6 Water 5 Poison 山風蠱 丁未 Fire Goat 29 十八 7	火2 Fire 6 Dispersing 風水渙 戊申 Earth Monkey 30 十九 6	

MAY 2021 癸巳

Xuan Kong Element 玄空五行	澤天夬 Eliminating	Period Luck 卦運	Monthly Star 月星
Metal 金4		6	2

SUNDAY	MONDAY	TUESDAY	WEDNESDAY	THURSDAY	FRIDAY	SATURDAY
木8 Wood Abundance 9 戊寅 Earth Tiger 雷火豐 **30** 十九 6	火7 Fire Regulate 1 己卯 Earth Rabbit 水澤節 **31** 二十 8					木3 Wood Travelling 7 己酉 Earth Rooster 火山旅 **1** 二十 8
金9 Metal Stagnation 8 庚戌 Metal Dog 天地否 **2** 廿一 9	火7 Fire Alliance 9 辛亥 Metal Pig 水地比 **3** 廿二 7	木8 Wood Thunder 1 壬子 Water Rat 震爲雷 **4** 廿三 1	水6 Water Beauty 2 癸丑 Water Ox 山火賁 **5** 廿四 8	火7 Fire Accomplished 3 甲寅 Wood Tiger 水火既濟 **6** 廿五 9	水1 Water Arriving 4 乙卯 Wood Rabbit 地澤臨 **7** 廿六 4	金4 Metal Marsh 5 丙辰 Fire Dragon 兑爲澤 **8** 廿七 1
火2 Fire Small Livestock 6 丁巳 Fire Snake 風天小畜 **9** 廿八 8	木3 Wood The Cauldron 7 戊午 Earth Horse 火風鼎 **10** 廿九 4	水1 Water Rising 8 己未 Earth Goat 地風升 **11** 三十 2	火7 Fire Water 9 庚申 Metal Monkey 坎爲水 **12** 四月初一 1	木8 Wood Lesser Exceeding 1 辛酉 Metal Rooster 雷山小過 **13** 初二 3	金4 Metal Gathering 2 壬戌 Water Dog 澤地萃 **14** 初三 4	水6 Water Peel 3 癸亥 Water Pig 山地剝 **15** 初四 6
水1 Water Earth 4 甲子 Wood Rat 坤爲地 **16** 初五 1	木3 Wood Biting 5 乙丑 Wood Ox 火雷噬嗑 **17** 初六 6	火2 Fire Family 6 丙寅 Fire Tiger 風火家人 **18** 初七 4	水6 Water Decreasing 7 丁卯 Fire Rabbit 山澤損 **19** 初八 9	金9 Metal Tread 8 戊辰 Earth Dragon 天澤履 **20** 初九 6	木8 Wood Great Strength 9 己巳 Earth Snake 雷天大壯 **21** 初十 2	木8 Wood Consistency 1 庚午 Metal Horse 雷風恒 **22** 十一 9
金9 Metal Litigation 2 辛未 Metal Goat 天水訟 **23** 十二 3	水1 Water Officer 3 壬申 Water Monkey 地水師 **24** 十三 7	火2 Fire Gradual Progress 4 癸酉 Water Rooster 風山漸 **25** 十四 7	火7 Fire Obstruction 5 甲戌 Wood Dog 水山蹇 **26** 十五 2	木3 Wood Advancement 6 乙亥 Wood Pig 火地晉 **27** 十六 3	水6 Water Nourish 7 丙子 Fire Rat 山雷頤 **28** 十七 3	金4 Metal Following 8 丁丑 Fire Ox 澤雷隨 **29** 十八 7

JUNE 2021 甲午

Xuan Kong Element 玄空五行	乾爲天 Heaven	Period Luck 卦運	Monthly Star 月星
Metal 金9		1	1

SUNDAY	MONDAY	TUESDAY	WEDNESDAY	THURSDAY	FRIDAY	SATURDAY
		水1 Water Unity 2 庚辰 Metal Dragon 地天泰 **1** 廿一 9	木3 Wood Great Reward 3 辛巳 Metal Snake 火天大有 **2** 廿二 7	火2 Fire Wind 4 壬午 Water Horse 巽爲風 **3** 廿三 1	金4 Metal Trap 5 癸未 Water Goat 澤水困 **4** 廿四 8	木3 Wood Not Yet Accomplished 6 甲申 Wood Monkey 火水未濟 **5** 廿五 9
金9 Metal Retreat 7 乙酉 Wood Rooster 天山遯 **6** 廿六 4	水6 Water Mountain 8 丙戌 Fire Dog 艮爲山 **7** 廿七 1	木8 Wood Delight 9 丁亥 Fire Pig 雷地豫 **8** 廿八 8	火7 Fire Beginning 1 戊子 Earth Rat 水雷屯 **9** 廿九 4	金9 Metal Without Wrongdoing 2 己丑 Earth Ox 天雷無妄 **10** 五月初一 2	木3 Wood Fire 3 庚寅 Metal Tiger 離爲火 **11** 初二 1	火2 Fire Sincerity 4 辛卯 Metal Rabbit 風澤中孚 **12** 初三 3
水6 Water Big Livestock 5 壬辰 Water Dragon 山天大畜 **13** 初四 4	金4 Metal Eliminating 6 癸巳 Water Snake 澤天夬 **14** 初五 6	金9 Metal Heaven 7 甲午 Wood Horse 乾爲天 **15** 初六 1	火7 Fire Well 8 乙未 Wood Goat 水風井 **16** 初七 6	木8 Wood Relief 9 丙申 Fire Monkey 雷水解 **17** 初八 4	金4 Metal Influence 1 丁酉 Fire Rooster 澤山咸 **18** 初九 9	水1 Water Humility 2 戊戌 Earth Dog 地山謙 **19** 初十 6
火2 Fire Observation 3 己亥 Earth Pig 風地觀 **20** 十一 2	火2 Fire Increasing 4/6 庚子 Metal Rat 風雷益 **21** 十二 9	水1 Water Dimming Light 5 辛丑 Metal Ox 地火明夷 **22** 十三 3	金9 Metal Fellowship 4 壬寅 Water Tiger 天火同人 **23** 十四 7	木8 Wood Marrying Maiden 3 癸卯 Water Rabbit 雷澤歸妹 **24** 十五 7	木3 Wood Opposition 2 甲辰 Wood Dragon 火澤睽 **25** 十六 2	火7 Fire Waiting 1 乙巳 Wood Snake 水天需 **26** 十七 3
金4 Metal Great Exceeding 9 丙午 Fire Horse 澤風大過 **27** 十八 3	水6 Water Poison 8 丁未 Fire Goat 山風蠱 **28** 十九 7	火2 Fire Dispersing 7 戊申 Earth Monkey 風水渙 **29** 二十 6	木3 Wood Travelling 6 己酉 Earth Rooster 火山旅 **30** 廿一 8			

JULY 2021 乙未

Xuan Kong Element 玄空五行	水風井 Well	Period Luck 卦運	Monthly Star 月星
Fire 火7		6	9

SUNDAY	MONDAY	TUESDAY	WEDNESDAY	THURSDAY	FRIDAY	SATURDAY
				1 廿二 金9 Metal 庚戌 Metal Dog 9 Stagnation 天地否 5	**2** 廿三 火7 Fire 辛亥 Metal Pig 7 Alliance 水地比 4	**3** 廿四 木8 Wood 壬子 Water Rat 1 Thunder 震為雷 3
4 廿五 水6 Water 癸丑 Water Ox 8 Beauty 山火賁 2	**5** 廿六 火7 Fire 甲寅 Wood Tiger 9 Accomplished 水火既濟 1	**6** 廿七 水1 Water 乙卯 Wood Rabbit 4 Arriving 地澤臨 9	**7** 廿八 金4 Metal 丙辰 Fire Dragon 1 Marsh 兌為澤 8	**8** 廿九 火2 Fire 丁巳 Fire Snake 8 Small Livestock 風天小畜 7	**9** 三十 木3 Wood 戊午 Earth Horse 4 The Cauldron 火風鼎 6	**10** 六月初一 水1 Water 己未 Earth Goat 2 Rising 地風升 5
11 初二 火7 Fire 庚申 Metal Monkey 1 Water 坎為水 4	**12** 初三 木8 Wood 辛酉 Metal Rooster 3 Lesser Exceeding 雷山小過 3	**13** 初四 金4 Metal 壬戌 Water Dog 4 Gathering 澤地萃 2	**14** 初五 水6 Water 癸亥 Water Pig 6 Peel 山地剝 1	**15** 初六 水1 Water 甲子 Wood Rat 1 Earth 坤為地 9	**16** 初七 木3 Wood 乙丑 Wood Ox 6 Biting 火雷噬嗑 8	**17** 初八 火2 Fire 丙寅 Fire Tiger 4 Family 風火家人 7
18 初九 水6 Water 丁卯 Fire Rabbit 9 Decreasing 山澤損 6	**19** 初十 金9 Metal 戊辰 Earth Dragon 6 Tread 天澤履 5	**20** 十一 木8 Wood 己巳 Earth Snake 2 Great Strength 雷天大壯 4	**21** 十二 木8 Wood 庚午 Metal Horse 9 Consistency 雷風恆 3	**22** 十三 金9 Metal 辛未 Metal Goat 3 Litigation 天水訟 2	**23** 十四 水1 Water 壬申 Water Monkey 7 Officer 地水師 1	**24** 十五 火2 Fire 癸酉 Water Rooster 7 Gradual Progress 風山漸 9
25 十六 火7 Fire 甲戌 Wood Dog 2 Obstruction 水山蹇 8	**26** 十七 木3 Wood 乙亥 Wood Pig 3 Advancement 火地晉 7	**27** 十八 水6 Water 丙子 Fire Rat 3 Nourish 山雷頤 6	**28** 十九 金4 Metal 丁丑 Fire Ox 7 Following 澤雷隨 5	**29** 二十 木8 Wood 戊寅 Earth Tiger 6 Abundance 雷火豐 4	**30** 廿一 火7 Fire 己卯 Earth Rabbit 8 Regulate 水澤節 3	**31** 廿二 水1 Water 庚辰 Metal Dragon 9 Unity 地天泰 2

AUGUST 2021 丙申

Xuan Kong Element 玄空五行	雷水解 Relief	Period Luck 卦運	Monthly Star 月星
Wood 木8		4	8

SUNDAY	MONDAY	TUESDAY	WEDNESDAY	THURSDAY	FRIDAY	SATURDAY
1 廿三 木3 Wood 辛巳 Metal Snake 7 Great Reward 火天大有 1	**2** 廿四 火2 Fire 壬午 Water Horse 1 Wind 巽為風 9	**3** 廿五 金4 Metal 癸未 Water Goat 8 Trap 澤水困 8	**4** 廿六 木3 Wood 甲申 Wood Monkey 9 Not Yet Accomplished 火水未濟 7	**5** 廿七 金9 Metal 乙酉 Wood Rooster 4 Retreat 天山遯 6	**6** 廿八 水6 Water 丙戌 Fire Dog 1 Mountain 艮為山 5	**7** 廿九 木8 Wood 丁亥 Fire Pig 8 Delight 雷地豫 4
8 七月初一 火7 Fire 戊子 Earth Rat 4 Beginning 水雷屯 3	**9** 初二 金9 Metal 己丑 Earth Ox 2 Without Wrongdoing 天雷無妄 2	**10** 初三 木3 Wood 庚寅 Metal Tiger 1 Fire 離為火 1	**11** 初四 火2 Fire 辛卯 Metal Rabbit 3 Sincerity 風澤中孚 9	**12** 初五 水6 Water 壬辰 Water Dragon 4 Big Livestock 山天大畜 8	**13** 初六 金4 Metal 癸巳 Water Snake 6 Eliminating 澤天夬 7	**14** 初七 金9 Metal 甲午 Wood Horse 1 Heaven 乾為天 6
15 初八 火7 Fire 乙未 Wood Goat 6 Well 水風井 5	**16** 初九 木8 Wood 丙申 Fire Monkey 4 Relief 雷水解 4	**17** 初十 金4 Metal 丁酉 Fire Rooster 9 Influence 澤山咸 3	**18** 十一 水1 Water 戊戌 Earth Dog 6 Humility 地山謙 2	**19** 十二 火2 Fire 己亥 Earth Pig 2 Observation 風地觀 1	**20** 十三 火2 Fire 庚子 Metal Rat 9 Increasing 風雷益 9	**21** 十四 水1 Water 辛丑 Metal Ox 3 Dimming Light 地火明夷 8
22 十五 金9 Metal 壬寅 Water Tiger 7 Fellowship 天火同人 7	**23** 十六 木8 Wood 癸卯 Water Rabbit 7 Marrying Maiden 雷澤歸妹 6	**24** 十七 木3 Wood 甲辰 Wood Dragon 2 Opposition 火澤睽 5	**25** 十八 火7 Fire 乙巳 Wood Snake 3 Waiting 水天需 4	**26** 十九 金4 Metal 丙午 Fire Horse 3 Great Exceeding 澤風大過 3	**27** 二十 水6 Water 丁未 Fire Goat 7 Poison 山風蠱 2	**28** 廿一 火2 Fire 戊申 Earth Monkey 6 Dispersing 風水渙 1
29 廿二 木3 Wood 己酉 Earth Rooster 8 Travelling 火山旅 9	**30** 廿三 金9 Metal 庚戌 Metal Dog 9 Stagnation 天地否 8	**31** 廿四 火7 Fire 辛亥 Metal Pig 7 Alliance 水地比 7				

SEPTEMBER 2021 丁酉

Xuan Kong Element 玄空五行	澤山咸 Influence	Period Luck 卦運	Monthly Star 月星
Metal 金4		9	7

SUNDAY	MONDAY	TUESDAY	WEDNESDAY	THURSDAY	FRIDAY	SATURDAY
			1 廿五 木8 Wood · 6 Thunder 震爲雷 壬子 Water Rat 1	**2** 廿六 水6 Water · 5 Beauty 山火賁 癸丑 Water Ox 8	**3** 廿七 火7 Fire · 4 Accomplished 水火既濟 甲寅 Wood Tiger 9	**4** 廿八 水1 Water · 3 Arriving 地澤臨 乙卯 Wood Rabbit 4
5 廿九 金4 Metal · 2 Marsh 兌爲澤 丙辰 Fire Dragon 1	**6** 三十 火2 Fire · 1 Small Livestock 風天小畜 丁巳 Fire Snake 8	**7** 八月初一 木3 Wood · 9 The Cauldron 火風鼎 戊午 Earth Horse 4	**8** 初二 水1 Water · 8 Rising 地風升 己未 Earth Goat 2	**9** 初三 火7 Fire · 7 Water 坎爲水 庚申 Metal Monkey 1	**10** 初四 木8 Wood · 6 Lesser Exceeding 雷山小過 辛酉 Metal Rooster 3	**11** 初五 金4 Metal · 5 Gathering 澤地萃 壬戌 Water Dog 4
12 初六 水6 Water · 4 Peel 山地剝 癸亥 Water Pig 6	**13** 初七 水1 Water · 3 Earth 坤爲地 甲子 Wood Rat 1	**14** 初八 木3 Wood · 2 Biting 火雷噬嗑 乙丑 Wood Ox 6	**15** 初九 火2 Fire · 1 Family 風火家人 丙寅 Fire Tiger 4	**16** 初十 水6 Water · 9 Decreasing 山澤損 丁卯 Fire Rabbit 9	**17** 十一 金9 Metal · 8 Tread 天澤履 戊辰 Earth Dragon 6	**18** 十二 木8 Wood · 7 Great Strength 雷天大壯 己巳 Earth Snake 2
19 十三 木8 Wood · 6 Consistency 雷風恆 庚午 Metal Horse 9	**20** 十四 金9 Metal · 5 Litigation 天水訟 辛未 Metal Goat 3	**21** 十五 水1 Water · 4 Officer 地水師 壬申 Water Monkey 7	**22** 十六 火2 Fire · 3 Gradual Progress 風山漸 癸酉 Water Rooster 7	**23** 十七 火7 Fire · 2 Obstruction 水山蹇 甲戌 Wood Dog 2	**24** 十八 木3 Wood · 1 Advancement 火地晉 乙亥 Wood Pig 3	**25** 十九 水6 Water · 9 Nourish 山雷頤 丙子 Fire Rat 3
26 二十 金4 Metal · 8 Following 澤雷隨 丁丑 Fire Ox 7	**27** 廿一 木8 Wood · 7 Abundance 雷火豐 戊寅 Earth Tiger 6	**28** 廿二 火7 Fire · 6 Regulate 水澤節 己卯 Earth Rabbit 8	**29** 廿三 水1 Water · 5 Unity 地天泰 庚辰 Metal Dragon 9	**30** 廿四 木3 Wood · 4 Great Reward 火天大有 辛巳 Metal Snake 7		

OCTOBER 2021 戊戌

Xuan Kong Element 玄空五行	地山謙 Humility	Period Luck 卦運	Monthly Star 月星
Water 水1		6	6

SUNDAY	MONDAY	TUESDAY	WEDNESDAY	THURSDAY	FRIDAY	SATURDAY
31 廿六 木8 Wood · 9 Thunder 震爲雷 壬子 Water Rat 1					**1** 廿五 火2 Fire · 3 Wind 巽爲風 壬午 Water Horse 1	**2** 廿六 金4 Metal · 2 Trap 澤水困 癸未 Water Goat 8
3 廿七 木3 Wood · 1 Not Yet Accomplished 火水未濟 甲申 Wood Monkey 9	**4** 廿八 金9 Metal · 9 Retreat 天山遯 乙酉 Wood Rooster 4	**5** 廿九 水6 Water · 8 Mountain 艮爲山 丙戌 Fire Dog 1	**6** 九月初一 木8 Wood · 7 Delight 雷地豫 丁亥 Fire Pig 8	**7** 初二 火7 Fire · 6 Beginning 水雷屯 戊子 Earth Rat 4	**8** 初三 金9 Metal · 5 Without Wrongdoing 天雷無妄 己丑 Earth Ox 2	**9** 初四 木3 Wood · 4 Fire 離爲火 庚寅 Metal Tiger 1
10 初五 火2 Fire · 3 Sincerity 風澤中孚 辛卯 Metal Rabbit 3	**11** 初六 水6 Water · 2 Big Livestock 山天大畜 壬辰 Water Dragon 4	**12** 初七 金4 Metal · 1 Eliminating 澤天夬 癸巳 Water Snake 6	**13** 初八 金9 Metal · 9 Heaven 乾爲天 甲午 Wood Horse 1	**14** 初九 火7 Fire · 8 Well 水風井 乙未 Wood Goat 6	**15** 初十 木8 Wood · 7 Relief 雷水解 丙申 Fire Monkey 4	**16** 十一 金4 Metal · 6 Influence 澤山咸 丁酉 Fire Rooster 9
17 十二 水1 Water · 5 Humility 地山謙 戊戌 Earth Dog 6	**18** 十三 火2 Fire · 4 Observation 風地觀 己亥 Earth Pig 2	**19** 十四 火2 Fire · 3 Increasing 風雷益 庚子 Metal Rat 9	**20** 十五 水1 Water · 2 Dimming Light 地火明夷 辛丑 Metal Ox 3	**21** 十六 金9 Metal · 1 Fellowship 天火同人 壬寅 Water Tiger 7	**22** 十七 木8 Wood · 9 Marrying Maiden 雷澤歸妹 癸卯 Water Rabbit 7	**23** 十八 木3 Wood · 8 Opposition 火澤睽 甲辰 Wood Dragon 2
24 十九 火7 Fire · 7 Waiting 水天需 乙巳 Wood Snake 3	**25** 二十 金4 Metal · 6 Great Exceeding 澤風大過 丙午 Fire Horse 3	**26** 廿一 水6 Water · 5 Poison 山風蠱 丁未 Fire Goat 7	**27** 廿二 火2 Fire · 4 Dispersing 風水渙 戊申 Earth Monkey 6	**28** 廿三 木3 Wood · 3 Travelling 火山旅 己酉 Earth Rooster 8	**29** 廿四 金9 Metal · 2 Stagnation 天地否 庚戌 Metal Dog 9	**30** 廿五 火7 Fire · 1 Alliance 水地比 辛亥 Metal Pig 7

NOVEMBER 2021 己亥

Xuan Kong Element 玄空五行	風地觀 Observation	Period Luck 卦運	Monthly Star 月星
Fire 火2		2	5

SUNDAY	MONDAY	TUESDAY	WEDNESDAY	THURSDAY	FRIDAY	SATURDAY
	1 水6 Water · 8 Beauty 山火賁 癸丑 Water Ox · 8 廿七	**2** 火7 Fire · 7 Accomplished 水火既濟 甲寅 Wood Tiger · 9 廿八	**3** 水1 Water · 6 Arriving 地澤臨 乙卯 Wood Rabbit · 4 廿九	**4** 金4 Metal · 5 Marsh 兌爲澤 丙辰 Fire Dragon · 1 三十	**5** 火2 Fire · 4 Small Livestock 風天小畜 丁巳 Fire Snake · 8 十月初一	**6** 木3 Wood · 3 The Cauldron 火風鼎 戊午 Earth Horse · 4 初二
7 水1 Water · 2 Rising 地風升 己未 Earth Goat · 2 初三	**8** 火7 Fire · 1 Water 坎爲水 庚申 Metal Monkey · 1 初四	**9** 木8 Wood · 9 Lesser Exceeding 雷山小過 辛酉 Metal Rooster · 3 初五	**10** 金4 Metal · 8 Gathering 澤地萃 壬戌 Water Dog · 4 初六	**11** 水6 Water · 7 Peel 山地剝 癸亥 Water Pig · 6 初七	**12** 水1 Water · 6 Earth 坤爲地 甲子 Wood Rat · 1 初八	**13** 木3 Wood · 5 Biting 火雷噬嗑 乙丑 Wood Ox · 6 初九
14 火2 Fire · 4 Family 風火家人 丙寅 Fire Tiger · 4 初十	**15** 水6 Water · 3 Decreasing 山澤損 丁卯 Fire Rabbit · 9 十一	**16** 金9 Metal · 2 Tread 天澤履 戊辰 Earth Dragon · 6 十二	**17** 木8 Wood · 1 Great Strength 雷天大壯 己巳 Earth Snake · 2 十三	**18** 木8 Wood · 9 Consistency 雷風恆 庚午 Metal Horse · 9 十四	**19** 金9 Metal · 8 Litigation 天水訟 辛未 Metal Goat · 3 十五	**20** 水1 Water · 7 Officer 地水師 壬申 Water Monkey · 7 十六
21 火2 Fire · 6 Gradual Progress 風山漸 癸酉 Water Rooster · 7 十七	**22** 火7 Fire · 5 Obstruction 水山蹇 甲戌 Wood Dog · 2 十八	**23** 木3 Wood · 4 Advancement 火地晉 乙亥 Wood Pig · 3 十九	**24** 水6 Water · 3 Nourish 山雷頤 丙子 Fire Rat · 3 二十	**25** 金4 Metal · 2 Following 澤雷隨 丁丑 Fire Ox · 7 廿一	**26** 木8 Wood · 1 Abundance 雷火豐 戊寅 Earth Tiger · 6 廿二	**27** 火7 Fire · 9 Regulate 水澤節 己卯 Earth Rabbit · 8 廿三
28 水1 Water · 8 Unity 地天泰 庚辰 Metal Dragon · 9 廿四	**29** 木3 Wood · 7 Great Reward 火天大有 辛巳 Metal Snake · 7 廿五	**30** 火2 Fire · 6 Wind 巽爲風 壬午 Water Horse · 1 廿六				

DECEMBER 2021 庚子

Xuan Kong Element 玄空五行	風雷益 Increasing	Period Luck 卦運	Monthly Star 月星
Fire 火2		9	4

SUNDAY	MONDAY	TUESDAY	WEDNESDAY	THURSDAY	FRIDAY	SATURDAY
			1 金4 Metal · 5 Trap 澤水困 癸未 Water Goat · 8 廿七	**2** 木3 Wood · 4 Not Yet Accomplished 火水未濟 甲申 Wood Monkey · 9 廿八	**3** 金9 Metal · 3 Retreat 天山遯 乙酉 Wood Rooster · 4 廿九	**4** 水6 Water · 2 Mountain 艮爲山 丙戌 Fire Dog · 1 十一月初一
5 木8 Wood · 1 Delight 雷地豫 丁亥 Fire Pig · 8 初二	**6** 火7 Fire · 9 Beginning 水雷屯 戊子 Earth Rat · 4 初三	**7** 金9 Metal · 8 Without Wrongdoing 天雷無妄 己丑 Earth Ox · 2 初四	**8** 木3 Wood · 7 Fire 離爲火 庚寅 Metal Tiger · 1 初五	**9** 火2 Fire · 6 Sincerity 風澤中孚 辛卯 Metal Rabbit · 3 初六	**10** 水6 Water · 5 Big Livestock 山天大畜 壬辰 Water Dragon · 4 初七	**11** 金4 Metal · 4 Eliminating 澤天夬 癸巳 Water Snake · 6 初八
12 金9 Metal · 3 Heaven 乾爲天 甲午 Wood Horse · 1 初九	**13** 火7 Fire · 2 Well 水風井 乙未 Wood Goat · 6 初十	**14** 木8 Wood · 1 Relief 雷水解 丙申 Fire Monkey · 4 十一	**15** 金4 Metal · 9 Influence 澤山咸 丁酉 Fire Rooster · 9 十二	**16** 水1 Water · 8 Humility 地山謙 戊戌 Earth Dog · 6 十三	**17** 火2 Fire · 7 Observation 風地觀 己亥 Earth Pig · 2 十四	**18** 火2 Fire · 6 Increasing 風雷益 庚子 Metal Rat · 9 十五
19 水1 Water · 5 Dimming Light 地火明夷 辛丑 Metal Ox · 3 十六	**20** 金9 Metal · 4 Fellowship 天火同人 壬寅 Water Tiger · 7 十七	**21** 木8 Wood · 3 Marrying Maiden 雷澤歸妹 癸卯 Water Rabbit · 7 十八	**22** 木3 Wood · 2/8 Opposition 火澤睽 甲辰 Wood Dragon · 2 十九	**23** 火7 Fire · 9 Waiting 水天需 乙巳 Wood Snake · 3 二十	**24** 金4 Metal · 1 Great Exceeding 澤風大過 丙午 Fire Horse · 3 廿一	**25** 水6 Water · 2 Poison 山風蠱 丁未 Fire Goat · 7 廿二
26 火2 Fire · 3 Dispersing 風水渙 戊申 Earth Monkey · 6 廿三	**27** 木3 Wood · 4 Travelling 火山旅 己酉 Earth Rooster · 8 廿四	**28** 金9 Metal · 5 Stagnation 天地否 庚戌 Metal Dog · 9 廿五	**29** 火7 Fire · 6 Alliance 水地比 辛亥 Metal Pig · 7 廿六	**30** 木8 Wood · 7 Thunder 震爲雷 壬子 Water Rat · 1 廿七	**31** 水6 Water · 8 Beauty 山火賁 癸丑 Water Ox · 8 廿八	

2022 壬寅

(*Ren Yin*) Water Tiger

2022 壬寅 *(Ren Yin)* Water Tiger

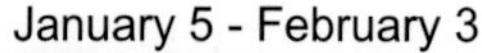

January 5 - February 3

February 4 - March 4

March 5 - April 4

April 5 - May 4

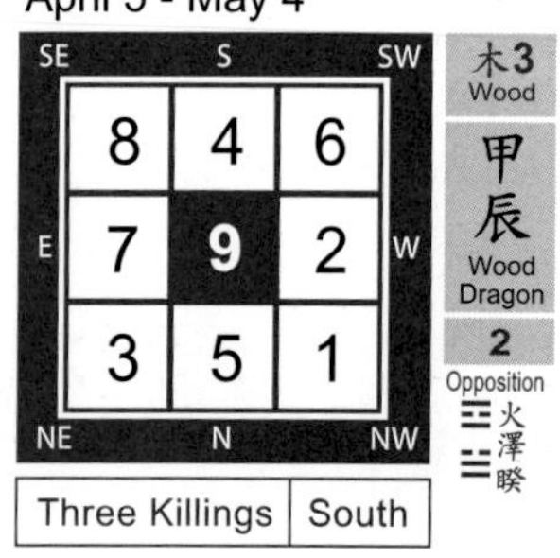

May 5 - June 5

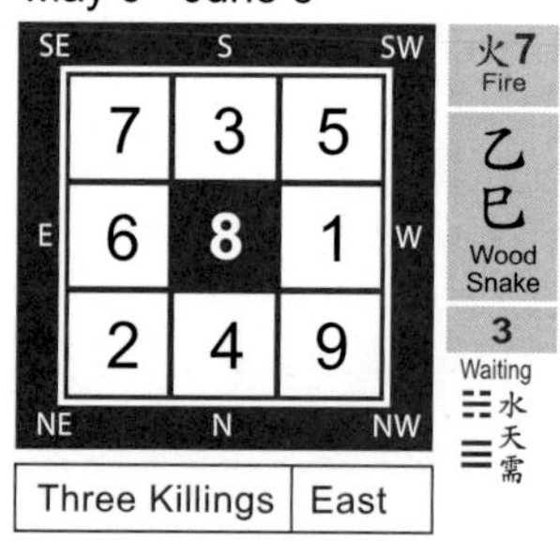

June 6 - July 6

July 7 - August 6

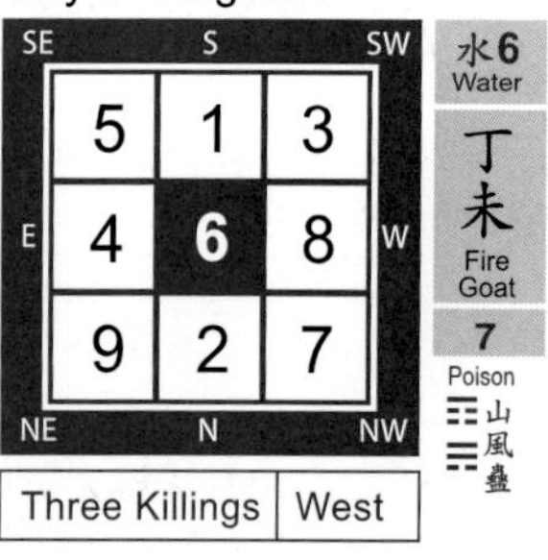

August 7 - September 6

September 7 - October 7

October 8 - November 6

November 7 - December 6

December 7 - January 4

JANUARY 2022 辛丑

Xuan Kong Element 玄空五行	地火明夷 Dimming Light	Period Luck 卦運	Monthly Star 月星
Water 水1		3	3

SUNDAY	MONDAY	TUESDAY	WEDNESDAY	THURSDAY	FRIDAY	SATURDAY
金4 Metal 2 Trap 澤水困 癸未 Water Goat 30 廿八 8	木3 Wood 3 Not Yet Accomplished 火水未濟 甲申 Wood Monkey 31 廿九 9					火7 Fire 9 Accomplished 水火既濟 甲寅 Wood Tiger 1 廿九 9
水1 Water 1 Arriving 地澤臨 乙卯 Wood Rabbit 2 三十 4	金4 Metal 2 Marsh 兌爲澤 丙辰 Fire Dragon 3 十二月初一 1	火2 Fire 3 Small Livestock 風天小畜 丁巳 Fire Snake 4 初二 8	木3 Wood 4 The Cauldron 火風鼎 戊午 Earth Horse 5 初三 4	水1 Water 5 Rising 地風升 己未 Earth Goat 6 初四 2	火7 Fire 6 Water 坎爲水 庚申 Metal Monkey 7 初五 1	木8 Wood 7 Lesser Exceeding 雷山小過 辛酉 Metal Rooster 8 初六 3
金4 Metal 8 Gathering 澤地萃 壬戌 Water Dog 9 初七 4	水6 Water 9 Peel 山地剝 癸亥 Water Pig 10 初八 6	水1 Water 1 Earth 坤爲地 甲子 Wood Rat 11 初九 1	木3 Wood 2 Biting 火雷噬嗑 乙丑 Wood Ox 12 初十 6	火2 Fire 3 Family 風火家人 丙寅 Fire Tiger 13 十一 4	水6 Water 4 Decreasing 山澤損 丁卯 Fire Rabbit 14 十二 9	金9 Metal 5 Tread 天澤履 戊辰 Earth Dragon 15 十三 6
木8 Wood 6 Great Strength 雷天大壯 己巳 Earth Snake 16 十四 2	木8 Wood 7 Consistency 雷風恒 庚午 Metal Horse 17 十五 9	金9 Metal 8 Litigation 天水訟 辛未 Metal Goat 18 十六 3	水1 Water 9 Officer 地水師 壬申 Water Monkey 19 十七 7	火2 Fire 1 Gradual Progress 風山漸 癸酉 Water Rooster 20 十八 7	火7 Fire 2 Obstruction 水山蹇 甲戌 Wood Dog 21 十九 2	木3 Wood 3 Advancement 火地晉 乙亥 Wood Pig 22 二十 3
水6 Water 4 Nourish 山雷頤 丙子 Fire Rat 23 廿一 3	金4 Metal 5 Following 澤雷隨 丁丑 Fire Ox 24 廿二 7	木8 Wood 6 Abundance 雷火豐 戊寅 Earth Tiger 25 廿三 6	火7 Fire 7 Regulate 水澤節 己卯 Earth Rabbit 26 廿四 8	水1 Water 8 Unity 地天泰 庚辰 Metal Dragon 27 廿五 9	木3 Wood 9 Great Reward 火天大有 辛巳 Metal Snake 28 廿六 7	火2 Fire 1 Wind 巽爲風 壬午 Water Horse 29 廿七 1

FEBRUARY 2022 壬寅

Xuan Kong Element 玄空五行	天火同人 Fellowship	Period Luck 卦運	Monthly Star 月星
Metal 金9		7	2

SUNDAY	MONDAY	TUESDAY	WEDNESDAY	THURSDAY	FRIDAY	SATURDAY
		金9 Metal 4 Retreat 天山遯 乙酉 Wood Rooster 1 正月初一 4	水6 Water 5 Mountain 艮爲山 丙戌 Fire Dog 2 初二 1	木8 Wood 6 Delight 雷地豫 丁亥 Fire Pig 3 初三 8	火7 Fire 7 Beginning 水雷屯 戊子 Earth Rat 4 初四 4	金9 Metal 8 Without Wrongdoing 天雷無妄 己丑 Earth Ox 5 初五 2
木3 Wood 9 Fire 離爲火 庚寅 Metal Tiger 6 初六 1	火2 Fire 1 Sincerity 風澤中孚 辛卯 Metal Rabbit 7 初七 3	水6 Water 2 Big Livestock 山天大畜 壬辰 Water Dragon 8 初八 4	金4 Metal 3 Eliminating 澤天夬 癸巳 Water Snake 9 初九 6	金9 Metal 4 Heaven 乾爲天 甲午 Wood Horse 10 初十 1	火7 Fire 5 Well 水風井 乙未 Wood Goat 11 十一 6	木8 Wood 6 Relief 雷水解 丙申 Fire Monkey 12 十二 4
金4 Metal 7 Influence 澤山咸 丁酉 Fire Rooster 13 十三 9	水1 Water 8 Humility 地山謙 戊戌 Earth Dog 14 十四 6	火2 Fire 9 Observation 風地觀 己亥 Earth Pig 15 十五 2	火2 Fire 1 Increasing 風雷益 庚子 Metal Rat 16 十六 9	水1 Water 2 Dimming Light 地火明夷 辛丑 Metal Ox 17 十七 3	金9 Metal 3 Fellowship 天火同人 壬寅 Water Tiger 18 十八 7	木8 Wood 4 Marrying Maiden 雷澤歸妹 癸卯 Water Rabbit 19 十九 7
木3 Wood 5 Opposition 火澤睽 甲辰 Wood Dragon 20 二十 2	火7 Fire 6 Waiting 水天需 乙巳 Wood Snake 21 廿一 3	金4 Metal 7 Great Exceeding 澤風大過 丙午 Fire Horse 22 廿二 3	水6 Water 8 Poison 山風蠱 丁未 Fire Goat 23 廿三 7	火2 Fire 9 Dispersing 風水渙 戊申 Earth Monkey 24 廿四 6	木3 Wood 1 Travelling 火山旅 己酉 Earth Rooster 25 廿五 8	金9 Metal 2 Stagnation 天地否 庚戌 Metal Dog 26 廿六 9
火7 Fire 3 Alliance 水地比 辛亥 Metal Pig 27 廿七 7	木8 Wood 4 Thunder 震爲雷 壬子 Water Rat 28 廿八 1					

MARCH 2022 癸卯

Xuan Kong Element 玄空五行	雷澤歸妹 Marrying Maiden	Period Luck 卦運	Monthly Star 月星
Wood 木8		7	1

SUNDAY	MONDAY	TUESDAY	WEDNESDAY	THURSDAY	FRIDAY	SATURDAY
		水6 Water 5 Beauty 癸丑 Water Ox 山火賁 1 8 廿九	火7 Fire 6 Accomplished 甲寅 Wood Tiger 水火既濟 2 9 三十	水1 Water 7 Arriving 乙卯 Wood Rabbit 地澤臨 3 4 二月初一	金4 Metal 8 Marsh 丙辰 Fire Dragon 兌為澤 4 1 初二	火2 Fire 9 Small Livestock 丁巳 Fire Snake 風天小畜 5 8 初三
木3 Wood 1 The Cauldron 戊午 Earth Horse 火風鼎 6 4 初四	水1 Water 2 Rising 己未 Earth Goat 地風升 7 2 初五	火7 Fire 3 Water 庚申 Metal Monkey 坎為水 8 1 初六	木8 Wood 4 Lesser Exceeding 辛酉 Metal Rooster 雷山小過 9 3 初七	金4 Metal 5 Gathering 壬戌 Water Dog 澤地萃 10 4 初八	水6 Water 6 Peel 癸亥 Water Pig 山地剝 11 6 初九	水1 Water 7 Earth 甲子 Wood Rat 坤為地 12 1 初十
木3 Wood 8 Biting 乙丑 Wood Ox 火雷噬嗑 13 6 十一	火2 Fire 9 Family 丙寅 Fire Tiger 風火家人 14 4 十二	水6 Water 1 Decreasing 丁卯 Fire Rabbit 山澤損 15 9 十三	金9 Metal 2 Tread 戊辰 Earth Dragon 天澤履 16 6 十四	木8 Wood 3 Great Strength 己巳 Earth Snake 雷天大壯 17 2 十五	木8 Wood 4 Consistency 庚午 Metal Horse 雷風恆 18 9 十六	金9 Metal 5 Litigation 辛未 Metal Goat 天水訟 19 3 十七
水1 Water 6 Officer 壬申 Water Monkey 地水師 20 7 十八	火2 Fire 7 Gradual Progress 癸酉 Water Rooster 風山漸 21 7 十九	火7 Fire 8 Obstruction 甲戌 Wood Dog 水山蹇 22 2 二十	木3 Wood 9 Advancement 乙亥 Wood Pig 火地晉 23 3 廿一	水6 Water 1 Nourish 丙子 Fire Rat 山雷頤 24 3 廿二	金4 Metal 2 Following 丁丑 Fire Ox 澤雷隨 25 7 廿三	木8 Wood 3 Abundance 戊寅 Earth Tiger 雷火豐 26 6 廿四
火7 Fire 4 Regulate 己卯 Earth Rabbit 水澤節 27 8 廿五	水1 Water 5 Unity 庚辰 Metal Dragon 地天泰 28 9 廿六	木3 Wood 6 Great Reward 辛巳 Metal Snake 火天大有 29 7 廿七	火2 Fire 7 Wind 壬午 Water Horse 巽為風 30 1 廿八	金4 Metal 8 Trap 癸未 Water Goat 澤水困 31 8 廿九		

APRIL 2022 甲辰

Xuan Kong Element 玄空五行	火澤睽 Opposition	Period Luck 卦運	Monthly Star 月星
Wood 木3		2	9

SUNDAY	MONDAY	TUESDAY	WEDNESDAY	THURSDAY	FRIDAY	SATURDAY
					木3 Wood 9 Not Yet Accomplished 甲申 Wood Monkey 火水未濟 1 9 三月初一	金9 Metal 1 Retreat 乙酉 Wood Rooster 天山遯 2 4 初二
水6 Water 2 Mountain 丙戌 Fire Dog 艮為山 3 1 初三	木8 Wood 3 Delight 丁亥 Fire Pig 雷地豫 4 8 初四	火7 Fire 4 Beginning 戊子 Earth Rat 水雷屯 5 4 初五	金9 Metal 5 Without Wrongdoing 己丑 Earth Ox 天雷無妄 6 2 初六	木3 Wood 6 Fire 庚寅 Metal Tiger 離為火 7 1 初七	火2 Fire 7 Sincerity 辛卯 Metal Rabbit 風澤中孚 8 3 初八	水6 Water 8 Big Livestock 壬辰 Water Dragon 山天大畜 9 4 初九
金4 Metal 9 Eliminating 癸巳 Water Snake 澤天夬 10 6 初十	金9 Metal 1 Heaven 甲午 Wood Horse 乾為天 11 1 十一	火7 Fire 2 Well 乙未 Wood Goat 水風井 12 6 十二	木8 Wood 3 Relief 丙申 Fire Monkey 雷水解 13 4 十三	金4 Metal 4 Influence 丁酉 Fire Rooster 澤山咸 14 9 十四	水1 Water 5 Humility 戊戌 Earth Dog 地山謙 15 6 十五	火2 Fire 6 Observation 己亥 Earth Pig 風地觀 16 2 十六
火2 Fire 7 Increasing 庚子 Metal Rat 風雷益 17 9 十七	水1 Water 8 Dimming Light 辛丑 Metal Ox 地火明夷 18 3 十八	金9 Metal 9 Fellowship 壬寅 Water Tiger 天火同人 19 7 十九	木8 Wood 1 Marrying Maiden 癸卯 Water Rabbit 雷澤歸妹 20 7 二十	木3 Wood 2 Opposition 甲辰 Wood Dragon 火澤睽 21 2 廿一	火7 Fire 3 Waiting 乙巳 Wood Snake 水天需 22 3 廿二	金4 Metal 4 Great Exceeding 丙午 Fire Horse 澤風大過 23 3 廿三
水6 Water 5 Poison 丁未 Fire Goat 山風蠱 24 7 廿四	火2 Fire 6 Dispersing 戊申 Earth Monkey 風水渙 25 6 廿五	木3 Wood 7 Travelling 己酉 Earth Rooster 火山旅 26 8 廿六	金9 Metal 8 Stagnation 庚戌 Metal Dog 天地否 27 9 廿七	火7 Fire 9 Alliance 辛亥 Metal Pig 水地比 28 7 廿八	木8 Wood 1 Thunder 壬子 Water Rat 震為雷 29 1 廿九	水6 Water 2 Beauty 癸丑 Water Ox 山火賁 30 8 三十

MAY 2022 乙巳

Xuan Kong Element 玄空五行	水天需	Period Luck 卦運	Monthly Star 月星
Fire 火7	Waiting	3	8

SUNDAY	MONDAY	TUESDAY	WEDNESDAY	THURSDAY	FRIDAY	SATURDAY
火7 Fire 甲寅 Wood Tiger 9 Accomplished 水火既濟 3 **1** 四月初一	水1 Water 乙卯 Wood Rabbit 4 Arriving 地澤臨 4 **2** 初二	金4 Metal 丙辰 Fire Dragon 1 Marsh 兑爲澤 5 **3** 初三	火2 Fire 丁巳 Fire Snake 8 Small Livestock 風天小畜 6 **4** 初四	木3 Wood 戊午 Earth Horse 4 The Cauldron 火風鼎 7 **5** 初五	水1 Water 己未 Earth Goat 2 Rising 地風升 8 **6** 初六	火7 Fire 庚申 Metal Monkey 1 Water 坎爲水 9 **7** 初七
木8 Wood 辛酉 Metal Rooster 3 Lesser Exceeding 雷山小過 1 **8** 初八	金4 Metal 壬戌 Water Dog 4 Gathering 澤地萃 2 **9** 初九	水6 Water 癸亥 Water Pig 6 Peel 山地剝 3 **10** 初十	水1 Water 甲子 Wood Rat 1 Earth 坤爲地 4 **11** 十一	木3 Wood 乙丑 Wood Ox 6 Biting 火雷噬嗑 5 **12** 十二	火2 Fire 丙寅 Fire Tiger 4 Family 風火家人 6 **13** 十三	水6 Water 丁卯 Fire Rabbit 9 Decreasing 山澤損 7 **14** 十四
金9 Metal 戊辰 Earth Dragon 6 Tread 天澤履 8 **15** 十五	木8 Wood 己巳 Earth Snake 2 Great Strength 雷天大壯 9 **16** 十六	木8 Wood 庚午 Metal Horse 9 Consistency 雷風恆 1 **17** 十七	金9 Metal 辛未 Metal Goat 3 Litigation 天水訟 2 **18** 十八	水1 Water 壬申 Water Monkey 7 Officer 地水師 3 **19** 十九	火2 Fire 癸酉 Water Rooster 7 Gradual Progress 風山漸 4 **20** 二十	火7 Fire 甲戌 Wood Dog 2 Obstruction 水山蹇 5 **21** 廿一
木3 Wood 乙亥 Wood Pig 3 Advancement 火地晉 6 **22** 廿二	水6 Water 丙子 Fire Rat 3 Nourish 山雷頤 7 **23** 廿三	金4 Metal 丁丑 Fire Ox 7 Following 澤雷隨 8 **24** 廿四	木8 Wood 戊寅 Earth Tiger 6 Abundance 雷火豐 9 **25** 廿五	火7 Fire 己卯 Earth Rabbit 8 Regulate 水澤節 1 **26** 廿六	水1 Water 庚辰 Metal Dragon 9 Unity 地天泰 2 **27** 廿七	木3 Wood 辛巳 Metal Snake 7 Great Reward 火天大有 3 **28** 廿八
火2 Fire 壬午 Water Horse 1 Wind 巽爲風 4 **29** 廿九	金4 Metal 癸未 Water Goat 8 Trap 澤水困 5 **30** 五月初一	木3 Wood 甲申 Wood Monkey 9 Not Yet Accomplished 火水未濟 6 **31** 初二				

JUNE 2022 丙午

Xuan Kong Element 玄空五行	澤風大過	Period Luck 卦運	Monthly Star 月星
Metal 金4	Great Exceeding	3	7

SUNDAY	MONDAY	TUESDAY	WEDNESDAY	THURSDAY	FRIDAY	SATURDAY
			金9 Metal 乙酉 Wood Rooster 4 Retreat 天山遯 7 **1** 初三	水6 Water 丙戌 Fire Dog 1 Mountain 艮爲山 8 **2** 初四	木8 Wood 丁亥 Fire Pig 8 Delight 雷地豫 9 **3** 初五	火7 Fire 戊子 Earth Rat 4 Beginning 水雷屯 1 **4** 初六
金9 Metal 己丑 Earth Ox 2 Without Wrongdoing 天雷無妄 2 **5** 初七	木3 Wood 庚寅 Metal Tiger 1 Fire 離爲火 3 **6** 初八	火2 Fire 辛卯 Metal Rabbit 3 Sincerity 風澤中孚 4 **7** 初九	水6 Water 壬辰 Water Dragon 4 Big Livestock 山天大畜 5 **8** 初十	金4 Metal 癸巳 Water Snake 6 Eliminating 澤天夬 6 **9** 十一	金9 Metal 甲午 Wood Horse 1 Heaven 乾爲天 7 **10** 十二	火7 Fire 乙未 Wood Goat 6 Well 水風井 8 **11** 十三
木8 Wood 丙申 Fire Monkey 4 Relief 雷水解 9 **12** 十四	金4 Metal 丁酉 Fire Rooster 9 Influence 澤山咸 1 **13** 十五	水1 Water 戊戌 Earth Dog 6 Humility 地山謙 2 **14** 十六	火2 Fire 己亥 Earth Pig 2 Observation 風地觀 3 **15** 十七	火2 Fire 庚子 Metal Rat 9 Increasing 風雷益 4 **16** 十八	水1 Water 辛丑 Metal Ox 3 Dimming Light 地火明夷 5 **17** 十九	金9 Metal 壬寅 Water Tiger 7 Fellowship 天火同人 6 **18** 二十
木8 Wood 癸卯 Water Rabbit 7 Marrying Maiden 雷澤歸妹 7 **19** 廿一	木3 Wood 甲辰 Wood Dragon 2 Opposition 火澤睽 8 **20** 廿二	火7 Fire 乙巳 Wood Snake 3 Waiting 水天需 9/1 **21** 廿三	金4 Metal 丙午 Fire Horse 3 Great Exceeding 澤風大過 9 **22** 廿四	水6 Water 丁未 Fire Goat 7 Poison 山風蠱 8 **23** 廿五	火2 Fire 戊申 Earth Monkey 6 Dispersing 風水渙 7 **24** 廿六	木3 Wood 己酉 Earth Rooster 8 Travelling 火山旅 6 **25** 廿七
金9 Metal 庚戌 Metal Dog 9 Stagnation 天地否 5 **26** 廿八	火7 Fire 辛亥 Metal Pig 7 Alliance 水地比 4 **27** 廿九	木8 Wood 壬子 Water Rat 1 Thunder 震爲雷 3 **28** 三十	水6 Water 癸丑 Water Ox 8 Beauty 山火賁 2 **29** 六月初一	火7 Fire 甲寅 Wood Tiger 9 Accomplished 水火既濟 1 **30** 初二		

JULY 2022 丁未

Xuan Kong Element 玄空五行	山風蠱 Poison	Period Luck 卦運	Monthly Star 月星
Water 水6		7	6

SUNDAY	MONDAY	TUESDAY	WEDNESDAY	THURSDAY	FRIDAY	SATURDAY
金9 Metal Retreat 6 乙酉 Wood Rooster 天山遯 31 4 初三					水1 Water Arriving 9 乙卯 Wood Rabbit 地澤臨 1 4 初三	金4 Metal Marsh 8 丙辰 Fire Dragon 兌爲澤 2 1 初四
火2 Fire Small Livestock 7 丁巳 Fire Snake 風天小畜 3 8 初五	木3 Wood The Cauldron 6 戊午 Earth Horse 火風鼎 4 4 初六	水1 Water Rising 5 己未 Earth Goat 地風升 5 2 初七	火7 Fire Water 4 庚申 Metal Monkey 坎爲水 6 1 初八	木8 Wood Lesser Exceeding 3 辛酉 Metal Rooster 雷山小過 7 3 初九	金4 Metal Gathering 2 壬戌 Water Dog 澤地萃 8 4 初十	水6 Water Peel 1 癸亥 Water Pig 山地剝 9 6 十一
水1 Water Earth 9 甲子 Wood Rat 坤爲地 10 1 十二	木3 Wood Biting 8 乙丑 Wood Ox 火雷噬嗑 11 6 十三	火2 Fire Family 7 丙寅 Fire Tiger 風火家人 12 4 十四	水6 Water Decreasing 6 丁卯 Fire Rabbit 山澤損 13 9 十五	金9 Metal Tread 5 戊辰 Earth Dragon 天澤履 14 6 十六	木8 Wood Great Strength 4 己巳 Earth Snake 雷天大壯 15 2 十七	木8 Wood Consistency 3 庚午 Metal Horse 雷風恆 16 9 十八
金9 Metal Litigation 2 辛未 Metal Goat 天水訟 17 3 十九	水1 Water Officer 1 壬申 Water Monkey 地水師 18 7 二十	火2 Fire Gradual Progress 9 癸酉 Water Rooster 風山漸 19 7 廿一	火7 Fire Obstruction 8 甲戌 Wood Dog 水山蹇 20 2 廿二	木3 Wood Advancement 7 乙亥 Wood Pig 火地晉 21 3 廿三	水6 Water Nourish 6 丙子 Fire Rat 山雷頤 22 3 廿四	金4 Metal Following 5 丁丑 Fire Ox 澤雷隨 23 7 廿五
木8 Wood Abundance 4 戊寅 Earth Tiger 雷火豐 24 6 廿六	火7 Fire Regulate 3 己卯 Earth Rabbit 水澤節 25 8 廿七	水1 Water Unity 2 庚辰 Metal Dragon 地天泰 26 9 廿八	木3 Wood Great Reward 1 辛巳 Metal Snake 火天大有 27 7 廿九	火2 Fire Wind 9 壬午 Water Horse 巽爲風 28 1 三十	金4 Metal Trap 8 癸未 Water Goat 澤水困 29 8 七月初一	木3 Wood Not Yet Accomplished 7 甲申 Wood Monkey 火水未濟 30 9 初二

AUGUST 2022 戊申

Xuan Kong Element 玄空五行	風水渙 Dispersing	Period Luck 卦運	Monthly Star 月星
Fire 火2		6	5

SUNDAY	MONDAY	TUESDAY	WEDNESDAY	THURSDAY	FRIDAY	SATURDAY
	水6 Water Mountain 5 丙戌 Fire Dog 艮爲山 1 1 初四	木8 Wood Delight 4 丁亥 Fire Pig 雷地豫 2 8 初五	火7 Fire Beginning 3 戊子 Earth Rat 水雷屯 3 4 初六	金9 Metal Without Wrongdoing 2 己丑 Earth Ox 天雷無妄 4 2 初七	木3 Wood Fire 1 庚寅 Metal Tiger 離爲火 5 1 初八	火2 Fire Sincerity 9 辛卯 Metal Rabbit 風澤中孚 6 3 初九
水6 Water Big Livestock 8 壬辰 Water Dragon 山天大畜 7 4 初十	金4 Metal Eliminating 7 癸巳 Water Snake 澤天夬 8 6 十一	金9 Metal Heaven 6 甲午 Wood Horse 乾爲天 9 1 十二	火7 Fire Well 5 乙未 Wood Goat 水風井 10 6 十三	木8 Wood Relief 4 丙申 Fire Monkey 雷水解 11 4 十四	金4 Metal Influence 3 丁酉 Fire Rooster 澤山咸 12 9 十五	水1 Water Humility 2 戊戌 Earth Dog 地山謙 13 6 十六
火2 Fire Observation 1 己亥 Earth Pig 風地觀 14 2 十七	火2 Fire Increasing 9 庚子 Metal Rat 風雷益 15 9 十八	水1 Water Dimming Light 8 辛丑 Metal Ox 地火明夷 16 3 十九	金9 Metal Fellowship 7 壬寅 Water Tiger 天火同人 17 7 二十	木8 Wood Marrying Maiden 6 癸卯 Water Rabbit 雷澤歸妹 18 7 廿一	木3 Wood Opposition 5 甲辰 Wood Dragon 火澤睽 19 2 廿二	火7 Fire Waiting 4 乙巳 Wood Snake 水天需 20 3 廿三
金4 Metal Great Exceeding 3 丙午 Fire Horse 澤風大過 21 3 廿四	水6 Water Poison 2 丁未 Fire Goat 山風蠱 22 7 廿五	火2 Fire Dispersing 1 戊申 Earth Monkey 風水渙 23 6 廿六	木3 Wood Travelling 9 己酉 Earth Rooster 火山旅 24 8 廿七	金9 Metal Stagnation 8 庚戌 Metal Dog 天地否 25 9 廿八	火7 Fire Alliance 7 辛亥 Metal Pig 水地比 26 7 廿九	木8 Wood Thunder 6 壬子 Water Rat 震爲雷 27 1 八月初一
水6 Water Beauty 5 癸丑 Water Ox 山火賁 28 8 初二	火7 Fire Accomplished 4 甲寅 Wood Tiger 水火既濟 29 9 初三	水1 Water Arriving 3 乙卯 Wood Rabbit 地澤臨 30 4 初四	金4 Metal Marsh 2 丙辰 Fire Dragon 兌爲澤 31 1 初五			

SEPTEMBER 2022 己酉

Xuan Kong Element 玄空五行	火山旅 Travelling	Period Luck 卦運	Monthly Star 月星
Wood 木3		8	4

SUNDAY	MONDAY	TUESDAY	WEDNESDAY	THURSDAY	FRIDAY	SATURDAY
				火2 Fire 1 Small Livestock 丁巳 Fire Snake 風天小畜 **1** 初六 8	木3 Wood 9 The Cauldron 戊午 Earth Horse 火風鼎 **2** 初七 4	水1 Water 8 Rising 己未 Earth Goat 地風升 **3** 初八 2
火7 Fire 7 Water 庚申 Metal Monkey 坎爲水 **4** 初九 1	木8 Wood 6 Lesser Exceeding 辛酉 Metal Rooster 雷山小過 **5** 初十 3	金4 Metal 5 Gathering 壬戌 Water Dog 澤地萃 **6** 十一 4	水6 Water 4 Peel 癸亥 Water Pig 山地剝 **7** 十二 6	水1 Water 3 Earth 甲子 Wood Rat 坤爲地 **8** 十三 1	木3 Wood 2 Biting 乙丑 Wood Ox 火雷噬嗑 **9** 十四 6	火2 Fire 1 Family 丙寅 Fire Tiger 風火家人 **10** 十五 4
水6 Water 9 Decreasing 丁卯 Fire Rabbit 山澤損 **11** 十六 9	金9 Metal 8 Tread 戊辰 Earth Dragon 天澤履 **12** 十七 6	木8 Wood 7 Great Strength 己巳 Earth Snake 雷天大壯 **13** 十八 2	木8 Wood 6 Consistency 庚午 Metal Horse 雷風恆 **14** 十九 9	金9 Metal 5 Litigation 辛未 Metal Goat 天水訟 **15** 二十 3	水1 Water 4 Officer 壬申 Water Monkey 地水師 **16** 廿一 7	火2 Fire 3 Gradual Progress 癸酉 Water Rooster 風山漸 **17** 廿二 7
火7 Fire 2 Obstruction 甲戌 Wood Dog 水山蹇 **18** 廿三 2	木3 Wood 1 Advancement 乙亥 Wood Pig 火地晉 **19** 廿四 3	水6 Water 9 Nourish 丙子 Fire Rat 山雷頤 **20** 廿五 3	金4 Metal 8 Following 丁丑 Fire Ox 澤雷隨 **21** 廿六 7	木8 Wood 7 Abundance 戊寅 Earth Tiger 雷火豐 **22** 廿七 6	火7 Fire 6 Regulate 己卯 Earth Rabbit 水澤節 **23** 廿八 8	水1 Water 5 Unity 庚辰 Metal Dragon 地天泰 **24** 廿九 9
木3 Wood 4 Great Reward 辛巳 Metal Snake 火天大有 **25** 三十 7	火2 Fire 3 Wind 壬午 Water Horse 巽爲風 **26** 九月初一 1	金4 Metal 2 Trap 癸未 Water Goat 澤水困 **27** 初二 8	木3 Wood 1 Not Yet Accomplished 甲申 Wood Monkey 火水未濟 **28** 初三 9	金9 Metal 9 Retreat 乙酉 Wood Rooster 天山遯 **29** 初四 4	水6 Water 8 Mountain 丙戌 Fire Dog 艮爲山 **30** 初五 1	

OCTOBER 2022 庚戌

Xuan Kong Element 玄空五行	天地否 Stagnation	Period Luck 卦運	Monthly Star 月星
Metal 金9		9	3

SUNDAY	MONDAY	TUESDAY	WEDNESDAY	THURSDAY	FRIDAY	SATURDAY
金4 Metal 5 Marsh 丙辰 Fire Dragon 兑爲澤 **30** 初六 1	火2 Fire 4 Small Livestock 丁巳 Fire Snake 風天小畜 **31** 初七 8					木8 Wood 7 Delight 丁亥 Fire Pig 雷地豫 **1** 初六 8
火7 Fire 6 Beginning 戊子 Earth Rat 水雷屯 **2** 初七 4	金9 Metal 5 Without Wrongdoing 己丑 Earth Ox 天雷無妄 **3** 初八 2	木3 Wood 4 Fire 庚寅 Metal Tiger 離爲火 **4** 初九 1	火2 Fire 3 Sincerity 辛卯 Metal Rabbit 風澤中孚 **5** 初十 3	水6 Water 2 Big Livestock 壬辰 Water Dragon 山天大畜 **6** 十一 4	金4 Metal 1 Eliminating 癸巳 Water Snake 澤天夬 **7** 十二 6	金9 Metal 9 Heaven 甲午 Wood Horse 乾爲天 **8** 十三 1
火7 Fire 8 Well 乙未 Wood Goat 水風井 **9** 十四 6	木8 Wood 7 Relief 丙申 Fire Monkey 雷水解 **10** 十五 4	金4 Metal 6 Influence 丁酉 Fire Rooster 澤山咸 **11** 十六 9	水1 Water 5 Humility 戊戌 Earth Dog 地山謙 **12** 十七 6	火2 Fire 4 Observation 己亥 Earth Pig 風地觀 **13** 十八 2	火2 Fire 3 Increasing 庚子 Metal Rat 風雷益 **14** 十九 9	水1 Water 2 Dimming Light 辛丑 Metal Ox 地火明夷 **15** 二十 3
金9 Metal 1 Fellowship 壬寅 Water Tiger 天火同人 **16** 廿一 7	木8 Wood 9 Marrying Maiden 癸卯 Water Rabbit 雷澤歸妹 **17** 廿二 7	木3 Wood 8 Opposition 甲辰 Wood Dragon 火澤睽 **18** 廿三 2	火7 Fire 7 Waiting 乙巳 Wood Snake 水天需 **19** 廿四 3	金4 Metal 6 Great Exceeding 丙午 Fire Horse 澤風大過 **20** 廿五 3	水6 Water 5 Poison 丁未 Fire Goat 山風蠱 **21** 廿六 7	火2 Fire 4 Dispersing 戊申 Earth Monkey 風水渙 **22** 廿七 6
木3 Wood 3 Travelling 己酉 Earth Rooster 火山旅 **23** 廿八 8	金9 Metal 2 Stagnation 庚戌 Metal Dog 天地否 **24** 廿九 9	火7 Fire 1 Alliance 辛亥 Metal Pig 水地比 **25** 十月初一 7	木8 Wood 9 Thunder 壬子 Water Rat 震爲雷 **26** 初二 1	水6 Water 8 Beauty 癸丑 Water Ox 山火賁 **27** 初三 8	火7 Fire 7 Accomplished 甲寅 Wood Tiger 水火既濟 **28** 初四 9	水1 Water 6 Arriving 乙卯 Wood Rabbit 地澤臨 **29** 初五 4

NOVEMBER 2022 辛亥

Xuan Kong Element 玄空五行	水地比 Alliance	Period Luck 卦運	Monthly Star 月星
Fire 火7		7	2

SUNDAY	MONDAY	TUESDAY	WEDNESDAY	THURSDAY	FRIDAY	SATURDAY
		1 初八 The Cauldron 火風鼎 木3 Wood 戊午 Earth Horse 4 [3]	2 初九 Rising 地風升 水1 Water 己未 Earth Goat 2 [2]	3 初十 Water 坎爲水 火7 Fire 庚申 Metal Monkey 1 [1]	4 十一 Lesser Exceeding 雷山小過 木8 Wood 辛酉 Metal Rooster 3 [9]	5 十二 Gathering 澤地萃 金4 Metal 壬戌 Water Dog 4 [8]
6 十三 Peel 山地剝 水6 Water 癸亥 Water Pig 6 [7]	7 十四 Earth 坤爲地 水1 Water 甲子 Wood Rat 1 [6]	8 十五 Biting 火雷噬嗑 木3 Wood 乙丑 Wood Ox 6 [5]	9 十六 Family 風火家人 火2 Fire 丙寅 Fire Tiger 4 [4]	10 十七 Decreasing 山澤損 水6 Water 丁卯 Fire Rabbit 9 [3]	11 十八 Tread 天澤履 金9 Metal 戊辰 Earth Dragon 6 [2]	12 十九 Great Strength 雷天大壯 木8 Wood 己巳 Earth Snake 2 [1]
13 二十 Consistency 雷風恒 木8 Wood 庚午 Metal Horse 9 [9]	14 廿一 Litigation 天水訟 金9 Metal 辛未 Metal Goat 3 [8]	15 廿二 Officer 地水師 水1 Water 壬申 Water Monkey 7 [7]	16 廿三 Gradual Progress 風山漸 火2 Fire 癸酉 Water Rooster 7 [6]	17 廿四 Obstruction 水山蹇 火7 Fire 甲戌 Wood Dog 2 [5]	18 廿五 Advancement 火地晉 木3 Wood 乙亥 Wood Pig 3 [4]	19 廿六 Nourish 山雷頤 水6 Water 丙子 Fire Rat 3 [3]
20 廿七 Following 澤雷隨 金4 Metal 丁丑 Fire Ox 7 [2]	21 廿八 Abundance 雷火豐 木8 Wood 戊寅 Earth Tiger 6 [1]	22 廿九 Regulate 水澤節 火7 Fire 己卯 Earth Rabbit 8 [9]	23 三十 Unity 地天泰 水1 Water 庚辰 Metal Dragon 9 [8]	24 十一月初一 Great Reward 火天大有 木3 Wood 辛巳 Metal Snake 7 [7]	25 初二 Wind 巽爲風 火2 Fire 壬午 Water Horse 1 [6]	26 初三 Trap 澤水困 金4 Metal 癸未 Water Goat 8 [5]
27 初四 Not Yet Accomplished 火水未濟 木3 Wood 甲申 Wood Monkey 9 [4]	28 初五 Retreat 天山遯 金9 Metal 乙酉 Wood Rooster 4 [3]	29 初六 Mountain 艮爲山 水6 Water 丙戌 Fire Dog 1 [2]	30 初七 Delight 雷地豫 木8 Wood 丁亥 Fire Pig 8 [1]			

DECEMBER 2022 壬子

Xuan Kong Element 玄空五行	震爲雷 Thunder	Period Luck 卦運	Monthly Star 月星
Wood 木8		1	1

SUNDAY	MONDAY	TUESDAY	WEDNESDAY	THURSDAY	FRIDAY	SATURDAY
				1 初八 Beginning 水雷屯 火7 Fire 戊子 Earth Rat 4 [9]	2 初九 Without Wrongdoing 天雷無妄 金9 Metal 己丑 Earth Ox 2 [8]	3 初十 Fire 離爲火 木3 Wood 庚寅 Metal Tiger 1 [7]
4 十一 Sincerity 風澤中孚 火2 Fire 辛卯 Metal Rabbit 3 [6]	5 十二 Big Livestock 山天大畜 水6 Water 壬辰 Water Dragon 4 [5]	6 十三 Eliminating 澤天夬 金4 Metal 癸巳 Water Snake 6 [4]	7 十四 Heaven 乾爲天 金9 Metal 甲午 Wood Horse 1 [3]	8 十五 Well 水風井 火7 Fire 乙未 Wood Goat 6 [2]	9 十六 Relief 雷水解 木8 Wood 丙申 Fire Monkey 4 [1]	10 十七 Influence 澤山咸 金4 Metal 丁酉 Fire Rooster 9 [9]
11 十八 Humility 地山謙 水1 Water 戊戌 Earth Dog 6 [8]	12 十九 Observation 風地觀 火2 Fire 己亥 Earth Pig 2 [7]	13 二十 Increasing 風雷益 火2 Fire 庚子 Metal Rat 9 [6]	14 廿一 Dimming Light 地火明夷 水1 Water 辛丑 Metal Ox 3 [5]	15 廿二 Fellowship 天火同人 金9 Metal 壬寅 Water Tiger 7 [4]	16 廿三 Marrying Maiden 雷澤歸妹 木8 Wood 癸卯 Water Rabbit 7 [3]	17 廿四 Opposition 火澤睽 木3 Wood 甲辰 Wood Dragon 2 [2]
18 廿五 Waiting 水天需 火7 Fire 乙巳 Wood Snake 3 [1]	19 廿六 Great Exceeding 澤風大過 金4 Metal 丙午 Fire Horse 3 [9]	20 廿七 Poison 山風蠱 水6 Water 丁未 Fire Goat 7 [8]	21 廿八 Dispersing 風水渙 火2 Fire 戊申 Earth Monkey 6 [7]	22 廿九 Travelling 火山旅 木3 Wood 己酉 Earth Rooster 8 [6/4]	23 十二月初一 Stagnation 天地否 金9 Metal 庚戌 Metal Dog 9 [5]	24 初二 Alliance 水地比 火7 Fire 辛亥 Metal Pig 7 [6]
25 初三 Thunder 震爲雷 木8 Wood 壬子 Water Rat 1 [7]	26 初四 Beauty 山火賁 水6 Water 癸丑 Water Ox 8 [8]	27 初五 Accomplished 水火既濟 火7 Fire 甲寅 Wood Tiger 9 [9]	28 初六 Arriving 地澤臨 水1 Water 乙卯 Wood Rabbit 4 [1]	29 初七 Marsh 兌爲澤 金4 Metal 丙辰 Fire Dragon 1 [2]	30 初八 Small Livestock 風天小畜 火2 Fire 丁巳 Fire Snake 8 [3]	31 初九 The Cauldron 火風鼎 木3 Wood 戊午 Earth Horse 4 [4]

2023 癸卯
(*Gui Mao*) **Water Rabbit**

2023 癸卯 *(Gui Mao)* Water Rabbit

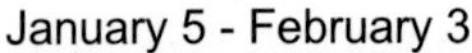

January 5 - February 3

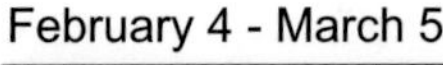

February 4 - March 5

March 6 - April 4

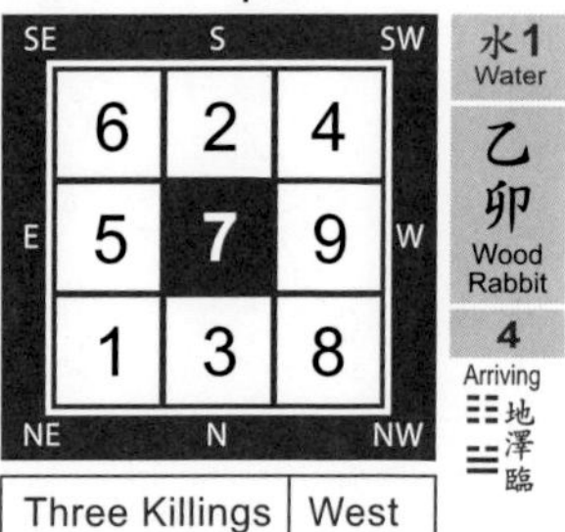

April 5 - May 5

May 6 - June 5

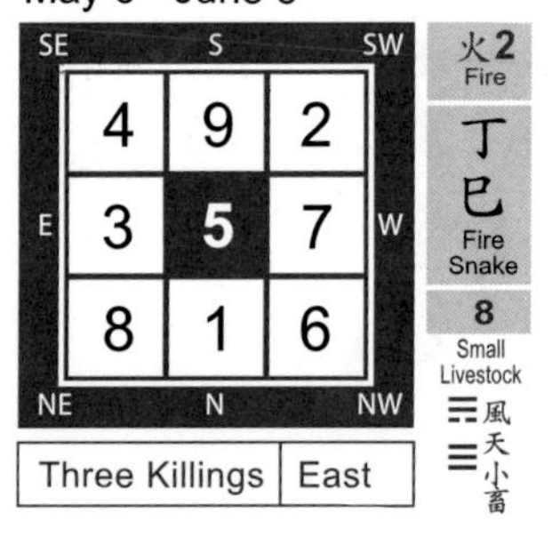

June 6 - July 6

July 7 - August 7

August 8 - September 7

September 8 - October 7

October 8 - November 7

November 8 - December 6

December 7 - January 5

JANUARY 2023 癸丑

Xuan Kong Element 玄空五行	山火賁 Beauty	Period Luck 卦運	Monthly Star 月星
Water 水6		8	9

SUNDAY	MONDAY	TUESDAY	WEDNESDAY	THURSDAY	FRIDAY	SATURDAY
水1 Water 5 Rising 地風升 己未 Earth Goat 2 1 初十	火7 Fire 6 Water 坎爲水 庚申 Metal Monkey 1 2 十一	木8 Wood 7 Lesser Exceeding 雷山小過 辛酉 Metal Rooster 3 3 十二	金4 Metal 8 Gathering 澤地萃 壬戌 Water Dog 4 4 十三	水6 Water 9 Peel 山地剝 癸亥 Water Pig 6 5 十四	水1 Water 1 Earth 坤爲地 甲子 Wood Rat 1 6 十五	木3 Wood 2 Biting 火雷噬嗑 乙丑 Wood Ox 6 7 十六
火2 Fire 3 Family 風火家人 丙寅 Fire Tiger 4 8 十七	水6 Water 4 Decreasing 山澤損 丁卯 Fire Rabbit 9 9 十八	金9 Metal 5 Tread 天澤履 戊辰 Earth Dragon 6 10 十九	木8 Wood 6 Great Strength 雷天大壯 己巳 Earth Snake 2 11 二十	木8 Wood 7 Consistency 雷風恆 庚午 Metal Horse 9 12 廿一	金9 Metal 8 Litigation 天水訟 辛未 Metal Goat 3 13 廿二	水1 Water 9 Officer 地水師 壬申 Water Monkey 7 14 廿三
火2 Fire 1 Gradual Progress 風山漸 癸酉 Water Rooster 7 15 廿四	火7 Fire 2 Obstruction 水山蹇 甲戌 Wood Dog 2 16 廿五	木3 Wood 3 Advancement 火地晉 乙亥 Wood Pig 3 17 廿六	水6 Water 4 Nourish 山雷頤 丙子 Fire Rat 3 18 廿七	金4 Metal 5 Following 澤雷隨 丁丑 Fire Ox 7 19 廿八	木8 Wood 6 Abundance 雷火豐 戊寅 Earth Tiger 6 20 廿九	火7 Fire 7 Regulate 水澤節 己卯 Earth Rabbit 8 21 三十
水1 Water 8 Unity 地天泰 庚辰 Metal Dragon 9 22 正月初一	木3 Wood 9 Great Reward 火天大有 辛巳 Metal Snake 7 23 初二	火2 Fire 1 Wind 巽爲風 壬午 Water Horse 1 24 初三	金4 Metal 2 Trap 澤水困 癸未 Water Goat 8 25 初四	木3 Wood 3 Not Yet Accomplished 火水未濟 甲申 Wood Monkey 9 26 初五	金9 Metal 4 Retreat 天山遯 乙酉 Wood Rooster 4 27 初六	水6 Water 5 Mountain 艮爲山 丙戌 Fire Dog 1 28 初七
木8 Wood 6 Delight 雷地豫 丁亥 Fire Pig 8 29 初八	火7 Fire 7 Beginning 水雷屯 戊子 Earth Rat 4 30 初九	金9 Metal 8 Without Wrongdoing 天雷無妄 己丑 Earth Ox 2 31 初十				

FEBRUARY 2023 甲寅

Xuan Kong Element 玄空五行	水火既濟 Accomplished	Period Luck 卦運	Monthly Star 月星
Fire 火7		9	8

SUNDAY	MONDAY	TUESDAY	WEDNESDAY	THURSDAY	FRIDAY	SATURDAY
			木3 Wood 9 Fire 離爲火 庚寅 Metal Tiger 1 1 十一	火2 Fire 1 Sincerity 風澤中孚 辛卯 Metal Rabbit 3 2 十二	水6 Water 2 Big Livestock 山天大畜 壬辰 Water Dragon 4 3 十三	金4 Metal 3 Eliminating 澤天夬 癸巳 Water Snake 6 4 十四
金9 Metal 4 Heaven 乾爲天 甲午 Wood Horse 1 5 十五	火7 Fire 5 Well 水風井 乙未 Wood Goat 6 6 十六	木8 Wood 6 Relief 雷水解 丙申 Fire Monkey 4 7 十七	金4 Metal 7 Influence 澤山咸 丁酉 Fire Rooster 9 8 十八	水1 Water 8 Humility 地山謙 戊戌 Earth Dog 6 9 十九	火2 Fire 9 Observation 風地觀 己亥 Earth Pig 2 10 二十	火2 Fire 1 Increasing 風雷益 庚子 Metal Rat 9 11 廿一
水1 Water 2 Dimming Light 地火明夷 辛丑 Metal Ox 3 12 廿二	金9 Metal 3 Fellowship 天火同人 壬寅 Water Tiger 7 13 廿三	木8 Wood 4 Marrying Maiden 雷澤歸妹 癸卯 Water Rabbit 7 14 廿四	木3 Wood 5 Opposition 火澤睽 甲辰 Wood Dragon 2 15 廿五	火7 Fire 6 Waiting 水天需 乙巳 Wood Snake 3 16 廿六	金4 Metal 7 Great Exceeding 澤風大過 丙午 Fire Horse 3 17 廿七	水6 Water 8 Poison 山風蠱 丁未 Fire Goat 7 18 廿八
火2 Fire 9 Dispersing 風水渙 戊申 Earth Monkey 6 19 廿九	木3 Wood 1 Travelling 火山旅 己酉 Earth Rooster 8 20 二月初一	金9 Metal 2 Stagnation 天地否 庚戌 Metal Dog 9 21 初二	火7 Fire 3 Alliance 水地比 辛亥 Metal Pig 7 22 初三	木8 Wood 4 Thunder 震爲雷 壬子 Water Rat 1 23 初四	水6 Water 5 Beauty 山火賁 癸丑 Water Ox 8 24 初五	火7 Fire 6 Accomplished 水火既濟 甲寅 Wood Tiger 9 25 初六
水1 Water 7 Arriving 地澤臨 乙卯 Wood Rabbit 4 26 初七	金4 Metal 8 Marsh 兌爲澤 丙辰 Fire Dragon 1 27 初八	火2 Fire 9 Small Livestock 風天小畜 丁巳 Fire Snake 8 28 初九				

MARCH 2023 乙卯

Xuan Kong Element 玄空五行	地澤臨 Arriving	Period Luck 卦運	Monthly Star 月星
Water 水1		4	7

SUNDAY	MONDAY	TUESDAY	WEDNESDAY	THURSDAY	FRIDAY	SATURDAY
			木3 Wood The Cauldron [1] 戊午 Earth Horse 火風鼎 **1** 初十 4	水1 Water Rising [2] 己未 Earth Goat 地風升 **2** 十一 2	火7 Fire Water [3] 庚申 Metal Monkey 坎爲水 **3** 十二 1	木8 Wood Lesser Exceeding [4] 辛酉 Metal Rooster 雷山小過 **4** 十三 3
金4 Metal Gathering [5] 壬戌 Water Dog 澤地萃 **5** 十四 4	水6 Water Peel [6] 癸亥 Water Pig 山地剝 **6** 十五 6	水1 Water Earth [7] 甲子 Wood Rat 坤爲地 **7** 十六 1	木3 Wood Biting [8] 乙丑 Wood Ox 火雷噬嗑 **8** 十七 6	火2 Fire Family [9] 丙寅 Fire Tiger 風火家人 **9** 十八 4	水6 Water Decreasing [1] 丁卯 Fire Rabbit 山澤損 **10** 十九 9	金9 Metal Tread [2] 戊辰 Earth Dragon 天澤履 **11** 二十 6
木8 Wood Great Strength [3] 己巳 Earth Snake 雷天大壯 **12** 廿一 2	木8 Wood Consistency [4] 庚午 Metal Horse 雷風恆 **13** 廿二 9	金9 Metal Litigation [5] 辛未 Metal Goat 天水訟 **14** 廿三 3	水1 Water Officer [6] 壬申 Water Monkey 地水師 **15** 廿四 7	火2 Fire Gradual Progress [7] 癸酉 Water Rooster 風山漸 **16** 廿五 7	火7 Fire Obstruction [8] 甲戌 Wood Dog 水山蹇 **17** 廿六 2	木3 Wood Advancement [9] 乙亥 Wood Pig 火地晉 **18** 廿七 3
水6 Water Nourish [1] 丙子 Fire Rat 山雷頤 **19** 廿八 3	金4 Metal Following [2] 丁丑 Fire Ox 澤雷隨 **20** 廿九 7	木8 Wood Abundance [3] 戊寅 Earth Tiger 雷火豐 **21** 三十 6	火7 Fire Regulate [4] 己卯 Earth Rabbit 水澤節 **22** 閏二月初一 8	水1 Water Unity [5] 庚辰 Metal Dragon 地天泰 **23** 初二 9	木3 Wood Great Reward [6] 辛巳 Metal Snake 火天大有 **24** 初三 7	火2 Fire Wind [7] 壬午 Water Horse 巽爲風 **25** 初四 1
金4 Metal Trap [8] 癸未 Water Goat 澤水困 **26** 初五 8	木3 Wood Not Yet Accomplished [9] 甲申 Wood Monkey 火水未濟 **27** 初六 9	金9 Metal Retreat [1] 乙酉 Wood Rooster 天山遯 **28** 初七 4	水6 Water Mountain [2] 丙戌 Fire Dog 艮爲山 **29** 初八 1	木8 Wood Delight [3] 丁亥 Fire Pig 雷地豫 **30** 初九 8	火7 Fire Beginning [4] 戊子 Earth Rat 水雷屯 **31** 初十 4	

APRIL 2023 丙辰

Xuan Kong Element 玄空五行	兌爲澤 Marsh	Period Luck 卦運	Monthly Star 月星
Metal 金4		1	6

SUNDAY	MONDAY	TUESDAY	WEDNESDAY	THURSDAY	FRIDAY	SATURDAY
木3 Wood The Cauldron [7] 戊午 Earth Horse 火風鼎 **30** 十一 4						金9 Metal Without Wrongdoing [5] 己丑 Earth Ox 天雷無妄 **1** 十一 2
木3 Wood Fire [6] 庚寅 Metal Tiger 離爲火 **2** 十二 1	火2 Fire Sincerity [7] 辛卯 Metal Rabbit 風澤中孚 **3** 十三 3	水6 Water Big Livestock [8] 壬辰 Water Dragon 山天大畜 **4** 十四 4	金4 Metal Eliminating [9] 癸巳 Water Snake 澤天夬 **5** 十五 6	金9 Metal Heaven [1] 甲午 Wood Horse 乾爲天 **6** 十六 1	火7 Fire Well [2] 乙未 Wood Goat 水風井 **7** 十七 6	木8 Wood Relief [3] 丙申 Fire Monkey 雷水解 **8** 十八 4
金4 Metal Influence [4] 丁酉 Fire Rooster 澤山咸 **9** 十九 9	水1 Water Humility [5] 戊戌 Earth Dog 地山謙 **10** 二十 6	火2 Fire Observation [6] 己亥 Earth Pig 風地觀 **11** 廿一 2	火2 Fire Increasing [7] 庚子 Metal Rat 風雷益 **12** 廿二 9	水1 Water Dimming Light [8] 辛丑 Metal Ox 地火明夷 **13** 廿三 3	金9 Metal Fellowship [9] 壬寅 Water Tiger 天火同人 **14** 廿四 7	木8 Wood Marrying Maiden [1] 癸卯 Water Rabbit 雷澤歸妹 **15** 廿五 7
木3 Wood Opposition [2] 甲辰 Wood Dragon 火澤睽 **16** 廿六 2	火7 Fire Waiting [3] 乙巳 Wood Snake 水天需 **17** 廿七 3	金4 Metal Great Exceeding [4] 丙午 Fire Horse 澤風大過 **18** 廿八 3	水6 Water Poison [5] 丁未 Fire Goat 山風蠱 **19** 廿九 7	火2 Fire Dispersing [6] 戊申 Earth Monkey 風水渙 **20** 三月初一 6	木3 Wood Travelling [7] 己酉 Earth Rooster 火山旅 **21** 初二 8	金9 Metal Stagnation [8] 庚戌 Metal Dog 天地否 **22** 初三 9
火7 Fire Alliance [9] 辛亥 Metal Pig 水地比 **23** 初四 7	木8 Wood Thunder [1] 壬子 Water Rat 震爲雷 **24** 初五 1	水6 Water Beauty [2] 癸丑 Water Ox 山火賁 **25** 初六 8	火7 Fire Accomplished [3] 甲寅 Wood Tiger 水火既濟 **26** 初七 9	水1 Water Arriving [4] 乙卯 Wood Rabbit 地澤臨 **27** 初八 4	金4 Metal Marsh [5] 丙辰 Fire Dragon 兌爲澤 **28** 初九 1	火2 Fire Small Livestock [6] 丁巳 Fire Snake 風天小畜 **29** 初十 8

MAY 2023 丁巳

Xuan Kong Element 玄空五行	風天小畜 Small Livestock	Period Luck 卦運	Monthly Star 月星
Fire 火2		8	5

SUNDAY	MONDAY	TUESDAY	WEDNESDAY	THURSDAY	FRIDAY	SATURDAY
	水1 Water 8 Rising 地風升 己未 Earth Goat **1** 十二 2	火7 Fire 9 Water 坎爲水 庚申 Metal Monkey **2** 十三 1	木8 Wood 1 Lesser Exceeding 雷山小過 辛酉 Metal Rooster **3** 十四 3	金4 Metal 2 Gathering 澤地萃 壬戌 Water Dog **4** 十五 4	水6 Water 3 Peel 山地剝 癸亥 Water Pig **5** 十六 6	水1 Water 4 Earth 坤爲地 甲子 Wood Rat **6** 十七 1
木3 Wood 5 Biting 火雷噬嗑 乙丑 Wood Ox **7** 十八 6	火2 Fire 6 Family 風火家人 丙寅 Fire Tiger **8** 十九 4	水6 Water 7 Decreasing 山澤損 丁卯 Fire Rabbit **9** 二十 9	金9 Metal 8 Tread 天澤履 戊辰 Earth Dragon **10** 廿一 6	木8 Wood 9 Great Strength 雷天大壯 己巳 Earth Snake **11** 廿二 2	木8 Wood 1 Consistency 雷風恒 庚午 Metal Horse **12** 廿三 9	金9 Metal 2 Litigation 天水訟 辛未 Metal Goat **13** 廿四 3
水1 Water 3 Officer 地水師 壬申 Water Monkey **14** 廿五 7	火2 Fire 4 Gradual Progress 風山漸 癸酉 Water Rooster **15** 廿六 7	火7 Fire 5 Obstruction 水山蹇 甲戌 Wood Dog **16** 廿七 2	木3 Wood 6 Advancement 火地晉 乙亥 Wood Pig **17** 廿八 3	水6 Water 7 Nourish 山雷頤 丙子 Fire Rat **18** 廿九 3	金4 Metal 8 Following 澤雷隨 丁丑 Fire Ox **19** 四月初一 7	木8 Wood 9 Abundance 雷火豐 戊寅 Earth Tiger **20** 初二 6
火7 Fire 1 Regulate 水澤節 己卯 Earth Rabbit **21** 初三 8	水1 Water 2 Unity 地天泰 庚辰 Metal Dragon **22** 初四 9	木3 Wood 3 Great Reward 火天大有 辛巳 Metal Snake **23** 初五 7	火2 Fire 4 Wind 巽爲風 壬午 Water Horse **24** 初六 1	金4 Metal 5 Trap 澤水困 癸未 Water Goat **25** 初七 8	木3 Wood 6 Not Yet Accomplished 火水未濟 甲申 Wood Monkey **26** 初八 9	金9 Metal 7 Retreat 天山遯 乙酉 Wood Rooster **27** 初九 4
水6 Water 8 Mountain 艮爲山 丙戌 Fire Dog **28** 初十 1	木8 Wood 9 Delight 雷地豫 丁亥 Fire Pig **29** 十一 8	火7 Fire 1 Beginning 水雷屯 戊子 Earth Rat **30** 十二 4	金9 Metal 2 Without Wrongdoing 天雷無妄 己丑 Earth Ox **31** 十三 2			

JUNE 2023 戊午

Xuan Kong Element 玄空五行	火風鼎 The Cauldron	Period Luck 卦運	Monthly Star 月星
Wood 木3		4	4

SUNDAY	MONDAY	TUESDAY	WEDNESDAY	THURSDAY	FRIDAY	SATURDAY
				木3 Wood 3 Fire 離爲火 庚寅 Metal Tiger **1** 十四 1	火2 Fire 4 Sincerity 風澤中孚 辛卯 Metal Rabbit **2** 十五 3	水6 Water 5 Big Livestock 山天大畜 壬辰 Water Dragon **3** 十六 4
金4 Metal 6 Eliminating 澤天夬 癸巳 Water Snake **4** 十七 6	金9 Metal 7 Heaven 乾爲天 甲午 Wood Horse **5** 十八 1	火7 Fire 8 Well 水風井 乙未 Wood Goat **6** 十九 6	木8 Wood 9 Relief 雷水解 丙申 Fire Monkey **7** 二十 4	金4 Metal 1 Influence 澤山咸 丁酉 Fire Rooster **8** 廿一 9	水1 Water 2 Humility 地山謙 戊戌 Earth Dog **9** 廿二 6	火2 Fire 3 Observation 風地觀 己亥 Earth Pig **10** 廿三 2
火2 Fire 4 Increasing 風雷益 庚子 Metal Rat **11** 廿四 9	水1 Water 5 Dimming Light 地火明夷 辛丑 Metal Ox **12** 廿五 3	金9 Metal 6 Fellowship 天火同人 壬寅 Water Tiger **13** 廿六 7	木8 Wood 7 Marrying Maiden 雷澤歸妹 癸卯 Water Rabbit **14** 廿七 7	木3 Wood 8 Opposition 火澤睽 甲辰 Wood Dragon **15** 廿八 2	火7 Fire 9 Waiting 水天需 乙巳 Wood Snake **16** 廿九 3	金4 Metal 1 Great Exceeding 澤風大過 丙午 Fire Horse **17** 三十 3
水6 Water 2 Poison 山風蠱 丁未 Fire Goat **18** 五月初一 7	火2 Fire 3 Dispersing 風水渙 戊申 Earth Monkey **19** 初二 6	木3 Wood 4 Travelling 火山旅 己酉 Earth Rooster **20** 初三 8	金9 Metal 55 Stagnation 天地否 庚戌 Metal Dog **21** 初四 9	火7 Fire 4 Alliance 水地比 辛亥 Metal Pig **22** 初五 7	木8 Wood 3 Thunder 震爲雷 壬子 Water Rat **23** 初六 1	水6 Water 2 Beauty 山火賁 癸丑 Water Ox **24** 初七 8
火7 Fire 1 Accomplished 水火既濟 甲寅 Wood Tiger **25** 初八 9	水1 Water 9 Arriving 地澤臨 乙卯 Wood Rabbit **26** 初九 4	金4 Metal 8 Marsh 兌爲澤 丙辰 Fire Dragon **27** 初十 1	火2 Fire 7 Small Livestock 風天小畜 丁巳 Fire Snake **28** 十一 8	木3 Wood 6 The Cauldron 火風鼎 戊午 Earth Horse **29** 十二 4	水1 Water 5 Rising 地風升 己未 Earth Goat **30** 十三 2	

JULY 2023 己未

Xuan Kong Element 玄空五行	地風升 Rising	Period Luck 卦運	Monthly Star 月星
Water 水1		2	3

SUNDAY	MONDAY	TUESDAY	WEDNESDAY	THURSDAY	FRIDAY	SATURDAY
金9 Metal Without Wrongdoing 2 己丑 Earth Ox 天雷無妄 30 十三 2	木3 Wood Fire 1 庚寅 Metal Tiger 離爲火 31 十四 1					火7 Fire Water 4 庚申 Metal Monkey 坎爲水 1 十四 1
木8 Wood Lesser Exceeding 3 辛酉 Metal Rooster 雷山小過 2 十五 3	金4 Metal Gathering 2 壬戌 Water Dog 澤地萃 3 十六 4	水6 Water Peel 1 癸亥 Water Pig 山地剝 4 十七 6	水1 Water Earth 9 甲子 Wood Rat 坤爲地 5 十八 1	木3 Wood Biting 8 乙丑 Wood Ox 火雷噬嗑 6 十九 6	火2 Fire Family 7 丙寅 Fire Tiger 風火家人 7 二十 4	水6 Water Decreasing 6 丁卯 Fire Rabbit 山澤損 8 廿一 9
金9 Metal Tread 5 戊辰 Earth Dragon 天澤履 9 廿二 6	木8 Wood Great Strength 4 己巳 Earth Snake 雷天大壯 10 廿三 2	木8 Wood Consistency 3 庚午 Metal Horse 雷風恆 11 廿四 9	金9 Metal Litigation 2 辛未 Metal Goat 天水訟 12 廿五 3	水1 Water Officer 1 壬申 Water Monkey 地水師 13 廿六 7	火2 Fire Gradual Progress 9 癸酉 Water Rooster 風山漸 14 廿七 7	火7 Fire Obstruction 8 甲戌 Wood Dog 水山蹇 15 廿八 2
木3 Wood Advancement 7 乙亥 Wood Pig 火地晉 16 廿九 3	水6 Water Nourish 6 丙子 Fire Rat 山雷頤 17 三十 3	金4 Metal Following 5 丁丑 Fire Ox 澤雷隨 18 六月初一 7	木8 Wood Abundance 4 戊寅 Earth Tiger 雷火豐 19 初二 6	火7 Fire Regulate 3 己卯 Earth Rabbit 水澤節 20 初三 8	水1 Water Unity 2 庚辰 Metal Dragon 地天泰 21 初四 9	木3 Wood Great Reward 1 辛巳 Metal Snake 火天大有 22 初五 7
火2 Fire Wind 9 壬午 Water Horse 巽爲風 23 初六 1	金4 Metal Trap 8 癸未 Water Goat 澤水困 24 初七 8	木3 Wood Not Yet Accomplished 7 甲申 Wood Monkey 火水未濟 25 初八 9	金9 Metal Retreat 6 乙酉 Wood Rooster 天山遯 26 初九 4	水6 Water Mountain 5 丙戌 Fire Dog 艮爲山 27 初十 1	木8 Wood Delight 4 丁亥 Fire Pig 雷地豫 28 十一 8	火7 Fire Beginning 3 戊子 Earth Rat 水雷屯 29 十二 4

AUGUST 2023 庚申

Xuan Kong Element 玄空五行	坎爲水 Water	Period Luck 卦運	Monthly Star 月星
Fire 火7		1	2

SUNDAY	MONDAY	TUESDAY	WEDNESDAY	THURSDAY	FRIDAY	SATURDAY
		火2 Fire Sincerity 9 辛卯 Metal Rabbit 風澤中孚 1 十五 3	水6 Water Big Livestock 8 壬辰 Water Dragon 山天大畜 2 十六 4	金4 Metal Eliminating 7 癸巳 Water Snake 澤天夬 3 十七 6	金9 Metal Heaven 6 甲午 Wood Horse 乾爲天 4 十八 1	火7 Fire Well 5 乙未 Wood Goat 水風井 5 十九 6
木8 Wood Relief 4 丙申 Fire Monkey 雷水解 6 二十 4	金4 Metal Influence 3 丁酉 Fire Rooster 澤山咸 7 廿一 9	水1 Water Humility 2 戊戌 Earth Dog 地山謙 8 廿二 6	火2 Fire Observation 1 己亥 Earth Pig 風地觀 9 廿三 2	火2 Fire Increasing 9 庚子 Metal Rat 風雷益 10 廿四 9	水1 Water Dimming Light 8 辛丑 Metal Ox 地火明夷 11 廿五 3	金9 Metal Fellowship 7 壬寅 Water Tiger 天火同人 12 廿六 7
木8 Wood Marrying Maiden 6 癸卯 Water Rabbit 雷澤歸妹 13 廿七 7	木3 Wood Opposition 5 甲辰 Wood Dragon 火澤睽 14 廿八 2	火7 Fire Waiting 4 乙巳 Wood Snake 水天需 15 廿九 3	金4 Metal Great Exceeding 3 丙午 Fire Horse 澤風大過 16 七月初一 3	水6 Water Poison 2 丁未 Fire Goat 山風蠱 17 初二 7	火2 Fire Dispersing 1 戊申 Earth Monkey 風水渙 18 初三 6	木3 Wood Travelling 9 己酉 Earth Rooster 火山旅 19 初四 8
金9 Metal Stagnation 8 庚戌 Metal Dog 天地否 20 初五 9	火7 Fire Alliance 7 辛亥 Metal Pig 水地比 21 初六 7	木8 Wood Thunder 6 壬子 Water Rat 震爲雷 22 初七 1	水6 Water Beauty 5 癸丑 Water Ox 山火賁 23 初八 8	火7 Fire Accomplished 4 甲寅 Wood Tiger 水火既濟 24 初九 9	水1 Water Arriving 3 乙卯 Wood Rabbit 地澤臨 25 初十 4	金4 Metal Marsh 2 丙辰 Fire Dragon 兌爲澤 26 十一 1
火2 Fire Small Livestock 1 丁巳 Fire Snake 風天小畜 27 十二 8	木3 Wood The Cauldron 9 戊午 Earth Horse 火風鼎 28 十三 4	水1 Water Rising 8 己未 Earth Goat 地風升 29 十四 2	火7 Fire Water 7 庚申 Metal Monkey 坎爲水 30 十五 1	木8 Wood Lesser Exceeding 6 辛酉 Metal Rooster 雷山小過 31 十六 3		

SEPTEMBER 2023 辛酉

Xuan Kong Element 玄空五行	雷山小過 Lesser Exceeding	Period Luck 卦運	Monthly Star 月星
Wood 木8		3	1

SUNDAY	MONDAY	TUESDAY	WEDNESDAY	THURSDAY	FRIDAY	SATURDAY
					金4 Metal 5 Gathering 澤地萃 壬戌 Water Dog 1 十七 4	水6 Water 4 Peel 山地剝 癸亥 Water Pig 2 十八 6
水1 Water 3 Earth 坤爲地 甲子 Wood Rat 3 十九 1	木3 Wood 2 Biting 火雷噬嗑 乙丑 Wood Ox 4 二十 6	火2 Fire 1 Family 風火家人 丙寅 Fire Tiger 5 廿一 4	水6 Water 9 Decreasing 山澤損 丁卯 Fire Rabbit 6 廿二 9	金9 Metal 8 Tread 天澤履 戊辰 Earth Dragon 7 廿三 6	木8 Wood 7 Great Strength 雷天大壯 己巳 Earth Snake 8 廿四 2	木8 Wood 6 Consistency 雷風恆 庚午 Metal Horse 9 廿五 9
金9 Metal 5 Litigation 天水訟 辛未 Metal Goat 10 廿六 3	水1 Water 4 Officer 地水師 壬申 Water Monkey 11 廿七 7	火2 Fire 3 Gradual Progress 風山漸 癸酉 Water Rooster 12 廿八 7	火7 Fire 2 Obstruction 水山蹇 甲戌 Wood Dog 13 廿九 2	木3 Wood 1 Advancement 火地晉 乙亥 Wood Pig 14 三十 3	水6 Water 9 Nourish 山雷頤 丙子 Fire Rat 15 八月初一 3	金4 Metal 8 Following 澤雷隨 丁丑 Fire Ox 16 初二 7
木8 Wood 7 Abundance 雷火豐 戊寅 Earth Tiger 17 初三 6	火7 Fire 6 Regulate 水澤節 己卯 Earth Rabbit 18 初四 8	水1 Water 5 Unity 地天泰 庚辰 Metal Dragon 19 初五 9	木3 Wood 4 Great Reward 火天大有 辛巳 Metal Snake 20 初六 7	火2 Fire 3 Wind 巽爲風 壬午 Water Horse 21 初七 1	金4 Metal 2 Trap 澤水困 癸未 Water Goat 22 初八 8	木3 Wood 1 Not Yet Accomplished 火水未濟 甲申 Wood Monkey 23 初九 9
金9 Metal 9 Retreat 天山遯 乙酉 Wood Rooster 24 初十 4	水6 Water 8 Mountain 艮爲山 丙戌 Fire Dog 25 十一 1	木8 Wood 7 Delight 雷地豫 丁亥 Fire Pig 26 十二 8	火7 Fire 6 Beginning 水雷屯 戊子 Earth Rat 27 十三 4	金9 Metal 5 Without Wrongdoing 天雷無妄 己丑 Earth Ox 28 十四 2	木3 Wood 4 Fire 離爲火 庚寅 Metal Tiger 29 十五 1	火2 Fire 3 Sincerity 風澤中孚 辛卯 Metal Rabbit 30 十六 3

OCTOBER 2023 壬戌

Xuan Kong Element 玄空五行	澤地萃 Gathering	Period Luck 卦運	Monthly Star 月星
Metal 金4		4	9

SUNDAY	MONDAY	TUESDAY	WEDNESDAY	THURSDAY	FRIDAY	SATURDAY
水6 Water 2 Big Livestock 山天大畜 壬辰 Water Dragon 1 十七 4	金4 Metal 1 Eliminating 澤天夬 癸巳 Water Snake 2 十八 6	金9 Metal 9 Heaven 乾爲天 甲午 Wood Horse 3 十九 1	火7 Fire 8 Well 水風井 乙未 Wood Goat 4 二十 6	木8 Wood 7 Relief 雷水解 丙申 Fire Monkey 5 廿一 4	金4 Metal 6 Influence 澤山咸 丁酉 Fire Rooster 6 廿二 9	水1 Water 5 Humility 地山謙 戊戌 Earth Dog 7 廿三 6
火2 Fire 4 Observation 風地觀 己亥 Earth Pig 8 廿四 2	火2 Fire 3 Increasing 風雷益 庚子 Metal Rat 9 廿五 9	水1 Water 2 Dimming Light 地火明夷 辛丑 Metal Ox 10 廿六 3	金9 Metal 1 Fellowship 天火同人 壬寅 Water Tiger 11 廿七 7	木8 Wood 9 Marrying Maiden 雷澤歸妹 癸卯 Water Rabbit 12 廿八 7	木3 Wood 8 Opposition 火澤睽 甲辰 Wood Dragon 13 廿九 2	火7 Fire 7 Waiting 水天需 乙巳 Wood Snake 14 三十 3
金4 Metal 6 Great Exceeding 澤風大過 丙午 Fire Horse 15 九月初一 3	水6 Water 5 Poison 山風蠱 丁未 Fire Goat 16 初二 7	火2 Fire 4 Dispersing 風水渙 戊申 Earth Monkey 17 初三 6	木3 Wood 3 Travelling 火山旅 己酉 Earth Rooster 18 初四 8	金9 Metal 2 Stagnation 天地否 庚戌 Metal Dog 19 初五 9	火7 Fire 1 Alliance 水地比 辛亥 Metal Pig 20 初六 7	木8 Wood 9 Thunder 震爲雷 壬子 Water Rat 21 初七 1
水6 Water 8 Beauty 山火賁 癸丑 Water Ox 22 初八 8	火7 Fire 7 Accomplished 水火既濟 甲寅 Wood Tiger 23 初九 9	水1 Water 6 Arriving 地澤臨 乙卯 Wood Rabbit 24 初十 4	金4 Metal 5 Marsh 兌爲澤 丙辰 Fire Dragon 25 十一 1	火2 Fire 4 Small Livestock 風天小畜 丁巳 Fire Snake 26 十二 8	木3 Wood 3 The Cauldron 火風鼎 戊午 Earth Horse 27 十三 4	水1 Water 2 Rising 地風升 己未 Earth Goat 28 十四 2
火7 Fire 1 Water 坎爲水 庚申 Metal Monkey 29 十五 1	木8 Wood 9 Lesser Exceeding 雷山小過 辛酉 Metal Rooster 30 十六 3	金4 Metal 8 Gathering 澤地萃 壬戌 Water Dog 31 十七 4				

NOVEMBER 2023 癸亥

Xuan Kong Element 玄空五行	山地剝 Peel	Period Luck 卦運	Monthly Star 月星
Water 水6		6	8

SUNDAY	MONDAY	TUESDAY	WEDNESDAY	THURSDAY	FRIDAY	SATURDAY
			水6 Water · Peel · 7 · 癸亥 Water Pig · 山地剝 · **1** · 十八 · 6	水1 Water · Earth · 6 · 甲子 Wood Rat · 坤為地 · **2** · 十九 · 1	木3 Wood · Biting · 5 · 乙丑 Wood Ox · 火雷噬嗑 · **3** · 二十 · 6	火2 Fire · Family · 4 · 丙寅 Fire Tiger · 風火家人 · **4** · 廿一 · 4
水6 Water · Decreasing · 3 · 丁卯 Fire Rabbit · 山澤損 · **5** · 廿二 · 9	金9 Metal · Tread · 2 · 戊辰 Earth Dragon · 天澤履 · **6** · 廿三 · 6	木8 Wood · Great Strength · 1 · 己巳 Earth Snake · 雷天大壯 · **7** · 廿四 · 2	木8 Wood · Consistency · 9 · 庚午 Metal Horse · 雷風恆 · **8** · 廿五 · 9	金9 Metal · Litigation · 8 · 辛未 Metal Goat · 天水訟 · **9** · 廿六 · 3	水1 Water · Officer · 7 · 壬申 Water Monkey · 地水師 · **10** · 廿七 · 7	火2 Fire · Gradual Progress · 6 · 癸酉 Water Rooster · 風山漸 · **11** · 廿八 · 7
火7 Fire · Obstruction · 5 · 甲戌 Wood Dog · 水山蹇 · **12** · 廿九 · 2	木3 Wood · Advancement · 4 · 乙亥 Wood Pig · 火地晉 · **13** · 十月初一 · 3	水6 Water · Nourish · 3 · 丙子 Fire Rat · 山雷頤 · **14** · 初二 · 3	金4 Metal · Following · 2 · 丁丑 Fire Ox · 澤雷隨 · **15** · 初三 · 7	木8 Wood · Abundance · 1 · 戊寅 Earth Tiger · 雷火豐 · **16** · 初四 · 6	火7 Fire · Regulate · 9 · 己卯 Earth Rabbit · 水澤節 · **17** · 初五 · 8	水1 Water · Unity · 8 · 庚辰 Metal Dragon · 地天泰 · **18** · 初六 · 9
木3 Wood · Great Reward · 7 · 辛巳 Metal Snake · 火天大有 · **19** · 初七 · 7	火2 Fire · Wind · 6 · 壬午 Water Horse · 巽為風 · **20** · 初八 · 1	金4 Metal · Trap · 5 · 癸未 Water Goat · 澤水困 · **21** · 初九 · 8	木3 Wood · Not Yet Accomplished · 4 · 甲申 Wood Monkey · 火水未濟 · **22** · 初十 · 9	金9 Metal · Retreat · 3 · 乙酉 Wood Rooster · 天山遯 · **23** · 十一 · 4	水6 Water · Mountain · 2 · 丙戌 Fire Dog · 艮為山 · **24** · 十二 · 1	木8 Wood · Delight · 1 · 丁亥 Fire Pig · 雷地豫 · **25** · 十三 · 8
火7 Fire · Beginning · 9 · 戊子 Earth Rat · 水雷屯 · **26** · 十四 · 4	金9 Metal · Without Wrongdoing · 8 · 己丑 Earth Ox · 天雷無妄 · **27** · 十五 · 2	木3 Wood · Fire · 7 · 庚寅 Metal Tiger · 離為火 · **28** · 十六 · 1	火2 Fire · Sincerity · 6 · 辛卯 Metal Rabbit · 風澤中孚 · **29** · 十七 · 3	水6 Water · Big Livestock · 5 · 壬辰 Water Dragon · 山天大畜 · **30** · 十八 · 4		

DECEMBER 2023 甲子

Xuan Kong Element 玄空五行	坤為地 Earth	Period Luck 卦運	Monthly Star 月星
Water 水1		1	7

SUNDAY	MONDAY	TUESDAY	WEDNESDAY	THURSDAY	FRIDAY	SATURDAY
水6 Water · Peel · 9 · 癸亥 Water Pig · 山地剝 · **31** · 十九 · 6					金4 Metal · Eliminating · 4 · 癸巳 Water Snake · 澤天夬 · **1** · 十九 · 6	金9 Metal · Heaven · 3 · 甲午 Wood Horse · 乾為天 · **2** · 二十 · 1
火7 Fire · Well · 2 · 乙未 Wood Goat · 水風井 · **3** · 廿一 · 6	木8 Wood · Relief · 1 · 丙申 Fire Monkey · 雷水解 · **4** · 廿二 · 4	金4 Metal · Influence · 9 · 丁酉 Fire Rooster · 澤山咸 · **5** · 廿三 · 9	水1 Water · Humility · 8 · 戊戌 Earth Dog · 地山謙 · **6** · 廿四 · 6	火2 Fire · Observation · 7 · 己亥 Earth Pig · 風地觀 · **7** · 廿五 · 2	火2 Fire · Increasing · 6 · 庚子 Metal Rat · 風雷益 · **8** · 廿六 · 9	水1 Water · Dimming Light · 5 · 辛丑 Metal Ox · 地火明夷 · **9** · 廿七 · 3
金9 Metal · Fellowship · 4 · 壬寅 Water Tiger · 天火同人 · **10** · 廿八 · 7	木8 Wood · Marrying Maiden · 3 · 癸卯 Water Rabbit · 雷澤歸妹 · **11** · 廿九 · 7	木3 Wood · Opposition · 2 · 甲辰 Wood Dragon · 火澤睽 · **12** · 三十 · 2	火7 Fire · Waiting · 1 · 乙巳 Wood Snake · 水天需 · **13** · 十一月初一 · 3	金4 Metal · Great Exceeding · 9 · 丙午 Fire Horse · 澤風大過 · **14** · 初二 · 3	水6 Water · Poison · 8 · 丁未 Fire Goat · 山風蠱 · **15** · 初三 · 7	火2 Fire · Dispersing · 7 · 戊申 Earth Monkey · 風水渙 · **16** · 初四 · 6
木3 Wood · Travelling · 6 · 己酉 Earth Rooster · 火山旅 · **17** · 初五 · 8	金9 Metal · Stagnation · 5 · 庚戌 Metal Dog · 天地否 · **18** · 初六 · 9	火7 Fire · Alliance · 4 · 辛亥 Metal Pig · 水地比 · **19** · 初七 · 7	木8 Wood · Thunder · 3 · 壬子 Water Rat · 震為雷 · **20** · 初八 · 1	水6 Water · Beauty · 2 · 癸丑 Water Ox · 山火賁 · **21** · 初九 · 8	火7 Fire · Accomplished · 1/9 · 甲寅 Wood Tiger · 水火既濟 · **22** · 初十 · 9	水1 Water · Arriving · 1 · 乙卯 Wood Rabbit · 地澤臨 · **23** · 十一 · 4
金4 Metal · Marsh · 2 · 丙辰 Fire Dragon · 兌為澤 · **24** · 十二 · 1	火2 Fire · Small Livestock · 3 · 丁巳 Fire Snake · 風天小畜 · **25** · 十三 · 8	木3 Wood · The Cauldron · 4 · 戊午 Earth Horse · 火風鼎 · **26** · 十四 · 4	水1 Water · Rising · 5 · 己未 Earth Goat · 地風升 · **27** · 十五 · 2	火7 Fire · Water · 6 · 庚申 Metal Monkey · 坎為水 · **28** · 十六 · 1	木8 Wood · Lesser Exceeding · 7 · 辛酉 Metal Rooster · 雷山小過 · **29** · 十七 · 3	金4 Metal · Gathering · 8 · 壬戌 Water Dog · 澤地萃 · **30** · 十八 · 4

2024 甲辰

(*Jia Chen*) Wood Dragon

2024 甲辰 *(Jia Chen)* Wood Dragon

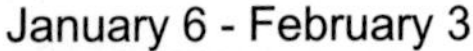

January 6 - February 3

February 4 - March 4

March 5 - April 3

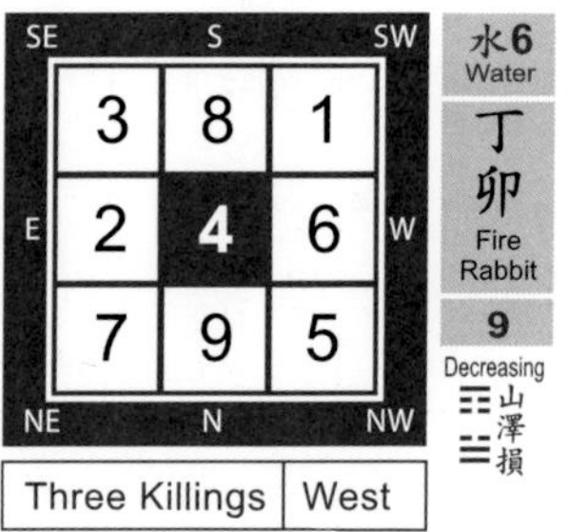

April 4 - May 4

May 5 - June 4

June 5 - July 5

July 6 - August 6

August 7 - September 6

September 7 - October 7

October 8 - November 6

November 7 - December 5

December 6 - January 4

JANUARY 2024 乙丑

Xuan Kong Element 玄空五行	火雷噬嗑 Biting	Period Luck 卦運	Monthly Star 月星
Wood 木3		6	6

SUNDAY	MONDAY	TUESDAY	WEDNESDAY	THURSDAY	FRIDAY	SATURDAY
	1 1 水1 Water Earth 甲子 Wood Rat 坤爲地 1 二十	2 2 木3 Wood Biting 乙丑 Wood Ox 火雷噬嗑 6 廿一	3 3 火2 Fire Family 丙寅 Fire Tiger 風火家人 4 廿二	4 4 水6 Water Decreasing 丁卯 Fire Rabbit 山澤損 9 廿三	5 5 金9 Metal Tread 戊辰 Earth Dragon 天澤履 6 廿四	6 6 木8 Wood Great Strength 己巳 Earth Snake 雷天大壯 2 廿五
7 7 木8 Wood Consistency 庚午 Metal Horse 雷風恆 9 廿六	8 8 金9 Metal Litigation 辛未 Metal Goat 天水訟 3 廿七	9 9 水1 Water Officer 壬申 Water Monkey 地水師 7 廿八	10 1 火2 Fire Gradual Progress 癸酉 Water Rooster 風山漸 7 廿九	11 2 火7 Fire Obstruction 甲戌 Wood Dog 水山蹇 2 十二月初一	12 3 木3 Wood Advancement 乙亥 Wood Pig 火地晉 3 初二	13 4 水6 Water Nourish 丙子 Fire Rat 山雷頤 3 初三
14 5 金4 Metal Following 丁丑 Fire Ox 澤雷隨 7 初四	15 6 木8 Wood Abundance 戊寅 Earth Tiger 雷火豐 6 初五	16 7 火7 Fire Regulate 己卯 Earth Rabbit 水澤節 8 初六	17 8 水1 Water Unity 庚辰 Metal Dragon 地天泰 9 初七	18 9 木3 Wood Great Reward 辛巳 Metal Snake 火天大有 7 初八	19 1 火2 Fire Wind 壬午 Water Horse 巽爲風 1 初九	20 2 金4 Metal Trap 癸未 Water Goat 澤水困 8 初十
21 3 木3 Wood Not Yet Accomplished 甲申 Wood Monkey 火水未濟 9 十一	22 4 金9 Metal Retreat 乙酉 Wood Rooster 天山遯 4 十二	23 5 水6 Water Mountain 丙戌 Fire Dog 艮爲山 1 十三	24 6 木8 Wood Delight 丁亥 Fire Pig 雷地豫 8 十四	25 7 火7 Fire Beginning 戊子 Earth Rat 水雷屯 4 十五	26 8 金9 Metal Without Wrongdoing 己丑 Earth Ox 天雷無妄 2 十六	27 9 木3 Wood Fire 庚寅 Metal Tiger 離爲火 1 十七
28 1 火2 Fire Sincerity 辛卯 Metal Rabbit 風澤中孚 3 十八	29 2 水6 Water Big Livestock 壬辰 Water Dragon 山天大畜 4 十九	30 3 金4 Metal Eliminating 癸巳 Water Snake 澤天夬 6 二十	31 4 金9 Metal Heaven 甲午 Wood Horse 乾爲天 1 廿一			

FEBRUARY 2024 丙寅

Xuan Kong Element 玄空五行	風火家人 Family	Period Luck 卦運	Monthly Star 月星
Fire 火2		4	5

SUNDAY	MONDAY	TUESDAY	WEDNESDAY	THURSDAY	FRIDAY	SATURDAY
				1 5 火7 Fire Well 乙未 Wood Goat 水風井 6 廿二	2 6 木8 Wood Relief 丙申 Fire Monkey 雷水解 4 廿三	3 7 金4 Metal Influence 丁酉 Fire Rooster 澤山咸 9 廿四
4 8 水1 Water Humility 戊戌 Earth Dog 地山謙 6 廿五	5 9 火2 Fire Observation 己亥 Earth Pig 風地觀 2 廿六	6 1 火2 Fire Increasing 庚子 Metal Rat 風雷益 9 廿七	7 2 水1 Water Dimming Light 辛丑 Metal Ox 地火明夷 3 廿八	8 3 金9 Metal Fellowship 壬寅 Water Tiger 天火同人 7 廿九	9 4 木8 Wood Marrying Maiden 癸卯 Water Rabbit 雷澤歸妹 7 三十	10 5 木3 Wood Opposition 甲辰 Wood Dragon 火澤睽 2 正月初一
11 6 火7 Fire Waiting 乙巳 Wood Snake 水天需 3 初二	12 7 金4 Metal Great Exceeding 丙午 Fire Horse 澤風大過 3 初三	13 8 水6 Water Poison 丁未 Fire Goat 山風蠱 7 初四	14 9 火2 Fire Dispersing 戊申 Earth Monkey 風水渙 6 初五	15 1 木3 Wood Travelling 己酉 Earth Rooster 火山旅 8 初六	16 2 金9 Metal Stagnation 庚戌 Metal Dog 天地否 9 初七	17 3 火7 Fire Alliance 辛亥 Metal Pig 水地比 7 初八
18 4 木8 Wood Thunder 壬子 Water Rat 震爲雷 1 初九	19 5 水6 Water Beauty 癸丑 Water Ox 山火賁 8 初十	20 6 火7 Fire Accomplished 甲寅 Wood Tiger 水火既濟 9 十一	21 7 水1 Water Arriving 乙卯 Wood Rabbit 地澤臨 4 十二	22 8 金4 Metal Marsh 丙辰 Fire Dragon 兌爲澤 1 十三	23 9 火2 Fire Small Livestock 丁巳 Fire Snake 風天小畜 8 十四	24 1 木3 Wood The Cauldron 戊午 Earth Horse 火風鼎 4 十五
25 2 水1 Water Rising 己未 Earth Goat 地風升 2 十六	26 3 火7 Fire Water 庚申 Metal Monkey 坎爲水 1 十七	27 4 木8 Wood Lesser Exceeding 辛酉 Metal Rooster 雷山小過 3 十八	28 5 金4 Metal Gathering 壬戌 Water Dog 澤地萃 4 十九	29 6 水6 Water Peel 癸亥 Water Pig 山地剝 6 二十		

MARCH 2024 丁卯

Xuan Kong Element 玄空五行	山澤損 Decreasing	Period Luck 卦運	Monthly Star 月星
Water 水6		9	4

SUNDAY	MONDAY	TUESDAY	WEDNESDAY	THURSDAY	FRIDAY	SATURDAY
金9 Metal Heaven 1 甲午 Wood Horse 乾為天 **31** 廿二 1					水1 Water Earth 7 甲子 Wood Rat 坤為地 **1** 廿一 1	木3 Wood Biting 8 乙丑 Wood Ox 火雷噬嗑 **2** 廿二 6
火2 Fire Family 9 丙寅 Fire Tiger 風火家人 **3** 廿三 4	水6 Water Decreasing 1 丁卯 Fire Rabbit 山澤損 **4** 廿四 9	金9 Metal Tread 2 戊辰 Earth Dragon 天澤履 **5** 廿五 6	木8 Wood Great Strength 3 己巳 Earth Snake 雷天大壯 **6** 廿六 2	木8 Wood Consistency 4 庚午 Metal Horse 雷風恒 **7** 廿七 9	金9 Metal Litigation 5 辛未 Metal Goat 天水訟 **8** 廿八 3	水1 Water Officer 6 壬申 Water Monkey 地水師 **9** 廿九 7
火2 Fire Gradual Progress 7 癸酉 Water Rooster 風山漸 **10** 二月初一 7	火7 Fire Obstruction 8 甲戌 Wood Dog 水山蹇 **11** 初二 2	木3 Wood Advancement 9 乙亥 Wood Pig 火地晉 **12** 初三 3	水6 Water Nourish 1 丙子 Fire Rat 山雷頤 **13** 初四 3	金4 Metal Following 2 丁丑 Fire Ox 澤雷隨 **14** 初五 7	木8 Wood Abundance 3 戊寅 Earth Tiger 雷火豐 **15** 初六 6	火7 Fire Regulate 4 己卯 Earth Rabbit 水澤節 **16** 初七 8
水1 Water Unity 5 庚辰 Metal Dragon 地天泰 **17** 初八 9	木3 Wood Great Reward 6 辛巳 Metal Snake 火天大有 **18** 初九 7	火2 Fire Wind 7 壬午 Water Horse 巽為風 **19** 初十 1	金4 Metal Trap 8 癸未 Water Goat 澤水困 **20** 十一 8	木3 Wood Not Yet Accomplished 9 甲申 Wood Monkey 火水未濟 **21** 十二 9	金9 Metal Retreat 1 乙酉 Wood Rooster 天山遯 **22** 十三 4	水6 Water Mountain 2 丙戌 Fire Dog 艮為山 **23** 十四 1
木8 Wood Delight 3 丁亥 Fire Pig 雷地豫 **24** 十五 8	火7 Fire Beginning 4 戊子 Earth Rat 水雷屯 **25** 十六 4	金9 Metal Without Wrongdoing 5 己丑 Earth Ox 天雷無妄 **26** 十七 2	木3 Wood Fire 6 庚寅 Metal Tiger 離為火 **27** 十八 1	火2 Fire Sincerity 7 辛卯 Metal Rabbit 風澤中孚 **28** 十九 3	水6 Water Big Livestock 8 壬辰 Water Dragon 山天大畜 **29** 二十 4	金4 Metal Eliminating 9 癸巳 Water Snake 澤天夬 **30** 廿一 6

APRIL 2024 戊辰

Xuan Kong Element 玄空五行	天澤履 Tread	Period Luck 卦運	Monthly Star 月星
Metal 金9		6	3

SUNDAY	MONDAY	TUESDAY	WEDNESDAY	THURSDAY	FRIDAY	SATURDAY
	火7 Fire Well 2 乙未 Wood Goat 水風井 **1** 廿三 6	木8 Wood Relief 3 丙申 Fire Monkey 雷水解 **2** 廿四 4	金4 Metal Influence 4 丁酉 Fire Rooster 澤山咸 **3** 廿五 9	水1 Water Humility 5 戊戌 Earth Dog 地山謙 **4** 廿六 6	火2 Fire Observation 6 己亥 Earth Pig 風地觀 **5** 廿七 2	火2 Fire Increasing 7 庚子 Metal Rat 風雷益 **6** 廿八 9
水1 Water Dimming Light 8 辛丑 Metal Ox 地火明夷 **7** 廿九 3	金9 Metal Fellowship 9 壬寅 Water Tiger 天火同人 **8** 三十 7	木8 Wood Marrying Maiden 1 癸卯 Water Rabbit 雷澤歸妹 **9** 三月初一 7	木3 Wood Opposition 2 甲辰 Wood Dragon 火澤睽 **10** 初二 2	火7 Fire Waiting 3 乙巳 Wood Snake 水天需 **11** 初三 3	金4 Metal Great Exceeding 4 丙午 Fire Horse 澤風大過 **12** 初四 3	水6 Water Poison 5 丁未 Fire Goat 山風蠱 **13** 初五 7
火2 Fire Dispersing 6 戊申 Earth Monkey 風水渙 **14** 初六 6	木3 Wood Travelling 7 己酉 Earth Rooster 火山旅 **15** 初七 8	金9 Metal Stagnation 8 庚戌 Metal Dog 天地否 **16** 初八 9	火7 Fire Alliance 9 辛亥 Metal Pig 水地比 **17** 初九 7	木8 Wood Thunder 1 壬子 Water Rat 震為雷 **18** 初十 1	水6 Water Beauty 2 癸丑 Water Ox 山火賁 **19** 十一 8	火7 Fire Accomplished 3 甲寅 Wood Tiger 水火既濟 **20** 十二 9
水1 Water Arriving 4 乙卯 Wood Rabbit 地澤臨 **21** 十三 4	金4 Metal Marsh 5 丙辰 Fire Dragon 兌為澤 **22** 十四 1	火2 Fire Small Livestock 6 丁巳 Fire Snake 風天小畜 **23** 十五 8	木3 Wood The Cauldron 7 戊午 Earth Horse 火風鼎 **24** 十六 4	水1 Water Rising 8 己未 Earth Goat 地風升 **25** 十七 2	火7 Fire Water 9 庚申 Metal Monkey 坎為水 **26** 十八 1	木8 Wood Lesser Exceeding 1 辛酉 Metal Rooster 雷山小過 **27** 十九 3
金4 Metal Gathering 2 壬戌 Water Dog 澤地萃 **28** 二十 4	水6 Water Peel 3 癸亥 Water Pig 山地剝 **29** 廿一 6	水1 Water Earth 4 甲子 Wood Rat 坤為地 **30** 廿二 1				

MAY 2024 己巳

Xuan Kong Element 玄空五行	雷天大壯	Period Luck 卦運	Monthly Star 月星
Wood 木8	Great Strength	2	2

SUNDAY	MONDAY	TUESDAY	WEDNESDAY	THURSDAY	FRIDAY	SATURDAY
			木3 Wood 5 乙丑 Wood Ox 6 Biting 火雷噬嗑 1 廿三	火2 Fire 6 丙寅 Fire Tiger 4 Family 風火家人 2 廿四	水6 Water 7 丁卯 Fire Rabbit 9 Decreasing 山澤損 3 廿五	金9 Metal 8 戊辰 Earth Dragon 6 Tread 天澤履 4 廿六
木8 Wood 9 己巳 Earth Snake 2 Great Strength 雷天大壯 5 廿七	木8 Wood 1 庚午 Metal Horse 9 Consistency 雷風恆 6 廿八	金9 Metal 2 辛未 Metal Goat 3 Litigation 天水訟 7 廿九	水1 Water 3 壬申 Water Monkey 7 Officer 地水師 8 四月初一	火2 Fire 4 癸酉 Water Rooster 7 Gradual Progress 風山漸 9 初二	火7 Fire 5 甲戌 Wood Dog 2 Obstruction 水山蹇 10 初三	木3 Wood 6 乙亥 Wood Pig 3 Advancement 火地晉 11 初四
水6 Water 7 丙子 Fire Rat 3 Nourish 山雷頤 12 初五	金4 Metal 8 丁丑 Fire Ox 7 Following 澤雷隨 13 初六	木8 Wood 9 戊寅 Earth Tiger 6 Abundance 雷火豐 14 初七	火7 Fire 1 己卯 Earth Rabbit 8 Regulate 水澤節 15 初八	水1 Water 2 庚辰 Metal Dragon 9 Unity 地天泰 16 初九	木3 Wood 3 辛巳 Metal Snake 7 Great Reward 火天大有 17 初十	火2 Fire 4 壬午 Water Horse 1 Wind 巽為風 18 十一
金4 Metal 5 癸未 Water Goat 8 Trap 澤水困 19 十二	木3 Wood 6 甲申 Wood Monkey 9 Not Yet Accomplished 火水未濟 20 十三	金9 Metal 7 乙酉 Wood Rooster 4 Retreat 天山遯 21 十四	水6 Water 8 丙戌 Fire Dog 1 Mountain 艮為山 22 十五	木8 Wood 9 丁亥 Fire Pig 8 Delight 雷地豫 23 十六	火7 Fire 1 戊子 Earth Rat 4 Beginning 水雷屯 24 十七	金9 Metal 2 己丑 Earth Ox 2 Without Wrongdoing 天雷無妄 25 十八
木3 Wood 3 庚寅 Metal Tiger 1 Fire 離為火 26 十九	火2 Fire 4 辛卯 Metal Rabbit 3 Sincerity 風澤中孚 27 二十	水6 Water 5 壬辰 Water Dragon 4 Big Livestock 山天大畜 28 廿一	金4 Metal 6 癸巳 Water Snake 6 Eliminating 澤天夬 29 廿二	金9 Metal 7 甲午 Wood Horse 1 Heaven 乾為天 30 廿三	火7 Fire 8 乙未 Wood Goat 6 Well 水風井 31 廿四	

JUNE 2024 庚午

Xuan Kong Element 玄空五行	雷風恆	Period Luck 卦運	Monthly Star 月星
Wood 木8	Consistency	9	1

SUNDAY	MONDAY	TUESDAY	WEDNESDAY	THURSDAY	FRIDAY	SATURDAY
木3 Wood 8 乙丑 Wood Ox 6 Biting 火雷噬嗑 30 廿五						木8 Wood 9 丙申 Fire Monkey 4 Relief 雷水解 1 廿五
金4 Metal 1 丁酉 Fire Rooster 9 Influence 澤山咸 2 廿六	水1 Water 2 戊戌 Earth Dog 6 Humility 地山謙 3 廿七	火2 Fire 3 己亥 Earth Pig 2 Observation 風地觀 4 廿八	火2 Fire 4 庚子 Metal Rat 9 Increasing 風雷益 5 廿九	水1 Water 5 辛丑 Metal Ox 3 Dimming Light 地火明夷 6 五月初一	金9 Metal 6 壬寅 Water Tiger 7 Fellowship 天火同人 7 初二	木8 Wood 7 癸卯 Water Rabbit 7 Marrying Maiden 雷澤歸妹 8 初三
木3 Wood 8 甲辰 Wood Dragon 2 Opposition 火澤睽 9 初四	火7 Fire 9 乙巳 Wood Snake 3 Waiting 水天需 10 初五	金4 Metal 1 丙午 Fire Horse 3 Great Exceeding 澤風大過 11 初六	水6 Water 2 丁未 Fire Goat 7 Poison 山風蠱 12 初七	火2 Fire 3 戊申 Earth Monkey 6 Dispersing 風水渙 13 初八	木3 Wood 4 己酉 Earth Rooster 8 Travelling 火山旅 14 初九	金9 Metal 5 庚戌 Metal Dog 9 Stagnation 天地否 15 初十
火7 Fire 6 辛亥 Metal Pig 7 Alliance 水地比 16 十一	木8 Wood 7 壬子 Water Rat 1 Thunder 震為雷 17 十二	水6 Water 8 癸丑 Water Ox 8 Beauty 山火賁 18 十三	火7 Fire 9 甲寅 Wood Tiger 9 Accomplished 水火既濟 19 十四	水1 Water 1 乙卯 Wood Rabbit 4 Arriving 地澤臨 20 十五	金4 Metal 2/8 丙辰 Fire Dragon 1 Marsh 兌為澤 21 十六	火2 Fire 7 丁巳 Fire Snake 8 Small Livestock 風天小畜 22 十七
木3 Wood 6 戊午 Earth Horse 4 The Cauldron 火風鼎 23 十八	水1 Water 5 己未 Earth Goat 2 Rising 地風升 24 十九	火7 Fire 4 庚申 Metal Monkey 1 Water 坎為水 25 二十	木8 Wood 3 辛酉 Metal Rooster 3 Lesser Exceeding 雷山小過 26 廿一	金4 Metal 2 壬戌 Water Dog 4 Gathering 澤地萃 27 廿二	水6 Water 1 癸亥 Water Pig 6 Peel 山地剝 28 廿三	水1 Water 9 甲子 Wood Rat 1 Earth 坤為地 29 廿四

JULY 2024 辛未

Xuan Kong Element 玄空五行	天水訟 Litigation	Period Luck 卦運	Monthly Star 月星
Metal 金9		3	9

SUNDAY	MONDAY	TUESDAY	WEDNESDAY	THURSDAY	FRIDAY	SATURDAY
	火2 Fire · Family · 7 丙寅 Fire Tiger · 風火家人 **1** 廿六 4	水6 Water · Decreasing · 6 丁卯 Fire Rabbit · 山澤損 **2** 廿七 9	金9 Metal · Tread · 5 戊辰 Earth Dragon · 天澤履 **3** 廿八 6	木8 Wood · Great Strength · 4 己巳 Earth Snake · 雷天大壯 **4** 廿九 2	木8 Wood · Consistency · 3 庚午 Metal Horse · 雷風恆 **5** 三十 9	金9 Metal · Litigation · 2 辛未 Metal Goat · 天水訟 **6** 六月初一 3
水1 Water · Officer · 1 壬申 Water Monkey · 地水師 **7** 初二 7	火2 Fire · Gradual Progress · 9 癸酉 Water Rooster · 風山漸 **8** 初三 7	火7 Fire · Obstruction · 8 甲戌 Wood Dog · 水山蹇 **9** 初四 2	木3 Wood · Advancement · 7 乙亥 Wood Pig · 火地晉 **10** 初五 3	水6 Water · Nourish · 6 丙子 Fire Rat · 山雷頤 **11** 初六 3	金4 Metal · Following · 5 丁丑 Fire Ox · 澤雷隨 **12** 初七 7	木8 Wood · Abundance · 4 戊寅 Earth Tiger · 雷火豐 **13** 初八 6
火7 Fire · Regulate · 3 己卯 Earth Rabbit · 水澤節 **14** 初九 8	水1 Water · Unity · 2 庚辰 Metal Dragon · 地天泰 **15** 初十 9	木3 Wood · Great Reward · 1 辛巳 Metal Snake · 火天大有 **16** 十一 7	火2 Fire · Wind · 9 壬午 Water Horse · 巽爲風 **17** 十二 1	金4 Metal · Trap · 8 癸未 Water Goat · 澤水困 **18** 十三 8	木3 Wood · Not Yet Accomplished · 7 甲申 Wood Monkey · 火水未濟 **19** 十四 9	金9 Metal · Retreat · 6 乙酉 Wood Rooster · 天山遯 **20** 十五 4
水6 Water · Mountain · 5 丙戌 Fire Dog · 艮爲山 **21** 十六 1	木8 Wood · Delight · 4 丁亥 Fire Pig · 雷地豫 **22** 十七 8	火7 Fire · Beginning · 3 戊子 Earth Rat · 水雷屯 **23** 十八 4	金9 Metal · Without Wrongdoing · 2 己丑 Earth Ox · 天雷無妄 **24** 十九 2	木3 Wood · Fire · 1 庚寅 Metal Tiger · 離爲火 **25** 二十 1	火2 Fire · Sincerity · 9 辛卯 Metal Rabbit · 風澤中孚 **26** 廿一 3	水6 Water · Big Livestock · 8 壬辰 Water Dragon · 山天大畜 **27** 廿二 4
金4 Metal · Eliminating · 7 癸巳 Water Snake · 澤天夬 **28** 廿三 6	金9 Metal · Heaven · 6 甲午 Wood Horse · 乾爲天 **29** 廿四 1	火7 Fire · Well · 5 乙未 Wood Goat · 水風井 **30** 廿五 6	木8 Wood · Relief · 4 丙申 Fire Monkey · 雷水解 **31** 廿六 4			

AUGUST 2024 壬申

Xuan Kong Element 玄空五行	地水師 Officer	Period Luck 卦運	Monthly Star 月星
Water 水1		7	8

SUNDAY	MONDAY	TUESDAY	WEDNESDAY	THURSDAY	FRIDAY	SATURDAY
				金4 Metal · Influence · 3 丁酉 Fire Rooster · 澤山咸 **1** 廿七 9	水1 Water · Humility · 2 戊戌 Earth Dog · 地山謙 **2** 廿八 6	火2 Fire · Observation · 1 己亥 Earth Pig · 風地觀 **3** 廿九 2
火2 Fire · Increasing · 9 庚子 Metal Rat · 風雷益 **4** 七月初一 9	水1 Water · Dimming Light · 8 辛丑 Metal Ox · 地火明夷 **5** 初二 3	金9 Metal · Fellowship · 7 壬寅 Water Tiger · 天火同人 **6** 初三 7	木8 Wood · Marrying Maiden · 6 癸卯 Water Rabbit · 雷澤歸妹 **7** 初四 7	木3 Wood · Opposition · 5 甲辰 Wood Dragon · 火澤睽 **8** 初五 2	火7 Fire · Waiting · 4 乙巳 Wood Snake · 水天需 **9** 初六 3	金4 Metal · Great Exceeding · 3 丙午 Fire Horse · 澤風大過 **10** 初七 3
水6 Water · Poison · 2 丁未 Fire Goat · 山風蠱 **11** 初八 7	火2 Fire · Dispersing · 1 戊申 Earth Monkey · 風水渙 **12** 初九 6	木3 Wood · Travelling · 9 己酉 Earth Rooster · 火山旅 **13** 初十 8	金9 Metal · Stagnation · 8 庚戌 Metal Dog · 天地否 **14** 十一 9	火7 Fire · Alliance · 7 辛亥 Metal Pig · 水地比 **15** 十二 7	木8 Wood · Thunder · 6 壬子 Water Rat · 震爲雷 **16** 十三 1	水6 Water · Beauty · 5 癸丑 Water Ox · 山火賁 **17** 十四 8
火7 Fire · Accomplished · 4 甲寅 Wood Tiger · 水火既濟 **18** 十五 9	水1 Water · Arriving · 3 乙卯 Wood Rabbit · 地澤臨 **19** 十六 4	金4 Metal · Marsh · 2 丙辰 Fire Dragon · 兑爲澤 **20** 十七 1	火2 Fire · Small Livestock · 1 丁巳 Fire Snake · 風天小畜 **21** 十八 8	木3 Wood · The Cauldron · 9 戊午 Earth Horse · 火風鼎 **22** 十九 4	水1 Water · Rising · 8 己未 Earth Goat · 地風升 **23** 二十 2	火7 Fire · Water · 7 庚申 Metal Monkey · 坎爲水 **24** 廿一 1
木8 Wood · Lesser Exceeding · 6 辛酉 Metal Rooster · 雷山小過 **25** 廿二 3	金4 Metal · Gathering · 5 壬戌 Water Dog · 澤地萃 **26** 廿三 4	水6 Water · Peel · 4 癸亥 Water Pig · 山地剝 **27** 廿四 6	水1 Water · Earth · 3 甲子 Wood Rat · 坤爲地 **28** 廿五 1	木3 Wood · Biting · 2 乙丑 Wood Ox · 火雷噬嗑 **29** 廿六 6	火2 Fire · Family · 1 丙寅 Fire Tiger · 風火家人 **30** 廿七 4	水6 Water · Decreasing · 9 丁卯 Fire Rabbit · 山澤損 **31** 廿八 9

SEPTEMBER 2024 癸酉

Xuan Kong Element 玄空五行	風山漸 Gradual Progress	Period Luck 卦運	Monthly Star 月星
Fire 火2		7	7

SUNDAY	MONDAY	TUESDAY	WEDNESDAY	THURSDAY	FRIDAY	SATURDAY
金9 Metal Tread 8 戊辰 Earth Dragon 天澤履 1 6 廿九	木8 Wood Great Strength 7 己巳 Earth Snake 雷天大壯 2 2 三十	木8 Wood Consistency 6 庚午 Metal Horse 雷風恆 3 9 八月初一	金9 Metal Litigation 5 辛未 Metal Goat 天水訟 4 3 初二	水1 Water Officer 4 壬申 Water Monkey 地水師 5 7 初三	火2 Fire Gradual Progress 3 癸酉 Water Rooster 風山漸 6 7 初四	火7 Fire Obstruction 2 甲戌 Wood Dog 水山蹇 7 2 初五
木3 Wood Advancement 1 乙亥 Wood Pig 火地晉 8 3 初六	水6 Water Nourish 9 丙子 Fire Rat 山雷頤 9 3 初七	金4 Metal Following 8 丁丑 Fire Ox 澤雷隨 10 7 初八	木8 Wood Abundance 7 戊寅 Earth Tiger 雷火豐 11 6 初九	火7 Fire Regulate 6 己卯 Earth Rabbit 水澤節 12 8 初十	水1 Water Unity 5 庚辰 Metal Dragon 地天泰 13 9 十一	木3 Wood Great Reward 4 辛巳 Metal Snake 火天大有 14 7 十二
火2 Fire Wind 3 壬午 Water Horse 巽為風 15 1 十三	金4 Metal Trap 2 癸未 Water Goat 澤水困 16 8 十四	木3 Wood Not Yet Accomplished 1 甲申 Wood Monkey 火水未濟 17 9 十五	金9 Metal Retreat 9 乙酉 Wood Rooster 天山遯 18 4 十六	水6 Water Mountain 8 丙戌 Fire Dog 艮為山 19 1 十七	木8 Wood Delight 7 丁亥 Fire Pig 雷地豫 20 8 十八	火7 Fire Beginning 6 戊子 Earth Rat 水雷屯 21 4 十九
金9 Metal Without Wrongdoing 5 己丑 Earth Ox 天雷無妄 22 2 二十	木3 Wood Fire 4 庚寅 Metal Tiger 離為火 23 1 廿一	火2 Fire Sincerity 3 辛卯 Metal Rabbit 風澤中孚 24 3 廿二	水6 Water Big Livestock 2 壬辰 Water Dragon 山天大畜 25 4 廿三	金4 Metal Eliminating 1 癸巳 Water Snake 澤天夬 26 6 廿四	金9 Metal Heaven 9 甲午 Wood Horse 乾為天 27 1 廿五	火7 Fire Well 8 乙未 Wood Goat 水風井 28 6 廿六
木8 Wood Relief 7 丙申 Fire Monkey 雷水解 29 4 廿七	金4 Metal Influence 6 丁酉 Fire Rooster 澤山咸 30 9 廿八					

OCTOBER 2024 甲戌

Xuan Kong Element 玄空五行	水山蹇 Obstruction	Period Luck 卦運	Monthly Star 月星
Fire 火7		2	6

SUNDAY	MONDAY	TUESDAY	WEDNESDAY	THURSDAY	FRIDAY	SATURDAY
		水1 Water Humility 5 戊戌 Earth Dog 地山謙 1 6 廿九	火2 Fire Observation 4 己亥 Earth Pig 風地觀 2 2 三十	火2 Fire Increasing 3 庚子 Metal Rat 風雷益 3 9 九月初一	水1 Water Dimming Light 2 辛丑 Metal Ox 地火明夷 4 3 初二	金9 Metal Fellowship 1 壬寅 Water Tiger 天火同人 5 7 初三
木8 Wood Marrying Maiden 9 癸卯 Water Rabbit 雷澤歸妹 6 7 初四	木3 Wood Opposition 8 甲辰 Wood Dragon 火澤睽 7 2 初五	火7 Fire Waiting 7 乙巳 Wood Snake 水天需 8 3 初六	金4 Metal Great Exceeding 6 丙午 Fire Horse 澤風大過 9 3 初七	水6 Water Poison 5 丁未 Fire Goat 山風蠱 10 7 初八	火2 Fire Dispersing 4 戊申 Earth Monkey 風水渙 11 6 初九	木3 Wood Travelling 3 己酉 Earth Rooster 火山旅 12 8 初十
金9 Metal Stagnation 2 庚戌 Metal Dog 天地否 13 9 十一	火7 Fire Alliance 1 辛亥 Metal Pig 水地比 14 7 十二	木8 Wood Thunder 9 壬子 Water Rat 震為雷 15 1 十三	水6 Water Beauty 8 癸丑 Water Ox 山火賁 16 8 十四	火7 Fire Accomplished 7 甲寅 Wood Tiger 水火既濟 17 9 十五	水1 Water Arriving 6 乙卯 Wood Rabbit 地澤臨 18 4 十六	金4 Metal Marsh 5 丙辰 Fire Dragon 兌為澤 19 1 十七
火2 Fire Small Livestock 4 丁巳 Fire Snake 風天小畜 20 8 十八	木3 Wood The Cauldron 3 戊午 Earth Horse 火風鼎 21 4 十九	水1 Water Rising 2 己未 Earth Goat 地風升 22 2 二十	火7 Fire Water 1 庚申 Metal Monkey 坎為水 23 1 廿一	木8 Wood Lesser Exceeding 9 辛酉 Metal Rooster 雷山小過 24 3 廿二	金4 Metal Gathering 8 壬戌 Water Dog 澤地萃 25 4 廿三	水6 Water Peel 7 癸亥 Water Pig 山地剝 26 6 廿四
水1 Water Earth 6 甲子 Wood Rat 坤為地 27 1 廿五	木3 Wood Biting 5 乙丑 Wood Ox 火雷噬嗑 28 6 廿六	火2 Fire Family 4 丙寅 Fire Tiger 風火家人 29 4 廿七	水6 Water Decreasing 3 丁卯 Fire Rabbit 山澤損 30 9 廿八	金9 Metal Tread 2 戊辰 Earth Dragon 天澤履 31 6 廿九		

NOVEMBER 2024 乙亥

Xuan Kong Element 玄空五行		Period Luck 卦運	Monthly Star 月星
Wood 木3	火地晉 Advancement	3	5

SUNDAY	MONDAY	TUESDAY	WEDNESDAY	THURSDAY	FRIDAY	SATURDAY
					1 十月初一 木8 Wood · 1 Great Strength 雷天大壯 己巳 Earth Snake 2	**2** 初二 木8 Wood · 9 Consistency 雷風恆 庚午 Metal Horse 9
3 初三 金9 Metal · 8 Litigation 天水訟 辛未 Metal Goat 3	**4** 初四 水1 Water · 7 Officer 地水師 壬申 Water Monkey 7	**5** 初五 火2 Fire · 6 Gradual Progress 風山漸 癸酉 Water Rooster 7	**6** 初六 火7 Fire · 5 Obstruction 水山蹇 甲戌 Wood Dog 2	**7** 初七 木3 Wood · 4 Advancement 火地晉 乙亥 Wood Pig 3	**8** 初八 水6 Water · 3 Nourish 山雷頤 丙子 Fire Rat 3	**9** 初九 金4 Metal · 2 Following 澤雷隨 丁丑 Fire Ox 7
10 初十 木8 Wood · 1 Abundance 雷火豐 戊寅 Earth Tiger 6	**11** 十一 火7 Fire · 9 Regulate 水澤節 己卯 Earth Rabbit 8	**12** 十二 水1 Water · 8 Unity 地天泰 庚辰 Metal Dragon 9	**13** 十三 木3 Wood · 7 Great Reward 火天大有 辛巳 Metal Snake 7	**14** 十四 火2 Fire · 6 Wind 巽為風 壬午 Water Horse 1	**15** 十五 金4 Metal · 5 Trap 澤水困 癸未 Water Goat 8	**16** 十六 木3 Wood · 4 Not Yet Accomplished 火水未濟 甲申 Wood Monkey 9
17 十七 金9 Metal · 3 Retreat 天山遯 乙酉 Wood Rooster 4	**18** 十八 水6 Water · 2 Mountain 艮為山 丙戌 Fire Dog 1	**19** 十九 木8 Wood · 1 Delight 雷地豫 丁亥 Fire Pig 8	**20** 二十 火7 Fire · 9 Beginning 水雷屯 戊子 Earth Rat 4	**21** 廿一 金9 Metal · 8 Without Wrongdoing 天雷無妄 己丑 Earth Ox 2	**22** 廿二 木3 Wood · 7 Fire 離為火 庚寅 Metal Tiger 1	**23** 廿三 火2 Fire · 6 Sincerity 風澤中孚 辛卯 Metal Rabbit 3
24 廿四 水6 Water · 5 Big Livestock 山天大畜 壬辰 Water Dragon 4	**25** 廿五 金4 Metal · 4 Eliminating 澤天夬 癸巳 Water Snake 6	**26** 廿六 金9 Metal · 3 Heaven 乾為天 甲午 Wood Horse 1	**27** 廿七 火7 Fire · 2 Well 水風井 乙未 Wood Goat 6	**28** 廿八 木8 Wood · 1 Relief 雷水解 丙申 Fire Monkey 4	**29** 廿九 金4 Metal · 9 Influence 澤山咸 丁酉 Fire Rooster 9	**30** 三十 水1 Water · 8 Humility 地山謙 戊戌 Earth Dog 6

DECEMBER 2024 丙子

Xuan Kong Element 玄空五行		Period Luck 卦運	Monthly Star 月星
Water 水6	山雷頤 Nourish	3	4

SUNDAY	MONDAY	TUESDAY	WEDNESDAY	THURSDAY	FRIDAY	SATURDAY
1 十一月初一 火2 Fire · 7 Observation 風地觀 己亥 Earth Pig 2	**2** 初二 火2 Fire · 6 Increasing 風雷益 庚子 Metal Rat 9	**3** 初三 水1 Water · 5 Dimming Light 地火明夷 辛丑 Metal Ox 3	**4** 初四 金9 Metal · 4 Fellowship 天火同人 壬寅 Water Tiger 7	**5** 初五 木8 Wood · 3 Marrying Maiden 雷澤歸妹 癸卯 Water Rabbit 7	**6** 初六 木3 Wood · 2 Opposition 火澤睽 甲辰 Wood Dragon 2	**7** 初七 火7 Fire · 1 Waiting 水天需 乙巳 Wood Snake 3
8 初八 金4 Metal · 9 Great Exceeding 澤風大過 丙午 Fire Horse 3	**9** 初九 水6 Water · 8 Poison 山風蠱 丁未 Fire Goat 7	**10** 初十 火2 Fire · 7 Dispersing 風水渙 戊申 Earth Monkey 6	**11** 十一 木3 Wood · 6 Travelling 火山旅 己酉 Earth Rooster 8	**12** 十二 金9 Metal · 5 Stagnation 天地否 庚戌 Metal Dog 9	**13** 十三 火7 Fire · 4 Alliance 水地比 辛亥 Metal Pig 7	**14** 十四 木8 Wood · 3 Thunder 震為雷 壬子 Water Rat 1
15 十五 水6 Water · 2 Beauty 山火賁 癸丑 Water Ox 8	**16** 十六 火7 Fire · 1 Accomplished 水火既濟 甲寅 Wood Tiger 9	**17** 十七 水1 Water · 9 Arriving 地澤臨 乙卯 Wood Rabbit 4	**18** 十八 金4 Metal · 8 Marsh 兌為澤 丙辰 Fire Dragon 1	**19** 十九 火2 Fire · 7 Small Livestock 風天小畜 丁巳 Fire Snake 8	**20** 二十 木3 Wood · 6 The Cauldron 火風鼎 戊午 Earth Horse 4	**21** 廿一 水1 Water · 5/5 Rising 地風升 己未 Earth Goat 2
22 廿二 火7 Fire · 6 Water 坎為水 庚申 Metal Monkey 1	**23** 廿三 木8 Wood · 7 Lesser Exceeding 雷山小過 辛酉 Metal Rooster 3	**24** 廿四 金4 Metal · 8 Gathering 澤地萃 壬戌 Water Dog 4	**25** 廿五 水6 Water · 9 Peel 山地剝 癸亥 Water Pig 6	**26** 廿六 水1 Water · 1 Earth 坤為地 甲子 Wood Rat 1	**27** 廿七 木3 Wood · 2 Biting 火雷噬嗑 乙丑 Wood Ox 6	**28** 廿八 火2 Fire · 3 Family 風火家人 丙寅 Fire Tiger 4
29 廿九 水6 Water · 4 Decreasing 山澤損 丁卯 Fire Rabbit 9	**30** 三十 金9 Metal · 5 Tread 天澤履 戊辰 Earth Dragon 6	**31** 十二月初一 木8 Wood · 6 Great Strength 雷天大壯 己巳 Earth Snake 2				

2025 乙巳

(*Yi Si*) Wood Snake

2025 乙巳 *(Yi Si)* Wood Snake

January 5 - February 2

February 3 - March 4

March 5 - April 3

April 4 - May 4

May 5 - June 4

June 5 - July 6

July 7 - August 6

August 7 - September 6

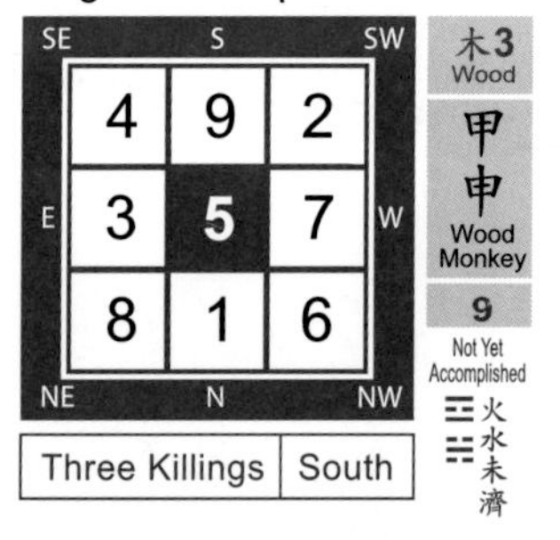

September 7 - October 7

October 8 - November 6

November 7 - December 6

December 7 - January 4

JANUARY 2025 丁丑

Xuan Kong Element 玄空五行	澤雷隨 Following	Period Luck 卦運	Monthly Star 月星
Metal 金4		7	3

SUNDAY	MONDAY	TUESDAY	WEDNESDAY	THURSDAY	FRIDAY	SATURDAY
			木8 Wood 7 Consistency 庚午 Metal Horse 雷風恒 **1** 初二 9	金9 Metal 8 Litigation 辛未 Metal Goat 天水訟 **2** 初三 3	水1 Water 9 Officer 壬申 Water Monkey 地水師 **3** 初四 7	火2 Fire 1 Gradual Progress 癸酉 Water Rooster 風山漸 **4** 初五 7
火7 Fire 2 Obstruction 甲戌 Wood Dog 水山蹇 **5** 初六 2	木3 Wood 3 Advancement 乙亥 Wood Pig 火地晉 **6** 初七 3	水6 Water 4 Nourish 丙子 Fire Rat 山雷頤 **7** 初八 3	金4 Metal 5 Following 丁丑 Fire Ox 澤雷隨 **8** 初九 7	木8 Wood 6 Abundance 戊寅 Earth Tiger 雷火豐 **9** 初十 6	火7 Fire 7 Regulate 己卯 Earth Rabbit 水澤節 **10** 十一 8	水1 Water 8 Unity 庚辰 Metal Dragon 地天泰 **11** 十二 9
木3 Wood 9 Great Reward 辛巳 Metal Snake 火天大有 **12** 十三 7	火2 Fire 1 Wind 壬午 Water Horse 巽為風 **13** 十四 1	金4 Metal 2 Trap 癸未 Water Goat 澤水困 **14** 十五 8	木3 Wood 3 Not Yet Accomplished 甲申 Wood Monkey 火水未濟 **15** 十六 9	金9 Metal 4 Retreat 乙酉 Wood Rooster 天山遯 **16** 十七 4	水6 Water 5 Mountain 丙戌 Fire Dog 艮為山 **17** 十八 1	木8 Wood 6 Delight 丁亥 Fire Pig 雷地豫 **18** 十九 8
火7 Fire 7 Beginning 戊子 Earth Rat 水雷屯 **19** 二十 4	金9 Metal 8 Without Wrongdoing 己丑 Earth Ox 天雷無妄 **20** 廿一 2	木3 Wood 9 Fire 庚寅 Metal Tiger 離為火 **21** 廿二 1	火2 Fire 1 Sincerity 辛卯 Metal Rabbit 風澤中孚 **22** 廿三 3	水6 Water 2 Big Livestock 壬辰 Water Dragon 山天大畜 **23** 廿四 4	金4 Metal 3 Eliminating 癸巳 Water Snake 澤天夬 **24** 廿五 6	金9 Metal 4 Heaven 甲午 Wood Horse 乾為天 **25** 廿六 1
火7 Fire 5 Well 乙未 Wood Goat 水風井 **26** 廿七 6	木8 Wood 6 Relief 丙申 Fire Monkey 雷水解 **27** 廿八 4	金4 Metal 7 Influence 丁酉 Fire Rooster 澤山咸 **28** 廿九 9	水1 Water 8 Humility 戊戌 Earth Dog 地山謙 **29** 正月初一 6	火2 Fire 9 Observation 己亥 Earth Pig 風地觀 **30** 初二 2	火2 Fire 1 Increasing 庚子 Metal Rat 風雷益 **31** 初三 9	

FEBRUARY 2025 戊寅

Xuan Kong Element 玄空五行	雷火豐 Abundance	Period Luck 卦運	Monthly Star 月星
Wood 木8		6	2

SUNDAY	MONDAY	TUESDAY	WEDNESDAY	THURSDAY	FRIDAY	SATURDAY
						水1 Water 2 Dimming Light 辛丑 Metal Ox 地火明夷 **1** 初四 3
金9 Metal 3 Fellowship 壬寅 Water Tiger 天火同人 **2** 初五 7	木8 Wood 4 Marrying Maiden 癸卯 Water Rabbit 雷澤歸妹 **3** 初六 7	木3 Wood 5 Opposition 甲辰 Wood Dragon 火澤睽 **4** 初七 2	火7 Fire 6 Waiting 乙巳 Wood Snake 水天需 **5** 初八 3	金4 Metal 7 Great Exceeding 丙午 Fire Horse 澤風大過 **6** 初九 3	水6 Water 8 Poison 丁未 Fire Goat 山風蠱 **7** 初十 7	火2 Fire 9 Dispersing 戊申 Earth Monkey 風水渙 **8** 十一 6
木3 Wood 1 Travelling 己酉 Earth Rooster 火山旅 **9** 十二 8	金9 Metal 2 Stagnation 庚戌 Metal Dog 天地否 **10** 十三 9	火7 Fire 3 Alliance 辛亥 Metal Pig 水地比 **11** 十四 7	木8 Wood 4 Thunder 壬子 Water Rat 震為雷 **12** 十五 1	水6 Water 5 Beauty 癸丑 Water Ox 山火賁 **13** 十六 8	火7 Fire 6 Accomplished 甲寅 Wood Tiger 水火既濟 **14** 十七 9	水1 Water 7 Arriving 乙卯 Wood Rabbit 地澤臨 **15** 十八 4
金4 Metal 8 Marsh 内辰 Fire Dragon 兑為澤 **16** 十九 1	火2 Fire 9 Small Livestock 丁巳 Fire Snake 風天小畜 **17** 二十 8	木3 Wood 1 The Cauldron 戊午 Earth Horse 火風鼎 **18** 廿 4	水1 Water 2 Rising 己未 Earth Goat 地風升 **19** 廿二 2	火7 Fire 3 Water 庚申 Metal Monkey 坎為水 **20** 廿三 1	木8 Wood 4 Lesser Exceeding 辛酉 Metal Rooster 雷山小過 **21** 廿四 3	金4 Metal 5 Gathering 壬戌 Water Dog 澤地萃 **22** 廿五 4
水6 Water 6 Peel 癸亥 Water Pig 山地剝 **23** 廿六 6	水1 Water 7 Earth 甲子 Wood Rat 坤為地 **24** 廿七 1	木3 Wood 8 Biting 乙丑 Wood Ox 火雷噬嗑 **25** 廿八 6	火2 Fire 9 Family 丙寅 Fire Tiger 風火家人 **26** 廿九 4	水6 Water 1 Decreasing 丁卯 Fire Rabbit 山澤損 **27** 三十 9	金9 Metal 2 Tread 戊辰 Earth Dragon 天澤履 **28** 二月初一 6	

MARCH 2025 己卯

Xuan Kong Element 玄空五行	水澤節 Regulate	Period Luck 卦運	Monthly Star 月星
Fire 火7		8	1

SUNDAY	MONDAY	TUESDAY	WEDNESDAY	THURSDAY	FRIDAY	SATURDAY
水1 Water 5 Humility 地山謙 戊戌 Earth Dog **30** 初二 6	火2 Fire 6 Observation 風地觀 己亥 Earth Pig **31** 初三 2					木8 Wood 3 Great Strength 雷天大壯 己巳 Earth Snake **1** 初二 2
木8 Wood 4 Consistency 雷風恒 庚午 Metal Horse **2** 初三 9	金9 Metal 5 Litigation 天水訟 辛未 Metal Goat **3** 初四 3	水1 Water 6 Officer 地水師 壬申 Water Monkey **4** 初五 7	火2 Fire 7 Gradual Progress 風山漸 癸酉 Water Rooster **5** 初六 7	火7 Fire 8 Obstruction 水山蹇 甲戌 Wood Dog **6** 初七 2	木3 Wood 9 Advancement 火地晉 乙亥 Wood Pig **7** 初八 3	水6 Water 1 Nourish 山雷頤 丙子 Fire Rat **8** 初九 3
金4 Metal 2 Following 澤雷隨 丁丑 Fire Ox **9** 初十 7	木8 Wood 3 Abundance 雷火豐 戊寅 Earth Tiger **10** 十一 6	火7 Fire 4 Regulate 水澤節 己卯 Earth Rabbit **11** 十二 8	水1 Water 5 Unity 地天泰 庚辰 Metal Dragon **12** 十三 9	木3 Wood 6 Great Reward 火天大有 辛巳 Metal Snake **13** 十四 7	火2 Fire 7 Wind 巽爲風 壬午 Water Horse **14** 十五 1	金4 Metal 8 Trap 澤水困 癸未 Water Goat **15** 十六 8
木3 Wood 9 Not Yet Accomplished 火水未濟 甲申 Wood Monkey **16** 十七 9	金9 Metal 1 Retreat 天山遯 乙酉 Wood Rooster **17** 十八 4	水6 Water 2 Mountain 艮爲山 丙戌 Fire Dog **18** 十九 1	木8 Wood 3 Delight 雷地豫 丁亥 Fire Pig **19** 二十 8	火7 Fire 4 Beginning 水雷屯 戊子 Earth Rat **20** 廿一 4	金9 Metal 5 Without Wrongdoing 天雷無妄 己丑 Earth Ox **21** 廿二 2	木3 Wood 6 Fire 離爲火 庚寅 Metal Tiger **22** 廿三 1
火2 Fire 7 Sincerity 風澤中孚 辛卯 Metal Rabbit **23** 廿四 3	水6 Water 8 Big Livestock 山天大畜 壬辰 Water Dragon **24** 廿五 4	金4 Metal 9 Eliminating 澤天夬 癸巳 Water Snake **25** 廿六 6	金9 Metal 1 Heaven 乾爲天 甲午 Wood Horse **26** 廿七 1	火7 Fire 2 Well 水風井 乙未 Wood Goat **27** 廿八 6	木8 Wood 3 Relief 雷水解 丙申 Fire Monkey **28** 廿九 4	金4 Metal 4 Influence 澤山咸 丁酉 Fire Rooster **29** 三月初一 9

APRIL 2025 庚辰

Xuan Kong Element 玄空五行	地天泰 Unity	Period Luck 卦運	Monthly Star 月星
Water 水1		9	9

SUNDAY	MONDAY	TUESDAY	WEDNESDAY	THURSDAY	FRIDAY	SATURDAY
		火2 Fire 7 Increasing 風雷益 庚子 Metal Rat **1** 初四 9	水1 Water 8 Dimming Light 地火明夷 辛丑 Metal Ox **2** 初五 3	金9 Metal 9 Fellowship 天火同人 壬寅 Water Tiger **3** 初六 7	木8 Wood 1 Marrying Maiden 雷澤歸妹 癸卯 Water Rabbit **4** 初七 7	木3 Wood 2 Opposition 火澤睽 甲辰 Wood Dragon **5** 初八 2
火7 Fire 3 Waiting 水天需 乙巳 Wood Snake **6** 初九 3	金4 Metal 4 Great Exceeding 澤風大過 丙午 Fire Horse **7** 初十 3	水6 Water 5 Poison 山風蠱 丁未 Fire Goat **8** 十一 7	火2 Fire 6 Dispersing 風水渙 戊申 Earth Monkey **9** 十二 6	木3 Wood 7 Travelling 火山旅 己酉 Earth Rooster **10** 十三 8	金9 Metal 8 Stagnation 天地否 庚戌 Metal Dog **11** 十四 9	火7 Fire 9 Alliance 水地比 辛亥 Metal Pig **12** 十五 7
木8 Wood 1 Thunder 震爲雷 壬子 Water Rat **13** 十六 1	水6 Water 2 Beauty 山火賁 癸丑 Water Ox **14** 十七 8	火7 Fire 3 Accomplished 水火既濟 甲寅 Wood Tiger **15** 十八 9	水1 Water 4 Arriving 地澤臨 乙卯 Wood Rabbit **16** 十九 4	金4 Metal 5 Marsh 兑爲澤 丙辰 Fire Dragon **17** 二十 1	火2 Fire 6 Small Livestock 風天小畜 丁巳 Fire Snake **18** 廿一 8	木3 Wood 7 The Cauldron 火風鼎 戊午 Earth Horse **19** 廿二 4
水1 Water 8 Rising 地風升 己未 Earth Goat **20** 廿三 2	火7 Fire 9 Water 坎爲水 庚申 Metal Monkey **21** 廿四 1	木8 Wood 1 Lesser Exceeding 雷山小過 辛酉 Metal Rooster **22** 廿五 3	金4 Metal 2 Gathering 澤地萃 壬戌 Water Dog **23** 廿六 4	水6 Water 3 Peel 山地剝 癸亥 Water Pig **24** 廿七 6	水1 Water 4 Earth 坤爲地 甲子 Wood Rat **25** 廿八 1	木3 Wood 5 Biting 火雷噬嗑 乙丑 Wood Ox **26** 廿九 6
火2 Fire 6 Family 風火家人 丙寅 Fire Tiger **27** 三十 4	水6 Water 7 Decreasing 山澤損 丁卯 Fire Rabbit **28** 四月初一 9	金9 Metal 8 Tread 天澤履 戊辰 Earth Dragon **29** 初二 6	木8 Wood 9 Great Strength 雷天大壯 己巳 Earth Snake **30** 初三 2			

MAY 2025 辛巳

Xuan Kong Element 玄空五行	火天大有 Great Reward	Period Luck 卦運	Monthly Star 月星
Wood 木3		7	8

SUNDAY	MONDAY	TUESDAY	WEDNESDAY	THURSDAY	FRIDAY	SATURDAY
				木8 Wood Consistency 1 庚午 Metal Horse 雷風恆 1 初四 9	金9 Metal Litigation 2 辛未 Metal Goat 天水訟 2 初五 3	水1 Water Officer 3 壬申 Water Monkey 地水師 3 初六 7
火2 Fire Gradual Progress 4 癸酉 Water Rooster 風山漸 4 初七 7	火7 Fire Obstruction 5 甲戌 Wood Dog 水山蹇 5 初八 2	木3 Wood Advancement 6 乙亥 Wood Pig 火地晉 6 初九 3	水6 Water Nourish 7 丙子 Fire Rat 山雷頤 7 初十 3	金4 Metal Following 8 丁丑 Fire Ox 澤雷隨 8 十一 7	木8 Wood Abundance 9 戊寅 Earth Tiger 雷火豐 9 十二 6	火7 Fire Regulate 1 己卯 Earth Rabbit 水澤節 10 十三 8
水1 Water Unity 2 庚辰 Metal Dragon 地天泰 11 十四 9	木3 Wood Great Reward 3 辛巳 Metal Snake 火天大有 12 十五 7	火2 Fire Wind 4 壬午 Water Horse 巽爲風 13 十六 1	金4 Metal Trap 5 癸未 Water Goat 澤水困 14 十七 8	木3 Wood Not Yet Accomplished 6 甲申 Wood Monkey 火水未濟 15 十八 9	金9 Metal Retreat 7 乙酉 Wood Rooster 天山遯 16 十九 4	水6 Water Mountain 8 丙戌 Fire Dog 艮爲山 17 二十 1
木8 Wood Delight 9 丁亥 Fire Pig 雷地豫 18 廿一 8	火7 Fire Beginning 1 戊子 Earth Rat 水雷屯 19 廿二 4	金9 Metal Without Wrongdoing 2 己丑 Earth Ox 天雷無妄 20 廿三 2	木3 Wood Fire 3 庚寅 Metal Tiger 離爲火 21 廿四 1	火2 Fire Sincerity 4 辛卯 Metal Rabbit 風澤中孚 22 廿五 3	水6 Water Big Livestock 5 壬辰 Water Dragon 山天大畜 23 廿六 4	金4 Metal Eliminating 6 癸巳 Water Snake 澤天夬 24 廿七 6
金9 Metal Heaven 7 甲午 Wood Horse 乾爲天 25 廿八 1	火7 Fire Well 8 乙未 Wood Goat 水風井 26 廿九 6	木8 Wood Relief 9 丙申 Fire Monkey 雷水解 27 五月初一 4	金4 Metal Influence 1 丁酉 Fire Rooster 澤山咸 28 初二 9	水1 Water Humility 2 戊戌 Earth Dog 地山謙 29 初三 6	火2 Fire Observation 3 己亥 Earth Pig 風地觀 30 初四 2	火2 Fire Increasing 4 庚子 Metal Rat 風雷益 31 初五 9

JUNE 2025 壬午

Xuan Kong Element 玄空五行	巽爲風 Wind	Period Luck 卦運	Monthly Star 月星
Fire 火2		1	7

SUNDAY	MONDAY	TUESDAY	WEDNESDAY	THURSDAY	FRIDAY	SATURDAY
水1 Water Dimming Light 5 辛丑 Metal Ox 地火明夷 1 初六 3	金9 Metal Fellowship 6 壬寅 Water Tiger 天火同人 2 初七 7	木8 Wood Marrying Maiden 7 癸卯 Water Rabbit 雷澤歸妹 3 初八 7	木3 Wood Opposition 8 甲辰 Wood Dragon 火澤睽 4 初九 2	火7 Fire Waiting 9 乙巳 Wood Snake 水天需 5 初十 3	金4 Metal Great Exceeding 1 丙午 Fire Horse 澤風大過 6 十一 3	水6 Water Poison 2 丁未 Fire Goat 山風蠱 7 十二 7
火2 Fire Dispersing 3 戊申 Earth Monkey 風水渙 8 十三 6	木3 Wood Travelling 4 己酉 Earth Rooster 火山旅 9 十四 8	金9 Metal Stagnation 5 庚戌 Metal Dog 天地否 10 十五 9	火7 Fire Alliance 6 辛亥 Metal Pig 水地比 11 十六 7	木8 Wood Thunder 7 壬子 Water Rat 震爲雷 12 十七 1	水6 Water Beauty 8 癸丑 Water Ox 山火賁 13 十八 8	火7 Fire Accomplished 9 甲寅 Wood Tiger 水火既濟 14 十九 9
水1 Water Arriving 1 乙卯 Wood Rabbit 地澤臨 15 二十 4	金4 Metal Marsh 2 丙辰 Fire Dragon 兑爲澤 16 廿一 1	火2 Fire Small Livestock 3 丁巳 Fire Snake 風天小畜 17 廿二 8	木3 Wood The Cauldron 4 戊午 Earth Horse 火風鼎 18 廿三 4	水1 Water Rising 5 己未 Earth Goat 地風升 19 廿四 2	火7 Fire Water 6 庚申 Metal Monkey 坎爲水 20 廿五 1	木8 Wood Lesser Exceeding 7/8 辛酉 Metal Rooster 雷山小過 21 廿六 3
金4 Metal Gathering 2 壬戌 Water Dog 澤地萃 22 廿七 4	水6 Water Peel 1 癸亥 Water Pig 山地剝 23 廿八 6	水1 Water Earth 9 甲子 Wood Rat 坤爲地 24 廿九 1	木3 Wood Biting 8 乙丑 Wood Ox 火雷噬嗑 25 六月初一 6	火2 Fire Family 7 丙寅 Fire Tiger 風火家人 26 初二 4	水6 Water Decreasing 6 丁卯 Fire Rabbit 山澤損 27 初三 9	金9 Metal Tread 5 戊辰 Earth Dragon 天澤履 28 初四 6
木8 Wood Great Strength 4 己巳 Earth Snake 雷天大壯 29 初五 2	木8 Wood Consistency 3 庚午 Metal Horse 雷風恆 30 初六 9					

JULY 2025 癸未

Xuan Kong Element 玄空五行	澤水困 Trap	Period Luck 卦運	Monthly Star 月星
Metal 金4		8	6

SUNDAY	MONDAY	TUESDAY	WEDNESDAY	THURSDAY	FRIDAY	SATURDAY
		金9 Metal 2 Litigation 天水訟 辛未 Metal Goat **1** 初七 3	水1 Water 1 Officer 地水師 壬申 Water Monkey **2** 初八 7	火2 Fire 9 Gradual Progress 風山漸 癸酉 Water Rooster **3** 初九 7	火7 Fire 8 Obstruction 水山蹇 甲戌 Wood Dog **4** 初十 2	木3 Wood 7 Advancement 火地晉 乙亥 Wood Pig **5** 十一 3
水6 Water 6 Nourish 山雷頤 丙子 Fire Rat **6** 十二 3	金4 Metal 5 Following 澤雷隨 丁丑 Fire Ox **7** 十三 7	木8 Wood 4 Abundance 雷火豐 戊寅 Earth Tiger **8** 十四 6	火7 Fire 3 Regulate 水澤節 己卯 Earth Rabbit **9** 十五 8	水1 Water 2 Unity 地天泰 庚辰 Metal Dragon **10** 十六 9	木3 Wood 1 Great Reward 火天大有 辛巳 Metal Snake **11** 十七 7	火2 Fire 9 Wind 巽爲風 壬午 Water Horse **12** 十八 1
金4 Metal 8 Trap 澤水困 癸未 Water Goat **13** 十九 8	木3 Wood 7 Not Yet Accomplished 火水未濟 甲申 Wood Monkey **14** 二十 9	金9 Metal 6 Retreat 天山遯 乙酉 Wood Rooster **15** 廿一 4	水6 Water 5 Mountain 艮爲山 丙戌 Fire Dog **16** 廿二 1	木8 Wood 4 Delight 雷地豫 丁亥 Fire Pig **17** 廿三 8	火7 Fire 3 Beginning 水雷屯 戊子 Earth Rat **18** 廿四 4	金9 Metal 2 Without Wrongdoing 天雷無妄 己丑 Earth Ox **19** 廿五 2
木3 Wood 1 Fire 離爲火 庚寅 Metal Tiger **20** 廿六 1	火2 Fire 9 Sincerity 風澤中孚 辛卯 Metal Rabbit **21** 廿七 3	水6 Water 8 Big Livestock 山天大畜 壬辰 Water Dragon **22** 廿八 4	金4 Metal 7 Eliminating 澤天夬 癸巳 Water Snake **23** 廿九 6	金9 Metal 6 Heaven 乾爲天 甲午 Wood Horse **24** 三十 1	火7 Fire 5 Well 水風井 乙未 Wood Goat **25** 閏六月初一 6	木8 Wood 4 Relief 雷水解 丙申 Fire Monkey **26** 初二 4
金4 Metal 3 Influence 澤山咸 丁酉 Fire Rooster **27** 初三 9	水1 Water 2 Humility 地山謙 戊戌 Earth Dog **28** 初四 6	火2 Fire 1 Observation 風地觀 己亥 Earth Pig **29** 初五 2	火2 Fire 9 Increasing 風雷益 庚子 Metal Rat **30** 初六 9	水1 Water 8 Dimming Light 地火明夷 辛丑 Metal Ox **31** 初七 3		

AUGUST 2025 甲申

Xuan Kong Element 玄空五行	火水未濟 Not Yet Accomplished	Period Luck 卦運	Monthly Star 月星
Wood 木3		9	5

SUNDAY	MONDAY	TUESDAY	WEDNESDAY	THURSDAY	FRIDAY	SATURDAY
水1 Water 4 Officer 地水師 壬申 Water Monkey **31** 初九 7					金9 Metal 7 Fellowship 天火同人 壬寅 Water Tiger **1** 初八 7	木8 Wood 6 Marrying Maiden 雷澤歸妹 癸卯 Water Rabbit **2** 初九 7
木3 Wood 5 Opposition 火澤睽 甲辰 Wood Dragon **3** 初十 2	火7 Fire 4 Waiting 水天需 乙巳 Wood Snake **4** 十一 3	金4 Metal 3 Great Exceeding 澤風大過 丙午 Fire Horse **5** 十二 3	水6 Water 2 Poison 山風蠱 丁未 Fire Goat **6** 十三 7	火2 Fire 1 Dispersing 風水渙 戊申 Earth Monkey **7** 十四 6	木3 Wood 9 Travelling 火山旅 己酉 Earth Rooster **8** 十五 8	金9 Metal 8 Stagnation 天地否 庚戌 Metal Dog **9** 十六 9
火7 Fire 7 Alliance 水地比 辛亥 Metal Pig **10** 十七 7	木8 Wood 6 Thunder 震爲雷 壬子 Water Rat **11** 十八 1	水6 Water 5 Beauty 山火賁 癸丑 Water Ox **12** 十九 8	火7 Fire 4 Accomplished 水火既濟 甲寅 Wood Tiger **13** 二十 9	水1 Water 3 Arriving 地澤臨 乙卯 Wood Rabbit **14** 廿一 4	金4 Metal 2 Marsh 兌爲澤 丙辰 Fire Dragon **15** 廿二 1	火2 Fire 1 Small Livestock 風天小畜 丁巳 Fire Snake **16** 廿三 8
木3 Wood 9 The Cauldron 火風鼎 戊午 Earth Horse **17** 廿四 4	水1 Water 8 Rising 地風升 己未 Earth Goat **18** 廿五 2	火7 Fire 7 Water 坎爲水 庚申 Metal Monkey **19** 廿六 1	木8 Wood 6 Lesser Exceeding 雷山小過 辛酉 Metal Rooster **20** 廿七 3	金4 Metal 5 Gathering 澤地萃 壬戌 Water Dog **21** 廿八 4	水6 Water 4 Peel 山地剝 癸亥 Water Pig **22** 廿九 6	水1 Water 3 Earth 坤爲地 甲子 Wood Rat **23** 七月初一 1
木3 Wood 2 Biting 火雷噬嗑 乙丑 Wood Ox **24** 初二 6	火2 Fire 1 Family 風火家人 丙寅 Fire Tiger **25** 初三 4	水6 Water 9 Decreasing 山澤損 丁卯 Fire Rabbit **26** 初四 9	金9 Metal 8 Tread 天澤履 戊辰 Earth Dragon **27** 初五 6	木8 Wood 7 Great Strength 雷天大壯 己巳 Earth Snake **28** 初六 2	木8 Wood 6 Consistency 雷風恆 庚午 Metal Horse **29** 初七 9	金9 Metal 5 Litigation 天水訟 辛未 Metal Goat **30** 初八 3

SEPTEMBER 2025 乙酉

Xuan Kong Element 玄空五行	天山遯 Retreat	Period Luck 卦運	Monthly Star 月星
Metal 金9		4	4

SUNDAY	MONDAY	TUESDAY	WEDNESDAY	THURSDAY	FRIDAY	SATURDAY
	火2 Fire Gradual Progress 3 癸酉 Water Rooster 風山漸 **1** 初十 7	火7 Fire Obstruction 2 甲戌 Wood Dog 水山蹇 **2** 十一 2	木3 Wood Advancement 1 乙亥 Wood Pig 火地晉 **3** 十二 3	水6 Water Nourish 9 丙子 Fire Rat 山雷頤 **4** 十三 3	金4 Metal Following 8 丁丑 Fire Ox 澤雷隨 **5** 十四 7	木8 Wood Abundance 7 戊寅 Earth Tiger 雷火豐 **6** 十五 6
火7 Fire Regulate 6 己卯 Earth Rabbit 水澤節 **7** 十六 8	水1 Water Unity 5 庚辰 Metal Dragon 地天泰 **8** 十七 9	木3 Wood Great Reward 4 辛巳 Metal Snake 火天大有 **9** 十八 7	火2 Fire Wind 3 壬午 Water Horse 巽爲風 **10** 十九 1	金4 Metal Trap 2 癸未 Water Goat 澤水困 **11** 二十 8	木3 Wood Not Yet Accomplished 1 甲申 Wood Monkey 火水未濟 **12** 廿一 9	金9 Metal Retreat 9 乙酉 Wood Rooster 天山遯 **13** 廿二 4
水6 Water Mountain 8 丙戌 Fire Dog 艮爲山 **14** 廿三 1	木8 Wood Delight 7 丁亥 Fire Pig 雷地豫 **15** 廿四 8	火7 Fire Beginning 6 戊子 Earth Rat 水雷屯 **16** 廿五 4	金9 Metal Without Wrongdoing 5 己丑 Earth Ox 天雷無妄 **17** 廿六 2	木3 Wood Fire 4 庚寅 Metal Tiger 離爲火 **18** 廿七 1	火2 Fire Sincerity 3 辛卯 Metal Rabbit 風澤中孚 **19** 廿八 3	水6 Water Big Livestock 2 壬辰 Water Dragon 山天大畜 **20** 廿九 4
金4 Metal Eliminating 1 癸巳 Water Snake 澤天夬 **21** 三十 6	金9 Metal Heaven 9 甲午 Wood Horse 乾爲天 **22** 八月初一 1	火7 Fire Well 8 乙未 Wood Goat 水風井 **23** 初二 6	木8 Wood Relief 7 丙申 Fire Monkey 雷水解 **24** 初三 4	金4 Metal Influence 6 丁酉 Fire Rooster 澤山咸 **25** 初四 9	水1 Water Humility 5 戊戌 Earth Dog 地山謙 **26** 初五 6	火2 Fire Observation 4 己亥 Earth Pig 風地觀 **27** 初六 2
火2 Fire Increasing 3 庚子 Metal Rat 風雷益 **28** 初七 9	水1 Water Dimming Light 2 辛丑 Metal Ox 地火明夷 **29** 初八 3	金9 Metal Fellowship 1 壬寅 Water Tiger 天火同人 **30** 初九 7				

OCTOBER 2025 丙戌

Xuan Kong Element 玄空五行	艮爲山 Mountain	Period Luck 卦運	Monthly Star 月星
Water 水6		1	3

SUNDAY	MONDAY	TUESDAY	WEDNESDAY	THURSDAY	FRIDAY	SATURDAY
			木8 Wood Marrying Maiden 9 癸卯 Water Rabbit 雷澤歸妹 **1** 初十 7	木3 Wood Opposition 8 甲辰 Wood Dragon 火澤睽 **2** 十一 2	火7 Fire Waiting 7 乙巳 Wood Snake 水天需 **3** 十二 3	金4 Metal Great Exceeding 6 丙午 Fire Horse 澤風大過 **4** 十三 3
水6 Water Poison 5 丁未 Fire Goat 山風蠱 **5** 十四 7	火2 Fire Dispersing 4 戊申 Earth Monkey 風水渙 **6** 十五 6	木3 Wood Travelling 3 己酉 Earth Rooster 火山旅 **7** 十六 8	金9 Metal Stagnation 2 庚戌 Metal Dog 天地否 **8** 十七 9	火7 Fire Alliance 1 辛亥 Metal Pig 水地比 **9** 十八 7	木8 Wood Thunder 9 壬子 Water Rat 震爲雷 **10** 十九 1	水6 Water Beauty 8 癸丑 Water Ox 山火賁 **11** 二十 8
火7 Fire Accomplished 7 甲寅 Wood Tiger 水火既濟 **12** 廿一 9	水1 Water Arriving 6 乙卯 Wood Rabbit 地澤臨 **13** 廿二 4	金4 Metal Marsh 5 丙辰 Fire Dragon 兑爲澤 **14** 廿三 1	火2 Fire Small Livestock 4 丁巳 Fire Snake 風天小畜 **15** 廿四 8	木3 Wood The Cauldron 3 戊午 Earth Horse 火風鼎 **16** 廿五 4	水1 Water Rising 2 己未 Earth Goat 地風升 **17** 廿六 2	火7 Fire Water 1 庚申 Metal Monkey 坎爲水 **18** 廿七 1
木8 Wood Lesser Exceeding 9 辛酉 Metal Rooster 雷山小過 **19** 廿八 3	金4 Metal Gathering 8 壬戌 Water Dog 澤地萃 **20** 廿九 4	水6 Water Peel 7 癸亥 Water Pig 山地剝 **21** 九月初一 6	水1 Water Earth 6 甲子 Wood Rat 坤爲地 **22** 初二 1	木3 Wood Biting 5 乙丑 Wood Ox 火雷噬嗑 **23** 初三 6	火2 Fire Family 4 丙寅 Fire Tiger 風火家人 **24** 初四 4	水6 Water Decreasing 3 丁卯 Fire Rabbit 山澤損 **25** 初五 9
金9 Metal Tread 2 戊辰 Earth Dragon 天澤履 **26** 初六 6	木8 Wood Great Strength 1 己巳 Earth Snake 雷天大壯 **27** 初七 2	木8 Wood Consistency 9 庚午 Metal Horse 雷風恆 **28** 初八 9	金9 Metal Litigation 8 辛未 Metal Goat 天水訟 **29** 初九 3	水1 Water Officer 7 壬申 Water Monkey 地水師 **30** 初十 7	火2 Fire Gradual Progress 6 癸酉 Water Rooster 風山漸 **31** 十一 7	

NOVEMBER 2025 丁亥

Xuan Kong Element 玄空五行	雷地豫 Delight	Period Luck 卦運	Monthly Star 月星
Wood 木8		8	2

SUNDAY	MONDAY	TUESDAY	WEDNESDAY	THURSDAY	FRIDAY	SATURDAY
木8 Wood 3 Marrying Maiden 癸卯 Water Rabbit 雷澤歸妹 30 十一 7						火7 Fire 5 Obstruction 甲戌 Wood Dog 水山蹇 1 十二 2
木3 Wood 4 Advancement 乙亥 Wood Pig 火地晉 2 十三 3	水6 Water 3 Nourish 丙子 Fire Rat 山雷頤 3 十四 3	金4 Metal 2 Following 丁丑 Fire Ox 澤雷隨 4 十五 7	木8 Wood 1 Abundance 戊寅 Earth Tiger 雷火豐 5 十六 6	火7 Fire 9 Regulate 己卯 Earth Rabbit 水澤節 6 十七 8	水1 Water 8 Unity 庚辰 Metal Dragon 地天泰 7 十八 9	木3 Wood 7 Great Reward 辛巳 Metal Snake 火天大有 8 十九 7
火2 Fire 6 Wind 壬午 Water Horse 巽為風 9 二十 1	金4 Metal 5 Trap 癸未 Water Goat 澤水困 10 廿一 8	木3 Wood 4 Not Yet Accomplished 甲申 Wood Monkey 火水未濟 11 廿二 9	金9 Metal 3 Retreat 乙酉 Wood Rooster 天山遯 12 廿三 4	水6 Water 2 Mountain 丙戌 Fire Dog 艮為山 13 廿四 1	木8 Wood 1 Delight 丁亥 Fire Pig 雷地豫 14 廿五 8	火7 Fire 9 Beginning 戊子 Earth Rat 水雷屯 15 廿六 4
金9 Metal 8 Without Wrongdoing 己丑 Earth Ox 天雷無妄 16 廿七 2	木3 Wood 7 Fire 庚寅 Metal Tiger 離為火 17 廿八 1	火2 Fire 6 Sincerity 辛卯 Metal Rabbit 風澤中孚 18 廿九 3	水6 Water 5 Big Livestock 壬辰 Water Dragon 山天大畜 19 三十 4	金4 Metal 4 Eliminating 癸巳 Water Snake 澤天夬 20 十月初一 6	金9 Metal 3 Heaven 甲午 Wood Horse 乾為天 21 初二 1	火7 Fire 2 Well 乙未 Wood Goat 水風井 22 初三 6
木8 Wood 1 Relief 丙申 Fire Monkey 雷水解 23 初四 4	金4 Metal 9 Influence 丁酉 Fire Rooster 澤山咸 24 初五 9	水1 Water 8 Humility 戊戌 Earth Dog 地山謙 25 初六 6	火2 Fire 7 Observation 己亥 Earth Pig 風地觀 26 初七 2	火2 Fire 6 Increasing 庚子 Metal Rat 風雷益 27 初八 9	水1 Water 5 Dimming Light 辛丑 Metal Ox 地火明夷 28 初九 3	金9 Metal 4 Fellowship 壬寅 Water Tiger 天火同人 29 初十 7

DECEMBER 2025 戊子

Xuan Kong Element 玄空五行	水雷屯 Beginning	Period Luck 卦運	Monthly Star 月星
Fire 火7		4	1

SUNDAY	MONDAY	TUESDAY	WEDNESDAY	THURSDAY	FRIDAY	SATURDAY
	木3 Wood 2 Opposition 甲辰 Wood Dragon 火澤睽 1 十二 2	火7 Fire 1 Waiting 乙巳 Wood Snake 水天需 2 十三 3	金4 Metal 9 Great Exceeding 丙午 Fire Horse 澤風大過 3 十四 3	水6 Water 8 Poison 丁未 Fire Goat 山風蠱 4 十五 7	火2 Fire 7 Dispersing 戊申 Earth Monkey 風水渙 5 十六 6	木3 Wood 6 Travelling 己酉 Earth Rooster 火山旅 6 十七 8
金9 Metal 5 Stagnation 庚戌 Metal Dog 天地否 7 十八 9	火7 Fire 4 Alliance 辛亥 Metal Pig 水地比 8 十九 7	木8 Wood 3 Thunder 壬子 Water Rat 震為雷 9 二十 1	水6 Water 2 Beauty 癸丑 Water Ox 山火賁 10 廿一 8	火7 Fire 1 Accomplished 甲寅 Wood Tiger 水火既濟 11 廿二 9	水1 Water 9 Arriving 乙卯 Wood Rabbit 地澤臨 12 廿三 4	金4 Metal 8 Marsh 丙辰 Fire Dragon 兌為澤 13 廿四 1
火2 Fire 7 Small Livestock 丁巳 Fire Snake 風天小畜 14 廿五 8	木3 Wood 6 The Cauldron 戊午 Earth Horse 火風鼎 15 廿六 4	水1 Water 5 Rising 己未 Earth Goat 地風升 16 廿七 2	火7 Fire 4 Water 庚申 Metal Monkey 坎為水 17 廿八 1	木8 Wood 3 Lesser Exceeding 辛酉 Metal Rooster 雷山小過 18 廿九 3	金4 Metal 2 Gathering 壬戌 Water Dog 澤地萃 19 三十 4	水6 Water 1 Peel 癸亥 Water Pig 山地剝 20 十一月初一 6
水1 Water 9/1 Earth 甲子 Wood Rat 坤為地 21 初二 1	木3 Wood 2 Biting 乙丑 Wood Ox 火雷噬嗑 22 初三 6	火2 Fire 3 Family 丙寅 Fire Tiger 風火家人 23 初四 4	水6 Water 4 Decreasing 丁卯 Fire Rabbit 山澤損 24 初五 9	金9 Metal 5 Tread 戊辰 Earth Dragon 天澤履 25 初六 6	木8 Wood 6 Great Strength 己巳 Earth Snake 雷天大壯 26 初七 2	木8 Wood 7 Consistency 庚午 Metal Horse 雷風恆 27 初八 9
金9 Metal 8 Litigation 辛未 Metal Goat 天水訟 28 初九 3	水1 Water 9 Officer 壬申 Water Monkey 地水師 29 初十 7	火2 Fire 1 Gradual Progress 癸酉 Water Rooster 風山漸 30 十一 7	火7 Fire 2 Obstruction 甲戌 Wood Dog 水山蹇 31 十二 2			

2026 丙午

(*Bing Wu*) Fire Horse

2026 丙午 *(Bing Wu)* Fire Horse

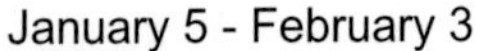

January 5 - February 3

February 4 - March 4

March 5 - April 4

April 5 - May 4

May 5 - June 4

June 5 - July 6

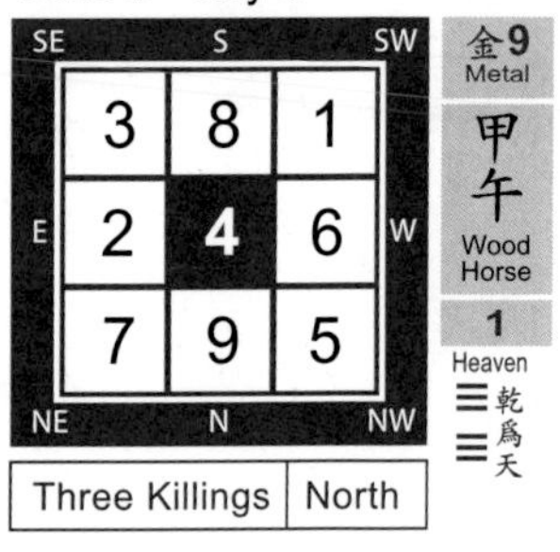

July 7 - August 6

August 7 - September 6

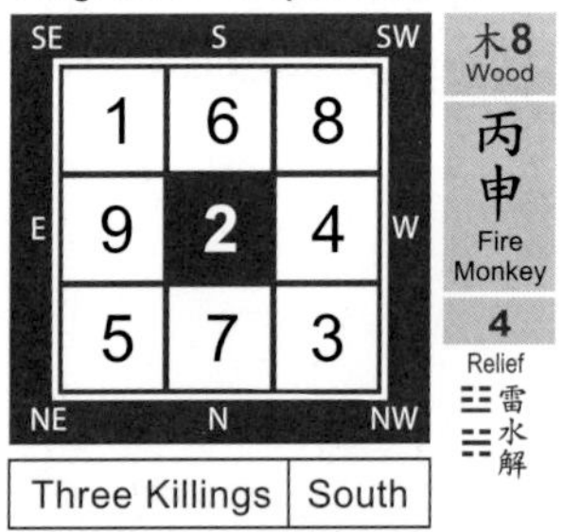

September 7 - October 7

October 8 - November 6

November 7 - December 6

December 7 - January 4

JANUARY 2026 己丑

Xuan Kong Element 玄空五行	天雷無妄 Without Wrongdoing	Period Luck 卦運	Monthly Star 月星
Metal 金9		2	9

SUNDAY	MONDAY	TUESDAY	WEDNESDAY	THURSDAY	FRIDAY	SATURDAY
				木3 Wood [3] Advancement 火地晉 乙亥 Wood Pig 3 1 十三	水6 Water [4] Nourish 山雷頤 丙子 Fire Rat 3 2 十四	金4 Metal [5] Following 澤雷隨 丁丑 Fire Ox 7 3 十五
木8 Wood [6] Abundance 雷火豐 戊寅 Earth Tiger 6 4 十六	火7 Fire [7] Regulate 水澤節 己卯 Earth Rabbit 8 5 十七	水1 Water [8] Unity 地天泰 庚辰 Metal Dragon 9 6 十八	木3 Wood [9] Great Reward 火天大有 辛巳 Metal Snake 7 7 十九	火2 Fire [1] Wind 巽爲風 壬午 Water Horse 1 8 二十	金4 Metal [2] Trap 澤水困 癸未 Water Goat 8 9 廿一	木3 Wood [3] Not Yet Accomplished 火水未濟 甲申 Wood Monkey 9 10 廿二
金9 Metal [4] Retreat 天山遯 乙酉 Wood Rooster 4 11 廿三	水6 Water [5] Mountain 艮爲山 丙戌 Fire Dog 1 12 廿四	木8 Wood [6] Delight 雷地豫 丁亥 Fire Pig 8 13 廿五	火7 Fire [7] Beginning 水雷屯 戊子 Earth Rat 4 14 廿六	金9 Metal [8] Without Wrongdoing 天雷無妄 己丑 Earth Ox 2 15 廿七	木3 Wood [9] Fire 離爲火 庚寅 Metal Tiger 1 16 廿八	火2 Fire [1] Sincerity 風澤中孚 辛卯 Metal Rabbit 3 17 廿九
水6 Water [2] Big Livestock 山天大畜 壬辰 Water Dragon 4 18 三十	金4 Metal [3] Eliminating 澤天夬 癸巳 Water Snake 6 19 十二月初一	金9 Metal [4] Heaven 乾爲天 甲午 Wood Horse 1 20 初二	火7 Fire [5] Well 水風井 乙未 Wood Goat 6 21 初三	木8 Wood [6] Relief 雷水解 丙申 Fire Monkey 4 22 初四	金4 Metal [7] Influence 澤山咸 丁酉 Fire Rooster 9 23 初五	水1 Water [8] Humility 地山謙 戊戌 Earth Dog 6 24 初六
火2 Fire [9] Observation 風地觀 己亥 Earth Pig 2 25 初七	火2 Fire [1] Increasing 風雷益 庚子 Metal Rat 9 26 初八	水1 Water [2] Dimming Light 地火明夷 辛丑 Metal Ox 3 27 初九	金9 Metal [3] Fellowship 天火同人 壬寅 Water Tiger 7 28 初十	木8 Wood [4] Marrying Maiden 雷澤歸妹 癸卯 Water Rabbit 7 29 十一	木3 Wood [5] Opposition 火澤睽 甲辰 Wood Dragon 2 30 十二	火7 Fire [6] Waiting 水天需 乙巳 Wood Snake 3 31 十三

FEBRUARY 2026 庚寅

Xuan Kong Element 玄空五行	離爲火 Fire	Period Luck 卦運	Monthly Star 月星
Wood 木3		1	8

SUNDAY	MONDAY	TUESDAY	WEDNESDAY	THURSDAY	FRIDAY	SATURDAY
金4 Metal [7] Great Exceeding 澤風大過 丙午 Fire Horse 3 1 十四	水6 Water [8] Poison 山風蠱 丁未 Fire Goat 7 2 十五	火2 Fire [9] Dispersing 風水渙 戊申 Earth Monkey 6 3 十六	木3 Wood [1] Travelling 火山旅 己酉 Earth Rooster 8 4 十七	金9 Metal [2] Stagnation 天地否 庚戌 Metal Dog 9 5 十八	火7 Fire [3] Alliance 水地比 辛亥 Metal Pig 7 6 十九	木8 Wood [4] Thunder 震爲雷 壬子 Water Rat 1 7 二十
水6 Water [5] Beauty 山火賁 癸丑 Water Ox 8 8 廿一	火7 Fire [6] Accomplished 水火既濟 甲寅 Wood Tiger 9 9 廿二	水1 Water [7] Arriving 地澤臨 乙卯 Wood Rabbit 4 10 廿三	金4 Metal [8] Marsh 兌爲澤 丙辰 Fire Dragon 1 11 廿四	火2 Fire [9] Small Livestock 風天小畜 丁巳 Fire Snake 8 12 廿五	木3 Wood [1] The Cauldron 火風鼎 戊午 Earth Horse 4 13 廿六	水1 Water [2] Rising 地風升 己未 Earth Goat 2 14 廿七
火7 Fire [3] Water 坎爲水 庚申 Metal Monkey 1 15 廿八	木8 Wood [4] Lesser Exceeding 雷山小過 辛酉 Metal Rooster 3 16 廿九	金4 Metal [5] Gathering 澤地萃 壬戌 Water Dog 4 17 正月初一	水6 Water [6] Peel 山地剝 癸亥 Water Pig 6 18 初二	水1 Water [7] Earth 坤爲地 甲子 Wood Rat 1 19 初三	木3 Wood [8] Biting 火雷噬嗑 乙丑 Wood Ox 6 20 初四	火2 Fire [9] Family 風火家人 丙寅 Fire Tiger 4 21 初五
水6 Water [1] Decreasing 山澤損 丁卯 Fire Rabbit 9 22 初六	金9 Metal [2] Tread 天澤履 戊辰 Earth Dragon 6 23 初七	木8 Wood [3] Great Strength 雷天大壯 己巳 Earth Snake 2 24 初八	木8 Wood [4] Consistency 雷風恒 庚午 Metal Horse 9 25 初九	金9 Metal [5] Litigation 天水訟 辛未 Metal Goat 3 26 初十	水1 Water [6] Officer 地水師 壬申 Water Monkey 7 27 十一	火2 Fire [7] Gradual Progress 風山漸 癸酉 Water Rooster 7 28 十二

MARCH 2026 辛卯

Xuan Kong Element 玄空五行	風澤中孚 Sincerity	Period Luck 卦運	Monthly Star 月星
Fire 火2		3	7

SUNDAY	MONDAY	TUESDAY	WEDNESDAY	THURSDAY	FRIDAY	SATURDAY
火7 Fire Obstruction 8 水山蹇 甲戌 Wood Dog **1** 十三 2	木3 Wood Advancement 9 火地晉 乙亥 Wood Pig **2** 十四 3	水6 Water Nourish 1 山雷頤 丙子 Fire Rat **3** 十五 3	金4 Metal Following 2 澤雷隨 丁丑 Fire Ox **4** 十六 7	木8 Wood Abundance 3 雷火豐 戊寅 Earth Tiger **5** 十七 6	火7 Fire Regulate 4 水澤節 己卯 Earth Rabbit **6** 十八 8	水1 Water Unity 5 地天泰 庚辰 Metal Dragon **7** 十九 9
木3 Wood Great Reward 6 火天大有 辛巳 Metal Snake **8** 二十 7	火2 Fire Wind 7 巽為風 壬午 Water Horse **9** 廿一 1	金4 Metal Trap 8 澤水困 癸未 Water Goat **10** 廿二 8	木3 Wood Not Yet Accomplished 9 火水未濟 甲申 Wood Monkey **11** 廿三 9	金9 Metal Retreat 1 天山遯 乙酉 Wood Rooster **12** 廿四 4	水6 Water Mountain 2 艮為山 丙戌 Fire Dog **13** 廿五 1	木8 Wood Delight 3 雷地豫 丁亥 Fire Pig **14** 廿六 8
火7 Fire Beginning 4 水雷屯 戊子 Earth Rat **15** 廿七 4	金9 Metal Without Wrongdoing 5 天雷無妄 己丑 Earth Ox **16** 廿八 2	木3 Wood Fire 6 離為火 庚寅 Metal Tiger **17** 廿九 1	火2 Fire Sincerity 7 風澤中孚 辛卯 Metal Rabbit **18** 三十 3	水6 Water Big Livestock 8 山天大畜 壬辰 Water Dragon **19** 二月初一 4	金4 Metal Eliminating 9 澤天夬 癸巳 Water Snake **20** 初二 6	金9 Metal Heaven 1 乾為天 甲午 Wood Horse **21** 初三 1
火7 Fire Well 2 水風井 乙未 Wood Goat **22** 初四 6	木8 Wood Relief 3 雷水解 丙申 Fire Monkey **23** 初五 4	金4 Metal Influence 4 澤山咸 丁酉 Fire Rooster **24** 初六 9	水1 Water Humility 5 地山謙 戊戌 Earth Dog **25** 初七 6	火2 Fire Observation 6 風地觀 己亥 Earth Pig **26** 初八 2	火2 Fire Increasing 7 風雷益 庚子 Metal Rat **27** 初九 9	水1 Water Dimming Light 8 地火明夷 辛丑 Metal Ox **28** 初十 3
金9 Metal Fellowship 9 天火同人 壬寅 Water Tiger **29** 十一 7	木8 Wood Marrying Maiden 1 雷澤歸妹 癸卯 Water Rabbit **30** 十二 7	木3 Wood Opposition 2 火澤睽 甲辰 Wood Dragon **31** 十三 2				

APRIL 2026 壬辰

Xuan Kong Element 玄空五行	山天大畜 Big Livestock	Period Luck 卦運	Monthly Star 月星
Water 水6		4	6

SUNDAY	MONDAY	TUESDAY	WEDNESDAY	THURSDAY	FRIDAY	SATURDAY
			火7 Fire Waiting 3 水天需 乙巳 Wood Snake **1** 十四 3	金4 Metal Great Exceeding 4 澤風大過 丙午 Fire Horse **2** 十五 3	水6 Water Poison 5 山風蠱 丁未 Fire Goat **3** 十六 7	火2 Fire Dispersing 6 風水渙 戊申 Earth Monkey **4** 十七 6
木3 Wood Travelling 7 火山旅 己酉 Earth Rooster **5** 十八 8	金9 Metal Stagnation 8 天地否 庚戌 Metal Dog **6** 十九 9	火7 Fire Alliance 9 水地比 辛亥 Metal Pig **7** 二十 7	木8 Wood Thunder 1 震為雷 壬子 Water Rat **8** 廿一 1	水6 Water Beauty 2 山火賁 癸丑 Water Ox **9** 廿二 8	火7 Fire Accomplished 3 水火既濟 甲寅 Wood Tiger **10** 廿三 9	水1 Water Arriving 4 地澤臨 乙卯 Wood Rabbit **11** 廿四 4
金4 Metal Marsh 5 兌為澤 丙辰 Fire Dragon **12** 廿五 1	火2 Fire Small Livestock 6 風天小畜 丁巳 Fire Snake **13** 廿六 8	木3 Wood The Cauldron 7 火風鼎 戊午 Earth Horse **14** 廿七 4	水1 Water Rising 8 地風升 己未 Earth Goat **15** 廿八 2	火7 Fire Water 9 坎為水 庚申 Metal Monkey **16** 廿九 1	木8 Wood Lesser Exceeding 1 雷山小過 辛酉 Metal Rooster **17** 三月初一 3	金4 Metal Gathering 2 澤地萃 壬戌 Water Dog **18** 初二 4
水6 Water Peel 3 山地剝 癸亥 Water Pig **19** 初三 6	水1 Water Earth 4 坤為地 甲子 Wood Rat **20** 初四 1	木3 Wood Biting 5 火雷噬嗑 乙丑 Wood Ox **21** 初五 6	火2 Fire Family 6 風火家人 丙寅 Fire Tiger **22** 初六 4	水6 Water Decreasing 7 山澤損 丁卯 Fire Rabbit **23** 初七 9	金9 Metal Tread 8 天澤履 戊辰 Earth Dragon **24** 初八 6	木8 Wood Great Strength 9 雷天大壯 己巳 Earth Snake **25** 初九 2
木8 Wood Consistency 1 雷風恆 庚午 Metal Horse **26** 初十 9	金9 Metal Litigation 2 天水訟 辛未 Metal Goat **27** 十一 3	水1 Water Officer 3 地水師 壬申 Water Monkey **28** 十二 7	火2 Fire Gradual Progress 4 風山漸 癸酉 Water Rooster **29** 十三 7	火7 Fire Obstruction 5 水山蹇 甲戌 Wood Dog **30** 十四 2		

MAY 2026 癸巳

Xuan Kong Element 玄空五行	澤天夬 Eliminating	Period Luck 卦運	Monthly Star 月星
Metal 金4		6	5

SUNDAY	MONDAY	TUESDAY	WEDNESDAY	THURSDAY	FRIDAY	SATURDAY
火7 Fire Waiting 9 乙巳 Wood Snake 水天需 **31** 十五 3					木3 Wood Advancement 6 乙亥 Wood Pig 火地晉 **1** 十五 3	水6 Water Nourish 7 丙子 Fire Rat 山雷頤 **2** 十六 3
金4 Metal Following 8 丁丑 Fire Ox 澤雷隨 **3** 十七 7	木8 Wood Abundance 9 戊寅 Earth Tiger 雷火豐 **4** 十八 6	火7 Fire Regulate 1 己卯 Earth Rabbit 水澤節 **5** 十九 8	水1 Water Unity 2 庚辰 Metal Dragon 地天泰 **6** 二十 9	木3 Wood Great Reward 3 辛巳 Metal Snake 火天大有 **7** 廿一 7	火2 Fire Wind 4 壬午 Water Horse 巽爲風 **8** 廿二 1	金4 Metal Trap 5 癸未 Water Goat 澤水困 **9** 廿三 8
木3 Wood Not Yet Accomplished 6 甲申 Wood Monkey 火水未濟 **10** 廿四 9	金9 Metal Retreat 7 乙酉 Wood Rooster 天山遯 **11** 廿五 4	水6 Water Mountain 8 丙戌 Fire Dog 艮爲山 **12** 廿六 1	木8 Wood Delight 9 丁亥 Fire Pig 雷地豫 **13** 廿七 8	火7 Fire Beginning 1 戊子 Earth Rat 水雷屯 **14** 廿八 4	金9 Metal Without Wrongdoing 2 己丑 Earth Ox 天雷無妄 **15** 廿九 2	木3 Wood Fire 3 庚寅 Metal Tiger 離爲火 **16** 三十 1
火2 Fire Sincerity 4 辛卯 Metal Rabbit 風澤中孚 **17** 四月初一 3	水6 Water Big Livestock 5 壬辰 Water Dragon 山天大畜 **18** 初二 4	金4 Metal Eliminating 6 癸巳 Water Snake 澤天夬 **19** 初三 6	金9 Metal Heaven 7 甲午 Wood Horse 乾爲天 **20** 初四 1	火7 Fire Well 8 乙未 Wood Goat 水風井 **21** 初五 6	木8 Wood Relief 9 丙申 Fire Monkey 雷水解 **22** 初六 4	金4 Metal Influence 1 丁酉 Fire Rooster 澤山咸 **23** 初七 9
水1 Water Humility 2 戊戌 Earth Dog 地山謙 **24** 初八 6	火2 Fire Observation 3 己亥 Earth Pig 風地觀 **25** 初九 2	火2 Fire Increasing 4 庚子 Metal Rat 風雷益 **26** 初十 9	水1 Water Dimming Light 5 辛丑 Metal Ox 地火明夷 **27** 十一 3	金9 Metal Fellowship 6 壬寅 Water Tiger 天火同人 **28** 十二 7	木8 Wood Marrying Maiden 7 癸卯 Water Rabbit 雷澤歸妹 **29** 十三 7	木3 Wood Opposition 8 甲辰 Wood Dragon 火澤睽 **30** 十四 2

JUNE 2026 甲午

Xuan Kong Element 玄空五行	乾爲天 Heaven	Period Luck 卦運	Monthly Star 月星
Metal 金9		1	4

SUNDAY	MONDAY	TUESDAY	WEDNESDAY	THURSDAY	FRIDAY	SATURDAY
	金4 Metal Great Exceeding 1 丙午 Fire Horse 澤風大過 **1** 十六 3	水6 Water Poison 2 丁未 Fire Goat 山風蠱 **2** 十七 7	火2 Fire Dispersing 3 戊申 Earth Monkey 風水渙 **3** 十八 6	木3 Wood Travelling 4 己酉 Earth Rooster 火山旅 **4** 十九 8	金9 Metal Stagnation 5 庚戌 Metal Dog 天地否 **5** 二十 9	火7 Fire Alliance 6 辛亥 Metal Pig 水地比 **6** 廿一 7
木8 Wood Thunder 7 壬子 Water Rat 震爲雷 **7** 廿二 1	水6 Water Beauty 8 癸丑 Water Ox 山火賁 **8** 廿三 8	火7 Fire Accomplished 9 甲寅 Wood Tiger 水火既濟 **9** 廿四 9	水1 Water Arriving 1 乙卯 Wood Rabbit 地澤臨 **10** 廿五 4	金4 Metal Marsh 2 丙辰 Fire Dragon 兌爲澤 **11** 廿六 1	火2 Fire Small Livestock 3 丁巳 Fire Snake 風天小畜 **12** 廿七 8	木3 Wood The Cauldron 4 戊午 Earth Horse 火風鼎 **13** 廿八 4
水1 Water Rising 5 己未 Earth Goat 地風升 **14** 廿九 2	火7 Fire Water 6 庚申 Metal Monkey 坎爲水 **15** 五月初一 1	木8 Wood Lesser Exceeding 7 辛酉 Metal Rooster 雷山小過 **16** 初二 3	金4 Metal Gathering 8 壬戌 Water Dog 澤地萃 **17** 初三 4	水6 Water Peel 9 癸亥 Water Pig 山地剝 **18** 初四 6	水1 Water Earth 1 甲子 Wood Rat 坤爲地 **19** 初五 1	木3 Wood Biting 2 乙丑 Wood Ox 火雷噬嗑 **20** 初六 6
火2 Fire Family 3/4 丙寅 Fire Tiger 風火家人 **21** 初七 4	水6 Water Decreasing 3 丁卯 Fire Rabbit 山澤損 **22** 初八 9	金9 Metal Tread 2 戊辰 Earth Dragon 天澤履 **23** 初九 6	木8 Wood Great Strength 1 己巳 Earth Snake 雷天大壯 **24** 初十 2	木8 Wood Consistency 9 庚午 Metal Horse 雷風恒 **25** 十一 9	金9 Metal Litigation 8 辛未 Metal Goat 天水訟 **26** 十二 3	水1 Water Officer 7 壬申 Water Monkey 地水師 **27** 十三 7
火2 Fire Gradual Progress 6 癸酉 Water Rooster 風山漸 **28** 十四 7	火7 Fire Obstruction 5 甲戌 Wood Dog 水山蹇 **29** 十五 2	木3 Wood Advancement 4 乙亥 Wood Pig 火地晉 **30** 十六 3				

JULY 2026 乙未

Xuan Kong Element 玄空五行	水風井 Well	Period Luck 卦運	Monthly Star 月星
Fire 火7		6	3

SUNDAY	MONDAY	TUESDAY	WEDNESDAY	THURSDAY	FRIDAY	SATURDAY
			水6 Water Nourish 3 丙子 Fire Rat 山雷頤 1 十七 3	金4 Metal Following 2 丁丑 Fire Ox 澤雷隨 2 十八 7	木8 Wood Abundance 1 戊寅 Earth Tiger 雷火豐 3 十九 6	火7 Fire Regulate 9 己卯 Earth Rabbit 水澤節 4 二十 8
水1 Water Unity 8 庚辰 Metal Dragon 地天泰 5 廿一 9	木3 Wood Great Reward 7 辛巳 Metal Snake 火天大有 6 廿二 7	火2 Fire Wind 6 壬午 Water Horse 巽爲風 7 廿三 1	金4 Metal Trap 5 癸未 Water Goat 澤水困 8 廿四 8	木3 Wood Not Yet Accomplished 4 甲申 Wood Monkey 火水未濟 9 廿五 9	金9 Metal Retreat 3 乙酉 Wood Rooster 天山遯 10 廿六 4	水6 Water Mountain 2 丙戌 Fire Dog 艮爲山 11 廿七 1
木8 Wood Delight 1 丁亥 Fire Pig 雷地豫 12 廿八 8	火7 Fire Beginning 9 戊子 Earth Rat 水雷屯 13 廿九 4	金9 Metal Without Wrongdoing 8 己丑 Earth Ox 天雷無妄 14 六月初一 2	木3 Wood Fire 7 庚寅 Metal Tiger 離爲火 15 初二 1	火2 Fire Sincerity 6 辛卯 Metal Rabbit 風澤中孚 16 初三 3	水6 Water Big Livestock 5 壬辰 Water Dragon 山天大畜 17 初四 4	金4 Metal Eliminating 4 癸巳 Water Snake 澤天夬 18 初五 6
金9 Metal Heaven 3 甲午 Wood Horse 乾爲天 19 初六 1	火7 Fire Well 2 乙未 Wood Goat 水風井 20 初七 6	木8 Wood Relief 1 丙申 Fire Monkey 雷水解 21 初八 4	金4 Metal Influence 9 丁酉 Fire Rooster 澤山咸 22 初九 9	水1 Water Humility 8 戊戌 Earth Dog 地山謙 23 初十 6	火2 Fire Observation 7 己亥 Earth Pig 風地觀 24 十一 2	火2 Fire Increasing 6 庚子 Metal Rat 風雷益 25 十二 9
水1 Water Dimming Light 5 辛丑 Metal Ox 地火明夷 26 十三 3	金9 Metal Fellowship 4 壬寅 Water Tiger 天火同人 27 十四 7	木8 Wood Marrying Maiden 3 癸卯 Water Rabbit 雷澤歸妹 28 十五 7	木3 Wood Opposition 2 甲辰 Wood Dragon 火澤睽 29 十六 2	火7 Fire Waiting 1 乙巳 Wood Snake 水天需 30 十七 3	金4 Metal Great Exceeding 9 丙午 Fire Horse 澤風大過 31 十八 3	

AUGUST 2026 丙申

Xuan Kong Element 玄空五行	雷水解 Relief	Period Luck 卦運	Monthly Star 月星
Wood 木8		4	2

SUNDAY	MONDAY	TUESDAY	WEDNESDAY	THURSDAY	FRIDAY	SATURDAY
水6 Water Nourish 6 丙子 Fire Rat 山雷頤 30 十八 3	金4 Metal Following 5 丁丑 Fire Ox 澤雷隨 31 十九 7					水6 Water Poison 8 丁未 Fire Goat 山風蠱 1 十九 7
火2 Fire Dispersing 7 戊申 Earth Monkey 風水渙 2 二十 6	木3 Wood Travelling 6 己酉 Earth Rooster 火山旅 3 廿一 8	金9 Metal Stagnation 5 庚戌 Metal Dog 天地否 4 廿二 9	火7 Fire Alliance 4 辛亥 Metal Pig 水地比 5 廿三 7	木8 Wood Thunder 3 壬子 Water Rat 震爲雷 6 廿四 1	水6 Water Beauty 2 癸丑 Water Ox 山火賁 7 廿五 8	火7 Fire Accomplished 1 甲寅 Wood Tiger 水火既濟 8 廿六 9
水1 Water Arriving 9 乙卯 Wood Rabbit 地澤臨 9 廿七 4	金4 Metal Marsh 8 丙辰 Fire Dragon 兌爲澤 10 廿八 1	火2 Fire Small Livestock 7 丁巳 Fire Snake 風天小畜 11 廿九 8	木3 Wood The Cauldron 6 戊午 Earth Horse 火風鼎 12 三十 4	水1 Water Rising 5 己未 Earth Goat 地風升 13 七月初一 2	火7 Fire Water 4 庚申 Metal Monkey 坎爲水 14 初二 1	木8 Wood Lesser Exceeding 3 辛酉 Metal Rooster 雷山小過 15 初三 3
金4 Metal Gathering 2 壬戌 Water Dog 澤地萃 16 初四 4	水6 Water Peel 1 癸亥 Water Pig 山地剝 17 初五 6	水1 Water Earth 9 甲子 Wood Rat 坤爲地 18 初六 1	木3 Wood Biting 8 乙丑 Wood Ox 火雷噬嗑 19 初七 6	火2 Fire Family 7 丙寅 Fire Tiger 風火家人 20 初八 4	水6 Water Decreasing 6 丁卯 Fire Rabbit 山澤損 21 初九 9	金9 Metal Tread 5 戊辰 Earth Dragon 天澤履 22 初十 6
木8 Wood Great Strength 4 己巳 Earth Snake 雷天大壯 23 十一 2	木8 Wood Consistency 3 庚午 Metal Horse 雷風恆 24 十二 9	金9 Metal Litigation 2 辛未 Metal Goat 天水訟 25 十三 3	水1 Water Officer 1 壬申 Water Monkey 地水師 26 十四 7	火2 Fire Gradual Progress 9 癸酉 Water Rooster 風山漸 27 十五 7	火7 Fire Obstruction 8 甲戌 Wood Dog 水山蹇 28 十六 2	木3 Wood Advancement 7 乙亥 Wood Pig 火地晉 29 十七 3

MAY 2026 癸巳

Xuan Kong Element 玄空五行	澤天夬 Eliminating	Period Luck 卦運	Monthly Star 月星
Metal 金4		6	5

SUNDAY	MONDAY	TUESDAY	WEDNESDAY	THURSDAY	FRIDAY	SATURDAY
火7 Fire 9 Waiting 乙巳 Wood Snake 水天需 31 十五 3					木3 Wood 6 Advancement 乙亥 Wood Pig 火地晉 1 十五 3	水6 Water 7 Nourish 丙子 Fire Rat 山雷頤 2 十六 3
金4 Metal 8 Following 丁丑 Fire Ox 澤雷隨 3 十七 7	木8 Wood 9 Abundance 戊寅 Earth Tiger 雷火豐 4 十八 6	火7 Fire 1 Regulate 己卯 Earth Rabbit 水澤節 5 十九 8	水1 Water 2 Unity 庚辰 Metal Dragon 地天泰 6 二十 9	木3 Wood 3 Great Reward 辛巳 Metal Snake 火天大有 7 廿一 7	火2 Fire 4 Wind 壬午 Water Horse 巽爲風 8 廿二 1	金4 Metal 5 Trap 癸未 Water Goat 澤水困 9 廿三 8
木3 Wood 6 Not Yet Accomplished 甲申 Wood Monkey 火水未濟 10 廿四 9	金9 Metal 7 Retreat 乙酉 Wood Rooster 天山遯 11 廿五 4	水6 Water 8 Mountain 丙戌 Fire Dog 艮爲山 12 廿六 1	木8 Wood 9 Delight 丁亥 Fire Pig 雷地豫 13 廿七 8	火7 Fire 1 Beginning 戊子 Earth Rat 水雷屯 14 廿八 4	金9 Metal 2 Without Wrongdoing 己丑 Earth Ox 天雷無妄 15 廿九 2	木3 Wood 3 Fire 庚寅 Metal Tiger 離爲火 16 三十 1
火2 Fire 4 Sincerity 辛卯 Metal Rabbit 風澤中孚 17 四月初一 3	水6 Water 5 Big Livestock 壬辰 Water Dragon 山天大畜 18 初二 4	金4 Metal 6 Eliminating 癸巳 Water Snake 澤天夬 19 初三 6	金9 Metal 7 Heaven 甲午 Wood Horse 乾爲天 20 初四 1	火7 Fire 8 Well 乙未 Wood Goat 水風井 21 初五 6	木8 Wood 9 Relief 丙申 Fire Monkey 雷水解 22 初六 4	金4 Metal 1 Influence 丁酉 Fire Rooster 澤山咸 23 初七 9
水1 Water 2 Humility 戊戌 Earth Dog 地山謙 24 初八 6	火2 Fire 3 Observation 己亥 Earth Pig 風地觀 25 初九 2	火2 Fire 4 Increasing 庚子 Metal Rat 風雷益 26 初十 9	水1 Water 5 Dimming Light 辛丑 Metal Ox 地火明夷 27 十一 3	金9 Metal 6 Fellowship 壬寅 Water Tiger 天火同人 28 十二 7	木8 Wood 7 Marrying Maiden 癸卯 Water Rabbit 雷澤歸妹 29 十三 7	木3 Wood 8 Opposition 甲辰 Wood Dragon 火澤睽 30 十四 2

JUNE 2026 甲午

Xuan Kong Element 玄空五行	乾爲天 Heaven	Period Luck 卦運	Monthly Star 月星
Metal 金9		1	4

SUNDAY	MONDAY	TUESDAY	WEDNESDAY	THURSDAY	FRIDAY	SATURDAY
	金4 Metal 1 Great Exceeding 丙午 Fire Horse 澤風大過 1 十六 3	水6 Water 2 Poison 丁未 Fire Goat 山風蠱 2 十七 7	火2 Fire 3 Dispersing 戊申 Earth Monkey 風水渙 3 十八 6	木3 Wood 4 Travelling 己酉 Earth Rooster 火山旅 4 十九 8	金9 Metal 5 Stagnation 庚戌 Metal Dog 天地否 5 二十 9	火7 Fire 6 Alliance 辛亥 Metal Pig 水地比 6 廿一 7
木8 Wood 7 Thunder 壬子 Water Rat 震爲雷 7 廿二 1	水6 Water 8 Beauty 癸丑 Water Ox 山火賁 8 廿三 8	火7 Fire 9 Accomplished 甲寅 Wood Tiger 水火既濟 9 廿四 9	水1 Water 1 Arriving 乙卯 Wood Rabbit 地澤臨 10 廿五 4	金4 Metal 2 Marsh 丙辰 Fire Dragon 兌爲澤 11 廿六 1	火2 Fire 3 Small Livestock 丁巳 Fire Snake 風天小畜 12 廿七 8	木3 Wood 4 The Cauldron 戊午 Earth Horse 火風鼎 13 廿八 4
水1 Water 5 Rising 己未 Earth Goat 地風升 14 廿九 2	火7 Fire 6 Water 庚申 Metal Monkey 坎爲水 15 五月初一 1	木8 Wood 7 Lesser Exceeding 辛酉 Metal Rooster 雷山小過 16 初二 3	金4 Metal 8 Gathering 壬戌 Water Dog 澤地萃 17 初三 4	水6 Water 9 Peel 癸亥 Water Pig 山地剝 18 初四 6	水1 Water 1 Earth 甲子 Wood Rat 坤爲地 19 初五 1	木3 Wood 2 Biting 乙丑 Wood Ox 火雷噬嗑 20 初六 6
火2 Fire 3/4 Family 丙寅 Fire Tiger 風火家人 21 初七 4	水6 Water 3 Decreasing 丁卯 Fire Rabbit 山澤損 22 初八 9	金9 Metal 2 Tread 戊辰 Earth Dragon 天澤履 23 初九 6	木8 Wood 1 Great Strength 己巳 Earth Snake 雷天大壯 24 初十 2	木8 Wood 9 Consistency 庚午 Metal Horse 雷風恆 25 十一 9	金9 Metal 8 Litigation 辛未 Metal Goat 天水訟 26 十二 3	水1 Water 7 Officer 壬申 Water Monkey 地水師 27 十三 7
火2 Fire 6 Gradual Progress 癸酉 Water Rooster 風山漸 28 十四 7	火7 Fire 5 Obstruction 甲戌 Wood Dog 水山蹇 29 十五 2	木3 Wood 4 Advancement 乙亥 Wood Pig 火地晉 30 十六 3				

JULY 2026 乙未

Xuan Kong Element 玄空五行	水風井 Well	Period Luck 卦運	Monthly Star 月星
Fire 火7		6	3

SUNDAY	MONDAY	TUESDAY	WEDNESDAY	THURSDAY	FRIDAY	SATURDAY
			水6 Water · 3 Nourish 丙子 Fire Rat 山雷頤 **1** 十七 3	金4 Metal · 2 Following 丁丑 Fire Ox 澤雷隨 **2** 十八 7	木8 Wood · 1 Abundance 戊寅 Earth Tiger 雷火豐 **3** 十九 6	火7 Fire · 9 Regulate 己卯 Earth Rabbit 水澤節 **4** 二十 8
水1 Water · 8 Unity 庚辰 Metal Dragon 地天泰 **5** 廿一 9	木3 Wood · 7 Great Reward 辛巳 Metal Snake 火天大有 **6** 廿二 7	火2 Fire · 6 Wind 壬午 Water Horse 巽為風 **7** 廿三 1	金4 Metal · 5 Trap 癸未 Water Goat 澤水困 **8** 廿四 8	木3 Wood · 4 Not Yet Accomplished 甲申 Wood Monkey 火水未濟 **9** 廿五 9	金9 Metal · 3 Retreat 乙酉 Wood Rooster 天山遯 **10** 廿六 4	水6 Water · 2 Mountain 丙戌 Fire Dog 艮為山 **11** 廿七 1
木8 Wood · 1 Delight 丁亥 Fire Pig 雷地豫 **12** 廿八 8	火7 Fire · 9 Beginning 戊子 Earth Rat 水雷屯 **13** 廿九 4	金9 Metal · 8 Without Wrongdoing 己丑 Earth Ox 天雷無妄 **14** 六月初一 2	木3 Wood · 7 Fire 庚寅 Metal Tiger 離為火 **15** 初二 1	火2 Fire · 6 Sincerity 辛卯 Metal Rabbit 風澤中孚 **16** 初三 3	水6 Water · 5 Big Livestock 壬辰 Water Dragon 山天大畜 **17** 初四 4	金4 Metal · 4 Eliminating 癸巳 Water Snake 澤天夬 **18** 初五 6
金9 Metal · 3 Heaven 甲午 Wood Horse 乾為天 **19** 初六 1	火7 Fire · 2 Well 乙未 Wood Goat 水風井 **20** 初七 6	木8 Wood · 1 Relief 丙申 Fire Monkey 雷水解 **21** 初八 4	金4 Metal · 9 Influence 丁酉 Fire Rooster 澤山咸 **22** 初九 9	水1 Water · 8 Humility 戊戌 Earth Dog 地山謙 **23** 初十 6	火2 Fire · 7 Observation 己亥 Earth Pig 風地觀 **24** 十一 2	火2 Fire · 6 Increasing 庚子 Metal Rat 風雷益 **25** 十二 9
水1 Water · 5 Dimming Light 辛丑 Metal Ox 地火明夷 **26** 十三 3	金9 Metal · 4 Fellowship 壬寅 Water Tiger 天火同人 **27** 十四 7	木8 Wood · 3 Marrying Maiden 癸卯 Water Rabbit 雷澤歸妹 **28** 十五 7	木3 Wood · 2 Opposition 甲辰 Wood Dragon 火澤睽 **29** 十六 2	火7 Fire · 1 Waiting 乙巳 Wood Snake 水天需 **30** 十七 3	金4 Metal · 9 Great Exceeding 丙午 Fire Horse 澤風大過 **31** 十八 3	

AUGUST 2026 丙申

Xuan Kong Element 玄空五行	雷水解 Relief	Period Luck 卦運	Monthly Star 月星
Wood 木8		4	2

SUNDAY	MONDAY	TUESDAY	WEDNESDAY	THURSDAY	FRIDAY	SATURDAY
水6 Water · 6 Nourish 丙子 Fire Rat 山雷頤 **30** 十八 3	金4 Metal · 5 Following 丁丑 Fire Ox 澤雷隨 **31** 十九 7					水6 Water · 8 Poison 丁未 Fire Goat 山風蠱 **1** 十九 7
火2 Fire · 7 Dispersing 戊申 Earth Monkey 風水渙 **2** 二十 6	木3 Wood · 6 Travelling 己酉 Earth Rooster 火山旅 **3** 廿一 8	金9 Metal · 5 Stagnation 庚戌 Metal Dog 天地否 **4** 廿二 9	火7 Fire · 4 Alliance 辛亥 Metal Pig 水地比 **5** 廿三 7	木8 Wood · 3 Thunder 壬子 Water Rat 震為雷 **6** 廿四 1	水6 Water · 2 Beauty 癸丑 Water Ox 山火賁 **7** 廿五 8	火7 Fire · 1 Accomplished 甲寅 Wood Tiger 水火既濟 **8** 廿六 9
水1 Water · 9 Arriving 乙卯 Wood Rabbit 地澤臨 **9** 廿七 4	金4 Metal · 8 Marsh 丙辰 Fire Dragon 兌為澤 **10** 廿八 1	火2 Fire · 7 Small Livestock 丁巳 Fire Snake 風天小畜 **11** 廿九 8	木3 Wood · 6 The Cauldron 戊午 Earth Horse 火風鼎 **12** 三十 4	水1 Water · 5 Rising 己未 Earth Goat 地風升 **13** 七月初一 2	火7 Fire · 4 Water 庚申 Metal Monkey 坎為水 **14** 初二 1	木8 Wood · 3 Lesser Exceeding 辛酉 Metal Rooster 雷山小過 **15** 初三 3
金4 Metal · 2 Gathering 壬戌 Water Dog 澤地萃 **16** 初四 4	水6 Water · 1 Peel 癸亥 Water Pig 山地剝 **17** 初五 6	水1 Water · 9 Earth 甲子 Wood Rat 坤為地 **18** 初六 1	木3 Wood · 8 Biting 乙丑 Wood Ox 火雷噬嗑 **19** 初七 6	火2 Fire · 7 Family 丙寅 Fire Tiger 風火家人 **20** 初八 4	水6 Water · 6 Decreasing 丁卯 Fire Rabbit 山澤損 **21** 初九 9	金9 Metal · 5 Tread 戊辰 Earth Dragon 天澤履 **22** 初十 6
木8 Wood · 4 Great Strength 己巳 Earth Snake 雷天大壯 **23** 十一 2	木8 Wood · 3 Consistency 庚午 Metal Horse 雷風恆 **24** 十二 9	金9 Metal · 2 Litigation 辛未 Metal Goat 天水訟 **25** 十三 3	水1 Water · 1 Officer 壬申 Water Monkey 地水師 **26** 十四 7	火2 Fire · 9 Gradual Progress 癸酉 Water Rooster 風山漸 **27** 十五 7	火7 Fire · 8 Obstruction 甲戌 Wood Dog 水山蹇 **28** 十六 2	木3 Wood · 7 Advancement 乙亥 Wood Pig 火地晉 **29** 十七 3

SEPTEMBER 2026 丁酉

Xuan Kong Element 玄空五行	澤山咸 Influence	Period Luck 卦運	Monthly Star 月星
Metal 金4		9	1

SUNDAY	MONDAY	TUESDAY	WEDNESDAY	THURSDAY	FRIDAY	SATURDAY
		木8 Wood 戊寅 Earth Tiger Abundance 雷火豐 4 **1** 二十 6	火7 Fire 己卯 Earth Rabbit Regulate 水澤節 3 **2** 廿一 8	水1 Water 庚辰 Metal Dragon Unity 地天泰 2 **3** 廿二 9	木3 Wood 辛巳 Metal Snake Great Reward 火天大有 1 **4** 廿三 7	火2 Fire 壬午 Water Horse Wind 巽爲風 9 **5** 廿四 1
金4 Metal 癸未 Water Goat Trap 澤水困 8 **6** 廿五 8	木3 Wood 甲申 Wood Monkey Not Yet Accomplished 火水未濟 7 **7** 廿六 9	金9 Metal 乙酉 Wood Rooster Retreat 天山遯 6 **8** 廿七 4	水6 Water 丙戌 Fire Dog Mountain 艮爲山 5 **9** 廿八 1	木8 Wood 丁亥 Fire Pig Delight 雷地豫 4 **10** 廿九 8	火7 Fire 戊子 Earth Rat Beginning 水雷屯 3 **11** 八月初一 4	金9 Metal 己丑 Earth Ox Without Wrongdoing 天雷無妄 2 **12** 初二 2
木3 Wood 庚寅 Metal Tiger Fire 離爲火 1 **13** 初三 1	火2 Fire 辛卯 Metal Rabbit Sincerity 風澤中孚 9 **14** 初四 3	水6 Water 壬辰 Water Dragon Big Livestock 山天大畜 8 **15** 初五 4	金4 Metal 癸巳 Water Snake Eliminating 澤天夬 7 **16** 初六 6	金9 Metal 甲午 Wood Horse Heaven 乾爲天 6 **17** 初七 1	火7 Fire 乙未 Wood Goat Well 水風井 5 **18** 初八 6	木8 Wood 丙申 Fire Monkey Relief 雷水解 4 **19** 初九 4
金4 Metal 丁酉 Fire Rooster Influence 澤山咸 3 **20** 初十 9	水1 Water 戊戌 Earth Dog Humility 地山謙 2 **21** 十一 6	火2 Fire 己亥 Earth Pig Observation 風地觀 1 **22** 十二 2	火2 Fire 庚子 Metal Rat Increasing 風雷益 9 **23** 十三 9	水1 Water 辛丑 Metal Ox Dimming Light 地火明夷 8 **24** 十四 3	金9 Metal 壬寅 Water Tiger Fellowship 天火同人 7 **25** 十五 7	木8 Wood 癸卯 Water Rabbit Marrying Maiden 雷澤歸妹 6 **26** 十六 7
木3 Wood 甲辰 Wood Dragon Opposition 火澤睽 5 **27** 十七 2	火7 Fire 乙巳 Wood Snake Waiting 水天需 4 **28** 十八 3	金4 Metal 丙午 Fire Horse Great Exceeding 澤風大過 3 **29** 十九 3	水6 Water 丁未 Fire Goat Poison 山風蠱 2 **30** 二十 7			

OCTOBER 2026 戊戌

Xuan Kong Element 玄空五行	地山謙 Humility	Period Luck 卦運	Monthly Star 月星
Water 水1		6	9

SUNDAY	MONDAY	TUESDAY	WEDNESDAY	THURSDAY	FRIDAY	SATURDAY
				火2 Fire 戊申 Earth Monkey Dispersing 風水渙 1 **1** 廿一 6	木3 Wood 己酉 Earth Rooster Travelling 火山旅 9 **2** 廿二 8	金9 Metal 庚戌 Metal Dog Stagnation 天地否 8 **3** 廿三 9
火7 Fire 辛亥 Metal Pig Alliance 水地比 7 **4** 廿四 7	木8 Wood 壬子 Water Rat Thunder 震爲雷 6 **5** 廿五 1	水6 Water 癸丑 Water Ox Beauty 山火賁 5 **6** 廿六 8	火7 Fire 甲寅 Wood Tiger Accomplished 水火既濟 4 **7** 廿七 9	水1 Water 乙卯 Wood Rabbit Arriving 地澤臨 3 **8** 廿八 4	金4 Metal 丙辰 Fire Dragon Marsh 兌爲澤 2 **9** 廿九 1	火2 Fire 丁巳 Fire Snake Small Livestock 風天小畜 1 **10** 九月初一 8
木3 Wood 戊午 Earth Horse The Cauldron 火風鼎 9 **11** 初二 4	水1 Water 己未 Earth Goat Rising 地風升 8 **12** 初三 2	火7 Fire 庚申 Metal Monkey Water 坎爲水 7 **13** 初四 1	木8 Wood 辛酉 Metal Rooster Lesser Exceeding 雷山小過 6 **14** 初五 3	金4 Metal 壬戌 Water Dog Gathering 澤地萃 5 **15** 初六 4	水6 Water 癸亥 Water Pig Peel 山地剝 4 **16** 初七 6	水1 Water 甲子 Wood Rat Earth 坤爲地 3 **17** 初八 1
木3 Wood 乙丑 Wood Ox Biting 火雷噬嗑 2 **18** 初九 6	火2 Fire 丙寅 Fire Tiger Family 風火家人 1 **19** 初十 4	水6 Water 丁卯 Fire Rabbit Decreasing 山澤損 9 **20** 十一 9	金9 Metal 戊辰 Earth Dragon Tread 天澤履 8 **21** 十二 6	木8 Wood 己巳 Earth Snake Great Strength 雷天大壯 7 **22** 十三 2	木8 Wood 庚午 Metal Horse Consistency 雷風恆 6 **23** 十四 9	金9 Metal 辛未 Metal Goat Litigation 天水訟 5 **24** 十五 3
水1 Water 壬申 Water Monkey Officer 地水師 4 **25** 十六 7	火2 Fire 癸酉 Water Rooster Gradual Progress 風山漸 3 **26** 十七 7	火7 Fire 甲戌 Wood Dog Obstruction 水山蹇 2 **27** 十八 2	木3 Wood 乙亥 Wood Pig Advancement 火地晉 1 **28** 十九 3	水6 Water 丙子 Fire Rat Nourish 山雷頤 9 **29** 二十 3	金4 Metal 丁丑 Fire Ox Following 澤雷隨 8 **30** 廿一 7	木8 Wood 戊寅 Earth Tiger Abundance 雷火豐 7 **31** 廿二 6

NOVEMBER 2026 己亥

Xuan Kong Element 玄空五行	風地觀 Observation	Period Luck 卦運	Monthly Star 月星
Fire 火2		2	8

SUNDAY	MONDAY	TUESDAY	WEDNESDAY	THURSDAY	FRIDAY	SATURDAY
火7 Fire 6 Regulate 水澤節 己卯 Earth Rabbit **1** 廿三 8	水1 Water 5 Unity 地天泰 庚辰 Metal Dragon **2** 廿四 9	木3 Wood 4 Great Reward 火天大有 辛巳 Metal Snake **3** 廿五 7	火2 Fire 3 Wind 巽為風 壬午 Water Horse **4** 廿六 1	金4 Metal 2 Trap 澤水困 癸未 Water Goat **5** 廿七 8	木3 Wood 1 Not Yet Accomplished 火水未濟 甲申 Wood Monkey **6** 廿八 9	金9 Metal 9 Retreat 天山遯 乙酉 Wood Rooster **7** 廿九 4
水6 Water 8 Mountain 艮為山 丙戌 Fire Dog **8** 三十 1	木8 Wood 7 Delight 雷地豫 丁亥 Fire Pig **9** 十月初一 8	火7 Fire 6 Beginning 水雷屯 戊子 Earth Rat **10** 初二 4	金9 Metal 5 Without Wrongdoing 天雷無妄 己丑 Earth Ox **11** 初三 2	木3 Wood 4 Fire 離為火 庚寅 Metal Tiger **12** 初四 1	火2 Fire 3 Sincerity 風澤中孚 辛卯 Metal Rabbit **13** 初五 3	水6 Water 2 Big Livestock 山天大畜 壬辰 Water Dragon **14** 初六 4
金4 Metal 1 Eliminating 澤天夬 癸巳 Water Snake **15** 初七 6	金9 Metal 9 Heaven 乾為天 甲午 Wood Horse **16** 初八 1	火7 Fire 8 Well 水風井 乙未 Wood Goat **17** 初九 6	木8 Wood 7 Relief 雷水解 丙申 Fire Monkey **18** 初十 4	金4 Metal 6 Influence 澤山咸 丁酉 Fire Rooster **19** 十一 9	水1 Water 5 Humility 地山謙 戊戌 Earth Dog **20** 十二 6	火2 Fire 4 Observation 風地觀 己亥 Earth Pig **21** 十三 2
火2 Fire 3 Increasing 風雷益 庚子 Metal Rat **22** 十四 9	水1 Water 2 Dimming Light 地火明夷 辛丑 Metal Ox **23** 十五 3	金9 Metal 1 Fellowship 天火同人 壬寅 Water Tiger **24** 十六 7	木8 Wood 9 Marrying Maiden 雷澤歸妹 癸卯 Water Rabbit **25** 十七 7	木3 Wood 8 Opposition 火澤睽 甲辰 Wood Dragon **26** 十八 2	火7 Fire 7 Waiting 水天需 乙巳 Wood Snake **27** 十九 3	金4 Metal 6 Great Exceeding 澤風大過 丙午 Fire Horse **28** 二十 3
水6 Water 5 Poison 山風蠱 丁未 Fire Goat **29** 廿一 7	火2 Fire 4 Dispersing 風水渙 戊申 Earth Monkey **30** 廿二 6					

DECEMBER 2026 庚子

Xuan Kong Element 玄空五行	風雷益 Increasing	Period Luck 卦運	Monthly Star 月星
Fire 火2		9	7

SUNDAY	MONDAY	TUESDAY	WEDNESDAY	THURSDAY	FRIDAY	SATURDAY
		木3 Wood 3 Travelling 火山旅 己酉 Earth Rooster **1** 廿三 8	金9 Metal 2 Stagnation 天地否 庚戌 Metal Dog **2** 廿四 9	火7 Fire 1 Alliance 水地比 辛亥 Metal Pig **3** 廿五 7	木8 Wood 9 Thunder 震為雷 壬子 Water Rat **4** 廿六 1	水6 Water 8 Beauty 山火賁 癸丑 Water Ox **5** 廿七 8
火7 Fire 7 Accomplished 水火既濟 甲寅 Wood Tiger **6** 廿八 9	水1 Water 6 Arriving 地澤臨 乙卯 Wood Rabbit **7** 廿九 4	金4 Metal 5 Marsh 兌為澤 丙辰 Fire Dragon **8** 三十 1	火2 Fire 4 Small Livestock 風天小畜 丁巳 Fire Snake **9** 十一月初一 8	木3 Wood 3 The Cauldron 火風鼎 戊午 Earth Horse **10** 初二 4	水1 Water 2 Rising 地風升 己未 Earth Goat **11** 初三 2	火7 Fire 1 Water 坎為水 庚申 Metal Monkey **12** 初四 1
木8 Wood 9 Lesser Exceeding 雷山小過 辛酉 Metal Rooster **13** 初五 3	金4 Metal 8 Gathering 澤地萃 壬戌 Water Dog **14** 初六 4	水6 Water 7 Peel 山地剝 癸亥 Water Pig **15** 初七 6	水1 Water 6 Earth 坤為地 甲子 Wood Rat **16** 初八 1	木3 Wood 5 Biting 火雷噬嗑 乙丑 Wood Ox **17** 初九 6	火2 Fire 4 Family 風火家人 丙寅 Fire Tiger **18** 初十 4	水6 Water 3 Decreasing 山澤損 丁卯 Fire Rabbit **19** 十一 9
金9 Metal 2 Tread 天澤履 戊辰 Earth Dragon **20** 十二 6	木8 Wood 1 Great Strength 雷天大壯 己巳 Earth Snake **21** 十三 2	木8 Wood 9/1 Consistency 雷風恆 庚午 Metal Horse **22** 十四 9	金9 Metal 2 Litigation 天水訟 辛未 Metal Goat **23** 十五 3	水1 Water 3 Officer 地水師 壬申 Water Monkey **24** 十六 7	火2 Fire 4 Gradual Progress 風山漸 癸酉 Water Rooster **25** 十七 7	火7 Fire 5 Obstruction 水山蹇 甲戌 Wood Dog **26** 十八 2
木3 Wood 6 Advancement 火地晉 乙亥 Wood Pig **27** 十九 3	水6 Water 7 Nourish 山雷頤 丙子 Fire Rat **28** 二十 3	金4 Metal 8 Following 澤雷隨 丁丑 Fire Ox **29** 廿一 7	木8 Wood 9 Abundance 雷火豐 戊寅 Earth Tiger **30** 廿二 6	火7 Fire 1 Regulate 水澤節 己卯 Earth Rabbit **31** 廿三 8		

2027 丁未

(*Ding Wei*) Fire Goat

2027 丁未 *(Ding Wei)* Fire Goat

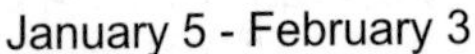
January 5 - February 3

February 4 - March 5

March 6 - April 4

April 5 - May 5

May 6 - June 5

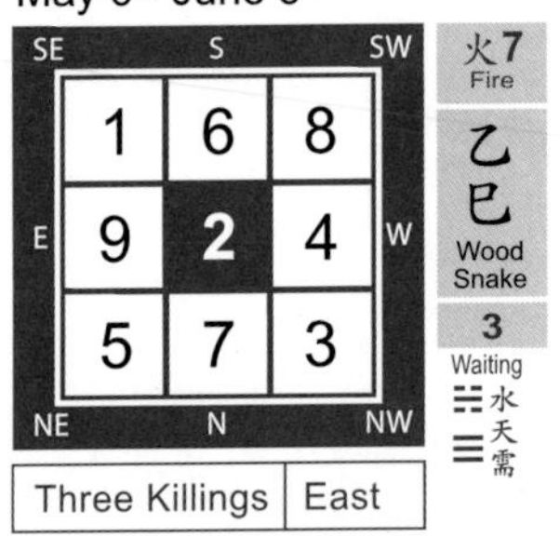

June 6 - July 6

July 7 - August 7

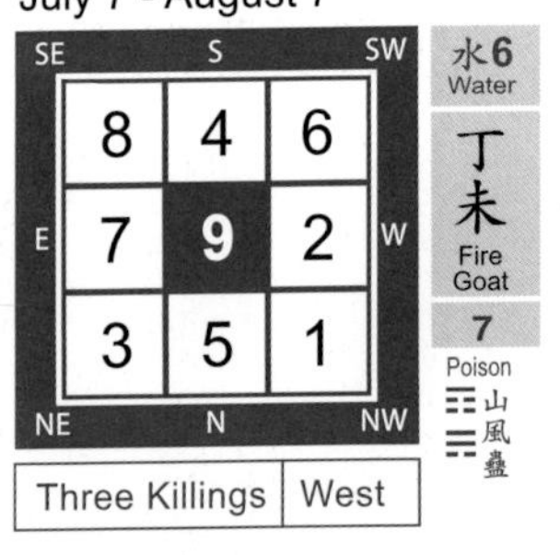

August 8 - September 7

September 8 - October 7

October 8 - November 6

November 7 - December 6

December 7 - January 5

JANUARY 2027 辛丑

Xuan Kong Element 玄空五行	地火明夷 Dimming Light	Period Luck 卦運	Monthly Star 月星
Water 水1		3	6

SUNDAY	MONDAY	TUESDAY	WEDNESDAY	THURSDAY	FRIDAY	SATURDAY
金9 Metal 5 Stagnation 天地否 庚戌 Metal Dog 9 31 廿四					水1 Water 2 Unity 地天泰 庚辰 Metal Dragon 9 1 廿四	木3 Wood 3 Great Reward 火天大有 辛巳 Metal Snake 7 2 廿五
火2 Fire 4 Wind 巽爲風 壬午 Water Horse 1 3 廿六	金4 Metal 5 Trap 澤水困 癸未 Water Goat 8 4 廿七	木3 Wood 6 Not Yet Accomplished 火水未濟 甲申 Wood Monkey 9 5 廿八	金9 Metal 7 Retreat 天山遯 乙酉 Wood Rooster 4 6 廿九	水6 Water 8 Mountain 艮爲山 丙戌 Fire Dog 1 7 三十	木8 Wood 9 Delight 雷地豫 丁亥 Fire Pig 8 8 十二月初一	火7 Fire 1 Beginning 水雷屯 戊子 Earth Rat 4 9 初二
金9 Metal 2 Without Wrongdoing 天雷無妄 己丑 Earth Ox 2 10 初三	木3 Wood 3 Fire 離爲火 庚寅 Metal Tiger 1 11 初四	火2 Fire 4 Sincerity 風澤中孚 辛卯 Metal Rabbit 3 12 初五	水6 Water 5 Big Livestock 山天大畜 壬辰 Water Dragon 4 13 初六	金4 Metal 6 Eliminating 澤天夬 癸巳 Water Snake 6 14 初七	金9 Metal 7 Heaven 乾爲天 甲午 Wood Horse 1 15 初八	火7 Fire 8 Well 水風井 乙未 Wood Goat 6 16 初九
木8 Wood 9 Relief 雷水解 丙申 Fire Monkey 4 17 初十	金4 Metal 1 Influence 澤山咸 丁酉 Fire Rooster 9 18 十一	水1 Water 2 Humility 地山謙 戊戌 Earth Dog 6 19 十二	火2 Fire 3 Observation 風地觀 己亥 Earth Pig 2 20 十三	火2 Fire 4 Increasing 風雷益 庚子 Metal Rat 9 21 十四	水1 Water 5 Dimming Light 地火明夷 辛丑 Metal Ox 3 22 十五	金9 Metal 6 Fellowship 天火同人 壬寅 Water Tiger 7 23 十六
木8 Wood 7 Marrying Maiden 雷澤歸妹 癸卯 Water Rabbit 7 24 十七	木3 Wood 8 Opposition 火澤睽 甲辰 Wood Dragon 2 25 十八	火7 Fire 9 Waiting 水天需 乙巳 Wood Snake 3 26 十九	金4 Metal 1 Great Exceeding 澤風大過 丙午 Fire Horse 3 27 二十	水6 Water 2 Poison 山風蠱 丁未 Fire Goat 7 28 廿一	火2 Fire 3 Dispersing 風水渙 戊申 Earth Monkey 6 29 廿二	木3 Wood 4 Travelling 火山旅 己酉 Earth Rooster 8 30 廿三

FEBRUARY 2027 壬寅

Xuan Kong Element 玄空五行	天火同人 Fellowship	Period Luck 卦運	Monthly Star 月星
Metal 金9		7	5

SUNDAY	MONDAY	TUESDAY	WEDNESDAY	THURSDAY	FRIDAY	SATURDAY
	火7 Fire 6 Alliance 水地比 辛亥 Metal Pig 7 1 廿五	木8 Wood 7 Thunder 震爲雷 壬子 Water Rat 1 2 廿六	水6 Water 8 Beauty 山火賁 癸丑 Water Ox 8 3 廿七	火7 Fire 9 Accomplished 水火既濟 甲寅 Wood Tiger 9 4 廿八	水1 Water 1 Arriving 地澤臨 乙卯 Wood Rabbit 4 5 廿九	金4 Metal 2 Marsh 兌爲澤 丙辰 Fire Dragon 1 6 正月初一
火2 Fire 3 Small Livestock 風天小畜 丁巳 Fire Snake 8 7 初二	木3 Wood 4 The Cauldron 火風鼎 戊午 Earth Horse 4 8 初三	水1 Water 5 Rising 地風升 己未 Earth Goat 2 9 初四	火7 Fire 6 Water 坎爲水 庚申 Metal Monkey 1 10 初五	木8 Wood 7 Lesser Exceeding 雷山小過 辛酉 Metal Rooster 3 11 初六	金4 Metal 8 Gathering 澤地萃 壬戌 Water Dog 4 12 初七	水6 Water 9 Peel 山地剝 癸亥 Water Pig 6 13 初八
水1 Water 1 Earth 坤爲地 甲子 Wood Rat 1 14 初九	木3 Wood 2 Biting 火雷噬嗑 乙丑 Wood Ox 6 15 初十	火2 Fire 3 Family 風火家人 丙寅 Fire Tiger 4 16 十一	水6 Water 4 Decreasing 山澤損 丁卯 Fire Rabbit 9 17 十二	金9 Metal 5 Tread 天澤履 戊辰 Earth Dragon 6 18 十三	木8 Wood 6 Great Strength 雷天大壯 己巳 Earth Snake 2 19 十四	木8 Wood 7 Consistency 雷風恆 庚午 Metal Horse 9 20 十五
金9 Metal 8 Litigation 天水訟 辛未 Metal Goat 3 21 十六	水1 Water 9 Officer 地水師 壬申 Water Monkey 7 22 十七	火2 Fire 1 Gradual Progress 風山漸 癸酉 Water Rooster 7 23 十八	火7 Fire 2 Obstruction 水山蹇 甲戌 Wood Dog 2 24 十九	木3 Wood 3 Advancement 火地晉 乙亥 Wood Pig 3 25 二十	水6 Water 4 Nourish 山雷頤 丙子 Fire Rat 3 26 廿一	金4 Metal 5 Following 澤雷隨 丁丑 Fire Ox 7 27 廿二
木8 Wood 6 Abundance 雷火豐 戊寅 Earth Tiger 6 28 廿三						

MARCH 2027 癸卯

Xuan Kong Element 玄空五行	雷澤歸妹 Marrying Maiden	Period Luck 卦運	Monthly Star 月星
Wood 木8		7	4

SUNDAY	MONDAY	TUESDAY	WEDNESDAY	THURSDAY	FRIDAY	SATURDAY
	火7 Fire · 7 Regulate 水澤節 己卯 Earth Rabbit **1** 廿四 8	水1 Water · 8 Unity 地天泰 庚辰 Metal Dragon **2** 廿五 9	木3 Wood · 9 Great Reward 火天大有 辛巳 Metal Snake **3** 廿六 7	火2 Fire · 1 Wind 巽爲風 壬午 Water Horse **4** 廿七 1	金4 Metal · 2 Trap 澤水困 癸未 Water Goat **5** 廿八 8	木3 Wood · 3 Not Yet Accomplished 火水未濟 甲申 Wood Monkey **6** 廿九 9
金9 Metal · 4 Retreat 天山遯 乙酉 Wood Rooster **7** 三十 4	水6 Water · 5 Mountain 艮爲山 丙戌 Fire Dog **8** 二月初一 1	木8 Wood · 6 Delight 雷地豫 丁亥 Fire Pig **9** 初二 8	火7 Fire · 7 Beginning 水雷屯 戊子 Earth Rat **10** 初三 4	金9 Metal · 8 Without Wrongdoing 天雷無妄 己丑 Earth Ox **11** 初四 2	木3 Wood · 9 Fire 離爲火 庚寅 Metal Tiger **12** 初五 1	火2 Fire · 1 Sincerity 風澤中孚 辛卯 Metal Rabbit **13** 初六 3
水6 Water · 2 Big Livestock 山天大畜 壬辰 Water Dragon **14** 初七 4	金4 Metal · 3 Eliminating 澤天夬 癸巳 Water Snake **15** 初八 6	金9 Metal · 4 Heaven 乾爲天 甲午 Wood Horse **16** 初九 1	火7 Fire · 5 Well 水風井 乙未 Wood Goat **17** 初十 6	木8 Wood · 6 Relief 雷水解 丙申 Fire Monkey **18** 十一 4	金4 Metal · 7 Influence 澤山咸 丁酉 Fire Rooster **19** 十二 9	水1 Water · 8 Humility 地山謙 戊戌 Earth Dog **20** 十三 6
火2 Fire · 9 Observation 風地觀 己亥 Earth Pig **21** 十四 2	火2 Fire · 1 Increasing 風雷益 庚子 Metal Rat **22** 十五 9	水1 Water · 2 Dimming Light 地火明夷 辛丑 Metal Ox **23** 十六 3	金9 Metal · 3 Fellowship 天火同人 壬寅 Water Tiger **24** 十七 7	木8 Wood · 4 Marrying Maiden 雷澤歸妹 癸卯 Water Rabbit **25** 十八 7	木3 Wood · 5 Opposition 火澤睽 甲辰 Wood Dragon **26** 十九 2	火7 Fire · 6 Waiting 水天需 乙巳 Wood Snake **27** 二十 3
金4 Metal · 7 Great Exceeding 澤風大過 丙午 Fire Horse **28** 廿一 3	水6 Water · 8 Poison 山風蠱 丁未 Fire Goat **29** 廿二 7	火2 Fire · 9 Dispersing 風水渙 戊申 Earth Monkey **30** 廿三 6	木3 Wood · 1 Travelling 火山旅 己酉 Earth Rooster **31** 廿四 8			

APRIL 2027 甲辰

Xuan Kong Element 玄空五行	火澤睽 Opposition	Period Luck 卦運	Monthly Star 月星
Wood 木3		2	3

SUNDAY	MONDAY	TUESDAY	WEDNESDAY	THURSDAY	FRIDAY	SATURDAY
				金9 Metal · 2 Stagnation 天地否 庚戌 Metal Dog **1** 廿五 9	火7 Fire · 3 Alliance 水地比 辛亥 Metal Pig **2** 廿六 7	木8 Wood · 4 Thunder 震爲雷 壬子 Water Rat **3** 廿七 1
水6 Water · 5 Beauty 山火賁 癸丑 Water Ox **4** 廿八 8	火7 Fire · 6 Accomplished 水火既濟 甲寅 Wood Tiger **5** 廿九 9	水1 Water · 7 Arriving 地澤臨 乙卯 Wood Rabbit **6** 三十 4	金4 Metal · 8 Marsh 兌爲澤 丙辰 Fire Dragon **7** 三月初一 1	火2 Fire · 9 Small Livestock 風天小畜 丁巳 Fire Snake **8** 初二 8	木3 Wood · 1 The Cauldron 火風鼎 戊午 Earth Horse **9** 初三 4	水1 Water · 2 Rising 地風升 己未 Earth Goat **10** 初四 2
火7 Fire · 3 Water 坎爲水 庚申 Metal Monkey **11** 初五 1	木8 Wood · 4 Lesser Exceeding 雷山小過 辛酉 Metal Rooster **12** 初六 3	金4 Metal · 5 Gathering 澤地萃 壬戌 Water Dog **13** 初七 4	水6 Water · 6 Peel 山地剝 癸亥 Water Pig **14** 初八 6	水1 Water · 7 Earth 坤爲地 甲子 Wood Rat **15** 初九 1	木3 Wood · 8 Biting 火雷噬嗑 乙丑 Wood Ox **16** 初十 6	火2 Fire · 9 Family 風火家人 丙寅 Fire Tiger **17** 十一 4
水6 Water · 1 Decreasing 山澤損 丁卯 Fire Rabbit **18** 十二 9	金9 Metal · 2 Tread 天澤履 戊辰 Earth Dragon **19** 十三 6	木8 Wood · 3 Great Strength 雷天大壯 己巳 Earth Snake **20** 十四 2	木8 Wood · 4 Consistency 雷風恒 庚午 Metal Horse **21** 十五 9	金9 Metal · 5 Litigation 天水訟 辛未 Metal Goat **22** 十六 3	水1 Water · 6 Officer 地水師 壬申 Water Monkey **23** 十七 7	火2 Fire · 7 Gradual Progress 風山漸 癸酉 Water Rooster **24** 十八 7
火7 Fire · 8 Obstruction 水山蹇 甲戌 Wood Dog **25** 十九 2	木3 Wood · 9 Advancement 火地晉 乙亥 Wood Pig **26** 二十 3	水6 Water · 1 Nourish 山雷頤 丙子 Fire Rat **27** 廿一 3	金4 Metal · 2 Following 澤雷隨 丁丑 Fire Ox **28** 廿二 7	木8 Wood · 3 Abundance 雷火豐 戊寅 Earth Tiger **29** 廿三 6	火7 Fire · 4 Regulate 水澤節 己卯 Earth Rabbit **30** 廿四 8	

MAY 2027 乙巳

Xuan Kong Element 玄空五行	水天需 Waiting	Period Luck 卦運	Monthly Star 月星
Fire 火7		3	2

SUNDAY	MONDAY	TUESDAY	WEDNESDAY	THURSDAY	FRIDAY	SATURDAY
木3 Wood 7 Travelling 火山旅 己酉 Earth Rooster **30** 廿五 8	金9 Metal 8 Stagnation 天地否 庚戌 Metal Dog **31** 廿六 9					水1 Water 5 Unity 地天泰 庚辰 Metal Dragon **1** 廿五 9
木3 Wood 6 Great Reward 火天大有 辛巳 Metal Snake **2** 廿六 7	火2 Fire 7 Wind 巽爲風 壬午 Water Horse **3** 廿七 1	金4 Metal 8 Trap 澤水困 癸未 Water Goat **4** 廿八 8	木3 Wood 9 Not Yet Accomplished 火水未濟 甲申 Wood Monkey **5** 廿九 9	金9 Metal 1 Retreat 天山遯 乙酉 Wood Rooster **6** 四月初一 4	水6 Water 2 Mountain 艮爲山 丙戌 Fire Dog **7** 初二 1	木8 Wood 3 Delight 雷地豫 丁亥 Fire Pig **8** 初三 8
火7 Fire 4 Beginning 水雷屯 戊子 Earth Rat **9** 初四 4	金9 Metal 5 Without Wrongdoing 天雷無妄 己丑 Earth Ox **10** 初五 2	木3 Wood 6 Fire 離爲火 庚寅 Metal Tiger **11** 初六 1	火2 Fire 7 Sincerity 風澤中孚 辛卯 Metal Rabbit **12** 初七 3	水6 Water 8 Big Livestock 山天大畜 壬辰 Water Dragon **13** 初八 4	金4 Metal 9 Eliminating 澤天夬 癸巳 Water Snake **14** 初九 6	金9 Metal 1 Heaven 乾爲天 甲午 Wood Horse **15** 初十 1
火7 Fire 2 Well 水風井 乙未 Wood Goat **16** 十一 6	木8 Wood 3 Relief 雷水解 丙申 Fire Monkey **17** 十二 4	金4 Metal 4 Influence 澤山咸 丁酉 Fire Rooster **18** 十三 9	水1 Water 5 Humility 地山謙 戊戌 Earth Dog **19** 十四 6	火2 Fire 6 Observation 風地觀 己亥 Earth Pig **20** 十五 2	火2 Fire 7 Increasing 風雷益 庚子 Metal Rat **21** 十六 9	水1 Water 8 Dimming Light 地火明夷 辛丑 Metal Ox **22** 十七 3
金9 Metal 9 Fellowship 天火同人 壬寅 Water Tiger **23** 十八 7	木8 Wood 1 Marrying Maiden 雷澤歸妹 癸卯 Water Rabbit **24** 十九 7	木3 Wood 2 Opposition 火澤睽 甲辰 Wood Dragon **25** 二十 2	火7 Fire 3 Waiting 水天需 乙巳 Wood Snake **26** 廿一 3	金4 Metal 4 Great Exceeding 澤風大過 丙午 Fire Horse **27** 廿二 3	水6 Water 5 Poison 山風蠱 丁未 Fire Goat **28** 廿三 7	火2 Fire 6 Dispersing 風水渙 戊申 Earth Monkey **29** 廿四 6

JUNE 2027 丙午

Xuan Kong Element 玄空五行	澤風大過 Great Exceeding	Period Luck 卦運	Monthly Star 月星
Metal 金4		3	1

SUNDAY	MONDAY	TUESDAY	WEDNESDAY	THURSDAY	FRIDAY	SATURDAY
		火7 Fire 9 Alliance 水地比 辛亥 Metal Pig **1** 廿七 7	木8 Wood 1 Thunder 震爲雷 壬子 Water Rat **2** 廿八 1	水6 Water 2 Beauty 山火賁 癸丑 Water Ox **3** 廿九 8	火7 Fire 3 Accomplished 水火既濟 甲寅 Wood Tiger **4** 三十 9	水1 Water 4 Arriving 地澤臨 乙卯 Wood Rabbit **5** 五月初一 4
金4 Metal 5 Marsh 兌爲澤 丙辰 Fire Dragon **6** 初二 1	火2 Fire 6 Small Livestock 風天小畜 丁巳 Fire Snake **7** 初三 8	木3 Wood 7 The Cauldron 火風鼎 戊午 Earth Horse **8** 初四 4	水1 Water 8 Rising 地風升 己未 Earth Goat **9** 初五 2	火7 Fire 9 Water 坎爲水 庚申 Metal Monkey **10** 初六 1	木8 Wood 1 Lesser Exceeding 雷山小過 辛酉 Metal Rooster **11** 初七 3	金4 Metal 2 Gathering 澤地萃 壬戌 Water Dog **12** 初八 4
水6 Water 3 Peel 山地剝 癸亥 Water Pig **13** 初九 6	水1 Water 4 Earth 坤爲地 甲子 Wood Rat **14** 初十 1	木3 Wood 5 Biting 火雷噬嗑 乙丑 Wood Ox **15** 十一 6	火2 Fire 6 Family 風火家人 丙寅 Fire Tiger **16** 十二 4	水6 Water 7 Decreasing 山澤損 丁卯 Fire Rabbit **17** 十三 9	金9 Metal 8 Tread 天澤履 戊辰 Earth Dragon **18** 十四 6	木8 Wood 9 Great Strength 雷天大壯 己巳 Earth Snake **19** 十五 2
木8 Wood 1 Consistency 雷風恆 庚午 Metal Horse **20** 十六 9	金9 Metal 2/8 Litigation 天水訟 辛未 Metal Goat **21** 十七 3	水1 Water 7 Officer 地水師 壬申 Water Monkey **22** 十八 7	火2 Fire 6 Gradual Progress 風山漸 癸酉 Water Rooster **23** 十九 7	火7 Fire 5 Obstruction 水山蹇 甲戌 Wood Dog **24** 二十 2	木3 Wood 4 Advancement 火地晉 乙亥 Wood Pig **25** 廿一 3	水6 Water 3 Nourish 山雷頤 丙子 Fire Rat **26** 廿二 3
金4 Metal 2 Following 澤雷隨 丁丑 Fire Ox **27** 廿三 7	木8 Wood 1 Abundance 雷火豐 戊寅 Earth Tiger **28** 廿四 6	火7 Fire 9 Regulate 水澤節 己卯 Earth Rabbit **29** 廿五 8	水1 Water 8 Unity 地天泰 庚辰 Metal Dragon **30** 廿六 9			

JULY 2027 丁未

Xuan Kong Element 玄空五行	山風蠱 Poison	Period Luck 卦運	Monthly Star 月星
Water 水6		7	9

SUNDAY	MONDAY	TUESDAY	WEDNESDAY	THURSDAY	FRIDAY	SATURDAY
				木3 Wood 7 Great Reward 辛巳 Metal Snake 火天大有 1 廿七 7	火2 Fire 6 Wind 壬午 Water Horse 巽爲風 2 廿八 1	金4 Metal 5 Trap 癸未 Water Goat 澤水困 3 廿九 8
木3 Wood 4 Not Yet Accomplished 甲申 Wood Monkey 火水未濟 4 六月初一 9	金9 Metal 3 Retreat 乙酉 Wood Rooster 天山遯 5 初二 4	水6 Water 2 Mountain 丙戌 Fire Dog 艮爲山 6 初三 1	木8 Wood 1 Delight 丁亥 Fire Pig 雷地豫 7 初四 8	火7 Fire 9 Beginning 戊子 Earth Rat 水雷屯 8 初五 4	金9 Metal 8 Without Wrongdoing 己丑 Earth Ox 天雷無妄 9 初六 2	木3 Wood 7 Fire 庚寅 Metal Tiger 離爲火 10 初七 1
火2 Fire 6 Sincerity 辛卯 Metal Rabbit 風澤中孚 11 初八 3	水6 Water 5 Big Livestock 壬辰 Water Dragon 山天大畜 12 初九 4	金4 Metal 4 Eliminating 癸巳 Water Snake 澤天夬 13 初十 6	金9 Metal 3 Heaven 甲午 Wood Horse 乾爲天 14 十一 1	火7 Fire 2 Well 乙未 Wood Goat 水風井 15 十二 6	木8 Wood 1 Relief 丙申 Fire Monkey 雷水解 16 十三 4	金4 Metal 9 Influence 丁酉 Fire Rooster 澤山咸 17 十四 9
水1 Water 8 Humility 戊戌 Earth Dog 地山謙 18 十五 6	火2 Fire 7 Observation 己亥 Earth Pig 風地觀 19 十六 2	火2 Fire 6 Increasing 庚子 Metal Rat 風雷益 20 十七 9	水1 Water 5 Dimming Light 辛丑 Metal Ox 地火明夷 21 十八 3	金9 Metal 4 Fellowship 壬寅 Water Tiger 天火同人 22 十九 7	木8 Wood 3 Marrying Maiden 癸卯 Water Rabbit 雷澤歸妹 23 二十 7	木3 Wood 2 Opposition 甲辰 Wood Dragon 火澤睽 24 廿一 2
火7 Fire 1 Waiting 乙巳 Wood Snake 水天需 25 廿二 3	金4 Metal 9 Great Exceeding 丙午 Fire Horse 澤風大過 26 廿三 3	水6 Water 8 Poison 丁未 Fire Goat 山風蠱 27 廿四 7	火2 Fire 7 Dispersing 戊申 Earth Monkey 風水渙 28 廿五 6	木3 Wood 6 Travelling 己酉 Earth Rooster 火山旅 29 廿六 8	金9 Metal 5 Stagnation 庚戌 Metal Dog 天地否 30 廿七 9	火7 Fire 4 Alliance 辛亥 Metal Pig 水地比 31 廿八 7

AUGUST 2027 戊申

Xuan Kong Element 玄空五行	風水渙 Dispersing	Period Luck 卦運	Monthly Star 月星
Fire 火2		6	8

SUNDAY	MONDAY	TUESDAY	WEDNESDAY	THURSDAY	FRIDAY	SATURDAY
木8 Wood 3 Thunder 壬子 Water Rat 震爲雷 1 廿九 1	水6 Water 2 Beauty 癸丑 Water Ox 山火賁 2 七月初一 8	火7 Fire 1 Accomplished 甲寅 Wood Tiger 水火既濟 3 初二 9	水1 Water 9 Arriving 乙卯 Wood Rabbit 地澤臨 4 初三 4	金4 Metal 8 Marsh 丙辰 Fire Dragon 兌爲澤 5 初四 1	火2 Fire 7 Small Livestock 丁巳 Fire Snake 風天小畜 6 初五 8	木3 Wood 6 The Cauldron 戊午 Earth Horse 火風鼎 7 初六 4
水1 Water 5 Rising 己未 Earth Goat 地風升 8 初七 2	火7 Fire 4 Water 庚申 Metal Monkey 坎爲水 9 初八 1	木8 Wood 3 Lesser Exceeding 辛酉 Metal Rooster 雷山小過 10 初九 3	金4 Metal 2 Gathering 壬戌 Water Dog 澤地萃 11 初十 4	水6 Water 1 Peel 癸亥 Water Pig 山地剝 12 十一 6	水1 Water 9 Earth 甲子 Wood Rat 坤爲地 13 十二 1	木3 Wood 8 Biting 乙丑 Wood Ox 火雷噬嗑 14 十三 6
火2 Fire 7 Family 丙寅 Fire Tiger 風火家人 15 十四 4	水6 Water 6 Decreasing 丁卯 Fire Rabbit 山澤損 16 十五 9	金9 Metal 5 Tread 戊辰 Earth Dragon 天澤履 17 十六 6	木8 Wood 4 Great Strength 己巳 Earth Snake 雷天大壯 18 十七 2	木8 Wood 3 Consistency 庚午 Metal Horse 雷風恆 19 十八 9	金9 Metal 2 Litigation 辛未 Metal Goat 天水訟 20 十九 3	水1 Water 1 Officer 壬申 Water Monkey 地水師 21 二十 7
火2 Fire 9 Gradual Progress 癸酉 Water Rooster 風山漸 22 廿一 7	火7 Fire 8 Obstruction 甲戌 Wood Dog 水山蹇 23 廿二 2	木3 Wood 7 Advancement 乙亥 Wood Pig 火地晉 24 廿三 3	水6 Water 6 Nourish 丙子 Fire Rat 山雷頤 25 廿四 3	金4 Metal 5 Following 丁丑 Fire Ox 澤雷隨 26 廿五 7	木8 Wood 4 Abundance 戊寅 Earth Tiger 雷火豐 27 廿六 6	火7 Fire 3 Regulate 己卯 Earth Rabbit 水澤節 28 廿七 8
水1 Water 2 Unity 庚辰 Metal Dragon 地天泰 29 廿八 9	木3 Wood 1 Great Reward 辛巳 Metal Snake 火天大有 30 廿九 7	火2 Fire 9 Wind 壬午 Water Horse 巽爲風 31 三十 1				

SEPTEMBER 2027 己酉

Xuan Kong Element 玄空五行	火山旅 Travelling	Period Luck 卦運	Monthly Star 月星
Wood 木3		8	7

SUNDAY	MONDAY	TUESDAY	WEDNESDAY	THURSDAY	FRIDAY	SATURDAY
			金4 Metal 8 Trap 癸未 Water Goat 澤水困 1 8 八月初一	木3 Wood 7 Not Yet Accomplished 甲申 Wood Monkey 火水未濟 2 9 初二	金9 Metal 6 Retreat 乙酉 Wood Rooster 天山遯 3 4 初三	水6 Water 5 Mountain 丙戌 Fire Dog 艮爲山 4 1 初四
木8 Wood 4 Delight 丁亥 Fire Pig 雷地豫 5 8 初五	火7 Fire 3 Beginning 戊子 Earth Rat 水雷屯 6 4 初六	金9 Metal 2 Without Wrongdoing 己丑 Earth Ox 天雷無妄 7 2 初七	木3 Wood 1 Fire 庚寅 Metal Tiger 離爲火 8 1 初八	火2 Fire 9 Sincerity 辛卯 Metal Rabbit 風澤中孚 9 3 初九	水6 Water 8 Big Livestock 壬辰 Water Dragon 山天大畜 10 4 初十	金4 Metal 7 Eliminating 癸巳 Water Snake 澤天夬 11 6 十一
金9 Metal 6 Heaven 甲午 Wood Horse 乾爲天 12 1 十二	火7 Fire 5 Well 乙未 Wood Goat 水風井 13 6 十三	木8 Wood 4 Relief 丙申 Fire Monkey 雷水解 14 4 十四	金4 Metal 3 Influence 丁酉 Fire Rooster 澤山咸 15 9 十五	水1 Water 2 Humility 戊戌 Earth Dog 地山謙 16 6 十六	火2 Fire 1 Observation 己亥 Earth Pig 風地觀 17 2 十七	火2 Fire 9 Increasing 庚子 Metal Rat 風雷益 18 9 十八
水1 Water 8 Dimming Light 辛丑 Metal Ox 地火明夷 19 3 十九	金9 Metal 7 Fellowship 壬寅 Water Tiger 天火同人 20 7 二十	木8 Wood 6 Marrying Maiden 癸卯 Water Rabbit 雷澤歸妹 21 7 廿一	木3 Wood 5 Opposition 甲辰 Wood Dragon 火澤睽 22 2 廿二	火7 Fire 4 Waiting 乙巳 Wood Snake 水天需 23 3 廿三	金4 Metal 3 Great Exceeding 丙午 Fire Horse 澤風大過 24 3 廿四	水6 Water 2 Poison 丁未 Fire Goat 山風蠱 25 7 廿五
火2 Fire 1 Dispersing 戊申 Earth Monkey 風水渙 26 6 廿六	木3 Wood 9 Travelling 己酉 Earth Rooster 火山旅 27 8 廿七	金9 Metal 8 Stagnation 庚戌 Metal Dog 天地否 28 9 廿八	火7 Fire 7 Alliance 辛亥 Metal Pig 水地比 29 7 廿九	木8 Wood 6 Thunder 壬子 Water Rat 震爲雷 30 1 九月初一		

OCTOBER 2027 庚戌

Xuan Kong Element 玄空五行	天地否 Stagnation	Period Luck 卦運	Monthly Star 月星
Metal 金9		9	6

SUNDAY	MONDAY	TUESDAY	WEDNESDAY	THURSDAY	FRIDAY	SATURDAY
金4 Metal 2 Trap 癸未 Water Goat 澤水困 31 8 初三					水6 Water 5 Beauty 癸丑 Water Ox 山火賁 1 8 初二	火7 Fire 4 Accomplished 甲寅 Wood Tiger 水火既濟 2 9 初三
水1 Water 3 Arriving 乙卯 Wood Rabbit 地澤臨 3 4 初四	金4 Metal 2 Marsh 丙辰 Fire Dragon 兑爲澤 4 1 初五	火2 Fire 1 Small Livestock 丁巳 Fire Snake 風天小畜 5 8 初六	木3 Wood 9 The Cauldron 戊午 Earth Horse 火風鼎 6 4 初七	水1 Water 8 Rising 己未 Earth Goat 地風升 7 2 初八	火7 Fire 7 Water 庚申 Metal Monkey 坎爲水 8 1 初九	木8 Wood 6 Lesser Exceeding 辛酉 Metal Rooster 雷山小過 9 3 初十
金4 Metal 5 Gathering 壬戌 Water Dog 澤地萃 10 4 十一	水6 Water 4 Peel 癸亥 Water Pig 山地剝 11 6 十二	水1 Water 3 Earth 甲子 Wood Rat 坤爲地 12 1 十三	木3 Wood 2 Biting 乙丑 Wood Ox 火雷噬嗑 13 6 十四	火2 Fire 1 Family 丙寅 Fire Tiger 風火家人 14 4 十五	水6 Water 9 Decreasing 丁卯 Fire Rabbit 山澤損 15 9 十六	金9 Metal 8 Tread 戊辰 Earth Dragon 天澤履 16 6 十七
木8 Wood 7 Great Strength 己巳 Earth Snake 雷天大壯 17 2 十八	木8 Wood 6 Consistency 庚午 Metal Horse 雷風恆 18 9 十九	金9 Metal 5 Litigation 辛未 Metal Goat 天水訟 19 3 二十	水1 Water 4 Officer 壬申 Water Monkey 地水師 20 7 廿一	火2 Fire 3 Gradual Progress 癸酉 Water Rooster 風山漸 21 7 廿二	火7 Fire 2 Obstruction 甲戌 Wood Dog 水山蹇 22 2 廿三	木3 Wood 1 Advancement 乙亥 Wood Pig 火地晉 23 3 廿四
水6 Water 9 Nourish 丙子 Fire Rat 山雷頤 24 3 廿五	金4 Metal 8 Following 丁丑 Fire Ox 澤雷隨 25 7 廿六	木8 Wood 7 Abundance 戊寅 Earth Tiger 雷火豐 26 6 廿七	火7 Fire 6 Regulate 己卯 Earth Rabbit 水澤節 27 8 廿八	水1 Water 5 Unity 庚辰 Metal Dragon 地天泰 28 9 廿九	木3 Wood 4 Great Reward 辛巳 Metal Snake 火天大有 29 7 十月初一	火2 Fire 3 Wind 壬午 Water Horse 巽爲風 30 1 初二

NOVEMBER 2027 辛亥

Xuan Kong Element 玄空五行	水地比 Alliance	Period Luck 卦運	Monthly Star 月星
Fire 火7		7	5

SUNDAY	MONDAY	TUESDAY	WEDNESDAY	THURSDAY	FRIDAY	SATURDAY
	木3 Wood 1 Not Yet Accomplished 甲申 Wood Monkey 火水未濟 1 初四 9	金9 Metal 9 Retreat 乙酉 Wood Rooster 天山遯 2 初五 4	水6 Water 8 Mountain 丙戌 Fire Dog 艮爲山 3 初六 1	木8 Wood 7 Delight 丁亥 Fire Pig 雷地豫 4 初七 8	火7 Fire 6 Beginning 戊子 Earth Rat 水雷屯 5 初八 4	金9 Metal 5 Without Wrongdoing 己丑 Earth Ox 天雷無妄 6 初九 2
木3 Wood 4 Fire 庚寅 Metal Tiger 離爲火 7 初十 1	火2 Fire 3 Sincerity 辛卯 Metal Rabbit 風澤中孚 8 十一 3	水6 Water 2 Big Livestock 壬辰 Water Dragon 山天大畜 9 十二 4	金4 Metal 1 Eliminating 癸巳 Water Snake 澤天夬 10 十三 6	金9 Metal 9 Heaven 甲午 Wood Horse 乾爲天 11 十四 1	火7 Fire 8 Well 乙未 Wood Goat 水風井 12 十五 6	木8 Wood 7 Relief 丙申 Fire Monkey 雷水解 13 十六 4
金4 Metal 6 Influence 丁酉 Fire Rooster 澤山咸 14 十七 9	水1 Water 5 Humility 戊戌 Earth Dog 地山謙 15 十八 6	火2 Fire 4 Observation 己亥 Earth Pig 風地觀 16 十九 2	火2 Fire 3 Increasing 庚子 Metal Rat 風雷益 17 二十 9	水1 Water 2 Dimming Light 辛丑 Metal Ox 地火明夷 18 廿一 3	金9 Metal 1 Fellowship 壬寅 Water Tiger 天火同人 19 廿二 7	木8 Wood 9 Marrying Maiden 癸卯 Water Rabbit 雷澤歸妹 20 廿三 7
木3 Wood 8 Opposition 甲辰 Wood Dragon 火澤睽 21 廿四 2	火7 Fire 7 Waiting 乙巳 Wood Snake 水天需 22 廿五 3	金4 Metal 6 Great Exceeding 丙午 Fire Horse 澤風大過 23 廿六 3	水6 Water 5 Poison 丁未 Fire Goat 山風蠱 24 廿七 7	火2 Fire 4 Dispersing 戊申 Earth Monkey 風水渙 25 廿八 6	木3 Wood 3 Travelling 己酉 Earth Rooster 火山旅 26 廿九 8	金9 Metal 2 Stagnation 庚戌 Metal Dog 天地否 27 三十 9
火7 Fire 1 Alliance 辛亥 Metal Pig 水地比 28 十一月初一 7	木8 Wood 9 Thunder 壬子 Water Rat 震爲雷 29 初二 1	水6 Water 8 Beauty 癸丑 Water Ox 山火賁 30 初三 8				

DECEMBER 2027 壬子

Xuan Kong Element 玄空五行	震爲雷 Thunder	Period Luck 卦運	Monthly Star 月星
Wood 木8		1	4

SUNDAY	MONDAY	TUESDAY	WEDNESDAY	THURSDAY	FRIDAY	SATURDAY
			火7 Fire 7 Accomplished 甲寅 Wood Tiger 水火既濟 1 初四 9	水1 Water 6 Arriving 乙卯 Wood Rabbit 地澤臨 2 初五 4	金4 Metal 5 Marsh 丙辰 Fire Dragon 兌爲澤 3 初六 1	火2 Fire 4 Small Livestock 丁巳 Fire Snake 風天小畜 4 初七 8
木3 Wood 3 The Cauldron 戊午 Earth Horse 火風鼎 5 初八 4	水1 Water 2 Rising 己未 Earth Goat 地風升 6 初九 2	火7 Fire 1 Water 庚申 Metal Monkey 坎爲水 7 初十 1	木8 Wood 9 Lesser Exceeding 辛酉 Metal Rooster 雷山小過 8 十一 3	金4 Metal 8 Gathering 壬戌 Water Dog 澤地萃 9 十二 4	水6 Water 7 Peel 癸亥 Water Pig 山地剝 10 十三 6	水1 Water 6 Earth 甲子 Wood Rat 坤爲地 11 十四 1
木3 Wood 5 Biting 乙丑 Wood Ox 火雷噬嗑 12 十五 6	火2 Fire 4 Family 丙寅 Fire Tiger 風火家人 13 十六 4	水6 Water 3 Decreasing 丁卯 Fire Rabbit 山澤損 14 十七 9	金9 Metal 2 Tread 戊辰 Earth Dragon 天澤履 15 十八 6	木8 Wood 1 Great Strength 己巳 Earth Snake 雷天大壯 16 十九 2	木8 Wood 9 Consistency 庚午 Metal Horse 雷風恆 17 二十 9	金9 Metal 8 Litigation 辛未 Metal Goat 天水訟 18 廿一 3
水1 Water 7 Officer 壬申 Water Monkey 地水師 19 廿二 7	火2 Fire 6 Gradual Progress 癸酉 Water Rooster 風山漸 20 廿三 7	火7 Fire 5 Obstruction 甲戌 Wood Dog 水山蹇 21 廿四 2	木3 Wood 4/6 Advancement 乙亥 Wood Pig 火地晉 22 廿五 3	水6 Water 7 Nourish 丙子 Fire Rat 山雷頤 23 廿六 3	金4 Metal 8 Following 丁丑 Fire Ox 澤雷隨 24 廿七 7	木8 Wood 9 Abundance 戊寅 Earth Tiger 雷火豐 25 廿八 6
火7 Fire 1 Regulate 己卯 Earth Rabbit 水澤節 26 廿九 8	水1 Water 2 Unity 庚辰 Metal Dragon 地天泰 27 三十 9	木3 Wood 3 Great Reward 辛巳 Metal Snake 火天大有 28 十二月初一 7	火2 Fire 4 Wind 壬午 Water Horse 巽爲風 29 初二 1	金4 Metal 5 Trap 癸未 Water Goat 澤水困 30 初三 8	木3 Wood 6 Not Yet Accomplished 甲申 Wood Monkey 火水未濟 31 初四 9	

2028 戊申

(*Wu Shen*) Earth Monkey

2028 戊申 *(Wu Shen)* Earth Monkey

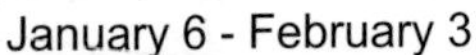

January 6 - February 3

February 4 - March 4

March 5 - April 3

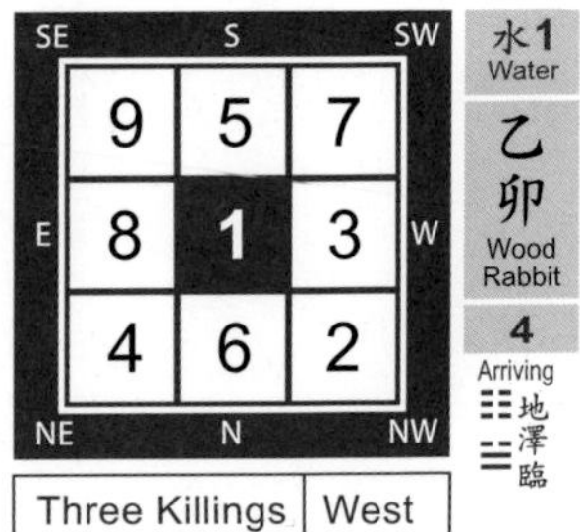

April 4 - May 4

May 5 - June 4

June 5 - July 5

July 6 - August 6

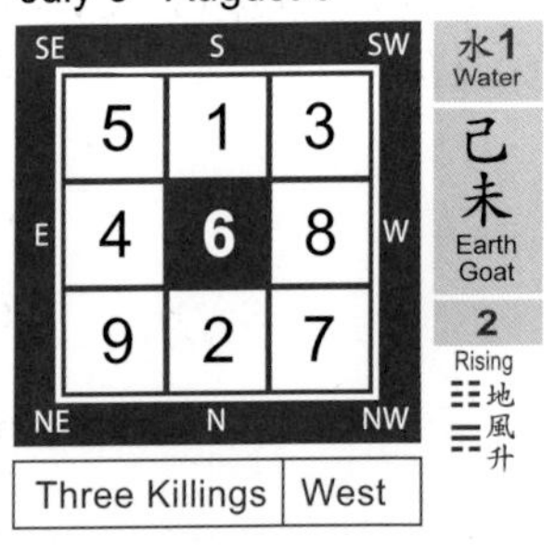

August 7 - September 6

September 7 - October 7

October 8 - November 6

November 7 - December 5

December 6 - January 4

JANUARY 2028 癸丑

Xuan Kong Element 玄空五行	山火賁 Beauty	Period Luck 卦運	Monthly Star 月星
Water 水6		8	3

SUNDAY	MONDAY	TUESDAY	WEDNESDAY	THURSDAY	FRIDAY	SATURDAY
火7 Fire 9 Accomplished 甲寅 Wood Tiger 水火既濟 30 初五 9	水1 Water 1 Arriving 乙卯 Wood Rabbit 地澤臨 31 初六 4					金9 Metal 7 Retreat 乙酉 Wood Rooster 天山遯 1 初五 4
水6 Water 8 Mountain 丙戌 Fire Dog 艮爲山 2 初六 1	木8 Wood 9 Delight 丁亥 Fire Pig 雷地豫 3 初七 8	火7 Fire 1 Beginning 戊子 Earth Rat 水雷屯 4 初八 4	金9 Metal 2 Without Wrongdoing 己丑 Earth Ox 天雷無妄 5 初九 2	木3 Wood 3 Fire 庚寅 Metal Tiger 離爲火 6 初十 1	火2 Fire 4 Sincerity 辛卯 Metal Rabbit 風澤中孚 7 十一 3	水6 Water 5 Big Livestock 壬辰 Water Dragon 山天大畜 8 十二 4
金4 Metal 6 Eliminating 癸巳 Water Snake 澤天夬 9 十三 6	金9 Metal 7 Heaven 甲午 Wood Horse 乾爲天 10 十四 1	火7 Fire 8 Well 乙未 Wood Goat 水風井 11 十五 6	木8 Wood 9 Relief 丙申 Fire Monkey 雷水解 12 十六 4	金4 Metal 1 Influence 丁酉 Fire Rooster 澤山咸 13 十七 9	水1 Water 2 Humility 戊戌 Earth Dog 地山謙 14 十八 6	火2 Fire 3 Observation 己亥 Earth Pig 風地觀 15 十九 2
火2 Fire 4 Increasing 庚子 Metal Rat 風雷益 16 二十 9	水1 Water 5 Dimming Light 辛丑 Metal Ox 地火明夷 17 廿一 3	金9 Metal 6 Fellowship 壬寅 Water Tiger 天火同人 18 廿二 7	木8 Wood 7 Marrying Maiden 癸卯 Water Rabbit 雷澤歸妹 19 廿三 7	木3 Wood 8 Opposition 甲辰 Wood Dragon 火澤睽 20 廿四 2	火7 Fire 9 Waiting 乙巳 Wood Snake 水天需 21 廿五 3	金4 Metal 1 Great Exceeding 丙午 Fire Horse 澤風大過 22 廿六 3
水6 Water 2 Poison 丁未 Fire Goat 山風蠱 23 廿七 7	火2 Fire 3 Dispersing 戊申 Earth Monkey 風水渙 24 廿八 6	木3 Wood 4 Travelling 己酉 Earth Rooster 火山旅 25 廿九 8	金9 Metal 5 Stagnation 庚戌 Metal Dog 天地否 26 正月初一 9	火7 Fire 6 Alliance 辛亥 Metal Pig 水地比 27 初二 7	木8 Wood 7 Thunder 壬子 Water Rat 震爲雷 28 初三 1	水6 Water 8 Beauty 癸丑 Water Ox 山火賁 29 初四 8

FEBRUARY 2028 甲寅

Xuan Kong Element 玄空五行	水火既濟 Accomplished	Period Luck 卦運	Monthly Star 月星
Fire 火7		9	2

SUNDAY	MONDAY	TUESDAY	WEDNESDAY	THURSDAY	FRIDAY	SATURDAY
		金4 Metal 2 Marsh 丙辰 Fire Dragon 兌爲澤 1 初七 1	火2 Fire 3 Small Livestock 丁巳 Fire Snake 風天小畜 2 初八 8	木3 Wood 4 The Cauldron 戊午 Earth Horse 火風鼎 3 初九 4	水1 Water 5 Rising 己未 Earth Goat 地風升 4 初十 2	火7 Fire 6 Water 庚申 Metal Monkey 坎爲水 5 十一 1
木8 Wood 7 Lesser Exceeding 辛酉 Metal Rooster 雷山小過 6 十二 3	金4 Metal 8 Gathering 壬戌 Water Dog 澤地萃 7 十三 4	水6 Water 9 Peel 癸亥 Water Pig 山地剝 8 十四 6	水1 Water 1 Earth 甲子 Wood Rat 坤爲地 9 十五 1	木3 Wood 2 Biting 乙丑 Wood Ox 火雷噬嗑 10 十六 6	火2 Fire 3 Family 丙寅 Fire Tiger 風火家人 11 十七 4	水6 Water 4 Decreasing 丁卯 Fire Rabbit 山澤損 12 十八 9
金9 Metal 5 Tread 戊辰 Earth Dragon 天澤履 13 十九 6	木8 Wood 6 Great Strength 己巳 Earth Snake 雷天大壯 14 二十 2	木8 Wood 7 Consistency 庚午 Metal Horse 雷風恆 15 廿一 9	金9 Metal 8 Litigation 辛未 Metal Goat 天水訟 16 廿二 3	水1 Water 9 Officer 壬申 Water Monkey 地水師 17 廿三 7	火2 Fire 1 Gradual Progress 癸酉 Water Rooster 風山漸 18 廿四 7	火7 Fire 2 Obstruction 甲戌 Wood Dog 水山蹇 19 廿五 2
木3 Wood 3 Advancement 乙亥 Wood Pig 火地晉 20 廿六 3	水6 Water 4 Nourish 丙子 Fire Rat 山雷頤 21 廿七 3	金4 Metal 5 Following 丁丑 Fire Ox 澤雷隨 22 廿八 7	木8 Wood 6 Abundance 戊寅 Earth Tiger 雷火豐 23 廿九 6	火7 Fire 7 Regulate 己卯 Earth Rabbit 水澤節 24 三十 8	水1 Water 8 Unity 庚辰 Metal Dragon 地天泰 25 二月初一 9	木3 Wood 9 Great Reward 辛巳 Metal Snake 火天大有 26 初二 7
火2 Fire 1 Wind 壬午 Water Horse 巽爲風 27 初三 1	金4 Metal 2 Trap 癸未 Water Goat 澤水困 28 初四 8	木3 Wood 3 Not Yet Accomplished 甲申 Wood Monkey 火水未濟 29 初五 9				

MARCH 2028 乙卯

Xuan Kong Element 玄空五行	地澤臨	Period Luck 卦運	Monthly Star 月星
Water 水1	Arriving	4	1

SUNDAY	MONDAY	TUESDAY	WEDNESDAY	THURSDAY	FRIDAY	SATURDAY
			金9 Metal 4 Retreat 天山遯 乙酉 Wood Rooster **1** 初六 4	水6 Water 5 Mountain 艮爲山 丙戌 Fire Dog **2** 初七 1	木8 Wood 6 Delight 雷地豫 丁亥 Fire Pig **3** 初八 8	火7 Fire 7 Beginning 水雷屯 戊子 Earth Rat **4** 初九 4
金9 Metal 8 Without Wrongdoing 天雷無妄 己丑 Earth Ox **5** 初十 2	木3 Wood 9 Fire 離爲火 庚寅 Metal Tiger **6** 十一 1	火2 Fire 1 Sincerity 風澤中孚 辛卯 Metal Rabbit **7** 十二 3	水6 Water 2 Big Livestock 山天大畜 壬辰 Water Dragon **8** 十三 4	金4 Metal 3 Eliminating 澤天夬 癸巳 Water Snake **9** 十四 6	金9 Metal 4 Heaven 乾爲天 甲午 Wood Horse **10** 十五 1	火7 Fire 5 Well 水風井 乙未 Wood Goat **11** 十六 6
木8 Wood 6 Relief 雷水解 丙申 Fire Monkey **12** 十七 4	金4 Metal 7 Influence 澤山咸 丁酉 Fire Rooster **13** 十八 9	水1 Water 8 Humility 地山謙 戊戌 Earth Dog **14** 十九 6	火2 Fire 9 Observation 風地觀 己亥 Earth Pig **15** 二十 2	火2 Fire 1 Increasing 風雷益 庚子 Metal Rat **16** 廿一 9	水1 Water 2 Dimming Light 地火明夷 辛丑 Metal Ox **17** 廿二 3	金9 Metal 3 Fellowship 天火同人 壬寅 Water Tiger **18** 廿三 7
木8 Wood 4 Marrying Maiden 雷澤歸妹 癸卯 Water Rabbit **19** 廿四 7	木3 Wood 5 Opposition 火澤睽 甲辰 Wood Dragon **20** 廿五 2	火7 Fire 6 Waiting 水天需 乙巳 Wood Snake **21** 廿六 3	金4 Metal 7 Great Exceeding 澤風大過 丙午 Fire Horse **22** 廿七 3	水6 Water 8 Poison 山風蠱 丁未 Fire Goat **23** 廿八 7	火2 Fire 9 Dispersing 風水渙 戊申 Earth Monkey **24** 廿九 6	木3 Wood 1 Travelling 火山旅 己酉 Earth Rooster **25** 三十 8
金9 Metal 2 Stagnation 天地否 庚戌 Metal Dog **26** 三月初一 9	火7 Fire 3 Alliance 水地比 辛亥 Metal Pig **27** 初二 7	木8 Wood 4 Thunder 震爲雷 壬子 Water Rat **28** 初三 1	水6 Water 5 Beauty 山火賁 癸丑 Water Ox **29** 初四 8	火7 Fire 6 Accomplished 水火既濟 甲寅 Wood Tiger **30** 初五 9	水1 Water 7 Arriving 地澤臨 乙卯 Wood Rabbit **31** 初六 4	

APRIL 2028 丙辰

Xuan Kong Element 玄空五行	兑爲澤	Period Luck 卦運	Monthly Star 月星
Metal 金4	Marsh	1	9

SUNDAY	MONDAY	TUESDAY	WEDNESDAY	THURSDAY	FRIDAY	SATURDAY
金9 Metal 1 Retreat 天山遯 乙酉 Wood Rooster **30** 初六 4						金4 Metal 8 Marsh 兑爲澤 丙辰 Fire Dragon **1** 初七 1
火2 Fire 9 Small Livestock 風天小畜 丁巳 Fire Snake **2** 初八 8	木3 Wood 1 The Cauldron 火風鼎 戊午 Earth Horse **3** 初九 4	水1 Water 2 Rising 地風升 己未 Earth Goat **4** 初十 2	火7 Fire 3 Water 坎爲水 庚申 Metal Monkey **5** 十一 1	木8 Wood 4 Lesser Exceeding 雷山小過 辛酉 Metal Rooster **6** 十二 3	金4 Metal 5 Gathering 澤地萃 壬戌 Water Dog **7** 十三 4	水6 Water 6 Peel 山地剝 癸亥 Water Pig **8** 十四 6
水1 Water 7 Earth 坤爲地 甲子 Wood Rat **9** 十五 1	木3 Wood 8 Biting 火雷噬嗑 乙丑 Wood Ox **10** 十六 6	火2 Fire 9 Family 風火家人 丙寅 Fire Tiger **11** 十七 4	水6 Water 1 Decreasing 山澤損 丁卯 Fire Rabbit **12** 十八 9	金9 Metal 2 Tread 天澤履 戊辰 Earth Dragon **13** 十九 6	木8 Wood 3 Great Strength 雷天大壯 己巳 Earth Snake **14** 二十 2	木8 Wood 4 Consistency 雷風恆 庚午 Metal Horse **15** 廿一 9
金9 Metal 5 Litigation 天水訟 辛未 Metal Goat **16** 廿二 3	水1 Water 6 Officer 地水師 壬申 Water Monkey **17** 廿三 7	火2 Fire 7 Gradual Progress 風山漸 癸酉 Water Rooster **18** 廿四 7	火7 Fire 8 Obstruction 水山蹇 甲戌 Wood Dog **19** 廿五 2	木3 Wood 9 Advancement 火地晉 乙亥 Wood Pig **20** 廿六 3	水6 Water 1 Nourish 山雷頤 丙子 Fire Rat **21** 廿七 3	金4 Metal 2 Following 澤雷隨 丁丑 Fire Ox **22** 廿八 7
木8 Wood 3 Abundance 雷火豐 戊寅 Earth Tiger **23** 廿九 6	火7 Fire 4 Regulate 水澤節 己卯 Earth Rabbit **24** 三十 8	水1 Water 5 Unity 地天泰 庚辰 Metal Dragon **25** 四月初一 9	木3 Wood 6 Great Reward 火天大有 辛巳 Metal Snake **26** 初二 7	火2 Fire 7 Wind 巽爲風 壬午 Water Horse **27** 初三 1	金4 Metal 8 Trap 澤水困 癸未 Water Goat **28** 初四 8	木3 Wood 9 Not Yet Accomplished 火水未濟 甲申 Wood Monkey **29** 初五 9

MAY 2028 丁巳

Xuan Kong Element 玄空五行	風天小畜 Small Livestock	Period Luck 卦運	Monthly Star 月星
Fire 火2		8	8

SUNDAY	MONDAY	TUESDAY	WEDNESDAY	THURSDAY	FRIDAY	SATURDAY
	水6 Water Mountain 2 丙戌 Fire Dog 艮爲山 1 初七 1	木8 Wood Delight 3 丁亥 Fire Pig 雷地豫 2 初八 8	火7 Fire Beginning 4 戊子 Earth Rat 水雷屯 3 初九 4	金9 Metal Without Wrongdoing 5 己丑 Earth Ox 天雷無妄 4 初十 2	木3 Wood Fire 6 庚寅 Metal Tiger 離爲火 5 十一 1	火2 Fire Sincerity 7 辛卯 Metal Rabbit 風澤中孚 6 十二 3
水6 Water Big Livestock 8 壬辰 Water Dragon 山天大畜 7 十三 4	金4 Metal Eliminating 9 癸巳 Water Snake 澤天夬 8 十四 6	金9 Metal Heaven 1 甲午 Wood Horse 乾爲天 9 十五 1	火7 Fire Well 2 乙未 Wood Goat 水風井 10 十六 6	木8 Wood Relief 3 丙申 Fire Monkey 雷水解 11 十七 4	金4 Metal Influence 4 丁酉 Fire Rooster 澤山咸 12 十八 9	水1 Water Humility 5 戊戌 Earth Dog 地山謙 13 十九 6
火2 Fire Observation 6 己亥 Earth Pig 風地觀 14 二十 2	火2 Fire Increasing 7 庚子 Metal Rat 風雷益 15 廿一 9	水1 Water Dimming Light 8 辛丑 Metal Ox 地火明夷 16 廿二 3	金9 Metal Fellowship 9 壬寅 Water Tiger 天火同人 17 廿三 7	木8 Wood Marrying Maiden 1 癸卯 Water Rabbit 雷澤歸妹 18 廿四 7	木3 Wood Opposition 2 甲辰 Wood Dragon 火澤睽 19 廿五 2	火7 Fire Waiting 3 乙巳 Wood Snake 水天需 20 廿六 3
金4 Metal Great Exceeding 4 丙午 Fire Horse 澤風大過 21 廿七 3	水6 Water Poison 5 丁未 Fire Goat 山風蠱 22 廿八 7	火2 Fire Dispersing 6 戊申 Earth Monkey 風水渙 23 廿九 6	木3 Wood Travelling 7 己酉 Earth Rooster 火山旅 24 五月初一 8	金9 Metal Stagnation 8 庚戌 Metal Dog 天地否 25 初二 9	火7 Fire Alliance 9 辛亥 Metal Pig 水地比 26 初三 7	木8 Wood Thunder 1 壬子 Water Rat 震爲雷 27 初四 1
水6 Water Beauty 2 癸丑 Water Ox 山火賁 28 初五 8	火7 Fire Accomplished 3 甲寅 Wood Tiger 水火既濟 29 初六 9	水1 Water Arriving 4 乙卯 Wood Rabbit 地澤臨 30 初七 4	金4 Metal Marsh 5 丙辰 Fire Dragon 兌爲澤 31 初八 1			

JUNE 2028 戊午

Xuan Kong Element 玄空五行	火風鼎 The Cauldron	Period Luck 卦運	Monthly Star 月星
Wood 木3		4	7

SUNDAY	MONDAY	TUESDAY	WEDNESDAY	THURSDAY	FRIDAY	SATURDAY
				火2 Fire Small Livestock 6 丁巳 Fire Snake 風天小畜 1 初九 8	木3 Wood The Cauldron 7 戊午 Earth Horse 火風鼎 2 初十 4	水1 Water Rising 8 己未 Earth Goat 地風升 3 十一 2
火7 Fire Water 9 庚申 Metal Monkey 坎爲水 4 十二 1	木8 Wood Lesser Exceeding 1 辛酉 Metal Rooster 雷山小過 5 十三 3	金4 Metal Gathering 2 壬戌 Water Dog 澤地萃 6 十四 4	水6 Water Peel 3 癸亥 Water Pig 山地剝 7 十五 6	水1 Water Earth 4 甲子 Wood Rat 坤爲地 8 十六 1	木3 Wood Biting 5 乙丑 Wood Ox 火雷噬嗑 9 十七 6	火2 Fire Family 6 丙寅 Fire Tiger 風火家人 10 十八 4
水6 Water Decreasing 7 丁卯 Fire Rabbit 山澤損 11 十九 9	金9 Metal Tread 8 戊辰 Earth Dragon 天澤履 12 二十 6	木8 Wood Great Strength 9 己巳 Earth Snake 雷天大壯 13 廿一 2	木8 Wood Consistency 1 庚午 Metal Horse 雷風恆 14 廿二 9	金9 Metal Litigation 2 辛未 Metal Goat 天水訟 15 廿三 3	水1 Water Officer 3 壬申 Water Monkey 地水師 16 廿四 7	火2 Fire Gradual Progress 4 癸酉 Water Rooster 風山漸 17 廿五 7
火7 Fire Obstruction 5 甲戌 Wood Dog 水山蹇 18 廿六 2	木3 Wood Advancement 6 乙亥 Wood Pig 火地晉 19 廿七 3	水6 Water Nourish 7 丙子 Fire Rat 山雷頤 20 廿八 3	金4 Metal Following 8/2 丁丑 Fire Ox 澤雷隨 21 廿九 7	木8 Wood Abundance 1 戊寅 Earth Tiger 雷火豐 22 三十 6	火7 Fire Regulate 9 己卯 Earth Rabbit 水澤節 23 閏五月初一 8	水1 Water Unity 8 庚辰 Metal Dragon 地天泰 24 初二 9
木3 Wood Great Reward 7 辛巳 Metal Snake 火天大有 25 初三 7	火2 Fire Wind 6 壬午 Water Horse 巽爲風 26 初四 1	金4 Metal Trap 5 癸未 Water Goat 澤水困 27 初五 8	木3 Wood Not Yet Accomplished 4 甲申 Wood Monkey 火水未濟 28 初六 9	金9 Metal Retreat 3 乙酉 Wood Rooster 天山遯 29 初七 4	水6 Water Mountain 2 丙戌 Fire Dog 艮爲山 30 初八 1	

JULY 2028 己未

Xuan Kong Element 玄空五行	地風升 Rising	Period Luck 卦運	Monthly Star 月星
Water 水1		2	6

SUNDAY	MONDAY	TUESDAY	WEDNESDAY	THURSDAY	FRIDAY	SATURDAY
金4 Metal 8 Marsh 兌爲澤 丙辰 Fire Dragon 30 初九 1	火2 Fire 7 Small Livestock 風天小畜 丁巳 Fire Snake 31 初十 8					木8 Wood 1 Delight 雷地豫 丁亥 Fire Pig 1 初九 8
火7 Fire 9 Beginning 水雷屯 戊子 Earth Rat 2 初十 4	金9 Metal 8 Without Wrongdoing 天雷無妄 己丑 Earth Ox 3 十一 2	木3 Wood 7 Fire 離爲火 庚寅 Metal Tiger 4 十二 1	火2 Fire 6 Sincerity 風澤中孚 辛卯 Metal Rabbit 5 十三 3	水6 Water 5 Big Livestock 山天大畜 壬辰 Water Dragon 6 十四 4	金4 Metal 4 Eliminating 澤天夬 癸巳 Water Snake 7 十五 6	金9 Metal 3 Heaven 乾爲天 甲午 Wood Horse 8 十六 1
火7 Fire 2 Well 水風井 乙未 Wood Goat 9 十七 6	木8 Wood 1 Relief 雷水解 丙申 Fire Monkey 10 十八 4	金4 Metal 9 Influence 澤山咸 丁酉 Fire Rooster 11 十九 9	水1 Water 8 Humility 地山謙 戊戌 Earth Dog 12 二十 6	火2 Fire 7 Observation 風地觀 己亥 Earth Pig 13 廿一 2	火2 Fire 6 Increasing 風雷益 庚子 Metal Rat 14 廿二 9	水1 Water 5 Dimming Light 地火明夷 辛丑 Metal Ox 15 廿三 3
金9 Metal 4 Fellowship 天火同人 壬寅 Water Tiger 16 廿四 7	木8 Wood 3 Marrying Maiden 雷澤歸妹 癸卯 Water Rabbit 17 廿五 7	木3 Wood 2 Opposition 火澤睽 甲辰 Wood Dragon 18 廿六 2	火7 Fire 1 Waiting 水天需 乙巳 Wood Snake 19 廿七 3	金4 Metal 9 Great Exceeding 澤風大過 丙午 Fire Horse 20 廿八 3	水6 Water 8 Poison 山風蠱 丁未 Fire Goat 21 廿九 7	火2 Fire 7 Dispersing 風水渙 戊申 Earth Monkey 22 六月初一 6
木3 Wood 6 Travelling 火山旅 己酉 Earth Rooster 23 初二 8	金9 Metal 5 Stagnation 天地否 庚戌 Metal Dog 24 初三 9	火7 Fire 4 Alliance 水地比 辛亥 Metal Pig 25 初四 7	木8 Wood 3 Thunder 震爲雷 壬子 Water Rat 26 初五 1	水6 Water 2 Beauty 山火賁 癸丑 Water Ox 27 初六 8	火7 Fire 1 Accomplished 水火既濟 甲寅 Wood Tiger 28 初七 9	水1 Water 9 Arriving 地澤臨 乙卯 Wood Rabbit 29 初八 4

AUGUST 2028 庚申

Xuan Kong Element 玄空五行	坎爲水 Water	Period Luck 卦運	Monthly Star 月星
Fire 火7		1	5

SUNDAY	MONDAY	TUESDAY	WEDNESDAY	THURSDAY	FRIDAY	SATURDAY
		木3 Wood 6 The Cauldron 火風鼎 戊午 Earth Horse 1 十一 4	水1 Water 5 Rising 地風升 己未 Earth Goat 2 十二 2	火7 Fire 4 Water 坎爲水 庚申 Metal Monkey 3 十三 1	木8 Wood 3 Lesser Exceeding 雷山小過 辛酉 Metal Rooster 4 十四 3	金4 Metal 2 Gathering 澤地萃 壬戌 Water Dog 5 十五 4
水6 Water 1 Peel 山地剝 癸亥 Water Pig 6 十六 6	水1 Water 9 Earth 坤爲地 甲子 Wood Rat 7 十七 1	木3 Wood 8 Biting 火雷噬嗑 乙丑 Wood Ox 8 十八 6	火2 Fire 7 Family 風火家人 丙寅 Fire Tiger 9 十九 4	水6 Water 6 Decreasing 山澤損 丁卯 Fire Rabbit 10 二十 9	金9 Metal 5 Tread 天澤履 戊辰 Earth Dragon 11 廿一 6	木8 Wood 4 Great Strength 雷天大壯 己巳 Earth Snake 12 廿二 2
木8 Wood 3 Consistency 雷風恒 庚午 Metal Horse 13 廿三 9	金9 Metal 2 Litigation 天水訟 辛未 Metal Goat 14 廿四 3	水1 Water 1 Officer 地水師 壬申 Water Monkey 15 廿五 7	火2 Fire 9 Gradual Progress 風山漸 癸酉 Water Rooster 16 廿六 7	火7 Fire 8 Obstruction 水山蹇 甲戌 Wood Dog 17 廿七 2	木3 Wood 7 Advancement 火地晉 乙亥 Wood Pig 18 廿八 3	水6 Water 6 Nourish 山雷頤 丙子 Fire Rat 19 廿九 3
金4 Metal 5 Following 澤雷隨 丁丑 Fire Ox 20 七月初一 7	木8 Wood 4 Abundance 雷火豐 戊寅 Earth Tiger 21 初二 6	火7 Fire 3 Regulate 水澤節 己卯 Earth Rabbit 22 初三 8	水1 Water 2 Unity 地天泰 庚辰 Metal Dragon 23 初四 9	木3 Wood 1 Great Reward 火天大有 辛巳 Metal Snake 24 初五 7	火2 Fire 9 Wind 巽爲風 壬午 Water Horse 25 初六 1	金4 Metal 8 Trap 澤水困 癸未 Water Goat 26 初七 8
木3 Wood 7 Not Yet Accomplished 火水未濟 甲申 Wood Monkey 27 初八 9	金9 Metal 6 Retreat 天山遯 乙酉 Wood Rooster 28 初九 4	水6 Water 5 Mountain 艮爲山 丙戌 Fire Dog 29 初十 1	木8 Wood 4 Delight 雷地豫 丁亥 Fire Pig 30 十一 8	火7 Fire 3 Beginning 水雷屯 戊子 Earth Rat 31 十二 4		

SEPTEMBER 2028 辛酉

Xuan Kong Element 玄空五行	雷山小過	Period Luck 卦運	Monthly Star 月星
Wood 木8	Lesser Exceeding	3	4

SUNDAY	MONDAY	TUESDAY	WEDNESDAY	THURSDAY	FRIDAY	SATURDAY
					1 十三 · 金9 Metal · 己丑 Earth Ox · Without Wrongdoing 天雷無妄 · 2 · 2	**2** 十四 · 木3 Wood · 庚寅 Metal Tiger · Fire 離爲火 · 1 · 1
3 十五 · 火2 Fire · 辛卯 Metal Rabbit · Sincerity 風澤中孚 · 9 · 3	**4** 十六 · 水6 Water · 壬辰 Water Dragon · Big Livestock 山天大畜 · 8 · 4	**5** 十七 · 金4 Metal · 癸巳 Water Snake · Eliminating 澤天夬 · 7 · 6	**6** 十八 · 金9 Metal · 甲午 Wood Horse · Heaven 乾爲天 · 6 · 1	**7** 十九 · 火7 Fire · 乙未 Wood Goat · Well 水風井 · 5 · 6	**8** 二十 · 木8 Wood · 丙申 Fire Monkey · Relief 雷水解 · 4 · 4	**9** 廿一 · 金4 Metal · 丁酉 Fire Rooster · Influence 澤山咸 · 3 · 9
10 廿二 · 水1 Water · 戊戌 Earth Dog · Humility 地山謙 · 2 · 6	**11** 廿三 · 火2 Fire · 己亥 Earth Pig · Observation 風地觀 · 1 · 2	**12** 廿四 · 火2 Fire · 庚子 Metal Rat · Increasing 風雷益 · 9 · 9	**13** 廿五 · 水1 Water · 辛丑 Metal Ox · Dimming Light 地火明夷 · 8 · 3	**14** 廿六 · 金9 Metal · 壬寅 Water Tiger · Fellowship 天火同人 · 7 · 7	**15** 廿七 · 木8 Wood · 癸卯 Water Rabbit · Marrying Maiden 雷澤歸妹 · 6 · 7	**16** 廿八 · 木3 Wood · 甲辰 Wood Dragon · Opposition 火澤睽 · 5 · 2
17 廿九 · 火7 Fire · 乙巳 Wood Snake · Waiting 水天需 · 4 · 3	**18** 三十 · 金4 Metal · 丙午 Fire Horse · Great Exceeding 澤風大過 · 3 · 3	**19** 八月初一 · 水6 Water · 丁未 Fire Goat · Poison 山風蠱 · 2 · 7	**20** 初二 · 火2 Fire · 戊申 Earth Monkey · Dispersing 風水渙 · 1 · 6	**21** 初三 · 木3 Wood · 己酉 Earth Rooster · Travelling 火山旅 · 9 · 8	**22** 初四 · 金9 Metal · 庚戌 Metal Dog · Stagnation 天地否 · 8 · 9	**23** 初五 · 火7 Fire · 辛亥 Metal Pig · Alliance 水地比 · 7 · 7
24 初六 · 木8 Wood · 壬子 Water Rat · Thunder 震爲雷 · 6 · 1	**25** 初七 · 水6 Water · 癸丑 Water Ox · Beauty 山火賁 · 5 · 8	**26** 初八 · 火7 Fire · 甲寅 Wood Tiger · Accomplished 水火既濟 · 4 · 9	**27** 初九 · 水1 Water · 乙卯 Wood Rabbit · Arriving 地澤臨 · 3 · 4	**28** 初十 · 金4 Metal · 丙辰 Fire Dragon · Marsh 兌爲澤 · 2 · 1	**29** 十一 · 火2 Fire · 丁巳 Fire Snake · Small Livestock 風天小畜 · 1 · 8	**30** 十二 · 木3 Wood · 戊午 Earth Horse · The Cauldron 火風鼎 · 9 · 4

OCTOBER 2028 壬戌

Xuan Kong Element 玄空五行	澤地萃	Period Luck 卦運	Monthly Star 月星
Metal 金4	Gathering	4	3

SUNDAY	MONDAY	TUESDAY	WEDNESDAY	THURSDAY	FRIDAY	SATURDAY
1 十三 · 水1 Water · 己未 Earth Goat · Rising 地風升 · 8 · 2	**2** 十四 · 火7 Fire · 庚申 Metal Monkey · Water 坎爲水 · 7 · 1	**3** 十五 · 木8 Wood · 辛酉 Metal Rooster · Lesser Exceeding 雷山小過 · 6 · 3	**4** 十六 · 金4 Metal · 壬戌 Water Dog · Gathering 澤地萃 · 5 · 4	**5** 十七 · 水6 Water · 癸亥 Water Pig · Peel 山地剝 · 4 · 6	**6** 十八 · 水1 Water · 甲子 Wood Rat · Earth 坤爲地 · 3 · 1	**7** 十九 · 木3 Wood · 乙丑 Wood Ox · Biting 火雷噬嗑 · 2 · 6
8 二十 · 火2 Fire · 丙寅 Fire Tiger · Family 風火家人 · 1 · 4	**9** 廿一 · 水6 Water · 丁卯 Fire Rabbit · Decreasing 山澤損 · 9 · 9	**10** 廿二 · 金9 Metal · 戊辰 Earth Dragon · Tread 天澤履 · 8 · 6	**11** 廿三 · 木8 Wood · 己巳 Earth Snake · Great Strength 雷天大壯 · 7 · 2	**12** 廿四 · 木8 Wood · 庚午 Metal Horse · Consistency 雷風恆 · 6 · 9	**13** 廿五 · 金9 Metal · 辛未 Metal Goat · Litigation 天水訟 · 5 · 3	**14** 廿六 · 水1 Water · 壬申 Water Monkey · Officer 地水師 · 4 · 7
15 廿七 · 火2 Fire · 癸酉 Water Rooster · Gradual Progress 風山漸 · 3 · 7	**16** 廿八 · 火7 Fire · 甲戌 Wood Dog · Obstruction 水山蹇 · 2 · 2	**17** 廿九 · 木3 Wood · 乙亥 Wood Pig · Advancement 火地晉 · 1 · 3	**18** 九月初一 · 水6 Water · 丙子 Fire Rat · Nourish 山雷頤 · 9 · 3	**19** 初二 · 金4 Metal · 丁丑 Fire Ox · Following 澤雷隨 · 8 · 7	**20** 初三 · 木8 Wood · 戊寅 Earth Tiger · Abundance 雷火豐 · 7 · 6	**21** 初四 · 火7 Fire · 己卯 Earth Rabbit · Regulate 水澤節 · 6 · 8
22 初五 · 水1 Water · 庚辰 Metal Dragon · Unity 地天泰 · 5 · 9	**23** 初六 · 木3 Wood · 辛巳 Metal Snake · Great Reward 火天大有 · 4 · 7	**24** 初七 · 火2 Fire · 壬午 Water Horse · Wind 巽爲風 · 3 · 1	**25** 初八 · 金4 Metal · 癸未 Water Goat · Trap 澤水困 · 2 · 8	**26** 初九 · 木3 Wood · 甲申 Wood Monkey · Not Yet Accomplished 火水未濟 · 1 · 9	**27** 初十 · 金9 Metal · 乙酉 Wood Rooster · Retreat 天山遯 · 9 · 4	**28** 十一 · 水6 Water · 丙戌 Fire Dog · Mountain 艮爲山 · 8 · 1
29 十二 · 木8 Wood · 丁亥 Fire Pig · Delight 雷地豫 · 7 · 8	**30** 十三 · 火7 Fire · 戊子 Earth Rat · Beginning 水雷屯 · 6 · 4	**31** 十四 · 金9 Metal · 己丑 Earth Ox · Without Wrongdoing 天雷無妄 · 5 · 2				

NOVEMBER 2028 癸亥

Xuan Kong Element 玄空五行	山地剝 Peel	Period Luck 卦運	Monthly Star 月星
Water 水6		6	2

SUNDAY	MONDAY	TUESDAY	WEDNESDAY	THURSDAY	FRIDAY	SATURDAY
			1 十五 木3 Wood 庚寅 Metal Tiger Fire 離為火 4 · 1	**2** 十六 火2 Fire 辛卯 Metal Rabbit Sincerity 風澤中孚 3 · 3	**3** 十七 水6 Water 壬辰 Water Dragon Big Livestock 山天大畜 2 · 4	**4** 十八 金4 Metal 癸巳 Water Snake Eliminating 澤天夬 1 · 6
5 十九 金9 Metal 甲午 Wood Horse Heaven 乾為天 9 · 1	**6** 二十 火7 Fire 乙未 Wood Goat Well 水風井 8 · 6	**7** 廿一 木8 Wood 丙申 Fire Monkey Relief 雷水解 7 · 4	**8** 廿二 金4 Metal 丁酉 Fire Rooster Influence 澤山咸 6 · 9	**9** 廿三 水1 Water 戊戌 Earth Dog Humility 地山謙 5 · 6	**10** 廿四 火2 Fire 己亥 Earth Pig Observation 風地觀 4 · 2	**11** 廿五 火2 Fire 庚子 Metal Rat Increasing 風雷益 3 · 9
12 廿六 水1 Water 辛丑 Metal Ox Dimming Light 地火明夷 2 · 3	**13** 廿七 金9 Metal 壬寅 Water Tiger Fellowship 天火同人 1 · 7	**14** 廿八 木8 Wood 癸卯 Water Rabbit Marrying Maiden 雷澤歸妹 9 · 7	**15** 廿九 木3 Wood 甲辰 Wood Dragon Opposition 火澤睽 8 · 2	**16** 十月初一 火7 Fire 乙巳 Wood Snake Waiting 水天需 7 · 3	**17** 初二 金4 Metal 丙午 Fire Horse Great Exceeding 澤風大過 6 · 3	**18** 初三 水6 Water 丁未 Fire Goat Poison 山風蠱 5 · 7
19 初四 火2 Fire 戊申 Earth Monkey Dispersing 風水渙 4 · 6	**20** 初五 木3 Wood 己酉 Earth Rooster Travelling 火山旅 3 · 8	**21** 初六 金9 Metal 庚戌 Metal Dog Stagnation 天地否 2 · 9	**22** 初七 火7 Fire 辛亥 Metal Pig Alliance 水地比 1 · 7	**23** 初八 木8 Wood 壬子 Water Rat Thunder 震為雷 9 · 1	**24** 初九 水6 Water 癸丑 Water Ox Beauty 山火賁 8 · 8	**25** 初十 火7 Fire 甲寅 Wood Tiger Accomplished 水火既濟 7 · 9
26 十一 水1 Water 乙卯 Wood Rabbit Arriving 地澤臨 6 · 4	**27** 十二 金4 Metal 丙辰 Fire Dragon Marsh 兌為澤 5 · 1	**28** 十三 火2 Fire 丁巳 Fire Snake Small Livestock 風天小畜 4 · 8	**29** 十四 木3 Wood 戊午 Earth Horse The Cauldron 火風鼎 3 · 4	**30** 十五 水1 Water 己未 Earth Goat Rising 地風升 2 · 2		

DECEMBER 2028 甲子

Xuan Kong Element 玄空五行	坤為地 Earth	Period Luck 卦運	Monthly Star 月星
Water 水1		1	1

SUNDAY	MONDAY	TUESDAY	WEDNESDAY	THURSDAY	FRIDAY	SATURDAY
31 十六 木3 Wood 庚寅 Metal Tiger Fire 離為火 3 · 1					**1** 十六 火7 Fire 庚申 Metal Monkey Water 坎為水 1 · 1	**2** 十七 木8 Wood 辛酉 Metal Rooster Lesser Exceeding 雷山小過 9 · 3
3 十八 金4 Metal 壬戌 Water Dog Gathering 澤地萃 8 · 4	**4** 十九 水6 Water 癸亥 Water Pig Peel 山地剝 7 · 6	**5** 二十 水1 Water 甲子 Wood Rat Earth 坤為地 6 · 1	**6** 廿一 木3 Wood 乙丑 Wood Ox Biting 火雷噬嗑 5 · 6	**7** 廿二 火2 Fire 丙寅 Fire Tiger Family 風火家人 4 · 4	**8** 廿三 水6 Water 丁卯 Fire Rabbit Decreasing 山澤損 3 · 9	**9** 廿四 金9 Metal 戊辰 Earth Dragon Tread 天澤履 2 · 6
10 廿五 木8 Wood 己巳 Earth Snake Great Strength 雷天大壯 1 · 2	**11** 廿六 木8 Wood 庚午 Metal Horse Consistency 雷風恆 9 · 9	**12** 廿七 金9 Metal 辛未 Metal Goat Litigation 天水訟 8 · 3	**13** 廿八 水1 Water 壬申 Water Monkey Officer 地水師 7 · 7	**14** 廿九 火2 Fire 癸酉 Water Rooster Gradual Progress 風山漸 6 · 7	**15** 三十 火7 Fire 甲戌 Wood Dog Obstruction 水山蹇 5 · 2	**16** 十一月初一 木3 Wood 乙亥 Wood Pig Advancement 火地晉 4 · 3
17 初二 水6 Water 丙子 Fire Rat Nourish 山雷頤 3 · 3	**18** 初三 金4 Metal 丁丑 Fire Ox Following 澤雷隨 2 · 7	**19** 初四 木8 Wood 戊寅 Earth Tiger Abundance 雷火豐 1 · 6	**20** 初五 火7 Fire 己卯 Earth Rabbit Regulate 水澤節 9 · 8	**21** 初六 水1 Water 庚辰 Metal Dragon Unity 地天泰 8/2 · 9	**22** 初七 木3 Wood 辛巳 Metal Snake Great Reward 火天大有 3 · 7	**23** 初八 火2 Fire 壬午 Water Horse Wind 巽為風 4 · 1
24 初九 金4 Metal 癸未 Water Goat Trap 澤水困 5 · 8	**25** 初十 木3 Wood 甲申 Wood Monkey Not Yet Accomplished 火水未濟 6 · 9	**26** 十一 金9 Metal 乙酉 Wood Rooster Retreat 天山遯 7 · 4	**27** 十二 水6 Water 丙戌 Fire Dog Mountain 艮為山 8 · 1	**28** 十三 木8 Wood 丁亥 Fire Pig Delight 雷地豫 9 · 8	**29** 十四 火7 Fire 戊子 Earth Rat Beginning 水雷屯 1 · 4	**30** 十五 金9 Metal 己丑 Earth Ox Without Wrongdoing 天雷無妄 2 · 2

2029 己酉

(*Ji You*) Earth Rooster

2029 己酉 *(Ji You)* Earth Rooster

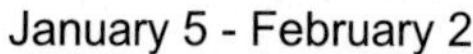

January 5 - February 2

February 3 - March 4

March 5 - April 3

April 4 - May 4

May 5 - June 4

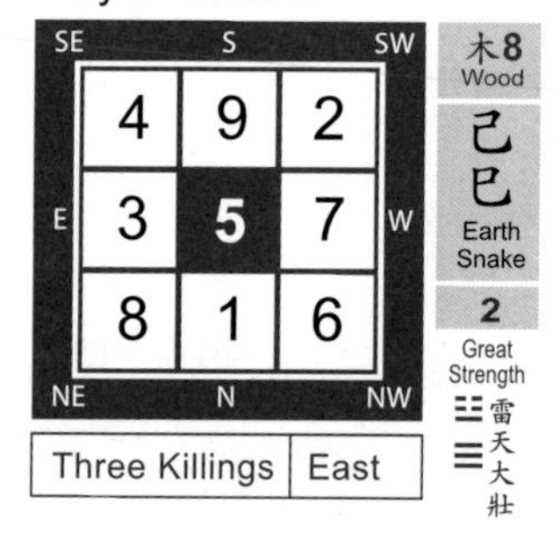

June 5 - July 6

July 7 - August 6

August 7 - September 6

September 7 - October 7

October 8 - November 6

November 7 - December 6

December 7 - January 4

JANUARY 2029 乙丑

Xuan Kong Element 玄空五行	火雷噬嗑 Biting	Period Luck 卦運	Monthly Star 月星
Wood 木3		6	9

SUNDAY	MONDAY	TUESDAY	WEDNESDAY	THURSDAY	FRIDAY	SATURDAY
	火2 Fire 辛卯 Metal Rabbit 3 Sincerity 風澤中孚 4 1 十七	水6 Water 壬辰 Water Dragon 4 Big Livestock 山天大畜 5 2 十八	金4 Metal 癸巳 Water Snake 6 Eliminating 澤天夬 6 3 十九	金9 Metal 甲午 Wood Horse 1 Heaven 乾爲天 7 4 二十	火7 Fire 乙未 Wood Goat 6 Well 水風井 8 5 廿一	木8 Wood 丙申 Fire Monkey 4 Relief 雷水解 9 6 廿二
金4 Metal 丁酉 Fire Rooster 9 Influence 澤山咸 1 7 廿三	水1 Water 戊戌 Earth Dog 6 Humility 地山謙 2 8 廿四	火2 Fire 己亥 Earth Pig 2 Observation 風地觀 3 9 廿五	火2 Fire 庚子 Metal Rat 9 Increasing 風雷益 4 10 廿六	水1 Water 辛丑 Metal Ox 3 Dimming Light 地火明夷 5 11 廿七	金9 Metal 壬寅 Water Tiger 7 Fellowship 天火同人 6 12 廿八	木8 Wood 癸卯 Water Rabbit 7 Marrying Maiden 雷澤歸妹 7 13 廿九
木3 Wood 甲辰 Wood Dragon 2 Opposition 火澤睽 8 14 三十	火7 Fire 乙巳 Wood Snake 3 Waiting 水天需 9 15 十二月初一	金4 Metal 丙午 Fire Horse 3 Great Exceeding 澤風大過 1 16 初二	水6 Water 丁未 Fire Goat 7 Poison 山風蠱 2 17 初三	火2 Fire 戊申 Earth Monkey 6 Dispersing 風水渙 3 18 初四	木3 Wood 己酉 Earth Rooster 8 Travelling 火山旅 4 19 初五	金9 Metal 庚戌 Metal Dog 9 Stagnation 天地否 5 20 初六
火7 Fire 辛亥 Metal Pig 7 Alliance 水地比 6 21 初七	木8 Wood 壬子 Water Rat 1 Thunder 震爲雷 7 22 初八	水6 Water 癸丑 Water Ox 8 Beauty 山火賁 8 23 初九	火7 Fire 甲寅 Wood Tiger 9 Accomplished 水火既濟 9 24 初十	水1 Water 乙卯 Wood Rabbit 4 Arriving 地澤臨 1 25 十一	金4 Metal 丙辰 Fire Dragon 1 Marsh 兑爲澤 2 26 十二	火2 Fire 丁巳 Fire Snake 8 Small Livestock 風天小畜 3 27 十三
木3 Wood 戊午 Earth Horse 4 The Cauldron 火風鼎 4 28 十四	水1 Water 己未 Earth Goat 2 Rising 地風升 5 29 十五	火7 Fire 庚申 Metal Monkey 1 Water 坎爲水 6 30 十六	木8 Wood 辛酉 Metal Rooster 3 Lesser Exceeding 雷山小過 7 31 十七			

FEBRUARY 2029 丙寅

Xuan Kong Element 玄空五行	風火家人 Family	Period Luck 卦運	Monthly Star 月星
Fire 火2		4	8

SUNDAY	MONDAY	TUESDAY	WEDNESDAY	THURSDAY	FRIDAY	SATURDAY
				金4 Metal 壬戌 Water Dog 4 Gathering 澤地萃 8 1 十八	水6 Water 癸亥 Water Pig 6 Peel 山地剝 9 2 十九	水1 Water 甲子 Wood Rat 1 Earth 坤爲地 1 3 二十
木3 Wood 乙丑 Wood Ox 6 Biting 火雷噬嗑 2 4 廿一	火2 Fire 丙寅 Fire Tiger 4 Family 風火家人 3 5 廿二	水6 Water 丁卯 Fire Rabbit 9 Decreasing 山澤損 4 6 廿三	金9 Metal 戊辰 Earth Dragon 6 Tread 天澤履 5 7 廿四	木8 Wood 己巳 Earth Snake 2 Great Strength 雷天大壯 6 8 廿五	木8 Wood 庚午 Metal Horse 9 Consistency 雷風恆 7 9 廿六	金9 Metal 辛未 Metal Goat 3 Litigation 天水訟 8 10 廿七
水1 Water 壬申 Water Monkey 7 Officer 地水師 9 11 廿八	火2 Fire 癸酉 Water Rooster 7 Gradual Progress 風山漸 1 12 廿九	火7 Fire 甲戌 Wood Dog 2 Obstruction 水山蹇 2 13 正月初一	木3 Wood 乙亥 Wood Pig 3 Advancement 火地晉 3 14 初二	水6 Water 丙子 Fire Rat 3 Nourish 山雷頤 4 15 初三	金4 Metal 丁丑 Fire Ox 7 Following 澤雷隨 5 16 初四	木8 Wood 戊寅 Earth Tiger 6 Abundance 雷火豐 6 17 初五
火7 Fire 己卯 Earth Rabbit 8 Regulate 水澤節 7 18 初六	水1 Water 庚辰 Metal Dragon 9 Unity 地天泰 8 19 初七	木3 Wood 辛巳 Metal Snake 7 Great Reward 火天大有 9 20 初八	火2 Fire 壬午 Water Horse 1 Wind 巽爲風 1 21 初九	金4 Metal 癸未 Water Goat 8 Trap 澤水困 2 22 初十	木3 Wood 甲申 Wood Monkey 9 Not Yet Accomplished 火水未濟 3 23 十一	金9 Metal 乙酉 Wood Rooster 4 Retreat 天山遯 4 24 十二
水6 Water 丙戌 Fire Dog 1 Mountain 艮爲山 5 25 十三	木8 Wood 丁亥 Fire Pig 8 Delight 雷地豫 6 26 十四	火7 Fire 戊子 Earth Rat 4 Beginning 水雷屯 7 27 十五	金9 Metal 己丑 Earth Ox 2 Without Wrongdoing 天雷無妄 8 28 十六			

MARCH 2029 丁卯

Xuan Kong Element 玄空五行	山澤損 Decreasing	Period Luck 卦運	Monthly Star 月星
Water 水6		9	7

SUNDAY	MONDAY	TUESDAY	WEDNESDAY	THURSDAY	FRIDAY	SATURDAY
				木3 Wood [9] Fire 離為火 庚寅 Metal Tiger **1** 十七 1	火2 Fire [1] Sincerity 風澤中孚 辛卯 Metal Rabbit **2** 十八 3	水6 Water [2] Big Livestock 山天大畜 壬辰 Water Dragon **3** 十九 4
金4 Metal [3] Eliminating 澤天夬 癸巳 Water Snake **4** 二十 6	金9 Metal [4] Heaven 乾為天 甲午 Wood Horse **5** 廿一 1	火7 Fire [5] Well 水風井 乙未 Wood Goat **6** 廿二 6	木8 Wood [6] Relief 雷水解 丙申 Fire Monkey **7** 廿三 4	金4 Metal [7] Influence 澤山咸 丁酉 Fire Rooster **8** 廿四 9	水1 Water [8] Humility 地山謙 戊戌 Earth Dog **9** 廿五 6	火2 Fire [9] Observation 風地觀 己亥 Earth Pig **10** 廿六 2
火2 Fire [1] Increasing 風雷益 庚子 Metal Rat **11** 廿七 9	水1 Water [2] Dimming Light 地火明夷 辛丑 Metal Ox **12** 廿八 3	金9 Metal [3] Fellowship 天火同人 壬寅 Water Tiger **13** 廿九 7	木8 Wood [4] Marrying Maiden 雷澤歸妹 癸卯 Water Rabbit **14** 三十 7	木3 Wood [5] Opposition 火澤睽 甲辰 Wood Dragon **15** 二月初一 2	火7 Fire [6] Waiting 水天需 乙巳 Wood Snake **16** 初二 3	金4 Metal [7] Great Exceeding 澤風大過 丙午 Fire Horse **17** 初三 3
水6 Water [8] Poison 山風蠱 丁未 Fire Goat **18** 初四 7	火2 Fire [9] Dispersing 風水渙 戊申 Earth Monkey **19** 初五 6	木3 Wood [1] Travelling 火山旅 己酉 Earth Rooster **20** 初六 8	金9 Metal [2] Stagnation 天地否 庚戌 Metal Dog **21** 初七 9	火7 Fire [3] Alliance 水地比 辛亥 Metal Pig **22** 初八 7	木8 Wood [4] Thunder 震為雷 壬子 Water Rat **23** 初九 1	水6 Water [5] Beauty 山火賁 癸丑 Water Ox **24** 初十 8
火7 Fire [6] Accomplished 水火既濟 甲寅 Wood Tiger **25** 十一 9	水1 Water [7] Arriving 地澤臨 乙卯 Wood Rabbit **26** 十二 4	金4 Metal [8] Marsh 兌為澤 丙辰 Fire Dragon **27** 十三 1	火2 Fire [9] Small Livestock 風天小畜 丁巳 Fire Snake **28** 十四 8	木3 Wood [1] The Cauldron 火風鼎 戊午 Earth Horse **29** 十五 4	水1 Water [2] Rising 地風升 己未 Earth Goat **30** 十六 2	火7 Fire [3] Water 坎為水 庚申 Metal Monkey **31** 十七 1

APRIL 2029 戊辰

Xuan Kong Element 玄空五行	天澤履 Tread	Period Luck 卦運	Monthly Star 月星
Metal 金9		6	6

SUNDAY	MONDAY	TUESDAY	WEDNESDAY	THURSDAY	FRIDAY	SATURDAY
木8 Wood [4] Lesser Exceeding 雷山小過 辛酉 Metal Rooster **1** 十八 3	金4 Metal [5] Gathering 澤地萃 壬戌 Water Dog **2** 十九 4	水6 Water [6] Peel 山地剝 癸亥 Water Pig **3** 二十 6	水1 Water [7] Earth 坤為地 甲子 Wood Rat **4** 廿一 1	木3 Wood [8] Biting 火雷噬嗑 乙丑 Wood Ox **5** 廿二 6	火2 Fire [9] Family 風火家人 丙寅 Fire Tiger **6** 廿三 4	水6 Water [1] Decreasing 山澤損 丁卯 Fire Rabbit **7** 廿四 9
金9 Metal [2] Tread 天澤履 戊辰 Earth Dragon **8** 廿五 6	木8 Wood [3] Great Strength 雷天大壯 己巳 Earth Snake **9** 廿六 2	木8 Wood [4] Consistency 雷風恆 庚午 Metal Horse **10** 廿七 9	金9 Metal [5] Litigation 天水訟 辛未 Metal Goat **11** 廿八 3	水1 Water [6] Officer 地水師 壬申 Water Monkey **12** 廿九 7	火2 Fire [7] Gradual Progress 風山漸 癸酉 Water Rooster **13** 三十 7	火7 Fire [8] Obstruction 水山蹇 甲戌 Wood Dog **14** 三月初一 2
木3 Wood [9] Advancement 火地晉 乙亥 Wood Pig **15** 初二 3	水6 Water [1] Nourish 山雷頤 丙子 Fire Rat **16** 初三 3	金4 Metal [2] Following 澤雷隨 丁丑 Fire Ox **17** 初四 7	木8 Wood [3] Abundance 雷火豐 戊寅 Earth Tiger **18** 初五 6	火7 Fire [4] Regulate 水澤節 己卯 Earth Rabbit **19** 初六 8	水1 Water [5] Unity 地天泰 庚辰 Metal Dragon **20** 初七 9	木3 Wood [6] Great Reward 火天大有 辛巳 Metal Snake **21** 初八 7
火2 Fire [7] Wind 巽為風 壬午 Water Horse **22** 初九 1	金4 Metal [8] Trap 澤水困 癸未 Water Goat **23** 初十 8	木3 Wood [9] Not Yet Accomplished 火水未濟 甲申 Wood Monkey **24** 十一 9	金9 Metal [1] Retreat 天山遯 乙酉 Wood Rooster **25** 十二 4	水6 Water [2] Mountain 艮為山 丙戌 Fire Dog **26** 十三 1	木8 Wood [3] Delight 雷地豫 丁亥 Fire Pig **27** 十四 8	火7 Fire [4] Beginning 水雷屯 戊子 Earth Rat **28** 十五 4
金9 Metal [5] Without Wrongdoing 天雷無妄 己丑 Earth Ox **29** 十六 2	木3 Wood [6] Fire 離為火 庚寅 Metal Tiger **30** 十七 1					

MAY 2029 己巳

Xuan Kong Element 玄空五行	雷天大壯	Period Luck 卦運	Monthly Star 月星
Wood 木8	Great Strength	2	5

SUNDAY	MONDAY	TUESDAY	WEDNESDAY	THURSDAY	FRIDAY	SATURDAY
		火2 Fire 7 Sincerity 風澤中孚 辛卯 Metal Rabbit 3 **1** 十八	水6 Water 8 Big Livestock 山天大畜 壬辰 Water Dragon 4 **2** 十九	金4 Metal 9 Eliminating 澤天夬 癸巳 Water Snake 6 **3** 二十	金9 Metal 1 Heaven 乾爲天 甲午 Wood Horse 1 **4** 廿一	火7 Fire 2 Well 水風井 乙未 Wood Goat 6 **5** 廿二
木8 Wood 3 Relief 雷水解 丙申 Fire Monkey 4 **6** 廿三	金4 Metal 4 Influence 澤山咸 丁酉 Fire Rooster 9 **7** 廿四	水1 Water 5 Humility 地山謙 戊戌 Earth Dog 6 **8** 廿五	火2 Fire 6 Observation 風地觀 己亥 Earth Pig 2 **9** 廿六	火2 Fire 7 Increasing 風雷益 庚子 Metal Rat 9 **10** 廿七	水1 Water 8 Dimming Light 地火明夷 辛丑 Metal Ox 3 **11** 廿八	金9 Metal 9 Fellowship 天火同人 壬寅 Water Tiger 7 **12** 廿九
木8 Wood 1 Marrying Maiden 雷澤歸妹 癸卯 Water Rabbit 7 **13** 四月初一	木3 Wood 2 Opposition 火澤睽 甲辰 Wood Dragon 2 **14** 初二	火7 Fire 3 Waiting 水天需 乙巳 Wood Snake 3 **15** 初三	金4 Metal 4 Great Exceeding 澤風大過 丙午 Fire Horse 3 **16** 初四	水6 Water 5 Poison 山風蠱 丁未 Fire Goat 7 **17** 初五	火2 Fire 6 Dispersing 風水渙 戊申 Earth Monkey 6 **18** 初六	木3 Wood 7 Travelling 火山旅 己酉 Earth Rooster 8 **19** 初七
金9 Metal 8 Stagnation 天地否 庚戌 Metal Dog 9 **20** 初八	火7 Fire 9 Alliance 水地比 辛亥 Metal Pig 7 **21** 初九	木8 Wood 1 Thunder 震爲雷 壬子 Water Rat 1 **22** 初十	水6 Water 2 Beauty 山火賁 癸丑 Water Ox 8 **23** 十一	火7 Fire 3 Accomplished 水火既濟 甲寅 Wood Tiger 9 **24** 十二	水1 Water 4 Arriving 地澤臨 乙卯 Wood Rabbit 4 **25** 十三	金4 Metal 5 Marsh 兑爲澤 丙辰 Fire Dragon 1 **26** 十四
火2 Fire 6 Small Livestock 風天小畜 丁巳 Fire Snake 8 **27** 十五	木3 Wood 7 The Cauldron 火風鼎 戊午 Earth Horse 4 **28** 十六	水1 Water 8 Rising 地風升 己未 Earth Goat 2 **29** 十七	火7 Fire 9 Water 坎爲水 庚申 Metal Monkey 1 **30** 十八	木8 Wood 1 Lesser Exceeding 雷山小過 辛酉 Metal Rooster 3 **31** 十九		

JUNE 2029 庚午

Xuan Kong Element 玄空五行	雷風恒	Period Luck 卦運	Monthly Star 月星
Wood 木8	Consistency	9	4

SUNDAY	MONDAY	TUESDAY	WEDNESDAY	THURSDAY	FRIDAY	SATURDAY
					金4 Metal 2 Gathering 澤地萃 壬戌 Water Dog 4 **1** 二十	水6 Water 3 Peel 山地剝 癸亥 Water Pig 6 **2** 廿一
水1 Water 4 Earth 坤爲地 甲子 Wood Rat 1 **3** 廿二	木3 Wood 5 Biting 火雷噬嗑 乙丑 Wood Ox 6 **4** 廿三	火2 Fire 6 Family 風火家人 丙寅 Fire Tiger 4 **5** 廿四	水6 Water 7 Decreasing 山澤損 丁卯 Fire Rabbit 9 **6** 廿五	金9 Metal 8 Tread 天澤履 戊辰 Earth Dragon 6 **7** 廿六	木8 Wood 9 Great Strength 雷天大壯 己巳 Earth Snake 2 **8** 廿七	木8 Wood 1 Consistency 雷風恒 庚午 Metal Horse 9 **9** 廿八
金9 Metal 2 Litigation 天水訟 辛未 Metal Goat 3 **10** 廿九	水1 Water 3 Officer 地水師 壬申 Water Monkey 7 **11** 三十	火2 Fire 4 Gradual Progress 風山漸 癸酉 Water Rooster 7 **12** 五月初一	火7 Fire 5 Obstruction 水山蹇 甲戌 Wood Dog 2 **13** 初二	木3 Wood 6 Advancement 火地晉 乙亥 Wood Pig 3 **14** 初三	水6 Water 7 Nourish 山雷頤 丙子 Fire Rat 3 **15** 初四	金4 Metal 8 Following 澤雷隨 丁丑 Fire Ox 7 **16** 初五
木8 Wood 9 Abundance 雷火豐 戊寅 Earth Tiger 6 **17** 初六	火7 Fire 1 Regulate 水澤節 己卯 Earth Rabbit 8 **18** 初七	水1 Water 2 Unity 地天泰 庚辰 Metal Dragon 9 **19** 初八	木3 Wood 3 Great Reward 火天大有 辛巳 Metal Snake 7 **20** 初九	火2 Fire 4/6 Wind 巽爲風 壬午 Water Horse 1 **21** 初十	金4 Metal 5 Trap 澤水困 癸未 Water Goat 8 **22** 十一	木3 Wood 4 Not Yet Accomplished 火水未濟 甲申 Wood Monkey 9 **23** 十二
金9 Metal 3 Retreat 天山遯 乙酉 Wood Rooster 4 **24** 十三	水6 Water 2 Mountain 艮爲山 丙戌 Fire Dog 1 **25** 十四	木8 Wood 1 Delight 雷地豫 丁亥 Fire Pig 8 **26** 十五	火7 Fire 9 Beginning 水雷屯 戊子 Earth Rat 4 **27** 十六	金9 Metal 8 Without Wrongdoing 天雷無妄 己丑 Earth Ox 2 **28** 十七	木3 Wood 7 Fire 離爲火 庚寅 Metal Tiger 1 **29** 十八	火2 Fire 6 Sincerity 風澤中孚 辛卯 Metal Rabbit 3 **30** 十九

JULY 2029 辛未

Xuan Kong Element 玄空五行	天水訟 Litigation	Period Luck 卦運	Monthly Star 月星
Metal 金9		3	3

SUNDAY	MONDAY	TUESDAY	WEDNESDAY	THURSDAY	FRIDAY	SATURDAY
水6 Water 5 Big Livestock 壬辰 Water Dragon 山天大畜 1 二十 4	金4 Metal 4 Eliminating 癸巳 Water Snake 澤天夬 2 廿一 6	金9 Metal 3 Heaven 甲午 Wood Horse 乾爲天 3 廿二 1	火7 Fire 2 Well 乙未 Wood Goat 水風井 4 廿三 6	木8 Wood 1 Relief 丙申 Fire Monkey 雷水解 5 廿四 4	金4 Metal 9 Influence 丁酉 Fire Rooster 澤山咸 6 廿五 9	水1 Water 8 Humility 戊戌 Earth Dog 地山謙 7 廿六 6
火2 Fire 7 Observation 己亥 Earth Pig 風地觀 8 廿七 2	火2 Fire 6 Increasing 庚子 Metal Rat 風雷益 9 廿八 9	水1 Water 5 Dimming Light 辛丑 Metal Ox 地火明夷 10 廿九 3	金9 Metal 4 Fellowship 壬寅 Water Tiger 天火同人 11 六月初一 7	木8 Wood 3 Marrying Maiden 癸卯 Water Rabbit 雷澤歸妹 12 初二 7	木3 Wood 2 Opposition 甲辰 Wood Dragon 火澤睽 13 初三 2	火7 Fire 1 Waiting 乙巳 Wood Snake 水天需 14 初四 3
金4 Metal 9 Great Exceeding 丙午 Fire Horse 澤風大過 15 初五 3	水6 Water 8 Poison 丁未 Fire Goat 山風蠱 16 初六 7	火2 Fire 7 Dispersing 戊申 Earth Monkey 風水渙 17 初七 6	木3 Wood 6 Travelling 己酉 Earth Rooster 火山旅 18 初八 8	金9 Metal 5 Stagnation 庚戌 Metal Dog 天地否 19 初九 9	火7 Fire 4 Alliance 辛亥 Metal Pig 水地比 20 初十 7	木8 Wood 3 Thunder 壬子 Water Rat 震爲雷 21 十一 1
水6 Water 2 Beauty 癸丑 Water Ox 山火賁 22 十二 8	火7 Fire 1 Accomplished 甲寅 Wood Tiger 水火既濟 23 十三 9	水1 Water 9 Arriving 乙卯 Wood Rabbit 地澤臨 24 十四 4	金4 Metal 8 Marsh 丙辰 Fire Dragon 兑爲澤 25 十五 1	火2 Fire 7 Small Livestock 丁巳 Fire Snake 風天小畜 26 十六 8	木3 Wood 6 The Cauldron 戊午 Earth Horse 火風鼎 27 十七 4	水1 Water 5 Rising 己未 Earth Goat 地風升 28 十八 2
火7 Fire 4 Water 庚申 Metal Monkey 坎爲水 29 十九 1	木8 Wood 3 Lesser Exceeding 辛酉 Metal Rooster 雷山小過 30 二十 3	金4 Metal 2 Gathering 壬戌 Water Dog 澤地萃 31 廿一 4				

AUGUST 2029 壬申

Xuan Kong Element 玄空五行	地水師 Officer	Period Luck 卦運	Monthly Star 月星
Water 水1		7	2

SUNDAY	MONDAY	TUESDAY	WEDNESDAY	THURSDAY	FRIDAY	SATURDAY
			水6 Water 1 Peel 癸亥 Water Pig 山地剝 1 廿二 6	水1 Water 9 Earth 甲子 Wood Rat 坤爲地 2 廿三 1	木3 Wood 8 Biting 乙丑 Wood Ox 火雷噬嗑 3 廿四 6	火2 Fire 7 Family 丙寅 Fire Tiger 風火家人 4 廿五 4
水6 Water 6 Decreasing 丁卯 Fire Rabbit 山澤損 5 廿六 9	金9 Metal 5 Tread 戊辰 Earth Dragon 天澤履 6 廿七 6	木8 Wood 4 Great Strength 己巳 Earth Snake 雷天大壯 7 廿八 2	木8 Wood 3 Consistency 庚午 Metal Horse 雷風恆 8 廿九 9	金9 Metal 2 Litigation 辛未 Metal Goat 天水訟 9 三十 3	水1 Water 1 Officer 壬申 Water Monkey 地水師 10 七月初一 7	火2 Fire 9 Gradual Progress 癸酉 Water Rooster 風山漸 11 初二 7
火7 Fire 8 Obstruction 甲戌 Wood Dog 水山蹇 12 初三 2	木3 Wood 7 Advancement 乙亥 Wood Pig 火地晉 13 初四 3	水6 Water 6 Nourish 丙子 Fire Rat 山雷頤 14 初五 3	金4 Metal 5 Following 丁丑 Fire Ox 澤雷隨 15 初六 7	木8 Wood 4 Abundance 戊寅 Earth Tiger 雷火豐 16 初七 6	火7 Fire 3 Regulate 己卯 Earth Rabbit 水澤節 17 初八 8	水1 Water 2 Unity 庚辰 Metal Dragon 地天泰 18 初九 9
木3 Wood 1 Great Reward 辛巳 Metal Snake 火天大有 19 初十 7	火2 Fire 9 Wind 壬午 Water Horse 巽爲風 20 十一 1	金4 Metal 8 Trap 癸未 Water Goat 澤水困 21 十二 8	木3 Wood 7 Not Yet Accomplished 甲申 Wood Monkey 火水未濟 22 十三 9	金9 Metal 6 Retreat 乙酉 Wood Rooster 天山遯 23 十四 4	水6 Water 5 Mountain 丙戌 Fire Dog 艮爲山 24 十五 1	木8 Wood 4 Delight 丁亥 Fire Pig 雷地豫 25 十六 8
火7 Fire 3 Beginning 戊子 Earth Rat 水雷屯 26 十七 4	金9 Metal 2 Without Wrongdoing 己丑 Earth Ox 天雷無妄 27 十八 2	木3 Wood 1 Fire 庚寅 Metal Tiger 離爲火 28 十九 1	火2 Fire 9 Sincerity 辛卯 Metal Rabbit 風澤中孚 29 二十 3	水6 Water 8 Big Livestock 壬辰 Water Dragon 山天大畜 30 廿一 4	金4 Metal 7 Eliminating 癸巳 Water Snake 澤天夬 31 廿二 6	

SEPTEMBER 2029 癸酉

Xuan Kong Element 玄空五行	風山漸 Gradual Progress	Period Luck 卦運	Monthly Star 月星
Fire 火2		7	1

SUNDAY	MONDAY	TUESDAY	WEDNESDAY	THURSDAY	FRIDAY	SATURDAY
水6 Water Peel 4 山地剝 癸亥 Water Pig 30 廿三 6						金9 Metal Heaven 6 乾爲天 甲午 Wood Horse 1 廿三 1
火7 Fire Well 5 水風井 乙未 Wood Goat 2 廿四 6	木8 Wood Relief 4 雷水解 丙申 Fire Monkey 3 廿五 4	金4 Metal Influence 3 澤山咸 丁酉 Fire Rooster 4 廿六 9	水1 Water Humility 2 地山謙 戊戌 Earth Dog 5 廿七 6	火2 Fire Observation 1 風地觀 己亥 Earth Pig 6 廿八 2	火2 Fire Increasing 9 風雷益 庚子 Metal Rat 7 廿九 9	水1 Water Dimming Light 8 地火明夷 辛丑 Metal Ox 8 八月初一 3
金9 Metal Fellowship 7 天火同人 壬寅 Water Tiger 9 初二 7	木8 Wood Marrying Maiden 6 雷澤歸妹 癸卯 Water Rabbit 10 初三 7	木3 Wood Opposition 5 火澤睽 甲辰 Wood Dragon 11 初四 2	火7 Fire Waiting 4 水天需 乙巳 Wood Snake 12 初五 3	金4 Metal Great Exceeding 3 澤風大過 丙午 Fire Horse 13 初六 3	水6 Water Poison 2 山風蠱 丁未 Fire Goat 14 初七 7	火2 Fire Dispersing 1 風水渙 戊申 Earth Monkey 15 初八 6
木3 Wood Travelling 9 火山旅 己酉 Earth Rooster 16 初九 8	金9 Metal Stagnation 8 天地否 庚戌 Metal Dog 17 初十 9	火7 Fire Alliance 7 水地比 辛亥 Metal Pig 18 十一 7	木8 Wood Thunder 6 震爲雷 壬子 Water Rat 19 十二 1	水6 Water Beauty 5 山火賁 癸丑 Water Ox 20 十三 8	火7 Fire Accomplished 4 水火既濟 甲寅 Wood Tiger 21 十四 9	水1 Water Arriving 3 地澤臨 乙卯 Wood Rabbit 22 十五 4
金4 Metal Marsh 2 兑爲澤 丙辰 Fire Dragon 23 十六 1	火2 Fire Small Livestock 1 風天小畜 丁巳 Fire Snake 24 十七 8	木3 Wood The Cauldron 9 火風鼎 戊午 Earth Horse 25 十八 4	水1 Water Rising 8 地風升 己未 Earth Goat 26 十九 2	火7 Fire Water 7 坎爲水 庚申 Metal Monkey 27 二十 1	木8 Wood Lesser Exceeding 6 雷山小過 辛酉 Metal Rooster 28 廿一 3	金4 Metal Gathering 5 澤地萃 壬戌 Water Dog 29 廿二 4

OCTOBER 2029 甲戌

Xuan Kong Element 玄空五行	水山蹇 Obstruction	Period Luck 卦運	Monthly Star 月星
Fire 火7		2	9

SUNDAY	MONDAY	TUESDAY	WEDNESDAY	THURSDAY	FRIDAY	SATURDAY
	水1 Water Earth 3 坤爲地 甲子 Wood Rat 1 廿四 1	木3 Wood Biting 2 火雷噬嗑 乙丑 Wood Ox 2 廿五 6	火2 Fire Family 1 風火家人 丙寅 Fire Tiger 3 廿六 4	水6 Water Decreasing 9 山澤損 丁卯 Fire Rabbit 4 廿七 9	金9 Metal Tread 8 天澤履 戊辰 Earth Dragon 5 廿八 6	木8 Wood Great Strength 7 雷天大壯 己巳 Earth Snake 6 廿九 2
木8 Wood Consistency 6 雷風恒 庚午 Metal Horse 7 三十 9	金9 Metal Litigation 5 天水訟 辛未 Metal Goat 8 九月初一 3	水1 Water Officer 4 地水師 壬申 Water Monkey 9 初二 7	火2 Fire Gradual Progress 3 風山漸 癸酉 Water Rooster 10 初三 7	火7 Fire Obstruction 2 水山蹇 甲戌 Wood Dog 11 初四 2	木3 Wood Advancement 1 火地晉 乙亥 Wood Pig 12 初五 3	水6 Water Nourish 9 山雷頤 丙子 Fire Rat 13 初六 3
金4 Metal Following 8 澤雷隨 丁丑 Fire Ox 14 初七 7	木8 Wood Abundance 7 雷火豐 戊寅 Earth Tiger 15 初八 6	火7 Fire Regulate 6 水澤節 己卯 Earth Rabbit 16 初九 8	水1 Water Unity 5 地天泰 庚辰 Metal Dragon 17 初十 9	木3 Wood Great Reward 4 火天大有 辛巳 Metal Snake 18 十一 7	火2 Fire Wind 3 巽爲風 壬午 Water Horse 19 十二 1	金4 Metal Trap 2 澤水困 癸未 Water Goat 20 十三 8
木3 Wood Not Yet Accomplished 1 火水未濟 甲申 Wood Monkey 21 十四 9	金9 Metal Retreat 9 天山遯 乙酉 Wood Rooster 22 十五 4	水6 Water Mountain 8 艮爲山 丙戌 Fire Dog 23 十六 1	木8 Wood Delight 7 雷地豫 丁亥 Fire Pig 24 十七 8	火7 Fire Beginning 6 水雷屯 戊子 Earth Rat 25 十八 4	金9 Metal Without Wrongdoing 5 天雷無妄 己丑 Earth Ox 26 十九 2	木3 Wood Fire 4 離爲火 庚寅 Metal Tiger 27 二十 1
火2 Fire Sincerity 3 風澤中孚 辛卯 Metal Rabbit 28 廿一 3	水6 Water Big Livestock 2 山天大畜 壬辰 Water Dragon 29 廿二 4	金4 Metal Eliminating 1 澤天夬 癸巳 Water Snake 30 廿三 6	金9 Metal Heaven 9 乾爲天 甲午 Wood Horse 31 廿四 1			

NOVEMBER 2029 乙亥

Xuan Kong Element 玄空五行	火地晉 Advancement	Period Luck 卦運	Monthly Star 月星
Wood 木3		3	8

SUNDAY	MONDAY	TUESDAY	WEDNESDAY	THURSDAY	FRIDAY	SATURDAY
				火7 Fire · 8 Well 水風井 乙未 Wood Goat 1 廿五 6	木8 Wood · 7 Relief 雷水解 丙申 Fire Monkey 2 廿六 4	金4 Metal · 6 Influence 澤山咸 丁酉 Fire Rooster 3 廿七 9
水1 Water · 5 Humility 地山謙 戊戌 Earth Dog 4 廿八 6	火2 Fire · 4 Observation 風地觀 己亥 Earth Pig 5 廿九 2	火2 Fire · 3 Increasing 風雷益 庚子 Metal Rat 6 十月初一 9	水1 Water · 2 Dimming Light 地火明夷 辛丑 Metal Ox 7 初二 3	金9 Metal · 1 Fellowship 天火同人 壬寅 Water Tiger 8 初三 7	木8 Wood · 9 Marrying Maiden 雷澤歸妹 癸卯 Water Rabbit 9 初四 7	木3 Wood · 8 Opposition 火澤睽 甲辰 Wood Dragon 10 初五 2
火7 Fire · 7 Waiting 水天需 乙巳 Wood Snake 11 初六 3	金4 Metal · 6 Great Exceeding 澤風大過 丙午 Fire Horse 12 初七 3	水6 Water · 5 Poison 山風蠱 丁未 Fire Goat 13 初八 7	火2 Fire · 4 Dispersing 風水渙 戊申 Earth Monkey 14 初九 6	木3 Wood · 3 Travelling 火山旅 己酉 Earth Rooster 15 初十 8	金9 Metal · 2 Stagnation 天地否 庚戌 Metal Dog 16 十一 9	火7 Fire · 1 Alliance 水地比 辛亥 Metal Pig 17 十二 7
木8 Wood · 9 Thunder 震爲雷 壬子 Water Rat 18 十三 1	水6 Water · 8 Beauty 山火賁 癸丑 Water Ox 19 十四 8	火7 Fire · 7 Accomplished 水火既濟 甲寅 Wood Tiger 20 十五 9	水1 Water · 6 Arriving 地澤臨 乙卯 Wood Rabbit 21 十六 4	金4 Metal · 5 Marsh 兑爲澤 丙辰 Fire Dragon 22 十七 1	火2 Fire · 4 Small Livestock 風天小畜 丁巳 Fire Snake 23 十八 8	木3 Wood · 3 The Cauldron 火風鼎 戊午 Earth Horse 24 十九 4
水1 Water · 2 Rising 地風升 己未 Earth Goat 25 二十 2	火7 Fire · 1 Water 坎爲水 庚申 Metal Monkey 26 廿一 1	木8 Wood · 9 Lesser Exceeding 雷山小過 辛酉 Metal Rooster 27 廿二 3	金4 Metal · 8 Gathering 澤地萃 壬戌 Water Dog 28 廿三 4	水6 Water · 7 Peel 山地剝 癸亥 Water Pig 29 廿四 6	水1 Water · 6 Earth 坤爲地 甲子 Wood Rat 30 廿五 1	

DECEMBER 2029 丙子

Xuan Kong Element 玄空五行	山雷頤 Nourish	Period Luck 卦運	Monthly Star 月星
Water 水6		3	7

SUNDAY	MONDAY	TUESDAY	WEDNESDAY	THURSDAY	FRIDAY	SATURDAY
金9 Metal · 7 Heaven 乾爲天 甲午 Wood Horse 30 廿六 1	火7 Fire · 8 Well 水風井 乙未 Wood Goat 31 廿七 6					木3 Wood · 5 Biting 火雷噬嗑 乙丑 Wood Ox 1 廿六 6
火2 Fire · 4 Family 風火家人 丙寅 Fire Tiger 2 廿七 4	水6 Water · 3 Decreasing 山澤損 丁卯 Fire Rabbit 3 廿八 9	金9 Metal · 2 Tread 天澤履 戊辰 Earth Dragon 4 廿九 6	木8 Wood · 1 Great Strength 雷天大壯 己巳 Earth Snake 5 十一月初一 2	木8 Wood · 9 Consistency 雷風恒 庚午 Metal Horse 6 初二 9	金9 Metal · 8 Litigation 天水訟 辛未 Metal Goat 7 初三 3	水1 Water · 7 Officer 地水師 壬申 Water Monkey 8 初四 7
火2 Fire · 6 Gradual Progress 風山漸 癸酉 Water Rooster 9 初五 7	火7 Fire · 5 Obstruction 水山蹇 甲戌 Wood Dog 10 初六 2	木3 Wood · 4 Advancement 火地晉 乙亥 Wood Pig 11 初七 3	水6 Water · 3 Nourish 山雷頤 丙子 Fire Rat 12 初八 3	金4 Metal · 2 Following 澤雷隨 丁丑 Fire Ox 13 初九 7	木8 Wood · 1 Abundance 雷火豐 戊寅 Earth Tiger 14 初十 6	火7 Fire · 9 Regulate 水澤節 己卯 Earth Rabbit 15 十一 8
水1 Water · 8 Unity 地天泰 庚辰 Metal Dragon 16 十二 9	木3 Wood · 7 Great Reward 火天大有 辛巳 Metal Snake 17 十三 7	火2 Fire · 6 Wind 巽爲風 壬午 Water Horse 18 十四 1	金4 Metal · 5 Trap 澤水困 癸未 Water Goat 19 十五 8	木3 Wood · 4 Not Yet Accomplished 火水未濟 甲申 Wood Monkey 20 十六 9	金9 Metal · 3/7 Retreat 天山遯 乙酉 Wood Rooster 21 十七 4	水6 Water · 8 Mountain 艮爲山 丙戌 Fire Dog 22 十八 1
木8 Wood · 9 Delight 雷地豫 丁亥 Fire Pig 23 十九 8	火7 Fire · 1 Beginning 水雷屯 戊子 Earth Rat 24 二十 4	金9 Metal · 2 Without Wrongdoing 天雷無妄 己丑 Earth Ox 25 廿一 2	木3 Wood · 3 Fire 離爲火 庚寅 Metal Tiger 26 廿二 1	火2 Fire · 4 Sincerity 風澤中孚 辛卯 Metal Rabbit 27 廿三 3	水6 Water · 5 Big Livestock 山天大畜 壬辰 Water Dragon 28 廿四 4	金4 Metal · 6 Eliminating 澤天夬 癸巳 Water Snake 29 廿五 6

2030 庚戌

(*Geng Xu*) Metal Dog

2030 庚戌 *(Geng Xu)* Metal Dog

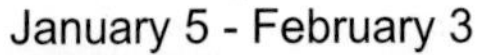

January 5 - February 3

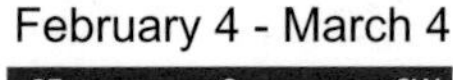

February 4 - March 4

March 5 - April 4

April 5 - May 4

May 5 - June 4

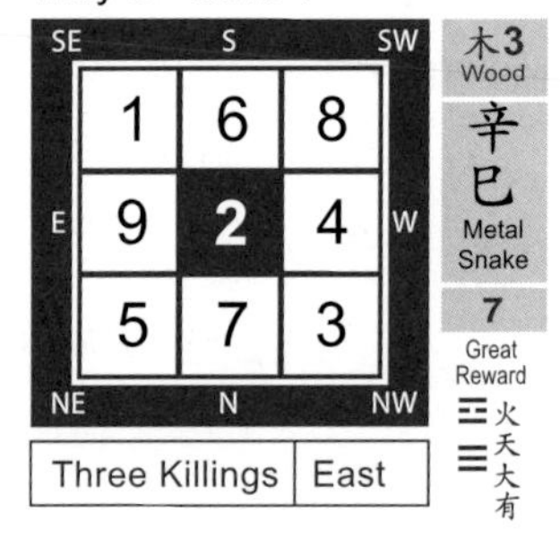

June 5 - July 6

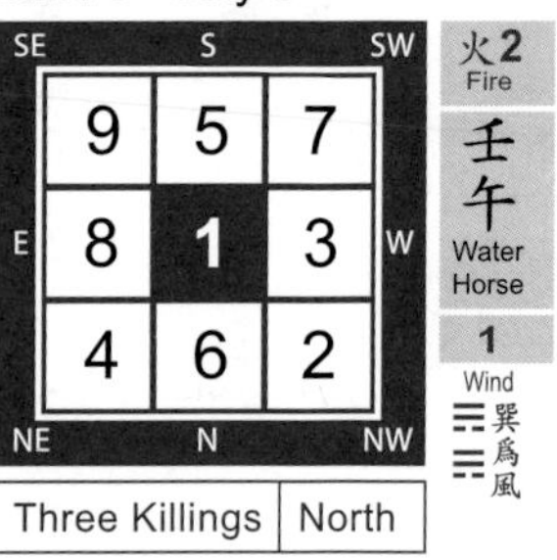

July 7 - August 6

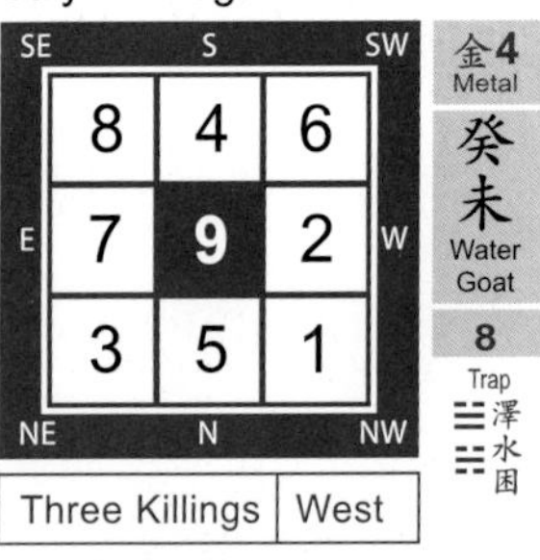

August 7 - September 6

September 7 - October 7

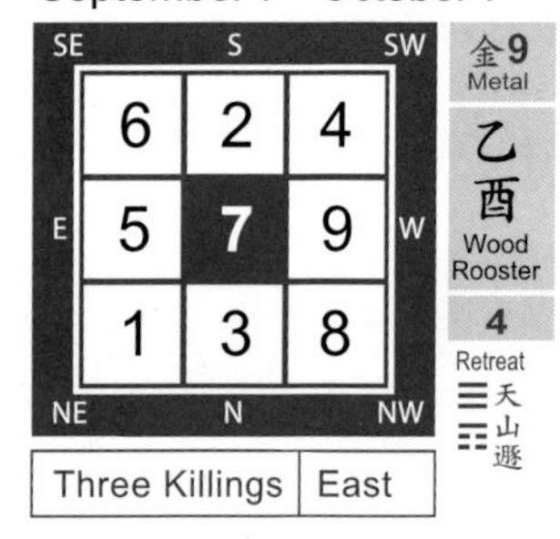

October 8 - November 6

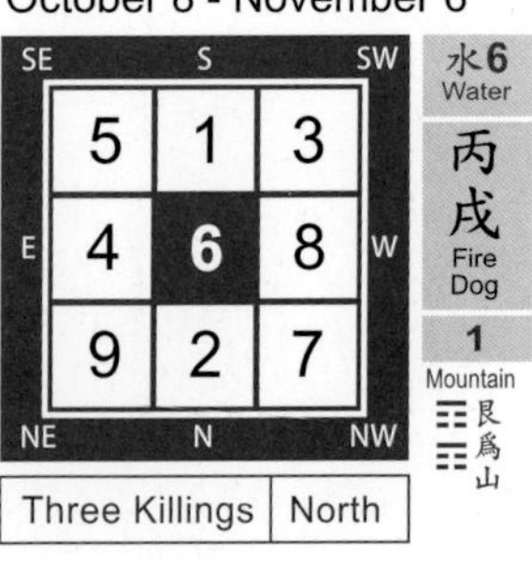

November 7 - December 6

December 7 - January 4

JANUARY 2030 丁丑

Xuan Kong Element 玄空五行	澤雷隨 Following	Period Luck 卦運	Monthly Star 月星
Metal 金4		7	6

SUNDAY	MONDAY	TUESDAY	WEDNESDAY	THURSDAY	FRIDAY	SATURDAY
		1 木8 Wood · 9 Relief 雷水解 丙申 Fire Monkey 4 · 廿八	**2** 金4 Metal · 1 Influence 澤山咸 丁酉 Fire Rooster 9 · 廿九	**3** 水1 Water · 2 Humility 地山謙 戊戌 Earth Dog 6 · 三十	**4** 火2 Fire · 3 Observation 風地觀 己亥 Earth Pig 2 · 十二月初一	**5** 火2 Fire · 4 Increasing 風雷益 庚子 Metal Rat 9 · 初二
6 水1 Water · 5 Dimming Light 地火明夷 辛丑 Metal Ox 3 · 初三	**7** 金9 Metal · 6 Fellowship 天火同人 壬寅 Water Tiger 7 · 初四	**8** 木8 Wood · 7 Marrying Maiden 雷澤歸妹 癸卯 Water Rabbit 7 · 初五	**9** 木3 Wood · 8 Opposition 火澤睽 甲辰 Wood Dragon 2 · 初六	**10** 火7 Fire · 9 Waiting 水天需 乙巳 Wood Snake 3 · 初七	**11** 金4 Metal · 1 Great Exceeding 澤風大過 丙午 Fire Horse 3 · 初八	**12** 水6 Water · 2 Poison 山風蠱 丁未 Fire Goat 7 · 初九
13 火2 Fire · 3 Dispersing 風水渙 戊申 Earth Monkey 6 · 初十	**14** 木3 Wood · 4 Travelling 火山旅 己酉 Earth Rooster 8 · 十一	**15** 金9 Metal · 5 Stagnation 天地否 庚戌 Metal Dog 9 · 十二	**16** 火7 Fire · 6 Alliance 水地比 辛亥 Metal Pig 7 · 十三	**17** 木8 Wood · 7 Thunder 震為雷 壬子 Water Rat 1 · 十四	**18** 水6 Water · 8 Beauty 山火賁 癸丑 Water Ox 8 · 十五	**19** 火7 Fire · 9 Accomplished 水火既濟 甲寅 Wood Tiger 9 · 十六
20 水1 Water · 1 Arriving 地澤臨 乙卯 Wood Rabbit 4 · 十七	**21** 金4 Metal · 2 Marsh 兑為澤 丙辰 Fire Dragon 1 · 十八	**22** 火2 Fire · 3 Small Livestock 風天小畜 丁巳 Fire Snake 8 · 十九	**23** 木3 Wood · 4 The Cauldron 火風鼎 戊午 Earth Horse 4 · 二十	**24** 水1 Water · 5 Rising 地風升 己未 Earth Goat 2 · 廿一	**25** 火7 Fire · 6 Water 坎為水 庚申 Metal Monkey 1 · 廿二	**26** 木8 Wood · 7 Lesser Exceeding 雷山小過 辛酉 Metal Rooster 3 · 廿三
27 金4 Metal · 8 Gathering 澤地萃 壬戌 Water Dog 4 · 廿四	**28** 水6 Water · 9 Peel 山地剝 癸亥 Water Pig 6 · 廿五	**29** 水1 Water · 1 Earth 坤為地 甲子 Wood Rat 1 · 廿六	**30** 木3 Wood · 2 Biting 火雷噬嗑 乙丑 Wood Ox 6 · 廿七	**31** 火2 Fire · 3 Family 風火家人 丙寅 Fire Tiger 4 · 廿八		

FEBRUARY 2030 戊寅

Xuan Kong Element 玄空五行	雷火豐 Abundance	Period Luck 卦運	Monthly Star 月星
Wood 木8		6	5

SUNDAY	MONDAY	TUESDAY	WEDNESDAY	THURSDAY	FRIDAY	SATURDAY
					1 水6 Water · 4 Decreasing 山澤損 丁卯 Fire Rabbit 9 · 廿九	**2** 金9 Metal · 5 Tread 天澤履 戊辰 Earth Dragon 6 · 三十
3 木8 Wood · 6 Great Strength 雷天大壯 己巳 Earth Snake 2 · 正月初一	**4** 木8 Wood · 7 Consistency 雷風恆 庚午 Metal Horse 9 · 初二	**5** 金9 Metal · 8 Litigation 天水訟 辛未 Metal Goat 3 · 初三	**6** 水1 Water · 9 Officer 地水師 壬申 Water Monkey 7 · 初四	**7** 火2 Fire · 1 Gradual Progress 風山漸 癸酉 Water Rooster 7 · 初五	**8** 火7 Fire · 2 Obstruction 水山蹇 甲戌 Wood Dog 2 · 初六	**9** 木3 Wood · 3 Advancement 火地晉 乙亥 Wood Pig 3 · 初七
10 水6 Water · 4 Nourish 山雷頤 丙子 Fire Rat 3 · 初八	**11** 金4 Metal · 5 Following 澤雷隨 丁丑 Fire Ox 7 · 初九	**12** 木8 Wood · 6 Abundance 雷火豐 戊寅 Earth Tiger 6 · 初十	**13** 火7 Fire · 7 Regulate 水澤節 己卯 Earth Rabbit 8 · 十一	**14** 水1 Water · 8 Unity 地天泰 庚辰 Metal Dragon 9 · 十二	**15** 木3 Wood · 9 Great Reward 火天大有 辛巳 Metal Snake 7 · 十三	**16** 火2 Fire · 1 Wind 巽為風 壬午 Water Horse 1 · 十四
17 金4 Metal · 2 Trap 澤水困 癸未 Water Goat 8 · 十五	**18** 木3 Wood · 3 Not Yet Accomplished 火水未濟 甲申 Wood Monkey 9 · 十六	**19** 金9 Metal · 4 Retreat 天山遯 乙酉 Wood Rooster 4 · 十七	**20** 水6 Water · 5 Mountain 艮為山 丙戌 Fire Dog 1 · 十八	**21** 木8 Wood · 6 Delight 雷地豫 丁亥 Fire Pig 8 · 十九	**22** 火7 Fire · 7 Beginning 水雷屯 戊子 Earth Rat 4 · 二十	**23** 金9 Metal · 8 Without Wrongdoing 天雷無妄 己丑 Earth Ox 2 · 廿一
24 木3 Wood · 9 Fire 離為火 庚寅 Metal Tiger 1 · 廿二	**25** 火2 Fire · 1 Sincerity 風澤中孚 辛卯 Metal Rabbit 3 · 廿三	**26** 水6 Water · 2 Big Livestock 山天大畜 壬辰 Water Dragon 4 · 廿四	**27** 金4 Metal · 3 Eliminating 澤天夬 癸巳 Water Snake 6 · 廿五	**28** 金9 Metal · 4 Heaven 乾為天 甲午 Wood Horse 1 · 廿六		

MARCH 2030 己卯

Xuan Kong Element 玄空五行	水澤節 Regulate	Period Luck 卦運	Monthly Star 月星
Fire 火7		8	4

SUNDAY	MONDAY	TUESDAY	WEDNESDAY	THURSDAY	FRIDAY	SATURDAY
木3 Wood 8 Biting 火雷噬嗑 乙丑 Wood Ox 6 31 廿八					火7 Fire 5 Well 水風井 乙未 Wood Goat 6 1	木8 Wood 6 Relief 雷水解 丙申 Fire Monkey 4 2 廿八
金4 Metal 7 Influence 澤山咸 丁酉 Fire Rooster 9 3 廿九	水1 Water 8 Humility 地山謙 戊戌 Earth Dog 6 4 二月初一	火2 Fire 9 Observation 風地觀 己亥 Earth Pig 2 5 初二	火2 Fire 1 Increasing 風雷益 庚子 Metal Rat 9 6 初三	水1 Water 2 Dimming Light 地火明夷 辛丑 Metal Ox 3 7 初四	金9 Metal 3 Fellowship 天火同人 壬寅 Water Tiger 7 8 初五	木8 Wood 4 Marrying Maiden 雷澤歸妹 癸卯 Water Rabbit 7 9 初六
木3 Wood 5 Opposition 火澤睽 甲辰 Wood Dragon 2 10 初七	火7 Fire 6 Waiting 水天需 乙巳 Wood Snake 3 11 初八	金4 Metal 7 Great Exceeding 澤風大過 丙午 Fire Horse 3 12 初九	水6 Water 8 Poison 山風蠱 丁未 Fire Goat 7 13 初十	火2 Fire 9 Dispersing 風水渙 戊申 Earth Monkey 6 14 十一	木3 Wood 1 Travelling 火山旅 己酉 Earth Rooster 8 15 十二	金9 Metal 2 Stagnation 天地否 庚戌 Metal Dog 9 16 十三
火7 Fire 3 Alliance 水地比 辛亥 Metal Pig 7 17 十四	木8 Wood 4 Thunder 震為雷 壬子 Water Rat 1 18 十五	水6 Water 5 Beauty 山火賁 癸丑 Water Ox 8 19 十六	火7 Fire 6 Accomplished 水火既濟 甲寅 Wood Tiger 9 20 十七	水1 Water 7 Arriving 地澤臨 乙卯 Wood Rabbit 4 21 十八	金4 Metal 8 Marsh 兌為澤 丙辰 Fire Dragon 1 22 十九	火2 Fire 9 Small Livestock 風天小畜 丁巳 Fire Snake 8 23 二十
木3 Wood 1 The Cauldron 火風鼎 戊午 Earth Horse 4 24 廿一	水1 Water 2 Rising 地風升 己未 Earth Goat 2 25 廿二	火7 Fire 3 Water 坎為水 庚申 Metal Monkey 1 26 廿三	木8 Wood 4 Lesser Exceeding 雷山小過 辛酉 Metal Rooster 3 27 廿四	金4 Metal 5 Gathering 澤地萃 壬戌 Water Dog 4 28 廿五	水6 Water 6 Peel 山地剝 癸亥 Water Pig 6 29 廿六	水1 Water 7 Earth 坤為地 甲子 Wood Rat 1 30 廿七

APRIL 2030 庚辰

Xuan Kong Element 玄空五行	地天泰 Unity	Period Luck 卦運	Monthly Star 月星
Water 水1		9	3

SUNDAY	MONDAY	TUESDAY	WEDNESDAY	THURSDAY	FRIDAY	SATURDAY
	火2 Fire 9 Family 風火家人 丙寅 Fire Tiger 4 1 廿九	水6 Water 1 Decreasing 山澤損 丁卯 Fire Rabbit 9 2 三十	金9 Metal 2 Tread 天澤履 戊辰 Earth Dragon 6 3 三月初一	木8 Wood 3 Great Strength 雷天大壯 己巳 Earth Snake 2 4 初二	木8 Wood 4 Consistency 雷風恆 庚午 Metal Horse 9 5 初三	金9 Metal 5 Litigation 天水訟 辛未 Metal Goat 3 6 初四
水1 Water 6 Officer 地水師 壬申 Water Monkey 7 7 初五	火2 Fire 7 Gradual Progress 風山漸 癸酉 Water Rooster 7 8 初六	火7 Fire 8 Obstruction 水山蹇 甲戌 Wood Dog 2 9 初七	木3 Wood 9 Advancement 火地晉 乙亥 Wood Pig 3 10 初八	水6 Water 1 Nourish 山雷頤 丙子 Fire Rat 3 11 初九	金4 Metal 2 Following 澤雷隨 丁丑 Fire Ox 7 12 初十	木8 Wood 3 Abundance 雷火豐 戊寅 Earth Tiger 6 13 十一
火7 Fire 4 Regulate 水澤節 己卯 Earth Rabbit 8 14 十二	水1 Water 5 Unity 地天泰 庚辰 Metal Dragon 9 15 十三	木3 Wood 6 Great Reward 火天大有 辛巳 Metal Snake 7 16 十四	火2 Fire 7 Wind 巽為風 壬午 Water Horse 1 17 十五	金4 Metal 8 Trap 澤水困 癸未 Water Goat 8 18 十六	木3 Wood 9 Not Yet Accomplished 火水未濟 甲申 Wood Monkey 9 19 十七	金9 Metal 1 Retreat 天山遯 乙酉 Wood Rooster 4 20 十八
水6 Water 2 Mountain 艮為山 丙戌 Fire Dog 1 21 十九	木8 Wood 3 Delight 雷地豫 丁亥 Fire Pig 8 22 二十	火7 Fire 4 Beginning 水雷屯 戊子 Earth Rat 4 23 廿一	金9 Metal 5 Without Wrongdoing 天雷無妄 己丑 Earth Ox 2 24 廿二	木3 Wood 6 Fire 離為火 庚寅 Metal Tiger 1 25 廿三	火2 Fire 7 Sincerity 風澤中孚 辛卯 Metal Rabbit 3 26 廿四	水6 Water 8 Big Livestock 山天大畜 壬辰 Water Dragon 4 27 廿五
金4 Metal 9 Eliminating 澤天夬 癸巳 Water Snake 6 28 廿六	金9 Metal 1 Heaven 乾為天 甲午 Wood Horse 1 29 廿七	火7 Fire 2 Well 水風井 乙未 Wood Goat 6 30 廿八				

MAY 2030 辛巳

Xuan Kong Element 玄空五行	火天大有 Great Reward	Period Luck 卦運	Monthly Star 月星
Wood 木3		7	2

SUNDAY	MONDAY	TUESDAY	WEDNESDAY	THURSDAY	FRIDAY	SATURDAY
			木8 Wood [3] Relief 雷水解 丙申 Fire Monkey **1** 廿九 4	金4 Metal [4] Influence 澤山咸 丁酉 Fire Rooster **2** 四月初一 9	水1 Water [5] Humility 地山謙 戊戌 Earth Dog **3** 初二 6	火2 Fire [6] Observation 風地觀 己亥 Earth Pig **4** 初三 2
火2 Fire [7] Increasing 風雷益 庚子 Metal Rat **5** 初四 9	水1 Water [8] Dimming Light 地火明夷 辛丑 Metal Ox **6** 初五 3	金9 Metal [9] Fellowship 天火同人 壬寅 Water Tiger **7** 初六 7	木8 Wood [1] Marrying Maiden 雷澤歸妹 癸卯 Water Rabbit **8** 初七 7	木3 Wood [2] Opposition 火澤睽 甲辰 Wood Dragon **9** 初八 2	火7 Fire [3] Waiting 水天需 乙巳 Wood Snake **10** 初九 3	金4 Metal [4] Great Exceeding 澤風大過 丙午 Fire Horse **11** 初十 3
水6 Water [5] Poison 山風蠱 丁未 Fire Goat **12** 十一 7	火2 Fire [6] Dispersing 風水渙 戊申 Earth Monkey **13** 十二 6	木3 Wood [7] Travelling 火山旅 己酉 Earth Rooster **14** 十三 8	金9 Metal [8] Stagnation 天地否 庚戌 Metal Dog **15** 十四 9	火7 Fire [9] Alliance 水地比 辛亥 Metal Pig **16** 十五 7	木8 Wood [1] Thunder 震爲雷 壬子 Water Rat **17** 十六 1	水6 Water [2] Beauty 山火賁 癸丑 Water Ox **18** 十七 8
火7 Fire [3] Accomplished 水火既濟 甲寅 Wood Tiger **19** 十八 9	水1 Water [4] Arriving 地澤臨 乙卯 Wood Rabbit **20** 十九 4	金4 Metal [5] Marsh 兑爲澤 丙辰 Fire Dragon **21** 二十 1	火2 Fire [6] Small Livestock 風天小畜 丁巳 Fire Snake **22** 廿一 8	木3 Wood [7] The Cauldron 火風鼎 戊午 Earth Horse **23** 廿二 4	水1 Water [8] Rising 地風升 己未 Earth Goat **24** 廿三 2	火7 Fire [9] Water 坎爲水 庚申 Metal Monkey **25** 廿四 1
木8 Wood [1] Lesser Exceeding 雷山小過 辛酉 Metal Rooster **26** 廿五 3	金4 Metal [2] Gathering 澤地萃 壬戌 Water Dog **27** 廿六 4	水6 Water [3] Peel 山地剝 癸亥 Water Pig **28** 廿七 6	水1 Water [4] Earth 坤爲地 甲子 Wood Rat **29** 廿八 1	木3 Wood [5] Biting 火雷噬嗑 乙丑 Wood Ox **30** 廿九 6	火2 Fire [6] Family 風火家人 丙寅 Fire Tiger **31** 三十 4	

JUNE 2030 壬午

Xuan Kong Element 玄空五行	巽爲風 Wind	Period Luck 卦運	Monthly Star 月星
Fire 火2		1	1

SUNDAY	MONDAY	TUESDAY	WEDNESDAY	THURSDAY	FRIDAY	SATURDAY
木8 Wood [1] Relief 雷水解 丙申 Fire Monkey **30** 三十 4						水6 Water [7] Decreasing 山澤損 丁卯 Fire Rabbit **1** 五月初一 9
金9 Metal [8] Tread 天澤履 戊辰 Earth Dragon **2** 初二 6	木8 Wood [9] Great Strength 雷天大壯 己巳 Earth Snake **3** 初三 2	木8 Wood [1] Consistency 雷風恒 庚午 Metal Horse **4** 初四 9	金9 Metal [2] Litigation 天水訟 辛未 Metal Goat **5** 初五 3	水1 Water [3] Officer 地水師 壬申 Water Monkey **6** 初六 7	火2 Fire [4] Gradual Progress 風山漸 癸酉 Water Rooster **7** 初七 7	火7 Fire [5] Obstruction 水山蹇 甲戌 Wood Dog **8** 初八 2
木3 Wood [6] Advancement 火地晉 乙亥 Wood Pig **9** 初九 3	水6 Water [7] Nourish 山雷頤 丙子 Fire Rat **10** 初十 3	金4 Metal [8] Following 澤雷隨 丁丑 Fire Ox **11** 十一 7	木8 Wood [9] Abundance 雷火豐 戊寅 Earth Tiger **12** 十二 6	火7 Fire [1] Regulate 水澤節 己卯 Earth Rabbit **13** 十三 8	水1 Water [2] Unity 地天泰 庚辰 Metal Dragon **14** 十四 9	木3 Wood [3] Great Reward 火天大有 辛巳 Metal Snake **15** 十五 7
火2 Fire [4] Wind 巽爲風 壬午 Water Horse **16** 十六 1	金4 Metal [5] Trap 澤水困 癸未 Water Goat **17** 十七 8	木3 Wood [6] Not Yet Accomplished 火水未濟 甲申 Wood Monkey **18** 十八 9	金9 Metal [7] Retreat 天山遯 乙酉 Wood Rooster **19** 十九 4	水6 Water [8] Mountain 艮爲山 丙戌 Fire Dog **20** 二十 1	木8 Wood [9/1] Delight 雷地豫 丁亥 Fire Pig **21** 廿一 8	火7 Fire [9] Beginning 水雷屯 戊子 Earth Rat **22** 廿二 4
金9 Metal [8] Without Wrongdoing 天雷無妄 己丑 Earth Ox **23** 廿三 2	木3 Wood [7] Fire 離爲火 庚寅 Metal Tiger **24** 廿四 1	火2 Fire [6] Sincerity 風澤中孚 辛卯 Metal Rabbit **25** 廿五 3	水6 Water [5] Big Livestock 山天大畜 壬辰 Water Dragon **26** 廿六 4	金4 Metal [4] Eliminating 澤天夬 癸巳 Water Snake **27** 廿七 6	金9 Metal [3] Heaven 乾爲天 甲午 Wood Horse **28** 廿八 1	火7 Fire [2] Well 水風井 乙未 Wood Goat **29** 廿九 6

JULY 2030 癸未

Xuan Kong Element 玄空五行	澤水困 Trap	Period Luck 卦運	Monthly Star 月星
Metal 金4		8	9

SUNDAY	MONDAY	TUESDAY	WEDNESDAY	THURSDAY	FRIDAY	SATURDAY
	金4 Metal Influence 澤山咸 9 丁酉 Fire Rooster 9 1 六月初一	水1 Water Humility 地山謙 8 戊戌 Earth Dog 6 2 初二	火2 Fire Observation 風地觀 7 己亥 Earth Pig 2 3 初三	火2 Fire Increasing 風雷益 6 庚子 Metal Rat 9 4 初四	水1 Water Dimming Light 地火明夷 5 辛丑 Metal Ox 3 5 初五	金9 Metal Fellowship 天火同人 4 壬寅 Water Tiger 7 6 初六
木8 Wood Marrying Maiden 雷澤歸妹 3 癸卯 Water Rabbit 7 7 初七	木3 Wood Opposition 火澤睽 2 甲辰 Wood Dragon 2 8 初八	火7 Fire Waiting 水天需 1 乙巳 Wood Snake 3 9 初九	金4 Metal Great Exceeding 澤風大過 9 丙午 Fire Horse 3 10 初十	水6 Water Poison 山風蠱 8 丁未 Fire Goat 7 11 十一	火2 Fire Dispersing 風水渙 7 戊申 Earth Monkey 6 12 十二	木3 Wood Travelling 火山旅 6 己酉 Earth Rooster 8 13 十三
金9 Metal Stagnation 天地否 5 庚戌 Metal Dog 9 14 十四	火7 Fire Alliance 水地比 4 辛亥 Metal Pig 7 15 十五	木8 Wood Thunder 震爲雷 3 壬子 Water Rat 1 16 十六	水6 Water Beauty 山火賁 2 癸丑 Water Ox 8 17 十七	火7 Fire Accomplished 水火既濟 1 甲寅 Wood Tiger 9 18 十八	水1 Water Arriving 地澤臨 9 乙卯 Wood Rabbit 4 19 十九	金4 Metal Marsh 兑爲澤 8 丙辰 Fire Dragon 1 20 二十
火2 Fire Small Livestock 風天小畜 7 丁巳 Fire Snake 8 21 廿一	木3 Wood The Cauldron 火風鼎 6 戊午 Earth Horse 4 22 廿二	水1 Water Rising 地風升 5 己未 Earth Goat 2 23 廿三	火7 Fire Water 坎爲水 4 庚申 Metal Monkey 1 24 廿四	木8 Wood Lesser Exceeding 雷山小過 3 辛酉 Metal Rooster 3 25 廿五	金4 Metal Gathering 澤地萃 2 壬戌 Water Dog 4 26 廿六	水6 Water Peel 山地剝 1 癸亥 Water Pig 6 27 廿七
水1 Water Earth 坤爲地 9 甲子 Wood Rat 1 28 廿八	木3 Wood Biting 火雷噬嗑 8 乙丑 Wood Ox 6 29 廿九	火2 Fire Family 風火家人 7 丙寅 Fire Tiger 4 30 七月初一	水6 Water Decreasing 山澤損 6 丁卯 Fire Rabbit 9 31 初二			

AUGUST 2030 甲申

Xuan Kong Element 玄空五行	火水未濟 Not Yet Accomplished	Period Luck 卦運	Monthly Star 月星
Wood 木3		9	8

SUNDAY	MONDAY	TUESDAY	WEDNESDAY	THURSDAY	FRIDAY	SATURDAY
				金9 Metal Tread 天澤履 5 戊辰 Earth Dragon 6 1 初三	木8 Wood Great Strength 雷天大壯 4 己巳 Earth Snake 2 2 初四	木8 Wood Consistency 雷風恆 3 庚午 Metal Horse 9 3 初五
金9 Metal Litigation 天水訟 2 辛未 Metal Goat 3 4 初六	水1 Water Officer 地水師 1 壬申 Water Monkey 7 5 初七	火2 Fire Gradual Progress 風山漸 9 癸酉 Water Rooster 7 6 初八	火7 Fire Obstruction 水山蹇 8 甲戌 Wood Dog 2 7 初九	木3 Wood Advancement 火地晉 7 乙亥 Wood Pig 3 8 初十	水6 Water Nourish 山雷頤 6 丙子 Fire Rat 3 9 十一	金4 Metal Following 澤雷隨 5 丁丑 Fire Ox 7 10 十二
木8 Wood Abundance 雷火豐 4 戊寅 Earth Tiger 6 11 十三	火7 Fire Regulate 水澤節 3 己卯 Earth Rabbit 8 12 十四	水1 Water Unity 地天泰 2 庚辰 Metal Dragon 9 13 十五	木3 Wood Great Reward 火天大有 1 辛巳 Metal Snake 7 14 十六	火2 Fire Wind 巽爲風 9 壬午 Water Horse 1 15 十七	金4 Metal Trap 澤水困 8 癸未 Water Goat 8 16 十八	木3 Wood Not Yet Accomplished 火水未濟 7 甲申 Wood Monkey 9 17 十九
金9 Metal Retreat 天山遯 6 乙酉 Wood Rooster 4 18 二十	水6 Water Mountain 艮爲山 5 丙戌 Fire Dog 1 19 廿一	木8 Wood Delight 雷地豫 4 丁亥 Fire Pig 8 20 廿二	火7 Fire Beginning 水雷屯 3 戊子 Earth Rat 4 21 廿三	金9 Metal Without Wrongdoing 天雷無妄 2 己丑 Earth Ox 2 22 廿四	木3 Wood Fire 離爲火 1 庚寅 Metal Tiger 1 23 廿五	火2 Fire Sincerity 風澤中孚 9 辛卯 Metal Rabbit 3 24 廿六
水6 Water Big Livestock 山天大畜 8 壬辰 Water Dragon 4 25 廿七	金4 Metal Eliminating 澤天夬 7 癸巳 Water Snake 6 26 廿八	金9 Metal Heaven 乾爲天 6 甲午 Wood Horse 1 27 廿九	火7 Fire Well 水風井 5 乙未 Wood Goat 6 28 三十	木8 Wood Relief 雷水解 4 丙申 Fire Monkey 4 29 八月初一	金4 Metal Influence 澤山咸 3 丁酉 Fire Rooster 9 30 初二	水1 Water Humility 地山謙 2 戊戌 Earth Dog 6 31 初三

SEPTEMBER 2030 乙酉

Xuan Kong Element 玄空五行	天山遯 Retreat	Period Luck 卦運	Monthly Star 月星
Metal 金9		4	7

SUNDAY	MONDAY	TUESDAY	WEDNESDAY	THURSDAY	FRIDAY	SATURDAY
火2 Fire · Observation · 1 乙亥 Earth Pig · 2 風地觀 **1** 初四	火2 Fire · Increasing · 9 庚子 Metal Rat · 9 風雷益 **2** 初五	水1 Water · Dimming Light · 8 辛丑 Metal Ox · 3 地火明夷 **3** 初六	金9 Metal · Fellowship · 7 壬寅 Water Tiger · 7 天火同人 **4** 初七	木8 Wood · Marrying Maiden · 6 癸卯 Water Rabbit · 7 雷澤歸妹 **5** 初八	木3 Wood · Opposition · 5 甲辰 Wood Dragon · 2 火澤睽 **6** 初九	火7 Fire · Waiting · 4 乙巳 Wood Snake · 3 水天需 **7** 初十
金4 Metal · Great Exceeding · 3 丙午 Fire Horse · 3 澤風大過 **8** 十一	水6 Water · Poison · 2 丁未 Fire Goat · 7 山風蠱 **9** 十二	火2 Fire · Dispersing · 1 戊申 Earth Monkey · 6 風水渙 **10** 十三	木3 Wood · Travelling · 9 己酉 Earth Rooster · 8 火山旅 **11** 十四	金9 Metal · Stagnation · 8 庚戌 Metal Dog · 9 天地否 **12** 十五	火7 Fire · Alliance · 7 辛亥 Metal Pig · 7 水地比 **13** 十六	木8 Wood · Thunder · 6 壬子 Water Rat · 1 震爲雷 **14** 十七
水6 Water · Beauty · 5 癸丑 Water Ox · 8 山火賁 **15** 十八	火7 Fire · Accomplished · 4 甲寅 Wood Tiger · 9 水火既濟 **16** 十九	水1 Water · Arriving · 3 乙卯 Wood Rabbit · 4 地澤臨 **17** 二十	金4 Metal · Marsh · 2 丙辰 Fire Dragon · 1 兌爲澤 **18** 廿一	火2 Fire · Small Livestock · 1 丁巳 Fire Snake · 8 風天小畜 **19** 廿二	木3 Wood · The Cauldron · 9 戊午 Earth Horse · 4 火風鼎 **20** 廿三	水1 Water · Rising · 8 己未 Earth Goat · 2 地風升 **21** 廿四
火7 Fire · Water · 7 庚申 Metal Monkey · 1 坎爲水 **22** 廿五	木8 Wood · Lesser Exceeding · 6 辛酉 Metal Rooster · 3 雷山小過 **23** 廿六	金4 Metal · Gathering · 5 壬戌 Water Dog · 4 澤地萃 **24** 廿七	水6 Water · Peel · 4 癸亥 Water Pig · 6 山地剝 **25** 廿八	水1 Water · Earth · 3 甲子 Wood Rat · 1 坤爲地 **26** 廿九	木3 Wood · Biting · 2 乙丑 Wood Ox · 6 火雷噬嗑 **27** 九月初一	火2 Fire · Family · 1 丙寅 Fire Tiger · 4 風火家人 **28** 初二
水6 Water · Decreasing · 9 丁卯 Fire Rabbit · 9 山澤損 **29** 初三	金9 Metal · Tread · 8 戊辰 Earth Dragon · 6 天澤履 **30** 初四					

OCTOBER 2030 丙戌

Xuan Kong Element 玄空五行	艮爲山 Mountain	Period Luck 卦運	Monthly Star 月星
Water 水6		1	6

SUNDAY	MONDAY	TUESDAY	WEDNESDAY	THURSDAY	FRIDAY	SATURDAY
		木8 Wood · Great Strength · 7 己巳 Earth Snake · 2 雷天大壯 **1** 初五	木8 Wood · Consistency · 6 庚午 Metal Horse · 9 雷風恒 **2** 初六	金9 Metal · Litigation · 5 辛未 Metal Goat · 3 天水訟 **3** 初七	水1 Water · Officer · 4 壬申 Water Monkey · 7 地水師 **4** 初八	火2 Fire · Gradual Progress · 3 癸酉 Water Rooster · 7 風山漸 **5** 初九
火7 Fire · Obstruction · 2 甲戌 Wood Dog · 2 水山蹇 **6** 初十	木3 Wood · Advancement · 1 乙亥 Wood Pig · 3 火地晉 **7** 十一	水6 Water · Nourish · 9 丙子 Fire Rat · 3 山雷頤 **8** 十二	金4 Metal · Following · 8 丁丑 Fire Ox · 7 澤雷隨 **9** 十三	木8 Wood · Abundance · 7 戊寅 Earth Tiger · 6 雷火豐 **10** 十四	火7 Fire · Regulate · 6 己卯 Earth Rabbit · 8 水澤節 **11** 十五	水1 Water · Unity · 5 庚辰 Metal Dragon · 9 地天泰 **12** 十六
木3 Wood · Great Reward · 4 辛巳 Metal Snake · 7 火天大有 **13** 十七	火2 Fire · Wind · 3 壬午 Water Horse · 1 巽爲風 **14** 十八	金4 Metal · Trap · 2 癸未 Water Goat · 8 澤水困 **15** 十九	木3 Wood · Not Yet Accomplished · 1 甲申 Wood Monkey · 9 火水未濟 **16** 二十	金9 Metal · Retreat · 9 乙酉 Wood Rooster · 4 天山遯 **17** 廿一	水6 Water · Mountain · 8 丙戌 Fire Dog · 1 艮爲山 **18** 廿二	木8 Wood · Delight · 7 丁亥 Fire Pig · 8 雷地豫 **19** 廿三
火7 Fire · Beginning · 6 戊子 Earth Rat · 4 水雷屯 **20** 廿四	金9 Metal · Without Wrongdoing · 5 己丑 Earth Ox · 2 天雷無妄 **21** 廿五	木3 Wood · Fire · 4 庚寅 Metal Tiger · 1 離爲火 **22** 廿六	火2 Fire · Sincerity · 3 辛卯 Metal Rabbit · 3 風澤中孚 **23** 廿七	水6 Water · Big Livestock · 2 壬辰 Water Dragon · 4 山天大畜 **24** 廿八	金4 Metal · Eliminating · 1 癸巳 Water Snake · 6 澤天夬 **25** 廿九	金9 Metal · Heaven · 9 甲午 Wood Horse · 1 乾爲天 **26** 三十
火7 Fire · Well · 8 乙未 Wood Goat · 6 水風井 **27** 十月初一	木8 Wood · Relief · 7 丙申 Fire Monkey · 4 雷水解 **28** 初二	金4 Metal · Influence · 6 丁酉 Fire Rooster · 9 澤山咸 **29** 初三	水1 Water · Humility · 5 戊戌 Earth Dog · 6 地山謙 **30** 初四	火2 Fire · Observation · 4 己亥 Earth Pig · 2 風地觀 **31** 初五		

NOVEMBER 2030 丁亥

Xuan Kong Element 玄空五行	雷地豫 Delight	Period Luck 卦運	Monthly Star 月星
Wood 木8		8	5

SUNDAY	MONDAY	TUESDAY	WEDNESDAY	THURSDAY	FRIDAY	SATURDAY
					火2 Fire 3 Increasing 風雷益 庚子 Metal Rat 9 1 初六	水1 Water 2 Dimming Light 地火明夷 辛丑 Metal Ox 3 2 初七
金9 Metal 1 Fellowship 天火同人 壬寅 Water Tiger 7 3 初八	木8 Wood 9 Marrying Maiden 雷澤歸妹 癸卯 Water Rabbit 7 4 初九	木3 Wood 8 Opposition 火澤睽 甲辰 Wood Dragon 2 5 初十	火7 Fire 7 Waiting 水天需 乙巳 Wood Snake 3 6 十一	金4 Metal 6 Great Exceeding 澤風大過 丙午 Fire Horse 3 7 十二	水6 Water 5 Poison 山風蠱 丁未 Fire Goat 7 8 十三	火2 Fire 4 Dispersing 風水渙 戊申 Earth Monkey 6 9 十四
木3 Wood 3 Travelling 火山旅 己酉 Earth Rooster 8 10 十五	金9 Metal 2 Stagnation 天地否 庚戌 Metal Dog 9 11 十六	火7 Fire 1 Alliance 水地比 辛亥 Metal Pig 7 12 十七	木8 Wood 9 Thunder 震爲雷 壬子 Water Rat 1 13 十八	水6 Water 8 Beauty 山火賁 癸丑 Water Ox 8 14 十九	火7 Fire 7 Accomplished 水火既濟 甲寅 Wood Tiger 9 15 二十	水1 Water 6 Arriving 地澤臨 乙卯 Wood Rabbit 4 16 廿一
金4 Metal 5 Marsh 兑爲澤 丙辰 Fire Dragon 1 17 廿二	火2 Fire 4 Small Livestock 風天小畜 丁巳 Fire Snake 8 18 廿三	木3 Wood 3 The Cauldron 火風鼎 戊午 Earth Horse 4 19 廿四	水1 Water 2 Rising 地風升 己未 Earth Goat 2 20 廿五	火7 Fire 1 Water 坎爲水 庚申 Metal Monkey 1 21 廿六	木8 Wood 9 Lesser Exceeding 雷山小過 辛酉 Metal Rooster 3 22 廿七	金4 Metal 8 Gathering 澤地萃 壬戌 Water Dog 4 23 廿八
水6 Water 7 Peel 山地剝 癸亥 Water Pig 6 24 廿九	水1 Water 6 Earth 坤爲地 甲子 Wood Rat 1 25 十一月初一	木3 Wood 5 Biting 火雷噬嗑 乙丑 Wood Ox 6 26 初二	火2 Fire 4 Family 風火家人 丙寅 Fire Tiger 4 27 初三	水6 Water 3 Decreasing 山澤損 丁卯 Fire Rabbit 9 28 初四	金9 Metal 2 Tread 天澤履 戊辰 Earth Dragon 6 29 初五	木8 Wood 1 Great Strength 雷天大壯 己巳 Earth Snake 2 30 初六

DECEMBER 2030 戊子

Xuan Kong Element 玄空五行	水雷屯 Beginning	Period Luck 卦運	Monthly Star 月星
Fire 火7		4	4

SUNDAY	MONDAY	TUESDAY	WEDNESDAY	THURSDAY	FRIDAY	SATURDAY
木8 Wood 9 Consistency 雷風恒 庚午 Metal Horse 9 1 初七	金9 Metal 8 Litigation 天水訟 辛未 Metal Goat 3 2 初八	水1 Water 7 Officer 地水師 壬申 Water Monkey 7 3 初九	火2 Fire 6 Gradual Progress 風山漸 癸酉 Water Rooster 7 4 初十	火7 Fire 5 Obstruction 水山蹇 甲戌 Wood Dog 2 5 十一	木3 Wood 4 Advancement 火地晉 乙亥 Wood Pig 3 6 十二	水6 Water 3 Nourish 山雷頤 丙子 Fire Rat 3 7 十三
金4 Metal 2 Following 澤雷隨 丁丑 Fire Ox 7 8 十四	木8 Wood 1 Abundance 雷火豐 戊寅 Earth Tiger 6 9 十五	火7 Fire 9 Regulate 水澤節 己卯 Earth Rabbit 8 10 十六	水1 Water 8 Unity 地天泰 庚辰 Metal Dragon 9 11 十七	木3 Wood 7 Great Reward 火天大有 辛巳 Metal Snake 7 12 十八	火2 Fire 6 Wind 巽爲風 壬午 Water Horse 1 13 十九	金4 Metal 5 Trap 澤水困 癸未 Water Goat 8 14 二十
木3 Wood 4 Not Yet Accomplished 火水未濟 甲申 Wood Monkey 9 15 廿一	金9 Metal 3 Retreat 天山遯 乙酉 Wood Rooster 4 16 廿二	水6 Water 2 Mountain 艮爲山 丙戌 Fire Dog 1 17 廿三	木8 Wood 1 Delight 雷地豫 丁亥 Fire Pig 8 18 廿四	火7 Fire 9 Beginning 水雷屯 戊子 Earth Rat 4 19 廿五	金9 Metal 8 Without Wrongdoing 天雷無妄 己丑 Earth Ox 2 20 廿六	木3 Wood 7 Fire 離爲火 庚寅 Metal Tiger 1 21 廿七
火2 Fire 6/4 Sincerity 風澤中孚 辛卯 Metal Rabbit 3 22 廿八	水6 Water 5 Big Livestock 山天大畜 壬辰 Water Dragon 4 23 廿九	金4 Metal 6 Eliminating 澤天夬 癸巳 Water Snake 6 24 三十	金9 Metal 7 Heaven 乾爲天 甲午 Wood Horse 1 25 十二月初一	火7 Fire 8 Well 水風井 乙未 Wood Goat 6 26 初二	木8 Wood 9 Relief 雷水解 丙申 Fire Monkey 4 27 初三	金4 Metal 1 Influence 澤山咸 丁酉 Fire Rooster 9 28 初四
水1 Water 2 Humility 地山謙 戊戌 Earth Dog 6 29 初五	火2 Fire 3 Observation 風地觀 己亥 Earth Pig 2 30 初六	火2 Fire 4 Increasing 風雷益 庚子 Metal Rat 9 31 初七				

2031 辛亥

(*Xin Hai*) Metal Pig

2031 辛亥 *(Xin Hai)* Metal Pig

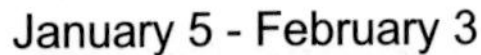

January 5 - February 3

February 4 - March 5

March 6 - April 4

April 5 - May 5

May 6 - June 5

June 6 - July 6

SE S SW
6 2 4
E 5 7 9 W
1 3 8
NE N NW
金9 Metal
甲午 Wood Horse
1 Heaven
乾爲天
Three Killings North

July 7 - August 7

August 8 - September 7

September 8 - October 7

October 8 - November 6

November 7 - December 6

December 7 - January 5

JANUARY 2031 己丑

Xuan Kong Element 玄空五行	天雷無妄 Without Wrongdoing	Period Luck 卦運	Monthly Star 月星
Metal 金9		2	3

SUNDAY	MONDAY	TUESDAY	WEDNESDAY	THURSDAY	FRIDAY	SATURDAY
			水1 Water · 5 Dimming Light 地火明夷 辛丑 Metal Ox · 3 **1** 初八	金9 Metal · 6 Fellowship 天火同人 壬寅 Water Tiger · 7 **2** 初九	木8 Wood · 7 Marrying Maiden 雷澤歸妹 癸卯 Water Rabbit · 7 **3** 初十	木3 Wood · 8 Opposition 火澤睽 甲辰 Wood Dragon · 2 **4** 十一
火7 Fire · 9 Waiting 水天需 乙巳 Wood Snake · 3 **5** 十二	金4 Metal · 1 Great Exceeding 澤風大過 丙午 Fire Horse · 3 **6** 十三	水6 Water · 2 Poison 山風蠱 丁未 Fire Goat · 7 **7** 十四	火2 Fire · 3 Dispersing 風水渙 戊申 Earth Monkey · 6 **8** 十五	木3 Wood · 4 Travelling 火山旅 己酉 Earth Rooster · 8 **9** 十六	金9 Metal · 5 Stagnation 天地否 庚戌 Metal Dog · 9 **10** 十七	火7 Fire · 6 Alliance 水地比 辛亥 Metal Pig · 7 **11** 十八
木8 Wood · 7 Thunder 震為雷 壬子 Water Rat · 1 **12** 十九	水6 Water · 8 Beauty 山火賁 癸丑 Water Ox · 8 **13** 二十	火7 Fire · 9 Accomplished 水火既濟 甲寅 Wood Tiger · 9 **14** 廿一	水1 Water · 1 Arriving 地澤臨 乙卯 Wood Rabbit · 4 **15** 廿二	金4 Metal · 2 Marsh 兌為澤 丙辰 Fire Dragon · 1 **16** 廿三	火2 Fire · 3 Small Livestock 風天小畜 丁巳 Fire Snake · 8 **17** 廿四	木3 Wood · 4 The Cauldron 火風鼎 戊午 Earth Horse · 4 **18** 廿五
水1 Water · 5 Rising 地風升 己未 Earth Goat · 2 **19** 廿六	火7 Fire · 6 Water 坎為水 庚申 Metal Monkey · 1 **20** 廿七	木8 Wood · 7 Lesser Exceeding 雷山小過 辛酉 Metal Rooster · 3 **21** 廿八	金4 Metal · 8 Gathering 澤地萃 壬戌 Water Dog · 4 **22** 廿九	水6 Water · 9 Peel 山地剝 癸亥 Water Pig · 6 **23** 正月初一	水1 Water · 1 Earth 坤為地 甲子 Wood Rat · 1 **24** 初二	木3 Wood · 2 Biting 火雷噬嗑 乙丑 Wood Ox · 6 **25** 初三
火2 Fire · 3 Family 風火家人 丙寅 Fire Tiger · 4 **26** 初四	水6 Water · 4 Decreasing 山澤損 丁卯 Fire Rabbit · 9 **27** 初五	金9 Metal · 5 Tread 天澤履 戊辰 Earth Dragon · 6 **28** 初六	木8 Wood · 6 Great Strength 雷天大壯 己巳 Earth Snake · 2 **29** 初七	木8 Wood · 7 Consistency 雷風恆 庚午 Metal Horse · 9 **30** 初八	金9 Metal · 8 Litigation 天水訟 辛未 Metal Goat · 3 **31** 初九	

FEBRUARY 2031 庚寅

Xuan Kong Element 玄空五行	離為火 Fire	Period Luck 卦運	Monthly Star 月星
Wood 木3		1	2

SUNDAY	MONDAY	TUESDAY	WEDNESDAY	THURSDAY	FRIDAY	SATURDAY
						水1 Water · 9 Officer 地水師 壬申 Water Monkey · 7 **1** 初十
火2 Fire · 1 Gradual Progress 風山漸 癸酉 Water Rooster · 7 **2** 十一	火7 Fire · 2 Obstruction 水山蹇 甲戌 Wood Dog · 2 **3** 十二	木3 Wood · 3 Advancement 火地晉 乙亥 Wood Pig · 3 **4** 十三	水6 Water · 4 Nourish 山雷頤 丙子 Fire Rat · 3 **5** 十四	金4 Metal · 5 Following 澤雷隨 丁丑 Fire Ox · 7 **6** 十五	木8 Wood · 6 Abundance 雷火豐 戊寅 Earth Tiger · 6 **7** 十六	火7 Fire · 7 Regulate 水澤節 己卯 Earth Rabbit · 8 **8** 十七
水1 Water · 8 Unity 地天泰 庚辰 Metal Dragon · 9 **9** 十八	木3 Wood · 9 Great Reward 火天大有 辛巳 Metal Snake · 7 **10** 十九	火2 Fire · 1 Wind 巽為風 壬午 Water Horse · 1 **11** 二十	金4 Metal · 2 Trap 澤水困 癸未 Water Goat · 8 **12** 廿一	木3 Wood · 3 Not Yet Accomplished 火水未濟 甲申 Wood Monkey · 9 **13** 廿二	金9 Metal · 4 Retreat 天山遯 乙酉 Wood Rooster · 4 **14** 廿三	水6 Water · 5 Mountain 艮為山 丙戌 Fire Dog · 1 **15** 廿四
木8 Wood · 6 Delight 雷地豫 丁亥 Fire Pig · 8 **16** 廿五	火7 Fire · 7 Beginning 水雷屯 戊子 Earth Rat · 4 **17** 廿六	金9 Metal · 8 Without Wrongdoing 天雷無妄 己丑 Earth Ox · 2 **18** 廿七	木3 Wood · 9 Fire 離為火 庚寅 Metal Tiger · 1 **19** 廿八	火2 Fire · 1 Sincerity 風澤中孚 辛卯 Metal Rabbit · 3 **20** 廿九	水6 Water · 2 Big Livestock 山天大畜 壬辰 Water Dragon · 4 **21** 二月初一	金4 Metal · 3 Eliminating 澤天夬 癸巳 Water Snake · 6 **22** 初二
金9 Metal · 4 Heaven 乾為天 甲午 Wood Horse · 1 **23** 初三	火7 Fire · 5 Well 水風井 乙未 Wood Goat · 6 **24** 初四	木8 Wood · 6 Relief 雷水解 丙申 Fire Monkey · 4 **25** 初五	金4 Metal · 7 Influence 澤山咸 丁酉 Fire Rooster · 9 **26** 初六	水1 Water · 8 Humility 地山謙 戊戌 Earth Dog · 6 **27** 初七	火2 Fire · 9 Observation 風地觀 己亥 Earth Pig · 2 **28** 初八	

MARCH 2031 辛卯

Xuan Kong Element 玄空五行	風澤中孚 Sincerity	Period Luck 卦運	Monthly Star 月星
Fire 火2		3	1

SUNDAY	MONDAY	TUESDAY	WEDNESDAY	THURSDAY	FRIDAY	SATURDAY
木8 Wood Great Strength 3 己巳 Earth Snake 雷天大壯 30 初八 2	木8 Wood Consistency 4 庚午 Metal Horse 雷風恆 31 初九 9					火2 Fire Increasing 1 庚子 Metal Rat 風雷益 1 初九 9
水1 Water Dimming Light 2 辛丑 Metal Ox 地火明夷 2 初十 3	金9 Metal Fellowship 3 壬寅 Water Tiger 天火同人 3 十一 7	木8 Wood Marrying Maiden 4 癸卯 Water Rabbit 雷澤歸妹 4 十二 7	木3 Wood Opposition 5 甲辰 Wood Dragon 火澤睽 5 十三 2	火7 Fire Waiting 6 乙巳 Wood Snake 水天需 6 十四 3	金4 Metal Great Exceeding 7 丙午 Fire Horse 澤風大過 7 十五 3	水6 Water Poison 8 丁未 Fire Goat 山風蠱 8 十六 7
火2 Fire Dispersing 9 戊申 Earth Monkey 風水渙 9 十七 6	木3 Wood Travelling 1 己酉 Earth Rooster 火山旅 10 十八 8	金9 Metal Stagnation 2 庚戌 Metal Dog 天地否 11 十九 9	火7 Fire Alliance 3 辛亥 Metal Pig 水地比 12 二十 7	木8 Wood Thunder 4 壬子 Water Rat 震爲雷 13 廿一 1	水6 Water Beauty 5 癸丑 Water Ox 山火賁 14 廿二 8	火7 Fire Accomplished 6 甲寅 Wood Tiger 水火既濟 15 廿三 9
水1 Water Arriving 7 乙卯 Wood Rabbit 地澤臨 16 廿四 4	金4 Metal Marsh 8 丙辰 Fire Dragon 兌爲澤 17 廿五 1	火2 Fire Small Livestock 9 丁巳 Fire Snake 風天小畜 18 廿六 8	木3 Wood The Cauldron 1 戊午 Earth Horse 火風鼎 19 廿七 4	水1 Water Rising 2 己未 Earth Goat 地風升 20 廿八 2	火7 Fire Water 3 庚申 Metal Monkey 坎爲水 21 廿九 1	木8 Wood Lesser Exceeding 4 辛酉 Metal Rooster 雷山小過 22 三十 3
金4 Metal Gathering 5 壬戌 Water Dog 澤地萃 23 三月初一 4	水6 Water Peel 6 癸亥 Water Pig 山地剝 24 初二 6	水1 Water Earth 7 甲子 Wood Rat 坤爲地 25 初三 1	木3 Wood Biting 8 乙丑 Wood Ox 火雷噬嗑 26 初四 6	火2 Fire Family 9 丙寅 Fire Tiger 風火家人 27 初五 4	水6 Water Decreasing 1 丁卯 Fire Rabbit 山澤損 28 初六 9	金9 Metal Tread 2 戊辰 Earth Dragon 天澤履 29 初七 6

APRIL 2031 壬辰

Xuan Kong Element 玄空五行	山天大畜 Big Livestock	Period Luck 卦運	Monthly Star 月星
Water 水6		4	9

SUNDAY	MONDAY	TUESDAY	WEDNESDAY	THURSDAY	FRIDAY	SATURDAY
		金9 Metal Litigation 5 辛未 Metal Goat 天水訟 1 初十 3	水1 Water Officer 6 壬申 Water Monkey 地水師 2 十一 7	火2 Fire Gradual Progress 7 癸酉 Water Rooster 風山漸 3 十二 7	火7 Fire Obstruction 8 甲戌 Wood Dog 水山蹇 4 十三 2	木3 Wood Advancement 9 乙亥 Wood Pig 火地晉 5 十四 3
水6 Water Nourish 1 丙子 Fire Rat 山雷頤 6 十五 3	金4 Metal Following 2 丁丑 Fire Ox 澤雷隨 7 十六 7	木8 Wood Abundance 3 戊寅 Earth Tiger 雷火豐 8 十七 6	火7 Fire Regulate 4 己卯 Earth Rabbit 水澤節 9 十八 8	水1 Water Unity 5 庚辰 Metal Dragon 地天泰 10 十九 9	木3 Wood Great Reward 6 辛巳 Metal Snake 火天大有 11 二十 7	火2 Fire Wind 7 壬午 Water Horse 巽爲風 12 廿一 1
金4 Metal Trap 8 癸未 Water Goat 澤水困 13 廿二 8	木3 Wood Not Yet Accomplished 9 甲申 Wood Monkey 火水未濟 14 廿三 9	金9 Metal Retreat 1 乙酉 Wood Rooster 天山遯 15 廿四 4	水6 Water Mountain 2 丙戌 Fire Dog 艮爲山 16 廿五 1	木8 Wood Delight 3 丁亥 Fire Pig 雷地豫 17 廿六 8	火7 Fire Beginning 4 戊子 Earth Rat 水雷屯 18 廿七 4	金9 Metal Without Wrongdoing 5 己丑 Earth Ox 天雷無妄 19 廿八 2
木3 Wood Fire 6 庚寅 Metal Tiger 離爲火 20 廿九 1	火2 Fire Sincerity 7 辛卯 Metal Rabbit 風澤中孚 21 三十 3	水6 Water Big Livestock 8 壬辰 Water Dragon 山天大畜 22 閏三月初一 4	金4 Metal Eliminating 9 癸巳 Water Snake 澤天夬 23 初二 6	金9 Metal Heaven 1 甲午 Wood Horse 乾爲天 24 初三 1	火7 Fire Well 2 乙未 Wood Goat 水風井 25 初四 6	木8 Wood Relief 3 丙申 Fire Monkey 雷水解 26 初五 4
金4 Metal Influence 4 丁酉 Fire Rooster 澤山咸 27 初六 9	水1 Water Humility 5 戊戌 Earth Dog 地山謙 28 初七 6	火2 Fire Observation 6 己亥 Earth Pig 風地觀 29 初八 2	火2 Fire Increasing 7 庚子 Metal Rat 風雷益 30 初九 9			

MAY 2031 癸巳

Xuan Kong Element 玄空五行	澤天夬 Eliminating	Period Luck 卦運	Monthly Star 月星
Metal 金4		6	8

SUNDAY	MONDAY	TUESDAY	WEDNESDAY	THURSDAY	FRIDAY	SATURDAY
				水1 Water 8 Dimming Light 地火明夷 辛丑 Metal Ox 3 1 初十	金9 Metal 9 Fellowship 天火同人 壬寅 Water Tiger 7 2 十一	木8 Wood 1 Marrying Maiden 雷澤歸妹 癸卯 Water Rabbit 7 3 十二
木3 Wood 2 Opposition 火澤睽 甲辰 Wood Dragon 2 4 十三	火7 Fire 3 Waiting 水天需 乙巳 Wood Snake 3 5 十四	金4 Metal 4 Great Exceeding 澤風大過 丙午 Fire Horse 3 6 十五	水6 Water 5 Poison 山風蠱 丁未 Fire Goat 7 7 十六	火2 Fire 6 Dispersing 風水渙 戊申 Earth Monkey 6 8 十七	木3 Wood 7 Travelling 火山旅 己酉 Earth Rooster 8 9 十八	金9 Metal 8 Stagnation 天地否 庚戌 Metal Dog 9 10 十九
火7 Fire 9 Alliance 水地比 辛亥 Metal Pig 7 11 二十	木8 Wood 1 Thunder 震爲雷 壬子 Water Rat 1 12 廿一	水6 Water 2 Beauty 山火賁 癸丑 Water Ox 8 13 廿二	火7 Fire 3 Accomplished 水火既濟 甲寅 Wood Tiger 9 14 廿三	水1 Water 4 Arriving 地澤臨 乙卯 Wood Rabbit 4 15 廿四	金4 Metal 5 Marsh 兌爲澤 丙辰 Fire Dragon 1 16 廿五	火2 Fire 6 Small Livestock 風天小畜 丁巳 Fire Snake 8 17 廿六
木3 Wood 7 The Cauldron 火風鼎 戊午 Earth Horse 4 18 廿七	水1 Water 8 Rising 地風升 己未 Earth Goat 2 19 廿八	火7 Fire 9 Water 坎爲水 庚申 Metal Monkey 1 20 廿九	木8 Wood 1 Lesser Exceeding 雷山小過 辛酉 Metal Rooster 3 21 四月初一	金4 Metal 2 Gathering 澤地萃 壬戌 Water Dog 4 22 初二	水6 Water 3 Peel 山地剝 癸亥 Water Pig 6 23 初三	水1 Water 4 Earth 坤爲地 甲子 Wood Rat 1 24 初四
木3 Wood 5 Biting 火雷噬嗑 乙丑 Wood Ox 6 25 初五	火2 Fire 6 Family 風火家人 丙寅 Fire Tiger 4 26 初六	水6 Water 7 Decreasing 山澤損 丁卯 Fire Rabbit 9 27 初七	金9 Metal 8 Tread 天澤履 戊辰 Earth Dragon 6 28 初八	木8 Wood 9 Great Strength 雷天大壯 己巳 Earth Snake 2 29 初九	木8 Wood 1 Consistency 雷風恆 庚午 Metal Horse 9 30 初十	金9 Metal 2 Litigation 天水訟 辛未 Metal Goat 3 31 十一

JUNE 2031 甲午

Xuan Kong Element 玄空五行	乾爲天 Heaven	Period Luck 卦運	Monthly Star 月星
Metal 金9		1	7

SUNDAY	MONDAY	TUESDAY	WEDNESDAY	THURSDAY	FRIDAY	SATURDAY
水1 Water 3 Officer 地水師 壬申 Water Monkey 7 1 十二	火2 Fire 4 Gradual Progress 風山漸 癸酉 Water Rooster 7 2 十三	火7 Fire 5 Obstruction 水山蹇 甲戌 Wood Dog 2 3 十四	木3 Wood 6 Advancement 火地晉 乙亥 Wood Pig 3 4 十五	水6 Water 7 Nourish 山雷頤 丙子 Fire Rat 3 5 十六	金4 Metal 8 Following 澤雷隨 丁丑 Fire Ox 7 6 十七	木8 Wood 9 Abundance 雷火豐 戊寅 Earth Tiger 6 7 十八
火7 Fire 1 Regulate 水澤節 己卯 Earth Rabbit 8 8 十九	水1 Water 2 Unity 地天泰 庚辰 Metal Dragon 9 9 二十	木3 Wood 3 Great Reward 火天大有 辛巳 Metal Snake 7 10 廿一	火2 Fire 4 Wind 巽爲風 壬午 Water Horse 1 11 廿二	金4 Metal 5 Trap 澤水困 癸未 Water Goat 8 12 廿三	木3 Wood 6 Not Yet Accomplished 火水未濟 甲申 Wood Monkey 9 13 廿四	金9 Metal 7 Retreat 天山遯 乙酉 Wood Rooster 4 14 廿五
水6 Water 8 Mountain 艮爲山 丙戌 Fire Dog 1 15 廿六	木8 Wood 9 Delight 雷地豫 丁亥 Fire Pig 8 16 廿七	火7 Fire 1 Beginning 水雷屯 戊子 Earth Rat 4 17 廿八	金9 Metal 2 Without Wrongdoing 天雷無妄 己丑 Earth Ox 2 18 廿九	木3 Wood 3 Fire 離爲火 庚寅 Metal Tiger 1 19 三十	火2 Fire 4 Sincerity 風澤中孚 辛卯 Metal Rabbit 3 20 五月初一	水6 Water 5/5 Big Livestock 山天大畜 壬辰 Water Dragon 4 21 初二
金4 Metal 4 Eliminating 澤天夬 癸巳 Water Snake 6 22 初三	金9 Metal 3 Heaven 乾爲天 甲午 Wood Horse 1 23 初四	火7 Fire 2 Well 水風井 乙未 Wood Goat 6 24 初五	木8 Wood 1 Relief 雷水解 丙申 Fire Monkey 4 25 初六	金4 Metal 9 Influence 澤山咸 丁酉 Fire Rooster 9 26 初七	水1 Water 8 Humility 地山謙 戊戌 Earth Dog 6 27 初八	火2 Fire 7 Observation 風地觀 己亥 Earth Pig 2 28 初九
火2 Fire 6 Increasing 風雷益 庚子 Metal Rat 9 29 初十	水1 Water 5 Dimming Light 地火明夷 辛丑 Metal Ox 3 30 十一					

JULY 2031 乙未

Xuan Kong Element 玄空五行	水風井 Well	Period Luck 卦運	Monthly Star 月星
Fire 火7		6	6

SUNDAY	MONDAY	TUESDAY	WEDNESDAY	THURSDAY	FRIDAY	SATURDAY
		金9 Metal 4 Fellowship 天火同人 壬寅 Water Tiger 1 十二 7	木8 Wood 3 Marrying Maiden 雷澤歸妹 癸卯 Water Rabbit 2 十三 7	木3 Wood 2 Opposition 火澤睽 甲辰 Wood Dragon 3 十四 2	火7 Fire 1 Waiting 水天需 乙巳 Wood Snake 4 十五 3	金4 Metal 9 Great Exceeding 澤風大過 丙午 Fire Horse 5 十六 3
水6 Water 8 Poison 山風蠱 丁未 Fire Goat 6 十七 7	火2 Fire 7 Dispersing 風水渙 戊申 Earth Monkey 7 十八 6	木3 Wood 6 Travelling 火山旅 己酉 Earth Rooster 8 十九 8	金9 Metal 5 Stagnation 天地否 庚戌 Metal Dog 9 二十 9	火7 Fire 4 Alliance 水地比 辛亥 Metal Pig 10 廿一 7	木8 Wood 3 Thunder 震爲雷 壬子 Water Rat 11 廿二 1	水6 Water 2 Beauty 山火賁 癸丑 Water Ox 12 廿三 8
火7 Fire 1 Accomplished 水火既濟 甲寅 Wood Tiger 13 廿四 9	水1 Water 9 Arriving 地澤臨 乙卯 Wood Rabbit 14 廿五 4	金4 Metal 8 Marsh 兑爲澤 丙辰 Fire Dragon 15 廿六 1	火2 Fire 7 Small Livestock 風天小畜 丁巳 Fire Snake 16 廿七 8	木3 Wood 6 The Cauldron 火風鼎 戊午 Earth Horse 17 廿八 4	水1 Water 5 Rising 地風升 己未 Earth Goat 18 廿九 2	火7 Fire 4 Water 坎爲水 庚申 Metal Monkey 19 六月初一 1
木8 Wood 3 Lesser Exceeding 雷山小過 辛酉 Metal Rooster 20 初二 3	金4 Metal 2 Gathering 澤地萃 壬戌 Water Dog 21 初三 4	水6 Water 1 Peel 山地剝 癸亥 Water Pig 22 初四 6	水1 Water 9 Earth 坤爲地 甲子 Wood Rat 23 初五 1	木3 Wood 8 Biting 火雷噬嗑 乙丑 Wood Ox 24 初六 6	火2 Fire 7 Family 風火家人 丙寅 Fire Tiger 25 初七 4	水6 Water 6 Decreasing 山澤損 丁卯 Fire Rabbit 26 初八 9
金9 Metal 5 Tread 天澤履 戊辰 Earth Dragon 27 初九 6	木8 Wood 4 Great Strength 雷天大壯 己巳 Earth Snake 28 初十 2	木8 Wood 3 Consistency 雷風恒 庚午 Metal Horse 29 十一 9	金9 Metal 2 Litigation 天水訟 辛未 Metal Goat 30 十二 3	水1 Water 1 Officer 地水師 壬申 Water Monkey 31 十三 7		

AUGUST 2031 丙申

Xuan Kong Element 玄空五行	雷水解 Relief	Period Luck 卦運	Monthly Star 月星
Wood 木8		4	5

SUNDAY	MONDAY	TUESDAY	WEDNESDAY	THURSDAY	FRIDAY	SATURDAY
木8 Wood 6 Marrying Maiden 雷澤歸妹 癸卯 Water Rabbit 31 十四 7					火2 Fire 9 Gradual Progress 風山漸 癸酉 Water Rooster 1 十四 7	火7 Fire 8 Obstruction 水山蹇 甲戌 Wood Dog 2 十五 2
木3 Wood 7 Advancement 火地晉 乙亥 Wood Pig 3 十六 3	水6 Water 6 Nourish 山雷頤 丙子 Fire Rat 4 十七 3	金4 Metal 5 Following 澤雷隨 丁丑 Fire Ox 5 十八 7	木8 Wood 4 Abundance 雷火豐 戊寅 Earth Tiger 6 十九 6	火7 Fire 3 Regulate 水澤節 己卯 Earth Rabbit 7 二十 8	水1 Water 2 Unity 地天泰 庚辰 Metal Dragon 8 廿一 9	木3 Wood 1 Great Reward 火天大有 辛巳 Metal Snake 9 廿二 7
火2 Fire 9 Wind 巽爲風 壬午 Water Horse 10 廿三 1	金4 Metal 8 Trap 澤水困 癸未 Water Goat 11 廿四 8	木3 Wood 7 Not Yet Accomplished 火水未濟 甲申 Wood Monkey 12 廿五 9	金9 Metal 6 Retreat 天山遯 乙酉 Wood Rooster 13 廿六 4	水6 Water 5 Mountain 艮爲山 丙戌 Fire Dog 14 廿七 1	木8 Wood 4 Delight 雷地豫 丁亥 Fire Pig 15 廿八 8	火7 Fire 3 Beginning 水雷屯 戊子 Earth Rat 16 廿九 4
金9 Metal 2 Without Wrongdoing 天雷無妄 己丑 Earth Ox 17 三十 2	木3 Wood 1 Fire 離爲火 庚寅 Metal Tiger 18 七月初一 1	火2 Fire 9 Sincerity 風澤中孚 辛卯 Metal Rabbit 19 初二 3	水6 Water 8 Big Livestock 山天大畜 壬辰 Water Dragon 20 初三 4	金4 Metal 7 Eliminating 澤天夬 癸巳 Water Snake 21 初四 6	金9 Metal 6 Heaven 乾爲天 甲午 Wood Horse 22 初五 1	火7 Fire 5 Well 水風井 乙未 Wood Goat 23 初六 6
木8 Wood 4 Relief 雷水解 丙申 Fire Monkey 24 初七 4	金4 Metal 3 Influence 澤山咸 丁酉 Fire Rooster 25 初八 9	水1 Water 2 Humility 地山謙 戊戌 Earth Dog 26 初九 6	火2 Fire 1 Observation 風地觀 己亥 Earth Pig 27 初十 2	火2 Fire 9 Increasing 風雷益 庚子 Metal Rat 28 十一 9	水1 Water 8 Dimming Light 地火明夷 辛丑 Metal Ox 29 十二 3	金9 Metal 7 Fellowship 天火同人 壬寅 Water Tiger 30 十三 7

SEPTEMBER 2031 丁酉

Xuan Kong Element 玄空五行	澤山咸 Influence	Period Luck 卦運	Monthly Star 月星
Metal 金4		9	4

SUNDAY	MONDAY	TUESDAY	WEDNESDAY	THURSDAY	FRIDAY	SATURDAY
	木3 Wood 5 Opposition 甲辰 Wood Dragon 火澤睽 1 十五 2	火7 Fire 4 Waiting 乙巳 Wood Snake 水天需 2 十六 3	金4 Metal 3 Great Exceeding 丙午 Fire Horse 澤風大過 3 十七 3	水6 Water 2 Poison 丁未 Fire Goat 山風蠱 4 十八 7	火2 Fire 1 Dispersing 戊申 Earth Monkey 風水渙 5 十九 6	木3 Wood 9 Travelling 己酉 Earth Rooster 火山旅 6 二十 8
金9 Metal 8 Stagnation 庚戌 Metal Dog 天地否 7 廿一 9	火7 Fire 7 Alliance 辛亥 Metal Pig 水地比 8 廿二 7	木8 Wood 6 Thunder 壬子 Water Rat 震爲雷 9 廿三 1	水6 Water 5 Beauty 癸丑 Water Ox 山火賁 10 廿四 8	火7 Fire 4 Accomplished 甲寅 Wood Tiger 水火既濟 11 廿五 9	水1 Water 3 Arriving 乙卯 Wood Rabbit 地澤臨 12 廿六 4	金4 Metal 2 Marsh 丙辰 Fire Dragon 兑爲澤 13 廿七 1
火2 Fire 1 Small Livestock 丁巳 Fire Snake 風天小畜 14 廿八 8	木3 Wood 9 The Cauldron 戊午 Earth Horse 火風鼎 15 廿九 4	水1 Water 8 Rising 己未 Earth Goat 地風升 16 三十 2	火7 Fire 7 Water 庚申 Metal Monkey 坎爲水 17 八月初一 1	木8 Wood 6 Lesser Exceeding 辛酉 Metal Rooster 雷山小過 18 初二 3	金4 Metal 5 Gathering 壬戌 Water Dog 澤地萃 19 初三 4	水6 Water 4 Peel 癸亥 Water Pig 山地剝 20 初四 6
水1 Water 3 Earth 甲子 Wood Rat 坤爲地 21 初五 1	木3 Wood 2 Biting 乙丑 Wood Ox 火雷噬嗑 22 初六 6	火2 Fire 1 Family 丙寅 Fire Tiger 風火家人 23 初七 4	水6 Water 9 Decreasing 丁卯 Fire Rabbit 山澤損 24 初八 9	金9 Metal 8 Tread 戊辰 Earth Dragon 天澤履 25 初九 6	木8 Wood 7 Great Strength 己巳 Earth Snake 雷天大壯 26 初十 2	木8 Wood 6 Consistency 庚午 Metal Horse 雷風恆 27 十一 9
金9 Metal 5 Litigation 辛未 Metal Goat 天水訟 28 十二 3	水1 Water 4 Officer 壬申 Water Monkey 地水師 29 十三 7	火2 Fire 3 Gradual Progress 癸酉 Water Rooster 風山漸 30 十四 7				

OCTOBER 2031 戊戌

Xuan Kong Element 玄空五行	地山謙 Humility	Period Luck 卦運	Monthly Star 月星
Water 水1		6	3

SUNDAY	MONDAY	TUESDAY	WEDNESDAY	THURSDAY	FRIDAY	SATURDAY
			火7 Fire 2 Obstruction 甲戌 Wood Dog 水山蹇 1 十五 2	木3 Wood 1 Advancement 乙亥 Wood Pig 火地晉 2 十六 3	水6 Water 9 Nourish 丙子 Fire Rat 山雷頤 3 十七 3	金4 Metal 8 Following 丁丑 Fire Ox 澤雷隨 4 十八 7
木8 Wood 7 Abundance 戊寅 Earth Tiger 雷火豐 5 十九 6	火7 Fire 6 Regulate 己卯 Earth Rabbit 水澤節 6 二十 8	水1 Water 5 Unity 庚辰 Metal Dragon 地天泰 7 廿一 9	木3 Wood 4 Great Reward 辛巳 Metal Snake 火天大有 8 廿二 7	火2 Fire 3 Wind 壬午 Water Horse 巽爲風 9 廿三 1	金4 Metal 2 Trap 癸未 Water Goat 澤水困 10 廿四 8	木3 Wood 1 Not Yet Accomplished 甲申 Wood Monkey 火水未濟 11 廿五 9
金9 Metal 9 Retreat 乙酉 Wood Rooster 天山遯 12 廿六 4	水6 Water 8 Mountain 丙戌 Fire Dog 艮爲山 13 廿七 1	木8 Wood 7 Delight 丁亥 Fire Pig 雷地豫 14 廿八 8	火7 Fire 6 Beginning 戊子 Earth Rat 水雷屯 15 廿九 4	金9 Metal 5 Without Wrongdoing 己丑 Earth Ox 天雷無妄 16 九月初一 2	木3 Wood 4 Fire 庚寅 Metal Tiger 離爲火 17 初二 1	火2 Fire 3 Sincerity 辛卯 Metal Rabbit 風澤中孚 18 初三 3
水6 Water 2 Big Livestock 壬辰 Water Dragon 山天大畜 19 初四 4	金4 Metal 1 Eliminating 癸巳 Water Snake 澤天夬 20 初五 6	金9 Metal 9 Heaven 甲午 Wood Horse 乾爲天 21 初六 1	火7 Fire 8 Well 乙未 Wood Goat 水風井 22 初七 6	木8 Wood 7 Relief 丙申 Fire Monkey 雷水解 23 初八 4	金4 Metal 6 Influence 丁酉 Fire Rooster 澤山咸 24 初九 9	水1 Water 5 Humility 戊戌 Earth Dog 地山謙 25 初十 6
火2 Fire 4 Observation 己亥 Earth Pig 風地觀 26 十一 2	火2 Fire 3 Increasing 庚子 Metal Rat 風雷益 27 十二 9	水1 Water 2 Dimming Light 辛丑 Metal Ox 地火明夷 28 十三 3	金9 Metal 1 Fellowship 壬寅 Water Tiger 天火同人 29 十四 7	木8 Wood 9 Marrying Maiden 癸卯 Water Rabbit 雷澤歸妹 30 十五 7	木3 Wood 8 Opposition 甲辰 Wood Dragon 火澤睽 31 十六 2	

NOVEMBER 2031 己亥

Xuan Kong Element 玄空五行	風地觀 Observation	Period Luck 卦運	Monthly Star 月星
Fire 火2		2	2

SUNDAY	MONDAY	TUESDAY	WEDNESDAY	THURSDAY	FRIDAY	SATURDAY
30 十六 火7 Fire Obstruction 5 水山蹇 甲戌 Wood Dog 2						**1** 十七 火7 Fire Waiting 7 水天需 乙巳 Wood Snake 3
2 十八 金4 Metal Great Exceeding 6 澤風大過 丙午 Fire Horse 3	**3** 十九 水6 Water Poison 5 山風蠱 丁未 Fire Goat 7	**4** 二十 火2 Fire Dispersing 4 風水渙 戊申 Earth Monkey 6	**5** 廿一 木3 Wood Travelling 3 火山旅 己酉 Earth Rooster 8	**6** 廿二 金9 Metal Stagnation 2 天地否 庚戌 Metal Dog 9	**7** 廿三 火7 Fire Alliance 1 水地比 辛亥 Metal Pig 7	**8** 廿四 木8 Wood Thunder 9 震爲雷 壬子 Water Rat 1
9 廿五 水6 Water Beauty 8 山火賁 癸丑 Water Ox 8	**10** 廿六 火7 Fire Accomplished 7 水火既濟 甲寅 Wood Tiger 9	**11** 廿七 水1 Water Arriving 6 地澤臨 乙卯 Wood Rabbit 4	**12** 廿八 金4 Metal Marsh 5 兑爲澤 丙辰 Fire Dragon 1	**13** 廿九 火2 Fire Small Livestock 4 風天小畜 丁巳 Fire Snake 8	**14** 三十 木3 Wood The Cauldron 3 火風鼎 戊午 Earth Horse 4	**15** 十月初一 水1 Water Rising 2 地風升 己未 Earth Goat 2
16 初二 火7 Fire Water 1 坎爲水 庚申 Metal Monkey 1	**17** 初三 木8 Wood Lesser Exceeding 9 雷山小過 辛酉 Metal Rooster 3	**18** 初四 金4 Metal Gathering 8 澤地萃 壬戌 Water Dog 4	**19** 初五 水6 Water Peel 7 山地剝 癸亥 Water Pig 6	**20** 初六 水1 Water Earth 6 坤爲地 甲子 Wood Rat 1	**21** 初七 木3 Wood Biting 5 火雷噬嗑 乙丑 Wood Ox 6	**22** 初八 火2 Fire Family 4 風火家人 丙寅 Fire Tiger 4
23 初九 水6 Water Decreasing 3 山澤損 丁卯 Fire Rabbit 9	**24** 初十 金9 Metal Tread 2 天澤履 戊辰 Earth Dragon 6	**25** 十一 木8 Wood Great Strength 1 雷天大壯 己巳 Earth Snake 2	**26** 十二 木8 Wood Consistency 9 雷風恒 庚午 Metal Horse 9	**27** 十三 金9 Metal Litigation 8 天水訟 辛未 Metal Goat 3	**28** 十四 水1 Water Officer 7 地水師 壬申 Water Monkey 7	**29** 十五 火2 Fire Gradual Progress 6 風山漸 癸酉 Water Rooster 7

DECEMBER 2031 庚子

Xuan Kong Element 玄空五行	風雷益 Increasing	Period Luck 卦運	Monthly Star 月星
Fire 火2		9	1

SUNDAY	MONDAY	TUESDAY	WEDNESDAY	THURSDAY	FRIDAY	SATURDAY
	1 十七 木3 Wood Advancement 4 火地晉 乙亥 Wood Pig 3	**2** 十八 水6 Water Nourish 3 山雷頤 丙子 Fire Rat 3	**3** 十九 金4 Metal Following 2 澤雷隨 丁丑 Fire Ox 7	**4** 二十 木8 Wood Abundance 1 雷火豐 戊寅 Earth Tiger 6	**5** 廿一 火7 Fire Regulate 9 水澤節 己卯 Earth Rabbit 8	**6** 廿二 水1 Water Unity 8 地天泰 庚辰 Metal Dragon 9
7 廿三 木3 Wood Great Reward 7 火天大有 辛巳 Metal Snake 7	**8** 廿四 火2 Fire Wind 6 巽爲風 壬午 Water Horse 1	**9** 廿五 金4 Metal Trap 5 澤水困 癸未 Water Goat 8	**10** 廿六 木3 Wood Not Yet Accomplished 4 火水未濟 甲申 Wood Monkey 9	**11** 廿七 金9 Metal Retreat 3 天山遯 乙酉 Wood Rooster 4	**12** 廿八 水6 Water Mountain 2 艮爲山 丙戌 Fire Dog 1	**13** 廿九 木8 Wood Delight 1 雷地豫 丁亥 Fire Pig 8
14 十一月初一 火7 Fire Beginning 9 水雷屯 戊子 Earth Rat 4	**15** 初二 金9 Metal Without Wrongdoing 8 天雷無妄 己丑 Earth Ox 2	**16** 初三 木3 Wood Fire 7 離爲火 庚寅 Metal Tiger 1	**17** 初四 火2 Fire Sincerity 6 風澤中孚 辛卯 Metal Rabbit 3	**18** 初五 水6 Water Big Livestock 5 山天大畜 壬辰 Water Dragon 4	**19** 初六 金4 Metal Eliminating 4 澤天夬 癸巳 Water Snake 6	**20** 初七 金9 Metal Heaven 3 乾爲天 甲午 Wood Horse 1
21 初八 火7 Fire Well 2 水風井 乙未 Wood Goat 6	**22** 初九 木8 Wood Relief 1/9 雷水解 丙申 Fire Monkey 4	**23** 初十 金4 Metal Influence 1 澤山咸 丁酉 Fire Rooster 9	**24** 十一 水1 Water Humility 2 地山謙 戊戌 Earth Dog 6	**25** 十二 火2 Fire Observation 3 風地觀 己亥 Earth Pig 2	**26** 十三 火2 Fire Increasing 4 風雷益 庚子 Metal Rat 9	**27** 十四 水1 Water Dimming Light 5 地火明夷 辛丑 Metal Ox 3
28 十五 金9 Metal Fellowship 6 天火同人 壬寅 Water Tiger 7	**29** 十六 木8 Wood Marrying Maiden 7 雷澤歸妹 癸卯 Water Rabbit 7	**30** 十七 木3 Wood Opposition 8 火澤睽 甲辰 Wood Dragon 2	**31** 十八 火7 Fire Waiting 9 水天需 乙巳 Wood Snake 3			

2032 壬子

(*Ren Zi*) Water Rat

2032 壬子 *(Ren Zi)* Water Rat

January 6 - February 3

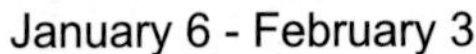

February 4 - March 4

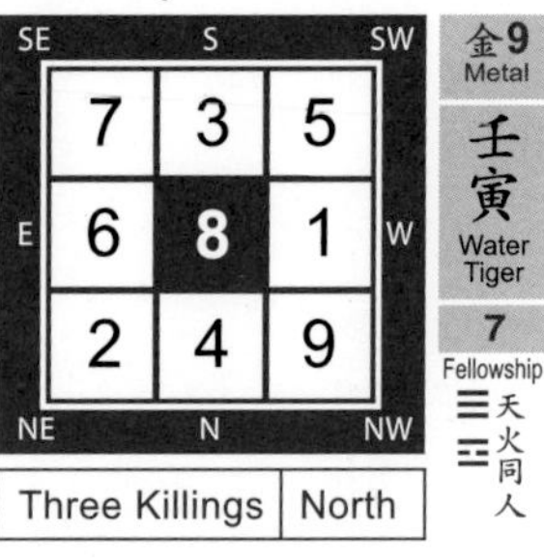

March 5 - April 3

April 4 - May 4

May 5 - June 4

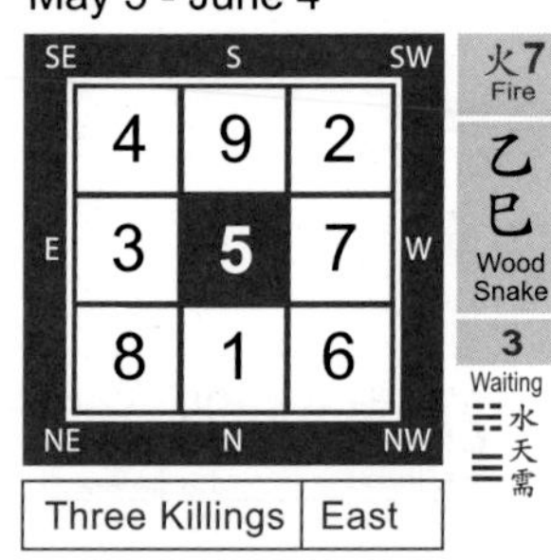

June 5 - July 5

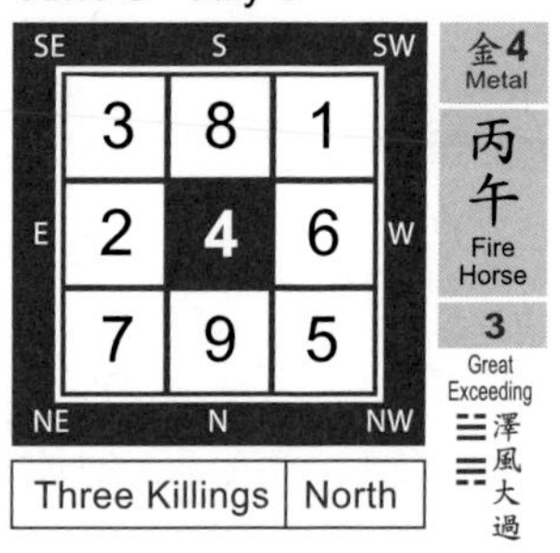

July 6 - August 6

August 7 - September 6

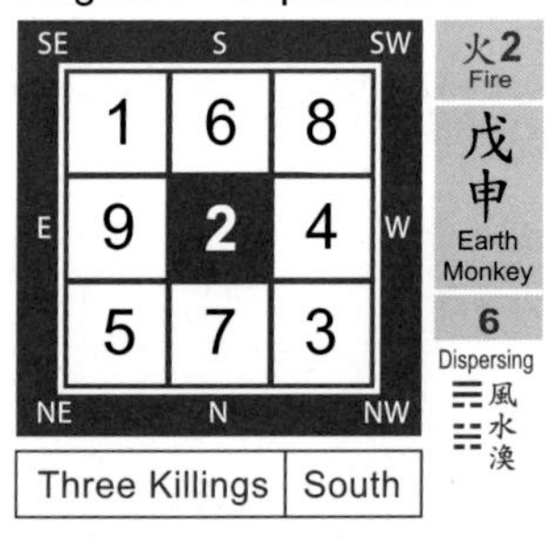

September 7 - October 7

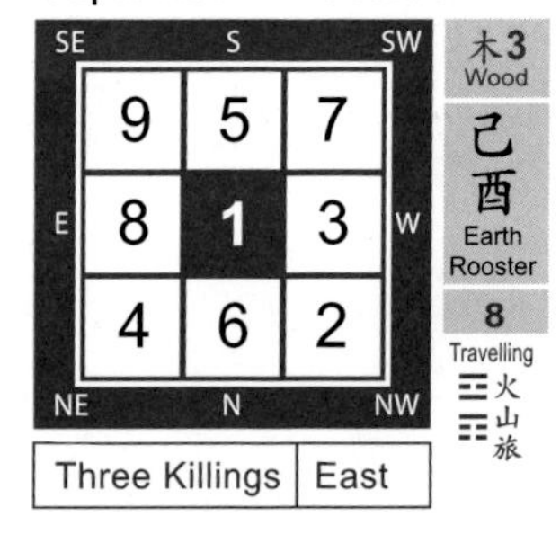

October 8 - November 6

November 7 - December 5

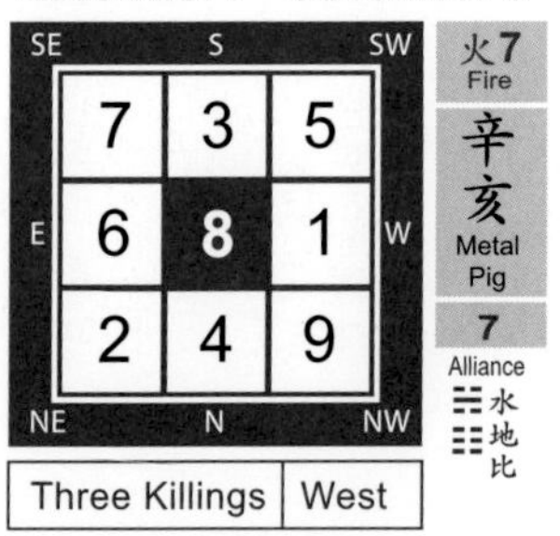

December 6 - January 4

JANUARY 2032 辛丑

Xuan Kong Element 玄空五行	地火明夷 Dimming Light	Period Luck 卦運	Monthly Star 月星
Water 水1		3	9

SUNDAY	MONDAY	TUESDAY	WEDNESDAY	THURSDAY	FRIDAY	SATURDAY
				金4 Metal · Great Exceeding [1] 丙午 Fire Horse · 澤風大過 1 十九 · 3	水6 Water · Poison [2] 丁未 Fire Goat · 山風蠱 2 二十 · 7	火2 Fire · Dispersing [3] 戊申 Earth Monkey · 風水渙 3 廿一 · 6
木3 Wood · Travelling [4] 己酉 Earth Rooster · 火山旅 4 廿二 · 8	金9 Metal · Stagnation [5] 庚戌 Metal Dog · 天地否 5 廿三 · 9	火7 Fire · Alliance [6] 辛亥 Metal Pig · 水地比 6 廿四 · 7	木8 Wood · Thunder [7] 壬子 Water Rat · 震爲雷 7 廿五 · 1	水6 Water · Beauty [8] 癸丑 Water Ox · 山火賁 8 廿六 · 8	火7 Fire · Accomplished [9] 甲寅 Wood Tiger · 水火既濟 9 廿七 · 9	水1 Water · Arriving [1] 乙卯 Wood Rabbit · 地澤臨 10 廿八 · 4
金4 Metal · Marsh [2] 丙辰 Fire Dragon · 兌爲澤 11 廿九 · 1	火2 Fire · Small Livestock [3] 丁巳 Fire Snake · 風天小畜 12 三十 · 8	木3 Wood · The Cauldron [4] 戊午 Earth Horse · 火風鼎 13 十二月初一 · 4	水1 Water · Rising [5] 己未 Earth Goat · 地風升 14 初二 · 2	火7 Fire · Water [6] 庚申 Metal Monkey · 坎爲水 15 初三 · 1	木8 Wood · Lesser Exceeding [7] 辛酉 Metal Rooster · 雷山小過 16 初四 · 3	金4 Metal · Gathering [8] 壬戌 Water Dog · 澤地萃 17 初五 · 4
水6 Water · Peel [9] 癸亥 Water Pig · 山地剝 18 初六 · 6	水1 Water · Earth [1] 甲子 Wood Rat · 坤爲地 19 初七 · 1	木3 Wood · Biting [2] 乙丑 Wood Ox · 火雷噬嗑 20 初八 · 6	火2 Fire · Family [3] 丙寅 Fire Tiger · 風火家人 21 初九 · 4	水6 Water · Decreasing [4] 丁卯 Fire Rabbit · 山澤損 22 初十 · 9	金9 Metal · Tread [5] 戊辰 Earth Dragon · 天澤履 23 十一 · 6	木8 Wood · Great Strength [6] 己巳 Earth Snake · 雷天大壯 24 十二 · 2
木8 Wood · Consistency [7] 庚午 Metal Horse · 雷風恆 25 十三 · 9	金9 Metal · Litigation [8] 辛未 Metal Goat · 天水訟 26 十四 · 3	水1 Water · Officer [9] 壬申 Water Monkey · 地水師 27 十五 · 7	火2 Fire · Gradual Progress [1] 癸酉 Water Rooster · 風山漸 28 十六 · 7	火7 Fire · Obstruction [2] 甲戌 Wood Dog · 水山蹇 29 十七 · 2	木3 Wood · Advancement [3] 乙亥 Wood Pig · 火地晉 30 十八 · 3	水6 Water · Nourish [4] 丙子 Fire Rat · 山雷頤 31 十九 · 3

FEBRUARY 2032 壬寅

Xuan Kong Element 玄空五行	天火同人 Fellowship	Period Luck 卦運	Monthly Star 月星
Metal 金9		7	8

SUNDAY	MONDAY	TUESDAY	WEDNESDAY	THURSDAY	FRIDAY	SATURDAY
金4 Metal · Following [5] 丁丑 Fire Ox · 澤雷隨 1 二十 · 7	木8 Wood · Abundance [6] 戊寅 Earth Tiger · 雷火豐 2 廿一 · 6	火7 Fire · Regulate [7] 己卯 Earth Rabbit · 水澤節 3 廿二 · 8	水1 Water · Unity [8] 庚辰 Metal Dragon · 地天泰 4 廿三 · 9	木3 Wood · Great Reward [9] 辛巳 Metal Snake · 火天大有 5 廿四 · 7	火2 Fire · Wind [1] 壬午 Water Horse · 巽爲風 6 廿五 · 1	金4 Metal · Trap [2] 癸未 Water Goat · 澤水困 7 廿六 · 8
木3 Wood · Not Yet Accomplished [3] 甲申 Wood Monkey · 火水未濟 8 廿七 · 9	金9 Metal · Retreat [4] 乙酉 Wood Rooster · 天山遯 9 廿八 · 4	水6 Water · Mountain [5] 丙戌 Fire Dog · 艮爲山 10 廿九 · 1	木8 Wood · Delight [6] 丁亥 Fire Pig · 雷地豫 11 正月初一 · 8	火7 Fire · Beginning [7] 戊子 Earth Rat · 水雷屯 12 初二 · 4	金9 Metal · Without Wrongdoing [8] 己丑 Earth Ox · 天雷無妄 13 初三 · 2	木3 Wood · Fire [9] 庚寅 Metal Tiger · 離爲火 14 初四 · 1
火2 Fire · Sincerity [1] 辛卯 Metal Rabbit · 風澤中孚 15 初五 · 3	水6 Water · Big Livestock [2] 壬辰 Water Dragon · 山天大畜 16 初六 · 4	金4 Metal · Ellminating [3] 癸巳 Water Snake · 澤天夬 17 初七 · 6	金9 Metal · Heaven [4] 甲午 Wood Horse · 乾爲天 18 初八 · 1	火7 Fire · Well [5] 乙未 Wood Goat · 水風井 19 初九 · 6	木8 Wood · Relief [6] 丙申 Fire Monkey · 雷水解 20 初十 · 4	金4 Metal · Influence [7] 丁酉 Fire Rooster · 澤山咸 21 十一 · 9
水1 Water · Humility [8] 戊戌 Earth Dog · 地山謙 22 十二 · 6	火2 Fire · Observation [9] 己亥 Earth Pig · 風地觀 23 十三 · 2	火2 Fire · Increasing [1] 庚子 Metal Rat · 風雷益 24 十四 · 9	水1 Water · Dimming Light [2] 辛丑 Metal Ox · 地火明夷 25 十五 · 3	金9 Metal · Fellowship [3] 壬寅 Water Tiger · 天火同人 26 十六 · 7	木8 Wood · Marrying Maiden [4] 癸卯 Water Rabbit · 雷澤歸妹 27 十七 · 7	木3 Wood · Opposition [5] 甲辰 Wood Dragon · 火澤睽 28 十八 · 2
火7 Fire · Waiting [6] 乙巳 Wood Snake · 水天需 29 十九 · 3						

MARCH 2032 癸卯

Xuan Kong Element 玄空五行	雷澤歸妹 Marrying Maiden	Period Luck 卦運	Monthly Star 月星
Wood 木8		7	7

SUNDAY	MONDAY	TUESDAY	WEDNESDAY	THURSDAY	FRIDAY	SATURDAY
	金4 Metal 7 Great Exceeding 澤風大過 丙午 Fire Horse 1 二十 3	水6 Water 8 Poison 山風蠱 丁未 Fire Goat 2 廿一 7	火2 Fire 9 Dispersing 風水渙 戊申 Earth Monkey 3 廿二 6	木3 Wood 1 Travelling 火山旅 己酉 Earth Rooster 4 廿三 8	金9 Metal 2 Stagnation 天地否 庚戌 Metal Dog 5 廿四 9	火7 Fire 3 Alliance 水地比 辛亥 Metal Pig 6 廿五 7
木8 Wood 4 Thunder 震爲雷 壬子 Water Rat 7 廿六 1	水6 Water 5 Beauty 山火賁 癸丑 Water Ox 8 廿七 8	火7 Fire 6 Accomplished 水火既濟 甲寅 Wood Tiger 9 廿八 9	水1 Water 7 Arriving 地澤臨 乙卯 Wood Rabbit 10 廿九 4	金4 Metal 8 Marsh 兌爲澤 丙辰 Fire Dragon 11 三十 1	火2 Fire 9 Small Livestock 風天小畜 丁巳 Fire Snake 12 二月初一 8	木3 Wood 1 The Cauldron 火風鼎 戊午 Earth Horse 13 初二 4
水1 Water 2 Rising 地風升 己未 Earth Goat 14 初三 2	火7 Fire 3 Water 坎爲水 庚申 Metal Monkey 15 初四 1	木8 Wood 4 Lesser Exceeding 雷山小過 辛酉 Metal Rooster 16 初五 3	金4 Metal 5 Gathering 澤地萃 壬戌 Water Dog 17 初六 4	水6 Water 6 Peel 山地剝 癸亥 Water Pig 18 初七 6	水1 Water 7 Earth 坤爲地 甲子 Wood Rat 19 初八 1	木3 Wood 8 Biting 火雷噬嗑 乙丑 Wood Ox 20 初九 6
火2 Fire 9 Family 風火家人 丙寅 Fire Tiger 21 初十 4	水6 Water 1 Decreasing 山澤損 丁卯 Fire Rabbit 22 十一 9	金9 Metal 2 Tread 天澤履 戊辰 Earth Dragon 23 十二 6	木8 Wood 3 Great Strength 雷天大壯 己巳 Earth Snake 24 十三 2	木8 Wood 4 Consistency 雷風恆 庚午 Metal Horse 25 十四 9	金9 Metal 5 Litigation 天水訟 辛未 Metal Goat 26 十五 3	水1 Water 6 Officer 地水師 壬申 Water Monkey 27 十六 7
火2 Fire 7 Gradual Progress 風山漸 癸酉 Water Rooster 28 十七 7	火7 Fire 8 Obstruction 水山蹇 甲戌 Wood Dog 29 十八 2	木3 Wood 9 Advancement 火地晉 乙亥 Wood Pig 30 十九 3	水6 Water 1 Nourish 山雷頤 丙子 Fire Rat 31 二十 3			

APRIL 2032 甲辰

Xuan Kong Element 玄空五行	火澤睽 Opposition	Period Luck 卦運	Monthly Star 月星
Wood 木3		2	6

SUNDAY	MONDAY	TUESDAY	WEDNESDAY	THURSDAY	FRIDAY	SATURDAY
				金4 Metal 2 Following 澤雷隨 丁丑 Fire Ox 1 廿一 7	木8 Wood 3 Abundance 雷火豐 戊寅 Earth Tiger 2 廿二 6	火7 Fire 4 Regulate 水澤節 己卯 Earth Rabbit 3 廿三 8
水1 Water 5 Unity 地天泰 庚辰 Metal Dragon 4 廿四 9	木3 Wood 6 Great Reward 火天大有 辛巳 Metal Snake 5 廿五 7	火2 Fire 7 Wind 巽爲風 壬午 Water Horse 6 廿六 1	金4 Metal 8 Trap 澤水困 癸未 Water Goat 7 廿七 8	木3 Wood 9 Not Yet Accomplished 火水未濟 甲申 Wood Monkey 8 廿八 9	金9 Metal 1 Retreat 天山遯 乙酉 Wood Rooster 9 廿九 4	水6 Water 2 Mountain 艮爲山 丙戌 Fire Dog 10 三月初一 1
木8 Wood 3 Delight 雷地豫 丁亥 Fire Pig 11 初二 8	火7 Fire 4 Beginning 水雷屯 戊子 Earth Rat 12 初三 4	金9 Metal 5 Without Wrongdoing 天雷無妄 己丑 Earth Ox 13 初四 2	木3 Wood 6 Fire 離爲火 庚寅 Metal Tiger 14 初五 1	火2 Fire 7 Sincerity 風澤中孚 辛卯 Metal Rabbit 15 初六 3	水6 Water 8 Big Livestock 山天大畜 壬辰 Water Dragon 16 初七 4	金4 Metal 9 Eliminating 澤天夬 癸巳 Water Snake 17 初八 6
金9 Metal 1 Heaven 乾爲天 甲午 Wood Horse 18 初九 1	火7 Fire 2 Well 水風井 乙未 Wood Goat 19 初十 6	木8 Wood 3 Relief 雷水解 丙申 Fire Monkey 20 十一 4	金4 Metal 4 Influence 澤山咸 丁酉 Fire Rooster 21 十二 9	水1 Water 5 Humility 地山謙 戊戌 Earth Dog 22 十三 6	火2 Fire 6 Observation 風地觀 己亥 Earth Pig 23 十四 2	火2 Fire 7 Increasing 風雷益 庚子 Metal Rat 24 十五 9
水1 Water 8 Dimming Light 地火明夷 辛丑 Metal Ox 25 十六 3	金9 Metal 9 Fellowship 天火同人 壬寅 Water Tiger 26 十七 7	木8 Wood 1 Marrying Maiden 雷澤歸妹 癸卯 Water Rabbit 27 十八 7	木3 Wood 2 Opposition 火澤睽 甲辰 Wood Dragon 28 十九 2	火7 Fire 3 Waiting 水天需 乙巳 Wood Snake 29 二十 3	金4 Metal 4 Great Exceeding 澤風大過 丙午 Fire Horse 30 廿一 3	

MAY 2032 乙巳

Xuan Kong Element 玄空五行	水天需 Waiting	Period Luck 卦運	Monthly Star 月星
Fire 火7		3	5

SUNDAY	MONDAY	TUESDAY	WEDNESDAY	THURSDAY	FRIDAY	SATURDAY
水6 Water 7 Nourish 丙子 Fire Rat 山雷頤 30 廿二 3	金4 Metal 8 Following 丁丑 Fire Ox 澤雷隨 31 廿三 7					水6 Water 5 Poison 丁未 Fire Goat 山風蠱 1 廿二 7
火2 Fire 6 Dispersing 戊申 Earth Monkey 風水渙 2 廿三 6	木3 Wood 7 Travelling 己酉 Earth Rooster 火山旅 3 廿四 8	金9 Metal 8 Stagnation 庚戌 Metal Dog 天地否 4 廿五 9	火7 Fire 9 Alliance 辛亥 Metal Pig 水地比 5 廿六 7	木8 Wood 1 Thunder 壬子 Water Rat 震爲雷 6 廿七 1	水6 Water 2 Beauty 癸丑 Water Ox 山火賁 7 廿八 8	火7 Fire 3 Accomplished 甲寅 Wood Tiger 水火既濟 8 廿九 9
水1 Water 4 Arriving 乙卯 Wood Rabbit 地澤臨 9 四月初一 4	金4 Metal 5 Marsh 丙辰 Fire Dragon 兑爲澤 10 初二 1	火2 Fire 6 Small Livestock 丁巳 Fire Snake 風天小畜 11 初三 8	木3 Wood 7 The Cauldron 戊午 Earth Horse 火風鼎 12 初四 4	水1 Water 8 Rising 己未 Earth Goat 地風升 13 初五 2	火7 Fire 9 Water 庚申 Metal Monkey 坎爲水 14 初六 1	木8 Wood 1 Lesser Exceeding 辛酉 Metal Rooster 雷山小過 15 初七 3
金4 Metal 2 Gathering 壬戌 Water Dog 澤地萃 16 初八 4	水6 Water 3 Peel 癸亥 Water Pig 山地剝 17 初九 6	水1 Water 4 Earth 甲子 Wood Rat 坤爲地 18 初十 1	木3 Wood 5 Biting 乙丑 Wood Ox 火雷噬嗑 19 十一 6	火2 Fire 6 Family 丙寅 Fire Tiger 風火家人 20 十二 4	水6 Water 7 Decreasing 丁卯 Fire Rabbit 山澤損 21 十三 9	金9 Metal 8 Tread 戊辰 Earth Dragon 天澤履 22 十四 6
木8 Wood 9 Great Strength 己巳 Earth Snake 雷天大壯 23 十五 2	木8 Wood 1 Consistency 庚午 Metal Horse 雷風恒 24 十六 9	金9 Metal 2 Litigation 辛未 Metal Goat 天水訟 25 十七 3	水1 Water 3 Officer 壬申 Water Monkey 地水師 26 十八 7	火2 Fire 4 Gradual Progress 癸酉 Water Rooster 風山漸 27 十九 7	火7 Fire 5 Obstruction 甲戌 Wood Dog 水山蹇 28 二十 2	木3 Wood 6 Advancement 乙亥 Wood Pig 火地晉 29 廿一 3

JUNE 2032 丙午

Xuan Kong Element 玄空五行	澤風大過 Great Exceeding	Period Luck 卦運	Monthly Star 月星
Metal 金4		3	4

SUNDAY	MONDAY	TUESDAY	WEDNESDAY	THURSDAY	FRIDAY	SATURDAY
		木8 Wood 9 Abundance 戊寅 Earth Tiger 雷火豐 1 廿四 6	火7 Fire 1 Regulate 己卯 Earth Rabbit 水澤節 2 廿五 8	水1 Water 2 Unity 庚辰 Metal Dragon 地天泰 3 廿六 9	木3 Wood 3 Great Reward 辛巳 Metal Snake 火天大有 4 廿七 7	火2 Fire 4 Wind 壬午 Water Horse 巽爲風 5 廿八 1
金4 Metal 5 Trap 癸未 Water Goat 澤水困 6 廿九 8	木3 Wood 6 Not Yet Accomplished 甲申 Wood Monkey 火水未濟 7 三十 9	金9 Metal 7 Retreat 乙酉 Wood Rooster 天山遯 8 五月初一 4	水6 Water 8 Mountain 丙戌 Fire Dog 艮爲山 9 初二 1	木8 Wood 9 Delight 丁亥 Fire Pig 雷地豫 10 初三 8	火7 Fire 1 Beginning 戊子 Earth Rat 水雷屯 11 初四 4	金9 Metal 2 Without Wrongdoing 己丑 Earth Ox 天雷無妄 12 初五 2
木3 Wood 3 Fire 庚寅 Metal Tiger 離爲火 13 初六 1	火2 Fire 4 Sincerity 辛卯 Metal Rabbit 風澤中孚 14 初七 3	水6 Water 5 Big Livestock 壬辰 Water Dragon 山天大畜 15 初八 4	金4 Metal 6 Eliminating 癸巳 Water Snake 澤天夬 16 初九 6	金9 Metal 7 Heaven 甲午 Wood Horse 乾爲天 17 初十 1	火7 Fire 8 Well 乙未 Wood Goat 水風井 18 十一 6	木8 Wood 9 Relief 丙申 Fire Monkey 雷水解 19 十二 4
金4 Metal 1 Influence 丁酉 Fire Rooster 澤山咸 20 十三 9	水1 Water 2/8 Humility 戊戌 Earth Dog 地山謙 21 十四 6	火2 Fire 7 Observation 己亥 Earth Pig 風地觀 22 十五 2	火2 Fire 6 Increasing 庚子 Metal Rat 風雷益 23 十六 9	水1 Water 5 Dimming Light 辛丑 Metal Ox 地火明夷 24 十七 3	金9 Metal 4 Fellowship 壬寅 Water Tiger 天火同人 25 十八 7	木8 Wood 3 Marrying Maiden 癸卯 Water Rabbit 雷澤歸妹 26 十九 7
木3 Wood 2 Opposition 甲辰 Wood Dragon 火澤睽 27 二十 2	火7 Fire 1 Waiting 乙巳 Wood Snake 水天需 28 廿一 3	金4 Metal 9 Great Exceeding 丙午 Fire Horse 澤風大過 29 廿二 3	水6 Water 8 Poison 丁未 Fire Goat 山風蠱 30 廿三 7			

JULY 2032 丁未

Xuan Kong Element 玄空五行	山風蠱 Poison	Period Luck 卦運	Monthly Star 月星
Water 水6		7	3

SUNDAY	MONDAY	TUESDAY	WEDNESDAY	THURSDAY	FRIDAY	SATURDAY
				火2 Fire Dispersing 7 戊申 Earth Monkey 風水渙 1 廿四 6	木3 Wood Travelling 6 己酉 Earth Rooster 火山旅 2 廿五 8	金9 Metal Stagnation 5 庚戌 Metal Dog 天地否 3 廿六 9
火7 Fire Alliance 4 辛亥 Metal Pig 水地比 4 廿七 7	木8 Wood Thunder 3 壬子 Water Rat 震爲雷 5 廿八 1	水6 Water Beauty 2 癸丑 Water Ox 山火賁 6 廿九 8	火7 Fire Accomplished 1 甲寅 Wood Tiger 水火既濟 7 六月初一 9	水1 Water Arriving 9 乙卯 Wood Rabbit 地澤臨 8 初二 4	金4 Metal Marsh 8 丙辰 Fire Dragon 兌爲澤 9 初三 1	火2 Fire Small Livestock 7 丁巳 Fire Snake 風天小畜 10 初四 8
木3 Wood The Cauldron 6 戊午 Earth Horse 火風鼎 11 初五 4	水1 Water Rising 5 己未 Earth Goat 地風升 12 初六 2	火7 Fire Water 4 庚申 Metal Monkey 坎爲水 13 初七 1	木8 Wood Lesser Exceeding 3 辛酉 Metal Rooster 雷山小過 14 初八 3	金4 Metal Gathering 2 壬戌 Water Dog 澤地萃 15 初九 4	水6 Water Peel 1 癸亥 Water Pig 山地剝 16 初十 6	水1 Water Earth 9 甲子 Wood Rat 坤爲地 17 十一 1
木3 Wood Biting 8 乙丑 Wood Ox 火雷噬嗑 18 十二 6	火2 Fire Family 7 丙寅 Fire Tiger 風火家人 19 十三 4	水6 Water Decreasing 6 丁卯 Fire Rabbit 山澤損 20 十四 9	金9 Metal Tread 5 戊辰 Earth Dragon 天澤履 21 十五 6	木8 Wood Great Strength 4 己巳 Earth Snake 雷天大壯 22 十六 2	木8 Wood Consistency 3 庚午 Metal Horse 雷風恆 23 十七 9	金9 Metal Litigation 2 辛未 Metal Goat 天水訟 24 十八 3
水1 Water Officer 1 壬申 Water Monkey 地水師 25 十九 7	火2 Fire Gradual Progress 9 癸酉 Water Rooster 風山漸 26 二十 7	火7 Fire Obstruction 8 甲戌 Wood Dog 水山蹇 27 廿一 2	木3 Wood Advancement 7 乙亥 Wood Pig 火地晉 28 廿二 3	水6 Water Nourish 6 丙子 Fire Rat 山雷頤 29 廿三 3	金4 Metal Following 5 丁丑 Fire Ox 澤雷隨 30 廿四 7	木8 Wood Abundance 4 戊寅 Earth Tiger 雷火豐 31 廿五 6

AUGUST 2032 戊申

Xuan Kong Element 玄空五行	風水渙 Dispersing	Period Luck 卦運	Monthly Star 月星
Fire 火2		6	2

SUNDAY	MONDAY	TUESDAY	WEDNESDAY	THURSDAY	FRIDAY	SATURDAY
火7 Fire Regulate 3 己卯 Earth Rabbit 水澤節 1 廿六 8	水1 Water Unity 2 庚辰 Metal Dragon 地天泰 2 廿七 9	木3 Wood Great Reward 1 辛巳 Metal Snake 火天大有 3 廿八 7	火2 Fire Wind 9 壬午 Water Horse 巽爲風 4 廿九 1	金4 Metal Trap 8 癸未 Water Goat 澤水困 5 三十 8	木3 Wood Not Yet Accomplished 7 甲申 Wood Monkey 火水未濟 6 七月初一 9	金9 Metal Retreat 6 乙酉 Wood Rooster 天山遯 7 初二 4
水6 Water Mountain 5 丙戌 Fire Dog 艮爲山 8 初三 1	木8 Wood Delight 4 丁亥 Fire Pig 雷地豫 9 初四 8	火7 Fire Beginning 3 戊子 Earth Rat 水雷屯 10 初五 4	金9 Metal Without Wrongdoing 2 己丑 Earth Ox 天雷無妄 11 初六 2	木3 Wood Fire 1 庚寅 Metal Tiger 離爲火 12 初七 1	火2 Fire Sincerity 9 辛卯 Metal Rabbit 風澤中孚 13 初八 3	水6 Water Big Livestock 8 壬辰 Water Dragon 山天大畜 14 初九 4
金4 Metal Eliminating 7 癸巳 Water Snake 澤天夬 15 初十 6	金9 Metal Heaven 6 甲午 Wood Horse 乾爲天 16 十一 1	火7 Fire Well 5 乙未 Wood Goat 水風井 17 十二 6	木8 Wood Relief 4 丙申 Fire Monkey 雷水解 18 十三 4	金4 Metal Influence 3 丁酉 Fire Rooster 澤山咸 19 十四 9	水1 Water Humility 2 戊戌 Earth Dog 地山謙 20 十五 6	火2 Fire Observation 1 己亥 Earth Pig 風地觀 21 十六 2
火2 Fire Increasing 9 庚子 Metal Rat 風雷益 22 十七 9	水1 Water Dimming Light 8 辛丑 Metal Ox 地火明夷 23 十八 3	金9 Metal Fellowship 7 壬寅 Water Tiger 天火同人 24 十九 7	木8 Wood Marrying Maiden 6 癸卯 Water Rabbit 雷澤歸妹 25 二十 7	木3 Wood Opposition 5 甲辰 Wood Dragon 火澤睽 26 廿一 2	火7 Fire Waiting 4 乙巳 Wood Snake 水天需 27 廿二 3	金4 Metal Great Exceeding 3 丙午 Fire Horse 澤風大過 28 廿三 3
水6 Water Poison 2 丁未 Fire Goat 山風蠱 29 廿四 7	火2 Fire Dispersing 1 戊申 Earth Monkey 風水渙 30 廿五 6	木3 Wood Travelling 9 己酉 Earth Rooster 火山旅 31 廿六 8				

SEPTEMBER 2032 己酉

Xuan Kong Element 玄空五行	火山旅 Travelling	Period Luck 卦運	Monthly Star 月星
Wood 木3		8	1

SUNDAY	MONDAY	TUESDAY	WEDNESDAY	THURSDAY	FRIDAY	SATURDAY
			金9 Metal [8] Stagnation 天地否 庚戌 Metal Dog 1 廿七 9	火7 Fire [7] Alliance 水地比 辛亥 Metal Pig 2 廿八 7	木8 Wood [6] Thunder 震爲雷 壬子 Water Rat 3 廿九 1	水6 Water [5] Beauty 山火賁 癸丑 Water Ox 4 三十 8
火7 Fire [4] Accomplished 水火既濟 甲寅 Wood Tiger 5 八月初一 9	水1 Water [3] Arriving 地澤臨 乙卯 Wood Rabbit 6 初二 4	金4 Metal [2] Marsh 兌爲澤 丙辰 Fire Dragon 7 初三 1	火2 Fire [1] Small Livestock 風天小畜 丁巳 Fire Snake 8 初四 8	木3 Wood [9] The Cauldron 火風鼎 戊午 Earth Horse 9 初五 4	水1 Water [8] Rising 地風升 己未 Earth Goat 10 初六 2	火7 Fire [7] Water 坎爲水 庚申 Metal Monkey 11 初七 1
木8 Wood [6] Lesser Exceeding 雷山小過 辛酉 Metal Rooster 12 初八 3	金4 Metal [5] Gathering 澤地萃 壬戌 Water Dog 13 初九 4	水6 Water [4] Peel 山地剝 癸亥 Water Pig 14 初十 6	水1 Water [3] Earth 坤爲地 甲子 Wood Rat 15 十一 1	木3 Wood [2] Biting 火雷噬嗑 乙丑 Wood Ox 16 十二 6	火2 Fire [1] Family 風火家人 丙寅 Fire Tiger 17 十三 4	水6 Water [9] Decreasing 山澤損 丁卯 Fire Rabbit 18 十四 9
金9 Metal [8] Tread 天澤履 戊辰 Earth Dragon 19 十五 6	木8 Wood [7] Great Strength 雷天大壯 己巳 Earth Snake 20 十六 2	木8 Wood [6] Consistency 雷風恆 庚午 Metal Horse 21 十七 9	金9 Metal [5] Litigation 天水訟 辛未 Metal Goat 22 十八 3	水1 Water [4] Officer 地水師 壬申 Water Monkey 23 十九 7	火2 Fire [3] Gradual Progress 風山漸 癸酉 Water Rooster 24 二十 7	火7 Fire [2] Obstruction 水山蹇 甲戌 Wood Dog 25 廿一 2
木3 Wood [1] Advancement 火地晉 乙亥 Wood Pig 26 廿二 3	水6 Water [9] Nourish 山雷頤 丙子 Fire Rat 27 廿三 3	金4 Metal [8] Following 澤雷隨 丁丑 Fire Ox 28 廿四 7	木8 Wood [7] Abundance 雷火豐 戊寅 Earth Tiger 29 廿五 6	火7 Fire [6] Regulate 水澤節 己卯 Earth Rabbit 30 廿六 8		

OCTOBER 2032 庚戌

Xuan Kong Element 玄空五行	天地否 Stagnation	Period Luck 卦運	Monthly Star 月星
Metal 金9		9	9

SUNDAY	MONDAY	TUESDAY	WEDNESDAY	THURSDAY	FRIDAY	SATURDAY
金9 Metal [2] Stagnation 天地否 庚戌 Metal Dog 31 廿八 9					水1 Water [5] Unity 地天泰 庚辰 Metal Dragon 1 廿七 9	木3 Wood [4] Great Reward 火天大有 辛巳 Metal Snake 2 廿八 7
火2 Fire [3] Wind 巽爲風 壬午 Water Horse 3 廿九 1	金4 Metal [2] Trap 澤水困 癸未 Water Goat 4 九月初一 8	木3 Wood [1] Not Yet Accomplished 火水未濟 甲申 Wood Monkey 5 初二 9	金9 Metal [9] Retreat 天山遯 乙酉 Wood Rooster 6 初三 4	水6 Water [8] Mountain 艮爲山 丙戌 Fire Dog 7 初四 1	木8 Wood [7] Delight 雷地豫 丁亥 Fire Pig 8 初五 8	火7 Fire [6] Beginning 水雷屯 戊子 Earth Rat 9 初六 4
金9 Metal [5] Without Wrongdoing 天雷無妄 己丑 Earth Ox 10 初七 2	木3 Wood [4] Fire 離爲火 庚寅 Metal Tiger 11 初八 1	火2 Fire [3] Sincerity 風澤中孚 辛卯 Metal Rabbit 12 初九 3	水6 Water [2] Big Livestock 山天大畜 壬辰 Water Dragon 13 初十 4	金4 Metal [1] Eliminating 澤天夬 癸巳 Water Snake 14 十一 6	金9 Metal [9] Heaven 乾爲天 甲午 Wood Horse 15 十二 1	火7 Fire [8] Well 水風井 乙未 Wood Goat 16 十三 6
木8 Wood [7] Relief 雷水解 丙申 Fire Monkey 17 十四 4	金4 Metal [6] Influence 澤山咸 丁酉 Fire Rooster 18 十五 9	水1 Water [5] Humility 地山謙 戊戌 Earth Dog 19 十六 6	火2 Fire [4] Observation 風地觀 己亥 Earth Pig 20 十七 2	火2 Fire [3] Increasing 風雷益 庚子 Metal Rat 21 十八 9	水1 Water [2] Dimming Light 地火明夷 辛丑 Metal Ox 22 十九 3	金9 Metal [1] Fellowship 天火同人 壬寅 Water Tiger 23 二十 7
木8 Wood [9] Marrying Maiden 雷澤歸妹 癸卯 Water Rabbit 24 廿一 7	木3 Wood [8] Opposition 火澤睽 甲辰 Wood Dragon 25 廿二 2	火7 Fire [7] Waiting 水天需 乙巳 Wood Snake 26 廿三 3	金4 Metal [6] Great Exceeding 澤風大過 丙午 Fire Horse 27 廿四 3	水6 Water [5] Poison 山風蠱 丁未 Fire Goat 28 廿五 7	火2 Fire [4] Dispersing 風水渙 戊申 Earth Monkey 29 廿六 6	木3 Wood [3] Travelling 火山旅 己酉 Earth Rooster 30 廿七 8

NOVEMBER 2032 辛亥

Xuan Kong Element 玄空五行	水地比 Alliance	Period Luck 卦運	Monthly Star 月星
Fire 火7		7	8

SUNDAY	MONDAY	TUESDAY	WEDNESDAY	THURSDAY	FRIDAY	SATURDAY
	火7 Fire [1] Alliance 水地比 辛亥 Metal Pig **1** 廿九 7	木8 Wood [9] Thunder 震為雷 壬子 Water Rat **2** 三十 1	水6 Water [8] Beauty 山火賁 癸丑 Water Ox **3** 十月初一 8	火7 Fire [7] Accomplished 水火既濟 甲寅 Wood Tiger **4** 初二 9	水1 Water [6] Arriving 地澤臨 乙卯 Wood Rabbit **5** 初三 4	金4 Metal [5] Marsh 兌為澤 丙辰 Fire Dragon **6** 初四 1
火2 Fire [4] Small Livestock 風天小畜 丁巳 Fire Snake **7** 初五 8	木3 Wood [3] The Cauldron 火風鼎 戊午 Earth Horse **8** 初六 4	水1 Water [2] Rising 地風升 己未 Earth Goat **9** 初七 2	火7 Fire [1] Water 坎為水 庚申 Metal Monkey **10** 初八 1	木8 Wood [9] Lesser Exceeding 雷山小過 辛酉 Metal Rooster **11** 初九 3	金4 Metal [8] Gathering 澤地萃 壬戌 Water Dog **12** 初十 4	水6 Water [7] Peel 山地剝 癸亥 Water Pig **13** 十一 6
水1 Water [6] Earth 坤為地 甲子 Wood Rat **14** 十二 1	木3 Wood [5] Biting 火雷噬嗑 乙丑 Wood Ox **15** 十三 6	火2 Fire [4] Family 風火家人 丙寅 Fire Tiger **16** 十四 4	水6 Water [3] Decreasing 山澤損 丁卯 Fire Rabbit **17** 十五 9	金9 Metal [2] Tread 天澤履 戊辰 Earth Dragon **18** 十六 6	木8 Wood [1] Great Strength 雷天大壯 己巳 Earth Snake **19** 十七 2	木8 Wood [9] Consistency 雷風恆 庚午 Metal Horse **20** 十八 9
金9 Metal [8] Litigation 天水訟 辛未 Metal Goat **21** 十九 3	水1 Water [7] Officer 地水師 壬申 Water Monkey **22** 二十 7	火2 Fire [6] Gradual Progress 風山漸 癸酉 Water Rooster **23** 廿一 7	火7 Fire [5] Obstruction 水山蹇 甲戌 Wood Dog **24** 廿二 2	木3 Wood [4] Advancement 火地晉 乙亥 Wood Pig **25** 廿三 3	水6 Water [3] Nourish 山雷頤 丙子 Fire Rat **26** 廿四 3	金4 Metal [2] Following 澤雷隨 丁丑 Fire Ox **27** 廿五 7
木8 Wood [1] Abundance 雷火豐 戊寅 Earth Tiger **28** 廿六 6	火7 Fire [9] Regulate 水澤節 己卯 Earth Rabbit **29** 廿七 8	水1 Water [8] Unity 地天泰 庚辰 Metal Dragon **30** 廿八 9				

DECEMBER 2032 壬子

Xuan Kong Element 玄空五行	震為雷 Thunder	Period Luck 卦運	Monthly Star 月星
Wood 木8		1	7

SUNDAY	MONDAY	TUESDAY	WEDNESDAY	THURSDAY	FRIDAY	SATURDAY
			木3 Wood [7] Great Reward 火天大有 辛巳 Metal Snake **1** 廿九 7	火2 Fire [6] Wind 巽為風 壬午 Water Horse **2** 三十 1	金4 Metal [5] Trap 澤水困 癸未 Water Goat **3** 十二月初一 8	木3 Wood [4] Not Yet Accomplished 火水未濟 甲申 Wood Monkey **4** 初二 9
金9 Metal [3] Retreat 天山遯 乙酉 Wood Rooster **5** 初三 4	水6 Water [2] Mountain 艮為山 丙戌 Fire Dog **6** 初四 1	木8 Wood [1] Delight 雷地豫 丁亥 Fire Pig **7** 初五 8	火7 Fire [9] Beginning 水雷屯 戊子 Earth Rat **8** 初六 4	金9 Metal [8] Without Wrongdoing 天雷無妄 己丑 Earth Ox **9** 初七 2	木3 Wood [7] Fire 離為火 庚寅 Metal Tiger **10** 初八 1	火2 Fire [6] Sincerity 風澤中孚 辛卯 Metal Rabbit **11** 初九 3
水6 Water [5] Big Livestock 山天大畜 壬辰 Water Dragon **12** 初十 4	金4 Metal [4] Eliminating 澤天夬 癸巳 Water Snake **13** 十一 6	金9 Metal [3] Heaven 乾為天 甲午 Wood Horse **14** 十二 1	火7 Fire [2] Well 水風井 乙未 Wood Goat **15** 十三 6	木8 Wood [1] Relief 雷水解 丙申 Fire Monkey **16** 十四 4	金4 Metal [9] Influence 澤山咸 丁酉 Fire Rooster **17** 十五 9	水1 Water [8] Humility 地山謙 戊戌 Earth Dog **18** 十六 6
火2 Fire [7] Observation 風地觀 己亥 Earth Pig **19** 十七 2	火2 Fire [6] Increasing 風雷益 庚子 Metal Rat **20** 十八 9	水1 Water [5/5] Dimming Light 地火明夷 辛丑 Metal Ox **21** 十九 3	金9 Metal [6] Fellowship 天火同人 壬寅 Water Tiger **22** 二十 7	木8 Wood [7] Marrying Maiden 雷澤歸妹 癸卯 Water Rabbit **23** 廿一 7	木3 Wood [8] Opposition 火澤睽 甲辰 Wood Dragon **24** 廿二 2	火7 Fire [9] Waiting 水天需 乙巳 Wood Snake **25** 廿三 3
金4 Metal [1] Great Exceeding 澤風大過 丙午 Fire Horse **26** 廿四 3	水6 Water [2] Poison 山風蠱 丁未 Fire Goat **27** 廿五 7	火2 Fire [3] Dispersing 風水渙 戊申 Earth Monkey **28** 廿六 6	木3 Wood [4] Travelling 火山旅 己酉 Earth Rooster **29** 廿七 8	金9 Metal [5] Stagnation 天地否 庚戌 Metal Dog **30** 廿八 9	火7 Fire [6] Alliance 水地比 辛亥 Metal Pig **31** 廿九 7	

2033 癸丑

(*Gui Chou*) Water Ox

2033 癸丑 *(Gui Chou)* Water Ox

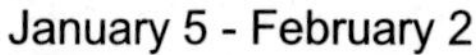

January 5 - February 2

February 3 - March 4

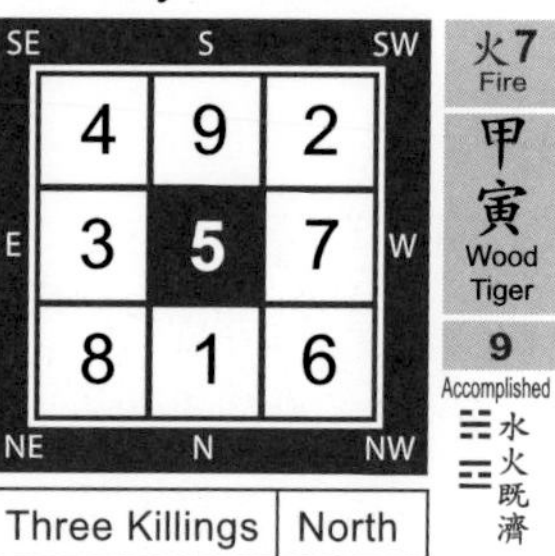

March 5 - April 3

April 4 - May 4

May 5 - June 4

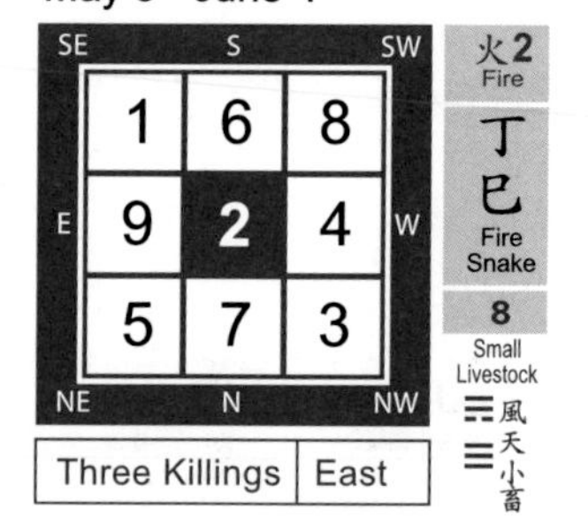

June 5 - July 6

July 7 - August 6

August 7 - September 6

September 7 - October 7

October 8 - November 6

November 7 - December 6

December 7 - January 4

JANUARY 2033 癸丑

Xuan Kong Element 玄空五行	山火賁 Beauty	Period Luck 卦運	Monthly Star 月星
Water 水6		8	6

SUNDAY	MONDAY	TUESDAY	WEDNESDAY	THURSDAY	FRIDAY	SATURDAY
木3 Wood 9 Great Reward 火天大有 辛巳 Metal Snake 7 **30** 三十	火2 Fire 1 Wind 巽為風 壬午 Water Horse 1 **31** 正月初一					木8 Wood 7 Thunder 震為雷 壬子 Water Rat 1 **1** 十二月初一
水6 Water 8 Beauty 山火賁 癸丑 Water Ox 8 **2** 初二	火7 Fire 9 Accomplished 水火既濟 甲寅 Wood Tiger 9 **3** 初三	水1 Water 1 Arriving 地澤臨 乙卯 Wood Rabbit 4 **4** 初四	金4 Metal 2 Marsh 兌為澤 丙辰 Fire Dragon 1 **5** 初五	火2 Fire 3 Small Livestock 風天小畜 丁巳 Fire Snake 8 **6** 初六	木3 Wood 4 The Cauldron 火風鼎 戊午 Earth Horse 4 **7** 初七	水1 Water 5 Rising 地風升 己未 Earth Goat 2 **8** 初八
火7 Fire 6 Water 坎為水 庚申 Metal Monkey 1 **9** 初九	木8 Wood 7 Lesser Exceeding 雷山小過 辛酉 Metal Rooster 3 **10** 初十	金4 Metal 8 Gathering 澤地萃 壬戌 Water Dog 4 **11** 十一	水6 Water 9 Peel 山地剝 癸亥 Water Pig 6 **12** 十二	水1 Water 1 Earth 坤為地 甲子 Wood Rat 1 **13** 十三	木3 Wood 2 Biting 火雷噬嗑 乙丑 Wood Ox 6 **14** 十四	火2 Fire 3 Family 風火家人 丙寅 Fire Tiger 4 **15** 十五
水6 Water 4 Decreasing 山澤損 丁卯 Fire Rabbit 9 **16** 十六	金9 Metal 5 Tread 天澤履 戊辰 Earth Dragon 6 **17** 十七	木8 Wood 6 Great Strength 雷天大壯 己巳 Earth Snake 2 **18** 十八	木8 Wood 7 Consistency 雷風恆 庚午 Metal Horse 9 **19** 十九	金9 Metal 8 Litigation 天水訟 辛未 Metal Goat 3 **20** 二十	水1 Water 9 Officer 地水師 壬申 Water Monkey 7 **21** 廿一	火2 Fire 1 Gradual Progress 風山漸 癸酉 Water Rooster 7 **22** 廿二
火7 Fire 2 Obstruction 水山蹇 甲戌 Wood Dog 2 **23** 廿三	木3 Wood 3 Advancement 火地晉 乙亥 Wood Pig 3 **24** 廿四	水6 Water 4 Nourish 山雷頤 丙子 Fire Rat 3 **25** 廿五	金4 Metal 5 Following 澤雷隨 丁丑 Fire Ox 7 **26** 廿六	木8 Wood 6 Abundance 雷火豐 戊寅 Earth Tiger 6 **27** 廿七	火7 Fire 7 Regulate 水澤節 己卯 Earth Rabbit 8 **28** 廿八	水1 Water 8 Unity 地天泰 庚辰 Metal Dragon 9 **29** 廿九

FEBRUARY 2033 甲寅

Xuan Kong Element 玄空五行	水火既濟 Accomplished	Period Luck 卦運	Monthly Star 月星
Fire 火7		9	5

SUNDAY	MONDAY	TUESDAY	WEDNESDAY	THURSDAY	FRIDAY	SATURDAY
		金4 Metal 2 Trap 澤水困 癸未 Water Goat 8 **1** 初二	木3 Wood 3 Not Yet Accomplished 火水未濟 甲申 Wood Monkey 9 **2** 初三	金9 Metal 4 Retreat 天山遯 乙酉 Wood Rooster 4 **3** 初四	水6 Water 5 Mountain 艮為山 丙戌 Fire Dog 1 **4** 初五	木8 Wood 6 Delight 雷地豫 丁亥 Fire Pig 8 **5** 初六
火7 Fire 7 Beginning 水雷屯 戊子 Earth Rat 4 **6** 初七	金9 Metal 8 Without Wrongdoing 天雷無妄 己丑 Earth Ox 2 **7** 初八	木3 Wood 9 Fire 離為火 庚寅 Metal Tiger 1 **8** 初九	火2 Fire 1 Sincerity 風澤中孚 辛卯 Metal Rabbit 3 **9** 初十	水6 Water 2 Big Livestock 山天大畜 壬辰 Water Dragon 4 **10** 十一	金4 Metal 3 Eliminating 澤天夬 癸巳 Water Snake 6 **11** 十二	金9 Metal 4 Heaven 乾為天 甲午 Wood Horse 1 **12** 十三
火7 Fire 5 Well 水風井 乙未 Wood Goat 6 **13** 十四	木8 Wood 6 Relief 雷水解 丙申 Fire Monkey 4 **14** 十五	金4 Metal 7 Influence 澤山咸 丁酉 Fire Rooster 9 **15** 十六	水1 Water 8 Humility 地山謙 戊戌 Earth Dog 6 **16** 十七	火2 Fire 9 Observation 風地觀 己亥 Earth Pig 2 **17** 十八	火2 Fire 1 Increasing 風雷益 庚子 Metal Rat 9 **18** 十九	水1 Water 2 Dimming Light 地火明夷 辛丑 Metal Ox 3 **19** 二十
金9 Metal 3 Fellowship 天火同人 壬寅 Water Tiger 7 **20** 廿一	木8 Wood 4 Marrying Maiden 雷澤歸妹 癸卯 Water Rabbit 7 **21** 廿二	木3 Wood 5 Opposition 火澤睽 甲辰 Wood Dragon 2 **22** 廿三	火7 Fire 6 Waiting 水天需 乙巳 Wood Snake 3 **23** 廿四	金4 Metal 7 Great Exceeding 澤風大過 丙午 Fire Horse 3 **24** 廿五	水6 Water 8 Poison 山風蠱 丁未 Fire Goat 7 **25** 廿六	火2 Fire 9 Dispersing 風水渙 戊申 Earth Monkey 6 **26** 廿七
木3 Wood 1 Travelling 火山旅 己酉 Earth Rooster 8 **27** 廿八	金9 Metal 2 Stagnation 天地否 庚戌 Metal Dog 9 **28** 廿九					

MARCH 2033 乙卯

Xuan Kong Element 玄空五行	地澤臨 Arriving	Period Luck 卦運	Monthly Star 月星
Water 水1		4	4

SUNDAY	MONDAY	TUESDAY	WEDNESDAY	THURSDAY	FRIDAY	SATURDAY
		火7 Fire 3 Alliance 辛亥 Metal Pig 水地比 **1** 二月初一 7	木8 Wood 4 Thunder 壬子 Water Rat 震爲雷 **2** 初二 1	水6 Water 5 Beauty 癸丑 Water Ox 山火賁 **3** 初三 8	火7 Fire 6 Accomplished 甲寅 Wood Tiger 水火既濟 **4** 初四 9	水1 Water 7 Arriving 乙卯 Wood Rabbit 地澤臨 **5** 初五 4
金4 Metal 8 Marsh 丙辰 Fire Dragon 兑爲澤 **6** 初六 1	火2 Fire 9 Small Livestock 丁巳 Fire Snake 風天小畜 **7** 初七 8	木3 Wood 1 The Cauldron 戊午 Earth Horse 火風鼎 **8** 初八 4	水1 Water 2 Rising 己未 Earth Goat 地風升 **9** 初九 2	火7 Fire 3 Water 庚申 Metal Monkey 坎爲水 **10** 初十 1	木8 Wood 4 Lesser Exceeding 辛酉 Metal Rooster 雷山小過 **11** 十一 3	金4 Metal 5 Gathering 壬戌 Water Dog 澤地萃 **12** 十二 4
水6 Water 6 Peel 癸亥 Water Pig 山地剝 **13** 十三 6	水1 Water 7 Earth 甲子 Wood Rat 坤爲地 **14** 十四 1	木3 Wood 8 Biting 乙丑 Wood Ox 火雷噬嗑 **15** 十五 6	火2 Fire 9 Family 丙寅 Fire Tiger 風火家人 **16** 十六 4	水6 Water 1 Decreasing 丁卯 Fire Rabbit 山澤損 **17** 十七 9	金9 Metal 2 Tread 戊辰 Earth Dragon 天澤履 **18** 十八 6	木8 Wood 3 Great Strength 己巳 Earth Snake 雷天大壯 **19** 十九 2
木8 Wood 4 Consistency 庚午 Metal Horse 雷風恆 **20** 二十 9	金9 Metal 5 Litigation 辛未 Metal Goat 天水訟 **21** 廿一 3	水1 Water 6 Officer 壬申 Water Monkey 地水師 **22** 廿二 7	火2 Fire 7 Gradual Progress 癸酉 Water Rooster 風山漸 **23** 廿三 7	火7 Fire 8 Obstruction 甲戌 Wood Dog 水山蹇 **24** 廿四 2	木3 Wood 9 Advancement 乙亥 Wood Pig 火地晉 **25** 廿五 3	水6 Water 1 Nourish 丙子 Fire Rat 山雷頤 **26** 廿六 3
金4 Metal 2 Following 丁丑 Fire Ox 澤雷隨 **27** 廿七 7	木8 Wood 3 Abundance 戊寅 Earth Tiger 雷火豐 **28** 廿八 6	火7 Fire 4 Regulate 己卯 Earth Rabbit 水澤節 **29** 廿九 8	水1 Water 5 Unity 庚辰 Metal Dragon 地天泰 **30** 三十 9	木3 Wood 6 Great Reward 辛巳 Metal Snake 火天大有 **31** 三月初一 7		

APRIL 2033 丙辰

Xuan Kong Element 玄空五行	兑爲澤 Marsh	Period Luck 卦運	Monthly Star 月星
Metal 金4		1	3

SUNDAY	MONDAY	TUESDAY	WEDNESDAY	THURSDAY	FRIDAY	SATURDAY
					火2 Fire 7 Wind 壬午 Water Horse 巽爲風 **1** 初二 1	金4 Metal 8 Trap 癸未 Water Goat 澤水困 **2** 初三 8
木3 Wood 9 Not Yet Accomplished 甲申 Wood Monkey 火水未濟 **3** 初四 9	金9 Metal 1 Retreat 乙酉 Wood Rooster 天山遯 **4** 初五 4	水6 Water 2 Mountain 丙戌 Fire Dog 艮爲山 **5** 初六 1	木8 Wood 3 Delight 丁亥 Fire Pig 雷地豫 **6** 初七 8	火7 Fire 4 Beginning 戊子 Earth Rat 水雷屯 **7** 初八 4	金9 Metal 5 Without Wrongdoing 己丑 Earth Ox 天雷無妄 **8** 初九 2	木3 Wood 6 Fire 庚寅 Metal Tiger 離爲火 **9** 初十 1
火2 Fire 7 Sincerity 辛卯 Metal Rabbit 風澤中孚 **10** 十一 3	水6 Water 8 Big Livestock 壬辰 Water Dragon 山天大畜 **11** 十二 4	金4 Metal 9 Eliminating 癸巳 Water Snake 澤天夬 **12** 十三 6	金9 Metal 1 Heaven 甲午 Wood Horse 乾爲天 **13** 十四 1	火7 Fire 2 Well 乙未 Wood Goat 水風井 **14** 十五 6	木8 Wood 3 Relief 丙申 Fire Monkey 雷水解 **15** 十六 4	金4 Metal 4 Influence 丁酉 Fire Rooster 澤山咸 **16** 十七 9
水1 Water 5 Humility 戊戌 Earth Dog 地山謙 **17** 十八 6	火2 Fire 6 Observation 己亥 Earth Pig 風地觀 **18** 十九 2	火2 Fire 7 Increasing 庚子 Metal Rat 風雷益 **19** 二十 9	水1 Water 8 Dimming Light 辛丑 Metal Ox 地火明夷 **20** 廿一 3	金9 Metal 9 Fellowship 壬寅 Water Tiger 天火同人 **21** 廿二 7	木8 Wood 1 Marrying Maiden 癸卯 Water Rabbit 雷澤歸妹 **22** 廿三 7	木3 Wood 2 Opposition 甲辰 Wood Dragon 火澤睽 **23** 廿四 2
火7 Fire 3 Waiting 乙巳 Wood Snake 水天需 **24** 廿五 3	金4 Metal 4 Great Exceeding 丙午 Fire Horse 澤風大過 **25** 廿六 3	水6 Water 5 Poison 丁未 Fire Goat 山風蠱 **26** 廿七 7	火2 Fire 6 Dispersing 戊申 Earth Monkey 風水渙 **27** 廿八 6	木3 Wood 7 Travelling 己酉 Earth Rooster 火山旅 **28** 廿九 8	金9 Metal 8 Stagnation 庚戌 Metal Dog 天地否 **29** 四月初一 9	火7 Fire 9 Alliance 辛亥 Metal Pig 水地比 **30** 初二 7

MAY 2033 丁巳

Xuan Kong Element 玄空五行	風天小畜 Small Livestock	Period Luck 卦運	Monthly Star 月星
Fire 火2		8	2

SUNDAY	MONDAY	TUESDAY	WEDNESDAY	THURSDAY	FRIDAY	SATURDAY
木8 Wood 1 Thunder 震爲雷 壬子 Water Rat 1 **1** 初三	水6 Water 2 Beauty 山火賁 癸丑 Water Ox 8 **2** 初四	火7 Fire 3 Accomplished 水火既濟 甲寅 Wood Tiger 9 **3** 初五	水1 Water 4 Arriving 地澤臨 乙卯 Wood Rabbit 4 **4** 初六	金4 Metal 5 Marsh 兌爲澤 丙辰 Fire Dragon 1 **5** 初七	火2 Fire 6 Small Livestock 風天小畜 丁巳 Fire Snake 8 **6** 初八	木3 Wood 7 The Cauldron 火風鼎 戊午 Earth Horse 4 **7** 初九
水1 Water 8 Rising 地風升 己未 Earth Goat 2 **8** 初十	火7 Fire 9 Water 坎爲水 庚申 Metal Monkey 1 **9** 十一	木8 Wood 1 Lesser Exceeding 雷山小過 辛酉 Metal Rooster 3 **10** 十二	金4 Metal 2 Gathering 澤地萃 壬戌 Water Dog 4 **11** 十三	水6 Water 3 Peel 山地剝 癸亥 Water Pig 6 **12** 十四	水1 Water 4 Earth 坤爲地 甲子 Wood Rat 1 **13** 十五	木3 Wood 5 Biting 火雷噬嗑 乙丑 Wood Ox 6 **14** 十六
火2 Fire 6 Family 風火家人 丙寅 Fire Tiger 4 **15** 十七	水6 Water 7 Decreasing 山澤損 丁卯 Fire Rabbit 9 **16** 十八	金9 Metal 8 Tread 天澤履 戊辰 Earth Dragon 6 **17** 十九	木8 Wood 9 Great Strength 雷天大壯 己巳 Earth Snake 2 **18** 二十	木8 Wood 1 Consistency 雷風恆 庚午 Metal Horse 9 **19** 廿一	金9 Metal 2 Litigation 天水訟 辛未 Metal Goat 3 **20** 廿二	水1 Water 3 Officer 地水師 壬申 Water Monkey 7 **21** 廿三
火2 Fire 4 Gradual Progress 風山漸 癸酉 Water Rooster 7 **22** 廿四	火7 Fire 5 Obstruction 水山蹇 甲戌 Wood Dog 2 **23** 廿五	木3 Wood 6 Advancement 火地晉 乙亥 Wood Pig 3 **24** 廿六	水6 Water 7 Nourish 山雷頤 丙子 Fire Rat 3 **25** 廿七	金4 Metal 8 Following 澤雷隨 丁丑 Fire Ox 7 **26** 廿八	木8 Wood 9 Abundance 雷火豐 戊寅 Earth Tiger 6 **27** 廿九	火7 Fire 1 Regulate 水澤節 己卯 Earth Rabbit 8 **28** 五月初一
水1 Water 2 Unity 地天泰 庚辰 Metal Dragon 9 **29** 初二	木3 Wood 3 Great Reward 火天大有 辛巳 Metal Snake 7 **30** 初三	火2 Fire 4 Wind 巽爲風 壬午 Water Horse 1 **31** 初四				

JUNE 2033 戊午

Xuan Kong Element 玄空五行	火風鼎 The Cauldron	Period Luck 卦運	Monthly Star 月星
Wood 木3		4	1

SUNDAY	MONDAY	TUESDAY	WEDNESDAY	THURSDAY	FRIDAY	SATURDAY
			金4 Metal 5 Trap 澤水困 癸未 Water Goat 8 **1** 初五	木3 Wood 6 Not Yet Accomplished 火水未濟 甲申 Wood Monkey 9 **2** 初六	金9 Metal 7 Retreat 天山遯 乙酉 Wood Rooster 4 **3** 初七	水6 Water 8 Mountain 艮爲山 丙戌 Fire Dog 1 **4** 初八
木8 Wood 9 Delight 雷地豫 丁亥 Fire Pig 8 **5** 初九	火7 Fire 1 Beginning 水雷屯 戊子 Earth Rat 4 **6** 初十	金9 Metal 2 Without Wrongdoing 天雷無妄 己丑 Earth Ox 2 **7** 十一	木3 Wood 3 Fire 離爲火 庚寅 Metal Tiger 1 **8** 十二	火2 Fire 4 Sincerity 風澤中孚 辛卯 Metal Rabbit 3 **9** 十三	水6 Water 5 Big Livestock 山天大畜 壬辰 Water Dragon 4 **10** 十四	金4 Metal 6 Eliminating 澤天夬 癸巳 Water Snake 6 **11** 十五
金9 Metal 7 Heaven 乾爲天 甲午 Wood Horse 1 **12** 十六	火7 Fire 8 Well 水風井 乙未 Wood Goat 6 **13** 十七	木8 Wood 9 Relief 雷水解 丙申 Fire Monkey 4 **14** 十八	金4 Metal 1 Influence 澤山咸 丁酉 Fire Rooster 9 **15** 十九	水1 Water 2 Humility 地山謙 戊戌 Earth Dog 6 **16** 二十	火2 Fire 3 Observation 風地觀 己亥 Earth Pig 2 **17** 廿一	火2 Fire 4 Increasing 風雷益 庚子 Metal Rat 9 **18** 廿二
水1 Water 5 Dimming Light 地火明夷 辛丑 Metal Ox 3 **19** 廿三	金9 Metal 6 Fellowship 天火同人 壬寅 Water Tiger 7 **20** 廿四	木8 Wood 7/3 Marrying Maiden 雷澤歸妹 癸卯 Water Rabbit 7 **21** 廿五	木3 Wood 2 Opposition 火澤睽 甲辰 Wood Dragon 2 **22** 廿六	火7 Fire 1 Waiting 水天需 乙巳 Wood Snake 3 **23** 廿七	金4 Metal 9 Great Exceeding 澤風大過 丙午 Fire Horse 3 **24** 廿八	水6 Water 8 Poison 山風蠱 丁未 Fire Goat 7 **25** 廿九
火2 Fire 7 Dispersing 風水渙 戊申 Earth Monkey 6 **26** 三十	木3 Wood 6 Travelling 火山旅 己酉 Earth Rooster 8 **27** 六月初一	金9 Metal 5 Stagnation 天地否 庚戌 Metal Dog 9 **28** 初二	火7 Fire 4 Alliance 水地比 辛亥 Metal Pig 7 **29** 初三	木8 Wood 3 Thunder 震爲雷 壬子 Water Rat 1 **30** 初四		

JULY 2033 己未

Xuan Kong Element 玄空五行	地風升 Rising	Period Luck 卦運	Monthly Star 月星
Water 水1		2	9

SUNDAY	MONDAY	TUESDAY	WEDNESDAY	THURSDAY	FRIDAY	SATURDAY
金4 Metal Trap 8 癸未 Water Goat 澤水困 31 初六 8					水6 Water Beauty 2 癸丑 Water Ox 山火賁 1 初五 8	火7 Fire Accomplished 1 甲寅 Wood Tiger 水火既濟 2 初六 9
水1 Water Arriving 9 乙卯 Wood Rabbit 地澤臨 3 初七 4	金4 Metal Marsh 8 丙辰 Fire Dragon 兌爲澤 4 初八 1	火2 Fire Small Livestock 7 丁巳 Fire Snake 風天小畜 5 初九 8	木3 Wood The Cauldron 6 戊午 Earth Horse 火風鼎 6 初十 4	水1 Water Rising 5 己未 Earth Goat 地風升 7 十一 2	火7 Fire Water 4 庚申 Metal Monkey 坎爲水 8 十二 1	木8 Wood Lesser Exceeding 3 辛酉 Metal Rooster 雷山小過 9 十三 3
金4 Metal Gathering 2 壬戌 Water Dog 澤地萃 10 十四 4	水6 Water Peel 1 癸亥 Water Pig 山地剝 11 十五 6	水1 Water Earth 9 甲子 Wood Rat 坤爲地 12 十六 1	木3 Wood Biting 8 乙丑 Wood Ox 火雷噬嗑 13 十七 6	火2 Fire Family 7 丙寅 Fire Tiger 風火家人 14 十八 4	水6 Water Decreasing 6 丁卯 Fire Rabbit 山澤損 15 十九 9	金9 Metal Tread 5 戊辰 Earth Dragon 天澤履 16 二十 6
木8 Wood Great Strength 4 己巳 Earth Snake 雷天大壯 17 廿一 2	木8 Wood Consistency 3 庚午 Metal Horse 雷風恒 18 廿二 9	金9 Metal Litigation 2 辛未 Metal Goat 天水訟 19 廿三 3	水1 Water Officer 1 壬申 Water Monkey 地水師 20 廿四 7	火2 Fire Gradual Progress 9 癸酉 Water Rooster 風山漸 21 廿五 7	火7 Fire Obstruction 8 甲戌 Wood Dog 水山蹇 22 廿六 2	木3 Wood Advancement 7 乙亥 Wood Pig 火地晉 23 廿七 3
水6 Water Nourish 6 丙子 Fire Rat 山雷頤 24 廿八 3	金4 Metal Following 5 丁丑 Fire Ox 澤雷隨 25 廿九 7	木8 Wood Abundance 4 戊寅 Earth Tiger 雷火豐 26 七月初一 6	火7 Fire Regulate 3 己卯 Earth Rabbit 水澤節 27 初二 8	水1 Water Unity 2 庚辰 Metal Dragon 地天泰 28 初三 9	木3 Wood Great Reward 1 辛巳 Metal Snake 火天大有 29 初四 7	火2 Fire Wind 9 壬午 Water Horse 巽爲風 30 初五 1

AUGUST 2033 庚申

Xuan Kong Element 玄空五行	坎爲水 Water	Period Luck 卦運	Monthly Star 月星
Fire 火7		1	8

SUNDAY	MONDAY	TUESDAY	WEDNESDAY	THURSDAY	FRIDAY	SATURDAY
	木3 Wood Not Yet Accomplished 7 甲申 Wood Monkey 火水未濟 1 初七 9	金9 Metal Retreat 6 乙酉 Wood Rooster 天山遯 2 初八 4	水6 Water Mountain 5 丙戌 Fire Dog 艮爲山 3 初九 1	木8 Wood Delight 4 丁亥 Fire Pig 雷地豫 4 初十 8	火7 Fire Beginning 3 戊子 Earth Rat 水雷屯 5 十一 4	金9 Metal Without Wrongdoing 2 己丑 Earth Ox 天雷無妄 6 十二 2
木3 Wood Fire 1 庚寅 Metal Tiger 離爲火 7 十三 1	火2 Fire Sincerity 9 辛卯 Metal Rabbit 風澤中孚 8 十四 3	水6 Water Big Livestock 8 壬辰 Water Dragon 山天大畜 9 十五 4	金4 Metal Eliminating 7 癸巳 Water Snake 澤天夬 10 十六 6	金9 Metal Heaven 6 甲午 Wood Horse 乾爲天 11 十七 1	火7 Fire Well 5 乙未 Wood Goat 水風井 12 十八 6	木8 Wood Relief 4 丙申 Fire Monkey 雷水解 13 十九 4
金4 Metal Influence 3 丁酉 Fire Rooster 澤山咸 14 二十 9	水1 Water Humility 2 戊戌 Earth Dog 地山謙 15 廿一 6	火2 Fire Observation 1 己亥 Earth Pig 風地觀 16 廿二 2	火2 Fire Increasing 9 庚子 Metal Rat 風雷益 17 廿三 9	水1 Water Dimming Light 8 辛丑 Metal Ox 地火明夷 18 廿四 3	金9 Metal Fellowship 7 壬寅 Water Tiger 天火同人 19 廿五 7	木8 Wood Marrying Maiden 6 癸卯 Water Rabbit 雷澤歸妹 20 廿六 7
木3 Wood Opposition 5 甲辰 Wood Dragon 火澤睽 21 廿七 2	火7 Fire Waiting 4 乙巳 Wood Snake 水天需 22 廿八 3	金4 Metal Great Exceeding 3 丙午 Fire Horse 澤風大過 23 廿九 3	水6 Water Poison 2 丁未 Fire Goat 山風蠱 24 三十 7	火2 Fire Dispersing 1 戊申 Earth Monkey 風水渙 25 閏七月初一 6	木3 Wood Travelling 9 己酉 Earth Rooster 火山旅 26 初二 8	金9 Metal Stagnation 8 庚戌 Metal Dog 天地否 27 初三 9
火7 Fire Alliance 7 辛亥 Metal Pig 水地比 28 初四 7	木8 Wood Thunder 6 壬子 Water Rat 震爲雷 29 初五 1	水6 Water Beauty 5 癸丑 Water Ox 山火賁 30 初六 8	火7 Fire Accomplished 4 甲寅 Wood Tiger 水火既濟 31 初七 9			

SEPTEMBER 2033 辛酉

Xuan Kong Element 玄空五行	雷山小過	Period Luck 卦運	Monthly Star 月星
Wood 木8	Lesser Exceeding	3	7

SUNDAY	MONDAY	TUESDAY	WEDNESDAY	THURSDAY	FRIDAY	SATURDAY
				水1 Water 3 Arriving 乙卯 Wood Rabbit 地澤臨 1 初八 4	金4 Metal 2 Marsh 丙辰 Fire Dragon 兌爲澤 2 初九 1	火2 Fire 1 Small Livestock 丁巳 Fire Snake 風天小畜 3 初十 8
木3 Wood 9 The Cauldron 戊午 Earth Horse 火風鼎 4 十一 4	水1 Water 8 Rising 己未 Earth Goat 地風升 5 十二 2	火7 Fire 7 Water 庚申 Metal Monkey 坎爲水 6 十三 1	木8 Wood 6 Lesser Exceeding 辛酉 Metal Rooster 雷山小過 7 十四 3	金4 Metal 5 Gathering 壬戌 Water Dog 澤地萃 8 十五 4	水6 Water 4 Peel 癸亥 Water Pig 山地剝 9 十六 6	水1 Water 3 Earth 甲子 Wood Rat 坤爲地 10 十七 1
木3 Wood 2 Biting 乙丑 Wood Ox 火雷噬嗑 11 十八 6	火2 Fire 1 Family 丙寅 Fire Tiger 風火家人 12 十九 4	水6 Water 9 Decreasing 丁卯 Fire Rabbit 山澤損 13 二十 9	金9 Metal 8 Tread 戊辰 Earth Dragon 天澤履 14 廿一 6	木8 Wood 7 Great Strength 己巳 Earth Snake 雷天大壯 15 廿二 2	木8 Wood 6 Consistency 庚午 Metal Horse 雷風恆 16 廿三 9	金9 Metal 5 Litigation 辛未 Metal Goat 天水訟 17 廿四 3
水1 Water 4 Officer 壬申 Water Monkey 地水師 18 廿五 7	火2 Fire 3 Gradual Progress 癸酉 Water Rooster 風山漸 19 廿六 7	火7 Fire 2 Obstruction 甲戌 Wood Dog 水山蹇 20 廿七 2	木3 Wood 1 Advancement 乙亥 Wood Pig 火地晉 21 廿八 3	水6 Water 9 Nourish 丙子 Fire Rat 山雷頤 22 廿九 3	金4 Metal 8 Following 丁丑 Fire Ox 澤雷隨 23 八月初一 7	木8 Wood 7 Abundance 戊寅 Earth Tiger 雷火豐 24 初二 6
火7 Fire 6 Regulate 己卯 Earth Rabbit 水澤節 25 初三 8	水1 Water 5 Unity 庚辰 Metal Dragon 地天泰 26 初四 9	木3 Wood 4 Great Reward 辛巳 Metal Snake 火天大有 27 初五 7	火2 Fire 3 Wind 壬午 Water Horse 巽爲風 28 初六 1	金4 Metal 2 Trap 癸未 Water Goat 澤水困 29 初七 8	木3 Wood 1 Not Yet Accomplished 甲申 Wood Monkey 火水未濟 30 初八 9	

OCTOBER 2033 壬戌

Xuan Kong Element 玄空五行	澤地萃	Period Luck 卦運	Monthly Star 月星
Metal 金4	Gathering	4	6

SUNDAY	MONDAY	TUESDAY	WEDNESDAY	THURSDAY	FRIDAY	SATURDAY
火7 Fire 7 Accomplished 甲寅 Wood Tiger 水火既濟 30 初八 9	水1 Water 6 Arriving 乙卯 Wood Rabbit 地澤臨 31 初九 4					金9 Metal 9 Retreat 乙酉 Wood Rooster 天山遯 1 初九 4
水6 Water 8 Mountain 丙戌 Fire Dog 艮爲山 2 初十 1	木8 Wood 7 Delight 丁亥 Fire Pig 雷地豫 3 十一 8	火7 Fire 6 Beginning 戊子 Earth Rat 水雷屯 4 十二 4	金9 Metal 5 Without Wrongdoing 己丑 Earth Ox 天雷無妄 5 十三 2	木3 Wood 4 Fire 庚寅 Metal Tiger 離爲火 6 十四 1	火2 Fire 3 Sincerity 辛卯 Metal Rabbit 風澤中孚 7 十五 3	水6 Water 2 Big Livestock 壬辰 Water Dragon 山天大畜 8 十六 4
金4 Metal 1 Eliminating 癸巳 Water Snake 澤天夬 9 十七 6	金9 Metal 9 Heaven 甲午 Wood Horse 乾爲天 10 十八 1	火7 Fire 8 Well 乙未 Wood Goat 水風井 11 十九 6	木8 Wood 7 Relief 丙申 Fire Monkey 雷水解 12 二十 4	金4 Metal 6 Influence 丁酉 Fire Rooster 澤山咸 13 廿一 9	水1 Water 5 Humility 戊戌 Earth Dog 地山謙 14 廿二 6	火2 Fire 4 Observation 己亥 Earth Pig 風地觀 15 廿三 2
火2 Fire 3 Increasing 庚子 Metal Rat 風雷益 16 廿四 9	水1 Water 2 Dimming Light 辛丑 Metal Ox 地火明夷 17 廿五 3	金9 Metal 1 Fellowship 壬寅 Water Tiger 天火同人 18 廿六 7	木8 Wood 9 Marrying Maiden 癸卯 Water Rabbit 雷澤歸妹 19 廿七 7	木3 Wood 8 Opposition 甲辰 Wood Dragon 火澤睽 20 廿八 2	火7 Fire 7 Waiting 乙巳 Wood Snake 水天需 21 廿九 3	金4 Metal 6 Great Exceeding 丙午 Fire Horse 澤風大過 22 三十 3
水6 Water 5 Poison 丁未 Fire Goat 山風蠱 23 九月初一 7	火2 Fire 4 Dispersing 戊申 Earth Monkey 風水渙 24 初二 6	木3 Wood 3 Travelling 己酉 Earth Rooster 火山旅 25 初三 8	金9 Metal 2 Stagnation 庚戌 Metal Dog 天地否 26 初四 9	火7 Fire 1 Alliance 辛亥 Metal Pig 水地比 27 初五 7	木8 Wood 9 Thunder 壬子 Water Rat 震爲雷 28 初六 1	水6 Water 8 Beauty 癸丑 Water Ox 山火賁 29 初七 8

NOVEMBER 2033 癸亥

Xuan Kong Element 玄空五行	山地剝 Peel	Period Luck 卦運	Monthly Star 月星
Water 水6		6	5

SUNDAY	MONDAY	TUESDAY	WEDNESDAY	THURSDAY	FRIDAY	SATURDAY
		金4 Metal 5 Marsh 兌爲澤 丙辰 Fire Dragon 1 **1** 初十	火2 Fire 4 Small Livestock 風天小畜 丁巳 Fire Snake 8 **2** 十一	木3 Wood 3 The Cauldron 火風鼎 戊午 Earth Horse 4 **3** 十二	水1 Water 2 Rising 地風升 己未 Earth Goat 2 **4** 十三	火7 Fire 1 Water 坎爲水 庚申 Metal Monkey 1 **5** 十四
木8 Wood 9 Lesser Exceeding 雷山小過 辛酉 Metal Rooster 3 **6** 十五	金4 Metal 8 Gathering 澤地萃 壬戌 Water Dog 4 **7** 十六	水6 Water 7 Peel 山地剝 癸亥 Water Pig 6 **8** 十七	水1 Water 6 Earth 坤爲地 甲子 Wood Rat 1 **9** 十八	木3 Wood 5 Biting 火雷噬嗑 乙丑 Wood Ox 6 **10** 十九	火2 Fire 4 Family 風火家人 丙寅 Fire Tiger 4 **11** 二十	水6 Water 3 Decreasing 山澤損 丁卯 Fire Rabbit 9 **12** 廿一
金9 Metal 2 Tread 天澤履 戊辰 Earth Dragon 6 **13** 廿二	木8 Wood 1 Great Strength 雷天大壯 己巳 Earth Snake 2 **14** 廿三	木8 Wood 9 Consistency 雷風恆 庚午 Metal Horse 9 **15** 廿四	金9 Metal 8 Litigation 天水訟 辛未 Metal Goat 3 **16** 廿五	水1 Water 7 Officer 地水師 壬申 Water Monkey 7 **17** 廿六	火2 Fire 6 Gradual Progress 風山漸 癸酉 Water Rooster 7 **18** 廿七	火7 Fire 5 Obstruction 水山蹇 甲戌 Wood Dog 2 **19** 廿八
木3 Wood 4 Advancement 火地晉 乙亥 Wood Pig 3 **20** 廿九	水6 Water 3 Nourish 山雷頤 丙子 Fire Rat 3 **21** 三十	金4 Metal 2 Following 澤雷隨 丁丑 Fire Ox 7 **22** 十月初一	木8 Wood 1 Abundance 雷火豐 戊寅 Earth Tiger 6 **23** 初二	火7 Fire 9 Regulate 水澤節 己卯 Earth Rabbit 8 **24** 初三	水1 Water 8 Unity 地天泰 庚辰 Metal Dragon 9 **25** 初四	木3 Wood 7 Great Reward 火天大有 辛巳 Metal Snake 7 **26** 初五
火2 Fire 6 Wind 巽爲風 壬午 Water Horse 1 **27** 初六	金4 Metal 5 Trap 澤水困 癸未 Water Goat 8 **28** 初七	木3 Wood 4 Not Yet Accomplished 火水未濟 甲申 Wood Monkey 9 **29** 初八	金9 Metal 3 Retreat 天山遯 乙酉 Wood Rooster 4 **30** 初九			

DECEMBER 2033 甲子

Xuan Kong Element 玄空五行	坤爲地 Earth	Period Luck 卦運	Monthly Star 月星
Water 水1		1	4

SUNDAY	MONDAY	TUESDAY	WEDNESDAY	THURSDAY	FRIDAY	SATURDAY
				水6 Water 2 Mountain 艮爲山 丙戌 Fire Dog 1 **1** 初十	木8 Wood 1 Delight 雷地豫 丁亥 Fire Pig 8 **2** 十一	火7 Fire 9 Beginning 水雷屯 戊子 Earth Rat 4 **3** 十二
金9 Metal 8 Without Wrongdoing 天雷無妄 己丑 Earth Ox 2 **4** 十三	木3 Wood 7 Fire 離爲火 庚寅 Metal Tiger 1 **5** 十四	火2 Fire 6 Sincerity 風澤中孚 辛卯 Metal Rabbit 3 **6** 十五	水6 Water 5 Big Livestock 山天大畜 壬辰 Water Dragon 4 **7** 十六	金4 Metal 4 Eliminating 澤天夬 癸巳 Water Snake 6 **8** 十七	金9 Metal 3 Heaven 乾爲天 甲午 Wood Horse 1 **9** 十八	火7 Fire 2 Well 水風井 乙未 Wood Goat 6 **10** 十九
木8 Wood 1 Relief 雷水解 丙申 Fire Monkey 4 **11** 二十	金4 Metal 9 Influence 澤山咸 丁酉 Fire Rooster 9 **12** 廿一	水1 Water 8 Humility 地山謙 戊戌 Earth Dog 6 **13** 廿二	火2 Fire 7 Observation 風地觀 己亥 Earth Pig 2 **14** 廿三	火2 Fire 6 Increasing 風雷益 庚子 Metal Rat 9 **15** 廿四	水1 Water 5 Dimming Light 地火明夷 辛丑 Metal Ox 3 **16** 廿五	金9 Metal 4 Fellowship 天火同人 壬寅 Water Tiger 7 **17** 廿六
木8 Wood 3 Marrying Maiden 雷澤歸妹 癸卯 Water Rabbit 7 **18** 廿七	木3 Wood 2 Opposition 火澤睽 甲辰 Wood Dragon 2 **19** 廿八	火7 Fire 1 Waiting 水天需 乙巳 Wood Snake 3 **20** 廿九	金4 Metal 9/1 Great Exceeding 澤風大過 丙午 Fire Horse 3 **21** 三十	水6 Water 2 Poison 山風蠱 丁未 Fire Goat 7 **22** 十二月初一	火2 Fire 3 Dispersing 風水渙 戊申 Earth Monkey 6 **23** 初二	木3 Wood 4 Travelling 火山旅 己酉 Earth Rooster 8 **24** 初三
金9 Metal 5 Stagnation 天地否 庚戌 Metal Dog 9 **25** 初四	火7 Fire 6 Alliance 水地比 辛亥 Metal Pig 7 **26** 初五	木8 Wood 7 Thunder 震爲雷 壬子 Water Rat 1 **27** 初六	水6 Water 8 Beauty 山火賁 癸丑 Water Ox 8 **28** 初七	火7 Fire 9 Accomplished 水火既濟 甲寅 Wood Tiger 9 **29** 初八	水1 Water 1 Arriving 地澤臨 乙卯 Wood Rabbit 4 **30** 初九	金4 Metal 2 Marsh 兌爲澤 丙辰 Fire Dragon 1 **31** 初十

2034 甲寅

(*Jia Yin*) Wood Tiger

2034 甲寅 *(Jia Yin)* Wood Tiger

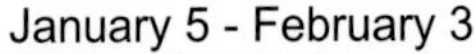

January 5 - February 3

Three Killings | East

February 4 - March 4

Three Killings | North

March 5 - April 4

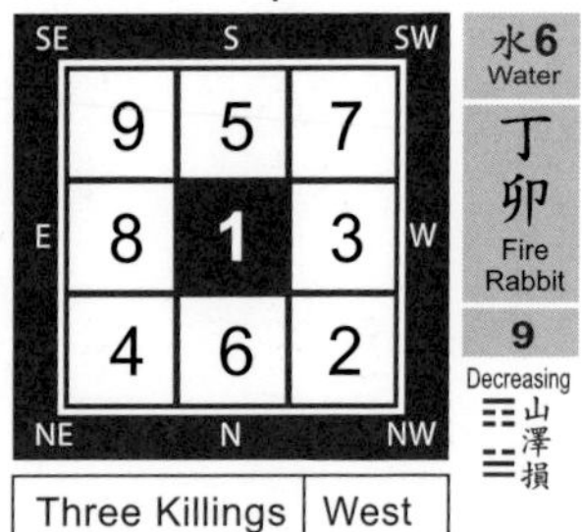

Three Killings | West

April 5 - May 4

Three Killings | South

May 5 - June 4

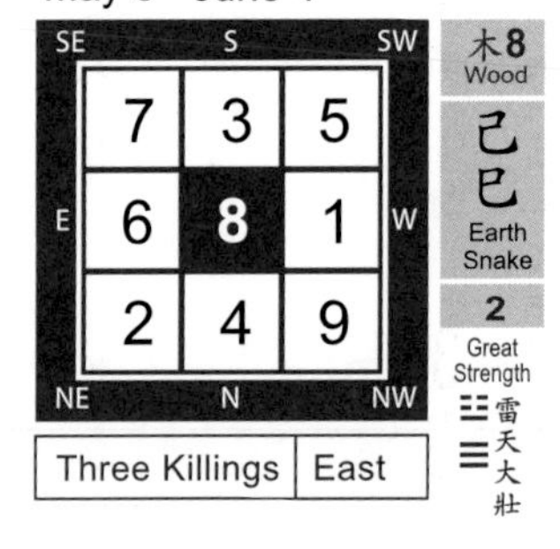

Three Killings | East

June 5 - July 6

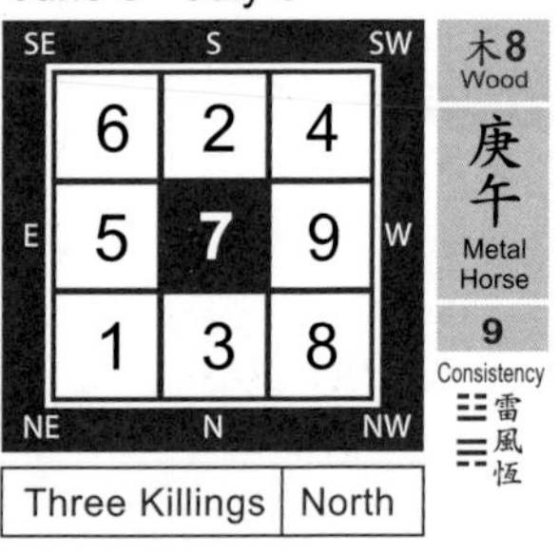

Three Killings | North

July 7 - August 6

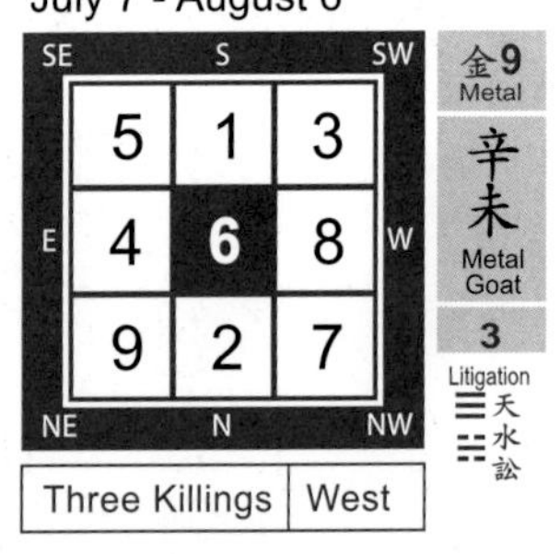

SE S SW
5 1 3
E 4 6 8 W
9 2 7
NE N NW
金9 Metal
辛未
Metal Goat
3
Litigation
天水訟

Three Killings | West

August 7 - September 6

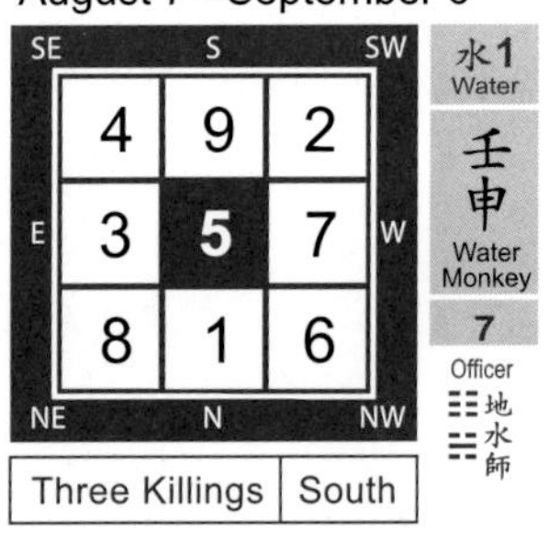

Three Killings | South

September 7 - October 7

Three Killings | East

October 8 - November 6

Three Killings | North

November 7 - December 6

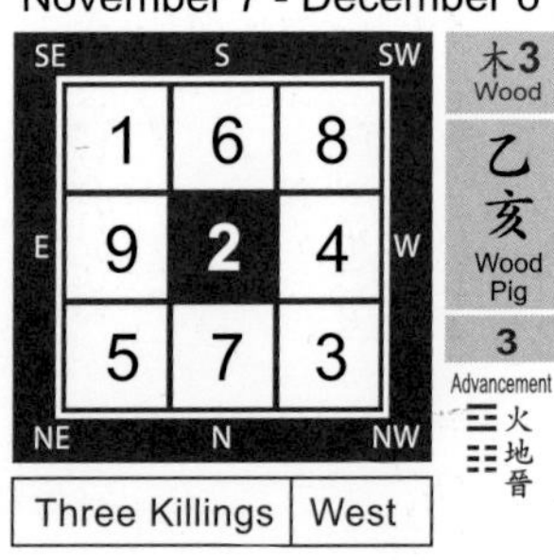

Three Killings | West

December 7 - January 4

Three Killings | South

JANUARY 2034 乙丑

Xuan Kong Element 玄空五行	火雷噬嗑 Biting	Period Luck 卦運	Monthly Star 月星
Wood 木3		6	3

SUNDAY	MONDAY	TUESDAY	WEDNESDAY	THURSDAY	FRIDAY	SATURDAY
火2 Fire Small Livestock 3 丁巳 Fire Snake 風天小畜 1 十一 8	木3 Wood The Cauldron 4 戊午 Earth Horse 火風鼎 2 十二 4	水1 Water Rising 5 己未 Earth Goat 地風升 3 十三 2	火7 Fire Water 6 庚申 Metal Monkey 坎爲水 4 十四 1	木8 Wood Lesser Exceeding 7 辛酉 Metal Rooster 雷山小過 5 十五 3	金4 Metal Gathering 8 壬戌 Water Dog 澤地萃 6 十六 4	水6 Water Peel 9 癸亥 Water Pig 山地剝 7 十七 6
水1 Water Earth 1 甲子 Wood Rat 坤爲地 8 十八 1	木3 Wood Biting 2 乙丑 Wood Ox 火雷噬嗑 9 十九 6	火2 Fire Family 3 丙寅 Fire Tiger 風火家人 10 二十 4	水6 Water Decreasing 4 丁卯 Fire Rabbit 山澤損 11 廿一 9	金9 Metal Tread 5 戊辰 Earth Dragon 天澤履 12 廿二 6	木8 Wood Great Strength 6 己巳 Earth Snake 雷天大壯 13 廿三 2	木8 Wood Consistency 7 庚午 Metal Horse 雷風恆 14 廿四 9
金9 Metal Litigation 8 辛未 Metal Goat 天水訟 15 廿五 3	水1 Water Officer 9 壬申 Water Monkey 地水師 16 廿六 7	火2 Fire Gradual Progress 1 癸酉 Water Rooster 風山漸 17 廿七 7	火7 Fire Obstruction 2 甲戌 Wood Dog 水山蹇 18 廿八 2	木3 Wood Advancement 3 乙亥 Wood Pig 火地晉 19 廿九 3	水6 Water Nourish 4 丙子 Fire Rat 山雷頤 20 十二月初一 3	金4 Metal Following 5 丁丑 Fire Ox 澤雷隨 21 初二 7
木8 Wood Abundance 6 戊寅 Earth Tiger 雷火豐 22 初三 6	火7 Fire Regulate 7 己卯 Earth Rabbit 水澤節 23 初四 8	水1 Water Unity 8 庚辰 Metal Dragon 地天泰 24 初五 9	木3 Wood Great Reward 9 辛巳 Metal Snake 火天大有 25 初六 7	火2 Fire Wind 1 壬午 Water Horse 巽爲風 26 初七 1	金4 Metal Trap 2 癸未 Water Goat 澤水困 27 初八 8	木3 Wood Not Yet Accomplished 3 甲申 Wood Monkey 火水未濟 28 初九 9
金9 Metal Retreat 4 乙酉 Wood Rooster 天山遯 29 初十 4	水6 Water Mountain 5 丙戌 Fire Dog 艮爲山 30 十一 1	木8 Wood Delight 6 丁亥 Fire Pig 雷地豫 31 十二 8				

FEBRUARY 2034 丙寅

Xuan Kong Element 玄空五行	風火家人 Family	Period Luck 卦運	Monthly Star 月星
Fire 火2		4	2

SUNDAY	MONDAY	TUESDAY	WEDNESDAY	THURSDAY	FRIDAY	SATURDAY
			火7 Fire Beginning 7 戊子 Earth Rat 水雷屯 1 十三 4	金9 Metal Without Wrongdoing 8 己丑 Earth Ox 天雷無妄 2 十四 2	木3 Wood Fire 9 庚寅 Metal Tiger 離爲火 3 十五 1	火2 Fire Sincerity 1 辛卯 Metal Rabbit 風澤中孚 4 十六 3
水6 Water Big Livestock 2 壬辰 Water Dragon 山天大畜 5 十七 4	金4 Metal Eliminating 3 癸巳 Water Snake 澤天夬 6 十八 6	金9 Metal Heaven 4 甲午 Wood Horse 乾爲天 7 十九 1	火7 Fire Well 5 乙未 Wood Goat 水風井 8 二十 6	木8 Wood Relief 6 丙申 Fire Monkey 雷水解 9 廿一 4	金4 Metal Influence 7 丁酉 Fire Rooster 澤山咸 10 廿二 9	水1 Water Humility 8 戊戌 Earth Dog 地山謙 11 廿三 6
火2 Fire Observation 9 己亥 Earth Pig 風地觀 12 廿四 2	火2 Fire Increasing 1 庚子 Metal Rat 風雷益 13 廿五 9	水1 Water Dimming Light 2 辛丑 Metal Ox 地火明夷 14 廿六 3	金9 Metal Fellowship 3 壬寅 Water Tiger 天火同人 15 廿七 7	木8 Wood Marrying Maiden 4 癸卯 Water Rabbit 雷澤歸妹 16 廿八 7	木3 Wood Opposition 5 甲辰 Wood Dragon 火澤睽 17 廿九 2	火7 Fire Waiting 6 乙巳 Wood Snake 水天需 18 三十 3
金4 Metal Great Exceeding 7 丙午 Fire Horse 澤風大過 19 正月初一 3	水6 Water Poison 8 丁未 Fire Goat 山風蠱 20 初二 7	火2 Fire Dispersing 9 戊申 Earth Monkey 風水渙 21 初三 6	木3 Wood Travelling 1 己酉 Earth Rooster 火山旅 22 初四 8	金9 Metal Stagnation 2 庚戌 Metal Dog 天地否 23 初五 9	火7 Fire Alliance 3 辛亥 Metal Pig 水地比 24 初六 7	木8 Wood Thunder 4 壬子 Water Rat 震爲雷 25 初七 1
水6 Water Beauty 5 癸丑 Water Ox 山火賁 26 初八 8	火7 Fire Accomplished 6 甲寅 Wood Tiger 水火既濟 27 初九 9	水1 Water Arriving 7 乙卯 Wood Rabbit 地澤臨 28 初十 4				

MARCH 2034 丁卯

Xuan Kong Element 玄空五行	山澤損 Decreasing	Period Luck 卦運	Monthly Star 月星
Water 水6		9	1

SUNDAY	MONDAY	TUESDAY	WEDNESDAY	THURSDAY	FRIDAY	SATURDAY
			金4 Metal Marsh 兌爲澤 丙辰 Fire Dragon **1** 十一 1 · 8	火2 Fire Small Livestock 風天小畜 丁巳 Fire Snake **2** 十二 8 · 9	木3 Wood The Cauldron 火風鼎 戊午 Earth Horse **3** 十三 4 · 1	水1 Water Rising 地風升 己未 Earth Goat **4** 十四 2 · 2
火7 Fire Water 坎爲水 庚申 Metal Monkey **5** 十五 1 · 3	木8 Wood Lesser Exceeding 雷山小過 辛酉 Metal Rooster **6** 十六 3 · 4	金4 Metal Gathering 澤地萃 壬戌 Water Dog **7** 十七 4 · 5	水6 Water Peel 山地剝 癸亥 Water Pig **8** 十八 6 · 6	水1 Water Earth 坤爲地 甲子 Wood Rat **9** 十九 1 · 7	木3 Wood Biting 火雷噬嗑 乙丑 Wood Ox **10** 二十 6 · 8	火2 Fire Family 風火家人 丙寅 Fire Tiger **11** 廿一 4 · 9
水6 Water Decreasing 山澤損 丁卯 Fire Rabbit **12** 廿二 9 · 1	金9 Metal Tread 天澤履 戊辰 Earth Dragon **13** 廿三 6 · 2	木8 Wood Great Strength 雷天大壯 己巳 Earth Snake **14** 廿四 2 · 3	木8 Wood Consistency 雷風恆 庚午 Metal Horse **15** 廿五 9 · 4	金9 Metal Litigation 天水訟 辛未 Metal Goat **16** 廿六 3 · 5	水1 Water Officer 地水師 壬申 Water Monkey **17** 廿七 7 · 6	火2 Fire Gradual Progress 風山漸 癸酉 Water Rooster **18** 廿八 7 · 7
火7 Fire Obstruction 水山蹇 甲戌 Wood Dog **19** 廿九 2 · 8	木3 Wood Advancement 火地晉 乙亥 Wood Pig **20** 二月初一 3 · 9	水6 Water Nourish 山雷頤 丙子 Fire Rat **21** 初二 3 · 1	金4 Metal Following 澤雷隨 丁丑 Fire Ox **22** 初三 7 · 2	木8 Wood Abundance 雷火豐 戊寅 Earth Tiger **23** 初四 6 · 3	火7 Fire Regulate 水澤節 己卯 Earth Rabbit **24** 初五 8 · 4	水1 Water Unity 地天泰 庚辰 Metal Dragon **25** 初六 9 · 5
木3 Wood Great Reward 火天大有 辛巳 Metal Snake **26** 初七 7 · 6	火2 Fire Wind 巽爲風 壬午 Water Horse **27** 初八 1 · 7	金4 Metal Trap 澤水困 癸未 Water Goat **28** 初九 8 · 8	木3 Wood Not Yet Accomplished 火水未濟 甲申 Wood Monkey **29** 初十 9 · 9	金9 Metal Retreat 天山遯 乙酉 Wood Rooster **30** 十一 4 · 1	水6 Water Mountain 艮爲山 丙戌 Fire Dog **31** 十二 1 · 2	

APRIL 2034 戊辰

Xuan Kong Element 玄空五行	天澤履 Tread	Period Luck 卦運	Monthly Star 月星
Metal 金9		6	9

SUNDAY	MONDAY	TUESDAY	WEDNESDAY	THURSDAY	FRIDAY	SATURDAY
金4 Metal Marsh 兌爲澤 丙辰 Fire Dragon **30** 十二 1 · 5						木8 Wood Delight 雷地豫 丁亥 Fire Pig **1** 十三 8 · 3
火7 Fire Beginning 水雷屯 戊子 Earth Rat **2** 十四 4 · 4	金9 Metal Without Wrongdoing 天雷無妄 己丑 Earth Ox **3** 十五 2 · 5	木3 Wood Fire 離爲火 庚寅 Metal Tiger **4** 十六 1 · 6	火2 Fire Sincerity 風澤中孚 辛卯 Metal Rabbit **5** 十七 3 · 7	水6 Water Big Livestock 山天大畜 壬辰 Water Dragon **6** 十八 4 · 8	金4 Metal Eliminating 澤天夬 癸巳 Water Snake **7** 十九 6 · 9	金9 Metal Heaven 乾爲天 甲午 Wood Horse **8** 二十 1 · 1
火7 Fire Well 水風井 乙未 Wood Goat **9** 廿一 6 · 2	木8 Wood Relief 雷水解 丙申 Fire Monkey **10** 廿二 4 · 3	金4 Metal Influence 澤山咸 丁酉 Fire Rooster **11** 廿三 9 · 4	水1 Water Humility 地山謙 戊戌 Earth Dog **12** 廿四 6 · 5	火2 Fire Observation 風地觀 己亥 Earth Pig **13** 廿五 2 · 6	火2 Fire Increasing 風雷益 庚子 Metal Rat **14** 廿六 9 · 7	水1 Water Dimming Light 地火明夷 辛丑 Metal Ox **15** 廿七 3 · 8
金9 Metal Fellowship 天火同人 壬寅 Water Tiger **16** 廿八 7 · 9	木8 Wood Marrying Maiden 雷澤歸妹 癸卯 Water Rabbit **17** 廿九 7 · 1	木3 Wood Opposition 火澤睽 甲辰 Wood Dragon **18** 三十 2 · 2	火7 Fire Waiting 水天需 乙巳 Wood Snake **19** 三月初一 3 · 3	金4 Metal Great Exceeding 澤風大過 丙午 Fire Horse **20** 初二 3 · 4	水6 Water Poison 山風蠱 丁未 Fire Goat **21** 初三 7 · 5	火2 Fire Dispersing 風水渙 戊申 Earth Monkey **22** 初四 6 · 6
木3 Wood Travelling 火山旅 己酉 Earth Rooster **23** 初五 8 · 7	金9 Metal Stagnation 天地否 庚戌 Metal Dog **24** 初六 9 · 8	火7 Fire Alliance 水地比 辛亥 Metal Pig **25** 初七 7 · 9	木8 Wood Thunder 震爲雷 壬子 Water Rat **26** 初八 1 · 1	水6 Water Beauty 山火賁 癸丑 Water Ox **27** 初九 8 · 2	火7 Fire Accomplished 水火既濟 甲寅 Wood Tiger **28** 初十 9 · 3	水1 Water Arriving 地澤臨 乙卯 Wood Rabbit **29** 十一 4 · 4

MAY 2034 己巳

Xuan Kong Element 玄空五行	雷天大壯 Great Strength	Period Luck 卦運	Monthly Star 月星
Wood 木8		2	8

SUNDAY	MONDAY	TUESDAY	WEDNESDAY	THURSDAY	FRIDAY	SATURDAY
	火2 Fire 6 Small Livestock 風天小畜 丁巳 Fire Snake 8 **1** 十三	木3 Wood 7 The Cauldron 火風鼎 戊午 Earth Horse 4 **2** 十四	水1 Water 8 Rising 地風升 己未 Earth Goat 2 **3** 十五	火7 Fire 9 Water 坎爲水 庚申 Metal Monkey 1 **4** 十六	木8 Wood 1 Lesser Exceeding 雷山小過 辛酉 Metal Rooster 3 **5** 十七	金4 Metal 2 Gathering 澤地萃 壬戌 Water Dog 4 **6** 十八
水6 Water 3 Peel 山地剝 癸亥 Water Pig 6 **7** 十九	水1 Water 4 Earth 坤爲地 甲子 Wood Rat 1 **8** 二十	木3 Wood 5 Biting 火雷噬嗑 乙丑 Wood Ox 6 **9** 廿一	火2 Fire 6 Family 風火家人 丙寅 Fire Tiger 4 **10** 廿二	水6 Water 7 Decreasing 山澤損 丁卯 Fire Rabbit 9 **11** 廿三	金9 Metal 8 Tread 天澤履 戊辰 Earth Dragon 6 **12** 廿四	木8 Wood 9 Great Strength 雷天大壯 己巳 Earth Snake 2 **13** 廿五
木8 Wood 1 Consistency 雷風恆 庚午 Metal Horse 9 **14** 廿六	金9 Metal 2 Litigation 天水訟 辛未 Metal Goat 3 **15** 廿七	水1 Water 3 Officer 地水師 壬申 Water Monkey 7 **16** 廿八	火2 Fire 4 Gradual Progress 風山漸 癸酉 Water Rooster 7 **17** 廿九	火7 Fire 5 Obstruction 水山蹇 甲戌 Wood Dog 2 **18** 四月初一	木3 Wood 6 Advancement 火地晉 乙亥 Wood Pig 3 **19** 初二	水6 Water 7 Nourish 山雷頤 丙子 Fire Rat 3 **20** 初三
金4 Metal 8 Following 澤雷隨 丁丑 Fire Ox 7 **21** 初四	木8 Wood 9 Abundance 雷火豐 戊寅 Earth Tiger 6 **22** 初五	火7 Fire 1 Regulate 水澤節 己卯 Earth Rabbit 8 **23** 初六	水1 Water 2 Unity 地天泰 庚辰 Metal Dragon 9 **24** 初七	木3 Wood 3 Great Reward 火天大有 辛巳 Metal Snake 7 **25** 初八	火2 Fire 4 Wind 巽爲風 壬午 Water Horse 1 **26** 初九	金4 Metal 5 Trap 澤水困 癸未 Water Goat 8 **27** 初十
木3 Wood 6 Not Yet Accomplished 火水未濟 甲申 Wood Monkey 9 **28** 十一	金9 Metal 7 Retreat 天山遯 乙酉 Wood Rooster 4 **29** 十二	水6 Water 8 Mountain 艮爲山 丙戌 Fire Dog 1 **30** 十三	木8 Wood 9 Delight 雷地豫 丁亥 Fire Pig 8 **31** 十四			

JUNE 2034 庚午

Xuan Kong Element 玄空五行	雷風恆 Consistency	Period Luck 卦運	Monthly Star 月星
Wood 木8		9	7

SUNDAY	MONDAY	TUESDAY	WEDNESDAY	THURSDAY	FRIDAY	SATURDAY
				火7 Fire 1 Beginning 水雷屯 戊子 Earth Rat 4 **1** 十五	金9 Metal 2 Without Wrongdoing 天雷無妄 己丑 Earth Ox 2 **2** 十六	木3 Wood 3 Fire 離爲火 庚寅 Metal Tiger 1 **3** 十七
火2 Fire 4 Sincerity 風澤中孚 辛卯 Metal Rabbit 3 **4** 十八	水6 Water 5 Big Livestock 山天大畜 壬辰 Water Dragon 4 **5** 十九	金4 Metal 6 Eliminating 澤天夬 癸巳 Water Snake 6 **6** 二十	金9 Metal 7 Heaven 乾爲天 甲午 Wood Horse 1 **7** 廿一	火7 Fire 8 Well 水風井 乙未 Wood Goat 6 **8** 廿二	木8 Wood 9 Relief 雷水解 丙申 Fire Monkey 4 **9** 廿三	金4 Metal 1 Influence 澤山咸 丁酉 Fire Rooster 9 **10** 廿四
水1 Water 2 Humility 地山謙 戊戌 Earth Dog 6 **11** 廿五	火2 Fire 3 Observation 風地觀 己亥 Earth Pig 2 **12** 廿六	火2 Fire 4 Increasing 風雷益 庚子 Metal Rat 9 **13** 廿七	水1 Water 5 Dimming Light 地火明夷 辛丑 Metal Ox 3 **14** 廿八	金9 Metal 6 Fellowship 天火同人 壬寅 Water Tiger 7 **15** 廿九	木8 Wood 7 Marrying Maiden 雷澤歸妹 癸卯 Water Rabbit 7 **16** 五月初一	木3 Wood 8 Opposition 火澤睽 甲辰 Wood Dragon 2 **17** 初二
火7 Fire 9 Waiting 水天需 乙巳 Wood Snake 3 **18** 初三	金4 Metal 1 Great Exceeding 澤風大過 丙午 Fire Horse 3 **19** 初四	水6 Water 2 Poison 山風蠱 丁未 Fire Goat 7 **20** 初五	火2 Fire 3/7 Dispersing 風水渙 戊申 Earth Monkey 6 **21** 初六	木3 Wood 6 Travelling 火山旅 己酉 Earth Rooster 8 **22** 初七	金9 Metal 5 Stagnation 天地否 庚戌 Metal Dog 9 **23** 初八	火7 Fire 4 Alliance 水地比 辛亥 Metal Pig 7 **24** 初九
木8 Wood 3 Thunder 震爲雷 壬子 Water Rat 1 **25** 初十	水6 Water 2 Beauty 山火賁 癸丑 Water Ox 8 **26** 十一	火7 Fire 1 Accomplished 水火既濟 甲寅 Wood Tiger 9 **27** 十二	水1 Water 9 Arriving 地澤臨 乙卯 Wood Rabbit 4 **28** 十三	金4 Metal 8 Marsh 兌爲澤 丙辰 Fire Dragon 1 **29** 十四	火2 Fire 7 Small Livestock 風天小畜 丁巳 Fire Snake 8 **30** 十五	

JULY 2034 辛未

Xuan Kong Element 玄空五行	天水訟 Litigation	Period Luck 卦運	Monthly Star 月星
Metal 金9		3	6

SUNDAY	MONDAY	TUESDAY	WEDNESDAY	THURSDAY	FRIDAY	SATURDAY
木8 Wood · 4 Delight 雷地豫 丁亥 Fire Pig 30 十五 8	火7 Fire · 3 Beginning 水雷屯 戊子 Earth Rat 31 十六 4				十五	木3 Wood · 6 The Cauldron 火風鼎 戊午 Earth Horse 1 十六 4
水1 Water · 5 Rising 地風升 己未 Earth Goat 2 十七 2	火7 Fire · 4 Water 坎爲水 庚申 Metal Monkey 3 十八 1	木8 Wood · 3 Lesser Exceeding 雷山小過 辛酉 Metal Rooster 4 十九 3	金4 Metal · 2 Gathering 澤地萃 壬戌 Water Dog 5 二十 4	水6 Water · 1 Peel 山地剝 癸亥 Water Pig 6 廿一 6	水1 Water · 9 Earth 坤爲地 甲子 Wood Rat 7 廿二 1	木3 Wood · 8 Biting 火雷噬嗑 乙丑 Wood Ox 8 廿三 6
火2 Fire · 7 Family 風火家人 丙寅 Fire Tiger 9 廿四 4	水6 Water · 6 Decreasing 山澤損 丁卯 Fire Rabbit 10 廿五 9	金9 Metal · 5 Tread 天澤履 戊辰 Earth Dragon 11 廿六 6	木8 Wood · 4 Great Strength 雷天大壯 己巳 Earth Snake 12 廿七 2	木8 Wood · 3 Consistency 雷風恒 庚午 Metal Horse 13 廿八 9	金9 Metal · 2 Litigation 天水訟 辛未 Metal Goat 14 廿九 3	水1 Water · 1 Officer 地水師 壬申 Water Monkey 15 三十 7
火2 Fire · 9 Gradual Progress 風山漸 癸酉 Water Rooster 16 六月初一 7	火7 Fire · 8 Obstruction 水山蹇 甲戌 Wood Dog 17 初二 2	木3 Wood · 7 Advancement 火地晉 乙亥 Wood Pig 18 初三 3	水6 Water · 6 Nourish 山雷頤 丙子 Fire Rat 19 初四 3	金4 Metal · 5 Following 澤雷隨 丁丑 Fire Ox 20 初五 7	木8 Wood · 4 Abundance 雷火豐 戊寅 Earth Tiger 21 初六 6	火7 Fire · 3 Regulate 水澤節 己卯 Earth Rabbit 22 初七 8
水1 Water · 2 Unity 地天泰 庚辰 Metal Dragon 23 初八 9	木3 Wood · 1 Great Reward 火天大有 辛巳 Metal Snake 24 初九 7	火2 Fire · 9 Wind 巽爲風 壬午 Water Horse 25 初十 1	金4 Metal · 8 Trap 澤水困 癸未 Water Goat 26 十一 8	木3 Wood · 7 Not Yet Accomplished 火水未濟 甲申 Wood Monkey 27 十二 9	金9 Metal · 6 Retreat 天山遯 乙酉 Wood Rooster 28 十三 4	水6 Water · 5 Mountain 艮爲山 丙戌 Fire Dog 29 十四 1

AUGUST 2034 壬申

Xuan Kong Element 玄空五行	地水師 Officer	Period Luck 卦運	Monthly Star 月星
Water 水1		7	5

SUNDAY	MONDAY	TUESDAY	WEDNESDAY	THURSDAY	FRIDAY	SATURDAY
		金9 Metal · 2 Without Wrongdoing 天雷無妄 己丑 Earth Ox 1 十七 2	木3 Wood · 1 Fire 離爲火 庚寅 Metal Tiger 2 十八 1	火2 Fire · 9 Sincerity 風澤中孚 辛卯 Metal Rabbit 3 十九 3	水6 Water · 8 Big Livestock 山天大畜 壬辰 Water Dragon 4 二十 4	金4 Metal · 7 Eliminating 澤天夬 癸巳 Water Snake 5 廿一 6
金9 Metal · 6 Heaven 乾爲天 甲午 Wood Horse 6 廿二 1	火7 Fire · 5 Well 水風井 乙未 Wood Goat 7 廿三 6	木8 Wood · 4 Relief 雷水解 丙申 Fire Monkey 8 廿四 4	金4 Metal · 3 Influence 澤山咸 丁酉 Fire Rooster 9 廿五 9	水1 Water · 2 Humility 地山謙 戊戌 Earth Dog 10 廿六 6	火2 Fire · 1 Observation 風地觀 己亥 Earth Pig 11 廿七 2	火2 Fire · 9 Increasing 風雷益 庚子 Metal Rat 12 廿八 9
水1 Water · 8 Dimming Light 地火明夷 辛丑 Metal Ox 13 廿九 3	金9 Metal · 7 Fellowship 天火同人 壬寅 Water Tiger 14 七月初一 7	木8 Wood · 6 Marrying Maiden 雷澤歸妹 癸卯 Water Rabbit 15 初二 7	木3 Wood · 5 Opposition 火澤睽 甲辰 Wood Dragon 16 初三 2	火7 Fire · 4 Waiting 水天需 乙巳 Wood Snake 17 初四 3	金4 Metal · 3 Great Exceeding 澤風大過 丙午 Fire Horse 18 初五 3	水6 Water · 2 Poison 山風蠱 丁未 Fire Goat 19 初六 7
火2 Fire · 1 Dispersing 風水渙 戊申 Earth Monkey 20 初七 6	木3 Wood · 9 Travelling 火山旅 己酉 Earth Rooster 21 初八 8	金9 Metal · 8 Stagnation 天地否 庚戌 Metal Dog 22 初九 9	火7 Fire · 7 Alliance 水地比 辛亥 Metal Pig 23 初十 7	木8 Wood · 6 Thunder 震爲雷 壬子 Water Rat 24 十一 1	水6 Water · 5 Beauty 山火賁 癸丑 Water Ox 25 十二 8	火7 Fire · 4 Accomplished 水火既濟 甲寅 Wood Tiger 26 十三 9
水1 Water · 3 Arriving 地澤臨 乙卯 Wood Rabbit 27 十四 4	金4 Metal · 2 Marsh 兌爲澤 丙辰 Fire Dragon 28 十五 1	火2 Fire · 1 Small Livestock 風天小畜 丁巳 Fire Snake 29 十六 8	木3 Wood · 9 The Cauldron 火風鼎 戊午 Earth Horse 30 十七 4	水1 Water · 8 Rising 地風升 己未 Earth Goat 31 十八 2		

SEPTEMBER 2034 癸酉

Xuan Kong Element 玄空五行	風山漸 Gradual Progress	Period Luck 卦運	Monthly Star 月星
Fire 火2		7	4

SUNDAY	MONDAY	TUESDAY	WEDNESDAY	THURSDAY	FRIDAY	SATURDAY
					1 火7 Fire · 7 Water 坎爲水 庚申 Metal Monkey 1 · 十九	**2** 木8 Wood · 6 Lesser Exceeding 雷山小過 辛酉 Metal Rooster 3 · 二十
3 金4 Metal · 5 Gathering 澤地萃 壬戌 Water Dog 4 · 廿一	**4** 水6 Water · 4 Peel 山地剝 癸亥 Water Pig 6 · 廿二	**5** 水1 Water · 3 Earth 坤爲地 甲子 Wood Rat 1 · 廿三	**6** 木3 Wood · 2 Biting 火雷噬嗑 乙丑 Wood Ox 6 · 廿四	**7** 火2 Fire · 1 Family 風火家人 丙寅 Fire Tiger 4 · 廿五	**8** 水6 Water · 9 Decreasing 山澤損 丁卯 Fire Rabbit 9 · 廿六	**9** 金9 Metal · 8 Tread 天澤履 戊辰 Earth Dragon 6 · 廿七
10 木8 Wood · 7 Great Strength 雷天大壯 己巳 Earth Snake 2 · 廿八	**11** 木8 Wood · 6 Consistency 雷風恆 庚午 Metal Horse 9 · 廿九	**12** 金9 Metal · 5 Litigation 天水訟 辛未 Metal Goat 3 · 三十	**13** 水1 Water · 4 Officer 地水師 壬申 Water Monkey 7 · 八月初一	**14** 火2 Fire · 3 Gradual Progress 風山漸 癸酉 Water Rooster 7 · 初二	**15** 火7 Fire · 2 Obstruction 水山蹇 甲戌 Wood Dog 2 · 初三	**16** 木3 Wood · 1 Advancement 火地晉 乙亥 Wood Pig 3 · 初四
17 水6 Water · 9 Nourish 山雷頤 丙子 Fire Rat 3 · 初五	**18** 金4 Metal · 8 Following 澤雷隨 丁丑 Fire Ox 7 · 初六	**19** 木8 Wood · 7 Abundance 雷火豐 戊寅 Earth Tiger 6 · 初七	**20** 火7 Fire · 6 Regulate 水澤節 己卯 Earth Rabbit 8 · 初八	**21** 水1 Water · 5 Unity 地天泰 庚辰 Metal Dragon 9 · 初九	**22** 木3 Wood · 4 Great Reward 火天大有 辛巳 Metal Snake 7 · 初十	**23** 火2 Fire · 3 Wind 巽爲風 壬午 Water Horse 1 · 十一
24 金4 Metal · 2 Trap 澤水困 癸未 Water Goat 8 · 十二	**25** 木3 Wood · 1 Not Yet Accomplished 火水未濟 甲申 Wood Monkey 9 · 十三	**26** 金9 Metal · 9 Retreat 天山遯 乙酉 Wood Rooster 4 · 十四	**27** 水6 Water · 8 Mountain 艮爲山 丙戌 Fire Dog 1 · 十五	**28** 木8 Wood · 7 Delight 雷地豫 丁亥 Fire Pig 8 · 十六	**29** 火7 Fire · 6 Beginning 水雷屯 戊子 Earth Rat 4 · 十七	**30** 金9 Metal · 5 Without Wrongdoing 天雷無妄 己丑 Earth Ox 2 · 十八

OCTOBER 2034 甲戌

Xuan Kong Element 玄空五行	水山蹇 Obstruction	Period Luck 卦運	Monthly Star 月星
Fire 火7		2	3

SUNDAY	MONDAY	TUESDAY	WEDNESDAY	THURSDAY	FRIDAY	SATURDAY
1 木3 Wood · 4 Fire 離爲火 庚寅 Metal Tiger 1 · 十九	**2** 火2 Fire · 3 Sincerity 風澤中孚 辛卯 Metal Rabbit 3 · 二十	**3** 水6 Water · 2 Big Livestock 山天大畜 壬辰 Water Dragon 4 · 廿一	**4** 金4 Metal · 1 Eliminating 澤天夬 癸巳 Water Snake 6 · 廿二	**5** 金9 Metal · 9 Heaven 乾爲天 甲午 Wood Horse 1 · 廿三	**6** 火7 Fire · 8 Well 水風井 乙未 Wood Goat 6 · 廿四	**7** 木8 Wood · 7 Relief 雷水解 丙申 Fire Monkey 4 · 廿五
8 金4 Metal · 6 Influence 澤山咸 丁酉 Fire Rooster 9 · 廿六	**9** 水1 Water · 5 Humility 地山謙 戊戌 Earth Dog 6 · 廿七	**10** 火2 Fire · 4 Observation 風地觀 己亥 Earth Pig 2 · 廿八	**11** 火2 Fire · 3 Increasing 風雷益 庚子 Metal Rat 9 · 廿九	**12** 水1 Water · 2 Dimming Light 地火明夷 辛丑 Metal Ox 3 · 九月初一	**13** 金9 Metal · 1 Fellowship 天火同人 壬寅 Water Tiger 7 · 初二	**14** 木8 Wood · 9 Marrying Maiden 雷澤歸妹 癸卯 Water Rabbit 7 · 初三
15 木3 Wood · 8 Opposition 火澤睽 甲辰 Wood Dragon 2 · 初四	**16** 火7 Fire · 7 Waiting 水天需 乙巳 Wood Snake 3 · 初五	**17** 金4 Metal · 6 Great Exceeding 澤風大過 丙午 Fire Horse 3 · 初六	**18** 水6 Water · 5 Poison 山風蠱 丁未 Fire Goat 7 · 初七	**19** 火2 Fire · 4 Dispersing 風水渙 戊申 Earth Monkey 6 · 初八	**20** 木3 Wood · 3 Travelling 火山旅 己酉 Earth Rooster 8 · 初九	**21** 金9 Metal · 2 Stagnation 天地否 庚戌 Metal Dog 9 · 初十
22 火7 Fire · 1 Alliance 水地比 辛亥 Metal Pig 7 · 十一	**23** 木8 Wood · 9 Thunder 震爲雷 壬子 Water Rat 1 · 十二	**24** 水6 Water · 8 Beauty 山火賁 癸丑 Water Ox 8 · 十三	**25** 火7 Fire · 7 Accomplished 水火既濟 甲寅 Wood Tiger 9 · 十四	**26** 水1 Water · 6 Arriving 地澤臨 乙卯 Wood Rabbit 4 · 十五	**27** 金4 Metal · 5 Marsh 兌爲澤 丙辰 Fire Dragon 1 · 十六	**28** 火2 Fire · 4 Small Livestock 風天小畜 丁巳 Fire Snake 8 · 十七
29 木3 Wood · 3 The Cauldron 火風鼎 戊午 Earth Horse 4 · 十八	**30** 水1 Water · 2 Rising 地風升 己未 Earth Goat 2 · 十九	**31** 火7 Fire · 1 Water 坎爲水 庚申 Metal Monkey 1 · 二十				

NOVEMBER 2034 乙亥

Xuan Kong Element 玄空五行	火地晉 Advancement	Period Luck 卦運	Monthly Star 月星
Wood 木3		3	2

SUNDAY	MONDAY	TUESDAY	WEDNESDAY	THURSDAY	FRIDAY	SATURDAY
			木8 Wood 9 Lesser Exceeding 雷山小過 1 辛酉 Metal Rooster 3 廿一	金4 Metal 8 Gathering 澤地萃 2 壬戌 Water Dog 4 廿二	水6 Water 7 Peel 山地剝 3 癸亥 Water Pig 6 廿三	水1 Water 6 Earth 坤爲地 4 甲子 Wood Rat 1 廿四
木3 Wood 5 Biting 火雷噬嗑 5 乙丑 Wood Ox 6 廿五	火2 Fire 4 Family 風火家人 6 丙寅 Fire Tiger 4 廿六	水6 Water 3 Decreasing 山澤損 7 丁卯 Fire Rabbit 9 廿七	金9 Metal 2 Tread 天澤履 8 戊辰 Earth Dragon 6 廿八	木8 Wood 1 Great Strength 雷天大壯 9 己巳 Earth Snake 2 廿九	木8 Wood 9 Consistency 雷風恆 10 庚午 Metal Horse 9 三十	金9 Metal 8 Litigation 天水訟 11 辛未 Metal Goat 3 十月初一
水1 Water 7 Officer 地水師 12 壬申 Water Monkey 7 初二	火2 Fire 6 Gradual Progress 風山漸 13 癸酉 Water Rooster 7 初三	火7 Fire 5 Obstruction 水山蹇 14 甲戌 Wood Dog 2 初四	木3 Wood 4 Advancement 火地晉 15 乙亥 Wood Pig 3 初五	水6 Water 3 Nourish 山雷頤 16 丙子 Fire Rat 3 初六	金4 Metal 2 Following 澤雷隨 17 丁丑 Fire Ox 7 初七	木8 Wood 1 Abundance 雷火豐 18 戊寅 Earth Tiger 6 初八
火7 Fire 9 Regulate 水澤節 19 己卯 Earth Rabbit 8 初九	水1 Water 8 Unity 地天泰 20 庚辰 Metal Dragon 9 初十	木3 Wood 7 Great Reward 火天大有 21 辛巳 Metal Snake 7 十一	火2 Fire 6 Wind 巽爲風 22 壬午 Water Horse 1 十二	金4 Metal 5 Trap 澤水困 23 癸未 Water Goat 8 十三	木3 Wood 4 Not Yet Accomplished 火水未濟 24 甲申 Wood Monkey 9 十四	金9 Metal 3 Retreat 天山遯 25 乙酉 Wood Rooster 4 十五
水6 Water 2 Mountain 艮爲山 26 丙戌 Fire Dog 1 十六	木8 Wood 1 Delight 雷地豫 27 丁亥 Fire Pig 8 十七	火7 Fire 9 Beginning 水雷屯 28 戊子 Earth Rat 4 十八	金9 Metal 8 Without Wrongdoing 天雷無妄 29 己丑 Earth Ox 2 十九	木3 Wood 7 Fire 離爲火 30 庚寅 Metal Tiger 1 二十		

DECEMBER 2034 丙子

Xuan Kong Element 玄空五行	山雷頤 Nourish	Period Luck 卦運	Monthly Star 月星
Water 水6		3	1

SUNDAY	MONDAY	TUESDAY	WEDNESDAY	THURSDAY	FRIDAY	SATURDAY
木8 Wood 7 Lesser Exceeding 雷山小過 31 辛酉 Metal Rooster 3 廿一					火2 Fire 6 Sincerity 風澤中孚 1 辛卯 Metal Rabbit 3 廿一	水6 Water 5 Big Livestock 山天大畜 2 壬辰 Water Dragon 4 廿二
金4 Metal 4 Eliminating 澤天夬 3 癸巳 Water Snake 6 廿三	金9 Metal 3 Heaven 乾爲天 4 甲午 Wood Horse 1 廿四	火7 Fire 2 Well 水風井 5 乙未 Wood Goat 6 廿五	木8 Wood 1 Relief 雷水解 6 丙申 Fire Monkey 4 廿六	金4 Metal 9 Influence 澤山咸 7 丁酉 Fire Rooster 9 廿七	水1 Water 8 Humility 地山謙 8 戊戌 Earth Dog 6 廿八	火2 Fire 7 Observation 風地觀 9 己亥 Earth Pig 2 廿九
火2 Fire 6 Increasing 風雷益 10 庚子 Metal Rat 9 三十	水1 Water 5 Dimming Light 地火明夷 11 辛丑 Metal Ox 3 十一月初一	金9 Metal 4 Fellowship 天火同人 12 壬寅 Water Tiger 7 初二	木8 Wood 3 Marrying Maiden 雷澤歸妹 13 癸卯 Water Rabbit 7 初三	木3 Wood 2 Opposition 火澤睽 14 甲辰 Wood Dragon 2 初四	火7 Fire 1 Waiting 水天需 15 乙巳 Wood Snake 3 初五	金4 Metal 9 Great Exceeding 澤風大過 16 丙午 Fire Horse 3 初六
水6 Water 8 Poison 山風蠱 17 丁未 Fire Goat 7 初七	火2 Fire 7 Dispersing 風水渙 18 戊申 Earth Monkey 6 初八	木3 Wood 6 Travelling 火山旅 19 己酉 Earth Rooster 8 初九	金9 Metal 5 Stagnation 天地否 20 庚戌 Metal Dog 9 初十	火7 Fire 4 Alliance 水地比 21 辛亥 Metal Pig 7 十一	木8 Wood 3/7 Thunder 震爲雷 22 壬子 Water Rat 1 十二	水6 Water 8 Beauty 山火賁 23 癸丑 Water Ox 8 十三
火7 Fire 9 Accomplished 水火既濟 24 甲寅 Wood Tiger 9 十四	水1 Water 1 Arriving 地澤臨 25 乙卯 Wood Rabbit 4 十五	金4 Metal 2 Marsh 兌爲澤 26 丙辰 Fire Dragon 1 十六	火2 Fire 3 Small Livestock 風天小畜 27 丁巳 Fire Snake 8 十七	木3 Wood 4 The Cauldron 火風鼎 28 戊午 Earth Horse 4 十八	水1 Water 5 Rising 地風升 29 己未 Earth Goat 2 十九	火7 Fire 6 Water 坎爲水 30 庚申 Metal Monkey 1 二十

2035 乙卯

(*Yi Mao*) Wood Rabbit

2035 乙卯 *(Yi Mao)* Wood Rabbit

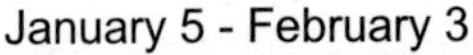

January 5 - February 3

February 4 - March 5

March 6 - April 4

April 5 - May 3

May 4 - June 5

June 6 - July 6

July 7 - August 6

August 7 - September 7

September 8 - October 7

October 8 - November 6

November 7 - December 6

December 7 - January 5

JANUARY 2035 丁丑

Xuan Kong Element 玄空五行	澤雷隨 Following	Period Luck 卦運	Monthly Star 月星
Metal 金4		7	9

SUNDAY	MONDAY	TUESDAY	WEDNESDAY	THURSDAY	FRIDAY	SATURDAY
	1 金4 Metal · 8 Gathering 澤地萃 壬戌 Water Dog 4 · 廿二	**2** 水6 Water · 9 Peel 山地剝 癸亥 Water Pig 6 · 廿三	**3** 水1 Water · 1 Earth 坤爲地 甲子 Wood Rat 1 · 廿四	**4** 木3 Wood · 2 Biting 火雷噬嗑 乙丑 Wood Ox 6 · 廿五	**5** 火2 Fire · 3 Family 風火家人 丙寅 Fire Tiger 4 · 廿六	**6** 水6 Water · 4 Decreasing 山澤損 丁卯 Fire Rabbit 9 · 廿七
7 金9 Metal · 5 Tread 天澤履 戊辰 Earth Dragon 6 · 廿八	**8** 木8 Wood · 6 Great Strength 雷天大壯 己巳 Earth Snake 2 · 廿九	**9** 木8 Wood · 7 Consistency 雷風恆 庚午 Metal Horse 9 · 十二月初一	**10** 金9 Metal · 8 Litigation 天水訟 辛未 Metal Goat 3 · 初二	**11** 水1 Water · 9 Officer 地水師 壬申 Water Monkey 7 · 初三	**12** 火2 Fire · 1 Gradual Progress 風山漸 癸酉 Water Rooster 7 · 初四	**13** 火7 Fire · 2 Obstruction 水山蹇 甲戌 Wood Dog 2 · 初五
14 木3 Wood · 3 Advancement 火地晉 乙亥 Wood Pig 3 · 初六	**15** 水6 Water · 4 Nourish 山雷頤 丙子 Fire Rat 3 · 初七	**16** 金4 Metal · 5 Following 澤雷隨 丁丑 Fire Ox 7 · 初八	**17** 木8 Wood · 6 Abundance 雷火豐 戊寅 Earth Tiger 6 · 初九	**18** 火7 Fire · 7 Regulate 水澤節 己卯 Earth Rabbit 8 · 初十	**19** 水1 Water · 8 Unity 地天泰 庚辰 Metal Dragon 9 · 十一	**20** 木3 Wood · 9 Great Reward 火天大有 辛巳 Metal Snake 7 · 十二
21 火2 Fire · 1 Wind 巽爲風 壬午 Water Horse 1 · 十三	**22** 金4 Metal · 2 Trap 澤水困 癸未 Water Goat 8 · 十四	**23** 木3 Wood · 3 Not Yet Accomplished 火水未濟 甲申 Wood Monkey 9 · 十五	**24** 金9 Metal · 4 Retreat 天山遯 乙酉 Wood Rooster 4 · 十六	**25** 水6 Water · 5 Mountain 艮爲山 丙戌 Fire Dog 1 · 十七	**26** 木8 Wood · 6 Delight 雷地豫 丁亥 Fire Pig 8 · 十八	**27** 火7 Fire · 7 Beginning 水雷屯 戊子 Earth Rat 4 · 十九
28 金9 Metal · 8 Without Wrongdoing 天雷無妄 己丑 Earth Ox 2 · 二十	**29** 木3 Wood · 9 Fire 離爲火 庚寅 Metal Tiger 1 · 廿一	**30** 火2 Fire · 1 Sincerity 風澤中孚 辛卯 Metal Rabbit 3 · 廿二	**31** 水6 Water · 2 Big Livestock 山天大畜 壬辰 Water Dragon 4 · 廿三			

FEBRUARY 2035 戊寅

Xuan Kong Element 玄空五行	雷火豐 Abundance	Period Luck 卦運	Monthly Star 月星
Wood 木8		6	8

SUNDAY	MONDAY	TUESDAY	WEDNESDAY	THURSDAY	FRIDAY	SATURDAY
				1 金4 Metal · 3 Eliminating 澤天夬 癸巳 Water Snake 6 · 廿四	**2** 金9 Metal · 4 Heaven 乾爲天 甲午 Wood Horse 1 · 廿五	**3** 火7 Fire · 5 Well 水風井 乙未 Wood Goat 6 · 廿六
4 木8 Wood · 6 Relief 雷水解 丙申 Fire Monkey 4 · 廿七	**5** 金4 Metal · 7 Influence 澤山咸 丁酉 Fire Rooster 9 · 廿八	**6** 水1 Water · 8 Humility 地山謙 戊戌 Earth Dog 6 · 廿九	**7** 火2 Fire · 9 Observation 風地觀 己亥 Earth Pig 2 · 三十	**8** 火2 Fire · 1 Increasing 風雷益 庚子 Metal Rat 9 · 正月初一	**9** 水1 Water · 2 Dimming Light 地火明夷 辛丑 Metal Ox 3 · 初二	**10** 金9 Metal · 3 Fellowship 天火同人 壬寅 Water Tiger 7 · 初三
11 木8 Wood · 4 Marrying Maiden 雷澤歸妹 癸卯 Water Rabbit 7 · 初四	**12** 木3 Wood · 5 Opposition 火澤睽 甲辰 Wood Dragon 2 · 初五	**13** 火7 Fire · 6 Waiting 水天需 乙巳 Wood Snake 3 · 初六	**14** 金4 Metal · 7 Great Exceeding 澤風大過 丙午 Fire Horse 3 · 初七	**15** 水6 Water · 8 Poison 山風蠱 丁未 Fire Goat 7 · 初八	**16** 火2 Fire · 9 Dispersing 風水渙 戊申 Earth Monkey 6 · 初九	**17** 木3 Wood · 1 Travelling 火山旅 己酉 Earth Rooster 8 · 初十
18 金9 Metal · 2 Stagnation 天地否 庚戌 Metal Dog 9 · 十一	**19** 火7 Fire · 3 Alliance 水地比 辛亥 Metal Pig 7 · 十二	**20** 木8 Wood · 4 Thunder 震爲雷 壬子 Water Rat 1 · 十三	**21** 水6 Water · 5 Beauty 山火賁 癸丑 Water Ox 8 · 十四	**22** 火7 Fire · 6 Accomplished 水火既濟 甲寅 Wood Tiger 9 · 十五	**23** 水1 Water · 7 Arriving 地澤臨 乙卯 Wood Rabbit 4 · 十六	**24** 金4 Metal · 8 Marsh 兌爲澤 丙辰 Fire Dragon 1 · 十七
25 火2 Fire · 9 Small Livestock 風天小畜 丁巳 Fire Snake 8 · 十八	**26** 木3 Wood · 1 The Cauldron 火風鼎 戊午 Earth Horse 4 · 十九	**27** 水1 Water · 2 Rising 地風升 己未 Earth Goat 2 · 二十	**28** 火7 Fire · 3 Water 坎爲水 庚申 Metal Monkey 1 · 廿一			

MARCH 2035 己卯

Xuan Kong Element 玄空五行	水澤節	Period Luck 卦運	Monthly Star 月星
Fire 火7	Regulate	8	7

SUNDAY	MONDAY	TUESDAY	WEDNESDAY	THURSDAY	FRIDAY	SATURDAY
				木8 Wood 4 Lesser Exceeding 雷山小過 辛酉 Metal Rooster **1** 廿二 3	金4 Metal 5 Gathering 澤地萃 壬戌 Water Dog **2** 廿三 4	水6 Water 6 Peel 山地剝 癸亥 Water Pig **3** 廿四 6
水1 Water 7 Earth 坤爲地 甲子 Wood Rat **4** 廿五 1	木3 Wood 8 Biting 火雷噬嗑 乙丑 Wood Ox **5** 廿六 6	火2 Fire 9 Family 風火家人 丙寅 Fire Tiger **6** 廿七 4	水6 Water 1 Decreasing 山澤損 丁卯 Fire Rabbit **7** 廿八 9	金9 Metal 2 Tread 天澤履 戊辰 Earth Dragon **8** 廿九 6	木8 Wood 3 Great Strength 雷天大壯 己巳 Earth Snake **9** 三十 2	木8 Wood 4 Consistency 雷風恆 庚午 Metal Horse **10** 二月初一 9
金9 Metal 5 Litigation 天水訟 辛未 Metal Goat **11** 初二 3	水1 Water 6 Officer 地水師 壬申 Water Monkey **12** 初三 7	火2 Fire 7 Gradual Progress 風山漸 癸酉 Water Rooster **13** 初四 7	火7 Fire 8 Obstruction 水山蹇 甲戌 Wood Dog **14** 初五 2	木3 Wood 9 Advancement 火地晉 乙亥 Wood Pig **15** 初六 3	水6 Water 1 Nourish 山雷頤 丙子 Fire Rat **16** 初七 3	金4 Metal 2 Following 澤雷隨 丁丑 Fire Ox **17** 初八 7
木8 Wood 3 Abundance 雷火豐 戊寅 Earth Tiger **18** 初九 6	火7 Fire 4 Regulate 水澤節 己卯 Earth Rabbit **19** 初十 8	水1 Water 5 Unity 地天泰 庚辰 Metal Dragon **20** 十一 9	木3 Wood 6 Great Reward 火天大有 辛巳 Metal Snake **21** 十二 7	火2 Fire 7 Wind 巽爲風 壬午 Water Horse **22** 十三 1	金4 Metal 8 Trap 澤水困 癸未 Water Goat **23** 十四 8	木3 Wood 9 Not Yet Accomplished 火水未濟 甲申 Wood Monkey **24** 十五 9
金9 Metal 1 Retreat 天山遯 乙酉 Wood Rooster **25** 十六 4	水6 Water 2 Mountain 艮爲山 丙戌 Fire Dog **26** 十七 1	木8 Wood 3 Delight 雷地豫 丁亥 Fire Pig **27** 十八 8	火7 Fire 4 Beginning 水雷屯 戊子 Earth Rat **28** 十九 4	金9 Metal 5 Without Wrongdoing 天雷無妄 己丑 Earth Ox **29** 二十 2	木3 Wood 6 Fire 離爲火 庚寅 Metal Tiger **30** 廿一 1	火2 Fire 7 Sincerity 風澤中孚 辛卯 Metal Rabbit **31** 廿二 3

APRIL 2035 庚辰

Xuan Kong Element 玄空五行	地天泰	Period Luck 卦運	Monthly Star 月星
Water 水1	Unity	9	6

SUNDAY	MONDAY	TUESDAY	WEDNESDAY	THURSDAY	FRIDAY	SATURDAY
水6 Water 8 Big Livestock 山天大畜 壬辰 Water Dragon **1** 廿三 4	金4 Metal 9 Eliminating 澤天夬 癸巳 Water Snake **2** 廿四 6	金9 Metal 1 Heaven 乾爲天 甲午 Wood Horse **3** 廿五 1	火7 Fire 2 Well 水風井 乙未 Wood Goat **4** 廿六 6	木8 Wood 3 Relief 雷水解 丙申 Fire Monkey **5** 廿七 4	金4 Metal 4 Influence 澤山咸 丁酉 Fire Rooster **6** 廿八 9	水1 Water 5 Humility 地山謙 戊戌 Earth Dog **7** 廿九 6
火2 Fire 6 Observation 風地觀 己亥 Earth Pig **8** 三月初一 2	火2 Fire 7 Increasing 風雷益 庚子 Metal Rat **9** 初二 9	水1 Water 8 Dimming Light 地火明夷 辛丑 Metal Ox **10** 初三 3	金9 Metal 9 Fellowship 天火同人 壬寅 Water Tiger **11** 初四 7	木8 Wood 1 Marrying Maiden 雷澤歸妹 癸卯 Water Rabbit **12** 初五 7	木3 Wood 2 Opposition 火澤睽 甲辰 Wood Dragon **13** 初六 2	火7 Fire 3 Waiting 水天需 乙巳 Wood Snake **14** 初七 3
金4 Metal 4 Great Exceeding 澤風大過 丙午 Fire Horse **15** 初八 3	水6 Water 5 Poison 山風蠱 丁未 Fire Goat **16** 初九 7	火2 Fire 6 Dispersing 風水渙 戊申 Earth Monkey **17** 初十 6	木3 Wood 7 Travelling 火山旅 己酉 Earth Rooster **18** 十一 8	金9 Metal 8 Stagnation 天地否 庚戌 Metal Dog **19** 十二 9	火7 Fire 9 Alliance 水地比 辛亥 Metal Pig **20** 十三 7	木8 Wood 1 Thunder 震爲雷 壬子 Water Rat **21** 十四 1
水6 Water 2 Beauty 山火賁 癸丑 Water Ox **22** 十五 8	火7 Fire 3 Accomplished 水火既濟 甲寅 Wood Tiger **23** 十六 9	水1 Water 4 Arriving 地澤臨 乙卯 Wood Rabbit **24** 十七 4	金4 Metal 5 Marsh 兌爲澤 丙辰 Fire Dragon **25** 十八 1	火2 Fire 6 Small Livestock 風天小畜 丁巳 Fire Snake **26** 十九 8	木3 Wood 7 The Cauldron 火風鼎 戊午 Earth Horse **27** 二十 4	水1 Water 8 Rising 地風升 己未 Earth Goat **28** 廿一 2
火7 Fire 9 Water 坎爲水 庚申 Metal Monkey **29** 廿二 1	木8 Wood 1 Lesser Exceeding 雷山小過 辛酉 Metal Rooster **30** 廿三 3					

MAY 2035 辛巳

Xuan Kong Element 玄空五行	火天大有 Great Reward	Period Luck 卦運	Monthly Star 月星
Wood 木3		7	5

SUNDAY	MONDAY	TUESDAY	WEDNESDAY	THURSDAY	FRIDAY	SATURDAY
		金4 Metal 2 Gathering 澤地萃 壬戌 Water Dog 1 廿四 4	水6 Water 3 Peel 山地剝 癸亥 Water Pig 2 廿五 6	水1 Water 4 Earth 坤爲地 甲子 Wood Rat 3 廿六 1	木3 Wood 5 Biting 火雷噬嗑 乙丑 Wood Ox 4 廿七 6	火2 Fire 6 Family 風火家人 丙寅 Fire Tiger 5 廿八 4
水6 Water 7 Decreasing 山澤損 丁卯 Fire Rabbit 6 廿九 9	金9 Metal 8 Tread 天澤履 戊辰 Earth Dragon 7 三十 6	木8 Wood 9 Great Strength 雷天大壯 己巳 Earth Snake 8 四月初一 2	木8 Wood 1 Consistency 雷風恆 庚午 Metal Horse 9 初二 9	金9 Metal 2 Litigation 天水訟 辛未 Metal Goat 10 初三 3	水1 Water 3 Officer 地水師 壬申 Water Monkey 11 初四 7	火2 Fire 4 Gradual Progress 風山漸 癸酉 Water Rooster 12 初五 7
火7 Fire 5 Obstruction 水山蹇 甲戌 Wood Dog 13 初六 2	木3 Wood 6 Advancement 火地晉 乙亥 Wood Pig 14 初七 3	水6 Water 7 Nourish 山雷頤 丙子 Fire Rat 15 初八 3	金4 Metal 8 Following 澤雷隨 丁丑 Fire Ox 16 初九 7	木8 Wood 9 Abundance 雷火豐 戊寅 Earth Tiger 17 初十 6	火7 Fire 1 Regulate 水澤節 己卯 Earth Rabbit 18 十一 8	水1 Water 2 Unity 地天泰 庚辰 Metal Dragon 19 十二 9
木3 Wood 3 Great Reward 火天大有 辛巳 Metal Snake 20 十三 7	火2 Fire 4 Wind 巽爲風 壬午 Water Horse 21 十四 1	金4 Metal 5 Trap 澤水困 癸未 Water Goat 22 十五 8	木3 Wood 6 Not Yet Accomplished 火水未濟 甲申 Wood Monkey 23 十六 9	金9 Metal 7 Retreat 天山遯 乙酉 Wood Rooster 24 十七 4	水6 Water 8 Mountain 艮爲山 丙戌 Fire Dog 25 十八 1	木8 Wood 9 Delight 雷地豫 丁亥 Fire Pig 26 十九 8
火7 Fire 1 Beginning 水雷屯 戊子 Earth Rat 27 二十 4	金9 Metal 2 Without Wrongdoing 天雷無妄 己丑 Earth Ox 28 廿一 2	木3 Wood 3 Fire 離爲火 庚寅 Metal Tiger 29 廿二 1	火2 Fire 4 Sincerity 風澤中孚 辛卯 Metal Rabbit 30 廿三 3	水6 Water 5 Big Livestock 山天大畜 壬辰 Water Dragon 31 廿四 4		

JUNE 2035 壬午

Xuan Kong Element 玄空五行	巽爲風 Wind	Period Luck 卦運	Monthly Star 月星
Fire 火2		1	4

SUNDAY	MONDAY	TUESDAY	WEDNESDAY	THURSDAY	FRIDAY	SATURDAY
					金4 Metal 6 Eliminating 澤天夬 癸巳 Water Snake 1 廿五 6	金9 Metal 7 Heaven 乾爲天 甲午 Wood Horse 2 廿六 1
火7 Fire 8 Well 水風井 乙未 Wood Goat 3 廿七 6	木8 Wood 9 Relief 雷水解 丙申 Fire Monkey 4 廿八 4	金4 Metal 1 Influence 澤山咸 丁酉 Fire Rooster 5 廿九 9	水1 Water 2 Humility 地山謙 戊戌 Earth Dog 6 五月初一 6	火2 Fire 3 Observation 風地觀 己亥 Earth Pig 7 初二 2	火2 Fire 4 Increasing 風雷益 庚子 Metal Rat 8 初三 9	水1 Water 5 Dimming Light 地火明夷 辛丑 Metal Ox 9 初四 3
金9 Metal 6 Fellowship 天火同人 壬寅 Water Tiger 10 初五 7	木8 Wood 7 Marrying Maiden 雷澤歸妹 癸卯 Water Rabbit 11 初六 7	木3 Wood 8 Opposition 火澤睽 甲辰 Wood Dragon 12 初七 2	火7 Fire 9 Waiting 水天需 乙巳 Wood Snake 13 初八 3	金4 Metal 1 Great Exceeding 澤風大過 丙午 Fire Horse 14 初九 3	水6 Water 2 Poison 山風蠱 丁未 Fire Goat 15 初十 7	火2 Fire 3 Dispersing 風水渙 戊申 Earth Monkey 16 十一 6
木3 Wood 4 Travelling 火山旅 己酉 Earth Rooster 17 十二 8	金9 Metal 5 Stagnation 天地否 庚戌 Metal Dog 18 十三 9	火7 Fire 6 Alliance 水地比 辛亥 Metal Pig 19 十四 7	木8 Wood 7 Thunder 震爲雷 壬子 Water Rat 20 十五 1	水6 Water 8/2 Beauty 山火賁 癸丑 Water Ox 21 十六 8	火7 Fire 1 Accomplished 水火既濟 甲寅 Wood Tiger 22 十七 9	水1 Water 9 Arriving 地澤臨 乙卯 Wood Rabbit 23 十八 4
金4 Metal 8 Marsh 兌爲澤 丙辰 Fire Dragon 24 十九 1	火2 Fire 7 Small Livestock 風天小畜 丁巳 Fire Snake 25 二十 8	木3 Wood 6 The Cauldron 火風鼎 戊午 Earth Horse 26 廿一 4	水1 Water 5 Rising 地風升 己未 Earth Goat 27 廿二 2	火7 Fire 4 Water 坎爲水 庚申 Metal Monkey 28 廿三 1	木8 Wood 3 Lesser Exceeding 雷山小過 辛酉 Metal Rooster 29 廿四 3	金4 Metal 2 Gathering 澤地萃 壬戌 Water Dog 30 廿五 4

JULY 2035 癸未

Xuan Kong Element 玄空五行	澤水困 Trap	Period Luck 卦運	Monthly Star 月星
Metal 金4		8	3

SUNDAY	MONDAY	TUESDAY	WEDNESDAY	THURSDAY	FRIDAY	SATURDAY
水6 Water · 1 Peel 山地剝 癸亥 Water Pig **1** 6 · 廿六	水1 Water · 9 Earth 坤爲地 甲子 Wood Rat **2** 1 · 廿七	木3 Wood · 8 Biting 火雷噬嗑 乙丑 Wood Ox **3** 6 · 廿八	火2 Fire · 7 Family 風火家人 丙寅 Fire Tiger **4** 4 · 廿九	水6 Water · 6 Decreasing 山澤損 丁卯 Fire Rabbit **5** 9 · 六月初一	金9 Metal · 5 Tread 天澤履 戊辰 Earth Dragon **6** 6 · 初二	木8 Wood · 4 Great Strength 雷天大壯 己巳 Earth Snake **7** 2 · 初三
木8 Wood · 3 Consistency 雷風恒 庚午 Metal Horse **8** 9 · 初四	金9 Metal · 2 Litigation 天水訟 辛未 Metal Goat **9** 3 · 初五	水1 Water · 1 Officer 地水師 壬申 Water Monkey **10** 7 · 初六	火2 Fire · 9 Gradual Progress 風山漸 癸酉 Water Rooster **11** 7 · 初七	火7 Fire · 8 Obstruction 水山蹇 甲戌 Wood Dog **12** 2 · 初八	木3 Wood · 7 Advancement 火地晉 乙亥 Wood Pig **13** 3 · 初九	水6 Water · 6 Nourish 山雷頤 丙子 Fire Rat **14** 3 · 初十
金4 Metal · 5 Following 澤雷隨 丁丑 Fire Ox **15** 7 · 十一	木8 Wood · 4 Abundance 雷火豐 戊寅 Earth Tiger **16** 6 · 十二	火7 Fire · 3 Regulate 水澤節 己卯 Earth Rabbit **17** 8 · 十三	水1 Water · 2 Unity 地天泰 庚辰 Metal Dragon **18** 9 · 十四	木3 Wood · 1 Great Reward 火天大有 辛巳 Metal Snake **19** 7 · 十五	火2 Fire · 9 Wind 巽爲風 壬午 Water Horse **20** 1 · 十六	金4 Metal · 8 Trap 澤水困 癸未 Water Goat **21** 8 · 十七
木3 Wood · 7 Not Yet Accomplished 火水未濟 甲申 Wood Monkey **22** 9 · 十八	金9 Metal · 6 Retreat 天山遯 乙酉 Wood Rooster **23** 4 · 十九	水6 Water · 5 Mountain 艮爲山 丙戌 Fire Dog **24** 1 · 二十	木8 Wood · 4 Delight 雷地豫 丁亥 Fire Pig **25** 8 · 廿一	火7 Fire · 3 Beginning 水雷屯 戊子 Earth Rat **26** 4 · 廿二	金9 Metal · 2 Without Wrongdoing 天雷無妄 己丑 Earth Ox **27** 2 · 廿三	木3 Wood · 1 Fire 離爲火 庚寅 Metal Tiger **28** 1 · 廿四
火2 Fire · 9 Sincerity 風澤中孚 辛卯 Metal Rabbit **29** 3 · 廿五	水6 Water · 8 Big Livestock 山天大畜 壬辰 Water Dragon **30** 4 · 廿六	金4 Metal · 7 Eliminating 澤天夬 癸巳 Water Snake **31** 6 · 廿七				

AUGUST 2035 甲申

Xuan Kong Element 玄空五行	火水未濟 Not Yet Accomplished	Period Luck 卦運	Monthly Star 月星
Wood 木3		9	2

SUNDAY	MONDAY	TUESDAY	WEDNESDAY	THURSDAY	FRIDAY	SATURDAY
			金9 Metal · 6 Heaven 乾爲天 甲午 Wood Horse **1** 1 · 廿八	火7 Fire · 5 Well 水風井 乙未 Wood Goat **2** 6 · 廿九	木8 Wood · 4 Relief 雷水解 丙申 Fire Monkey **3** 4 · 三十	金4 Metal · 3 Influence 澤山咸 丁酉 Fire Rooster **4** 9 · 七月初一
水1 Water · 2 Humility 地山謙 戊戌 Earth Dog **5** 6 · 初二	火2 Fire · 1 Observation 風地觀 己亥 Earth Pig **6** 2 · 初三	火2 Fire · 9 Increasing 風雷益 庚子 Metal Rat **7** 9 · 初四	水1 Water · 8 Dimming Light 地火明夷 辛丑 Metal Ox **8** 3 · 初五	金9 Metal · 7 Fellowship 天火同人 壬寅 Water Tiger **9** 7 · 初六	木8 Wood · 6 Marrying Maiden 雷澤歸妹 癸卯 Water Rabbit **10** 7 · 初七	木3 Wood · 5 Opposition 火澤睽 甲辰 Wood Dragon **11** 2 · 初八
火7 Fire · 4 Waiting 水天需 乙巳 Wood Snake **12** 3 · 初九	金4 Metal · 3 Great Exceeding 澤風大過 丙午 Fire Horse **13** 3 · 初十	水6 Water · 2 Poison 山風蠱 丁未 Fire Goat **14** 7 · 十一	火2 Fire · 1 Dispersing 風水渙 戊申 Earth Monkey **15** 6 · 十二	木3 Wood · 9 Travelling 火山旅 己酉 Earth Rooster **16** 8 · 十三	金9 Metal · 8 Stagnation 天地否 庚戌 Metal Dog **17** 9 · 十四	火7 Fire · 7 Alliance 水地比 辛亥 Metal Pig **18** 7 · 十五
木8 Wood · 6 Thunder 震爲雷 壬子 Water Rat **19** 1 · 十六	水6 Water · 5 Beauty 山火賁 癸丑 Water Ox **20** 8 · 十七	火7 Fire · 4 Accomplished 水火既濟 甲寅 Wood Tiger **21** 9 · 十八	水1 Water · 3 Arriving 地澤臨 乙卯 Wood Rabbit **22** 4 · 十九	金4 Metal · 2 Marsh 兌爲澤 丙辰 Fire Dragon **23** 1 · 二十	火2 Fire · 1 Small Livestock 風天小畜 丁巳 Fire Snake **24** 8 · 廿一	木3 Wood · 9 The Cauldron 火風鼎 戊午 Earth Horse **25** 4 · 廿二
水1 Water · 8 Rising 地風升 己未 Earth Goat **26** 2 · 廿三	火7 Fire · 7 Water 坎爲水 庚申 Metal Monkey **27** 1 · 廿四	木8 Wood · 6 Lesser Exceeding 雷山小過 辛酉 Metal Rooster **28** 3 · 廿五	金4 Metal · 5 Gathering 澤地萃 壬戌 Water Dog **29** 4 · 廿六	水6 Water · 4 Peel 山地剝 癸亥 Water Pig **30** 6 · 廿七	水1 Water · 3 Earth 坤爲地 甲子 Wood Rat **31** 1 · 廿八	

SEPTEMBER 2035 乙酉

Xuan Kong Element 玄空五行	天山遯 Retreat	Period Luck 卦運	Monthly Star 月星
Metal 金9		4	1

SUNDAY	MONDAY	TUESDAY	WEDNESDAY	THURSDAY	FRIDAY	SATURDAY
金9 Metal 9 Heaven 乾爲天 甲午 Wood Horse 30 廿九 1						木3 Wood 2 Biting 火雷噬嗑 乙丑 Wood Ox 1 廿九 6
火2 Fire 1 Family 風火家人 丙寅 Fire Tiger 2 八月初一 4	水6 Water 9 Decreasing 山澤損 丁卯 Fire Rabbit 3 初二 9	金9 Metal 8 Tread 天澤履 戊辰 Earth Dragon 4 初三 6	木8 Wood 7 Great Strength 雷天大壯 己巳 Earth Snake 5 初四 2	木8 Wood 6 Consistency 雷風恆 庚午 Metal Horse 6 初五 9	金9 Metal 5 Litigation 天水訟 辛未 Metal Goat 7 初六 3	水1 Water 4 Officer 地水師 壬申 Water Monkey 8 初七 7
火2 Fire 3 Gradual Progress 風山漸 癸酉 Water Rooster 9 初八 7	火7 Fire 2 Obstruction 水山蹇 甲戌 Wood Dog 10 初九 2	木3 Wood 1 Advancement 火地晉 乙亥 Wood Pig 11 初十 3	水6 Water 9 Nourish 山雷頤 丙子 Fire Rat 12 十一 3	金4 Metal 8 Following 澤雷隨 丁丑 Fire Ox 13 十二 7	木8 Wood 7 Abundance 雷火豐 戊寅 Earth Tiger 14 十三 6	火7 Fire 6 Regulate 水澤節 己卯 Earth Rabbit 15 十四 8
水1 Water 5 Unity 地天泰 庚辰 Metal Dragon 16 十五 9	木3 Wood 4 Great Reward 火天大有 辛巳 Metal Snake 17 十六 7	火2 Fire 3 Wind 巽爲風 壬午 Water Horse 18 十七 1	金4 Metal 2 Trap 澤水困 癸未 Water Goat 19 十八 8	木3 Wood 1 Not Yet Accomplished 火水未濟 甲申 Wood Monkey 20 十九 9	金9 Metal 9 Retreat 天山遯 乙酉 Wood Rooster 21 二十 4	水6 Water 8 Mountain 艮爲山 丙戌 Fire Dog 22 廿一 1
木8 Wood 7 Delight 雷地豫 丁亥 Fire Pig 23 廿二 8	火7 Fire 6 Beginning 水雷屯 戊子 Earth Rat 24 廿三 4	金9 Metal 5 Without Wrongdoing 天雷無妄 己丑 Earth Ox 25 廿四 2	木3 Wood 4 Fire 離爲火 庚寅 Metal Tiger 26 廿五 1	火2 Fire 3 Sincerity 風澤中孚 辛卯 Metal Rabbit 27 廿六 3	水6 Water 2 Big Livestock 山天大畜 壬辰 Water Dragon 28 廿七 4	金4 Metal 1 Eliminating 澤天夬 癸巳 Water Snake 29 廿八 6

OCTOBER 2035 丙戌

Xuan Kong Element 玄空五行	艮爲山 Mountain	Period Luck 卦運	Monthly Star 月星
Water 水6		1	9

SUNDAY	MONDAY	TUESDAY	WEDNESDAY	THURSDAY	FRIDAY	SATURDAY
	火7 Fire 8 Well 水風井 乙未 Wood Goat 1 九月初一 6	木8 Wood 7 Relief 雷水解 丙申 Fire Monkey 2 初二 4	金4 Metal 6 Influence 澤山咸 丁酉 Fire Rooster 3 初三 9	水1 Water 5 Humility 地山謙 戊戌 Earth Dog 4 初四 6	火2 Fire 4 Observation 風地觀 己亥 Earth Pig 5 初五 2	火2 Fire 3 Increasing 風雷益 庚子 Metal Rat 6 初六 9
水1 Water 2 Dimming Light 地火明夷 辛丑 Metal Ox 7 初七 3	金9 Metal 1 Fellowship 天火同人 壬寅 Water Tiger 8 初八 7	木8 Wood 9 Marrying Maiden 雷澤歸妹 癸卯 Water Rabbit 9 初九 7	木3 Wood 8 Opposition 火澤睽 甲辰 Wood Dragon 10 初十 2	火7 Fire 7 Waiting 水天需 乙巳 Wood Snake 11 十一 3	金4 Metal 6 Great Exceeding 澤風大過 丙午 Fire Horse 12 十二 3	水6 Water 5 Poison 山風蠱 丁未 Fire Goat 13 十三 7
火2 Fire 4 Dispersing 風水渙 戊申 Earth Monkey 14 十四 6	木3 Wood 3 Travelling 火山旅 己酉 Earth Rooster 15 十五 8	金9 Metal 2 Stagnation 天地否 庚戌 Metal Dog 16 十六 9	火7 Fire 1 Alliance 水地比 辛亥 Metal Pig 17 十七 7	木8 Wood 9 Thunder 震爲雷 壬子 Water Rat 18 十八 1	水6 Water 8 Beauty 山火賁 癸丑 Water Ox 19 十九 8	火7 Fire 7 Accomplished 水火既濟 甲寅 Wood Tiger 20 二十 9
水1 Water 6 Arriving 地澤臨 乙卯 Wood Rabbit 21 廿一 4	金4 Metal 5 Marsh 兌爲澤 丙辰 Fire Dragon 22 廿二 1	火2 Fire 4 Small Livestock 風天小畜 丁巳 Fire Snake 23 廿三 8	木3 Wood 3 The Cauldron 火風鼎 戊午 Earth Horse 24 廿四 4	水1 Water 2 Rising 地風升 己未 Earth Goat 25 廿五 2	火7 Fire 1 Water 坎爲水 庚申 Metal Monkey 26 廿六 1	木8 Wood 9 Lesser Exceeding 雷山小過 辛酉 Metal Rooster 27 廿七 3
金4 Metal 8 Gathering 澤地萃 壬戌 Water Dog 28 廿八 4	水6 Water 7 Peel 山地剝 癸亥 Water Pig 29 廿九 6	水1 Water 6 Earth 坤爲地 甲子 Wood Rat 30 三十 1	木3 Wood 5 Biting 火雷噬嗑 乙丑 Wood Ox 31 十月初一 6			

NOVEMBER 2035 丁亥

Xuan Kong Element 玄空五行	雷地豫	Period Luck 卦運	Monthly Star 月星
Wood 木8	Delight	8	8

SUNDAY	MONDAY	TUESDAY	WEDNESDAY	THURSDAY	FRIDAY	SATURDAY
				火2 Fire 4 Family 丙寅 Fire Tiger 風火家人 **1** 初二 4	水6 Water 3 Decreasing 丁卯 Fire Rabbit 山澤損 **2** 初三 9	金9 Metal 2 Tread 戊辰 Earth Dragon 天澤履 **3** 初四 6
木8 Wood 1 Great Strength 己巳 Earth Snake 雷天大壯 **4** 初五 2	木8 Wood 9 Consistency 庚午 Metal Horse 雷風恒 **5** 初六 9	金9 Metal 8 Litigation 辛未 Metal Goat 天水訟 **6** 初七 3	水1 Water 7 Officer 壬申 Water Monkey 地水師 **7** 初八 7	火2 Fire 6 Gradual Progress 癸酉 Water Rooster 風山漸 **8** 初九 7	火7 Fire 5 Obstruction 甲戌 Wood Dog 水山蹇 **9** 初十 2	木3 Wood 4 Advancement 乙亥 Wood Pig 火地晉 **10** 十一 3
水6 Water 3 Nourish 丙子 Fire Rat 山雷頤 **11** 十二 3	金4 Metal 2 Following 丁丑 Fire Ox 澤雷隨 **12** 十三 7	木8 Wood 1 Abundance 戊寅 Earth Tiger 雷火豐 **13** 十四 6	火7 Fire 9 Regulate 己卯 Earth Rabbit 水澤節 **14** 十五 8	水1 Water 8 Unity 庚辰 Metal Dragon 地天泰 **15** 十六 9	木3 Wood 7 Great Reward 辛巳 Metal Snake 火天大有 **16** 十七 7	火2 Fire 6 Wind 壬午 Water Horse 巽為風 **17** 十八 1
金4 Metal 5 Trap 癸未 Water Goat 澤水困 **18** 十九 8	木3 Wood 4 Not Yet Accomplished 甲申 Wood Monkey 火水未濟 **19** 二十 9	金9 Metal 3 Retreat 乙酉 Wood Rooster 天山遯 **20** 廿一 4	水6 Water 2 Mountain 丙戌 Fire Dog 艮為山 **21** 廿二 1	木8 Wood 1 Delight 丁亥 Fire Pig 雷地豫 **22** 廿三 8	火7 Fire 9 Beginning 戊子 Earth Rat 水雷屯 **23** 廿四 4	金9 Metal 8 Without Wrongdoing 己丑 Earth Ox 天雷無妄 **24** 廿五 2
木3 Wood 7 Fire 庚寅 Metal Tiger 離為火 **25** 廿六 1	火2 Fire 6 Sincerity 辛卯 Metal Rabbit 風澤中孚 **26** 廿七 3	水6 Water 5 Big Livestock 壬辰 Water Dragon 山天大畜 **27** 廿八 4	金4 Metal 4 Eliminating 癸巳 Water Snake 澤天夬 **28** 廿九 6	金9 Metal 3 Heaven 甲午 Wood Horse 乾為天 **29** 三十 1	火7 Fire 2 Well 乙未 Wood Goat 水風井 **30** 十一月初一 6	

DECEMBER 2035 戊子

Xuan Kong Element 玄空五行	水雷屯	Period Luck 卦運	Monthly Star 月星
Fire 火7	Beginning	4	7

SUNDAY	MONDAY	TUESDAY	WEDNESDAY	THURSDAY	FRIDAY	SATURDAY
木3 Wood 2 Biting 乙丑 Wood Ox 火雷噬嗑 **30** 初二 6	火2 Fire 3 Family 丙寅 Fire Tiger 風火家人 **31** 初三 4					木8 Wood 1 Relief 丙申 Fire Monkey 雷水解 **1** 初二 4
金4 Metal 9 Influence 丁酉 Fire Rooster 澤山咸 **2** 初三 9	水1 Water 8 Humility 戊戌 Earth Dog 地山謙 **3** 初四 6	火2 Fire 7 Observation 己亥 Earth Pig 風地觀 **4** 初五 2	火2 Fire 6 Increasing 庚子 Metal Rat 風雷益 **5** 初六 9	水1 Water 5 Dimming Light 辛丑 Metal Ox 地火明夷 **6** 初七 3	金9 Metal 4 Fellowship 壬寅 Water Tiger 天火同人 **7** 初八 7	木8 Wood 3 Marrying Maiden 癸卯 Water Rabbit 雷澤歸妹 **8** 初九 7
木3 Wood 2 Opposition 甲辰 Wood Dragon 火澤睽 **9** 初十 2	火7 Fire 1 Waiting 乙巳 Wood Snake 水天需 **10** 十一 3	金4 Metal 9 Great Exceeding 丙午 Fire Horse 澤風大過 **11** 十二 3	水6 Water 8 Poison 丁未 Fire Goat 山風蠱 **12** 十三 7	火2 Fire 7 Dispersing 戊申 Earth Monkey 風水渙 **13** 十四 6	木3 Wood 6 Travelling 己酉 Earth Rooster 火山旅 **14** 十五 8	金9 Metal 5 Stagnation 庚戌 Metal Dog 天地否 **15** 十六 9
火7 Fire 4 Alliance 辛亥 Metal Pig 水地比 **16** 十七 7	木8 Wood 3 Thunder 壬子 Water Rat 震為雷 **17** 十八 1	水6 Water 2 Beauty 癸丑 Water Ox 山火賁 **18** 十九 8	火7 Fire 1 Accomplished 甲寅 Wood Tiger 水火既濟 **19** 二十 9	水1 Water 9 Arriving 乙卯 Wood Rabbit 地澤臨 **20** 廿一 4	金4 Metal 8 Marsh 丙辰 Fire Dragon 兌為澤 **21** 廿二 1	火2 Fire 7/8 Small Livestock 丁巳 Fire Snake 風天小畜 **22** 廿三 8
木3 Wood 4 The Cauldron 戊午 Earth Horse 火風鼎 **23** 廿四 4	水1 Water 5 Rising 己未 Earth Goat 地風升 **24** 廿五 2	火7 Fire 6 Water 庚申 Metal Monkey 坎為水 **25** 廿六 1	木8 Wood 7 Lesser Exceeding 辛酉 Metal Rooster 雷山小過 **26** 廿七 3	金4 Metal 8 Gathering 壬戌 Water Dog 澤地萃 **27** 廿八 4	水6 Water 9 Peel 癸亥 Water Pig 山地剝 **28** 廿九 6	水1 Water 1 Earth 甲子 Wood Rat 坤為地 **29** 十二月初一 1

2036 丙辰

(*Bing Chen*) Fire Dragon

2036 丙辰 *(Bing Chen)* Fire Dragon

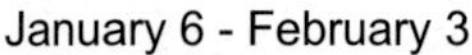

January 6 - February 3

February 4 - March 4

March 5 - April 3

April 4 - May 4

May 5 - June 4

June 5 - July 5

July 6 - August 6

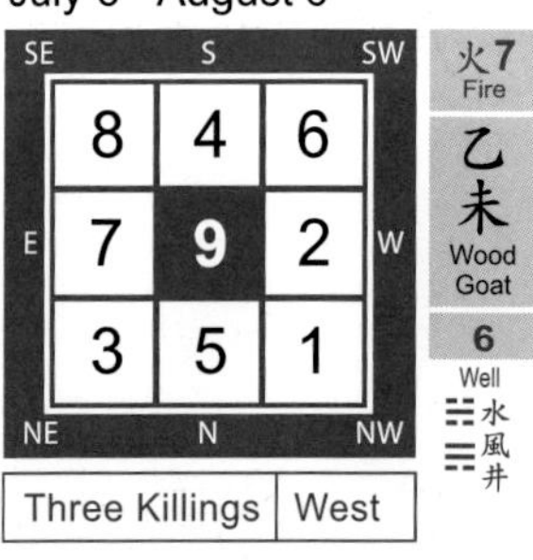

August 7 - September 6

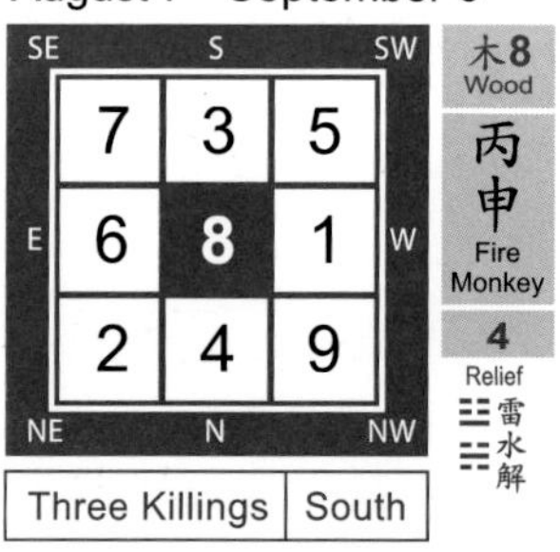

September 7 - October 7

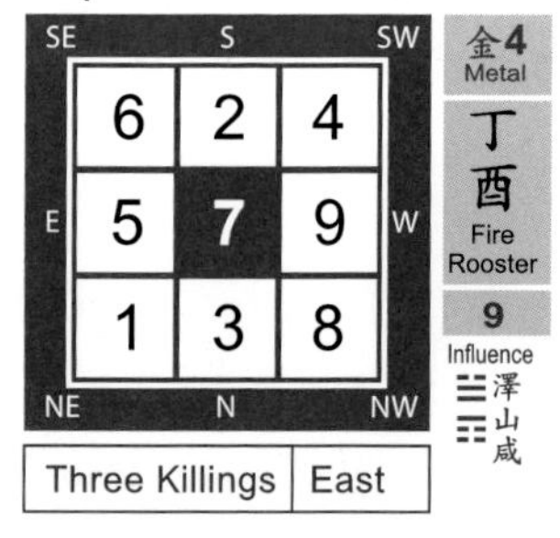

October 8 - November 6

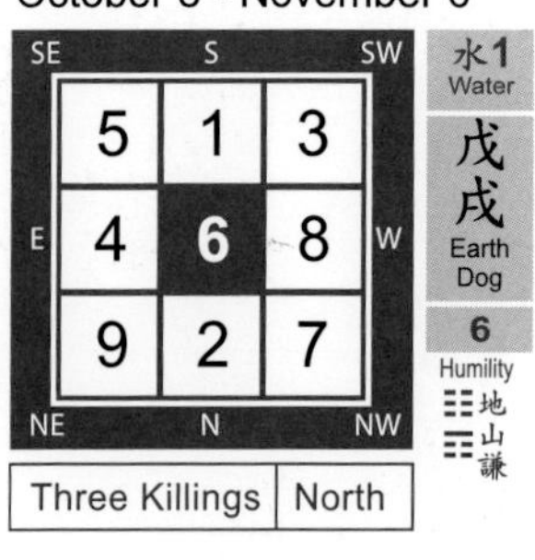

November 7 - December 5

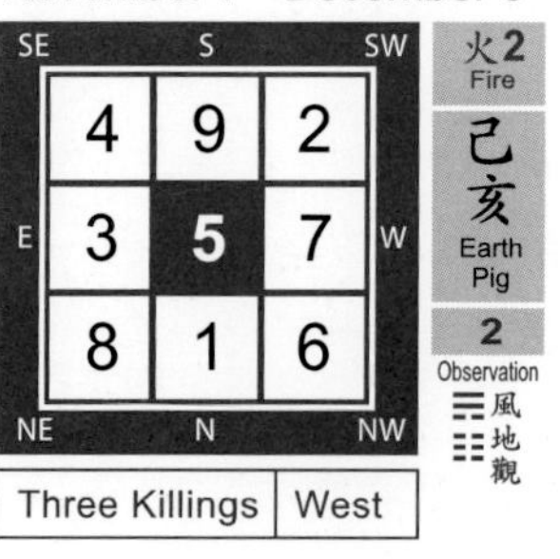

December 6 - January 4

JANUARY 2036 己丑

Xuan Kong Element 玄空五行	天雷無妄 Without Wrongdoing	Period Luck 卦運	Monthly Star 月星
Metal 金9		2	6

SUNDAY	MONDAY	TUESDAY	WEDNESDAY	THURSDAY	FRIDAY	SATURDAY
		水6 Water Decreasing 4 丁卯 Fire Rabbit 山澤損 **1** 初四 9	金9 Metal Tread 5 戊辰 Earth Dragon 天澤履 **2** 初五 6	木8 Wood Great Strength 6 己巳 Earth Snake 雷天大壯 **3** 初六 2	木8 Wood Consistency 7 庚午 Metal Horse 雷風恆 **4** 初七 9	金9 Metal Litigation 8 辛未 Metal Goat 天水訟 **5** 初八 3
水1 Water Officer 9 壬申 Water Monkey 地水師 **6** 初九 7	火2 Fire Gradual Progress 1 癸酉 Water Rooster 風山漸 **7** 初十 7	火7 Fire Obstruction 2 甲戌 Wood Dog 水山蹇 **8** 十一 2	木3 Wood Advancement 3 乙亥 Wood Pig 火地晉 **9** 十二 3	水6 Water Nourish 4 丙子 Fire Rat 山雷頤 **10** 十三 3	金4 Metal Following 5 丁丑 Fire Ox 澤雷隨 **11** 十四 7	木8 Wood Abundance 6 戊寅 Earth Tiger 雷火豐 **12** 十五 6
火7 Fire Regulate 7 己卯 Earth Rabbit 水澤節 **13** 十六 8	水1 Water Unity 8 庚辰 Metal Dragon 地天泰 **14** 十七 9	木3 Wood Great Reward 9 辛巳 Metal Snake 火天大有 **15** 十八 7	火2 Fire Wind 1 壬午 Water Horse 巽爲風 **16** 十九 1	金4 Metal Trap 2 癸未 Water Goat 澤水困 **17** 二十 8	木3 Wood Not Yet Accomplished 3 甲申 Wood Monkey 火水未濟 **18** 廿一 9	金9 Metal Retreat 4 乙酉 Wood Rooster 天山遯 **19** 廿二 4
水6 Water Mountain 5 丙戌 Fire Dog 艮爲山 **20** 廿三 1	木8 Wood Delight 6 丁亥 Fire Pig 雷地豫 **21** 廿四 8	火7 Fire Beginning 7 戊子 Earth Rat 水雷屯 **22** 廿五 4	金9 Metal Without Wrongdoing 8 己丑 Earth Ox 天雷無妄 **23** 廿六 2	木3 Wood Fire 9 庚寅 Metal Tiger 離爲火 **24** 廿七 1	火2 Fire Sincerity 1 辛卯 Metal Rabbit 風澤中孚 **25** 廿八 3	水6 Water Big Livestock 2 壬辰 Water Dragon 山天大畜 **26** 廿九 4
金4 Metal Eliminating 3 癸巳 Water Snake 澤天夬 **27** 三十 6	金9 Metal Heaven 4 甲午 Wood Horse 乾爲天 **28** 正月初一 1	火7 Fire Well 5 乙未 Wood Goat 水風井 **29** 初二 6	木8 Wood Relief 6 丙申 Fire Monkey 雷水解 **30** 初三 4	金4 Metal Influence 7 丁酉 Fire Rooster 澤山咸 **31** 初四 9		

FEBRUARY 2036 庚寅

Xuan Kong Element 玄空五行	離爲火 Fire	Period Luck 卦運	Monthly Star 月星
Wood 木3		1	5

SUNDAY	MONDAY	TUESDAY	WEDNESDAY	THURSDAY	FRIDAY	SATURDAY
					水1 Water Humility 8 戊戌 Earth Dog 地山謙 **1** 初五 6	火2 Fire Observation 9 己亥 Earth Pig 風地觀 **2** 初六 2
火2 Fire Increasing 1 庚子 Metal Rat 風雷益 **3** 初七 9	水1 Water Dimming Light 2 辛丑 Metal Ox 地火明夷 **4** 初八 3	金9 Metal Fellowship 3 壬寅 Water Tiger 天火同人 **5** 初九 7	木8 Wood Marrying Maiden 4 癸卯 Water Rabbit 雷澤歸妹 **6** 初十 7	木3 Wood Opposition 5 甲辰 Wood Dragon 火澤睽 **7** 十一 2	火7 Fire Waiting 6 乙巳 Wood Snake 水天需 **8** 十二 3	金4 Metal Great Exceeding 7 丙午 Fire Horse 澤風大過 **9** 十三 3
水6 Water Poison 8 丁未 Fire Goat 山風蠱 **10** 十四 7	火2 Fire Dispersing 9 戊申 Earth Monkey 風水渙 **11** 十五 6	木3 Wood Travelling 1 己酉 Earth Rooster 火山旅 **12** 十六 8	金9 Metal Stagnation 2 庚戌 Metal Dog 天地否 **13** 十七 9	火7 Fire Alliance 3 辛亥 Metal Pig 水地比 **14** 十八 7	木8 Wood Thunder 4 壬子 Water Rat 震爲雷 **15** 十九 1	水6 Water Beauty 5 癸丑 Water Ox 山火賁 **16** 二十 8
火7 Fire Accomplished 6 甲寅 Wood Tiger 水火既濟 **17** 廿一 9	水1 Water Arriving 7 乙卯 Wood Rabbit 地澤臨 **18** 廿二 4	金4 Metal Marsh 8 丙辰 Fire Dragon 兌爲澤 **19** 廿三 1	火2 Fire Small Livestock 9 丁巳 Fire Snake 風天小畜 **20** 廿四 8	木3 Wood The Cauldron 1 戊午 Earth Horse 火風鼎 **21** 廿五 4	水1 Water Rising 2 己未 Earth Goat 地風升 **22** 廿六 2	火7 Fire Water 3 庚申 Metal Monkey 坎爲水 **23** 廿七 1
木8 Wood Lesser Exceeding 4 辛酉 Metal Rooster 雷山小過 **24** 廿八 3	金4 Metal Gathering 5 壬戌 Water Dog 澤地萃 **25** 廿九 4	水6 Water Peel 6 癸亥 Water Pig 山地剝 **26** 三十 6	水1 Water Earth 7 甲子 Wood Rat 坤爲地 **27** 二月初一 1	木3 Wood Biting 8 乙丑 Wood Ox 火雷噬嗑 **28** 初二 6	火2 Fire Family 9 丙寅 Fire Tiger 風火家人 **29** 初三 4	

MARCH 2036 辛卯

Xuan Kong Element 玄空五行	風澤中孚 Sincerity	Period Luck 卦運	Monthly Star 月星
Fire 火2		3	4

SUNDAY	MONDAY	TUESDAY	WEDNESDAY	THURSDAY	FRIDAY	SATURDAY
木8 Wood Relief 3 丙申 Fire Monkey 雷水解 30 初三 4	金4 Metal Influence 4 丁酉 Fire Rooster 澤山咸 31 初四 9					水6 Water Decreasing 1 丁卯 Fire Rabbit 山澤損 1 初四 9
金9 Metal Tread 2 戊辰 Earth Dragon 天澤履 2 初五 6	木8 Wood Great Strength 3 己巳 Earth Snake 雷天大壯 3 初六 2	木8 Wood Consistency 4 庚午 Metal Horse 雷風恒 4 初七 9	金9 Metal Litigation 5 辛未 Metal Goat 天水訟 5 初八 3	水1 Water Officer 6 壬申 Water Monkey 地水師 6 初九 7	火2 Fire Gradual Progress 7 癸酉 Water Rooster 風山漸 7 初十 7	火7 Fire Obstruction 8 甲戌 Wood Dog 水山蹇 8 十一 2
木3 Wood Advancement 9 乙亥 Wood Pig 火地晉 9 十二 3	水6 Water Nourish 1 丙子 Fire Rat 山雷頤 10 十三 3	金4 Metal Following 2 丁丑 Fire Ox 澤雷隨 11 十四 7	木8 Wood Abundance 3 戊寅 Earth Tiger 雷火豐 12 十五 6	火7 Fire Regulate 4 己卯 Earth Rabbit 水澤節 13 十六 8	水1 Water Unity 5 庚辰 Metal Dragon 地天泰 14 十七 9	木3 Wood Great Reward 6 辛巳 Metal Snake 火天大有 15 十八 7
火2 Fire Wind 7 壬午 Water Horse 巽爲風 16 十九 1	金4 Metal Trap 8 癸未 Water Goat 澤水困 17 二十 8	木3 Wood Not Yet Accomplished 9 甲申 Wood Monkey 火水未濟 18 廿一 9	金9 Metal Retreat 1 乙酉 Wood Rooster 天山遯 19 廿二 4	水6 Water Mountain 2 丙戌 Fire Dog 艮爲山 20 廿三 1	木8 Wood Delight 3 丁亥 Fire Pig 雷地豫 21 廿四 8	火7 Fire Beginning 4 戊子 Earth Rat 水雷屯 22 廿五 4
金9 Metal Without Wrongdoing 5 己丑 Earth Ox 天雷無妄 23 廿六 2	木3 Wood Fire 6 庚寅 Metal Tiger 離爲火 24 廿七 1	火2 Fire Sincerity 7 辛卯 Metal Rabbit 風澤中孚 25 廿八 3	水6 Water Big Livestock 8 壬辰 Water Dragon 山天大畜 26 廿九 4	金4 Metal Eliminating 9 癸巳 Water Snake 澤天夬 27 三十 6	金9 Metal Heaven 1 甲午 Wood Horse 乾爲天 28 三月初一 1	火7 Fire Well 2 乙未 Wood Goat 水風井 29 初二 6

APRIL 2036 壬辰

Xuan Kong Element 玄空五行	山天大畜 Big Livestock	Period Luck 卦運	Monthly Star 月星
Water 水6		4	3

SUNDAY	MONDAY	TUESDAY	WEDNESDAY	THURSDAY	FRIDAY	SATURDAY
		水1 Water Humility 5 戊戌 Earth Dog 地山謙 1 初五 6	火2 Fire Observation 6 己亥 Earth Pig 風地觀 2 初六 2	火2 Fire Increasing 7 庚子 Metal Rat 風雷益 3 初七 9	水1 Water Dimming Light 8 辛丑 Metal Ox 地火明夷 4 初八 3	金9 Metal Fellowship 9 壬寅 Water Tiger 天火同人 5 初九 7
木8 Wood Marrying Maiden 1 癸卯 Water Rabbit 雷澤歸妹 6 初十 7	木3 Wood Opposition 2 甲辰 Wood Dragon 火澤睽 7 十一 2	火7 Fire Waiting 3 乙巳 Wood Snake 水天需 8 十二 3	金4 Metal Great Exceeding 4 丙午 Fire Horse 澤風大過 9 十三 3	水6 Water Poison 5 丁未 Fire Goat 山風蠱 10 十四 7	火2 Fire Dispersing 6 戊申 Earth Monkey 風水渙 11 十五 6	木3 Wood Travelling 7 己酉 Earth Rooster 火山旅 12 十六 8
金9 Metal Stagnation 8 庚戌 Metal Dog 天地否 13 十七 9	火7 Fire Alliance 9 辛亥 Metal Pig 水地比 14 十八 7	木8 Wood Thunder 1 壬子 Water Rat 震爲雷 15 十九 1	水6 Water Beauty 2 癸丑 Water Ox 山火賁 16 二十 8	火7 Fire Accomplished 3 甲寅 Wood Tiger 水火既濟 17 廿一 9	水1 Water Arriving 4 乙卯 Wood Rabbit 地澤臨 18 廿二 4	金4 Metal Marsh 5 丙辰 Fire Dragon 兑爲澤 19 廿三 1
火2 Fire Small Livestock 6 丁巳 Fire Snake 風天小畜 20 廿四 8	木3 Wood The Cauldron 7 戊午 Earth Horse 火風鼎 21 廿五 4	水1 Water Rising 8 己未 Earth Goat 地風升 22 廿六 2	火7 Fire Water 9 庚申 Metal Monkey 坎爲水 23 廿七 1	木8 Wood Lesser Exceeding 1 辛酉 Metal Rooster 雷山小過 24 廿八 3	金4 Metal Gathering 2 壬戌 Water Dog 澤地萃 25 廿九 4	水6 Water Peel 3 癸亥 Water Pig 山地剝 26 四月初一 6
水1 Water Earth 4 甲子 Wood Rat 坤爲地 27 初二 1	木3 Wood Biting 5 乙丑 Wood Ox 火雷噬嗑 28 初三 6	火2 Fire Family 6 丙寅 Fire Tiger 風火家人 29 初四 4	水6 Water Decreasing 7 丁卯 Fire Rabbit 山澤損 30 初五 9			

MAY 2036 癸巳

Xuan Kong Element 玄空五行	澤天夬 Eliminating	Period Luck 卦運	Monthly Star 月星
Metal 金4	☱☰	6	2

SUNDAY	MONDAY	TUESDAY	WEDNESDAY	THURSDAY	FRIDAY	SATURDAY
				金9 Metal Tread 8 戊辰 Earth Dragon 天澤履 1 初六 6	木8 Wood Great Strength 9 己巳 Earth Snake 雷天大壯 2 初七 2	木8 Wood Consistency 1 庚午 Metal Horse 雷風恆 3 初八 9
金9 Metal Litigation 2 辛未 Metal Goat 天水訟 4 初九 3	水1 Water Officer 3 壬申 Water Monkey 地水師 5 初十 7	火2 Fire Gradual Progress 4 癸酉 Water Rooster 風山漸 6 十一 7	火7 Fire Obstruction 5 甲戌 Wood Dog 水山蹇 7 十二 2	木3 Wood Advancement 6 乙亥 Wood Pig 火地晉 8 十三 3	水6 Water Nourish 7 丙子 Fire Rat 山雷頤 9 十四 3	金4 Metal Following 8 丁丑 Fire Ox 澤雷隨 10 十五 7
木8 Wood Abundance 9 戊寅 Earth Tiger 雷火豐 11 十六 6	火7 Fire Regulate 1 己卯 Earth Rabbit 水澤節 12 十七 8	水1 Water Unity 2 庚辰 Metal Dragon 地天泰 13 十八 9	木3 Wood Great Reward 3 辛巳 Metal Snake 火天大有 14 十九 7	火2 Fire Wind 4 壬午 Water Horse 巽爲風 15 二十 1	金4 Metal Trap 5 癸未 Water Goat 澤水困 16 廿一 8	木3 Wood Not Yet Accomplished 6 甲申 Wood Monkey 火水未濟 17 廿二 9
金9 Metal Retreat 7 乙酉 Wood Rooster 天山遯 18 廿三 4	水6 Water Mountain 8 丙戌 Fire Dog 艮爲山 19 廿四 1	木8 Wood Delight 9 丁亥 Fire Pig 雷地豫 20 廿五 8	火7 Fire Beginning 1 戊子 Earth Rat 水雷屯 21 廿六 4	金9 Metal Without Wrongdoing 2 己丑 Earth Ox 天雷無妄 22 廿七 2	木3 Wood Fire 3 庚寅 Metal Tiger 離爲火 23 廿八 1	火2 Fire Sincerity 4 辛卯 Metal Rabbit 風澤中孚 24 廿九 3
水6 Water Big Livestock 5 壬辰 Water Dragon 山天大畜 25 三十 4	金4 Metal Eliminating 6 癸巳 Water Snake 澤天夬 26 五月初一 6	金9 Metal Heaven 7 甲午 Wood Horse 乾爲天 27 初二 1	火7 Fire Well 8 乙未 Wood Goat 水風井 28 初三 6	木8 Wood Relief 9 丙申 Fire Monkey 雷水解 29 初四 4	金4 Metal Influence 1 丁酉 Fire Rooster 澤山咸 30 初五 9	水1 Water Humility 2 戊戌 Earth Dog 地山謙 31 初六 6

JUNE 2036 甲午

Xuan Kong Element 玄空五行	乾爲天 Heaven	Period Luck 卦運	Monthly Star 月星
Metal 金9	☰☰	1	1

SUNDAY	MONDAY	TUESDAY	WEDNESDAY	THURSDAY	FRIDAY	SATURDAY
火2 Fire Observation 3 己亥 Earth Pig 風地觀 1 初七 2	火2 Fire Increasing 4 庚子 Metal Rat 風雷益 2 初八 9	水1 Water Dimming Light 5 辛丑 Metal Ox 地火明夷 3 初九 3	金9 Metal Fellowship 6 壬寅 Water Tiger 天火同人 4 初十 7	木8 Wood Marrying Maiden 7 癸卯 Water Rabbit 雷澤歸妹 5 十一 7	木3 Wood Opposition 8 甲辰 Wood Dragon 火澤睽 6 十二 2	火7 Fire Waiting 9 乙巳 Wood Snake 水天需 7 十三 3
金4 Metal Great Exceeding 1 丙午 Fire Horse 澤風大過 8 十四 3	水6 Water Poison 2 丁未 Fire Goat 山風蠱 9 十五 7	火2 Fire Dispersing 3 戊申 Earth Monkey 風水渙 10 十六 6	木3 Wood Travelling 4 己酉 Earth Rooster 火山旅 11 十七 8	金9 Metal Stagnation 5 庚戌 Metal Dog 天地否 12 十八 9	火7 Fire Alliance 6 辛亥 Metal Pig 水地比 13 十九 7	木8 Wood Thunder 7 壬子 Water Rat 震爲雷 14 二十 1
水6 Water Beauty 8 癸丑 Water Ox 山火賁 15 廿一 8	火7 Fire Accomplished 9 甲寅 Wood Tiger 水火既濟 16 廿二 9	水1 Water Arriving 1 乙卯 Wood Rabbit 地澤臨 17 廿三 4	金4 Metal Marsh 2 丙辰 Fire Dragon 兌爲澤 18 廿四 1	火2 Fire Small Livestock 3 丁巳 Fire Snake 風天小畜 19 廿五 8	木3 Wood The Cauldron 4 戊午 Earth Horse 火風鼎 20 廿六 4	水1 Water Rising 5/5 己未 Earth Goat 地風升 21 廿七 2
火7 Fire Water 4 庚申 Metal Monkey 坎爲水 22 廿八 1	木8 Wood Lesser Exceeding 3 辛酉 Metal Rooster 雷山小過 23 廿九 3	金4 Metal Gathering 2 壬戌 Water Dog 澤地萃 24 六月初一 4	水6 Water Peel 1 癸亥 Water Pig 山地剝 25 初二 6	水1 Water Earth 9 甲子 Wood Rat 坤爲地 26 初三 1	木3 Wood Biting 8 乙丑 Wood Ox 火雷噬嗑 27 初四 6	火2 Fire Family 7 丙寅 Fire Tiger 風火家人 28 初五 4
水6 Water Decreasing 6 丁卯 Fire Rabbit 山澤損 29 初六 9	金9 Metal Tread 5 戊辰 Earth Dragon 天澤履 30 初七 6					

JULY 2036 乙未

Xuan Kong Element 玄空五行	水風井 Well	Period Luck 卦運	Monthly Star 月星
Fire 火7		6	9

SUNDAY	MONDAY	TUESDAY	WEDNESDAY	THURSDAY	FRIDAY	SATURDAY
		木8 Wood 4 己巳 Earth Snake Great Strength 雷天大壯 1 初八 2	木8 Wood 3 庚午 Metal Horse Consistency 雷風恆 2 初九 9	金9 Metal 2 辛未 Metal Goat Litigation 天水訟 3 初十 3	水1 Water 1 壬申 Water Monkey Officer 地水師 4 十一 7	火2 Fire 9 癸酉 Water Rooster Gradual Progress 風山漸 5 十二 7
火7 Fire 8 甲戌 Wood Dog Obstruction 水山蹇 6 十三 2	木3 Wood 7 乙亥 Wood Pig Advancement 火地晉 7 十四 3	水6 Water 6 丙子 Fire Rat Nourish 山雷頤 8 十五 3	金4 Metal 5 丁丑 Fire Ox Following 澤雷隨 9 十六 7	木8 Wood 4 戊寅 Earth Tiger Abundance 雷火豐 10 十七 6	火7 Fire 3 己卯 Earth Rabbit Regulate 水澤節 11 十八 8	水1 Water 2 庚辰 Metal Dragon Unity 地天泰 12 十九 9
木3 Wood 1 辛巳 Metal Snake Great Reward 火天大有 13 二十 7	火2 Fire 9 壬午 Water Horse Wind 巽為風 14 廿一 1	金4 Metal 8 癸未 Water Goat Trap 澤水困 15 廿二 8	木3 Wood 7 甲申 Wood Monkey Not Yet Accomplished 火水未濟 16 廿三 9	金9 Metal 6 乙酉 Wood Rooster Retreat 天山遯 17 廿四 4	水6 Water 5 丙戌 Fire Dog Mountain 艮為山 18 廿五 1	木8 Wood 4 丁亥 Fire Pig Delight 雷地豫 19 廿六 8
火7 Fire 3 戊子 Earth Rat Beginning 水雷屯 20 廿七 4	金9 Metal 2 己丑 Earth Ox Without Wrongdoing 天雷無妄 21 廿八 2	木3 Wood 1 庚寅 Metal Tiger Fire 離為火 22 廿九 1	火2 Fire 9 辛卯 Metal Rabbit Sincerity 風澤中孚 23 閏六月初一 3	水6 Water 8 壬辰 Water Dragon Big Livestock 山天大畜 24 初二 4	金4 Metal 7 癸巳 Water Snake Eliminating 澤天夬 25 初三 6	金9 Metal 6 甲午 Wood Horse Heaven 乾為天 26 初四 1
火7 Fire 5 乙未 Wood Goat Well 水風井 27 初五 6	木8 Wood 4 丙申 Fire Monkey Relief 雷水解 28 初六 4	金4 Metal 3 丁酉 Fire Rooster Influence 澤山咸 29 初七 9	水1 Water 2 戊戌 Earth Dog Humility 地山謙 30 初八 6	火2 Fire 1 己亥 Earth Pig Observation 風地觀 31 初九 2		

AUGUST 2036 丙申

Xuan Kong Element 玄空五行	雷水解 Relief	Period Luck 卦運	Monthly Star 月星
Wood 木8		4	8

SUNDAY	MONDAY	TUESDAY	WEDNESDAY	THURSDAY	FRIDAY	SATURDAY
木8 Wood 6 庚午 Metal Horse Consistency 雷風恆 31 初十 9					火2 Fire 9 庚子 Metal Rat Increasing 風雷益 1 初十 9	水1 Water 8 辛丑 Metal Ox Dimming Light 地火明夷 2 十一 3
金9 Metal 7 壬寅 Water Tiger Fellowship 天火同人 3 十二 7	木8 Wood 6 癸卯 Water Rabbit Marrying Maiden 雷澤歸妹 4 十三 7	木3 Wood 5 甲辰 Wood Dragon Opposition 火澤睽 5 十四 2	火7 Fire 4 乙巳 Wood Snake Waiting 水天需 6 十五 3	金4 Metal 3 丙午 Fire Horse Great Exceeding 澤風大過 7 十六 3	水6 Water 2 丁未 Fire Goat Poison 山風蠱 8 十七 7	火2 Fire 1 戊申 Earth Monkey Dispersing 風水渙 9 十八 6
木3 Wood 9 己酉 Earth Rooster Travelling 火山旅 10 十九 8	金9 Metal 8 庚戌 Metal Dog Stagnation 天地否 11 二十 9	火7 Fire 7 辛亥 Metal Pig Alliance 水地比 12 廿一 7	木8 Wood 6 壬子 Water Rat Thunder 震為雷 13 廿二 1	水6 Water 5 癸丑 Water Ox Beauty 山火賁 14 廿三 8	火7 Fire 4 甲寅 Wood Tiger Accomplished 水火既濟 15 廿四 9	水1 Water 3 乙卯 Wood Rabbit Arriving 地澤臨 16 廿五 4
金4 Metal 2 丙辰 Fire Dragon Marsh 兌為澤 17 廿六 1	火2 Fire 1 丁巳 Fire Snake Small Livestock 風天小畜 18 廿七 8	木3 Wood 9 戊午 Earth Horse The Cauldron 火風鼎 19 廿八 4	水1 Water 8 己未 Earth Goat Rising 地風升 20 廿九 2	火7 Fire 7 庚申 Metal Monkey Water 坎為水 21 三十 1	木8 Wood 6 辛酉 Metal Rooster Lesser Exceeding 雷山小過 22 七月初一 3	金4 Metal 5 壬戌 Water Dog Gathering 澤地萃 23 初二 4
水6 Water 4 癸亥 Water Pig Peel 山地剝 24 初三 6	水1 Water 3 甲子 Wood Rat Earth 坤為地 25 初四 1	木3 Wood 2 乙丑 Wood Ox Biting 火雷噬嗑 26 初五 6	火2 Fire 1 丙寅 Fire Tiger Family 風火家人 27 初六 4	水6 Water 9 丁卯 Fire Rabbit Decreasing 山澤損 28 初七 9	金9 Metal 8 戊辰 Earth Dragon Tread 天澤履 29 初八 6	木8 Wood 7 己巳 Earth Snake Great Strength 雷天大壯 30 初九 2

SEPTEMBER 2036 丁酉

Xuan Kong Element 玄空五行	澤山咸 Influence	Period Luck 卦運	Monthly Star 月星
Metal 金4		9	7

SUNDAY	MONDAY	TUESDAY	WEDNESDAY	THURSDAY	FRIDAY	SATURDAY
	金9 Metal 辛未 Metal Goat Litigation 天水訟 **1** 十一 3 / 5	水1 Water 壬申 Water Monkey Officer 地水師 **2** 十二 7 / 4	火2 Fire 癸酉 Water Rooster Gradual Progress 風山漸 **3** 十三 7 / 3	火7 Fire 甲戌 Wood Dog Obstruction 水山蹇 **4** 十四 2 / 2	木3 Wood 乙亥 Wood Pig Advancement 火地晉 **5** 十五 3 / 1	水6 Water 丙子 Fire Rat Nourish 山雷頤 **6** 十六 3 / 9
金4 Metal 丁丑 Fire Ox Following 澤雷隨 **7** 十七 7 / 8	木8 Wood 戊寅 Earth Tiger Abundance 雷火豐 **8** 十八 6 / 7	火7 Fire 己卯 Earth Rabbit Regulate 水澤節 **9** 十九 8 / 6	水1 Water 庚辰 Metal Dragon Unity 地天泰 **10** 二十 9 / 5	木3 Wood 辛巳 Metal Snake Great Reward 火天大有 **11** 廿一 7 / 4	火2 Fire 壬午 Water Horse Wind 巽爲風 **12** 廿二 1 / 3	金4 Metal 癸未 Water Goat Trap 澤水困 **13** 廿三 8 / 2
木3 Wood 甲申 Wood Monkey Not Yet Accomplished 火水未濟 **14** 廿四 9 / 1	金9 Metal 乙酉 Wood Rooster Retreat 天山遯 **15** 廿五 4 / 9	水6 Water 丙戌 Fire Dog Mountain 艮爲山 **16** 廿六 1 / 8	木8 Wood 丁亥 Fire Pig Delight 雷地豫 **17** 廿七 8 / 7	火7 Fire 戊子 Earth Rat Beginning 水雷屯 **18** 廿八 4 / 6	金9 Metal 己丑 Earth Ox Without Wrongdoing 天雷無妄 **19** 廿九 2 / 5	木3 Wood 庚寅 Metal Tiger Fire 離爲火 **20** 八月初一 1 / 4
火2 Fire 辛卯 Metal Rabbit Sincerity 風澤中孚 **21** 初二 3 / 3	水6 Water 壬辰 Water Dragon Big Livestock 山天大畜 **22** 初三 4 / 2	金4 Metal 癸巳 Water Snake Eliminating 澤天夬 **23** 初四 6 / 1	金9 Metal 甲午 Wood Horse Heaven 乾爲天 **24** 初五 1 / 9	火7 Fire 乙未 Wood Goat Well 水風井 **25** 初六 6 / 8	木8 Wood 丙申 Fire Monkey Relief 雷水解 **26** 初七 4 / 7	金4 Metal 丁酉 Fire Rooster Influence 澤山咸 **27** 初八 9 / 6
水1 Water 戊戌 Earth Dog Humility 地山謙 **28** 初九 6 / 5	火2 Fire 己亥 Earth Pig Observation 風地觀 **29** 初十 2 / 4	火2 Fire 庚子 Metal Rat Increasing 風雷益 **30** 十一 9 / 3				

OCTOBER 2036 戊戌

Xuan Kong Element 玄空五行	地山謙 Humility	Period Luck 卦運	Monthly Star 月星
Water 水1		6	6

SUNDAY	MONDAY	TUESDAY	WEDNESDAY	THURSDAY	FRIDAY	SATURDAY
			水1 Water 辛丑 Metal Ox Dimming Light 地火明夷 **1** 十二 3 / 2	金9 Metal 壬寅 Water Tiger Fellowship 天火同人 **2** 十三 7 / 1	木8 Wood 癸卯 Water Rabbit Marrying Maiden 雷澤歸妹 **3** 十四 7 / 9	木3 Wood 甲辰 Wood Dragon Opposition 火澤睽 **4** 十五 2 / 8
火7 Fire 乙巳 Wood Snake Waiting 水天需 **5** 十六 3 / 7	金4 Metal 丙午 Fire Horse Great Exceeding 澤風大過 **6** 十七 3 / 6	水6 Water 丁未 Fire Goat Poison 山風蠱 **7** 十八 7 / 5	火2 Fire 戊申 Earth Monkey Dispersing 風水渙 **8** 十九 6 / 4	木3 Wood 己酉 Earth Rooster Travelling 火山旅 **9** 二十 8 / 3	金9 Metal 庚戌 Metal Dog Stagnation 天地否 **10** 廿一 9 / 2	火7 Fire 辛亥 Metal Pig Alliance 水地比 **11** 廿二 7 / 1
木8 Wood 壬子 Water Rat Thunder 震爲雷 **12** 廿三 1 / 9	水6 Water 癸丑 Water Ox Beauty 山火賁 **13** 廿四 8 / 8	火7 Fire 甲寅 Wood Tiger Accomplished 水火既濟 **14** 廿五 9 / 7	水1 Water 乙卯 Wood Rabbit Arriving 地澤臨 **15** 廿六 4 / 6	金4 Metal 丙辰 Fire Dragon Marsh 兌爲澤 **16** 廿七 1 / 5	火2 Fire 丁巳 Fire Snake Small Livestock 風天小畜 **17** 廿八 8 / 4	木3 Wood 戊午 Earth Horse The Cauldron 火風鼎 **18** 廿九 4 / 3
水1 Water 己未 Earth Goat Rising 地風升 **19** 九月初一 2 / 2	火7 Fire 庚申 Metal Monkey Water 坎爲水 **20** 初二 1 / 1	木8 Wood 辛酉 Metal Rooster Lesser Exceeding 雷山小過 **21** 初三 3 / 9	金4 Metal 壬戌 Water Dog Gathering 澤地萃 **22** 初四 4 / 8	水6 Water 癸亥 Water Pig Peel 山地剝 **23** 初五 6 / 7	水1 Water 甲子 Wood Rat Earth 坤爲地 **24** 初六 1 / 6	木3 Wood 乙丑 Wood Ox Biting 火雷噬嗑 **25** 初七 6 / 5
火2 Fire 丙寅 Fire Tiger Family 風火家人 **26** 初八 4 / 4	水6 Water 丁卯 Fire Rabbit Decreasing 山澤損 **27** 初九 9 / 3	金9 Metal 戊辰 Earth Dragon Tread 天澤履 **28** 初十 6 / 2	木8 Wood 己巳 Earth Snake Great Strength 雷天大壯 **29** 十一 2 / 1	木8 Wood 庚午 Metal Horse Consistency 雷風恆 **30** 十二 9 / 9	金9 Metal 辛未 Metal Goat Litigation 天水訟 **31** 十三 3 / 8	

NOVEMBER 2036 己亥

Xuan Kong Element 玄空五行	風地觀 Observation	Period Luck 卦運	Monthly Star 月星
Fire 火2		2	5

SUNDAY	MONDAY	TUESDAY	WEDNESDAY	THURSDAY	FRIDAY	SATURDAY
水1 Water 5 Dimming Light 地火明夷 辛丑 Metal Ox 30 十三 3						水1 Water 7 Officer 地水師 壬申 Water Monkey 1 十四 7
火2 Fire 6 Gradual Progress 風山漸 癸酉 Water Rooster 2 十五 7	火7 Fire 5 Obstruction 水山蹇 甲戌 Wood Dog 3 十六 2	木3 Wood 4 Advancement 火地晉 乙亥 Wood Pig 4 十七 3	水6 Water 3 Nourish 山雷頤 丙子 Fire Rat 5 十八 3	金4 Metal 2 Following 澤雷隨 丁丑 Fire Ox 6 十九 7	木8 Wood 1 Abundance 雷火豐 戊寅 Earth Tiger 7 二十 6	火7 Fire 9 Regulate 水澤節 己卯 Earth Rabbit 8 廿一 8
水1 Water 8 Unity 地天泰 庚辰 Metal Dragon 9 廿二 9	木3 Wood 7 Great Reward 火天大有 辛巳 Metal Snake 10 廿三 7	火2 Fire 6 Wind 巽為風 壬午 Water Horse 11 廿四 1	金4 Metal 5 Trap 澤水困 癸未 Water Goat 12 廿五 8	木3 Wood 4 Not Yet Accomplished 火水未濟 甲申 Wood Monkey 13 廿六 9	金9 Metal 3 Retreat 天山遯 乙酉 Wood Rooster 14 廿七 4	水6 Water 2 Mountain 艮為山 丙戌 Fire Dog 15 廿八 1
木8 Wood 1 Delight 雷地豫 丁亥 Fire Pig 16 廿九 8	火7 Fire 9 Beginning 水雷屯 戊子 Earth Rat 17 三十 4	金9 Metal 8 Without Wrongdoing 天雷無妄 己丑 Earth Ox 18 十月初一 2	木3 Wood 7 Fire 離為火 庚寅 Metal Tiger 19 初二 1	火2 Fire 6 Sincerity 風澤中孚 辛卯 Metal Rabbit 20 初三 3	水6 Water 5 Big Livestock 山天大畜 壬辰 Water Dragon 21 初四 4	金4 Metal 4 Eliminating 澤天夬 癸巳 Water Snake 22 初五 6
金9 Metal 3 Heaven 乾為天 甲午 Wood Horse 23 初六 1	火7 Fire 2 Well 水風井 乙未 Wood Goat 24 初七 6	木8 Wood 1 Relief 雷水解 丙申 Fire Monkey 25 初八 4	金4 Metal 9 Influence 澤山咸 丁酉 Fire Rooster 26 初九 9	水1 Water 8 Humility 地山謙 戊戌 Earth Dog 27 初十 6	火2 Fire 7 Observation 風地觀 己亥 Earth Pig 28 十一 2	火2 Fire 6 Increasing 風雷益 庚子 Metal Rat 29 十二 9

DECEMBER 2036 庚子

Xuan Kong Element 玄空五行	風雷益 Increasing	Period Luck 卦運	Monthly Star 月星
Fire 火2		9	4

SUNDAY	MONDAY	TUESDAY	WEDNESDAY	THURSDAY	FRIDAY	SATURDAY
	金9 Metal 4 Fellowship 天火同人 壬寅 Water Tiger 1 十四 7	木8 Wood 3 Marrying Maiden 雷澤歸妹 癸卯 Water Rabbit 2 十五 7	木3 Wood 2 Opposition 火澤睽 甲辰 Wood Dragon 3 十六 2	火7 Fire 1 Waiting 水天需 乙巳 Wood Snake 4 十七 3	金4 Metal 9 Great Exceeding 澤風大過 丙午 Fire Horse 5 十八 3	水6 Water 8 Poison 山風蠱 丁未 Fire Goat 6 十九 7
火2 Fire 7 Dispersing 風水渙 戊申 Earth Monkey 7 二十 6	木3 Wood 6 Travelling 火山旅 己酉 Earth Rooster 8 廿一 8	金9 Metal 5 Stagnation 天地否 庚戌 Metal Dog 9 廿二 9	火7 Fire 4 Alliance 水地比 辛亥 Metal Pig 10 廿三 7	木8 Wood 3 Thunder 震為雷 壬子 Water Rat 11 廿四 1	水6 Water 2 Beauty 山火賁 癸丑 Water Ox 12 廿五 8	火7 Fire 1 Accomplished 水火既濟 甲寅 Wood Tiger 13 廿六 9
水1 Water 9 Arriving 地澤臨 乙卯 Wood Rabbit 14 廿七 4	金4 Metal 8 Marsh 兌為澤 丙辰 Fire Dragon 15 廿八 1	火2 Fire 7 Small Livestock 風天小畜 丁巳 Fire Snake 16 廿九 8	木3 Wood 6 The Cauldron 火風鼎 戊午 Earth Horse 17 十一月初一 4	水1 Water 5 Rising 地風升 己未 Earth Goat 18 初二 2	火7 Fire 4 Water 坎為水 庚申 Metal Monkey 19 初三 1	木8 Wood 3 Lesser Exceeding 雷山小過 辛酉 Metal Rooster 20 初四 3
金4 Metal 2/8 Gathering 澤地萃 壬戌 Water Dog 21 初五 4	水6 Water 9 Peel 山地剝 癸亥 Water Pig 22 初六 6	水1 Water 1 Earth 坤為地 甲子 Wood Rat 23 初七 1	木3 Wood 2 Biting 火雷噬嗑 乙丑 Wood Ox 24 初八 6	火2 Fire 3 Family 風火家人 丙寅 Fire Tiger 25 初九 4	水6 Water 4 Decreasing 山澤損 丁卯 Fire Rabbit 26 初十 9	金9 Metal 5 Tread 天澤履 戊辰 Earth Dragon 27 十一 6
木8 Wood 6 Great Strength 雷天大壯 己巳 Earth Snake 28 十二 2	木8 Wood 7 Consistency 雷風恆 庚午 Metal Horse 29 十三 9	金9 Metal 8 Litigation 天水訟 辛未 Metal Goat 30 十四 3	水1 Water 9 Officer 地水師 壬申 Water Monkey 31 十五 7			

2037 丁巳

(*Ding Si*) Fire Snake

2037 丁巳 *(Ding Si)* Fire Snake

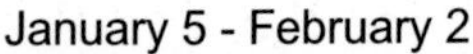

January 5 - February 2

February 3 - March 4

March 5 - April 3

April 4 - May 4

May 5 - June 4

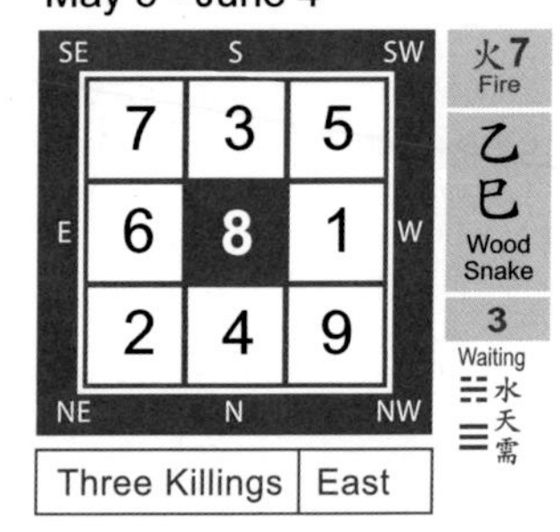

June 5 - July 6

July 7 - August 6

August 7 - September 6

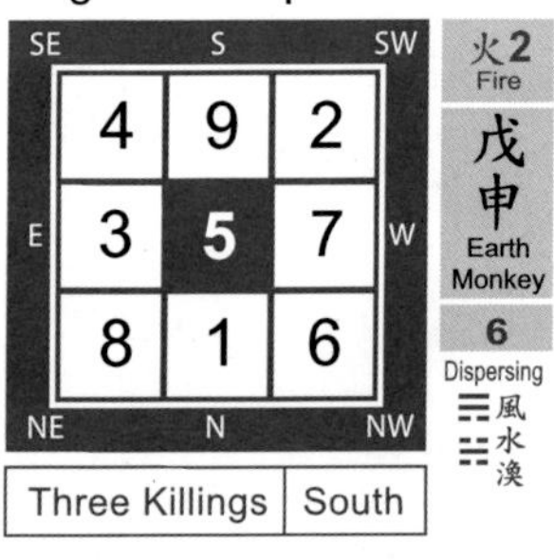

September 7 - October 6

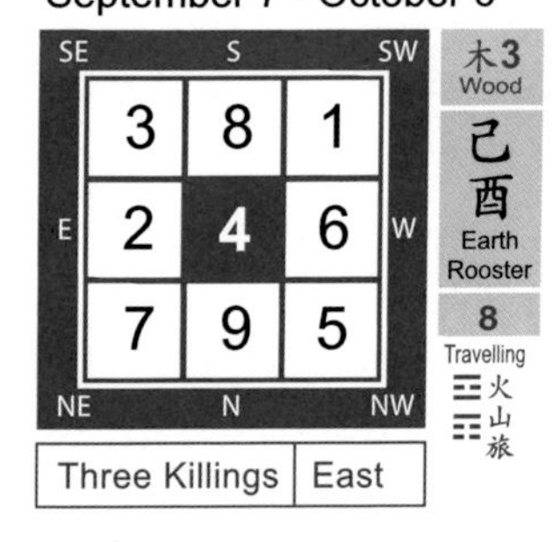

October 7 - November 6

November 7 - December 6

December 7 - January 4

JANUARY 2037 辛丑

Xuan Kong Element 玄空五行	地火明夷 Dimming Light	Period Luck 卦運	Monthly Star 月星
Water 水1		3	3

SUNDAY	MONDAY	TUESDAY	WEDNESDAY	THURSDAY	FRIDAY	SATURDAY
				火2 Fire 1 Gradual Progress 風山漸 癸酉 Water Rooster 1 十六 7	火7 Fire 2 Obstruction 水山蹇 甲戌 Wood Dog 2 十七 2	木3 Wood 3 Advancement 火地晉 乙亥 Wood Pig 3 十八 3
水6 Water 4 Nourish 山雷頤 丙子 Fire Rat 4 十九 3	金4 Metal 5 Following 澤雷隨 丁丑 Fire Ox 5 二十 7	木8 Wood 6 Abundance 雷火豐 戊寅 Earth Tiger 6 廿一 6	火7 Fire 7 Regulate 水澤節 己卯 Earth Rabbit 7 廿二 8	水1 Water 8 Unity 地天泰 庚辰 Metal Dragon 8 廿三 9	木3 Wood 9 Great Reward 火天大有 辛巳 Metal Snake 9 廿四 7	火2 Fire 1 Wind 巽爲風 壬午 Water Horse 10 廿五 1
金4 Metal 2 Trap 澤水困 癸未 Water Goat 11 廿六 8	木3 Wood 3 Not Yet Accomplished 火水未濟 甲申 Wood Monkey 12 廿七 9	金9 Metal 4 Retreat 天山遯 乙酉 Wood Rooster 13 廿八 4	水6 Water 5 Mountain 艮爲山 丙戌 Fire Dog 14 廿九 1	木8 Wood 6 Delight 雷地豫 丁亥 Fire Pig 15 三十 8	火7 Fire 7 Beginning 水雷屯 戊子 Earth Rat 16 十二月初一 4	金9 Metal 8 Without Wrongdoing 天雷無妄 己丑 Earth Ox 17 初二 2
木3 Wood 9 Fire 離爲火 庚寅 Metal Tiger 18 初三 1	火2 Fire 1 Sincerity 風澤中孚 辛卯 Metal Rabbit 19 初四 3	水6 Water 2 Big Livestock 山天大畜 壬辰 Water Dragon 20 初五 4	金4 Metal 3 Eliminating 澤天夬 癸巳 Water Snake 21 初六 6	金9 Metal 4 Heaven 乾爲天 甲午 Wood Horse 22 初七 1	火7 Fire 5 Well 水風井 乙未 Wood Goat 23 初八 6	木8 Wood 6 Relief 雷水解 丙申 Fire Monkey 24 初九 4
金4 Metal 7 Influence 澤山咸 丁酉 Fire Rooster 25 初十 9	水1 Water 8 Humility 地山謙 戊戌 Earth Dog 26 十一 6	火2 Fire 9 Observation 風地觀 己亥 Earth Pig 27 十二 2	火2 Fire 1 Increasing 風雷益 庚子 Metal Rat 28 十三 9	水1 Water 2 Dimming Light 地火明夷 辛丑 Metal Ox 29 十四 3	金9 Metal 3 Fellowship 天火同人 壬寅 Water Tiger 30 十五 7	木8 Wood 4 Marrying Maiden 雷澤歸妹 癸卯 Water Rabbit 31 十六 7

FEBRUARY 2037 壬寅

Xuan Kong Element 玄空五行	天火同人 Fellowship	Period Luck 卦運	Monthly Star 月星
Metal 金9		7	2

SUNDAY	MONDAY	TUESDAY	WEDNESDAY	THURSDAY	FRIDAY	SATURDAY
木3 Wood 5 Opposition 火澤睽 甲辰 Wood Dragon 1 十七 2	火7 Fire 6 Waiting 水天需 乙巳 Wood Snake 2 十八 3	金4 Metal 7 Great Exceeding 澤風大過 丙午 Fire Horse 3 十九 3	水6 Water 8 Poison 山風蠱 丁未 Fire Goat 4 二十 7	火2 Fire 9 Dispersing 風水渙 戊申 Earth Monkey 5 廿一 6	木3 Wood 1 Travelling 火山旅 己酉 Earth Rooster 6 廿二 8	金9 Metal 2 Stagnation 天地否 庚戌 Metal Dog 7 廿三 9
火7 Fire 3 Alliance 水地比 辛亥 Metal Pig 8 廿四 7	木8 Wood 4 Thunder 震爲雷 壬子 Water Rat 9 廿五 1	水6 Water 5 Beauty 山火賁 癸丑 Water Ox 10 廿六 8	火7 Fire 6 Accomplished 水火既濟 甲寅 Wood Tiger 11 廿七 9	水1 Water 7 Arriving 地澤臨 乙卯 Wood Rabbit 12 廿八 4	金4 Metal 8 Marsh 兑爲澤 丙辰 Fire Dragon 13 廿九 1	火2 Fire 9 Small Livestock 風天小畜 丁巳 Fire Snake 14 三十 8
木3 Wood 1 The Cauldron 火風鼎 戊午 Earth Horse 15 正月初一 4	水1 Water 2 Rising 地風升 己未 Earth Goat 16 初二 2	火7 Fire 3 Water 坎爲水 庚申 Metal Monkey 17 初三 1	木8 Wood 4 Lesser Exceeding 雷山小過 辛酉 Metal Rooster 18 初四 3	金4 Metal 5 Gathering 澤地萃 壬戌 Water Dog 19 初五 4	水6 Water 6 Peel 山地剝 癸亥 Water Pig 20 初六 6	水1 Water 7 Earth 坤爲地 甲子 Wood Rat 21 初七 1
木3 Wood 8 Biting 火雷噬嗑 乙丑 Wood Ox 22 初八 6	火2 Fire 9 Family 風火家人 丙寅 Fire Tiger 23 初九 4	水6 Water 1 Decreasing 山澤損 丁卯 Fire Rabbit 24 初十 9	金9 Metal 2 Tread 天澤履 戊辰 Earth Dragon 25 十一 6	木8 Wood 3 Great Strength 雷天大壯 己巳 Earth Snake 26 十二 2	木8 Wood 4 Consistency 雷風恆 庚午 Metal Horse 27 十三 9	金9 Metal 5 Litigation 天水訟 辛未 Metal Goat 28 十四 3

MARCH 2037 癸卯

Xuan Kong Element 玄空五行	雷澤歸妹 Marrying Maiden	Period Luck 卦運	Monthly Star 月星
Wood 木8		7	1

SUNDAY	MONDAY	TUESDAY	WEDNESDAY	THURSDAY	FRIDAY	SATURDAY
水1 Water Officer 地水師 壬申 Water Monkey 6 · 7 **1** 十五	火2 Fire Gradual Progress 風山漸 癸酉 Water Rooster 7 · 7 **2** 十六	火7 Fire Obstruction 水山蹇 甲戌 Wood Dog 8 · 2 **3** 十七	木3 Wood Advancement 火地晉 乙亥 Wood Pig 9 · 3 **4** 十八	水6 Water Nourish 山雷頤 丙子 Fire Rat 1 · 3 **5** 十九	金4 Metal Following 澤雷隨 丁丑 Fire Ox 2 · 7 **6** 二十	木8 Wood Abundance 雷火豐 戊寅 Earth Tiger 3 · 6 **7** 廿一
火7 Fire Regulate 水澤節 己卯 Earth Rabbit 4 · 8 **8** 廿二	水1 Water Unity 地天泰 庚辰 Metal Dragon 5 · 9 **9** 廿三	木3 Wood Great Reward 火天大有 辛巳 Metal Snake 6 · 7 **10** 廿四	火2 Fire Wind 巽爲風 壬午 Water Horse 7 · 1 **11** 廿五	金4 Metal Trap 澤水困 癸未 Water Goat 8 · 8 **12** 廿六	木3 Wood Not Yet Accomplished 火水未濟 甲申 Wood Monkey 9 · 9 **13** 廿七	金9 Metal Retreat 天山遯 乙酉 Wood Rooster 1 · 4 **14** 廿八
水6 Water Mountain 艮爲山 丙戌 Fire Dog 2 · 1 **15** 廿九	木8 Wood Delight 雷地豫 丁亥 Fire Pig 3 · 8 **16** 三十	火7 Fire Beginning 水雷屯 戊子 Earth Rat 4 · 4 **17** 二月初一	金9 Metal Without Wrongdoing 天雷無妄 己丑 Earth Ox 5 · 2 **18** 初二	木3 Wood Fire 離爲火 庚寅 Metal Tiger 6 · 1 **19** 初三	火2 Fire Sincerity 風澤中孚 辛卯 Metal Rabbit 7 · 3 **20** 初四	水6 Water Big Livestock 山天大畜 壬辰 Water Dragon 8 · 4 **21** 初五
金4 Metal Eliminating 澤天夬 癸巳 Water Snake 9 · 6 **22** 初六	金9 Metal Heaven 乾爲天 甲午 Wood Horse 1 · 1 **23** 初七	火7 Fire Well 水風井 乙未 Wood Goat 2 · 6 **24** 初八	木8 Wood Relief 雷水解 丙申 Fire Monkey 3 · 4 **25** 初九	金4 Metal Influence 澤山咸 丁酉 Fire Rooster 4 · 9 **26** 初十	水1 Water Humility 地山謙 戊戌 Earth Dog 5 · 6 **27** 十一	火2 Fire Observation 風地觀 己亥 Earth Pig 6 · 2 **28** 十二
火2 Fire Increasing 風雷益 庚子 Metal Rat 7 · 9 **29** 十三	水1 Water Dimming Light 地火明夷 辛丑 Metal Ox 8 · 3 **30** 十四	金9 Metal Fellowship 天火同人 壬寅 Water Tiger 9 · 7 **31** 十五				

APRIL 2037 甲辰

Xuan Kong Element 玄空五行	火澤睽 Opposition	Period Luck 卦運	Monthly Star 月星
Wood 木3		2	9

SUNDAY	MONDAY	TUESDAY	WEDNESDAY	THURSDAY	FRIDAY	SATURDAY
			木8 Wood Marrying Maiden 雷澤歸妹 癸卯 Water Rabbit 1 · 7 **1** 十六	木3 Wood Opposition 火澤睽 甲辰 Wood Dragon 2 · 2 **2** 十七	火7 Fire Waiting 水天需 乙巳 Wood Snake 3 · 3 **3** 十八	金4 Metal Great Exceeding 澤風大過 丙午 Fire Horse 4 · 3 **4** 十九
水6 Water Poison 山風蠱 丁未 Fire Goat 5 · 7 **5** 二十	火2 Fire Dispersing 風水渙 戊申 Earth Monkey 6 · 6 **6** 廿一	木3 Wood Travelling 火山旅 己酉 Earth Rooster 7 · 8 **7** 廿二	金9 Metal Stagnation 天地否 庚戌 Metal Dog 8 · 9 **8** 廿三	火7 Fire Alliance 水地比 辛亥 Metal Pig 9 · 7 **9** 廿四	木8 Wood Thunder 震爲雷 壬子 Water Rat 1 · 1 **10** 廿五	水6 Water Beauty 山火賁 癸丑 Water Ox 2 · 8 **11** 廿六
火7 Fire Accomplished 水火既濟 甲寅 Wood Tiger 3 · 9 **12** 廿七	水1 Water Arriving 地澤臨 乙卯 Wood Rabbit 4 · 4 **13** 廿八	金4 Metal Marsh 兌爲澤 丙辰 Fire Dragon 5 · 1 **14** 廿九	火2 Fire Small Livestock 風天小畜 丁巳 Fire Snake 6 · 8 **15** 三十	木3 Wood The Cauldron 火風鼎 戊午 Earth Horse 7 · 4 **16** 三月初一	水1 Water Rising 地風升 己未 Earth Goat 8 · 2 **17** 初二	火7 Fire Water 坎爲水 庚申 Metal Monkey 9 · 1 **18** 初三
木8 Wood Lesser Exceeding 雷山小過 辛酉 Metal Rooster 1 · 3 **19** 初四	金4 Metal Gathering 澤地萃 壬戌 Water Dog 2 · 4 **20** 初五	水6 Water Peel 山地剝 癸亥 Water Pig 3 · 6 **21** 初六	水1 Water Earth 坤爲地 甲子 Wood Rat 4 · 1 **22** 初七	木3 Wood Biting 火雷噬嗑 乙丑 Wood Ox 5 · 6 **23** 初八	火2 Fire Family 風火家人 丙寅 Fire Tiger 6 · 4 **24** 初九	水6 Water Decreasing 山澤損 丁卯 Fire Rabbit 7 · 9 **25** 初十
金9 Metal Tread 天澤履 戊辰 Earth Dragon 8 · 6 **26** 十一	木8 Wood Great Strength 雷天大壯 己巳 Earth Snake 9 · 2 **27** 十二	木8 Wood Consistency 雷風恆 庚午 Metal Horse 1 · 9 **28** 十三	金9 Metal Litigation 天水訟 辛未 Metal Goat 2 · 3 **29** 十四	水1 Water Officer 地水師 壬申 Water Monkey 3 · 7 **30** 十五		

MAY 2037 乙巳

Xuan Kong Element 玄空五行	水天需 Waiting	Period Luck 卦運	Monthly Star 月星
Fire 火7		3	8

SUNDAY	MONDAY	TUESDAY	WEDNESDAY	THURSDAY	FRIDAY	SATURDAY
木8 Wood [7] Marrying Maiden 雷澤歸妹 癸卯 Water Rabbit **31** 十七 7					火2 Fire [4] Gradual Progress 風山漸 癸酉 Water Rooster **1** 十六 7	火7 Fire [5] Obstruction 水山蹇 甲戌 Wood Dog **2** 十七 2
木3 Wood [6] Advancement 火地晉 乙亥 Wood Pig **3** 十八 3	水6 Water [7] Nourish 山雷頤 丙子 Fire Rat **4** 十九 3	金4 Metal [8] Following 澤雷隨 丁丑 Fire Ox **5** 二十 7	木8 Wood [9] Abundance 雷火豐 戊寅 Earth Tiger **6** 廿一 6	火7 Fire [1] Regulate 水澤節 己卯 Earth Rabbit **7** 廿二 8	水1 Water [2] Unity 地天泰 庚辰 Metal Dragon **8** 廿三 9	木3 Wood [3] Great Reward 火天大有 辛巳 Metal Snake **9** 廿四 7
火2 Fire [4] Wind 巽為風 壬午 Water Horse **10** 廿五 1	金4 Metal [5] Trap 澤水困 癸未 Water Goat **11** 廿六 8	木3 Wood [6] Not Yet Accomplished 火水未濟 甲申 Wood Monkey **12** 廿七 9	金9 Metal [7] Retreat 天山遯 乙酉 Wood Rooster **13** 廿八 4	水6 Water [8] Mountain 艮為山 丙戌 Fire Dog **14** 廿九 1	木8 Wood [9] Delight 雷地豫 丁亥 Fire Pig **15** 四月初一 8	火7 Fire [1] Beginning 水雷屯 戊子 Earth Rat **16** 初二 4
金9 Metal [2] Without Wrongdoing 天雷無妄 己丑 Earth Ox **17** 初三 2	木3 Wood [3] Fire 離為火 庚寅 Metal Tiger **18** 初四 1	火2 Fire [4] Sincerity 風澤中孚 辛卯 Metal Rabbit **19** 初五 3	水6 Water [5] Big Livestock 山天大畜 壬辰 Water Dragon **20** 初六 4	金4 Metal [6] Eliminating 澤天夬 癸巳 Water Snake **21** 初七 6	金9 Metal [7] Heaven 乾為天 甲午 Wood Horse **22** 初八 1	火7 Fire [8] Well 水風井 乙未 Wood Goat **23** 初九 6
木8 Wood [9] Relief 雷水解 丙申 Fire Monkey **24** 初十 4	金4 Metal [1] Influence 澤山咸 丁酉 Fire Rooster **25** 十一 9	水1 Water [2] Humility 地山謙 戊戌 Earth Dog **26** 十二 6	火2 Fire [3] Observation 風地觀 己亥 Earth Pig **27** 十三 2	火2 Fire [4] Increasing 風雷益 庚子 Metal Rat **28** 十四 9	水1 Water [5] Dimming Light 地火明夷 辛丑 Metal Ox **29** 十五 3	金9 Metal [6] Fellowship 天火同人 壬寅 Water Tiger **30** 十六 7

JUNE 2037 丙午

Xuan Kong Element 玄空五行	澤風大過 Great Exceeding	Period Luck 卦運	Monthly Star 月星
Metal 金4		3	7

SUNDAY	MONDAY	TUESDAY	WEDNESDAY	THURSDAY	FRIDAY	SATURDAY
	木3 Wood [8] Opposition 火澤睽 甲辰 Wood Dragon **1** 十八 2	火7 Fire [9] Waiting 水天需 乙巳 Wood Snake **2** 十九 3	金4 Metal [1] Great Exceeding 澤風大過 丙午 Fire Horse **3** 二十 3	水6 Water [2] Poison 山風蠱 丁未 Fire Goat **4** 廿一 7	火2 Fire [3] Dispersing 風水渙 戊申 Earth Monkey **5** 廿二 6	木3 Wood [4] Travelling 火山旅 己酉 Earth Rooster **6** 廿三 8
金9 Metal [5] Stagnation 天地否 庚戌 Metal Dog **7** 廿四 9	火7 Fire [6] Alliance 水地比 辛亥 Metal Pig **8** 廿五 7	木8 Wood [7] Thunder 震為雷 壬子 Water Rat **9** 廿六 1	水6 Water [8] Beauty 山火賁 癸丑 Water Ox **10** 廿七 8	火7 Fire [9] Accomplished 水火既濟 甲寅 Wood Tiger **11** 廿八 9	水1 Water [1] Arriving 地澤臨 乙卯 Wood Rabbit **12** 廿九 4	金4 Metal [2] Marsh 兑為澤 丙辰 Fire Dragon **13** 三十 1
火2 Fire [3] Small Livestock 風天小畜 丁巳 Fire Snake **14** 五月初一 8	木3 Wood [4] The Cauldron 火風鼎 戊午 Earth Horse **15** 初二 4	水1 Water [5] Rising 地風升 己未 Earth Goat **16** 初三 2	火7 Fire [6] Water 坎為水 庚申 Metal Monkey **17** 初四 1	木8 Wood [7] Lesser Exceeding 雷山小過 辛酉 Metal Rooster **18** 初五 3	金4 Metal [8] Gathering 澤地萃 壬戌 Water Dog **19** 初六 4	水6 Water [9] Peel 山地剝 癸亥 Water Pig **20** 初七 6
水1 Water [1/9] Earth 坤為地 甲子 Wood Rat **21** 初八 1	木3 Wood [8] Biting 火雷噬嗑 乙丑 Wood Ox **22** 初九 6	火2 Fire [7] Family 風火家人 丙寅 Fire Tiger **23** 初十 4	水6 Water [6] Decreasing 山澤損 丁卯 Fire Rabbit **24** 十一 9	金9 Metal [5] Tread 天澤履 戊辰 Earth Dragon **25** 十二 6	木8 Wood [4] Great Strength 雷天大壯 己巳 Earth Snake **26** 十三 2	木8 Wood [3] Consistency 雷風恒 庚午 Metal Horse **27** 十四 9
金9 Metal [2] Litigation 天水訟 辛未 Metal Goat **28** 十五 3	水1 Water [1] Officer 地水師 壬申 Water Monkey **29** 十六 7	火2 Fire [9] Gradual Progress 風山漸 癸酉 Water Rooster **30** 十七 7				

JULY 2037 丁未

Xuan Kong Element 玄空五行	山風蠱 Poison	Period Luck 卦運	Monthly Star 月星
Water 水6		7	6

SUNDAY	MONDAY	TUESDAY	WEDNESDAY	THURSDAY	FRIDAY	SATURDAY
			火7 Fire · 8 Obstruction 水山蹇 甲戌 Wood Dog **1** 十八 · 2	木3 Wood · 7 Advancement 火地晉 乙亥 Wood Pig **2** 十九 · 3	水6 Water · 6 Nourish 山雷頤 丙子 Fire Rat **3** 二十 · 3	金4 Metal · 5 Following 澤雷隨 丁丑 Fire Ox **4** 廿一 · 7
木8 Wood · 4 Abundance 雷火豐 戊寅 Earth Tiger **5** 廿二 · 6	火7 Fire · 3 Regulate 水澤節 己卯 Earth Rabbit **6** 廿三 · 8	水1 Water · 2 Unity 地天泰 庚辰 Metal Dragon **7** 廿四 · 9	木3 Wood · 1 Great Reward 火天大有 辛巳 Metal Snake **8** 廿五 · 7	火2 Fire · 9 Wind 巽爲風 壬午 Water Horse **9** 廿六 · 1	金4 Metal · 8 Trap 澤水困 癸未 Water Goat **10** 廿七 · 8	木3 Wood · 7 Not Yet Accomplished 火水未濟 甲申 Wood Monkey **11** 廿八 · 9
金9 Metal · 6 Retreat 天山遯 乙酉 Wood Rooster **12** 廿九 · 4	水6 Water · 5 Mountain 艮爲山 丙戌 Fire Dog **13** 六月初一 · 1	木8 Wood · 4 Delight 雷地豫 丁亥 Fire Pig **14** 初二 · 8	火7 Fire · 3 Beginning 水雷屯 戊子 Earth Rat **15** 初三 · 4	金9 Metal · 2 Without Wrongdoing 天雷無妄 己丑 Earth Ox **16** 初四 · 2	木3 Wood · 1 Fire 離爲火 庚寅 Metal Tiger **17** 初五 · 1	火2 Fire · 9 Sincerity 風澤中孚 辛卯 Metal Rabbit **18** 初六 · 3
水6 Water · 8 Big Livestock 山天大畜 壬辰 Water Dragon **19** 初七 · 4	金4 Metal · 7 Eliminating 澤天夬 癸巳 Water Snake **20** 初八 · 6	金9 Metal · 6 Heaven 乾爲天 甲午 Wood Horse **21** 初九 · 1	火7 Fire · 5 Well 水風井 乙未 Wood Goat **22** 初十 · 6	木8 Wood · 4 Relief 雷水解 丙申 Fire Monkey **23** 十一 · 4	金4 Metal · 3 Influence 澤山咸 丁酉 Fire Rooster **24** 十二 · 9	水1 Water · 2 Humility 地山謙 戊戌 Earth Dog **25** 十三 · 6
火2 Fire · 1 Observation 風地觀 己亥 Earth Pig **26** 十四 · 2	火2 Fire · 9 Increasing 風雷益 庚子 Metal Rat **27** 十五 · 9	水1 Water · 8 Dimming Light 地火明夷 辛丑 Metal Ox **28** 十六 · 3	金9 Metal · 7 Fellowship 天火同人 壬寅 Water Tiger **29** 十七 · 7	木8 Wood · 6 Marrying Maiden 雷澤歸妹 癸卯 Water Rabbit **30** 十八 · 7	木3 Wood · 5 Opposition 火澤睽 甲辰 Wood Dragon **31** 十九 · 2	

AUGUST 2037 戊申

Xuan Kong Element 玄空五行	風水渙 Dispersing	Period Luck 卦運	Monthly Star 月星
Fire 火2		6	5

SUNDAY	MONDAY	TUESDAY	WEDNESDAY	THURSDAY	FRIDAY	SATURDAY
火7 Fire · 2 Obstruction 水山蹇 甲戌 Wood Dog **30** 二十 · 2	木3 Wood · 1 Advancement 火地晉 乙亥 Wood Pig **31** 廿一 · 3					火7 Fire · 4 Waiting 水天需 乙巳 Wood Snake **1** 二十 · 3
金4 Metal · 3 Great Exceeding 澤風大過 丙午 Fire Horse **2** 廿一 · 3	水6 Water · 2 Poison 山風蠱 丁未 Fire Goat **3** 廿二 · 7	火2 Fire · 1 Dispersing 風水渙 戊申 Earth Monkey **4** 廿三 · 6	木3 Wood · 9 Travelling 火山旅 己酉 Earth Rooster **5** 廿四 · 8	金9 Metal · 8 Stagnation 天地否 庚戌 Metal Dog **6** 廿五 · 9	火7 Fire · 7 Alliance 水地比 辛亥 Metal Pig **7** 廿六 · 7	木8 Wood · 6 Thunder 震爲雷 壬子 Water Rat **8** 廿七 · 1
水6 Water · 5 Beauty 山火賁 癸丑 Water Ox **9** 廿八 · 8	火7 Fire · 4 Accomplished 水火既濟 甲寅 Wood Tiger **10** 廿九 · 9	水1 Water · 3 Arriving 地澤臨 乙卯 Wood Rabbit **11** 七月初一 · 4	金4 Metal · 2 Marsh 兑爲澤 丙辰 Fire Dragon **12** 初二 · 6	火2 Fire · 1 Small Livestock 風天小畜 丁巳 Fire Snake **13** 初三 · 8	木3 Wood · 9 The Cauldron 火風鼎 戊午 Earth Horse **14** 初四 · 4	水1 Water · 8 Rising 地風升 己未 Earth Goat **15** 初五 · 2
火7 Fire · 7 Water 坎爲水 庚申 Metal Monkey **16** 初六 · 1	木8 Wood · 6 Lesser Exceeding 雷山小過 辛酉 Metal Rooster **17** 初七 · 3	金4 Metal · 5 Gathering 澤地萃 壬戌 Water Dog **18** 初八 · 4	水6 Water · 4 Peel 山地剝 癸亥 Water Pig **19** 初九 · 6	水1 Water · 3 Earth 坤爲地 甲子 Wood Rat **20** 初十 · 1	木3 Wood · 2 Biting 火雷噬嗑 乙丑 Wood Ox **21** 十一 · 6	火2 Fire · 1 Family 風火家人 丙寅 Fire Tiger **22** 十二 · 4
水6 Water · 9 Decreasing 山澤損 丁卯 Fire Rabbit **23** 十三 · 9	金9 Metal · 8 Tread 天澤履 戊辰 Earth Dragon **24** 十四 · 6	木8 Wood · 7 Great Strength 雷天大壯 己巳 Earth Snake **25** 十五 · 2	木8 Wood · 6 Consistency 雷風恒 庚午 Metal Horse **26** 十六 · 9	金9 Metal · 5 Litigation 天水訟 辛未 Metal Goat **27** 十七 · 3	水1 Water · 4 Officer 地水師 壬申 Water Monkey **28** 十八 · 7	火2 Fire · 3 Gradual Progress 風山漸 癸酉 Water Rooster **29** 十九 · 7

SEPTEMBER 2037 己酉

Xuan Kong Element 玄空五行	火山旅 Travelling	Period Luck 卦運	Monthly Star 月星
Wood 木3		8	4

SUNDAY	MONDAY	TUESDAY	WEDNESDAY	THURSDAY	FRIDAY	SATURDAY
		水6 Water 9 Nourish 丙子 Fire Rat 山雷頤 1 3 廿二	金4 Metal 8 Following 丁丑 Fire Ox 澤雷隨 2 7 廿三	木8 Wood 7 Abundance 戊寅 Earth Tiger 雷火豐 3 6 廿四	火7 Fire 6 Regulate 己卯 Earth Rabbit 水澤節 4 8 廿五	水1 Water 5 Unity 庚辰 Metal Dragon 地天泰 5 9 廿六
木3 Wood 4 Great Reward 辛巳 Metal Snake 火天大有 6 7 廿七	火2 Fire 3 Wind 壬午 Water Horse 巽爲風 7 1 廿八	金4 Metal 2 Trap 癸未 Water Goat 澤水困 8 8 廿九	木3 Wood 1 Not Yet Accomplished 甲申 Wood Monkey 火水未濟 9 9 三十	金9 Metal 9 Retreat 乙酉 Wood Rooster 天山遯 10 4 八月初一	水6 Water 8 Mountain 丙戌 Fire Dog 艮爲山 11 1 初二	木8 Wood 7 Delight 丁亥 Fire Pig 雷地豫 12 8 初三
火7 Fire 6 Beginning 戊子 Earth Rat 水雷屯 13 4 初四	金9 Metal 5 Without Wrongdoing 己丑 Earth Ox 天雷無妄 14 2 初五	木3 Wood 4 Fire 庚寅 Metal Tiger 離爲火 15 1 初六	火2 Fire 3 Sincerity 辛卯 Metal Rabbit 風澤中孚 16 3 初七	水6 Water 2 Big Livestock 壬辰 Water Dragon 山天大畜 17 4 初八	金4 Metal 1 Eliminating 癸巳 Water Snake 澤天夬 18 6 初九	金9 Metal 9 Heaven 甲午 Wood Horse 乾爲天 19 1 初十
火7 Fire 8 Well 乙未 Wood Goat 水風井 20 6 十一	木8 Wood 7 Relief 丙申 Fire Monkey 雷水解 21 4 十二	金4 Metal 6 Influence 丁酉 Fire Rooster 澤山咸 22 9 十三	水1 Water 5 Humility 戊戌 Earth Dog 地山謙 23 6 十四	火2 Fire 4 Observation 己亥 Earth Pig 風地觀 24 2 十五	火2 Fire 3 Increasing 庚子 Metal Rat 風雷益 25 9 十六	水1 Water 2 Dimming Light 辛丑 Metal Ox 地火明夷 26 3 十七
金9 Metal 1 Fellowship 壬寅 Water Tiger 天火同人 27 7 十八	木8 Wood 9 Marrying Maiden 癸卯 Water Rabbit 雷澤歸妹 28 7 十九	木3 Wood 8 Opposition 甲辰 Wood Dragon 火澤睽 29 2 二十	火7 Fire 7 Waiting 乙巳 Wood Snake 水天需 30 3 廿一			

OCTOBER 2037 庚戌

Xuan Kong Element 玄空五行	天地否 Stagnation	Period Luck 卦運	Monthly Star 月星
Metal 金9		9	3

SUNDAY	MONDAY	TUESDAY	WEDNESDAY	THURSDAY	FRIDAY	SATURDAY
				金4 Metal 6 Great Exceeding 丙午 Fire Horse 澤風大過 1 3 廿二	水6 Water 5 Poison 丁未 Fire Goat 山風蠱 2 7 廿三	火2 Fire 4 Dispersing 戊申 Earth Monkey 風水渙 3 6 廿四
木3 Wood 3 Travelling 己酉 Earth Rooster 火山旅 4 8 廿五	金9 Metal 2 Stagnation 庚戌 Metal Dog 天地否 5 9 廿六	火7 Fire 1 Alliance 辛亥 Metal Pig 水地比 6 7 廿七	木8 Wood 9 Thunder 壬子 Water Rat 震爲雷 7 1 廿八	水6 Water 8 Beauty 癸丑 Water Ox 山火賁 8 8 廿九	火7 Fire 7 Accomplished 甲寅 Wood Tiger 水火既濟 9 9 九月初一	水1 Water 6 Arriving 乙卯 Wood Rabbit 地澤臨 10 4 初二
金4 Metal 5 Marsh 丙辰 Fire Dragon 兌爲澤 11 1 初三	火2 Fire 4 Small Livestock 丁巳 Fire Snake 風天小畜 12 8 初四	木3 Wood 3 The Cauldron 戊午 Earth Horse 火風鼎 13 4 初五	水1 Water 2 Rising 己未 Earth Goat 地風升 14 2 初六	火7 Fire 1 Water 庚申 Metal Monkey 坎爲水 15 1 初七	木8 Wood 9 Lesser Exceeding 辛酉 Metal Rooster 雷山小過 16 3 初八	金4 Metal 8 Gathering 壬戌 Water Dog 澤地萃 17 4 初九
水6 Water 7 Peel 癸亥 Water Pig 山地剝 18 6 初十	水1 Water 6 Earth 甲子 Wood Rat 坤爲地 19 1 十一	木3 Wood 5 Biting 乙丑 Wood Ox 火雷噬嗑 20 6 十二	火2 Fire 4 Family 丙寅 Fire Tiger 風火家人 21 4 十三	水6 Water 3 Decreasing 丁卯 Fire Rabbit 山澤損 22 9 十四	金9 Metal 2 Tread 戊辰 Earth Dragon 天澤履 23 6 十五	木8 Wood 1 Great Strength 己巳 Earth Snake 雷天大壯 24 2 十六
木8 Wood 9 Consistency 庚午 Metal Horse 雷風恆 25 9 十七	金9 Metal 8 Litigation 辛未 Metal Goat 天水訟 26 3 十八	水1 Water 7 Officer 壬申 Water Monkey 地水師 27 7 十九	火2 Fire 6 Gradual Progress 癸酉 Water Rooster 風山漸 28 7 二十	火7 Fire 5 Obstruction 甲戌 Wood Dog 水山蹇 29 2 廿一	木3 Wood 4 Advancement 乙亥 Wood Pig 火地晉 30 3 廿二	水6 Water 3 Nourish 丙子 Fire Rat 山雷頤 31 3 廿三

NOVEMBER 2037 辛亥

Xuan Kong Element 玄空五行	水地比 Alliance	Period Luck 卦運	Monthly Star 月星
Fire 火7		7	2

SUNDAY	MONDAY	TUESDAY	WEDNESDAY	THURSDAY	FRIDAY	SATURDAY
金4 Metal Following 澤雷隨 2 丁丑 Fire Ox **1** 7 廿四	木8 Wood Abundance 雷火豐 1 戊寅 Earth Tiger **2** 6 廿五	火7 Fire Regulate 水澤節 9 己卯 Earth Rabbit **3** 8 廿六	水1 Water Unity 地天泰 8 庚辰 Metal Dragon **4** 9 廿七	木3 Wood Great Reward 火天大有 7 辛巳 Metal Snake **5** 7 廿八	火2 Fire Wind 巽為風 6 壬午 Water Horse **6** 1 廿九	金4 Metal Trap 澤水困 5 癸未 Water Goat **7** 8 十月初一
木3 Wood Not Yet Accomplished 火水未濟 4 甲申 Wood Monkey **8** 9 初二	金9 Metal Retreat 天山遯 3 乙酉 Wood Rooster **9** 4 初三	水6 Water Mountain 艮為山 2 丙戌 Fire Dog **10** 1 初四	木8 Wood Delight 雷地豫 1 丁亥 Fire Pig **11** 8 初五	火7 Fire Beginning 水雷屯 9 戊子 Earth Rat **12** 4 初六	金9 Metal Without Wrongdoing 天雷無妄 8 己丑 Earth Ox **13** 2 初七	木3 Wood Fire 離為火 7 庚寅 Metal Tiger **14** 1 初八
火2 Fire Sincerity 風澤中孚 6 辛卯 Metal Rabbit **15** 3 初九	水6 Water Big Livestock 山天大畜 5 壬辰 Water Dragon **16** 4 初十	金4 Metal Eliminating 澤天夬 4 癸巳 Water Snake **17** 6 十一	金9 Metal Heaven 乾為天 3 甲午 Wood Horse **18** 1 十二	火7 Fire Well 水風井 2 乙未 Wood Goat **19** 6 十三	木8 Wood Relief 雷水解 1 丙申 Fire Monkey **20** 4 十四	金4 Metal Influence 澤山咸 9 丁酉 Fire Rooster **21** 9 十五
水1 Water Humility 地山謙 8 戊戌 Earth Dog **22** 6 十六	火2 Fire Observation 風地觀 7 己亥 Earth Pig **23** 2 十七	火2 Fire Increasing 風雷益 6 庚子 Metal Rat **24** 9 十八	水1 Water Dimming Light 地火明夷 5 辛丑 Metal Ox **25** 3 十九	金9 Metal Fellowship 天火同人 4 壬寅 Water Tiger **26** 7 二十	木8 Wood Marrying Maiden 雷澤歸妹 3 癸卯 Water Rabbit **27** 7 廿一	木3 Wood Opposition 火澤睽 2 甲辰 Wood Dragon **28** 2 廿二
火7 Fire Waiting 水天需 1 乙巳 Wood Snake **29** 3 廿三	金4 Metal Great Exceeding 澤風大過 9 丙午 Fire Horse **30** 3 廿四					

DECEMBER 2037 壬子

Xuan Kong Element 玄空五行	震為雷 Thunder	Period Luck 卦運	Monthly Star 月星
Wood 木8		1	1

SUNDAY	MONDAY	TUESDAY	WEDNESDAY	THURSDAY	FRIDAY	SATURDAY
		水6 Water Poison 山風蠱 8 丁未 Fire Goat **1** 7 廿五	火2 Fire Dispersing 風水渙 7 戊申 Earth Monkey **2** 6 廿六	木3 Wood Travelling 火山旅 6 己酉 Earth Rooster **3** 8 廿七	金9 Metal Stagnation 天地否 5 庚戌 Metal Dog **4** 9 廿八	火7 Fire Alliance 水地比 4 辛亥 Metal Pig **5** 7 廿九
木8 Wood Thunder 震為雷 3 壬子 Water Rat **6** 1 三十	水6 Water Beauty 山火賁 2 癸丑 Water Ox **7** 8 十一月初一	火7 Fire Accomplished 水火既濟 1 甲寅 Wood Tiger **8** 9 初二	水1 Water Arriving 地澤臨 9 乙卯 Wood Rabbit **9** 4 初三	金4 Metal Marsh 兌為澤 8 丙辰 Fire Dragon **10** 1 初四	火2 Fire Small Livestock 風天小畜 7 丁巳 Fire Snake **11** 8 初五	木3 Wood The Cauldron 火風鼎 6 戊午 Earth Horse **12** 4 初六
水1 Water Rising 地風升 5 己未 Earth Goat **13** 2 初七	火7 Fire Water 坎為水 4 庚申 Metal Monkey **14** 1 初八	木8 Wood Lesser Exceeding 雷山小過 3 辛酉 Metal Rooster **15** 3 初九	金4 Metal Gathering 澤地萃 2 壬戌 Water Dog **16** 4 初十	水6 Water Peel 山地剝 1 癸亥 Water Pig **17** 6 十一	水1 Water Earth 坤為地 9 甲子 Wood Rat **18** 1 十二	木3 Wood Biting 火雷噬嗑 8 乙丑 Wood Ox **19** 6 十三
火2 Fire Family 風火家人 7 丙寅 Fire Tiger **20** 4 十四	水6 Water Decreasing 山澤損 6/7 丁卯 Fire Rabbit **21** 9 十五	金9 Metal Tread 天澤履 8 戊辰 Earth Dragon **22** 6 十六	木8 Wood Great Strength 雷天大壯 9 己巳 Earth Snake **23** 2 十七	木8 Wood Consistency 雷風恒 1 庚午 Metal Horse **24** 9 十八	金9 Metal Litigation 天水訟 2 辛未 Metal Goat **25** 3 十九	水1 Water Officer 地水師 3 壬申 Water Monkey **26** 7 二十
火2 Fire Gradual Progress 風山漸 4 癸酉 Water Rooster **27** 7 廿一	火7 Fire Obstruction 水山蹇 5 甲戌 Wood Dog **28** 2 廿二	木3 Wood Advancement 火地晉 6 乙亥 Wood Pig **29** 3 廿三	水6 Water Nourish 山雷頤 7 丙子 Fire Rat **30** 3 廿四	金4 Metal Following 澤雷隨 8 丁丑 Fire Ox **31** 7 廿五		

2038 戊午

(*Wu Wu*) Earth Horse

2038 戊午 *(Wu Wu)* Earth Horse

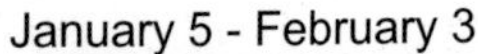

January 5 - February 3

February 4 - March 4

March 5 - April 3

April 4 - May 4

May 5 - June 4

June 5 - July 6

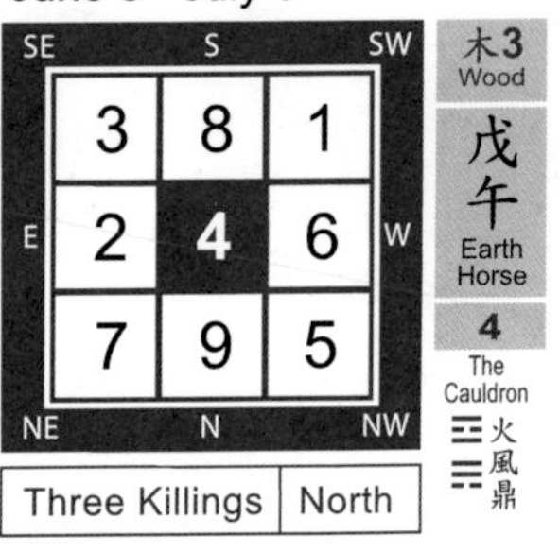

July 7 - August 6

August 7 - September 6

September 7 - October 7

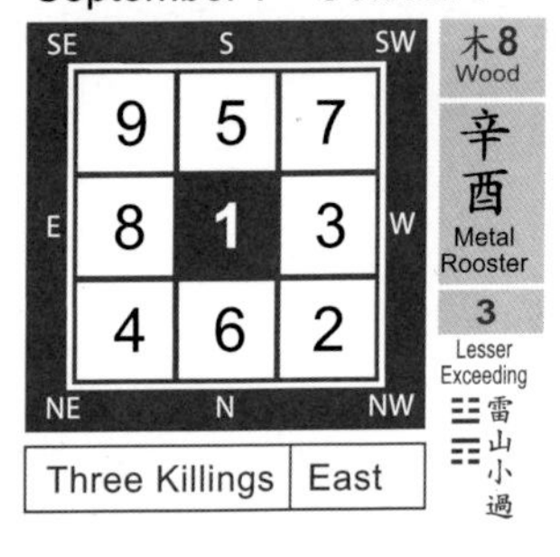

October 8 - November 6

November 7 - December 6

December 7 - January 4

JANUARY 2038 癸丑

Xuan Kong Element 玄空五行	山火賁 Beauty	Period Luck 卦運	Monthly Star 月星
Water 水6		8	9

SUNDAY	MONDAY	TUESDAY	WEDNESDAY	THURSDAY	FRIDAY	SATURDAY
火2 Fire Dispersing 3 戊申 Earth Monkey 風水渙 6 31 廿七					木8 Wood Abundance 9 戊寅 Earth Tiger 雷火豐 6 1 廿六	火7 Fire Regulate 1 己卯 Earth Rabbit 水澤節 8 2 廿七
水1 Water Unity 2 庚辰 Metal Dragon 地天泰 9 3 廿八	木3 Wood Great Reward 3 辛巳 Metal Snake 火天大有 7 4 廿九	火2 Fire Wind 4 壬午 Water Horse 巽爲風 1 5 十二月初一	金4 Metal Trap 5 癸未 Water Goat 澤水困 8 6 初二	木3 Wood Not Yet Accomplished 6 甲申 Wood Monkey 火水未濟 9 7 初三	金9 Metal Retreat 7 乙酉 Wood Rooster 天山遯 4 8 初四	水6 Water Mountain 8 丙戌 Fire Dog 艮爲山 1 9 初五
木8 Wood Delight 9 丁亥 Fire Pig 雷地豫 8 10 初六	火7 Fire Beginning 1 戊子 Earth Rat 水雷屯 4 11 初七	金9 Metal Without Wrongdoing 2 己丑 Earth Ox 天雷無妄 2 12 初八	木3 Wood Fire 3 庚寅 Metal Tiger 離爲火 1 13 初九	火2 Fire Sincerity 4 辛卯 Metal Rabbit 風澤中孚 3 14 初十	水6 Water Big Livestock 5 壬辰 Water Dragon 山天大畜 4 15 十一	金4 Metal Eliminating 6 癸巳 Water Snake 澤天夬 6 16 十二
金9 Metal Heaven 7 甲午 Wood Horse 乾爲天 1 17 十三	火7 Fire Well 8 乙未 Wood Goat 水風井 6 18 十四	木8 Wood Relief 9 丙申 Fire Monkey 雷水解 4 19 十五	金4 Metal Influence 1 丁酉 Fire Rooster 澤山咸 9 20 十六	水1 Water Humility 2 戊戌 Earth Dog 地山謙 6 21 十七	火2 Fire Observation 3 己亥 Earth Pig 風地觀 2 22 十八	火2 Fire Increasing 4 庚子 Metal Rat 風雷益 9 23 十九
水1 Water Dimming Light 5 辛丑 Metal Ox 地火明夷 3 24 二十	金9 Metal Fellowship 6 壬寅 Water Tiger 天火同人 7 25 廿一	木8 Wood Marrying Maiden 7 癸卯 Water Rabbit 雷澤歸妹 7 26 廿二	木3 Wood Opposition 8 甲辰 Wood Dragon 火澤睽 2 27 廿三	火7 Fire Waiting 9 乙巳 Wood Snake 水天需 3 28 廿四	金4 Metal Great Exceeding 1 丙午 Fire Horse 澤風大過 3 29 廿五	水6 Water Poison 2 丁未 Fire Goat 山風蠱 7 30 廿六

FEBRUARY 2038 甲寅

Xuan Kong Element 玄空五行	水火既濟 Accomplished	Period Luck 卦運	Monthly Star 月星
Fire 火7		9	8

SUNDAY	MONDAY	TUESDAY	WEDNESDAY	THURSDAY	FRIDAY	SATURDAY
	木3 Wood Travelling 4 己酉 Earth Rooster 火山旅 8 1 廿八	金9 Metal Stagnation 5 庚戌 Metal Dog 天地否 9 2 廿九	火7 Fire Alliance 6 辛亥 Metal Pig 水地比 7 3 三十	木8 Wood Thunder 7 壬子 Water Rat 震爲雷 1 4 正月初一	水6 Water Beauty 8 癸丑 Water Ox 山火賁 8 5 初二	火7 Fire Accomplished 9 甲寅 Wood Tiger 水火既濟 9 6 初三
水1 Water Arriving 1 乙卯 Wood Rabbit 地澤臨 4 7 初四	金4 Metal Marsh 2 丙辰 Fire Dragon 兌爲澤 1 8 初五	火2 Fire Small Livestock 3 丁巳 Fire Snake 風天小畜 8 9 初六	木3 Wood The Cauldron 4 戊午 Earth Horse 火風鼎 4 10 初七	水1 Water Rising 5 己未 Earth Goat 地風升 2 11 初八	火7 Fire Water 6 庚申 Metal Monkey 坎爲水 1 12 初九	木8 Wood Lesser Exceeding 7 辛酉 Metal Rooster 雷山小過 3 13 初十
金4 Metal Gathering 8 壬戌 Water Dog 澤地萃 4 14 十一	水6 Water Peel 9 癸亥 Water Pig 山地剝 6 15 十二	水1 Water Earth 1 甲子 Wood Rat 坤爲地 1 16 十三	木3 Wood Biting 2 乙丑 Wood Ox 火雷噬嗑 6 17 十四	火2 Fire Family 3 丙寅 Fire Tiger 風火家人 4 18 十五	水6 Water Decreasing 4 丁卯 Fire Rabbit 山澤損 9 19 十六	金9 Metal Tread 5 戊辰 Earth Dragon 天澤履 6 20 十七
木8 Wood Great Strength 6 己巳 Earth Snake 雷天大壯 2 21 十八	木8 Wood Consistency 7 庚午 Metal Horse 雷風恆 9 22 十九	金9 Metal Litigation 8 辛未 Metal Guat 天水訟 3 23 二十	水1 Water Officer 9 壬申 Water Monkey 地水師 7 24 廿一	火2 Fire Gradual Progress 1 癸酉 Water Rooster 風山漸 7 25 廿二	火7 Fire Obstruction 2 甲戌 Wood Dog 水山蹇 2 26 廿三	木3 Wood Advancement 3 乙亥 Wood Pig 火地晉 3 27 廿四
水6 Water Nourish 4 丙子 Fire Rat 山雷頤 3 28 廿五						

MARCH 2038 乙卯

Xuan Kong Element 玄空五行	地澤臨 Arriving	Period Luck 卦運	Monthly Star 月星
Water 水1		4	7

SUNDAY	MONDAY	TUESDAY	WEDNESDAY	THURSDAY	FRIDAY	SATURDAY
	金4 Metal 5 Following 澤雷隨 丁丑 Fire Ox **1** 7 廿六	木8 Wood 6 Abundance 雷火豐 戊寅 Earth Tiger **2** 6 廿七	火7 Fire 7 Regulate 水澤節 己卯 Earth Rabbit **3** 8 廿八	水1 Water 8 Unity 地天泰 庚辰 Metal Dragon **4** 9 廿九	木3 Wood 9 Great Reward 火天大有 辛巳 Metal Snake **5** 7 三十	火2 Fire 1 Wind 巽爲風 壬午 Water Horse **6** 1 二月初一
金4 Metal 2 Trap 澤水困 癸未 Water Goat **7** 8 初二	木3 Wood 3 Not Yet Accomplished 火水未濟 甲申 Wood Monkey **8** 9 初三	金9 Metal 4 Retreat 天山遯 乙酉 Wood Rooster **9** 4 初四	水6 Water 5 Mountain 艮爲山 丙戌 Fire Dog **10** 1 初五	木8 Wood 6 Delight 雷地豫 丁亥 Fire Pig **11** 8 初六	火7 Fire 7 Beginning 水雷屯 戊子 Earth Rat **12** 4 初七	金9 Metal 8 Without Wrongdoing 天雷無妄 己丑 Earth Ox **13** 2 初八
木3 Wood 9 Fire 離爲火 庚寅 Metal Tiger **14** 1 初九	火2 Fire 1 Sincerity 風澤中孚 辛卯 Metal Rabbit **15** 3 初十	水6 Water 2 Big Livestock 山天大畜 壬辰 Water Dragon **16** 4 十一	金4 Metal 3 Eliminating 澤天夬 癸巳 Water Snake **17** 6 十二	金9 Metal 4 Heaven 乾爲天 甲午 Wood Horse **18** 1 十三	火7 Fire 5 Well 水風井 乙未 Wood Goat **19** 6 十四	木8 Wood 6 Relief 雷水解 丙申 Fire Monkey **20** 4 十五
金4 Metal 7 Influence 澤山咸 丁酉 Fire Rooster **21** 9 十六	水1 Water 8 Humility 地山謙 戊戌 Earth Dog **22** 6 十七	火2 Fire 9 Observation 風地觀 己亥 Earth Pig **23** 2 十八	火2 Fire 1 Increasing 風雷益 庚子 Metal Rat **24** 9 十九	水1 Water 2 Dimming Light 地火明夷 辛丑 Metal Ox **25** 3 二十	金9 Metal 3 Fellowship 天火同人 壬寅 Water Tiger **26** 7 廿一	木8 Wood 4 Marrying Maiden 雷澤歸妹 癸卯 Water Rabbit **27** 7 廿二
木3 Wood 5 Opposition 火澤睽 甲辰 Wood Dragon **28** 2 廿三	火7 Fire 6 Waiting 水天需 乙巳 Wood Snake **29** 3 廿四	金4 Metal 7 Great Exceeding 澤風大過 丙午 Fire Horse **30** 3 廿五	水6 Water 8 Poison 山風蠱 丁未 Fire Goat **31** 7 廿六			

APRIL 2038 丙辰

Xuan Kong Element 玄空五行	兌爲澤 Marsh	Period Luck 卦運	Monthly Star 月星
Metal 金4		1	6

SUNDAY	MONDAY	TUESDAY	WEDNESDAY	THURSDAY	FRIDAY	SATURDAY
				火2 Fire 9 Dispersing 風水渙 戊申 Earth Monkey **1** 6 廿七	木3 Wood 1 Travelling 火山旅 己酉 Earth Rooster **2** 8 廿八	金9 Metal 2 Stagnation 天地否 庚戌 Metal Dog **3** 9 廿九
火7 Fire 3 Alliance 水地比 辛亥 Metal Pig **4** 7 三十	木8 Wood 4 Thunder 震爲雷 壬子 Water Rat **5** 1 三月初一	水6 Water 5 Beauty 山火賁 癸丑 Water Ox **6** 8 初二	火7 Fire 6 Accomplished 水火既濟 甲寅 Wood Tiger **7** 9 初三	水1 Water 7 Arriving 地澤臨 乙卯 Wood Rabbit **8** 4 初四	金4 Metal 8 Marsh 兌爲澤 丙辰 Fire Dragon **9** 1 初五	火2 Fire 9 Small Livestock 風天小畜 丁巳 Fire Snake **10** 8 初六
木3 Wood 1 The Cauldron 火風鼎 戊午 Earth Horse **11** 4 初七	水1 Water 2 Rising 地風升 己未 Earth Goat **12** 2 初八	火7 Fire 3 Water 坎爲水 庚申 Metal Monkey **13** 1 初九	木8 Wood 4 Lesser Exceeding 雷山小過 辛酉 Metal Rooster **14** 3 初十	金4 Metal 5 Gathering 澤地萃 壬戌 Water Dog **15** 4 十一	水6 Water 6 Peel 山地剝 癸亥 Water Pig **16** 6 十二	水1 Water 7 Earth 坤爲地 甲子 Wood Rat **17** 1 十三
木3 Wood 8 Biting 火雷噬嗑 乙丑 Wood Ox **18** 6 十四	火2 Fire 9 Family 風火家人 丙寅 Fire Tiger **19** 4 十五	水6 Water 1 Decreasing 山澤損 丁卯 Fire Rabbit **20** 9 十六	金9 Metal 2 Tread 天澤履 戊辰 Earth Dragon **21** 6 十七	木8 Wood 3 Great Strength 雷天大壯 己巳 Earth Snake **22** 2 十八	木8 Wood 4 Consistency 雷風恆 庚午 Metal Horse **23** 9 十九	金9 Metal 5 Litigation 天水訟 辛未 Metal Goat **24** 3 二十
水1 Water 6 Officer 地水師 壬申 Water Monkey **25** 7 廿一	火2 Fire 7 Gradual Progress 風山漸 癸酉 Water Rooster **26** 7 廿二	火7 Fire 8 Obstruction 水山蹇 甲戌 Wood Dog **27** 2 廿三	木3 Wood 9 Advancement 火地晉 乙亥 Wood Pig **28** 3 廿四	水6 Water 1 Nourish 山雷頤 丙子 Fire Rat **29** 3 廿五	金4 Metal 2 Following 澤雷隨 丁丑 Fire Ox **30** 7 廿六	

MAY 2038 丁巳

Xuan Kong Element 玄空五行	風天小畜 Small Livestock	Period Luck 卦運	Monthly Star 月星
Fire 火2		8	5

SUNDAY	MONDAY	TUESDAY	WEDNESDAY	THURSDAY	FRIDAY	SATURDAY
水6 Water · Poison · 5 · 山風蠱 · 丁未 Fire Goat · **30** 廿七 · 7	火2 Fire · Dispersing · 6 · 風水渙 · 戊申 Earth Monkey · **31** 廿八 · 6					木8 Wood · Abundance · 3 · 雷火豐 · 戊寅 Earth Tiger · **1** 廿七 · 6
火7 Fire · Regulate · 4 · 水澤節 · 己卯 Earth Rabbit · **2** 廿八 · 8	水1 Water · Unity · 5 · 地天泰 · 庚辰 Metal Dragon · **3** 廿九 · 9	木3 Wood · Great Reward · 6 · 火天大有 · 辛巳 Metal Snake · **4** 四月初一 · 7	火2 Fire · Wind · 7 · 巽爲風 · 壬午 Water Horse · **5** 初二 · 1	金4 Metal · Trap · 8 · 澤水困 · 癸未 Water Goat · **6** 初三 · 8	木3 Wood · Not Yet Accomplished · 9 · 火水未濟 · 甲申 Wood Monkey · **7** 初四 · 9	金9 Metal · Retreat · 1 · 天山遯 · 乙酉 Wood Rooster · **8** 初五 · 4
水6 Water · Mountain · 2 · 艮爲山 · 丙戌 Fire Dog · **9** 初六 · 1	木8 Wood · Delight · 3 · 雷地豫 · 丁亥 Fire Pig · **10** 初七 · 8	火7 Fire · Beginning · 4 · 水雷屯 · 戊子 Earth Rat · **11** 初八 · 4	金9 Metal · Without Wrongdoing · 5 · 天雷無妄 · 己丑 Earth Ox · **12** 初九 · 2	木3 Wood · Fire · 6 · 離爲火 · 庚寅 Metal Tiger · **13** 初十 · 1	火2 Fire · Sincerity · 7 · 風澤中孚 · 辛卯 Metal Rabbit · **14** 十一 · 3	水6 Water · Big Livestock · 8 · 山天大畜 · 壬辰 Water Dragon · **15** 十二 · 4
金4 Metal · Eliminating · 9 · 澤天夬 · 癸巳 Water Snake · **16** 十三 · 6	金9 Metal · Heaven · 1 · 乾爲天 · 甲午 Wood Horse · **17** 十四 · 1	火7 Fire · Well · 2 · 水風井 · 乙未 Wood Goat · **18** 十五 · 6	木8 Wood · Relief · 3 · 雷水解 · 丙申 Fire Monkey · **19** 十六 · 4	金4 Metal · Influence · 4 · 澤山咸 · 丁酉 Fire Rooster · **20** 十七 · 9	水1 Water · Humility · 5 · 地山謙 · 戊戌 Earth Dog · **21** 十八 · 6	火2 Fire · Observation · 6 · 風地觀 · 己亥 Earth Pig · **22** 十九 · 2
火2 Fire · Increasing · 7 · 風雷益 · 庚子 Metal Rat · **23** 二十 · 9	水1 Water · Dimming Light · 8 · 地火明夷 · 辛丑 Metal Ox · **24** 廿一 · 3	金9 Metal · Fellowship · 9 · 天火同人 · 壬寅 Water Tiger · **25** 廿二 · 7	木8 Wood · Marrying Maiden · 1 · 雷澤歸妹 · 癸卯 Water Rabbit · **26** 廿三 · 7	木3 Wood · Opposition · 2 · 火澤睽 · 甲辰 Wood Dragon · **27** 廿四 · 2	火7 Fire · Waiting · 3 · 水天需 · 乙巳 Wood Snake · **28** 廿五 · 3	金4 Metal · Great Exceeding · 4 · 澤風大過 · 丙午 Fire Horse · **29** 廿六 · 3

JUNE 2038 戊午

Xuan Kong Element 玄空五行	火風鼎 The Cauldron	Period Luck 卦運	Monthly Star 月星
Wood 木3		4	4

SUNDAY	MONDAY	TUESDAY	WEDNESDAY	THURSDAY	FRIDAY	SATURDAY
		木3 Wood · Travelling · 7 · 火山旅 · 己酉 Earth Rooster · **1** 廿九 · 8	金9 Metal · Stagnation · 8 · 天地否 · 庚戌 Metal Dog · **2** 三十 · 9	火7 Fire · Alliance · 9 · 水地比 · 辛亥 Metal Pig · **3** 五月初一 · 7	木8 Wood · Thunder · 1 · 震爲雷 · 壬子 Water Rat · **4** 初二 · 1	水6 Water · Beauty · 2 · 山火賁 · 癸丑 Water Ox · **5** 初三 · 8
火7 Fire · Accomplished · 3 · 水火既濟 · 甲寅 Wood Tiger · **6** 初四 · 9	水1 Water · Arriving · 4 · 地澤臨 · 乙卯 Wood Rabbit · **7** 初五 · 4	金4 Metal · Marsh · 5 · 兌爲澤 · 丙辰 Fire Dragon · **8** 初六 · 1	火2 Fire · Small Livestock · 6 · 風天小畜 · 丁巳 Fire Snake · **9** 初七 · 8	木3 Wood · The Cauldron · 7 · 火風鼎 · 戊午 Earth Horse · **10** 初八 · 4	水1 Water · Rising · 8 · 地風升 · 己未 Earth Goat · **11** 初九 · 2	火7 Fire · Water · 9 · 坎爲水 · 庚申 Metal Monkey · **12** 初十 · 1
木8 Wood · Lesser Exceeding · 1 · 雷山小過 · 辛酉 Metal Rooster · **13** 十一 · 3	金4 Metal · Gathering · 2 · 澤地萃 · 壬戌 Water Dog · **14** 十二 · 4	水6 Water · Peel · 3 · 山地剝 · 癸亥 Water Pig · **15** 十三 · 6	水1 Water · Earth · 4 · 坤爲地 · 甲子 Wood Rat · **16** 十四 · 1	木3 Wood · Biting · 5 · 火雷噬嗑 · 乙丑 Wood Ox · **17** 十五 · 6	火2 Fire · Family · 6 · 風火家人 · 丙寅 Fire Tiger · **18** 十六 · 4	水6 Water · Decreasing · 7 · 山澤損 · 丁卯 Fire Rabbit · **19** 十七 · 9
金9 Metal · Tread · 8 · 天澤履 · 戊辰 Earth Dragon · **20** 十八 · 6	木8 Wood · Great Strength · 9/1 · 雷天大壯 · 己巳 Earth Snake · **21** 十九 · 2	木8 Wood · Consistency · 9 · 雷風恆 · 庚午 Metal Horse · **22** 二十 · 9	金9 Metal · Litigation · 8 · 天水訟 · 辛未 Metal Goat · **23** 廿一 · 3	水1 Water · Officer · 7 · 地水師 · 壬申 Water Monkey · **24** 廿二 · 7	火2 Fire · Gradual Progress · 6 · 風山漸 · 癸酉 Water Rooster · **25** 廿三 · 7	火7 Fire · Obstruction · 5 · 水山蹇 · 甲戌 Wood Dog · **26** 廿四 · 2
木3 Wood · Advancement · 4 · 火地晉 · 乙亥 Wood Pig · **27** 廿五 · 3	水6 Water · Nourish · 3 · 山雷頤 · 丙子 Fire Rat · **28** 廿六 · 3	金4 Metal · Following · 2 · 澤雷隨 · 丁丑 Fire Ox · **29** 廿七 · 7	木8 Wood · Abundance · 1 · 雷火豐 · 戊寅 Earth Tiger · **30** 廿八 · 6			

JULY 2038 己未

Xuan Kong Element 玄空五行	地風升 Rising	Period Luck 卦運	Monthly Star 月星
Water 水1		2	3

SUNDAY	MONDAY	TUESDAY	WEDNESDAY	THURSDAY	FRIDAY	SATURDAY
				火7 Fire 9 Regulate 己卯 Earth Rabbit 水澤節 1 廿九 8	水1 Water 8 Unity 庚辰 Metal Dragon 地天泰 2 六月初一 9	木3 Wood 7 Great Reward 辛巳 Metal Snake 火天大有 3 初二 7
火2 Fire 6 Wind 壬午 Water Horse 巽爲風 4 初三 1	金4 Metal 5 Trap 癸未 Water Goat 澤水困 5 初四 8	木3 Wood 4 Not Yet Accomplished 甲申 Wood Monkey 火水未濟 6 初五 9	金9 Metal 3 Retreat 乙酉 Wood Rooster 天山遯 7 初六 4	水6 Water 2 Mountain 丙戌 Fire Dog 艮爲山 8 初七 1	木8 Wood 1 Delight 丁亥 Fire Pig 雷地豫 9 初八 8	火7 Fire 9 Beginning 戊子 Earth Rat 水雷屯 10 初九 4
金9 Metal 8 Without Wrongdoing 己丑 Earth Ox 天雷無妄 11 初十 2	木3 Wood 7 Fire 庚寅 Metal Tiger 離爲火 12 十一 1	火2 Fire 6 Sincerity 辛卯 Metal Rabbit 風澤中孚 13 十二 3	水6 Water 5 Big Livestock 壬辰 Water Dragon 山天大畜 14 十三 4	金4 Metal 4 Eliminating 癸巳 Water Snake 澤天夬 15 十四 6	金9 Metal 3 Heaven 甲午 Wood Horse 乾爲天 16 十五 1	火7 Fire 2 Well 乙未 Wood Goat 水風井 17 十六 6
木8 Wood 1 Relief 丙申 Fire Monkey 雷水解 18 十七 4	金4 Metal 9 Influence 丁酉 Fire Rooster 澤山咸 19 十八 9	水1 Water 8 Humility 戊戌 Earth Dog 地山謙 20 十九 6	火2 Fire 7 Observation 己亥 Earth Pig 風地觀 21 二十 2	火2 Fire 6 Increasing 庚子 Metal Rat 風雷益 22 廿一 9	水1 Water 5 Dimming Light 辛丑 Metal Ox 地火明夷 23 廿二 3	金9 Metal 4 Fellowship 壬寅 Water Tiger 天火同人 24 廿三 7
木8 Wood 3 Marrying Maiden 癸卯 Water Rabbit 雷澤歸妹 25 廿四 7	木3 Wood 2 Opposition 甲辰 Wood Dragon 火澤睽 26 廿五 2	火7 Fire 1 Waiting 乙巳 Wood Snake 水天需 27 廿六 3	金4 Metal 9 Great Exceeding 丙午 Fire Horse 澤風大過 28 廿七 3	水6 Water 8 Poison 丁未 Fire Goat 山風蠱 29 廿八 7	火2 Fire 7 Dispersing 戊申 Earth Monkey 風水渙 30 廿九 6	木3 Wood 6 Travelling 己酉 Earth Rooster 火山旅 31 三十 8

AUGUST 2038 庚申

Xuan Kong Element 玄空五行	坎爲水 Water	Period Luck 卦運	Monthly Star 月星
Fire 火7		1	2

SUNDAY	MONDAY	TUESDAY	WEDNESDAY	THURSDAY	FRIDAY	SATURDAY
金9 Metal 5 Stagnation 庚戌 Metal Dog 天地否 1 七月初一 9	火7 Fire 4 Alliance 辛亥 Metal Pig 水地比 2 初二 7	木8 Wood 3 Thunder 壬子 Water Rat 震爲雷 3 初三 1	水6 Water 2 Beauty 癸丑 Water Ox 山火賁 4 初四 8	火7 Fire 1 Accomplished 甲寅 Wood Tiger 水火既濟 5 初五 9	水1 Water 9 Arriving 乙卯 Wood Rabbit 地澤臨 6 初六 4	金4 Metal 8 Marsh 丙辰 Fire Dragon 兑爲澤 7 初七 1
火2 Fire 7 Small Livestock 丁巳 Fire Snake 風天小畜 8 初八 8	木3 Wood 6 The Cauldron 戊午 Earth Horse 火風鼎 9 初九 4	水1 Water 5 Rising 己未 Earth Goat 地風升 10 初十 2	火7 Fire 4 Water 庚申 Metal Monkey 坎爲水 11 十一 1	木8 Wood 3 Lesser Exceeding 辛酉 Metal Rooster 雷山小過 12 十二 3	金4 Metal 2 Gathering 壬戌 Water Dog 澤地萃 13 十三 4	水6 Water 1 Peel 癸亥 Water Pig 山地剝 14 十四 6
水1 Water 9 Earth 甲子 Wood Rat 坤爲地 15 十五 1	木3 Wood 8 Biting 乙丑 Wood Ox 火雷噬嗑 16 十六 6	火2 Fire 7 Family 丙寅 Fire Tiger 風火家人 17 十七 4	水6 Water 6 Decreasing 丁卯 Fire Rabbit 山澤損 18 十八 9	金9 Metal 5 Tread 戊辰 Earth Dragon 天澤履 19 十九 6	木8 Wood 4 Great Strength 己巳 Earth Snake 雷天大壯 20 二十 2	木8 Wood 3 Consistency 庚午 Metal Horse 雷風恒 21 廿一 9
金9 Metal 2 Litigation 辛未 Metal Goat 天水訟 22 廿二 3	水1 Water 1 Officer 壬申 Water Monkey 地水師 23 廿三 7	火2 Fire 9 Gradual Progress 癸酉 Water Rooster 風山漸 24 廿四 7	火7 Fire 8 Obstruction 甲戌 Wood Dog 水山蹇 25 廿五 2	木3 Wood 7 Advancement 乙亥 Wood Pig 火地晉 26 廿六 3	水6 Water 6 Nourish 丙子 Fire Rat 山雷頤 27 廿七 3	金4 Metal 5 Following 丁丑 Fire Ox 澤雷隨 28 廿八 7
木8 Wood 4 Abundance 戊寅 Earth Tiger 雷火豐 29 廿九 6	火7 Fire 3 Regulate 己卯 Earth Rabbit 水澤節 30 八月初一 8	水1 Water 2 Unity 庚辰 Metal Dragon 地天泰 31 初二 9				

SEPTEMBER 2038 辛酉

Xuan Kong Element 玄空五行	雷山小過 Lesser Exceeding	Period Luck 卦運	Monthly Star 月星
Wood 木8		3	1

SUNDAY	MONDAY	TUESDAY	WEDNESDAY	THURSDAY	FRIDAY	SATURDAY
			木3 Wood 1 Great Reward 火天大有 辛巳 Metal Snake 1 初三 7	火2 Fire 9 Wind 巽爲風 壬午 Water Horse 2 初四 1	金4 Metal 8 Trap 澤水困 癸未 Water Goat 3 初五 8	木3 Wood 7 Not Yet Accomplished 火水未濟 甲申 Wood Monkey 4 初六 9
金9 Metal 6 Retreat 天山遯 乙酉 Wood Rooster 5 初七 4	水6 Water 5 Mountain 艮爲山 丙戌 Fire Dog 6 初八 1	木8 Wood 4 Delight 雷地豫 丁亥 Fire Pig 7 初九 8	火7 Fire 3 Beginning 水雷屯 戊子 Earth Rat 8 初十 4	金9 Metal 2 Without Wrongdoing 天雷無妄 己丑 Earth Ox 9 十一 2	木3 Wood 1 Fire 離爲火 庚寅 Metal Tiger 10 十二 1	火2 Fire 9 Sincerity 風澤中孚 辛卯 Metal Rabbit 11 十三 3
水6 Water 8 Big Livestock 山天大畜 壬辰 Water Dragon 12 十四 4	金4 Metal 7 Eliminating 澤天夬 癸巳 Water Snake 13 十五 6	金9 Metal 6 Heaven 乾爲天 甲午 Wood Horse 14 十六 1	火7 Fire 5 Well 水風井 乙未 Wood Goat 15 十七 6	木8 Wood 4 Relief 雷水解 丙申 Fire Monkey 16 十八 4	金4 Metal 3 Influence 澤山咸 丁酉 Fire Rooster 17 十九 9	水1 Water 2 Humility 地山謙 戊戌 Earth Dog 18 二十 6
火2 Fire 1 Observation 風地觀 己亥 Earth Pig 19 廿一 2	火2 Fire 9 Increasing 風雷益 庚子 Metal Rat 20 廿二 9	水1 Water 8 Dimming Light 地火明夷 辛丑 Metal Ox 21 廿三 3	金9 Metal 7 Fellowship 天火同人 壬寅 Water Tiger 22 廿四 7	木8 Wood 6 Marrying Maiden 雷澤歸妹 癸卯 Water Rabbit 23 廿五 7	木3 Wood 5 Opposition 火澤睽 甲辰 Wood Dragon 24 廿六 2	火7 Fire 4 Waiting 水天需 乙巳 Wood Snake 25 廿七 3
金4 Metal 3 Great Exceeding 澤風大過 丙午 Fire Horse 26 廿八 3	水6 Water 2 Poison 山風蠱 丁未 Fire Goat 27 廿九 7	火2 Fire 1 Dispersing 風水渙 戊申 Earth Monkey 28 三十 6	木3 Wood 9 Travelling 火山旅 己酉 Earth Rooster 29 九月初一 8	金9 Metal 8 Stagnation 天地否 庚戌 Metal Dog 30 初二 9		

OCTOBER 2038 壬戌

Xuan Kong Element 玄空五行	澤地萃 Gathering	Period Luck 卦運	Monthly Star 月星
Metal 金4		4	9

SUNDAY	MONDAY	TUESDAY	WEDNESDAY	THURSDAY	FRIDAY	SATURDAY
木3 Wood 4 Great Reward 火天大有 辛巳 Metal Snake 31 初四 7					火7 Fire 7 Alliance 水地比 辛亥 Metal Pig 1 初三 7	木8 Wood 6 Thunder 震爲雷 壬子 Water Rat 2 初四 1
水6 Water 5 Beauty 山火賁 癸丑 Water Ox 3 初五 8	火7 Fire 4 Accomplished 水火既濟 甲寅 Wood Tiger 4 初六 9	水1 Water 3 Arriving 地澤臨 乙卯 Wood Rabbit 5 初七 4	金4 Metal 2 Marsh 兌爲澤 丙辰 Fire Dragon 6 初八 1	火2 Fire 1 Small Livestock 風天小畜 丁巳 Fire Snake 7 初九 8	木3 Wood 9 The Cauldron 火風鼎 戊午 Earth Horse 8 初十 4	水1 Water 8 Rising 地風升 己未 Earth Goat 9 十一 2
火7 Fire 7 Water 坎爲水 庚申 Metal Monkey 10 十二 1	木8 Wood 6 Lesser Exceeding 雷山小過 辛酉 Metal Rooster 11 十三 3	金4 Metal 5 Gathering 澤地萃 壬戌 Water Dog 12 十四 4	水6 Water 4 Peel 山地剝 癸亥 Water Pig 13 十五 6	水1 Water 3 Earth 坤爲地 甲子 Wood Rat 14 十六 1	木3 Wood 2 Biting 火雷噬嗑 乙丑 Wood Ox 15 十七 6	火2 Fire 1 Family 風火家人 丙寅 Fire Tiger 16 十八 4
水6 Water 9 Decreasing 山澤損 丁卯 Fire Rabbit 17 十九 9	金9 Metal 8 Tread 天澤履 戊辰 Earth Dragon 18 二十 6	木8 Wood 7 Great Strength 雷天大壯 己巳 Earth Snake 19 廿一 2	木8 Wood 6 Consistency 雷風恆 庚午 Metal Horse 20 廿二 9	金9 Metal 5 Litigation 天水訟 辛未 Metal Goat 21 廿三 3	水1 Water 4 Officer 地水師 壬申 Water Monkey 22 廿四 7	火2 Fire 3 Gradual Progress 風山漸 癸酉 Water Rooster 23 廿五 7
火7 Fire 2 Obstruction 水山蹇 甲戌 Wood Dog 24 廿六 2	木3 Wood 1 Advancement 火地晉 乙亥 Wood Pig 25 廿七 3	水6 Water 9 Nourish 山雷頤 丙子 Fire Rat 26 廿八 3	金4 Metal 8 Following 澤雷隨 丁丑 Fire Ox 27 廿九 7	木8 Wood 7 Abundance 雷火豐 戊寅 Earth Tiger 28 十月初一 6	火7 Fire 6 Regulate 水澤節 己卯 Earth Rabbit 29 初二 8	水1 Water 5 Unity 地天泰 庚辰 Metal Dragon 30 初三 9

NOVEMBER 2038 癸亥

Xuan Kong Element 玄空五行	山地剝 Peel	Period Luck 卦運	Monthly Star 月星
Water 水6		6	8

SUNDAY	MONDAY	TUESDAY	WEDNESDAY	THURSDAY	FRIDAY	SATURDAY
	火2 Fire 3 Wind 壬午 Water Horse 巽爲風 1 1 初五	金4 Metal 2 Trap 癸未 Water Goat 澤水困 2 8 初六	木3 Wood 1 Not Yet Accomplished 甲申 Wood Monkey 火水未濟 3 9 初七	金9 Metal 9 Retreat 乙酉 Wood Rooster 天山遯 4 4 初八	水6 Water 8 Mountain 丙戌 Fire Dog 艮爲山 5 1 初九	木8 Wood 7 Delight 丁亥 Fire Pig 雷地豫 6 8 初十
火7 Fire 6 Beginning 戊子 Earth Rat 水雷屯 7 4 十一	金9 Metal 5 Without Wrongdoing 己丑 Earth Ox 天雷無妄 8 2 十二	木3 Wood 4 Fire 庚寅 Metal Tiger 離爲火 9 1 十三	火2 Fire 3 Sincerity 辛卯 Metal Rabbit 風澤中孚 10 3 十四	水6 Water 2 Big Livestock 壬辰 Water Dragon 山天大畜 11 4 十五	金4 Metal 1 Eliminating 癸巳 Water Snake 澤天夬 12 6 十六	金9 Metal 9 Heaven 甲午 Wood Horse 乾爲天 13 1 十七
火7 Fire 8 Well 乙未 Wood Goat 水風井 14 6 十八	木8 Wood 7 Relief 丙申 Fire Monkey 雷水解 15 4 十九	金4 Metal 6 Influence 丁酉 Fire Rooster 澤山咸 16 9 二十	水1 Water 5 Humility 戊戌 Earth Dog 地山謙 17 6 廿一	火2 Fire 4 Observation 己亥 Earth Pig 風地觀 18 2 廿二	火2 Fire 3 Increasing 庚子 Metal Rat 風雷益 19 9 廿三	水1 Water 2 Dimming Light 辛丑 Metal Ox 地火明夷 20 3 廿四
金9 Metal 1 Fellowship 壬寅 Water Tiger 天火同人 21 7 廿五	木8 Wood 9 Marrying Maiden 癸卯 Water Rabbit 雷澤歸妹 22 7 廿六	木3 Wood 8 Opposition 甲辰 Wood Dragon 火澤睽 23 2 廿七	火7 Fire 7 Waiting 乙巳 Wood Snake 水天需 24 3 廿八	金4 Metal 6 Great Exceeding 丙午 Fire Horse 澤風大過 25 3 廿九	水6 Water 5 Poison 丁未 Fire Goat 山風蠱 26 7 十一月初一	火2 Fire 4 Dispersing 戊申 Earth Monkey 風水渙 27 6 初二
木3 Wood 3 Travelling 己酉 Earth Rooster 火山旅 28 8 初三	金9 Metal 2 Stagnation 庚戌 Metal Dog 天地否 29 9 初四	火7 Fire 1 Alliance 辛亥 Metal Pig 水地比 30 7				

DECEMBER 2038 甲子

Xuan Kong Element 玄空五行	坤爲地 Earth	Period Luck 卦運	Monthly Star 月星
Water 水1		1	7

SUNDAY	MONDAY	TUESDAY	WEDNESDAY	THURSDAY	FRIDAY	SATURDAY
		初五	木8 Wood 9 Thunder 壬子 Water Rat 震爲雷 1 1 初六	水6 Water 8 Beauty 癸丑 Water Ox 山火賁 2 8 初七	火7 Fire 7 Accomplished 甲寅 Wood Tiger 水火既濟 3 9 初八	水1 Water 6 Arriving 乙卯 Wood Rabbit 地澤臨 4 4 初九
金4 Metal 5 Marsh 丙辰 Fire Dragon 兌爲澤 5 1 初十	火2 Fire 4 Small Livestock 丁巳 Fire Snake 風天小畜 6 8 十一	木3 Wood 3 The Cauldron 戊午 Earth Horse 火風鼎 7 4 十二	水1 Water 2 Rising 己未 Earth Goat 地風升 8 2 十三	火7 Fire 1 Water 庚申 Metal Monkey 坎爲水 9 1 十四	木8 Wood 9 Lesser Exceeding 辛酉 Metal Rooster 雷山小過 10 3 十五	金4 Metal 8 Gathering 壬戌 Water Dog 澤地萃 11 4 十六
水6 Water 7 Peel 癸亥 Water Pig 山地剝 12 6 十七	水1 Water 6 Earth 甲子 Wood Rat 坤爲地 13 1 十八	木3 Wood 5 Biting 乙丑 Wood Ox 火雷噬嗑 14 6 十九	火2 Fire 4 Family 丙寅 Fire Tiger 風火家人 15 4 二十	水6 Water 3 Decreasing 丁卯 Fire Rabbit 山澤損 16 9 廿一	金9 Metal 2 Tread 戊辰 Earth Dragon 天澤履 17 6 廿二	木8 Wood 1 Great Strength 己巳 Earth Snake 雷天大壯 18 2 廿三
木8 Wood 9 Consistency 庚午 Metal Horse 雷風恆 19 9 廿四	金9 Metal 8 Litigation 辛未 Metal Goat 天水訟 20 3 廿五	水1 Water 7 Officer 壬申 Water Monkey 地水師 21 7 廿六	火2 Fire 6/4 Gradual Progress 癸酉 Water Rooster 風山漸 22 7 廿七	火7 Fire 5 Obstruction 甲戌 Wood Dog 水山蹇 23 2 廿八	木3 Wood 6 Advancement 乙亥 Wood Pig 火地晉 24 3 廿九	水6 Water 7 Nourish 丙子 Fire Rat 山雷頤 25 3 三十
金4 Metal 8 Following 丁丑 Fire Ox 澤雷隨 26 7 十二月初一	木8 Wood 9 Abundance 戊寅 Earth Tiger 雷火豐 27 6 初二	火7 Fire 1 Regulate 己卯 Earth Rabbit 水澤節 28 8 初三	水1 Water 2 Unity 庚辰 Metal Dragon 地天泰 29 9 初四	木3 Wood 3 Great Reward 辛巳 Metal Snake 火天大有 30 7 初五	火2 Fire 4 Wind 壬午 Water Horse 巽爲風 31 1 初六	

2039 己未

(*Ji Wei*) Earth Goat

2039 己未 *(Ji Wei)* Earth Goat

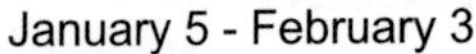

January 5 - February 3

February 4 - March 5

March 6 - April 4

April 5 - May 4

May 5 - June 5

June 6 - July 6

July 7 - August 6

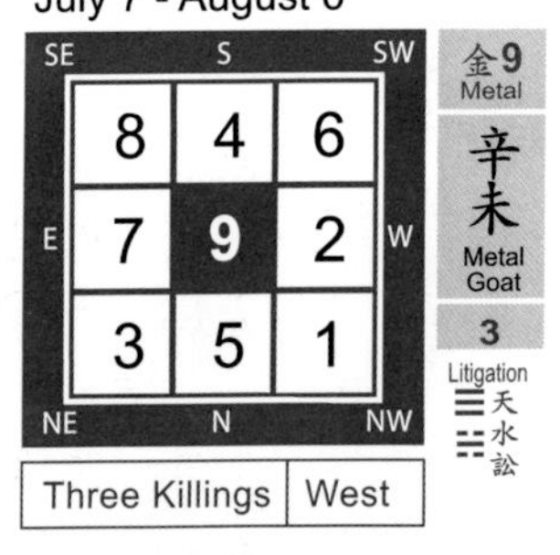

August 7 - September 7

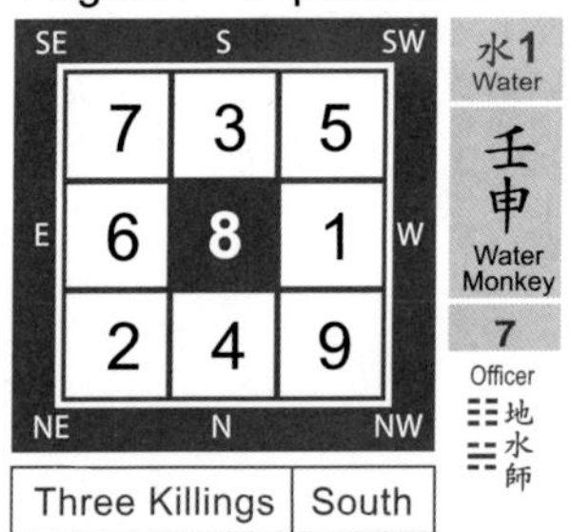

September 8 - October 7

October 8 - November 6

November 7 - December 6

December 7 - January 5

JANUARY 2039 乙丑

Xuan Kong Element 玄空五行	火雷噬嗑 Biting	Period Luck 卦運	Monthly Star 月星
Wood 木3		6	6

SUNDAY	MONDAY	TUESDAY	WEDNESDAY	THURSDAY	FRIDAY	SATURDAY
木8 Wood 7 Thunder 震爲雷 壬子 Water Rat 30 初七 1	水6 Water 8 Beauty 山火賁 癸丑 Water Ox 31 初八 8					金4 Metal 5 Trap 澤水困 癸未 Water Goat 1 初七 8
木3 Wood 6 Not Yet Accomplished 火水未濟 甲申 Wood Monkey 2 初八 9	金9 Metal 7 Retreat 天山遯 乙酉 Wood Rooster 3 初九 4	水6 Water 8 Mountain 艮爲山 丙戌 Fire Dog 4 初十 1	木8 Wood 9 Delight 雷地豫 丁亥 Fire Pig 5 十一 8	火7 Fire 1 Beginning 水雷屯 戊子 Earth Rat 6 十二 4	金9 Metal 2 Without Wrongdoing 天雷無妄 己丑 Earth Ox 7 十三 2	木3 Wood 3 Fire 離爲火 庚寅 Metal Tiger 8 十四 1
火2 Fire 4 Sincerity 風澤中孚 辛卯 Metal Rabbit 9 十五 3	水6 Water 5 Big Livestock 山天大畜 壬辰 Water Dragon 10 十六 4	金4 Metal 6 Eliminating 澤天夬 癸巳 Water Snake 11 十七 6	金9 Metal 7 Heaven 乾爲天 甲午 Wood Horse 12 十八 1	火7 Fire 8 Well 水風井 乙未 Wood Goat 13 十九 6	木8 Wood 9 Relief 雷水解 丙申 Fire Monkey 14 二十 4	金4 Metal 1 Influence 澤山咸 丁酉 Fire Rooster 15 廿一 9
水1 Water 2 Humility 地山謙 戊戌 Earth Dog 16 廿二 6	火2 Fire 3 Observation 風地觀 己亥 Earth Pig 17 廿三 2	火2 Fire 4 Increasing 風雷益 庚子 Metal Rat 18 廿四 9	水1 Water 5 Dimming Light 地火明夷 辛丑 Metal Ox 19 廿五 3	金9 Metal 6 Fellowship 天火同人 壬寅 Water Tiger 20 廿六 7	木8 Wood 7 Marrying Maiden 雷澤歸妹 癸卯 Water Rabbit 21 廿七 7	木3 Wood 8 Opposition 火澤睽 甲辰 Wood Dragon 22 廿八 2
火7 Fire 9 Waiting 水天需 乙巳 Wood Snake 23 廿九 3	金4 Metal 1 Great Exceeding 澤風大過 丙午 Fire Horse 24 正月初一 3	水6 Water 2 Poison 山風蠱 丁未 Fire Goat 25 初二 7	火2 Fire 3 Dispersing 風水渙 戊申 Earth Monkey 26 初三 6	木3 Wood 4 Travelling 火山旅 己酉 Earth Rooster 27 初四 8	金9 Metal 5 Stagnation 天地否 庚戌 Metal Dog 28 初五 9	火7 Fire 6 Alliance 水地比 辛亥 Metal Pig 29 初六 7

FEBRUARY 2039 丙寅

Xuan Kong Element 玄空五行	風火家人 Family	Period Luck 卦運	Monthly Star 月星
Fire 火2		4	5

SUNDAY	MONDAY	TUESDAY	WEDNESDAY	THURSDAY	FRIDAY	SATURDAY
		火7 Fire 9 Accomplished 水火既濟 甲寅 Wood Tiger 1 初九 9	水1 Water 1 Arriving 地澤臨 乙卯 Wood Rabbit 2 初十 4	金4 Metal 2 Marsh 兌爲澤 丙辰 Fire Dragon 3 十一 1	火2 Fire 3 Small Livestock 風天小畜 丁巳 Fire Snake 4 十二 8	木3 Wood 4 The Cauldron 火風鼎 戊午 Earth Horse 5 十三 4
水1 Water 5 Rising 地風升 己未 Earth Goat 6 十四 2	火7 Fire 6 Water 坎爲水 庚申 Metal Monkey 7 十五 1	木8 Wood 7 Lesser Exceeding 雷山小過 辛酉 Metal Rooster 8 十六 3	金4 Metal 8 Gathering 澤地萃 壬戌 Water Dog 9 十七 4	水6 Water 9 Peel 山地剝 癸亥 Water Pig 10 十八 6	水1 Water 1 Earth 坤爲地 甲子 Wood Rat 11 十九 1	木3 Wood 2 Biting 火雷噬嗑 乙丑 Wood Ox 12 二十 6
火2 Fire 3 Family 風火家人 丙寅 Fire Tiger 13 廿一 4	水6 Water 4 Decreasing 山澤損 丁卯 Fire Rabbit 14 廿二 9	金9 Metal 5 Tread 天澤履 戊辰 Earth Dragon 15 廿三 6	木8 Wood 6 Great Strength 雷天大壯 己巳 Earth Snake 16 廿四 2	木8 Wood 7 Consistency 雷風恆 庚午 Metal Horse 17 廿五 9	金9 Metal 8 Litigation 天水訟 辛未 Metal Goat 18 廿六 3	水1 Water 9 Officer 地水師 壬申 Water Monkey 19 廿七 7
火2 Fire 1 Gradual Progress 風山漸 癸酉 Water Rooster 20 廿八 7	火7 Fire 2 Obstruction 水山蹇 甲戌 Wood Dog 21 廿九 2	木3 Wood 3 Advancement 火地晉 乙亥 Wood Pig 22 三十 3	水6 Water 4 Nourish 山雷頤 丙子 Fire Rat 23 二月初一 3	金4 Metal 5 Following 澤雷隨 丁丑 Fire Ox 24 初二 7	木8 Wood 6 Abundance 雷火豐 戊寅 Earth Tiger 25 初三 6	火7 Fire 7 Regulate 水澤節 己卯 Earth Rabbit 26 初四 8
水1 Water 8 Unity 地天泰 庚辰 Metal Dragon 27 初五 9	木3 Wood 9 Great Reward 火天大有 辛巳 Metal Snake 28 初六 7					

MARCH 2039 丁卯

Xuan Kong Element 玄空五行	山澤損 Decreasing	Period Luck 卦運	Monthly Star 月星
Water 水6		9	4

SUNDAY	MONDAY	TUESDAY	WEDNESDAY	THURSDAY	FRIDAY	SATURDAY
		1 初七 火2 Fire 1 Wind 巽爲風 壬午 Water Horse 1	2 初八 金4 Metal 2 Trap 澤水困 癸未 Water Goat 8	3 初九 木3 Wood 3 Not Yet Accomplished 火水未濟 甲申 Wood Monkey 9	4 初十 金9 Metal 4 Retreat 天山遯 乙酉 Wood Rooster 4	5 十一 水6 Water 5 Mountain 艮爲山 丙戌 Fire Dog 1
6 十二 木8 Wood 6 Delight 雷地豫 丁亥 Fire Pig 8	7 十三 火7 Fire 7 Beginning 水雷屯 戊子 Earth Rat 4	8 十四 金9 Metal 8 Without Wrongdoing 天雷無妄 己丑 Earth Ox 2	9 十五 木3 Wood 9 Fire 離爲火 庚寅 Metal Tiger 1	10 十六 火2 Fire 1 Sincerity 風澤中孚 辛卯 Metal Rabbit 3	11 十七 水6 Water 2 Big Livestock 山天大畜 壬辰 Water Dragon 4	12 十八 金4 Metal 3 Eliminating 澤天夬 癸巳 Water Snake 6
13 十九 金9 Metal 4 Heaven 乾爲天 甲午 Wood Horse 1	14 二十 火7 Fire 5 Well 水風井 乙未 Wood Goat 6	15 廿一 木8 Wood 6 Relief 雷水解 丙申 Fire Monkey 4	16 廿二 金4 Metal 7 Influence 澤山咸 丁酉 Fire Rooster 9	17 廿三 水1 Water 8 Humility 地山謙 戊戌 Earth Dog 6	18 廿四 火2 Fire 9 Observation 風地觀 己亥 Earth Pig 2	19 廿五 火2 Fire 1 Increasing 風雷益 庚子 Metal Rat 9
20 廿六 水1 Water 2 Dimming Light 地火明夷 辛丑 Metal Ox 3	21 廿七 金9 Metal 3 Fellowship 天火同人 壬寅 Water Tiger 7	22 廿八 木8 Wood 4 Marrying Maiden 雷澤歸妹 癸卯 Water Rabbit 7	23 廿九 木3 Wood 5 Opposition 火澤睽 甲辰 Wood Dragon 2	24 三十 火7 Fire 6 Waiting 水天需 乙巳 Wood Snake 3	25 三月初一 金4 Metal 7 Great Exceeding 澤風大過 丙午 Fire Horse 3	26 初二 水6 Water 8 Poison 山風蠱 丁未 Fire Goat 7
27 初三 火2 Fire 9 Dispersing 風水渙 戊申 Earth Monkey 6	28 初四 木3 Wood 1 Travelling 火山旅 己酉 Earth Rooster 8	29 初五 金9 Metal 2 Stagnation 天地否 庚戌 Metal Dog 9	30 初六 火7 Fire 3 Alliance 水地比 辛亥 Metal Pig 7	31 初七 木8 Wood 4 Thunder 震爲雷 壬子 Water Rat 1		

APRIL 2039 戊辰

Xuan Kong Element 玄空五行	天澤履 Tread	Period Luck 卦運	Monthly Star 月星
Metal 金9		6	3

SUNDAY	MONDAY	TUESDAY	WEDNESDAY	THURSDAY	FRIDAY	SATURDAY
					1 初八 水6 Water 5 Beauty 山火賁 癸丑 Water Ox 8	2 初九 火7 Fire 6 Accomplished 水火既濟 甲寅 Wood Tiger 9
3 初十 水1 Water 7 Arriving 地澤臨 乙卯 Wood Rabbit 4	4 十一 金4 Metal 8 Marsh 兌爲澤 丙辰 Fire Dragon 1	5 十二 火2 Fire 9 Small Livestock 風天小畜 丁巳 Fire Snake 8	6 十三 木3 Wood 1 The Cauldron 火風鼎 戊午 Earth Horse 4	7 十四 水1 Water 2 Rising 地風升 己未 Earth Goat 2	8 十五 火7 Fire 3 Water 坎爲水 庚申 Metal Monkey 1	9 十六 木8 Wood 4 Lesser Exceeding 雷山小過 辛酉 Metal Rooster 3
10 十七 金4 Metal 5 Gathering 澤地萃 壬戌 Water Dog 4	11 十八 水6 Water 6 Peel 山地剝 癸亥 Water Pig 6	12 十九 水1 Water 7 Earth 坤爲地 甲子 Wood Rat 1	13 二十 木3 Wood 8 Biting 火雷噬嗑 乙丑 Wood Ox 6	14 廿一 火2 Fire 9 Family 風火家人 丙寅 Fire Tiger 4	15 廿二 水6 Water 1 Decreasing 山澤損 丁卯 Fire Rabbit 9	16 廿三 金9 Metal 2 Tread 天澤履 戊辰 Earth Dragon 6
17 廿四 木8 Wood 3 Great Strength 雷天大壯 己巳 Earth Snake 2	18 廿五 木8 Wood 4 Consistency 雷風恒 庚午 Metal Horse 9	19 廿六 金9 Metal 5 Litigation 天水訟 辛未 Metal Goat 3	20 廿七 水1 Water 6 Officer 地水師 壬申 Water Monkey 7	21 廿八 火2 Fire 7 Gradual Progress 風山漸 癸酉 Water Rooster 7	22 廿九 火7 Fire 8 Obstruction 水山蹇 甲戌 Wood Dog 2	23 四月初一 木3 Wood 9 Advancement 火地晉 乙亥 Wood Pig 3
24 初二 水6 Water 1 Nourish 山雷頤 丙子 Fire Rat 3	25 初三 金4 Metal 2 Following 澤雷隨 丁丑 Fire Ox 7	26 初四 木8 Wood 3 Abundance 雷火豐 戊寅 Earth Tiger 6	27 初五 火7 Fire 4 Regulate 水澤節 己卯 Earth Rabbit 8	28 初六 水1 Water 5 Unity 地天泰 庚辰 Metal Dragon 9	29 初七 木3 Wood 6 Great Reward 火天大有 辛巳 Metal Snake 7	30 初八 火2 Fire 7 Wind 巽爲風 壬午 Water Horse 1

MAY 2039 己巳

Xuan Kong Element 玄空五行	雷天大壯 Great Strength	Period Luck 卦運	Monthly Star 月星
Wood 木8		2	2

SUNDAY	MONDAY	TUESDAY	WEDNESDAY	THURSDAY	FRIDAY	SATURDAY
金4 Metal [8] Trap 澤水困 癸未 Water Goat 8 1 初九	木3 Wood [9] Not Yet Accomplished 火水未濟 甲申 Wood Monkey 9 2 初十	金9 Metal [1] Retreat 天山遯 乙酉 Wood Rooster 4 3 十一	水6 Water [2] Mountain 艮爲山 丙戌 Fire Dog 1 4 十二	木8 Wood [3] Delight 雷地豫 丁亥 Fire Pig 8 5 十三	火7 Fire [4] Beginning 水雷屯 戊子 Earth Rat 4 6 十四	金9 Metal [5] Without Wrongdoing 天雷無妄 己丑 Earth Ox 2 7 十五
木3 Wood [6] Fire 離爲火 庚寅 Metal Tiger 1 8 十六	火2 Fire [7] Sincerity 風澤中孚 辛卯 Metal Rabbit 3 9 十七	水6 Water [8] Big Livestock 山天大畜 壬辰 Water Dragon 4 10 十八	金4 Metal [9] Eliminating 澤天夬 癸巳 Water Snake 6 11 十九	金9 Metal [1] Heaven 乾爲天 甲午 Wood Horse 1 12 二十	火7 Fire [2] Well 水風井 乙未 Wood Goat 6 13 廿一	木8 Wood [3] Relief 雷水解 丙申 Fire Monkey 4 14 廿二
金4 Metal [4] Influence 澤山咸 丁酉 Fire Rooster 9 15 廿三	水1 Water [5] Humility 地山謙 戊戌 Earth Dog 6 16 廿四	火2 Fire [6] Observation 風地觀 己亥 Earth Pig 2 17 廿五	火2 Fire [7] Increasing 風雷益 庚子 Metal Rat 9 18 廿六	水1 Water [8] Dimming Light 地火明夷 辛丑 Metal Ox 3 19 廿七	金9 Metal [9] Fellowship 天火同人 壬寅 Water Tiger 7 20 廿八	木8 Wood [1] Marrying Maiden 雷澤歸妹 癸卯 Water Rabbit 7 21 廿九
木3 Wood [2] Opposition 火澤睽 甲辰 Wood Dragon 2 22 三十	火7 Fire [3] Waiting 水天需 乙巳 Wood Snake 3 23 五月初一	金4 Metal [4] Great Exceeding 澤風大過 丙午 Fire Horse 3 24 初二	水6 Water [5] Poison 山風蠱 丁未 Fire Goat 7 25 初三	火2 Fire [6] Dispersing 風水渙 戊申 Earth Monkey 6 26 初四	木3 Wood [7] Travelling 火山旅 己酉 Earth Rooster 8 27 初五	金9 Metal [8] Stagnation 天地否 庚戌 Metal Dog 9 28 初六
火7 Fire [9] Alliance 水地比 辛亥 Metal Pig 7 29 初七	木8 Wood [1] Thunder 震爲雷 壬子 Water Rat 1 30 初八	水6 Water [2] Beauty 山火賁 癸丑 Water Ox 8 31 初九				

JUNE 2039 庚午

Xuan Kong Element 玄空五行	雷風恆 Consistency	Period Luck 卦運	Monthly Star 月星
Wood 木8		9	1

SUNDAY	MONDAY	TUESDAY	WEDNESDAY	THURSDAY	FRIDAY	SATURDAY
			火7 Fire [3] Accomplished 水火既濟 甲寅 Wood Tiger 9 1 初十	水1 Water [4] Arriving 地澤臨 乙卯 Wood Rabbit 4 2 十一	金4 Metal [5] Marsh 兌爲澤 丙辰 Fire Dragon 1 3 十二	火2 Fire [6] Small Livestock 風天小畜 丁巳 Fire Snake 8 4 十三
木3 Wood [7] The Cauldron 火風鼎 戊午 Earth Horse 4 5 十四	水1 Water [8] Rising 地風升 己未 Earth Goat 2 6 十五	火7 Fire [9] Water 坎爲水 庚申 Metal Monkey 1 7 十六	木8 Wood [1] Lesser Exceeding 雷山小過 辛酉 Metal Rooster 3 8 十七	金4 Metal [2] Gathering 澤地萃 壬戌 Water Dog 4 9 十八	水6 Water [3] Peel 山地剝 癸亥 Water Pig 6 10 十九	水1 Water [4] Earth 坤爲地 甲子 Wood Rat 1 11 二十
木3 Wood [5] Biting 火雷噬嗑 乙丑 Wood Ox 6 12 廿一	火2 Fire [6] Family 風火家人 丙寅 Fire Tiger 4 13 廿二	水6 Water [7] Decreasing 山澤損 丁卯 Fire Rabbit 9 14 廿三	金9 Metal [8] Tread 天澤履 戊辰 Earth Dragon 6 15 廿四	木8 Wood [9] Great Strength 雷天大壯 己巳 Earth Snake 2 16 廿五	木8 Wood [1] Consistency 雷風恆 庚午 Metal Horse 9 17 廿六	金9 Metal [2] Litigation 天水訟 辛未 Metal Goat 3 18 廿七
水1 Water [3] Officer 地水師 壬申 Water Monkey 7 19 廿八	火2 Fire [4] Gradual Progress 風山漸 癸酉 Water Rooster 7 20 廿九	火7 Fire [5] Obstruction 水山蹇 甲戌 Wood Dog 2 21 三十	木3 Wood [4] Advancement 火地晉 乙亥 Wood Pig 3 22 閏五月初一	水6 Water [3] Nourish 山雷頤 丙子 Fire Rat 3 23 初二	金4 Metal [2] Following 澤雷隨 丁丑 Fire Ox 7 24 初三	木8 Wood [1] Abundance 雷火豐 戊寅 Earth Tiger 6 25 初四
火7 Fire [9] Regulate 水澤節 己卯 Earth Rabbit 8 26 初五	水1 Water [8] Unity 地天泰 庚辰 Metal Dragon 9 27 初六	木3 Wood [7] Great Reward 火天大有 辛巳 Metal Snake 7 28 初七	火2 Fire [6] Wind 巽爲風 壬午 Water Horse 1 29 初八	金4 Metal [5] Trap 澤水困 癸未 Water Goat 8 30 初九		

JULY 2039 辛未

Xuan Kong Element 玄空五行	天水訟 Litigation	Period Luck 卦運	Monthly Star 月星
Metal 金9		3	9

SUNDAY	MONDAY	TUESDAY	WEDNESDAY	THURSDAY	FRIDAY	SATURDAY
火7 Fire Accomplished 1 甲寅 Wood Tiger 水火既濟 31 十一 9					木3 Wood Not Yet Accomplished 4 甲申 Wood Monkey 火水未濟 1 初十 9	金9 Metal Retreat 3 乙酉 Wood Rooster 天山遯 2 十一 4
水6 Water Mountain 2 丙戌 Fire Dog 艮為山 3 十二 1	木8 Wood Delight 1 丁亥 Fire Pig 雷地豫 4 十三 8	火7 Fire Beginning 9 戊子 Earth Rat 水雷屯 5 十四 4	金9 Metal Without Wrongdoing 8 己丑 Earth Ox 天雷無妄 6 十五 2	木3 Wood Fire 7 庚寅 Metal Tiger 離為火 7 十六 1	火2 Fire Sincerity 6 辛卯 Metal Rabbit 風澤中孚 8 十七 3	水6 Water Big Livestock 5 壬辰 Water Dragon 山天大畜 9 十八 4
金4 Metal Eliminating 4 癸巳 Water Snake 澤天夬 10 十九 6	金9 Metal Heaven 3 甲午 Wood Horse 乾為天 11 二十 1	火7 Fire Well 2 乙未 Wood Goat 水風井 12 廿一 6	木8 Wood Relief 1 丙申 Fire Monkey 雷水解 13 廿二 4	金4 Metal Influence 9 丁酉 Fire Rooster 澤山咸 14 廿三 9	水1 Water Humility 8 戊戌 Earth Dog 地山謙 15 廿四 6	火2 Fire Observation 7 己亥 Earth Pig 風地觀 16 廿五 2
火2 Fire Increasing 6 庚子 Metal Rat 風雷益 17 廿六 9	水1 Water Dimming Light 5 辛丑 Metal Ox 地火明夷 18 廿七 3	金9 Metal Fellowship 4 壬寅 Water Tiger 天火同人 19 廿八 7	木8 Wood Marrying Maiden 3 癸卯 Water Rabbit 雷澤歸妹 20 廿九 7	木3 Wood Opposition 2 甲辰 Wood Dragon 火澤睽 21 六月初一 2	火7 Fire Waiting 1 乙巳 Wood Snake 水天需 22 初二 3	金4 Metal Great Exceeding 9 丙午 Fire Horse 澤風大過 23 初三 3
水6 Water Poison 8 丁未 Fire Goat 山風蠱 24 初四 7	火2 Fire Dispersing 7 戊申 Earth Monkey 風水渙 25 初五 6	木3 Wood Travelling 6 己酉 Earth Rooster 火山旅 26 初六 8	金9 Metal Stagnation 5 庚戌 Metal Dog 天地否 27 初七 9	火7 Fire Alliance 4 辛亥 Metal Pig 水地比 28 初八 7	木8 Wood Thunder 3 壬子 Water Rat 震為雷 29 初九 1	水6 Water Beauty 2 癸丑 Water Ox 山火賁 30 初十 8

AUGUST 2039 壬申

Xuan Kong Element 玄空五行	地水師 Officer	Period Luck 卦運	Monthly Star 月星
Water 水1		7	8

SUNDAY	MONDAY	TUESDAY	WEDNESDAY	THURSDAY	FRIDAY	SATURDAY
	水1 Water Arriving 9 乙卯 Wood Rabbit 地澤臨 1 十二 4	金4 Metal Marsh 8 丙辰 Fire Dragon 兌為澤 2 十三 1	火2 Fire Small Livestock 7 丁巳 Fire Snake 風天小畜 3 十四 8	木3 Wood The Cauldron 6 戊午 Earth Horse 火風鼎 4 十五 4	水1 Water Rising 5 己未 Earth Goat 地風升 5 十六 2	火7 Fire Water 4 庚申 Metal Monkey 坎為水 6 十七 1
木8 Wood Lesser Exceeding 3 辛酉 Metal Rooster 雷山小過 7 十八 3	金4 Metal Gathering 2 壬戌 Water Dog 澤地萃 8 十九 4	水6 Water Peel 1 癸亥 Water Pig 山地剝 9 二十 6	水1 Water Earth 9 甲子 Wood Rat 坤為地 10 廿一 1	木3 Wood Biting 8 乙丑 Wood Ox 火雷噬嗑 11 廿二 6	火2 Fire Family 7 丙寅 Fire Tiger 風火家人 12 廿三 4	水6 Water Decreasing 6 丁卯 Fire Rabbit 山澤損 13 廿四 9
金9 Metal Tread 5 戊辰 Earth Dragon 天澤履 14 廿五 6	木8 Wood Great Strength 4 己巳 Earth Snake 雷天大壯 15 廿六 2	木8 Wood Consistency 3 庚午 Metal Horse 雷風恒 16 廿七 9	金9 Metal Litigation 2 辛未 Metal Goat 天水訟 17 廿八 3	水1 Water Officer 1 壬申 Water Monkey 地水師 18 廿九 7	火2 Fire Gradual Progress 9 癸酉 Water Rooster 風山漸 19 三十 7	火7 Fire Obstruction 8 甲戌 Wood Dog 水山蹇 20 七月初一 2
木3 Wood Advancement 7 乙亥 Wood Pig 火地晉 21 初二 3	水6 Water Nourish 6 丙子 Fire Rat 山雷頤 22 初三 3	金4 Metal Following 5 丁丑 Fire Ox 澤雷隨 23 初四 7	木8 Wood Abundance 4 戊寅 Earth Tiger 雷火豐 24 初五 6	火7 Fire Regulate 3 己卯 Earth Rabbit 水澤節 25 初六 8	水1 Water Unity 2 庚辰 Metal Dragon 地天泰 26 初七 9	木3 Wood Great Reward 1 辛巳 Metal Snake 火天大有 27 初八 7
火2 Fire Wind 9 壬午 Water Horse 巽為風 28 初九 1	金4 Metal Trap 8 癸未 Water Goat 澤水困 29 初十 8	木3 Wood Not Yet Accomplished 7 甲申 Wood Monkey 火水未濟 30 十一 9	金9 Metal Retreat 6 乙酉 Wood Rooster 天山遯 31 十二 4			

SEPTEMBER 2039 癸酉

Xuan Kong Element 玄空五行	風山漸 Gradual Progress	Period Luck 卦運	Monthly Star 月星
Fire 火2		7	7

SUNDAY	MONDAY	TUESDAY	WEDNESDAY	THURSDAY	FRIDAY	SATURDAY
				水6 Water 5 Mountain 丙戌 Fire Dog 艮爲山 1 十三 1	木8 Wood 4 Delight 丁亥 Fire Pig 雷地豫 2 十四 8	火7 Fire 3 Beginning 戊子 Earth Rat 水雷屯 3 十五 4
金9 Metal 2 Without Wrongdoing 己丑 Earth Ox 天雷無妄 4 十六 2	木3 Wood 1 Fire 庚寅 Metal Tiger 離爲火 5 十七 1	火2 Fire 9 Sincerity 辛卯 Metal Rabbit 風澤中孚 6 十八 3	水6 Water 8 Big Livestock 壬辰 Water Dragon 山天大畜 7 十九 4	金4 Metal 7 Eliminating 癸巳 Water Snake 澤天夬 8 二十 6	金9 Metal 6 Heaven 甲午 Wood Horse 乾爲天 9 廿一 1	火7 Fire 5 Well 乙未 Wood Goat 水風井 10 廿二 6
木8 Wood 4 Relief 丙申 Fire Monkey 雷水解 11 廿三 4	金4 Metal 3 Influence 丁酉 Fire Rooster 澤山咸 12 廿四 9	水1 Water 2 Humility 戊戌 Earth Dog 地山謙 13 廿五 6	火2 Fire 1 Observation 己亥 Earth Pig 風地觀 14 廿六 2	火2 Fire 9 Increasing 庚子 Metal Rat 風雷益 15 廿七 9	水1 Water 8 Dimming Light 辛丑 Metal Ox 地火明夷 16 廿八 3	金9 Metal 7 Fellowship 壬寅 Water Tiger 天火同人 17 廿九 7
木8 Wood 6 Marrying Maiden 癸卯 Water Rabbit 雷澤歸妹 18 八月初一 7	木3 Wood 5 Opposition 甲辰 Wood Dragon 火澤睽 19 初二 2	火7 Fire 4 Waiting 乙巳 Wood Snake 水天需 20 初三 3	金4 Metal 3 Great Exceeding 丙午 Fire Horse 澤風大過 21 初四 3	水6 Water 2 Poison 丁未 Fire Goat 山風蠱 22 初五 7	火2 Fire 1 Dispersing 戊申 Earth Monkey 風水渙 23 初六 6	木3 Wood 9 Travelling 己酉 Earth Rooster 火山旅 24 初七 8
金9 Metal 8 Stagnation 庚戌 Metal Dog 天地否 25 初八 9	火7 Fire 7 Alliance 辛亥 Metal Pig 水地比 26 初九 7	木8 Wood 6 Thunder 壬子 Water Rat 震爲雷 27 初十 1	水6 Water 5 Beauty 癸丑 Water Ox 山火賁 28 十一 8	火7 Fire 4 Accomplished 甲寅 Wood Tiger 水火既濟 29 十二 9	水1 Water 3 Arriving 乙卯 Wood Rabbit 地澤臨 30 十三 4	

OCTOBER 2039 甲戌

Xuan Kong Element 玄空五行	水山蹇 Obstruction	Period Luck 卦運	Monthly Star 月星
Fire 火7		2	6

SUNDAY	MONDAY	TUESDAY	WEDNESDAY	THURSDAY	FRIDAY	SATURDAY
金9 Metal 9 Retreat 乙酉 Wood Rooster 天山遯 30 十三 4	水6 Water 8 Mountain 丙戌 Fire Dog 艮爲山 31 十四 1					金4 Metal 2 Marsh 丙辰 Fire Dragon 兌爲澤 1 十四 1
火2 Fire 1 Small Livestock 丁巳 Fire Snake 風天小畜 2 十五 8	木3 Wood 9 The Cauldron 戊午 Earth Horse 火風鼎 3 十六 4	水1 Water 8 Rising 己未 Earth Goat 地風升 4 十七 2	火7 Fire 7 Water 庚申 Metal Monkey 坎爲水 5 十八 1	木8 Wood 6 Lesser Exceeding 辛酉 Metal Rooster 雷山小過 6 十九 3	金4 Metal 5 Gathering 壬戌 Water Dog 澤地萃 7 二十 4	水6 Water 4 Peel 癸亥 Water Pig 山地剝 8 廿一 6
水1 Water 3 Earth 甲子 Wood Rat 坤爲地 9 廿二 1	木3 Wood 2 Biting 乙丑 Wood Ox 火雷噬嗑 10 廿三 6	火2 Fire 1 Family 丙寅 Fire Tiger 風火家人 11 廿四 4	水6 Water 9 Decreasing 丁卯 Fire Rabbit 山澤損 12 廿五 9	金9 Metal 8 Tread 戊辰 Earth Dragon 天澤履 13 廿六 6	木8 Wood 7 Great Strength 己巳 Earth Snake 雷天大壯 14 廿七 2	木8 Wood 6 Consistency 庚午 Metal Horse 雷風恒 15 廿八 9
金9 Metal 5 Litigation 辛未 Metal Goat 天水訟 16 廿九 3	水1 Water 4 Officer 壬申 Water Monkey 地水師 17 三十 7	火2 Fire 3 Gradual Progress 癸酉 Water Rooster 風山漸 18 九月初一 7	火7 Fire 2 Obstruction 甲戌 Wood Dog 水山蹇 19 初二 2	木3 Wood 1 Advancement 乙亥 Wood Pig 火地晉 20 初三 3	水6 Water 9 Nourish 丙子 Fire Rat 山雷頤 21 初四 3	金4 Metal 8 Following 丁丑 Fire Ox 澤雷隨 22 初五 7
木8 Wood 7 Abundance 戊寅 Earth Tiger 雷火豐 23 初六 6	火7 Fire 6 Regulate 己卯 Earth Rabbit 水澤節 24 初七 8	水1 Water 5 Unity 庚辰 Metal Dragon 地天泰 25 初八 9	木3 Wood 4 Great Reward 辛巳 Metal Snake 火天大有 26 初九 7	火2 Fire 3 Wind 壬午 Water Horse 巽爲風 27 初十 1	金4 Metal 2 Trap 癸未 Water Goat 澤水困 28 十一 8	木3 Wood 1 Not Yet Accomplished 甲申 Wood Monkey 火水未濟 29 十二 9

NOVEMBER 2039 乙亥

Xuan Kong Element 玄空五行	火地晉 Advancement	Period Luck 卦運	Monthly Star 月星
Wood 木3		3	5

SUNDAY	MONDAY	TUESDAY	WEDNESDAY	THURSDAY	FRIDAY	SATURDAY
		木8 Wood 7 Delight 雷地豫 丁亥 Fire Pig 1 十五 8	火7 Fire 6 Beginning 水雷屯 戊子 Earth Rat 2 十六 4	金9 Metal 5 Without Wrongdoing 天雷無妄 己丑 Earth Ox 3 十七 2	木3 Wood 4 Fire 離爲火 庚寅 Metal Tiger 4 十八 1	火2 Fire 3 Sincerity 風澤中孚 辛卯 Metal Rabbit 5 十九 3
水6 Water 2 Big Livestock 山天大畜 壬辰 Water Dragon 6 二十 4	金4 Metal 1 Eliminating 澤天夬 癸巳 Water Snake 7 廿一 6	金9 Metal 9 Heaven 乾爲天 甲午 Wood Horse 8 廿二 1	火7 Fire 8 Well 水風井 乙未 Wood Goat 9 廿三 6	木8 Wood 7 Relief 雷水解 丙申 Fire Monkey 10 廿四 4	金4 Metal 6 Influence 澤山咸 丁酉 Fire Rooster 11 廿五 9	水1 Water 5 Humility 地山謙 戊戌 Earth Dog 12 廿六 6
火2 Fire 4 Observation 風地觀 己亥 Earth Pig 13 廿七 2	火2 Fire 3 Increasing 風雷益 庚子 Metal Rat 14 廿八 9	水1 Water 2 Dimming Light 地火明夷 辛丑 Metal Ox 15 廿九 3	金9 Metal 1 Fellowship 天火同人 壬寅 Water Tiger 16 十月初一 7	木8 Wood 9 Marrying Maiden 雷澤歸妹 癸卯 Water Rabbit 17 初二 7	木3 Wood 8 Opposition 火澤睽 甲辰 Wood Dragon 18 初三 2	火7 Fire 7 Waiting 水天需 乙巳 Wood Snake 19 初四 3
金4 Metal 6 Great Exceeding 澤風大過 丙午 Fire Horse 20 初五 3	水6 Water 5 Poison 山風蠱 丁未 Fire Goat 21 初六 7	火2 Fire 4 Dispersing 風水渙 戊申 Earth Monkey 22 初七 6	木3 Wood 3 Travelling 火山旅 己酉 Earth Rooster 23 初八 8	金9 Metal 2 Stagnation 天地否 庚戌 Metal Dog 24 初九 9	火7 Fire 1 Alliance 水地比 辛亥 Metal Pig 25 初十 7	木8 Wood 9 Thunder 震爲雷 壬子 Water Rat 26 十一 1
水6 Water 8 Beauty 山火賁 癸丑 Water Ox 27 十二 8	火7 Fire 7 Accomplished 水火既濟 甲寅 Wood Tiger 28 十三 9	水1 Water 6 Arriving 地澤臨 乙卯 Wood Rabbit 29 十四 4	金4 Metal 5 Marsh 兌爲澤 丙辰 Fire Dragon 30 十五 1			

DECEMBER 2039 丙子

Xuan Kong Element 玄空五行	山雷頤 Nourish	Period Luck 卦運	Monthly Star 月星
Water 水6		3	4

SUNDAY	MONDAY	TUESDAY	WEDNESDAY	THURSDAY	FRIDAY	SATURDAY
				火2 Fire 4 Small Livestock 風天小畜 丁巳 Fire Snake 1 十六 8	木3 Wood 3 The Cauldron 火風鼎 戊午 Earth Horse 2 十七 4	水1 Water 2 Rising 地風升 己未 Earth Goat 3 十八 2
火7 Fire 1 Water 坎爲水 庚申 Metal Monkey 4 十九 1	木8 Wood 9 Lesser Exceeding 雷山小過 辛酉 Metal Rooster 5 二十 3	金4 Metal 8 Gathering 澤地萃 壬戌 Water Dog 6 廿一 4	水6 Water 7 Peel 山地剝 癸亥 Water Pig 7 廿二 6	水1 Water 6 Earth 坤爲地 甲子 Wood Rat 8 廿三 1	木3 Wood 5 Biting 火雷噬嗑 乙丑 Wood Ox 9 廿四 6	火2 Fire 4 Family 風火家人 丙寅 Fire Tiger 10 廿五 4
水6 Water 3 Decreasing 山澤損 丁卯 Fire Rabbit 11 廿六 9	金9 Metal 2 Tread 天澤履 戊辰 Earth Dragon 12 廿七 6	木8 Wood 1 Great Strength 雷天大壯 己巳 Earth Snake 13 廿八 2	木8 Wood 9 Consistency 雷風恆 庚午 Metal Horse 14 廿九 9	金9 Metal 8 Litigation 天水訟 辛未 Metal Goat 15 三十 3	水1 Water 7 Officer 地水師 壬申 Water Monkey 16 十一月初一 7	火2 Fire 6 Gradual Progress 風山漸 癸酉 Water Rooster 17 初二 7
火7 Fire 5 Obstruction 水山蹇 甲戌 Wood Dog 18 初三 2	木3 Wood 4 Advancement 火地晉 乙亥 Wood Pig 19 初四 3	水6 Water 3 Nourish 山雷頤 丙子 Fire Rat 20 初五 3	金4 Metal 2 Following 澤雷隨 丁丑 Fire Ox 21 初六 7	木8 Wood 1/9 Abundance 雷火豐 戊寅 Earth Tiger 22 初七 6	火7 Fire 1 Regulate 水澤節 己卯 Earth Rabbit 23 初八 8	水1 Water 2 Unity 地天泰 庚辰 Metal Dragon 24 初九 9
木3 Wood 3 Great Reward 火天大有 辛巳 Metal Snake 25 初十 7	火2 Fire 4 Wind 巽爲風 壬午 Water Horse 26 十一 1	金4 Metal 5 Trap 澤水困 癸未 Water Goat 27 十二 8	木3 Wood 6 Not Yet Accomplished 火水未濟 甲申 Wood Monkey 28 十三 9	金9 Metal 7 Retreat 天山遯 乙酉 Wood Rooster 29 十四 4	水6 Water 8 Mountain 艮爲山 丙戌 Fire Dog 30 十五 1	木8 Wood 9 Delight 雷地豫 丁亥 Fire Pig 31 十六 8

2040 庚申

(*Geng Shen*) Metal Monkey

2040 庚申 *(Geng Shen)* Metal Monkey

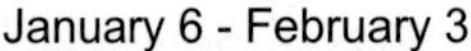

January 6 - February 3

February 4 - March 4

March 5 - April 3

April 4 - May 4

May 5 - June 4

June 5 - July 5

July 6 - August 6

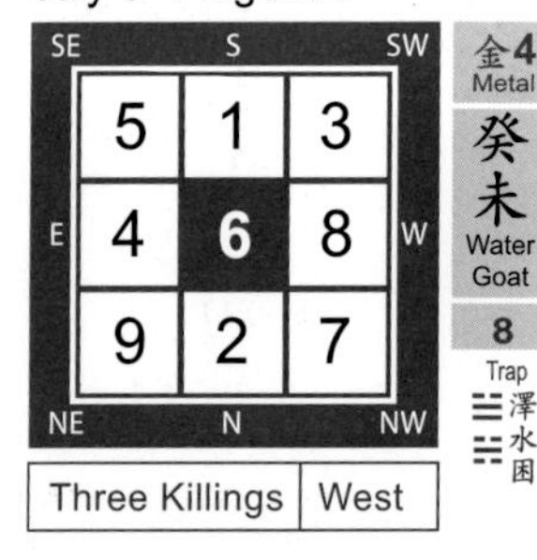

August 7 - September 6

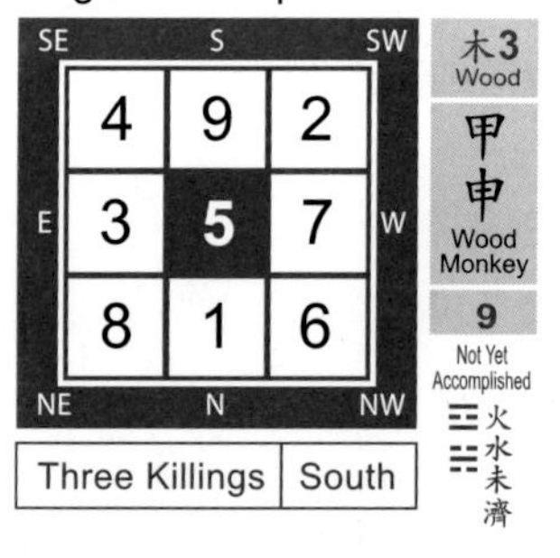

September 7 - October 7

October 8 - November 6

November 7 - December 5

December 6 - January 4

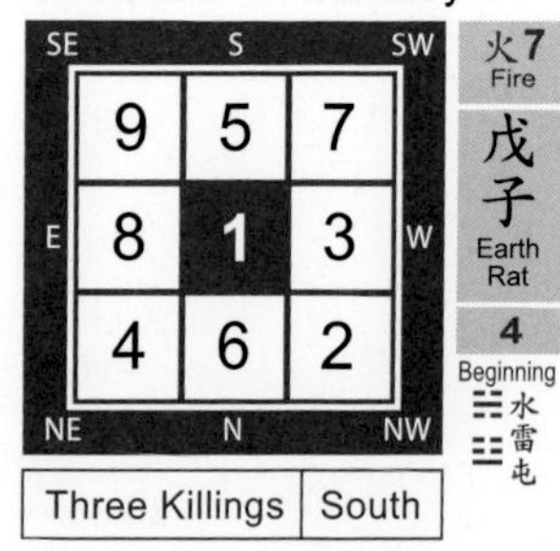

JANUARY 2040 丁丑

Xuan Kong Element 玄空五行	澤雷隨 Following	Period Luck 卦運	Monthly Star 月星
Metal 金4		7	3

SUNDAY	MONDAY	TUESDAY	WEDNESDAY	THURSDAY	FRIDAY	SATURDAY
火7 Fire 戊子 Earth Rat Beginning 水雷屯 [1] **1** 十七 4	金9 Metal 己丑 Earth Ox Without Wrongdoing 天雷無妄 [2] **2** 十八 2	木3 Wood 庚寅 Metal Tiger Fire 離爲火 [3] **3** 十九 1	火2 Fire 辛卯 Metal Rabbit Sincerity 風澤中孚 [4] **4** 二十 3	水6 Water 壬辰 Water Dragon Big Livestock 山天大畜 [5] **5** 廿一 4	金4 Metal 癸巳 Water Snake Eliminating 澤天夬 [6] **6** 廿二 6	金9 Metal 甲午 Wood Horse Heaven 乾爲天 [7] **7** 廿三 1
火7 Fire 乙未 Wood Goat Well 水風井 [8] **8** 廿四 6	木8 Wood 丙申 Fire Monkey Relief 雷水解 [9] **9** 廿五 4	金4 Metal 丁酉 Fire Rooster Influence 澤山咸 [1] **10** 廿六 9	水1 Water 戊戌 Earth Dog Humility 地山謙 [2] **11** 廿七 6	火2 Fire 己亥 Earth Pig Observation 風地觀 [3] **12** 廿八 2	火2 Fire 庚子 Metal Rat Increasing 風雷益 [4] **13** 廿九 9	水1 Water 辛丑 Metal Ox Dimming Light 地火明夷 [5] **14** 十二月初一 3
金9 Metal 壬寅 Water Tiger Fellowship 天火同人 [6] **15** 初二 7	木8 Wood 癸卯 Water Rabbit Marrying Maiden 雷澤歸妹 [7] **16** 初三 7	木3 Wood 甲辰 Wood Dragon Opposition 火澤睽 [8] **17** 初四 2	火7 Fire 乙巳 Wood Snake Waiting 水天需 [9] **18** 初五 3	金4 Metal 丙午 Fire Horse Great Exceeding 澤風大過 [1] **19** 初六 3	水6 Water 丁未 Fire Goat Poison 山風蠱 [2] **20** 初七 7	火2 Fire 戊申 Earth Monkey Dispersing 風水渙 [3] **21** 初八 6
木3 Wood 己酉 Earth Rooster Travelling 火山旅 [4] **22** 初九 8	金9 Metal 庚戌 Metal Dog Stagnation 天地否 [5] **23** 初十 9	火7 Fire 辛亥 Metal Pig Alliance 水地比 [6] **24** 十一 7	木8 Wood 壬子 Water Rat Thunder 震爲雷 [7] **25** 十二 1	水6 Water 癸丑 Water Ox Beauty 山火賁 [8] **26** 十三 8	火7 Fire 甲寅 Wood Tiger Accomplished 水火既濟 [9] **27** 十四 9	水1 Water 乙卯 Wood Rabbit Arriving 地澤臨 [1] **28** 十五 4
金4 Metal 丙辰 Fire Dragon Marsh 兌爲澤 [2] **29** 十六 1	火2 Fire 丁巳 Fire Snake Small Livestock 風天小畜 [3] **30** 十七 8	木3 Wood 戊午 Earth Horse The Cauldron 火風鼎 [4] **31** 十八 4				

FEBRUARY 2040 戊寅

Xuan Kong Element 玄空五行	雷火豐 Abundance	Period Luck 卦運	Monthly Star 月星
Wood 木8		6	2

SUNDAY	MONDAY	TUESDAY	WEDNESDAY	THURSDAY	FRIDAY	SATURDAY
			水1 Water 己未 Earth Goat Rising 地風升 [5] **1** 十九 2	火7 Fire 庚申 Metal Monkey Water 坎爲水 [6] **2** 二十 1	木8 Wood 辛酉 Metal Rooster Lesser Exceeding 雷山小過 [7] **3** 廿一 3	金4 Metal 壬戌 Water Dog Gathering 澤地萃 [8] **4** 廿二 4
水6 Water 癸亥 Water Pig Peel 山地剝 [9] **5** 廿三 6	水1 Water 甲子 Wood Rat Earth 坤爲地 [1] **6** 廿四 1	木3 Wood 乙丑 Wood Ox Biting 火雷噬嗑 [2] **7** 廿五 6	火2 Fire 丙寅 Fire Tiger Family 風火家人 [3] **8** 廿六 4	水6 Water 丁卯 Fire Rabbit Decreasing 山澤損 [4] **9** 廿七 9	金9 Metal 戊辰 Earth Dragon Tread 天澤履 [5] **10** 廿八 6	木8 Wood 己巳 Earth Snake Great Strength 雷天大壯 [6] **11** 廿九 2
木8 Wood 庚午 Metal Horse Consistency 雷風恆 [7] **12** 正月初一 9	金9 Metal 辛未 Metal Goat Litigation 天水訟 [8] **13** 初二 3	水1 Water 壬申 Water Monkey Officer 地水師 [9] **14** 初三 7	火2 Fire 癸酉 Water Rooster Gradual Progress 風山漸 [1] **15** 初四 7	火7 Fire 甲戌 Wood Dog Obstruction 水山蹇 [2] **16** 初五 2	木3 Wood 乙亥 Wood Pig Advancement 火地晉 [3] **17** 初六 3	水6 Water 丙子 Fire Rat Nourish 山雷頤 [4] **18** 初七 3
金4 Metal 丁丑 Fire Ox Following 澤雷隨 [5] **19** 初八 7	木8 Wood 戊寅 Earth Tiger Abundance 雷火豐 [6] **20** 初九 6	火7 Fire 己卯 Earth Rabbit Regulate 水澤節 [7] **21** 初十 8	水1 Water 庚辰 Metal Dragon Unity 地天泰 [8] **22** 十一 9	木3 Wood 辛巳 Metal Snake Great Reward 火天大有 [9] **23** 十二 7	火2 Fire 壬午 Water Horse Wind 巽爲風 [1] **24** 十三 1	金4 Metal 癸未 Water Goat Trap 澤水困 [2] **25** 十四 8
木3 Wood 甲申 Wood Monkey Not Yet Accomplished 火水未濟 [3] **26** 十五 9	金9 Metal 乙酉 Wood Rooster Retreat 天山遯 [4] **27** 十六 4	水6 Water 丙戌 Fire Dog Mountain 艮爲山 [5] **28** 十七 1	木8 Wood 丁亥 Fire Pig Delight 雷地豫 [6] **29** 十八 8			

MARCH 2040 己卯

Xuan Kong Element 玄空五行	水澤節 Regulate	Period Luck 卦運	Monthly Star 月星
Fire 火7		8	1

SUNDAY	MONDAY	TUESDAY	WEDNESDAY	THURSDAY	FRIDAY	SATURDAY
				火7 Fire 7 Beginning 水雷屯 戊子 Earth Rat 1 十九 4	金9 Metal 8 Without Wrongdoing 天雷無妄 己丑 Earth Ox 2 二十 2	木3 Wood 9 Fire 離為火 庚寅 Metal Tiger 3 廿一 1
火2 Fire 1 Sincerity 風澤中孚 辛卯 Metal Rabbit 4 廿二 3	水6 Water 2 Big Livestock 山天大畜 壬辰 Water Dragon 5 廿三 4	金4 Metal 3 Eliminating 澤天夬 癸巳 Water Snake 6 廿四 6	金9 Metal 4 Heaven 乾為天 甲午 Wood Horse 7 廿五 1	火7 Fire 5 Well 水風井 乙未 Wood Goat 8 廿六 6	木8 Wood 6 Relief 雷水解 丙申 Fire Monkey 9 廿七 4	金4 Metal 7 Influence 澤山咸 丁酉 Fire Rooster 10 廿八 9
水1 Water 8 Humility 地山謙 戊戌 Earth Dog 11 廿九 6	火2 Fire 9 Observation 風地觀 己亥 Earth Pig 12 三十 2	火2 Fire 1 Increasing 風雷益 庚子 Metal Rat 13 二月初一 9	水1 Water 2 Dimming Light 地火明夷 辛丑 Metal Ox 14 初二 3	金9 Metal 3 Fellowship 天火同人 壬寅 Water Tiger 15 初三 7	木8 Wood 4 Marrying Maiden 雷澤歸妹 癸卯 Water Rabbit 16 初四 7	木3 Wood 5 Opposition 火澤睽 甲辰 Wood Dragon 17 初五 2
火7 Fire 6 Waiting 水天需 乙巳 Wood Snake 18 初六 3	金4 Metal 7 Great Exceeding 澤風大過 丙午 Fire Horse 19 初七 3	水6 Water 8 Poison 山風蠱 丁未 Fire Goat 20 初八 7	火2 Fire 9 Dispersing 風水渙 戊申 Earth Monkey 21 初九 6	木3 Wood 1 Travelling 火山旅 己酉 Earth Rooster 22 初十 8	金9 Metal 2 Stagnation 天地否 庚戌 Metal Dog 23 十一 9	火7 Fire 3 Alliance 水地比 辛亥 Metal Pig 24 十二 7
木8 Wood 4 Thunder 震為雷 壬子 Water Rat 25 十三 1	水6 Water 5 Beauty 山火賁 癸丑 Water Ox 26 十四 8	火7 Fire 6 Accomplished 水火既濟 甲寅 Wood Tiger 27 十五 9	水1 Water 7 Arriving 地澤臨 乙卯 Wood Rabbit 28 十六 4	金4 Metal 8 Marsh 兑為澤 丙辰 Fire Dragon 29 十七 1	火2 Fire 9 Small Livestock 風天小畜 丁巳 Fire Snake 30 十八 8	木3 Wood 1 The Cauldron 火風鼎 戊午 Earth Horse 31 十九 4

APRIL 2040 庚辰

Xuan Kong Element 玄空五行	地天泰 Unity	Period Luck 卦運	Monthly Star 月星
Water 水1		9	9

SUNDAY	MONDAY	TUESDAY	WEDNESDAY	THURSDAY	FRIDAY	SATURDAY
水1 Water 2 Rising 地風升 己未 Earth Goat 1 二十 2	火7 Fire 3 Water 坎為水 庚申 Metal Monkey 2 廿一 1	木8 Wood 4 Lesser Exceeding 雷山小過 辛酉 Metal Rooster 3 廿二 3	金4 Metal 5 Gathering 澤地萃 壬戌 Water Dog 4 廿三 4	水6 Water 6 Peel 山地剝 癸亥 Water Pig 5 廿四 6	水1 Water 7 Earth 坤為地 甲子 Wood Rat 6 廿五 1	木3 Wood 8 Biting 火雷噬嗑 乙丑 Wood Ox 7 廿六 6
火2 Fire 9 Family 風火家人 丙寅 Fire Tiger 8 廿七 4	水6 Water 1 Decreasing 山澤損 丁卯 Fire Rabbit 9 廿八 9	金9 Metal 2 Tread 天澤履 戊辰 Earth Dragon 10 廿九 6	木8 Wood 3 Great Strength 雷天大壯 己巳 Earth Snake 11 三月初一 2	木8 Wood 4 Consistency 雷風恒 庚午 Metal Horse 12 初二 9	金9 Metal 5 Litigation 天水訟 辛未 Metal Goat 13 初三 3	水1 Water 6 Officer 地水師 壬申 Water Monkey 14 初四 7
火2 Fire 7 Gradual Progress 風山漸 癸酉 Water Rooster 15 初五 7	火7 Fire 8 Obstruction 水山蹇 甲戌 Wood Dog 16 初六 2	木3 Wood 9 Advancement 火地晉 乙亥 Wood Pig 17 初七 3	水6 Water 1 Nourish 山雷頤 丙子 Fire Rat 18 初八 3	金4 Metal 2 Following 澤雷隨 丁丑 Fire Ox 19 初九 7	木8 Wood 3 Abundance 雷火豐 戊寅 Earth Tiger 20 初十 6	火7 Fire 4 Regulate 水澤節 己卯 Earth Rabbit 21 十一 8
水1 Water 5 Unity 地天泰 庚辰 Metal Dragon 22 十二 9	木3 Wood 6 Great Reward 火天大有 辛巳 Metal Snake 23 十三 7	火2 Fire 7 Wind 巽為風 壬午 Water Horse 24 十四 1	金4 Metal 8 Trap 澤水困 癸未 Water Goat 25 十五 8	木3 Wood 9 Not Yet Accomplished 火水未濟 甲申 Wood Monkey 26 十六 9	金9 Metal 1 Retreat 天山遯 乙酉 Wood Rooster 27 十七 4	水6 Water 2 Mountain 艮為山 丙戌 Fire Dog 28 十八 1
木8 Wood 3 Delight 雷地豫 丁亥 Fire Pig 29 十九 8	火7 Fire 4 Beginning 水雷屯 戊子 Earth Rat 30 二十 4					

MAY 2040 辛巳

Xuan Kong Element 玄空五行	火天大有 Great Reward	Period Luck 卦運	Monthly Star 月星
Wood 木3		7	8

SUNDAY	MONDAY	TUESDAY	WEDNESDAY	THURSDAY	FRIDAY	SATURDAY
		1 廿一 金9 Metal · 5 己丑 Earth Ox · 2 Without Wrongdoing 天雷無妄	**2** 廿二 木3 Wood · 6 庚寅 Metal Tiger · 1 Fire 離爲火	**3** 廿三 火2 Fire · 7 辛卯 Metal Rabbit · 3 Sincerity 風澤中孚	**4** 廿四 水6 Water · 8 壬辰 Water Dragon · 4 Big Livestock 山天大畜	**5** 廿五 金4 Metal · 9 癸巳 Water Snake · 6 Eliminating 澤天夬
6 廿六 金9 Metal · 1 甲午 Wood Horse · 1 Heaven 乾爲天	**7** 廿七 火7 Fire · 2 乙未 Wood Goat · 6 Well 水風井	**8** 廿八 木8 Wood · 3 丙申 Fire Monkey · 4 Relief 雷水解	**9** 廿九 金4 Metal · 4 丁酉 Fire Rooster · 9 Influence 澤山咸	**10** 三十 水1 Water · 5 戊戌 Earth Dog · 6 Humility 地山謙	**11** 四月初一 火2 Fire · 6 己亥 Earth Pig · 2 Observation 風地觀	**12** 初二 火2 Fire · 7 庚子 Metal Rat · 9 Increasing 風雷益
13 初三 水1 Water · 8 辛丑 Metal Ox · 3 Dimming Light 地火明夷	**14** 初四 金9 Metal · 9 壬寅 Water Tiger · 7 Fellowship 天火同人	**15** 初五 木8 Wood · 1 癸卯 Water Rabbit · 7 Marrying Maiden 雷澤歸妹	**16** 初六 木3 Wood · 2 甲辰 Wood Dragon · 2 Opposition 火澤睽	**17** 初七 火7 Fire · 3 乙巳 Wood Snake · 3 Waiting 水天需	**18** 初八 金4 Metal · 4 丙午 Fire Horse · 3 Great Exceeding 澤風大過	**19** 初九 水6 Water · 5 丁未 Fire Goat · 7 Poison 山風蠱
20 初十 火2 Fire · 6 戊申 Earth Monkey · 6 Dispersing 風水渙	**21** 十一 木3 Wood · 7 己酉 Earth Rooster · 8 Travelling 火山旅	**22** 十二 金9 Metal · 8 庚戌 Metal Dog · 9 Stagnation 天地否	**23** 十三 火7 Fire · 9 辛亥 Metal Pig · 7 Alliance 水地比	**24** 十四 木8 Wood · 1 壬子 Water Rat · 1 Thunder 震爲雷	**25** 十五 水6 Water · 2 癸丑 Water Ox · 8 Beauty 山火賁	**26** 十六 火7 Fire · 3 甲寅 Wood Tiger · 9 Accomplished 水火既濟
27 十七 水1 Water · 4 乙卯 Wood Rabbit · 4 Arriving 地澤臨	**28** 十八 金4 Metal · 5 丙辰 Fire Dragon · 1 Marsh 兌爲澤	**29** 十九 火2 Fire · 6 丁巳 Fire Snake · 8 Small Livestock 風天小畜	**30** 二十 木3 Wood · 7 戊午 Earth Horse · 4 The Cauldron 火風鼎	**31** 廿一 水1 Water · 8 己未 Earth Goat · 2 Rising 地風升		

JUNE 2040 壬午

Xuan Kong Element 玄空五行	巽爲風 Wind	Period Luck 卦運	Monthly Star 月星
Fire 火2		1	7

SUNDAY	MONDAY	TUESDAY	WEDNESDAY	THURSDAY	FRIDAY	SATURDAY
					1 廿二 火7 Fire · 9 庚申 Metal Monkey · 1 Water 坎爲水	**2** 廿三 木8 Wood · 1 辛酉 Metal Rooster · 3 Lesser Exceeding 雷山小過
3 廿四 金4 Metal · 2 壬戌 Water Dog · 4 Gathering 澤地萃	**4** 廿五 水6 Water · 3 癸亥 Water Pig · 6 Peel 山地剝	**5** 廿六 水1 Water · 4 甲子 Wood Rat · 1 Earth 坤爲地	**6** 廿七 木3 Wood · 5 乙丑 Wood Ox · 6 Biting 火雷噬嗑	**7** 廿八 火2 Fire · 6 丙寅 Fire Tiger · 4 Family 風火家人	**8** 廿九 水6 Water · 7 丁卯 Fire Rabbit · 9 Decreasing 山澤損	**9** 三十 金9 Metal · 8 戊辰 Earth Dragon · 6 Tread 天澤履
10 五月初一 木8 Wood · 9 己巳 Earth Snake · 2 Great Strength 雷天大壯	**11** 初二 木8 Wood · 1 庚午 Metal Horse · 9 Consistency 雷風恆	**12** 初三 金9 Metal · 2 辛未 Metal Goat · 3 Litigation 天水訟	**13** 初四 水1 Water · 3 壬申 Water Monkey · 7 Officer 地水師	**14** 初五 火2 Fire · 4 癸酉 Water Rooster · 7 Gradual Progress 風山漸	**15** 初六 火7 Fire · 5 甲戌 Wood Dog · 2 Obstruction 水山蹇	**16** 初七 木3 Wood · 6 乙亥 Wood Pig · 3 Advancement 火地晉
17 初八 水6 Water · 7 丙子 Fire Rat · 3 Nourish 山雷頤	**18** 初九 金4 Metal · 8 丁丑 Fire Ox · 7 Following 澤雷隨	**19** 初十 木8 Wood · 9 戊寅 Earth Tiger · 6 Abundance 雷火豐	**20** 十一 火7 Fire · 1 己卯 Earth Rabbit · 8 Regulate 水澤節	**21** 十二 水1 Water · 2/8 庚辰 Metal Dragon · 9 Unity 地天泰	**22** 十三 木3 Wood · 7 辛巳 Metal Snake · 7 Great Reward 火天大有	**23** 十四 火2 Fire · 6 壬午 Water Horse · 1 Wind 巽爲風
24 十五 金4 Metal · 5 癸未 Water Goat · 8 Trap 澤水困	**25** 十六 木3 Wood · 4 甲申 Wood Monkey · 9 Not Yet Accomplished 火水未濟	**26** 十七 金9 Metal · 3 乙酉 Wood Rooster · 4 Retreat 天山遯	**27** 十八 水6 Water · 2 丙戌 Fire Dog · 1 Mountain 艮爲山	**28** 十九 木8 Wood · 1 丁亥 Fire Pig · 8 Delight 雷地豫	**29** 二十 火7 Fire · 9 戊子 Earth Rat · 4 Beginning 水雷屯	**30** 廿一 金9 Metal · 8 己丑 Earth Ox · 2 Without Wrongdoing 天雷無妄

JULY 2040 癸未

Xuan Kong Element 玄空五行	澤水困 Trap	Period Luck 卦運	Monthly Star 月星
Metal 金4		8	6

SUNDAY	MONDAY	TUESDAY	WEDNESDAY	THURSDAY	FRIDAY	SATURDAY
木3 Wood · 7 Fire 離爲火 庚寅 Metal Tiger **1** 1 · 廿二	火2 Fire · 6 Sincerity 風澤中孚 辛卯 Metal Rabbit **2** 3 · 廿三	水6 Water · 5 Big Livestock 山天大畜 壬辰 Water Dragon **3** 4 · 廿四	金4 Metal · 4 Eliminating 澤天夬 癸巳 Water Snake **4** 6 · 廿五	金9 Metal · 3 Heaven 乾爲天 甲午 Wood Horse **5** 1 · 廿六	火7 Fire · 2 Well 水風井 乙未 Wood Goat **6** 6 · 廿七	木8 Wood · 1 Relief 雷水解 丙申 Fire Monkey **7** 4 · 廿八
金4 Metal · 9 Influence 澤山咸 丁酉 Fire Rooster **8** 9 · 廿九	水1 Water · 8 Humility 地山謙 戊戌 Earth Dog **9** 6 · 六月初一	火2 Fire · 7 Observation 風地觀 己亥 Earth Pig **10** 2 · 初二	火2 Fire · 6 Increasing 風雷益 庚子 Metal Rat **11** 9 · 初三	水1 Water · 5 Dimming Light 地火明夷 辛丑 Metal Ox **12** 3 · 初四	金9 Metal · 4 Fellowship 天火同人 壬寅 Water Tiger **13** 7 · 初五	木8 Wood · 3 Marrying Maiden 雷澤歸妹 癸卯 Water Rabbit **14** 7 · 初六
木3 Wood · 2 Opposition 火澤睽 甲辰 Wood Dragon **15** 2 · 初七	火7 Fire · 1 Waiting 水天需 乙巳 Wood Snake **16** 3 · 初八	金4 Metal · 9 Great Exceeding 澤風大過 丙午 Fire Horse **17** 3 · 初九	水6 Water · 8 Poison 山風蠱 丁未 Fire Goat **18** 7 · 初十	火2 Fire · 7 Dispersing 風水渙 戊申 Earth Monkey **19** 6 · 十一	木3 Wood · 6 Travelling 火山旅 己酉 Earth Rooster **20** 8 · 十二	金9 Metal · 5 Stagnation 天地否 庚戌 Metal Dog **21** 9 · 十三
火7 Fire · 4 Alliance 水地比 辛亥 Metal Pig **22** 7 · 十四	木8 Wood · 3 Thunder 震爲雷 壬子 Water Rat **23** 1 · 十五	水6 Water · 2 Beauty 山火賁 癸丑 Water Ox **24** 8 · 十六	火7 Fire · 1 Accomplished 水火既濟 甲寅 Wood Tiger **25** 9 · 十七	水1 Water · 9 Arriving 地澤臨 乙卯 Wood Rabbit **26** 4 · 十八	金4 Metal · 8 Marsh 兌爲澤 丙辰 Fire Dragon **27** 1 · 十九	火2 Fire · 7 Small Livestock 風天小畜 丁巳 Fire Snake **28** 8 · 二十
木3 Wood · 6 The Cauldron 火風鼎 戊午 Earth Horse **29** 4 · 廿一	水1 Water · 5 Rising 地風升 己未 Earth Goat **30** 2 · 廿二	火7 Fire · 4 Water 坎爲水 庚申 Metal Monkey **31** 1 · 廿三				

AUGUST 2040 甲申

Xuan Kong Element 玄空五行	火水未濟 Not Yet Accomplished	Period Luck 卦運	Monthly Star 月星
Wood 木3		9	5

SUNDAY	MONDAY	TUESDAY	WEDNESDAY	THURSDAY	FRIDAY	SATURDAY
			木8 Wood · 3 Lesser Exceeding 雷山小過 辛酉 Metal Rooster **1** 3 · 廿四	金4 Metal · 2 Gathering 澤地萃 壬戌 Water Dog **2** 4 · 廿五	水6 Water · 1 Peel 山地剝 癸亥 Water Pig **3** 6 · 廿六	水1 Water · 9 Earth 坤爲地 甲子 Wood Rat **4** 1 · 廿七
木3 Wood · 8 Biting 火雷噬嗑 乙丑 Wood Ox **5** 6 · 廿八	火2 Fire · 7 Family 風火家人 丙寅 Fire Tiger **6** 4 · 廿九	水6 Water · 6 Decreasing 山澤損 丁卯 Fire Rabbit **7** 9 · 三十	金9 Metal · 5 Tread 天澤履 戊辰 Earth Dragon **8** 6 · 七月初一	木8 Wood · 4 Great Strength 雷天大壯 己巳 Earth Snake **9** 2 · 初二	木8 Wood · 3 Consistency 雷風恆 庚午 Metal Horse **10** 9 · 初三	金9 Metal · 2 Litigation 天水訟 辛未 Metal Goat **11** 3 · 初四
水1 Water · 1 Officer 地水師 壬申 Water Monkey **12** 7 · 初五	火2 Fire · 9 Gradual Progress 風山漸 癸酉 Water Rooster **13** 7 · 初六	火7 Fire · 8 Obstruction 水山蹇 甲戌 Wood Dog **14** 2 · 初七	木3 Wood · 7 Advancement 火地晉 乙亥 Wood Pig **15** 3 · 初八	水6 Water · 6 Nourish 山雷頤 丙子 Fire Rat **16** 3 · 初九	金4 Metal · 5 Following 澤雷隨 丁丑 Fire Ox **17** 7 · 初十	木8 Wood · 4 Abundance 雷火豐 戊寅 Earth Tiger **18** 6 · 十一
火7 Fire · 3 Regulate 水澤節 己卯 Earth Rabbit **19** 8 · 十二	水1 Water · 2 Unity 地天泰 庚辰 Metal Dragon **20** 9 · 十三	木3 Wood · 1 Great Reward 火天大有 辛巳 Metal Snake **21** 7 · 十四	火2 Fire · 9 Wind 巽爲風 壬午 Water Horse **22** 1 · 十五	金4 Metal · 8 Trap 澤水困 癸未 Water Goat **23** 8 · 十六	木3 Wood · 7 Not Yet Accomplished 火水未濟 甲申 Wood Monkey **24** 9 · 十七	金9 Metal · 6 Retreat 天山遯 乙酉 Wood Rooster **25** 4 · 十八
水6 Water · 5 Mountain 艮爲山 丙戌 Fire Dog **26** 1 · 十九	木8 Wood · 4 Delight 雷地豫 丁亥 Fire Pig **27** 8 · 二十	火7 Fire · 3 Beginning 水雷屯 戊子 Earth Rat **28** 4 · 廿一	金9 Metal · 2 Without Wrongdoing 天雷無妄 己丑 Earth Ox **29** 2 · 廿二	木3 Wood · 1 Fire 離爲火 庚寅 Metal Tiger **30** 1 · 廿三	火2 Fire · 9 Sincerity 風澤中孚 辛卯 Metal Rabbit **31** 3 · 廿四	

SEPTEMBER 2040 乙酉

Xuan Kong Element 玄空五行	天山遯 Retreat	Period Luck 卦運	Monthly Star 月星
Metal 金9		4	4

SUNDAY	MONDAY	TUESDAY	WEDNESDAY	THURSDAY	FRIDAY	SATURDAY
木8 Wood 6 Lesser Exceeding 雷山小過 辛酉 Metal Rooster 3 **30** 廿五						水6 Water 8 Big Livestock 山天大畜 壬辰 Water Dragon 4 **1** 廿五
金4 Metal 7 Eliminating 澤天夬 癸巳 Water Snake 6 **2** 廿六	金9 Metal 6 Heaven 乾爲天 甲午 Wood Horse 1 **3** 廿七	火7 Fire 5 Well 水風井 乙未 Wood Goat 6 **4** 廿八	木8 Wood 4 Relief 雷水解 丙申 Fire Monkey 4 **5** 廿九	金4 Metal 3 Influence 澤山咸 丁酉 Fire Rooster 9 **6** 八月初一	水1 Water 2 Humility 地山謙 戊戌 Earth Dog 6 **7** 初二	火2 Fire 1 Observation 風地觀 己亥 Earth Pig 2 **8** 初三
火2 Fire 9 Increasing 風雷益 庚子 Metal Rat 9 **9** 初四	水1 Water 8 Dimming Light 地火明夷 辛丑 Metal Ox 3 **10** 初五	金9 Metal 7 Fellowship 天火同人 壬寅 Water Tiger 7 **11** 初六	木8 Wood 6 Marrying Maiden 雷澤歸妹 癸卯 Water Rabbit 7 **12** 初七	木3 Wood 5 Opposition 火澤睽 甲辰 Wood Dragon 2 **13** 初八	火7 Fire 4 Waiting 水天需 乙巳 Wood Snake 3 **14** 初九	金4 Metal 3 Great Exceeding 澤風大過 丙午 Fire Horse 3 **15** 初十
水6 Water 2 Poison 山風蠱 丁未 Fire Goat 7 **16** 十一	火2 Fire 1 Dispersing 風水渙 戊申 Earth Monkey 6 **17** 十二	木3 Wood 9 Travelling 火山旅 己酉 Earth Rooster 8 **18** 十三	金9 Metal 8 Stagnation 天地否 庚戌 Metal Dog 9 **19** 十四	火7 Fire 7 Alliance 水地比 辛亥 Metal Pig 7 **20** 十五	木8 Wood 6 Thunder 震爲雷 壬子 Water Rat 1 **21** 十六	水6 Water 5 Beauty 山火賁 癸丑 Water Ox 8 **22** 十七
火7 Fire 4 Accomplished 水火既濟 甲寅 Wood Tiger 9 **23** 十八	水1 Water 3 Arriving 地澤臨 乙卯 Wood Rabbit 4 **24** 十九	金4 Metal 2 Marsh 兌爲澤 丙辰 Fire Dragon 1 **25** 二十	火2 Fire 1 Small Livestock 風天小畜 丁巳 Fire Snake 8 **26** 廿一	木3 Wood 9 The Cauldron 火風鼎 戊午 Earth Horse 4 **27** 廿二	水1 Water 8 Rising 地風升 己未 Earth Goat 2 **28** 廿三	火7 Fire 7 Water 坎爲水 庚申 Metal Monkey 1 **29** 廿四

OCTOBER 2040 丙戌

Xuan Kong Element 玄空五行	艮爲山 Mountain	Period Luck 卦運	Monthly Star 月星
Water 水6		1	3

SUNDAY	MONDAY	TUESDAY	WEDNESDAY	THURSDAY	FRIDAY	SATURDAY
	金4 Metal 5 Gathering 澤地萃 壬戌 Water Dog 4 **1** 廿六	水6 Water 4 Peel 山地剝 癸亥 Water Pig 6 **2** 廿七	水1 Water 3 Earth 坤爲地 甲子 Wood Rat 1 **3** 廿八	木3 Wood 2 Biting 火雷噬嗑 乙丑 Wood Ox 6 **4** 廿九	火2 Fire 1 Family 風火家人 丙寅 Fire Tiger 4 **5** 三十	水6 Water 9 Decreasing 山澤損 丁卯 Fire Rabbit 9 **6** 九月初一
金9 Metal 8 Tread 天澤履 戊辰 Earth Dragon 6 **7** 初二	木8 Wood 7 Great Strength 雷天大壯 己巳 Earth Snake 2 **8** 初三	木8 Wood 6 Consistency 雷風恆 庚午 Metal Horse 9 **9** 初四	金9 Metal 5 Litigation 天水訟 辛未 Metal Goat 3 **10** 初五	水1 Water 4 Officer 地水師 壬申 Water Monkey 7 **11** 初六	火2 Fire 3 Gradual Progress 風山漸 癸酉 Water Rooster 7 **12** 初七	火7 Fire 2 Obstruction 水山蹇 甲戌 Wood Dog 2 **13** 初八
木3 Wood 1 Advancement 火地晉 乙亥 Wood Pig 3 **14** 初九	水6 Water 9 Nourish 山雷頤 丙子 Fire Rat 3 **15** 初十	金4 Metal 8 Following 澤雷隨 丁丑 Fire Ox 7 **16** 十一	木8 Wood 7 Abundance 雷火豐 戊寅 Earth Tiger 6 **17** 十二	火7 Fire 6 Regulate 水澤節 己卯 Earth Rabbit 8 **18** 十三	水1 Water 5 Unity 地天泰 庚辰 Metal Dragon 9 **19** 十四	木3 Wood 4 Great Reward 火天大有 辛巳 Metal Snake 7 **20** 十五
火2 Fire 3 Wind 巽爲風 壬午 Water Horse 1 **21** 十六	金4 Metal 2 Trap 澤水困 癸未 Water Goat 8 **22** 十七	木3 Wood 1 Not Yet Accomplished 火水未濟 甲申 Wood Monkey 9 **23** 十八	金9 Metal 9 Retreat 天山遯 乙酉 Wood Rooster 4 **24** 十九	水6 Water 8 Mountain 艮爲山 丙戌 Fire Dog 1 **25** 二十	木8 Wood 7 Delight 雷地豫 丁亥 Fire Pig 8 **26** 廿一	火7 Fire 6 Beginning 水雷屯 戊子 Earth Rat 4 **27** 廿二
金9 Metal 5 Without Wrongdoing 天雷無妄 己丑 Earth Ox 2 **28** 廿三	木3 Wood 4 Fire 離爲火 庚寅 Metal Tiger 1 **29** 廿四	火2 Fire 3 Sincerity 風澤中孚 辛卯 Metal Rabbit 3 **30** 廿五	水6 Water 2 Big Livestock 山天大畜 壬辰 Water Dragon 4 **31** 廿六			

NOVEMBER 2040 丁亥

Xuan Kong Element 玄空五行	雷地豫 Delight	Period Luck 卦運	Monthly Star 月星
Wood 木8		8	2

SUNDAY	MONDAY	TUESDAY	WEDNESDAY	THURSDAY	FRIDAY	SATURDAY
				金4 Metal 1 Eliminating 澤天夬 癸巳 Water Snake 1 6 廿七	金9 Metal 9 Heaven 乾為天 甲午 Wood Horse 2 1 廿八	火7 Fire 8 Well 水風井 乙未 Wood Goat 3 6 廿九
木8 Wood 7 Relief 雷水解 丙申 Fire Monkey 4 4 三十	金4 Metal 6 Influence 澤山咸 丁酉 Fire Rooster 5 9 十月初一	水1 Water 5 Humility 地山謙 戊戌 Earth Dog 6 6 初二	火2 Fire 4 Observation 風地觀 己亥 Earth Pig 7 2 初三	火2 Fire 3 Increasing 風雷益 庚子 Metal Rat 8 9 初四	水1 Water 2 Dimming Light 地火明夷 辛丑 Metal Ox 9 3 初五	金9 Metal 1 Fellowship 天火同人 壬寅 Water Tiger 10 7 初六
木8 Wood 9 Marrying Maiden 雷澤歸妹 癸卯 Water Rabbit 11 7 初七	木3 Wood 8 Opposition 火澤睽 甲辰 Wood Dragon 12 2 初八	火7 Fire 7 Waiting 水天需 乙巳 Wood Snake 13 3 初九	金4 Metal 6 Great Exceeding 澤風大過 丙午 Fire Horse 14 3 初十	水6 Water 5 Poison 山風蠱 丁未 Fire Goat 15 7 十一	火2 Fire 4 Dispersing 風水渙 戊申 Earth Monkey 16 6 十二	木3 Wood 3 Travelling 火山旅 己酉 Earth Rooster 17 8 十三
金9 Metal 2 Stagnation 天地否 庚戌 Metal Dog 18 9 十四	火7 Fire 1 Alliance 水地比 辛亥 Metal Pig 19 7 十五	木8 Wood 9 Thunder 震為雷 壬子 Water Rat 20 1 十六	水6 Water 8 Beauty 山火賁 癸丑 Water Ox 21 8 十七	火7 Fire 7 Accomplished 水火既濟 甲寅 Wood Tiger 22 9 十八	水1 Water 6 Arriving 地澤臨 乙卯 Wood Rabbit 23 4 十九	金4 Metal 5 Marsh 兑為澤 丙辰 Fire Dragon 24 1 二十
火2 Fire 4 Small Livestock 風天小畜 丁巳 Fire Snake 25 8 廿一	木3 Wood 3 The Cauldron 火風鼎 戊午 Earth Horse 26 4 廿二	水1 Water 2 Rising 地風升 己未 Earth Goat 27 2 廿三	火7 Fire 1 Water 坎為水 庚申 Metal Monkey 28 1 廿四	木8 Wood 9 Lesser Exceeding 雷山小過 辛酉 Metal Rooster 29 3 廿五	金4 Metal 8 Gathering 澤地萃 壬戌 Water Dog 30 4 廿六	

DECEMBER 2040 戊子

Xuan Kong Element 玄空五行	水雷屯 Beginning	Period Luck 卦運	Monthly Star 月星
Fire 火7		4	1

SUNDAY	MONDAY	TUESDAY	WEDNESDAY	THURSDAY	FRIDAY	SATURDAY
水6 Water 5 Big Livestock 山天大畜 壬辰 Water Dragon 30 4 廿七	金4 Metal 6 Eliminating 澤天夬 癸巳 Water Snake 31 6 廿八					水6 Water 7 Peel 山地剝 癸亥 Water Pig 1 6 廿七
水1 Water 6 Earth 坤為地 甲子 Wood Rat 2 1 廿八	木3 Wood 5 Biting 火雷噬嗑 乙丑 Wood Ox 3 6 廿九	火2 Fire 4 Family 風火家人 丙寅 Fire Tiger 4 4 十一月初一	水6 Water 3 Decreasing 山澤損 丁卯 Fire Rabbit 5 9 初二	金9 Metal 2 Tread 天澤履 戊辰 Earth Dragon 6 6 初三	木8 Wood 1 Great Strength 雷天大壯 己巳 Earth Snake 7 2 初四	木8 Wood 9 Consistency 雷風恒 庚午 Metal Horse 8 9 初五
金9 Metal 8 Litigation 天水訟 辛未 Metal Goat 9 3 初六	水1 Water 7 Officer 地水師 壬申 Water Monkey 10 7 初七	火2 Fire 6 Gradual Progress 風山漸 癸酉 Water Rooster 11 7 初八	火7 Fire 5 Obstruction 水山蹇 甲戌 Wood Dog 12 2 初九	木3 Wood 4 Advancement 火地晉 乙亥 Wood Pig 13 3 初十	水6 Water 3 Nourish 山雷頤 丙子 Fire Rat 14 3 十一	金4 Metal 2 Following 澤雷隨 丁丑 Fire Ox 15 7 十二
木8 Wood 1 Abundance 雷火豐 戊寅 Earth Tiger 16 6 十三	火7 Fire 9 Regulate 水澤節 己卯 Earth Rabbit 17 8 十四	水1 Water 8 Unity 地天泰 庚辰 Metal Dragon 18 9 十五	木3 Wood 7 Great Reward 火天大有 辛巳 Metal Snake 19 7 十六	火2 Fire 6 Wind 巽為風 壬午 Water Horse 20 1 十七	金4 Metal 5/5 Trap 澤水困 癸未 Water Goat 21 8 十八	木3 Wood 6 Not Yet Accomplished 火水未濟 甲申 Wood Monkey 22 9 十九
金9 Metal 7 Retreat 天山遯 乙酉 Wood Rooster 23 4 二十	水6 Water 8 Mountain 艮為山 丙戌 Fire Dog 24 1 廿一	木8 Wood 9 Delight 雷地豫 丁亥 Fire Pig 25 8 廿二	火7 Fire 1 Beginning 水雷屯 戊子 Earth Rat 26 4 廿三	金9 Metal 2 Without Wrongdoing 天雷無妄 己丑 Earth Ox 27 2 廿四	木3 Wood 3 Fire 離為火 庚寅 Metal Tiger 28 1 廿五	火2 Fire 4 Sincerity 風澤中孚 辛卯 Metal Rabbit 29 3 廿六

2041 辛酉

(*Xin You*) Metal Rooster

2041 辛酉 *(Xin You)* Metal Rooster

January 5 - February 2

February 3 - March 4

March 5 - April 3

April 4 - May 4

May 5 - June 4

June 5 - July 6

July 7 - August 6

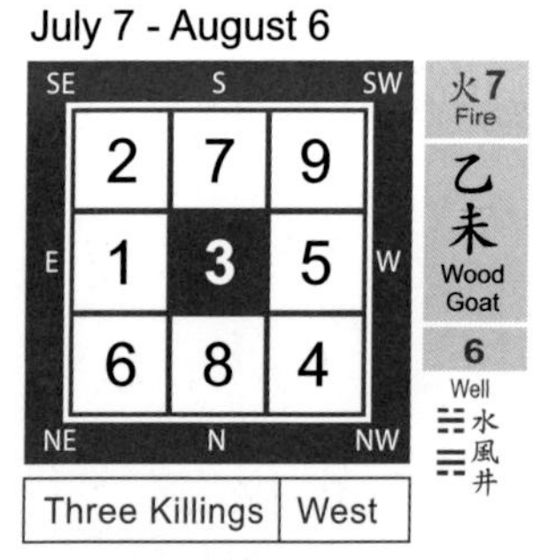

August 7 - September 6

September 7 - October 7

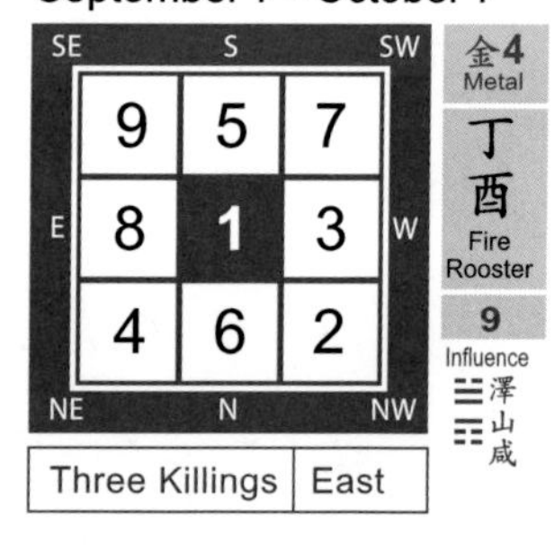

October 8 - November 6

November 7 - December 6

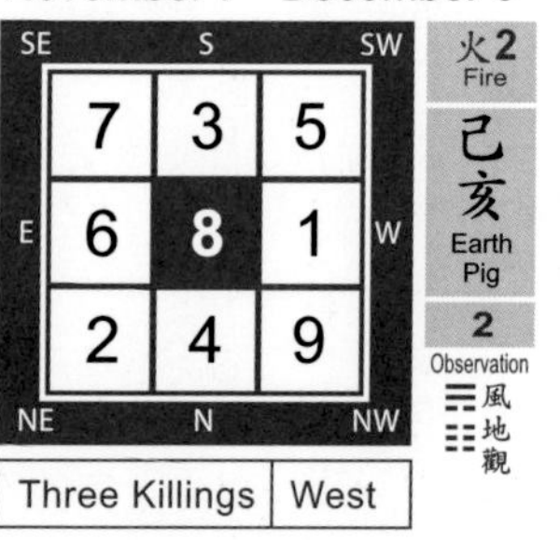

December 7 - January 4

JANUARY 2041 己丑

Xuan Kong Element 玄空五行	天雷無妄 Without Wrongdoing	Period Luck 卦運	Monthly Star 月星
Metal 金9		2	9

SUNDAY	MONDAY	TUESDAY	WEDNESDAY	THURSDAY	FRIDAY	SATURDAY
		金9 Metal · 7 Heaven 乾爲天 甲午 Wood Horse **1** 廿九 1	火7 Fire · 8 Well 水風井 乙未 Wood Goat **2** 三十 6	木8 Wood · 9 Relief 雷水解 丙申 Fire Monkey **3** 十二月初一 4	金4 Metal · 1 Influence 澤山咸 丁酉 Fire Rooster **4** 初二 9	水1 Water · 2 Humility 地山謙 戊戌 Earth Dog **5** 初三 6
火2 Fire · 3 Observation 風地觀 己亥 Earth Pig **6** 初四 2	火2 Fire · 4 Increasing 風雷益 庚子 Metal Rat **7** 初五 9	水1 Water · 5 Dimming Light 地火明夷 辛丑 Metal Ox **8** 初六 3	金9 Metal · 6 Fellowship 天火同人 壬寅 Water Tiger **9** 初七 7	木8 Wood · 7 Marrying Maiden 雷澤歸妹 癸卯 Water Rabbit **10** 初八 7	木3 Wood · 8 Opposition 火澤睽 甲辰 Wood Dragon **11** 初九 2	火7 Fire · 9 Waiting 水天需 乙巳 Wood Snake **12** 初十 3
金4 Metal · 1 Great Exceeding 澤風大過 丙午 Fire Horse **13** 十一 3	水6 Water · 2 Poison 山風蠱 丁未 Fire Goat **14** 十二 7	火2 Fire · 3 Dispersing 風水渙 戊申 Earth Monkey **15** 十三 6	木3 Wood · 4 Travelling 火山旅 己酉 Earth Rooster **16** 十四 8	金9 Metal · 5 Stagnation 天地否 庚戌 Metal Dog **17** 十五 9	火7 Fire · 6 Alliance 水地比 辛亥 Metal Pig **18** 十六 7	木8 Wood · 7 Thunder 震爲雷 壬子 Water Rat **19** 十七 1
水6 Water · 8 Beauty 山火賁 癸丑 Water Ox **20** 十八 8	火7 Fire · 9 Accomplished 水火既濟 甲寅 Wood Tiger **21** 十九 9	水1 Water · 1 Arriving 地澤臨 乙卯 Wood Rabbit **22** 二十 4	金4 Metal · 2 Marsh 兌爲澤 丙辰 Fire Dragon **23** 廿一 1	火2 Fire · 3 Small Livestock 風天小畜 丁巳 Fire Snake **24** 廿二 8	木3 Wood · 4 The Cauldron 火風鼎 戊午 Earth Horse **25** 廿三 4	水1 Water · 5 Rising 地風升 己未 Earth Goat **26** 廿四 2
火7 Fire · 6 Water 坎爲水 庚申 Metal Monkey **27** 廿五 1	木8 Wood · 7 Lesser Exceeding 雷山小過 辛酉 Metal Rooster **28** 廿六 3	金4 Metal · 8 Gathering 澤地萃 壬戌 Water Dog **29** 廿七 4	水6 Water · 9 Peel 山地剝 癸亥 Water Pig **30** 廿八 6	水1 Water · 1 Earth 坤爲地 甲子 Wood Rat **31** 廿九 1		

FEBRUARY 2041 庚寅

Xuan Kong Element 玄空五行	離爲火 Fire	Period Luck 卦運	Monthly Star 月星
Wood 木3		1	8

SUNDAY	MONDAY	TUESDAY	WEDNESDAY	THURSDAY	FRIDAY	SATURDAY
					木3 Wood · 2 Biting 火雷噬嗑 乙丑 Wood Ox **1** 正月初一 6	火2 Fire · 3 Family 風火家人 丙寅 Fire Tiger **2** 初二 4
水6 Water · 4 Decreasing 山澤損 丁卯 Fire Rabbit **3** 初三 9	金9 Metal · 5 Tread 天澤履 戊辰 Earth Dragon **4** 初四 6	木8 Wood · 6 Great Strength 雷天大壯 己巳 Earth Snake **5** 初五 2	木8 Wood · 7 Consistency 雷風恆 庚午 Metal Horse **6** 初六 9	金9 Metal · 8 Litigation 天水訟 辛未 Metal Goat **7** 初七 3	水1 Water · 9 Officer 地水師 壬申 Water Monkey **8** 初八 7	火2 Fire · 1 Gradual Progress 風山漸 癸酉 Water Rooster **9** 初九 7
火7 Fire · 2 Obstruction 水山蹇 甲戌 Wood Dog **10** 初十 2	木3 Wood · 3 Advancement 火地晉 乙亥 Wood Pig **11** 十一 3	水6 Water · 4 Nourish 山雷頤 丙子 Fire Rat **12** 十二 3	金4 Metal · 5 Following 澤雷隨 丁丑 Fire Ox **13** 十三 7	木8 Wood · 6 Abundance 雷火豐 戊寅 Earth Tiger **14** 十四 6	火7 Fire · 7 Regulate 水澤節 己卯 Earth Rabbit **15** 十五 8	水1 Water · 8 Unity 地天泰 庚辰 Metal Dragon **16** 十六 9
木3 Wood · 9 Great Reward 火天大有 辛巳 Metal Snake **17** 十七 7	火2 Fire · 1 Wind 巽爲風 壬午 Water Horse **18** 十八 1	金4 Metal · 2 Trap 澤水困 癸未 Water Goat **19** 十九 8	木3 Wood · 3 Not Yet Accomplished 火水未濟 甲申 Wood Monkey **20** 二十 9	金9 Metal · 4 Retreat 天山遯 乙酉 Wood Rooster **21** 廿一 4	水6 Water · 5 Mountain 艮爲山 丙戌 Fire Dog **22** 廿二 1	木8 Wood · 6 Delight 雷地豫 丁亥 Fire Pig **23** 廿三 8
火7 Fire · 7 Beginning 水雷屯 戊子 Earth Rat **24** 廿四 4	金9 Metal · 8 Without Wrongdoing 天雷無妄 己丑 Earth Ox **25** 廿五 2	木3 Wood · 9 Fire 離爲火 庚寅 Metal Tiger **26** 廿六 1	火2 Fire · 1 Sincerity 風澤中孚 辛卯 Metal Rabbit **27** 廿七 3	水6 Water · 2 Big Livestock 山天大畜 壬辰 Water Dragon **28** 廿八 4		

MARCH 2041 辛卯

Xuan Kong Element 玄空五行	風澤中孚 Sincerity	Period Luck 卦運	Monthly Star 月星
Fire 火2		3	7

SUNDAY	MONDAY	TUESDAY	WEDNESDAY	THURSDAY	FRIDAY	SATURDAY
水6 Water Peel 山地剝 6 癸亥 Water Pig 6 31 三十					金4 Metal Eliminating 澤天夬 3 癸巳 Water Snake 6 1 廿九	金9 Metal Heaven 乾爲天 4 甲午 Wood Horse 1 2 二月初一
火7 Fire Well 水風井 5 乙未 Wood Goat 6 3 初二	木8 Wood Relief 雷水解 6 丙申 Fire Monkey 4 4 初三	金4 Metal Influence 澤山咸 7 丁酉 Fire Rooster 9 5 初四	水1 Water Humility 地山謙 8 戊戌 Earth Dog 6 6 初五	火2 Fire Observation 風地觀 9 己亥 Earth Pig 2 7 初六	火2 Fire Increasing 風雷益 1 庚子 Metal Rat 9 8 初七	水1 Water Dimming Light 地火明夷 2 辛丑 Metal Ox 3 9 初八
金9 Metal Fellowship 天火同人 3 壬寅 Water Tiger 7 10 初九	木8 Wood Marrying Maiden 雷澤歸妹 4 癸卯 Water Rabbit 7 11 初十	木3 Wood Opposition 火澤睽 5 甲辰 Wood Dragon 2 12 十一	火7 Fire Waiting 水天需 6 乙巳 Wood Snake 3 13 十二	金4 Metal Great Exceeding 澤風大過 7 丙午 Fire Horse 3 14 十三	水6 Water Poison 山風蠱 8 丁未 Fire Goat 7 15 十四	火2 Fire Dispersing 風水渙 9 戊申 Earth Monkey 6 16 十五
木3 Wood Travelling 火山旅 1 己酉 Earth Rooster 8 17 十六	金9 Metal Stagnation 天地否 2 庚戌 Metal Dog 9 18 十七	火7 Fire Alliance 水地比 3 辛亥 Metal Pig 7 19 十八	木8 Wood Thunder 震爲雷 4 壬子 Water Rat 1 20 十九	水6 Water Beauty 山火賁 5 癸丑 Water Ox 8 21 二十	火7 Fire Accomplished 水火既濟 6 甲寅 Wood Tiger 9 22 廿一	水1 Water Arriving 地澤臨 7 乙卯 Wood Rabbit 4 23 廿二
金4 Metal Marsh 兑爲澤 8 丙辰 Fire Dragon 1 24 廿三	火2 Fire Small Livestock 風天小畜 9 丁巳 Fire Snake 8 25 廿四	木3 Wood The Cauldron 火風鼎 1 戊午 Earth Horse 4 26 廿五	水1 Water Rising 地風升 2 己未 Earth Goat 2 27 廿六	火7 Fire Water 坎爲水 3 庚申 Metal Monkey 1 28 廿七	木8 Wood Lesser Exceeding 雷山小過 4 辛酉 Metal Rooster 3 29 廿八	金4 Metal Gathering 澤地萃 5 壬戌 Water Dog 4 30 廿九

APRIL 2041 壬辰

Xuan Kong Element 玄空五行	山天大畜 Big Livestock	Period Luck 卦運	Monthly Star 月星
Water 水6		4	6

SUNDAY	MONDAY	TUESDAY	WEDNESDAY	THURSDAY	FRIDAY	SATURDAY
	水1 Water Earth 坤爲地 7 甲子 Wood Rat 1 1 三月初一	木3 Wood Biting 火雷噬嗑 8 乙丑 Wood Ox 6 2 初二	火2 Fire Family 風火家人 9 丙寅 Fire Tiger 4 3 初三	水6 Water Decreasing 山澤損 1 丁卯 Fire Rabbit 9 4 初四	金9 Metal Tread 天澤履 2 戊辰 Earth Dragon 6 5 初五	木8 Wood Great Strength 雷天大壯 3 己巳 Earth Snake 2 6 初六
木8 Wood Consistency 雷風恆 4 庚午 Metal Horse 9 7 初七	金9 Metal Litigation 天水訟 5 辛未 Metal Goat 3 8 初八	水1 Water Officer 地水師 6 壬申 Water Monkey 7 9 初九	火2 Fire Gradual Progress 風山漸 7 癸酉 Water Rooster 7 10 初十	火7 Fire Obstruction 水山蹇 8 甲戌 Wood Dog 2 11 十一	木3 Wood Advancement 火地晉 9 乙亥 Wood Pig 3 12 十二	水6 Water Nourish 山雷頤 1 丙子 Fire Rat 3 13 十三
金4 Metal Following 澤雷隨 2 丁丑 Fire Ox 7 14 十四	木8 Wood Abundance 雷火豐 3 戊寅 Earth Tiger 6 15 十五	火7 Fire Regulate 水澤節 4 己卯 Earth Rabbit 8 16 十六	水1 Water Unity 地天泰 5 庚辰 Metal Dragon 9 17 十七	木3 Wood Great Reward 火天大有 6 辛巳 Metal Snake 7 18 十八	火2 Fire Wind 巽爲風 7 壬午 Water Horse 1 19 十九	金4 Metal Trap 澤水困 8 癸未 Water Goat 8 20 二十
木3 Wood Not Yet Accomplished 火水未濟 9 甲申 Wood Monkey 9 21 廿一	金9 Metal Retreat 天山遯 1 乙酉 Wood Rooster 4 22 廿二	水6 Water Mountain 艮爲山 2 丙戌 Fire Dog 1 23 廿三	木8 Wood Delight 雷地豫 3 丁亥 Fire Pig 8 24 廿四	火7 Fire Beginning 水雷屯 4 戊子 Earth Rat 4 25 廿五	金9 Metal Without Wrongdoing 天雷無妄 5 己丑 Earth Ox 2 26 廿六	木3 Wood Fire 離爲火 6 庚寅 Metal Tiger 1 27 廿七
火2 Fire Sincerity 風澤中孚 7 辛卯 Metal Rabbit 3 28 廿八	水6 Water Big Livestock 山天大畜 8 壬辰 Water Dragon 4 29 廿九	金4 Metal Eliminating 澤天夬 9 癸巳 Water Snake 6 30 四月初一				

MAY 2041 癸巳

Xuan Kong Element 玄空五行	澤天夬 Eliminating	Period Luck 卦運	Monthly Star 月星
Metal 金4		6	5

SUNDAY	MONDAY	TUESDAY	WEDNESDAY	THURSDAY	FRIDAY	SATURDAY
			金9 Metal [1] Heaven 乾爲天 甲午 Wood Horse **1** 初二 1	火7 Fire [2] Well 水風井 乙未 Wood Goat **2** 初三 6	木8 Wood [3] Relief 雷水解 丙申 Fire Monkey **3** 初四 4	金4 Metal [4] Influence 澤山咸 丁酉 Fire Rooster **4** 初五 9
水1 Water [5] Humility 地山謙 戊戌 Earth Dog **5** 初六 6	火2 Fire [6] Observation 風地觀 己亥 Earth Pig **6** 初七 2	火2 Fire [7] Increasing 風雷益 庚子 Metal Rat **7** 初八 9	水1 Water [8] Dimming Light 地火明夷 辛丑 Metal Ox **8** 初九 3	金9 Metal [9] Fellowship 天火同人 壬寅 Water Tiger **9** 初十 7	木8 Wood [1] Marrying Maiden 雷澤歸妹 癸卯 Water Rabbit **10** 十一 7	木3 Wood [2] Opposition 火澤睽 甲辰 Wood Dragon **11** 十二 2
火7 Fire [3] Waiting 水天需 乙巳 Wood Snake **12** 十三 3	金4 Metal [4] Great Exceeding 澤風大過 丙午 Fire Horse **13** 十四 3	水6 Water [5] Poison 山風蠱 丁未 Fire Goat **14** 十五 7	火2 Fire [6] Dispersing 風水渙 戊申 Earth Monkey **15** 十六 6	木3 Wood [7] Travelling 火山旅 己酉 Earth Rooster **16** 十七 8	金9 Metal [8] Stagnation 天地否 庚戌 Metal Dog **17** 十八 9	火7 Fire [9] Alliance 水地比 辛亥 Metal Pig **18** 十九 7
木8 Wood [1] Thunder 震爲雷 壬子 Water Rat **19** 二十 1	水6 Water [2] Beauty 山火賁 癸丑 Water Ox **20** 廿一 8	火7 Fire [3] Accomplished 水火既濟 甲寅 Wood Tiger **21** 廿二 9	水1 Water [4] Arriving 地澤臨 乙卯 Wood Rabbit **22** 廿三 4	金4 Metal [5] Marsh 兑爲澤 丙辰 Fire Dragon **23** 廿四 1	火2 Fire [6] Small Livestock 風天小畜 丁巳 Fire Snake **24** 廿五 8	木3 Wood [7] The Cauldron 火風鼎 戊午 Earth Horse **25** 廿六 4
水1 Water [8] Rising 地風升 己未 Earth Goat **26** 廿七 2	火7 Fire [9] Water 坎爲水 庚申 Metal Monkey **27** 廿八 1	木8 Wood [1] Lesser Exceeding 雷山小過 辛酉 Metal Rooster **28** 廿九 3	金4 Metal [2] Gathering 澤地萃 壬戌 Water Dog **29** 三十 4	水6 Water [3] Peel 山地剝 癸亥 Water Pig **30** 五月初一 6	水1 Water [4] Earth 坤爲地 甲子 Wood Rat **31** 初二 1	

JUNE 2041 甲午

Xuan Kong Element 玄空五行	乾爲天 Heaven	Period Luck 卦運	Monthly Star 月星
Metal 金9		1	4

SUNDAY	MONDAY	TUESDAY	WEDNESDAY	THURSDAY	FRIDAY	SATURDAY
金9 Metal [3] Heaven 乾爲天 甲午 Wood Horse **30** 初三 1						木3 Wood [5] Biting 火雷噬嗑 乙丑 Wood Ox **1** 初三 6
火2 Fire [6] Family 風火家人 丙寅 Fire Tiger **2** 初四 4	水6 Water [7] Decreasing 山澤損 丁卯 Fire Rabbit **3** 初五 9	金9 Metal [8] Tread 天澤履 戊辰 Earth Dragon **4** 初六 6	木8 Wood [9] Great Strength 雷天大壯 己巳 Earth Snake **5** 初七 2	木8 Wood [1] Consistency 雷風恆 庚午 Metal Horse **6** 初八 9	金9 Metal [2] Litigation 天水訟 辛未 Metal Goat **7** 初九 3	水1 Water [3] Officer 地水師 壬申 Water Monkey **8** 初十 7
火2 Fire [4] Gradual Progress 風山漸 癸酉 Water Rooster **9** 十一 7	火7 Fire [5] Obstruction 水山蹇 甲戌 Wood Dog **10** 十二 2	木3 Wood [6] Advancement 火地晉 乙亥 Wood Pig **11** 十三 3	水6 Water [7] Nourish 山雷頤 丙子 Fire Rat **12** 十四 3	金4 Metal [8] Following 澤雷隨 丁丑 Fire Ox **13** 十五 7	木8 Wood [9] Abundance 雷火豐 戊寅 Earth Tiger **14** 十六 6	火7 Fire [1] Regulate 水澤節 己卯 Earth Rabbit **15** 十七 8
水1 Water [2] Unity 地天泰 庚辰 Metal Dragon **16** 十八 9	木3 Wood [3] Great Reward 火天大有 辛巳 Metal Snake **17** 十九 7	火2 Fire [4] Wind 巽爲風 壬午 Water Horse **18** 二十 1	金4 Metal [5] Trap 澤水困 癸未 Water Goat **19** 廿一 8	木3 Wood [4] Not Yet Accomplished 火水未濟 甲申 Wood Monkey **20** 廿二 9	金9 Metal [7/8] Retreat 天山遯 乙酉 Wood Rooster **21** 廿三 4	水6 Water [2] Mountain 艮爲山 丙戌 Fire Dog **22** 廿四 1
木8 Wood [1] Delight 雷地豫 丁亥 Fire Pig **23** 廿五 8	火7 Fire [9] Beginning 水雷屯 戊子 Earth Rat **24** 廿六 4	金9 Metal [8] Without Wrongdoing 天雷無妄 己丑 Earth Ox **25** 廿七 2	木3 Wood [7] Fire 離爲火 庚寅 Metal Tiger **26** 廿八 1	火2 Fire [6] Sincerity 風澤中孚 辛卯 Metal Rabbit **27** 廿九 3	水6 Water [5] Big Livestock 山天大畜 壬辰 Water Dragon **28** 六月初一 4	金4 Metal [4] Eliminating 澤天夬 癸巳 Water Snake **29** 初二 6

JULY 2041 乙未

Xuan Kong Element 玄空五行	水風井 Well	Period Luck 卦運	Monthly Star 月星
Fire 火7		6	3

SUNDAY	MONDAY	TUESDAY	WEDNESDAY	THURSDAY	FRIDAY	SATURDAY
	1 火7 Fire · Well · 2 乙未 Wood Goat 水風井 6 · 初四	2 木8 Wood · Relief · 1 丙申 Fire Monkey 雷水解 4 · 初五	3 金4 Metal · Influence · 9 丁酉 Fire Rooster 澤山咸 9 · 初六	4 水1 Water · Humility · 8 戊戌 Earth Dog 地山謙 6 · 初七	5 火2 Fire · Observation · 7 己亥 Earth Pig 風地觀 2 · 初八	6 火2 Fire · Increasing · 6 庚子 Metal Rat 風雷益 9 · 初九
7 水1 Water · Dimming Light · 5 辛丑 Metal Ox 地火明夷 3 · 初十	8 金9 Metal · Fellowship · 4 壬寅 Water Tiger 天火同人 7 · 十一	9 木8 Wood · Marrying Maiden · 3 癸卯 Water Rabbit 雷澤歸妹 7 · 十二	10 木3 Wood · Opposition · 2 甲辰 Wood Dragon 火澤睽 2 · 十三	11 火7 Fire · Waiting · 1 乙巳 Wood Snake 水天需 3 · 十四	12 金4 Metal · Great Exceeding · 9 丙午 Fire Horse 澤風大過 3 · 十五	13 水6 Water · Poison · 8 丁未 Fire Goat 山風蠱 7 · 十六
14 火2 Fire · Dispersing · 7 戊申 Earth Monkey 風水渙 6 · 十七	15 木3 Wood · Travelling · 6 己酉 Earth Rooster 火山旅 8 · 十八	16 金9 Metal · Stagnation · 5 庚戌 Metal Dog 天地否 9 · 十九	17 火7 Fire · Alliance · 4 辛亥 Metal Pig 水地比 7 · 二十	18 木8 Wood · Thunder · 3 壬子 Water Rat 震爲雷 1 · 廿一	19 水6 Water · Beauty · 2 癸丑 Water Ox 山火賁 8 · 廿二	20 火7 Fire · Accomplished · 1 甲寅 Wood Tiger 水火既濟 9 · 廿三
21 水1 Water · Arriving · 9 乙卯 Wood Rabbit 地澤臨 4 · 廿四	22 金4 Metal · Marsh · 8 丙辰 Fire Dragon 兑爲澤 1 · 廿五	23 火2 Fire · Small Livestock · 7 丁巳 Fire Snake 風天小畜 8 · 廿六	24 木3 Wood · The Cauldron · 6 戊午 Earth Horse 火風鼎 4 · 廿七	25 水1 Water · Rising · 5 己未 Earth Goat 地風升 2 · 廿八	26 火7 Fire · Water · 4 庚申 Metal Monkey 坎爲水 1 · 廿九	27 木8 Wood · Lesser Exceeding · 3 辛酉 Metal Rooster 雷山小過 3 · 三十
28 金4 Metal · Gathering · 2 壬戌 Water Dog 澤地萃 4 · 七月初一	29 水6 Water · Peel · 1 癸亥 Water Pig 山地剝 6 · 初二	30 水1 Water · Earth · 9 甲子 Wood Rat 坤爲地 1 · 初三	31 木3 Wood · Biting · 8 乙丑 Wood Ox 火雷噬嗑 6 · 初四			

AUGUST 2041 丙申

Xuan Kong Element 玄空五行	雷水解 Relief	Period Luck 卦運	Monthly Star 月星
Wood 木8		4	2

SUNDAY	MONDAY	TUESDAY	WEDNESDAY	THURSDAY	FRIDAY	SATURDAY
				1 火2 Fire · Family · 7 丙寅 Fire Tiger 風火家人 4 · 初五	2 水6 Water · Decreasing · 6 丁卯 Fire Rabbit 山澤損 9 · 初六	3 金9 Metal · Tread · 5 戊辰 Earth Dragon 天澤履 6 · 初七
4 木8 Wood · Great Strength · 4 己巳 Earth Snake 雷天大壯 2 · 初八	5 木8 Wood · Consistency · 3 庚午 Metal Horse 雷風恆 9 · 初九	6 金9 Metal · Litigation · 2 辛未 Metal Goat 天水訟 3 · 初十	7 水1 Water · Officer · 1 壬申 Water Monkey 地水師 7 · 十一	8 火2 Fire · Gradual Progress · 9 癸酉 Water Rooster 風山漸 7 · 十二	9 火7 Fire · Obstruction · 8 甲戌 Wood Dog 水山蹇 2 · 十三	10 木3 Wood · Advancement · 7 乙亥 Wood Pig 火地晉 3 · 十四
11 水6 Water · Nourish · 6 丙子 Fire Rat 山雷頤 3 · 十五	12 金4 Metal · Following · 5 丁丑 Fire Ox 澤雷隨 7 · 十六	13 木8 Wood · Abundance · 4 戊寅 Earth Tiger 雷火豐 6 · 十七	14 火7 Fire · Regulate · 3 己卯 Earth Rabbit 水澤節 8 · 十八	15 水1 Water · Unity · 2 庚辰 Metal Dragon 地天泰 9 · 十九	16 木3 Wood · Great Reward · 1 辛巳 Metal Snake 火天大有 7 · 二十	17 火2 Fire · Wind · 9 壬午 Water Horse 巽爲風 1 · 廿一
18 金4 Metal · Trap · 8 癸未 Water Goat 澤水困 8 · 廿二	19 木3 Wood · Not Yet Accomplished · 7 甲申 Wood Monkey 火水未濟 9 · 廿三	20 金9 Metal · Retreat · 6 乙酉 Wood Rooster 天山遯 4 · 廿四	21 水6 Water · Mountain · 5 丙戌 Fire Dog 艮爲山 1 · 廿五	22 木8 Wood · Delight · 4 丁亥 Fire Pig 雷地豫 8 · 廿六	23 火7 Fire · Beginning · 3 戊子 Earth Rat 水雷屯 4 · 廿七	24 金9 Metal · Without Wrongdoing · 2 己丑 Earth Ox 天雷無妄 2 · 廿八
25 木3 Wood · Fire · 1 庚寅 Metal Tiger 離爲火 1 · 廿九	26 火2 Fire · Sincerity · 9 辛卯 Metal Rabbit 風澤中孚 3 · 三十	27 水6 Water · Big Livestock · 8 壬辰 Water Dragon 山天大畜 4 · 八月初一	28 金4 Metal · Eliminating · 7 癸巳 Water Snake 澤天夬 6 · 初二	29 金9 Metal · Heaven · 6 甲午 Wood Horse 乾爲天 1 · 初三	30 火7 Fire · Well · 5 乙未 Wood Goat 水風井 6 · 初四	31 木8 Wood · Relief · 4 丙申 Fire Monkey 雷水解 4 · 初五

SEPTEMBER 2041 丁酉

Xuan Kong Element 玄空五行	澤山咸 Influence	Period Luck 卦運	Monthly Star 月星
Metal 金4		9	1

SUNDAY	MONDAY	TUESDAY	WEDNESDAY	THURSDAY	FRIDAY	SATURDAY
金4 Metal Influence 3 丁酉 Fire Rooster 澤山咸 **1** 初六 9	水1 Water Humility 2 戊戌 Earth Dog 地山謙 **2** 初七 6	火2 Fire Observation 1 己亥 Earth Pig 風地觀 **3** 初八 2	火2 Fire Increasing 9 庚子 Metal Rat 風雷益 **4** 初九 9	水1 Water Dimming Light 8 辛丑 Metal Ox 地火明夷 **5** 初十 3	金9 Metal Fellowship 7 壬寅 Water Tiger 天火同人 **6** 十一 7	木8 Wood Marrying Maiden 6 癸卯 Water Rabbit 雷澤歸妹 **7** 十二 7
木3 Wood Opposition 5 甲辰 Wood Dragon 火澤睽 **8** 十三 2	火7 Fire Waiting 4 乙巳 Wood Snake 水天需 **9** 十四 3	金4 Metal Great Exceeding 3 丙午 Fire Horse 澤風大過 **10** 十五 3	水6 Water Poison 2 丁未 Fire Goat 山風蠱 **11** 十六 7	火2 Fire Dispersing 1 戊申 Earth Monkey 風水渙 **12** 十七 6	木3 Wood Travelling 9 己酉 Earth Rooster 火山旅 **13** 十八 8	金9 Metal Stagnation 8 庚戌 Metal Dog 天地否 **14** 十九 9
火7 Fire Alliance 7 辛亥 Metal Pig 水地比 **15** 二十 7	木8 Wood Thunder 6 壬子 Water Rat 震爲雷 **16** 廿一 1	水6 Water Beauty 5 癸丑 Water Ox 山火賁 **17** 廿二 8	火7 Fire Accomplished 4 甲寅 Wood Tiger 水火既濟 **18** 廿三 9	水1 Water Arriving 3 乙卯 Wood Rabbit 地澤臨 **19** 廿四 4	金4 Metal Marsh 2 丙辰 Fire Dragon 兑爲澤 **20** 廿五 1	火2 Fire Small Livestock 1 丁巳 Fire Snake 風天小畜 **21** 廿六 8
木3 Wood The Cauldron 9 戊午 Earth Horse 火風鼎 **22** 廿七 4	水1 Water Rising 8 己未 Earth Goat 地風升 **23** 廿八 2	火7 Fire Water 7 庚申 Metal Monkey 坎爲水 **24** 廿九 1	木8 Wood Lesser Exceeding 6 辛酉 Metal Rooster 雷山小過 **25** 九月初一 3	金4 Metal Gathering 5 壬戌 Water Dog 澤地萃 **26** 初二 4	水6 Water Peel 4 癸亥 Water Pig 山地剝 **27** 初三 6	水1 Water Earth 3 甲子 Wood Rat 坤爲地 **28** 初四 1
木3 Wood Biting 2 乙丑 Wood Ox 火雷噬嗑 **29** 初五 6	火2 Fire Family 1 丙寅 Fire Tiger 風火家人 **30** 初六 4					

OCTOBER 2041 戊戌

Xuan Kong Element 玄空五行	地山謙 Humility	Period Luck 卦運	Monthly Star 月星
Water 水1		6	9

SUNDAY	MONDAY	TUESDAY	WEDNESDAY	THURSDAY	FRIDAY	SATURDAY
		水6 Water Decreasing 9 丁卯 Fire Rabbit 山澤損 **1** 初七 9	金9 Metal Tread 8 戊辰 Earth Dragon 天澤履 **2** 初八 6	木8 Wood Great Strength 7 己巳 Earth Snake 雷天大壯 **3** 初九 2	木8 Wood Consistency 6 庚午 Metal Horse 雷風恒 **4** 初十 9	金9 Metal Litigation 5 辛未 Metal Goat 天水訟 **5** 十一 3
水1 Water Officer 4 壬申 Water Monkey 地水師 **6** 十二 7	火2 Fire Gradual Progress 3 癸酉 Water Rooster 風山漸 **7** 十三 7	火7 Fire Obstruction 2 甲戌 Wood Dog 水山蹇 **8** 十四 2	木3 Wood Advancement 1 乙亥 Wood Pig 火地晉 **9** 十五 3	水6 Water Nourish 9 丙子 Fire Rat 山雷頤 **10** 十六 3	金4 Metal Following 8 丁丑 Fire Ox 澤雷隨 **11** 十七 7	木8 Wood Abundance 7 戊寅 Earth Tiger 雷火豐 **12** 十八 6
火7 Fire Regulate 6 己卯 Earth Rabbit 水澤節 **13** 十九 8	水1 Water Unity 5 庚辰 Metal Dragon 地天泰 **14** 二十 9	木3 Wood Great Reward 4 辛巳 Metal Snake 火天大有 **15** 廿一 7	火2 Fire Wind 3 壬午 Water Horse 巽爲風 **16** 廿二 1	金4 Metal Trap 2 癸未 Water Goat 澤水困 **17** 廿三 8	木3 Wood Not Yet Accomplished 1 甲申 Wood Monkey 火水未濟 **18** 廿四 9	金9 Metal Retreat 9 乙酉 Wood Rooster 天山遯 **19** 廿五 4
水6 Water Mountain 8 丙戌 Fire Dog 艮爲山 **20** 廿六 1	木8 Wood Delight 7 丁亥 Fire Pig 雷地豫 **21** 廿七 8	火7 Fire Beginning 6 戊子 Earth Rat 水雷屯 **22** 廿八 4	金9 Metal Without Wrongdoing 5 己丑 Earth Ox 天雷無妄 **23** 廿九 2	木3 Wood Fire 4 庚寅 Metal Tiger 離爲火 **24** 三十 1	火2 Fire Sincerity 3 辛卯 Metal Rabbit 風澤中孚 **25** 十月初一 3	水6 Water Big Livestock 2 壬辰 Water Dragon 山天大畜 **26** 初二 4
金4 Metal Eliminating 1 癸巳 Water Snake 澤天夬 **27** 初三 6	金9 Metal Heaven 9 甲午 Wood Horse 乾爲天 **28** 初四 1	火7 Fire Well 8 乙未 Wood Goat 水風井 **29** 初五 6	木8 Wood Relief 7 丙申 Fire Monkey 雷水解 **30** 初六 4	金4 Metal Influence 6 丁酉 Fire Rooster 澤山咸 **31** 初七 9		

NOVEMBER 2041 己亥

Xuan Kong Element 玄空五行	風地觀 Observation	Period Luck 卦運	Monthly Star 月星
Fire 火2		2	8

SUNDAY	MONDAY	TUESDAY	WEDNESDAY	THURSDAY	FRIDAY	SATURDAY
					1 水1 Water · 5 Humility 地山謙 戊戌 Earth Dog 6 · 初八	**2** 火2 Fire · 4 Observation 風地觀 己亥 Earth Pig 2 · 初九
3 火2 Fire · 3 Increasing 風雷益 庚子 Metal Rat 9 · 初十	**4** 水1 Water · 2 Dimming Light 地火明夷 辛丑 Metal Ox 3 · 十一	**5** 金9 Metal · 1 Fellowship 天火同人 壬寅 Water Tiger 7 · 十二	**6** 木8 Wood · 9 Marrying Maiden 雷澤歸妹 癸卯 Water Rabbit 7 · 十三	**7** 木3 Wood · 8 Opposition 火澤睽 甲辰 Wood Dragon 2 · 十四	**8** 火7 Fire · 7 Waiting 水天需 乙巳 Wood Snake 3 · 十五	**9** 金4 Metal · 6 Great Exceeding 澤風大過 丙午 Fire Horse 3 · 十六
10 水6 Water · 5 Poison 山風蠱 丁未 Fire Goat 7 · 十七	**11** 火2 Fire · 4 Dispersing 風水渙 戊申 Earth Monkey 6 · 十八	**12** 木3 Wood · 3 Travelling 火山旅 己酉 Earth Rooster 8 · 十九	**13** 金9 Metal · 2 Stagnation 天地否 庚戌 Metal Dog 9 · 二十	**14** 火7 Fire · 1 Alliance 水地比 辛亥 Metal Pig 7 · 廿一	**15** 木8 Wood · 9 Thunder 震爲雷 壬子 Water Rat 1 · 廿二	**16** 水6 Water · 8 Beauty 山火賁 癸丑 Water Ox 8 · 廿三
17 火7 Fire · 7 Accomplished 水火既濟 甲寅 Wood Tiger 9 · 廿四	**18** 水1 Water · 6 Arriving 地澤臨 乙卯 Wood Rabbit 4 · 廿五	**19** 金4 Metal · 5 Marsh 兑爲澤 丙辰 Fire Dragon 1 · 廿六	**20** 火2 Fire · 4 Small Livestock 風天小畜 丁巳 Fire Snake 8 · 廿七	**21** 木3 Wood · 3 The Cauldron 火風鼎 戊午 Earth Horse 4 · 廿八	**22** 水1 Water · 2 Rising 地風升 己未 Earth Goat 2 · 廿九	**23** 火7 Fire · 1 Water 坎爲水 庚申 Metal Monkey 1 · 三十
24 木8 Wood · 9 Lesser Exceeding 雷山小過 辛酉 Metal Rooster 3 · 十一月初一	**25** 金4 Metal · 8 Gathering 澤地萃 壬戌 Water Dog 4 · 初二	**26** 水6 Water · 7 Peel 山地剝 癸亥 Water Pig 6 · 初三	**27** 水1 Water · 6 Earth 坤爲地 甲子 Wood Rat 1 · 初四	**28** 木3 Wood · 5 Biting 火雷噬嗑 乙丑 Wood Ox 6 · 初五	**29** 火2 Fire · 4 Family 風火家人 丙寅 Fire Tiger 4 · 初六	**30** 水6 Water · 3 Decreasing 山澤損 丁卯 Fire Rabbit 9 · 初七

DECEMBER 2041 庚子

Xuan Kong Element 玄空五行	風雷益 Increasing	Period Luck 卦運	Monthly Star 月星
Fire 火2		9	7

SUNDAY	MONDAY	TUESDAY	WEDNESDAY	THURSDAY	FRIDAY	SATURDAY
1 金9 Metal · 2 Tread 天澤履 戊辰 Earth Dragon 6 · 初八	**2** 木8 Wood · 1 Great Strength 雷天大壯 己巳 Earth Snake 2 · 初九	**3** 木8 Wood · 9 Consistency 雷風恆 庚午 Metal Horse 9 · 初十	**4** 金9 Metal · 8 Litigation 天水訟 辛未 Metal Goat 3 · 十一	**5** 水1 Water · 7 Officer 地水師 壬申 Water Monkey 7 · 十二	**6** 火2 Fire · 6 Gradual Progress 風山漸 癸酉 Water Rooster 7 · 十三	**7** 火7 Fire · 5 Obstruction 水山蹇 甲戌 Wood Dog 2 · 十四
8 木3 Wood · 4 Advancement 火地晉 乙亥 Wood Pig 3 · 十五	**9** 水6 Water · 3 Nourish 山雷頤 丙子 Fire Rat 3 · 十六	**10** 金4 Metal · 2 Following 澤雷隨 丁丑 Fire Ox 7 · 十七	**11** 木8 Wood · 1 Abundance 雷火豐 戊寅 Earth Tiger 6 · 十八	**12** 火7 Fire · 9 Regulate 水澤節 己卯 Earth Rabbit 8 · 十九	**13** 水1 Water · 8 Unity 地天泰 庚辰 Metal Dragon 9 · 二十	**14** 木3 Wood · 7 Great Reward 火天大有 辛巳 Metal Snake 7 · 廿一
15 火2 Fire · 6 Wind 巽爲風 壬午 Water Horse 1 · 廿二	**16** 金4 Metal · 5 Trap 澤水困 癸未 Water Goat 8 · 廿三	**17** 木3 Wood · 4 Not Yet Accomplished 火水未濟 甲申 Wood Monkey 9 · 廿四	**18** 金9 Metal · 3 Retreat 天山遯 乙酉 Wood Rooster 4 · 廿五	**19** 水6 Water · 2 Mountain 艮爲山 丙戌 Fire Dog 1 · 廿六	**20** 木8 Wood · 1 Delight 雷地豫 丁亥 Fire Pig 8 · 廿七	**21** 火7 Fire · 9/1 Beginning 水雷屯 戊子 Earth Rat 4 · 廿八
22 金9 Metal · 2 Without Wrongdoing 天雷無妄 己丑 Earth Ox 2 · 廿九	**23** 木3 Wood · 3 Fire 離爲火 庚寅 Metal Tiger 1 · 十二月初一	**24** 火2 Fire · 4 Sincerity 風澤中孚 辛卯 Metal Rabbit 3 · 初二	**25** 水6 Water · 5 Big Livestock 山天大畜 壬辰 Water Dragon 4 · 初三	**26** 金4 Metal · 6 Eliminating 澤天夬 癸巳 Water Snake 6 · 初四	**27** 金9 Metal · 7 Heaven 乾爲天 甲午 Wood Horse 1 · 初五	**28** 火7 Fire · 8 Well 水風井 乙未 Wood Goat 6 · 初六
29 木8 Wood · 9 Relief 雷水解 丙申 Fire Monkey 4 · 初七	**30** 金4 Metal · 1 Influence 澤山咸 丁酉 Fire Rooster 9 · 初八	**31** 水1 Water · 2 Humility 地山謙 戊戌 Earth Dog 6 · 初九				

2042 壬戌

(*Ren Xu*) Water Dog

2042 壬戌 *(Ren Xu)* Water Dog

January 5 - February 3
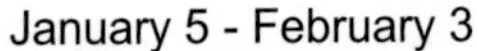

水1 Water
辛丑 Metal Ox
3 Dimming Light
地火明夷

February 4 - March 4

金9 Metal
壬寅 Water Tiger
7 Fellowship
天火同人

March 5 - April 3

April 4 - May 4

木3 Wood
甲辰 Wood Dragon
2 Opposition
火澤睽

May 5 - June 4

火7 Fire
乙巳 Wood Snake
3 Waiting
水天需

June 5 - July 6
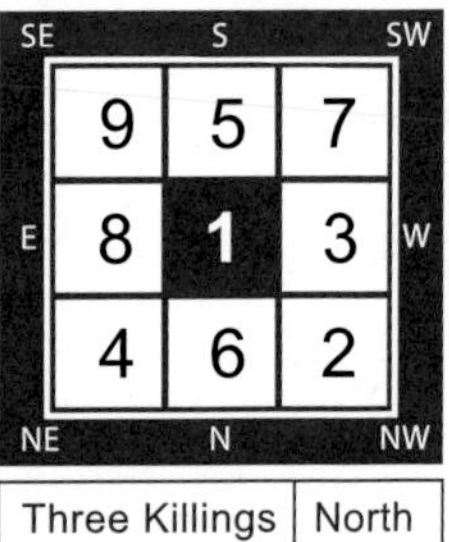

July 7 - August 6

水6 Water
丁未 Fire Goat
7 Poison
山風蠱

August 7 - September 6

火2 Fire
戊申 Earth Monkey
6 Dispersing
風水渙

September 7 - October 7

October 8 - November 6

金9 Metal
庚戌 Metal Dog
9 Stagnation
天地否

November 7 - December 6
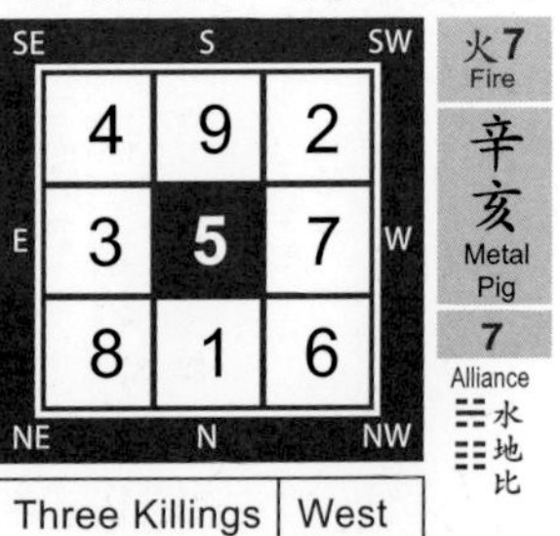

火7 Fire
辛亥 Metal Pig
7 Alliance
水地比

December 7 - January 4

木8 Wood
壬子 Water Rat
1 Thunder
震爲雷

JANUARY 2042 辛丑

Xuan Kong Element 玄空五行	地火明夷 Dimming Light	Period Luck 卦運	Monthly Star 月星
Water 水1		3	6

SUNDAY	MONDAY	TUESDAY	WEDNESDAY	THURSDAY	FRIDAY	SATURDAY
			火2 Fire 3 Observation 己亥 Earth Pig 風地觀 **1** 初十 2	火2 Fire 4 Increasing 庚子 Metal Rat 風雷益 **2** 十一 9	水1 Water 5 Dimming Light 辛丑 Metal Ox 地火明夷 **3** 十二 3	金9 Metal 6 Fellowship 壬寅 Water Tiger 天火同人 **4** 十三 7
木8 Wood 7 Marrying Maiden 癸卯 Water Rabbit 雷澤歸妹 **5** 十四 7	木3 Wood 8 Opposition 甲辰 Wood Dragon 火澤睽 **6** 十五 2	火7 Fire 9 Waiting 乙巳 Wood Snake 水天需 **7** 十六 3	金4 Metal 1 Great Exceeding 丙午 Fire Horse 澤風大過 **8** 十七 3	水6 Water 2 Poison 丁未 Fire Goat 山風蠱 **9** 十八 7	火2 Fire 3 Dispersing 戊申 Earth Monkey 風水渙 **10** 十九 6	木3 Wood 4 Travelling 己酉 Earth Rooster 火山旅 **11** 二十 8
金9 Metal 5 Stagnation 庚戌 Metal Dog 天地否 **12** 廿一 9	火7 Fire 6 Alliance 辛亥 Metal Pig 水地比 **13** 廿二 7	木8 Wood 7 Thunder 壬子 Water Rat 震爲雷 **14** 廿三 1	水6 Water 8 Beauty 癸丑 Water Ox 山火賁 **15** 廿四 8	火7 Fire 9 Accomplished 甲寅 Wood Tiger 水火既濟 **16** 廿五 9	水1 Water 1 Arriving 乙卯 Wood Rabbit 地澤臨 **17** 廿六 4	金4 Metal 2 Marsh 丙辰 Fire Dragon 兑爲澤 **18** 廿七 1
火2 Fire 3 Small Livestock 丁巳 Fire Snake 風天小畜 **19** 廿八 8	木3 Wood 4 The Cauldron 戊午 Earth Horse 火風鼎 **20** 廿九 4	水1 Water 5 Rising 己未 Earth Goat 地風升 **21** 三十 2	火7 Fire 6 Water 庚申 Metal Monkey 坎爲水 **22** 正月初一 1	木8 Wood 7 Lesser Exceeding 辛酉 Metal Rooster 雷山小過 **23** 初二 3	金4 Metal 8 Gathering 壬戌 Water Dog 澤地萃 **24** 初三 4	水6 Water 9 Peel 癸亥 Water Pig 山地剝 **25** 初四 6
水1 Water 1 Earth 甲子 Wood Rat 坤爲地 **26** 初五 1	木3 Wood 2 Biting 乙丑 Wood Ox 火雷噬嗑 **27** 初六 6	火2 Fire 3 Family 丙寅 Fire Tiger 風火家人 **28** 初七 4	水6 Water 4 Decreasing 丁卯 Fire Rabbit 山澤損 **29** 初八 9	金9 Metal 5 Tread 戊辰 Earth Dragon 天澤履 **30** 初九 6	木8 Wood 6 Great Strength 己巳 Earth Snake 雷天大壯 **31** 初十 2	

FEBRUARY 2042 壬寅

Xuan Kong Element 玄空五行	天火同人 Fellowship	Period Luck 卦運	Monthly Star 月星
Metal 金9		7	5

SUNDAY	MONDAY	TUESDAY	WEDNESDAY	THURSDAY	FRIDAY	SATURDAY
						木8 Wood 7 Consistency 庚午 Metal Horse 雷風恆 **1** 十一 9
金9 Metal 8 Litigation 辛未 Metal Goat 天水訟 **2** 十二 3	水1 Water 9 Officer 壬申 Water Monkey 地水師 **3** 十三 7	火2 Fire 1 Gradual Progress 癸酉 Water Rooster 風山漸 **4** 十四 7	火7 Fire 2 Obstruction 甲戌 Wood Dog 水山蹇 **5** 十五 2	木3 Wood 3 Advancement 乙亥 Wood Pig 火地晉 **6** 十六 3	水6 Water 4 Nourish 丙子 Fire Rat 山雷頤 **7** 十七 3	金4 Metal 5 Following 丁丑 Fire Ox 澤雷隨 **8** 十八 7
木8 Wood 6 Abundance 戊寅 Earth Tiger 雷火豐 **9** 十九 6	火7 Fire 7 Regulate 己卯 Earth Rabbit 水澤節 **10** 二十 8	水1 Water 8 Unity 庚辰 Metal Dragon 地天泰 **11** 廿一 9	木3 Wood 9 Great Reward 辛巳 Metal Snake 火天大有 **12** 廿二 7	火2 Fire 1 Wind 壬午 Water Horse 巽爲風 **13** 廿三 1	金4 Metal 2 Trap 癸未 Water Goat 澤水困 **14** 廿四 8	木3 Wood 3 Not Yet Accomplished 甲申 Wood Monkey 火水未濟 **15** 廿五 9
金9 Metal 4 Retreat 乙酉 Wood Rooster 天山遯 **16** 廿六 4	水6 Water 5 Mountain 丙戌 Fire Dog 艮爲山 **17** 廿七 1	木8 Wood 6 Delight 丁亥 Fire Pig 雷地豫 **18** 廿八 8	火7 Fire 7 Beginning 戊子 Earth Rat 水雷屯 **19** 廿九 4	金9 Metal 8 Without Wrongdoing 己丑 Earth Ox 天雷無妄 **20** 二月初一 2	木3 Wood 9 Fire 庚寅 Metal Tiger 離爲火 **21** 初二 1	火2 Fire 1 Sincerity 辛卯 Metal Rabbit 風澤中孚 **22** 初三 3
水6 Water 2 Big Livestock 壬辰 Water Dragon 山天大畜 **23** 初四 4	金4 Metal 3 Eliminating 癸巳 Water Snake 澤天夬 **24** 初五 6	金9 Metal 4 Heaven 甲午 Wood Horse 乾爲天 **25** 初六 1	火7 Fire 5 Well 乙未 Wood Goat 水風井 **26** 初七 6	木8 Wood 6 Relief 丙申 Fire Monkey 雷水解 **27** 初八 4	金4 Metal 7 Influence 丁酉 Fire Rooster 澤山咸 **28** 初九 9	

MARCH 2042 癸卯

Xuan Kong Element 玄空五行	雷澤歸妹 Marrying Maiden	Period Luck 卦運	Monthly Star 月星
Wood 木8		7	4

SUNDAY	MONDAY	TUESDAY	WEDNESDAY	THURSDAY	FRIDAY	SATURDAY
水6 Water 1 Decreasing 山澤損 丁卯 Fire Rabbit 30 初九 9	金9 Metal 2 Tread 天澤履 戊辰 Earth Dragon 31 初十 6					水1 Water 8 Humility 地山謙 戊戌 Earth Dog 1 初十 6
火2 Fire 9 Observation 風地觀 己亥 Earth Pig 2 十一 2	火2 Fire 1 Increasing 風雷益 庚子 Metal Rat 3 十二 9	水1 Water 2 Dimming Light 地火明夷 辛丑 Metal Ox 4 十三 3	金9 Metal 3 Fellowship 天火同人 壬寅 Water Tiger 5 十四 7	木8 Wood 4 Marrying Maiden 雷澤歸妹 癸卯 Water Rabbit 6 十五 7	木3 Wood 5 Opposition 火澤睽 甲辰 Wood Dragon 7 十六 2	火7 Fire 6 Waiting 水天需 乙巳 Wood Snake 8 十七 3
金4 Metal 7 Great Exceeding 澤風大過 丙午 Fire Horse 9 十八 3	水6 Water 8 Poison 山風蠱 丁未 Fire Goat 10 十九 7	火2 Fire 9 Dispersing 風水渙 戊申 Earth Monkey 11 二十 6	木3 Wood 1 Travelling 火山旅 己酉 Earth Rooster 12 廿一 8	金9 Metal 2 Stagnation 天地否 庚戌 Metal Dog 13 廿二 9	火7 Fire 3 Alliance 水地比 辛亥 Metal Pig 14 廿三 7	木8 Wood 4 Thunder 震爲雷 壬子 Water Rat 15 廿四 1
水6 Water 5 Beauty 山火賁 癸丑 Water Ox 16 廿五 8	火7 Fire 6 Accomplished 水火既濟 甲寅 Wood Tiger 17 廿六 9	水1 Water 7 Arriving 地澤臨 乙卯 Wood Rabbit 18 廿七 4	金4 Metal 8 Marsh 兑爲澤 丙辰 Fire Dragon 19 廿八 1	火2 Fire 9 Small Livestock 風天小畜 丁巳 Fire Snake 20 廿九 8	木3 Wood 1 The Cauldron 火風鼎 戊午 Earth Horse 21 三十 4	水1 Water 2 Rising 地風升 己未 Earth Goat 22 閏二月初一 2
火7 Fire 3 Water 坎爲水 庚申 Metal Monkey 23 初二 1	木8 Wood 4 Lesser Exceeding 雷山小過 辛酉 Metal Rooster 24 初三 3	金4 Metal 5 Gathering 澤地萃 壬戌 Water Dog 25 初四 4	水6 Water 6 Peel 山地剝 癸亥 Water Pig 26 初五 6	水1 Water 7 Earth 坤爲地 甲子 Wood Rat 27 初六 1	木3 Wood 8 Biting 火雷噬嗑 乙丑 Wood Ox 28 初七 6	火2 Fire 9 Family 風火家人 丙寅 Fire Tiger 29 初八 4

APRIL 2042 甲辰

Xuan Kong Element 玄空五行	火澤睽 Opposition	Period Luck 卦運	Monthly Star 月星
Wood 木3		2	3

SUNDAY	MONDAY	TUESDAY	WEDNESDAY	THURSDAY	FRIDAY	SATURDAY
		木8 Wood 3 Great Strength 雷天大壯 己巳 Earth Snake 1 十一 2	木8 Wood 4 Consistency 雷風恆 庚午 Metal Horse 2 十二 9	金9 Metal 5 Litigation 天水訟 辛未 Metal Goat 3 十三 3	水1 Water 6 Officer 地水師 壬申 Water Monkey 4 十四 7	火2 Fire 7 Gradual Progress 風山漸 癸酉 Water Rooster 5 十五 7
火7 Fire 8 Obstruction 水山蹇 甲戌 Wood Dog 6 十六 2	木3 Wood 9 Advancement 火地晉 乙亥 Wood Pig 7 十七 3	水6 Water 1 Nourish 山雷頤 丙子 Fire Rat 8 十八 3	金4 Metal 2 Following 澤雷隨 丁丑 Fire Ox 9 十九 7	木8 Wood 3 Abundance 雷火豐 戊寅 Earth Tiger 10 二十 6	火7 Fire 4 Regulate 水澤節 己卯 Earth Rabbit 11 廿一 8	水1 Water 5 Unity 地天泰 庚辰 Metal Dragon 12 廿二 9
木3 Wood 6 Great Reward 火天大有 辛巳 Metal Snake 13 廿三 7	火2 Fire 7 Wind 巽爲風 壬午 Water Horse 14 廿四 1	金4 Metal 8 Trap 澤水困 癸未 Water Goat 15 廿五 8	木3 Wood 9 Not Yet Accomplished 火水未濟 甲申 Wood Monkey 16 廿六 9	金9 Metal 1 Retreat 天山遯 乙酉 Wood Rooster 17 廿七 4	水6 Water 2 Mountain 艮爲山 丙戌 Fire Dog 18 廿八 1	木8 Wood 3 Delight 雷地豫 丁亥 Fire Pig 19 廿九 8
火7 Fire 4 Beginning 水雷屯 戊子 Earth Rat 20 三月初一 4	金9 Metal 5 Without Wrongdoing 天雷無妄 己丑 Earth Ox 21 初二 2	木3 Wood 6 Fire 離爲火 庚寅 Metal Tiger 22 初三 3	火2 Fire 7 Sincerity 風澤中孚 辛卯 Metal Rabbit 23 初四 3	水6 Water 8 Big Livestock 山天大畜 壬辰 Water Dragon 24 初五 4	金4 Metal 9 Eliminating 澤天夬 癸巳 Water Snake 25 初六 6	金9 Metal 1 Heaven 乾爲天 甲午 Wood Horse 26 初七 1
火7 Fire 2 Well 水風井 乙未 Wood Goat 27 初八 6	木8 Wood 3 Relief 雷水解 丙申 Fire Monkey 28 初九 4	金4 Metal 4 Influence 澤山咸 丁酉 Fire Rooster 29 初十 9	水1 Water 5 Humility 地山謙 戊戌 Earth Dog 30 十一 6			

MAY 2042 乙巳

Xuan Kong Element 玄空五行	水天需 Waiting	Period Luck 卦運	Monthly Star 月星
Fire 火7		3	2

SUNDAY	MONDAY	TUESDAY	WEDNESDAY	THURSDAY	FRIDAY	SATURDAY
				火2 Fire 6 Observation 己亥 Earth Pig 風地觀 **1** 十二 2	火2 Fire 7 Increasing 庚子 Metal Rat 風雷益 **2** 十三 9	水1 Water 8 Dimming Light 辛丑 Metal Ox 地火明夷 **3** 十四 3
金9 Metal 9 Fellowship 壬寅 Water Tiger 天火同人 **4** 十五 7	木8 Wood 1 Marrying Maiden 癸卯 Water Rabbit 雷澤歸妹 **5** 十六 7	木3 Wood 2 Opposition 甲辰 Wood Dragon 火澤睽 **6** 十七 2	火7 Fire 3 Waiting 乙巳 Wood Snake 水天需 **7** 十八 3	金4 Metal 4 Great Exceeding 丙午 Fire Horse 澤風大過 **8** 十九 3	水6 Water 5 Poison 丁未 Fire Goat 山風蠱 **9** 二十 7	火2 Fire 6 Dispersing 戊申 Earth Monkey 風水渙 **10** 廿一 6
木3 Wood 7 Travelling 己酉 Earth Rooster 火山旅 **11** 廿二 8	金9 Metal 8 Stagnation 庚戌 Metal Dog 天地否 **12** 廿三 9	火7 Fire 9 Alliance 辛亥 Metal Pig 水地比 **13** 廿四 7	木8 Wood 1 Thunder 壬子 Water Rat 震爲雷 **14** 廿五 1	水6 Water 2 Beauty 癸丑 Water Ox 山火賁 **15** 廿六 8	火7 Fire 3 Accomplished 甲寅 Wood Tiger 水火既濟 **16** 廿七 9	水1 Water 4 Arriving 乙卯 Wood Rabbit 地澤臨 **17** 廿八 4
金4 Metal 5 Marsh 丙辰 Fire Dragon 兌爲澤 **18** 廿九 1	火2 Fire 6 Small Livestock 丁巳 Fire Snake 風天小畜 **19** 四月初一 8	木3 Wood 7 The Cauldron 戊午 Earth Horse 火風鼎 **20** 初二 4	水1 Water 8 Rising 己未 Earth Goat 地風升 **21** 初三 2	火7 Fire 9 Water 庚申 Metal Monkey 坎爲水 **22** 初四 1	木8 Wood 1 Lesser Exceeding 辛酉 Metal Rooster 雷山小過 **23** 初五 3	金4 Metal 2 Gathering 壬戌 Water Dog 澤地萃 **24** 初六 4
水6 Water 3 Peel 癸亥 Water Pig 山地剝 **25** 初七 6	水1 Water 4 Earth 甲子 Wood Rat 坤爲地 **26** 初八 1	木3 Wood 5 Biting 乙丑 Wood Ox 火雷噬嗑 **27** 初九 6	火2 Fire 6 Family 丙寅 Fire Tiger 風火家人 **28** 初十 4	水6 Water 7 Decreasing 丁卯 Fire Rabbit 山澤損 **29** 十一 9	金9 Metal 8 Tread 戊辰 Earth Dragon 天澤履 **30** 十二 6	木8 Wood 9 Great Strength 己巳 Earth Snake 雷天大壯 **31** 十三 2

JUNE 2042 丙午

Xuan Kong Element 玄空五行	澤風大過 Great Exceeding	Period Luck 卦運	Monthly Star 月星
Metal 金4		3	1

SUNDAY	MONDAY	TUESDAY	WEDNESDAY	THURSDAY	FRIDAY	SATURDAY
木8 Wood 1 Consistency 庚午 Metal Horse 雷風恒 **1** 十四 9	金9 Metal 2 Litigation 辛未 Metal Goat 天水訟 **2** 十五 3	水1 Water 3 Officer 壬申 Water Monkey 地水師 **3** 十六 7	火2 Fire 4 Gradual Progress 癸酉 Water Rooster 風山漸 **4** 十七 7	火7 Fire 5 Obstruction 甲戌 Wood Dog 水山蹇 **5** 十八 2	木3 Wood 6 Advancement 乙亥 Wood Pig 火地晉 **6** 十九 3	水6 Water 7 Nourish 丙子 Fire Rat 山雷頤 **7** 二十 3
金4 Metal 8 Following 丁丑 Fire Ox 澤雷隨 **8** 廿一 7	木8 Wood 9 Abundance 戊寅 Earth Tiger 雷火豐 **9** 廿二 6	火7 Fire 1 Regulate 己卯 Earth Rabbit 水澤節 **10** 廿三 8	水1 Water 2 Unity 庚辰 Metal Dragon 地天泰 **11** 廿四 9	木3 Wood 3 Great Reward 辛巳 Metal Snake 火天大有 **12** 廿五 7	火2 Fire 4 Wind 壬午 Water Horse 巽爲風 **13** 廿六 1	金4 Metal 5 Trap 癸未 Water Goat 澤水困 **14** 廿七 8
木3 Wood 6 Not Yet Accomplished 甲申 Wood Monkey 火水未濟 **15** 廿八 9	金9 Metal 7 Retreat 乙酉 Wood Rooster 天山遯 **16** 廿九 4	水6 Water 8 Mountain 丙戌 Fire Dog 艮爲山 **17** 三十 1	木8 Wood 9 Delight 丁亥 Fire Pig 雷地豫 **18** 五月初一 8	火7 Fire 1 Beginning 戊子 Earth Rat 水雷屯 **19** 初二 4	金9 Metal 2 Without Wrongdoing 己丑 Earth Ox 天雷無妄 **20** 初三 2	木3 Wood 3/7 Fire 庚寅 Metal Tiger 離爲火 **21** 初四 1
火2 Fire 6 Sincerity 辛卯 Metal Rabbit 風澤中孚 **22** 初五 3	水6 Water 5 Big Livestock 壬辰 Water Dragon 山天大畜 **23** 初六 4	金4 Metal 4 Eliminating 癸巳 Water Snake 澤天夬 **24** 初七 6	金9 Metal 3 Heaven 甲午 Wood Horse 乾爲天 **25** 初八 1	火7 Fire 2 Well 乙未 Wood Goat 水風井 **26** 初九 6	木8 Wood 1 Relief 丙申 Fire Monkey 雷水解 **27** 初十 4	金4 Metal 9 Influence 丁酉 Fire Rooster 澤山咸 **28** 十一 9
水1 Water 8 Humility 戊戌 Earth Dog 地山謙 **29** 十二 6	火2 Fire 7 Observation 己亥 Earth Pig 風地觀 **30** 十三 2					

JULY 2042 丁未

Xuan Kong Element 玄空五行	山風蠱 Poison	Period Luck 卦運	Monthly Star 月星
Water 水6		7	9

SUNDAY	MONDAY	TUESDAY	WEDNESDAY	THURSDAY	FRIDAY	SATURDAY
		1 火2 Fire [6] Increasing 風雷益 庚子 Metal Rat 9 十四	**2** 水1 Water [5] Dimming Light 地火明夷 辛丑 Metal Ox 3 十五	**3** 金9 Metal [4] Fellowship 天火同人 壬寅 Water Tiger 7 十六	**4** 木8 Wood [3] Marrying Maiden 雷澤歸妹 癸卯 Water Rabbit 7 十七	**5** 木3 Wood [2] Opposition 火澤睽 甲辰 Wood Dragon 2 十八
6 火7 Fire [1] Waiting 水天需 乙巳 Wood Snake 3 十九	**7** 金4 Metal [9] Great Exceeding 澤風大過 丙午 Fire Horse 3 二十	**8** 水6 Water [8] Poison 山風蠱 丁未 Fire Goat 7 廿一	**9** 火2 Fire [7] Dispersing 風水渙 戊申 Earth Monkey 6 廿二	**10** 木3 Wood [6] Travelling 火山旅 己酉 Earth Rooster 8 廿三	**11** 金9 Metal [5] Stagnation 天地否 庚戌 Metal Dog 9 廿四	**12** 火7 Fire [4] Alliance 水地比 辛亥 Metal Pig 7 廿五
13 木8 Wood [3] Thunder 震爲雷 壬子 Water Rat 1 廿六	**14** 水6 Water [2] Beauty 山火賁 癸丑 Water Ox 8 廿七	**15** 火7 Fire [1] Accomplished 水火既濟 甲寅 Wood Tiger 9 廿八	**16** 水1 Water [9] Arriving 地澤臨 乙卯 Wood Rabbit 4 廿九	**17** 金4 Metal [8] Marsh 兌爲澤 丙辰 Fire Dragon 1 六月初一	**18** 火2 Fire [7] Small Livestock 風天小畜 丁巳 Fire Snake 8 初二	**19** 木3 Wood [6] The Cauldron 火風鼎 戊午 Earth Horse 4 初三
20 水1 Water [5] Rising 地風升 己未 Earth Goat 2 初四	**21** 火7 Fire [4] Water 坎爲水 庚申 Metal Monkey 1 初五	**22** 木8 Wood [3] Lesser Exceeding 雷山小過 辛酉 Metal Rooster 3 初六	**23** 金4 Metal [2] Gathering 澤地萃 壬戌 Water Dog 4 初七	**24** 水6 Water [1] Peel 山地剝 癸亥 Water Pig 6 初八	**25** 水1 Water [9] Earth 坤爲地 甲子 Wood Rat 1 初九	**26** 木3 Wood [8] Biting 火雷噬嗑 乙丑 Wood Ox 6 初十
27 火2 Fire [7] Family 風火家人 丙寅 Fire Tiger 4 十一	**28** 水6 Water [6] Decreasing 山澤損 丁卯 Fire Rabbit 9 十二	**29** 金9 Metal [5] Tread 天澤履 戊辰 Earth Dragon 6 十三	**30** 木8 Wood [4] Great Strength 雷天大壯 己巳 Earth Snake 2 十四	**31** 木8 Wood [3] Consistency 雷風恒 庚午 Metal Horse 9 十五		

AUGUST 2042 戊申

Xuan Kong Element 玄空五行	風水渙 Dispersing	Period Luck 卦運	Monthly Star 月星
Fire 火2		6	8

SUNDAY	MONDAY	TUESDAY	WEDNESDAY	THURSDAY	FRIDAY	SATURDAY
31 水1 Water [8] Dimming Light 地火明夷 辛丑 Metal Ox 3 十六					**1** 金9 Metal [2] Litigation 天水訟 辛未 Metal Goat 3 十六	**2** 水1 Water [1] Officer 地水師 壬申 Water Monkey 7 十七
3 火2 Fire [9] Gradual Progress 風山漸 癸酉 Water Rooster 7 十八	**4** 火7 Fire [8] Obstruction 水山蹇 甲戌 Wood Dog 2 十九	**5** 木3 Wood [7] Advancement 火地晉 乙亥 Wood Pig 3 二十	**6** 水6 Water [6] Nourish 山雷頤 丙子 Fire Rat 3 廿一	**7** 金4 Metal [5] Following 澤雷隨 丁丑 Fire Ox 7 廿二	**8** 木8 Wood [4] Abundance 雷火豐 戊寅 Earth Tiger 6 廿三	**9** 火7 Fire [3] Regulate 水澤節 己卯 Earth Rabbit 8 廿四
10 水1 Water [2] Unity 地天泰 庚辰 Metal Dragon 9 廿五	**11** 木3 Wood [1] Great Reward 火天大有 辛巳 Metal Snake 7 廿六	**12** 火2 Fire [9] Wind 巽爲風 壬午 Water Horse 1 廿七	**13** 金4 Metal [8] Trap 澤水困 癸未 Water Goat 8 廿八	**14** 木3 Wood [7] Not Yet Accomplished 火水未濟 甲申 Wood Monkey 9 廿九	**15** 金9 Metal [6] Retreat 天山遯 乙酉 Wood Rooster 4 三十	**16** 水6 Water [5] Mountain 艮爲山 丙戌 Fire Dog 1 七月初一
17 木8 Wood [4] Delight 雷地豫 丁亥 Fire Pig 8 初二	**18** 火7 Fire [3] Beginning 水雷屯 戊子 Earth Rat 4 初三	**19** 金9 Metal [2] Without Wrongdoing 天雷無妄 己丑 Earth Ox 2 初四	**20** 木3 Wood [1] Fire 離爲火 庚寅 Metal Tiger 1 初五	**21** 火2 Fire [9] Sincerity 風澤中孚 辛卯 Metal Rabbit 3 初六	**22** 水6 Water [8] Big Livestock 山天大畜 壬辰 Water Dragon 4 初七	**23** 金4 Metal [7] Eliminating 澤天夬 癸巳 Water Snake 6 初八
24 金9 Metal [6] Heaven 乾爲天 甲午 Wood Horse 1 初九	**25** 火7 Fire [5] Well 水風井 乙未 Wood Goat 6 初十	**26** 木8 Wood [4] Relief 雷水解 丙申 Fire Monkey 4 十一	**27** 金4 Metal [3] Influence 澤山咸 丁酉 Fire Rooster 9 十二	**28** 水1 Water [2] Humility 地山謙 戊戌 Earth Dog 6 十三	**29** 火2 Fire [1] Observation 風地觀 己亥 Earth Pig 2 十四	**30** 火2 Fire [9] Increasing 風雷益 庚子 Metal Rat 9 十五

SEPTEMBER 2042 己酉

Xuan Kong Element 玄空五行	火山旅 Travelling	Period Luck 卦運	Monthly Star 月星
Wood 木3		8	7

SUNDAY	MONDAY	TUESDAY	WEDNESDAY	THURSDAY	FRIDAY	SATURDAY
	1 金9 Metal · Fellowship · 7 壬寅 Water Tiger 天火同人 十七 · 7	**2** 木8 Wood · Marrying Maiden · 6 癸卯 Water Rabbit 雷澤歸妹 十八 · 7	**3** 木3 Wood · Opposition · 5 甲辰 Wood Dragon 火澤睽 十九 · 2	**4** 火7 Fire · Waiting · 4 乙巳 Wood Snake 水天需 二十 · 3	**5** 金4 Metal · Great Exceeding · 3 丙午 Fire Horse 澤風大過 廿一 · 3	**6** 水6 Water · Poison · 2 丁未 Fire Goat 山風蠱 廿二 · 7
7 火2 Fire · Dispersing · 1 戊申 Earth Monkey 風水渙 廿三 · 6	**8** 木3 Wood · Travelling · 9 己酉 Earth Rooster 火山旅 廿四 · 8	**9** 金9 Metal · Stagnation · 8 庚戌 Metal Dog 天地否 廿五 · 9	**10** 火7 Fire · Alliance · 7 辛亥 Metal Pig 水地比 廿六 · 7	**11** 木8 Wood · Thunder · 6 壬子 Water Rat 震爲雷 廿七 · 1	**12** 水6 Water · Beauty · 5 癸丑 Water Ox 山火賁 廿八 · 8	**13** 火7 Fire · Accomplished · 4 甲寅 Wood Tiger 水火既濟 廿九 · 9
14 水1 Water · Arriving · 3 乙卯 Wood Rabbit 地澤臨 八月初一 · 4	**15** 金4 Metal · Marsh · 2 丙辰 Fire Dragon 兑爲澤 初二 · 1	**16** 火2 Fire · Small Livestock · 1 丁巳 Fire Snake 風天小畜 初三 · 8	**17** 木3 Wood · The Cauldron · 9 戊午 Earth Horse 火風鼎 初四 · 4	**18** 水1 Water · Rising · 8 己未 Earth Goat 地風升 初五 · 2	**19** 火7 Fire · Water · 7 庚申 Metal Monkey 坎爲水 初六 · 1	**20** 木8 Wood · Lesser Exceeding · 6 辛酉 Metal Rooster 雷山小過 初七 · 3
21 金4 Metal · Gathering · 5 壬戌 Water Dog 澤地萃 初八 · 4	**22** 水6 Water · Peel · 4 癸亥 Water Pig 山地剝 初九 · 6	**23** 水1 Water · Earth · 3 甲子 Wood Rat 坤爲地 初十 · 1	**24** 木3 Wood · Biting · 2 乙丑 Wood Ox 火雷噬嗑 十一 · 6	**25** 火2 Fire · Family · 1 丙寅 Fire Tiger 風火家人 十二 · 4	**26** 水6 Water · Decreasing · 9 丁卯 Fire Rabbit 山澤損 十三 · 9	**27** 金9 Metal · Tread · 8 戊辰 Earth Dragon 天澤履 十四 · 6
28 木8 Wood · Great Strength · 7 己巳 Earth Snake 雷天大壯 十五 · 2	**29** 木8 Wood · Consistency · 6 庚午 Metal Horse 雷風恆 十六 · 9	**30** 金9 Metal · Litigation · 5 辛未 Metal Goat 天水訟 十七 · 3				

OCTOBER 2042 庚戌

Xuan Kong Element 玄空五行	天地否 Stagnation	Period Luck 卦運	Monthly Star 月星
Metal 金9		9	6

SUNDAY	MONDAY	TUESDAY	WEDNESDAY	THURSDAY	FRIDAY	SATURDAY
			1 水1 Water · Officer · 4 壬申 Water Monkey 地水師 十八 · 7	**2** 火2 Fire · Gradual Progress · 3 癸酉 Water Rooster 風山漸 十九 · 7	**3** 火7 Fire · Obstruction · 2 甲戌 Wood Dog 水山蹇 二十 · 2	**4** 木3 Wood · Advancement · 1 乙亥 Wood Pig 火地晉 廿一 · 3
5 水6 Water · Nourish · 9 丙子 Fire Rat 山雷頤 廿二 · 3	**6** 金4 Metal · Following · 8 丁丑 Fire Ox 澤雷隨 廿三 · 7	**7** 木8 Wood · Abundance · 7 戊寅 Earth Tiger 雷火豐 廿四 · 6	**8** 火7 Fire · Regulate · 6 己卯 Earth Rabbit 水澤節 廿五 · 8	**9** 水1 Water · Unity · 5 庚辰 Metal Dragon 地天泰 廿六 · 9	**10** 木3 Wood · Great Reward · 4 辛巳 Metal Snake 火天大有 廿七 · 7	**11** 火2 Fire · Wind · 3 壬午 Water Horse 巽爲風 廿八 · 1
12 金4 Metal · Trap · 2 癸未 Water Goat 澤水困 廿九 · 8	**13** 木3 Wood · Not Yet Accomplished · 1 甲申 Wood Monkey 火水未濟 三十 · 9	**14** 金9 Metal · Retreat · 9 乙酉 Wood Rooster 天山遯 九月初一 · 4	**15** 水6 Water · Mountain · 8 丙戌 Fire Dog 艮爲山 初二 · 1	**16** 木8 Wood · Delight · 7 丁亥 Fire Pig 雷地豫 初三 · 8	**17** 火7 Fire · Beginning · 6 戊子 Earth Rat 水雷屯 初四 · 4	**18** 金9 Metal · Without Wrongdoing · 5 己丑 Earth Ox 天雷無妄 初五 · 2
19 木3 Wood · Fire · 4 庚寅 Metal Tiger 離爲火 初六 · 1	**20** 火2 Fire · Sincerity · 3 辛卯 Metal Rabbit 風澤中孚 初七 · 3	**21** 水6 Water · Big Livestock · 2 壬辰 Water Dragon 山天大畜 初八 · 4	**22** 金4 Metal · Eliminating · 1 癸巳 Water Snake 澤天夬 初九 · 6	**23** 金9 Metal · Heaven · 9 甲午 Wood Horse 乾爲天 初十 · 1	**24** 火7 Fire · Well · 8 乙未 Wood Goat 水風井 十一 · 6	**25** 木8 Wood · Relief · 7 丙申 Fire Monkey 雷水解 十二 · 4
26 金4 Metal · Influence · 6 丁酉 Fire Rooster 澤山咸 十三 · 9	**27** 水1 Water · Humility · 5 戊戌 Earth Dog 地山謙 十四 · 6	**28** 火2 Fire · Observation · 4 己亥 Earth Pig 風地觀 十五 · 2	**29** 火2 Fire · Increasing · 3 庚子 Metal Rat 風雷益 十六 · 9	**30** 水1 Water · Dimming Light · 2 辛丑 Metal Ox 地火明夷 十七 · 3	**31** 金9 Metal · Fellowship · 1 壬寅 Water Tiger 天火同人 十八 · 7	

NOVEMBER 2042 辛亥

Xuan Kong Element 玄空五行	水地比 Alliance	Period Luck 卦運	Monthly Star 月星
Fire 火7		7	5

SUNDAY	MONDAY	TUESDAY	WEDNESDAY	THURSDAY	FRIDAY	SATURDAY
水1 Water Officer 7 壬申 Water Monkey 地水師 30 十八 7						木8 Wood Marrying Maiden 9 癸卯 Water Rabbit 雷澤歸妹 1 十九 7
木3 Wood Opposition 8 甲辰 Wood Dragon 火澤睽 2 二十 2	火7 Fire Waiting 7 乙巳 Wood Snake 水天需 3 廿一 3	金4 Metal Great Exceeding 6 丙午 Fire Horse 澤風大過 4 廿二 3	水6 Water Poison 5 丁未 Fire Goat 山風蠱 5 廿三 7	火2 Fire Dispersing 4 戊申 Earth Monkey 風水渙 6 廿四 6	木3 Wood Travelling 3 己酉 Earth Rooster 火山旅 7 廿五 8	金9 Metal Stagnation 2 庚戌 Metal Dog 天地否 8 廿六 9
火7 Fire Alliance 1 辛亥 Metal Pig 水地比 9 廿七 7	木8 Wood Thunder 9 壬子 Water Rat 震為雷 10 廿八 1	水6 Water Beauty 8 癸丑 Water Ox 山火賁 11 廿九 8	火7 Fire Accomplished 7 甲寅 Wood Tiger 水火既濟 12 三十 9	水1 Water Arriving 6 乙卯 Wood Rabbit 地澤臨 13 十月初一 4	金4 Metal Marsh 5 丙辰 Fire Dragon 兌為澤 14 初二 1	火2 Fire Small Livestock 4 丁巳 Fire Snake 風天小畜 15 初三 8
木3 Wood The Cauldron 3 戊午 Earth Horse 火風鼎 16 初四 4	水1 Water Rising 2 己未 Earth Goat 地風升 17 初五 2	火7 Fire Water 1 庚申 Metal Monkey 坎為水 18 初六 1	木8 Wood Lesser Exceeding 9 辛酉 Metal Rooster 雷山小過 19 初七 3	金4 Metal Gathering 8 壬戌 Water Dog 澤地萃 20 初八 4	水6 Water Peel 7 癸亥 Water Pig 山地剝 21 初九 6	水1 Water Earth 6 甲子 Wood Rat 坤為地 22 初十 1
木3 Wood Biting 5 乙丑 Wood Ox 火雷噬嗑 23 十一 6	火2 Fire Family 4 丙寅 Fire Tiger 風火家人 24 十二 4	水6 Water Decreasing 3 丁卯 Fire Rabbit 山澤損 25 十三 9	金9 Metal Tread 2 戊辰 Earth Dragon 天澤履 26 十四 6	木8 Wood Great Strength 1 己巳 Earth Snake 雷天大壯 27 十五 2	木8 Wood Consistency 9 庚午 Metal Horse 雷風恆 28 十六 9	金9 Metal Litigation 8 辛未 Metal Goat 天水訟 29 十七 3

DECEMBER 2042 壬子

Xuan Kong Element 玄空五行	震為雷 Thunder	Period Luck 卦運	Monthly Star 月星
Wood 木8		1	4

SUNDAY	MONDAY	TUESDAY	WEDNESDAY	THURSDAY	FRIDAY	SATURDAY
	火2 Fire Gradual Progress 6 癸酉 Water Rooster 風山漸 1 十九 7	火7 Fire Obstruction 5 甲戌 Wood Dog 水山蹇 2 二十 2	木3 Wood Advancement 4 乙亥 Wood Pig 火地晉 3 廿一 3	水6 Water Nourish 3 丙子 Fire Rat 山雷頤 4 廿二 3	金4 Metal Following 2 丁丑 Fire Ox 澤雷隨 5 廿三 7	木8 Wood Abundance 1 戊寅 Earth Tiger 雷火豐 6 廿四 6
火7 Fire Regulate 9 己卯 Earth Rabbit 水澤節 7 廿五 8	水1 Water Unity 8 庚辰 Metal Dragon 地天泰 8 廿六 9	木3 Wood Great Reward 7 辛巳 Metal Snake 火天大有 9 廿七 7	火2 Fire Wind 6 壬午 Water Horse 巽為風 10 廿八 1	金4 Metal Trap 5 癸未 Water Goat 澤水困 11 廿九 8	木3 Wood Not Yet Accomplished 4 甲申 Wood Monkey 火水未濟 12 十一月初一 9	金9 Metal Retreat 3 乙酉 Wood Rooster 天山遯 13 初二 4
水6 Water Mountain 2 丙戌 Fire Dog 艮為山 14 初三 1	木8 Wood Delight 1 丁亥 Fire Pig 雷地豫 15 初四 8	火7 Fire Beginning 9 戊子 Earth Rat 水雷屯 16 初五 4	金9 Metal Without Wrongdoing 8 己丑 Earth Ox 天雷無妄 17 初六 2	木3 Wood Fire 7 庚寅 Metal Tiger 離為火 18 初七 1	火2 Fire Sincerity 6 辛卯 Metal Rabbit 風澤中孚 19 初八 3	水6 Water Big Livestock 5 壬辰 Water Dragon 山天大畜 20 初九 4
金4 Metal Eliminating 4 癸巳 Water Snake 澤天夬 21 初十 6	金9 Metal Heaven 3/7 甲午 Wood Horse 乾為天 22 十一 1	火7 Fire Well 8 乙未 Wood Goat 水風井 23 十二 6	木8 Wood Relief 9 丙申 Fire Monkey 雷水解 24 十三 4	金4 Metal Influence 1 丁酉 Fire Rooster 澤山咸 25 十四 9	水1 Water Humility 2 戊戌 Earth Dog 地山謙 26 十五 6	火2 Fire Observation 3 己亥 Earth Pig 風地觀 27 十六 2
火2 Fire Increasing 4 庚子 Metal Rat 風雷益 28 十七 9	水1 Water Dimming Light 5 辛丑 Metal Ox 地火明夷 29 十八 3	金9 Metal Fellowship 6 壬寅 Water Tiger 天火同人 30 十九 7	木8 Wood Marrying Maiden 7 癸卯 Water Rabbit 雷澤歸妹 31 二十 7			

2043 癸亥

(*Gui Hai*) Water Pig

2043 癸亥 *(Gui Hai)* Water Pig

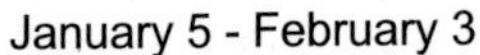

January 5 - February 3

February 4 - March 5

March 6 - April 4

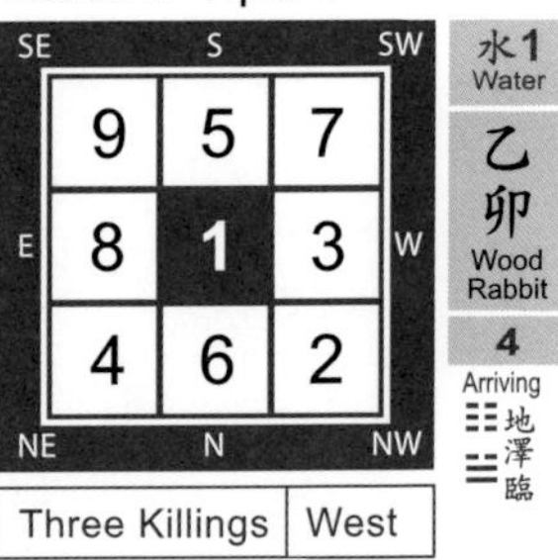

April 5 - May 4

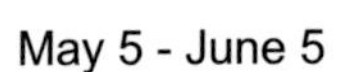

May 5 - June 5

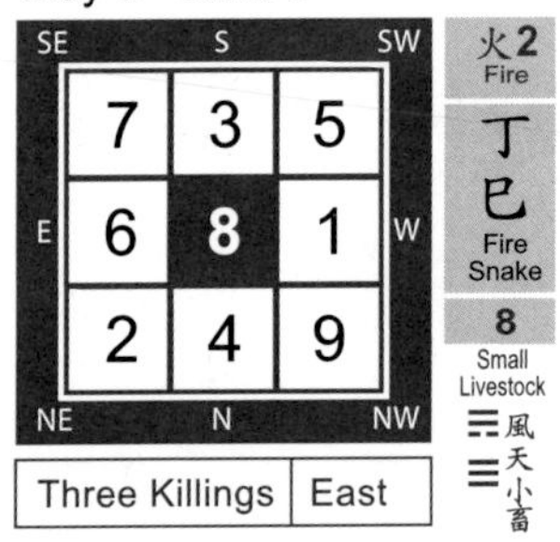

June 6 - July 6

July 7 - August 6

August 7 - September 7

September 8 - October 7

October 8 - November 6

November 7 - December 6

December 7 - January 5

JANUARY 2043 癸丑

Xuan Kong Element 玄空五行	山火賁 Beauty	Period Luck 卦運	Monthly Star 月星
Water 水6		8	3

SUNDAY	MONDAY	TUESDAY	WEDNESDAY	THURSDAY	FRIDAY	SATURDAY
				木3 Wood 8 Opposition 甲辰 Wood Dragon 火澤睽 **1** 廿一 2	火7 Fire 9 Waiting 乙巳 Wood Snake 水天需 **2** 廿二 3	金4 Metal 1 Great Exceeding 丙午 Fire Horse 澤風大過 **3** 廿三 3
水6 Water 2 Poison 丁未 Fire Goat 山風蠱 **4** 廿四 7	火2 Fire 3 Dispersing 戊申 Earth Monkey 風水渙 **5** 廿五 6	木3 Wood 4 Travelling 己酉 Earth Rooster 火山旅 **6** 廿六 8	金9 Metal 5 Stagnation 庚戌 Metal Dog 天地否 **7** 廿七 9	火7 Fire 6 Alliance 辛亥 Metal Pig 水地比 **8** 廿八 7	木8 Wood 7 Thunder 壬子 Water Rat 震為雷 **9** 廿九 1	水6 Water 8 Beauty 癸丑 Water Ox 山火賁 **10** 三十 8
火7 Fire 9 Accomplished 甲寅 Wood Tiger 水火既濟 **11** 十二月初一 9	水1 Water 1 Arriving 乙卯 Wood Rabbit 地澤臨 **12** 初二 4	金4 Metal 2 Marsh 丙辰 Fire Dragon 兌為澤 **13** 初三 1	火2 Fire 3 Small Livestock 丁巳 Fire Snake 風天小畜 **14** 初四 8	木3 Wood 4 The Cauldron 戊午 Earth Horse 火風鼎 **15** 初五 4	水1 Water 5 Rising 己未 Earth Goat 地風升 **16** 初六 2	火7 Fire 6 Water 庚申 Metal Monkey 坎為水 **17** 初七 1
木8 Wood 7 Lesser Exceeding 辛酉 Metal Rooster 雷山小過 **18** 初八 3	金4 Metal 8 Gathering 壬戌 Water Dog 澤地萃 **19** 初九 4	水6 Water 9 Peel 癸亥 Water Pig 山地剝 **20** 初十 6	水1 Water 1 Earth 甲子 Wood Rat 坤為地 **21** 十一 1	木3 Wood 2 Biting 乙丑 Wood Ox 火雷噬嗑 **22** 十二 6	火2 Fire 3 Family 丙寅 Fire Tiger 風火家人 **23** 十三 4	水6 Water 4 Decreasing 丁卯 Fire Rabbit 山澤損 **24** 十四 9
金9 Metal 5 Tread 戊辰 Earth Dragon 天澤履 **25** 十五 6	木8 Wood 6 Great Strength 己巳 Earth Snake 雷天大壯 **26** 十六 2	木8 Wood 7 Consistency 庚午 Metal Horse 雷風恆 **27** 十七 9	金9 Metal 8 Litigation 辛未 Metal Goat 天水訟 **28** 十八 3	水1 Water 9 Officer 壬申 Water Monkey 地水師 **29** 十九 7	火2 Fire 1 Gradual Progress 癸酉 Water Rooster 風山漸 **30** 二十 7	火7 Fire 2 Obstruction 甲戌 Wood Dog 水山蹇 **31** 廿一 2

FEBRUARY 2043 甲寅

Xuan Kong Element 玄空五行	水火既濟 Accomplished	Period Luck 卦運	Monthly Star 月星
Fire 火7		9	2

SUNDAY	MONDAY	TUESDAY	WEDNESDAY	THURSDAY	FRIDAY	SATURDAY
木3 Wood 3 Advancement 乙亥 Wood Pig 火地晉 **1** 廿二 3	水6 Water 4 Nourish 丙子 Fire Rat 山雷頤 **2** 廿三 3	金4 Metal 5 Following 丁丑 Fire Ox 澤雷隨 **3** 廿四 7	木8 Wood 6 Abundance 戊寅 Earth Tiger 雷火豐 **4** 廿五 6	火7 Fire 7 Regulate 己卯 Earth Rabbit 水澤節 **5** 廿六 8	水1 Water 8 Unity 庚辰 Metal Dragon 地天泰 **6** 廿七 9	木3 Wood 9 Great Reward 辛巳 Metal Snake 火天大有 **7** 廿八 7
火2 Fire 1 Wind 壬午 Water Horse 巽為風 **8** 廿九 1	金4 Metal 2 Trap 癸未 Water Goat 澤水困 **9** 三十 8	木3 Wood 3 Not Yet Accomplished 甲申 Wood Monkey 火水未濟 **10** 正月初一 9	金9 Metal 4 Retreat 乙酉 Wood Rooster 天山遯 **11** 初二 4	水6 Water 5 Mountain 丙戌 Fire Dog 艮為山 **12** 初三 1	木8 Wood 6 Delight 丁亥 Fire Pig 雷地豫 **13** 初四 8	火7 Fire 7 Beginning 戊子 Earth Rat 水雷屯 **14** 初五 4
金9 Metal 8 Without Wrongdoing 己丑 Earth Ox 天雷無妄 **15** 初六 2	木3 Wood 9 Fire 庚寅 Metal Tiger 離為火 **16** 初七 1	火2 Fire 1 Sincerity 辛卯 Metal Rabbit 風澤中孚 **17** 初八 3	水6 Water 2 Big Livestock 壬辰 Water Dragon 山天大畜 **18** 初九 4	金4 Metal 3 Eliminating 癸巳 Water Snake 澤天夬 **19** 初十 6	金9 Metal 4 Heaven 甲午 Wood Horse 乾為天 **20** 十一 1	火7 Fire 5 Well 乙未 Wood Goat 水風井 **21** 十二 6
木8 Wood 6 Relief 丙申 Fire Monkey 雷水解 **22** 十三 4	金4 Metal 7 Influence 丁酉 Fire Rooster 澤山咸 **23** 十四 9	水1 Water 8 Humility 戊戌 Earth Dog 地山謙 **24** 十五 6	火2 Fire 9 Observation 己亥 Earth Pig 風地觀 **25** 十六 2	火2 Fire 1 Increasing 庚子 Metal Rat 風雷益 **26** 十七 9	水1 Water 2 Dimming Light 辛丑 Metal Ox 地火明夷 **27** 十八 3	金9 Metal 3 Fellowship 壬寅 Water Tiger 天火同人 **28** 十九 7

MARCH 2043 乙卯

Xuan Kong Element 玄空五行	地澤臨 Arriving	Period Luck 卦運	Monthly Star 月星
Water 水1		4	1

SUNDAY	MONDAY	TUESDAY	WEDNESDAY	THURSDAY	FRIDAY	SATURDAY
1 二十 木8 Wood · 4 癸卯 Water Rabbit · 7 Marrying Maiden 雷澤歸妹	**2** 廿一 木3 Wood · 5 甲辰 Wood Dragon · 2 Opposition 火澤睽	**3** 廿二 火7 Fire · 6 乙巳 Wood Snake · 3 Waiting 水天需	**4** 廿三 金4 Metal · 7 丙午 Fire Horse · 3 Great Exceeding 澤風大過	**5** 廿四 水6 Water · 8 丁未 Fire Goat · 7 Poison 山風蠱	**6** 廿五 火2 Fire · 9 戊申 Earth Monkey · 6 Dispersing 風水渙	**7** 廿六 木3 Wood · 1 己酉 Earth Rooster · 8 Travelling 火山旅
8 廿七 金9 Metal · 2 庚戌 Metal Dog · 9 Stagnation 天地否	**9** 廿八 火7 Fire · 3 辛亥 Metal Pig · 7 Alliance 水地比	**10** 廿九 木8 Wood · 4 壬子 Water Rat · 1 Thunder 震爲雷	**11** 二月初一 水6 Water · 5 癸丑 Water Ox · 8 Beauty 山火賁	**12** 初二 火7 Fire · 6 甲寅 Wood Tiger · 9 Accomplished 水火既濟	**13** 初三 水1 Water · 7 乙卯 Wood Rabbit · 4 Arriving 地澤臨	**14** 初四 金4 Metal · 8 丙辰 Fire Dragon · 1 Marsh 兑爲澤
15 初五 火2 Fire · 9 丁巳 Fire Snake · 8 Small Livestock 風天小畜	**16** 初六 木3 Wood · 1 戊午 Earth Horse · 4 The Cauldron 火風鼎	**17** 初七 水1 Water · 2 己未 Earth Goat · 2 Rising 地風升	**18** 初八 火7 Fire · 3 庚申 Metal Monkey · 1 Water 坎爲水	**19** 初九 木8 Wood · 4 辛酉 Metal Rooster · 3 Lesser Exceeding 雷山小過	**20** 初十 金4 Metal · 5 壬戌 Water Dog · 4 Gathering 澤地萃	**21** 十一 水6 Water · 6 癸亥 Water Pig · 6 Peel 山地剝
22 十二 水1 Water · 7 甲子 Wood Rat · 1 Earth 坤爲地	**23** 十三 木3 Wood · 8 乙丑 Wood Ox · 6 Biting 火雷噬嗑	**24** 十四 火2 Fire · 9 丙寅 Fire Tiger · 4 Family 風火家人	**25** 十五 水6 Water · 1 丁卯 Fire Rabbit · 9 Decreasing 山澤損	**26** 十六 金9 Metal · 2 戊辰 Earth Dragon · 6 Tread 天澤履	**27** 十七 木8 Wood · 3 己巳 Earth Snake · 2 Great Strength 雷天大壯	**28** 十八 木8 Wood · 4 庚午 Metal Horse · 9 Consistency 雷風恒
29 十九 金9 Metal · 5 辛未 Metal Goat · 3 Litigation 天水訟	**30** 二十 水1 Water · 6 壬申 Water Monkey · 7 Officer 地水師	**31** 廿一 火2 Fire · 7 癸酉 Water Rooster · 7 Gradual Progress 風山漸				

APRIL 2043 丙辰

Xuan Kong Element 玄空五行	兑爲澤 Marsh	Period Luck 卦運	Monthly Star 月星
Metal 金4		1	9

SUNDAY	MONDAY	TUESDAY	WEDNESDAY	THURSDAY	FRIDAY	SATURDAY
			1 廿二 火7 Fire · 8 甲戌 Wood Dog · 2 Obstruction 水山蹇	**2** 廿三 木3 Wood · 9 乙亥 Wood Pig · 3 Advancement 火地晉	**3** 廿四 水6 Water · 1 丙子 Fire Rat · 3 Nourish 山雷頤	**4** 廿五 金4 Metal · 2 丁丑 Fire Ox · 7 Following 澤雷隨
5 廿六 木8 Wood · 3 戊寅 Earth Tiger · 6 Abundance 雷火豐	**6** 廿七 火7 Fire · 4 己卯 Earth Rabbit · 8 Regulate 水澤節	**7** 廿八 水1 Water · 5 庚辰 Metal Dragon · 9 Unity 地天泰	**8** 廿九 木3 Wood · 6 辛巳 Metal Snake · 7 Great Reward 火天大有	**9** 三十 火2 Fire · 7 壬午 Water Horse · 1 Wind 巽爲風	**10** 三月初一 金4 Metal · 8 癸未 Water Goat · 8 Trap 澤水困	**11** 初二 木3 Wood · 9 甲申 Wood Monkey · 9 Not Yet Accomplished 火水未濟
12 初三 金9 Metal · 1 乙酉 Wood Rooster · 4 Retreat 天山遯	**13** 初四 水6 Water · 2 丙戌 Fire Dog · 1 Mountain 艮爲山	**14** 初五 木8 Wood · 3 丁亥 Fire Pig · 8 Delight 雷地豫	**15** 初六 火7 Fire · 4 戊子 Earth Rat · 4 Beginning 水雷屯	**16** 初七 金9 Metal · 5 己丑 Earth Ox · 2 Without Wrongdoing 天雷無妄	**17** 初八 木3 Wood · 6 庚寅 Metal Tiger · 1 Fire 離爲火	**18** 初九 火2 Fire · 7 辛卯 Metal Rabbit · 3 Sincerity 風澤中孚
19 初十 水6 Water · 8 壬辰 Water Dragon · 4 Big Livestock 山天大畜	**20** 十一 金4 Metal · 9 癸巳 Water Snake · 6 Eliminating 澤天夬	**21** 十二 金9 Metal · 1 甲午 Wood Horse · 1 Heaven 乾爲天	**22** 十三 火7 Fire · 2 乙未 Wood Goat · 6 Well 水風井	**23** 十四 木8 Wood · 3 丙申 Fire Monkey · 4 Relief 雷水解	**24** 十五 金4 Metal · 4 丁酉 Fire Rooster · 9 Influence 澤山咸	**25** 十六 水1 Water · 5 戊戌 Earth Dog · 6 Humility 地山謙
26 十七 火2 Fire · 6 己亥 Earth Pig · 2 Observation 風地觀	**27** 十八 火2 Fire · 7 庚子 Metal Rat · 9 Increasing 風雷益	**28** 十九 水1 Water · 8 辛丑 Metal Ox · 3 Dimming Light 地火明夷	**29** 二十 金9 Metal · 9 壬寅 Water Tiger · 7 Fellowship 天火同人	**30** 廿一 木8 Wood · 1 癸卯 Water Rabbit · 7 Marrying Maiden 雷澤歸妹		

MAY 2043 丁巳

Xuan Kong Element 玄空五行	風天小畜 Small Livestock	Period Luck 卦運	Monthly Star 月星
Fire 火2		8	8

SUNDAY	MONDAY	TUESDAY	WEDNESDAY	THURSDAY	FRIDAY	SATURDAY
火7 Fire 甲戌 Wood Dog 2 Obstruction 5 水山蹇 31 廿三					木3 Wood 甲辰 Wood Dragon 2 Opposition 2 火澤睽 1 廿二	火7 Fire 乙巳 Wood Snake 3 Waiting 3 水天需 2 廿三
金4 Metal 丙午 Fire Horse 3 Great Exceeding 4 澤風大過 3 廿四	水6 Water 丁未 Fire Goat 7 Poison 5 山風蠱 4 廿五	火2 Fire 戊申 Earth Monkey 6 Dispersing 6 風水渙 5 廿六	木3 Wood 己酉 Earth Rooster 8 Travelling 7 火山旅 6 廿七	金9 Metal 庚戌 Metal Dog 9 Stagnation 8 天地否 7 廿八	火7 Fire 辛亥 Metal Pig 7 Alliance 9 水地比 8 廿九	木8 Wood 壬子 Water Rat 1 Thunder 1 震爲雷 9 四月初一
水6 Water 癸丑 Water Ox 8 Beauty 2 山火賁 10 初二	火7 Fire 甲寅 Wood Tiger 9 Accomplished 3 水火既濟 11 初三	水1 Water 乙卯 Wood Rabbit 4 Arriving 4 地澤臨 12 初四	金4 Metal 丙辰 Fire Dragon 1 Marsh 5 兑爲澤 13 初五	火2 Fire 丁巳 Fire Snake 8 Small Livestock 6 風天小畜 14 初六	木3 Wood 戊午 Earth Horse 4 The Cauldron 7 火風鼎 15 初七	水1 Water 己未 Earth Goat 2 Rising 8 地風升 16 初八
火7 Fire 庚申 Metal Monkey 1 Water 9 坎爲水 17 初九	木8 Wood 辛酉 Metal Rooster 3 Lesser Exceeding 1 雷山小過 18 初十	金4 Metal 壬戌 Water Dog 4 Gathering 2 澤地萃 19 十一	水6 Water 癸亥 Water Pig 6 Peel 3 山地剝 20 十二	水1 Water 甲子 Wood Rat 1 Earth 4 坤爲地 21 十三	木3 Wood 乙丑 Wood Ox 6 Biting 5 火雷噬嗑 22 十四	火2 Fire 丙寅 Fire Tiger 4 Family 6 風火家人 23 十五
水6 Water 丁卯 Fire Rabbit 9 Decreasing 7 山澤損 24 十六	金9 Metal 戊辰 Earth Dragon 6 Tread 8 天澤履 25 十七	木8 Wood 己巳 Earth Snake 2 Great Strength 9 雷天大壯 26 十八	木8 Wood 庚午 Metal Horse 9 Consistency 1 雷風恆 27 十九	金9 Metal 辛未 Metal Goat 3 Litigation 2 天水訟 28 二十	水1 Water 壬申 Water Monkey 7 Officer 3 地水師 29 廿一	火2 Fire 癸酉 Water Rooster 7 Gradual Progress 4 風山漸 30 廿二

JUNE 2043 戊午

Xuan Kong Element 玄空五行	火風鼎 The Cauldron	Period Luck 卦運	Monthly Star 月星
Wood 木3		4	7

SUNDAY	MONDAY	TUESDAY	WEDNESDAY	THURSDAY	FRIDAY	SATURDAY
	木3 Wood 乙亥 Wood Pig 3 Advancement 6 火地晉 1 廿四	水6 Water 丙子 Fire Rat 3 Nourish 7 山雷頤 2 廿五	金4 Metal 丁丑 Fire Ox 7 Following 8 澤雷隨 3 廿六	木8 Wood 戊寅 Earth Tiger 6 Abundance 9 雷火豐 4 廿七	火7 Fire 己卯 Earth Rabbit 8 Regulate 1 水澤節 5 廿八	水1 Water 庚辰 Metal Dragon 9 Unity 2 地天泰 6 廿九
木3 Wood 辛巳 Metal Snake 7 Great Reward 3 火天大有 7 五月初一	火2 Fire 壬午 Water Horse 1 Wind 4 巽爲風 8 初二	金4 Metal 癸未 Water Goat 8 Trap 5 澤水困 9 初三	木3 Wood 甲申 Wood Monkey 9 Not Yet Accomplished 6 火水未濟 10 初四	金9 Metal 乙酉 Wood Rooster 4 Retreat 7 天山遯 11 初五	水6 Water 丙戌 Fire Dog 1 Mountain 8 艮爲山 12 初六	木8 Wood 丁亥 Fire Pig 8 Delight 9 雷地豫 13 初七
火7 Fire 戊子 Earth Rat 4 Beginning 1 水雷屯 14 初八	金9 Metal 己丑 Earth Ox 2 Without Wrongdoing 2 天雷無妄 15 初九	木3 Wood 庚寅 Metal Tiger 1 Fire 3 離爲火 16 初十	火2 Fire 辛卯 Metal Rabbit 3 Sincerity 4 風澤中孚 17 十一	水6 Water 壬辰 Water Dragon 4 Big Livestock 5 山天大畜 18 十二	金4 Metal 癸巳 Water Snake 6 Eliminating 6 澤天夬 19 十三	金9 Metal 甲午 Wood Horse 1 Heaven 7 乾爲天 20 十四
火7 Fire 乙未 Wood Goat 6 Well 8/2 水風井 21 十五	木8 Wood 丙申 Fire Monkey 4 Relief 1 雷水解 22 十六	金4 Metal 丁酉 Fire Rooster 9 Influence 9 澤山咸 23 十七	水1 Water 戊戌 Earth Dog 6 Humility 8 地山謙 24 十八	火2 Fire 己亥 Earth Pig 2 Observation 7 風地觀 25 十九	火2 Fire 庚子 Metal Rat 9 Increasing 6 風雷益 26 二十	水1 Water 辛丑 Metal Ox 3 Dimming Light 5 地火明夷 27 廿一
金9 Metal 壬寅 Water Tiger 7 Fellowship 4 天火同人 28 廿二	木8 Wood 癸卯 Water Rabbit 7 Marrying Maiden 3 雷澤歸妹 29 廿三	木3 Wood 甲辰 Wood Dragon 2 Opposition 2 火澤睽 30 廿四				

JULY 2043 己未

Xuan Kong Element 玄空五行	地風升 Rising	Period Luck 卦運	Monthly Star 月星
Water 水1		2	6

SUNDAY	MONDAY	TUESDAY	WEDNESDAY	THURSDAY	FRIDAY	SATURDAY
			火7 Fire · Waiting · 1 乙巳 Wood Snake 水天需 1 廿五 3	金4 Metal · Great Exceeding · 9 丙午 Fire Horse 澤風大過 2 廿六 3	水6 Water · Poison · 8 丁未 Fire Goat 山風蠱 3 廿七 7	火2 Fire · Dispersing · 7 戊申 Earth Monkey 風水渙 4 廿八 6
木3 Wood · Travelling · 6 己酉 Earth Rooster 火山旅 5 廿九 8	金9 Metal · Stagnation · 5 庚戌 Metal Dog 天地否 6 三十 9	火7 Fire · Alliance · 4 辛亥 Metal Pig 水地比 7 六月初一 7	木8 Wood · Thunder · 3 壬子 Water Rat 震爲雷 8 初二 1	水6 Water · Beauty · 2 癸丑 Water Ox 山火賁 9 初三 8	火7 Fire · Accomplished · 1 甲寅 Wood Tiger 水火既濟 10 初四 9	水1 Water · Arriving · 9 乙卯 Wood Rabbit 地澤臨 11 初五 4
金4 Metal · Marsh · 8 丙辰 Fire Dragon 兑爲澤 12 初六 1	火2 Fire · Small Livestock · 7 丁巳 Fire Snake 風天小畜 13 初七 8	木3 Wood · The Cauldron · 6 戊午 Earth Horse 火風鼎 14 初八 4	水1 Water · Rising · 5 己未 Earth Goat 地風升 15 初九 2	火7 Fire · Water · 4 庚申 Metal Monkey 坎爲水 16 初十 1	木8 Wood · Lesser Exceeding · 3 辛酉 Metal Rooster 雷山小過 17 十一 3	金4 Metal · Gathering · 2 壬戌 Water Dog 澤地萃 18 十二 4
水6 Water · Peel · 1 癸亥 Water Pig 山地剝 19 十三 6	水1 Water · Earth · 9 甲子 Wood Rat 坤爲地 20 十四 1	木3 Wood · Biting · 8 乙丑 Wood Ox 火雷噬嗑 21 十五 6	火2 Fire · Family · 7 丙寅 Fire Tiger 風火家人 22 十六 4	水6 Water · Decreasing · 6 丁卯 Fire Rabbit 山澤損 23 十七 9	金9 Metal · Tread · 5 戊辰 Earth Dragon 天澤履 24 十八 6	木8 Wood · Great Strength · 4 己巳 Earth Snake 雷天大壯 25 十九 2
木8 Wood · Consistency · 3 庚午 Metal Horse 雷風恒 26 二十 9	金9 Metal · Litigation · 2 辛未 Metal Goat 天水訟 27 廿一 3	水1 Water · Officer · 1 壬申 Water Monkey 地水師 28 廿二 7	火2 Fire · Gradual Progress · 9 癸酉 Water Rooster 風山漸 29 廿三 7	火7 Fire · Obstruction · 8 甲戌 Wood Dog 水山蹇 30 廿四 2	木3 Wood · Advancement · 7 乙亥 Wood Pig 火地晉 31 廿五 3	

AUGUST 2043 庚申

Xuan Kong Element 玄空五行	坎爲水 Water	Period Luck 卦運	Monthly Star 月星
Fire 火7		1	5

SUNDAY	MONDAY	TUESDAY	WEDNESDAY	THURSDAY	FRIDAY	SATURDAY
火7 Fire · Waiting · 4 乙巳 Wood Snake 水天需 30 廿六 3	金4 Metal · Great Exceeding · 3 丙午 Fire Horse 澤風大過 31 廿七 3					水6 Water · Nourish · 6 丙子 Fire Rat 山雷頤 1 廿六 3
金4 Metal · Following · 5 丁丑 Fire Ox 澤雷隨 2 廿七 7	木8 Wood · Abundance · 4 戊寅 Earth Tiger 雷火豐 3 廿八 6	火7 Fire · Regulate · 3 己卯 Earth Rabbit 水澤節 4 廿九 8	水1 Water · Unity · 2 庚辰 Metal Dragon 地天泰 5 七月初一 9	木3 Wood · Great Reward · 1 辛巳 Metal Snake 火天大有 6 初二 7	火2 Fire · Wind · 9 壬午 Water Horse 巽爲風 7 初三 1	金4 Metal · Trap · 8 癸未 Water Goat 澤水困 8 初四 8
木3 Wood · Not Yet Accomplished · 7 甲申 Wood Monkey 火水未濟 9 初五 9	金9 Metal · Retreat · 6 乙酉 Wood Rooster 天山遯 10 初六 4	水6 Water · Mountain · 5 丙戌 Fire Dog 艮爲山 11 初七 1	木8 Wood · Delight · 4 丁亥 Fire Pig 雷地豫 12 初八 8	火7 Fire · Beginning · 3 戊子 Earth Rat 水雷屯 13 初九 4	金9 Metal · Without Wrongdoing · 2 己丑 Earth Ox 天雷無妄 14 初十 2	木3 Wood · Fire · 1 庚寅 Metal Tiger 離爲火 15 十一 1
火2 Fire · Sincerity · 9 辛卯 Metal Rabbit 風澤中孚 16 十二 3	水6 Water · Big Livestock · 8 壬辰 Water Dragon 山天大畜 17 十三 4	金4 Metal · Eliminating · 7 癸巳 Water Snake 澤天夬 18 十四 6	金9 Metal · Heaven · 6 甲午 Wood Horse 乾爲天 19 十五 1	火7 Fire · Well · 5 乙未 Wood Goat 水風井 20 十六 6	木8 Wood · Relief · 4 丙申 Fire Monkey 雷水解 21 十七 4	金4 Metal · Influence · 3 丁酉 Fire Rooster 澤山咸 22 十八 9
水1 Water · Humility · 2 戊戌 Earth Dog 地山謙 23 十九 6	火2 Fire · Observation · 1 己亥 Earth Pig 風地觀 24 二十 2	火2 Fire · Increasing · 9 庚子 Metal Rat 風雷益 25 廿一 9	水1 Water · Dimming Light · 8 辛丑 Metal Ox 地火明夷 26 廿二 3	金9 Metal · Fellowship · 7 壬寅 Water Tiger 天火同人 27 廿三 7	木8 Wood · Marrying Maiden · 6 癸卯 Water Rabbit 雷澤歸妹 28 廿四 7	木3 Wood · Opposition · 5 甲辰 Wood Dragon 火澤睽 29 廿五 2

SEPTEMBER 2043 辛酉

Xuan Kong Element 玄空五行	雷山小過 Lesser Exceeding	Period Luck 卦運	Monthly Star 月星
Wood 木8		3	4

SUNDAY	MONDAY	TUESDAY	WEDNESDAY	THURSDAY	FRIDAY	SATURDAY
		水6 Water [2] Poison 丁未 Fire Goat 山風蠱 **1** 廿八 7	火2 Fire [1] Dispersing 戊申 Earth Monkey 風水渙 **2** 廿九 6	木3 Wood [9] Travelling 己酉 Earth Rooster 火山旅 **3** 八月初一 8	金9 Metal [8] Stagnation 庚戌 Metal Dog 天地否 **4** 初二 9	火7 Fire [7] Alliance 辛亥 Metal Pig 水地比 **5** 初三 7
木8 Wood [6] Thunder 壬子 Water Rat 震爲雷 **6** 初四 1	水6 Water [5] Beauty 癸丑 Water Ox 山火賁 **7** 初五 8	火7 Fire [4] Accomplished 甲寅 Wood Tiger 水火既濟 **8** 初六 9	水1 Water [3] Arriving 乙卯 Wood Rabbit 地澤臨 **9** 初七 4	金4 Metal [2] Marsh 丙辰 Fire Dragon 兌爲澤 **10** 初八 1	火2 Fire [1] Small Livestock 丁巳 Fire Snake 風天小畜 **11** 初九 8	木3 Wood [9] The Cauldron 戊午 Earth Horse 火風鼎 **12** 初十 4
水1 Water [8] Rising 己未 Earth Goat 地風升 **13** 十一 2	火7 Fire [7] Water 庚申 Metal Monkey 坎爲水 **14** 十二 1	木8 Wood [6] Lesser Exceeding 辛酉 Metal Rooster 雷山小過 **15** 十三 3	金4 Metal [5] Gathering 壬戌 Water Dog 澤地萃 **16** 十四 4	水6 Water [4] Peel 癸亥 Water Pig 山地剝 **17** 十五 6	水1 Water [3] Earth 甲子 Wood Rat 坤爲地 **18** 十六 1	木3 Wood [2] Biting 乙丑 Wood Ox 火雷噬嗑 **19** 十七 6
火2 Fire [1] Family 丙寅 Fire Tiger 風火家人 **20** 十八 4	水6 Water [9] Decreasing 丁卯 Fire Rabbit 山澤損 **21** 十九 9	金9 Metal [8] Tread 戊辰 Earth Dragon 天澤履 **22** 二十 6	木8 Wood [7] Great Strength 己巳 Earth Snake 雷天大壯 **23** 廿一 2	木8 Wood [6] Consistency 庚午 Metal Horse 雷風恆 **24** 廿二 9	金9 Metal [5] Litigation 辛未 Metal Goat 天水訟 **25** 廿三 3	水1 Water [4] Officer 壬申 Water Monkey 地水師 **26** 廿四 7
火2 Fire [3] Gradual Progress 癸酉 Water Rooster 風山漸 **27** 廿五 7	火7 Fire [2] Obstruction 甲戌 Wood Dog 水山蹇 **28** 廿六 2	木3 Wood [1] Advancement 乙亥 Wood Pig 火地晉 **29** 廿七 3	水6 Water [9] Nourish 丙子 Fire Rat 山雷頤 **30** 廿八 3			

OCTOBER 2043 壬戌

Xuan Kong Element 玄空五行	澤地萃 Gathering	Period Luck 卦運	Monthly Star 月星
Metal 金4		4	3

SUNDAY	MONDAY	TUESDAY	WEDNESDAY	THURSDAY	FRIDAY	SATURDAY
				金4 Metal [8] Following 丁丑 Fire Ox 澤雷隨 **1** 廿九 7	木8 Wood [7] Abundance 戊寅 Earth Tiger 雷火豐 **2** 三十 6	火7 Fire [6] Regulate 己卯 Earth Rabbit 水澤節 **3** 九月初一 8
水1 Water [5] Unity 庚辰 Metal Dragon 地天泰 **4** 初二 9	木3 Wood [4] Great Reward 辛巳 Metal Snake 火天大有 **5** 初三 7	火2 Fire [3] Wind 壬午 Water Horse 巽爲風 **6** 初四 1	金4 Metal [2] Trap 癸未 Water Goat 澤水困 **7** 初五 8	木3 Wood [1] Not Yet Accomplished 甲申 Wood Monkey 火水未濟 **8** 初六 9	金9 Metal [9] Retreat 乙酉 Wood Rooster 天山遯 **9** 初七 4	水6 Water [8] Mountain 丙戌 Fire Dog 艮爲山 **10** 初八 1
木8 Wood [7] Delight 丁亥 Fire Pig 雷地豫 **11** 初九 8	火7 Fire [6] Beginning 戊子 Earth Rat 水雷屯 **12** 初十 4	金9 Metal [5] Without Wrongdoing 己丑 Earth Ox 天雷無妄 **13** 十一 2	木3 Wood [4] Fire 庚寅 Metal Tiger 離爲火 **14** 十二 1	火2 Fire [3] Sincerity 辛卯 Metal Rabbit 風澤中孚 **15** 十三 3	水6 Water [2] Big Livestock 壬辰 Water Dragon 山天大畜 **16** 十四 4	金4 Metal [1] Eliminating 癸巳 Water Snake 澤天夬 **17** 十五 6
金9 Metal [9] Heaven 甲午 Wood Horse 乾爲天 **18** 十六 1	火7 Fire [8] Well 乙未 Wood Goat 水風井 **19** 十七 6	木8 Wood [7] Relief 丙申 Fire Monkey 雷水解 **20** 十八 4	金4 Metal [6] Influence 丁酉 Fire Rooster 澤山咸 **21** 十九 9	水1 Water [5] Humility 戊戌 Earth Dog 地山謙 **22** 二十 6	火2 Fire [4] Observation 己亥 Earth Pig 風地觀 **23** 廿一 2	火2 Fire [3] Increasing 庚子 Metal Rat 風雷益 **24** 廿二 9
水1 Water [2] Dimming Light 辛丑 Metal Ox 地火明夷 **25** 廿三 3	金9 Metal [1] Fellowship 壬寅 Water Tiger 天火同人 **26** 廿四 7	木8 Wood [9] Marrying Maiden 癸卯 Water Rabbit 雷澤歸妹 **27** 廿五 7	木3 Wood [8] Opposition 甲辰 Wood Dragon 火澤睽 **28** 廿六 2	火7 Fire [7] Waiting 乙巳 Wood Snake 水天需 **29** 廿七 3	金4 Metal [6] Great Exceeding 丙午 Fire Horse 澤風大過 **30** 廿八 3	水6 Water [5] Poison 丁未 Fire Goat 山風蠱 **31** 廿九 7

NOVEMBER 2043 癸亥

Xuan Kong Element 玄空五行	山地剝 Peel	Period Luck 卦運	Monthly Star 月星
Water 水6		6	2

SUNDAY	MONDAY	TUESDAY	WEDNESDAY	THURSDAY	FRIDAY	SATURDAY
火2 Fire 4 Dispersing 風水渙 戊申 Earth Monkey 1 三十 6	木3 Wood 3 Travelling 火山旅 己酉 Earth Rooster 2 十月初一 8	金9 Metal 2 Stagnation 天地否 庚戌 Metal Dog 3 初二 9	火7 Fire 1 Alliance 水地比 辛亥 Metal Pig 4 初三 7	木8 Wood 9 Thunder 震為雷 壬子 Water Rat 5 初四 1	水6 Water 8 Beauty 山火賁 癸丑 Water Ox 6 初五 8	火7 Fire 7 Accomplished 水火既濟 甲寅 Wood Tiger 7 初六 9
水1 Water 6 Arriving 地澤臨 乙卯 Wood Rabbit 8 初七 4	金4 Metal 5 Marsh 兌為澤 丙辰 Fire Dragon 9 初八 1	火2 Fire 4 Small Livestock 風天小畜 丁巳 Fire Snake 10 初九 8	木3 Wood 3 The Cauldron 火風鼎 戊午 Earth Horse 11 初十 4	水1 Water 2 Rising 地風升 己未 Earth Goat 12 十一 2	火7 Fire 1 Water 坎為水 庚申 Metal Monkey 13 十二 1	木8 Wood 9 Lesser Exceeding 雷山小過 辛酉 Metal Rooster 14 十三 3
金4 Metal 8 Gathering 澤地萃 壬戌 Water Dog 15 十四 4	水6 Water 7 Peel 山地剝 癸亥 Water Pig 16 十五 6	水1 Water 6 Earth 坤為地 甲子 Wood Rat 17 十六 1	木3 Wood 5 Biting 火雷噬嗑 乙丑 Wood Ox 18 十七 6	火2 Fire 4 Family 風火家人 丙寅 Fire Tiger 19 十八 4	水6 Water 3 Decreasing 山澤損 丁卯 Fire Rabbit 20 十九 9	金9 Metal 2 Tread 天澤履 戊辰 Earth Dragon 21 二十 6
木8 Wood 1 Great Strength 雷天大壯 己巳 Earth Snake 22 廿一 2	木8 Wood 9 Consistency 雷風恆 庚午 Metal Horse 23 廿二 9	金9 Metal 8 Litigation 天水訟 辛未 Metal Goat 24 廿三 3	水1 Water 7 Officer 地水師 壬申 Water Monkey 25 廿四 7	火2 Fire 6 Gradual Progress 風山漸 癸酉 Water Rooster 26 廿五 7	火7 Fire 5 Obstruction 水山蹇 甲戌 Wood Dog 27 廿六 2	木3 Wood 4 Advancement 火地晉 乙亥 Wood Pig 28 廿七 3
水6 Water 3 Nourish 山雷頤 丙子 Fire Rat 29 廿八 3	金4 Metal 2 Following 澤雷隨 丁丑 Fire Ox 30 廿九 7					

DECEMBER 2043 甲子

Xuan Kong Element 玄空五行	坤為地 Earth	Period Luck 卦運	Monthly Star 月星
Water 水1		1	1

SUNDAY	MONDAY	TUESDAY	WEDNESDAY	THURSDAY	FRIDAY	SATURDAY
		木8 Wood 1 Abundance 雷火豐 戊寅 Earth Tiger 1 十一月初一 6	火7 Fire 9 Regulate 水澤節 己卯 Earth Rabbit 2 初二 8	水1 Water 8 Unity 地天泰 庚辰 Metal Dragon 3 初三 9	木3 Wood 7 Great Reward 火天大有 辛巳 Metal Snake 4 初四 7	火2 Fire 6 Wind 巽為風 壬午 Water Horse 5 初五 1
金4 Metal 5 Trap 澤水困 癸未 Water Goat 6 初六 8	木3 Wood 4 Not Yet Accomplished 火水未濟 甲申 Wood Monkey 7 初七 9	金9 Metal 3 Retreat 天山遯 乙酉 Wood Rooster 8 初八 4	水6 Water 2 Mountain 艮為山 丙戌 Fire Dog 9 初九 1	木8 Wood 1 Delight 雷地豫 丁亥 Fire Pig 10 初十 8	火7 Fire 9 Beginning 水雷屯 戊子 Earth Rat 11 十一 4	金9 Metal 8 Without Wrongdoing 天雷無妄 己丑 Earth Ox 12 十二 2
木3 Wood 7 Fire 離為火 庚寅 Metal Tiger 13 十三 1	火2 Fire 6 Sincerity 風澤中孚 辛卯 Metal Rabbit 14 十四 3	水6 Water 5 Big Livestock 山天大畜 壬辰 Water Dragon 15 十五 4	金4 Metal 4 Eliminating 澤天夬 癸巳 Water Snake 16 十六 6	金9 Metal 3 Heaven 乾為天 甲午 Wood Horse 17 十七 1	火7 Fire 2 Well 水風井 乙未 Wood Goat 18 十八 6	木8 Wood 1 Relief 雷水解 丙申 Fire Monkey 19 十九 4
金4 Metal 9 Influence 澤山咸 丁酉 Fire Rooster 20 二十 9	水1 Water 8 Humility 地山謙 戊戌 Earth Dog 21 廿一 6	火2 Fire 7/3 Observation 風地觀 己亥 Earth Pig 22 廿二 2	火2 Fire 4 Increasing 風雷益 庚子 Metal Rat 23 廿三 9	水1 Water 5 Dimming Light 地火明夷 辛丑 Metal Ox 24 廿四 3	金9 Metal 6 Fellowship 天火同人 壬寅 Water Tiger 25 廿五 7	木8 Wood 7 Marrying Maiden 雷澤歸妹 癸卯 Water Rabbit 26 廿六 7
木3 Wood 8 Opposition 火澤睽 甲辰 Wood Dragon 27 廿七 2	火7 Fire 9 Waiting 水天需 乙巳 Wood Snake 28 廿八 3	金4 Metal 1 Great Exceeding 澤風大過 丙午 Fire Horse 29 廿九 3	水6 Water 2 Poison 山風蠱 丁未 Fire Goat 30 三十 7	火2 Fire 3 Dispersing 風水渙 戊申 Earth Monkey 31 十二月初一 6		

2044 甲子

(*Jia Zi*) Wood Rat

2044 甲子 *(Jia Zi)* Wood Rat

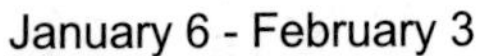

January 6 - February 3

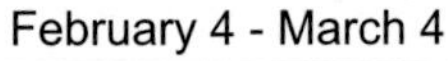

February 4 - March 4

March 5 - April 3

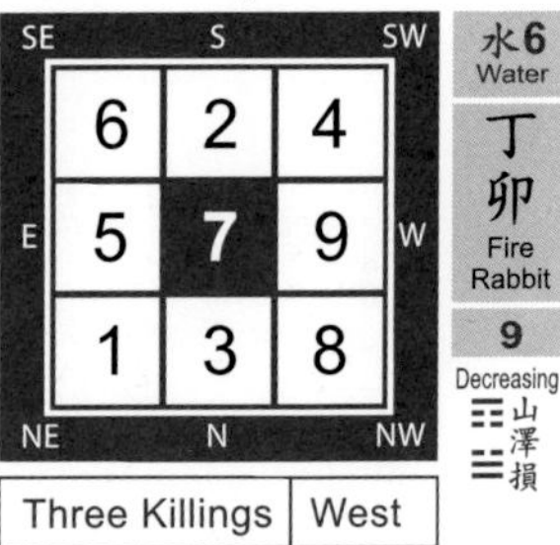

April 4 - May 4

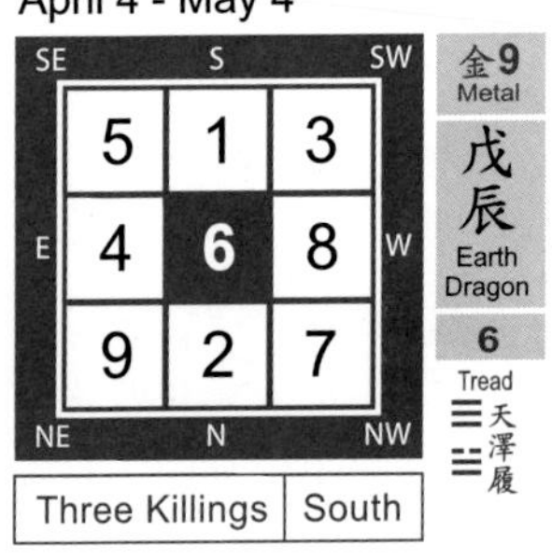

May 5 - June 4

June 5 - July 5

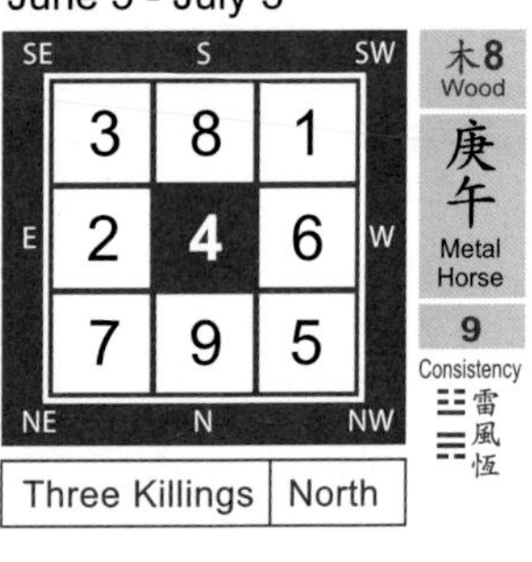

July 6 - August 6

August 7 - September 6

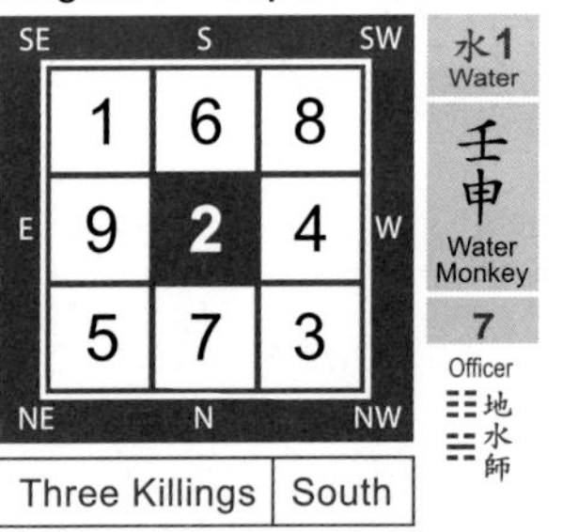

September 7 - October 6

October 7 - November 6

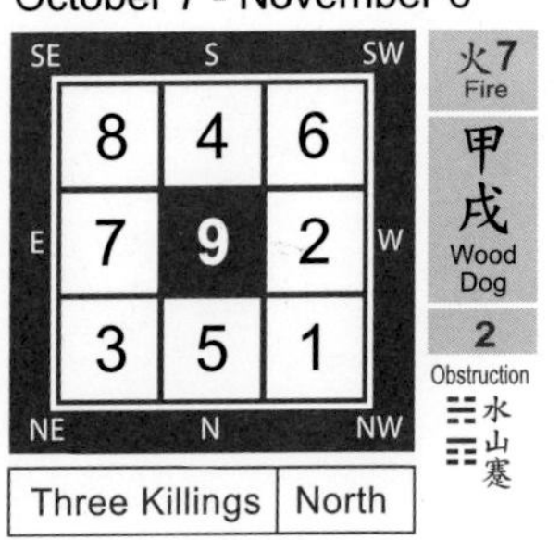

November 7 - December 5

December 6 - January 4

JANUARY 2044 乙丑

Xuan Kong Element 玄空五行	火雷噬嗑 Biting	Period Luck 卦運	Monthly Star 月星
Wood 木3		6	9

SUNDAY	MONDAY	TUESDAY	WEDNESDAY	THURSDAY	FRIDAY	SATURDAY
火7 Fire [7] Regulate 水澤節 己卯 Earth Rabbit 8 **31** 初二					木3 Wood [4] Travelling 火山旅 己酉 Earth Rooster 8 **1** 初二	金9 Metal [5] Stagnation 天地否 庚戌 Metal Dog 9 **2** 初三
火7 Fire [6] Alliance 水地比 辛亥 Metal Pig 7 **3** 初四	木8 Wood [7] Thunder 震爲雷 壬子 Water Rat 1 **4** 初五	水6 Water [8] Beauty 山火賁 癸丑 Water Ox 8 **5** 初六	火7 Fire [9] Accomplished 水火既濟 甲寅 Wood Tiger 9 **6** 初七	水1 Water [1] Arriving 地澤臨 乙卯 Wood Rabbit 4 **7** 初八	金4 Metal [2] Marsh 兌爲澤 丙辰 Fire Dragon 1 **8** 初九	火2 Fire [3] Small Livestock 風天小畜 丁巳 Fire Snake 8 **9** 初十
木3 Wood [4] The Cauldron 火風鼎 戊午 Earth Horse 4 **10** 十一	水1 Water [5] Rising 地風升 己未 Earth Goat 2 **11** 十二	火7 Fire [6] Water 坎爲水 庚申 Metal Monkey 1 **12** 十三	木8 Wood [7] Lesser Exceeding 雷山小過 辛酉 Metal Rooster 3 **13** 十四	金4 Metal [8] Gathering 澤地萃 壬戌 Water Dog 4 **14** 十五	水6 Water [9] Peel 山地剝 癸亥 Water Pig 6 **15** 十六	水1 Water [1] Earth 坤爲地 甲子 Wood Rat 1 **16** 十七
木3 Wood [2] Biting 火雷噬嗑 乙丑 Wood Ox 6 **17** 十八	火2 Fire [3] Family 風火家人 丙寅 Fire Tiger 4 **18** 十九	水6 Water [4] Decreasing 山澤損 丁卯 Fire Rabbit 9 **19** 二十	金9 Metal [5] Tread 天澤履 戊辰 Earth Dragon 6 **20** 廿一	木8 Wood [6] Great Strength 雷天大壯 己巳 Earth Snake 2 **21** 廿二	木8 Wood [7] Consistency 雷風恆 庚午 Metal Horse 9 **22** 廿三	金9 Metal [8] Litigation 天水訟 辛未 Metal Goat 3 **23** 廿四
水1 Water [9] Officer 地水師 壬申 Water Monkey 7 **24** 廿五	火2 Fire [1] Gradual Progress 風山漸 癸酉 Water Rooster 7 **25** 廿六	火7 Fire [2] Obstruction 水山蹇 甲戌 Wood Dog 2 **26** 廿七	木3 Wood [3] Advancement 火地晉 乙亥 Wood Pig 3 **27** 廿八	水6 Water [4] Nourish 山雷頤 丙子 Fire Rat 3 **28** 廿九	金4 Metal [5] Following 澤雷隨 丁丑 Fire Ox 7 **29** 三十	木8 Wood [6] Abundance 雷火豐 戊寅 Earth Tiger 6 **30** 正月初一

FEBRUARY 2044 丙寅

Xuan Kong Element 玄空五行	風火家人 Family	Period Luck 卦運	Monthly Star 月星
Fire 火2		4	8

SUNDAY	MONDAY	TUESDAY	WEDNESDAY	THURSDAY	FRIDAY	SATURDAY
	水1 Water [8] Unity 地天泰 庚辰 Metal Dragon 9 **1** 初三	木3 Wood [9] Great Reward 火天大有 辛巳 Metal Snake 7 **2** 初四	火2 Fire [1] Wind 巽爲風 壬午 Water Horse 1 **3** 初五	金4 Metal [2] Trap 澤水困 癸未 Water Goat 8 **4** 初六	木3 Wood [3] Not Yet Accomplished 火水未濟 甲申 Wood Monkey 9 **5** 初七	金9 Metal [4] Retreat 天山遯 乙酉 Wood Rooster 4 **6** 初八
水6 Water [5] Mountain 艮爲山 丙戌 Fire Dog 1 **7** 初九	木8 Wood [6] Delight 雷地豫 丁亥 Fire Pig 8 **8** 初十	火7 Fire [7] Beginning 水雷屯 戊子 Earth Rat 4 **9** 十一	金9 Metal [8] Without Wrongdoing 天雷無妄 己丑 Earth Ox 2 **10** 十二	木3 Wood [9] Fire 離爲火 庚寅 Metal Tiger 1 **11** 十三	火2 Fire [1] Sincerity 風澤中孚 辛卯 Metal Rabbit 3 **12** 十四	水6 Water [2] Big Livestock 山天大畜 壬辰 Water Dragon 4 **13** 十五
金4 Metal [3] Eliminating 澤天夬 癸巳 Water Snake 6 **14** 十六	金9 Metal [4] Heaven 乾爲天 甲午 Wood Horse 1 **15** 十七	火7 Fire [5] Well 水風井 乙未 Wood Goat 6 **16** 十八	木8 Wood [6] Relief 雷水解 丙申 Fire Monkey 4 **17** 十九	金4 Metal [7] Influence 澤山咸 丁酉 Fire Rooster 9 **18** 二十	水1 Water [8] Humility 地山謙 戊戌 Earth Dog 6 **19** 廿一	火2 Fire [9] Observation 風地觀 己亥 Earth Pig 2 **20** 廿二
火2 Fire [1] Increasing 風雷益 庚子 Metal Rat 9 **21** 廿三	水1 Water [2] Dimming Light 地火明夷 辛丑 Metal Ox 3 **22** 廿四	金9 Metal [3] Fellowship 天火同人 壬寅 Water Tiger 7 **23** 廿五	木8 Wood [4] Marrying Maiden 雷澤歸妹 癸卯 Water Rabbit 7 **24** 廿六	木3 Wood [5] Opposition 火澤睽 甲辰 Wood Dragon 2 **25** 廿七	火7 Fire [6] Waiting 水天需 乙巳 Wood Snake 3 **26** 廿八	金4 Metal [7] Great Exceeding 澤風大過 丙午 Fire Horse 3 **27** 廿九
水6 Water [8] Poison 山風蠱 丁未 Fire Goat 7 **28** 三十	火2 Fire [9] Dispersing 風水渙 戊申 Earth Monkey 6 **29** 二月初一					

MARCH 2044 丁卯

Xuan Kong Element 玄空五行	山澤損 Decreasing	Period Luck 卦運	Monthly Star 月星
Water 水6		9	7

SUNDAY	MONDAY	TUESDAY	WEDNESDAY	THURSDAY	FRIDAY	SATURDAY
		木3 Wood · 1 Travelling 火山旅 己酉 Earth Rooster **1** 初二 8	金9 Metal · 2 Stagnation 天地否 庚戌 Metal Dog **2** 初三 9	火7 Fire · 3 Alliance 水地比 辛亥 Metal Pig **3** 初四 7	木8 Wood · 4 Thunder 震爲雷 壬子 Water Rat **4** 初五 1	水6 Water · 5 Beauty 山火賁 癸丑 Water Ox **5** 初六 8
火7 Fire · 6 Accomplished 水火既濟 甲寅 Wood Tiger **6** 初七 9	水1 Water · 7 Arriving 地澤臨 乙卯 Wood Rabbit **7** 初八 4	金4 Metal · 8 Marsh 兌爲澤 丙辰 Fire Dragon **8** 初九 1	火2 Fire · 9 Small Livestock 風天小畜 丁巳 Fire Snake **9** 初十 8	木3 Wood · 1 The Cauldron 火風鼎 戊午 Earth Horse **10** 十一 4	水1 Water · 2 Rising 地風升 己未 Earth Goat **11** 十二 2	火7 Fire · 3 Water 坎爲水 庚申 Metal Monkey **12** 十三 1
木8 Wood · 4 Lesser Exceeding 雷山小過 辛酉 Metal Rooster **13** 十四 3	金4 Metal · 5 Gathering 澤地萃 壬戌 Water Dog **14** 十五 4	水6 Water · 6 Peel 山地剝 癸亥 Water Pig **15** 十六 6	水1 Water · 7 Earth 坤爲地 甲子 Wood Rat **16** 十七 1	木3 Wood · 8 Biting 火雷噬嗑 乙丑 Wood Ox **17** 十八 6	火2 Fire · 9 Family 風火家人 丙寅 Fire Tiger **18** 十九 4	水6 Water · 1 Decreasing 山澤損 丁卯 Fire Rabbit **19** 二十 9
金9 Metal · 2 Tread 天澤履 戊辰 Earth Dragon **20** 廿一 6	木8 Wood · 3 Great Strength 雷天大壯 己巳 Earth Snake **21** 廿二 2	木8 Wood · 4 Consistency 雷風恆 庚午 Metal Horse **22** 廿三 9	金9 Metal · 5 Litigation 天水訟 辛未 Metal Goat **23** 廿四 3	水1 Water · 6 Officer 地水師 壬申 Water Monkey **24** 廿五 7	火2 Fire · 7 Gradual Progress 風山漸 癸酉 Water Rooster **25** 廿六 7	火7 Fire · 8 Obstruction 水山蹇 甲戌 Wood Dog **26** 廿七 2
木3 Wood · 9 Advancement 火地晉 乙亥 Wood Pig **27** 廿八 3	水6 Water · 1 Nourish 山雷頤 丙子 Fire Rat **28** 廿九 3	金4 Metal · 2 Following 澤雷隨 丁丑 Fire Ox **29** 三月初一 7	木8 Wood · 3 Abundance 雷火豐 戊寅 Earth Tiger **30** 初二 6	火7 Fire · 4 Regulate 水澤節 己卯 Earth Rabbit **31** 初三 8		

APRIL 2044 戊辰

Xuan Kong Element 玄空五行	天澤履 Tread	Period Luck 卦運	Monthly Star 月星
Metal 金9		6	6

SUNDAY	MONDAY	TUESDAY	WEDNESDAY	THURSDAY	FRIDAY	SATURDAY
					水1 Water · 5 Unity 地天泰 庚辰 Metal Dragon **1** 初四 9	木3 Wood · 6 Great Reward 火天大有 辛巳 Metal Snake **2** 初五 7
火2 Fire · 7 Wind 巽爲風 壬午 Water Horse **3** 初六 1	金4 Metal · 8 Trap 澤水困 癸未 Water Goat **4** 初七 8	木3 Wood · 9 Not Yet Accomplished 火水未濟 甲申 Wood Monkey **5** 初八 9	金9 Metal · 1 Retreat 天山遯 乙酉 Wood Rooster **6** 初九 4	水6 Water · 2 Mountain 艮爲山 丙戌 Fire Dog **7** 初十 1	木8 Wood · 3 Delight 雷地豫 丁亥 Fire Pig **8** 十一 8	火7 Fire · 4 Beginning 水雷屯 戊子 Earth Rat **9** 十二 4
金9 Metal · 5 Without Wrongdoing 天雷無妄 己丑 Earth Ox **10** 十三 2	木3 Wood · 6 Fire 離爲火 庚寅 Metal Tiger **11** 十四 1	火2 Fire · 7 Sincerity 風澤中孚 辛卯 Metal Rabbit **12** 十五 3	水6 Water · 8 Big Livestock 山天大畜 壬辰 Water Dragon **13** 十六 4	金4 Metal · 9 Eliminating 澤天夬 癸巳 Water Snake **14** 十七 6	金9 Metal · 1 Heaven 乾爲天 甲午 Wood Horse **15** 十八 1	火7 Fire · 2 Well 水風井 乙未 Wood Goat **16** 十九 6
木8 Wood · 3 Relief 雷水解 丙申 Fire Monkey **17** 二十 4	金4 Metal · 4 Influence 澤山咸 丁酉 Fire Rooster **18** 廿一 9	水1 Water · 5 Humility 地山謙 戊戌 Earth Dog **19** 廿二 6	火2 Fire · 6 Observation 風地觀 己亥 Earth Pig **20** 廿三 2	火2 Fire · 7 Increasing 風雷益 庚子 Metal Rat **21** 廿四 9	水1 Water · 8 Dimming Light 地火明夷 辛丑 Metal Ox **22** 廿五 3	金9 Metal · 9 Fellowship 天火同人 壬寅 Water Tiger **23** 廿六 7
木8 Wood · 1 Marrying Maiden 雷澤歸妹 癸卯 Water Rabbit **24** 廿七 7	木3 Wood · 2 Opposition 火澤睽 甲辰 Wood Dragon **25** 廿八 2	火7 Fire · 3 Waiting 水天需 乙巳 Wood Snake **26** 廿九 3	金4 Metal · 4 Great Exceeding 澤風大過 丙午 Fire Horse **27** 三十 3	水6 Water · 5 Poison 山風蠱 丁未 Fire Goat **28** 四月初一 7	火2 Fire · 6 Dispersing 風水渙 戊申 Earth Monkey **29** 初二 6	木3 Wood · 7 Travelling 火山旅 己酉 Earth Rooster **30** 初三 8

MAY 2044 己巳

Xuan Kong Element 玄空五行	雷天大壯 Great Strength	Period Luck 卦運	Monthly Star 月星
Wood 木8		2	5

SUNDAY	MONDAY	TUESDAY	WEDNESDAY	THURSDAY	FRIDAY	SATURDAY
金9 Metal 8 Stagnation 天地否 庚戌 Metal Dog 1 初四 9	火7 Fire 9 Alliance 水地比 辛亥 Metal Pig 2 初五 7	木8 Wood 1 Thunder 震爲雷 壬子 Water Rat 3 初六 1	水6 Water 2 Beauty 山火賁 癸丑 Water Ox 4 初七 8	火7 Fire 3 Accomplished 水火既濟 甲寅 Wood Tiger 5 初八 9	水1 Water 4 Arriving 地澤臨 乙卯 Wood Rabbit 6 初九 4	金4 Metal 5 Marsh 兌爲澤 丙辰 Fire Dragon 7 初十 1
火2 Fire 6 Small Livestock 風天小畜 丁巳 Fire Snake 8 十一 8	木3 Wood 7 The Cauldron 火風鼎 戊午 Earth Horse 9 十二 4	水1 Water 8 Rising 地風升 己未 Earth Goat 10 十三 2	火7 Fire 9 Water 坎爲水 庚申 Metal Monkey 11 十四 1	木8 Wood 1 Lesser Exceeding 雷山小過 辛酉 Metal Rooster 12 十五 3	金4 Metal 2 Gathering 澤地萃 壬戌 Water Dog 13 十六 4	水6 Water 3 Peel 山地剝 癸亥 Water Pig 14 十七 6
水1 Water 4 Earth 坤爲地 甲子 Wood Rat 15 十八 1	木3 Wood 5 Biting 火雷噬嗑 乙丑 Wood Ox 16 十九 6	火2 Fire 6 Family 風火家人 丙寅 Fire Tiger 17 二十 4	水6 Water 7 Decreasing 山澤損 丁卯 Fire Rabbit 18 廿一 9	金9 Metal 8 Tread 天澤履 戊辰 Earth Dragon 19 廿二 6	木8 Wood 9 Great Strength 雷天大壯 己巳 Earth Snake 20 廿三 2	木8 Wood 1 Consistency 雷風恆 庚午 Metal Horse 21 廿四 9
金9 Metal 2 Litigation 天水訟 辛未 Metal Goat 22 廿五 3	水1 Water 3 Officer 地水師 壬申 Water Monkey 23 廿六 7	火2 Fire 4 Gradual Progress 風山漸 癸酉 Water Rooster 24 廿七 7	火7 Fire 5 Obstruction 水山蹇 甲戌 Wood Dog 25 廿八 2	木3 Wood 6 Advancement 火地晉 乙亥 Wood Pig 26 廿九 3	水6 Water 7 Nourish 山雷頤 丙子 Fire Rat 27 五月初一 3	金4 Metal 8 Following 澤雷隨 丁丑 Fire Ox 28 初二 7
木8 Wood 9 Abundance 雷火豐 戊寅 Earth Tiger 29 初三 6	火7 Fire 1 Regulate 水澤節 己卯 Earth Rabbit 30 初四 8	水1 Water 2 Unity 地天泰 庚辰 Metal Dragon 31 初五 9				

JUNE 2044 庚午

Xuan Kong Element 玄空五行	雷風恆 Consistency	Period Luck 卦運	Monthly Star 月星
Wood 木8		9	4

SUNDAY	MONDAY	TUESDAY	WEDNESDAY	THURSDAY	FRIDAY	SATURDAY
			木3 Wood 3 Great Reward 火天大有 辛巳 Metal Snake 1 初六 7	火2 Fire 4 Wind 巽爲風 壬午 Water Horse 2 初七 1	金4 Metal 5 Trap 澤水困 癸未 Water Goat 3 初八 8	木3 Wood 6 Not Yet Accomplished 火水未濟 甲申 Wood Monkey 4 初九 9
金9 Metal 7 Retreat 天山遯 乙酉 Wood Rooster 5 初十 4	水6 Water 8 Mountain 艮爲山 丙戌 Fire Dog 6 十一 1	木8 Wood 9 Delight 雷地豫 丁亥 Fire Pig 7 十二 8	火7 Fire 1 Beginning 水雷屯 戊子 Earth Rat 8 十三 4	金9 Metal 2 Without Wrongdoing 天雷無妄 己丑 Earth Ox 9 十四 2	木3 Wood 3 Fire 離爲火 庚寅 Metal Tiger 10 十五 1	火2 Fire 4 Sincerity 風澤中孚 辛卯 Metal Rabbit 11 十六 3
水6 Water 5 Big Livestock 山天大畜 壬辰 Water Dragon 12 十七 4	金4 Metal 6 Eliminating 澤天夬 癸巳 Water Snake 13 十八 6	金9 Metal 7 Heaven 乾爲天 甲午 Wood Horse 14 十九 1	火7 Fire 8 Well 水風井 乙未 Wood Goat 15 二十 6	木8 Wood 9 Relief 雷水解 丙申 Fire Monkey 16 廿一 4	金4 Metal 1 Influence 澤山咸 丁酉 Fire Rooster 17 廿二 9	水1 Water 2 Humility 地山謙 戊戌 Earth Dog 18 廿三 6
火2 Fire 3 Observation 風地觀 己亥 Earth Pig 19 廿四 2	火2 Fire 4 Increasing 風雷益 庚子 Metal Rat 20 廿五 9	水1 Water 5/5 Dimming Light 地火明夷 辛丑 Metal Ox 21 廿六 3	金9 Metal 4 Fellowship 天火同人 壬寅 Water Tiger 22 廿七 7	木8 Wood 3 Marrying Maiden 雷澤歸妹 癸卯 Water Rabbit 23 廿八 7	木3 Wood 2 Opposition 火澤睽 甲辰 Wood Dragon 24 廿九 2	火7 Fire 1 Waiting 水天需 乙巳 Wood Snake 25 六月初一 3
金4 Metal 9 Great Exceeding 澤風大過 丙午 Fire Horse 26 初二 3	水6 Water 8 Poison 山風蠱 丁未 Fire Goat 27 初三 7	火2 Fire 7 Dispersing 風水渙 戊申 Earth Monkey 28 初四 6	木3 Wood 6 Travelling 火山旅 己酉 Earth Rooster 29 初五 8	金9 Metal 5 Stagnation 天地否 庚戌 Metal Dog 30 初六 9		

JULY 2044 辛未

Xuan Kong Element 玄空五行	天水訟 Litigation	Period Luck 卦運	Monthly Star 月星
Metal 金9		3	3

SUNDAY	MONDAY	TUESDAY	WEDNESDAY	THURSDAY	FRIDAY	SATURDAY
31 初七 Great Reward 火天大有 1 木3 Wood 辛巳 Metal Snake 7					1 初七 Alliance 水地比 4 火7 Fire 辛亥 Metal Pig 7	2 初八 Thunder 震為雷 3 木8 Wood 壬子 Water Rat 1
3 初九 Beauty 山火賁 2 水6 Water 癸丑 Water Ox 8	4 初十 Accomplished 水火既濟 1 火7 Fire 甲寅 Wood Tiger 9	5 十一 Arriving 地澤臨 9 水1 Water 乙卯 Wood Rabbit 4	6 十二 Marsh 兌為澤 8 金4 Metal 丙辰 Fire Dragon 1	7 十三 Small Livestock 風天小畜 7 火2 Fire 丁巳 Fire Snake 8	8 十四 The Cauldron 火風鼎 6 木3 Wood 戊午 Earth Horse 4	9 十五 Rising 地風升 5 水1 Water 己未 Earth Goat 2
10 十六 Water 坎為水 4 火7 Fire 庚申 Metal Monkey 1	11 十七 Lesser Exceeding 雷山小過 3 木8 Wood 辛酉 Metal Rooster 3	12 十八 Gathering 澤地萃 2 金4 Metal 壬戌 Water Dog 4	13 十九 Peel 山地剝 1 水6 Water 癸亥 Water Pig 6	14 二十 Earth 坤為地 9 水1 Water 甲子 Wood Rat 1	15 廿一 Biting 火雷噬嗑 8 木3 Wood 乙丑 Wood Ox 6	16 廿二 Family 風火家人 7 火2 Fire 丙寅 Fire Tiger 4
17 廿三 Decreasing 山澤損 6 水6 Water 丁卯 Fire Rabbit 9	18 廿四 Tread 天澤履 5 金9 Metal 戊辰 Earth Dragon 6	19 廿五 Great Strength 雷天大壯 4 木8 Wood 己巳 Earth Snake 2	20 廿六 Consistency 雷風恒 3 木8 Wood 庚午 Metal Horse 9	21 廿七 Litigation 天水訟 2 金9 Metal 辛未 Metal Goat 3	22 廿八 Officer 地水師 1 水1 Water 壬申 Water Monkey 7	23 廿九 Gradual Progress 風山漸 9 火2 Fire 癸酉 Water Rooster 7
24 三十 Obstruction 水山蹇 8 火7 Fire 甲戌 Wood Dog 2	25 七月初一 Advancement 火地晉 7 木3 Wood 乙亥 Wood Pig 3	26 初二 Nourish 山雷頤 6 水6 Water 丙子 Fire Rat 3	27 初三 Following 澤雷隨 5 金4 Metal 丁丑 Fire Ox 7	28 初四 Abundance 雷火豐 4 木8 Wood 戊寅 Earth Tiger 6	29 初五 Regulate 水澤節 3 火7 Fire 己卯 Earth Rabbit 8	30 初六 Unity 地天泰 2 水1 Water 庚辰 Metal Dragon 9

AUGUST 2044 壬申

Xuan Kong Element 玄空五行	地水師 Officer	Period Luck 卦運	Monthly Star 月星
Water 水1		7	2

SUNDAY	MONDAY	TUESDAY	WEDNESDAY	THURSDAY	FRIDAY	SATURDAY
	1 初八 Wind 巽為風 9 火2 Fire 壬午 Water Horse 1	2 初九 Trap 澤水困 8 金4 Metal 癸未 Water Goat 8	3 初十 Not Yet Accomplished 火水未濟 7 木3 Wood 甲申 Wood Monkey 9	4 十一 Retreat 天山遯 6 金9 Metal 乙酉 Wood Rooster 4	5 十二 Mountain 艮為山 5 水6 Water 丙戌 Fire Dog 1	6 十三 Delight 雷地豫 4 木8 Wood 丁亥 Fire Pig 8
7 十四 Beginning 水雷屯 3 火7 Fire 戊子 Earth Rat 4	8 十五 Without Wrongdoing 天雷無妄 2 金9 Metal 己丑 Earth Ox 2	9 十六 Fire 離為火 1 木3 Wood 庚寅 Metal Tiger 1	10 十七 Sincerity 風澤中孚 9 火2 Fire 辛卯 Metal Rabbit 3	11 十八 Big Livestock 山天大畜 8 水6 Water 壬辰 Water Dragon 4	12 十九 Eliminating 澤天夬 7 金4 Metal 癸巳 Water Snake 6	13 二十 Heaven 乾為天 6 金9 Metal 甲午 Wood Horse 1
14 廿一 Well 水風井 5 火7 Fire 乙未 Wood Goat 6	15 廿二 Relief 雷水解 4 木8 Wood 丙申 Fire Monkey 4	16 廿三 Influence 澤山咸 3 金4 Metal 丁酉 Fire Rooster 9	17 廿四 Humility 地山謙 2 水1 Water 戊戌 Earth Dog 6	18 廿五 Observation 風地觀 1 火2 Fire 己亥 Earth Pig 2	19 廿六 Increasing 風雷益 9 火2 Fire 庚子 Metal Rat 9	20 廿七 Dimming Light 地火明夷 8 水1 Water 辛丑 Metal Ox 3
21 廿八 Fellowship 天火同人 7 金9 Metal 壬寅 Water Tiger 7	22 廿九 Marrying Maiden 雷澤歸妹 6 木8 Wood 癸卯 Water Rabbit 7	23 閏七月初一 Opposition 火澤睽 5 木3 Wood 甲辰 Wood Dragon 2	24 初二 Waiting 水天需 4 火7 Fire 乙巳 Wood Snake 3	25 初三 Great Exceeding 澤風大過 3 金4 Metal 丙午 Fire Horse 3	26 初四 Poison 山風蠱 2 水6 Water 丁未 Fire Goat 7	27 初五 Dispersing 風水渙 1 火2 Fire 戊申 Earth Monkey 6
28 初六 Travelling 火山旅 9 木3 Wood 己酉 Earth Rooster 8	29 初七 Stagnation 天地否 8 金9 Metal 庚戌 Metal Dog 9	30 初八 Alliance 水地比 7 火7 Fire 辛亥 Metal Pig 7	31 初九 Thunder 震為雷 6 木8 Wood 壬子 Water Rat 1			

SEPTEMBER 2044 癸酉

Xuan Kong Element 玄空五行	風山漸 Gradual Progress	Period Luck 卦運	Monthly Star 月星
Fire 火2		7	1

SUNDAY	MONDAY	TUESDAY	WEDNESDAY	THURSDAY	FRIDAY	SATURDAY
				水6 Water 5 Beauty 山火賁 癸丑 Water Ox **1** 初十 8	火7 Fire 4 Accomplished 水火既濟 甲寅 Wood Tiger **2** 十一 9	水1 Water 3 Arriving 地澤臨 乙卯 Wood Rabbit **3** 十二 4
金4 Metal 2 Marsh 兌為澤 丙辰 Fire Dragon **4** 十三 1	火2 Fire 1 Small Livestock 風天小畜 丁巳 Fire Snake **5** 十四 8	木3 Wood 9 The Cauldron 火風鼎 戊午 Earth Horse **6** 十五 4	水1 Water 8 Rising 地風升 己未 Earth Goat **7** 十六 2	火7 Fire 7 Water 坎為水 庚申 Metal Monkey **8** 十七 1	木8 Wood 6 Lesser Exceeding 雷山小過 辛酉 Metal Rooster **9** 十八 3	金4 Metal 5 Gathering 澤地萃 壬戌 Water Dog **10** 十九 4
水6 Water 4 Peel 山地剝 癸亥 Water Pig **11** 二十 6	水1 Water 3 Earth 坤為地 甲子 Wood Rat **12** 廿一 1	木3 Wood 2 Biting 火雷噬嗑 乙丑 Wood Ox **13** 廿二 6	火2 Fire 1 Family 風火家人 丙寅 Fire Tiger **14** 廿三 4	水6 Water 9 Decreasing 山澤損 丁卯 Fire Rabbit **15** 廿四 9	金9 Metal 8 Tread 天澤履 戊辰 Earth Dragon **16** 廿五 6	木8 Wood 7 Great Strength 雷天大壯 己巳 Earth Snake **17** 廿六 2
木8 Wood 6 Consistency 雷風恆 庚午 Metal Horse **18** 廿七 9	金9 Metal 5 Litigation 天水訟 辛未 Metal Goat **19** 廿八 3	水1 Water 4 Officer 地水師 壬申 Water Monkey **20** 廿九 7	火2 Fire 3 Gradual Progress 風山漸 癸酉 Water Rooster **21** 八月初一 7	火7 Fire 2 Obstruction 水山蹇 甲戌 Wood Dog **22** 初二 2	木3 Wood 1 Advancement 火地晉 乙亥 Wood Pig **23** 初三 3	水6 Water 9 Nourish 山雷頤 丙子 Fire Rat **24** 初四 3
金4 Metal 8 Following 澤雷隨 丁丑 Fire Ox **25** 初五 7	木8 Wood 7 Abundance 雷火豐 戊寅 Earth Tiger **26** 初六 6	火7 Fire 6 Regulate 水澤節 己卯 Earth Rabbit **27** 初七 8	水1 Water 5 Unity 地天泰 庚辰 Metal Dragon **28** 初八 9	木3 Wood 4 Great Reward 火天大有 辛巳 Metal Snake **29** 初九 7	火2 Fire 3 Wind 巽為風 壬午 Water Horse **30** 初十 1	

OCTOBER 2044 甲戌

Xuan Kong Element 玄空五行	水山蹇 Obstruction	Period Luck 卦運	Monthly Star 月星
Fire 火7		2	9

SUNDAY	MONDAY	TUESDAY	WEDNESDAY	THURSDAY	FRIDAY	SATURDAY
木8 Wood 9 Thunder 震為雷 壬子 Water Rat **30** 初十 1	水6 Water 8 Beauty 山火賁 癸丑 Water Ox **31** 十一 8					金4 Metal 2 Trap 澤水困 癸未 Water Goat **1** 十一 8
木3 Wood 1 Not Yet Accomplished 火水未濟 甲申 Wood Monkey **2** 十二 9	金9 Metal 9 Retreat 天山遯 乙酉 Wood Rooster **3** 十三 4	水6 Water 8 Mountain 艮為山 丙戌 Fire Dog **4** 十四 1	木8 Wood 7 Delight 雷地豫 丁亥 Fire Pig **5** 十五 8	火7 Fire 6 Beginning 水雷屯 戊子 Earth Rat **6** 十六 4	金9 Metal 5 Without Wrongdoing 天雷無妄 己丑 Earth Ox **7** 十七 2	木3 Wood 4 Fire 離為火 庚寅 Metal Tiger **8** 十八 1
火2 Fire 3 Sincerity 風澤中孚 辛卯 Metal Rabbit **9** 十九 3	水6 Water 2 Big Livestock 山天大畜 壬辰 Water Dragon **10** 二十 4	金4 Metal 1 Eliminating 澤天夬 癸巳 Water Snake **11** 廿一 6	金9 Metal 9 Heaven 乾為天 甲午 Wood Horse **12** 廿二 1	火7 Fire 8 Well 水風井 乙未 Wood Goat **13** 廿三 6	木8 Wood 7 Relief 雷水解 丙申 Fire Monkey **14** 廿四 4	金4 Metal 6 Influence 澤山咸 丁酉 Fire Rooster **15** 廿五 9
水1 Water 5 Humility 地山謙 戊戌 Earth Dog **16** 廿六 6	火2 Fire 4 Observation 風地觀 己亥 Earth Pig **17** 廿七 2	火2 Fire 3 Increasing 風雷益 庚子 Metal Rat **18** 廿八 9	水1 Water 2 Dimming Light 地火明夷 辛丑 Metal Ox **19** 廿九 3	金9 Metal 1 Fellowship 天火同人 壬寅 Water Tiger **20** 三十 7	木8 Wood 9 Marrying Maiden 雷澤歸妹 癸卯 Water Rabbit **21** 九月初一 7	木3 Wood 8 Opposition 火澤睽 甲辰 Wood Dragon **22** 初二 2
火7 Fire 7 Waiting 水天需 乙巳 Wood Snake **23** 初三 3	金4 Metal 6 Great Exceeding 澤風大過 丙午 Fire Horse **24** 初四 3	水6 Water 5 Poison 山風蠱 丁未 Fire Goat **25** 初五 7	火2 Fire 4 Dispersing 風水渙 戊申 Earth Monkey **26** 初六 6	木3 Wood 3 Travelling 火山旅 己酉 Earth Rooster **27** 初七 8	金9 Metal 2 Stagnation 天地否 庚戌 Metal Dog **28** 初八 9	火7 Fire 1 Alliance 水地比 辛亥 Metal Pig **29** 初九 7

NOVEMBER 2044 乙亥

Xuan Kong Element 玄空五行	火地晉 Advancement	Period Luck 卦運	Monthly Star 月星
Wood 木3		3	8

SUNDAY	MONDAY	TUESDAY	WEDNESDAY	THURSDAY	FRIDAY	SATURDAY
		火7 Fire 7 Accomplished 甲寅 Wood Tiger 水火既濟 1 十二 9	水1 Water 6 Arriving 乙卯 Wood Rabbit 地澤臨 2 十三 4	金4 Metal 5 Marsh 丙辰 Fire Dragon 兑爲澤 3 十四 1	火2 Fire 4 Small Livestock 丁巳 Fire Snake 風天小畜 4 十五 8	木3 Wood 3 The Cauldron 戊午 Earth Horse 火風鼎 5 十六 4
水1 Water 2 Rising 己未 Earth Goat 地風升 6 十七 2	火7 Fire 1 Water 庚申 Metal Monkey 坎爲水 7 十八 1	木8 Wood 9 Lesser Exceeding 辛酉 Metal Rooster 雷山小過 8 十九 3	金4 Metal 8 Gathering 壬戌 Water Dog 澤地萃 9 二十 4	水6 Water 7 Peel 癸亥 Water Pig 山地剝 10 廿一 6	水1 Water 6 Earth 甲子 Wood Rat 坤爲地 11 廿二 1	木3 Wood 5 Biting 乙丑 Wood Ox 火雷噬嗑 12 廿三 6
火2 Fire 4 Family 丙寅 Fire Tiger 風火家人 13 廿四 4	水6 Water 3 Decreasing 丁卯 Fire Rabbit 山澤損 14 廿五 9	金9 Metal 2 Tread 戊辰 Earth Dragon 天澤履 15 廿六 6	木8 Wood 1 Great Strength 己巳 Earth Snake 雷天大壯 16 廿七 2	木8 Wood 9 Consistency 庚午 Metal Horse 雷風恆 17 廿八 9	金9 Metal 8 Litigation 辛未 Metal Goat 天水訟 18 廿九 3	水1 Water 7 Officer 壬申 Water Monkey 地水師 19 十月初一 7
火2 Fire 6 Gradual Progress 癸酉 Water Rooster 風山漸 20 初二 7	火7 Fire 5 Obstruction 甲戌 Wood Dog 水山蹇 21 初三 2	木3 Wood 4 Advancement 乙亥 Wood Pig 火地晉 22 初四 3	水6 Water 3 Nourish 丙子 Fire Rat 山雷頤 23 初五 3	金4 Metal 2 Following 丁丑 Fire Ox 澤雷隨 24 初六 7	木8 Wood 1 Abundance 戊寅 Earth Tiger 雷火豐 25 初七 6	火7 Fire 9 Regulate 己卯 Earth Rabbit 水澤節 26 初八 8
水1 Water 8 Unity 庚辰 Metal Dragon 地天泰 27 初九 9	木3 Wood 7 Great Reward 辛巳 Metal Snake 火天大有 28 初十 7	火2 Fire 6 Wind 壬午 Water Horse 巽爲風 29 十一 1	金4 Metal 5 Trap 癸未 Water Goat 澤水困 30 十二 8			

DECEMBER 2044 丙子

Xuan Kong Element 玄空五行	山雷頤 Nourish	Period Luck 卦運	Monthly Star 月星
Water 水6		3	7

SUNDAY	MONDAY	TUESDAY	WEDNESDAY	THURSDAY	FRIDAY	SATURDAY
				木3 Wood 4 Not Yet Accomplished 甲申 Wood Monkey 火水未濟 1 十三 9	金9 Metal 3 Retreat 乙酉 Wood Rooster 天山遯 2 十四 4	水6 Water 2 Mountain 丙戌 Fire Dog 艮爲山 3 十五 1
木8 Wood 1 Delight 丁亥 Fire Pig 雷地豫 4 十六 8	火7 Fire 9 Beginning 戊子 Earth Rat 水雷屯 5 十七 4	金9 Metal 8 Without Wrongdoing 己丑 Earth Ox 天雷無妄 6 十八 2	木3 Wood 7 Fire 庚寅 Metal Tiger 離爲火 7 十九 1	火2 Fire 6 Sincerity 辛卯 Metal Rabbit 風澤中孚 8 二十 3	水6 Water 5 Big Livestock 壬辰 Water Dragon 山天大畜 9 廿一 4	金4 Metal 4 Eliminating 癸巳 Water Snake 澤天夬 10 廿二 6
金9 Metal 3 Heaven 甲午 Wood Horse 乾爲天 11 廿三 1	火7 Fire 2 Well 乙未 Wood Goat 水風井 12 廿四 6	木8 Wood 1 Relief 丙申 Fire Monkey 雷水解 13 廿五 4	金4 Metal 9 Influence 丁酉 Fire Rooster 澤山咸 14 廿六 9	水1 Water 8 Humility 戊戌 Earth Dog 地山謙 15 廿七 6	火2 Fire 7 Observation 己亥 Earth Pig 風地觀 16 廿八 2	火2 Fire 6 Increasing 庚子 Metal Rat 風雷益 17 廿九 9
水1 Water 5 Dimming Light 辛丑 Metal Ox 地火明夷 18 三十 3	金9 Metal 4 Fellowship 壬寅 Water Tiger 天火同人 19 十一月初一 7	木8 Wood 3 Marrying Maiden 癸卯 Water Rabbit 雷澤歸妹 20 初二 7	木3 Wood 2/8 Opposition 甲辰 Wood Dragon 火澤睽 21 初三 2	火7 Fire 9 Waiting 乙巳 Wood Snake 水天需 22 初四 3	金4 Metal 1 Great Exceeding 丙午 Fire Horse 澤風大過 23 初五 3	水6 Water 2 Poison 丁未 Fire Goat 山風蠱 24 初六 7
火2 Fire 3 Dispersing 戊申 Earth Monkey 風水渙 25 初七 6	木3 Wood 4 Travelling 己酉 Earth Rooster 火山旅 26 初八 8	金9 Metal 5 Stagnation 庚戌 Metal Dog 天地否 27 初九 9	火7 Fire 6 Alliance 辛亥 Metal Pig 水地比 28 初十 7	木8 Wood 7 Thunder 壬子 Water Rat 震爲雷 29 十一 1	水6 Water 8 Beauty 癸丑 Water Ox 山火賁 30 十二 8	火7 Fire 9 Accomplished 甲寅 Wood Tiger 水火既濟 31 十三 9

2045 乙丑

(*Yi Chou*) Wood Ox

2045 乙丑 *(Yi Chou)* Wood Ox

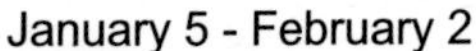

January 5 - February 2

February 3 - March 4

March 5 - April 3

April 4 - May 4

May 5 - June 4

June 5 - July 6

July 7 - August 6

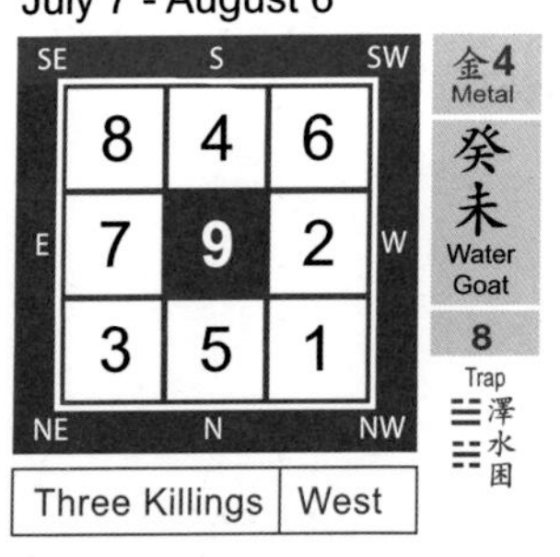

August 7 - September 6

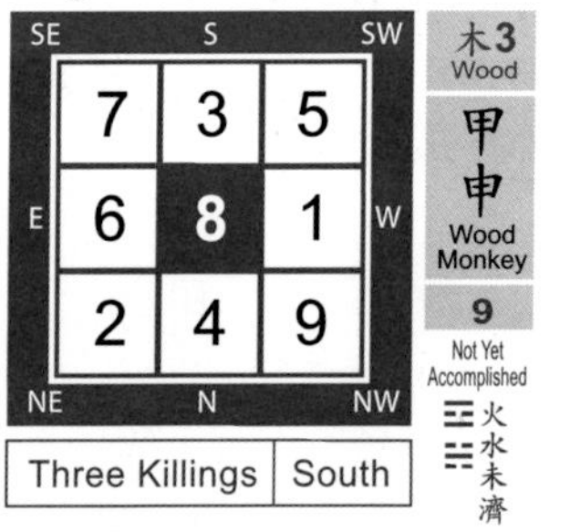

September 7 - October 7

October 8 - November 6

November 7 - December 6

December 7 - January 4

JANUARY 2045 丁丑

Xuan Kong Element 玄空五行	澤雷隨 Following	Period Luck 卦運	Monthly Star 月星
Metal 金4		7	6

SUNDAY	MONDAY	TUESDAY	WEDNESDAY	THURSDAY	FRIDAY	SATURDAY
水1 Water · 1 Arriving 乙卯 Wood Rabbit 地澤臨 **1** 十四 4	金4 Metal · 2 Marsh 丙辰 Fire Dragon 兌爲澤 **2** 十五 1	火2 Fire · 3 Small Livestock 丁巳 Fire Snake 風天小畜 **3** 十六 8	木3 Wood · 4 The Cauldron 戊午 Earth Horse 火風鼎 **4** 十七 4	水1 Water · 5 Rising 己未 Earth Goat 地風升 **5** 十八 2	火7 Fire · 6 Water 庚申 Metal Monkey 坎爲水 **6** 十九 1	木8 Wood · 7 Lesser Exceeding 辛酉 Metal Rooster 雷山小過 **7** 二十 3
金4 Metal · 8 Gathering 壬戌 Water Dog 澤地萃 **8** 廿一 4	水6 Water · 9 Peel 癸亥 Water Pig 山地剝 **9** 廿二 6	水1 Water · 1 Earth 甲子 Wood Rat 坤爲地 **10** 廿三 1	木3 Wood · 2 Biting 乙丑 Wood Ox 火雷噬嗑 **11** 廿四 6	火2 Fire · 3 Family 丙寅 Fire Tiger 風火家人 **12** 廿五 4	水6 Water · 4 Decreasing 丁卯 Fire Rabbit 山澤損 **13** 廿六 9	金9 Metal · 5 Tread 戊辰 Earth Dragon 天澤履 **14** 廿七 6
木8 Wood · 6 Great Strength 己巳 Earth Snake 雷天大壯 **15** 廿八 2	木8 Wood · 7 Consistency 庚午 Metal Horse 雷風恆 **16** 廿九 9	金9 Metal · 8 Litigation 辛未 Metal Goat 天水訟 **17** 三十 3	水1 Water · 9 Officer 壬申 Water Monkey 地水師 **18** 十二月初一 7	火2 Fire · 1 Gradual Progress 癸酉 Water Rooster 風山漸 **19** 初二 7	火7 Fire · 2 Obstruction 甲戌 Wood Dog 水山蹇 **20** 初三 2	木3 Wood · 3 Advancement 乙亥 Wood Pig 火地晉 **21** 初四 3
水6 Water · 4 Nourish 丙子 Fire Rat 山雷頤 **22** 初五 3	金4 Metal · 5 Following 丁丑 Fire Ox 澤雷隨 **23** 初六 7	木8 Wood · 6 Abundance 戊寅 Earth Tiger 雷火豐 **24** 初七 6	火7 Fire · 7 Regulate 己卯 Earth Rabbit 水澤節 **25** 初八 8	水1 Water · 8 Unity 庚辰 Metal Dragon 地天泰 **26** 初九 9	木3 Wood · 9 Great Reward 辛巳 Metal Snake 火天大有 **27** 初十 7	火2 Fire · 1 Wind 壬午 Water Horse 巽爲風 **28** 十一 1
金4 Metal · 2 Trap 癸未 Water Goat 澤水困 **29** 十二 8	木3 Wood · 3 Not Yet Accomplished 甲申 Wood Monkey 火水未濟 **30** 十三 9	金9 Metal · 4 Retreat 乙酉 Wood Rooster 天山遯 **31** 十四 4				

FEBRUARY 2045 戊寅

Xuan Kong Element 玄空五行	雷火豐 Abundance	Period Luck 卦運	Monthly Star 月星
Wood 木8		6	5

SUNDAY	MONDAY	TUESDAY	WEDNESDAY	THURSDAY	FRIDAY	SATURDAY
			水6 Water · 5 Mountain 丙戌 Fire Dog 艮爲山 **1** 十五 1	木8 Wood · 6 Delight 丁亥 Fire Pig 雷地豫 **2** 十六 8	火7 Fire · 7 Beginning 戊子 Earth Rat 水雷屯 **3** 十七 4	金9 Metal · 8 Without Wrongdoing 己丑 Earth Ox 天雷無妄 **4** 十八 2
木3 Wood · 9 Fire 庚寅 Metal Tiger 離爲火 **5** 十九 1	火2 Fire · 1 Sincerity 辛卯 Metal Rabbit 風澤中孚 **6** 二十 3	水6 Water · 2 Big Livestock 壬辰 Water Dragon 山天大畜 **7** 廿一 4	金4 Metal · 4 Eliminating 癸巳 Water Snake 澤天夬 **8** 廿二 6	金9 Metal · 4 Heaven 甲午 Wood Horse 乾爲天 **9** 廿三 1	火7 Fire · 5 Well 乙未 Wood Goat 水風井 **10** 廿四 6	木8 Wood · 6 Relief 丙申 Fire Monkey 雷水解 **11** 廿五 4
金4 Metal · 7 Influence 丁酉 Fire Rooster 澤山咸 **12** 廿六 9	水1 Water · 8 Humility 戊戌 Earth Dog 地山謙 **13** 廿七 6	火2 Fire · 9 Observation 己亥 Earth Pig 風地觀 **14** 廿八 2	火2 Fire · 1 Increasing 庚子 Metal Rat 風雷益 **15** 廿九 9	水1 Water · 2 Dimming Light 辛丑 Metal Ox 地火明夷 **16** 三十 3	金9 Metal · 3 Fellowship 壬寅 Water Tiger 天火同人 **17** 正月初一 7	木8 Wood · 4 Marrying Maiden 癸卯 Water Rabbit 雷澤歸妹 **18** 初二 7
木3 Wood · 5 Opposition 甲辰 Wood Dragon 火澤睽 **19** 初三 2	火7 Fire · 6 Waiting 乙巳 Wood Snake 水天需 **20** 初四 8	金4 Metal · 7 Great Exceeding 丙午 Fire Horse 澤風大過 **21** 初五 3	水6 Water · 8 Poison 丁未 Fire Goat 山風蠱 **22** 初六 7	火2 Fire · 9 Dispersing 戊申 Earth Monkey 風水渙 **23** 初七 6	木3 Wood · 1 Travelling 己酉 Earth Rooster 火山旅 **24** 初八 8	金9 Metal · 2 Stagnation 庚戌 Metal Dog 天地否 **25** 初九 9
火7 Fire · 3 Alliance 辛亥 Metal Pig 水地比 **26** 初十 7	木8 Wood · 4 Thunder 壬子 Water Rat 震爲雷 **27** 十一 1	水6 Water · 5 Beauty 癸丑 Water Ox 山火賁 **28** 十二 8				

MARCH 2045 己卯

Xuan Kong Element 玄空五行	水澤節 Regulate	Period Luck 卦運	Monthly Star 月星
Fire 火7		8	4

SUNDAY	MONDAY	TUESDAY	WEDNESDAY	THURSDAY	FRIDAY	SATURDAY
			火7 Fire 6 甲寅 Wood Tiger Accomplished 水火既濟 1 十三 9	水1 Water 7 乙卯 Wood Rabbit Arriving 地澤臨 2 十四 4	金4 Metal 8 丙辰 Fire Dragon Marsh 兌爲澤 3 十五 1	火2 Fire 9 丁巳 Fire Snake Small Livestock 風天小畜 4 十六 8
木3 Wood 1 戊午 Earth Horse The Cauldron 火風鼎 5 十七 4	水1 Water 2 己未 Earth Goat Rising 地風升 6 十八 2	火7 Fire 3 庚申 Metal Monkey Water 坎爲水 7 十九 1	木8 Wood 4 辛酉 Metal Rooster Lesser Exceeding 雷山小過 8 二十 3	金4 Metal 5 壬戌 Water Dog Gathering 澤地萃 9 廿一 4	水6 Water 6 癸亥 Water Pig Peel 山地剝 10 廿二 6	水1 Water 7 甲子 Wood Rat Earth 坤爲地 11 廿三 1
木3 Wood 8 乙丑 Wood Ox Biting 火雷噬嗑 12 廿四 6	火2 Fire 9 丙寅 Fire Tiger Family 風火家人 13 廿五 4	水6 Water 1 丁卯 Fire Rabbit Decreasing 山澤損 14 廿六 9	金9 Metal 2 戊辰 Earth Dragon Tread 天澤履 15 廿七 6	木8 Wood 3 己巳 Earth Snake Great Strength 雷天大壯 16 廿八 2	木8 Wood 4 庚午 Metal Horse Consistency 雷風恆 17 廿九 9	金9 Metal 5 辛未 Metal Goat Litigation 天水訟 18 三十 3
水1 Water 6 壬申 Water Monkey Officer 地水師 19 二月初一 7	火2 Fire 7 癸酉 Water Rooster Gradual Progress 風山漸 20 初二 7	火7 Fire 8 甲戌 Wood Dog Obstruction 水山蹇 21 初三 2	木3 Wood 9 乙亥 Wood Pig Advancement 火地晉 22 初四 3	水6 Water 1 丙子 Fire Rat Nourish 山雷頤 23 初五 3	金4 Metal 2 丁丑 Fire Ox Following 澤雷隨 24 初六 7	木8 Wood 3 戊寅 Earth Tiger Abundance 雷火豐 25 初七 6
火7 Fire 4 己卯 Earth Rabbit Regulate 水澤節 26 初八 8	水1 Water 5 庚辰 Metal Dragon Unity 地天泰 27 初九 9	木3 Wood 6 辛巳 Metal Snake Great Reward 火天大有 28 初十 7	火2 Fire 7 壬午 Water Horse Wind 巽爲風 29 十一 1	金4 Metal 8 癸未 Water Goat Trap 澤水困 30 十二 8	木3 Wood 9 甲申 Wood Monkey Not Yet Accomplished 火水未濟 31 十三 9	

APRIL 2045 庚辰

Xuan Kong Element 玄空五行	地天泰 Unity	Period Luck 卦運	Monthly Star 月星
Water 水1		9	3

SUNDAY	MONDAY	TUESDAY	WEDNESDAY	THURSDAY	FRIDAY	SATURDAY
火7 Fire 3 甲寅 Wood Tiger Accomplished 水火既濟 30 十四 9						金9 Metal 1 乙酉 Wood Rooster Retreat 天山遯 1 十四 4
水6 Water 2 丙戌 Fire Dog Mountain 艮爲山 2 十五 1	木8 Wood 3 丁亥 Fire Pig Delight 雷地豫 3 十六 8	火7 Fire 4 戊子 Earth Rat Beginning 水雷屯 4 十七 4	金9 Metal 5 己丑 Earth Ox Without Wrongdoing 天雷無妄 5 十八 2	木3 Wood 6 庚寅 Metal Tiger Fire 離爲火 6 十九 1	火2 Fire 7 辛卯 Metal Rabbit Sincerity 風澤中孚 7 二十 3	水6 Water 8 壬辰 Water Dragon Big Livestock 山天大畜 8 廿一 4
金4 Metal 9 癸巳 Water Snake Eliminating 澤天夬 9 廿二 6	金9 Metal 1 甲午 Wood Horse Heaven 乾爲天 10 廿三 1	火7 Fire 2 乙未 Wood Goat Well 水風井 11 廿四 6	木8 Wood 3 丙申 Fire Monkey Relief 雷水解 12 廿五 4	金4 Metal 4 丁酉 Fire Rooster Influence 澤山咸 13 廿六 9	水1 Water 5 戊戌 Earth Dog Humility 地山謙 14 廿七 6	火2 Fire 6 己亥 Earth Pig Observation 風地觀 15 廿八 2
火2 Fire 7 庚子 Metal Rat Increasing 風雷益 16 廿九 9	水1 Water 8 辛丑 Metal Ox Dimming Light 地火明夷 17 三月初一 3	金9 Metal 9 壬寅 Water Tiger Fellowship 天火同人 18 初二 7	木8 Wood 1 癸卯 Water Rabbit Marrying Maiden 雷澤歸妹 19 初三 7	木3 Wood 2 甲辰 Wood Dragon Opposition 火澤睽 20 初四 2	火7 Fire 3 乙巳 Wood Snake Waiting 水天需 21 初五 3	金4 Metal 4 丙午 Fire Horse Great Exceeding 澤風大過 22 初六 3
水6 Water 5 丁未 Fire Goat Poison 山風蠱 23 初七 7	火2 Fire 6 戊申 Earth Monkey Dispersing 風水渙 24 初八 6	木3 Wood 7 己酉 Earth Rooster Travelling 火山旅 25 初九 8	金9 Metal 8 庚戌 Metal Dog Stagnation 天地否 26 初十 9	火7 Fire 9 辛亥 Metal Pig Alliance 水地比 27 十一 7	木8 Wood 1 壬子 Water Rat Thunder 震爲雷 28 十二 1	水6 Water 2 癸丑 Water Ox Beauty 山火賁 29 十三 8

MAY 2045 辛巳

Xuan Kong Element 玄空五行	火天大有 Great Reward	Period Luck 卦運	Monthly Star 月星
Wood 木3		7	2

SUNDAY	MONDAY	TUESDAY	WEDNESDAY	THURSDAY	FRIDAY	SATURDAY
	水1 Water 4 Arriving 地澤臨 乙卯 Wood Rabbit 1 十五 4	金4 Metal 5 Marsh 兌爲澤 丙辰 Fire Dragon 2 十六 1	火2 Fire 6 Small Livestock 風天小畜 丁巳 Fire Snake 3 十七 8	木3 Wood 7 The Cauldron 火風鼎 戊午 Earth Horse 4 十八 4	水1 Water 8 Rising 地風升 己未 Earth Goat 5 十九 2	火7 Fire 9 Water 坎爲水 庚申 Metal Monkey 6 二十 1
木8 Wood 1 Lesser Exceeding 雷山小過 辛酉 Metal Rooster 7 廿一 3	金4 Metal 2 Gathering 澤地萃 壬戌 Water Dog 8 廿二 4	水6 Water 3 Peel 山地剝 癸亥 Water Pig 9 廿三 6	水1 Water 4 Earth 坤爲地 甲子 Wood Rat 10 廿四 1	木3 Wood 5 Biting 火雷噬嗑 乙丑 Wood Ox 11 廿五 6	火2 Fire 6 Family 風火家人 丙寅 Fire Tiger 12 廿六 4	水6 Water 7 Decreasing 山澤損 丁卯 Fire Rabbit 13 廿七 9
金9 Metal 8 Tread 天澤履 戊辰 Earth Dragon 14 廿八 6	木8 Wood 9 Great Strength 雷天大壯 己巳 Earth Snake 15 廿九 2	木8 Wood 1 Consistency 雷風恆 庚午 Metal Horse 16 三十 9	金9 Metal 2 Litigation 天水訟 辛未 Metal Goat 17 四月初一 3	水1 Water 3 Officer 地水師 壬申 Water Monkey 18 初二 7	火2 Fire 4 Gradual Progress 風山漸 癸酉 Water Rooster 19 初三 7	火7 Fire 5 Obstruction 水山蹇 甲戌 Wood Dog 20 初四 2
木3 Wood 6 Advancement 火地晉 乙亥 Wood Pig 21 初五 3	水6 Water 7 Nourish 山雷頤 丙子 Fire Rat 22 初六 3	金4 Metal 8 Following 澤雷隨 丁丑 Fire Ox 23 初七 7	木8 Wood 9 Abundance 雷火豐 戊寅 Earth Tiger 24 初八 6	火7 Fire 1 Regulate 水澤節 己卯 Earth Rabbit 25 初九 8	水1 Water 2 Unity 地天泰 庚辰 Metal Dragon 26 初十 9	木3 Wood 3 Great Reward 火天大有 辛巳 Metal Snake 27 十一 7
火2 Fire 4 Wind 巽爲風 壬午 Water Horse 28 十二 1	金4 Metal 5 Trap 澤水困 癸未 Water Goat 29 十三 8	木3 Wood 6 Not Yet Accomplished 火水未濟 甲申 Wood Monkey 30 十四 9	金9 Metal 7 Retreat 天山遯 乙酉 Wood Rooster 31 十五 4			

JUNE 2045 壬午

Xuan Kong Element 玄空五行	巽爲風 Wind	Period Luck 卦運	Monthly Star 月星
Fire 火2		1	1

SUNDAY	MONDAY	TUESDAY	WEDNESDAY	THURSDAY	FRIDAY	SATURDAY
				水6 Water 8 Mountain 艮爲山 丙戌 Fire Dog 1 十六 1	木8 Wood 9 Delight 雷地豫 丁亥 Fire Pig 2 十七 8	火7 Fire 1 Beginning 水雷屯 戊子 Earth Rat 3 十八 4
金9 Metal 2 Without Wrongdoing 天雷無妄 己丑 Earth Ox 4 十九 2	木3 Wood 3 Fire 離爲火 庚寅 Metal Tiger 5 二十 1	火2 Fire 4 Sincerity 風澤中孚 辛卯 Metal Rabbit 6 廿一 3	水6 Water 5 Big Livestock 山天大畜 壬辰 Water Dragon 7 廿二 4	金4 Metal 6 Eliminating 澤天夬 癸巳 Water Snake 8 廿三 6	金9 Metal 7 Heaven 乾爲天 甲午 Wood Horse 9 廿四 1	火7 Fire 8 Well 水風井 乙未 Wood Goat 10 廿五 6
木8 Wood 9 Relief 雷水解 丙申 Fire Monkey 11 廿六 4	金4 Metal 1 Influence 澤山咸 丁酉 Fire Rooster 12 廿七 9	水1 Water 2 Humility 地山謙 戊戌 Earth Dog 13 廿八 6	火2 Fire 3 Observation 風地觀 己亥 Earth Pig 14 廿九 2	火2 Fire 4 Increasing 風雷益 庚子 Metal Rat 15 五月初一 9	水1 Water 5 Dimming Light 地火明夷 辛丑 Metal Ox 16 初二 3	金9 Metal 6 Fellowship 天火同人 壬寅 Water Tiger 17 初三 7
木8 Wood 7 Marrying Maiden 雷澤歸妹 癸卯 Water Rabbit 18 初四 7	木3 Wood 8 Opposition 火澤睽 甲辰 Wood Dragon 19 初五 2	火7 Fire 9 Waiting 水天需 乙巳 Wood Snake 20 初六 3	金4 Metal 1/9 Great Exceeding 澤風大過 丙午 Fire Horse 21 初七 3	水6 Water 8 Poison 山風蠱 丁未 Fire Goat 22 初八 7	火2 Fire 7 Dispersing 風水渙 戊申 Earth Monkey 23 初九 6	木3 Wood 6 Travelling 火山旅 己酉 Earth Rooster 24 初十 8
金9 Metal 5 Stagnation 天地否 庚戌 Metal Dog 25 十一 9	火7 Fire 4 Alliance 水地比 辛亥 Metal Pig 26 十二 7	木8 Wood 3 Thunder 震爲雷 壬子 Water Rat 27 十三 1	水6 Water 2 Beauty 山火賁 癸丑 Water Ox 28 十四 8	火7 Fire 1 Accomplished 水火既濟 甲寅 Wood Tiger 29 十五 9	水1 Water 9 Arriving 地澤臨 乙卯 Wood Rabbit 30 十六 4	

JULY 2045 癸未

Xuan Kong Element 玄空五行	澤水困 Trap	Period Luck 卦運	Monthly Star 月星
Metal 金4		8	9

SUNDAY	MONDAY	TUESDAY	WEDNESDAY	THURSDAY	FRIDAY	SATURDAY
30 金9 Metal Retreat 天山遯 乙酉 Wood Rooster 十七 6 / 4	**31** 水6 Water Mountain 艮爲山 丙戌 Fire Dog 十八 5 / 1					**1** 金4 Metal Marsh 兌爲澤 丙辰 Fire Dragon 十七 8 / 1
2 火2 Fire Small Livestock 風天小畜 丁巳 Fire Snake 十八 7 / 8	**3** 木3 Wood The Cauldron 火風鼎 戊午 Earth Horse 十九 6 / 4	**4** 水1 Water Rising 地風升 己未 Earth Goat 二十 5 / 2	**5** 火7 Fire Water 坎爲水 庚申 Metal Monkey 廿一 4 / 1	**6** 木8 Wood Lesser Exceeding 雷山小過 辛酉 Metal Rooster 廿二 3 / 3	**7** 金4 Metal Gathering 澤地萃 壬戌 Water Dog 廿三 2 / 4	**8** 水6 Water Peel 山地剝 癸亥 Water Pig 廿四 1 / 6
9 水1 Water Earth 坤爲地 甲子 Wood Rat 廿五 9 / 1	**10** 木3 Wood Biting 火雷噬嗑 乙丑 Wood Ox 廿六 8 / 6	**11** 火2 Fire Family 風火家人 丙寅 Fire Tiger 廿七 7 / 4	**12** 水6 Water Decreasing 山澤損 丁卯 Fire Rabbit 廿八 6 / 9	**13** 金9 Metal Tread 天澤履 戊辰 Earth Dragon 廿九 5 / 6	**14** 木8 Wood Great Strength 雷天大壯 己巳 Earth Snake 六月初一 4 / 2	**15** 木8 Wood Consistency 雷風恒 庚午 Metal Horse 初二 3 / 9
16 金9 Metal Litigation 天水訟 辛未 Metal Goat 初三 2 / 3	**17** 水1 Water Officer 地水師 壬申 Water Monkey 初四 1 / 7	**18** 火2 Fire Gradual Progress 風山漸 癸酉 Water Rooster 初五 9 / 7	**19** 火7 Fire Obstruction 水山蹇 甲戌 Wood Dog 初六 8 / 2	**20** 木3 Wood Advancement 火地晉 乙亥 Wood Pig 初七 7 / 3	**21** 水6 Water Nourish 山雷頤 丙子 Fire Rat 初八 6 / 3	**22** 金4 Metal Following 澤雷隨 丁丑 Fire Ox 初九 5 / 7
23 木8 Wood Abundance 雷火豐 戊寅 Earth Tiger 初十 4 / 6	**24** 火7 Fire Regulate 水澤節 己卯 Earth Rabbit 十一 3 / 8	**25** 水1 Water Unity 地天泰 庚辰 Metal Dragon 十二 2 / 9	**26** 木3 Wood Great Reward 火天大有 辛巳 Metal Snake 十三 1 / 7	**27** 火2 Fire Wind 巽爲風 壬午 Water Horse 十四 9 / 1	**28** 金4 Metal Trap 澤水困 癸未 Water Goat 十五 8 / 8	**29** 木3 Wood Not Yet Accomplished 火水未濟 甲申 Wood Monkey 十六 7 / 9

AUGUST 2045 甲申

Xuan Kong Element 玄空五行	火水未濟 Not Yet Accomplished	Period Luck 卦運	Monthly Star 月星
Wood 木3		9	8

SUNDAY	MONDAY	TUESDAY	WEDNESDAY	THURSDAY	FRIDAY	SATURDAY
		1 木8 Wood Delight 雷地豫 丁亥 Fire Pig 十九 4 / 8	**2** 火7 Fire Beginning 水雷屯 戊子 Earth Rat 二十 3 / 4	**3** 金9 Metal Without Wrongdoing 天雷無妄 己丑 Earth Ox 廿一 2 / 2	**4** 木3 Wood Fire 離爲火 庚寅 Metal Tiger 廿二 1 / 1	**5** 火2 Fire Sincerity 風澤中孚 辛卯 Metal Rabbit 廿三 9 / 3
6 水6 Water Big Livestock 山天大畜 壬辰 Water Dragon 廿四 8 / 4	**7** 金4 Metal Eliminating 澤天夬 癸巳 Water Snake 廿五 7 / 6	**8** 金9 Metal Heaven 乾爲天 甲午 Wood Horse 廿六 6 / 1	**9** 火7 Fire Well 水風井 乙未 Wood Goat 廿七 5 / 6	**10** 木8 Wood Relief 雷水解 丙申 Fire Monkey 廿八 4 / 4	**11** 金4 Metal Influence 澤山咸 丁酉 Fire Rooster 廿九 3 / 9	**12** 水1 Water Humility 地山謙 戊戌 Earth Dog 三十 2 / 6
13 火2 Fire Observation 風地觀 己亥 Earth Pig 七月初一 1 / 2	**14** 火2 Fire Increasing 風雷益 庚子 Metal Rat 初二 9 / 9	**15** 水1 Water Dimming Light 地火明夷 辛丑 Metal Ox 初三 8 / 3	**16** 金9 Metal Fellowship 天火同人 壬寅 Water Tiger 初四 7 / 7	**17** 木8 Wood Marrying Maiden 雷澤歸妹 癸卯 Water Rabbit 初五 6 / 7	**18** 木3 Wood Opposition 火澤睽 甲辰 Wood Dragon 初六 5 / 2	**19** 火7 Fire Waiting 水天需 乙巳 Wood Snake 初七 4 / 3
20 金4 Metal Great Exceeding 澤風大過 丙午 Fire Horse 初八 3 / 3	**21** 水6 Water Poison 山風蠱 丁未 Fire Goat 初九 2 / 7	**22** 火2 Fire Dispersing 風水渙 戊申 Earth Monkey 初十 1 / 6	**23** 木3 Wood Travelling 火山旅 己酉 Earth Rooster 十一 9 / 8	**24** 金9 Metal Stagnation 天地否 庚戌 Metal Dog 十二 8 / 9	**25** 火7 Fire Alliance 水地比 辛亥 Metal Pig 十三 7 / 7	**26** 木8 Wood Thunder 震爲雷 壬子 Water Rat 十四 6 / 1
27 水6 Water Beauty 山火賁 癸丑 Water Ox 十五 5 / 8	**28** 火7 Fire Accomplished 水火既濟 甲寅 Wood Tiger 十六 4 / 9	**29** 水1 Water Arriving 地澤臨 乙卯 Wood Rabbit 十七 3 / 4	**30** 金4 Metal Marsh 兌爲澤 丙辰 Fire Dragon 十八 2 / 1	**31** 火2 Fire Small Livestock 風天小畜 丁巳 Fire Snake 十九 1 / 8		

SEPTEMBER 2045 乙酉

Xuan Kong Element 玄空五行	天山遯 Retreat	Period Luck 卦運	Monthly Star 月星
Metal 金9		4	7

SUNDAY	MONDAY	TUESDAY	WEDNESDAY	THURSDAY	FRIDAY	SATURDAY
					木3 Wood · 9 The Cauldron 火風鼎 戊午 Earth Horse **1** 二十 4	水1 Water · 8 Rising 地風升 己未 Earth Goat **2** 廿一 2
火7 Fire · 7 Water 坎爲水 庚申 Metal Monkey **3** 廿二 1	木8 Wood · 6 Lesser Exceeding 雷山小過 辛酉 Metal Rooster **4** 廿三 3	金4 Metal · 5 Gathering 澤地萃 壬戌 Water Dog **5** 廿四 4	水6 Water · 4 Peel 山地剝 癸亥 Water Pig **6** 廿五 6	水1 Water · 3 Earth 坤爲地 甲子 Wood Rat **7** 廿六 1	木3 Wood · 2 Biting 火雷噬嗑 乙丑 Wood Ox **8** 廿七 6	火2 Fire · 1 Family 風火家人 丙寅 Fire Tiger **9** 廿八 4
水6 Water · 9 Decreasing 山澤損 丁卯 Fire Rabbit **10** 廿九 9	金9 Metal · 8 Tread 天澤履 戊辰 Earth Dragon **11** 八月初一 6	木8 Wood · 7 Great Strength 雷天大壯 己巳 Earth Snake **12** 初二 2	木8 Wood · 6 Consistency 雷風恆 庚午 Metal Horse **13** 初三 9	金9 Metal · 5 Litigation 天水訟 辛未 Metal Goat **14** 初四 3	水1 Water · 4 Officer 地水師 壬申 Water Monkey **15** 初五 7	火2 Fire · 3 Gradual Progress 風山漸 癸酉 Water Rooster **16** 初六 7
火7 Fire · 2 Obstruction 水山蹇 甲戌 Wood Dog **17** 初七 2	木3 Wood · 1 Advancement 火地晉 乙亥 Wood Pig **18** 初八 3	水6 Water · 9 Nourish 山雷頤 丙子 Fire Rat **19** 初九 3	金4 Metal · 8 Following 澤雷隨 丁丑 Fire Ox **20** 初十 7	木8 Wood · 7 Abundance 雷火豐 戊寅 Earth Tiger **21** 十一 6	火7 Fire · 6 Regulate 水澤節 己卯 Earth Rabbit **22** 十二 8	水1 Water · 5 Unity 地天泰 庚辰 Metal Dragon **23** 十三 9
木3 Wood · 4 Great Reward 火天大有 辛巳 Metal Snake **24** 十四 7	火2 Fire · 3 Wind 巽爲風 壬午 Water Horse **25** 十五 1	金4 Metal · 2 Trap 澤水困 癸未 Water Goat **26** 十六 8	木3 Wood · 1 Not Yet Accomplished 火水未濟 甲申 Wood Monkey **27** 十七 9	金9 Metal · 9 Retreat 天山遯 乙酉 Wood Rooster **28** 十八 4	水6 Water · 8 Mountain 艮爲山 丙戌 Fire Dog **29** 十九 1	木8 Wood · 7 Delight 雷地豫 丁亥 Fire Pig **30** 二十 8

OCTOBER 2045 丙戌

Xuan Kong Element 玄空五行	艮爲山 Mountain	Period Luck 卦運	Monthly Star 月星
Water 水6		1	6

SUNDAY	MONDAY	TUESDAY	WEDNESDAY	THURSDAY	FRIDAY	SATURDAY
火7 Fire · 6 Beginning 水雷屯 戊子 Earth Rat **1** 廿一 4	金9 Metal · 5 Without Wrongdoing 天雷無妄 己丑 Earth Ox **2** 廿二 2	木3 Wood · 4 Fire 離爲火 庚寅 Metal Tiger **3** 廿三 1	火2 Fire · 3 Sincerity 風澤中孚 辛卯 Metal Rabbit **4** 廿四 3	水6 Water · 2 Big Livestock 山天大畜 壬辰 Water Dragon **5** 廿五 4	金4 Metal · 1 Eliminating 澤天夬 癸巳 Water Snake **6** 廿六 6	金9 Metal · 9 Heaven 乾爲天 甲午 Wood Horse **7** 廿七 1
火7 Fire · 8 Well 水風井 乙未 Wood Goat **8** 廿八 6	木8 Wood · 7 Relief 雷水解 丙申 Fire Monkey **9** 廿九 4	金4 Metal · 6 Influence 澤山咸 丁酉 Fire Rooster **10** 九月初一 9	水1 Water · 5 Humility 地山謙 戊戌 Earth Dog **11** 初二 6	火2 Fire · 4 Observation 風地觀 己亥 Earth Pig **12** 初三 2	火2 Fire · 3 Increasing 風雷益 庚子 Metal Rat **13** 初四 9	水1 Water · 2 Dimming Light 地火明夷 辛丑 Metal Ox **14** 初五 3
金9 Metal · 1 Fellowship 天火同人 壬寅 Water Tiger **15** 初六 7	木8 Wood · 9 Marrying Maiden 雷澤歸妹 癸卯 Water Rabbit **16** 初七 7	木3 Wood · 8 Opposition 火澤睽 甲辰 Wood Dragon **17** 初八 2	火7 Fire · 7 Waiting 水天需 乙巳 Wood Snake **18** 初九 3	金4 Metal · 6 Great Exceeding 澤風大過 丙午 Fire Horse **19** 初十 3	水6 Water · 5 Poison 山風蠱 丁未 Fire Goat **20** 十一 7	火2 Fire · 4 Dispersing 風水渙 戊申 Earth Monkey **21** 十二 6
木3 Wood · 3 Travelling 火山旅 己酉 Earth Rooster **22** 十三 8	金9 Metal · 2 Stagnation 天地否 庚戌 Metal Dog **23** 十四 9	火7 Fire · 1 Alliance 水地比 辛亥 Metal Pig **24** 十五 7	木8 Wood · 9 Thunder 震爲雷 壬子 Water Rat **25** 十六 1	水6 Water · 8 Beauty 山火賁 癸丑 Water Ox **26** 十七 8	火7 Fire · 7 Accomplished 水火既濟 甲寅 Wood Tiger **27** 十八 9	水1 Water · 6 Arriving 地澤臨 乙卯 Wood Rabbit **28** 十九 4
金4 Metal · 5 Marsh 兌爲澤 丙辰 Fire Dragon **29** 二十 1	火2 Fire · 4 Small Livestock 風天小畜 丁巳 Fire Snake **30** 廿一 8	木3 Wood · 3 The Cauldron 火風鼎 戊午 Earth Horse **31** 廿二 4				

NOVEMBER 2045 丁亥

Xuan Kong Element 玄空五行	雷地豫 Delight	Period Luck 卦運	Monthly Star 月星
Wood 木8		8	5

SUNDAY	MONDAY	TUESDAY	WEDNESDAY	THURSDAY	FRIDAY	SATURDAY
			水1 Water 2 Rising 己未 Earth Goat 地風升 1 廿三 2	火7 Fire 1 Water 庚申 Metal Monkey 坎爲水 2 廿四 1	木8 Wood 9 Lesser Exceeding 辛酉 Metal Rooster 雷山小過 3 廿五 3	金4 Metal 8 Gathering 壬戌 Water Dog 澤地萃 4 廿六 4
水6 Water 7 Peel 癸亥 Water Pig 山地剝 5 廿七 6	水1 Water 6 Earth 甲子 Wood Rat 坤爲地 6 廿八 1	木3 Wood 5 Biting 乙丑 Wood Ox 火雷噬嗑 7 廿九 6	火2 Fire 4 Family 丙寅 Fire Tiger 風火家人 8 三十 4	水6 Water 3 Decreasing 丁卯 Fire Rabbit 山澤損 9 十月初一 9	金9 Metal 2 Tread 戊辰 Earth Dragon 天澤履 10 初二 6	木8 Wood 1 Great Strength 己巳 Earth Snake 雷天大壯 11 初三 2
木8 Wood 9 Consistency 庚午 Metal Horse 雷風恆 12 初四 9	金9 Metal 8 Litigation 辛未 Metal Goat 天水訟 13 初五 3	水1 Water 7 Officer 壬申 Water Monkey 地水師 14 初六 7	火2 Fire 6 Gradual Progress 癸酉 Water Rooster 風山漸 15 初七 7	火7 Fire 5 Obstruction 甲戌 Wood Dog 水山蹇 16 初八 2	木3 Wood 4 Advancement 乙亥 Wood Pig 火地晉 17 初九 3	水6 Water 3 Nourish 丙子 Fire Rat 山雷頤 18 初十 3
金4 Metal 2 Following 丁丑 Fire Ox 澤雷隨 19 十一 7	木8 Wood 1 Abundance 戊寅 Earth Tiger 雷火豐 20 十二 6	火7 Fire 9 Regulate 己卯 Earth Rabbit 水澤節 21 十三 8	水1 Water 8 Unity 庚辰 Metal Dragon 地天泰 22 十四 9	木3 Wood 7 Great Reward 辛巳 Metal Snake 火天大有 23 十五 7	火2 Fire 6 Wind 壬午 Water Horse 巽爲風 24 十六 1	金4 Metal 5 Trap 癸未 Water Goat 澤水困 25 十七 8
木3 Wood 4 Not Yet Accomplished 甲申 Wood Monkey 火水未濟 26 十八 9	金9 Metal 3 Retreat 乙酉 Wood Rooster 天山遯 27 十九 4	水6 Water 2 Mountain 丙戌 Fire Dog 艮爲山 28 二十 1	木8 Wood 1 Delight 丁亥 Fire Pig 雷地豫 29 廿一 8	火7 Fire 9 Beginning 戊子 Earth Rat 水雷屯 30 廿二 4		

DECEMBER 2045 戊子

Xuan Kong Element 玄空五行	水雷屯 Beginning	Period Luck 卦運	Monthly Star 月星
Fire 火7		4	4

SUNDAY	MONDAY	TUESDAY	WEDNESDAY	THURSDAY	FRIDAY	SATURDAY
水1 Water 5 Rising 己未 Earth Goat 地風升 31 廿四 2					金9 Metal 8 Without Wrongdoing 己丑 Earth Ox 天雷無妄 1 廿三 2	木3 Wood 7 Fire 庚寅 Metal Tiger 離爲火 2 廿四 1
火2 Fire 6 Sincerity 辛卯 Metal Rabbit 風澤中孚 3 廿五 3	水6 Water 5 Big Livestock 壬辰 Water Dragon 山天大畜 4 廿六 4	金4 Metal 4 Eliminating 癸巳 Water Snake 澤天夬 5 廿七 6	金9 Metal 3 Heaven 甲午 Wood Horse 乾爲天 6 廿八 1	火7 Fire 2 Well 乙未 Wood Goat 水風井 7 廿九 6	木8 Wood 1 Relief 丙申 Fire Monkey 雷水解 8 十一月初一 4	金4 Metal 9 Influence 丁酉 Fire Rooster 澤山咸 9 初二 9
水1 Water 8 Humility 戊戌 Earth Dog 地山謙 10 初三 6	火2 Fire 7 Observation 己亥 Earth Pig 風地觀 11 初四 2	火2 Fire 6 Increasing 庚子 Metal Rat 風雷益 12 初五 9	水1 Water 5 Dimming Light 辛丑 Metal Ox 地火明夷 13 初六 3	金9 Metal 4 Fellowship 壬寅 Water Tiger 天火同人 14 初七 7	木8 Wood 3 Marrying Maiden 癸卯 Water Rabbit 雷澤歸妹 15 初八 7	木3 Wood 2 Opposition 甲辰 Wood Dragon 火澤睽 16 初九 2
火7 Fire 1 Waiting 乙巳 Wood Snake 水天需 17 初十 3	金4 Metal 9 Great Exceeding 丙午 Fire Horse 澤風大過 18 十一 3	水6 Water 8 Poison 丁未 Fire Goat 山風蠱 19 十二 7	火2 Fire 7 Dispersing 戊申 Earth Monkey 風水渙 20 十三 6	木3 Wood 6/4 Travelling 己酉 Earth Rooster 火山旅 21 十四 8	金9 Metal 5 Stagnation 庚戌 Metal Dog 天地否 22 十五 9	火7 Fire 6 Alliance 辛亥 Metal Pig 水地比 23 十六 7
木8 Wood 7 Thunder 壬子 Water Rat 震爲雷 24 十七 1	水6 Water 8 Beauty 癸丑 Water Ox 山火賁 25 十八 8	火7 Fire 9 Accomplished 甲寅 Wood Tiger 水火既濟 26 十九 9	水1 Water 1 Arriving 乙卯 Wood Rabbit 地澤臨 27 二十 4	金4 Metal 2 Marsh 丙辰 Fire Dragon 兌爲澤 28 廿一 1	火2 Fire 3 Small Livestock 丁巳 Fire Snake 風天小畜 29 廿二 8	木3 Wood 4 The Cauldron 戊午 Earth Horse 火風鼎 30 廿三 4

2046 丙寅

(*Bing Yin*) Fire Tiger

2046 丙寅 *(Bing Yin)* Fire Tiger

January 5 - February 3

February 4 - March 4

March 5 - April 3

April 4 - May 4

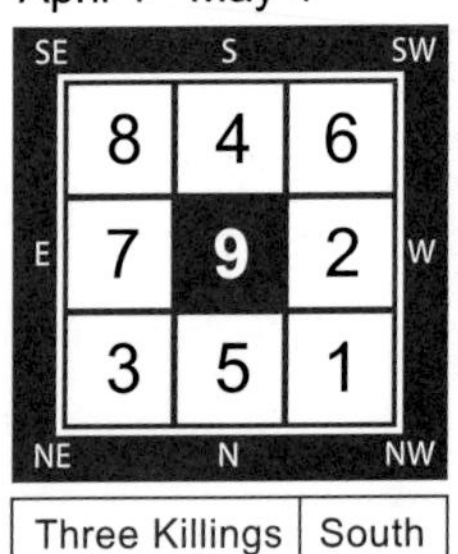

May 5 - June 4

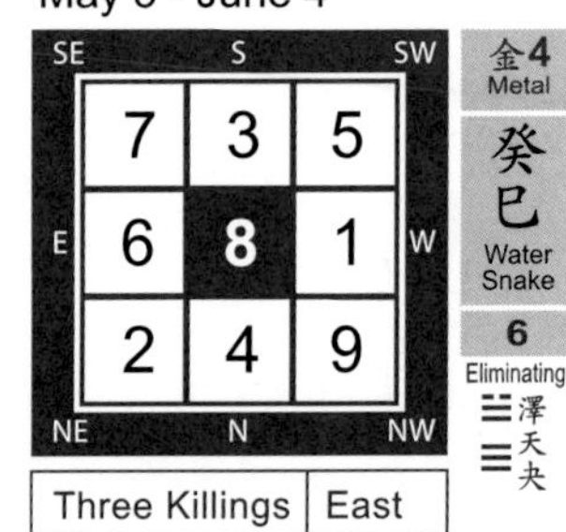

June 5 - July 6

July 7 - August 6

August 7 - September 6

September 7 - October 7

October 8 - November 6

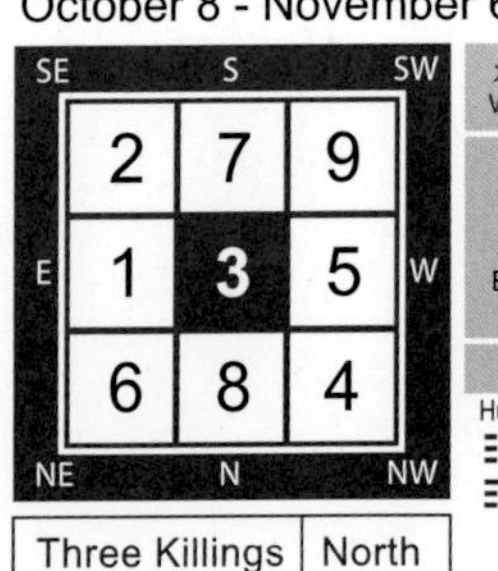

November 7 - December 6

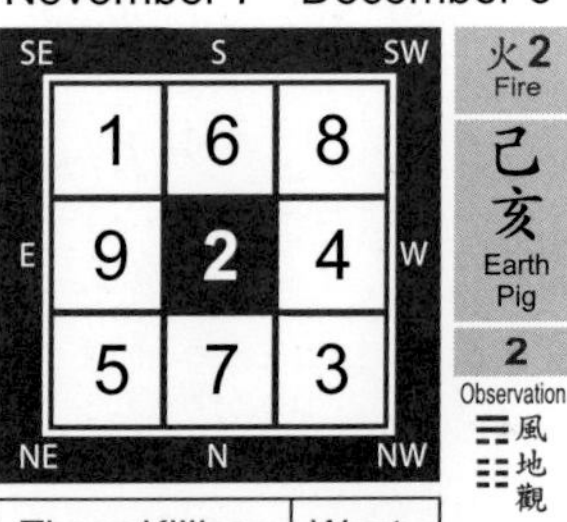

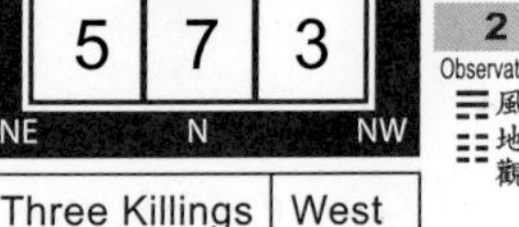

December 7 - January 4

JANUARY 2046 己丑

Xuan Kong Element 玄空五行	天雷無妄 Without Wrongdoing	Period Luck 卦運	Monthly Star 月星
Metal 金9		2	3

SUNDAY	MONDAY	TUESDAY	WEDNESDAY	THURSDAY	FRIDAY	SATURDAY
	火7 Fire 6 Water 坎爲水 庚申 Metal Monkey 1 **1** 廿五	木8 Wood 7 Lesser Exceeding 雷山小過 辛酉 Metal Rooster 3 **2** 廿六	金4 Metal 8 Gathering 澤地萃 壬戌 Water Dog 4 **3** 廿七	水6 Water 9 Peel 山地剝 癸亥 Water Pig 6 **4** 廿八	水1 Water 1 Earth 坤爲地 甲子 Wood Rat 1 **5** 廿九	木3 Wood 2 Biting 火雷噬嗑 乙丑 Wood Ox 6 **6** 三十
火2 Fire 3 Family 風火家人 丙寅 Fire Tiger 4 **7** 十二月初一	水6 Water 4 Decreasing 山澤損 丁卯 Fire Rabbit 9 **8** 初二	金9 Metal 5 Tread 天澤履 戊辰 Earth Dragon 6 **9** 初三	木8 Wood 6 Great Strength 雷天大壯 己巳 Earth Snake 2 **10** 初四	木8 Wood 7 Consistency 雷風恆 庚午 Metal Horse 9 **11** 初五	金9 Metal 8 Litigation 天水訟 辛未 Metal Goat 3 **12** 初六	水1 Water 9 Officer 地水師 壬申 Water Monkey 7 **13** 初七
火2 Fire 1 Gradual Progress 風山漸 癸酉 Water Rooster 7 **14** 初八	火7 Fire 2 Obstruction 水山蹇 甲戌 Wood Dog 2 **15** 初九	木3 Wood 3 Advancement 火地晉 乙亥 Wood Pig 3 **16** 初十	水6 Water 4 Nourish 山雷頤 丙子 Fire Rat 3 **17** 十一	金4 Metal 5 Following 澤雷隨 丁丑 Fire Ox 7 **18** 十二	木8 Wood 6 Abundance 雷火豐 戊寅 Earth Tiger 6 **19** 十三	火7 Fire 7 Regulate 水澤節 己卯 Earth Rabbit 8 **20** 十四
水1 Water 8 Unity 地天泰 庚辰 Metal Dragon 9 **21** 十五	木3 Wood 9 Great Reward 火天大有 辛巳 Metal Snake 7 **22** 十六	火2 Fire 1 Wind 巽爲風 壬午 Water Horse 1 **23** 十七	金4 Metal 2 Trap 澤水困 癸未 Water Goat 8 **24** 十八	木3 Wood 3 Not Yet Accomplished 火水未濟 甲申 Wood Monkey 9 **25** 十九	金9 Metal 4 Retreat 天山遯 乙酉 Wood Rooster 4 **26** 二十	水6 Water 5 Mountain 艮爲山 丙戌 Fire Dog 1 **27** 廿一
木8 Wood 6 Delight 雷地豫 丁亥 Fire Pig 8 **28** 廿二	火7 Fire 7 Beginning 水雷屯 戊子 Earth Rat 4 **29** 廿三	金9 Metal 8 Without Wrongdoing 天雷無妄 己丑 Earth Ox 2 **30** 廿四	木3 Wood 9 Fire 離爲火 庚寅 Metal Tiger 1 **31** 廿五			

FEBRUARY 2046 庚寅

Xuan Kong Element 玄空五行	離爲火 Fire	Period Luck 卦運	Monthly Star 月星
Wood 木3		1	2

SUNDAY	MONDAY	TUESDAY	WEDNESDAY	THURSDAY	FRIDAY	SATURDAY
				火2 Fire 1 Sincerity 風澤中孚 辛卯 Metal Rabbit 3 **1** 廿六	水6 Water 2 Big Livestock 山天大畜 壬辰 Water Dragon 4 **2** 廿七	金4 Metal 3 Eliminating 澤天夬 癸巳 Water Snake 6 **3** 廿八
金9 Metal 4 Heaven 乾爲天 甲午 Wood Horse 1 **4** 廿九	火7 Fire 5 Well 水風井 乙未 Wood Goat 6 **5** 三十	木8 Wood 6 Relief 雷水解 丙申 Fire Monkey 4 **6** 正月初一	金4 Metal 7 Influence 澤山咸 丁酉 Fire Rooster 9 **7** 初二	水1 Water 8 Humility 地山謙 戊戌 Earth Dog 6 **8** 初三	火2 Fire 9 Observation 風地觀 己亥 Earth Pig 2 **9** 初四	火2 Fire 1 Increasing 風雷益 庚子 Metal Rat 9 **10** 初五
水1 Water 2 Dimming Light 地火明夷 辛丑 Metal Ox 3 **11** 初六	金9 Metal 3 Fellowship 天火同人 壬寅 Water Tiger 7 **12** 初七	木8 Wood 4 Marrying Maiden 雷澤歸妹 癸卯 Water Rabbit 7 **13** 初八	木3 Wood 5 Opposition 火澤睽 甲辰 Wood Dragon 2 **14** 初九	火7 Fire 6 Waiting 水天需 乙巳 Wood Snake 3 **15** 初十	金4 Metal 7 Great Exceeding 澤風大過 丙午 Fire Horse 3 **16** 十一	水6 Water 8 Poison 山風蠱 丁未 Fire Goat 7 **17** 十二
火2 Fire 9 Dispersing 風水渙 戊申 Earth Monkey 6 **18** 十三	木3 Wood 1 Travelling 火山旅 己酉 Earth Rooster 8 **19** 十四	金9 Metal 2 Stagnation 天地否 庚戌 Metal Dog 9 **20** 十五	火7 Fire 3 Alliance 水地比 辛亥 Metal Pig 7 **21** 十六	木8 Wood 4 Thunder 震爲雷 壬子 Water Rat 1 **22** 十七	水6 Water 5 Beauty 山火賁 癸丑 Water Ox 8 **23** 十八	火7 Fire 6 Accomplished 水火既濟 甲寅 Wood Tiger 9 **24** 十九
水1 Water 7 Arriving 地澤臨 乙卯 Wood Rabbit 4 **25** 二十	金4 Metal 8 Marsh 兌爲澤 丙辰 Fire Dragon 1 **26** 廿一	火2 Fire 9 Small Livestock 風天小畜 丁巳 Fire Snake 8 **27** 廿二	木3 Wood 1 The Cauldron 火風鼎 戊午 Earth Horse 4 **28** 廿三			

MARCH 2046 辛卯

Xuan Kong Element 玄空五行	風澤中孚 Sincerity	Period Luck 卦運	Monthly Star 月星
Fire 火2		3	1

SUNDAY	MONDAY	TUESDAY	WEDNESDAY	THURSDAY	FRIDAY	SATURDAY
				水1 Water 2 Rising 地風升 己未 Earth Goat 2 1 廿四	火7 Fire 3 Water 坎爲水 庚申 Metal Monkey 1 2 廿五	木8 Wood 4 Lesser Exceeding 雷山小過 辛酉 Metal Rooster 3 3 廿六
金4 Metal 5 Gathering 澤地萃 壬戌 Water Dog 4 4 廿七	水6 Water 6 Peel 山地剝 癸亥 Water Pig 6 5 廿八	水1 Water 7 Earth 坤爲地 甲子 Wood Rat 1 6 廿九	木3 Wood 8 Biting 火雷噬嗑 乙丑 Wood Ox 6 7 三十	火2 Fire 9 Family 風火家人 丙寅 Fire Tiger 4 8 二月初一	水6 Water 1 Decreasing 山澤損 丁卯 Fire Rabbit 9 9 初二	金9 Metal 2 Tread 天澤履 戊辰 Earth Dragon 6 10 初三
木8 Wood 3 Great Strength 雷天大壯 己巳 Earth Snake 2 11 初四	木8 Wood 4 Consistency 雷風恆 庚午 Metal Horse 9 12 初五	金9 Metal 5 Litigation 天水訟 辛未 Metal Goat 3 13 初六	水1 Water 6 Officer 地水師 壬申 Water Monkey 7 14 初七	火2 Fire 7 Gradual Progress 風山漸 癸酉 Water Rooster 7 15 初八	火7 Fire 8 Obstruction 水山蹇 甲戌 Wood Dog 2 16 初九	木3 Wood 9 Advancement 火地晉 乙亥 Wood Pig 3 17 初十
水6 Water 1 Nourish 山雷頤 丙子 Fire Rat 3 18 十一	金4 Metal 2 Following 澤雷隨 丁丑 Fire Ox 7 19 十二	木8 Wood 3 Abundance 雷火豐 戊寅 Earth Tiger 6 20 十三	火7 Fire 4 Regulate 水澤節 己卯 Earth Rabbit 8 21 十四	水1 Water 5 Unity 地天泰 庚辰 Metal Dragon 9 22 十五	木3 Wood 6 Great Reward 火天大有 辛巳 Metal Snake 7 23 十六	火2 Fire 7 Wind 巽爲風 壬午 Water Horse 1 24 十七
金4 Metal 8 Trap 澤水困 癸未 Water Goat 8 25 十八	木3 Wood 9 Not Yet Accomplished 火水未濟 甲申 Wood Monkey 9 26 十九	金9 Metal 1 Retreat 天山遯 乙酉 Wood Rooster 4 27 二十	水6 Water 2 Mountain 艮爲山 丙戌 Fire Dog 1 28 廿一	木8 Wood 3 Delight 雷地豫 丁亥 Fire Pig 8 29 廿二	火7 Fire 4 Beginning 水雷屯 戊子 Earth Rat 4 30 廿三	金9 Metal 5 Without Wrongdoing 天雷無妄 己丑 Earth Ox 2 31 廿四

APRIL 2046 壬辰

Xuan Kong Element 玄空五行	山天大畜 Big Livestock	Period Luck 卦運	Monthly Star 月星
Water 水6		4	9

SUNDAY	MONDAY	TUESDAY	WEDNESDAY	THURSDAY	FRIDAY	SATURDAY
木3 Wood 6 Fire 離爲火 庚寅 Metal Tiger 1 1 廿五	火2 Fire 7 Sincerity 風澤中孚 辛卯 Metal Rabbit 3 2 廿六	水6 Water 8 Big Livestock 山天大畜 壬辰 Water Dragon 4 3 廿七	金4 Metal 9 Eliminating 澤天夬 癸巳 Water Snake 6 4 廿八	金9 Metal 1 Heaven 乾爲天 甲午 Wood Horse 1 5 廿九	火7 Fire 2 Well 水風井 乙未 Wood Goat 6 6 三月初一	木8 Wood 3 Relief 雷水解 丙申 Fire Monkey 4 7 初二
金4 Metal 4 Influence 澤山咸 丁酉 Fire Rooster 9 8 初三	水1 Water 5 Humility 地山謙 戊戌 Earth Dog 6 9 初四	火2 Fire 6 Observation 風地觀 己亥 Earth Pig 2 10 初五	火2 Fire 7 Increasing 風雷益 庚子 Metal Rat 9 11 初六	水1 Water 8 Dimming Light 地火明夷 辛丑 Metal Ox 3 12 初七	金9 Metal 9 Fellowship 天火同人 壬寅 Water Tiger 7 13 初八	木8 Wood 1 Marrying Maiden 雷澤歸妹 癸卯 Water Rabbit 7 14 初九
木3 Wood 2 Opposition 火澤睽 甲辰 Wood Dragon 2 15 初十	火7 Fire 3 Waiting 水天需 乙巳 Wood Snake 3 16 十一	金4 Metal 4 Great Exceeding 澤風大過 丙午 Fire Horse 3 17 十二	水6 Water 5 Poison 山風蠱 丁未 Fire Goat 7 18 十三	火2 Fire 6 Dispersing 風水渙 戊申 Earth Monkey 6 19 十四	木3 Wood 7 Travelling 火山旅 己酉 Earth Rooster 8 20 十五	金9 Metal 8 Stagnation 天地否 庚戌 Metal Dog 9 21 十六
火7 Fire 9 Alliance 水地比 辛亥 Metal Pig 7 22 十七	木8 Wood 1 Thunder 震爲雷 壬子 Water Rat 1 23 十八	水6 Water 2 Beauty 山火賁 癸丑 Water Ox 8 24 十九	火7 Fire 3 Accomplished 水火既濟 甲寅 Wood Tiger 9 25 二十	水1 Water 4 Arriving 地澤臨 乙卯 Wood Rabbit 4 26 廿一	金4 Metal 5 Marsh 兑爲澤 丙辰 Fire Dragon 1 27 廿二	火2 Fire 6 Small Livestock 風天小畜 丁巳 Fire Snake 8 28 廿三
木3 Wood 7 The Cauldron 火風鼎 戊午 Earth Horse 4 29 廿四	水1 Water 8 Rising 地風升 己未 Earth Goat 2 30 廿五					

MAY 2046 癸巳

Xuan Kong Element 玄空五行	澤天夬 Eliminating	Period Luck 卦運	Monthly Star 月星
Metal 金4		6	8

SUNDAY	MONDAY	TUESDAY	WEDNESDAY	THURSDAY	FRIDAY	SATURDAY
		火7 Fire 9 Water 坎爲水 庚申 Metal Monkey 1 **1** 廿六	木8 Wood 1 Lesser Exceeding 雷山小過 辛酉 Metal Rooster 3 **2** 廿七	金4 Metal 2 Gathering 澤地萃 壬戌 Water Dog 4 **3** 廿八	水6 Water 3 Peel 山地剝 癸亥 Water Pig 6 **4** 廿九	水1 Water 4 Earth 坤爲地 甲子 Wood Rat 1 **5** 三十
木3 Wood 5 Biting 火雷噬嗑 乙丑 Wood Ox 6 **6** 四月初一	火2 Fire 6 Family 風火家人 丙寅 Fire Tiger 4 **7** 初二	水6 Water 7 Decreasing 山澤損 丁卯 Fire Rabbit 9 **8** 初三	金9 Metal 8 Tread 天澤履 戊辰 Earth Dragon 6 **9** 初四	木8 Wood 9 Great Strength 雷天大壯 己巳 Earth Snake 2 **10** 初五	木8 Wood 1 Consistency 雷風恒 庚午 Metal Horse 9 **11** 初六	金9 Metal 2 Litigation 天水訟 辛未 Metal Goat 3 **12** 初七
水1 Water 3 Officer 地水師 壬申 Water Monkey 7 **13** 初八	火2 Fire 4 Gradual Progress 風山漸 癸酉 Water Rooster 7 **14** 初九	火7 Fire 5 Obstruction 水山蹇 甲戌 Wood Dog 2 **15** 初十	木3 Wood 6 Advancement 火地晉 乙亥 Wood Pig 3 **16** 十一	水6 Water 7 Nourish 山雷頤 丙子 Fire Rat 3 **17** 十二	金4 Metal 8 Following 澤雷隨 丁丑 Fire Ox 7 **18** 十三	木8 Wood 9 Abundance 雷火豐 戊寅 Earth Tiger 6 **19** 十四
火7 Fire 1 Regulate 水澤節 己卯 Earth Rabbit 8 **20** 十五	水1 Water 2 Unity 地天泰 庚辰 Metal Dragon 9 **21** 十六	木3 Wood 3 Great Reward 火天大有 辛巳 Metal Snake 7 **22** 十七	火2 Fire 4 Wind 巽爲風 壬午 Water Horse 1 **23** 十八	金4 Metal 5 Trap 澤水困 癸未 Water Goat 8 **24** 十九	木3 Wood 6 Not Yet Accomplished 火水未濟 甲申 Wood Monkey 9 **25** 二十	金9 Metal 7 Retreat 天山遯 乙酉 Wood Rooster 4 **26** 廿一
水6 Water 8 Mountain 艮爲山 丙戌 Fire Dog 1 **27** 廿二	木8 Wood 9 Delight 雷地豫 丁亥 Fire Pig 8 **28** 廿三	火7 Fire 1 Beginning 水雷屯 戊子 Earth Rat 4 **29** 廿四	金9 Metal 2 Without Wrongdoing 天雷無妄 己丑 Earth Ox 2 **30** 廿五	木3 Wood 3 Fire 離爲火 庚寅 Metal Tiger 1 **31** 廿六		

JUNE 2046 甲午

Xuan Kong Element 玄空五行	乾爲天 Heaven	Period Luck 卦運	Monthly Star 月星
Metal 金9		1	7

SUNDAY	MONDAY	TUESDAY	WEDNESDAY	THURSDAY	FRIDAY	SATURDAY
					火2 Fire 4 Sincerity 風澤中孚 辛卯 Metal Rabbit 3 **1** 廿七	水6 Water 5 Big Livestock 山天大畜 壬辰 Water Dragon 4 **2** 廿八
金4 Metal 6 Eliminating 澤天夬 癸巳 Water Snake 6 **3** 廿九	金9 Metal 7 Heaven 乾爲天 甲午 Wood Horse 1 **4** 五月初一	火7 Fire 8 Well 水風井 乙未 Wood Goat 6 **5** 初二	木8 Wood 9 Relief 雷水解 丙申 Fire Monkey 4 **6** 初三	金4 Metal 1 Influence 澤山咸 丁酉 Fire Rooster 9 **7** 初四	水1 Water 2 Humility 地山謙 戊戌 Earth Dog 6 **8** 初五	火2 Fire 3 Observation 風地觀 己亥 Earth Pig 2 **9** 初六
火2 Fire 4 Increasing 風雷益 庚子 Metal Rat 9 **10** 初七	水1 Water 5 Dimming Light 地火明夷 辛丑 Metal Ox 3 **11** 初八	金9 Metal 6 Fellowship 天火同人 壬寅 Water Tiger 7 **12** 初九	木8 Wood 7 Marrying Maiden 雷澤歸妹 癸卯 Water Rabbit 7 **13** 初十	木3 Wood 8 Opposition 火澤睽 甲辰 Wood Dragon 2 **14** 十一	火7 Fire 9 Waiting 水天需 乙巳 Wood Snake 3 **15** 十二	金4 Metal 1 Great Exceeding 澤風大過 丙午 Fire Horse 3 **16** 十三
水6 Water 2 Poison 山風蠱 丁未 Fire Goat 7 **17** 十四	火2 Fire 3 Dispersing 風水渙 戊申 Earth Monkey 6 **18** 十五	木3 Wood 4 Travelling 火山旅 己酉 Earth Rooster 8 **19** 十六	金9 Metal 5 Stagnation 天地否 庚戌 Metal Dog 9 **20** 十七	火7 Fire 6/4 Alliance 水地比 辛亥 Metal Pig 7 **21** 十八	木8 Wood 3 Thunder 震爲雷 壬子 Water Rat 1 **22** 十九	水6 Water 2 Beauty 山火賁 癸丑 Water Ox 8 **23** 二十
火7 Fire 1 Accomplished 水火既濟 甲寅 Wood Tiger 9 **24** 廿一	水1 Water 9 Arriving 地澤臨 乙卯 Wood Rabbit 4 **25** 廿二	金4 Metal 8 Marsh 兌爲澤 丙辰 Fire Dragon 1 **26** 廿三	火2 Fire 7 Small Livestock 風天小畜 丁巳 Fire Snake 8 **27** 廿四	木3 Wood 6 The Cauldron 火風鼎 戊午 Earth Horse 4 **28** 廿五	水1 Water 5 Rising 地風升 己未 Earth Goat 2 **29** 廿六	火7 Fire 4 Water 坎爲水 庚申 Metal Monkey 1 **30** 廿七

JULY 2046 乙未

Xuan Kong Element 玄空五行	水風井 Well	Period Luck 卦運	Monthly Star 月星
Fire 火7		6	6

SUNDAY	MONDAY	TUESDAY	WEDNESDAY	THURSDAY	FRIDAY	SATURDAY
木8 Wood 3 Lesser Exceeding 雷山小過 辛酉 Metal Rooster 3 1 廿八	金4 Metal 2 Gathering 澤地萃 壬戌 Water Dog 4 2 廿九	水6 Water 1 Peel 山地剝 癸亥 Water Pig 6 3 三十	水1 Water 9 Earth 坤爲地 甲子 Wood Rat 1 4 六月初一	木3 Wood 8 Biting 火雷噬嗑 乙丑 Wood Ox 6 5 初二	火2 Fire 7 Family 風火家人 丙寅 Fire Tiger 4 6 初三	水6 Water 6 Decreasing 山澤損 丁卯 Fire Rabbit 9 7 初四
金9 Metal 5 Tread 天澤履 戊辰 Earth Dragon 6 8 初五	木8 Wood 4 Great Strength 雷天大壯 己巳 Earth Snake 2 9 初六	木8 Wood 3 Consistency 雷風恒 庚午 Metal Horse 9 10 初七	金9 Metal 2 Litigation 天水訟 辛未 Metal Goat 3 11 初八	水1 Water 1 Officer 地水師 壬申 Water Monkey 7 12 初九	火2 Fire 9 Gradual Progress 風山漸 癸酉 Water Rooster 7 13 初十	火7 Fire 8 Obstruction 水山蹇 甲戌 Wood Dog 2 14 十一
木3 Wood 7 Advancement 火地晉 乙亥 Wood Pig 3 15 十二	水6 Water 6 Nourish 山雷頤 丙子 Fire Rat 3 16 十三	金4 Metal 5 Following 澤雷隨 丁丑 Fire Ox 7 17 十四	木8 Wood 4 Abundance 雷火豐 戊寅 Earth Tiger 6 18 十五	火7 Fire 3 Regulate 水澤節 己卯 Earth Rabbit 8 19 十六	水1 Water 2 Unity 地天泰 庚辰 Metal Dragon 9 20 十七	木3 Wood 1 Great Reward 火天大有 辛巳 Metal Snake 7 21 十八
火2 Fire 9 Wind 巽爲風 壬午 Water Horse 1 22 十九	金4 Metal 8 Trap 澤水困 癸未 Water Goat 8 23 二十	木3 Wood 7 Not Yet Accomplished 火水未濟 甲申 Wood Monkey 9 24 廿一	金9 Metal 6 Retreat 天山遯 乙酉 Wood Rooster 4 25 廿二	水6 Water 5 Mountain 艮爲山 丙戌 Fire Dog 1 26 廿三	木8 Wood 4 Delight 雷地豫 丁亥 Fire Pig 8 27 廿四	火7 Fire 3 Beginning 水雷屯 戊子 Earth Rat 4 28 廿五
金9 Metal 2 Without Wrongdoing 天雷無妄 己丑 Earth Ox 2 29 廿六	木3 Wood 1 Fire 離爲火 庚寅 Metal Tiger 1 30 廿七	火2 Fire 9 Sincerity 風澤中孚 辛卯 Metal Rabbit 3 31 廿八				

AUGUST 2046 丙申

Xuan Kong Element 玄空五行	雷水解 Relief	Period Luck 卦運	Monthly Star 月星
Wood 木8		4	5

SUNDAY	MONDAY	TUESDAY	WEDNESDAY	THURSDAY	FRIDAY	SATURDAY
			水6 Water 8 Big Livestock 山天大畜 壬辰 Water Dragon 4 1 廿九	金4 Metal 7 Eliminating 澤天夬 癸巳 Water Snake 6 2 七月初一	金9 Metal 6 Heaven 乾爲天 甲午 Wood Horse 1 3 初二	火7 Fire 5 Well 水風井 乙未 Wood Goat 6 4 初三
木8 Wood 4 Relief 雷水解 丙申 Fire Monkey 4 5 初四	金4 Metal 3 Influence 澤山咸 丁酉 Fire Rooster 9 6 初五	水1 Water 2 Humility 地山謙 戊戌 Earth Dog 6 7 初六	火2 Fire 1 Observation 風地觀 己亥 Earth Pig 2 8 初七	火2 Fire 9 Increasing 風雷益 庚子 Metal Rat 9 9 初八	水1 Water 8 Dimming Light 地火明夷 辛丑 Metal Ox 3 10 初九	金9 Metal 7 Fellowship 天火同人 壬寅 Water Tiger 7 11 初十
木8 Wood 6 Marrying Maiden 雷澤歸妹 癸卯 Water Rabbit 7 12 十一	木3 Wood 5 Opposition 火澤睽 甲辰 Wood Dragon 2 13 十二	火7 Fire 4 Waiting 水天需 乙巳 Wood Snake 3 14 十三	金4 Metal 3 Great Exceeding 澤風大過 丙午 Fire Horse 3 15 十四	水6 Water 2 Poison 山風蠱 丁未 Fire Goat 7 16 十五	火2 Fire 1 Dispersing 風水渙 戊申 Earth Monkey 6 17 十六	木3 Wood 9 Travelling 火山旅 己酉 Earth Rooster 8 18 十七
金9 Metal 8 Stagnation 天地否 庚戌 Metal Dog 9 19 十八	火7 Fire 7 Alliance 水地比 辛亥 Metal Pig 7 20 十九	木8 Wood 6 Thunder 震爲雷 壬子 Water Rat 1 21 二十	水6 Water 5 Beauty 山火賁 癸丑 Water Ox 8 22 廿一	火7 Fire 4 Accomplished 水火既濟 甲寅 Wood Tiger 9 23 廿二	水1 Water 3 Arriving 地澤臨 乙卯 Wood Rabbit 4 24 廿三	金4 Metal 2 Marsh 兑爲澤 丙辰 Fire Dragon 1 25 廿四
火2 Fire 1 Small Livestock 風天小畜 丁巳 Fire Snake 8 26 廿五	木3 Wood 9 The Cauldron 火風鼎 戊午 Earth Horse 4 27 廿六	水1 Water 8 Rising 地風升 己未 Earth Goat 2 28 廿七	火7 Fire 7 Water 坎爲水 庚申 Metal Monkey 1 29 廿八	木8 Wood 6 Lesser Exceeding 雷山小過 辛酉 Metal Rooster 3 30 廿九	金4 Metal 5 Gathering 澤地萃 壬戌 Water Dog 4 31 三十	

SEPTEMBER 2046 丁酉

Xuan Kong Element 玄空五行	澤山咸 Influence	Period Luck 卦運	Monthly Star 月星
Metal 金4		9	4

SUNDAY	MONDAY	TUESDAY	WEDNESDAY	THURSDAY	FRIDAY	SATURDAY
水6 Water 壬辰 Water Dragon 4 Big Livestock 山天大畜 30 九月初一 2						水6 Water 癸亥 Water Pig 6 Peel 山地剝 1 八月初一 4
水1 Water 甲子 Wood Rat 1 Earth 坤爲地 2 初二 3	木3 Wood 乙丑 Wood Ox 6 Biting 火雷噬嗑 3 初三 2	火2 Fire 丙寅 Fire Tiger 4 Family 風火家人 4 初四 1	水6 Water 丁卯 Fire Rabbit 9 Decreasing 山澤損 5 初五 9	金9 Metal 戊辰 Earth Dragon 6 Tread 天澤履 6 初六 8	木8 Wood 己巳 Earth Snake 2 Great Strength 雷天大壯 7 初七 7	木8 Wood 庚午 Metal Horse 9 Consistency 雷風恆 8 初八 6
金9 Metal 辛未 Metal Goat 3 Litigation 天水訟 9 初九 5	水1 Water 壬申 Water Monkey 7 Officer 地水師 10 初十 4	火2 Fire 癸酉 Water Rooster 7 Gradual Progress 風山漸 11 十一 3	火7 Fire 甲戌 Wood Dog 2 Obstruction 水山蹇 12 十二 2	木3 Wood 乙亥 Wood Pig 3 Advancement 火地晉 13 十三 1	水6 Water 丙子 Fire Rat 3 Nourish 山雷頤 14 十四 9	金4 Metal 丁丑 Fire Ox 7 Following 澤雷隨 15 十五 8
木8 Wood 戊寅 Earth Tiger 6 Abundance 雷火豐 16 十六 7	火7 Fire 己卯 Earth Rabbit 8 Regulate 水澤節 17 十七 6	水1 Water 庚辰 Metal Dragon 9 Unity 地天泰 18 十八 5	木3 Wood 辛巳 Metal Snake 7 Great Reward 火天大有 19 十九 4	火2 Fire 壬午 Water Horse 1 Wind 巽爲風 20 二十 3	金4 Metal 癸未 Water Goat 8 Trap 澤水困 21 廿一 2	木3 Wood 甲申 Wood Monkey 9 Not Yet Accomplished 火水未濟 22 廿二 1
金9 Metal 乙酉 Wood Rooster 4 Retreat 天山遯 23 廿三 9	水6 Water 丙戌 Fire Dog 1 Mountain 艮爲山 24 廿四 8	木8 Wood 丁亥 Fire Pig 8 Delight 雷地豫 25 廿五 7	火7 Fire 戊子 Earth Rat 4 Beginning 水雷屯 26 廿六 6	金9 Metal 己丑 Earth Ox 2 Without Wrongdoing 天雷無妄 27 廿七 5	木3 Wood 庚寅 Metal Tiger 1 Fire 離爲火 28 廿八 4	火2 Fire 辛卯 Metal Rabbit 3 Sincerity 風澤中孚 29 廿九 3

OCTOBER 2046 戊戌

Xuan Kong Element 玄空五行	地山謙 Humility	Period Luck 卦運	Monthly Star 月星
Water 水1		6	3

SUNDAY	MONDAY	TUESDAY	WEDNESDAY	THURSDAY	FRIDAY	SATURDAY
	金4 Metal 癸巳 Water Snake 6 Eliminating 澤天夬 1 初二 1	金9 Metal 甲午 Wood Horse 1 Heaven 乾爲天 2 初三 9	火7 Fire 乙未 Wood Goat 6 Well 水風井 3 初四 8	木8 Wood 丙申 Fire Monkey 4 Relief 雷水解 4 初五 7	金4 Metal 丁酉 Fire Rooster 9 Influence 澤山咸 5 初六 6	水1 Water 戊戌 Earth Dog 6 Humility 地山謙 6 初七 5
火2 Fire 己亥 Earth Pig 2 Observation 風地觀 7 初八 4	火2 Fire 庚子 Metal Rat 9 Increasing 風雷益 8 初九 3	水1 Water 辛丑 Metal Ox 3 Dimming Light 地火明夷 9 初十 2	金9 Metal 壬寅 Water Tiger 7 Fellowship 天火同人 10 十一 1	木8 Wood 癸卯 Water Rabbit 7 Marrying Maiden 雷澤歸妹 11 十二 9	木3 Wood 甲辰 Wood Dragon 2 Opposition 火澤睽 12 十三 8	火7 Fire 乙巳 Wood Snake 3 Waiting 水天需 13 十四 7
金4 Metal 丙午 Fire Horse 3 Great Exceeding 澤風大過 14 十五 6	水6 Water 丁未 Fire Goat 7 Poison 山風蠱 15 十六 5	火2 Fire 戊申 Earth Monkey 6 Dispersing 風水渙 16 十七 4	木3 Wood 己酉 Earth Rooster 8 Travelling 火山旅 17 十八 3	金9 Metal 庚戌 Metal Dog 9 Stagnation 天地否 18 十九 2	火7 Fire 辛亥 Metal Pig 7 Alliance 水地比 19 二十 1	木8 Wood 壬子 Water Rat 1 Thunder 震爲雷 20 廿一 9
水6 Water 癸丑 Water Ox 8 Beauty 山火賁 21 廿二 8	火7 Fire 甲寅 Wood Tiger 9 Accomplished 水火既濟 22 廿三 7	水1 Water 乙卯 Wood Rabbit 4 Arriving 地澤臨 23 廿四 6	金4 Metal 丙辰 Fire Dragon 1 Marsh 兑爲澤 24 廿五 5	火2 Fire 丁巳 Fire Snake 8 Small Livestock 風天小畜 25 廿六 4	木3 Wood 戊午 Earth Horse 4 The Cauldron 火風鼎 26 廿七 3	水1 Water 己未 Earth Goat 2 Rising 地風升 27 廿八 2
火7 Fire 庚申 Metal Monkey 1 Water 坎爲水 28 廿九 1	木8 Wood 辛酉 Metal Rooster 3 Lesser Exceeding 雷山小過 29 十月初一 9	金4 Metal 壬戌 Water Dog 4 Gathering 澤地萃 30 初二 8	水6 Water 癸亥 Water Pig 6 Peel 山地剝 31 初三 7			

NOVEMBER 2046 己亥

Xuan Kong Element 玄空五行	風地觀 Observation	Period Luck 卦運	Monthly Star 月星
Fire 火2		2	2

SUNDAY	MONDAY	TUESDAY	WEDNESDAY	THURSDAY	FRIDAY	SATURDAY
				水1 Water Earth 坤爲地 6 甲子 Wood Rat 1 **1** 初四	木3 Wood Biting 火雷噬嗑 5 乙丑 Wood Ox 6 **2** 初五	火2 Fire Family 風火家人 4 丙寅 Fire Tiger 4 **3** 初六
水6 Water Decreasing 山澤損 3 丁卯 Fire Rabbit 9 **4** 初七	金9 Metal Tread 天澤履 2 戊辰 Earth Dragon 6 **5** 初八	木8 Wood Great Strength 雷天大壯 1 己巳 Earth Snake 2 **6** 初九	木8 Wood Consistency 雷風恆 9 庚午 Metal Horse 9 **7** 初十	金9 Metal Litigation 天水訟 8 辛未 Metal Goat 3 **8** 十一	水1 Water Officer 地水師 7 壬申 Water Monkey 7 **9** 十二	火2 Fire Gradual Progress 風山漸 6 癸酉 Water Rooster 7 **10** 十三
火7 Fire Obstruction 水山蹇 5 甲戌 Wood Dog 2 **11** 十四	木3 Wood Advancement 火地晉 4 乙亥 Wood Pig 3 **12** 十五	水6 Water Nourish 山雷頤 3 丙子 Fire Rat 3 **13** 十六	金4 Metal Following 澤雷隨 2 丁丑 Fire Ox 7 **14** 十七	木8 Wood Abundance 雷火豐 1 戊寅 Earth Tiger 6 **15** 十八	火7 Fire Regulate 水澤節 9 己卯 Earth Rabbit 8 **16** 十九	水1 Water Unity 地天泰 8 庚辰 Metal Dragon 9 **17** 二十
木3 Wood Great Reward 火天大有 7 辛巳 Metal Snake 7 **18** 廿一	火2 Fire Wind 巽爲風 6 壬午 Water Horse 1 **19** 廿二	金4 Metal Trap 澤水困 5 癸未 Water Goat 8 **20** 廿三	木3 Wood Not Yet Accomplished 火水未濟 4 甲申 Wood Monkey 9 **21** 廿四	金9 Metal Retreat 天山遯 3 乙酉 Wood Rooster 4 **22** 廿五	水6 Water Mountain 艮爲山 2 丙戌 Fire Dog 1 **23** 廿六	木8 Wood Delight 雷地豫 1 丁亥 Fire Pig 8 **24** 廿七
火7 Fire Beginning 水雷屯 9 戊子 Earth Rat 4 **25** 廿八	金9 Metal Without Wrongdoing 天雷無妄 8 己丑 Earth Ox 2 **26** 廿九	木3 Wood Fire 離爲火 7 庚寅 Metal Tiger 1 **27** 三十	火2 Fire Sincerity 風澤中孚 6 辛卯 Metal Rabbit 3 **28** 十一月初一	水6 Water Big Livestock 山天大畜 5 壬辰 Water Dragon 4 **29** 初二	金4 Metal Eliminating 澤天夬 4 癸巳 Water Snake 6 **30** 初三	

DECEMBER 2046 庚子

Xuan Kong Element 玄空五行	風雷益 Increasing	Period Luck 卦運	Monthly Star 月星
Fire 火2		9	1

SUNDAY	MONDAY	TUESDAY	WEDNESDAY	THURSDAY	FRIDAY	SATURDAY
水6 Water Peel 山地剝 9 癸亥 Water Pig 6 **30** 初四	水1 Water Earth 坤爲地 1 甲子 Wood Rat 1 **31** 初五					金9 Metal Heaven 乾爲天 3 甲午 Wood Horse 1 初四
火7 Fire Well 水風井 2 乙未 Wood Goat 6 **2** 初五	木8 Wood Relief 雷水解 1 丙申 Fire Monkey 4 **3** 初六	金4 Metal Influence 澤山咸 9 丁酉 Fire Rooster 9 **4** 初七	水1 Water Humility 地山謙 8 戊戌 Earth Dog 6 **5** 初八	火2 Fire Observation 風地觀 7 己亥 Earth Pig 2 **6** 初九	火2 Fire Increasing 風雷益 6 庚子 Metal Rat 9 **7** 初十	水1 Water Dimming Light 地火明夷 5 辛丑 Metal Ox 3 **8** 十一
金9 Metal Fellowship 天火同人 4 壬寅 Water Tiger 7 **9** 十二	木8 Wood Marrying Maiden 雷澤歸妹 3 癸卯 Water Rabbit 7 **10** 十三	木3 Wood Opposition 火澤睽 2 甲辰 Wood Dragon 2 **11** 十四	火7 Fire Waiting 水天需 1 乙巳 Wood Snake 3 **12** 十五	金4 Metal Great Exceeding 澤風大過 9 丙午 Fire Horse 3 **13** 十六	水6 Water Poison 山風蠱 8 丁未 Fire Goat 7 **14** 十七	火2 Fire Dispersing 風水渙 7 戊申 Earth Monkey 6 **15** 十八
木3 Wood Travelling 火山旅 6 己酉 Earth Rooster 8 **16** 十九	金9 Metal Stagnation 天地否 5 庚戌 Metal Dog 9 **17** 二十	火7 Fire Alliance 水地比 4 辛亥 Metal Pig 7 **18** 廿一	木8 Wood Thunder 震爲雷 3 壬子 Water Rat 1 **19** 廿二	水6 Water Beauty 山火賁 2 癸丑 Water Ox 8 **20** 廿三	火7 Fire Accomplished 水火既濟 1 甲寅 Wood Tiger 9 **21** 廿四	水1 Water Arriving 地澤臨 9/1 乙卯 Wood Rabbit 4 **22** 廿五
金4 Metal Marsh 兌爲澤 2 丙辰 Fire Dragon 1 **23** 廿六	火2 Fire Small Livestock 風天小畜 3 丁巳 Fire Snake 8 **24** 廿七	木3 Wood The Cauldron 火風鼎 4 戊午 Earth Horse 4 **25** 廿八	水1 Water Rising 地風升 5 己未 Earth Goat 2 **26** 廿九	火7 Fire Water 坎爲水 6 庚申 Metal Monkey 1 **27** 十二月初一	木8 Wood Lesser Exceeding 雷山小過 7 辛酉 Metal Rooster 3 **28** 初二	金4 Metal Gathering 澤地萃 8 壬戌 Water Dog 4 **29** 初三

2047 丁卯

(*Ding Mao*) Fire Rabbit

2047 丁卯 *(Ding Mao)* Fire Rabbit

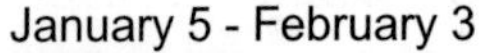

February 4 - March 5

March 6 - April 4

April 5 - May 4

May 5 - June 5

June 6 - July 6

July 7 - August 6

August 7 - September 7

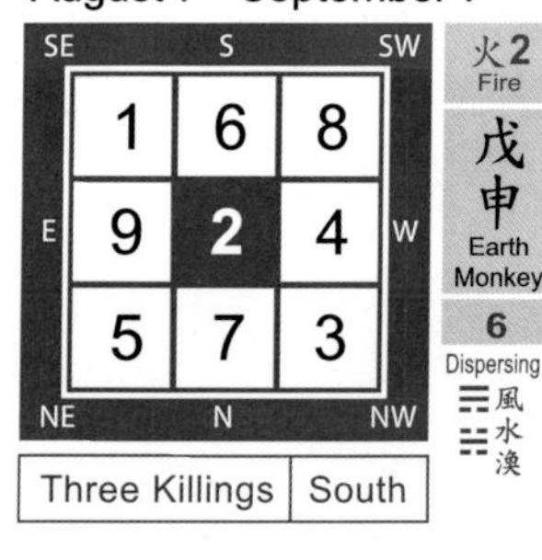

September 8 - October 7

October 8 - November 6

November 7 - December 6

December 7 - January 5

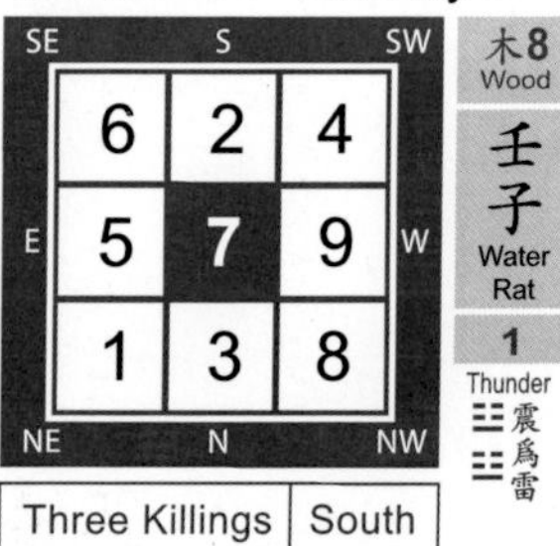

JANUARY 2047 辛丑

Xuan Kong Element 玄空五行	地火明夷 Dimming Light	Period Luck 卦運	Monthly Star 月星
Water 水1		3	9

SUNDAY	MONDAY	TUESDAY	WEDNESDAY	THURSDAY	FRIDAY	SATURDAY
		木3 Wood 2 Biting 火雷噬嗑 乙丑 Wood Ox **1** 初六 6	火2 Fire 3 Family 風火家人 丙寅 Fire Tiger **2** 初七 4	水6 Water 4 Decreasing 山澤損 丁卯 Fire Rabbit **3** 初八 9	金9 Metal 5 Tread 天澤履 戊辰 Earth Dragon **4** 初九 6	木8 Wood 6 Great Strength 雷天大壯 己巳 Earth Snake **5** 初十 2
木8 Wood 7 Consistency 雷風恆 庚午 Metal Horse **6** 十一 9	金9 Metal 8 Litigation 天水訟 辛未 Metal Goat **7** 十二 3	水1 Water 9 Officer 地水師 壬申 Water Monkey **8** 十三 7	火2 Fire 1 Gradual Progress 風山漸 癸酉 Water Rooster **9** 十四 7	火7 Fire 2 Obstruction 水山蹇 甲戌 Wood Dog **10** 十五 2	木3 Wood 3 Advancement 火地晉 乙亥 Wood Pig **11** 十六 3	水6 Water 4 Nourish 山雷頤 丙子 Fire Rat **12** 十七 3
金4 Metal 5 Following 澤雷隨 丁丑 Fire Ox **13** 十八 7	木8 Wood 6 Abundance 雷火豐 戊寅 Earth Tiger **14** 十九 6	火7 Fire 7 Regulate 水澤節 己卯 Earth Rabbit **15** 二十 8	水1 Water 8 Unity 地天泰 庚辰 Metal Dragon **16** 廿一 9	木3 Wood 9 Great Reward 火天大有 辛巳 Metal Snake **17** 廿二 7	火2 Fire 1 Wind 巽爲風 壬午 Water Horse **18** 廿三 1	金4 Metal 2 Trap 澤水困 癸未 Water Goat **19** 廿四 8
木3 Wood 3 Not Yet Accomplished 火水未濟 甲申 Wood Monkey **20** 廿五 9	金9 Metal 4 Retreat 天山遯 乙酉 Wood Rooster **21** 廿六 4	水6 Water 5 Mountain 艮爲山 丙戌 Fire Dog **22** 廿七 1	木8 Wood 6 Delight 雷地豫 丁亥 Fire Pig **23** 廿八 8	火7 Fire 7 Beginning 水雷屯 戊子 Earth Rat **24** 廿九 4	金9 Metal 8 Without Wrongdoing 天雷無妄 己丑 Earth Ox **25** 三十 2	木3 Wood 9 Fire 離爲火 庚寅 Metal Tiger **26** 正月初一 1
火2 Fire 1 Sincerity 風澤中孚 辛卯 Metal Rabbit **27** 初二 3	水6 Water 2 Big Livestock 山天大畜 壬辰 Water Dragon **28** 初三 4	金4 Metal 3 Eliminating 澤天夬 癸巳 Water Snake **29** 初四 6	金9 Metal 4 Heaven 乾爲天 甲午 Wood Horse **30** 初五 1	火7 Fire 5 Well 水風井 乙未 Wood Goat **31** 初六 6		

FEBRUARY 2047 壬寅

Xuan Kong Element 玄空五行	天火同人 Fellowship	Period Luck 卦運	Monthly Star 月星
Metal 金9		7	8

SUNDAY	MONDAY	TUESDAY	WEDNESDAY	THURSDAY	FRIDAY	SATURDAY
					木8 Wood 6 Relief 雷水解 丙申 Fire Monkey **1** 初七 4	金4 Metal 7 Influence 澤山咸 丁酉 Fire Rooster **2** 初八 9
水1 Water 8 Humility 地山謙 戊戌 Earth Dog **3** 初九 6	火2 Fire 9 Observation 風地觀 己亥 Earth Pig **4** 初十 2	火2 Fire 1 Increasing 風雷益 庚子 Metal Rat **5** 十一 9	水1 Water 2 Dimming Light 地火明夷 辛丑 Metal Ox **6** 十二 3	金9 Metal 3 Fellowship 天火同人 壬寅 Water Tiger **7** 十三 7	木8 Wood 4 Marrying Maiden 雷澤歸妹 癸卯 Water Rabbit **8** 十四 7	木3 Wood 5 Opposition 火澤睽 甲辰 Wood Dragon **9** 十五 2
火7 Fire 6 Waiting 水天需 乙巳 Wood Snake **10** 十六 3	金4 Metal 7 Great Exceeding 澤風大過 丙午 Fire Horse **11** 十七 3	水6 Water 8 Poison 山風蠱 丁未 Fire Goat **12** 十八 7	火2 Fire 9 Dispersing 風水渙 戊申 Earth Monkey **13** 十九 6	木3 Wood 1 Travelling 火山旅 己酉 Earth Rooster **14** 二十 8	金9 Metal 2 Stagnation 天地否 庚戌 Metal Dog **15** 廿一 9	火7 Fire 3 Alliance 水地比 辛亥 Metal Pig **16** 廿二 7
木8 Wood 4 Thunder 震爲雷 壬子 Water Rat **17** 廿三 1	水6 Water 5 Beauty 山火賁 癸丑 Water Ox **18** 廿四 8	火7 Fire 6 Accomplished 水火既濟 甲寅 Wood Tiger **19** 廿五 9	水1 Water 7 Arriving 地澤臨 乙卯 Wood Rabbit **20** 廿六 4	金4 Metal 8 Marsh 兌爲澤 丙辰 Fire Dragon **21** 廿七 1	火2 Fire 9 Small Livestock 風天小畜 丁巳 Fire Snake **22** 廿八 8	木3 Wood 1 The Cauldron 火風鼎 戊午 Earth Horse **23** 廿九 4
水1 Water 2 Rising 地風升 己未 Earth Goat **24** 三十 2	火7 Fire 3 Water 坎爲水 庚申 Metal Monkey **25** 二月初一 1	木8 Wood 4 Lesser Exceeding 雷山小過 辛酉 Metal Rooster **26** 初二 3	金4 Metal 5 Gathering 澤地萃 壬戌 Water Dog **27** 初三 4	水6 Water 6 Peel 山地剝 癸亥 Water Pig **28** 初四 6		

MARCH 2047 癸卯

Xuan Kong Element 玄空五行	雷澤歸妹 Marrying Maiden	Period Luck 卦運	Monthly Star 月星
Wood 木8		7	7

SUNDAY	MONDAY	TUESDAY	WEDNESDAY	THURSDAY	FRIDAY	SATURDAY
金9 Metal [1] Heaven 乾爲天 甲午 Wood Horse 31 初六 1					水1 Water [7] Earth 坤爲地 甲子 Wood Rat 1 初五 1	木3 Wood [8] Biting 火雷噬嗑 乙丑 Wood Ox 2 初六 6
火2 Fire [9] Family 風火家人 丙寅 Fire Tiger 3 初七 4	水6 Water [1] Decreasing 山澤損 丁卯 Fire Rabbit 4 初八 9	金9 Metal [2] Tread 天澤履 戊辰 Earth Dragon 5 初九 6	木8 Wood [3] Great Strength 雷天大壯 己巳 Earth Snake 6 初十 2	木8 Wood [4] Consistency 雷風恆 庚午 Metal Horse 7 十一 9	金9 Metal [5] Litigation 天水訟 辛未 Metal Goat 8 十二 3	水1 Water [6] Officer 地水師 壬申 Water Monkey 9 十三 7
火2 Fire [7] Gradual Progress 風山漸 癸酉 Water Rooster 10 十四 7	火7 Fire [8] Obstruction 水山蹇 甲戌 Wood Dog 11 十五 2	木3 Wood [9] Advancement 火地晉 乙亥 Wood Pig 12 十六 3	水6 Water [1] Nourish 山雷頤 丙子 Fire Rat 13 十七 3	金4 Metal [2] Following 澤雷隨 丁丑 Fire Ox 14 十八 7	木8 Wood [3] Abundance 雷火豐 戊寅 Earth Tiger 15 十九 6	火7 Fire [4] Regulate 水澤節 己卯 Earth Rabbit 16 二十 8
水1 Water [5] Unity 地天泰 庚辰 Metal Dragon 17 廿一 9	木3 Wood [6] Great Reward 火天大有 辛巳 Metal Snake 18 廿二 7	火2 Fire [7] Wind 巽爲風 壬午 Water Horse 19 廿三 1	金4 Metal [8] Trap 澤水困 癸未 Water Goat 20 廿四 8	木3 Wood [9] Not Yet Accomplished 火水未濟 甲申 Wood Monkey 21 廿五 9	金9 Metal [1] Retreat 天山遯 乙酉 Wood Rooster 22 廿六 4	水6 Water [2] Mountain 艮爲山 丙戌 Fire Dog 23 廿七 1
木8 Wood [3] Delight 雷地豫 丁亥 Fire Pig 24 廿八 8	火7 Fire [4] Beginning 水雷屯 戊子 Earth Rat 25 廿九 4	金9 Metal [5] Without Wrongdoing 天雷無妄 己丑 Earth Ox 26 三月初一 2	木3 Wood [6] Fire 離爲火 庚寅 Metal Tiger 27 初二 1	火2 Fire [7] Sincerity 風澤中孚 辛卯 Metal Rabbit 28 初三 3	水6 Water [8] Big Livestock 山天大畜 壬辰 Water Dragon 29 初四 4	金4 Metal [9] Eliminating 澤天夬 癸巳 Water Snake 30 初五 6

APRIL 2047 甲辰

Xuan Kong Element 玄空五行	火澤睽 Opposition	Period Luck 卦運	Monthly Star 月星
Wood 木3		2	6

SUNDAY	MONDAY	TUESDAY	WEDNESDAY	THURSDAY	FRIDAY	SATURDAY
	火7 Fire [2] Well 水風井 乙未 Wood Goat 1 初七 6	木8 Wood [3] Relief 雷水解 丙申 Fire Monkey 2 初八 4	金4 Metal [4] Influence 澤山咸 丁酉 Fire Rooster 3 初九 9	水1 Water [5] Humility 地山謙 戊戌 Earth Dog 4 初十 6	火2 Fire [6] Observation 風地觀 己亥 Earth Pig 5 十一 2	火2 Fire [7] Increasing 風雷益 庚子 Metal Rat 6 十二 9
水1 Water [8] Dimming Light 地火明夷 辛丑 Metal Ox 7 十三 3	金9 Metal [9] Fellowship 天火同人 壬寅 Water Tiger 8 十四 7	木8 Wood [1] Marrying Maiden 雷澤歸妹 癸卯 Water Rabbit 9 十五 7	木3 Wood [2] Opposition 火澤睽 甲辰 Wood Dragon 10 十六 2	火7 Fire [3] Waiting 水天需 乙巳 Wood Snake 11 十七 3	金4 Metal [4] Great Exceeding 澤風大過 丙午 Fire Horse 12 十八 3	水6 Water [5] Poison 山風蠱 丁未 Fire Goat 13 十九 7
火2 Fire [6] Dispersing 風水渙 戊申 Earth Monkey 14 二十 6	木3 Wood [7] Travelling 火山旅 己酉 Earth Rooster 15 廿一 8	金9 Metal [8] Stagnation 天地否 庚戌 Metal Dog 16 廿二 9	火7 Fire [9] Alliance 水地比 辛亥 Metal Pig 17 廿三 7	木8 Wood [1] Thunder 震爲雷 壬子 Water Rat 18 廿四 1	水6 Water [2] Beauty 山火賁 癸丑 Water Ox 19 廿五 8	火7 Fire [3] Accomplished 水火既濟 甲寅 Wood Tiger 20 廿六 9
水1 Water [4] Arriving 地澤臨 乙卯 Wood Rabbit 21 廿七 4	金4 Metal [5] Marsh 兌爲澤 丙辰 Fire Dragon 22 廿八 1	火2 Fire [6] Small Livestock 風天小畜 丁巳 Fire Snake 23 廿九 8	木3 Wood [7] The Cauldron 火風鼎 戊午 Earth Horse 24 三十 4	水1 Water [8] Rising 地風升 己未 Earth Goat 25 四月初一 2	火7 Fire [9] Water 坎爲水 庚申 Metal Monkey 26 初二 1	木8 Wood [1] Lesser Exceeding 雷山小過 辛酉 Metal Rooster 27 初三 3
金4 Metal [2] Gathering 澤地萃 壬戌 Water Dog 28 初四 4	水6 Water [3] Peel 山地剝 癸亥 Water Pig 29 初五 6	水1 Water [4] Earth 坤爲地 甲子 Wood Rat 30 初六 1				

MAY 2047 乙巳

Xuan Kong Element 玄空五行	水天需 Waiting	Period Luck 卦運	Monthly Star 月星
Fire 火7		3	5

SUNDAY	MONDAY	TUESDAY	WEDNESDAY	THURSDAY	FRIDAY	SATURDAY
			木3 Wood 5 Biting 火雷噬嗑 乙丑 Wood Ox 6 1 初七	火2 Fire 6 Family 風火家人 丙寅 Fire Tiger 4 2 初八	水6 Water 7 Decreasing 山澤損 丁卯 Fire Rabbit 9 3 初九	金9 Metal 8 Tread 天澤履 戊辰 Earth Dragon 6 4 初十
木8 Wood 9 Great Strength 雷天大壯 己巳 Earth Snake 2 5 十一	木8 Wood 1 Consistency 雷風恆 庚午 Metal Horse 9 6 十二	金9 Metal 2 Litigation 天水訟 辛未 Metal Goat 3 7 十三	水1 Water 3 Officer 地水師 壬申 Water Monkey 7 8 十四	火2 Fire 4 Gradual Progress 風山漸 癸酉 Water Rooster 7 9 十五	火7 Fire 5 Obstruction 水山蹇 甲戌 Wood Dog 2 10 十六	木3 Wood 6 Advancement 火地晉 乙亥 Wood Pig 3 11 十七
水6 Water 7 Nourish 山雷頤 丙子 Fire Rat 3 12 十八	金4 Metal 8 Following 澤雷隨 丁丑 Fire Ox 7 13 十九	木8 Wood 9 Abundance 雷火豐 戊寅 Earth Tiger 6 14 二十	火7 Fire 1 Regulate 水澤節 己卯 Earth Rabbit 8 15 廿一	水1 Water 2 Unity 地天泰 庚辰 Metal Dragon 9 16 廿二	木3 Wood 3 Great Reward 火天大有 辛巳 Metal Snake 7 17 廿三	火2 Fire 4 Wind 巽爲風 壬午 Water Horse 1 18 廿四
金4 Metal 5 Trap 澤水困 癸未 Water Goat 8 19 廿五	木3 Wood 6 Not Yet Accomplished 火水未濟 甲申 Wood Monkey 9 20 廿六	金9 Metal 7 Retreat 天山遯 乙酉 Wood Rooster 4 21 廿七	水6 Water 8 Mountain 艮爲山 丙戌 Fire Dog 1 22 廿八	木8 Wood 9 Delight 雷地豫 丁亥 Fire Pig 8 23 廿九	火7 Fire 1 Beginning 水雷屯 戊子 Earth Rat 4 24 三十	金9 Metal 2 Without Wrongdoing 天雷無妄 己丑 Earth Ox 2 25 五月初一
木3 Wood 3 Fire 離爲火 庚寅 Metal Tiger 1 26 初二	火2 Fire 4 Sincerity 風澤中孚 辛卯 Metal Rabbit 3 27 初三	水6 Water 5 Big Livestock 山天大畜 壬辰 Water Dragon 4 28 初四	金4 Metal 6 Eliminating 澤天夬 癸巳 Water Snake 6 29 初五	金9 Metal 7 Heaven 乾爲天 甲午 Wood Horse 1 30 初六	火7 Fire 8 Well 水風井 乙未 Wood Goat 6 31 初七	

JUNE 2047 丙午

Xuan Kong Element 玄空五行	澤風大過 Great Exceeding	Period Luck 卦運	Monthly Star 月星
Metal 金4		3	4

SUNDAY	MONDAY	TUESDAY	WEDNESDAY	THURSDAY	FRIDAY	SATURDAY
木3 Wood 8 Biting 火雷噬嗑 乙丑 Wood Ox 6 30 初八						木8 Wood 9 Relief 雷水解 丙申 Fire Monkey 4 1 初八
金4 Metal 1 Influence 澤山咸 丁酉 Fire Rooster 9 2 初九	水1 Water 2 Humility 地山謙 戊戌 Earth Dog 6 3 初十	火2 Fire 3 Observation 風地觀 己亥 Earth Pig 2 4 十一	火2 Fire 4 Increasing 風雷益 庚子 Metal Rat 9 5 十二	水1 Water 5 Dimming Light 地火明夷 辛丑 Metal Ox 3 6 十三	金9 Metal 6 Fellowship 天火同人 壬寅 Water Tiger 7 7 十四	木8 Wood 7 Marrying Maiden 雷澤歸妹 癸卯 Water Rabbit 7 8 十五
木3 Wood 8 Opposition 火澤睽 甲辰 Wood Dragon 2 9 十六	火7 Fire 9 Waiting 水天需 乙巳 Wood Snake 3 10 十七	金4 Metal 1 Great Exceeding 澤風大過 丙午 Fire Horse 3 11 十八	水6 Water 2 Poison 山風蠱 丁未 Fire Goat 7 12 十九	火2 Fire 3 Dispersing 風水渙 戊申 Earth Monkey 6 13 二十	木3 Wood 4 Travelling 火山旅 己酉 Earth Rooster 8 14 廿一	金9 Metal 5 Stagnation 天地否 庚戌 Metal Dog 9 15 廿二
火7 Fire 6 Alliance 水地比 辛亥 Metal Pig 7 16 廿三	木8 Wood 7 Thunder 震爲雷 壬子 Water Rat 1 17 廿四	水6 Water 8 Beauty 山火賁 癸丑 Water Ox 8 18 廿五	火7 Fire 9 Accomplished 水火既濟 甲寅 Wood Tiger 9 19 廿六	水1 Water 1 Arriving 地澤臨 乙卯 Wood Rabbit 4 20 廿七	金4 Metal 2/8 Marsh 兌爲澤 丙辰 Fire Dragon 1 21 廿八	火2 Fire 7 Small Livestock 風天小畜 丁巳 Fire Snake 8 22 廿九
木3 Wood 6 The Cauldron 火風鼎 戊午 Earth Horse 4 23 閏五月初一	水1 Water 5 Rising 地風升 己未 Earth Goat 2 24 初二	火7 Fire 4 Water 坎爲水 庚申 Metal Monkey 1 25 初三	木8 Wood 3 Lesser Exceeding 雷山小過 辛酉 Metal Rooster 3 26 初四	金4 Metal 2 Gathering 澤地萃 壬戌 Water Dog 4 27 初五	水6 Water 1 Peel 山地剝 癸亥 Water Pig 6 28 初六	水1 Water 9 Earth 坤爲地 甲子 Wood Rat 1 29 初七

JULY 2047 丁未

Xuan Kong Element 玄空五行	山風蠱 Poison	Period Luck 卦運	Monthly Star 月星
Water 水6		7	3

SUNDAY	MONDAY	TUESDAY	WEDNESDAY	THURSDAY	FRIDAY	SATURDAY
	火2 Fire 7 Family 丙寅 Fire Tiger 風火家人 1 初九 4	水6 Water 6 Decreasing 丁卯 Fire Rabbit 山澤損 2 初十 9	金9 Metal 5 Tread 戊辰 Earth Dragon 天澤履 3 十一 6	木8 Wood 4 Great Strength 己巳 Earth Snake 雷天大壯 4 十二 2	木8 Wood 3 Consistency 庚午 Metal Horse 雷風恒 5 十三 9	金9 Metal 2 Litigation 辛未 Metal Goat 天水訟 6 十四 3
水1 Water 1 Officer 壬申 Water Monkey 地水師 7 十五 7	火2 Fire 9 Gradual Progress 癸酉 Water Rooster 風山漸 8 十六 7	火7 Fire 8 Obstruction 甲戌 Wood Dog 水山蹇 9 十七 2	木3 Wood 7 Advancement 乙亥 Wood Pig 火地晉 10 十八 3	水6 Water 6 Nourish 丙子 Fire Rat 山雷頤 11 十九 3	金4 Metal 5 Following 丁丑 Fire Ox 澤雷隨 12 二十 7	木8 Wood 4 Abundance 戊寅 Earth Tiger 雷火豐 13 廿一 6
火7 Fire 3 Regulate 己卯 Earth Rabbit 水澤節 14 廿二 8	水1 Water 2 Unity 庚辰 Metal Dragon 地天泰 15 廿三 9	木3 Wood 1 Great Reward 辛巳 Metal Snake 火天大有 16 廿四 7	火2 Fire 9 Wind 壬午 Water Horse 巽爲風 17 廿五 1	金4 Metal 8 Trap 癸未 Water Goat 澤水困 18 廿六 8	木3 Wood 7 Not Yet Accomplished 甲申 Wood Monkey 火水未濟 19 廿七 9	金9 Metal 6 Retreat 乙酉 Wood Rooster 天山遯 20 廿八 4
水6 Water 5 Mountain 丙戌 Fire Dog 艮爲山 21 廿九 1	木8 Wood 4 Delight 丁亥 Fire Pig 雷地豫 22 三十 8	火7 Fire 3 Beginning 戊子 Earth Rat 水雷屯 23 六月初一 4	金9 Metal 2 Without Wrongdoing 己丑 Earth Ox 天雷無妄 23 初二 2	木3 Wood 1 Fire 庚寅 Metal Tiger 離爲火 25 初三 1	火2 Fire 9 Sincerity 辛卯 Metal Rabbit 風澤中孚 26 初四 3	水6 Water 8 Big Livestock 壬辰 Water Dragon 山天大畜 27 初五 4
金4 Metal 7 Eliminating 癸巳 Water Snake 澤天夬 28 初六 6	金9 Metal 6 Heaven 甲午 Wood Horse 乾爲天 29 初七 1	火7 Fire 5 Well 乙未 Wood Goat 水風井 30 初八 6	木8 Wood 4 Relief 丙申 Fire Monkey 雷水解 31 初九 4			

AUGUST 2047 戊申

Xuan Kong Element 玄空五行	風水渙 Dispersing	Period Luck 卦運	Monthly Star 月星
Fire 火2		6	2

SUNDAY	MONDAY	TUESDAY	WEDNESDAY	THURSDAY	FRIDAY	SATURDAY
				金4 Metal 3 Influence 丁酉 Fire Rooster 澤山咸 1 初十 9	水1 Water 2 Humility 戊戌 Earth Dog 地山謙 2 十一 6	火2 Fire 1 Observation 己亥 Earth Pig 風地觀 3 十二 2
火2 Fire 9 Increasing 庚子 Metal Rat 風雷益 4 十三 9	水1 Water 8 Dimming Light 辛丑 Metal Ox 地火明夷 5 十四 3	金9 Metal 7 Fellowship 壬寅 Water Tiger 天火同人 6 十五 7	木8 Wood 6 Marrying Maiden 癸卯 Water Rabbit 雷澤歸妹 7 十六 2	木3 Wood 5 Opposition 甲辰 Wood Dragon 火澤睽 8 十七 2	火7 Fire 4 Waiting 乙巳 Wood Snake 水天需 9 十八 3	金4 Metal 3 Great Exceeding 丙午 Fire Horse 澤風大過 10 十九 3
水6 Water 2 Poison 丁未 Fire Goat 山風蠱 11 二十 7	火2 Fire 1 Dispersing 戊申 Earth Monkey 風水渙 12 廿一 6	木3 Wood 9 Travelling 己酉 Earth Rooster 火山旅 13 廿二 8	金9 Metal 8 Stagnation 庚戌 Metal Dog 天地否 14 廿三 9	火7 Fire 7 Alliance 辛亥 Metal Pig 水地比 15 廿四 7	木8 Wood 6 Thunder 壬子 Water Rat 震爲雷 16 廿五 1	水6 Water 5 Beauty 癸丑 Water Ox 山火賁 17 廿六 8
火7 Fire 4 Accomplished 甲寅 Wood Tiger 水火既濟 18 廿七 9	水1 Water 3 Arriving 乙卯 Wood Rabbit 地澤臨 19 廿八 4	金4 Metal 2 Marsh 丙辰 Fire Dragon 兌爲澤 20 廿九 1	火2 Fire 1 Small Livestock 丁巳 Fire Snake 風天小畜 21 七月初一 8	木3 Wood 9 The Cauldron 戊午 Earth Horse 火風鼎 22 初二 4	水1 Water 8 Rising 己未 Earth Goat 地風升 23 初三 2	火7 Fire 7 Water 庚申 Metal Monkey 坎爲水 24 初四 1
木8 Wood 6 Lesser Exceeding 辛酉 Metal Rooster 雷山小過 25 初五 3	金4 Metal 5 Gathering 壬戌 Water Dog 澤地萃 26 初六 4	水6 Water 4 Peel 癸亥 Water Pig 山地剝 27 初七 6	水1 Water 3 Earth 甲子 Wood Rat 坤爲地 28 初八 1	木3 Wood 2 Biting 乙丑 Wood Ox 火雷噬嗑 29 初九 6	火2 Fire 1 Family 丙寅 Fire Tiger 風火家人 30 初十 4	水6 Water 9 Decreasing 丁卯 Fire Rabbit 山澤損 31 十一 9

SEPTEMBER 2047 己酉

Xuan Kong Element 玄空五行	火山旅 Travelling	Period Luck 卦運	Monthly Star 月星
Wood 木3		8	1

SUNDAY	MONDAY	TUESDAY	WEDNESDAY	THURSDAY	FRIDAY	SATURDAY
金9 Metal 8 Tread 戊辰 Earth Dragon 天澤履 **1** 十二 6	木8 Wood 7 Great Strength 己巳 Earth Snake 雷天大壯 **2** 十三 2	木8 Wood 6 Consistency 庚午 Metal Horse 雷風恆 **3** 十四 9	金9 Metal 5 Litigation 辛未 Metal Goat 天水訟 **4** 十五 3	水1 Water 4 Officer 壬申 Water Monkey 地水師 **5** 十六 7	火2 Fire 3 Gradual Progress 癸酉 Water Rooster 風山漸 **6** 十七 7	火7 Fire 2 Obstruction 甲戌 Wood Dog 水山蹇 **7** 十八 2
木3 Wood 1 Advancement 乙亥 Wood Pig 火地晉 **8** 十九 3	水6 Water 9 Nourish 丙子 Fire Rat 山雷頤 **9** 二十 3	金4 Metal 8 Following 丁丑 Fire Ox 澤雷隨 **10** 廿一 7	木8 Wood 7 Abundance 戊寅 Earth Tiger 雷火豐 **11** 廿二 6	火7 Fire 6 Regulate 己卯 Earth Rabbit 水澤節 **12** 廿三 8	水1 Water 5 Unity 庚辰 Metal Dragon 地天泰 **13** 廿四 9	木3 Wood 4 Great Reward 辛巳 Metal Snake 火天大有 **14** 廿五 7
火2 Fire 3 Wind 壬午 Water Horse 巽為風 **15** 廿六 1	金4 Metal 2 Trap 癸未 Water Goat 澤水困 **16** 廿七 8	木3 Wood 1 Not Yet Accomplished 甲申 Wood Monkey 火水未濟 **17** 廿八 9	金9 Metal 9 Retreat 乙酉 Wood Rooster 天山遯 **18** 廿九 4	水6 Water 8 Mountain 丙戌 Fire Dog 艮為山 **19** 三十 1	木8 Wood 7 Delight 丁亥 Fire Pig 雷地豫 **20** 八月初一 8	火7 Fire 6 Beginning 戊子 Earth Rat 水雷屯 **21** 初二 4
金9 Metal 5 Without Wrongdoing 己丑 Earth Ox 天雷無妄 **22** 初三 2	木3 Wood 4 Fire 庚寅 Metal Tiger 離為火 **23** 初四 1	火2 Fire 3 Sincerity 辛卯 Metal Rabbit 風澤中孚 **24** 初五 3	水6 Water 2 Big Livestock 壬辰 Water Dragon 山天大畜 **25** 初六 4	金4 Metal 1 Eliminating 癸巳 Water Snake 澤天夬 **26** 初七 6	金9 Metal 9 Heaven 甲午 Wood Horse 乾為天 **27** 初八 1	火7 Fire 8 Well 乙未 Wood Goat 水風井 **28** 初九 6
木8 Wood 7 Relief 丙申 Fire Monkey 雷水解 **29** 初十 4	金4 Metal 6 Influence 丁酉 Fire Rooster 澤山咸 **30** 十一 9					

OCTOBER 2047 庚戌

Xuan Kong Element 玄空五行	天地否 Stagnation	Period Luck 卦運	Monthly Star 月星
Metal 金9		9	9

SUNDAY	MONDAY	TUESDAY	WEDNESDAY	THURSDAY	FRIDAY	SATURDAY
		水1 Water 5 Humility 戊戌 Earth Dog 地山謙 **1** 十二 6	火2 Fire 4 Observation 己亥 Earth Pig 風地觀 **2** 十三 2	火2 Fire 3 Increasing 庚子 Metal Rat 風雷益 **3** 十四 9	水1 Water 2 Dimming Light 辛丑 Metal Ox 地火明夷 **4** 十五 3	金9 Metal 1 Fellowship 壬寅 Water Tiger 天火同人 **5** 十六 7
木8 Wood 9 Marrying Maiden 癸卯 Water Rabbit 雷澤歸妹 **6** 十七 7	木3 Wood 8 Opposition 甲辰 Wood Dragon 火澤睽 **7** 十八 2	火7 Fire 7 Waiting 乙巳 Wood Snake 水天需 **8** 十九 3	金4 Metal 6 Great Exceeding 丙午 Fire Horse 澤風大過 **9** 二十 3	水6 Water 5 Poison 丁未 Fire Goat 山風蠱 **10** 廿一 7	火2 Fire 4 Dispersing 戊申 Earth Monkey 風水渙 **11** 廿二 6	木3 Wood 3 Travelling 己酉 Earth Rooster 火山旅 **12** 廿三 8
金9 Metal 2 Stagnation 庚戌 Metal Dog 天地否 **13** 廿四 9	火7 Fire 1 Alliance 辛亥 Metal Pig 水地比 **14** 廿五 7	木8 Wood 9 Thunder 壬子 Water Rat 震為雷 **15** 廿六 1	水6 Water 8 Beauty 癸丑 Water Ox 山火賁 **16** 廿七 8	火7 Fire 7 Accomplished 甲寅 Wood Tiger 水火既濟 **17** 廿八 9	水1 Water 6 Arriving 乙卯 Wood Rabbit 地澤臨 **18** 廿九 4	金4 Metal 5 Marsh 丙辰 Fire Dragon 兌為澤 **19** 九月初一 1
火2 Fire 4 Small Livestock 丁巳 Fire Snake 風天小畜 **20** 初二 8	木3 Wood 3 The Cauldron 戊午 Earth Horse 火風鼎 **21** 初三 4	水1 Water 2 Rising 己未 Earth Goat 地風升 **22** 初四 2	火7 Fire 1 Water 庚申 Metal Monkey 坎為水 **23** 初五 1	木8 Wood 9 Lesser Exceeding 辛酉 Metal Rooster 雷山小過 **24** 初六 3	金4 Metal 8 Gathering 壬戌 Water Dog 澤地萃 **25** 初七 4	水6 Water 7 Peel 癸亥 Water Pig 山地剝 **26** 初八 6
水1 Water 6 Earth 甲子 Wood Rat 坤為地 **27** 初九 1	木3 Wood 5 Biting 乙丑 Wood Ox 火雷噬嗑 **28** 初十 6	火2 Fire 4 Family 丙寅 Fire Tiger 風火家人 **29** 十一 4	水6 Water 3 Decreasing 丁卯 Fire Rabbit 山澤損 **30** 十二 9	金9 Metal 2 Tread 戊辰 Earth Dragon 天澤履 **31** 十三 6		

NOVEMBER 2047 辛亥

Xuan Kong Element 玄空五行	水地比 Alliance	Period Luck 卦運	Monthly Star 月星
Fire 火7		7	8

SUNDAY	MONDAY	TUESDAY	WEDNESDAY	THURSDAY	FRIDAY	SATURDAY
					木8 Wood 1 己巳 Earth Snake Great Strength 雷天大壯 **1** 十四 2	木8 Wood 9 庚午 Metal Horse Consistency 雷風恆 **2** 十五 9
金9 Metal 8 辛未 Metal Goat Litigation 天水訟 **3** 十六 3	水1 Water 7 壬申 Water Monkey Officer 地水師 **4** 十七 7	火2 Fire 6 癸酉 Water Rooster Gradual Progress 風山漸 **5** 十八 7	火7 Fire 5 甲戌 Wood Dog Obstruction 水山蹇 **6** 十九 2	木3 Wood 4 乙亥 Wood Pig Advancement 火地晉 **7** 二十 3	水6 Water 3 丙子 Fire Rat Nourish 山雷頤 **8** 廿一 3	金4 Metal 2 丁丑 Fire Ox Following 澤雷隨 **9** 廿二 7
木8 Wood 1 戊寅 Earth Tiger Abundance 雷火豐 **10** 廿三 6	火7 Fire 9 己卯 Earth Rabbit Regulate 水澤節 **11** 廿四 8	水1 Water 8 庚辰 Metal Dragon Unity 地天泰 **12** 廿五 9	木3 Wood 7 辛巳 Metal Snake Great Reward 火天大有 **13** 廿六 7	火2 Fire 6 壬午 Water Horse Wind 巽爲風 **14** 廿七 1	金4 Metal 5 癸未 Water Goat Trap 澤水困 **15** 廿八 8	木3 Wood 4 甲申 Wood Monkey Not Yet Accomplished 火水未濟 **16** 廿九 9
金9 Metal 3 乙酉 Wood Rooster Retreat 天山遯 **17** 十月初一 4	水6 Water 2 丙戌 Fire Dog Mountain 艮爲山 **18** 初二 1	木8 Wood 1 丁亥 Fire Pig Delight 雷地豫 **19** 初三 8	火7 Fire 9 戊子 Earth Rat Beginning 水雷屯 **20** 初四 4	金9 Metal 8 己丑 Earth Ox Without Wrongdoing 天雷無妄 **21** 初五 2	木3 Wood 7 庚寅 Metal Tiger Fire 離爲火 **22** 初六 1	火2 Fire 6 辛卯 Metal Rabbit Sincerity 風澤中孚 **23** 初七 3
水6 Water 5 壬辰 Water Dragon Big Livestock 山天大畜 **24** 初八 4	金4 Metal 4 癸巳 Water Snake Eliminating 澤天夬 **25** 初九 6	金9 Metal 3 甲午 Wood Horse Heaven 乾爲天 **26** 初十 1	火7 Fire 2 乙未 Wood Goat Well 水風井 **27** 十一 6	木8 Wood 1 丙申 Fire Monkey Relief 雷水解 **28** 十二 4	金4 Metal 9 丁酉 Fire Rooster Influence 澤山咸 **29** 十三 9	水1 Water 8 戊戌 Earth Dog Humility 地山謙 **30** 十四 6

DECEMBER 2047 壬子

Xuan Kong Element 玄空五行	震爲雷 Thunder	Period Luck 卦運	Monthly Star 月星
Wood 木8		1	7

SUNDAY	MONDAY	TUESDAY	WEDNESDAY	THURSDAY	FRIDAY	SATURDAY
火2 Fire 7 己亥 Earth Pig Observation 風地觀 **1** 十五 2	火2 Fire 6 庚子 Metal Rat Increasing 風雷益 **2** 十六 9	水1 Water 5 辛丑 Metal Ox Dimming Light 地火明夷 **3** 十七 3	金9 Metal 4 壬寅 Water Tiger Fellowship 天火同人 **4** 十八 7	木8 Wood 3 癸卯 Water Rabbit Marrying Maiden 雷澤歸妹 **5** 十九 7	木3 Wood 2 甲辰 Wood Dragon Opposition 火澤睽 **6** 二十 2	火7 Fire 1 乙巳 Wood Snake Waiting 水天需 **7** 廿一 3
金4 Metal 9 丙午 Fire Horse Great Exceeding 澤風大過 **8** 廿二 3	水6 Water 8 丁未 Fire Goat Poison 山風蠱 **9** 廿三 7	火2 Fire 7 戊申 Earth Monkey Dispersing 風水渙 **10** 廿四 6	木3 Wood 6 己酉 Earth Rooster Travelling 火山旅 **11** 廿五 8	金9 Metal 5 庚戌 Metal Dog Stagnation 天地否 **12** 廿六 9	火7 Fire 4 辛亥 Metal Pig Alliance 水地比 **13** 廿七 7	木8 Wood 3 壬子 Water Rat Thunder 震爲雷 **14** 廿八 1
水6 Water 2 癸丑 Water Ox Beauty 山火賁 **15** 廿九 8	火7 Fire 1 甲寅 Wood Tiger Accomplished 水火既濟 **16** 三十 9	水1 Water 9 乙卯 Wood Rabbit Arriving 地澤臨 **17** 十一月初一 4	金4 Metal 8 丙辰 Fire Dragon Marsh 兌爲澤 **18** 初二 1	火2 Fire 7 丁巳 Fire Snake Small Livestock 風天小畜 **19** 初三 8	木3 Wood 6 戊午 Earth Horse The Cauldron 火風鼎 **20** 初四 4	水1 Water 5 己未 Earth Goat Rising 地風升 **21** 初五 2
火7 Fire 4/6 庚申 Metal Monkey Water 坎爲水 **22** 初六 1	木8 Wood 7 辛酉 Metal Rooster Lesser Exceeding 雷山小過 **23** 初七 3	金4 Metal 8 壬戌 Water Dog Gathering 澤地萃 **24** 初八 4	水6 Water 9 癸亥 Water Pig Peel 山地剝 **25** 初九 6	水1 Water 1 甲子 Wood Rat Earth 坤爲地 **26** 初十 1	木3 Wood 2 乙丑 Wood Ox Biting 火雷噬嗑 **27** 十一 6	火2 Fire 3 丙寅 Fire Tiger Family 風火家人 **28** 十二 4
水6 Water 4 丁卯 Fire Rabbit Decreasing 山澤損 **29** 十三 9	金9 Metal 5 戊辰 Earth Dragon Tread 天澤履 **30** 十四 6	木8 Wood 6 己巳 Earth Snake Great Strength 雷天大壯 **31** 十五 2				

2048 戊辰

(*Wu Chen*) Earth Dragon

2048 戊辰 *(Wu Chen)* Earth Dragon

January 6 - February 3

水6 Water
癸丑 Water Ox
8 Beauty
山火賁

SE	S	SW
5	1	3
4	6	8
9	2	7

February 4 - March 4

火7 Fire
甲寅 Wood Tiger
9 Accomplished
水火既濟

SE	S	SW
4	9	2
3	5	7
8	1	6

March 5 - April 3

水1 Water
乙卯 Wood Rabbit
4 Arriving
地澤臨

SE	S	SW
3	8	1
2	4	6
7	9	5

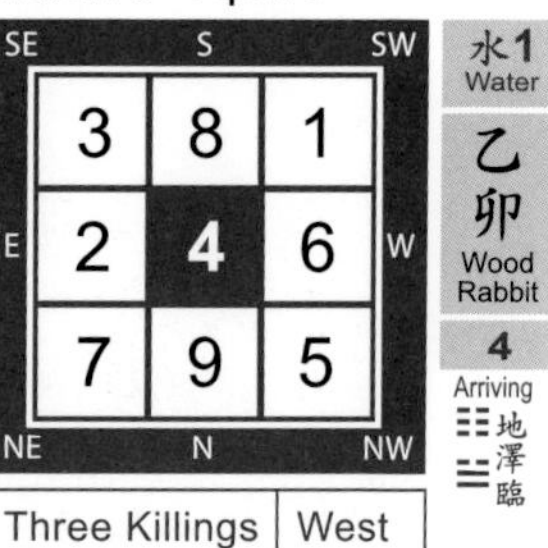

April 4 - May 4

金4 Metal
丙辰 Fire Dragon
1 Marsh
兌爲澤

SE	S	SW
2	7	9
1	3	5
6	8	4

May 5 - June 4

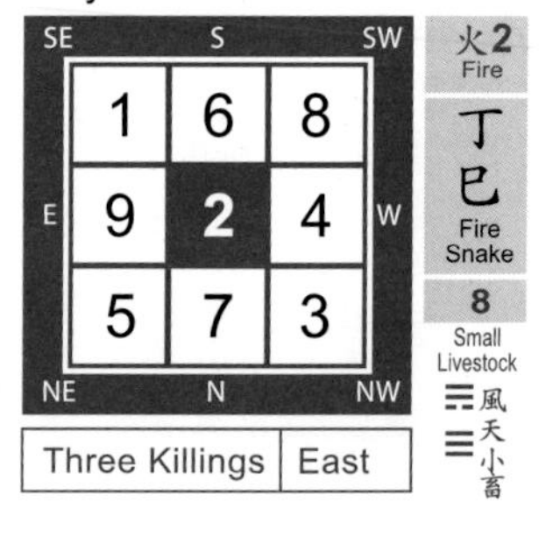

火2 Fire
丁巳 Fire Snake
8 Small Livestock
風天小畜

SE	S	SW
1	6	8
9	2	4
5	7	3

June 5 - July 5

木3 Wood
戊午 Earth Horse
4 The Cauldron
火風鼎

SE	S	SW
9	5	7
8	1	3
4	6	2

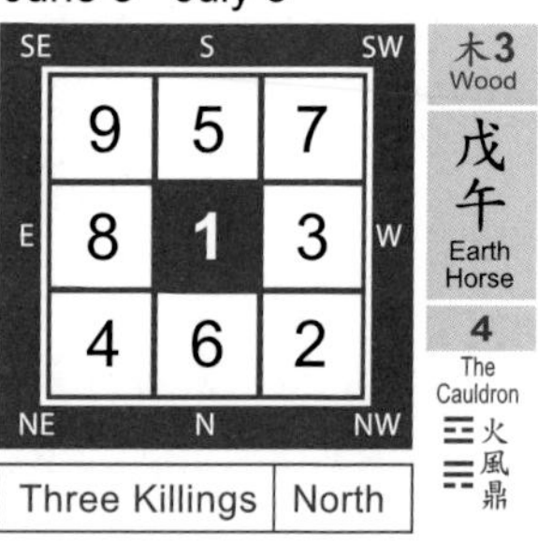

July 6 - August 6

水1 Water
己未 Earth Goat
2 Rising
地風升

SE	S	SW
8	4	6
7	9	2
3	5	1

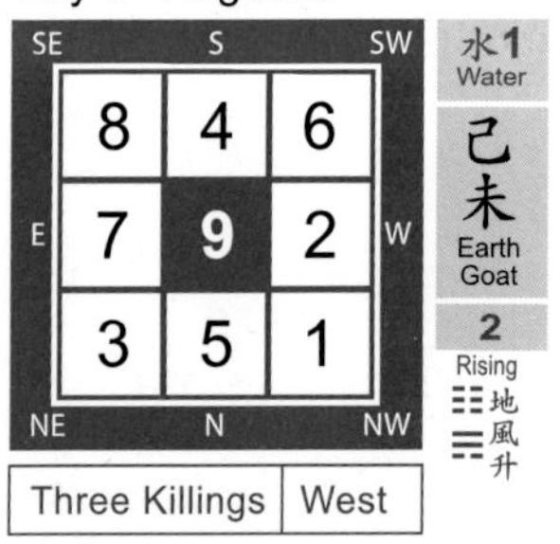

August 7 - September 5

火7 Fire
庚申 Metal Monkey
1 Water
坎爲水

SE	S	SW
7	3	5
6	8	1
2	4	9

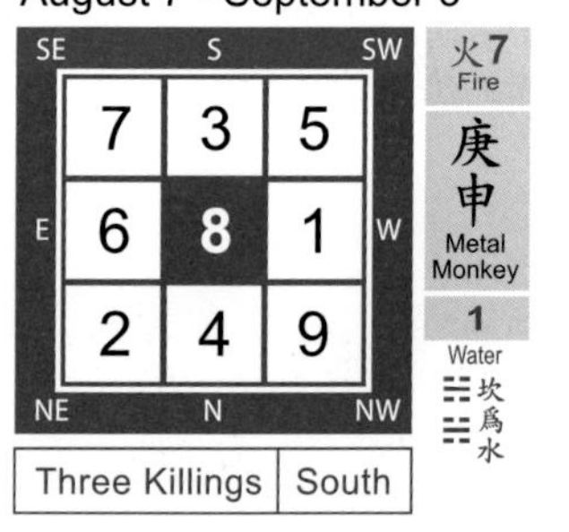

September 6 - October 6

木8 Wood
辛酉 Metal Rooster
3 Lesser Exceeding
雷山小過

SE	S	SW
6	2	4
5	7	9
1	3	8

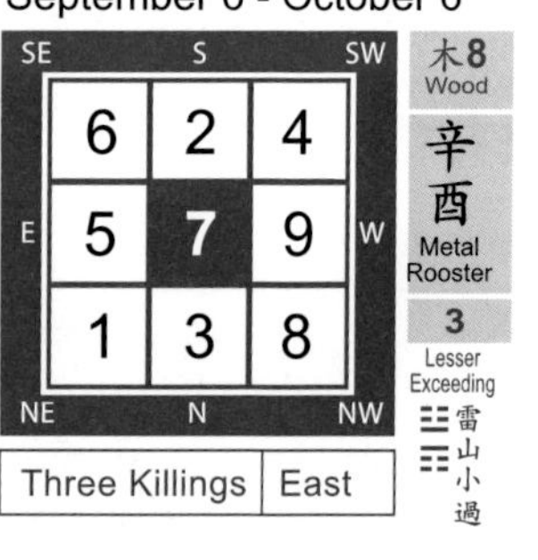

October 7 - November 6

金4 Metal
壬戌 Water Dog
4 Gathering
澤地萃

SE	S	SW
5	1	3
4	6	8
9	2	7

November 7 - December 5

水6 Water
癸亥 Water Pig
6 Peel
山地剝

SE	S	SW
4	9	2
3	5	7
8	1	6

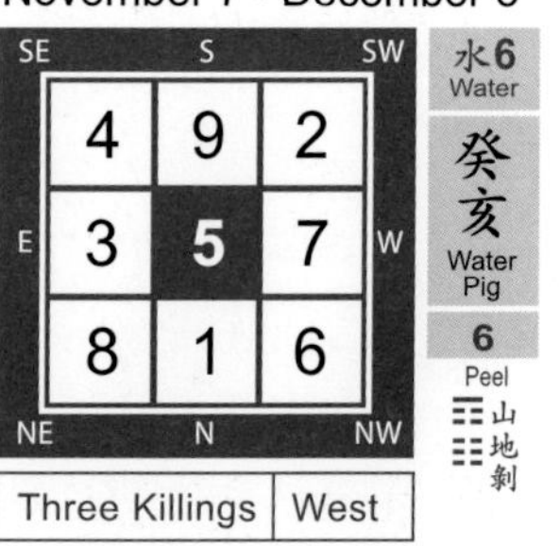

December 6 - January 4

水1 Water
甲子 Wood Rat
1 Earth
坤爲地

SE	S	SW
3	8	1
2	4	6
7	9	5

JANUARY 2048 癸丑

Xuan Kong Element 玄空五行	山火賁 Beauty	Period Luck 卦運	Monthly Star 月星
Water 水6		8	6

SUNDAY	MONDAY	TUESDAY	WEDNESDAY	THURSDAY	FRIDAY	SATURDAY
			木8 Wood 7 Consistency 庚午 Metal Horse 雷風恆 **1** 9 十六	金9 Metal 8 Litigation 辛未 Metal Goat 天水訟 **2** 3 十七	水1 Water 9 Officer 壬申 Water Monkey 地水師 **3** 7 十八	火2 Fire 1 Gradual Progress 癸酉 Water Rooster 風山漸 **4** 7 十九
火7 Fire 2 Obstruction 甲戌 Wood Dog 水山蹇 **5** 2 二十	木3 Wood 3 Advancement 乙亥 Wood Pig 火地晉 **6** 3 廿一	水6 Water 4 Nourish 丙子 Fire Rat 山雷頤 **7** 3 廿二	金4 Metal 5 Following 丁丑 Fire Ox 澤雷隨 **8** 7 廿三	木8 Wood 6 Abundance 戊寅 Earth Tiger 雷火豐 **9** 6 廿四	火7 Fire 7 Regulate 己卯 Earth Rabbit 水澤節 **10** 8 廿五	水1 Water 8 Unity 庚辰 Metal Dragon 地天泰 **11** 9 廿六
木3 Wood 9 Great Reward 辛巳 Metal Snake 火天大有 **12** 7 廿七	火2 Fire 1 Wind 壬午 Water Horse 巽爲風 **13** 1 廿八	金4 Metal 2 Trap 癸未 Water Goat 澤水困 **14** 8 廿九	木3 Wood 3 Not Yet Accomplished 甲申 Wood Monkey 火水未濟 **15** 9 十二月初一	金9 Metal 4 Retreat 乙酉 Wood Rooster 天山遯 **16** 4 初二	水6 Water 5 Mountain 丙戌 Fire Dog 艮爲山 **17** 1 初三	木8 Wood 6 Delight 丁亥 Fire Pig 雷地豫 **18** 8 初四
火7 Fire 7 Beginning 戊子 Earth Rat 水雷屯 **19** 4 初五	金9 Metal 8 Without Wrongdoing 己丑 Earth Ox 天雷無妄 **20** 2 初六	木3 Wood 9 Fire 庚寅 Metal Tiger 離爲火 **21** 1 初七	火2 Fire 1 Sincerity 辛卯 Metal Rabbit 風澤中孚 **22** 3 初八	水6 Water 2 Big Livestock 壬辰 Water Dragon 山天大畜 **23** 4 初九	金4 Metal 3 Eliminating 癸巳 Water Snake 澤天夬 **24** 6 初十	金9 Metal 4 Heaven 甲午 Wood Horse 乾爲天 **25** 1 十一
火7 Fire 5 Well 乙未 Wood Goat 水風井 **26** 6 十二	木8 Wood 6 Relief 丙申 Fire Monkey 雷水解 **27** 4 十三	金4 Metal 7 Influence 丁酉 Fire Rooster 澤山咸 **28** 9 十四	水1 Water 8 Humility 戊戌 Earth Dog 地山謙 **29** 6 十五	火2 Fire 9 Observation 己亥 Earth Pig 風地觀 **30** 2 十六	火2 Fire 1 Increasing 庚子 Metal Rat 風雷益 **31** 9 十七	

FEBRUARY 2048 甲寅

Xuan Kong Element 玄空五行	水火既濟 Accomplished	Period Luck 卦運	Monthly Star 月星
Fire 火7		9	5

SUNDAY	MONDAY	TUESDAY	WEDNESDAY	THURSDAY	FRIDAY	SATURDAY
						水1 Water 2 Dimming Light 辛丑 Metal Ox 地火明夷 **1** 3 十八
金9 Metal 3 Fellowship 壬寅 Water Tiger 天火同人 **2** 7 十九	木8 Wood 4 Marrying Maiden 癸卯 Water Rabbit 雷澤歸妹 **3** 7 二十	木3 Wood 5 Opposition 甲辰 Wood Dragon 火澤睽 **4** 2 廿一	火7 Fire 6 Waiting 乙巳 Wood Snake 水天需 **5** 3 廿二	金4 Metal 7 Great Exceeding 丙午 Fire Horse 澤風大過 **6** 3 廿三	水6 Water 8 Poison 丁未 Fire Goat 山風蠱 **7** 7 廿四	火2 Fire 9 Dispersing 戊申 Earth Monkey 風水渙 **8** 6 廿五
木3 Wood 1 Travelling 己酉 Earth Rooster 火山旅 **9** 8 廿六	金9 Metal 2 Stagnation 庚戌 Metal Dog 天地否 **10** 9 廿七	火7 Fire 3 Alliance 辛亥 Metal Pig 水地比 **11** 7 廿八	木8 Wood 4 Thunder 壬子 Water Rat 震爲雷 **12** 1 廿九	水6 Water 5 Beauty 癸丑 Water Ox 山火賁 **13** 8 三十	火7 Fire 6 Accomplished 甲寅 Wood Tiger 水火既濟 **14** 9 正月初一	水1 Water 7 Arriving 乙卯 Wood Rabbit 地澤臨 **15** 4 初二
金4 Metal 8 Marsh 丙辰 Fire Dragon 兌爲澤 **16** 1 初三	火2 Fire 9 Small Livestock 丁巳 Fire Snake 風天小畜 **17** 8 初四	木3 Wood 1 The Cauldron 戊午 Earth Horse 火風鼎 **18** 4 初五	水1 Water 2 Rising 己未 Earth Goat 地風升 **19** 2 初六	火7 Fire 3 Water 庚申 Metal Monkey 坎爲水 **20** 1 初七	木8 Wood 4 Lesser Exceeding 辛酉 Metal Rooster 雷山小過 **21** 3 初八	金4 Metal 5 Gathering 壬戌 Water Dog 澤地萃 **22** 4 初九
水6 Water 6 Peel 癸亥 Water Pig 山地剝 **23** 6 初十	水1 Water 7 Earth 甲子 Wood Rat 坤爲地 **24** 1 十一	木3 Wood 8 Biting 乙丑 Wood Ox 火雷噬嗑 **25** 6 十二	火2 Fire 9 Family 丙寅 Fire Tiger 風火家人 **26** 4 十三	水6 Water 1 Decreasing 丁卯 Fire Rabbit 山澤損 **27** 9 十四	金9 Metal 2 Tread 戊辰 Earth Dragon 天澤履 **28** 6 十五	木8 Wood 3 Great Strength 己巳 Earth Snake 雷天大壯 **29** 2 十六

MARCH 2048 乙卯

Xuan Kong Element 玄空五行	地澤臨 Arriving	Period Luck 卦運	Monthly Star 月星
Water 水1		4	4

SUNDAY	MONDAY	TUESDAY	WEDNESDAY	THURSDAY	FRIDAY	SATURDAY
木8 Wood [4] Consistency 雷風恆 庚午 Metal Horse **1** 十七 9	金9 Metal [5] Litigation 天水訟 辛未 Metal Goat **2** 十八 3	水1 Water [6] Officer 地水師 壬申 Water Monkey **3** 十九 7	火2 Fire [7] Gradual Progress 風山漸 癸酉 Water Rooster **4** 二十 7	火7 Fire [8] Obstruction 水山蹇 甲戌 Wood Dog **5** 廿一 2	木3 Wood [9] Advancement 火地晉 乙亥 Wood Pig **6** 廿二 3	水6 Water [1] Nourish 山雷頤 丙子 Fire Rat **7** 廿三 3
金4 Metal [2] Following 澤雷隨 丁丑 Fire Ox **8** 廿四 7	木8 Wood [3] Abundance 雷火豐 戊寅 Earth Tiger **9** 廿五 6	火7 Fire [4] Regulate 水澤節 己卯 Earth Rabbit **10** 廿六 8	水1 Water [5] Unity 地天泰 庚辰 Metal Dragon **11** 廿七 9	木3 Wood [6] Great Reward 火天大有 辛巳 Metal Snake **12** 廿八 7	火2 Fire [7] Wind 巽爲風 壬午 Water Horse **13** 廿九 1	金4 Metal [8] Trap 澤水困 癸未 Water Goat **14** 二月初一 8
木3 Wood [9] Not Yet Accomplished 火水未濟 甲申 Wood Monkey **15** 初二 9	金9 Metal [1] Retreat 天山遯 乙酉 Wood Rooster **16** 初三 4	水6 Water [2] Mountain 艮爲山 丙戌 Fire Dog **17** 初四 1	木8 Wood [3] Delight 雷地豫 丁亥 Fire Pig **18** 初五 8	火7 Fire [4] Beginning 水雷屯 戊子 Earth Rat **19** 初六 4	金9 Metal [5] Without Wrongdoing 天雷無妄 己丑 Earth Ox **20** 初七 2	木3 Wood [6] Fire 離爲火 庚寅 Metal Tiger **21** 初八 1
火2 Fire [7] Sincerity 風澤中孚 辛卯 Metal Rabbit **22** 初九 3	水6 Water [8] Big Livestock 山天大畜 壬辰 Water Dragon **23** 初十 4	金4 Metal [9] Eliminating 澤天夬 癸巳 Water Snake **24** 十一 6	金9 Metal [1] Heaven 乾爲天 甲午 Wood Horse **25** 十二 1	火7 Fire [2] Well 水風井 乙未 Wood Goat **26** 十三 6	木8 Wood [3] Relief 雷水解 丙申 Fire Monkey **27** 十四 4	金4 Metal [4] Influence 澤山咸 丁酉 Fire Rooster **28** 十五 9
水1 Water [5] Humility 地山謙 戊戌 Earth Dog **29** 十六 6	火2 Fire [6] Observation 風地觀 己亥 Earth Pig **30** 十七 2	火2 Fire [7] Increasing 風雷益 庚子 Metal Rat **31** 十八 9				

APRIL 2048 丙辰

Xuan Kong Element 玄空五行	兌爲澤 Marsh	Period Luck 卦運	Monthly Star 月星
Metal 金4		1	3

SUNDAY	MONDAY	TUESDAY	WEDNESDAY	THURSDAY	FRIDAY	SATURDAY
			水1 Water [8] Dimming Light 地火明夷 辛丑 Metal Ox **1** 十九 3	金9 Metal [9] Fellowship 天火同人 壬寅 Water Tiger **2** 二十 7	木8 Wood [1] Marrying Maiden 雷澤歸妹 癸卯 Water Rabbit **3** 廿一 7	木3 Wood [2] Opposition 火澤睽 甲辰 Wood Dragon **4** 廿二 2
火7 Fire [3] Waiting 水天需 乙巳 Wood Snake **5** 廿三 3	金4 Metal [4] Great Exceeding 澤風大過 丙午 Fire Horse **6** 廿四 3	水6 Water [5] Poison 山風蠱 丁未 Fire Goat **7** 廿五 7	火2 Fire [6] Dispersing 風水渙 戊申 Earth Monkey **8** 廿六 6	木3 Wood [7] Travelling 火山旅 己酉 Earth Rooster **9** 廿七 8	金9 Metal [8] Stagnation 天地否 庚戌 Metal Dog **10** 廿八 9	火7 Fire [9] Alliance 水地比 辛亥 Metal Pig **11** 廿九 7
木8 Wood [1] Thunder 震爲雷 壬子 Water Rat **12** 三十 1	水6 Water [2] Beauty 山火賁 癸丑 Water Ox **13** 三月初一 8	火7 Fire [3] Accomplished 水火既濟 甲寅 Wood Tiger **14** 初二 9	水1 Water [4] Arriving 地澤臨 乙卯 Wood Rabbit **15** 初三 4	金4 Metal [5] Marsh 兌爲澤 丙辰 Fire Dragon **16** 初四 1	火2 Fire [6] Small Livestock 風天小畜 丁巳 Fire Snake **17** 初五 8	木3 Wood [7] The Cauldron 火風鼎 戊午 Earth Horse **18** 初六 4
水1 Water [8] Rising 地風升 己未 Earth Goat **19** 初七 2	火7 Fire [9] Water 坎爲水 庚申 Metal Monkey **20** 初八 1	木8 Wood [1] Lesser Exceeding 雷山小過 辛酉 Metal Rooster **21** 初九 3	金4 Metal [2] Gathering 澤地萃 壬戌 Water Dog **22** 初十 4	水6 Water [3] Peel 山地剝 癸亥 Water Pig **23** 十一 6	水1 Water [4] Earth 坤爲地 甲子 Wood Rat **24** 十二 1	木3 Wood [5] Biting 火雷噬嗑 乙丑 Wood Ox **25** 十三 6
火2 Fire [6] Family 風火家人 丙寅 Fire Tiger **26** 十四 4	水6 Water [7] Decreasing 山澤損 丁卯 Fire Rabbit **27** 十五 9	金9 Metal [8] Tread 天澤履 戊辰 Earth Dragon **28** 十六 6	木8 Wood [9] Great Strength 雷天大壯 己巳 Earth Snake **29** 十七 2	木8 Wood [1] Consistency 雷風恆 庚午 Metal Horse **30** 十八 9		

MAY 2048 丁巳

Xuan Kong Element 玄空五行	風天小畜	Period Luck 卦運	Monthly Star 月星
Fire 火2	Small Livestock	8	2

SUNDAY	MONDAY	TUESDAY	WEDNESDAY	THURSDAY	FRIDAY	SATURDAY
水1 Water · 5 Dimming Light 地火明夷 辛丑 Metal Ox · 3 **31** 十九					金9 Metal · 2 Litigation 天水訟 辛未 Metal Goat · 3 **1** 十九	水1 Water · 3 Officer 地水師 壬申 Water Monkey · 7 **2** 二十
火2 Fire · 4 Gradual Progress 風山漸 癸酉 Water Rooster · 7 **3** 廿一	火7 Fire · 5 Obstruction 水山蹇 甲戌 Wood Dog · 2 **4** 廿二	木3 Wood · 6 Advancement 火地晉 乙亥 Wood Pig · 3 **5** 廿三	水6 Water · 7 Nourish 山雷頤 丙子 Fire Rat · 3 **6** 廿四	金4 Metal · 8 Following 澤雷隨 丁丑 Fire Ox · 7 **7** 廿五	木8 Wood · 9 Abundance 雷火豐 戊寅 Earth Tiger · 6 **8** 廿六	火7 Fire · 1 Regulate 水澤節 己卯 Earth Rabbit · 8 **9** 廿七
水1 Water · 2 Unity 地天泰 庚辰 Metal Dragon · 9 **10** 廿八	木3 Wood · 3 Great Reward 火天大有 辛巳 Metal Snake · 7 **11** 廿九	火2 Fire · 4 Wind 巽爲風 壬午 Water Horse · 1 **12** 三十	金4 Metal · 5 Trap 澤水困 癸未 Water Goat · 8 **13** 四月初一	木3 Wood · 6 Not Yet Accomplished 火水未濟 甲申 Wood Monkey · 9 **14** 初二	金9 Metal · 7 Retreat 天山遯 乙酉 Wood Rooster · 4 **15** 初三	水6 Water · 8 Mountain 艮爲山 丙戌 Fire Dog · 1 **16** 初四
木8 Wood · 9 Delight 雷地豫 丁亥 Fire Pig · 8 **17** 初五	火7 Fire · 1 Beginning 水雷屯 戊子 Earth Rat · 4 **18** 初六	金9 Metal · 2 Without Wrongdoing 天雷無妄 己丑 Earth Ox · 2 **19** 初七	木3 Wood · 3 Fire 離爲火 庚寅 Metal Tiger · 1 **20** 初八	火2 Fire · 4 Sincerity 風澤中孚 辛卯 Metal Rabbit · 3 **21** 初九	水6 Water · 5 Big Livestock 山天大畜 壬辰 Water Dragon · 4 **22** 初十	金4 Metal · 6 Eliminating 澤天夬 癸巳 Water Snake · 6 **23** 十一
金9 Metal · 7 Heaven 乾爲天 甲午 Wood Horse · 1 **24** 十二	火7 Fire · 8 Well 水風井 乙未 Wood Goat · 6 **25** 十三	木8 Wood · 9 Relief 雷水解 丙申 Fire Monkey · 4 **26** 十四	金4 Metal · 1 Influence 澤山咸 丁酉 Fire Rooster · 9 **27** 十五	水1 Water · 2 Humility 地山謙 戊戌 Earth Dog · 6 **28** 十六	火2 Fire · 3 Observation 風地觀 己亥 Earth Pig · 2 **29** 十七	火2 Fire · 4 Increasing 風雷益 庚子 Metal Rat · 9 **30** 十八

JUNE 2048 戊午

Xuan Kong Element 玄空五行	火風鼎	Period Luck 卦運	Monthly Star 月星
Wood 木3	The Cauldron	4	1

SUNDAY	MONDAY	TUESDAY	WEDNESDAY	THURSDAY	FRIDAY	SATURDAY
	金9 Metal · 6 Fellowship 天火同人 壬寅 Water Tiger · 7 **1** 二十	木8 Wood · 7 Marrying Maiden 雷澤歸妹 癸卯 Water Rabbit · 7 **2** 廿一	木3 Wood · 8 Opposition 火澤睽 甲辰 Wood Dragon · 2 **3** 廿二	火7 Fire · 9 Waiting 水天需 乙巳 Wood Snake · 3 **4** 廿三	金4 Metal · 1 Great Exceeding 澤風大過 丙午 Fire Horse · 3 **5** 廿四	水6 Water · 2 Poison 山風蠱 丁未 Fire Goat · 7 **6** 廿五
火2 Fire · 3 Dispersing 風水渙 戊申 Earth Monkey · 6 **7** 廿六	木3 Wood · 4 Travelling 火山旅 己酉 Earth Rooster · 8 **8** 廿七	金9 Metal · 5 Stagnation 天地否 庚戌 Metal Dog · 9 **9** 廿八	火7 Fire · 6 Alliance 水地比 辛亥 Metal Pig · 7 **10** 廿九	木8 Wood · 7 Thunder 震爲雷 壬子 Water Rat · 1 **11** 五月初一	水6 Water · 8 Beauty 山火賁 癸丑 Water Ox · 8 **12** 初二	火7 Fire · 9 Accomplished 水火既濟 甲寅 Wood Tiger · 9 **13** 初三
水1 Water · 1 Arriving 地澤臨 乙卯 Wood Rabbit · 4 **14** 初四	金4 Metal · 2 Marsh 兌爲澤 丙辰 Fire Dragon · 1 **15** 初五	火2 Fire · 3 Small Livestock 風天小畜 丁巳 Fire Snake · 8 **16** 初六	木3 Wood · 4 The Cauldron 火風鼎 戊午 Earth Horse · 4 **17** 初七	水1 Water · 5 Rising 地風升 己未 Earth Goat · 2 **18** 初八	火7 Fire · 6 Water 坎爲水 庚申 Metal Monkey · 1 **19** 初九	木8 Wood · 7/3 Lesser Exceeding 雷山小過 辛酉 Metal Rooster · 3 **20** 初十
金4 Metal · 2 Gathering 澤地萃 壬戌 Water Dog · 4 **21** 十一	水6 Water · 1 Peel 山地剝 癸亥 Water Pig · 6 **22** 十二	水1 Water · 9 Earth 坤爲地 甲子 Wood Rat · 1 **23** 十三	木3 Wood · 8 Biting 火雷噬嗑 乙丑 Wood Ox · 6 **24** 十四	火2 Fire · 7 Family 風火家人 丙寅 Fire Tiger · 4 **25** 十五	水6 Water · 6 Decreasing 山澤損 丁卯 Fire Rabbit · 9 **26** 十六	金9 Metal · 5 Tread 天澤履 戊辰 Earth Dragon · 6 **27** 十七
木8 Wood · 4 Great Strength 雷天大壯 己巳 Earth Snake · 2 **28** 十八	木8 Wood · 3 Consistency 雷風恒 庚午 Metal Horse · 9 **29** 十九	金9 Metal · 2 Litigation 天水訟 辛未 Metal Goat · 3 **30** 二十				

JULY 2048 己未

Xuan Kong Element 玄空五行	地風升 Rising	Period Luck 卦運	Monthly Star 月星
Water 水1		2	9

SUNDAY	MONDAY	TUESDAY	WEDNESDAY	THURSDAY	FRIDAY	SATURDAY
			水1 Water Officer 1 壬申 Water Monkey 地水師 **1** 廿一 7	火2 Fire Gradual Progress 9 癸酉 Water Rooster 風山漸 **2** 廿二 7	火7 Fire Obstruction 8 甲戌 Wood Dog 水山蹇 **3** 廿三 2	木3 Wood Advancement 7 乙亥 Wood Pig 火地晉 **4** 廿四 3
水6 Water Nourish 6 丙子 Fire Rat 山雷頤 **5** 廿五 3	金4 Metal Following 5 丁丑 Fire Ox 澤雷隨 **6** 廿六 7	木8 Wood Abundance 4 戊寅 Earth Tiger 雷火豐 **7** 廿七 6	火7 Fire Regulate 3 己卯 Earth Rabbit 水澤節 **8** 廿八 8	水1 Water Unity 2 庚辰 Metal Dragon 地天泰 **9** 廿九 9	木3 Wood Great Reward 1 辛巳 Metal Snake 火天大有 **10** 三十 7	火2 Fire Wind 9 壬午 Water Horse 巽為風 **11** 六月初一 1
金4 Metal Trap 8 癸未 Water Goat 澤水困 **12** 初二 8	木3 Wood Not Yet Accomplished 7 甲申 Wood Monkey 火水未濟 **13** 初三 9	金9 Metal Retreat 6 乙酉 Wood Rooster 天山遯 **14** 初四 4	水6 Water Mountain 5 丙戌 Fire Dog 艮為山 **15** 初五 1	木8 Wood Delight 4 丁亥 Fire Pig 雷地豫 **16** 初六 8	火7 Fire Beginning 3 戊子 Earth Rat 水雷屯 **17** 初七 4	金9 Metal Without Wrongdoing 2 己丑 Earth Ox 天雷無妄 **18** 初八 2
木3 Wood Fire 1 庚寅 Metal Tiger 離為火 **19** 初九 1	火2 Fire Sincerity 9 辛卯 Metal Rabbit 風澤中孚 **20** 初十 3	水6 Water Big Livestock 8 壬辰 Water Dragon 山天大畜 **21** 十一 4	金4 Metal Eliminating 7 癸巳 Water Snake 澤天夬 **22** 十二 6	金9 Metal Heaven 6 甲午 Wood Horse 乾為天 **23** 十三 1	火7 Fire Well 5 乙未 Wood Goat 水風井 **24** 十四 6	木8 Wood Relief 4 丙申 Fire Monkey 雷水解 **25** 十五 4
金4 Metal Influence 3 丁酉 Fire Rooster 澤山咸 **26** 十六 9	水1 Water Humility 2 戊戌 Earth Dog 地山謙 **27** 十七 6	火2 Fire Observation 1 己亥 Earth Pig 風地觀 **28** 十八 2	火2 Fire Increasing 9 庚子 Metal Rat 風雷益 **29** 十九 9	水1 Water Dimming Light 8 辛丑 Metal Ox 地火明夷 **30** 二十 3	金9 Metal Fellowship 7 壬寅 Water Tiger 天火同人 **31** 廿一 7	

AUGUST 2048 庚申

Xuan Kong Element 玄空五行	坎為水 Water	Period Luck 卦運	Monthly Star 月星
Fire 火7		1	8

SUNDAY	MONDAY	TUESDAY	WEDNESDAY	THURSDAY	FRIDAY	SATURDAY
水1 Water Officer 4 壬申 Water Monkey 地水師 **30** 廿一 7	火2 Fire Gradual Progress 3 癸酉 Water Rooster 風山漸 **31** 廿二 7					木8 Wood Marrying Maiden 6 癸卯 Water Rabbit 雷澤歸妹 **1** 廿二 7
木3 Wood Opposition 5 甲辰 Wood Dragon 火澤睽 **2** 廿三 2	火7 Fire Waiting 4 乙巳 Wood Snake 水天需 **3** 廿四 3	金4 Metal Great Exceeding 3 丙午 Fire Horse 澤風大過 **4** 廿五 3	水6 Water Poison 2 丁未 Fire Goat 山風蠱 **5** 廿六 7	火2 Fire Dispersing 1 戊申 Earth Monkey 風水渙 **6** 廿七 6	木3 Wood Travelling 9 己酉 Earth Rooster 火山旅 **7** 廿八 8	金9 Metal Stagnation 8 庚戌 Metal Dog 天地否 **8** 廿九 9
火7 Fire Alliance 7 辛亥 Metal Pig 水地比 **9** 三十 7	木8 Wood Thunder 6 壬子 Water Rat 震為雷 **10** 七月初一 1	水6 Water Beauty 5 癸丑 Water Ox 山火賁 **11** 初二 8	火7 Fire Accomplished 4 甲寅 Wood Tiger 水火既濟 **12** 初三 9	水1 Water Arriving 3 乙卯 Wood Rabbit 地澤臨 **13** 初四 4	金4 Metal Marsh 2 丙辰 Fire Dragon 兌為澤 **14** 初五 1	火2 Fire Small Livestock 1 丁巳 Fire Snake 風天小畜 **15** 初六 8
木3 Wood The Cauldron 9 戊午 Earth Horse 火風鼎 **16** 初七 4	水1 Water Rising 8 己未 Earth Goat 地風升 **17** 初八 2	火7 Fire Water 7 庚申 Metal Monkey 坎為水 **18** 初九 1	木8 Wood Lesser Exceeding 6 辛酉 Metal Rooster 雷山小過 **19** 初十 3	金4 Metal Gathering 5 壬戌 Water Dog 澤地萃 **20** 十一 4	水6 Water Peel 4 癸亥 Water Pig 山地剝 **21** 十二 6	水1 Water Earth 3 甲子 Wood Rat 坤為地 **22** 十三 1
木3 Wood Biting 2 乙丑 Wood Ox 火雷噬嗑 **23** 十四 6	火2 Fire Family 1 丙寅 Fire Tiger 風火家人 **24** 十五 4	水6 Water Decreasing 9 丁卯 Fire Rabbit 山澤損 **25** 十六 9	金9 Metal Tread 8 戊辰 Earth Dragon 天澤履 **26** 十七 6	木8 Wood Great Strength 7 己巳 Earth Snake 雷天大壯 **27** 十八 2	木8 Wood Consistency 6 庚午 Metal Horse 雷風恆 **28** 十九 9	金9 Metal Litigation 5 辛未 Metal Goat 天水訟 **29** 二十 3

SEPTEMBER 2048 辛酉

Xuan Kong Element 玄空五行	雷山小過 Lesser Exceeding	Period Luck 卦運	Monthly Star 月星
Wood 木8		3	7

SUNDAY	MONDAY	TUESDAY	WEDNESDAY	THURSDAY	FRIDAY	SATURDAY
		1 火7 Fire · 2 Obstruction 水山蹇 甲戌 Wood Dog 2 · 廿三	**2** 木3 Wood · 1 Advancement 火地晉 乙亥 Wood Pig 3 · 廿四	**3** 水6 Water · 9 Nourish 山雷頤 丙子 Fire Rat 3 · 廿五	**4** 金4 Metal · 8 Following 澤雷隨 丁丑 Fire Ox 7 · 廿六	**5** 木8 Wood · 7 Abundance 雷火豐 戊寅 Earth Tiger 6 · 廿七
6 火7 Fire · 6 Regulate 水澤節 己卯 Earth Rabbit 8 · 廿八	**7** 水1 Water · 5 Unity 地天泰 庚辰 Metal Dragon 9 · 廿九	**8** 木3 Wood · 4 Great Reward 火天大有 辛巳 Metal Snake 7 · 八月初一	**9** 火2 Fire · 3 Wind 巽爲風 壬午 Water Horse 1 · 初二	**10** 金4 Metal · 2 Trap 澤水困 癸未 Water Goat 8 · 初三	**11** 木3 Wood · 1 Not Yet Accomplished 火水未濟 甲申 Wood Monkey 9 · 初四	**12** 金9 Metal · 9 Retreat 天山遯 乙酉 Wood Rooster 4 · 初五
13 水6 Water · 8 Mountain 艮爲山 丙戌 Fire Dog 1 · 初六	**14** 木8 Wood · 7 Delight 雷地豫 丁亥 Fire Pig 8 · 初七	**15** 火7 Fire · 6 Beginning 水雷屯 戊子 Earth Rat 4 · 初八	**16** 金9 Metal · 5 Without Wrongdoing 天雷無妄 己丑 Earth Ox 2 · 初九	**17** 木3 Wood · 4 Fire 離爲火 庚寅 Metal Tiger 1 · 初十	**18** 火2 Fire · 3 Sincerity 風澤中孚 辛卯 Metal Rabbit 3 · 十一	**19** 水6 Water · 2 Big Livestock 山天大畜 壬辰 Water Dragon 4 · 十二
20 金4 Metal · 1 Eliminating 澤天夬 癸巳 Water Snake 6 · 十三	**21** 金9 Metal · 9 Heaven 乾爲天 甲午 Wood Horse 1 · 十四	**22** 火7 Fire · 8 Well 水風井 乙未 Wood Goat 6 · 十五	**23** 木8 Wood · 7 Relief 雷水解 丙申 Fire Monkey 4 · 十六	**24** 金4 Metal · 6 Influence 澤山咸 丁酉 Fire Rooster 9 · 十七	**25** 水1 Water · 5 Humility 地山謙 戊戌 Earth Dog 6 · 十八	**26** 火2 Fire · 4 Observation 風地觀 己亥 Earth Pig 2 · 十九
27 火2 Fire · 3 Increasing 風雷益 庚子 Metal Rat 9 · 二十	**28** 水1 Water · 2 Dimming Light 地火明夷 辛丑 Metal Ox 3 · 廿一	**29** 金9 Metal · 1 Fellowship 天火同人 壬寅 Water Tiger 7 · 廿二	**30** 木8 Wood · 9 Marrying Maiden 雷澤歸妹 癸卯 Water Rabbit 7 · 廿三			

OCTOBER 2048 壬戌

Xuan Kong Element 玄空五行	澤地萃 Gathering	Period Luck 卦運	Monthly Star 月星
Metal 金4		4	6

SUNDAY	MONDAY	TUESDAY	WEDNESDAY	THURSDAY	FRIDAY	SATURDAY
				1 木3 Wood · 8 Opposition 火澤睽 甲辰 Wood Dragon 2 · 廿四	**2** 火7 Fire · 7 Waiting 水天需 乙巳 Wood Snake 3 · 廿五	**3** 金4 Metal · 6 Great Exceeding 澤風大過 丙午 Fire Horse 3 · 廿六
4 水6 Water · 5 Poison 山風蠱 丁未 Fire Goat 7 · 廿七	**5** 火2 Fire · 4 Dispersing 風水渙 戊申 Earth Monkey 6 · 廿八	**6** 木3 Wood · 3 Travelling 火山旅 己酉 Earth Rooster 8 · 廿九	**7** 金9 Metal · 2 Stagnation 天地否 庚戌 Metal Dog 9 · 三十	**8** 火7 Fire · 1 Alliance 水地比 辛亥 Metal Pig 7 · 九月初一	**9** 木8 Wood · 9 Thunder 震爲雷 壬子 Water Rat 1 · 初二	**10** 水6 Water · 8 Beauty 山火賁 癸丑 Water Ox 8 · 初三
11 火7 Fire · 7 Accomplished 水火既濟 甲寅 Wood Tiger 9 · 初四	**12** 水1 Water · 6 Arriving 地澤臨 乙卯 Wood Rabbit 4 · 初五	**13** 金4 Metal · 5 Marsh 兑爲澤 丙辰 Fire Dragon 1 · 初六	**14** 火2 Fire · 4 Small Livestock 風天小畜 丁巳 Fire Snake 8 · 初七	**15** 木3 Wood · 3 The Cauldron 火風鼎 戊午 Earth Horse 4 · 初八	**16** 水1 Water · 2 Rising 地風升 己未 Earth Goat 2 · 初九	**17** 火7 Fire · 1 Water 坎爲水 庚申 Metal Monkey 1 · 初十
18 木8 Wood · 9 Lesser Exceeding 雷山小過 辛酉 Metal Rooster 3 · 十一	**19** 金4 Metal · 8 Gathering 澤地萃 壬戌 Water Dog 4 · 十二	**20** 水6 Water · 7 Peel 山地剝 癸亥 Water Pig 6 · 十三	**21** 水1 Water · 6 Earth 坤爲地 甲子 Wood Rat 1 · 十四	**22** 木3 Wood · 5 Biting 火雷噬嗑 乙丑 Wood Ox 6 · 十五	**23** 火2 Fire · 4 Family 風火家人 丙寅 Fire Tiger 4 · 十六	**24** 水6 Water · 3 Decreasing 山澤損 丁卯 Fire Rabbit 9 · 十七
25 金9 Metal · 2 Tread 天澤履 戊辰 Earth Dragon 6 · 十八	**26** 木8 Wood · 1 Great Strength 雷天大壯 己巳 Earth Snake 2 · 十九	**27** 木8 Wood · 9 Consistency 雷風恆 庚午 Metal Horse 9 · 二十	**28** 金9 Metal · 8 Litigation 天水訟 辛未 Metal Goat 3 · 廿一	**29** 水1 Water · 7 Officer 地水師 壬申 Water Monkey 7 · 廿二	**30** 火2 Fire · 6 Gradual Progress 風山漸 癸酉 Water Rooster 7 · 廿三	**31** 火7 Fire · 5 Obstruction 水山蹇 甲戌 Wood Dog 2 · 廿四

NOVEMBER 2048 癸亥

Xuan Kong Element 玄空五行	山地剝 Peel	Period Luck 卦運	Monthly Star 月星
Water 水6		6	5

SUNDAY	MONDAY	TUESDAY	WEDNESDAY	THURSDAY	FRIDAY	SATURDAY
木3 Wood 4 Advancement 火地晉 乙亥 Wood Pig 1 3 廿五	水6 Water 3 Nourish 山雷頤 丙子 Fire Rat 2 3 廿六	金4 Metal 2 Following 澤雷隨 丁丑 Fire Ox 3 7 廿七	木8 Wood 1 Abundance 雷火豐 戊寅 Earth Tiger 4 6 廿八	火7 Fire 9 Regulate 水澤節 己卯 Earth Rabbit 5 8 廿九	水1 Water 8 Unity 地天泰 庚辰 Metal Dragon 6 9 十月初一	木3 Wood 7 Great Reward 火天大有 辛巳 Metal Snake 7 7 初二
火2 Fire 6 Wind 巽爲風 壬午 Water Horse 8 1 初三	金4 Metal 5 Trap 澤水困 癸未 Water Goat 9 8 初四	木3 Wood 4 Not Yet Accomplished 火水未濟 甲申 Wood Monkey 10 9 初五	金9 Metal 3 Retreat 天山遯 乙酉 Wood Rooster 11 4 初六	水6 Water 2 Mountain 艮爲山 丙戌 Fire Dog 12 1 初七	木8 Wood 1 Delight 雷地豫 丁亥 Fire Pig 13 8 初八	火7 Fire 9 Beginning 水雷屯 戊子 Earth Rat 14 4 初九
金9 Metal 8 Without Wrongdoing 天雷無妄 己丑 Earth Ox 15 2 初十	木3 Wood 7 Fire 離爲火 庚寅 Metal Tiger 16 1 十一	火2 Fire 6 Sincerity 風澤中孚 辛卯 Metal Rabbit 17 3 十二	水6 Water 5 Big Livestock 山天大畜 壬辰 Water Dragon 18 4 十三	金4 Metal 4 Eliminating 澤天夬 癸巳 Water Snake 19 6 十四	金9 Metal 3 Heaven 乾爲天 甲午 Wood Horse 20 1 十五	火7 Fire 2 Well 水風井 乙未 Wood Goat 21 6 十六
木8 Wood 1 Relief 雷水解 丙申 Fire Monkey 22 4 十七	金4 Metal 9 Influence 澤山咸 丁酉 Fire Rooster 23 9 十八	水1 Water 8 Humility 地山謙 戊戌 Earth Dog 24 6 十九	火2 Fire 7 Observation 風地觀 己亥 Earth Pig 25 2 二十	火2 Fire 6 Increasing 風雷益 庚子 Metal Rat 26 9 廿一	水1 Water 5 Dimming Light 地火明夷 辛丑 Metal Ox 27 3 廿二	金9 Metal 4 Fellowship 天火同人 壬寅 Water Tiger 28 7 廿三
木8 Wood 3 Marrying Maiden 雷澤歸妹 癸卯 Water Rabbit 29 7 廿四	木3 Wood 2 Opposition 火澤睽 甲辰 Wood Dragon 30 2 廿五					

DECEMBER 2048 甲子

Xuan Kong Element 玄空五行	坤爲地 Earth	Period Luck 卦運	Monthly Star 月星
Water 水1		1	4

SUNDAY	MONDAY	TUESDAY	WEDNESDAY	THURSDAY	FRIDAY	SATURDAY
		火7 Fire 1 Waiting 水天需 乙巳 Wood Snake 1 3 廿六	金4 Metal 9 Great Exceeding 澤風大過 丙午 Fire Horse 2 3 廿七	水6 Water 8 Poison 山風蠱 丁未 Fire Goat 3 7 廿八	火2 Fire 7 Dispersing 風水渙 戊申 Earth Monkey 4 6 廿九	木3 Wood 6 Travelling 火山旅 己酉 Earth Rooster 5 8 十一月初一
金9 Metal 5 Stagnation 天地否 庚戌 Metal Dog 6 9 初二	火7 Fire 4 Alliance 水地比 辛亥 Metal Pig 7 7 初三	木8 Wood 3 Thunder 震爲雷 壬子 Water Rat 8 1 初四	水6 Water 2 Beauty 山火賁 癸丑 Water Ox 9 8 初五	火7 Fire 1 Accomplished 水火既濟 甲寅 Wood Tiger 10 9 初六	水1 Water 9 Arriving 地澤臨 乙卯 Wood Rabbit 11 4 初七	金4 Metal 8 Marsh 兌爲澤 丙辰 Fire Dragon 12 1 初八
火2 Fire 7 Small Livestock 風天小畜 丁巳 Fire Snake 13 8 初九	木3 Wood 6 The Cauldron 火風鼎 戊午 Earth Horse 14 4 初十	水1 Water 5 Rising 地風升 己未 Earth Goat 15 2 十一	火7 Fire 4 Water 坎爲水 庚申 Metal Monkey 16 1 十二	木8 Wood 3 Lesser Exceeding 雷山小過 辛酉 Metal Rooster 17 3 十三	金4 Metal 2 Gathering 澤地萃 壬戌 Water Dog 18 4 十四	水6 Water 1 Peel 山地剝 癸亥 Water Pig 19 6 十五
水1 Water 9 Earth 坤爲地 甲子 Wood Rat 20 1 十六	木3 Wood 8/5 Biting 火雷噬嗑 乙丑 Wood Ox 21 6 十七	火2 Fire 6 Family 風火家人 丙寅 Fire Tiger 22 4 十八	水6 Water 7 Decreasing 山澤損 丁卯 Fire Rabbit 23 9 十九	金9 Metal 8 Tread 天澤履 戊辰 Earth Dragon 24 6 二十	木8 Wood 9 Great Strength 雷天大壯 己巳 Earth Snake 25 2 廿一	木8 Wood 1 Consistency 雷風恆 庚午 Metal Horse 26 9 廿二
金9 Metal 2 Litigation 天水訟 辛未 Metal Goat 27 3 廿三	水1 Water 3 Officer 地水師 壬申 Water Monkey 28 7 廿四	火2 Fire 4 Gradual Progress 風山漸 癸酉 Water Rooster 29 7 廿五	火7 Fire 5 Obstruction 水山蹇 甲戌 Wood Dog 30 2 廿六	木3 Wood 6 Advancement 火地晉 乙亥 Wood Pig 31 3 廿七		

2049 己巳

(*Ji Si*) Earth Snake

2049 己巳 *(Ji Si)* Earth Snake

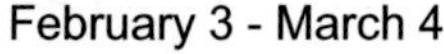

January 5 - February 2

木3 Wood
乙丑 Wood Ox
6
Biting
火雷噬嗑

Three Killings | East

February 3 - March 4

火2 Fire
丙寅 Fire Tiger
4
Family
風火家人

Three Killings | North

March 5 - April 3

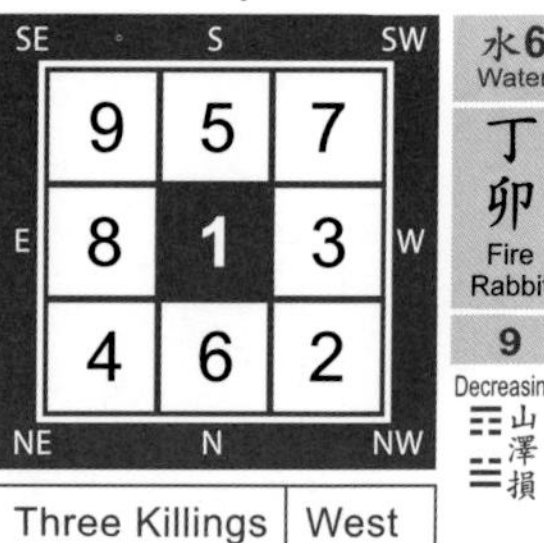

Three Killings | West

April 4 - May 4

金9 Metal
戊辰 Earth Dragon
6
Tread
天澤履

Three Killings | South

May 5 - June 4

木8 Wood
己巳 Earth Snake
2
Great Strength
雷天大壯

Three Killings | East

June 5 - July 5

木8 Wood
庚午 Metal Horse
9
Consistency
雷風恆

Three Killings | North

July 6 - August 6

金9 Metal
辛未 Metal Goat
3
Litigation
天水訟

Three Killings | West

August 7 - September 6

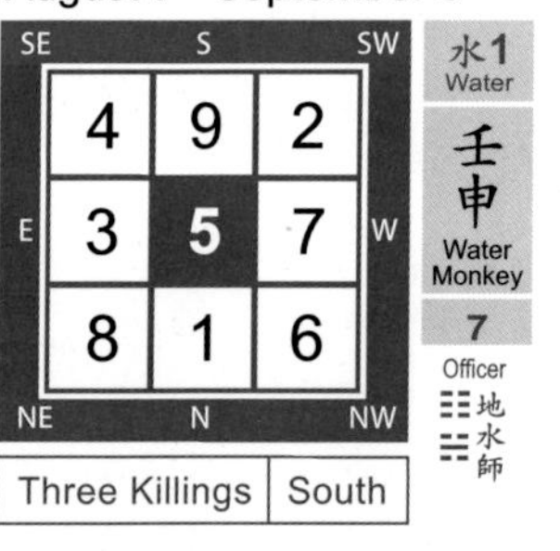

水1 Water
壬申 Water Monkey
7
Officer
地水師

Three Killings | South

September 7 - October 7

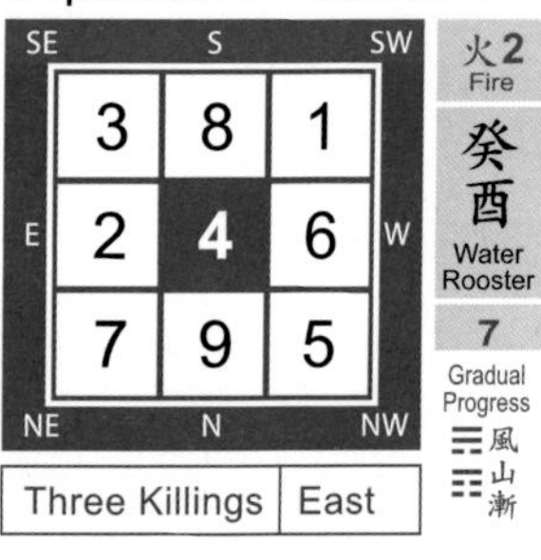

火2 Fire
癸酉 Water Rooster
7
Gradual Progress
風山漸

Three Killings | East

October 8 - November 6

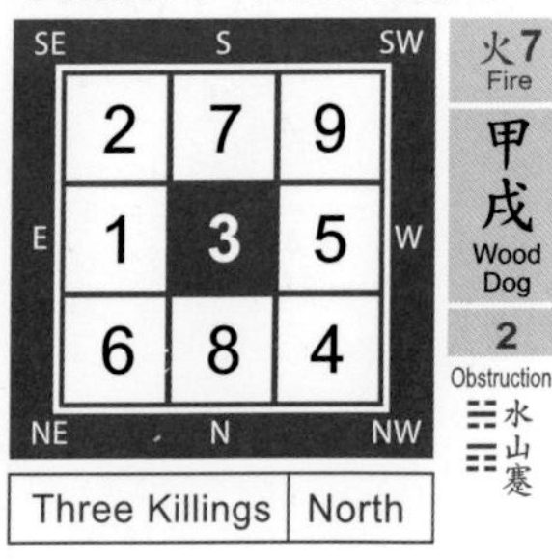

火7 Fire
甲戌 Wood Dog
2
Obstruction
水山蹇

Three Killings | North

November 7 - December 6

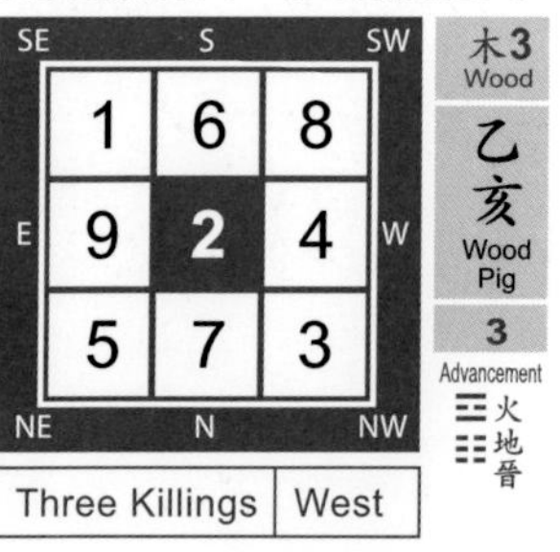

木3 Wood
乙亥 Wood Pig
3
Advancement
火地晉

Three Killings | West

December 7 - January 4

水6 Water
丙子 Fire Rat
3
Nourish
山雷頤

Three Killings | South

JANUARY 2049 乙丑

Xuan Kong Element 玄空五行	火雷噬嗑 Biting	Period Luck 卦運	Monthly Star 月星
Wood 木3		6	3

SUNDAY	MONDAY	TUESDAY	WEDNESDAY	THURSDAY	FRIDAY	SATURDAY
金4 Metal · 1 Great Exceeding 丙午 Fire Horse 澤風大過 31 3 · 廿八					水6 Water · 7 Nourish 丙子 Fire Rat 山雷頤 1 3 · 廿八	金4 Metal · 8 Following 丁丑 Fire Ox 澤雷隨 2 7 · 廿九
木8 Wood · 9 Abundance 戊寅 Earth Tiger 雷火豐 3 6 · 三十	火7 Fire · 1 Regulate 己卯 Earth Rabbit 水澤節 4 8 · 十二月初一	水1 Water · 2 Unity 庚辰 Metal Dragon 地天泰 5 9 · 初二	木3 Wood · 3 Great Reward 辛巳 Metal Snake 火天大有 6 7 · 初三	火2 Fire · 4 Wind 壬午 Water Horse 巽爲風 7 1 · 初四	金4 Metal · 5 Trap 癸未 Water Goat 澤水困 8 8 · 初五	木3 Wood · 6 Not Yet Accomplished 甲申 Wood Monkey 火水未濟 9 9 · 初六
金9 Metal · 7 Retreat 乙酉 Wood Rooster 天山遯 10 4 · 初七	水6 Water · 8 Mountain 丙戌 Fire Dog 艮爲山 11 1 · 初八	木8 Wood · 9 Delight 丁亥 Fire Pig 雷地豫 12 8 · 初九	火7 Fire · 1 Beginning 戊子 Earth Rat 水雷屯 13 4 · 初十	金9 Metal · 2 Without Wrongdoing 己丑 Earth Ox 天雷無妄 14 2 · 十一	木3 Wood · 3 Fire 庚寅 Metal Tiger 離爲火 15 1 · 十二	火2 Fire · 4 Sincerity 辛卯 Metal Rabbit 風澤中孚 16 3 · 十三
水6 Water · 5 Big Livestock 壬辰 Water Dragon 山天大畜 17 4 · 十四	金4 Metal · 6 Eliminating 癸巳 Water Snake 澤天夬 18 6 · 十五	金9 Metal · 7 Heaven 甲午 Wood Horse 乾爲天 19 1 · 十六	火7 Fire · 8 Well 乙未 Wood Goat 水風井 20 6 · 十七	木8 Wood · 9 Relief 丙申 Fire Monkey 雷水解 21 4 · 十八	金4 Metal · 1 Influence 丁酉 Fire Rooster 澤山咸 22 9 · 十九	水1 Water · 2 Humility 戊戌 Earth Dog 地山謙 23 6 · 二十
火2 Fire · 3 Observation 己亥 Earth Pig 風地觀 24 2 · 廿一	火2 Fire · 4 Increasing 庚子 Metal Rat 風雷益 25 9 · 廿二	水1 Water · 5 Dimming Light 辛丑 Metal Ox 地火明夷 26 3 · 廿三	金9 Metal · 6 Fellowship 壬寅 Water Tiger 天火同人 27 7 · 廿四	木8 Wood · 7 Marrying Maiden 癸卯 Water Rabbit 雷澤歸妹 28 7 · 廿五	木3 Wood · 8 Opposition 甲辰 Wood Dragon 火澤睽 29 2 · 廿六	火7 Fire · 9 Waiting 乙巳 Wood Snake 水天需 30 3 · 廿七

FEBRUARY 2049 丙寅

Xuan Kong Element 玄空五行	風火家人 Family	Period Luck 卦運	Monthly Star 月星
Fire 火2		4	2

SUNDAY	MONDAY	TUESDAY	WEDNESDAY	THURSDAY	FRIDAY	SATURDAY
	水6 Water · 2 Poison 丁未 Fire Goat 山風蠱 1 7 · 廿九	火2 Fire · 3 Dispersing 戊申 Earth Monkey 風水渙 2 6 · 正月初一	木3 Wood · 4 Travelling 己酉 Earth Rooster 火山旅 3 8 · 初二	金9 Metal · 5 Stagnation 庚戌 Metal Dog 天地否 4 9 · 初三	火7 Fire · 6 Alliance 辛亥 Metal Pig 水地比 5 7 · 初四	木8 Wood · 7 Thunder 壬子 Water Rat 震爲雷 6 1 · 初五
水6 Water · 8 Beauty 癸丑 Water Ox 山火賁 7 8 · 初六	火7 Fire · 9 Accomplished 甲寅 Wood Tiger 水火既濟 8 9 · 初七	水1 Water · 1 Arriving 乙卯 Wood Rabbit 地澤臨 9 4 · 初八	金4 Metal · 2 Marsh 丙辰 Fire Dragon 兌爲澤 10 1 · 初九	火2 Fire · 3 Small Livestock 丁巳 Fire Snake 風天小畜 11 8 · 初十	木3 Wood · 4 The Cauldron 戊午 Earth Horse 火風鼎 12 4 · 十一	水1 Water · 5 Rising 己未 Earth Goat 地風升 13 2 · 十二
火7 Fire · 6 Water 庚申 Metal Monkey 坎爲水 14 1 · 十三	木8 Wood · 7 Lesser Exceeding 辛酉 Metal Rooster 雷山小過 15 3 · 十四	金4 Metal · 8 Gathering 壬戌 Water Dog 澤地萃 16 4 · 十五	水6 Water · 9 Peel 癸亥 Water Pig 山地剝 17 6 · 十六	水1 Water · 1 Earth 甲子 Wood Rat 坤爲地 18 1 · 十七	木3 Wood · 2 Biting 乙丑 Wood Ox 火雷噬嗑 19 6 · 十八	火2 Fire · 3 Family 丙寅 Fire Tiger 風火家人 20 4 · 十九
水6 Water · 4 Decreasing 丁卯 Fire Rabbit 山澤損 21 9 · 二十	金9 Metal · 5 Tread 戊辰 Earth Dragon 天澤履 22 6 · 廿一	木8 Wood · 6 Great Strength 己巳 Earth Snake 雷天大壯 23 2 · 廿二	木8 Wood · 7 Consistency 庚午 Metal Horse 雷風恒 24 9 · 廿三	金9 Metal · 8 Litigation 辛未 Metal Goat 天水訟 25 3 · 廿四	水1 Water · 9 Officer 壬申 Water Monkey 地水師 26 7 · 廿五	火2 Fire · 1 Gradual Progress 癸酉 Water Rooster 風山漸 27 7 · 廿六
火7 Fire · 2 Obstruction 甲戌 Wood Dog 水山蹇 28 2 · 廿七						

MARCH 2049 丁卯

Xuan Kong Element 玄空五行	山澤損 Decreasing	Period Luck 卦運	Monthly Star 月星
Water 水6		9	1

SUNDAY	MONDAY	TUESDAY	WEDNESDAY	THURSDAY	FRIDAY	SATURDAY
	木3 Wood 3 Advancement 乙亥 Wood Pig 火地晉 1 廿八 3	水6 Water 4 Nourish 丙子 Fire Rat 山雷頤 2 廿九 3	金4 Metal 5 Following 丁丑 Fire Ox 澤雷隨 3 三十 7	木8 Wood 6 Abundance 戊寅 Earth Tiger 雷火豐 4 二月初一 6	火7 Fire 7 Regulate 己卯 Earth Rabbit 水澤節 5 初二 8	水1 Water 8 Unity 庚辰 Metal Dragon 地天泰 6 初三 9
木3 Wood 9 Great Reward 辛巳 Metal Snake 火天大有 7 初四 7	火2 Fire 1 Wind 壬午 Water Horse 巽為風 8 初五 1	金4 Metal 2 Trap 癸未 Water Goat 澤水困 9 初六 8	木3 Wood 3 Not Yet Accomplished 甲申 Wood Monkey 火水未濟 10 初七 9	金9 Metal 4 Retreat 乙酉 Wood Rooster 天山遯 11 初八 4	水6 Water 5 Mountain 丙戌 Fire Dog 艮為山 12 初九 1	木8 Wood 6 Delight 丁亥 Fire Pig 雷地豫 13 初十 8
火7 Fire 7 Beginning 戊子 Earth Rat 水雷屯 14 十一 4	金9 Metal 8 Without Wrongdoing 己丑 Earth Ox 天雷無妄 15 十二 2	木3 Wood 9 Fire 庚寅 Metal Tiger 離為火 16 十三 1	火2 Fire 1 Sincerity 辛卯 Metal Rabbit 風澤中孚 17 十四 3	水6 Water 2 Big Livestock 壬辰 Water Dragon 山天大畜 18 十五 4	金4 Metal 3 Eliminating 癸巳 Water Snake 澤天夬 19 十六 6	金9 Metal 4 Heaven 甲午 Wood Horse 乾為天 20 十七 1
火7 Fire 5 Well 乙未 Wood Goat 水風井 21 十八 6	木8 Wood 6 Relief 丙申 Fire Monkey 雷水解 22 十九 4	金4 Metal 7 Influence 丁酉 Fire Rooster 澤山咸 23 二十 9	水1 Water 8 Humility 戊戌 Earth Dog 地山謙 24 廿一 6	火2 Fire 9 Observation 己亥 Earth Pig 風地觀 25 廿二 2	火2 Fire 1 Increasing 庚子 Metal Rat 風雷益 26 廿三 9	水1 Water 2 Dimming Light 辛丑 Metal Ox 地火明夷 27 廿四 3
金9 Metal 3 Fellowship 壬寅 Water Tiger 天火同人 28 廿五 7	木8 Wood 4 Marrying Maiden 癸卯 Water Rabbit 雷澤歸妹 29 廿六 7	木3 Wood 5 Opposition 甲辰 Wood Dragon 火澤睽 30 廿七 2	火7 Fire 6 Waiting 乙巳 Wood Snake 水天需 31 廿八 3			

APRIL 2049 戊辰

Xuan Kong Element 玄空五行	天澤履 Tread	Period Luck 卦運	Monthly Star 月星
Metal 金9		6	9

SUNDAY	MONDAY	TUESDAY	WEDNESDAY	THURSDAY	FRIDAY	SATURDAY
				金4 Metal 7 Great Exceeding 丙午 Fire Horse 澤風大過 1 廿九 3	水6 Water 8 Poison 丁未 Fire Goat 山風蠱 2 三月初一 7	火2 Fire 9 Dispersing 戊申 Earth Monkey 風水渙 3 初二 6
木3 Wood 1 Travelling 己酉 Earth Rooster 火山旅 4 初三 8	金9 Metal 2 Stagnation 庚戌 Metal Dog 天地否 5 初四 9	火7 Fire 3 Alliance 辛亥 Metal Pig 水地比 6 初五 7	木8 Wood 4 Thunder 壬子 Water Rat 震為雷 7 初六 1	水6 Water 5 Beauty 癸丑 Water Ox 山火賁 8 初七 8	火7 Fire 6 Accomplished 甲寅 Wood Tiger 水火既濟 9 初八 9	水1 Water 7 Arriving 乙卯 Wood Rabbit 地澤臨 10 初九 4
金4 Metal 8 Marsh 丙辰 Fire Dragon 兌為澤 11 初十 1	火2 Fire 9 Small Livestock 丁巳 Fire Snake 風天小畜 12 十一 8	木3 Wood 1 The Cauldron 戊午 Earth Horse 火風鼎 13 十二 4	水1 Water 2 Rising 己未 Earth Goat 地風升 14 十三 2	火7 Fire 3 Water 庚申 Metal Monkey 坎為水 15 十四 1	木8 Wood 4 Lesser Exceeding 辛酉 Metal Rooster 雷山小過 16 十五 3	金4 Metal 5 Gathering 壬戌 Water Dog 澤地萃 17 十六 4
水6 Water 6 Peel 癸亥 Water Pig 山地剝 18 十七 6	水1 Water 7 Earth 甲子 Wood Rat 坤為地 19 十八 1	木3 Wood 8 Biting 乙丑 Wood Ox 火雷噬嗑 20 十九 6	火2 Fire 9 Family 丙寅 Fire Tiger 風火家人 21 二十 4	水6 Water 1 Decreasing 丁卯 Fire Rabbit 山澤損 22 廿一 9	金9 Metal 2 Tread 戊辰 Earth Dragon 天澤履 23 廿二 6	木8 Wood 3 Great Strength 己巳 Earth Snake 雷天大壯 24 廿三 2
木8 Wood 4 Consistency 庚午 Metal Horse 雷風恆 25 廿四 9	金9 Metal 5 Litigation 辛未 Metal Goat 天水訟 26 廿五 3	水1 Water 6 Officer 壬申 Water Monkey 地水師 27 廿六 7	火2 Fire 7 Gradual Progress 癸酉 Water Rooster 風山漸 28 廿七 7	火7 Fire 8 Obstruction 甲戌 Wood Dog 水山蹇 29 廿八 2	木3 Wood 9 Advancement 乙亥 Wood Pig 火地晉 30 廿九 3	

MAY 2049 己巳

Xuan Kong Element 玄空五行	雷天大壯 Great Strength	Period Luck 卦運	Monthly Star 月星
Wood 木8		2	8

SUNDAY	MONDAY	TUESDAY	WEDNESDAY	THURSDAY	FRIDAY	SATURDAY
火7 Fire [3] 乙巳 Wood Snake Waiting 水天需 30 廿九 3	金4 Metal [4] 丙午 Fire Horse Great Exceeding 澤風大過 31 五月初一 3					水6 Water [1] 丙子 Fire Rat Nourish 山雷頤 1 三十 3
金4 Metal [2] 丁丑 Fire Ox Following 澤雷隨 2 四月初一 7	木8 Wood [3] 戊寅 Earth Tiger Abundance 雷火豐 3 初二 6	火7 Fire [4] 己卯 Earth Rabbit Regulate 水澤節 4 初三 8	水1 Water [5] 庚辰 Metal Dragon Unity 地天泰 5 初四 9	木3 Wood [6] 辛巳 Metal Snake Great Reward 火天大有 6 初五 7	火2 Fire [7] 壬午 Water Horse Wind 巽為風 7 初六 1	金4 Metal [8] 癸未 Water Goat Trap 澤水困 8 初七 8
木3 Wood [9] 甲申 Wood Monkey Not Yet Accomplished 火水未濟 9 初八 9	金9 Metal [1] 乙酉 Wood Rooster Retreat 天山遯 10 初九 4	水6 Water [2] 丙戌 Fire Dog Mountain 艮為山 11 初十 1	木8 Wood [3] 丁亥 Fire Pig Delight 雷地豫 12 十一 8	火7 Fire [4] 戊子 Earth Rat Beginning 水雷屯 13 十二 4	金9 Metal [5] 己丑 Earth Ox Without Wrongdoing 天雷無妄 14 十三 2	木3 Wood [6] 庚寅 Metal Tiger Fire 離為火 15 十四 1
火2 Fire [7] 辛卯 Metal Rabbit Sincerity 風澤中孚 16 十五 3	水6 Water [8] 壬辰 Water Dragon Big Livestock 山天大畜 17 十六 4	金4 Metal [9] 癸巳 Water Snake Eliminating 澤天夬 18 十七 6	金9 Metal [1] 甲午 Wood Horse Heaven 乾為天 19 十八 1	火7 Fire [2] 乙未 Wood Goat Well 水風井 20 十九 6	木8 Wood [3] 丙申 Fire Monkey Relief 雷水解 21 二十 4	金4 Metal [4] 丁酉 Fire Rooster Influence 澤山咸 22 廿一 9
水1 Water [5] 戊戌 Earth Dog Humility 地山謙 23 廿二 6	火2 Fire [6] 己亥 Earth Pig Observation 風地觀 24 廿三 2	火2 Fire [7] 庚子 Metal Rat Increasing 風雷益 25 廿四 9	水1 Water [8] 辛丑 Metal Ox Dimming Light 地火明夷 26 廿五 3	金9 Metal [9] 壬寅 Water Tiger Fellowship 天火同人 27 廿六 7	木8 Wood [1] 癸卯 Water Rabbit Marrying Maiden 雷澤歸妹 28 廿七 7	木3 Wood [2] 甲辰 Wood Dragon Opposition 火澤睽 29 廿八 2

JUNE 2049 庚午

Xuan Kong Element 玄空五行	雷風恆 Consistency	Period Luck 卦運	Monthly Star 月星
Wood 木8		9	7

SUNDAY	MONDAY	TUESDAY	WEDNESDAY	THURSDAY	FRIDAY	SATURDAY
		水6 Water [5] 丁未 Fire Goat Poison 山風蠱 1 初二 7	火2 Fire [6] 戊申 Earth Monkey Dispersing 風水渙 2 初三 6	木3 Wood [7] 己酉 Earth Rooster Travelling 火山旅 3 初四 8	金9 Metal [8] 庚戌 Metal Dog Stagnation 天地否 4 初五 9	火7 Fire [9] 辛亥 Metal Pig Alliance 水地比 5 初六 7
木8 Wood [1] 壬子 Water Rat Thunder 震為雷 6 初七 1	水6 Water [2] 癸丑 Water Ox Beauty 山火賁 7 初八 8	火7 Fire [3] 甲寅 Wood Tiger Accomplished 水火既濟 8 初九 9	水1 Water [4] 乙卯 Wood Rabbit Arriving 地澤臨 9 初十 4	金4 Metal [5] 丙辰 Fire Dragon Marsh 兑為澤 10 十一 1	火2 Fire [6] 丁巳 Fire Snake Small Livestock 風天小畜 11 十二 8	木3 Wood [7] 戊午 Earth Horse The Cauldron 火風鼎 12 十三 4
水1 Water [8] 己未 Earth Goat Rising 地風升 13 十四 2	火7 Fire [9] 庚申 Metal Monkey Water 坎為水 14 十五 1	木8 Wood [1] 辛酉 Metal Rooster Lesser Exceeding 雷山小過 15 十六 3	金4 Metal [2] 壬戌 Water Dog Gathering 澤地萃 16 十七 4	水6 Water [3] 癸亥 Water Pig Peel 山地剝 17 十八 6	水1 Water [4] 甲子 Wood Rat Earth 坤為地 18 十九 1	木3 Wood [5] 乙丑 Wood Ox Biting 火雷噬嗑 19 二十 6
火2 Fire [6] 丙寅 Fire Tiger Family 風火家人 20 廿一 4	水6 Water [7/3] 丁卯 Fire Rabbit Decreasing 山澤損 21 廿二 9	金9 Metal [2] 戊辰 Earth Dragon Tread 天澤履 22 廿三 6	木8 Wood [1] 己巳 Earth Snake Great Strength 雷天大壯 23 廿四 2	木8 Wood [9] 庚午 Metal Horse Consistency 雷風恆 24 廿五 9	金9 Metal [8] 辛未 Metal Goat Litigation 天水訟 25 廿六 3	水1 Water [7] 壬申 Water Monkey Officer 地水師 26 廿七 7
火2 Fire [6] 癸酉 Water Rooster Gradual Progress 風山漸 27 廿八 7	火7 Fire [5] 甲戌 Wood Dog Obstruction 水山蹇 28 廿九 2	木3 Wood [4] 乙亥 Wood Pig Advancement 火地晉 29 三十 3	水6 Water [3] 丙子 Fire Rat Nourish 山雷頤 30 六月初一 3			

JULY 2049 辛未

Xuan Kong Element 玄空五行	天水訟 Litigation	Period Luck 卦運	Monthly Star 月星
Metal 金9		3	6

SUNDAY	MONDAY	TUESDAY	WEDNESDAY	THURSDAY	FRIDAY	SATURDAY
				金4 Metal 2 Following 澤雷隨 丁丑 Fire Ox **1** 初二 7	木8 Wood 1 Abundance 雷火豐 戊寅 Earth Tiger **2** 初三 6	火7 Fire 9 Regulate 水澤節 己卯 Earth Rabbit **3** 初四 8
水1 Water 8 Unity 地天泰 庚辰 Metal Dragon **4** 初五 9	木3 Wood 7 Great Reward 火天大有 辛巳 Metal Snake **5** 初六 7	火2 Fire 6 Wind 巽為風 壬午 Water Horse **6** 初七 1	金4 Metal 5 Trap 澤水困 癸未 Water Goat **7** 初八 8	木3 Wood 4 Not Yet Accomplished 火水未濟 甲申 Wood Monkey **8** 初九 9	金9 Metal 3 Retreat 天山遯 乙酉 Wood Rooster **9** 初十 4	水6 Water 2 Mountain 艮為山 丙戌 Fire Dog **10** 十一 1
木8 Wood 1 Delight 雷地豫 丁亥 Fire Pig **11** 十二 8	火7 Fire 9 Beginning 水雷屯 戊子 Earth Rat **12** 十三 4	金9 Metal 8 Without Wrongdoing 天雷無妄 己丑 Earth Ox **13** 十四 2	木3 Wood 7 Fire 離為火 庚寅 Metal Tiger **14** 十五 1	火2 Fire 6 Sincerity 風澤中孚 辛卯 Metal Rabbit **15** 十六 3	水6 Water 5 Big Livestock 山天大畜 壬辰 Water Dragon **16** 十七 4	金4 Metal 4 Eliminating 澤天夬 癸巳 Water Snake **17** 十八 6
金9 Metal 3 Heaven 乾為天 甲午 Wood Horse **18** 十九 1	火7 Fire 2 Well 水風井 乙未 Wood Goat **19** 二十 6	木8 Wood 1 Relief 雷水解 丙申 Fire Monkey **20** 廿一 4	金4 Metal 9 Influence 澤山咸 丁酉 Fire Rooster **21** 廿二 9	水1 Water 8 Humility 地山謙 戊戌 Earth Dog **22** 廿三 6	火2 Fire 7 Observation 風地觀 己亥 Earth Pig **23** 廿四 2	火2 Fire 6 Increasing 風雷益 庚子 Metal Rat **24** 廿五 9
水1 Water 5 Dimming Light 地火明夷 辛丑 Metal Ox **25** 廿六 3	金9 Metal 4 Fellowship 天火同人 壬寅 Water Tiger **26** 廿七 7	木8 Wood 3 Marrying Maiden 雷澤歸妹 癸卯 Water Rabbit **27** 廿八 7	木3 Wood 2 Opposition 火澤睽 甲辰 Wood Dragon **28** 廿九 2	火7 Fire 1 Waiting 水天需 乙巳 Wood Snake **29** 三十 3	金4 Metal 9 Great Exceeding 澤風大過 丙午 Fire Horse **30** 七月初一 3	水6 Water 8 Poison 山風蠱 丁未 Fire Goat **31** 初二 7

AUGUST 2049 壬申

Xuan Kong Element 玄空五行	地水師 Officer	Period Luck 卦運	Monthly Star 月星
Water 水1		7	5

SUNDAY	MONDAY	TUESDAY	WEDNESDAY	THURSDAY	FRIDAY	SATURDAY
火2 Fire 7 Dispersing 風水渙 戊申 Earth Monkey **1** 初三 6	木3 Wood 6 Travelling 火山旅 己酉 Earth Rooster **2** 初四 8	金9 Metal 5 Stagnation 天地否 庚戌 Metal Dog **3** 初五 9	火7 Fire 4 Alliance 水地比 辛亥 Metal Pig **4** 初六 7	木8 Wood 3 Thunder 震為雷 壬子 Water Rat **5** 初七 1	水6 Water 2 Beauty 山火賁 癸丑 Water Ox **6** 初八 8	火7 Fire 1 Accomplished 水火既濟 甲寅 Wood Tiger **7** 初九 9
水1 Water 9 Arriving 地澤臨 乙卯 Wood Rabbit **8** 初十 4	金4 Metal 8 Marsh 兌為澤 丙辰 Fire Dragon **9** 十一 1	火2 Fire 7 Small Livestock 風天小畜 丁巳 Fire Snake **10** 十二 8	木3 Wood 6 The Cauldron 火風鼎 戊午 Earth Horse **11** 十三 4	水1 Water 5 Rising 地風升 己未 Earth Goat **12** 十四 2	火7 Fire 4 Water 坎為水 庚申 Metal Monkey **13** 十五 1	木8 Wood 3 Lesser Exceeding 雷山小過 辛酉 Metal Rooster **14** 十六 3
金4 Metal 2 Gathering 澤地萃 壬戌 Water Dog **15** 十七 4	水6 Water 1 Peel 山地剝 癸亥 Water Pig **16** 十八 6	水1 Water 9 Earth 坤為地 甲子 Wood Rat **17** 十九 1	木3 Wood 8 Biting 火雷噬嗑 乙丑 Wood Ox **18** 二十 6	火2 Fire 7 Family 風火家人 丙寅 Fire Tiger **19** 廿一 4	水6 Water 6 Decreasing 山澤損 丁卯 Fire Rabbit **20** 廿二 9	金9 Metal 5 Tread 天澤履 戊辰 Earth Dragon **21** 廿三 6
木8 Wood 4 Great Strength 雷天大壯 己巳 Earth Snake **22** 廿四 2	木8 Wood 3 Consistency 雷風恆 庚午 Metal Horse **23** 廿五 9	金9 Metal 2 Litigation 天水訟 辛未 Metal Goat **24** 廿六 3	水1 Water 1 Officer 地水師 壬申 Water Monkey **25** 廿七 7	火2 Fire 9 Gradual Progress 風山漸 癸酉 Water Rooster **26** 廿八 7	火7 Fire 8 Obstruction 水山蹇 甲戌 Wood Dog **27** 廿九 2	木3 Wood 7 Advancement 火地晉 乙亥 Wood Pig **28** 八月初一 3
水6 Water 6 Nourish 山雷頤 丙子 Fire Rat **29** 初二 3	金4 Metal 5 Following 澤雷隨 丁丑 Fire Ox **30** 初三 7	木8 Wood 4 Abundance 雷火豐 戊寅 Earth Tiger **31** 初四 6				

SEPTEMBER 2049 癸酉

Xuan Kong Element 玄空五行	風山漸 Gradual Progress	Period Luck 卦運	Monthly Star 月星
Fire 火2		7	4

SUNDAY	MONDAY	TUESDAY	WEDNESDAY	THURSDAY	FRIDAY	SATURDAY
			1 初五 火7 Fire Regulate 水澤節 己卯 Earth Rabbit 8	**2** 初六 水1 Water Unity 地天泰 庚辰 Metal Dragon 9	**3** 初七 木3 Wood Great Reward 火天大有 辛巳 Metal Snake 7	**4** 初八 火2 Fire Wind 巽爲風 壬午 Water Horse 1
5 初九 金4 Metal Trap 澤水困 癸未 Water Goat 8	**6** 初十 木3 Wood Not Yet Accomplished 火水未濟 甲申 Wood Monkey 9	**7** 十一 金9 Metal Retreat 天山遯 乙酉 Wood Rooster 4	**8** 十二 水6 Water Mountain 艮爲山 丙戌 Fire Dog 1	**9** 十三 木8 Wood Delight 雷地豫 丁亥 Fire Pig 8	**10** 十四 火7 Fire Beginning 水雷屯 戊子 Earth Rat 4	**11** 十五 金9 Metal Without Wrongdoing 天雷無妄 己丑 Earth Ox 2
12 十六 木3 Wood Fire 離爲火 庚寅 Metal Tiger 1	**13** 十七 火2 Fire Sincerity 風澤中孚 辛卯 Metal Rabbit 3	**14** 十八 水6 Water Big Livestock 山天大畜 壬辰 Water Dragon 4	**15** 十九 金4 Metal Eliminating 澤天夬 癸巳 Water Snake 6	**16** 二十 金9 Metal Heaven 乾爲天 甲午 Wood Horse 1	**17** 廿一 火7 Fire Well 水風井 乙未 Wood Goat 6	**18** 廿二 木8 Wood Relief 雷水解 丙申 Fire Monkey 4
19 廿三 金4 Metal Influence 澤山咸 丁酉 Fire Rooster 9	**20** 廿四 水1 Water Humility 地山謙 戊戌 Earth Dog 6	**21** 廿五 火2 Fire Observation 風地觀 己亥 Earth Pig 2	**22** 廿六 火2 Fire Increasing 風雷益 庚子 Metal Rat 9	**23** 廿七 水1 Water Dimming Light 地火明夷 辛丑 Metal Ox 3	**24** 廿八 金9 Metal Fellowship 天火同人 壬寅 Water Tiger 7	**25** 廿九 木8 Wood Marrying Maiden 雷澤歸妹 癸卯 Water Rabbit 7
26 三十 木3 Wood Opposition 火澤睽 甲辰 Wood Dragon 2	**27** 九月初一 火7 Fire Waiting 水天需 乙巳 Wood Snake 3	**28** 初二 金4 Metal Great Exceeding 澤風大過 丙午 Fire Horse 3	**29** 初三 水6 Water Poison 山風蠱 丁未 Fire Goat 7	**30** 初四 火2 Fire Dispersing 風水渙 戊申 Earth Monkey 6		

OCTOBER 2049 甲戌

Xuan Kong Element 玄空五行	水山蹇 Obstruction	Period Luck 卦運	Monthly Star 月星
Fire 火7		2	3

SUNDAY	MONDAY	TUESDAY	WEDNESDAY	THURSDAY	FRIDAY	SATURDAY
31 初五 火7 Fire Regulate 水澤節 己卯 Earth Rabbit 8					**1** 初五 木3 Wood Travelling 火山旅 己酉 Earth Rooster 8	**2** 初六 金9 Metal Stagnation 天地否 庚戌 Metal Dog 9
3 初七 火7 Fire Alliance 水地比 辛亥 Metal Pig 7	**4** 初八 木8 Wood Thunder 震爲雷 壬子 Water Rat 1	**5** 初九 水6 Water Beauty 山火賁 癸丑 Water Ox 8	**6** 初十 火7 Fire Accomplished 水火既濟 甲寅 Wood Tiger 9	**7** 十一 水1 Water Arriving 地澤臨 乙卯 Wood Rabbit 4	**8** 十二 金4 Metal Marsh 兌爲澤 丙辰 Fire Dragon 1	**9** 十三 火2 Fire Small Livestock 風天小畜 丁巳 Fire Snake 8
10 十四 木3 Wood The Cauldron 火風鼎 戊午 Earth Horse 4	**11** 十五 水1 Water Rising 地風升 己未 Earth Goat 2	**12** 十六 火7 Fire Water 坎爲水 庚申 Metal Monkey 1	**13** 十七 木8 Wood Lesser Exceeding 雷山小過 辛酉 Metal Rooster 3	**14** 十八 金4 Metal Gathering 澤地萃 壬戌 Water Dog 4	**15** 十九 水6 Water Peel 山地剝 癸亥 Water Pig 6	**16** 二十 水1 Water Earth 坤爲地 甲子 Wood Rat 1
17 廿一 木3 Wood Biting 火雷噬嗑 乙丑 Wood Ox 6	**18** 廿二 火2 Fire Family 風火家人 丙寅 Fire Tiger 4	**19** 廿三 水6 Water Decreasing 山澤損 丁卯 Fire Rabbit 9	**20** 廿四 金9 Metal Tread 天澤履 戊辰 Earth Dragon 6	**21** 廿五 木8 Wood Great Strength 雷天大壯 己巳 Earth Snake 2	**22** 廿六 木8 Wood Consistency 雷風恆 庚午 Metal Horse 9	**23** 廿七 金9 Metal Litigation 天水訟 辛未 Metal Goat 3
24 廿八 水1 Water Officer 地水師 壬申 Water Monkey 7	**25** 廿九 火2 Fire Gradual Progress 風山漸 癸酉 Water Rooster 7	**26** 三十 火7 Fire Obstruction 水山蹇 甲戌 Wood Dog 2	**27** 十月初一 木3 Wood Advancement 火地晉 乙亥 Wood Pig 3	**28** 初二 水6 Water Nourish 山雷頤 丙子 Fire Rat 3	**29** 初三 金4 Metal Following 澤雷隨 丁丑 Fire Ox 7	**30** 初四 木8 Wood Abundance 雷火豐 戊寅 Earth Tiger 6

NOVEMBER 2049 乙亥

Xuan Kong Element 玄空五行	火地晉 Advancement	Period Luck 卦運	Monthly Star 月星
Wood 木3		3	2

SUNDAY	MONDAY	TUESDAY	WEDNESDAY	THURSDAY	FRIDAY	SATURDAY
	1 初六 水1 Water · 5 Unity 地天泰 庚辰 Metal Dragon 9	**2** 初七 木3 Wood · 4 Great Reward 火天大有 辛巳 Metal Snake 7	**3** 初八 火2 Fire · 3 Wind 巽爲風 壬午 Water Horse 1	**4** 初九 金4 Metal · 2 Trap 澤水困 癸未 Water Goat 8	**5** 初十 木3 Wood · 1 Not Yet Accomplished 火水未濟 甲申 Wood Monkey 9	**6** 十一 金9 Metal · 9 Retreat 天山遯 乙酉 Wood Rooster 4
7 十二 水6 Water · 8 Mountain 艮爲山 丙戌 Fire Dog 1	**8** 十三 木8 Wood · 7 Delight 雷地豫 丁亥 Fire Pig 8	**9** 十四 火7 Fire · 6 Beginning 水雷屯 戊子 Earth Rat 4	**10** 十五 金9 Metal · 5 Without Wrongdoing 天雷無妄 己丑 Earth Ox 2	**11** 十六 木3 Wood · 4 Fire 離爲火 庚寅 Metal Tiger 1	**12** 十七 火2 Fire · 3 Sincerity 風澤中孚 辛卯 Metal Rabbit 3	**13** 十八 水6 Water · 2 Big Livestock 山天大畜 壬辰 Water Dragon 4
14 十九 金4 Metal · 1 Eliminating 澤天夬 癸巳 Water Snake 6	**15** 二十 金9 Metal · 9 Heaven 乾爲天 甲午 Wood Horse 1	**16** 廿一 火7 Fire · 8 Well 水風井 乙未 Wood Goat 6	**17** 廿二 木8 Wood · 7 Relief 雷水解 丙申 Fire Monkey 4	**18** 廿三 金4 Metal · 6 Influence 澤山咸 丁酉 Fire Rooster 9	**19** 廿四 水1 Water · 5 Humility 地山謙 戊戌 Earth Dog 6	**20** 廿五 火2 Fire · 4 Observation 風地觀 己亥 Earth Pig 2
21 廿六 火2 Fire · 3 Increasing 風雷益 庚子 Metal Rat 9	**22** 廿七 水1 Water · 2 Dimming Light 地火明夷 辛丑 Metal Ox 3	**23** 廿八 金9 Metal · 1 Fellowship 天火同人 壬寅 Water Tiger 7	**24** 廿九 木8 Wood · 9 Marrying Maiden 雷澤歸妹 癸卯 Water Rabbit 7	**25** 十一月初一 木3 Wood · 8 Opposition 火澤睽 甲辰 Wood Dragon 2	**26** 初二 火7 Fire · 7 Waiting 水天需 乙巳 Wood Snake 3	**27** 初三 金4 Metal · 6 Great Exceeding 澤風大過 丙午 Fire Horse 3
28 初四 水6 Water · 5 Poison 山風蠱 丁未 Fire Goat 7	**29** 初五 火2 Fire · 4 Dispersing 風水渙 戊申 Earth Monkey 6	**30** 初六 木3 Wood · 3 Travelling 火山旅 己酉 Earth Rooster 8				

DECEMBER 2049 丙子

Xuan Kong Element 玄空五行	山雷頤 Nourish	Period Luck 卦運	Monthly Star 月星
Water 水6		3	1

SUNDAY	MONDAY	TUESDAY	WEDNESDAY	THURSDAY	FRIDAY	SATURDAY
			1 初七 金9 Metal · 2 Stagnation 天地否 庚戌 Metal Dog 9	**2** 初八 火7 Fire · 1 Alliance 水地比 辛亥 Metal Pig 7	**3** 初九 木8 Wood · 9 Thunder 震爲雷 壬子 Water Rat 1	**4** 初十 水6 Water · 8 Beauty 山火賁 癸丑 Water Ox 8
5 十一 火7 Fire · 7 Accomplished 水火既濟 甲寅 Wood Tiger 9	**6** 十二 水1 Water · 6 Arriving 地澤臨 乙卯 Wood Rabbit 4	**7** 十三 金4 Metal · 5 Marsh 兌爲澤 丙辰 Fire Dragon 1	**8** 十四 火2 Fire · 4 Small Livestock 風天小畜 丁巳 Fire Snake 8	**9** 十五 木3 Wood · 3 The Cauldron 火風鼎 戊午 Earth Horse 4	**10** 十六 水1 Water · 2 Rising 地風升 己未 Earth Goat 2	**11** 十七 火7 Fire · 1 Water 坎爲水 庚申 Metal Monkey 1
12 十八 木8 Wood · 9 Lesser Exceeding 雷山小過 辛酉 Metal Rooster 3	**13** 十九 金4 Metal · 8 Gathering 澤地萃 壬戌 Water Dog 4	**14** 二十 水6 Water · 7 Peel 山地剝 癸亥 Water Pig 6	**15** 廿一 水1 Water · 6 Earth 坤爲地 甲子 Wood Rat 1	**16** 廿二 木3 Wood · 5 Biting 火雷噬嗑 乙丑 Wood Ox 6	**17** 廿三 火2 Fire · 4 Family 風火家人 丙寅 Fire Tiger 4	**18** 廿四 水6 Water · 3 Decreasing 山澤損 丁卯 Fire Rabbit 9
19 廿五 金9 Metal · 2 Tread 天澤履 戊辰 Earth Dragon 6	**20** 廿六 木8 Wood · 1 Great Strength 雷天大壯 己巳 Earth Snake 2	**21** 廿七 木8 Wood · 9 Consistency 雷風恆 庚午 Metal Horse 9	**22** 廿八 金9 Metal · 8 Litigation 天水訟 辛未 Metal Goat 3	**23** 廿九 水1 Water · 7/3 Officer 地水師 壬申 Water Monkey 7	**24** 三十 火2 Fire · 4 Gradual Progress 風山漸 癸酉 Water Rooster 7	**25** 十二月初一 火7 Fire · 5 Obstruction 水山蹇 甲戌 Wood Dog 2
26 初二 木3 Wood · 6 Advancement 火地晉 乙亥 Wood Pig 3	**27** 初三 水6 Water · 7 Nourish 山雷頤 丙子 Fire Rat 3	**28** 初四 金4 Metal · 8 Following 澤雷隨 丁丑 Fire Ox 7	**29** 初五 木8 Wood · 9 Abundance 雷火豐 戊寅 Earth Tiger 6	**30** 初六 火7 Fire · 1 Regulate 水澤節 己卯 Earth Rabbit 8	**31** 初七 水1 Water · 2 Unity 地天泰 庚辰 Metal Dragon 9	

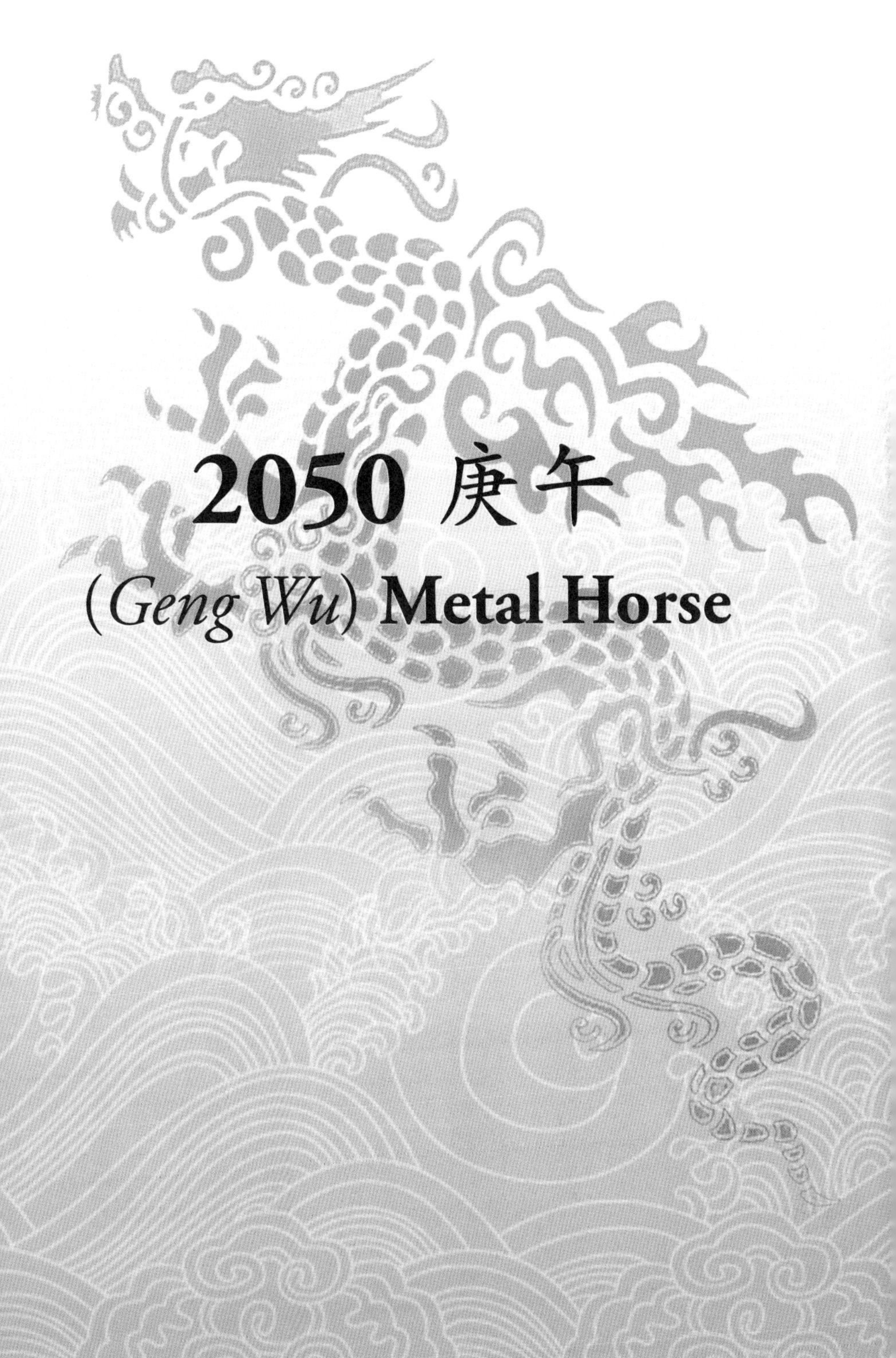

2050 庚午

(*Geng Wu*) Metal Horse

2050 庚午 *(Geng Wu)* Metal Horse

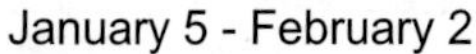

February 3 - March 4

March 5 - April 3

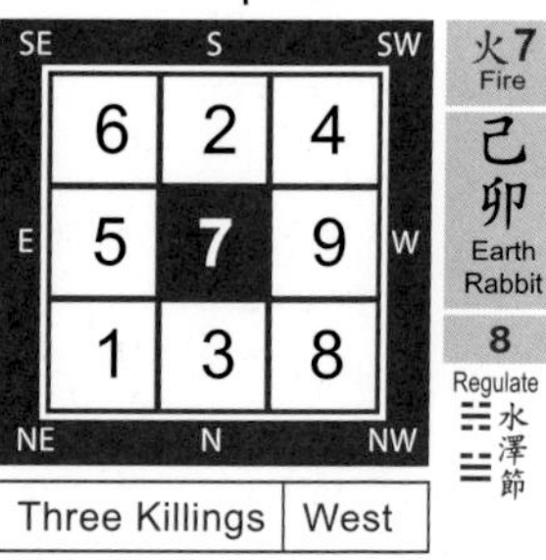

April 4 - May 4

May 5 - June 4

June 5 - July 6

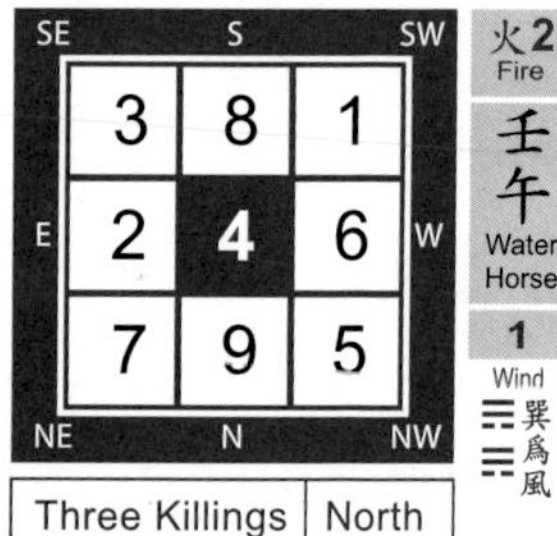

July 7 - August 6

August 7 - September 6

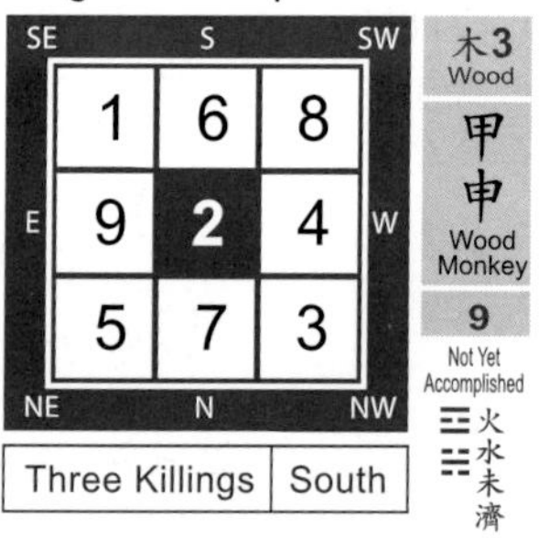

September 7 - October 7

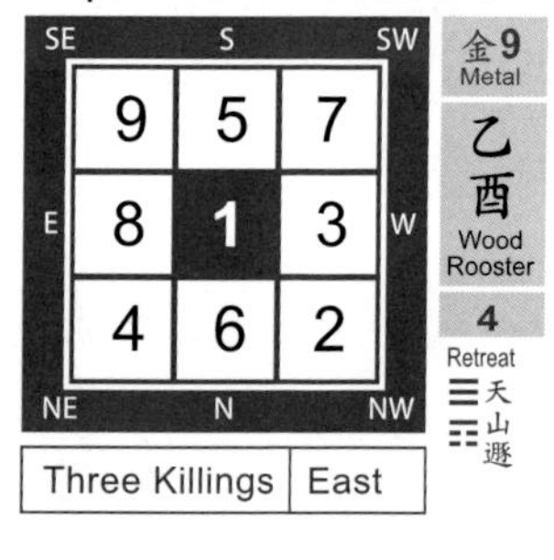

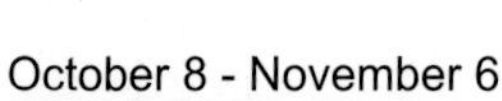

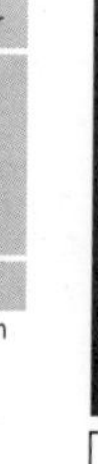

November 7 - December 6

December 7 - January 4

JANUARY 2050 丁丑

Xuan Kong Element 玄空五行	澤雷隨 Following	Period Luck 卦運	Monthly Star 月星
Metal 金4		7	9

SUNDAY	MONDAY	TUESDAY	WEDNESDAY	THURSDAY	FRIDAY	SATURDAY
金9 Metal Stagnation 5 庚戌 Metal Dog 天地否 30 9 初八	火7 Fire Alliance 6 辛亥 Metal Pig 水地比 31 7 初九					木3 Wood Great Reward 3 辛巳 Metal Snake 火天大有 1 7 初八
火2 Fire Wind 4 壬午 Water Horse 巽為風 2 1 初九	金4 Metal Trap 5 癸未 Water Goat 澤水困 3 8 初十	木3 Wood Not Yet Accomplished 6 甲申 Wood Monkey 火水未濟 4 9 十一	金9 Metal Retreat 7 乙酉 Wood Rooster 天山遯 5 4 十二	水6 Water Mountain 8 丙戌 Fire Dog 艮為山 6 1 十三	木8 Wood Delight 9 丁亥 Fire Pig 雷地豫 7 8 十四	火7 Fire Beginning 1 戊子 Earth Rat 水雷屯 8 4 十五
金9 Metal Without Wrongdoing 2 己丑 Earth Ox 天雷無妄 9 2 十六	木3 Wood Fire 3 庚寅 Metal Tiger 離為火 10 1 十七	火2 Fire Sincerity 4 辛卯 Metal Rabbit 風澤中孚 11 3 十八	水6 Water Big Livestock 5 壬辰 Water Dragon 山天大畜 12 4 十九	金4 Metal Eliminating 6 癸巳 Water Snake 澤天夬 13 6 二十	金9 Metal Heaven 7 甲午 Wood Horse 乾為天 14 1 廿一	火7 Fire Well 8 乙未 Wood Goat 水風井 15 6 廿二
木8 Wood Relief 9 丙申 Fire Monkey 雷水解 16 4 廿三	金4 Metal Influence 1 丁酉 Fire Rooster 澤山咸 17 9 廿四	水1 Water Humility 2 戊戌 Earth Dog 地山謙 18 6 廿五	火2 Fire Observation 3 己亥 Earth Pig 風地觀 19 2 廿六	火2 Fire Increasing 4 庚子 Metal Rat 風雷益 20 9 廿七	水1 Water Dimming Light 5 辛丑 Metal Ox 地火明夷 21 3 廿八	金9 Metal Fellowship 6 壬寅 Water Tiger 天火同人 22 7 廿九
木8 Wood Marrying Maiden 7 癸卯 Water Rabbit 雷澤歸妹 23 7 正月初一	木3 Wood Opposition 8 甲辰 Wood Dragon 火澤睽 24 2 初二	火7 Fire Waiting 9 乙巳 Wood Snake 水天需 25 3 初三	金4 Metal Great Exceeding 1 丙午 Fire Horse 澤風大過 26 3 初四	水6 Water Poison 2 丁未 Fire Goat 山風蠱 27 7 初五	火2 Fire Dispersing 3 戊申 Earth Monkey 風水渙 28 6 初六	木3 Wood Travelling 4 己酉 Earth Rooster 火山旅 29 8 初七

FEBRUARY 2050 戊寅

Xuan Kong Element 玄空五行	雷火豐 Abundance	Period Luck 卦運	Monthly Star 月星
Wood 木8		6	8

SUNDAY	MONDAY	TUESDAY	WEDNESDAY	THURSDAY	FRIDAY	SATURDAY
		木8 Wood Thunder 7 壬子 Water Rat 震為雷 1 1 初十	水6 Water Beauty 8 癸丑 Water Ox 山火賁 2 8 十一	火7 Fire Accomplished 9 甲寅 Wood Tiger 水火既濟 3 9 十二	水1 Water Arriving 1 乙卯 Wood Rabbit 地澤臨 4 4 十三	金4 Metal Marsh 2 丙辰 Fire Dragon 兌為澤 5 1 十四
火2 Fire Small Livestock 3 丁巳 Fire Snake 風天小畜 6 8 十五	木3 Wood The Cauldron 4 戊午 Earth Horse 火風鼎 7 4 十六	水1 Water Rising 5 己未 Earth Goat 地風升 8 2 十七	火7 Fire Water 6 庚申 Metal Monkey 坎為水 9 1 十八	木8 Wood Lesser Exceeding 7 辛酉 Metal Rooster 雷山小過 10 3 十九	金4 Metal Gathering 8 壬戌 Water Dog 澤地萃 11 4 二十	水6 Water Peel 9 癸亥 Water Pig 山地剝 12 6 廿一
水1 Water Earth 1 甲子 Wood Rat 坤為地 13 1 廿二	木3 Wood Biting 2 乙丑 Wood Ox 火雷噬嗑 14 6 廿三	火2 Fire Family 3 丙寅 Fire Tiger 風火家人 15 4 廿四	水6 Water Decreasing 4 丁卯 Fire Rabbit 山澤損 16 9 廿五	金9 Metal Tread 5 戊辰 Earth Dragon 天澤履 17 6 廿六	木8 Wood Great Strength 6 己巳 Earth Snake 雷天大壯 18 2 廿七	木8 Wood Consistency 7 庚午 Metal Horse 雷風恒 19 9 廿八
金9 Metal Litigation 8 辛未 Metal Goat 天水訟 20 3 廿九	水1 Water Officer 9 壬申 Water Monkey 地水師 21 7 二月初一	火2 Fire Gradual Progress 1 癸酉 Water Rooster 風山漸 22 7 初二	火7 Fire Obstruction 2 甲戌 Wood Dog 水山蹇 23 2 初三	木3 Wood Advancement 3 乙亥 Wood Pig 火地晉 24 3 初四	水6 Water Nourish 4 丙子 Fire Rat 山雷頤 25 3 初五	金4 Metal Following 5 丁丑 Fire Ox 澤雷隨 26 7 初六
木8 Wood Abundance 6 戊寅 Earth Tiger 雷火豐 27 6 初七	火7 Fire Regulate 7 己卯 Earth Rabbit 水澤節 28 8 初八					

MARCH 2050 己卯

Xuan Kong Element 玄空五行	水澤節 Regulate	Period Luck 卦運	Monthly Star 月星
Fire 火7		8	7

SUNDAY	MONDAY	TUESDAY	WEDNESDAY	THURSDAY	FRIDAY	SATURDAY
		水1 Water · Unity · 8 庚辰 Metal Dragon · 地天泰 1 初九 9	木3 Wood · Great Reward · 9 辛巳 Metal Snake · 火天大有 2 初十 7	火2 Fire · Wind · 1 壬午 Water Horse · 巽爲風 3 十一 1	金4 Metal · Trap · 2 癸未 Water Goat · 澤水困 4 十二 8	木3 Wood · Not Yet Accomplished · 3 甲申 Wood Monkey · 火水未濟 5 十三 9
金9 Metal · Retreat · 4 乙酉 Wood Rooster · 天山遯 6 十四 4	水6 Water · Mountain · 5 丙戌 Fire Dog · 艮爲山 7 十五 1	木8 Wood · Delight · 6 丁亥 Fire Pig · 雷地豫 8 十六 8	火7 Fire · Beginning · 7 戊子 Earth Rat · 水雷屯 9 十七 4	金9 Metal · Without Wrongdoing · 8 己丑 Earth Ox · 天雷無妄 10 十八 2	木3 Wood · Fire · 9 庚寅 Metal Tiger · 離爲火 11 十九 1	火2 Fire · Sincerity · 1 辛卯 Metal Rabbit · 風澤中孚 12 二十 3
水6 Water · Big Livestock · 2 壬辰 Water Dragon · 山天大畜 13 廿一 4	金4 Metal · Eliminating · 3 癸巳 Water Snake · 澤天夬 14 廿二 6	金9 Metal · Heaven · 4 甲午 Wood Horse · 乾爲天 15 廿三 1	火7 Fire · Well · 5 乙未 Wood Goat · 水風井 16 廿四 6	木8 Wood · Relief · 6 丙申 Fire Monkey · 雷水解 17 廿五 4	金4 Metal · Influence · 7 丁酉 Fire Rooster · 澤山咸 18 廿六 9	水1 Water · Humility · 8 戊戌 Earth Dog · 地山謙 19 廿七 6
火2 Fire · Observation · 9 己亥 Earth Pig · 風地觀 20 廿八 2	火2 Fire · Increasing · 1 庚子 Metal Rat · 風雷益 21 廿九 9	水1 Water · Dimming Light · 2 辛丑 Metal Ox · 地火明夷 22 三十 3	金9 Metal · Fellowship · 3 壬寅 Water Tiger · 天火同人 23 三月初一 7	木8 Wood · Marrying Maiden · 4 癸卯 Water Rabbit · 雷澤歸妹 24 初二 7	木3 Wood · Opposition · 5 甲辰 Wood Dragon · 火澤睽 25 初三 2	火7 Fire · Waiting · 6 乙巳 Wood Snake · 水天需 26 初四 3
金4 Metal · Great Exceeding · 7 丙午 Fire Horse · 澤風大過 27 初五 3	水6 Water · Poison · 8 丁未 Fire Goat · 山風蠱 28 初六 7	火2 Fire · Dispersing · 9 戊申 Earth Monkey · 風水渙 29 初七 6	木3 Wood · Travelling · 1 己酉 Earth Rooster · 火山旅 30 初八 8	金9 Metal · Stagnation · 2 庚戌 Metal Dog · 天地否 31 初九 9		

APRIL 2050 庚辰

Xuan Kong Element 玄空五行	地天泰 Unity	Period Luck 卦運	Monthly Star 月星
Water 水1		9	6

SUNDAY	MONDAY	TUESDAY	WEDNESDAY	THURSDAY	FRIDAY	SATURDAY
					火7 Fire · Alliance · 3 辛亥 Metal Pig · 水地比 1 初十 7	木8 Wood · Thunder · 4 壬子 Water Rat · 震爲雷 2 十一 1
水6 Water · Beauty · 5 癸丑 Water Ox · 山火賁 3 十二 8	火7 Fire · Accomplished · 6 甲寅 Wood Tiger · 水火既濟 4 十三 9	水1 Water · Arriving · 7 乙卯 Wood Rabbit · 地澤臨 5 十四 4	金4 Metal · Marsh · 8 丙辰 Fire Dragon · 兑爲澤 6 十五 1	火2 Fire · Small Livestock · 9 丁巳 Fire Snake · 風天小畜 7 十六 8	木3 Wood · The Cauldron · 1 戊午 Earth Horse · 火風鼎 8 十七 4	水1 Water · Rising · 2 己未 Earth Goat · 地風升 9 十八 2
火7 Fire · Water · 3 庚申 Metal Monkey · 坎爲水 10 十九 1	木8 Wood · Lesser Exceeding · 4 辛酉 Metal Rooster · 雷山小過 11 二十 3	金4 Metal · Gathering · 5 壬戌 Water Dog · 澤地萃 12 廿一 4	水6 Water · Peel · 6 癸亥 Water Pig · 山地剝 13 廿二 6	水1 Water · Earth · 7 甲子 Wood Rat · 坤爲地 14 廿三 1	木3 Wood · Biting · 8 乙丑 Wood Ox · 火雷噬嗑 15 廿四 6	火2 Fire · Family · 9 丙寅 Fire Tiger · 風火家人 16 廿五 4
水6 Water · Decreasing · 1 丁卯 Fire Rabbit · 山澤損 17 廿六 9	金9 Metal · Tread · 2 戊辰 Earth Dragon · 天澤履 18 廿七 6	木8 Wood · Great Strength · 3 己巳 Earth Snake · 雷天大壯 19 廿八 2	木8 Wood · Consistency · 4 庚午 Metal Horse · 雷風恆 20 廿九 9	金9 Metal · Litigation · 5 辛未 Metal Goat · 天水訟 21 閏三月初一 3	水1 Water · Officer · 6 壬申 Water Monkey · 地水師 22 初二 7	火2 Fire · Gradual Progress · 7 癸酉 Water Rooster · 風山漸 23 初三 7
火7 Fire · Obstruction · 8 甲戌 Wood Dog · 水山蹇 24 初四 2	木3 Wood · Advancement · 9 乙亥 Wood Pig · 火地晉 25 初五 3	水6 Water · Nourish · 1 丙子 Fire Rat · 山雷頤 26 初六 3	金4 Metal · Following · 2 丁丑 Fire Ox · 澤雷隨 27 初七 7	木8 Wood · Abundance · 3 戊寅 Earth Tiger · 雷火豐 28 初八 6	火7 Fire · Regulate · 4 己卯 Earth Rabbit · 水澤節 29 初九 8	水1 Water · Unity · 5 庚辰 Metal Dragon · 地天泰 30 初十 9

MAY 2050 辛巳

Xuan Kong Element 玄空五行	火天大有 Great Reward	Period Luck 卦運	Monthly Star 月星
Wood 木3		7	5

SUNDAY	MONDAY	TUESDAY	WEDNESDAY	THURSDAY	FRIDAY	SATURDAY
木3 Wood 6 Great Reward 辛巳 Metal Snake 火天大有 1 十一 7	火2 Fire 7 Wind 壬午 Water Horse 巽爲風 2 十二 1	金4 Metal 8 Trap 癸未 Water Goat 澤水困 3 十三 8	木3 Wood 9 Not Yet Accomplished 甲申 Wood Monkey 火水未濟 4 十四 9	金9 Metal 1 Retreat 乙酉 Wood Rooster 天山遯 5 十五 4	水6 Water 2 Mountain 丙戌 Fire Dog 艮爲山 6 十六 1	木8 Wood 3 Delight 丁亥 Fire Pig 雷地豫 7 十七 8
火7 Fire 4 Beginning 戊子 Earth Rat 水雷屯 8 十八 4	金9 Metal 5 Without Wrongdoing 己丑 Earth Ox 天雷無妄 9 十九 2	木3 Wood 6 Fire 庚寅 Metal Tiger 離爲火 10 二十 1	火2 Fire 7 Sincerity 辛卯 Metal Rabbit 風澤中孚 11 廿一 3	水6 Water 8 Big Livestock 壬辰 Water Dragon 山天大畜 12 廿二 4	金4 Metal 9 Eliminating 癸巳 Water Snake 澤天夬 13 廿三 6	金9 Metal 1 Heaven 甲午 Wood Horse 乾爲天 14 廿四 1
火7 Fire 2 Well 乙未 Wood Goat 水風井 15 廿五 6	木8 Wood 3 Relief 丙申 Fire Monkey 雷水解 16 廿六 4	金4 Metal 4 Influence 丁酉 Fire Rooster 澤山咸 17 廿七 9	水1 Water 5 Humility 戊戌 Earth Dog 地山謙 18 廿八 6	火2 Fire 6 Observation 己亥 Earth Pig 風地觀 19 廿九 2	火2 Fire 7 Increasing 庚子 Metal Rat 風雷益 20 三十 9	水1 Water 8 Dimming Light 辛丑 Metal Ox 地火明夷 21 四月初一 3
金9 Metal 9 Fellowship 壬寅 Water Tiger 天火同人 22 初二 7	木8 Wood 1 Marrying Maiden 癸卯 Water Rabbit 雷澤歸妹 23 初三 7	木3 Wood 2 Opposition 甲辰 Wood Dragon 火澤睽 24 初四 2	火7 Fire 3 Waiting 乙巳 Wood Snake 水天需 25 初五 3	金4 Metal 4 Great Exceeding 丙午 Fire Horse 澤風大過 26 初六 3	水6 Water 5 Poison 丁未 Fire Goat 山風蠱 27 初七 7	火2 Fire 6 Dispersing 戊申 Earth Monkey 風水渙 28 初八 6
木3 Wood 7 Travelling 己酉 Earth Rooster 火山旅 29 初九 8	金9 Metal 8 Stagnation 庚戌 Metal Dog 天地否 30 初十 9	火7 Fire 9 Alliance 辛亥 Metal Pig 水地比 31 十一 7				

JUNE 2050 壬午

Xuan Kong Element 玄空五行	巽爲風 Wind	Period Luck 卦運	Monthly Star 月星
Fire 火2		1	4

SUNDAY	MONDAY	TUESDAY	WEDNESDAY	THURSDAY	FRIDAY	SATURDAY
			木8 Wood 1 Thunder 壬子 Water Rat 震爲雷 1 十二 1	水6 Water 2 Beauty 癸丑 Water Ox 山火賁 2 十三 8	火7 Fire 3 Accomplished 甲寅 Wood Tiger 水火既濟 3 十四 9	水1 Water 4 Arriving 乙卯 Wood Rabbit 地澤臨 4 十五 4
金4 Metal 5 Marsh 丙辰 Fire Dragon 兌爲澤 5 十六 1	火2 Fire 6 Small Livestock 丁巳 Fire Snake 風天小畜 6 十七 8	木3 Wood 7 The Cauldron 戊午 Earth Horse 火風鼎 7 十八 4	水1 Water 8 Rising 己未 Earth Goat 地風升 8 十九 2	火7 Fire 9 Water 庚申 Metal Monkey 坎爲水 9 二十 1	木8 Wood 1 Lesser Exceeding 辛酉 Metal Rooster 雷山小過 10 廿一 3	金4 Metal 2 Gathering 壬戌 Water Dog 澤地萃 11 廿二 4
水6 Water 3 Peel 癸亥 Water Pig 山地剝 12 廿三 6	水1 Water 4 Earth 甲子 Wood Rat 坤爲地 13 廿四 1	木3 Wood 5 Biting 乙丑 Wood Ox 火雷噬嗑 14 廿五 6	火2 Fire 6 Family 丙寅 Fire Tiger 風火家人 15 廿六 4	水6 Water 7 Decreasing 丁卯 Fire Rabbit 山澤損 16 廿七 9	金9 Metal 8 Tread 戊辰 Earth Dragon 天澤履 17 廿八 6	木8 Wood 9 Great Strength 己巳 Earth Snake 雷天大壯 18 廿九 2
木8 Wood 1 Consistency 庚午 Metal Horse 雷風恆 19 五月初一 9	金9 Metal 2 Litigation 辛未 Metal Goat 天水訟 20 初二 3	水1 Water 3/7 Officer 壬申 Water Monkey 地水師 21 初三 7	火2 Fire 6 Gradual Progress 癸酉 Water Rooster 風山漸 22 初四 7	火7 Fire 5 Obstruction 甲戌 Wood Dog 水山蹇 23 初五 2	木3 Wood 4 Advancement 乙亥 Wood Pig 火地晉 24 初六 3	水6 Water 3 Nourish 丙子 Fire Rat 山雷頤 25 初七 3
金4 Metal 2 Following 丁丑 Fire Ox 澤雷隨 26 初八 7	木8 Wood 1 Abundance 戊寅 Earth Tiger 雷火豐 27 初九 6	火7 Fire 9 Regulate 己卯 Earth Rabbit 水澤節 28 初十 8	水1 Water 8 Unity 庚辰 Metal Dragon 地天泰 29 十一 9	木3 Wood 7 Great Reward 辛巳 Metal Snake 火天大有 30 十二 7		

JULY 2050 癸未

Xuan Kong Element 玄空五行	澤水困 Trap	Period Luck 卦運	Monthly Star 月星
Metal 金4		8	3

SUNDAY	MONDAY	TUESDAY	WEDNESDAY	THURSDAY	FRIDAY	SATURDAY
31 十三 木8 Wood 3 Thunder 震爲雷 壬子 Water Rat 1					1 十三 火2 Fire 6 Wind 巽爲風 壬午 Water Horse 1	2 十四 金4 Metal 5 Trap 澤水困 癸未 Water Goat 8
3 十五 木3 Wood 4 Not Yet Accomplished 火水未濟 甲申 Wood Monkey 9	4 十六 金9 Metal 3 Retreat 天山遯 乙酉 Wood Rooster 4	5 十七 水6 Water 2 Mountain 艮爲山 丙戌 Fire Dog 1	6 十八 木8 Wood 1 Delight 雷地豫 丁亥 Fire Pig 8	7 十九 火7 Fire 9 Beginning 水雷屯 戊子 Earth Rat 4	8 二十 金9 Metal 8 Without Wrongdoing 天雷無妄 己丑 Earth Ox 2	9 廿一 木3 Wood 7 Fire 離爲火 庚寅 Metal Tiger 1
10 廿二 火2 Fire 6 Sincerity 風澤中孚 辛卯 Metal Rabbit 3	11 廿三 水6 Water 5 Big Livestock 山天大畜 壬辰 Water Dragon 4	12 廿四 金4 Metal 4 Eliminating 澤天夬 癸巳 Water Snake 6	13 廿五 金9 Metal 3 Heaven 乾爲天 甲午 Wood Horse 1	14 廿六 火7 Fire 2 Well 水風井 乙未 Wood Goat 6	15 廿七 木8 Wood 1 Relief 雷水解 丙申 Fire Monkey 4	16 廿八 金4 Metal 9 Influence 澤山咸 丁酉 Fire Rooster 9
17 廿九 水1 Water 8 Humility 地山謙 戊戌 Earth Dog 6	18 三十 火2 Fire 7 Observation 風地觀 己亥 Earth Pig 2	19 六月初一 火2 Fire 6 Increasing 風雷益 庚子 Metal Rat 9	20 初二 水1 Water 5 Dimming Light 地火明夷 辛丑 Metal Ox 3	21 初三 金9 Metal 4 Fellowship 天火同人 壬寅 Water Tiger 7	22 初四 木8 Wood 3 Marrying Maiden 雷澤歸妹 癸卯 Water Rabbit 7	23 初五 木3 Wood 2 Opposition 火澤睽 甲辰 Wood Dragon 2
24 初六 火7 Fire 1 Waiting 水天需 乙巳 Wood Snake 3	25 初七 金4 Metal 9 Great Exceeding 澤風大過 丙午 Fire Horse 3	26 初八 水6 Water 8 Poison 山風蠱 丁未 Fire Goat 7	27 初九 火2 Fire 7 Dispersing 風水渙 戊申 Earth Monkey 6	28 初十 木3 Wood 6 Travelling 火山旅 己酉 Earth Rooster 8	29 十一 金9 Metal 5 Stagnation 天地否 庚戌 Metal Dog 9	30 十二 火7 Fire 4 Alliance 水地比 辛亥 Metal Pig 7

AUGUST 2050 甲申

Xuan Kong Element 玄空五行	火水未濟 Not Yet Accomplished	Period Luck 卦運	Monthly Star 月星
Wood 木3		9	2

SUNDAY	MONDAY	TUESDAY	WEDNESDAY	THURSDAY	FRIDAY	SATURDAY
	1 十四 水6 Water 2 Beauty 山火賁 癸丑 Water Ox 8	2 十五 火7 Fire 1 Accomplished 水火既濟 甲寅 Wood Tiger 9	3 十六 水1 Water 9 Arriving 地澤臨 乙卯 Wood Rabbit 4	4 十七 金4 Metal 8 Marsh 兑爲澤 丙辰 Fire Dragon 1	5 十八 火2 Fire 7 Small Livestock 風天小畜 丁巳 Fire Snake 8	6 十九 木3 Wood 6 The Cauldron 火風鼎 戊午 Earth Horse 4
7 二十 水1 Water 5 Rising 地風升 己未 Earth Goat 2	8 廿一 火7 Fire 4 Water 坎爲水 庚申 Metal Monkey 1	9 廿二 木8 Wood 3 Lesser Exceeding 雷山小過 辛酉 Metal Rooster 3	10 廿三 金4 Metal 2 Gathering 澤地萃 壬戌 Water Dog 4	11 廿四 水6 Water 1 Peel 山地剝 癸亥 Water Pig 6	12 廿五 水1 Water 9 Earth 坤爲地 甲子 Wood Rat 1	13 廿六 木3 Wood 8 Biting 火雷噬嗑 乙丑 Wood Ox 6
14 廿七 火2 Fire 7 Family 風火家人 丙寅 Fire Tiger 4	15 廿八 水6 Water 6 Decreasing 山澤損 丁卯 Fire Rabbit 9	16 廿九 金9 Metal 5 Tread 天澤履 戊辰 Earth Dragon 6	17 七月初一 木8 Wood 4 Great Strength 雷天大壯 己巳 Earth Snake 2	18 初二 木8 Wood 3 Consistency 雷風恆 庚午 Metal Horse 9	19 初三 金9 Metal 2 Litigation 天水訟 辛未 Metal Goat 3	20 初四 水1 Water 1 Officer 地水師 壬申 Water Monkey 7
21 初五 火2 Fire 9 Gradual Progress 風山漸 癸酉 Water Rooster 7	22 初六 火7 Fire 8 Obstruction 水山蹇 甲戌 Wood Dog 2	23 初七 木3 Wood 7 Advancement 火地晉 乙亥 Wood Pig 3	24 初八 水6 Water 6 Nourish 山雷頤 丙子 Fire Rat 3	25 初九 金4 Metal 5 Following 澤雷隨 丁丑 Fire Ox 7	26 初十 木8 Wood 4 Abundance 雷火豐 戊寅 Earth Tiger 6	27 十一 火7 Fire 3 Regulate 水澤節 己卯 Earth Rabbit 8
28 十二 水1 Water 2 Unity 地天泰 庚辰 Metal Dragon 9	29 十三 木3 Wood 1 Great Reward 火天大有 辛巳 Metal Snake 7	30 十四 火2 Fire 9 Wind 巽爲風 壬午 Water Horse 1	31 十五 金4 Metal 8 Trap 澤水困 癸未 Water Goat 8			

SEPTEMBER 2050 乙酉

Xuan Kong Element 玄空五行	天山遯 Retreat	Period Luck 卦運	Monthly Star 月星
Metal 金9		4	1

SUNDAY	MONDAY	TUESDAY	WEDNESDAY	THURSDAY	FRIDAY	SATURDAY
				木3 Wood · Not Yet Accomplished · 7 甲申 Wood Monkey · 火水未濟 1 · 十六 · 9	金9 Metal · Retreat · 6 乙酉 Wood Rooster · 天山遯 2 · 十七 · 4	水6 Water · Mountain · 5 丙戌 Fire Dog · 艮爲山 3 · 十八 · 1
木8 Wood · Delight · 4 丁亥 Fire Pig · 雷地豫 4 · 十九 · 8	火7 Fire · Beginning · 3 戊子 Earth Rat · 水雷屯 5 · 二十 · 4	金9 Metal · Without Wrongdoing · 2 己丑 Earth Ox · 天雷無妄 6 · 廿一 · 2	木3 Wood · Fire · 1 庚寅 Metal Tiger · 離爲火 7 · 廿二 · 1	火2 Fire · Sincerity · 9 辛卯 Metal Rabbit · 風澤中孚 8 · 廿三 · 3	水6 Water · Big Livestock · 8 壬辰 Water Dragon · 山天大畜 9 · 廿四 · 4	金4 Metal · Eliminating · 7 癸巳 Water Snake · 澤天夬 10 · 廿五 · 6
金9 Metal · Heaven · 6 甲午 Wood Horse · 乾爲天 11 · 廿六 · 1	火7 Fire · Well · 5 乙未 Wood Goat · 水風井 12 · 廿七 · 6	木8 Wood · Relief · 4 丙申 Fire Monkey · 雷水解 13 · 廿八 · 4	金4 Metal · Influence · 3 丁酉 Fire Rooster · 澤山咸 14 · 廿九 · 9	水1 Water · Humility · 2 戊戌 Earth Dog · 地山謙 15 · 三十 · 6	火2 Fire · Observation · 1 己亥 Earth Pig · 風地觀 16 · 八月初一 · 2	火2 Fire · Increasing · 9 庚子 Metal Rat · 風雷益 17 · 初二 · 9
水1 Water · Dimming Light · 8 辛丑 Metal Ox · 地火明夷 18 · 初三 · 3	金9 Metal · Fellowship · 7 壬寅 Water Tiger · 天火同人 19 · 初四 · 7	木8 Wood · Marrying Maiden · 6 癸卯 Water Rabbit · 雷澤歸妹 20 · 初五 · 7	木3 Wood · Opposition · 5 甲辰 Wood Dragon · 火澤睽 21 · 初六 · 2	火7 Fire · Waiting · 4 乙巳 Wood Snake · 水天需 22 · 初七 · 3	金4 Metal · Great Exceeding · 3 丙午 Fire Horse · 澤風大過 23 · 初八 · 3	水6 Water · Poison · 2 丁未 Fire Goat · 山風蠱 24 · 初九 · 7
火2 Fire · Dispersing · 1 戊申 Earth Monkey · 風水渙 25 · 初十 · 6	木3 Wood · Travelling · 9 己酉 Earth Rooster · 火山旅 26 · 十一 · 8	金9 Metal · Stagnation · 8 庚戌 Metal Dog · 天地否 27 · 十二 · 9	火7 Fire · Alliance · 7 辛亥 Metal Pig · 水地比 28 · 十三 · 7	木8 Wood · Thunder · 6 壬子 Water Rat · 震爲雷 29 · 十四 · 1	水6 Water · Beauty · 5 癸丑 Water Ox · 山火賁 30 · 十五 · 8	

OCTOBER 2050 丙戌

Xuan Kong Element 玄空五行	艮爲山 Mountain	Period Luck 卦運	Monthly Star 月星
Water 水6		1	9

SUNDAY	MONDAY	TUESDAY	WEDNESDAY	THURSDAY	FRIDAY	SATURDAY
金4 Metal · Trap · 2 癸未 Water Goat · 澤水困 30 · 十五 · 8	木3 Wood · Not Yet Accomplished · 1 甲申 Wood Monkey · 火水未濟 31 · 十六 · 9					火7 Fire · Accomplished · 4 甲寅 Wood Tiger · 水火既濟 1 · 十六 · 9
水1 Water · Arriving · 3 乙卯 Wood Rabbit · 地澤臨 2 · 十七 · 4	金4 Metal · Marsh · 2 丙辰 Fire Dragon · 兌爲澤 3 · 十八 · 1	火2 Fire · Small Livestock · 1 丁巳 Fire Snake · 風天小畜 4 · 十九 · 8	木3 Wood · The Cauldron · 9 戊午 Earth Horse · 火風鼎 5 · 二十 · 4	水1 Water · Rising · 8 己未 Earth Goat · 地風升 6 · 廿一 · 2	火7 Fire · Water · 7 庚申 Metal Monkey · 坎爲水 7 · 廿二 · 1	木8 Wood · Lesser Exceeding · 6 辛酉 Metal Rooster · 雷山小過 8 · 廿三 · 3
金4 Metal · Gathering · 5 壬戌 Water Dog · 澤地萃 9 · 廿四 · 4	水6 Water · Peel · 4 癸亥 Water Pig · 山地剝 10 · 廿五 · 6	水1 Water · Earth · 3 甲子 Wood Rat · 坤爲地 11 · 廿六 · 1	木3 Wood · Biting · 2 乙丑 Wood Ox · 火雷噬嗑 12 · 廿七 · 6	火2 Fire · Family · 1 丙寅 Fire Tiger · 風火家人 13 · 廿八 · 4	水6 Water · Decreasing · 9 丁卯 Fire Rabbit · 山澤損 14 · 廿九 · 9	金9 Metal · Tread · 8 戊辰 Earth Dragon · 天澤履 15 · 三十 · 6
木8 Wood · Great Strength · 7 己巳 Earth Snake · 雷天大壯 16 · 九月初一 · 2	木8 Wood · Consistency · 6 庚午 Metal Horse · 雷風恒 17 · 初二 · 9	金9 Metal · Litigation · 5 辛未 Metal Goat · 天水訟 18 · 初三 · 3	水1 Water · Officer · 4 壬申 Water Monkey · 地水師 19 · 初四 · 7	火2 Fire · Gradual Progress · 3 癸酉 Water Rooster · 風山漸 20 · 初五 · 7	火7 Fire · Obstruction · 2 甲戌 Wood Dog · 水山蹇 21 · 初六 · 2	木3 Wood · Advancement · 1 乙亥 Wood Pig · 火地晉 22 · 初七 · 3
水6 Water · Nourish · 9 丙子 Fire Rat · 山雷頤 23 · 初八 · 3	金4 Metal · Following · 8 丁丑 Fire Ox · 澤雷隨 24 · 初九 · 7	木8 Wood · Abundance · 7 戊寅 Earth Tiger · 雷火豐 25 · 初十 · 6	火7 Fire · Regulate · 6 己卯 Earth Rabbit · 水澤節 26 · 十一 · 8	水1 Water · Unity · 5 庚辰 Metal Dragon · 地天泰 27 · 十二 · 9	木3 Wood · Great Reward · 4 辛巳 Metal Snake · 火天大有 28 · 十三 · 7	火2 Fire · Wind · 3 壬午 Water Horse · 巽爲風 29 · 十四 · 1

NOVEMBER 2050 丁亥

Xuan Kong Element 玄空五行	雷地豫	Period Luck 卦運	Monthly Star 月星
Wood 木8	Delight	8	8

SUNDAY	MONDAY	TUESDAY	WEDNESDAY	THURSDAY	FRIDAY	SATURDAY
		金9 Metal 9 Retreat 天山遯 乙酉 Wood Rooster 1 十七 4	水6 Water 8 Mountain 艮爲山 丙戌 Fire Dog 2 十八 1	木8 Wood 7 Delight 雷地豫 丁亥 Fire Pig 3 十九 8	火7 Fire 6 Beginning 水雷屯 戊子 Earth Rat 4 二十 4	金9 Metal 5 Without Wrongdoing 天雷無妄 己丑 Earth Ox 5 廿一 2
木3 Wood 4 Fire 離爲火 庚寅 Metal Tiger 6 廿二 1	火2 Fire 3 Sincerity 風澤中孚 辛卯 Metal Rabbit 7 廿三 3	水6 Water 2 Big Livestock 山天大畜 壬辰 Water Dragon 8 廿四 4	金4 Metal 1 Eliminating 澤天夬 癸巳 Water Snake 9 廿五 6	金9 Metal 9 Heaven 乾爲天 甲午 Wood Horse 10 廿六 1	火7 Fire 8 Well 水風井 乙未 Wood Goat 11 廿七 6	木8 Wood 7 Relief 雷水解 丙申 Fire Monkey 12 廿八 4
金4 Metal 6 Influence 澤山咸 丁酉 Fire Rooster 13 廿九 9	水1 Water 5 Humility 地山謙 戊戌 Earth Dog 14 十月初一 6	火2 Fire 4 Observation 風地觀 己亥 Earth Pig 15 初二 2	火2 Fire 3 Increasing 風雷益 庚子 Metal Rat 16 初三 9	水1 Water 2 Dimming Light 地火明夷 辛丑 Metal Ox 17 初四 3	金9 Metal 1 Fellowship 天火同人 壬寅 Water Tiger 18 初五 7	木8 Wood 9 Marrying Maiden 雷澤歸妹 癸卯 Water Rabbit 19 初六 7
木3 Wood 8 Opposition 火澤睽 甲辰 Wood Dragon 20 初七 2	火7 Fire 7 Waiting 水天需 乙巳 Wood Snake 21 初八 3	金4 Metal 6 Great Exceeding 澤風大過 丙午 Fire Horse 22 初九 3	水6 Water 5 Poison 山風蠱 丁未 Fire Goat 23 初十 7	火2 Fire 4 Dispersing 風水渙 戊申 Earth Monkey 24 十一 6	木3 Wood 3 Travelling 火山旅 己酉 Earth Rooster 25 十二 8	金9 Metal 2 Stagnation 天地否 庚戌 Metal Dog 26 十三 9
火7 Fire 1 Alliance 水地比 辛亥 Metal Pig 27 十四 7	木8 Wood 9 Thunder 震爲雷 壬子 Water Rat 28 十五 1	水6 Water 8 Beauty 山火賁 癸丑 Water Ox 29 十六 8	火7 Fire 7 Accomplished 水火既濟 甲寅 Wood Tiger 30 十七 9			

DECEMBER 2050 戊子

Xuan Kong Element 玄空五行	水雷屯	Period Luck 卦運	Monthly Star 月星
Fire 火7	Beginning	4	7

SUNDAY	MONDAY	TUESDAY	WEDNESDAY	THURSDAY	FRIDAY	SATURDAY
				水1 Water 6 Arriving 地澤臨 乙卯 Wood Rabbit 1 十八 4	金4 Metal 5 Marsh 兌爲澤 丙辰 Fire Dragon 2 十九 1	火2 Fire 4 Small Livestock 風天小畜 丁巳 Fire Snake 3 二十 8
木3 Wood 3 The Cauldron 火風鼎 戊午 Earth Horse 4 廿一 4	水1 Water 2 Rising 地風升 己未 Earth Goat 5 廿二 2	火7 Fire 1 Water 坎爲水 庚申 Metal Monkey 6 廿三 1	木8 Wood 9 Lesser Exceeding 雷山小過 辛酉 Metal Rooster 7 廿四 3	金4 Metal 8 Gathering 澤地萃 壬戌 Water Dog 8 廿五 4	水6 Water 7 Peel 山地剝 癸亥 Water Pig 9 廿六 6	水1 Water 6 Earth 坤爲地 甲子 Wood Rat 10 廿七 1
木3 Wood 5 Biting 火雷噬嗑 乙丑 Wood Ox 11 廿八 6	火2 Fire 4 Family 風火家人 丙寅 Fire Tiger 12 廿九 4	水6 Water 3 Decreasing 山澤損 丁卯 Fire Rabbit 13 三十 9	金9 Metal 2 Tread 天澤履 戊辰 Earth Dragon 14 十一月初一 6	木8 Wood 1 Great Strength 雷天大壯 己巳 Earth Snake 15 初二 2	木8 Wood 9 Consistency 雷風恆 庚午 Metal Horse 16 初三 9	金9 Metal 8 Litigation 天水訟 辛未 Metal Goat 17 初四 3
水1 Water 7 Officer 地水師 壬申 Water Monkey 18 初五 7	火2 Fire 6 Gradual Progress 風山漸 癸酉 Water Rooster 19 初六 7	火7 Fire 5 Obstruction 水山蹇 甲戌 Wood Dog 20 初七 2	木3 Wood 4 Advancement 火地晉 乙亥 Wood Pig 21 初八 3	水6 Water 3/7 Nourish 山雷頤 丙子 Fire Rat 22 初九 3	金4 Metal 8 Following 澤雷隨 丁丑 Fire Ox 23 初十 7	木8 Wood 9 Abundance 雷火豐 戊寅 Earth Tiger 24 十一 6
火7 Fire 1 Regulate 水澤節 己卯 Earth Rabbit 25 十二 8	水1 Water 2 Unity 地天泰 庚辰 Metal Dragon 26 十三 9	木3 Wood 3 Great Reward 火天大有 辛巳 Metal Snake 27 十四 7	火2 Fire 4 Wind 巽爲風 壬午 Water Horse 28 十五 1	金4 Metal 5 Trap 澤水困 癸未 Water Goat 29 十六 8	木3 Wood 6 Not Yet Accomplished 火水未濟 甲申 Wood Monkey 30 十七 9	金9 Metal 7 Retreat 天山遯 乙酉 Wood Rooster 31 十八 4

About Joey Yap

Joey Yap is the Founder and Master Trainer of the Mastery Academy of Chinese Metaphysics, a global organisation devoted to the worldwide teaching of Feng Shui, BaZi, Mian Xiang, Yi Jing and other Chinese Metaphysics subjects. Joey is also the Chief Consultant of Yap Global Consulting, an international Feng Shui and Chinese Astrology consulting firm offering audit and consultation services to corporations and individuals all over the world.

Joey received his formal education in Malaysia and Australia. He has combined the best of Eastern learning and Western education systems in the teaching methodology practiced at the Academy. Students of the Mastery Academy study traditional syllabuses of Chinese Metaphysics but through Western-style modular programs that are structured and systematic, enabling individuals to easily and quickly learn, grasp and master complex Chinese Metaphysics subjects like Feng Shui and BaZi. These unique structured learning systems are also utilized by Mastery Academy instructors all over the world to teach BaZi and Feng Shui.

The Mastery Academy is also the first international educational organisation to fully utilize the benefits of the Internet to promote continuous education, encourage peer-to-peer learning, enable mentoring and distance learning. Students interact with each other live, and continue to learn and improve their knowledge.

Joey Yap is also the bestselling author of various books, including ***Stories and Lessons on Feng Shui***, ***BaZi – The Destiny Code*** and its sequel, **BaZi – The Destiny Code Revealed**, **Mian Xiang – Discover Face Reading**, ***Feng Shui for Homebuyers – Exterior***, ***Feng Shui for Homebuyers – Interior***, and ***The Art of Date Selection – Personal Date Selection***, all of which topped the Malaysian MPH bookstores' bestseller lists. He is also the producer of the first comprehensive reference source of Chinese Metaphysics, ***The Chinese Metaphysics Compendium***, a compilation of all the essential formulas and applications known and practiced in Chinese Metaphysics today. Besides being a regular guest of various radio and TV talk shows, Joey is also a regular columnist for a national newspaper and various magazines in Malaysia. In fact, he hosted his own TV series, Discover Feng Shui with Joey Yap, on Malaysia's 8TV channel in 2005; a popular program that focused on heightening awareness of Feng Shui and Chinese Metaphysics.

A firm believer in innovation being the way forward, Joey recently released the BaZi Ming Pan 2.0 software, which allows users to generate configurable, detailed BaZi charts.

Author's personal website: www.joeyyap.com | www.fengshuilogy.com
Academy website: www.masteryacademy.com | www.masteryjournal.com | www.maelearning.com

EDUCATION

The Mastery Academy of Chinese Metaphysics: the first choice for practitioners and aspiring students of the art and science of Chinese Classical Feng Shui and Astrology.

For thousands of years, Eastern knowledge has been passed from one generation to another through the system of discipleship. A venerated master would accept suitable individuals at a young age as his disciples, and informally through the years, pass on his knowledge and skills to them. His disciples in turn, would take on their own disciples, as a means to perpetuate knowledge or skills.

This system served the purpose of restricting the transfer of knowledge to only worthy honourable individuals and ensuring that outsiders or Westerners would not have access to thousands of years of Eastern knowledge, learning and research.

However, the disciple system has also resulted in Chinese Metaphysics and Classical Studies lacking systematic teaching methods. Knowledge garnered over the years has not been accumulated in a concise, systematic manner, but scattered amongst practitioners, each practicing his/her knowledge, art and science, in isolation.

The disciple system, out of place in today's modern world, endangers the advancement of these classical fields that continue to have great relevance and application today.

At the Mastery Academy of Chinese Metaphysics, our Mission is to bring Eastern Classical knowledge in the fields of metaphysics, Feng Shui and Astrology sciences and the arts to the world. These Classical teachings and knowledge, previously shrouded in secrecy and passed on only through the discipleship system, are adapted into structured learning, which can easily be understood, learnt and mastered. Through modern learning methods, these renowned ancient arts, sciences and practices can be perpetuated while facilitating more extensive application and understanding of these classical subjects.

The Mastery Academy espouses an educational philosophy that draws from the best of the East and West. It is the world's premier educational institution for the study of Chinese Metaphysics Studies offering a wide range and variety of courses, ensuring that students have the opportunity to pursue their preferred field of study and enabling existing practitioners and professionals to gain cross-disciplinary knowledge that complements their current field of practice.

Courses at the Mastery Academy have been carefully designed to ensure a comprehensive yet compact syllabus. The modular nature of the courses enables students to immediately begin to put their knowledge into practice while pursuing continued study of their field and complementary fields. Students thus have the benefit of developing and gaining practical experience in tandem with the expansion and advancement of their theoretical knowledge.

Students can also choose from a variety of study options, from a distance learning program, the Homestudy Series, that enables study at one's own pace or intensive foundation courses and compact lecture-based courses, held in various cities around the world by Joey Yap or our licensed instructors. The Mastery Academy's faculty and make-up is international in nature, thus ensuring that prospective students can attend courses at destinations nearest to their country of origin or with a licensed Mastery Academy instructor in their home country.

The Mastery Academy provides 24x7 support to students through its Online Community, with a variety of tools, documents, forums and e-learning materials to help students stay at the forefront of research in their fields and gain invaluable assistance from peers and mentoring from their instructors.

MASTERY ACADEMY
OF CHINESE METAPHYSICS

www.masteryacademy.com

MALAYSIA
19-3, The Boulevard
Mid Valley City
59200 Kuala Lumpur, Malaysia
Tel : +603-2284 8080
Fax : +603-2284 1218
Email : info@masteryacademy.com

SINGAPORE
14, Robinson Road # 13-00
Far East Finance Building
Singapore 048545
Tel : +65-6494 9147
Email : singapore@masteryacademy.com

AUSTRALIA
Unit 3 / 61 Belmont Avenue,
Belmont WA 6104.
Australia.
Tel : +618-9467 3626
Fax : +618-9479 3388
Email : australia@masteryacademy.com

Represented in:
Australia, Austria, Brazil, Canada, China, Cyprus, France, Germany, Greece, Hungary, India, Japan, Indonesia, Italy, Malaysia, Mexico, Netherlands, New Zealand, Philippines, Russian Federation, Poland, Singapore, South Africa, Switzerland, Turkey, U.S.A., Ukraine, United Kingdom

Introducing...
The Mastery Academy's E-Learning Center!

The Mastery Academy's goal has always been to share authentic knowledge of Chinese Metaphysics with the whole world.

Nevertheless, we do recognize that distance, time, and hotel and traveling costs – amongst many other factors – could actually hinder people from enrolling for a classroom-based course. But with the advent and amazing advance of IT today, NOT any more!

With this in mind, we have invested heavily in IT, to conceive what is probably the first and only E-Learning Center in the world today that offers a full range of studies in the field of Chinese Metaphysics.

Convenient

Study from Your Own Home

Easy Enrollment

The Mastery Academy's E-Learning Center

Now, armed with your trusty computer or laptop, and Internet access, knowledge of classical Feng Shui, BaZi (Destiny Analysis) and Mian Xiang (Face Reading) are but a literal click away!

Study at your own pace, and interact with your Instructor and fellow students worldwide, from anywhere in the world. With our E-Learning Center, knowledge of Chinese Metaphysics is brought DIRECTLY to you in all its clarity – topic-by-topic, and lesson-by-lesson; with illustrated presentations and comprehensive notes expediting your learning curve!

Your education journey through our E-Learning Center may be done via any of the following approaches:

Mastery Academy around the world

Canada
United States
Mexico
Brazil
United Kingdom
Switzerland
Netherlands
France
Cyprus
Italy
Germany
Austria
Poland
Hungary
Greece
South Africa
Russian Federation
Ukraine
Turkey
India
China
Japan
Philippines
Kuala Lumpur
Malaysia
Indonesia
Singapore
Australia
New Zealand

www.joeyyap.com

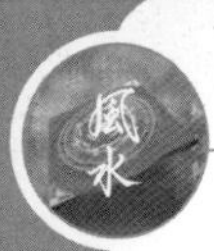

Feng Shui Consultations

For Residential Properties
- Initial Land/Property Assessment
- Residential Feng Shui Consultations
- Residential Land Selection
- End-to-End Residential Consultation

For Commercial Properties
- Initial Land/Property Assessment
- Commercial Feng Shui Consultations
- Commercial Land Selection
- End-to-End Commercial Consultation

For Property Developers
- End-to-End Consultation
- Post-Consultation Advisory Services
- Panel Feng Shui Consultant

For Property Investors
- Your Personal Feng Shui Consultant
- Tailor-Made Packages

For Memorial Parks & Burial Sites
- Yin House Feng Shui

BaZi Consultations

Personal Destiny Analysis
- Personal Destiny Analysis for Individuals
- Children's BaZi Analysis
- Family BaZi Analysis

Strategic Analysis for Corporate Organizations
- Corporate BaZi Consultations
- BaZi Analysis for Human Resource Management

Entrepreneurs & Business Owners
- BaZi Analysis for Entrepreneurs

Career Pursuits
- BaZi Career Analysis

Relationships
- Marriage and Compatibility Analysis
- Partnership Analysis

For Everyone
- Annual BaZi Forecast
- Your Personal BaZi Coach

Date Selection Consultations

- **Marriage Date Selection**
- **Caesarean Birth Date Selection**
- **House-Moving Date Selection**
- **Renovation & Groundbreaking Dates**
- **Signing of Contracts**
- **Official Openings**
- **Product Launches**

Yi Jing Assessment

A Time-Tested, Accurate Science

- With a history predating 4 millennia, the Yi Jing - or Classic of Change - is one of the oldest Chinese texts surviving today. Its purpose as an oracle, in predicting the outcome of things, is based on the variables of Time, Space and Specific Events.

- A Yi Jing Assessment provides specific answers to any specific questions you may have about a specific event or endeavor. This is something that a Destiny Analysis would not be able to give you.

Basically, what a Yi Jing Assessment does is focus on only ONE aspect or item at a particular point in your life, and give you a calculated prediction of the details that will follow suit, if you undertake a particular action. It gives you an insight into a situation, and what course of action to take in order to arrive at a satisfactory outcome at the end of the day.

Please Contact YGC for a personalized Yi Jing Assessment!

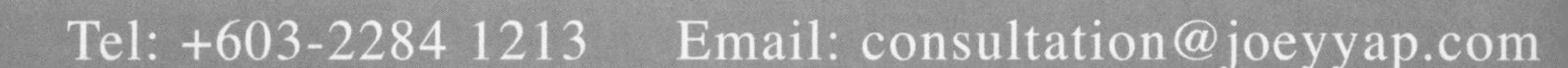

Chinese Metaphysics Reference Series

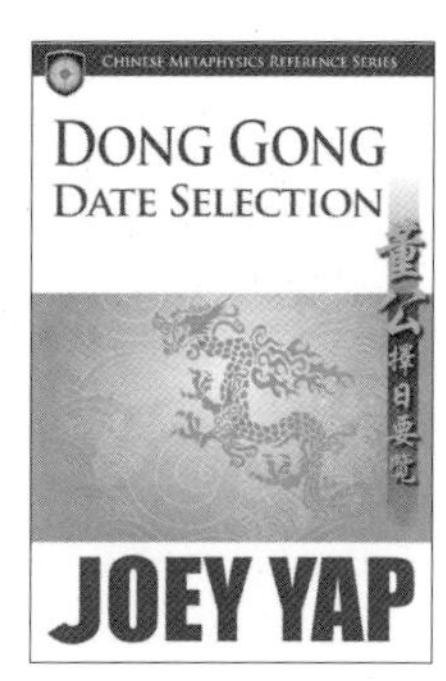

Dong Gong
Date Selection

The Chinese
Metaphysics
Compendium

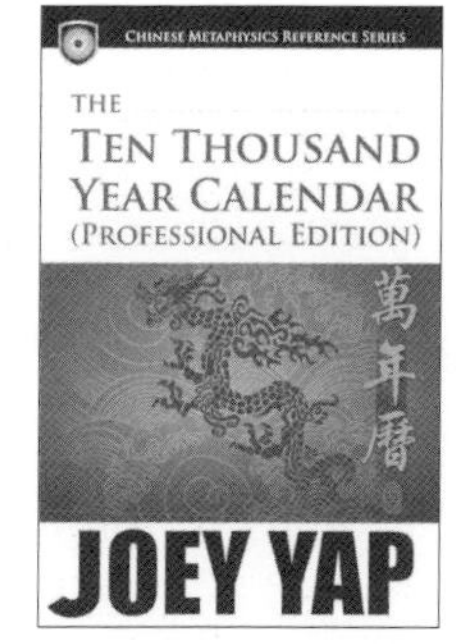

The Ten Thousand
Year Calendar
(Professional Edition)

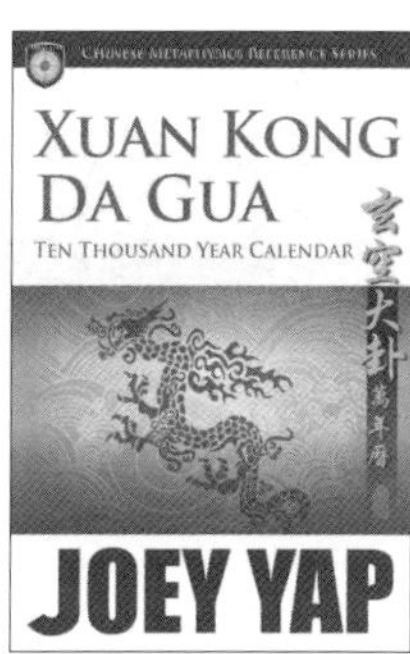

Xuan Kong Da Gua
Ten Thousand Year
Calendar

Xuan Kong Da Gua
Structures Reference
Book

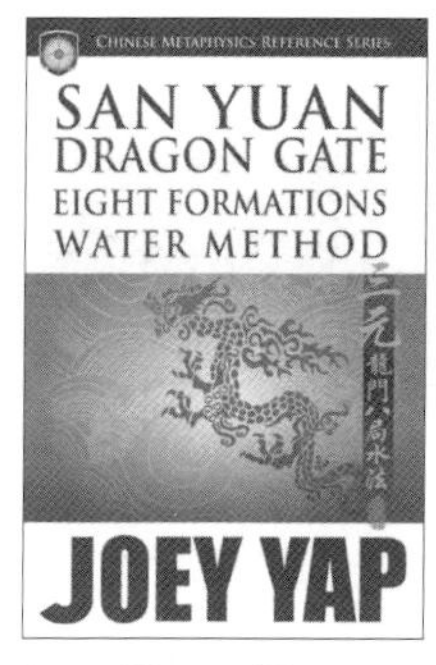

San Yuan Dragon
Gate Eight Formations
Water Method

Qi Men Dun Jia
1080 Charts

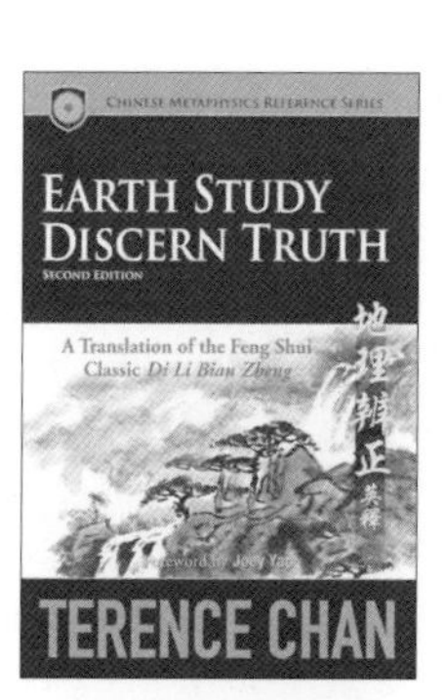

Earth Study
Discern Truth
Second Edition

Latest DVDs Release by Joey Yap
Feng Shui for Homebuyers DVD Series

Best-selling Author, and international Master Trainer and Consultant Joey Yap reveals in these DVDs the significant Feng Shui features that every homebuyer should know when evaluating a property.

Joey will guide you on how to customise your home to maximise the Feng Shui potential of your property and gain the full benefit of improving your health, wealth and love life using the 9 Palace Grid. He will show you how to go about applying the classical applications of the Life Gua and House Gua techniques to get attuned to your Sheng Qi (positive energies).

In these DVDs, you will also learn how to identify properties with good Feng Shui features that will help you promote a fulfilling life and achieve your full potential. Discover how to avoid properties with negative Feng Shui that can bring about detrimental effects to your health, wealth and relationships.

Joey will also elaborate on how to fix the various aspects of your home that may have an impact on the Feng Shui of your property and give pointers on how to tap into the positive energies to support your goals.

Discover Feng Shui with Joey Yap (TV Series)

Discover Feng Shui with Joey Yap: Set of 4 DVDs

Informative and entertaining, classical Feng Shui comes alive in *Discover Feng Shui with Joey Yap!*

Dying to know how you can use Feng Shui to improve your house or office, but simply too busy attend for formal classes?

You have the questions. Now let Joey personally answer them in this 4-set DVD compilation! Learn how to ensure the viability of your residence or workplace, Feng Shui-wise, without having to convert it into a Chinese antiques' shop. Classical Feng Shui is about harnessing the natural power of your environment to improve quality of life. It's a systematic and subtle metaphysical science.

And that's not all. Joey also debunks many a myth about classical Feng Shui, and shares with viewers Face Reading tips as well!

Own the series that national channel 8TV did a re-run of in 2005, today!

Feng Shui for Homebuyers Series

Feng Shui For Homebuyers - Exterior

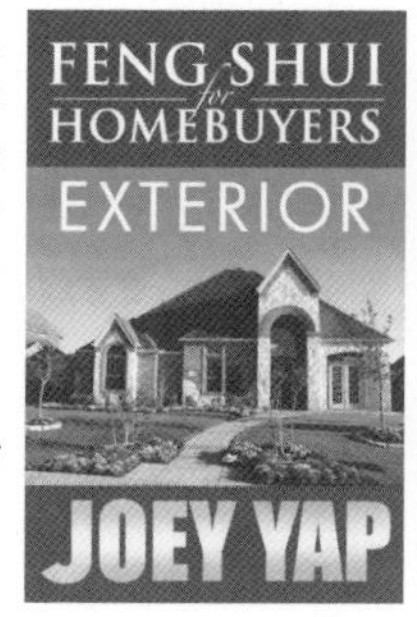

Best selling Author and international Feng Shui Consultant, Joey Yap, will guide you on the various important features in your external environment that have a bearing on the Feng Shui of your home. For homeowners, those looking to build their own home or even investors who are looking to apply Feng Shui to their homes, this book provides valuable information from the classical Feng Shui theories and applications.

This book will assist you in screening and eliminating unsuitable options with negative FSQ (Feng Shui Quotient) should you acquire your own land or if you are purchasing a newly built home. It will also help you in determining which plot of land to select and which to avoid when purchasing an empty parcel of land.

Feng Shui for Homebuyers - Interior

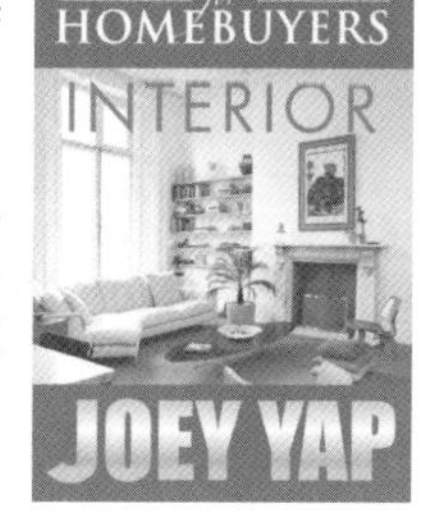

A book every homeowner or potential house buyer should have. The Feng Shui for Homebuyers (Interior) is an informative reference book and invaluable guide written by best selling Author and international Feng Shui Consultant, Joey Yap.

This book provides answers to the important questions of what really does matter when looking at the internal Feng Shui of a home or office. It teaches you how to analyze your home or office floor plans and how to improve their Feng Shui. It will answer all your questions about the positive and negative flow of Qi within your home and ways to utilize them to your maximum benefit.

Providing you with a guide to calculating your Life Gua and House Gua to fine-tune your Feng Shui within your property, Joey Yap focuses on practical, easily applicable ideas on what you can implement internally in a property.

Feng Shui for Apartment Buyers - Home Owners

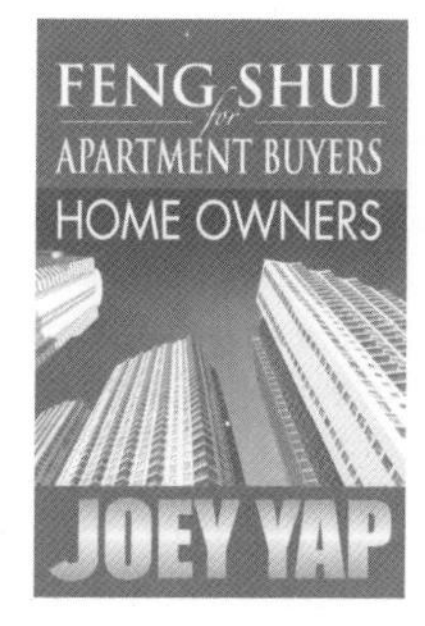

Finding a good apartment or condominium is never an easy task but who do you ensure that is also has good Feng Shui? And how exactly do you apply Feng Shui to an apartment or condominium or high-rise residence?

These questions and more are answered by renowned Feng Shui Consultant and Master Trainer Joey Yap in **Feng Shui for Apartment Buyers - Home Owners**. Joey answers the key questions about Feng Shui and apartments, then guides you through the bare basics like taking a direction and superimposing a Flying Stars chart onto a floor plan. Joey also walks you through the process of finding an apartment with favorable Feng Shui, sharing with you some of the key methods and techniques that are employed by professional Feng Shui consultants in assesing apartment Feng Shui.

In his trademark straight-to-the-point manner, Joey shares with you the Feng Shui do's and dont's when it comes to finding an apartment with favorable Feng Shui and which is conducive for home living.

Educational Tools & Software

Mini Feng Shui Compass

This Mini Feng Shui Compass with the accompanying Companion Booklet written by leading Feng Shui and Chinese Astrology Master Trainer Joey Yap is a must-have for any Feng Shui enthusiast.

The Mini Feng Shui Compass is a self-aligning compass that is not only light at 100gms but also built sturdily to ensure it will be convenient to use anywhere. The rings on the Mini Feng Shui Compass are bi-lingual and incorporate the 24 Mountain Rings that is used in your traditional Luo Pan.

The comprehensive booklet included will guide you in applying the 24 Mountain Directions on your Mini Feng Shui Compass effectively and the 8 Mansions Feng Shui to locate the most auspicious locations within your home, office and surroundings. You can also use the Mini Feng Shui Compass when measuring the direction of your property for the purpose of applying Flying Stars Feng Shui.

BaZi Ming Pan Software Version 2.0

Professional Four Pillars Calculator for Destiny Analysis

The BaZi Ming Pan Version 2.0 Professional Four Pillars Calculator for Destiny Analysis is the most technically advanced software of its kind in the world today. It allows even those without any knowledge of BaZi to generate their own BaZi Charts, and provides virtually every detail required to undertake a comprehensive Destiny Analysis.

This Professional Four Pillars Calculator allows you to even undertake a day-to-day analysis of your Destiny. What's more, all BaZi Charts generated by this software are fully printable and configurable! Designed for both enthusiasts and professional practitioners, this state-of-the-art software blends details with simplicity, and is capable of generating 4 different types of BaZi charts: **BaZi Professional Charts, BaZi Annual Analysis Charts, BaZi Pillar Analysis Charts and BaZi Family Relationship Charts.**

Additional references, configurable to cater to all levels of BaZi knowledge and usage, include: • Dual Age & Bilingual Option (Western & Chinese) • Na Yin narrations • 12 Life Stages evaluation • Death & Emptiness • Gods & Killings • Special Days • Heavenly Virtue Nobles

This software also comes with a Client Management feature that allows you to save and trace clients' records instantly, navigate effortlessly between BaZi charts, and file your clients' information in an organized manner.

The BaZi Ming Pan Version 2.0 Calculator sets a new standard by combining the best of BaZi and technology.

Accelerate Your Face Reading Skills With Joey Yap's Face Reading Revealed DVD Series

Mian Xiang, the Chinese art of Face Reading, is an ancient form of physiognomy and entails the use of the face and facial characteristics to evaluate key aspects of a person's life, luck and destiny. In his Face Reading DVDs series, Joey Yap shows you how the facial features reveal a wealth of information about a person's luck, destiny and personality.

Mian Xiang also tell us the talents, quirks and personality of an individual. Do you know that just by looking at a person's face, you can ascertain his or her health, wealth, relationships and career? Let Joey Yap show you how the 12 Palaces can be utilised to reveal a person's inner talents, characteristics and much more.

Each facial feature on the face represents one year in a person's life. Your face is a 100-year map of your life and each position reveals your fortune and destiny at a particular age as well as insights and information about your personality, skills, abilities and destiny.

Using Mian Xiang, you will also be able to plan your life ahead by identifying, for example, the right business partner and knowing the sort of person that you need to avoid. By knowing their characteristics through the facial features, you will be able to gauge their intentions and gain an upper hand in negotiations.

Do you know what moles signify? Do they bring good or bad luck? Do you want to build better relationships with your partner or family members or have your ever wondered why you seem to be always bogged down by trivial problems in your life?

In these highly entertaining DVDs, Joey will help you answer all these questions and more. You will be able to ascertain the underlying meaning of moles, birthmarks or even the type of your hair in Face Reading. Joey will also reveal the guidelines to help you foster better and stronger relationships with your loved ones through Mian Xiang.

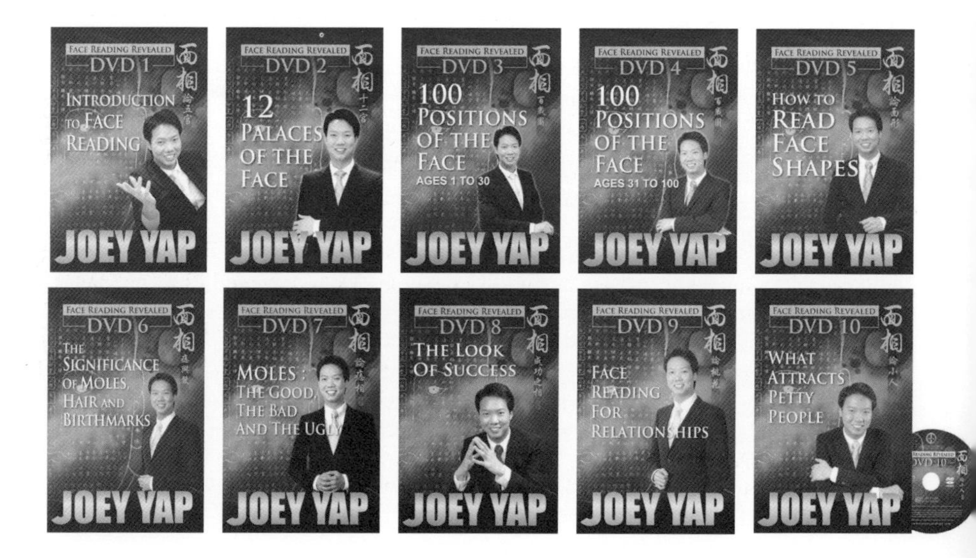

Continue Your Journey with Joey Yap's Books

BaZi - The Destiny Code (English & Chinese versions)

Leading Chinese Astrology Master Trainer Joey Yap makes it easy to learn how to unlock your Destiny through your BaZi with this book. BaZi or Four Pillars of Destiny is an ancient Chinese science which enables individuals to understand their personality, hidden talents and abilities as well as their luck cycle, simply by examining the information contained within their birth data. *The Destiny Code* is the first book that shows readers how to plot and interpret their own Destiny Charts and lays the foundation for more in-depth BaZi studies. Written in a lively entertaining style, the Destiny Code makes BaZi accessible to the layperson. Within 10 chapters, understand and appreciate more about this astoundingly accurate ancient Chinese Metaphysical science.

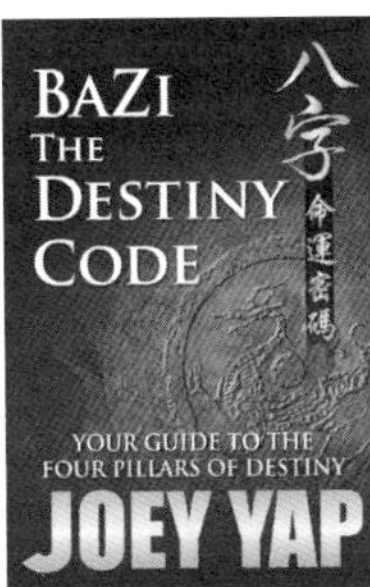

BaZi - The Destiny Code Revealed

In this follow up to Joey Yap's best-selling *The Destiny Code*, delve deeper into your own Destiny chart through an understanding of the key elemental relationships that affect the Heavenly Stems and Earthly Branches. Find out how Combinations, Clash, Harm, Destructions and Punishments bring new dimension to a BaZi chart. Complemented by extensive real-life examples, *The Destiny Code Revealed* takes you to the next level of BaZi, showing you how to unlock the Codes of Destiny and to take decisive action at the right time, and capitalise on the opportunities in life.

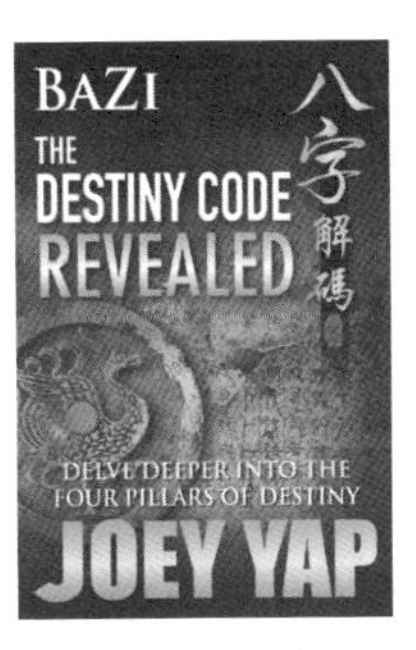

The Ten Thousand Year Calendar

The Ten Thousand Year Calendar or 萬年曆 Wan Nian Li is a regular reference book and an invaluable tool used by masters, practitioners and students of Feng Shui, BaZi (Four Pillars of Destiny), Chinese Zi Wei Dou Shu Astrology (Purple Star), Yi Jing (I-Ching) and Date Selection specialists.

JOEY YAP's *Ten Thousand Year Calendar* provides the Gregorian (Western) dates converted into both the Chinese Solar and Lunar calendar in both the English and Chinese language.

It also includes a comprehensive set of key Feng Shui and Chinese Astrology charts and references, including Xuan Kong Nine Palace Flying Star Charts, Monthly and Daily Flying Stars, Water Dragon Formulas Reference Charts, Zi Wei Dou Shu (Purple Star) Astrology Reference Charts, BaZi (Four Pillars of Destiny) Heavenly Stems, Earthly Branches and all other related reference tables for Chinese Metaphysical Studies.

Annual Releases

Chinese Astrology for 2008

This information-packed annual guide to the Chinese Astrology for 2008 goes way beyond the conventional `animal horoscope' book. To begin with, author Joey Yap includes a personalized outlook for 2008 based on the individual's BaZi Day Pillar (Jia Zi) and a 12-month micro-analysis for each of the 60 Day Pillars – in addition to the annual outlook for all 12 animal signs and the 12-month outlook for each animal sign in 2008. Find out what awaits you in 2008 from the four key aspects of Health, Wealth, Career and Relationships... with Joey Yap's **Chinese Astrology for 2008**!

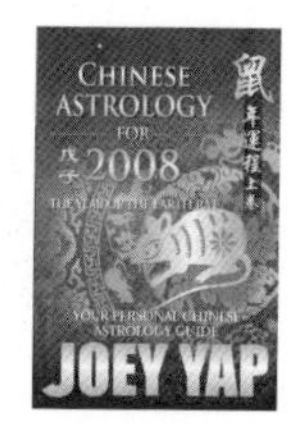

Feng Shui for 2008

Maximize the Qi of the Year of the Earth Rat for your home and office, with Joey Yap's **Feng Shui for 2008** book. Learn how to tap into the positive sectors of the year, and avoid the negative ones and those with the Annual Afflictions, as well as ascertain how the annual Flying Stars affect your property by comparing them against the Eight Mansions (Ba Zhai) for 2008. Flying Stars enthusiasts will also find this book handy, as it includes the monthly Flying Stars charts for the year, accompanied by detailed commentaries on what sectors to use and avoid – to enable you to optimize your Academic, Relationships and Wealth Luck in 2008.

Tong Shu Diary 2008

Organize your professional and personal lives with the **Tong Shu Diary 2008**, with a twist... it also allows you to determine the most suitable dates on which you can undertake important activities and endeavors throughout the year! This compact Diary integrates the Chinese Solar and Lunar Calendars with the universal lingua franca of the Gregorian Calendar.

Tong Shu Monthly Planner 2008

Tailor-made for the Feng Shui or BaZi enthusiast in you, or even professional Chinese Metaphysics consultants who want a compact planner with useful information incorporated into it. In the **Tong Shu Monthly Planner 2008**, you will find the auspicious and inauspicious dates for the year marked out for you, alongside the most suitable activities to be undertaken on each day. As a bonus, there is also a reference section containing all the monthly Flying Stars charts and Annual Afflictions for 2008.

Tong Shu Desktop Calendar 2008

Get an instant snapshot of the suitable and unsuitable activities for each day of the Year of the Earth Rat, with the icons displayed on this lightweight Desktop Calendar. Elegantly presenting the details of the Chinese Solar Calendar in the form of the standard Gregorian one, the **Tong Shu Desktop Calendar 2008** is perfect for Chinese Metaphysics enthusiasts and practitioners alike. Whether it a business launching or meeting, ground breaking ceremony, travel or house-moving that you have in mind, this Calendar is designed to fulfill your information needs.

Tong Shu Year Planner 2008

This one-piece Planner presents you all the essential information you need for significant activities or endeavors...with just a quick glance! In a nutshell, it allows you to identify the favorable and unfavorable days, which will in turn enable you to schedule your year's activities so as to make the most of good days, and avoid the ill-effects brought about by inauspicious ones.

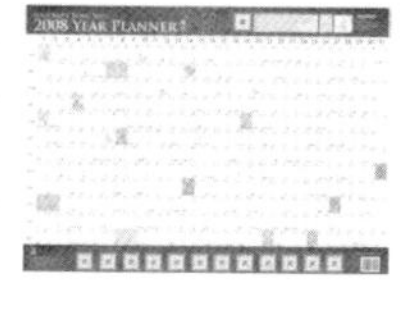

Continue Your Journey with Joey Yap's Books

Stories and Lessons on Feng Shui (English & Chinese versions)

Stories and Lessons on Feng Shui is a compilation of essays and stories written by leading Feng Shui and Chinese Astrology trainer and consultant Joey Yap about Feng Shui and Chinese Astrology.

In this heart-warming collection of easy to read stories, find out why it's a myth that you should never have Water on the right hand side of your house, the truth behind the infamous 'love' and 'wealth' corners and that the sudden death of a pet fish is really NOT due to bad luck!

More Stories and Lessons on Feng Shui

Finally, the long-awaited sequel to *Stories & Lessons on Feng Shui*!

If you've read the best-selling Stories & Lessons on Feng Shui, you won't want to miss this book. And even if you haven't read *Stories & Lessons on Feng Shui*, there's always a time to rev your Feng Shui engine up.

The time is NOW.

And the book? *More Stories & Lessons on Feng Shui* – the 2nd compilation of the most popular articles and columns penned by Joey Yap; **specially featured in national and international publications, magazines and newspapers.**

All in all, *More Stories & Lessons on Feng Shui* is a delightful chronicle of Joey's articles, thoughts and vast experience - as a professional Feng Shui consultant and instructor - that have been purposely refined, edited and expanded upon to make for a light-hearted, interesting yet educational read. And with Feng Shui, BaZi, Mian Xiang and Yi Jing all thrown into this one dish, there's something for everyone…so all you need to serve or accompany *More Stories & Lessons on Feng Shui* with is your favorite cup of tea or coffee!

Even More Stories and Lessons on Feng Shui

In this third release in the Stories and Lessons series, Joey Yap continues his exploration on the study and practice of Feng Shui in the modern age through a series of essays and personal anecdotes. Debunking superstition, offering simple and understandable "Feng Shui-It-Yourself" tips, and expounding on the history and origins of classical Feng Shui, Joey takes readers on a journey that is always refreshing and exciting.

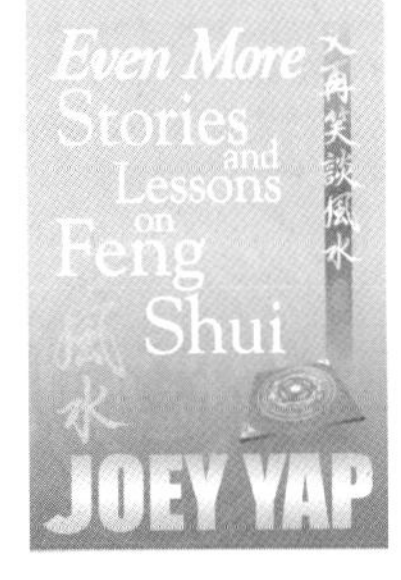

Besides 'behind-the-scenes' revelations of actual Feng Shui audits, there are also chapters on how beginners can easily and accurately incorporate Feng Shui practice into their lives, as well as travel articles that offer proof that when it comes to Feng Shui, the Qi literally knows no boundaries.

In his trademark lucid and forthright style, Joey covers themes and topics that will strike a chord with all readers who have an interest in Feng Shui.

Continue Your Journey with Joey Yap's Books

Xuan Kong: Flying Stars Feng Shui

Xuan Kong Flying Stars Feng Shui is an essential introductory book to the subject of Xuan Kong Fei Xing, a well-known and popular system of Feng Shui, written by International Feng Shui Master Trainer Joey Yap.

In his down-to-earth, entertaining and easy to read style, Joey Yap takes you through the essential basics of Classical Feng Shui, and the key concepts of Xuan Kong Fei Xing (Flying Stars). Learn how to fly the stars, plot a Flying Star chart for your home or office and interpret the stars and star combinations. Find out how to utilise the favourable areas of your home or office for maximum benefit and learn 'tricks of the trade' and 'trade secrets' used by Feng Shui practitioners to enhance and maximise Qi in your home or office.

An essential integral introduction to the subject of Classical Feng Shui and the Flying Stars System of Feng Shui!

Xuan Kong Flying Stars: Structures and Combinations

Delve deeper into Flying Stars through a greater understanding of the 81 Combinations and the influence of the Annual and Monthly Stars on the Base, Sitting and Facing Stars in this 2nd book in the Xuan Kong Feng Shui series. Learn how Structures like the Combination of 10, Up the Mountain and Down the River, Pearl and Parent String Structures are used to interpret a Flying Star chart.

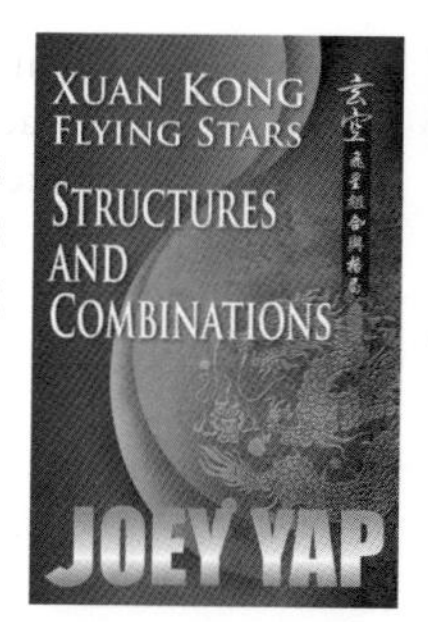

(Available in 2008)

Xuan Kong Flying Stars: Advanced Techniques

Take your knowledge of Xuan Kong Flying Stars to a higher level and learn how to apply complex techniques and advanced formulas such as Castle Gate Technique, Seven Star Robbery Formation, Advancing the Dragon Formation and Replacement Star technique amongst others. Joey Yap also shows you how to use the Life Palace technique to combine Gua Numbers with Flying Star numbers and utilise the predictive facets of Flying Stars Feng Shui.

(Available in 2009)

Continue Your Journey with Joey Yap's Books

Mian Xiang - Discover Face Reading

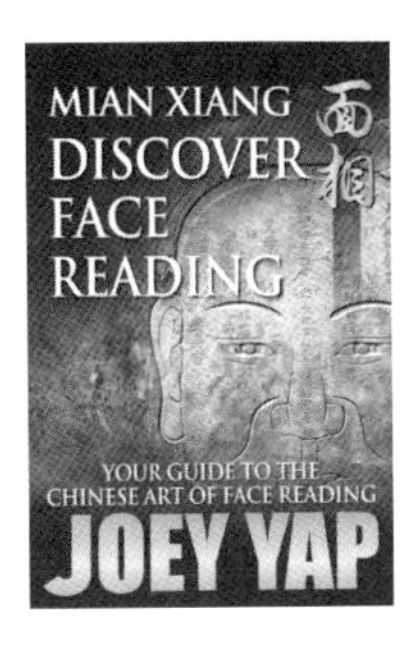

Need to identify a suitable business partner? How about understanding your staff or superiors better? Or even choosing a suitable spouse? These mind boggling questions can be answered in Joey Yap's introductory book to Face Reading titled *Mian Xiang – Discover Face Reading*. This book will help you discover the hidden secrets in a person's face.

Mian Xiang – Discover Face Reading is comprehensive book on all areas of Face Reading, covering some of the most important facial features, including the forehead, mouth, ears and even the philtrum above your lips. This book will help you analyse not just your Destiny but help you achieve your full potential and achieve life fulfillment.

The Art of Date Selection: Personal Date Selection

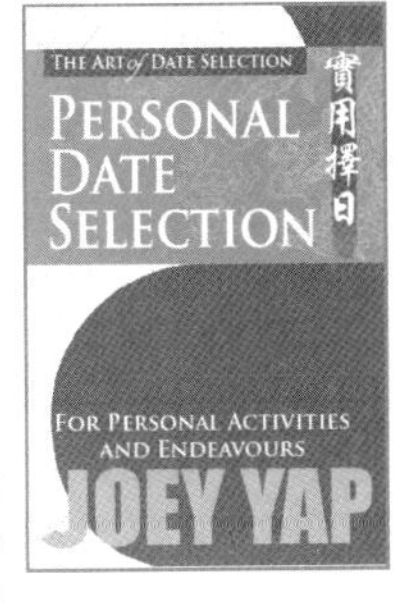

In today's modern world, it is not good enough to just do things effectively – we need to do them efficiently, as well. From the signing of business contracts and moving into a new home, to launching a product or even tying the knot; everything has to move, and move very quickly too. There is a premium on Time, where mistakes can indeed be costly.

The notion of doing the Right Thing, at the Right Time and in the Right Place is the very backbone of Date Selection. Because by selecting a suitable date specially tailored to a specific activity or endeavor, we infuse it with the most positive energies prevalent in our environment during that particular point in time; and that could well make the difference between `make-and-break'! With the *Art of Date Selection: Personal Date Selection*, learn simple, practical methods you can employ to select not just good dates, but personalized good dates. Whether it's a personal activity such as a marriage or professional endeavor such as launching a business, signing a contract or even acquiring assets, this book will show you how to pick the good dates and tailor them to suit the activity in question, as well as avoid the negative ones too!

The Art of Date Selection: Feng Shui Date Selection

(Available in 2008)

Date Selection is the Art of selecting the most suitable date, where the energies present on the day support the specific activities or endeavors we choose to undertake on that day. Feng Shui is the Chinese Metaphysical study of the Physiognomy of the Land – landforms and the Qi they produce, circulate and conduct. Hence, anything that exists on this Earth is invariably subject to the laws of Feng Shui. So what do we get when Date Selection and Feng Shui converge?

Feng Shui Date Selection, of course! Say you wish to renovate your home, or maybe buy or rent one. Or perhaps, you're a developer, and wish to know WHEN is the best date possible to commence construction works on your project. In any case – and all cases – you certainly wish to ensure that your endeavors are well supported by the positive energies present on a good day, won't you? And this is where Date Selection supplements the practice of Feng Shui. At the end of the day, it's all about making the most of what's good, and minimizing what's bad.

Elevate Your Feng Shui Skills With Joey Yap's Home Study Course And Educational DVDs

Xuan Kong Vol.1
An Advanced Feng Shui Home Study Course

Learn the Xuan Kong Flying Star Feng Shui system in just 20 lessons! Joey Yap's specialised notes and course work have been written to enable distance learning without compromising on the breadth or quality of the syllabus. Learn at your own pace with the same material students in a live class would use. The most comprehensive distance learning course on Xuan Kong Flying Star Feng Shui in the market. Xuan Kong Flying Star Vol.1 comes complete with a special binder for all your course notes.

Feng Shui for Period 8 - (DVD)

Don't miss the Feng Shui Event of the next 20 years! Catch Joey Yap LIVE and find out just what Period 8 is all about. This DVD boxed set zips you through the fundamentals of Feng Shui and the impact of this important change in the Feng Shui calendar. Joey's entertaining, conversational style walks you through the key changes that Period 8 will bring and how to tap into Wealth Qi and Good Feng Shui for the next 20 years.

Xuan Kong Flying Stars Beginners Workshop - (DVD)

Take a front row seat in Joey Yap's Xuan Kong Flying Stars workshop with this unique LIVE RECORDING of Joey Yap's Xuan Kong Flying Stars Feng Shui workshop, attended by over 500 people. This DVD program provides an effective and quick introduction of Xuan Kong Feng Shui essentials for those who are just starting out in their study of classical Feng Shui. Learn to plot your own Flying Star chart in just 3 hours. Learn 'trade secret' methods, remedies and cures for Flying Stars Feng Shui. This boxed set contains 3 DVDs and 1 workbook with notes and charts for reference.

BaZi Four Pillars of Destiny Beginners Workshop - (DVD)

Ever wondered what Destiny has in store for you? Or curious to know how you can learn more about your personality and inner talents? BaZi or Four Pillars of Destiny is an ancient Chinese science that enables us to understand a person's hidden talent, inner potential, personality, health and wealth luck from just their birth data. This specially compiled DVD set of Joey Yap's BaZi Beginners Workshop provides a thorough and comprehensive introduction to BaZi. Learn how to read your own chart and understand your own luck cycle. This boxed set contains 3 DVDs and 1 workbook with notes and reference charts.

Interested in learning MORE about Feng Shui? Advance Your Feng Shui Knowledge with the Mastery Academy Courses.

Feng Shui Mastery Series™
LIVE COURSES (MODULES ONE TO FOUR)

Feng Shui Mastery – Module One
Beginners Course

Designed for students seeking an entry-level intensive program into the study of Feng Shui , Module One is an intensive foundation course that aims not only to provide you with an introduction to Feng Shui theories and formulas and equip you with the skills and judgments to begin practicing and conduct simple Feng Shui audits upon successful completion of the course. Learn all about Forms, Eight Mansions Feng Shui and Flying Star Feng Shui in just one day with a unique, structured learning program that makes learning Feng Shui quick and easy!

Feng Shui Mastery – Module Two
Practitioners Course

Building on the knowledge and foundation in classical Feng Shui theory garnered in M1, M2 provides a more advanced and in-depth understanding of Eight Mansions, Xuan Kong Flying Star and San He and introduces students to theories that are found only in the classical Chinese Feng Shui texts. This 3-Day Intensive course hones analytical and judgment skills, refines Luo Pan (Chinese Feng Shui compass) skills and reveals 'trade secret' remedies. Module Two covers advanced Forms Analysis, San He's Five Ghost Carry Treasure formula, Advanced Eight Mansions and Xuan Kong Flying Stars and equips you with the skills needed to undertake audits and consultations for residences and offices.

Feng Shui Mastery – Module Three
Advanced Practitioners Course

Module Three is designed for Professional Feng Shui Practitioners. Learn advanced topics in Feng Shui and take your skills to a cutting edge level. Be equipped with the knowledge, techniques and confidence to conduct large scale audits (like estate and resort planning). Learn how to apply different systems appropriately to remedy situations or cases deemed inauspicious by one system and reconcile conflicts in different systems of Feng Shui. Gain advanced knowledge of San He (Three Harmony) systems and San Yuan (Three Cycles) systems, advanced Luan Tou (Forms Feng Shui) and specialist Water Formulas.

Feng Shui Mastery – Module Four
Master Course

The graduating course of the Feng Shui Mastery (FSM) Series, this course takes the advanced practitioner to the Master level. Power packed M4 trains students to 'walk the mountains' and identify superior landform, superior grade structures and make qualitative evaluations of landform, structures, Water and Qi and covers advanced and exclusive topics of San He, San Yuan, Xuan Kong, Ba Zhai, Luan Tou (Advanced Forms and Water Formula) Feng Shui. Master Internal, External and Luan Tou (Landform) Feng Shui methodologies to apply Feng Shui at every level and undertake consultations of every scale and magnitude, from houses and apartments to housing estates, townships, shopping malls and commercial districts.

BaZi Mastery Series™

LIVE COURSES (MODULES ONE TO FOUR)

BaZi Mastery – Module One

Intensive Foundation Course

This Intensive One Day Foundation Course provides an introduction to the principles and fundamentals of BaZi (Four Pillars of Destiny) and Destiny Analysis methods such as Ten Gods, Useful God and Strength of Qi. Learn how to plot a BaZi chart and interpret your Destiny and your potential. Master BaZi and learn to capitalize on your strengths, minimize risks and downturns and take charge of your Destiny.

BaZi Mastery – Module Two

Practical BaZi Applications

BaZi Module Two teaches students advanced BaZi analysis techniques and specific analysis methods for relationship luck, health evaluation, wealth potential and career potential. Students will learn to identify BaZi chart structures, sophisticated methods for applying the Ten Gods, and how to read Auxiliary Stars. Students who have completed Module Two will be able to conduct professional BaZi readings.

BaZi Mastery – Module Three

Advanced Practitioners Program

Designed for the BaZi practitioner, learn how to read complex cases and unique events in BaZi charts and perform Big and Small assessments. Discover how to analyze personalities and evaluate talents precisely, as well as special formulas and classical methodologies for BaZi from classics such as Di Tian Sui and Qiong Tong Bao Jian.

BaZi Mastery – Module Four

Master Course in BaZi

The graduating course of the BaZi Mastery Series, this course takes the advanced practitioner to the Masters' level. BaZi M4 focuses on specialized techniques of BaZi reading, unique special structures and advance methods from ancient classical texts. This program includes techniques on date selection and ancient methodologies from the Qiong Tong Bao Jian and Yuan Hai Zi Ping classics.

XUAN KONG MASTERY SERIES™
LIVE COURSES (MODULES ONE TO THREE)
* Advanced Courses For Master Practitioners

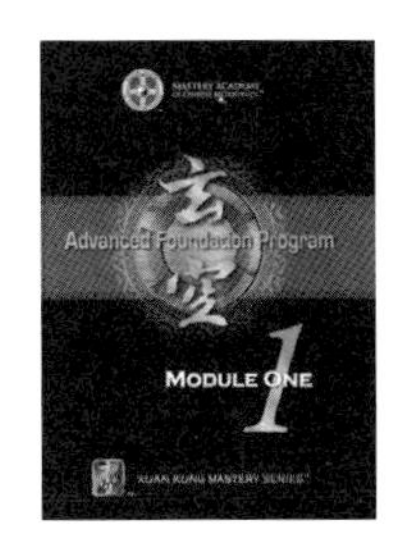

Xuan Kong Mastery – Module One
Advanced Foundation Program

This course is for the experienced Feng Shui professionals who wish to expand their knowledge and skills in the Xuan Kong system of Feng Shui, covering important foundation methods and techniques from the Wu Chang and Guang Dong lineages of Xuan Kong Feng Shui.

Xuan Kong Mastery – Module Two A
Advanced Xuan Kong Methodologies

Designed for Feng Shui practitioners seeking to specialise in the Xuan Kong system, this program focuses on methods of application and Joey Yap's unique Life Palace and Shifting Palace Methods, as well as methods and techniques from the Wu Chang lineage.

Xuan Kong Mastery – Module Two B
Purple White

Explore in detail and in great depth the star combinations in Xuan Kong. Learn how each different combination reacts or responds in different palaces, under different environmental circumstances and to whom in the property. Learn methods, theories and techniques extracted from ancient classics such as Xuan Kong Mi Zhi, Xuan Kong Fu, Fei Xing Fu and Zi Bai Jue.

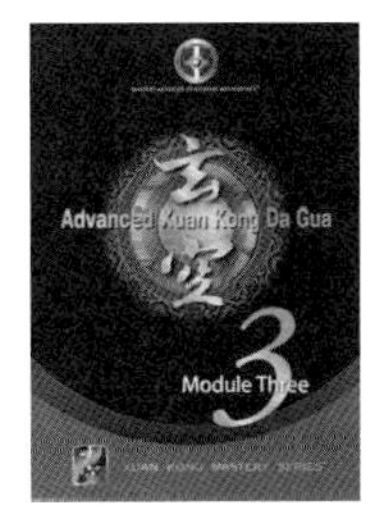

Xuan Kong Mastery – Module Three
Advanced Xuan Kong Da Gua

This intensive course focuses solely on the Xuan Kong Da Gua system covering the theories, techniques and methods of application of this unique 64-Hexagram based system of Xuan Kong including Xuan Kong Da Gua for landform analysis.

Mian Xiang Mastery Series™
LIVE COURSES (MODULES ONE AND TWO)

Mian Xiang Mastery – Module One
Basic Face Reading

A person's face is their fortune – learn more about the ancient Chinese art of Face Reading. In just one day, be equipped with techniques and skills to read a person's face and ascertain their character, luck, wealth and relationship luck.

Mian Xiang Mastery – Module Two
Practical Face Reading

Mian Xiang Module Two covers face reading techniques extracted from the ancient classics Shen Xiang Quan Pian and Shen Xiang Tie Guan Dau. Gain a greater depth and understanding of Mian Xiang and learn to recognize key structures and characteristics in a person's face.

Yi Jing Mastery Series™
LIVE COURSES (MODULES ONE AND TWO)

Yi Jing Mastery – Module One
Traditional Yi Jing

'Yi', relates to change. Change is the only constant in life and the universe, without exception to this rule. The Yi Jing is hence popularly referred to as the Book or Classic of Change. Discoursed in the language of Yin and Yang, the Yi Jing is one of the oldest Chinese classical texts surviving today. With Traditional Yi Jing, learnn how this Classic is used to divine the outcomes of virtually every facet of life; from your relationships to seeking an answer to the issues you may face in your daily life.

Yi Jing Mastery – Module Two
Plum Blossom Numerology

Shao Yong, widely regarded as one of the greatest scholars of the Sung Dynasty, developed Mei Hua Yi Shu (Plum Blossom Numerology) as a more advanced means for divination purpose using the Yi Jing. In Plum Blossom Numerology, the results of a hexagram are interpreted by referring to the Gua meanings, where the interaction and relationship between the five elements, stems, branches and time are equally taken into consideration. This divination method, properly applied, allows us to make proper decisions whenever we find ourselves in a predicament.

Ze Ri Mastery Series™

LIVE COURSES (MODULES ONE AND TWO)

Ze Ri Mastery Series Module 1
Personal and Feng Shui Date Selection

The Mastery Academy's Date Selection Mastery Series Module 1 is specifically structured to provide novice students with an exciting introduction to the Art of Date Selection. Learn the rudiments and tenets of this intriguing metaphysical science. What makes a good date, and what makes a bad date? What dates are suitable for which activities, and what dates simply aren't? And of course, the mother of all questions: WHY aren't all dates created equal. All in only one Module – Module 1!

Ze Ri Mastery Series Module 2
Xuan Kong Da Gua Date Selection

In Module 2, discover advanced Date Selection techniques that will take your knowledge of this Art to a level equivalent to that of a professional's! This is the Module where Date Selection infuses knowledge of the ancient metaphysical science of Feng Shui and BaZi (Chinese Astrology, or Four Pillars of Destiny). Feng Shui, as a means of maximizing Human Luck (i.e. our luck on Earth), is often quoted as the cure to BaZi, which allows us to decipher our Heaven (i.e. inherent) Luck. And one of the most potent ways of making the most of what life has to offer us is to understand our Destiny, know how we can use the natural energies of our environment for our environments and MOST importantly, WHEN we should use these energies and for WHAT endeavors!

You will learn specific methods on how to select suitable dates, tailored to specific activities and events. More importantly, you will also be taught how to suit dates to a person's BaZi (Chinese Astrology, or Four Pillars of Destiny), in order to maximize his or her strengths, and allow this person to surmount any challenges that lie in wait. Add in the factor of 'place', and you would have satisfied the notion of 'doing the right thing, at the right time and in the right place'! A basic knowledge of BaZi and Feng Shui will come in handy in this Module, although these are not pre-requisites to successfully undergo Module 2.

Walk the Mountains! Learn Feng Shui in a Practical and Hands-on Program

Feng Shui Mastery Excursion Series™ : CHINA

Learn landform (Luan Tou) Feng Shui by walking the mountains and chasing the Dragon's vein in China. This Program takes the students in a study tour to examine notable Feng Shui landmarks, mountains, hills, valleys, ancient palaces, famous mansions, houses and tombs in China. The Excursion is a 'practical' hands-on course where students are shown to perform readings using the formulas they've learnt and to recognize and read Feng Shui Landform (Luan Tou) formations.

Read about China Excursion here:
http://www.masteryacademy.com/Education/schoolfengshui/fengshuimasteryexcursion.asp

Mastery Academy courses are conducted around the world. Find out when will Joey Yap be in your area by visiting **www.masteryacademy.com** or call our office at **+603-2284 8080**.